personal ^{14e}
Financial Planning

Randall S. Billingsley
Virginia Tech

Lawrence J. Gitman
San Diego State University

Michael D. Joehnk
Arizona State University

CENGAGE
Learning·

Australia • Brazil • Mexico • Singapore • United Kingdom • United States

CENGAGE
Learning®

Personal Financial Planning, Fourteenth Edition
Randall S. Billingsley, Lawrence J. Gitman,
Michael D. Joehnk

Vice President, General Manager Science, Math and
Quantitative Business: Balraj Kalsi

Product Director: Mike Schenk

Senior Product Manager: Mike Reynolds

Content Developer: Conor Allen

Senior Product Assistant: Adele Scholtz

Marketing Manager: Nate Anderson

Marketing Coordinator: Eileen Corcoran

Associate Media Producer: Mark Hopkinson

Manufacturing Planner: Kevin Kluck

Art and Cover Direction, Production Management,
and Composition: Lumina Datamatics, Inc.

Cover Images: Macrovector/Shutterstock.com,
©graphixmania/Shutterstock.com, ©Incomible/
Shutterstock.com

Intellectual Property

Analyst: Christina Ciaramella, Brittani Morgan

Project Manager: Erika Mugavin

For product information and technology assistance, contact us at
Cengage Learning Customer & Sales Support, 1-800-354-9706

For permission to use material from this text or product,
submit all requests online at **www.cengage.com/permissions**
Further permissions questions can be emailed to
permissionrequest@cengage.com

Library of Congress Control Number: 2015950159

Student Edition:
ISBN: 978-1-305-63661-3

Loose-leaf Edition:
ISBN: 978-1-305-86233-3

Cengage Learning
20 Channel Center Street
Boston, MA 02210
USA

Cengage Learning is a leading provider of customized learning
solutions with employees residing in nearly 40 different countries
and sales in more than 125 countries around the world. Find your
local representative at **www.cengage.com**.

Cengage Learning products are represented in Canada by Nelson Education, Ltd.

To learn more about Cengage Learning Solutions, visit **www.cengage.com**

Purchase any of our products at your local college store or at our
preferred online store **www.cengagebrain.com**

Unless otherwise noted, all items are © Cengage Learning

Printed in the United States of America

Print Number: 02 Print Year: 2016

For Bonnie, Lauren, and Evan
RSB

For our children:
Zachary, Jessica, and Caren
LJG

For Colwyn,
Grace, and Rhett
MDJ

Brief Contents

Contents

ARIEL SKELLEY/JUPITER IMAGES

ALIKEYOU/SHUTTERSTOCK.COM

- Why can't I budget more effectively and what should I do about it?
- How much money should I set aside for emergencies?
- How do I pick the best credit card and best manage it?
- Would I be better off renting or buying a home?
- How much of a mortgage can I afford?
- What are the implications of the Affordable Care Act for my health insurance?
- What features do I need in car and homeowner's insurance and how do I get the best prices?
- What do I need to know about stocks and bonds to make good investments?
- How do I choose the best mutual funds and exchange traded funds (ETFs)?
- How do I plan for retirement?
- How do tax-deferred investment vehicles work and what should I do about them?
- Do I really need a will if I'm young and just getting started?
- Isn't estate planning just for rich people?

So many questions about managing our personal finances—and the stakes are so high! *Personal Financial Planning*, 14th edition, provides a framework for answering these questions and more. Careful planning allows us to best adapt to changes in the financial environment and the associated changes in our own lives. This book provides tools for preparing personal financial plans that serve as road maps for achieving goals. It emphasizes the dynamics of the financial planning process by considering the impact of life changes—birth, marriage, divorce, job and career, and death.

Personal Financial Planning addresses all of the major financial planning issues and problems that individuals and families encounter. It links together all of the major elements of effective money management. All of the latest financial planning tools and techniques are discussed. This comprehensive text is written in a personal style that uses state-of-the-art pedagogy to present the key concepts and procedures used in sound personal financial planning and effective money management. The roles of various financial decisions in the overall personal financial planning process are clearly delineated.

The book serves individuals who are, or will be, actively developing their own personal financial plans. It meets the needs of instructors and students in a first course in personal financial planning (often called "personal finance") offered at colleges and universities, junior and community colleges, professional certification programs, and continuing education courses. The experiences of individuals and families are used to demonstrate successes and failures in various aspects of personal financial planning. A conversational style and liberal use of examples and worksheets guide students through the material and emphasize important points. The benefits of the book's readability accrue not only to students but also to their instructors.

ORGANIZATION OF THE BOOK

Personal Financial Planning is divided into six parts. Part 1 presents the foundations of personal financial planning, beginning with the financial planning process and then covering financial statements and budgets and also taxes. Part 2 concerns the management of basic assets, including cash and savings instruments, automobiles, and housing. Part 3 covers credit management, including the various types of open account borrowing and consumer loans. Part 4 deals with managing insurance needs and considers life insurance, health care insurance, and property insurance. Part 5 covers investments—including stocks, bonds, mutual funds, ETFs, and real estate—and how to make transactions in securities markets. Part 6 is devoted to retirement and estate planning.

Pedagogy

Each chapter opens with six learning goals that link the material covered to specific learning outcomes and anchor the text's *integrated learning system*. The learning goal numbers are tied to major chapter headings and restated and reviewed point by point in the end-of-chapter summary. New to the 14th edition, each chapter also opens with a series of statements presented as *Financial Fact or Fantasy* in the related chapter material. Each statement is critically evaluated as fact or fantasy in the context of the relevant material. Then, at the end of each of the major sections, *Test Yourself* questions allow readers to reinforce their understanding of the material before moving on to the next section. As students read through the chapters, these *Test Yourself* questions allow them to test their understanding of the material in each section. Students can find the answers to the *Test Yourself* questions on the book's companion website by going to www.cengagebrain.com and searching for this book by its author or ISBN, and then adding it to the dashboard. They're also found in the instructor's manual. Also new to the 14th edition, at the end of select chapters is a summary of all key financial relationships along with a problem set illustrating their application.

Each chapter contains several *Financial Planning Tips* and *Financial Road Signs*, which provide important hints or suggestions to consider when implementing certain parts of a financial plan. *Worksheets* are included to simplify demonstration of various calculations and procedures and to provide students with helpful materials that they can use in managing their own personal finances. The worksheets are numbered for convenient reference in end-of-chapter problems, and they include descriptive captions. Numerous exhibits, each including a descriptive caption, are used throughout to more fully illustrate key points in the text. Also included in each chapter is a *running glossary* that appears in the margin and provides brief definitions of all highlighted terms in the accompanying text. Most chapters discuss how the Internet can be used in various phases of personal financial planning. End-of-chapter material includes a *Summary*, which restates each learning goal and follows it with a brief paragraph that summarizes the material related to it. The next element is the new *Financial Impact of Personal Choices* feature, which presents a personal financial planning decision related to an important topic in each chapter and evaluates the outcome. Selected chapters also provide a new feature, *Key Financial Relationships*, which concisely summarizes the analytical frameworks used and provides related practice problems and their solutions. Then each chapter provides *Financial Planning Exercises*, which include questions and problems that students can use to test their grasp of the material. Following this feature is *Applying Personal Finance*, which generally involves some type of outside project or exercise. Two *Critical Thinking Cases* that highlight the important analytical topics and concepts are also provided.

Major Changes in the 14th Edition

The 14th edition has been thoroughly updated to consider the most up-to-date techniques of contemporary personal financial planning. We emphasize that the key principles of personal financial planning remain valid: save, diversify your investments, watch your expenditures, and borrow carefully. This edition reflects feedback from past users, practicing financial planners, finance industry experts, students, and our own research. It provides helpful new approaches, expanded coverage in certain areas, streamlined coverage in others, and enhanced pedagogy anchored by a state-of-the-art integrated learning system. The basic organizational structure, topical coverage, superior readability, and useful instructional aids that marked the success of the first 13 editions have been retained and extended. Important changes in this edition are described below, first as general changes and then as specific chapter-by-chapter changes.

General Changes and Hallmark Features

- The 14th edition includes in each chapter a series of highlighted practical examples illustrating everyday applications of the covered material. The featured examples include "The Sooner You Start an IRA, the Better" (Chapter 1), "Determining the Value of an Investment" and Keeping Track of Loans" (Chapter 2), "Applying Tax Rates" and "Determining the Amount Owed or Refunded" (Chapter 3), "Determining the Extent of FDIC Insurance Protection" (Chapter 4), "Calculating the Maximum Affordable Mortgage Loan" (Chapter 5), "Credit Card Choice Trade-offs" and "Paying Only the Minimum on Your Credit Card" (Chapter 6), "Calculating the Total Finance Charge and Payment on a Simple Interest Loan" (Chapter 7), "Appropriate Use of Term Life Insurance" and "Using Low-Load Whole Life Insurance—Building Cash Value" (Chapter 8), "Effect of Per-Illness, Per-Accident Deductible" (Chapter 9), "Effect of Co-insurance," and "Homeowner's Policy Coverage Limits" (Chapter 10), "Limit Orders" and "Using Margin Trades to Magnify Returns" (Chapter 11), "Inflation-Adjustment of TIPS Bonds" and "Calculating the Approximate Yield to Maturity" (Chapter 12), "Calculating a Mutual Fund's NAV" and "Calculating the Value of Income-Producing Property" (Chapter 13), "Effect of Inflation on Future Retirement Needs" and "Measuring the Benefits of a Roth IRA Over a Taxable Account" (Chapter 14), and "Disadvantage of Joint Tenancy with the Right of Survivorship" and "Use of Life Insurance in an Estate" (Chapter 15).
- The 14th edition includes a new feature in each chapter, *You Can Do It Now*, which allows the reader to act on the presented material on the spot. The *You Can Do It Now* features include "Start a List of Your Financial Goals" and "Recognize that YOU are Your Most Important Asset" (Chapter 1), "Track Your Expenses" and "Save Automatically" (Chapter 2), "Tax Planning" (Chapter 3), "Shop for the Best Short-Term Rates" and "Reconcile Your Checkbook" (Chapter 4), "What's Your Car Worth?" and "Rent vs. Buy a Home?" (Chapter 5), "How Does Your Credit Report Look?" and "Is Your Credit Card a Good Deal?" (Chapter 6), "Current Auto Loan Rates" (Chapter 7), "Shop for a Customized Life Insurance Policy" and "Check Out the Best Life Insurance Companies" (Chapter 8), "Compare Policies on an ACA Health Insurance Exchange" (Chapter 9), "Check Out the Best Homeowner's Insurance Companies" and "Evaluate the Best Auto insurance Companies" (Chapter 10), "How's the Market Doing Right Now?" and "Get a Quick Perspective on Your Asset Allocation" (Chapter 11), "What's the Market P/E Ratio Telling You?" and "How Do Stock and Bond Market Returns Compare This Year?" (Chapter 12), "Objective Mutual Fund Resources" and "How to Choose the Best ETF for You" (Chapter 13), "Get a Rough Estimate of Your Future Social Security Benefits" and "Calculating the Benefits of a Traditional IRA" (Chapter 14), and "Estate Planning Conversations" and "Importance of Naming Alternative Beneficiaries" (Chapter 15).
- New to the 14th edition is the *Financial Impact of Personal Choices* feature, which presents a personal financial planning decision related to an important topic in each chapter and evaluates the outcome. The *Financial Impact of Personal Choices* feature includes "Bob Cuts Back on Lunch Out and Lattes" (Chapter 1), "No Budget, No Plan: Sean Bought a Boat!" (Chapter 2), "Angela and Tim's Tax Management Strategy" (Chapter 3), "Stella Likes Cash—Too Much?" (Chapter 4), "Vivian Wants to Buy a House but Doesn't Want a Roommate Now" (Chapter 5), "Stan Has Had It and Files for Bankruptcy" (Chapter 6), "John and Mary Calculate Their Auto Loan Backwards" (Chapter 7), "Matt and Jan Consider 'Buying Term and Investing the Rest'" (Chapter 8), "Josh Expands His Health Insurance

Coverage" (Chapter 9), "Wade Saves on His Car Insurance" (Chapter 10), "Trey and April Get Serious About Their Retirement Asset Allocation" (Chapter 11), "Landon and Kirsten Like High Flying Stocks" (Chapter 12), "Virginia Finds a Simple Retirement Investment Plan" (Chapter 13), "Carl and Brian's Different Approaches to a Traditional IRA" (Chapter 14), and "The (Un)intended Effects of Corbin's Beneficiary Designations" (Chapter 15).

- The 14th edition adds a summary of *Key Financial Relationships* at the end of selected chapters. Practice problems illustrating the application of these key analytical frameworks are also provided.

- The highly regarded *Worksheets* are provided in a user-friendly Excel® format that students can download from the book's companion Internet site. Students have the option of using the Worksheets multiple times and having some of the calculations within the Worksheets completed electronically.

- The book has been *completely updated and redesigned* to allow improved presentation of each of the text's pedagogical features.

- The 14th edition continues to place emphasis on *using the Internet*. Included are a number of features that either link students to relevant Internet sites or describe how the Internet can be incorporated into the personal financial planning process.

- Step-by-step *use of a handheld financial calculator* to make time value calculations continues to be integrated into relevant discussions in this edition. To improve understanding, relevant keystrokes are highlighted in these demonstrations. Basics of the time value of money are introduced in Chapter 2, "Using Financial Statements and Budgets," and Appendix E now explains how financial calculators can be used to make time value calculations. The use of a financial calculator is reinforced in later chapters, where the time value techniques are applied. For example, using a calculator to find the future value of a deposit given various compounding periods is shown in Chapter 4, "Managing Your Cash and Savings," and calculating estimates of future retirement needs is demonstrated in Chapter 14, "Planning for Retirement." The inclusion of calculator keystrokes should help the reader learn how to develop financial plans more effectively by using this important tool of the trade.

- The 14th edition continues and updates the well-received *Behavior Matters*, which relates each chapter's topic to the reader's everyday behavior and shows how readers might adapt their behavior to become more financially savvy. The *Behavior Matters* features show how all-too-common behavioral biases can adversely affect how we process financial information and make financial decisions. The feature helps link the text discussions to actual financial planning ideas, experiences, and practices—all intended to fully engage readers in the personal financial planning process. The *Behavior Matters* features include "Practicing Financial Self-Awareness" (Chapter 1), "Don't Fool Yourself...Pessimistic Budgeting Wins" (Chapter 2), "Do We Really Value Paying Taxes After All?" (Chapter 3), "Why Can't I Save More—And What Can I Do About It?" (Chapter 4), "Watch Out for 'Anchoring': The Case of the Used Car Salesperson Strategy," (Chapter 5), "Behavioral Biases and Credit Card Use" (Chapter 6), "The Paradox of More Financial Choices" (Chapter 7), "Whole Life vs. Term Life Insurance and Behavioral Biases" (Chapter 8), "Behavioral Biases in Making Health Insurance Decisions" (Chapter 9), "Behavioral Tips in Buying Property Insurance" (Chapter 10), "Do We Live in the Present Too Much? Looking for Patterns That Aren't There..." (Chapter 11), "Dealing with Investor Overreaction" (Chapter 12), "Behavioral Biases in Mutual Fund Investing" (Chapter 13), "Behavioral Biases in Retirement Planning" (Chapter 14), and "Recognizing and Overcoming Aversion to Ambiguity in Estate Planning" (Chapter 15).

- Exhibits and Worksheets, and end-of-chapter *Financial Planning Exercises* and *Critical Thinking Cases*—have been retained and improved as part of the integrated learning system. The *Planning Over a Lifetime* feature continues to highlight how the chapter's topic is important to readers in different life stages.

Specific Chapter-by-Chapter Changes and Summaries

Because instructors often like to know where new material appears, the significant changes that have been made in the 14th edition are summarized next.

Chapter 1 on understanding the financial planning process, has been carefully revised to focus on the most important themes in the book. Emphasis is placed on setting realistic goals for your finances, helpful ways to save money by changing everyday habits, and being more financially self-aware.

Chapter 2 on using your financial statements and budgeting has been restructured, streamlined, and updated. Calculator keystrokes and time lines continue to appear in discussions of the time value of money. There are new discussions on setting realistic budgeting plans and avoiding potential budgeting mistakes, how to choose the right personal finance software, and practical ways to change your behavior to spend less.

Chapter 3 on preparing your taxes has been updated to reflect the changes in tax laws, rates, procedures, and forms in effect at the time we revised the chapter. The material emphasizes current tax practices and explains the nature of progressive tax rates, average tax rates, itemized deductions, individual retirement accounts (IRAs), and other types of tax issues. The chapter continues to provide readers with sidebar advice on finding commonly missed tax deductions, avoiding common tax-form errors, tax tips, and audit triggers. There are new features about what documents you'll need to collect to prepare for tax time, effective ways to reduce your tax liability, and tips for choosing the most appropriate tax preparer for you.

Chapter 4 on managing your cash and savings, has been revised to reflect up-to-date capital market conditions. The potential use of I bonds to manage inflation risk is emphasized. There are practical explanations of why you should start saving *now*, what to look for when choosing a new bank, planning tips for when and when not to use your debit card, and tips for what you should and shouldn't store in a safety deposit box.

Chapter 5 on making automobile and housing decisions considers new market developments and sources of information. The chapter discusses when it makes sense to lease a car, when to buy versus rent a house, how to know when it's time to buy your first home, how to tell what kind of house you need (prioritizing your needs and being practical), and the top ten home improvement projects based on the percentage of the investment recovered at the sale of a home.

Chapter 6 on consumer credit and credit cards, focuses on the positive aspects of using credit and what it takes to build and maintain a strong credit history. The chapter explores the dangers of making only the minimum payment on your credit cards and why "mental accounting" can be dangerous, tips for choosing the right credit card, risky situations for using your debit card, protecting yourself from identity theft, and how to use credit through the different stages of your life.

Chapter 7 on using consumer loans, analyzes the benefits and uses of consumer credit for both single-payment and installment loans. The discussion concentrates on the key issues surrounding loan provisions, finance charges, and other credit considerations. There are suggested questions to ask before you loan money to family and friends, a discussion about 0 percent annual percentage rate (APR) loans and their potential limitations, and a discussion of what lenders are looking at when you submit a loan application—your credit report, debt history, employment history, and savings.

Chapter 8 on insuring your life, discusses how to choose the right life insurance, the benefits of buying a whole-life policy, the differences between whole life and term life insurance, knowing what to expect during your life insurance medical exam, potential conflicts of interest in dealing with insurance agents, and key considerations for life insurance use in each stage of life.

Chapter 9 on insuring your health, has been updated and includes a discussion of the new rules and guidelines for student health care, Medicare Advantage plans, how to save on health insurance, and how to choose the right plan for you. There's also a new discussion about the rationale for health-care reform and the controversy over the Affordable Health Care Act of 2010. The chapter also includes tips on buying disability income insurance, buying long-term care insurance, and health-care apps for your smart phone.

Chapter 10 on protecting your property, discusses behavioral biases when buying property insurance, how to handle a denied insurance claim, and buying auto insurance—getting multiple quotes, how the car itself affects the price of the policy, and how much auto insurance you need. We continue to emphasize practical advice for reducing homeowner's insurance premiums, filing auto insurance claims, preventing auto theft, strategies to avoid liability, and obtaining discounts for auto safety and good driving.

Chapter 11 on investment planning has been revised and updated with discussions of why people are more likely to make short-term investments (and why you might want to avoid this tendency), the importance of saving for retirement, and how to begin investing online.

Chapter 12 on investing in stocks and bonds continues to emphasize the risk–return characteristics of these securities. As part of the revision process, we present new information on successful stock and bond investing, analysis of Apple's financial performance and valuation, tips for avoiding common investing mistakes, properly interpreting overly optimistic equity analysis, how accrued interest affects bond prices, and how to invest in stocks and bonds at each stage of life.

Chapter 13 on investing has been updated and discusses target-date mutual funds, choosing the best mutual funds, avoiding "dog" funds, choosing between exchange traded funds (ETFs) and mutual funds, and a lengthy new discussion and exhibit about how to evaluate ETF performance. There's also a *Behavior Matters* feature about behavioral biases in mutual fund investing—how educating yourself can help you break harmful investing tendencies.

Chapter 14 on planning for retirement, has several valuable features discussing behavioral biases in retirement planning, an app for your smart phone that will help you plan for retirement, a discussion about protecting private-sector defined benefit retirement plans, tips for managing your 401(k) account, and coverage about converting a traditional IRA to a Roth IRA and the implications of doing so.

Chapter 15 on preserving your estate, has been updated to reflect the most recent estate tax laws and tax rates. The chapter discusses online estate planning resources, the details of choosing a suitable guardian for minor children in case of death, tips for writing a will, reasons to use a trust, and a feature about recognizing and overcoming aversion to ambiguity in estate planning.

SUPPLEMENTARY MATERIALS

Because we recognize the importance of outstanding support materials to the instructor and the student, we have continued to improve and expand our supplements package.

Instructor Supplements

CengageNOW

CengageNOW is a powerful course management and online homework tool that provides robust instructor control and customization to optimize the student learning experience and meet desired outcomes. CengageNOW offers:

- Auto-graded homework (static and algorithmic varieties), a test bank, and an eBook, all in one resource.
- Easy-to-use course management options offering flexibility and continuity from one semester to another.
- New! Expanded post-submission feedback explains each problem to students. The instructor decides when this solution is delivered to the students. The 14th edition of *Personal Financial Planning* is the first to offer post-submission feedback to students using CengageNOW.
- The most robust and flexible assignment options in the industry.
- The ability to analyze student work from the gradebook and generate reports on learning outcomes. Each problem is tagged to Business Program (AACSB) and Bloom's Taxonomy outcomes so that you can measure student performance.
- Contact your sales representative for more details if you are interested in offering CengageNOW to your students.

Instructor's Manual and Test Bank

A comprehensive *Instructor's Manual* has been prepared to assist the instructor. For each chapter, the manual includes:

- An outline
- Discussion of major topics
- A list of key concepts
- Solutions to all *Test Yourself* questions, end-of-chapter *Financial Planning Exercises*, and *Critical Thinking Cases*

The *Test Bank* has been revised, updated, and expanded, and all solutions have been checked for accuracy. It includes true–false and multiple-choice questions, as well as four to six short problems for nearly every chapter. Each question is tagged with the corresponding learning objective and learning outcomes. The *Instructor's Manual* has been revised by Professor Sam Hicks, CPA, of VirginiaTech.

Testing with Cognero

Cengage Learning Testing Powered by Cognero is a flexible, online system that allows you to author, edit, and manage test bank content, create multiple test versions in an instant, and deliver tests from your LMS, in your classroom or through CengageNOW.

Microsoft PowerPoint®

Enhance lectures and simplify class preparation. Chapter PowerPoint® presentations are available to instructors both on the Instructor's Resource CD and on the text's instructor Web site. Each presentation consists of a general outline of key concepts from the book. The PowerPoints were revised by Professor Sam Hicks, CPA, of VirginiaTech.

STUDENT SUPPLEMENTS

Interactive Worksheets

Interactive *Worksheets* identical to those presented in the text can be downloaded from this text's student companion Internet site. Each Worksheet provides a logical format for dealing with some aspect of personal financial planning, such as preparing a cash budget, assessing home affordability, or deciding whether to lease or purchase an automobile. Providing worksheets electronically in Excel® format allows students to complete them multiple times for mastery, and many of the worksheets can actually be used to calculate figures needed to make financial decisions.

ACKNOWLEDGMENTS

In addition to the many individuals who made significant contributions to this book by their expertise, classroom experience, guidance, general advice, and reassurance, we also appreciate the students and faculty who used the book and provided valuable feedback, confirming our conviction that a truly teachable personal financial planning text could be developed.

Of course, we are indebted to all the academicians and practitioners who have created the body of knowledge contained in this text. We particularly wish to thank several people who gave the most significant help in developing and revising it. They include Professor John Brozovsky, CPA, of VirginiaTech, for assistance in the chapter on taxes; Professor Sam Hicks, CPA, of VirginiaTech, for his thorough review of the entire book; Thomas C. Via Jr., CLU, for his help in the chapters on life and property insurance; Kent Dodge for his help in the chapter on health insurance; Professor Hongbok Lee, of Western Illinois University, for helpful observations, and Marlene Bellamy of Writeline Associates for her help with the real estate material.

Cengage Learning shared our objective of producing a truly teachable text and relied on the experience and advice of numerous excellent reviewers for the 14th edition:

Ed Anthony, Trevecca Nazarene University
John Bedics, DeSales University
Omar Benkato, Ball State University
Ross E. Blankenship, State Fair Community College
Tim Chesnut, Mt. Vernon Nazarene University
Joseph C. Eppolito, Syracuse University
Jonathan Fox, Ohio State University
Laurie Hensley, Cornell University
John Guess, Delgado Community College
Dianne Morrison, University of Wisconsin—La Crosse
Kathy Mountjoy, Illinois State University
Eric Munshower, University of Dubuque
Muhammad Mustafa, South Carolina State University
Thomas Paczkowski, Cayuga Community College
Ohaness Paskelian, University of Houston—Downtown
Joan Ryan, Clackamas Community College
Amy Scott, DeSales University
Donna Scarlett, Iowa Western Community College—Clarinda Campus
Rahul Verma, University of Houston—Downtown

We also appreciate the many suggestions from previous reviewers, all of whom have had a significant impact on the earlier editions of this book. Our thanks go to the following: Linda Afdahl, Micheal J. Ahern III, Robert J. Angell, H. Kent Baker, Harold David Barr, Catherine L. Bertelson, Steve Blank, Kathleen K. Bromley, D. Gary

Carman, Dan Casey, P. R. Chandy, Tony Cherin, Larry A. Cox, Maurice L. Crawford, Carlene Creviston, Rosa Lea Danielson, William B. Dillon, David Durst, Jeanette A. Eberle, Mary Ellen Edmundson, Ronald Ehresman, Jim Farris, Stephen Ferris, Sharon Hatten Garrison, Wayne H. Gawlick, Alan Goldfarb, Carol Zirnheld Green, Joseph D. Greene, C. R. Griffen, John L. Grimm, Chris Hajdas, James Haltman, Vickie L. Hampton, Forest Harlow, Eric W. Hayden, Henry C. Hill, Kendall B. Hill, Darrell D. Hilliker, Arlene Holyoak, Marilynn E. Hood, Frank Inciardi, Ray Jackson, Kenneth Jacques, Dixie Porter Johnson, Ted Jones, William W. Jones, Judy Kamm, Gordon Karels, Peggy Keck, Gary L. Killion, Earnest W. King, Karol Kitt, George Klander, Xymena S. Kulsrud, Carole J. Makela, Paul J. Maloney, David Manifold, Charles E. Maxwell, Charles W. McKinney, Robert W. McLeod, George Muscal, Robert Nash, Ed Nelling, Charles O'Conner, Albert Pender, Aaron L. Phillips, Armand Picou, Franklin Potts, Fred Power, Alan Raedels, Margaret P. Reed, Charles F. Richardson, Arnold M. Rieger, Vivian Rippentrop, Gayle M. Ross, Kenneth H. St. Clair, Brent T. Sjaardema, Thomas M. Springer, Frank A. Thompson, Dick Verrone, Rosemary Walker, Peggy Bergmeier Ward, Tom Warschauer, Gary Watts, Grant J. Wells, Brock Williams, Janet Bear Wolverton, Betty Wright, and R. R. Zilkowski.

Because of the wide variety of topics covered in this book, we called on many experts for whose insight on recent developments we are deeply grateful. We would like to thank them and their firms for allowing us to draw on their knowledge and resources, particularly Robert Andrews, Willis M. Allen Co. Realtors; Bill Bachrach, Bachrach & Associates; Mark D. Erwin, Commonwealth Financial Network; Robin Gitman, Willis M. Allen Co. Realtors; Craig Gussin, CLU, Auerbach & Gussin; Frank Hathaway, CFA, Chief Economist, NASDAQ; John Markese, former President of the American Association of Individual Investors; Mark Nussbaum, CFP®, Wells Fargo Advisors, Inc.; Sherri Tobin, Farmers Insurance Group; and Deila Mangold, Ideal Homes Realty.

The editorial staff of Cengage Learning has been most helpful in our endeavors. We wish to thank Joe Sabatino, Senior Product Team Manager; Mike Reynolds, Senior Product Manager; Conor Allen, Content Developer; and Adele Scholtz, Senior Product Assistant.

Finally, our wives—Bonnie, Robin, and Charlene—have provided needed support and understanding during the writing of this book. We are forever grateful to them.

Randall S. Billingsley, FRM, CFA
VirginiaTech

Lawrence J. Gitman, CFP®
San Diego State University

Michael D. Joehnk, CFA
Arizona State University

About the Authors

Randall S. Billingsley is a finance professor at VirginiaTech. He received his bachelor's degree in economics from Texas Tech University and received both an M.S. in economics and a Ph.D. in finance from Texas A&M University. Professor Billingsley holds the Chartered Financial Analyst (CFA), Financial Risk Manager (FRM), and Certified Rate of Return Analyst (CRRA) professional designations. An award-winning teacher at the undergraduate and graduate levels, his research, consulting, and teaching focus on investment analysis and issues relevant to practicing financial advisors. Formerly a vice president at the Association for Investment Management and Research (now the CFA Institute), Professor Billingsley's published equity valuation case study of Merck & Company was assigned reading in the CFA curriculum for several years. In 2006 the Wharton School published his book, *Understanding Arbitrage: An Intuitive Approach to Financial Analysis*. In addition, his research has been published in refereed journals that include the *Journal of Portfolio Management*, the *Journal of Banking and Finance*, *Financial Management*, the *Journal of Financial Research*, and the *Journal of Futures Markets*. Professor Billingsley advises the Student-Managed Endowment for Educational Development (SEED) at Virginia Tech, which manages an equity portfolio of about $5 million on behalf of the Virginia Tech Foundation.

Professor Billingsley's consulting to date has focused on two areas of expertise. First, he has acted extensively as an expert witness on financial issues. Second, he has taught seminars and published materials that prepare investment professionals for the CFA examinations. This has afforded him the opportunity to explore and discuss the relationships among diverse areas of investment analysis. His consulting endeavors have taken him across the United States and to Canada, Europe, and Asia. A primary goal of Professor Billingsley's consulting is to apply the findings of academic financial research to practical investment decision making and personal financial planning.

Lawrence J. Gitman is an emeritus professor of finance at San Diego State University. He received his bachelor's degree from Purdue University, his M.B.A. from the University of Dayton, and his Ph.D. from the University of Cincinnati. Professor Gitman is a prolific textbook author and has more than 50 articles appearing in various finance journals.

His other major textbooks include *Fundamentals of Investing*, 12th edition, which is co-authored with Scott B. Smart and Michael D. Joehnk; and *Principles of Managerial Finance*, 7th Brief edition, and *Principles of Managerial Finance*, 14th edition, both co-authored with Chad J. Zutter.

An active member of numerous professional organizations, Professor Gitman is past president of the Academy of Financial Services, the San Diego Chapter of the Financial Executives Institute, the Midwest Finance Association, and the FMA National Honor Society. In addition, he is a Certified Financial Planner® (CFP®). Gitman formerly served as a director on the CFP® Board of Governors, as vice-president–financial education for the Financial Management Association, and as director of the San Diego MIT Enterprise Forum. He has two grown children and lives with his wife in La Jolla, California, where he is an avid bicyclist.

Michael D. Joehnk is an emeritus professor of finance at Arizona State University (ASU). In addition to his academic appointments at ASU, Professor Joehnk spent a year (1999) as a visiting professor of finance at the University of Otago in New Zealand. He received his bachelor's and Ph.D. degrees from the University of Arizona and his M.B.A. from Arizona State University. A Chartered Financial Analyst (CFA), he has served as a member of the Candidate Curriculum Committee and of the Council of Examiners of the Institute of Chartered Financial Analysts. He has also served as a director of the Phoenix Society of Financial Analysts and as secretary-treasurer of the Western Finance Association, and he was elected to two terms as a vice-president of the Financial Management Association. Professor Joehnk is the author or co-author of some 50 articles, five books, and numerous monographs. His articles have appeared in *Financial Management*, the *Journal of Finance*, the *Journal of Bank Research*, the *Journal of Portfolio Management*, the *Journal of Consumer Affairs*, the *Journal of Financial and Quantitative Analysis*, the *AAII Journal,* the *Journal of Financial Research*, the *Bell Journal of Economics*, the *Daily Bond Buyer*, *Financial Planner,* and other publications.

In addition to co-authoring several books with Lawrence J. Gitman, Professor Joehnk was the author of a highly successful paperback trade book, *Investing for Safety's Sake*. In addition, Dr. Joehnk was the editor of *Institutional Asset Allocation*, which was sponsored by the Institute of Chartered Financial Analysts and published by Dow Jones–Irwin. He also was a contributor to the *Handbook for Fixed Income Securities* and to *Investing and Risk Management*, volume 1 of the Library of Investment Banking. In addition, he served a six-year term as executive co-editor of the *Journal of Financial Research*. He and his wife live in Flagstaff, Arizona, where they enjoy hiking and other activities in the nearby mountains and canyons.

PART 1

Foundations of Financial Planning

CHAPTERS

1 Understanding the Financial Planning Process
2 Using Financial Statements and Budgets
3 Preparing Your Taxes

Understanding the Financial Planning Process

LEARNING GOALS

LG1 Identify the benefits of using personal financial planning techniques to manage your finances.

LG2 Describe the personal financial planning process and define your goals.

LG3 Explain the life cycle of financial plans, their role in achieving your financial goals, how to deal with special planning concerns, and the use of professional financial planners.

LG4 Examine the economic environment's influence on personal financial planning.

LG5 Evaluate the impact of age, education, and geographic location on personal income.

LG6 Understand the importance of career choices and their relationship to personal financial planning.

How Will This Affect Me?

The heart of financial planning is making sure your values line up with how you spend and save. That means knowing where you are financially and planning on how to get where you want to be in the future no matter what life throws at you. For example, how should your plan handle the projection that Social Security costs may exceed revenues by 2037? And what if the government decides to raise tax rates to help cover the federal deficit? An informed financial plan should reflect such uncertainties and more.

This chapter overviews the financial planning process and explains its context. Topics include how financial plans change to accommodate your current stage in life and the role that financial planners can play in helping you achieve your objectives. After reading this chapter you will have a good perspective on how to organize your overall personal financial plan.

Financial Fact or Fantasy?

Are the following statements Financial Facts (true) or Fantasies (false)? Consider these statements as you read through this chapter.

- An improved standard of living is one of the payoffs of sound personal financial planning.
- A savings account is an example of a tangible asset because it represents something on deposit at a bank or other financial institution.
- Personal financial planning involves translating personal financial goals into specific plans and strategies that put these plans into action.
- Over the long-run, gaining only an extra percent or two on an investment makes little difference in the amount of earnings generated.
- Inflation generally has little effect on personal financial planning.
- Your income level depends on your age, education, and career choice.

1-1 THE REWARDS OF SOUND FINANCIAL PLANNING

What does living "the good life" mean to you? Does it mean having the flexibility to pursue your dreams and goals in life? Is it owning a home in a certain part of town, starting a company, being debt free, driving a particular type of car, taking luxury vacations, or having a large investment portfolio? Today's complex, fast-paced world offers a bewildering array of choices. Rapidly changing economic, political, technological, and social environments make it increasingly difficult to develop solid financial strategies that will improve your lifestyle consistently. Moreover, the recent financial crisis dramatizes the need to plan for financial contingencies. Today, a couple may need two incomes just to maintain an acceptable standard of living, and they may have to wait longer to buy a home. Clearly, no matter how you define it, the good life requires sound planning to turn financial goals into reality.

The best way to achieve financial objectives is through *personal financial planning*, which helps define financial goals and develop appropriate strategies to reach them. We should not depend solely on employee or government benefits—such as steady salary increases or adequate funding from employer-paid pensions or Social Security—to retire comfortably. Creating flexible plans and regularly revising them is the key to building a sound financial future. Successful financial planning also brings rewards that include greater flexibility, an improved standard of living, wise spending habits, and increased wealth. Of course, planning alone does not guarantee success; but having an effective, consistent plan can help you use your resources wisely. Careful financial planning increases the chance that your financial goals will be achieved and that you will have sufficient flexibility to handle such contingencies as illness, job loss, and even financial crises.

The goal of this book is to remove the mystery from the personal financial planning process and replace it with the tools you need to take charge of your personal finances and your life. To organize this process, the text is divided into six parts as follows.

- Part 1: Foundations of Financial Planning
- Part 2: Managing Basic Assets
- Part 3: Managing Credit
- Part 4: Managing Insurance Needs
- Part 5: Managing Investments
- Part 6: Retirement and Estate Planning

FINANCIAL PLANNING TIPS

Be SMART in Planning Your Financial Goals

Success is most likely if your goals are:

Specific: What do I want to achieve? What is required of me and what are my constraints?

Measurable: How much money is needed? How will I know if I am succeeding?

Attainable: How can I do this? Is this consistent with my other financial goals?

Realistic: Am I willing and able to do this?

Timely: What is my target date? What short-term goals must be achieved along the way to achieve my longer term goals?

Source: Inspired by Paul J. Meyer's, *Attitude Is Everything*, The Meyer Resource Group, 2003.

Each part explains a different aspect of personal financial planning, as shown in Exhibit 1.1. This organizational scheme revolves around financial decision making that's firmly based on an operational set of financial plans. We believe that sound financial planning enables individuals to make decisions that will yield their desired results. Starting with Part 1—where we look at personal financial statements, plans, and taxes—we move through the various types of decisions you'll make when implementing a financial plan.

1-1a Improving Your Standard of Living

standard of living
The necessities, comforts, and luxuries enjoyed or desired by an individual or family.

With personal financial planning we learn to acquire, use, and control our financial resources more efficiently. It allows us to gain more enjoyment from our income and thus to improve our standard of living—the necessities, comforts, and luxuries we have or desire.

Americans view standards of living, and what constitute necessities or luxuries, differently depending on their level of affluence. For example, 45 percent of Americans consider a second or vacation home the ultimate symbol of affluence, while others see taking two or more annual vacations or living in an exclusive neighborhood as an indicator of wealth.

So our quality of life is closely tied to our standard of living. Although other factors—geographic location, public facilities, local cost of living, pollution, traffic, and population density—also affect quality of life, wealth is commonly viewed as a key determinant. Material items such as a house, car, and clothing, as well as money available for health care, education, art, music, travel, and entertainment, all contribute to our quality of life. Of course, many so-called wealthy people live "plain" lives, choosing to save, invest, or support philanthropic organizations with their money rather than indulge themselves with luxuries.

One trend with a profound effect on our standard of living is the *two-income family*. What was relatively rare in the early 1970s has become commonplace today, and the incomes of millions of families have risen sharply as a result. About 75 percent

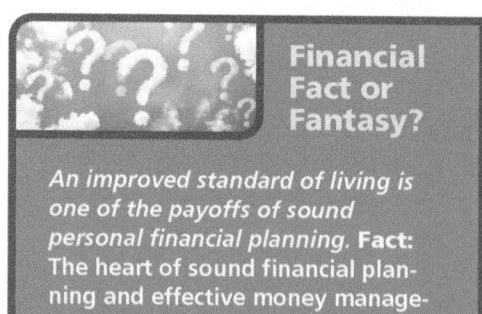

Financial Fact or Fantasy?

An improved standard of living is one of the payoffs of sound personal financial planning. **Fact:** The heart of sound financial planning and effective money management is the greater enjoyment of the money one makes by improving one's standard of living.

EXHIBIT 1.1   **Organizational Planning Model**

This text emphasizes making financial decisions regarding assets, credit, insurance, investments, and retirement and estates.

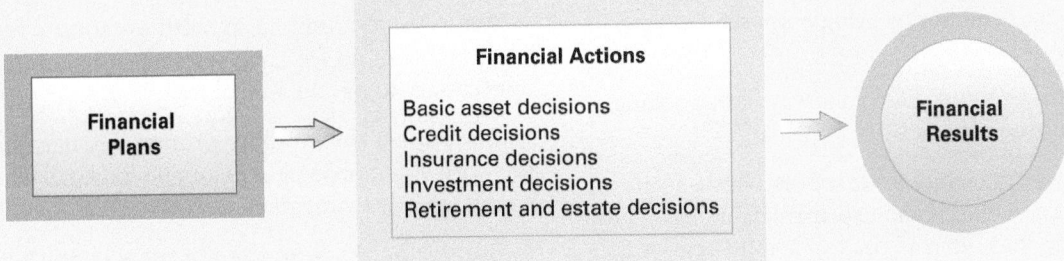

of married adults say that they and their mate share all their money, while some partners admit to having a secret stash of cash. Two incomes buy more, but they also require greater responsibility to manage the money wisely.

1-1b Spending Money Wisely

Using money wisely is a major benefit of financial planning. Whatever your income, you can either spend it now or save some of it for the future. Determining your current and future spending patterns is an important part of personal money management. The goal, of course, is to spend your money so that you get the most satisfaction from each dollar.

Current Needs

average propensity to consume
The percentage of each dollar of income, on average, that a person spends for current needs rather than savings.

Your current spending level is based on the necessities of life and your average propensity to consume, which is the percentage of each dollar of income, on average, that is spent for current needs rather than savings. A minimum level of spending would allow you to obtain only the necessities of life: food, clothing, and shelter. Although the quantity and type of food, clothing, and shelter purchased may differ among individuals depending on their wealth, we all need these items to survive. Some people with high average propensities to consume earn low incomes and spend a large portion of it on basic necessities. On the other hand, many "ultra-consumers" choose to splurge on a few items and scrimp elsewhere; these people also exhibit high average propensities to consume. Conversely, individuals earning large amounts quite often have low average propensities to consume, in part because the cost of necessities represents only a small portion of their income.

Still, two people with significantly different incomes could have the same average propensity to consume because of differences in their standard of living. The person making more money may believe it is essential to buy better-quality items or more items and will thus, on average, spend the same percentage of each dollar of income as the person making far less.

Future Needs

A carefully developed financial plan should set aside a portion of current income for deferred, future spending. Placing these funds in various savings and investment vehicles allows you to generate a return on your funds until you need them. For example, you may want to build up a retirement fund to maintain a desirable

FINANCIAL PLANNING TIPS

Ways to Save More Money

You can save more money by being purposeful in your spending.

- **Cook at home more.** Ease your way in by cooking at home at least once a week.

- **Make rather than buy your coffee.** While a latte is great, we all know that it's an expensive habit. Don't stop cold—just skip it as often as you can and make your coffee at home instead.

- **Take your lunch to work.** Lunch with coworkers may be the norm and a wise way to build helpful relationships. So it may not be practical to take your lunch all of the time. But it will save you money to take your lunch at least occasionally.

- **Avoid late fees by paying your bills on time.** You can have many bills like utilities paid automatically so there is no reason to pay late fees.

- **Avoid ATM fees.** Many banks do not waive ATM withdrawal fees. Be sure to use ATMs that do not charge a fee.

- **Avoid using credit cards with an annual fee.** The number of no-fee cards with reward plans makes it unnecessary to pay an annual fee.

- **Disconnect the landline phone.** You may do just fine with you mobile phones and no landline, which would save you some money.

- **Borrow books from the library and don't buy them.** Library cards are free and the book and media selection is usually up-to-date.

- **Don't buy bottled water, bottle your own.** Buy bottled water only occasionally just so you can get the bottle to fill with your own water.

- **Drive your car a long time.** Keep your car until the repair costs and questionable reliability make it necessary to find a replacement.

Source: Adapted from Sam Baker of GradMoneyMatters.com, republished June 19, 2011, http://www.dumblittleman.com/2008/01/30-easy-ways-to-save-money-and-no-you.html, accessed July 2015.

standard of living in your later years. Instead of spending the money now, you defer actual spending until the future when you retire. Nearly 35 percent of Americans say retirement planning is their most pressing financial concern. Other examples of deferred spending include saving for a child's education, a primary residence or vacation home, a major acquisition (such as a car or home entertainment center), or even a vacation.

The portion of current income we commit to future needs depends on how much we earn and also on our average propensity to consume. About two-thirds of affluent Americans say they need at least $5 million to feel rich. The more we earn and the less we devote to current spending, the more we can commit to meeting future needs. In any case, some portion of current income should be set aside regularly for future use. This practice creates good saving habits.

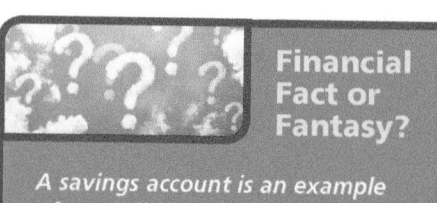

Financial Fact or Fantasy?

A savings account is an example of a tangible asset because it represents something on deposit at a bank or other financial institution.

Fantasy: A savings account, like stocks, bonds, and mutual funds, is an example of a financial asset—an intangible, a "paper" asset. Real assets, in contrast, refer to tangibles—physical items like houses, cars, and appliances.

1-1c Accumulating Wealth

In addition to using current income to pay for everyday living expenses, we often spend it to acquire assets such as cars, a home, or stocks and bonds. Our assets largely determine how wealthy we are. Personal financial planning plays a critical role in the accumulation of wealth by directing our financial resources to the most productive areas.

EXHIBIT 1.2 **The Average American, Financially Speaking**

This financial snapshot of the "average American" gives you an idea of where you stand in terms of income, net worth, and other measures. It should help you set some goals for the future.

	Income and Assets
What Do We Earn? (*median*)	
All families	$ 46,700
What Are We Worth? (*median*)	
All families	81,200
Home Ownership (*median*)	
Value of primary residence	170,000
Mortgage on primary residence	115,000
How Much Savings Do We Have? (*median*)	80,000
Pooled investment funds (excluding money market)	27,000
Individual stocks	94,500
Bonds	20,100
Bank accounts/CDs	
Retirement accounts	59,000

Source: Adapted from Jesse Bricker, Lisa J. Dettling, Alice Henriques, Joanne W. Hsu, Kevin B. Moore, John Sabelhaus, Jeffrey Thompson, and Richard A. Windle, "Changes in U.S. Family Finances from 2010 to 2013: Evidence from the Survey of Consumer Finances," Board of Governors of the Federal Reserve System, Washington, DC, (October 24, 2014, data is for 2013), http://www.federalreserve.gov/pubs/bulletin/2014/pdf/scf14.pdf, Tables 1–4, accessed July 2015.

wealth
The total value of all items owned by an individual, such as savings accounts, stocks, bonds, home, and automobiles.

financial assets
Intangible assets, such as savings accounts and securities, that are acquired for some promised future return.

tangible assets
Physical assets, such as real estate and automobiles that can be held for either consumption or investment purposes.

One's **wealth** is the net total value of all the items the individual owns. Wealth consists of financial and tangible assets. **Financial assets** are intangible, paper assets, such as savings accounts and securities (stocks, bonds, mutual funds, and so forth). They are *earning assets* that are held for the returns they promise. **Tangible assets**, in contrast, are physical assets, such as real estate and automobiles. These assets can be held for either consumption (e.g., your home, car, artwork, or jewelry) or investment purposes (e.g., a duplex purchased for rental income). In general, the goal of most people is to accumulate as much wealth as possible while maintaining current consumption at a level that provides the desired standard of living. To see how you compare with the typical American in financial terms, check out the statistics in Exhibit 1.2.

TEST YOURSELF

1-1 What is a *standard of living*? What factors affect the quality of life?

1-2 Are consumption patterns related to quality of life? Explain.

1-3 What is *average propensity to consume*? Is it possible for two people with very different incomes to have the same average propensity to consume? Why?

1-4 Discuss the various forms in which wealth can be accumulated.

personal financial planning
A systematic process that considers important elements of an individual's financial affairs in order to fulfill financial goals.

Many people mistakenly assume that personal financial planning is only for the wealthy. However, nothing could be further from the truth. Whether you have a lot of money or not enough, you still need personal financial planning. If you have enough money, planning can help you spend and invest it wisely. If your income seems inadequate, taking steps to plan your financial activities will lead to an improved lifestyle. **Personal financial planning** is a systematic process that considers the important elements of an individual's financial affairs and is aimed at fulfilling his or her financial goals.

Everyone—including recent college graduates, single professionals, young married couples, single parents, mid-career married couples, and senior corporate executives—needs to develop a personal financial plan. Knowing what you need to accomplish financially, and how you intend to do it, gives you an edge over someone who merely reacts to financial events as they unfold. Just think of the example provided by the recent financial crisis. Do you think that a financial plan would have helped in weathering the financial storm?

Purchasing a new car immediately after graduation may be an important goal for you. But buying a car is a major expenditure involving a large initial cash outlay and additional consumer debt that must be repaid over time. It therefore warrants careful planning. Evaluating (and possibly even arranging) financing before your shopping trip, as opposed to simply accepting the financing arrangements offered by an auto dealer, could save you a considerable amount of money. Moreover, some dealers advertise low-interest loans but charge higher prices for their cars. Knowing all your costs in advance can help you find the best deal. Using personal financial planning concepts to reach all your financial goals will bring similar positive benefits.

Behavior Matters

Practicing Financial Self-Awareness

Are you aware of your financial behavior, its causes, and its consequences? For example, are you routinely relying too heavily on your credit card, which puts you more in debt? Are you saving enough to buy a new car or to fund your retirement? And the bottom line: Are you continuing the same financial behavior you have in the past and yet expecting different results?

The first decisive step in taking control of your life is to be aware of what you're thinking, feeling, and doing. Be financially self-aware: observe your own thoughts, feelings, and behavior concerning your finances. Take notes on things that affect how you feel and what you do about financial decisions. Watch yourself and be honest about your feelings concerning money and your future.

Then ask yourself two critically important questions:

- **Is the way I spend money consistent with what I believe?** Financial planning that works is taking the time to develop a plan that purposely lines up your values and your use of money.

- **Have I clearly stated the financial goals that are important to me and, if so, what am I doing today to make sure I achieve them?** The heart of financial planning is determining where you are today and where you want to be in the future. This implies the need for a financial plan: limited resources sometimes bring painful trade-offs.

Source: Adapted from Carl Richards, "Practicing Radical Self-Awareness," Behaviorgap.com. http://us2.campaign-archive1.com/?u=23ce2ac179e8158f 7583c4e3f&id=86f42577bc&e=b50e826a9e, accessed July 2015.

| EXHIBIT 1.3 | The Six-Step Financial Planning Process |

The financial planning process translates personal financial goals into specific financial plans and strategies, implements them, and then uses budgets and financial statements to monitor, evaluate, and revise plans and strategies as needed. This process typically involves the six steps shown in sequence here:

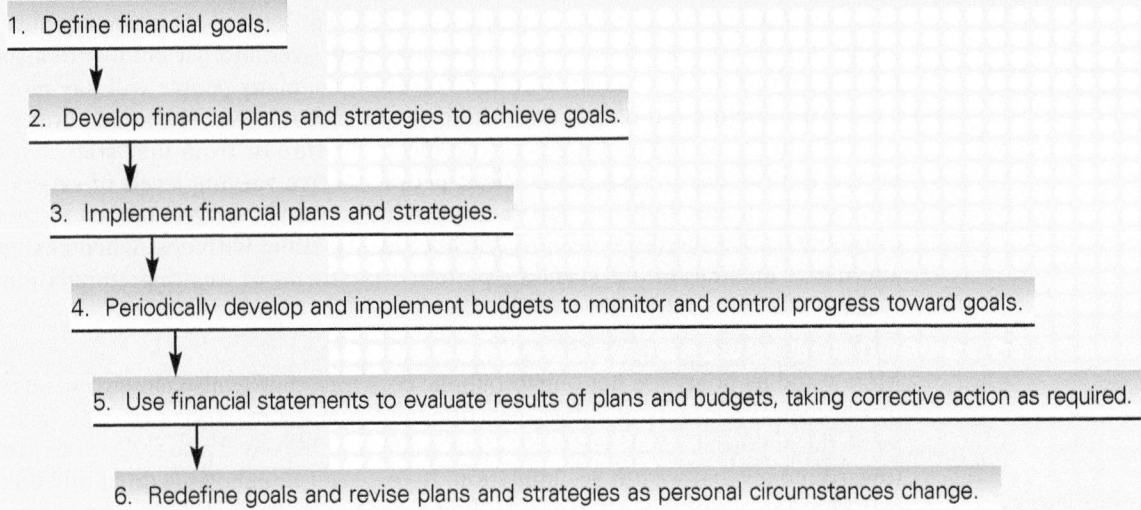

1. Define financial goals.

2. Develop financial plans and strategies to achieve goals.

3. Implement financial plans and strategies.

4. Periodically develop and implement budgets to monitor and control progress toward goals.

5. Use financial statements to evaluate results of plans and budgets, taking corrective action as required.

6. Redefine goals and revise plans and strategies as personal circumstances change.

1-2a Steps in the Financial Planning Process

If you take a closer look at financial planning, you'll see that the process translates personal financial goals into specific financial plans, which then helps you implement those plans through financial strategies. The financial planning process involves the six steps shown in Exhibit 1.3.

The financial planning process runs full circle. You start with financial goals, formulate and implement financial plans and strategies to reach them, monitor and control progress toward goals through budgets, and use financial statements to evaluate the plan and budget results. This leads you back to redefining your goals so that they better meet your current needs and to revising your financial plans and strategies accordingly.

Let's now look at how goal setting fits into the planning process. In Chapters 2 and 3, we'll consider other information essential to creating your financial plans: personal financial statements, budgets, and taxes.

1-2b Defining Your Financial Goals

financial goals
Results that an individual wants to attain, such as buying a home, building a college fund, or achieving financial independence.

Financial goals are the results that an individual wants to attain. Examples include buying a home, building a college fund, or achieving financial independence. What are your financial goals? Have you spelled them out? It's impossible to effectively manage your financial resources without financial goals. We need to know where we are going, in a financial sense, to effectively meet the major financial events in our lives. Perhaps achieving financial independence at a relatively early age is important to you. If so, then saving, investing, and retirement planning will be an important part of your financial life. Your financial goals or preferences must be stated in monetary terms because money and the satisfaction it can bring are an integral part of financial planning.

The Role of Money

money
The medium of exchange used as a measure of value in financial transactions.

About 75 percent of Americans believe that money is freedom. **Money** is the medium of exchange used to measure value in financial transactions. It would be difficult to set specific personal financial goals and to measure progress toward achieving them without the standard unit of exchange provided by the dollar. Money, as we know it today, is the key consideration in establishing financial goals. Yet it's not money, as such, that most people want. Rather, we want the **utility**, which is the amount of satisfaction received from buying quantities of goods and services of a given quality that money makes possible. People may choose one item over another because of a special feature that provides additional utility. For example, many people will pay more for a car with satellite radio than one with only an audio player. The added utility may result from the actual usefulness of the special feature or from the "status" it's expected to provide, or both. Regardless, people receive varying levels of satisfaction from similar items, and their satisfaction isn't necessarily directly related to the cost of the items. We therefore need to consider utility along with cost when evaluating alternative qualities of life, spending patterns, and forms of wealth accumulation.

utility
The amount of satisfaction received from purchasing certain types or quantities of goods and services.

The Psychology of Money

Money and its utility are not only economic concepts; they're also closely linked to the psychological concepts of values, emotion, and personality. Your personal value system—the important ideals and beliefs that guide your life—will also shape your attitude toward money and wealth accumulation. If you place a high value on family life, you may choose a career that offers regular hours and less stress or choose an employer who offers flextime rather than a higher-paying position that requires travel and lots of overtime. You may have plenty of money but choose to live frugally and do things yourself rather than hire someone to do them for you. Or you may spend a high proportion of your current income on acquiring luxuries. Financial goals and decisions should be consistent with your personal values. You can formulate financial plans that provide the greatest personal satisfaction and quality of life by identifying your values.

Money is an important motivator of personal behavior because it has a strong effect on self-image. Each person's unique personality and emotional makeup determine the importance and role of money in his or her life. Depending on timing and circumstances, emotional responses to money may be positive (love, happiness, security) or negative (fear, greed, insecurity). For example, some people feel satisfaction in their work when they receive a paycheck. Others feel relief in knowing that they can pay past-due bills. You should become aware of your own attitudes toward money because they are the basis of your "money personality" and money management style. Exhibit 1.4 explores attitudes toward money.

Some questions to ask yourself include: How important is money to me? Why? What types of spending give me satisfaction? Am I a risk taker? Do I need large financial reserves to feel secure? Knowing the answers to these questions is a prerequisite for developing realistic and effective financial goals and plans. For example, if you prefer immediate satisfaction, then you will find it more difficult to achieve long-term net worth or savings goals than if you are highly disciplined and primarily concerned with achieving a comfortable retirement at an early age. Trade-offs between current and future benefits are strongly affected by values, emotions, and personality. Effective financial plans are both economically and psychologically sound. They must not only consider your wants, needs, and financial resources, but must also realistically reflect your personality and emotional reactions to money.

1-2c Money and Relationships

The average couple spends between 250 and 700 hours planning their wedding. While most couples spend less than $10,000 on the big day, the average cost has risen to almost $30,000, depending on where they live. But with all the hoopla surrounding the wedding day, many couples overlook one of the most important aspects

Our attitudes toward money influence how we spend, save, and invest. Which of the following attitudes toward money best describes you? You may be predominately one type or a combination of types.

The Spender: You only live once
Spenders see shopping as entertainment. They would rather have something tangible than something intangible like savings or an investment. Spenders have a hard time saving money.

The Builder: Make it so
Builders see money as a tool. They use money to achieve their goals and dreams. Examples include self-made millionaires, entrepreneurs, corporate leaders, and dedicated hobbyists. Builders can miscalculate risks or ignore the need for a margin of error. They may start projects simply for the challenge but not finish them as the next new thing beckons.

The Giver: It's better to give than to receive
Givers enjoy taking care of other people. They volunteer and give to charities. Givers commit their time, energy, and money to their beliefs. Most givers simply enjoy making other people happy and doing good deeds. Givers sometimes ignore their own needs, and their long-term financial plans can suffer as a result.

The Saver: A bird in the hand is worth two in the bush
Savers can accumulate significant wealth even on a modest income. They tend to be organized and to avoid money-wasting activities. Although savers can be good investors, they can be too risk averse and prefer holding too much cash. Such conservatism means that their investments often grow too slowly.

Source: Adapted from Diane McCurdy, CFP, *How Much Is Enough?* (John Wiley & Sons, 2005). Copyright © 2005 by John Wiley & Sons. All rights reserved. Reproduced by permission.

of marriage: financial compatibility. Money can be one of the most emotional issues in any relationship, including that with a partner, your parents, or children. Most people are uncomfortable talking about money matters and avoid such discussions, even with their partners. However, differing opinions on how to spend money may threaten the stability of a marriage or cause arguments between parents and children. Learning to communicate with your partner about money is a critical step in developing effective financial plans.

Your parents should play an important role in your financial planning. As they age, you may have to assume greater responsibility for their care. Do you know what health care coverage and financial plans they have in place? Where do they keep important financial and legal documents? What preferences do they have for health care should they become incapacitated? Asking these questions may be difficult, but having the answers will save you many headaches.

The best way to resolve money disputes is to be aware of your partner's financial style, consistently communicate openly, and be willing to compromise. It's unlikely that you can change your partner's style, but you can work out your differences. Financial planning is an especially important part of the conflict resolution process.

1-2d Types of Financial Goals

Financial goals cover a wide range of financial aspirations: controlling living expenses, meeting retirement needs, setting up a savings and investment program, and minimizing your taxes. Other important financial goals include having enough money to live as well as possible now, being financially independent, sending children to college, and providing for retirement.

EXHIBIT 1.5 | **Check Your Financial Planning Assumptions**

It's important to make sure that your financial planning assumptions are realistic. Consider these common assumptions.

Assumption 1: Saving a few thousand dollars a year should provide enough to fund my child's college education.

Reality: The College Board reports that the average increase in tuition and fees over the last decade has been 5 percent, which is about twice the rate of inflation. If this rate of increase continues, the average 4-year cost of tuition and fees for a child born in 2014 will be about $323,900 for a private school and $94,800 for an in-state public education. And that doesn't consider the cost of room and board. That's more than a few thousand dollars to save each year!

Assumption 2: An emergency fund lasting 3 months should be adequate.

Reality: Tell that to the average unemployed person in the United States in 2011 who looked for work for over 9 months. While this is the longest average duration of unemployment since 1948, it would be wise to keep an emergency fund that covers 6 to 9 months.

Assumption 3: I will be able to retire at 65 and should have plenty to live on in retirement.

Reality: The average 65-year old man can expect to live to about 84 and a 65-year old woman can expect to live to about 87. That planning horizon could easily leave you short on funding. So it would be wise to determine how much you need to set aside to fund a realistic life expectancy horizon. This might imply saving more now, retiring later, or working part-time after retirement.

Assumption 4: I'm relying on the rule of thumb that I will need only 70 percent of my pre-retirement income to manage nicely in retirement.

Reality: Like all rules of thumb, one size does not necessarily fit all. While it's true that you won't have work-related expenses in retirement, you're likely to have much higher health care costs. And it's important to consider long-term care insurance to protect against such high costs. So betting on 70 percent could leave you short.

Sources: Adapted from http://www.savingforcollege.com/tutorial101/the_real_cost_of_higher_education.php, http://economix.blogs.nytimes.com/2011/06/03/average-length-of-unemployment-at-all-time-high/, accessed July 2015.

Financial goals should be defined as specifically as possible. Saying that you want to save money next year is not a specific goal. How much do you want to save, and for what purpose? A goal such as "save 10 percent of my take-home pay each month to start an investment program" states clearly what you want to do and why.

Because they are the basis of your financial plans, your goals should be realistic and attainable. If you set your savings goals too high—for example, 25 percent of your take-home pay when your basic living expenses already account for 85 percent of it—then your goal is unattainable and there's no way to meet it. But if savings goals are set too low, you may not accumulate enough for a meaningful investment program. If your goals are unrealistic, they'll put the basic integrity of your financial plan at risk and be a source of ongoing financial frustration. You must also use realistic assumptions when setting goals. Exhibit 1.5 will help you do a reality check.

It's important to involve your immediate family in the goal-setting process. When family members "buy into" the goals, it eliminates the potential for future conflicts and improves the family's chances for financial success. After defining and approving your goals, you can prepare appropriate cash budgets. Finally, you should assign priorities and a time frame to financial goals. Are they short-term goals for the next year, or are they intermediate or long-term goals that will not be achieved for many

EXHIBIT 1.6 — How Financial Goals Change with a Person's Life Situation

Financial goals are not static; they change continually over a lifetime. Here are some typical long-term, intermediate, and short-term goals for a number of different personal situations.

Personal Situation	Long-Term Goals (6+ years)	Intermediate Goals (2–5 years)	Short-Term Goals (1 year)
College senior	Begin an investment program Buy a townhouse Earn a master's degree	Repay college loans Trade in car and upgrade to a nicer model Buy new furniture	Find a job Rent an apartment Get a bank credit card Buy a new stereo
Single, mid-20s	Begin law school Build an investment portfolio Save enough for a down payment on a home	Begin regular savings program Take a Caribbean vacation Buy life insurance Start a retirement fund	Prepare a budget Buy a new flat-screen television Get additional job training Build an emergency fund Reduce expenses by 10 percent
Married couple with children, late 30s	Diversify investment portfolio Buy a larger home	Buy a second car Increase college fund contributions Increase second income from part-time to full-time	Repaint house Get braces for children Review life and disability insurance
Married couple with grown children, mid-50s	Decide whether to relocate when retired Retire at age 62 Travel to Europe and the Far East	Take cruise Shift investment portfolio into income-producing securities Sell house and buy smaller residence	Buy new furniture Review skills for possible career change

more years? For example, saving for a vacation might be a medium-priority short-term goal, whereas buying a larger home may be a high-priority intermediate goal and purchasing a vacation home a low-priority long-term goal. Normally, long-term financial goals are set first, followed by a series of corresponding short-term and intermediate goals. Your goals will continue to change with your life situation, as Exhibit 1.6 demonstrates.

1-2e Putting Target Dates on Financial Goals

goal dates
Target dates in the future when certain financial objectives are expected to be completed.

Financial goals are most effective when they are set with goal dates. Goal dates are target points in the future when you expect to have achieved or completed certain financial objectives. They may serve as progress checkpoints toward some longer-term financial goals and/or as deadlines for others.

EXAMPLE: Target Dates for Financial Goals

Jim and Stacy Thompson are both 28 and have been married for one year. They have set financial goals of buying a boat for $3,000 in 2018, accumulate a net worth of $10,000 by 2022, and accumulate a net worth of $50,000 by 2030.

Long-Term Goals

Long-term financial goals should indicate wants and desires for a period covering about 6 years out to the next 30 or 40 years. Although it's difficult to pinpoint exactly what you will want 30 years from now, it's useful to establish some tentative long-term financial goals. However, you should recognize that long-term goals will change over time and that you'll need to revise them accordingly. If the goals seem too ambitious, you'll want to make them more realistic. If they're too conservative, you'll want to adjust them to a level that encourages you to make financially responsible decisions rather than squander surplus funds.

Short-Term Goals and Intermediate Goals

Short-term financial goals are set each year and cover a 12-month period. They include making substantial, regular contributions to savings or investments in order to accumulate your desired net worth. Intermediate goals bridge the gap between short- and long-term goals, and both intermediate and short-term goals should be consistent with those long-term goals. Short-term goals become the key input for the cash budget, a tool used to plan for short-term income and expenses. To define your short-term goals, consider your immediate goals, expected income for the year, and long-term goals. Short-term planning should also include establishing an emergency fund with at least 6 to 9 months' worth of income. This special savings account serves as a safety reserve in case of financial emergencies such as a temporary loss of income.

Unless you attain your short-term goals, you probably won't achieve your intermediate or long-term goals. It's tempting to let the desire to spend now take priority over the need to save for the future. But by making some short-term sacrifices now, you're more likely to have a comfortable future. If you don't realize this for another 10 or 20 years, then you may discover that it's too late to reach some of your most important financial goals.

Worksheet 1.1 is a convenient way to summarize your personal financial goals. It groups them by time frame (short-term, intermediate, or long-term) and lists a priority for each goal (high, medium, or low), a target date to reach the goal, and an estimated cost.

We have filled out the form showing the goals that Simon and Meghan Kane set in December 2016. The Kanes were married in 2017, own a condominium in a Midwestern suburb, and have no children. Because Simon and Meghan are 28 and 26 years old, respectively, they have set their longest-term financial goal 33 years from now, when they want to retire. Simon has just completed his fifth year as an electrical engineer. Meghan, a former elementary school teacher, finished her MBA in May

Financial Fact or Fantasy?

Personal financial planning involves translating personal financial goals into specific plans and arrangements that put these plans into action.
Fact: Personal financial plans are based on the specific financial goals that you set for yourself and your family. Once in place, the plans are put into action using the various financial strategies explained in this book.

Do It Now

Start a List of Your Financial Goals

Yogi Berra summed it up: "If you don't know where you're going, you might not get there." And so it is with your financial goals. Pick up some paper now and start a list of your financial goals. May be it's as simple as saving $25 by the end of the month or as lofty as saving $200,000 for retirement by the time you're 50. You'll never achieve your goals if you don't know what they are, much less know whether they're realistic. Go ahead and dream. List your goals (short-term, intermediate, and long-term) and start laying out how you'll get there. You can do it now.

2015 and began working at a local advertising agency. Simon and Meghan love to travel and ski. They plan to start a family in a few years, but for now they want to develop some degree of financial stability and independence. Their goals include purchasing assets (clothes, stereo, furniture, and car), reducing debt, reviewing insurance, increasing savings, and planning for retirement.

| WORKSHEET 1.1 | Summary of Personal Financial Goals |

Set financial goals carefully and realistically, because they form the basis for your personal financial plans. Each goal should be clearly defined and have a priority, time frame, and cost estimate.

Personal Financial Goals

Name(s) Simon and Meghan Kane   Date December 27, 2016

Short-Term Goals (1 year or less)

Goal	Priority	Target Date	Cost Estimate $
Buy new tires and brakes for Ford Focus	High	Feb. 2017	500
Take Colorado ski trip	Medium	Mar. 2017	1,800
Buy career clothes for Meghan	High	May 2017	1,200
Buy new work cloths for Simon	Medium	June 2017	750
Replace stereo components	Low	Sept. 2017	1,100

Intermediate Goals (2 to 5 years)

Goal	Priority	Target Date	Cost Estimate $
Start family	High	2018	–
Take 2-week Hawaiian vacation	Medium	2018 – 19	5,000
Repay all loans except mortgage	High	2019	7,500
Trade Focus and buy larger car	High	2019	10,500
Review insurance needs	High	2019	–
Accumulate $10,000 net worth	High	2019	–
Buy new bedroom furniture	Low	2021	4,000

Long-Term Goals (61 years)

Goal	Priority	Target Date	Cost Estimate $
Begin college fund for children	High	2022	? /year
Diversify/increase investment portfolio	High	2023	varies
Take European vacation	Low	2024	10,000
Increase college fund contributions	High	2024	–
Accumulate $50,000 net worth	High	2024	–
Buy larger home	High	2025	250,000
Accumulate $100,000 net worth	High	2034	–
Retire from jobs	High	2049	?

1-3 FROM GOALS TO PLANS: A LIFETIME OF PLANNING

LG3

How will you achieve the financial goals you set for yourself? The answer, of course, lies in the financial plans you establish. Financial plans provide the roadmap for achieving your financial goals. The six-step financial planning process (introduced in Exhibit 1.3) results in separate yet interrelated components covering all the important financial elements in your life. Some elements deal with the more immediate aspects of money management, such as preparing a budget to help manage spending. Others focus on acquiring major assets, controlling borrowing, reducing financial risk, providing for emergency funds and future wealth accumulation, taking advantage of and managing employer-sponsored benefits, deferring and minimizing taxes, providing for financial security when you stop working, and ensuring an orderly and cost-effective transfer of assets to your heirs.

In addition to discussing your financial goals and attitudes toward money with your partner, you must allocate responsibility for money management tasks and decisions. Many couples make major decisions jointly and divide routine financial decision-making on the basis of expertise and interest. Others believe it is important for their entire family to work together as a team to manage the family finances. They hold family financial meetings once every few months to help their children understand how the household money is spent. These meetings also serve as a forum for children to request a raise in allowance, a new bike, or funds for a school trip. The entire family is involved in the decision-making process on how surplus funds will be allocated.

ARIEL SKELLEY/JUPITER IMAGES

Giving children an allowance is a good way to start teaching them to budget and save. By setting their own financial goals and taking steps to reach them, they will develop their own money management skills.

1-3a The Life Cycle of Financial Plans

Financial planning is a dynamic process. As you move through different stages of your life, your needs and goals will change. Yet certain financial goals are important regardless of age. Having extra resources to fall back on in an economic downturn or period of unemployment should be a priority whether you are 25, 45, or 65. Some changes—a new job, marriage, children, moving to a new area—may be part of your original plan.

More often than not, you'll face unexpected "financial shocks" during your life: loss of a job, a car accident, divorce or death of a spouse, a long illness, or the need to support adult children or aging parents. With careful planning, you can get through tough times and prosper in good times. You need to plan ahead and take steps to weather life's financial storms successfully. For example, setting up an emergency fund or reducing monthly expenses will help protect you and your family financially if a setback occurs.

As we move from childhood to retirement age, we traditionally go through different life stages. Exhibit 1.7 illustrates the various components of a typical *personal financial planning life cycle* as they relate to these different life stages. This exhibit presents the organizing framework of the entire financial planning process. We will refer to it in every chapter of the book—as we suggest that you do for the rest of your life. As we pass from one stage of maturation to the next, our patterns of income, home ownership, and debt also change. From early childhood, when we rely on our parents for support, to early adulthood, when we hold our first jobs and start our families, we can see a noticeable change in income patterns. For example, those in the 45–64 age range tend to have higher income than those younger than age 45. Thus, as our emphasis in life changes, so do the kinds of financial plans we need to pursue.

Today, new career strategies—planned and unplanned job changes—are common and may require that financial plans be revised. Many young people focus on their careers and building a financial base before marrying and having children. The families of women who interrupt their careers to stay home with their children, whether for

EXHIBIT 1.7   The Personal Financial Planning Life Cycle

As you move through life and your income patterns change, you'll typically have to pursue a variety of financial plans. For instance, after graduating from college your focus likely will be on buying a car and a house, and you'll be concerned about health and automobile insurance to protect against loss.

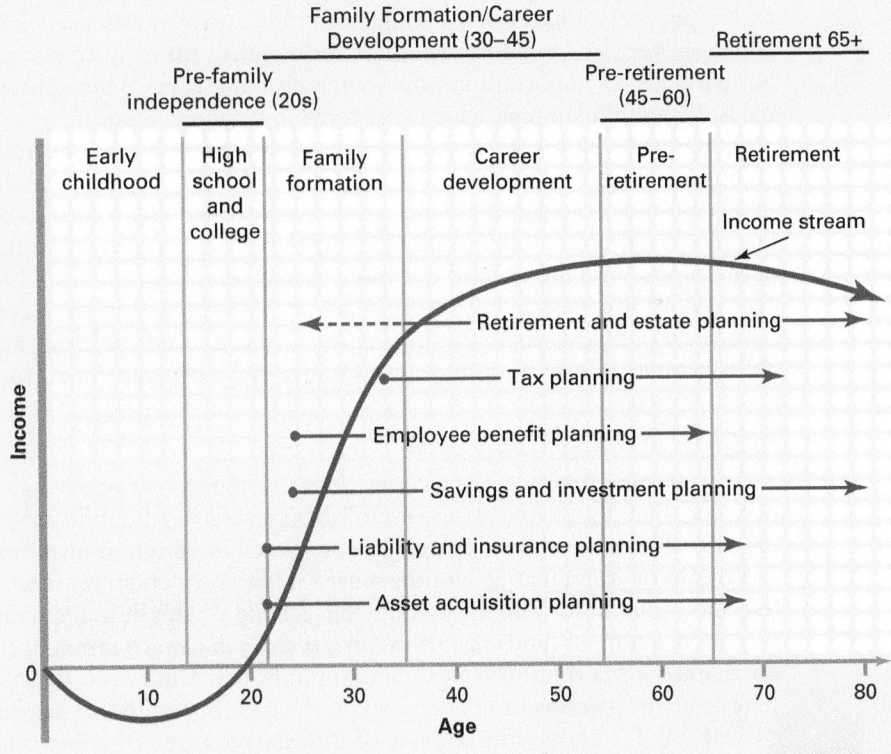

6 months or 6 years, will experience periods of reduced income. A divorce, a spouse's death, or remarriage can also drastically change your financial circumstances. Many people in their 40s and 50s find themselves in the "sandwich generation," supporting their elderly parents while still raising their own children and paying for college. And some people must cope with reduced income due to jobs lost because of corporate downsizing or early retirement. We'll look at these and other special planning concerns next.

1-3b Plans to Achieve Your Financial Goals

As discussed earlier, financial goals can range from short-term goals such as saving for a new stereo to long-term goals such as saving enough to start your own business. Reaching your particular goals requires different types of financial planning. Let's take a brief look at what each major plan category includes.

Asset Acquisition Planning

One of the first categories of financial planning is asset acquisition. We accumulate *assets*—things we own—throughout our lives. These include *liquid assets* (cash, savings accounts, and money market funds) used to pay everyday expenses, *investments* (stocks, bonds, and mutual funds) acquired to earn a return, *personal property* (movable property such as automobiles, household furnishings, appliances, clothing, jewelry, home electronics, and similar items), and *real property* (immovable property; land and anything fixed to it, such as a house). Chapters 4 and 5 focus on important considerations for managing liquid assets and other major assets such as automobiles and housing.

Liability and Insurance Planning

Another category of financial planning is liability planning. A *liability* is something we owe, which is measured by the amount of debt we incur. We create liabilities by borrowing money. By the time most of us graduate from college, we have debts of some sort: education loans, car loans, credit card balances, and so on. Our borrowing needs typically increase as we acquire other assets such as a home, furnishings, and appliances. Whatever the source of credit, such transactions have one thing in common: *the debt must be repaid at some future time*. How we manage our debt burden is just as important as how we manage our assets. Managing credit effectively requires careful planning, which is covered in Chapters 6 and 7.

Obtaining adequate *insurance coverage* is also essential. Like borrowing money, obtaining insurance is generally introduced relatively early in our life cycle (usually in the family formation stage). Insurance is a way to reduce financial risk and protect both income (life, health, and disability insurance) and assets (property and liability insurance). Most consumers regard insurance as absolutely essential—and for good reason. One serious illness or accident can wipe out everything you have accumulated over many years of hard work. But having the wrong amount of insurance can be costly. We'll examine how to manage your insurance needs in Chapters 8, 9 and 10.

Savings and Investment Planning

As your income begins to increase, so does the importance of savings and investment planning. Initially, people save to establish an emergency fund for meeting unexpected expenses. Eventually, however, they devote greater attention to investing excess income as a means of accumulating wealth, either for major expenditures (such as a child's college education) or for retirement. Individuals build wealth through savings and the subsequent investing of funds in various investment vehicles: common or preferred stocks, government or corporate bonds, mutual funds, real estate, and so on. The higher the returns on the investment of excess funds, the greater wealth they accumulate.

Exhibit 1.8 shows the impact of alternative rates of return on accumulated wealth. The graph shows that if you had $1,000 today and could keep it invested at

EXHIBIT 1.8   How a $1,000 Investment Grows Over Time

Four percent or 6 percent: How big a deal is a 2 percent difference? The deal is more than twice the money over a 40-year period! Through the power of compound interest, a higher return means dramatically more money as time goes on.

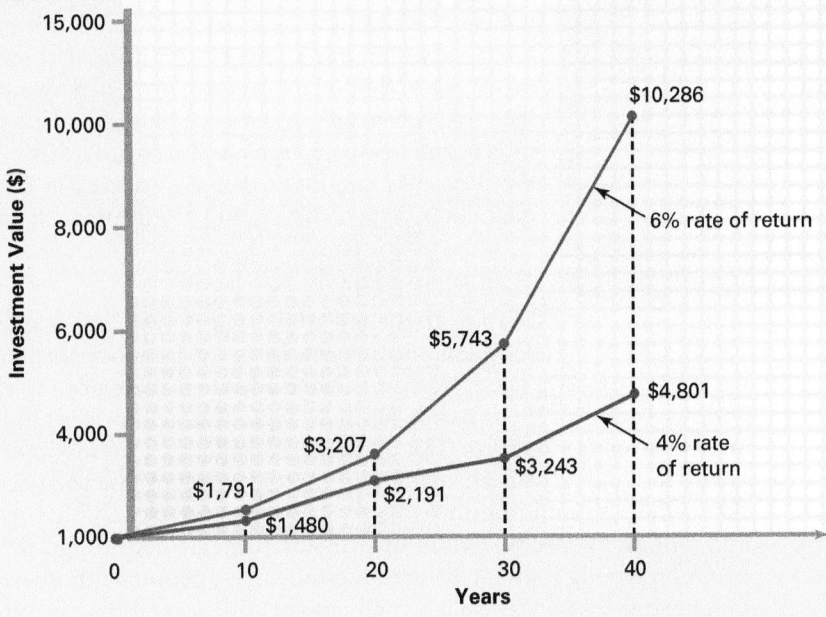

4 percent, then you would accumulate a considerable sum of money over time. For example, at the end of 40 years, you'd have about $4,801 from your original $1,000. Earning a higher rate of return provides even greater rewards. Some might assume that earning, say, only 2 percentage points more (i.e., 6 percent rather than 4 percent) would not matter much. But it certainly would! Observe that if you could earn 6 percent over the 40 years, then you'd accumulate $10,286, or *more than twice as much* as you'd accumulate at 4 percent. This powerful observation is important to keep in mind when comparing competing investment and savings alternatives.

As we'll explore in Part 5 on managing investments, seemingly small differences in various investment management fees can translate into significant differences in net investment returns over long periods of time. The length of time you keep your money invested is just as important as the rate of return you earn on your investments. You can accumulate more than twice as much capital by investing for 40 rather than 30 years with either rate of return (4 percent or 6 percent). This is the magic of compound interest, which explains why it's so important to create strong savings and investment habits early in life. We'll examine compounding more fully in Chapter 2, savings in Chapter 4, and investments in Chapters 11, 12, and 13.

Employee Benefit Planning

Your employer may offer a wide variety of employee benefit plans, especially if you work for a large firm. These could include life, health, and disability insurance; tuition reimbursement programs for continuing education; pension and profit-sharing plans, and 401(k) retirement plans; flexible spending accounts for child care and health care expenses; stock options; sick leave, personal time, and vacation days; and miscellaneous benefits such as employee discounts and subsidized meals or parking. Employee benefit plans are described more fully in later chapters.

Managing your employee benefit plans and coordinating them with your other plans are an important part of the overall financial planning process. For example, tax-deferred retirement plans and flexible spending accounts offer tax advantages. Some retirement plans allow you to borrow against them. Employer-sponsored insurance programs may need to be supplemented with personal policies. In addition, in today's volatile labor market, you can no longer assume that you'll be working at the same company for many years. If you change jobs, your new company may not offer the same benefits. Your personal financial plans should include contingency plans to replace employer-provided benefits as required. We'll discuss employee benefits in greater detail in Chapters 2 (planning); 3 (taxes); 8, 9, and 10 (insurance); and 14 (retirement).

Tax Planning

Despite all the talk about tax reform, our tax code remains highly complex. Income can be taxed as active (ordinary), portfolio (investment), passive, tax-free, or tax-deferred. Then there are tax shelters, which use various aspects of the tax code (such as depreciation expenses) to legitimately reduce an investor's tax liability. Tax planning considers all these factors and more. It involves looking at your current and projected earnings and then developing strategies that will defer and minimize taxes. Tax plans are closely tied to investment plans and will often specify certain investment strategies. Although tax planning is most common among individuals with high incomes, people with lower incomes can also obtain sizable savings. We'll examine taxes and tax planning in Chapter 3.

Retirement and Estate Planning

While you're still working, you should be managing your finances to attain those goals you feel are important after you retire. These might include maintaining your standard of living, extensive travel, visiting children, frequent dining at better restaurants, and perhaps a vacation home or boat. Retirement planning should begin long before you retire. Most people don't start thinking about retirement until well into their 40s or 50s. This is unfortunate, because it usually results in a substantially reduced level of retirement income. The sooner you start, the better off you'll be. Take, for instance, the IRA (individual retirement account), whereby certain wage earners were allowed to invest up to $6,500 per year in 2015. We'll look at IRAs and other aspects of retirement planning in Chapter 14.

> **EXAMPLE: The Sooner You Start an IRA, the Better**
>
> If you start investing for retirement at age 40 and put only $2,000 a year in an IRA earning 5 percent for 25 years, you will have $95,454 at age 65. However, if you start the same retirement plan 10 years earlier at age 30, you'll have $180,641 at age 65!

Accumulating assets to enjoy in retirement is only part of the long-term financial planning process. As people grow older, they must also consider how they can most effectively pass their wealth on to their heirs, an activity known as *estate planning*. We'll examine this complex subject—which includes such topics as wills, trusts, and the effects of gift and estate taxes—in Chapter 15.

1-3c Special Planning Concerns

Students may not spend much time on financial planning. Yet the sooner you start, the better prepared you'll be to adapt your plans to changing personal circumstances. Such changes include changing or losing a job, relocating to a new state,

Common Misconceptions About Financial Planning

- **A professional financial planner is an unnecessary expense.** The answer depends on you. A lot of good financial planning can be done on your own. But honestly ask yourself: Do I have the discipline, time, and financial experience to manage these complicated tasks effectively and confidently? If the answer is no, see a financial planner to get a decent idea of the planning process.

- **A little credit card debt is just fine.** Define "a little." A modest amount of credit card debt is OK. The problem is that for all too many people, "a little" leads to a lot. As discussed in Part 3 of this book, "Managing Credit," credit card debt is often one of the biggest problems in managing your personal finances. Just consider the high interest rates on credit cards and how easy it is to build up a big balance.

- **I don't need a budget because I have a general idea of what I earn and spend.** There is a natural tendency to overspend because expenses are easy to underestimate without a formal budget. And if you spend first and only save what's left over, the probability of achieving your financial goals is much lower. Sticking to a budget is the key.

- **Retirement is a lifetime away.** While that may be true, that doesn't justify focusing only on short-term goals, like coming up with the down payment on a house. When retirement is a "lifetime away," that's the time to exploit the compounding of returns over a long period of time by taking full advantage of retirement investments in your employer's 401(k) plan and in IRAs. An early start can put you well ahead.

Source: Adapted from Kimberly J. Howard, CFP®, CRPC, "Financial Fiascos Every Young Couple with Debts Should Avoid," NAPFA Planning Perspectives, volume 6, issue 5, Sept./Oct. 2011, www.NAPFA.org, accessed July 2015.

getting married, having children, being in a serious accident, getting a chronic illness, losing a spouse through divorce or death, retiring, or taking responsibility for dependent parents. These and other stressful events are "financial shocks" that require reevaluation of your financial goals and plans.

It is important not to rush to make major financial decisions at these times, when you're most vulnerable. Postpone any action until you have had time to recover from the event and evaluate all your options carefully. This can be difficult because some financial salespeople will rush to contact you in these circumstances. For example, when you have a child, you will find that insurance agents, financial planners, and stockbrokers actively encourage you to buy insurance and start investing in a college fund. Although these are valid objectives, don't be pushed into any expensive decisions. People who get large sums of money—from severance packages, retirement benefits, or insurance policies when a loved one dies—are also likely to hear from financial salespeople eager to help them invest the funds. This is another time to wait. Face it—some professionals may have a greater interest in selling their own products than advising you on the best strategy for your needs.

Managing Two Incomes

Did you know that the earnings of the average dual-income family will add up to more than $1 million over the wage earners' lives? Today, two-income couples account for the majority of U.S. households and many depend on the second income to make ends meet. For others, it provides financial security and a way to afford "extras." Often, however, a second income doesn't add as much as expected to the bottom line. Higher expenses such as child care, taxes, clothing, dry cleaning, transportation, and lunches may consume a large part of the second paycheck. And two-income families tend to spend what they earn rather than save it.

When Alicia Cisneros was offered a job as a credit analyst, she and her husband, Luis, filled out Worksheet 1.2 to assess the net monthly income from her paycheck, both with and without the impact of employer-paid benefits. Alicia had been staying home with their three children, but now two were in school all day. The couple listed only those expenses that *directly related to the second job* and made sure not to

WORKSHEET 1.2	Analyzing the Benefit of a Second Income

Use this worksheet to estimate the contribution of a second paycheck. Without the employer-paid benefits of $1,632 (line 2), the Cisneros family would realize a net monthly income of $1,808 (line 1 - line 3); with those benefits, their net monthly income would be $3,440 (line 4).

Second Income Analysis

Name(s) _Alicia and Luis Cisneros_   Date _December 27, 2016_

MONTHLY CASH INCOME

Gross pay	$5,000
Pretax employer contributions (401(k) plans, dependent-care reimbursement account(s))	400
Additional job-related income (bonuses, overtime, commissions)	0
(1) Total Cash Income	$5,400

EMPLOYER-PAID BENEFITS

Health insurance	$550
Life insurance	100
Pension contributions	600
Thrift-plan contributions	0
Social Security	382
Profit sharing	0
Other deferred compensation	0
(2) Total Benefits	$1,632

MONTHLY JOB-RELATED EXPENSES

Federal income tax	$1,500
Social Security tax	382
State income tax	250
Child care	640
Clothing; personal care; dry cleaning	400
Meals away from home	200
Public transportation	0
Auto-related expenses (gas, parking, maintenance)	220
Other	0
(3) Total Expenses	$3,592
(4) Net Income (Deficit) = Total Cash Income + Total Benefits − Total Expenses	$3,440

include personal expenses that would exist even without the second job. Alicia's job offer included good employer-paid benefits, with a better health insurance plan than the one Luis' employer offered. Taking these benefits and the job-related expenses into account, the Cisneros family's net monthly income would increase by $3,440 a month, or $41,280 a year. Without benefits, this amount drops to $1,808, or $21,696 a year. These numbers provided the information that the Cisneros family needed to discuss the pros and cons of Alicia's job offer. They took into account not just the higher total income and out-of-pocket costs, but also the intangible costs (additional demands on their lives, less time with family, and higher stress) and benefits (career development, job satisfaction, and sense of worth). They decided that the timing was right and agreed that they'd use the second income to increase their college savings accounts and build up their other investments. This would provide greater financial security in these uncertain times if Luis were laid off from his research job at a bio-technology company.

Like the Cisneros family, partners in two-income households need to approach discussions on financial matters with an open mind and be willing to compromise. Spouses need to decide together how to allocate income to household expenses, family financial goals, and personal spending goals. Will you use a second income to meet basic expenses, afford a more luxurious lifestyle, save for a special vacation, or invest in retirement accounts? You may need to try several money management strategies to find the one that works best for you. Some couples place all income into a single joint account. Others have each spouse contribute *equal* amounts into a joint account to pay bills, but retain individual discretion over remaining income. Still others contribute a *proportional* share of each income to finance joint expenses and goals. In any case, both spouses should have money of their own to spend without accountability.

Managing Employee Benefits

As we've already discussed, if you hold a full-time job, then your employer probably provides various employee benefits, ranging from health and life insurance to pension plans. As we saw when analyzing the Cisneros family's case, these benefits can have a major financial impact on family income. Most American families depend solely on employer-sponsored group plans for their health insurance coverage and also for a big piece of their life insurance coverage and retirement needs.

Today's well-defined employee benefits packages cover a full spectrum of benefits that may include:

- Health and life insurance
- Disability insurance
- Long-term care insurance
- Pension and profit-sharing plans
- Supplemental retirement programs, such as 401(k) plans
- Dental and vision care
- Child care, elder care, and educational assistance programs
- Subsidized employee food services

Each company's benefit package is different. Some companies and industries are known for generous benefit plans; others offer far less attractive packages. In general, large firms can afford more benefits than small ones can. Because employee benefits can increase your total compensation by 30 percent or more, you should thoroughly investigate your employee benefits to choose those appropriate for your personal situation. Be sure to coordinate your benefits with your partner's to avoid paying for duplicate coverage. Companies change their benefit packages often and today are shifting more costs to employees. Although an employer may pay for some benefits in full, typically employees pay for part of the cost of group health insurance, supplemental life insurance, long-term care insurance, and participation in voluntary retirement programs.

Due to the prevalence of two-income families and an increasingly diverse workforce, many employers today are replacing traditional programs, where the company sets the type and amounts of benefits, with **flexible-benefit (cafeteria) plans**. In flexible-benefit programs, the employer allocates a certain amount of money to each employee and then lets the employee "spend" that money for benefits that suit his or her age, marital status, number of dependent children, level of income, and so on. These plans usually cover everything from child care to retirement benefits, offer several levels of health and life insurance coverage, and have some limits on the minimum and maximum amounts of coverage. Within these constraints, you can select the benefits that do you the most good. In some plans, you can even take part of the benefits in the form of more take-home pay or extra vacation time!

Managing Your Finances in Tough Economic Times

Tough economic times can be due to broad macroeconomic trends like a recession, or they can be brought on by more personal, local developments. The effects of recessions and financial crises divide people into three groups: (1) those who are directly and severely hurt through job loss, (2) those who are marginally hurt by reduced income, and (3) those who are not directly hurt. If you are in either of the first two groups, you must make significant lifestyle changes to reduce spending. Even if you are in the last group, a recession affects you indirectly. For example, retirement accounts typically drop in value and financial plans must be revised. And everyone's expectations are at least temporarily affected, which causes most people to be more cautious about their expenditures during a recession or crisis.

The financial crisis of 2008 and 2009 and the subsequent long period of high unemployment was a macroeconomic challenge of historic global proportions. It drives home the benefits of having a sound financial plan—and dramatized the cost of not having one. The precipitous decline in stock and home prices and the many people laid off from their jobs made everyone think a lot more about financial planning in general and how to survive a financial crisis in particular. Although we all hope that such broad crises will be rare, it is important to plan for a possible recurrence. All of the financial planning principles explained in this book remained valid during the recent global financial crisis and should continue to serve us well in any future similar situations.

So how do you best plan to survive a broad-based financial crisis? First, you remind yourself of the key principles of financial planning presented in this book:

- Spend less than you earn.
- Keep investing so your money continues to work toward your goals.
- Know where you are and plan for the unexpected. You cannot know where you are financially unless you carefully, and frequently, update your family's budget. And it is important to set aside money for an emergency fund. As discussed earlier in this chapter, you should set aside enough cash to last at least 6 to 9 months.

Second, don't panic when financial markets crash! This means that you shouldn't try to time the market by buying when the experts say it's at a low or by selling when they say it's at a high. Continue to invest for the long-term but keep in mind how close you are to achieving your financial objectives. For example, if you pull all of your

Do It Now

Start Building an Emergency Fund

What would happen if you lost your job, got hurt, or had an unexpected big expense? Even if you're not making much money now, you could start building an emergency fund by putting aside even $10 a month. As this chapter points out, your goal is to eventually set aside enough to last at least 6 to 9 months. Considering the risk of not doing so, you can do it now.

money out of the stock market when it has fallen, you will not be positioned to take advantage of its eventual recovery. Part 5 of the book focuses on investment management.

You can take specific actions in your day-to-day life to deal effectively with a financial crisis or recession. Consider the following ways to manage expenses in times of stress:

- Postpone large expenses. For example, hold on to your old car rather than buying a new one. And you could wait on that new refrigerator or big-screen TV.
- Cut back on the number of times you eat out.
- Take your vacation at or around home.
- If you rely mostly on a cell phone, consider canceling your landline phone and/or the extras like caller ID.
- Cancel nonessential magazine subscriptions.

Recessions and financial crises can be challenging. A financial plan that considers such contingencies will help you weather the storm.

Adapting to Other Major Life Changes

Economic hardships are not always the result of adverse macroeconomic developments. Even in the best of times, people can lose their job or face other hardships. Situations that require special consideration include changes in marital status and the need to support grown children or elderly relatives. Marriage, divorce, or the death of a spouse results in the need to revise financial plans and money management strategies.

FINANCIAL PLANNING TIPS

Planning for Critical Life Events

Just like you, financial plans go through stages and must adapt to changes over your lifetime. Here are some of the critical life events that may make you reconsider and possibly revise an existing financial plan:

- **Marriage.** Finances must be merged, and there may be a need for life insurance.

- **Children.** It's time to start a college savings plan and revise your budget accordingly. A will is needed that makes provisions for guardianship if both parents die while the children are minors.

- **Divorce.** Financial plans based on two incomes are no longer applicable. Revised plans must reflect any property settlements, alimony, and/or child support.

- **Moving into middle age.** Although having started a savings and investing plan early in life should be paying off, the number of working years is declining, along with future earning ability. The shorter horizon implies that you may want to take less risk and keep less money in the stock market. While the greater safety is appealing, the reduced expected returns are also sobering. In addition, this could be the time to consider long-term-care insurance for possible use in retirement.

- **Death of a parent.** The estate must be settled, and you may need help managing a possible inheritance.

- **Retirement.** If you set it up right, your financial plan generated the amount needed to fund your retirement. During retirement, you will try to preserve your capital, relying as much as possible on the income generated by your investments to fund your living expenses. Although investment risk should be reduced greatly, it cannot be eliminated because inflation risk must be managed. Money can be withdrawn from tax-deferred retirement accounts beginning at age 59 1/2 without penalty, but taxes will be due. You *must* start taking out such money at age 70 1/2 at a rate that is based on the average life expectancy for that age. The risk of increases in future tax rates can be managed, in part, with Roth IRAs, which are retirement accounts where your original contributions are not tax-deductible. However, there is no requirement that you take out the money and it is not taxed when you do. Estate planning and long-term care issues must also be addressed.

As we mentioned previously, couples should discuss their money attitudes and financial goals and decide how to manage joint financial affairs *before* they get married. Take an inventory of your financial assets and liabilities, including savings and checking accounts; credit card accounts and outstanding bills; auto, health, and life insurance policies; and investment portfolios. You may want to eliminate some credit cards. Too many cards can hurt your credit rating, and most people need only one or two. Each partner should have a card in his or her name to establish a credit record. Compare employee benefit plans to figure out the lowest-cost source of health insurance coverage, and coordinate other benefits. Change the beneficiary on your life insurance policies as desired. Adjust withholding amounts as necessary based on your new filing category.

In the event of divorce, income may decrease because alimony and child-support payments may cause one salary to be divided between two households. Single parents may have to stretch limited financial resources further to meet added expenses such as child care. Remarriage brings additional financial considerations, including decisions involving children from prior marriages and managing the assets that each spouse brings to the marriage. Some couples develop a prenuptial contract that outlines their agreement on financial matters, such as the control of assets, their disposition in event of death or divorce, and other important money issues.

The death of a spouse is another change that greatly affects financial planning. The surviving spouse is typically faced with decisions on how to receive and invest life insurance proceeds and manage other assets. In families where the deceased made most of the financial decisions with little or no involvement of the surviving spouse, the survivor may be overwhelmed by the need to take on financial responsibilities. Advance planning can minimize many of these problems.

Couples should regularly review all aspects of their finances. Each spouse should understand what is owned and owed, participate in formulating financial goals and investment strategies, and fully understand estate plans (covered in detail in Chapter 15).

1-3d Technology in Financial Planning

Using personal computers and the Internet streamlines the number crunching and information gathering involved in budgeting, tax planning, and investment management. Many reasonably priced, user-friendly programs are available for personal financial planning and money management, including the popular Microsoft Money and Quicken packages. And the number of free and reasonably priced online and smart-phone apps for this purpose continues to grow at an amazing rate.

The Internet puts a wealth of financial information literally at your fingertips. Comprehensive sites that consistently get good reviews include Yahoo! Finance (**http://finance.yahoo.com**), Microsoft's MSN MoneyCentral (**http://moneycentral.msn.com**), and Intuit's Quicken.com (**http://www.quicken.com**). Where applicable, we'll point out ways to use the computer and Internet resources to simplify and reduce the time required to manage your personal finances.

1-3e Using Professional Financial Planners

professional financial planners
An individual or firm that helps clients establish financial goals and develop and implement financial plans to achieve those goals.

Does developing your own financial plans seem like an overwhelming task? Help is at hand! Professional financial planners will guide you through establishing goals, plan preparation, and the increasingly complex maze of financial products and investment opportunities. This field has experienced tremendous growth, and there are now more than 300,000 financial planners in the United States.

Financial planners offer a wide range of services, including preparing comprehensive financial plans that evaluate a client's total personal financial situation or abbreviated plans focusing on a specific concern, such as managing a client's assets and investments and retirement planning. Where once only the wealthy used professional planners, now financial firms such as H&R Block's Financial Advisors and the Personal Advisors of Ameriprise Financial compete for the business of middle-income people as well.

Why do people turn to financial advisors? Surveys indicate that retirement needs motivated 50 percent, while 23 percent were unhappy with the results of trying to manage their own finances. Estate and inheritance planning caused another 13 percent to seek help; saving for college and tax issues were also mentioned as reasons.

1-3f Types of Planners

Most financial planners fall into one of two categories based on how they are paid: commissions or fees. *Commission-based planners* earn commissions on the financial products they sell, whereas *fee-only planners* charge fees based on the complexity of the plan they prepare. Many financial planners take a hybrid approach and charge fees and collect commissions on products they sell, offering lower fees if you make product transactions through them.

Insurance salespeople and securities brokers who continue to sell the same financial products (life insurance, stocks, bonds, mutual funds, and annuities) often now call themselves "financial planners." Other advisors work for large, established financial institutions that recognize the enormous potential in the field and compete with the best financial planners. Still others work in small firms, promising high-quality advice for a flat fee or an hourly rate. Regardless of their affiliation, full-service financial planners help their clients articulate their long- and short-term financial goals, systematically plan for their financial needs, and help implement various aspects of the plans. Exhibit 1.9 provides a guide to some of the different planning designations.

EXHIBIT 1.9	Financial Planning Designations

Confused about what the letters after a financial advisor's name signify? Here's a summary of the most common certifications so you can choose the one that best suits your needs.

Credential	Description	Internet Address
Chartered Financial Analyst (CFA)	Focuses primarily on securities analysis not financial planning	http://www.cfainstitute.org
Certified Financial Planner® (CFP®)	Requires a comprehensive education in financial planning	http://www.cfp.net
Chartered Financial Consultant (ChFC)	Financial planning designation for insurance agents	http://www.theamerican college.edu/
Certified Trust & Financial Advisor (CTFA)	Estate planning and trusts expertise, found mostly in the banking industry	http://aba.com/ICB/ CTFA.htm
Personal Financial Specialist (PFS)	Comprehensive planning credential only for CPAs	http://www.pfp.aicpa.org
Chartered Life Underwriter (CLU)	Insurance agent designation, often accompanied by the ChFC credential	http://www.theamerican college.edu
Certified Investment Management Analyst	Consulting designation for professional investment managers	http://www.imca.org/
Registered Financial Associate (RFA)	Designation granted only to recent graduates of an approved academic curriculum in financial services	http://www.iarfc.org

Source: Adapted from http://apps.finra.org/DataDirectory/1/prodesignations.aspx, accessed July 2015.

In addition to one-on-one financial planning services, some institutions offer computerized financial plans. Merrill Lynch/Bank of America, Ameriprise Financial, T. Rowe Price, and other major investment firms provide these computerized plans on the Internet to help clients develop plans to save for college or retirement, reduce taxes, or restructure investment portfolios.

Personal finance programs such as Quicken and Microsoft Money also have a financial planning component that can help you set a path to your goals and do tax and retirement planning. As you'll see in later chapters, some Internet sites provide planning advice on one topic, such as taxes, insurance, or estate planning. Although these plans are relatively inexpensive or even free, they are somewhat impersonal. However, they are a good solution for those who need help getting started and for do-it-yourself planners who want some guidance.

The cost of financial planning services depends on the type of planner, the complexity of your financial situation, and the services you want. The cost may be well worth the benefits, especially for people who have neither the time, inclination, discipline, nor expertise to plan on their own. Remember, however, that the best advice is worthless if you're not willing to change your financial habits.

1-3g Choosing a Financial Planner

Planners who have completed the required course of study and earned the Certified Financial Planner® (CFP®) or Chartered Financial Consultant (ChFC) designation are often a better choice than the many self-proclaimed "financial planners." Of course, CPAs, attorneys, investment managers, and other professionals without such certifications in many instances also provide sound financial planning advice.

FINANCIAL ROAD SIGN

Potential Financial Advisor Conflicts of Interest

When interviewing a prospective financial advisor, keep in mind the following and ask questions.

How is the advisor paid? Financial advisors can be paid by product sale commissions and/or by client-paid fees. Client-paid fees can include an hourly fee, an annual retainer, a fee that is based on the amount invested with the advisor, or a flat fee for each service provided. And some advisors are paid using a combination of commissions and fees. While most advisors are honest, opportunities for conflicts of interest abound. Advisors who get a commission have an incentive to sell you the products that generate the most money for them, but those are not necessarily the best products for you. Advisors who are paid an hourly fee have an incentive to add hours to your bill. And advisors who earn a fee based on the amount of assets under management tend to encourage you to invest more with them.

Good questions to ask: Ask a prospective advisor how he or she is paid. If an advisor receives commissions, ask for a description of the commissions on the company's products. Alternatively, ask a fee-paid advisor for a schedule of fees for each type of service provided. Consider using the questionnaire provided on the National Association of Personal Financial Advisors (NAPFA) Internet site, which is **www.napfa.org**. The questionnaire has good questions to ask when interviewing a prospective advisor and provides a form that your advisor can use to disclose the commissions that he or she receives.

Source: Adapted from Jennifer Lane, CFP, with Bill Lane, "Advisor Fees and Conflicts," http://www.netplaces.com/money-for-40s-50s/do-you-need-an-advisor/advisor-fees-and-conflicts.htm, accessed July 2015.

Unlike accounting and law, the field is still largely unregulated, and almost anyone can call himself or herself a financial planner. Most financial planners are honest and reputable, but there have been cases of fraudulent practice. So it's critical to thoroughly check out a potential financial advisor—and preferably to interview two or three.

The way a planner is paid—commissions, fees, or both—should be one of your major concerns. Obviously, you need to be aware of potential conflicts of interest when using a planner with ties to a brokerage firm, insurance company, or bank. Many planners now provide clients with disclosure forms outlining fees and commissions for various transactions. In addition to asking questions of the planner, you should also check with your state securities department and the Securities and Exchange Commission (for planners registered to sell securities). Ask if the planner has any pending lawsuits, complaints by state or federal regulators, personal bankruptcies, or convictions for investment-related crimes. However, even these agencies may not have accurate or current information; simply being properly registered and having no record of disciplinary actions don't guarantee that an advisor's track record is good. You may also want to research the planner's reputation in the local financial community. Clearly, you should do your homework before engaging the services of a professional financial planner.

TEST YOURSELF

1-9 What types of financial planning concerns does a complete set of financial plans cover?

1-10 Discuss the relationship of life-cycle considerations to personal financial planning. What are some factors to consider when revising financial plans to reflect changes in the life cycle?

1-11 Don Smitham's investments over the past several years have not lived up to his full return expectations. He is not particularly concerned, however, because his return is only about 2 percentage points below his expectations. Do you have any advice for Don?

1-12 Describe employee benefit and tax planning. How do they fit into the financial planning framework?

1-13 "There's no sense in worrying about retirement until you reach middle age." Discuss this point of view.

1-14 Discuss briefly how the following situations affect personal financial planning:

   a. Being part of a dual-income couple
   b. Major life changes, such as marriage or divorce
   c. Death of a spouse

1-15 What is a *professional financial planner*? Does it make any difference whether the financial planner earns money from commissions made on products sold as opposed to the fees he or she charges?

1-4 THE PLANNING ENVIRONMENT

Financial planning takes place in a dynamic economic environment created by the actions of government, business, and consumers. Your purchase, saving, investment, and retirement plans and decisions are influenced by both the present and future state of the economy. Understanding the economic environment will allow you to make better financial decisions.

Consider that a strong economy can lead to high returns in the stock market, which in turn can positively affect your investment and retirement programs. The economy also affects the interest rates you pay on your mortgage and credit cards as well as those you earn on savings accounts and bonds. Periods of high inflation can lead to rapid price increases that make it difficult to make ends meet. Here we look at two important aspects of the planning environment: the major financial planning players and the economy.

1-4a The Players

The financial planning environment contains various interrelated groups of players, each attempting to fulfill certain goals. Although their objectives are not necessarily incompatible, they do impose some constraints on one another. There are three vital groups: government, business, and consumers. Exhibit 1.10 shows the relationships among these groups.

Government

Federal, state, and local governments provide us with many essential public goods and services, such as police and fire protection, national defense, highways, public education, and health care. The federal government plays a major role in regulating economic activity. Government is also a customer of business and an employer of consumers, so it's a source of revenue for business and of wages for consumers. The two major constraints from the perspective of personal financial planning are taxation and regulation.

EXHIBIT 1.10   The Financial Planning Environment

Government, business, and consumers are the major players in our economic system. They interact with one another to produce the environment in which we carry out our financial plans.

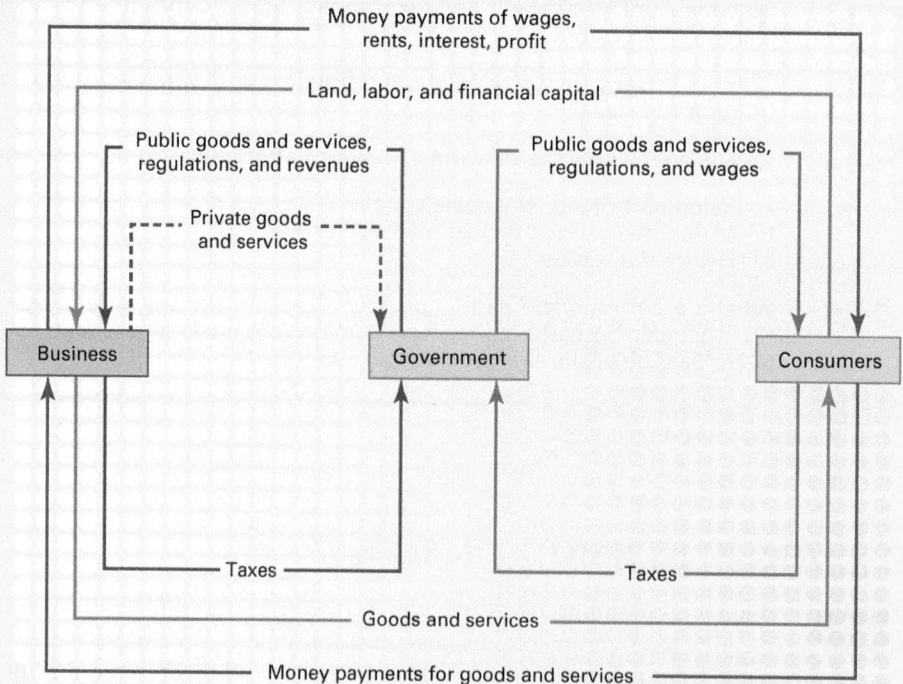

Taxation The federal government levies taxes on income, state governments levy taxes on sales and income, and local governments levy taxes primarily on real estate and personal property. The largest tax bite for consumers is federal income taxes, which are *progressive* in that (up to a point) the greater the taxable income, the higher the tax rate. Changes in tax rates and procedures will increase or decrease the amount of income consumers have to spend, so you should factor the effects of taxes into your personal money management activities. Because of tax structure constraints and the potential magnitude of taxes, financial decisions should be evaluated on an after-tax basis. Taxes are discussed in Chapter 3.

Regulation Federal, state, and local governments place many regulations on activities that affect consumers and businesses. Aimed at protecting the consumer from fraudulent and undesirable actions by sellers and lenders, these regulations require certain types of businesses to have licenses, maintain specified hygiene standards, adequately disclose financial charges, and warrant their goods and services. Other laws protect sellers from adverse activities such as shoplifting and nonpayment for services rendered. Decisions related to achieving personal financial goals should consider the legal requirements that protect consumers and those that constrain their activities.

Business

As Exhibit 1.10 shows, business provides consumers with goods and services and, in return, receives payment in the form of money. Firms must hire labor and use land and financial capital (economists call these *factors of production*) to produce these goods and services. In return, firms pay out wages, rents, interest, and profits to the various factors of production. Thus, businesses are an important part of the circular flow of income that sustains our free enterprise system. In general, they create a competitive environment in which consumers may select from an array of goods and services. As noted previously, all businesses are limited in some way by federal, state, and local laws.

Consumers

The consumer is the central player in the financial planning environment. Consumer choices ultimately determine the kinds of goods and services that businesses will provide. The consumer's choice of whether to spend or save also has a direct impact on present and future circular flows of money. Cutbacks in consumer spending are usually associated with a decline in economic activity, whereas increases in consumer spending help the economy to recover.

Consumers are often thought to have free choices in the marketplace, but they must operate in an environment that includes government and business. Although they can affect these parties by voting and by their purchasing actions, consumers need lobbyists and consumer groups in order to have a significant impact. The individual consumer should not expect to change government or business and instead plan transactions within the existing financial environment.

1-4b The Economy

Our economy is influenced by interactions among government, business, and consumers, as well as by world economic conditions. Through specific policy decisions, the government's goal is to manage the economy to provide economic stability and a high level of employment. Government decisions have a major impact on the economic and financial planning environment. The federal government's *monetary policy*—programs for controlling the amount of money in circulation (the money supply)—is used to stimulate or moderate economic growth. For example, increases in the money supply tend to lower interest rates. This typically leads to a higher level of consumer and business borrowing and spending that increases overall economic activity. The reverse is also true. Reducing the money supply raises interest rates, which reduces consumer and business borrowing and spending and thus slows economic activity. The historically low interest rates in the wake of the financial crisis of 2008 and 2009 and beyond reflect efforts by the Federal Reserve (Fed) to bolster the sagging economy and decrease unemployment.

The government's other principal tool for managing the economy is *fiscal policy*—its programs of spending and taxation. Increased spending for social services, education, defense, and other programs stimulates the economy, while decreased spending slows economic activity. Increasing taxes, on the other hand, gives businesses and individuals less to spend and, as a result, negatively affects economic activity. Conversely, decreasing taxes stimulates the economy. The importance of fiscal policy is illustrated by the government's massive spending to stimulate the U.S. economy in 2008 and 2009 as a way to address the greatest financial crisis since the Great Depression of the 1930s in the United States.

Economic Cycles

Although the government uses monetary and fiscal policy to manage the economy and provide economic stability, the level of economic activity changes constantly. The upward and downward movement creates *economic cycles* (also called *business cycles*), which vary in length and in extent. An economic cycle typically contains four stages: *expansion, peak, contraction,* and *trough.*

Exhibit 1.11 shows how each of these stages relates to real (inflation-adjusted) gross domestic product (GDP), which is an important indicator of economic activity. The stronger the economy, the higher the levels of real GDP and employment. During an expansion, real GDP increases until it hits a peak, which usually signals the end of the expansion and the beginning of a contraction. During a contraction (also known as *recession*), real GDP falls into a trough, which is the end of a contraction and the beginning of an expansion. For about 75 years, the government has been reasonably successful in keeping the economy out of a depression, although we have experienced periods of rapid expansion and high inflation, followed by periods of deep recession. And some would argue that the financial crisis of 2008 and 2009 came close to precipitating a depression.

Economic growth is measured by changes in GDP, the total of all goods and services produced within the country. The broadest measure of economic activity, GDP is reported quarterly and is used to compare trends in national output. A rising GDP means that the economy is growing. The *rate* of GDP growth is also important. Although the long-term trend in nominal GDP typically is positive, the annual rate of GDP growth varies widely. For example, while nominal GDP grew an average of about 6.6 percent between 1950 and 2014, its minimum value was –2 percent and its maximum value was 15.7 percent. And real GDP only grew about 3.3 percent over that time period, with a minimum of 2.8 percent and a maximum of 8.7 percent. Another important measure of economic health is the *unemployment rate.* The swings in unemployment from one phase of the cycle to the next can be substantial. For example, between 1950 and 2014, the civilian unemployment rate fluctuated between a low of 2.9 percent and a high of 9.7 percent. In addition to GDP growth and the unemployment rate, numerous economic statistics such as inflation, interest rates, bank failures, corporate profits, taxes, and government deficits directly and profoundly affect our financial well-being. These factors affect our financial plans: our level of income, investment returns, interest earned and paid, taxes paid, and prices paid for goods and services we buy.

Inflation, Prices, and Planning

As we've discussed, our economy is based on the exchange of goods and services between businesses and their customers—consumers, government, and other businesses—for a medium of exchange called money. The mechanism that facilitates

gross domestic product (GDP)
The total of all goods and services produced in a country; used to monitor economic growth.

expansion
The phase of the economic cycle when levels of employment and production are high and the economy is growing, generally accompanied by rising prices for goods and services.

peak
The phase of the economic cycle when an expansion ends and a contraction begins.

contraction
The phase of the economic cycle when real GDP falls.

trough
The phase of the economic cycle when a contraction ends and an expansion begins.

EXHIBIT 1.11   The Business Cycle

The business cycle consists of four stages: expansion, peak, contraction, and trough.

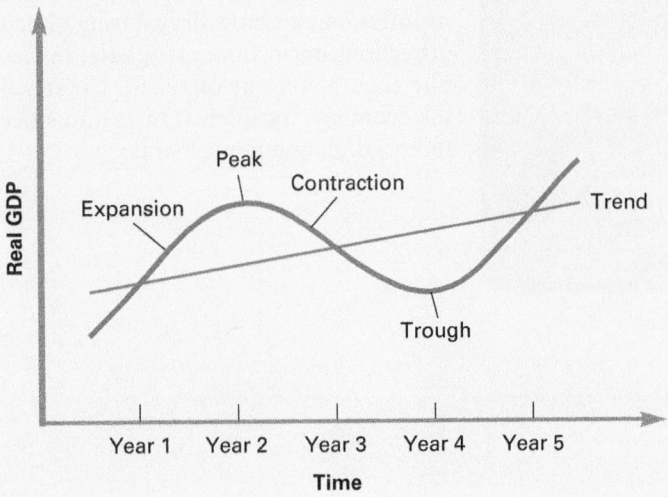

Source: Adapted from William Boyes and Michael Melvin, *Economics*, 8th ed. (Cengage, 2011), p. 35.

inflation
A state of the economy in which the general price level is increasing.

consumer price index (CPI)
A measure of inflation based on changes in the cost of consumer goods and services.

this exchange is a system of *prices*. Technically speaking, the price of something is *the amount of money the seller is willing to accept in exchange for a given quantity of some good or service*—for instance, $3 for a pound of meat or $10 for an hour of work. The economy is said to be experiencing a period of inflation when the general level of prices *increases* over time. The most common measure of inflation, the consumer price index (CPI), is based on changes in the cost of consumer goods and services. At times, the rate of inflation has been substantial. In 1980, for instance, prices went up by 13.6 percent. Fortunately, inflation has dropped dramatically in this country, and the annual rate of inflation has remained below 5 percent every year since 1983, except in 1990, when it was 5.4 percent. While there was mild deflation of –0.34 percent during the financial crisis in 2009, inflation moved up to about 3.2 percent in 2011 and fell below 2 percent for the next few years.

Inflation is of vital concern to financial planning. It affects not only what we pay for our goods and services but also what we earn in our jobs. Inflation tends to give an illusion of something that doesn't exist. That is, though we seem to be making more money, we really aren't. As prices rise, we need more income because our purchasing power—the amount of goods and services each dollar buys at a given time—declines. So be sure to look at what you earn in terms of its purchasing power, not just in absolute dollars.

EXAMPLE: Impact of Inflation on Financial Planning

Carla earned $48,000 in 2015 and expected to receive annual raises so that her salary would be $52,000 by 2018. While the annual growth rate in her salary is 2.7 percent, assume that inflation averaged 3 percent per year. Carla's salary needed to growth to $52,451 just to keep pace with inflation. So her real salary declined.

Chapter 1 | Understanding the Financial Planning Process   **33**

Inflation also directly affects interest rates. High rates of inflation drive up the cost of borrowing money as lenders demand compensation for their eroding purchasing power. Higher interest rates mean higher mortgage payments, higher monthly car payments, and so on. High inflation rates also have a detrimental effect on stock and bond prices. Finally, sustained high rates of inflation can have devastating effects on retirement plans and other long-term financial goals. Indeed, for many people it can put such goals out of reach. Clearly, low inflation is good for the economy, for interest rates and stock and bond prices, and for financial planning in general.

TEST YOURSELF

1-16 Discuss the following statement: "The interactions among government, business, and consumers determine the environment in which personal financial plans must be made."

1-17 What are the stages of an economic cycle? Explain their significance for your personal finances.

1-18 What is *inflation*, and why should it be a concern in financial planning?

1-5 WHAT DETERMINES YOUR PERSONAL INCOME?

LG5, LG6

An obvious and important factor in determining how well we live is the amount of income we earn. In the absence of any inheritance or similar financial windfall, your income will largely depend on such factors as your age, marital status, education, geographic location, and choice of career. A significant level of income—whether derived from your job, your own business, or your investments—is within your reach if you have the necessary dedication, a commitment to hard work, and a well-thought-out set of financial plans. The data in Exhibit 1.12 show how income changes with age and education.

1-5a Demographics and Your Income

Typically, people with low incomes fall into the very young or very old age groups, with the highest earnings generally occurring between the ages of 45 and 64. Those below age 45 are developing careers or beginning to move up in their jobs, and many over 64 are working only part time or are retired. In the 35–44 age group, the median annual income of household heads is about $60,900, and then falls to about $28,500 in the 75 or older age group. Your own income will vary over time, too, so you should incorporate anticipated shifts in earnings into your financial plans.

1-5b Your Education

Your level of formal education is a controllable factor that significantly affects your income. As Exhibit 1.12 illustrates, individuals who have more formal education earn higher annual incomes than do those with lesser degrees. Specifically, the average

EXHIBIT 1.12   How Age and Education Affect Annual Income

The amount of money you earn is closely tied to your age and education. Generally, the closer you are to middle age (45–65) and the more education you have, the greater your income will be.

ANNUAL INCOME (HEAD OF HOUSEHOLD)

Age	Median Income ($)*
Less than 35	35,300
35–44	60,900
45–54	60,900
55–64	55,100
65–74	45,900
75 or older	28,500

Education	Median Income ($)**
No high school diploma	20,150
High school diploma	29,770
Bachelor's degree	50,280
Master's degree	61,040
Professional degree	97,200
Dr. degree	82,880

*Data for 2013.
** Data for 2012.

Source: Adapted from Jesse Bricker, Lisa J. Dettling, Alice Henriques, Joanne W. Hsu, Kevin B. Moore, John Sabelhaus, Jeffrey Thompson, and Richard A. Windle, "Changes in U.S. Family Finances from 2010 to 2013: Evidence from the Survey of Consumer Finances," Board of Governors of the Federal Reserve System, Washington, DC, http://www.federalreserve.gov/pubs/bulletin/2014/pdf/scf14.pdf, Table 1, accessed July 2015; and Institute of Education Statistics, National Center for Education Statistics, Digest of Education Statistics: 2013, http://nces.ed.gov/programs/digest/d13/tables/dt13_502.40.asp, Table 502.40, Table 440, accessed July 2015.

(median) salary of a high school graduate in 2013 was about $29,770, compared to $50,280 for the holder of a bachelor's degree. Add a master's or other professional degree and earnings rise substantially. Over a lifetime, these differences really add up! Education alone cannot guarantee a high income, but these statistics suggest that a solid formal education greatly enhances your earning power. And it makes sense to consider the cost of getting a degree while making your decision to get one.

Do It Now

Recognize That YOU Are Your Most Important Asset

Your greatest asset is YOU. So it's important to build the value of your best asset by investing in your education and career. The amount you can consume, save, and invest is directly related to your earning ability. Consider that over an entire career, the average bachelor's degree holder will earn $1.19 million, which is about twice what the typical high school grad earns and $335,000 more than the typical associate degree holder. (For additional motivating information, see the source of these statistics: The Hamilton Project at the Brookings Institution, http://hamiltonproject.org/earnings_by_major/). It's so important to realize you're your greatest asset and act on it—you can do it now.

1-5c Where You Live

Geographic factors can also affect your earning power. Salaries vary regionally, tending to be higher in the Northeast and West than in the South. Typically, your salary will also be higher if you live in a large metropolitan area rather than a small town or rural area. Such factors as economic conditions, labor supply, and industrial base also affect salary levels in different areas.

Living costs also vary considerably throughout the country. You'd earn more in Los Angeles than in Memphis, Tennessee, but your salary would probably not go as far because of the much higher cost of living in Los Angeles. Like many others, you may decide that lifestyle considerations take priority over earning potential. Your local chamber of commerce or the Internet can provide an intercity cost-of-living index that shows living costs in major cities and serves as a useful resource for comparing jobs in different areas. The overall index is developed by tracking costs in six major categories: groceries, housing, utilities, transportation, health care, and miscellaneous goods and services.

1-5d Your Career

A critical determinant of your lifetime earnings is your career. The career you choose is closely related to your level of education and your particular skills, interests, lifestyle preferences, and personal values. Social, demographic, economic, and technological trends also influence your decision as to what fields offer the best opportunities for your future. It's not a prerequisite for many types of careers (e.g., sales, service, and certain types of manufacturing and clerical work), but a formal education generally leads to greater decision-making responsibility—and consequently increased income potential—within a career. Exhibit 1.13 presents a list of average salaries for various careers.

EXHIBIT 1.13   Representative Salaries for Selected Careers

Professional and managerial workers, who typically have a college degree, tend to earn the highest salaries.

Career	Average Annual Salary ($)
Accountants and auditors	73,760
Architects and engineers	81,520
Computer programmer	82,690
Family and general practice physicians	186,320
Financial analyst	92,250
Human resources manager	114,140
Lawyer	133,470
Paralegal	51,840
Pharmacist	118,470
Police officer	59,530
Psychiatrist	182,700
Registered nurse	69,790
Teacher, elementary school	56,830

Source: "Occupational Employment and Wages - May 2014," News Release, March 25, 2015, Table 1, U.S. Department of Labor, Bureau of Labor Statistics, http://www.bls.gov/news.release/ocwage.nr0.htm, accessed July 2015.

1-5e Planning Your Career

Career planning and personal financial planning are closely related activities, so the decisions you make in one area affect the other. Like financial planning, career planning is a lifelong process that includes short- and long-term goals. Since your career goals are likely to change several times, you should not expect to stay in one field, or to remain with one company, for your whole life.

You might graduate with a computer science degree and accept a job with a software company. Your financial plan might include furnishing your apartment, saving for a vacation or new car, and starting an investment program. If five years later, you decide to attend law school, you'll have to revise your financial plan and include strategies to cover living expenses and finance your tuition. You may decide that you need to go to school at night while earning a living during the day.

The average American starting a career today can expect to have at least ten jobs with five or more employers, and many of us will have three, four, or even more careers during our lifetimes. Some of these changes will be based on personal decisions; others may result from layoffs or corporate downsizing. For example, a branch manager for a regional bank who feels that bank mergers have reduced her job prospects in banking may start her own business and become her own boss. Job security is practically a thing of the past, and corporate loyalty has given way to a more self-directed career approach that requires new career strategies.

Through careful career planning, you can improve your work situation to gain greater personal and professional satisfaction. Some of the steps are similar to the financial planning process described earlier.

- Identify your interests, skills, needs, and values.
- Set specific long- and short-term career goals.
- Develop and use an action plan to achieve those goals.
- Review and revise your career plans as your situation changes.

Your action plan depends on your job situation. For example, if you're unemployed then it should focus on your job search. If you have a job but want to change careers, your action plan might include researching career options, networking to develop a broad base of contacts, listing companies to contact for information, and getting special training to prepare for your chosen career.

A personal portfolio of skills, both general and technical, will protect your earning power during economic downturns and advance it during prosperous times. It's important to keep your skills current with on-the-job training programs and continuing education. Adding proficiency in technology or languages puts you ahead of the pack in keeping up with changing workplace requirements.

Good job-hunting skills will serve you well throughout your career. Learn how to research new career opportunities and investigate potential jobs, taking advantage of online resources as well as traditional ones. Develop a broad base of career resources, starting with your college placement office, the public library, and personal contacts such as family and friends. Know how to market your qualifications to your advantage in your résumé and cover letters, on the phone, and in person during a job interview.

Financial Fact or Fantasy?

Your income level depends on your age, education, and career choice.
Fact: All three of these variables are important determinants of your income level, particularly when accompanied by adequate ambition and disciplined work habits.

TEST YOURSELF

1-19 "All people who have equivalent formal education earn similar incomes." Do you agree or disagree with this statement? Explain your position.

1-20 Discuss the need for career planning throughout the life cycle and its relationship to financial planning. What are some of your personal career goals?

Financial Impact of Personal Choices
Bob Cuts Back on Lunch Out and Lattes

Bob buys lunch out most days and buys a latte every morning. He believes he could cut back a bit and save $5 a day, which is $35 a week and $140 a month. So what's the impact of this seemingly modest cutback?

If Bob invests his $35 savings a week every month at 5 percent, he will have the following in the future:

20 years: $ 57,545
30 years: $116,516
40 years: $213,643

So the seemingly small act of investing only $5 a day would have a dramatic long-term effect on Bob's future accumulated wealth.

Summary

LG1 **Identify the benefits of using personal financial planning techniques to manage your finances. p. 3**
Personal financial planning helps you marshal and control your financial resources. It should allow you to improve your standard of living, to enjoy your money more by spending it wisely, and to accumulate wealth. By setting short- and long-term financial goals, you'll enhance your quality of life both now and in the future.

LG2 **Describe the personal financial planning process and define your goals. p. 8**
Personal financial planning is a six-step process that helps you achieve your financial goals: (1) define financial goals; (2) develop financial plans and strategies to achieve those goals; (3) implement financial plans and strategies; (4) periodically develop and implement budgets to monitor and control progress toward goals; (5) use financial statements to evaluate results of plans and budgets, taking corrective action as required; and (6) redefine goals and revise plans and strategies as personal circumstances change. It is critical to realistically spell out your short-term, intermediate, and long-term financial goals. Your goals, which reflect your values and circumstances, may change owing to personal circumstances.

LG3 **Explain the life cycle of financial plans, their role in achieving your financial goals, how to**
deal with special planning concerns, and the use of professional financial planners. p. 16
In moving through various life-cycle stages, you must revise your financial plans to include goals and strategies appropriate to each stage. Income and expense patterns change with age. Changes in your life due to marriage, children, divorce, remarriage, and job status also necessitate adapting financial plans to meet current needs. Although these plans change over time, they are the road map you'll follow to achieve your financial goals. After defining your goals, you can develop and implement an appropriate personal financial plan. A complete set of financial plans covers asset acquisition, liability and insurance, savings and investments, employee benefits, taxes, and retirement and estate planning. Review these plans regularly and revise them accordingly. Situations that require special attention include managing two incomes, managing employee benefits, and adapting to changes in your personal situation, such as marital status or taking responsibility for elderly relatives' care. Professional financial planners can help you with the planning process.

LG4 **Examine the economic environment's influence on personal financial planning. p. 29**
Financial planning occurs in an environment where government, business, and consumers are all influential participants. Personal financial decisions are affected by economic cycles (expansion, recession,

depression, and recovery) and the impact of inflation on prices (purchasing power and personal income).

LG5 **Evaluate the impact of age, education, and geographic location on personal income. p. 34** Demographics, education, and career are all important factors affecting your income level. People between 45 and 64 years old tend to earn more than others, as do those who are married. Equally important, statistics show that income generally increases with the level of education. Where you live is an additional consideration, because salaries and living costs are higher in some areas than in others. Career choices also affect your level of income: those in professional and managerial positions tend to earn the highest salaries.

LG6 **Understand the importance of career choices and their relationship to personal financial planning. p. 34** Career planning is a lifetime process that involves goal setting as well as career development strategies. A career plan should be flexible enough to adapt to new workplace requirements. When making career plans, identify your interests, skills, needs, and values; set specific long- and short-term career goals; develop and use an action plan to achieve your goals; and review and revise your career plans as your situation changes. Coordinate your career plans with your personal financial plans.

Key Terms

average propensity to consume, 5

consumer price index (CPI), 33

contraction, 32

expansion, 32

financial assets, 7

financial goals, 9

flexible-benefit (cafeteria) plan, 24

goal dates, 13

gross domestic product (GDP), 32

inflation, 33

money, 10

peak, 32

personal financial planning, 8

professional financial planner, 26

standard of living, 4

tangible assets, 7

trough, 32

utility, 10

wealth, 7

Answers to Test Yourself

You can find answers to these questions on this book's companion website. Look for it at *www.cengagebrain.com*. Search for this book by its title, and then add it to your dashboard.

Financial Planning Exercises

LG1, p. 3

1. *Benefits of Personal Financial Planning.* How can using personal financial planning tools help you improve your financial situation? Describe changes you can make in at least three areas.

LG2, 3 p. 8, 16

2. *Personal Financial Goals and the Life Cycle. Use Worksheet 1.1.* Describe your current status based on the personal financial planning life cycle shown in Exhibit 1.7. Fill out Worksheet 1.1, "Summary of Personal Financial Goals," with goals reflecting your current situation and your expected life situation in 5 and 10 years. Discuss the reasons for the changes in your goals and how you'll need to adapt your financial plans as a result. Which types of financial plans do you need for your current situation, and why?

LG2, p. 8

3. *Personal Financial Goals.* Recommend three financial goals and related activities for someone in each of the following circumstances:
   - A junior in college
   - A 30-year-old computer programmer who plans to earn an MBA degree

- A couple in their 30s with two children, ages 3 and 6
- A divorced 52-year-old man with a 16-year-old child and a 78-year-old father who is ill

LG3, p. 16
4. **Life Cycle of Financial Plans.** Ben Saunders and Ashley Tinsdale are planning to get married in six months. Both are 30 years old have been out of college for several years. Ben uses three credit cards and has a bank account balance of $7,500 while Ashely only uses one credit card and has $9,500 in her bank account. What financial planning advice would you give the couple?

LG4, p. 29
5. **Impact of Economic Environment on Financial Planning.** Summarize current and projected trends in the economy with regard to GDP growth, unemployment, and inflation. How should you use this information to make personal financial and career planning decisions?

LG5, p. 34
6. **Financial Impact of Career Decisions.** Alice Reynolds and Tricia Bostwick, both freshman and friends at a major university, are interested in going into a health sciences career. While they're not just interested in the money they can make, they do want to have a sense of the compensation in different health sciences careers. What do the data in Exhibit 1.13 tell Alice and Tricia?

LG6, p. 34
7. **Career Choices and Financial Planning.** Assume that you graduated from college with a major in marketing and took a job with a large consumer products company. After three years, you are laid off when the company downsizes. Describe the steps you'd take to "repackage" yourself for another field.

Applying Personal Finance

Watch Your Attitude!

Many people's *attitude* toward money has as much or more to do with their ability to accumulate wealth as it does with the *amount* of money they earn. As observed in Exhibit 1.4, your attitude toward money influences the entire financial planning process and often determines whether financial goals become reality or end up being pipe dreams. This project will help you examine your attitude toward money and wealth so that you can formulate realistic goals and plans.

Use the following questions to stimulate your thought process.

a. Am I a saver, or do I spend almost all the money I receive?
b. Does it make me feel good just to spend money, regardless of what it's for?
c. Is it important for me to have new clothes or a new car just for the sake of having them?
d. Do I have clothes hanging in my closet with the price tags still on them?
e. Do I buy things because they are a bargain or because I need them?
f. Do I save for my vacations, or do I charge everything and take months paying off my credit card at high interest?
g. If I have a balance on my credit card, can I recall what the charges were for without looking at my statement?
h. Where do I want to be professionally and financially in 5 years? In 10 years?
i. Will my attitude toward money help get me there? If not, what do I need to do?
j. If I dropped out of school today or lost my job, what would I do?

Does your attitude toward money help or hinder you? How can you adjust your attitude so that you are more likely to accomplish your financial goals?

CRITICAL THINKING CASES

LG1, 2, 3, 4, p. 3, 8, 16, 29
1.1 Jim's Need to Know: Personal Finance or Golf?

During the Christmas break of his final year at the University of Maryland (UMD), Jim Malone plans to put together his résumé in order to seek full-time employment as a software engineer during the spring semester. To help Jim prepare for the job interview process, his older brother has arranged for him to meet with a friend, Lisa Bancroft, who has worked as a software engineer since her graduation from UMD two years earlier. Lisa gives him numerous pointers on résumé preparation, the interview process, and possible job opportunities.

After answering Jim's many questions, Lisa asks Jim to update her on what he's up to at UMD. As they discuss courses, Lisa indicates that of all the electives she took, the personal financial planning course was most useful. Jim says that, although he had considered personal financial planning for his last elective, he's currently leaning toward a beginning golf course. He feels that the course will be fun because some of his friends are taking it. He points out that he doesn't expect to get rich and already knows how to balance his checkbook. Lisa tells him that personal financial planning involves much more than balancing a checkbook, and that the course is highly relevant regardless of income level. She strongly believes that the personal financial planning course will benefit Jim more than beginning golf—a course that she also took while at UMD.

Critical Thinking Questions

1. Describe to Jim the goals and rewards of the personal financial planning process.
2. Explain to Jim what is meant by the term *financial planning* and why it is important regardless of income.
3. Describe the financial planning environment to Jim. Explain the role of the consumer and the impact of economic conditions on financial planning.
4. What arguments would you present to convince Jim that the personal financial planning course would benefit him more than beginning golf?

LG5, 6, p. 34

1.2 Brad's Dilemma: Finding a New Job

Brad Thomas, a 53-year-old retail store manager earning $75,000 a year, has worked for the same company during his entire 28-year career. Brad was recently laid off and is still unemployed 10 months later, and his severance pay and 6 months' unemployment compensation have run out. Because he has consistently observed careful financial planning practices, he now has sufficient savings and investments to carry him through several more months of unemployment.

Brad is actively seeking work but finds that he is overqualified for available lower-paying jobs and under-qualified for higher-paying, more desirable positions. There are no openings for positions equivalent to the manager's job he lost. He lost his wife several years earlier and is close to his two grown children, who live in the same city.

Brad has these options:

- Wait out the recession until another retail store manager position opens up.
- Move to another area of the country where store manager positions are more plentiful.
- Accept a lower-paying job for two or three years and then go back to school evenings to finish his college degree and qualify for a better position.
- Consider other types of jobs that could benefit from his managerial skills.

Critical Thinking Questions

1. What important career factors should Brad consider when evaluating his options?
2. What important personal factors should Brad consider when deciding among his career options?
3. What recommendations would you give Brad in light of both the career and personal dimensions of his options noted in Questions 1 and 2?
4. What career strategies should today's workers employ in order to avoid Brad's dilemma?

CHAPTER 2

Using Financial Statements and Budgets

LEARNING GOALS

LG1   Understand the relationship between financial plans and statements.

LG2   Prepare a personal balance sheet.

LG3   Generate a personal income and expense statement.

LG4   Develop a good record-keeping system and use ratios to evaluate personal financial statements.

LG5   Construct a cash budget and use it to monitor and control spending.

LG6   Apply time value of money concepts to put a monetary value on financial goals.

How Will This Affect Me?

Recent polls show that up to 70 percent of Americans do not prepare a detailed household budget and about 75 percent do not have enough savings to cover 6 to 9 months of expenses.* These are scary numbers ... and this chapter shows what you can do to avoid being part of these alarming statistics.

Everyone knows it's hard to get where you need to go if you don't know where you are. Financial goals describe your destination, and financial statements and budgets are the tools that help you determine exactly where you are in the journey. This chapter helps you define your financial goals and explains how to gauge your progress carefully over time.

*Gallup's annual Economy and Personal Finance poll, June 2013, and CNNMoney, 2013.

2-1 MAPPING OUT YOUR FINANCIAL FUTURE

personal financial statements
Balance sheets and income and expense statements that serve as essential planning tools for developing and monitoring personal financial plans.

balance sheet
A financial statement that describes a person's financial position at a *given point* in time.

income and expense statement
A financial statement that measures financial performance *over* time.

On your journey to financial security, you need navigational tools to guide you to your destination: namely, the fulfillment of your financial goals. Operating without a plan is like traveling without a road map. Financial plans, financial statements, and budgets provide direction by helping you work toward specific financial goals. Financial plans are the road maps that show you the way, whereas personal financial statements let you know where you stand. Budgets, detailed short-term financial forecasts that compare estimated income with estimated expenses, allow you to monitor and control expenses and purchases in a manner that is consistent with your financial plans. All three tools are essential to sound personal financial management and the achievement of goals. They provide control by bringing the various dimensions of your personal financial affairs into focus.

2-1a The Role of Financial Statements in Financial Planning

Before you can set realistic goals, develop your financial plans, or effectively manage your money, you must take stock of your current financial situation. You'll also need tools to monitor your progress. **Personal financial statements** are planning tools that provide an up-to-date evaluation of your financial well-being, help you identify potential financial problems, and help you make better-informed financial decisions. They measure your financial condition so you can establish realistic financial goals and evaluate your progress toward those goals. Knowing how to prepare and interpret personal financial statements is a cornerstone of personal financial planning.

Two types of personal financial statements—the balance sheet and income and expense statement—are essential to developing and monitoring personal financial plans. They show your financial position as it *actually* exists and report on financial transactions that have *really* occurred.

The **balance sheet** describes your financial position—the assets you hold, less the debts you owe, equal your net worth (general level of wealth)—at a *given point in time.* This planning tool helps you track the progress you're making in building up your assets and reducing your debt.

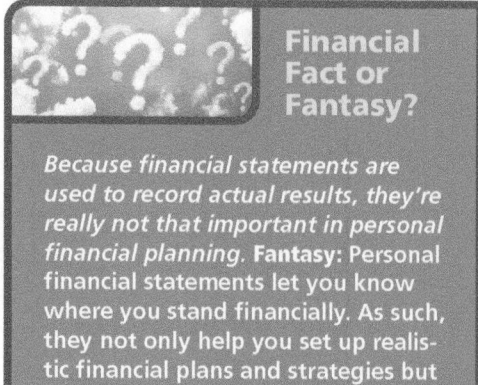
budgets
A detailed financial report that looks *forward*, based on expected income and expenses.

In contrast, the income and expense statement measures financial performance *over* time. It tracks income earned, as well as expenses made, during a given period (usually a month or a year). You use this tool to compare your actual expenses and purchases with the amounts budgeted and then make the necessary changes to correct discrepancies between the actual and budgeted amounts. This information helps you control your future expenses and purchases so you'll have the funds needed to carry out your financial plans.

Budgets, another type of financial report, are *forward* looking. Budgets allow you to monitor and control spending because they are based on expected income and expenses.

Exhibit 2.1 summarizes the various financial statements and reports and their relationship to each other in the personal financial planning process. Note that financial plans provide direction to annual budgets, whereas budgets directly affect both your balance sheet and your income and expense statement. As you move from plans to budgets to actual statements, you can compare your actual results with your plans. This will show you how well you are meeting your financial goals and staying within your budget.

EXHIBIT 2.1 | **The Interlocking Network of Financial Plans and Statements**

Personal financial planning involves a network of financial reports that link future goals and plans with actual results. Such a network provides direction, control, and feedback.

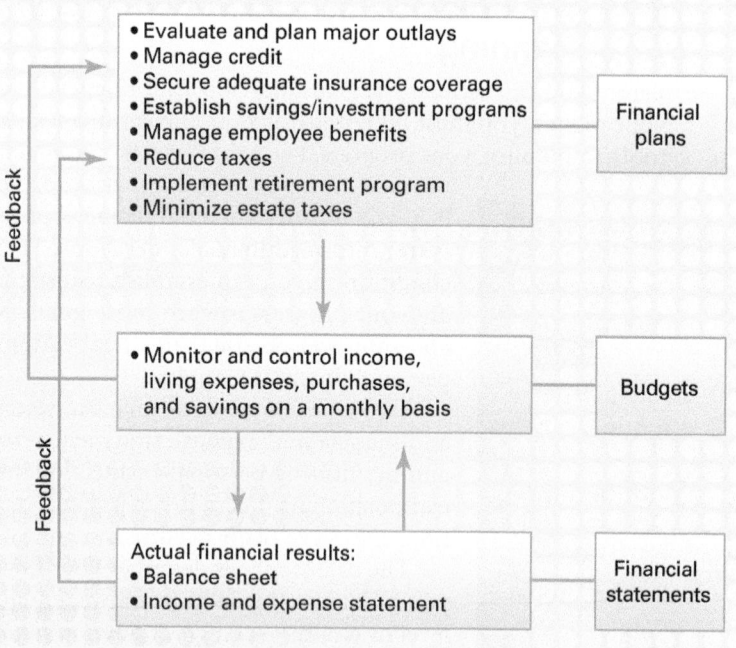

FINANCIAL ROAD SIGN

How to Have a Realistic Budget

- So what if it's on sale? Don't buy it if you wouldn't have bought it anyway.
- Spend less than you earn. You'll need to pay off debt, design a realistic budget, and save some of your income each month.
- Make more and buy less. Make your own lunches, coffee, and anything else you can without great effort. Why spend the money if you can make it yourself without spending a lot of time?
- Live one raise behind. When you get a raise, continue living and spending as you did before and put that additional income into savings.
- Make 30-day lists. When you see something you really want to buy, put it on a 30-day list and only buy it if you still want it in 30 days.

Source: http://www.careeroverview.com/blog/2010/the-psychology-of-spending-money-25-tricks-you-need-to-know/, accessed July 2015.

2-1b Assessing Your Financial Situation, Plans, and Goals

As you learned in Chapter 1, the financial planning process includes six steps that translate personal financial goals into specific financial plans and the strategies to achieve these goals. In addition to clearly defining your financial goals in measurable terms, you need to put target dates and a monetary value on your short-term, intermediate, and long-term goals. We'll discuss the various types of financial statements and plans in this chapter. Then we'll look at how to use "time value of money" concepts to calculate the value of a financial goal that occurs years into the future.

TEST YOURSELF

2-1 What are the two types of personal financial statements? What is a budget, and how does it differ from personal financial statements? What role do these reports play in a financial plan?

2-2 THE BALANCE SHEET: HOW MUCH ARE YOU WORTH TODAY?

Because you should track your progress toward your financial goals, you need a starting point that shows how much you're worth today. Preparing a personal balance sheet, or statement of financial position, will give you this important information. This financial statement represents a person's (or family's) financial condition at a given point in time. Think of a balance sheet as a snapshot taken of your financial position on one day out of the year.

A balance sheet has three parts that, taken together, summarize your financial picture:

- Assets: What you own
- Liabilities, or debts: What you owe
- Net worth: The difference between your assets and liabilities

The accounting relationship among these three categories is called the balance sheet equation and is expressed as follows:

$$\text{Total Assets} = \text{Total Liabilities} + \text{Net Worth}$$

or

$$\text{Net Worth} = \text{Total Assets} - \text{Total Liabilities}$$

> **EXAMPLE: The Balance Sheet Identity**
>
> Courtney has total liabilities of $150,000 and a net worth of $75,000. This implies that she has total assets of $325,000 (total liabilities of $150,000 + net worth of $75,000 = $325,000 in total assets).

Let's now look at the components of each section of the balance sheet.

2-2a Assets: The Things You Own

assets
Items that one owns.

Assets are the items you own. An item is classified as an asset whether it was purchased with cash or financed using debt. In other words, even if you haven't fully paid for an asset, you should list it on the balance sheet. In contrast, an item that's leased is not shown as an asset because someone else actually owns it.

A useful way to group assets is on the basis of their underlying characteristics and uses. This results in four broad categories: liquid assets, investments, real property, and personal property.

liquid assets
Assets that are held in the form of cash or that can readily be converted to cash with little or no loss in value.

investments
Assets such as stocks, bonds, mutual funds, and real estate that are acquired in order to earn a return rather than provide a service.

real property
Tangible assets that are immovable: land and anything fixed to it, such as a house.

personal property
Tangible assets that are movable and used in everyday life.

- **Liquid assets:** Low-risk financial assets held in the form of cash or instruments that can be converted to cash quickly, with little or no loss in value. They are used to meet the everyday needs of life and provide for emergencies and unexpected opportunities. Cash on hand or in a checking or savings account, money market deposit accounts, money market mutual funds, or certificates of deposit that mature within 1 year are all examples of liquid assets.
- **Investments:** Assets acquired to earn a return rather than provide a service. These assets are mostly intangible financial assets (stocks, bonds, mutual funds, and other types of securities), typically acquired to achieve long-term personal financial goals. Business ownership, the cash value of life insurance and pensions, retirement funds such as IRAs and 401(k) plans, and other investment vehicles such as commodities, financial futures, and options represent still other forms of investment assets. (For retirement fund accounts, only those balances that are eligible to be withdrawn should be shown as an asset on the balance sheet. Alternatively, those balances could be shown on an after-tax basis.) They vary in marketability (the ability to sell quickly) from high (stocks and bonds) to low (real estate and business ownership investments).
- **Real and personal property:** Tangible assets that we use in our everyday lives. **Real property** refers to immovable property: land and anything fixed to it, such as a house. Real property generally has a relatively long life and high cost, and it may appreciate, or increase in value. **Personal property** is movable property, such as automobiles, recreational equipment, household furnishings and appliances, clothing, jewelry, home electronics, and similar items. Most types of personal property depreciate, or decline in value, shortly after being put into use.

About 40 percent of the average household's assets consists of financial assets (liquid assets and investments); nearly half is real property (including housing); and the rest is other nonfinancial assets. The left side of Worksheet 2.1 lists some of the typical assets you'd find on a personal balance sheet.

fair market value
The actual value of an asset, or the price for which it can reasonably be expected to sell in the open market.

All assets, regardless of category, should be recorded on the balance sheet at their current **fair market value**, which may differ considerably from their original purchase price. Fair market value is either the actual value of the asset (such as money in a checking account) or the price for which the asset can reasonably be expected to sell in the open market (as with a used car or a home).

If you've taken an accounting course, you will notice a difference between the way assets are recorded on a personal balance sheet and a business balance sheet. Under generally accepted accounting principles (GAAP), the accounting profession's guiding rules, assets appear on a company's balance sheet at cost, not at fair market value. One reason for the disparity is that in business, an asset's value is often subject to debate and uncertainty. The users of the statements may have different goals, and accountants like to be conservative in their measurements. For purposes of personal financial planning, the user and the preparer of the statement are one and the same. Besides, most personal assets have market values that can be estimated easily.

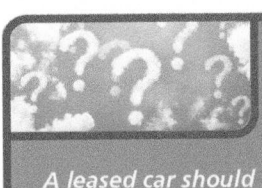

Financial Fact or Fantasy?

A leased car should be listed as an asset on your personal balance sheet. **Fantasy:** You are only "using" the leased car and do not own it. Consequently, it should not be included as an asset on the balance sheet.

2-2b Liabilities: The Money You Owe

liabilities
Debts such as credit card charges, loans, and mortgages.

Liabilities represent an individual's or family's debts. They could result from department-store charges, bank credit card charges, installment loans, or mortgages on housing and other real estate. A liability, regardless of its source, is something that you owe and must repay in the future.

Liabilities are generally classified according to maturity.

current (short-term) liability
Any debt due within 1 year of the date of the balance sheet.

open account credit obligations
Current liabilities that represent the balances outstanding against established credit lines.

- **Current, or short-term, liability:** Any debt currently owed and due within 1 year of the date of the balance sheet. Examples include charges for consumable goods, utility bills, rent, insurance premiums, taxes, medical bills, repair bills, and total **open account credit obligations**—the outstanding balances against established credit lines (usually through credit card purchases).
- **Long-term liability:** Debt due 1 year or more from the date of the balance sheet. These liabilities typically include real estate mortgages, most consumer installment loans, education loans, and margin loans used to purchase securities.

long-term liability
Any debt due 1 year or more from the date of the balance sheet.

You must show all types of loans on your balance sheet. Although most loans will fall into the category of long-term liabilities, any loans that come due within a year should be shown as current liabilities. Examples of short-term loans include a 6-month, single-payment bank loan and a 9-month consumer installment loan for a refrigerator.

Regardless of the type of loan, only the latest outstanding loan balance should be shown as a liability on the balance sheet, because at any given time, it is the balance still due that matters, not the initial loan balance. Another important and closely related point is that only the outstanding principal portion of a loan or mortgage should be listed as a liability on the balance sheet. In other words, you should not include the interest portion of your payments as part of your balance sheet debt. The **principal** is the amount of debt you owe at a given time, and future interest payments are not accounted for separately as long-term liabilities on the balance sheet.

Financial Fact or Fantasy?

Only the principal portion of a loan should be recorded on the liability side of a balance sheet. **Fact:** The principal portion of a loan represents the unpaid balance and is the amount of money you owe. In contrast, interest is a charge that will be levied over time for the use of the money.

Lenders evaluate a prospective borrower's liabilities carefully. High levels of debt and overdue debts are both viewed with disfavor. You'll find the most common categories of liabilities on Worksheet 2.1.

A balance sheet is set up to show what you own on one side (your assets) and how you pay for them on the other (debt or net worth). As you can see, the Kanes have more assets than liabilities.

BALANCE SHEET

Name(s) _Simon and Meghan Kane_   Date _December 31, 2017_

ASSETS			LIABILITIES		
Liquid Assets			**Current Liabilities**		
Cash on hand	$	150	Utilities	$	175
In checking		575	Rent		
Savings accounts		760	Insurance premiums		
Money market funds and deposits		800	Taxes		
Certificates of deposit			Medical/dental bills		125
Total Liquid Assets	$	2,285	Repair bills		
			Bank credit card balances		425
Investments			Dept. store credit card balances		165
Stocks		3,750	Travel and entertainment card balances		135
Bonds		1,000	Gas and other credit card balances		
Certificates of deposit			Bank line of credit balances		
Mutual funds		2,250	Other current liabilities		45
Real estate			**Total Current Liabilities**	$	1,070
Retirement funds, IRA		4,000			
Other			**Long-Term Liabilities**		
Total Investments	$	11,000	Primary residence mortgage	$160,000	
			Second home mortgage		
Real Property			Real estate investment mortgage		
Primary residence	$225,000		Auto loans		4,350
Second home			Appliance/furniture loans		800
Other			Home improvement loans		
Total Real Property	$	225,000	Single-payment loans		
			Education loans		3,800
Personal Property			Margin loans		
Auto(s): '12 Toyota Corolla	$	10,600	Other long-term loans (from parents)		4,000
Auto(s): '10 Ford Focus		7,400	**Total Long-Term Liabilities**	$	172,950
Recreational vehicles					
Household furnishings		3,700	**(II) Total Liabilities**	$	174,020
Jewelry and artwork		1,500			
Other					
Other			**Net Worth [(I) – (II)]**	$	87,465
Total Personal Property	$	23,200			
(I)Total Assets	$	261,485	**Total Liabilities and Net Worth**	$	261,485

2-2c Net Worth: A Measure of Your Financial Worth

net worth
An individual's or family's actual wealth; determined by subtracting total liabilities from total assets.

equity
The actual ownership interest in a specific asset or group of assets.

Now that you've listed what you own and what you owe, you can calculate your **net worth**, the amount of actual wealth or **equity** that an individual or family has in owned assets. It represents the amount of money you'd have left after selling all your owned assets at their estimated fair market values and paying off all your liabilities (assuming there are no transaction costs). As noted earlier, every balance sheet must "balance" so that total assets equal total liabilities plus net worth. Rearranging this equation, we see that net worth equals total assets minus total liabilities. Once you establish the fair market value of assets and the level of liabilities, you can easily calculate net worth by subtracting total liabilities from total assets. If net worth is less than zero, the family is technically insolvent. Although this form of insolvency doesn't necessarily mean that the family will end up in bankruptcy proceedings, it likely shows insufficient financial planning.

Net worth typically increases over the life cycle of an individual or family, as Exhibit 2.2 illustrates. For example, the balance sheet of a college student will probably be fairly simple. Assets would include modest liquid assets (cash, checking, and savings accounts) and personal property, which may include a car. Liabilities might include utility bills, perhaps some open account credit obligations, and automobile and education loans. At this point in life, net worth would typically be low because assets are small in comparison with liabilities. In contrast, a 32-year-old single schoolteacher would have more liquid assets and personal property, may have started an investment program, and may have purchased a condominium. Net worth would be rising but may still be low due to the increased liabilities associated with real and personal property purchases. The higher net worth of a two-career couple in their late 30s with children reflects a greater proportion of assets relative to liabilities as they save for college expenses and retirement.

The level of net worth is important in the long-term financial planning process. Once you have established a goal of accumulating a certain level and type of wealth, you can track progress toward that goal by monitoring net worth.

> **EXAMPLE: Calculating Net Worth**
>
> A family has total assets of $225,000 and total liabilities of $175,000. Net worth is total assets of $225,000 less total liabilities of $175,000, which equals $50,000. This is effectively the amount of assets the family "owns" after paying off its liabilities.

2-2d Balance Sheet Format and Preparation

You should prepare your personal balance sheet at least once a year, preferably every 3 to 6 months. Here's how to do it, using the categories in Worksheet 2.1 as a guide.

1. **List your assets at their fair market value as of the date you are preparing the balance sheet.** You'll find the fair market value of liquid and investment assets on checking and savings account records and investment account statements. Estimate the values of homes and cars using published sources of information, such as advertisements for comparable homes and the *Kelley Blue Book* for used car values. Certain items—for example, homes, jewelry, and artwork—may appreciate, or increase in value, over time. The values of assets like cars and most other types of personal property will depreciate, or decrease in value, over time.
2. **List all current and long-term liabilities.** Show all outstanding charges, even if you haven't received the bill, as current liabilities on the balance sheet. For example, assume that on April 25, you used your MasterCard to charge $600 for a set of tires. You typically receive your MasterCard bill around the 10th of the following month. If you were preparing a balance sheet dated April 30, you should include the $600 as a current liability, even though the bill won't arrive until May 10. Remember to list only the principal balance of any loan obligation.
3. **Calculate net worth.** Subtract your total liabilities from your total assets. This is your net worth, which reflects the equity you have in your total assets.

2-2e A Balance Sheet for Simon and Meghan Kane

What can you learn from a balance sheet? Let's examine a hypothetical balance sheet as of December 31, 2017, prepared for Simon and Meghan Kane, the young couple (ages 28 and 26) we met in Chapter 1 (see Worksheet 2.1). Assets are listed on the left side, with the most liquid first; liabilities are on the right, starting with the most recent. The net worth entry is at the bottom right of the statement, just below the

EXHIBIT 2.2 | **Median Net Worth by Age**

Net worth starts to build in the younger-than-35 age bracket and continues to climb, peaking at the 65–74 age bracket. As indicated for the 75 and older age bracket, net worth declines after a person has been retired for a few years and has consequently used some of his or her assets to meet living expenses.

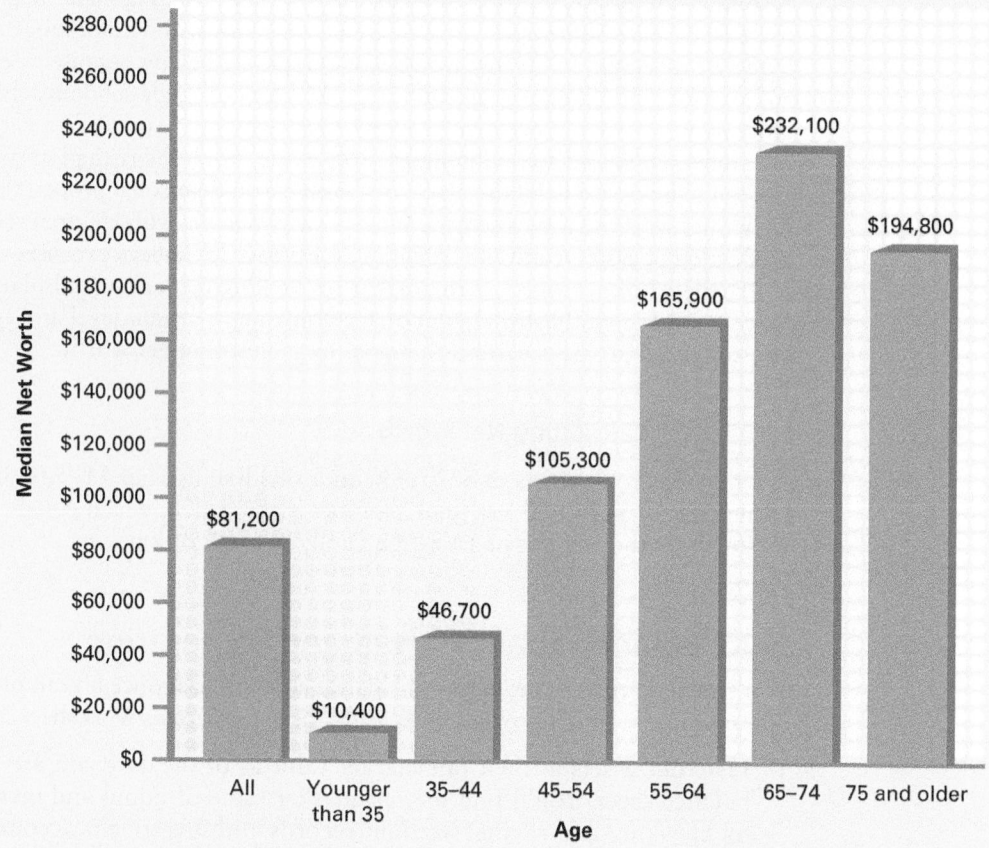

Source: Adapted from Jesse Bricker, Lisa J. Dettling, Alice Henriques, Joanne W. Hsu, Kevin B. Moore, John Sabelhaus, Jeffrey Thompson, and Richard A. Windle, "Changes in U.S. Family Finances from 2010 to 2013: Evidence from the Survey of Consumer Finances," Board of Governors of the Federal Reserve System, Washington, DC (October 24, 2014; data are for 2013), http://www.federalreserve.gov/pubs/bulletin/2014/pdf/scf14.pdf, Table 2, accessed July 2015.

liabilities. The statement should balance: total assets should equal the sum of total liabilities and net worth, as in the balance sheet equation on page 46. Here's what this financial statement tells us about the Kanes' financial condition:

- **Assets:** Given their ages, the Kanes' asset position looks quite good. The dominant asset is their house. They also have $11,000 in investments, which include retirement funds and appear to have adequate liquid assets to meet their bill payments and cover small, unexpected expenses.
- **Liabilities:** The Kanes' primary liability is the $160,000 mortgage on their house. Their equity, or actual ownership interest, in the house is approximately $65,000 ($225,000 market value minus the $160,000 outstanding mortgage loan). Their current liabilities are $1,070, with other debts of $12,950 representing auto, furniture, and education loans, as well as a loan from their parents to help with the down payment on their home.
- **Net worth:** The Kanes' net worth ($261,485 in total assets minus total liabilities of $174,020) is $87,465—a respectable amount that is enviably above the median for their age group shown in Exhibit 2.2.

Comparing the Kanes' total liabilities to their total assets gives a more realistic view of their current wealth position than merely looking at assets or liabilities alone. By calculating their net worth periodically, the Kanes can measure their progress toward achieving their financial goals.

TEST YOURSELF

2-2 Describe the balance sheet, its components, and how you would use it in personal financial planning. Differentiate between investments and real and personal property.

2-3 What is the balance sheet equation? Explain when a family may be viewed as technically insolvent.

2-4 Explain two ways in which net worth could increase (or decrease) from one period to the next.

2-3 THE INCOME AND EXPENSE STATEMENT: WHAT WE EARN AND WHERE IT GOES

LG3 When confronted with a lack of funds, the first question people ask themselves is, "Where does all the money go?" Preparing an income and expense statement would answer this question. Whereas the balance sheet describes a person's or family's financial position at a given time, the income and expense statement captures the various financial transactions that have occurred over the stated period of time, which is usually a year or a month. Think of this statement as a motion picture that not only shows actual results over time but also lets you compare them with budgeted financial goals. Equally important, the statement allows you to evaluate the amount of saving and investing during the period it covers.

Like the balance sheet, the income and expense statement has three major parts: income, expenses, and cash surplus (or deficit). A cash surplus (or deficit) is merely the difference between income and expenses. The statement is prepared on a cash basis, which means that only transactions involving actual cash inflows or actual cash outlays are recorded. The term cash is used in this case to include not only coin and currency but also checks and debit card transactions drawn against checking and certain types of savings accounts.

Income and expense patterns change over the individual's or family's life cycle. Income and spending levels typically rise steadily to a peak in the 45–54 age bracket. On average, people in this age group, whose children are typically in college or no longer at home, have the highest level of income. They also spend more than other age groups on entertainment, dining out, transportation, education, insurance, and charitable contributions. Families in the 35–44 age range have slightly lower average levels of income and expenses and very different spending patterns. Because they tend to have school-age children, they spend more on groceries, housing, clothing, and other personal needs. Yet the average percentage of pre-tax income spent is about the same—at around 75 percent to 80 percent—for all age ranges through age 64. It rises sharply to about 97 percent, however, for persons age 65 and over.

cash basis
A method of preparing financial statements in which only transactions involving actual cash receipts or actual cash outlays are recorded.

2-3a Income: Cash In

income
Earnings received as wages, salaries, bonuses, commissions, interest and dividends, or proceeds from the sale of assets.

Common sources of income include earnings received as wages, salaries, self-employment income, bonuses, and commissions; interest and dividends received from savings and investments; and proceeds from the sale of assets such as stocks and bonds or an auto. Other income items include pension, annuity, and Social Security income; rent received from leased assets; alimony and child support; scholarships or grants; tax refunds; and miscellaneous types of income. Worksheet 2.2, Income and Expense Statement for Simon and Meghan Kane, has general categories for recording income.

Note also that the proper figure to use is *gross* wages, salaries, and commissions, which constitute the amount of income you receive from your employer *before* taxes and other payroll deductions. The gross value is used because the taxes and payroll deductions will be itemized and deducted as expenses later in the income and expense statement. Therefore, you should not use take-home pay, because it understates your income by the amount of these deductions.

2-3b Expenses: Cash Out

expenses
Money spent on living costs and to pay taxes, purchase assets, or repay debt.

Expenses represent money used for outlays. Worksheet 2.2, Income and Expense Statement for Simon and Meghan Kane categorizes them by the types of benefits they provide: (1) living expenses (such as housing, utilities, food, transportation, medical, clothing, and insurance); (2) tax payments; (3) asset purchases (such as autos, stereos, furniture, appliances, and loan payments on them); and (4) other payments for personal care, recreation and entertainment, and other expenses. Some are fixed expenses—usually contractual, predetermined, and involving equal payments each period (typically each month). Examples include mortgage and installment loan payments, insurance premiums, professional or union dues, club dues, monthly savings or investment programs, and cable TV fees. Others (such as food, clothing, utilities, entertainment, and medical expenses) are variable expenses, because their amounts change from one time period to the next.

fixed expenses
Contractual, predetermined expenses involving equal payments each period.

variable expenses
Expenses involving payment amounts that change from one time period to the next.

Exhibit 2.3 shows the average annual expenses by major category as a percentage of after-tax income. It's a useful benchmark to see how you compare with national averages. However, your own expenses will vary according to your age, lifestyle, and where you live. For example, it costs considerably more to buy a home in San Diego than in Charlotte. Similarly, if you live in the suburbs, your commuting expenses will be higher than those of city dwellers.

2-3c Cash Surplus (or Deficit)

The third component of the income and expense statement shows the net result of the period's financial activities. Subtracting total expenses from total income gives you the cash surplus (or deficit) for the period. At a glance, you can see how you did financially over the period. A positive figure indicates that expenses were less than income, resulting in a cash surplus. A value of zero indicates that expenses were exactly equal to income for the period, while a negative value means that your expenses exceeded income and you have a cash deficit.

cash surplus
An excess amount of income over expenses that results in *increased* net worth.

cash deficit
An excess amount of expenses over income, resulting in insufficient funds as well as in *decreased* net worth.

You can use a cash surplus for savings or investment purposes, to acquire assets, or to reduce debt. Adding to savings or investments should increase your future income and net worth, and making payments on debt affects cash flow favorably by reducing future expenses. In contrast, when a cash deficit occurs, you must cover the shortfall from your savings or investments, reduce assets, or borrow. All of these strategies will reduce net worth and negatively affect your financial future.

EXAMPLE: Calculating a Cash Surplus or Deficit

Will had cash income this year of $50,000 and cash expenses of $47,500. Consequently, his cash surplus is $2,500, which is income of $50,000 less expenses of $47,500. Had Will's expenses been $51,200 while earning the same income, he would have generated a cash deficit of $1,200, which is $50,000 minus $51,200.

The income and expense statement shows what you earned, how you spent your money, and how much you were left with (or, if you spent more than you took in, how much you went "in the hole").

INCOME AND EXPENSE STATEMENT

Name(s) _Simon and Meghan Kane_

For the _Year_ _____ Ended _December 31, 2017_

INCOME

Wages and salaries	Name: Simon Kane	$	65,000
	Name: Meghan Kane		18,350
	Name:		
Self-employment income			
Bonuses and commissions	Simon-sales commissions		3,050
Investment income	Interest received		195
	Dividends received		120
	Rents received		
	Sale of securities		
	Other		
Pensions and annuities			
Other income			
	(I) Total Income	$	86,715

EXPENSES

Housing	Rent/mortgage payment (include insurance and taxes, if applicable)	$	11,820
	Repairs, maintenance, improvements		1,050
Utilities	Gas, electric, water		1,750
	Phone		480
	Cable TV and other		240
Food	Groceries		2,425
	Dining out		3,400
Transportation	Auto loan payments		2,520
	License plates, fees, etc.		250
	Gas, oil, repairs, tires, maintenance		2,015
Medical	Health, major medical, disability insurance (payroll deductions or not provided by employer)		2,250
	Doctor, dentist, hospital, medicines		305
Clothing	Clothes, shoes, and accessories		1,700
Insurance	Homeowner's (if not covered by mortgage payment)		1,200
	Life (not provided by employer)		1,865
	Auto		1,780
Taxes	Income and social security		18,319
	Property (if not included in mortgage)		2,100
Appliances, furniture, and other major purchases	Loan payments		800
	Purchases and repairs		450
Personal care	Laundry, cosmetics, hair care		700
Recreation and entertainment	Vacations		2,000
	Other recreation and entertainment		2,630
Other items	Tuition and books: Meghan		1,400
	Gifts		215
	Loan payments: Education loans		900
	Loan payments: Parents		600
	(II) Total Expenses	$	65,164
	CASH SURPLUS (OR DEFICIT) [(I) − (II)]	$	21,551

EXHIBIT 2.3   **How We Spend Our Income**

Almost three-quarters of expenditures made with pre-tax income fall into one of four categories: housing, transportation, food, and personal insurance and pensions.

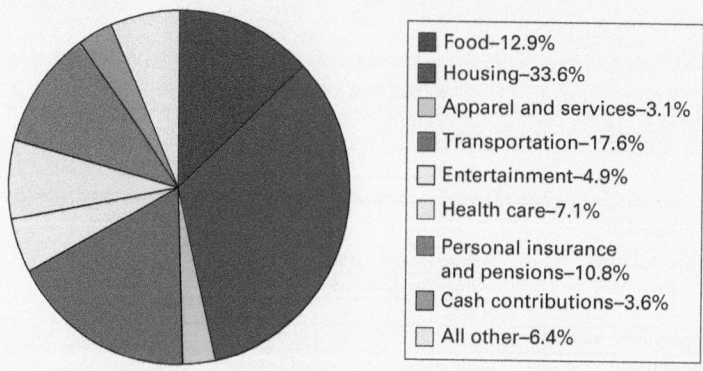

- Food–12.9%
- Housing–33.6%
- Apparel and services–3.1%
- Transportation–17.6%
- Entertainment–4.9%
- Health care–7.1%
- Personal insurance and pensions–10.8%
- Cash contributions–3.6%
- All other–6.4%

Source: "Consumer Expenditures—2013," Washington, DC: U.S. Department of Labor, Bureau of Labor Statistics, News Release, USDL-14-1671, based on Table A, September 9, 2014.

It is important to keep in mind that a cash surplus does not necessarily mean that funds are simply lying around waiting to be used. The actual disposition of the surplus (or deficit) is shown in the asset, liability, and net worth accounts on the balance sheet. For example, if you used the surplus to make investments, this would increase the appropriate asset account. If you used the surplus to pay off a loan, the payment would reduce that liability account. Of course, if you used the surplus to increase cash balances, you'd have the funds to use. In each case, your net worth *increases*. Surpluses *increase* net worth; deficits *decrease* it, whether the shortfall is financed by reducing an asset (e.g., drawing down a savings account) or by borrowing.

2-3d Preparing the Income and Expense Statement

As shown in Worksheet 2.2, the income and expense statement is dated to define the period covered. To prepare the statement, follow these steps.

1. **Record your income from all sources for the chosen period.** Use your paycheck stubs to verify your gross pay for the period, and be sure to include bonuses, commission checks, and overtime pay. You'll find interest earned, securities bought and sold, interest and dividends received, and other investment matters on your bank and investment account statements. Keep a running list of other income sources, such as rents, tax refunds, and asset sales.
2. **Establish meaningful expense categories.** Those shown on Worksheet 2.2 are a good starting point. Information on monthly house (or rent) payments, loan payments, and other fixed payments (such as insurance premiums and cable TV) is readily available from either the payment book or your checkbook (or, in the case of payroll deductions, your check stubs). (Be careful with adjustable-rate loans because the amount of monthly loan payments will eventually change when the interest rate changes.)
3. **Subtract total expenses from total income to get the cash surplus (a positive number) or deficit (a negative number).** This "bottom line" summarizes the net cash flow resulting from your financial activities during the period.

You'll probably pay for most major variable expenses by check, debit card, or credit card, so it's easy to keep track of them. It's harder to keep tabs on all the items in a month that you pay for with cash, such as parking, lunches, movies, and incidentals. Try to remember what you spent during the week, and write it down on your calendar to the nearest $5. If you can't remember, then try the exercise over shorter and shorter periods of time until you can.

Just as you show only the amounts of cash actually received as income, record only the amounts of money you actually pay out in cash as expenses. If you borrow to buy an item, particularly an asset, include only the actual cash payment—purchase price minus amount borrowed—as an expense, as well as payments on the loan in the period you actually make them. You show credit purchases of this type as an asset and corresponding liability on the balance sheet. Record only the cash payments on loans, not the actual amounts of the loans themselves, on the income and expense statement.

> **EXAMPLE: Keeping Track of Loans**
>
> Carter bought a car for $20,000 in September. He made a down payment of $3,000 and financed the remaining $17,000 with a 4-year, 5.5 percent loan, payable monthly.
>
> On Carter's September 30th income and expense statement he showed a cash expenditure of $3,000, and each subsequent monthly statement would show a loan payment expense of $395. Carter's September 30th balance sheet would show the car as an asset worth $20,000 and the $17,000 loan as a long-term liability. The values of the car and the loan will be adjusted going forward.

Finally, when making your list of expenses for the year, remember to include the amount of income tax and Social Security taxes withheld from your paycheck, as well as any other payroll deductions (health insurance, savings plans, retirement and pension contributions, and professional/union dues). These deductions (from gross wages, salaries, bonuses, and commissions) represent personal expenses, even if they don't involve a direct cash payment.

You might be shocked when listing what's taken out of your paycheck. Even if you're in a fairly low federal income tax bracket, your paycheck could easily be reduced by more than 25 percent for taxes alone. Your federal tax could be withheld at 15 percent, your state income tax could be withheld at 5 percent, and your Social Security and Medicare tax could be withheld at 7.65 percent. That doesn't even count health and disability income insurance.

Preparing income and expense statements can involve a lot of number crunching. Fortunately, some good computer software packages, such as Quicken and Microsoft Money, can simplify the job of preparing personal financial statements and doing other personal financial planning tasks.

2-3e An Income and Expense Statement for Simon and Meghan Kane

Simon and Meghan Kane's balance sheet in Worksheet 2.1 shows us their financial condition *as of* December 31, 2017. Worksheet 2.2, their income and expense statement for the *year ended* December 31, 2017, was prepared using the background material presented earlier, along with the Kanes' balance sheet. This statement shows how money flowed into and out of their "pockets."

- Income: Total income for the year ended December 31, 2017, is $86,715. Simon's wages represent the family's chief source of income, although Meghan has finished her MBA and will now be making a major contribution. Other sources of income include $195 in interest on their savings accounts and bond investments and $120 in dividends from their common stock holdings.

- Expenses: Total expenses for this year of $65,164 include their home mortgage, food, auto loan, clothing, and income and Social Security taxes. Other sizable expenses during the year include home repairs and improvements, gas and electricity, auto license and operating expenses, insurance, tuition, and education loan payments.
- Cash surplus: The Kanes end the year with a cash surplus of $21,551 (total income of $86,715 minus total expenses of $65,164).

The Kanes can use their surplus to increase savings, invest in stocks, bonds, or other vehicles, or make payments on some outstanding debts. The best strategy depends on their financial goals. If they had a cash deficit, the Kanes would have to withdraw savings, liquidate investments, or borrow an amount equal to the deficit to meet their financial commitments (i.e., to "make ends meet"). With their surplus of $21,551, the Kanes have made a positive contribution to their net worth.

TEST YOURSELF

2-5 What is an income and expense statement? What role does it serve in personal financial planning?

2-6 Explain what cash basis means in this statement: "An income and expense statement should be prepared on a cash basis." How and where are credit purchases shown when statements are prepared on a cash basis?

2-7 Distinguish between fixed and variable expenses, and give examples of each.

2-8 Is it possible to have a cash deficit on an income and expense statement? If so, how?

2-4 USING YOUR PERSONAL FINANCIAL STATEMENTS

Whether you're just starting out and have a minimal net worth or are farther along the path toward achieving your goals, your balance sheet and income and expense statement provide insight into your current financial status. You now have the information you need to examine your financial position, monitor your financial activities, and track the progress you're making toward your financial goals. Let's now look at ways to help you create better personal financial statements and analyze them to better understand your financial situation.

2-4a Keeping Good Records

Although record keeping doesn't rank high on most "to do" lists, a good record-keeping system helps you manage and control your personal financial affairs. With organized, up-to-date financial records, you'll prepare more accurate personal financial statements and budgets, pay less to your tax preparer, not miss any tax deductions, and save on taxes when you sell a house or securities or withdraw retirement funds. Also, good records make it easier for a spouse or relative to manage your financial affairs in an emergency. To that end, you should prepare a comprehensive list of these records, their locations, and your key advisors (financial planner, banker, accountant, attorney, doctors) for family members.

Prepare your personal financial statements at least once each year, ideally when drawing up your budget. Many people update their financial statements every 3 or

6 months. You may want to keep a **ledger**, or financial record book, to summarize all your financial transactions. The ledger has sections for assets, liabilities, sources of income, and expenses; these sections contain separate accounts for each item. Whenever any accounts change, make an appropriate ledger entry. For example, if you bought headphones for $100 in cash, you'd show the headphones on your balance sheet as an asset (at its fair market value) and as a $100 expenditure on your income and expense statement. If you borrowed to pay for the headphones, the loan amount would be a liability on the balance sheet, and any loan payments made during the period would be shown on the income and expense statement. You'd keep similar records for asset sales, loan repayments, income sources, and so on.

Managing Your Financial Records

Your system doesn't have to be fancy to be effective. You'll need the ledger book just described and a set of files with general categories such as banking and credit cards, taxes, home, insurance, investments, and retirement accounts. An expandable file, with a dozen or so compartments for incoming bills, receipts, paycheck stubs, or anything you might need later, works well. You can easily keep a lot of this kind of information in a computer spreadsheet—but if so, be sure to back it up from time to time. Also, keep in mind that a bank safe-deposit box is a great place to store important documents and files.

Start by taking an inventory. Make a list of everything you own and owe. Check it at least once a year to make sure it's up-to-date and to review your financial progress. Then, record transactions manually in your ledger or with financial planning software. Exhibit 2.4 offers general guidelines for keeping and organizing your personal financial records.

You'll want to set up separate files for tax planning records, with one for income (paycheck stubs, interest on savings accounts, etc.) and another for deductions, as well as for individual mutual fund and brokerage account records. Once you set up your files, be sure to go through them at least once a year and throw out unnecessary items.

2-4b Tracking Financial Progress: Ratio Analysis

Each time you prepare your financial statements, you should analyze them to see how well you're doing on your financial goals. For example, with an income and expense statement, you can compare actual financial results with budgeted figures to make sure that your spending is under control. Likewise, comparing a set of financial plans with a balance sheet will reveal whether you're meeting your savings and investment goals, reducing your debt, or building up a retirement reserve. You can compare current performance with historical performance to find out if your financial situation is improving or getting worse.

Calculating certain financial ratios can help you evaluate your financial performance over time. What's more, if you apply for a loan, the lender probably will look at these ratios to judge your ability to carry additional debt. Four important money management ratios are (1) solvency ratio, (2) liquidity ratio, (3) savings ratio, and (4) debt service ratio. The first two are associated primarily with the balance sheet, the last two with the income and expense statement. Exhibit 2.5 defines these ratios and illustrates their calculation for Simon and Meghan Kane.

Balance Sheet Ratios

When evaluating your balance sheet, you should be most concerned with your net worth at a given time. As explained earlier in this chapter, you are technically insolvent when your total liabilities exceed your total assets—that is, when you have a

EXHIBIT 2.4 | **Managing Your Financial Records**

Here are some key steps to managing your financial records effectively.

Keep a list of key financial documents. These include records of all bank accounts, credit cards, investment accounts, home deed, vehicle registrations, all insurance policies, will and all legal documents, tax records, birth certificate, driver's license copy, passport, marriage and death certificates, and car titles. Store these in a safe place like a fireproof box or a safe-deposit box at a bank.

Renew key documents. Many important documents have an expiration date. Make sure you don't miss important renewal dates for your driver's license, passport, and automobile and homeowners insurance.

Save records for tax and insurance purposes. The Internal Revenue Service requires you to keep most tax records and related receipts for 3 to 7 years. Don't throw away any financial documents without checking whether you'll need them in the future. For example, receipts for home renovations can be needed to support insurance claims. Scanning important documents is a great way to reduce clutter.

Review your financial plans. Review how your investments are doing at least once a quarter and evaluate whether you are well on your way to meeting key financial goals like retirement. Organize your records so that you can complete the financial statements discussed in this chapter, making sure to calculate your net worth.

Ensure your family can locate important documents. If you are injured or die, your family will appreciate being able to find your insurance records or will easily. Electronic records can be saved online with services such as www.assetlock. net and www.legacylocker.com, which can be accessed by your family. It's also important to keep up-to-date records of important computer accounts and passwords in a secure location. Consider a safe-deposit box at a bank.

Dispose of documents safely. Shred unneeded documents that have identifying and/or financial information on them.

Re-organize your finances at least once a year. This is not a one-time event. Schedule a date that's easy to remember.

---

solvency ratio
Total net worth divided by total assets; measures the degree of exposure to insolvency.

negative net worth. The solvency ratio shows, as a percentage, your degree of exposure to insolvency, or how much "cushion" you have as a protection against insolvency. Simon and Meghan's solvency ratio is 33.4 percent, which means that they could withstand about a 33 percent decline in the market value of their assets before they would be insolvent. Consider that the stock market, as measured by the S&P 500 index, fell about 37 percent during the financial crisis of 2008. Also, the average home's value fell about 18 percent during that crisis year, as measured by the S&P/Case-Shiller U.S. National Home Price Index. The value of Simon and Meghan's solvency ratio suggests that they are in good shape for now, but they may want to consider increasing it a bit in the future to manage a potential decline in the value of their assets even better.

Although the solvency ratio indicates the potential to withstand financial problems, it does not deal directly with the ability to pay current debts. This issue is addressed with the liquidity ratio, which shows how long you could continue to pay current debts (any bills or charges that must be paid within 1 year) with existing liquid assets in the event of income loss.

liquidity ratio
Total liquid assets divided by total current debts; measures the ability to pay current debts.

The calculated liquidity ratio indicates that the Kanes can cover only about 13 percent of their existing 1-year debt obligations with their current liquid assets. In other words, they have 1½ months of coverage (a month is one-twelfth, or 8.3 percent, of a year). If an unexpected event cut off their income, their liquid reserves would quickly be exhausted. Although there's no hard-and-fast rule for what this ratio should be, it seems too low for the Kanes. They should consider strengthening it along with their solvency ratio. They should be able to add to their cash surpluses now that Meghan is working full-time.

EXHIBIT 2.5   Ratios for Personal Financial Statement Analysis

Ratio	Formula	2017 Calculation for the Kanes
Solvency ratio	$\dfrac{\text{Total net worth}}{\text{Total assets}}$	$\dfrac{\$87,465}{\$261,485} = 0.334$, or 33.4%
Liquidity ratio	$\dfrac{\text{Total liquid assets}}{\text{Total current debts}}$	$\dfrac{\$2,285}{\$17,710^{(a)}} = 0.129$, or 12.90%
Savings ratio	$\dfrac{\text{Cash surplus}}{\text{Income after taxes}}$	$\dfrac{\$21,551}{\$86,715 - \$18,319} = \dfrac{\$21,551}{\$68,396} = 0.315$, or 31.5%
Debt service ratio	$\dfrac{\text{Total monthly loan payments}}{\text{Monthly gross (before-tax) income}}$	$\dfrac{\$1,387^{(b)}}{\$7,226^{(c)}} = 0.192$, or 19.2%

(a) You'll find the Kanes' total liquid assets ($2,285) and total current liabilities ($1,070) on Worksheet 2.1. The current debt totals $17,710: current liabilities of $1,070 (from Worksheet 2.1) plus loan payments due within 1 year of $16,640 (from Worksheet 2.2). Note that loan payments due within 1 year consist of $11,820 in mortgage payments, $2,520 in auto loan payments, $800 in furniture loan payments, $900 in education loan payments, and $600 in loan payments to parents.

(b) On an annual basis, the Kanes' debt obligations total $16,640 ($11,820 in mortgage payments, $2,520 in auto loan payments, $800 in furniture loan payments, $900 in education loan payments, and $600 in loan payments to parents; all from Worksheet 2.2). The Kanes' total monthly loan payments are about $1,387 ($16,640 ÷ 12 months).

(c) Dividing the Kanes' annual gross income (also found in Worksheet 2.2) of $86,715 by 12 equals $7,226 per month.

The amount of liquid reserves will vary with your personal circumstances and "comfort level." Another useful liquidity guideline is to have a reserve fund equal to at least 6 to 9 months of after-tax income available to cover living expenses. The Kanes' after-tax income for 2017 was $5,700 per month [($86,715 total income – $18,319 income and Social Security taxes) ÷ 12]. Therefore, this guideline suggests that they should have at least $34,200 in total liquid assets—considerably more than the $2,285 on their latest balance sheet. If you feel that your job is secure or you have other potential sources of income, you may be comfortable with three or four months in reserve. In troubled economic times, such as the recent recession, you may want to keep more than six to nine months of income in this fund as protection in case you lose your job.

Income and Expense Statement Ratios

When evaluating your income and expense statement, you should be concerned with the bottom line, which shows the cash surplus (or deficit) resulting from the period's activities. You can relate the cash surplus (or deficit) to income by calculating a **savings ratio**, which is done most effectively with after-tax income.

savings ratio
Cash surplus divided by net income (after tax); indicates relative amount of cash surplus achieved during a given period.

Simon and Meghan saved about 31 percent of their after-tax income, which is excellent (American families, on average, save about 5 percent to 8 percent). How much to save is a personal choice. Some families would plan much higher levels, particularly if they're saving to achieve an important goal, such as buying a home.

Although maintaining an adequate level of savings is obviously important to personal financial planning, so is the ability to pay debts promptly. In fact, debt payments have a higher priority. The **debt service ratio** allows you to make sure you can comfortably meet your debt obligations. This ratio excludes current liabilities and considers only mortgage, installment, and personal loan obligations.

debt service ratio
Total monthly loan payments divided by monthly gross (before-tax) income; provides a measure of the ability to pay debts promptly.

Monthly loan payments account for about 19 percent of Simon and Meghan's monthly gross income. This relatively low debt service ratio indicates that the

Kanes should have little difficulty in meeting their monthly loan payments. In your financial planning, try to keep your debt service ratio somewhere under 35 percent or so, because that's generally viewed as a manageable level of debt. Of course, the lower the debt service ratio, the easier it is to meet loan payments as they come due.

TEST YOURSELF

2-9 How can accurate records and control procedures be used to ensure the effectiveness of the personal financial planning process?

2-10 Describe some of the areas or items you would consider when evaluating your balance sheet and income and expense statement. Cite several ratios that could help in this effort.

2-5 CASH IN AND CASH OUT: PREPARING AND USING BUDGETS

LG5 Many of us avoid budgeting as if it were the plague. After all, do you really want to know that 30 percent of your take-home pay is going to restaurant meals? Yet preparing, analyzing, and monitoring your personal budget are essential steps for successful personal financial planning.

After defining your short-term financial goals, you can prepare a cash budget for the coming year. Recall that a budget is a short-term financial planning report that helps you achieve your short-term financial goals. By taking the time to evaluate your current financial situation, spending patterns, and goals, you can develop a realistic budget that is consistent with your personal lifestyle, family situation, and values. A cash budget is a valuable money management tool that helps you:

BUBBLES PHOTOLIBRARY/ALAMY

- Maintain the necessary information to monitor and control your finances
- Decide how to allocate your income to reach your financial goals
- Implement a system of disciplined spending—as opposed to just existing from one paycheck to the next
- Reduce needless spending so you can increase the funds allocated to savings and investments
- Achieve your long-term financial goals

Just as your goals will change over your lifetime, so too will your budget as your financial situation becomes more complex. Typically, the number of income and expense categories increases as you accumulate more assets and debts and have more family responsibilities. For example, the budget of a college student should be quite simple, with limited income from part-time jobs, parental contributions, and scholarships and grants. Expenses might include room and board, clothes, books,

FINANCIAL PLANNING TIPS

Tips on Budgeting

• **Gather every financial statement and receipt you can find.** This includes bank statements, investment accounts, recent utility bills, and any documents on income or expenses. The purpose of collecting this information is to create a monthly average of income and expenses.

• **Record all of your sources of income.** Record your total income as a monthly amount.

• **Create a list of usual monthly expenses.** This should include any mortgage payments, car payments, auto insurance, groceries, utilities, entertainment, dry cleaning, auto insurance, retirement or college savings, and anything else you spend money on.

• **Categorize expenses as fixed or variable.** Fixed expenses stay about the same each month. Examples include your mortgage or rent, car payments, cable and/or Internet service, and trash pickup. Variable expenses change from month to month and include groceries, gasoline, entertainment, eating out, gifts and credit card payments. Variable expenses provide some room to maneuver when trying to balance your budget.

• **Total your monthly income and monthly expenses and project them over the next year.** If you have more income than expenses, then you're well on your way. You can allocate this excess to areas of your budget such as saving for retirement or paying more on credit cards to pay off outstanding debt. If your expenses exceed your income, changes have to be made.

• **Make adjustments to expenses if necessary.** The overall goal of your budget is to have your income equal your expenses, which should include your savings expense allocation.

• **Review your budget monthly.** It is important to review your budget on a regular basis to make sure you know how things are going. At the end of each month, compare the actual expenses with what you budgeted.

Source: Adapted from Jerry Vohwinkle, http://financialplan.about.com/od/budgetingyourmoney/ht/createbudget.htm, accessed July 2015.

auto expenses, and entertainment. Once a student graduates and goes to work full-time, his or her budget will include additional expenses, such as rent, insurance, work clothes, and commuting costs. For most people, this process does not become simpler until retirement.

2-5a The Budgeting Process

cash budget
A budget that takes into account estimated monthly cash receipts and cash expenses for the coming year.

Like the income and expense statement, a budget should be prepared on a cash basis; thus, we call this document a **cash budget** because it deals with estimated cash receipts and cash expenses, including savings and investments, that are expected to occur in the coming year. Because you receive and pay most bills monthly, you'll probably want to estimate income as well as expenses on a monthly basis.

The cash budget preparation process has three stages: forecasting income, forecasting expenses, and finalizing the cash budget. When you're forecasting income and expenses, take into account any anticipated changes in the cost of living and their impact on your budget components. If your income is fixed—not expected to change over the budgetary period—then increases in various expense items will probably decrease the purchasing power of your income. Worksheet 2.3, the Kanes' Annual Cash Budget by Month, has separate sections to record income (cash receipts) and expenses (cash expenses) and lists the most common categories for each.

The Kanes' annual cash budget shows several months in which substantial cash deficits are expected to occur; they can use this information to develop plans for covering those monthly shortfalls.

ANNUAL CASH BUDGET BY MONTH

Name(s) _Simon and Meghan Kane_

For the _Year_   Ended _December 31, 2017_

	Jan.	Feb.	Mar.	April	May	June	July	Aug.	Sep.	Oct.	Nov.	Dec.	Total for the Year
INCOME													
Take-home pay	$4,800	$4,800	$4,800	$4,800	$4,800	$5,200	$5,200	$5,200	$5,200	$5,200	$5,200	$5,200	$60,400
Bonuses and commissions						1,350						1,300	2,650
Pensions and annuities													
Investment income			50			50			50			50	200
Other income													
(I) Total Income	$4,800	$4,800	$4,850	$4,800	$4,800	$6,600	$5,200	$5,200	$5,250	$5,200	$5,200	$6,550	$63,250
EXPENSES													
Housing (rent/mortgage, repairs)	$1,185	$1,485	$1,185	$1,185	$1,185	$1,185	$1,185	$1,185	$1,185	$1,185	$1,185	$1,185	$14,520
Utilities (phone, elec., gas, water)	245	245	245	175	180	205	230	245	205	195	230	250	2,650
Food (home and away)	696	696	1,200	696	696	696	696	696	696	696	696	696	8,856
Transportation (auto/public)	375	620	375	355	375	375	575	375	375	425	375	375	4,975
Medical/dental, incl. insurance	50	50	50	50	50	75	50	50	50	50	50	50	625
Clothing	150	150	670	200	200	200	300	600	200	300	300	300	3,570
Insurance (life, auto, home)				660	1,598					660	1,598		4,516
Taxes (property)		550							550				1,100
Appliances, furniture, and other (purchases/loans)	60	60	60	60	60	60	60	60	60	60	60	60	720
Personal care	100	100	100	100	100	100	100	100	100	100	100	100	1,200
Recreation and entertainment	250	300	3,200	200	200	400	300	200	200	200	200	2,050	7,700
Savings and investments	575	575	575	575	575	575	575	575	575	575	575	575	6,900
Other expenses	135	200	175	135	510	180	135	235	235	135	405	325	2,805
Fun money	200	200	230	130	200	200	200	200	200	200	200	230	2,390
(II) Total Expenses	$4,021	$5,231	$8,065	$4,521	$5,929	$4,251	$4,406	$5,071	$4,081	$4,781	$5,974	$6,196	$62,527
CASH SURPLUS (OR DEFICIT) [(I)-(II)]	$779	($431)	($3,215)	$279	($1,129)	$2,349	$794	$129	$1,169	$419	($774)	$354	$723
CUMULATIVE CASH SURPLUS (OR DEFICIT)	$779	$348	($2,867)	($2,588)	($3,717)	($1,368)	($574)	($445)	$724	$1,143	$369	$723	$723

Forecasting Income

The first step in preparing your cash budget is to forecast your income for the coming year. Include all income expected for the year: the take-home pay of both spouses, expected bonuses or commissions, pension or annuity income, and investment income—interest, dividend, rental, and asset (particularly security) sale income. When estimating income, keep in mind that any amount you receive for which repayment is required is not considered income. For instance, loan proceeds are treated not as a source of income but as a liability for which scheduled repayments are required.

Unlike the income and expense statement, in the cash budget you should use take-home pay (rather than gross income). Your cash budget focuses on those areas that you can control—and most people have limited control over things like taxes withheld, contributions to company insurance and pension plans, and the like. In effect, take-home pay represents the amount of disposable income you receive from your employer.

Forecasting Expenses

The second step in the cash budgeting process is by far the most difficult: preparing a schedule of estimated expenses for the coming year. This is usually done using actual expenses from previous years (as found on income and expense statements and in supporting information for those periods), along with predetermined short-term financial goals. Good financial records, as discussed earlier, make it easier to develop realistic expense estimates. If you do not have past expense data, you could reexamine old checkbook registers and credit card statements to approximate expenses, or take a "needs approach" and attach dollar values to projected expenses. Pay close attention to expenses associated with medical disabilities, divorce and child support, and similar special circumstances.

When preparing your budget, be aware of your expenditure patterns and how you spend money. After tracking your expenses over several months, study your spending habits to see if you are doing things that should be eliminated. For example, you may become aware that you are going to the ATM too often or using credit cards too freely.

You'll probably find it easier to budget expenses if you group them into several general categories rather than trying to estimate each item. Worksheet 2.3 is an example of one such grouping scheme, patterned after the categories used in the income and expense statement. You may also want to refer to the average expense percentages given in Exhibit 2.3. Choose categories that reflect your priorities and allow you to monitor areas of concern.

Your expense estimates should include the transactions necessary to achieve your short-term goals. You should also quantify any current or short-term contributions toward your long-term goals and schedule them into the budget. Equally important are scheduled additions to savings and investments, because planned savings should be high on everyone's list of goals. If your budget doesn't balance with all these items, you will have to make some adjustments in the final budget.

Base estimated expenses on current price levels and then increase them by a percentage that reflects the anticipated rate of inflation. For example, if you estimate the current monthly food bill at $500 and expect 4 percent inflation next year, you should budget your monthly food expenditure next year at $520, or $500 + $20 (4 percent × $500).

Do It Now

Track Your Expenses

It's easy for spending to become so automatic that we're not aware we're doing it. So where does your money go? The only way to find out is to keep track of it. Writing down what you spend in a paper journal or using an app like Expensify (www.expensify.com) is simple and will make you more aware of where your money goes. Knowing where you are will probably make you feel better too—so do it now.

Don't forget an allowance for "fun money," which family members can spend as they wish. This gives each person some financial independence and helps form a healthy family budget relationship.

Finalizing the Cash Budget

After estimating income and expenses, finalize your budget by comparing projected income to projected expenses. Show the difference in the third section as a surplus or deficit. In a balanced budget, the total income for the year equals or exceeds total expenses. If you find that you have a deficit at year end, you'll have to go back and adjust your expenses. If you have several months of large surpluses, you should be able to cover any shortfall in a later month, as explained later. Budget preparation is complete once all monthly deficits are resolved and the total annual budget balances.

Admittedly, there's a lot of number crunching in personal cash budgeting. As discussed earlier, personal financial planning software can greatly streamline the budget preparation process.

2-5b Dealing with Deficits

Even if the annual budget balances, in certain months expenses may exceed income, causing a monthly budget deficit. Likewise, a budget surplus occurs when income in some months exceeds expenses. Two remedies exist:

- Shift expenses from months with budget deficits to months with surpluses (or, alternatively, transfer income, if possible, from months with surpluses to those with deficits).
- Use savings, investments, or borrowing to cover temporary deficits.

Because the budget balances for the year, the need for funds to cover shortages is only temporary. In months with budget surpluses, you should return funds taken from savings or investments or repay loans. Either remedy is feasible for curing a monthly budget deficit in a balanced annual budget, although the second is probably more practical.

What can you do if your budget shows an annual budget deficit even after you've made a few expense adjustments? You have three options, as follows:

- **Liquidate enough savings and investments or borrow enough to meet the total budget shortfall for the year.** Obviously, this option is not preferred, because it violates the objective of budgeting: to set expenses at a level that allows you to enjoy a reasonable standard of living *and* progress toward achieving your long-term goals. Reducing savings and investments or increasing debt to balance the budget reduces net worth. People who use this approach are *not* living within their means.
- **Cut low-priority expenses from the budget.** This option is clearly preferable to the first one. It balances the budget without using external funding sources by eliminating expenses associated with your least important short-term goals, such as flexible or discretionary expenses for nonessential items (e.g., recreation, entertainment, some types of clothing).
- **Increase income.** Finding a higher-paying job or perhaps a second, part-time job is the most difficult option; it takes more planning and may result in significant lifestyle changes. However, people who can't liquidate savings or investments or borrow funds to cover necessary expenses may have to choose this route to balance their budgets.

2-5c A Cash Budget for Simon and Meghan Kane

Using their short-term financial goals (Worksheet 1.1 in Chapter 1) and past financial statements (Worksheets 2.1 and 2.2), Simon and Meghan Kane have prepared their cash budget for the 2018 calendar year. Worksheet 2.3 shows the Kanes' estimated total 2018 annual take-home income and expenses by month, as well as their monthly and annual cash surplus or deficit.

The Kanes list their total 2018 take-home income of $63,250 by source for each month. By using take-home pay, they eliminate the need to show income-based taxes, Social Security payments, and other payroll deductions as expenses. The take-home pay reflects Simon and Meghan's expected salary increases.

In estimating annual expenses for 2018, the Kanes anticipate a small amount of inflation and have factored some price increases into their expense projections.

They have also allocated $6,900 to savings and investments, a wise budgeting strategy, and included an amount for fun money to be divided between them.

During their budgeting session, Simon and Meghan discovered that their first estimate resulted in expenses of $63,877, compared with their estimated income of $63,250. To eliminate the $627 deficit to balance their budget and allow for unexpected expenses, Simon and Meghan made these decisions:

- Omit some low-priority goals: spend less on stereo components, take a shorter Hawaiian vacation instead of the Colorado ski trip shown in Worksheet 1.1.

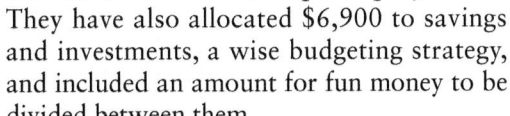

- Reschedule some of the loan repayment to their parents.
- Reduce their fun money slightly.

These reductions lower Simon and Meghan's total scheduled expenses to $62,527, giving them a surplus of $723 ($63,250 − $62,527) and balancing the budget on an annual basis with some money left over. Of course, the Kanes can reduce other discretionary expenses to further increase the budget surplus and have a cushion for unexpected expenses.

The Kanes' final step is to analyze monthly surpluses and deficits and determine whether to use savings, investments, or borrowing to cover monthly shortfalls. The bottom line of their annual cash budget lists the cumulative, or running, totals of monthly cash surpluses and deficits. Despite their $723 year-end cumulative cash surplus, they have cumulative deficits from March to August, primarily because of their March Hawaiian vacation and insurance payments. To help cover these deficits, Simon and Meghan have arranged an interest-free loan from their parents. If they had dipped into savings to finance the deficits, they would have lost some interest earnings, which are included as income. They could delay clothing and recreation and entertainment expenses until later in the year to reduce the deficits more quickly. If they weren't able to obtain funds to cover the deficits, they would have to reduce expenses further or increase income. At year end, they should use their surplus to increase savings or investments or to repay part of a loan.

2-5d Using Your Budgets

In the final analysis, a cash budget has value only if (1) you use it and (2) you keep careful records of actual income and expenses. These records show whether you are staying within your budget limits. Record this information in a budget record book or an Excel spreadsheet often enough that you don't overlook anything significant, yet not so often that it becomes a nuisance. A loose-leaf binder with separate pages for each income and expense category works quite well. So does a well-organized spreadsheet. Rounding entries to the nearest dollar simplifies the arithmetic.

At the beginning of each month, record the budgeted amount for each category and enter income received and money spent on the appropriate pages. At month's end, total each account and calculate the surplus or deficit. Except for certain income accounts (such as salary) and fixed expense accounts (such as mortgage or loan payments), most categories will end the month with a positive or negative variance, indicating a cash surplus or deficit. You can then transfer your total spending by category to a budget control schedule that compares actual income and expenses with the various categories and shows the budget variance,

budget control schedule
A summary that shows how actual income and expenses compare with the various budget categories and where variances (surpluses or deficits) exist.

budget variance
The difference between the budgeted and actual amount paid out or received.

Behavior Matters

How to Really Spend Less

Spending less means changing your behavior, which is hard to do. These concrete steps will help.

- **Make a budget and use it to help set financial goals.** Decide how much less you want to spend and set a savings goal.

- **Use your savings account first and your checking account last.** Set up two bank accounts so that money can be transferred between them. Deposit your income into savings and transfer your budgeted amount into checking—not the other way around.

- **Spend cash—don't rely on credit cards.** It's harder to use cash for everything, so you'll spend less.

- **Have someone hold you accountable.** Let someone you trust—your spouse, friend, or parent, for instance—know your goals and have them follow your progress.

- **Before you buy, consider the alternatives.** Always wait at least two days before making a big purchase. Think about how it fits into your budget. Really think about your alternatives.

Source: Adapted from Brian Reed, "6 New Behavioral Strategies to Curb Your Spending in 2012," http://www.investinganswers.com/personal-finance/savings-budget/6-new-behavioral-strategies-curb-your-spending-2012-3963, accessed July 2015.

which is the difference between the budgeted and actual amount paid out or received.

This monthly comparison makes it easy to identify major budget categories where income falls far short of—or spending far exceeds—desired levels (variances of 5 percent to 10 percent or more). After pinpointing these areas, you can take corrective action to keep your budget on course. Don't just look at the size of the variances. Analyze them, particularly the larger ones, to discover *why* they occurred. An account deficit that occurs in only one period is obviously less of a problem than one that occurs in several periods. If recurring deficits indicate that an account was underbudgeted, you may need to adjust the budget to cover the outlays, reducing over-budgeted or nonessential accounts. Only in exceptional situations should you finance budget adjustments by using savings and investments or by borrowing.

> **EXAMPLE: Calculating Budget Variance**
>
> Angie budgeted $125 last month for transportation but actually spent $150. She consequently had a variance that was a budget deficit of $25. Had Angie actually spent only $115, the variance would have been a $10 budget surplus.

Looking at the Kanes' budget control schedule for a representative month in Worksheet 2.4, you can see that actual income and expense levels are reasonably close to their targets and have a net positive variance for the month shown. The biggest variances were in medical/dental and recreation and entertainment, which presumably occurred because these expenses are paid unevenly over the months of the year.

The monthly budget provides important feedback on how the actual cash flow stacks up against the forecasted monthly cash budget. If the variances are significant enough and/or continue month after month, the Kanes should consider altering either their spending habits or their cash budget.

MONTHLY BUDGET

Name(s) _Simon and Meghan Kane_

	Budgeted Amount	Actual Amount	Variance
INCOME	(1)	(2)	(3)*
Take-home pay	$4,800	$4,817	$17
Bonuses and commissions			0
Pensions and annuities			0
Investment income			0
Other income			0
(I) Total Income	$4,800	$4,817	$17
EXPENSES			
Housing (rent/mtge, repairs)	$1,185	1,185	0
Utilities (phone, elec., gas, water)	245	237	(8)
Food (home and away)	696	680	(16)
Transportation (auto/public)	375	385	10
Medical/dental, incl. insurance	50	0	(50)
Clothing	150	190	40
Insurance (life, auto, home)	0	0	0
Taxes (property)	0	0	0
Appliances, furniture, and other (purchases/loans)	60	60	0
Personal care	100	85	(15)
Recreation and entertainment	250	210	(40)
Savings and investments	575	575	0
Other expenses	135	118	(17)
Fun money	200	200	0
(II) Total Expenses	$4,021	$3,925	($96)
CASH SURPLUS (OR DEFICIT) [(I)-(II)]	$779	$892	$113

* Col. (3) = Col. (2) – Col. (1).

TEST YOURSELF

2-11 Describe the cash budget and its three parts. How does a budget deficit differ from a budget surplus?

2-12 The Rivera family has prepared their annual cash budget for 2018. They have divided it into 12 monthly budgets. Although only 1 monthly budget balances, they have managed to balance the overall budget for the year. What remedies are available to the Rivera family for meeting the monthly budget deficits?

2-13 Why is it important to analyze budget variances and their implied surpluses or deficits at the end of each month?

2-6 THE TIME VALUE OF MONEY: PUTTING A DOLLAR VALUE ON FINANCIAL GOALS

Assume that one of your financial goals is to buy your first home in 6 years. Then your first question is how much you want to spend on that home. Let's say you've done some "window shopping" and feel that, taking future inflation into consideration, you can buy a condominium for about $200,000 in 6 years. Of course, you won't need the full amount, but assuming that you'll make a 20 percent down payment of $40,000 (0.20 × $200,000 = $40,000) and pay $5,000 in closing costs, you'll need $45,000. You now have a well-defined long-term financial goal: To accumulate $45,000 in 6 years to buy a home costing about $200,000.

The next question is how to get all that money. You'll probably accumulate it by saving or investing a set amount each month or year. You can easily estimate how much to save or invest each year if you know your goal and what you expect to earn on your savings or investments. In this case, if you have to start from scratch (i.e., if nothing has already been saved) and estimate that you can earn about 5 percent on your money, you'll have to save or invest about $6,616 per year for each of the next 6 years to accumulate $45,000 over that time. Now you have another vital piece of information: You know what you must do over the next 6 years to reach your financial goal.

How did we arrive at the $6,616 figure? We used a concept called the **time value of money**, the idea that a dollar today is worth more than a dollar received in the future. With time value concepts, we can correctly compare dollar values occurring at different points in time. So long as you can earn a positive rate of return (interest rate) on your investments (ignoring taxes and other behavioral factors), in a strict financial sense, you should always prefer to receive equal amounts of money sooner rather than later. The two key time value concepts, future value and present value, are discussed separately next. We'll use **timelines**, graphical representations of cash flows, to visually depict the time value calculations. They will appear in the text margin near the related discussion. (*Note:* The time value discussions and demonstrations initially rely on the use of financial tables. Appendix E explains how to use financial calculators, which have tables built into them, to conveniently make time value calculations.) The calculator keystrokes for each calculation are shown in the text margin near the related discussion. Because of rounding in the tables, the calculator values will always be more precise.

time value of money
The concept that a dollar today is worth more than a dollar received in the future.

timeline
A graphical presentation of cash flows.

2-6a Future Value

To calculate how much to save to buy the $200,000 condominium, we used **future value**, the value to which an amount today will grow if it earns a specific rate of interest over a given period. Assume, for example, that you make annual deposits of $2,000 into a savings account that pays 5 percent interest per year. At the end of 20 years, your deposits would total $40,000 (20 × $2,000). If you made no withdrawals, your account balance would have increased to $66,132! This growth in value occurs not only because of earning interest but also because of **compounding**—the interest earned each year is left in the account and becomes part of the balance (or principal) on which interest is earned in subsequent years.

future value
The value to which an amount today will grow if it earns a specific rate of interest over a given period.

compounding
When interest earned each year is left in an account and becomes part of the balance (or principal) on which interest is earned in subsequent years.

Future Value of a Single Amount

To demonstrate future value, let's return to the goal of accumulating $45,000 for a down payment to buy a home in 6 years. You might be tempted to solve this problem by simply dividing the $45,000 goal by the 6-year period: $45,000/6 = $7,500. This procedure would be incorrect, however, because it fails to take into account the time value of money. The correct way to approach this problem is to use the **future value**

I = 5%

0 1 2 3 4 5 ↑
                  6
$5,000 $6,700

End of Year

INPUTS	FUNCTIONS
5000	PV
6	N
5	I
	CPT
	FV
	SOLUTION
	6,700.48

See Appendix E for details.

concept. For instance, if you can invest $100 today at 5 percent, you will have $105 in a year. You will earn $5 on your investment (0.05 × $100 = $5) and get your original $100 back. Once you know the length of time and rate of return involved, you can find the future value of any investment by using the following simple formula:

Future Value = Amount Invested × Future Value Factor

Tables of future value factors simplify the computations in this formula (see Appendix A). The table is easy to use; simply find the factor that corresponds to a given year and interest rate.

EXAMPLE: Calculating the Future Value of a Single Amount

You've saved $5,000 toward the down payment for the purchase of a home. You plan to invest this single amount at 5 percent for 6 years. The interest factor in Appendix A is 1.340. In 6 years you should have:

Future Value = $5,000 × 1.340 = $6,700

In 6 years, then, you will have about $6,700 if you invest the $5,000 at 5 percent. Because you feel you are going to need $45,000, you are still $38,300 short of your goal.

Future Value of an Annuity

annuity
A fixed sum of money that occurs annually.

How are you going to accumulate the additional $38,300? You'll again use the future value concept, but this time you'll use the future value annuity factor. An **annuity** is a fixed sum of money that occurs annually, for example, a deposit of $1,000 per year for each of the next 5 years, with payment to be made at the end of each year. To find out how much you need to save each year in order to accumulate a given amount, use this equation:

$$\text{Yearly Savings} = \frac{\text{Future Amount of Money Desired}}{\text{Future Value Annuity Factor}}$$

I = 5%
                        $38,300
   1   2   3   4   5
0 ↓   ↓   ↓   ↓   ↓   ↑
                      6
$5,631 $5,631 $5,631 $5,631 $5,631 $5,631

End of Year

When dealing with an annuity, you need to use a different table of factors, such as that in Appendix B. Note that it's very much like the table of future value factors and, in fact, is used in exactly the same way: the proper future value annuity factor is the one that corresponds to a given year *and* interest rate.

INPUTS	FUNCTIONS
38,300	FV
6	N
5	I
	CPT
	PMT
	SOLUTION
	5,630.77

See Appendix E for details.

EXAMPLE: Calculating the Future Value of an Annuity

You want to make equal annual investments that will grow to the additional $38,300 needed for the down payment on a home in 6 years while earning 5 percent a year. Appendix B provides an annuity factor of 6.802. The needed equal annual investment is:

$$\text{Yearly Savings} = \frac{\$38,300}{6.802} = \$5,630.70$$

You'll need to save about $5,630.70 a year to reach your goal. Note in this example that you must add $5,630.70 each year to the $5,000 you initially invested in order to build up a pool of $45,000 in 6 years. At a 5 percent rate of return, the $5,630.70 per year will grow to $38,300 and the $5,000 will grow to about $6,700, so in 6 years you'll have $38,300 + $6,700 = $45,000.

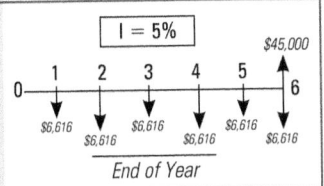

Timeline

| = 5% $45,000

0 — 1 — 2 — 3 — 4 — 5 — 6

$6,616 $6,616 $6,616 $6,616 $6,616 $6,616

End of Year

Calculator

INPUTS	FUNCTIONS
45,000	FV
6	N
5	I
	CPT
	PMT
	SOLUTION
	6,615.79

See Appendix E for details.

rule of 72
A useful formula for estimating about how long it will take to double a sum at a given interest rate.

present value
The value today of an amount to be received in the future; it's the amount that would have to be invested today at a given interest rate over a specified time period to accumulate the future amount.

discounting
The process of finding present value; the inverse of *compounding* to find future value.

How much, you may ask, would you need to save each year if you didn't have the $5,000 to start with? In this case, your goal would still be the same (to accumulate $45,000 in 6 years), but because you'd be starting from scratch, the full $45,000 would need to come from yearly savings. Assuming you can still earn 5 percent over the 6-year period, you can use the same future value annuity factor (6.802) and compute the amount of yearly savings as follows:

$$\text{Yearly Savings} = \frac{\$45,000}{6.802} = \$6,615.70$$

or approximately $6,616. Note that this amount corresponds to the $6,616 figure cited at the beginning of this section.

Using the future value concept, you can readily find either the future value to which an investment will grow over time or the amount that you must save each year to accumulate a given amount of money by a specified future date. In either case, the procedures allow you to put monetary values on long-term financial goals.

2-6b The Rule of 72

Suppose that you don't have access to time value of money tables or a financial calculator but want to know how long it takes for your money to double. There's an easy way to approximate this using the rule of 72. Simply divide the number 72 by the percentage rate you're earning on your investment:

$$\text{Number of Years to Double Money} = \frac{72}{\text{Annual Compound Interest Rate}}$$

EXAMPLE: Applying the Rule of 72

You recently opened a savings account with $1,000 that earns 4.5 percent annually. Its value will double to $2,000 in 16 years (72 ÷ 4.5 = 16).

The rule of 72 also applies to debts. Your debts can quickly double with high interest rates, such as those charged on most credit card accounts. So keep the rule of 72 in mind whether you invest or borrow!

2-6c Present Value

Lucky you! You've just won $100,000 in your state lottery. You want to spend part of it now, but because you're 30 years old, you also want to use part of it for your retirement fund. Your goal is to accumulate $300,000 in the fund by the time you're age 55 (25 years from now). How much do you need to invest if you estimate that you can earn 5 percent annually on your investments during the next 25 years?

Using **present value**, the value today of an amount to be received in the future, you can calculate the answer. It represents the amount you'd have to invest today at a given interest rate over the specified time period to accumulate the future amount. The process of finding present value is called **discounting**, which is the inverse of compounding to find future value.

Present Value of a Single Amount

Assuming you wish to create the retirement fund (future value) by making a single lump-sum deposit today, you can use this formula to find the amount you need to deposit:

$$\text{Present Value} = \text{Future Value} \times \text{Present Value Factor}$$

Tables of present value factors make this calculation easy (see Appendix C).

$I = 5\%$

$300,000

0 1 2 ... 24 25

$88,500

End of Year

INPUTS	FUNCTIONS
300000	FV
25	N
5	I
	CPT
	PV
	SOLUTION
	88,590.83

See Appendix E for details.

EXAMPLE: Calculating the Present Value of a Single Amount

You want to have a retirement fund of $300,000 in 25 years by making a lump-sum deposit today that will earn 5 percent a year. Appendix C provides a present value factor of 0.295. Your deposit will be:

$$\text{Present Value} = \$300,000 \times 0.295 = \$88,500$$

The $88,500 is the amount you'd have to deposit today into an account paying 5 percent annual interest in order to accumulate $300,000 at the end of 25 years.

Present Value of an Annuity

You can also use present value techniques to determine how much you can withdraw from your retirement fund each year over a specified time horizon. This calls for the **present value annuity factor**. Assume that at age 55 you wish to begin making equal annual withdrawals over the next 30 years from your $300,000 retirement fund. At first, you might think you could withdraw $10,000 per year ($300,000/30 years). However, the funds still on deposit would continue to earn 5 percent annual interest. To find the amount of the equal annual withdrawal, you again need to consider the time value of money. Specifically, you would use this formula:

$$\text{Annual Withdrawal} = \frac{\text{Initial Deposit}}{\text{Present Value Annuity Factor}}$$

$I = 5\%$

0 1 2 ... 29 30

$300,000 $19,515 $19,515 $19,515 $19,515

End of Year

INPUTS	FUNCTIONS
300000	PV
30	N
5	I
	CPT
	PMT
	SOLUTION
	19,515.43

See Appendix E for details.

EXAMPLE: Calculating the Present Value of an Annuity

You've successfully accumulated $300,000 for retirement and want to make equal annual withdrawals over the next 30 years while earning 5 percent. Using the present value annuity factor of 15.373 in Appendix D, the equal annual withdrawal is:

$$\text{Annual Withdrawal} = \frac{\$300,000}{15.372} = \$19,514.73$$

Therefore, you can withdraw $19,514.73 each year for 30 years. This value is clearly much larger than the $10,000 annual withdrawal mentioned earlier.

Other Applications of Present Value

You can also use present value techniques to analyze investments. Suppose you have an opportunity to purchase an annuity investment that promises to pay $700 per year for 5 years. You know that you'll receive a total of $3,500 ($700 × 5 years) over the 5-year period. However, you wish to earn a minimum annual return of 5 percent on your investments. What's the most you should pay for this annuity today? You can answer this question by rearranging the terms in the formula to get:

$$\text{Initial Deposit} = \text{Annual Withdrawal} \times \text{Present Value Annuity Factor}$$

Adapting the equation to this situation, "initial deposit" represents the maximum price to pay for the annuity, and "annual withdrawal" represents the annual annuity payment of $700.

Timeline

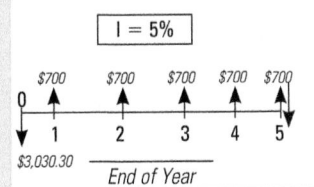

I = 5%

$700 $700 $700 $700 $700
0   1   2   3   4   5
$3,030.30
End of Year

Calculator

INPUTS	FUNCTIONS
700	PMT
5	N
5	I
	CPT
	PV
	SOLUTION
	3,030.63

See Appendix E for details.

EXAMPLE: Determining the Value of an Investment

What should you be willing to pay up front for an investment that will pay $700 a year for 5 years when you want to earn at least a 5 percent return?

This is calculated as the present value of an annuity, which Appendix D shows to have a factor of 4.329.

$$\text{Initial Deposit} = \$700 \times 4.329 = \$3,030.30$$

The most you should pay for the $700, 5-year annuity, given your 5 percent annual return, is about $3,031. At this price, you'd earn 5 percent on the investment.

Using the present value concept, you can easily determine the present value of a sum to be received in the future, equal annual future withdrawals available from an initial deposit, and the initial deposit that would generate a given stream of equal annual withdrawals. These procedures, like future value concepts, allow you to place monetary values on long-term financial goals.

EXAMPLE: Comparing the Value of Money Over Time

Why would you be willing to pay about $9,524 for the right to receive $10,000 in about a year when the interest rate is 5 percent a year? You'd pay $9,542 today because, if invested at 5%, it would grow to $10,000 in a year. Alternatively viewed, $9,542 is the *present value* of the $10,000 *future value* to be received in a year given that you can invest at 5 percent. Thus, monetary values at different points in time may be compared by considering the present amount that would need to be invested to produce the given future amount.

TEST YOURSELF

2-14   Why is it important to use time value of money concepts in setting personal financial goals?

2-15   What is compounding? Explain the rule of 72.

2-16   When might you use future value? Present value? Give specific examples.

Planning Over a Lifetime: *Budgeting*

While budgeting is important across all stages of the life cycle, here are some key considerations in each stage.

Independent Lifestyle (20s)	Family and Career Development (30s–40s)	Mature Lifestyle (50s–60s)	Retirement (65+)
✓ Develop financial record-keeping system.	✓ Revise budget in light of family and career financial changes.	✓ Revise budget to reflect typically higher income relative to expenses.	✓ Revise budget to adapt to retirement living expenses, health costs, insurance needs, and income.
✓ Develop a budget and carefully track expenses.	✓ Budget amount to save for children's education.	✓ Evaluate projected expenses and housing for retirement planning.	✓ Draw on retirement income sources and accumulated assets.
✓ Budget savings each month and build up an emergency fund.	✓ Determine and set aside retirement contribution.	✓ More aggressively budget to increase retirement contributions.	✓ Spend to meet previously determined long-term financial goals.
✓ Develop personal balance sheet and income statement, and calculate net worth at least annually.	✓ Spend to meet previously determined short- and medium-term financial goals.	✓ Spend to meet previously determined medium-term financial goals.	✓ Update personal balance sheet and income statement, and calculate net worth at least annually.
✓ Develop short-, medium-, and long- term financial goals.	✓ Update personal balance sheet and income statement, and calculate net worth at least annually.	✓ Update personal balance sheet and income statement, and calculate net worth at least annually.	

Financial Impact of Personal Choices
No Budget, No Plan: Sean Bought a Boat!

Sean is 28 and has a good job as a sales rep. He's always found budgeting boring and has been intending to start a financial plan for years.

Recently Sean went out with some friends on a rented boat to fish. He had a great time and saw a boat sale on his way home. Before he knew it, the salesman convinced Sean that the deal was just too good to pass up. So Sean bought a $10,000 boat and financed 80 percent of the cost for the next 5 years. Sean now finds himself relying more on his credit card to get by each month.

What if Sean had kept track of his money, used a budget, and had a set of financial goals? Knowing where his money went and having a financial plan would have increased the chance that Sean would make more deliberate, informed financial decisions.

LG1 **Understand the relationship between financial plans and statements, p. 43**
Preparing and using the balance sheet and the income and expense statement is important to personal financial planning. These tools help you to keep track of your current financial position and to monitor progress toward achieving financial goals. A budget allows you to monitor and control your spending in light of your financial plans.

LG2 **Prepare a personal balance sheet, p. 45**
A balance sheet reports on your financial position at a specific time. It summarizes the things you own (assets), the money you owe (liabilities), and your financial worth (net worth). Net worth represents your actual wealth and is the difference between your total assets and total liabilities.

LG3 **Generate a personal income and expense statement, p. 51**
The income and expense statement summarizes the income you received and the money you spent over a specific period. It's prepared on a cash basis and thus reflects your actual cash flow. Expenses consist of cash outflows to (1) meet living expenses, (2) pay taxes, (3) purchase various kinds of assets, and (4) pay debts. A cash surplus (or deficit) is the difference between income and expenses.

LG4 **Develop a good record-keeping system and use ratios to evaluate personal financial statements, p. 56**
Good records make it easier to prepare accurate personal financial statements, simplify tax return preparation, and provide the necessary documentation for tax deductions. Ratio analysis allows you to assess how well you are doing relative to your past performance. Four important financial ratios are the solvency, liquidity, savings, and debt service ratios.

LG5 **Construct a cash budget and use it to monitor and control spending, p. 60**
A cash budget helps you to carry out a system of disciplined spending. Household budgets identify planned monthly cash income and cash expenses for the coming year. The objective is to take in more money than you spend, so you'll save money and add to your net worth over time.

LG6 **Apply time value of money concepts to put a monetary value on financial goals, p. 69**
When putting a dollar value on financial goals, be sure to consider the time value of money and, if appropriate, use the notion of future value or present value to prepare your estimates.

Key Terms

Answers to Test Yourself

You can find answers to these questions on this book's companion website. Look for it at *www. cengagebrain.com*. Search for this book by its title, and then add it to your dashboard.

Key Financial Relationships

Concept	Financial Relationship	Page Number
Balance Sheet Identity	Total Assets = Total Liabilities + Net Worth	46
Income & Expenditures Identity	Income − Expenses = Cash Surplus (or Deficit)	51
Future Value of a Single Amount	Future Value = Amount Invested × Future Value Factor	70
Future Value of an Annuity	Yearly Savings = Future Amount of Money Desired/Future Value Annuity Factor	70
Rule of 72	Number of Years to Double Money = 72/Annual Compound Interest Rate	71
Present Value of a Single Amount	Present Value = Future Value × Present Value Factor	71
Present Value of an Annuity	Annual Withdrawal = Initial Deposit/Present Value Annuity Factor	72

Key Financial Relationship Problem Set

1. **Balance Sheet Identity.** David Allen would like to better understand where he stands financially. He has total assets of $175,000 and total liabilities of $95,000. What is David's net worth?

   Solution: Total Assets = Total Liabilities + Net Worth, which implies that Net Worth = Total Assets − Total Liabilities = $175,000 − $95,000 = $80,000.

2. **Income & Expenditures Identity.** Ashley Warren earned $48,500 last year while paying $12,000 in housing expenses, $2,400 on utilities, $2,000 on food, $15,000 in miscellaneous expenses, and $7,663 in taxes. What cash surplus or deficit did Ashley earn last year?

   Solution: Income − Expenses = Cash Surplus (or Deficit). In Ashley's case, Income = $48,500 and Expenses = $12,000 + $2,400 + $2,000 + $15,000 + $7,663 = $39,063. Thus, Ashley generated a cash surplus of $48,500 − $39,063 = $9,437.

3. **Future Value of a Single Amount.** Stan Davis has saved $8,000 and wants to invest this single amount for the next 10 years. He believes that he can earn a 7 percent annual return in a moderately risky portfolio. How much should Stan's portfolio be worth in 10 years?

    Solution: Future value = Amount Invested × Future Value Factor. The future value interest factor for 10 years and 7 percent in Appendix A is 1.967. Thus, in 10 years Stan's portfolio is expected to be worth $8,000 × 1.967 = $15,736.

4. **Future Value of an Annuity.** Alice Tobias is 30 years of age and wants to know how much she needs to invest every year to have $100,000 in her account by the time she turns 60. She expects to earn 6 percent per year. What answer can you provide to Alice?

    Solution: Yearly Savings = Future Amount of Money Desired/Future Value Annuity Factor. The future value annuity factor for 30 years and 6 percent in Appendix B is 79.058. Alice should invest a yearly amount of $100,000/79.058 = $1,264.89 if she wants to have $100,000 in her account at the age of 60.

5. **Rule of 72.** Carla Martinez has saved $6,500. How long will it take for Carla's savings to double if she is able to earn 4 percent a year?

    Solution: Number of Years to Double Money = 72/Annual Compound Interest Rate. Carla's savings should double to $13,000 in 72/4 = 18 years.

6. **Present Value of a Single Amount.** Van Tran would like to have $150,000 in his investment account in 20 years. He would like to invest a single sum that will grow to that goal at 4 percent a year. What amount should Van invest?

    Solution: Present Value = Future Value × Present Value Factor. The present value interest factor for 20 years and 4 percent in Appendix C is 0.456. Van would consequently need to invest $150,000 × 0.456 = $68,400 in order for this sum to grow to $150,000 in 20 years.

7. **Present Value of an Annuity.** Lee Zorn wants to help his parents plan for their retirement. They're about to retire and have built up a nest egg of $425,000. Lee would like to let his parents know how much they could plan to withdraw from this fund each year over the next 25 years of retirement if they can earn 6 percent.

    Solution: Annual Withdrawal = Initial Deposit/Present Value Annuity Factor. The present value annuity factor for 25 years and 6 percent in Appendix D is 12.783. Lee can tell his parents that they should be able to withdraw $425,000/12.873 = $33,014.84 per year for the next 25 years.

Financial Planning Exercises

LG2, 3,
p. 45, 51

1. **Preparing financial statements.** Chad Livingston is preparing his balance sheet and income and expense statement for the year ending June 30, 2017. He is having difficulty classifying six items and asks for your help. Which, if any, of the following transactions are assets, liabilities, income, or expense items?
    a. Chad rents a house for $1,350 a month.
    b. On June 21, 2017, Chad bought diamond earrings for his wife and charged them using his MasterCard. The earrings cost $900, but he hasn't yet received the bill.
    c. Chad borrowed $3,500 from his parents last fall, but so far, he has made no payments to them.
    d. Chad makes monthly payments of $225 on an installment loan; about half of it is interest, and the balance is repayment of principal. He has 20 payments left, totaling $4,500.
    e. Chad paid $3,800 in taxes during the year and is due a tax refund of $650, which he hasn't yet received.
    f. Chad invested $2,300 in some common stock.

2. ***Projecting financial statements.*** Put yourself 10 years into the future. Construct a fairly detailed and realistic balance sheet and income and expense statement reflecting what you would like to achieve by that time.

3. ***Preparing personal balance sheet. Use Worksheet 2.1.*** Denise Fisher's banker has asked her to submit a personal balance sheet as of June 30, 2017, in support of an application for a $6,000 home improvement loan. She comes to you for help in preparing it. So far, she has made the following list of her assets and liabilities as of June 30, 2017:

Cash on hand	$70	
Balance in checking account	180	
Balance in money market deposit account with		
Southwest Savings	650	
Bills outstanding:		
Telephone	$20	
Electricity	70	
Charge account balance	190	
Visa	180	
MasterCard	220	
Taxes	400	
Insurance	<u>220</u>	1,300
Condo and property		68,000
Condo mortgage loan		52,000
Automobile: 2012 Honda Civic		12,000
Installment loan balances:		
Auto loans	3,000	
Furniture loan	<u>500</u>	3,500
Personal property:		
Furniture	1,050	
Clothing	<u>900</u>	1,950
Investments:		
U.S. government savings bonds	500	
Stock of Harvester Corp.	<u>3,000</u>	3,500

From the data given, prepare Denise Fisher's balance sheet, dated June 30, 2017 (follow the balance sheet form shown in Worksheet 2.1). Then evaluate her balance sheet relative to the following factors: (a) solvency, (b) liquidity, and (c) equity in her dominant asset.

4. ***Preparing income and expense statement. Use Worksheet 2.2.*** Bill and Nancy Ballinger are about to construct their income and expense statement for the year ending December 31, 2017. Bill is finishing up college and currrently has no income. They have put together the following income and expense information for 2017:

Nancy's salary	$47,000
Reimbursement for travel expenses	1,950
Interest on:	
Savings account	110
Bonds of Alpha Corporation	70
Groceries	4,150
Rent	9,600
Utilities	960

Gas and auto expenses	650
Bill's tuition, books, and supplies	3,300
Books, magazines, and periodicals	280
Clothing and other miscellaneous expenses	2,700
Cost of photographic equipment purchased with charge card	2,200
Amount paid to date on photographic equipment	1,600
Nancy's travel expenses	1,950
Purchase of a used car (cost)	9,750
Outstanding loan balance on car	7,300
Purchase of bonds in Alpha Corporation	4,900

Using the information provided, prepare an income and expense statement for the Ballingers for the year ending December 31, 2017 (follow the form shown in Worksheet 2.2).

LG5, p. 60

5. **Preparing cash budget.** Richard and Elizabeth Walker are preparing their cash budget. Help the Walkers reconcile the following differences, giving reasons to support your answers.

   a. Their only source of income is Richard's salary, which amounts to $5,000 a month before taxes. Elizabeth wants to show the $5,000 as their monthly income, whereas Richard argues that his take-home pay of $3,917 is the correct value to show.

   b. Elizabeth wants to make a provision for fun money, an idea that Richard cannot understand. He asks, "Why do we need fun money when everything is provided for in the budget?"

LG5, p. 60

6. **Identifying missing budget items.** Here is a portion of Chuck Schwartz's budget record for a recent month. Fill in the blanks in columns 5 and 6.

Item (1)	Amount Budgeted (2)	Amount Spent (3)	Beginning Balance (4)	Surplus (Deficit) (5)	Cumulative Surplus (Deficit) (6)
Rent	$550	$575	$50	$_____	$_____
Utilities	150	145	15	_____	_____
Food	510	475	−45	_____	_____
Auto	75	95	−25	_____	_____
Recreation and entertainment	100	110	−50	_____	_____

LG5, p. 60

7. **Personal cash budget. Use Worksheet 2.3.** Prepare a record of your income and expenses for the last 30 days; then prepare a personal cash budget for the next three months. (Use the format in Worksheet 2.3, but fill out only three months and the Total column.) Use the cash budget to control and regulate your expenses during the next month. Discuss the impact of the budget on your spending behavior, as well as any differences between your expected and actual spending patterns.

LG6, p. 69

8. **Calculating present and future values.** Use future or present value techniques to solve the following problems.

   a. Starting with $15,000, how much will you have in 10 years if you can earn 6 percent on your money? If you can earn only 4 percent?

   b. If you inherited $45,000 today and invested all of it in a security that paid a 7 percent rate of return, how much would you have in 25 years?

   c. If the average new home costs $275,000 today, how much will it cost in 10 years if the price increases by 5 percent each year?

   d. You think that in 15 years, it will cost $212,000 to provide your child with a 4-year college education. Will you have enough if you take $70,000 today and invest it for the next 15 years at 5 percent? If you start from scratch, how much will you have to save each year to have $212,000 in 15 years if you can earn a 4 percent rate of return on your investments?

e. If you can earn 4 percent, how much will you have to save each year if you want to retire in 35 years with $1 million?

f. You plan to have $750,000 in savings and investments when you retire at age 60. Assuming that you earn an average of 8 percent on this portfolio, what is the maximum annual withdrawal you can make over a 25-year period of retirement?

9. ***Evaluating a savings goal.*** Over the past several years, Catherine Lee has been able to save regularly. As a result, she has $54,188 in savings and investments today. She wants to establish her own business in 5 years and feels she will need $100,000 to do so.

a. If she can earn 4 percent on her money, how much will her $54,188 in savings/investments be worth in 5 years? Will Catherine have the $100,000 she needs? If not, how much more money will she need?

b. Given your answer to part **a,** how much will Catherine have to save each year over the next 5 years to accumulate the additional money? Assume that she can earn interest at a rate of 4 percent.

c. If Catherine can afford to save only $4,000 a year, then given your answer to part a, will she have the $100,000 she needs to start her own business in 5 years?

10. ***Funding a retirement goal.*** Chris Jones wishes to have $800,000 in a retirement fund 20 years from now. He can create the retirement fund by making a single lump-sum deposit today.

a. If he can earn 6 percent on his investments, how much must Chris deposit today to create the retirement fund? If he can earn only 4 percent on his investments? Compare and discuss the results of your calculations.

b. If, upon retirement in 20 years, Chris plans to invest the $800,000 in a fund that earns 4 percent, what is the maximum annual withdrawal he can make over the following 15 years?

c. How much would Chris need to have on deposit at retirement to annually withdraw $35,000 over the 15 years if the retirement fund earns 4 percent?

d. To achieve his annual withdrawal goal of $35,000 calculated in part **c,** how much more than the amount calculated in part **a** must Chris deposit today in an investment earning 4 percent annual interest?

11. ***Funding a college goal.*** Dan Weaver wants to set up a fund to pay for his daughter's education. In order to pay her expenses, he will need $23,000 in four years, $24,300 in five years, $26,000 in six years, and $28,000 in seven years. If he can put money into a fund that pays 4 percent interest, what lump-sum payment must Dan place in the fund today to meet his college funding goals?

12. ***Calculating expected future value of investments.*** Jessica Wright has always been interested in stocks. She has decided to invest $2,000 once every year into an equity mutual fund that is expected to produce a return of 6 percent a year for the foreseeable future. Jessica is really curious how much money she can reasonably expect her investment to be worth in 20 years. What would you tell her?

Applying Personal Finance

What's Your Condition?

Financial statements reflect your financial condition. They help you measure where you are now. Then, as time passes and you prepare your financial statements periodically, you can use them to track your progress toward financial goals. Good financial statements are also a must when you apply for a loan. This project will help you to evaluate your current financial condition.

Look back at the discussion in this chapter on balance sheets and income and expense statements, and prepare your own. If you're doing this for the first time, it may not be as easy as it sounds! Use the following questions to help you along.

1. Have you included all your assets at fair market value (not historical cost) on your balance sheet?

2. Have you included all your debt balances as liabilities on your balance sheet? (Don't take your monthly payment amounts multiplied by the number of payments you have left—this total includes future interest.)

3. Have you included all items of income on your income and expense statement? (Remember, your paycheck is income and not an asset on your balance sheet.)

4. Have you included all debt payments as expenses on your income and expense statement? (Your phone bill is an expense for this month if you've already paid it. If the bill is still sitting on your desk staring you in the face, it's a liability on your balance sheet.)

5. Are there occasional expenses that you've forgotten about, or hidden expenses such as entertainment that you have overlooked? Look back through your checkbook, spending diary, or any other financial records to find these occasional or infrequent expenses.

6. Remember that items go on either the balance sheet or the income and expense statement, but not on both. For example, the $350 car payment you made this month is an expense on your income and expense statement. The remaining $15,000 balance on your car loan is a liability on your balance sheet, while the fair market value of your car at $17,500 is an asset.

After completing your statements, calculate your solvency, liquidity, savings, and debt service ratios. Now, use your statements and ratios to assess your current financial condition. Do you like where you are? If not, how can you get where you want to be? Use your financial statements and ratios to help you formulate plans for the future.

CRITICAL THINKING CASES

2.1 The Beckers' Version of Financial Planning

Terry and Evelyn Becker are a married couple in their mid-20s. Terry has a good start as an electrical engineer and Evelyn works as a sales representative. Since their marriage four years ago, Terry and Evelyn have been living comfortably. Their income has exceeded their expenses, and they have accumulated an enviable net worth. This includes $10,000 that they have built up in savings and investments. Because their income has always been more than enough for them to have the lifestyle they desire, the Beckers have done no financial planning.

Evelyn has just learned that she's pregnant. She's concerned about how they'll make ends meet if she quits work after their child is born. Each time she and Terry discuss the matter, he tells her not to worry because "we've always managed to pay our bills on time." Evelyn can't understand his attitude because her income will be completely eliminated. To convince Evelyn that there's no need for concern, Terry points out that their expenses last year, but for the common stock purchase, were about equal to his take-home pay. With an anticipated promotion and an expected 10 percent pay raise, his income next year should exceed this amount. Terry also points out that they can reduce luxuries (trips, recreation, and entertainment) and can always draw down their savings or sell some of their stock if they get in a bind. When Evelyn asks about the long-run implications for their finances, Terry says there will be "no problems" because his boss has assured him that he has a bright future with the engineering firm. Terry also emphasizes that Evelyn can go back to work in a few years if necessary.

Despite Terry's arguments, Evelyn feels that they should carefully examine their financial condition in order to do some serious planning. She has gathered the following financial information for the year ending December 31, 2017:

Salaries	Take-Home Pay	Gross Salary
Terry	*$52,500*	*$76,000*
Evelyn	*29,200*	*42,000*

Item	Amount
Food	$5,902
Clothing	2,300
Mortgage payments, including property taxes of $1,400	11,028
Travel and entertainment card balances	2,000
Gas, electric, water expenses	1,990
Household furnishings	4,500
Telephone	640
Auto loan balance	4,650
Common stock investments	7,500
Bank credit card balances	675
Federal income taxes	22,472
State income tax	5,040
Social security contributions	9,027
Credit card loan payments	2,210
Cash on hand	85
2012 Nissan Sentra	10,500
Medical expenses (unreimbursed)	600
Homeowner's insurance premiums paid	1,300
Checking account balance	485
Auto insurance premiums paid	1,600
Transportation	2,800
Cable television	680
Estimated value of home	185,000
Trip to Europe	5,000
Recreation and entertainment	4,000
Auto loan payments	2,150
Money market account balance	2,500
Purchase of common stock	7,500
Addition to money market account	500
Mortgage on home	148,000

Critical Thinking Questions

1. Using this information and Worksheets 2.1 and 2.2, construct the Beckers' balance sheet and income and expense statement for the year ending December 31, 2017.
2. Comment on the Beckers' financial condition regarding (a) solvency, (b) liquidity, (c) savings, and (d) ability to pay debts promptly. If the Beckers continue to manage their finances as described, what do you expect the long-run consequences to be? Discuss.
3. Critically evaluate the Beckers' approach to financial planning. Point out any fallacies in Terry's observations, and be sure to mention (a) implications for the long term, as well as (b) the potential impact of inflation in general and specifically on their net worth. What procedures should they use to get their financial house in order? Be sure to discuss the role that long- and short-term financial plans and budgets might play.

2.2 Brooke Stauffer Learns to Budget

Brooke Stauffer recently graduated from college and moved to Atlanta to take a job as a market research analyst. She was pleased to be financially independent and was sure that, with her $45,000 salary, she could cover her living expenses and have plenty of money left over to furnish her studio apartment and enjoy the wide variety of social and recreational activities available in Atlanta. She opened several department-store charge accounts and obtained a bank credit card.

For a while, Brooke managed pretty well on her monthly take-home pay of $2,893, but by the end of 2017, she was having trouble fully paying all her credit card charges each month. Concerned that her spending had gotten out of control and that she was barely making it from paycheck to paycheck, she decided to list her expenses for the past calendar year and develop a budget. She hoped not only to reduce her credit card debt but also to begin a regular savings program.

Brooke prepared the following summary of expenses for 2017:

Item	Annual Expenditure
Rent	$12,000
Auto insurance	1,855
Auto loan payments	3,840
Auto expenses (gas, repairs, and fees)	1,560
Clothing	3,200
Installment loan for stereo	540
Personal care	424
Phone	600
Cable TV	440
Gas and electricity	1,080
Medical care	120
Dentist	70
Groceries	2,500
Dining out	2,600
Furniture purchases	1,200
Recreation and entertainment	2,900
Other expenses	600

After reviewing her 2017 expenses, Brooke made the following assumptions about her expenses for 2018:

1. All expenses will remain at the same levels, with these exceptions:
   a. Auto insurance, auto expenses, gas and electricity, and groceries will increase 5 percent.
   b. Clothing purchases will decrease to $2,250.
   c. Phone and cable TV will increase $5 per month.
   d. Furniture purchases will decrease to $660, most of which is for a new television.
   e. She will take a one-week vacation to Colorado in July, at a cost of $2,100.
2. All expenses will be budgeted in equal monthly installments except for the vacation and these items:
   a. Auto insurance is paid in two installments due in June and December.
   b. She plans to replace the brakes on his car in February, at a cost of $220.
   c. Visits to the dentist will be made in March and September.
3. She will eliminate his bank credit card balance by making extra monthly payments of $75 during each of the first six months.
4. Regarding her income, Brooke has just received a small raise, so her take-home pay will be $3,200 per month.

Critical Thinking Questions

1. a. Prepare a preliminary cash budget for Brooke for the year ending December 31, 2018, using the format shown in Worksheet 2.3.
    b. Compare Brooke's estimated expenses with her expected income and make recommendations that will help her balance his budget.
2. Make any necessary adjustments to Brooke's estimated monthly expenses, and revise her annual cash budget for the year ending December 31, 2018, using Worksheet 2.3.
3. Analyze the budget and advise Brooke on her financial situation. Suggest some long-term, intermediate, and short-term financial goals for Brooke, and discuss some steps she can take to reach them.

CHAPTER 3

Preparing Your Taxes

LEARNING GOALS

LG1   Discuss the basic principles of income taxes and determine your filing status.

LG2   Describe the sources of gross income and adjustments to income, differentiate between standard and itemized deductions and exemptions, and calculate taxable income.

LG3   Prepare a basic tax return using the appropriate tax forms and rate schedules.

LG4   Explain who needs to pay estimated taxes, when to file or amend your return, and how to handle an audit.

LG5   Know where to get help with your taxes and how software can make tax return preparation easier.

LG6   Implement an effective tax planning strategy.

How Will This Affect Me?

There's an old joke that people who complain about taxes can be divided into two groups: men and women. This chapter helps you pursue the tax-planning goal of maximizing the money that you get to keep by legally minimizing the taxes you have to pay. Income, various adjustments to income, deductions, and credits are considered in computing taxes. The chapter walks through the steps in completing representative tax returns. The impact of Social Security taxes and tax shelters are considered. And a framework for choosing a professional tax preparer or tax preparation software is provided. After reading this chapter you should be able to prepare your own taxes or to better understand and evaluate how your taxes are prepared by software or a tax professional.

Jose Luis Pelaez Inc/Blend Images/Jupiter Images

3-1 UNDERSTANDING FEDERAL INCOME TAX PRINCIPLES

taxes
The dues paid for membership in our society; a cost of living in this country.

Taxes are dues that we pay for membership in our society; they're the cost of living in this country. Federal, state, and local tax receipts fund government activities and a wide variety of public services, from national defense to local libraries. Administering and enforcing federal tax laws is the responsibility of the Internal Revenue Service (IRS), a part of the U.S. Department of Treasury.

Because federal income tax is generally the largest tax you'll pay, you are wise to make tax planning an important part of personal financial planning. A typical American family currently pays *more than one-third of its gross income in taxes:* federal income and Social Security taxes and numerous state and local income, sales, and property taxes. You may think of tax planning as an activity to do between the beginning of the year and April 15, the usual filing deadline, but you should make tax planning a year-round activity. It's always wise to consider tax consequences when preparing and revising your financial plans and making major financial decisions, such as buying a home and making any investment decisions at all.

The overriding objective of tax planning is simple: *to maximize the amount of money that you can keep legally by minimizing the amount of taxes you pay.* So long as it's done honestly and within the tax codes, there is nothing immoral, illegal, or unethical about trying to minimize your tax bill. Most tax planning focuses on ways to minimize income and estate taxes. In this chapter, we concentrate on *income taxes paid by individuals*—particularly the federal income tax, the largest and most important tax for most taxpayers. Although you may currently pay little or no taxes, we use a mid-career couple to demonstrate the key aspects of individual taxation. This approach will give you a good understanding of your future tax situation and allow you to develop realistic financial plans.

In addition to federal income tax, there are other forms of taxes to contend with. For example, additional federal taxes may be levied on self-employment or outside consulting income and on certain types of transactions. At the state and local levels, sales transactions, income, property ownership, and licenses may be taxed. Because most individuals have to pay many of these other types of taxes, you should evaluate their impact on your financial decisions. Thus, a person saving to purchase a new automobile costing $25,000 should realize that the state and local sales taxes, as well as the cost of license plates and registration, may add another $2,000 or more to the total cost of the car.

Behavior Matters

Do We Really Value Paying Taxes After All?

Surprisingly, your brain may like paying taxes! Recent research suggests that people can feel good about paying taxes that improve others' well-being. While most people would prefer to keep their money rather than pay taxes, paying taxes still is not the same thing as throwing the money away. Taxes can be viewed, even if only subconsciously, as a social good. And people don't like inequality and seek to preserve a positive self-image, which means that most are unlikely to cheat on their taxes. Interestingly, there is evidence that many people work harder when they realize they will be taxed. In a recent experiment, participants worked harder when paid $100 and there was a $10 tax than when they were paid $90 with no taxes due.

So what could explain this? It's important for people to feel that their taxes actually do some good. When people clearly know what their taxes are used for—and if it appears to be for the common good—they can actually find paying taxes somewhat satisfying. This challenges governments everywhere to make their tax systems fully transparent and to explicitly show that the money is being spent in a positive way. Doing so makes sense in a democracy and creates the right incentives for taxpayers.

Source: Adapted from Patrick Temple-West, "Surprise, Your Brain Might Value Paying Taxes," http://blogs.reuters.com/unstructuredfinance/2012/04/02/surprise-your-brain-might-value-paying-taxes/, accessed July 2015; based on a research article by Iwan Djanali and Damien Sheehan-Connor, "Tax affinity hypothesis: Do we really hate paying taxes?" *Journal of Economic Psychology*, August 2012.

Because tax laws are complicated and subject to frequent revision, we'll present key concepts and show how they apply to common tax situations. Provisions of the tax code may change annually for tax rates, amounts and types of deductions and personal exemptions, and similar items. The tax tables, calculations, and sample tax returns presented in this chapter are based on the tax laws applicable to the calendar year 2014. Nonetheless, *although tax rates and other provisions will change, the basic procedures will remain the same.* Before preparing your tax returns, be sure to review the current regulations; IRS publications and other tax preparation guides may be helpful.

3-1a The Economics of Income Taxes

Unsurprisingly, most people simply don't like paying taxes. Some of this feeling likely stems from the widely held perception that a lot of government spending amounts to little more than bureaucratic waste. But a good deal of this feeling is probably because taxpayers don't always perceive that they receive tangible benefits for their money. After all, paying taxes isn't like spending $7,000 on a European vacation. We too often tend to overlook or take for granted the many services provided by the taxes we pay—public schools and state colleges, roads and highways, and parks and recreational facilities, not to mention police and fire protection, retirement benefits, and many other health and social services.

Income taxes are the major source of revenue for the federal government. Personal income taxes are scaled on progressive rates. To illustrate how this **progressive tax structure** works, consider the following data for single taxpayers filing 2014 returns:

income taxes
A type of tax levied on taxable income by the federal government and by many state and local governments.

progressive tax structure
A tax structure in which the larger the amount of taxable income, the higher the rate at which it is taxed.

Taxable Income	Tax Rate
$1 to $9,075	10%
$9,076 to $36,900	15%
$36,901 to $89,350	25%
$89,351 to $186,350	28%
$186,351 to $405,100	33%
$405,101 to $406,750	35%
Over $406,750	39.6%

Of course, any nontaxable income can be viewed as being in the 0 percent tax bracket. As taxable income moves from a lower to a higher bracket, the higher rate applies *only to the additional taxable income in that bracket,* not to the entire taxable income.

EXAMPLE: Applying Tax Rates

Two single brothers, Finn and Connor, have taxable incomes of $50,000 and $100,000, respectively. They calculate their tax liabilities as follows:

Name	Taxable Income	Tax Calculation	Tax Liability
Finn	$50,000	= [($50,000 − $36,900) × 0.25]	
		+ [($36,900 − $9,075) × 0.15]	
		+ [$9,075 × 0.10]	
		= $3,275 + $4,173.75 + $907.50 =	$8,356.25
Connor	$100,000	= [($100,000 − $89,350) × 0.28]	
		+ [(89,350 − $36,900) × 0.25]	
		+ [(36,900 − $9,075) × 0.15]	
		+ [$9,075 × 0.10]	
		= $2,982 + $13,112.5 + $4,173.75 + $907.5	$21,175.75

Note that Finn pays the 25 percent rate only on the portion of his $50,000 taxable income that exceeds $36,900. Due to this kind of progressive scale, the more money you make, the progressively more you pay in taxes. Although Connor's taxable income is twice that of Finn's, his income tax is about 2½ times higher than his brother's.

The tax rate for each bracket—10 percent, 15 percent, 25 percent, 28 percent, 33 percent, 35 percent, and 39.6 percent—is called the marginal tax rate, or the rate applied to the next dollar of taxable income. When you relate the tax liability to the level of taxable income earned, the tax rate, called the average tax rate, drops considerably.

marginal tax rate
The tax rate that you pay on the next dollar of taxable income.

average tax rate
The rate at which each dollar of taxable income is taxed on average; calculated by dividing the tax liability by taxable income.

EXAMPLE: Calculating an Average Tax Rate

Finn paid taxes of $8,356.25 on taxable income of $50,000, which implies an average tax rate of $8,356.25/$50,000 = 16.7 percent. His brother, Connor, paid taxes of $21,175.75 on income of $100,000 for an average tax rate of $21,175.75/$100,000) = 21.2 percent. While taxes are progressive, the average size of the bite is not as bad as the stated tax rate might suggest.

3-1b Your Filing Status

The taxes you pay depend in part on your *filing status,* which is based on your marital status and family situation on the last day of your tax year (usually December 31). Filing status affects whether you're required to file an income tax return, the amount of your standard deduction, and your tax rate. If you have a choice of filing status, you should calculate your taxes both ways and choose the status that results in the lower tax liability.

There are five different filing status categories:

- **Single taxpayers:** Unmarried or legally separated from their spouses by either a separation or final divorce decree.
- **Married filing jointly:** Married couples who combine their income and allowable deductions and file one tax return.
- **Married filing separately:** Each spouse files his or her own return, reporting only his or her income, deductions, and exemptions.
- **Head of household:** A taxpayer who is unmarried or considered unmarried and pays more than half of the cost of keeping up a home for himself or herself and an eligible dependent child or relative.
- **Qualifying widow or widower with dependent child:** A person whose spouse died within two years of the tax year (e.g., in 2012 or 2013 for the 2014 tax year) and who supports a dependent child may use joint return tax rates and is eligible for the highest standard deduction. (After the two-year period, such a person may file under the head of household status if he or she qualifies.)

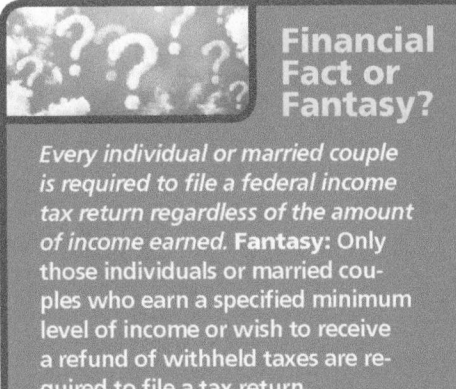

Financial Fact or Fantasy?

Every individual or married couple is required to file a federal income tax return regardless of the amount of income earned. **Fantasy:** Only those individuals or married couples who earn a specified minimum level of income or wish to receive a refund of withheld taxes are required to file a tax return.

The tax brackets (rates) and payments for married couples filing separately are now typically close to the same as for joint filers. However, because the spouses rarely account for equal amounts of taxable income and deductions, it may be advantageous in some cases for spouses to file separate returns. For instance, if one spouse has a moderate income and substantial medical expenses and the other has a low income and no medical expenses, then filing separately may provide a tax savings. It's worth your time to calculate your taxes using both scenarios to see which results in the lower amount.

Every individual or married couple who earns a specified level of income is required to file a tax return. For example: for those under 65, a single person who earned more than $10,150 and a married couple with a combined income of more than $20,300 must file a tax return (for 2014). Like the personal tax rates, these minimums are adjusted annually based on the annual rate of inflation, and they're published in the instructions accompanying each year's tax forms. If your income falls below the current minimum levels, you're not required to file a tax return. But if you had any income tax withheld during the year, you must file a tax return—even if your income falls *below* the minimum filing amount—to receive a refund of the income tax withheld.

3-1c Your Take-Home Pay

Although many of us don't give much thought to taxes until April 15 approaches, we actually are required to pay taxes as we earn income throughout the year. Under this *pay-as-you-go* system, your employer withholds (deducts) a portion of your income every pay period and sends it to the IRS to be credited to your own tax account. Self-employed persons must also prepay their taxes by forwarding part of their income to the IRS at four dates each year (referred to as quarterly estimated tax payments). The amounts withheld are based on a taxpayer's estimated tax liability. After the close of the taxable year, you calculate the actual taxes you owe and file your tax return. When you file, you receive full credit for the amount of taxes withheld (including estimated tax payments) from your income during the year and either (1) receive a refund from the IRS (if too much tax was withheld from your paycheck and/or pre-paid in estimated taxes) or (2) pay additional taxes (if the amount withheld/prepaid didn't cover your tax liability). Your employer normally withholds funds not only for federal income taxes but also for Federal Insurance Contributions Act (FICA, or **Social Security** and **Medicare**) taxes and, if applicable, state and local income taxes. In addition to taxes, you may have other tax deductions for items such as life and health insurance, savings plans, retirement programs, professional or union dues, or charitable

Federal Insurance Contributions Act (FICA) or social security tax
The law establishing the combined Old-Age, Survivor's, Disability, and Hospital Insurance tax levied on both employer and employee.

contributions—all of which lower your take-home pay. Your *take-home pay* is what you're left with after subtracting the amount withheld from your *gross earnings*.

Federal Withholding Taxes

federal withholding taxes
Taxes—based on the level of earnings and the number of withholding allowances claimed—that an employer deducts from the employee's gross earnings each pay period.

The amount of **federal withholding taxes** deducted from your gross earnings each pay period depends on both the level of your earnings and the number of withholding allowances you have claimed on a form called a *W-4*, which you must complete for your employer. Withholding allowances reduce the amount of taxes withheld from your income. A taxpayer is entitled to one allowance for himself or herself, one for a nonworking spouse (if filing jointly), and one for each dependent claimed (children or parents being supported mainly by the taxpayers). In addition, you may qualify for a *special allowance* or *additional withholding allowances* under certain circumstances. Taxpayers may have to change their withholding allowances during the tax year if their employment or marital status changes.

FICA and Other Withholding Taxes

In addition to income tax withholding on earnings, all employed workers (except certain federal employees) have to pay a combined old-age, survivor's, disability, and hospital insurance tax under provisions of the FICA. Known more commonly as the Social Security tax, it is paid equally by employer and employee. In 2014, the total Social Security tax rate was 15.3 percent, allocating 12.4 percent to Social Security and 2.9 percent to Medicare. The 12.4 percent applies only to the first $117,000 of an employee's earnings (this number rises with national average wages), whereas the Medicare component is paid on all earnings. In 2014, self-employed persons pay the full 15.3 percent tax but can deduct 50 percent of it on their tax returns.

Most states have their own income taxes, which differ from state to state. Some cities assess income taxes as well. These state and local income taxes will also be withheld from earnings. They are deductible on federal returns, but deductibility of federal taxes on the state or local return depends on state and local laws.

Financial Fact or Fantasy?

The amount of federal income tax withheld depends on both your level of earnings and the number of withholding allowances claimed. **Fact:** The more you make and the fewer withholding allowances you claim, the more will be withheld from your paycheck.

TEST YOURSELF

3-1 What is a *progressive tax structure* and the economic rationale for it?

3-2 Briefly define the five filing categories available to taxpayers. When might married taxpayers choose to file separately?

3-3 Distinguish between *gross earnings* and *take-home pay*. What does the employer do with the difference?

3-4 What two factors determine the amount of federal withholding taxes that will be deducted from gross earnings each pay period? Explain.

3-2 IT'S TAXABLE INCOME THAT MATTERS

taxable income
The amount of income subject to taxes; it is calculated by subtracting adjustments, the larger of itemized or standard deductions, and exemptions from gross income.

As you've no doubt gathered by now, paying your income taxes is a complex process involving several steps and many calculations. Exhibit 3.1 depicts the procedure to compute your **taxable income** and total tax liability. It looks simple enough—just subtract certain adjustments from your gross income to get your adjusted gross income; then subtract either the standard deduction or your itemized deductions and your total personal exemptions to get taxable income; and finally, calculate your taxes, subtract any tax credits from that amount, and add any other taxes to it to get your

EXHIBIT 3.1   Calculating Your Taxable Income and Total Tax Liability Owed

To find taxable income, you must first subtract all adjustments from gross income and then subtract deductions and personal exemptions. Your total tax liability owed includes tax on this taxable income amount, less any tax credits, plus other taxes owed.

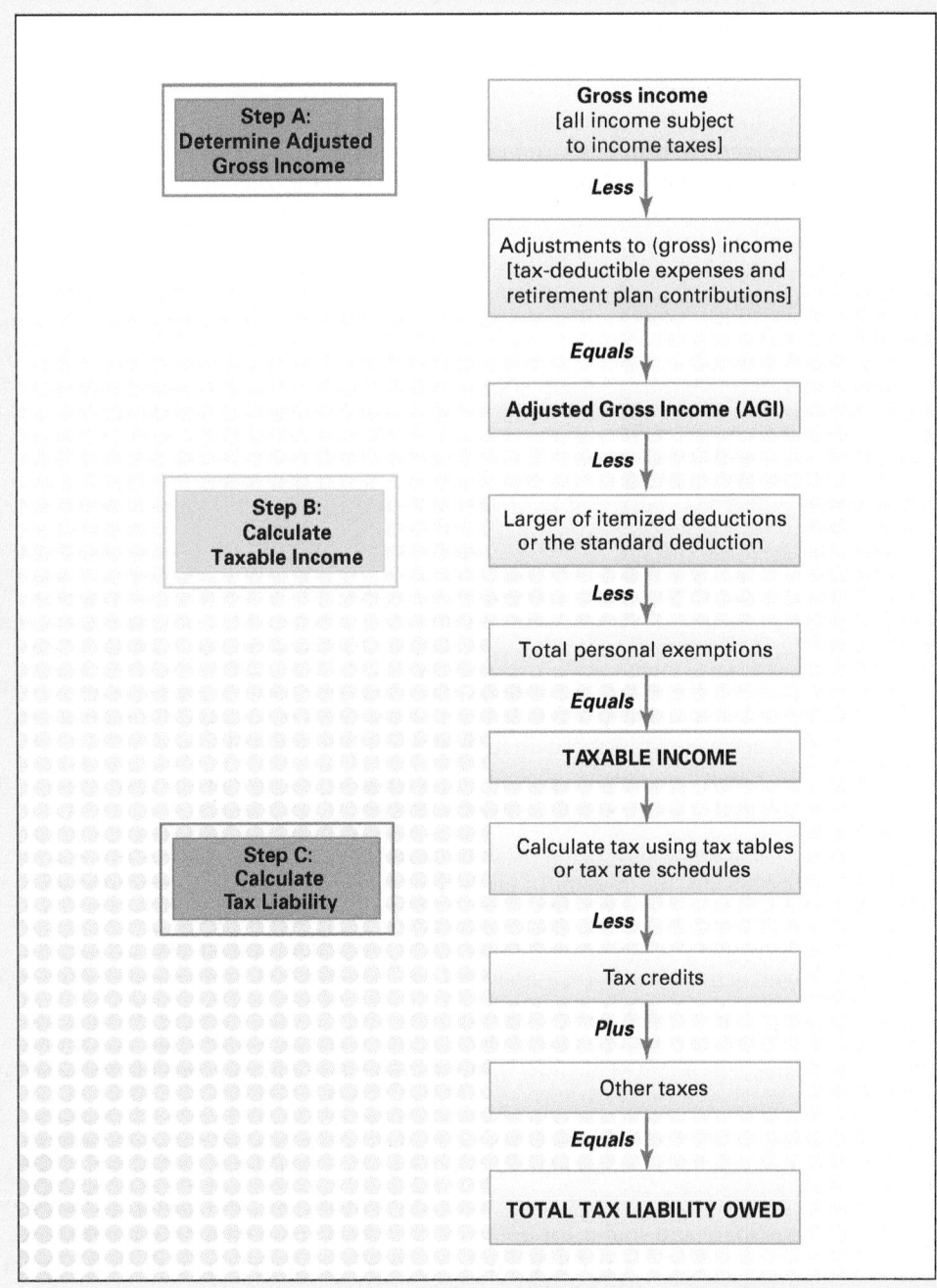

total tax liability. This isn't as easy as it sounds, however! Various sections of the Internal Revenue Code place numerous conditions and exceptions on the tax treatment and deductibility of certain income and expense items and also define certain types of income as tax exempt. As we'll see, some problems can arise in defining what you may subtract.

3-2a Gross Income

gross income
The total of all of a taxpayer's income (before any adjustments, deductions, or exemptions) subject to federal taxes; it includes active, portfolio, and passive income.

Gross income essentially includes any and all income subject to federal taxes. Here are some common forms of gross income:

- Wages and salaries
- Bonuses, commissions, and tips
- Interest and dividends received
- Alimony received
- Business and farm income
- Gains from the sale of assets
- Income from pensions and annuities
- Income from rents and partnerships
- Prizes, lottery, and gambling winnings

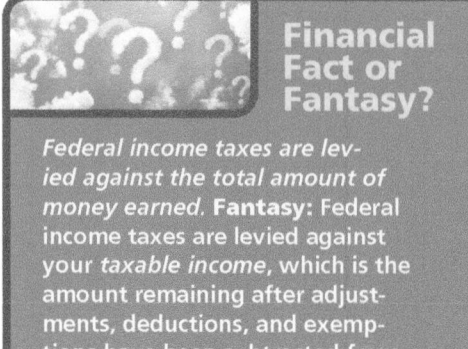

Financial Fact or Fantasy?

Federal income taxes are levied against the total amount of money earned. **Fantasy:** Federal income taxes are levied against your *taxable income,* which is the amount remaining after adjustments, deductions, and exemptions have been subtracted from gross income.

In addition to these sources of income, there are others that are considered *tax exempt* and consequently are excluded—totally or partially—from gross income. Common types of tax-exempt income include child-support payments; municipal bond interest payments; certain types of employee fringe benefits; compensation from accident, health, and life insurance policies; federal income tax refunds; gifts, inheritances, scholarships, and fellowships (limited as to amount and time); and veterans' benefits.

Three Kinds of Income

Individual income falls into one of three basic categories:

- **Active income:** Income *earned* on the job, such as wages and salaries, bonuses and tips; most other forms of *noninvestment* income, including pension income and alimony
- **Portfolio income:** Earnings (interest, dividends, and capital gains [profits on the sale of investments]) generated from most types of investment holdings; includes savings accounts, stocks, bonds, mutual funds, options, and futures
- **Passive income:** A special category that includes income derived from real estate, limited partnerships, and other forms of tax shelters

These categories limit the amount of deductions and write-offs that taxpayers can take. Specifically, the amount of allowable, deductible expenses associated with portfolio and passive income *is limited to the amount of income derived from these two sources.* For deduction purposes, you cannot combine portfolio and passive income with each other or with active income. *Investment-related expenses can be used only with portfolio income,* and with a few exceptions, *passive investment expenses can be used only to offset the income from passive investments.* All the other allowances and deductions we'll describe later are written off against the total amount of *active* income the taxpayer generates.

Capital Gains

Technically, a *capital gain* occurs whenever a capital asset (such as a stock, a bond, or real estate) is sold for more than its original cost. So, if you purchased stock for $50 per share and sold it for $60, you'd have a capital gain of $10 per share.

Capital gains are taxed at different rates, depending on the holding period. Exhibit 3.2 shows the different holding periods and applicable tax rates based on the 2014 tax brackets. As a rule, taxpayers include most capital gains as part of *portfolio income.* They will add any capital gains to the amount of dividends, interest, and rents they generate to arrive at total investment income. In addition to the rates shown in Exhibit 3.2, some higher income earners may also have to pay a 3.8 percent Medicare surtax.

Although there are no limits on the amount of capital gains taxpayers can generate, the IRS imposes some restrictions on the amount of capital losses taxpayers can take in a given year. Specifically, a taxpayer can write off capital losses, dollar for dollar, against any capital gains. After that, he or she can write off a maximum of $3,000

EXHIBIT 3.2   Capital Gains Tax Categories as of 2014

Capital gains tax rates are as low as 0 percent for low-income levels or as high as 28 percent for higher income levels and certain types of assets, so long as the holding period is more than 12 months.

Holding Period	Tax Brackets/Asset Sold (2014)	Tax on Capital Gains
Less than 12 months	All (10%, 15%, 25%, 28%, 33%, 35%, and 39.6%) - any asset sold	Same as ordinary income
Over 12 months	10% and 15% - assets other than real estate and collectibles	0%,
	25%, 33%, 35%, 39.6%	15%, or 20% (later only if in 39.6% tax bracket)
	Sale of depreciable real estate	25% on gain up to depreciation amount
	Collectibles	28% all gains from collectibles

in additional capital losses against other (active, earned) income. For example, if a taxpayer had $10,000 in capital gains and $18,000 in capital losses in 2014, only $13,000 could be written off on 2014 taxes: $10,000 against the capital gains generated in 2014 and another $3,000 against active income. The remainder—$5,000 in this case—will have to be written off in later years, in the same order as just indicated: first against any capital gains and then up to $3,000 against active income.

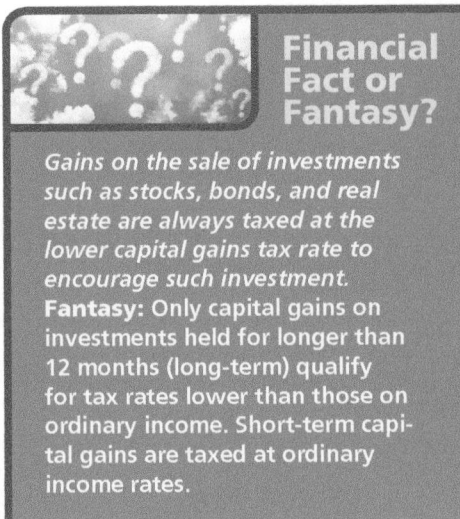

Financial Fact or Fantasy?

Gains on the sale of investments such as stocks, bonds, and real estate are always taxed at the lower capital gains tax rate to encourage such investment.

Fantasy: Only capital gains on investments held for longer than 12 months (long-term) qualify for tax rates lower than those on ordinary income. Short-term capital gains are taxed at ordinary income rates.

Selling Your Home: A Special Case Homeowners, for various reasons, receive special treatment in the tax codes, including the taxation of capital gains on the sale of a home. Under current law, single taxpayers can exclude from income the first $250,000 of gain on the sale of a principal residence. Married taxpayers can exclude the first $500,000. To get this favorable tax treatment, the taxpayer must own and occupy the residence as a principal residence for at least two of the five years prior to the sale. This exclusion is available on only one sale every two years. A loss on the sale of a principal residence is not deductible. This law is generally quite favorable to homeowners.

EXAMPLE: Taxes on the Sale of a Home

The Jacobs are married taxpayers who just sold their principal residence for $475,000. They had purchased their home four years earlier for $325,000. They may exclude their $150,000 gain ($475,000 − $325,000) from their income because they occupied the residence for more than two years, and the gain is less than $500,000.

3-2b Adjustments to (Gross) Income

adjustments to (gross) income
Allowable deductions from gross income, including certain employee, personal retirement, insurance, and support expenses.

Now that you've totaled your gross income, you can deduct your adjustments to (gross) income. These are allowable deductions from gross income, including certain employee, personal retirement, insurance, and support expenses. Most of these deductions are nonbusiness in nature.

Here are some items that can be treated as adjustments to income:

- Educator expenses (limited)
- Higher education tuition costs (limited)
- IRA contributions (limited)

- Self-employment taxes paid (limited to 50 percent of the amount paid)
- Self-employed health insurance payments
- Penalty on early withdrawal of savings
- Alimony paid
- Reimbursed moving expenses (some limits)

(*Note:* The limitations on deductions for self-directed retirement plans, such as individual retirement accounts (IRAs) and Simplified Employee Pensions (SEPs), are discussed in Chapter 14.)

After subtracting the total of all allowable adjustments to income from your gross income, you're left with adjusted gross income (AGI). AGI is an important value, because it's used to calculate limits for certain itemized deductions.

adjusted gross income (AGI)
The amount of income remaining after subtracting all allowable adjustments to income from gross income.

3-2c Deductions: Standard or Itemized?

As we see from Exhibit 3.1, the next step in calculating your taxes is to subtract allowable deductions from your AGI. This may be the most complex part of the tax preparation process. You have two options: take the *standard deduction*, a fixed amount that depends on your filing status, or list your *itemized deductions* (specified tax-deductible personal expenses). Obviously, you should use the method that results in larger allowable deductions.

standard deduction
A blanket deduction that depends on the taxpayer's filing status, age, and vision and can be taken by a taxpayer whose total itemized deductions are too small.

Standard Deduction

Instead of itemizing personal deductions, a taxpayer can take the standard deduction, a blanket deduction that includes the various deductible expenses that taxpayers normally incur. People whose total itemized deductions are less than the standard

FINANCIAL PLANNING TIPS

Ways to Reduce Your Taxes

It is all too common for some taxpayers to overlook the following tax deductions and credits that would decrease their tax bill. While there are qualifications and limitations on these tax deductions and credits, it's worth your time to be aware of these opportunities. Keep in mind that all of these deductions are reduced by 2 percent of AGI before adding them to the other itemized deductions.

- **Medical travel expenses.** The costs of traveling to visit health care providers to receive medical care are deductible if the visits are recommended by a doctor. There is a standard mileage deduction if you drive, and you can deduct direct expenses like taxis, parking fees, and tolls.

- **Health insurance and medical expenses.** Health insurance premiums are deductible. Similarly, the cost of prescriptions and separate charges for medical coverage included in a dependent child's college fees are deductible. Medical bills that you pay for a person who is your dependent are also deductible.

- **Real estate taxes and home sale costs.** Real estate taxes paid are deductible, as are any "point" fees associated with a mortgage. Annual maintenance fees for a

condo also may be deducted because they are your share of the overall property's real estate taxes.

- **Volunteer and donation-related expenses.** When you donate to a charity or volunteer your time, the associated expenses are tax-deductible. For example, if you donate cookies to be sold by a charity, you can deduct the cost of baking them. Transportation costs can also be deducted.

- **Job search expenses.** The costs associated with looking for a new job are generally deductible. So you can write off employment placement agency fees, resume printing costs, and related travel expenses.

- **Tax and investment-related expenses.** The expenses paid for preparing your tax return are deductible. Further, any expenses associated with managing your investments are generally deductible. For example, you can write off financial advisors' fees and investment publication subscription costs.

- **College tuition tax credit.** You can get up to a $2,500 tax credit in college tuition for family members if your adjusted gross income falls within certain limits.

deduction take the standard deduction, which varies depending on the taxpayer's filing status (single, married filing jointly, and so on), age (65 or older), and vision (blind). In 2014, the standard deduction ranged from $6,200 to $17,200. For single filers, it is $6,200, and for married people filing jointly, it is $12,400. Those over 65 and those who are blind are eligible for a higher standard deduction. Each year, the standard deduction amounts are usually adjusted in response to any changes in the cost of living.

Itemized Deductions

itemized deductions
Personal expenditures that can be deducted from AGI when determining taxable income.

Itemized deductions allow taxpayers to reduce their AGI by the amount of their allowable personal expenditures. The Internal Revenue Code defines the types of nonbusiness items that can be deducted from AGI. Here are some of the more common ones:

- Medical and dental expenses (*in excess* of 10 percent of AGI for those under the age of 65)
- State, local, and foreign income and property taxes; state and local personal property taxes
- Residential mortgage interest and investment interest (limited)
- Charitable contributions (limited to 50 percent, 30 percent, or 20 percent of AGI depending on certain factors)
- Casualty and theft losses (in excess of 10 percent of AGI; reduced by $100 per loss)
- Job, investment, and other expenses (in excess of 2 percent of AGI)
- Moving expenses (some restrictions; also reimbursed expenses are deductible for those who don't itemize)

Read the instructions accompanying the tax forms for detailed descriptions of allowable deductions in each category and of qualifying factors such as distance from previous residence.

Choosing the Better Option

Your decision to take the standard deduction or itemize deductions may change from year to year, or even in the same year. Taxpayers who find they've chosen the wrong option and paid too much may recalculate their tax using the other method and claim a refund for the difference. For example, suppose that you computed and paid your taxes, which amounted to $2,450, using the standard deduction. A few months later you find that had you itemized your deductions, your taxes would have been only $1,950. Using the appropriate forms, you can file an *amended return (Form 1040X)* showing a $500 refund ($2,450 − $1,950). To avoid having to file an amended return because you used the wrong deduction technique, estimate your deductions using both the standard and itemized deduction amounts and then choose the one that results in lower taxes. Most taxpayers use the standard deduction, but homeowners who pay home mortgage interest and property taxes generally itemize because those expenses alone typically exceed the allowable standard deduction.

3-2d Exemptions

exemptions
Deductions from AGI based on the number of persons supported by the taxpayer's income.

There's one more calculation for determining your taxable income. Deductions from AGI based on the number of persons supported by the taxpayer's income are called **exemptions**. A taxpayer can claim an exemption for himself or herself, his or her spouse, and any *dependents*. A dependent must be either a qualified child or a qualified relative. A major requirement for a qualified child is the age test—the child must less than 18 or, if a full-time student, 24. A major requirement for a qualified relative is the gross income test—gross income must be less than the amount of the exemption, which was $3,950 in 2014. All dependents must have a social security number, which can be a problem in the year of adoption for parents of adopted children.

MONKEY BUSINESS IMAGES/SHUTTERSTOCK.COM

So a college student, for example, could be 20 years old and still be claimed as an exemption by her parents, so long as all other dependency requirements are met. In 2014, each exemption claimed was worth $3,950. The personal exemption amount is tied to the cost of living and changes annually based on the prevailing rate of inflation.

A personal exemption can be claimed only once. If a child is *eligible* to be claimed as an exemption by her parents, then she doesn't have the choice of using a personal exemption on her own tax return, regardless of whether the parents use her exemption.

In 2014, a family of four could take total exemptions of $15,800—that is, 4 × $3,950. Subtracting the amount claimed for itemized deductions (or the standard deduction) and exemptions from AGI results in the amount of *taxable income,* which is the basis on which taxes are calculated. A taxpayer who makes $50,000 a year may have only, say, $25,000 in taxable income after adjustments, deductions, and exemptions. It is the *lower,* taxable income figure that determines how much tax an individual must pay.

TEST YOURSELF

3-5   Define and differentiate between *gross income* and *AGI.* Name several types of tax-exempt income. What is *passive income?*

3-6   What is a *capital gain,* and how is it treated for tax purposes?

3-7   If you itemize your deductions, you may include certain expenses as part of your itemized deductions. Discuss five types of itemized deductions and the general rules that apply to them.

3-8   Dan Caldwell was married on January 15, 2014. His wife, Catherine, is a full-time student at the university and earns $625 a month working in the library. How many personal exemptions will Dan and Catherine be able to claim on their joint return? Would it make any difference if Catherine's parents paid for more than 50 percent of her support? Explain.

3-3 CALCULATING AND FILING YOUR TAXES

Now that we've reviewed the general principles of federal income taxes and the components of taxable income, we can direct our attention to calculating the amount of income tax due. To do this, we need to address several key aspects of measuring taxable income and taxes: (1) the tax rates applicable to various types of personal income, (2) tax credits, (3) the basic tax forms and schedules, and (4) the procedures for determining tax liability.

3-3a Tax Rates

As we saw earlier in this chapter, to find the amount of *taxable income,* we subtract itemized deductions (or the standard deduction for non-itemizers) *and* personal exemptions from AGI. *Both itemizers and non-itemizers* use this procedure, which is a key calculation in determining your tax liability. It is *reported taxable income* that determines the amount of income subject to federal income taxes. Once you know the amount of your taxable income, you can refer to *tax rate tables* to find the amount of taxes you owe. (When actually filing a tax return, taxpayers with taxable income of more than $100,000 must instead use the tax rate schedules.)

Tax rates vary not only with the amount of reported taxable income but also with filing status. Thus, different tax rate schedules apply to each filing category, as shown in Exhibit 3.3. The vast majority of taxpayers fall into the first three brackets and are subject to tax rates of either 10 percent, 15 percent, or 25 percent.

EXHIBIT 3.3   Sample Tax Rate Schedules

Tax rates levied on personal income vary with the amount of reported taxable income and the taxpayer's filing status.

2014
Tax Rate
Schedules

Schedule X—If your filing status is **Single**

If your taxable income is: Over—	But not over—	The tax is:	of the amount over—
$0	$9,075	- - - - - - 10%	$0
9,075	36,900	$907.50 + 15	9,075
36,900	89,350	5,081.25 + 25	36,900
89,350	186,350	18,193.75 + 28	89,350
186,350	405,100	45,353.75 + 33	186,350
405,100	406,750	117,541.25 + 35	405,100
406,750	- - - - - -	118,118.75 + 39.6	406,750

Schedule Y-1—If your filing status is **Married filing jointly** or **Qualifying widow(er)**

If your taxable income is: Over—	But not over—	The tax is:	of the amount over—
$0	$18,150	- - - - - - 10%	$0
18,150	73,800	$1,815.00 + 15	18,150
73,800	148,850	10,162.50 + 25	73,800
148,850	226,850	28,925.00 + 28	148,850
226,850	405,100	50,765.00 + 33	226,850
405,100	457,600	109,587.50 + 35	405,100
457,600	- - - - - -	127,962.50 + 39.6	457,600

Schedule Y-2—If your filing status is **Married filing separately**

If your taxable income is: Over—	But not over—	The tax is:	of the amount over—
$0	$9,075	- - - - - - 10%	$0
9,075	36,900	$907.50 + 15	9,075
36,900	74,425	5,081.25 + 25	36,900
74,425	113,425	14,462.50 + 28	74,425
113,425	202,550	25,382.50 + 33	113,425
202,550	228,800	54,793.75 + 35	202,550
228,800	- - - - - -	63,981.25 + 39.6	228,800

Schedule Z—If your filing status is **Head of household**

If your taxable income is: Over—	But not over—	The tax is:	of the amount over—
$0	$12,950	- - - - - - 10%	$0
12,950	49,400	$1,295.00 + 15	12,950
49,400	127,550	6,762.50 + 25	49,400
127,550	206,600	26,300.00 + 28	127,550
206,600	405,100	48,434.00 + 33	206,600
405,100	432,200	113,939.00 + 35	405,100
432,200	- - - - - -	123,424.00 + 39.6	432,200

Source: Internal Revenue Service.

To see how the tax rates in Exhibit 3.3 work, consider two single taxpayers: one has taxable income of $12,500; the other, $38,600. Here's how we would calculate their respective tax liabilities:

- For taxable income of $12,500: $907.50 + [($12,500−$9,075) × 0.15] = $907.50 + $513.75 = $1,421.25
- For taxable income of $38,600: $5,081.25 + [($38,600−$36,900) × 0.25] = $5,081.25 + $425.00 = $5,506.25

The income of $12,500 is partially taxed at the 10 percent rate and partially taxed at the 15 percent rate. The first $9,075 of the $38,600 is taxed at 10 percent, the next $27,825 at 15 percent, and the remaining $1,700 at 25 percent. Keep in mind that taxpayers use the same procedures at this point whether they itemize or not. To show how the amount of tax liability will vary with the level of taxable income, Exhibit 3.4 lists the taxes due on a range of taxable incomes, from $1,500 to $460,000, for individual and joint returns.

Returning to our example involving the taxpayer with an income of $38,600, we see that this individual had an average tax rate of 14.3 percent ($5,506.25/$38,600), which is considerably less than the stated tax rate of 25 percent. Actually, the 25 percent represents the taxpayer's *marginal tax rate*—the rate at which the next dollar

EXHIBIT 3.4 **Taxable Income and the Amount of Income Taxes Due (2014)**

Given the progressive tax structure used in this country, it follows that the larger your income, the more you can expect to pay in taxes.

	Taxes Due (Rounded)	
Taxable Income	Individual Returns	Joint Returns
$ 1,500	$ 150[a]	$ 150[a]
8,000	800[a]	800[a]
15,000	1,796[b]	1,500[a]
30,000	4,046[b]	3,592[b]
60,000	10,856[c]	8,902[b]
100,000	21,176[c]	16,712[c]
200,000	49,858[d]	43,247[d]
410,000	119,256[f]	111,302[f]
460,000	139,206[g]	128,913[f]

[a] Income is taxed at 10 percent.
[b] 15 percent tax rate now applies.
[c] 25 percent tax rate now applies.
[d] 28 percent tax rate now applies.
[e] 33 percent tax rate now applies.
[f] 35 percent tax rate now applies.
[g] 39.6 percent tax rate now applies.

Source: Internal Revenue Service.

of taxable income is taxed. Notice in our calculations that the marginal 25 percent tax rate applies only to that portion of the single person's income that exceeds $36,900, which is $1,700 in this example.

Some taxpayers are subject to the *alternative minimum tax (AMT)*, currently 26 percent of the first $182,500 and 28 percent of the excess. A taxpayer's tax liability is the higher of the AMT or the regular tax. The AMT is designed to ensure that high-income taxpayers with many deductions and tax shelter investments that provide attractive tax write-offs are paying their fair share of taxes. The AMT includes in alternative minimum taxable income certain types of deductions otherwise allowed, such as state and local income and property taxes, miscellaneous itemized deductions, unreimbursed medical expenses, and depreciation. Therefore, taxpayers with moderate levels of taxable income, including those living in states with high tax rates and self-employed persons with depreciation deductions, may be subject to the AMT calculation and additional tax.

3-3b Tax Credits

After determining amount of taxes some taxpayers are allowed to reduce their tax using tax credits, directly from their tax liability.

tax credits
Deductions from a taxpayer's tax liability that directly reduce his or her *taxes due* rather than *taxable income.*

A tax credit is much more valuable than a deduction or an exemption because it directly reduces, dollar for dollar, the amount of *taxes due,* whereas a deduction or an exemption merely reduces the amount of *taxable income.* In Exhibit 3.5, we see how this difference affects the tax liability of two single taxpayers with $34,000 of gross income and $6,000 of other deductions/exemptions (in the 15 percent tax bracket). One has $1,000 in deductions, and the other has a $1,000 tax credit. Look at what happens to the amount of taxes due. In effect, the tax credit in this example has reduced taxes (and therefore *increased* after-tax income) by $850.

EXHIBIT 3.5	How Deductions and Tax Credits Affect Taxes Due

As this example shows, a $1,000 tax credit reduces taxes due by far more than a $1,000 tax deduction.

Calculation	$1,000 Deduction	$1,000 Tax Credit
Gross income	$34,000	$34,000
Less: Other deductions/exemptions	6,000	6,000
Less: $1,000 deduction	1,000	—
Taxable income	$27,000	$28,000
Tax liability*	3,596	3,746
Less $1,000 tax credit	—	1,000
Taxes due	$ 3,596	$ 2,746

*Tax liability is figured as follows: the first $9,075 of taxable income is taxed at 10 percent, the balance at 15 percent.

An often-used tax credit is for *child and dependent care expenses*. This credit is based on the amount spent for dependent care while a taxpayer (and spouse, if married) works or goes to school. An *adoption tax credit* of up to $13,190 is available for the qualifying costs of adopting a child under age 18. Here are some other common tax credits:

- Credit for the elderly or the disabled
- Foreign tax credit
- Credit for prior year minimum tax
- Retirement savings credit
- Credit for qualified electric vehicle

To receive one of these credits, the taxpayer must file a return along with a separate schedule in support of the tax credit claimed.

3-3c Tax Forms and Schedules

The IRS requires taxpayers to file their returns using specified tax forms. As noted earlier, these forms and various instruction booklets on how to prepare them are available to taxpayers free of charge. Generally, all persons who filed tax returns in the previous year are automatically sent a booklet containing tax forms and instructions for preparing returns for the current year. Inside the booklet is a form that can be used to obtain additional tax forms for filing various tax-related returns and information. Tax forms and instructions can be downloaded from **http://www.irs.gov.**

Variations of Form 1040

All individuals use some variation of Form 1040 to file their tax returns. *Form 1040EZ* is a simple, one-page form. You qualify to use this form if you are single or married filing a joint return; under age 65 (both if filing jointly); not blind; do not claim any dependents; have taxable income of less than $100,000 from only wages, salaries, tips, or taxable scholarships or grants; have interest income of less than $1,500; and do not claim any adjustments to income, itemize deductions, or claim any tax credits. Worksheet 3.1 shows the Form 1040EZ filed in 2014 by Anna Bhatia, a full-time graduate student at State University. Keep in mind that the tax form only shows dollar amounts and not cents, which is permissible in filing the form with the IRS. Her sources of income include a $12,500 scholarship, of which $4,900 was used for room and board; $7,600 earned from part-time and summer jobs; and $50 interest earned on a savings account deposit. Because scholarships used for tuition and fees are not taxed, she should include as income only the portion used for room and board. She had a total of $475 withheld for federal income taxes during the year. Although Anna would also complete a Salaries & Wages Report form, it is omitted for simplicity because it only lists the $4,900 of her scholarship that went toward her room and board, her part-time income of $7,600, and the details of her withholdings.

To use *Form 1040A*, a two-page form, your income must be less than $100,000 and be derived only from specified sources. Using this form, you may deduct certain IRA contributions and claim certain tax credits, but you cannot itemize your deductions. If your income is over $100,000 or you itemize deductions, you must use the standard Form 1040 along with appropriate schedules.

The use of these schedules, which provide detailed guidelines for calculating certain entries on the first two pages of *Form 1040*, varies among taxpayers depending on the relevance of these entries to their situations. Pages 1 and 2 of Form 1040, which summarize all items of income and deductions detailed on the accompanying schedules, are used to determine and report the taxable income and associated tax liability.

Form 1040EZ is easy to use, and most of the instructions are printed on the form itself. Anna Bhatia qualifies to use it because she is single, under age 65, not blind, and meets its income and deduction restrictions.

Department of the Treasury—Internal Revenue Service

Form 1040EZ

Income Tax Return for Single and Joint Filers With No Dependents (99)

2014

OMB No. 1545-0074

Your first name and initial	Last name	Your social security number
Anna	Bhatia	1 2 3 45 6 7 8 9

If a joint return, spouse's first name and initial	Last name	Spouse's social security number

Home address (number and street). If you have a P.O. box, see instructions.
1000 State University Drive   Apt. no.

▲ Make sure the SSN(s) above are correct.

City, town or post office, state, and ZIP code. If you have a foreign address, also complete spaces below (see instructions).
Anytown, Anystate 10001

Presidential Election Campaign
Check here if you, or your spouse if filing jointly, want $3 to go to this fund. Checking a box below will not change your tax or refund. ☑ You ☐ Spouse

Foreign country name	Foreign province/state/county	Foreign postal code

Income

Attach Form(s) W-2 here.

Enclose, but do not attach, any payment.

1	Wages, salaries, and tips. This should be shown in box 1 of your Form(s) W-2. Attach your Form(s) W-2.	**1**	12,500
2	Taxable interest. If the total is over $1,500, you cannot use Form 1040EZ.	**2**	50
3	Unemployment compensation and Alaska Permanent Fund dividends (see instructions).	**3**	
4	Add lines 1, 2, and 3. This is your **adjusted gross income.**	**4**	12,550
5	If someone can claim you (or your spouse if a joint return) as a dependent, check the applicable box(es) below and enter the amount from the worksheet on back. ☐ You ☐ Spouse If no one can claim you (or your spouse if a joint return), enter $10,150 if **single;** $20,300 if **married filing jointly.** See back for explanation.	**5**	10,150
6	Subtract line 5 from line 4. If line 5 is larger than line 4, enter -0-. This is your **taxable income.** ▶	**6**	2,400

Payments, Credits, and Tax

7	Federal income tax withheld from Form(s) W-2 and 1099.	**7**	495
8a	**Earned income credit (EIC)** (see instructions)	**8a**	
b	Nontaxable combat pay election. 8b		
9	Add lines 7 and 8a. These are your **total payments and credits.** ▶	**9**	495
10	**Tax.** Use the amount on **line 6 above** to find your tax in the tax table in the instructions. Then, enter the tax from the table on this line.	**10**	241
11	Health care: individual responsibility (see instructions) Full-year coverage ☑	**11**	
12	Add lines 10 and 11. This is your **total tax.**	**12**	254

Refund

Have it directly deposited! See instructions and fill in 13b, 13c, and 13d, or Form 8888.

13a	If line 9 is larger than line 12, subtract line 12 from line 9. This is your **refund.** If Form 8888 is attached, check here ▶ ☐	**13a**	254
▶ b	Routing number ▶ c Type: ☐ Checking ☐ Savings		
▶ d	Account number		

Amount You Owe

14	If line 12 is larger than line 9, subtract line 9 from line 12. This is the **amount you owe.** For details on how to pay, see instructions. ▶	**14**	

Third Party Designee

Do you want to allow another person to discuss this return with the IRS (see instructions)? ☐ **Yes.** Complete below.   ☐ **No**

Designee's name ▶	Phone no. ▶	Personal identification number (PIN) ▶

Sign Here

Joint return? See instructions.

Keep a copy for your records.

Under penalties of perjury, I declare that I have examined this return and, to the best of my knowledge and belief, it is true, correct, and accurately lists all amounts and sources of income I received during the tax year. Declaration of preparer (other than the taxpayer) is based on all information of which the preparer has any knowledge.

Your signature	Date	Your occupation	Daytime phone number
Anna Bhatia	4/14/15	Student	(555) 555-1212
Spouse's signature. If a joint return, **both** must sign.	Date	Spouse's occupation	If the IRS sent you an Identity Protection PIN, enter it here (see inst.)

Paid Preparer Use Only

Print/Type preparer's name	Preparer's signature	Date	Check ☐ if self-employed	PTIN
Firm's name ▶			Firm's EIN ▶	
Firm's address ▶			Phone no.	

For Disclosure, Privacy Act, and Paperwork Reduction Act Notice, see instructions.   Cat. No. 11329W   FORM **1040EZ** (2014)

(Continued)

FINANCIAL PLANNING TIPS

Best Ways to Spend Your Tax Refund

While it may be tempting to celebrate your tax refund by just spending it all on stuff, consider how a refund could constructively enter into your overall financial plan.

- **Add to an emergency fund.** Who knows when an emergency will happen? Consider starting a new fund or adding to your present emergency fund.

- **Pay off some debt.** Using your refund to pay off some debt will save you interest charges. Start with any credit card debt because it carries the highest rates.

- **Add to your retirement savings.** Consider putting some of your refund into an IRA.

- **Invest in your career.** Your refund could help pay for going back to school or taking some courses that will upgrade your skills.

- **Get healthier.** You could use your refund to buy a gym membership or to pay for needed dental work, which is often not fully covered by health insurance.

- **Do house repairs.** Your refund could help pay for needed repairs or upgrades, such as painting or plumbing.

- **Improve your home's energy efficiency.** You could make your house more energy-efficient by putting in energy-efficient appliances, installing double-paned windows, or by replacing traditional light bulbs with light-emitting diodes (LEDs) or fluorescent bulbs.

- **Buy life insurance.** If you don't already own some life insurance, use your tax refund to protect your loved ones if you die prematurely. Term life insurance policies are usually the cheapest to buy.

- **Save for family vacations.** While they can be expensive, vacations can bring a family closer. Consider adding your refund to a vacation savings account.

- **Donate to charity.** Donating at least part of your refund to a charity will help others. And it's also tax-deductible!

Source: Adapted from Rose Kivi, "10 Tips on How to Spend Your Tax Refund Money," http://www.candofinance.com/taxes/how-to-spend-your-tax-refund-money/, accessed July 2015.

Despite detailed instructions that accompany the tax forms, taxpayers still make a lot of mistakes when filling them out. Common errors include missing information and arithmetic errors. So check and recheck your forms *before submitting them to the IRS*.

3-3d The 2014 Tax Return of Terry and Evelyn Becker

Let's now put all the pieces of the tax preparation puzzle together to see how Terry and Evelyn Becker calculate and file their income taxes. The Beckers own their own home and are both 35 years old. Married for 11 years, they have three children—Thomas (age 9), Richard (age 7), and Harriet (age 3). Terry is a manager for an insurance company headquartered in their hometown. Evelyn works part-time as a sales clerk in a retail store. During 2014, Terry's salary totaled $60,415, while Evelyn earned $9,750. Terry's employer withheld taxes of $6,260, and Evelyn's withheld $1,150. During the year, the Beckers earned $800 interest on their joint savings account and realized $1,250 in capital gains on the sale of securities that they had owned for 11 months. In addition, Terry kept the books for his brother's car dealership, from which he netted $5,800 during the year. Because no taxes were withheld from any of their outside income, during the year they made estimated tax payments totaling $1,000. The Beckers' records indicate that they had $14,713 of potential itemized deductions during the year. Finally, the Beckers plan to contribute $4,000 to Evelyn's traditional IRA account. Beginning next year, the Beckers plan to switch Terry's account to a Roth IRA (see Chapter 14 for more information about that topic).

Finding the Beckers' Tax Liability: Form 1040

Looking at the Beckers' 2014 tax return (Worksheet 3.2), we can get a feel for the basic calculations required in the preparation of a Form 1040. Although we don't include the supporting schedules here, we illustrate the basic calculations that they require. As in the above example, keep in mind that the tax form only shows dollar amounts and not cents, which is permissible in filing the form with the IRS. The Beckers have detailed records of their income and expenses, which they use not only for tax purposes, but as important input to their budgeting process. Using this information, the Beckers intend to prepare their 2014 tax return so that their total tax liability is as low as possible. Like most married couples, the Beckers file a *joint return*.

Gross Income The Beckers' gross income in 2014 amounted to $78,015—the amount shown as "total income" on line 22 of their tax return. They have both active income and portfolio income, as follows:

Active Income	
Terry's earnings	$60,415
Evelyn's earnings	9,750
Terry's business income (Net)	5,800
Total active income	$75,965

Portfolio Income	
Interest from savings account	$ 800
Capital gains realized*	1,250
Total portfolio income	$ 2,050
Total income ($75,965 + $2,050)	$78,015

* Because this gain was realized on stock held for less than 12 months, the full amount is taxable as ordinary income.

They have no investment expenses to offset their portfolio income, so they'll be liable for taxes on the full amount of portfolio income. Although they have interest income, the Beckers don't have to file Schedule B (for interest and dividend income) with the Form 1040, because the interest is less than $1,500 and they earned no dividends. (If they receive dividends on stock in the future, they will have to complete a Qualified Dividends and Capital Gains Tax Worksheet, provided in the Form 1040 instruction booklet. Qualified dividends are taxed at the lower capital gains rates.) In addition, Terry will have to file Schedule C, detailing the income earned and expenses incurred in his bookkeeping business, and Schedule D to report capital gains income.

Adjustments to Gross Income The Beckers have only two adjustments to income: Evelyn's IRA contribution and 50 percent of the self-employment tax on Terry's net business income. Since Evelyn isn't covered by a retirement plan and since Terry's and her combined modified AGI is below $181,000, they can deduct her entire $4,000 contribution (the maximum contribution to an IRA is $5,500 or, depending on age, $6,500 in 2014) to an IRA account even though Terry is already covered by a company-sponsored retirement program (see Chapter 14). Terry's self-employment tax will be 15.3 percent of 0.9235 of his $5,800 net business income, and he will be able to deduct one-half that amount—$409.76 [(0.153 × 0.9235 × $5,800) ÷ 2], which is rounded to $410 on line 27. As noted in working through the prior tax return example for an individual, keep in mind that the tax form in Worksheet 3.2 only shows dollar amounts and not cents, which is permissible in filing the form with the IRS.

Because they itemize deductions, the Beckers use standard Form 1040 to file their tax return. When filed with the IRS, their return will include not only Form 1040, but also other schedules and forms detailing many of their expenses and deductions.

Form **1040**	Department of the Treasury—Internal Revenue Service (99) **U.S. Individual Income Tax Return** 20**14**	OMB No. 1545-0074	IRS Use Only—Do not write or staple in this space.

For the year Jan. 1–Dec. 31, 2014, or other tax year beginning _____ , 2014, ending _____ , 20____   See separate instructions.

Your first name and initial	Last name	Your social security number
Terry S.	Becker	123 45 6789

If a joint return, spouse's first name and initial	Last name	Spouse's social security number
Evelyn M.	Becker	987 65 4321

Home address (number and street). If you have a P.O. box, see instructions.   Apt. no.
1234 Success Circle

▲ Make sure the SSN(s) above and on line 6c are correct.

City, town or post office, state, and ZIP code. If you have a foreign address, also complete spaces below (see instructions).
Anytown, Anystate 10001

Presidential Election Campaign
Check here if you, or your spouse if filing jointly, want $3 to go to this fund. Checking a box below will not change your tax or refund.   ☑ You ☐ Spouse

Foreign country name	Foreign province/state/county	Foreign postal code

Filing Status

Check only one box.

1 ☐ Single
2 ☑ Married filing jointly (even if only one had income)
3 ☐ Married filing separately. Enter spouse's SSN above and full name here. ▶
4 ☐ Head of household (with qualifying person). (See instructions.) If the qualifying person is a child but not your dependent, enter this child's name here. ▶
5 ☐ Qualifying widow(er) with dependent child

Exemptions

6a ☑ **Yourself.** If someone can claim you as a dependent, **do not** check box 6a . . . . . }
b ☑ **Spouse** . . . . }

Boxes checked on 6a and 6b   **2**

c **Dependents:**

(1) First name Last name	(2) Dependent's social security number	(3) Dependent's relationship to you	(4) ✓ if child under age 17 qualifying for child tax credit (see instructions)
Thomas C. Becker	065 01 2347	Son	☑
Richard E. Becker	012 34 5678	Son	☑
Harriet G. Becker	034 65 1234	Daughter	☑
			☐

If more than four dependents, see instructions and check here ▶ ☐

No. of children on 6c who:
• lived with you   **3**
• did not live with you due to divorce or separation (see instructions)
Dependents on 6c not entered above

Add numbers on lines above ▶   **5**

d Total number of exemptions claimed . . . .

Income

Attach Form(s) W-2 here. Also attach Forms W-2G and 1099-R if tax was withheld.

If you did not get a W-2, see instructions.

7	Wages, salaries, tips, etc. Attach Form(s) W-2	7	70,165 00
8a	**Taxable** interest. Attach Schedule B if required	8a	800 00
b	**Tax-exempt** interest. **Do not** include on line 8a . . . 8b		
9a	Ordinary dividends. Attach Schedule B if required	9a	
b	Qualified dividends 9b		
10	Taxable refunds, credits, or offsets of state and local income taxes	10	
11	Alimony received	11	
12	Business income or (loss). Attach Schedule C or C-EZ	12	5,800 00
13	Capital gain or (loss). Attach Schedule D if required. If not required, check here ▶ ☐	13	1,250 00
14	Other gains or (losses). Attach Form 4797	14	
15a	IRA distributions . 15a _____ b Taxable amount . . .	15b	
16a	Pensions and annuities 16a _____ b Taxable amount . . .	16b	
17	Rental real estate, royalties, partnerships, S corporations, trusts, etc. Attach Schedule E	17	
18	Farm income or (loss). Attach Schedule F	18	
19	Unemployment compensation	19	
20a	Social security benefits 20a _____ b Taxable amount . . .	20b	
21	Other income. List type and amount _____	21	
22	Combine the amounts in the far right column for lines 7 through 21. This is your **total income** ▶	22	78,015 00

Adjusted Gross Income

23	Educator expenses 23		
24	Certain business expenses of reservists, performing artists, and fee-basis government officials. Attach Form 2106 or 2106-EZ 24		
25	Health savings account deduction. Attach Form 8889 . 25		
26	Moving expenses. Attach Form 3903 26		
27	Deductible part of self-employment tax. Attach Schedule SE . 27 410 00		
28	Self-employed SEP, SIMPLE, and qualified plans . . 28		
29	Self-employed health insurance deduction . . . 29		
30	Penalty on early withdrawal of savings 30		
31a	Alimony paid b Recipient's SSN ▶ _____ 31a		
32	IRA deduction 32 4,000 00		
33	Student loan interest deduction 33		
34	Tuition and fees. Attach Form 8917 34		
35	Domestic production activities deduction. Attach Form 8903 35		
36	Add lines 23 through 35	36	4,410 00
37	Subtract line 36 from line 22. This is your **adjusted gross income** . . . . ▶	37	73,605 00

For Disclosure, Privacy Act, and Paperwork Reduction Act Notice, see separate instructions.   Cat. No. 11320B   Form **1040** (2014)

Tax and Credits	38	Amount from line 37 (adjusted gross income)	38	73,605	00
	39a	Check if: ☐ **You** were born before January 2, 1950, ☐ Blind. ☐ **Spouse** was born before January 2, 1950, ☐ Blind. } Total boxes checked ▶ 39a			
	b	If your spouse itemizes on a separate return or you were a dual-status alien, check here▶ 39b☐			
Standard Deduction for— • People who check any box on line 39a or 39b **or** who can be claimed as a dependent, see instructions. • All others: Single or Married filing separately, $6,200 Married filing jointly or Qualifying widow(er), $12,400 Head of household, $9,100	40	**Itemized deductions** (from Schedule A) **or** your **standard deduction** (see left margin) . .	40	12,978	00
	41	Subtract line 40 from line 38	41	60,627	00
	42	**Exemptions.** If line 38 is $152,525 or less, multiply $3,950 by the number on line 6d. Otherwise, see instructions	42	19,750	00
	43	**Taxable income.** Subtract line 42 from line 41. If line 42 is more than line 41, enter -0- . .	43	40,877	00
	44	**Tax** (see instructions). Check if any from: **a** ☐ Form(s) 8814 **b** ☐ Form 4972 **c** ☐ _____	44	5,224	00
	45	**Alternative minimum tax** (see instructions). Attach Form 6251	45		
	46	Excess advance premium tax credit repayment. Attach Form 8962 . .	46		
	47	Add lines 44, 45, and 46 . . . . ▶	47	5,224	00
	48	Foreign tax credit. Attach Form 1116 if required . . .	48		
	49	Credit for child and dependent care expenses. Attach Form 2441	49		
	50	Education credits from Form 8863, line 19 . .	50		
	51	Retirement savings contributions credit. Attach Form 8880	51		
	52	Child tax credit. Attach Schedule 8812, if required . . .	52	3,000	
	53	Residential energy credits. Attach Form 5695 . . .	53		
	54	Other credits from Form: **a** ☐ 3800 **b** ☐ 8801 **c** ☐	54		
	55	Add lines 48 through 54. These are your **total credits**	55	3,000	00
	56	Subtract line 55 from line 47. If line 55 is more than line 47, enter -0- . . . . . ▶	56	2,224	00
Other Taxes	57	Self-employment tax. Attach Schedule SE	57	819	00
	58	Unreported social security and Medicare tax from Form: **a** ☐ 4137 **b** ☐ 8919 . .	58		
	59	Additional tax on IRAs, other qualified retirement plans, etc. Attach Form 5329 if required . .	59		
	60a	Household employment taxes from Schedule H	60a		
	b	First-time homebuyer credit repayment. Attach Form 5405 if required . .	60b		
	61	Health care: individual responsibility (see instructions) Full-year coverage ☑	61		
	62	Taxes from: **a** ☐ Form 8959 **b** ☐ Form 8960 **c** ☐ Instructions; enter code(s) ___	62		
	63	Add lines 56 through 62. This is your **total tax** . . . . . . ▶	63	3,043	00
Payments If you have a qualifying child, attach Schedule EIC.	64	Federal income tax withheld from Forms W-2 and 1099 . .	64 7,410	00	
	65	2014 estimated tax payments and amount applied from 2013 return	65 1,000	00	
	66a	**Earned income credit (EIC)**	66a		
	b	Nontaxable combat pay election 66b			
	67	Additional child tax credit. Attach Schedule 8812	67		
	68	American opportunity credit from Form 8863, line 8 . . .	68		
	69	Net premium tax credit. Attach Form 8962	69		
	70	Amount paid with request for extension to file	70		
	71	Excess social security and tier 1 RRTA tax withheld . . .	71		
	72	Credit for federal tax on fuels. Attach Form 4136 . . .	72		
	73	Credits from Form: **a** ☐ 2439 **b** ☐ Reserved **c** ☐ Reserved **d** ☐	73		
	74	Add lines 64, 65, 66a, and 67 through 73. These are your **total payments** . . . . ▶	74	8,410	00
Refund Direct deposit? See instructions.	75	If line 74 is more than line 63, subtract line 63 from line 74. This is the amount you **overpaid**	75	5,367	00
	76a	Amount of line 75 you want **refunded to you.** If Form 8888 is attached, check here . . ▶ ☐	76a	5,367	00
	b	Routing number ||||||||| ▶ **c** Type: ☐ Checking ☐ Savings			
	d	Account number ||||||||||||||||			
	77	Amount of line 75 you want **applied to your 2015 estimated tax** ▶ 77			
Amount You Owe	78	**Amount you owe.** Subtract line 74 from line 63. For details on how to pay, see instructions ▶	78		
	79	Estimated tax penalty (see instructions) 79			

Third Party Designee

Do you want to allow another person to discuss this return with the IRS (see instructions)? ☐ **Yes.** Complete below.   ☐ **No**

Designee's name ▶	Phone no. ▶	Personal identification number (PIN) ▶

Sign Here

Joint return? See instructions. Keep a copy for your records.

Under penalties of perjury, I declare that I have examined this return and accompanying schedules and statements, and to the best of my knowledge and belief, they are true, correct, and complete. Declaration of preparer (other than taxpayer) is based on all information of which preparer has any knowledge.

Your signature	Date	Your occupation	Daytime phone number
Terry S. Becker	4/10/15	Manager	(555) 555-1234
Spouse's signature. If a joint return, **both** must sign.	Date	Spouse's occupation	If the IRS sent you an Identity Protection PIN, enter it here (see inst.)
Evelyn M. Becker	4/10/15	Sales Clerk	

Paid Preparer Use Only

Print/Type preparer's name	Preparer's signature	Date	Check ☐ if self-employed	PTIN
Firm's name ▶			Firm's EIN ▶	
Firm's address ▶			Phone no.	

www.irs.gov/form1040   Form **1040** (2014)

Source : Internal Revenue Service.

Adjusted Gross Income (AGI) After deducting the $410 self-employment tax and Evelyn's $4,000 IRA contribution from their gross income, the Beckers are left with an AGI of $73,605, as reported on line 37.

Itemized Deductions or Standard Deduction? The Beckers are filing a joint return, and neither is over age 65 or blind; so according to the box on page 2 of Form 1040, they are entitled to a standard deduction of $12,400. However, they want to evaluate their itemized deductions before deciding which type of deduction to take—obviously they'll take the higher deduction because it will result in the lowest amount of taxable income and keep their tax liability to a minimum. Their preliminary paperwork resulted in the following deductions:

Medical and dental expenses	$ 1,223
State income and property taxes paid	2,560
Mortgage interest	8,893
Charitable contributions	475
Job and other expenses	2,522
Total	$15,673

The taxes, mortgage interest, and charitable contributions are deductible in full; so at the minimum, the Beckers will have itemized deductions amounting to $11,928 ($2,560 + $8,893 + $475). However, to be deductible, the medical and dental expenses and job and other expenses must exceed stipulated minimum levels of AGI—only that portion exceeding the specified minimum levels of AGI can be included as part of their itemized deductions. For medical and dental expenses, the minimum is 10 percent of AGI, and for job and other expenses, it is 2 percent of AGI. Because 10 percent of the Beckers' AGI is about $7,360 (0.10 × $73,605), they fall short of the minimum and cannot deduct any medical and dental expenses. In contrast, because 2 percent of the Beckers' AGI is about $1,472 (0.02 × $73,605), they can deduct any job and other expenses exceeding that amount, or $2,522 − $1,472 = $1,050. Adding that amount to their other allowable deductions ($11,928) results in total itemized deductions of $12,978. This amount exceeds the standard deduction of $12,400, so the Beckers should strongly consider itemizing their deductions. They would enter the details of these deductions on Schedule A and attach it to their Form 1040. (The total amount of the Beckers' itemized deductions is listed on line 40 of Form 1040.)

The Beckers are entitled to claim two exemptions for themselves and another three for their three dependent children, for a total of five (see line 6d). Because each exemption is worth $3,950, they receive a total personal exemption of $19,750 (5 × $3,950), which is the amount listed on line 42 of their Form 1040.

The Beckers' Taxable Income and Tax Liability Taxable income is found by subtracting itemized deductions and personal exemptions from AGI. In the Beckers' case, taxable income (rounded) amounts to $73,605 − $12,978 − $19,750 = $40,877, as shown on line 43. Given this information, the Beckers can now refer to the tax rate schedule (like the one in Exhibit 3.3) to find their appropriate tax rate and, ultimately, the amount of taxes they'll have to pay. (Because the Beckers' taxable income is less than $100,000, they could use the *tax tables* [not shown in this chapter] to find their tax. For clarity and convenience, we use the schedules here.) As we can see, Beckers' $40,877 in taxable income places them in the 15 percent marginal tax bracket. Using the schedule in Exhibit 3.3, they calculate their tax as follows: $1,815 + [0.15 × ($40,877− $18,150] = $5,224. They enter this amount on line 44.

The Beckers also qualify for the child tax credit: $1,000 for each child under age 17. They enter $3,000 on lines 52 and 55 and subtract that amount from the tax on line 47, entering $2,224 on line 56. In addition, the Beckers owe self-employment

(Social Security) tax on Terry's $5,800 net business income. This will increase their tax liability by $819 (0.153 × .9235 × $5,800) and would be reported on Schedule SE and entered on line 57 of Form 1040. (Recall that the Beckers deducted 50 percent of this amount, or $410, on line 27 as an adjustment to income.) The Beckers enter their total tax liability on line 63: $3,043 ($2,224 + 819).

Do They Get a Tax Refund? Because the total amount of taxes withheld of $7,410 ($6,260 from Terry's salary and $1,150 from Evelyn's wages) shown on line 64 plus estimated tax payments of $1,000 shown on line 65 total $8,410, as shown on line 74, the Beckers total tax payments exceed their tax liability. As a result, they are entitled to a refund of $ 5,367: the $8,410 withholding less their $3,043 tax liability. (Over 75 percent of all taxpayers receive refunds each year.) Instead of paying the IRS, they'll be getting money back. (Generally, it takes 1 to 2 months after a tax return has been filed to receive a refund check or electronic deposit. If filed electronically, it usually takes about three weeks to get a refund.)

All the Beckers have to do now is sign and date their completed Form 1040 and send it, along with any supporting forms and schedules, to the nearest IRS Center that serves their state on or before April 15, 2015.

One reason for the Beckers' large refund was the child tax credit. With such a sizable refund, the Beckers may want to stop making estimated tax payments because their combined withholding more than covers the amount of taxes they owe. Another option is to change their withholding to reduce the amount withheld.

Note that if total tax payments had been less than the Beckers' tax liability, they would have owed the IRS money—the amount owed is found by subtracting total tax payments made from the tax liability. If they owed money, they would include a check in the amount due with Form 1040 when filing their tax return.

TEST YOURSELF

3-9 Define and differentiate between the *average tax rate* and the *marginal tax rate*. How does a *tax credit* differ from an *itemized deduction*?

3-10 Explain how the following are used in filing a tax return: (a) Form 1040, (b) various schedules that accompany Form 1040, and (c) tax rate schedules.

3-4 OTHER FILING CONSIDERATIONS

LG4, LG5

Preparing and filing your tax returns involves more than merely filling out and filing a form on or before April 15th (the traditional date for filing taxes, although as the example in this chapter shows, that date sometimes changes, for various reasons). Other considerations include the need to pay estimated taxes, file for extensions, or amend the return; the possibility of a tax audit; and whether to use a tax preparation service or computer software to assist you in preparing your return.

3-4a Estimates, Extensions, and Amendments

Like Terry Becker, who provided accounting services to his brother's business, you may have income that's not subject to withholding. You may need to file a declaration of estimated taxes with your return and to pay quarterly taxes. Or perhaps you are unable to meet the normal filing deadline or need to correct a previously filed return. Let's look at the procedures for handling these situations.

Estimated Taxes

estimated taxes
Tax payments required on income not subject to withholding that are paid in four installments.

Because federal withholding taxes are regularly taken only from employment income, such as that paid in the form of wages or salaries, the IRS requires certain people to pay estimated taxes on income earned from other sources. This requirement allows the pay-as-you-go principle to be applied not only to employment income subject to withholding, but also to other sources of income. Four payments of estimated taxes are most commonly required of investors, consultants, lawyers, business owners, and various other professionals who are likely to receive income in a form that is not subject to withholding. Generally, if all your income is subject to withholding, you probably do not need to make estimated tax payments.

The declaration of estimated taxes (Form 1040-ES) is not filed with the tax return. Estimated taxes must be paid in four installments on April 15, June 15, and September 15 of the current year, and January 15 of the following year. Failure to estimate and pay these taxes in accordance with IRS guidelines can result in a penalty levied by the IRS.

April 15th: Filing Deadline

As we've seen from the Becker family example, at the end of each tax year, those taxpayers required to file a return must determine the amount of their *tax liability*—the amount of taxes they owe due to the past year's activities. The tax year corresponds to the calendar year and covers the period January 1 through December 31. Taxpayers may file their returns any time after the end of the tax year and *must* file no later than April 15th of the year immediately following the tax year (or by the first business day after that date if it falls on a weekend or federal holiday). If you have a computer, an Internet connection, and tax preparation software, you can probably use the IRS's *e-file* and *e-pay* to file your return and pay your taxes electronically either by using a credit card or by authorizing an electronic withdrawal from your checking or savings account. You can use an "Authorized *e-file* Provider," who may charge a fee to file for you, or do it yourself using commercial tax preparation software. (We'll discuss computer-based tax returns in greater detail later.)

Depending on whether the total of taxes withheld and any estimated tax payments is greater or less than the computed tax liability, the taxpayer either receives a refund or must pay additional taxes. Taxpayers can pay their taxes using a credit card; however, because the IRS cannot pay credit card companies an issuing fee, taxpayers must call a special provider and pay a service charge to arrange for the payment.

TOPSELLER/SHUTTERSTOCK.COM

> **EXAMPLE: Determining the Amount Owed or Refunded**
>
> Ashok had $2,000 withheld and paid estimated taxes of $1,200 during the year. After filling out the appropriate tax forms, he had a tax liability of only $2,800. Consequently, Ashok overpaid his taxes by $400 ($2,000 + $1,200 − $2,800) and will receive a $400 refund from the IRS. On the other hand, if Ashok's tax liability had been $4,000, then he would owe the IRS an additional $800 ($4,000 − $2,000 − $1,200).

Filing Extensions and Amended Returns

It's possible to receive an extension of time for filing your federal tax return. You can apply for an automatic six-month filing extension, which makes the due date October 15, simply by submitting Form 4868. In filing for an extension, however, the taxpayer must estimate the taxes due and remit that amount with the application. The extension does *not* give taxpayers more time to pay their taxes.

amended return
A tax return filed to adjust for information received after the filing date of the taxpayer's original return or to correct errors.

After filing a return, you may discover that you overlooked some income or a major deduction or made a mistake, so you paid too little or too much in taxes. You can easily correct this by filing an amended return (Form 1040X) showing the corrected amount of income or deductions and the amount of taxes you should have paid, along with the amount of any tax refund or additional taxes owed. You generally have three years from the date you file your original return or two years from the date you paid the taxes, whichever is later, to file an amended return. If you prepare and file your amended return properly and it reflects nothing out of the ordinary, it generally won't trigger an audit. By all means, don't "correct" an oversight in one year by "adjusting" the following year's tax return—the IRS frowns on that.

3-4b Audited Returns

tax audit
An examination by the IRS to validate the accuracy of a given tax return.

Because taxpayers themselves provide the key information and fill out the necessary tax forms, the IRS has no proof that taxes have been correctly calculated. In addition to returns that stand out in some way and warrant further investigation, the IRS also randomly selects some returns for a tax audit—an examination to validate the return's accuracy. Despite the traditionally scary aura that surrounds the audit concept, the outcome of an audit is not *always* additional tax owed to the IRS. In fact, about 5 percent of all audits result in a refund to the taxpayer, and in 15 percent of all audits, the IRS finds that returns are correctly prepared.

FINANCIAL PLANNING TIPS

Watch Out for Tax Audit Red Flags

While the IRS typically only audits about 1 percent of tax returns, there are some practices that significantly increase your chance of being audited. It's wise to be aware of the following possible triggers:

- **High income.** The more income you make, the more likely you are to experience an audit. For example, if you make more than $200,000, you chance is about 3 percent, and if you make $1 million or more, your chance rises to about 11 percent.

- **Unreported taxable income.** If your 1099s and W-2s add up to more than the income reported on your tax return, expect a bill from the IRS—and a possible audit.

- **Higher-than-average deductions.** If your deductions are large relative to your income, the IRS can flag your return for a potential audit. Make sure that you know the IRS regulations for deductions and donations and keep all supporting documents and receipts.

- **Home office deductions.** A home office is supposed to be used exclusively for business. The IRS

has found that this requirement is frequently not met, and the deduction is consequently denied. Thus, this is a red flag for an audit. If you take this deduction, be ready to prove it.

- **Business meals, travel, and entertainment.** IRS experience shows that the self-employed are responsible for most of the underreporting of income and overstating of deductions. Large deductions for meals, travel, and entertainment are an audit flag. Make sure to keep good records if you plan to take these kinds of deductions.

- **Business use of a vehicle.** Claiming 100 percent business use of a car is a red flag to the IRS because it's rare for an individual to really use a car exclusively for business. Make sure that you keep detailed mileage logs.

- **Unreported foreign bank account.** You are required to disclose offshore accounts. If the IRS finds an unreported account, it's an audit flag.

Source: Adapted from Joy Taylor, "IRS Audit Red Flags: The Dirty Dozen," http://www.kiplinger.com/article/taxes/T054-C000-S001-irs-audit-red-flags-the-dirty-dozen.html, accessed July 2015.

Typically, audits question (1) whether all income received has been properly reported and (2) if the deductions claimed are legitimate and the correct amount. The IRS can take as many as three years—and in some cases, six years—from the date of filing to audit your return, so you should retain records and receipts used in preparing returns for about seven years. Severe financial penalties, even prison sentences, can result from violating tax laws.

In summary, you should take advantage of all legitimate deductions to minimize your tax liability, but you must also be sure to properly report all items of income and expense as required by the Internal Revenue Code.

3-4c Tax Preparation Services: Getting Help on Your Returns

Many people prepare their own tax returns. These "do-it-yourselfers" typically have fairly simple returns that can be prepared without much difficulty. Of course, some taxpayers with quite complicated financial affairs may also invest their time in preparing their own returns. The IRS offers many informational publications to help you prepare your tax return. You can order them directly from the IRS by mail, from the IRS Web site (**http://www.irs.gov**), or by calling the IRS toll-free number (800-829-3676, or special local numbers in some areas). An excellent (and free) comprehensive tax preparation reference book is *Your Federal Income Tax*. Other publications cover special topics, such as the earned income credit, self-employment taxes, and business use of your home. Each form and schedule comes with detailed instructions to guide you, step-by-step, in completing the form accurately.

Help from the IRS

The IRS, in addition to issuing various publications for use in preparing tax returns, also provides direct assistance to taxpayers. The IRS will compute taxes for those whose taxable income is less than $100,000 and who do not itemize deductions. Persons who use this IRS service must fill in certain data, sign and date the return, and send it to the IRS on or before April 15 of the year immediately following the tax year. The IRS attempts to calculate taxes to result in the "smallest" tax bite. It then sends taxpayers a refund (if their withholding exceeds their tax liability) or a bill (if their tax liability is greater than the amount of withholding). People who either fail to qualify for or do not want to use this total tax preparation service can still obtain IRS assistance in preparing their returns from a toll-free service. Consult your telephone directory for the toll-free number of the IRS office closest to you.

Private Tax Preparers

More than half of all taxpayers believe that the complexity of the tax forms makes preparation too difficult and time-consuming. They prefer to use professional *tax preparation services* to improve accuracy and minimize their tax liability as much as possible. The fees charged by professional tax preparers can range from at least $100 for simple returns to $1,000 or more for complicated returns that include many itemized deductions, partnership income or losses, or self-employment income. You can select from the following types of tax preparation services.

- **National and local tax services:** These include national services such as H&R Block and independent local firms. These services are best for taxpayers with relatively common types of income and expenditures.
- **Certified public accountants (CPAs):** Tax professionals who prepare returns and can advise taxpayers on planning.
- **Enrolled agents (EAs):** Federally licensed individual tax practitioners who have passed a difficult, 2-day, IRS-administered exam. They are fully qualified to handle tax preparation at various levels of complexity.
- **Tax attorneys:** Lawyers who specialize in tax planning.

The services of CPAs, EAs, and tax attorneys can be expensive and are best suited to taxpayers with relatively complicated financial situations.

Always check your own completed tax returns carefully before signing them. Remember that *taxpayers themselves must accept primary responsibility for the accuracy of their returns*. The IRS requires professional tax preparers to sign each return as the preparer, enter their own Preparers Tax Identification Number (PTIN), firm's Employer Identification number (EIN), and give the taxpayer a copy of the return being filed. Tax preparers with the necessary hardware and software can electronically file their clients' tax returns so that eligible taxpayers can receive refunds more quickly.

There's no guarantee that your professional tax preparer will correctly determine your tax liability. To reduce the chance of error, you should become familiar with the basic tax principles and regulations, check all documents (such as *W-2s* and *1099s*) for accuracy, maintain good communication with your tax preparer, and request an explanation of any entries on your tax return that you don't understand.

3-4d Computer-Based Tax Returns

Many people use their computers to help with tax planning and preparing tax returns. Several good tax software packages will save hours when you're filling out the forms and schedules involved in filing tax returns. The programs often identify tax-saving opportunities you might otherwise miss. These computer programs aren't for everyone, however. Simple returns, like the *Form 1040EZ*, don't require them. And for complex returns, there's no substitute for the skill and expertise of a tax accountant or attorney. Tax preparation software will be most helpful for taxpayers who itemize deductions but don't need tax advice.

There are two general kinds of software: tax planning and tax preparation. Planning programs such as Quicken let you experiment with different strategies to see their effects on the amount of taxes you must pay. The other category of tax software focuses on helping you complete and file your tax return. These programs take much of the tedium out of tax preparation, reducing the time you spend from days to hours. If you file the *Form 1040* and some supporting forms, invest in the stock market, own real estate, or have foreign income or a home-based business, you'll probably benefit from using tax preparation programs.

The two major software players are Intuit's TurboTax and H&R Block's TaxCut, both available for either Windows or Macintosh. TurboTax also has a Web-based version that lets you work on your returns from any computer. Both major companies also offer an add-on program that accurately assigns fair market value to the household items most commonly donated to charity. Both programs feature a clean interface and guide you through the steps in preparing your return by asking you the questions that apply to your situation. In addition to the primary tax-form preparation section, they include extensive resources and links to additional Internet references, video clips to make tricky concepts easier to understand, tax planning questionnaires, deduction finders, and more. State tax return packages cost more. All major software providers have free online versions for preparing federal taxes for people who meet specific requirements, which vary by provider. See **http://apps.irs .gov/app/freeFile/jsp/index.jsp** for a listing of providers of free federal software with their individual restrictions.

The IRS has "fill-in forms," which allow you to enter information while the form is displayed on your computer by Adobe Acrobat Reader. After entering the requested information, you can print out the completed form. Fill-in forms give you a cleaner, crisper printout for your records and for filing with the IRS. Unlike tax preparation software, these fill-in forms have no computational capabilities, so you must do all your calculations before starting. These forms are labeled "Fill-in forms" at the IRS Internet site.

FINANCIAL PLANNING TIPS

Working with the Best Tax Preparer

As already stated, you are legally responsible for your tax returns, even if someone else prepared them. Thus, it's important to choose the right person or firm to prepare them for you. Keep in mind the following tips in making this major decision and working with your preparer:

- **Qualifications.** All paid tax return preparers are required to have a Preparer Tax Identification Number (PTIN). Make sure that a prospective preparer has a PTIN.

- **Preparer's history.** Check with the Better Business Bureau for the preparer's history of problems. Make sure that there have been no disciplinary actions, and check the status of any CPA's license through the state boards of accountancy. The same check should be made for state bar associations for attorneys and with the IRS Office of Enrollment for Enrolled Agents (EAs).

- **Understand the fees that the preparer will charge you.** Make sure that you understand and accept the fee for services rendered and compare

preparers' fees. It does not make sense to use preparers who ask for a percentage of your refund.

- **Electronic filing.** Be certain that the prospective preparer offers IRS e-file. You can opt to file a paper return instead, but it is typically easiest to file electronically—and if you're getting a refund, you'll get it faster that way.

- **Accessibility.** Make sure that you can get hold of the tax preparer easily in case you have questions *before* or *after* the return is filed.

- **Requests for records and receipts.** Good preparers will ask to see your records and receipts. They will also ask questions about your total income, tax-deductible expenses, and more. It's best to avoid preparers who are willing to file your return electronically without seeing your W-2 form and other records.

- **Return signature.** Never use a preparer who asks you to sign a blank tax form. Similarly, review the entire return, verify its accuracy, and make sure that preparer has supplied his or her PTIN before you sign it.

Source: Adapted from Internal Revenue Publication, "Tips for Choosing a Tax Return Preparer," http://www.irs.gov/newsroom/article/0,,id=251962,00.html, accessed July 2015.

TEST YOURSELF

3-11 Define *estimated taxes*, and explain under what conditions such tax payments are required.

3-12 What is the purpose of a *tax audit*? Describe some things you can do to be prepared if your return is audited.

3-13 What types of assistance and tax preparation services does the IRS provide?

3-14 What are the advantages of using tax preparation software?

3-5 EFFECTIVE TAX PLANNING

Tax planning is a key ingredient of your overall personal financial planning. The overriding objective of effective tax planning is to maximize total after-tax income by reducing, shifting, and deferring taxes to as low a level as legally possible.

Keep in mind that *avoiding taxes* is one thing, but *evading* them is another matter altogether. By all means, don't confuse tax avoidance with tax evasion, which includes such illegal activities as omitting income or overstating deductions. Tax evasion, in effect, involves a failure to accurately report income or deductions and, in extreme cases, a failure to pay taxes altogether. Persons found guilty of tax evasion are subject to severe financial penalties—and even prison terms. Tax avoidance, in contrast, focuses on reducing taxes in ways that are legal and compatible with the intent of Congress.

3-5a Fundamental Objectives of Tax Planning

Tax planning involves the use of various investment vehicles, retirement programs, and estate distribution procedures to (1) reduce, (2) shift, and (3) defer taxes. You can *reduce* taxes, for instance, by using techniques that create tax deductions or credits, or that receive preferential tax treatment—such as investments that produce depreciation (such as real estate) or that generate tax-free income (such as municipal bonds). You can *shift* taxes by using gifts or trusts to transfer some of your income to other family members who are in lower tax brackets and to whom you intend to provide some level of support anyway, such as a retired, elderly parent.

The idea behind *deferring* taxes is to reduce or eliminate your taxes today by postponing them to some time in the future, when you may be in a lower tax bracket. Perhaps more important, *deferring taxes gives you use of the money that would otherwise go to taxes*—thereby allowing you to invest it to make even more money. Deferring taxes is usually done through various types of retirement plans, such as IRAs, or by investing in certain types of annuities, variable life insurance policies, or even Series EE bonds (U.S. savings bonds).

The fundamentals of tax planning include making sure that you take all the deductions to which you're entitled and also take full advantage of the various tax provisions that will minimize your tax liability. Thus, comprehensive tax planning is an ongoing activity with both an immediate and a long-term perspective. *It plays a key role in personal financial planning.* In fact, a major component of a comprehensive personal financial plan is a summary of the potential tax impacts of various recommended financial strategies. Tax planning is closely interrelated with many financial planning activities, including investment, retirement, and estate planning.

3-5b Some Popular Tax Strategies

Many tax strategies are fairly straightforward and can be used by the average middle-income taxpayer. For example, the interest income on Series EE bonds is free from state income tax, and the holder can elect to delay payment of federal taxes until (1) the year the bonds are redeemed for cash or (2) the year in which they finally mature, whichever occurs first. This feature makes Series EE bonds an excellent vehicle for earning tax-deferred income.

There are other strategies that can cut your tax bill. Accelerating or bunching deductions into a single year may permit itemizing deductions. Shifting income from one year to another is one way to cut your tax liability. If you expect to be in the same or a higher-income tax bracket this year than you will be next year, defer income until next year and shift expenses to this year so you can accelerate your deductions and reduce taxes this year.

Maximizing Deductions

Review a comprehensive list of possible deductions for ideas, because even small deductions can add up to big tax savings. Accelerate or bunch deductions into one tax year if this allows you to itemize rather than take the standard deduction. For example, make your fourth-quarter estimated state tax payment before December 31 rather than on January 15 to deduct it in the current taxable year. Group miscellaneous expenses—and schedule unreimbursed elective medical procedures—to fall into one tax year so that they exceed the required "floor" for deductions (2 percent of AGI for miscellaneous expenses; 10 percent of AGI for medical expenses). Increase discretionary deductions such as charitable contributions.

Income Shifting

income shifting
A technique used to reduce taxes in which a taxpayer shifts a portion of income to relatives in lower tax brackets.

One way of reducing income taxes is to use a technique known as income shifting. Here, the taxpayer shifts a portion of his or her income, and thus taxes, to relatives in lower tax brackets. This can be done by creating trusts or custodial accounts or by making outright gifts of income-producing property to family members. For instance, parents with $125,000 of taxable income (28 percent marginal tax rate) and $18,000 in corporate bonds paying $2,000 in annual interest might give the bonds to their 15-year-old child—with the understanding that such income is to be used ultimately for the child's college education. The $2,000 would then belong to the child, who would probably be assumed to be able to pay $100 [0.10 × ($2,000 − $1,000 minimum standard deduction for a dependent)] in taxes on this income, and the parents' taxable income would be reduced by $2,000, thereby reducing their taxes by $560 (0.28 × $2,000).

Unfortunately, this strategy is not as simple as it might seem. A number of restrictions surround the strategy for children under 19, so it's possible to employ such techniques with older children (and with other older relatives, such as elderly parents). Parents need to be aware that shifting assets into a child's name to save taxes could affect the amount of college financial aid for which the child qualifies. Additional tax implications of gifts to dependents are discussed in Chapter 15.

YOU CAN DO IT NOW

Tax Planning

Consider whether you expect your tax rate to be lower, the same, or higher next year. Then do some simple but effective tax planning:

- If your tax rate is expected to be lower or the same next year, if you can, delay receiving income until next year so it will be taxed at the lower rate—or just later at the same rate.
- If your tax rate is expected to be higher next year, try to speed up the receipt of income so it will be taxed at the currently lower rate. And consider waiting to take some deductions until next year when the higher rate will shield you better from the higher rate.

Tax-Free and Tax-Deferred Income

tax deferred
Income that is not subject to taxes immediately but that will be subject to taxes later.

Some investments provide tax-free income; in most cases, however, the tax on the income is only deferred (or delayed) to a later day. Although there aren't many forms of tax-free investments left today, probably the best example would be the *interest* income earned on *municipal bonds*. Such income is free from federal income tax and possibly state income taxes. No matter how much municipal bond interest income you earn, you don't have to pay any federal taxes on it. (Tax-free municipal bonds are discussed in Chapter 12.) Income that is tax deferred, in contrast, only delays the payment of taxes to a future date. Until that time arrives, however, tax-deferred investment vehicles allow you to *accumulate tax-free earnings*. This results in much higher savings than would occur in a taxed account. A good example of tax-deferred income would be income earned in a *traditional IRA*. Chapter 14 provides a detailed discussion of this and other similar arrangements.

Most any wage earner can open an IRA and contribute up to $5,500 (or possibly $6,500, depending on age) each year to the account (in 2014). So why have an IRA? *Because all the income that you earn in your IRA accumulates tax free.*

This is a *tax-deferred* investment, so you'll eventually have to pay taxes on these earnings, but not until you start drawing down your account. *Roth IRAs* provide a way for people to contribute after-tax dollars. Not only do earnings grow tax free, but so do withdrawals if the account has been open for five or more years and the individual is over 59 ½. However, keep in mind that using after-tax dollars for a Roth IRA means that the contribution is not tax-deductible. In addition to IRAs, tax-deferred income can also be obtained from other types of pension and retirement plans and annuities. See Chapter 14 for more information on these financial products and strategies.

TEST YOURSELF

3-15 Differentiate between *tax evasion* and *tax avoidance*.

3-16 Explain each of the following strategies for reducing current taxes: (a) maximizing deductions, (b) income shifting, (c) tax-free income, and (d) tax-deferred income.

Planning Over a Lifetime: *Tax Preparation and Planning*

Here are some key considerations for life insurance use in each stage of the life cycle.

Pre-family Independence: 20s	Family Formation/ Career Development: 30–45	Pre-Retirement: 45–65	Retirement: 65 and Beyond
✓ Manage your withholding amount so that it is about equal to your tax bill. Avoid large amounts owed or refunded.	✓ When you marry and/or have family changes, revise your withholding amount accordingly.	✓ As your income grows, consider tax-exempt investments like municipal bonds.	✓ Estimate Social Security benefits and plan when you will start receiving payments.
✓ Maintain a careful record of income and tax-deductible expenses.	✓ Acquire tax shelters like a mortgage, which has tax-deductible interest expenses.	✓ Consider increasing your average contributions to tax-sheltered retirement plans.	✓ Plan orderly withdrawals from tax-sheltered retirement accounts and associated tax bill.
✓ Consider using tax preparation software.	✓ Make regular contributions to your employer's tax-sheltered retirement plan and consider IRAs.	✓ Consider "catch up" larger retirement plan contributions.	✓ Consider the use of life insurance to manage potential estate taxes. This is covered in more detail in Chapter 15.

WILLIAM HUBER/PHOTONICA/GETTY IMAGES

Financial Impact of Personal Choices
Angela and Tim's Tax Management Strategy

Angela and Tim are a married couple in their late 20s. Angela is an electrical engineer and Tim is a free-lance computer programmer. They recently saw a newscast about the budget deficit in the United States and believe it's likely tax rates will increase significantly by the time they retire. Tim expects to finish a large programming job toward the end of this year and is preparing to bill his client. The couple expects their marginal tax rate to increase from 15 percent to 25 percent next year. What tax management strategies should they pursue?

Angela and Tim decided that they should get more serious about retirement planning given the prospect of a larger tax bite next year and going forward. So they each invested $3,000 in an IRA this year and plan to invest the maximum next year. Angela invested in a traditional IRA that reduces their taxable income by $3,000 this year. Her plan to invest more next year will provide even more of a benefit given their higher expected tax rate. Tim invested in a Roth IRA, which provides no tax benefit this year but will shield the future value of the IRA from ever being taxed. This addresses their long-term concerns. Finally, Tim decided to bill his client immediately to speed the receipt of the consulting income to this year when their tax rate is expected to be lower than next year. Tim and Angela are well on their way to managing their taxes effectively.

Summary

LG1 Discuss the basic principles of income taxes and determine your filing status, p. 86

The dominant tax in our country today is the federal income tax, a levy that provides the government with most of the funds it needs to cover its operating costs. Federal income tax rates are progressive, so that your tax rate increases as your income rises. Other types of taxes include state and local income taxes, sales taxes, and property taxes. The administration and enforcement of federal tax laws is the responsibility of the IRS, a part of the U.S. Department of the Treasury. The amount of taxes that you owe depends on your filing status—single, married filing jointly, married filing separately, head of household, or qualifying widow(er) with dependent child—and the amount of taxable income that you report. Because the government collects taxes on a pay-as-you-go basis, employers are required to withhold taxes from their employees' paychecks.

LG2 Describe the sources of gross income and adjustments to income, differentiate between standard and itemized deductions and exemptions, and calculate taxable income, p. 90

Gross income includes active income (such as wages, bonuses, pensions, alimony), portfolio income (dividends, interest, and capital gains), and passive income (income derived from real estate, limited partnerships, and other tax shelters). You must decide whether to take the standard deduction or itemize your various deductions. Some allowable deductions for those who itemize include mortgage interest, medical expenses, and certain job-related expenses. To calculate taxable income, deduct allowable adjustments, such as IRA contributions and alimony paid, from gross income to get AGI; then subtract from AGI the amount of deductions and personal exemptions claimed.

LG3 Prepare a basic tax return using the appropriate tax forms and rate schedules, p. 96

After determining your taxable income, you can find the amount of taxes owed using either the tax rate tables or, if your taxable income is over $100,000, the tax rate schedules. Tax rates vary with the level of taxable income and filing status. Personal tax returns are filed using one of these forms: *1040EZ*, *1040A*, or *1040*. Certain taxpayers must include schedules with their *Form 1040*.

LG4 **Explain who needs to pay estimated taxes, when to file or amend your return, and how to handle an audit, p. 107**
Persons with income not subject to withholding may need to file a declaration of estimated taxes and make tax payments in four installments. Annual returns must usually be filed on or before April 15, unless the taxpayer requests an automatic 6-month filing extension. The IRS audits selected returns to confirm their validity by carefully examining the data reported in them.

LG5 **Know where to get help with your taxes and how software can make tax return preparation easier, p. 107**
Assistance in preparing returns is available from the IRS and private tax preparers such as national and local tax firms, certified public accountants, enrolled agents, and tax attorneys. Computer programs can help do-it-yourselfers with both tax planning and tax preparation.

LG6 **Implement an effective tax planning strategy, p, 112**
The objectives of tax planning are to reduce, shift, or defer taxes so that the taxpayer gets maximum use of and benefits from the money he or she earns. Some of the more popular tax strategies include maximizing deductions, shifting income to relatives in lower tax brackets, investing in tax-exempt municipal bonds, setting up IRAs, and using other types of pension and retirement plans and annuities to generate tax-deferred income.

Key Terms

adjusted gross income (AGI), 94

adjustments to (gross) income, 93

amended return, 109

average tax rate, 88

estimated taxes, 108

exemptions, 95

Federal Insurance Contributions Act (FICA, or social security), 89

federal withholding taxes, 90

gross income, 92

income shifting, 114

income taxes, 87

itemized deductions, 95

marginal tax rate, 88

progressive tax structure, 87

standard deduction, 94

taxable income, 90

taxes, 86

tax audit, 109

tax avoidance, 113

tax credits, 99

tax deferred, 114

tax evasion, 113

Answers to Test Yourself

You can find answers to these questions on this book's companion website. Look for it at *www.cengagebrain.com*. Search for this book by its title, and then add it to your dashboard.

LG2, 3,
p. 90, 96

1. ***Estimating taxable income, tax liability, and potential refund.*** Sophia Johnson is 24 years old and single, lives in an apartment, and has no dependents. Last year she earned $55,000 as a sales assistant for Office Furniture Rentals, $6,910 of her wages were withheld for federal income taxes. In addition, she had interest income of $142. She takes the standard deduction. Calculate her taxable income, tax liability, and tax refund or tax owed.

LG2, p. 90

2. ***Calculating gross income and tax exempt income.*** Emma Williams received the following items and amounts of income during 2014. Help her calculate (a) her gross income and (b) that portion (dollar amount) of her income that is tax exempt.

Salary	*$33,500*
Dividends	*800*
Gift from mother	*500*
Child support from ex-husband	*3,600*
Interest on savings account	*250*
Rent	*900*
Loan from bank	*2,000*
Interest on state government bonds	*300*

LG2, p. 90

3. ***Calculating taxes on security transactions.*** If Olivia Garcia is single and in the 28 percent tax bracket, calculate the tax associated with each of the following transactions. (Use the IRS regulations for capital gains in effect in 2014.)
   a. She sold stock for $1,200 that she purchased for $1,000 5 months earlier.
   b. She sold bonds for $4,000 that she purchased for $3,000 3 years earlier.
   c. She sold stock for $1,000 that she purchased for $1,500 15 months earlier.

LG2, p. 90

4. ***Effect of tax credit vs. tax exemption.*** Explain and calculate the differences resulting from a $2,000 tax credit versus a $2,000 tax deduction for a single taxpayer in the 25 percent tax bracket with $40,000 of pre-tax income.

LG3, p. 96

5. ***Choosing and preparing an individual's tax form. Use Worksheets 3.1 and 3.2.*** Henry Zhao graduated from college in 2014 and began work as a systems analyst in July 2014. He is preparing to file his income tax return for 2014, and has collected the following financial information for calendar year 2014:

Tuition, scholarships, and grants	*$ 5,750*
Scholarship, room, and board	*1,850*
Salary	*30,250*
Interest income	*185*
Deductible expenses, total	*3,000*
Income taxes withheld	*2,600*

   a. Prepare Henry's 2014 tax return, using a $6,200 standard deduction, a personal exemption of $3,950, and the tax rates given in Exhibit 3.3. Which tax form should Henry use, and why?
   b. Prepare Henry's 2014 tax return using the data in part a, along with the following information:

IRA contribution	*$5,000*
Cash dividends received	*150*

   Which tax form should he use in this case? Why?

6. **_Calculating taxable income for a married couple filing jointly._** Ethan and Zoe Wilson are married and have one child. Ethan is putting together some figures so that he can prepare the Wilson's joint 2014 tax return. He can claim three personal exemptions (including himself). So far, he's been able to determine the following with regard to income and possible deductions:

Total unreimbursed medical expenses incurred	$ 1,155
Gross wages and commissions earned	50,770
IRA contribution	5,000
Mortgage interest paid	5,200
Capital gains realized on assets held less than 12 months	1,450
Income from limited partnership	200
Job expenses and other allowable deductions	875
Interest paid on credit cards	380
Dividend and interest income earned	610
Sales taxes paid	2,470
Charitable contributions made	1,200
Capital losses realized	3,475
Interest paid on a car loan	570
Alimony paid by Ethan to his first wife	6,000
Social Security taxes paid	2,750
Property taxes paid	700
State income taxes paid	1,700

Given this information, how much taxable income will the Wilsons have in 2014? (_Note:_ Assume that Ethan is covered by a pension plan where he works, the standard deduction of $12,400 for married filing jointly applies, and each exemption claimed is worth $3,950.)

7. **_Preparing for a tax audit._** Jacob and Mia Davis have been notified that they are being audited. What should they do to prepare for the audit?

Applying Personal Finance

Tax Relief

Even though many were eliminated by the Tax Reform Act of 1986, tax shelters are still around. Beware, however, because some are legitimate, while others are not. American taxpayers have the right to lower their tax burdens, so long as they do it by legal means. This project will help you to learn about any tax shelters currently allowed by law.

Where can you go to find tax shelter opportunities? First, try the financial section of your newspaper. There may be advertisements or articles on tax shelters, such as tax-free bond funds. A bank is another source. Simply ask at the "new accounts" department for tax shelter information. Another major source of new tax shelters is the brokerage houses that sell stocks, bonds, and other securities to the investing public. If you have access to a brokerage house, ask them for tax shelter information. Also, you might want to search for "tax shelters" on the Internet.

List the tax shelters you've found. Do any apply to you now, or are there any that you'd like to use in the future? Finally, pull up the IRS Web site at **http://www.irs.gov** and search for "abusive tax shelters" to determine if the tax shelters you have found are allowed by current tax laws.

CRITICAL THINKING CASES

LG1, 2, 3,
p. 86, 90, 96

3.1 The Andersons Tackle Their Tax Return

Noah and Olivia Anderson are a married couple in their early 20s living in Dallas. Noah Anderson earned $73,000 in 2014 from his sales job. During the year, his employer withheld $9,172 for income tax purposes. In addition, the Andersons received interest of $350 on a joint savings account, $750 interest on tax-exempt municipal bonds, and dividends of $400 on common stocks. At the end of 2014, the Andersons sold two stocks, A and B. Stock A was sold for $700 and had been purchased four months earlier for $800. Stock B was sold for $1,500 and had been purchased three years earlier for $1,100. Their only child, Logan, age 2, received (as his sole source of income) dividends of $200 from Hershey stock.

Although Noah is covered by his company's pension plan, he plans to contribute $5,000 to a traditional deductible IRA for 2014. Here are the amounts of money paid out during the year by the Andersons:

Medical and dental expenses (unreimbursed)	$ 200
State and local property taxes	831
Interest paid on home mortgage	4,148
Charitable contributions	1,360
Total	$6,539

In addition, Noah incurred some unreimbursed travel costs for an out-of-town business trip:

Airline ticket	$250
Taxis	20
Lodging	60
Meals (as adjusted to 50 percent of cost)	36
Total	$366

Critical Thinking Questions

1. Using the Andersons' information, determine the total amount of their itemized deductions. Assume that they'll use the filing status of married filing jointly, the standard deduction for that status is $12,400, and each exemption claimed is worth $3,950. Should they itemize or take the standard deduction? Prepare a joint tax return for Noah and Olivia Anderson for the year ended December 31, 2014, that gives them the smallest tax liability. Use the appropriate tax rate schedule provided in Exhibit 3.3 to calculate their taxes owed.
2. How much have you saved the Andersons through your treatment of their deductions?
3. Discuss whether the Andersons need to file a tax return for their son.
4. Suggest some tax strategies that the Andersons might use to reduce their tax liability for next year.

3.2 Kendra Thayer: Waitress or Tax Expert?

Kendra Thayer, who is single, goes to graduate school part-time and works as a waitress at the Backwater Grill in New York. During the past year (2014), her gross income was $18,700 in wages and tips. She has decided to prepare her own tax return because she cannot afford the services of a tax expert. After preparing her return, she comes to you for advice. Here's a summary of the figures that she has prepared thus far:

Gross income:	
Wages	$10,500
Tips	+8,200
Adjusted gross income (AGI)	$18,700
Less: Itemized deductions	−2,300
	$16,400
Less: Standard deduction	−6,200
Taxable income	$10,600

Kendra believes that if an individual's income falls below $20,350, the federal government considers him or her "poor" and allows both itemized deductions and a standard deduction.

Critical Thinking Questions

1. Calculate Kendra Thayer's taxable income, being sure to consider her exemption. Assume that the standard deduction for a single taxpayer is $6,200, and that each exemption claimed is worth $3,950.
2. Discuss Kendra's errors in interpreting the tax laws, and explain the difference between itemized deductions and the standard deduction.
3. Kendra has been dating Joe Keating for nearly four years, and they are seriously thinking about getting married. Joe has income and itemized deductions that are identical to Kendra's. How much tax would they pay as a married couple (using the filing status of married filing jointly and a standard deduction of $12,400) versus the total amount the two would pay as single persons (each using the filing status of single)? Strictly from a tax perspective, does it make any difference whether Kendra and Joe stay single or get married? Explain.

Managing Basic Assets

CHAPTER 4

Managing Your Cash and Savings

LEARNING GOALS

LG1 Understand the role of cash management in the personal financial planning process.

LG2 Describe today's financial services marketplace, both depository and nondepository financial institutions.

LG3 Select the checking, savings, electronic banking, and other bank services that meet your needs.

LG4 Open and use a checking account.

LG5 Calculate the interest earned on your money using compound interest and future value techniques.

LG6 Develop a cash management strategy that incorporates a variety of savings plans.

How Will This Affect Me?

Finding the best mix of alternative cash management accounts and assets requires careful cost/benefit analysis based on your personal objectives and constraints.

This chapter presents a variety of different alternatives and focuses on key characteristics that include minimum balances, interest rate returns and costs, liquidity, and safety. Cash management alternatives examined include checking and savings accounts, money market deposit accounts, certificates of deposit (CDs), money market mutual funds, U.S. Treasury bills, U.S. Series EE bonds, and U.S. Series I bonds. After reading this chapter you should be able to design an effective cash management strategy, which is an integral part of your comprehensive financial plan.

4-1 THE ROLE OF CASH MANAGEMENT IN PERSONAL FINANCIAL PLANNING

cash management
The routine, day-to-day administration of cash and near-cash resources, also known as *liquid assets*, by an individual or family.

Establishing good financial habits involves managing cash as well as other areas of personal finance. In this chapter we focus on **cash management**—the routine, day-to-day administration of cash and near-cash resources, also known as *liquid assets*, by an individual or family. These assets are considered liquid because they're either held in cash or can be readily converted into cash with little or no loss in value.

In addition to cash, there are several other kinds of liquid assets, including checking accounts, savings accounts, money market deposit accounts, money market mutual funds, and other short-term investment vehicles. As a rule, near-term needs are met using cash on hand, and unplanned or future needs are met using some type of savings or short-term investment vehicle. Exhibit 4.1 briefly describes some popular types of liquid assets and the representative rates of return they earned in mid-2015. The rates reflect the Federal Reserve's (the Fed's) policy goal of keeping rates low to help stimulate the economy during the fragile period following the global financial crisis of 2008–2009. As detailed below, these low interest rates pose difficult problems for some consumers.

In personal financial planning, efficient cash management ensures adequate funds for both household use and an effective savings program. The success of your financial plans depends on your ability to develop and follow cash budgets like those discussed in Chapter 2.

You Can Do It Now

Shop for the Best Short-Term Interest Rates

Most of us get in the habit of choosing the most conveniently located bank, and its ATMs. But that doesn't mean you're getting the best-priced checking account and competitive short-term investment rates of return. It's easy to shop for the best online and local rates via your postal zip code using **www.bankrate.com**. In minutes you'll have a good sense of where you and your current bank stand—so you can do it now.

EXHIBIT 4.1   Where to Stash the Cash

The wide variety of liquid assets available meets just about any savings or short-term investment need. Rates vary considerably both by type of asset and point in time, so shop around for the best interest rate.

REPRESENTATIVE RATES OF RETURN

Type	Mid-2015	Description
Cash	0%	Pocket money; the coin and currency in one's possession.
Checking account	0%–0.37%	A substitute for cash. Offered by commercial banks and other financial institutions such as savings and loans and credit unions.
Savings account/ Money market deposit	0.05%–1.25%	Savings accounts are available at any time, but funds cannot be withdrawn by check. Money market deposit accounts (MMDAs) require a fairly large (typically $1,000 or more) minimum deposit, and offer check-writing privileges.
Certificate of deposit (CD)	0.33%–1.25% (1-year)	A savings instrument where funds are left on deposit for a stipulated period (1 week to 1 year or more); imposes a penalty for withdrawing funds early. Market yields vary by size and maturity; no check-writing privileges.
U.S. Treasury bill (T-bill)	0.06% (3-month)	Short-term, highly marketable security issued by the U.S. Treasury (originally issued with maturities of 13 and 26 weeks); smallest denomination is $100.
U.S. savings bond (EE)	0.30%	Issued at a discount from face value by the U.S. Treasury; rate of interest is tied to U.S. Treasury securities. Long a popular savings vehicle (widely used with payroll deduction plans). Matures to face value in approximately 5 years; sold in denominations of $25 and more.

A good way to keep your spending in line is to make all household transactions (even fun money or weekly cash allowances) using a tightly controlled *checking account*. Write checks only at certain times of the week or month and, just as important, avoid carrying your checkbook (or debit card) when you might be tempted to write checks (or make debits) for unplanned purchases. If you're going shopping, set a maximum spending limit beforehand—an amount consistent with your cash budget.

This system not only helps you avoid frivolous, impulsive expenditures but also documents how and where you spend your money. If your financial outcomes aren't consistent with your plans, you can better identify causes and take corrective actions.

Another aspect of cash management is establishing an ongoing savings program, which is an important part of personal financial planning. Savings are not only a cushion against financial emergencies but also a way to accumulate funds to meet future financial goals. You may want to put money aside so you can go back to school in a few years to earn a graduate degree, or buy a new home, or take a vacation. Savings will help you meet these specific financial objectives.

4-1a The Problem with Low Interest Rates

Just how low did interest rates fall in the wake of the financial crisis under the Fed's policies? Consider how some key interest rates in mid-2015 compare with their historical averages from 1980 to

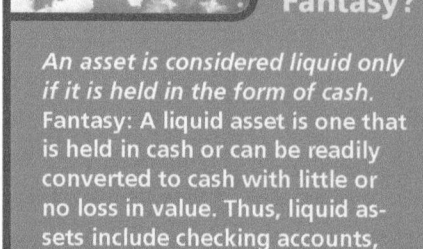

Financial Fact or Fantasy?

An asset is considered liquid only if it is held in the form of cash.

Fantasy: A liquid asset is one that is held in cash or can be readily converted to cash with little or no loss in value. Thus, liquid assets include checking accounts, savings accounts, money market accounts and funds, and other short-term investment vehicles.

mid-2015. The average interest rates on 5- and 10-year Treasury bonds over this time period were 6.03 percent and 6.50 percent, respectively. In mid-2015, these rates had fallen to only 1.68 percent and 2.36 percent! And a prudent saver looking for a short-term return on a 3-month negotiable CD could only get less than 1 percent in mid-2015!

These massive drops in interest rates have important implications for your personal finances. For a sense of the significance of the drop in interest rates, consider the effect of investing $25,000 for 5 years at the low rate of only 1.68 percent in mid-2015 vs. investing at the historical average rate of 6.03 percent. After 5 years, you would have earned about $33,503 at the average rate and only about $28,982 at the lower rate.

There are benefits and costs to the unprecedentedly low interest rates that have persisted for years after the financial crisis of 2008–2009. Whether they are a net benefit or a net cost depends on your perspective. While financial markets generally reacted positively to this low rate policy by pushing up asset prices, low interest rates also tend to signal sluggish economic growth and the risk of deflation. The benefits of lower interest rates include the reduced costs of financing the massive federal budget deficit, which is a significant savings given that interest on the federal debt was $430.8 billion in 2014. And lower rates have helped support the "too big to fail" banks. Indeed, the Fed's low interest rate policy has allowed banks to pay less than 1 percent interest on savings. But the costs are equally impressive. Low interest rates reduce income to retirees and to pension funds. Some retirees have had to dip into their principal, which could put more stress on welfare programs for the elderly and may prompt the government to increase its financial support of underfunded pension funds.

The recent extremely low interest rates favor borrowers and dampen the incentive to save. While keeping big banks afloat has advantages, many argue that low interest rates have helped protect banks from absorbing the consequences of their actions and redistribute wealth away from prudent savers. Indeed, the inflation-adjusted real interest rate has been negative, which means that savers are not keeping up with inflation and will either have to tap into their principal or cut their spending. This is bad for retirees and for the overall economy. People are also giving less to charity as they seek to cover income shortfalls resulting from lower interest rates. The percentage of savings out of income is decreasing. It has fallen from a high of 8.2 percent in 1985 to a low of only 1.5 percent in 2005 and settled around 4.9 percent in late 2014.

Low interest rates also create economic distortions, especially when real, inflation-adjusted interest rates are negative. Low rates discourage savings and discourage the reduction of overall debt levels in the economy. Low interest rates also encourage investors to search for investments that pay higher income, which increases the demand for stocks paying high dividends and for lower-grade, riskier bonds. Low interest rates imply low opportunity costs for holding assets that pay no income. Investors consequently hope for asset price increases, which push up demand for commodities like gold and alternative assets (such as art) and can encourage the mispricing of risk and thereby create asset bubbles. Unfortunately, low interest rates do not seem to increase the supply of credit. Being fearful of taking much risk during and after the financial crisis, banks have tended to invest more in government securities and less in risky loans.

So what's a prudent saver to do in a low-interest-rate environment? Unfortunately, the search for higher current returns has led many people to make higher risk investments. Some move into higher-quality corporate bonds. But when rates are so low, they are likely to go up. And bond prices fall when rates rise, which poses substantial risk to longer-term bonds. More moderate strategies involve buying stocks that pay higher dividends and buying preferred stocks, which will be discussed more in Chapter 12. But stocks are generally riskier than bonds, so the pursuit of higher returns in a low-interest-rate environment must be tempered by careful consideration of the suitability of the higher risk.

TEST YOURSELF

4-1   What is *cash management*, and what are its major functions?

4-2   Give at least two reasons for holding liquid assets. Identify and briefly describe the popular types of liquid assets.

4-3   Explain the effects that historically low interest rates have on borrowers, lenders, savers, and retirees.

4-2 TODAY'S FINANCIAL SERVICES MARKETPLACE

Emily Davis hasn't been inside her bank for years. Her company pays her salary into her checking account each month by direct deposit, and she regularly does all her banking from her home computer: with the click of a mouse, she can check her account balances, pay her bills, even search for the best rates on savings instruments. And by pushing a few buttons, she is able to withdraw money from her U.S. bank account using an automated teller machine (ATM) in Geneva!

Financial Fact or Fantasy?

Today's financial marketplace offers consumers a full range of financial products and services, many times all under one roof.
Fact: The financial marketplace offers financial products such as checking and savings accounts, credit cards, loans and mortgages, insurance, and mutual funds, and financial services concerned with financial planning, taxes, real estate, trusts, retirement, and estate planning. Such products and services are offered by banks and savings institutions, insurance companies, brokerage firms, mutual funds, and even nonfinancial companies like Kroger and General Motors.

The pace of change in the financial services industry is accelerating, thanks to advanced technology and less restrictive regulations. Consumers can now choose from many financial institutions competing for their business. No longer must you go to one place for your checking accounts, another for credit cards or loans, and yet another for stock brokerage services. Today, financial institutions are expanding services and are competitively pricing products by bundling different accounts. For example, if you have $25,000 in Bank of America/Merrill Lynch accounts, you're eligible for reduced or zero-cost commissions on stock trades, free checking, free bill-pay, a credit card, and free ATM debit card transactions. And online banking allows you to easily access all of these services. It's your choice: you can choose an institution like Bank of America that provides "one-stop shopping," or you can have accounts with a variety of financial service providers, depending on what's best for you.

The *financial services industry*, comprises all institutions that market various kinds of *financial products* (such as checking and savings accounts, credit cards, loans and mortgages, insurance, and mutual funds) and *financial services* (such as financial planning, securities brokerage, tax filing and planning, estate planning, real estate, trusts, and retirement). What 30 years ago were several distinct (though somewhat related) industries is now, in essence, one industry in which firms are differentiated more by organizational structure than by name or product offerings.

4-2a Types of Financial Institutions

Financial institutions can be classified into two broad groups—depository and nondepository—based on whether or not they accept deposits as traditional banks do.

Depository Financial Institutions

The vast majority of financial transactions take place at *depository financial institutions*—commercial banks (both brick-and-mortar and Internet), savings and loan associations

Behavior Matters

Why Can't I Seem to Save More— and What Can I Do about It?

There's a well-worn joke about meaning to read a book about procrastination ... but you just can't get around to it. Similarly, procrastination is a common behavioral bias that often keeps us from saving more because we just keep putting it off. People are most likely to procrastinate when they make decisions that are perceived as complex. For example, if you view the saving decision more broadly as a set of complex investment decisions, you're more likely to put off the decision to save more. So what's the best way to save more? Simplify the decision by adopting an easy plan, like saving 10 percent of your income by directing your bank to automatically transfer the money each month from your checking to savings account. Putting basic decisions like this on autopilot combats our natural tendency to procrastinate. That's a start that you can build on before approaching more complex investing decisions. But no savings means nothing to invest ... it's best to act now and not worry about specific savings decisions every month.

VLADGRIN/SHUTTERSTOCK.COM

(S&Ls), savings banks, and credit unions. Although they're regulated by different agencies, depository financial institutions are commonly referred to as "banks" because of their similar products and services. What sets these institutions apart from others is their ability to accept deposits; most people use them for checking and savings account needs. These depository financial institutions are briefly described in Exhibit 4.2.

EXHIBIT 4.2 | Depository Financial Institutions

Depository financial institutions differ from their nonbank counterparts, such as stock brokerages and mutual funds, in their ability to accept deposits. Most consumers use these institutions to meet their checking and savings account needs.

Institution	Description
Commercial bank	Offers checking and savings accounts and a full range of financial products and services; the only institution that can offer *non-interest-paying checking accounts (demand deposits)*. The most popular of the depository financial institutions. Most are traditional *brick-and-mortar banks*, but **Internet banks**—online commercial banks—are becoming more popular because of their convenience, lower service fees, and higher interest paid on account balances.
Savings and loan association (S&L)	Channels the savings of depositors primarily into mortgage loans for purchasing and improving homes. Also offers many of the same checking, saving, and lending products as commercial banks. Often pays slightly higher interest on savings than do commercial banks.
Savings bank	Similar to S&Ls, but located primarily in the New England states. Most are *mutual associations*—their depositors are their owners and thus receive a portion of the profits in the form of interest on their savings.
Credit union	A nonprofit, member-owned financial cooperative that provides a full range of financial products and services to its *members*, who must belong to a common occupation, religious or fraternal order, or residential area. Generally small institutions when compared with commercial banks and S&Ls. Offer interest-paying checking accounts—called **share draft accounts**—and a variety of saving and lending programs. Because they are run to benefit their members, they pay higher interest on savings and charge lower rates on loans than do other depository financial institutions.

Nondepository Financial Institutions

Other types of financial institutions that offer banking services, but don't accept deposits like traditional banks, are considered *nondepository institutions.* Today you can hold a credit card issued by a stock brokerage firm or have an account with a mutual fund that allows you to write a limited number of checks.

- *Stock brokerage firms* offer several cash management options, including money market mutual funds that invest in short-term securities and earn a higher rate of interest than bank accounts, special "wrap" accounts, and credit cards.
- *Mutual funds,* discussed in detail in Chapter 13, provide yet another alternative to bank savings accounts. Like stockbrokers, mutual fund companies offer money market mutual funds.

Other nondepository financial institutions include life insurance and finance companies.

4-2b How Safe Is Your Money?

Today, the main reason that a bank goes out of business is its purchase by another bank. Almost all commercial banks, S&Ls, savings banks, and credit unions are federally insured by U.S. government agencies. The few that are not federally insured usually obtain insurance through either a state-chartered or private insurance agency. Most experts believe that these privately insured institutions have less protection against loss than those that are federally insured. Exhibit 4.3 lists the insuring agencies and maximum insurance amounts provided under the various federal deposit insurance programs.

deposit insurance
A type of insurance that protects funds on deposit against failure of the institution; can be insured by the FDIC and the NCUA.

Deposit insurance protects the funds you have on deposit at banks and other depository institutions against institutional failure. In effect, the insuring agency stands behind the financial institution and guarantees the safety of your deposits up to a specified maximum amount. The ordinary amount covered per depositor by federal insurance was $100,000 prior to the financial crisis, and it was increased to $250,000 in 2009. Deposit insurance is provided to the *depositor* rather than a *deposit account.* Thus, the checking *and* savings accounts of each depositor are insured and, *as long as the maximum insurable amount is not exceeded,* the depositor can have any number of accounts and still be fully protected. This is an important feature to keep in mind because many people mistakenly believe that the maximum insurance applies to *each* of their accounts.

EXHIBIT 4.3	Federal Deposit Insurance Programs

If your checking and savings accounts are at a federally insured institution, you are covered up to $250,000.

Savings Institution	Insuring Agency	Insurance Amounts
Commercial bank	Federal Deposit Insurance Corporation (FDIC)	$250,000/depositor through the Bank Insurance Fund (BIF)
Savings and loan association	FDIC	$250,000/depositor through the Savings Association Insurance Fund (SAIF)
Savings bank	FDIC	$250,000/depositor through the BIF
Credit union	National Credit Union Administration (NCUA)	$250,000/depositor through the National Credit Union Share Insurance Fund (NCUSIF)

> **EXAMPLE: Determining the Extent of FDIC Insurance Protection**
>
> Beth has a $15,000 checking account balance at a branch office of First National Bank, an MMDA of $135,000 at First National Bank's main office, and a $50,000 CD issued by First National Bank. Does FDIC insurance protect Beth completely?
>
> Yes! Beth is entirely covered by the FDIC's deposit insurance amount of $250,000 per depositor. If the CD was for $150,000, however, then Beth's total would be $300,000 and thus not entirely covered under the plan. However, purchasing the CD from *another bank*, which also provides $250,000 of deposit insurance, would fully protect all of Beth's funds.

Now that banks are offering a greater variety of products, including mutual funds, it's important to remember that only deposit accounts, including CDs, are covered by deposit insurance. *Securities purchased through your bank are not protected by any form of deposit insurance.*

As a depositor, it's possible to increase your $250,000 of deposit insurance if necessary by opening accounts in different depositor names at the same institution. For example, a married couple can obtain $1,500,000 or more in coverage, apart from the coverage of CDs noted below, by setting up several accounts:

- One in the name of each spouse ($500,000 in coverage)
- A *joint* account in both names (good for $500,000, which is $250,000 per account owner)
- *Separate trust or self-directed retirement (IRA, Keogh, etc.) accounts* in the name of each spouse (good for an additional $250,000 per spouse)

In this case, each depositor name is treated as a separate legal entity, receiving full insurance coverage—the husband alone is considered one legal entity, the wife another, and the husband and wife as a couple a third. The trust and self-directed retirement accounts are also viewed as separate legal entities. The Certificate of Deposit Account Registry Service (CDARS) allows a bank to provide customers with full FDIC insurance on CDs up to $50 million. This is available to businesses, non-profit companies, public funds, and consumers.

TEST YOURSELF

4-4 Briefly describe the basic operations of—and the products and services offered by—each of the following financial institutions: (a) commercial bank, (b) savings and loan association, (c) savings bank, (d) credit union, (e) stock brokerage firm, and (f) mutual fund.

4-5 What role does the FDIC play in insuring financial institutions? What other federal insurance program exists? Explain.

4-6 Would it be possible for an *individual* to have, say, six or seven checking and savings accounts at the same bank and still be fully protected under federal deposit insurance? Explain. Describe how it would be possible for a *married couple* to obtain $1,500,000 in federal deposit insurance coverage at a single bank.

4-3 A FULL MENU OF CASH MANAGEMENT PRODUCTS

LG3 After meeting with an officer at his local bank, Raul Rodriguez was confused. As a student on a tight budget, working to pay his way through college, Raul knew how important it was to plan his saving and spending, and he wanted to make the right decisions about managing his financial resources. By using a checking account comparison chart, like to the one in Exhibit 4.4, Raul could compare information on daily balance requirements, service fees, interest rates, and the services his bank offers to college students and others. As Exhibit 4.4 demonstrates, banks offer a variety of convenient checking account services.

4-3a Checking and Savings Accounts

People hold cash and other forms of liquid assets, such as checking and savings accounts, for the convenience they offer in making purchase transactions, meeting normal living expenses, and providing a safety net, or cushion, to meet unexpected expenses or take advantage of unanticipated opportunities. Financial institutions compete to offer a wide array of products meeting every liquid-asset need.

The federal *Truth-in-Savings Act of 1993* helps consumers evaluate the terms and costs of banking products. Depository financial institutions must clearly disclose fees, interest rates, and terms—of both checking and savings accounts. The Act places strict controls on bank advertising and on what constitutes a "free" account. For example, banks cannot advertise free checking if there are minimum balance requirements or

EXHIBIT 4.4	Checking Accounts Comparison Chart

Most banks offer a variety of checking account options, typically differentiated by minimum balances, fees, and other services.

REPRESENTATIVE BANK USA

Features	College Checking	Custom Checking	Advantage Checking	Advantage Plus Checking
Minimum daily balance (to waive monthly service fee)	None	$750 in checking	$5,000 in checking	$7,500 combined balance
Monthly service fee	$5.95	$9 with direct deposit	$11 without direct deposit; no fee with Homeowner's Option	$12 ($2 discount with direct deposit)
Interest	No	No	Yes	Yes
Online statements	Free	Free	Free	Free
Check safekeeping	Free	Free	Free	Free
Monthly check return	$3.00	$3.00	$3.00	Free
ATM and check card	Free	Free	Free	Free
Bank by phone	Free automated calls	Free automated calls	Free automated calls	Free banker-assisted calls
Overdraft protection	Credit card	Credit card	Credit card, line of credit account, and select deposit accounts	Credit card, line of credit account, and select deposit accounts
Direct deposit advance service	Not available	Yes, with a direct deposit of $100 a month or more	Yes, with a direct deposit of $100 a month or more	Yes, with a direct deposit of $100 a month or more

per-check charges. Banks must use a standard *annual percentage yield (APY)* formula that considers compounding (discussed later) when stating the interest paid on accounts. This makes it easier for consumers to compare each bank's offerings. The law also requires banks to pay interest on a customer's full daily or monthly average deposit balance. Banks are prohibited from paying interest on only the lowest daily balance and from paying no interest if the account balance falls below the minimum balance for just 1 day. In addition, banks must notify customers 30 days in advance before lowering rates on deposit accounts or CDs.

Checking Accounts

demand deposit
An account held at a financial institution from which funds can be withdrawn on demand by the account holder; same as a *checking account*.

A checking account held at a financial institution is a demand deposit, meaning, that the bank must permit these funds to be withdrawn whenever the account holder demands. You put money into your checking account by *depositing* funds; you withdraw it by *writing a check, using a debit card,* or *making a cash withdrawal.* As long as you have sufficient funds in your account, the bank, when presented with a valid check or an electronic debit, must immediately pay the amount indicated by deducting it from your account. Money held in checking accounts is liquid, so you can easily use it to pay bills and make purchases.

Regular checking is the most common type of checking account. Traditionally, it pays no interest, and any service charges can be waived if you maintain a minimum balance (usually between $500 and $1,500). Many banks are moving away from such minimum balance requirements. Technically, only commercial banks can offer non-interest-paying regular checking accounts. Savings banks, S&Ls, and credit unions also offer checking accounts; but these accounts, which must pay interest, are called *negotiable order of withdrawal (NOW) accounts* or, in the case of credit unions, *share draft accounts.* Demand deposit balances are an important type of cash balance, and using checks to pay bills or electronic debits to make purchases gives you a convenient payment record.

Savings Accounts

time deposits
A savings deposit at a financial institution; remains on deposit for a longer time than a demand deposit.

A savings account is another type of liquid asset available at commercial banks, S&Ls, savings banks, credit unions, and other types of financial institutions. Savings deposits are referred to as time deposits because they are expected to remain on deposit for longer periods of time than demand deposits. Because savings deposits earn higher rates of interest, savings accounts are typically preferable to checking accounts when the depositor's goal is to accumulate money for a future expenditure or to maintain balances for meeting unexpected expenses. Most banks pay higher interest rates on larger savings account balances. For example, a bank might pay 0.5 percent on balances up to $2,500, 0.65 percent on balances between $2,500 and $10,000, and 0.75 percent on balances of more than $10,000. As noted above, current interest rates are extremely low by historical standards due to the Fed's post-crisis policy initiatives.

Although financial institutions generally have the right to require a savings account holder to wait a certain number of days before receiving payment of a withdrawal, most are willing to pay withdrawals immediately. In addition to withdrawal policies and deposit insurance, the stated interest rate and the method of calculating interest paid on savings accounts are important considerations when choosing the financial institution in which to place your savings.

Interest-Paying Checking Accounts

Depositors can choose from NOW accounts, money market deposit accounts, and money market mutual funds.

negotiable order of withdrawal (NOW) account
A checking account on which the financial institution pays interest; NOWs have no legal minimum balance.

Now Accounts Negotiable order of withdrawal (NOW) accounts are checking accounts on which the financial institution pays interest. There is no legal minimum balance for a NOW, but many institutions impose their own requirement, often between $500 and $1,000. Some pay interest on any balance in the account, but most institutions pay a higher rate of interest for balances above a specified amount.

money market deposit account (MMDA)
A federally insured savings account, offered by banks and other depository institutions that competes with money market mutual funds.

Money Market Deposit Accounts Money market deposit accounts (MMDAs) are a popular offering at banks and other financial institutions and compete for deposits with money market mutual funds. MMDAs are popular with savers and investors because of their convenience and safety, because deposits in MMDAs (unlike those in money funds) are *federally insured*. Most banks require a minimum MMDA balance of $1,000 or more.

Depositors can use check-writing privileges or ATMs to access MMDA accounts. They receive a limited number (usually six) of free monthly checks and transfers but pay a fee on additional transactions. Although this reduces the flexibility of these accounts, most depositors view MMDAs as savings rather than convenience accounts and do not consider these restrictions a serious obstacle. Moreover, MMDAs pay the highest interest rate of any bank account on which checks can be written.

A major problem with the growing popularity of interest-paying checking accounts has been a rise in monthly bank charges, which can easily amount to more than the interest earned on all but the highest account balances. So the higher rates of interest offered by MMDAs can be misleading.

money market mutual fund (MMMF)
A mutual fund that pools the funds of many small investors and purchases high-return, short-term marketable securities.

Money Market Mutual Funds Money market mutual funds have become the most successful type of mutual fund ever offered. A money market mutual fund (MMMF) pools the funds of many small investors to purchase high-return, short-term marketable securities offered by the U.S. Treasury, major corporations, large commercial banks, and various government organizations. (Mutual funds are discussed in greater detail in Chapter 13.)

MMMFs have historically paid interest at rates of 1 percent to 3 percent above those paid on regular savings accounts. Moreover, investors have instant access to their funds through check-writing privileges, although these must be written for a stipulated minimum amount (often $500). The checks look like, and are treated like, any other check drawn on a demand deposit account. As with all interest-bearing checking accounts, you continue to earn interest on your money while the checks make their way through the banking system.

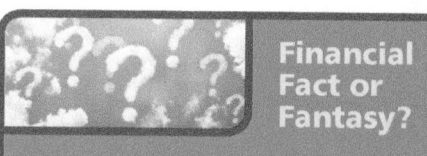

Financial Fact or Fantasy?

Unlike money market mutual funds, money market deposit accounts are federally insured. **Fact:** Money market deposit accounts are funds deposited in special, higher-paying savings accounts at banks, S&Ls, and other depository institutions and thus are covered by the same federal deposit insurance as any other checking or savings account. Money market mutual funds don't have this coverage.

Asset Management Accounts

Perhaps the best example of a banking service also offered by a nondepository financial institution is the asset management account (AMA), or *central asset account*. The AMA is a comprehensive deposit account that combines checking, investing, and borrowing activities and is offered primarily by brokerage houses and mutual funds. AMAs appeal to investors because they can consolidate most of their financial transactions at one institution and on one account statement.

asset management account (AMA)
A comprehensive deposit account, offered primarily by brokerage houses and mutual funds.

A typical AMA account includes an MMDA with unlimited free checking, a Visa or MasterCard debit card, use of ATMs, and brokerage and loan accounts. Annual fees and account charges, such as a per-transaction charge for ATM withdrawals, vary; so it pays to shop around. AMAs have increased in popularity as more institutions have lowered minimum balance requirements to $5,000, and they pay higher interest rates on checking account deposits than banks do. Their distinguishing feature is that they automatically "sweep" excess balances—for example, those more than $500—into a higher-return MMMF daily or weekly. When the account holder needs funds to purchase securities or cover checks written on the MMDA, the funds are transferred back to the MMDA. If the amount of securities purchased or checks presented for payment exceeds the account balance, the needed funds are supplied automatically through a loan.

Although AMAs are an attractive alternative to a traditional bank account, they have some drawbacks. Compared with banks, there are fewer "branch" locations. However, AMAs are typically affiliated with ATM networks, making it easy to withdraw funds. Yet ATM transactions are more costly; checks can take longer to clear; and some bank services, such as traveler's and certified checks, may not be offered. AMAs are not covered by deposit insurance, although these deposits are protected by the *Securities Investor Protection Corporation* (explained in Chapter 11) and the firm's private insurance.

4-3b Electronic Banking Services

The fastest-changing area in cash management today is electronic banking services. Whether you're using an ATM or checking your account balance online, electronic banking services make managing your money easier and more convenient. Electronic funds transfer systems allow you to conduct many types of banking business at any hour of the day or night.

Electronic Funds Transfer Systems

Electronic funds transfer systems (EFTSs) use the latest telecommunications and computer technology to electronically transfer funds into and out of your account. For example, your employer may use an EFTS to electronically transfer your pay from the firm's bank account directly into your personal bank account at the same or a different bank. This eliminates the employer's need to prepare and process checks and the employee's need to deposit them. Electronic transfer systems make possible such services as debit cards and ATMs, preauthorized deposits and payments, bank-by-phone accounts, and online banking.

Debit Cards and Automated Teller Machines This form of EFTS uses specially coded plastic cards, called **debit cards**, to transfer funds from the customer's bank account (a debit) to the recipient's account. A debit card may be used to make purchases at any place of business set up with the point-of-sale terminals required to accept debit card payments. The personal identification number (PIN) issued with your debit card verifies that you are authorized to access the account.

Visa and MasterCard issue debit cards linked to your checking account that give you even more flexibility. In addition to using the card to purchase goods and services, you can use it at ATMs, which have become a popular way to make banking transactions. **Automated teller machines (ATMs)** are remote computer terminals that customers of a bank or other depository institution can use to make deposits, withdrawals, and other transactions such as loan payments or transfers between accounts—24 hours a day, 7 days a week. Most banks have ATMs outside their offices, and some place freestanding ATMs in shopping malls, airports, and grocery stores; at colleges and universities; and in other high-traffic areas to enhance their competitive position. If your bank belongs to an EFTS network, such as Cirrus, Star, or Interlink, you can get cash from the ATM of any bank in the United States or overseas that is a member of that network. (In fact, the easiest way to get foreign currency when you travel overseas is through an ATM on your bank's network! It

electronic funds transfer systems (EFTSs)
Systems using the latest telecommunications and computer technology to electronically transfer funds into and out of customers' accounts.

debit cards
Specially coded plastic cards used to transfer funds from a customer's bank account to the recipient's account to pay for goods or services.

automated teller machines (ATM)
A remote computer terminal that customers of depository institutions can use to make basic transactions 24 hours a day, 7 days a week.

ALIKEYOU/SHUTTERSTOCK.COM

also gives you the best exchange rate for your dollar.) Banks charge an average per-transaction fee of $2.60 for using the ATM of another bank, and some also charge when you use your ATM card to pay certain merchants. However, to be more competitive some banks now reimburse the fees associated with using the ATMs of other banks.

The total dollar volume of purchases made using Visa's branded debit cards surpassed credit-card purchases for the first time late in 2008. This is likely related to more cautious use of credit cards during a recession. Yet the trend was becoming clear before this because combined credit- and debit-card purchases of retail goods and services exceeded purchases via checks in 2003. Thus, plastic is growing more popular among U.S. consumers in general, with debit cards starting to overtake credit cards.

Security concerns are increasing pressure for financial institutions to replace the common magnetic strip on credit cards with EMV chips, named for its developers—Europay, MasterCard, Visa. The cardholder information is entered on a chip embedded in the card in an encrypted form. Card issuers hope to require use of EMV cards by late 2015. However, many ATMs and merchants' credit card readers are not expected to be converted by that time. In the interim, cards with both a magnetic strip and the EMV chip are being offered by issuers.

Debit card use is increasing because these cards are convenient both for retailers, who don't have to worry about bounced checks, and for consumers, who don't have to write checks and can often get cash back when they make a purchase. ATM and other debit cards are accepted by supermarkets, gas stations, and convenience stores as well as many other retail and service outlets. The convenience of debit cards may, in fact, be their biggest drawback: it can be easy to overspend. To avoid problems, make sure to record all debit card purchases immediately in your checkbook ledger and deduct them from your checkbook balance. Also be aware that if there's a problem with a purchase, you can't stop payment—an action you could take if you had paid by check or credit card.

Preauthorized Deposits and Payments Two related EFTS services are *preauthorized deposits and payments*. They allow you to receive automatic deposits or make payments that occur regularly. For example, you can arrange to have your paycheck or monthly pension or Social Security benefits deposited directly into your account. Regular, fixed-amount payments, such as mortgage and consumer loan payments or monthly retirement fund contributions, can be preauthorized to be made automatically from your account. You can also preauthorize regular payments of varying amounts such as monthly utility bills. In this case, each month you would specify by phone the amount to be paid.

Charges for preauthorized payments vary from bank to bank. Typically, customers must maintain a specified minimum deposit balance and pay fees ranging from nothing to less than $1 per transaction. This system better allows the customer to earn interest on deposits used to pay bills, and it's a convenient payment method that eliminates postage costs.

Bank-by-Phone Accounts Bank customers can make various banking transactions by telephone, either by calling a customer service operator who handles the transaction or by using the keypad on a touch-tone telephone to instruct the bank's computer. After the customer provides a passcode to access the account, the system provides the appropriate prompts to perform various transactions, such as obtaining an account balance, finding out what checks have cleared, transferring funds to other accounts, and dispatching payments to participating merchants. To encourage banking by phone, many banks today charge no fee on basic account transactions or allow a limited number of free transactions per month. However, online banking options are replacing bank-by-phone accounts.

The Pew Internet & American Life Project found that over 61 percent of Internet users rely on some form of *online banking* services. The number has grown steadily as banks make online services easier to use and as people become more comfortable using the Internet for financial transactions. Many individuals just check their balances, but more than half use the Internet to transfer funds as well. Thanks to improved security procedures, most online bank services are delivered through the Internet, although some may use direct dial-up connections with the customer's bank. Today, most banks will compete for your online banking business because it's in their best financial interests to do so. A recent study showed that the cost of a full-service teller transaction is about $1, an ATM transaction is less than 30 cents, and an Internet transaction is less than 1 cent.

FINANCIAL PLANNING TIPS

Using a Debit Card Wisely

A debit card seems like a substitute for a credit card. But the way transactions are processed and the protections afforded the cardholder are significantly different. Remember that unlike a credit card, a debit card is a direct link to your bank account. You may want to use a credit card over a debit card in some situations, like the following:

• **Online and phone orders:** While your liability for fraudulent transactions is limited to $50 if you report it to your bank within two days and perhaps to zero under your bank's policies, you still face significant inconveniences. Getting money put back into your account is not easy, and your balance could drop and cause returned checks and extra fees.

• **Expensive items and delayed delivery:** While credit cards generally provide dispute rights if there is a problem with a purchase, debit cards do not generally do so. A credit card is safer to use for big purchases and items that will be delivered later. And you can sometimes get extended warranties and additional property insurance on car rentals with credit cards, which you can't for debit cards.

• **Required deposits:** Let's say that you are renting a power washer and a deposit is required. If you use a credit card to make the deposit, you retain access to the funds in your bank account and will hopefully never have to give up the money. You lose access to the money with a debit card.

• **Restaurants:** Many argue that you shouldn't let your debit card out of your sight, which always happens at a restaurant. And restaurants often authorize your card for more than the purchase amount because they expect you to add a tip. It may be for more than you actually pay, and you'll lose the use of that difference for a few days.

• **Recurring payments:** It's common to have problems stopping recurring payments like magazine subscriptions and fitness club memberships. Getting your money back is typically easier with credit cards than debit cards.

• **Future travel:** If you book airline and hotel reservations with a debit card, your money is paid out immediately. A credit card often will not be charged until close to the time you use the service (that is, when you arrive at the hotel or take the flight).

• **Hotels:** Upon check-in, some hotels place holds on your card to cover expenses for clients who may leave without settling the entire bill. This involves extra charges on a debit card that must be reversed. You probably won't even notice extra charges that will be voided on a credit card.

• **At ATMs:** Criminals are getting better at adding "skimmers" to ATMs, which read your debit card information. If you do decide to use your debit card at an ATM, make sure that the ATM looks like it's in good shape and that nothing unusual seems added.

Source: Adapted from Dana Dratch, "10 Places NOT to Use Your Debit Card," http://www.creditcards.com/credit-card-news/10-places-not-to-use-debit-card-1271.php, accessed July 2015.

Although computer-based bank-at-home systems and mobile banking don't replace the use of an ATM to obtain cash or deposit money, they can save both time and postage when you're paying bills. Other benefits include convenience and the potential to earn higher interest rates and pay lower fees. Customers like being able to check their account balances at any time of the day or night, not just when their printed statement comes once a month.

While some banks still charge for online bill payment services, they are now free at most banks. But online banking doesn't always live up to its promises. You can't make cash deposits, checks may get lost in the mail, and you don't know when the funds will reach your account. Most consumers prefer the security of a bank with a physical presence and a variety of other banking options such as branches, ATMs, and phone services. Your current "traditional" bank probably offers online and mobile banking services.

4-3c Regulation of EFTS Services

The federal *Electronic Fund Transfer Act of 1978* describes your rights and responsibilities as an EFTS user. Under this law, you cannot stop payment on a defective or questionable purchase, although individual banks and state laws have more lenient provisions. If there's an error, you must notify the bank within 60 days of its occurrence. The bank must investigate and tell you the results within 10 days. The bank can then take up to 45 more days to investigate the error but must return the disputed money to your account until the issue is resolved.

If you fail to notify the bank of the error within 60 days, the bank has no obligation under federal law to conduct an investigation or return your money. You must notify the bank immediately about the theft, loss, or unauthorized use of your EFTS card. Notification within 2 business days after you discover the card missing limits your loss to $50. After 2 business days, you may lose up to $500 (but never more than the amount that was withdrawn by the thief). If you don't report the loss within 60 days after your periodic statement was mailed, you can lose all the money in your account. When reporting errors or unauthorized transactions, it's best to notify your bank by telephone and follow up with a letter. Keep a copy of the letter in your file.

Many state regulations offer additional consumer protection regarding your use of EFTS. However, your best protection is to carefully guard the PIN used to access your accounts. Don't write the PIN on your EFTS card, and be sure to check your periodic statements regularly for possible errors or unauthorized transactions.

4-3d Other Bank Services

In addition to the services described earlier in this chapter, many banks offer other types of money management services, such as safe-deposit boxes and trust services.

- Safe-deposit boxes: A *safe-deposit* box is a rented drawer in a bank's vault. Boxes can be rented for an average of about $30 per year, depending on their size. When you rent a box, you receive one key to it, and the bank keeps another key. The box can be opened only when both keys are used. This arrangement protects items in the box from theft and serves as an excellent storage place for jewelry, contracts, stock certificates, titles, and other important documents. Keeping valuables in a safe-deposit box may also reduce your homeowner's insurance by eliminating the "riders" that are often needed to cover such items.

- Trust services: Bank trust departments provide investment and estate planning advice. They manage and administer the investments in a trust account or from an estate.

FINANCIAL PLANNING TIPS

Be Careful What You Store in a Safe-Deposit Box

- **What Should I Keep in a Safe-Deposit Box?**

Important papers include original deeds, titles, mortgages, contracts, and insurance policies. Family records, such as birth, marriage, and death certificates, can be time consuming to replace. Valuables that deserve space in a safe-deposit box include expensive jewels, medals, rare stamps, and other collectibles. It's important to keep videos or pictures of your home's contents to provide your insurance company in case of theft or damage to your house.

- **What Should I NOT Keep in a Safety Deposit Box?**

Don't keep anything in a safe-deposit box that you might need in an emergency when your bank is closed. Examples include the originals of a "power of attorney" (written authorization for another person to transact business on your behalf), passports (for an emergency trip), medical care directives if

you become ill and incapacitated, and funeral or burial instructions. It's also reasonable to give the originals of important documents to your attorney and keep copies in your safe-deposit box.

- **Protect Your Property**

If a safe-deposit box is apparently unused for a number of years, your state can view it as abandoned and its contents as unclaimed property. And the majority of states do not return unclaimed property to the rightful owners. So it's important to make documented contact with your bank at least once a year and to make sure that it has your current address. Insure valuables even though they are in your safe-deposit box. This will assure that your valuables are protected even if the bank or state mistakenly takes your property or if a fire or flood destroys the contents of your box.

Source: Adapted from "Helpful Guide to Bank Safe-Deposit Boxes—Use, Access, and Safety of Safe-Deposit Boxes in U.S. Banks," http://foreignborn.com/self-help/banking/10-sd_boxes.htm, accessed July 2015; Elisabeth Leamy, "Not-So-Safe-Deposit Boxes: States Seize Citizens' Property to Balance Their Budgets," http://abcnews.go.com/GMA/story?id=4832471, accessed July 2015.

TEST YOURSELF

4-7 Distinguish between a checking account and a savings account.

4-8 Define and discuss (a) demand deposits, (b) time deposits, (c) interest-paying checking accounts.

4-9 Briefly describe the key characteristics of each of the following forms of interest-paying checking accounts: (a) NOW account, (b) MMDA, and (c) MMMF.

4-10 Describe the features of an AMA, its advantages, and its disadvantages.

4-11 Briefly describe (a) debit cards, (b) banking at ATMs, (c) preauthorized deposits and payments, (d) bank-by-phone accounts, and (e) online banking and bill-paying services.

4-12 What are your legal rights and responsibilities when using EFTSs?

4-4 MAINTAINING A CHECKING ACCOUNT

By the time Alison Brown started college, she had a thriving car-detailing business that earned her several hundred dollars per week. Some customers paid her in advance, some paid after the fact, and some forgot (or otherwise neglected) to pay at all. But by depositing each check or cash payment into her checking account, Alison was able to keep track of her earnings without complicated bookkeeping. A checking account is one of the most useful cash management tools you can have. It's a safe and convenient way to hold money and streamline point-of-sale purchases, debt payments, and other basic transactions. You can have regular or interest-paying checking accounts at commercial banks, S&Ls, savings banks, credit unions, and even brokerage houses through asset management accounts. For convenience, we'll focus on commercial bank checking accounts, although our discussion also applies to checking accounts maintained at other types of financial institutions.

4-4a Opening and Using Your Checking Account

Factors that typically influence the choice of where to maintain a checking account are convenience, services, and cost. Many people choose a bank based solely on convenience factors: business hours, location, number of drive-thru windows, and number and location of branch offices and ATMs. Ease of access is obviously an important consideration because most people prefer to bank near home or work. Although services differ from bank to bank, today most banks offer several types of accounts: debit, ATM, credit cards, and loans. Many banks also offer online and telephone banking and bill-paying services, safe-deposit box rental, provision for direct deposits and withdrawals, and mutual-fund sales.

After determining the banking services you need, evaluate the offerings of conveniently located, federally insured financial institutions. In addition to convenience and safety, consider interest rates, types of accounts (including special accounts that combine such features as credit cards, free checks, and reduced fees), structure and level of fees and charges, and quality of customer service.

The Cost of a Checking Account

Bank service charges have increased sharply owing to deregulation and the growth of interest-paying checking accounts. Today few, if any, banks and other depository institutions allow unlimited free check-writing privileges. Most banks levy monthly and per-check fees when your checking account balance drops below a required minimum, and some may charge for checking no matter how large a balance you carry.

Some banks are moving away from minimum balance requirements, but a common requirement is to maintain a minimum balance of $500 to $1,000 (or even more) to avoid service charges. Although some banks use the *average monthly* balance in an account to determine whether to levy a service charge, most use the *daily* balance procedure. This means that if your account should happen to fall just $1 below the minimum balance *just once* during the month, you'll be hit with the full service charge—even if your average balance is three times the minimum requirement.

Service charges take two forms: (1) a base service charge of, say, $7.50 a month, and (2) additional charges of, say, 25 cents for each check you write and 10 cents for each ATM or bank-by-phone transaction. Using these fees as an illustration, assume you write 20 checks and make 7 ATM transactions in a given month. If your balance falls below the minimum, you'll have to pay a service charge of $7.50 + (20 × $0.25) + (7 × $0.10) = $13.20.

In addition to the service charges on checking accounts, banks have increased most other check-related charges and raised the minimum balances required for free checking and waivers of specified fees. The average charge on a returned check is between $25 and $30, and stop-payment orders typically cost $20 to $35. Some banks charge fees for ATM or bank-by-phone transactions that exceed a specified number. Most also charge for using the

Financial Fact or Fantasy?

At most banks and other depository institutions, you will be hit with a hefty service charge if your checking account balance falls even just $1 below the stipulated minimum amount for just one day out of the month. **Fact:** Many depository institutions use the *daily* balance in your account, rather than the *average* monthly balance, to determine whether you must pay a service charge. Thus, letting it fall below the minimum even once can have a significant cost.

Choosing a Bank

If you're looking for a bank, here are some important factors to consider.

- **Convenient location, online, and mobile services.** Find a bank that is conveniently located *and* has online services, because online service providing banks tend to pay more competitive savings rates.

- **Free checking and free money transfers.** "Free checking" usually means that you aren't required to keep a minimum balance in your account and can write as many checks a month as you like. Even if it isn't labeled as such, look for free checking. Also look for banks that let you transfer funds between different accounts for free.

- **Convenient ATMs.** The average fee for using the ATM of another bank is over $4. Although some banks are starting to refund such fees, by visiting only ATMs that belong to your bank, you can avoid all surcharges and the hassle of refunds. It is best to have an ATM close to your work and home.

- **Overdraft and FDIC protection.** Given that fees for bounced checks average about $35, it is important to know what the charges are and what kind of overdraft protection is offered. Also make sure that your deposits are insured by the FDIC.

- **Competitive interest income.** Find out if the bank pays interest on your balance. You can shop for the most competitive rates at **www.bankrate.com** and **www.bankingmyway.com.**

Source: Adapted from Farnoosh Torabi, "Back to Basics: Choosing a New Bank," http://www.mainstreet.com/article/back-to-basics-choosing-a-new-bank, accessed July 2015.

ATM of another bank that is not a member of the same network. It's not surprising that smart consumers use cost as the single most important variable when choosing where to set up a checking account.

Individual or Joint Account

Two people wishing to open a checking account may do so in one of three ways:

1. They can each open individual checking accounts (on which the other cannot write checks).
2. They can open a joint account that requires both signatures on all checks.
3. They can open a joint account that allows either one to write checks (the most common type of joint account).

One advantage of the joint account over two individual accounts is lower service charges. In addition, the account has rights of survivorship: for a married couple, this means that if one spouse dies, the surviving spouse, after fulfilling a specified legal requirement, can draw checks on the account. If account owners are treated as tenants in common rather than having rights of survivorship, then the survivor gets only his or her share of the account. Thus, when you're opening a joint account, be sure to specify the rights you prefer.

General Checking Account Procedures

After you select the bank that meets your needs and has the type of account you want, it's a simple matter to open the account. The application form asks for basic personal information such as name, date of birth, Social Security number, address, phone, and place of employment. You'll also have to provide identification, sign signature cards, and make an initial deposit. The bank will give you a supply of checks to use until your personalized checks arrive.

After opening a checking account, follow these basic procedures:

- Always write checks in ink.
- Include the name of the person being paid, the date, and the amount of the check—written in both numerals and words for accuracy.
- Sign the check the same way as on the signature card you filled out when opening the account.
- Note the check's purpose on the check—usually on the line provided in the lower left corner. This information is helpful for both budgeting and tax purposes.

Make sure to enter all checking account transactions—checks written, deposits, point-of-sale debit purchases, ATM transactions, and preauthorized automatic payments and deposits—in the **checkbook ledger** provided with your supply of checks. Then, subtract the amount of each check, debit card purchase, ATM cash withdrawal, or payment, and add the amount of each deposit to the previous balance to keep track of your current account balance. Good transaction records and an accurate balance prevent overdrawing the account.

With each deposit, write a deposit slip (generally included with your checks and also available at your bank) listing the currency, coins, and checks being deposited. List checks by the *transit ID number* printed on the check, usually at the top right. Also properly endorse all checks that you're depositing. Federal regulations require your endorsement to be made in black or blue ink, within 1½ inches of the check's trailing edge (left end of the check when viewed from the front) so as not to interfere with bank endorsements. If you don't comply, you'll still get your money but it may take longer.

To protect against possible loss of endorsed checks, it is common practice to use a special endorsement, such as "Pay to the order of XYZ Bank," or a restrictive endorsement, such as "For deposit only." If the way your name is written on the check differs from the way that you signed the signature card, you should sign your correct signature below your endorsement. To further ensure that the deposit is properly entered into your account, write your account number below your endorsement.

When depositing checks, you may encounter a delay in funds' availability that is due to the time required for them to clear. To avoid overdrawing your account, know your bank's "hold" policy on deposits, which are capped by federal maximum funds-availability delays. It generally takes between 1 and 5 business days for funds to become available. For example, on a check drawn on another local bank, funds must be made available no later than the second business day after deposit. An out-of-town check, however, may take up to 5 business days to clear. Longer holds—up to 9 business days—can be applied by banks under special circumstances, such as when large amounts (over $5,000) are deposited in a single day or when the depositor has repeatedly overdrawn his or her account during the immediately preceding 6 months.

Overdrafts

When a check is written for an amount greater than the current account balance, the result is an **overdraft**. If the overdraft is proven to be intentional, the bank can initiate legal proceedings against the account holder. The action taken by a bank on an overdraft depends on the strength of its relationship with the account holder and the amount involved. In many cases, the bank stamps the overdrawn check with the words "insufficient balance (or funds)" and returns it to the party to whom it was written. This is often called a "bounced check." The account holder is notified of this action, and the holder's bank deducts an average overdraft fee of $35 from his checking account. The depositor of a "bad check" may also be charged by her bank, which explains why merchants typically charge customers who give them bad checks $15 to $25 or more and often refuse to accept future checks from them.

When you have a good relationship with your bank or arrange **overdraft protection**, the bank will pay a check that overdraws the account. In cases where overdraft protection has not been prearranged but the bank pays the check, the account holder is

checkbook ledger
A booklet, provided with a supply of checks, used to maintain accurate records of all checking account transactions.

overdraft
The result of writing a check for an amount greater than the current account balance.

overdraft protection
An arrangement between the account holder and the depository institution wherein the institution automatically pays a check that overdraws the account.

usually notified by the bank and charged a penalty fee for the inconvenience. However, the check does not bounce, and the check writer's creditworthiness is not damaged.

There are several ways to arrange overdraft protection. Many banks offer an overdraft line of credit, which automatically extends a loan to cover the amount of an overdraft. In most cases, however, the loans are made only in specified increments, such as $50 or $100, and interest (or a fee) is levied against the loan amount, not the actual amount of the overdraft. This can be an expensive form of protection, particularly if you do not promptly repay such a loan.

For example, if you had a $110 overdraft and the bank made overdraft loans in $100 increments, it would automatically deposit $200 in your account. If the bank charged 12 percent annually (or 1 percent per month) and you repaid the loan within a month, you would incur total interest of $2 ([$200 × 12%]/12). But remember, you paid interest on $90 ($200 – $110) that you didn't need, and the annualized rate of interest on this overdraft loan is *21.8 percent* ([$2/$110] × 12)!

Another way to cover overdrafts is with an *automatic transfer program,* which automatically transfers funds from your savings account into your checking account in the event of an overdraft. Under this program, some banks charge both an annual fee and a fee on each transfer. Of course, the best form of overdraft protection is to use good cash management techniques and regularly balance your checking account.

Stopping Payment

stop payment
An order made by an account holder instructing the depository institution to refuse payment on an already issued check.

Occasionally it's necessary to **stop payment** on a check that has been issued because a good or service paid for by check is found to be faulty (though some states prohibit you from stopping payment on faulty goods or services) or on a check issued as part of a contract that is not carried out. If your checks or checkbook are lost or stolen, there's no need to stop payment on them because you have no personal liability. Stopping payment in this case only incurs expense; it doesn't change your personal liability.

To stop payment on a check, you must notify the bank and fill out a form indicating the check number and date, amount, and the name of the person to whom it was written. You can initiate stop-payment orders online or by phone. Once you place a stop-payment order, the bank refuses payment on the affected check, and the check will be rejected if another bank presents it in the check-clearing process. Banks typically charge a fee ranging from $20 to $35 to stop payment on a check.

4-4b Monthly Statements

Once a month, your bank provides a statement—an itemized listing of all transactions in your checking account (checks written, ATM transactions, debit purchases, automatic payments, and deposits made). Also included are bank service charges and interest earned (see Jackson Smith's May 2017 bank statement in Exhibit 4.5). Some banks include your original canceled checks with your bank statement, although most are abandoning this practice as we move closer to a "paperless society." Many banks now let you view canceled checks online, free of charge. It's important to review your monthly bank statement to verify the accuracy of your account records and to reconcile differences between the statement balance and the balance shown in your checkbook ledger. The monthly statement is also a valuable source of information for your tax records.

Account Reconciliation

account reconciliation
Verifying the accuracy of your checking account balance in relation to the bank's records as reflected in the bank statement, which is an itemized listing of all transactions in the checking account.

You should reconcile your bank account as soon as possible after receiving your monthly statement. The **account reconciliation** process, or *balancing the checkbook,* can uncover errors in recording checks or deposits, in addition or subtraction, and, occasionally, in the bank's processing of a check. It can also help you avoid overdrafts by forcing you to verify your account balance monthly. Assuming that neither you nor the bank has made any errors, discrepancies between your checkbook ledger account balance and your bank statement can be attributed to one of four factors:

EXHIBIT 4.5   A Bank Statement

Each month, you receive a statement from your bank or depository financial institution that summarizes the month's transactions and shows your latest account balance. This sample statement for Jackson Smith not only shows the checks that have been paid, but it also lists all ATM transactions, point-of-sale transactions using his ATM card (e.g., the Interlink payments at Lucky Stores), and direct payroll deposits.

```
        YOUR BANK                      #240
        P.O. BOX 516   ANY CITY, USA   90000-0000

        JACKSON G. SMITH
        1765 SHERIDAN DRIVE            N        CALL (800) 222-0000
        YOUR CITY, STATE 12091         21       24 HOURS/DAY, 7 DAYS/WEEK
                                                FOR ASSISTANCE WITH
                                                YOUR ACCOUNT.

PAGE 1 OF 1       THIS STATEMENT COVERS: 4/30/2017 THROUGH 5/29/2017

PREMIUM           SUMMARY
ACCOUNT
                  PREVIOUS BALANCE        473.68     MINIMUM BALANCE    21.78
0123-45678        DEPOSITS              1,302.83+
                  WITHDRAWALS           1,689.02-
                  SERVICE CHARGES           7.50-
                  DIRECT DEPOSIT DISCOUNT    1.00+
                  NEW BALANCE              80.99

CHECKS AND        CHECK   DATE PAID   AMOUNT    CHECK   DATE PAID   AMOUNT
WITHDRAWALS       203     5/01        10.00     213     5/08        40.00
                  204     4/30        15.00     214     5/09         9.58
                  205     5/10       635.00     215     5/20        66.18
                  206     5/08        25.00     216     5/20        64.92
                  207     5/07        19.00     217     5/21        25.03
                  208     5/07        50.00     218     5/21        37.98
                  209     5/08        15.00     219     5/22        35.00
                  210     5/10        83.00     220     5/22       105.00
                  211     5/10        10.00     222*    5/22       100.00
                  212     5/08        70.00     223     5/21        40.00
                                               224     5/29        40.82

                  PREMIUM ACCOUNT FEE LESS $1.00 DISCOUNT    4/30        6.50
ATM
TRANSACTIONS      INTERLINK PURCHASE #572921 ON 04/30 AT     5/01       50.00
                  LUCKY STORE NO 043
                  WITHDRAWAL #08108 AT 00165A ON 05/04       5/06       20.00
                  INTERLINK PURCHASE #807409 ON 05/11 AT     5/13       12.51
                  LUCKY STORE NO 056
                  WITHDRAWAL #01015 AT 00240C ON 05/17       5/17       20.00
                  WITHDRAWAL #04792 AT 00167C ON 05/20       5/20       20.00
                  WITHDRAWAL #04386 AT 00240D ON 05/21       5/21       40.00
                  INTERLINK PURCHASE #880318 ON 05/28 AT     5/29       30.00
                  LUCKY STORE #043

DEPOSITS                                             DATE POSTED   AMOUNT
                  AVS RNT CAR SYST PAYROLL G2 000000035382    5/03      618.69
                  AVS RNT CAR SYST PAYROLL G2 000000035382    5/17       83.39
                  AVS RNT CAR SYST PAYROLL G2 000000035382    5/17      600.75

ATM               00165A: 249 PRIMROSE RD, ANY CITY, USA
LOCATIONS USED    00240C: 490 BROADWAY, ANY CITY, USA
                  00167C: 1145 BROADWAY, ANY CITY, USA
                  00240D: 490 BROADWAY, ANY CITY, USA
```

1. Checks that you've written, ATM withdrawals, debit purchases, or other automatic payments subtracted from your checkbook balance haven't yet been received and processed by your bank and therefore remain outstanding.
2. Deposits that you've made and added to your checkbook balance haven't yet been credited to your account.
3. Any service (activity) charges levied on your account by the bank haven't yet been deducted from your checkbook balance.
4. Interest earned on your account (if it's a NOW or an MMDA account) hasn't yet been added to your checkbook balance.

You Can Do It Now

Reconcile Your Checkbook

In this era of online and mobile banking, it's easy to keep up with the *current* balance in your checking account. So many people don't bother to reconcile their checking accounts. But it's all too easy to forget about outstanding checks, delayed payments, and ATM withdrawals when you just focus on your current balance. And reconciling your checkbook provides insight into how you spend your money each month, which will inform your budgeting and overall financial planning. So pick up your most recent bank statement and get reconciled—you can do it now.

Exhibit 4.6 lists the steps to reconcile your checkbook each month.

The reverse side of your bank statement usually provides a form for reconciling your account along with step-by-step instructions. Worksheet 4.1 includes an account reconciliation form that Jackson Smith completed for the month of May 2017 using the reconciliation procedures we have described. You can use the form to reconcile either regular or interest-paying checking accounts such as NOWs or MMDAs.

4-4c Special Types of Checks

In some circumstances, sellers of goods or services may not accept personal checks because they can't be absolutely sure that the check is good. This is common for large purchases or when the buyer's bank is not located in the same area where the purchase is being made. A form of check that guarantees payment may be required instead: cashier's checks, traveler's checks, or certified checks.

cashier's check
A check payable to a third party that is drawn by a bank on itself in exchange for the amount specified plus, in most cases, a service fee (of about $5).

- **Cashier's check**: Anyone can buy a cashier's check from a bank. These checks are often used by people who don't have checking accounts. They can be purchased

EXHIBIT 4.6 Make That Checkbook Balance!

Take the following steps to reconcile your account:

1. On receipt of your bank statement, arrange all canceled checks in ascending numerical order based on their sequence numbers or issuance dates. (Skip this step if your bank doesn't return canceled checks.)
2. Compare each check or its bank statement information with the corresponding entry in your checkbook ledger to make sure there are no recording errors. Mark off in your checkbook ledger each check and any other withdrawals such as from ATMs, point-of-sale debit transactions, or automatic payments.
3. List the checks and other deductions (ATM withdrawals or debit purchases) still *outstanding*—that is, those deducted in your checkbook but not returned with your bank statement (see Step 2). Total their amount.
4. Compare the deposits indicated on the statement with deposits shown in your checkbook ledger. Total the amount of deposits still outstanding—that is, those shown in your checkbook ledger but not yet received by the bank. Be sure to include all automatic deposits and deposits made at ATMs in your calculations.
5. *Subtract* the total amount of checks outstanding (from Step 3) from your bank statement balance, and *add* to this balance the amount of outstanding deposits (from Step 4). The resulting amount is your *adjusted bank balance*.
6. Deduct the amount of any bank service charges from your checkbook ledger balance, and add any interest earned to that balance. Make sure that you include all service charges for the period, including those for any returned checks, stop payments, or new checks ordered. The resulting amount is your *new checkbook balance*. This amount should equal your adjusted bank balance (from Step 5). If it doesn't, check all addition and subtraction in your checkbook ledger, because you've probably made an error.

Jackson Smith used this form to reconcile his checking account for the month of May 2017. Because line A equals line B, he has fully reconciled the difference between the $80.99 bank statement balance and his $339.44 checkbook balance. Accounts should be reconciled each month—as soon as possible after receiving the bank statement.

CHECKING ACCOUNT RECONCILIATION

For the Month of ___ May ___ , 20 _17_

Accountholder Name (s) ___ Jackson Smith ___

Type of Account ___ Regular Checking ___

1. Ending balance shown on bank statement _____ $ 80.99

Add up checks and withdrawals still outstanding:

Check Number or Date	Amount	Check Number or Date	Amount
221	$ 81.55		
225	196.50		
Lucky—5/28	25.00		
ATM—5/29	40.00		
	TOTAL	$ 343.05	

2. Deduct total checks/withdrawals still outstanding from bank balance _____ − $343.05

Add up deposits not shown on bank statement:

Date	Amount	Date	Amount
5/29/17	$ 595.00		
	TOTAL	$ 595.00	

3. Add total deposits still outstanding to bank balance _____ + $595.00

A   **Adjusted Bank Balance (1 − 2 + 3)** _____ $332.94

4. Ending balance shown in checkbook _____ $339.44

5. Deduct any bank service charges for the period ___ (−$ 7.50 + $ 1.00) ___ − $ 6.50

6. Add interest earned for the period _____ + $ 0

B   **New Checkbook Balance (4 − 5 + 6)** _____ $332.94

Note: Your account is reconciled when line A equals line B.

for the face amount of the check plus a service fee that averages around $9, although under some circumstances they're issued at no charge to bank customers. The bank issues a check payable to a third party and drawn on itself, not you—the best assurance you can give that the check is good.

traveler's check
A check sold (for a fee of about 1 to 2 percent) by many large financial institutions, typically in denominations ranging from $20 to $100, that can be used for making purchases and exchanged for local currencies in most parts of the world.

- **Traveler's check:** Some large financial organizations—such as Citibank, American Express, MasterCard, Visa, and Bank of America—issue traveler's checks, which can be purchased at commercial banks and most other financial institutions, typically in denominations ranging from $20 to $100. A fee of 1 to 2 percent or more can be charged on the purchase.

  Properly endorsed and countersigned traveler's checks are accepted by most U.S. businesses and can be exchanged for local currencies in most parts of the world. Because they're insured against loss or theft by the issuing agency, they provide a safe, convenient, and popular form of money for travel. However, the large number of counterfeit traveler's checks has made them less popular with many businesses, which is making them less commonly used.

certified check
A personal check that is guaranteed by the bank on which it is drawn.

- **Certified check:** A certified check is a personal check that the bank certifies, with a stamp, to guarantee that the funds are available. The bank immediately deducts the amount of the check from your account. There's usually only a minimal or no charge for this service if you are the bank's customer.

MONKEY BUSINESS IMAGES/DREAMSTIME.COM

TEST YOURSELF

4-13 What are the key factors to consider when opening a checking account? Discuss the advantages and disadvantages of individual versus joint accounts.

4-14 Is it possible to bounce a check because of insufficient funds when the checkbook ledger shows a balance available to cover it? Explain what happens when a check bounces. Can you obtain protection against overdrafts?

4-15 Describe the procedure used to stop payment on a check. Why might you wish to initiate this process?

4-16 What type of information is found in the monthly bank statement, and how is it used? Explain the basic steps involved in reconciling an account.

4-17 Briefly describe each of these special types of checks:

   a. Cashier's check

   b. Traveler's check

   c. Certified check

4-5 ESTABLISHING A SAVINGS PROGRAM

LG5, LG6

The vast majority of American households have some money put away in savings, making it clear that most of us understand the value of saving for the future. In the wake of the recent financial crisis, the U.S. personal saving rate increased to an average of almost 5 percent of after-tax income, after hitting a low of around 1 percent in 2005. The act of saving is a deliberate, well-thought-out activity designed to preserve the value of money, ensure liquidity, and earn a competitive rate of return. Almost by definition, *smart savers are smart investors.* They regard saving as more than putting loose change into a piggy bank; rather, they recognize the importance of saving and know that savings must be managed as astutely as any security.

After all, what we normally think of as "savings" is really a form of investment—a short-term, highly liquid investment—that's subject to minimal risk. Establishing and maintaining an ongoing savings program is a vital element of personal financial planning. To get the most from your savings, however, you must understand your options and how different savings vehicles pay interest.

4-5a Starting Your Savings Program

Careful financial planning dictates that you hold a portion of your assets to meet liquidity needs and accumulate wealth. Although opinions differ as to how much you should keep as liquid reserves, the post-crisis consensus is that most families should have an amount equal to at least 6 to 9 months of after-tax income. Therefore, if you take home $3,000 a month, you should have between $18,000 and $27,000 in liquid reserves. If your employer has a strong salary continuation program covering extended periods of illness, or if you have a sizable line of credit available, then a somewhat lower amount is probably adequate.

A specific savings plan should be developed to accumulate funds. Saving should be a priority item in your budget, not something that occurs only when income happens to exceed expenditures. Some people manage this by arranging to have savings directly withheld from their paychecks. Not only do direct deposit arrangements help your savings effort, but they also enable your funds to earn interest sooner. Or you can transfer funds regularly to other financial institutions such as commercial banks, savings and loans, savings banks, credit unions, and even mutual funds. But the key to success is to establish a *regular* pattern of saving.

You should make it a practice to set aside an amount you can comfortably afford *each month,* even if it's only $50 to $100. (Keep in mind that $100 monthly deposits earning 4 percent interest will grow to more than $36,500 in 20 years!) Exhibit 4.7 lists some strategies that you can use to increase your savings and build a nest egg.

You must also decide which savings products best meet your needs. Many savers prefer to keep their emergency funds in a regular savings or money market deposit account at an institution with federal deposit insurance. Although these accounts are safe, convenient, and highly liquid, they tend to pay relatively low rates of interest. Other important considerations include your risk preference, the length of time you can leave your money on deposit, and the level of current and anticipated interest rates.

Suppose that one year from now, you plan to use $5,000 of your savings to make the down payment on a new car, and you expect interest rates to drop during that period. You should lock in today's higher rate by purchasing a 1-year CD. On the other hand, if you're unsure about when you'll actually need the funds or believe that interest rates will rise, then you're better off with an MMDA or MMMF because their rates change with market conditions, and you can access your funds at any time without penalty.

Short-term interest rates generally fluctuate more than long-term rates, so it pays to monitor interest rate movements, shop around for the best rates, and place your funds in savings vehicles consistent with your needs. If short-term interest rates drop, you won't be able to reinvest the proceeds from maturing CDs at comparable rates. You'll need to reevaluate your savings plans and may choose to move funds into other savings vehicles with higher rates of interest but greater risk.

Many financial planning experts recommend keeping a minimum of 10 percent to 25 percent of your investment portfolio in savings-type instruments in addition to the 6 to 9 months of liquid reserves noted earlier. Someone with $50,000 in investments should probably have a minimum of $5,000 to $12,500—and possibly more—in short-term vehicles such as MMDAs, MMMFs, or CDs. At times, the amount invested in short-term vehicles could far exceed the recommended minimum, approaching 50 percent or more of the portfolio. This generally depends on expected interest rate movements. If interest rates are relatively high and you expect them to fall, you would invest in longer-term vehicles in order to lock in the attractive interest rates. On the other hand, if rates are relatively low and you expect them to rise, you might invest in shorter-term vehicles so you can more quickly reinvest when rates do rise.

4-5b Earning Interest on Your Money

Interest earned is the reward for putting your money in a savings account or short-term investment vehicle, and it's important for you to understand how that interest is earned. But unfortunately, even in the relatively simple world of savings, not all interest rates are created equal.

The Effects of Compounding

Interest can be earned in one of two ways. First, some short-term investments are sold on a *discount basis*. This means the security is sold for a price that's lower than its redemption value; the difference is the amount of interest earned. Treasury bills, for instance, are issued on a discount basis. Another way to earn interest on short-term investments is by *direct payment*, which occurs when interest is applied to a regular savings account. Although this is a simple process, determining the actual rate of return can be complicated.

| EXHIBIT 4.7 | Strategies to Build Up Your Savings |

Having trouble getting your savings program started? Here are some strategies to begin building up your savings:

- **Pay yourself first, then pay your bills.** Write a check to yourself each month as if it were another invoice and deposit it in a savings account.
- **Examine your spending habits** for places to cut back. Bring your lunch to work or school. Comparison shop. Carpool. Cut back on trips to the ATM.
- **Set up a payroll deduction** and have your employer deduct money from your paycheck to be deposited directly into your savings account. It's painless because you never see the money in your checking account.
- **Save your raise or bonus.** Keep your lifestyle where it is and put the difference in your savings account.
- **Keep making those loan payments,** and you'll feel rich when those obligations finally end. When the loans are paid off, deposit the same amount to your savings account.
- **Be aware of the return paid on your savings account.** You might do a bit better by moving your money to an asset management account at a brokerage firm.
- **Reinvest interest and dividends.** You won't miss the money, and your account will grow more rapidly. If you have a savings account, make sure the interest is reinvested rather than paid into your non-interest-bearing checking account. If you own stocks or mutual funds, virtually all offer dividend reinvestment plans.
- **Set up a retirement plan** to make sure you contribute to your company's retirement program. Your contributions are tax-deductible, and many employers match your contributions. Check out available individual retirement account options such as IRAs and 401(k)s (see Chapter 14).
- **Splurge once in a while**—the boost you get will make saving money a little easier. All work and no play makes for a dull life, so once you've reached a savings goal, take some money and enjoy yourself.

Calculator

INPUTS	FUNCTIONS
1000	PV
365	N
7	÷
365	=
	I
	CPT
	FV
SOLUTION	
1,072.50	

See Appendix E for details.

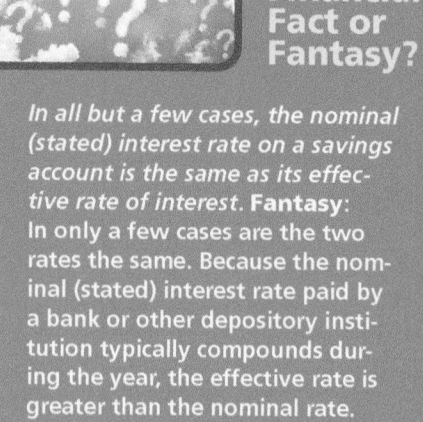

Financial Fact or Fantasy?

In all but a few cases, the nominal (stated) interest rate on a savings account is the same as its effective rate of interest. **Fantasy:** In only a few cases are the two rates the same. Because the nominal (stated) interest rate paid by a bank or other depository institution typically compounds during the year, the effective rate is greater than the nominal rate.

The first complication is in the method used to set the amount and rate of **compound interest** earned annually. You've probably read or seen advertisements by banks or other depository institutions declaring that they pay daily, rather than annual, interest. Consider an example to understand what this means. Assume that you invest $1,000 in a savings account advertised as paying annual **simple interest** at a rate of 5 percent. The interest is paid only on the initial amount of the deposit with simple interest. This means that if you leave the $1,000 on deposit for 1 year, you'll earn $50 in interest, and the account balance will total $1,050 at year's end. In this case, the **nominal (stated) rate of interest** (the promised rate of interest paid on a savings deposit or charged on a loan) is 5 percent.

In contrast, the **effective rate of interest** is the annual rate of return that's *actually earned* (or *charged*) during the period the funds are held (or borrowed). You can calculate it with the following formula:

$$\text{Effective Rate of Interest} = \frac{\text{Amount of Interest Earned}}{\text{Amount of Money Invested or Deposited}}$$

In our example, because $50 was earned during the year on an investment of $1,000, the effective rate is $50/$1,000 or 5 percent, which is the same as the nominal rate of interest. (Notice in the preceding formula that it's interest earned during the *year* that matters; if you wanted to calculate the effective rate of interest on an account held for 6 months, you'd double the amount of interest earned.)

EXAMPLE: Calculating Earnings When Interest Is Compounded Semiannually

Suppose Ramon can invest $1,000 at 5 percent, compounded *semiannually*. Because interest is applied midyear, his dollar earnings will be:

First 6 months' interest = $1,000 × 0.05 × 6/12 = $25.00

Second 6 months' interest = $1,025 × 0.05 × 6/12 = $25.63

Total annual interest = $50.63

Interest is generated on a larger investment in the second half of the year because the amount of money on deposit has increased by the amount of interest earned in the first half ($25). Although the nominal rate on this account is still 5 percent, the effective rate is 5.06 percent ($50.63/$1,000). As you may have guessed, *the more frequently interest is compounded, the greater the effective rate for any given nominal rate.* Exhibit 4.8 shows these relationships for a sample of interest rates and compounding periods. Note, for example, that with a 7 percent nominal rate, daily compounding adds one-fourth of a percent to the total return—not a trivial amount.

You can calculate the interest compounded daily by using a financial calculator similar to that described in Appendix E. Let's assume you want to invest $1,000 at 7 percent interest compounded daily. How much money will you have in the account at the end of the year? Using a calculator, we get $1,072.50. This value is clearly greater than the $1,070 that annual compounding would return. The effective interest rate would have been 7.25 percent ($72.50 interest earned ÷ $1,000 initially invested), as noted in Exhibit 4.8.

EXHIBIT 4.8   The Magic of Compounding

The effective rate of interest you earn on a savings account will exceed the nominal (stated) rate if interest is compounded more than once a year (as are most savings and interest-paying accounts).

Nominal Rate	Effective Rate				
	Annually	Semiannually	Quarterly	Monthly	Daily
3%	3.00%	3.02%	3.03%	3.04%	3.05%
4	4.00	4.04	4.06	4.07	4.08
5	5.00	5.06	5.09	5.12	5.13
6	6.00	6.09	6.14	6.17	6.18
7	7.00	7.12	7.19	7.23	7.25
8	8.00	8.16	8.24	8.30	8.33
9	9.00	9.20	9.31	9.38	9.42
10	10.00	10.25	10.38	10.47	10.52
11	11.00	11.30	11.46	11.57	11.62
12	12.00	12.36	12.55	12.68	12.74

Compound Interest Generates Future Value

Compound interest is consistent with the *future value* concept introduced in Chapter 2. You can use the procedures described there to find out how much an investment or deposit will grow over time at a compounded rate of interest. You can use the same basic procedure to find the future value of an *annuity*.

Calculator

INPUTS	FUNCTIONS
1000	PV
4	N
5	I
	CPT
	FV
	SOLUTION
	1,215.51

See Appendix E for details.

EXAMPLE: Calculating the Future Value of a Savings Deposit

Brandon would like to know how much $1,000 will be worth in 4 years if he deposits it into a savings account paying 5 percent interest per year compounded annually. Using the future value formula and the future value factor from Appendix A (see Chapter 2 if you need a reminder):

$$\text{Future Value} = \text{Amount Deposited} \times \text{Future Value Factor}$$
$$= \$1,000 \times 1.216$$
$$= \$1,216$$

Calculator

INPUTS	FUNCTIONS
1000	PV
4	N
5	I
	CPT
	FV
	SOLUTION
	4,310.13

See Appendix E for details on calculator use.

EXAMPLE: Calculating the Future Value of Ongoing Savings

Caroline deposits $1,000 a year into a savings account paying 5% per year, compounded annually. Using the future value interest factor for an annuity in Appendix B, in 4 years Caroline will have:

$$\text{Future Value} = \text{Amount Deposited Yearly} \times \text{Future Value Annuity Factor}$$
$$= \$1,000 \times 4.310$$
$$= \$4,310$$

4-5c A Variety of Ways to Save

During the past decade or so, there has been a huge growth of savings and short-term investment vehicles, particularly for people of modest means. And because of the flexibility it provides, there'll always be a place in your portfolio for cash savings.

Today, investors can choose from savings accounts, money market deposit accounts, money market mutual funds, NOW accounts, CDs, U.S. Treasury bills, Series EE bonds, and asset management accounts. We examined several of these savings vehicles earlier in this chapter. Now let's look at the three remaining types of deposits and securities.

Certificates of Deposit

certificates of deposit (CDs)
A type of savings instrument issued by certain financial institutions in exchange for a deposit; typically requires a minimum deposit and has a maturity ranging from 7 days to as long as 7 or more years.

Certificates of deposit (CDs) differ from the savings instruments discussed earlier in that CD funds (except for CDs purchased through brokerage firms) must remain on deposit for a specified period (from 7 days to as long as 7 or more years). Although it's possible to withdraw funds prior to maturity, an interest penalty usually makes withdrawal somewhat costly. The bank or other depository institution is free to charge whatever penalty it likes, but most require you to forfeit some interest. Banks, S&Ls, and other depository institutions can offer any rate and maturity CD they wish. As a result, a wide variety of CDs are offered by most banks, depository institutions, and other financial institutions such as brokerage firms. Most pay higher rates for larger deposits and longer periods of time. CDs are convenient to buy and hold because they offer attractive and highly competitive yields plus federal deposit insurance protection.

U.S. Treasury Bills

U.S. Treasury bill (T-bill)
A short-term (3- or 6-month maturity) debt instrument issued at a discount by the U.S. Treasury in the ongoing process of funding the national debt.

The **U.S. Treasury bill (T-bill)** is considered the ultimate safe haven for savings and investments. T-bills are issued by the U.S. Treasury as part of its ongoing process of funding the national debt. They are sold on a discount basis in minimum denominations of $100 and are issued with 3-month (13-week) or 6-month (26-week) maturities. The bills are auctioned off every Monday. Backed by the full faith and credit of the U.S. government, T-bills pay an attractive and safe return that is free from state and local income taxes.

T-bills are almost as liquid as cash because they can be sold at any time (in a very active secondary market) with no interest penalty. However, should you have to sell before maturity, you may lose some money on your investment if interest rates have risen, and you'll have to pay a broker's fee. Treasury bills pay interest on a *discount basis* and thus are different from other savings or short-term investment vehicles—that is, their interest is equal to the difference between the purchase price paid and their stated value at maturity.

EXAMPLE: Interest Earned on a Treasury Bill

Kevin paid $980 for a Treasury bill that will be worth $1,000 at maturity. How much interest will Kevin earn?

Because a T-bill is a discount instrument, Kevin will earn interest of $1,000 − $980 = $20.

An individual investor may purchase T-bills directly by participating in the weekly Treasury auctions or indirectly through a commercial bank or a securities dealer who buys bills for investors on a commission basis. T-bills may now be purchased over the Internet (**www.treasurydirect.gov**) or by phone (call 800-722-2678 and follow the interactive menu to complete transactions).

Outstanding Treasury bills can also be purchased in the secondary market through banks or dealers. This approach gives the investor a much wider selection of maturities, ranging from less than a week to as long as 6 months.

Series EE Bonds

Although they are issued by the U.S. Treasury on a discount basis and are free of state and local income taxes, Series EE bonds are quite different from T-bills. Savings bonds are *accrual-type securities*, which means that interest is paid when they're cashed in or before maturity, rather than periodically during their lives. The government does issue Series HH bonds; they have a 10-year maturity and are available in denominations of $50 to $10,000. Unlike EE bonds, HH bonds are issued at their full face value and pay interest semiannually at the current fixed rate.

Series EE savings bonds are backed by the full faith and credit of the U.S. government and can be replaced without charge in case of loss, theft, or destruction. Now also designated as "Patriot Bonds" in honor of September 11, 2001, they present an opportunity for all Americans to contribute to the government's efforts and save for their own futures as well. You can purchase them at banks or other depository institutions or through payroll deduction plans. Issued in denominations from $25 through $10,000, their purchase price is a uniform 50 percent of the face amount (thus a $100 bond will cost $50 and be worth $100 at maturity).

Series EE bonds earn interest at a fixed rate for 30 years. Their long life lets investors use them for truly long-term goals like education and retirement. The higher the rate of interest being paid, the shorter the time it takes for the bond to accrue from its discounted purchase price to its maturity value. Bonds can be redeemed any time after the first 12 months, although redeeming EE bonds in less than 5 years results in a penalty of the last 3 months of interest earned. The fixed interest rate is set every 6 months in May and November and changes with prevailing Treasury security market yields. EE bonds increase in value every month, and the fixed interest rate is compounded semiannually. To obtain current rates on Series EE bonds, it's easiest to use the Internet link for the savings bond site.

In addition to being exempt from state and local taxes, Series EE bonds give their holders an appealing tax twist: *Savers need not report interest earned on their federal tax returns until the bonds are redeemed.* Although interest can be reported annually (for example, when the bonds are held in the name of a child who has limited interest income), most investors choose to defer it. A second attractive tax feature allows partial or complete tax avoidance of EE bond earnings when proceeds are used to pay education expenses, such as college tuition, for the bond purchaser, a spouse, or another IRS-defined dependent. To qualify, the purchaser must be age 24 or older and must have income below a given maximum that is adjusted annually. The rationale for the later requirement is to provide tax relief only to low- and middle-income people.

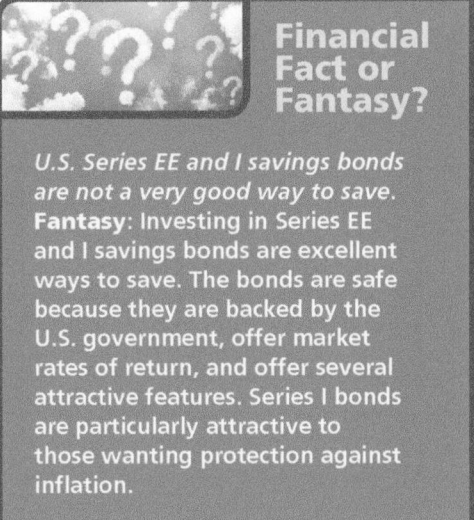

I Savings Bonds

I savings bonds are similar to Series EE bonds in numerous ways. Both are issued by the U.S. Treasury and are accrual-type securities. I bonds are available in denominations between $25 and $10,000. Interest compounds semiannually for 30 years on both securities. Like Series EE bonds, I savings bonds' interest remains exempt from state and local income taxes but does face state and local estate, inheritance, gift, and other excise taxes. Interest earnings are subject to federal income tax but may be excluded when used to finance education, with some limitations.

There are some significant differences between the two savings vehicles. Whereas Series EE bonds are sold at a discount, I bonds are sold at face value. I savings bonds differ from Series EE bonds in that their annual interest rate combines a fixed rate that remains the same for the life of the bond with a semi-annual inflation rate that changes with the Consumer Price Index for all Urban Consumers (CPI-U). In contrast, the rate on Series EE bonds is based on the 6-month averages of 5-year Treasury security market yields. Thus, the key

FINANCIAL ROAD SIGN

Determining How Much Interest You Will Earn

Before opening a deposit account, investigate the following factors, which determine the amount of interest you'll earn on your savings or interest-bearing checking account:

- **Frequency of compounding.** The more often interest is compounded, the higher your return.
- **Balance on which interest is paid.** For balances that qualify to earn interest, most banks now use the *actual balance, or day of deposit to day of withdrawal,* method. The actual balance method is fairest because it pays depositors interest on all funds on deposit for the actual amount of time they remain there.
- **Interest rate paid.** As mentioned earlier, the Truth in Savings Act standardized the way that banks calculate the rate of interest they pay on deposit accounts. This makes it easy to compare each bank's annual percentage yield (APY) and to choose the bank offering the highest APY.

difference between Series EE bonds and I bonds is that I bond returns are adjusted for inflation. Note in particular that the earnings rate cannot go below zero and that the value of I bonds cannot drop below their redemption value. Like Series EE bonds, I bonds can be bought on the Internet or via phone. I bonds offer the opportunity to "inflation-protect" your savings somewhat. I bonds cannot be bought or sold in the secondary market; transactions are only with the U.S. Treasury.

TEST YOURSELF

4-18 In general, how much of your annual income should you save in the form of liquid reserves? What portion of your investment portfolio should you keep in savings and other short-term investment vehicles? Explain.

4-19 Define and distinguish between the *nominal (stated) rate of interest* and the *effective rate of interest.* Explain why a financial institution that pays a nominal rate of 4.5 percent interest, compounded daily, actually pays an effective rate of 4.6 percent.

4-20 What factors determine the amount of interest you will earn on a deposit account? Which combination provides the best return?

4-21 Briefly describe the basic features of each of the following savings vehicles: (a) CDs, (b) U.S. Treasury bills, (c) Series EE bonds, and (d) I savings bonds.

Planning Over a Lifetime: *Managing Cash and Savings*

Here are some key considerations for managing your cash and savings in each stage of the life cycle.

Pre-family Independence: 20s	Family Formation/ Career Development: 30–45	Pre-Retirement: 45–65	Retirement: 65 and Beyond
✓ Build up savings in general and emergency fund in particular.	✓ Increase savings to fund future financial goals.	✓ Maintain emergency fund.	✓ Maintain list of bank accounts that are easily accessible by spouse and family.
✓ Pay off any outstanding college loans.	✓ Broaden variety of cash management vehicles and reliance on financial planners for strategy development.	✓ Relate savings strategies more directly to retirement planning.	✓ Take advantage of bank accounts with senior discounts on fees.
✓ Find best mix of financial institution accounts based on fees, returns, and convenience. Make comparisons across banks.	✓ Carefully relate savings program to funding children's future educational needs.	✓ Start being sensitive to the presence of "senior" discounts.	✓ Integrate cash management and savings with retirement spending and estate plan.
	✓ Get an estimate of your Social Security benefits based on your expected retirement date.		

WILLIAM HUBER/PHOTONICA/GETTY IMAGES

Financial Impact of Personal Choices
Stella Likes Cash—Too Much?

Stella has a good job that pays $65,000 a year. She invests the maximum amount allowable in her work-based retirement plan. During the financial crisis a few years ago her retirement investments fell about 40 percent in value! While her investments have more than recovered, Stella is very risk conscious and has consequently built up an emergency fund of $60,000, which she keeps in a savings account that pays 0.5 percent, compounded monthly. Is Stella's approach to handling her emergency funds the best way to go?

Stella has done a great job setting aside a $60,000 emergency fund. And contributing the maximum will serve her well. However, the recommended emergency fund for 6 to 9 months of income for her $65,000 annual income is only $32,500 to $48,750. So Stella has set aside much more than is recommended. Further, Stella is leaving it in a savings account only paying 0.5 percent a year, which generates interest income of only about $325 a year. It would make sense for Stella to invest more aggressively—even a CD would provide a higher return with comparable risk. And she should at least shop around for a better savings rate than 0.5 percent for her hopefully reduced emergency fund. Stella could find another savings vehicle with a rate of at least 1 percent a year, which would about double her annual return. Stella is doing great—but she likes cash too much for her own good. She could do even better.

Summary

LG1 Understand the role of cash management in the personal financial planning process. p.125
Cash management plays a vital role in personal financial planning. It involves the administration and control of liquid assets—cash, checking accounts, savings, and other short-term investment vehicles. With good cash management practices, you'll have the necessary funds to cover your expenses and establish a regular savings program.

LG2 Describe today's financial services marketplace, both depository and nondepository financial institutions. p.128
Today's financial services marketplace is highly competitive and offers consumers expanded product offerings at attractive prices. Individuals and families continue to rely heavily on traditional depository financial institutions for most of their financial services needs. Nondepository financial institutions also offer some banking services such as credit cards and money market fund accounts with check-writing privileges. You should make sure your bank has federal deposit insurance and is financially sound. Most depository institutions are federally insured for up to $250,000 per depositor name.

LG3 Select the checking, savings, electronic banking, and other bank services that meet your needs. p.131
Financial institutions provide a variety of accounts to help you manage your cash: regular checking accounts; savings accounts; and interest-paying checking accounts, such as NOW accounts, money market deposit accounts, and money market mutual funds. Asset management accounts offered by brokerage firms and mutual funds combine checking, investment, and borrowing activities and pay higher interest on deposits than do other, more traditional, checking accounts. Other money management services include electronic funds transfer systems (EFTSs) that use telecommunications and computer technology to electronically transfer funds. Popular EFTS services include debit cards, ATMs, preauthorized deposits and payments, bank-by-phone accounts, and online banking and bill-paying services. Many banks also provide safe-deposit boxes, which serve as a storage place for valuables and important documents.

LG4 Open and use a checking account. p.139
A checking account is a convenient way to hold cash and pay for goods and services. The sharp increase in bank service charges makes it important to evaluate different types of checking accounts and their service charges, minimum balance requirements, and other fees. You should understand how to write and endorse checks, make deposits, keep good checking account records, prevent overdrafts, and stop payment on checks. The account reconciliation, or checkbook balancing, process confirms the accuracy of your account records and monthly bank statement. Other special types of checks that you may occasionally use include cashier's, traveler's, and certified checks.

LG5 Calculate the interest earned on your money using compound interest and future value techniques. p.148
Once you know the interest rate, frequency of compounding, and how the bank determines the balance on which interest is paid, you can calculate how much interest you'll earn on your money. Use future value and future value of an annuity formulas to find out how your savings will grow. The more often interest is compounded, the greater the effective rate for a given nominal rate of interest. Most banks use the actual balance (or "day of deposit to day of withdrawal") method to determine which balances qualify to earn interest, which is the fairest method for depositors.

LG6 Develop a cash management strategy that incorporates a variety of savings plans. p.148
Your cash management strategy should include establishing a regular pattern of saving with liquid reserves equal to at least 6 to 9 months of after-tax income. The choice of savings products depends on your needs, your risk preference, the length of time you plan to leave money on deposit, and current and expected interest rates. You may wish to put some of your savings into vehicles that pay a higher rate of interest than savings or NOW accounts, such as CDs, U.S. Treasury bills, Series EE bonds, and I savings bonds.

Key Terms

account reconciliation, 143

asset management account (AMA), 134

automated teller machines (ATMs), 135

cash management, 125

cashier's check, 145

certificates of deposit (CDs), 152

certified check, 147

checkbook ledger, 142

compound interest, 150

debit cards, 135

demand deposit, 133

deposit insurance, 130

effective rate of interest, 150

electronic funds transfer systems (EFTSs), 135

I savings bonds, 153

internet banks, 130

money market deposit account (MMDA), 134

money market mutual fund (MMMF), 134

negotiable order of withdrawal (NOW) account, 133

nominal (stated) rate of interest, 150

overdraft, 142

overdraft protection, 142

series EE bonds, 153

share draft accounts, 130

simple interest, 150

stop payment, 143

time deposits, 133

traveler's checks, 147

U.S. Treasury bill (T-bill), 152

Answers to Test Yourself

You can find answers to these questions on this book's companion website. Look for it at *www.cengagebrain.com*. Search for this book by its title, and then add it to your dashboard.

Key Financial Relationships

Concept	Financial Relationship	Page Number
Effective Rate of Interest	Effective Rate of Interest = $\dfrac{\text{Amount of Interest Earned}}{\text{Amount of Money Invested or Deposited}}$	150
Future Value of a Savings Deposit	Future Value = Amount Deposited × Future Value Factor	151
Future Value of Ongoing Savings	Future Value = Amount Deposited Yearly × Future Value Annuity Factor	151

Key Financial Relationships Problem Set

1. **Effective Rate of Interest.** Hannah Reed invested $5,000 in a short-term investment that yielded interest of $203.71 after one year. What effective rate of interest did Hannah earn?

   Solution:

   $$\text{Effective Rate of Interest} = \frac{\text{Amount of Interest Earned}}{\text{Amount of Money Invested or Deposited}} = \frac{\$203.71}{\$5,000.00} = 4.07 \text{ percent}$$

2. **Future Value of a Savings Deposit.** Nolan Adams just got a $7,500 bonus and plans to invest it in a CD paying 6 percent interest compounded annually. What value can Nolan expect his investment to grow to after five years?

   Solution: Future Value = Amount Deposited × Future Value Factor. The future value interest factor for 5 years and 6 percent in Appendix A is 1.338. Thus, in 5 years Nolan's CD is expected to be worth $7,500 × 1.338 = $10,035.

3. **Future Value of Ongoing Savings.** Abigail Lewis deposits $2,500 a year into a savings account paying 4 percent per year, compounded annually. Her goal is to accumulate an emergency fund of $20,000 in 8 years. Is Abigail likely to achieve her financial goal?

Solution: Future Value = Amount Deposited Yearly × Future Value Annuity Factor. The future value interest factor for an annuity for 8 years and 4 percent in Appendix B is 9.214. In 8 years Abigail should consequently have accumulated $2,500 × 9.214 = $23,035.57.

Financial Planning Exercises

LG1, p. 125

1. **Adapting to a low interest rate environment.** Your parents are retired and have expressed concern about the really low interest rates they're earning on their savings. They've been approached by an advisor who says he has a "sure-fire" way to get them higher returns. What would you tell your parents about the low-interest-rate environment, and how would you advise them to view the advisor's new prospective investments?

LG2, 3, 4, p. 128, 131, 139

2. **Comparing banks online.** What type of bank serves your needs best? Visit the Internet sites of the following institutions and prepare a chart comparing the services offered, such as traditional and online banking, investment services, and personal financial advice. Which one would you choose to patronize, and why?
   a. Wells Fargo (**https://www.wellsfargo.com**)—a nationwide full-service bank
   b. A leading local commercial bank in your area
   c. A local savings institution
   d. A local credit union

LG3, p. 131

3. **Exposure from stolen ATM card.** Suppose that someone stole your ATM card and withdrew $950 from your checking account. How much money could you lose according to federal legislation if you reported the stolen card to the bank: (a) the day the card was stolen, (b) 6 days after the theft, (c) 65 days after receiving your periodic statement?

LG2, 3, 4, p. 128, 131, 139

4. **Choosing a new bank.** You're getting married and are unhappy with your present bank. Discuss your strategy for choosing a new bank and opening an account. Consider the factors that are important to you in selecting a bank—such as the type and ownership of new accounts and bank fees and charges.

LG4, p. 139

5. **Calculating the net costs of checking accounts.** Determine the annual net cost of these checking accounts:
   a. Monthly fee $4, check-processing fee of 20 cents, average of 23 checks written per month
   b. Annual interest of 2.5 percent paid if balance exceeds $750, $8 monthly fee if account falls below minimum balance, average monthly balance $815, account falls below $750 during 4 months

LG4, p. 139

6. **Checking account reconciliation. Use Worksheet 4.1.** Carlos Perez has a NOW account at the First National Bank. His checkbook ledger lists the following checks:

Check Number	Amount
654	$206.05
658	55.22
662	103.00
668	99.00
670	6.10
671	50.25
672	24.90
673	32.45

Check Number	Amount
674	44.50
675	30.00
676	30.00
677	111.23
678	38.04
679	97.99
680	486.70
681	43.50
682	75.00
683	98.50

Carlos also made the following withdrawals and deposits at an ATM near his home:

Date	Amount	Transaction
11/1	$50.00	Withdrawal
11/2	$525.60	Deposit
11/6	$100.00	Deposit
11/14	$75.00	Withdrawal
11/21	$525.60	Deposit
11/24	$150.00	Withdrawal
11/27	$225.00	Withdrawal
11/30	$400.00	Deposit

Carlos' checkbook ledger shows an ending balance of $286.54. He has just received his bank statement for the month of November. It shows an ending balance of $622.44; it also shows that he earned interest for November of $3.28, had a check service charge of $8 for the month, and had another $12 charge for a returned check. His bank statement indicates the following checks have cleared: 654, 662, 672, 674, 675, 676, 677, 678, 679, and 681. ATM withdrawals on 11/1 and 11/14 and deposits on 11/2 and 11/6 have cleared; no other checks or ATM activities are listed on his statement, so anything remaining should be treated as outstanding. Use a checking account reconciliation form like the one in Worksheet 4.1 to reconcile Carlos' checking account.

LG5, 6, p. 148

7. ***Determining the right amount of short-term, liquid investments.*** Owen and Audrey Nelson together earn approximately $82,000 a year after taxes. Through an inheritance and some wise investing, they also have an investment portfolio with a value of almost $150,000.
   a. How much of their annual income do you recommend they hold in some form of liquid savings as reserves? Explain.
   b. How much of their investment portfolio do you recommend they hold in savings and other short-term investment vehicles? Explain.
   c. How much, in total, should they hold in short-term liquid assets?

LG5, 6, p. 148

8. ***Calculating interest earned and future value of savings account.*** If you put $6,000 in a savings account that pays interest at the rate of 4 percent, compounded annually, how much will you have in 5 years? (*Hint:* Use the *future value* formula.) How much interest will you earn during the 5 years? If you put $6,000 *each* year into a savings account that pays interest at the rate of 4 percent a year, how much would you have after 5 years?

LG6, p. 148

9. ***Short-term investments and inflation.*** Describe some of the short-term investment vehicles that can be used to manage your cash resources. What would you focus on if you were concerned that inflation will increase significantly in the future?

Applying Personal Finance

Manage Your Cash!

What difference does it make where you keep your money? The returns are so low on checking and savings accounts that you certainly won't grow rich on their earnings! It's no wonder that many people tend to overlook the importance of managing their cash and liquid assets. This project will help you evaluate your cash management needs and the various financial service providers available so that you can select the one best suited to your needs.

First, spend some time making a list of your needs and preferences. Do you like to visit your banking institution in person, or would you rather do your banking electronically or by mail? Is a high yield important to you, or is your typical balance usually pretty low so that any earnings would be minimal? What other services might you need, such as a safe-deposit box, brokerage account, trust services, or financial and estate planning?

Next, go back through this chapter and review all the types of financial institutions and the services they provide. Then, beside each need on your list, write down the institutions that would best meet that need. Is there one banking institution that would meet all your needs, or do you think you'd require several? After identifying the type or types that are appropriate for you, survey your community via the phone book, interviews with finance professionals, and other methods to identify the various financial institutions in your area. Look beyond your area as well, and consider what services are available over the Internet or from other regions of the country. Make a list of your top choices and find out more information concerning their services, products, and fees charged to help you decide where you'd like to do business. Bring your findings to class to compare and discuss with your classmates.

CRITICAL THINKING CASES

LG4, 5, 6, p. 139, 148

4.1 June Xu's Savings and Banking Plans

June Xu is a registered nurse who earns $3,250 per month after taxes. She has been reviewing her savings strategies and current banking arrangements to determine if she should make any changes. June has a regular checking account that charges her a flat fee per month, writes an average of 18 checks a month, and carries an average balance of $795 (although it has fallen below $750 during 3 months of the past year). Her only other account is a money market deposit account with a balance of $4,250. She tries to make regular monthly deposits of $50–$100 into her money market account but has done so only about every other month.

Of the many checking accounts June's bank offers, here are the three that best suit her needs.

- *Regular checking, per-item plan*: Service charge of $3 per month plus 35 cents per check.
- *Regular checking, flat-fee plan (the one* June *currently has)*: Monthly fee of $7 regardless of how many checks written. With either of these regular checking accounts, she can avoid any charges by keeping a minimum daily balance of $750.
- *Interest checking*: Monthly service charge of $7; interest of 3 percent, compounded daily (refer to Exhibit 4.8). With a minimum balance of $1,500, the monthly charge is waived.

June's bank also offers CDs for a minimum deposit of $500; the current annual interest rates are 3.5 percent for 6 months, 3.75 percent for 1 year, and 4 percent for 2 years.

Critical Thinking Questions

1. Calculate the annual cost of each of the three accounts, assuming that June's banking habits remain the same. Which plan would you recommend and why?
2. Should June consider opening the interest checking account and increasing her minimum balance to at least $1,500 to avoid service charges? Explain your answer.
3. What other advice would you give June about her checking account and savings strategy?

4.2 Reconciling the Campbells' Checking Account

Caleb and Eva Campbell are college students who opened their first joint checking account together at the American Bank on September 14, 2017. They've just received their first bank statement for the period ending October 5, 2017. The statement and checkbook ledger are shown in the table following the *Critical Thinking Questions*.

Critical Thinking Questions

1. From this information, prepare a bank reconciliation for the Campbells as of October 5, 2017, using a form like the one in Worksheet 4.1.
2. Given your answer to Question 1, what, if any, adjustments will the Campbells need to make in their checkbook ledger? Comment on the procedures used to reconcile their checking account and their findings.
3. If the Campbells earned interest on their idle balances because the account is a money market deposit account, what impact would this have on the reconciliation process? Explain.

CALEB AND EVA CAMPBELL 2128 E. ARBOR ST. DENVER, COLORADO				THE AMERICAN BANK 800-000-0000 STATEMENT PERIOD SEPT. 6—OCT. 5, 2017
	Opening Balance	**Total Deposits for Period**	**Total Checks/Withdrawals for Period**	**Ending Balance**
	$ 0.00	$569.25	$473.86	$95.39
Date	**Withdrawals (Debits)**		**Deposits (Credits)**	**Balance**
Sept. 14			$360.00	$360.00
Sept. 15			97.00	457.00
Sept. 25	$45.20		9.25	421.05
Oct. 1			103.00	524.05
Oct. 1	3.00 BC			521.05
Oct. 4	65.90	$49.76	$45.00	360.39
Oct. 5	265.00			95.39
RT = Returned Check	DM = Debit Memo	BC = Bank Charges		
FC = Finance Charges	CM = Credit Memo			

Checkbook Ledger						
Check Number	**Date 2017**	**Details**	✓	**Check Amount**	**Deposit Amount**	**Account Balance**
—	Sept. 14	Cash—gift from birthday			$360.00	$360.00
—	Sept. 15	Scott's wages			97.00	457.00
101	Sept. 24	Kroger's—groceries		$45.20		411.80
102	Sept. 27	Telephone bill		28.40		383.40
—	Oct. 1	Scott's wages			103.00	486.40
103	Oct. 1	Univ. Bk. Sto.—college books		65.90		420.50

Checkbook Ledger						
Check Number	Date 2017	Details	✓	Check Amount	Deposit Amount	Account Balance
104	Oct. 1	Walmart—sewing material		16.75		403.75
105	Oct. 1	B. Hadley—apartment rent		265.00		138.75
106	Oct. 2	Anthem—health insurance		17.25		121.50
107	Oct. 3	Kroger's—groceries		49.76		71.74
108	Oct. 4	Cash: gas, entertain., laundry		45.00		26.74
—	Oct. 5	Angela's salary			450.00	476.74

CHAPTER 5

Making Automobile and Housing Decisions

LEARNING GOALS

LG1 Design a plan to research and select a new or used automobile.

LG2 Decide whether to buy or lease a car.

LG3 Identify housing alternatives, assess the rental option, and perform a rent-or-buy analysis.

LG4 Evaluate the benefits and costs of homeownership and estimate how much you can afford to pay for a home.

LG5 Describe the home-buying process.

LG6 Choose mortgage financing that meets your needs.

How Will This Affect Me?

A home is typically the largest single investment you'll ever make, and a car is usually the second largest. As a result, the decisions to buy and finance these assets are important, personal, and complicated.

This chapter presents frameworks for deciding when to buy a first home, how to finance a home, and when to rent rather than to purchase a home. It also discusses the best way to go about buying a new or a used car and how to decide between leasing and purchasing a car. Given the large costs of such assets, the frameworks provided in this chapter can significantly improve your short- and long-term financial well-being. After reading this chapter you should be able to make more informed decisions in purchasing and financing your home and car.

5-1 BUYING AN AUTOMOBILE

Buying an automobile is probably the first major expenditure that many of us make. The car purchase is second only to housing in the amount of money the typical consumer spends. Because you'll buy a car many times during your life—most people buy one every two to five years—a systematic approach to selecting and financing a vehicle can mean significant savings. Before making any major purchase—whether it's a car, house, or large appliance—consider some basic guidelines to wise purchasing decisions.

- *Research* your purchase thoroughly, considering not only the market but also your personal needs and preferences.
- *Select* the best item for your needs and preferences.
- *Buy* the item after negotiating the best price and arranging financing on favorable terms. Be sure you understand all the terms of the sale before signing any contracts.
- *Maintain* your purchase and make necessary repairs promptly.

Exhibit 5.1 summarizes the steps in the car-buying process.

5-1a Choosing a Car

Hybrid, diesel, or gas? Sport utility vehicle (SUV) or pickup truck? Sedan, convertible, or coupe? Car buyers today have more choices than ever before, so more than one category of vehicle may be of interest. A good way to start your research is by tapping into the many available sources of information about cars, their prices, features, and reliability. Industry resources include manufacturers' brochures and dealer personnel. Car magazines, such as *Car and Driver, Motor Trend,* and *Road and Track,* and consumer magazines, such as *Consumer Reports* and *Consumer Guide,* regularly compare and rate cars. In addition, *Consumer Reports* and *Kiplinger's Personal Finance* magazine publish annual buying guides that include comparative statistics and ratings on most domestic and foreign cars. Kiplinger's Personal Finance also has an online Find the Right Car Tool at **http://www.kiplinger.com** (go to the "Spending section," then "Car Buying Guide"). *Consumer Reports* includes information on used cars in its guide

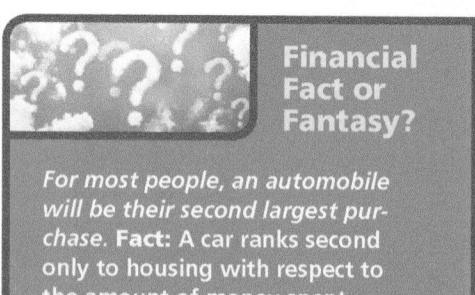

Financial Fact or Fantasy?

For most people, an automobile will be their second largest purchase. **Fact:** A car ranks second only to housing with respect to the amount of money spent.

EXHIBIT 5.1   **Key Steps in Buying a New Car**

These steps summarize the car-buying process discussed in this chapter:

- Research which car best meets your needs and determine how much you can afford to spend on it. Choose the best way to pay for your new car—cash, financing, or lease. Ask your insurance agent for annual premium quotes for insuring various cars, as auto insurance is another significant expense of owning a car.
- Check Internet sites like Edmunds.com and TV and newspapers for incentives and rebates on the car you would like to buy. This could include a cash rebate or low-cost financing.
- Decide on a price based on the dealer's cost for the car and options, plus a markup for the dealer's profit, minus rebates and incentives.
- Find the exact car for you in terms of size, performance, safety, and styling. Choose at least three "target cars" to consider buying. Get online quotes from multiple car dealers.
- Test-drive the car—and the car salesperson. Test-drive the car at least once, both on local streets and on highways. Determine if the car salesperson is someone you want to do business with. Is he or she relaxed, open, and responsive to your questions?
- If you are trading in your old car, you are not likely to get as high a price as if you sell it yourself. Look up your car's trade-in-value at Edmunds.com or kkb.com. Get bids from several dealers.
- Negotiate the lowest price on your new car by getting bids from at least three dealers. Hold firm on your target price before closing the deal.
- Close the deal after looking not just at the cost of the car but also the related expenses. Consider the sales tax and various fees. Get the salesperson to fax you a worksheet and invoice before you go to the dealership.
- Review and sign the paperwork. If you have a worksheet for the deal, the contract should match it. Make sure the numbers match and there are no additional charges or fees.
- Inspect the car for scratches and dents. If anything is missing—like floor mats, for example—ask for a "Due Bill" that states it in writing.

Source: Adapted from Philip Read, "10 Steps to Buying a New Car," http://www.edmunds.com/car-buying/10-steps-to-buying-a-new-car.html, accessed August 2015.

and offers a fee-based service called the *Consumer Reports* New & Used Car Price Service (for more information, see **http://www.consumerreports.org**), which provides the list price and dealer cost on a new car, and its available options.

The Internet has made it especially easy to do your homework before ever setting foot in a dealer's showroom. In addition to finding online versions of automotive magazines, you can visit one of the many comprehensive Internet sites for car shoppers, offering pricing and model information, as well as links to other useful sites. And don't forget the Internet sites of the automobile companies themselves. For example, Ford Motor Company is online at **http://www.ford.com**, and Toyota is at **http://www.toyota.com**. Once you've done the research, you'll be in a better position to negotiate with the dealer. Knowing what you want and can afford before purchasing either a new or used car will prevent a persuasive auto salesperson from talking you into buying a car you don't need.

5-1b Affordability

Before shopping for a car, determine how much you can afford to spend. You'll need to calculate two numbers unless you can pay cash for the entire cost of the car.

- Amount of down payment: This money will come from savings, so be sure not to deplete your emergency fund.
- Size of the monthly loan payment you can afford: Analyze your available resources—for example, your other expenses, including housing—and your transportation requirements. Don't forget to include insurance. Your monthly car payment should be no more than 20 percent of your monthly net income.

Calculator

INPUTS	FUNCTIONS
48	N
5	I
500	PMT
	CPT
	PV
	SOLUTION
	21,711.48

See Appendix E for details.

depreciation
The loss in the value of an asset, such as an automobile, that occurs over its period of ownership; calculated as the difference between the price initially paid and the subsequent sale price.

Operating Costs

The out-of-pocket cost of operating an automobile includes not only car payments but also insurance, license, fuel, oil, tires, and other operating and maintenance outlays. Some of these costs are *fixed* regardless of how much you drive; others are *variable,* depending on the number of miles you drive. The biggest fixed cost is likely to be the *installment payments* associated with the loan or lease used to acquire the car; the biggest variable cost will probably be fuel.

Another purchase cost is depreciation, which is the loss in value that occurs over its period of ownership. In effect, depreciation is the difference between the price you paid for the car and what you can sell it for. If you paid $20,000 for an automobile that can be sold 3 years later for $14,000, the car will cost you $6,000 in depreciation. Although depreciation may not be a recurring out-of-pocket cost, it's an important operating expense that shouldn't be overlooked.

Gas, Diesel, or Hybrid?

Given the cost of fuel, it's important to determine the type of fuel you prefer. If you're a "green" who's concerned about the environmental impact of the fuel your car uses, you may be interested only in a hybrid or an electric car. In this case, price differences may not matter. Although you'll want to consider fuel economy when car shopping, comparable gas-fueled, internal combustion engines and diesel-powered cars have similar fuel economy. Generally diesels are a bit noisier, accelerate slower but have more power, and have longer engine lives than do traditional gas-powered cars.

Hybrids, which blend gas and battery power, have experienced rapid sales growth due to historically increasing gas prices, improved technology and availability, and greater public awareness of environmental issues. Although they're more economical and less polluting than gas- and diesel-powered vehicles, hybrids do have some disadvantages: high cost of battery replacement, generally higher repair costs, and typically

FINANCIAL ROAD SIGN

Where Can You Find Used Cars?

In addition to trade-ins and privately sold vehicles, here are some other sources of used cars.

- Certified used ("pre-owned") cars. Near-new cars that are inspected, certified, and warrantied by the dealer.
- Off-lease cars. Typically single-driver, fully equipped cars that have been inspected after lease return and prior to resale.
- Rental cars ("program cars"). Attractive rental cars, often with some remaining factory warranty, relatively high miles, and limited options.
- Corporate fleet cars. Typically well-maintained, high-mileage cars that are two to three years old.

EXHIBIT 5.2   Pros and Cons of Buying a Used Car

Thinking of buying a used car? Consider both the advantages and disadvantages. Here are some of the *advantages*.

- It's less expensive than a comparable new car, and the recent popularity of short-term car leases has increased the availability of late-model, attractively priced used cars.
- It won't depreciate in value as quickly as a new car—purchasing a used car that is fewer than 18 months old often means saving the 20 percent to 25 percent depreciation in value typically experienced during that part of a car's life.
- Because used cars are less expensive, buyers don't have to put down as much money as they would for a new car.
- Today's used cars are more reliable. The quality and durability of well-maintained 2- to 4-year-old cars makes them more reliable and less expensive to maintain than the new cars of 10 years ago.
- The *federal odometer disclosure law*, requiring sellers to give buyers a signed statement attesting that the mileage shown on the odometer of their used cars is accurate, protects consumers. Penalties for violating this law are stringent.

The main *disadvantage* of buying a used car is the uncertainty about its mechanical condition. It might look good and have low mileage, but it could still have mechanical problems requiring future maintenance and repair expenditures. Having your prospective used car purchase checked out by a reputable mechanic or independent inspection service is money well spent that could save you hundreds of dollars and much aggravation later on.

a higher initial purchase price. It's important to consider the differences between the costs and performance of differently fueled vehicles and decide on the vehicle you want before shopping for a specific new or used car.

New, Used, or "Nearly New"?

One decision you must make is whether to buy a new, used, or "nearly new" car. If you can't afford to buy a new car, the decision is made for you. Some people who can afford to buy a new car choose to buy a used car so they can have a better model—a used luxury car such as a BMW, Lexus, or Mercedes—rather than a less-expensive brand of new car such as a Ford. With the increasing popularity of used cars, car dealers are trying to dispel the negative image associated with buying a used, or "preowned," car. You'll find used cars advertised in local or nearby city newspapers, publications like *AutoTrader,* and their Web sites. These provide an excellent source of information on used cars for sale. Exhibit 5.2 offers advice for buying a used car.

Once you know what you want, shop at these places.

- Franchise dealerships: Offer the latest-model used cars, provide financing, and will negotiate on price. Be sure to research values before shopping.
- Superstores: AutoNation, CarMax, and similar dealers offer no-haggle pricing and a large selection. They certify cars and may offer a limited short-term warranty. May cost slightly more than at a dealer who will negotiate.
- Independent used car lots: Usually offer older (four- to six-year-old) cars and have lower overhead than franchise dealers do. There are no uniform industry standards, so be sure to check with the Better Business Bureau before buying.
- Private individuals: Generally cost less because there's no dealer overhead; may have maintenance records. Be sure that the seller holds the title of the car.

Size, Body Style, and Features

Your first consideration should be what type of car you need. More than one style category may work for you. For example, a family of five can buy a mid-size or full-size sedan, station wagon, minivan, or compact or full-size SUV. When considering size, body style, and features, think about your needs, likes, and dislikes, as well as

Behavior Matters

Watch out for "Anchoring": The Case of the Used Car Salesperson Strategy

While we try to be logical and objective in making purchases, psychologists find that people make estimates of the appropriate price of an item by starting from an initial estimate. We tend to make biased decisions because we often **anchor** on that initial value and have a hard time moving away from it in negotiating transactions.

Consider a common strategy of used car salespersons. Why do you think that they start negotiating with a high price and then work their way down? Salespeople are trying to get the consumer anchored on the initial high price so that when a lower price is offered, the consumer views the lower price as a good value, even if that is not the case. Combine this behavioral bias with our tendency to be a bit too overconfident about our negotiating skills, and you have a potential problem.

So what should you do about the anchoring behavioral bias? Recognize the tendency, do your homework about a reasonable price for a used car, and take into account the used car salesperson's strategy.

anchoring
A behavioral bias in which an individual tends to allow an initial estimate (of value or price) to dominate one's subsequent assessment (of value or price) regardless of new information to the contrary.

the cost. In most cases, there's a direct relationship between size and cost: In general, the larger the car, the more expensive it will be to purchase and to operate. Also consider performance, handling, appearance, fuel economy, reliability, repair problems, and the resale value of the car. And don't try to adapt your needs to fit the car you want—a two-passenger sports car may not be appropriate if you need the car for business or if you have children.

By listing all of the options you want before shopping for a new car, you can avoid paying for features you really don't need. Literally hundreds of options are available, ranging in price from a few dollars up to $2,000 or more, including automatic transmission, a bigger engine, air conditioning, high-performance brakes, an audio system, clock, power windows, power seats, electric door locks, leather seats, navigation systems, a rear window defroster, and special suspension. Some appearance-related options are two-tone or metallic paint, electric sunroof, special tires, sport wheels, and various interior and exterior trim packages.

Most cars have at least some options, but you can select additional optional features that provide a broad range of conveniences and luxuries—for a price. On new cars, a window sticker details each option and its price, but on used cars, only close observation serves to determine the options. Window stickers quite often list standard features that might be considered optional on other models, and vice versa. When shopping for a new car, it's important to be sure that you're comparing comparably equipped models.

Reliability and Warranties

Assess the *reliability* of a car by talking with friends who own similar cars and reading objective assessments published by consumer magazines and buying guides such as *Consumer Reports*. Study the *warranty* offered by new car manufacturers, comparing those for cars that interest you. Significant differences may exist. Be sure to read the warranty booklet included with a new car to understand the warranty terms. Most warranties are void if the owner has not performed routine maintenance or has somehow abused the car.

On new cars, the manufacturer guarantees the general reliability and quality of construction of the vehicle for a specified period in a written warranty, obligating it to repair or replace, at little or no cost to the owner, any defective parts and/or flaws in workmanship. Today, most new car warranties cover a minimum of the first three years of ownership or 36,000 miles, whichever comes first, and some provide coverage for as long as seven years or 70,000 miles. However, most warranties have limitations. For example, longer warranty periods may apply to only the engine and drive train. Auto manufacturers and private insurers also sell extended warranties and service contracts, sometimes called "buyer protection plans." Most experts consider these unnecessary and not worth their cost, given the relatively long initial warranty periods now being offered by most manufacturers.

Other Considerations

Here are some other factors that affect affordability:

- **Trading in or selling your existing car:** Although trading in is convenient, it's generally a better deal to sell your old car outright. If you're willing to take the time, you can usually sell your car for more than the wholesale price typically offered by a dealer on a trade-in.
- **Fuel economy:** The *Environmental Protection Agency (EPA) mileage ratings* are especially useful on new vehicles, which carry a sticker indicating the number of miles per gallon each model is expected to get (as determined by EPA tests) for both city and highway driving. You can check out those ratings at **http://www.fueleconomy.gov.**
- **Safety features:** Government regulations ensure that these features are likely to be similar in new cars, but older used cars may not have some features, such as side-impact airbags. Don't forget to include *auto insurance costs,* which vary depending on make, model, safety features, and other factors (and are discussed in detail in Chapter 10).

5-1c The Purchase Transaction

Once you've determined what you can afford to spend and the features that you want, you're ready to begin car shopping. If you plan to buy a new car, visit all dealers with cars that meet your requirements. Look the cars over and ask questions—but don't make any offers until you've found two or three cars with the desired features that are priced within your budget. Also, if you can be flexible about the model and options you want, you can sometimes negotiate a better deal than if you're determined to have a particular model and options. Make an appointment to test-drive the cars you're interested in. Drive—then leave! You need time to evaluate the car without pressure to buy from the salesperson.

Image Source/Getty Images

Comparison shopping is essential, because a dealer selling the same brand as another may give you a better deal. Be aware of the sales technique called *lowballing,* where the salesperson quotes a low price for the car to get you to make an offer, and then negotiates the price upward prior to your signing the sales contract. Exhibit 5.3 lists some other factors to consider once you begin looking at cars.

Because lowballing, price haggling, and other high-pressure sales tactics can make car buying an unpleasant experience, many dealers have refocused their sales practices to emphasize customer satisfaction. Some manufacturers offer firm prices, so if you buy today, you can be sure that no one will get a better deal tomorrow. However, you should still research prices, as described in the next section, because a firm selling price doesn't guarantee the lowest cost.

EXHIBIT 5.3   **Finding the Best Car for You**

Start by inspecting the key points of the car. Don't overlook the obvious.

1. *How easy is it to get people and things into and out of the car?*
    - Do the doors open easily?
    - Is the trunk large enough for your needs?
    - Does the car offer a pass-through or fold-down rear seat to accommodate larger items?

2. *Comfort and visibility.*
    - Are the seats comfortable?
    - Can you adjust the driver's seat and steering wheel properly?
    - What are the car's blind spots for a person of your height?
    - Can you see all the gauges clearly?
    - Can you reach the controls for the radio, audio player, heater, air conditioner, and other features easily while driving?
    - Does it have the options you want?

Then take the car for a test drive.

1. Set aside at least 20 minutes and drive it on highways and local roads.

2. To test acceleration, merge into traffic getting onto the freeway and try passing another car.

3. If possible, drive home and make sure the car fits into your garage—especially if you're interested in a larger SUV or truck!

4. For a used car, test the heater and air conditioner. Then turn the fan off and listen for any unusual engine noises.

5. Check out overall handling. Parallel park, make a U-turn, brake hard, and so on. Do the gears shift smoothly? If testing a standard transmission, try to determine if the clutch is engaging too high or too low, which might indicate excessive wear or a problem.

As soon as you return to the car lot, take notes on how well the car handled and how comfortable you felt driving it.

This is especially important if you are test driving several cars.

Negotiating Price

Choosing among various makes, models, and options can make comparisons difficult. The price you pay for a car, whether new or used, can consequently vary widely. The more you narrow your choices to a particular car, the easier it is to get price quotes from dealers to make an "apples-to-apples" comparison.

The "sticker price" on a new car represents the manufacturer's *suggested retail price* for that particular car with its listed options. This price means very little. The key to negotiating a good price is knowing the *dealer's cost* for the car. The easiest and quickest way to find the dealer's invoice cost is going to the Edmunds and Kelley Blue Book Internet sites mentioned in this chapter or by checking car-buying guides available at your library or bookstore.

Before making an offer, prepare a worksheet with the cost versus the list price for the exact car you want. This will help you avoid high pressure by the salesperson and paying for options you don't want or need. Try to negotiate the lowest acceptable markup (3 percent to 4 percent for cars priced under $20,000; 6 percent to 7 percent for higher-priced models), push for a firm quote, and make it clear that you are comparison shopping. Don't let the salesperson pressure you into signing a sales contract or leaving a deposit until you're sure that you have negotiated the best deal. Good cost information will improve your bargaining position and possibly allow you to negotiate a price that is only several hundred dollars above the dealer's cost.

If you want to avoid negotiating entirely, you can buy your car through a buying service, either by phone or over the Internet. These include independent companies—such as AutoVantage (**http://www.autovantage.com**), Autobytel (**http://www.autobytel.com**), and AutoWeb (**http://www.autoweb.com**)—or services offered through credit unions, motor clubs, and discount warehouses such as Costco. Buying services work in a variety of ways. They may have an arrangement with a network of dealers to sell cars at a predetermined price above invoice, provide you with competitive bids from several local dealers, find the car you want and negotiate the price with the dealer, or place an order with the factory for a made-to-order car. You'll get a good price through a service—although you can't assume that it will be the best price.

It's best not to discuss your plan to finance the purchase or the value of your trade-in until you've settled the question of price. These should be separate issues. Salespeople will typically want to find out how much you can afford monthly and then offer financing deals with payments close to that amount. In the case of trade-ins, the dealer might offer you a good price for your old car and raise the price of the new car to compensate. The dealer may offer financing terms that sound attractive, but be sure to compare them with the cost of bank loans. Sometimes dealers increase the price of the car to make up for a low interest rate, or attractive financing may apply only to certain models. Often financing charges include unneeded extras such as credit life insurance, accident insurance, an extended warranty, or a service package.

Manufacturers and dealers often offer buyers special incentives, such as rebates and cut-rate financing, particularly when car sales are slow. (Deduct rebates from the dealer's cost when you negotiate price.) You may have a choice between a rebate and low-cost financing. To determine which is the better deal, calculate the difference between the monthly payments on a market-rate bank loan and the special dealer loan for the same term. Multiply the payment difference by the loan maturity, in months, and compare it with the rebate.

> **EXAMPLE: Is That Rebate a Good Deal?**
>
> A car dealer offers either a $1,000 rebate or a 4 percent interest rate on a $10,000, 4-year loan. Your monthly payments would be $226 with dealer financing and $234 on a 6 percent bank loan with similar terms. The payment savings over the life of the loan are $384 ($8 per month 3 48 months), which is less than the $1,000 rebate. So in this case you would be better off with the rebate.

Closing the Deal

Whether you're buying a new or used car, to make a legally binding offer, you must sign a **sales contract** that specifies the offering price and all the conditions of your offer. The sales contract also specifies whether the offer includes a trade-in. If it does,

sales contract
An agreement to purchase an automobile that states the offering price and all conditions of the offer; when signed by the buyer and seller, the contract legally binds them to its terms.

You Can Do It Now

What's Your Car Worth?

If you have a car, it's good to know what it's worth from time-to-time. That way you'll have a better sense of your net worth and you'll know how much your car is depreciating over time. Just go to the Kelley Blue book site at **http://www.kbb.com** and go to the "Price New/Used Cars"—you can do it now.

the offering price will include both the payment amount and the trade-in allowance. Because this agreement contractually binds you to purchase the car at the offering price, be sure that you want and can afford the car before signing this agreement. You may be required to include a deposit of around $200 or more with the contract to show that you're making an offer in good faith.

Once the dealer accepts your offer, you complete the purchase transaction and take delivery of the car. If you're not paying cash for the car, you can arrange financing through the dealer, at your bank, a credit union, or a consumer finance company. The key aspects of these types of installment loans, which can be quickly negotiated if your credit is good, are discussed in Chapter 7. Prior to delivery, the dealer is responsible for cleaning the car and installing any optional equipment. It's a good idea to make sure that all equipment you are paying for has been installed and that the car is ready for use before paying the dealer. When you pay for the car in full, you should receive a title or appropriate evidence that you own the car.

Refinancing Your Auto Loan

Refinancing your auto loan can pay off—but only under particular circumstances. First, you need to have enough equity in the car to serve as collateral for what is essentially a used car loan. If you made a large down payment or are well into a loan, then you may be a candidate for refinancing. If you can cut your interest rate by at least 2 percentage points without stretching the final payment date of your current loan, you could enjoy substantial savings.

Banks generally aren't interested in refinancing car loans, so online lenders such as E-Loan (**http://www.eloan.com**) and HSBC Auto Finance (**http://www.auto-loan-center.com/lenders-hsbc.php**) get most of that business. If you're a member of a credit union, see what it can do for you. If you own a home, consider tapping a home equity line of credit to pay off a high-interest auto loan. Unlike consumer loans, the interest paid on a home equity loan is tax deductible. Wherever you choose to refinance, you'll probably have to pay $5 to $50 for a title change listing the new lien holder. And forget about refinancing your auto loan if you have bad credit.

Traditionally, car loans were for three or four years, but loan terms are lengthening as buyers stretch to afford cars that can top $40,000 or even $50,000. These loans typically carry higher interest rates. It is common for six-year loan rates to exceed four-year loan rates by 0.75 percent or more. However, the monthly payments are smaller than those on the shorter-term loans. So far, only a handful of banks and credit unions are offering eight-year loans, but many now offer seven-year loans. Today, five-year and longer loans account for over half of all new car loans. Long-term loans are most commonly used to buy high-end luxury vehicles and are not available for all vehicles. By the end of the loan term, you'll still be making payments on a vehicle that has used up most of its life and is practically worthless—a major downside of longer-term car loans.

JUICE IMAGES/GETTY IMAGES

5-1 Briefly discuss how each of these purchase considerations would affect your choice of a car:

a. Affordability

b. Operating costs

c. Gas, diesel, hybrid, or electric?

d. New, used, or "nearly new"?

e. Size, body style, and features

f. Reliability and warranty protection

5-2 Describe the purchase transaction process, including shopping, negotiating price, and closing the deal on a car.

5-2 LEASING A CAR

lease
An arrangement in which the lessee receives the use of a car (or other asset) in exchange for making monthly lease payments over a specified period.

Don't worry about temperamental engines or transmissions—you could just get a new car every few years using a leasing arrangement. Put a small amount down, make easy payments. No wonder leasing is popular, accounting for about 25 percent of all new vehicles delivered. When you **lease**, you (the lessee) receive the use of a car in exchange for monthly lease payments over a specified period, usually two to four years. Leasing appeals to a wide range of car buyers, even though the total cost of leasing is generally more than buying a car with a loan, and at the end of the lease, you have nothing. The car—and the money you paid to rent it—are gone. So why do so many car buyers lease their cars? Reasons include rising new car prices, the nondeductibility of consumer loan interest, lower monthly payments, driving a more expensive car for the same monthly payment, and minimizing the down payment to preserve cash.

With all the advertisements promising low monthly lease payments, it's easy to focus on only the payment. Unlike a loan purchase, with a lease you're paying not for the whole car but only for its use during a specified period. Leasing is a more complex arrangement than borrowing money to buy a car. Until you understand how leasing works and compare lease terms with bank financing, you won't know if leasing is the right choice for you.

closed-end lease
The most popular form of automobile lease; often called a *walk-away lease*, because at the end of its term the lessee simply turns in the car (assuming the preset mileage limit has not been exceeded and the car hasn't been abused).

open-end (finance) lease
An automobile lease under which the estimated *residual value* of the car is used to determine lease payments; if the car is actually worth less than this value at the end of the lease, the lessee must pay the difference.

residual value
The remaining value of a leased car at the end of the lease term.

5-2a The Leasing Process

The first step is the same for leasing and purchasing: research car types and brands, comparison shop at several dealers, and find the car you want at the best price. Don't ask the dealer about leasing or any financing incentives until *after* you've negotiated the final price. Then compare the lease terms offered by the dealer to those of at least one independent leasing firm. As with a purchase, try to negotiate lower lease payments—a payment reduction of $20 a month saves nearly $1,000 on a four-year lease. And don't reveal what you can afford to pay per month; doing so can lead you to a poor lease deal. Once you agree on leasing terms, be sure to get everything in writing.

The majority of car lessees choose the **closed-end lease**, often called the *walk-away lease*, because at the end of its term you simply turn in the car, assuming that you have neither exceeded the preset mileage limit nor abused the car. This is the dominant type of lease used by consumers. Under the less popular **open-end** or **finance lease**, if the car is worth less than the estimated **residual value**—the remaining value of the car at the end of the lease term—then you must pay the difference. These leases are used primarily for commercial business leasing.

A commonly cited benefit of leasing is the absence of a down payment. However, most leases require a "capital cost reduction," which is a down payment that lowers the potential depreciation and therefore your monthly lease payments. You may be able to negotiate a lower capital cost reduction or find a lease that doesn't require one.

The lease payment calculation is based on four variables:

capitalized cost
The price of a car that is being leased.

money factor
The financing rate on a lease; similar to the interest rate on a loan.

1. The capitalized cost of the car (the price of the car you are leasing)
2. The forecast *residual value* of the car at the end of the lease
3. The money factor, or financing rate on the lease (similar to the interest rate on a loan)
4. The *lease term*

The *depreciation* during the lease term (which is what you are financing) is the capitalized cost minus the residual value. Dividing the sum of the depreciation and the sales tax (on the financed portion only) by the number of months in the lease term and then adding the lessor's required monthly return (at the money factor) results in the monthly payment. (To convert the money factor to an annual percentage rate, multiply it by 2,400; for example, a money factor of 0.0025 is the equivalent of paying 6 percent interest on a loan.) The lower the capitalized cost and higher the residual value, the lower your payment. Residual values quoted by different dealers can vary, so check several sources to find the highest residual value to minimize depreciation.

Lease terms typically run two to four years. Terminating a lease early is often difficult and costly, so be reasonably sure that you can keep the car for the full lease term. The lease contract should outline any costs and additional fees associated with early termination. Early termination clauses also apply to cars that are stolen or totaled in an accident. Some leases require "gap insurance" to cover the lost lease payments that would result from early termination caused by one of these events.

Under most leases, you are responsible for insuring and maintaining the car. At the end of the lease, you are obligated to pay for any "unreasonable wear and tear." A good lease contract should clearly define what is considered unreasonable. In addition, most leases require the lessee to pay a disposition fee of about $150 to $250 when the car is returned.

purchase option
A price specified in a lease at which the lessee can buy the car at the end of the lease term.

Most auto leases include a purchase option (either a fixed price, the market price at the end of the lease term, or the residual value of the car) that specifies the price at which the lessee can buy the car at the end of the lease term. A lower residual results in a lower purchase price but raises monthly payments. Experts recommend negotiating a fixed-price purchase option, if possible.

The annual mileage allowance—typically, about 10,000 to 15,000 miles per year for the lease term—is another important lease consideration. Usually the lessee must pay between 10 and 25 cents per mile for additional miles. If you expect to exceed the allowable mileage, you would be wise to negotiate a more favorable rate for extra miles before signing the lease contract.

FINANCIAL ROAD SIGN

Auto Leasing Checklist

Smart buyers will know the following figures before attempting to negotiate a car lease:

- List price for the car and options
- Capitalized cost (the value on which monthly payments are based)
- Money factor (interest rate assumption)
- Total interest paid
- Total sales tax
- Residual value for which the car can be purchased at the lease's end
- Depreciation (the capitalized cost minus the residual value)
- Lease term (period)

5-2b Lease versus Purchase Analysis

To decide whether it is less costly to lease rather than purchase a car, you need to perform a *lease versus purchase analysis* to compare the total cost of leasing to the total cost of purchasing a car over equal periods. In this analysis, the purchase is assumed to be financed with an installment loan over the same period as the lease.

For example, assume that Mary Dixon is considering either leasing or purchasing a new Toyota Prius costing $29,990. The four-year, closed-end lease that she is considering requires a $2,900 down payment (capital cost reduction), a $500 security deposit, and monthly payments of $440, including sales tax. If she purchases the car, she will make a $4,500 down payment and finance the balance with a four-year, 4 percent loan requiring monthly payments of about $576. She will also have to pay 5 percent sales tax ($1,500) on the purchase, and she expects the car to have a residual value of $16,500 at the end of 4 years. Mary can earn 3 percent interest on her savings with short-term CDs. After filling in Worksheet 5.1, Mary concludes that purchasing is better because its *total cost* of $17,665.42 is $6,762.58 less than the $24,428.00 total cost of leasing—even though the monthly lease payment is about $136 lower. Clearly, all else being equal, the least costly alternative of purchasing is preferred to leasing.

If you're fortunate enough to be able to pay cash for your car, you may still want to investigate leasing. Sometimes dealers offer such good lease terms that you can come out ahead by leasing and then investing the money you would have paid for the car. The decision to make a cash purchase rather than to finance it depends on the cost of the car, the financing cost, the rate of return that could be earned on investing the purchase price, and the trade-in value of the car at the end of the lease period. More specifically, to compare the total cost of a cash purchase, simply take the cost of the car (including sales tax), add to it the opportunity cost of using all cash, and deduct the car's value at the end of the lease or loan period. At 3 percent per year on her savings, Mary's total cost of the car is as follows: $31,489.50 cost + $3,778.74 lost interest ($4 \times 0.03 \times \$31,489.50$) − $16,500 trade-in value = $18,768.24. Compare this with the previously determined cost of buying the car using financing, which is $17,665.42. Thus, in this case, the cost of purchasing the car for cash is about $1,102.82 more than its purchase cost with financing. So Mary would be better off using the financing.

5-2c When the Lease Ends

At the end of the lease, you'll be faced with a major decision. Should you return the car and walk away, or should you buy the car? If you turn in the car and move on to a new model, you may be hit with "excess wear and damage" and "excess mileage" charges and disposition fees. To minimize these, replace worn tires, get repairs done yourself,

FINANCIAL
ROAD
SIGN

When Does It Make Sense to Lease a Car?

The most important question to ask yourself is why you need a new car every few years. Leasing may make sense if:

- **You value purchasing flexibility.** A lease allows you to put off the purchasing decision while using the car. It's like having a test drive that lasts several years instead of a few minutes.
- **You value the convenience of not having to deal with significant auto repairs.**
- **You're self-employed and can take the leasing payment as a tax-deductible business expense.**
- **You want to drive a luxury car for less, but you don't want to put up that much money.**

The key is being honest about why you want to lease and being informed about the costs and benefits of a leasing arrangement.

This worksheet illustrates Mary Dixon's lease versus purchase analysis for a new Toyota Prius costing $29,990. The four-year closed-end lease requires an initial payment of $3,400 ($2,900 down payment + $500 security deposit) and monthly payments of $440. Purchasing requires a $4,500 down payment, sales tax of 5 percent ($1,499.50), and 48 monthly payments of $575.45. The trade-in value of the new car at the end of four years is estimated to be $16,500. *Because the total cost of leasing of $24,428 is greater than the $17,665.42 total cost of purchasing, Mary should purchase rather than lease the car.*

AUTOMOBILE LEASE VERSUS PURCHASE ANALYSIS*

Name _Mary Dixon_   Date _Sep 11, 2017_

Item Description		Amount
LEASE		
1 Initial payment:		
a. Down payment (capital cost reduction):	$ 2,900.00	
b. Security deposit:	500.00	$ 3,400.00
2 Term of lease and loan (years)*		4
3 Term of lease and loan (months) (Item 2 × 12)		48
4 Monthly lease payment		$ 440.00
5 Total payments over term of lease (Item 3 × Item 4)		$ 21,120.00
6 Interest rate earned on savings (in decimal form)		$ 0.030
7 Opportunity cost of initial payment (Item 1 × Item 2 × Item 6)		$ 408.00
8 Payment/refund for market value adjustment at end of lease ($0 for closed-end leases) and/or estimated end-of-term charges		$ 0.00
9 Total cost of leasing (Item 1a + Item 5 + Item 7 + Item 8)		$ 24,428.00
PURCHASE		
10 Purchase price		$ 29,990.00
11 Down payment		$ 4,500.00
12 Sales tax rate (in decimal form)		$ 0.50
13 Sales tax (Item 10 × Item 12)		$ 1,499.50
14 Monthly loan payment (Terms: _25,490.00_ , _48_ months, _4_ %)		$ 575.54
15 Total payments over term of loan (Item 3 × Item 14)		$ 27,625.92
16 Opportunity cost of down payment (Item 2 × Item 6 × Item 11)		$ 540.00
17 Estimated value of car at end of loan		$ 16,500.00
18 Total cost of purchasing (Item 11 + Item 13 + Item 15 + Item 16 − Item 17)		$ 17,665.42

DECISION

If the value of Item 9 is less than the value of Item 18, leasing is preferred; otherwise, the *purchase alternative is preferred.*

*Note: This form is based on assumed equal terms for the lease and the installment loan, which is assumed to be used to finance the purchase.

and document the car's condition before returning it. You may be able to negotiate a lower disposition fee. If you can't return the car without high repair charges or greatly exceeded mileage allowances, you may come out ahead by buying the car.

Whether the purchase option makes sense depends largely on the residual value. With popular cars, the residual value in your lease agreement may be lower than the car's trade-in value. Buying the car then makes sense. Even if you want a different car, you can exercise the purchase option and sell the car on the open market to net the difference, which could be $1,000 or more. If the reverse is true and the residual is higher than the price of a comparable used car, just let the lease expire. Find your car's market value by looking in used car price guides and newspaper ads and comparing it with the residual value of your car in the lease agreement.

TEST YOURSELF

5-3   What are the advantages and disadvantages of leasing a car?

5-4   Given your personal financial circumstances, if you were buying a car today, would you probably pay cash, lease, or finance it, and why? Which factors are most important to you in making this decision?

5-3   MEETING HOUSING NEEDS: BUY OR RENT?

LG3

5-3a Housing Prices and the Recent Financial Crisis

Before considering how and when to buy or rent a home, it is important to consider the recent rough history of housing prices during and after the financial crisis of 2008–2009. After examining this context in which housing decisions are made, we'll consider how to know when you should buy your first home. There are many factors to consider before taking on such a large financial responsibility. In the remainder of this chapter, we'll explore some of these factors and discuss how to approach the home-buying and renting process.

From early 2001 through 2006, home prices in the United States rose rapidly. The median nominal sales price of existing homes rose from $141,600 to $230,400. Existing home prices started dropping and fell to a median price of $154,600 in early 2012. Prices had fallen because the real estate bubble had popped and the financial crisis of 2008–2009 had vastly depressed home sales. This period of recession was characterized by high unemployment, low consumer confidence, and tighter credit. Indeed, about 1 in 7 American homeowners had *negative equity*: owing more on their mortgage than their homes were worth.

The bubble in real estate prices had several important side effects. It encouraged a massive increase in construction and the extraction of a lot of home equity through home equity loans and refinancings, about two-thirds of which went into increased consumption. Net worth increased with home prices as well. Yet those side effects went in the opposite direction during the financial crisis. Between 2007 and 2009, the crisis reduced the average family's net worth by about 23 percent and dampened consumption, which slowed the macroeconomy. Home foreclosures, the process whereby lenders attempt to recover loan balances from borrowers who have quit making payments by forcing the sale of the home pledged as collateral, increased significantly.

Although housing prices and the number of home sales result from a variety of economic and behavioral factors, it's generally agreed that increasing interest rates tend to slow the volume (and prices) of home sales. Conversely, declines in mortgage rates tend to increase the volume of home sales (and prices). However, as shown in Exhibit 5.4, prices vary widely from one part of the country to another.

foreclosure
The process whereby lenders attempt to recover loan balances from borrowers who have quit making payments by forcing the sale of the home pledged as collateral.

5-3b What Type of Housing Meets Your Needs?

Because you have your own unique set of likes and dislikes, the best way to start your search for housing is to list your preferences and classify them according to whether their satisfaction is essential, desirable, or merely a "plus." This exercise is important for three reasons. First, it screens out housing that doesn't meet your minimum

Behavior Matters

Did the Real Estate Bubble Result from Behavioral Biases?

There's a tendency for us to sometimes exhibit herding behavior. Well-known Yale behavioral economist and Nobel laureate Robert Shiller argues that after the rapid run-up in real estate prices between 2001 and 2006, a "social epidemic" encouraged the belief that housing was a critical investment opportunity that shouldn't be missed. And there is a behavioral bias, known as the *conservatism bias*, which encourages us to rely too heavily on past experience and to revise our expectations for the future too slowly in light of new, relevant information. These psychological biases only fed additional housing price increases apart from the underlying real estate investment fundamentals, which supported the development of the real estate bubble.

Others argue that households generally have trouble distinguishing between real (inflation-adjusted) and nominal (unadjusted for inflation) changes in interest rates and rents. Thus, when expected inflation drops, consumers buy homes to take advantage of apparently low nominal financing costs, without realizing that future home price and rent appreciation rates will fall by comparable amounts. The falling inflation and the associated "inflation illusion" in the early 2000s consequently brought unjustified real estate price spikes, which culminated in the housing bubble and it's subsequent dramatic pop.

EXHIBIT 5.4 **Home Prices in Different Regions of the U.S.**

The median sales price of existing homes varies widely from one part of the country to another—$299,600 in the Western states, $159,100 in the Midwest, $184,100 in the South, and $246,600 in the Northeast.

West: median price $299,600

Midwest: median price $159,100

Northeast: median price $246,600

South: median price $184,100

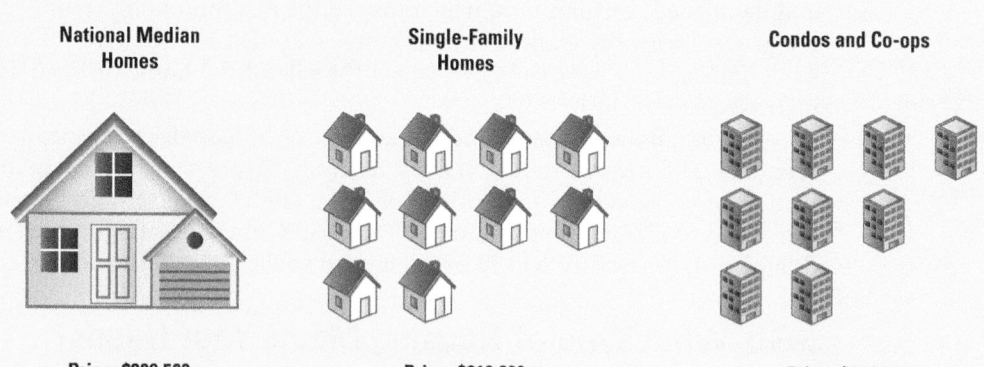

National Median Homes	Single-Family Homes	Condos and Co-ops
Price: $209,500	Price: $210,200	Price: $204,000

Source: National Association of Realtors, "Infographic: December 2014 Existing-Home Sales," http://www.realtor.org/infographics/infographic-december-2014-existing-home-sales, accessed August 2015.

requirements. Second, it helps you recognize that you may have to make trade-offs, because seldom will you find a single home that meets all your needs. Third, it will help you focus on those needs for which you are willing and able to pay.

One of the first decisions you'll have to make is the type of housing unit that you want and need. Several of the following may be suitable:

- **Single-family homes:** These are the most popular choice. They can be stand-alone homes on their own legally defined lots or *row houses* or *townhouses* that share a common wall. As a rule, single-family homes offer buyers privacy, prestige, pride of ownership, and maximum property control.

condominium (condo)
A form of direct ownership of an individual unit in a multiunit project in which lobbies, swimming pools, and other common areas and facilities are jointly owned by all property owners in the project.

- **Condominiums:** The term condominium, or condo, describes a form of ownership rather than a type of building. Condominiums can be apartments, townhouses, or cluster housing. The condominium buyer receives title to an individual residential unit and joint ownership of common areas and facilities such as lobbies, swimming pools, lakes, and tennis courts. Buyers arrange their own mortgages and pay their own taxes for their units. They are assessed a monthly *homeowner's fee* for their proportionate share of common facility maintenance costs. The *homeowners' association* elects a board of managers to supervise the buildings and grounds. Condominiums generally cost less than single-family detached homes because they're designed for more efficient land use and lower construction costs. Many home buyers are attracted to condominiums because they don't want the responsibility of maintaining and caring for a property. Exhibit 5.5 lists some of the key things to check before buying a condominium.

cooperative apartment (co-op)
An apartment in a building in which each tenant owns a share of the nonprofit corporation that owns the building.

- **Cooperative apartments:** In a cooperative apartment, or co-op, building, each tenant owns a share of the nonprofit corporation that owns the building. Residents lease their units from the corporation and pay a monthly assessment in proportion to ownership shares, based on the space they occupy. These assessments cover the cost of services, maintenance, taxes, and the mortgage on the entire building and are subject to change, depending on the actual costs of operating the building and the actions of the board of directors, which determines the corporation's policies. The cooperative owner receives the tax benefits resulting from interest and property taxes attributable to his or her

| EXHIBIT 5.5 | Condo Buyer's Checklist |

It pays to carefully check out the various operating and occupancy features of a condo before you buy.

- Thoroughly investigate the developer's reputation—through local real estate brokers, banks, or the Better Business Bureau—whether the building is brand new, under construction, or being converted.
- Investigate the condo homeowners' association, the restrictions on condo owners, and the quality of the property management. Read the rules of the organization.
- Check the construction of the building and its physical condition. If the building is being converted to condos, ask to see an independent inspection firm's report on the building's condition.
- Insist that any planned changes to the property be detailed in writing.
- Talk to the current occupants to see if they are satisfied with the living conditions.
- Determine how many units are rented; generally, owner-occupied units are better maintained.
- Determine if there is sufficient parking space.
- Watch for unusually low maintenance fees that may have to be increased soon.
- Consider the resale value.

For new developments, compare the projected monthly homeowner's fees with those of similar buildings already in operation. For older developments, check to see when capital improvements such as exterior painting and roof replacement were last made. Special assessments are usually levied on all unit owners for major costly improvements.

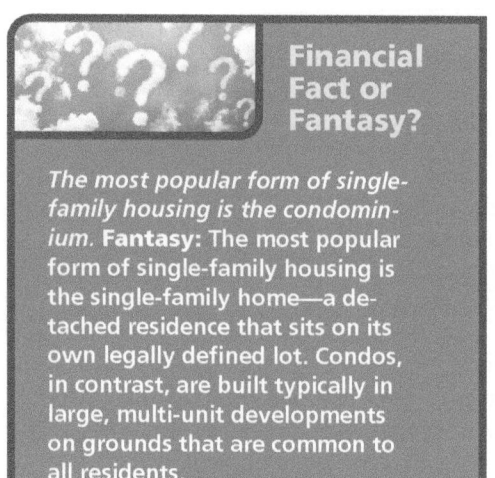
proportionate ownership interest. Drawbacks of co-op ownership include difficulty in obtaining a mortgage (because many financial institutions don't like taking shares of a corporation rather than property as collateral), rent increases to cover maintenance costs of vacant units, and the need to abide by the capital improvement decisions of the co-op board of directors, which can increase the monthly assessment.

- **Rental units:** Some individuals and families choose to *rent* or *lease* their place of residence rather than own it. They may be just starting out and have limited funds for housing, or they may be uncertain where they want to live. Perhaps they like the short-term commitment and limited maintenance responsibilities. The cost and availability of rental units varies from one geographic area to another. Rental units range from duplexes, fourplexes, and even single-family homes to large, high-rise apartment complexes containing several hundred units. Renting does come with restrictions, however. For example, you may not be allowed to have a pet or make changes to the unit's appearance.

5-3c The Rental Option

Many people choose to rent rather than buy their home. For example, young adults usually rent for one or more of the following reasons: (1) they don't have the funds for a down payment and closing costs, (2) they're unsettled in their jobs and family status, (3) they don't want the additional responsibilities associated with homeownership, or (4) they believe they can afford a nicer home later by renting now because housing market conditions or mortgage rates are currently unattractive. A big drawback of renting is that the payments are *not* tax deductible.

The Rental Contract (Lease Agreement)

**rental contract
lease agreement**

A legal instrument that protects both the *lessor* and the *lessee* from an adverse action by the other party; it specifies the *amount* of the monthly payment, the payment *due date, penalties* for late payment, the *length* of the lease agreement, *deposit* requirements, *fair wear and tear* definitions and provisions, the distribution of *expenses, renewal* options and *early termination penalties,* and any *restrictions* on children, pets, subleasing or using the facilities.

When you rent an apartment, duplex, house, or any other type of residence, you'll be required to sign a rental contract or lease agreement. Although oral agreements are generally binding, a written contract is a legal instrument that better protects both the *lessor* (the person who owns the property) and the *lessee* (the person who leases the property). Because the rental contract binds you, the lessee, to various actions, be sure that you fully understand it before signing it. As a rule, the contract specifies the *amount* of the monthly payment, the payment *due date, penalties* for late payment, the *length* of the lease agreement, security and/or advance rent (*deposit*) requirements, *fair wear and tear* definitions and provisions, the distribution of *expenses, lease renewal* options and *early termination penalties,* and any *restrictions* on children, pets, subleasing, or using the facilities.

Most leases have a minimum term of either six months or one year and require payments at the beginning of each month. They may initially require a security deposit and/or payment of the last month's rent in advance as security against damages or violation of the lease agreement. If there's no serious damage, most of the deposit should be refunded to the lessee shortly after the lease expires. A portion of the deposit is sometimes retained by the lessor to cover the cost of cleaning and minor repairs, regardless of how clean and well kept the unit was. Because the landlord controls the deposit, a written statement describing any preexisting damage, *prior to* occupancy, may help the lessee avoid losing their entire deposit. Renters should also clarify who bears expenses such as utilities and trash collection and exactly what, if any, restrictions are placed on the use of the property. It's also a good idea for renters to check the renter–landlord laws in their state to fully understand their *rights* and responsibilities.

Evaluating the General Attractiveness of Renting versus Buying a Home

rent ratio
The ratio of the average house price to the average annual rent, which provides insight into the relative attractiveness of buying a house versus renting in a given area of potential interest.

You can get a general sense of the relative cost of renting versus buying a home by considering the so-called **rent ratio**, which is the ratio of the average house price to the average annual rent in the area that you are considering. Given the bursting of the housing bubble in the late 2000s, the inflation-adjusted rent ratio steadily fell to around late-1990 levels. Thus, the relative attractiveness of renting has decreased in recent years. Exhibit 5.6 shows the nominal rent ratios for major U.S. cities, which differ significantly in the relative attractiveness of buying versus renting. Rent ratios between 31 and 35 indicate that it is more attractive to rent than to buy. At the other extreme, a rent ratio between 6 and 10 indicates that it is more attractive to buy than to rent. And a moderate rent ratio (between 16 and 20) suggests that while renting is expensive, it may still be better to buy. Exhibit 5.6 shows that nationally in late 2014 it was generally 38 percent cheaper to buy than to rent. However, the decision

---

| EXHIBIT 5.6 | **Relative Attractiveness of Renting versus Buying a House** |

The Trulia Rent vs. Buy Index portrays the average list price of homes versus the average annual rent on two-bedroom apartments, condos, and townhomes in America's 50 largest cities by population listed on Trulia.com. Note the highlighted mortgage rate, tax bracket, and expected home holding period assumptions.

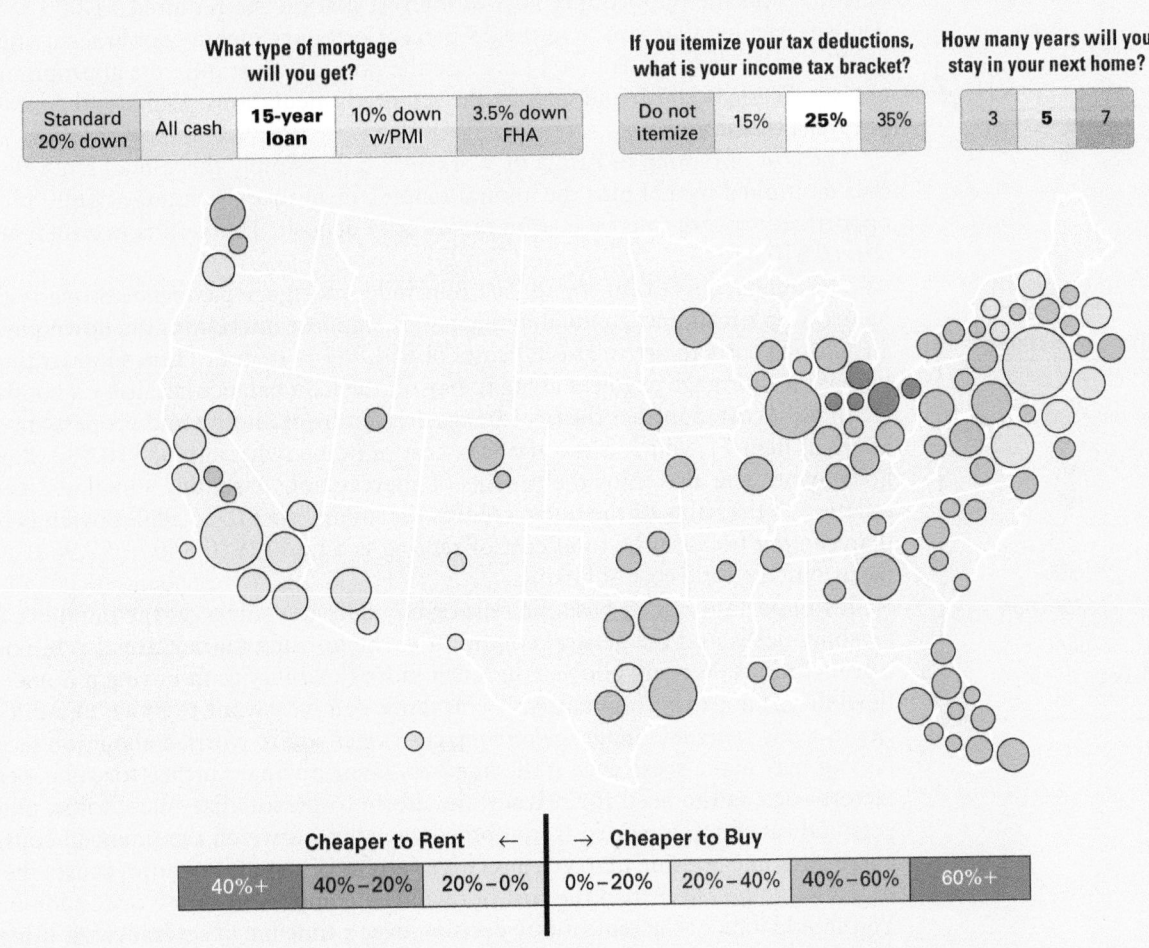

Source: "Rent vs. Buy: Which Is Cheaper for You?" http://www.trulia.com/trends/vis/rentvsbuy-q3-2014/, accessed August 2015.

was closer in California and New York City. The gap between the benefits of buying vs. renting was widest in the Midwest and the South. You may want to consider the rent ratio when considering where to relocate or to form some basic expectations if you've decided where to move.

Analyzing the Rent-or-Buy Decision

Owning a home is not always more costly on a monthly basis than renting, although there are many other factors to consider before making this important decision. The economics of renting or buying a place to live depends on four main factors: (1) housing prices and mortgage interest rates, (2) tax write-offs for homeowners, (3) the expected increase or decrease in home values over time, and (4) how many years you expect to stay in your home.

To choose the lowest-cost alternative, compare the cost of renting with the cost of buying, as illustrated by the rent-or-buy analysis in Worksheet 5.2. Note that because the interest deduction nearly always exceeds the amount of the standard deduction ($6,300 for single and $12,600 for married filing jointly in 2015), the form assumes that the taxpayer will itemize deductions. Suppose that you must decide between renting an apartment for $850 a month or buying a similar-sized condominium for $150,000. Purchasing the condo involves a $30,000 down payment; a $120,000, 6 percent, 30-year mortgage with monthly mortgage payments of $719; $4,500 in closing costs; and property taxes, insurance, and maintenance. With renting, the only costs are the $850 monthly rental payment, an annual renter's insurance premium of $600, and the opportunity cost of interest lost on the required $1,000 security deposit. Assume that you're in the 25 percent ordinary income tax bracket and that you'll itemize deductions if you purchase the home. Substituting the appropriate values into Worksheet 5.2 and making the required calculations results in the total cost of each alternative.

The cost of renting in Part A of Worksheet 5.2 is simply the annual rent (monthly rent multiplied by 12) plus the annual renter's insurance premium of $600 plus the opportunity cost of interest lost on the security deposit. This results in a total annual cost of $10,840.

The annual cost of buying in Part B includes mortgage payments, property taxes, homeowner's insurance, annual maintenance, and lost interest on the down payment and closing costs to arrive at total costs of $14,964 in Item 6. Then, subtract the portion of the mortgage payment going to pay off the loan balance because it's not part of the interest cost. Subtract the tax savings derived from interest and property taxes to arrive at Item 11, which is the after-tax cost of homeownership of $10,980. But as a homeowner, you also enjoy the benefits of appreciation. Assuming a modest 2 percent inflation in the value of the home reduces the annual cost to $7,980. Buying is better than renting because the total cost of renting is $2,860 ($10,840 − $7,980) a year more than the total cost of buying.

It's important *not* to base the rent-or-buy decision solely on the numbers. Your personal needs and the general condition of the housing market are also important considerations. Renting allows you much more flexibility than buying a home—but flexibility is not easy to quantify. If you think you may want to move to a different city in a few years and incur the moving costs or if you're worried about job security, renting may make sense even if the numbers favor buying. Further, for some people, factors such as the need for privacy, the desire to personalize one's home, and the personal satisfaction gained from homeownership outweigh the financial considerations. In some housing markets, a relative surplus of rental properties causes the cost of renting to be lower than the cost of owning a comparable house or condominium. You should look at the rent-or-buy decision over a timeline of several years, using different assumptions regarding rent increases, mortgage rates, home appreciation rates in the area, and the rate of return that you can earn on the funds you could invest (if you rent) rather than use toward a down payment on a house (if you buy).

Calculator

INPUTS	FUNCTIONS
120000	PV
360	N
6	÷
12	=
	I
	CPT
	PMT
	SOLUTION
	719.46

See Appendix E for details.

Calculator

INPUTS	FUNCTIONS
180000	PV
360	N
6	÷
12	=
	I
	CPT
	PMT
	SOLUTION
	1079.19

See Appendix E for details.

With this procedure for making the rent-or-buy decision, you should *rent* if the total cost of renting is less than the total cost of buying, or *buy* if the total cost of renting is more than the total cost of buying. In this example, the rental option requires monthly payments of $850. The purchase option is a $150,000 condo, financed with a $30,000 down payment and a $120,000, 6 percent, 30-year mortgage, with additional closing costs of $4,500.

RENT-OR-BUY ANALYSIS

A. COST OF RENTING

1. Annual rental costs
   (12 × monthly rental rate of $ 850) .... $ 10,200

2. Renter's insurance 600

3. Opportunity cost of security deposit: $ 1,000 × after-tax savings rate 0.040 40
   Total cost of renting (line A.1 + line A.2 + line A.3) .... $ 10,840

B. COST OF BUYING

1. Annual mortgage payments (Terms: $ 120,000 , 360 months, 6 %) $ 8,634
   (12 × monthly mortgage payment of $ 719)

2. Property taxes 3,000
   (2.0% of price of home)

3. Homeowner's insurance 750
   (0.5% of price of home)

4. Maintenance 1,200
   (0.8% of price of home)

5. After-tax cost of interest on down payment and closing costs 1,380
   ($ 34,500 × 4.0 % after-tax rate of return)

6. Total costs (sum of lines B.1 through B.5) .... $ 14,964

Less:

7. Principal reduction in loan balance (see note below) .... $ 1,434

8. Tax savings due to interest deductions* 1,800
   (Interest portion of mortgage payments $ 7,200 × tax rate of 25 %)

9. Tax savings due to property tax deductions* 750
   (line B.2 × tax rate of 25 %)

10. Total deductions (sum of lines B.7 through B.9) 3,984

11. Annual after-tax cost of homeownership .... $ 10,980
    (line B.6 − line B.10)

12. Estimated annual appreciation in value of home 3,000
    (2 % of price of home)
    Total cost of buying (line B.11 − line B.12) .... $ 7,980

Note: Find monthly mortgage payments using a calculator or from Exhibit 5.9. An easy way to approximate the portion of the annual loan payment that goes to interest (line B.8) is to multiply the interest rate by the size of the loan (in this case, $120,000 × 0.06 = $7,200). To find the principal reduction in the loan balance (line B.7), subtract the amount that goes to interest from total annual mortgage payments ($8,634 − $7,200 = $1,434).

*Tax-shelter items.

TEST YOURSELF

5-5 In addition to single-family homes, what other forms of housing are available in the United States? Briefly describe each of them.

5-6 What type of housing would you choose for yourself now, and why? Why might you choose to rent instead of buy?

5-7 Why is it important to have a written lease? What should a rental contract include?

5-4 HOW MUCH HOUSING CAN YOU AFFORD?

Buying a home obviously involves lots of careful planning and analysis. Not only must you decide on the kind of home you want (its location, number of bedrooms, and other features), you must also consider its cost, what kind of mortgage to get, how large a monthly payment you can afford, what kind of homeowner's insurance coverage to have, and so forth.

Buying a home (or any other major, big-ticket item) touches on many elements of personal financial planning. The money you use for a down payment will likely be drawn from your *savings program;* the homeowner's policy you choose is a part of your *insurance planning;* and your monthly mortgage payments will have an enormous impact on your *cash budget* and *tax plans.*

Sound financial planning dictates caution when buying a home or any other major item. Knowing how much housing you can afford goes a long way toward helping you achieve balanced financial goals.

5-4a Benefits of Owning a Home

Homeownership is important to most people, whether they own a detached home or a condominium. It offers the security and peace of mind derived from living in one's own home and the feeling of permanence and sense of stability that ownership brings. This so-called psychological reward is not the only reason people enjoy owning their home. There are also financial payoffs from homeownership.

- Tax shelter: As noted in Chapter 3, you can deduct both mortgage interest and property taxes when calculating your federal and, in most states, state income taxes, reducing your taxable income and thus your tax liability. The only requirement is that you itemize your deductions. This tax break is so good that people who have never itemized usually begin doing so after they buy their first house. Also keep in mind that, for the first 15 to 20 years of ownership (assuming a 30-year mortgage), most of your monthly mortgage payment is made up of interest and property taxes—in fact, during the first 5 to 10 years or so, these could well account for *85 percent to 90 percent of your total payment.* This allows you to write off nearly all of your monthly mortgage payment.

- Inflation hedge: Homeownership usually provides an inflation hedge because your home appreciates in value at a rate equal to or greater than the rate of inflation. For example, from 2001 through 2006, a home became one of the best investments that you could make, generating a far better return than stocks, bonds, or mutual funds. However, housing values on average dropped by around a third between 2006 and 2012. Whether a real estate market is "hot" or "cold" is literally a matter of supply and demand. For long-term planning purposes, it makes sense to expect that housing prices will roughly keep pace with the rate of inflation.

5-4b The Cost of Homeownership

Although there definitely are some strong emotional and financial reasons for owning a home, there's still the question of whether you can afford to own one. There are two important aspects to the consideration of affordability: You must come up with the down payment and other closing costs, and you must be able to meet the cash-flow requirements associated with monthly mortgage payments and home maintenance expenses. In particular, you should consider these five costs of homeownership in determining how much home you can afford: the down payment, points and closing costs, mortgage payments, property taxes and insurance, and maintenance and operating expenses.

The Down Payment

down payment
A portion of the full purchase price provided by the purchaser when a house or other major asset is purchased; often called *equity*.

loan-to-value ratio
The maximum percentage of the value of a property that the lender is willing to loan.

The first major hurdle is the down payment. Most buyers finance a major part of the purchase price of the home, but they're required by lenders to invest money of their own, called *equity*. The actual amount of down payment required varies among lenders, mortgage types, and properties. To determine the amount of down payment required in specific instances, lenders use the loan-to-value ratio, which specifies the maximum percentage of the value of a property that the lender is willing to loan. For example, if the loan-to-value ratio is 80 percent, the buyer will have to come up with a down payment equal to the remaining 20 percent.

Most first-time home buyers spend several years accumulating enough money to afford the down payment and other costs associated with a home purchase. You can best accumulate these funds if you plan ahead, using future value techniques (presented in Chapters 2, 4, 11, and 14) to determine the monthly or annual savings necessary to have the needed amount by a specified future date. A detailed demonstration of this process is included in Chapter 11 (see Worksheet 11.1, part B). A disciplined savings program is the best way to obtain the funds needed to purchase a home or any other big-ticket item requiring a sizable down payment or cash outlay.

If you don't have enough savings to cover the down payment and closing costs, you can consider several other sources. You may be able to obtain some funds by withdrawing (subject to legal limitations) your contributions from your company's profit-sharing or thrift plan. Your IRA is another option; first-time home buyers are permitted to withdraw $10,000 without penalty before age 59½. However, using retirement money should be a last resort because you must still pay income tax on retirement distributions. Thus, if you're in the 25 percent income tax bracket, your $10,000 IRA withdrawal would net you only $7,500 ($10,000 − $2,500) for your down payment. And you would be reducing your retirement funds.

The Federal National Mortgage Association ("Fannie Mae") has programs to help buyers who have limited cash for a down payment and closing costs. The "Fannie 3/2" Program is available from local lenders to limit required down payments for qualified buyers. "Fannie 97" helps the home buyer who can handle monthly mortgage payments but doesn't have cash for the down payment. It requires only a 3 percent down payment from the borrower's own funds, and the borrower needs to have only one month's mortgage payment in cash savings, or reserves, after closing. Programs have also developed to help banks liquidate homes owned by Fannie Mae because of the foreclosures resulting from the financial crisis

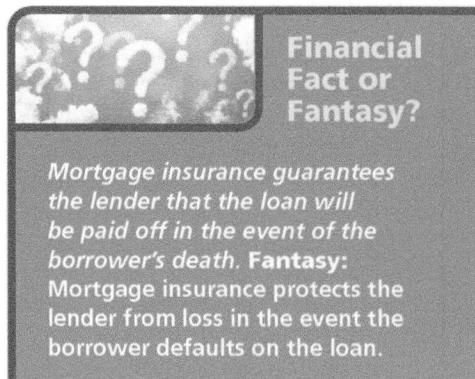
private mortgage insurance (PMI) An insurance policy that protects the mortgage lender from loss in the event the borrower defaults on the loan; typically required by lenders when the down payment is less than 20 percent.

mortgage points Fees (one point equals 1 percent of the amount borrowed) charged by lenders at the time they grant a mortgage loan; they are related to the lender's supply of loanable funds and the demand for mortgages.

in 2008–2009. The HomePath Mortgage Financing program is available from local and national lenders. Borrowers who meet certain income criteria may qualify for a 97 percent loan-to-value mortgage and may obtain their down payment from a gift, grant, or loan from a nonprofit organization, state or local government, or employer. The HomePath Renovation Mortgage Financing program is a comparable program available only on homes that will be a primary residence that are in need of light renovations.

When the down payment is less than 20 percent, the lender usually requires the buyer to obtain private mortgage insurance (PMI), which protects the lender from loss if the borrower defaults on the loan. Usually PMI covers the lender's risk above 80 percent of the house price. Thus, with a 10 percent down payment, the mortgage will be a 90 percent loan, and mortgage insurance will cover 10 percent of the home's price. The average cost of mortgage insurance is about 0.50 percent, ranging between 0.20 percent and 0.80 percent of the loan balance each year, depending on the size of your down payment. It can be included in your monthly payment, and the average cost ranges from about $40 to $70 per month. You should contact your lender to cancel the mortgage insurance once the equity in your home reaches 20 to 25 percent. However, under federal law, PMI on most loans made after mid-1999 ends automatically once the mortgage is paid down to 78 percent of the home's original value.

Points and Closing Costs

A second hurdle to homeownership relates to mortgage points and closing costs. Mortgage points are fees charged by lenders at the time that they grant a mortgage loan. In appearance, points are like interest in that they are a charge for borrowing money. They're related to the lender's supply of loanable funds and the demand for mortgages; the greater the demand relative to the supply, the more points you can expect to pay. One point equals 1 percent of the amount borrowed.

> **EXAMPLE: Calculating Mortgage Points**
>
> If you borrow $100,000 and loan fees equal 3 points, the amount of money you'll pay in points is:
>
> $100,000 × 0.03 = $3,000.

Lenders typically use points as an alternative way of charging interest on their loans. They can vary the interest rate along with the number of points they charge to create loans with comparable effective rates. For example, a lender might be willing to give you a 5 percent rather than a 6 percent mortgage if you're willing to pay more points; that is, you choose between a 6 percent mortgage rate with 1 point or a 5 percent mortgage rate with 3 points. If you choose the 5 percent loan, you'll pay a lot more *at closing* (although the amount of interest paid *over the life of the mortgage* may be considerably less).

Points increase the *effective rate of interest* or APR on a mortgage. The amount you pay in points and the length of time you hold a mortgage determine the increase in the effective interest rate. For example, on an 8 percent, 30-year, fixed-rate mortgage, each point increases the annual percentage rate by about 0.11 percent if the loan is held for 30 years, 0.17 percent if held 15 years, 0.32 percent if held 7 years, and 0.70 percent if held 3 years. You pay the same amount in points regardless of how long you keep your home. So, the longer you hold the mortgage, the longer the period over which you spread out (amortize) the fixed cost of the points and the smaller the effect of the points on the effective annual interest rate.

According to IRS rulings, the points paid on a mortgage at the time a home is originally purchased are usually considered immediately tax deductible. The same points are *not* considered immediately tax deductible if they're incurred when *refinancing a mortgage*; in this case, the amount paid in points must be written off (*amortized*) over the life of the new mortgage loan.

closing costs
All expenses (including mortgage points) that borrowers ordinarily pay when a mortgage loan is closed and they receive title to the purchased property.

Closing costs are all expenses that borrowers ordinarily pay when a mortgage loan is closed and they receive title to the purchased property. Closing costs are like down payments: they represent money you must come up with *at the time you buy the house*. Closing costs are made up of such items as loan application and loan origination fees paid to the lender, mortgage points, title search and insurance fees, attorneys' fees, appraisal fees, and other miscellaneous fees for things such as mortgage taxes, filing fees, inspections, credit reports, and so on. As Exhibit 5.7 shows, these costs can total 50 percent or more of the down payment amount. For example, with a 10 percent down payment on a $200,000 home, the closing costs, as shown in Exhibit 5.7, are about 56 percent of the down payment, or $11,130. The exhibit indicates that this buyer will need about $31,130 to buy the house (the $20,000 down payment plus another $11,130 in closing costs).

EXHIBIT 5.7 **Closing Costs: The Hidden Costs of Buying a Home**

The closing costs on a home mortgage loan can be substantial—as much as 5 percent to 7 percent of the price of the home. Except for the real estate commission (generally paid by the seller), the buyer incurs the biggest share of the closing costs and must pay them—in addition to the down payment—when the loan is closed and title to the property is conveyed.

Item	SIZE OF DOWN PAYMENT	
	20%	10%
Loan application fee	$300	$300
Loan origination fee	1,600	1,800
Points	4,160	5,400
Mortgage and homeowner's insurance	—	675
Title search and insurance	665	665
Attorneys' fees	400	400
Appraisal fees	425	425
Home inspection	350	350
Mortgage tax	665	725
Filing fees	80	80
Credit reports	35	35
Miscellaneous	200	200
Total closing costs	$9,530	$11,130

Note: Typical closing costs for a $200,000 home—2.6 points charged with 20 percent down, 3 points with 10 percent down. Actual amounts will vary by lender and location.

Mortgage Payments

Each mortgage payment is made up partly of principal repayment on the loan and partly of interest charges on the loan. However, as Exhibit 5.8 shows, for much of the life of the mortgage, the vast majority of each monthly payment goes to *interest*. The loan illustrated in the exhibit is a $100,000, 30-year, 5 percent mortgage with monthly payments of $536.82, for a total of $6,441.84 per year. Note that it is not until the 16th year of this 30-year mortgage that the principal portion of the monthly loan payment exceeds the amount that goes to interest.

In practice, most mortgage lenders and realtors use their calculator to obtain monthly payments. Some of them still use *comprehensive mortgage payment tables,* which provide monthly payments for virtually every combination of loan size, interest rate, and maturity. Exhibit 5.9 provides an excerpt from one such comprehensive mortgage payment table (with values rounded to the nearest cent). It lists the *monthly payments* associated with a $10,000, fixed-rate loan for selected maturities of 10 to 30 years and for various interest rates ranging from 5 percent to 10 percent. This table can be used to find the monthly payment for a loan of any size. Preferably, you can use a business calculator to quickly and precisely calculate monthly mortgage payments.

EXHIBIT 5.8 | **Typical Principal and Interest Payment Patterns on a Mortgage Loan**

For much of the life of a fixed rate mortgage loan, the majority of each monthly payment goes to interest and only a small portion goes toward repaying the principal. Over the 30-year life of the 5 percent, $100,000 mortgage illustrated here, the homeowner will pay about $93,255 in interest.

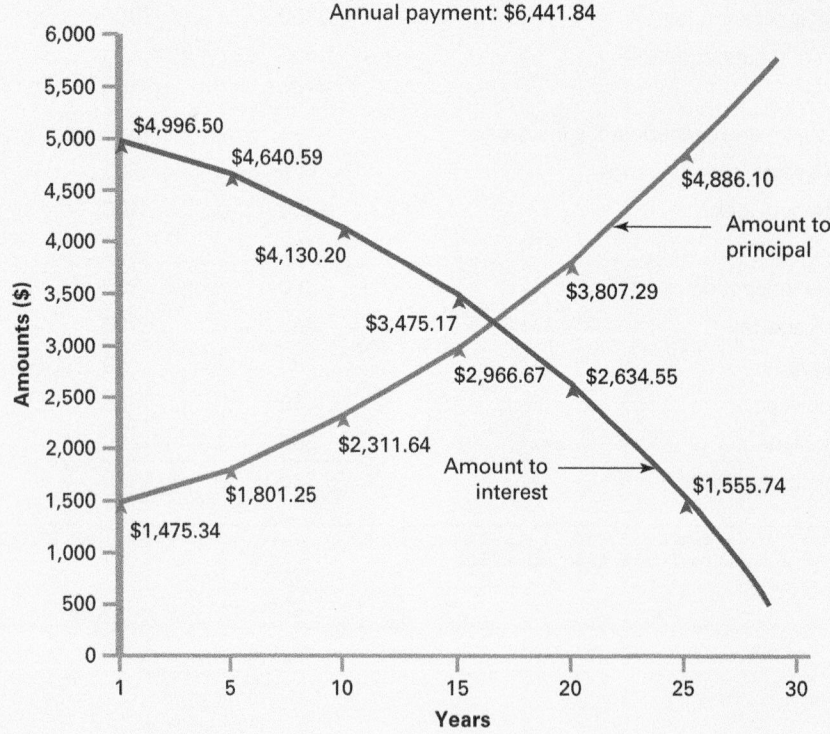

Note: Dollar amounts in the graph represent the amount of principal repaid and interest from the $6,441.84 annual payment made during the given year.

INPUTS	FUNCTIONS
180000	PV
360	N
6	÷
12	=
	I
	CPT
	PMT
	SOLUTION
	1079.19

See Appendix E for details.

EXAMPLE: Calculating Monthly Mortgage Payment

You'd like to use the mortgage payment tables to find the monthly loan payment on an $180,000, 6 percent, 30-year mortgage.

Divide the amount of the loan ($180,000) by $10,000 and then multiply this factor (18.0) by the payment amount shown in Exhibit 5.9 for a 6 percent, 30-year loan ($59.96):

$$\text{Mortgage Payment} = \frac{\text{Amount of Loan}}{\$10,000} \times \text{Monthly Payment on } \$10,000 \text{ Loan}$$

$$= \frac{\$180,000}{\$10,000} \times \$59.96 = \$1,079.28$$

The resulting monthly mortgage payment is thus $1,079.28.

The calculator keystrokes shown in the margin can be used to more easily calculate mortgage payments in the above example. Note that the mortgage payment of $1,079.19 generated by the calculator is considered to be more precise than the value calculated using the table of monthly mortgage payments but they're close.

Affordability Ratios. The key issue regarding mortgage payments is *affordability*: How large a monthly mortgage payment can you afford, given your budget? This amount determines how much you can borrow to finance the purchase of a home.

To obtain a mortgage, a potential borrower must be "qualified"—demonstrate that he or she has adequate income and an acceptable credit record to reliably make

---

EXHIBIT 5.9 | **A Table of Monthly Mortgage Payments (Monthly Payments Necessary to Repay a $10,000 Loan)**

The monthly loan payments on a mortgage vary not only by the amount of the loan, but also by the rate of interest and loan maturity.

Rate of Interest	LOAN MATURITY				
	10 Years	15 Years	20 Years	25 Years	30 Years
5.0%	$106.07	$79.08	$66.00	$58.46	$53.68
5.5	108.53	81.71	68.79	61.41	56.79
6.0	111.02	84.39	71.64	64.43	59.96
6.5	113.55	87.11	74.56	67.52	63.21
7.0	116.11	89.88	77.53	70.68	66.53
7.5	118.71	92.71	80.56	73.90	69.93
8.0	121.33	95.57	83.65	77.19	73.38
8.5	123.99	98.48	86.79	80.53	76.90
9.0	126.68	101.43	89.98	83.92	80.47
9.5	129.40	104.43	93.22	87.37	84.09
10.0	132.16	107.47	96.51	90.88	87.76

Instructions: (1) Divide amount of the loan by $10,000; (2) find the loan payment amount in the table for the specific interest rate and maturity; and (3) multiply the amount from step 1 by the amount from step 2.
Example: Using the steps just described, the monthly payment for a $98,000, 5.5 percent, 30-year loan would be determined as: (1) $98,000/$10,000 5 9.8; (2) the payment associated with a 5.5 percent, 30-year loan, from the table, is $56.79; (3) the monthly payment required to repay a $98,000, 5.5 percent, 30-year loan is 9.8 × $56.79 = $556.54.

scheduled loan payments. Federal and private mortgage insurers and institutional mortgage investors have certain standards they expect borrowers to meet to reduce the borrower's risk of default.

The most important affordability guidelines relate both *monthly mortgage payments* and *total monthly installment loan payments* (including the monthly mortgage payment and monthly payments on auto, furniture, and other consumer installment loans) to *monthly borrower gross income*. Customary ratios for a *conventional mortgage* stipulate that monthly mortgage payments cannot exceed 25 to 30 percent of the borrower's monthly *gross* (before-tax) income, and the borrower's total monthly installment loan payments (including the mortgage payment) cannot exceed 33 percent to 38 percent of monthly gross income. Because both conditions stipulate a range, the lender has some leeway in choosing the most appropriate ratio for a particular loan applicant.

Let's look at how these affordability ratios work. Assume that your monthly gross income is $4,500. Applying the lower end of the ranges (i.e., 25 and 33 percent), we see that this income level supports mortgage payments of $1,125 a month ($4,500 × 0.25 = $1,125) *so long as total monthly installment loan payments do not exceed $1,485* ($4,500 × 0.33 = $1,485). If your nonmortgage monthly installment loan payments exceeded $360 (the difference between $1,485 and $1,125), then your mortgage payment would have to be reduced accordingly or the other installment loan payments reduced or paid off. For instance, if you had $500 in other installment payments, your maximum monthly mortgage payment would be $1,485 − $500 = $985.

Property Taxes and Insurance

Aside from loan costs, mortgage payments often include property tax and insurance payments. The mortgage payment therefore consists of *p*rincipal, *i*nterest, property *t*axes, and homeowner's *i*nsurance (or PITI for short). Actually, that portion of the loan payment that goes for taxes and insurance is paid into an *escrow account,* where it accumulates until the lender pays property taxes and homeowner insurance premiums that are due. Some lenders pay interest—typically at no higher than the regular savings rate—on escrow account balances. However, it's preferable to pay insurance and taxes yourself, if you have the financial discipline. This strategy provides greater cash flexibility and an opportunity to earn a higher rate of return on funds than the escrow account pays.

The level of property taxes differs from one community to another because they're local taxes levied to fund schools, law enforcement, and other local services. In addition, within a given community, individual property taxes will vary according to the *assessed value* of the real estate—the larger and/or more expensive the home, the higher the property taxes, and vice versa. Annual property taxes typically vary from less than 0.5 percent to more than 2 percent of a home's approximate market value. Thus, the property taxes on a $100,000 home could vary from about $500 to more than $2,000 a year, depending on location and geographic area.

The other component of the monthly mortgage payment is homeowner's insurance. Its cost varies with such factors as the age of the house, location, materials used in construction, and geographic area. Homeowner's insurance is required by mortgage lenders and covers only the replacement value of the home and its contents, not the land. Annual insurance costs usually amount to approximately 0.25 percent to 0.5 percent of the home's market value, or from $500 to $1,000 for a $200,000 house. The types, characteristics, and features of homeowner's insurance policies are discussed in more detail in Chapter 10.

Maintenance and Operating Expenses

In addition to monthly mortgage payments, homeowners incur maintenance and operating expenses. Maintenance costs should be anticipated even on new homes. Painting, mechanical and plumbing repairs, and lawn maintenance, for example, are inescapable facts of homeownership. Such costs are likely to be greater for larger, older homes. Thus, although a large, established home may have an attractive purchase price, a new, smaller home may be a better buy in view of its lower

PITI
Acronym that refers to a mortgage payment including stipulated portions of *p*rincipal, *i*nterest, property *t*axes, and homeowner's *i*nsurance.

property taxes
Taxes levied by local governments on the *assessed value* of real estate for the purpose of funding schools, law enforcement, and other local services.

homeowner's insurance
Insurance that is required by mortgage lenders and covers the replacement value of a home and its contents.

When Is It Time to Buy a First Home?

The timing of when to buy a first home depends on your current and expected income and expenses, future plans, and your preferred lifestyle.

It's probably a good time to buy a home if you have the following:

- Reliable income and a good credit history, both of which you should be able to document
- Ability to make at least a 5 percent down payment and to cover closing costs
- The desire to build equity and to be eligible for homeowner tax breaks and credits
- Ability to finance home-maintenance and improvement projects
- Adequate savings and a cash reserve sufficient to handle the loss of your job or another financial challenge for at least a few months
- A plan to stay in your home for at least four years

Source: Adapted from http://www.freddiemac.com/homeownership/rent_or_buy/right_for_you.html, accessed August 2015.

maintenance and operating costs. Also consider the cost of operating the home, specifically the cost of utilities such as electricity, gas, water, and sewage. These costs have skyrocketed over the past 20 years and today are a large part of home ownership costs, so obtain estimates of utilities when evaluating a home for purchase.

5-4c Performing a Home Affordability Analysis

Worksheet 5.3 helps you determine your maximum price for a home purchase based on your monthly income and down payment amount after meeting estimated closing costs. In our example, Rene and Pierre Goulet have a combined annual income of $75,200 and savings of $30,000 for a down payment and closing costs. They estimate monthly property taxes and homeowner's insurance at $375 and expect the mortgage lender to use a 28 percent monthly mortgage payment affordability ratio, to lend at an average interest rate of 6 percent on a 30-year (360-month) mortgage, and to require a 10 percent minimum down payment. The Goulets' analysis shows that they can afford to purchase a home for about $201,000.

Worksheet 5.3 walks us through the steps that the Goulet family took to reach this conclusion. The maximum purchase price is determined from two perspectives: the maximum based on monthly income and the maximum based on the minimum acceptable down payment. The lower of the two estimates determines the maximum purchase price. Based on their monthly income and the 28 percent affordability ratio, their monthly payment could be $1,755 ($6,267 × 0.28), shown as Item 4. After deducting taxes and insurance, the maximum monthly mortgage payment amount is $1,380 (Item 6).

Calculator

INPUTS	FUNCTIONS
1380	PMT
360	N
6	÷
12	=
	I
	CPT
	PV
	SOLUTION
	230172.43

See Appendix E for details.

EXAMPLE: Calculating the Maximum Affordable Mortgage Loan

The Goulets want to determine the maximum loan they can carry given that they can afford a maximum monthly mortgage payment of $1,380. Exhibit 5.9 indicates that a $10,000 loan for 30 years at 6 percent would result in a monthly payment of $59.96, as indicated in Item 9 of Worksheet 5.3. This would support loan of:

$$\text{Maximum Mortgage Loan} = \$10,000 \times \frac{\text{Maximum Monthly Payment}}{\text{Present Value Interest Factor}}$$

$$= \$10,000 \times \frac{\$1,380}{\$59.96} = \$230,153.44$$

The calculator result in the margin indicates a maximum purchase price of $230,172.43, which is more precise than the approximation provided using Exhibit 5.9.

By using the following variables in the home affordability analysis form, the Goulets estimate a maximum home purchase price of $201,000: their combined annual income of $75,200; the $30,000 available for a down payment and paying all closing costs; estimated monthly property taxes and homeowner's insurance of $375; the lender's 28 percent monthly mortgage payment affordability ratio; an average interest rate of 6 percent and expected loan maturity of 30 years; and a minimum down payment of 10 percent.

HOME AFFORDABILITY ANALYSIS*

Name _Rene and Pierre Goulet_   Date _August 14, 2017_

Item	Description	Amount
1	Amount of annual income	$ 75,200
2	Monthly income (Item 1 ÷ 12)	$ 6,267
3	Lender's affordability ratio (in decimal form)	0.28
4	Maximum monthly mortgage payment (PITI) (Item 2 × Item 3)	$ 1,755
5	Estimated monthly prop tax and homeowner's insurance payment	$ 375
6	Maximum monthly loan payment (Item 4 − Item 5)	$ 1,380
7	Approximate average interest rate on loan	6 %
8	Planned loan maturity (years)	30
9	Monthly mortgage payment per $10,000 (using Item 7 and Item 8 and Table of Monthly Mortgage Payments in Exhibit 5.9)	$ 59.96
10	Maximum loan based on monthly income ($10,000 × Item 6 ÷ Item 9)	$230,000
11	Funds available for making a down payment and paying closing costs	$ 30,000
12	Funds available for making a down payment (Item 11 × .67)	$ 20,100
13	Maximum purchase price based on available monthly income (Item 10 + Item 12)	$250,100
14	Minimum acceptable down payment (in decimal form)	0.10
15	Maximum purchase price based on down payment (Item 12 ÷ Item 14)	$201,000
16	Maximum home purchase price (lower of Item 13 and Item 15)	$201,000

*Note: This analysis assumes that one-third of the funds available for making the down payment and paying closing costs are used to meet closing costs and that the remaining two-thirds are available for a down payment. This means that closing costs will represent an amount equal to 50 percent of the down payment.

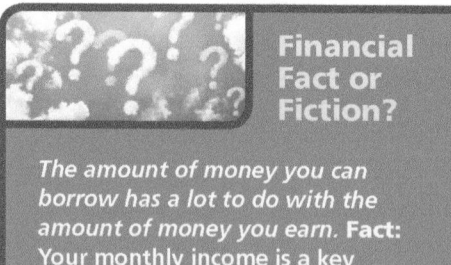

Financial Fact or Fiction?

The amount of money you can borrow has a lot to do with the amount of money you earn. **Fact:** Your monthly income is a key determinate of how large a mortgage loan you can afford. Also important are your credit record and the level of your total monthly installment loan payment.

With a down payment of $30,000 and monthly income of $6,267, the Goulet family can afford a home costing $250,100 (Item 13). The Goulets then look at the maximum purchase price based on their $30,000 down payment, or $150,000 (Item 15). Their maximum home purchase price is the lower of Items 13 and 15, or $201,000 (Item 16), and is limited by the amount available for a down payment.

You can use Exhibit 5.10 to quickly estimate the size of mortgage you can afford based on various assumptions about interest rates and the monthly mortgage payment. First, determine the maximum monthly mortgage payment you can handle, then follow that line across to find the approximate size of the mortgage your payment will buy at each mortgage interest rate.

EXHIBIT 5.10 **How Much Mortgage Will Your Payment Buy?**

This table lets you quickly estimate the size of the mortgage that you can afford based on the monthly mortgage payment and mortgage interest rate. It assumes a 30-year, fixed-rate loan. Remember that this amount is only for mortgage principal and interest; you must have funds available for paying property taxes and homeowner's insurance as well.

Monthly Mortgage Payment	Mortgage Interest Rate					
	5%	6%	7%	8%	9%	10%
$ 500	$ 93,141	$ 83,396	$ 75,154	$68,142	$ 62,141	$ 56,975
600	111,769	100,075	90,185	81,770	74,569	68,370
700	130,397	116,754	105,215	95,398	86,997	79,766
800	149,025	133,433	120,246	109,027	99,425	91,161
900	167,653	150,112	135,277	122,655	111,854	102,556
1,000	186,282	166,792	150,308	136,283	124,282	113,951
1,100	204,910	183,471	165,338	149,912	136,710	125,346
1,200	223,538	200,150	180,369	163,540	149,138	136,741
1,300	242,166	216,829	195,400	177,169	161,566	148,136
1,400	260,794	233,508	210,431	190,797	173,995	159,531
1,500	279,422	250,187	225,461	204,425	186,423	170,926

Instructions: (1) Find the amount of monthly mortgage payment you can afford, to the nearest $100. Then find the current mortgage interest rate to the nearest percent. The approximate mortgage amount will be at the intersection of the two columns. (2) To estimate the mortgage size if the interest rate ends in ".5," add the mortgage amounts for the lower and higher mortgage interest rates and divide by 2. (3) To estimate the mortgage size for a payment ending in "50," add the mortgage amounts for the lower and higher monthly mortgage payments and divide by 2.

Example: (1) The estimated mortgage size if you have a monthly mortgage payment of $900 on a 30-year, 6% loan is $150,112. (2) To find the estimated mortgage size if you have a monthly mortgage payment of $900 and the mortgage interest rate is 5.5%, add the mortgage sizes for $900 at 5% and at 6% and divide by 2: ($167,653 + $150,112) ÷ 2 = $317,765 ÷ 2 = $158,882. (3) To find the estimated mortgage size if you have a monthly mortgage payment of $950 and the mortgage interest rate is 6%, add the mortgage sizes for $900 and $1,000 at 6% and divide by 2: ($150,112 + $166,792) ÷ 2 = $316,904 ÷ 2 = $158,402.

(This figure assumes a 30-year, fixed-rate loan and does *not* include property taxes and homeowner's insurance.) For example, if you estimate that you have $1,000 available per month and the prevailing mortgage interest rate is 6 percent, you can afford a mortgage of about $166,792.

TEST YOURSELF

5-8 Briefly describe the various benefits of owning a home. Which one is most important to you? Which is least important?

5-9 What does the *loan-to-value ratio* on a home represent? Is the down payment on a home related to its loan-to-value ratio? Explain.

5-10 What are *mortgage points?* How much would a home buyer have to pay if the lender wanted to charge 2.5 points on a $250,000 mortgage? When would this amount have to be paid? What effect do points have on the mortgage's rate of interest?

5-11 What are *closing costs,* and what items do they include? Who pays these costs, and when?

5-12 What are the most common guidelines used to determine the monthly mortgage payment one can afford?

5-13 Why is it advisable for the prospective home buyer to investigate property taxes?

5-5 THE HOME-BUYING PROCESS

Buying a home requires time, effort, and money. You'll want to educate yourself about available properties and prevailing prices by doing a systematic search and careful analysis. And you'll also need a basic understanding of the role of a real estate agent, the mortgage application process, the real estate sales contract, and other documents required to close a deal.

5-5a Shop the Market First

Most people who shop the housing market rely on real estate agents for information, access to properties, and advice. Many of them also shop via the Internet, visiting various real estate sites to learn about available properties. Other sources of information, such as newspaper ads, are also widely used to find available properties. Occasionally a person seeking to buy or rent property will advertise his or her needs and wait for sellers to initiate contact.

Buying a home involves many factors, both financial and emotional, and the emotional factors often carry the greatest weight. As noted earlier, you must begin your home search project by figuring out what *you* require for your particular lifestyle needs—in terms of living space, style, and other special features. The property's location, neighborhood, and school district are usually important considerations as well. It's helpful to divide your list into *necessary* features, such as the number of bedrooms and baths, and *optional*—but desirable—features, such as fireplaces, whirlpool tubs, and so on. And of course, an affordability analysis is a critical part of the housing search.

Keep an open mind as you start looking. Be flexible and look at a variety of homes in your price range. This can be invaluable in helping to define your wants and needs more clearly.

If you already own a house but want or need a larger or different type of home, you can either trade up or remodel it. You may choose to remodel it if you like your neighborhood and can make the desired changes to your current home. In some cases, the cost to remodel will be less than the transaction costs of buying another house. The best remodeling projects are those whose costs you can recover when you sell the house. Kitchen improvements, additional bathrooms, and family rooms tend to best enhance a home's market value. Although a swimming pool may give you pleasure, you may not recover its cost when you sell the house.

Real Estate Short Sales

real estate short sale
Sale of real estate property in which the proceeds are less than the balance owed on a loan secured by the property sold.

The bursting of the real estate bubble associated with the financial crisis of 2008–2009 increased the use of real estate short sales. A **real estate short sale** is the sale of property in which the proceeds are less than the balance owed on a loan secured by the property sold. This procedure is an effort by mortgage lenders to come to terms with homeowners who are about to default or are defaulting on their mortgage loans. A broker's price opinion or an appraisal is obtained to estimate the probable selling price of the property for the purposes of the short sale. The short sale typically occurs to prevent home foreclosure by finding the most economic means for the mortgage lender—often a bank—to recover as much of the loan balance owed on the property as possible. In a **foreclosure**, the borrower typically cannot make scheduled mortgage payments and the lender repossesses the property in an effort to recover the loan balance owed. Mortgage holders will agree to a short sale only if they believe that the proceeds generated by the sale will bring a smaller loss than foreclosing on the property. A real estate short sale may consequently be viewed as a negotiated effort to mitigate the losses of the mortgage lender.

foreclosure
A borrower typically cannot make scheduled mortgage payments and the lender repossesses the property in an effort to recover the loan balance owed.

You may be wondering if a short sale works only for the benefit of the mortgage lender. Although it certainly can reduce a lender's losses, it can also be beneficial for the homeowner. A real estate short sale will avoid having a foreclosure appear on the

FINANCIAL PLANNING TIPS

Top Home Remodeling Projects

The National Association of Realtors found that the value of home remodeling projects declined by only about half as much as home prices during the recent financial crisis. While it's best to expect that you will not get all of your money back from home improvements when you sell your home, keep in mind that you will likely enjoy the improvements until that time and will probably recover most of the money if you stay in your home for some years to come. Here's a list of the top remodeling projects in terms of the percentage of the investment recovered at the sale of the home.

Midrange Project	Cost Recovered
Entry door replacement (steel)	101.8%
Manufactured stone veneer	92.2%
Garage door replacement	88.4%
Siding replacement (vinyl)	80.7%
Deck addition (wood)	80.5%
Minor kitchen remodel	79.3%
Window replacement (wood)	78.8%
Attic bedroom	77.2%
Window replacement (vinyl)	72.9%
Basement remodel	72.8%
Entry door replacement (fiberglass)	72.0%
Roofing replacement	71.6%

Source: Adapted from "Cost vs. Value Report: 2015," http://www.remodeling.hw.net/cost-vs-value/2015/, accessed August 2015.

homeowner's credit history. Short sales should also help homeowners manage the costs that got them into trouble in the first place. Finally, a short sale is usually faster and cheaper for the homeowner than a foreclosure. Most short sales fully satisfy the debt owed, but this is not always the case, so homeowners should confirm this in the settlement.

5-5b Using an Agent

Multiple Listing Service (MLS) A comprehensive listing, updated daily, of properties for sale in a given community or metropolitan area; includes a brief description of each property with a photo and its asking price but can be accessed only by realtors who work for an MLS member.

Most home buyers rely on real estate agents because they're professionals who are in daily contact with the housing market. Once you describe your needs to an agent, he or she can begin to search for appropriate properties. Your agent will also help you negotiate with the seller, obtain satisfactory financing, and, although not empowered to give explicit legal advice, prepare the real estate sales contract.

Most real estate firms belong to a local **Multiple Listing Service (MLS)**, a comprehensive listing, updated daily, of properties for sale in a given community or metropolitan area. A brief description of each property and its asking price are included, with a photo of the property. Only realtors who work for an MLS member firm have access to this major segment of the market.

Buyers should remember that *agents typically are employed by sellers.* Unless you've agreed to pay a fee to a sales agent to act as a buyer's agent, a realtor's primary responsibility, by law, is to sell listed properties at the highest possible prices. Agents are paid only if they make a sale, so some might pressure you to "sign now or miss the chance of a lifetime." But most agents will listen to your needs and work to match you with the right property and under terms that will benefit both you and the seller. Good agents recognize that their interests are best served when all parties to a transaction are satisfied.

Real estate commissions generally range from 5 percent to 6 percent for new homes and from 6 percent to 7 percent for previously occupied homes or *resales.* It may be possible to negotiate a lower commission with your agent or to find a discount broker or one who charges a flat fee. Commissions are typically paid only by the seller, but because the price of a home is often inflated by the size of the real estate commission—many builders are believed to factor commission costs into the prices of their new homes—it follows that the buyer probably absorbs some or even all of the commission. Of course, you may be able to find a suitable property that is "for sale by owner" and therefore eliminate the need for a realtor. This approach is generally not recommended, however, because of the many legal and financial complexities of the real estate transaction.

Whereas traditional agents represent the seller's interests, *buyer's agents,* as the term implies, are hired by buyers to negotiate on their behalf. Commissions to buyer's agents are negotiated and may ultimately be paid by the seller. A *facilitator,* on the other hand, represents neither the buyer nor the seller but is typically paid by both parties to serve as a neutral intermediary between them.

5-5c Prequalifying and Applying for a Mortgage

Before beginning your home search, you may want to meet with one or more mortgage lenders to prearrange a mortgage loan. **Prequalification** can work to your advantage in several ways. You'll know ahead of time the specific mortgage amount that you qualify for—subject, of course, to changes in rates and terms—and can focus your search on homes within an affordable price range.

Prequalification also provides estimates of the required down payment and closing costs for different types of mortgages. It identifies in advance any problems, such as credit report errors, that might arise from your application and allows you time to correct them. Finally, prequalification enhances your bargaining power with the seller of a house you want by letting her or him know that the deal won't fall through because you can't afford the property or obtain suitable financing. And since you will have already gone through the mortgage application process, the time required to close the sale should be relatively short.

There are many sources of mortgage loans, and you should begin investigating them while looking for a house. When you actually apply for a mortgage loan on a particular home, you'll need to give the lender information on your income, assets, and outstanding debts. Documents the lender may request include proof of your monthly income (paycheck stubs, W-2 forms, etc.), statements showing all debt balances (credit cards, car and education loans, bank lines of credit, and so on), lists of financial assets such as savings accounts and securities, several months' bank account statements, and at least two years' income tax returns. Financing your home is covered in detail later in this chapter.

5-5d The Real Estate Sales Contract

After selecting a home to buy, you must enter into a sales contract. State laws generally specify that, to be enforceable in court, real estate buy–sell agreements must be in writing and contain certain information, including: (1) the names of buyers and sellers, (2) a description of the property sufficient for positive identification, (3) specific price and other terms, and (4) usually the signatures of the buyers and sellers.

prequalification
The process of arranging with a mortgage lender, in advance of buying a home, to obtain the amount of mortgage financing the lender deems affordable to the home buyer.

Real estate sales transactions often take weeks and sometimes months to complete. Because they involve a fair amount of legal work, they require expert assistance in preparation. Contract requirements help keep the facts straight and reduce the chance for misunderstanding, misrepresentation, or fraud.

Although these requirements fulfill the minimums necessary for court enforcement, in practice real estate sales contracts usually contain several other contractual clauses relating to earnest money deposits, contingencies, personal property, and closing costs. An earnest money deposit is the money that you pledge to show good faith when you make an offer. If, after signing a sales contract, you withdraw from the transaction without a valid reason, you might have to forfeit this deposit. A valid reason for withdrawal would be stated in the contract as a contingency clause. With a contingency clause, you can condition your agreement to buy on such factors as the availability of financing, a satisfactory termite inspection or other physical inspection of the property, or the advice of a lawyer or real estate expert. Your lawyer should review and approve all agreements before you sign them.

5-5e Closing the Deal

After you obtain financing and your loan is approved, the closing process begins. Although closing costs may climb into the thousands of dollars, home buyers can often save significant amounts if they shop for financing, insurance, and other closing items rather than merely accepting the costs quoted by any one lender or provider of closing services.

The Real Estate Settlement Procedures Act (RESPA) governs closings on owner-occupied houses, condominiums, and apartment buildings of four units or fewer. This act reduced closing costs by prohibiting kickbacks made to real estate agents and others from lenders or title insurance companies. It also requires clear, advance disclosure of all closing costs to home buyers. Lenders must give potential borrowers a U.S. Department of Housing and Urban Development booklet entitled *Settlement Costs and You: A HUD Guide for Homebuyers*. The booklet sets forth the specific requirements of RESPA, and can take much of the mystery out of the closing process. An overview of these closing requirements may be found on HUD's Web site (go to the "Homes" section of **http://www.hud.gov**). Exhibit 5.11 provides some tips to help you sail smoothly through the home-buying process in general and the closing process in particular.

Title Check

Numerous legal interests can exist in real estate simultaneously: for example, those of the owners, lenders, lien holders (such as an unpaid roofing contractor), and easement holders. Before taking title to a property, make sure that the seller (who is conveying title to you) actually has the legal interest he or she claims and that the title is free of all liens and encumbrances (except those specifically referred to in the sales contract).

Although it's up to you to question the integrity of the title to the property you're buying, in most cases, an attorney or title insurance company performs a title check, consisting of the necessary research of legal documents and courthouse records. The customary practices and procedures and costs vary widely throughout the country. Regardless of the specific custom in your area, be sure to make some form of title check an essential part of your closing process.

Closing Statement

A *closing statement,* provided to both buyer and seller at or before the actual closing, accounts for monies that change hands during the transaction. The statement reconciles the borrower's and seller's costs and shows how much the borrower owes and the seller receives from the transaction. Before closing a home purchase, you should be given an opportunity to review the closing statement and have your questions

earnest money deposit
Money pledged by a buyer to show good faith when making an offer to buy a home.

contingency clause
A clause in a real estate sales contract that makes the agreement conditional on such factors as the availability of financing, property inspections, or obtaining expert advice.

Real Estate Settlement Procedures Act (RESPA)
A federal law requiring mortgage lenders to give potential borrowers a government publication describing the closing process and providing clear, advance disclosure of all closing costs to home buyers.

title check
The research of legal documents and courthouse records to verify that the seller conveying title actually has the legal interest he or she claims and that the title is free of all liens and encumbrances.

EXHIBIT 5.11 | Effective Home-Buying Strategies

Keeping in mind the following pitfalls will improve your chances of becoming a happy, successful homeowner:

- **Don't wipe out your savings.** While it makes sense to put down the largest down payment that you can afford, it is important to keep your emergency reserves intact, hold money for closing costs, and set aside funds to handle possible repairs and future maintenance.
- **Pick the right neighborhood.** You've heard that the three most important factors in valuing real estate are location, location, and location. This is no joke. Drive through a neighborhood, ask the police department about crime statistics, and talk to neighbors before you buy. If they don't want to talk, that tells you something too!
- **Stay away from the most expensive home in the neighborhood.** While having the largest and most expensive home in the neighborhood might be appealing, it doesn't bode well for resale value. If you need three bedrooms, don't consider a five-bedroom that looks good but costs more and meets your needs less.
- **Interview your agent and ask hard questions.** Make sure that he or she is experienced. Consider signing a buyer's broker agreement, which gives both you and the broker responsibilities and reasonable performance expectations.
- **Rely on professional advice.** Pay attention to what your agent or mortgage broker tells you. Look up information on the Internet, read real estate books, and ask for a second opinion. Lawyers and accountants are excellent resources.
- **Use traditional financing.** One of the biggest lessons of the financial crisis a few years ago is that real estate prices don't always go up. And what you don't know about your mortgage can hurt you! Don't sign off on your mortgage until you understand every detail. Terms like indexes, margins, caps, and negative amortization should make you nervous.
- **Don't change the financial picture before closing.** While waiting for loan funding, there is no need to buy a new car to match your new home. Your excellent credit report does not give you free rein to buy whatever you want. Borrowing too much more at this time could adversely affect the funding of a mortgage.
- **Be sure to do the home inspection.** Home inspections are *not* a waste of time and money. Qualified home inspectors can find problems that most of us would miss.
- **Be careful about taking on additional debt after closing.** After you become a homeowner, you'll be offered many deals on a home equity loan. Although it may be tempting to pull out all your equity and use this newfound money to buy all sorts of new toys, you should stick to a reasonable financial plan. It is critically important to cover the contingency of losing a job or an emergency by setting aside some money.

Source: Adapted from Elizabeth Weintraub, "Top 10 Ways to Lose Your Home," http://homebuying.about.com/od/buyingahome/tp/072007LoseHome.htm, accessed August 2015. Used with permission of About, Inc., which can be found online at www.about.com. All rights reserved.

answered. Carefully and critically review the statement to make sure that it is accurate and consistent with the contractual terms of the transaction; if not, have the statement corrected before closing the deal.

TEST YOURSELF

5-14 Describe some of the steps home buyers can take to improve the home-buying process and increase their overall satisfaction with their purchases.

5-15 What role does a real estate agent play in the purchase of a house? What is the benefit of the *MLS*? How is the real estate agent compensated, and by whom?

5-16 Describe a real estate short sales transaction. What are the potential benefits and costs from the perspective of the homeowner?

5-17 Why should you investigate mortgage loans and prequalify for a mortgage early in the home-buying process?

5-18 What information is normally included in a real estate sales contract? What is an *earnest money deposit*? What is a *contingency clause*?

5-19 Describe the steps involved in closing the purchase of a home.

5-6 FINANCING THE TRANSACTION

mortgage loan
A loan secured by the property: If the borrower defaults, the lender has the legal right to liquidate the property to recover the funds it is owed.

Earlier in the chapter, we saw that mortgage terms can dramatically affect the amount you can afford to spend on a home. The success of a real estate transaction often hinges on obtaining a mortgage with favorable terms. A mortgage loan is secured by the property: If the borrower defaults, the lender has the legal right to liquidate the property to recover the funds it is owed. Before you obtain such a loan, it's helpful to understand the sources and types of mortgages and their underlying economics.

5-6a Sources of Mortgage Loans

The major sources of home mortgages today are commercial banks, thrift institutions, and mortgage bankers or brokers; also, some credit unions make mortgage loans available to their members. Commercial banks are also an important source of *interim construction loans,* providing short-term financing during the construction process for individuals who are building or remodeling a home. After the home is completed, the homeowner obtains *permanent financing,* in the form of a standard mortgage loan, and then uses the proceeds from it to repay the construction loan.

Another way to obtain a mortgage loan is through a mortgage banker or mortgage broker. Both solicit borrowers, originate loans, and place them with traditional mortgage lenders, as well as life insurance companies and pension funds. Whereas mortgage bankers often use their own money to initially fund mortgages they later resell, mortgage brokers take loan applications and then seek lenders willing to grant the mortgage loans under the desired terms. Mortgage bankers deal primarily in government-insured and government-guaranteed loans, whereas mortgage brokers concentrate on finding conventional loans for consumers. Most brokers also have ongoing relationships with different lenders, thereby increasing your chances of finding a loan even if you don't qualify at a commercial bank or thrift institution. Brokers can often simplify the financing process by cutting through red tape, negotiating more favorable terms, and reducing the amount of time to close the loan. Mortgage brokers earn their income from commissions and origination fees paid by the lender, costs that are typically passed on to the borrower in the points charged on a loan. The borrower must often pay application, processing, and document preparation fees to the lender at closing. Exhibit 5.12 offers advice for finding a good mortgage broker. You may prefer to shop for a mortgage on your own or with your realtor, who is knowledgeable about various lenders and is legally prohibited from collecting fees or kickbacks for helping to arrange financing.

mortgage banker
A firm that solicits borrowers, originates primarily government-insured and government-guaranteed loans, and places them with mortgage lenders; often uses its own money to initially fund mortgages that it later resells.

mortgage broker
A firm that solicits borrowers, originates primarily conventional loans, and places them with mortgage lenders; the broker merely takes loan applications and then finds lenders willing to grant the mortgage loans under the desired terms.

5-6b Online Mortgage Resources

Shopping for the best mortgage rate and terms has become easier thanks to the Internet. Many sites allow you to search for the best fixed-rate or adjustable-rate mortgage in your area. HSH Associates, a mortgage consulting firm with a Web site at **http://www.hsh.com**, lists mortgages offered by banks, mortgage companies, and brokerage firms across the country, along with information on prevailing interest rates, terms, and points. Bankrate (**http://www.bankrate.com**) and similar sites also offer mortgage comparisons. Shopping via the Internet gives you great leverage when dealing with a lender. For example, if a local mortgage lender offers a three-year adjustable-rate mortgage (ARM) with 1.20 points and a 5.75 percent rate, while a lender in a different state offers the same terms with the same rate and only 1 point, you can negotiate with your local lender to get a better deal.

Although the Internet is still primarily a source of comparative information, online lenders such as E-Loan (**http://www.eloan.com**), a large online-only mortgage bank, hope that home buyers will choose to apply for and close a loan online. Or submit your information to LendingTree at **http://www.lendingtree.com**; within 24 hours you'll receive bids from four lenders interested in making your loan. You can also visit MSN Real Estate at **http://realestate.msn.com** for loan and general home-buying information.

EXHIBIT 5.12 **Should I Use a Mortgage Broker or My Bank?**

You've decided to buy a home and it's time to shop for a mortgage. Is it better to get your mortgage from your bank or from a mortgage broker? Here's how to best approach the decision.

It is common to find the best deal at the bank where you have your checking and savings accounts. Importantly, this is not the same as a mortgage company with the same name as your local bank. This is because your bank tends to do a volume business, is lending out its own money, and doesn't have as many middlemen who charge for dealing with your loan. Banks also tend to be cheaper than mortgage brokers because they focus on borrowers with good credit, established jobs with decent income, and long-term residence in the area. By implication, mortgage brokers tend to attract prospective borrowers with less appealing creditworthiness. That usually brings higher fees and mortgage interest rates.

So how should you organize your search for a mortgage?

Focus on finding a mortgage broker when you:
- don't have the best credit history
- are self-employed and/or can't document your income
- have just changed professions
- have a large amount of debt

Focus on your bank when you:
- have a good credit history
- have an established job and lengthy work history
- have a modest amount of debt
- are self-employed but can provide at least two years of income tax returns and other documents that prove your income

Even in light of the above general rules, some mortgage brokers may have rates and fees that compare favorably with your bank. So it's important to compare the deals that you can get with your bank vs. at least a couple of mortgage brokers.

Source: Adapted from "Mortgage Broker or My Bank—Which Is Better?" http://www.creditinfocenter.com/mortgage/brokeRbank.shtml, accessed August 2015.

5-6c Types of Mortgage Loans

There is no single way to classify mortgages. For our purposes, we'll group them in two ways: (1) terms of payment and (2) whether they're conventional, insured, or guaranteed.

There are literally dozens of different types of home mortgages from which to choose. The most common types of mortgage loans made today are fixed-rate and adjustable-rate mortgages. Let's take a closer look at their features, advantages, and disadvantages.

Fixed-Rate Mortgages

fixed-rate mortgage
The traditional type of mortgage, in which both the rate of interest and the monthly mortgage payment are fixed over the full term of the loan.

The fixed-rate mortgage still accounts for a large portion of all home mortgages. Both the rate of interest and the monthly mortgage payment are fixed over the full term of the loan. The most common type of fixed-rate mortgage is the *30-year fixed-rate* loan, although *10- and 15-year loans* are becoming more popular as homeowners recognize the advantages of paying off their loan over a shorter period of time. Because of the risks that the lender assumes with a 30-year loan, it's usually the most expensive form of home financing.

Gaining in popularity is the *15-year fixed-rate* loan. Its chief appeal is that it is repaid twice as fast (15 years versus 30) and yet the monthly payments don't increase twofold. To pay off a loan in less time, the homeowner must pay more each month, but the monthly payment on a 15-year loan is generally only about 20 percent larger than the payment on a 30-year loan. The following table shows the difference in monthly payment and total interest paid for 30- and 15-year fixed-rate mortgages. In both cases, the purchaser borrows $160,000 at a 5 percent fixed rate of interest:

Term of Loan	Regular Monthly Payment	Total Interest Paid over Life of Loan
30 years	$ 858.91	$149,209.25
15 years	$1,265.27	$ 67,748.56

Perhaps the most startling feature is the substantial difference in the total amount of interest paid over the term of the loan. In effect, you can save *about $81,460* just by financing your home with a 15-year mortgage rather than over the traditional 30 years! Note that this amount of savings is possible even though monthly payments differ by only about $406. In practice, the difference in the monthly payment would be even less, because 15-year mortgages are usually available at interest rates that are about half a percentage point below comparable 30-year loans.

Although the idea of paying off a mortgage in 15 years instead of 30 may seem like a good one, you should consider how long you plan to stay in the house. While paying off the loan faster always increases your home equity faster, you might not feel as motivated to do this if you plan to sell the house in a few years. In addition, the tax deductibility of mortgage interest makes a mortgage one of the least expensive sources of borrowing. If you can earn a higher rate of return than the rate of interest on a 30-year loan, then you'd be better off taking the 30-year loan and investing the difference in the payment between it and the comparable 15-year loan.

Another way to shorten the mortgage term without committing to an initially shorter term is by making extra principal payments regularly or when you have extra funds. If you can earn exactly the mortgage interest rate (5 percent annually, in our example), then you could take the 30-year loan and invest the $406 that you save each month over the 15-year mortgage; then, at any time, subtracting the sum of the saved mortgage payments and the interest earned on them from the outstanding 30-year mortgage balance would exactly equal the outstanding balance on the 15-year loan. In other words, you could use the 30-year loan to exactly replicate the 15-year loan. Because of this relationship, some people recommend "taking the 30-year loan and investing the savings over a comparable 15-year loan." However, the success of this strategy depends on (1) sufficient discipline for you to invest the difference every month and, more importantly, (2) an ability to consistently earn the mortgage interest rate on your investments. Because both of these conditions are unlikely, you're best off taking the mortgage that most closely meets your financial needs.

balloon-payment mortgage
A mortgage with a single large principal payment due at a specified future date.

Some lenders offer other types of fixed-rate loans. Balloon-payment mortgages offer terms of 5, 7, or 10 years where the interest rate is fixed, typically at 0.25 to 0.5 percent below the 30-year fixed rate. The monthly payments are the same as for a 30-year loan at the given rate. When the loan matures, the remaining principal balance comes due and must be refinanced. Although the lower rate results in lower monthly payments, these loans do carry some risk because refinancing may be difficult, particularly if rates have risen.

You Can Do It Now
Current Mortgage Rates

If you're considering buying a home, you need to know current mortgage rates to determine prospective monthly payments and what price you can pay for the home. Up-to-date market rates for different maturities of fixed and adjustable rate mortgages are available at **http://www.bankrate.com**. And you can also obtain refinancing rates there when you already have a mortgage and are considering refinancing it. It's so accessible—you can do it now.

adjustable-rate mortgage (ARM)
A mortgage on which the rate of interest, and therefore the size of the monthly payment, is adjusted based on market interest rate movements.

adjustment period
On an adjustable-rate mortgage, the period of time between rate or payment changes.

index rate
On an adjustable-rate mortgage, the baseline index rate that captures interest rate movements.

margin
On an adjustable-rate mortgage, the percentage points a lender adds to the *index rate* to determine the rate of interest.

interest rate cap
On an adjustable-rate mortgage, the limit on the amount that the interest rate can increase each adjustment period and over the life of the loan.

payment cap
On an adjustable-rate mortgage, the limit on the monthly payment increase that may result from a rate adjustment.

Calculator

INPUTS	FUNCTIONS
100000	PV
360	N
6.5	÷
12	=
	/
	CPT
	PMT
	SOLUTION
	632.07

See Appendix E for details.

negative amortization
When the principal balance on a mortgage loan increases because the monthly loan payment is lower than the amount of monthly interest being charged; some ARMs are subject to this undesirable condition.

Adjustable-Rate Mortgages (ARMs)

Another popular form of home loan is the adjustable-rate mortgage (ARM). The rate of interest, and therefore the size of the monthly payment, is adjusted based on market interest rate movements. The mortgage interest rate is linked to a specific *interest rate index* and is adjusted at specific intervals (usually once or twice a year) based on changes in the index. When the index moves up, so does the interest rate on the mortgage and, in turn, the size of the monthly mortgage payment increases. The new interest rate and monthly mortgage payment remain in effect until the next adjustment date.

The term of an ARM can be 15 or 30 years. Because the size of the monthly payments will vary with interest rates, there's no way to tell what your future payments will be. However, because the borrower assumes most or all of the interest rate risk in these mortgages, the *initial rate of interest* on an adjustable-rate mortgage is normally well below—typically by 2 to 3 percentage points—the rate of a standard 30-year fixed-rate loan. Of course, whether the borrower actually ends up paying less interest depends on the behavior of market interest rates during the term of the loan.

Features of ARMs. It's important for home buyers to understand the following basic features of an ARM:

- Adjustment period: Although the period of time between rate or payment changes is typically six months to one year, adjustment periods can range from three months to three or five years.
- Index rate: A baseline rate that captures the movement in interest rates, tied to six-month U.S. Treasury securities, six-month CDs, or the average cost of funds to savings institutions as commonly measured by the 11th Federal Home Loan Bank District Cost of Funds.
- Margin: The percentage points that a lender adds to the index to determine the rate of interest on an ARM, usually a fixed amount over the life of the loan. Thus, the rate of interest on an ARM equals the index rate plus the margin.
- Interest rate caps: Limits on the amount the interest rate can increase over a given period. *Periodic caps* limit interest rate increases from one adjustment to the next (typically, lenders cap annual rate adjustments at 1 to 2 percentage points), and *overall caps* limit the interest rate increase over the life of the loan (lifetime interest rate caps are typically set at 5 to 8 percentage points). Many ARMs have both periodic and overall interest rate caps.
- Payment caps: Limits on monthly payment increases that may result from a rate adjustment—usually a percentage of the previous payment. If your ARM has a 5 percent payment cap, your monthly payments can increase no more than 5 percent from one year to the next—regardless of what happens to interest rates.

Because most ARMs are 30-year loans (360 payments), you can determine the initial monthly payment in the same manner as for any other 30-year mortgage. For example, for a $100,000 loan at 6.5 percent (4.5 percent index rate + 2 percent margin), we can use a calculator as shown in the margin to find the first-year monthly payments of $632.07. Assuming a 1-year adjustment period, if the index rate rises to 5.5 percent, then the interest rate for the second year will be 7.5 percent (5.5 percent + 2 percent = 7.5 percent). The size of the monthly payment for the next 12 months will then be adjusted upward to about $697.83. This process is repeated each year thereafter until the loan matures.

Beware of Negative Amortization. Some ARMs are subject to negative amortization—an increase in the principal balance resulting from monthly loan payments that are lower than the amount of monthly interest being charged. In other words, you could end up with a larger mortgage balance on the next anniversary of your loan than on the previous one. This occurs when the payment is intentionally set below the interest charge, or when the ARM has interest rates that are adjusted monthly—with monthly payments that adjust annually. In the latter case, when rates are rising on these loans, the current monthly payment can be less than the interest being charged, and the difference is added to the principal, thereby increasing the size of the loan.

ARMs with a cap on the dollar amount of monthly payments can also lead to negative amortization. For example, assume that the monthly payment on a 5.5 percent, 30-year, $100,000 loan is $568, with its next annual adjustment in 10 months. If rising interest rates cause the mortgage rate to increase to 7 percent, therefore increasing the monthly payment to $663, then negative amortization of $95 per month would occur. If no other interest rate change occurred over the remaining 10 months until its next adjustment, then the mortgage balance would be $100,950, with the increase of $950 attributable to the $95 per month negative amortization over 10 months.

When considering an ARM, be sure to learn whether negative amortization is allowed in the mortgage document. Generally, loans without the potential for negative amortization are available, although they tend to have slightly higher initial rates and interest rate caps.

Here are other types of ARMs lenders may offer.

convertible ARM
An adjustable-rate mortgage loan that allows borrowers to convert from an adjustable-rate to a fixed-rate loan, usually at any time between the 13th and the 60th month.

two-step ARM
An adjustable-rate mortgage with just two interest rates: one for the first five to seven years of the loan, and a higher one for the remaining term of the loan.

- Convertible ARMs allow borrowers to convert from an adjustable-rate to a fixed-rate loan during a specified time period, usually any time between the 13th and 60th month. Although these loans seldom provide the lowest initial rate, they allow the borrower to convert to a fixed-rate loan if interest rates decline. A conversion fee of about $500 is typical, and the fixed rate is normally set at 0.25 percent to 0.5 percent above the going rate on fixed-rate loans at the time you convert.
- Two-step ARMs have just two interest rates, the first for an initial period of 5 to 7 years and a higher one for the remaining term of the loan.

Implications of the ARM Index. The index on your ARM significantly affects the level and stability of your mortgage payments over the term of your loan. Lenders use short-term indexes such as the Six-Month Treasury Bill; the *London Interbank Offered Rate,* or LIBOR, a base rate similar to the prime rate and used in the international marketplace; CD-based indexes; and the 11th Federal Home Loan Bank District Cost of Funds.

The most important difference between the indexes is their volatility. LIBOR and CD rates are volatile because they quickly respond to changes in the financial markets. The 11th Federal Home Loan Bank District Cost of Funds index is less volatile because it represents an average of the cost of funds to S&Ls in the district. It tends to lag other short-term rate movements, both up and down, and exhibits a fairly smooth pattern over time. You may want to compare index rates over the past several years to more fully understand how one index behaves relative to another.

So what does this mean for the home buyer considering an ARM? If your mortgage is tied to a LIBOR or CD index, you can expect sharper and more frequent upward and downward interest rate movements compared to cost of funds indexes, which move more slowly in both directions. To see which index is better for you, consider the annual rate cap on the mortgage, the level of interest rates, and future interest rate expectations. If you have a low rate cap of 1 to 2 percentage points and you think that rates might go down, you may be comfortable with a more volatile index.

Some lenders offer special first-year "teaser" rates that are below the index rate on the loan. Be wary of lenders with very low rates. Ask them if the first-year rate is based on the index and verify the rate yourself. Be sure you can comfortably make the monthly mortgage payment when the interest rate steps up to the indexed rate.

Monitoring Your Mortgage Payments. You should carefully monitor your mortgage over its life. Always verify the calculation of your loan payment when rate or payment adjustments are made. To verify your payment amount, you need to know the index rate, the margin, and the formula used to adjust the loan; all are found in the loan agreement. Interest rates for the most commonly used indexes are readily available in the financial press and are published weekly in the real estate section of most newspapers. The loan formula tells you when the rate is set—for example, 45 days before the adjustment date—and the margin on the loan. You can use a handheld business calculator (as demonstrated earlier) to calculate the payment once you know the new

rate, the number of years until the loan is paid off, and the current principal balance.

If you suspect you're being overcharged, call your lender and ask for an explanation of the rate and payment calculations. Special mortgage-checking services will review your ARM for a fee of about $70 to $100.

Fixed Rate or Adjustable Rate?

Fixed-rate mortgages are popular with home buyers who plan to stay in their homes for at least 5 to 7 years and want to know what their payments will be. Of course, the current level of interest rates and your expectations about future interest rates will influence your choice of a fixed-rate or adjustable-rate mortgage. When the average interest rate on a 30-year mortgage loan is high, people choose ARMs to avoid being locked into prevailing high rates. When interest rates are low, many home buyers opt for fixed-rate mortgages to lock in these attractive rates. In such situations, many homeowners with existing ARMs refinance them with fixed-rate loans to take advantage of favorable current fixed rates.

Other Mortgage Payment Options

In addition to standard fixed-rate and adjustable-rate mortgage loans, some lenders offer variations designed to help first-time home buyers.

interest-only mortgage
A mortgage that requires the borrower to pay only interest; typically used to finance the purchase of more expensive properties.

- **Interest-only mortgages** are loans requiring the borrower to pay only the interest. The popularity of these mortgages increased in response to the rapidly rising prices of the real estate boom between 2001 and 2006. Rather than amortizing the loan into equal monthly payments over the term of the loan, the borrower merely pays the accrued interest each month. These mortgages allow the borrower, typically on more expensive properties, to make lower payments that are fully tax deductible. Most interest-only mortgages are offered as ARMs.

graduated-payment mortgage
A mortgage that starts with unusually low payments that rise over several years to a fixed payment.

- **Graduated-payment mortgages** are loans offering low payments for the first few years, gradually increasing until year 3 or 5 and then remaining fixed. The low initial payments appeal to people who are just starting out and expect their income to rise. If this doesn't occur, however, it could result in a higher debt load than the borrower can handle.

growing-equity mortgage
Fixed-rate mortgage with payments that increase over a specific period. Extra funds are applied to the principal so that the loan is paid off more quickly.

- **Growing-equity mortgages** are fixed-rate mortgages with payments that increase over a specific period. The extra funds are applied to the principal, so a conventional 30-year loan is paid off in about 20 years. However, you can accomplish the same thing without locking yourself into a set schedule by taking a fixed-rate mortgage that allows prepayments.

shared-appreciation mortgage
A loan that allows a lender or other party to share in the appreciated value when the home is sold.

- **Shared-appreciation mortgages** are loans that have a below-market interest rate because the lender or other party shares from 30 percent to 50 percent of the appreciated value when the home is sold. This can be a useful tool if you absolutely can't afford the higher rates of a conventional loan; but keep in mind that, with appreciation of only 2 percent per year for just five years, such a loan could cost you up to $5,000 in shared equity on a $100,000 property.

biweekly mortgage
A loan on which payments equal to half the regular monthly payment are made every two weeks.

- **Biweekly mortgages** are loans on which payments equal to half of a regular monthly payment are made every two weeks rather than once a month. Because you make 26 payments (52 weeks ÷ 2), which is the equivalent of 13 monthly payments, the principal balance declines faster and you pay less interest over the life of the loan. Once again, with most 30-year mortgages, you can make extra principal payments at any time without penalty. This may be preferable to committing to a biweekly loan that can charge an additional processing fee.

buydown
Financing made available by a builder or seller to a potential new-home buyer at well below market interest rates, often only for a short period.

- **Buydowns** are a type of seller financing sometimes offered on new homes. A builder or seller arranges for mortgage financing with a financial institution at interest rates well below market rates. For example, a builder may offer 5 percent financing when the market rate of interest is around 6 percent or 6.5 percent. Typically, the builder or seller subsidizes the loan for the buyer at a special low interest rate. However, the reduced interest rate may be for only a short period, or the buyer may pay for the reduced interest in the form of a higher purchase price.

Conventional, Insured, and Guaranteed Loans

conventional mortgage

A mortgage offered by a lender who assumes all the risk of loss; typically requires a down payment of at least 20 percent of the value of the mortgaged property.

A **conventional mortgage** is a mortgage offered by a lender who assumes all the risk of loss. To protect themselves, lenders usually require a down payment of at least 20 percent of the value of the mortgaged property. For lower down payments, the lender usually requires *PMI*, as described earlier in the chapter. High borrower equity greatly reduces the likelihood of default on a mortgage and subsequent loss to the lender. However, a high down payment requirement makes home buying more difficult for many families and individuals.

To promote homeownership, the federal government, through the Federal Housing Administration (FHA), offers lenders mortgage insurance on loans with a high loan-to-value ratio. These loans usually feature low down payments, below-market interest rates, few if any points, and relaxed income or debt-ratio qualifications.

FHA mortgage insurance

A program under which the Federal Housing Administration (FHA) offers lenders mortgage insurance on loans having a high loan-to-value ratio; its intent is to encourage loans to home buyers who have very little money available for a down payment and closing costs.

The **FHA mortgage insurance** program helps people buy homes even when they have very little money available for a down payment and closing costs. As of mid-2015, the up-front mortgage insurance premium for a 15- or 30-year mortgage was 1.75 percent of the loan amount—paid by the borrower at closing or included in the mortgage—plus another 0.80 to 1.05 percent annual renewal premium, paid monthly, depending on the maturity of the loan and the amount of the down payment. The FHA agrees to reimburse lenders for losses up to a specified maximum amount if the buyer defaults. The interest rate on an FHA loan is generally about 0.5 percent to 1 percent lower than that on conventional fixed-rate loans. The affordability ratios that are used to qualify applicants for these loans are typically less stringent than those used for conventional loans. The maximum mortgage amount that the FHA can insure is based on the national *median* price of homes and varies depending on location. To learn more about FHA mortgages, visit **http://www.fha.com**.

VA loan guarantee

A guarantee offered by the U.S. Veterans Administration to lenders who make qualified mortgage loans to eligible veterans of the U.S. armed forces and their unmarried surviving spouses.

Guaranteed loans are similar to insured loans, but better—if you qualify. **VA loan guarantees** are provided by the U.S. Veterans Administration to lenders who make qualified mortgage loans to eligible veterans of the U.S. armed forces and their unmarried surviving spouses. This program, however, does not require lenders or veterans to pay a premium for the guarantee. In many instances, an eligible veteran must pay only closing costs; in effect, under such a program, a veteran can buy a home with no down payment. (This can be done *only once* with a VA loan.) The mortgage loan—subject to a maximum of about $417,000 for a no-money-down loan (or more in high-cost areas as of 2015)—can amount to as much as 100 percent of a purchased property's appraised value. It is important to note that there are some regional differences in VA loan requirements. VA loans include a funding fee of about 2.15 percent on first-time, no-down-payment loans for regular military members (the fee is lower if the down payment is 10 percent or more). The VA sets the maximum interest rate, which (as with FHA loans) is usually about 0.5 percent below the rate on conventional fixed-rate loans. To qualify, the veteran must meet VA credit guidelines. You can find more information at **http://www.homeloans.va.gov**.

5-6d Refinancing Your Mortgage

After you've purchased a home and closed the transaction, interest rates on similar loans may drop. If rates drop by 1 percent to 2 percent or more, then you should consider the economics of refinancing after carefully comparing the terms of the old and new mortgages, the anticipated number of years you expect to remain in the home, any prepayment penalty on the old mortgage, and closing costs associated with the new mortgage.

Worksheet 5.4 provides a form for analyzing the impact of refinancing. The data for the Varela family's analysis is shown. Their original $80,000, 10-year-old,

8 percent mortgage has a current balance of $70,180 and monthly payments of $587 for 20 more years. If they refinance the $70,180 balance at the prevailing rate of 5 percent then, over the remaining 20-year life of the current mortgage, the monthly payment would drop to $463. The Varelas plan to live in their house for at least five more years. They won't have to pay a penalty for prepaying their current mortgage, and closing and other costs associated with the new mortgage are $2,400 after taxes. Entering these values into Worksheet 5.4 reveals (in Item 7) that it will take the Varelas 26 months to break even with the new mortgage. Because 26 months is considerably less than their anticipated minimum five years (60 months) in the home, the economics easily support refinancing their mortgage under the specified terms.

There are two basic reasons to refinance—to reduce the monthly payment or to reduce the total interest cost over the term of the loan. If a lower monthly payment is the objective, then the analysis is relatively simple: determine how long it will take for the monthly savings to equal your closing costs (see Worksheet 5.4).

If your objective is to reduce the total interest cost over the life of the loan, then the analysis is more complex. The term of the new loan versus the existing loan is a critical element. If you refinance a 30-year loan that's already 10 years old with another 30-year loan, you're extending the total loan maturity to 40 years. Consequently, even with a lower interest rate, you may pay more interest over the life of the newly extended loan. So you should refinance with a shorter-term loan, ideally one that matures no later than the original loan maturity date. (The example in Worksheet 5.4 is prepared on this basis.)

Many homeowners want to pay off their loans more quickly to free up funds for their children's college education or for their own retirement. By refinancing at a lower rate and continuing to make the same monthly payment, a larger portion of each payment will go toward reducing the principal, so the loan will be paid off more quickly. Alternately, the borrower can make extra principal payments whenever possible. Paying only an additional $25 per month on a 30-year, 6 percent, $100,000 mortgage reduces the term to about 26 years and saves about $18,500 in interest.

WORKSHEET 5.4	Mortgage Refinancing Analysis for the Varela Family

Using this form, the Varelas find that—by refinancing the $70,180 balance on their 10-year-old, $80,000, 8 percent, 30-year mortgage (which has no prepayment penalty and requires payments of $587 per month) with a 5 percent, 20-year mortgage requiring $463 monthly payments and $2,400 in total after-tax closing costs—it will take 26 months to break even. Because the Varelas plan to stay in their home for at least 60 more months, the refinancing is easily justified.

MORTGAGE REFINANCING ANALYSIS

Name _Demi and Nicholas Varela_   Date _October 8, 2017_

Item	Description		Amount
1	Current monthly payment (Terms: _$80,000, 8%, 30 years_)		$ 587
2	New monthly payment (Terms: _$70,180, 5%, 20 years_)		463
3	Monthly savings, pretax (Item 1 − Item 2)		$ 124
4	Tax on monthly savings [Item 3 × tax rate (_25_%)]		31
5	Monthly savings, after-tax (Item 3 − Item 4)		$ 93
6	Costs to refinance:		
	a. Prepayment penalty	$ 0	
	b. Total closing costs (after-tax)	2,400	
	c. Total refinancing costs (Item 6a + Item 6b)		$2,400
7	Months to break even (Item 6c ÷ Item 5)		26

Some people consider the reduced tax deduction associated with a smaller mortgage interest deduction as a disadvantage of refinancing. Although the interest deduction may indeed be reduced because of refinancing, the more important concern is the amount of the actual after-tax cash payments. In this regard, refinancing with a lower-interest-rate mortgage (with all other terms assumed unchanged) will always result in lower after-tax cash outflows and is therefore economically appealing. Of course, as demonstrated in Worksheet 5.4, the monthly savings should be compared with the refinancing costs before making the final decision.

Remember that when you refinance, most lenders require you to have at least 20 percent equity in your home, based on a current market appraisal. Many financial institutions are willing to refinance their existing loans, often charging fewer points and lower closing costs than a new lender would charge, so be sure to check with your existing lender first.

TEST YOURSELF

5-20 Describe the various sources of mortgage loans. What role might a *mortgage broker* play in obtaining mortgage financing?

5-21 Briefly describe the two basic types of mortgage loans. Which has the lowest initial rate of interest? What is *negative amortization*, and which type of mortgage can experience it? Discuss the advantages and disadvantages of each mortgage type.

5-22 Differentiate among conventional, insured, and guaranteed mortgage loans.

Planning Over a Lifetime: *Auto and Housing Decisions*

Here are some key considerations in making auto and housing decisions in each stage of the life cycle.

Pre-family Independence: 20s	Family Formation/ Career Development: 30–45	Pre-Retirement: 45–65	Retirement: 65 and Beyond
✓ Start saving for a down payment on a house.	✓ Compare current mortgage rates with yours and evaluate the value of refinancing.	✓ Periodically re-evaluate the attractiveness of refinancing your mortgage.	✓ Re-evaluate housing choices and location. Consider downsizing but watch transactions costs.
✓ Compare renting vs. buying a house.	✓ Budget to make additional payments on your mortgage to gain greater financial flexibility in the future.	✓ Budget to pay off your mortgage prior to retirement.	✓ Pay off your mortgage.
✓ Familiarize yourself with the various types of mortgages.	✓ Save to finance the replacement of your current car.	✓ Consider whether a different type of car(s) is (are) appropriate.	✓ Consider whether more than one family car is needed in retirement.

Financial Impact of Personal Choices
Vivian Wants to Buy a House but Doesn't Want a Roommate Now

Vivian has saved $10,000 toward a $20,000 down payment on buying a home. She puts aside $300 a month in her house fund and is currently renting a one-bedroom apartment on her own for $1,300 a month. If she rented a two-bedroom apartment with a roommate, she could reduce her rent to $900 a month. While having a roommate is not Vivian's favorite solution, she'd be able to build up her down payment for buying a house a lot faster if she were able to save an extra $400 a month. If Vivian stays on her own and her finances remain the same, it will take her about 2¾ years to put aside the needed additional $10,000. In contrast, if she set aside the rent saved by getting a roommate, she would have the needed $10,000 in about only 14 months. Doing without a roommate at this stage in Vivian's life is costly.

Summary

LG1 **Design a plan to research and select a new or used automobile. p. 164**
The purchase of an automobile should be based on thorough market research and comparison shopping. Important purchase considerations include affordability; operating costs; whether to buy a gas-, diesel-, or hybrid-fueled car; whether to buy a new versus a used or nearly new car; the type of car and its features; and its reliability and warranties. Knowing the dealer's cost is the key to negotiating a good price.

LG2 **Decide whether to buy or lease a car. p. 173**
Before leasing a vehicle you should consider all the terms of the lease, including the annual mileage allowance and early termination penalties. The economics of leasing versus purchasing a car with an installment loan should not be considered until the price is set. The four components of the lease payment are the capitalized cost, residual value, money factor, and lease term.

LG3 **Identify housing alternatives, assess the rental option, and perform a rent-or-buy analysis. p. 177**
In addition to single-family homes, there are condominiums, cooperative apartments, and rental units. Evaluate the advantages and disadvantages of each for your current lifestyle. Many people rent because they can't afford to buy a home; others rent because it's more convenient for their lifestyle and economic situation. The rental contract, or lease agreement, describes the terms under which you can rent the property, including the monthly rental amount, lease term, restrictions, and so forth. The rent ratio—the relationship between renting and buying a comparable house—quantifies the relative attractiveness of renting versus buying. A rent-or-buy analysis will identify the least costly alternative. Also consider qualitative factors, such as how long you plan to stay in an area, and perform the analysis over a several-year timeline.

LG4 **Evaluate the benefits and costs of homeownership and estimate how much you can afford to pay for a home. p. 184**
In addition to the emotional rewards, other benefits of homeownership are the tax shelter and inflation hedge it provides. Homeownership costs include the down payment, points and closing costs, monthly mortgage payments, property taxes and insurance, and normal home maintenance and operating expenses. Carefully consider all of these costs when estimating how much you can afford to spend on a home.

LG5 **Describe the home-buying process. p. 194**
Most people shopping for a home seek the help of a real estate agent to obtain access to properties and to provide needed information and advice. The agents involved in the transaction usually split a commission of 5 percent to 7 percent, paid by the seller, when the transaction is closed. Today, the Internet is a valuable resource that allows home buyers to conveniently search for the best available properties. It's a good idea

to prequalify yourself for a mortgage before starting to house-hunt. A real estate sales contract is used to confirm in writing all terms of the transaction between buyer and seller. After a mortgage loan is approved, the loan is closed. A closing statement shows how much the borrower owes and the seller receives in the transaction.

LG6 **Choose mortgage financing that meets your needs. p. 199**
Mortgage loans can be obtained from commercial banks, from thrift institutions, or through a mortgage banker or mortgage broker. Although many types of mortgage loans are available, the most widely used are 30- and 15-year fixed-rate mortgages and adjustable-rate mortgages (ARMs). Sometimes interest rates will drop several years after closing, and mortgage refinancing will become attractive. The refinancing analysis considers the difference in terms between the old and new mortgages, any prepayment penalty on the old mortgage, closing costs, and how long you plan to stay in the home.

Key Terms

anchor, 168

adjustable-rate mortgage (ARM), 202

adjustment period, 202

balloon-payment mortgage, 201

biweekly mortgage, 204

buydown, 204

capitalized cost, 174

closing costs, 187

condominium (condo), 179

cooperative apartment (co-op), 179

convertible ARM, 203

closed-end lease, 173

conventional mortgage, 205

contingency clause, 197

depreciation, 166

down payment, 185

earnest money deposit,197

foreclosure, 194

foreclosures, 177

fixed-rate mortgage, 200

FHA mortgage insurance, 205

graduated-payment mortgage, 204

growing-equity mortgage, 204

homeowner's insurance, 190

interest-only mortgage, 204

index rate, 202

interest rate cap, 202

lease, 173

loan-to-value ratio, 185

margin, 202

Multiple Listing Service (MLS), 195

mortgage points, 186

money factor, 174

mortgage loan, 199

mortgage banker, 199

mortgage broker, 199

negative amortization, 202

open-end (finance) lease, 173

payment cap, 202

Prequalification, 196

purchase option, 174

private mortgage insurance (PMI), 186

PITI, 190

property taxes, 190

residual value 173

rental contract lease agreement, 180

rent ratio,181

Real Estate Settlement Procedures Act (RESPA), 197

sales contract, 171

shared-appreciation mortgage, 204

real estate short sale, 194

title check, 197

two-step ARM, 203

VA loan guarantees, 205

Answers to Test Yourself

You can find answers to these questions on this book's companion website. Look for it at *www.cengagebrain.com*. Search for this book by its title, and then add it to your dashboard.

Key Financial Relationships

Concept	Financial Relationship	Page Number
Mortgage Payment	Mortgage Payment = $\dfrac{\text{Amount of Loan}}{\$10,000} \times$ Monthly Payment on \$10,000 Loan	189
Maximum Affordable Mortgage Loan	Maximum Mortgage Loan = \$10,000 $\times \dfrac{\text{Maximum Monthly Payment}}{\text{Present Value Interest Factor}}$	191

Key Financial Relationships Problem Set

1. **Mortgage Payment.** Evelyn Ward wants to find the monthly payment on a \$150,000, 5 percent, 30-year mortgage.

   Solution: Using the monthly mortgage payments provided in Exhibit 5.9 to repay a \$10,000, 5 percent, 15-year loan:

   $$\text{Mortgage Payment} = \frac{\text{Amount of Loan}}{\$10,000} \times \text{Monthly Payment on } \$10,000 \text{ Loan}$$

   $$= \frac{\$150,000}{\$10,000} \times \$79.08 = 15 \times \$79.08 = \$1,186.20$$

   Evelyn could also use a financial calculator with the following key strokes:

Inputs	Functions
15000	PV
180	N
5	÷
12	=
	I
	CPT
	PMT
	SOLUTION
	1186.19

2. **Maximum Affordable Mortgage Loan.** Alex and Lucy Riley have saved a \$25,000 down payment and are considering buying a home. Based on their monthly income and affordability analysis, the Rileys can handle a maximum mortgage payment of \$1,500 a month. The Riley's want to determine the amount of the maximum 30-year, 6 percent mortgage they can obtain.

   Solution: Using the monthly mortgage payments provided in Exhibit 5.9 to repay a \$10,000, 6 percent, 30-year loan:

   $$\text{Maximum Mortgage Loan} = \$10,000 \times \frac{\text{Maximum Monthly Payment}}{\text{Monthly Payment on } \$10,000 \text{ Loan}}$$

   $$= \$10,000 \times \frac{\$1,500}{\$59.96} = \$250,166.78$$

Alex and Lucy Riley could also use a financial calculator with the following key strokes:

Inputs	Functions
1500	*PMT*
360	*N*
6	÷
12	=
	I
	CPT
	PV
	SOLUTION
	250187.42

Further, the quick estimate provided in Exhibit 5.10 indicates a maximum mortgage of $250,187.

Thus, given their $25,000 down payment, the Riley's could afford to pay about $280,000 mortgage.

Financial Planning Exercises

LG1, 2, p. 164, 173

1. ***Planning a new car purchase.*** Janet Wilhite has just graduated from college and needs to buy a car to commute to work. She estimates that she can afford to pay about $450 per month for a loan or lease and has about $2,000 in savings to use for a down payment. Develop a plan to guide her through her first car-buying experience, including researching car type, deciding whether to buy a new or used car, negotiating the price and terms, and financing the transaction.

LG2, p. 173

2. ***Lease vs. purchase car decision. Use Worksheet 5.1.*** Chris Svenson is trying to decide whether to lease or purchase a new car costing $18,000. If he leases, he'll have to pay a $600 security deposit and monthly payments of $425 over the 36-month term of the closed-end lease. On the other hand, if he buys the car then he'll have to make a $2,400 down payment and will finance the balance with a 36-month loan requiring monthly payments of $515; he'll also have to pay a 6 percent sales tax ($1,080) on the purchase price, and he expects the car to have a residual value of $6,500 at the end of 3 years. Chris can earn 4 percent interest on his savings. Use the automobile lease versus purchase analysis form in Worksheet 5.1 to find the total cost of both the lease and the purchase and then recommend the best strategy for Chris.

LG3, p. 177

3. ***Interpreting the rent ratio.*** Art Patton has equally attractive job offers in Miami and Los Angeles. The rent ratios in the cities are 8 and 20, respectively. Art would really like to buy rather than rent a home after he moves. Explain how to interpret the rent ratio and what it tells Art about the relative attractiveness of moving to Miami rather than Los Angeles, given his stated goal.

LG3, 4, p. 177, 184

4. ***Rent vs. buy home. Use Worksheet 5.2.*** Denise Green is currently renting an apartment for $725 per month and paying $275 annually for renter's insurance. She just found a small townhouse that she can buy for $185,000. She has enough cash for a $10,000 down payment and $4,000 in closing costs. Her bank is offering 30-year mortgages at 6 percent per year. Denise estimated the following costs as a percentage of the home's price: property taxes, 2.5 percent; homeowner's insurance, 0.5 percent; and maintenance, 0.7 percent. She is in the 25 percent tax bracket and has an after-tax rate of return on invested funds of 4 percent. Using Worksheet 5.2, calculate the cost of each alternative and recommend the less costly option—rent or buy—for Denise.

LG4, p. 184

5. ***Calculating required down payment on home purchase.*** How much would you have to put down on a house costing $100,000 if the house had an appraised value of $105,000 and the lender required an 80 percent loan-to-value ratio?

LG4, p. 184

6. ***Determining maximum affordable mortgage.*** Using the maximum ratios for a conventional mortgage, how big a monthly payment could the Danforth family afford if their gross (before-tax) monthly income amounted to $4,000? Would it make any difference if they were already making monthly installment loan payments totaling $750 on two car loans?

| LG4, p. 184 | 7. | **_Changes in mortgage principal and interest over time._** Explain how the composition of the principal and interest components of a fixed-rate mortgage change over the life of the mortgage. What are the implications of this change? |

| LG4, p. 184 | 8. | **_Calculating monthly mortgage payments._** Find the _monthly_ mortgage payments on the following mortgage loans using either your calculator or the table in Exhibit 5.8: |

    a. $80,000 at 6.5 percent for 30 years
    b. $105,000 at 5.5 percent for 20 years
    c. $95,000 at 5 percent for 15 years

| LG4, p. 184 | 9. | **_Home affordability analysis. Use Worksheet 5.3._** Selma and Rodney Jackson need to calculate the amount that they can afford to spend on their first home. They have a combined annual income of $47,500 and have $27,000 available for a down payment and closing costs. The Jacksons estimate that homeowner's insurance and property taxes will be $250 per month. They expect the mortgage lender to use a 30 percent (of monthly gross income) mortgage payment affordability ratio, to lend at an interest rate of 6 percent on a 30-year mortgage, and to require a 15 percent down payment. Based on this information, use the home affordability analysis form in Worksheet 5.3 to determine the highest-priced home that the Jacksons can afford. |

| LG4, 5, p. 184, 194 | 10. | **_Estimating closing costs on home purchase._** How much might a home buyer expect to pay in closing costs on a $220,000 house with a 10 percent down payment? How much would the home buyer have to pay at the time of closing, taking into account closing costs, down payment, and a loan fee of 3 points? |

| LG6, p. 199 | 11. | **_Conventional vs. ARM mortgage payments._** What would the monthly payments be on a $150,000 loan if the mortgage were set up as: |

    a. A 15-year, 6 percent fixed-rate loan?
    b. A 30-year ARM in which the lender adds a margin of 2.5 to the index rate, which now stands at 4.5 percent? Find the monthly mortgage payments for the first year only.

| LG6, p. 199 | 12. | **_Adding to monthly mortgage payments._** What are the pros and cons of adding $100 a month to your fixed-rate mortgage payment? |

| LG6, p. 199 | 13. | **_Refinancing a mortgage. Use Worksheet 5.4._** Latha Yang purchased a condominium four years ago for $180,000, paying $1,250 per month on her $162,000, 8 percent, 25-year mortgage. The current loan balance is $152,401. Recently, interest rates have dropped sharply, causing Latha to consider refinancing her condo at the prevailing rate of 6 percent. She expects to remain in the condo for at least four more years and has found a lender that will make a 6 percent, 21-year, $152,401 loan requiring monthly payments of $1,065. Although there is no prepayment penalty on her current mortgage, Latha will have to pay $1,500 in closing costs on the new mortgage. She is in the 15 percent tax bracket. Based on this information, use the mortgage refinancing analysis form in Worksheet 5.4 to determine whether she should refinance her mortgage under the specified terms. |

Applying Personal Finance

How's Your Local Housing Market?

What's the best source of information about available housing in your community? The answer is a well-informed professional real estate agent whose business is helping buyers find and negotiate the purchase of the most suitable property at the best price. However, there's another readily available source of information: the local newspaper—in paper or online. Almost anything you want to know about the local housing scene can be found in the real estate section of the paper. For this project, you'll gather information concerning your local housing market.

Review recent issues of your local newspaper and describe the market for both purchased homes and rental units. Look for useful information such as location, size of property, price or rent, lease requirements, and so forth. You should observe that the housing market is very fragmented, which makes good purchase and rent decisions more difficult. See if you can answer questions such as: What is the average size of a house or apartment in your community? What is the typical sales price or monthly rent per square foot? Is the purchase market competitive? How about the rental market? How great a difference exists in prices and rents between the most and least desirable areas of the community? Also check online for other sources of information, such as the county tax office, and try to find out how much property taxes and homeowner's insurance premiums average in your area. From your study of the local market, summarize its conditions and be prepared to participate in a class discussion of the local housing market.

CRITICAL THINKING CASES

LG1, 2,
p. 164, 173

5.1 The Newtons' New Car Decision: Lease vs. Purchase

Farrah and Sam Newton, a dual-income couple in their late 20s, want to replace their seven-year-old car, which has 90,000 miles on it and needs some expensive repairs. After reviewing their budget, the Newtons conclude that they can afford auto payments of not more than $350 per month and a down payment of $2,000. They enthusiastically decide to visit a local dealer after reading its newspaper ad offering a closed-end lease on a new car for a monthly payment of $245. After visiting with the dealer, test-driving the car, and discussing the lease terms with the salesperson, they remain excited about leasing the car but decide to wait until the following day to finalize the deal. Later that day, the Newtons begin to question their approach to the new car acquisition process and decide to reevaluate their decision carefully.

Critical Thinking Questions

1. What are some basic purchasing guidelines that the Newtons should consider when choosing which new car to buy or lease? How can they find the information they need?
2. How would you advise the Newtons to research the lease-versus-purchase decision before visiting the dealer? What are the advantages and disadvantages of each alternative?
3. Assume that the Newtons can get the following terms on a lease or a bank loan for the car, which they could buy for $17,000. This amount includes tax, title, and license fees.
   - **Lease:** 48 months, $245 monthly payment, 1 month's payment required as a security deposit, $350 end-of-lease charges; a residual value of $6,775 is the purchase option price at the end of the lease.
   - **Loan:** $2,000 down payment, $15,000, 48-month loan at 5 percent interest requiring a monthly payment of $345.44; assume that the car's value at the end of 48 months will be the same as the residual value and that sales tax is 6 percent.

The Newtons can currently earn interest of 3 percent annually on their savings. They expect to drive about the same number of miles per year as they do now.
   a. Use the format given in Worksheet 5.1 to determine which deal is best for the Newtons.
   b. What other costs and terms of the lease option might affect their decision?
   c. Based on the available information, should the Newtons lease or purchase the car? Why?

LG4, 6,
p. 184, 199

5.2 Evaluating a Mortgage Loan for the Gerrards

Ben and Marie Gerrard, both in their mid-20s, have been married for four years and have two pre-school-age children. Ben has an accounting degree and is employed as a cost accountant at an annual salary of $62,000. They're now renting a duplex but wish to buy a home in the suburbs of their rapidly developing city. They've decided they can afford a $215,000 house and hope to find one with the features they desire in a good neighborhood.

The insurance costs on such a home are expected to be $800 per year, taxes are expected to be $2,500 per year, and annual utility bills are estimated at $1,440—an increase of $500 over those they pay in the duplex. The Gerrards are considering financing their home with a fixed-rate, 30-year, 6 percent mortgage. The lender charges 2 points on mortgages with 20 percent down and 3 points if less than 20 percent is put down (the commercial bank that the Gerrards will deal with requires a minimum of 10 percent down). Other closing costs are estimated at 5 percent of the home's purchase price. Because of their excellent credit record, the bank will probably be willing to let the Gerrards' monthly mortgage payments (principal and interest portions) equal as much as 28 percent of their monthly gross income. Since getting married, the Gerrards have been saving for the purchase of a home and now have $44,000 in their savings account.

Critical Thinking Questions

1. How much would the Gerrards have to put down if the lender required a minimum 20 percent down payment? Could they afford it?
2. Given that the Gerrards want to put only $25,000 down, how much would their closing costs be? Considering only principal and interest, how much would their monthly mortgage payments be? Would they qualify for a loan using a 28 percent affordability ratio?
3. Using a $25,000 down payment on a $215,000 home, what would the Gerrards' loan-to-value ratio be? Calculate the monthly mortgage payments on a PITI basis.
4. What recommendations would you make to the Gerrards? Explain.

LG3, 4,
p. 177, 184

5.3 Julie's Rent-or-Buy Decision

Julie Brown is in her late 20s. She is renting an apartment in the fashionable part of town for $1,200 a month. After much thought, she's seriously considering buying a condominium for $175,000. She intends to put 20 percent down and expects that closing costs will amount to another $5,000; a commercial bank has agreed to lend her money at the fixed rate of 6 percent on a 15-year mortgage. Julie would have to pay an annual condominium owner's insurance premium of $600 and property taxes of $1,200 a year (she's now paying renter's insurance of $550 per year). In addition, she estimates that annual maintenance expenses will be about 0.5 percent of the price of the condo (which includes a $30 monthly fee to the property owners' association). Julie's income puts her in the 25 percent tax bracket (she itemizes her deductions on her tax returns), and she earns an after-tax rate of return on her investments of around 4 percent.

Critical Thinking Questions

1. Given the information provided, use Worksheet 5.2 to evaluate and compare Julie's alternatives of remaining in the apartment or purchasing the condo.
2. Working with a friend who is a realtor, Julie has learned that condos like the one that she's thinking of buying are appreciating in value at the rate of 3.5 percent a year and are expected to continue doing so. Would such information affect the rent-or-buy decision made in Question 1? Explain.
3. Discuss any other factors that should be considered when making a rent-or-buy decision.
4. Which alternative would you recommend for Julie in light of your analysis?

PART 3

Managing Credit

CHAPTERS

6   Using Credit

7   Using Consumer Loans

CHAPTER 6

Using Credit

LEARNING GOALS

LG1 Describe the reasons for using consumer credit, and identify its benefits and problems.

LG2 Develop a plan to establish a strong credit history.

LG3 Distinguish among the different forms of open account credit.

LG4 Apply for, obtain, and manage open forms of credit.

LG5 Choose the right credit cards and recognize their advantages and disadvantages.

LG6 Avoid credit problems, protect yourself against credit card fraud, and understand the personal bankruptcy process.

How Will This Affect Me?

The ability to borrow funds to buy goods and services is as convenient as it is seductive. It is important to understand how to get and maintain access to credit and convenient transactions via credit cards, debit cards, lines of credit, and other means. This chapter reviews the common sources of consumer credit and provides a framework for choosing among them. It also discusses the importance of developing a good credit history, achieving and maintaining a good credit score, and protecting against identity theft and credit fraud. The chapter will help you understand the need to use credit intentionally, in a way that is consistent with your overall financial objectives.

6-1 THE BASIC CONCEPTS OF CREDIT

LG1, LG2

It's so easy. Just slide that credit card through the reader and you can buy gas for your car, have a gourmet meal at an expensive restaurant, or furnish an apartment. It happens *several hundred million times a day* across the United States. Credit, in fact, has become an entrenched part of our everyday lives, and we as consumers use it in one form or another to purchase just about every type of good or service imaginable. Indeed, because of the ready availability and widespread use of credit, our economy is often called a "credit economy." And for good reason: as of the end of 2014, households in this country had run up almost *$11.83 trillion dollars* in debt—and that doesn't even include home mortgages.

Consumer credit is important in the personal financial planning process because of the impact it can have on (1) attaining financial goals and (2) cash budgets. For one thing, various forms of consumer credit can help you reach your financial objectives by enabling you to acquire some of the more expensive items in a systematic fashion, without throwing your whole budget into disarray. But there's another side to consumer credit: it has to be paid back! Unless credit is used intelligently, the "buy now, pay later" attitude can quickly turn an otherwise orderly budget into a budgetary nightmare and lead to some serious problems—even bankruptcy! So, really, the issue is one of moderation and affordability.

In today's economy, consumers, businesses, and governments alike use credit to make transactions. Credit helps businesses supply the goods and services needed to satisfy consumer demand. Business credit also provides higher levels of employment and helps raise our overall standard of living. Local, state, and federal governments borrow for various projects and programs that also increase our standard of living and create additional employment opportunities. Clearly, borrowing helps fuel our economy and enhance the overall quality of our lives. Consequently, *consumers in a credit economy need to know how to establish credit and how to avoid the dangers of using it improperly.*

6-1a Why We Use Credit

People typically use credit as a way to pay for goods and services that cost more than they can afford to pay out of their current income. This is particularly true for those in the 25–44 age group, who simply have not had time to accumulate the liquid assets required to pay cash outright for major purchases and expenditures. As people begin to approach their mid-40s, however, their savings and investments start to build up and their debt loads tend to decline, which is really not too surprising when you consider that the median household net worth for those in the 45–54 age group is considerably higher than for those aged 35–44.

Whatever their age group, people tend to borrow for several major reasons.

- To avoid paying cash for large outlays: Rather than pay cash for large purchases such as houses and cars, most people borrow part of the purchase price and then repay the loan on some scheduled basis. Spreading payments over time makes big-ticket items more affordable, and consumers get the use of an expensive asset right away. In their minds, at least, the benefits of current consumption outweigh the interest costs on the loan. Unfortunately, while the initial euphoria of the purchase may wear off over time, the loan payments remain—perhaps for many more years to come.

- To meet a financial emergency: For example, people may need to borrow to cover living expenses during a period of unemployment or to purchase plane tickets to visit a sick relative. As indicated in Chapter 4, however, using savings is preferable to using credit for financial emergencies.

- For convenience: Merchants as well as banks offer a variety of charge accounts and credit cards that allow consumers to charge just about anything—from gas or clothes and stereos to doctor and dental bills and even college tuition. Further, in many places—restaurants, for instance—using a credit card is far easier than writing a check. Although such transactions usually incur no interest (at least not initially), these credit card purchases are still a form of borrowing. This is because payment is not made at the time of the transaction.

- For investment purposes: As we'll see in Chapter 11, it's relatively easy for an investor to partially finance the purchase of many different kinds of investments with borrowed funds.

Financial Fact or Fantasy?

One of the benefits of using credit is that it allows you to purchase expensive goods and services while spreading the payment for them over time. **Fact:** One of the major benefits of buying on credit is that expensive purchases are made more affordable because the consumer is able to pay for them systematically over time.

6-1b Improper Uses of Credit

Many people use consumer credit to live beyond their means. For some people, overspending becomes a way of life, and it is perhaps the biggest danger in borrowing—especially because it's so easy to do. And nowhere did that become more apparent than in the wake of the credit crisis of 2007–2009. Indeed, as credit became more readily available and easier to obtain, it also became increasingly clear that many consumers were, in fact, severely overusing it. All this resulted in a credit meltdown unlike anything this country had ever seen.

Once hooked on "plastic," people may use their credit cards to make even routine purchases and all too often don't realize they have overextended themselves until it's too late. And by making only the minimum payment, borrowers pay a huge price in the long run. Exhibit 6.1 shows the amount of time and interest charges required to repay credit card balances if you make only minimum payments of 3 percent of the outstanding balance. Paying only the minimum balance is a costly decision.

> **EXAMPLE: Paying Only the Minimum on Your Credit Card**
>
> If you carry a $3,000 balance—which is about *one-fifth* of the national average—on a credit card that charges 15.0 percent annually and only pay the minimum amount due, it would take you 14 years to retire the debt, and your interest charges would total some $2,000—*or more than 66 percent of the original balance!*

EXHIBIT 6.1   Minimum Payments Mean Maximum Years

Paying off credit card balances at the minimum monthly amount required by the card issuer will take a long time and cost you a great deal of interest, as this table demonstrates. *The calculations here are based on a minimum 3 percent payment and 15 percent annual interest rate.*

Original Balance	Years to Repay	Interest Paid	Total Interest Paid, as Percentage of Original Balance
$5,000	16.4	$3,434	68.7%
4,000	15.4	2,720	68.0
3,000	14.0	2,005	66.8
2,000	12.1	1,291	64.5
1,000	8.8	577	57.7

Some cards offer even lower minimum payments of just 2 percent of the outstanding balance. Although such small payments may seem like a good deal, clearly they don't work to your advantage and only increase the time and amount of interest required to repay the debt. For example, by making minimum 2 percent payments, it would take *more than 32 years* to pay off a $5,000 balance on a credit card that carries a 15 percent rate of interest. In contrast, as can be seen in Exhibit 6.1, that same $5,000 balance could be paid off in *just 16.4 years* if you had made 3 percent minimum payments. Just think, making an additional 1 percent payment can save you nearly 16 years of interest! That's why the federal banking regulators issued guidelines stating that minimum monthly credit card payments should now cover at least 1 percent of the outstanding balance, plus all monthly finance charges and any other fees.

Avoid the possibility of future repayment shock by keeping in mind the following types of transactions for which you should *not* (routinely, at least) use credit: (1) to meet basic living expenses; (2) to make impulse purchases, especially expensive ones; and (3) to purchase nondurable (short-lived) goods and services. Except in situations where credit cards are used occasionally for convenience (such as for gasoline, groceries, and entertainment) or where payments on recurring credit purchases are built into the monthly budget, a good rule to remember when considering the use of credit is that *the product purchased on credit should outlive the amount of time it takes to pay it off.*

Unfortunately, people who overspend eventually must choose to either become delinquent in their payments or sacrifice necessities, such as food and clothing. If payment obligations aren't met, the consequences are likely to be a damaged credit rating, lawsuits, or even personal bankruptcy. Exhibit 6.2 lists some common signals that indicate it may be time to stop buying on credit. *Ignoring the telltale signs that you are overspending can only lead to more serious problems.*

6-1c Establishing Credit

The willingness of lenders to extend credit depends on their assessment of your creditworthiness—that is, your ability to promptly repay the debt. Lenders look at various factors in making this decision, such as your present earnings and net worth. Equally important, they look at your current debt position and your credit history. Thus, it's worth your while to do what you can to build a strong credit rating.

EXHIBIT 6.2 **Watch for Credit Danger Signs**

If one or more of these signs exist, it's time to proceed with caution in your credit spending. Be prepared to revise and update your spending patterns, cut back on the use of credit, and be alert for other signs of overspending.

Serious trouble may be ahead if you:

- Regularly use credit cards to buy on impulse
- Postdate checks to keep them from bouncing
- Regularly exceed the borrowing limits on your credit cards
- Never add up all your bills, to avoid facing grim realities
- Now take 60 or 90 days to pay bills that you once paid in 30
- Have to borrow just to meet normal living expenses
- Often use one form of credit—such as a cash advance from a credit card—to make payments on other debt
- Can barely make the minimum required payments on bills
- Are using more than 20 percent of your take-home income to pay credit card bills and personal loans (excluding mortgage payments)
- Have little or no savings
- Are so far behind on credit payments that collection agencies are calling you

First Steps in Establishing Credit

First, open checking and savings accounts. They signal stability to lenders and indicate that you handle your financial affairs in a businesslike way. Second, use credit: open one or two charge accounts and use them periodically, even if you prefer paying cash. For example, get a *MasterCard* and make a few credit purchases each month (don't overdo it, of course). You might pay an annual fee or interest on some (or all) of your account balances, but in the process, you'll build a record of being a reliable credit customer. Third, obtain a small loan, even if you don't need one. If you don't actually need the money, put it in a liquid investment, such as a money market account or certificate of deposit. The interest you earn should offset some of the interest expense on the loan; you can view the difference as a cost of building good credit. You should repay the loan promptly, perhaps even a little ahead of schedule, to minimize the difference in interest rates. However, don't pay off the loan too quickly because lenders like to see how you perform over an extended period of time. Keep in mind that your ability to obtain a large loan in the future will depend, in part, on how you managed smaller ones in the past.

Build a Strong Credit History

From a financial perspective, maintaining a strong credit history is just as important as developing a solid employment record! Don't take credit lightly, and don't assume that getting the loan or the credit card is the toughest part. It's not. That's just the first step; servicing it (i.e., making payments) in a timely fashion—month in and month out—is the really tough part of the consumer credit process. By using credit wisely and repaying it on time, you're establishing a *credit history* that tells lenders you're a dependable, reliable, and responsible borrower.

The consumer credit industry watches your credit and your past payment performance closely (more on this when we discuss *credit bureaus* later in this chapter). So the more responsible you are as a borrower, the easier it will be to get credit when and where you want it. The best way to build a strong credit history and maintain your creditworthiness is to *consistently make payments on time,* month after month. Being late occasionally—say, two or three times a year—might label you a "late payer." When you take on credit, you have an *obligation* to live up to the terms of the loan, including how and when the credit will be repaid.

If you foresee difficulty in meeting a monthly payment, let the lender know. Usually arrangements can be made to help you through the situation. This is especially true with installment loans that require fixed monthly payments. If you have one or two of these loans and see a month coming that's going to be really tight, the first thing you should try to do (other than trying to borrow some money from a family member) is get an extension on your loan. Don't just skip a payment, because that's going to put your account into *late status until you make up the missed payment*. In other words, until you make a *double* payment, your account/loan will remain in a late status, which is subject to a monthly late penalty. Trying to work out an extension with your lender obviously makes a lot more sense.

Here's what you do. Explain the situation to the loan officer and ask for an extension of one (or two) months on your loan. In most cases, so long as this hasn't occurred before, the extension is almost automatically granted. The maturity of the loan is formally extended for a month (or two), and the extra interest of carrying the loan for another month (or two) is either added to the loan balance or, more commonly, paid at the time the extension is granted (such an extension fee generally amounts to a fraction of the normal monthly payment). Then, in a month or two, you pick up where you left off and resume your normal monthly payments on the loan. This is the most sensible way of making it through those rough times because it doesn't harm your credit record. Just don't do it too often.

How Much Credit Can You Handle?

Sound financial planning dictates that you need a good idea of how much credit you can comfortably tolerate. The easiest way to avoid repayment problems and ensure that your borrowing won't place an undue strain on your monthly budget is to *limit the use*

Financial Fact or Fantasy?

It's a good idea to contact your creditors immediately if, for some reason, you can't make payments as agreed. **Fact:** Let the lenders know and they'll often give you a credit extension. This is one of the smartest things you can do to build a sound credit history. However, except for those occasional tight spots, it's important to make credit payments on time consistently!

FINANCIAL ROAD SIGN

The 5 Cs of Credit

Lenders often look to the "5 Cs of Credit" as a way to assess the willingness and ability of a borrower to repay a loan.

1. Character. A key factor in defining the borrower's willingness to live up to the terms of the loan.
2. Capacity. The ability of the borrower to service the loan in a timely fashion.
3. Collateral. Something of value that's used to secure a loan and that the lender can claim in case of default.
4. Capital. The amount of unencumbered assets owned by the borrower, used as another indicator of the borrower's ability to repay the loan.
5. Condition. The extent to which prevailing economic conditions could affect the borrower's ability to service a loan.

Here are some things you can do to build a strong credit history:

- Use credit only when you can afford it and only when the repayment schedule fits comfortably into the family budget—in short, don't overextend yourself.
- Fulfill all the terms of the credit.
- Be *consistent* in making payments *promptly*.
- Consult creditors immediately if you cannot meet payments as agreed.
- Be truthful when applying for credit. Lies are not likely to go undetected.

debt safety ratio
The proportion of total
monthly consumer credit
obligations to monthly
take-home pay.

of credit to your ability to repay the debt! A useful *credit guideline* (and one widely used by lenders) is to make sure your monthly repayment burden doesn't exceed 20 percent of your monthly *take-home pay.* Most experts, however, regard the 20 percent figure as the *maximum* debt burden and strongly recommend a debt safety ratio closer to 10 or 15 percent—perhaps even lower if you plan on applying for a new mortgage in the near future. Note that the monthly repayment burden here *does include* payments on your credit cards, but it *excludes* your monthly mortgage obligation.

To illustrate, consider someone who takes home $2,500 a month. Using a 20 percent ratio, she should have monthly consumer credit payments of no more than $500—that is, $2,500 × 0.20 = $500. This is the maximum amount of her monthly disposable income that she should need to pay off both personal loans and other forms of consumer credit (such as credit cards and education loans). This, of course, is not the maximum amount of consumer credit that she can have outstanding—in fact, her total consumer indebtedness can, and likely would, be considerably larger. The key factor is that with her income level, her *payments* on this type of debt should not exceed $500 a month. (*Caution:* This doesn't mean that credit terms should be lengthened just to accommodate this guideline; rather, in all cases, it's assumed that standard credit terms apply.)

Exhibit 6.3 provides a list of low (10 percent), manageable (15 percent), and maximum (20 percent) monthly credit payments for various income levels. Obviously, the closer your total monthly payments are to your desired debt safety ratio, the less future borrowing you can do. Conversely, *the lower the debt safety ratio, the better shape you're in, creditwise, and the easier it should be for you to service your outstanding consumer debt.*

You can compute the debt safety ratio as follows:

$$\text{Debt Safety Ratio} = \frac{\text{Total Monthly Consumer Credit Payments}}{\text{Monthly Take} - \text{Home Pay}}$$

EXHIBIT 6.3   Credit Guidelines Based on Ability to Repay

According to the debt safety ratio, the amount of consumer credit you should have outstanding depends on the monthly payments you can afford to make.

Monthly Take-Home Pay	MONTHLY CONSUMER CREDIT PAYMENTS		
	Low Debt Safety Ratio (10%)	*Manageable* Debt Safety Ratio (15%)	*Maximum* Debt Safety Ratio (20%)
$1,000	$100	$150	$200
1,250	125	188	250
1,500	150	225	300
2,000	200	300	400
2,500	250	375	500
3,000	300	450	600
3,500	350	525	700
4,000	400	600	800
5,000	500	750	1,000

Financial Fact or Fantasy?

Excluding mortgage payments, most families will have little or no credit problems so long as they limit their monthly credit payments to 25 to 30 percent of their monthly take-home pay. **Fantasy:** Most experts suggest that you keep your monthly debt repayment burden, excluding mortgage payments, to 20 percent or less of your take-home pay. Letting it get as high as 25 to 30 percent can lead to serious credit problems.

This measure is the focus of Worksheet 6.1, which you can use for keeping close tabs on your own debt safety ratio. It shows the impact that each new loan you take out, or credit card you sign up for, can have on this important measure of creditworthiness. Consider, for example, Winston and Victoria Chang. As seen in Worksheet 6.1, they have five outstanding consumer loans, plus they're carrying balances on three credit cards. All told, these eight obligations require monthly payments of almost $740, which accounts for about one-fifth of their combined take-home pay and gives them a debt safety ratio of 18 percent. And note the information at the bottom of the worksheet that says if the Changs want to lower this ratio to, say, 15 percent, then they'll either have to reduce their monthly payments to $615 or increase their take-home pay to at least $4,927 a month.

TEST YOURSELF

6-1 Why do people borrow? What are some improper uses of credit?

6-2 Describe the general guidelines that lenders use to calculate an applicant's maximum debt burden.

6-3 How can you use the *debt safety ratio* to determine whether your debt obligations are within reasonable limits?

6-4 What steps can you take to establish a good credit rating?

6-2 CREDIT CARDS AND OTHER TYPES OF OPEN ACCOUNT CREDIT

open account credit
A form of credit extended to a consumer in advance of any transaction.

credit limit
A specified amount beyond which a customer may not borrow or purchase on credit.

credit statement
A monthly statement summarizing the transactions, interest charges, fees, and payments in a consumer credit account.

Open account credit is a form of credit extended to a consumer in advance of any transactions. Typically, a retail outlet or bank agrees to allow the consumer to buy or borrow up to a specified amount on open account. Credit is extended so long as the consumer does not exceed the established **credit limit** and makes payments in accordance with the specified terms. Open account credit issued by a retail outlet, such as a department store or oil company, is usually applicable only in that establishment or one of its locations. In contrast, open account credit issued by banks, such as *MasterCard* and *Visa* accounts, can be used to make purchases at a wide variety of businesses. For the rest of this chapter, we'll direct our attention to the various types and characteristics of open account credit; in Chapter 7, we'll look at various forms of single-payment and installment loans.

Having open account credit is a lot like having a personal line of credit—it's there when you need it. But unlike most other types of debt, consumers who use open forms of credit can often avoid paying interest charges *if they promptly pay the full amount of their account balance.* For example, assume that in a given month you charge $75.58 on an open account at a department store. Sometime within the next month or so, you'll receive a **credit statement** from the store that summarizes recent transactions on your account. Now, if there are no other charges and the total

A worksheet like this one will help a household stay on top of their monthly credit card and consumer loan payments, as well as their *debt safety ratio*—an important measure of creditworthiness. The key is to keep the debt safety ratio as low as (reasonably) possible, something that can be done by keeping monthly loan payments in line with monthly take-home pay.

MONTHLY CONSUMER LOAN PAYMENTS & DEBT SAFETY RATIO

Name Winston and Victoria Chang   **Date** June 21, 2017

■ Type of Loan*	Lender	Current Monthly (or Min.) Payment
• Auto and personal loans	Ford Motor Credit	$ 360.00
	Bank of America	115.00
• Education loans	U.S. Dept. of Education	75.00
• Overdraft protection line	Bank of America	30.00
• Personal line of credit		
• Credit cards	Bank of America Visa	28.00
	Fidelity MC	31.00
	JC Penney	28.00
• Home equity line	Bank of America	72.00
	TOTAL MONTHLY PAYMENTS	$ 739.00

*Note: List only those loans that require regular monthly payments.

■ Monthly Take-Home Pay	1. Winston	$ 1,855.00
	2. Victoria	2,250.00
	TOTAL MONTHLY TAKE-HOME PAY	$ 4,105.00

■ **Debt Safety Ratio:**

$$\frac{\text{Total monthly payments}}{\text{Total monthly take-home pay}} \times 100 = \frac{\$\ 739.00}{\$4,105.00} \times 100 = \underline{18.0}\ \%$$

• **Changes needed to reach a new debt safety ratio**

1. New (Target) debt safety ratio: 15.0 %

2. At current take-home pay of $4,105.00 ,
   total monthly payments must equal:

$$\text{Total monthly take-home pay} \times \text{Target debt safety ratio**}$$

$$\underline{\$4,105.00} \times \underline{0.150} = \underline{\$\ 615.75}$$
New Monthly Payments

OR

3. With current monthly payments of $739.00 ,
   total take-home pay must equal:

$$\frac{\text{Total monthly payments}}{\text{New (target) debt safety ratio}} \times 100 = \frac{\$\ 739.00}{0.150} = \underline{\$4,926.67}$$
New take-home pay

**Note: Enter debt safety ratio as a decimal (e.g., 15% = 0.15).

account balance is $75.58, you can (usually) avoid any finance charges by paying the account in full before the next billing date.

Open account credit generally is available from two broadly defined sources: (1) financial institutions and (2) retail stores/merchants. *Financial institutions* issue general-purpose credit cards, as well as secured and unsecured revolving lines of credit and overdraft protection lines. Commercial banks have long been the major providers of consumer credit; and, since deregulation, so have S&Ls, credit unions, major stock-brokerage firms, and consumer finance companies. *Retail stores and merchants* make up the other major source of open account credit. They provide this service as a way to promote the sales of their products, and their principal form of credit is the charge (or credit) card. Let's now take a look at these two forms of credit, along with *debit cards* and *revolving lines of credit*.

6-2a Bank Credit Cards

bank credit card
A credit card issued by a bank or other financial institution that allows the holder to charge purchases at any establishment that accepts it.

Probably the most popular form of open account credit is the bank credit card issued by commercial banks and other financial institutions—*Visa* and *MasterCard* are the two dominant types. These cards allow their holders to charge purchases worldwide at literally millions of stores, restaurants, shops, and gas stations as well as at state and municipal governments, colleges and universities, medical groups, and mail-order houses—not to mention the Internet, where they've become the currency of choice. They can be used to pay for almost anything. The volume of credit and debit card purchases moved beyond cash and check transactions in 2003. Thousands of banks, S&Ls, credit unions, brokerage houses, and other financial services institutions issue *Visa* and *MasterCard*; and each issuer, within reasonable limits, can set its own credit terms and conditions.

Bank credit cards can be used to borrow money as well as buy goods and services on credit. Because of their potential for use in literally thousands of businesses and banks, they can be of great convenience and value to consumers. However, individuals who use them should be thoroughly familiar with their basic features.

The financial crisis in 2008–2009 brought tighter credit standards to the bank credit card business. This includes higher standards for personal credit history. Standards tend to tighten quickly in a crisis, and it can take several years before they move back to their pre-crisis levels. As a result, consumers find it harder to get new credit cards, and the limits on many existing cards are reduced markedly.

Line of Credit

line of credit
The maximum amount of credit a customer is allowed to have outstanding at any point in time.

The line of credit provided to the holder of a bank credit card is set by the issuer for each card. It's the maximum amount that the cardholder can owe at any time. The size of the credit line depends on both the applicant's request and the results of the issuer's investigation of the applicant's credit and financial status. Lines of credit offered by issuers of bank cards can reach $50,000 or more, but for the most part they range from about $500 to $2,500. Although card issuers fully expect you to keep your credit within the specified limits, most won't take any action unless you extend your account balance a certain percentage beyond the account's stated maximum. For example, if you had a $1,000 credit limit, you probably wouldn't hear from the card issuer until your outstanding account balance exceeded, say, $1,200 (i.e., 20 percent above the $1,000 line of credit). On the other hand, don't count on getting off for free, because most card issuers assess *over-the-limit* fees whenever you go over your credit limit.

Cash Advances

cash advance
A loan that can be obtained by a bank credit cardholder at any participating bank or financial institution.

In addition to purchasing merchandise and services, the holder of a bank credit card can obtain a cash advance from any participating bank. Cash advances are loans on which interest begins to accrue immediately. They're transacted in the same way as merchandise purchases, except that they take place at a commercial bank or some other financial institution and involve the receipt of cash (or a check) instead of goods and services. Another way to get a cash advance is to use the "convenience checks" that you receive from the card issuer to pay for purchases. You can even use your credit card to draw cash from an ATM, any time of the day or night. Usually, the size of the cash advance from an ATM is limited to some nominal amount (a common amount is $500 or less), although the amount you can obtain from the teller window at a bank is limited only by the unused credit in your account. Thus, if you've used only $1,000 of a $5,000 credit limit, you can take out a cash advance of up to $4,000.

Interest Charges

The average *annual rate of interest* charged on standard fixed-rate bank credit cards was 13.01 percent in mid-2015, while the average rate on standard variable-rate cards was 15.76 percent. You'll find that most bank cards have one rate for merchandise purchases and a much higher rate for cash advances. For example, the rate on merchandise purchases might be 12 percent, while the rate on cash advances could be 19 percent or 20 percent. And when shopping for a credit card, watch out for those *special low introductory rates* that many banks offer. Known as "teaser rates," they're usually only good for the first 6 to 12 months. Then, just as soon as the introductory period ends, so do the low interest rates.

base rate
The rate of interest a bank uses as a base for loans to individuals and small to midsize businesses.

Most of these cards have variable interest rates that are tied to an index that moves with market rates. The most popular is the prime or base rate: the rate a bank uses as a base for loans to individuals and small or midsize businesses. These cards adjust their interest rate monthly or quarterly and usually have minimum and maximum rates. Given the widespread use of variable interest rates, bank cardholders should be aware that—just as falling rates bring down interest rates on credit cards—rising market rates are guaranteed to lead to much higher interest charges!

> **EXAMPLE: Bank Credit Card Index Interest Rates**
>
> Consider a bank card whose terms are *prime plus 7.5 percent,* with a minimum of 10 percent and a maximum of 15.25 percent. If the prime rate is 3.25 percent, then the rate of interest charged on this card would be 3.25 percent + 7.5 percent = 10.75 percent.

Generally speaking, *the interest rates on credit cards are higher than any other form of consumer credit.* However, because competition has become so intense, a growing number of banks today are actually willing to negotiate their fees as a way to retain their customers. Whether this trend will have any significant impact on permanently reducing interest rates and fees remains to be seen, but at least most consumers would agree it's a step in the right direction.

grace period
A short period of time, usually 20 to 30 days, during which you can pay your credit card bill in full and not incur any interest charges.

Bank credit card issuers must disclose interest costs and related information to consumers *before* extending credit. In the case of purchases of merchandise and services, the specified interest rate may not apply to charges until after the grace period. During this short period, usually 20 to 30 days, you have historically been able to pay your credit card bill in full and avoid any interest charges. Once you carry a balance—that is, when you don't pay your card in full during the grace period—the interest rate is usually applied to any unpaid balances carried from previous periods, as well as to any new purchases made. Interest on cash advances, however, *begins the day that the advance is taken out.*

Those Other Fees

Besides the interest charged on bank credit cards, there are a few other fees you should be aware of. To begin with, many (though not all) bank cards charge *annual fees* just for the "privilege" of being able to use the card. In most cases, the fee is around $25 to $40 a year, though it can amount to much more for prestige cards. Sometimes, this annual fee is waived in the first year, but you'll be stuck with it for the second and every other year you hold the card. As a rule, the larger the bank or S&L, the more likely it is to charge an annual fee for its credit cards. What's more, many issuers also charge a *transaction fee* for each (non-ATM) cash advance; this fee usually amounts to about $5 per cash advance or 3 percent of the amount obtained in the transaction, whichever is more.

Historically, card issuers have come up with many ways to squeeze additional revenue from you. These have included late-payment fees, over-the-limit charges, foreign transaction fees, and balance transfer fees. For example, if you were a bit late in making your payment, then some banks will hit you with a late-payment fee, which is really a redundant charge because you were already paying interest on the unpaid balance. Similarly, if you happened to go over your credit limit, then you'd be hit with a charge for that, too (again, this is in addition to the interest you're already paying). The card issuers have justified these charges by saying it costs money to issue and administer these cards, so they have a right to charge these fees if you don't use their cards. Of course, you have the right to let the issuer know what you think of these charges by canceling your card! Regardless of when or why any of these fees are levied, the net effect is that *they add to the true cost of using bank credit cards.*

These onerous credit card issuer practices and extra fees led to the passage of the Credit Card Act of 2009. In the past, credit card companies could change interest rates and other aspects of the agreement without notice. They could even change terms retroactively such that they applied two months before you were notified. The new law requires credit card companies to give 45 days' notice before changing your agreement. Similarly, credit card companies previously could raise your interest rate if your credit report deteriorated or if you were late on even just one payment. The new law allows credit card companies to apply a new interest rate only to new balances after you are 60 days delinquent paying on your account. And just as important is that your old balance can only be charged your old interest rate. Exhibit 6.4 summarizes some of the key provisions of the law. In the year after the law went into effect in 2010, credit card balances fell, late payments dropped, payment defaults declined, and there was increased use of debit over credit cards.

Balance Transfers

balance transfer
A program that enables cardholders to readily transfer credit balances from one card to another.

One feature of bank credit cards that some users find attractive is the ability to transfer balances from one card to another. Known as balance transfers, the card issuers make a big deal out of allowing you to transfer the balances from one or more (old) cards to their (new) card. The idea is to dump the old card(s) by putting everything, including current balances, on the issuer's (new) card. There are two potential advantages to these balance transfer programs. First, there's the convenience of being able to consolidate your credit card payments. Second, there's the potential savings in interest that accompanies the transfer, since such deals usually come with very low (introductory) rates. But these transfers also have their drawbacks. For starters, although you may benefit (initially) from a low rate on all transferred funds, the issuer will often charge a much higher rate on new purchases. On top of that, your monthly payment is usually applied first to the transferred balance and not the *new purchases,* which incur the higher rate. In addition, some banks will charge a flat fee on all transferred funds.

> **EXAMPLE: Cost of Transferring a Credit Card Balance**
>
> Suppose you transfer a balance of $5,000 to a new credit card that imposes a 4 percent fee for the transfer. This would result in a charge of $200, and that's in addition to any other interest charges! Although many balance transfer programs offer relatively low introductory rates, those low rates usually don't last very long.

EXHIBIT 6.4   How the Credit Card Act of 2009 Affects You

The Credit Card Act of 2009 provides sweeping and significant credit card reform. Its goal is to protect consumers from some of the harsher practices of credit card companies. While it provides some protection, it's no substitute for responsible credit card habits. Here are some of the major provisions of the new law:

Finance Charges and Interest Rate Increases
- Credit card companies must give you notice 45 days before increasing your interest rate or changing your agreement. Prior to passage of the new law, the requirement was only 15 days' notice. Promotional rates must last at least six months.
- Finance charges can no longer be calculated using the double-cycle billing approach, which takes into account not only the average daily balance of the current billing cycle, but also the average daily balance of the prior period. This billing approach can increase interest charges significantly for consumers whose average balance varies a lot from month to month.
- If your card company increases your rate, the new rate can be applied only to new balances, not to preexisting balances.

Payment Allocation and Fees
- Fees for making your credit card payment are prohibited unless you're making a last-minute payment by phone when your payment is due.
- If your balances have different interest rates, any payment above the minimum due must be allocated to your highest-interest rate balance first.
- Over-the-limit fees cannot be charged unless you direct the credit card company to process the over-the-limit transactions. Only one over-the-limit fee is allowed per billing cycle.

Billing Statements and Payment Processing
- Credit card statements must be sent out 21 days before the due date.
- Payments received the next business day after a holiday or a weekend are considered on time.

Credit Cards for Minors and College Students
- Minors under 18 cannot have credit cards unless they are emancipated or are authorized to use a parent's or guardian's account.
- College students without verifiable income cannot be issued credit cards.

Credit Card Disclosures
- Billing statements must include payoff information, including the number of months it will take to pay off the balance while making only minimum payments.
- Credit card solicitations must explain that numerous credit report inquiries can lower your credit score.

Source: Adapted from Miranda Marquit, "Credit Card Act of 2009: How It Affects You," http://personaldividends.com/credit-card-act-of-2009-how-it-affects-you/, accessed August 2015; LaToya Irby, "The Credit Cardholder's Bill of Rights Act of 2009: New Rules for the Credit Card Industry," http://credit.about.com/od/consumercreditlaws/a/creditbillright.htm, accessed August 2015.

6-2b Special Types of Bank Credit Cards

Today, in addition to standard, "plain vanilla" bank cards, you can obtain cards that offer rebates and special incentive programs, cards that are sponsored by nonprofit organizations, even credit cards aimed specifically at college and high-school students. We'll now look at several of these special types of bank credit cards, including reward cards, affinity cards, secured credit cards, and student credit cards.

reward (co-branded) credit card
A bank credit card that combines features of a traditional bank credit card with an additional incentive, such as rebates and airline mileage.

Reward Cards

One of the fastest-growing segments of the bank card market is the reward (co-branded) credit card, which combines features of a traditional bank credit card with an incentive: cash, merchandise rebates, airline tickets, or even investments. About half of credit cards are rebate cards, and new types are introduced almost every day. Here are some of the many incentive programs.

- **Frequent flyer programs:** In this program, the cardholder earns free frequent flyer miles for each dollar charged on his or her credit card. These frequent flyer miles can then be used with airline-affiliated programs for free tickets, first-class upgrades, and other travel-related benefits. Examples include the Delta Sky Miles Card and United Airlines Mileage Plus *Visa* Card; with the American Express and Chase Travel Plus programs, the miles can be used on any one of numerous airlines.

- **Automobile rebate programs:** A number of credit cards allow the cardholder to earn annual rebates of up to 5 percent for new car purchases or leases and gas and auto maintenance purchases up to specified limits. For example, Citibank's ThankYou Preferred Card provides rebates that can be applied to the purchase of any vehicle brand, new or used. Cardholders can earn 1 percent on most all purchases (notably excluding gas) and 6 percent during the year. Most of the major car companies offer some kind of rewards-related credit card that can be used to buy a car or related items.

- **Other merchandise rebates:** An increasing number of companies are participating in bank card reward programs, including, for example, Norwegian Cruise Line, NASCAR, Starbucks, Marriott Hotels, and Hard Rock Café. Some major oil companies also offer rebate cards, where the cardholder earns credit that can be applied to the purchase of the company's gasoline. Several regional phone companies even offer rebates on phone calls. (A good site for finding information about these and other rebate card offers is **http://www.cardtrak.com**.)

Are rebate cards a good deal? Well, yes and no. To see if they make sense for you, evaluate these cards carefully by looking at your usage patterns and working out the annual cost of the cards before and after the rebate. Don't get so carried away with the gimmick that you lose sight of the total costs. Most incentive cards carry higher interest rates than regular bank cards do. These cards work best for those who can use the rebates, charge a lot, and don't carry high monthly balances.

Affinity Cards

affinity card
A standard bank credit card issued in conjunction with some charitable, political, or other nonprofit organization.

"Credit cards with a cause" is the way to describe **affinity cards**. These cards are nothing more than standard *Visa* or *MasterCard* that are issued in conjunction with a sponsoring group—most commonly some type of charitable, political, or professional organization. So-named because of the bond between the sponsoring group and its members, affinity cards are sponsored by such nonprofit organizations as Mothers Against Drunk Driving (MADD), the American Association of Individual Investors, the American Wildlife Fund, AARP, and the Special Olympics. In addition, they are issued by college and university alumni groups, labor organizations, religious and fraternal groups, and professional societies. In many cases, all you have to do is support the cause to obtain one of these cards (as in the case of MADD). In other cases, you'll

You Can Do It Now

Is Your Credit Card a Good Deal?

While your credit card might have been a good deal when you first got it, that may not still be the case. Go to a credit card Internet site like **http://www.creditcards.com**, which allows you to evaluate numerous credit cards by type. For example, you can focus on 0% APR, rewards, cash back, travel & airline, cards for students, and more types of cards. It's worth a look—you can do it now.

Behavior Matters

Behavioral Biases and Credit Card Use

Be wary of the minimum payment in your monthly credit card statement. Many people focus unduly or "anchor" on the stated minimum payment and as a result, pay a lower amount than they would otherwise. And the effect is obvious—they end up paying more interest.

Another tendency is to fall victim to "mental accounting," which refers to inappropriately viewing interdependent decisions as independent. For example, some people hold short-term, low-yield investments and costly credit card debt at the same time. It would obviously make sense to liquidate the investments and use the proceeds to pay off the credit card debt, which reduces interest charges. But many people don't do this because they view these as separate, unrelated transactions.

You should always consider how your financial decisions relate to one another and take into account common behavioral biases like anchoring and mental accounting, especially as they relate to managing credit card debt.

have to belong to a certain group in order to get one of their cards (for example, be a graduate of the school or member of a particular professional group to qualify).

Why even bother with one of these cards? Well, unlike traditional bank cards, affinity cards make money for the group backing the card as well as for the bank, because the sponsoring groups receive a share of the profits (usually 0.5 percent to 1 percent of retail purchases made with the card). So, for the credit cardholder, it's a form of "painless philanthropy." But to cover the money that goes to the sponsoring organization, the cardholder usually pays higher fees or higher interest costs. Even so, some may view these cards as a great way to contribute to a worthy cause. Others, however, may feel it makes more sense to use a traditional credit card and then write a check to their favorite charity.

Secured Credit Cards

secured (collateralized) credit cards
A type of credit card that's secured with some form of collateral, such as a bank CD.

You may have seen the ad on TV where the announcer says that no matter how bad your credit, you can still qualify for one of their credit cards. The pitch may sound too good to be true; and in some respects it is, because there's a catch. Namely, the credit is "secured"—meaning that you have to put up *collateral* in order to get the card! These are so-called secured or collateralized credit cards, where the amount of credit is determined by the amount of liquid collateral you're able to put up. These cards are targeted at people with no credit or bad credit histories, who don't qualify for conventional credit cards. Issued as *Visa* or *MasterCard*, they're like any other credit card except for the collateral. To qualify, a customer must deposit a certain amount (usually $500 or more) into a 12- to 18-month certificate of deposit that the issuing bank holds as collateral. The cardholder then gets a credit line equal to the deposit. If the customer defaults, the bank has the CD to cover its losses. By making payments on time, it's hoped that these cardholders will establish (or reestablish) a credit history that may qualify them for a conventional (unsecured) credit card. Even though fully secured, these cards still carry annual fees and finance charges that are equal to, or greater than, those of regular credit cards.

Student Credit Cards

student credit card
A credit card marketed specifically to college-students.

Some large banks, through their *Visa* and *MasterCard* programs, have special credit cards that target college students (in some cases, even high-school students). These student credit cards often come packaged with special promotional programs that

FINANCIAL PLANNING TIPS

Choosing a Credit Card

You'll get the best credit card for you by considering the following factors:

- **Spending habits.** How do you plan to use the card? If you'll pay off the card's balance every month, then the interest rate doesn't matter. Thus, just look for a card with no annual fee and a grace period that makes it easy to stay current. In contrast, if you're going to carry a balance, then find a card with the lowest interest rate *and* a low introductory rate. If you will use the card only for emergencies, get the lowest interest rate you can find and low or no fees.

- **Type of interest rate.** The annual percentage rate (APR) can be fixed or variable, which means adjusted relative to another rate such as prime. Are you comfortable with the prospect that the interest rate you pay could vary?

- **Credit limit.** Your credit history will determine how much the card will let you borrow. Be careful not to get a card with such a low credit limit that you could frequently max it out, which can hurt your credit score.

- **Fees and penalties.** Card issuers often charge fees for balance transfers, cash advances, exceeding your credit limit, or for making payments by phone. Compare the fees on cards to make sure that you get a card with reasonable charges. And don't pay extra for rewards programs, which often can be had for free.

- **Balance computation method.** If you plan to carry a balance, it's important to know how the finance charge is calculated. The most common approach is the average daily balance (ADB), which adds the daily balances and then divides by the number of days in the billing cycle. Avoid cards that compute the balance using two billing cycles because that approach increases financing fees.

- **Incentives.** Some card issuers offer reward programs to encourage their customers to use the card. If you plan to make the purchases anyway and don't have to pay extra for the card, this can be a useful benefit. Make sure the program offers flexibility, such as cash or travel, benefits that you will actually use, and benefits that are easy to earn and to redeem. Watch out for program restrictions, and note whether rewards expire and if there are limits on the benefits that you can earn.

Source: Adapted from Pat Curry, "6 Things to Consider before Choosing a Credit Card," http://www.creditcards.com/credit-card-news/help/6-consider-before-choosing-picking-credit-card-6000.php, accessed August 2015.

©SEYOMEDO/SHUTTERSTOCK.COM

are meant to appeal to this segment of the market—such as free music, movie tickets, and the like. Some even offer special discounts on pizzas, clothing, computer software, and so on. Except for these features, there's really nothing unusual about these cards or their terms. Most simply require that you be enrolled in a two- or four-year college or university and have some source of income, whatever that may be. In particular, they usually *do not require* any parental or guardian guarantees, nor do they require that you hold a full-time (or even a part-time) job.

So what's in it for the card issuers? While they know that most college students don't earn much money, they also know that's likely to change after they graduate—which is why they're so willing to offer the cards. Their logic seems to be that students obviously have some source of income and are going to be spending money anyway, so why not spend it with one of their credit cards? From the student's perspective, these cards not only offer convenience but are also great for building up a solid credit history. Just *remember to use them responsibly;* that's the way to get the most from these cards—or any other form of credit, for that matter!

6-2c Retail Charge Cards

retail charge card
A type of credit card issued by retailers that allows customers to charge goods and services up to a preestablished amount.

Retail charge cards are the second-largest category of credit card and are issued by department stores, oil companies, car rental agencies, and so on. These cards are popular with merchants because they build consumer loyalty and enhance sales; consumers like them because they offer a convenient way to shop. These cards carry a preset credit limit—a line of credit—that varies with the creditworthiness of the cardholder.

This form of credit is most common in department and clothing stores and other high-volume outlets, where customers are likely to make several purchases each month. Most large oil companies also offer charge cards that allow customers to buy gas and oil products, *but they're expected to pay for such purchases in full upon receipt of the monthly bill.* However, to promote the sale of their more expensive products, oil companies frequently offer revolving credit for use in purchasing items such as tires, batteries, and accessories. Many families have—and regularly use—five or six different retail charge cards. Interest on most retail charge cards is typically fixed at 1.5 percent to 1.85 percent monthly, or 18 percent to 22 percent per year. These cards are generally more expensive than bank credit cards.

6-2d Debit Cards

It looks like a credit card, it works like a credit card, it even has the familiar *MasterCard* and *Visa* credit card markings. But it's not a *credit* card—rather, it's a *debit* card. Simply put, a debit card provides direct access to your checking account and thus *works like writing a check.* For example, when you use a debit card to make a purchase, the amount of the transaction is charged directly to your checking account. Using a debit card isn't the same thing as buying on credit. It may appear that you're charging it, but actually *you're paying with cash.* Accordingly, there are no finance charges to pay.

Debit cards are becoming more popular, especially with consumers who want the convenience of a credit card but not the high cost of interest that comes with them. In fact, in 2006, debit card use exceeded credit card use for the first time. Debit cards are accepted at most establishments displaying the *Visa* or *MasterCard* logo but function as an alternative to writing checks. If you use a debit card to make a purchase at a department store or restaurant, the transaction will show up on your next monthly *checking account* statement. Needless to say, to keep your records straight, you should enter debit card transactions directly into your checkbook ledger as they occur and treat them as withdrawals, or checks, by subtracting them from your checking account balance. Debit cards can also be used to gain access to your account through 24-hour teller machines or ATMs—which is the closest thing to a cash advance that these cards have to offer.

A big disadvantage of a debit card, of course, is that it doesn't provide a line of credit. In addition, it can cause overdraft problems if you fail to make the proper entries to your checking account or inadvertently use it when you think you're using a credit card. Also, some debit card issuers charge a transaction fee or a flat annual fee; and some *merchants* may even charge you just for using your debit card. On the plus side, a debit card enables you to avoid the potential credit problems and high costs of credit cards. Further, it's as convenient to use as a credit card. In fact, if convenience is the major reason you use a credit card, you might want to consider switching to a debit card for at least some transactions, especially at outlets such as gas stations that give discounts for cash purchases and consider a debit card to be as good as cash.

Another difference between debit and credit cards involves the level of protection for the user when a card is lost or stolen. When a credit card is lost or stolen, federal banking laws state that the cardholder is not liable for any fraudulent charges if the loss or theft is reported before that card is used. If reported after the card is used, the cardholder's maximum liability is $50. Unfortunately, *this protection does not extend to debit cards typically.* Instead, your liability resulting from a lost or stolen debit card is limited to between $50 and $500, "depending on the circumstances of the loss." In practice, most banks provide the same level of protection for debit cards as for credit cards, but check with your bank to be sure.

Prepaid Cards

prepaid card
A plastic card with a magnetic strip or microchip that stores the amount of money the purchaser has to spend and from which is deducted the value of each purchase.

Tired of fumbling for change to buy a candy bar from a vending machine or to use a pay phone? Buy a **prepaid card** and your pockets won't jingle with coins anymore. Or you can use a smartphone app that effectively provides a prepaid card for purchases at coffee shop chains and the like. These "smart cards" can now be used to purchase a variety of items—phone calls, coffee, meals in some employee cafeterias, vending machine snacks—and their use is increasing. You pay a fixed amount, which is then stored on either a magnetic strip or rechargeable microchip on the card. Each time you make a purchase, the amount is electronically deducted from the card. The popularity of these "electronic wallets" is increasing, as consumers and merchants alike find them convenient. And they're likely to become even more popular, since the microchips now being embedded in these smart cards can be used not only to execute

FINANCIAL PLANNING TIPS

Risky Places to Use Your Debit Card

Yes, debit cards are convenient to use and generally accepted by most establishments. But unlike credit cards, debit cards provide a thief with direct access to your checking account. If you find a fraudulent charge on your credit card bill, you can just decline or dispute the charge. In contrast, by the time you find a fraudulent charge on your debit card, your money—not the bank's money—is already gone, and it's up to *you* to get it back, not the bank. While it usually takes only a few days to deal with fraudulent credit card transactions, it can take months to get your money back from fraudulent debit transactions.

You are most vulnerable to debit card fraud in the following situations:

- **Be careful using outdoor ATMs.** "Skimming" is the capturing of card information by a magnetic strip reader. Such skimmers can be placed over the real card slots at ATMs. Watch for apparently beaten-up or old-looking ATMs, which might indicate that a skimmer has been added. Surprisingly, outdoor ATMs are one of the most dangerous places to use a debit card. Public places provide criminals with the ability to add skimmers, point cameras at the ATM, or to even watch transactions with

binoculars. It's much safer to use ATMs inside retail stores or other well-lighted, high-traffic areas.

- **Protect your personal identification number (PIN) at gas stations.** Gas stations are another vulnerable spot for using debit cards. Given that there's not much supervision, it's easy for a criminal to install a skimmer or to point a camera at the gas pump. Credit cards are much safer to use.

- **The Internet is a dangerous place to use a debit card.** Your debit card information is vulnerable to capture at many points: malware could be on your computer, your data could be intercepted by wireless eavesdropping on the way to the vendor, or your merchant's database could be compromised. The site may say it's safe, but so what? You have no idea how many people are handling your private debit card data, or who they are.

- **Some restaurants keep debit card data on file.** And restaurants routinely take your card out of your sight to process a transaction, which creates the opportunity for someone to inappropriately keep the information. Ethical or not, few small businesses take adequate steps to protect your private data.

Source: Adapted from Claes Bell, "4 Risky Places to Swipe Your Debit Card," http://www.bankrate.com/finance/checking/risky-places-swipe-debit-card-1.aspx, accessed August 2015.

transactions but also to store such things as electronic plane tickets or theater tickets. It's also easier to control Internet fraud, because the cards have electronic readers that plug easily into your computer for authenticity verification.

Prepaid cards and comparable smartphone apps are a lot like *debit cards*. Each time you use one, you're actually debiting the amount purchased to what you have stored on the card (or in your checking account). But don't confuse prepaid cards with prepaid *credit cards,* which you can use again and again. With prepaid cards, once the card is used up, you either toss it or get it recharged—there's no line of credit here, and no monthly bills with their minimum monthly payments.

6-2e Revolving Credit Lines

revolving lines of credit
A type of open account credit offered by banks and other financial institutions that can be accessed by writing checks against demand deposit or specially designated credit line accounts.

Revolving lines of credit are offered by banks, brokerage houses, and other financial institutions. These credit lines normally don't involve the use of credit cards. Rather, they're accessed by writing checks on regular checking accounts or specially designated credit line accounts. They are a form of open account credit and often represent a far better deal than credit cards, not only because they offer more credit but also because they can be a lot less expensive. And there may even be a tax advantage to using one of these other kinds of credit. These lines basically provide their users with ready access to borrowed money (i.e., cash advances) through revolving lines of credit. The three major forms of open (non-credit card) credit are overdraft protection lines, unsecured personal lines of credit, and home equity credit lines.

Overdraft Protection

overdraft protection line
A line of credit linked to a checking account that allows a depositor to overdraw the account up to a specified amount.

An **overdraft protection line** is simply a line of credit linked to a checking account that enables a depositor to overdraw his or her checking account up to a predetermined limit. These lines are usually set up with credit limits of $500 to $1,000, but they can be for as much as $10,000 or more. The consumer taps this line of credit by writing a check. If that particular check happens to overdraw the account, the overdraft protection line will automatically advance funds in an amount necessary to put the account back in the black. In some cases, overdraft protection is provided by *linking*

FINANCIAL PLANNING TIPS

Debit Card Signature Transactions: The Best of Both Worlds

When you put a debit card in the reader, you don't have to press the "debit" button and enter your PIN (a PIN transaction). Instead, you can choose "credit" and sign the receipt (a signature transaction). The benefits of doing so are:

• *Avoid fees.* While some banks charge for PIN transactions, they typically do not charge for signature transactions.

• *Reward points.* You're more likely to get reward points on a signature than on a PIN transaction.

• *Liability protection.* Signature transactions go through credit card networks that provide some fraud protection.

PIN transactions are processed through electronic funds transfer systems that don't provide liability protection.

If you use a debit transaction, your money will be taken out of your account the same day. However, if you use credit, your money will not be removed for two or three days.

So why would you ever do a debit PIN transaction? If you want cash back, you should use a debit PIN transaction rather than using the ATM of another bank. Otherwise, both the ATM and your bank will charge you more than enough to offset any benefit from signing for the transaction.

the bank's credit card to your checking account. These arrangements act like regular overdraft lines except that, when the account is overdrawn, the bank automatically taps your credit card line and transfers the money into your checking account. It's treated as a cash advance from your credit card, but the result is the same as a regular overdraft protection line; it automatically covers overdrawn checks.

If you're not careful, you can quickly exhaust this type of credit by writing a lot of overdraft checks. As with any line of credit, there's a limit to how much you can obtain. Be careful with such a credit line, and by all means, *Don't use it to routinely overdraw your account!* Doing so on a regular basis is a signal that you're probably mismanaging your cash and/or living beyond your budget. It's best to view an overdraft protection line strictly as an *emergency* source of credit—and any funds advanced should be repaid as quickly as possible.

Unsecured Personal Lines

unsecured personal credit line
A line of credit made available to an individual on an as-needed basis.

Another form of revolving credit is the **unsecured personal credit line**, which basically makes a line of credit available to an individual on an as-needed basis. In essence, it's a way of borrowing money from a bank, S&L, credit union, savings bank, or brokerage firm any time you wish and without going through all the hassle of setting up a new loan.

Here's how it works. Suppose you apply for and are approved for a personal line of credit at your bank. Once you've been approved and the credit line is established, you'll be issued *checks* that you can write against it. If you need a cash advance, all you need to do is write a check (against your credit line account) and deposit it into your checking account. Or, if you need the money to buy some big-ticket item—say, an expensive personal electronics—you can just make the credit line check out to the dealer and, when it clears, it will be charged against your unsecured personal credit line as an advance. (While these credit line checks look and "spend" just like regular checks, they are not channeled through your normal checking account.) Personal lines of credit are usually set up for minimums of $2,000 to $5,000 and often amount to $25,000 or more. As with an overdraft protection line, once an advance is made, repayment is set up on a monthly installment basis. Depending on the amount outstanding, repayment is normally structured over a period of two to five years; to keep the monthly payments low, larger amounts of debt are usually given longer repayment periods.

Financial Fact or Fantasy?

You use a check rather than a credit card to obtain funds from an unsecured personal line of credit. **Fact:** Credit cards are not issued with unsecured personal credit lines. Instead, if you want to borrow money through such a line, you do it by simply writing a check directly against it.

Although these credit lines do offer attractive terms to the consumer, they come with their share of problems, perhaps the biggest of which is how easily cash advances can be obtained. These lines also normally involve *substantial* amounts of credit and are nearly as easy to use as credit cards. This combination can have devastating effects on a family's budget if it leads to overspending or excessive reliance on credit. To be safe, these lines should be used only for emergency purposes or to make *planned credit expenditures.* Systematic repayment of the debt should be built into the budget, and every effort should be made to ensure that using this kind of credit will not overly strain the family finances.

Home Equity Credit Lines

home equity credit line
A line of credit issued against the existing equity in a home.

Here's a familiar situation. A couple buys a home for $285,000; some 10 years later, it's worth $365,000. The couple now has an asset worth $365,000 on which all they owe is the original mortgage, which may now have a balance of, say, $220,000. The couple clearly has built up a substantial amount of equity in their home: $365,000 − $220,000 = $145,000. But how can they tap that equity without having to sell their home? The answer is a **home equity credit line.** Such lines are much like unsecured personal credit lines except that they're *secured with a second mortgage on the home.* These lines of credit allow you to tap up to 100 percent (or more) of the equity in your home by merely writing a check. Although some banks and financial institutions allow their customers to borrow up to 100 percent of the *equity* in their homes—or, in some cases, even more—most lenders set their maximum credit lines at 75 percent to 80 percent of the *market value* of the home, which reduces the amount of money they'll lend.

Here's how these lines work. Recall the couple in our example that has built up equity of $145,000 in their home—equity against which they can borrow through a home equity credit line. Assuming that they have a good credit record and using a 75 percent loan-to-market-value ratio, a bank would be willing to lend up to $273,750; that is, 75 percent of the value of the house is 0.75 × $365,000 = $273,750. Subtracting the $220,000 still due on the first mortgage, we see that our couple could qualify for a home equity credit line of $53,750. Note, in this case, that if the bank had been willing to lend the couple *100 percent of the equity* in their home, it would have given them a (much higher) credit line of $145,000, which is the difference between what the house is worth and what they still owe on it. Most lenders don't do this because it results in very large credit lines and, more importantly, it provides the lender with much less of a cushion should the borrower default. Even worse, from the borrowers' perspective, it provides access to a lot of relatively inexpensive credit, which can lead some homeowners to overextend themselves and thus encounter serious debt service problems down the road—even bankruptcy or loss of their home!

Home equity lines also have a tax feature that you should be aware of: the annual interest charges on such lines may be fully deductible for those who itemize. This is the only type of consumer loan that still qualifies for such tax treatment. According to the latest provisions of the tax code, a homeowner is allowed to *fully deduct the interest charges on home equity loans up to $100,000,* regardless of the original cost of the house or use of the proceeds. Indeed, the only restriction is that *the amount of total indebtedness on the house cannot exceed its fair market value,* which is highly unlikely because homeowners usually cannot borrow more than 75 percent to 80 percent of the home's market value anyway. (In effect, the interest on that portion of the loan that exceeds $100,000—or 100 percent of the home's market value, if this amount is lower—*cannot* be treated as a tax-deductible expense.)

> **EXAMPLE: Tax Deductibility of Home Equity Credit Line Interest**
>
> The homeowners in the prior discussion could take out the full amount of their credit line ($53,750), and every dime that they paid in interest would be tax deductible. If they paid, say, $3,225 in interest and if they were in the 28 percent tax bracket, then this feature would reduce their tax liability by some $903 (i.e., $3,225 × 0.28)—assuming, of course, that they itemize their deductions.

Not only do home equity credit lines offer shelter from taxes, they're also among *the cheapest forms of consumer credit.* For example, while the average rate on standard fixed rate credit cards in mid-2015 was about 13.01 percent, the average rate on home equity credit lines was considerably less than that, at about 4 percent depending on the amount of the line and the borrower's credit score. To see what that can mean to you as a borrower, assume you have $10,000 in consumer debt outstanding. If you had borrowed that money through a standard consumer loan at 13.01 percent, then you'd pay interest of $1,301 per year—none of which would be tax deductible. But borrow the same amount through a home equity credit line at 4.00 percent, and you'll pay only $400 in interest. And because that's all tax deductible, if you're in the 28 percent tax bracket, then the after-tax cost to you would be $400 × (1 − 0.28) = $288.00. This is about a fifth of the cost of the other loan! So, which would you rather pay for a $10,000 loan: $1,301 or $288.00? That's really not a tough decision, and it explains why these lines have become so popular and are today one of the fastest-growing forms of consumer credit.

Home equity credit lines are offered by a variety of financial institutions, from banks and S&Ls to major brokerage houses. All sorts of credit terms and credit lines are available, and most of them carry repayment periods of 10 to 15 years, or longer. Perhaps most startling, however, is the maximum amount of credit available under these lines—indeed, $100,000 figures are not at all unusual. And it's precisely because of the enormous amount of money available that this form of credit should be used with caution. *The fact that you have equity in your home does not necessarily mean that you have the cash flow necessary to service the debt that such a credit line imposes.* Remember that your house is the collateral. If you can't repay the loan, you could lose your home! At the minimum, paying for major expenditures through a home equity credit line should be done only after you have determined that you can afford the purchase and the required monthly payments will fit comfortably within your budget. Equally important, don't be tempted to use a 15-year home equity credit line to finance, say, a new car that you may be driving for only 5 or 6 years—the last thing you want to be doing is paying for that car 8 to 10 years after you've traded it in. If a 15-year loan is the only way you can afford the car, then face it: you can't afford the car!

FINANCIAL ROAD SIGN

And Then There Are These Other Lenders ...

Various "shadow" lenders exist outside of the traditional banking system. They are most commonly used by low-income consumers who do not have good enough credit histories to borrow money from traditional lenders. These alternative lenders tend to have two sobering common characteristics: high interest rates and high fees. Here are some example loans:

- *Payday Loans*
  In the average loan, a consumer borrows $350 for 14 days and writes the lender a check for $402.50. The lender agrees to hold the check until the next payday in two weeks. While this might seem like a 15 percent interest rate, the annual percentage rate is actually almost 400 percent! The average borrower does this 10 times a year and is indebted to the lender for 199 days. So the average borrower is keeping the loan open rather than paying it off after the first two weeks. About 12 million households borrow money with payday loans.

- *Pawnshops*
  Pawnshops offer loans that are secured by personal property as collateral. Consumers who cannot get a loan from a bank will often borrow against jewelry, electronics, and precious metals. The loans are typically for 30 to 45 days and are often for less than $100. If the loan and fees are paid by the deadline, the property is returned. Yet the finance charges range from 5 to 25 percent *per month,* depending on state regulations. Annual interest rates of 100 percent are not unusual.

- *Car Title Loans*
  Car title loans use your car as collateral to secure a short-term loan for a fraction of the value of the car. If the borrower misses a payment, doesn't pay the fees, or doesn't pay the interest and principal on the loan by the end of the term, the car could be sold or repossessed. The average loan is for about 30 days and the annual percentage rate can approach 300 percent!

The high fees and interest rate costs make the above alternative loan sources extremely expensive. Proper planning and building a good credit history should allow you to avoid them.

Source: Payday loan statistics and example obtained from Consumer Financial Protection Bureau, http://files .consumerfinance.gov/f/201304_cfpb_payday-factsheet.pdf, accessed August 2015.

TEST YOURSELF

6-5 What is *open account credit*? Name several different types of open account credit.

6-6 What is the attraction of *reward cards*?

6-7 How is the interest rate typically set on bank credit cards?

6-8 Many bank card issuers impose different types of fees; briefly describe three of these fees.

6-9 What is a *debit card*? How is it similar to a credit card? How does it differ?

6-10 Describe how *revolving credit lines* provide open account credit.

6-11 What are the basic features of a *home equity credit line*?

6-3 OBTAINING AND MANAGING OPEN FORMS OF CREDIT

Consumers love to use their charge cards. In 2014, *Visa* alone handled about $7.3 trillion in transactions. Consumers find credit and debit cards more convenient than cash or checks, and the number of other benefits (e.g., rebates and frequent flyer miles) continues to grow.

For the sake of convenience, people often maintain several different kinds of open credit. Nearly every household, for example, uses 30-day charge accounts to pay their utility bills, phone bills, and so on. In addition, most families have one or more retail charge cards and a couple of bank cards. And that's not all—families can also have revolving credit lines in the form of overdraft protection or a home equity line. When all these cards and lines are totaled together, a family conceivably can have tens of thousands of dollars of readily available credit. It's easy to see why consumer credit has become such a popular way of making relatively routine purchases. Although open account credit can increase the risk of budgetary overload, these accounts can also serve as a useful way of keeping track of expenditures.

6-3a Opening an Account

What do retail charge cards, bank credit cards, and revolving lines of credit all have in common? *Answer:* They all require you to go through a formal credit application. Let's now look at how you'd go about obtaining open forms of credit, including the normal credit application, investigation, and decision process. We'll focus our discussion on credit cards, but keep in mind that similar procedures apply to other revolving lines of credit as well.

The Credit Application

Credit applications are usually available at the store or bank involved. Sometimes they can be found at the businesses that accept these cards or obtained on request from the issuing companies. Exhibit 6.5 provides an example of a bank credit card application. As you can see, the type of information requested in a typical credit application covers little more than personal/family matters, housing, employment and income, and existing charge accounts. Such information is intended to give the lender insight about the applicant's creditworthiness. In essence, the lender is trying to determine whether the applicant has the *character* and *capacity* to handle the debt in a prompt and timely manner.

The Credit Investigation

credit investigation
An investigation that involves contacting credit references or corresponding with a credit bureau to verify information on a credit application.

Once the credit application has been completed and returned to the establishment issuing the card, it is subject to a **credit investigation**. The purpose is to evaluate the kind of credit risk that you pose to the lender (the party issuing the credit or charge card). So be

EXHIBIT 6.5   An Online Credit Card Application

You can apply for many credit cards today right on the Internet. This credit application, like most, seeks information about the applicant's place of employment, monthly income, place of residence, credit history, and other financial matters that are intended to help the lender decide whether or not to extend credit.

Credit Card Application   YOUR BANK

Read Privacy Policy and Pricing and Terms for important information about rates, fees and other costs.

🔒 **All application pages are secure.**

* indicates a required field.

Application Information

Before completing the application, you should be able to answer "Yes" to the following statements by checking the boxes:

☐ Yes, my credit history is clear of bankruptcy.

☐ Yes, my credit history is clear of seriously delinquent accounts.

☐ Yes, I have NOT been denied credit within the last 6 months.

Personal Information

	Title	First* (Required)	M.I.	Last* (Required)
Name:				

Residential Address Line 1:   **Unit/Apt #:**

Residential Address Line 2:

City: **State:**

Zip Code: -   **Home Phone:** - -

Lived There: Years   Months

SSN: - -

Date of Birth: / / (MM/DD/YYYY)

Mother's Maiden Name:

E-mail Address:

Employment Information

(If retired, note previous employer. If self-employed, note nature of business.)

Employer: **Position:**

Worked There: years   months

Work Phone: - -

Financial Information

Alimony, child support, or separate maintenance income need not be revealed if you do not wish it to be considered as a basis for repaying this obligation.

Annual Household Income: $ .00 (Please do not use commas.)

Please select the type(s) of bank account(s) you have:

Select Residence:

Monthly Rent or Mortgage: $ .00 (Please do not use commas.)

JOHNNY LYE/SHUTTERSTOCK.COM

sure to fill out your credit application carefully. Believe it or not, they really do look at those things closely. The key items that lenders look at are how much money you make, how much debt you have outstanding and how well you handle it, and how stable you are (for example, your age, employment history, whether you own or rent a home, and so on). Obviously, the higher your income and the better your credit history, the greater the chance that your credit application will be approved.

During the credit investigation, the lender attempts to verify much of the information you've provided on the credit application. Obviously, false or misleading information will almost certainly result in outright rejection of your application. For example, the lender may verify your place of employment, level of income, current debt load, debt service history, and so forth. If you've lived in the area for several years and have established relations with a local bank, a call to your banker may be all it takes to confirm your creditworthiness. If you haven't established such bank relations—and most young people have not—the lender is likely to turn to the local credit bureau for a *credit report* on you.

The Credit Bureau

credit bureau
An organization that collects and stores credit information about individual borrowers.

A credit bureau is a type of reporting agency that gathers and sells information about individual borrowers. If, as is often the case, the lender doesn't know you personally, it must rely on a cost-effective way of verifying your employment and credit history. It would be far too expensive and time-consuming for individual creditors to confirm your credit application on their own, so they turn to credit bureaus that maintain fairly detailed credit files about you. Information in your file comes from one of three sources: creditors who subscribe to the bureau, other creditors who supply information at your request, and publicly recorded court documents (such as tax liens or bankruptcy records).

Contrary to popular opinion, your credit file does *not* contain everything anyone would ever want to know about you—there's nothing on your lifestyle, friends, habits, or religious or political affiliations. Instead, most of the information is pretty dull stuff and covers such things as name, social security number, age, number of dependents, employment record and salary data, public records of bankruptcies, and the names of those who have recently requested copies of your file.

Although one late credit card payment probably won't make much of a difference on an otherwise clean credit file, a definite pattern of delinquencies (consistently being 30 to 60 days late with your payments) or a personal bankruptcy certainly will. Unfortunately, poor credit traits will stick with you for a long time, because delinquencies remain on your credit file for as long as 7 years and bankruptcies for 10 years. An example of an actual credit bureau report (or at least a part of one) is provided in Exhibit 6.6. It shows the kind of information you can expect to find in one of these reports.

You Can Do It Now

How Does Your Credit Report Look?

When did you last check your credit report? It's a good idea to look at it at least once a year to know where you stand and to assure that there are no errors. The Fair Credit Reporting Act (FCRA) requires each of the national credit reporting firms—Experian, Equifax Credit Information Services, and TransUnion—to provide a free copy of your credit report once a year. These three companies have set up an Internet site where you can get your free annual report at **https://www.annualcreditreport.com**. Be careful about using other Internet sites that offer free credit reports, free credit monitoring, or free credit scores. Such sites are not authorized to meet the legal requirements of the FCRA and often have strings attached. Just go to the authorized site—you can do it now.

EXHIBIT 6.6 **An Example of a Credit Bureau Report**

Credit bureau reports have been revised and are now easier to understand. Notice that, in addition to some basic information, the report deals strictly with credit information—including payment records, past-due status, and types of credit.

Your Credit Report as of 04/09/2017

This Credit Report is available for you to view for 30 days. If you would like a current Credit Report, you may order another from MyEquifax.

ID # XXXXXXXXXXXX

• Personal Data

John Q. Public
2351 N 85th Ave
Phoenix, AZ 85037

Social Security Number: 022-22-2222
Date of Birth: 1/11/1980

• Previous Address(es):

133 Third Avenue
Phoenix, AZ 85037

• Employment History

Cendant Hospitality FR

	Location:	Employment Date:	Verified Date:
	Phoenix, AZ	2/1/2005	1/3/2017

Previous Employment(s):

SOFTWARE Support Hospitality Franch

	Location:	Employment Date:	Verified Date:
	Atlanta, GA	1/3/2003	1/3/2004

• Public Records

No bankruptcies on file
No liens on file
No foreclosures on file

• Collection Accounts

No collections on file.

• Credit Information

Company Name	Account Number and Whose Account	Date Opened	Last Activity	Type of Account and Status	High Credit	Items as of Date Reported Terms Balance		Past Due	Date Reported
Americredit Financial Services	40404XXXX JOINT ACCOUNT	03/2010	03/2016	Installment REPOSSESSION	$16933	$430	$9077	$128	3/2016

Prior Paying History
30 days past due 07 times; 60 days past due 05 times; 90+ days past due 03 times
INVOLUNTARY REPOSSESSION AUTO

Capital One	412174147128XXXX INDIVIDUAL ACCOUNT	10/2014	01/2017	Revolving PAYS AS AGREED	$777	15	$514		01/2017

Prior Paying History
30 days past due 02 times; 60 days past due 1 times; 90+ days past due 00 times
CREDIT CARD

Desert Schools FCU	423325003406XXXX INDIVIDUAL ACCOUNT	07/2003	06/2013	Revolving PAYS AS AGREED	$500		$0		07/2013

Prior Paying History
30 days past due 02 times; 60 days past due 00 times; 90+ days past due 00 times
ACCOUNT PAID   CLOSED ACCOUNT

• Credit Inquiries

Companies that Requested your Credit File

04/09/2017 EFX Credit Profile Online
06/30/2016 Automotive
01/18/2014 Desert Schools Federal C.U.
07/02/2013 Time Life, Inc.

Local credit bureaus (there are about a thousand of them) are established and mutually owned by local merchants and banks. They collect and store credit information on people living within the community and make it available, for a fee, to members who request it. Local bureaus are linked together nationally through one of the "big three" national bureaus—TransUnion, Equifax Credit Information Services, and Experian—each of which provides the mechanism for obtaining credit information from almost any place in the United States. Traditionally, credit bureaus did little more than collect and provide credit information; they neither analyzed the information nor used it to make final credit decisions. In 2006, however, the three major credit bureaus announced that they had jointly developed a new credit-scoring system, called *VantageScore,* that would incorporate data from all three bureaus—Equifax, Experian, and TransUnion. Thus, for the first time, each of the three national bureaus began assigning uniform credit ratings to individual credit files. The VantageScore system is supposed to simplify and enhance the credit-granting process, because all three bureaus will now be reporting, among other things, the same credit score—although they're still obligated to report other credit scores, such as the widely used FICO scores. Of course, whether adding still another credit score to the four or five that already exist actually simplifies matters or not remains to be seen. (We'll examine credit scores and FICO scores in more detail later in this text.)

Credit bureaus in the past were heavily criticized because of the large numbers of reporting errors they made and their poor record in promptly and efficiently correcting these errors. Fortunately, things have changed dramatically in recent years as the major credit bureaus have taken a more consumer-oriented approach. According to the amended Fair Credit Reporting Act, credit bureaus must provide you with low-cost copies of your own credit report and they must have toll-free phone numbers. Disputes must be resolved in 30 days and must take the consumer's documentation into account, not just the creditor's.

All Americans are entitled to receive *a free copy of their credit report once a year.* To get your free report, go to the Internet site set up by the Federal Trade Commission (FTC) at **http://www .annualcreditreport.com.** You should ensure that your credit report accurately reflects your credit history. The best way to do that is to obtain a copy of your own credit report and then go through it carefully. If you do find a mistake, let the credit bureau know immediately—and by all means, put it in writing. *Then request a copy of the corrected file to make sure that the mistake has been eliminated.* Most consumer advisors recommend that you review your credit files annually. Here are the Internet sites for the three national credit bureaus:

- Equifax Credit Information Services
  http://www.equifax.com
- TransUnion LLC Consumer Disclosure Center
  http://www.tuc.com
- Experian National Consumer Assistance Center
  http://www.experian.com

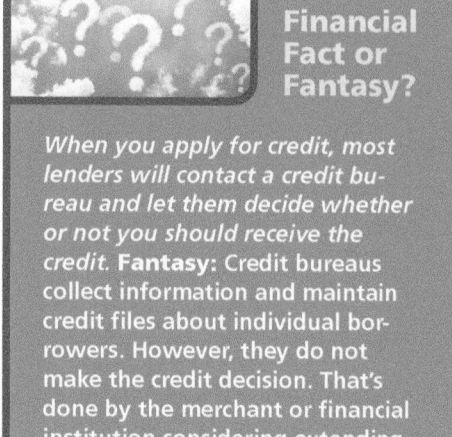

Financial Fact or Fantasy?

When you apply for credit, most lenders will contact a credit bureau and let them decide whether or not you should receive the credit. **Fantasy:** Credit bureaus collect information and maintain credit files about individual borrowers. However, they do not make the credit decision. That's done by the merchant or financial institution considering extending the credit.

6-3b The Credit Decision

Using the data provided by the credit applicant, along with any information obtained from the credit bureau, the store or bank must decide whether to grant credit. Very likely, some type of credit scoring scheme will be used to make the decision. An overall credit score is developed for you by assigning values to such factors as your annual income, whether you rent or own your home, number and types of credit cards you hold, level of your existing debts, whether you have savings accounts, and general credit references. Fifteen or 20 different factors may be

credit scoring
A method of evaluating an applicant's creditworthiness by assigning values to such factors as income, existing debts, and credit references.

considered, and each characteristic receives a score based on some predetermined standard. For example, if you're 26 years old, single, earn $32,500 a year (on a job that you've had for only two years), and rent an apartment, you might receive the following scores:

1. Age (25–30)	5 points
2. Marital status (single)	−2 points
3. Annual income ($30–35,000)	12 points
4. Length of employment (2 years or less)	4 points
5. Rent or own a home (rent)	0 points
	19 points

Based on information obtained from your credit application, similar scores would be assigned to another 10 to 15 factors.

In all cases, the stronger your personal traits or characteristics, the higher the score you'll receive. For instance, if you were 46 years old (rather than 26), you might receive 18 points for your age factor, being married rather than single would give you 9 points, and earning $75,000 a year would obviously be worth a lot more than earning $32,500! The idea is that the more stable you are *perceived* to be, the more income you make, the better your credit record, and so on, the higher the score you should receive. In essence, statistical studies have shown that certain personal and financial traits can be used to determine your creditworthiness. Indeed, the whole credit scoring system is based on extensive statistical studies that identify the characteristics to look at and the scores to assign.

The largest provider of credit scores is, by far, Fair Isaac & Co.—the firm that produces the widely used *FICO scores*. Unlike some credit score providers, *Fair Isaac uses only credit information in its calculations*. There's nothing in them about your age, marital status, salary, occupation, employment history, or where you live. Instead, FICO scores are derived from the following five major components, which are listed along with their respective weights: payment history (35 percent), amounts owed (30 percent), length of credit history (15 percent), new credit (10 percent), and types of credit used (10 percent). FICO scores, which are reported by all three of the major credit bureaus, range from a low of 300 to a max of 850. A representative reported distribution of FICO scores is as follows:

300–499	5.8%
500–549	8.4%
550–599	9.8%
600–649	10.2%
650–699	12.7%
700–749	16.3%
750–799	18.4%
800–850	18.6%

FICO scores are meant to be an indication of a borrower's credit risk; the higher the score, the lower the risk. While few, if any, credit decisions are based solely on FICO scores, you can be sure that higher scores are likely to result in lower interest rates on loans and, as a result, lower loan payments. For example, in mid-2015, if you were taking out a 30-year fixed-rate mortgage, you could expect to borrow at an interest rate of around 3.664 percent if you had a FICO score of 760–850, compared with 5.253 percent if your score was in the range of 620–639. That translates into monthly mortgage payments of around $1,375 a month versus $1,657 a month. Granted, a lot more goes into a credit decision than a simple credit score. But as you can see, it definitely pays to keep your FICO score as high as possible.

6-3c Computing Finance Charges

Because card issuers don't know in advance how much you'll charge on your account, they cannot specify the dollar amount of interest you will be charged. But they can—and must, according to the Truth in Lending Act—disclose the *rate of interest* that they charge and their method of computing finance charges. This is the **annual percentage rate (APR)**, the true or actual rate of interest paid, which must include all fees and costs and be calculated as defined by law. Remember, it's your right as a consumer to know—and it is the lender's obligation to tell you—the dollar amount of charges (where applicable) and the APR on any financing you consider.

The amount of interest you pay for open credit depends partly on the method the lender uses to calculate the balances on which they apply finance charges. Most bank and retail charge card issuers use one of two variations of the **average daily balance (ADB) method**, which applies the interest rate to the ADB of the account over the billing period. The most common method (used by an estimated 95 percent of bank card issuers) is the *ADB, including new purchases*. Card issuers can also use an ADB method that *excludes* new purchases. Balance calculations under each of these methods are as follows:

- ADB, including new purchases: For each day in the billing cycle, take the outstanding balance, including new purchases, and subtract payments and credits; then divide by the number of days in the billing cycle.
- ADB, excluding new purchases: Same as the first method, but excluding new purchases.

These different calculations can obviously affect a card's credit balance, and therefore the amount of finance charges you'll have to pay. Also be aware that the finance charges on two cards with the same APR but different methods of calculating balances may differ dramatically. It's important to know the method your card issuer uses. The comparisons in Exhibit 6.7 show how the method used to calculate the ADB affects the amount of finance charges you pay. In the situation illustrated here, monthly finance charges are between $66 and $132. It is clear that carrying a balance on a credit card can be expensive and that the way in which the finance charge is calculated can be important.

annual percentage rate (APR)
The actual or true rate of interest paid over the life of a loan; includes all fees and costs.

average daily balance (ADB) method
A method of computing finance charges by applying interest charges to the ADB of the account over the billing period.

Consider how to calculate balances and finance charges under the most popular method, *the ADB including new purchases.* Assume that you have a FirstBank *Visa* card with a monthly interest rate of 1.5 percent. Your statement for the billing period extending from October 10, 2017, through November 10, 2017—a total of 31 days— show, that your beginning balance was $1,582, you made purchases of $750 on October 15 and $400 on October 22, and you made a $275 payment on November 6. Therefore, the outstanding balance for the first 5 days of the period (October 11 through 15) was $1,582; for the next 7 days (October 16 through 22), it was $2,332 ($1,582 + $750); for the next 15 days (October 23 through November 6), it was $2,732 ($2,332 + $400); and for the last 4 days (November 7 through November 10), it was $2,457 ($2,732 minus the $275 payment). We can now calculate the ADB using the procedure shown in Exhibit 6.8. Note that the outstanding balances are weighted by the number of days that the balance existed and then averaged (divided) by the number of days in the billing period. By multiplying the ADB of $2,420.71 by the 1.5 percent interest rate, we get a finance charge of $36.31.

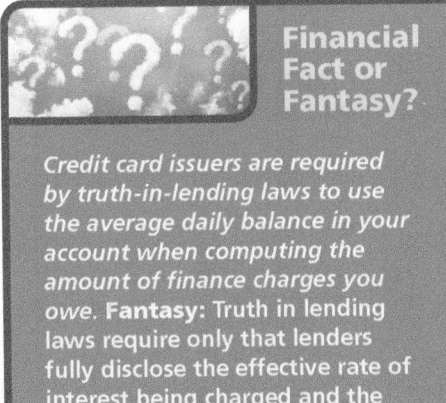

Financial Fact or Fantasy?

Credit card issuers are required by truth-in-lending laws to use the average daily balance in your account when computing the amount of finance charges you owe. **Fantasy:** Truth in lending laws require only that lenders fully disclose the effective rate of interest being charged and the method used to compute finance charges. Lenders can choose the specific method used to calculate the balances on which they apply finance charges. The average daily balance method is the most widely used.

6-3d Managing Your Credit Cards

Congratulations! You have applied for and been granted a bank credit card, as well as a retail charge card from your favorite department store. You carefully reviewed the terms of the credit agreement and have at least a basic understanding of how finance charges are computed for each account. Now you must manage your accounts efficiently, which involves using the monthly statement to help you make the required payments on time, as well as to track purchases and returned items.

The Statement

If you use a credit card, you'll receive monthly statements similar to the sample bank card statement in Exhibit 6.9, showing billing cycle and payment due dates, interest rate, minimum payment, and all account activity during the current period. Retail charge cards have similar monthly statements, but without a section for cash advances. (Revolving line of credit lenders will also send you a monthly statement showing the amount borrowed, payments, and finance charges.) The statement summarizes your account activity: the previous balance (the amount of credit outstanding at the beginning of the month—not to be confused with past-due, or late, payments); new charges made (four, in this case) during the past month; any finance charges (interest) on the unpaid balance; the preceding period's payment; any other credits (such as those for returns); and the new balance (previous balance plus new purchases and finance charges, less any payments and credits).

Although merchandise and cash transactions are separated on the statement, the finance charge in each case is calculated at the rate of 1.5 percent per month (18 percent annually). This procedure works fine for illustration but it's a bit out of the ordinary, because most card issuers charge a higher rate for cash advances than for purchases. Note that the ADB method is used to compute the finance charge in this statement.

You should review your statements promptly each month. Save your receipts and use them to verify statement entries for purchases and returns *before* paying. If you find any errors or suspect fraudulent use of your card, first use the issuer's toll-free number to report any problems. Then always follow up *in writing* within 60 days of the postmark on the bill.

EXHIBIT 6.7 **Finance Charges for Different Balance Calculation Methods**

The way a credit card issuer calculates the ADB on which the consumer pays finance charges has a big effect on the amount of interest you actually pay, as this table demonstrates. Note that the Credit Card Act of 2009 prohibits the use of the two-cycle method.

Example: A consumer starts the first month with a zero *balance* and charges $1,000, of which he pays off only the minimum amount due (1/36 of balance due). The next month, he charges another $1,000. He then pays off the entire balance due. This same pattern is repeated three more times during the year. The interest rate is 19.8 percent.

	Annual Finance Charges
ADB (including new purchases):	$132.00
ADB (excluding new purchases):	$66.00

Source: Based on "How Do Credit Card Companies Determine the Balance on Which Interest Is Charged?" http://www.extension.org/faq/29098, accessed August 2015.

EXHIBIT 6.8 **Finding the Average Daily Balance and Finance Charge**

The average daily balance including new purchases is the method most widely used by credit card issuers to determine the monthly finance charge on an account.

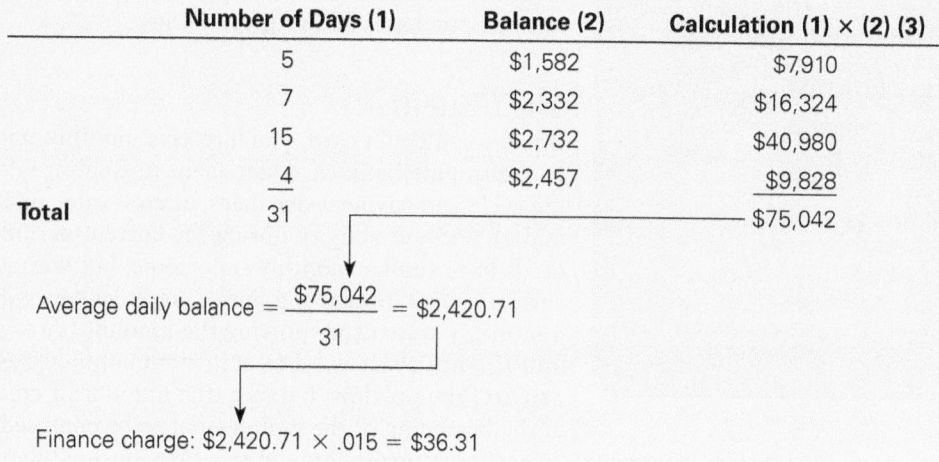

	Number of Days (1)	**Balance (2)**	**Calculation (1) × (2) (3)**
	5	$1,582	$7,910
	7	$2,332	$16,324
	15	$2,732	$40,980
	4	$2,457	$9,828
Total	31		$75,042

Average daily balance = $\dfrac{\$75,042}{31}$ = $2,420.71

Finance charge: $2,420.71 × .015 = $36.31

Payments

minimum monthly payment
In open account credit, a minimum specified percentage of the new account balance that must be paid in order to remain current.

Credit card users can avoid *future* finance charges by paying the total new balance shown on their statement each month. For example, if the $534.08 total new balance shown in Exhibit 6.9 is paid by the due date of September 21, 2017, then no additional finance charges will be incurred. (The cardholder, however, is still liable for the $4.40 in finance charges incurred to date.) If cardholders cannot pay the total new balance, they can pay any amount that is equal to or greater than the minimum monthly payment specified on the statement. If they do this, however, they will incur

| EXHIBIT 6.9 | A Bank Credit Card Monthly Statement |

Each month, a bank credit cardholder receives a statement that provides an itemized list of charges and credits, as well as a summary of previous activity and finance charges.

Please detach the above portion and return it with your payment to insure proper credit.

Bank Card Statement

Retain this statement for your records.

Account Number 123-XYZ-45678	Name(s) Mr. Scott Lataste Mrs. Emily Lataste	8-24-17 Statement Date	09-21-17 Payment Due Date

ACCOUNT ACTIVITY				FINANCE CHARGE CALCULATION			
Previous Balance	203.64	Credit Status		Amounts Subject to Finance Charge		This Month's Charge	
Payments −	119.89	Your Credit		A. *Average			ENTIRE BAL.
Credits −	.00	Limit is:		Daily Balance	293.25	4.40	1.5% 18.00%
Subtotal	83.75			B. *Cash Advance	.00	.00	Monthly Nominal
New Transaction +	445.93	2000.00		C. *Loan Advance	.00	.00	Periodic Annual
Finance Charge +	4.40	Your Available					Rate Rate
Late Charge +	.00	Credit is:				4.40	18.00%
NEW BALANCE	534.08	1465.92		*Finance Charges explained on reverse side		Finance Charge	Annual Percentage Rate

Mail Billing Inquiries to: Post Office Box 7890, Van Niles, California, 85258, or call   800/000-0000
For Inquiries on Past Due Accounts, Overlimits or Credit Line Increase, call   800/000-0000

Posted Mo./Day	Transaction Description or Merchant Name and Location		Purchase Mo./Day	Bank Reference Number	Purchases/ Advances/Debits	Payments Credits
8-08	AMERICA WEST AIRLINES	LOS ANGELES	07-25	850000008823395192	42.00	
8-13	HACIENDA MOTORS	COSTA MESA	08-05	015400018537022316	166.86	
8-15	RICOS RESTAURANT	PALM SPRG	08-10	114500018856161722	132.47	
8-12	PAYMENT—THANK YOU		08-11	4501000182MD02139		119.89
8-24	RENEES RESTAURANT	NEWPORT	08-13	114500068201632483	104.60	

Notice See reverse side for important information

					Total Debits 445.93	Total Credits 119.89
MIN. PAYMENT: 27.00	NEW BALANCE: 534.08					

additional finance charges in the following month. Note that the account in Exhibit 6.9 has a minimum payment of 5 percent of the new balance, rounded to the nearest full dollar. As shown at the bottom of the statement, this month's minimum payment is $27.00 (i.e., $534.08 × 0.05 = $26.70 ≈ $27.00). This $27.00 works out to be a *principal payment* of $22.60; that is, $27.00 − $4.40 (interest charges) = $22.60. That's actually about 4.25 percent of the "new balance." Now if the new balance had been less than $200, the bank would have required a payment of $10 (which is the absolute minimum dollar payment) or of the total new balance, if less than $10. Cardholders who fail to make the minimum payment are considered to be in default on their account, and the bank issuing the card can take whatever legal action it deems necessary.

6-4 USING CREDIT WISELY

LG5, LG6

As we've discussed, credit cards and revolving lines of credit can simplify your life financially. Unfortunately, you can also get into real trouble unless you use them wisely. That's why you should carefully shop around to choose the right credit cards for your personal situation, understand the advantages and disadvantages of credit cards, learn how to resolve credit problems, and know how to avoid the ultimate cost of credit abuse—bankruptcy.

6-4a Shop Around for the Best Deal

They say it pays to shop around, and when it comes to credit cards, that's certainly true. With all the fees and high interest costs, it pays to get the best deal possible. So, where do you start? Most credit experts suggest the first thing you should do is step back and take a look at yourself. What kind of "spender" are you, and how do you pay your bills? In fact, no single credit card is right for everyone. If you pay off your card balance each month, then you'll want a card that's different from the one that's right for someone who carries a credit balance from month to month and may pay only the minimum due.

Regardless of which category you fall into, there are basically four card features to look for:

- Annual fees
- Rate of interest charged on account balance
- Length of the grace period
- Method of calculating balances

Now, if you normally pay your account balance in full each month, get a card with *no annual fees and a long grace period*. The rate of interest on the card is irrelevant, since you don't carry account balances from month to month anyway. In contrast, if you don't pay your account in full, then look for cards that charge *a low rate of interest on unpaid balances*. The length of the grace period isn't all that important here, but obviously, other things being equal, you're better off with low (or no) annual fees.

Sometimes, however, "other things aren't equal," and you have to decide between interest rates and annual fees. If you're not a big spender and don't build up big balances on your credit card (i.e., the card balance rarely goes above $400 or $500), then *avoid* cards with annual fees and get one with as *low* a rate of interest as possible. This situation often applies to college students. On the other hand, if you do carry big balances (say, $1,000 or more), then you'll probably be better off *paying an annual fee* (even a relatively high one) *to keep the rate of interest on the card as low as possible.*

The bottom line is: don't take the first credit card that comes along. Instead, get the one that's right for you. To do that, learn as much as you can about the credit cards you've been offered or are considering. Be sure to read (or at least review) the credit agreement, and look for information about annual fees, grace periods, interest rates, and how finance charges are calculated. Don't overlook all those other charges and fees you may be assessed if you're ever late with a payment or go over your credit limit. Also, if local credit card deals aren't great, you might consider cards that are offered nationally. To help you do that, look at publications like *Money* magazine and *Kiplinger's Personal Finance* magazine, whose respective Internet sites are located at **http://www.money.com** and **http://www.kiplinger.com**. These magazines and Internet sites regularly publish information about banks and other financial institutions that offer low-cost credit cards nationally; an example is given in Exhibit 6.10.

One final point: Some people spend a lot of time and energy shopping for deals, jumping from one card to another to take advantage of low introductory rates. Although a strategy like this may result in lower interest payments, it can backfire if the low rates rise significantly after the introductory period or if you miss a payment. A wiser approach is to shop around, check for better deals from time to time, and then *direct the rest of your energy toward working to reduce (or even eliminate) any monthly balances*.

6-4b Avoiding Credit Problems

As more places accept credit cards, and as shopping online becomes more widely accepted, the volume of credit card purchases has grown tremendously—and so has the level of credit card debt. As a result, it's not unusual to find people using credit cards to solve cash-flow problems. Even the most careful consumers occasionally find themselves with mounting credit card debt, especially after the year-end holiday buying season. The real problems occur when the situation is no longer temporary and the debt continues to increase. If overspending is not curtailed, then the size of the unpaid balance may seriously strain the budget. Essentially, people who let their credit balances build up are *limiting their future flexibility*. By using credit, they're actually committing a part of their future income to make payments on the debt.

FINANCIAL ROAD SIGN

Should You Switch Credit Cards?

Shopping for a better deal on a credit card can be confusing because card issuers frequently change their offers. Here's how to figure out if it's time to switch.

- Review your card terms about every six months. Visit the Internet site of the card issuer to learn of current offers for new customers. If it's better than what you have, call the company and ask for the better deal. They may be willing to offer you the same terms to keep your business.
- Compare offers from competing companies at one of the credit card sites mentioned in the chapter, such as **http://www.bankrate.com**.
- Know what you need. If you carry balances, you'll want a lower introductory rate; if you pay in full each month, look for ways to reduce fees or earn rewards.

EXHIBIT 6.10   **Average Interest Rates for Different Types of Credit Cards**

Information about low-cost credit cards is readily available in the financial media. Pay particular attention to the *cards with the lowest rates* (probably best for people who regularly carry an account balance) and *no-fee cards with the lowest rates* (probably best for people who pay their accounts in full each month).

Type of Credit Card	Average Annual Percentage Rate (APR)
Balance transfer cards	14.12%
Cash back cards	15.27%
Low interest cards	11.62%

These rates are as of August 5, 2015; rates are adjustable. Banks sometimes offer lower introductory rates, many charge no annual fee, and the cards vary in credit score requirements. Most of these cards have variable rates. Data compiled from http://www.bankrate.com, accessed August 2015.

The best way to avoid credit problems is to be disciplined when using credit. Reduce the number of cards you carry, and don't rush to accept the tempting preapproved credit card offers filling your mailbox. A wallet full of cards can work against you in two ways. Obviously, the ready availability of credit can tempt you to overspend and incur too much credit card debt. But there's another, less obvious, danger: when you apply for a loan, lenders look at the *total amount* of credit you have available as well as at the outstanding balances on your credit cards. If you have a lot of unused credit capacity, it may be harder to get a loan because of lender concerns that you could become overextended. Two cards is the most that financial advisors suggest you carry: perhaps one rebate card, if you charge enough to make the benefit worthwhile, and a low-rate card for purchases you want to repay over time. And should you decide to start using a new card (because their offer was just too good to pass up), then *get rid of one of your old cards*—physically cut up the old card and inform the issuer in writing that you're canceling your account.

Suppose that, despite all your efforts, you find that your credit card balances are higher than you'd like and you anticipate having problems reducing them to a more manageable level. The first thing you can do is stop making any new charges until you pay off (or pay down) the existing balances. Then, commit to a repayment plan. One good strategy is to pay off the highest-interest cards first, keeping the original payment rather than reducing it as your balance drops. Or, even better, pay more than the minimum—even if it's just $10 more. You'd be surprised how much difference that makes.

You may also want to consider transferring your balances to a card with a low introductory rate and paying off as much as possible before the rate increases. Another option is to consolidate all your credit card debt and pay it off as quickly as possible using a lower-rate loan, such as a revolving personal line of credit. This can be a risky strategy, however. If you continue to be undisciplined about repaying your debts, then you could end up with one big credit problem instead of a bunch of small ones! Even worse, cleaning up your credit card debt may tempt you to start the credit card borrowing cycle all over again, putting you even farther behind than you were before.

6-4c Credit Card Fraud

Despite the efforts of law enforcement officials, plastic has become the vehicle of choice among crooks as a way of defrauding and stealing from both you and the merchants who honor credit cards. No doubt about it: credit card crime is a big business, with estimated losses in the United States at billions of dollars a year. Stolen account numbers are the biggest source of credit card fraud. Be especially careful where you use your credit card on the Internet. Most, if not all, of the big-name sites are about as secure as they can get, but when you go to one of the less reputable sites, you could be asking for trouble by giving them your credit card number!

Basically, "it's us against them," and the first thing you have to understand is that the credit card you're carrying around is a powerful piece of plastic. To reduce your chances of being defrauded, here are some suggestions:

- Never, ever, give your account number to people or organizations *who call you.* No matter how legitimate it sounds, if you didn't initiate the call then don't give out the information!
- If you initiated the call, it's acceptable to give your account number over the phone when ordering or purchasing something from a major catalog house, airline, hotel, and so on, but don't do it for any other reason.
- Use the same precautions *when purchasing something over the Internet* with your credit card—don't do it *unless* you're dealing at the site of a major retailer who uses state-of-the-art protection against fraud and thievery.
- When paying for something *by check,* don't put your credit card account number on the check and don't let the store clerk do it—show the clerk a check guarantee card (if you have one), a driver's license, or some other form of identification— but *not* your Social Security number.
- Don't put your phone number or address (and certainly not your Social Security number) on credit/charge slips, even if the merchant asks for it—they're *not* entitled to it.
- When using your card to make a purchase, *always keep your eye on it* (so the clerk can't make an extra imprint). If the clerk makes a mistake and wants to make another imprint, ask for the first imprint, and tear it up on the spot.
- Always draw a line on the credit slip through any blank spaces above the total, so the amount can't be altered.
- *Destroy* all old credit slips. And when you receive your monthly statement, be sure to *go over it promptly* to make sure there are no errors. If you find a mistake, call or send a letter immediately, detailing the error.
- If you lose a card or it's stolen, *report it to the card issuer immediately*—the most you're ever liable for with a lost or stolen card is $50 (per card), but if you report the loss *before* the card can be used, you won't be liable for any unauthorized charges (the phone number to call is listed on the back of your statement).
- Destroy old cards or those that you no longer use.

6-4d Bankruptcy: Paying the Price for Credit Abuse

It certainly isn't an overstatement to say that during the 1980s and 1990s, *debt was in*! In fact, the explosion of debt that has occurred since 1980 is almost incomprehensible. The national debt rose from less than a trillion dollars when the 1980s began to about $18.7 trillion by mid-2015. Businesses also took on debt rapidly. Not to be outdone, consumers were using credit like there was no tomorrow. So it should come as no surprise that when you couple this heavy debt load with a serious economic recession like that in 2009, you have all the ingredients of a real financial crisis. In 2014 about 910,000 people filed for **personal bankruptcy.**

personal bankruptcy
A form of legal recourse open to insolvent debtors, who may petition a court for protection from creditors and arrange for the orderly liquidation and distribution of their assets.

When too many people are too heavily in debt, a recession (or some other economic reversal) can come along and push many of them over the edge. But let's face it, the recession is not the main culprit here; the only way a recession can push you over the edge is if you're already sitting on it! The real culprit is excess debt. Some people simply abuse credit by taking on more than they can afford. Maybe they're pursuing a lifestyle beyond their means, or perhaps an unfortunate event—like the loss of a job—occurs.

Whatever the cause, sooner or later, these debtors start missing payments and their credit rating begins to deteriorate. Unless corrective actions are taken, this is followed by repossession of property and, eventually, even bankruptcy. These people

FINANCIAL PLANNING TIPS

Protect Against Identity Theft

Watch out for the following methods that thieves use to get your information:

- **Dumpster diving.** Don't leave bills or anything with personal information in your trash. Shredding such documents is a good idea.

- **Skimming.** Watch for unusual "additions" to credit and debit card readers that can steal your numbers.

- **Phishing.** Thieves can pretend to be financial institutions or companies and can use Internet pop-ups or send e-mail messages that ask you to disclose personal information.

- **Changing your address.** Thieves can re-route your bills to them by completing a change of address form.

- **Old-fashioned stealing.** Simple still works. Thieves continue to steal wallets and purses, mail, and new checks or tax information. Also, they sometimes bribe store employees to provide access to your personal information.

- **Pretexting.** Thieves can obtain your personal information from financial institutions, telephone companies, and other sources under false pretenses.

So what should you do? The FTC recommends the following:

- **Deter** thefts by protecting your information. Be aware of the above mentioned ways in which information is stolen.

- **Detect** suspicious activity by consistently checking your financial and billing statements.

- **Defend** against identity theft as soon as you suspect a possible problem. Place a "fraud alert" on your credit reports by contacting one of the consumer reporting companies noted earlier in this chapter (Experian, TransUnion, or Equifax). Contact the security departments of each company where an unauthorized account was opened.

Source: Adapted from http://www.finra.org/web/groups/sai/@sai/documents/sai_original_content/p036799.pdf, accessed August 2015.

---

have reached the end of a long line of deteriorating financial affairs. Households that cannot resolve serious credit problems on their own need help from the courts. Two of the most widely used legal procedures (employed by well over 95 percent of those who file for bankruptcy) are (1) the Wage Earner Plan and (2) straight bankruptcy.

Wage Earner Plan

Wage Earner Plan
An arrangement for scheduled debt repayment over future years that is an alternative to straight bankruptcy; used when a person has a steady source of income and there is a reasonable chance of repayment within 3 to 5 years.

The **Wage Earner Plan** (as defined in *Chapter 13* of the U.S. Bankruptcy Code) is a workout procedure involving some type of debt restructuring—usually by establishing a debt repayment schedule that's more compatible with the person's income. It may be a viable alternative for someone who has a steady source of income, not more than $1,149,525 in secured debt and $383,175 in unsecured debt, and a reasonably good chance of being able to repay the debts in three to five years. A majority of creditors must agree to the plan, and interest charges, along with late-payment penalties, are waived for the repayment period. Creditors usually will go along with this plan because they stand to lose more in a straight bankruptcy. After the plan is approved, the individual makes periodic payments to the court, which then pays off the creditors. Throughout the process, the individual retains the use of, and keeps title to, all of his or her assets.

Straight Bankruptcy

Straight bankruptcy, which is allowed under Chapter 7 of the bankruptcy code, can be viewed as a legal procedure that results in "wiping the slate clean and starting anew." *About 70 percent of those filing personal bankruptcy choose this route.* However, straight bankruptcy does not eliminate all the debtor's obligations, nor does the debtor necessarily lose all of his or her assets. For example, the debtor must make certain tax payments and keep up alimony and child-support payments but is allowed to retain certain payments from Social Security, retirement, veterans', and disability benefits. The debtor also may retain the equity in a home (based on established exemptions), a car (once again, based on established exemptions), and some other personal assets. Minimum values of what you can keep are established by federal regulations, though state laws are generally much more generous regarding the amount the debtor is allowed to keep. The choice of filing for bankruptcy under federal versus state regulations depends on the debtor's assets.

6-4e Using Credit Counselor Services

Filing for bankruptcy is a serious step that should be taken only as a last resort. For one thing, it's going to stick with you for a long time (it will stay in your credit file for up to 10 years) and certainly won't help your chances of getting credit in the future. It often makes more sense to work problems out before they get so bad that bankruptcy is the only option. Some people can do that on their own, but in many cases, it may be a good idea to seek the help of a qualified *credit counselor*.

credit counselor
A professional financial advisor who assists overextended consumers in repairing budgets for both spending and debt repayment.

Credit counselors work with a family to set up a budget and may even negotiate with creditors to establish schedules for repaying debts. The counseling service will often go so far as to collect money from the debtor and distribute it to creditors. Some private firms will, for a fee, act as intermediaries between borrowers and creditors and provide counseling services. These counselors generally try to reduce the size of payments, the size of outstanding debt, or both. However, their fees can run as much as 20 percent of the amount owed.

Another option is a nonprofit agency, such as those affiliated with the nationwide network of Consumer Credit Counseling Services (CCCS) (**http://credit.org/cccs/**). You'll get many of the services that private agencies provide, but at a lower cost. Of course, as with any financial advisor, you should check out a credit counselor's credentials, fees, services provided, and track record *before* using his or her services. But before even going to a credit counselor, try contacting your creditors yourself. You may be able to work out a deal on your own, especially if you have just a few lenders and need only two to three months to catch up. If, however, you have six or more creditors, then you should probably see a credit counselor. Make sure to ask your counselor for several *debt-reduction options* appropriate for your financial situation. More important, face up to credit and debt problems as soon as they occur, and do everything possible to avoid ruining your credit record.

TEST YOURSELF

6-16 What are some key factors that you should consider when choosing a credit card?

6-17 Discuss the steps that you would take to avoid and/or resolve credit problems.

6-18 What's the biggest source of credit card fraud? List at least five things you can do to reduce your chances of being a victim of credit card fraud.

6-19 Distinguish between a Wage Earner Plan and straight bankruptcy.

Planning Over a Lifetime: *Using Credit*

Here are some key considerations for using credit in each stage of the life cycle.

Pre-family Independence: 20s	Family Formation/ Career Development: 30–45	Pre-Retirement: 45 –65	Retirement: 65 and Beyond
✓ Obtain a credit card to start building a credit history. Consider a secured card first.	✓ Watch consumer credit use carefully to avoid overspending.	✓ Re-evaluate use of consumer credit in light of revised expenditures and income.	✓ Budget to eliminate reliance on consumer credit in retirement.
✓ Plan to pay all consumer credit bills in full.	✓ Periodically evaluate credit card costs, and change cards if you are not getting the best deal.	✓ Check your credit score periodically.	✓ Maintain credit score to assure credit access.
✓ Carefully monitor all charges and financial statements for unauthorized transactions.	✓ Continue to monitor all accounts for unauthorized transactions and possible identity theft.	✓ Continue to watch for unauthorized transactions and identity theft.	✓ Be particularly careful about releasing personal financial information.

Financial Impact of Personal Choices
Stan Has Had It and Files for Bankruptcy

Stan Thompson is overwhelmed by his bills. While making $60,000 a year, he has amassed credit card debt of $24,000, has an $80,000 college loan, holds a $150,000 mortgage, and pays monthly on his leased Jetta. He's having trouble paying the mortgage monthly and can never seem to pay more than the minimum on his credit card debt. Stan's wife, Zoe, is currently unemployed. Stan has heard that declaring bankruptcy can eliminate some of his debt commitments and give him extra time to deal with others. He's had it and just filed for bankruptcy. What can Stan look forward to as a result of his decision?

Stan can expect some short-term cash flow relief and filing for bankruptcy will likely prevent or at least delay foreclosure on his home. However, the bankruptcy filing will adversely affect his credit report for up to the next 10 years. Stan will probably have trouble getting a loan or a new credit card. And if he can borrow money or get a new credit card, he'll probably have to pay the highest allowable interest rate. By not having managed his family's indebtedness, Stan has exercised the bankruptcy "nuclear option." This provides short-term relief at the expense of longer-term access to credit on reasonable terms.

Summary

LG1 **Describe the reasons for using consumer credit, and identify its benefits and problems. p. 217**
Families and individuals use credit as a way to pay for relatively expensive items and, occasionally, to deal with a financial emergency. Consumer credit is also used because it's so convenient. Finally, it's used to partially finance the purchase of various types of investments. Consumer credit can be misused to the point where people live beyond their means by purchasing goods and services that they simply can't afford. Such overspending can get so bad that it eventually leads to bankruptcy.

LG2 **Develop a plan to establish a strong credit history. p. 217**
Establishing a strong credit history is an important part of personal financial planning. Opening checking and savings accounts, obtaining one or two credit cards and using them judiciously, and taking out a small loan and repaying it on schedule are ways to show potential lenders that you can handle credit wisely. Be sure to use credit only when you're sure you can repay the obligation, make payments promptly, and notify a lender immediately if you can't meet payments as agreed. The debt safety ratio is used to calculate how much of your monthly take-home pay is going toward consumer credit payments. One widely used credit capacity guideline is that total monthly consumer credit payments (exclusive of your mortgage payment) should not exceed 20 percent of your monthly take-home pay.

LG3 **Distinguish among the different forms of open account credit. p. 223**
Open account credit is one of the most popular forms of consumer credit; it's available from various types of financial institutions and from many retail stores and merchants. Major types of open account credit include bank credit cards; retail charge cards; and revolving lines of credit such as overdraft protection lines, home equity credit lines, and unsecured personal lines of credit. Many financial institutions issue special types of credit cards, such as rewards cards, affinity cards, or secured credit cards. Instead of using only credit cards, a growing number of consumers are turning to debit cards, which give their users a way to "write checks" with plastic.

LG4 **Apply for, obtain, and manage open forms of credit. p. 238**
Most types of revolving credit require formal application, which generally involves an extensive investigation of your credit background and an evaluation of your creditworthiness. This usually includes checking credit bureau reports. You should verify the accuracy of these reports regularly and promptly correct any errors. The amount of finance charges, if any, due on consumer credit depends largely on the technique used to compute the account balance; the ADB method that includes new purchases is the most common today. Managing your accounts involves understanding the monthly statement and making payments on time.

LG5 **Choose the right credit cards and recognize their advantages and disadvantages. p. 248**
With so many different types of credit cards available, it pays to shop around to choose the best one for your needs. Consider your spending habits and then compare the fees, interest rates, grace period, and any incentives. If you pay off your balance each month, you'll want a card with low annual fees; if you carry a balance, a low interest rate is your best bet. Advantages of credit cards include interest-free loans, simplified record-keeping, ease of making returns and resolving unsatisfactory purchase disputes, convenience and security, and use in emergencies. The disadvantages are the tendency to overspend and high interest costs on unpaid balances.

LG6 **Avoid credit problems, protect yourself against credit card fraud, and understand the personal bankruptcy process. p. 248**
Avoiding credit problems requires self-discipline. Keep the number of cards you use to a minimum, and be sure you can repay any balances quickly. When credit card debt gets out of control, adopt a payment strategy to pay off the debt as fast as possible by looking for a low-rate card, paying

more than the minimum payment, and not charging any additional purchases until the debt is repaid or substantially paid down. Another option is a consolidation loan. To protect yourself against credit card fraud, don't give out your card number unnecessarily; destroy old cards and receipts, verify your credit card transactions, and report a lost card or suspicious activity immediately. A solution to credit abuse, albeit a drastic one, is personal bankruptcy. Those who file for bankruptcy work out a debt restructuring program under Chapter 13's Wage Earner Plan or Chapter 7's straight bankruptcy. If you have serious problems in managing personal credit, a credit counselor may be able to help you learn to control spending and work out a repayment strategy.

Key Terms

affinity card, 229

annual percentage rate (APR), 244

average daily balance (ADB) method, 244

balance transfer, 227

bank credit card, 225

base rate, 226

cash advance, 225

credit bureau, 240

credit counselor, 253

credit investigation, 238

credit limit, 223

credit scoring, 242

credit statement, 223

debt safety ratio, 222

grace period, 226

home equity credit line, 235

line of credit, 225

minimum monthly payment, 246

open account credit, 223

overdraft protection line, 234

personal bankruptcy, 251

prepaid card, 233

retail charge card, 232

revolving lines of credit, 234

reward (co-branded) credit card, 228

secured (collateralized) credit cards, 230

straight bankruptcy, 252

student credit card, 230

unsecured personal credit line, 235

Wage Earner Plan, 252

Answers to Test Yourself

You can find answers to these questions on this book's companion website. Look for it at *www.cengagebrain.com*. Search for this book by its title, and then add it to your dashboard.

Financial Planning Exercises

LG1, p. 217

1. ***Establishing credit history.*** After graduating from college last fall, Nicole Butler took a job as a consumer credit analyst at a local bank. From her work reviewing credit applications, she realizes that she should begin establishing her own credit history. Describe for Nicole several steps that she could take to begin building a strong credit record. Does the fact that she took out a student loan for her college education help or hurt her credit record?

LG2, p. 217

2. ***Evaluating debt burden.*** Isaac Wright has a monthly take-home pay of $1,685; he makes payments of $410 a month on his outstanding consumer credit (excluding the mortgage on his home). How would you characterize Isaac's debt burden? What if his take-home pay was $850 a month and he had monthly credit payments of $150?

LG2, p. 217   3. **Calculating and interpreting personal debt safety ratio.** Calculate your own debt safety ratio. What does it tell you about your current credit situation and your debt capacity? Does this information indicate a need to make any changes in your credit use patterns? If so, what steps should you take?

LG2, p. 217   4. **Evaluating debt safety ratio. Use Worksheet 6.1.** Alyssa Clark is evaluating her debt safety ratio. Her monthly take-home pay is $3,320. Each month, she pays $380 for an auto loan, $120 on a personal line of credit, $60 on a department store charge card, and $85 on her bank credit card. Complete Worksheet 6.1 by listing Alyssa's outstanding debts, and then calculate her debt safety ratio. Given her current take-home pay, what is the maximum amount of monthly debt payments that Alyssa can have if she wants her debt safety ratio to be 12.5 percent? Given her current monthly debt payment load, what would Alyssa's take-home pay have to be if she wanted a 12.5 percent debt safety ratio?

LG2, p. 217   5. **Implications of Credit Card Act.** What are the main features and implications of the Credit Card Act of 2009?

LG4, p. 238   6. **Using overdraft protection line.** Isabella Harris has an overdraft protection line. Assume that her October 2017 statement showed a latest (new) balance of $862. If the line had a minimum monthly payment requirement of 5 percent of the latest balance (rounded to the nearest $5 figure), then what would be the minimum amount that she'd have to pay on her overdraft protection line?

LG3, p. 223   7. **Home equity line interest.** Sean and Amy Anderson have a home with an appraised value of $180,000 and a mortgage balance of only $90,000. Given that an S&L is willing to lend money at a loan-to-value ratio of 75 percent, how big a home equity credit line can Sean and Amy obtain? How much, if any, of this line would qualify as tax-deductible interest if their house originally cost $100,000?

LG4, p. 238   8. **Calculating credit card interest.** Ryan Gray, a student at State College, has a balance of $380 on his retail charge card; if the store levies a finance charge of 21 percent per year, how much monthly interest will be added to his account?

LG4, p. 238   9. **Choosing between credit cards.** Wyatt Collins recently graduated from college and is evaluating two credit cards. Card A has an annual fee of $75 and an interest rate of 9 percent. Card B has no annual fee and an interest rate of 16 percent. Assuming that Wyatt intends to carry no balance and to pay off his charges in full each month, which card represents the better deal? If Wyatt expected to carry a significant balance from one month to the next, which card would be better? Explain.

LG4, p. 238   10. **Balance transfer credit cards.** Martina Lopez has several credit cards, on which she is carrying a total current balance of $14,500. She is considering transferring this balance to a new card issued by a local bank. The bank advertises that, for a 2 percent fee, she can transfer her balance to a card that charges a 0 percent interest rate on transferred balances for the first nine months. Calculate the fee that Martina would pay to transfer the balance, and describe the benefits and drawbacks of balance transfer cards.

LG4, p. 238   11. **Calculating credit card finance charge.** Parker Young recently received his monthly *MasterCard* bill for the period June 1–30, 2017, and wants to verify the monthly finance charge calculation, which is assessed at a rate of 15 percent per year and based on ADBs, including new purchases. His outstanding balance, purchases, and payments are as follows:

> *Previous Balance:*
>
> | | Purchases: | $386 | Payments: | |
> |---|---|---|---|---|
> | | June 4 | $137 | June 21 | $35 |
> | | June 12 | 78 | | |
> | | June 20 | 98 | | |
> | | June 26 | 75 | | |

What are his ADB and finance charges for the period? (Use a table like the one in Exhibit 6.8 for your calculations.)

LG3, p. 223 12. **Credit vs. debit card.** Henry Stewart is trying to decide whether to apply for a credit card or a debit card. He has $8,500 in a savings account at the bank and spends his money frugally. What advice would you have for Henry? Describe the benefits and drawbacks of each type of card.

LG5, p. 248 13. **Credit card liability.** Christine Lin was reviewing her credit card statement and noticed several charges that didn't look familiar to her. Christine is unsure whether she should pay the bill in full and forget about the unfamiliar charges, or "make some noise." If some of these charges aren't hers, is she still liable for the full amount? Is she liable for any part of these charges, even if they're fraudulent?

LG2, p. 217 14. **Evaluating loan request.** Carter Hall recently graduated from college and wants to borrow $50,000 to start a business, which he believes will produce a cash flow of at least $10,000 per year. As a student, Carter was active in clubs, held leadership positions, and did a lot of community service. He currently has no other debts. He owns a car worth about $10,000 and has $6,000 in a savings account. Although the economy is currently in a recession, economic forecasters expect the recession to end soon. If you were a bank loan officer, how would you evaluate Carter's loan request within the context of the "5 C's of Credit"? Briefly describe each characteristic and indicate whether it has *favorable or unfavorable* implications for Carter's loan request.

Applying Personal Finance

How's Your Credit?

Establishing credit and maintaining your creditworthiness are essential to your financial well-being. Good credit allows you to obtain loans and acquire assets that you otherwise might not be able to attain. This project will help you to examine your credit.

If you've already established credit, get a copy of your credit report from one of the credit bureaus mentioned in this chapter. (If you've applied for a loan recently, your lender may already have sent you a copy of your credit report.) Carefully examine your report for any inaccuracies, and take the necessary steps to correct them. Then look over your report and evaluate your creditworthiness. If you feel you need to improve your creditworthiness, what steps do you need to take?

If you haven't yet established credit, find an application for a card such as *Visa*, *MasterCard*, or a department store or gasoline company credit card. Places to look might be at a department store, banking institution, gas station, or the Internet. Take the application home and fill it out. Then look it over and try to do a self-evaluation of your creditworthiness. Based on the information that you've provided, do you think you would qualify for the credit card? What do you see as your major strengths? What are your major weaknesses? Is there anything you can do about them?

CRITICAL THINKING CASES

LG2, 4, p. 217, 238

6.1 The Ramirez Family Seeks Some Credit Card Information

Felipe and Lucia Ramirez are a newly married couple in their mid-20s. Felipe is a senior at a state university and expects to graduate in the summer of 2017. Lucia graduated last spring with a degree in marketing and recently started working as a sales rep for the Fulcrum Systems Corporation. She supports both of them on her monthly salary of $4,250 after taxes. The Ramirez family currently pay all their expenses by cash or check. They would, however, like to use a bank credit card for some of their transactions. Because neither Felipe nor Lucia has ever applied for a credit card, they approach you for help.

Critical Thinking Questions

1. Advise the couple on how to fill out a credit application.
2. Explain to them the procedure that the bank will probably follow in processing their application.

3. Tell them about credit scoring and how the bank will arrive at a credit decision.
4. What kind of advice would you offer the Ramirez family on the best use of their card? What would you tell them about building a strong credit record?

LG2, 3, 4, p. 217, 223, 238

6.2 June Starts Over After Bankruptcy

A year after declaring bankruptcy and moving with her daughter back into her parents' home, June Maffeo is about to get a degree in nursing. As she starts out in a new career, she also wants to begin a new life—one built on a solid financial base. June will be starting out as a full-time nurse at a salary of $52,000 a year, and she plans to continue working at a second (part-time) nursing job with an annual income of $10,500. She'll be paying back $24,000 in bankruptcy debts and wants to be able to move into an apartment within a year and then buy a condo or house in five years.

June won't have to pay rent for the time that she lives with her parents. She also will have child care at no cost, which will continue after she and her daughter are able to move out on their own. While the living arrangement with her parents is great financially, the accommodations are "tight," and June's work hours interfere with her parents' routines. Everyone agrees that one more year of this is about all the family can take. However, before June is able to make a move—even into a rented apartment—she'll have to reestablish credit over and above paying off her bankruptcy debts. To rent the kind of place she'd like, she needs to have a good credit record for a year; to buy a home she must sustain that credit standing for at least three to five years.

Critical Thinking Questions

1. In addition to opening checking and savings accounts, what else might June do to begin establishing credit with a bank?
2. Although June is unlikely to be able to obtain a major bank credit card for at least a year, how might she begin establishing credit with local merchants?
3. What's one way she might be able to obtain a bank credit card? Explain.
4. How often should June monitor her credit standing with credit reporting services?
5. What general advice would you offer for getting June back on track to a new life financially?

CHAPTER 7

Using Consumer Loans

LEARNING GOALS

LG1   Know when to use consumer loans, and be able to differentiate between the major types.

LG2   Identify the various sources of consumer loans.

LG3   Choose the best loans by comparing finance charges, maturity, collateral, and other loan terms.

LG4   Describe the features of, and calculate the finance charges on, single payment loans.

LG5   Evaluate the benefits of an installment loan.

LG6   Determine the costs of installment loans, and analyze whether it is better to pay cash or take out a loan.

How Will This Affect Me?

Consumer loan sources abound, and their terms vary significantly. The primary types are single-payment and installment consumer loans. It's important to understand when to use each credit source, to be able to calculate and compare their costs, and to determine the circumstances in which it is best to take out a loan or pay cash. Practical examples considered in this chapter include taking out a car loan and borrowing to pay for a college education. The chapter provides you with an applied framework for evaluating the best ways to choose among and obtain consumer loans.

7-1 BASIC FEATURES OF CONSUMER LOANS

LG1, LG2

In previous chapters, we've discussed the different types of financial goals that individuals and families can set for themselves. These goals often involve large sums of money and may include such things as a college education or the purchase of a new car. One way to reach these goals is to systematically save the money. Another is to use a loan to at least partially finance the transaction. Consumer loans are important to the personal financial planning process because they can help you reach certain types of financial goals. The key, of course, is to successfully manage the credit by keeping the amount of debt used and debt-repayment burden *well within your budget!*

7-1a Using Consumer Loans

As we saw in Chapter 6, using open or revolving credit can be helpful to those who plan and live within their personal financial budgets. More important to the long-term achievement of personal financial goals, however, are single-payment and installment consumer loans. These long-term liabilities are widely used to finance the purchase of goods that are far too expensive to buy from current income, to help fund a college education, or to pay for certain types of nondurable items, such as expensive vacations. Of course, the extent to which this type of borrowing is used should be governed by personal financial plans and budgets.

These loans differ from open forms of credit in several ways, including the formality of their lending arrangements. That is, while open account credit results from a rather informal process, consumer loans are *formal, negotiated contracts* that specify both the terms for borrowing and the repayment schedule. Another difference is that an open line of credit can be used again and again, but consumer loans are one-shot transactions made for specific purposes. Because there's no revolving credit with a consumer loan, no more credit is available (from that particular loan) once it's paid off. Furthermore, no credit cards or checks are issued with this form of credit. Finally, whereas open account credit is used chiefly to make repeated purchases of relatively low-cost *goods and services*, consumer loans are used mainly to *borrow money* to pay for big-ticket items.

consumer loans
Loans made for specific purposes using formally negotiated contracts that specify the borrowing terms and repayment.

FINANCIAL PLANNING TIPS

Arranging an Auto Loan

It's important to do the following things *before* you go to the car dealership:

- Review your credit report and correct any errors that could increase your borrowing costs. Bring your credit report to the dealership when it's time to talk about financing.

- Know the maximum amount that you can spend on the car. Work backward from the maximum monthly payment to the implied maximum car price.

- Visit the car manufacturer's Internet site to see available special incentives or other deals. Print them out and take to the dealer when negotiating.

- Visit the Web sites of Kelley Blue Book (**http://kbb.com**) and Edmunds (**http://edmunds.com**) to get the value of your current car. Sell the car yourself if the dealer won't give you a fair trade-in price.

- Print out all of the pricing information on the car you want from the Internet and take it with you to the dealership.

- Get loan quotes from banks, credit unions, and online financial institutions and take the information with you to the dealership. Compare rates, application fees, loan terms, and prepayment penalties. If the terms look better, get the best loan and go to the dealership as a cash buyer.

- Increasing your down payment with rebate money to reduce the financed amount is often a better deal than 0 percent financing.

- Ask to have any rebates mailed directly to you. Don't let the dealership apply them to your down payment. Make the down payment yourself and then deposit the rebate in your account when you receive the check in the mail from the manufacturer.

Source: Adapted from Lee Anne Obringer, "How Car Financing Works," http://auto.howstuffworks.com/buying-selling/car-financing2.htm, accessed August 2015.

7-1b Different Types of Loans

Although they can be used for just about any purpose imaginable, most consumer loans fall into one of the following categories.

- Auto loans: Financing a new car, truck, SUV, or minivan is the single most common reason for borrowing money through a consumer loan. Indeed, auto loans account for about 35 percent of all consumer credit outstanding. Typically, about 80 percent to 90 percent of the cost of a new vehicle (somewhat less with used cars) can be financed with credit. The buyer must provide the rest through a *down payment*. The loan is *secured* with the auto, meaning that the vehicle serves as **collateral** for the loan and can be repossessed by the lender should the buyer fail to make payments. These loans generally have maturities ranging from 36 to 60 months.

collateral
An item of value used to secure the principal portion of a loan.

You Can Do It Now

Current Auto Loan Rates

If you're considering buying a car, you need to know current auto loan rates to estimate prospective monthly payments and what price you can afford to pay for an auto. Up-to-date market rates are available at **http://www.bankrate.com**. You'll see how much higher used auto loan rates are than new auto loan rates. And you'll get a sense of the trade-off between auto loan rates and maturity, for example, between 48- and 60-month loan rates. Getting familiar with auto loan rates will help you be a more informed shopper—you can do it now.

- Loans for other durable goods: Consumer loans can also be used to finance other kinds of *costly durable goods*, such as furniture, home appliances, TVs, home computers, recreational vehicles, and even small airplanes and mobile homes. These loans are also secured by the items purchased and generally require some down payment. Maturities vary with the type of asset purchased: 9- to 12-month loans are common for less costly items, such as TVs and audio equipment, whereas 10- to 15-year loans (or even longer) are normal with mobile homes.
- Education loans: Getting a college education is another important reason for taking out a consumer loan. Such loans can be used to finance either undergraduate or graduate studies, and special government-subsidized loan programs are available to students and parents. We'll discuss student loans in more detail in the following section.
- Personal loans: These loans are typically used for nondurable expenditures, such as an expensive European vacation or to cover temporary cash shortfalls. Many personal loans are *unsecured*, which means there's no collateral with the loan other than the borrower's good name.
- Consolidation loans: This type of loan is used to straighten out an unhealthy credit situation. When consumers overuse credit cards, credit lines, or consumer loans and can no longer promptly service their debt, a consolidation loan may help control this deteriorating credit situation. By borrowing money from one source to pay off other forms of credit, borrowers can replace, say, five or six monthly payments that total $400 with one payment amounting to $250. *Consolidation loans are usually expensive, and people who use them must be careful to stop using credit cards and other forms of credit until they repay the loans. Otherwise, they may end up right back where they started.*

Student Loans

The recent average annual budget for tuition, fees, books and supplies, and room and board ranges from $23,410 at four-year public colleges for state residents to over $46,000 at private colleges. Alarmingly, after adjusting for inflation, students are paying about 3 times what they paid 30 years ago for a public college education and about 2.5 times what they paid for a private college education. Many families, even those who started saving for college when their children were young, are faced with higher-than-expected bills. Fortunately, there are many types of financial aid programs available, including some federal programs described later in this chapter, as well as state, private, and college-sponsored programs.

Paying for a college education is one of the most legitimate reasons for going into debt. Although you could borrow money for college through normal channels—that is, take out a regular consumer loan from your bank and use the proceeds to finance an education—there are better ways to go about getting education loans. That's because the federal government (and some state governments) have available several different types of subsidized educational loan programs. The federally sponsored programs are:

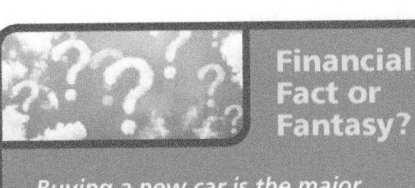

Financial Fact or Fantasy?

Buying a new car is the major reason that people borrow money through consumer loans.

Fact: Buying a new car accounts for about 35 percent of all consumer loans outstanding, which is the single most common reason for taking out a consumer loan.

- Stafford loans (Direct and Federal Family Education Loans—FFELs)
- Perkins loans
- Parent Loans (PLUS)

The Stafford and Perkins loans have the best terms and are the foundation of the government's student loan program. In contrast, PLUS (which stands for *Parent Loans for Undergraduate Students*) loans are *supplemental loans* for *undergraduate students* who demonstrate a need but, for one reason or another, don't qualify for Stafford or Perkins loans or need more aid than they're receiving. Under this program, parents can take out loans to meet or

©SYDA PRODUCTIONS/SHUTTERSTOCK.COM

supplement the costs of their children's college education, *up to the full cost of attendance.* Whereas Stafford and Perkins loans are made directly to students, PLUS loans are made to the parents or legal guardians of college students. Probably the best place to look for information about these and other programs is the Internet. For example, look up FASTWEB (which stands for *Financial Aid Search Through the WEB*). This site, which is free, not only provides details on all the major, and some of the not-so-major, student loan programs but also has a service that matches individuals with scholarships and loans, even going so far as to provide form letters to use in requesting more information. (The address for this Internet site is **http://www.fastweb.com.**)

Let's look at the Stafford loan program to see how student loans work. There are two types of Stafford loans. In the subsidized loan program, the U.S. Department of Education pays interest while the student is in school and also during grace and deferment periods. In the unsubsidized program, the borrower is responsible for all interest, whether in or out of school. (Except where noted, the other two federally subsidized programs have much the same standards and follow the same procedures as discussed here.) Stafford loans carry low, possibly government-subsidized interest rates; most major banks, as well as some of the bigger S&Ls and credit unions, participate in the program. Actually, the loans are made directly by one of the participating financial institutions (in the case of the Stafford FFEL loan program), although the student has no direct contact with the lending institution. Instead, the whole process—which really is quite simple—begins with a visit to the school's financial aid office, where a financial aid counselor will help you determine your eligibility.

To be eligible, you must demonstrate a *financial need,* where the amount of your financial need is defined as the cost of attending school *less* the amount that can be paid by you or your family. Thus, in these programs, students are expected to contribute something to their educational expense regardless of their income. You must also be making *satisfactory progress in your academic program,* and you cannot be in default on any other student loans. Each academic year, you'll have to fill out a Free Application for Federal Student Aid (FAFSA) statement to attest that these qualifications are being met. The financial aid office will have the forms available in hard copy, or you can complete and submit the form on the Internet at **http://www.fafsa. ed.gov.** In short, so long as you can demonstrate a financial need and are making satisfactory academic progress, you'll probably qualify for a Stafford loan.

Obtaining a Student Loan. All you have to do to obtain a Stafford loan is complete a simple application form, which is then submitted to *your school's financial aid office.* You do *not* have to deal with the bank (your school will submit all the necessary papers to the institution actually making the loan in the case of an FFEL loan, or directly to the federal government in the case of a Stafford Direct loan), and you won't be subject to credit checks—although with PLUS loans, the borrower (parent) may be subject to a credit judgment by the lender. The latest innovation in this procedure involves transmitting the application electronically to the necessary parties, thus reducing paperwork and speeding up the processing (see, for example, **http:// www.staffordloan.com**). Most schools are converting to this method, if they haven't already done so.

Each program has specific loan limits. For example, with subsidized Stafford loans for dependent students, you can borrow up to $3,500 per academic year for first-year studies, $4,500 for the second year, and $5,500 per academic year thereafter, up to a subsidized loan maximum of $23,000 for undergraduate studies—you can obtain even more if you can show that you're no longer dependent on your parents; in other words, that you're an *independent* undergraduate student paying for your college education on your own. Graduate students can qualify for up to $8,500 per academic year for independent students. The maximum for both undergraduate and graduate subsidized loans combined is $65,500 (or $224,000 for health professionals). There's no limit on the *number* of loans you can have, only on the maximum dollar amount that you can receive annually from each program. Exhibit 7.1 compares the major loan provisions (borrower, interest rates, guarantee and/or origination fees, borrowing limits, and loan terms) of the three federally sponsored student loan programs—Stafford, Perkins, and PLUS loans.

Each year, right on through graduate school, a student can take out a loan from one or more of these government programs. Over time, that can add up to a lot of loans. Indeed, the average graduating senior leaves school about $30,000 in debt—all of which must be repaid. But here's another nice feature of these loans: in addition to carrying low (government-subsidized) interest rates, loan repayment doesn't begin until after you're out of school (for the Stafford and Perkins programs only—repayment on PLUS loans normally begins within 60 days of loan disbursement). In addition, interest doesn't begin accruing until you get out of school (except, of course, with PLUS loans, where interest starts accumulating with the first disbursement). While you're in school, the lenders will receive interest on their loans, but it's paid by the federal government! Once repayment begins, you start paying interest on the loans, which may be tax deductible, depending on your income.

Student loans are usually amortized with monthly (principal and interest) payments over a period of 5 to 10 years. To help you service the debt, if you have several student loans outstanding, then you can *consolidate* the loans, at a single blended rate, and extend the repayment period to as long as 20 years. You also can ask for

EXHIBIT 7.1	Federal Government Student Loan Programs at a Glance

More and more college students rely on loans subsidized by the federal government to finance all or part of their educations. There are three types of federally subsidized loan programs, the basic loan provisions of which are listed here. These loans all have low interest rates and provide various deferment options and extended repayment terms. (*Note: Loan rates and terms shown here are for the 2015–2016 school year.*)

	TYPE OF FEDERAL LOAN PROGRAM		
Loan Provisions	**Stafford Loans***	**Perkins Loans**	**PLUS Loans**
Borrower	Student	Student	Parent
Interest rate	4.29% (undergrad) 5.84% (grad/professional)	5%	7.21%
Cumulative borrow limits	*Dependent and independent undergraduate students:* $23,000; *Grad/professional students:* $138,500 (including a max of $65,500 in subsidized loans) or $224,000 for medical school/health professionals	$27,500 (undergrad) $60,000 (grad/ professional)	*No total dollar limit:* Cost of attendance minus any other financial aid received.
Loan fees	1.073% of loan origination fee	None	4.272% of loan amount
Loan term	Up to 10 years	10 years	10 years

*Data are for subsidized Stafford loans and unsubsidized graduate or professional Stafford loans, and interest rates are as of mid-2015. Stafford loans can be subsidized and unsubsidized and the lifetime limits can differ. Subsidized Stafford loans also have annual borrowing limits. Perkins loans have annual limits of $5,550 per year of undergraduate study and $8,000 per year of graduate school.

Source: http://www.fastweb.com and http://www.staffordloan.com; accessed August 2015.

either an *extended repayment* for a longer term of up to 30 years; a *graduated repayment schedule*, which will give you low payments in the early years and then higher payments later on; or an *income-contingent repayment plan*, with payments that fluctuate annually according to your income and debt levels. But no matter what you do, *take the repayment provisions seriously, because defaults will be reported to credit bureaus and become a part of your credit records!* What's more, due to recent legislation, you can't get out of repaying your student loans by filing for bankruptcy: whether you file under Chapter 7 or Chapter 13, *student loans are no longer dischargeable in a bankruptcy proceeding.*

In addition to the government programs just described, there are other ways to pay for a college education. One of the most innovative is the so-called 529 College Savings Plan. These plans aren't based on borrowing money to pay for college but rather on using a special tax-sheltered *savings and investment program.*

529 college savings plan
A government-sponsored investment vehicle that allows earnings to grow free from federal taxes, so long as they are used to meet college education expenses.

Are Student Loans "Too Big to Fail"? During the recent financial crisis, some banks were deemed "too big to fail" by virtue of their importance to the operation of the entire financial system. Their size consequently became the rationale for providing massive public financial assistance. Education is important to the economy, and, as discussed in this chapter, the federal government provides loans to finance undergraduate and graduate education. The financial crisis obviously put more pressure on households seeking to pay the increasing cost of college educations. So how large have student loans grown? Student loans now total more than $1.2 trillion! So the federal government has taken on a significant liability to support higher education that is important to the overall economy. This recently prompted a representative of the newly created Consumer Finance Protection Bureau (CFPB) to observe that the student loan program has possibly become "too big to fail" as well.

While this chapter discusses the limits on public loans, there is no limit on private student loans. While the average student debt is about $30,000, around 5 percent of student borrowers owe more than $100,000. And about 25 percent of all student borrowers have a past-due balance! Exhibit 7.2 portrays the distribution of loan balances for young families. These balances take on particular significance given that the average starting salary of a recent college graduate is about $48,700.

EXHIBIT 7.2 | **Distribution of Education Loan Balances for Young Families**

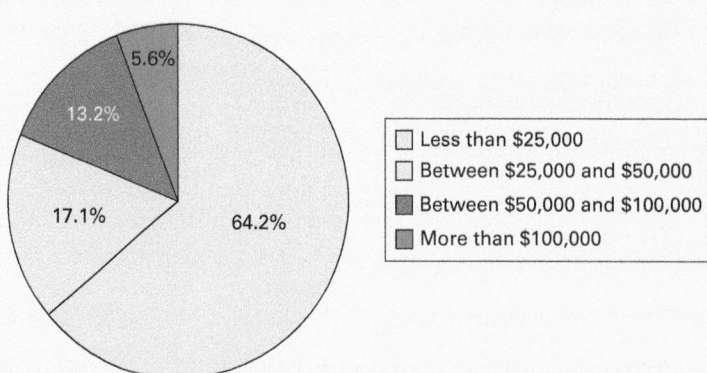

- ☐ Less than $25,000
- ☐ Between $25,000 and $50,000
- ■ Between $50,000 and $100,000
- ■ More than $100,000

Source: Jesse Bricker, Lisa J. Dettling, Alice Henriques, Joanne W. Hsu, Kevin B. Moore, John Sabelhaus, Jeffrey Thompson, and Richard A. Windle, "Changes in U.S. Family Finances from 2010 to 2013: Evidence from the Survey of Consumer Finances," Board of Governors of the Federal Reserve System, Washington, DC, (October 24, 2014, data is for 2013), http://www.federalreserve.gov/pubs/bulletin/2014/pdf/scf14.pdf, Box 10, Figure B, accessed August 2015.

A survey by the Young Invincibles, a nonprofit group focusing on issues affecting 18- to 34-year-olds (**http://www.younginvincibles.org**), found that about two-thirds of student borrowers with private loans did not understand the differences between public and private student loans. This is significant because public lenders are often more flexible than private lenders in providing financial relief when borrowers are under pressure. For example, federal programs provide public service loan forgiveness, income-based repayment, and loan repayment assistance programs. Public service loan forgiveness allows those who borrowed under the previously discussed FFEL program to make no more than 120 payments on their loans if they work for a federal, state, or local government agency, entity, or organization. The remaining balance is forgiven.

Strategies for Reducing Student Loan Costs. It's important to borrow as little as possible to cover college costs. This common-sense goal can be quantified by borrowing in light of the student's expected future salary. Based on that expected future salary, figure out what monthly payment the student will be able to afford and then use a loan repayment calculator to determine the maximum amount that can be borrowed at the expected interest rate on the loan. For example, consider using the following online student loan calculator: **http://www.bankrate.com/calculators/college-planning/loan-calculator.aspx**. The analysis should also include looking for the lowest interest rate. Before borrowing, it makes sense to explore all possibly available grants and scholarships and to apply for federal student aid. And upon graduation, it is wise to explore the Public Service Loan Forgiveness and Loan Repayment Assistance programs. There could also be the option to consolidate federal student loans and to participate in an income-based repayment program.

Single-Payment or Installment Loans

Consumer loans can also be broken into categories based on the type of repayment arrangement—single-payment or installment. Single-payment loans are made for a specified period of time, at the end of which payment in full (principal plus interest) is due. They generally have maturities ranging from 30 days to a year; rarely do these loans run for more than a year. Sometimes single-payment loans are made to finance purchases or pay bills when the cash to be used for repayment is known to be forthcoming in the near future; in this case, they serve as a form of interim financing. In other situations, single-payment loans are used by consumers who want to avoid being strapped with monthly installment payments and choose instead to make one large payment at the end of the loan.

Installment loans, in contrast, are repaid in a series of fixed, scheduled payments rather than in one lump sum. The payments are almost always set up on a monthly basis, with each installment made up partly of principal and partly of interest. For example, out of a $75 monthly payment, $50 might be credited to principal and the balance to interest. These loans are typically made to finance the purchase of a good or service for which current resources are inadequate. The repayment period can run from six months to six years or more. Installment loans have become a way of life for many consumers. They're popular because they provide a convenient way to "buy now and pay later" in fixed monthly installments that can be readily incorporated into a family budget.

Fixed- or Variable-Rate Loans

Most consumer loans are made at fixed rates of interest—that is, the interest rate charged and the monthly payment remain the same over the life of the obligation. However, variable-rate loans are also being made with increasing frequency, especially on *longer-term installment loans*. As with an adjustable-rate home mortgage, the rate of interest charged on such loans changes periodically in keeping with prevailing market conditions. If market interest rates go up, the rate of interest on the loan goes up accordingly, as does the monthly loan payment. These loans have periodic

single-payment loan
A loan made for a specified period, at the end of which payment is due in full.

interim financing
The use of a single-payment loan to finance a purchase or pay bills in situations where the funds to be used for repayment are known to be forthcoming in the near future.

installment loan
A loan that is repaid in a series of fixed, scheduled payments rather than a lump sum.

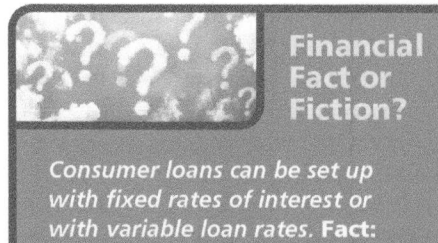
adjustment dates (for example, monthly, quarterly, or semiannually), at which time the interest rate and monthly payment are adjusted as necessary. Once an adjustment is made, the new rate remains in effect until the next adjustment date (sometimes the payment amount remains the same, but the number of payments changes). Many variable-rate loans have caps on the maximum increase per adjustment period as well as over the life of the loan. Generally speaking, variable-rate loans are desirable *if interest rates are expected to fall* over the course of the loan. In contrast, fixed-rate loans are preferable *if interest rates are expected to rise*.

Whether the loans are fixed or variable, their cost tends to vary with market conditions. As a rule, when interest rates move up or down in the market, so will the cost of consumer loans. Inevitably, there will be times when *the cost of credit simply becomes too high to justify borrowing* as a way of making major purchases. So when market rates start climbing, you should ask yourself whether the cost is really worth it. Financially, you may be far better off delaying the purchase until rates come down.

7-1c Where Can You Get Consumer Loans?

Consumer loans can be obtained from a number of sources, including commercial banks, consumer finance companies, credit unions, S&Ls, sales finance companies, and life insurance companies—even brokerage firms, pawnshops, or friends and relatives. *Commercial banks* dominate the field and provide nearly half of all consumer loans. Second to banks are *consumer finance companies* and then *credit unions*. Together, about 75 percent of all consumer loans are originated by these three financial institutions! The S&Ls are not much of a force in this market since they tend to focus on mortgage loans rather than consumer loans. Selection of a lender often depends on both the rate of interest being charged and how easily the loan can be negotiated. Of course, today it's becoming easier than ever to obtain consumer loans online. Just go to Google and search for "installment loans," and you'll get hundreds of Internet sites. Some of these sites will actually accept applications online; others offer a brief description of their services along with a toll-free phone number.

Commercial Banks

Because they offer various types of loans at attractive rates of interest, commercial banks are a popular source of consumer loans. Commercial banks typically charge lower rates than most other lenders, largely because they take only the best credit risks and are able to obtain relatively inexpensive funds from their depositors. The demand for their loans is generally high, and they can be selective in making consumer loans. Commercial banks usually lend only to customers with good credit ratings who can readily demonstrate an ability to repay a loan according to the specified terms. They also give preference to loan applicants who are account holders. Although banks prefer to make loans secured by some type of collateral, they also make unsecured loans to their better customers. The interest rate charged on a bank loan may be affected by the loan's size, terms, and whether it's secured by some type of collateral.

Consumer Finance Companies

consumer finance company
A firm that makes secured and unsecured personal loans to qualified individuals; also called a *small loan company*.

Sometimes called *small loan companies*, **consumer finance companies** make secured and unsecured (signature) loans to qualified individuals. These companies do not accept deposits but obtain funds from their stockholders and through open market borrowing. Because they don't have the inexpensive sources of funds that banks and other deposit-type institutions do, their interest rates are generally quite high. Actual rates charged by consumer finance companies are regulated by interest-rate ceilings (or usury laws) set by the states in which they operate. The maximum allowable interest rate may vary with the size of the loan, and the state regulatory authorities may also limit the length of the repayment period. Loans made by consumer finance companies typically are for $5,000 or less and are secured by some type of collateral. Repayment is required in installments, usually within five years or less.

Consumer finance companies specialize in small loans to high-risk borrowers. These loans are quite costly, but they may be the only alternative for people with poor credit ratings. Because of the high rates of interest charged, individuals should consider this source only after exhausting other alternatives.

Credit Unions

A credit union is a cooperative financial institution that is owned and controlled by the people ("members") who use its services. Only the members can obtain installment loans and other types of credit from these institutions, but credit unions can offer membership to just about anyone they want, not merely to certain groups of people. Because they are nonprofit organizations with minimal operating costs, credit unions charge relatively low rates on their loans. They make either unsecured or secured loans, depending on the size and type of loan requested. Membership in a credit union generally provides the most attractive borrowing opportunities available because their interest rates and borrowing requirements are usually more favorable than other sources of consumer loans.

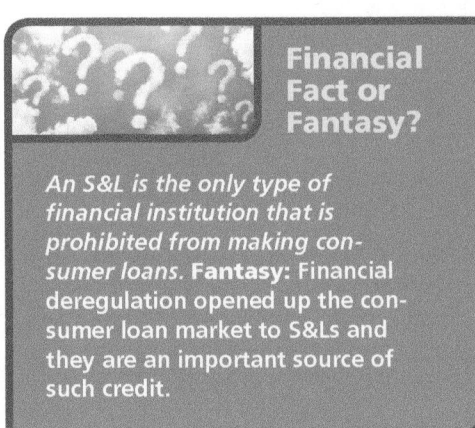

S&L Associations

S&L associations (as well as savings banks) primarily make mortgage loans. While they aren't major players in the consumer loan field, S&Ls can make loans on such consumer durables as automobiles, televisions, refrigerators, and other appliances. They can also make certain types of home improvement and mobile-home loans, as well as some personal and educational loans. Rates of interest on consumer loans at S&Ls are fairly close to the rates charged by commercial banks; if anything, they tend to be a bit more expensive. Like their banking counterparts, the rates charged at S&Ls will, in the final analysis, depend on such factors as type and purpose of the loan, duration and type of repayment, and the borrower's overall creditworthiness.

Sales Finance Companies

sales finance company
A firm that purchases notes drawn up by sellers of certain types of merchandise, typically big-ticket items.

captive finance company
A sales finance company that is owned by a manufacturer of big-ticket merchandise. GMAC is a captive finance company.

Businesses that sell relatively expensive items—such as automobiles, furniture, and appliances—often provide installment financing to their customers. Because dealers can't afford to tie up their funds in installment contracts, they sell them to a sales finance company for cash. This procedure is often called "selling paper" because the merchants are, in effect, selling their loans to a third party. When the sales finance company purchases these notes, customers are usually notified to make payments directly to it.

The largest sales finance organizations are the captive finance companies owned by the manufacturers of big-ticket items—automobiles and appliances. General Motors Acceptance Corporation (GMAC) and General Electric Credit Corporation (GECC) are just two examples of captive finance companies that purchase the installment loans made by the dealers of their products. Also, most commercial banks act as sales finance companies by buying paper from auto dealers and other businesses. The cost of financing through a sales finance company is generally higher than the rates charged by banks and S&Ls, particularly when you let the dealer do all the work in arranging the financing. This is because dealers normally get a cut of the finance income, so it's obviously in their best interest to secure as high a rate as possible. That's certainly not true in all cases, however; automakers today will frequently use interest rates on new car loans (or leases) as a marketing tool. They do this by dropping the rate of interest (*usually for selected models*) to levels that are well below the market—even 0 percent financing! Auto manufacturers use these loan rates (along with rebates) to stimulate sales by keeping the cost of buying a new car down. Clearly, cutting the cost of borrowing for a new car can result in big savings.

Life Insurance Companies

Life insurance policyholders may be able to obtain loans from their insurance companies. That's because certain types of policies not only provide death benefits but also have a savings function, so they can be used as collateral for loans. (*Be careful with these loans, however, as they could involve a tax penalty if certain conditions are not met.* A detailed discussion of life insurance is presented in Chapter 8.) Life insurance companies are required by law to make loans against the **cash value**—the amount of accumulated savings—of certain types of life insurance policies. The rate of interest on this type of loan is stated in the policy and usually carries a variable rate that goes up and down with prevailing market conditions. Although you'll be charged interest for as long as the policy loan is outstanding, these loans don't have repayment dates—in other words, *you don't have to pay them back*. When you take out a loan against the cash value of your life insurance policy, you're really borrowing from yourself. Thus, the amount of the loan outstanding, plus any accrued interest,

cash value (of life insurance)
An accumulation of savings in an insurance policy that can be used as a source of loan collateral.

FINANCIAL PLANNING TIPS

Lending to Family and Friends

Before you lend money to family or friends, it's helpful to answer the following questions:

• **Has your friend or family member explored other funding sources?** Starting with a bank or a credit union makes sense. If that doesn't work, non-financial-institution, peer-to-peer lending organizations like Prosper (**http://prosper.com**) or Lending Club (**http://lendingclub.com**) are worth looking into. Every other resource should be exhausted before you consider giving a loan to friends or relatives.

• **Can you help other than with money?** For example, if a friend or relative is out of work, perhaps you could help by providing an introduction or by arranging an interview.

• **Will the loan be repaid?** It's a cliché for a reason: Don't lend any money that you can't afford to lose. If you really think repayment is unlikely, you may want to consider just offering cash as a gift, without any obligation to repay.

• **What will happen to your relationship if the loan isn't repaid?** How hard would you push your friend or relative for repayment, and how far would you be willing to go? Could you just forget about the money without

bearing a grudge? Is the risk of losing a friend worth any interest that you might earn on the loan?

• **What if the loan is not used as you'd hoped?** Resist the urge to direct how the money is used. While you should be repaid, you have no control over how the money is used. Don't lend the money if you have concerns about how it will be used.

• **Is the interest rate fair?** It is sometimes awkward to charge interest to a relative or friend. If you do decide to do that, though, a good rule is to charge interest at a rate comparable to that on a high-yield savings account. If you didn't make the loan, it's likely you'd keep it in a savings account anyway. If you charge interest, it should be a fair, legal rate.

• **Should this be a formal, legal transaction?** Even though this is your friend or relative, it's wise to formalize the loan with a contract. A contract shows that you're serious about the arrangement and expect to be repaid. Search online for "promissory note" and you'll find Internet sites where you can buy one at a reasonable price. If you wouldn't consider taking legal action against a friend or a relative, consider just giving some money instead of extending a loan.

Source: Adapted from Luke Landes, "Lending Money to Friends and Family," *Consumerism Commentary*, http://www.consumerismcommentary.com/lending-money-to-friends-and-family/, accessed August 2015.

is deducted from the amount of coverage provided by the policy—*effectively lowering your insurance coverage* and endangering your beneficiaries with a lower payout should you die before repayment. The chief danger in life insurance loans is that they don't have a firm maturity date, so *borrowers may lack the motivation to repay them.* Also, many insurers put borrowed policies in a different (less attractive) investment return category, based on the lower cash value in the policy.

Friends and Relatives

Sometimes, rather than going to a bank or some other financial institution, you may know of a close friend or relative who's willing to lend you money. Such loans often are attractive because little or no interest is charged. The terms will, of course, vary depending on the borrower's financial needs; but they should be specified in some type of loan agreement that states the costs, conditions, and maturity date of the loan as well as the obligations of both borrower and lender. Not only does a written loan agreement reduce opportunities for disagreement and unhappiness, it also protects both borrower and lender should either of them die or if other unexpected events occur. *Still, given the potential for disagreement and conflict, borrowing from friends or relatives is not advisable.* Consider doing so only when there are no other viable alternatives. Remember, a loan to or from a friend or family member is far more than a run-of-the-mill banking transaction: the interest is emotional, and the risks are the relationship itself!

TEST YOURSELF

7-1   List and briefly discuss the five major reasons for borrowing money through a consumer loan.

7-2   Identify several different types of federally sponsored student loan programs.

7-3   As a college student, what aspects of these student loan programs appeal to you the most?

7-4   Explain some strategies for reducing the cost of student loans.

7-5   Define and differentiate between (a) fixed- and variable-rate loans and (b) a *single-payment loan* and an *installment loan*.

7-6   Compare the consumer lending activities of (a) *consumer finance companies* and (b) *sales finance companies*. Describe a *captive finance company*.

7-7   Discuss the role in consumer lending of (a) credit unions and (b) savings and loan associations. Point out any similarities or differences in their lending activities. How do they compare with commercial banks?

7-2 MANAGING YOUR CREDIT

Borrowing money to make major purchases—and, in general, using consumer loans—is a sound and perfectly legitimate way to conduct your financial affairs. From a financial planning perspective, you should ask yourself two questions when considering the use of a consumer loan: (1) does making this purchase fit into your financial plans; and (2) do the required debt payments on the loan fit into your monthly cash budget? Indeed, when *full consideration is given not only to the need for the asset or item in question but also to the repayment of the ensuing debt,* sound credit management is the result. In contrast, if the expenditure in question will seriously jeopardize your financial plans or if repaying of the loan is likely to strain your cash budget, then you should definitely reconsider the purchase! Perhaps it can be postponed, or you can liquidate some assets in order to come up with more down payment.

You may even have to alter some other area of your financial plan in order to work in the expenditure. Whatever route you choose, the key point is to make sure that the debt will be fully compatible with your financial plans and cash budget *before* the loan is taken out and the money spent.

7-2a Shopping for Loans

Once you've decided to use credit, it's equally important that you shop around and evaluate the various costs and terms available. You may think the only thing you need do to make a sound credit decision is determine which source offers the lowest finance charge. But this could not be farther from the truth—as we'll see below, finance charges are just one of the factors to consider when shopping for a loan.

Finance Charges

What's it going to cost me? That's one of the first things most people want to know when taking out a loan. And that's appropriate, because borrowers should know what they'll have to pay to get the money. Lenders are required by law to explicitly disclose *all* finance charges and other loan fees. Find out the effective (or true) *rate* of interest you'll have to pay on the loan as well as whether the loan carries a fixed or variable rate. Obviously, *as long as everything else is equal*, it's in your best interest to secure the least expensive loan. In this regard, ask the lender what the *annual rate of interest* on the loan will be, because it's easier (and far more relevant) to compare percentage rates on alternative borrowing arrangements than the dollar amount of the loan charges. This rate of interest, known as the *APR* (annual percentage rate), includes not only the basic cost of money but also any additional fees that might be required on the loan (APR is more fully discussed later). Also, if it's a variable-rate loan, find out what the interest rate is pegged to, how many "points" are added to the base rate, how often the loan rate can be changed, and if rate caps exist. Just as important is how the lender makes the periodic adjustments: will the *size* of the monthly payment change or the *number* of monthly payments? To avoid any future shock, it's best to find out these things before making the loan.

Behavior Matters
The Paradox of More Financial Choices

More choices are better than fewer choices, right? That sounds like common sense. Yet behavioral finance studies show that when presented with too many financial choices, people tend to get overwhelmed and fall back on what they already know or to just make the simplest choice by default. This is called the *paradox of choice.* Complexity can overwhelm the average consumer. Our brains are just not wired to analyze lots of choices. The best defense is to be financially literate: do your homework, develop a framework for making such decisions, and be prepared to ask for help.

Consider the complicated choice among various mortgage types and terms. You have to choose between 15- and 30-year maturities and between fixed- and adjustable-rate mortgages; decide on the amount of the down payment, the amount of "points" (percent of the loan amount) to pay in order to reduce your mortgage rate, and when to "lock in" your rate; and you must choose the best array of up-front mortgage-related fees. Some consumers, when facing so many decisions, wind up making bad ones, borrowing too much, or holding mortgages that are inconsistent with their best interests. And research shows that lower financial literacy and analytical abilities are directly related to higher mortgage default rates.

This book in general, and the chapters on managing credit in particular, should help prepare you to make these complicated financial decisions.

Loan Maturity

Try to make sure that the size and number of payments will fit comfortably into your spending and savings plans. As a rule, the cost of credit increases with the length of the repayment period. Thus, to lower your cost, you should consider shortening the loan maturity—but only to the point where doing so won't place an unnecessary strain on your cash flow. Although a shorter maturity may reduce the cost of the loan, it also increases the size of the monthly loan payment. Indeed, finding a monthly loan payment you'll be comfortable with is a critical dimension of sound credit management. Altering the loan maturity is just one way of coming up with an affordable monthly payment; there are scores of Internet sites where you can quickly run through all sorts of alternatives to find the monthly payment that will best fit your monthly budget. (The "tools" section of most major financial services sites on the Internet have "calculators" that enable you to quickly and easily figure interest rates and monthly loan payments for all sorts of loans; generally, all you need to do is plug in a few key pieces of information—such as the interest rate and loan term—and then hit "calculate" and let the computer do the rest. For example, go to **http://www .finaid.org** and try out their "Loan Payments Calculator.")

Total Cost of the Transaction

When comparison shopping for credit, always look at the total cost of both the price of the item purchased *and* the price of the credit. Retailers often manipulate both sticker prices and interest rates, so you really won't know what kind of deal you're getting until you look at the total cost of the transaction. Along this line, comparing *monthly payments* is a good way to get a handle on total cost. It's a simple matter to compare total costs: *just add the amount put down on the purchase to the total of all the monthly loan payments;* other things being equal, the one with the lowest total is the one you should pick.

Collateral

Make sure you know up front what collateral (if any) you'll have to pledge on the loan and what you stand to lose if you default on your payments. Actually, if it makes no difference to you and if it's not too inconvenient, using collateral often makes sense. It may result in *lower* finance charges—perhaps half a percentage point or so.

Other Loan Considerations

In addition to following the guidelines just described, here are some questions that you should also ask. Can you choose a *payment date* that will be compatible with your spending patterns? Can you obtain the loan *promptly and conveniently?* What are the charges for late payments, and are they reasonable? Will you receive a refund on credit charges if you prepay your loan, or are there prepayment penalties? Taking the time to look around for the best credit deal will pay off, not only in reducing the cost of such debt but also in keeping the burden of credit in line with your cash budget and financial plans. In the long run, you're the one who has the most to gain (or lose). Thus, *you should see to it that the consumer debt you undertake does, in fact, have the desired effects on your financial condition.* You're paying for the loan, so you might as well make the most of it!

7-2b Keeping Track of Your Consumer Debt

To stay abreast of your financial condition, it's a good idea to periodically take inventory of the consumer debt you have outstanding. Ideally you should do this every three or four months, but at least once a year. To take inventory of what you owe, simply list all your outstanding consumer debt. Include *everything except your home*

FINANCIAL PLANNING TIPS

Is a 0 Percent APR Loan Really a Great Deal? Watch the Rebate ...

Many 0 percent APR loan deals also give you the alternative of a cash-back rebate. You can have one or the other, but not both. Taking the cash-back rebate means that you finance your loan at a normal interest rate. Accepting the rebate will allow you to borrow less, although you pay a higher interest rate.

Consider an example in which you buy a car and finance $15,000 for 48 months at a 6.7 percent APR interest rate, which requires a monthly payment of $357.11. Your total payments over the life of the loan are $17,141. Interest is $17,141 − $15,000 = $2,141. Alternatively, a 0 percent APR loan deal for the same car at the same price would cost you only $312.50 per month, which is a savings of $2,141 over the life of the

loan. Assume that both loans are for 48 months and that your down payment is the same.

Now, assume that the car dealer offers a $2,000 cash-back rebate as an alternative to the 0 percent APR loan deal. This would reduce the loan amount to $13,000, which would mean a monthly payment of $309.49 at 6.7 percent APR. So the cash-back rebate provides a lower monthly payment than the 0 percent APR loan!

So what can we take away from this example? If you have the choice, it is almost always better to accept a rebate than a 0 percent APR loan. This is especially the case if you don't have much down payment money, because the rebate effectively acts as a down payment.

Source: Adapted from "0 percent APR Loan Deals—Good Deal or Not?" http://best-car-deals.buyerreports.org/0-apr-loan-deals, accessed August 2015.

mortgage—installment loans, single-payment loans, credit cards, revolving credit lines, overdraft protection lines, even home equity credit lines.

Worksheet 7.1 should be helpful in preparing a list of your debts. To use it, simply list the current monthly payment and the latest balance due for each type of consumer credit outstanding; then, total both columns to see how much you're paying each month and how large a debt load you have built up. Hopefully, when you've totaled all the numbers, you won't be surprised to learn just how much you really do owe.

A way to assess your debt position quickly is to compute your *debt safety ratio* (we discussed this ratio in Chapter 6) by dividing the total monthly payments (from the worksheet) by your monthly take-home pay. If 20 percent or more of your take-home pay is going to monthly credit payments, then you're relying too heavily on credit; but if your debt safety ratio works out to 10 percent or less, you're in a strong credit position. *Keeping track of your credit and holding the amount of outstanding debt to a reasonable level is the surest way to maintain your creditworthiness.*

TEST YOURSELF

7-8 What two questions should be answered before taking out a consumer loan? Explain.

7-9 List and briefly discuss the different factors to consider when shopping for a loan. How would you determine the total cost of the transaction?

7-3 SINGLE-PAYMENT LOANS

 Unlike most types of consumer loans, a single-payment loan is repaid in full with a single payment on a given due date. The payment usually consists of principal and all interest charges. Sometimes, however, interim interest payments must be made (e.g., every quarter), in which case the payment at maturity is made up of principal plus any unpaid interest. Although installment loans are far more popular, single-payment loans still have their place in the consumer loan market.

| WORKSHEET 7.1 | Tracking Your Consumer Debt |

Use a worksheet like this one to keep track of your outstanding credit along with your monthly debt service requirements. Such information is a major component of sound credit management.

AN INVENTORY OF CONSUMER DEBT

Name   Dan and Rebecca Watson   Date   June 14, 2017

Type of Consumer Debt	Creditor	Current Monthly Payment*	Latest Balance Due
Auto loans	Ford	$ 342.27	$13,796.00
Education loans	U.S. Dept of Education	117.00	7,986.00
Personal installment loans	Chase Bank	183.00	5,727.00
	Bank of America	92.85	2,474.00
Home improvement loan			
Other installment loans			
Single-payment loans			
Credit cards (retail charge cards, bank cards, etc.)	CapitalOne Visa	42.00	826.00
	Amex	35.00	600.00
	Sears	40.00	1,600.00
Overdraft protection line	Smith County Schools Credit Union	15.00	310.00
Personal line of credit			
Home equity credit line	Wells Fargo	97.00	9,700.00
Loan on life insurance			
Margin loan from broker			
Other loans	Mom & Dad		2,500.00
Totals		$ 964.12	$45,519.00

$$\text{Debt safety ratio} = \frac{\text{Total monthly payments}}{\text{Monthly take-home pay}} \times 100 = \frac{\$ \ 964.12}{\$ \ 5,200.00} \times 100 = \underline{18.5\%}$$

*Leave the space blank if there is **no** monthly payment required on a loan (e.g., as with a single-payment or education loan).

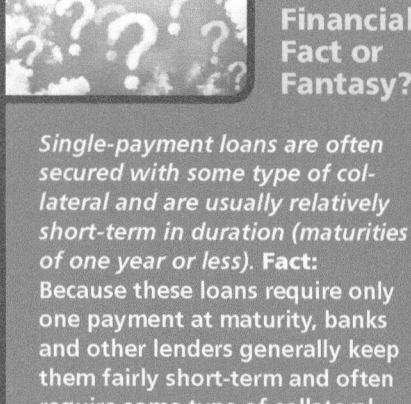
Single-payment loans can be secured or unsecured and can be taken out for just about any purpose, from buying a new car to paying for a vacation. They're perhaps most useful when the funds needed for a given purchase or transaction are temporarily unavailable but are expected to be forthcoming in the near future. By helping you cope with a temporary cash shortfall, these loans can serve as a form of interim financing until more permanent arrangements can be made.

Single-payment loans can also be used to help establish or rebuild an individual's credit rating. Often a bank will agree to a single-payment loan for a higher-credit-risk customer if an equal amount is deposited into an account at the bank, where both the loan and deposit have the same maturity. In this way, the bank has the principal of the loan fully secured and need only be concerned about the difference between the rate charged for the loan and the rate paid on the deposit.

7-3a Important Loan Features

When applying for either a single-payment or installment loan, you must first submit a loan application, an example of which is shown in Exhibit 7.3. The loan application gives the lending institution information about the purpose of the loan, whether it will be secured or unsecured, and the applicant's financial condition. The loan officer uses this document, along with other information (such as a credit report from the local credit bureau and income verification) to determine whether you should be granted the loan. Here again, some type of *credit scoring* (as discussed in Chapter 6) may be used to make the decision. As part of the loan application process, you should also consider various features of the debt, the three most important of which are loan collateral, loan maturity, and loan repayment.

Loan Collateral

Most single-payment loans are secured by certain specified assets. For *collateral*, lenders prefer items they feel are readily marketable at a price that's high enough to cover the principal portion of the loan—for example, an automobile, jewelry, or stocks and bonds. If a loan is obtained to purchase some personal asset, then that asset may be used to secure it. In most cases, lenders don't take physical possession of the collateral but instead file a lien, which is a legal claim that permits them to liquidate the collateral to satisfy the loan if the borrower defaults. The lien is filed in the county courthouse and is a matter of public record. If the borrowers maintain possession or title to *movable* property—such as cars, TVs, and jewelry—then the instrument that gives lenders title to the property in event of default is called a chattel mortgage. If lenders hold title to the collateral—or actually take possession of it, as in the case of stocks and bonds—then the agreement giving them the right to sell these items in case of default is a collateral note.

Loan Maturity

As indicated previously, the maturity (or term) on a single-payment loan is usually for a period of one year or less; it very rarely extends to two years or longer. When you request a single-payment loan, be sure that the term is long enough to allow you to obtain the funds for repaying the loans *but* not any longer than necessary. Don't stretch the maturity out too far, since the amount of the finance charges paid will increase with time. Because the loan is retired in a single payment, the lender must be assured that you'll be able to repay it even if unexpected events occur in the future. So, the term of your single-payment loan must be consistent with your budget and your ability to pay. If the money you plan to use for repayment will be received periodically over the term of the loan, then an installment-type loan may be more suitable.

loan application
An application that gives a lender information about the purpose of the loan as well as the applicant's financial condition.

lien
A legal claim permitting the lender, in case the borrower defaults, to liquidate the items serving as collateral to satisfy the obligation.

chattel mortgage
A mortgage on personal property given as security for the payment of an obligation.

collateral note
A legal note giving the lender the right to sell collateral if the borrower defaults on the obligation.

EXHIBIT 7.3   **A Consumer Loan Credit Application**

A typical loan application, like this one, contains information about the persons applying for the loan, including source(s) of income, current debt load, and a brief record of employment.

CONSUMER CREDIT APPLICATION

LOAN INFORMATION

Amount Requested $	Purpose		Application Type ☐Individual ☐Joint

COLLATERAL INFORMATION

☐Motor Vehicle: Year_____ Make_____ Model_____ Miles_____
☐Personal Property   ☐Other (Describe)

APPLICANT INFORMATION

Name (Last, First, M.I.)   E-mail Address

Social Security #	Date of Birth	☐Married ☐Unmarried ☐Separated	# of Dependents

CO-APPLICANT INFORMATION

Name (Last, First, M.I.)   E-mail Address

Social Security #	Date of Birth	☐Married ☐Unmarried ☐Separated	# of Dependents

APPLICANT RESIDENCE INFORMATION

Address (Number, St, and Apt. or Lot # if applicable)   Telephone #

City, State, Zip Code   Time At Residence Years / Months

Previous Address   Time At Residence Years / Months

☐Rent ☐Live with Parents   Landlord or Mortgage Holder   Monthly Payment
☐Own ☐Other_____   Name: Phone #: $

CO-APPLICANT RESIDENCE INFORMATION

Address (Number, St, and Apt. or Lot # if applicable)   Telephone #

City, State, Zip Code   Time At Residence Years / Months

Previous Address   Time At Residence Years / Months

☐Rent ☐Live with Parents   Landlord or Mortgage Holder   Monthly Payment
☐Own ☐Other_____   Name: Phone #: $

APPLICANT EMPLOYMENT INFORMATION

Employer   Employer Telephone

Employer Address   Position

Gross Income: $ ☐Weekly ☐Bi-weekly ☐Monthly   Time At Job Years / Months

Other Income: $ Source

Previous Employer & location   Previous Emp. Phone #

Position   Time At Job Years / Months

CO-APPLICANT EMPLOYMENT

Employer   Employer Telephone

Employer Address   Position

Gross Income: $ ☐Weekly ☐Bi-weekly ☐Monthly   Time At Job Years / Months

Other Income: $ Source   Alimony, Child support, or separate maintenance income need not be revealed if you do not wish to have it considered as a basis for repaying this obligation.

Previous Employer & Location   Previous Emp. Phone #

Position   Time At Job Years / Months

APPLICANT CREDIT REFERENCES

Creditor	Payment	Balance

☐Checking Bank Name_____ Acct#_____
☐Savings Bank Name_____ Acct#_____

CO-APPLICANT CREDIT REFERENCES

Creditor	Payment	Balance

☐Checking Bank Name_____ Acct#_____
☐Savings Bank Name_____ Acct#_____

AUTHORIZATION AND SIGNATURES

By signing this application, you promise that all information provided is true and complete. You also promise that you have revealed any pending lawsuits or unpaid judgements against you. You intend the lender and/or assignee to rely upon these promises in deciding whether to extend credit to you. You authorize a full investigation of your credit record and your employment history. You also authorize the seller and/or assignee to release information about your credit experience with them. You understand that the lender will retain this application whether or not it is approved. I understand that if the application is for a secured loan additional information may be required.

Applicant Signature   Date

Co-Applicant Signature   Date

Loan Repayment

Repayment of a single-payment loan is expected at a single point in time: on its maturity date. Occasionally, the funds needed to repay this type of loan will be received prior to maturity. Depending on the lender, the borrower might be able to repay the loan early and thus reduce the finance charges. Many credit unions permit early repayment of these loans with *reduced* finance charges. However, commercial banks and other single-payment lenders may not accept early repayments or, if they do, may charge a prepayment penalty. This penalty normally amounts to a set percentage of the interest that would have been paid over the remaining life of the loan. The Truth in Lending Act requires lenders to disclose in the loan agreement whether, and in what amount, prepayment penalties are charged on a single-payment loan.

Occasionally, an individual will borrow money using a single-payment loan and then discover that he or she is short of money when the loan comes due—after all, making one big loan payment can cause a real strain on one's cash flow. Should this happen to you, don't just let the payment go past due; instead, *inform the lender in advance so that a partial payment, loan extension, or some other arrangement can be made.* Under such circumstances, the lender will often agree to a loan rollover, in which case the original loan is paid off by taking out another loan. The lender will usually require that all the interest, and at least part of the principal, be paid at the time of the rollover. So if you originally borrowed $5,000 for 12 months, then the bank might be willing to lend you a lower amount, such as $3,500, for another 6 to 9 months as part of a loan rollover. In this case, you'll have to "pay down" $1,500 of the original loan, along with all interest due. However, you can expect the interest rate on a rollover loan to go up a bit; that's the price you pay for falling short on the first loan. Also, you should not expect to get more than one, or at the most two, loan rollovers—a bank's patience tends to grow short after a while!

ISTOCKPHOTO.COM/JULIE BIRCH

prepayment penalty
An additional charge you may owe if you pay off your loan prior to maturity.

loan rollover
The process of paying off a loan by taking out another loan.

loan disclosure statement
A document, which lenders are required to supply borrowers, that states both the dollar amount of finance charges and the APR applicable to a loan.

simple interest method
A method of computing finance charges in which interest is charged on the actual loan balance outstanding.

7-3b Finance Charges and the Annual Percentage Rate

As indicated in Chapter 6, lenders are required to disclose both the dollar amount of finance charges and the APR of interest. A sample loan disclosure statement applicable to either a single-payment or installment loan is in Exhibit 7.4. Note that such a statement discloses not only interest costs but also other fees and expenses that may be tacked onto the loan. Although disclosures like this one allow you to compare the various borrowing alternatives, you still need to understand the methods used to compute finance charges, because similar loans with the same *stated* interest rates may have different finance charges and APRs. The two basic procedures used to calculate the finance charges on single-payment loans are the *simple interest method* and the *discount method*.

Simple Interest Method

Interest is charged only on the *actual loan balance outstanding* in the simple interest method. This method is commonly used on revolving credit lines by commercial banks, S&Ls, and credit unions. To see how it's applied to a single-payment loan, assume that you borrow $1,000 for two years at an 8 percent annual rate of interest. On a single-payment loan, the actual loan balance outstanding for the two years will be the full $1,000 because no principal payments will be made until this period ends.

EXHIBIT 7.4 **A Loan Disclosure Statement**

The loan disclosure statement informs the borrower of all charges (finance and otherwise) associated with the loan and the APR. It also specifies the payment terms, as well as the existence of any balloon payments.

FEDERAL TRUTH IN LENDING DISCLOSURE STATEMENT

Creditor: YOUR FAVORITE MORTGAGE CORPORATION
Borrower(s):

Account Number: 1111111

ANNUAL PERCENTAGE RATE	FINANCE CHARGE	Amount Financed	Total of Payments
The cost of your credit as a yearly rate	The dollar amount the credit will cost you	The amount of credit provided to you or on your behalf	The amount you will have paid after you have made all payments as scheduled
7.337 %	$ 205,017.52	$ 138,796.50	$ 343,814.02

Your payment schedule will be:

NUMBER OF PAYMENTS	AMOUNT OF PAYMENTS	WHEN PAYMENTS ARE DUE
359	$955.05	Monthly beginning 09/01/17
1	951.07	Monthly beginning 08/01/48

Variable Rate: If checked, your loan contains a variable rate feature. Disclosures about the variable rate feature have been provided to you earlier.

Demand Feature: If checked, this obligation has a demand feature.

Insurance: You may obtain property insurance from anyone you want that is acceptable to the creditor.

If checked, you can get insurance through Your Favorite Mortgage Corporation. You will pay $____ for 12 months hazard insurance coverage. You will pay $ ____ for 12 months flood insurance coverage.

Security: You are giving a security interest in   property being purchased   property located at
1234 118TH STREET, NW, WASHINGTON, DC 20009
   Assignment of brokerage account and pledge of securities   Personal property: stocks and lease
   Assignment of life insurance policy   Other:
Late Charges: If a payment is late, you will be charged **5.000 %** of the payment.

Prepayment: If you pay off early, you   may   will not have to pay a penalty. You   may   will not be entitled to a refund of part of the finance charge.

Assumption: Someone buying your house   may, subject to conditions, be allowed to   cannot assume the remainder of the mortgage on the original terms.

See your contract documents for any additional information about nonpayment, default, any required repayment in full before the scheduled date, prepayment refunds and penalties and assumption policy.

ACKNOWLEDGMENT
By signing below you acknowledge that you have received a completed copy of this Federal Truth in Lending Statement prior to the execution *of* any closing documents.

_____   _____
Borrower/Date of Acknowledgment   Borrower/Date of Acknowledgment

Source: Adapted from http://www.entitledirect.com/sites/default/files/fed_truth_in_lending.pdf, accessed August 2015.

With simple interest, the finance charge is obtained by multiplying the outstanding *principal* by the stated annual rate of interest and then multiplying this amount by the term of the loan:

$$\text{Finance Charge (Simple Interest)} = \text{Amount of Loan} \times \text{Interest Rate} \times \text{Term of Loan}$$

Note that the term of the loan is stated in years. For example, the term would equal 0.5 for a 6-month loan, 1.25 for a 15-month loan, and 2.0 for a 2-year loan.

EXAMPLE: **Calculating the Total Finance Charge and Payment on a Simple Interest Loan**

You have taken out a $1,000, 8 percent, two-year simple interest loan. Using the above equation, the total finance charge on the loan equals $160 (i.e., $1,000 × 0.08 per year × 2 years). With this type of credit arrangement, the loan payment is found by adding the finance charges to the principal amount of the loan, so you'd have to make a loan payment of $1,000 + $160 = $1,160 at maturity to pay off this debt.

EXAMPLE: **Calculating the Annual Percentage Rate on a Simple Interest Loan**

Continuing the prior simple loan method example, the true, or annual, percentage rate of interest is the average annual finance charge divided by the average loan balance outstanding, as follows:

$$\text{APR} = \frac{\text{Average Annual Finance Charge}}{\text{Average Loan Balance Outstanding}}$$

The average annual finance charge is found by dividing the total finance charge by the life of the loan (in years), which is $80 in this example ($160/2). Because the loan

FINANCIAL PLANNING TIPS

How Do Lenders Look at Your Loan Application?

When you're planning to take out a loan for a purchase (large or small), it helps to understand how lenders will evaluate your loan application. Here are the items they look at and what you can do to make them as good as possible:

• **Credit report.** Lenders will review your credit report from two or three of the credit reporting companies (Experian, Equifax, and TransUnion) to assure that they have all the facts. Make sure to check at least one of your reports so you'll know what the lender is seeing and can fix any potential errors that could delay or prevent approval of your loan.

• **Debt history.** When looking over your credit report, the lender will consider how much debt you already owe, how much unused credit is available to you, how promptly you pay your bills, and whether you've applied for more credit lately. Be prepared to answer questions about these points.

• **Job history.** Lenders will look at your job history in order to evaluate your financial stability and associated capacity to repay the loan.

• **Savings.** The lender will want to know if you have enough money for a down payment, funds to cover an emergency, and where these funds are (e.g., savings account, checking account, and mutual funds).

Keep in mind that whether you're hoping to finance a house or a new car, you'll be in the best bargaining position when shopping if you have obtained a pre-approval (pre-qualification) for a specific loan amount. Knowing the above points should help your loan application move along smoothly.

balance outstanding remains at $1,000 over the life of the loan, the average loan balance is $1,000. Thus, the APR is:

$$\$80/\$1,000 = 8 \text{ percent}$$

The APR and the stated rate of interest are equivalent: they both equal 8 percent. *This is always the case when the simple interest method is used to calculate finance charges, regardless of whether loans are single-payment or installment.*

Discount Method

discount method
A method of calculating finance charges in which interest is computed and then subtracted from the principal, with the remainder being disbursed to the borrower.

The **discount method** calculates total finance charges on the full principal amount of the loan, which is then subtracted from the amount of the loan. The difference between the amount of the loan and the finance charge is then paid to the borrower. In other words, finance charges are paid in advance and represent a discount from the principal portion of the loan. The finance charge on a single-payment loan using the discount method is calculated in exactly the same way as for a simple interest loan:

$$\text{Finance Charge (Discount Method)} = \text{Amount of Loan} \times \text{Interest Rate} \times \text{Term of Loan}$$

Using this formula, the finance charge on the $1,000, 8 percent, 2-year, single-payment discount method loan is (of course) the same $160 we calculated earlier. However, in sharp contrast to simple interest loans, the loan payment with a discount loan is based on the original amount of the loan, and the finance charges on the loan are deducted up front from the loan proceeds. Thus, the discount method yields a much higher APR on single-payment loans than does the simple interest method. Exhibit 7.5 contrasts the results from both methods for the single-payment loan example discussed here.

Financial Fact or Fantasy?

Using the discount method to calculate interest is one way of lowering the effective cost of a consumer loan. **Fantasy:** Because the interest is paid in advance on discount loans, the net effect is to substantially raise the cost of borrowing. Specifically, a discount loan results in a true interest rate (APR) that is much higher than the stated rate.

EXAMPLE: Calculating the Annual Percentage Rate on a Discount Loan

You have taken out a $1,000, 8 percent, two-year discount loan. To find the APR on this discount loan, substitute the appropriate values into the APR equation shown previously. For this 2-year loan, the average annual finance charge is $80 ($160 ÷ 2). However, because this is a discount loan, the borrower will receive only $840. And because this is a single-payment loan, the average amount of debt outstanding is also $840. When these figures are used in the APR equation, we find the true rate for this 8 percent discount loan is:

$$\$80/\$840 = 9.52\%.$$

EXHIBIT 7.5	Finance Charges and APRs for a Single-Payment Loan ($1,000 Loan for Two Years at 8 percent Interest)

Sometimes what you see is not what you get—such as when you borrow money through a discount loan and end up paying quite a bit more than the quoted rate.

Method	Stated Rate on Loan	Finance Charges	APR
Simple interest	8.0%	$160	8.00%
Discount	8.0	160	9.52

7-4 INSTALLMENT LOANS

LG5, LG6

Installment loans differ from single-payment loans in that they require the borrower to repay the debt in a series of installment payments (usually monthly) over the life of the loan. Installment loans have long been one of the most popular forms of consumer credit—right up there with credit cards! Much of this popularity is due to how conveniently the loan repayment is set up. Unsurprisingly, most people find it easier on their checkbooks to make a series of small payments than one big one.

7-4a A Real Consumer Credit Workhorse

As a source of financing, there are few things that installment loans can't do—which explains, in large part, why this form of consumer credit is so widely used. They can be used to finance just about any type of big-ticket item imaginable. New car loans are the dominant type of installment loan, but this form of credit is also used to finance home furnishings, appliances and entertainment centers, camper trailers and other recreational vehicles, and even expensive vacations. Also, more and more college students are turning to this type of credit as the way to finance their education.

Not only can installment loans be used to finance all sorts of things, they can also be obtained at many locations. You'll find them at banks and other financial institutions, as well as at major department stores and merchants that sell relatively expensive products. These loans can be taken out for just a few hundred dollars, or they can involve thousands of dollars—indeed, installment loans of $25,000 or more are common. In addition, installment loans can be set up with maturities as short as 6 months or as long as 7 to 10 years—or even 15 years.

Most installment loans are secured with some kind of collateral. For example, the car or home entertainment center you purchased with the help of an installment loan usually serves as collateral on the loan. Even personal loans used to finance things like expensive vacations can be secured—in these cases, the collateral could be securities, CDs, or some other type of financial asset. One rapidly growing segment of this market is installment loans secured by second mortgages. These so-called *home equity loans* are similar to the home equity credit lines discussed in Chapter 6, except they involve a set amount of money loaned over a set period of time (often as long as 15 years) rather than a revolving credit line from which you can borrow, repay, and reborrow. For example, if a borrower needs $25,000 to help pay for an expensive new boat, he can simply take out a loan in that amount and *secure it with a second mortgage on his home*. This loan would be like any other installment loan in the sense that it's for a set amount of money and is to be repaid over a set period of time in monthly installments. Besides their highly competitive interest rates, a big attraction of *home equity loans* is that the interest paid on them usually can be taken as a tax deduction. Thus, borrowers get the double benefit of *low interest rates* and *tax deductibility*. However, as with home equity credit lines, failure to repay could result in the loss of your home.

7-4b Finance Charges, Monthly Payments, and the APR

We previously discussed the simple interest and discount methods of determining finance charges on single-payment loans. In this section, we look at the use of simple and add-on interest to compute finance charges and monthly payments for installment loans (technically, discount interest can also be used with installment loans; but because this is rare, we ignore it here). To illustrate, we'll use an 8 percent, $1,000 installment loan that is to be paid off in 12 monthly payments. As in the earlier illustration for single-payment loans, we assume that interest is the only component of the finance charge; there are no other fees and charges.

Using Simple Interest

When simple interest is used with installment loans, interest is charged only on the outstanding balance of the loan. Thus, as the loan principal declines with monthly payments, the amount of interest being charged also decreases. Because finance charges change each month, the procedure used to find the interest expense is mathematically complex. Fortunately, this isn't much of a problem in practice because of the widespread use of computers, handheld financial calculators (which we'll illustrate later), and preprinted finance tables—an example of which is provided in Exhibit 7.6. The tables show the *monthly payment* required to retire an installment loan carrying a given simple rate of interest with a given term to maturity. Because

EXHIBIT 7.6	A Table of Monthly Installment Loan Payments to Repay a $1,000, Simple Interest Loan

You can use a table like this to find the monthly payments on a wide variety of simple interest installment loans. Although it's set up to show payments on a $1,000 loan, with a little modification, you can easily use it with any size loan (the principal can be more or less than $1,000).

LOAN MATURITY

Rate of Interest	6 Months	12 Months	18 Months	24 Months	36 Months	48 Months	60 Months
6.0	$169.60	$86.07	$58.23	$44.32	$30.42	$23.49	$19.33
6.5	169.84	86.30	58.46	44.55	30.65	23.71	19.57
7.0	170.09	86.53	58.68	44.77	30.88	23.95	19.80
7.5	170.33	86.76	58.92	45.00	31.11	24.18	20.05
8.0	170.58	86.99	59.15	45.23	31.34	24.42	20.28
8.5	170.82	87.22	59.37	45.46	31.57	24.65	20.52
9.0	171.07	87.46	59.60	45.69	31.80	24.89	20.76
9.5	171.32	87.69	59.83	45.92	32.04	25.13	21.01
10.0	171.56	87.92	60.06	46.15	32.27	25.37	21.25
11.0	172.05	88.50	60.64	46.73	32.86	25.97	21.87
12.0	172.50	88.85	60.99	47.08	33.22	26.34	22.25
13.0	173.04	89.32	61.45	47.55	33.70	26.83	22.76
14.0	173.54	89.79	61.92	48.02	34.18	27.33	23.27
15.0	174.03	90.26	62.39	48.49	34.67	27.84	23.79
16.0	174.53	90.74	62.86	48.97	35.16	28.35	24.32
17.0	175.03	91.21	63.34	49.45	35.66	28.86	24.86
18.0	175.53	91.68	63.81	49.93	36.16	29.38	25.40

these tables (sometimes referred to as *amortization schedules*) have interest charges built right into them, the monthly payments shown cover both principal and interest.

Notice that the loan payments shown in Exhibit 7.6 cover a variety of interest rates (from 6 percent to 18 percent) and loan maturities (from 6 to 60 months). The table values represent the monthly payments required to retire a $1,000 loan. Although it's assumed that you're borrowing $1,000, you can use the table with any size loan. For example, if you're looking at a $5,000 loan, just multiply the monthly loan payment from the table by 5 (since $5,000/$1,000 = 5); or, if you have a $500 loan, multiply the loan payment by 0.5 ($500/$1,000 = 0.5). In many respects, this table is just like the mortgage loan payment schedule introduced in Chapter 5, except we use much shorter loan maturities here than with mortgages.

> **EXAMPLE: Determining Installment Loan Payment Amounts Using Financial Tables**
>
> Suppose you want to find the monthly installment payment required on our example $1,000, 8 percent, 12-month loan using Exhibit 7.6. Looking under the 12-month column and across from the 8 percent rate of interest, we find a value of $86.99. That is the monthly payment it will take to pay off the $1,000 loan in 12 months. When we multiply the monthly payments ($86.99) by the term of the loan in months (12), the result is total payments of $86.99 × 12 = $1,043.88. The difference between the total payments on the loan and the principal portion represents the *total finance charges on the loan*—in this case, $1,043.88 − $1,000 = $43.88 in interest charges.

Calculator

INPUTS	FUNCTIONS
12	N
8	I/Y
−1000	PV
	CPT
	PMT
	SOLUTION
	86.99

See Appendix E for details.

Calculator Keystrokes. Instead of using a table like the one in Exhibit 7.6, you could just as easily have used a handheld financial calculator to *find the monthly payments on an installment loan*. Here's what you'd do. First, set the payments per year (P/Y) key to 12 to put the calculator in a monthly payment mode. Now, to find the monthly payment needed to pay off an 8 percent, 12-month, $1,000 installment loan, use the keystrokes shown here, where

N = length of the loan, *in months*
I/Y = the *annual* rate of interest being charged on the loan
PV = the amount of the loan, entered as a *negative* number

As seen, to pay off this installment loan, you'll have to make payments of $86.99 per month for the next 12 months.

From each monthly payment (of $86.99), a certain portion goes to interest and the balance is used to reduce the principal. Because the principal balance declines with each payment, the amount that goes to interest also *decreases* while the amount that goes to principal *increases*. Exhibit 7.7 illustrates this cash-flow stream. Because *monthly* payments are used with the loan, the interest column in Exhibit 7.7 is also based on a *monthly* rate of interest—that is, the annual rate is divided by 12 to obtain a monthly rate (8 percent per year ÷ 12 months per year = 0.67 percent per month). This monthly rate is then applied to the outstanding loan balance to find the monthly interest charges in column 3. Because interest is charged only on the outstanding balance, *the annual percentage rate (APR) on a simple interest installment loan will always equal the stated rate*—in this case, 8 percent.

add-on method
A method of calculating interest by computing finance charges on the original loan balance and then adding the interest to that balance.

Add-on Method

Some installment loans, particularly those obtained directly from retail merchants or made at finance companies and the like, are made using the **add-on method**. Add-on

EXHIBIT 7.7

Monthly Payment Analysis for a Simple Interest Installment Loan (Assumes a $1,000, 8%, 12-Month Loan)

Part of each monthly payment on an installment loan goes to interest and part to principal. As the loan is paid down over time, less and less of each payment goes to interest and more and more goes to principal.

Month	Outstanding Loan Balance at Beginning of Month (1)	Monthly Payment (2)	Interest Charges [(1) × 0.00667] (3)	Principal [(2) − (3)] (4)
1	$1,000.00	$86.99	$6.67	$80.32
2	919.68	86.99	6.13	80.86
3	838.82	86.99	5.59	81.40
4	757.42	86.99	5.05	81.94
5	675.49	86.99	4.50	82.49
6	593.00	86.99	3.95	83.03
7	509.97	86.99	3.40	83.59
8	426.38	86.99	2.84	84.15
9	342.23	86.99	2.28	84.71
10	257.52	86.99	1.72	85.27
11	172.25	86.99	1.15	85.84
12	86.41	86.99	0.58	86.41
Total		$1,043.88	$43.88	$1,000.00

Note: The monthly interest rate is 0.08/12 = 0.00667. Column 1 values for months 2 through 12 are obtained by subtracting the principal payment shown in column 4 for the preceding month from the outstanding loan balance shown in column 1 for the preceding month; thus, $1,000 − $80.32 = $919.68, which is the outstanding loan balance at the beginning of month 2.

loans generally rank as one of the most costly forms of consumer credit, with APRs that are often well above the rates charged even on many credit cards. With add-on interest, the finance charges are calculated using the *original* balance of the loan; this amount (of the total finance charges) is then added on to the original loan balance to determine the total amount to be repaid. Thus, the amount of finance charges on an add-on loan can be found by using the familiar simple interest formula:

Finance Charge (Add-on Method) = Amount of Loan × Interest Rate × Term of Loan

Given the $1,000 loan we've been using for illustrative purposes, the total finance charges on an 8 percent, 1-year add-on loan would be

Finance Charge (Add-on Method) = $1,000 × 0.08 × 1 = $80

Compared to the finance charges for the same installment loan on a simple interest basis ($43.88), an add-on installment loan is a lot more expensive—a fact that also shows up in monthly payments and in the APR. Keep in mind that both of these loans would be quoted as "8 percent" loans. Thus, you may think you're getting an 8 percent loan, but looks can be deceiving—especially when you're dealing with add-on interest! So, when you're taking out an installment loan, be sure to find out whether simple or add-on interest is being used to compute finance charges. (And if it's add-on, you might want to consider looking elsewhere for the loan.)

To find the monthly payments on an add-on loan, add the finance charge to the original principal amount of the loan and then divide this sum by the number of monthly payments to be made:

$$\text{Monthly Payment} = \frac{(\text{Amount of Loan} + \text{Finance Charge})}{\text{Number of Payments}}$$

> **EXAMPLE: Calculating Monthly Payments on an Add-On Installment Loan**
>
> You want to calculate the monthly payments a $1,000, 8 percent, 12-month add-on interest loan. The previously-calculated finance charge is $80. Applying the above expression:
>
> $$\text{Monthly Payment} = \frac{(\$1,000 + \$80)}{12} = \$90$$
>
> As expected, these monthly payments are higher than those on an otherwise comparable simple interest installment loan.

Because the actual rate of interest with an add-on loan is considerably higher than the stated rate, it's particularly important to calculate the loan's APR. That can easily be done with a financial calculator, as shown below. As you can see, the APR on this 8 percent add-on loan is more like 14.45 percent. Clearly, when viewed from an APR perspective, the add-on loan is an expensive form of financing! (A rough but reasonably accurate rule of thumb is that the APR on an add-on loan is about *twice* the stated rate. Thus, if the loan is quoted at an add-on rate of 9 percent, you'll probably be paying a true rate that's closer to 18 percent.) This is because when add-on interest is applied to an installment loan, the interest included in each payment is charged on the *initial principal* even though the outstanding loan balance declines as installment payments are made. A summary of comparative finance charges and APRs for simple interest and add-on interest methods is presented in Exhibit 7.8.

Calculator

INPUTS	FUNCTIONS
12	N
–1000	PV
90.00	PMT
	CPT
	I/Y
	SOLUTION
	14.45

See Appendix E for details.

Calculator Keystrokes. Here's how you *find the APR on an add-on installment loan* using a financial calculator. First, make sure the payments per year (P/Y) key is set to 12, so the calculator is in the monthly payment mode. Then, to find the APR on a $1,000, 12-month, 8 percent add-on installment loan, use the following keystrokes, where

> N = Length of the loan, in months
> PV = Size of the loan, entered as a negative number
> PMT = Size of the monthly installment loan payments

You'll find that the APR on the 8 percent add-on loan is a whopping 14.45 percent!

EXHIBIT 7.8 **Comparative Finance Charges and APRs on a $1,000, 8 Percent, 12-Month Installment Loan**

In sharp contrast to simple interest loans, the APR with add-on installment loans is much higher than the stated rate.

	Simple Interest	Add-on Interest
Stated rate on loan	8%	8%
Finance charges	$43.88	$80.00
Monthly payments	$86.99	$90.00
Total payments made	$1,043.88	$1,080.00
APR	8%	14.45%

Federal banking regulations require that the exact APR (accurate to the nearest 0.25 percent) must be disclosed to borrowers. And note that not only interest but also any other fees required to obtain a loan are considered part of the finance charges and must be included in the computation of APR.

Prepayment Penalties

Another type of finance charge that's often found in installment loan contracts is the *prepayment penalty*, an additional charge you may owe if you decide to pay off your loan prior to maturity. When you pay off a loan early, you may find that you owe quite a bit more than expected, especially if the lender uses the **Rule of 78s** (or sum-of-the-digits method) to calculate the amount of interest paid and the principal balance to date. You might think that paying off a $1,000, 8 percent, 1-year loan at the end of 6 months would mean that you've paid about half of the principal and owe somewhere around $500 to the lender. That's just not so with a loan that uses the Rule of 78s! This method charges more interest in the early months of the loan on the theory that the borrower has use of more money in the loan's early stages and so should pay more finance charges in the early months and progressively less later. There's nothing wrong with that, of course; it's how all loans operate. But what's wrong is that the Rule of 78s front-loads an inordinate amount of interest charges to the early months of the loan, thereby producing a much higher principal balance than you'd normally expect (remember: the more of the loan payment that goes to interest, the less that goes to the repayment of principal).

Let's assume that we want to pay off the $1,000, 8 percent, 1-year add-on loan after six months. Using the Rule of 78s, you would owe $518.46. So, even though you've made payments for half of the life of the loan, you still owe more than half of the principal. In contrast, with the same loan under simple interest, you'd owe only $509.97 in principal after six months. Thus, the Rule of 78s benefits the lender at the expense of the borrower.

Credit Life Insurance

Sometimes, as a condition of receiving an installment loan, a borrower is required to buy **credit life insurance** and possibly **credit disability insurance**. Credit life (and disability) insurance is tied to a particular installment loan and provides insurance that the loan will be paid off if the borrower dies (or becomes disabled) before the loan matures. These policies insure the borrower for an amount sufficient to repay the outstanding loan balance. The seller's (or lender's) ability to dictate the terms of these insurance requirements is either banned or restricted by law in many states. If this type of insurance is required as a condition of the loan, then its cost must be added to the finance charges and included as part of the APR. From the borrower's perspective, credit life and disability insurance is not a good deal: *It's very costly and does little more than give lenders an additional lucrative source of income.* Unsurprisingly, because it's so lucrative, some lenders aggressively push it on unsuspecting borrowers and, in some cases, even require it as a condition for granting a loan. The best advice is to avoid it if at all possible!

7-4c Buy on Time or Pay Cash?

When buying a big-ticket item, you often have little choice but to take out a loan—the purchase (perhaps it's a new car) is just so expensive that you can't afford to pay cash. And even if you do have the money, you may still be better off using something like an installment loan *if the cash purchase would end up severely depleting your liquid reserves.* But don't just automatically take

Rule of 78s (sum-of-the-digits method)
A method of calculating interest that has extra-heavy interest charges in the early months of the loan.

credit life (or disability) insurance
A type of life (or disability) insurance in which the coverage decreases at the same rate as the loan balance.

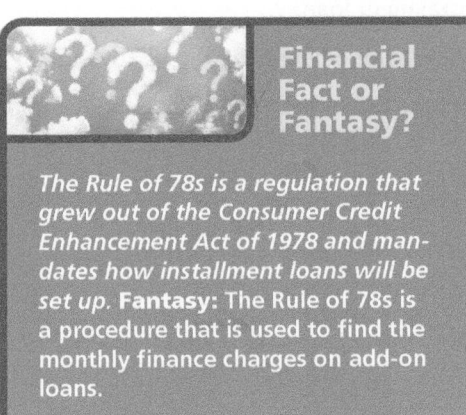

Financial Fact or Fantasy?

The Rule of 78s is a regulation that grew out of the Consumer Credit Enhancement Act of 1978 and mandates how installment loans will be set up. **Fantasy:** The Rule of 78s is a procedure that is used to find the monthly finance charges on add-on loans.

out a loan. Rather, take the time to find out if that is, in fact, the best thing to do. Such a decision can easily be made by using Worksheet 7.2, which considers the cost of the loan relative to the after-tax earnings generated from having your money in some type of short-term investment. It's assumed that the consumer has an adequate level of liquid reserves and that these reserves are being held in some type of savings account. (Obviously, if this is not the case, then there's little reason to go through the exercise because you have no choice but to borrow the money.) Essentially, it all boils down to this: *If it costs more to borrow the money than you can earn in interest, then withdraw the money from your savings to pay cash for the purchase; if not, you should consider taking out a loan.*

Consider this situation: You're thinking about buying a second car (a nice, low-mileage used vehicle) but, after the normal down payment, you still need to come up with $12,000. This balance can be taken care of in one of two ways: (1) you can take out a 36-month, 8 percent installment loan (for a monthly payment of $376.04), or (2) you can pay cash by drawing the money from a money fund (paying 4 percent interest today and for the foreseeable future). We can now run the numbers to decide whether to buy on time or pay cash—see Worksheet 7.2 for complete details. In this case, we assume the loan is a standard installment loan (where the interest does not qualify as a tax deduction) and that you're in the 28 percent tax bracket. The worksheet shows that, by borrowing the money, you'll end up paying about $1,537 in interest (line 4), none of which is tax deductible. In contrast, by leaving your money on deposit in the money fund, you'll receive only $1,038 in interest, after taxes (see line 11). Taken together, we see the net cost of borrowing (line 12) is nearly $500—so you'll be paying $1,537 to earn only $1,038, which certainly doesn't make much sense! Clearly, it's far more cost-effective in this case to take the money from savings and pay cash for the car, because you'll save nearly $500.

Although saving $500 is a convincing reason for avoiding a loan, sometimes the actual dollar spread between the cost of borrowing and interest earned is very small, perhaps only $100 or less. Being able to deduct the interest on a loan can lead to a relatively small spread, but it can also occur, for example, if the amount being financed is relatively small—say, you want $1,500 or $2,000 for a ski trip to Colorado. In this case—and so long as the spread stays small enough—you may decide it's still worthwhile to borrow the money in order to maintain a higher level of liquidity. Although this decision is perfectly legitimate when very small spreads exist, it makes less sense as the gap starts to widen.

TEST YOURSELF

7-13 Briefly describe the basic features of an installment loan.

7-14 What is a home equity loan, and what are its major advantages and disadvantages?

7-15 Explain why a borrower is often required to purchase *credit life* and *disability insurance* as a condition of receiving an installment loan.

7-16 Define simple interest as it relates to an installment loan. Are you better off with add-on interest? Explain.

7-17 When does it make more sense to pay cash for a big-ticket item than to borrow the money to finance the purchase?

Using a worksheet like this, you can decide whether to buy on time or pay cash by comparing the after-tax cost of interest paid on a loan with the after-tax interest income lost by taking the money out of savings and using it to pay cash for the purchase.

BUY ON TIME OR PAY CASH

Name __Glen Bronson__   Date __2/28/2017__

■ **Cost of Borrowing**		
1. Terms of the loan		
a. Amount of the loan	$ 12,000.00	
b. Length of the loan (in years)	3.00	
c. Monthly payment	$ 376.04	
2. Total loan payments made (monthly loan payment × length of loan in months) $ _376.04_ per month × _36_ months		$ 13,537.44
3. Less: Principal amount of the loan		$ 12,000.00
4. Total interest paid over life of loan (line 2 — 3)		$ 1,537.44
5. Tax considerations: • Is this a home equity loan (where interest expenses can be deducted from taxes)? . . . . • Do you itemize deductions on your federal tax returns? • If you answered yes to BOTH questions, then proceed to line 6; if you answered no to *either one* or *both* of the questions, then proceed to *line 8* and use *line 4* as the after-tax interest cost of the loan.	☐ yes ☑ no ☑ yes ☐ no	
6. What federal tax bracket are you in? (use either 10, 15, 25, 28, 33, or 35%)	_28_%	
7. Taxes saved due to interest deductions (line 4 × tax rate, from line 6: $ _____ × _____ %)		$ 0.00
8. Total after-tax interest cost on the loan (line 4 − line 7)		$ 1,537.44
■ **Cost of Paying Cash**		
9. Annual interest earned on savings (annual rate of interest earned on savings × amount of loan: _4_ % × _12,000.00_)		$ 480.00
10. Annual after-tax interest earnings (line 9 × [1 − tax rate] — e.g., 1 − 28% = 72%: $ _480.00_ × _72_ %)		$ 346.00
11. Total after-tax interest earnings over life of loan (line 10 × line 1b: $ _346.00_ × _3_ years)		$ 1,038.00
■ **Net Cost of Borrowing**		
12. Difference in cost of borrowing vs. cost of paying cash (line 8 minus line 11)		$ 499.44

BASIC DECISION RULE: *Pay cash* if line 12 is positive; *borrow the money* if line 12 is negative.

Note: For simplicity, compounding is ignored in calculating *both* the cost of interest and interest earnings.

Planning Over a Lifetime: *Using Consumer Loans*

Here are some key considerations for using credit in each stage of the life cycle.

Pre-family Independence: 20s	Family Formation/ Career Development: 30–45	Pre-Retirement: 45–65	Retirement: 65 and Beyond
✓ Make sure your emergency fund is adequate.	✓ Start selectively relying on savings rather than credit for large purchases.	✓ If you must make credit payments late, inform the lender.	✓ Consider a second mortgage or home equity line of credit to reduce borrowing costs.
✓ If you are married, maintain your individual credit history by not borrowing exclusively as a couple.	✓ Budget to keep credit account balances easy to pay each month.	✓ Monitor your credit card and bank statements for unauthorized transactions.	✓ Budget to limit dependence on consumer credit.
✓ Review your credit report at least once a year.	✓ Monitor your credit report at least once a year.	✓ Monitor your credit report at least once a year.	✓ Monitor your credit report at least once a year.

Financial Impact of Personal Choices

John and Mary Calculate their Auto Loan Backward

John and Mary Brunner budget and spend their money carefully. Their Honda CRV has over 150,000 miles and needs to be replaced. Because they drive their cars so long, John and Mary have decided to buy a new car and have saved a $5,000 down payment. They are willing to make a monthly car payment of about $350 while 48-month loans are at 3 percent. Before they choose a new car, they want to determine how much they can afford to spend.

John and Mary do their auto loan calculations backward to figure out the size of the auto loan implied by a 48-month maturity and 3 percent interest. Using a calculator and the approach explained in this chapter, that loan amount is about $15,813. Thus, given their down payment of $5,000, John and Mary can afford a car selling for about $20,813 net of tax, title and licensing fees ($15,813 + $5,000). They are indeed careful, if not "backward," car shoppers who explore the angles.

Summary

LG1 **Know when to use consumer loans, and be able to differentiate between the major types. p. 261**
Single-payment and installment loans are formally negotiated consumer loan arrangements used mainly to finance big-ticket items. Most of these consumer loans are taken out as auto loans, loans for other durable goods, education loans, personal loans, and consolidation loans.

LG2 **Identify the various sources of consumer loans. p. 261**
Consumer loans can be obtained from various sources, including commercial banks (the biggest providers of such credit), consumer finance companies, credit unions, S&Ls, sales finance (and captive finance) companies, life insurance companies (and other financial services organizations), and, as a last resort, your friends and relatives.

LG3 **Choose the best loans by comparing finance charges, maturity, collateral, and other loan terms. p. 271**
Before taking out a consumer loan, you should be sure the purchase is compatible with your financial plans and that you can service the debt without straining your budget. When shopping for credit, it's in your best interest to compare such loan features as finance charges (APRs), loan maturities, monthly payments, and collateral requirements; then choose loans with terms that are fully compatible with your financial plans and cash budget.

LG4 **Describe the features of, and calculate the finance charges on, single-payment loans. p. 275**
In a single-payment loan, the borrower makes just one principal payment (at the maturity of the loan), although there may be one or more interim interest payments. Such loans are usually made for one year or less, and they're normally secured by some type of collateral. A major advantage of the single-payment loan is that it doesn't require monthly payments and won't tie up the borrower's cash flow. Finance charges can be calculated in one of two ways: (1) the simple interest method, which applies the interest rate to the outstanding loan balance; or (2) the discount method, in which interest is calculated just as in the previous method but is then deducted from the loan principal, yielding a higher APR.

LG5 **Evaluate the benefits of an installment loan. p. 282**
In an installment loan, the borrower agrees to repay the loan through a series of equal installment payments (usually monthly) until the obligation is fully repaid; in this way, the borrower can receive a loan repayment schedule that fits neatly into his or her financial plans and cash budget. This highly popular form of consumer credit can be used to finance just about any type of big-ticket asset or expenditure. Many installment loans are taken out as home equity loans to capture tax advantages.

LG6 **Determine the costs of installment loans, and analyze whether it is better to pay cash or take out a loan. p. 282**
Most single-payment loans are made with either simple or discount interest, whereas most installment loans are made with either simple or add-on interest. When simple interest is used, the actual finance charge always corresponds to the stated rate of interest; in contrast, when add-on or discount rates are used, the APR is always more than the stated rate. In the end, whether it makes sense to borrow rather than to pay cash is a matter of which alternative costs less.

Key Terms

529 college savings plan, 266

add-on method, 284

captive finance company, 269

cash value (of life insurance), 270

chattel mortgage, 276

collateral note, 276

collateral, 262

consumer finance company, 268

consumer loans, 261

credit disability insurance, 287

Answers Test Yourself

You can find answers to these questions on this book's companion website. Look for it at *www.cengagebrain.com*. Search for this book by its title, and then add it to your dashboard.

Key Financial Relationships

Concept	Financial Relationship	Page Num
Simple Interest Method Finance Charges on a Single-Payment Loan	Finance Charge (Simple Interest method) = Amount of Loan × Interest Rate × Term of Loan	280
Discount Method Finance Charges on a Single-Payment Loan	Finance Charge (Discount method) = Amount of Loan × Interest Rate × Term of Loan	281
Annual Percentage Rate (APR)	$APR = \dfrac{\text{Average Annual Finance Charge}}{\text{Average Loan Balance Outstanding}}$	280
Add-on Loan Monthly Payment	$\text{Monthly Payment (Add-on Method)} = \dfrac{\text{Amount of Loan} + \text{Finance Charge}}{\text{Number of Payments}}$	285

Key Financial Relationships Problem Set

1. **Simple Interest Method Finance Charges.** Todd Gardner wants to calculate the total finance charge on a 2-year, 4 percent simple interest, single-payment loan for $3,000.

    Solution: The total finance charge is calculated as:

    Finance Charge (Simple Interest) = Amount of Loan × Interest Rate × Term of Loan

    $$= \$3{,}000 \times 0.04 \times 2 = \$240.00$$

2. **Discount Method Finance Charges.** Nicole Holmes has taken out a 1 and a half-year, 3 percent discount, single-payment loan for $4,000. What is the total finance charge on the loan?

    Solution: The total finance charge is calculated as:

    Finance Charge (Discount method) = Amount of Loan × Interest Rate × Term of Loan

    $$= \$4{,}000 \times 0.03 \times 1.5 = \$180.00$$

    Notice that the approach to calculating the total finance charge is the same as that used for the simple interest approach.

3. ***Annual Percentage Rate (APR).*** Wayne Snyder is considering taking out a 2-year, 4 percent, single-payment discount loan for $3,500. He's heard that the APR for discount loans is greater than the stated rate and wants to confirm exactly how much higher it is before considering an otherwise comparable simple interest loan.

   Solution: Wayne must first determine the total finance charge, which is:

   Finance Charge (Discount method) = Amount of Loan × Interest Rate × Term of Loan

   $$= \$3,500 \times 0.04 \times 2 = \$280.00$$

   Because it's a discount loan, at the time the loan is extended Wayne will only receive $3,500 − $280.00 = $3,220. As a 2-year single-payment loan, the average amount of debt outstanding is also $3,220. The APR is calculated as:

   $$\text{APR} = \frac{\text{Average Annual Finance Charge}}{\text{Average Loan Balance Outstanding}} = \frac{\$280.00/2}{\$3,220.00} = 4.35 \text{ percent}$$

   Wayne is correct that the APR of the discount loan is somewhat higher than the rate on an otherwise comparable simple interest loan.

4. ***Add-on Loan Monthly Payment and APR.*** Craig Sims has decided to borrow $4,500 using a 1-year, 4 percent, monthly installment loan. He wants to calculate the amount of the monthly payments and the APR on the loan.

   Solution: Craig must first determine the total finance charge, which is:

   Finance Charge (Discount) = Amount of Loan × Interest Rate × Term of Loan

   $$= \$4,500 \times 0.04 \times 1 = \$180.00$$

   The monthly payments are calculated as:

   $$\text{Monthly Payment (Add-on Method)} = \frac{\text{Amount of Loan} + \text{Finance Charge}}{\text{Number of Payments}}$$

   $$= \frac{\$4,500 + \$180}{12} = \$390.00$$

   Craig could use a financial calculator with the following key strokes to estimate the APR on the add-on loan:

Inputs	Functions
12	N
−1450	PV
390	PMT
	CPT
	CPT
	I/Y
	SOLUTION
	7.30

   Thus, using a 4 percent add-on installment loan will really cost Craig about 7.3 percent while an otherwise comparable simple-interest installment loan would have a stated interest rate and an APR of 4 percent.

Financial Planning Exercises

LG1, 2, p. 261   1.   ***Student loan options.*** Marilyn Seacrest is a sophomore at State College and is running out of money. Wanting to continue her education, Marilyn is considering a student loan. Explain her options. How can she minimize her borrowing costs and maximize her flexibility?

LG3, 6, p. 271, 282   2.   ***Evaluating finance packages.*** Assume that you've been shopping for a new car and intend to finance part of it through an installment loan. The car you're looking for has a sticker price of $18,000. The local dealership has offered to sell it to you for $3,000 down and finance the balance with a loan that will require 48 monthly payments of $333.67; Adventure Vehicles will sell you the exact same vehicle for $3,500 down, plus a 60-month loan for the balance, with monthly payments of $265.02. Which of these two finance packages is the better deal? Explain.

LG3, p. 271   3.   ***Calculating debt safety ratio. Use Worksheet 7.1.*** Every six months, Larry Sun takes an inventory of the consumer debts that he has outstanding. His latest tally shows that he still owes $4,000 on a home improvement loan (monthly payments of $125); he is making $85 monthly payments on a personal loan with a remaining balance of $750; he has a $2,000, secured, single-payment loan that's due late next year; he has a $70,000 home mortgage on which he's making $750 monthly payments; he still owes $8,600 on a new car loan (monthly payments of $375); and he has a $960 balance on his *MasterCard* (minimum payment of $40), a $70 balance on his Exxon credit card (balance due in 30 days), and a $1,200 balance on a personal line of credit ($60 monthly payments). Use Worksheet 7.1 to prepare an inventory of Larry's consumer debt. Find his debt safety ratio given that his take-home pay is $2,500 per month. Would you consider this ratio to be good or bad? Explain.

LG4, p. 275   4.   ***Calculating single payment loan amount due at maturity.*** Jim Grant plans to borrow $8,000 for five years. The loan will be *repaid with a single payment after five years*, and the interest on the loan will be computed using the simple interest method at an annual rate of 6 percent. How much will Jim have to pay in five years? How much will he have to pay at maturity if he's required to make *annual interest payments* at the end of each year?

LG4, p. 275   5.   ***Calculating the APR on simple interest and discount loans.*** Find the finance charges on a 6.5 percent, 18-month, single-payment loan when interest is computed using the simple interest method. Find the finance charges on the same loan when interest is computed using the discount method. Determine the APR in each case.

LG4, p. 275   6.   ***Comparing the costs of single-payment discount and simple interest loans.*** Sara Boquist needs to borrow $4,000. First State Bank will lend her the money for 12 months through a single-payment loan at 8 percent, discount; Home Savings and Loan will make her a $4,000, single-payment, 12-month loan at 10 percent, simple interest. From where should Sara borrow the money? Explain.

LG5, 6, p. 282   7.   ***Calculating monthly installment loan payments.*** Using the simple interest method, find the monthly payments on a $3,000 installment loan if the funds are borrowed for 24 months at an annual interest rate of 6 percent. How much interest will be paid during the first year of this loan? (Use a monthly payment analysis similar to the one in Exhibit 7.7.)

LG5, 6, p. 282   8.   ***Calculating and comparing add-on and simple interest loans.*** Chris Jenkins is borrowing $10,000 for five years at 7 percent. Payments are made on a monthly basis, which are determined using the add-on method.
   a.   How much total interest will Chris pay on the loan if it is held for the full five-year term?
   b.   What are Chris' monthly payments?
   c.   How much higher are the monthly payments under the add-on method than under the simple interest method?

LG5, 6, p. 282   9.   ***Calculating interest and APR of installment loan.*** Assuming that interest is the only finance charge, how much interest would be paid on a $5,000 installment loan to be repaid in 36 monthly installments of $166.10? What is the APR on this loan?

LG5, 6, p. 282 10. *Calculating payments, interest, and APR on auto loan.* After careful comparison shopping, Bill Withers decides to buy a new Toyota Camry. With some options added, the car has a price of $23,558—including plates and taxes. Because he can't afford to pay cash for the car, he will use some savings and his old car as a trade-in to put down $8,500. Bill plans to finance the rest with a $20,000, 60-month loan at a simple interest rate of 4 percent.

   a. What will his monthly payments be?

   b. How much total interest will Bill pay in the first year of the loan? (Use a monthly payment analysis procedure similar to the one in Exhibit 7.7.)

   c. How much interest will Bill pay over the full (60-month) life of the loan?

   d. What is the APR on this loan?

LG5, 6, p. 282 11. *Calculating and comparing APRs of competing financing alternatives.* Lina Martinez wants to buy a new high-end audio system for her car. The system is being sold by two dealers in town, both of whom sell the equipment for the same price of $2,000. Lina can buy the equipment from Dealer A, with no money down, by making payments of $119.20 a month for 18 months; she can buy the same equipment from Dealer B by making 36 monthly payments of $69.34 (again, with no money down). Lina is considering purchasing the system from Dealer B because of the lower payment. Find the APR for each alternative. What do you recommend?

LG5, 6, p. 282 12. *Calculating interest and APR of add-on loan.* Sherman Jacobs plans to borrow $5,000 and to repay it in 36 monthly installments. This loan is being made at an annual add-on interest rate of 7.5 percent.

   a. Calculate the finance charge on this loan, assuming that the only component of the finance charge is interest.

   b. Use your finding in part (a) to calculate the monthly payment on the loan.

   c. Using a financial calculator, determine the APR on this loan.

LG6, p. 282 13. *Deciding whether to pay cash or finance a purchase. Use* **Worksheet 7.2**. Elizabeth Ehrlich wants to buy a home entertainment center. Complete with a big-screen TV, DVD, and sound system, the unit would cost $4,500. Elizabeth has over $15,000 in a money fund, so she can easily afford to pay cash for the whole thing (the fund is currently paying 5 percent interest, and Elizabeth expects that yield to hold for the foreseeable future). To stimulate sales, the dealer is offering to finance the full cost of the unit with a 36-month installment loan at 5 percent, simple. (*Note:* Assume Elizabeth is in the 28 percent tax bracket and that she itemizes deductions on her tax returns.) Briefly explain your answer.

   a. Should she pay cash for the entertainment center?

   b. Rework the problem, assuming that Elizabeth has the option of using a 48-month, 6 percent *home equity loan* to finance the full cost of this entertainment center. Again, use Worksheet 7.2 to determine if Elizabeth should pay cash or buy on time. Does your answer change from the one you came up with in part (a)? Explain.

LG5, 6, p. 282 14. *Comparing payments and APRs of financing alternatives.* Because of a job change, Ben Hardesty has just relocated to the southeastern United States. He sold his furniture before he moved, so he's now shopping for new furnishings. At a local furniture store, he's found an assortment of couches, chairs, tables, and beds that he thinks would look great in his new two-bedroom apartment; the total cost for everything is $6,400. Because of moving costs, Ben is a bit short of cash right now, so he's decided to take out an installment loan for $6,400 to pay for the furniture. The furniture store offers to lend him the money for 48 months at an add-on interest rate of 6.5 percent. The credit union at Ben's firm also offers to lend him the money—they'll give him the loan at an interest rate of 6 percent simple, but only for a term of 24 months.

   a. Compute the monthly payments for both of the loan offers.

   b. Determine the APR for both loans.

   c. Which is more important: low payments or a low APR? Explain.

Applying Personal Finance

Making the Payments!

For many of us, new cars can be so appealing! We get bitten by the "new car bug" and think how great it would be to have a new car. Then we tell ourselves that we *really need* a new car because our old one is just a piece of junk waiting to fall apart in the middle of the road. Of course, we don't have the money to purchase a new car outright, so we'll have to get a loan. That means car payments. The trouble is, car payments often turn out to be a lot less affordable *after* we actually get the loan than we thought they would be *before* we signed on the dotted line. And they last way beyond the time the new car aura wears off. This project will help you understand how loan payments are determined, as well as the obligation that they place on you as the borrower.

Let's assume for this project that your parents have promised to make the down payment on a new car once you have your degree in hand. They have agreed to pay 30 percent of the cost of any car you choose, so long as you are able to obtain a loan and make the payments on the remainder. Find the price of the vehicle you would like by visiting a car dealership or pulling up a Web site such as **http://www.edmunds.com**. Add another 4 percent to the price for tax, title, license, and so on (or ask a dealer to estimate these costs for you). Take 70 percent of the total to determine how much you'll have to finance from your car loan. Then find out what the going rate is for car loans in your area by calling or visiting your bank or by consulting a Internet site such as **http://www.bankrate.com**. Calculate what your monthly payments would be at this rate if you financed the loan for three, five, and six years. How well do you think these car payments would fit into your budget? What kind of income would you have to make to afford such payments comfortably? If the payments are more than you thought they would be, what can you do to bring them down?

CRITICAL THINKING CASES

7.1 Financing Tessa's Education

At age 19, Tessa Trainor is in the middle of her second year of studies at a community college in Savannah. She has done well in her course work; majoring in pre-business studies, she currently has a 3.75 grade point average. Tessa lives at home and works part-time as a filing clerk for a nearby electronics distributor. Her parents can't afford to pay any of her tuition and college expenses, so she's virtually on her own as far as college goes. Tessa plans to transfer to the University of Tennessee next year. (She has already been accepted.) After talking with her counselor, Tessa feels she won't be able to hold down a part-time job and still manage to complete her bachelor's degree program at UT in two years. Knowing that on her 22nd birthday, she will receive approximately $35,000 from a trust fund left her by her grandmother; Tessa has decided to borrow against the trust fund to support herself during the next two years. She estimates that she'll need $25,000 to cover tuition, room and board, books and supplies, travel, personal expenditures, and so on during that period. Unable to qualify for any special loan programs, Tessa has found two sources of single-payment loans, each requiring a security interest in the trust proceeds as collateral. The terms required by each potential lender are as follows:

a. Tennessee State Bank will lend $30,000 at 6 percent discount interest. The loan principal would be due at the end of two years.
b. National Bank of Knoxville will lend $25,000 under a two-year note. The note would carry a 7 percent simple interest rate and would also be due in a single payment at the end of two years.

Critical Thinking Questions

1. How much would Tessa (a) receive in initial loan proceeds and (b) be required to repay at maturity under the Tennessee State Bank loan?
2. Compute (a) the finance charges and (b) the APR on the loan offered by Tennessee State Bank.

3. Compute (a) the finance charges and (b) the APR on the loan offered by the National Bank of Knoxville. How big a loan payment would be due at the end of two years?
4. Compare your findings in Questions 2 and 3, and recommend one of the loans to Tessa. Explain your recommendation.
5. What other recommendations might you offer Tessa regarding disposition of the loan proceeds?

7.2 Grant Gets His Outback

Grant Tyson, a 27-year-old living in Arlington, Virginia, has been a high-school teacher for five years. For the past four months, he's been thinking about buying a Subaru Outback, but he feels that he can't afford a brand-new one. Recently, however, his friend Martin Grubbs has offered to sell Grant his fully loaded Subaru Outback 3.6R. Martin wants $26,900 for his Outback, which has been driven only 8,000 miles and is in very good condition. Grant is eager to buy the vehicle but has only $10,000 in his savings account at Central Bank. He expects to net $8,000 from the sale of his Chevrolet Malibu, but this will still leave him about $8,900 short. He has two alternatives for obtaining the money:

a. Borrow $8,900 from the First National Bank of Arlington at a fixed rate of 6 percent per annum, simple interest. The loan would be repaid in equal monthly installments over a three-year (36-month) period.

b. Obtain an $8,900 installment loan requiring 36 monthly payments from the Arlington Teacher's Credit Union at a 4.5 percent stated rate of interest. The add-on method would be used to calculate the finance charges on this loan.

Critical Thinking Questions

1. Using Exhibit 7.6 or a financial calculator, determine the required monthly payments if the loan is taken out at First National Bank of Arlington.
2. Compute (a) the finance charges and (b) the APR on the loan offered by First National Bank of Arlington.
3. Determine the size of the monthly payment required on the loan from the Arlington Teacher's Credit Union.
4. Compute (a) the finance charges and (b) the APR on the loan offered by the Arlington Teacher's Credit Union.
5. Compare the two loans and recommend one of them to Grant. Explain your recommendation.

Managing Insurance Needs

CHAPTER 8

Insuring Your Life

LEARNING GOALS

LG1 Explain the concept of risk and the basics of insurance underwriting.

LG2 Discuss the primary reasons for life insurance and identify those who need coverage.

LG3 Calculate how much life insurance you need.

LG4 Distinguish among the various types of life insurance policies and describe their advantages and disadvantages.

LG5 Choose the best life insurance policy for your needs at the lowest cost.

LG6 Become familiar with the key features of life insurance policies.

How Will This Affect Me?

Insurance should be used only to protect against potentially catastrophic losses, not for small-risk exposures. It should cover losses that could derail your family's future. Insurance balances the relatively small, certain loss of ongoing premiums against low-probability, high-cost risks. This chapter focuses on how to buy life insurance. Premature death is a catastrophic loss that could endanger your family's financial future. We start by explaining how to determine the amount of life insurance that is right for you. Then we consider how to choose among key insurance products, which include term life, whole life, universal life, variable life, and group life policies. The key features of life insurance contracts are explained, and frameworks for choosing an insurance agent and an insurance company are presented. The chapter should prepare you to make informed life insurance decisions.

8-1 BASIC INSURANCE CONCEPTS

As most people discover, life is full of unexpected events that can have far-reaching consequences. Your car is sideswiped on the highway and damaged beyond repair. A family member falls ill and can no longer work. A fire or other disaster destroys your home. Your spouse dies suddenly. Although most people don't like to think about such events, protecting yourself and your family against unforeseen disasters is part of sound financial planning. Insurance plays a central role in providing that protection. *Auto and homeowner's insurance,* for example, reimburses you if your car or home is destroyed or damaged. *Life insurance* helps replace lost income if premature death occurs, providing funds so that your loved ones can keep their home, maintain an acceptable lifestyle, pay for education, and meet other needs. *Hospitalization and health insurance* covers medical costs when you get sick or injured, and *disability insurance* protects your income while you're ill.

All of these types of insurance are intended *to protect you and your family from the financial consequences of losing assets or income when an accident, illness, or death occurs.* By anticipating the potential risks to which your assets and income could be exposed and by weaving insurance protection into your financial plan, you lend a degree of certainty to your financial future. This chapter begins by introducing important insurance concepts, such as risk and underwriting, before focusing on how to make decisions regarding life insurance. In Chapters 9 and 10, we'll discuss other important types of insurance, including health insurance and property insurance.

8-1a The Concept of Risk

An important concept in any discussion of insurance is *risk*. In insurance terms, risk is defined as uncertainty concerning a potential economic loss. Whenever you and your family have a financial interest in something—whether it's your life, health, home, car, or business—there's a risk of significant financial loss if that item is lost or damaged. Because such losses can be devastating to your financial security, you must devise strategies for anticipating and dealing with such risk exposures, including risk avoidance, loss prevention and control, risk assumption, and insurance.

Risk Avoidance

The simplest way to deal with risk is to avoid the act that creates it. For example, people who are afraid they might lose everything they own because of a lawsuit resulting from an automobile accident could avoid driving. Or avid skydivers or bungee jumpers might choose another recreational activity to avoid life and health risks!

Although **risk avoidance** can be an effective way to handle some risks, it has its costs. People who avoid driving have to face considerable inconvenience as well, and the retired skydiver may find she now suffers *more* stress, which can lead to different types of health risks. Risk avoidance is an attractive way to deal with risk only when the estimated cost of avoidance is less than the estimated cost of handling it in some other way.

risk avoidance
Avoiding an act that would create a risk.

Loss Prevention and Control

Generally, **loss prevention** is any activity that reduces the probability that a loss will occur (such as driving within the speed limit to lessen the chance of being in a car accident). **Loss control**, in contrast, is any activity that lessens the severity of loss once it occurs (such as wearing a safety belt or buying a car with air bags). Loss prevention and loss control should be important parts of the risk management program of every individual and family. In fact, insurance is a reasonable way of handling risk only when people use effective loss prevention and control measures.

loss prevention
Any activity that reduces the probability that a loss will occur.

loss control
Any activity that lessens the severity of loss once it occurs.

Risk Assumption

With **risk assumption**, you choose to accept and bear the risk of loss. Risk assumption can be an effective way to handle many types of potentially small exposures to loss when insurance would be too expensive. For example, the risk of having your *Personal Financial Planning* text stolen probably doesn't justify buying insurance. Risk assumption is also a reasonable approach for dealing with very large risks that you can't ordinarily prevent or secure insurance for (e.g., a nuclear holocaust). Unfortunately, people often assume risks unknowingly. They may be unaware of various exposures to loss or think that their insurance policy offers adequate protection when, in fact, it doesn't.

risk assumption
The choice to accept and bear the risk of loss.

Insurance

An **insurance policy** is a contract between you (the insured) and an insurance company (the insurer) under which the insurance company agrees to reimburse you for the losses you suffer according to specified terms. From your perspective, *you are transferring your risk of loss to the insurance company*. You pay a relatively small *certain* amount (the insurance premium) in exchange for the insurance company's promise that they'll reimburse you if you suffer an *uncertain* loss covered by the insurance policy.

Why are insurance companies willing to accept this risk? They combine the loss experiences of large numbers of people and use statistical information, called *actuarial data*, to estimate the risk—frequency and magnitude—of loss for the given population. They set and collect premiums, which they invest and use to pay out losses and cover expenses. If they pay out less than the sum of the premiums and the earnings on them, they make a profit.

insurance policy
A contract between the insured and the insurer under which the insurer agrees to reimburse the insured for any losses suffered according to specified terms.

8-1b Underwriting Basics

Insurance companies take great pains to decide whom they will insure and the applicable premiums they will charge. This function is called **underwriting**. Underwriters design rate-classification schedules so that people pay premiums that reflect their chance of loss. Through underwriting, insurance companies try to guard against *adverse selection*, which happens when only high-risk clients apply for and get insurance coverage. Insurers are always trying to improve their underwriting capabilities in order to set premium rates that will adequately protect policyholders and yet be attractive and reasonable.

Because underwriting practices and standards also vary among insurance companies, you can often save money by shopping around for the company offering the most favorable underwriting policies for your specific characteristics and needs. The discussion of life insurance that follows in this chapter—and in succeeding chapters that discuss other types of insurance—will help you accomplish these goals.

underwriting
The process used by insurers to decide who can be insured and to determine applicable rates that will be charged for premiums.

8-2 WHY BUY LIFE INSURANCE?

Life insurance planning is an important part of every successful financial plan. Its primary purpose is *to protect your dependents from financial loss in the event of your untimely death*. It's an umbrella of protection for your loved ones, protecting the assets you've built up during your life and providing funds to help your family reach important financial goals even after you die. The key idea is that life insurance protects your family from the potentially catastrophic financial damage caused by the premature death of the major breadwinner(s).

8-2a Benefits of Life Insurance

Despite the importance of life insurance to sound financial planning, many people put off the decision to buy it. This happens partly because life insurance is associated with something unpleasant in most people's minds—namely, death. People don't like to think or talk about death or the things associated with it, so they often put off considering their life insurance needs. Life insurance is also intangible. You can't see, smell, touch, or taste its benefits—and those benefits mainly are realized after you've died. However, life insurance has some important benefits that should not be ignored in the financial planning process. These benefits include:

- **Financial protection for dependents:** If your family or loved ones depend on your income, what would happen to them after you die? Would they be able to maintain their current lifestyle, stay in their home, or afford a college education? Life insurance provides a financial cushion for your dependents, giving them a set amount of money after your death that they can use for many purposes. In short, the most important benefit of life insurance is providing financial protection for your dependents after your death.

> **EXAMPLE: Using Life Insurance to Protect Dependents**
> If you were to unfortunately die prematurely, your spouse could use your life insurance proceeds to pay off the mortgage on your home, so your family can continue living there comfortably, or set aside funds for your child's college education.

- **Protection from creditors:** A life insurance policy can be structured so that death benefits are paid directly to a named beneficiary rather than being considered as part of your estate. This means that even if you have outstanding bills and debts at the time of your death, creditors cannot claim the cash benefits from your life insurance policy, which provides further financial protection for your dependents.

- Tax benefits: Life insurance proceeds paid to your heirs, aren't generally subject to state or federal income taxes. Furthermore, if certain requirements are met, policy proceeds can pass to named beneficiaries free of any *estate taxes*.
- Savings vehicle: Some types of life insurance policies can serve as a savings vehicle, particularly for those who are looking for safety of principal. *Variable life policies,* which we'll discuss later in this chapter, are more investment vehicles than they are life insurance products. But don't assume that all life insurance products can be considered savings instruments. As we'll see later in this chapter, this is often inappropriate.

Just as with other aspects of personal financial planning, life insurance decisions can be made easier by following a step-by-step approach. You will need answers to the following questions:

- Do you need life insurance?
- If so, how much life insurance do you need?
- Which type of life insurance is best, given your financial objectives?
- What factors should you consider in making the final purchase decision?

8-2b Do You Need Life Insurance?

The first question to ask when considering the purchase of life insurance is whether you need it. Not everyone does. Many factors, including your personal situation and other financial resources, play a role in determining your need for life insurance. Remember, the major purpose of life insurance is to provide financial security for your dependents in the event of your death. As we've discussed, life insurance provides other benefits, but they're all a distant second to this one.

Who needs life insurance? In general, life insurance should be considered if you have dependents counting on you for financial support. Therefore, a single adult who doesn't have children or other relatives to support may not need life insurance at all. Children also usually don't require insurance on their life.

Once you marry, your life insurance requirements should be reevaluated, depending on your spouse's earning potential and assets—such as a house—that you want to protect. The need for life insurance increases the most when children enter the picture because young families stand to suffer the greatest financial hardship from the premature death of a parent. Even a non-wage-earning parent may require some life insurance to ensure that children are cared for adequately if the parent dies.

As families build assets, their life insurance requirements continue to change, both in terms of the amount of insurance needed and the type of policy necessary to meet their financial objectives and protect their assets. Other life changes will also affect your life insurance needs. For example, if you divorce or your spouse dies, you may need additional life insurance to protect your children. Once your children finish school and are on their own, the need for life insurance may end. In later years, life insurance needs vary depending on the availability of other financial resources, such as pensions and investments, to provide for your dependents.

TEST YOURSELF

8-4   Discuss some benefits of life insurance in addition to protecting family members financially after the primary wage earner's death.

8-5   Explain the circumstances under which a single college graduate would or would not need life insurance. What life-cycle events would change this initial evaluation, and how might they affect the graduate's life insurance needs?

8-3 HOW MUCH LIFE INSURANCE IS RIGHT FOR YOU?

After confirming your need for life insurance, you'll need to make more decisions to find the life insurance product that best fits your needs. First, you must determine how much life insurance you need for adequate coverage. Buying too much life insurance can be costly; buying too little may prove disastrous. To avoid these problems, you can use one of two methods to estimate how much insurance is necessary: the *multiple-of-earnings method* and the *needs analysis method*.

multiple-of-earnings method
A method of determining the amount of life insurance coverage needed by multiplying gross annual earnings by some selected number.

The multiple-of-earnings method takes your gross annual earnings and multiplies it by some selected (often arbitrary) number to arrive at an estimate of adequate life insurance coverage. The rule of thumb used by many insurance agents is that your insurance coverage should be equal to 5 to 10 times your current income. Although simple to use, the multiple-of-earnings method fails to fully recognize the financial obligations and resources of the individual and his or her family. Therefore, the multiple-of-earnings method should be used only to roughly approximate life insurance needs.

> **EXAMPLE: Determining the Amount of Life Insurance Using the Multiple-of-Earnings Method**
>
> You plan to rely on the rule that your life insurance coverage should be between 5 and 10 times your current income. Thus, if you currently earn $70,000 a year, using the multiple-of-earnings method you'd need between $350,000 and $700,000 worth of life insurance.

needs analysis method
A method of determining the amount of life insurance coverage needed by considering a person's financial obligations and available financial resources *in addition to life insurance.*

A more detailed approach is the needs analysis method. This method considers both the financial obligations and financial resources of the insured and his or her dependents. It involves three steps, as shown in Exhibit 8.1:

1. Estimate the total economic resources needed if the individual were to die.
2. Determine all financial resources that would be available after death, including existing life insurance and pension plan death benefits.
3. Subtract available resources from the amount needed to determine how much additional life insurance is required.

8-3a Step 1: Assess Your Family's Total Economic Needs

The first question that the needs analysis method asks is: *What financial resources will my survivors need should I die tomorrow?* When answering this question, you should consider the following five items:

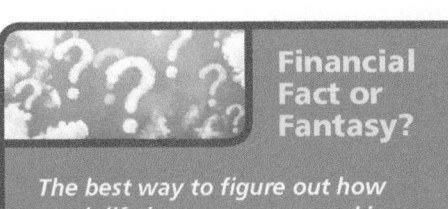

Financial Fact or Fantasy?

The best way to figure out how much life insurance you need is to use a multiple of your earnings. **Fantasy:** While the multiple earnings approach is probably the simplest procedure, it suffers from a number of serious shortcomings. A better choice is the needs approach.

1. Income needed to maintain an adequate lifestyle: If you died, how much money would your dependents need each month in order to live a comfortable life? Estimate this amount by looking at your family's current monthly budget, including expenses for housing costs, utilities, food, clothing, and medical and dental needs. Other expenses to consider include property taxes, insurance, recreation and travel, and savings. Try to take into account that the amount needed may change over time. For example, once children are grown, monthly household expenses should decrease substantially, but the surviving spouse may still need monthly support. Therefore, the survivor's life expectancy and the income required should be considered.

EXHIBIT 8.1   How Much Life Insurance Do You Need?

The needs analysis method uses three steps to estimate life insurance needs.

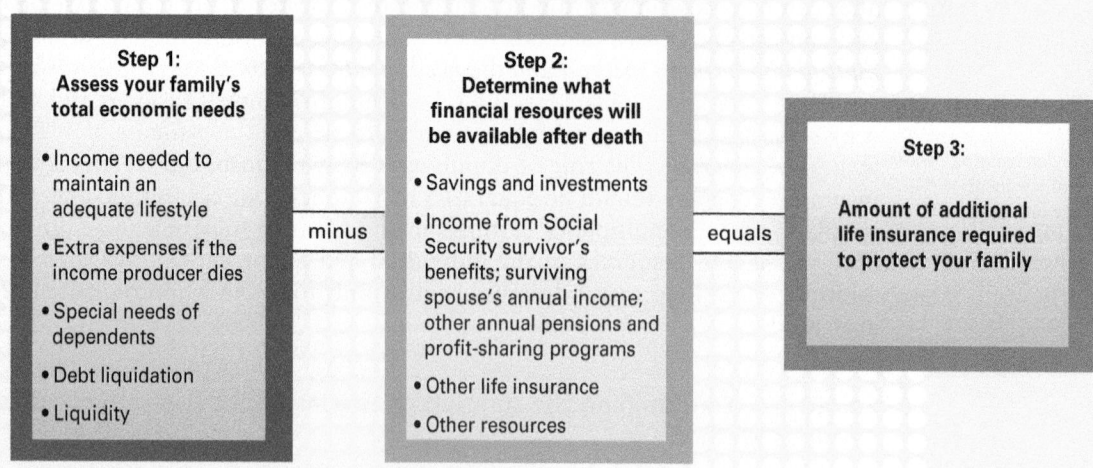

2. **Extra expenses if the primary income producer dies:** These expenses include funeral costs and any expenses that might be incurred to replace services that you currently provide. For example, a mother who doesn't work outside the home provides critically important child care, cooking, cleaning, and other services. If she were to die, or if her spouse died and she had to return to work, then these services likely would have to be replaced using the family's income. Because such expenses can stretch a family budget to the breaking point, include them when you're estimating insurance needs.

3. **Special needs of dependents:** In addition to daily economic needs, you may want to provide for special needs of your dependents. These needs might include long-term nursing care for a disabled or chronically ill dependent, an emergency fund for unexpected financial burdens, or a college education fund for your children.

4. **Debt liquidation:** In the event of their death, most breadwinners prefer to leave their families relatively debt free. To accomplish this, it's necessary to calculate the average amount due for outstanding bills. This amount would include the balances on credit cards, department store accounts, and other similar obligations. In addition, some will want to leave enough money to allow their dependents to pay off the home mortgage.

5. **Liquidity:** After your death, it may take time for your dependents to sell noncash assets. Real estate, for example, is difficult to convert into cash quickly. If a high percentage of your wealth is in illiquid assets, the cash proceeds from life insurance can be used to pay the bills until those assets can be sold at a fair market value.

8-3b Step 2: Determine What Financial Resources Will Be Available After Death

Once you've estimated the lifetime financial needs of dependents, the next step is to list all current resources that will be available for meeting those needs. For most families, money from savings, investments, and Social Security survivor's benefits make up the largest non–life insurance financial resources. Additional resources may include proceeds from employer-sponsored group life insurance policies and the death benefits payable from accumulated pension plans and profit-sharing programs. Another important source is income that can be earned by the surviving spouse or children. The earnings of a surviving spouse who is skilled and readily employable could be a family's largest available resource. After developing a complete list of available resources, you should make a reasonable estimate of their value. Although this step can be difficult because of the changing values of many assets, coming up with a set of reasonably accurate estimates is certainly within reach.

8-3c Step 3: Subtract Resources from Needs to Calculate How Much Life Insurance You Require

Finally, subtract the total available resources from the total needed to satisfy all of the family's financial objectives. If available resources are greater than anticipated needs, then no additional life insurance is required. If the resources are less than the needs—as is the case in most families with children—then the difference is the amount of life insurance necessary to provide the family with its desired standard of living.

FINANCIAL PLANNING TIPS

Buying the Right Life Insurance for You

The following tips will help you get the right insurance policy at the right price:

• **Don't let an insurance agent tell you how much insurance you need.** Use the methods in this chapter to determine the right amount of insurance for you. Agents often have a strong motivation to sell large policies—the larger, the better.

• **Consult an independent insurance broker.** Independent brokers have access to more products than the representative of any single company.

• **Just say no to one-meeting recommendations.** A broker who makes a recommendation in the first meeting is moving too fast and probably is not considering all of your best options.

• **Know how your agent is compensated.** Is he or she compensated by a commission-alone, fee-plus-commission, or fee-only structure? If you don't know how your broker is paid, you cannot recognize possible conflicts of interest.

• **Keep your insurance and investment decisions separate.** Term insurance provides protection against premature death alone, without a savings element. Whole life and universal life policies provide both insurance and savings; consequently, they cost much more. If you combine insurance and investing, make sure you understand why and the costs of doing so. Most people buy separate insurance and investment products.

• **Always do some comparison shopping.** There are lots of alternatives, with major price differences for essentially the same product.

• **Avoid replacing old whole-life insurance policies.** After holding a whole-life policy for years, you may lose the premiums that you've paid and pay more administration fees if you replace it. Just buy more insurance if your circumstances warrant doing so.

• **Avoid buying expensive riders.** Insurance agents often try to sell riders that provide special extra coverage. Make sure that you need any riders that you buy.

• **Consider your budget when buying insurance.** Make sure you understand and can afford new insurance before you buy it.

Source: Adapted from J. D. Roth, "14 Tips for Purchasing Life Insurance," http://www.getrichslowly.org/blog/2009/04/28/14-tips-for-purchasing-life-insurance/, accessed August 2015.

The needs analysis method may seem complex, but technology has made it simpler to use. Insurance companies now have computer software that can quickly determine the insurance needs of individuals and families. Many Internet sites and software programs also let you do your own analysis.

Regardless of the procedure you use, remember that *life insurance needs will likely change over time*. The amount and type of life insurance you need today will probably differ from the amount and type suitable for you 10 or 20 years from now. As with other areas of your personal financial plan, you should review and adjust life insurance programs (as necessary) at least every 5 years or after any major changes in the family (e.g., the birth of a child, the purchase of a home, or a job change).

Needs Analysis in Action: The Brewer Family

Let's take a closer look at how the needs analysis method works by considering the hypothetical case of Spencer and Erica Brewer. Spencer Brewer is 37 and the primary breadwinner in the family; his current earnings are $85,000. Spencer and his wife, Erica, want to be sure that his life insurance policy will provide enough proceeds to take care of Erica and their two children, ages 6 and 8, if he should die. You can follow their analysis of needs and resources in Worksheet 8.1.

Financial Resources Needed after Death (Step 1)

Spencer and Erica Brewer review their budget and decide that monthly living expenses for Erica and the two children would be about $3,500 in current dollars

© STOCKLITE/SHUTTERSTOCK.COM

while the children are still living at home (Period 1), or $42,000 annually. After both children leave home (Period 2), Erica, now 35, will need monthly income of $3,000—or $36,000 a year—until she retires at age 65. At that point (Period 3), the Brewers estimate that Erica's living expenses would fall to $2,750 a month, or $33,000 annually. The life expectancy of a woman Erica's age is 87 years, so the Brewers calculate that Erica will spend about 22 years in retirement. Therefore, as shown in the first section of the worksheet, the total income necessary to meet the Brewers' living expenses over the next 52 years is $1,878,000.

Although Erica previously worked as a stockbroker, they planned for her to stay home until the children graduated from high school. The Brewers are concerned that her previous education may be somewhat outdated at that point, so they include $25,000 for Erica to update her education and skills. Spencer and Erica also want to fund their children's college educations. After researching the current cost of their state's public university, they decide to establish a college fund of $100,000 for this purpose. Last, they estimate final expenses (e.g., funeral costs and estate taxes) of $15,000.

The Brewers use credit sparingly, so their outstanding debts are limited to a mortgage (with a current balance of $150,000), an automobile loan ($4,000), and miscellaneous charge accounts ($1,000). Spencer and Erica, therefore, estimate that $155,000 would pay off all of their existing debts.

All of these estimates are shown in the top half of Spencer and Erica's insurance calculations in Worksheet 8.1. Note that $2,173,000 is the total amount they estimate would be necessary to meet their financial goals if Spencer were to die.

Financial Resources Available After Death (Step 2)

Social Security survivor's benefits
Benefits under Social Security intended to provide basic, minimum support to families faced with the loss of a principal wage earner.

If Spencer died, Erica would be eligible to receive Social Security survivor's benefits for both herself and her children. Social Security survivor's benefits are intended to provide basic, minimum support to families faced with the loss of their principal wage

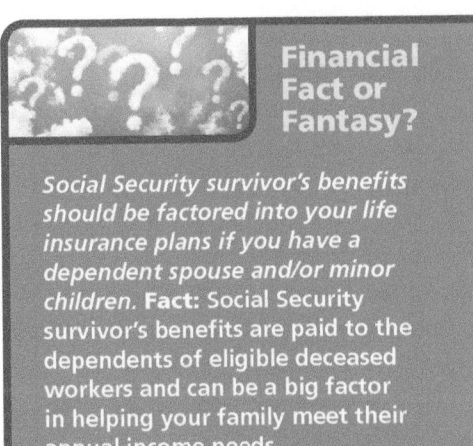
earner. The benefits are paid to unmarried children until age 18 (or 19 if they are still in high school) and to nonworking surviving spouses until their children reach age 16. The surviving spouse would also receive individual survivor's benefits upon turning 65. Limits are placed on the total amount of survivor's benefits that can be paid to a household, and if the surviving spouse returns to work, then the amount of benefits would be reduced if earnings exceed certain limits. We'll discuss Social Security and its benefits in more detail in Chapter 14.

Erica and Spencer visit the Social Security Administration's Internet site for an estimate of the survivor's benefits Erica will receive. Based on the number of years that Spencer has worked, his income, and the number of children they have, the Brewers estimate that Erica would receive approximately $3,200 a month, or $38,400 a year, in Social Security survivor's benefits for herself and the children until the youngest child graduates from high school in 12 years.

In the 18 years between when the children leave home and Erica retires, the Brewers expect Erica to be employed full-time and earn about $35,000 after taxes. After Erica turns 65, she'd receive approximately $2,250 a month ($27,000 a year) from Spencer's survivor's benefits, her own Social Security benefits, and her own retirement benefits. However, Erica will have some other resources available if Spencer should die prematurely. The couple has invested $65,000 in a mutual fund, and Spencer's employer provides a $100,000 life insurance policy for him. Adding these amounts to Erica's expected income means she'd have $1,849,800 in total resources available.

Additional Life Insurance Needed (Step 3)

How much life insurance should the Brewers buy for Spencer in order to be sure Erica and the children would be adequately cared for? To find out, the Brewers subtract the total financial resources available ($1,849,800) from the total financial resources needed ($2,173,000). The difference is $323,200, so the additional life insurance Spencer should buy to protect his family is about $325,000.

Of course, Spencer and Erica will need to examine their insurance situation periodically as their children grow and the family's financial circumstances change. But for now, they feel satisfied that they have a good estimate of the amount of additional life insurance they need to buy for Spencer. Next, they can begin to consider which type of policy is best.

8-3d Life Insurance Underwriting Considerations

As we discussed earlier, insurance companies use a process called *underwriting* to determine whom they will insure and what they will charge for insurance coverage. Underwriting policies are particularly important to understand when choosing life insurance products, so let's briefly examine some of the factors that life insurance underwriters consider.

Life insurance underwriting begins by asking potential insureds to complete an application designed to gather information about their risk potential. In other words, underwriters consider the likelihood the insured will die while the life insurance policy is in effect. Underwriters use life expectancy figures to look at overall longevity for various age groups. They also consider specific factors related to the applicant's health. Someone who smokes, is obese, has a history of heart disease, or has a dangerous job or hobby is considered a greater risk than someone who doesn't. Applicants who have been charged with driving under the influence of drugs or alcohol or who have had their driver's license suspended may also be viewed as riskier.

All these factors are then used to determine whether to accept you and, based on your risk factors, what premium to charge. For example, someone in excellent health

LIFE INSURANCE NEEDS ANALYSIS METHOD

Insured's Name Spencer and Erica Brewer   **Date** April 12, 2017

Step 1: Financial resources needed after death

1. Annual living expenses and other needs:

		Period 1	Period 2	Period 3	
a.	Monthly living expenses	$ 3,500	$ 3,000	$ 2,750	
b.	Net yearly income needed (a × 12)	$ 42,000	$ 36,000	$ 33,000	
c.	Number of years in time period	12	18	22	
d.	Total living need per time period (b × c)	$ 504,000	$ 648,000	$ 726,000	

TOTAL LIVING EXPENSES (add line d for each period): $ 1,878,000

2. Special needs

a.	Spouse education fund	$ 25,000
b.	Children's college fund	$ 100,000
c.	Other needs	0

3. Final expenses (funeral, estate costs, etc.) $ 15,000

4. Debt liquidation

a.	House mortgage	$ 150,000			
b.	Other loans	5,000			
c.	Total debt (4 a + 4 b)				$ 155,000

5. Other financial needs   0

TOTAL FINANCIAL RESOURCES NEEDED (add right column) $ 2,173,000

Step 2: Financial resources available after death

1. Income

		Period 1	Period 2	Period 3	
a.	Annual Social Security survivor's benefits	$ 38,400	0	0	
b.	Surviving spouse's annual income	0	$ 35,000	0	
c.	Other annual pensions and Social Security benefits	0	0	$ 27,000	
d.	Annual income	$ 38,400	$ 35,000	$ 27,000	
e.	Number of years in time period	12	18	22	
f.	Total period income (d × e)	$ 460,800	$ 630,000	$ 594,000	

g.	TOTAL INCOME	$ 1,684,800
2.	Savings and investments	$ 65,000
3.	Other life insurance	$ 100,000
4.	Other resources	0

TOTAL FINANCIAL RESOURCES AVAILABLE (1g + 2 + 3 + 4) $ 1,849,800

Step 3: Additional Life Insurance needed

Step 1: Total financial resources needed	$ 2,173,000
Step 2: Total financial resources available	$ 1,849,800

ADDITIONAL LIFE INSURANCE NEEDED $ 323,200

is usually considered "preferred" and pays the lowest premium. Other typical categories include standard, preferred smoker, and smoker. Those with special medical conditions—high cholesterol or diabetes, for example—fall into rated categories and pay considerably higher premiums if they're accepted.

The bottom line: If you have any of the risks commonly considered in life insurance underwriting—such as obesity, heart disease, or a high-risk hobby or job—then it's especially important to shop carefully and compare the cost implications of different types of insurance policies and the underwriting standards used by different companies. For example, an overweight hang-gliding enthusiast with a history of heart disease who walks tightropes for a living should expect to pay more for life insurance.

TEST YOURSELF

8-6 Discuss the two most commonly used ways to determine a person's life insurance needs.

8-7 Name and explain the most common financial resources needed after the death of a family breadwinner.

8-8 What are some factors that underwriters consider when evaluating a life insurance application? Which, if any, apply to you or your family members?

8-4 WHAT KIND OF POLICY IS RIGHT FOR YOU?

After determining the amount of life insurance you need to cover your family's financial requirements and considering how various underwriting policies might affect you, your next step is to decide on the type of insurance policy. Although a variety of life insurance products are available, three major types account for 90 percent to 95 percent of life insurance sales: term life, whole life, and universal life.

8-4a Term Life Insurance

term life insurance
Insurance that provides only death benefits, for a specified period, and does not provide for the accumulation of cash value.

Term life insurance is the simplest type of insurance policy. You purchase a specified amount of insurance protection for a set period. If you die during that time, your beneficiaries will receive the full amount specified in your policy. Term insurance can be bought for many different time increments, such as 5 years, 10 years, even 30 years. Depending on the policy, premiums can be paid annually, semi-annually, or quarterly.

Types of Term Insurance
The most common types of term insurance are straight (or level) term and decreasing term.

straight term policy
A term insurance policy written for a given number of years, with coverage remaining unchanged throughout the effective period.

Straight Term. A straight term life insurance policy is written for a set number of years, during which time the amount of life insurance coverage remains unchanged. The *annual premium* on a **straight term policy** may increase each year, as with *annual renewable term policies*, or remain level throughout the policy period, as with *level premium term policies*. Due to the convenience of knowing the future premiums for at least a few years at a time, level premium term policies have become much more popular than annual renewable term policies in recent years.

Exhibits 8.2 and 8.3 list representative annual premiums for annual renewable term and level premium term life policies, respectively. (*Note:* The premiums

EXHIBIT 8.2

Representative Annual Renewable Term Life Insurance Premiums: $100,000 Policy, Preferred Nonsmoker Rates

When you buy term life insurance, you're buying a product that provides life insurance coverage and nothing more. This table shows representative rates for several age categories and selected policy years; actual premiums increase every year. As you can see, females pay less than males for coverage, and premiums increase sharply with age.

	AGE 25		AGE 40		AGE 60	
Policy Year	Male ($)	Female ($)	Male ($)	Female ($)	Male ($)	Female ($)
1	95	49	145	117	429	366
5	97	63	177	151	732	570
10	107	88	237	194	1,278	864
15	145	117	299	236	2,307	1,620
20	177	151	429	366	3,988	2,902

EXHIBIT 8.3

Representative Level Premium Term Life Rates: $100,000 Preferred Nonsmoker Policy

This table shows representative annual premiums for $100,000 of level premium term life insurance. Although level premium costs less than annual renewable term for the same period, you must requalify at the end of each term to retain the lower premium.

Age	10 YEAR Male/Female ($)	15 YEAR Male/Female ($)	20 YEAR Male/Female ($)	30 YEAR Male/Female ($)
25	106/102	116/110	128/116	161/143
35	108/102	117/112	134/125	175/152
40	122/115	135/129	157/145	222/185
50	203/171	250/199	298/233	475/341
60	403/300	539/373	669/502	Not Available

Financial Fact or Fantasy?

Term insurance provides nothing more than a stipulated amount of death benefits and, as a result, is considered the purest form of life insurance. **Fact:** Term insurance provides a given amount of life insurance (i.e., death benefits) for a stipulated period of time and nothing more—no investment feature or cash value.

are for nonsmokers; rates for similar smoker policies would be higher in view of the greater risk and shorter life expectancies of smokers.) Until recently, annual renewable term premiums were less expensive in the early years but increased rapidly over time. These policies, however, aren't popular today. Because people now live longer, the rates for level premium term have fallen sharply and are well below those on annual renewable term from year 1 on, so they're a better value and, as noted above, more popular.

Decreasing Term. Because the death rate increases with each year of life, the premiums on annual renewable straight term policies for each successive period of coverage will also increase. As an alternative, some term policies *maintain a level premium* throughout all periods of coverage *while the amount of protection*

decreasing term policy
A term insurance policy that *maintains a level premium* throughout all periods of coverage while *the amount of protection decreases.*

decreases. Such a policy is called a decreasing term policy because the amount of protection decreases over its life. Decreasing term is used when the amount of needed coverage declines over time. For example, decreasing term policies are popular with homeowners who want a level of life insurance coverage that will decline at about the same rate as the balances on their home mortgages. Families with young children use these policies to ensure a sufficient level of family income while the kids are growing up. As they grow older, the amount of coverage needed decreases until the last child becomes independent and the need expires.

Again, remember that the type and length of term policy you choose affects the amount of premiums you'll pay over time. For a given person, the annual premium for a specified initial amount of coverage, say $250,000, would be lowest for straight term, higher for decreasing term, and highest for annual renewable term. The only reason that the premium on decreasing term is higher than the premium on straight term is that most major insurance companies don't offer decreasing term policies, so the small number of companies offering these policies operate in a less competitive market that allows them to charge high premiums. Of course, the death benefit on the decreasing term policy will, by design, decline during the policy's term.

Advantages and Disadvantages of Term Life

One of the biggest advantages of term life is cost. Term life usually offers lower initial premiums than other types of insurance, especially for younger people. Term life is an economical way to buy a large amount of life insurance protection over a given, relatively short period, making it particularly advantageous for covering needs that will disappear over time.

> **EXAMPLE: Appropriate Use of Term Life Insurance**
>
> Term life insurance is particularly useful for covering needs that will disappear over time. For example, a family with young children can use term life insurance to provide coverage until the children are grown.

The main disadvantage, however, is that term insurance offers only temporary coverage. Once the policy term expires, you must renew the policy. This can be a problem if you develop underwriting factors in the future that make it difficult to qualify for insurance. Many term life policies overcome part of this drawback by offering a renewability provision that gives you the option to renew your policy at the end of its term without having to show evidence of insurability. A guaranteed renewal provision allows you to renew the policy even if you have become uninsurable because of an accident or other illness during the original policy period. Generally, term policies are renewable at the end of each term until the insured reaches age 65 or 70. However, the premium will still increase to reflect the greater chance of death at older ages.

renewability
A term life policy provision allowing the insured to renew the policy at the end of its term without having to show evidence of insurability.

convertibility
A term life policy provision allowing the insured to convert the policy into a comparable whole life policy.

Another option that can help overcome some of the limitations of term insurance is a convertibility provision. This lets you convert your term insurance policy into a comparable whole life policy at a future time. A whole life policy, as we'll discuss next, provides lifelong protection, eliminating the need to consistently renew your life insurance. Convertibility is particularly useful if you need a large amount of relatively low-cost, short-term protection immediately, but in the future, you expect to have greater income that will allow you to purchase permanent insurance. Convertibility options are standard on most term policies today, but many place specific limits on when the conversion can take place.

One way to overcome the drawback of having to pay increased premiums at the end of each term is to purchase a longer-term policy. The insurance industry offers 30-year straight term policies that lock in a set premium. For example, a 35-year-old man who qualifies for preferred rates could lock in a $250,000 death benefit for 30 years in a row and pay only a set premium of $360 a year. As with all insurance policies, however, make sure before signing up that the rate is fully locked in for the duration of the policy.

Who Should Buy Term Insurance?

For most young families on limited budgets, the need for death protection greatly exceeds their need to save. If you fall into this category, guaranteed renewable and convertible term insurance should account for the largest portion of your insurance protection. These policies provide the most life insurance coverage for the least cost, thereby preserving financial resources for meeting immediate and future consumption and savings goals. Healthy older people with many other financial resources may also prefer to use term policies to meet specific coverage needs.

A strategy used by some is to buy term insurance and invest in a retirement plan the difference between the premium for whole life and the premium for term insurance. The short name for this is "buy term and invest the difference." As the cost of term insurance increases, the value of the investment will also increase, hopefully to the level needed at that stage of life. That is, the investment replaces the need for lifetime insurance.

8-4b Whole Life Insurance

whole life insurance
Life insurance designed to offer ongoing insurance coverage over the course of an insured's entire life.

cash value
The accumulated refundable value of an insurance policy; results from the investment earnings on paid-in insurance premiums.

Unlike term insurance, which offers financial protection for only a certain period, whole life insurance is designed to provide ongoing insurance coverage during an individual's entire life. In other words, it's considered a permanent insurance product. In addition to death protection, whole life insurance has a *savings* feature, called cash value, that results from the investment earnings on paid-in insurance premiums. Thus, *whole life provides not only insurance coverage, but also a modest return on your investment*. The idea behind cash value is to provide the insurance buyer with a tangible return while also receiving insurance coverage; the savings rates on whole life policies are normally *fixed* and *guaranteed* to be more than a certain rate (historically, 4 to 6 percent). Exhibit 8.4 illustrates how the cash value in a whole life policy builds up over time. Obviously, the longer the insured keeps the policy in force, the greater the cash value. Whole life can be purchased through several different payment plans—including continuous premium, limited payment, and single premium—all of which provide for accumulating cash values.

The cash value of a policy increases over time to reflect the greater chance of death that comes with age. If a policyholder cancels his contract prior to death, then that portion of the assets set aside to provide payment for the death claim is available to him. This right to a cash value is termed the policyholder's nonforfeiture right. By terminating their insurance contracts, policyholders forfeit their rights to death benefits. Likewise, the company must forfeit its claim to the monies paid by these policyholders for a future death benefit that it is no longer required to pay.

nonforfeiture right
A life insurance feature giving the whole life policyholder, upon policy cancellation, the portion of those assets that were set aside to provide payment for the future death claim.

Types of Whole Life Policies

Three major types of whole life policies are available: continuous premium, limited payment, and single premium. To develop a sense for the costs of these policies, look at the representative rates shown in Exhibit 8.5.

Continuous Premium. Under a *continuous premium whole life* policy—or *straight life,* as it's more commonly called—individuals pay a level premium each year until they either die or exercise a nonforfeiture right. The earlier in life the coverage is purchased, the lower the annual premium. Life insurance agents often use this as a selling point to convince younger people to buy now. Their argument is that the sooner you buy, the less you pay *annually*. Of course, the sooner people purchase whole life, the longer they have coverage in force, but (all other things being equal) the *more* they pay in total. There are good reasons (such as securing needed protection, savings, and insurability) for many young people to buy whole life insurance, but it should seldom be purchased by anyone simply because the *annual* premium will be lower now than if it's purchased later.

Of the various whole life policies available, continuous premium (straight life) offers the greatest amount of permanent death protection and the least amount of

Here is an example of the projected cash value for an actual $200,000 whole life policy issued by a major life insurer to a male, age 30. For *each year* of the illustration, the difference between the $200,000 death benefit and the projected cash value represents the *death protection* offered by the insurer.

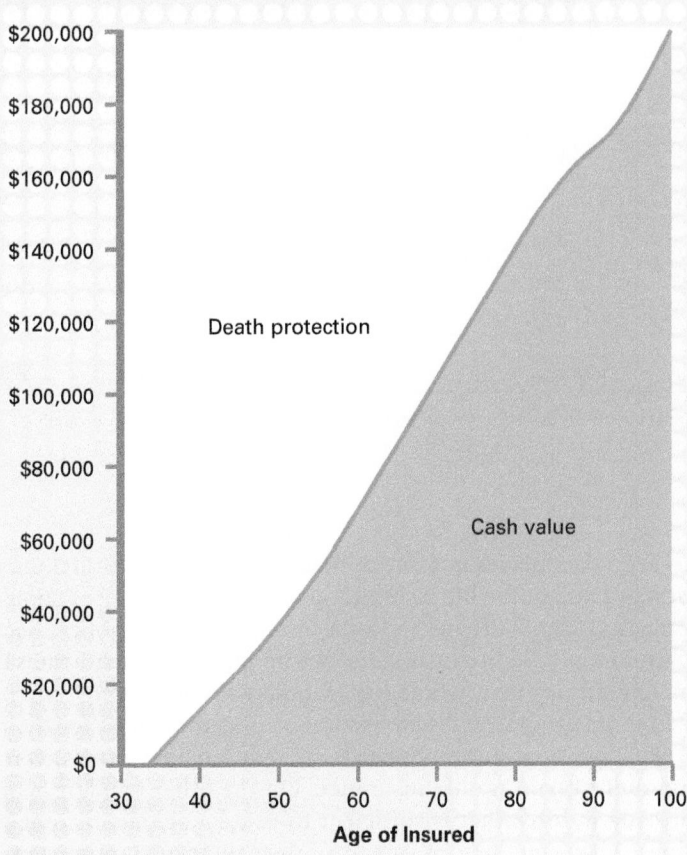

savings per premium dollar. This emphasis on *death protection* makes it the wisest choice to fill a permanent life insurance need.

Limited Payment. With a *limited payment whole life* policy, you're covered for your entire life, but the premium payment is based on a specified period—for example, so-called 20-pay life and 30-pay life require level premium payments for a period of 20 and 30 years, respectively. For stipulated age policies such as those paid up at age 55 or 65, you pay premiums until you reach the stated age. In all of these cases, on completion of the scheduled payments, *the insurance remains in force, at its face value, for the rest of the insured's life.*

Some insurance companies try to convince consumers to buy limited payment policies by stressing the "large" savings element that will develop and by emphasizing that the policyholder won't have to pay premiums for an entire lifetime. This logic fails on two counts. First, for most people, the primary purpose of whole life insurance is permanent protection against financial loss resulting from death, not the accumulation of savings. Second, even if people buy continuous premium whole life (straight life) policies, they need to pay the premium only so long as they wish

Like any life insurance product, whole life is more expensive the older you are. Also, whole life is more costly than term because you're getting an investment/savings account, represented by the "total cash value" column, in addition to life insurance coverage.

	ANNUAL PREMIUM		PREMIUMS PAID THROUGH YEAR 20		TOTAL CASH VALUE AT YEAR 20*		PAID UP INSURANCE AT YEAR 20	
Age	Male ($)	Female ($)	Male ($)	Female ($)	Male ($)	Female ($)	Male ($)	Female ($)
25	603	$ 525	$12,060	$10,580	$10,670	$12,360	$55,700	$56,200
30	727	$ 683	$14,540	$12,760	$13,518	$15,768	$57,500	$58,600
35	891	$ 775	$17,820	$15,500	$16,908	$19,842	$58,900	$60,600
40	1,078	$ 931	$21,560	$18,620	$20,518	$24,473	$60,000	$62,300
50	1,590	$1,367	$31,800	$27,340	$29,796	$35,382	$62,300	$65,300
60	2,418	$2,050	$48,360	$41,000	$41,796	$41,796	$66,260	$68,800

*The whole life policy in this example does not pay dividends, so the cash values and guaranteed paid-up insurance amounts are fixed (guaranteed).

to keep the policies in force at their full face value. If lifelong death protection is the primary aim of the life insurance policy, then the insured should purchase continuous premium whole life instead of a limited payment policy. Because more continuous premium whole life insurance can be purchased with the same number of dollars as limited payment whole life, people who need whole life insurance are probably better off using straight life insurance to get the most for their life insurance dollars. Then, once their insurance needs are reduced, they can convert the policy to a smaller amount of paid-up life insurance. On the other hand, if people have life insurance already in force that is sufficient to protect against income loss, then they can use limited payment policies as part of their savings or retirement plans.

Single Premium. Continuous premium and limited payment whole life policies represent methods of acquiring life insurance on an installment basis. In contrast, a *single premium whole life* policy is purchased with one cash premium payment at the inception of the contract, thus buying life insurance coverage for the rest of your life. The single premium policy has only limited usefulness in the life insurance programs of most families. However, because of its investment attributes, single premium life insurance, or *SPLI* for short, appeals to those looking for a *tax-sheltered investment vehicle*. Like any whole life insurance policy, interest/investment earnings within the policy are tax deferred. There is a catch, however: any cash withdrawals or loans taken against the SPLI cash value before you reach age 59 1/2 are not only taxed as capital gains, but also are subject to a 10 percent penalty for early withdrawal.

Advantages and Disadvantages of Whole Life

The most noteworthy advantage of whole life insurance is that premium payments contribute toward building an estate, regardless of how long the insured lives. The face value of the policy is paid on death; alternatively, the insured can borrow against it or withdraw cash value when the need for insurance protection has expired. As the final column of Exhibit 8.5 shows, the amount of this cash value can be significant.

A corresponding benefit of whole life (except SPLI) is that individuals who need insurance for an entire lifetime can budget their premium payments over a relatively long period. This eliminates the affordability and uninsurability problems often encountered with term insurance in later years.

Another benefit of whole life policies is shown in the "Paid Up Insurance at Year 20" column of Exhibit 8.5. This indicates how much insurance coverage the policyholder can retain if the policy premiums are no longer paid beyond that point and the total cash value at that time is exchanged for the indicated amount of coverage. For example, Exhibit 8.5 shows that a male buying insurance at the age of 40 would pay a premium of $1,078 a year. After 20 years, the cash value of the policy would be $20,518. If he decided to quit paying the premiums from then on, he could sacrifice the $20,518 cash value in return for life insurance coverage of $60,000 up to a maximum age specified in the policy, which is often 65. This flexibility of whole life policies is viewed as a benefit by some insurance buyers.

Some people like whole life policies because the periodic payments force them to save regularly and because favorable tax treatment is given to accumulated earnings. This is because your earnings build up on a tax-sheltered basis, which means that the underlying cash value of the policy increases at a much faster rate than it otherwise would. Insurance experts also point out that the whole life policy offers other potentially valuable options in addition to death protection and cash value. Some of these options include the continuation of coverage after allowing the policy to lapse because premiums were not paid (nonforfeiture option) and the ability to revive an older, favorably priced policy that has lapsed (policy reinstatement). These and other options are discussed in a later section on life insurance contract features.

One disadvantage of whole life insurance is its cost. It provides less death protection per premium dollar than term insurance does. Contrast the premiums paid for various whole life products with those paid for term insurance by comparing Exhibits 8.2, 8.3, and 8.5. You can readily see how much more expensive whole life is than term life. The reason for the difference is that you pay extra for the savings/investment feature included with whole life. Another disadvantage of whole life is that its investment feature provides lower yields than many otherwise comparable vehicles. The returns on most whole life insurance policies are just not very competitive. As with term insurance, the negative aspects of whole life often arise from misuse of the policy. In other words, a *whole life policy should not be used to obtain maximum return on investment*. However, if a person wishes to combine a given amount of death protection for the entire life of the insured (or until the policy is terminated) with a savings plan that provides a *moderate* tax-sheltered rate of return, then whole life insurance may be a wise purchase.

One way to keep the cost of whole life down is to consider purchasing *low-load* whole life insurance. Low-load products are sold directly by insurers to consumers, sometimes over the Internet or via a toll-free phone number, thereby eliminating sales agents from the transaction. With traditional whole life policies sold by an agent, sales commissions and marketing expenses account for between 100 percent and 150 percent of the first year's premium and from 20 percent to 25 percent of total premiums paid over the life of the policy. In comparison, only about 5 percent to 10 percent of low-load policy premiums go toward selling and marketing expenses. As a result, cash values grow much more quickly.

EXAMPLE: Using Low-Load Whole Life Insurance—Building Cash Value

Consider the case of a 50-year-old male who purchased a low-load policy with a $500,000 death benefit for an annual premium of $7,500. Within 5 years his cash surrender value was projected to be more than $36,000. In contrast, a comparable, fully-loaded policy was projected to produce a cash value of only $24,000.

Behavior Matters

Whole Life vs. Term Life Insurance and Behavioral Biases

A whole life insurance policy accumulates cash value over time based on the difference in the premiums on whole life and term life policies for a given individual. Whole life policies are consequently more expensive than term life. Let's consider how whole life insurance policies can be marketed to exploit behavioral biases.

Whole life insurance can be marketed to appeal to the mental accounting behavioral bias. Many people will think of life insurance and saving for retirement as separate though related "mental accounts," both of which have merit. Yet it's easy to confound the investment and life insurance components of a whole life policy when an agent pitches it as a mandated savings plan. Thus, the policy is marketed as offering protection for your family in the event of premature death, as well as providing a mandatory savings plan that will help you consistently pursue retirement savings goals. Some agents will even argue that the whole life policy will eventually be "free" when the cash value has grown large enough to cover the insurance premium. Many cannot resist the apparent appeal of protecting the family today in the event of premature death combined with embarking on a disciplined savings plan that helps save for retirement and will provide "free" insurance in the future.

A rational decision maker knows that there is no such thing as "free" insurance. And such a person would separate the need to have a savings plan from the need to have adequate life insurance coverage. So what causes people to confound these decisions? The concept of premature death, protecting one's family, and planning for retirement are emotional issues. A fully aware person would likely commit to a savings plan, buy term life insurance, and invest the difference between the whole life and term life premiums. Saving and investing for retirement are separate issues that need not be combined in a whole life insurance policy. This is not to say that there are no people for whom whole life insurance is appropriate. However, life insurance and investing for retirement should not be considered without separate analyses.

Source: Adapted from Justin Reckers and Robert Simon, "Behavioral Finance and Life Insurance," http://www.morningstar.com/advisor/t/42987554/behavioral-finance-and-life-insurance.htm#axzz2i25ZJlmG, accessed August 2015.

Who Should Buy Whole Life Insurance?

Most families also need some amount of permanent insurance and savings, which a continuous premium whole life policy can satisfy. Some financial advisors recommend that you use cash-value insurance to cover your *permanent need for insurance*—the amount your dependents will need regardless of the age at which you die. (Although term insurance is less expensive, you may not be able to buy term insurance as you grow older, or it may become too expensive.) Such needs may include final expenses and either the survivor's retirement need (Period 3 in Worksheet 8.1) or additional insurance coverage, whichever is less. This amount is different for every person. Using these guidelines, the Brewers in our earlier example would need about $147,000 in whole life insurance (in Worksheet 8.1: $15,000 final expenses [Step 1, line 3] plus about $132,000 of Period 3 living expenses [Period 3 resources needed vs. resources available, which is Step 1, line 1d for Period 3 minus Step 2, line 1f for Period 3—i.e., $726,000 − $594,000]) and another $176,200 (say $176,000 or $177,000) in term life (in Worksheet 8.1: $323,200 [Step 3] minus about $147,000 in permanent insurance just calculated). Limited payment whole life and single premium whole life policies should be purchased only when the primary goal is savings or additional tax-deferred investments and not protection against financial loss resulting from death.

Whole life may make sense in several other situations. For example, a family history of heart disease, cancer, or similar conditions may increase your risk of developing health problems and make it hard to qualify for term insurance at a later date. If you're already over 50, term life insurance may be too expensive. Or, perhaps you've "maxed out" your other tax-deferred savings options and want to buy cash-value insurance to accumulate additional retirement funds.

8-4c Universal Life Insurance

universal life insurance
Permanent cash-value insurance that combines term insurance (death benefits) with a tax-sheltered savings/investment account that pays interest, usually at competitive money market rates.

Universal life insurance is another form of permanent cash-value insurance that combines term insurance, which provides death benefits, with a tax-sheltered savings/investment account that pays interest, usually at competitive money market rates. The death protection (or pure insurance) portion and the savings portion are identified separately in its premium. This is referred to as *unbundling*. Exhibit 8.6 shows representative annual outlays, premiums, and cash values for a $100,000 universal life policy.

Traditionally, for whole life insurance, you pay a premium to purchase a stated face amount of coverage in a policy with a *fixed cash-value schedule*. With universal life, part of your premium pays administrative fees, and the remainder is put into the cash-value (savings) portion of the policy, where it earns a certain rate of return. This rate of earnings varies with market yields but is guaranteed to be more than some stipulated minimum rate (say, 3 percent). Then, each month the cost of 1 month's term insurance is withdrawn from the cash value to purchase the required death protection. So long as there's enough in the savings portion to buy death protection, the policy will stay in force. Should the cash value grow to an unusually large amount, the amount of insurance coverage must be increased in order for the policy to retain its favorable tax treatment (tax laws require that the death benefits in a universal life policy *must always exceed the cash value* by a stipulated amount).

The explicit separation of the protection and savings elements in universal policies has raised the question of whether this type of insurance is, in fact, whole life insurance. This question is important because the accumulation of cash values in whole life policies arises partly from the interest credited to them. Under

| EXHIBIT 8.6 | **Representative Universal Life Insurance Annual Outlays: $100,000 Policy, Preferred Nonsmoker Rates** |

Universal life premiums are lower than whole life and can vary over the policy's life. After deducting the cost of the death benefit and any administrative fees from your annual contribution, the rest goes into an accumulation account and builds at a variable rate—in this example, the current rate is 3.5 percent. However, the guaranteed rate is only 3 percent, so your actual cash value may be less.

	ANNUAL OUTLAY		PREMIUMS PAID THROUGH YEAR 20		CASH SURRENDER VALUE AT YEAR 20*	
Age	Male ($)	Female ($)	Male ($)	Female ($)	Male ($)	Female ($)
25	701	628	14,027	12,574	16,206	14,495
30	830	742	16,590	14,833	19,480	17,302
35	995	885	19,896	17,702	23,169	20,481
40	1,205	1,067	24,108	21,340	27,366	24,234
50	1,806	1,579	36,127	31,573	38,468	34,368
60	2,808	2,402	56,155	48,034	56,365	47,912

*Based on an assumed annual rate of 3.5 percent.

today's tax laws, *this accumulation occurs tax-free so long as the cash value does not exceed the total premiums paid to the insurer*. However, if a whole life policy is surrendered for its cash value and that cash value exceeds the premiums paid, then *the gain* is taxed. Universal life policies enjoy the same favorable tax treatment as do other forms of whole life insurance: death benefits are tax-free and, prior to the insured's death, amounts credited to the cash value (including investment earnings) accumulate on a tax-deferred basis. The insurance company sends the insured an annual statement summarizing the monthly credits of interest and deductions of expenses.

A universal life insurance policy provides two types of death protection. The first type, known as Option A, provides a level death benefit. As the cash value increases, the amount of pure insurance protection *decreases*. The second type, Option B, provides a stated amount of insurance plus the accumulated cash value. Therefore, the death benefit at any time varies with the rate of earnings on the savings plan and will increase along with the accumulated cash value.

Advantages and Disadvantages of Universal Life

As with any insurance policy, universal life has its pros and cons. There are two principal advantages.

- Flexibility: The annual premium you pay can be increased or decreased from year to year, because the cost of the death protection *may be covered from either the annual premium or the accumulation account* (i.e., the cash value). If the accumulation account is adequate, you can use it to pay the annual premium. The death benefit also can be increased or decreased, and you can change from the level benefit type of policy to the cash value plus a stated amount of insurance. Note, however, that evidence of insurability is usually required if the death benefit is to be increased. This flexibility allows you to adapt the death benefit to your life-cycle needs—for example, increasing the death benefit when you have another child and decreasing it when your children are grown.
- Savings feature: A universal life insurance policy credits cash value at the "current" rate of interest, and this *current* rate of interest may well be higher than the guaranteed *minimum* rate. Find out what benchmark is used to determine the current rate of interest; the 90-day U.S. Treasury bill rate is often used.

Universal life's flexibility in making premium payments, although an attractive feature, is also one of its two major drawbacks.

- Changing premiums and protection levels: A policyholder who economizes on premium payments in early years may find that premiums must be higher than originally planned in later policy years to keep the policy in force. Indeed, some policyholders buy universal life expecting their premiums to vanish once cash value builds to a certain level. All too often, however, the premiums never disappear altogether. Or if they do, they reappear when interest rates fall below the rate in effect when the policy was purchased.
- Charges or fees: Universal life usually carries heavy fees compared to other policy types. These fees include the front-end load or commission on the first premium, the expense charge on each annual premium, investment expense charged by the insurer in determining the "current" rate of return, and other charges. Most states require the insurance company to issue an annual disclosure statement spelling out premiums paid, all expenses and mortality costs, interest earned, and beginning and ending cash values.

Who Should Buy Universal Life Insurance?

Universal life is a suitable choice if you're looking for a savings vehicle with greater potential returns than a whole life policy offers. Its flexible nature makes it particularly useful for people anticipating changes from their current need for death protection. For example, if you're recently married and expect to have children, a universal life policy will allow you to increase the death benefit as your family grows.

8-4d Other Types of Life Insurance

Besides term, whole life, and universal life, you can buy several other types of life insurance products, including variable life insurance, group life, and other special-purpose life policies such as credit life, mortgage life, and industrial life insurance. These insurance products serve diverse needs. Some may help you meet specific needs; others are simply comparable alternatives to traditional types of life insurance.

Variable Life Insurance

variable life insurance
Life insurance in which the benefits are a function of the returns being generated on the investments selected by the policyholder.

A **variable life insurance** policy goes further than whole and universal life policies in combining death benefits and savings. The policyholder decides how to invest the money in the savings (cash-value) component. The investment accounts are set up just like *mutual funds,* and most firms that offer variable life policies let you choose from a full menu of different funds, ranging from money market accounts and bond funds to international investments or aggressively managed stock funds. Unlike whole or universal life policies, however, variable life insurance policies do not guarantee a *minimum return*. Also, as the name implies, the amount of insurance coverage provided varies with the profits (and losses) generated in the investment account. Thus, the amount of death benefits payable in variable life insurance policies is, for the most part, related to the policies' investment returns. Exhibit 8.7 demonstrates how two possible investment return scenarios would affect the cash value and death benefits of a variable life insurance policy for a 45-year-old, nonsmoking male over a 20-year period.

Although all these features may sound great, variable life puts more emphasis on investments than any other life insurance product. Indeed, many observers view variable life more as an investment vehicle than a life insurance policy. It's an investment product wrapped around just enough life insurance coverage to make it legal. If you want the benefits of higher investment returns, then you must also be willing to assume the risks of reduced insurance coverage. So what does this mean for you? *It means you should use extreme care when buying variable life insurance.*

EXHIBIT 8.7	REPRESENTATIVE VARIABLE Life Insurance Values: $100,000 Policy, Preferred Nonsmoker, Male, Age 45

Variable life insurance pays a death benefit whose amount is tied to the policy's investment returns. The cash value created over the life of the policy is also related to investment returns. This table shows the effects of 6 percent and 12 percent annual returns over a 20-year period. Of course, a 12 percent return is quite optimistic. Lower returns result in lower cash value and death benefits; higher returns result in higher cash value and death benefits.

Policy Year	Total Premiums Paid	6% RETURN		12% RETURN	
		Cash Value	Death Benefit	Cash Value	Death Benefit
1	$1,575	$995	$100,995	$1,064	$101,064
5	8,705	5,244	105,244	5,705	105,705
10	19,810	10,592	110,592	15,365	115,365
15	33,986	15,093	115,093	27,688	127,688
20	52,079	17,080	117,080	43,912	143,912

Group Life Insurance

group life insurance
Life insurance that provides a master policy for a group; each eligible group member receives a certificate of insurance.

Under **group life insurance**, one master policy is issued and each eligible group member receives a certificate of insurance. Group life is nearly always term insurance, and the premium is based on the group's characteristics as a whole rather than the characteristics of any specific individual. Employers often provide group life insurance as a fringe benefit for their employees. However, just about any type of group (e.g., a labor union, a professional association, an alumni organization) can secure a group life policy as long as the insurance is only incidental to the reason for the group's existence.

Accounting for about one-third of all life insurance in the United States, group life insurance is one of the fastest-growing areas of insurance. Many group life policies now offer coverage for dependents as well as group members. What's more, group life policies generally provide that individual members who leave the group may continue the coverage by converting their protection to individually issued whole life policies. It is important to note that conversion normally doesn't require evidence of insurability as long as it occurs within a specified period. Of course, after conversion, the individual pays all premiums. Before buying additional coverage purchased through a group plan or converting a group policy to an individual one, it's important to compare rates. Often the premiums are more expensive than other readily available sources of term insurance.

As noted in Chapters 1 and 2, the availability of group coverage through employee benefit programs should be considered when developing a life insurance program. However, because of its potentially temporary nature and relatively low benefit amount (often equal to about 1 year's salary), it should be used only to fulfill low-priority insurance needs. Only in rare cases should a family rely solely on group life insurance to fulfill its primary income-protection requirements.

Other Special-Purpose Life Policies

Use caution before buying one of the following types of life insurance:

credit life insurance
Life insurance sold in conjunction with installment loans.

- Credit life insurance: Banks, finance companies, and other lenders generally sell credit life insurance in conjunction with installment loans. Usually, credit life is a term policy of less than five years with a face value corresponding to the outstanding balance on the loan. Although liquidating debts on the death of a family breadwinner is often desirable, it's usually preferable to do so through an individual's term or whole life insurance, rather than buying a separate credit life insurance policy. This is because credit life is one of the most expensive forms of life insurance—and one you should therefore avoid.

mortgage life insurance
A term policy designed to pay off the mortgage balance in the event of the borrower's death.

- Mortgage life insurance: Mortgage life insurance is a term policy designed to pay off the mortgage balance on a home in the event of the borrower's death. As in the case of credit life, this need can usually be met less expensively by shopping the market for a suitable decreasing term policy.

industrial life insurance (home service life insurance)
Whole life insurance issued in policies with relatively small face amounts, often $1,000 or less.

- Industrial life insurance: Sometimes called **home service life insurance**, this whole life insurance is issued in policies with small face amounts, often $1,000 or less. Agents call on policyholders weekly or monthly to collect the premiums. The term *industrial* became popular when the policies were first sold primarily to low-paid industrial wage earners. Industrial life insurance costs a good deal more per $1,000 of coverage than regular whole life policies, primarily because of its high marketing costs. Even so, some insurance authorities believe that industrial life insurance offers the only practical way to deliver coverage to low-income families.

8-5 BUYING LIFE INSURANCE

Once you have evaluated your personal financial needs and have become familiar with the basic life insurance options, you're ready to begin shopping for a life insurance policy. Exhibit 8.8 summarizes the major advantages and disadvantages of the most popular types of life insurance discussed so far in this chapter.

Several factors should be considered when making the final purchase decision: (1) comparing the costs and features of competitive products, (2) selecting a financially healthy insurance company, and (3) choosing a good agent.

8-5a Compare Costs and Features

The cost of a life insurance policy can vary considerably from company to company, even for the same amount and type of coverage. By comparison shopping, you can save thousands of dollars over the life of your policy. For example, the total cost for a 10-year, $250,000, term life policy at preferred rates for a 25-year-old can range from $1,170 to more than $2,000. Exhibit 8.9 gives a quick overview of differences in the key features of various types of life insurance.

If you smoke or have a health problem such as high cholesterol or high blood pressure, then spending time to check out several companies can really pay off. Some companies are more willing to accept these risks than others. They may even give you preferred rates if you correct the problem within a certain period of time. But until you do your homework, you won't know which policy offers you the coverage that you need at the lowest cost. If you have an unusual health problem or some other type of complication, a policy bought through an agent may actually be the cheapest alternative.

It's not enough to look only at current rates. You'll also need to ask how long the rates are locked-in and to find out the maximum you can be charged when you renew. A guaranteed policy may cost another $20 a year, but you won't be hit with unexpected, larger rate increases later. Establish for how long you'll need the coverage, and then find the best rates for the total period; low premiums for a five-year policy may jump when you renew for additional coverage. Also be sure you're getting the features you need, like the convertibility of term policies.

Major advantages and disadvantages of the most popular types of life insurance are summarized here. They should be considered when shopping for life insurance.

Type of Policy	Advantages	Disadvantages
Term	• Low initial premiums: simple, easy to buy.	• Provides only temporary coverage for a set period. • May have to pay higher premiums when policy is renewed.
Whole life	• Permanent coverage • Savings vehicle: cash value builds as premiums are paid. • Some tax advantages on accumulated earnings.	• Cost: provides less death protection per premium dollar than term. • Often provides lower yields than other investment vehicles. • Sales commissions and marketing expenses can increase costs of fully loaded policy.
Universal life	• Permanent coverage • Flexible: allows insured adapt level of protection and cost of premiums. • Savings vehicle: cash value builds at current rate of interest. • Savings and death protection identified separately.	• Can be difficult to evaluate true cost at time of purchase; insurance carrier may levy costly fees and charges.
Variable life	• Investment vehicle: insured decides how cash value will be invested.	• Higher risk.

Finally, be sure the policies that you are comparing *have similar provisions and amounts*. In other words, don't compare a $100,000 term life policy from one company with a $150,000 universal life policy from another. Instead, *first decide how much and what kind of policy you want, and then compare costs*. For similar cash-value policies, you may find it useful to compare interest-adjusted cost indexes that are often shown on policy illustrations. The *surrender cost index* measures the policy's cost if you surrender it after a certain period, typically 10 or 20 years, assuming that premiums and dividends earn 5 percent interest. The *net payment cost index* is calculated in a similar way but assumes that the policy is kept in force.

It's easy to gather the information that allows you to compare costs and features. Term life quote services, available over the Internet or the phone, can streamline the selection process by providing you, free of charge, with the names of several companies offering the lowest-cost policies based on your specifications. Probably the fastest-growing source of life insurance quotes and policies in recent years is the Internet. You can not only obtain quick, real-time quotes but also can buy insurance electronically. Buying on the Internet allows you to avoid dealing with insurance salespeople, and you can purchase the policies (usually term insurance only) on cost-effective terms. For example, one major life insurer offers discounts of up to 20 percent for term life policies purchased online. Of course, you'll still need a physical exam, but often the insurance company will send a qualified technician/nurse to your home or office to take a blood sample and other basic readings. Efinancial (**http://www.efinancial.com**), Select Quote Insurance Services (**http://www.selectquote.com**), Insure.com (**http://www.insure.com**), and Matrix Direct Insurance Services (**http://matrixdirect.com**)

EXHIBIT 8.9 **Key Features of Various Types of Life Insurance**

Differences in the key features of various types of life insurance are listed here. It's important to compare both costs and features when shopping for life insurance.

Feature	Term	Whole Life	Universal Life
Death protection	High	Moderate	Low to high
Coverage period	Temporary for set period	Ongoing	Ongoing
Costs	Low fixed premiums, no fees	High fixed premiums; may also be charged fees	Can vary from high to low; may also be charged fees
Return on investment?	None	Yes, moderate	Yes; return can vary
Tax advantages	No	Yes	Yes

maintain databases of life insurance policy costs for various companies and will also act as your agent to buy the policy if you wish. Insure.com and Matrix Direct provide quotes for both term insurance and whole life. Also, don't overlook companies that sell directly to the public or offer low-load policies, such as Ameritas, Lincoln Benefit, and USAA (for the military and their families).

8-5b Select an Insurance Company

Selecting a life insurance company is an important part of shopping for life insurance. Besides looking for a firm that offers reasonably priced products, attractive contract features, and good customer service, it's vital to consider the financial health of any insurance firm before buying a life insurance policy. You want to be sure that the company will be around and have the assets to pay your beneficiaries should you die. Even before you die, however, your insurance company's financial stability is important. If the company fails, you may be forced to buy a new policy at less favorable rates.

The age and size of insurance companies are useful indicators in narrowing your choices. Unless there's a good reason to do otherwise, you should probably limit the companies you consider to those that have been doing business for 25 years or more and that have annual premium volume of more than $100 million. These criteria will rule out a lot of smaller firms, but there are still plenty of companies left to choose from. You may also find that one company is preferable for your term protection and another for your whole life needs.

Factors to consider before making the final choice include the firm's reputation, financial history, commissions and other fees, and the specifics of its policy provisions. If you're choosing a company for a cash value life insurance policy, the company's investment performance and dividend history is also an important consideration.

You Can Do It Now
Shop for a Customized Life Insurance Policy

Let's make life insurance more concrete and personal. You can easily get an insurance quote online. Go to the popular Internet site noted in this chapter, **http://www.insure .com/life-insurance/**, and provide the requested personal information. Then request a quote for, say, a 20-year, $200,000 term life insurance policy—you can do it now.

FINANCIAL PLANNING TIPS

Breezing through Your Life Insurance Medical Exam

You're more likely to pass your life insurance medical exam if you keep the following tips in mind:

• **Know what to expect.** The examiner will measure and record your height, weight, blood pressure, and pulse rate, and will collect blood and urine samples. Also, expect the examiner to confirm the answers that you provided on your life insurance application. The test results will be sent to the insurance company and the underwriter, which will assess your risk and determine your life insurance premiums.

• **Drink water before the exam.** This makes it easier to draw blood.

• **Fast before the exam.** Eating within four to eight hours before the exam could elevate your glucose levels.

• **Don't do a rigorous workout for at least 12 hours prior to the exam.** Take it easy, and avoid even a fast walk or a workout on an aerobic machine. Strenuous exercise before a physical can elevate the protein found in your urine to a point of concern.

• **Avoid alcohol for at least 12 hours before the exam.** Drinking too much alcohol can dehydrate you and possibly elevate liver function test flags, which can push you into a riskier category.

• **Avoid caffeine and nicotine for at least a couple of hours prior to the exam.** Caffeine and nicotine tend to elevate blood pressure. If you simply cannot make it without coffee, be sure to drink it black—no cream or sugar.

• **Bring a list of your medications.** Examiners typically take a medical history during the exam, which requires a list of your current prescriptions and over-the-counter medications.

• **Get to bed early the night before the exam.** While it might not directly affect your test results, you'll be more relaxed, and this should help moderate your blood pressure if you have "white coat anxiety."

Source: Adapted from Jeffrey Steele, "Ace Your Life Insurance Medical Exam," http://www.insurance.com/life-insurance/life-insurance-basics/life-insurance-medical-exam .aspx, accessed August 2015.

How do you find all of this information? Luckily, private rating agencies have done much of the work for you. The four most commonly used agencies are A. M. Best, Fitch, Moody's, and Standard & Poor's (see Exhibit 8-10). These agencies use publicly available financial data from insurance companies to analyze their debt structure, pricing practices, and management strategies in an effort to assess their financial stability. The purpose is to evaluate the insurance company's ability to pay future claims made by policyholders, which is known as its *claims paying ability*. In most cases, insurance firms pay ratings agencies a fee for this service. The ratings agencies then give each insurance firm a "grade" based on their analysis of the firm's financial data. Most public libraries and insurance agents have these ratings. Each rating firm has an Internet site where some insurance company ratings may also be found.

> **You Can Do It Now**
>
> *Check Out the Best Life Insurance Companies*
>
> The ratings of the best life insurance companies and an overall ranking, known as the Comdex rank, are provided online at **http://toplifeinsurancereviews.com/ comdex-ranking-life-insurance/**. Go to the site and jot down the top five life insurance companies. Now you have a great start when you are ready to shop for life insurance—you can do it now.

FINANCIAL PLANNING TIPS

Potential Conflicts of Interest in Dealing with Insurance Agents

Most insurance agents are ethical and professional. However, in order to help you identify the others and protect yourself from the few who are not, it's important to keep in mind some potential conflicts of interest between you and insurance agents and brokers. Most have to do with sales commission incentives that can conflict with you getting the best advice.

- Agents only rarely disclose their commissions—and likely will do so only if you ask. Ask agents about the commissions that they receive on competing insurance products. If they balk at the request, it's time to find another agent.

- Agents have an incentive to recommend policies that provide the greatest commissions. Alternatively stated, agents have no financial incentive to recommend policies that pay no commissions.

- Agents often avoid bringing up the negative aspects of a policy because they don't want to blow the sale. This also tempts some agents to oversimplify policy features. You need to ask the hard questions.

- While some existing policies should be kept and some replaced, agents only get paid for giving advice when it leads to commissions. So agents can be unreliable sources of advice about the performance of an existing policy. Getting a second opinion from an agent with another firm is always a good idea.

- Watch out when agents present company illustrations and projections of future policy performance. Don't accept the projections and assumptions uncritically.

- Be aware that some lawyers, accountants, and financial planners don't ask hard questions about life insurance proposals because they depend on life insurance agents for business referrals. Thus, it can be hard to find objective sources of advice concerning life insurance proposals. Consider using a fee-only insurance advisor.

Notwithstanding these potential conflicts of interest, you can accomplish a lot by doing your own homework and by relying on recommended advisors who are true fiduciaries who put their clients first.

Source: Life Insurance Advisors, Inc., "Conflicts and Limitations of Life Insurance Agents," http://www.lifeinsuranceadvisorsinc.com/conflicts.html, accessed August 2015.

Most experts agree that it's wise to purchase life insurance only from insurance companies that are assigned ratings by at least two of the major rating agencies and are consistently rated in the top two or three categories (e.g., Aaa, Aa1, or Aa2 by Moody's) by each of the major agencies from which they received ratings. The easiest way to comprehensively evaluate an insurance company is to rely on the Comdex ranking, which considers the ratings established by A. M. Best, Standard & Poor's, Moody's Investors Services, and Fitch. (See **http://www.ebixlife.com/vitalsigns/comdexcalc.aspx** for more information.)

Financial Fact or Fantasy?

Selecting an insurance company is the first thing you should do when buying life insurance. **Fantasy:** The first thing you should do is determine the amount of life insurance you need and then select the type of policy that is best for you. Only after you have taken these steps should you address where you will buy the insurance.

8-5c Choosing an Agent

There's an old axiom in the life insurance business that life insurance is sold, not bought. Life insurance agents play a major role in most people's decision to buy life insurance. Unless you plan to buy all of your life insurance via the Internet, selecting a good life insurance agent is important because you'll be relying on him or her for guidance in making some important financial decisions. Don't assume that just because agents are licensed, they are competent and will serve your best interests. Consider an agent's formal and professional level of educational attainment. Does the agent have a college degree with a major in business or insurance?

EXHIBIT 8.10 **Major Insurance Rating Agencies**

The three biggest insurance rating agencies are A. M. Best Company, Moody's Investor Services, and Standard & Poor's Corporation. A smaller (but growing) agency is Fitch Inc. Contact information for each of these agencies is given here.*

A.M. Best Company
Internet address: **http://www.ambest.com**
Top three grades: A++, A+, and A

Standard & Poor's Corporation
Internet address: **http://www.standardandpoors.com**
Top three grades: AAA, AA+, and AA

Moody's Investor Services
Internet address: **http://www.moodys.com**
Top three grades: Aaa, Aa1, and Aa2

Fitch Inc.
Internet address: **http://www.fitchratings.com**
Top three grades: AAA, AA+, and AA

*The Comdex ranking shows how an insurance company compares to other companies based on the ratings assigned by the above four agencies. Internet address: http://www.ebixlife.com/vitalsigns/comdexcalc.aspx.

CORBIS/JUPITER IMAGES

Does the agent have a professional designation, such as Chartered Life Underwriter (CLU), Chartered Financial Consultant (ChFC), or Certified Financial Planner® (CFP®)? These designations are awarded only to those who meet certain experience requirements and pass comprehensive examinations in such fields as life and health insurance, estate and pension planning, investments, and federal income tax law.

Observe how an agent reacts to your questions. Does the agent use fancy buzzwords and generic answers, or does she really listen attentively and, after some thought, logically answer your questions? These and other personal characteristics should be considered. In most cases, you should talk with several agents and discuss the pros and cons of each agent with your spouse or other trusted person before committing yourself. Then, when you've decided, call the agent again and finish your business.

When seeking a good life insurance agent, try to obtain recommendations from other professionals who work with agents. Bankers in trust departments, attorneys, and accountants who are specialists in estate planning are usually good sources. In contrast, be a bit wary of selecting an agent simply because of the agent's aggressiveness in soliciting your patronage.

TEST YOURSELF

8-17 Briefly describe the steps to take when you shop for and buy life insurance.

8-18 Briefly describe the insurance company ratings assigned by A. M. Best, Moody's, Fitch, Standard & Poor's, and Comdex. Why is it important to know how a company is rated? What ratings would you look for when selecting a life insurance company? Explain.

8-19 What characteristics would be most important to you when choosing an insurance agent?

8-6 KEY FEATURES OF LIFE INSURANCE POLICIES

When buying a life insurance policy, you are entering into a contract with the insurance company. The provisions in this contract spell out the policyholder's and the insurer's rights and obligations as well as the features of the policy being purchased. Unfortunately, there's no such thing as a standard life insurance policy. Each insurance company uses its own wording. Policies can also vary from state to state, depending on the law of the state where the policy is sold. Even so, certain elements are common in most life insurance contracts.

8-6a Life Insurance Contract Features

Key features found in most life insurance contracts are the beneficiary clause, settlement options, policy loans, premium payments, grace period, nonforfeiture options, policy reinstatement, and change of policy.

Beneficiary Clause

beneficiary
A person who receives the death benefits of a life insurance policy after the insured's death.

The beneficiary is the person who will receive the death benefits of the policy on the insured's death. All life insurance policies should have one or more beneficiaries. Otherwise, death benefits are paid to the deceased's estate and are subject to the often lengthy and expensive legal procedure of going through probate. An insured person is able to name both a *primary beneficiary* and various *contingent beneficiaries*. The primary beneficiary receives the entire death benefit if he or she is surviving when the insured dies. If the primary beneficiary does not survive the insured, then the insurer will distribute the death benefits to the contingent beneficiary or beneficiaries. If neither primary nor contingent beneficiaries are living at the death of the insured, then the death benefits pass to the estate of the insured and are distributed by the probate court according to the insured's will or, if no will exists, according to state law.

The identification of named beneficiaries should be clear. For example, a man could buy a policy and simply designate the beneficiary as "my wife." But if he later divorces and remarries, there could be a controversy as to which "wife" is entitled to the benefits. Obviously, you should consider changing your named beneficiary if circumstances, such as marital status, change. The person you name as a beneficiary can be changed at any time as long as you didn't indicate an *irrevocable beneficiary* when you took out the policy. Thus, if your wishes change, all you need to do is notify the insurance company—easy to do, but also easy to forget.

Settlement Options

Insurance companies generally offer several ways of paying life insurance policy death proceeds. How the insurance benefits will be distributed can either be permanently established by the policyholder before death or left up to the beneficiary when the policy proceeds are paid out.

- Lump sum: This is the most common settlement option, chosen by more than 95 percent of policyholders. The entire death benefit is paid in a single amount, allowing beneficiaries to use or invest the proceeds soon after death occurs.
- Interest only: The insurance company keeps policy proceeds for a specified time; the beneficiary receives interest payments, usually at some guaranteed rate. This option can be useful when there's no current need for the principal. For example, proceeds could be left on deposit until children go to college, with interest supplementing family income. Typically, however, interest rates paid by insurers are lower than those available with other savings vehicles.
- Fixed period: The face amount of the policy, along with interest earned, is paid to the beneficiary over a fixed time period. For example, a 55-year-old beneficiary may need additional income until Social Security benefits start.

- Fixed amount: The beneficiary receives policy proceeds in regular payments of a fixed amount until the proceeds run out.
- Life income: The insurer guarantees to pay the beneficiary a certain payment for the rest of his or her life, based on the beneficiary's sex, age when benefits start, life expectancy, policy face value, and interest rate assumptions. This option appeals to beneficiaries who don't want to outlive the income from policy proceeds and so become dependent on others for support. An interesting variation of this settlement option is the *life-income-with-period-certain option,* whereby the company guarantees a specified number of payments that would pass to a secondary beneficiary if the original beneficiary dies before the period ends.

Policy Loans

An advance made by a life insurance company to a policyholder against a whole life policy is called a policy loan. These loans are secured by the cash value of the life insurance policy. Although these loans do *not* have to be repaid, any balance plus interest on the loan remaining at the insured's death is *subtracted from the proceeds of the policy*. Typically policies offer either a fixed-rate loan or a rate that varies with market interest rates on high-quality bonds. Some policies let the insured choose whether the loans will be at fixed or variable rates. Take out a policy loan only if your estate is large enough to cover the accompanying loss of death proceeds when the loan is not repaid. Remember that life insurance is intended to provide basic financial protection for your dependents, and spending those proceeds prematurely defeats the purpose of life insurance. A word of caution: *Be careful with these loans; unless certain conditions are met, the IRS may treat them as withdrawals, meaning they could be subject to tax penalties*. If you're in any way unsure, consult your insurance agent or a tax advisor.

Premium Payments

All life insurance contracts have a provision specifying when premiums, which are normally paid in advance, are due. With most insurers, the policyholder may elect to pay premiums annually, semiannually, quarterly, or monthly. In most cases, insurance companies charge a fee if you decide to pay more often than annually.

Grace Period

The *grace period* permits the policyholder to retain full death protection for a short period (usually 31 days) after missing a premium payment date. In other words, you won't lose your insurance protection just because you're a little late in making the premium payment. If the insured dies during the grace period, the face amount of the policy less the unpaid premium is paid to the beneficiary.

Nonforfeiture Options

As discussed earlier, a *nonforfeiture option* gives a cash value life insurance policyholder some benefits even when a policy is terminated before its maturity. State laws require that all permanent whole, universal, or variable life policies (and term contracts covering an extended period) contain a nonforfeiture provision. Rather than taking a check in the amount of the policy's cash value, insurance companies usually offer the two options—*paid-up insurance* and *extended term insurance*—described here.

- Paid-up insurance: The policyholder receives a policy exactly like the terminated one, but with a lower face value. In effect, the policyholder uses the cash value to buy a new, single premium policy. For example, a policy canceled after 10 years might have a cash value of $90.84 per $1,000 of face value, which could be used to buy $236 of paid-up whole life insurance. This paid-up insurance is useful, as the cash value continues to grow because of future interest earnings, even though the policyholder makes no further premium payments. This option is useful when a person's income and need for death protection decline—when he or she reaches age 60 or 65, for example—yet that person still wants some coverage.

- **Extended term insurance:** The insured uses the accumulated cash value to buy a term life policy for the same face value as the lapsed policy. The coverage period is based on the amount of term protection a single premium payment (equal to the total cash value) buys at the insured's present age. This option usually goes into effect automatically if the policyholder quits paying premiums and gives no instructions to the insurer.

Policy Reinstatement

So long as a whole life policy is under the reduced paid-up insurance option or the extended term insurance option, the policyholder may reinstate the original policy by paying all back premiums plus interest at a stated rate and by providing evidence that he or she can pass a physical examination and meet any other insurability requirements. *Reinstatement* revives the original contractual relationship between the company and the policyholder. Most often, the policyholder must reinstate the policy within a specified period (three to five years) after the policy has lapsed. However, before exercising a reinstatement option, a policyholder should determine whether buying a new policy (from the same or a different company) might be less costly.

Change of Policy

Many life insurance contracts contain a provision that permits the insured to switch from one policy form to another. For instance, a policyholder may decide that he'd rather have a policy that is paid up at age 65 rather than his current continuous premium whole life policy. A change-of-policy provision would allow this change without penalty. When policyholders change from high- to lower-premium policies, they may need to prove insurability. This requirement reduces the insurance company's exposure to adverse selection.

8-6b Other Policy Features

Along with the key contractual features described earlier, here are some other policy features to consider:

- **Multiple indemnity clause:** Multiple indemnity clauses increase the face amount of the policy, most often doubling or tripling it, if the insured dies in an accident. This benefit is usually offered to the policyholder at a small additional cost. Many insurance authorities dismiss the use of a multiple indemnity benefit as irrational. This coverage should be ignored as a source of funds when determining insurance needs because it offers no protection if the insured's death is due to illness.

- **Disability clause:** A disability clause may contain a waiver-of-premium benefit alone or coupled with disability income. A *waiver-of-premium benefit* excuses the payment of premiums on the life insurance policy if the insured becomes totally and permanently disabled prior to age 60 (or sometimes age 65). Under the *disability income portion,* the insured not only is granted a waiver of premium but also receives a monthly income equal to $5 or $10 per $1,000 of policy face value. Some insurers will continue these payments for the life of the insured; others terminate them at age 65. Disability riders for a waiver of premium and disability income protection are relatively inexpensive and can be added to most whole life policies but generally not to term policies.

multiple indemnity clause
A clause in a life insurance policy that typically doubles or triples the policy's face amount if the insured dies in an accident.

disability clause
A clause in a life insurance contract containing a *waiver-of-premium benefit* alone or coupled with *disability income.*

Financial Fact or Fantasy?

Because most life insurance policies are largely the same, you need not concern yourself with differences in specific contract provisions. **Fantasy:** All insurance policies are not the same. Thus, it is important to familiarize yourself with the provisions of the contract, including the beneficiary clauses and settlement options.

guaranteed purchase option
An option in a life insurance contract giving the policyholder the right to purchase additional coverage at stipulated intervals without providing evidence of insurability.

- Guaranteed purchase option: The policyholder who has a guaranteed purchase option may purchase additional coverage at stipulated intervals without providing evidence of insurability. This option is frequently offered to buyers of a whole life policy who are under age 40. Increases in coverage usually can be purchased every three, four, or five years in sums equal to the amount of the original policy or $10,000, whichever is lower. This option should be attractive to individuals whose life insurance needs and ability to pay are expected to increase over a 5- to 15-year period.

- Suicide clause: Nearly all life insurance policies have a *suicide clause* that voids the contract if an insured commits suicide within a certain period, normally two years after the policy's inception. In these cases, the company simply returns the premiums that have been paid. If an insured commits suicide after this initial period has elapsed, the policy proceeds are paid regardless.

- Exclusions: Although all private insurance policies exclude some types of losses, life policies offer broad protection. Other than the suicide clause, the only common exclusions are aviation, war, and hazardous occupation or hobby. However, a company would rarely be able to modify the premium charged or coverage offered should the insured take up, say, Formula One racing or hang gliding *after* a policy is issued.

participating policy
A life insurance policy that pays *policy dividends* reflecting the difference between the premiums that are charged and the amount of premium necessary to fund the actual mortality experience of the company.

- Participation: In a participating policy, the policyholder is entitled to receive *policy dividends* reflecting the difference between the premiums that are charged and the amount of premium necessary to fund the actual mortality experience of the company. When the base premium schedule for participating policies is established, a company estimates what it believes its mortality and investment experience will be and then adds a generous margin of safety to these figures. The premiums charged the policyholder are based on these conservative estimates.

- Living benefits: Also called *accelerated benefits,* this feature allows the insured to receive a percentage of the death benefit from a whole or universal life policy prior to death. Some insurers offer this option at no charge to established policyholders if the insured suffers a terminal illness that is expected to result in death within a specified period (such as six months to a year) or needs an expensive treatment (such as an organ transplant) to survive. These benefits can also be added as a *living benefit rider* that pays a portion of a policy's death benefit in advance, usually about 2 percent per month, for long-term health care such as nursing home expenses. This rider can add an extra 5 percent to 15 percent to the normal life insurance premium, and benefits are capped at some fixed percentage of the death benefit.

- Viatical settlement: Like a living benefits feature, this option allows a terminally ill insurance holder to receive a percentage of the insurance policy's death benefit for immediate use. But unlike the living benefits feature, this isn't handled through the insurance company but rather through a third-party investor. The insured sells an interest in the life insurance policy to the investor, who then becomes the policy's beneficiary, and then receives a cash amount from that investor—most commonly 60 percent of the policy value. After the insured dies, the investor receives the balance from the policy. Approach viatical settlements carefully, because they mean giving up all future claims on the life insurance policy and can also affect a patient's Medicare eligibility in some cases. Note also that some viatical settlement companies—the firms that arrange the transfer between insureds and investors—have been scrutinized by government agencies for unethical practices.

8-6c Understanding Life Insurance Policy Illustrations

life insurance policy illustration
A hypothetical representation of a life insurance policy's performance that reflects the most important assumptions that the insurance company relies on when presenting the policy results to a prospective client.

A **life insurance policy illustration** is a hypothetical representation of a policy's performance that reflects the most important assumptions that the company relies on when presenting the policy results to a prospective client. Insurance illustrations are complicated and often contain more than 20 pages of numbers and legal disclaimers. The insurance illustration specifies the inflows from premiums paid and interest credits, both of which increase the cash value of the policy. The illustration also states mortality charges and expenses, both of which decrease the cash value. An illustration typically consists of two main parts:

- **Guaranteed illustration:** The insurance company is required by law to disclose the worst-case scenario, which shows the effects of the insurer crediting the minimum interest and charging the maximum amount based on standard mortality tables. It's safe to assume that the benefits, cash surrender value, and accumulated values will never be lower than what this scenario presents.
- **Current illustration:** This is the insurance company's representation of policy performance based on the credit rates and mortality charges *currently* in effect.

When you look at an insurance illustration, focus first on the basic assumptions that the company used to compute it, including your age, sex, and underwriting health status. As noted above, the illustration will indicate the premiums, cash surrender value, and death benefits. Double-check all the information. Ask the insurance agent to provide an *inforce reprojection* that shows any changes in credits or charges that the insurance company has declared for the next policy year. These changes in credits and charges will affect premiums or benefits. Most agents will not provide this unless you ask them. Watch for any unanticipated premium increases.

Check to make sure that all the following sections are present in the narrative summary of the illustration and that no pages are missing:

- **Policy description, terms, and features:** This section overviews the main components of the policy. Double-check that the policy's premiums and benefit projections match your needs.
- **Underwriting discussion:** This provides a detailed description of the policy's benefits, premiums, and tax information.
- **Column definitions and key terms:** This defines the terms used in the illustration. Make sure that you understand all the definitions and terms.
- **Disclaimer:** This section informs the prospective client that the illustration's portrayal of future values could vary from actual results.
- **Signature page:** This section provides a numerical summary of the illustration in 5- and 10-year increments. The insurance agent's signature here acknowledges that he or she has explained that the nonguaranteed elements are subject to change, and your signature acknowledges that you understand this.

TEST YOURSELF

8-20 What is a *beneficiary*? A *contingent beneficiary*? Explain why it's essential to designate a beneficiary for your policy.

8-21 Explain the basic settlement options available for the payment of life insurance proceeds upon a person's death.

8-22 What do *nonforfeiture options* accomplish? Differentiate between *paid-up insurance* and *extended term insurance*.

8-23 Explain the following clauses often found in life insurance policies: (a) *multiple indemnity clause*, (b) *disability clause*, and (c) *suicide clause*. Give some examples of common exclusions.

8-24 Describe what is meant by a *participating policy*, and explain the role of *policy dividends* in these policies.

8-25 Describe the key elements of an *insurance policy illustration* and explain what a prospective client should focus on in evaluating an illustration.

Planning Over a Lifetime: *Life Insurance*

Here are some key considerations for life insurance use in each stage of the life cycle.

Pre-family Independence: 20s	Family Formation/ Career Development: 30–45	Pre-Retirement: 45–65	Retirement: 65 and Beyond
✓ Term life insurance is needed only if you have dependents relying on you financially.	✓ If you marry, add life insurance to cover the financial needs of your spouse and other dependents.	✓ Re-evaluate insurance coverage if you change jobs or move to a higher-paying job.	✓ Assure adequate financial protection of your surviving spouse.
	✓ Consider increasing insurance coverage as additional children are born.	✓ Consider reducing insurance coverage as children leave home and graduate from college. More insurance coverage may be needed if you are supporting aging parents. Consider possible use of life insurance in estate planning, which is covered in detail in Chapter 15.	✓ Consider possible use of life insurance in estate planning, which is covered in detail in Chapter 15.
		✓ Evaluate the magnitude of your accumulated assets relative to needs of dependents. Insurance may no longer be needed or could be dramatically decreased.	✓ It may be possible to discontinue coverage for grown dependents. May need to maintain some life insurance to help dependents with special needs.

Financial Impact of Personal Choices

Matt and Jan Consider "Buying Term and Investing the Rest"

Matt and Jan Horton have two young children and believe it's time to buy a life insurance policy to protect their family. They've both heard the life insurance advice to "buy term and invest the rest." In order to evaluate this advice they've collected quotes for 20-year term and whole life policies on Matt, both with a payoff of $250,000. The whole life policy premium is $347 a month while the term policy premium is only $23 a month. In 20 years the whole life policy will have a guaranteed cash value of $70,018 but at current rates would be worth $105,721. The death benefit will have grown to $326,352. If the Hortons buy the term policy and invest the $324 difference in monthly premiums at 8% for 20 years, they could have a portfolio worth about $190,843! The Hortons wonder about the financial consequences of their decision.

It looks like buying term and investing the difference leaves the Hortons better off. Yet the financial consequences can only be fully evaluated in light of the Hortons' objectives and attitude towards risk. The whole life insurance policy provides a *guaranteed* cash value in 20 years while the invested difference produces a higher expected but *risky*, unguaranteed payoff. And the Hortons must consider whether they will have the discipline to keep "investing the difference" over the next 20 years. Once the whole life policy's cash value builds up, they could stop paying the premium by accepting some trade-offs in the value of the policy. And in 20 years the term life insurance coverage will go away, which might be fine if the kids are independent and the mortgage is paid off. In contrast, the Hortons could stop paying the whole life policy premiums then and accept a reduced paid-up amount of coverage.

The personal financial consequences of "buy term and invest the rest" suggest the advice may well work for the Hortons. But the best decision depends on their objectives, discipline, and attitude towards the risks of "investing the rest."

Source: Adapted from Chris Arnold, "Life Insurance: Is Buying Term and Investing the Difference Your Best Approach?" http://www.nerdwallet.com/blog/finance/advisorvoices/difference-term-life-insuranc/, accessed August 2015.

Summary

LG1 Explain the concept of risk and the basics of insurance underwriting. p. 301

Adequate life insurance coverage is vital to sound personal financial planning because it not only protects what you've already acquired but also helps ensure the attainment of unfulfilled financial goals. The whole notion of insurance is based on the concept of risk and the different methods of handling it, including risk avoidance, loss prevention and control, risk assumption, and insurance (a cost-effective procedure that allows families to reduce financial risks by sharing losses). Through the underwriting process, insurance companies decide whom they consider an acceptable risk and the premiums to charge for coverage.

LG2 Discuss the primary reasons for life insurance and identify those who need coverage. p. 303

Life insurance fills the gap between the financial resources available to your dependents if you should die prematurely and what they need to maintain a given lifestyle. Some policies provide only a death benefit; others also have a savings component. If you have children or elderly relatives who count on your income to support them, you should include life insurance as one of several financial resources to meet their requirements. If you have no dependents, you probably don't need life insurance. Your life insurance needs change over your life cycle and should be reviewed regularly.

LG3 Calculate how much life insurance you need. p. 305

There are several ways to determine the amount of life insurance a family should have. Although the multiple-of-earnings method is simple to use, most experts agree that the needs analysis method is the better procedure. It systematically considers such variables as family income, household and other expenses, special needs, final expenses, debt liquidation, and other financial needs, which are then compared with the financial resources available to meet these needs.

LG4   Distinguish among the various types of life insurance policies and describe their advantages and disadvantages. p. 311
The three basic types of life insurance policies are term life, whole life, and universal life. Term life insurance provides a stipulated amount of death benefits; whole life combines death benefits with a modest savings program; and universal life combines term insurance with a tax-sheltered savings/investment account that pays interest at competitive money market rates. Other types of life insurance include variable life, group life, credit life, mortgage life, and industrial life.

LG5   Choose the best life insurance policy for your needs at the lowest cost. p. 323
To get as much coverage as possible from your insurance dollar, it's important not only to compare costs but also to buy the proper amount of life insurance and pick the right type of insurance policy.

Beyond the cost and features of the insurance policy, carefully consider the financial stability of the insurer who offers it, paying special attention to the ratings assigned by major rating agencies. The Internet has become an excellent resource for comparison shopping. In addition to selecting a company, you must also choose an agent who understands your needs.

LG6   Become familiar with the key features of life insurance policies. p. 329
Some important contract features of life insurance policies you should become familiar with are the beneficiary clause, settlement options, policy loans, premium payments, grace period, nonforfeiture options, policy reinstatement, and change of policy. Other policy features include multiple indemnity and disability clauses, guaranteed purchase options, a suicide clause, exclusions, participation, living benefits, and viatical settlements. Life insurance policy illustrations provide insight into the assumptions relied on by an insurance company and the potential performance of the policy.

Key Terms

beneficiary, 329

cash value, 314

convertibility, 313

credit life insurance, 322

decreasing term policy, 313

disability clause, 331

group life insurance, 322

guaranteed purchase option, 332

industrial life insurance (home service life insurance), 322

insurance policy, 302

life insurance policy illustration, 332

loss control, 302

loss prevention, 302

mortgage life insurance, 322

multiple indemnity clause, 331

multiple-of-earnings method, 305

needs analysis method, 305

nonforfeiture right, 314

participating policy, 332

policy loan, 330

renewability, 313

risk assumption, 302

risk avoidance, 302

Social Security survivor's benefits, 308

straight term policy, 311

term life insurance, 311

underwriting, 302

universal life insurance, 319

variable life insurance, 321

whole life insurance, 314

Financial Planning Exercises

LG2, 3, 4, p. 303, 305, 311

1. ***Estimating life insurance needs. Use Worksheet 8.1.*** Katie Holt is a 72-year-old widow who has recently been diagnosed with Alzheimer's disease. She has limited financial assets of her own and has been living with her daughter Laurie for two years. Her income is only $850 a month in Social Security survivor's benefits. Laurie wants to make sure her mother will be taken care of if Laurie should die. Laurie, 40, is single and earns $55,000 a year as a human resources manager for a small manufacturing firm. She owns a condo with a current market value of $100,000 and has a $70,000 mortgage. Other debts include a $5,000 auto loan and $500 in various credit card balances. Her 401(k) plan has a current balance of $24,500, and she keeps $7,500 in a money market account for emergencies. After talking with her mother's doctor, Laurie believes that her mother will be able to continue living independently for another two to three years. She estimates that her mother would need about $2,000 a month to cover her living expenses and medical costs during this time. After that, Laurie's mother will probably need nursing home care. Laurie calls several local nursing homes and finds that it will cost about $5,000 a month when her mother enters a nursing home. Her mother's doctor says it is difficult to estimate her mother's life expectancy but indicates that with proper care some Alzheimer's patients can live 10 or more years after diagnosis. Laurie also estimates that her personal final expenses would be around $5,000, and she'd like to provide a $25,000 contingency fund that would be used to pay a trusted friend to supervise her mother's care if Laurie were no longer alive. Use Worksheet 8.1 to calculate Laurie's total life insurance requirements and recommend the type of policy that she should buy.

LG2, 3, p. 303, 305

2. ***Deciding if life insurance is needed. Use Worksheet 8.1.*** Given your current personal financial situation, do you feel you need life insurance coverage? Why or why not? Use Worksheet 8.1 to confirm your answer and calculate how much additional insurance (if any) you might need to purchase.

LG2, 3, 4, p. 303, 305, 311

3. ***Deciding if additional life insurance is needed and, if so, appropriate type.*** Use Worksheet 8.1. Rudy Steele, 43, is a recently divorced father of two children, ages 9 and 7. He currently earns $95,000 a year as an operations manager for a utility company. The divorce settlement requires him to pay $1,500 a month in child support and $400 a month in alimony to his ex-wife, who currently earns $35,000 annually as a preschool teacher. Rudy is now renting an apartment, and the divorce settlement left him with about $100,000 in savings and retirement benefits. His employer provides a $75,000 life insurance policy. Rudy's ex-wife is currently the beneficiary listed on the policy. What advice would you give to Rudy? What factors should he consider in deciding whether to buy additional life insurance at this point in his life? If he does need additional life insurance, what type of policy or policies should he buy? Use Worksheet 8.1 to help answer these questions for Rudy.

LG4, p. 311

4. ***Life insurance premiums and comparison of types.*** Using the premium schedules provided in Exhibits 8.2, 8.3, and 8.5, how much in *annual* premiums would a 25-year-old male have to pay for $100,000 of annual renewable term, level premium term, and whole life insurance? (Assume a five-year term or period of coverage.) How much would a 25-year-old woman have to pay for the same coverage? Consider a 40-year-old male (or female): Using annual premiums, compare the cost of 10 years of coverage under annual renewable and level premium term options and whole life insurance coverage. Relate the advantages and disadvantages of each policy type to their price differences.

LG2, 3, 4, 5,
p. 303, 305,
311, 323

5. ***Appropriateness of whole life insurance.*** Ramona and Pablo Valdez are a dual-career couple who just had their first child. Pablo, age 29, already has a group life insurance policy, but Ramona's employer does not offer a life insurance benefit. A financial planner is recommending that the 25-year-old Ramona buy a $250,000 whole life policy with an annual premium of $1,670 (the policy has an assumed rate of earnings of 5 percent a year). Help Ramona evaluate this advice and decide on an appropriate course of action.

LG2, 3, 4, 6,
p. 303, 305,
311, 329

6. ***Appropriateness of variable life insurance.*** While at lunch with a group of coworkers, one of your friends mentions that he plans to buy a variable life insurance policy because it provides a good annual return and is a good way to build savings for his 5-year-old's college education. Another colleague says that she's adding coverage through the group plan's additional insurance option. What advice would you give them?

Applying Personal Finance

Insure Your Life!

Providing for our loved ones in the event of our death is a serious concern for most of us. The problem is that planning for such an event is not pleasant, and most of us would just as soon put off thinking about it. This project will help you determine your current and future life insurance needs.

Life insurance can be put in place to provide income for your family, educate your children, or pay off debt. Life insurance can also be used in estate planning or to benefit a cause that's important to you. Make a list of your present life insurance needs and another list of what you expect your needs to be 10 years down the road. Estimate the dollar amount for each of your needs. Use Worksheet 8.1 to determine the amount of life insurance you need now and in the future. Consider the features of different types of life insurance. Which type of life insurance would be most appropriate for you? What would the cost be to provide these amounts of life insurance? You may use the premium schedules in this chapter or obtain actual quotes from an agent or the Internet. Use these estimates to help you with your personal financial planning.

CRITICAL THINKING CASES

LG3, 4, 5,
p. 305, 311,
323

8.1 Jun Hsieh's Insurance Decision: Whole Life, Variable Life, or Term Life?

Jun Hsieh, a 38-year-old widowed mother of three children (ages 12, 10, and 4), works as a product analyst for Panama Hats. Although she's covered by a group life insurance policy at work, she feels, based on some rough calculations, that she needs additional protection. Phil Griffin, an insurance agent from Safety First Insurance, has been trying to persuade Jun to buy a $150,000, 25-year, limited payment whole life policy. However, Jun favors a variable life policy. To further complicate matters, Jun's father feels that term life insurance is more suitable to the needs of her young family.

Critical Thinking Questions

1. Explain to Jun the differences between (a) a whole life policy, (b) a variable life policy, and (c) a term life policy.
2. What are the major advantages and disadvantages of each type of policy?
3. In what way is a whole life policy superior to either a variable life or term life policy? In what way is a variable life policy superior? How about term life insurance?
4. Given the limited information in the case, which type of policy would you recommend for Ms. Hsieh? Defend and explain your recommendations.

8.2 The Jennings Want to Know: How Much Is Enough?

Darrell and Lena Jennings are a two-income couple in their early 30s. They have two children, ages 6 and 3. Darrell's monthly take-home pay is $3,600, and Lena's is $4,200. The Jennings feel that, because they're a two-income family, they both should have adequate life insurance coverage. Accordingly, they are now trying to decide how much *life insurance each one of them* needs.

To begin with, they'd like to set up an education fund for their children in the amount of $120,000 to provide college funds of $15,000 a year—in today's dollars—for four years for each child. Moreover, if either spouse should die, they want the surviving spouse to have the funds to pay off all outstanding debts, including the $210,000 mortgage on their house. They estimate that they have $25,000 in consumer installment loans and credit cards. They also project that if either of them dies, the other probably will be left with about $10,000 in final estate and burial expenses.

Regarding their annual income needs, Darrell and Lena both feel strongly that each should have enough insurance to replace her or his respective current income level until the youngest child turns 18 (a period of 15 years). Although neither Darrell nor Lena would be eligible for Social Security survivor's benefits because they both intend to continue working, both children would qualify in the (combined) amount of around $1,800 a month. The Jennings have accumulated about $75,000 in investments, and they have a decreasing term life policy on each other in the amount of $100,000, which could be used to partially pay off the mortgage. Darrell also has an $80,000 group life insurance policy at work and Lena a $100,000 group life insurance policy.

Critical Thinking Questions

1. Assume that Darrell's gross annual income is $54,000 and Lena's is $64,000. Their insurance agent has given them a multiple earnings table showing that the earnings multiple to replace 75 percent of their lost earnings is 8.7 for Darrell and 7.4 for Lena. Use this approach to find the amount of life insurance each should have if they want to replace 75 percent of their lost earnings.

2. Use Worksheet 8.1 to find the additional insurance needed on both Darrell's and Lena's lives. (Because Darrell and Lena hold secure, well-paying jobs, both agree that they won't need any additional help once the kids are grown; both also agree that they'll have plenty of income from Social Security and company pension benefits to take care of themselves in retirement. Thus, when preparing the worksheet, assume "funding needs" of zero in Periods 2 and 3.)

3. Is there a difference in your answers to Questions 1 and 2? If so, why? Which number do you think is more indicative of the Jennings' life insurance needs? Using the amounts computed in Question 2 (employing the needs approach), what kind of life insurance policy would you recommend for Darrell? For Lena? Briefly explain your answers.

CHAPTER 9

Insuring Your Health

LEARNING GOALS

LG1 Discuss why having adequate health insurance is important and identify the factors contributing to the growing cost of health insurance.

LG2 Differentiate among the major types of health insurance plans and identify major private and public health insurance providers and their programs.

LG3 Analyze your own health insurance needs and explain how to shop for appropriate coverage.

LG4 Explain the basic types of medical expenses covered by and the policy provisions of health insurance plans.

LG5 Assess the need for and features of long-term-care insurance.

LG6 Discuss the features of disability income insurance and how to determine your need for it.

How Will This Affect Me?

Having adequate health insurance is critically important to your financial plan. Health care costs have grown dramatically in recent years, and a major illness or accident could wipe you and your family out financially if you are uninsured. Yet health insurance policies are complicated to price and to compare. This chapter explains the importance of health insurance and the key determinants of its costs. The various types of public and private health insurance are described and a framework for decision making is provided. This includes discussions of how to analyze your health insurance needs, how to make sense of common policy features, and policy buying tips. The implications of the Patient Protection and Affordable Care Act of 2010 are considered. This chapter also discusses how to determine whether you need long-term care insurance or disability income insurance. After reading this chapter, you should understand how to insure your health most effectively and economically.

Financial Facts or Fantasies?

Are the following statements Financial Facts (true) or Fantasies (false)? Consider the answers to the questions below as you read through this chapter.

- Health care insurance coverage should be viewed as an essential component of your personal financial plans.
- The difference between a health maintenance organization (HMO) and a preferred provider organization (PPO) is that the HMO offers a wider range of choices of physicians, hospitals, and related services.
- With health care insurance that covers the whole family, children may be included up to age 26 as long as they are full-time students.
- Health reimbursement accounts (HRAs) and health savings accounts (HSAs) are both funded by employers to help their employees cover health-related costs—and any unused money is the employee's to keep.
- Hospital insurance is the most comprehensive type of medical insurance you can buy.
- Disability insurance is helpful only if you make a lot of money—and then only if you are out of work for a long period of time (at least six months to a year).
- The cost of coverage and the quality of the agent and insurance company are two important variables to consider when shopping for health care insurance.

9-1 THE IMPORTANCE OF HEALTH INSURANCE COVERAGE

The next best thing to good health is probably a good health insurance plan. In recent years, the price of medical treatment has risen dramatically. As a result, a serious illness or accident can involve not only physical pain from sickness and injury, but also economic pain. A major illness can easily cost tens (or even hundreds) of thousands of dollars once you consider hospitalization and medical expenses and the loss of income while you recover. Even routine medical care, such as doctors' office visits and health care screenings, can add up quickly. Health insurance helps you pay for the costs associated with both routine and major medical care so that your financial accomplishments and plans are not seriously damaged or even destroyed. Indeed, about 62 percent of all U.S. personal bankruptcies are due, at least in part, to medical costs.

Despite the financial importance of health insurance, many Americans remain underinsured or uninsured. About 13 percent of the population doesn't have health insurance. And about 6.5 percent of children are without health insurance. Exhibit 9.1 helps explain why so many are uninsured: health insurance premiums have skyrocketed between 1999 and 2014. The average annual premium for families has increased by about 290 percent! In 2014, the average annual premium was $6,025 for single coverage and $16,834 for family coverage. The average percentage of health care premiums paid by covered workers is 29 percent for family plans.

Costly advances in medical technology, an aging U.S. population, and a poor demand-and-supply distribution of health care facilities and services have fueled rapidly rising health care costs. In addition, administrative costs, excessive paperwork, increased regulation, and insurance fraud are contributing to rising health care costs.

Concerns over health care costs and the number of uninsured Americans has made health care reform a major priority of Congress and the administration. Policy

solutions concerning the proper mix between government-run and privately run health insurance programs continue to prompt vigorous debate even after the passage of the Patient Protection and Affordable Care Act and the Reconciliation Act of 2010, which is discussed in detail below. The high cost of public health insurance, the desire by most to preserve patient choices, and the effects of reform on competition make this issue as contentious as it is important. Becoming familiar with current health insurance options and the issues associated with the new legislation should help you make better decisions, as well as provide a useful perspective on the health care reform debate and how it could affect you.

| EXHIBIT 9.1 | Average Annual Health Insurance Premiums for Single and Family Coverage, 1999–2014 |

As the chart shows, health insurance premiums have risen dramatically in recent years.

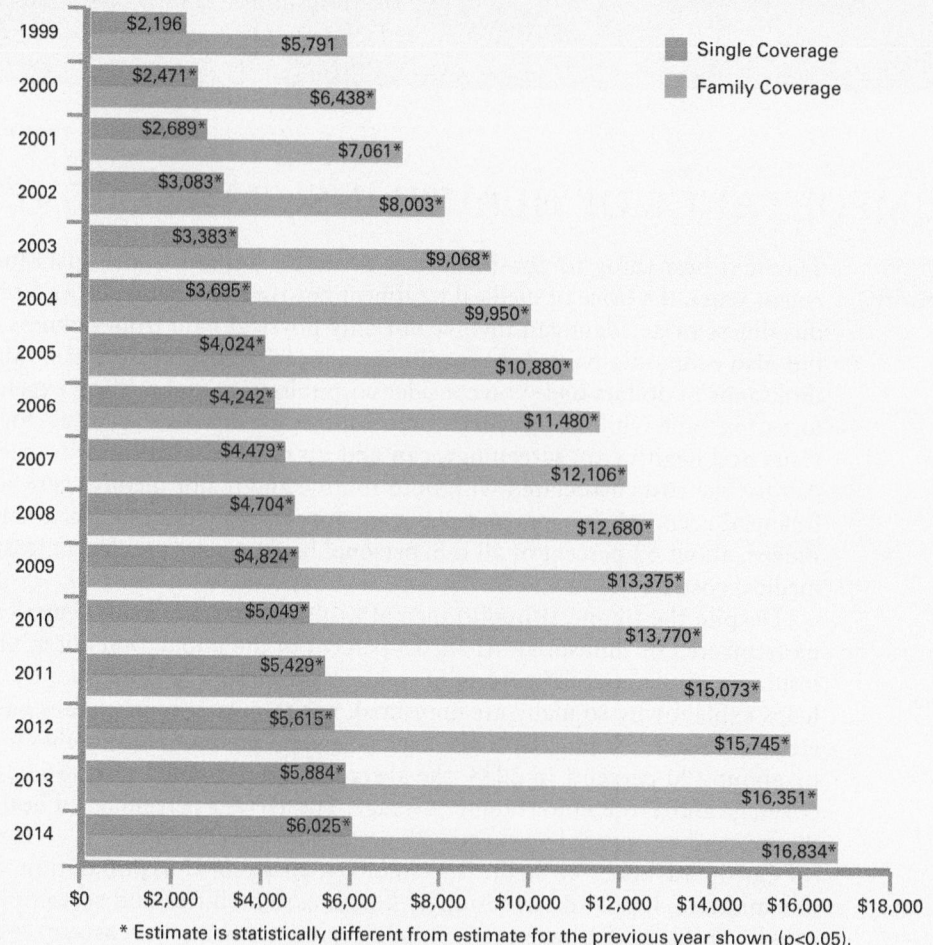

* Estimate is statistically different from estimate for the previous year shown (p<0.05).

Source: Kaiser/HRET Survey of Employer-Sponsored Health Benefits, 1999–2014.

TEST YOURSELF

9-1 Why should health insurance planning be included in your personal financial plan?

9-2 What factors have contributed to today's high costs of health care and health insurance?

9-2 HEALTH INSURANCE PLANS

Health insurance coverage is available from two main sources: private and government-sponsored programs. Regardless of the source of the plan, the Patient Protection and Affordable Care Act has significantly affected the expenses covered, the method of purchasing the plan, and the related taxes. In recent years, 28 percent of national health care expenditures were paid for by households, private businesses paid 21 percent, state and local governments paid 16 percent, the federal government paid 27 percent, and the rest was presumably paid by the self-insured.

9-2a Private Health Insurance Plans

group health insurance
Health insurance consisting of contracts written between a group (employer, union, etc.) and the health care provider.

Private companies sell a variety of health insurance plans to both groups and individuals. **Group health insurance** refers to health insurance contracts written between a group (such as an employer, union, credit union, or other organization) and the health care provider: a private insurance company, Blue Cross/Blue Shield plan, or a managed care organization. Typically, group plans provide comprehensive medical expense coverage and may also offer prescription drug, dental, and vision care service. The coverage provided by any given plan is subject to negotiation between the group and the insurer, and the group may offer several options for health insurance coverage.

If you work for an employer that has more than just a few employees, you'll probably have access to some type of group health plan. To control rising costs, many employers no longer provide universal coverage but merely underwrite employee applications, much as insurers do. Employers are also shifting a larger percentage of the cost to employees. As a result, you may want to compare group and individual policies before deciding which coverage to buy.

Most private health insurance plans fall into one of two categories: traditional *indemnity (fee-for-service) plans* and *managed care plans,* which include health maintenance organizations (HMOs), preferred provider organizations (PPOs), and similar plans. Both types of plans provide financial aid for the cost of medical care arising from illness or accidents, but they do so in somewhat different ways. Exhibit 9.2 compares some features of the three most common types of health plans.

Traditional Indemnity (Fee-for-Service) Plans

indemnity (fee-for-service) plan
A health insurance plan in which the health care provider is separate from the insurer, who pays the provider or reimburses you for a specified percentage of expenses after a deductible amount has been met.

With a traditional **indemnity (fee-for-service) plan**, the person or organization from which you obtain health care services is separate from your insurer. Your insurer either pays the health service provider directly or reimburses your expenses when you submit claims for medical treatment. Typically, indemnity plans pay 80 percent of the eligible health care expenses and the insured pays the other 20 percent. The health insurance company will begin paying its share after you pay a deductible amount of expenses. The deductible can range from $100 to over $2,000. The lower your deductible, the higher your premium.

The amount the insurance company pays is commonly based on the usual, customary, and reasonable (UCR) charges—what the insurer considers to be the prevailing fees within your area, not what your doctor or hospital actually charges. If your doctor charges more than the UCR, you may be responsible for the full amount

FINANCIAL PLANNING TIPS

Student Health Care Insurance in the New Era

Active students have a high injury rate, and viruses often move quickly through college campuses and dorms. It is essential to be insured, even when you are young and think you're healthy. No one knows when an expensive medical procedure may be required. For these reasons, colleges often require students to have health insurance. Under the new ACA, many parents can meet that requirement by keeping their children on their health insurance plan until the age of 26 (and this actually applies whether they are in school or not). Here are some key trends and issues to consider in arranging student health care insurance:

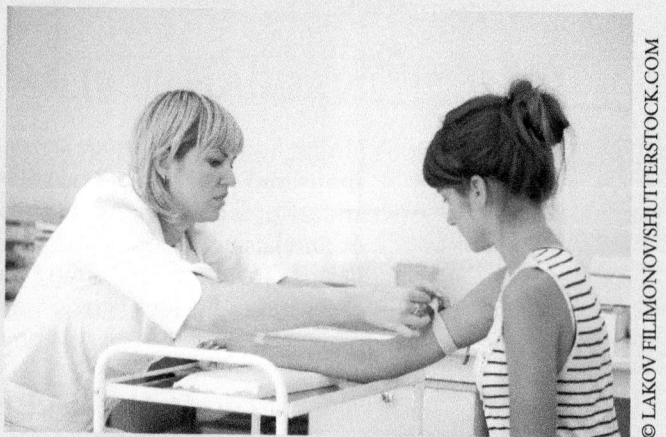

© LAKOV FILIMONOV/SHUTTERSTOCK.COM

- **Escalating costs.** The ACA requires students to have a level of coverage that exceeds the plans historically offered by most colleges. Consequently, premiums are rising by several hundred dollars a year, to around $2,000 per student currently. Indeed, some colleges are dropping student health insurance plans due to their higher costs. Students who are not covered under their parents' health care plan should consider buying an individual health insurance plan. You can compare prices and coverage using an Internet provider like **http://www.eHealthInsurance.com** or **http://www.StudentHealthPlan.com**.

- **Network coverage.** If you are a student relying on your parents' policy, be careful if your college is in another state. Make sure that your plan's network of preferred doctors and hospitals extends there. If not, the highest level of coverage may not be available.

- **Parent policy choices.** Parents should choose a family plan that covers their children for all medical emergencies and associated care. Most plans have basic out-of-state coverage for children. However, if out-of-state coverage is limited, as noted above, consider a high-deductible student health plan. It makes sense for students to return home for all routine care and prescriptions.

- **Good effects of the new law.** The ACA may make some student health plans more appealing. It prohibits all plans from having "lifetime coverage limits" that could put a cap on the maximum coverage in the case of a serious illness or accident. The new law also prohibits insurers from excluding students under 19 for pre-existing conditions.

Source: Adapted from Quentin Fottrell, "How to Save on College Health Care," http://blogs.smartmoney.com/advice/2012/06/04/ how-to-save-on-college-health-care, accessed August 2015.

EXHIBIT 9.2   **How the Most Common Types of Health Plans Compare**

This table highlights some of the key differences among the three most common types of health plans.

Type	Choice of Service Providers	Premium Cost	Out-of-Pocket Costs	Annual Deductible
Indemnity	Yes	Low if high-deductible plan, high if low-deductible plan	Usually 20% of medical expenses plus deductible	Yes
HMO	No	Low	Low co-pay	No
PPO	Some	Higher than HMO	Low if using network providers, higher if provider is outside the network	No

of the excess. UCR charges vary significantly among insurers, so you should compare your doctor's fees with what a plan pays. Many carriers offer indemnity plans wherein physicians who accept the insurance agree to accept the UCR payments set by the insurer. However, it should be noted that there are few indemnity plans left in the United States.

Managed Care Plans

Today, employers are moving away from traditional indemnity plans and adopting managed care plans. In a managed care plan, subscribers/users contract with and make monthly payments directly to the organization that provides the health care service. An insurance company may not even be involved, although today most major health insurance companies offer both indemnity and managed care plans. Managed care plan members receive comprehensive health care services from a designated group of doctors, hospitals, and other providers who must meet the managed care provider's specific selection standards.

With a managed care plan, the insured pays no deductibles and only a small fee, or co-payment, for office visits and medications. Most medical services—including preventive and routine care that indemnity plans may not cover—are fully covered when obtained from plan providers. Managed care plans include HMOs and PPOs (as already mentioned), exclusive provider organizations (EPOs), and point-of-service (POS) plans.

Health Maintenance Organizations. A health maintenance organization (HMO) is an organization of hospitals, physicians, and other health care providers who have joined to provide comprehensive health care services to its members. As an HMO member, you pay a monthly fee that varies according to the number of people in your family. You may also pay a co-payment typically of $5 to $40 each time that you use some of the services provided by the HMO or fill a prescription. The services provided to HMO members include doctors' office visits, imaging and laboratory services, preventive care, health screenings, hospital inpatient care and surgery, maternity care, mental health care, and drug prescriptions. The advantages of HMO membership include a lack of deductibles, few or no exclusions, and not having to file insurance claims. In the past, the primary disadvantage was that HMO members couldn't always choose their physicians and may have faced limitations if they needed care outside of the geographic area of their HMO. However, in recent years, many HMOs don't require members to pick one primary care physician, some don't require referrals, and almost all offer some flexibility to get out-of-network coverage.

There are two main types of HMOs: group and individual practice associations. A group HMO employs a group of doctors to provide health care services to members *from a central facility*. Group HMO members obtain medical care from the doctors and other medical personnel who practice there. Often, the group HMO's hospital facilities are located in the same building. Group HMOs are most prevalent in larger cities.

An individual practice association (IPA) is the most popular type of HMO. IPA members receive medical care from individual physicians practicing *from their own offices and from community hospitals* that are affiliated with the IPA. As a member of an IPA, you have some choice of which doctors and hospitals to use.

Preferred Provider Organizations. A preferred provider organization (PPO) is a managed care plan that has the characteristics of both an IPA and an indemnity plan. An insurance company or provider group contracts with a network of physicians and hospitals that agree to accept a negotiated fee for medical services provided to the PPO customers. Unlike the HMO, however, a PPO also provides insurance coverage for medical services not provided by the PPO network, so you can choose to go to other doctors or hospitals. However, you will pay a higher price for medical services provided by out-of-network doctors and hospitals.

---

managed care plan
A health care plan in which subscribers/users contract with the provider organization, which uses a designated group of providers meeting specific selection standards to furnish health care services for a monthly fee.

health maintenance organization (HMO)
An organization of hospitals, physicians, and other health care providers that have joined to provide comprehensive health care services to its members, who pay a monthly fee.

group HMO
An HMO that provides health care services *from a central facility*; most prevalent in larger cities.

individual practice association (IPA)
A form of HMO in which subscribers receive services from physicians practicing *from their own offices and from community hospitals* affiliated with the IPA.

preferred provider organization (PPO)
A health provider that combines the characteristics of the IPA form of HMO with an indemnity plan to provide comprehensive health care services to its subscribers within a network of physicians and hospitals.

exclusive provider organization (EPO)
A managed care plan that is similar to a PPO but reimburses members only when affiliated providers are used.

point-of-service (POS) plan
A hybrid form of HMO that allows members to go outside the HMO network for care and reimburses them at a specified percentage of the cost.

Other Managed Care Plans. Besides the plans just described, you may encounter two other forms of managed care plans. An exclusive provider organization (EPO) contracts with medical providers to offer services to members at reduced costs, but it reimburses members only when affiliated providers are used. Plan members who use a nonaffiliated provider must bear the entire cost. The point-of-service (POS) plan is a hybrid form of HMO that allows members to go outside of the HMO network for care. Payment for nonaffiliated physician services is similar to indemnity plan payments: the plan pays a specified percentage of the cost after your medical costs reach an annual deductible.

Blue Cross/Blue Shield Plans

In a technical sense, Blue Cross/Blue Shield plans are not insurance policies, but rather are prepaid hospital and medical expense plans. Today, there are about 38 independent local Blue Cross/Blue Shield organizations, all of them for-profit corporations, which collectively cover over 105 million people.

Blue Cross contracts with hospitals that agree to provide specified hospital services to members of groups covered by Blue Cross in exchange for a specified fee or payment. Blue Cross also contracts for surgical and medical services. Blue Cross serves as the intermediary between the groups that want these services and the physicians who contractually agree to provide them. Today, many Blue Cross and Blue Shield plans have combined to form one provider, and they compete for business with other private insurance companies. Because Blue Cross/Blue Shield is a producer cooperative, payments for health care services are seldom made to the subscriber but rather directly to the participating hospital or physician.

Financial Fact or Fantasy?

The difference between a health maintenance organization (HMO) and a preferred provider organization (PPO) is that the HMO offers a wider range of choices of physicians, hospitals, and so forth. **Fantasy:** One of the drawbacks of an HMO is that it is common to be treated at its central facility and by its own doctors. More options are, however, being offered. In a PPO, on the other hand, there are typically more opportunities to choose your health care providers from a network of designated physicians and hospitals.

Blue Cross/Blue Shield plans
Prepaid hospital and medical expense plans under which health care services are provided to plan participants by member hospitals and physicians.

Medicare
A health insurance plan administered by the federal government to help persons age 65 and over, and others receiving monthly Social Security disability benefits, to meet their health care costs.

9-2b Government Health Insurance Plans

In addition to health insurance coverage provided by private sources, federal and state agencies provide health care coverage to eligible individuals. About 34 percent of the U.S. population is covered by some form of government health insurance program. For example, prior to the implementation of the ACA, the government offered the Pre-Existing Condition Insurance Plan (PCIP), which provided health coverage to U.S. citizens or others residing in the United States legally who have been denied health insurance because of a pre-existing condition, so long as the person has been uninsured for at least six months. The program was administered by both the states and by the federal government. In addition, some states provide health insurance for children who do not qualify for Medicaid (discussed later), but whose family still has very low income.

Medicare

Medicare is a health insurance program administered under the Social Security Administration. It's primarily designed to help persons 65 and over meet their health care costs, but it also covers many people under 65 who receive monthly Social Security disability benefits. Funds for Medicare benefits come from Social Security taxes paid by covered workers and their employers. Traditionally, Medicare has provided two primary health care components, basic hospital insurance and supplementary medical insurance as well as prescription drug coverage.

- Basic hospital insurance: This coverage (commonly called *Part A*) provides inpatient hospital services such as room, board, and other customary inpatient service for the first 90 days of illness. A deductible is applied during the first 60 days of illness. Co-insurance provisions, applicable to days 61–90 of the hospital stay, can further reduce benefits. Medicare also covers all or part of the cost of up to 100 days in post-hospital extended-care facilities that provide skilled care, such as nursing homes. However, it doesn't cover the most common types of nursing home care—intermediate and custodial care. Medicare basic hospital insurance also covers some post-hospital medical services, such as intermittent nursing care, therapy, rehabilitation, and home health care. Medicare deductibles and co-insurance amounts are revised annually to reflect changing medical costs.

supplementary medical insurance (SMI)
A voluntary program under Medicare (commonly called *Part B*) that provides payments for services not covered under basic hospital insurance (*Part A*).

- **Supplementary medical insurance:** The **supplementary medical insurance (SMI)** program (commonly called *Part B*) covers the services of physicians and surgeons in addition to the costs of medical and health services such as imaging, laboratory tests, prosthetic devices, rental of medical equipment, and ambulance transportation. It also covers some home health services (such as in-home visits by a registered nurse) and limited psychiatric care. Unlike the basic Medicare hospital plan, SMI is a *voluntary program* for which participants pay premiums, which are then matched with government funds. Anyone age 65 or over can enroll in SMI.

Medicare Advantage plans
Commonly called *Plan C*, these plans provide Medicare benefits to eligible people, but they differ in that they are administered by private providers rather than by the government. Common supplemental benefits include vision, hearing, dental, general checkups, and health and wellness programs.

- **Medicare Advantage plans:** Medicare Advantage (commonly called *Plan C*) plans provide Medicare benefits to eligible people, but they differ in that they are administered by private providers rather than by the government. Common supplemental benefits include vision, hearing, dental, general checkups, and health and wellness programs. These supplemental benefits are a major reason for interest in these plans. Medicare pays the private health plan a fixed amount every month for each member. The members may pay a monthly premium in addition to the Medicare Part B premium. However, many of the private providers don't charge a premium beyond the Medicare Part B premium, which the member pays directly to Medicare. Members usually pay a fixed amount (e.g., a co-payment of $30), every time they visit a doctor, rather than pay a deductible and buy co-insurance (typically 20 percent) under original Medicare. Private plans may use some of the excess payments that they receive from the government to offer supplemental benefits. Most of the plans also include Medicare prescription drug coverage, discussed next. Because Medicare Advantage plans cost the federal government more than standard Medicare, the subsidies paid to these plans will start to decline under the ACA, which may lead to higher premiums or reduced benefits. However, the benefits cannot be reduced if they could normally be received from standard Medicare.

prescription drug coverage
A voluntary program under Medicare (commonly called *Part D*), insurance that covers both brand-name and generic prescription drugs at participating pharmacies. Participants pay a monthly fee and a yearly deductible and must also pay part of the cost of prescriptions, including a co-payment or co-insurance.

- **Prescription drug coverage:** The **prescription drug coverage** program (commonly called *Part D*) is insurance covering both brand-name and generic prescription drugs at participating pharmacies. It's intended to provide protection for people who have very high drug costs. All Medicare recipients are eligible for this coverage, regardless of their income and resources, health status, or existing prescription expenses. There are several ways to obtain this coverage. Participants in this *voluntary program* pay a monthly fee and a yearly deductible, which vary by provider. In 2015, the national monthly fee was based on income and was the overall plan premium plus no more than $70.80. The average monthly premium was $33.13 and most plans had a deductible of $320. They also pay part of the cost of prescriptions, including a co-payment or co-insurance. The plan provides extra help—paying almost all prescription drug costs—for the 1 in 3 Medicare recipients who have limited income and resources.

Although Medicare pays for many health care expenses for the disabled and those over 65, there are still gaps in its coverage. Many Medicare enrollees buy private insurance policies to fill in these gaps.

Medicaid

Medicaid
A state-run public assistance program that provides health insurance benefits only to those who are unable to pay for health care.

Medicaid is a state-run public assistance program that provides health insurance benefits only to those who are unable to pay for health care. Each state has its own regulations about who is eligible for Medicaid coverage and the types of medical services that are covered. Although Medicaid is primarily funded by each state, the federal government also contributes funds. More than 65 million people are covered by Medicaid.

Workers' Compensation Insurance

Workers' compensation insurance is designed to compensate workers who are injured on the job or become ill through work-related causes. Although mandated by the federal government, each state is responsible for setting workers' compensation legislation and regulating its own program. Specifics vary from state to state, but typical workers' compensation benefits include medical and rehabilitation expenses, disability income, and scheduled lump-sum amounts for death and certain injuries, such as dismemberment. Employers bear nearly the entire cost of workers' compensation insurance in most states. Premiums are based on historical usage; employers who file the most claims pay the highest rates. Self-employed people are required to contribute to workers' compensation for themselves and their employees.

9-2c Rationale for Health Care Reform

The goal of health care reform is to provide more people access to needed services at affordable rates. Before considering the implications of the ACA, it's important to understand the problems in the U.S. health care system that prompted the development of the new legislation.

Historical cost-benefit analysis reveals that the U.S. health care system looks pretty anemic. The U.S. economy spends about 17 cents of every dollar on health care, which is about twice the average for other rich economies. And what do we get in return? Outcomes for infant mortality, life expectancy, and heart attack survival rates are all worse than the average for members of the Organization for Economic Cooperation and Development (OECD). And, about 41 million citizens were not covered by health insurance as recently as 2013.

Health care in the United States has been more expensive because of two significant economic distortions. First, the cost of employer-provided health care insurance is tax-deductible. This has encouraged overly generous programs in which the true costs are hard to determine. The tax deductibility of health care programs is estimated to cost the government at least $250 billion annually. Second, most U.S. physicians are compensated on a fee-for-service basis. This creates an incentive for excessive health care expenses that do not always lead to better outcomes. Although this problem is not unique to the United States, it is thought to be worse there than in any other rich country. Reducing unnecessarily expensive procedures and prescriptions could save from 10 percent to 30 percent on health care costs.

High health care costs hurt the United States in three important ways. First, taxpayer burdens are already high. More than half of the U.S. population relies on the government for health care, which presses federal and state budgets. Second, private insurance programs are costly for employers. Consider that the cost of health insurance has been prominent in the financial troubles of General Motors. And many small firms are being forced to give up funding employee health care insurance because of its cost. Third, high health care insurance premiums reduce workers' wages.

9-2d The Patient Protection and Affordable Care Act of 2010

Provisions of the Act

The **Patient Protection and Affordable Care Act (ACA)** is extensive and remains controversial. The ACA has significantly changed the offering of health insurance plans available to citizens of the United States. While its legality was contested,

workers' compensation insurance
Health insurance required by state and federal governments and paid nearly in full by employers in most states; it compensates workers for job-related illness or injury.

Patient Protection and Affordable Care Act and the Reconciliation Act of 2010 (ACA)
Health care reform legislation that requires all Americans to have or buy health insurance, requires insurers to cover the children of those they insure up to the age of 26, prohibits insurers from denying coverage or setting unrealistically high premiums for pre-existing medical conditions, establishes health care insurance exchanges, and requires small firms to provide health insurance coverage for its employees.

the U.S. Supreme Court affirmed the ACA's constitutionality in 2012. In making health care insurance decisions, it's important to understand the key provisions of the new law.

The ACA has two key goals:

- Reduce the number of uninsured citizens in the country.
- Reduce the increases in health care costs by providing a "state based" health insurance exchange in each state.

The ACA is designed to reach these goals by requiring the purchase of health insurance and by assuring that health insurance provides "essential health benefits." All individuals who are not covered by Medicaid or Medicare are required to purchase health insurance or pay a penalty that will amount to the greater of $695 per adult (and $347.50 per child) or 2.5% of the family income in 2016. Businesses that employ more than 50 full time employees must provide health insurance for their employees or pay a penalty of $2,000 times the number of employees less 30. For example, if a business has 130 full-time employees but does not provide insurance, the penalty would be $2,000 × (130 − 30) or $200,000 per year.

The essential health benefits required by the ACA include the following:

- Ambulatory patient services
- Emergency services
- Hospitalization
- Maternity and newborn care
- Mental health and substance use disorder services, including behavioral health treatment
- Prescription drugs
- Rehabilitative and habilitative services and devices
- Laboratory services
- Preventive and wellness services and chronic disease management
- Pediatric services, including oral and vision care

In addition, the ACA requires that health insurance plans provide the following features:

- Cover pre-existing conditions
- Parents must have the option to carry their children on their plan until age 26
- Life time dollar limits on total insurance coverage are prohibited
- Plans must cover preventive care and medical screenings
- Insurers must spend at least 80% of premiums on claims

Insurance Exchanges

Under the ACA health care insurance exchanges are available in each state. The exchanges are competitive marketplaces where health insurance may be purchased by individuals and small firms. All insurance plans listed on the insurance exchanges must provide the essential health benefits described above. Similarly, all plans offered by employers must provide the indicated essential health benefits. The ACA provides four levels of benefits, each of which are identified by a metal label.

Metal label	Percentage of benefit costs (%)
Bronze	60
Silver	70
Gold	80
Platinum	90

The areas where insurance companies can compete are quite limited. The rates that companies charge are allowed to vary largely upon whether or not the insured uses tobacco products and the geographical area. The hope is that by increasing the amount of competition among insurers, the cost of insurance will go down.

Premium Assistance and Taxes

The ACA provides a tax credit to assist low income consumers in the purchase of health insurance. The credit is based upon the federal poverty level in the rating area and the cost of the benchmark (bronze) plan. In order to help pay for the costs associated with the ACA, the law added some taxes. For example, those earning more than $250,000 who file joint returns are subject to a 0.9% Medicare tax and a net investment tax of 3.8% that is added to income from investments (e.g., dividends and capital gains). Beginning in 2018, there is also an excise tax levied on the insurance companies providing "Cadillac" plans, which are those plans that cost more than $27,500 for a family.

You Can Do It Now

Compare Policies on an ACA Health Insurance Exchange

It's worth taking the time to survey the policies and premiums available to you on an ACA health insurance marketplace. Just go to **https://www.healthcare.gov/see-plans**. All you have to do is put in your zip code and some basic information on yourself. If you're shopping, it provides useful information. And if you already have a plan through your job, it'll be interesting to see how it compares. It's easy and you can do it now.

TEST YOURSELF

9-3 What are the two main sources of health insurance coverage in the United States?

9-4 What is *group health insurance*? Differentiate between group and individual health insurance.

9-5 Describe the features of traditional *indemnity (fee-for-service) plans* and explain the differences between them and *managed care plans*.

9-6 Briefly explain how an HMO works. Compare and contrast group HMOs, IPAs, and PPOs.

9-7 Discuss the basics of the Blue Cross/Blue Shield plans.

9-8 Who is eligible for Medicare and Medicaid benefits? What do those benefits encompass?

9-9 What is the objective of workers' compensation insurance? Explain its benefits for employees who are injured on the job or become ill through work-related causes.

9-10 What are the key provisions of the ACA? How is it likely to affect your health care insurance?

9-3 HEALTH INSURANCE DECISIONS

With all these options, how can you systematically plan your health insurance purchases? As with other insurance decisions, you'll need to consider potential areas of loss, types of coverage and other resources available to you and your family, and any gaps in protection. Once you've done all three, you can choose a health insurance plan that's best for you.

9-3a Evaluate Your Health Care Cost Risk

Most people need protection against two types of losses that can result from illness or accidents: (1) expenses for medical care and rehabilitation and (2) loss of income or household services caused by an inability to work. The cost of medical care can't be estimated easily; but in cases of long-term, serious illness, medical bills and related expenses can easily run into hundreds of thousands of dollars. An adequate amount of protection against these costs for most people would be at least $300,000 and, with a protracted illness or disability, as high as $1 million. In contrast, lost income is relatively easy to calculate: it's a percentage of your (or your spouse's) current monthly earnings. Most experts believe that 60 percent to 75 percent is sufficient.

A good health insurance plan considers more than financing medical expenses, lost income, and replacement services. It should also incorporate other means of risk reduction. Recall from Chapter 8 that you can deal with risk in four ways: risk avoidance, loss prevention and control, risk assumption, and insurance. So, in deciding on health insurance, you should consider these other ways of minimizing your risk.

- **Risk avoidance:** Look for ways to avoid exposure to health care loss before it occurs. For example, people who don't take illegal drugs never have to worry about disability from overdose, people who refuse to ride on motorcycles avoid the risk of injury from this relatively dangerous means of transportation, and people who don't smoke in bed are a lot less likely to doze off and start a fire in their house.

- **Loss prevention and control:** People who accept responsibility for their own well-being and live healthier lifestyles can prevent illness and reduce high medical costs. Smoking, alcohol and drug dependency, improper diet, inadequate sleep, and lack of regular exercise contribute to more than 60 percent of all diagnosed illnesses. Eliminating some or all of these factors from your lifestyle can reduce your chances of becoming ill. Similarly, following highway safety laws, not driving while intoxicated, and wearing a seat belt help prevent injury from car accidents.

- **Risk assumption:** Consider the risks that you're willing to retain as you deal with health insurance decisions. Some risks pose relatively small loss potential; you can budget for them rather than insure against them. For example, choosing insurance plans with deductibles and waiting periods is a form of risk assumption because it's more economical to pay small losses from savings than to pay higher premiums to cover them.

9-3b Determine Available Coverage and Resources

Some employers offer employees a *flexible-benefit ("cafeteria") plan* offering a choice of benefits. Typically, the menu of benefits includes more than one health insurance option, as well as life insurance, disability income insurance, and other benefits. As we discussed in Chapter 2, the employer specifies a set dollar amount that it will provide, and employees choose a combination from these benefits, depending on their preferences and circumstances. If, after choosing your benefits from the menu offered, you decide you want or need additional insurance benefits, most employers will set up a salary reduction agreement with the employee. The employee agrees to reduce his or her salary by the amount of the additional cost of the desired benefit.

Some employers offer consumer-directed health plans that go one step beyond a flexible-benefit caféteria plan. Typically, these plans combine a high-deductible health insurance policy with a tax-free **health reimbursement account (HRA)**, a plan funded by employers for each participating employee. When the account is used up, you must pay the remaining deductible of the health insurance policy before insurance begins to pay. If you don't use the money by the end of the year, you can "roll over" the amount; after several years of rolling it over, you could accumulate quite a bit of cash to pay for medical expenses. If you change jobs, the money stays with the employer. The Internal Revenue Service (IRS) considers employer contributions to medical reimbursement accounts to be tax-free income.

Another similar type of account is the **health savings account (HSA)**. The HSA is also a tax-free account, but the money is funded by employees, employers, or both to spend on routine medical costs. An HSA is also combined with a high-deductible insurance policy to pay for catastrophic care in case of major accident or illness, and—as with an HRA—can be rolled over each year. If you change jobs, the money in your HSA belongs only to you and is yours to keep. In addition to the HSA and HRA, there are many other consumer-directed health plans. And there are also **flexible spending accounts (FSAs)** that allow employees to contribute pre-tax dollars to an account that must be spent on qualified medical (or dependent care) expenses. If the account balance is not spent during the year, it is not carried over to the next year.

If you're married and your spouse is employed, you should also evaluate his or her benefit package before making any decisions. You may, for example, already be covered under your spouse's group health insurance plan or be able to purchase coverage for yourself and family members at a cheaper rate than through your own employer's plan.

If you're laid off from or leave a job where you've had health benefits, then you are legally eligible to continue your coverage for a period of 18 months under federal COBRA regulations (discussed later in the chapter). You'll be responsible for paying the full cost of the insurance if you decide to continue your coverage during this time, but you'll still pay group insurance rates that are often less expensive than buying individual insurance. However, you must arrange to continue your coverage before leaving your former employer. Importantly, under the ACA losing your job triggers a "qualifying life event" that allows you to obtain health insurance under COBRA or you can buy a policy in the private health insurance market. But there are critical enrollment windows and policy coverage details to compare. You'll need to do the math to identify the best option for you.

Another important area of group coverage to consider is retiree benefits. The number of companies providing health insurance to retirees has decreased sharply, so you may not be able to count on receiving employer-paid benefits once you retire. Know what your options are to ensure continued coverage for both you and your family after you retire. Medicare will cover basic medical expenses, but you'll probably want to supplement this coverage with one of the 12 standard Medigap plans, which are termed plans "A" through "L."

There are several other possible sources of health care coverage. As we'll discuss in Chapter 10, homeowner's and automobile insurance policies often contain limited amounts of medical expense protections. Your automobile policy, for example, may cover you if you're involved in an auto accident regardless of whether you're in a car, on foot, or on a bicycle when the accident occurs. In addition to Social Security's Medicare program, various other government programs help pay medical expenses. For instance, medical care is provided for people who've served in the armed services and were honorably discharged. Public health programs exist to treat communicable diseases, handicapped children, and mental health disorders.

If you need or want to purchase additional medical insurance coverage on an individual basis, you can buy a variety of policies from private insurance companies such as Aetna, CIGNA, and United Healthcare. You should buy plans from an insurance agent who will listen to your needs and provide well-thought-out responses to your questions. You should also research the carrier that will be providing your

insurance. Look for a carrier that is rated highly by at least two of the major ratings agencies and that has a reputation for settling claims fairly and promptly. The National Committee for Quality Assurance (NCQA) is another source of information. This non-profit, unbiased organization issues annual "report cards" that rate the service quality of various health plans.

9-3c Choose a Health Insurance Plan

After familiarizing yourself with the different health insurance plans and providers and reviewing your needs, you must choose one or more plans to provide coverage for you and your dependents. If you're employed, first review the various health insurance plans that your company offers. If you can't get coverage from an employer, get plan descriptions and policy costs from several providers, including a group plan from a professional or trade organization, if available, for both indemnity and managed care plans. You should also check the state or federal insurance exchange available to you. Then take your time and carefully read the plan materials to understand exactly what is covered, and at what cost. Next, add up what you've spent on medical costs over the past few years and what you might expect to spend in the future, so you can see what your costs would be under various plans.

Before choosing a particular plan, you should ask yourself some important questions to decide whether you want an indemnity plan or a managed care plan.

- **How important is cost compared with having freedom of choice?** You may have to pay more to stay with your current doctor if he or she is not part of a managed care plan that you're considering. Also, you have to decide if you can tolerate the managed care plan's approach to health care.

    Some states have experimented in recent years with the **community rating approach to health insurance premium pricing**, which prohibits insurance companies from varying rates based on health status or claim history. The "community" is defined as the area in which the insurance is offered. In the "pure" approach, all policyholders in an area pay the same premium without regard to their personal health, age, gender, or other factors. Under the adjusted (modified) community rating approach, insurers can adjust premiums based only on your family size, where you live, whether you use tobacco, and your age. The ACA requires insurance companies to adhere to the adjusted community rating approach for individuals and small businesses.

- **Will you be reimbursed if you choose a managed care plan and want to see an out-of-network provider?** For most people, the managed care route is cheaper, even if you visit a doctor only once a year, because of indemnity plans' "reasonable charge" provisions.

- **What types of coverage do you need?** Everyone has different needs; one person may want a plan with good maternity and pediatric care, whereas another may want outpatient mental health benefits. Make sure the plans that you consider offer what you want.

- **How good is the managed care network?** Look at the participating doctors and hospitals to see how many of your providers are part of the plan. Check out the credentials of participating providers; a good sign is accreditation from the NCQA. Are the providers' locations convenient for you? What preventive medical programs does it provide? Has membership grown? Talk to friends and associates to see what their experiences have been with the plan.

- **How old are you, and how's your health?** Many financial advisors recommend buying the lowest-cost plan—which may be an indemnity plan with a high deductible—if you're young and healthy.

community rating approach to health insurance premium pricing
Policyholders in a community (area) pay the same premium without regard to their personal health, age, gender, or other factors.

FINANCIAL PLANNING TIPS

Saving on Health Insurance

Health insurance is not equally affordable by all people. And there are still plenty of decisions for you to make concerning health insurance. It's important to consider how to save on the cost of obtaining and using health insurance. Consider the following tips to manage your costs:

- **Stay in the network.** You can save a lot of money by staying within the insurer's network.

- **Check on alternative facilities.** Some physicians work at outpatient surgery centers as well as hospitals. And the charges can vary significantly by location. Ask your physician—you may be able to save by choosing a cheaper facility for surgery or treatment. This could save you thousands of dollars.

- **Look for lower-cost after-hours care.** Visiting a convenience care clinic, like a MinuteClinic at CVS, may well cost only a tenth of an emergency-room visit. If you don't really need an ER, consider this alternative.

- **Consider independent facilities.** The prices of X-rays and lab tests can vary a lot across different facilities. For example, having a magnetic resonance imaging (MRI) done at a hospital can easily cost twice as much as having the same procedure done at an independent radiology facility. The procedure is the same using a qualified radiologist—only the place differs.

- **Ask for generic drugs and buy your drugs through the mail.** Generic drugs are much cheaper than branded drugs, and mail-order pharmacies often offer a three-month supply of drugs for the same price as a one-month supply at a local pharmacy.

- **Know the fair prices of medical procedures.** Check out **http://www.healthcarebluebook.com**, which posts the average fee that providers in your area accept as payment from insurers for surgery, hospital stays, doctor visits, and medical tests.

Source: Adapted from Kimberly Lankford, "30 Ways to Cut Health Care Costs," http://www.kiplinger.com/article/spending/T027-C000-S002-30-ways-to-cut-health-care-costs.html, accessed August 2015.

FINANCIAL ROAD SIGN

Choosing a Health Insurance Plan

Ask the following questions when choosing among health care insurance plans:

- Can I choose to use any doctor, hospital, clinic, or pharmacy?
- What coverage, if any, is provided for seeing specialists like eye doctors and dentists?
- Does the plan cover special conditions or treatments like psychiatric care, pregnancy, and physical therapy?
- Does the plan cover home care or nursing home care?
- What kind of limitations are there on the coverage of prescribed medications?
- What are the deductible and any co-payment amounts?
- What is the maximum I would have to pay out of health care expenses, either in a calendar year or during my lifetime?
- How are billing or service disputes handled under the plan?

Source: Adapted from "Choosing a Health Insurance Plan," http://www.usa.gov/topics/health/health-insurance/choosing.shtml, accessed August 2015.

After considering all of the coverage and resources available to you, consider where gaps in your health insurance coverage may lie and how best to fill them. Doing this requires an understanding of the features, policy provisions, and coverage provided by various insurance carriers and policies. We'll discuss these in detail in the next section.

TEST YOURSELF

9-11 Explain four methods for controlling the risks associated with health care expenses.

9-12 Explain what factors should be considered in evaluating available employer-sponsored health insurance plans.

9-13 Discuss possible sources of health insurance available to supplement employer-sponsored health insurance plans.

9-14 Answer the key questions posed to help you choose a plan, based on your current situation. What type of plan do you think will best suit your needs?

9-4 MEDICAL EXPENSE COVERAGE AND POLICY PROVISIONS

So far, we've discussed the major types of health insurance plans, their providers, and the factors that should be considered in evaluating the need for health insurance. To evaluate different insurance plan options, however, you must be able to compare and contrast what they cover and how each plan's policy provisions may affect you and your family. By doing so, you can decide which health plan offers the best protection at the most reasonable cost. Worksheet 9.1 provides a convenient checklist for comparing the costs and benefits of competing health insurance plans. You may want to refer to it while reading the following sections.

9-4a Types of Medical Expense Coverage

The medical services covered vary from health plan to health plan. You can purchase narrowly defined plans that cover only what you consider to be the most important medical services or, if you can afford it and want the comfort of broader coverage, you can purchase insurance coverage to help you pay for most or all of your health care needs. Here are the medical expenses most commonly covered by health insurance.

Hospitalization

If you must spend time in the hospital, a *hospitalization insurance policy* will reimburse you for the cost of your stay. Hospitalization policies usually pay for a portion of: (1) the hospital's daily semiprivate room rate, which typically includes meals, nursing care, and other routine services; and (2) the cost of ancillary services, such as laboratory tests, imaging, and medications you receive while hospitalized. Many hospitalization plans also cover some outpatient and out-of-hospital services once you're discharged, such as in-home rehabilitation, diagnostic treatment, and preadmission testing. Some hospitalization plans simply pay a flat daily amount for each day the insured is in the hospital, regardless of actual charges. Most policies set a limit on the number of days of hospitalization and a maximum dollar amount on ancillary services that they will pay for.

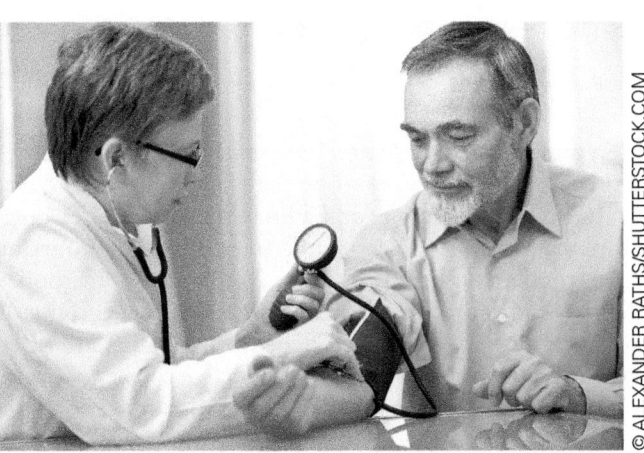

© ALEXANDER RATHS/SHUTTERSTOCK.COM

Surgical Expenses

Surgical expense insurance covers the cost of surgery in or out of the hospital. Usually, surgical expense coverage is provided as part of a hospitalization insurance policy or as a rider to such a

Here is a convenient checklist that you can use to compare the costs and benefits of competing health care plans.
Check those services in the first column that are most important to you, determine how these services are handled in each policy, and then decide which policy best meets your needs. The most important covered service is hospitalization.

Service	Policy #1	Policy #2	Policy #3
Hospital care			
Surgery (inpatient and outpatient)			
Office visits to your doctor			
Maternity/well-baby care			
Pediatric care			
Immunizations			
Mammograms			
Medical tests, X-rays			
Mental health care			
Dental care, braces, and cleaning			
Vision care, eyeglasses, and exams			
Prescription drugs			
Home health care			
Nursing home care			
Services you need that are excluded			
Choice of doctors			
Location of doctors and hospitals			
Ease of getting an appointment			
Minimal paperwork			
Waiting period for coverage			
Copays and deductibles			
Premiums			
Totals			

Source: Adapted from http://www.pahealthoptions.com/docs/compare_coverage_checklist.pdf, accessed August 2015.

policy. Most plans reimburse you for *reasonable and customary* surgical expenses based on a survey of surgical costs during the previous year. They may also cover anesthesia, nonemergency treatment using imaging, and a limited allowance for diagnostic tests. Some plans still pay according to a *schedule of benefits,* reimbursing up to a fixed maximum for a particular surgical procedure. For example, the policy might state that you would receive no more than $1,500 for an appendectomy or $1,200 for diagnostic arthroscopic surgery on a knee. Scheduled benefits are often inadequate when compared with typical surgical costs. Most elective cosmetic surgeries, such as a "nose job" or "tummy tuck," are typically excluded from reimbursement unless they are deemed medically necessary.

Physician Expenses

Physicians expense insurance, also called *regular medical expense*, covers the cost of visits to a doctor's office or for a doctor's hospital visits, including consultation with a specialist. Also covered are imaging and laboratory tests performed outside of a hospital. Plans are offered on either a reasonable and customary or scheduled benefit basis. Sometimes, the first few visits with the physician for any single cause are excluded. This exclusion serves the same purpose as the deductible and waiting-period features found in other types of insurance. Often, these plans specify a maximum payment per visit as well as a maximum number of visits per injury or illness.

major medical plan
An insurance plan designed to supplement the basic coverage of hospitalization, surgical, and physician expenses; used to finance more catastrophic medical costs.

Major Medical Insurance

Major medical plans provide broad coverage for nearly all types of medical expenses resulting from either illnesses or accidents. In the past, it was common to have lifetime limits of $500,000 or $1,000,000. However, the ACA eliminates lifetime limits on total health care insurance payments by insurers. Because hospitalization, surgical, and physician coverage meets the smaller medical costs, major medical is used to finance more catastrophic medical costs. Many people use major medical with a high deductible to protect them in case they have a catastrophic illness.

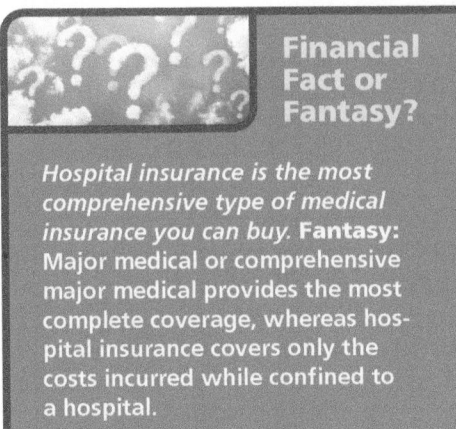

Financial Fact or Fantasy?

Hospital insurance is the most comprehensive type of medical insurance you can buy. **Fantasy:** Major medical or comprehensive major medical provides the most complete coverage, whereas hospital insurance covers only the costs incurred while confined to a hospital.

Comprehensive Major Medical Insurance

A comprehensive major medical insurance plan combines basic hospitalization, surgical, and physician expense coverage with major medical protection into a single policy, usually with a low deductible. Comprehensive major medical insurance is often written under a group contract. However, some efforts have been made to make this type of coverage available to individuals.

comprehensive major medical insurance
A health insurance plan that combines into a single policy the coverage for basic hospitalization, surgical, and physician expenses along with major medical protection.

Dental Services

Dental insurance covers necessary dental care and some dental injuries sustained through accidents. (Expenses for accidental damage to natural teeth are normally covered under standard surgical expense and major medical policies.) Depending on the policy, covered services may include examinations, X-rays, dental cleanings, fillings, extractions, dentures, root canal therapy, orthodontics, and oral surgery. The maximum limit on most dental policies is often low—$1,000 to $2,500 per patient—so these plans don't fully protect against unusually high dental work costs.

Limited Protection Policies

The types of health plans already discussed are sufficient to meet the protection needs of most individuals and families. But insurance companies offer other options that provide limited protection against certain types of perils:

- *Accident policies* that pay a specified sum to an insured injured in a certain type of accident
- *Sickness policies,* sometimes called *dread disease policies,* that pay a specified sum for a named disease, such as cancer
- *Hospital income policies* that promise to guarantee a specific daily, weekly, or monthly amount as long as the insured is hospitalized

Remember that sound insurance planning seldom dictates the purchase of such policies. Also, be aware that the extra cost of purchasing these insurance options typically outweighs the limited coverage that they provide. The problem with buying policies that cover only a certain type of accident, illness, or financial need is that

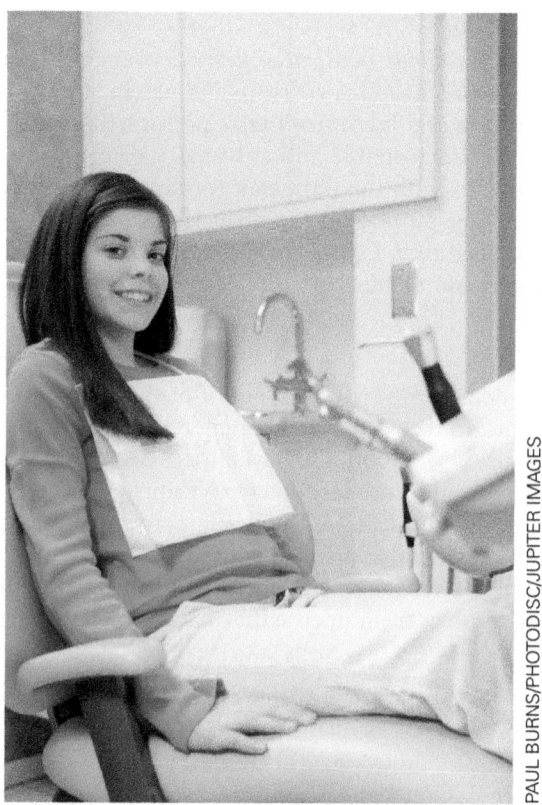

PAUL BURNS/PHOTODISC/JUPITER IMAGES

major gaps in coverage will often occur. The financial loss can be just as great if the insured falls down a flight of stairs or if she contracts cancer, lung disease, or heart disease. Most limited-peril policies should be used only to supplement a comprehensive insurance program if the coverage is not overlapping.

9-4b Policy Provisions of Medical Expense Plans

To compare the health insurance plans offered by different insurers, evaluate whether they contain liberal or restrictive provisions. Generally, policy provisions can be divided into two groups: terms of payment and terms of coverage.

Terms of Payment

Four provisions govern how much your health insurance plan will pay: (1) deductibles, (2) the participation (co-insurance) clause, (3) the policy's internal limits, and (4) the coordination of benefits clause, if any.

Deductibles. Because major medical insurance plans are designed to supplement basic hospitalization, surgical, and physicians' expense plans, those offered under an indemnity (fee-for-service) plan often have a relatively large *deductible,* typically $500 or $1,000. The deductible represents the initial amount that's not covered by the policy and is thus the insured's responsibility. Comprehensive major medical plans tend to offer lower deductibles, sometimes $100 or less. Most plans offer a calendar-year, all-inclusive deductible. In effect, this allows a person to accumulate the deductible from more than one incident of use. Some plans also include a *carryover provision,* whereby any part of the deductible that occurs during the final three months of the year can be applied to the current year's deductible and can *also* be applied to the following calendar year's deductible. In a few plans, the deductible is on a per-illness or per-accident basis.

> **EXAMPLE: Effect of Per-Illness, Per-Accident Deductible**
>
> You're covered by a health insurance policy that has a $1,000 per-illness, per-accident deductible. How much would the policy pay if you suffered three separate accidents in one year, each requiring $1,000 of medical expenses? None! Unfortunately you wouldn't be eligible to collect any benefits from the major medical plan.

Participation (Co-insurance). A participation or co-insurance clause stipulates that the company will pay some portion—say, 80 percent or 90 percent—of the amount of the covered loss in excess of the deductible rather than the entire amount. Co-insurance helps reduce the incentive for policyholders to fake an illness and discourages them from incurring unnecessary medical expenses. Many major medical plans also have a *stop-loss provision* that places a cap on the amount of participation required. Without a stop-loss provision, a $1 million medical bill would leave the insured with $200,000 of costs under an 80 percent plan. Often such provisions limit the insured's participation to less than $10,000 and sometimes to as little as $2,000.

Internal Limits. Most major medical plans are written with internal limits that control the amounts paid for certain specified expenses—even if the claim *doesn't* exceed overall policy limits. Charges commonly subject to internal limits are hospital

deductible
The initial amount *not* covered by an insurance policy and thus the insured's responsibility; it's usually determined on a calendar-year basis or on a per-illness or per-accident basis.

participation (co-insurance) clause
A provision in many health insurance policies stipulating that the insurer will pay some portion—say, 80 or 90 percent—of the amount of the covered loss in excess of the deductible.

internal limits
A feature commonly found in health insurance policies that limits the amounts that will be paid for certain specified expenses, even if the claim does *not* exceed overall policy limits.

room and board, surgical fees, mental and nervous conditions, and nursing services. If an insured chooses an expensive physician or medical facility, then he or she is responsible for paying the portion of the charges that are above a "reasonable and customary" level or beyond a specified maximum amount. The following example shows how deductibles, co-insurance, and internal limits constrain the amount a company is obligated to pay under a major medical plan.

Major Medical Policy: An Example. Assume that Fred Woods, a graduate student, has coverage under a major medical insurance policy that specifies a $500,000 lifetime limit of protection, a $1,000 deductible, an 80 percent co-insurance clause, internal limits of $350 per day on hospital room and board, and $6,000 as the maximum payable surgical fee. When Fred was hospitalized for three days to remove a small tumor, he incurred these costs:

Hospitalization: 3 days at $500 a day	$1,500
Surgical expense	5,800
Other covered medical expenses	3,800
Total medical expenses	$11,100

By the terms of the policy's co-insurance clause, the maximum that the company must pay is 80 percent of the covered loss in excess of the deductible. Without internal limits, the company would pay $8,080 [0.80 × ($11,100 − $1,000)]. The internal limits further restrict the payment. Even though 80 percent of the $500-per-day hospitalization charge is $400, the most the company would have to pay is $350 per day. Thus Fred, the insured, becomes liable for $50 per day for three days, or $150. The surgical expense is below the $6,000 internal limit, so the 80 percent co-insurance clause applies and the insurer will pay $4,640 (0.80 × $5,800). The company's total obligation is reduced to $7,930 ($8,080 − $150), and Fred must pay a total of $3,170 [$1,000 deductible + 0.20($11,100 − $1,000) co-insurance + $150 excess hospital room and board charges]. This example shows that, although major medical insurance can offer large amounts of reimbursement, you may still be responsible for substantial payments.

coordination of benefits provision
A provision often included in health insurance policies to prevent the insured from collecting more than 100 percent of covered charges; it requires that benefit payments be coordinated if the insured is eligible for benefits under more than one policy.

Coordination of Benefits. Health insurance policies are not contracts of *indemnity*. This means that the insured party can collect multiple payments for the same illness or accident unless health insurance policies include a coordination of benefits provision. This clause prevents you from collecting more than 100 percent of covered charges by collecting benefits from more than one policy. For example, many private health insurance policies coordinate benefit provisions with medical benefits paid under workers' compensation. In contrast, some companies widely advertise that their policies will pay claims regardless of other coverage the policyholder has. Of course, these latter types of insurance policies often charge more per dollar of protection. From the standpoint of insurance planning, using policies with coordination of benefits clauses can help you prevent coverage overlaps and, ideally, reduce your premiums.

Considering the complexity of medical expense contracts, the various clauses limiting payments, and coordination of benefits with other policies, one might expect that insurers often pay only partial claims and sometimes completely deny claims. However, if you make a claim and don't receive the payment you expected, don't give up. Exhibit 9.3 provides some guidelines on how you might go about getting your health insurance claims paid.

Terms of Coverage

Several contract provisions affect a health insurance plan's value to you. Some important provisions address (1) the persons and places covered, (2) cancellation,

EXHIBIT 9.3   **How to Get Paid on a Health Insurance Claim**

The following steps will help you to get paid for health insurance claims.

1. *Keep detailed records of all visits to physicians and medical professionals.* Even though medical facilities are supposed to keep medical records, it is also important for you to keep a copy for your own records. This includes all bills, dates of service, and insurance company approvals. Your records provide the proof you need when filing a claim with the insurance company.

2. *Contact the physician or medical professional's office yourself rather than waiting for the insurance company to do so.* Sometimes a claim is held up because the insurance company is waiting for documentation. Take the initiative and find out who needs what and make a call or two. This will reduce the wait for a claim to be paid.

3. *If the insurance company isn't paying the claim, ask them to explain why not.* Most companies will provide an explanation. This will allow you to quickly determine your next step in assuring that your claim is paid.

4. *If a claim is denied, make sure to call your physician or medical professional.* Such professionals deal with insurance companies frequently and can often cut to the essence of the problem quickly.

5. *Keep all documents provided by your insurance company.* This includes the company's Explanation of Benefits statement. Check them to make sure that you are contacting the proper departments at the company and asking the relevant questions. It may well be that your solution is buried in the fine print.

6. *If your claim is denied, it may be worthwhile to hire a private claims advocate.* Find one through the Alliance of Claims Assistance Professionals Web site, **http://www.claims.org.**

Sources: Adapted from "Choosing a Health Insurance Plan," http://www.usa.gov/topics/health/health-insurance/choosing.shtml, accessed August 2015; Sheila Guilloton, "What to Do If Your Health Insurance Company Won't Pay," http://www.examiner.com/article/what-to-do-if-your-health-insurance-company-won-t-pay, accessed August 2015.

(3) preexisting conditions, (4) pregnancy and abortion, (5) mental illness, (6) rehabilitation coverage, and (7) continuation of group coverage.

Persons and Places Covered. Under the ACA, family health care insurers must allow parents to retain their children on their health insurance policies up to the age of 26. Some policies protect you only while you're in the United States or Canada; others offer worldwide coverage but exclude named countries.

Cancellation. Many health insurance policies are written to permit *cancellation* at the insurer's option at any time. Some policies explicitly state this; others don't. To protect yourself against premature cancellation, buy policies that specifically state that the insurer won't cancel coverage so long as premiums are paid.

pre-existing condition clause

A clause that used to be included in most individual health insurance policies permitting permanent or temporary exclusion of coverage for any physical or mental problems the insured had at the time the policy was purchased; under the ACA, insurers now are prohibited from denying coverage for pre-existing conditions, making this clause moot.

Pre-existing Conditions. In the past, most health insurance policies sold to individuals (as opposed to group/employer-sponsored plans) contained a **pre-existing condition clause.** This means the policy might exclude coverage for physical or mental problems that you had at the time you bought it. In some policies, the exclusion was permanent; in others, it lasted only for the first year or two that the coverage is in force. Group insurance plans in the past may also have had pre-existing condition clauses, but they tended to be less restrictive than those in individually written policies. The ACA has changed this. The new legislation prohibits insurers from denying coverage due to the presence of pre-existing conditions.

Employees who have recently left a job or retired are covered by the *Health Insurance Portability and Accountability Act, or HIPAA.* This federal law, implemented in 1996, is designed to protect people's ability to obtain continued health insurance after they leave a job or retire, even if they have a serious health problem. Under HIPAA, if you've already been covered by a health plan without a break in coverage of more than 63 days and you apply for new insurance, insurers cannot turn you down, charge you higher premiums, or enforce an exclusionary period because of your health status. HIPAA doesn't guarantee you group coverage, but it does protect your ability to buy individual health insurance even if you have a preexisting health condition. HIPAA now applies only to "grandfathered" plans that existed when the ACA went into effect in March 2010 and have not been changed significantly since then. The ACA deals with some of the issues previously addressed by HIPAA.

Pregnancy and Abortion. Many individual and group health insurance plans include special clauses for medical expenses incurred through pregnancy or abortion. Some liberal policies pay for all related expenses, including sick-leave pay during the final months of pregnancy, whereas others pay for medical expenses that result from pregnancy or abortion complications, but not for routine procedure expenses. In the most restrictive cases, policies offer no coverage for any costs of pregnancy or abortion.

Mental Illness. Many health insurance plans omit or offer only reduced benefits for treatment of mental disorders. For example, a health insurance policy may offer hospitalization benefits that continue to pay so long as you remain hospitalized—except for mental illness. It may restrict payment for mental illness to one-half the normally provided payment amounts and for a period not to exceed 30 days. Unfortunately, mental illness is the number one sickness requiring long-term hospital care. Because coverage for mental illness is an important insurance protection, check your policies to learn how liberal—or how restrictive—they are regarding this feature.

Rehabilitation Coverage. In the past, health insurance plans focused almost exclusively on reasonable and necessary medical expenses. If an illness or accident left an insured partially or totally disabled, then normally no funds would be available to help the person retrain for employment and a more productive life. Now, though, many policies include *rehabilitation coverage* for counseling, occupational therapy, and even some educational or job training programs. This is a good feature to look for in major medical and disability income policies.

Consolidated Omnibus Budget Reconciliation Act (COBRA)
A federal law that allows an employee who leaves the insured group to continue coverage for up to 18 months by paying premiums to his or her former employer on time; the employee retains all benefits previously available, except for disability income coverage.

Continuation of Group Coverage. Under the Consolidated Omnibus Budget Reconciliation Act (COBRA) passed by Congress in 1986, an employee who leaves the insured group voluntarily or involuntarily (except in the case of "gross misconduct") may elect to continue coverage for up to 18 months by paying premiums to his or her former employer on time (up to 102 percent of the company cost). The employee retains all benefits previously available, except for disability income coverage.

Similar continuation coverage is available for retirees and their families for up to 18 months or until they become eligible for Medicare, whichever occurs first. An employee's dependents may be covered for up to 36 months under COBRA under special circumstances, such as divorce or death of the employee. After COBRA coverage expires, most states provide for conversion of the group coverage to an individual policy regardless of the insured's current health and without evidence of insurability. Premium charges and benefits of the converted policy are determined at the time of conversion. As noted above, under the ACA losing your job triggers a "qualifying life event" that allows you to obtain health insurance under COBRA or you can buy a policy in the private health insurance market.

9-4c Cost Containment Provisions for Medical Expense Plans

Considering the continued inflation in medical costs, it's hardly surprising that insurers, along with employers that sponsor medical expense plans, are looking for ways to limit their incurred costs. Today, various cost containment provisions are included in almost all medical expense plans, both indemnity and managed care policies. These cost containment provisions include the following.

- Preadmission certification: This requires you to receive approval from your insurer before entering the hospital for a scheduled stay. Such approval is not normally required for emergency stays.
- Continued stay review: To receive normal reimbursement, the insured must secure approval from the insurer for any stay that exceeds the originally approved limits.
- Second surgical opinions: Many plans require second opinions on specific non-emergency procedures and, in their absence, may reduce the surgical benefits paid. Most surgical expense plans now fully reimburse the cost of second opinions.
- Waiver of co-insurance: Because insurers can save money on hospital room-and-board charges by encouraging outpatient surgery, many now agree to waive the co-insurance clause and pay 100 percent of surgical costs for outpatient

Behavior Matters

Behavioral Biases in Making Health Insurance Decisions

Research in behavioral economics indicates that individuals have difficulty making decisions involving uncertainty, trade-offs between current and future benefits and costs, or significant complexity. These decisions require estimating the probabilities, financial costs, and quality of life and happiness associated with possible future health events such as having cancer or a heart attack. People find it hard to do this well.

Research shows that individuals tend to make systematic mistakes in estimating probabilities. For example, they are inclined to overestimate the likelihood of low-probability events, such as dying in a plane crash. And it's almost impossible for most people to estimate the financial costs associated with various health conditions. This is because, for the most part, there is no place to look up health service prices. And people tend to overestimate how much their quality of life and happiness will decline if they become sick.

Health care choices often require bearing costs today in the hope of future benefits. This is as much the case for preventative care as it is for more costly and invasive procedures designed to reduce the probability of cancer among high-risk patients. Yet research shows that people tend to invest too little in such activities because they put too much weight on current costs and too little weight on future benefits.

Health care insurance decisions can also be quite complex. Insurance policies include many facets such as deductibles, co-payments, and different levels of coverage for different providers. And health insurance includes trade-offs that many people don't seem to understand. For example, employees may not fully appreciate that they are sacrificing some wages in return for employer health care insurance premium subsidies.

What are the implications of the above biases?

- It's important to be aware of common behavioral biases when making health insurance decisions. For example, realize that most people don't pay sufficient attention to preventive health care measures.
- Most of us would be better off if our health insurance plans were mediated by some entity that would screen and restrict health insurance choices down to a manageable number. Research suggests that employers would perform this role better than the government or private insurance agents, which is a provocative finding in light of the ACA.

Source: "Lessons for Health Care from Behavioral Economics," http://www.nber.org/bah/2008no4/w14330.html (see referenced study by Jeffrey Liebman and Richard Zeckhauser, "Simple Humans, Complex Insurance, Subtle Subsidies," Working Paper 14330, http://www.nber.org/papers/w14330, 2008), accessed August 2015.

procedures. A similar waiver is sometimes applied to generic pharmaceuticals. For example, the patient may choose between an 80 percent payment for a brand-name pharmaceutical costing $35 or 100 percent reimbursement for its $15 generic equivalent.

- Limitation of insurer's responsibility: Many policies also have provisions limiting the insurer's financial responsibility to reimbursing only for costs that are considered "reasonable and customary." This provision can sometimes place limitations on the type and place of medical care for which the insurer will pay.

TEST YOURSELF

9-15 Explain the differences between hospitalization insurance and surgical expense insurance.

9-16 What are the features of a *major medical* plan? Compare major medical to *comprehensive major medical* insurance.

9-17 Describe these policy provisions commonly found in medical expense plans: (a) deductibles, (b) co-insurance, and (c) coordination of benefits.

9-18 What are the key provisions of COBRA? How do they relate to continuation of group coverage when an employee voluntarily or involuntarily leaves the insured group?

9-19 Explain the cost containment provisions commonly found in medical expense plans. How might the provision for second surgical opinions help an insurer contain its costs?

9-5 LONG-TERM-CARE INSURANCE

LG5

long-term care
The delivery of medical and personal care, other than hospital care, to persons with chronic medical conditions resulting from either illness or frailty.

Long-term care involves the delivery of medical and personal care, other than hospitalization, to persons with chronic medical conditions. Whether in a nursing home, in an assisted-living community, or through care provided in the patient's home, it can have a major financial impact. A year's stay in a private nursing home, for example, averages over $91,250, according to a 2015 cost-of-care survey by Genworth Financial. About 44 percent of men and 58 percent of women over 65 are expected to need long-term care at some time. And yet, less than 3 percent of American adults have purchased long-term care insurance. This is a potential concern because the average long-term stay is over one year.

Consumers pay about 25 percent of long-term care costs out of their own pockets. Government programs such as Medicare and Medicaid cover less than half of the total cost, and eligibility for their benefits is strictly defined. Major medical insurance plans also exclude most of the costs related to long-term care. When a person receiving nursing home care cannot afford to cover such a large personal expense out-of-pocket, the younger generation often ends up footing the bill.

The ACA has provisions that relate to long-term care. It includes the Community Living Assistance Services and Support Program (CLASS), which is a voluntary, consumer-financed insurance plan designed to cover long-term-care expenses. This is similar to long-term-care programs currently available in the private market. However, it differs in that the program will be administered by the government. Further, any working adult who is 18 or older will be able to enroll, regardless of any pre-existing medical condition. And the benefits will be good for as long as someone needs long-term care. However, the fate of the long-term-care parts of the ACA remain unclear. The U.S. Department of Health and Human Services has questioned the financial viability of implementing the long-term-care program presented in the ACA.

Fortunately, special insurance policies are available to cover long-term care. Most are indemnity policies that pay a fixed dollar amount for each day that you receive specified care either in a nursing home or at home. The decision to buy long-term-care insurance is an important part of health insurance and retirement financial planning.

Most people purchase individual long-term-care products either through organizations like the AARP or directly from the more than 100 insurance companies that offer them. Employer-sponsored long-term-care insurance is also growing in popularity. Many businesses now offer some type of long-term-care insurance to their employees. Usually, however, employees pay the full cost of premiums, although employer-sponsored plans can often cost less than purchasing long-term care on an individual basis. Whether you purchase long-term-care insurance as an individual or through an employer-sponsored plan, however, it's important to evaluate policy provisions and costs.

9-5a Do You Need Long-Term-Care Insurance?

The odds of needing more than a year of nursing home care before you reach age 65 are 1 in 33. And yet, the expense of a prolonged nursing home stay can cause severe financial hardship. How do you decide if you need long-term-care insurance? Answer the following questions.

- Do you have many assets to preserve for your dependents? Because you must deplete most of your assets before Medicaid will pay for nursing home care, some financial advisors recommend that people over 65 whose net worth is more than $100,000 and income exceeds $50,000 a year consider long-term-care

FINANCIAL PLANNING TIPS

Buying Long-Term-Care Insurance

Consider the following tips when shopping for a long-term-care insurance policy:

- **Buy the right amount and the right kind of coverage.** Long-term-care insurance benefits are usually stated as a fixed daily amount over a certain period, up to a given maximum amount of coverage. Access to the benefits is usually triggered by a "long-term-care event" like breaking a hip or having a stroke. The key is that physicians expect you to need help with daily living tasks for at least 90 days. Many salespeople will try to sell you a policy that covers the cost of several years of nursing home care. However, consider the more affordable alternative of a policy that includes time with a home health aide or adult day care, both of which are much cheaper than nursing home care.

- **Buy at the right time.** You'll save significantly over the lifetime of the policy if you buy a policy when you're under 60 and healthy. About 25 percent of people wait until they are much older and have health issues that can greatly increase the cost of obtaining a policy.

- **Be aware of the "restoration of benefits" rider, as well as the rest of the policy's fine print.** The "restoration of benefits" rider should be considered because it allows you to stop the clock on your policy. For example, assume that you fall down the stairs at the age of 83. The right policy will allow you to start spending the benefits immediately on a home health aide. And when you recover, a "restoration of benefits" rider allows you to stop the clock on the policy. If you stay well for six months, the overall total benefits are restored as if you never had fallen.

- **Take inflation into account.** It makes sense to buy a policy that provides at least 5 percent compound inflation protection.

Source: Adapted in part from Anya Kamenetz, "Tips for Buying Long-term Care Insurance," http://articles.chicagotribune.com/2012-04-24/business/sns-201204241730—tms—savingsgctnzy-a20120424apr24_1_long-term-care-insurance-home-health-affordable-policy, accessed August 2015.

insurance—*if* they can afford the premiums. The very wealthy, however, may prefer to self-insure.

- Can you afford the premiums? Premiums of many good-quality policies can be 5 percent to 7 percent of annual income, or even more. Such high premiums may cause more financial hardship than the cost of a potential nursing home stay. You may be better off investing the amount you'd spend in premiums; it would then be available for *any* future need, including long-term health care.
- Is there a family history of disabling disease? This factor increases your odds of needing long-term care. If there's a history of Alzheimer's, neurological disorders, or other potentially debilitating diseases, the need for long-term care insurance may increase.
- Are you male or female? Women tend to live longer and are more likely to require long-term care. They're also the primary caregivers for other family members, which may mean that when they need care, help won't be available.
- Do you have family who can care for you? The availability of relatives or home health services to provide care can reduce the cost of long-term care.

9-5b Long-Term-Care Insurance Provisions and Costs

Whether you purchase long-term-care insurance as an individual or through an employer-sponsored plan, it's important to understand what you're buying. Substantial variation exists between product offerings, so you must be especially careful to evaluate the provisions of each policy. Exhibit 9.4 summarizes the typical provisions of policies offered by leading insurers. Of course, policy provisions are important factors in determining the premium for each policy. Let's take a closer look at the most important policy provisions to consider in purchasing long-term-care insurance.

- Type of care: Some long-term-care policies offer benefits only for nursing home care, whereas others pay only for services in the insured's home, such as skilled or unskilled nursing care, physical therapy, homemakers, and home health aides. Because it's hard to predict whether a person might need to be in a nursing home, most financial planners recommend policies covering both. Many of these policies focus on nursing home care, and any expenses for health care in the insured's

---

EXHIBIT 9.4 **Typical Provisions in Long-Term-Care Insurance Policies**

Long-term-care insurers offer a wide range of provisions in their policies. A typical policy includes the following:

Services covered	Skilled, intermediate, and custodial care; home health care; adult day care (often)
Benefit eligibility	Physician certification/medically necessary
Daily benefit	$100–$450/day, nursing home; $50–$250/day, home health care
Benefit period	3–4 years
Maximum benefit period	5 years; unlimited
Waiting period	0–100 days
Renewability	Guaranteed
Preexisting conditions	Conditions existing 6–12 months prior to policy coverage
Inflation protection	Yes, for an additional premium
Deductibility periods	0, 20, 30, 90, 100 days
Alzheimer's disease coverage	Yes
Age limits for purchasing	40–84

home are covered in a rider to the basic policy. Many policies also cover assisted living, adult day care and other community care programs, alternative care, and respite care for the caregiver.

- Eligibility requirements: Some important provisions determine whether the insured will receive payment for claims. These are known as *gatekeeper* provisions. The most liberal policies state that the insured will qualify for benefits so long as his or her physician orders the care. A common and much more restrictive provision pays only for long-term care that's medically necessary because of sickness or injury.

  One common gatekeeper provision requires the insured's inability to perform a given number of *activities of daily living (ADLs)* such as bathing, dressing, or eating. Some policies also provide care for cognitive impairment or when medically necessary and prescribed by the patient's physician. In the case of an Alzheimer's patient who remains physically healthy, inclusion of cognitive abilities as ADLs would be extremely important. Newer policies no longer require a certain period of nursing home care before covering home health care services.

- Services covered: Most policies today cover several levels of service in state-licensed nursing homes: skilled, intermediate, and custodial care. *Skilled care* is needed when a patient requires constant attention from a medical professional, such as a physician or registered nurse. *Intermediate care* is provided when the patient needs medical attention or supervision but not the constant attention of a medical professional. *Custodial care* provides assistance in the normal activities of daily living but no medical attention or supervision; a physician or nurse may be on call, however. Most long-term-care policies also cover home care services, such as skilled or unskilled nursing care, physical therapy, homemakers, and home health aides provided by state-licensed or Medicare-certified home health agencies. Newer policies no longer require a certain period of nursing home care before covering home health care services.

- Daily benefits: Long-term-care policies reimburse the insured for services incurred up to a daily maximum. For nursing home care policies, the daily maximums generally range from $100 to $450, depending on the amount of premium the insured is willing to pay. For combination nursing home and home care policies, the maximum home care benefit is normally half the nursing home maximum.

- Benefit duration: The maximum duration of benefits ranges from 1 year to the insured's lifetime. Lifetime coverage is expensive, however. Most financial planners recommend the purchase of a policy with a duration of three to six years to give the insured protection for a longer-than-average period of care.

- Waiting period: Even if the policy's eligibility requirements are met, the insured must pay long-term-care expenses during the waiting or elimination period. Typical waiting periods are 90 to 100 days. Although premiums are much lower for policies with longer waiting periods, the insured must have liquid assets to cover his or her expenses during that period. An insured individual who is still receiving care after the waiting period expires will begin to receive benefits for the duration of the policy so long as its eligibility requirements continue to be met.

- Renewability: Most long-term-care insurance policies now include a guaranteed renewability provision to ensure continued coverage for your lifetime as long as you continue to pay the premiums. This clause does not ensure a level premium over time, however. Nearly all policies allow the insurer to raise premiums if the claims experience for your peer group of policyholders is unfavorable. Watch out for policies with an optional renewability clause. These policies are renewable *only at the insurer's option*.

- Pre-existing conditions: Many long-term care policies include a *pre-existing conditions clause,* whose effect ranges from 6 to 12 months. On the other hand, many policies have no such clause, which effectively eliminates one important source of possible claim disputes. If someone has already been diagnosed with Parkinson's or Alzheimer's disease, takes memory drugs, uses any type of assistance in walking, has had a stroke, or has osteoporosis, an insurance company may well not be willing to sell that person a long-term insurance policy.

waiting (elimination) period
The period after an insured meets the policy's eligibility requirements, during which he or she must pay expenses out-of-pocket; when the waiting period expires, the insured begins to receive benefits.

guaranteed renewability
A policy provision ensuring continued insurance coverage for the insured's lifetime, so long as the premiums continue to be paid.

optional renewability
A contractual clause allowing the insured to continue insurance *only at the insurer's option.*

- Inflation protection: Many policies offer riders that, for an additional premium, let you increase your benefits over time so that benefits roughly match the rising cost of nursing home and home health care. Most inflation protection riders let you increase benefits by a flat amount, often 5 percent, per year. Others offer benefits linked to the rise in the consumer price index (CPI). Most policies discontinue inflation adjustments after either 10 or 20 years. Inflation protection riders can add between 25 percent and 40 percent to the basic premium for a long-term-care insurance policy.

- Premium levels: Long-term-care insurance is rather expensive, and premiums vary widely among insurance companies. For example, an average healthy 55-year-old male may pay about $5,100 per year for a policy that pays for three years of care at $250 per day for nursing home care with a 90-day waiting period and a 3 percent inflation rider. The cost of the same coverage drops substantially with the ages of the insured. Because of this marked rise in premium with age, some financial planners recommend buying long-term-care insurance when you are fairly young. But keep in mind that, although the annual premiums are lower, you'll be paying for a lot longer time before you are likely to actually need the benefits. And remember that insurance companies can and do get permission to increase premiums significantly over the life of a policy. So future premiums are uncertain, which is not comforting.

9-5c How to Buy Long-Term-Care Insurance

If you decide that you or a relative should have long-term-care insurance, be sure to buy from a financially sound company (based on ratings from the major ratings agencies) that has experience in this market segment. Here are some additional guidelines to help you choose the right policy:

- Buy the policy when you're healthy: Once you have a disease (such as Alzheimer's or multiple sclerosis) or have a stroke, you become uninsurable. The best time to buy is when you're in your mid-50s or 60s.

- Buy the right types of coverage—but don't buy more coverage than you need: Your policy should cover skilled, intermediate, and custodial care as well as adult day care centers and assisted living facilities. If you have access to family caregivers or home health services, opt for only nursing home coverage; if not, select a policy with generous home health care benefits. To reduce costs, increase the waiting period before benefits start; the longer you can cover the costs yourself, the lower your premiums. You may also choose a shorter benefit payment period; 3 years is a popular choice, but the average nursing home stay is about one year. Lifetime coverage increases the premium for a 65-year-old by as much as 40 percent.

- Understand what the policy covers and when it pays benefits: The amounts paid, benefit periods, and services covered vary among insurers. One rule of thumb is to buy a policy covering 80 percent to 100 percent of current nursing home costs in your area. Some policies pay only for licensed health care providers, whereas others include assistance with household chores. Know how the policy defines benefit eligibility.

TEST YOURSELF

9-20   Why should a consumer consider purchasing a long-term care insurance policy?

9-21   Describe the differences among long-term-care policies regarding (a) type of care, (b) eligibility requirements, and (c) services covered. List and discuss some other important policy provisions.

9-22   Discuss some of the questions one should ask before buying long-term-care insurance. What guidelines can be used to choose the right policy?

9-6 DISABILITY INCOME INSURANCE

LG6

When a family member becomes sick for an extended period, the effect on the family goes beyond medical bills. About one-third of people between the ages of 35 and 65 will be disabled for 90 days or longer before age 65, and about one in seven people between the ages of 35 and 65 will become disabled for five years or more. During the working years, becoming disabled is more likely than death. For a 35-year-old male, the odds are nearly 2 to 1, and for a 35-year-old female, the odds are nearly 3 to 1. Although most Americans have life insurance, few have taken steps to protect their family should a serious illness or accident prevent them from working for an extended period.

Disability income insurance
Insurance that provides families with weekly or monthly payments to replace income when the insured is unable to work because of a covered illness, injury, or disease.

The best way to protect against the potentially devastating financial consequences of a health-related disability is with disability income insurance. Disability income insurance provides families with weekly or monthly payments to replace income when the insured is unable to work because of a covered illness, injury, or disease. Some companies also offer disability income protection for a spousal homemaker; such coverage helps pay for the services that the spouse would normally provide.

Almost all employers offer disability income insurance at advantageous rates. However, coverage is often voluntary, and you may have to pay the entire premium yourself. Group coverage is usually a good buy, and premiums for employer-sponsored group coverage average $300 to $500 a year depending on age and income—about one-third less than the cost of comparable private coverage. A disadvantage is that if you change jobs, you may lose the coverage. The benefits from a group plan in which you pay the premiums are tax free (unless paid through a flexible spending account). As a safeguard, you'd be well advised to run a needs analysis, as described in the instructions for Worksheet 9.2, to be sure you have enough coverage for your needs.

Financial Fact or Fantasy?

Disability insurance is helpful only if you make a lot of money—and then only if you are out of work for a long period of time (at least six months to a year). **Fantasy:** Disability income insurance replaces some or all of the weekly earnings lost in case you are physically unable to work. The coverage usually begins after a short waiting period and is just as valuable—perhaps more so—to the low-income family as it is to those with high incomes.

Social Security offers disability income benefits, but you must be unable to do *any* job whatsoever to receive benefits. Benefits are payable only if your disability is expected to last at least one year (or to be fatal), and they don't begin until you've been disabled for at least five months. The actual amount paid is a percentage of your previous monthly earnings, with some statistical adjustments. The percentage is higher for people with low earnings. Most recipients receive between $300 and $2,200 a month with a maximum monthly payment in 2015 of $2,663.

The need for disability income coverage is great but is generally ignored by the public. Although most workers receive some disability insurance benefits from their employer, in many cases, the group plan falls short and pays only about 60 to 70 percent of salary for a limited period. The first step in considering disability income insurance is to determine the dollar amount your family would need (typically monthly) if an earner becomes disabled. Then you can buy the coverage that you need or supplement existing coverage if necessary.

9-6a Estimating Your Disability Insurance Needs

The main purpose of disability income insurance is to replace all (or most) of the income—that is, earnings—that would be lost if you became disabled and physically unable to hold a job. In essence, it should enable you to maintain a standard of living at or near your present level. To help decide how much disability income insurance is right for you, use Worksheet 9.2 to estimate your monthly disability benefit needs. Here is all you have to do.

1. Calculate take-home pay. Disability benefits are generally, but not always, tax free, so you typically need to replace only your *take-home (after-tax) pay*. Benefits from employer-paid policies are fully or partially taxable. To estimate

Using a worksheet like this makes the job of estimating disability benefit insurance needs a lot easier.

DISABILITY BENEFIT NEEDS

Name(s) _____ Date _____

1. Estimate current monthly take-home pay $ _____

2. Estimate existing monthly benefits

   a. Social Security benefits $ _____

   b. Other government program benefits   _____

   c. Company disability benefits   _____

   d. Group disability policy benefits   _____

3. Total existing monthly disability benefits (2a + 2b + 2c + 2d) $ _____   _____

4. **Estimated monthly disability benefits needed ([1] – [3])** $ _____

---

take-home pay, subtract income and Social Security taxes paid from your gross earned income (salary only). Divide this total by 12 to calculate your monthly take-home pay.

2. Estimate the monthly amounts of disability benefits from government or employer programs.

   a. *Social Security benefits*. Obtain an estimate of your benefits by using the online calculators provided by the Social Security Administration on their Internet site. The average Social Security disability benefit is about $1,200 per month.

   b. *Other government program benefits* with disability benefits for which you qualify (armed services, Veterans Administration, civil service, the Federal Employees Compensation Act, state workers' compensation systems). There are also special programs for railroad workers, longshoremen, and people with black-lung disease.

   c. *Company disability benefits*. Ask your company benefits supervisor to help you calculate company-provided benefits, including sick pay or wage continuation plans (these are essentially short-term disability income insurance) and plans formally designated as disability insurance. For each benefit that your employer offers, check on its tax treatment.

   d. *Group disability policy benefits*. A private insurer provides the coverage, and you pay for it, often through payroll deduction.

3. Add up your existing monthly disability benefits.

4. Subtract your existing monthly disability benefits from your current monthly take-home pay. The result shows the estimated monthly disability benefits you'll need in order to maintain your present after-tax income. Note that investment income and spousal income (if the spouse is presently employed) are ignored because it's assumed this income will continue and is necessary to maintain your current standard of living. If your spouse is now unemployed but would enter the workforce if you ever became disabled, then his or her estimated monthly income (take-home pay) could be subtracted from item 4 of Worksheet 9.2 to determine your net monthly disability benefit needs.

9-6b Disability Income Insurance Provisions and Costs

The scope and cost of your disability income coverage depend on its contractual provisions. Although disability income insurance policies can be complex, certain features are important: (1) definition of disability, (2) benefit amount and duration, (3) probationary period, (4) waiting period, (5) renewability, and (6) other provisions.

Definition of Disability

Disability policies vary in the standards you must meet to receive benefits. Some pay benefits if you're unable to perform the duties of your customary occupation—the *own occupation* (or "Own Occ") definition—whereas others pay only if you can engage in no gainful employment at all—the *any occupation* (or "Any Occ") definition. Under the "Own Occ" definition, a professor who lost his voice—yet could still be paid to write or do research—would receive full benefits because he couldn't lecture, a primary function of his occupation. With a *residual benefit option,* you would be paid partial benefits if you can only work part-time or at a lower salary. The "Any Occ" definition is considerably less expensive because it gives the insurer more leeway in determining whether the insured should receive benefits.

Individual disability policies may contain a *presumptive disability* clause that supersedes the previously discussed definition of disability when certain types of

FINANCIAL PLANNING TIPS

Buying Disability Income Insurance

Consider the following tips in evaluating disability income insurance policies:

- **Know what the government can do for you.** Social Security disability benefits are available only to those with a condition that makes them unable to work of at least a year or that is terminal. The average benefit payout is only about 40 percent of pre-disability income. Qualified applicants should expect to wait between three and five months to get Social Security disability benefits. Only a few states provide additional benefits, although it's worth checking that. If you buy a private disability income insurance policy, be aware that most require you to apply for Social Security benefits, which will be subtracted from the benefit that you receive from the insurer.

- **Buying a policy at work is usually cheapest.** Many employers provide disability income insurance and pay part of the premiums. If you go this route, make sure that you have both short- and long-term coverage. Short-term coverage usually lasts for a few months, and long-term coverage often starts paying after 90 to 180 days. Make

sure that you're not exposed to a significant gap between the two. If you buy a policy through your employer, you may be able to pay the premiums directly out of your paycheck on a pretax basis. However, this means that your benefits would be taxable.

- **Determine if a policy purchased through your employer is portable.** It's good to know if you can keep the policy if you leave your current company.

- **Understand the circumstances in which the disability insurance benefit will be paid.** The best trigger is when you cannot do your current job. However, some policies only pay if you cannot do any comparable job, which is a much more complicated constraint.

- **Read the fine print.** It's important to know what percentage of pre-disability income is paid out by the policy. And does it include just base salary or additional compensation like commissions or bonuses? Are there limits on benefit payouts for certain conditions like mental illness? You'll want to know the ins and outs of each policy that you consider.

Source: Anna Wilde Mathews, "Just in Case: The Skinny on Buying Disability Insurance," http://www.wsj.com/articles/SB10001424052748704561004575013073100310 794, accessed August 2015.

losses occur. Loss of both hands, sight in both eyes, and hearing in both ears are examples where the insured may be *presumed* totally disabled and may receive full benefits even though he or she still can be employed in some capacity.

Benefit Amount and Duration

Most individual disability income policies pay a flat monthly benefit, which is stated in the policy, whereas group plans pay a fixed percentage of gross income. In either case, insurers normally won't agree to amounts of more than 60 percent to 70 percent of the insured's gross income. Insurers won't issue policies for the full amount of gross income because this would give some people an incentive to fake a disability (e.g., "bad back") and possibly collect more in insurance benefits than they normally would receive as take-home pay.

Monthly benefits can be paid for a few months or a lifetime. If you're assured a substantial defined benefit pension, Social Security, or other benefits at retirement, then a policy that pays benefits until age 65 is adequate. Most people, however, will need to continue their occupations for many more years and should consider a policy offering lifetime benefits. Many policies offer benefits for periods as short as two or five years. Although these policies may be better than nothing, they don't protect against the major financial losses associated with long-term disabilities.

Probationary Period

Both group and individual disability income policies are likely to include a probationary period, usually 7 to 30 days, which is a time delay from the date the policy is issued until benefit privileges are available. Any disability stemming from an illness, injury, or disease that occurs during the probationary period is *not* covered—even if it continues beyond this period. This feature keeps costs down.

Waiting Period

The waiting, or elimination, period provisions in a disability income policy are similar to those discussed for long-term-care insurance. Typical waiting periods range from 30 days to a year. If you have an adequate emergency fund to provide family income during the early months of disability, you can choose a longer waiting period and substantially reduce your premiums, as shown in Exhibit 9.5.

With most insurers, you can trade off an increase in the waiting period—say, from 60 days to 90 days—for an increase in the duration of benefits from five years to age 65. In fact, as Exhibit 9.5 shows, the premium charged by this insurer for a

---

EXHIBIT 9.5　**Representative Disability Income Insurance Premium Costs**

The cost of disability income insurance varies with the terms of payment as well as the length of the waiting period. Women pay substantially higher rates than men do. This table shows representative premiums for basic disability income coverage for a 35-year-old that pays $2,000 per month in benefits, with guaranteed premiums to age 65. The policy also includes a 3 percent inflation rider.

Benefit Period	2 Years		5 Years		10 Years		To Age 65	
Waiting Period	Male	Female	Male	Female	Male	Female	Male	Female
60 days	$378	$486	$546	$740	$731	$1,122	$974	$1,575
90 days	294	357	412	532	552	828	747	1,189
6 months	269	317	393	487	519	758	713	1,136
One year	N/A	N/A	361	441	488	720	689	1,084

policy covering a 35-year-old male with a 60-day waiting period and two-year benefit period ($378) is about the same as one charged for a five-year benefit period with a six-month waiting period ($393). Accepting this type of trade-off usually makes sense because the primary purpose of insurance is to protect the insured against a catastrophic loss, not from smaller losses that are better handled through proper budgeting and saving.

Renewability

Most individual disability income insurance is either *guaranteed renewable* or *noncancelable*. As with long-term-care policies, guaranteed renewability ensures that you can renew the policy until you reach the age stated in the clause, usually age 65. Premiums can be raised over time if justified by the loss experience of all those in the same class (usually based on age, sex, and occupational category). Noncancelable policies offer guaranteed renewability, but they also guarantee that future premiums will remain the same as those stated in the policy at issuance. Because of this stable premium guarantee, noncancelable policies generally are more expensive than those with only a guaranteed renewability provision.

Other Provisions

The purchasing power of income from a long-term disability policy that pays, say, $2,000 per month could be severely affected by inflation. In fact, a 3 percent inflation rate would reduce the purchasing power of this $2,000 benefit to less than $1,500 in 10 years. To counteract such a reduction, many insurers offer a *cost-of-living adjustment (COLA)*. With a COLA provision, the monthly benefit is adjusted upward each year, often in line with the CPI, although these annual adjustments are often capped at a given rate (say, 8 percent). Although some financial advisors suggest buying COLA riders, others feel the 10 percent to 25 percent additional premium is too much to pay for it.

Although the COLA provision applies only once the insured is disabled, the *guaranteed insurability option (GIO)* can allow you to purchase additional disability income insurance in line with inflation increases while you're still healthy. Under the GIO, the price of this additional insurance is fixed at the contract's inception, and you don't have to prove insurability.

A *waiver of premium* is standard in disability income policies. If you're disabled for a minimum period, normally 60 or 90 days, then the insurer will waive any future premiums that come due while you remain disabled. In essence, the waiver of premium gives you additional disability income insurance in the amount of your regular premium payment.

Remember that disability income insurance is just one part of your overall personal financial plan. You'll need to find your own balance between cost and coverage.

TEST YOURSELF

9-23 What is disability income insurance? Explain the waiting-period provisions found in such policies.

9-24 Describe both the liberal and strict definitions used to establish whether an insured is disabled.

9-25 Why is it important to consider benefit duration when shopping for disability income coverage?

Planning Over a Lifetime: *Insuring Your Health*

Here are some key ideas concerning how insuring your health changes over the stages in the life cycle.

Independent Lifestyle (20s)	Family and Career Development (30s–40s)	Mature Lifestyle (50s–60s)	Retirement (65+)
✓ Assess your health and take steps to stay healthy: exercise, eat well, and avoid smoking and too much alcohol.	✓ Consider HMOs and PPOs to lower deductibles and to maximize flexibility of choices.	✓ Evaluate the need for long-term-care insurance.	✓ Consider the best way to get prescription benefits in light of Medicare options.
✓ While in school or unemployed, take advantage of your opportunity to stay on your parents' health insurance until the age of 26.	✓ Re-evaluate the need for disability income insurance.	✓ Re-evaluate the need for long-term-care insurance.	✓ Re-evaluate the need for long-term-care insurance.
✓ When employed, take out health care insurance coverage with your employer and/or check out policies available on an ACA insurance exchange.	✓ Re-evaluate your health insurance policy and its premiums.	✓ Familiarize yourself with Medicare benefits.	
✓ Evaluate the appropriateness of disability income insurance.			
✓ Consider pre-tax accounts like flexibility spending to save money.			

Financial Impact of Personal Choices
Josh Expands His Health Insurance Coverage

Josh Wallace is 27 years old. He works for a company with a good comprehensive major medical health insurance plan. Indeed, Josh has heard it's priced better than most plans and has consequently taken out the optional expanded dental and vision plans. While he doesn't currently wear glasses or contact lenses, he does go for an annual eye exam and wants the extra vision plan in case he ends up needing corrective lens or has any eye problems. His plan has a $40 co-payment for an annual eye exam and pays $100 toward eye glass frames plus 20 percent of the rest of the cost. Contact lenses have similar coverage. Josh pays just an additional $15 monthly premium for the vision plan. Josh feels more comfortable having expanded health insurance coverage.

While Josh feels better having expanded health insurance coverage in general and vision coverage in particular, it isn't currently a cost effective decision. Josh makes a $40 co-payment for an annual eye exam, which is probably cheaper than the full cost of an eye exam. But he doesn't wear glasses or contact lenses. His $15 monthly premium costs him $180 per year. It's extremely unlikely that he saves anywhere near that much on the cost of his exam under the vision plan. And if Josh has a significant medical problem with his eyes, his major medical insurance plan should cover the costs well. It could make sense for him to have such expanded vision coverage in the future if corrective lenses are needed. So it appears that Josh's comfort over having expanded vision coverage is costly.

Summary

LG1 Discuss why having adequate health insurance is important and identify the factors contributing to the growing cost of health insurance. p. 341
A serious illness or major injury can have devastating financial consequences, easily costing tens of thousands of dollars in medical care and lost income. Even routine medical care can be costly. Adequate health insurance protects you from having to pay all of these costs out of pocket. However, many Americans are uninsured or underinsured because the cost of health insurance has skyrocketed. Trends pushing medical expenses and health insurance higher include the growth of new drugs and treatments that save lives but also cost more to provide. Administrative costs, excessive paperwork, increased regulation, and insurance fraud are also contributing to rising costs.

LG2 Differentiate among the major types of health insurance plans and identify major private and public health insurance providers and their programs. p. 343
Health insurance is available from both private and government-sponsored programs. Private health insurance plans include indemnity (fee-for-service) plans and managed care plans. Indemnity plans pay a share of health care costs directly to a medical provider, who is usually separate from the insurer. The insured pays the remaining amount. In a managed care plan, subscribers contract with and make monthly payments directly to the organization providing the health services. Examples of managed care plans include health maintenance organizations (HMOs) and preferred provider organizations (PPOs). Blue Cross/Blue Shield plans are prepaid hospital and medical expense plans. Federal and state agencies also provide health insurance coverage to eligible individuals. Medicare, Medicaid, and workers' compensation insurance are all forms of government health insurance plans.

LG3 Analyze your own health insurance needs and explain how to shop for appropriate coverage. p. 351
From a health insurance perspective, most people need protection from two types of losses: (1) the cost of medical bills and other associated expenses, and (2) loss of income or household services caused by an inability to work. A good

health care plan should use risk avoidance, loss prevention and control, and risk assumption strategies to reduce risk and the associated need and cost of insurance. The best way to buy health insurance is to determine your current coverage and resources and then match your needs with the various types of coverage available. When shopping for health insurance, consider the cost of coverage, its availability as an employee benefit, the quality of both the agent and the insurer or managed care provider, and your own medical needs and care preferences.

LG4 **Explain the basic types of medical expenses covered by and the policy provisions of health insurance plans. p. 355**
The basic types of medical expenses covered by insurance are hospitalization, surgical expenses, physician expenses (nonsurgical medical care), and major medical insurance (which covers all types of medical expenses). Some health insurers offer comprehensive major medical policies that combine basic hospitalization, surgical, and physician expense coverage with a major medical plan to form a single policy.

The most important provisions in medical insurance policies pertain to terms of payment, terms of coverage, and cost containment. How much your plan will pay depends on deductibles, participation (co-insurance), internal limits, and coordination of benefits. Terms of coverage encompass the persons and places covered, cancellation, pregnancy and abortion, mental illness, rehabilitation, and group coverage continuation. The most common cost containment provisions are preadmission certification, continued stay review, second surgical opinions, waiver of co-insurance, and limitations of insurer's responsibility.

LG5 **Assess the need for and features of long-term-care insurance. p. 363**
Long-term-care insurance covers nonhospital expenses, such as nursing home care or home health care, caused by chronic illness or frailty. Coverage availability depends on provisions addressing type of care, eligibility requirements, services covered, renewability, and preexisting conditions. Terms-of-payment provisions include daily benefits, benefit duration, waiting period, and inflation protection. Premium levels result from differences in coverage and payment provisions, and they vary widely among insurance companies.

LG6 **Discuss the features of disability income insurance and how to determine your need for it. p. 368**
The loss of family income caused by the disability of a principal wage earner can be at least partially replaced by disability income insurance. Disability insurance needs can be estimated by subtracting the amount of existing monthly disability benefits from current monthly take-home pay. Important coverage terms include the definition of disability, probationary period, renewability, guaranteed insurability, and waiver of premium. Provisions pertaining to benefit amount and duration, waiting period, and cost-of-living adjustments define the terms of payment. Because these policies are expensive, you should choose as long a waiting period as possible given your other available financial resources.

Key Terms

Answers to Test Yourself

You can find answers to these questions on this book's companion website. Look for it at *www.cengagebrain.com*. Search for this book by its title, and then add it to your dashboard.

Financial Planning Exercises

LG2, 3, 4
p. 343, 351, 355

1. ***Choosing a health insurance plan.*** Joe and Whitney Alexander have two children, with ages of 6 years and 5 months. Their younger child, Nathan, was born with a congenital heart defect that will require several major surgeries in the next few years to correct fully. Joe is employed as a salesperson for a major pharmaceutical firm, and Whitney does not work outside the home. Joe's employer offers employees a choice between two health benefit plans:

   - A plan that allows the Alexanders to choose health services from a wide range of doctors and hospitals. The plan pays 80 percent of all medical costs, and the Alexanders are responsible for the other 20 percent. There's a deductible of $500 per person. Joe's employer will pay 100 percent of the cost of this plan for Joe, but the Alexanders will be responsible for paying $380 a month to cover Whitney and the children under this plan.
   - A group HMO. If the Alexanders choose this plan, the company still pays 100 percent of the plan's cost for Joe, but insurance for Whitney and the children will cost $295 a month. They'll also have to make a $20 co-payment for any doctor's office visits and prescription drugs. They will be restricted to using the HMO's doctors and hospital for medical services. Which plan would you recommend that the Alexanders choose? Why? What other health coverage options should the Alexanders consider?

LG2, 3, 4
p. 343, 351, 355

2. ***Out-of-pocket plan costs.*** John Chang was seriously injured in a snowboarding accident that broke both his legs and an arm. His medical expenses included five days of hospitalization at $900 a day, $6,200 in surgical fees, $4,300 in physician's fees (including time in the hospital and eight follow-up office visits), $520 in prescription medications, and $2,100 for physical therapy treatments. All of these charges fall within customary and reasonable payment amounts.
   a. If John had an indemnity plan that pays 80 percent of his charges with a $500 deductible and a $5,000 stop-loss provision, how much would he have to pay out of pocket?
   b. What would John's out-of-pocket expenses be if he belonged to an HMO with a $20 co-pay for office visits?
   c. Monthly premiums are $155 for the indemnity plan and $250 for the HMO. If he had no other medical expenses this year, which plan would have provided more cost-effective coverage for John? What other factors should be considered when deciding between the two plans?

LG2, 3, 4
p. 343, 351, 355

3. ***Comparing health insurance policies. Use Worksheet 9.1.*** Erika Willis, a recent college graduate, has decided to accept a job offer from a nonprofit organization. She'll earn $40,000 a year but will receive no employee health benefits. Erika estimates that her monthly living expenses will be about $2,000 a month, including rent, food, transportation, and clothing. She has no health problems and expects to remain in good health in the near future. Using the Internet or other

resources, gather information about three health insurance policies that Erika could purchase on her own. Use Worksheet 9.1 to compare the policies' features. Which of the three policies would you recommend Erika buy, and why?

LG5 p. 363

4. ***Pros and cons of long-term care insurance.*** Discuss the pros and cons of long-term care insurance. Does it make sense for anyone in your family right now? Why or why not? What factors might change this assessment in the future?

LG6 p. 368

5. ***Calculating need for disability income insurance. Use Worksheet 9.2.*** Ben West, a 35-year-old computer programmer, earns $72,000 a year. His monthly take-home pay is $3,750. His wife, Ashley, works part-time at their children's elementary school but receives no benefits. Under state law, Ashley's employer contributes to a workers' compensation insurance fund that would provide $2,250 per month for six months if Ben were disabled and unable to work.

   a. Use Worksheet 9.2 to calculate Ben's disability insurance needs, assuming that he won't qualify for Medicare under his Social Security benefits.

   b. Based on your answer in part **a**, what would you advise Ben about his need for additional disability income insurance? Discuss the type and size of disability income insurance coverage he should consider, including possible provisions he might want to include. What other factors should he take into account if he decides to purchase a policy?

LG6 p. 368

6. ***Calculating your need for disability income insurance. Use Worksheet 9.2.*** Do you need disability income insurance? Calculate your need using Worksheet 9.2. Discuss how you'd go about purchasing this coverage.

LG1, 2, 3, 4 p. 341, 343, 351, 355

7. ***Assess your health insurance situation.*** Do you have any health insurance now? What does your policy cover? What is excluded? Are there any gaps that you think need to be filled? Are there any risks in your current lifestyle or situation that might make additional coverage necessary? If you were to purchase health insurance for yourself in the near future, what type of plan would you select, and why? What steps can you take to keep your health costs down?

Applying Personal Finance

Insure Your Health!

Health care costs have increased dramatically in recent years, and many insurance providers have reduced their coverage, leaving the individual to foot more of the bill. In this project, you'll examine your health insurance needs and determine the coverage that's appropriate for you.

First, make a list of the possible health care needs you're likely to have during the year. Be sure to include the potential accident risks to which you're typically exposed in pursuit of your lifestyle activities. Then, if you currently have health insurance, make a list of the coverage it provides, including deductibles, co-insurance amounts, prescription coverage, policy limits and exclusions, and so forth. Is your coverage adequate in light of your needs? Are there ways you can reduce your costs? If you don't currently have health insurance, research possible providers. Can you obtain insurance through your university, place of employment, or through an organization to which you belong? What options are available to you on an ACA insurance exchange? Consider all of your feasible alternatives, the coverages that would be provided, and the cost of each.

CRITICAL THINKING CASES

LG2, 3, 4, 5, 6 p. 343, 351, 355, 363, 368

9.1 Evaluating Walter's Health Care Coverage

Walter Burton was a self-employed window washer earning approximately $700 per week. One day, while cleaning windows on the eighth floor of the Commercial Bank Building, he tripped and fell from the scaffolding to the pavement below. He sustained severe multiple injuries but miraculously survived the accident. He was immediately rushed to the local hospital for surgery. He remained there for 60 days of treatment, after which he was allowed to go home for further recuperation. During his hospital stay, he incurred the following expenses: surgeon, $2,500; physician, $1,000; hospital bill for room and board, $250 per day; nursing services, $1,200; anesthetics, $600; wheelchair rental, $100; ambulance, $150; and drugs, $350. Walter has a major medical policy that has a $3,000 deductible clause, an 80 percent co-insurance clause, internal limits of $180 per day on hospital room and board, and $1,500 as a maximum surgical fee. The policy provides no disability income benefits.

Critical Thinking Questions

1. Explain the policy provisions as they relate to deductibles, co-insurance, and internal limits.
2. How much should Walter recover from the insurance company? How much must he pay out of his own pocket?
3. Would any other policies have offered Walter additional protection? What about his inability to work while recovering from his injury?
4. Based on the information presented, how would you assess Walter's health care insurance coverage? Explain.

LG5 p. 363 ## 9.2 Luis and Dora Barillas Evaluate Their Disability Income Needs

Luis Barillas and his wife, Dora, have been married for two years and have a 1-year-old son. They live in Charlotte, North Carolina, where Luis works for Advanced Marketing Analytics. He earns $3,200 per month, of which he takes home $2,300. Luis and his family are entitled to receive the benefits provided by the company's group health insurance policy. In addition to major medical coverage, the policy provides a monthly disability income benefit amounting to 20 percent of the employee's average monthly take-home pay for the most recent 12 months prior to incurring the disability. (*Note:* Luis' average monthly take-home pay for the most recent year is equal to his current monthly take-home pay.) In case of complete disability, Luis would also be eligible for Social Security payments of $700 per month.

Dora is also employed. She earns $700 per month after taxes by working part-time at a nearby grocery store. As a part-time employee, the store gives her no benefits. Should Luis become disabled, Dora would continue to work at her part-time job. If she became disabled, Social Security would provide monthly income of $400. Luis and Dora spend 90 percent of their combined take-home pay to meet their bills and provide for a variety of necessary items. They use the remaining 10 percent to fulfill their entertainment and savings goals.

Critical Thinking Questions

1. How much, if any, additional disability income insurance does Luis require to ensure adequate protection against his becoming completely disabled? Use Worksheet 9.2 to assess his needs.
2. Does Dora need any disability income coverage? Explain.
3. What specific recommendations regarding disability income insurance would you give Luis and Dora to provide adequate protection for themselves and their child?

CHAPTER 10

Protecting Your Property

LEARNING GOALS

LG1 Discuss the importance and basic principles of property insurance, including types of exposure, indemnity, and co-insurance.

LG2 Identify the types of coverage provided by homeowner's insurance.

LG3 Select the right homeowner's insurance policy for your needs.

LG4 Analyze the coverage in a personal automobile policy (PAP) and choose the most cost-effective policy.

LG5 Describe other types of property and liability insurance.

LG6 Choose a property and liability insurance agent and company, and settle claims.

How Will This Affect Me?

The chapter explains the key property insurance concepts of indemnity, subrogation, and co-insurance. It then describes the common sources of property and liability risk exposures and the insurance coverage available to address them. The main characteristics of homeowner's and auto insurance are covered, as well as how to choose the version of each policy type that's best for you. Supplemental insurance to protect against floods and earth-quakes and personal liability umbrella policies are also described. Especially practical tips can be found in the discussions of how to choose an insurance agent and how to settle property and liability insurance claims. When you finish this chapter, you should understand the best and most cost-effective ways to use insurance to protect your property and associated liability exposures.

10-1 BASIC PRINCIPLES OF PROPERTY INSURANCE

LG1

Suppose that a severe storm destroyed your home. Could you afford to replace it? Most people couldn't. To protect yourself from this and other similar types of property loss, you need property insurance. What's more, every day you face some type of risk of negligence. For example, you might be distraught over a personal problem and unintentionally run a red light, seriously injuring a pedestrian. Could you pay for the medical and other costs? Because consequences like this and other potentially negligent acts could cause financial ruin, having appropriate liability insurance is essential.

Property and liability insurance should be as much a part of your personal financial plans as life and health insurance. Such coverage protects the assets you've already acquired and safeguards your progress toward financial goals. **Property insurance** guards against catastrophic losses of real and personal property caused by such perils as fire, theft, vandalism, windstorms, and other calamities. **Liability insurance** offers protection against the financial consequences that may arise from the insured's responsibility for property loss or personal injuries to others.

People spend lots of money for insurance coverage, but few really understand what they're getting for their premium dollars. The vast majority of people consequently are totally unaware of any gaps, overinsurance, or underinsurance in their property and liability insurance policies. Ineffective insurance protection is at odds with the objectives of personal financial planning. It is thus important to become familiar with the principles of property and liability insurance. The basic principles of property and liability insurance pertain to types of exposure, indemnity, and co-insurance. We'll discuss each of these principles in the following sections.

property insurance
Insurance coverage that protects real and personal property from catastrophic losses caused by a variety of perils, such as fire, theft, vandalism, and windstorms.

liability insurance
Insurance that protects against the financial consequences that may arise from the insured's responsibility for property loss or injuries to others.

10-1a Types of Exposure

Most individuals face two types of exposure: physical loss of property and loss through liability.

Exposure to Property Loss

peril
A cause of loss.

Most property insurance contracts define the property covered and name the perils—the causes of loss—for which the insured will be compensated in case of a claim against their policy. As a rule, most property insurance contracts impose two obligations on the property owner: (1) developing a complete inventory of the property being insured; and (2) identifying the perils against which protection is desired. Some property contracts limit coverage by excluding certain types of property and perils, while others offer more comprehensive protection.

Property Inventory. Taking inventory of property is part of the financial planning process. It is especially important in the case of a total loss—if your home is destroyed by fire, for example. All property insurance companies require you to show *proof of loss* when making a claim. Your personal property inventory, along with corresponding values at the time of inventory, can serve as evidence to satisfy the company. A comprehensive property inventory not only helps you settle a claim when a loss occurs, but also serves as a useful guide for selecting the most appropriate coverage for your particular needs.

Most families have a home, household furnishings, clothing and personal belongings, lawn and garden equipment, and motor vehicles, all of which need to be insured. Fortunately, most homeowner's and automobile insurance policies provide coverage for these types of belongings. But many families also own such items as motorboats and trailers, various types of off-road vehicles, business property and inventories, jewelry, stamp or coin collections, musical instruments, guns, antiques, paintings, bonds, securities, and other items of special value, such as cameras, golf clubs, electronic equipment, and personal computers. Coverage for these belongings (and those that accompany you when you travel) often require special types of insurance.

Many insurance companies have easy-to-complete personal property inventory forms available to help policyholders prepare inventories. A partial sample of one such form is shown in Exhibit 10.1. These inventory forms can be supplemented with photographs or videos of household contents and belongings. For insurance purposes, a picture may truly be worth a thousand words. Regardless of whether inventory forms are supplemented with photographs or videotapes, *every effort should be made to keep these documents in a safe place*, where they can't be destroyed—such as a bank safe-deposit box. Also consider keeping a *duplicate copy* with a parent or trusted relative. Remember, you may need these photographs and inventories if something serious does happen and you have to come up with an authenticated list of property losses.

Identifying Perils. Many people feel a false sense of security after buying insurance because they believe they're safeguarded against all contingencies. However, certain *perils* cannot be reasonably insured. For example, most homeowner's or automobile insurance policies limit or exclude damage or loss caused by flood (remember Hurricane Katrina in New Orleans in 2005), earthquake, backing up of sewers and drains, mudslides, mysterious disappearance, war, nuclear radiation, and ordinary wear and tear. In addition, property insurance contracts routinely limit coverage based on the location of the property, time of loss, persons involved, and types of hazards to which the property is exposed.

Liability Exposures

We all encounter a variety of liability exposures daily. Driving a car, entertaining guests at home, volunteer activities, or being careless in performing professional duties are some common liability risks. Loss exposures result from negligence, which is failing to act in a reasonable manner or take necessary steps to protect others from harm. Even if you're never negligent and always prudent, someone might *believe* that you are the cause of a loss and bring a costly lawsuit against you. Losing the judgment could cost you thousands—or even millions—of dollars. A debt that size could force you into bankruptcy or financial ruin.

negligence
Failing to act in a reasonable manner or to take necessary steps to protect others from harm.

EXHIBIT 10.1 **A Personal Property Inventory Form**

Using a form like this will help you keep track of your personal property, including date of purchase, original purchase price, and replacement cost.

Living Room

Stereo System

Brand	
Model	
Serial #	Date purchased
Purchase price $	Replacement cost $

Large-Screen TV

Brand	
Model	
Serial #	Date purchased
Purchase price $	Replacement cost $

Personal Computer

Brand	
Model	
Serial #	Date purchased
Purchase price $	Replacement cost $

Home Theater System

Brand	
Model	
Serial #	Date purchased
Purchase price $	Replacement cost $

DVD Player

Brand	
Model	
Serial #	Date purchased
Purchase price $	Replacement cost $

Living Room

Article	Qty.	Date Purchased	Purchase Price	Replacement Cost
Air conditioners (window)				
Blinds/shades				
Bookcases				
Books				
Cabinets				
Carpets/rugs				
Chairs				
Chests				
Clocks				
Couches/sofas				
Curtains/draperies				
Fireplace fixtures				
Lamps/lighting fixtures				
Mirrors				
Pictures/paintings				
Audio recordings				
Planters				
Stereo equipment				
Tables				
Television sets				
Other				
Other				

Fortunately, *liability insurance* coverage will protect you against losses resulting from these risks, *including the high legal fees* required to defend yourself against suits that may, or may not, have merit. It's important to include adequate liability insurance in your overall insurance program, either through your homeowner's and automobile policies or through a separate umbrella policy.

10-1b Principle of Indemnity

principle of indemnity
An insurance principle stating that an insured may not be compensated by the insurance company in an amount exceeding the insured's economic loss.

The **principle of indemnity** states that the insured may not be compensated by the insurance company in an amount exceeding the insured's economic loss. Most property and liability insurance contracts are based on this principle—although, as noted in Chapters 8 and 9, this *principle does not apply to life and health insurance*. Several important concepts related to the principle of indemnity include actual cash value, subrogation, and other insurance.

Actual Cash Value versus Replacement Cost

actual cash value
A value assigned to an insured property that is determined by subtracting the amount of physical depreciation from its replacement cost.

The principle of indemnity limits the amount that an insured may collect to the **actual cash value** of the property: the replacement cost minus the value of physical depreciation. Some insurers pay replacement cost without taking depreciation into account—for example, most homeowner's policies will settle building losses on a replacement cost basis if the proper type and amount of insurance is purchased. Without a replacement-cost provision, it's common practice to deduct the amount of depreciation to obtain the actual cash value. If an insured property is damaged, then the insurer is obligated to pay no more than the property would cost new today (its replacement cost) less the amount of depreciation from wear and tear.

> **EXAMPLE: Recovery of Replacement Cost**
>
> A fire has destroyed two rooms of furniture that were 6 years old with an estimated useful life of 10 years. The replacement cost is $5,000. At the time of loss, the furniture was subject to an assumed physical depreciation of 60 percent (6 years ÷ 10 years)—in this case, $3,000. Because the actual cash value is estimated at $2,000 ($5,000 replacement cost minus $3,000 of depreciation), the maximum that the insurer would have to pay is $2,000. Importantly, the original cost of the property has no bearing on the settlement.

Subrogation

right of subrogation
The right of an insurer, who has paid an insured's claim, to request reimbursement from either the person who caused the loss or that person's insurer.

After an insurance company pays a claim, its **right of subrogation** allows it to request reimbursement from either the person who caused the loss or that person's insurance company. For example, assume you're in an automobile accident in which the other party damages your car. You may collect from your insurer or the at-fault party's insurer, but not from both (not for the same loss). Clearly, to collect the full amount of the loss from both parties would leave you better off after the loss than before it. However, this violates the principle of indemnity. Because the party who caused the accident (or loss) is ultimately responsible for paying the damages, your insurance company can go after the responsible party to collect its loss, which is the amount it paid out to you.

Other Insurance

Nearly all property and liability insurance contracts have an *other-insurance clause*, prohibiting insured persons from insuring their property with two or more insurance companies and collecting from multiple companies for the same loss. The other-insurance clause normally states that if a person has more than one insurance policy on a property, then each company need only pay an amount prorated for its share of all insurance covering the property. Without this provision, insured persons could use duplicate property insurance policies to profit from their losses.

10-1c Co-insurance

co-insurance
In property insurance, a provision requiring a policyholder to buy insurance of an amount equal to a specified percentage of the replacement value of their property.

Co-insurance, a provision commonly found in property insurance contracts, requires policyholders to buy insurance in an amount equal to a specified percentage of the replacement value of their property, or else the *policyholder* is required to pay for a proportional share of the loss. In essence, the co-insurance provision stipulates that if a property isn't sufficiently covered, the property owner will become the "co-insurer" and bear part of the loss. If the policyholder has the stipulated amount of coverage (usually 80 percent of the value of the property), then the insurance company will reimburse for covered losses, dollar-for-dollar, up to the amount of the policy limits.

Obviously, you should evaluate closely the co-insurance clause of any property insurance policy so you won't have an unexpected additional burden in the case of a loss.

EXAMPLE: Effect of Co-insurance

Joel and Anna have a fire insurance policy on their $300,000 home with an 80 percent co-insurance clause. The policy limits must equal or exceed 80 percent of the replacement value of their home. They ran short of money and decided to save by buying a $180,000 policy instead of $240,000 (80 percent of $300,000), as required by the co-insurance clause. If a loss occurs, then the company would be obligated to pay only 75 percent (180,000/240,000) of the loss, up to the amount of the policy limit. Thus, on damages of $40,000, the insurer would pay only $30,000 (75 percent of $40,000).

TEST YOURSELF

10-1 Briefly explain the fundamental concepts related to property and liability insurance.

10-2 Explain the principle of indemnity. Are any limits imposed on the amount that an insured may collect under this principle?

10-3 Explain the right of subrogation. How does this feature help lower insurance costs?

10-4 Describe how the co-insurance feature works.

10-2 HOMEOWNER'S INSURANCE

LG2, LG3

Although homeowner's insurance is often thought of as a single type of insurance policy, homeowners can choose from five different forms (HO-1, HO-2, HO-3, HO-5, and HO-8). Two other forms (HO-4 and HO-6) meet the needs of renters and owners of condominiums (see Exhibit 10.2). An HO-4 renter's policy offers essentially the same broad protection as an HO-2 homeowner's policy, but the coverage doesn't apply to the rented dwelling unit because tenants usually don't have a financial interest in the real property.

All HO forms are divided into two sections. Section I applies to the dwelling, accompanying structures, and personal property of the insured. Section II deals with comprehensive coverage for personal liability and for medical payments to others. The scope of coverage under Section I is least with an HO-1 policy and greatest with an HO-5 policy. HO-8 is a modified coverage policy for older homes, which is used to insure houses that have market values well below the cost to rebuild. The coverage in Section II is the same for all forms.

In the following paragraphs, we'll explain the important features of homeowner's forms HO-3 and HO-5, the most commonly sold policies. (As Exhibit 10.2 shows, HO-1 is a basic, seldom-used policy with relatively narrow coverage.) The coverage offered under the HO-3 and HO-5 forms is basically the same; the differences lie only in the number of perils against which protection applies to the personal property coverage.

comprehensive policy Property and liability insurance policy covering all perils unless they are specifically excluded.

named peril policy Property and liability insurance policy that individually names the perils covered.

10-2a Perils Covered

Some property and liability insurance agreements, called comprehensive policies, cover all perils except those specifically excluded, whereas named peril policies name particular, individual perils covered.

MELISSA BRANDES/SHUTTERSTOCK.COM

Section I Perils

The perils against which the home and its contents are insured are shown in Exhibit 10.2. Coverage on the dwelling is the same for the HO-3 and HO-5 forms, but coverage on the house itself and other structures (e.g., a detached garage) is comprehensive under HO-5 and a named peril in HO-3. An HO-5 provides comprehensive coverage on the personal property, where an HO-3 covers only named perils. Whether homeowners should buy an HO-3 or an HO-5 form depends primarily on how much they're willing to spend to secure the additional protection. The size of premiums for HO-3 and HO-5 policies can differ substantially among insurance companies. In some states, an HO-5 policy is the better buy because the premium differential is small. In other states, the HO-3 form has a much lower premium. Buying an HO-1 or HO-2 policy is not recommended because of its more limited coverage.

Note in Exhibit 10.2 that the types of Section I perils covered include just about every situation, from fire and explosions to lightning and wind damage to theft and vandalism. Although the list of perils is extensive, some are specifically excluded from most homeowner's contracts—in particular, *most policies (even HO-5 and HO-3 forms) exclude earthquakes and floods*. Many areas of the country are not susceptible to earthquakes and floods, and homeowners in those areas shouldn't have to pay premiums for coverage that they don't need. But even if you live in an area where the risk of an earthquake or a flood is relatively high, you'll find that *standard homeowner's policies do not provide protection against these perils* because the catastrophic nature of such events causes widespread and costly damage. As we'll see later in this chapter, you can obtain coverage for earthquakes and floods under a separate policy or a rider.

Section II Perils

The perils insured against under Section II of the homeowner's contract are the (alleged) negligence of an insured. The coverage is called *comprehensive personal liability coverage* because it offers protection against personal liability (major exclusions are noted later) resulting from negligence. It does not insure against other losses for which one may become liable, such as libel, slander, defamation of character, and contractual or intentional wrongdoing. For example, coverage would apply if you unintentionally knocked someone down your stairs. If you purposely struck and injured another person, however, or harmed someone's reputation either orally or in writing, homeowner's liability coverage would not protect you.

Section II also provides a limited amount of medical coverage for persons other than the homeowner's family in certain types of minor accidents on or off the insured's premises. This coverage helps homeowners to meet their moral obligations and helps deter possible lawsuits. The limited medical payment coverage pays irrespective of negligence or fault.

10-2b Factors Affecting Home Insurance Costs

Several factors affect premiums for home and property insurance.

- Type of structure: Do you live in a home made from wood or brick? The construction materials used in your home affect the cost of insuring it. A home built from brick costs less to insure than a similar home made of wood, yet the reverse is true when it comes to earthquake insurance—brick homes are more expensive

EXHIBIT 10.2   **A Guide to Homeowner's Policies**

The amount of insurance coverage you receive depends on the type of homeowner's (HO) policy you buy. You can also obtain coverage if you're a renter or a condominium owner.

Form	Coverages*	Covered perils
Basic Form (HO-1)	A—$15,000 minimum; B—10% of A; C—50% of A; D—10% of A; E—$100,000; F—$1,000 per person	Fire, smoke, lightning, windstorm, hail, volcanic eruption, explosion, glass breakage, aircraft, vehicles, riot or civil commotion, theft, vandalism or malicious mischief
Broad Form (HO-2)	Minimum varies; other coverages in same percentages or amounts except D—20% of A	Covers all basic-form risks plus weight of ice, snow, sleet; freezing; accidental discharge of water or steam; falling objects; accidental tearing, cracking, or burning of heating/cooling/sprinkler system or appliance; damage from electrical current
Special Form (HO-3)	Minimum varies; other coverages in same percentages or amounts except D—20% of A	Dwelling and other structures covered against risks of direct physical loss to property except losses specifically excluded; personal property covered by same perils as HO-2 plus damage by glass or safety glazing material, which is part of a building, storm door, or storm window
Renter's Form (HO-4)	Coverages A and B—Not applicable C—Minimum varies by company D—20% of C E—$100,000 F—$1,000 per person	Covers same perils covered by HO-2 for personal property
Comprehensive Form (HO-5)	Coverages A and B—Not applicable B—Not applicable C—Minimum varies by company D—40% of C E—$100,000 F—$1,000 per person	Covers same perils as HO-4, but covered perils are dwelling, other structures, and personal property covered against risks of direct physical loss except losses that are excluded specifically
Condominium Form (HO-6)	Coverage A—Minimum $1,000 B—Not applicable C—Minimum varies by company D—40% of C E—$100,000 F—$1,000 per person	Covers same perils covered by HO-2 for personal property
Modified Coverage Form (HO-8)	Same as HO-1, except losses are paid based on the amount required to repair or replace the property using common construction materials and methods	Same perils as HO-1, except theft coverage applies to losses only on the residential premises up to a maximum of $1,000; certain other coverage restrictions also apply

*Coverages:
A. Dwelling
B. Other structures
C. Personal Property
D. Loss of use
E. Personal liability
F. Medical Payments to Others

to insure. The style and age of the house also contribute to its potential insurance risk, thereby affecting insurance costs.

- Credit score: Research shows that people with lower credit scores tend to file more insurance claims. Credit scores affect premiums more than any other factor. If you have a poor credit score, you may pay two or three times more than an otherwise comparable person with an excellent credit score. So if your credit score improves, it's important to let your insurance company know because this could lower your premiums.
- Location of home: Local crime rates, weather, and proximity to a fire hydrant all affect your home's insurance premium costs. If many claims are filed from your area, insurance premiums for all the homeowners there will be higher. The local frequency of hailstorms and hurricanes will affect rates too.
- Other factors: If you have a swimming pool, trampoline, large dog, or other potentially hazardous risk factors on your property, your homeowner's premiums will be higher. Deductibles and the type and amount of coverage also affect the cost.

You Can Do It Now

Check Out the Best Homeowners Insurance Companies

When you're considering buying new homeowners insurance, it's good to know how the various insurance companies are rated. A good Internet site is **http://www.consumeraffairs.com/insurance/home.html#buyers-guide**, which summarizes industry ratings by A.M. Best, Standard & Poors, and J.D. Power & Associates. You can do it now.

10-2c Property Covered

The homeowner's policy offers property protection under Section I for the dwelling unit, accompanying structures, and personal property of homeowners and their families. Coverage for certain types of loss also applies to lawns, trees, plants, and shrubs. However, the policy excludes structures on the premises used for business purposes (except incidentally), animals (pets or otherwise), and motorized vehicles not used in maintaining the premises (such as autos, motorcycles, golf carts, or snowmobiles). *Business inventory* (e.g., goods held by an insured who is a traveling salesperson, or other goods held for sale) is not covered. Although the policy doesn't cover business inventory, it does cover *business property* (such as books, computers, copiers, office furniture, and supplies), typically up to a maximum of $2,500, while it is on the insured premises.

If you work at home, either full- or part-time, then you may need to increase your policy's limits to protect your home office. This insurance is critical because damage to your home affects not only where you live, but also your source of income. In many cases, adding a rider to your homeowner's policy can increase your home business limits to adequate levels for your computer and office equipment and provide additional limited liability coverage. The cost for these riders is low, often as low as $75 per year, depending on what coverage you include. If you need greater protection, you should investigate a separate business owner's policy that offers broader coverage for business liability, all-risk protection for equipment, and business income protection if damage to your home results in lost income.

personal property floater (PPF)
An insurance endorsement or policy providing either blanket or scheduled coverage of expensive personal property not adequately covered in a standard homeowner's policy.

10-2d Personal Property Floater

As we'll see later in this chapter, policies limit the type and amount of coverage provided. Your homeowner's policy may not protect your expensive personal property adequately. To overcome this deficiency, you can either add the **personal property floater (PPF)** as an endorsement to your homeowner's policy or take out a separate floater policy. *The PPF provides either blanket or scheduled coverage of items that are not covered adequately in a standard homeowner's policy.*

A *blanket*, or *unscheduled, PPF* provides the maximum protection available for virtually all the insured's personal property. *Scheduled PPFs* list the items to be covered and provide supplemental coverage under a homeowner's contract. This coverage is especially useful for expensive property and it includes loss, damage, and theft. Some popular uses of PPFs are for furs, jewelry, personal computers and peripheral equipment, photographic equipment, silverware, fine art and antiques, collections.

> **EXAMPLE: Personal Property Floaters**
>
> Angela owns a diamond ring valued at $7,500. She should itemize it under a personal property floater because it's worth more than the standard $1,000 coverage C (discussed later) allowance for all jewelry stolen. Generally, insurance companies require appraisals to determine value before scheduling items.

Financial Fact or Fantasy?

Homeowner's insurance provides protection not only on the home itself but also most of its contents. **Fact:** Homeowner's insurance covers the home itself and most of the contents in it, including furniture, stereos and TVs, computers, and clothing. On the other hand, cars, motorcycles, golf carts, high value jewelry, and the like usually are not covered under a homeowner's policy.

10-2e Renter's Insurance: Don't Move In Without It

If you live in an apartment (or some other type of rental unit), be aware that although the building you live in is likely to be fully insured, *your furnishings and other personal belongings are not.* As a renter (or even the owner of a condominium unit), you need a special type of HO policy to obtain insurance coverage on your personal possessions.

Consider, for example, Sally Caldwell's predicament. She never got around to insuring her personal possessions in the apartment that she rented in Chicago. One wintry night, a water pipe ruptured, and the escaping water damaged her furniture, rugs, and other belongings. When the building owner refused to pay for the loss, Sally hauled him into court—and lost. Why did she lose her case? Simple: *Unless a landlord can be proven negligent—and this one wasn't— he or she isn't responsible for a tenant's property.* The moral of this story is clear: once you've accumulated valuable personal belongings (from clothing and home furnishings to stereo equipment, TVs, computers, and video players), make sure that they're covered adequately by insurance, even if you're only renting a place to live! Otherwise, you could risk losing everything you own.

Apparently many tenants don't realize this, because surveys show that most of them aren't insured, even though renter's insurance is available at reasonable rates. The policy, called Renter's Form HO-4, is a scaled-down version of homeowner's insurance. It covers the contents of a house, apartment, or cooperative unit, but not the structure itself. Owners of condominium units need Form HO-6; it's similar, but it includes a minimum of $1,000 in protection for any building alterations, additions, and decorations paid for by the policyholder. Like regular homeowner's insurance, HO-4 and HO-6 policies include liability coverage and protect you at home and away. For example, if somebody is injured and sues you, the policy would pay for damages up to a specified limit, generally $100,000, although some insurers go as high as $500,000.

A standard renter's insurance policy covers furniture, carpets, appliances, clothing, and most other personal items for their cash value at the time of loss. Expect to pay around $150 to $250 a year for about $30,000 in personal property coverage and $100,000 in liability coverage, depending on where you live. For maximum protection, you can buy *replacement-cost insurance* (discussed again later in this chapter), which pays the actual cost of replacing articles with comparable ones, though some policies limit the payout to four times the cash value. You'll pay more

for this—perhaps as little as another 10 percent, but perhaps much more—depending on the insurer. Also, the standard renter's policy provides limited coverage of such valuables as jewelry, furs, and silverware. Coverage varies, although some insurers pay up to $1,000 for the loss of watches, gems, and furs and up to $2,500 for silverware. For larger amounts, you need an endorsement or a separate PPF policy, as discussed previously.

Renter's insurance pays for losses caused by fire or lightning, explosion, windstorms, hail, theft, civil commotion, aircraft, vehicles, smoke, vandalism and malicious mischief, falling objects, building collapse, and the weight of ice and snow. Certain damages caused by water, steam, electricity, appliances, and frozen pipes are covered as well. Plus, if your residence can't be occupied because of damage from any of those perils, the insurer will pay for any increase in living expenses resulting from staying at a hotel and eating in restaurants. The liability coverage also pays for damages and legal costs arising from injuries or damage caused by you, a member of your family, or a pet—either on or off your premises.

10-2f Coverage: What Type, Who, and Where?

We've discussed what types of property are covered by a homeowner's policy. These policies also define the types of losses that they cover and the persons and locations covered.

Types of Losses Covered

There are three types of property-related losses when misfortune occurs:

1. Direct loss of property
2. Indirect loss occurring due to loss of damaged property
3. Additional expenses resulting from direct and indirect losses

Homeowner's insurance contracts offer compensation for each type of loss.

Section I Coverage. When a house is damaged by an insured peril, the insurance company will pay reasonable living expenses that a family might incur. One such covered expense would be the cost of renting alternative accommodations while the insured's home is being repaired or rebuilt. Also, in many instances, the insurer will pay for damages caused by perils other than those mentioned in the policy if a named peril is determined to be the underlying cause of the loss. Assume, for instance, that lightning (a covered peril) strikes a house while a family is away and knocks out the power, causing $400 worth of food in the freezer and refrigerator to spoil. Insurance will pay for the loss even though temperature change (the direct cause) is not mentioned in the policy.

Section II Coverage. Besides paying successfully pursued liability claims against an insured, a homeowner's policy includes coverage for (1) the cost of defending the insured, (2) reasonable expenses incurred by an insured in helping the insurance company's defense, and (3) the payment of court costs. Because these costs apply even when the liability suit is found to be without merit, this coverage can save you thousands of dollars in attorney fees.

Persons Covered

A homeowner's policy covers the persons named in the policy and members of their families who are residents of the household. A person can be a resident of the household even while temporarily living away from home. For example, college students who live at school part of the year and at home during vacations are normally classified as household residents. Their parents' homeowner's policy may cover their belongings at school—including such items as stereo equipment, TVs, personal computers, and microwave ovens. But there could be limits and exceptions to the coverage, so check the policy to find out what's covered. For example, some companies may consider students living off-campus to be independent and therefore ineligible for coverage under their parents' insurance. The standard homeowner's contract also extends limited coverage to guests of the insured.

Locations Covered

Most homeowner's policies offer coverage worldwide. Consequently, an insured's personal property is fully covered even if it is lent to the next-door neighbor or kept in a hotel room in London. The only exception is property left at a second home (such as a beach house or resort condominium), where coverage is reduced to 10 percent of the policy limit on personal property unless the loss occurs while the insured is residing there.

Homeowners and their families have liability protection for their negligent acts wherever they occur. Excluded are negligent acts involving certain types of motorized vehicles (such as large boats and aircraft) or those occurring in the course of employment or professional practice. It does include golf carts (when used for golfing purposes) and recreational vehicles such as snowmobiles and "four-wheelers," provided that they're used on the insured's premises.

10-2g Limitations on Payment

In addition to the principle of indemnity, actual cash value, subrogation, and other insurance features restricting the amount paid out under a property and liability insurance contract, replacement-cost provisions, policy limits, and deductibles influence the amount an insurance company will pay for a loss.

Replacement Cost

replacement cost
The amount necessary to repair, rebuild, or replace an asset at today's prices.

The amount necessary to repair, rebuild, or replace an asset at today's prices is the **replacement cost**. When replacement-cost coverage is in effect, a homeowner's reimbursement for damage to a house or accompanying structures is based on the cost of repairing or replacing those structures. This means that the insurer will repair or replace damaged items without deducting for depreciation. Exhibit 10.3 illustrates a replacement-cost calculation for a 2,400-square-foot home with a two-car garage.

Homeowners are eligible for reimbursement on a full replacement-cost basis only if they keep their homes insured for at least 80 percent of the amount that it would cost to build them today, not including the value of the land. In periods of inflation, homeowners must either increase their coverage limits on the dwelling unit every

---

EXHIBIT 10.3	Calculating Replacement Cost

Here's a typical example of how an insurance company calculates replacement cost. It would take $374,400 to fully replace this home today.

Dwelling cost: 2,400 sq. ft. at $125 per sq. ft.	$300,000
Extra features: built-in appliances, mahogany cabinets, 3 ceiling fans	15,000
Porches, patios: screened and trellised patio	3,700
Two-car garage: 900 sq. ft. at $55 per sq. ft.	49,500
Other site improvements: driveway, storage, landscaping	6,200
Total replacement cost	$374,400

year or take a chance on falling below the 80 percent requirement. Alternatively, for a nominal cost, homeowners can purchase an inflation protection rider that automatically adjusts the amount of coverage based on prevailing inflation rates. Without the rider, maximum compensation for losses thus would be based on a specified percentage of loss. With the inflation protection rider, this won't happen.

Even if a home is in an excellent state of repair, its market value may be lessened by functional obsolescence within the structure—for example, when a house doesn't have enough electrical power to run a dishwasher, microwave, and hair dryer at the same time. The HO-8 homeowner's form (for older homes) was adopted as a partial response to this problem. A 2,200-square-foot home in an older neighborhood might have a market value (excluding land) of $195,000, yet the replacement cost might be $260,000. The HO-8 policy solves this problem so that homeowners don't have to buy more expensive coverage based on replacement cost. This policy covers property in full, up to the amount of the loss or up to the property's market value, whichever is less.

Although coverage on a house is often on a *replacement-cost basis*, standard coverage on its contents may be on an *actual cash-value basis*, which deducts depreciation from the *current replacement cost* for claims involving furniture, clothing, and other belongings. Some policies offer, for a slight increase in premium, replacement-cost coverage on contents. You should seriously consider this option—as well as an inflation protection rider on the dwelling—when buying homeowner's insurance.

FINANCIAL PLANNING TIPS

Lowering Your Homeowner's Insurance Premiums

Having the right amount of homeowner's insurance is important. But there's no need to overpay. Here are some ways to reduce your insurance premiums.

• **Increase your deductible.** A primary goal of insurance is to protect your family's financial resources from cataclysmic losses, not to totally insulate you from having to pay out much of anything under any circumstances. Think of your insurance as risk sharing, not risk elimination. Increasing your deductible from $500 to $1,000 could reduce your insurance premiums by 25 percent.

• **Bundle your homeowner's and auto insurance.** Buying your homeowner's and auto insurance from the same insurer can provide a discount of 5 percent to 15 percent. First, get quotes from separate companies for each policy, and then compare them with bundled quotes.

• **Check on the discounts that you may get from insurers.** Some relatively minor improvements to your home can earn you discounts. Examples include discounts for smoke detectors, deadbolt locks, security and fire alarms, and fire extinguishers. Often, seniors also can get an additional 10 percent discount.

• **Ask your insurance agent what you can do to reduce the risk of your home from the insurer's perspective.** For example, updating an old heating system or replacing old wiring can reduce your insurance premiums.

• **Avoid risks that insurers don't like to insure.** Owning dogs more frequently involved in claims (such as pit bulls) can limit or void your policy. Similarly, having a swimming pool or a trampoline can increase your insurance premium. You may have to buy additional coverage to protect yourself against certain risk exposures.

• **Manage your credit score.** Allowing your credit score to get too low can increase your insurance premiums.

• **Shop carefully for homeowner's insurance.** While it's worthwhile to shop around from time to time, keep in mind that you may be getting a longevity discount if you've been with your insurer for a few years. It's common to get a 5 percent discount if you've been with your company for three to five years and a 10 percent discount if you've been with the company for at least six years.

Source: Adapted from Deborah Fowles, "Ten Ways to Cut the Cost of Your Homeowner's Insurance," http://financialplan.about.com/od/homeownersinsurance/a/Homeowners.htm, accessed August 2015.

Policy Limits

In Section I of the homeowner's policy, the amount of coverage on the dwelling unit (coverage A) establishes the amounts applicable to the accompanying structures (coverage B), the unscheduled personal property (coverage C), and the temporary living expenses (coverage D). Generally, the limits under coverage B, C, and D are 10 percent, 50 percent, and 10 percent to 20 percent, respectively, of the amount of coverage under A.

> **EXAMPLE: Homeowner's Policy Coverage Limits**
>
> If a house is insured for $150,000, then the respective limits for coverage B, C, and D would be $15,000, $75,000, and $30,000 (i.e., 10 percent of $150,000, 50 percent of $150,000, and 20 percent of $150,000). These limits can be increased if either is considered insufficient to cover the exposure. Also, for a small reduction in premium, some companies will permit a homeowner to reduce coverage on unscheduled personal property to 40 percent of the amount on the dwelling unit.

Remember that homeowner's policies usually specify limits for certain types of personal property included under the coverage C category. These coverage limits are *within the total dollar amount* of coverage C and in no way act to increase that total. For example, the dollar limit for losses of money, bank notes, bullion, and related items is $200; securities, accounts, deeds, evidences of debt, manuscripts, passports, tickets, and stamps have a $1,000 limit. As mentioned earlier, loss from jewelry theft is limited to $1,000, and payment for theft of silverware, goldware, and pewterware has a $2,500 limit. Some policies also offer $5,000 coverage for home computer equipment. You can increase these limits by increasing coverage C.

In Section II the personal liability coverage (coverage E) often starts at $100,000, and the medical payments portion (coverage F) normally has a limit of $1,000 per person. Additional coverage included in Section II consists of claim expenses, such as court costs and attorney fees; first aid and medical expenses, including ambulance costs; and damage to others' property of up to $500 per occurrence.

Although these are the most common limits, most homeowners need additional protection, especially liability coverage. In these days of high damage awards by juries, a $100,000 liability limit may not be adequate. The cost to increase the liability limit with most companies is nominal. For example, the annual premium difference between a $100,000 personal liability limit and a $300,000 limit is likely to be only $20 to $30. You can also increase personal liability coverage with a personal liability umbrella policy, discussed later in the chapter.

Deductibles

Each of the preceding limits on recovery constrains the maximum amount an insurance company must pay under the policy. *Deductibles*, which limit what a company must pay for small losses, help reduce insurance premiums by doing away with the frequent small loss claims that are proportionately more expensive to administer. The standard deductible in most states is $250 on the physical damage protection covered in Section I. However, choosing higher deductible amounts of $500 or $1,000 results in considerable premium savings—as much as 10 percent to 20 percent in some states. Deductibles don't apply to liability and medical payments coverage because insurers want to be notified of all claims, no matter how trivial. Otherwise, they could be notified too late to investigate properly and prepare adequate defenses for resulting lawsuits.

10-2h Homeowner's Insurance Premiums

As you might expect, the size of insurance premiums varies widely depending on the insurance provider (company) and the location of the property (neighborhood/city/state). It pays to shop around! When you're shopping, be sure to state clearly the type of insurance you're looking for and to obtain and compare the cost, net of any discounts, offered by a number of agents or insurance companies. Remember, each type of property damage coverage is subject to a deductible of $250 or more.

Most people need to modify the basic package of coverage by adding an inflation rider and increasing the coverage on their homes to 100 percent of the replacement cost. Changing the contents protection from actual cash value to replacement cost and scheduling some items of expensive personal property may be desirable. Most insurance professionals also advise homeowners to increase their liability and medical payments limits. Each of these changes results in an additional premium charge.

At the same time, you can reduce your total premium by increasing the amount of your deductible. Because it's better to budget for small losses than to insure against them, larger deductibles are becoming more popular. You may also qualify for discounts for deadbolt locks, monitored security systems, and other safety features such as smoke alarms and sprinkler systems.

Behavior Matters

Behavioral Biases in Buying Property Insurance

What are the best property insurance policies for you? The answer to that question depends on your various risk exposures, your attitude toward risk, and the costs of competing insurance policies. There are some well-known behavioral biases that can lead you into making decisions that aren't in your best interest. It's a good idea to keep the following in mind when buying property insurance:

- **Don't just automatically renew your property insurance.** *Anchoring* is the behavioral bias in which people tend to rely unduly on past prices or estimates without considering new information. Just because your property insurance premiums were competitive in the past does not mean that they're still that way when your policy comes up for renewal. Be sure to shop around—don't just renew your current policy.

- **Be careful to weigh recent evidence properly before buying insurance.** The *representativeness bias* is the tendency to place too much weight on recent experience when making financial decisions. Guess what happens the day after an area is hit by an earthquake? Despite the fact that this is a relatively rare event almost everywhere, a lot of people run out to get it, and the price of earthquake insurance goes up! So be careful about buying insurance right after an adverse event occurs. Weigh the evidence carefully, assess your true risk exposures, and buy insurance deliberately and accordingly.

TEST YOURSELF

10-5 What are the *perils* that most properties are insured for under various types of homeowner's policies?

10-6 What types of property are covered under a homeowner's policy? When should you consider adding a PPF to your policy? Indicate which of the following are included in a standard policy's coverage: (a) an African parrot, (b) a motorbike, (c) Avon cosmetics held for sale, (d) Tupperware® for home use.

10-7 Describe (a) types of losses, (b) persons, and (c) locations that are covered under a homeowner's policy.

10-8 Describe *replacement-cost* coverage and compare this to *actual cash value* coverage. Which is preferable?

10-9 What are *deductibles?* Do they apply to either liability or medical payments coverage under the homeowner's policy?

10-3 AUTOMOBILE INSURANCE

Automobiles also involve risk because damage to them or negligence in their use can result in significant loss. Fortunately, insurance can protect individuals against a big part of these costs. Automobile insurance includes several types of coverage packaged together. We begin by describing the major features of a private passenger automobile policy. Then we explain no-fault laws, followed by discussions of auto insurance premiums and financial responsibility laws.

10-3a Types of Auto Insurance Coverage

personal automobile policy (PAP)
A comprehensive automobile insurance policy designed to be easily understood by the "typical" insurance purchaser.

The **personal automobile policy (PAP)** is a comprehensive, six-part automobile insurance policy designed to be easily understood by the "typical" insurance purchaser. The policy's first four parts identify the coverage provided.

- Part A: Liability coverage
- Part B: Medical payments coverage
- Part C: Uninsured motorists coverage
- Part D: Coverage for damage to your vehicle

Part E pertains to your duties and responsibilities if you're involved in an accident, and Part F defines basic provisions of the policy, including the policy coverage period and the right of termination. We'll focus mostly on the types of coverage in parts A through D of the policy.

You're almost sure to purchase liability, medical payments, and uninsured motorists protection. You may, however, choose *not* to buy protection against damage to your automobile if it's an older vehicle of relatively little value. On the other hand, if you have a loan against your car, then you'll probably be required to have physical damage coverage—part D—at least equal to the loan amount. Exhibit 10.4 illustrates how the four basic parts of a PAP might be displayed in a typical automobile insurance policy. The premiums shown are for a six-month period.

Part A: Liability Coverage

Most states require you to buy at least a minimum amount of liability insurance. As part of the liability provisions of a PAP, the insurer agrees to:

- Pay damages for bodily injury and/or property damage for which you are legally responsible as a result of an automobile accident
- Settle or defend any claim or suit asking for such damages

The provision for legal defense is important and could mean savings of thousands of dollars. Even if you're not at fault in an automobile accident, you may be compelled to prove your innocence in court, incurring expensive legal fees. The policy does *not* cover defense of criminal charges against the insured due to an accident (such as a drunk driver who's involved in an accident).

Part A of your insurance policy includes certain supplemental payments for items such as expenses incurred in settling the claim, reimbursement of premiums for appeal bonds, bonds to release attachments of the insured's property, and bail bonds required as a result of an accident. These supplemental payments are not restricted by the applicable policy limits.

Policy Limits. Although the insurance company provides both bodily injury and property damage liability insurance under part A, it typically sets *a dollar limit up to which it will pay for damages from any one accident.* Typical limits are $50,000, $100,000, $300,000, and $500,000. You'd be well advised to consider no less than $300,000 coverage in today's legal liability environment. Damage awards are increasing, and the insurer's duty to defend you *ends when the coverage limit has been exhausted.* It's easy to "exhaust" $50,000 or $100,000, leaving you to pay any

EXHIBIT 10.4 The Four Parts of a Personal Automobile Policy (PAP)

This automobile insurance statement for six months of coverage shows how the four major parts of a PAP might be incorporated. Notice that the premium for collision/comprehensive damage is relatively low because of the age and type of car (a 2012 Honda CRV); these drivers also enjoyed a premium reduction of more than $130 for the six months due to having other insurance with the same provider, a car alarm system, and a good driving record.

ANYSTATE INSURANCE COMPANIES   **AUTO RENEWAL**

Anystate Automobile Insurance Company
1665 West Anywhere Drive
Yourtown, CO 80209   2012 Honda CRV

POLICY NUMBER	PERIOD COVERED	DATE DUE	PLEASE PAY THIS AMOUNT
ABC-123-XYZ-456	MAY 26 2017 to NOV 26 2017	MAY 26 2017	$505

1 H -1582   A

Griffin, Nicholas S. and Allison B.
1643 Thunder Rd. #32
Yourtown, CO 80209

Coverages and Limits			Premiums
Part A	A	Liability	
		Bodily Injury 250,000/500,000	$219
		Property Damage 100,000	
Part B	M	Medical 5,000	19
Part C	U	Uninsured Motor Vehicle	
		Bodily Injury 100,000/300,000	71
Part D	G	500 Deductible Collision	140
	D-WG	500 Deductible Comprehensive	50
	H	Emergency Road Service	6
Amount Due			**$505**

Your premium has already been adjusted by the following:

Premium Reductions	
Multiple Line	22
Antitheft devices	40
Good driver	70

Your premium is based on the following ...
If not correct, contact your agent.

2012 Honda CRV
Serial number: 4 ABCD12M3NP456789

Drivers of vehicle in your household ...
There are no male or unmarried female drivers under age 25.
Younger drivers included if rated on another car insured with us.

Ordinary use of vehicle ...
To and from work or school, more than 100 miles weekly.
Driven more than 7,500 miles annually.
(National average is 10,000 miles annually.)

Source: Adapted from a major automobile insurance company quote.

additional costs above the policy limit. So be sure to purchase adequate coverage—*regardless of the minimum requirements in your state.* Otherwise, you place your personal assets at risk. As Exhibit 10.4 shows, the Griffin family obtained fairly high coverage limits.

bodily injury liability losses
A PAP provision that protects the insured against claims made for bodily injury.

Some insurers make so-called *split limits* of liability coverage available, with the first amount in each combination the per-individual limit and the second the per-accident limit. Some policy limit combinations for protecting individuals against claims made for bodily injury liability losses are $25,000/$50,000, $50,000/$100,000, $100,000/$300,000, $250,000/$500,000, and $500,000/$1,000,000. Because the

Griffins purchased the $250,000/$500,000 policy limits (Exhibit 10.4), the maximum amount any one person negligently injured in an accident could receive from the insurance company would be $250,000. Further, the total amount the insurer would pay to all injured victims in one accident would not exceed $500,000. If a jury awarded a claimant $80,000, the defendant whose insurance policy limits were $50,000/$100,000 could be required to pay $30,000 out of his or her pocket ($80,000 award minus $50,000 paid by insurance). For the defendant, this could mean loss of home, cars, bank accounts, and other assets. In many states, if the value of these assets is too little to satisfy a claim then the defendant's wages may be garnished (taken by the court and used to satisfy the outstanding debt).

The policy limits available to cover property damage liability losses are typically $10,000, $25,000, $50,000, and $100,000. In contrast to bodily injury liability limits, property damage limits are stated as a per-accident limit, without specifying limits applicable on a per-item or per-person basis.

property damage liability losses
A PAP provision that protects the insured against claims made for damage to property.

Persons Insured. Two basic definitions in the PAP determine who is covered under part A: insured person and covered auto. Essentially, an *insured person* includes you (the named insured) and any family member, any person using a covered auto, and any person or organization that may be held responsible for your actions. The *named insured* is the person named in the declarations page of the policy. The spouse of the person named is considered a named insured if he or she resides in the same household. Family members are persons related by blood, marriage, or adoption and residing in the same household. An unmarried college student living away from home usually is considered a family member. *Covered autos* are the vehicles shown in the declarations page of your PAP, autos acquired during the policy period, any trailer owned, and any auto or trailer used as a temporary substitute while your auto or trailer is being repaired or serviced. An automobile that you lease for an extended time can be included as a covered automobile.

The named insured and family members have part A liability coverage regardless of the automobile they are driving. However, for persons other than the named insured and family members to have liability coverage, they must be driving a covered auto.

When a motorist who is involved in an automobile accident is covered under two or more liability insurance contracts, the coverage *on the automobile* is primary and the other coverage is secondary. For example, if Dennis Ellis, a named insured in his own right, was involved in an accident while driving Kaitlin Wei's car (with permission), then a claim settlement exceeding the limits of Kaitlin's liability policy would be necessary before Dennis' liability insurance would apply. If Kaitlin's insurance had lapsed, Dennis' policy would then offer primary protection (but it would apply to Dennis only, not to Kaitlin.).

Part B: Medical Payments Coverage

Medical payments coverage insures a covered individual for reasonable and necessary medical expenses incurred within three years of an automobile accident in an amount not to exceed the policy limits. It provides for reimbursement even if other sources of recovery, such as health or accident insurance, also make payments. What's more, in most states, the insurer reimburses the insured for medical payments even if the insured proves that another person was negligent in the accident and receives compensation from that party's liability insurer.

A person need not be occupying an automobile when the accidental injury occurs to be eligible for benefits. Injuries sustained as a pedestrian, or on a bicycle in a traffic accident, are also covered. (Motorcycle accidents are normally not covered.) Part B insurance also pays on an excess basis. For instance, if you're a passenger in a friend's automobile during an accident and suffer $8,000 in medical expenses, you can collect under his medical payments insurance up to his policy limits. Further, you can collect (up to the amount of your policy limits) from your insurer the amount exceeding what the other medical payments provide.

Policy Limits. Medical payments insurance usually has per-person limits of $1,000, $2,000, $3,000, $5,000, or $10,000. Thus, an insurer could conceivably pay $60,000 or more in medical payments benefits for one accident involving a named insured and five passengers. Most families are advised to buy the $5,000 or $10,000 limit because, even though they may have other health insurance available, they can't be sure that their passengers are as well protected. Having automobile medical payments insurance also reduces the probability that a passenger in your auto will sue you and try to collect under your liability insurance coverage (in those states that permit it).

Persons Insured. Coverage under an automobile medical payments insurance policy applies to the named insured and to family members who are injured while occupying an automobile (whether owned by the named insured or not) or when struck by an automobile or trailer of any type. Part B also applies to any other person occupying a covered automobile.

Part C: Uninsured Motorists Coverage

uninsured motorists coverage
Automobile insurance designed to meet the needs of "innocent" victims of accidents who are negligently injured by uninsured, underinsured, or hit-and-run motorists.

Uninsured motorists coverage is available to meet the needs of "innocent" victims of accidents who are negligently injured by uninsured, underinsured, or hit-and-run motorists. Nearly all states require uninsured motorists insurance to be included in each liability insurance policy issued. The insured is allowed, however, to reject this coverage in most of these states. Because about 16 percent of drivers are uninsured and because many others meet only minimum insurance coverage requirements, rejecting uninsured motorists coverage is not a good idea. In many states, a person may also collect even if the negligent motorist's insurance company is insolvent. With uninsured motorists insurance, an insured is legally entitled to collect an amount equal to the sum that could have been collected from the negligent motorist's liability insurance, had such coverage been available, up to a maximum amount equal to the policy's stated *uninsured motorists limit.*

Three points must be proven to receive payment through uninsured motorists insurance: (1) another motorist must be at fault, (2) the motorist has no available insurance or is underinsured, and (3) damages were incurred. Because property damage is not included in this coverage in most states, with uninsured motorists coverage, you generally can collect only for losses arising from bodily injury.

Policy Limits. Uninsured motorists insurance is fairly low in cost (usually around $100 to $150 per year). Because the cost of this coverage is low compared to the amount of protection it provides, drivers should purchase at least the minimum available limits of uninsured motorists insurance. The Griffins purchased $100,000/$300,000 coverage for $71 per six months.

Persons Insured. Uninsured motorists protection covers the named insured, family members, and any other person occupying a covered auto.

underinsured motorists coverage
Optional automobile insurance coverage, available in some states, that protects the insured against damages caused by being in an accident with an underinsured motorist who is found liable.

Underinsured Motorists Coverage. In addition to *uninsured motorists,* in some states, for a nominal premium you can obtain underinsured motorists coverage, which protects the insured against damages caused by being in an accident with an underinsured motorist who is found liable. Underinsured motorists insurance has become increasingly popular and *can be purchased for both bodily injury and property damage.* If an at-fault driver causes more damage to you than the limit of her liability, your insurance company makes up the difference (up to the limits of your coverage) and then goes

after the negligent driver for the deficiency. If it's available in your state, you should consider purchasing this optional coverage.

EXAMPLE: Underinsured Motorists Coverage

If you have underinsured motorists coverage of $50,000 for bodily injury and incur medical expenses of $40,000 because of an accident caused by an at-fault insured driver with the minimum compulsory bodily injury limit of $25,000, then your insurer will cover the $15,000 gap ($40,000 medical expenses minus $25,000 liability limit of at-fault driver).

Part D: Coverage for Physical Damage to a Vehicle

This part of the PAP provides coverage for damage to your auto. The two basic types of coverage are collision and comprehensive (or "other than collision").

collision insurance
Automobile insurance that pays for collision damage to an insured automobile *regardless of who is at fault.*

Collision Insurance. Collision insurance is automobile insurance that pays for collision damage to an insured automobile *regardless of who is at fault.* The amount of insurance payable is the actual cash value of the loss in excess of your deductible. Remember that *actual cash value is defined as replacement cost less depreciation.* So, if a car is demolished, the insured is paid an amount equal to the car's depreciated value minus any deductible. Deductibles typically range between $50 and $1,000, and selecting a higher deductible, as did the Griffins, will reduce your premium.

LORAKS/SHUTTERSTOCK.COM

Lenders typically require collision insurance on cars they finance. In some cases, especially when the auto dealer is handling the financing, it will try to sell you this insurance. *Avoid buying automobile insurance from car dealers or finance companies.* It is best to buy such insurance from your regular insurance agent and include collision insurance as part of your full auto insurance policy (i.e., the PAP). A full-time insurance agent is better able to assess and meet your insurance needs. The collision provision of your insurance policy often fully protects you in a rental car, so be sure to check before purchasing supplemental collision insurance when renting a car. Also, when you charge your car rental to your credit card, collision insurance may be offered under the umbrella of the credit card.

comprehensive automobile insurance
Coverage that protects against loss to an insured automobile caused by any peril (with a few exceptions) *other than collision.*

Comprehensive Automobile Insurance. Comprehensive automobile insurance protects against loss to an insured automobile caused by any peril (with a few exceptions) *other than collision.* The maximum compensation provided under this coverage is the actual cash value of the automobile. This broad coverage includes, but is not limited to, damage caused by fire, theft, glass breakage, falling objects, malicious mischief, vandalism, riot, and earthquake. Contrary to popular belief, the automobile insurance policy normally does *not* cover the theft of personal property left in the insured vehicle. However, the off-premises coverage of the homeowner's policy may cover such a loss if the auto was locked when the theft occurred.

no-fault automobile insurance
Automobile insurance that reimburses the parties involved in an accident without regard to negligence.

10-3b No-Fault Automobile Insurance

No-fault automobile insurance is a system under which each insured party is compensated by his or her own company, regardless of which party caused the accident. In return, legal remedies and payments for pain and suffering are restricted. Under the concept of *pure* no-fault insurance, the driver, passengers, and injured pedestrians are reimbursed by the insurer of the car for economic losses stemming from bodily injury. The insurer doesn't have to cover claims for losses to other motorists who are covered by their own policies.

Advocates of no-fault automobile insurance apparently forget that the sole purpose of liability insurance is to protect the assets of the insured—not to pay losses, *per se*. State laws governing no-fault insurance vary widely as to both the amount of no-fault benefits provided and the degree to which restrictions for legal actions apply. Most states provide from $2,000 to $10,000 in personal injury protection and restrict legal recovery for pain and suffering to cases where medical or economic losses exceed some threshold level, such as $500 or $1,000. In all states, recovery based on negligence is permitted for economic losses exceeding the amount payable by no-fault insurance.

10-3c Automobile Insurance Premiums

The cost of car insurance depends on many things, including your age, where you live, the car you drive, your driving record, the coverage you have, and the amount of your deductible. Consequently, car insurance premiums—even for the same coverage—vary all over the map.

Factors Affecting Premiums

Factors that influence how auto insurance premiums are set include (1) rating territory, (2) amount of use the automobile receives, (3) personal characteristics of the driver, (4) type of automobile, and (5) insured's driving record.

- Rating territory: Rates are higher in geographic areas where accident rates, number of claims filed, and average cost of claims paid are higher. Rates reflect auto repair costs, hospital and medical expenses, jury awards, and theft and vandalism in the area. Even someone with a perfect driving record will be charged the going rate for the area where the automobile is garaged. Exhibit 10.5 gives some helpful tips for protecting your vehicle wherever you live. Some jurisdictions prohibit the use of rating territories, age, and gender factors because it's believed these factors unfairly discriminate against the urban, the young, and the male.
- Use of the automobile: Drive less, pay less! Low annual miles translate into a smaller probability of being in an accident, so you pay lower rates. Rates are also lower if the insured automobile isn't usually driven to work or is driven less than

---

| EXHIBIT 10.5 | Preventing Your Car from Being Stolen |

You can help prevent your car from being stolen by taking the following precautions:
- Keep your car doors locked, even while driving. Close all windows.
- Never leave your keys in an unattended car.
- Never leave your car running and unattended.
- Avoid leaving valuables inside your car where they can be seen.
- Do not leave your vehicle title or proof of insurance in the car.
- Avoid high crime areas even if the alternate route takes more time.
- Install anti-theft devices like a burglar alarm or a steering wheel lock.
- Etch your car's vehicle identification number (VIN) on more than one of the windows.
- When parking on an incline, turn the wheels toward the curb and set the emergency brake.
- Do not resist a carjacker. You can't be replaced; your car can.

Sources: Adapted from "How to Prevent Your Car from Being Stolen," https://www.geico.com/information/safety/auto/preventing-auto-theft/, accessed August 2015.

3 miles one way. Premiums rise slightly if you drive more than 3 but fewer than 15 miles to work and increase if your commute exceeds 15 miles each way.

- **Drivers' personal characteristics:** The insured's age, sex, and marital status can also affect automobile insurance premiums. Insurance companies base premium differentials on the number of accidents involving certain age groups. For example, drivers aged 25 and under make up only about 15 percent of the total driving population, but they are involved in nearly 30 percent of auto accidents and in 26 percent of all fatal accidents. Male drivers are involved in a larger percentage of fatal crashes, so unmarried males under age 30 (and married males under 25) pay higher premiums than do older individuals. Females over age 24, as well as married females of any age, are exempt from the youthful operator classification and pay lower premiums.

- **Type of automobile:** Insurance companies charge higher rates for automobiles classified as intermediate-performance, high-performance, and sports vehicles and also for rear-engine models. Some states even rate four-door cars differently from two-door models.

- **Driving record:** The driving records—traffic violations and accidents—of those insured and the people who live with them affect premium levels. More severe traffic convictions—driving under the influence of alcohol or drugs, leaving the scene of an accident, homicide or assault arising from the operation of a motor vehicle, and driving with a revoked or suspended driver's license—result in higher insurance premiums. Any conviction for a moving traffic violation that results in the accumulation of points under a state point system also may incur a premium surcharge. In most states, accidents determined to be the insured's fault also incur points and a premium surcharge.

automobile insurance plan
An arrangement providing automobile insurance to drivers who have been refused regular coverage under normal procedures.

You Can Do It Now

Evaluate the Best Auto Insurance Companies

When you're considering buying new car insurance, it's helpful to know which insurance companies are considered the best. A good Internet site is **http://www.consumeraffairs.com/insurance/car.html**. The site discusses the key elements of auto insurance policies, which include liability, comprehensive coverage, uninsured motorist protection, collusion coverage, and personal injury protection. You can do it now.

Many states place drivers with multiple traffic violations in an **automobile insurance plan** (formerly called an *assigned-risk plan*), providing automobile insurance to those refused regular coverage. The automobile insurance plan generally offers less coverage for a higher premium. Even with high premiums, however, insurers lost billions of dollars on this type of business in a recent 5-year period.

Financial Fact or Fantasy?

The type of car you drive is a personal matter that has no bearing on how much you will have to pay for automobile insurance. **Fantasy:** The type of car you drive is one of the major determinants of auto insurance premiums. You can expect to pay a lot more for insurance on a sporty model than on a more " sedate" one.

Driving Down the Cost of Car Insurance

Comparison shopping for car insurance can really pay off, yet only about one-third of car owners shop around for auto coverage. One of the best ways to reduce the cost of car insurance is to take advantage of the discounts auto insurers offer. Taken together, such discounts can knock from 5 percent to 50 percent off your annual premium. Some give overall *safe-driving* (accident-free) discounts, and most give youthful operators lower rates if they've had *driver's training*. High school and college students may also receive *good-student* discounts for maintaining a B average or making the dean's list at their school.

Nearly all insurance companies give discounts to families with two or more automobiles insured by the same company (the *multicar* discount). Most insurers also offer discounts to owners who install *antitheft devices* in their cars. Likewise, some insurers offer *nonsmoker* and *nondrinker* discounts. And some insurers accept only persons who are educators or executives; others accept only government employees. Through more selective underwriting these companies are able to reduce losses and operating expenses, which results in lower premiums.

It's to your advantage to look for and use as many of these discounts as you can. Take another look at the auto insurance statement in Exhibit 10.4, and you'll see that the insured reduced his overall cost of coverage by 25 percent by qualifying for just three of the discounts (labeled "Premium Reductions"). Another effective way to drive down the cost of car insurance is to *raise your deductibles* (as discussed earlier in this chapter). This frequently overlooked tactic can affect the cost of your insurance premium dramatically. For example, the difference between a $100 deductible and a $500 deductible may be as much as 25 percent on collision coverage and 30 percent on comprehensive coverage; request a $1,000 deductible, and you may save as much as 50 percent on both collision and comprehensive coverage.

financial responsibility laws Laws requiring motorists to buy a specified minimum amount of automobile liability insurance or to provide other proof of comparable financial responsibility.

10-3d Financial Responsibility Laws

Annual losses from automobile accidents in the United States run into billions of dollars. For this reason, most states have financial responsibility laws, whereby motorists *must buy a specified minimum amount of automobile liability insurance* or provide other proof of comparable financial responsibility. The required limits are low in most states—well below what you should carry.

FINANCIAL PLANNING TIPS

How to Buy Auto Insurance

The cost of auto insurance can vary greatly. It pays to keep the following in mind while shopping around:

- **Get at least a few quotes.** Start with the largest insurers, such as State Farm and Allstate. Then ask a couple of independent agents to provide quotes from more than one company. Finally, get quotes from direct marketers, GEICO (http://www.geico.com) and Progressive (http://www.progressive.com) being two of the most competitive. Make sure to ask for an itemized list of coverages and costs so that you can compare policies and prices.

- **The car you buy affects your premium.** The price of the car affects the replacement cost if it is stolen or destroyed in an accident. And the cost of repairing the car can affect your premium. Check the statistics on injury claims, collision repair costs, and theft rates by vehicle model available from the Highway Loss Data Institute (http://www.carsafety.org/) before making your final car purchase decision.

- **Decide how much insurance you need.** While it's risky to be underinsured, it's also costly to carry too much insurance. However, don't pay attention to the minimum amount of insurance required in your state—it's rarely enough. Think about the cost of plowing into a Mercedes-Benz! A common recommendation is to have liability coverage of at least $100,000 per person, $300,000 per accident, and $50,000 in property damage coverage.

- **Take advantage of available discounts.** When you get insurance quotes, ask what kind of discounts you can get. For example, a common discount is for those who drive less than 7,500 miles a year. And you can reduce your premium significantly if you increase your deductible for collision or if you drop the medical payments portion of your policy if your health insurance provides good coverage.

Source: Adapted from "5 Car Insurance Tips," http://auto.howstuffworks.com/buying-selling/cg-car-insurance-tips.htm, accessed August 2015.

Financial responsibility laws fall into two categories. *Compulsory auto insurance laws* require motorists to show evidence of insurance coverage *before* receiving their license plates. Penalties for not having liability insurance include fines and suspension of your driver's license. The second category requires motorists to show evidence of their insurance coverage only *after* being involved in an accident. If they then fail to demonstrate compliance with the law, their registrations and driver's licenses are suspended. Although motorists who aren't able to fulfill their financial responsibility lose their driving privileges, victims may never recover their losses.

TEST YOURSELF

10-10 Briefly explain the major types of coverage available under the personal auto policy (PAP). Which persons are insured under (a) automobile medical payments coverage and (b) uninsured motorists coverage?

10-11 Explain the nature of (a) automobile collision insurance and (b) automobile comprehensive insurance.

10-12 Define *no-fault insurance* and discuss its pros and cons.

10-13 Describe the important factors that influence the availability and cost of auto insurance.

10-14 Discuss the role of financial responsibility laws and describe the two basic types currently employed.

10-4 OTHER PROPERTY AND LIABILITY INSURANCE

Homeowner's and automobile insurance policies provide the basic protection needed by most families, but some need other, more specialized types of insurance. Popular forms of other insurance include supplemental property insurance—earthquake, flood, and other forms of transportation—as well as the personal liability umbrella policy.

10-4a Supplemental Property Insurance Coverage

Because homeowner's policies exclude certain types of damage, you may want to consider some of the following types of supplemental coverage.

- Earthquake insurance: In addition to California, areas in other states are also subject to this type of loss. Very few homeowners buy this coverage because these policies typically carry a 15 percent deductible on the replacement cost of a home damaged or destroyed by earthquake. So even though the premiums are relatively inexpensive, you have to pay a lot out of pocket before you can collect on the policy.
- Flood insurance: The federal government has established a subsidized flood insurance program in cooperation with private insurance agents, who can sell this low-cost coverage to homeowners and tenants living in designated communities. The flood insurance program also encourages communities to initiate land-use controls to reduce future flood losses.
- Other forms of transportation insurance: In addition to automobile insurance, you may wish to insure other types of vehicles, such as mobile homes, recreational vehicles, or boats.

personal liability umbrella policy
An insurance policy providing excess liability coverage for homeowner's and automobile insurance as well as additional coverage not provided by either policy.

10-4b Personal Liability Umbrella Policy

Persons with moderate to high levels of income and net worth may want to take out a personal liability umbrella policy. It provides added liability coverage for homeowner's and automobile insurance as well as additional coverage not provided by either of

those policies. Umbrella policies often include limits of $1 million or more. Some also provide added amounts of coverage for a family's major medical insurance.

The premiums are usually quite reasonable for the broad coverage offered—$150 to $300 a year for as much as $1 million in coverage. Although the protection is comprehensive, it does contain some exclusions. The insured party must already have relatively high liability limits ($100,000 to $300,000) on their homeowner's and auto coverage in order to purchase a personal liability umbrella policy.

Do you need the extra protection that a personal liability umbrella policy provides? The answer is yes if you have sizable assets that could be seized to pay a judgment against you that is not fully covered by your homeowner's and automobile policies. But you may also need this coverage if you rent your home to others, have house sitters, or hire unbonded help such as gardeners or babysitters because you're responsible for any injuries that they incur or cause. You may also need this coverage if you work from home and clients visit you at your home office.

TEST YOURSELF

10-15 Briefly describe the following supplemental property insurance coverage: (a) earthquake insurance, (b) flood insurance, and (c) other forms of transportation insurance.

10-16 What is a *personal liability umbrella policy?* Under what circumstances might it be a wise purchase?

10-5 BUYING INSURANCE AND SETTLING CLAIMS

The first step when buying property and liability insurance is to develop an inventory of exposures to loss and then arrange them from highest to lowest priority. Losses that lend themselves to insurance protection are those that seldom occur but are potentially substantial—for example, damage to a home and its contents or liability arising from a negligence claim. Somewhat less important, but still desirable, is insurance to cover losses that could disrupt a family's financial plans, even if the losses might not result in insolvency. Such risks include physical damage to automobiles, boats, and other personal property of moderate value. Lowest-priority exposures can be covered by savings or from current income.

10-5a Property and Liability Insurance Agents

captive agent
An insurance agent who represents only one insurance company and who is, in effect, an employee of that company.

independent agent
An insurance agent who may place coverage with any company with which he or she has an agency relationship, as long as the insured meets that company's underwriting standards.

A good property insurance agent can make the purchase process much easier. Most property insurance agents fall into either the captive or independent category. A captive agent represents only one insurance company and is more or less an employee of that company. Allstate, Nationwide, and State Farm are major insurance companies that market their products through captive agents. In contrast, independent agents typically represent from 2 to 10 different insurance companies. These agents may place your coverage with any of the companies with whom they have an agency relationship, so long as you meet the underwriting standards of that company. Some well-known companies that operate through independent agents include The Hartford, Kemper, Chubb, and Travelers. Either type of agent can serve your needs well and should take the time to do the following:

- Review your total property and liability insurance exposures
- Inventory property and identify exposures
- Determine appropriate covered perils, limits, deductibles, and floater policies

Because of large variations in premiums and services, it pays to comparison shop.

Property insurance agents who meet various experiential and educational requirements, including passing a series of written examinations, qualify for the *Chartered Property and Casualty Underwriter (CPCU)* or *Certified Insurance Counselor (CIC)* designation. Another alternative to consider is companies that sell directly to the consumer through an 800 number or online. Generally, their premiums are lower. Examples of direct sellers are Amica, Erie, GEICO, and USAA.

10-5b Property and Liability Insurance Companies

Selecting an agent is an important step when purchasing property and liability insurance, but you should also ask questions about the company's financial soundness, its claims settlement practices, and the geographic range of its operations (this could be important if you're involved in an accident 1,000 miles from home). As with any form of insurance, you should check the company's ratings (see Chapter 8) and stick with those rated in the top categories. The agent should be a good source of information about the technical aspects of a company's operations; friends and acquaintances often can provide insight into its claims settlement policy. The Internet offers lots of information about various property and liability insurance products. Many insurance companies now have elaborate home pages on the Internet containing basic information about the provider and its products, directions to local agents, or calculators to crunch the numbers and generate sample premiums.

10-5c Settling Property and Liability Claims

Insurance companies typically settle claims promptly and fairly—especially life and health care claims. But in settling property and liability claims, there is often some claimant–insurer disagreement. In this section, we'll review the claims settlement process beginning with what you should do immediately following an accident.

First Steps Following an Accident

After an accident, record the names, addresses, and phone numbers of all witnesses, drivers, occupants, and injured parties, along with the license numbers of the automobiles involved. *Never leave the scene of an accident, even if the other party says it's acceptable to do so.* Immediately notify law enforcement officers and your insurance agent of the accident. Never discuss liability at the scene of an accident or with anyone other than the police and your insurer. The duty of the police is to assess the probability of a law violation and maintain order at the scene of an accident—not to make judgments about liability.

Steps in Claims Settlement

If you're involved in an accident, one of the first things to decide is whether you want to file a claim. Most experts agree that unless it's a very minor or insignificant accident, the best course of action is to file a claim. Be aware, though, that if you've made several claims, then your insurance company may decide to drop you after settling the current one. The claims settlement process typically involves these steps:

1. Notice to your insurance company: You must notify your insurance company that a loss (or potential for loss) has occurred. Timely notice is extremely important.
2. Investigation: Insurance company personnel may talk to witnesses or law enforcement officers and gather physical evidence to determine whether the claimed loss is

FINANCIAL PLANNING TIPS

How to Handle a Denied Insurance Claim

If your homeowner's or automobile insurance company refuses to pay all or part of your claim, that can be an upsetting. Here are some key steps to take if you decide to contest a denied claim:

• **Review the claim and the insurer's stated reason for denying it.** Determine whether there is a discrepancy between the terms stated in your policy and the rationale provided in the denial. Make sure that you know your policy maximums. You can't fight the denial effectively if you can't point out the discrepancy to your insurance company.

• **Document every step.** Obtain written copies of police or fire department reports and outside appraisals, and take lots of photos.

• **Request a review of the claim denial immediately.** Complain to your insurance company and ask for a review of your case. Do this as soon as possible, because some companies require you to file an appeal within one year of the date of the first decision.

• **If the insurance company does not honor your claim or takes weeks to respond, then go to your state's insurance department.** In most states, insurers have about six weeks to resolve a dispute.

• **Weigh the costs and the benefits carefully before you file a lawsuit.** The legal fees and hassle might be worth it if you have a homeowner's claim for $25,000 or $50,000. But a denied auto claim for a few thousand dollars may not be worth pursuing in light of the legal costs.

Source: Based, in part, on Kalen Smith, "What to Do If Your Homeowners Insurance Claim Is Denied," http://www.moneycrashers.com/homeowners-insurance-claim-denied/, accessed August 2015.

---

covered by the policy, and they'll check to make sure that the date of the loss falls within the policy period. If you delay filing your claim, you hinder the insurer's ability to check the facts. All policies specify the period within which you must give notice. Failure to report an accident can result in losing your right to collect on it.

3. Proof of loss: This proof requires you to give a sworn statement. You may have to show medical bills, submit an inventory, and certify the value of lost property (e.g., a written inventory, photographs, and purchase receipts). You may also have to submit an employer statement of lost wages and, if possible, physical evidence of damage (e.g., X-rays if you claim a back injury; show a broken window or pried door if you claim a break-in and theft at your home). After reviewing your proof of loss, the insurer may (1) pay you the amount you asked for, (2) offer you a lesser amount, or (3) deny that the company has any legal responsibility under the terms of your policy.

If the amount is disputed, most policies provide for some form of claims arbitration. You hire a third party, the company hires a third party, and these two arbitrators jointly select one more person. When any two of the three arbitrators reach agreement, their decision binds you and the company to their solution. When a company denies responsibility, you do not get the right of arbitration. In such cases, the company is saying that the loss does not fall under the policy coverage. You must then either forget the claim or bring in an attorney or, perhaps, a public adjustor (discussed next).

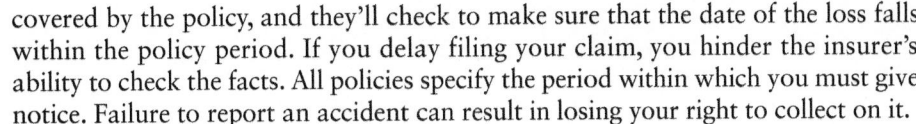

Financial Fact or Fantasy?

Filing a property or liability claim is quick and easy to do. Just call your agent, provide a few basic details, and look for your check in a few days. **Fantasy:** Filing a property or liability claim is often a detailed and time-consuming process wherein you must prove your loss. The insurance company can offer you an amount less than the loss you claim or deny your claim altogether.

Claims Adjustment

Usually the first person to call when you need to file a claim is your insurance agent. If your loss is relatively minor, the agent can process it quickly and, in fact, often gives you a check right on the spot. If your loss is more complex, your company will probably assign a claims adjustor to the case. A claims adjustor is an insurance specialist who works for the insurance company either as an independent adjustor or for an adjustment bureau. The adjustor investigates claims, looking out for the company's interests—which might very well be to keep you, its customer, satisfied. However, many claimants are out to collect all they can from insurance companies, which they think have "deep pockets." Thus adjustors walk a fine line: they must diligently question and investigate while at the same time offering service to minimize settlement delays and financial hardship. To promote your own interest in the claim, cooperate with your adjustor and answer inquiries honestly—keeping in mind that the insurance company writes the adjustor's paycheck.

TEST YOURSELF

10-17 Differentiate between *captive* and *independent* insurance agents. What characteristics should you look for in an insurance agent and an insurance company when you're buying property or liability insurance?

10-18 Briefly describe key aspects of the claims settlement process, explaining what to do after an accident, the steps in claim settlement, and the role of claims adjustors.

Planning Over a Lifetime: *Protecting Your Property*

Here are some suggestions on how to insure your property and protect against liability exposures over the different stages of your life.

Independent Lifestyle (20s)	Family and Career Development (30s–40s)	Mature Lifestyle (50s–60s)	Retirement (65+)
✓ Evaluate renter's insurance to protect your personal property and to limit liability exposure.	✓ Buy homeowner's insurance with appropriate property and liability coverage.	✓ Review homeowner's insurance coverage. Keep in mind the possible need for riders on expensive, otherwise insufficiently uncovered personal items.	✓ Revise homeowner's and liability coverage in light of retirement situation.
✓ Make sure to get adequate auto insurance. Don't try to save by buying too little liability coverage.	✓ Document your personal items with photos and purchase receipts.	✓ Consider bundling your homeowner's and auto policies with the same insurer for a discount.	✓ Revise auto insurance in light of your retirement situation.
	✓ Re-evaluate auto insurance coverage.	✓ Consider getting policy discounts by buying anti-theft systems for your home and/or car.	

Financial Impact of Personal Choices
Wade Saves on His Car Insurance

Wade Bradley is a frugal and careful financial planner. One of his money-saving decisions is to continue driving his nine year-old car, which is now worth about $7,500. In order to save money on his car insurance, Wade increased his deductible from $500 to $1,000, which reduced his annual premium by $200. He has just decided that he no longer needs the collision coverage on his policy, which pays for the repair or replacement of his car if damaged. Wade has consequently decided that he should take the risk that he would have to pay for the repair or replacement of his low-value car rather than to continue taking the certain loss of the higher-priced insurance coverage. This decision will save him several hundred dollars a year.

Summary

LG1   **Discuss the importance and basic principles of property insurance, including types of exposure, indemnity, and co-insurance, p. 380.**

Property and liability insurance protects against the loss of real and personal property that can occur from exposure to various perils. Such insurance also protects against loss from lawsuits based on alleged negligence by the insured. The principle of indemnity limits the insured's compensation to the amount of economic loss. The co-insurance provision requires the policyholder to buy insurance coverage that equals a set percentage of the property's value in order to receive full compensation under the policy's terms.

LG2   **Identify the types of coverage provided by homeowner's insurance, p. 384.**

Most homeowner's insurance policies are divided into two sections. Section I covers the insured's dwelling unit, accompanying structures, and personal property. Section II provides comprehensive coverage for personal liability and medical payments to others. The most commonly sold homeowner's policies (Forms HO-2 and HO-3) cover a broad range of perils, including damage from fire or lightning, windstorms, explosions, aircraft, vehicles, smoke, vandalism, theft, freezing, and so on. Personal property coverage is typically set at 50 percent of the coverage on the dwelling.

LG3   **Select the right homeowner's insurance policy for your needs, p. 384.**

Everyone should have some form of homeowner's insurance, whether you own a single-family house or a condominium or rent an apartment. Renter's insurance covers your personal possessions. Except for the house and garage, which are covered on a replacement-cost basis, homeowner's or renter's insurance normally reimburses all losses on an actual cash-value basis, subject to applicable deductibles and policy limits. For an additional premium, you can usually obtain replacement-cost coverage on personal belongings. In Section I, internal limits are set for various classes of property. You may wish to increase these limits if you have valuable property. One way to do so is with a personal property floater (PPF). Because the standard Section II liability limit is only $100,000, it's a good idea to buy additional liability coverage, generally available at minimal cost. Choose a policy with a higher deductible to reduce premiums.

LG4   **Analyze the coverage in a personal automobile policy (PAP) and choose the most cost-effective policy, p. 394.**

Automobile insurance policies usually protect the insured from loss due to personal liability, medical payments, uninsured (and underinsured) motorists, collision (property damage to the vehicle), and comprehensive coverage (which applies to nearly any other type of noncollision damage a car might suffer, such as theft or vandalism). Where you live, the type of car, your driving record, how much you drive, and your personal characteristics influence the policy premium cost. Most automobile insurers offer discounts for good driving records, safety and antitheft devices, driver's training courses, and so on. Other ways to reduce premiums are through higher deductibles and eliminating collision coverage if your car is old.

LG5 **Describe other types of property and liability insurance, p. 402.**
Besides the major forms of homeowner's and automobile insurance, you can obtain other property and liability coverage, including supplemental property insurance coverage—earthquake insurance, flood insurance, and other forms of transportation insurance (mobile-home, recreational vehicle, and boat insurance)—and personal liability umbrella policies.

LG6 **Choose a property and liability insurance agent and company, and settle claims, p. 403.**
Before buying property and liability coverage, evaluate your exposure to loss and determine the coverage needed. Also, select your insurance agent and insurance company carefully to obtain appropriate coverage at a reasonable price. Equally important, make sure that the agent and company you deal with have reputations for fair claims settlement practices. Before filing a claim, decide whether the amount of damage warrants a claim. Document all claims properly and file promptly. If you have a complex loss claim, expect your insurer to assign a claims adjustor to the case.

Key Terms

actual cash value, 383

automobile insurance plan, 400

bodily injury liability losses, 395

captive agent, 403

claims adjustor, 406

co-insurance, 383

collision insurance, 398

comprehensive automobile insurance, 398

comprehensive policy, 384

financial responsibility laws, 401

independent agent, 403

liability insurance, 380

named peril policy, 384

negligence, 381

no-fault automobile insurance, 398

peril, 380

personal automobile policy (PAP), 394

personal liability umbrella policy, 402

personal property floater (PPF), 387

principle of indemnity, 382

property damage liability losses, 396

property insurance, 380

replacement cost, 390

right of subrogation, 383

underinsured motorists coverage, 397

uninsured motorists coverage, 397

Answers to Test Yourself

You can find answers to these questions on this book's companion website. Look for it at *www.cengagebrain.com*. Search for this book by its title, and then add it to your dashboard.

Financial Planning Exercises

LG1, p. 380

1. *Co-insurance clauses.* Assume that Tina Walsh had a homeowner's insurance policy with $100,000 of coverage on the dwelling. Would a 90 percent co-insurance clause be better than an 80 percent clause in such a policy? Give reasons to support your answer.

LG2, p. 384

2. *Evaluating homeowner's policy coverage.* Last year, Brett and Amber Walsh bought a home with a dwelling replacement value of $250,000 and insured it (via an HO-5 policy) for $210,000. The policy reimburses for actual cash value and has a $500 deductible, standard limits for coverage C items, and no scheduled property. Recently, burglars broke into the house and stole a

two-year-old television set with a current replacement value of $600 and an estimated useful life of eight years. They also took jewelry valued at $1,850 and silver flatware valued at $3,000.

a. If the Walsh's policy has an 80 percent co-insurance clause, do they have enough insurance?

b. Assuming a 50 percent coverage C limit, calculate how much the Walshes would receive if they filed a claim for the stolen items.

c. What advice would you give the Walshes about their homeowner's coverage?

LG3, p. 384   3. ***Payout on homeowner's insurance policy.*** Eva Stone's home in Chicago was recently gutted in a fire. Her living and dining rooms were destroyed completely, and the damaged personal property had a replacement price of $32,000. The average age of the damaged personal property was 5 years, and its useful life was estimated to be 15 years. What is the maximum amount the insurance company would pay Eva, assuming that it reimburses losses on an actual cash-value basis?

LG3, p. 384   4. ***Need for renter's insurance.*** Tyler and Sherry Hughes both graduate students, moved into an apartment near the university. Sherry wants to buy renter's insurance, but Tyler thinks that they don't need it because their furniture isn't worth much. Sherry points out that, among other things, they have some expensive computer and stereo equipment. To help the Hughes resolve their dilemma, suggest a plan for deciding how much insurance to buy and give them some ideas for finding a policy.

LG4, p. 394   5. ***Personal automobile policy coverage.*** Marc Rose has a PAP with coverage of $25,000/$50,000 for bodily injury liability, $25,000 for property damage liability, $5,000 for medical payments, and a $500 deductible for collision insurance. How much will his insurance cover in each of the following situations? Will he have any out-of-pocket costs?

a. Marc loses control and skids on ice, running into a parked car and causing $3,785 damage to the unoccupied vehicle and $2,350 damage to his own car.

b. Marc runs a stop sign and causes a serious auto accident, badly injuring two people. The injured parties win lawsuits against him for $30,000 each.

c. Marc's 18-year old son borrows his car. He backs into a telephone pole and causes $450 damage to the car.

LG4, p. 394   6. ***Evaluating personal automobile policy features.*** Jose Ruiz is a single 40-year-old loan officer at large regional bank; he has a 16-year-old son. He has decided to use his annual bonus as a down payment on a new car. One Saturday afternoon in late September, he visits Unique Motors and buys a new car for $32,000. To obtain insurance on the car, Jose calls his agent, Carrie Ruffin, who represents Brown's Insurance Agency, and explains his auto insurance needs. Carrie says that she'll investigate the various options for him. Three days later, Jose and Carrie get together to review his coverage options. Carrie offers several proposals, including various combinations of the following coverages: (i) basic automobile liability insurance, (ii) uninsured motorists coverage, (iii) automobile medical payments insurance, (iv) automobile collision insurance, and (v) comprehensive automobile insurance.

a. Describe the key features of these insurance coverages.

b. Are there any limitations on these coverages? Explain.

c. Indicate the persons who would be protected under each type of coverage.

d. What kind of insurance coverages would you recommend that Jose purchase? Explain your recommendation.

LG5, p. 402   7. ***Supplemental property insurance.*** Chandler and Frances Cornett are a high-net worth couple. They have appropriate auto and homeowner's insurance but are concerned that they could be sued by someone visiting or working at their home. What type of supplemental insurance might be appropriate for the Cornetts in light of their expressed concern? Explain your answer.

LG6, p. 403   8. ***Auto insurance claims.*** Zach and Jane Rendon recently went out for dinner on a rainy night. When the traffic unexpectedly slowed down, they were rear-ended by an inexperienced driver. Describe what steps the Rendons should have taken after the accident to assure that their auto insurance claim would be settled properly.

Applying Personal Finance

Insure Your Property!

Adequate property insurance is a vital part of financial planning. It helps protect our hard-earned investments in a home, car, or other property. This project will help you determine your property insurance needs.

List the property for which you'd need insurance coverage. Your list may include such things as a home, car, boat, motorcycle, or household items. Beside each entry, list the insurance that you currently have in place on each. Then examine the depth of coverage of your policies. Is this coverage adequate? What are its exclusions and limits? What are the costs? Can you do something to lower these costs? If you don't have coverage or if your coverage is inadequate, research various policies. If you rent a place to live, do you have renter's insurance? If not, tally up what it would cost you to replace all your household items, and then find several quotes for renter's insurance.

CRITICAL THINKING CASES

10.1 The Perkins' Homeowners' Insurance Decision

Calvin and Danielle Perkins, ages 30 and 28, were recently married in Kansas City. Calvin is an electrical engineer with Analytical Solutions, a computer component design firm. Danielle has a master's degree in education and teaches at a local middle school. After living in an apartment for six months, the Perkins have negotiated the purchase of a new home in a rapidly growing Kansas City suburb. Kansas City Savings and Loan Association has approved their loan request for $270,000, which represents 90 percent of the $300,000 purchase price. Before closing the loan, the Perkins must obtain homeowner's insurance for the home. The Perkins currently have an HO-4 renter's insurance policy, which they purchased from Calvin's bridge partner, Gene Patterson, who is an agent with the Roberts Insurance Company. To learn about the types of available homeowner's insurance, Calvin has discussed their situation with Gene, who has offered them several homeowner's policies for their consideration. He has recommended that the Perkins purchase an HO-5 policy because it would provide them with comprehensive coverage.

Critical Thinking Questions

1. What forms of homeowner's insurance are available? Which forms should the Perkins consider?
2. What are the perils against which the home and its contents should be insured?
3. Discuss the types of loss protection provided by the homeowner's policies under consideration.
4. What advice would you give the Perkins regarding Gene's suggestion? What coverage should they buy?

LG2, 3,
p. 384

10.2 Auto Insurance for Dwight Fox

Dwight Fox is a 40-year-old loan officer at a large regional bank; he has a 16-year-old son. He has decided to use his annual bonus as a down payment on a new car. One Saturday afternoon he visits Unique Motors and buys a new car for $32,000. To obtain insurance on the car, Dwight calls his agent, Carla Dawson, who represents Brown's Insurance Company, and explains his auto insurance needs. Carla says that she'll investigate the various options for him. Three days later, Dwight and carla get together to review his coverage options. carla offers several proposals, including various combinations of the following coverages: (a) basic automobile liability insurance, (b) uninsured motorist's coverage, (c) automobile medical payments insurance, (d) automobile collision insurance, and (e) comprehensive automobile insurance.

Critical Thinking Questions

1. Describe the key features of these insurance coverages.
2. Are there any limitations on these coverages? Explain.
3. Indicate the persons who would be protected under each type of coverage.
4. What kind of insurance coverages would you recommend that Dwight purchase? Explain your recommendation.

411

CHAPTER 11

Investment Planning

LEARNING GOALS

LG1 Discuss the role that investing plays in the personal financial planning-process and identify several different investment objectives.

LG2 Distinguish between primary and secondary markets, as well as between broker and dealer markets.

LG3 Explain the process of buying and selling securities and recognize the different types of orders.

LG4 Develop an appreciation of how various forms of investment information can lead to better investing skills and returns.

LG5 Gain a basic understanding of the impact of the Internet on the field of investments.

LG6 Describe an investment portfolio and how you'd go about developing, monitoring, and managing a portfolio of securities.

How Will This Affect Me?

Investing is the means by which many important financial goals in life are achieved. This chapter discusses how to determine the amount of investment capital needed to reach common financial goals and explains how to invest for retirement, to fund major expenditures, to earn needed income, and to establish tax shelters. The market context in which investing occurs is described, and how to buy and sell investments is explained. A framework for evaluating investments is also presented, which includes how to describe, monitor, and manage a portfolio. Sources of investment information are discussed, as well as some of the useful investing tools available online. After reading this chapter you should be able to plan your investments to better meet your financial goals.

11-1 THE OBJECTIVES AND REWARDS OF INVESTING

People invest their money for all sorts of reasons. Some do it as a way to accumulate the down payment on a new home; others do it as a way to supplement their income; still others invest to build up a nest egg for retirement. Actually, the term *investment* means different things to different people; that is, while millions of people *invest* regularly in securities like stocks, bonds, and mutual funds, others *speculate* in commodities or options. Investing is generally considered to take a long-term perspective and is viewed as a process of purchasing securities wherein stability of value and level of return are somewhat predictable. Speculating, on the other hand, is viewed as the short-term buying and selling of securities in which future value and expected return are highly uncertain. The average investor is risk averse and requires higher expected returns as compensation for taking on greater risk. Think of an investor as someone wearing a belt *and* suspenders, whereas the speculator might wear neither.

If you're like most investors, at first you'll probably keep your funds in some type of savings vehicle (as described in Chapter 4). Once you have *sufficient savings*—for emergencies and other purposes—you can start building up a *pool of invested capital*. This often means making sacrifices and doing what you can to *live within your budget*. Granted, it's far easier to spend money than to save it, but if you're really serious about getting into investments, you'll have to accumulate the necessary capital to invest! In addition to a savings and capital accumulation program, it's also important to have adequate *insurance coverage* to provide protection against the unexpected (we discussed different kinds of insurance in Chapters 8, 9, and 10). In this chapter we'll assume that you're adequately insured and that the cost of insurance coverage is built into your family's monthly cash budget. Ample insurance and liquidity (cash and savings) with which to meet life's emergencies are two *investment prerequisites* that are absolutely essential to developing a successful investment program. Once these conditions are met, you're ready to start investing.

11-1a How Do I Get Started?

Contrary to what you may believe, there's really nothing magical about the topic of investments. In fact, so long as you have the capital to do so, it's really quite easy to start investing. The terminology may seem baffling at times, and some of the procedures and techniques may seem quite complicated. But don't let that mislead you into

investing
The process of placing money in some medium such as stocks or bonds in the expectation of receiving some future benefit.

speculating
A form of investing in which future value and expected returns are highly uncertain.

risk averse
The average investor's attitude toward risk is such that, when presented with two investments having the same expected return, the one with the lowest risk will be chosen.

thinking there's no room for the small, individual investor. Nothing could be farther from the truth! As we'll see in this and the next two chapters, individual investors can choose from a wide array of securities and investment vehicles. What's more, opening an investment account is no more difficult than opening a checking account.

How, then, do you get started? First, you need some money—not a lot; $500 to $1,000 will do. And remember, this is *investment capital* we're talking about here—money you've accumulated above and beyond basic emergency savings. Besides the money, you need knowledge and know-how. Never invest in something you don't understand—that's the quickest way to lose money. Instead, learn as much as you can about the market, different types of securities, and various trading strategies. This course you're taking on personal finance is a good start, but you may want to do more, such as becoming a regular reader of publications such as *Money, The Wall Street Journal, Barron's*, and *Forbes*. We strongly suggest that, after you've learned a few things about stocks and bonds, you set up a portfolio of securities on paper and make *paper trades* in and out of your portfolio, for six months to a year, to get a feel for what it's like to make (and lose) money in the market. Start out with an imaginary sum of, say, $50,000 (if you're going to dream, you might as well dream big). Then keep track of the stocks and bonds you hold, record the number of shares bought and sold, dividends received, and so on. Throughout this exercise, be sure to use actual prices (as obtained from *The Wall Street Journal*, **CNN.com**, or your local newspaper) and keep it as realistic as possible. You might even want to use one of the *portfolio tracking* programs offered at such sites as **http://www.quicken.com** or **http://moneycentral.msn.com**.

You'll also need a way to invest—more specifically, a brokerage firm (person or online) and some investment vehicle in which to invest. As we'll see later in this chapter, the brokerage is the means whereby you'll be buying and selling stocks, bonds, and other securities. As a beginning investor with limited funds, it's probably best to confine your investment activity to the basics. Stick to stocks, bonds, mutual funds, and exchange-traded funds. Avoid getting fancy. Further, *be patient!* Don't expect the price of the stock to double overnight, and don't panic when things don't work out as expected in the short run (after all, security prices do occasionally go down). Finally, remember that you don't need spectacular returns in order to make a significant amount of money in the market. Instead, be consistent and let compound interest work for you. Do that and you'll find that just $2,000 a year invested at a fairly conservative rate of 5 percent will grow to over $66,000 in 20 years! Although the type of security you invest in is a highly personal decision, you might want to seriously consider some sort of mutual fund as your first investment (see Chapter 13). Mutual funds and exchange-traded funds provide professional management and diversification that individual investors—especially those with limited resources—can rarely obtain on their own.

11-1b The Role of Investing in Personal Financial Planning

Buy a car, build a house, enjoy a comfortable retirement—these are goals we'd all like to attain some day and, in many cases, they're the centerpieces of well-developed financial plans. As a rule, a financial goal such as building a house is not something we pay for out of our cash reserves. Instead, we must accumulate the funds over time, which is where investment planning and the act of investing enters into the personal financial planning process. By investing our money, we are letting it work for us.

It all starts with an objective: a particular financial goal that you'd like to achieve within a certain period of time. Take the case of the Dwyers. Shortly after the birth of their first child, they decided to start a college education fund. After doing some rough calculations, they concluded they'd need to accumulate about $330,000 over the next 18 years to have enough money for their daughter's education. Does that seem like a big number to you? Well, consider that public college tuition, fees, room, and board expenses are currently running around $24,000 a year. Then consider that college costs are expected to increase by more than the general level of inflation. Common estimates are between 5 percent and 7 percent a year for planning purposes.

Simply by setting that objective, the Dwyers created a well-defined, specific financial goal. The purpose is to meet their child's educational needs, and the amount of money involved is $330,000 in 18 years. But how do they reach their goal? First, they must decide where the money will come from. While part of it will come from the return (profit) on their investments, they still have to come up with the initial *investment capital*.

Coming Up with the Capital

So far, the Dwyers know how much money they want to accumulate ($330,000) and how long they have to accumulate it (18 years). The only other thing they need to determine at this point is the *rate of return* that they think they can earn on their money. Having taken a financial planning course in college, the Dwyers know that the amount of money they'll have to put into their investment program largely depends on *how much they can earn from their investments*: the higher their rate of return, the less they'll have to put up. Let's say they feel comfortable using a 6 percent rate of return. That's a fairly conservative number—one that won't require them to put all or most of their money into high-risk investments—and they're reasonably certain they can reach that level of return, *on average*, over the long haul. It's important to use some care in coming up with a projected rate of return. Don't saddle yourself with an unreasonably high rate because that will simply reduce the chance of reaching your targeted financial goal.

A reasonable way to project future returns is to look at what the market has done over the past and then use the average return performance over various historical periods as your estimates. To help you in this regard, take a look at the statistics in the following table; they show the average annual returns on stocks, bonds, and U.S. Treasury bills along with portfolios made up of two or three of these asset classes over holding periods of 5, 10, 15, and 87 years.

Holding Period	Stock Returns (S&P 500)	U.S. Treasury Bond Returns (10-year)	Stocks and Treasury Bonds Together (1/2, 1/2)	Returns on Short-Term U.S. Treasury Bills	Stocks, Bonds, and T-Bills Combined (1/3, 1/3, 1/3)
5 years: 2010–2014	15.69%	5.82%	10.75%	0.07%	7.19%
10 years: 2005–2014	9.37%	5.31%	7.34%	1.44%	5.38%
15 years: 2000–2014	6.00%	6.36%	6.18%	1.85%	4.73%
87 years: 1928–2014	11.53%	5.28%	8.40%	3.53%	6.78%

You Can Do It Now

How's the Market Doing Right Now?

It's easy to find out how the stock market is doing anytime during trading hours as well as its performance so far during the current year. For example, if you want to see how the S&P 500 index is doing, go to **http://www.bloomberg.com/quote/SPX:IND**. You'll be able to see how the index is doing and if you look at the "year-to-date" section, you'll see what the S&P 500 stocks have returned so far in this year. You can do it now.

The average return on stocks over the 15-year period from 2000 to 2014 was 6 percent, and the average return from 1928 to 2014 was 11.53 percent. Thus, even in light of the financial crisis of 2008, long-term stock market performance suggests that average returns of at least 6 percent have not been unusual. The two portrayed portfolios of stocks and T-bonds and of stocks, T-bonds, and T-bills show the effect of diversification. When the stock market does well, its returns tend to exceed bond and bill returns. However, the relative stability of bonds and bills provides some protection when the stock market falters. Of course, there's no guarantee that these historical returns will occur again in the next 10 to 15 years, but the past does at least give us a basis for making projections into the future.

Now, returning to our problem at hand, there are two ways of coming up with the capital needed to reach a targeted sum of money: (1) you can make a lump-sum investment up front and let that amount grow over time; or (2) you can set up a systematic savings plan and put away a certain amount of money each year. Worksheet 11.1 is designed to help you find the amount of investment capital that you'll need to reach a given financial goal. It employs the *compound value* concept discussed in Chapter 2 and is based on a given financial target (line 1) and a projected average rate of return on your investments (line 2). By way of brief review of the chapter 2 framework, the yearly savings required to fund the target goal is computed as:

$$\text{Yearly Savings} = \frac{\text{Future Amount of Money Desired}}{\text{Future Value Annuity Factor}}$$

You can use this worksheet to find either a required lump-sum investment (part A) or an amount that will have to be put away each year in a savings plan (part B). We'll assume the Dwyers have $10,000 to start with (this comes mostly from gifts their daughter received from her grandparents). Since they know they'll need a lot more than that to reach their target, the Dwyers decide to use part B of the worksheet to find out how much they'll have to save annually.

Behavior Matters

Do We Live in the Present Too Much? Looking for Patterns That Aren't There ...

Evidence indicates that frequent trading damages the average investor's wealth. A patient, long-term orientation works best. However, neuroscience researchers find that short-term thinking may well be hard-wired into our brains. Using a clever experiment that involved four slot machines with *random payoffs*, participants could choose among machines based on how much a given slot machine paid off. As soon as the payoffs changed, participants moved to the machine that had the most favorable *recent* payoffs. Thus, participants appeared to make choices largely by extrapolating from their most recent experience. This is consistent with so-called *recency cognitive bias*, in which undue emphasis is placed on recent experience in decision making. Thus, it appears that our brains are hard-wired to create patterns even when they don't exist in random data.

The random structure of the experiment is comparable to the returns in financial markets. Recent research finds that among the mutual funds that performed in the top half relative to the Standard & Poor's 500 index, only 49 percent were still in the upper half a year later. And a year after that, only 24 percent remained in the top half of mutual fund performers. Thus, the results seem to be no better than flipping a coin, which is a matter of pure luck. So if our brains are hard-wired to act on patterns that don't really exist, it's no surprise that most investors find it hard to pursue a long-term, buy-and-hold investing strategy.

Given this built-in bias, what should you do with your investments? Recognize that you may well have this bias yourself and be deliberate in your investment decision making. Make a list of criteria that every investment must meet before you buy or sell. Don't buy or sell only because of recent price moves. List three reasons for making the investment that have nothing to do with recent price performance. It's also critically important to follow the performance of an investment *after* you sell it as well. That lets you know if what you bought did better or worse than if you'd held the original investment. Understanding built-in behavioral biases is the start of more informed and consistent investing.

Source: Adapted from Jason Zweig, "Why We're Driven to Trade," http://professional.wsj.com/article/SB10000872396390444097904577538924031591882.html, accessed August 2015.

The first thing to do is find the future value of the $10,000 initial investment at the assumed 6 percent average rate of return. The specific question here is: How much will that initial lump-sum investment grow to over an 18-year period? Using the compound value concept and the appropriate "future value factor" (from Appendix A) for 6 percent and 18 years, we see in line 7 that this deposit will grow to about $28,540. That's only about 9 percent of the target amount of $330,000. Thus, by subtracting the terminal value of the initial investment (line 7) from our target (line 1), we find the amount that must be generated from some sort of annual savings plan—see line 8. (*Note*: If you were starting from scratch then you'd enter a zero in line 5, and the amount in line 8 would be equal to the amount in line 1.) Again, using the appropriate future value factor (this time from Appendix B), we find that the Dwyers will have to put away about $9,754 a year in order to reach their target of $330,000 in 18 years. That is, the $9,754 a year will grow to $301,460, and this amount plus $28,540 (the amount to which the initial $10,000 will grow) equals the Dwyers targeted financial goal of $330,000. (By the way, they can also reach their target by making an up-front lump-sum investment of $115,613—try working out part A of the worksheet on your own to see if you can come up with that number.) As you might have suspected, the last few steps in the worksheet can just as easily be done on a financial calculator. That is, after determining the size of the nest egg (as in step 8, for example), you can use a financial calculator to find the amount of money that must be put away each year to fund the nest egg.

Calculator

INPUTS	FUNCTIONS
18	N
6	I/Y
−301,460	FV
	CPT
	PMT
	SOLUTION
	9,754.20

See Appendix E for details.

Calculator Keystrokes. You can use a financial calculator to *find the annual payments necessary to fund a target amount* by first putting the calculator in the *annual compounding* mode. Then, to determine the amount of money that must be put away each year, at a 6 percent rate of return, to accumulate $301,460 in 18 years, make the keystrokes shown here, where:

N = number of *years* in investment horizon
I/Y = expected average *annual* rate of return on investments
FV = the targeted amount of money you want to accumulate, entered as a *negative* number

The calculator should then display a value of $9,754.20 (net of the $ sign on most calculators), which is the amount of money that must be put away each year to reach the targeted amount of $301,460 in 18 years. (*Note:* The calculator keystrokes take you from steps 8 to 10 in Worksheet 11.1. You can also do steps 5 to 7 on the calculator by letting N = 18, I/Y = 6.0, and PV = −10000; then solve for (CPT) FV. Try it—you should come up with a number fairly close to the amount shown on line 7 of Worksheet 11.1.)

An Investment Plan Provides Direction

Now that the Dwyers know how much they have to save each year, their next step is deciding how they'll save it. For many investors, it's best to follow some type of *systematic routine*—for example, build a set amount of savings each month or quarter into the household budget and then stick with it. But whatever procedure is followed, keep in mind that all we're doing here is accumulating the required investment capital. That money still has to be put to work in some kind of investment program, and that's where an investment plan enters the picture. An **investment plan** is nothing

investment plan
A statement—preferably written—that specifies how investment capital will be invested to achieve a specified goal.

You can use a worksheet like this one to find out how much money you must come up with to reach a given financial goal. This worksheet is based on the same future value concepts we first introduced in Chapter 2

DETERMINING AMOUNT OF INVESTMENT CAPITAL	
Financial goal: _To accumulate $330,000 in 18 years for the purpose of meeting the cost of daughter's college education._	
1. Targeted Financial Goal (see Note 1)	$ 330,000
2. Projected Average Return on Investments	6%
A. Finding a Lump Sum Investment:	
3. Future Value Factor, from Appendix A ■ based on _____ years to target date and a projected average return on investment of ___%___	0.000
4. Required Lump Sum Investment ■ line 1 ÷ line 3	$ 0
B. Making a Series of Investments over Time:	
5. Amount of Initial Investment, if any (see Note 2)	$ 10,000
6. Future Value Factor, from Appendix A ■ based on _18_ years of target date and a projected average return on investment of _6%_	2.854
7. Terminal Value of Initial Investment ■ line 5 × line 6	$ 28,540
8. Balance to Come from Savings Plan ■ line 1 − line 7	$ 301,460
9. Future Value Annuity Factor, from Appendix B ■ based on _18_ years to target date and a projected average return on investment of _6%_	30.906
10. Series of Annual Investments Required over Time ■ line 8 ÷ line 9	$ 9,754

Note 1: The "targeted financial goal" is the amount of money you want to accumulate by some target date in the future.

Note 2: If you're starting from scratch—that is, there is *no* initial investment—enter zero on line 5, *skip* lines 6 and 7, and then use the total targeted financial goal (from line 1) as the amount to be funded from a savings plan; now proceed with the rest of the worksheet.

more than a simple—preferably written—statement explaining how the accumulated investment capital will be invested in order to reach the targeted goal. In the Dwyers case, their capital accumulation plan calls for a 6 percent rate of return as a target they feel they can achieve. Now they need to find a way to obtain that 6 percent return on their money—meaning they have to specify, in general terms at least, the kinds of investment vehicles they intend to use. When completed, *an investment plan is a way of translating an abstract investment target* (in this case, a 6 percent return) *into a specific investment program.*

11-1c What Are Your Investment Objectives?

Some people buy securities for the protection they provide from taxes, which is what tax shelters are all about. Others want to have money put aside for that proverbial rainy day or, perhaps, to build up a nice retirement nest egg. *Your goals tend to set the tone for your investment program, and they play a major role in determining how conservative (or aggressive) you're likely to be in making investment decisions.* These goals define the purpose for your investments. Given that you have adequate savings and insurance to cover any emergencies, the most frequent investment objectives are to (1) accumulate funds for retirement, (2) save for a major purchase, (3) enhance current income, and (4) seek shelter from taxes.

Retirement

Accumulating funds for retirement is *the single most important reason for investing.* Too often, though, retirement planning occupies only a small amount of our time because we tend to rely too heavily on employers and Social Security for our retirement needs. As many people learn too late in life, that can be a serious mistake. A much better approach is to review the amounts of income you can realistically expect to receive from Social Security and your employee pension plan, and then decide, based on your retirement goals, *whether they'll be adequate to meet your needs.* You'll probably find that you'll have to supplement them through personal investing. (Retirement plans are discussed in Chapter 14.)

Major Expenditures

People often put money aside, sometimes for years, to save up enough to make just one major expenditure. Here are the most common ones:

- Down payment on a home
- Money for a child's college education
- Capital for going into business
- Expensive (perhaps once-in-a-lifetime) vacation
- Purchase of a special, expensive item
- Funds for retirement

Whatever your goal, the idea is to set your sights on something and then go about building your capital with that objective in mind. Once you know about how much money you're going to need to attain one of these goals (following a procedure like the one illustrated in Worksheet 11.1), you can specify the types of investment vehicles that you intend to use. For example, you might follow a low-risk approach by making a single lump-sum investment in a high-grade bond that matures the same year that you'll need the funds; or you could follow a riskier investment plan that calls for investing a set amount of money over time in something like a growth-oriented mutual fund (where there's little assurance of the investment's terminal value). Of course, for some purposes—such as the down payment on a home or a child's education—you'll probably want to take a lot less risk than for others, because attaining these goals should not be jeopardized by the types of investment vehicles that you choose to employ.

Current Income

The idea with current income is to put your money into investments that will enable you to supplement your income. In other words, it's for people who want to live off their investment income. A secure source of high current income, from dividends or interest, is the primary concern of such investors. Retired people, for example, often choose investments offering high current income at low risk. Another common reason for seeking supplemental income is that a family member requires extended, costly medical care. Even after insurance, such recurring costs can heavily burden a family budget without this vital income supplement.

Shelter from Taxes

As explained in Chapter 3, federal income taxes do not treat all sources of income equally. For example, if you own real estate then you may be able to take depreciation deductions against certain other sources of income, thereby reducing the amount of your taxable income. This tax write-off feature can make real estate an attractive investment vehicle for some investors, even though its pre-tax rate of return may not appear very high. The goal of sheltering income from taxes is a legitimate one that, for some investors, often goes hand in hand with the goals of saving for a major outlay or for retirement. If you can avoid paying taxes on the income from an investment then you will, all other things considered, have more funds available for reinvestment during the period.

11-1d Different Ways to Invest

After establishing your investment objectives, you can use a variety of investment vehicles to fulfill those goals. In this section, we'll briefly describe various types of investments that are popular with (and widely used by) individual investors.

Common Stock

Common stocks are a form of *equity*—as an investment, they represent an ownership interest in a corporation. Each share of stock symbolizes a fractional ownership position in a firm; for example, one share of common stock in a corporation that has 10,000 shares outstanding would denote a 1/10,000 ownership interest in the firm. A share of stock typically entitles the holder to equal participation in the corporation's earnings and dividends as well as an equal vote to elect the management of the corporation. From the investor's perspective, the return to stockholders comes from dividends and/or appreciation in share price. Common stock has no maturity date and, as a result, remains outstanding indefinitely (common stocks are discussed in Chapter 12).

Bonds

In contrast to stocks, *bonds* are *liabilities*—they're IOUs of the issuer. Governments and corporations issue bonds that pay a stated return, called *interest*. An individual who invests in a bond receives a stipulated interest income, typically paid every six months, plus the return of the principal (face) value of the bond at maturity. For example, if you purchased a $1,000 bond that paid 5 percent interest in semiannual installments, then you could expect to receive $25 every six months (i.e., 5 percent × 0.5 years × $1,000) and at maturity, recover the $1,000 face value of the bond. Of course, a bond can be bought or sold prior to maturity at a price that may differ from its face value because bond prices, like common stock prices, fluctuate in the marketplace (see Chapter 12).

Preferreds and Convertibles

These are forms of *hybrid securities* in that each has the characteristics of both stocks and bonds; they're a cross between the two. *Preferred securities* are issued as stock and, as such, represent an equity position in a corporation. But unlike common stock, preferreds have a stated (fixed) dividend rate that is paid before the dividends to holders of common stock are paid. Like bonds, preferred stocks are usually purchased for the current income (dividends) they pay. A *convertible security*, in contrast, is a fixed-income obligation (usually a bond, but sometimes a preferred stock) that carries a conversion feature permitting the investor to convert it into a specified number of shares of common stock. Thus convertible securities provide the fixed-income benefits (interest) of a bond while offering the price appreciation (capital gains) potential of common stock. (Convertibles are discussed in Chapter 12.)

Mutual Funds, Exchange-Traded Funds, and Exchange Traded Notes

An organization that invests in and professionally manages a diversified portfolio of securities is called a *mutual fund*. A mutual fund sells shares to investors, who then become part owners of the fund's securities portfolio. Most mutual funds issue and repurchase shares at a price that reflects the underlying value of the portfolio at the time the transaction is made. Mutual funds have become popular with individual investors because they offer a wide variety of investment opportunities and a full array of services that many investors find particularly appealing (these securities are discussed in Chapter 13).

Exchange-traded funds (ETFs) are similar to mutual funds in that they are portfolios of securities. They are commonly designed to track a basket or index of equity securities like the S&P 500 or a particular sector, such as telecommunications or utility stocks. They can also include other types of investments, which include bonds and real estate. Whereas mutual funds can be bought or sold only at the end of the day, investors can trade ETFs throughout the trading day just like individual shares of stock. ETFs offer certain advantages over mutual funds. For example, unlike mutual funds, they trade continuously throughout the trading day and can be purchased with borrowed money or sold short. Further, ETFs provide more favorable tax treatment than mutual funds.

Exchange-traded notes (ETNs) are more similar to ETFs than to mutual funds. They are senior, unsecured, unsubordinated debt securities issued by an underwriting bank. As such, ETNs are debt securities that have a maturity date and are backed only by the credit of the issuer. Like ETFs, most ETNs are designed to reproduce the returns on a market benchmark, net of investment management fees. Thus, the underwriting bank promises to pay an amount based on the value of the index, net of fees, upon maturity. It's important to realize that an ETN bears a different risk than an ETF. If the bank underwriting the ETN goes bankrupt, the ETN might lose value just as a senior debt security would. Consequently, ETFs only face the risk of market fluctuations, while ETNs face both market risk and the risk that the issuing bank will default. Unfortunately, this credit risk is hard for investors to evaluate. Like ETFs, ETNs are traded on an exchange and can be sold short. Also like ETFs, ETNs provide tax advantages over mutual funds. (More information on these advantages, and disadvantages, will be given in Chapter 13.)

Real Estate

Investments in *real estate* can take many forms, ranging from raw land speculation to limited-partnership shares in commercial property, even real estate mutual funds. The returns on real estate come from rents, capital gains, and certain tax benefits. (Various types of real estate investments are discussed in Chapter 13.)

TEST YOURSELF

11-1   Briefly discuss the relationship between investing and personal financial planning.

11-2   What's the difference between an investment plan and a capital accumulation plan?

11-3   Why is it important to have investment objectives when embarking on an investment program?

11-2 SECURITIES MARKETS

securities markets
The marketplace in which stocks, bonds, and other financial instruments are traded.

The term **securities markets** generally describes the arena where stocks, bonds, and other financial instruments are traded. Such markets can be physical places, but they can just as easily be *electronic networks* that allow buyers and sellers to come together to execute trades. Securities markets can be broken into two parts: capital markets and money markets. The *capital market* is where long-term securities like stocks and bonds are traded. The *money market* is the marketplace for short-term, low-risk credit instruments with maturities of 1 year or less; these include U.S. Treasury bills, commercial paper, negotiable certificates of deposit, and so on. Both types of markets provide a vital mechanism for bringing the buyers and sellers of securities together. Some of the more popular money market securities were discussed in Chapter 4, where we looked at short-term investment vehicles. In this chapter, we consider the capital markets.

11-2a Primary and Secondary Markets

Securities markets can also be divided into primary and secondary segments. In the *primary market*, new securities are sold to the public, and one party to the transaction is always the issuer. In contrast, old (outstanding) securities are bought and sold in the *secondary market*, where the securities are "traded" between investors. A security is sold in the primary market just once, when it's originally issued by a corporation or a governmental body (e.g., a state or municipality). Subsequent transactions, in which securities are sold by one investor to another, take place in the secondary market.

Primary Markets

When a corporation sells a new issue to the public, several financial institutions will participate in the transaction. To begin with, the corporation will probably use an *investment banking firm*, which specializes in *underwriting* (selling) new security issues. The investment banker will give the corporation advice on pricing and other aspects of the issue and will either sell the new security itself or arrange for a *selling group* to do so. The selling group is normally made up of several brokerage firms, each responsible for selling a certain portion of the new issue. On large issues, the originating investment banker will bring in other underwriting firms as partners and form an *underwriting syndicate* in order to spread the risks associated with underwriting and selling the new securities. A potential investor in a new issue must be given a **prospectus**, which is a document describing the firm and the issue. Certain federal agencies are responsible for ensuring that all the information included in a prospectus accurately represents the facts.

prospectus
A document made available to prospective security buyers that describes the firm and a new security issue.

Secondary Markets

The secondary markets permit investors to execute transactions among themselves; it's the marketplace where an investor can easily sell his or her holdings to someone else. Unlike primary market transactions, the secondary market does not generate cash for the underlying company (issuer). Included among the secondary markets are the various *securities exchanges*, in which the buyers and sellers of securities are brought together for the purpose of executing trades. Another major segment of the market is made up of those securities that are listed and traded on the *National Association of Securities Dealers Automated Quotation System (NASDAQ)* market, which employs an all-electronic trading platform to execute trades. Finally, the *over-the-counter (OTC)* market deals in smaller, unlisted securities.

11-2b Broker Markets and Dealer Markets

By far, the vast majority of trades made by small individual investors take place in the secondary market, so we'll focus on it for the rest of this chapter. When you look at the secondary market *on the basis of how securities are traded*, you'll find you can essentially divide the market into two segments: broker markets and dealer markets. Exhibit 11.1 shows the structure of the secondary market in terms of broker or dealer markets. As you can see, the *broker market* consists of national and regional "securities exchanges," while the *dealer market* is made up of both the NASDAQ market and the OTC market.

EXHIBIT 11.1   Broker and Dealer Markets

On a typical trading day, the secondary market is a beehive of activity, where literally billions of shares change hands. This market consists of two parts, the broker market and the dealer market. As can be seen, each of these markets is made up of various exchanges and trading venues.

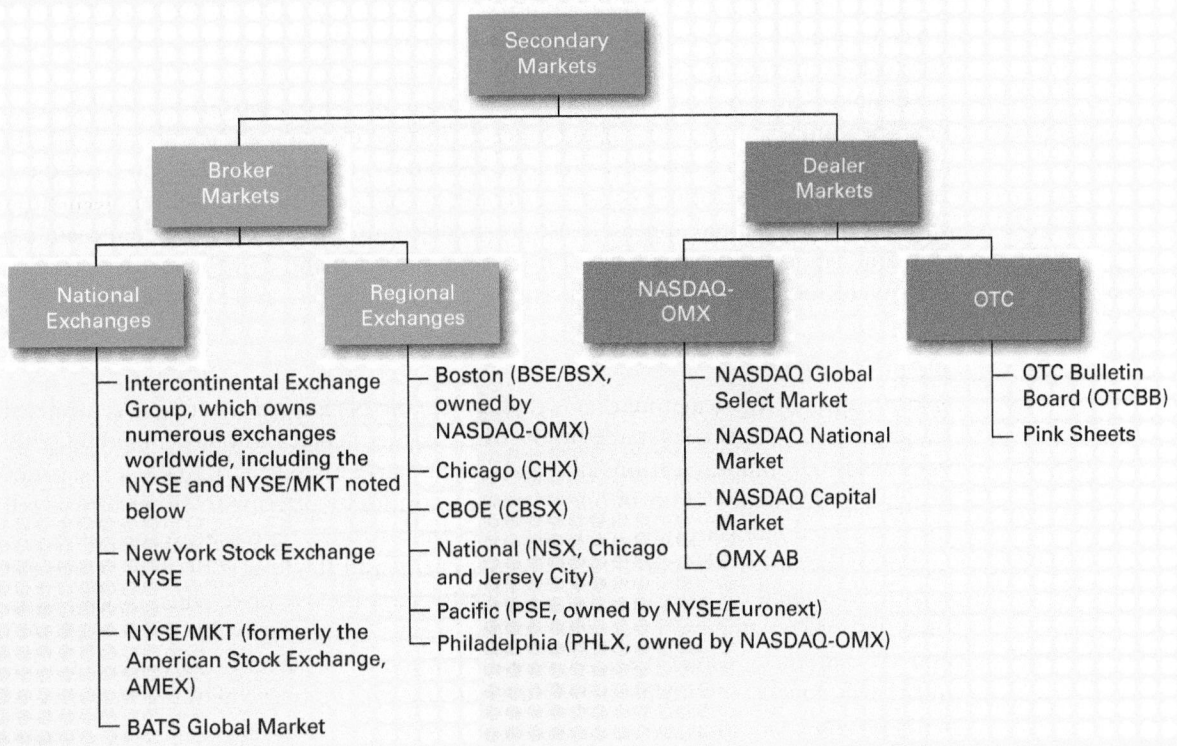

It's important to understand that a key *difference between the two markets is how the trades are executed*. That is, when a trade occurs in a *broker market* (on one of the so-called securities exchanges), the two sides to the transaction—the buyer and the seller—are brought together and the trade takes place at that point: Party A sells his securities directly to the buyer, Party B. In a sense, with the help of a *broker*, the securities change hands right there on the floor of the exchange. In contrast, when trades are made in one of the *dealer markets*, the buyer and seller are never brought together directly; instead, their buy/sell orders are executed separately through *securities dealers*, who act as *market makers*. Essentially, two separate trades are made: Party A sells his securities (in, say, the XYZ Corp.) to one dealer, and Party B buys her securities (in the same XYZ Corp.) from the same dealer or another dealer. Thus, there is always a dealer (market maker) on one side of the transaction.

Broker Markets

When you think of the stock market, if you're like most individual investors, then the first name to come to mind is the New York Stock Exchange (NYSE), which has been the largest stock exchange in the United States. In 2007, the NYSE combined with Euronext, which is the combination of stock exchanges in Amsterdam, Brussels, Lisbon, and Paris. The combined entity, NYSE Euronext, operates six cash equities exchanges in seven countries. And in late 2013 NYSE Euronext was acquired by the Intercontinental Exchange Group (ICE). ICE operates 11 regulated exchanges and numerous central clearing houses. In late 2014 its listings included companies with an aggregate market value in excess of $28 trillion. It includes about 90 percent of the firms in the Dow Jones Industrial Average (DJIA) and about 80 percent of the firms in the S&P 500 index. ICE also owns the American Stock Exchange (AMEX), which was formerly the second-largest U.S. exchange. The AMEX had less restrictive listing requirements than the NYSE, so the acquisition allowed the NYSE to broaden the types of companies falling under its umbrella. The organization is also referred to as NYSE MKT. In mid-2014 ICE spun off Euronext as a standalone European company. The ICE entity is a part of the broker market—indeed, it's their biggest player! BATS Global Market merged with Direct Edge in 2014. This created one of the largest stock exchange operators in the United States.

Besides ICE, a handful of *regional exchanges* are also a part of the broker market. The number of securities listed on each of these exchanges typically ranges from about 100 to 500 companies. The best known of these are the Boston, National, Pacific, and Philadelphia exchanges. These exchanges deal primarily in securities with local and regional appeal. Most are modeled after the NYSE, but their membership and listing requirements are considerably more lenient. To enhance their trading activity, regional exchanges often list securities that are also listed on the NYSE.

Dealer Markets

A key feature of the dealer market is that, unlike the NYSE, it doesn't have centralized trading floors. Instead, it's made up of many market makers who are linked together via a mass telecommunications network. Each market maker is actually a securities dealer who makes a market in one or more securities by offering to either buy or sell them at stated bid/ask prices. (The **bid price** and **ask price** represent, respectively, the highest price offered to purchase a given security and the lowest price at which the security is offered for sale; in effect, an investor pays the ask price when *buying* securities and receives the bid price when *selling* them.) Consisting of both the NASDAQ and OTC markets, dealer markets account for about 40 percent of all shares traded in the U.S. market—with NASDAQ accounting for the overwhelming majority of those trades.

The biggest dealer market, hands down, is made up of a select list of stocks that are listed and traded on the *NASDAQ*. Founded in 1971, NASDAQ had its origins in the OTC market, but today it is considered *a totally separate entity that's no longer*

bid price
The price at which one can sell a security.

ask price
The price at which one can purchase a security.

a part of the OTC market. In fact, in 2006, the Securities and Exchange Commission (SEC) formally recognized NASDAQ as a "listed exchange," giving it much the same stature and prestige as the NYSE. To be traded on NASDAQ, all stocks must have at least two market makers—although the bigger, more actively traded stocks (such as Apple) will have many more than that. These dealers electronically post all their bid/ask prices so that, when investors place (market) orders, they're immediately filled at the best available price. In 2008, NASDAQ combined its business with OMX AB, which owned and operated the largest securities market in northern Europe. It also acquired the Philadelphia and Boston stock exchanges. Across its markets, NASDAQ lists about 3,500 companies with an aggregate market value of $9.5 trillion from all over the world.

NASDAQ sets various listing standards, the most comprehensive of which are for the 2,000 or so stocks traded on the *NASDAQ National Market (NNM)* and the roughly 1,000 stocks traded on the *NASDAQ Global Select Market* (this market is reserved for the biggest and bluest NASDAQ stocks). Stocks included on these two markets are all actively traded and, in general, have a *national following*. These securities are widely quoted, and the trades, all executed electronically, are just as efficient as they are on the floor of the NYSE. Indeed, just as the NYSE has its list of big-name players (e.g., ExxonMobil, Wal-Mart, Pfizer, IBM, Coca-Cola, Home Depot, and UPS), so too does NASDAQ—including names like Apple, Microsoft, Intel, Cisco Systems, eBay, and Google.

The other part of the dealer market is made up of securities that trade in the *OTC market.* This market is separate from NASDAQ and includes mostly small companies that either can't or don't wish to comply with NASDAQ listing requirements. They trade on either the *OTC Bulletin Board (OTCBB)* or in the so-called *Pink Sheets.* The OTCBB is an electronic quotation system that links the market makers who trade the shares of small companies. The OTCBB is regulated by the SEC, which requires (among other things) that all companies traded on this market file audited financial statements and comply with federal securities law. In sharp contrast, the OTC Pink Sheets represent the *unregulated* segment of the market, where the companies aren't even required to file with the SEC. Actually, this market is broken into two tiers. The larger (bottom) tier is populated by all those small and oftentimes questionable companies that provide little or no information about their operations, while the top (albeit smaller) tier is reserved for companies that choose to provide audited financial statements and other required information. Their name comes from the color of paper these quotes used to be printed on, but today the Pinks use an electronic quotation system. Even so, liquidity is often minimal or almost nonexistent; and the market, especially the bottom tier, is littered with scores of nearly worthless stocks—definitely not a market for the uninitiated!

Financial Fact or Fantasy?

Stocks listed on the New York Stock Exchange are traded in the over-the-counter market. **Fantasy:** Stocks not listed on organized exchanges are traded in the over-the-counter (OTC) market. Listed securities are traded on stock exchanges, which are not part of the OTC market.

11-2c Foreign Securities Markets

In addition to those in the United States, more than 100 other countries worldwide have organized securities exchanges. Indeed, actively traded markets can be found not only in the major industrialized nations like Japan, Great Britain, Germany, and Canada but also in emerging economies. In terms of market capitalization (total market value of all shares traded), the NYSE is the biggest stock market in the world, followed by the Tokyo stock market and then the NASDAQ market. After these three markets comes the London market, then Toronto and Frankfurt. Other major exchanges are located in Sydney, Zurich, Hong Kong, Singapore, Rome, and Amsterdam. Besides these markets, you'll find developing markets all over the globe—from Argentina and Armenia to Egypt and Fiji; from Iceland, Israel, and Malaysia to New Zealand, Russia, and Zimbabwe.

11-2d Regulating the Securities Markets

Several laws have been enacted to regulate the activities of various participants in the securities markets and to provide for adequate and accurate disclosure of information to potential and existing investors. State laws, regulating the sale of securities within state borders, typically establish procedures that apply to the sellers of securities doing business within the state. However, the most important and far-reaching securities laws are those enacted by the federal government.

Securities and Exchange Commission (SEC)
An agency of the federal government that regulates the disclosure of information about securities and generally oversees the operation of securities exchanges and markets.

- Securities Act of 1933: This act was passed by Congress to ensure full disclosure of information with respect to new security issues and to prevent a stock market collapse similar to the one that occurred during 1929–1932. The Act requires the issuer of a new security to file a registration statement containing information about the new issue with the Securities and Exchange Commission (SEC), an agency of the U.S. government established to enforce federal securities laws.

- Securities Exchange Act of 1934: This act expanded the scope of federal regulation and formally established the SEC as the agency in charge of the administration of federal securities laws. The Act gives the SEC power to regulate organized securities exchanges and the OTC market by extending disclosure requirements to outstanding securities. It requires the stock exchanges and the stocks traded on them to be registered with the SEC.

- Investment Company Act of 1940: This act protects those purchasing investment company (mutual fund) shares. It established rules and regulations for investment companies and formally authorized the SEC to regulate the companies' practices and procedures. It requires investment companies to register with the SEC and to fulfill certain disclosure requirements. The Act was amended in 1970 to prohibit investment companies from paying excessive fees to their advisors and from charging excessive commissions to purchasers of company shares.

- Sarbanes–Oxley Act of 2002: The purpose of this act (known as "SOX" for short) is to eliminate corporate fraud as related to accounting practices and other information released to investors. Among other things, SOX requires an annual evaluation of internal controls and procedures for financial reporting; it also requires the top executives of the corporation, as well as its auditors, to certify the accuracy of its financial statements and disclosures. What's more, it prohibits audit/accounting firms from engaging in consulting activities with its clients and establishes ethical guidelines for financial officers and security analysts.

- Dodd–Frank Wall Street Reform and Consumer Protection Act of 2010: Prompted by the financial crisis of 2008–2009, this legislation is designed primarily to improve accountability and transparency in the U.S. financial system, to discontinue the "too big to fail" regulatory approach, to protect American taxpayers from costly government bailouts, and to protect consumers from exploitative financial services practices. The Act is the most significant change in financial regulation since the Great Depression. The legislation contains the so-called Volcker Rule, which prohibits depository banks from proprietary trading. Finally, the Act created new federal agencies, which include the Financial Stability Oversight Council, the Office of Financial Research, and the Bureau of Consumer Financial Protection.

National Association of Securities Dealers (NASD)
An agency made up of brokers and dealers in over-the-counter securities that regulates OTC market operations.

- Other significant federal legislation: The *Maloney Act of 1938* provided for the establishment of trade associations for the purpose of self-regulation within the securities industry. This act led to the creation of the National Association of Securities Dealers (NASD), which is made up of all brokers and dealers who participate in the OTC market. The NASD is a self-regulatory organization that polices the activities of brokers and dealers to ensure that its standards are upheld. The SEC supervises NASD activities, thus further protecting investors from fraudulent activities. *The Securities Investor Protection Act of 1970* created the Securities

Investor Protection Corporation (SIPC), an organization that protects investors against the financial failure of brokerage firms, much as the Federal Deposit Insurance Corporation (FDIC) protects depositors against bank failures (we'll examine the SIPC later in this chapter).

11-2e Bull Market or Bear?

The general condition of the market is termed as either *bullish* or *bearish*, depending on whether securities prices are rising or falling over extended periods. Changing market conditions generally stem from changing investor attitudes, changes in economic activity, and certain governmental actions aimed at stimulating or slowing down the economy. Prices go *up* in **bull markets**; these favorable markets are normally associated with investor optimism, economic recovery, and growth. In contrast, prices go *down* in **bear markets**, which are normally associated with investor pessimism and economic slowdowns. These terms are used to describe conditions in the bond and other securities markets as well as the stock market. As a rule, investors can earn attractive rates of return during bull markets and only low (or negative) returns during bear markets. Exhibit 11.2 shows historical U.S. stock market performance going all the way back to 1825.

Look closely at the exhibit and you'll notice that, over the past 50 years or so, stock market behavior has been generally bullish, reflecting the growth and prosperity of the economy (the market was up about 75 percent of the last 50 years). Since World War II, the longest bull market lasted 125 months—from November 1990 through March 2000. This bull market is probably as well known for *how it ended* as it is for the returns it generated. That record-breaking bull market ended abruptly in the spring of 2000, when a nasty bear market took over. After recovering in October 2002, the market generally advanced until about October 2007, when the full effects of the financial crisis started to become apparent. The S&P 500 lost about 37 percent in 2008 yet rose by about 40 percent between March and May of 2009. The S&P 500 has varied significantly since, producing a low return of only about 2 percent in 2011 but a return in excess of 32 percent in 2013 and about 13.7 percent in 2014. The index produced a return of about 3 percent during the first six months of 2015.

Let's put recent developments in general and the financial crisis in particular in perspective. As Exhibit 11.2 shows, the 2008 decline was the second-worst stock market performance since 1825. Losses that bad occurred only in 1931 and 1937. Since 1825, returns increased in 134 years and decreased in 56 years.

bull market
A market condition normally associated with investor optimism, economic recovery, and expansion; characterized by generally rising securities prices.

bear market
A condition of the market typically associated with investor pessimism and economic slowdown; characterized by generally falling securities prices.

TEST YOURSELF

11-4 How does a primary market differ from a secondary market? Where are most securities traded: in the primary or the secondary market?

11-5 What is the difference between the broker and dealer markets?

11-6 What are regional exchanges, and what role do they play?

11-7 Describe the operations of the NASDAQ market. Compare it with an exchange, such as the NYSE.

11-8 Contrast the NASDAQ and National Market System with the OTCBB.

11-9 Explain the difference between a *bull* market and a *bear* market. Discuss the frequency with which returns as bad as those during 2008–2009 occur. How would you characterize the current state of the stock market?

This graphical portrayal of U.S. stock market performance since 1825 shows the variability in returns.

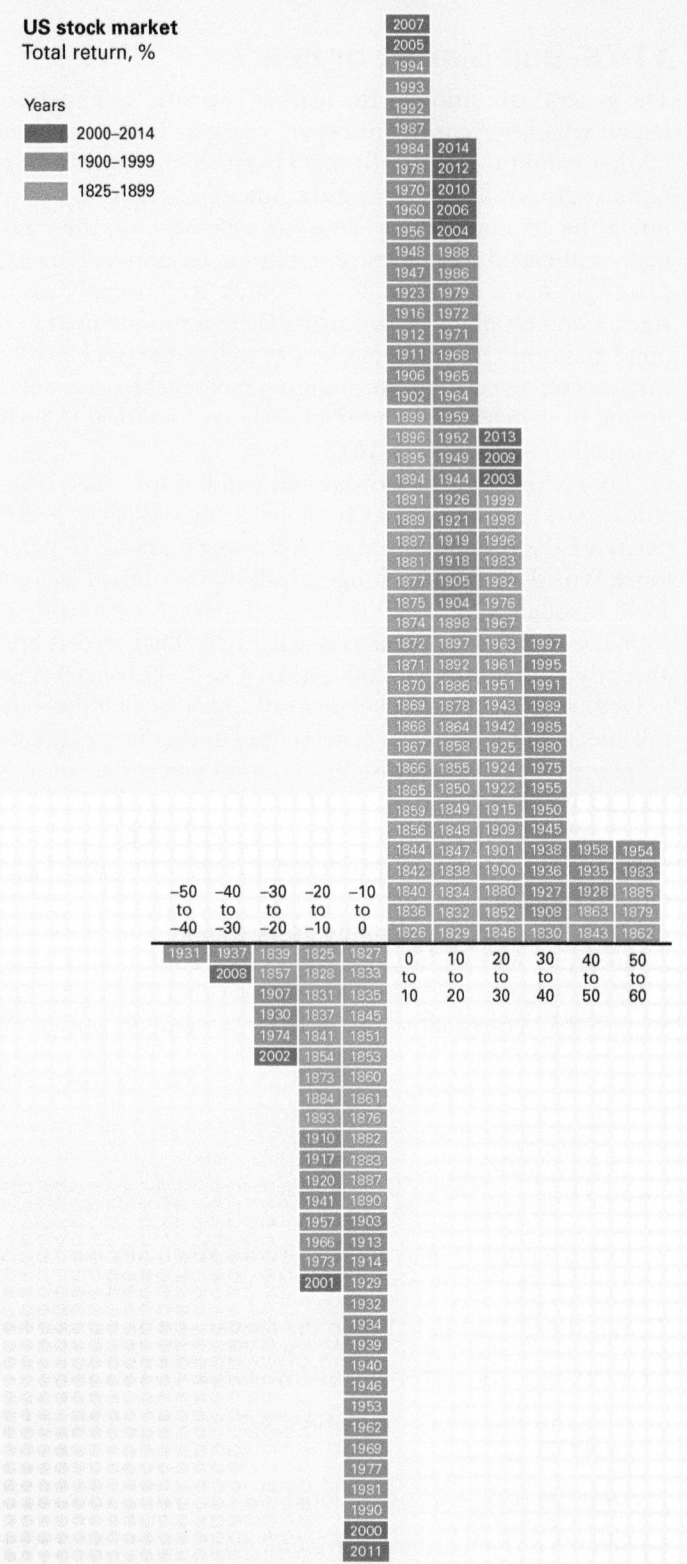

Source: Adapted from "U.S. Stockmarket Returns: Booms and Busts," http://www.economist.com/node/12811306. Based in part on data from Value Square Asset Management, "A New Historical Database of the NYSE 1815 to 1925: Performance and Predictability," Yale School of Management Working Paper, July 2000; data updated by authors.

11-3 MAKING TRANSACTIONS IN THE SECURITIES MARKETS

 In many respects, dealing in the securities markets almost seems like operating in another world, one with all kinds of unusual orders and strange-sounding transactions. Actually, making securities transactions is relatively simple once you understand the basics—in fact, you'll probably find it's no harder than using a checking account!

11-3a Stockbrokers

Stockbroker (account executive, financial consultant)
A person who buys and sells securities on behalf of clients and gives them investment advice and information.

Stockbrokers, or **account executives** and **financial consultants**, as they're also called, buy and sell securities for their customers. Although deeply ingrained in our language, the term *stockbroker* is really somewhat of a misnomer, as they help investors buy and sell not only stocks but also bonds, convertibles, mutual funds, options, and many other types of securities. Brokers must be licensed by the exchanges and must abide by the ethical guidelines of the exchanges and SEC regulations. They work for brokerage firms and in essence are there to execute the orders placed. As discussed earlier, procedures for executing orders in broker markets differ a bit from those in dealer markets; but you as an investor would never know the difference because you'd place your order in exactly the same way.

Selecting a Broker

If you decide to start investing with a *full-service broker*, it's important to select someone *who understands your investment objectives and who can effectively help you pursue them*. If you choose a broker whose own disposition toward investing is similar to yours, then you should be able to avoid conflict and establish a solid working relationship. A good place to start the search is to ask friends, relatives, or business associates to recommend a broker. It's not important to know your stockbroker

FINANCIAL PLANNING TIPS

Is It Time to Get a Robo Investment Advisor?

Robo investment advisers are Internet-based platforms that typically use algorithms to recommend portfolios of low-cost exchange-traded funds across multiple asset classes based on online questionnaires completed by investors. In the last few years, more than 200 companies have entered the market to help investors plan their portfolios online. These include fund giants Fidelity Investments, Vanguard Group, and brokerage firms such as Charles Schwab. While currently only a fraction of the wealth management market, digital wealth-management assets are projected to reach $60 billion soon.

The average robo-adviser customer is millennial, self-directed, and comfortable with technology. Robo-advisers charge annual management fees usually ranging between 0.25 percent and 0.75 percent of assets plus fund expenses. In contrast, traditional advisers tend to

charge an average of 1 percent. The rationale for robo investment advisers is that investors are best served by low fees and broadly diversified portfolios.

Should you be tempted to use a robo-adviser? Low expenses and simplified investment management are positives. However, surveys indicate that investors with the same investment objectives can receive markedly different advice from the broad array of robo-advisers. Keep in mind that you can get a bit of hand-holding from companies like Vanguard's Personal Advisor Services (**https://investor.vanguard. com/advice/personal-advisor**) and Personal Capital (**https://www.personalcapital.com/**). It makes sense to sample a number of robo-advisors' platforms and read their reviews carefully. And it's wise to do your homework before putting your investment portfolio on (semi-) automatic pilot.

Source: Adapted, from Liz Moyer, "Putting Robo Advisers to the Test," *The Wall Street Journal*, http://www.wsj.com/articles/putting-robo-advisers-to-the-test-1429887456, accessed August 2015.

socially because most, if not all, of your transactions/orders will probably be placed online or by phone. But a broker should be far more than just a salesperson; *a good broker is someone who's more interested in your investments than in his or her own commissions.* Should you find you're dealing with someone who's always trying to get you to trade your stocks or who's pushing new investments on you, then by all means dump that broker and find a new one!

Full-Service, Discount, and Online Brokers

Just a few years ago, there were three distinct types of brokers—full-service, discount, and online—and each occupied a well-defined market niche. Today, the lines between these three types of brokers are blurred. Most brokerage firms, even the more traditional ones, now offer online services to compete with the increasingly popular online firms. And many discount brokers now offer services, such as research reports for clients, that once were available only from a full-service broker.

The traditional full-service broker offers investors a wide array of brokerage services, including investment advice and information, trade execution, holding securities for safekeeping, online brokerage services, and margin loans. Such services are fine for investors who want such help—and are willing to pay for it. In contrast, investors who simply want to execute trades and aren't interested in obtaining all those brokerage services should consider either a *discount broker* or *an online broker.* Discount brokers tend to have low-overhead operations and offer fewer customer services than do full-service brokers. Transactions are initiated by calling a toll-free number—or visiting the broker's Web site—and placing the desired buy or sell order. The brokerage firm then executes the order at the best possible price and confirms the transaction details by phone, e-mail, or regular mail. Depending on the transaction size, *discount brokers can save investors from 30 percent to 80 percent of the commissions charged by full-service brokers.*

With the technology that's available to almost everyone today, it's not surprising that investors can more easily trade securities online than on the phone. All you need is an online broker (also called *Internet* or *electronic brokers*) and you, too, can execute trades electronically. The investor merely accesses the online broker's Internet site to open an account, review the commission schedule, or see a demonstration of available transaction services and procedures. Confirmation of electronic trades can take as little as a few seconds, and most occur within a minute. Online investing is increasingly popular, particularly among young investors who enjoy surfing the Internet—so popular, in fact, that it has prompted virtually every traditional full-service broker (and many discount brokers) to offer online trading to their clients. Some of the major full-service, discount, and online brokers are shown below.

Brokerage Fees

Brokerage firms receive commissions for executing buy and sell orders for their clients. These commissions are said to be *negotiated,* meaning they're not fixed. In practice, however, most firms have *established fee schedules* that they use with small transactions. Fees definitely do differ from one brokerage firm to another, so it pays to shop around. If you're an "active trader" who generates a couple thousand dollars (or more) in annual commissions, then by all means try to negotiate a reduced commission schedule with your broker. Chances are, they'll probably agree to a deal with you: brokers much prefer active traders to buy-and-hold investors, because traders generate a lot more commissions. Generally speaking, brokerage fees on a round lot (100 shares) of common stock will amount to roughly 1 percent of the transaction value.

Because there are so many discount brokers today, there is significant variation in the fees charged and services offered. The way commissions are calculated also varies; some firms base them on the dollar value of the transaction, some on the number of shares, and some use both. Exhibit 11.3 ranks the best online brokers using

full-service broker
A broker who, in addition to executing clients' transactions, offers a full array of brokerage services.

discount broker
A broker with low overhead who charges low commissions and offers little or no services to investors.

online broker
Typically a discount broker through whom investors can execute trades electronically/online through a commercial service or on the Internet; also called *Internet broker* or *electronic broker.*

comprehensive criteria. The firms with higher commissions generally offer more services. Similarly, some discounters charge clients extra for their research services.

Brokerage commissions on *bond transactions* differ from those on stock transactions. Brokerage firms typically charge a minimum fee between $5 and $30, regardless of the number of bonds involved. For multiple bond transactions, the brokerage cost per $1,000 corporate bond typically drops to $10 or below. Commission schedules for other securities, such as mutual funds and options, differ from those used with stocks and bonds (we'll look at some of these in the next two chapters). The magnitude of brokerage commissions is obviously an important consideration when making security transactions, because these fees tend to raise the overall cost of purchasing securities and lower the overall proceeds from their sale. In recent years, competition and the increasing use of online brokers have decreased trading commissions significantly.

Type of Broker		
Full-Service	**Discount**	**Online**
Raymond James	Bank of America	AccuTrade
Edward Jones	Charles Schwab	TD Ameritrade
Morgan Stanley	J.D. Seibert	E*Trade
Merrill Lynch	Muriel Siebert	Fidelity Brokerage Services
Wachovia	Vanguard Brokerage Services	Scotttrade
UBS	York Securities	TD Waterhouse

odd lot
A quantity of fewer than 100 shares of a stock.

round lot
A quantity of 100 shares of stock, or multiples thereof.

Security transactions can be made in either odd or round lots. An odd lot consists of fewer than 100 shares of stock, while a round lot represents a 100-share unit or multiples thereof. The sale of 400 shares of stock would be considered a round-lot transaction, but the purchase of 75 shares would be an odd-lot transaction; trading 250 shares of stock would involve two round lots and an odd lot. Because the purchase or sale of odd lots requires additional processing, an added fee—known as an *odd-lot differential*—is often tacked on to the normal commission charge, driving up the costs of these small trades. Indeed, the relatively high cost of an odd-lot trade is why it's best to deal in round lots whenever possible.

Investor Protection

Securities Investor Protection Corporation (SIPC)
A nonprofit corporation, created by Congress and subject to SEC and congressional oversight, that insures customer accounts against the financial failure of a brokerage firm.

As a client, you're protected against the loss of securities or cash held by your broker by the Securities Investor Protection Corporation (SIPC), a nonprofit corporation authorized by the Securities Investor Protection Act of 1970 to protect customer accounts against the financial failure of a brokerage firm. Although subject to SEC and Congressional oversight, the SIPC is *not* an agency of the U.S. government.

SIPC insurance covers each account for up to $500,000 (of which up to $100,000 may be in cash balances held by the firm). Note, however, that SIPC insurance does not guarantee that the dollar value of the securities will be recovered. It ensures only that *the securities themselves will be returned*. So what happens if your broker gives you bad advice and you lose a lot of money on an investment? The SIPC won't help you, because it's not intended to insure you against bad investment advice, stock market risk, or broker fraud. If you have a dispute with your broker, first discuss the situation with the managing officer at the branch where you do your business. If that doesn't help, then write or talk to the firm's compliance officer and contact the securities office in your home state. If you still aren't satisfied, you may have to take the case to arbitration, a process whereby you and your broker present the two sides of the argument before an arbitration panel, which then decides how the case will be resolved. If it's *binding* arbitration, and it usually is, then you have no choice but to

arbitration
A procedure used to settle disputes between a brokerage firm and its clients; both sides present their positions to a board of arbitration, which makes a final and often binding decision on the matter.

It's important to find the online broker that best meets your specific needs. Barron's ratings are based on the following criteria for an online broker's Internet site: 1) usability, availability, and quality of mobile trading; 2) range of investment offerings; 3) quality and accessibility of research, quotes, and charting; 4) timely and effectively organized portfolio analysis and reports; 5) customer service and education features like live chat capability, user guides, frequently-asked questions, and security features, and 6) costs, which include trading commissions and margin (borrowing) costs.

BEST FOR LONG-TERM INVESTING	STARS	BEST FOR INTERNATIONAL TRADERS	STARS
TD Ameritrade (Website)	★★★★ ½	Interactive Brokers	★★★★ ½
Fidelity	★★★★ ½	TradeStation	★★★★ ½
Charles Schwab	★★★★	Fidelity	★★★★
Merrill Edge	★★★★	E*Trade	★★★★
E*Trade	★★★★	Charles Schwab	★★★ ½

BEST FOR FREQUENT TRADERS	STARS	BEST FOR NOVICES	STARS
Interactive Brokers	★★★★ ½	TD Ameritrade (Website)	★★★★ ½
TradeStation	★★★★ ½	Fidelity	★★★★
Lightspeed Trading	★★★★ ½	E*Trade	★★★★
TD Ameritrade (thinkorswim)	★★★★	Capital One Sharebuilder	★★★★
Livevol	★★★★	Merrill Edge	★★★★

BEST FOR OPTIONS TRADERS	STARS	BEST FOR IN-PERSON SERVICE	STARS
OptionsHouse	★★★★ ½	Scottrade	★★★★
TD Ameritrade (thinkorswim)	★★★★ ½	Merrill Edge	★★★★
Interactive Brokers	★★★★ ½	Charles Schwab	★★★★
TradeStation	★★★★	Fidelity	★★★★
Livevol	★★★★	TD Ameritrade (firmwide)	★★★★

Source: Theresa W. Carey, "Barron's Best Online Broker Ranking of 2015," http://online.barrons.com/articles/SB51367578116875004693704580502703510707706, accessed August 2015.

accept the decision—you cannot go to court to appeal your case. In fact, many brokerage firms require that you resolve disputes using binding arbitration. So before you open an account, check the brokerage agreement to see if it contains a binding arbitration clause.

11-3b Executing Trades

For most individual investors, a securities transaction involves placing a buy or sell order, usually by phone or on the Internet, and later receiving confirmation that the order has been completed. These investors have no idea what happens to their orders. In fact, a lot goes on—and very quickly—once the order is placed. It has to, because on a typical day the NYSE alone executes *millions* of trades, and many more occur on the NASDAQ and the rest of the market. In most cases, if the investor places a market order (which we will explain later), then it should take *less than two minutes* to place, execute, and confirm a trade.

The process starts with a phone call to the broker or an online order. The order is then transmitted to the stock exchange floor, the NASDAQ market, or the OTCBB, where it's promptly executed. Confirmation that the order has been executed is transmitted to the originating broker and then to the customer. Once the trade takes place, the investor has three (business) days to "settle" his or her account with the broker—that is, to pay for the securities.

Financial Fact or Fantasy?

If you lose a lot of money because a broker gave you a poor investment recommendation, you can recover all or most of your loss by filing a claim with the Securities Investor Protection Corporation. **Fantasy:** SIPC insurance applies only if you are dealing with a *brokerage firm* that goes out of business. If the brokerage firm fails, you are protected against the loss of securities or cash held by the broker. Importantly, that has nothing to do with getting bad advice from a broker; the SIPC does not cover such situations.

In an online trade, your order goes via the Internet from your computer to the brokerage computer, which checks the type of order and confirms that it's in compliance with regulations. It is then transmitted to the exchange floor or a NASDAQ (or OTC) dealer for execution. The time for the whole process, including a confirmation that's sent back to your computer, is usually less than a minute.

11-3c Types of Orders

Investors may choose from several different kinds of orders when buying or selling securities. The type of order chosen normally depends on the investor's goals and expectations regarding the given transaction. The three basic types of orders are the market order, limit order, and stop-loss order.

Market Order

market order
An order to buy or sell a security at the best price available at the time it is placed.

An order to buy or sell a security at the best price available at the time it's placed is a market order. It's usually the quickest way to have orders filled because market orders are executed as soon as they reach the trading floor. In fact, on small trades of less than a few thousand shares, it takes less than 10 seconds to fill a market order once it hits the trading floor. These orders are executed through a process that attempts to allow *buy orders* to be filled at the lowest price and *sell orders* at the highest, thereby providing the best possible deal to both the buyers and sellers of a security.

Limit Order

limit order
An order to either buy a security at a specified or lower price or to sell a security at or above a specified price.

An order to buy at a specified price (or lower), or sell at a specified price (or higher) is known as a limit order. The broker transmits a limit order to a *specialist* dealing in the given security on the floor of the exchange. The order is executed as soon as the specified market price is reached and all other such orders with precedence have been filled. Although a limit order can be quite effective, it can also cost you money. If, for instance, you want to buy at $20 or less and the stock price moves from its current $20.50 to $32 while you're waiting, your limit order for $20 will have caused you to forgo an opportunity to make a profit of $11.50 ($32.00 − $20.50) per share. Had you placed a market order, this profit would have been yours.

> **EXAMPLE: Limit Orders**
>
> You've placed a limit order to buy 100 shares of a stock at a price of $20, even though the stock is currently selling at $20.50. Once the stock hits $20 and the specialist has cleared all similar orders received before yours, the specialist will execute the order.

Stop-Loss Order

stop-loss (stop order)
An order to sell a stock when the market price reaches or drops below a specified level.

An order to *sell a stock* when the market price reaches or drops below a specified level is called a stop-loss, or stop order. Used to protect the investor against rapid declines in stock prices, the stop order is placed on the specialist's book and activated when the stop price is reached. At that point, the stop order becomes a *market order* to sell. This means that the stock is offered for sale at the prevailing market price, which could be less than the price at which the order was initiated by the stop.

> **EXAMPLE: Stop-Loss Orders**
>
> Imagine that you own 100 shares of DEF, which is currently selling for $25. Because of the high uncertainty associated with the price movements of the stock, you decide to place a stop order to sell at $21. If the stock price drops to $21, your stop order is activated and the specialist will sell all your DEF stock at the best price available, which may be below $21 a share. Of course, if the market price increases, or stays at or about $25 a share, nothing will have been lost by placing the stop-loss order.

Types of Limit Orders

With a limit order, you set not only the price you want but also the time period you want the order to remain outstanding. Here are some choices.

- *Fill-or-kill order.* An order that is executed immediately (at the specified price or better), or else it is canceled.
- *Day order.* An order that expires at the end of the day, even if it hasn't been executed.
- *Good-till-canceled (GTC) order.* An order that will remain open until it's either executed or canceled.
- *All-or-none order.* An order to buy or sell a *specified quantity* of stocks (at a given price, or better), which remains open until executed or canceled.

11-3d Calculating Investment Returns

The reason you invest is to earn an expected rate of return that compensates you for the risk you take on. Indeed, the only way to earn a higher rate of return is to face higher risk, which involves a higher chance that you won't get the return you'd hoped for. So it's important to know how to determine the rate of return you earned over a given period of time. For example, perhaps you took your uncle's advice and invested $500 in a mutual fund two years ago. You should know how to calculate the rate of return on the investment so you can decide whether to keep it there or move it elsewhere.

rate of return
The increase or decrease in the price of an investment as well as any income received over the investment period, both stated as a percentage of the initial investment.

The rate of return on an investment depends on the increase or decrease in the price of an investment as well as any income received over the investment period, both stated as a percentage of the initial investment. The rate of return is consequently the amount earned on an investment per dollar invested. It is calculated as:

$$\text{Rate of Return} = \frac{\text{Ending Value} - \text{Beginning Value} + \text{Income}}{\text{Beginning Value}}$$

Thus, the rate of return on a stock is the change in the price of the stock plus any dividends received over the investment period, both divided by the original price paid for the stock.

> **EXAMPLE: Calculating the Rate of Return on a Stock Investment**
>
> You bought 100 shares of The Walt Disney Company (DIS) one year ago at $81.22 a share. The stock is currently selling at $111.40. Over the year Disney paid dividends of $1.15 per share. What rate of return did you earn?
>
> $$\text{Rate of Return} = \frac{\text{Ending Value} - \text{Beginning Value} + \text{Income}}{\text{Beginning Value}}$$
>
> $$= \frac{(100 \times \$111.40) - (100 \times \$81.22) + (100 \times \$1.15)}{(100 \times \$81.22)}$$
>
> $$= 38.57 \text{ percent}$$

After you've calculated the return over the investment's time horizon, you can compare it with other investments of similar risk that you could have made. And you can also use this calculation approach to project future rates of return for competing investment alternatives.

11-3e Margin Trades and Short Sales

When you're ready to buy securities, you can do so by putting up your own money or by borrowing some of the money. *Buying on margin*, as it's called, is a practice that allows investors to use borrowed money to make security transactions. Margin trading is closely regulated and is carried out under strict *margin requirements* set by the Federal Reserve Board. These requirements specify the amount of *equity* that an investor must put up when buying stocks, bonds, and other securities. The most recent requirement is 50 percent for common stock, which means that at least 50 percent of each dollar invested must be the investor's own; the remaining 50 percent may be borrowed.

The use of margin allows you to increase the return on your investment when stock prices increase. A major attribute of margin trading is that it allows you to *magnify your returns*—that is, you can use margin to reduce your equity in an investment and thereby magnify the returns from invested capital when security prices go up. Importantly, the use of margin magnifies *both* profits and losses. And if the price of a margined stock continues to drop, you'll eventually reach the point where your equity in the investment will be so low that the brokerage house will liquidate the investment unless you provide more collateral (*margin call*).

> **EXAMPLE: Using Margin Trades to Magnify Returns**
>
> Assume you buy 100 shares of stock that increase from $50 to $70 a share—that's a $2,000 profit from a $5,000 investment, which translates into a 40 percent return on investment (i.e., $2,000 profit ÷ $5,000 investment = 40 percent). However, if that trade had been made on 50 percent margin (so you put up only $2,500 of the $5,000 and borrow the rest), then your return would be twice that amount, or a whopping 80 percent (i.e., $2,000 profit ÷ $2,500 investment = 80 percent). Now if the price of the stock had *fallen* $20, from $50 to $30 a share, then the return on your investment would have been a *negative* 40 percent (without the margin) or a *negative* 80 percent (with margin).

Investors can go long or short when they trade stocks. By far, the vast majority of trades are *long transactions*, like the margin trade just illustrated. That is, they're made in anticipation of *stock prices going up*, so the investor can make money by buying low and selling high. A **short sale** transaction, in contrast, is made in anticipation of a decline in the price of a stock. When an investor sells a security short, the broker borrows the security and then sells it on behalf of the short seller's account— short sellers actually *sell securities they don't own!* The borrowed shares must, of course, be replaced in the future, and if the investor can repurchase the shares at a lower price, then a profit will result.

short sale
A transaction that involves selling borrowed securities with the expectation that they can be replaced at a lower price at some future date; made in anticipation of a decline in the security's price.

The objective of a short sale is to take advantage of a *drop in price* by first selling high and then buying low—just like the adage, "buy low, sell high," except in reverse. Falling prices are good news to short-sellers, but the worst thing that can happen to them is for the price of the stock to go up. Make no mistake about it, *both margin trades and short sales involve a lot of risk, so it's important that you become thoroughly familiar with these techniques and their risk before using them.*

Financial Fact or Fantasy?

An aggressive investor would short sell a stock if he or she expects its price to go down. **Fact:** Short sales are made in anticipation of a drop in the price of a security; an investor makes money on a short sale when prices decline. However, selling short is quite risky and should only be done by risk-hardy, well-informed investors.

> **EXAMPLE: Short Sales**
>
> If an investor short-sells 100 shares of stock at $50 a share and then some time later, *after the price of the stock has dropped*, buys them back at, say, $30 a share, then she'll generate a profit of $20 a share, or $2,000 (i.e., ($50 − $30) × 100 shares = $2,000]. Of course, the investor will have to make a margin deposit equal to 50 percent of the value of the stock when the short sale was made. So a short transaction will require the investor to come up with some capital before the trade can be made.

FINANCIAL PLANNING TIPS

Understanding the Long and the Short of Investing

One of the best ways to understand an investment is to identify three factors:

- What's the most I could make?

- What's the most I could lose?

- At what price would I break even?

Consider the example of entering a stock investment at $60 per share. Let's compare the possible outcomes of long and short investments. To keep it simple, we'll ignore transaction costs and margin requirements. Graphs make it easier to understand what's going on.

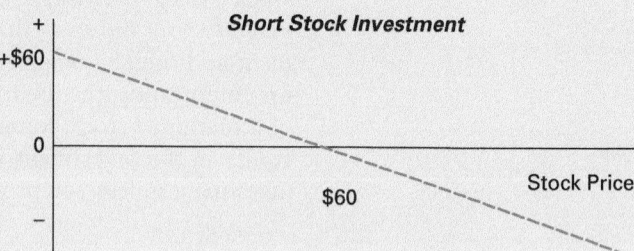

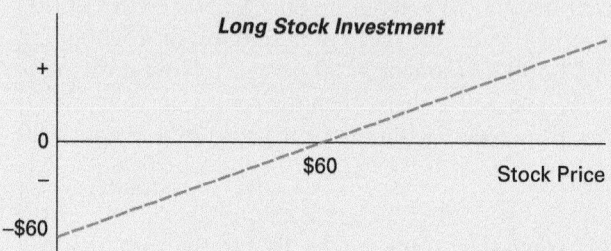

We can observe the following about these positions:

- **Long positions:** Maximum gain is unlimited; maximum loss is limited to the purchase price ($60), and the breakeven price is the purchase price ($60).

- **Short positions:** Maximum gain is limited to the purchase price ($60); maximum loss is unlimited, and the breakeven price is the short sale price ($60).

So what's the primary takeaway from this analysis? Determining these key price points is essential if you want to understand your potential investment gains and losses. And an unprotected short position can be very risky!

TEST YOURSELF

11-10 Describe the role that discount brokers play in carrying out security transactions. To whom are their services especially appealing?

11-11 What are *online brokers*, and what kinds of investors are most likely to use them?

11-12 What is the SIPC, and how does it protect investors?

11-13 What is *arbitration?* Does SIPC require the use of arbitration in investor disputes?

11-14 Name and describe three basic types of orders.

11-15 Why might an investor buy securities on margin?

11-16 Describe how the return on an investment is calculated.

11-17 What is a *short sale*? Explain the logic behind it. How much could be gained or lost on a short sale investment?

11-4 BECOMING AN INFORMED INVESTOR

Face it: Some people know more about investing than others. As a result, they may use certain investment vehicles or tactics that aren't even in another investor's vocabulary. Investor know-how, in short, defines the playing field. It helps determine how well you'll meet your investment objectives. Although being an informed investor can't guarantee you success, it can help you avoid unnecessary losses—as happens all too often when people put their money into investments they don't fully understand. These investors violate the first rule of investing: *Never start an investment program, or buy an investment vehicle, unless you thoroughly understand what you're getting into!* Thus, before making any major investment decision, thoroughly investigate the security and its merits. Formulate some basic expectations about its future performance, and gain an understanding of the sources of risk and return. This can usually be done by reading the popular financial press and referring to other print or Internet sources of investment information.

Here are the four types of investment information that you should follow on a regular basis:

- Economic developments and current events: To help you evaluate the underlying investment environment
- Alternative investment vehicles: To keep you abreast of market developments
- Current interest rates and prices: To monitor your investments and stay alert for developing investment opportunities
- Personal investment strategies: To help you hone your skills and stay alert for new techniques as they develop

11-4a Annual Stockholders' Reports

Every publicly traded corporation is required to provide its stockholders and other interested parties with annual stockholders' reports. These documents contain a wealth of information about the companies, including balance sheets, income statements, and other financial reports for the latest fiscal year, as well as for several prior years. Annual reports usually describe the firm's business activities, recent developments, and future plans and outlook. Financial ratios describing past performance are also included, along with other relevant statistics. In fact, annual reports offer a great deal of insight into the company's past, present, and future operations. You can obtain them for free directly from the companies, through a brokerage firm, or at most large libraries. And most companies also post their annual reports on the Internet, so you can obtain them online.

Here are some suggestions to help you get the most information when reading an annual report:

- Start with the highlights or selected financial data sections. These provide a quick overview of performance by summarizing key information, such as the past two years' revenues, net income, assets, earnings per share (EPS), and dividends.
- Read the chief executive's letter. But read it with a careful eye, looking for euphemisms like "a slowing of growth" to describe a drop in earnings.
- Move on to the discussion of operations in management's discussion and analysis. This section provides information on sales, earnings, debt, ongoing litigation, and so on.
- Review the financial statements, including the notes. These will tell you about the company's financial condition and performance. Look for trends in sales, costs, profit, cash position, and net working capital.
- Read the auditor's report. Look for phrases like "except for" or "subject to," as they mean just one thing: *there may be problems you need to understand.*

Financial Fact or Fantasy?

You should pay little attention to annual stockholders' reports because they are so biased. **Fantasy:** While they do tend to accentuate the positive, annual stockholders' reports are nonetheless an excellent source of information and are widely used by informed investors to obtain financial information about specific companies.

11-4b The Financial Press

The most common sources of financial news are the Internet and the local newspaper. Other common sources of financial news include *The Wall Street Journal, Barron's, Investor's Business Daily,* and the "Money" section of *USA Today.* These are all national publications that include articles on the behavior of the economy, the market, various industries, and individual companies. The most comprehensive and up-to-date coverage of financial news is provided Monday through

Saturday by *The Wall Street Journal*. Other excellent sources of investment information include magazines, such as *Money, Forbes, Fortune, Business Week*, and *Kiplinger's Personal Finance*. These publications are available online and as traditional hard copy publications.

Market Data

Usually presented in the form of averages, or indexes, *market data* describe the general behavior of the securities markets. The averages and indexes are based on the price movements of a select group of securities over an extended period. They're used to capture the overall performance of the market as a whole. You would want to follow one or more of these measures *to get a feel for how the market is doing over time* and, perhaps, an indication of what lies ahead. The absolute level of the index at a specific time (or on a given day) is far less important than *what's been happening to that index over a given period*. The most commonly cited market measures are those calculated by Dow Jones, Standard & Poor's, the NYSE, and NASDAQ. These measures are all intended to track the behavior of the stock market, particularly NYSE stocks (the Dow, S&P, and NYSE averages all follow stocks on the "big board," which is the NYSE).

Dow Jones Industrial Averages. The granddaddy of them all, and probably the most widely followed measure of stock market performance, is the Dow Jones Industrial Average (DJIA). Actually, the Dow Jones averages, which began in 1896, are made up of four parts: (1) an industrial average, the DJIA, which is based on 30 stocks; (2) a transportation average based on 20 stocks; (3) a utility average based on 15 stocks; and (4) a composite average based on all 65 industrial, transportation, and utility stocks. Most of the stocks in the DJIA are picked from the NYSE; but a few NASDAQ shares, such as Intel and Microsoft, are included as well. Although these stocks are intended to represent a cross section of companies, there's a strong bias toward blue chips, which is a major criticism of the DJIA. However, the facts show that, as a rule, the DJIA behavior closely reflects that of other broadly based stock market measures—with the possible exception of NASDAQ. Exhibit 11.4 lists the 30 stocks in the DJIA.

Standard & Poor's Indexes. The Standard & Poor's (S&P) indexes are similar to the Dow Jones averages in that both are used to capture the overall performance of the market. However, some important differences exist between the two measures. For

Dow Jones Industrial Average (DJIA)
The most widely followed measure of stock market performance; consists of 30 blue-chip stocks listed mostly on NYSE.

Standard & Poor's (S&P) indexes
Indexes compiled by Standard & Poor's that are similar to the DJIA but employ different computational methods and consist of far more stocks.

EXHIBIT 11.4   The Dow Jones Industrial Average

The DJIA is made up of 30 of the bluest of blue-chip stocks and has been closely followed by investors for the past 100 years or so.

The 30 Stocks in the DJIA (as of August 2015)

American Express	General Electric	Minnesota M&M (3M)
Apple	Goldman Sachs	Nike
Boeing	Home Depot	Pfizer
Caterpillar	IBM	Procter & Gamble
Chevron	Intel	Travelers
Cisco	Johnson & Johnson	United Health
Coca-Cola	J.P. Morgan Chase	United Technologies
Disney	McDonald's	Verizon
DuPont	Merck	Visa
ExxonMobil	Microsoft	Wal-Mart

one thing, the S&P uses a lot more stocks: the popular S&P 500 composite index is based on 500 different stocks, whereas the DJIA uses only 30. What's more, the S&P index is made up of all large NYSE stocks in addition to some major AMEX and NASDAQ stocks, so there are not only more issues in the S&P sample but also a greater breadth of representation. Finally, there are some technical differences in the mathematical procedures used to compute the two measures; the Dow Jones is an *average*, whereas the S&P is an *index*. Despite the technical differences, movements in these two measures are, in fact, *highly correlated*. Even so, the S&P has a much lower value than the DJIA—for example, in August 2015, the Dow stood at almost 17,000, whereas the S&P index of 500 stocks was just around 2,000. Now, this doesn't mean that the S&P consists of less valuable stocks; rather, the disparity is due solely to the different methods used to compute the measures. In addition to the S&P 500, two other widely followed S&P indexes are the *MidCap 400* (made up of 400 medium-sized companies with market values ranging from about $1.4 billion to $5.9 billion.) and the *SmallCap 600* (consisting of companies with market caps of around $400 million to $1.8 billion).

The NYSE, NASDAQ, and Other Market Indexes. The most widely followed exchange-based indexes are those of the NYSE and NASDAQ. The NYSE index includes all the stocks listed on the "big board" and provides a measure of performance in that market. Behavior in the NASDAQ market is also measured by several indexes, the most comprehensive of which is the *NASDAQ Composite index*, which is calculated using virtually all the stocks traded on NASDAQ. In addition, there's the *NASDAQ 100 index*, which tracks the price behavior of the biggest 100 (nonfinancial) firms traded on NASDAQ—companies like Apple, Microsoft, Intel, Oracle, Cisco, Staples, and Dell. The NASDAQ Composite is often used as a benchmark in assessing the price behavior of *high-tech* stocks. This index is far more volatile than either the Dow or the S&P, which means that it tends to outperform those indices in up markets and to underperform them in down markets.

Besides these major indexes, there are a couple of other measures of market performance, one of which is the Dow Jones Wilshire 5000 index. It's estimated that the Wilshire index reflects the *total market value of 98 percent to 99 percent of all publicly traded stocks in the United States*. In essence, it shows what's happening in the stock market as a whole—the dollar amount of market value added or lost as the market moves up and down. Thus, the Wilshire can be used not only to track the behavior of the U.S. stock market but also to give you a pretty accurate reading on the size of that market on any given day. For example, in August 2015, the Wilshire index stood at about 21,200. That translates into a total market value over $24 *trillion!* Another widely followed measure is the *Russell 2000*, which tracks the behavior of 2,000 relatively small companies and is widely considered to be a fairly accurate measure of the small-cap segment of the market.

Industry Data

Local newspapers, *The Wall Street Journal*, *Barron's*, and various financial publications regularly contain articles and data about different industries. For example, Standard & Poor's *Industry Surveys* provides detailed descriptions and statistics for all the major industries; on a smaller scale, *Bloomberg Business Week* and other magazines regularly include indexes of industry performance and price levels.

Company Data

Articles about new developments and the performance of companies are included in local newspapers, *The Wall Street Journal*, *Barron's*, and most investment magazines—both online and in hard copy form. The prices of many securities are quoted daily in *The Wall Street Journal*, *Investor's Business Daily*, and *USA Today*, as well as weekly in *Barron's*. Many daily newspapers also contain stock price quotations, though in the smaller dailies the listing may be selective; in some cases, only stocks of local interest are included.

NYSE index
An index of the performance of all stocks listed on the New York Stock Exchange.

Dow Jones Wilshire 5000 index
An index of the total market value of the approximately 6,000–7,000 most actively traded stocks in the United States.

Stock Quotes

Stock price quotes appear daily online on many sites, which include Yahoo! Finance (**http://finance.yahoo.com**), the *Wall Street Journal* (**http://wsj.com**), and CNN (**www.cnn.com**). Most online quotations provide not only current prices but a great deal of additional information as well.

Consider representative information available on numerous Internet sites. Exhibit 11.5 shows that Apple's stock price was at $127.96 on the afternoon of May 1, 2015, which was an increase of $2.81 from the prior day's closing price. The shares are shown as listed on the NASDAQ market. We see that Apple's trading symbol is AAPL. Its annual cash dividend yield is 1.50 percent, which is found by dividing the annual dividend by the indicated market price. The firm's recent P/E ratio is also shown, which is the current market price divided by the per-share earnings for

EXHIBIT 11.5	Listed Stock Quote for Apple

This exhibit provides information on one day's trading activity and the price quote for Apple, which is traded on NASDAQ. Note that, in addition to the latest stock price, a typical online stock quote provides an array of other information.

Apple Inc (NASDAQ:AAPL)

127.96
Real-Time Quote

▲ **2.81 (2.24%)**
Today's Change

Today's Trading

Previous close	125.15
Today's open	126.10
Day's range	125.30 – 128.12
Volume	42,157,492
Average volume (3 months)	52,746,100
Market cap	$745.31B
Dividend and yield	$1.88 (1.50%)

Growth & Valuation

Earnings growth (last 5 years)	28.39%
Earnings growth (this year)	38.90%
Earnings growth (next 5 years)	13.20%
P/E ratio	17.33
Price/Sales	3.65
Price/Book	5.91

Data as of 3:16 p.m. EDT, 5/1/2015

Source: From http://finance.yahoo.com/q?s=AAPL, accessed May 1, 2015.

the most recent 12-month period. As can be seen, Apple is trading at a P/E of 17.33 times earnings. And the exhibit shows that Apple's overall market capitalization (stock price times the number of shares) is $745.31 billion. This makes it the largest company in the world, as measured by market capitalization.

11-4c Brokerage Reports

Reports produced by the research staffs of major (full-service) brokerage firms provide still another important source of investor information. These reports cover a wide variety of topics, from economic and market analyses to industry and company reports, news of special situations, and reports on interest rates and the bond market. Reports on certain industries or securities prepared by the house's research staff may be issued regularly and contain lists of securities within certain industries classified by the type of market behavior they are expected to exhibit. Brokerage houses also regularly issue reports, prepared by their security analysts, on specific securities; these reports include, among other things, recommendations for the type of investment returns expected and whether to buy, hold, or sell specific securities.

11-4d Advisory Services

Subscription advisory services provide information and recommendations on various industries and specific securities. The services normally cost from $50 to several hundred dollars a year, although you can usually review such materials (for free) at your broker's office, at university and public libraries, or online. Probably the best-known investment advisory services are those provided by Standard & Poor's, Moody's Investors Service, and Value Line. Both Standard & Poor's and Moody's publish manuals containing historical facts and financial data on thousands of corporations, broken down by industry groups. Standard & Poor's publishes a monthly stock guide and bond guide, each summarizing the financial conditions of a few thousand issues; Moody's also publishes stock and bond guides. And the *Value Line Investment Survey* is a popular source of firm and industry analysis. Some reports are also prepared weekly, like Standard & Poor's *Outlook*.

An example of a subscription service stock report is provided in Exhibit 11.6. Prepared by Standard & Poor's this report presents a concise summary of a company's financial history, current finances, and future prospects; similar stock reports are available from Value Line and Morningstar. Recommended lists of securities, broken down into groups based on investment objectives, constitute still another type of service. Besides these popular subscription services, many *investment letters*, which periodically advise subscribers on buying and selling securities, are available.

TEST YOURSELF

11-18   Briefly discuss the four basic types of information that you, as an investor, should follow.

11-19   What role do market averages and indexes play in the investment process?

11-20   Briefly describe the *DJIA, S&P 400, S&P 500, NASDAQ Composite, Russell 2000*, and *Dow Jones Wilshire 5000* indexes. Which segments of the market does each index track?

EXHIBIT 11.6   An S&P Stock Report

An S&P report like this one provides a wealth of information about the operating results and financial condition of the company and is an invaluable source of information to investors.

Stock Report | April 30, 2015 | NNM Symbol: **AAPL** | **AAPL** is in the S&P 500

S&P Capital IQ

Apple Inc

S&P Capital IQ Recommendation **HOLD** ★★★☆☆	**Price** $125.15 (as of Apr 30, 2015 4:00 PM ET)	**12-Mo. Target Price** $150.00	**Report Currency** USD	**Investment Style** Large-Cap Growth

S&P Capital IQ Equity Analyst Angelo Zino, CFA

UPDATE: PLEASE SEE THE ANALYST'S LATEST RESEARCH NOTE IN THE COMPANY NEWS SECTION

GICS Sector Information Technology
Sub-Industry Technology Hardware, Storage & Peripherals

Summary This company is a prominent provider of hardware including iPhone smartphones, iPad tablets, Mac computers and iPod digital media players.

Key Stock Statistics (Source S&P Capital IQ, Vickers, company reports)

52-Wk Range	$134.54–82.90	S&P Oper. EPS 2015E	8.95	Market Capitalization(B)	$728.967	Beta	0.81
Trailing 12-Month EPS	$8.05	S&P Oper. EPS 2016E	9.54	Yield (%)	1.66	S&P 3-Yr. Proj. EPS CAGR(%)	15
Trailing 12-Month P/E	15.6	P/E on S&P Oper. EPS 2015E	14.0	Dividend Rate/Share	$2.08	S&P Quality Ranking	B+
$10K Invested 5 Yrs Ago	$35,573	Common Shares Outstg. (M)	5,824.7	Institutional Ownership (%)	61		

Price Performance

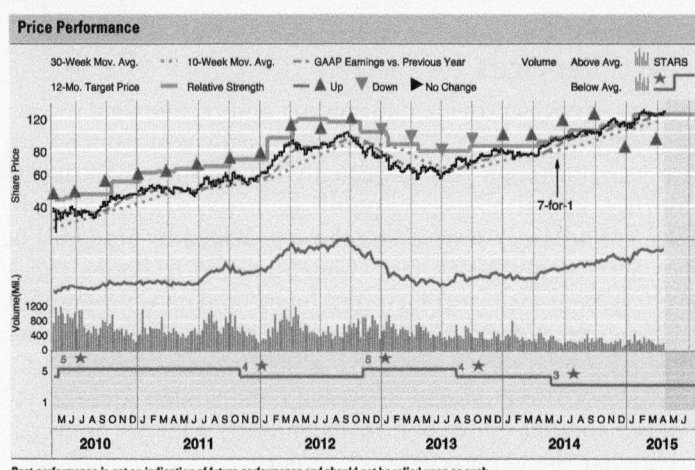

30-Week Mov. Avg. --- 10-Week Mov. Avg. --- GAAP Earnings vs. Previous Year   Volume   Above Avg. ▦ STARS
12-Mo. Target Price — Relative Strength — ▲ Up ▼ Down ▶ No Change   Below Avg. ▮

7-for-1

Past performance is not an indication of future performance and should not be relied upon as such.

Analysis prepared by Equity Analyst **Angelo Zino, CFA** on Apr 28, 2015 09:03 AM, when the stock traded at **$132.65**.

Highlights

➤ We project 39% revenue growth for FY 15 (Sep.) and a 6.6% gain for FY 16. AAPL's move to large screen iPhones (iPhone 6 at 4.7 inches and iPhone 6 Plus at 5.5 inches) is helping the company to capture share at the high-end of the smartphone market, we believe. We anticipate steady Mac sales, despite a challenging PC landscape, but lackluster iPad sales ahead of a new launch. In the March quarter, revenue was broken down as follows: 69% iPhone, 9% iPad, 10% Mac, 12% Services/Other. We positively view growth potential from the Apple Watch, but revenue contribution is likely to be minimal in the coming quarters.

➤ We see the annual gross margin widening to about 40% in FY 15 and FY 16, compared to a 39% margin in FY 14 and 38% margin in FY 13. iPhone and iPad margins will be aided by efficiencies, we think, offset somewhat by risks related to average selling prices. The Apple Watch commands higher margins than the corporate average, which could provide an upside in the coming years.

➤ We estimate operating EPS of $8.95 in FY 15 and $9.54 in FY 16. As of the end of March, AAPL had $194 billion in cash and investments.

Investment Rationale/Risk

➤ We note AAPL's significant market position in key areas, and high customer satisfaction and switching costs, in our view. Higher volumes, a focus on common components and a greater emphasis on software and services should aid profitability. AAPL's superior ecosystem and new product launches will be enough to sustain high iPhone customer retention rates, we think. The Apple Watch will see success over time, we believe, and we are optimistic about the potential for AAPL to expand its addressable market in the coming years. We positively view free cash flow generation, and believe the balance sheet will be increasingly employed for dividends and stock repurchases, as well as M&A.

➤ Risks to our recommendation and target price include weaker end-market demand, pricing pressures, competitive handset and tablet offerings gaining traction, carrier efforts to reduce or eliminate subsidy payments and less success with product launches/innovations.

➤ Our 12-month target price of $150 is based on a P/E of 15.7X our FY 16 EPS estimate, above hardware peers, but near the S&P 500 Technology sector.

Analyst's Risk Assessment

LOW	**MEDIUM**	HIGH

Our risk assessment reflects our view of a seemingly ever-evolving market for consumer-oriented technology products, potential challenges associated with the company's growing size and offerings and possible changes in the pace or success of product innovations following recent management changes.

Revenue/Earnings Data

Revenue (Million U.S. $)

	1Q	2Q	3Q	4Q	Year
2015	74,599	58,010	--	--	--
2014	57,594	45,646	37,432	42,123	182,795
2013	54,512	43,603	35,323	37,472	170,910
2012	46,333	39,186	35,023	35,966	156,508
2011	26,741	24,667	28,571	28,270	108,249
2010	15,683	13,499	15,700	20,343	65,225

Earnings Per Share (U.S. $)

2015	3.06	2.33	E1.74	E1.84	E8.95
2014	2.07	1.66	1.28	1.42	6.45
2013	1.97	1.44	1.07	1.18	5.68
2012	1.98	1.76	1.33	1.24	6.31
2011	0.92	0.91	1.11	1.01	3.95
2010	0.52	0.48	0.50	0.66	2.16

Fiscal year ended Sep. 30. Next earnings report expected: Late July. EPS Estimates based on S&P Capital IQ Operating Earnings; historical GAAP earnings are as reported in Company reports.

Dividend Data

Amount ($)	Date Decl.	Ex-Div. Date	Stk. of Record	Payment Date
0.470	Jul 22	Aug 7	Aug 11	Aug 14 '14
0.470	Oct 20	Nov 6	Nov 10	Nov 13 '14
0.470	Jan 27	Feb 5	Feb 9	Feb 12 '15
0.520	Apr 27	May 7	May 11	May 14 '15

Dividends have been paid since 2012. Source: Company reports.

Past performance is not an indication of future performance and should not be relied upon as such.

Please read the Required Disclosures and Analyst Certification on the last page of this report.

EXHIBIT 11.6 (Continued)

Stock Report | April 30, 2015 | NNM Symbol: **AAPL**

Apple Inc

S&P CAPITAL IQ
McGRAW HILL FINANCIAL

Quantitative Evaluations

S&P Capital IQ   5+
Fair Value
Rank

| 1 | 2 | 3 | 4 | 5 |

LOWEST   HIGHEST
Based on S&P Capital IQ's proprietary quantitative model, stocks are ranked from most overvalued (1) to most undervalued (5).

Fair Value $163.50   Analysis of the stock's current worth, based on S&P Capital IQ's
Calculation   proprietary quantitative model suggests that AAPL is Undervalued by $38.35 or 30.6%.

Investability   **99**
Quotient
Percentile   LOWEST = 1   HIGHEST = 100
AAPL scored higher than 99% of all companies for which an S&P Capital IQ Report is available.

Volatility | LOW | AVERAGE | HIGH |

Technical   **BULLISH**   Since April, 2015, the technical indicators for AAPL have been
Evaluation   BULLISH.

Insider Activity | UNFAVORABLE | NEUTRAL | FAVORABLE |

For further clarification on the terms used in this report, please visit www.standardandpoors.com/stockreportguide

Expanded Ratio Analysis

	2014	2013	2012	2011
Price/Sales	3.70	3.06	3.21	3.50
Price/EBITDA	11.18	9.37	8.60	10.65
Price/Pretax Income	12.64	10.42	9.02	11.09
P/E Ratio	17.11	14.11	12.06	14.63
Avg. Diluted Shares Outstg (M)	6,122.7	6,521.6	6,617.5	6,556.5

Figures based on calendar year-end price

Key Growth Rates and Averages

Past Growth Rate (%)	1 Year	3 Years	5 Years	9 Years
Sales	6.95	18.06	35.01	36.91
Net Income	6.68	12.13	37.84	51.85
Ratio Analysis (Annual Avg.)				
Net Margin (%)	21.61	23.32	23.08	19.37
% LT Debt to Capitalization	20.63	10.90	6.54	3.63
Return on Equity (%)	33.61	35.70	37.16	32.76

Company Financials   Fiscal Year Ended Sep. 30

Per Share Data (U.S. $)	2014	2013	2012	2011	2010	2009	2008	2007	2006	2005
Tangible Book Value	17.52	18.71	17.17	11.10	7.28	4.95	3.29	2.32	1.64	1.26
Cash Flow	7.75	6.72	6.80	4.23	2.32	1.41	0.84	0.61	0.36	0.25
Earnings	6.45	5.68	6.31	3.95	2.16	1.30	0.77	0.56	0.32	0.22
S&P Capital IQ Core Earnings	6.47	5.68	6.29	3.94	2.16	1.30	0.77	0.56	0.32	0.21
Dividends	Nil	1.63	0.38	Nil	Nil	Nil	Nil	Nil	Nil	Nil
Payout Ratio	Nil	29%	6%	Nil	Nil	Nil	Nil	Nil	Nil	Nil
Prices:High	119.75	82.16	100.72	60.96	46.67	30.56	28.61	28.99	13.31	10.78
Prices:Low	70.51	55.01	58.43	44.36	27.18	11.17	11.31	11.70	7.17	4.47
P/E Ratio:High	19	14	16	15	22	24	37	52	41	48
P/E Ratio:Low	11	10	9	11	13	9	15	21	22	20

Income Statement Analysis (Million U.S. $)	2014	2013	2012	2011	2010	2009	2008	2007	2006	2005
Revenue	182,795	170,910	156,508	108,249	65,225	42,905	32,479	24,006	19,315	13,931
Operating Income	60,449	55,756	58,518	35,604	19,412	12,474	6,748	4,726	2,645	1,829
Depreciation	7,946	6,757	3,277	1,814	1,027	734	473	317	225	179
Interest Expense	384	136	Nil	Nil	Nil	Nil	Nil	Nil	Nil	Nil
Pretax Income	53,483	50,155	55,763	34,205	18,540	12,066	6,895	5,008	2,818	1,815
Effective Tax Rate	26.1%	26.2%	25.2%	24.2%	24.4%	31.8%	29.9%	30.2%	29.4%	26.4%
Net Income	39,510	37,037	41,733	25,922	14,013	8,235	4,834	3,496	1,989	1,335
S&P Capital IQ Core Earnings	39,643	37,037	41,614	25,851	14,013	8,235	4,834	3,496	1,989	1,259

Balance Sheet & Other Financial Data (Million U.S. $)	2014	2013	2012	2011	2010	2009	2008	2007	2006	2005
Cash	25,158	40,590	29,129	25,952	25,620	23,464	24,490	9,352	6,392	3,491
Current Assets	68,531	73,286	57,653	44,988	41,678	31,555	34,690	21,956	14,509	10,300
Total Assets	231,839	207,000	176,064	116,371	75,183	47,501	39,572	25,347	17,205	11,551
Current Liabilities	63,448	43,658	38,542	27,970	20,722	11,506	14,092	9,299	6,471	3,484
Long Term Debt	28,987	16,960	Nil	Nil	Nil	Nil	Nil	Nil	Nil	Nil
Common Equity	111,547	123,549	118,210	76,615	47,791	31,640	21,030	14,532	9,984	7,466
Total Capital	140,534	140,509	118,210	76,615	47,791	31,640	21,705	15,151	10,365	7,466
Capital Expenditures	9,571	8,165	8,295	4,260	2,005	1,144	1,091	735	657	260
Cash Flow	47,456	43,794	45,010	27,736	15,040	8,969	5,307	3,813	2,214	1,514
Current Ratio	1.1	1.7	1.5	1.6	2.0	2.7	2.5	2.4	2.2	3.0
% Long Term Debt of Capitalization	20.6	12.1	Nil	Nil	Nil	Nil	Nil	Nil	Nil	Nil
% Net Income of Revenue	21.6	21.7	26.7	24.0	21.5	19.2	14.9	14.6	10.3	9.6
% Return on Assets	18.0	19.3	28.5	27.1	21.7	19.7	14.9	16.4	13.9	13.6
% Return on Equity	33.6	30.6	42.8	41.7	37.1	30.5	27.2	28.5	22.8	21.3

Data as originally reported in Company reports.; bef. results of disc opers/spec. items. Per share data adj. for stk. divs.; EPS diluted. E-Estimated. NA-Not Available. NM-Not Meaningful. NR-Not Ranked. UR-Under Review.

Source: Reprinted by permission of Standard & Poor's Financial Services LLC, a division of the McGraw-Hill Companies © 2015.

11-5 ONLINE INVESTING

The Internet is a major force in the investing environment. It has opened the world of investing to individual investors, leveling the playing field and providing access to tools and market information formerly restricted to professionals. Not only can you trade all types of securities online, you can also find a wealth of information, from real-time stock quotes to security analysts' research reports. However, online investing also carries risks. The Internet requires investors to exercise the same—and possibly more—caution as they would if they were getting information from and placing orders with a human broker. You don't have the safety net of a live broker suggesting that you rethink your trade. Online or off, the basic rules for smart investing are still the same: *know what you're buying, from whom, and at what level of risk.*

How can you successfully navigate through this cyberinvesting universe? Typically one site includes a combination of resources for novice and sophisticated investors alike. For example, the next time you're online, go to the home page for *E*Trade*, a major online brokerage firm (**http://www.etrade.com**). With a few clicks of the mouse, you can learn about E*Trade's services, open an account, or place an order to trade securities. You can also get a quick overview of recent market activity, obtain price quotes and research reports, or use their services to track a whole portfolio of securities. At their site you can select stocks, bonds, and mutual funds; get advice on retirement planning and saving for college; go to "Ideas, Education, and Guidance" under "Investing and Trading" to learn about the markets; and even do your banking at the *E*Trade Bank*.

11-5a Online Investor Services

As the E*Trade Internet site reveals, the Internet offers a full array of online investor services, from up-to-the-minute stock quotes and research reports to charting services and portfolio tracking. When it comes to investing, you name it and you can probably find it online! Unfortunately, although many of these are truly high-quality sites offering valuable information, many others are pure garbage, so be careful when entering the world of online investing. It takes time and effort to use the Internet wisely. Let's now review the kinds of investor services you can find online, starting with investor education sites.

Investor Education

The Internet offers a wide array of tutorials, online classes, and articles to educate the novice investor. Even experienced investors will find sites that expand their investing knowledge. Although most good investment-oriented Internet sites include many educational resources, here are a few good sites featuring *investment fundamentals*.

- *The Motley Fool* (**http://www.fool.com**) *Fool's School* has sections on fundamentals of investing, mutual fund investing, choosing a broker, investment strategies and styles, lively discussion boards, and more.
- Morningstar (**http://www.morningstar.com**) provides comprehensive information on stocks, mutual funds, ETFs, and more.
- Zacks Investment Research (**http://www.zacks.com**) is an excellent starting place to learn what the Internet can offer investors.
- NASDAQ (**http://www.nasdaq.com**) has an Investor Resource section that helps with financial planning and choosing a broker.

Other good educational sites include, as noted above, leading personal finance magazines like *Money* (**http://money.cnn.com**) and *Kiplinger's Personal Finance Magazine* (**http://www.kiplinger.com**).

Investment Tools

Once you're familiar with the basics of investing, you can use the Internet to develop financial plans and set investment goals, find securities that meet your investment objectives, analyze potential investments, and organize your portfolio. Many of these tools, once used only by professional money managers, are free to anyone who wants to go online. You'll find financial calculators and worksheets, screening and charting tools, and portfolio trackers at the Internet sites of large brokerage firms and on other financial sites. You can set up a personal calendar to notify you of forthcoming earnings announcements and receive alerts when one of your stocks hits a predetermined price target.

Investment Planning. Online calculators and worksheets can help you find answers to your financial planning and investing questions. With them, you can figure out how much to save each month for a particular goal, such as the down payment for your first home, a college education for your children, or to be able to retire by the time you reach 55. For example, Fidelity (**http://www.fidelity.com**) has a wide selection of planning tools that deal with such topics as investment growth, college planning, and retirement planning. One of the best sites for financial calculators is *Kiplinger's Personal Finance* (**http://www.kiplinger.com**). Go to their personal finance page, click on "Tools & Calculators," and you'll find over 100 calculators dealing with everything from stocks, bonds, and mutual funds to retirement planning, home buying, and taxes.

Investment Research and Screening. One of the best investor services offered online is the ability to conduct in-depth research on stocks, bonds, mutual funds, exchange-traded funds and other types of investment vehicles. Go to a site like **http://www.kiplinger.com**, click on "Investing," and you can obtain literally dozens of pages of financial and market information about a specific stock or mutual fund. For example, you can find historical and forecasted information about a firm's earnings, earnings per share, dividend yields, growth rates, and more in both tabular and graphic formats; you can also track the behavior of a specific stock relative to a market index or to one or more of its major competitors. Many of these sites have links to the company itself, so with a few mouse clicks you can obtain the company's annual report, detailed financial statements, and historical summaries of a full array of financial and market ratios. In addition, you'll find various *online screening tools*

FINANCIAL PLANNING TIPS

Starting Online Investing

• **Set aside some money to get started and choose a broker.** You don't need much—your initial deposit can be as little as $50. Choose an online broker with no minimum deposit. Consider the results of the Barron's online broker rankings provided in Exhibit 11.3 earlier in this chapter.

• **Learn the key investing jargon.** Some useful sources are Investopedia (**http://www.investopedia.com**) and InvestorWords (**http://www.investorwords.com**).

• **Practice with a paper account before investing real money.** Try out the Investing Simulator Center (**http://www.investingonline.org/isc/index.html**) and then practice with different investment strategies using online

trading simulators like Icarra (**http://www.icarra.com**) or paperTrade (**https://www.trademonster.com/Difference/Online-Paper-Trading.jsp**).

• **Gradually add more money to your brokerage account.** Add amounts regularly that are consistent with your investment goals.

• **Monitor your portfolio's performance.** Data can be obtained easily using Yahoo! Finance (**http://finance.yahoo.com/**) or Google Finance (**http://www.google.com/finance**).

• **Keep up with financial news.** In addition, read as much as you can on how to invest.

Source: Adapted from Matt Krantz, "How to Get Started Investing Online," http://www.dummies.com/how-to/content/investing-online-for-dummies-cheat-sheet.html, accessed August 2015.

that can be used to identify attractive and potentially rewarding investment vehicles. These tools (available at the Internet sites of Quicken, Morningstar, MSN Money Central, and elsewhere) enable you to sort quickly through huge databases of stocks and mutual funds to find those that meet specific characteristics, such as stocks with low or high P/E multiples, small market capitalizations, high dividend yields, specific revenue growth, and low debt-to-equity ratios. You answer a series of questions to specify the type of stock or fund you're looking for, performance criteria you desire, cost parameters, and so on. The screen then provides a list of stocks (or funds) that have met the standards that you've set.

Portfolio Tracking. Almost every investment-oriented Web site includes *portfolio tracking tools*. Simply enter the number of shares held and the symbol for those stocks or mutual funds you wish to follow, and the tracker automatically updates the value of your portfolio in real time. What's more, you can usually click on one of the provided links and quickly obtain detailed information about each stock or mutual fund in your portfolio. But be careful; the features, quality, and ease of using these portfolio trackers vary widely, so check several to find the one that meets your needs. Quicken.com, MSN MoneyCentral (**http://money.msn.com**), Google (**http://google.com/finance/portfolio**) and E*Trade (**http://www.etrade.com**) all have portfolio trackers that are easy to set up and use. For example, Quicken's tracker alerts you whenever an analyst changes the rating on one of your stocks or funds and tells you how well you're diversified among the major asset classes or sectors you hold.

Online Trading

As discussed earlier, trading stocks (and other securities) online has become popular among investors—if for no other reason than the rock-bottom cost of executing such trades. After all, it's an easy, convenient, and low-cost way of trading securities. But for some investors, the attraction of trading stocks online is so compelling that they become day traders. The opposite of buy-and-hold investors with a long-term perspective, **day traders** buy and sell stocks quickly throughout the trading day. They hope their stocks will continue to rise in value for the short time they own them—sometimes just seconds or minutes—so they can make quick profits. Day trading is neither illegal nor unethical, but *it is highly risky*. To compound their risk, day traders usually buy on margin to earn even higher returns. But as we've seen, margin trading also increases the risk of larger losses. Day traders typically incur major financial losses when they start trading. Some never reach profitability. Day traders also have high expenses for brokerage commissions, training, and computer equipment. By some estimates, they must make a 50 percent to 60 percent profit just to break even on fees and commissions.

day trader
An investor who buys and sells stocks (and other securities) rapidly throughout the trading day in hopes of making quick profits.

TEST YOURSELF

11-21 Describe the Internet's impact on the world of investing.

11-22 What are some products and services that you, as an individual investor, can now obtain online?

11-23 Briefly describe several types of online investment tools, and note how they can help you become a better investor.

11-24 What is *day trading*, and how is it different from the more traditional approach to investing?

11-6 MANAGING YOUR INVESTMENT HOLDINGS

portfolio
A collection of securities assembled for the purpose of meeting common investment goals.

Buying and selling securities is not difficult; the hard part is finding securities that will provide the kind of return that you're looking for. Like most individual investors, you too will be buying, selling, and trading securities with ease in time. Eventually, your investment holdings will increase to the point where you're managing a whole portfolio of securities. A **portfolio** is a collection of investment vehicles assembled to meet a common investment goal. But a portfolio is far more than a collection of investments. It breathes life into your investment program as it combines your personal and financial traits with your investment objectives to give some structure to your investments.

Seasoned investors often devote much attention to constructing diversified portfolios of securities. Such portfolios consist of stocks and bonds selected not only for their returns but also for their combined risk–return behavior. The idea behind **diversification** is that, by combining securities with dissimilar risk–return characteristics, you can produce a portfolio of reduced risk and more predictable levels of return. In recent years, investment researchers have shown that you can achieve a noticeable reduction in risk simply by diversifying your investment holdings. For the small investor with a moderate amount of money to invest, this means that *investing in several securities rather than a single one should be beneficial*. The payoff from diversification comes in the form of reduced risk without a significant impact on return. For example, Joanne Ortiz, who has all of her $30,000 portfolio invested in just one stock (Stock A), might find that—by selling two-thirds of her holdings and using the proceeds to buy equal amounts of Stocks B and C—she'll continue to earn the same level of return (say, 8 percent) while greatly decreasing the associated risk. Professional money managers emphasize that investors should not put all their eggs in one basket but instead should hold portfolios that are diversified across a broad segment of businesses.

diversification
The process of choosing securities with dissimilar risk–return characteristics in order to create a portfolio that provides an acceptable level of return and an acceptable exposure to risk.

11-6a Building a Portfolio of Securities

In developing a portfolio of investment holdings, it's assumed that diversification is a desirable investment attribute that leads to improved return and/or reduced risk. Again, as emphasized previously, holding a variety of investments is far more desirable than concentrating all your investments in a single security or industry. For example, a portfolio made up of nothing but drug stocks, such as Merck and Eli Lilly, would hardly be well diversified. As you build up your investment funds, your opportunities (and need) for diversification will increase dramatically. Certainly, by the time you have $10,000 to $15,000 to invest, you should make sure your holdings are well-diversified. To get an idea of the kind of portfolio diversification employed by investors, look at the following numbers, which show the types of investments held by average *individual investors*.

Type of Investment Product	Percentage of Portfolio (July 2015)
Stocks and stock funds	67%
Bonds and bond funds	16%
Short-term investments (CDs, money mkt. dep. accts., etc.)	17%
Total	100%

This portfolio reflects the results of a monthly asset allocation survey conducted by the *American Association of Individual Investors*. Whether this is what your portfolio should look like depends on various factors, including your own needs and objectives.

Investor Characteristics

To formulate an effective portfolio strategy, begin with an honest evaluation of your own financial condition and family situation. Pay particular attention to variables like these:

- Level and stability of income
- Family factors
- Investment horizon
- Net worth
- Investment experience and age
- Disposition toward risk

These are the variables that set the tone for your investments. They determine the kinds of investments you should consider and how long you can tie up your money. For your portfolio to work, it must be tailored to meet your personal financial needs. Your income, family responsibilities, relative financial security, experience, and age all enter into the delicate equation that yields a sound portfolio strategy.

For example, the size and predictability of an investor's employment income has a significant bearing on portfolio strategy. An investor with a secure job is more likely to embark on a more aggressive investment program than is an investor with a less secure position. Income taxes also bear on the investment decision. The higher an investor's income, the more important the tax ramifications of an investment program become. Consider that municipal bonds normally yield about 25 percent to 30 percent less in annual interest than corporate bonds, because the interest income on municipal bonds is tax-free. On an after-tax basis, however, municipal bonds may provide a superior return if an investor is in a tax bracket of 28 percent or higher.

In addition, an individual's investment experience also influences the type of investment strategy. Normally, investors assume higher levels of investment risk gradually over time. It's best to "get your feet wet" in the investment market by slipping into it slowly rather than leaping in head first. Investors who make risky initial investments often suffer heavy losses, damaging the long-run potential of the entire investment program. A cautiously developed investment program will likely provide more favorable long-run results than an impulsive, risky one. Finally, investors should carefully consider risk. High-risk investments have not only high return potential but also high risk of loss. Remember, when going for the home run (via a high-risk, high-return

Common Investing Mistakes

Avoiding these common mistakes will make you a better and more successful investor:

- Not defining objectives and priorities, which include risk tolerance, appropriate benchmarks, asset allocation, and diversification.
- Not rebalancing your portfolio every year or so to keep asset allocation percentages in line.
- Owning too many different stocks, bonds, exchange-traded funds, and mutual funds.
- Inefficient use of tax strategies.
- Paying too much in mutual fund fees.
- Not enough use of index funds, which are lower-cost and perform on average better than most actively-managed funds.
- Paying too much attention to financial media—almost nothing covered will help you achieve your goals.

Sources: Adapted, in part, from Jay Yoder, "7 common Investor Mistakes," http://www.investopedia.com/articles/stocks/07/mistakes.asp, accessed August 2015.

investment), the odds of striking out are much higher than when simply going for a base hit (a more conservative investment posture). A good rule to remember is that *an investor's exposure to risk should never exceed the ability to bear that risk*.

Investor Objectives

After developing a personal financial profile, the investor's next question is: "What do I want from my portfolio?" This seems like an easy question to answer. Ideally, we would all like to double our money every year by making low-risk investments. However, the realities of the highly competitive investment environment make this outcome unlikely, so the question must be answered more realistically. There's generally a trade-off between earning a high current income from an investment and obtaining significant capital appreciation from it. An investor must choose one or the other; it's hard to obtain both from a single investment vehicle. Of course, in a portfolio it's possible to have a *balance* of both income and growth (capital gains), but most often that involves "tilting" the portfolio in one direction (e.g., toward income) or the other (toward growth).

An investor's needs should determine which approach to choose. For instance, a retired investor whose income depends a lot on her portfolio will probably choose a lower-risk, current-income-oriented approach for financial survival. In contrast, a high-income, financially secure investor may be much more willing to take on risky investments in hopes of improving her net worth. Likewise, a young investor with a secure job may be less concerned about current income and more able to bear risk. This type of investor will likely be more capital gains oriented and may choose speculative investments. As an investor approaches age 60, the desired level of income likely rises as retirement approaches. The more senior investor is typically less willing to bear risk and will focus on preserving principal, because these investments will soon be needed as a source of retirement income.

11-6b Asset Allocation and Portfolio Management

A portfolio must be built around an individual's needs, which in turn depend on income, family responsibilities, financial resources, age, retirement plans, and ability to bear risk. These needs shape one's financial goals. But to create a portfolio geared to those goals, you need to develop an asset allocation strategy. Asset allocation is the decision on *how to divide your portfolio among different types of securities*. For example, what portion of your portfolio will be devoted to short-term securities, to long-term bonds and bond funds, and to individual common stocks and equity funds? In asset allocation, the emphasis is often on *preserving capital* using careful diversification. The idea is to position your assets in such a way that you can protect your portfolio from potential negative developments in the market while still taking advantage of potential positive developments. Asset allocation is one of the most overlooked yet most important aspects of investing. There's overwhelming evidence that, over the long run, *the total return on a portfolio is influenced far more by its asset allocation than by specific security selections*.

Asset allocation deals in broad categories and *does not tell you which individual securities to buy or sell*. It might look something like this:

asset allocation
A plan for dividing a portfolio among different classes of securities in order to preserve capital by protecting the portfolio against negative market developments.

Type of Investment	Asset Mix
Short-term securities	*5%*
Intermediate-term bonds (7- to 10-year maturities)	*20%*
Equity funds	*75%*
Total portfolio	*100%*

As you can see, all you're really doing here is deciding how to cut up the pie. You still have to decide which particular securities to invest in. Once you've decided that you want to put, say, 20 percent of your money into intermediate-term (7- to 10-year)

bonds, your next step is to select those specific securities. After establishing your asset allocation strategy, you should check it regularly for two reasons: first, to make sure that your portfolio is in line with your desired asset mix; and second, to see if that mix is still appropriate for your investment objectives. Here are some reasons to reevaluate your asset allocation:

- A major change in personal circumstances—marriage, birth of a child, loss of a spouse to divorce or death, child graduating from college, loss of job, or family illness—that changes your investment goals.
- The proportion of an asset category rises or falls considerably and thereby deviates from your target allocation for that class by more than, say, 5 percent.
- You're close to reaching a certain goal (such as saving for your child's college education or for your retirement).

Periodically, you'll likely find it necessary to *rebalance* your portfolio—that is, to reallocate the assets in your portfolio. For example, suppose that your asset allocation plan calls for 75 percent equities, but then the stock market falls, so stocks represent only 65 percent of your total portfolio value. If you're still bullish on the (long-term) market and if stocks are still appropriate for your portfolio, then you may view this as a good time to buy stocks and, in so doing, bring your portfolio back up to 75 percent in equities. If your personal goals change, or if you think the market may not recover in the near future, then you may decide to change your percentages so as to hold fewer stocks. But don't be too quick to rebalance every time your portfolio gets a little out of whack; you should allow for some variation in the actual allocations because market fluctuations will make it impossible to constantly maintain exact percentages. And don't forget to consider tax implications and the costs from trading commissions.

Portfolio management involves the buying, selling, and holding of various securities in order to meet a set of predetermined investment needs and objectives. To give you an idea of portfolio management in action, Exhibit 11.7 provides examples of four portfolios, each developed with a particular financial situation in mind. Notice that in each case, the asset allocation strategies and portfolio structures change with the different financial objectives. The first one is the *newlywed couple;* in their late 20s, they earn $65,000 a year and spend just about every cent. They have managed to put away some money, however, and are quickly beginning to appreciate the need to develop a savings program. Next is the *two-income couple;* in their early 40s, they earn $115,000 a year and are concerned about college costs for their children, ages

Financial Fact or Fantasy?

Coming up with a sound asset allocation plan will likely have more of an impact on long-term investment returns than the specific securities you hold in your portfolio. **Fact:** Research shows that, over the long-run, the total return on a portfolio is influenced more by its asset allocation plan—its mix of assets—than by specific security selections.

EXHIBIT 11.7 | Four Model Portfolios

The type of portfolio that you put together will depend on your financial and family situation as well as on your investment objectives. Clearly, what is right for one family may be totally inappropriate for another.

Family Situation	Portfolio
Newlywed couple	80 percent to 90 percent in common stocks, with three-quarters of that in mutual funds aiming for maximum capital gains and the rest in growth-and-income or equity-income funds
	10 percent to 20 percent in a money market fund or other short-term money market securities
Two-income couple	60 percent to 70 percent in common stocks, with three-quarters of that in blue chips or growth mutual funds and the rest in more aggressive issues or mutual funds aiming for maximum capital gains
	25 percent to 30 percent in discount Treasury notes whose maturities correspond with the bills for college tuition
	5 percent to 10 percent in money market funds or other short-term money market securities
Single parent	40 percent to 50 percent in money market funds or other short-term money market securities
	50 percent to 60 percent in growth and income mutual funds
Older couple	60 percent to 70 percent in blue-chip common stocks, growth funds, or value funds
	25 percent to 30 percent in municipal bonds or short- and intermediate-term discount bonds that will mature as the couple starts needing the money to live on
	5 percent to 10 percent in CDs and money market funds

17 and 12. Then there is the *single parent;* she is 34, has custody of her children, ages 7 and 4, and receives $50,000 a year in salary and child support. Finally, we have the *older couple;* in their mid-50s, they're planning for retirement in 10 years, when the husband will retire from his $95,000-a-year job.

11-6c Keeping Track of Your Investments

Just as you need investment objectives to provide direction for your portfolio, so too do you need to *monitor* it by keeping track of what your investment holdings consist of, how they've performed over time, and whether they've lived up to your expectations. Sometimes investments don't perform the way you thought they would. Their return may be well below what you'd like, or you may even have suffered a loss. In either case, it may be time to sell the investments and put the money elsewhere. A monitoring system should allow you to identify such securities in your portfolio. It should also enable you to stay on top of the holdings that are performing to your satisfaction. Knowing when to sell and when to hold can significantly affect the amount of return you're able to generate from your investments.

You can use a tool like Worksheet 11.2 to keep an inventory of your investment holdings. All types of investments can be included on this worksheet—from stocks, bonds, and mutual funds to real estate and savings accounts. To see how it works, consider the investment portfolio that has been built up since 2004 by Drew and Renee Porter, a two-income couple in their early 40s. Worksheet 11.2 shows that, as of May 1, 2015, Drew and Renee hold common stock in three companies, one bond exchange-traded fund, two equity mutual funds, and a savings account. While not shown, they also own a home that they bought in 2005, which has appreciated from an original cost of $280,000 to about $400,000. And they hold an emergency fund of $25,000 in an account that pays less than 1 percent a year. Using such a worksheet in conjunction with an online portfolio tracker would give an investor plenty of information about the performance of his or her portfolio—the *worksheet* providing long-term information from the date of purchase of an

A worksheet like this one will enable you to keep track of your investment holdings and to identify investments that aren't performing up to expectations.

AN INVENTORY OF INVESTMENT HOLDINGS

Name(s): Drew and Renee Porter   Date: May 1, 2015

Type of Investment	Description of Investment	Date Purchased	Amount of Original Investment	Latest Market Value	Cumulative Return
Common stock	250 shares–McDonalds	12/7/2005	$8,815.00	$24,450.00	+177.37%
Common stock	300 shares–Disney	10/19/2007	$10,143.00	$33,156.00	+226.89%
Common stock	150 shares–Intel	8/11/2010	$2,914.50	$5,013.00	+72.00%
Exchange-traded fund	400 shares–Vanguard Total International Bond ETF	8/12/2014	$20,444.00	$221,368.00	+4.52%
Mutual fund	200 shares–Vanguard Health Care	6/16/2004	$25,142.00	$45,426.00	+80.68%
Mutual fund	725 shares–Fidelity Contrafund	6/16/2004	$37,149.00	$73,384.50	+97.54%
	Portfolio Totals		**$104,607.50**	**$231,683.36**	**+93.87%**

asset, and the *online portfolio tracker* providing year-to-date or annual returns. Note that the Porters' holdings have grown from around $104,608 to about $231,683. A report like this should be prepared at least once a year. When completed, it provides a quick overview of your investment holdings and lets you know where you stand at a given point in time.

You Can Do It Now

Track Your Portfolio for Free

You can track your portfolio for free. And you can track a "paper" portfolio as well just to test out investment ideas. Just go to **https://www.google.com/finance/portfolio?action=view** – you can do it now.

TEST YOURSELF

11-25 Explain why it might be preferable for a person to invest in a *portfolio* of securities rather than in a *single* security.

11-26 Briefly describe the concept of *asset allocation* and note how it works.

11-27 Discuss the role of asset allocation in portfolio management.

11-28 What, if anything, can be gained from keeping track of your investment holdings?

Planning Over a Lifetime: *Investing*

Here are some key considerations for investment planning in each stage of the life cycle.

Pre-family Independence: 20s	Family Formation/ Career Development: 30–45	Pre-Retirement: 45–65	Retirement: 65 and Beyond
✓ Describe specific, tangible investments goals concerning retirement, major purchases, ways to enhance current income, and tax shelters.	✓ Revise investment plan to focus more on retirement and funding children's education, if applicable.	✓ Revise investment plan in light of recent developments.	✓ Revise investment plan to include more conservative assets.
✓ Align your investment goals with an amount regularly set aside from your income.	✓ Consider rebalancing investment portfolio consistent with long-term strategy.	✓ Monitor portfolio performance and consider rebalancing asset exposures.	✓ Monitor portfolio performance and match current income to expenditures.
✓ Establish an emergency fund equal to six months of income.	✓ Gradually increase the amount set aside for investments and savings.	✓ Continue to gradually increase the amount you invest and save.	✓ Integrate investment strategy with estate planning.
✓ Make paying off college loans a priority. They limit your financial flexibility.			

Financial Impact of Personal Choices
Trey and April Get Serious About Their Retirement Asset Allocation

Trey and April Addison are married and are both 32 years old. While they want to save for their children's future college educations, they also want to be plan carefully for their retirement. They know it's important to be adequately diversified and to be properly positioned in the various asset categories in their 401(k) retirement plans and IRAs. So one recent Saturday afternoon they found a free online asset allocation calculator (**http://money.cnn.com/tools/assetallocwizard/assetallocwizard.html**) and got some initial guidance on their proper asset allocation.

The online survey asked them about their investment time horizon, how much risk they were comfortable with, the flexibility of their retirement date, and whether they're tempted to sell stocks during a downturn or buy more. They indicated a 20+ year investment time horizon, medium risk tolerance, flexible retirement dates, and an inclination to leave their investments alone during a downturn. The recommended asset allocation was:

10% bonds
50% large stocks
20% small stocks
20% foreign stocks

Given that this recommends they invest 90% of their money in stocks, Trey and April have decided to get some more recommendations for a broader perspective on their asset allocation decision. This recommendation strikes them as a bit too risky for their tastes. However, this recommendation confirms their interest in having a significant amount invested in stocks with decent international diversification for the long haul. Trey and April are well on their way to managing their retirement investments effectively.

Summary

LG1 **Discuss the role that investing plays in the personal financial planning process and identify several different investment objectives, p. 413**
Investing plays an important part in personal financial planning; it's the means of reaching many of your financial goals. Your investment activities should be based on a sound investment plan that's linked to an ongoing savings plan. Most people invest their money to enhance their current income, accumulate funds for a major expenditure, save for retirement, or shelter some of their income from taxes.

LG2 **Distinguish between primary and secondary markets as well as between broker and dealer markets, p. 422**
Stocks, bonds, and other long-term securities are traded in the capital, or long-term, markets. Newly issued securities are sold in the primary markets, whereas transactions between investors occur in the secondary markets; the secondary market can be further divided into broker and dealer markets. Broker markets are made up of various securities exchanges, like the NYSE as well as some smaller regional exchanges. In contrast, the dealer market is where you'll find both the NASDAQ markets (like the NASDAQ Global Select and National Markets) as well as the OTC markets.

LG3 **Explain the process of buying and selling securities, and recognize the different types of orders, p. 429**
The securities transaction process starts when you call and place an order with your broker, who then transmits it via sophisticated telecommunications equipment to the floor of the stock exchange or the OTC market, where it's promptly executed and confirmed. Investors can buy or sell securities in odd or round lots by simply placing one of the three basic types of orders: a market order, limit order, or stop-loss order.

LG4 **Develop an appreciation of how various forms of investment information can lead to better investing skills and returns, p. 436**
Becoming an informed investor is essential to developing a sound investment program. Vital information about specific companies and industries,

the securities markets, the economy, and different investment vehicles and strategies can be obtained from such sources as annual stockholders' reports, brokerage and advisory service reports, the financial press, and the Internet. Various averages and indexes—such as the DJIA, the Standard & Poor's indexes, and the NYSE and NASDAQ indexes—provide information about daily market performance. These averages and indexes not only measure performance in the overall market but also provide standards of performance.

LG5 **Gain a basic understanding of the impact of the Internet on the field of investments, p. 444**
The computer and the Internet have empowered individual investors by providing information and tools formerly available only to investing professionals. The savings they offer in time and money are huge. Investors get the most current information, including real-time stock price quotes, market activity data, research reports, educational articles, and discussion forums. Tools such as financial planning calculators, stock screening programs, and portfolio tracking are free at many sites. Buying and selling securities online is convenient, simple, inexpensive, and fast.

LG6 **Describe an investment portfolio and how you'd go about developing, monitoring, and managing a portfolio of securities, p. 447**
An investment portfolio represents a collection of the securities/investments you hold, and it also gives focus and purpose to your investing activities. Developing a well-diversified portfolio of investment holdings enables an investor not only to achieve given investment objectives but also to enjoy reduced risk exposure and a more predictable level of return. To develop such a portfolio, the investor must carefully consider his or her level and stability of income, family factors, financial condition, experience and age, and disposition toward risk. Designing an asset allocation strategy, or mix of securities, that's based on these personal needs and objectives is also an important part of portfolio management. You should monitor your investment portfolio regularly to measure its performance and make changes as required by return data and life-cycle factors.

Key Terms

Answers to Test Yourself

You can find answers to these questions on this book's companion website. Look for it at *www.cengagebrain.com*. Search for this book by its title, and then add it to your dashboard.

Key Financial Relationships

Concept	Financial Relationship	Page Number
Payments to Fund Future Target Amount	Yearly Savings = Future Amount of Money Desired/Future Value Annuity Factor	416
Rate of Return	$\text{Rate of Return} = \dfrac{\text{Ending Value} - \text{Beginning Value} + \text{Income}}{\text{Beginning Value}}$	434

Key Financial Relationships Problem Set

1. ***Payments to Fund Future Target Amount.*** Liam and Tara Gleason want to have $275,000 available to fund their daughter's college education in 16 years. They are relatively conservative investors and expect to earn 5 percent per year on their portfolio. How much would the Gleason's need to invest every year to have the desired $275,000 available in 16 years?

   Solution: Yearly Savings = Future Amount of Money Desired/Future Value Annuity Factor. The future value annuity factor for 16 years and 5 percent in Appendix B is 23.657. Consequently, the

Gleasons should invest a yearly amount of $275,000/23.657 = $11,624.47 if they want to have $275,000 available to fund their daughter's education in 16 years

2. **Rate of Return.** Valerie Goldsmith bought a stock for $95 two years ago. Over this time period she received $3.00 in dividends while the price increased to $125. Valerie wants to find the rate of return on her investment.

    Solution: The rate of return is calculated as:

    $$\text{Rate of Return} = \frac{\text{Ending Value} - \text{Beginning Value} + \text{Income}}{\text{Beginning Value}} = \frac{(\$125 - \$95) + \$3.000}{\$95.00}$$
    $$= 34.74 \text{ percent}$$

Financial Planning Exercises

LG1, p. 413

1. **Amount to invest to meet objectives. Use Worksheet 11.1** Alison Conroy is early in her career and is now employed as the managing editor of a well-known business journal. Although she thoroughly enjoys her job and the people she works with, she would really like to be a literary agent. She would like to go on her own in about eight years and figures she'll need about $50,000 in capital to do so. Given that she thinks she can make about 10 percent on her money, use Worksheet 11.1 to answer the following questions.
    a. How much would Alison have to invest today, in one lump sum, to end up with $50,000 in eight years?
    b. If she's starting from scratch, how much would she have to put away annually to accumulate the needed capital in eight years?
    c. How about if she already has $10,000 socked away; how much would she have to put away annually to accumulate the required capital in eight years?
    d. Given that Alison has an idea of how much she needs to save, briefly explain how she could use an *investment plan* to help reach her objective.

LG2, p. 422

2. **Rationale for stock exchange listings.** Why do you suppose that large, well-known companies such as Apple, Starbucks, and Facebook prefer to have their shares traded on the NASDAQ rather than on one of the major listed exchanges, such as the NYSE (for which they'd easily meet all listing requirements)? What's in it for them? What would they gain by switching over to the NYSE?

LG3, p. 429

3. **Market and limit orders.** Suppose Gary Hooker places an order to buy 100 shares of The Gap. Explain how the order will be processed if it's a market order. Would it make any difference if it had been a limit order? Explain.

LG3, p. 429

4. **Calculating profits on margined and unmargined investments.** Claire Gerber wants to buy 300 shares of Google, which is selling in the market for $537.34 a share. Rather than liquidate all her savings, she decides to borrow through her broker at 5 percent a year. Assume that the margin requirement on common stock is 50 percent. If the stock rises to $625 a share over the next year, calculate the dollar profit and percentage return that Claire would earn if she makes the investment with 50 percent margin. Contrast these figures to what she'd make if she uses no margin.

LG3, p. 429

5. **Calculating return on investment.** Which of the following would offer the best return on investment? Assume that you buy $5,000 in stock in all three cases, and ignore interest and transaction costs in all your calculations.
    a. Buy a stock at $60 without margin, and sell it a year later at $90.
    b. Buy a stock at $20 with 50 percent margin, and sell it a year later at $30.
    c. Buy a stock at $40 with 75 percent margin, and sell it a year later at $55.

LG3, p. 429

6. **Calculating short position profit.** How much profit (if any) would Max Adler make if he short-sold 300 shares of a stock at $100 a share and the price of the stock suddenly tumbled to $70?

7. *Calculating long and short position profits.* Given that Hometown Care, Inc.'s stock is currently selling for $40 a share, calculate the amount of money that Calvin Haskins will make (or lose) on each of the following transactions. Assume all transactions involve 100 shares of stock, and ignore brokerage commissions.

    a.   He short-sells the stock and then repurchases the borrowed shares at $50.

    b.   He buys the stock and then sells it some time later at $50.

    c.   He short-sells the stock and then repurchases the borrowed shares at $25.

8. *Calculating short position cash flows and returns.* Assume that an investor short-sells 500 shares of stock at a price of $85 a share, making a 50 percent margin deposit. A year later, she repurchases the borrowed shares at $50 a share.

    a.   How much of her money did the short-seller have to put up to make this transaction?

    b.   How much money did the investor make, or lose, on this transaction?

    c.   What rate of return did she make on her *invested capital* (see part a)?

9. *Interpreting stock quotes.* The following quote for The Walt Disney Company, a NYSE stock, appeared on May 1, 2015 (Friday) on Yahoo! Finance (**http://finance.yahoo.com/q?s=DIS&ql=1**):

The Walt Disney Company (DIS)—NYSE			
110.52 ↑ 1.80 (1.66%) May 1, 4:01PM EDT			
Prev Close:	108.72	Day's Range:	109.27–110.67
Open:	109.79	52wk Range:	78.54–111.66
Bid:	110.81 × 400	Volume:	6,205,116
Ask:	110.95 × 500	Avg Vol (3m):	6,394,880
1y Target Est:	110.23	Market Cap:	187.84B
Beta:	1.1	P/E (ttm):	24.57
Next Earnings Date:	5-May-15	EPS (ttm):	4.50
		Div & Yield:	1.15 (1.10%)

Given this information, answer the following questions.

    a.   At what price did the stock sell at the time of the quote?

    b.   What is the stock's price/earnings ratio? What does that indicate?

    c.   What is the last price at which the stock traded on the prior trading day?

    d.   What is the stock's dividend yield?

    e.   What are the highest and lowest prices at which the stock traded during the latest 52-week period?

    f.   How large is the market capitalization of the company?

10. *Finding and interpreting stock quotes.* Listed below are three pairs of stocks. Look at each pair and select the security you'd like to own, given that you want to *select the one with the highest market value.* Then, *after* making all three of your selections, use *The Wall Street Journal* or some other source to find the latest market value of the two securities in each pair.

    a.   50 shares of Berkshire Hathaway (stock symbol BRKA) or 150 shares of JP Morgan Chase (stock symbol JPM). (Both stocks are listed on the NYSE.)

    b.   100 shares of Home Depot (symbol HD), a NYSE stock; or 100 shares of Apple (symbol AAPL), a NASDAQ stock and a member of the Dow Jones Industrial Average.

    c.   150 shares of Wal-Mart (symbol WMT) or 50 shares of Facebook (symbol FB).

How many times did you pick the one that was worth more money? Did the price of any of these stocks surprise you? If so, which one(s)? Does the price of a stock represent its value? Explain.

11. *Finding and using market index quotes.* Using a resource like *The Wall Street Journal or Barron's* (either in print or online), find the latest values for each of the following market averages and indexes, and indicate how each has performed over the past six months:

    a.   DJIA

    b.   Dow Jones Global Titans 50

    c.   S&P 500

d.   NYSE Composite

e.   NASDAQ Composite

f.   S&P MidCap 400

g.   Dow Jones Wilshire 5000

h.   Russell 2000

LG4, p. 436   12. **Finding stock quote information.** Using the Internet site for Yahoo! Finance (**http://finance. yahoo.com**), find the 52-week high and low for Coca-Cola's common stock (symbol KO). What is the stock's latest dividend yield? What was Coca-Cola's most recent closing price, and at what P/E ratio was the stock trading?

LG4, p. 436   13. **Interpreting stock report information.** Using the S&P report in Exhibit 11.6, find the following information for Apple.

a.   What was the amount of revenues (i.e., sales) generated by the company in 2014?

b.   What were the latest annual dividends per share and dividend yield?

c.   What were the earnings (per share) projections for 2015?

d.   How many common shareholders were there?

e.   What were the book value per share and earnings per share in 2014?

f.   Where is the stock traded?

g.   How much long-term debt did the company have in 2014?

h.   What was the company's effective tax rate in 2014?

LG6, p. 447   14. **Tracking portfolio performance. Use Worksheet 11.2** to help Clayton and Julie Grover, a married couple in their late 40s, evaluate their securities portfolio, which includes these holdings.

a.   *IBM.* (NYSE; symbol IBM): 100 shares bought in 2011 for $170.40 per share.

b.   *Verizon* (NYSE; symbol VZ): 250 shares purchased in 2007 for $40.62 per share.

c.   *Procter & Gamble* (NYSE; symbol PG): 150 shares purchased in 2010 at $61.85 per share.

d.   *Google* (NASDAQ; symbol, GOOG): 200 shares purchased in 2014 at $519.98 per share.

e.   The Grovers also have $8,000 in a bank savings account that pays 1.25 percent annual interest.

   1.   Based on the latest quotes and portfolio tracking tools obtained from the Internet, complete Worksheet 11.2.

   2.   What's the total amount the Grovers have invested in these securities, the annual income they now receive, and the latest market value of their investments?

Applying Personal Finance

Research Your Investments!

Investing involves making informed decisions, which means researching companies and industries *before* plunking down your hard-earned money! An excellent source of information about a company is the company itself, particularly its annual report to stockholders. In this project, you'll examine the annual stockholders' report of a company in which you are interested.

The annual report is a document that provides financial and operating information about a company to its owners, the stockholders. Obtain a copy of the latest annual report of the company you are researching. Copies can be found in many public and college libraries, at local brokerage offices, or on the company's Internet site. Carefully study the annual report and then prepare a corporate profile of the firm you selected. Your profile should include the following elements:

a.   Name of the company, its ticker symbol, and the exchange on which it trades

b.   Current market price of the stock and its percentage change from 1, 3, and 5 years ago (try to find a chart of its stock price)

c.   Location of its corporate headquarters, names of its officers, and percentage of inside ownership

d.   Brief description of the company, including its major products or services

e.   Brief history of the company

f.   Major competitors

g. Sales and profit summaries

h. Other relevant financial ratios and measures

i. Recent developments and future plans

Based on your findings, would you consider this company for a potential investment? Why or why not?

CRITICAL THINKING CASES

LG6, p. 447

11.1 The Woodsons Struggle with Two Investment Goals

Like many married couples, Damian and Brandi Woodson are trying their best to save for two important investment objectives: (1) an education fund to put their two children through college; and (2) a retirement nest egg for themselves. They want to set aside $100,000 per child by the time each one starts college. Given that their children are now 10 and 12 years old, Damian and Brandi have 6 years remaining for one child and 8 for the other. As far as their retirement plans are concerned, the Woodsons both hope to retire in 20 years, when they reach age 65. Both Damian and Brandi work, and together, they currently earn about $90,000 a year.

The Woodsons started a college fund some years ago by investing $6,000 a year in bank CDs. That fund is now worth $65,000. They also have $50,000 that they received from an inheritance invested in several mutual funds and another $20,000 in a tax-sheltered retirement account. Damian and Brandi believe that they'll be able to continue putting away $6,000 a year for the next 20 years. In fact, Brandi thinks they'll be able to put away even more, particularly after the children are out of school. The Woodsons are fairly conservative investors and feel they can probably earn about 6 percent on their money. (Ignore taxes for the purpose of this exercise.)

Critical Thinking Questions

1. **Use Worksheet 11.1** to determine whether the Woodsons have enough money right now to meet their children's educational needs. That is, will the $65,000 they've accumulated so far be enough to put their children through school, given they can invest their money at 6 percent? Remember, they want to have $100,000 set aside for each child by the time each one starts college.

2. Regarding their retirement nest egg, assume that no additions are made to either the $50,000 they now have in mutual funds or to the $20,000 in the retirement account. How much would these investments be worth in 20 years, given that they can earn 6 percent?

3. Now, if the Woodsons can invest $6,000 a year for the next 20 years and apply all of that to their retirement nest egg, how much would they be able to accumulate given their 6 percent rate of return?

4. How do you think the Woodsons are doing with regard to meeting their twin investment objectives? Explain.

LG6, p. 447

11.2 Russ Alonzo Takes Stock of His Securities

Russ Alonzo is 42 years old, single, and works as a designer for a major architectural firm. He is well paid and has built up a sizable portfolio of investments. He considers himself an aggressive investor and, because he has no dependents to worry about, likes to invest in high-risk/high-return securities. His records show the following information.

1. In 2006, Russ bought 200 shares of eBay (NASDAQ; symbol EBAY) at $29.77 a share.

2. In 2013 he bought 250 shares of Facebook (NASDAQ; symbol FB) at $26.89 a share.

3. In 2008, Russ bought 200 shares of United Technologies Corp. (NYSE; symbol UTX) at $74.92 a share.

4. In early 2009, he bought 450 shares of JPMorgan Chase (NYSE; symbol JPM) at $16 a share.

5. Also in 2009, Russ bought 400 shares of PepsiCo (NYSE; symbol PEP) at $52.50 a share.

6. He has $12,000 in a 1 percent money market mutual fund.

Every three months or so, Russ prepares a complete, up-to-date report on his investment holdings.

Critical Thinking Questions

1. **Use a form like Worksheet 11.2** to prepare a complete inventory of Russ' investment holdings. (*Note*: Look in the latest issue of *The Wall Street Journal*, or pull up an online source such as **http://finance.yahoo.com**, to find the most recent closing price of the five stocks in Russ' portfolio.)

2. What is your overall assessment of Russ' investment portfolio? Does it appear that his personal net worth is improving because of his investments?

3. Based on the worksheet you prepared in Question 1, do you see any securities that you think Russ should consider selling? What other investment advice might you give Russ?

CHAPTER 12

Investing in Stocks and Bonds

LEARNING GOALS

LG1 Describe the various types of risks to which investors are exposed, as well as the sources of return.

LG2 Know how to search for an acceptable investment on the basis of risk, total return, and yield.

LG3 Discuss the merits of investing in common stock and be able to distinguish among the different types of stocks.

LG4 Become familiar with the various measures of performance and how to use them in placing a value on stocks.

LG5 Describe the basic issue characteristics of bonds, as well as how these securities are used as investment vehicles.

LG6 Distinguish between the different types of bonds, gain an understanding of how bond prices behave, and know how to compute different measures of yield.

How Will This Affect Me?

Once you've figured out how much you need to invest to meet important financial goals, it's time to decide which specific investments to buy. This chapter describes the basic characteristics of stocks and bonds, explains their potential returns and risks, and provides a framework for choosing among stocks and bonds to meet your financial objectives. Care is taken to explore how stock and bond prices behave and how to evaluate their performance over time. After reading this chapter you should be able to choose the most appropriate stocks and bonds for your portfolio in light of your goals and constraints.

Financial Facts or Fantasies?

Are the following statements Financial Facts (true) or Fantasies (false)? Consider the answers to the questions below as you read through this chapter.

- A good investment is one that offers a positive expected rate of return.

- Income stocks have relatively high dividend yields and, as such, appeal to individuals who seek a high level of current income.

- Putting your money into stocks that offer dividend reinvestment plans is a great way of building up your investment capital.

- When interest rates go down, bond prices also go down because such securities become less valuable.

- Convertible bonds are so named because they can be exchanged for a set number of shares of common stock.

12-1 THE RISKS AND REWARDS OF INVESTING

Most rational investors are motivated to buy or sell a security based on its expected return: buy if the return looks good, sell if it doesn't. But a security's return is just part of the story; you can't consider the return on an investment without also looking at its *risk*—the chance that the actual return from an investment may differ from what was expected (i.e., fall short—you wouldn't mind if it exceeded expectations, after all). Generally speaking, you expect riskier investments to provide higher levels of return. Otherwise, what incentive is there for an investor to risk his or her capital? This is referred to as the risk–return trade-off. The concepts of risk and return are of vital concern to investors, so, before taking up the issue of investing in stocks and bonds, let's look more closely at the risks of investing and the various components of return. Equally important, we'll see how these two components can be used together to find potentially attractive investments.

12-1a The Risks of Investing

Just about any type of investment is subject to some risk—some investment types more than others. The basic types of investment risk are business risk, financial risk, market risk, purchasing power risk, interest rate risk, liquidity risk, and event risk. Other things being equal, you'd like to reduce your exposure to these risks as much as possible.

Business Risk

business risk
The variability associated with a firm's cash flows and with its subsequent ability to meet its operating expenses on time.

When investing in a company, you accept the possibility that the firm will not be able to maintain sales and profits, or even to stay in business. Such failure is due either to economic or industry factors or, as is more often the case, to poor management decisions. Business risk is the variability surrounding the firm's cash flows and subsequent ability to meet operating expenses on time. Companies that are subject to high degrees of business risk may experience wide fluctuations in sales, may have widely erratic earnings, and can experience substantial operating losses every now and then.

Financial Risk

financial risk
A type of risk associated with the amount of debt used to finance the firm and its ability to meet these obligations on time.

Financial risk concerns the amount of debt used to finance a firm, as well as the possibility that the firm will not have sufficient cash flows to meet these obligations on time.

Look to the company's balance sheet in order to get a handle on a firm's financial risk. As a rule, companies that have little or no long-term debt are fairly low in financial risk. This is the case particularly if the company also has a healthy earnings picture. The problem with debt financing is that it creates principal and interest obligations that must be met regardless of how much profit the company is generating.

Market Risk

market risk
A type of risk associated with the price volatility of a security.

Market risk results from the behavior of investors in the securities markets that can lead to swings in security prices. These price changes can be due to underlying intrinsic factors, as well as to changes in political, economic, and social conditions or in investor tastes and preferences. Essentially, market risk is reflected in the *price volatility* of a security: the more volatile the price of a security relative to the overall market, the greater its market risk.

Purchasing Power Risk

purchasing power risk
A type of risk, resulting from possible changes in price levels, which can significantly affect investment returns.

Changes in the general level of prices within the economy also produce **purchasing power risk**. In periods of rising prices (inflation), the purchasing power of the dollar declines. This means that a smaller quantity of goods and services can be purchased with a given number of dollars. In general, investments (such as stocks and real estate) whose values tend to move with general price levels are most profitable during periods of rising prices, whereas investments (such as bonds) that pay fixed cash flows are preferred during periods of low or declining price levels.

Interest Rate Risk

fixed-income securities
Securities such as bonds, notes, and preferred stocks that offer purchasers fixed periodic income.

interest rate risk
A type of risk, resulting from changing market interest rates, that mainly affects fixed-income securities.

Fixed-income securities—which include notes, bonds, and preferred stocks—pay investors a fixed periodic cash flow and, as such, are most affected by **interest rate risk**. As interest rates change, the prices of these securities fluctuate, decreasing with rising interest rates and increasing with falling rates. The prices of fixed-income securities drop when interest rates increase because investors require rates of return that are competitive with securities offering higher levels of interest income.

Liquidity Risk

liquidity risk
A type of risk associated with the inability to liquidate an investment conveniently and at a reasonable price.

The risk of not being able to liquidate (i.e., sell) an investment conveniently and at a reasonable price is called **liquidity risk**. In general, investments traded in *thin markets*, where supply and demand are relatively small, tend to be less liquid than those traded in *broad markets*. However, to be liquid, an investment not only must be easy to sell, but also must be so *at a reasonable price*. The liquidity of an investment can generally be enhanced merely by cutting its price. For example, a security recently purchased for $1,000 wouldn't be viewed as highly liquid if it could be sold only at a significantly reduced price, such as $500. Vehicles such as mutual funds, common stocks, and U.S. Treasury securities are generally highly liquid; others, such as an isolated parcel of raw land, are not.

Event Risk

event risk
The risk that some major, unexpected event will occur that leads to a sudden and substantial change in the value of an investment.

Event risk occurs when something substantial happens to a company and that event, in itself, has a sudden impact on the company's financial condition. It involves an unexpected event that has a significant and usually immediate effect on the underlying value of an investment. A good example of event risk was the action by the Food and Drug Administration (FDA) years ago to halt the use of silicone breast implants. The share price of Dow Corning—the dominant producer of this product—quickly fell due to this single event! Another comparable example is the controversy over Vioxx, a drug produced by Merck, which was eventually withdrawn from the market and brought civil and criminal litigation that ultimately cost the company at least $5.8 billion. Fortunately, event risk tends to be confined to specific companies, securities, or market segments.

12–1b The Returns from Investing

Any investment—whether it's a share of stock, a bond, a piece of real estate, or a mutual fund—has two basic sources of return: *current income* and *capital gains*. Some investments offer only one source of return (for example, non-dividend-paying stocks provide only capital gains), but many others offer both income and capital gains, which together make up what's known as the *total return* from an investment. Of course, when both elements of return are present, the relative importance of each will vary among investments. For example, whereas current income is more important with bonds, capital gains are usually a larger portion of the total return from common stocks.

Current Income

Current income is generally received with some degree of regularity over the course of the year. It may take the form of dividends on stock, interest from bonds, or rents from real estate. People who invest to obtain income look for investments that will provide regular and predictable patterns of income. Preferred stocks and bonds, which are expected to pay established amounts at specified times (e.g., quarterly or semiannually), are usually viewed as good income investments.

Capital Gains

The other type of return available from investments is capital appreciation (or growth), which is reflected as an increase in the market value of an investment vehicle. Capital gains occur when you're able to sell a security for more than you paid for it. Investments that provide greater growth potential through capital appreciation normally have lower levels of current income, because the firm achieves its growth by reinvesting its earnings instead of paying dividends to the owners. Many common stocks, for example, are bought for their capital gains potential.

Earning Interest on Interest: Another Source of Return

When does a 4 percent investment end up yielding only 3 percent? Probably more often than you think! Obviously, it can happen when investment performance fails to live up to expectations. But it can also happen *even when everything goes right*. That is, so long as at least part of the return from an investment involves the periodic receipt of current income (such as dividends or interest payments), then that income must be *reinvested* at a given rate of return in order to achieve the yield you thought you had going into the investment. For example, consider an investor who buys a 4 percent U.S. Treasury bond and holds it to the maturity date in 20 years. Each year, the bondholder receives $40 in interest, and at maturity, the $1,000 in principal is repaid. There's no loss in capital, no default; everything is paid right on time. Yet this sure-fire investment ends up yielding only 3 percent. Why? Because the investor failed to reinvest the semiannual interest payments received at the original interest rate of 4 percent. By not plowing back all the investment earnings, the bondholder failed to earn any interest on interest.

Take a look at Exhibit 12.1. It shows the three elements of return for a 4 percent, 20-year bond: (1) the recovery of principal, (2) periodic interest income, and (3) the interest on interest earned from reinvesting the semiannual interest payments. Note that because the bond was originally bought at par ($1,000), you start off with a 4 percent investment. *Where you end up depends, in large part, on what you do with the interest earnings from this investment.* If you don't reinvest the interest income at the original 4 percent, then you could end up at the 3 percent line—or even lower.

You have to earn interest on interest from your investments in order to move to the 4 percent line. Specifically, because you started with a 4 percent investment, that's the rate of return that you need to earn when reinvesting your income. Keep in mind that, even though we used a bond in our illustration, *this same concept applies to any type of long-term investment* so long as current income is part of an

FINANCIAL PLANNING TIPS

Keys to Successful Stock and Bond Investing: Asset Allocation, Diversification, and Rebalancing

Here are some key concepts that will help you manage your portfolio successfully:

• **Asset allocation.** This is the decision on how to divide your investments among the different major asset classes, which include stocks, bonds, and cash. The best mix depends on your *tolerance for risk* and on your *time horizon*. Longer-term investors, like someone in their 20s saving for retirement, are often more comfortable investing in riskier assets like stocks. In contrast, shorter-term investors, like someone saving for a house down payment or a child's education, often will prefer less risk. Many such people will invest less in stocks and more in bonds. And most investors change their asset allocation as their time horizon changes—for instance, as they approach retirement. Thus, most investors tend to have less money in stocks and more money in bonds and cash as they get older.

• **Diversification.** This is the strategy of spreading your money among different investments so that losses on some investments will be offset, at least somewhat, by gains on other investments in your portfolio. Your portfolio should be diversified both *among* and *within* asset classes. This means that your asset allocation strategy should spread out your money among stocks, bonds, and cash, and that your money should be spread out among different securities within *each* asset class. For example, within the equity asset class, it's important to identify stocks that perform distinctly under different equity market conditions. This often involves investing in stocks in different sectors and industries.

• **Rebalancing.** Over time, changes in market values could make your portfolio inconsistent with your financial goals. For example, what if you have decided that your portfolio should consist of 70 percent stocks, but a market turndown has reduced the value of your stock holdings to only 60 percent of your portfolio? In order to rebalance your holdings, you'll need to buy more equities or sell some bonds and/or use some cash to fund the additional exposure to stocks. But before you rebalance, you should consider carefully the transaction costs and any possible tax consequences. Many financial advisors suggest that you consider rebalancing your portfolio every 6 to 12 months, and whenever the asset allocation gets out of kilter by a significant percentage, like 5 percent or 10 percent.

Source: "Beginners' Guide to Asset Allocation, Diversification, and Rebalancing," http://www.sec.gov/investor/pubs/assetallocation.htm, accessed August 2015.

investment's return. In other words, it's just as relevant to common stocks and mutual funds as it is to long-term bond instruments. This notion of earning interest on interest is what the market refers to as a *fully compounded rate of return*. It's an important concept because you can't reap the full potential from your investments unless you earn a fully compounded return on your money.

If periodic investment income is a part of your investment return, then the reinvestment of that income and interest on interest are important matters. In fact, *interest on interest is a particularly important element of return for investment programs involving a lot of current income.* This is so because, in contrast to capital gains, current income must be reinvested by the individual investor. (With capital gains, the investment itself does all the reinvesting automatically.) It follows, then, that if your investment program tends to lean toward income-oriented securities, then interest on interest—and the continued reinvestment of income—will play an important role in defining the amount of investment success you have. Of course, *the length of your investment horizon* also plays a key role in defining the amount of interest on interest embedded in a security's return. In particular, *long-term investments* (e.g., 20-year bonds) are subject to a lot more interest on interest than are short-term investments (e.g., six-month T-bills or dividend-paying stocks that you hold for only 2 or 3 years).

EXHIBIT 12.1 **Three Elements of Return for a 4 Percent, 20-Year Bond**

As seen here, the long-term return from an investment (in this case, a bond) is made up of three parts: recovery of capital, current income, and interest on interest; of the three components, interest on interest is particularly important, *especially for long-term investments.*

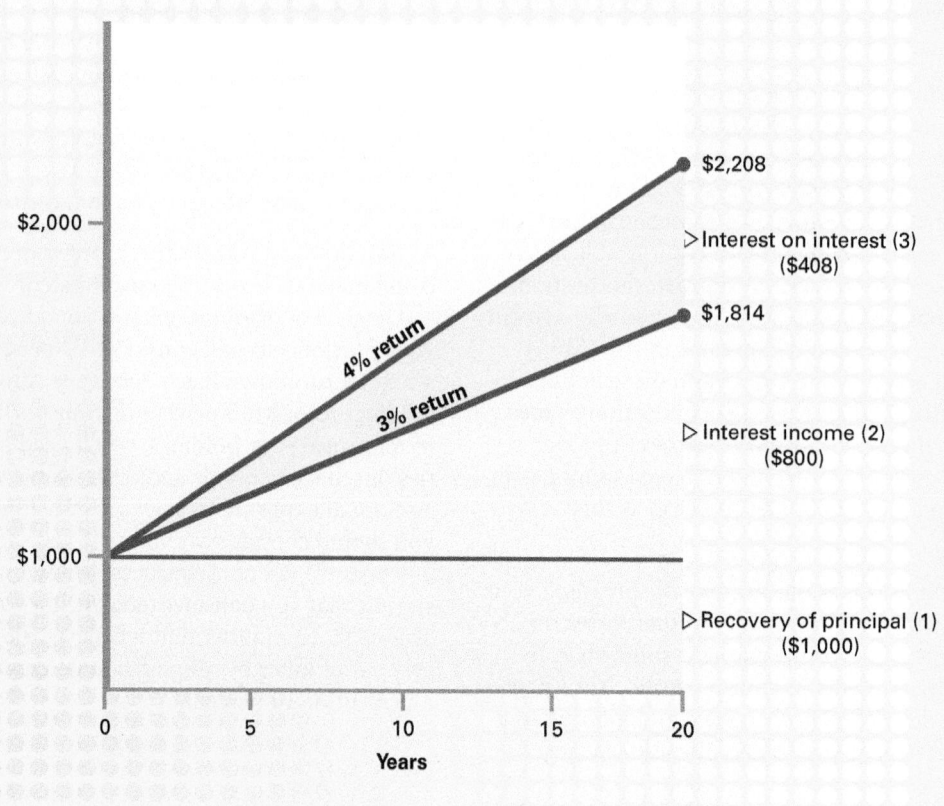

12–1c The Risk-Return Trade-off

The amount of risk associated with a given investment is directly related to its expected return. This universal rule of investing means that if you want a higher level of return, you'll probably have to accept greater exposure to risk. Yet, you can't invest in a high-risk security and earn a high rate of return automatically. Unfortunately, it doesn't work that way—risk isn't, by definition, that predictable!

Because most people are *risk averse* (they dislike taking risks), some incentive for taking risks must be offered. If a low-risk investment offered the same return as a high-risk one, then investors would naturally opt for the former; put another way, investors will choose the investment with the least risk for a given level of return. Exhibit 12.2 portrays the expected risk-return trade-off for some popular investment vehicles. Note that it's possible to receive a positive return for zero risk, such as at point A. This is referred to as the risk-free rate of return, which is often measured by the return on a short-term government security, such as a 90-day Treasury bill (T-bill).

risk-free rate of return The rate of return on short-term government securities, such as Treasury bills, that is free from any type of risk.

12–1d What Makes a Good Investment?

In keeping with the preceding risk-return discussion, it follows that the value of any investment depends on the amount and timing of benefits it's expected to

EXHIBIT 12.2 **The Risk–Return Relationship**

For investments, there's generally a direct relationship between risk and return: the more risk you face, the greater the return you should expect from the investment.

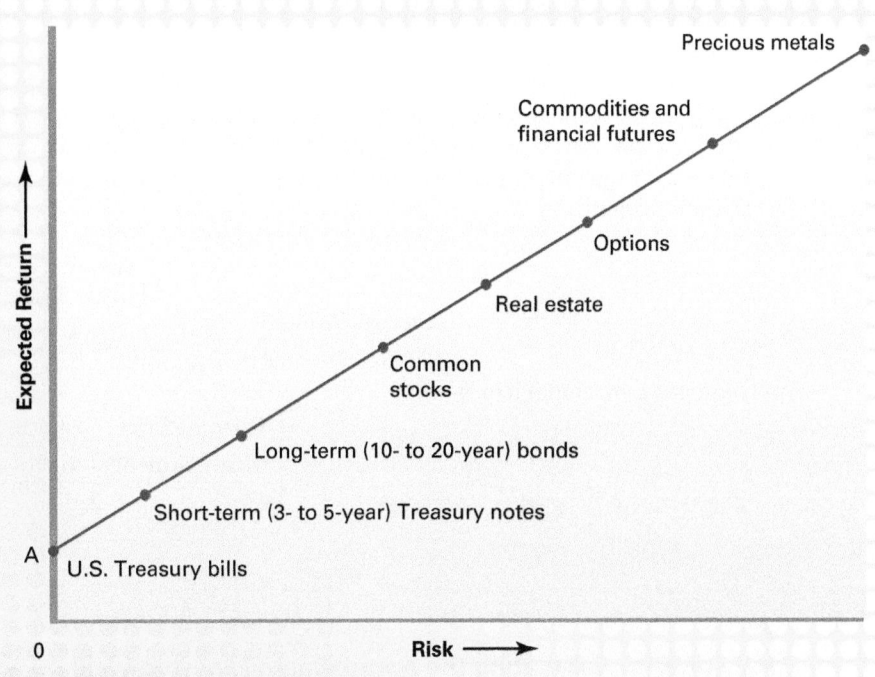

provide relative to the amount of perceived risk involved. This applies to all types of investments, including stocks, bonds, convertibles, options, real estate, and commodities.

Future Return

In investments, it's the *expected future return* that matters. Aside from the help that they can provide in getting a handle on future returns, past returns are of little value to investors. After all, it's not what the security did last year that matters, but rather, what it's expected to do next year.

To get an idea of the future return on an investment, we must *formulate expectations of its future income and future capital appreciation.* As an illustration, assume you're thinking of buying some stock in CTA Strategic Group, Inc. (CTA). After reviewing several financial reports, you've estimated the future dividends and price behavior of CTA as follows:

Expected average annual dividends, 2017–2019	$2.15 a share
Expected market price of the stock, 2019	$95.00 a share

Because the stock is now selling for $60 a share, the difference between its current and expected future market price ($95 − $60) represents the amount of *capital gains* that you expect to receive over the next three years—in this case, $35 a share. The projected future price, along with expected average annual dividends, gives you an estimate of the stock's *future income stream;* what you need now is a way to measure the *expected return.*

Approximate Expected Yield

Finding the exact rate of return on an investment involves an iterative mathematical procedure—one that's hard to solve without using a handheld financial calculator (which we'll demonstrate shortly). There is, however, a fairly easy way to obtain a reasonably close estimation of expected return, and that is to compute an investment's *approximate expected yield*. It's useful when dealing with forecasted numbers (that are subject to some degree of uncertainty anyway). The measure considers not only income and capital gains, but interest on interest as well. Hence, *approximate expected yield provides a measure of the fully compounded rate of return* from an investment. Finding the approximate expected yield on an investment is shown in the following equation. If you briefly study the formula, you'll see it's really not as formidable as it may appear. All it does is relate average current income and average capital gains to the average amount of the investment.

$$\text{Approximate Expected Yield} = \cfrac{\text{Average Annual Current Income} + \left[\cfrac{\substack{\text{Future Price} \\ \text{of Investment}} - \substack{\text{Current Price} \\ \text{of Investment}}}{\text{Number of Years in Investment Period}}\right]}{\left[\cfrac{\substack{\text{Current Price} \\ \text{of Investment}} + \substack{\text{Future Price} \\ \text{of Investment}}}{2}\right]}$$

EXAMPLE: Calculating the Approximate Expected Yield on a Stock

To illustrate, let's use the CTA example again. Given the average current income from annual dividends of $2.15, current stock price of $60, future stock price of $95, and an investment period of three years (you expect to hold the stock from the beginning of 2017 through the end of 2019), you can use this equation to find the approximate expected yield on CTA as follows:

$$\text{Approximate Yield} = \cfrac{\$2.15 + \left[\cfrac{\$95 - \$60}{3}\right]}{\left[\cfrac{\$60 + \$95}{2}\right]}$$

$$= \cfrac{\$2.15 + \left[\cfrac{\$35}{3}\right]}{\left[\cfrac{\$155}{2}\right]}$$

$$= \cfrac{\$2.15 + \$11.67}{\$77.50} = \cfrac{\$13.82}{\$77.50}$$

$$= \underline{17.8\%}$$

In this case, if your forecasts of annual dividends and capital gains hold up, an investment in CTA should provide a return of around 17.8 percent per year.

See Appendix E for details.

Calculator

INPUTS	FUNCTIONS
3	N
−60	PV
2.15	PMT
95.00	FV
	CPT
	I/Y
	SOLUTION
	19.66

Calculator Keystrokes. You can easily find the *exact* expected return on this example investment using a handheld financial calculator. Here's what you do. First, put the calculator in the *annual compounding* mode. Then—to find the expected return on a stock that you buy at $60 a share, hold for three years (during which time you receive average annual dividends of $2.15 a share), and then sell at $95—use the keystrokes shown in the margin, where:

N = number of *years* that you hold the stock
PV = the price that you pay for the stock (entered as a *negative* number)
PMT = *average* amount of dividends received *each year*
FV = the price that you expect to receive when you *sell* the stock (in three years)

You'll notice that there is a difference in the computed yield measures (17.8 percent with the approximate procedure, versus 19.66 percent here). That's to be expected because one is only an approximate measure of performance, whereas the calculator gives an exact measure.

required rate of return
The minimum rate of return an investor feels should be earned in compensation for the amount of risk assumed.

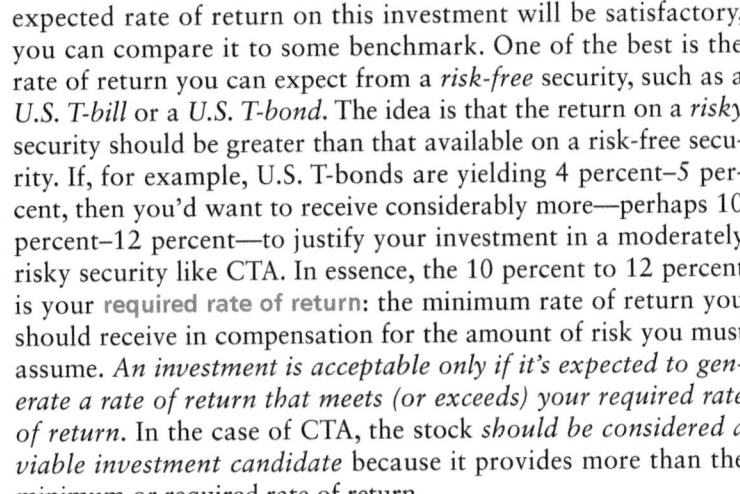

Financial Fact or Fantasy?

A good investment is one that offers a positive expected rate of return.
Fantasy: *A good investment is one that offers an expected return that equals or exceeds the investor's required rate of return, which is defined relative to the risk of the investment. Thus, what might be a good return in one case may be totally inadequate in another.*

Whether you should consider CTA a viable investment candidate depends on how the expected return stacks up to the amount of risk that you would assume. Suppose you've decided the stock is moderately risky. To determine whether the expected rate of return on this investment will be satisfactory, you can compare it to some benchmark. One of the best is the rate of return you can expect from a *risk-free* security, such as a U.S. *T-bill* or a U.S. *T-bond*. The idea is that the return on a *risky* security should be greater than that available on a risk-free security. If, for example, U.S. T-bonds are yielding 4 percent–5 percent, then you'd want to receive considerably more—perhaps 10 percent–12 percent—to justify your investment in a moderately risky security like CTA. In essence, the 10 percent to 12 percent is your **required rate of return**: the minimum rate of return you should receive in compensation for the amount of risk you must assume. *An investment is acceptable only if it's expected to generate a rate of return that meets (or exceeds) your required rate of return.* In the case of CTA, the stock *should be considered a viable investment candidate* because it provides more than the minimum or required rate of return.

TEST YOURSELF

12-1 Describe the various types of risk to which investors are exposed.

12-2 What is meant by the *risk-return trade-off?* What is the *risk-free rate of return?*

12-3 Briefly describe the two basic sources of return to investors.

12-4 What is *interest on interest*, and why is it such an important element of return?

12-5 What is the *desired rate of return*, and how would it be used to make an investment decision?

12-2 INVESTING IN COMMON STOCK

Common stocks appeal to investors for various reasons. To some, investing in stocks is a way to hit it big if the issue shoots up in price. To others, it's the level of current income that stocks offer. A share of common stock enables the investor to participate in the profits of the firm. Every shareholder is, in effect, a part owner of the firm and, as such, is entitled to a piece of its profit. Common stockholders are really the **residual owners** of the company, meaning that they're entitled to dividend income and a prorated share of the company's earnings, but only after all the firm's other obligations have been met.

residual owners
Shareholders of the company; they are entitled to dividend income and a share of the company's profits only after all of the firm's other obligations have been met.

12-2a Common Stocks as a Form of Investing

Given the nature of common stocks, if the market is strong, then investors can generally expect to benefit from steady price appreciation. A good example is the performance in 2013, when the market, as measured by the Dow Jones Industrial Average (DJIA), went up more than 26 percent. Unfortunately, when markets falter, so do investor returns. For example, over the three-year period from early 2000 through late 2002, the market (again, as measured by the DJIA) fell some 38 percent. Excluding dividends, that means a $100,000 investment would have declined in value to a little over $60,000. And in 2008, the Dow fell yet again, this time by almost 34 percent, while the S&P 500 Composite Index (S&P 500) fell by about 38 percent.

Make no mistake, the market does have its bad days, and sometimes those bad days seem to go on for months. It may not always seem that way, but those bad days *really are the exception, not the rule.* That was certainly the case from 1929 through 2015, when the Dow went down (for the year) just 21 times. That's only about 25 percent of the time; the other 75 percent the market was up—anywhere from around 2 percent to nearly 40 percent! True, there's some risk and price volatility (even in good markets), but that's the price you have to pay for all the upside potential. Consider, for example, the behavior of the market from 1982 through early 2000. Starting in August 1982, when the Dow stood at 777, this market saw the DJIA climb nearly 11,000 points to reach a high of 11,723 in January 2000. This turned out to be one of the longest bull markets in history, as the DJIA grew at an annual rate of nearly 17 percent.

Unfortunately, all that came to a screeching halt in early 2000, when each of the three major market measures peaked—the Dow at 11,723, the NASDAQ at 5,048, and the S&P 500 at 1,527. Over the course of the next 32 months, through September 2002, these market measures fell flat on their collective faces. While the Dow recovered from 2003 through mid-2007, it fell big time from that point on through early 2009. In fact, it fell from about 14,000 in July 2007 to around 6,500 in March 2009, with most of that loss occurring in 2008, when the Dow dropped by nearly 34 percent. Not to be outdone, the S&P 500 fell by 38 percent, which was the second-worst performance on record. Only 1931 was worse, when the S&P 500 fell by more than 49 percent.

Take a look at Exhibit 12.3, which tracks the behavior of the DJIA and the NASDAQ Composite from 2005 to mid-2015, and you'll quickly get a feel for just how volatile this market was! As the exhibit shows, despite all those market gyrations, both the Dow and the NASDAQ—which track two totally different segments of the market—ended up with decent returns (7.93 percent and 9.44 percent, respectively). Specifically, a $10,000 investment in the DJIA in January 2005 would have grown to about $22,031 by May 2015, while $10,000 invested in the NASDAQ would have grown to about $25,450. Given the high volatility of stock returns over time, investors who pull their money out of the market in bad times tend to lose the opportunity to make up their losses in good times. The possible effect of trying to time the market is discussed more fully later in this chapter.

The market entered one of the worst bear markets in history during 2007 and 2008, as the markets experienced the impact of the global financial crisis. Fortunately, the market recovered from 2009 to mid-2015. This graph shows how the value of a $10,000 investment changed between 2005 and mid-2015.

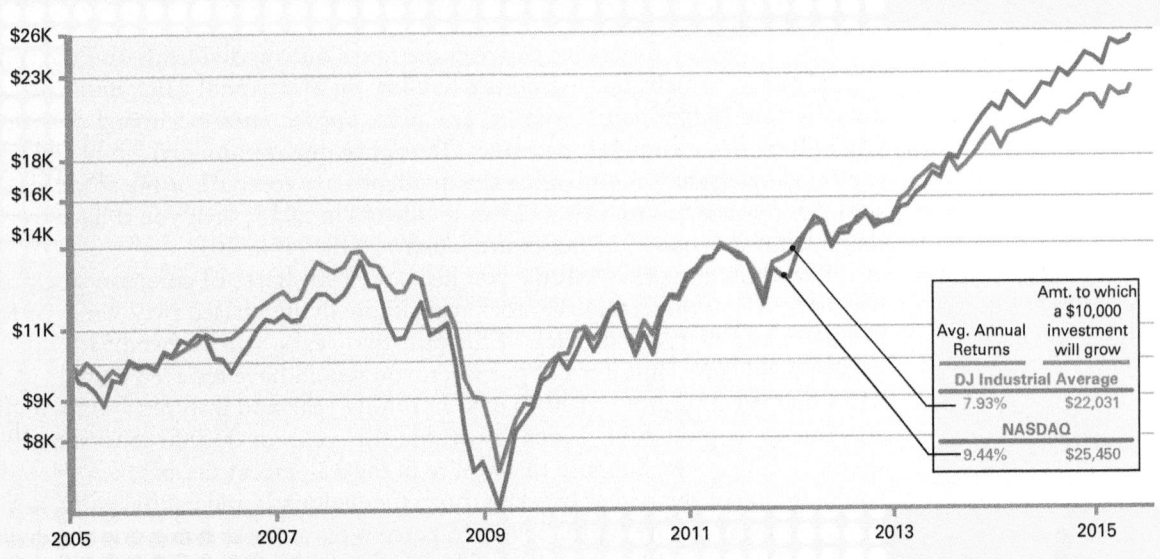

	Avg. Annual Returns	Amt. to which a $10,000 investment will grow
DJ Industrial Average		
	7.93%	$22,031
NASDAQ		
	9.44%	$25,450

Issuers of Common Stock

Shares of common stock can be issued by any corporation in any line of business. All corporations have stockholders, but not all of them have publicly traded shares. The stocks of interest to us in this book are the so-called *publicly traded issues*—the shares that are readily available to the general public and that are bought and sold in the open market. Aside from the initial distribution of common stock when the corporation is formed, subsequent sales of additional shares may be made through a procedure known as a *public offering*. In a public offering, the corporation, working with its underwriter, simply offers the investing public a certain number of shares of its stock at a certain price. When issued, the new shares are commingled with the outstanding shares (assuming they're all the same class of stock), and the net result will be an increase in the number of shares outstanding.

Voting Rights

The holders of common stock normally receive *voting rights*, which means that for each share of stock held, they receive one vote. In some cases, common stock may be designated as nonvoting at the time of issue, but this is the exception rather than the rule. Although different voting systems exist, small stockholders need not concern themselves with them because, regardless of the system used, their chances of affecting corporate control with their votes are quite slim.

Corporations have annual stockholders' meetings, at which time new directors are elected and special issues are voted on. Because most small stockholders can't attend these meetings, they can use a proxy to assign their votes to another person, who will vote for them. A proxy is a written statement assigning voting rights to another party.

Basic Tax Considerations

Common stocks provide income in the form of dividends, usually paid quarterly, and/or capital gains, which occur when the price of the stock goes up over time. From a tax *rate* perspective, it really makes no difference whether the investment return comes in the form of dividends or long-term capital gains—in 2015, they're both taxed at 15 or 20 percent, or less (it's 0 percent for those filers in the 10 percent and 15 percent tax brackets).

There's one key difference between the taxes due on dividends and those due on capital gains: namely, there is no tax liability on any capital gains until the stock is actually sold (*paper gains*—that is, any price appreciation occurring on stock that you still own—accumulate tax free). Taxes are due on any dividends and realized capital gains in the year in which the dividends are received or the stock is actually sold. So if you received, say, $125 in dividends in 2015, then you'd have to include that income on your 2015 tax return when you filed it in 2016.

Here's how it works: Assume you just sold 100 shares of common stock for $50 per share. Also assume that the stock was originally purchased two years ago for $20 per share and that, during each of the past two years, you received $1.25 per share in cash dividends. Thus, for tax purposes, you would have received cash dividends of $125 (i.e., $1.25/share × 100 shares) *both* this year and last, plus you would have generated a capital gain, which is taxable this year, of $3,000 ($50/share − $20/share) × 100 shares. Suppose that you're in the 33 percent tax bracket. Even though you're in one of the higher brackets, both the dividends and capital gains earned on this investment qualify for the lower 15 percent tax rate. Therefore, on the dividends, you'll pay taxes of $125 × 0.15 = $18.75 (for each of the past two years), and on the capital gains, you'll owe $3,000 × 0.15 = $450 (for this year only). Therefore, your tax liability will be $18.75 (for the dividends last year), plus $468.75 (for the dividends and capital gains this year). Bottom line: out of the $3,250 you earned on this investment over the past two years, you keep $2,762.50 after taxes.

12–2b Dividends

Corporations pay dividends to their common stockholders in the form of cash and/or additional stock. *Cash dividends* are the most common. Cash dividends are normally distributed quarterly in an amount determined by the firm's board of directors. For example, if the directors declared a quarterly cash dividend of 50 cents a share and if you owned 200 shares of stock, then you'd receive a check for $100.

A popular way of assessing the amount of dividends received is to measure the stock's dividend yield. Dividend yield is a measure of common stock dividends on a relative (percentage) basis—that is, the dollar amount of dividends received is compared to the market price of the stock. As such, dividend yield measures the rate of current income being earned on the investment. It's computed as follows:

$$\text{Dividend Yield} = \frac{\text{Annual Dividend Received per Share}}{\text{Market Price per Share of Stock}}$$

For example, a company that pays $2 per share in annual dividends and whose stock is trading at $50 a share will have a dividend yield of 4 percent ($2/$50 = 0.04). Dividend yield is widely used by income-oriented investors looking for (reasonably priced) stocks with a long and sustained record of regularly paying higher-than-average dividends.

Occasionally, the directors may declare a stock dividend as a supplement to or in place of cash dividends. Stock dividends are paid in the form of additional shares of stock. That is, rather than receiving cash, shareholders receive additional shares of the company's stock—say, 1/10 of a share of new stock for each share owned (as in a *10 percent stock dividend*). For example, if you owned 100 shares of stock in a company that declared a 10 percent stock dividend, you'd receive 10 new shares of stock. Unfortunately, you'll be no better off after the stock dividend than you were before. That's because the total market value of the shares owned would be (roughly) the same after the stock dividend as before. This is because the price of the stock usually falls in direct proportion to the size of a stock dividend. Thus, in this example, a drop in price will bring the total market value of 110 shares (after the stock dividend) to about the same as the total market value of the 100 shares that existed before the dividend.

12-2c Some Key Measures of Performance

Seasoned investors use a variety of financial ratios and measures when making common stock investment decisions. Fortunately, most of the widely followed ratios can be found in published reports—like those produced by Morningstar or Standard & Poor's (see Exhibit 11.6 in Chapter 11 for an example of an S&P stock report)—so you don't have to compute them yourself. Even so, if you're thinking about buying a stock or already have some stocks, there are a few measures of performance you'll want to keep track of: dividend yield (mentioned earlier), book value (or book value per share), net profit margin, return on equity, earnings per share, price/earnings ratio, and beta.

Book Value

book value
The amount of stockholders' equity in a firm; determined by subtracting the company's liabilities and preferred stock from its assets.

The amount of stockholders' equity in a firm is measured by book value. This accounting measure is found by subtracting the firm's liabilities and preferred stock value from the value of its assets. Book value indicates the net amount of stockholder funds used to finance the firm. For instance, assume that our example company (CTA) had assets of $8 million, liabilities of $2 million, and preferred stock valued at $1 million. The book value of the firm's common stock would be $5 million ($8 million − $2 million − $1 million). If the book value is divided by the number of shares outstanding, the result is *book value per share*. So if CTA had 100,000 shares of common stock outstanding, then its book value per share would be $50 ($5,000,000/100,000 shares). Because it usually reflects attractive growth, you'd like to see book value per share steadily increasing over time. Also, look for stocks whose market prices are comfortably above their book values.

Net Profit Margin

net profit margin
A key measure of profitability that relates a firm's net profits to its sales; shows the rate of return the company is earning on its sales.

As a yardstick of profitability, net profit margin is one of the most widely followed measures of corporate performance. Measured as a firm's net profit divided by its sales, this ratio indicates how well the company translates sales into profits. It also captures how well the company manages its cost structure. The higher the net profit margin, the more money the company earns. Look for a relatively stable—or, even better, an increasing—net profit margin.

Return on Equity

return on equity (ROE)
A measure that captures the firm's overall profitability; it is important because of its impact on the firm's growth, profits, and dividends.

Another important and widely-followed measure, return on equity (ROE), reflects the firm's overall profitability from the equityholders' perspective. Measured as net income divided by shareholders' equity, this captures how effectively the firm manages its assets, operations, and capital structure. ROE is important because it is significantly related to the profits, growth, and dividends of the firm. So long as a firm is not borrowing too much money, the better the ROE and the better the company's financial and competitive positions. Look for a stable or increasing ROE. Watch out for a falling ROE because that could spell trouble.

Earnings per Share

earnings per share (EPS)
The dollar return earned by each share of common stock; calculated by dividing all earnings remaining after paying preferred dividends by the number of common shares outstanding.

With stocks, the firm's annual earnings are usually measured and reported in terms of earnings per share (EPS). EPS translates total corporate profits into profits on a per-share basis and provides a convenient measure of the amount of earnings available to stockholders. EPS is found by using this simple formula:

$$\text{EPS} = \frac{\text{Net Profit After Taxes} - \text{Preferred Dividends Paid}}{\text{Number of Shares of Common Stock Outstanding}}$$

For example, if CTA reported a net profit of $600,000, paid $100,000 in dividends to preferred stockholders, and had 100,000 shares of common outstanding, then it would have an EPS of $5.00 [($600,000 − $100,000)/100,000]. Note that preferred dividends are *subtracted* from profits because they must be paid before any monies can be distributed to common stockholders. Stockholders follow EPS closely because it represents the amount that the firm has earned on behalf of each outstanding share of common stock. Here, too, look for steady growth in EPS.

> ### You Can Do It Now
>
> #### *What's the Market P/E Ratio Telling You?*
>
> Nobel Prize–winning Professor Robert Shiller came up with the Shiller P/E ratio, which is based on average inflation-adjusted price multiples over ten-year intervals. Many investors use it to get a sense of whether the overall stock market is properly valued. You can check out the current Shiller P/E ratio vs. historical averages for the U.S. and several other major stock markets at the interesting Research Affiliates site: https://www.researchaffiliates.com/AssetAllocation/Pages/Equities.aspx. You can do it now.

Price/Earnings Ratio

price/earnings (P/E) ratio
A measure of investors' confidence in a given security or the overall market; calculated by dividing market price per share by EPS.

When the prevailing market price of a share of common stock is divided by the annual EPS, the result is the price/earnings (P/E) ratio, which is viewed as an indication of investor confidence and expectations. The higher the P/E multiple, the more confidence that investors are presumed to have in a given security. In the case of CTA, whose shares are currently selling for $60, the P/E ratio is 12 ($60 per share/$5.00 per share). This means that CTA stock is selling for 12 times its earnings. P/E ratios are important to investors because they reveal how aggressively the stock is being priced in the market. Watch out for very high P/Es—that is, P/Es that are way out of line with the market—because that could indicate the stock is overpriced. P/E ratios tend to move with the market: when the market is soft, a stock's P/E will be lower; when the market heats up, the stock's P/E will typically rise. For perspective, the long-term average P/E ratio for the S&P 500 index is about 15.

Beta

beta
An index of the price volatility for a share of common stock; a reflection of how the stock price responds to overall market forces.

A stock's beta is an indication of its *price volatility;* it shows how responsive the stock is to changes in the overall stock market. Published betas are available from most brokerage firms and investment services. The market (often measured by the S&P index of 500 stocks) is used as a benchmark of performance, which has a beta of 1.0. From there, everything is relative: low-beta stocks—those with betas of less than 1.0—have low price volatility (their prices are relatively stable), whereas high-beta stocks—those with betas of more than 1.0—are considered to be highly volatile. In short, the higher a stock's beta, the riskier the stock. Most stock betas are positive, which means the stocks move in the same general direction as the market.

Beta is an *index* of relative price performance. If CTA has a beta of, say, 0.8, then it should rise (or fall) only 80 percent as much as the market. Thus, if the market goes up by 10 percent, then CTA should go up only 8 percent (10 percent × 0.8). In contrast, if the stock had a beta of 1.8, then it would go up or down 1.8 times as fast—the price of the stock would rise higher and fall harder than the general market. Other things being equal, if you're looking for a relatively conservative investment, then you should stick with low-beta stocks; on the other hand, if it's potentially high capital gains and price volatility you're after, go with high-beta securities.

12–2d Types of Common Stock

Common stocks are often classified on the basis of their dividends or their rate of growth in EPS. Some popular types of common stock are blue-chip, growth, tech stocks, income, speculative, cyclical, defensive, large-cap, mid-cap, and small-cap stocks.

Blue-Chip Stocks

blue-chip stock
A stock generally issued by companies expected to provide an uninterrupted stream of dividends and good long-term growth prospects.

Blue-chip stocks are the cream of the common stock crop; these stocks are unsurpassed in quality and have a long and stable record of earnings and dividends. They're issued by large, well-established firms that have impeccable financial credentials—firms such as Apple, Nike, Wal-Mart, IBM, Microsoft, Merck, and ExxonMobil. These companies hold important, if not leading, positions in their industries, and they often determine the standards by which other firms are measured. Blue chips are particularly attractive to investors who seek high-quality investments offering decent dividend yields and respectable growth potential. Blue-chip stocks are popular with a large segment of the investing public and, as a result, are often relatively high priced, especially when the market is unsettled and investors become more quality-conscious.

Growth Stocks

growth stock
A stock whose earnings and market price have increased over time at a rate that is well above average.

Stocks that have experienced—and are expected to continue experiencing—consistently high rates of growth in operations and earnings are known as **growth stocks**. A good growth stock might exhibit a *sustained* rate of growth in earnings of 15 percent–20 percent (or more) over a period when common stocks are averaging only 6 percent–8 percent. In mid-2015, prime examples of large capitalization growth stocks include Apple, SAP, Intel, and Wal-Mart. Internet sites like Seeking Alpha (**http://seekingalpha.com**) try to predict the next growth stocks. For example, some of their mid-2015 projections of stocks that could prove to be the next crop of big growth stocks include: Monsanto, Gilead Sciences, Ensco, Michael Kors, and Matthews International. These stocks often pay little or nothing in dividends because the firms' rapid growth potential require them to retain and reinvest most, if not all, of their earnings. The high growth expectations for such stocks usually cause them to sell at relatively high P/E ratios, and they typically have betas in excess of 1.0. Because of their potential for dramatic price appreciation, they appeal mostly to investors who are seeking capital gains rather than dividend income.

Tech Stocks

tech stock
A stock from the technology sector of the market.

Tech stocks represent the technology sector of the market and include all those companies that produce or provide technology-based products and services such as computers, semiconductors, data storage devices, computer software and hardware, peripherals, Internet services, content providers, networking, and wireless communications. Thousands of companies fall into the tech stock category, including everything from very small firms providing some service on the Internet to huge multinational companies. These stocks often fall into either the *growth stock* category (described earlier) or the *speculative stock* class (discussed next), although some of them are legitimate *blue chips*. Tech stocks may offer the potential for attractive, even phenomenal, returns, but they also involve considerable risk and so are probably most suitable for investors with high tolerance for such risk. Included in the tech stock category are some big names—Microsoft, Cisco, Apple, and Google—as well as many not-so-big names, such as Infosonics, Freescale Semiconductor, and Amkor Technology.

Income Stocks versus Speculative Stocks

income stock
A stock whose primary appeal is the higher dividends it pays out; offers dividend payments that can be expected to increase over time.

Stocks whose appeal is based primarily on the dividends they pay are known as **income stocks**. They have a fairly stable stream of earnings, a large portion of which is

speculative stock
Stock that is purchased on little more than the hope that its price per share will increase.

cyclical stock
Stock whose price movements tend to parallel the various stages of the business cycle.

defensive stock
Stock whose price movements are usually *contrary* to movements in the business cycle.

Financial Fact or Fantasy?

Income stocks have relatively high dividend yields and, as such, appeal to individuals who seek a high level of current income. **Fact:** Income shares are have a long and sustained record of regularly paying a much higher than average level of dividends. Because of this, they are highly sought after by investors seeking a safe and steady source of current income.

distributed in the form of dividends. Income shares have relatively high dividend yields and thus are ideally suited for investors seeking a relatively safe and high level of current income from their investment capital. An added (and often overlooked) feature of these stocks is that, unlike bonds and preferred stock, holders of income stock can expect *the amount of dividends paid to increase over time*. Examples of income stocks include Philip Morris International, Johnson & Johnson, PepsiCo, and Proctor & Gamble. Reflecting their low risk, these stocks commonly have betas of less than 1.0.

Rather than basing their investment decisions on a proven record of earnings, investors in speculative stocks gamble that some new information, discovery, or production technique will favorably affect the firm's growth and inflate its stock price. For example, a company whose stock is considered speculative may recently have discovered a new drug or located a valuable resource, such as oil. They are also often small, not well-known firms in industries that could turn around. The value of speculative stocks and their P/E ratios tend to fluctuate widely as additional information about the firm's future is received. Betas for speculative stocks are nearly always well in excess of 1.0. Investors in speculative stocks should be prepared to experience losses as well as gains, since *these are high-risk securities*. In mid-2015, they include companies like Bona Film Group, Destination Maternity, Global Power Equipment Group, and Iridium Communications.

Cyclical and Defensive Stocks

Stocks whose price movements tend to follow the business cycle are called cyclical stocks. This means that when the economy is in an expansionary stage, the prices of cyclical stocks tend to increase; during a contractionary stage (recession), they decline. Most cyclical stocks are found in the basic industries—automobiles, steel, and lumber, for example—which are generally sensitive to changes in economic activity. Investors try to purchase cyclical stocks just before an expansionary phase and to sell just before the contraction occurs. Because they tend to move with the market, these stocks always have positive betas. Alcoa, eBay, Kohl's, Goodyear Tire & Rubber, Dow Chemical, and Ford Motor are all examples of cyclical stocks.

The prices and returns from defensive stocks, unlike those of cyclical stocks, are expected to remain stable during periods of contraction in business activity. For this reason, they're often called *countercyclical*. The shares of consumer goods companies, certain public utilities, and gold mining companies are good examples of defensive stocks. Because they're basically income stocks, their earnings and dividends tend to keep their market prices up during periods of economic decline. Betas on these stocks are typically quite low. Coca-Cola, McDonald's, Wal-Mart, Procter & Gamble, and Merck are all examples of defensive stocks.

Large-Caps, Mid-Caps, and Small-Caps

In the stock market, a stock's size is based on its market value—or, more commonly, on what's known as its *market capitalization* or *market cap*. A stock's market cap is found by multiplying its market price by the number of shares outstanding. Generally speaking, the market can be broken into three major segments, as measured by a stock's market "cap":

> Large-cap—Market caps of more than $10 billion
> Mid-cap—Market caps of $2 to $10 billion
> Small-cap—Stocks with market caps of less than $2 billion

In addition to these three segments, another is reserved for the *really small* stocks, known as *micro-caps*. Many of these stocks have market capitalizations of well below $250 million (some as low as $50 million); they should be purchased only by investors who fully understand the risks involved and can tolerate such risk exposure.

Of the three major categories, the large-cap stocks are the real biggies—the Apples, Wal-Marts, GEs, and Microsofts of the world—and many are considered to be blue-chip stocks. Although there are far fewer large-cap stocks than any of the other market cap categories, these companies account for about 80 percent–90 percent of the total market value of all U.S. equity markets. Just because they're big, however, doesn't mean they're better. Indeed, both the small- and mid-cap segments of the market tend to hold their own with, or even outperform, large stocks over time.

Mid-cap stocks offer investors some attractive return opportunities. They provide much of the sizzle of small-stock returns, but without all the price volatility. At the same time, because these are fairly good-sized companies and many have been around for a long time, they offer some of the safety of the big, established stocks. Among the ranks of the mid-caps are Accuity, Advance Auto Parts, Avery Dennison, Oshkosh, and USG. These securities offer a nice alternative to large cap stocks without all the drawbacks and uncertainties of small-caps, although they're probably most appropriate for investors who are willing to tolerate a bit more risk and price volatility.

Some investors consider small companies to be in a class by themselves. They believe these firms hold especially attractive return opportunities, and in many cases, this has turned out to be true. Known as small-cap stocks, these companies often have annual revenues of less than $250 million; because of their size, spurts of growth can dramatically affect their earnings and stock prices. Immunogen, Hecla Mining, Vaalco Energy, Western Refining, and Zynga are just a few of the interesting small-cap stocks out there. Although some small-caps are solid companies with equally solid financials, that's definitely not the case with most of them! Because many of these companies are so small, they don't have a lot of stock outstanding and their shares aren't widely traded. What's more, small-company stocks have a tendency to be "here today and gone tomorrow." These stocks may hold the potential for high returns, but investors should also be aware of the high risk exposure associated with many of them.

12–2e Market Globalization and Foreign Stocks

Besides investing in many of the different types of stocks already mentioned, a growing number of American investors are turning to foreign markets as a way to earn attractive returns. Ironically, as our world is becoming smaller, our universe of investment opportunities is growing by leaps and bounds! Consider, for example, that in 1970, the U.S. stock market accounted for fully *two-thirds of the world market*. In essence, our stock market was twice as big as the rest of the world's stock markets *combined*. That's no longer true; the U.S. share of the world equity market is now more like 36 percent.

Foreign stocks can offer investors not only attractive return opportunities but also attractive geographic diversification opportunities. Among the various ways of investing in foreign shares, three stand out: mutual funds, exchange-traded funds, and

large-cap stock
A stock with a total market value of equity of more than $10 billion.

mid-cap stock
A stock whose total market value falls somewhere between $2 billion and $10 billion.

small-cap stock
A stock with a total market value of equity of less than $2 billion.

American Depositary Receipts (ADRs). Without a doubt, the best and easiest way to invest in foreign markets is through *international mutual funds or exchange-traded funds*—we'll discuss such funds in Chapter 13. An alternative to mutual funds is to buy ADRs, which are *denominated in dollars and are traded directly on U.S. markets* (such as the NYSE). They're just like common stock, except that each ADR represents a stated number of shares in a specific foreign company. The shares of more than 1,000 companies from some 50 foreign countries are traded on U.S. exchanges as ADRs; these companies include Honda Motor Co., Sony, Nestlé, Nokia, Ericsson, Tata Motors, and Vodafone, to mention just a few. ADRs are a great way to invest in foreign stocks because their prices are quoted in dollars, not in British pounds, Swiss francs, or euros. What's more, all dividends are paid in dollars.

12–2f Investing in Common Stock

There are three basic reasons for investing in common stock: (1) to use the stock as a warehouse of value, (2) to accumulate capital, and (3) to provide a source of income. Some investors are more concerned about storage of value than others, and they put safety of principal first in their stock selection process. These investors are more quality-conscious and tend to gravitate toward blue chips and other low-risk securities. Accumulation of capital generally is an important goal to individuals with long-term investment horizons. These investors use the capital gains and dividends that stocks provide to build up their wealth. Some use growth stocks for such purposes; others do it with income shares; still others use a little of both. Finally, some people use stocks as a source of income; to them, a dependable flow of dividends is essential. High-yielding, good-quality income shares are usually their preferred investment vehicle.

Advantages and Disadvantages of Stock Ownership

Ownership of common stock has both advantages and disadvantages. Its advantages are threefold. First, the potential returns, in the form of both dividend income and price appreciation, can be substantial. Second, many stocks are actively traded and so are a highly liquid form of investment, which means that they can be bought and sold quickly without having to take a significant price concession. Finally, they involve no direct management (or unusual management problems), and market/company information is usually widely published and readily available.

The disadvantages of owning common stock include risk, the problem of timing purchases and sales, and the uncertainty of dividends. Although potential common stock returns may be high, the risk and uncertainty associated with the actual receipt of that return is also great. Even though the careful selection of stocks may reduce the amount of risk to which the investor is exposed, a significant risk–return trade-off still exists. When it comes to common stock, not even dividends are guaranteed. If things turn bad, the company can always shut off the stream of dividends and suffer no legal ramifications. Finally, there's the timing of purchases and sales. Human nature being what it is, we don't always do it right. Unfortunately, all too many investors purchase a stock, hold it for a period of time during which the price drops, and then sell it below the original purchase price—that is, at a loss. The proper strategy, of course, is to buy low and sell high; but the problem of predicting price movements makes it difficult to implement such a plan.

12–2g Making the Investment Decision

The first step in investing is to know where to put your money; the second is to know when to make your moves. The first question basically involves matching your risk and return objectives with the available investment vehicles. *A stock (or any other investment vehicle) should be considered a viable investment candidate only as long as it looks likely to generate a sufficiently attractive rate of return* and, importantly, one that fully compensates for the risks you take. Thus, if you're considering the purchase of a stock, you should expect to earn more than what you can get from T-bills or high-grade corporate bonds. This is because stocks are riskier than bills or bonds and you consequently deserve a higher return from stocks. Indeed, if you can't get enough expected return from the security to offset the risk, then you shouldn't invest in the stock!

Putting a Value on Stock

Every investor faces one of the most difficult questions in the field of investments: *How much should you be willing to pay for a stock?* To answer this question, you must place a value on the stock. As noted earlier in this chapter, we know that the value of a stock depends on its expected stream of future earnings, expected future market price appreciation, and the associated risk. Once you have a handle on the expected stream of future earnings and price appreciation, you can use that information to find the *expected rate of return on the investment*. If the expected return from the investment exceeds your minimum required rate of return, then you should make the investment. If the return that you expect from the investment is less than your required rate of return, then you should not buy the stock because it's currently "overpriced," and thus you won't be able to earn your required rate of return.

FINANCIAL PLANNING TIPS

Recognize These Common Investing Myths

Here are some myths that you should be aware of when investing:

• **During volatile markets, it makes sense to sell your stocks and wait for calmer conditions.** While it sounds so reasonable, investors who remain in the market outperform those who move in and out to manage their market exposure. When trading in and out, you pay more commissions and, more importantly, you tend to miss the upturns in the market that can make you whole—or even more than whole—again.

• **Gold is a good addition to any portfolio.** It's true that gold can be a good asset to add because its returns tend to move opposite those of stocks, which is good for diversification. However, few advisors would recommend allocating more than 5 or 10 percent of a portfolio to gold in most cases. There have been long periods when gold generated poor returns.

• **The S&P 500 is the best place for long-term stock investors.** The large stocks in the S&P 500 do not always pay the best returns. While riskier, small cap and value stocks tend to outperform the S&P 500 over the long haul.

• **Far less should be invested in stocks during retirement.** While it may make sense to reduce equity exposure as retirement *approaches*, there is evidence that gradually increasing equity exposure *during retirement* may best manage the risk of running out of money.

So, how do you go about finding a stock that's right for you? The answer is by doing a little digging and crunching a few numbers. Here's what you should do. First, find a company you like and then take a look at how it has performed *over the past three to five years*. Find out what kind of growth in sales it has experienced, if it has a strong ROE and has been able to maintain or improve its profit margin, and how much it has been paying out to stockholders in the form of dividends. This kind of information is readily available in publications like *Value Line Investment Survey* and *S&P Stock Reports* or from a number of Internet sites. The idea is to find stocks that are financially strong, have done well in the past, and continue to hold prominent positions in a given industry or market segment. But looking at the past is only the beginning; what's really important to stock valuation is the *future!*

So let's turn our attention to the expected future performance of a stock. The idea is to assess the *outlook* for the stock, thereby *gaining some insight into the benefits to be derived from investing in it.* The key benefits are future dividends and share price behavior. It usually doesn't make much sense to go out more than two

© ENDERMASALI / SHUTTERSTOCK.COM

or three years—five, at the most—because the accuracy of most forecasts begins to deteriorate rapidly after that. Thus, using a three-year investment horizon, you'd want to forecast annual dividends per share for each of the next three years *plus* the future price of the stock at the end of the three-year holding period. You can try to generate these forecasts yourself, or you can check such publications as *Value Line Investment Survey* to obtain projections (*Value Line* projects dividends and share prices three to five years into the future). After projecting dividends and share price, you can use the approximate expected yield equation or a handheld calculator to determine the expected return from the investment as discussed earlier in this chapter.

Consider the example of Apple, some data for which was provided in Exhibit 11.6. The calculations in the example below indicate that if Apple's stock performance lives up to the projections made by *Value Line Investment Survey* at the time this was written, it should provide a return between 13 and 14 percent. In today's market, that would be an attractive return and one that likely *exceeds* our risk-adjusted required rate of return (which probably should be around 8 or 9 percent under normal market conditions). If that's the case, then this should be considered a viable investment candidate. According to our standards, the stock is currently undervalued and thus should be seriously considered as a possible addition to our portfolio.

EXAMPLE: Calculating the Expected Return on Apple's Stock

To see how this can be done, consider the common shares of Apple, Inc., which provides hardware and software that includes Mac computers, iPod digital media players, iPhone smart phones, and iPad tablets. According to several financial reporting services, the company has strong financials; its sales have been growing at a bit more than 40 percent per year for the past five years, its recent net profit margin is almost 22 percent, and its ROE is around 28 percent. Thus, historically, the company has performed astoundingly well and is definitely a market leader in its field. Indeed, it's currently the largest company in the world! In April 2015, the stock was trading at around $127 a share and was expected to pay annual dividends of about $1.94 a share in 2015. Around that time Value Line was projecting dividends to grow to $2.10 per share the next year (2016), and to an average of about $4 a share between 2018 and 2020. It was also estimating that the price of the stock could rise to an average of $177.50 per share over that period. For simplicity, we'll look at these forecasts as applying to a planned holding period of about three years and average the data accordingly.

Because the approximate expected yield equation shown here uses "average annual current income" as one of the inputs, we use a rough average of our projected dividends ($2.68 a share) as a proxy for average annual dividends. Because this stock was trading at $127 a share and had a projected average future price of $177.50 per share, we can find the expected return (for our three-year investment horizon) as follows:

$$\text{Approximate Yield (Expected Return)} = \frac{\$2.68 + \left[\dfrac{\$177.50 - \$127.00}{3} \right]}{\left[\dfrac{\$177.50 + \$127.00}{2} \right]}$$

$$= \frac{\$2.68 + \$16.83}{\$152.25} = \underline{\underline{12.81\%}}$$

Timing Your Investments

Once you find a stock that you think will give you the kind of return that you're looking for, then you're ready to deal with the matter of timing your investments. So long as the prospects for the market and the economy are positive, the time may be right to invest in stocks. On the other hand, sometimes investing in stocks makes no sense at all—in particular, *don't* invest in stocks under either of the following conditions:

- You believe *strongly* that the market is headed down in the short run. If you're confident the market's in for a big fall (or will continue to fall, if it's already doing so), then wait until the market drops and buy the stock when it's cheaper.

Calculator

INPUTS	FUNCTIONS
3	N
−127.00	PV
2.68	PMT
177.50	FV
	CPT
	I/Y
	SOLUTION
	13.70

See Appendix E for details.

Calculator Keystrokes. You can use a handheld financial calculator—set in the *annual compounding mode*—to find the expected return on a stock that you purchase at $127.00 per share, hold for three years (during which time you receive average annual dividends of $2.68 per share), and then sell at an average of $177.50 per share. Simply use the keystrokes shown in the margin, where:

N = number of *years* you hold the stock
PV = the price you pay for the stock (entered as a *negative* value)
PMT = average amount of dividends received each *year*
FV = the price you expect to receive when you sell the stock (in three years)

The expected return (of 13.70 percent) is a bit higher here, but even so, it's still in the ballpark with the return (of 12.81 percent) that we computed using the approximate expected yield method. Of course, one would expect an approximation to be somewhat less precise, but it is nonetheless informative.

- You feel uncomfortable with the general tone of the market—it lacks direction, or there's way too much price volatility to suit you. Once again, wait for the market to settle down before buying stocks.

Research shows that most investors are better off investing steadily than trying to time the market. It is exceedingly difficult to buy consistently at market bottoms and sell at market tops. Many investors pulled out of the stocks during the financial crisis of 2008–2009. Yet as of mid-2015, the S&P 500 index had more than tripled since the worst of the stock market crisis in 2009. Consider the example of an investor who put $10,000 into the S&P 500 at the bottom of the market in 2009 and left

FINANCIAL PLANNING TIPS

Equity Analysts Are Too Optimistic—Invest with Caution!

Researchers at McKinsey & Company did a long-term study of the accuracy of equity analysts' forecasts. They find strong evidence that analysts are usually overly optimistic, far too slow to revise their forecasts in light of new economic developments, and likely to make even less accurate forecasts when the economy's growth is falling. This is particularly troubling given the numerous new rules and regulations developed over the last 10 years that are designed to improve the quality of analysts' forecasts, enhance investor confidence in these forecasts, and minimize conflicts of interest that could affect the forecasting process.

Consider analysts' earnings forecasts for the firms in the S&P 500 index. Analysts have been consistently too optimistic over the past 25 years. While their average earnings growth rate forecast was between 10 percent and 12 percent a year, actual earnings growth averaged only

about 6 percent. Indeed, during this time period, actual earnings growth exceed forecasts in only two cases, both of which were during the earnings recovery after a recession. Amazingly, analysts' average forecasts have been almost 100 percent too high!

So what's an investor to do? First, consider that long-term steady-state growth for the stock market as a whole is unlikely to differ much from growth in overall gross domestic product (GDP), which has historically been between 3 percent and 4 percent on average in nominal terms in the United States. Only firms with significant non-U.S. business should be able to sustain growth rates much beyond that. Second, recognize that overly optimistic analyst forecasts imply that analysts tend to overvalue stocks. Consequently, it makes sense to view analysts' forecasts as overly optimistic, particularly during an economic downturn, and to invest accordingly.

Source: Adapted from Marc Goedhart, Rishi Raj, and Abhishek Saxena, "Equity Analysts: Still Too Bullish," https://www.mckinseyquarterly.com/Equity_analysts_Still_too_bullish_2565, accessed August 2015. (Note that to gain full online access to the article, you'll have to register on the Internet site, which is free.)

it there untouched until the middle of 2015. The initial investment would have grown to about $34,000, which is an annualized return of about 22 percent. Indeed, even those who invested in the S&P 500 at the beginning of 2008 and early in 2009 had recouped their losses by the end of 2009. There's a high potential cost of being out of the equity market during its best-performing times. This is because pulling money out of the market exposes you to the significant risk that you'll miss the months of good returns that could help you recoup prior losses.

Be Sure to Plow Back Your Earnings

dividend reinvestment plan (DRP)
A program whereby stockholders can choose to take their cash dividends in the form of more shares of the company's stock.

Unless you're living off the income, the basic investment objective with stocks is the same as it is with any other security: to earn an attractive, fully compounded rate of return. This requires regular reinvestment of dividend income. And there's no better way to accomplish such reinvestment than through a dividend reinvestment plan (DRP). The investment philosophy at work here is this: if the company is good enough to invest in, then it's good enough to reinvest in. In a DRP, shareholders can sign up to have their cash dividends automatically reinvested in additional shares of the company's common stock—in essence, it's like taking your cash dividends in the form of more shares of common stock. Such an approach can have a tremendous impact on your investment position over time, as seen in Exhibit 12.4.

Today, many companies have DRPs, and each one gives investors a convenient and inexpensive way to accumulate capital. Stocks in most DRPs are acquired free of any brokerage commissions, and most plans allow *partial participation*. That is, rather than committing all of their cash dividends to these plans, participants may

Financial Fact or Fantasy?

Putting your money into stocks that offer dividend reinvestment plans is a great way of building up your investment capital. **Fact:** In a dividend reinvestment plan, you receive additional shares of stock, rather than cash every time the company pays a dividend. It's a great way to reap the benefits of compounding and watch your money grow over time.

EXHIBIT 12.4   Cash or Reinvested Dividends

Participating in a dividend reinvestment plan is a simple yet highly effective way of building up capital over time. Over the long haul, it can prove to be a great way of earning a fully compounded rate of return on your money.

Situation: Buy 100 shares of stock at $25 a share (total investment $2,500); stock currently pays $1 a share in annual dividends. Price of the stock increases at 8 percent per year; dividends grow at 5 percent per year.

Investment Period	Number of Shares Held	Market Value of Stock Holdings	Total Cash Dividends Received
Take Dividends in Cash			
5 years	100	$3,672	$552
10 years	100	$5,397	$1,258
15 years	100	$7,930	$2,158
20 years	100	$11,652	$3,307
Participate in a DRP			
5 years	115.59	$4,245	$0
10 years	135.66	$7,322	$0
15 years	155.92	$12,364	$0
20 years	176.00	$20,508	$0

specify a portion of their shares for dividend reinvestment and receive cash dividends on the rest. Some plans even sell their shares in their programs at discounts of 3 percent to 5 percent. Most plans also credit fractional shares to the investors' accounts. There's a catch, however: even though these dividends take the form of additional shares of stock, *reinvested dividends are taxable in the year they're received, just as if they had been received in cash.*

TEST YOURSELF

12-6   From a tax perspective, would it make any difference to an investor whether the return on a stock took the form of dividends or capital gains? Explain.

12-7   What's the difference between a *cash* dividend and a *stock* dividend? Which would you rather receive?

12-8   Define and briefly discuss each of these common stock measures: (a) book value, (b) ROE, (c) EPS, (d) P/E ratio, and (e) beta.

12-9   Briefly discuss some of the different types of common stock. Which types would be most appealing to you, and why?

12-10   Summarize the evidence on the potential cost of being out of the stock market during its best months.

12-11   What are *DRPs*, and how do they fit into a stock investment program?

12–3 INVESTING IN BONDS

LG5, LG6   In contrast to stocks, *bonds are liabilities*—they're publicly traded IOUs where the bondholders are actually *lending money* to the issuer. Bonds are often referred to as *fixed-income securities* because the debt service obligations of the issuer are usually fixed—that is, the issuing organization agrees to pay a *fixed amount of interest periodically and to repay a fixed amount of principal at or before maturity*. In the United States, bonds usually have face values of $1,000 or $5,000 and have maturities of 10 to 30 years or more.

12–3a Why Invest in Bonds?

Bonds provide investors with two kinds of income: (1) Most provide current income, and (2) they can generate substantial capital gains. The current income, of course, comes from the interest payments received periodically over the life of the issue. Indeed, this regular and predictable source of income is a key factor that draws investors to bonds. But these securities can also produce capital gains, which occur whenever market interest rates fall. A basic rule in the bond market is that *interest rates and bond prices move in opposite directions*: when interest rates rise, bond prices fall; conversely, when interest rates fall, bond prices rise. Thus, it's possible to buy bonds at one price and, if interest rate conditions are right, to sell them sometime later at a higher price. Taken together, the current income and capital gains earned from bonds can lead to competitive investor returns.

Bonds are also a versatile investment outlet. They can be used conservatively by those seeking high current income or aggressively by those actively seeking capital gains. And because of the high quality of many bond issues, they can also be used for the preservation and long-term accumulation of capital. In fact, some investors regularly commit all or a good deal of their investment funds to bonds because of this single attribute.

12–3b Bonds versus Stocks

Although bonds definitely do have their good points—lower risk and attractive levels of current income, along with *desirable diversification properties*. However, they also have a significant downside: their *comparative* returns. The fact is, *relative to stocks*, there's usually a big sacrifice in returns when investing in bonds—which, of course, is the price that you pay for the even bigger reduction in risk! But just because there's a deficit in long-term returns, it doesn't mean that bonds are always the underachievers. Consider, for example, what's happened over the past 20 years in general, and during and since the recent financial crisis of 2007–2009 in particular. Starting in the 1980s, fixed-income securities held their own and continued to do so through the early 1990s, only to fall far behind stocks for the rest of the decade. But then along came a couple of nasty bear markets in stocks (2000–2002 and 2007–2008) and the subsequent stock market recovery in 2009 and beyond. The net results of all this can be seen in Exhibit 12.5, which tracks the comparative returns of stocks (via the S&P 500 index) and bonds (using the BofA Merrill Lynch U.S. Treasuries 15+ year maturity total return index) from 1995 through mid-2015.

Over the roughly 20-year period from 1995 to mid-2015, the S&P 500 overperformed long-term Treasury bonds by 1.53 percent (9.83 percent versus 8.30 percent). The net result was that a $10,000 investment in 1995 would have generated a terminal value in mid-2015 of about $67,429 for stocks, compared with about $50,666 for bonds. Although historically, the long-term performance of stocks typically outstrips that of bonds, there have been times when that just wasn't so. And the margin was particularly small over this time period owing to the effects of the financial crisis.

EXHIBIT 12.5   Comparative Performance of Stocks and Bonds: 1995–mid-2015

This graph shows what happened to $10,000 invested in bonds over the (roughly) 20-year period from January 1995 through mid-2015, versus the same amount invested in stocks. While stocks held a commanding lead through early 2000 and then again in 2003–2006, the bear markets of 2000–2002 and 2008 limited the higher relative performance of stocks. Yet the strong bull market from 2009 to mid-2015 left stocks performing significantly better than bonds for the entire period.

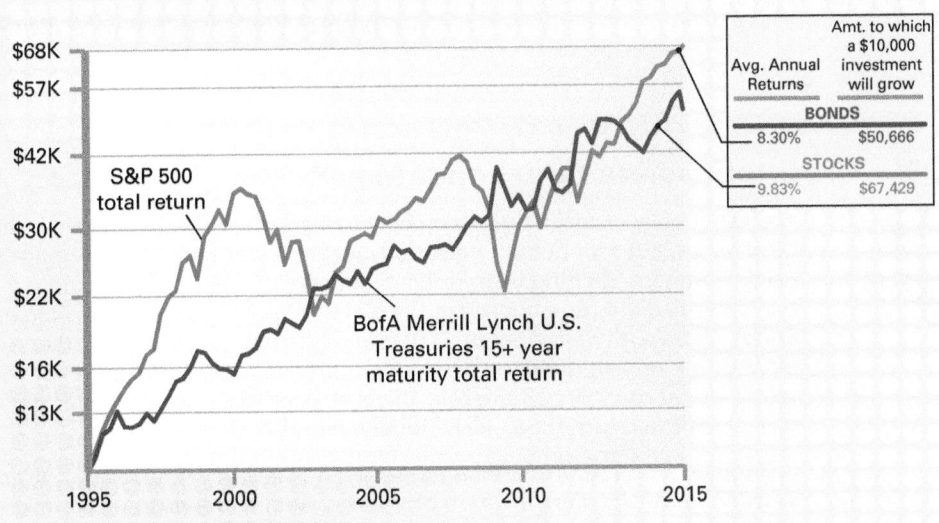

12–3c Basic Issue Characteristics

A bond is a negotiable, long-term debt instrument that carries certain obligations on the part of the issuer. Unlike the holders of common stock, bondholders have no ownership or equity position in the issuing firm or organization. This is so because bonds are debt and thus the bondholders, in a roundabout way, are only lending money to the issuer.

YOU CAN DO IT NOW

How Do Stock and Bond Market Returns Compare This Year?

If you want a broad sense of how stock and bond returns compare so far this year, take a look at the returns on two broad-based exchange-traded funds (ETFs, which we discuss in detail in Chapter 13). Vanguard's Total Stock Market ETF (ticker VTI) seeks to track the overall performance of U.S. stocks traded on the New York Stock Exchange and NASDAQ. And Vanguard's Total Bond Market ETF (ticker BND) seeks to track investment grade U.S. bonds. Take a look at the year-to-date (YTD) returns, which were, for example, 3.61 percent for VTI and 0.78 percent for BND on July 1, 2015. Just go to http://finance.yahoo.com/ and type VTI and then BND into the Quote Lookup box. You can do it now.

---

coupon
Bond feature that defines the annual interest income the issuer will pay the bondholder.

U.S. bonds typically pay interest every six months. The amount of interest paid depends on the coupon, which defines the annual interest that the issuer will pay to the bondholder. For instance, a $1,000 bond with an 8 percent coupon would pay $80 in interest every year ($1,000 : 0.08 = $80), generally in the form of two $40 semiannual payments. The principal amount of a bond, also known as its *par value*, specifies the amount of capital that must be repaid at maturity—there's $1,000 of principal in a $1,000 bond.

Debt securities regularly trade at market prices that differ from their principal (or par) values. This occurs whenever an issue's coupon differs from the prevailing market rate of interest because the price of an issue will change until its yield is compatible with prevailing market yields. For example, such behavior explains why a 7 percent coupon issue will carry a market price of only $825 when the market yield is 9 percent. The drop in price is necessary to raise the yield on this bond from 7 percent to 9 percent. Issues with market values lower than par are known as *discount bonds*

FINANCIAL ROAD SIGN

Intermediate Term Bonds May Be the "Sweet Spot"

You can usually expect longer-term bonds to provide higher yields than shorter-term bonds. But that doesn't necessarily mean longer-term bonds are always the best investment. It's long been common knowledge that, for most individual investors, intermediate-term bonds are the place to be. The reason: *Intermediate-term bonds (those with maturities of 7–10 years) typically deliver about 80 percent or more of the returns obtained from long-term bonds (with maturities of 25–30 years), but at roughly half the risk.* This is an excellent risk–return trade-off: you give up a little return for a much bigger cut in risk.

In addition, bond returns are far more stable than stock returns and they possess *excellent portfolio diversification properties.* Adding bonds to a portfolio will generally—up to a point—have a much greater impact on (lowering) risk than it will on (reducing) returns. Face it: you don't buy bonds for high expected returns (except when you think interest rates are heading down). Rather, you buy them for their current income and the stability they bring to a portfolio.

and carry coupons that are less than those on new issues. In contrast, issues with market values above par are called *premium bonds* and have coupons greater than those currently being offered on new issues.

Types of Issues

In addition to their coupons and maturities, bonds can be differentiated from one another by the type of collateral behind them. In this regard, the issues can be viewed as having either junior or senior standing. *Senior bonds are secured obligations* because they're backed by a legal claim on some specific property of the issuer that acts as *collateral* for the bonds. Such issues include mortgage bonds, which are secured by real estate, and equipment trust certificates, which are backed by certain types of equipment and are popular with railroads and airlines. *Junior bonds*, on the other hand, are backed only with a promise by the issuer to pay interest and principal on a timely basis. There are several classes of *unsecured* bonds, the most popular of which is known as a debenture. Issued as either notes (with maturities of 2 to 10 years) or bonds (maturities of more than 10 years), debentures are totally unsecured in the sense that there's no collateral backing them up—other than the issuer's good name.

Sinking Fund

Another provision that's important to investors is the sinking fund, which describes how a bond will be paid off over time. Not all bonds have these requirements; but for those that do, a sinking fund specifies the annual repayment schedule to be used in paying off the issue and indicates how much principal will be retired each year. Sinking fund requirements generally begin one to five years after the date of issue and continue annually thereafter until all or most of the issue has been paid off. Any amount not repaid by maturity is then retired with a single balloon payment.

Call Feature

Every bond has a call feature, which stipulates whether a bond can be called (i.e., retired) before its regularly scheduled maturity date and, if so, under what conditions. Basically, there are three types of call features:

- A bond can be *freely callable*, which means the issuer can retire the bond prematurely at any time.
- A bond can be *noncallable*, which means the issuer is prohibited from retiring the bond prior to maturity.
- The issue could carry a *deferred call*, which means the issue cannot be called until after a certain length of time has passed from the date of issue. In essence, the issue is not callable during the deferment period and then becomes freely callable thereafter.

Call features are usually used to retire a bond prematurely and replace it with one that carries a lower coupon rate. In this way, the issuer benefits by being able to reduce its annual interest costs. In an attempt to at least partially compensate investors who have their bonds called out from under them, a *call premium* (usually equal to about six months to one year of interest) is tacked onto the par value of the bond and paid to investors, along with the issue's par value, at the time the bond is called. For example, if a company decides to call its 7 percent bonds some 15 years before they mature, then it might pay $1,052.50 for every $1,000 bond outstanding (i.e., a call premium equal to nine months' interest—$70 : 0.75 = $52.50—would be added to the par value of $1,000). Although this might sound like a good deal, it's really not for the investor. The bondholder may indeed get a few extra bucks when the bond is called; but in turn, she loses a source of high current income. For example, the investor may have a 7 percent bond called away at a time when the best she can do in the market is maybe 4 percent or 5 percent.

mortgage bond
A bond secured by a claim on real assets, such as a manufacturing plant.

equipment trust certificate
A bond secured by certain types of equipment, such as railroad cars and airplanes.

debenture
An unsecured bond issued on the general credit of the firm.

sinking fund
A bond provision specifying the annual repayment schedule to be used in paying off the issue.

call feature
Bond feature that allows the issuer to retire the security prior to maturity.

12–3d The Bond Market

One thing that really stands out about the bond market is its size—the U.S. bond market is huge and getting bigger almost daily. Indeed, from a $250 billion market in 1950 it has grown to the point where, in 2014, the dollar value of bonds outstanding in this country was around $39 *trillion!* Given such size, it's not surprising that today's bond market offers securities to meet just about any type of investment objective and suit virtually any type of investor, no matter how conservative or aggressive. The bond market is usually divided into four segments, according to type of issuer: Treasury, agency, municipal, and corporate.

Treasury Bonds

Treasury bond
A bond issued and backed up by the full faith and credit of the U.S. government.

Treasury bonds (sometimes called *Treasuries* or *governments*) are a dominant force in the bond market and, if not the most popular, are certainly the best known. The U.S. Treasury issues bonds, notes, and other types of debt securities (such as the T-bills discussed in Chapter 4) as a means of meeting the federal government's ever-increasing needs. All Treasury obligations are of the highest quality (backed by the full faith and credit of the U.S. government), a feature that, along with their liquidity, makes them extremely popular with individual and institutional investors both domestically and abroad. Indeed, U.S. Treasury securities are traded in all of the world's major markets, from New York to London to Tokyo.

Treasury notes are issued with maturities of 2, 3, 5, and 10 years, whereas *Treasury bonds* carry 20- and 30-year maturities. (Note that, although the Treasury is authorized to issue these securities, it hasn't issued any 20-year bonds since January 1986, and it did not resume issuing 30-year bonds until February 2006.) The Treasury issues its securities at regularly scheduled auctions. And it's through this auction process that the Treasury establishes the initial yields and coupons on the securities it issues. All Treasury notes and bonds are sold in minimum denominations of $1,000; although interest income is subject to normal federal income tax, *it is exempt from state and local taxes.* Also, the Treasury today issues only *noncallable* securities—the last time the U.S. Treasury issued callable debt was in 1984.

The newest type of Treasury issue is the

Treasury inflation-indexed bond
A bond, issued by the U.S. government, whose principal payments are adjusted to provide protection again inflation, as measured by the Consumer Price Index (CPI).

Treasury inflation-indexed bond (or *TIPS*, which stands for Treasury Inflation-Protected Security). These securities—which are issued with maturities of 5, 10, or 20 years—give the investor the opportunity to keep up with inflation by periodically adjusting their returns for any

GOODLUZ/SHUTTERSTOCK.COM

inflation that has occurred. Unfortunately, the coupons on these securities are set very low because they're meant to provide investors with *real (inflation-adjusted) returns*. So one of these bonds might carry a coupon of only 1.5 percent (when regular T-bonds are paying, say, 3.5 percent or 4 percent). But there's an upside even to this: in the event of inflation, the actual *size of the coupon payment will increase over time as the par value on the bond increases*. For investors who seek protection against inflation, these securities may be just the ticket.

> **EXAMPLE: Inflation-Adjustment of TIPS Bonds**
>
> Assume that inflation is running at an annual rate of 3 percent. At the end of the year, the par (or maturity) value of your TIPS bond will increase by 3 percent (actually, adjustments to par value are made every six months). Thus, the $1,000 par value will grow to $1,030 at the end of the first year and, if the 3 percent inflation rate continues for the second year, the par value will once again move up, this time from $1,030 to $1,061 (or $1,030 × 1.03).

Agency and Mortgage-Backed Bonds

agency bond
An obligation of a political subdivision of the U.S. government.

Agency bonds are an important segment of the U.S. bond market. Although issued by political subdivisions of the U.S. government, *these securities are not obligations of the U.S. Treasury*. An important feature of these securities is that they customarily provide yields that are comfortably above the market rates for Treasuries and thus offer investors a way to increase returns with little or no real difference in risk. Some actively traded and widely quoted agency issues include those sold by the Federal Farm Credit Bank, the Federal National Mortgage Association (or "Fannie Mae," as it's more commonly known), the Federal Land Bank, the Student Loan Marketing Association, and the Federal Home Loan Mortgage Corporation (FHLMC, or Freddie Mac). Although various agencies issue traditional unsecured notes and bonds, they are perhaps best known for their mortgage-backed securities. Two of the biggest issuers of such securities are Fannie Mae and Freddie Mac, who package and issue bonds backed by mortgages that have no government guarantee.

mortgage-backed securities
Securities that are a claim on the cash flows generated by mortgage loans; bonds backed by mortgages as collateral.

Another participant in the mortgage market is the Government National Mortgage Association (GNMA, or Ginnie Mae). It is owned by the U.S. government and insures bonds that are backed by Veterans Administration (VA) and Federal Housing Administration (FHA) home loans. As a result, these GNMA-insured bonds are backed by the full faith and credit of the U.S. government. Some agency issues have unusual interest-payment provisions (i.e., interest is paid monthly in a few instances, and yearly in one case), and in some cases, the interest is exempt from state and local taxes.

Municipal Bonds

municipal bond
A bond issued by state or local governments; interest income is usually exempt from federal taxes.

Municipal bonds are the issues of states, counties, cities, and other political subdivisions, such as school districts and water and sewer districts. Historically, these have generally been considered high-grade securities. However, these days you should be careful when selecting municipal bonds because they can and sometimes do go into default. When a municipality goes into bankruptcy, you essentially end up holding a "junk" bond. While defaults are rare, there are more defaults than are reported by the rating agencies. Usually, only the most financially secure municipalities request bond ratings.

Municipal bonds are unlike other bonds in that their interest income is usually free from federal income tax (which is why they're known as *tax-free bonds*). However, this tax-free status does not apply to any capital gains that may be earned on these securities—such gains are subject to the usual federal taxes. A tax-free yield is probably the most important feature of municipal bonds and is certainly a major reason why individuals invest in them. Exhibit 12.6 shows what a taxable bond (such as a Treasury issue) would have to yield to equal the take-home yield of a tax-free municipal bond. It demonstrates how the yield attractiveness of municipal bonds varies with an investor's income level. The higher the individual's tax bracket, the more attractive municipal bonds become.

The yields on municipal bonds are usually lower than the returns available from fully taxable issues. So unless the tax effect is sufficient to raise the yield on a municipal to a level that equals or exceeds the yields on taxable issues, it obviously doesn't make sense to buy municipal bonds. You can determine the return that a fully taxable bond must provide in order to match the after-tax return on a lower-yielding tax-free bond by computing the municipal's **fully taxable equivalent yield**:

$$\text{Fully Taxable Equivalent Yield} = \frac{\text{Yield on Municipal Bond}}{1 - \text{Tax Rate}}$$

EXAMPLE: Calculating the Fully Taxable Equivalent Yield

If a municipal bond offered a yield of 6 percent, then an individual in the 35 percent federal tax bracket would have to find a fully taxable bond with a yield of more than 9 percent to reap the same after-tax return: 6 percent / (1 − 0.35) = 6 percent / 0.65 = 9.23 percent.

fully taxable equivalent yield
The return that a fully taxable bond must provide in order to match the after-tax return on a lower-yielding tax-free bond.

serial obligation
An issue that is broken down into a series of smaller bonds, each with its own maturity date and coupon rate.

revenue bond
A municipal bond serviced from the income generated by a specific project.

general obligation bond
A municipal bond backed by the full faith and credit of the issuing municipality.

corporate bond
A bond issued by a corporation.

zero coupon bond
A bond that pays no annual interest but sells at a deep discount to its par value.

Municipal bonds are generally issued as **serial obligations**, meaning that the issue is broken into a series of smaller bonds, each with its own maturity date and coupon rate. Thus, instead of the bond having just one maturity date 20 years from now, it will have a series of (say) 20 maturity dates over the 20-year time frame. Although it may not seem that municipal issuers would default on either interest or principal payments, it does occur! Investors should be especially cautious when investing in **revenue bonds**, which are municipal bonds serviced from the income generated by specific income-producing projects, such as toll roads. Unlike issuers of so-called **general obligation bonds**—which are backed by the full faith and credit of the municipality—the issuer of a revenue bond is obligated to pay principal and interest *only if a sufficient level of revenue* is generated. General obligation municipal bonds, in contrast, are required to be serviced in a prompt and timely fashion regardless of the level of tax income generated by the municipality.

Corporate Bonds

The major nongovernmental issuers of bonds are corporations. The market for **corporate bonds** is customarily subdivided into several segments, which include *industrials* (the most diverse of the group), *public utilities* (the dominant group in terms of the volume of new issues), *rail and transportation bonds*, and *financial issues* (such as banks and finance companies). In this market, you'll find the widest range of different types of issues, from *first-mortgage bonds and convertible bonds* (discussed below) to *debentures, subordinated debentures*, and *income bonds*. Interest on corporate bonds is paid semiannually, and sinking funds are common. The bonds usually come in $1,000 denominations, and maturities usually range from 5 to 10 years but can be up to 30 years or more. Many of the issues carry call provisions that prohibit prepayment of the issue during the first 5 to 10 years. Corporate issues are popular with individuals because of their relatively high yields.

The Special Appeal of Zero Coupon Bonds

In addition to the standard bond vehicles already described, investors can also choose from several types of *specialty issues*—bonds that, for the most part, have unusual coupon or repayment provisions. That's certainly the case with **zero coupon bonds**, which, as the name implies, are bonds issued without coupons. To compensate for their lack of coupons, these bonds are sold at a deep discount from their par values and then increase in value over time, at a compound rate of return, so at maturity they're worth much more than their initial investment. Other things being equal, the cheaper the bond, the greater the return you can earn. For example, whereas a 7 percent 15-year zero bond might sell for $362, a 15-year issue with a 5 percent yield will cost a lot more—say, $481.

EXHIBIT 12.6   Table of Taxable Equivalent Yields

Tax-exempt securities generally yield less than fully taxable obligations. As a result, you have to be in a sufficiently high tax bracket (25 percent or more) to make up for the yield shortfall.

			TO MATCH A TAX-FREE YIELD OF:			
	5%	6%	7%	8%	9%	10%
Tax Bracket*	**You Must Earn This Yield on a Taxable Investment:**					
10%	5.55%	6.66%	7.77%	8.88%	10.00%	11.11%
15	5.88	7.06	8.24	9.41	10.59	11.76
25	6.67	8.00	9.33	10.67	12.00	13.33
28	6.94	8.33	9.72	11.11	12.50	13.89
33	7.46	8.96	10.45	11.94	13.43	14.92
35	7.69	9.23	10.77	12.31	13.85	15.38
39.6	8.28	9.93	11.59	13.25	14.9	16.56

*Federal tax rates in effect in 2015.

Because they have no coupons, these bonds pay nothing to the investor until they mature. In this regard, zero coupon bonds are like the Series EE savings bonds discussed in Chapter 4. Strange as it may seem, this is the main attraction of zero coupon bonds. Investors need not worry about reinvesting coupon income twice a year because there are no interest payments. Instead, the fully compounded rate of return on a zero coupon bond is virtually guaranteed at the rate that existed when the issue was purchased as long as the investor holds it to full maturity. For example, in August 2015, U.S. Treasury zero coupon bonds with 10-year maturities were available at yields of about 2.16 percent. Thus, these bonds *lock in* a 2.16 percent compound rate of return on their investment capital for the full 10-year life of the issue. Because of their unusual tax exposure (even though the bonds don't pay regular yearly interest, the Internal Revenue Service treats the annually accrued interest as taxable income), zeros are best used in tax-sheltered investments, such as individual retirement accounts (IRAs), or held by minor children who are likely to be taxed at low rates, if at all.

Zeros are issued by corporations, municipalities, and federal agencies; you can even buy U.S. Treasury notes and bonds in the form of zero coupon securities. During the 1980s, major brokerage houses packaged U.S. Treasury securities as zeros and sold them to the investing public in the form of unit investment trusts. These securities became so popular with investors that the Treasury decided to eliminate the middleman and "issue" its own form of zero coupon bond, known as *Treasury STRIPS*, or *STRIP-Ts*, for short. Actually, the Treasury doesn't issue zero coupon bonds; instead, *they allow government securities dealers to take regular coupon-bearing notes and bonds in stripped form*, which can then be sold to the public as zero-coupon securities. Essentially, the coupons are stripped from the bond, repackaged, and then sold separately as zero coupon bonds. For instance, a 10-year Treasury bond has 20 semiannual coupon payments plus 1 principal payment—and each of these 21 cash flows can be repackaged and sold as 21 different zero coupon securities with maturities ranging from six months to 10 years.

Convertible Bonds

Another popular type of specialty issue is the convertible bond. Found only in the corporate market, these issues are a *hybrid security* that possess the features of both corporate bonds and common stocks. That is, though they're initially issued as debentures (unsecured debt), they carry a provision that enables them to *be converted into a certain number of shares of the issuing company's common stock*.

The key element of any convertible issue is its **conversion privilege**, which describes the conditions and specific nature of the conversion feature. First, it states exactly when the bond can be converted. Sometimes there'll be an initial waiting period of six months to perhaps two years after the date of issue, during which time the issue cannot be converted. The *conversion period* then begins, after which the issue can be converted at any time. From the investor's point of view, the most important feature is the **conversion ratio**, which specifies the number of shares of common stock into which the bond can be converted. For example, one of these bonds might carry a conversion ratio of 20, meaning that you can exchange one convertible bond for 20 shares of the company's stock.

Given the significance of the price behavior of the underlying common stock to the value of a convertible security, one of the most important measures is conversion value. **Conversion value** indicates what a convertible issue would trade for *if it were priced to sell based only on its stock value*. Conversion value is easy to determine: simply multiply the conversion ratio of the issue by the current market price of the underlying common stock. Convertibles seldom trade precisely at their conversion value. Instead, they usually trade at **conversion premiums**, which means that the convertibles are priced in the market at more than their conversion values. Convertible securities appeal to investors who want *the price potential of a common stock along with the downside risk protection of a corporate bond*.

EXAMPLE: Calculating the Conversion Value of a Convertible Bond

A convertible bond carrying a conversion ratio of 20 would have a conversion value of $1,200 if the firm's stock traded at a current market price of $60 per share ($20 \times \$60 = \$1,200$).

12–3e Bond Ratings

Bond ratings are like grades: A letter grade is assigned to a bond, which designates its investment quality. Ratings are widely used and are an important part of the municipal and corporate bond markets. The two largest and best-known rating agencies are Moody's and Standard & Poor's. Every time a large, new corporate or municipal issue comes to the market, a staff of professional bond analysts determines its default risk exposure and investment quality. The financial records of the issuing organization are thoroughly examined and its future prospects assessed. The result of all this is the assignment of a bond rating at the time of issue that indicates *the ability of the issuing organization to service its debt in a prompt and timely manner*. Exhibit 12.7 lists the various ratings assigned to bonds by each of the two major agencies. Note that the top four ratings (Aaa through Baa, or AAA through BBB) designate *investment-grade bonds*—such ratings are highly coveted by issuers because they indicate

financially strong, well-run companies or municipalities. The next two ratings (Ba/B or BB/B) are where you'll find most junk bonds. These ratings indicate that, although the principal and interest payments on the bonds are still being paid, the risk of default is relatively high because the issuers lack the financial strength found with investment-grade issues. Although junk bonds—or *high-yield bonds*, as they're also known—are popular with some investors, it should be understood that they involve substantial risk. In particular, there's a very real likelihood that the issue may encounter some difficulties.

Once a new issue is rated, the process doesn't stop there. Older, outstanding bonds are also regularly reviewed to ensure that their assigned ratings are still valid. Although most issues will carry a single rating to maturity, ratings can change over time as new information becomes available. Finally, although it may appear that the issuing

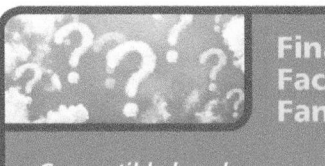

Financial Fact or Fantasy?

Convertible bonds are so named because they can be exchanged for a set number of shares of common stock. **Fact:** Convertible bonds carry the provision that they may, within a stipulated time period, be converted into a certain number of shares of the issuing company's common stock.

EXHIBIT 12.7   Moody's and Standard & Poor's Bond Ratings

Agencies like Moody's and Standard & Poor's rate corporate and municipal bonds; these ratings provide an indication of the bonds' investment quality (particularly regarding an issue's default risk exposure).

BOND RATINGS*

Moody's	S&P	Description
Aaa	AAA	*Prime-Quality Investment Bonds*—This is the highest rating assigned, denoting extremely strong capacity to pay.
AaA	AA	*High-Grade Investment Bonds*—These are also considered very safe bonds, though they're not quite as safe as Aaa/AAA issues; double-A-rated bonds (Aa/AA) are safer (have less risk of default) than single-A-rated issues.
A	A	
Baa	BBB	*Medium-Grade Investment Bonds*—These are the lowest of the investment-grade issues; they're felt to lack certain protective elements against adverse economic conditions.
Ba	BB	*Junk Bonds*—With little protection against default, these are viewed as highly speculative securities.
B	B	
Caa	CCC	*Poor-Quality Bonds*—These are either in default or very close to it; they're often referred to as "Zombie Bonds."
Ca	CC	
C	C	
	D	

*Some ratings may be modified to show relative standing within a major rating category; for example, Moody's uses numerical modifiers (1, 2, 3), whereas S&P uses plus (+) or minus (−) signs.

firm or municipality is receiving the rating, it's actually the *individual* issue that is being rated. As a result, a firm (or municipality) can have different ratings assigned to its issues; the senior securities, for example, might carry one rating and the junior issues a slightly lower rating. Most investors pay careful attention to ratings, because they affect comparative market yields. Other things being equal, *the higher the rating, the lower the yield of an obligation*. Thus, whereas an A-rated bond might offer a 5 percent yield, a comparable AAA issue would probably yield something like 4.25 percent or 4.50 percent.

12–3f Pricing a Bond

Unlike stocks, bonds aren't widely quoted in the financial press, not even in *The Wall Street Journal*. So, rather than looking at how bonds are quoted, let's look at how they're priced in the marketplace. Regardless of the type, *all bonds are priced as a percentage of par*, meaning that a quote of, say, 85 translates into a price of 85 percent of the bond's par value. In the bond market, 1 point = $10, so a quote of 85 does not mean $85, but rather $850. This is so because market convention assumes that bonds carry par values of $1,000. Keep in mind that the price of any bond is always related to the issue's coupon and maturity—those two features are always a part of any listed price because of their effect on the price of a bond. (We'll explain more about the impact of coupons and maturities on bond price behavior in the section entitled "Bond Prices and Yields," later in this chapter.)

In the corporate and municipal markets, bonds are priced in decimals, using three places to the right of the decimal point. Thus, a quote of 87.562, as a percentage of a $1,000 par bond, converts to a price of $875.62. Similarly, a quote of 121.683 translates into a price of 1.21683 × $1,000 = $1,216.83. In contrast, U.S. Treasury and agency bond quotes are stated in *32s of a point* (where, again, 1 point = $10). For example, you might see the price of a T-bond listed at "94:16." This means that the bond is being priced at $94^{16}/_{32}$, or 94.5 percent of par—in other words, it's being priced at $945.00. With government bonds, the figures to the right of the colon (:) show the number of 32s embedded in the price. Consider another bond that's trading at 141:08. This bond is being priced at $141^8/_{32}$, or 141.25% of par. Thus, if you wanted to buy 15 of these bonds (with a par value of $15,000), you'd have to pay $21,187.50 (i.e., 1.4125 × $15,000).

Bond Prices and Accrued Interest

The price of a bond quoted on your favorite financial Internet site is unlikely to be the price that you would actually pay as a buyer. This is because such quoted prices usually do not include the interest that accrues between the coupon payment dates of the bond. **Accrued interest** is the amount of interest that's been earned since the last coupon payment date by the bond holder/seller, but which will be received by the new owner/buyer of the bond at the next regularly scheduled coupon payment date. When a bond is sold between coupon payment dates, the buyer pays the seller for the accrued interest, which is the prorated share of the upcoming coupon payment.

Consider a specific example of how accrued interest affects the price paid for a bond between coupon payments. Assume that you're selling a corporate bond with $1,000 par value and paying a 4 percent coupon semiannually, which is $20 every six months. The bond is quoted on the Internet at $1,000, and it's three months after the last coupon payment. Because the bond is halfway between coupon payments, accrued interest is $20 × 3/6 = $10. Thus, the buyer's actual price paid to the seller will be the $1,000 quoted price plus the accrued interest of $10, for a total of $1,010.

In market jargon, how accrued interest is treated in bond pricing is the basis for the distinction between **clean price** and **dirty (full) price**. This can be summarized as:

> Clean price = quoted price
> Dirty (full) price = quoted price + accrued interest

So what's the significance of the distinction between dirty and clean prices for bond investors? It's important to realize that the commonly cited prices in the financial

accrued interest
The amount of interest that's been earned since the last coupon payment date by the bond holder/seller, but which will be received by the new owner/buyer of the bond at the next regularly scheduled coupon payment date.

clean price
The quoted price of a bond, which understates the true price of a bond by any accrued interest.

dirty (full) price
The quoted price of a bond plus accrued interest, the total of which is the relevant price to be paid by a bond buyer.

press and on the Internet are typically net of accrued interest and are so-called clean bond prices. The relevant sale or invoice price of a bond to the buyer is the dirty price, which adds the accrued interest to the quoted price. In terms of the earlier example, the buyer of the 4 percent coupon bond would pay the dirty price of $1,010, not the clean price of $1,000. In summary, the quoted clean price *understates* the true (dirty) price that must be paid to actually purchase the bond in the open market.

Bond Prices and Yields

The price of a bond depends on its coupon, maturity, and the movement of market interest rates. As previously noted, *when interest rates go down, bond prices go up, and vice versa.* The relationship of bond prices to market rates is captured in Exhibit 12.8. The graph serves to reinforce the *inverse* relationship between bond prices and market interest rates; note that *lower* rates lead to *higher* bond prices. The exhibit also shows the difference between premium and discount bonds. A premium bond is one that sells for more than its par value, which occurs whenever market interest rates drop below the coupon rate on the bond; a discount bond, in contrast, sells for less than par and is the result of market rates being greater than the issue's coupon rate. So the 4 percent bond in our illustration traded as a premium bond when market rates were at 2 percent but as a discount bond when rates stood at 6 percent.

premium bond
A bond whose market value is higher than par.

discount bond
A bond whose market value is lower than par.

When a bond is first issued, it's usually sold to the public at a price that equals (or is very close to) its par value. Likewise, when the bond matures—some 15, 20, or 30 years later—it will once again be priced at its par value. What happens to the price of the bond over time is of considerable concern to bond investors who may wish to trade the bond over its life. We know that how much bond prices move depends not only on the direction of interest rate changes but also on the *magnitude* of such changes. The greater the moves in interest rates, the greater the swings in bond prices. Bond prices will also vary according to the coupon and maturity of the issue. Bonds with *lower coupons* and/or *longer maturities* will respond more vigorously to changes in market rates and undergo *greater price swings.* Thus, if interest rates are moving up, then the investor should seek high coupon bonds with short maturities, because this will dampen price variation and *preserve as much capital as possible.* In contrast, if rates are heading down, that's the time to be in long-term bonds. If you're a speculator looking for lots of capital gains, then go with long-term, *low coupon bonds.* In contrast, if you're trying to lock in a high level of coupon (interest) income, then stick with long-term, *high coupon* bonds that offer plenty of call protection.

Financial Fact or Fantasy?

When interest rates go down, bond prices also go down because such securities become less valuable.

Fantasy: Bond prices and interest rates move in the opposite direction. As a result, when interest rates go down, bond prices go up.

Current Yield and Yield to Maturity

The two most commonly cited bond yields are current yield and yield to maturity. Current yield reflects the amount of annual interest income the bond provides relative to its current market price. Here's the formula for current yield:

Current yield
The amount of current income a bond provides relative to its market price.

$$\text{Current Yield} = \frac{\text{Annual Interest Income}}{\text{Market Price of Bond}}$$

As you can see, the current yield on a bond is comparable to the dividend yield on a stock. This measure would be of interest to *investors seeking current income.* Other things being equal, the higher the current yield, the more attractive a bond would be to such an investor.

> **EXAMPLE: Calculating the Current Yield on a Bond**
>
> A 6 percent bond with a $1,000 face value is currently selling for $910. Because annual interest income is $60 (i.e., 0.06 × $1,000) and because the current market price of the bond is $910, its current yield would be 6.59 percent ($60/$910).

EXHIBIT 12.8   **Price Behavior** of a Bond with a 4 Percent Coupon

A bond sells at its par value so long as the prevailing market interest rate remains the same as the bond's coupon (for example, when both coupon and market rates equal 4 percent). But if market rates drop, then bond prices rise, and vice versa. Moreover, as a bond approaches its maturity, the issue price always moves toward its par value no matter what happens to interest rates.

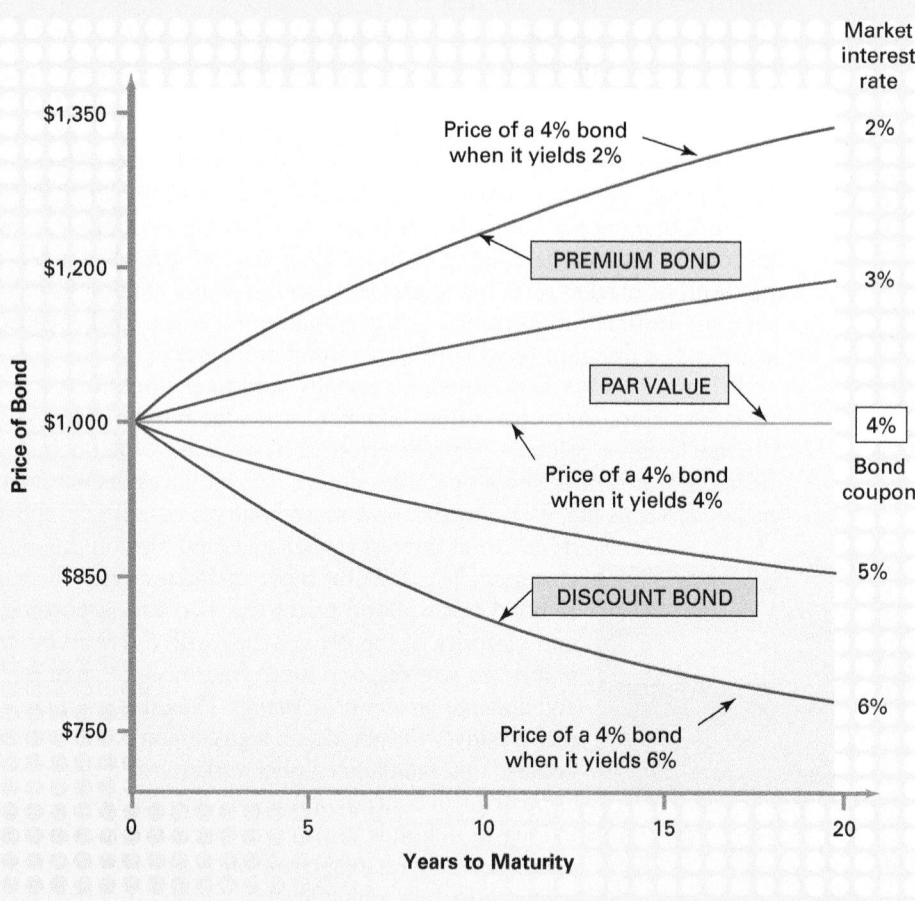

The annual rate of return that a bondholder would receive *if she held the issue to its maturity* is captured in the bond's **yield to maturity**. This measure captures both the annual interest income and the recovery of principal at maturity. It also includes the impact of interest on interest and therefore provides a fully compounded rate of return. If a bond is purchased at its face value, then its yield to maturity will equal the coupon, or stated, rate of interest. On the other hand, if the bond is purchased at a discount or a premium then its yield to maturity will vary according to the prevailing level of market yields.

yield to maturity
The fully compounded rate of return that a bond would yield if it were held to maturity.

You can find the yield to maturity on discount or premium bonds using the *approximate yield* formula introduced earlier in this chapter. Or you can use a hand-held financial calculator (which we'll demonstrate soon) to obtain a yield to maturity that's a bit more accurate and is, in fact, very close to the measure used in the market. The only difference is that market participants normally use semiannual compounding in their calculations, whereas we use annual compounding for simplicity to illustrate the basic concept. Bonds are normally priced in the market using semiannual compounding because the vast majority of U.S. bonds pay interest semiannually. The difference in yields using annual versus semiannual compounding usually amounts to no more than 5 or 6 basis points, where 1 basis point = 1/100 of 1 percent. Now that might be a big deal to institutional investors, but not to the small individual investor. So we'll stick with annual compounding here, though we'll show how you can use your handheld calculator to find yield to maturity on a semiannual basis. So, employing the approximate yield approach for now, by setting the future maturity value of the investment equal to the bond's face value ($1,000), you can use the following version of the equation to find the *approximate yield to maturity on a bond*:

$$\text{Approximate Yield to Maturity} = \frac{\text{Annual Coupon Income} + \left[\dfrac{\$1,000 - \text{Current Bond Price}}{\text{Number of Years to Maturity}}\right]}{\left[\dfrac{\text{Current Price of Bond} + \$1,000}{2}\right]}$$

EXAMPLE: Calculating the Approximate Yield to Maturity

Assume you're contemplating the purchase of a $1,000, 6 percent annual coupon income bond with 15 years remaining to maturity and that the bond currently is trading at a price of $910. The approximate yield to maturity on this bond will be:

$$\text{Approximate Yield to Maturity} = \frac{\$60 + \left[\dfrac{\$1,000 - \$910}{15}\right]}{\left[\dfrac{\$910 + \$1,000}{2}\right]}$$

$$= \frac{\$60 + \left[\dfrac{\$90}{15}\right]}{\left[\dfrac{\$1,910}{2}\right]} = \underline{6.91\%}$$

This is above both the 6 percent stated (coupon) rate and the 6.59 percent current yield. That's because the bond is trading at a discount to its face value.

Calculator

INPUTS	FUNCTIONS
15	N
−910	PV
60	PMT
1000	FV
	CPT
	I/Y
	SOLUTION
	6.99

See Appendix E for details.

Calculator Keystrokes. You can also *find the yield to maturity on a bond* by using a financial calculator; here's what you'd do. With the calculator in the *annual mode*, to find the yield to maturity on our 6 percent (annual pay coupon), 15-year bond that's currently trading at $910, use the keystrokes shown here, where:

N = number of *years* to maturity
PV = the current market price of the bond (entered as a negative)
PMT = the size of the annual coupon payments (in *dollars*)
FV = the par value of the bond

A value of 6.99 should appear in the calculator display, which is the bond's yield to maturity using annual compounding; note that it's very close to the approximate yield of 6.91 percent we just computed.

You can also use your handheld calculator to find the slightly more accurate *yield to maturity based on semiannual compounding.* Here's how: Keeping the calculator in the *annual mode, multiply* the number of years to maturity by 2 (to obtain the number of 6-month periods to maturity) and *divide* the coupon by 2 (to determine the size of the semiannual coupon payments). Now input the appropriate data: N = 15 × 2 = 30, PMT = 60/2 = 30, PV = −910; and FV = 1000; then hit CPT I/Y and you should end up with 3.49, which is the semi-annual yield. Then double that value (3.49 × 2) and you'll have 6.98 percent, *the bond's yield to maturity using semiannual compounding.* Notice in this case that the difference in the annual (6.99 percent) versus semiannual (6.98 percent) yields to maturity is just 1 basis point!

Measures of yield to maturity are used by investors to assess the attractiveness of a bond. The higher the yield to maturity, the more attractive the investment, other things being equal. *If a bond provided a yield to maturity that equaled or exceeded an investor's desired rate of return, then it would be considered a worthwhile investment candidate* because it would promise a yield that should adequately compensate the investor for the perceived amount of risk involved.

TEST YOURSELF

12-12 Go to the asset allocation tool provided at: **http://www.ipers.org/calcs/AssetAllocator.html**. Enter assumptions that fit your current and anticipated situation and produce an asset allocation recommendation. Then add 20 years to your age and redo the calculations. Finally, redo the calculations assuming minimal risk tolerance. Explain the results of changing these key assumptions.

12-13 What's the difference between a *secured* bond and an *unsecured* bond?

12-14 Are *junk bonds* and *zero coupon bonds* the same? Explain. What are the basic tax features of a tax-exempt *municipal* bond?

12-15 What is a *convertible* bond, and why do investors buy convertible securities?

12-16 Describe the conversion privilege on a convertible security. Explain how the market price of the underlying common stock affects the market price of a convertible bond.

12-17 Explain the system of bond ratings used by Moody's and Standard & Poor's. Why would it make sense to ever buy junk bonds?

12-18 Explain the difference between dirty (full) and clean bond prices? What is the significance of the difference in the prices for a bond buyer?

12-19 What effects do market interest rates have on the price behavior of outstanding bonds?

Financial Impact of Personal Choices
Landon and Kirsten Like High Flying Stocks

Landon and Kirsten Malloy are both 33 years old and invest 15 percent of their after-tax annual income in stocks. They hate missing out on great returns when the stock of a company doing great things starts going through the roof. For example, Landon and Kirsten feel they should have invested in Electronic Arts in 2014 when it earned around a 60 percent return! So any time a company they know well earns more than 20 percent in a year, they try to invest in it. And because they believe in the stocks they buy, the Malloys always hold their stocks until they at least break-even. What do you make of the Malloys' approach to stock investing?

The Malloys decision to invest 15 percent of their after-tax income is great. However, Landon and Kirsten shouldn't invest just in stocks and should adopt an asset allocation strategy that provides diversified exposure to bonds, real estate, and more. Their current exclusive focus on stocks is likely too risky. Further, their rule to buy well-known stocks that earn more than 20 percent in a year likely leaves them insufficiently diversified. And their 20 percent return rule also focuses too much on *past* returns and not enough on a careful forecast of *future* returns. The Malloys could end up with overvalued stocks with their best performance behind them. Finally, their rule to not sell until they at least break-even suggests the behavioral bias of unduly "anchoring" on purchase prices. It could be that a company has changed for the worse and it's simply time to sell, even if it implies a loss. Investing 15 percent of their income is great, but the Malloys could do even better.

Planning Over a Lifetime: *Investing in Stocks and Bonds*

Here are some key considerations for investment planning in each stage of the life cycle.

Pre-family Independence: 20s	Family Formation/Career Development: 30–45	Pre-Retirement: 45–65	Retirement: 65 and Beyond
✓ Determine major investment goals and how much money needs to be invested each month to achieve them.	✓ Revise investment plan to focus more on retirement and funding children's education, if applicable.	✓ Revise investment plan in light of recent developments.	✓ Revise investment plan to lean more towards debt and cash instruments than to stocks.
✓ Determine your asset allocation among stocks, bonds, and cash based on your time horizon and attitude towards risk.	✓ Review your asset allocation and rebalance if it is inconsistent with your goals.	✓ Review your asset allocation and rebalance if it is inconsistent with your goals.	✓ Review your asset allocation and rebalance if it is inconsistent with your goals.
✓ Make sure to participate in any employer-sponsored 401(k) retirement plan and match your asset allocation plan.	✓ Gradually increase the amount invested in any employer-sponsored 401(k) retirement plan and reevaluate how it relates to your asset allocation plan.	✓ Continue to gradually increase the amount you invest in any employer sponsored 401(k) retirement plan and reevaluate how it relates to your asset allocation plan.	✓ Integrate investment asset allocation strategy with estate planning.
✓ Consider opening traditional and/or a Roth IRAs.	✓ Consider increasing your contribution to traditional and/or a Roth IRAs.	✓ Consider increasing your contribution to traditional and/or a Roth IRAs.	✓ Carefully plan for mandatory withdrawals from tax shelter accounts and associated tax consequences.

WILLIAM HUBER/PHOTONICA/GETTY IMAGES

Summary

LG1 Describe the various types of risks to which investors are exposed, as well as the sources of return, p. 462

Although investing offers returns in the form of current income and/or capital gains, it also involves risk. The basic types of investment risk are business risk, financial risk, market risk, purchasing power risk, interest rate risk, liquidity risk, and event risk—all of which combine to affect the level of return from an investment.

LG2 Know how to search for an acceptable investment on the basis of risk, total return, and yield, p. 462

The value, and therefore the acceptability, of any investment depends on the return it's expected to produce relative to the amount of risk involved in the investment. Investors are entitled to be compensated for the risks that they must accept in an investment. Therefore, the more risk there is in an investment, the more return you should expect to earn. This risk–return trade-off is generally captured in the "desired rate of return," which is that rate of return you feel you should receive in compensation for the amount of risk you must assume. As long as the expected return on an investment (the return you *think* you'll earn) is greater than the desired rate of return (the return you *should* earn), it should be considered an acceptable investment candidate—one worthy of your attention.

LG3 **Discuss the merits of investing in common stock and be able to distinguish among the different types of stocks, p. 470**

Common stocks are a popular form of investing that can be used to meet just about any investment objective—from capital gains or current income to some combination of both. Investors can choose from blue chips, growth, or tech stocks; income, speculative, cyclical, or defensive stocks; and small- or mid-cap stocks. If they're so inclined, they can even buy foreign stocks by investing in American Depositary Receipts (ADRs).

LG4 **Become familiar with the various measures of performance and how to use them in placing a value on stocks, p. 470**

The value of a share of stock is largely based on performance measures: dividend yield, book value, net profit margin, return on equity (ROE), earnings per share, price/earnings (P/E) ratio, and beta. Investors look at these measures to gain insights about a firm's financial condition and operating results and ultimately to obtain the input needed to measure the expected return on the firm's stock.

LG5 **Describe the basic issue characteristics of bonds, as well as how these securities are used as investment vehicles, p. 484**

Bonds are a popular form of investing; they're often referred to as *fixed-income* securities because the debt service obligations of the issuer are fixed. The coupon that the bond carries defines the amount of annual interest income that the investor will receive over time, while the par value defines the amount of capital to be repaid at maturity. Bonds may be issued with or without collateral, and most bonds allow the issuer to retire the issue before its maturity. As investment vehicles, bonds can be used to generate either current income or capital gains (which occur when market rates go down).

LG6 **Distinguish between the different types of bonds, gain an understanding of how bond prices behave, and know how to compute different measures of yield, p. 484**

Bonds are the publicly issued debt of corporations and various types of government—from the U.S. Treasury and various agencies of the U.S. government to state and local (municipal) governments. Regardless of the issuer, the price of a bond moves inversely with market interest rates: the lower the market rate, the higher the price of the bond. There are basically two ways to measure the yield performance of a bond: one is current yield, which looks only at the coupon income on a bond; the other is yield to maturity, which provides a fully compounded rate of return that considers not only interest income but also capital gains (or loss) and interest on interest.

Key Terms

Answers to Test Yourself

You can find answers to these questions on this book's companion website. Look for it at *www.cengagebrain.com*. Search for this book by its title, and then add it to your dashboard.

Key Financial Relationships

Concept	Financial Relationship	Page Number
Approximate Expected Yield	$$\text{Approximate Yield} = \frac{\text{Average Annual Current Income} + \left[\dfrac{\dfrac{\text{Future Price of Investment} - \text{Current Price of Investment}}{\text{Number of Years in Investment Period}}}{}\right]}{\left[\dfrac{\text{Current Price of Investment} + \text{Future Price of Investment}}{2}\right]}$$	468
Dividend Yield	$$\text{Dividend Yield} = \frac{\text{Annual Dividend Received per Share}}{\text{Market Price per Share of Stock}}$$	472
Book Value per Share	$$\text{Book Value per Share} = \frac{\text{Total Assets} - \text{Total Liabilities} - \text{Preferred Stock}}{\text{Number of Shares of Common Stock Outstanding}}$$	473
Net Profit Margin	$$\text{Net Profit Margin} = \frac{\text{Net Profit}}{\text{Sales}}$$	473
Return on Equity	$$\text{Return on Equity} = \frac{\text{Net Profit}}{\text{Shareholders' Equity}}$$	473
Earnings per Share	$$\text{Earnings per Share} = \frac{\text{Net Profit} - \text{Preferred Dividends Paid}}{\text{Number of Shares of Common Stock Outstanding}}$$	474
Price/Earnings Ratio	$$\frac{\text{Price}}{\text{Earnings}} = \frac{\text{Market Price per Share of Common Stock}}{\text{Annual Earnings per Share}}$$	474

Concept	Financial Relationship	Page Number
Fully taxable Equivalent Yield	$$\text{Fully Taxable Equivalent Yield} = \frac{\text{Yield on Municipal Bond}}{1 - \text{Tax Rate}}$$	490
Current Yield	$$\text{Current Yield} = \frac{\text{Annual Interest Income}}{\text{Market Price of Bond}}$$	495
Approximate Yield to Maturity	$$\text{Approximate Yield to Maturity} = \frac{\text{Annual Coupon Income} + \dfrac{\$1{,}000 - \text{Current Bond Price}}{\text{Number of Years to Maturity}}}{\left[\dfrac{\text{Current Price of Bond} + \$1{,}000}{2}\right]}$$	497

Key Financial Relationships Problem Set

1. **Approximate expected yield.** Britney Cottrell is evaluating a small stock that's been recommended to her. The average annual dividend is $1.75, the current stock price is $72.50, the projected future stock price is $90.00, and she expects to hold the stock for four years. What is the expected approximate expected yield on the stock?

   Solution:

   $$\text{Approximate Yield} = \frac{\begin{array}{c}\text{Average Annual} \\ \text{Current Income}\end{array} + \dfrac{\begin{array}{c}\text{Future Price} \\ \text{of Investment}\end{array} - \begin{array}{c}\text{Current Price} \\ \text{of Investment}\end{array}}{\text{Number of Years in Investment Period}}}{\dfrac{\begin{array}{c}\text{Current Price} \\ \text{of Investment}\end{array} + \begin{array}{c}\text{Future Price} \\ \text{of Investment}\end{array}}{2}}$$

   $$= \frac{\$1.75 + \dfrac{\$90.00 - \$72.50}{4}}{\dfrac{\$72.50 + \$90.00}{2}}$$

   $$= 7.54 \text{ Percent}$$

2. **Dividend yield.** In mid-2015 Merck's stock was selling for $60.10 and had an annual dividend of $1.80. Kaleb Aleman is looking for stocks that pay attractive current income. The average dividend yield on dividend-paying S&P 500 stocks at the time was 2.31 percent. What is Merck's dividend yield and how attractive is it?

   Solution:

   $$\text{Dividend yield} = \frac{\text{Annual Dividend Received per Share}}{\text{Market Price per Share of Stock}}$$

   $$= \frac{\$1.80}{\$60.10}$$

   $$= 3 \text{ Percent}$$

   This is a bit above the average dividend yield for S&P 500 stocks, which may make Merck attractive to Kaleb.

3. **Book value per share.** At the end of 2014 Facebook had total assets of $40.184 billion and total liabilities of $4.088 billion. Given that the firm has 2.25 billion shares of common stock outstanding and no preferred stock, what is Facebook's book value per share?

   Solution:

   $$\text{Book Value per Share} = \frac{\text{Total Assets} - \text{Total Liabilities} - \text{Preferred Stock}}{\text{Number of Shares of Common Stock Outstanding}}$$

   $$= \frac{\$40.184 - \$4.088}{2.25}$$

   $$= \$16.04 \text{ per Share}$$

4. **Net profit margin.** In 2014 Facebook earned a net profit of $2.925 billion on sales of $12.466 billion. What was Facebook's net profit margin in 2014?

Solution:

$$\text{Net Profit Margin} = \frac{\text{Net Profit}}{\text{Sales}} = \frac{\$2.925}{\$12.466} = 23.46 \text{ Percent}$$

5. **Return on equity.** In 2014 Facebook had net income (net profit) of $2.925 billion and had stockholders' equity of $36.096 billion. What was Facebook's return on equity in 2014?

Solution:

$$\text{Return on Equity} = \frac{\text{Net Profit}}{\text{Shareholders' Equity}} = \frac{\$2.925}{\$36.096} = 8.1 \text{ Percent}$$

6. **Earnings per share.** In 2014 Facebook had net profit of $2.925 and 2.25 billion shares outstanding. What was Facebook's earnings per share in 2014?

Solution:

$$\text{Earnings per Share} = \frac{\text{Net Profit} - \text{Preferred Dividends Paid}}{\text{Number of Shares of Common Stock Outstanding}}$$
$$= \frac{\$2.925}{2.25}$$
$$= \$1.30 \text{ per Share}$$

7. **Price/Earnings ratio.** In 2014 Facebook had earnings per share of $1.30 and on May 21, 2015, its share price closed at $80.48 per share. What was its price/earnings ratio at that time using its 2014 earnings per share as the base?

Solution:

$$\text{Price/Earnings Ratio} = \frac{\text{Market Price per Share of Common Stock}}{\text{Annual Earnings per Share}}$$
$$= \frac{\$80.48}{\$1.30}$$
$$= 16.91$$

8. **Fully taxable equivalent yield.** A municipal bond is offering a yield of 5 percent. Darren Haskins is in the 35 percent marginal federal tax bracket. He is wondering what yield he would need to earn on a fully taxable corporate bond to earn the same after-tax return as that expected on the municipal bond. What should you tell Darren?

Solution:

$$\text{Fully Taxable Yield} = \frac{\text{Yield on Municipal Bond}}{1 - \text{Tax Rate}}$$
$$= \frac{5 \text{ Percent}}{1 - 35 \text{ Percent}}$$
$$= 7.69 \text{ Percent.}$$

Thus, you should tell Darren that he would have to earn more than 7.69 percent on a fully taxable corporate bond in order to earn an after tax return greater than the 5 percent return on the municipal bond.

9. **Current yield.** You're considering buying a bond that pays an annual interest (coupon) income of 4 percent that is selling for $925. What is the current yield on the bond?

Solution:

$$\text{Current Yield} = \frac{\text{Annual Interest Income}}{\text{Market Price of Bond}}$$
$$= \frac{\$40}{\$925}$$
$$= 4.32\%.$$

10. **Approximate yield to maturity.** Anna Schmidt is considering buying a bond that has a face value of $1,000, a 5% coupon, 12 years to maturity, and is trading at a price of $875. In order to decide on the purchase, Ann has asked you to calculate the bond's approximate yield to maturity. What should you tell Anna?

Solution:

$$\text{Approximate Yield to Maturity} = \frac{\text{Annual Coupon Income} + \dfrac{\$1,000 - \text{Current Bond Price}}{\text{Number of Years to Maturity}}}{\dfrac{\text{Current Bond Price} + \$1,000}{2}}$$

$$= \frac{\$50 + \dfrac{\$1,000 - \$875}{12}}{\dfrac{\$875 + \$1,000}{2}}$$

$$= 6.44 \text{ Percent}$$

Financial Planning Exercises

LG1,2, p. 462   1.   **Ranking investments by expected returns.** What makes for a good investment? Use the approximate yield formula or a financial calculator to rank the following investments according to their expected returns.
a.   Buy a stock for $30 a share, hold it for three years, and then sell it for $60 a share (the stock pays annual dividends of $2 a share).
b.   Buy a security for $40, hold it for two years, and then sell it for $100 (current income on this security is zero).
c.   Buy a one-year, 5 percent note for $1,000 (assume that the note has a $1,000 par value and that it will be held to maturity).

LG3,4, p. 470   2.   **Calculating key financial ratios.** Selected financial information about Backpacking Resources, Inc. is as follows:

Total assets	$20,000,000
Total liabilities	$8,000,000
Total preferred stock	$3,000,000
Total annual preferred stock dividends	$240,000
Net profits after tax	$2,500,000
Number of shares of common stock outstanding	500,000 shares
Current market price of common stock	$50.00 a share
Annual common stock dividends	$2.50 a share

Using the company's financial information, compute the following:
a.   Dividend yield
b.   Book value per share
c.   EPS
d.   P/E ratio

LG3,4, p. 470   3.   **Choosing appropriate stocks.** Assume that you've just inherited $500,000 and have decided to invest a big chunk of it ($350,000, to be exact) in common stocks. Your objective is to build up as much capital as you can over the next 15 to 20 years, and you're willing to tolerate a "good deal" of risk.
a.   What *types* of stocks (blue chips, income stocks, and so on) do you think you'd be most interested in, and why? Select at least three types of stocks and briefly explain the rationale for selecting each.
b.   Would your selections change if you were dealing with a smaller amount of money—say, only $50,000? What if you were a more risk-averse investor?

LG3,4, p. 470   4.   **Effectiveness of stock market timing.** Discuss the evidence regarding the ability of most investors to effectively time getting in and out of the stock market. How sensitive are returns to being out of the market for just a few months of good stock market performance?

LG3,4, p. 470 5. ***Calculating expected return on investment.*** An investor is thinking about buying some shares of Health Monitoring, Inc., at $75 a share. She expects the price of the stock to rise to $115 a share over the next three years. During that time, she also expects to receive annual dividends of $4 per share. Given that the investor's expectations (about the future price of the stock and the dividends it pays) hold up, what rate of return can the investor expect to earn on this investment? (*Hint*: Use either the approximate yield formula or a financial calculator to solve this problem.)

LG3,4, p. 470 6. ***Calculating book value.*** A company has total assets of $2.5 billion, total liabilities of $1.8 billion, and $200 million worth of 8 percent preferred stock outstanding. What is the firm's total book value? What would its book value per share be if the firm had 100 million shares of common stock outstanding?

LG3,4, p. 470 7. ***Calculating key stock performance metrics.*** The Morton Company recently reported net profits after taxes of $15.8 million. It has 2.5 million shares of common stock outstanding and pays preferred dividends of $1 million a year. The company's stock currently trades at $60 per share.
   a. Compute the stock's EPS.
   b. What is the stock's P/E ratio?
   c. Determine what the stock's dividend yield would be if it paid $1.75 per share to common stockholders.

LG3,4, p. 470 8. ***Calculating expected return on a stock.*** The price of Green Mountain Homes, Inc. is now $85. The company pays no dividends. Trey Hamlin expects the price four years from now to be $125 a share. Should Trey buy Green Mountain Homes if he wants a 15 percent rate of return? Explain.

LG3,4,5,6, p. 470, 484 9. ***Collect key data on actual stocks, bonds, and convertible bonds.*** Using the resources available at your campus or public library, work the following problems. (*Note:* Show your work for all your calculations.)
   a. Select any two *common* stocks and then determine the dividend yield, EPS, and P/E ratio for each.
   b. Select any two *bonds* and then determine the current yield and yield to maturity of each.
   c. Select any two *convertible bonds* and then determine the conversion ratio, conversion value, and conversion premium for each.

LG5,6, p. 484 10. ***Tax treatment of bond returns.*** An investor in the 28 percent tax bracket is trying to decide which of two bonds to select: one is a 5.5 percent U.S. Treasury bond selling at par; the other is a municipal bond with a 4.25 percent coupon, which is also selling at par. Which of these two bonds should the investor select? Why?

LG5,6, p. 484 11. ***Calculating current yield and yield to maturity.*** Describe and differentiate between a bond's (a) current yield and (b) yield to maturity. Why are these yield measures important to the bond investor? Find the yield to maturity of a 20-year, 9 percent, $1,000 par value bond trading at a price of $850. What's the current yield on this bond?

LG5,6, p. 484 12. ***Calculating and comparing current yields.*** Which of these two bonds offers the highest current yield? Which one has the highest yield to maturity?
   a. A 6.55 percent, 22-year bond quoted at 52.000
   b. A 10.25 percent, 27-year bond quoted at 103.625

LG5,6, p. 484 13. ***Calculating and interpreting current yield and yield to maturity.*** Find the current yield of a 5.65 percent, 8-year bond that's currently priced in the market at $853.75. Now, use a financial calculator to find the yield to maturity on this bond (use annual compounding). What's the current yield and yield to maturity on this bond if it trades at $1,000? If it's priced at $750? Comment on your findings.

LG5,6, p. 484 14. ***Calculating current yield and yield to maturity.*** A 25-year, zero coupon bond was recently quoted at 6.500. Find the current yield and yield to maturity of this issue, given the bond has a par value of $1,000. (Assume annual compounding for the yield to maturity measure.)

LG5,6, p. 484 15. ***Calculating current yield and return on investment.*** Assume that an investor pays $850 for a long-term bond that carries a 7.5 percent coupon. During the next 12 months, interest rates drop sharply, and the investor sells the bond at a price of $962.50.
   a. Find the current yield that existed on this bond at the beginning of the year. What was it by the end of the one-year holding period?
   b. Calculate the return on this investment using the approximate yield formula and a one-year investment period.

LG5,6, p. 484 16. **Calculating conversion value and conversion premium.** Find the conversion value of a convertible bond that carries a conversion ratio of 24, given that the market price of the underlying common stock is $55 a share. Would there be any conversion premium if the convertible bond had a market price of $1,500? If so, how much?

LG5,6, p. 484 17. **Calculate current yield, conversion ratio, conversion price, and yield to maturity.** A 6 percent convertible bond (maturing in 20 years) is convertible into 25 shares of the company's common stock. The bond has a par value of $1,000 and is currently trading at $800; the stock (which pays a dividend of 95 cents a share) is currently trading in the market at $35 a share. Use this information to answer the following questions:
   a. What is the current yield on the convertible bond? What is the dividend yield on the company's common stock? Which provides more current income: the convertible bond or the common stock? Explain.
   b. What is the bond's conversion ratio? Its conversion price?
   c. What is the conversion value of this issue? Is there any conversion premium in this issue? If so, how much?
   d. What is the (approximate) yield to maturity on the convertible bond?

LG6, p. 484 18. **Clean and dirty bond prices.** You have decided to sell a 5 percent semiannual coupon bond two months after the last coupon payment. The bond is currently selling for $951.25. Answer the following questions about the bond:
   a. What is the clean price of the bond?
   b. What is the dirty (full) price of the bond?
   c. Explain how the clean and dirty prices of the bond are relevant to the buyer of the bond.

Applying Personal Finance

Choosing the Best Type of Stock

In this chapter, we learned that common stock is often placed into various categories—blue-chip, growth, income, and so forth—and referred to by its size, such as large-, mid-, or small-cap. In this project, you'll examine and compare the returns on various types of common stock.
   Common comparisons include:

- Large-cap versus mid- or small-cap
- Blue-chip versus speculative
- Growth versus income
- Cyclical versus defensive

   Pick any two combinations from the foregoing list, and then select a stock to represent each of the categories included in your choices. For all four of your stocks, obtain information on:

- The company's EPS
- Growth in dividends per share
- Dividend yield
- P/E ratio
- The stock's beta

   In addition, use the formula given in this chapter to compute each stock's approximate yield for the past year, based on what the stock is trading for today versus the price it sold for a year ago. Be sure to include any dividends paid over the past 12 months. You can obtain this information from financial newspapers or from online sources, such as **http://finance.yahoo.com**.
   Compare and contrast the performance and characteristics of the stocks you've chosen. Based on your findings, does the type of stock you own make a difference? Which type or types are the most suitable for your investment purposes?

CRITICAL THINKING CASES

LG3,5,
p. 470, 484

12.1 The Madsen's Problem: What to Do with "Extra" Money?

A couple in their early 30s, Rodney and Carly Madsen recently inherited $90,000 from a relative. Rodney earns a comfortable income as a sales manager for System Analytics, Inc., and Carly does equally well as an attorney with a major law firm. Because they have no children and don't need the money, they've decided to invest all of the inheritance in stocks, bonds, and perhaps even some money market instruments. However, because they're not very familiar with the market, they turn to you for help.

Critical Thinking Questions

1. What kind of investment approach do you think the Madsens should adopt—that is, should they be conservative with their money or aggressive? Explain.
2. What kind of stocks do you think the Madsens should invest in? How important is current income (i.e., dividends or interest income) to them? Should they be putting any of their money into bonds? Explain.
3. Construct an investment portfolio that you feel would be right for the Madsens and invest the full $90,000. Put actual stocks, bonds, and/or convertible securities in the portfolio; you may also put up to one-third of the money into short-term securities such as CDs, Treasury bills, money funds, or MMDAs. Select any securities you want, so long as you feel they'd be suitable for the Madsens. Make sure that the portfolio consists of six or more different securities, and use the latest issue of *The Wall Street Journal* or an online source such as **http://finance.yahoo.com** to determine the market prices of the securities you select. Show the amount invested in each security along with the amount of current income (from dividends and/or interest) that will be generated from the investments. Briefly explain why you selected these particular securities for the Madsens' portfolio.

LG3,5,
p. 470, 484

12.2 Natasha Explores Investing

Natasha Cormier is a 28-year-old management trainee at a large chemical company. She is single, has an annual salary of $34,000 (placing her in the 15 percent tax bracket), and her monthly expenditures come to approximately $1,500. During the past year or so, Natasha has managed to save around $8,000, and she expects to continue saving at least that amount each year for the foreseeable future. Her company pays the premium on her $35,000 life insurance policy. Because Natasha's entire education was financed by scholarships, she was able to save money from the summer and part-time jobs she held as a student. Altogether, she has a nest egg of nearly $18,000, out of which she'd like to invest about $15,000. She'll keep the remaining $3,000 in a bank CD that pays 3 percent interest and will use this money only in an emergency. Natasha can afford to take more risks than someone with family obligations can, but she doesn't wish to be a speculator; she simply wants to earn an attractive rate of return on her investments.

Critical Thinking Questions

1. What investment options are open to Natasha?
2. What chance does she have of earning a satisfactory return if she invests her $15,000 in (a) blue-chip stocks, (b) growth stocks, (c) speculative stocks, (d) corporate bonds, or (e) municipal bonds?
3. Discuss the factors you would consider when analyzing these alternate investment vehicles.
4. What recommendation would you make to Natasha regarding her available investment alternatives? Explain.

Investing in Mutual Funds, ETFs, and Real Estate

LEARNING GOALS

LG1 Describe the basic features and operating characteristics of mutual funds and exchange-traded funds.

LG2 Differentiate between open- and closed-end mutual funds as well as exchange-traded funds, and discuss the various types of fund loads and charges.

LG3 Discuss the types of funds available to investors and the different kinds of investor services offered by mutual funds and exchange-traded funds.

LG4 Gain an understanding of the variables that should be considered when selecting funds for investment purposes.

LG5 Identify the sources of return and calculate the rate of return earned on an investment in a mutual fund, as well as evaluate the performance of an exchange-traded fund.

LG6 Understand the role that real estate plays in a diversified investment portfolio, along with the basics of investing in real estate, either directly or indirectly.

How Will This Affect Me?

Having a financial plan, and being aware that diversification is crucial is a great start to the task of investment planning. The next step is figuring out how to implement your plan by deciding what to invest in. For most people, diversification is best achieved using mutual funds and exchange-traded funds (ETFs). This chapter describes the key characteristics of each type of fund, sorts through the various options you have, shows how to calculate rates of return and evaluate performance, and explains how to choose among funds. The essential elements of investing in real estate and its role in diversifying your overall investment portfolio are also covered. After reading this chapter, you should be in a good position to invest in mutual funds, ETFs, and real estate in a way that will help you achieve your financial objectives.

13-1 MUTUAL FUNDS AND EXCHANGE-TRADED FUNDS: SOME BASICS

LG1, LG2

Sound investment planning involves finding investments with risk–return characteristics that are compatible with your financial objectives. In this chapter, we'll look beyond stocks and bonds and consider other types of investment products that enjoy widespread use among individual investors: mutual funds, exchange-traded funds (ETFs), and real estate. These investment outlets offer risk–return opportunities that you may not be able to obtain from just buying stocks or bonds on your own. For example, investors interested in receiving the benefits of professional portfolio management, but who don't have the funds to purchase a diversified portfolio of securities, may find mutual funds attractive. ETFs, on the other hand, are similar to mutual funds but offer a degree of flexibility that standard mutual funds don't have. Still other investors may be drawn to real estate, either because of its perceived return potential or perhaps to obtain some preferential tax treatment. Let's now take a closer look at each of these investments.

mutual fund
A financial services organization that receives money from its shareholders and invests those funds on their behalf in a diversified portfolio of securities.

A **mutual fund** is a financial services organization that receives money from its shareholders and invests those funds on their behalf in a diversified portfolio of securities. An **exchange-traded fund (ETF)** is an investment company whose shares trade on stock exchanges. Unlike mutual funds, ETF shares can be bought or sold (or sold short) throughout the day. When investors buy shares in a mutual fund or an ETF, they usually become *part owners of a widely diversified portfolio of securities*. A mutual fund or an ETF share can be thought of as the *financial product* that's sold to the public by an investment company. That is, the investment company builds and manages a portfolio of securities and sells ownership interests—shares of stock—in that portfolio through a vehicle known as a mutual fund. This concept underlies the whole mutual fund structure and is depicted in Exhibit 13.1. For individual investors today, mutual funds are the investment vehicle of choice. In fact, more people invest in mutual funds than any other type of investment product.

exchange-traded fund (ETF)
An investment company whose shares trade on stock exchanges; unlike mutual funds, ETF shares can be bought or sold (or sold short) throughout the day. ETFs are usually structured as an index fund that's set up to match the performance of a certain market segment.

Mutual funds are popular because they offer not only a variety of interesting investment opportunities, but also a wide array of services that many investors find appealing. They're an easy and convenient way to invest—one that's especially suited to beginning investors and those with limited investment capital. And as we'll see later in the chapter, ETFs have become an increasingly popular alternative to mutual funds.

EXHIBIT 13.1   Basic Mutual Fund Structure

A mutual fund brings together the funds from many individual investors and uses this pool of money to acquire a diversified portfolio of stocks, bonds, and other securities.

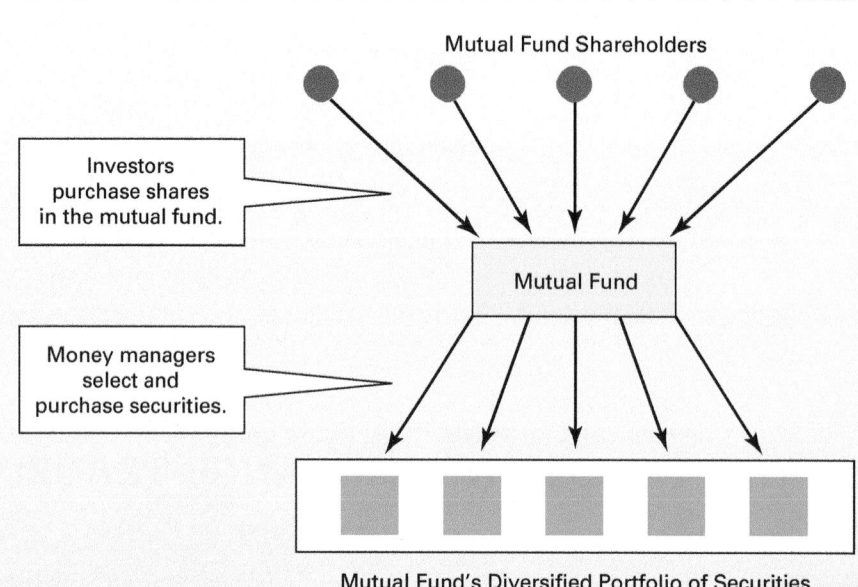

Mutual Fund Shareholders

Investors purchase shares in the mutual fund.

Mutual Fund

Money managers select and purchase securities.

Mutual Fund's Diversified Portfolio of Securities

13-1a The Mutual Fund Concept

The first mutual fund in this country was started in Boston in 1924. By 1980, 564 mutual funds were in operation. But that was only the beginning—by the end of 2014, mutual fund assets under management grew to some $15.9 trillion in the United States. Indeed, in 2014, *there were nearly 8,000 publicly traded mutual funds in the United States*. Actually, counting duplicate or multiple fund offerings from the same investment company, there were closer to *30,000 funds* available; such duplication occurs because sometimes two or three versions of the same fund are offered, with each "fund" having a different type of load charge or fee structure. To put that number in perspective, *there are more mutual funds in existence today than there are stocks listed on all the stock exchanges in the United States!*

Mutual funds are big business in the United States and, indeed, all over the world. In 2014, registered investment companies managed 24 percent of households' financial assets, and about 53.2 million, or about 43 percent, of those households owned mutual funds. Mutual funds appeal to a lot of investors, who all share one view: they've decided, for one reason or another, to turn the problems of security selection and portfolio management over to professional money managers. Questions of which stock or bond to select, when to buy, and when to sell have plagued investors for about as long as there have been organized securities markets. Such concerns lie at the heart of the mutual fund concept and are largely behind the growth in funds. The fact is that many people simply lack the time, the know-how, or the commitment to manage their own securities, so they turn to others. And most often, that means mutual funds.

Pooled Diversification

The mutual fund concept is based on the simple idea of delegating security selection and portfolio management to professional money managers. A mutual fund combines the investment capital of many people with similar investment goals and invests those funds in a wide variety of securities. Investors receive shares of stock in the mutual fund and, through the fund, enjoy much wider investment diversification than they could otherwise achieve. Indeed, some mutual funds commonly hold hundreds of different stocks or bonds. For example, in the middle of 2015, the Fidelity Contrafund held about 319 different securities, and the Dreyfus GNMA bond fund had about 830 holdings. For all but the super-rich, that's far more diversification than most investors could ever hope to attain. Yet each investor who owns shares in a fund is, in effect, a part owner of that fund's diversified portfolio of securities.

Regardless of the fund size, as the securities held by it move up and down in price, the market value of the mutual fund shares moves accordingly. And when the fund receives dividend and interest payments, they too are passed on to the mutual fund shareholders and distributed on the basis of prorated ownership. For example, if you own 1,000 shares of stock in a mutual fund and that represents, say, 1 percent of all shares outstanding, then you would receive 1 percent of the dividends paid by the fund. When a security held by the fund is sold for a profit, the capital gain is also passed on to fund shareholders. The whole mutual fund idea, in fact, rests on the concept of pooled diversification and works much like insurance, whereby individuals pool their resources for the collective benefit of all contributors.

pooled diversification
A process whereby investors buy into a diversified portfolio of securities for the collective benefit of individual investors.

13-1b Why Invest in Mutual Funds or ETFs?

Mutual funds and ETFs can be used by individual investors in various ways. One investor may buy a fund because of the substantial capital gains opportunities that it provides; another may buy a totally different fund not for its capital gains, but instead for its current income. Whatever kind of income a fund provides, individuals tend to use these investment vehicles for one or more of these reasons: (1) to achieve diversification in their investment holdings, (2) to obtain the services of professional money managers, (3) to generate an attractive rate of return on their investment capital, and (4) for the convenience that they offer.

Diversification

As we just discussed, diversification is a primary motive for investing in mutual funds and ETFs. This ability to diversify allows investors to reduce their exposure to risk sharply by indirectly investing in several types of securities and numerous companies, rather than just one or two. If you have only $500 or $1,000 to invest, you obviously won't achieve much diversification on your own. But if you invest that money in a mutual fund or an ETF, you'll end up owning part of a well-diversified portfolio of securities.

Professional Management

While management is paid a fee for its services, the contributions of a full-time expert manager should be well worth the fee. These pros know where to look for return and how to avoid unnecessary risk; at the minimum, their decisions should result in better returns than the average individual investor can achieve.

Financial Returns

Although professional managers *may* be able to achieve better returns than small investors can generate, the relatively high purchase fees, coupled with the management and operating costs, tend to reduce the returns actually earned on mutual fund investments. But the mutual fund industry hasn't attracted millions of investors by generating substandard returns. Quite the contrary; over the long haul, mutual funds have provided relatively attractive returns. Exhibit 13.2 shows the average return performance on a

EXHIBIT 13.2

Comparative Performance of Selected Mutual Funds Categories by Holding Period: 2011–2015

The type of fund you invest in and your holding period have a lot to do with the kind of return you can expect. While the selected funds below are sorted by 5-year returns within each fund type, it is clear that the 1- and 3-year returns can be substantially different as well.

Fund Type	Average Annual Returns (%)		
	1 Year	3 Year	5 Year
Domestic Sector Stock Funds			
Consumer defensive	12.74	16.51	15.97
Health	40.62	33.25	25.80
Consumer cyclical	16.10	20.64	18.45
Technology	20.14	19.71	15.94
Real estate	12.72	12.04	14.12
Utilities	6.32	13.60	13.83
Industrials	7.50	20.67	16.26
Natural resources	−13.40	3.20	4.29
Equity energy	−18.81	5.57	4.92
Communications	7.15	15.14	13.24
Financial	10.27	19.40	11.48
Allocation Funds			
Convertibles	7.51	13.89	11.08
World allocation	2.97	8.92	8.68
International Stock Funds			
Pacific/Asia ex-Japan stock	10.80	11.98	9.39
Latin America stock	−20.34	−5.30	−2.85
Europe stock	0.51	15.96	11.86
Fixed-Income Funds			
Long-term government	8.00	1.59	6.56
High-yield bond	1.19	7.05	8.18
Inflation-protected bond	−1.54	−1.04	2.67
Intermediate-term bond	2.34	2.82	4.08
Short-term government	0.70	0.38	0.98

Source: Adapted from http://news.morningstar.com/fund-category-returns/, accessed May 2015. The Morningstar data contained herein (1) is proprietary to Morningstar; (2) may not be copied or distributed without written permission; and (3) is not warranted to be accurate, complete, or timely. Morningstar is not responsible for any damages or losses arising from any use of this information and has not granted its consent to be considered or deemed an "expert" under the Securities Act of 1933.

variety of mutual funds and suggests the kind of returns that investors were able to achieve over one-, three-, and five-year holding periods ending in May 2015. Given the range of returns across the different fund types and holding periods, it's clear that investors should do their homework before putting money into mutual funds.

Convenience

Mutual fund shares can be purchased from various sources, which is another reason for their appeal. Mutual funds make it easy to invest, and most don't require much capital to get started. They handle all the paperwork and recordkeeping, their prices are widely quoted, and it's usually possible to deal in fractional shares. Opening a mutual fund account is about as easy as opening a checking account. Just fill out an investor form, send in the minimum amount of money, and you're in business!

13-1c How Mutual Funds Are Organized and Run

Although it's tempting to think of a mutual fund as a monolithic entity, that's really not the case. Various functions—investing, recordkeeping, safekeeping, and others—are split among two or more companies. Besides the fund itself, which is organized as a separate corporation or trust and *is owned by the shareholders*, there are several other major players.

- The *management company* runs the fund's daily operations. These include the firms such as Fidelity, Vanguard, and T. Rowe Price. Usually, the management firm also serves as the investment advisor.
- The *investment advisor* buys and sells the stocks or bonds and otherwise oversees the portfolio. Three parties participate in this phase of the operation: the *portfolio manager*, who actually runs the portfolio and makes the buy and sell decisions; *securities analysts*, who analyze securities and look for attractive investment candidates; and *traders*, who try to buy and sell blocks of securities at the best possible price.
- The *distributor* sells the fund shares, either directly to the public or through certain authorized dealers (such as major brokerage houses and commercial banks).
- The *custodian* physically safeguards the securities and other assets of a fund, but without taking an active role in the investment decisions. To discourage foul play, an independent party (such as a bank) serves in this capacity.
- The *transfer agent* executes transactions, keeps track of purchase and redemption requests from shareholders, and maintains other shareholder records.

All this separation of duties is designed for just one thing—to protect the mutual fund investor/shareholder. Obviously, you can always lose money if your fund's stock or bond holdings go down in value. But that's really the only risk of loss you face, because the chance of ever losing money from fraud or a mutual fund collapse is almost nonexistent. Besides the separation of duties noted earlier, the only formal link between the mutual fund and the management company is a contract that must be regularly renewed—and approved by shareholders. The fund's assets *can never be in the hands of the management company*. As still another safeguard, each fund must have a board of directors, or trustees, who are elected by shareholders and charged with keeping tabs on the management company and renewing its contract.

13-1d Open-End versus Closed-End Funds

It may seem that all mutual funds are organized in roughly the same way, but investors should be aware of some major differences. One way that funds differ is in how they are structured. Funds can be set up either as *open-end companies*, which can sell an unlimited number of ownership shares, or as *closed-end companies*, which can issue only a limited number of shares.

Open-End Investment Companies

open-end investment company
A firm that can issue an unlimited number of shares that it buys and sells at a price based on the current market value of the securities it owns; also called a *mutual fund.*

The term *mutual fund* commonly denotes an open-end investment company. Such organizations are the dominant type of investment company and account for well over 95 percent of assets under management. In an open-end investment company, investors actually buy their shares from, and sell them back to, the mutual fund itself. When they buy shares in the fund, the fund issues new shares of stock and fills the purchase order with these new shares. There's no limit to the number of shares that the fund can issue, other than investor demand. Further, all open-end mutual funds stand behind their shares and buy them back when investors decide to sell. So there's never any trading among individuals. Many of these funds are huge and hold billions of dollars' worth of securities.

net asset value (NAV)
The current market value of all the securities the fund owns, less any liabilities, on a per-share basis.

Buy and sell transactions in an open-end mutual fund are carried out at prices based on the current value of all the securities held in the fund's portfolio. This is known as the fund's net asset value (NAV); it is calculated at least once a day and represents the underlying value of a share of stock in a particular fund. NAV is found by taking the total market value of all securities held by the fund, subtracting any liabilities, and dividing the result by the number of shares outstanding. The NAV would be used to derive the price at which the fund's shares could be bought and sold. (As we'll see later, NAV is generally included in the fund's quoted price and indicates the price at which an investor can *sell shares*—or the price that an investor would pay to *buy no-load funds*.)

> ### EXAMPLE: Calculating a Mutual Fund's NAV
>
> On a recent day, the market value of all the securities held by the XYZ mutual fund equaled $10 million and XYZ had 500,000 shares outstanding. Consequently, the fund's NAV per share would be $20, which is calculated as:
>
> $$\frac{\text{Total Market Value of All Securities} - \text{Liabilities}}{\text{Number of Shares Outstanding}} = \frac{\$10,000,000}{500,000}$$

Closed-End Investment Companies

closed-end investment company
An investment company that issues a fixed number of shares, which are themselves listed and traded like any other share of stock.

The term *mutual fund* is supposed to be used only with open-end funds, but as a practical matter, it's regularly used with closed-end investment companies as well. Basically, closed-end investment companies operate with a fixed number of shares outstanding and do *not* regularly issue new shares of stock. In effect, they are like any other corporation, except that the corporation's business happens to be investing in marketable securities. Like open-end funds, closed-end investment companies have enjoyed remarkable growth in the past decade or so. Only 34 of these funds existed in 1980. By the end of 2014, there were about 570 closed-end funds with total net assets of $289 billion—though still just a fraction of the $15.9 trillion invested in the mutual fund industry. Shares in closed-end investment companies are actively traded in the secondary market, just like any other common stock; but unlike open-end funds, *all trading is done between investors in the open market*. The fund itself plays no role in either buy or sell transactions; once the shares are issued, the fund is out of the picture.

There are some major differences that exist between open- and closed-end funds. Because closed-end funds have a fixed amount of capital to work with, they don't have to worry about stock redemptions or new money coming into the fund. So they don't have to be concerned about keeping cash on hand to meet redemptions. Equally important, because closed-end funds don't have new money flowing in all the time, they don't have to worry about finding new investments for that money. Instead, they can concentrate on a set portfolio of securities and do the best job they can in managing it. The share prices of closed-end companies are determined not only by their NAVs, but also by general supply-and-demand conditions in the market. Depending on the market outlook and investor expectations, closed-end companies generally trade at a *discount* or *premium* to their NAVs.

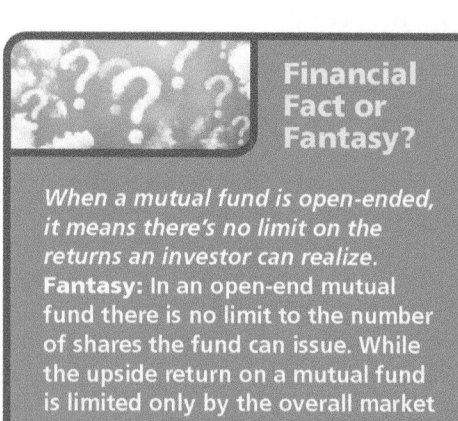

Financial Fact or Fantasy?

When a mutual fund is open-ended, it means there's no limit on the returns an investor can realize.
Fantasy: In an open-end mutual fund there is no limit to the number of shares the fund can issue. While the upside return on a mutual fund is limited only by the overall market and the skill of its managers, investors cannot lose more than they invested.

13-1e ETFs

Combine some of the operating characteristics of an open-end fund with some of the trading characteristics of a closed-end fund, and you'll end up with something called an *ETF*. As defined above, an ETF is an investment company whose shares trade on one of the stock exchanges. Most all ETFs are structured as *index funds*, set up to match the performance of a certain market segment. They do this by owning all or a representative sample of the stocks (or bonds) in a targeted market segment or index (we'll examine traditional index funds in more detail later in this chapter). Thus, ETFs offer the professional money management of traditional mutual funds and the liquidity of an exchange-traded stock.

However, the passive indexing of early ETFs is giving way to the creation of actively managed ETFs.

As pointed out in Chapter 11, *exchange-traded notes (ETNs)* are more similar to ETFs than to mutual funds. Like ETFs, most ETNs are designed to reproduce the returns on a market benchmark, net of investment management fees. Also like ETFs, ETNs provide tax advantages over mutual funds. However, they differ from ETFs in being senior, unsecured, unsubordinated debt securities issued by an underwriting bank. While our discussion in this chapter focuses on ETFs, ETNs are in many cases close, but not perfect substitutes for ETFs. ETNs should consequently be kept in mind when you choose among the different investments that can help you achieve your financial goals.

Even though ETFs are like closed-end funds (they're traded on listed exchanges), *they are actually open-end mutual funds* whose number of shares outstanding can be increased or decreased in response to market demand. That is, ETFs can be bought or sold like any other stock, and *the ETF distributor can also create new shares or redeem old shares*. This is done to prevent the fund from trading at (much of) a premium or discount to the underlying value of its holdings, thereby avoiding a pitfall of closed-end funds. In 1998, there were only 29 ETFs in the United States, with about $16 billion under management. By the end of 2014, there were over 1,400 ETFs in existence, with assets under management of nearly $2.0 trillion. ETFs have become more popular as institutional investors use them to exploit or hedge against broad movements in the stock market. It's estimated that about 4 percent (5.2 million) of U.S. households owned ETFs in 2014. About 9 percent of households that own mutual funds also own ETFs.

These funds cover a wide array of domestic and international stock indexes and submarkets as well as a handful of U.S. Treasury and corporate bond indexes. The biggest and oldest ETFs (dating back to 1993) are based on the S&P 500 and are known as *Spiders* (SPDRs). In addition, there are *Qubes* (based on the NASDAQ 100; this is the most actively traded ETF—in fact, it's the most actively traded stock in the world), *Diamonds* (based on the DJIA), and ETFs based on dozens of international markets (from Australia and Canada to Germany, Japan, and the United Kingdom). Just about every major U.S. index, in fact, has its own ETF, along with lots of minor indexes covering specialized market segments. The NAVs of ETFs are set at a fraction of the underlying index value at any given time. In June 2015, for example, when the S&P 500 index was 2,124.20, the ETF on that index traded at $212.04 (or about 1/10 of the index); likewise, the ETF on the Dow is set at about 1/100 of the DJIA (so when the Dow closed at 18,144.07 at this time, the ETF closed at $181.12).

ETFs combine many advantages of closed-end funds with those of traditional (open-end) index funds. That is, like closed-end funds, ETFs can be bought and sold at *any time of the day;* you can place an order through your broker (and pay a standard commission, just as you would with any other stock). In contrast, you *cannot* trade a traditional open-end fund on an intraday basis because all buy and sell orders for these funds are filled, at closing prices, at the end of the trading day. What's more, because most ETFs are passively managed, they offer all the advantages of any index fund: low costs, low portfolio turnover, and low taxes. The fund's tax liability is kept low because ETFs rarely distribute any capital gains to shareholders. However, actively managed ETFs could well have higher costs, portfolio turnover, and taxes than passively managed ETFs. It remains to be seen whether actively managed ETFs will take significant market share away from mutual funds.

There are many types of ETFs. The most common type tracks a major market index like the S&P 500 or the NASDAQ-100 index. Foreign market ETFs track non-U.S. market indexes, like Japan's Nikkei index or the MSCI index for Germany. Foreign-currency ETFs provide exposure to an individual foreign currency or to a basket to currencies. There are also sector and industry ETFs that allow investors access to specific segments of the market like high-tech or

pharmaceuticals. ETFs also provide exposure to commodities like gold or oil. You can even buy ETFs that invest in real estate, or are composed of derivatives like options and futures. *Style* ETFs typically follow either certain market capitalization stocks (small-, mid-, or large-cap) or value or growth stocks. The latter types of ETFs are often tied to style indexes developed by S&P, BARRA, or Frank Russell. There are also ETFs that track bonds. The trend toward customization of ETFs even provides inverse ETFs that effectively create short positions. These ETFs appreciate in value when the market falls, and vice versa. There are also a variety of new innovations that include actively managed ETFs and leveraged ETFs. As the name suggests, an actively managed ETF manages assets toward a goal of outperforming, rather than merely tracking, a given index. Leveraged ETFs seek to outperform a benchmark, which is usually achieved by using derivatives like options, futures, and swaps. If you're thinking that this can be extremely risky, you're right. Innovation continues in the ETF market to provide investors with more choices so that they can either moderate or enhance their risk exposure. Exhibit 13.3 lists some available ETFs.

13-1f Some Important Cost Considerations

When you buy or sell shares in a *closed-end* investment company, or in *ETFs* for that matter, you pay a commission just as you would with any other type of listed or over the counter (OTC) common stock transaction. This isn't so with *open-end* funds, however. In particular, the cost of investing in an open-end mutual fund depends on the types of fees and load charges that the fund levies on its investors.

Load Funds

load fund
A fund that charges a fee at time of purchase.

Most open-end mutual funds are so-called load funds because they charge a commission *when the shares are purchased* (such charges are often referred to as *front-end loads*). However, few funds today charge the maximum. Instead, many funds charge commissions of only 2 percent or 3 percent—such funds are known as low-load funds. The good news on front-end load funds is that there's normally no charge or commission to pay when you *sell* your shares! Occasionally, however, you'll run into funds that charge a commission—or a *redemption fee*—when you sell your shares. Known as back-end load funds, these charges tend to decline over time and usually disappear altogether after five or six years. The purpose of such charges is to discourage investors from trading in and out of the funds over short periods of time. According to the latest regulations, a mutual fund cannot charge more than 8.5 percent in *total sales charges and fees*, and that includes front- and back-end loads, as well as 12b-1 fees, which will be discussed later in the chapter. This means that, if a fund charges a 5 percent front-end load and a 1 percent 12b-1 fee, then it can charge a maximum of only 2.5 percent in back-end load charges—otherwise, it will violate the 8.5 percent cap.

low-load fund
A fund that has a low purchase fee.

back-end load
A commission charged for redeeming fund shares.

No-Load Funds

no-load fund
A fund on which no transaction fees are charged.

Some open-end investment companies charge you nothing at all to buy their funds; these are known as no-load funds. Less than half of the funds sold today are true no-loads; all the rest charge some type of load or fee. Even funds that don't have front-end loads (and so may be categorized as no-loads) can have back-end load charges that you must pay when selling your fund shares—or something called a 12b-1 fee, which you'd pay for as long as you hold your shares.

Behavior Matters

Behavioral Biases in Mutual Fund Investing

In theory, rational investors should pursue a simple investment strategy that involves well-diversified, low-expense mutual funds, accompanied by only minimal portfolio rebalancing. The time-tested approach is to choose index mutual funds with low fees and low portfolio turnover. In contrast, current research indicates that many individual investors exhibit the following puzzling behaviors:

- Investors tend to sell winners too quickly and hold losers too long.

- Investors often buy mutual funds with high fees and even pay high fees for index funds that passively hold the components of indexes like the S&P 500.

- Individual investors often chase funds with high past returns.

What does behavioral finance research have to say about the above biased behavior?

- **Disposition effect.** People dislike taking losses much more than they enjoy realizing gains. Consequently, they tend to hold assets that have lost value too long and tend to take gains too soon. In mutual fund investing, this bias may encourage some investors to overestimate their expected holding periods and mistakenly select high-expense (front-end load) funds, the effect of which declines with the expected holding period. This often leads to overly frequent trading.

- **Narrow framing.** It's possible that investors buy and sell mutual funds without adequately considering the effects of the costs on their *total* portfolio. Similarly, if investors tend to view mutual funds as much safer than buying individual stocks, they may spend less time than they should evaluating mutual fund performance and costs.

- **Representativeness.** There is evidence that investors view recent performance as overly representative of a mutual fund's future performance (despite those warning statements we've probably all seen if we've read a prospectus). This could cause them to buy mutual funds inappropriately, just because of their past records. This bias may be partially explained by investor services companies' ratings of funds based on *past* returns.

So what's the remedy for the above behavioral biases? The answer is clear: education! There is evidence that sophisticated investors are far less likely to fall into these behavioral traps. "Sophisticated" investors are better informed about key investment principles, understand these behavioral tendencies, are more experienced, and have higher incomes. They use mutual funds effectively, which means that they hold most funds for a long time, avoid high expense funds, and consequently enjoy relatively good performance. And based on what you now know, this could be you.

Source: Adapted from Warren Bailey, Alok Kumar, and David Ng, 2011, "Behavioral Biases of Mutual Fund Investors," *Journal of Financial Economics,* v. 102, pp. 1–27.

12b-1 Fees

12b-1 fee
An annual fee that's supposed to be used to offset promotion and selling expenses.

Also known as *hidden loads*, 12b-1 fees are allowed by the Securities and Exchange Commission (SEC) and were originally designed to help no-load funds cover their distribution and marketing expenses. Unsurprisingly, the popularity of these fees spread rapidly among fund distributors, so they're now used by nearly 70 percent of all open-end mutual funds. The fees are assessed annually and can amount to as much as 1 percent of assets under management. In good markets and bad, the fee is paid right off the top—and that takes its toll. Consider, for instance, $10,000 in a fund that charges a 1 percent 12b-1 fee. That translates into an annual charge of *$100 a year*, which is a significant amount of money. The SEC set a 1 percent

EXHIBIT 13.3 **Examples of Exchange-Traded Funds (ETFs)**

The ETF market remains dominated by products that seek to track various domestic and international indexes. However, actively managed ETFs that focus on selecting and trading a dynamic mix of securities are growing. Below are representative examples of available ETFs.

Type of ETF	Ticker	Tracking Goal
U.S. Equity Indexes		
SPDR S&P 500 ETF	SPY	S&P 500 index.
PowerShares QQQ Trust, Ser 1	QQQ	Nasdaq-100 index.
SPDR Dow Jones Industrial Average ETF	DIA	Dow Jones Industrial Average index.
iShares Russell 2000	IWM	Russell 2000 index.
Vanguard Total Stock market ETF	VTI	Overall stock market.
U.S. Equity Sector Indexes		
Energy Select Sector SPDR ETF*	XLE	Energy Select Sector Index.
Financial Select Sector SPDR ETF	XLF	Financial Select Sector Index.
Technology Select Sector SPDR ETF	XLK	Technology Select Sector Index.
U.S. Bond Market		
iShares Core U.S. Aggregate Bond ETF	AGG	Index of U.S. investment-grade bond market.
Vanguard Short-Term Bond ETF	BSV	Market-weighted bond index with short-term dollar-weighted average maturity.
iShares Core 10+Year USD Bond ETF	ILTB	Index of U.S. dollar-denominated, investment-grade U.S. corporate and government bonds with maturities of at least 10 years.
International Markets		
MSCI EAFE ETF	EFA	MSCI European, Australasian, and Far Eastern "EAFE" Index.
iShares MSCI Emerging Markets ETF	EEM	MSCI Emerging Markets Index.
Actively Managed Funds		
PIMCO Enhanced Short Maturity Active ETF	MINT	Seeks greater income and total return than money market funds.
PowerShares Active U.S. Real Estate ETF	PSR	Selects securities in the FTSE NAREIT Equity REIT index
iShares Enhanced U.S. Small-Cap ETF	IESM	Pursues long-term capital gains by investing in U.S. small cap stocks

*SPDRS are available on all of the S&P 500 sectors as well as on variously defined industries.

cap on annual 12b-1 fees and, perhaps more significantly, stated that true no-load funds cannot charge more than 0.25 percent in annual 12b-1 fees (otherwise, they must drop the "no-load" label in their sales and promotional material).

A trend in mutual fund fees is the *multiple-class sales charge*. You'll find such arrangements at firms like Dreyfus, Merrill Lynch, MFS, Scudder, Putnam, and others. The way it works is that the mutual fund will issue different classes of shares on the same fund or portfolio of securities. So, rather than having just one class of stock outstanding, there might be three of them: Class A shares might have normal (modest) front-end loads; Class B stock might have no front-end loads but substantial back-end loads along with maximum annual 12b-1 fees; and Class C shares might carry a small back-end load and modest 12b-1 fees. In other words, you pick your own poison.

Management Fees

management fee
A fee paid to the professional money managers who administer a mutual fund's portfolio.

The **management fee** is the cost that you incur to hire professional money managers to run the fund's portfolio of investments. These fees are also assessed annually and usually range from less than 0.5 percent to as much as 3 percent or 4 percent of assets under management. All funds—whether they're load or no-load, open- or closed-end—have these fees; and, like 12b-1 fees, they bear watching because high management fees will take their toll on performance. The size of the management fee is usually unrelated to the fund's performance. In addition to these management fees, some funds may charge an *exchange fee* whenever an investor transfers money from one fund to another within the same fund family and/or an *annual maintenance fee* to help defer the costs of providing service to low-balance accounts.

Keeping Track of Fund Fees and Loads

Fortunately, steps have been taken to bring fund fees and loads out into the open. For one thing, fund charges are more widely reported now than they were in the past. Most notably, today you can find detailed information about the types and amounts of fees and charges on just about any mutual fund by going to one of the dozens of Internet sites that report on mutual funds, including **Quicken.com**, **Kiplinger.com**, **Morningstar.com**, Yahoo! (at **http://finance.yahoo.com**), and a host of others. Or you could use the mutual fund quotes that appear daily in (most) major newspapers and in *The Wall Street Journal*. For example, take a look at *The Wall Street Journal*'s online quotations in Exhibit 13.4; right after the (abbreviated) name of the fund, you'll often find the letters *r*, *p*, or *t*. If you see an *r* after a fund's name, it means that the fund charges some type of redemption fee, or back-end load, when you sell your shares. The use of a *p* means the fund levies a 12b-1 fee. Finally, a *t* indicates funds that charge redemption fees *and* 12b-1 fees. The quotations, of course, tell you only *what kinds of fees* are charged by the funds; they don't tell you *how much* is charged. What's more, these quotes *tell you nothing about the front-end loads*, if any, charged by the funds. You can access Internet (or other) sources to find out whether a particular fund charges a front-end load or to obtain specifics on any amounts charged.

> ## You Can Do It Now
> ### Objective Mutual Fund Resources
> Looking for information on mutual fund investing from a source that isn't trying to sell you a financial product? Then try the Mutual Fund Investor's Center at http://mfea.com/. It's sponsored by the Mutual Fund Education Alliance (MFEA), which is a national trade organization for mutual funds. You can do it now.

Mutual funds are required by the SEC to *disclose fully* all their fees and expenses in a standardized, easy-to-understand format. Every fund prospectus must contain, right up front, a fairly detailed *fee table*, much like the one illustrated in Exhibit 13.5. Notice that this table has three parts. The first specifies all *shareholder transaction costs*. This section tells you what it's going to cost to buy and sell shares in the mutual fund. The next section lists all *annual operating expenses* of the fund. Showing these expenses as a percentage of average net assets, the fund must break out management fees, those elusive 12b-1 fees, and any other expenses. The third section gives the *total*

EXHIBIT 13.4 **Mutual Fund Quotes**

Open-end mutual funds are listed separately from other securities and have their own quotation system; an example is shown here in online quotes from *The Wall Street Journal*. Note that these securities are also quoted in dollars and cents and that the quotes include not only the fund's NAV but also year-to-date (YTD) returns. Also included as part of the quotes is an indication of whether the fund charges redemption and/or 12b-1 fees.

Family/Fund	Symbol	NAV	Chg	YTD % return	3-year % chg
American Century A					
CorePis p	ACCQX	10.87	–0.01	0.9	2.2
EmgMktA t	AEMMX	9.31	0.04	11.9	9.6
Growth p	TCRAX	29.68	...	5.7	16.7
IntlBnd t	AIBDX	12.41	–0.10	–5.1	–3.5
LtTf	MMBAX	11.41	0.01	–0.5	0.01
Artisan Funds					
EmgMktsInv	ARTZX	13.03	0.04	8.9	13.03
EmgMktsInst	APHEX	12.93	0.03	8.7	5.3
IntlVal Inv	ARTKX	36.81	–0.21	7.6	18.8
MidCapInv	ARTMX	48.20	–0.01	6.1	17.9
MidCapVal Inv	ARTQX	25.61	–0.07	3.9	16.5
SmCapVal Inv	ARTVX	14.30	–0.09	1.1	8.0
ValueInv	ARTLX	13.87	–0.04	6.0	15.4

American Century Core Plus Fund, class A shares; a fund with a front-end load fee (p).

American Century Emerging Markets, class A shares; a fund with both 12b-1 and front-end load fees (t).

American Century International Bond Fund, class A shares; a fund with a front-end load fee and possible redemption fee (p).

American Century Long-Term Tax-Free Fund, class A shares; a fund with a front-end fee (p).

Artisan International Value Fund; a true no-load fund (no front-end, back-end, or 12b-1 fees)

p—Distribution costs apply, 12b-1.

r—Redemption charge may apply.

t—Footnotes p and r apply.

Source: *The Wall Street Journal*, http://online.wsj.com/mdc/public/page/2_3048-usmfunds_A-usmfunds.html, accessed May 22, 2015; NAV-net asset value. Chg-change in NAV from previous trading day. 3-year % chg-is trailing three-year annualized.

cost over time of buying, selling, and owning the fund. This part of the table contains both transaction and operating expenses and shows what the total costs would be over hypothetical 1-, 3-, 5-, and 10-year holding periods. To ensure consistency and comparability, the funds must follow a rigid set of guidelines when presenting the example costs.

13-1g Buying and Selling Funds

Buying and selling shares of closed-end investment companies or ETFs is no different from buying shares of common stock. The transactions are executed through brokers or dealers who handle the orders in the usual way. They're subject to the normal transaction costs, and because they're treated like any other listed or OTC stock, their shares can even be margined or sold short, which are discussed in Chapter 11.

The situation is considerably different, however, with *open-end funds*. Such funds can be bought through a discount or full-service broker or directly from the mutual fund company itself. And, of course, at most funds, you can open an account online. Once your account is open and the company has your initial deposit, you are ready to buy shares. Selling shares in a fund is a do-it-yourself affair that simply requires

EXHIBIT 13.5   Example of a Mutual Fund Fee Table

The SEC requires mutual funds to disclose fully load charges, redemption fees, and annual expenses in a three-part table like the one shown here. The table must be conspicuously placed near the front of the prospectus, not hidden somewhere in the back.

Fee table

The following table describes the fees and expenses that are incurred when you buy, hold, or sell shares of the fund.

Shareholder fees (paid by the investor directly)

Maximum sales charge (load) on purchases (as a % of offering price)	3.00
Sales charge (load) on reinvested distributions	None
Deferred sales charge (load) on redemptions	None
Exchange fees	None
Annual account maintenance fee (for accounts under $2,500)	$12.00

Annual fund operating expenses (paid from fund assets)

Management fee	0.45%
Distribution and service (12b-1) fee	None
Other expenses	0.20%
Total annual fund operating expenses	0.65%

Example

This example is intended to help an investor compare the cost of investing in different funds. The example assumes a $10,000 investment in the fund for 1, 3, 5, and 10 years and then redemption of all fund shares at the end of those periods. The example also assumes that an investment returns 5 percent each year and that the fund's operating expenses remain the same. Although actual costs may be higher or lower, based on these assumptions an investor's costs would be:

1 year	$ 364
3 years	$ 502
5 years	$ 651
10 years	$1,086

using an online account or an 800 telephone number. When selling, it is wise to see if your company offers the ability to switch funds. A common feature is the ability to go online (or pick up the phone) to move money from one fund to another—the only constraint is that the funds must be managed by the same "family" of funds. Most companies charge little or nothing for these shifts, although funds that offer free exchange privileges often limit the number of times you can switch each year. (We'll discuss this service in more detail when we cover *conversion privileges* later in the chapter.)

Should you want more information than what is provided in either the profile or prospectus, you can always request a copy of the fund's *Statement of Additional Information*, which contains detailed information on the fund's investment objectives, portfolio composition, management, and past performance. Whether it's the fund profile (which should be good enough for most investors), the fund's prospectus, or its Statement of Additional Information, the bottom line is these publications should be required reading for anybody who's thinking about investing in a mutual fund.

13-2 TYPES OF FUNDS AND FUND SERVICES

Categorizing mutual funds and ETFs according to their investment policies and objectives is widely practiced in the investment industry. This is because it tends to reflect similarities not only in how the funds manage their money, but also in their risk and return characteristics. Every fund has a particular stated investment objective, of which the most common are capital appreciation, income, tax-exempt income, preserving investment capital, or some combination thereof. Some popular types of mutual funds include growth, aggressive growth, value, equity-income, balanced, growth-and-income, bond, money market, index, sector, socially responsible, international, and asset allocation funds. Disclosure of a fund's investment objective is required by the SEC, and each fund is expected to conform to its stated investment policy and objective. Let's now look at these funds to see what they are and what they have to offer investors. After that, we'll look at the kinds of investor services these funds offer.

13-2a Types of Funds

Growth Funds

The objective of a *growth fund* is simple—capital appreciation. Long-term growth and capital gains are the primary goals of such funds, so they invest principally in common stocks with above-average growth potential. Because of the uncertainty concerning their future capital gains, growth funds involve a fair amount of risk exposure. They're usually viewed as long-term investment vehicles that are most suitable for the aggressive investor who wants to build capital and has little interest in current income.

Aggressive Growth Funds

Aggressive growth funds are highly speculative investments that seek large profits from capital gains; in many ways, they're really an extension of the growth fund concept. Many are fairly small with average assets under management of less than $300 million. Also known as "capital appreciation" funds, they often buy stocks of small, unseasoned companies; stocks with relatively high price/earnings multiples; and stocks whose prices are highly volatile. Some of these funds even go so far as to buy stocks on margin by borrowing part of the purchase price. Such leverage is designed to yield big returns. However, aggressive growth funds are perhaps the most volatile of all the fund types. When the markets are good, these funds do well; when the markets are bad, they typically experience substantial losses.

Value Funds

Value funds invest in stocks considered to be *undervalued* in the market. Consequently, the funds look for stocks that are fundamentally sound but have yet to be discovered, and as such, remain undervalued by the market. In stark contrast to growth funds, value funds look for stocks with relatively low price/earnings (P/E) ratios, high dividend yields, and moderate amounts of financial leverage. They prefer undiscovered companies that offer the *potential* for growth, rather than those that are already experiencing rapid growth. Value investing involves extensive evaluation of corporate financial statements and any other documents that will help fund managers *uncover value (i.e., investment opportunities) before the rest of the market does—* that's the key to getting low P/Es. And the approach seems to work. For even though value investing is generally regarded as being *less risky* than growth investing (lower P/Es, higher dividend yields, and fundamentally stronger companies all translate into reduced risk exposure), the long-term returns to investors in value funds are quite competitive with those earned from growth or even aggressive growth funds. Thus, value funds are often viewed as a viable alternative for relatively conservative investors who are looking for the attractive returns offered by common stocks, yet want to keep share price volatility and investment risk in check.

Equity-Income Funds

Equity-income funds emphasize current income, which they provide by investing primarily in high-yielding common stocks. Preserving capital is also a goal of these funds; so is increasing capital gains, although it's not their primary objective. These funds invest heavily in high-grade common stocks, some convertible securities and preferred stocks, and occasionally even junk bonds or certain types of high-grade foreign bonds. In general, because of their emphasis on dividends and current income, these funds tend to hold higher-quality securities that are subject to less price volatility than seen in the market as a whole. They're generally viewed as a fairly low-risk way of investing in stocks.

Balanced Funds

Balanced funds are so named because they tend to hold a balanced portfolio of both stocks and bonds, and they do so to generate a well-balanced return of current income and long-term capital gains. In many ways, they're like equity-income funds except that balanced funds usually put much more into fixed-income securities. Generally, they keep 30 percent to 40 percent (and sometimes more) of their portfolios in bonds. The bonds are used primarily to provide current income, and stocks are selected mainly for their long-term growth potential. The more the fund leans toward fixed-income securities, the more income-oriented it will be. Balanced funds tend to confine their investing mainly to high-grade securities and therefore are usually considered a relatively safe form of investing—one that can earn you a competitive rate of return without a lot of price volatility.

Growth-and-Income Funds

Like balanced funds, *growth-and-income funds* seek a balanced return made up of current income and long-term capital gains, but they put greater emphasis on growth of capital. Moreover, unlike balanced funds, growth-and-income funds put most of their money into equities—it's not unusual for these funds to have 80 percent to 90 percent of their capital in common stocks. They tend to confine most of their investing to high-quality issues, so you can expect to find lots of growth-oriented blue-chip stocks in their portfolios, along with a fair number of high-quality income stocks. These funds do involve a fair amount of risk, if for no other reason than their emphasis on stocks and capital gains. Growth-and-income funds are most suitable for investors who can tolerate their risk and price volatility.

Bond Funds

As their name implies, *bond funds* invest in various kinds of fixed-income securities. Income is their primary investment objective, although they don't ignore capital gains. There are three important advantages to buying shares in bond funds rather than investing directly in bonds. First, bond funds generally are more liquid; second, they offer a cost-effective way of achieving a high degree of diversification in an otherwise expensive investment (most bonds carry minimum denominations of $1,000 to $5,000 or more); and third, bond funds automatically reinvest interest and other income, thereby allowing the investor to earn fully compounded rates of return. Bond funds are considered a fairly conservative form of investment, but they're not totally without risk because the prices of the bonds held in the funds' portfolios will fluctuate with changing interest rates. In 2014, bond mutual funds had $3.46 trillion under management, while bond ETFs had about $296.4 billion under management.

No matter what your tastes, you'll find a full menu of bond funds available, including these:

- Government bond funds, which invest in U.S. Treasury and agency securities.
- Mortgage-backed bond funds, which put their money into various types of mortgage-backed securities issued by agencies of the U.S. government, such as Government National Mortgage Association (GNMA) issues. These funds appeal to investors because they provide diversification and a more affordable way to get into mortgage-backed securities. They also have a provision that allows investors (if they so choose) to reinvest the *principal* portion of the monthly cash flow—thereby enabling them to preserve, rather than consume, their capital.
- High-grade corporate bond funds, which invest chiefly in investment-grade securities rated BBB or better.
- High-yield corporate bond funds, which are risky investments that buy *junk bonds* for the yields that they offer, which can be higher than standard bonds.
- Convertible bond funds, which invest primarily in (domestic and possibly foreign) securities that can be converted or exchanged into common stocks. By investing in convertible bonds and preferred stocks, the funds offer investors some of the price stability of bonds, along with the capital appreciation potential of stocks.
- Municipal bond funds, which invest in tax-exempt securities and are suitable for investors looking for tax-free income. Like their corporate counterparts, municipals can also be in either high-grade or high-yield funds. A special type of municipal bond fund is the *single-state* fund, which invests in the municipal issues of only one state and so produces (for residents of that state) interest income that's *fully* exempt from federal taxes as well as state (and possibly even local/city) taxes.
- Intermediate-term bond funds, which invest in bonds with maturities of 7 to 10 years or less, and offer not only attractive yields but also relatively low price volatility. Shorter (2- to 5-year) funds are also available and can be used as substitutes for money market investments by investors looking for higher returns on their money, especially when short-term rates are way down.

Money Market Mutual Funds

Money market mutual funds invest in a widely diversified portfolio of short-term money market instruments. These funds are very popular with investors, and for good reason: They give investors with modest amounts of capital access to the higher-yielding end of the money market, where many instruments require minimum investments of $100,000 or more. Today, there are about 530 publicly traded money market funds that, together, hold nearly $2.73 *trillion* in assets.

There are several different kinds of money market mutual funds. **General-purpose money funds** invest in any and all types of money market investments, from Treasury bills to corporate commercial paper and bank certificates of deposit. They invest their

general-purpose money fund
A money fund that invests in virtually any type of short-term investment vehicle.

money wherever they can find attractive short-term returns. Most money funds are of this type. The **tax-exempt money fund** limits its investments to tax-exempt municipal securities with very short (30- to 90-day) maturities. Because their income is free from federal income tax, they appeal predominantly to investors in high tax brackets. **Government securities money funds** were established as a way of meeting investors' need for safety. These funds eliminate any risk of default by confining their investments to Treasury bills and other short-term securities of the U.S. government or its agencies (such as the GNMA).

Money funds are highly liquid investment vehicles that are very low in risk because they're virtually immune to capital loss. However, the interest income they produce tends to follow interest rate conditions, so the returns to shareholders are subject to the ups and downs of market interest rates. (Money funds were discussed more fully in Chapter 4, along with other short-term investments.)

Index Funds

"If you can't beat 'em, join 'em." That's the idea behind the *index fund*, which is a type of fund that buys and holds a portfolio of stocks (or bonds) equivalent to those in a market index such as the S&P 500. An index fund that's trying to match the S&P 500, for example, would hold the same 500 stocks that are held in that index and in the same proportion. Rather than trying to beat the market, *index funds simply try to match the market*—that is, to match the performance of the index on which the fund is based. They do this through low-cost investment management. In many cases, the whole portfolio is run almost entirely by a computer that matches the fund's holdings with those of the targeted index. Besides the S&P 500, several other market indexes are used, including the S&P MidCap 400, Russell 2000, and Wilshire 5000, as well as value stock indexes, growth stock indexes, international stock indexes, and even bond indexes. While index funds form only a part of the overall mutual fund market, they comprise the vast majority of ETFs.

The approach of index funds is strictly buy and hold. About the only time there's a change to the portfolio of an index fund is when the targeted market index alters its "market basket" of securities. A pleasant by-product of this buy-and-hold approach is that the funds have low portfolio turnover rates and therefore little in *realized* capital gains. As a result, aside from a modest amount of dividend income, these funds produce little taxable income from year to year, which leads many high-income investors to view them as a type of tax-sheltered investment. But these funds provide something else—namely, they produce *highly competitive returns* for investors! It's tough to outperform the market consistently, so the index funds don't even try. The net result is that, on average, index funds tend to produce better returns than do most other types of stock funds. Granted, every now and then the fully managed funds will have a year (or two) when they outperform index funds, but those are the exception rather than the rule.

Sector Funds

As the name implies, a *sector fund* restricts its investments to a particular sector of the market. These funds concentrate their investment holdings in the one or more industries that make up the targeted sector. For example, a *health care* sector fund would confine its investments to those industries that make up this segment of the market: drug companies, hospital management firms, medical

DARREN BAKER/ DREAMSTIME.COM

suppliers, and biotech concerns. The underlying investment objective of most sector funds is *capital gains*. In many ways, they're similar to growth funds and should be considered speculative. The idea behind sector funds is that the really attractive returns come from small segments of the market. So, rather than diversifying the portfolio across wide segments of the market, you can put your money where the action currently is. Some popular sector funds concentrate their investments in real estate (real estate investment trusts, or REITs), technology, financial services, natural resources, electronics, telecommunications, and, of course, health care.

Socially Responsible Funds

socially responsible fund (SRF)
A fund that invests only in companies meeting certain moral, ethical, and/or environmental criteria.

For some investors, the security selection process doesn't end with bottom lines, P/E ratios, growth rates, and betas; rather, it also includes the *active, explicit consideration of moral, ethical, and environmental issues*. The idea is that social concerns should play just as big a role in the investment decision as profits and other financial matters. socially responsible funds (SRFs) consider only what they view as socially responsible companies for inclusion in their portfolios. If a company doesn't meet certain moral, ethical, or environmental tests, they simply won't consider buying the stock, no matter how good the bottom line looks. Generally speaking, these funds abstain from investing in companies that derive revenues from tobacco, alcohol, or gambling; that are weapons contractors; or that operate nuclear power plants. The funds also tend to favor firms that produce "responsible" products and services, have strong employee relations, have positive environmental records, and are socially responsive to the communities in which they operate. According to the Forum for Sustainable and Responsible Investment, SRF funds under management grew to about $6.6 trillion by early 2014.

International Funds

international fund
A mutual fund that does all or most of its investing in foreign securities.

In searching for higher returns and better diversification, American investors have shown increased interest in foreign securities, and the mutual fund industry has responded with a full array of international funds. In 1985, there were only about 40 of these funds; by 2015, that number had grown to several thousand. The fact is, many people would like to invest in foreign securities but simply don't have the experience or know-how. International funds may be just the ticket for such investors. Technically, the term *international fund* is used to describe a type of fund that *invests exclusively in foreign securities*, often confining the fund's activities to specific geographical regions (such as Mexico, Australia, Europe, or the Pacific Rim). In contrast, there's another class of international funds, known as *global funds*, that invests not only in foreign securities *but also in U.S. companies*—usually multinational firms. As a rule, global funds provide more diversity and, with access to both foreign and domestic markets, can go wherever the action is.

Asset Allocation Funds

Studies have shown that the most important decision an investor can make is where to allocate his or her investment assets. This is known as *asset allocation*, and (as we saw in Chapter 11) it involves deciding how you're going to divide your investments among different types of securities. For example, what portion of your money will be devoted to money market securities, what portion to stocks, and what portion to bonds? Asset allocation deals in broad terms and doesn't address individual security selection. Even so, as strange as it may sound, asset allocation has been found to be a far more important determinant of total returns on a well-diversified portfolio than has individual security selection.

Because a lot of individual investors have a tough time making asset allocation decisions, the mutual fund industry has created a product to do the job for them. Known as *asset allocation funds*, these funds spread investors' money across all different types of markets. That is, whereas most mutual funds concentrate on one type of investment—whether it is stocks, bonds, or money market securities—asset allocation funds put money into all these markets. Many of them also include foreign securities in their asset allocation scheme, and some may even include inflation-resistant investments such as gold or real estate.

These funds are designed for people who want to hire fund managers not only to select individual securities for them, but also to make the strategic decisions concerning asset allocation over time. The money manager will establish a desired allocation mix, which might look something like this: 50 percent of the portfolio goes to U.S. stocks, 10 percent to foreign securities, 30 percent to bonds, and 10 percent to money market securities. Securities are then purchased for the fund in this proportion, and the overall portfolio maintains the desired mix. Actually, each segment of the fund is managed almost as a separate portfolio, so that securities within (say) the stock portion are bought, sold, and held as the market dictates. *As market conditions change over time, the asset allocation mix also changes.* So, if the U.S. stock market starts to soften, then funds will be moved out of stocks to some other area. As a result, the stock portion of the portfolio may drop to 35 percent and the foreign securities portion may increase to 25 percent, for example. Of course, there's no assurance that the money manager will make the right moves at the right time, but that's the idea behind these funds.

FINANCIAL PLANNING TIPS

Target-Date Funds: One Size Does *Not* Fit All

Target-date mutual funds and ETFs are relatively new types of asset allocation funds. The funds select a year in which an investor expects to retire, and then gradually shift the asset allocation to become more conservative as that retirement date approaches and most investors' risk tolerance decreases. Notwithstanding their growing popularity, you should be aware of the following issues in using target-date funds:

• **Target-date funds don't suit every investor.** While they meet the needs of most investors, some people might want a different asset allocation depending on special circumstances. For example, if you have significantly different net worth than the average person your age, you might have different needs.

• **Asset classes can differ across funds.** Many target-date fund families use large-cap, small-cap, and mid-cap domestic equity funds; international and emerging markets equity funds; and domestic fixed-income funds. And yet others also include inflation-protected Treasury Inflation-Protected Securities (TIPs), high-yield bonds, international fixed-income, emerging-markets debt, real estate, commodities, and long or short funds. You need to know how the fund defines its asset classes because this has significant risk implications.

• **Different target-date fund companies can use different asset allocations for the same target date.** Let's say you're planning to retire in 2045. One 2045 target date fund might have 90 percent in stocks, while another company's 2045 fund might have only 60 percent in stocks. You have to look at the details and make sure that you're comfortable with the riskiness of a fund's underlying asset allocation.

• **Target-date fund costs vary significantly.** For example, one popular target-date fund provider has several versions of the same retirement-year fund. The catch is that the expense ratio varies from 0.42 percent to 1.5 percent for the same target retirement-year fund! And yet the comparable fund offered by Vanguard had an expense ratio of 0.18 percent. You need to shop around and make comparisons.

• **Target-date glide path.** The glide path is the point in time at which the allocation to stocks drops to steady-state retirement mode. Some funds go into the glide-path stage after the average investor hits age 65. In contrast, other funds assume that you will stay invested in their fund until you die. This assumption can have a big effect on the asset allocation and risk.

Source: Adapted from Daniel Solin, "The Hidden Dangers of Target-Date Funds," http://money.usnews.com/money/blogs/on-retirement/2012/06/21/the,-hidden-dangers-of-target-date-funds, accessed September 2015; and Roger Wohlner, "Evaluating Your Target-Date Fund Options," http://money.usnews.com/money/blogs/the-smarter-mutual-fund-investor/2012/03/07/evaluating-your-target-date-fund-options, accessed September 2015.

13-2b Services Offered by Mutual Funds

Ask most investors why they buy a particular mutual fund, and they'll probably tell you that the fund offers the kind of income and return that they're looking for. Now, no one would question the importance of return in the investment decision, but there are other reasons for investing in mutual funds, not the least of which are the valuable services they provide. Some of the most sought-after *mutual fund services* are automatic investment and reinvestment plans, regular income programs, conversion privileges, and retirement programs. Unfortunately, many of these services are not available with ETFs, as they are basically nothing more than shares of common stock, which customarily do not offer such programs.

Automatic Investment Plans

automatic investment plan
An automatic savings program that enables an investor to channel a set amount of money systematically into a given mutual fund.

Mutual funds provide a program that makes savings and capital accumulation as painless as possible. The automatic investment plan allows fund shareholders to funnel fixed amounts of money *from their paychecks or bank accounts* automatically into a mutual fund. It's much like a payroll deduction plan that treats savings a lot like insurance coverage—that is, just as insurance premiums are automatically deducted from your paycheck (or bank account), so too are investments to your mutual fund.

Just about every major fund group offers some kind of automatic investment plan. To enroll, a shareholder simply fills out a form authorizing the fund to transfer a set amount (usually it must be a minimum of $25 to $100 per period) from your bank account or paycheck at regular intervals—typically monthly or quarterly. Once enrolled, you'll be buying shares in the funds of your choice every month or quarter (most funds deal in fractional shares). Of course, if it's a load fund, you'll still have to pay normal sales charges on your periodic investments. You can get out of the program anytime you like, without penalty, simply by contacting the fund. Convenience may be the chief advantage of these plans, but they make solid investment sense as well because one of the best ways of building up a sizable amount of capital is to *add funds to your investment program systematically over time*. The importance of making regular contributions to your investment program cannot be overstated—it ranks right up there with compound interest!

Automatic Reinvestment Plans

automatic reinvestment plan
A plan that gives share owners the option of electing to have dividends and capital gains distributions reinvested in additional fund shares.

Automatic reinvestment is one of the real draws of mutual funds, and it's offered by just about every open-ended mutual fund. Whereas automatic investment plans deal with money shareholders put into a fund, automatic reinvestment plans deal with the dividends and other distributions that the funds pay to their shareholders. Much like the dividend reinvestment plans we looked at with stocks, the automatic reinvestment plans of mutual funds enable you to keep all your capital fully employed. Through this service, dividend and capital gains income is *used to buy additional shares in the fund automatically*, which enables the investor to earn a fully compounded rate of return. Keep in mind, however, that even though you reinvest your dividends and capital gains, the Internal Revenue Service (IRS) still treats them as cash receipts and taxes them in the year that they're paid.

The important point is that by plowing profits (reinvested dividends and capital gains distributions) back into a fund, investors can put this money to work generating even more earnings. Indeed, the effects of these plans on total accumulated capital over the long haul can be substantial. Exhibit 13.6 shows the long-term impact of one such plan, which provides the actual performance numbers for a real-life mutual fund, Fidelity Contrafund. In the illustration, we assume that the investor starts with $10,000 and, except for reinvesting dividends and capital gains distributions, *adds no new capital over time*. Even so, the initial investment of $10,000 grew to about $30,941 over the roughly 15-year period from 2000 to mid-2015 (which, by the way, amounts to a fully compounded rate of return of 7.6 percent). So long as care is taken in selecting an appropriate fund, *attractive benefits can be derived from the systematic accumulation of capital offered by automatic reinvestment plans.*

Regular Income

systematic withdrawal plan
A plan offered by mutual funds that allows shareholders to be paid specified amounts of money each period.

Automatic reinvestment plans are great for the long-term investor, but how about the investor who's looking for a steady stream of income? Mutual funds also have a service to meet this need. It's called a systematic withdrawal plan, and it's offered by most open-ended funds. Once enrolled in one of these plans, you'll automatically receive a predetermined amount of money every month or quarter. To participate, shareholders are usually required to have a minimum investment of $5,000 to $10,000, and the size of the withdrawal must usually be $50 or more per month. Depending on how well the fund is doing, the annual return generated by the fund may actually be greater than the withdrawals, thus allowing the investor not only to receive regular income, but also to enjoy an automatic accumulation of *additional* shares in the plan. On the other hand, if the fund isn't performing well, then the withdrawals could eventually deplete the original investment.

EXHIBIT 13.6   **Effects of Reinvesting Income**

Reinvesting dividends and/or capital gains can have tremendous effects on your investment position. This graph shows the results of a hypothetical investor who initially invested $10,000 and, for a period of about 15 years, reinvested all dividends and capital gains distributions in additional fund shares. [No adjustment has been made for any fees or for any income taxes payable by the shareholder, which would be appropriate provided that the fund was held in a tax-deferred account like an individual retirement account (IRA) or a 401(k) account.] This example is for the Fidelity Contrafund.

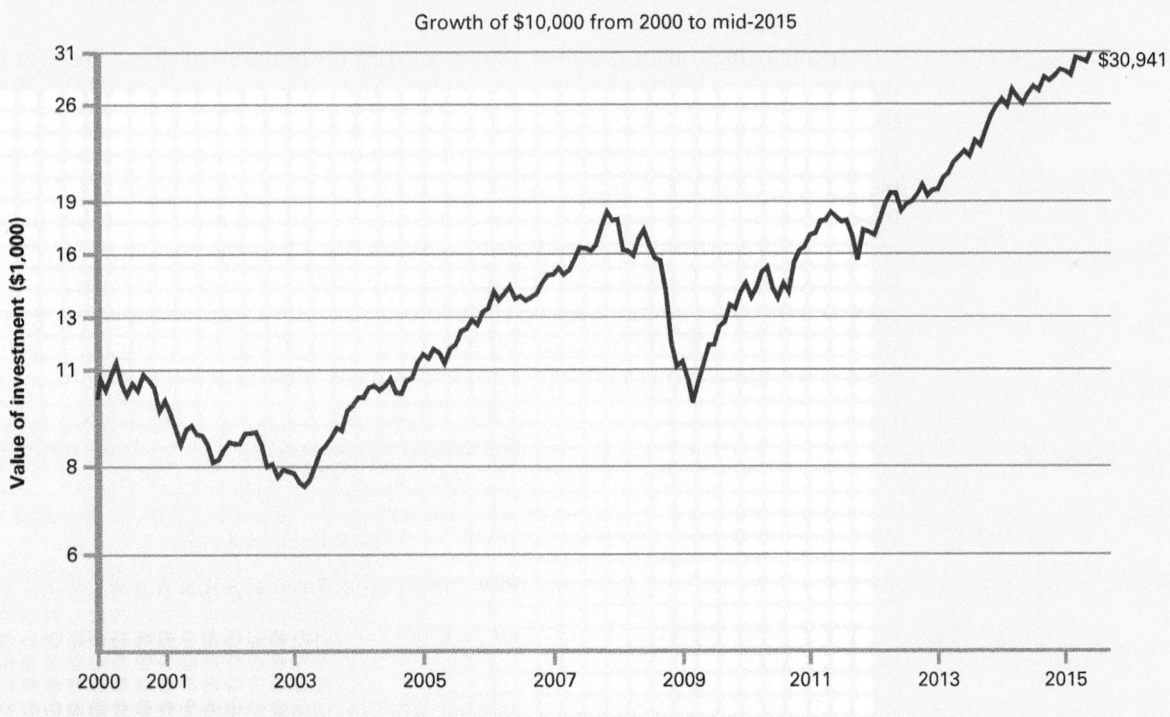

Growth of $10,000 from 2000 to mid-2015

Conversion Privileges

Sometimes investors find it necessary to switch out of one fund and into another; for example, their investment objectives may change or the investment environment itself may have changed. **Conversion (or exchange) privileges** conveniently and economically meet the needs of these investors. Investment companies that offer a number of different funds to the investing public—known as *fund families*—usually provide conversion privileges that enable shareholders to move easily from one fund to another; this can be done either online or by phone. The only limitation is that the investor must confine the switches to the same *family* of funds. For example, an investor can switch from a Fidelity growth fund to a Fidelity money fund, or to its income fund, or to any other fund managed by Fidelity. Most fund families, especially the bigger ones, offer investors a full range of investment products as part of providing one-stop mutual fund shopping. Whether you want an equity fund, a bond fund, or a money fund, these fund families have something for you.

Conversion privileges are attractive because they permit investors to manage their holdings more aggressively by allowing them to move in and out of funds as the investment environment changes. Indeed, there is some evidence that stocks that have done well in one time period are likely to do well in the next period, all of which may be an effect of industry momentum. Regardless of what causes it, mutual fund families with conversion privileges make it easier and less costly to shift money across sectors and industries. Unfortunately, there's one major drawback; although you never see the cash, the exchange of shares from one fund to another is regarded, for tax purposes, as a sale followed by the purchase of a new security. As a result, if any capital gains exist at the time of the exchange, the investor is liable for the taxes on that profit.

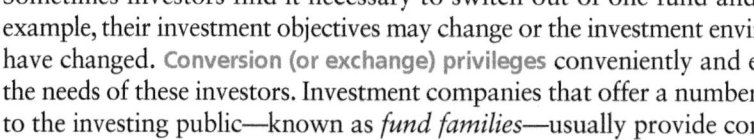

Financial Fact or Fantasy?

Online and phone switching are services that enable you to move money from one fund to another, so long as you stay within the same family of funds. **Fact:** Online and phone switching are conversion (or exchange) privileges that allow you to sell one fund and buy another, with the only condition being that you confine your switches to the same family of funds.

Retirement Plans

Government legislation permits self-employed individuals to divert part of their income into self-directed retirement plans. And all working Americans, whether they're self-employed or not, are allowed to establish individual retirement accounts—in the form of either a standard, tax-deductible IRA or the newest type of retirement account, the Roth IRA (all of which we'll look at in the next chapter). Today, all mutual funds provide a special service that allows individuals to set up tax-deferred retirement programs quickly and easily as either IRA or Keogh accounts—or, through their place of employment, to participate in a qualified tax-sheltered retirement plan, such as a 401(k). The funds set up the plans and handle all the administrative details so that the shareholders can take full advantage of available tax savings. We will discuss these issues further in Chapter 14, which deals with retirement planning.

TEST YOURSELF

13-8 What's the difference between a growth fund and a balanced fund?

13-9 What's an international fund, and how does it differ from a global fund?

13-10 What's an asset allocation fund? How do these funds differ from other types of mutual funds?

13-11 If growth, income, and capital preservation are the primary objectives of mutual funds, why do we bother to categorize them by type?

13-12 What are fund families? What advantages do these families offer investors?

13-13 What are automatic reinvestment plans, and how do they differ from automatic investment plans?

13-3 MAKING MUTUAL FUND AND ETF INVESTMENTS

LG4, LG5

Suppose you have money to invest and are trying to select the right place to put it. You obviously want to pick an investment that not only meets your idea of an acceptable risk, but also generates an attractive rate of return. The problem is that you have to choose from literally thousands of investments. But perhaps if you approach the problem systematically, it may not be so formidable after all. For as we'll see, it is possible to whittle down the list of alternatives by matching your investment needs with the investment objectives of the funds.

13-3a The Selection Process

When it comes to mutual funds and ETFs, one question that every investor must answer is: Why invest in a mutual fund or an ETF to begin with; why not just go it alone (that is, buy individual stocks and bonds directly)? For beginning investors, or investors with little capital, the answer is pretty simple—mutual funds and ETFs provide far more diversification than such investors could ever get on their own, plus they get the help of professional money managers, and at a reasonable cost to boot.

Certainly, the diversification and professional money management come into play, but there are other reasons to invest in a mutual fund or an ETF. The competitive returns offered by mutual funds and ETFs have to be a factor with many investors, and so do the services they provide. A lot of well-to-do investors have decided that they can get better returns over the long haul by carefully selecting mutual funds than by trying to invest in individual stocks on their own. So they put all, or a big chunk, of their money into funds. Many of these investors will use part of their capital to buy and sell individual securities on their own, and they'll use the rest *to buy mutual funds or ETFs that invest in areas they don't fully understand or aren't well informed about*. For example, they'll use mutual funds or ETFs to get into foreign markets or as a way to buy mortgage-backed securities.

After deciding to use mutual funds or ETFs, the investor must then decide which funds to buy. The selection process itself (especially regarding the *types* of funds to purchase) obviously plays an important role in defining the amount of success you'll have with mutual funds or ETFs. It means putting into action all you know about investing in order to gain as much return as possible at an acceptable level of risk. Given that you have an asset allocation strategy in place and that you're trying to select funds compatible with your targeted mix, the selection process begins with an assessment of your own investment needs; this sets the tone for your investment program. Obviously, you'll want to select from those thousands of funds the one or two (or three or four) that will best meet your investment needs.

Objectives and Motives for Using Funds

The place to start is with your own investment objectives. In other words, why do you want to invest in a mutual fund or an ETF, and what are you looking for in a fund? Obviously, an attractive rate of return would be desirable, but there's also the matter of ensuring a tolerable amount of risk exposure. More than likely, when looking at your own risk temperament in relation to the various types of mutual funds and ETFs available, you'll discover that certain types of funds are more appealing to you than others. For instance, aggressive growth or sector funds will probably *not* be attractive to individuals wishing to avoid high exposure to risk.

Another important factor in the selection process is the intended use of the mutual fund or ETF. Do you want to invest in mutual funds or ETFs as a way of *accumulating capital* over an extended time, to *speculate* with your money in the hopes of generating high rates of return, or to *conserve your capital* by investing in low-risk securities where preservation of capital is no less important than return on capital. Finally, there's the matter of the services provided by the fund. If you're particularly interested in some services, be sure to look for them in the funds that you select.

How to Choose the Best Mutual Funds

Choosing the best mutual funds to achieve your financial objectives is mostly about doing your homework and focusing on a few key elements. Here are the steps and the main considerations:

- **Decide how much money you want to invest in mutual funds.** That depends on how much money you need in the future, when you need it, and where your other money is invested. For example, are you hoping to fund a child's college education in 18 years, or are you investing for retirement?

- **Decide on your asset allocation.** This depends a lot on the length of time until you need the money, your capacity to take risk, and your risk tolerance. Let's say that you're investing for retirement. A reasonable starting point is the common rule of thumb that the percentage in bonds should equal your age, and the residual percentage should be in stocks. So if you're 25, it makes sense to have 25 percent of your money in bonds and 75 percent in stocks. You can fine-tune the percentages based on how comfortable you are with the risk implications of this rule-of-thumb allocation.

- **Diversify your investments over different types of mutual funds.** Research supports having some money invested in small-cap and value stocks, as well as in both domestic and foreign stocks. And you'll want to diversify your bond fund holdings at least across maturities, ratings, and possibly tax exposure. For many people,

the best choice in each fund category is a low-cost index fund, if available.

- **Put together a list of available mutual funds.** Compare each fund's historical performance with an appropriate benchmark. (**Morningstar.com** is a convenient source for such comparisons.) Then compare the expense ratios of each fund in the category that you are considering, which show how much the fund's returns are reduced by trading and operating expenses. Obviously, you would prefer the fund with the lowest expense ratio; over time, the higher net return will affect the amount of money in the fund significantly. Similarly, it's helpful to compare mutual funds' turnover ratios, which indicate the percentage of the assets held by the fund that were sold during the year. *Higher turnover ratios bring both higher expenses and higher taxes,* which will depress net returns in the same way as higher expense ratios.

- **Avoid "dog" funds.** Many people just pick the fund with the best historical performance and figure that's the star. Doesn't that make sense—who wouldn't want to reach for the stars? However, that strategy is often misguided. Although it's hard to identify the stars, past performance does appear to be a reliable way of identifying the true losers. The worst funds often stay at the bottom of their category in terms of performance for years. And that can be measured using their returns, expense ratios, and turnover. So here's the best approach: *Don't search for the stars—just avoid the dogs!*

Having assessed what you're looking for in a fund, now you can look at what the funds have to offer.

What Funds Have to Offer

The ideal mutual fund or ETF would achieve maximum capital growth when security prices rise, provide complete protection against capital loss when prices decline, and achieve high levels of current income at all times. Unfortunately, such funds don't exist. Instead, just as each individual has a set of investment needs, each fund has its own *investment objective*, its own *manner or style of operation*, and its own *range of services*. These three factors are useful in helping you assess investment alternatives. But where does the investor look for such information? One obvious place is the fund's *profile* (or its prospectus), where information on investment objectives, portfolio composition, management, and past performance can be obtained. In addition, publications such as *The Wall Street Journal, Barron's, Money, Fortune,* and *Forbes* provide all sorts of useful data and information about mutual funds. These sources publish a wealth of operating and performance statistics in a convenient, easy-to-read format. Services are also available that provide background information and assessments on a wide variety of funds. Among the best in this category are Morningstar's online (**http://morningstar.com**) and other vendors' software-based products (see Exhibit 13.7), *The Value Line Fund Advisor, and The Value Line ETF Survey* (these reports are similar to Value Line's stock reports, but they apply to mutual funds and ETFs). And, of course, all sorts of performance statistics are available on the Internet. For example, there are scores of free finance Internet sites, such as **http://finance.yahoo.com**, where you can obtain historical information on a fund's performance, security holdings, risk profile, load charges, and purchase information. Or you can buy, usually at reasonable prices, quarterly or annually updated software from organizations like Morningstar or the American Association of Individual Investors (AAII).

Whittling Down the Alternatives

At this point, fund selection becomes a process of elimination as you weigh your investment needs against the types of funds available. Many funds can be eliminated from consideration simply because they don't meet your needs. Some may be too risky; others may be unsuitable as a storehouse of value. So, rather than trying to evaluate thousands of different funds, you can use a process of elimination to narrow the list down to two or three *types* of funds that best match your investment (and asset allocation) needs.

From here, you can whittle the list down a bit more by introducing other constraints. For example, because of cost considerations, you may want to deal only in no-load or low-load funds (more on this later), or you may be seeking certain services that are important to your investment goals.

Now we're ready to introduce the final (but certainly not the least important) element in the selection process: *the fund's investment performance.* Useful information includes (1) how the fund has performed over the past five to seven years; (2) the type of return that it has generated in good markets as well as bad; (3) the level of dividend and capital gains distributions, which is an important indication not only of how much current income the fund distributes annually but also of the fund's *tax efficiency* (funds with low dividends and low asset turnovers typically expose their shareholders to lower taxes and consequently have higher tax-efficiency ratings); and (4) the level of investment stability the fund has enjoyed over time (or, put another way, the amount of volatility/risk in the fund's return). By evaluating such information, you can identify some of the more successful mutual funds—those that not only offer the investment objectives and services you seek but also provide the best payoffs. And while you're doing this, you might want to consider some of the fund facts listed in Exhibit 13.8.

Stick with No-Loads or Low-Load Mutual Funds

There's a longstanding "debate" in the mutual fund industry regarding load funds and no-load funds. The question is, do load funds add enough value to overcome the load fees? And if not, why pay the load charges? The evidence indicates that load fund returns generally aren't, on a risk-adjusted basis, any higher than the returns from no-load funds. In fact, the funds with abnormally high loads and 12b-1 fees often produce returns that are far *less* than what you can get from no-loads, after taking risk into account! Moreover, because of compounding, the differential returns tend to widen with longer holding periods.

That shouldn't be surprising, though, because big load charges and/or 12b-1 fees do nothing more than *reduce your invested capital*, thus reducing the amount of money you have working for you. In fact, the only way that a load fund can overcome this handicap is to *produce superior returns*—which is not easy to do year in

EXHIBIT 13.7 **Mutual Fund Information**

Investors who want in-depth information about the operating characteristics, investment holdings, and market performance of mutual funds can usually find what they're looking for in Morningstar publications or, as shown here, from online and software-based information sources such as *MorningstarDirect*.

Fidelity® Contrafund® FCNTX

Morningstar Analyst Rating
Under Review

NAV $	NAV Day Change %	Yield TTM %	Total Assets $ Bil	Status	Min. Inv.	Load	Expenses	Morningstar Rating™	Category	Investment Style
103.24	↓-0.07 | -0.07	0.24	110.7	Open	$2,500	None	0.64%	★★★★	Large Growth	Large Growth

Growth of 10,000 05-23-2005 - 05-23-2015

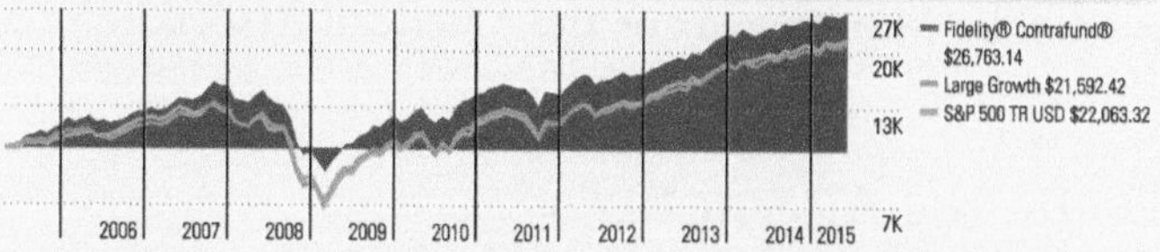

— Fidelity® Contrafund® $26,763.14
— Large Growth $21,592.42
— S&P 500 TR USD $22,063.32

2006 2007 2008 2009 2010 2011 2012 2013 2014 2015

3 Year Average Morningstar Risk Measures

| Risk vs. Category (1577) | Low |
| Return vs. Category (1577) | +Avg |

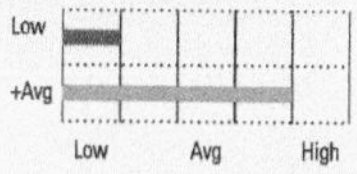

Low · Avg · High

Pillars

Process	⊕ Positive
Performance	⊕ Positive
People	⊕ Positive
Parent	⊕ Positive
Price	⊕ Positive
Rating	🛡 Silver

Investment Strategy

The investment seeks capital appreciation. The fund normally invests primarily in common stocks. It invests in securities of companies whose value the advisor believes is not fully recognized by the public. The fund invests in domestic and foreign issuers. It invests in either "growth" stocks or "value" stocks or both. The fund uses fundamental analysis of factors such as each issuer's financial condition and industry position, as well as market and economic conditions to select investments.

Performance

	YTD	1 Mo	1 Yr	3Yr Ann	5Yr Ann	10Yr Ann

* Currency is displayed in BASE

Style Map

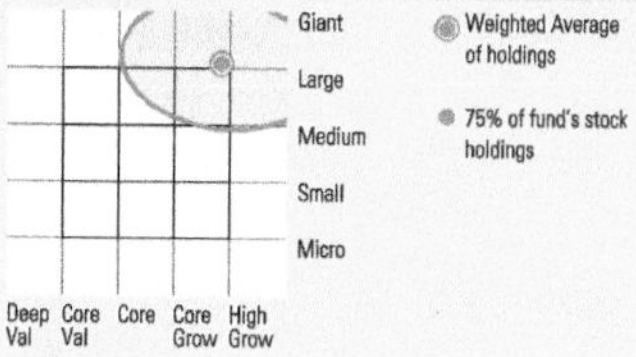

Giant
Large
Medium
Small
Micro

Deep Core Core Core High
Val Val Grow Grow

⊙ Weighted Average of holdings
● 75% of fund's stock holdings

Top Holdings 03-31-2015

	Weight %	Last Price	Day Chg %	52 Week Range
⊖ Berkshire Hathaway Inc Class A	4.65	— BASE	-0.59 ↓	185,005.00 - 229,374.00
⊖ Apple Inc	3.74	132.54 BASE	0.88 ↑	86.64 - 134.54
⊕ Facebook Inc Class A	3.50	80.54 BASE	0.08 ↑	60.15 - 86.07
⊖ Wells Fargo & Co	3.43	56.00 BASE	-0.02 ↓	46.44 - 56.70
⊕ Biogen Inc	3.25	398.68 BASE	-0.62 ↓	290.85 - 480.18
% Assets in Top 5 Holdings	18.57			

⊕ Increase ⊖ Decrease ✿ New to Portfolio

Top Sectors 03-31-2015

	Fund	3 Yr High	3 Yr Low	Cat Avg
Technology	24.12	24.24	23.06	25.02
Healthcare	19.93	19.93	11.63	19.55
Financial Services	19.02	21.50	19.02	10.07
Consumer Cyclical	15.93	19.23	14.68	17.11
Industrials	8.62	8.62	7.60	10.67

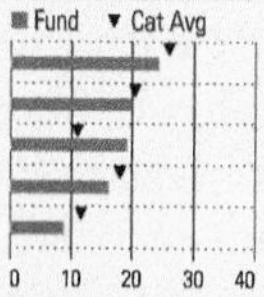

■ Fund ▼ Cat Avg
0 10 20 30 40

Asset Allocation

	% Net	% Short	% Long	Bench mark	Cat Avg
● Cash	1.94	0.00	1.94	0.00	2.00
● US Stock	88.66	0.00	88.66	98.42	89.96
● Non US Stock	8.68	0.00	8.68	1.59	7.79
● Bond	0.10	0.00	0.10	0.00	0.10
● Other	0.62	0.00	0.62	0.00	0.15

Management

	Start Date
William Danoff	09-17-1990

Dividend and Capital Gains Distributions

Distribution Date	Distribution NAV	Long-Term Capital Gain	Long-Term Short Gain	Return of Capital	Dividend Income	Distribution Total
02-06-2015	97.92	0.9500	0.0000	0.0000	0.0000	0.9500
12-12-2014	96.19	5.9200	0.0000	0.0000	0.2500	6.1700
02-07-2014	94.21	0.9700	0.0000	0.0000	0.0000	0.9700
12-13-2013	92.57	6.5800	0.0000	0.0000	0.1300	6.7100
02-08-2013	81.25	0.7400	0.0000	0.0000	0.0000	0.7400

Source: MorningstarDirect, May 24, 2015. © 2012 Morningstar, Inc. All rights reserved. The Morningstar data contained herein (1) is proprietary to Morningstar; (2) may not be copied or distributed without written permission; and (3) is not warranted to be accurate, complete, or timely. Morningstar is not responsible for any damages or losses arising from any use of this information and has not granted its consent to be considered or deemed an "expert" under the Securities Act of 1933.

EXHIBIT 13.8	Some Mutual Fund Facts Every Investor Should Know

Mutual funds are meant to give investors a simple yet effective way of buying into the stock and bond markets. Unfortunately, fund investing isn't always as simple as it looks. Here are a few fund facts every investor should keep in mind when making mutual fund investments:

- Stock funds that get hit hard in market crashes aren't necessarily bad investments.
- Even great funds have bad years now and then.
- Most stock (and bond) funds fail to beat the market.
- You don't need a broker to buy mutual funds.
- A fund that doesn't charge a sales commission isn't necessarily a no-load fund. Watch out for 12b-1 charges.
- If you own a dozen or more funds, you probably own too many.
- Mutual fund names are often misleading. Look beyond the name to the actual performance. Morningstar-style categories are more useful than the fund's name. Consistency is important.
- Bond funds with high current yields don't necessarily produce high *total* returns.
- Money market funds are not risk-free (you never know what kind of return they'll earn).
- If the market crashes, it will be too late to sell your fund shares (the damage probably will already have been done).
- Even bad funds sometimes rank as top performers. And the same goes for good funds—sometimes they come in at the bottom of the pack. Once again, consistency is important.

and year out. Granted, a handful of load funds have produced attractive returns over extended periods, but they're the exception rather than the rule.

Obviously, it's in your best interest to pay close attention to load charges (and other fees) whenever you're considering an investment in a mutual fund. In order to maximize returns, *you should seriously consider sticking to no-load funds, or low-loads* (funds with total load charges, including 12b-1 fees, of 3 percent or less). At the very least, you should consider a more expensive load fund *only* if it has a much better performance record (and offers more return potential) than a less expensive fund. It shouldn't be all that hard to stick mostly with no-load funds because there are literally thousands of no-load and low-load funds to choose from, and they come in all types.

Choosing Between ETFs and Mutual Funds

The preceding discussion identifies the relative advantages and disadvantages of investing in funds. Yet this begs the question of how you choose between ETFs and mutual funds. The answer depends on what you want to invest in and how sensitive you are to taxes and costs. Consider the following criteria suggested by Morningstar:

- *Broad or narrow focus?* ETFs have been developed to accommodate investors pursuing narrow market segments. If you want to focus on a single market sector, industry, or geographic region, there's likely an ETF for you. Furthermore, there are far more ETFs that track single foreign countries than mutual funds that do so. The downside is that narrowly focused ETFs are not as well diversified as are many mutual funds. So, while there are mutual funds and ETFs for broad index investing, some ETFs offer more narrow, targeted investing.
- *Tax management.* ETFs are set up to protect investors from capital gains taxes better than most mutual funds can. Most ETFs are index funds that trade less than the average actively managed mutual fund, which means that they should generate fewer taxable gains.
- *Costs.* ETFs have lower overhead expenses than most mutual funds because they don't have to manage customer accounts or staff call centers. This means that ETFs tend to have lower expense ratios than mutual funds. ETFs are often the most cost-effective choice for investors using discount brokers, for those investing a large sum of money, and for those with a long-term horizon.

13-3b Getting a Handle on Fund Performance

If you were to believe all the sales literature, you'd think that there was no way you could go wrong by investing in mutual funds or ETFs. Just put your money into one of these funds and let the good times roll! Unfortunately, the hard facts of life are that, *when it comes to investing, performance is never guaranteed.* And that applies just as much to mutual funds as it does to any other form of investing—perhaps even more so, because with mutual funds, the single variable driving a fund's market price and return behavior is the performance of the fund's portfolio of securities.

Measuring Fund Performance

Any mutual fund (open- or closed-end) or any ETF has three potential sources of return: (1) dividend income, (2) capital gains distribution, and (3) change in the fund's share price. Depending on the type of fund, some will derive more income from one source than another. For example, we'd normally expect income-oriented funds to generate higher dividend income than capital gains-oriented funds do. Mutual funds regularly publish reports that recap investment performance. One such report is *The Summary of Income and Capital Changes;* an example of which is provided in Exhibit 13.9. This statement gives a brief overview of a fund's investment activities, including expense ratios and portfolio turnover rates. Of interest to us in this discussion is the top part of the report (from "Net asset value, beginning of period" through "Net asset value, end of period"—lines 1 to 10). This part reveals the amount of dividend income and capital gains distributed to the shareholders, along with any change in the fund's NAV.

Dividend income (see line 7 of Exhibit 13.9) is the amount derived from the dividend and interest income earned on the security holdings of the mutual fund. When the fund receives dividends or interest payments, it passes these on to shareholders in the form of dividend payments. The fund accumulates all the current income that it has received for the period and then pays it out on a prorated basis. Because the mutual fund itself is tax exempt, any taxes due on dividend earnings are payable by the individual investor. For funds that are not held in tax-deferred accounts [e.g., IRAs and 401(k)s], the amount of taxes due on dividends will depend on the source of such dividends. That is, *if these distributions are derived from dividends earned on the fund's common stock holdings, then they're subject to the preferential tax rate of 15 or 20 percent or less.* But, if these distributions are derived from interest earnings on bonds, dividends from REITs, or dividends from most types of preferred stocks, then such dividends *do not qualify for preferential tax treatment* and instead are taxed as ordinary income (see Chapter 3 for details).

Capital gains distributions (see line 8) work on the same principle as dividends, except that they're derived from the *capital gains actually earned* by the fund. (From a tax perspective, if the capital gains are long-term, then they qualify for the preferential tax rate of 15 or 20 percent or less; if not, they're treated as ordinary income.) Note that these (capital gains) distributions apply only to *realized* capital gains—that is, when the securities holdings are actually sold and capital gains actually earned. *Unrealized* capital gains (or "paper profits") make up the third

EXHIBIT 13.9   A Summary of Mutual Fund Income and Capital Changes

The return on a mutual fund is made up of (1) the (net) investment income the fund earns from dividends and interest and (2) the realized and unrealized capital gains the fund earns on its security transactions. Mutual funds provide such information to their shareholders in a standardized format (like the statement here) that highlights, among other things, income, expenses, and capital gains.

	2017	2016	2015
1. **Net asset value, beginning of period:**	$ 24.47	$ 27.03	$ 24.26
2. **Income from investment operations:**			
3. Net investment income	$ 0.60	$ 0.66	$ 0.50
4. Net gains on securities (realized and unrealized)	6.37	(1.74)	3.79
5. Total from investment operations	6.97	(1.08)	4.29
6. **Less distributions:**			
7. Dividends from net investment income	($0.55)	($0.64)	($0.50)
8. Distributions from realized gains	(1.75)	(.84)	(1.02)
9. Total distributions	(2.30)	(1.48)	(1.52)
10. **Net asset value, end of period:**	$ 29.14	$ 24.47	$ 27.03
11. **Total return:**	28.48%	(4.00%)	17.68%
12. **Ratios/supplemental data:**			
13. Net assets, end of period ($000)	$307,951	$153,378	$108,904
14. Ratio of expenses to average net assets	1.04%	0.85%	0.94%
15. Ratio of net investment income to average net assets	1.47%	2.56%	2.39%
16. Portfolio turnover rate*	85%	144%	74%

Portfolio turnover rate measures the number of shares bought and sold by the fund against the total number of shares held in the fund's portfolio; a high turnover rate (e.g., one exceeding 100%) would mean the fund has been doing a lot of trading.

and final element in a mutual fund's return, for *when the fund's securities holdings go up or down in price, its NAV moves accordingly*. This change (or movement) in the NAV is what makes up the unrealized capital gains of the fund. It represents the profit that shareholders would receive (and are entitled to) if the fund were to sell its holdings.

EXAMPLE: Calculating the Approximate Yield on a Mutual Fund

A simple but effective way of measuring performance is to describe mutual fund returns based on the three major sources of return noted above—dividends earned, capital gains distributions received, and change in share price. These payoffs can be converted to a convenient return figure by using the standard *approximate yield* formula that was first introduced in Chapter 12. The calculations necessary for finding such a return measure can be shown using the 2017 figures from Exhibit 13.9. Referring to the exhibit, we can see that this hypothetical no-load fund paid $0.55 per share in dividends and another $1.75 in capital gains distributions; also, its price (NAV) at the beginning of the year (that is, at the end of 2016) of $24.47 rose to $29.14 by the end of the year (see lines 1 and 10, respectively). Putting this data into the familiar approximate yield formula, we see that the hypothetical mutual fund provided an annual rate of return of 26 percent.

$$\text{Approximate Yield} = \frac{\text{Dividends and Capital Gains Distributions} + \left[\dfrac{\text{Ending Price} - \text{Beginning Price}}{\text{Length of Time Period}}\right]}{\left[\dfrac{\text{Ending Price} - \text{Beginning Price}}{2}\right]}$$

$$= \frac{(\$0.55 + \$1.75) + \left[\dfrac{\$29.14 - \$24.47}{1}\right]}{\left[\dfrac{\$29.14 - \$24.47}{2}\right]}$$

$$= \frac{\$2.30 + \$4.67}{\$26.80} = \frac{\$6.97}{\$26.80} = \underline{\underline{26.0\%}}$$

Calculator

INPUTS	FUNCTIONS
1	N
−24.47	PV
2.30	PMT
29.14	FV
	CPT
	I/Y
	SOLUTION
	28.48

See Appendix E for details.

Calculator Keystrokes. You can just as easily find the exact return on this investment with a handheld financial calculator. Here's what you'd do: Using *annual compounding*, to find the return on this mutual fund in 2017, we use the same input data as given before. Namely, we start with a price at the beginning of the year of $24.47; add in total dividends and capital gains distributions of $2.30 a share (i.e., $0.55 + $1.75); and then, using a year-end price of $29.14, punch the keystrokes shown in the margin, where:

N = number of *years* you hold the fund
PV = the *initial* price of the fund (entered as a *negative number*)
PMT = *total* amount of dividends and capital gains distributions received
FV = the *ending* price of the fund

Note that our computed return (of 28.48 percent) is exactly the same as the "Total Return" shown on line 11 of Exhibit 13.9—that's because this is basically the same procedure that the mutual funds must use to report their return performance. The approximate yield measure (26 percent) may be close to the actual return, but clearly it's not close enough for fund-reporting purposes.

Evaluating ETF Performance ETFs and mutual funds are similar in that their prices depend on the value of the funds' underlying investments. Both have NAVs and depend on dividends and capital gains to generate returns. So let's focus on the aspects that are particularly important in ETF performance evaluation. As discussed previously, while there are some actively managed ETFs, the vast majority are designed to replicate an index. Thus, for our purposes here, we'll consider the issues associated with evaluating the index-based form of ETF.

The primary reason for investing in an index-based ETF, of course, is to replicate the performance of the index. It follows that an important aspect of ETF performance is how well it tracks the performance of the underlying index. You can determine this by checking the so-called R-Squared (R^2) statistical measure, which shows how much of the variability in an ETF's total returns is explained by the variability in the total returns of the underlying index. The R^2 varies between 0 percent and a maximum of 100 percent. Obviously, the higher the R^2, the closer the relationship between the ETF and the associated target index. It also makes sense to know how the ETF's style is described and how consistently it pursues this style. Finally, it's wise to check how the ETF's performance compares to its peers and how the ETF's expense ratio compares with reasonable benchmarks.

Consider the Morningstar information on the PowerShares QQQ ETF (QQQ) in Exhibit 13.10. This ETF is designed to replicate the performance of the NASDAQ 100 index, which includes the 100 largest domestic and international non-financial firms trading on the NASDAQ stock exchange. The index includes companies from the following industries: health care, retail, transportation, telecommunications, biotechnology, technology, services, media, and industrial. The exhibit portrays various performance metrics for the ETF.

EXHIBIT 13.10 | **Evaluating ETF Performance**

Index-based ETF performance evaluation depends on how well the ETF's returns track the underlying index, the consistency with which it follows its investment style, its performance relative to its peers, and the competitiveness of its expenses. This example provides a page from a Morningstar report on the PowerShares QQQ ETF.

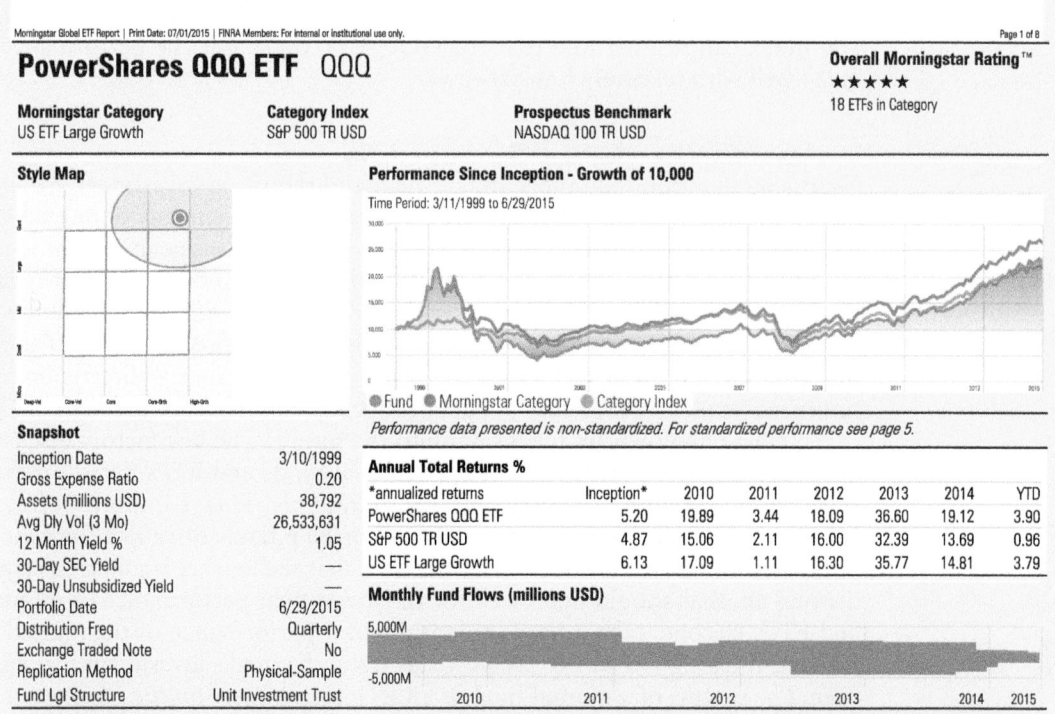

Morningstar Global ETF Report | Print Date: 07/01/2015 | FINRA Members: For internal or institutional use only.   Page 1 of 8

PowerShares QQQ ETF QQQ

Overall Morningstar Rating™
★★★★★
18 ETFs in Category

Morningstar Category	Category Index	Prospectus Benchmark
US ETF Large Growth	S&P 500 TR USD	NASDAQ 100 TR USD

Style Map

Performance Since Inception - Growth of 10,000

Time Period: 3/11/1999 to 6/29/2015

● Fund ● Morningstar Category ● Category Index

Performance data presented is non-standardized. For standardized performance see page 5.

Snapshot

Inception Date	3/10/1999
Gross Expense Ratio	0.20
Assets (millions USD)	38,792
Avg Dly Vol (3 Mo)	26,533,631
12 Month Yield %	1.05
30-Day SEC Yield	—
30-Day Unsubsidized Yield	—
Portfolio Date	6/29/2015
Distribution Freq	Quarterly
Exchange Traded Note	No
Replication Method	Physical-Sample
Fund Lgl Structure	Unit Investment Trust

Annual Total Returns %

*annualized returns	Inception*	2010	2011	2012	2013	2014	YTD
PowerShares QQQ ETF	5.20	19.89	3.44	18.09	36.60	19.12	3.90
S&P 500 TR USD	4.87	15.06	2.11	16.00	32.39	13.69	0.96
US ETF Large Growth	6.13	17.09	1.11	16.30	35.77	14.81	3.79

Monthly Fund Flows (millions USD)

5,000M

-5,000M

2010   2011   2012   2013   2014   2015

Performance Disclosure: *The performance data quoted represents past performance and does not guarantee future results. The investment return and principal value of an investment will fluctuate; thus an investor's shares, when sold, may be worth more or less than their original cost. Current performance may be lower or higher than return data quoted herein. For performance data current to the most recent month-end, please call +1 8009830903 or visit www.invescopowershares.com. The Overall Morningstar Rating is based on risk-adjusted returns, derived from a weighted average of the three-, five-, and 10-year (if applicable) Morningstar metrics.*

Annual Income Return %

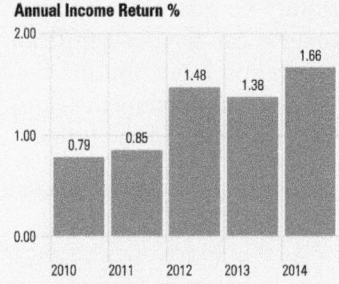

Year	Value
2010	0.79
2011	0.85
2012	1.48
2013	1.38
2014	1.66

Risk/Return Analysis (3 years)

	ETF	Cat Index	Cat Avg
Standard Deviation %	10.25	8.47	10.05
Arithmetic Mean %	1.76	1.54	1.56
Sharpe Ratio	2.06	2.17	—
R-Squared	71.10	—	—
Beta	1.02	—	—
Alpha %	2.28	—	—
Treynor Ratio	22.15	—	—
Sortino Ratio	4.67	4.97	—

Suitability

By Robert Goldsborough 5/11/2015

PowerShares QQQ ETF QQQ, the 11th most actively traded and sixth-largest U.S. exchange-traded fund offers a large helping of large-cap growth stocks with a strong tilt toward the technology sector. QQQ, which tracks the cap-weighted Nasdaq-100 Index of the 100 largest nonfinancial stocks in the Nasdaq Composite Index, also includes leading consumer discretionary (19.5% of assets) and biotech (15% of assets) firms. Given its focus on a few sectors, this ETF works best as a satellite holding in a diversified portfolio.

Given this fund's sector tilts, it is more volatile than a broad portfolio of large-cap stocks. For example, over the past 10 years, it has had a standard deviation of 17.9% compared with 14.7% for the S&P 500.

Many of the stocks in this fund are already in other more diversified funds. This ETF's tech holdings comprise almost the S&P 500's entire 20% tech component. Indeed, QQQ's performance correlates highly with the S&P 500 (90% over the past 10 years) and has an even higher correlation with Technology Select Sector SDPR XLK (97% over the past 10 years).

Source: MorningstarDirect, July 2015. © 2012 Morningstar, Inc. All rights reserved.

The Morningstar investment style category is "Large Growth." The exhibit shows that the ETF's performance compares favorably with other funds in its category. In addition, notice that the R^2 ("R-Squared" in the exhibit) of the QQQ ETF relative to the S&P 500 is 71.10 percent. The "alpha" of 2.28 percent shows that the QQQ ETF generated about 2.3 percent more than expected for its degree of market risk. While not shown in the exhibit, Morningstar indicates elsewhere that the net expense ratio for the QQQ ETF is only 0.20 percent. In summary, an investor wanting consistent exposure to the large non-financial growth stocks that characterize the NASDAQ 100 index can rest assured that the QQQ ETF replicates the performance of that index well with relatively low expenses.

What About Future Performance?

There's no question that approximate yield and return on investment are simple yet highly effective measures that capture all the important elements of mutual fund and ETF returns. Unfortunately, looking at past performance is one thing, but what about the future? Ideally, we'd want to evaluate the same three elements of return over the future much as we did for the past. Yet it's difficult—if not impossible—to get a handle on what the *future* holds for dividends, capital gains, and NAV. The reason is that a mutual fund's or ETF's future investment performance is directly linked to the future makeup of its securities portfolio, which is impossible to predict.

So where do you look for insight into the future? The key factors discussed here apply equally to the evaluation of both mutual funds and ETFs. First, carefully consider the *future direction of the market as a whole*. This is important because the behavior of a well-diversified mutual fund or ETF tends to reflect the general tone of the market. So, if the consensus forecast is that the market is going to be generally drifting up, that should bode well for the investment performance of mutual funds and ETFs. Second, take a hard look at the past performance of the mutual fund or ETF itself. It's a good way to see how successful the fund's investment managers have been. The success of a mutual fund or an ETF rests largely *on the investment skills of the fund managers*. So, when investing in a fund, look for consistently good performance in up as well as down markets, as well as over extended periods (five to seven years, or more). Most important, check to see whether the same key people are still running the fund. Although past success is certainly no guarantee of future performance, a strong, consistent team of money managers can have a significant bearing on the level of fund returns. Put another way, when you buy a mutual fund or ETF, you're buying a formula (investment policy + money management team) that has worked in the past, in the expectation that it will work again in the future.

TEST YOURSELF

13-14 What are the most common reasons for buying mutual funds and ETFs?

13-15 Briefly describe the steps in the mutual fund selection process.

13-16 Why does it pay to invest in no-load funds rather than load funds? Under what conditions might it make sense to invest in a load fund?

13-17 Identify three potential sources of return to mutual fund and ETF investors, and briefly discuss how each could affect total return to shareholders.

13-18 Which would you rather have: $100 in dividend income or $100 in capital gains distribution? $100 in realized capital gains or $100 in unrealized capital gains?

13-19 Describe how to evaluate the attractiveness of investing in an index-based ETF.

13-20 How important is the overall market in affecting the price performance of mutual funds and ETFs?

13-4 INVESTING IN REAL ESTATE

For many years, investing in real estate was quite lucrative. Real estate, it seemed, was one of the few investment vehicles that just couldn't go wrong. Of course, as with any investment, the market for real estate fluctuates over time, and investors must do their homework before making real estate investments. When the economy is growing and inflation is relatively high, as it was in the 1970s and early 1980s, real estate prices were also strong. But in the early 1990s, the market weakened, and prices started to level off. That didn't last long, however, as real estate values began to climb again in the latter part of the 1990s. One example of this behavior was housing prices, which rose rapidly—indeed, shot almost straight up—from 2001 through 2006. But then, from a market peak in 2006, housing prices fell almost as quickly as they had risen, with the average price of a home plummeting nearly 33 percent by early 2011, which was the bottom when prices had fallen by more than during the Great Depression. Housing prices recovered significantly from 2012 to 2014. While still below 2006 peak levels in 2015, housing prices were expected to rise at an average rate of 4 to 5 percent in the near term.

ANTHONY BERENYI /DREAMSTIME.COM

Real estate includes everything from homes and raw land to different types of income-producing properties such as warehouses, commercial and retail space, office and apartment buildings, and condominiums. Investments in real estate can take several forms. For example, investors can buy land or property directly, or they may prefer to invest in various types of real estate securities such as real estate mutual funds (discussed earlier in this chapter), REITs, mortgages, stocks of real estate-related companies, or real estate limited partnerships. Adding real estate to your investment portfolio *provides greater diversification than does holding just stocks or bonds.* That's because *real estate typically exhibits less volatility than stocks and it doesn't usually move in tandem with stocks.* Before deciding to buy real estate for your portfolio, however, it's essential for you to evaluate such issues as the outlook for the national economy, interest rate levels, supply and demand for space, and regional considerations. Then you must choose the right properties or investment vehicles for your financial needs—and manage them well.

13-4a Some Basic Considerations

The attractiveness of a real estate investment depends on the expected cash flows over the planned holding period and the riskiness of those cash flows. The expected ongoing cash flows are determined by rent, depreciation, and taxes—and, of course, the all-important expected future sales price. The expected return on a real estate investment is determined by the relationship between the expected future cash flows relative to the initial investment, which is typically reduced by using a significant amount of borrowed funds. The value of the investment is assessed in light of the returns available on alternative investments of comparable risk (such as stocks, bonds, and mutual funds). Far more than with most other types of investment vehicles, financial leverage (borrowing) is a key determinant of real estate investment returns. We'll now briefly describe the basic factors affecting the value of real estate investments, including after-tax cash flows, appreciation in value, and the use of leverage.

Cash Flow and Taxes

The after-tax *cash flow* on a real estate investment depends on the revenues generated by the property, on any operating expenses, and on depreciation and taxes. Real estate typically provides large depreciation write-offs that tend to lower the taxable income of certain (*qualified*) investors. Depreciation gives the property owner an allowance for the decline in the physical condition of real estate over time. Although it's a bookkeeping entry that's considered an expense for tax purposes, it involves no actual cash outflow. Depreciation can result in lower taxes; for this reason, it's viewed as a *tax shelter*. But there's a catch: depreciation can be used only up to a certain amount and only by investors who meet certain income qualifications, as we'll explain next.

Keep in mind that, for tax purposes, real estate is considered a *passive* investment. Therefore, the amount of expenses, *including depreciation*, that can be written off is generally limited to the amount of income generated by this and any other passive investments owned by the investor. For example, if you owned some apartments that generated $25,000 a year in rental income and if (in the absence of any other passive investments) you had mortgage interest and other operating expenses (such as property taxes and minor repairs) of $20,000 annually, then you might be able to write off up to $5,000 in depreciation ($25,000 income minus $20,000 other expenses). However, if your *adjusted gross income* (AGI) is less than $100,000 a year, then you may be able to write off even more depreciation—specifically, as much as $25,000 in losses on *rented real estate* can be used to offset the ordinary income of people who "actively participate" in the rental activity of the buildings *and* whose AGI is less than $100,000. (This provision is phased out at $150,000.) In this example, if you had $90,000 in AGI and $15,000 in depreciation expenses, then $5,000 of it could be written off against the remaining $5,000 of net rental income, as discussed before. The other $10,000 could be charged directly against your ordinary income, thereby reducing your taxable income and your taxes. Because of its effect on taxes, *depreciation is considered an important component of real estate investments*. Because depreciation and taxes are such important elements in measuring cash flow, an individual investor should have a tax consultant evaluate proposed real estate investments.

Appreciation in Value

An investment evaluation of a proposed piece of real estate should include not only the recurring cash flows from the property (e.g., rents), but also expected changes in property values. In many cases, such appreciation has a much greater impact on the rate of return than does the net annual cash flow from the property. Hence, if the market price of the real estate is expected to increase by $100,000, then that price appreciation should be treated as capital gains and included as part of the return from the investment (minus, of course, the capital gains taxes paid).

Use of Leverage

A big attraction for investing in real estate is the high degree of financial leverage that it permits. Leverage involves using borrowed money to magnify returns. Because real estate is a tangible asset, investors can borrow as much as 75 percent to 90 percent of its cost. As a result, if the profit rate on the investment is greater than the cost of borrowing, then the return on a leveraged investment will be *proportionally greater* than the return generated from an otherwise comparable unleveraged investment.

EXAMPLE: The Effect of Leverage on Real Estate Returns

You're considering a real estate investment costing $100,000—like the one in Exhibit 13.11. You can purchase the property in one of two ways: you can either pay cash for it or you can put up $20,000 of your own money and borrow the remaining $80,000 at 5 percent annual interest. If the property earns $13,000 per year after all expenses, including property taxes and depreciation but *before interest and income taxes are deducted*, then the leveraged investment will provide a much better rate of return than the cash deal, as seen in Exhibit 13.11. Observe that your return on investment in the no-leverage case will be 9.36 percent but that, with leverage, you stand to make a return of 32.40 percent! And the higher expected return is the compensation for taking on the higher risk implied by using leverage.

| EXHIBIT 13.11 | Using Leverage in Real Estate Investments |

Although earnings after taxes are lower with the leveraged investment, the return on investment is considerably higher because the investor puts a lot less of his or her own money into the deal.

	No Leverage		Leverage
Owner investment	$100,000		$ 20,000
Borrowed money	0		80,000
Total investment	$100,000		$100,000
Earnings before interest and income taxes*	$ 13,000		$ 13,000
Less: Interest	0	(0.05)($80,000) =	4,000
Earnings before taxes	$ 13,000		$ 9,000
Less: Income taxes (assumed 28% rate)	3,640		2,520
Earnings after taxes	$ 9,360		$ 6,480

$$\text{Return on Investment} = \frac{\text{Earnings After Taxes}}{\text{Amount of Owner Investment}} = \frac{\$9,630}{\$100,000} = 9.36\% \qquad \frac{\$6,480}{\$20,000} = 32.40\%$$

*All expenses, including property taxes and depreciation, are assumed to have been deducted from earnings.

Financial Fact or Fantasy?

In many types of real estate investments, appreciation in the value of the property affects return more than annual rental income. **Fact:** Like most forms of investing, the biggest bang for your buck usually comes from capital gains. You'll find that's the way the really big money is made, and real estate is certainly no exception to that rule.

Because some of the leveraged investment is made with borrowed money, the return on investment in Exhibit 13.11 reflects *only the amount of money that you put up* to buy it. So, even though the leveraged investment provides *less in earnings after taxes*, it has a lower investment base. The net result is a *higher return on investment*. By leveraging your investment, you'll get a bigger bang from your investment bucks. However, when no borrowing is involved, you have no risk of default; on the other hand, when you use leverage, minimum earnings (before interest and taxes) of $4,000 are necessary to pay the interest and thereby avoid default. The risk that comes with leverage, therefore, must be considered along with the potential benefits. Indeed, many people have been driven into bankruptcy because they used too much leverage.

13-4b Speculating in Raw Land

Investing in real estate can take several forms. One approach that's popular with many investors is to *speculate in raw land*. In this approach, *which is often viewed as highly risky*, investors seek to generate high rates of return by investing in property that they *hope* will undergo dramatic increases in value. The key to such speculation is to isolate areas of potential population growth and/or real estate demand (ideally, before anyone else does) and purchase property in these areas in anticipation of their eventual development. Undeveloped acreage with no utilities or improvements is often purchased by land speculators either to hold for future development or to sell, as is, at a higher price later. Given the high degree of uncertainty involved, raw land speculation should be reserved for real estate investors who understand and can accept the inherent risks.

13-4c Investing in Income Property

income (income-producing) property Real estate purchased for leasing or renting to tenants in order to generate ongoing monthly/annual income in the form of rent receipts.

One of the most popular forms of real estate investing is income (or income-producing) property, which includes commercial and residential properties. Investments in income properties offer both attractive returns and tax advantages for investors. The purchased real estate is leased to tenants to generate income from rent. And although the primary purpose of investing in income property is to produce an attractive annual cash flow, certain types of strategically located income properties also offer attractive opportunities for appreciation in value. Before buying income property, be sure you know what you're getting into. The owner of income property is responsible for leasing the units and maintaining the property. This means fixing leaky roofs and appliances, painting and other repairs, cleaning after a tenant leaves, and similar responsibilities.

Calculating the value of income-producing property requires estimating the annual net operating income (NOI), which *equals gross rental income (less an allowance for vacancies and bad debts) minus all operating expenses, such as property (but not income) taxes, insurance, maintenance, and so on.* Once you have a property's NOI, you can apply a *cap rate* (the expected annual rate of return on the property) to arrive at an estimated value for the property. A typical cap rate for income property is around 9 percent or 10 percent.

> **EXAMPLE: Calculating the Value of Income-Producing Property**
>
> You're thinking about buying an office building that generates an estimated $50,000 per year in NOI. With a 9 percent cap rate, that property would have an estimated value of $555,556 = $50,000/0.09.

Commercial Properties

The commercial property category consists of many types of properties, including office buildings, industrial space, warehouses, retail space (from freestanding stores to strip shopping centers to malls), and hotels. The risks and returns on commercial real estate investments are tied to business conditions and location. The value of commercial property, especially retail businesses, is enhanced by a location in a high-traffic area. Because commercial properties call for professional management and involve significant expenses, investing in this category of income property is generally the domain of more seasoned (often professional) real estate investors.

Residential Properties

First-time investors often choose income-producing *residential properties* such as homes, apartments, and smaller multifamily buildings. This category of income property is available in various sizes, prices, and types ranging from single family homes, duplexes, and triplexes to large apartment buildings. Aside from the considerations of purchase and financing costs, major factors influencing the profitability of these investments are the occupancy rates—the percentage of available space rented over the year—and maintenance and management costs. Other factors to consider are the neighborhood where the units are located, local regulations regarding tenants, and supply and demand trends for the type of property.

13-4d Other Ways to Invest in Real Estate

What if the idea of owning and managing property doesn't appeal to you? Or perhaps you don't have enough money to buy income property outright. Another way to own real estate is by purchasing specialized securities. For example, you can buy shares in a *real estate mutual fund* (discussed earlier in this chapter). Or you can buy stock in *publicly traded real estate-related companies.* These include residential homebuilders, construction companies, mortgage lenders, home improvement retailers, property managers, real estate brokerage firms, and engineering companies. Let's now look at two other options: REITs and real estate limited partnerships (LPs; otherwise known as *limited liability companies,* or *LLCs*).

Real Estate Investment Trusts

real estate investment trust (REIT)
An investment company that accumulates money by selling shares to investors, in order to invest that money in various forms of real estate, including mortgages; this type of fund is similar to a mutual fund, but a REIT invests only in specific types of real estate or real estate-related firms.

Arguably, the best way for most individuals to invest in real estate is through a real estate investment trust (REIT), which is a type of closed-end investment company that invests money in various types of real estate and real estate mortgages. A REIT is like a mutual fund in that it sells shares of stock to the investing public and uses the proceeds, along with borrowed funds, to invest in a portfolio of real estate investments. The investor therefore owns part of the real estate portfolio held by the REIT. REITs appeal to investors because they offer the benefits of real estate ownership—both capital appreciation and current income—without the headaches of property management.

REITs have become popular with investors seeking portfolio diversification because these trusts generally have relatively low correlations with other market sectors, such as common stocks and bonds. They also provide attractive dividend yields—well above the yields on common stocks. (In fact, about 65 percent of the total return from REITs comes from their dividends.) REITs have also produced competitive returns: the compound annual return from REITs (dividends plus stock price appreciation on the FTSE REIT U.S. Real Estate Index) for the last 30 years was 11.36 percent, compared with 12.51 percent for the S&P 500. The performance of REITs over this period is significantly influenced by the real estate losses resulting from the financial crisis of 2007–2009. However, the return on REITs was 27.15 percent in 2014 and the three-year return from 2012 to 2014 was 16.83 percent. REITs can be particularly attractive investments during periods of high inflation, which is projected by many to eventually result from the large deficit spending induced by the financial crisis of 2007–2009.

Like any investment fund, each REIT has stated investment objectives, which should be considered carefully before acquiring shares. There are three basic types of REITs:

- Equity REITs: They own and operate income-producing real estate such as apartments, office buildings, shopping centers, and hotels.
- Mortgage REITs: These make both construction and mortgage loans to real estate investors.
- Hybrid REITs: They invest in both income-producing properties and mortgage loans.

Equity REITs produce both attractive current yields and the potential to earn excellent capital gains as their properties appreciate in value. In contrast, mortgage REITs tend to be more income oriented; they emphasize the high current yields they generate by investing in debt. Listed equity REITs hold more than $1 trillion in U.S. real estate assets and constitute about 90 percent of the $700 billion listed REIT market. Most of the rest of the market involves mortgage REITs. The income earned by a REIT isn't taxed, but the income distributed to owners is designated and taxed as ordinary income. Whereas dividends on common stocks normally are taxed at preferential rates (of 15 or 20 percent or less), this is not the case with REITs, whose cash dividends are treated as ordinary income and taxed accordingly.

Financial Fact or Fantasy?

A real estate investment trust (REIT) is a popular form of limited partnership that enables individuals to invest directly in income-producing property. Fantasy: A REIT is a type of closed-end investment company (like a mutual fund) that issues stocks and invests the proceeds in various kinds of real estate properties, including mortgages.

Real Estate Limited Partnerships or Limited Liability Companies

Special-purpose syndicates organized to invest in real estate are another type of real estate investment. These can be structured as LPs or LLCs. With LPs, the managers assume the role of *general partner*, which means that their liability is unlimited and that the other investors are *limited partners* who are legally liable only for the amount of their initial investment. In recent years, the LLC has become a more popular way to form these entities. Rather than general and limited partners, the LLC has a managing member and other members—none of which have any liability. Investors buy *units* in an LP or LLC; a unit represents an ownership position, similar to a share of stock. Real estate LPs and LLCs are riskier investments than REITs, and they appeal to more affluent investors who can afford the typical unit cost of $100,000 or more.

TEST YOURSELF

13-21 Define and briefly discuss the role of each of these factors in evaluating a proposed real estate investment:

 a. Cash flow and taxes
 b. Appreciation in value
 c. Use of leverage

13-22 Why is speculating in raw land considered a high-risk venture?

13-23 Describe the major categories of income property, and explain the advantages and disadvantages of investing in income property. How can a single-family home be used to generate income?

13-24 Describe how the following securities allow investors to participate in the real estate market.

 a. Stock in real estate-related companies
 b. Real estate limited partnerships (LPs) or limited liability companies (LLCs)

13-25 Briefly describe the basic structure and investment considerations associated with a REIT. What are the three basic types of REITs?

Planning Over a Lifetime: *Investing in Mutual Funds, ETFs, and Real Estate*

Here are some key considerations for investment planning in each stage of the life cycle.

Pre-family Independence: 20s	Family Formation/ Career Development: 30–45	Pre-Retirement: 45–65	Retirement: 65 and Beyond
✓ Determine your major investment goals and how much money needs to be invested each month to achieve them.	✓ Revise investments in mutual funds, ETFs, and real estate to focus more on retirement and funding children's education, if applicable.	✓ Revise your investment plan in light of recent developments.	✓ Revise your investment plan to lean more toward debt and cash instruments than to stocks in your mutual funds and ETFs.
✓ Determine your asset allocation among stocks, bonds, real estate, and cash based on your time horizon and attitude towards risk. Choose mutual funds and ETFs accordingly.	✓ Review your asset allocation and rebalance it to be more consistent with your goals.	✓ Review your asset allocation and rebalance investments among mutual funds, ETFs, and real estate if it is inconsistent with your goals.	✓ Review your asset allocation, and rebalance it if it is inconsistent with your goals.

Planning Over a Lifetime: *Investing in Mutual Funds, ETFs, and Real Estate (continued)*

Here are some key considerations for investment planning in each stage of the life cycle.

Pre-family Independence: 20s	Family Formation/ Career Development: 30–45	Pre-Retirement: 45–65	Retirement: 65 and Beyond
✓ Match your investments in any employer-sponsored 401(k) retirement plan with your overall asset allocation plan.	✓ Gradually increase the amount invested in any employer-sponsored 401(k) retirement plan and reevaluate how it relates to your asset allocation plan.	✓ Continue to gradually increase the amount you invest in any employer-sponsored 401(k) retirement plan and reevaluate how it relates to your asset allocation plan.	✓ Integrate investment asset allocation strategy with estate planning.
✓ Consider investing in mutual funds and ETFs under a traditional IRA, a Roth IRA, or both.	✓ Consider increasing your contribution to traditional IRA, a Roth IRA, or both.	✓ Consider increasing your contribution to traditional and/or Roth IRAs using mutual funds and ETFs.	✓ Plan carefully for mandatory withdrawals from tax-sheltered accounts and associated tax consequences.

WILLIAM HUBER/PHOTONICA/GETTY IMAGES

Financial Impact of Personal Choices
Virginia Finds a Simple Retirement Investment Plan

Virginia Woodall, 27 years old, wants to get her retirement investing portfolio up and running. But she has a demanding job and little time to manage a portfolio closely. In doing some research, she read a short (16-page) booklet by William J. Bernstein, "If You Can" (**www.etf.com/docs/IfYouCan.pdf**). Bernstein argues that by age 25 it's important to invest at least 15 percent of your income annually in a 401(k), an IRA, or a taxable account (or all three) in just three mutual funds or ETFs:

- U.S. total stock market index fund
- International total stock market fund
- U.S. total bond market index fund

These funds will earn different rates of return over time, so once a year it makes sense to rebalance the amount in each account so they're equal. Bernstein convincingly argues that following this simple investment plan will beat most professional investors and would likely provide enough savings for Virginia to retire comfortably.

Virginia was indeed convinced and estimated that keeping the plan in place would take about 30 minutes a year. So she invested equal amounts in the following ETFs:

- Vanguard Total International Stock ETF (VXUS)
- Vanguard Total Stock Market ETF (VXUS)
- Vanguard Total Bond Market ETF (BND)

Virginia will invest 15 percent of her income each year in these ETFs and rebalance them annually. Her research and simple, systematic approach will no doubt serve her well.

Summary

LG1 **Describe the basic features and operating characteristics of mutual funds and exchange-traded funds, p. 509.**
Mutual fund shares represent ownership in a diversified, professionally managed portfolio of securities that do not trade on stock exchanges. In contrast, exchange-traded funds (ETFs) are investment company shares that trade throughout the day on stock exchanges. Many investors who lack the time, know-how, or commitment to manage their own money turn to these investments. By investing in mutual funds or ETFs, shareholders benefit from a level of diversification and investment performance that otherwise they might find difficult to achieve.

LG2 **Differentiate between open- and closed-end mutual funds as well as exchange-traded funds, and discuss the various types of fund loads and charges, p. 509.**
Investors can buy either open-end funds, which can issue an unlimited number of shares, or closed-end funds, which have a fixed number of shares outstanding and which trade in the secondary markets like any other share of common stock. Investors also can buy ETFs, which are typically structured like index funds and operate much like open-end funds but trade in the market like closed-end funds. There's a cost, however, to investing in mutual funds (and other types of professionally managed investment products). Mutual fund investors face a full array of loads, fees, and charges, including front-end loads, back-end loads, annual 12b-1 charges, and annual management fees. Some of these costs (e.g., front-end loads) are one-time charges, but others [such as 12b-1 and management fees] must be paid annually.

LG3 **Discuss the types of funds available to investors and the different kinds of investor services offered by mutual funds and exchange-traded funds, p. 522.**
Each fund has an established investment objective that determines its investment policy and identifies it as a certain type of fund. Some popular types of funds are growth, aggressive growth, value, equity-income, balanced, growth-and-income, bond, money market, index, sector, socially responsible, asset allocation, and international funds. The different categories of funds have different risk-return characteristics, which are important variables in the fund selection process. Many investors buy mutual funds not only for their investment returns, but also to take advantage of the various investor services that the funds offer, such as automatic investment and reinvestment plans, systematic withdrawal programs, low-cost conversion and phone or online switching privileges, and retirement programs.

LG4 **Gain an understanding of the variables that should be considered when selecting funds for investment purposes, p. 531.**
The fund selection process usually starts by assessing your own needs and wants. This sets the tone for your investment program and helps you decide on the types of funds to consider. Next, look at what the funds have to offer, particularly regarding their investment objectives and investor services; then, narrow down the alternatives by aligning your needs with the types of funds available. From this list of funds, conduct the final selection tests: fund performance and cost. Other things being equal, look for higher performance and lower costs.

LG5 **Identify the sources of return and calculate the rate of return earned on a mutual fund investment, as well as evaluate the performance of an exchange-traded fund, p. 531.**
The investment performance of mutual funds and ETFs largely depends on the returns that the money managers are able to generate from their securities portfolios. Strong markets usually translate into attractive returns for mutual fund and ETF investors. Mutual funds and ETFs have three basic sources of return: (1) dividends, (2) capital gains distributions, and (3) changes in the fund's NAV (accruing from unrealized capital gains). Both the approximate yield and total return measures recognize these three elements and provide simple yet effective ways of measuring the annual rate of return from a mutual fund or an ETF. Index-based ETF performance considers the fund's returns, as well as how closely it tracks the performance of its underlying index, how consistently it pursues its investment style, how its performance compares with its peers, and how the fund's expense ratio compares with reasonable benchmarks.

LG6 Understand the role that real estate plays in a diversified investment portfolio along with the basics of investing in real estate, either directly or indirectly, p. 541.

Investing in real estate—be it raw land, income property (such as office buildings, apartments, and retail space), or even homes—provides an opportunity to earn attractive returns and further diversify an investment portfolio. Investors can buy property directly or invest in several types of real estate securities. Speculating in raw land is a high-risk type of real estate investment. Income-producing property, on the other hand, offers attractive returns from income and price appreciation as well as certain tax advantages. Investors not wishing to own real estate directly can invest indirectly through real estate mutual funds, as well as in the common shares of real estate-related companies, REITs, or real estate LPs or LLCs. REITs, which are closed-end investment companies that invest in real estate, are the most popular type of real estate security and have a track record of solid returns.

Key Terms

12b-1 fee, 517

automatic investment plan, 528

automatic reinvestment plan, 528

back-end load, 516

closed-end investment company, 514

conversion (exchange) privileges, 530

exchange-traded fund (ETF), 509

general-purpose money fund, 524

government securities money fund, 525

income (income-producing) property, 543

international fund, 526

load fund, 516

low-load fund, 516

management fee, 519

mutual fund, 509

net asset value (NAV), 513

no-load fund, 516

open-end investment company, 513

pooled diversification, 511

real estate investment trust (REIT), 545

socially responsible fund (SRF), 526

systematic withdrawal plan, 529

tax-exempt money fund, 525

Answers to Test Yourself

You can find answers to these questions on this book's companion website. Look for it at *www.cengagebrain.com*. Search for this book by its title, and then add it to your dashboard.

Key Financial Relationships

Concept	Financial Relationship	Page Number
Net Asset Value per Share	Net Asset Value per Share = $\dfrac{\text{Total Market Value of All Securities} - \text{Liabilities}}{\text{Number of Fund Shares Outstanding}}$	514
Approximate Yield	Approximate Yield = $\dfrac{\text{Dividends and Capital Gains Distribution} + \dfrac{\text{Ending Price} - \text{Beginning Price}}{\text{Length of Time Period}}}{\dfrac{\text{Ending Price} + \text{Beginning Price}}{2}}$	537

Key Financial Relationships Problem Set

1. **Net asset value.** The market value of all of the securities held by a mutual fund is $5 billion. It's an open-end mutual fund with 750 million shares outstanding. What is the mutual fund's net asset value (NAV) per share?

   Solution:

   $$\text{Net Asset Value per Share} = \frac{\text{Total Market Value of All Securities} - \text{Liabilities}}{\text{Number of Fund Shares Outstanding}} = \frac{\$5 \text{ billion}}{\$750 \text{ million}}$$

   $$= \$6.67 \text{ per Share}$$

2. **Approximate yield.** Owen Chow wants to better understand how his mutual fund generated its return over the last year. The fund paid dividends of $0.85 per share, distributed capital gains of $3.25 per share and started the year with a net asset value of $32.25 per share and ended the year with a net asset value of $39.83 per share. What is the mutual fund's approximate yield and what is the primary source of its return?

   Solution:

   So Owen's mutual fund generated an attractive return. Most of the return was generated by the appreciation in the share price (NAV) of the fund. The NAV increased by $7.58 while dividends and capital gains distributed only contributed $4.10 to the return this year.

   $$\text{Approximate Yield} = \frac{\text{Dividends and Capital Gains Distribution} + \dfrac{\text{Ending Price} - \text{Beginning Price}}{\text{Length of Time Period}}}{\dfrac{\text{Ending Price} + \text{Beginning Price}}{2}}$$

   $$= \frac{(\$0.85 + \$3.25) + \dfrac{\$39.83 - \$32.25}{1}}{\dfrac{\$39.83 + \$32.25}{2}}$$

   $$= \frac{\$4.10 + \$7.58}{\$36.04} = 32.41\%$$

Financial Planning Exercises

LG2, p. 509

1. **Estimating cost of mutual fund investments.** Using the mutual fund quotes in Exhibit 13.4, and assuming that you can buy these funds at their quoted NAVs, how much would you have to pay to buy each of the following funds?
   a. American Century Emerging Markets Fund, A shares (AEMMX)
   b. American Century Growth Fund, A shares (TCRAX)
   c. American Century International Bond Fund, A shares (AIBDX)
   d. Artisan Small Cap Value Fund Investor Shares (ARTVX)

   According to the quotes, which of these four funds have 12b-1 fees? Which have redemption fees? Are any of them no-loads? Which fund has the highest year-to-date return? Which has the lowest?

LG2,3,
p. 509, 522

2. ***Building a mutual fund portfolio.*** Imagine you've just inherited $40,000 from a rich uncle. Now you're faced with the problem of deciding how to spend it. You could make a down payment on a condo—or better yet, on that BMW that you've always wanted; or you could spend your windfall more profitably by building a mutual fund portfolio. Let's say that, after a lot of soul-searching, you decide to build a mutual fund portfolio. Your task is to develop a $40,000 mutual fund portfolio. Use actual funds and actual quoted prices, invest as much of the $40,000 as you possibly can, and be specific! Briefly describe the portfolio that you end up with, including the investment objectives that you're trying to achieve.

LG2,3,
p. 509, 522

3. ***Comparing ETF with mutual fund.*** Describe an ETF and explain how these funds combine the characteristics of open- and closed-end funds. Within the Vanguard family of funds, which would most closely resemble a "Spider" (SPDR)? In what respects are the Vanguard fund (that you selected) and SPDRs the same, and how are they different? If you could invest in only one of them, which would it be? Explain.

LG3, p. 522

4. ***Mutual fund family services.*** What investor service is most closely linked to the notion of a fund family? If a fund is not part of a family of mutual funds, can it still offer a full range of investor services? Explain. Using a source such as *The Wall Street Journal* or perhaps your local newspaper, find two examples of fund families and list some of the mutual funds that they offer.

LG3, p. 522

5. ***Comparing different types of mutual funds.*** Using a source like *Barron's, Forbes, Money,* or *Morningstar*, along with any related Internet sites, select five mutual funds—a growth fund, an index fund, a sector fund, an international fund, and a high-yield corporate bond fund—that you believe would make good investments. Briefly explain why you selected each of the funds.

LG4, p. 531

6. ***Contrasting direct and mutual fund or ETF investing.*** Contrast *mutual fund or ETF ownership* with *direct investment in stocks and bonds*. Assume that you've been asked to debate the merits of investing through mutual funds versus investing directly in stocks and bonds. Develop some pro and con arguments for this debate, and be prepared to discuss them. If you had to choose a side, which one would it be? Explain.

LG4, p. 531

7. ***Comparing risks of different mutual fund/ETF types.*** For *each pair* of funds listed below, select the fund that would be *less* risky and briefly explain your answer.
   a. Growth versus growth-and-income
   b. Equity-income versus high-grade corporate bonds
   c. Intermediate-term bonds versus high-yield municipals
   d. International versus balanced

LG4, 5, p. 531

8. ***Evaluating an ETF.*** Using the Morningstar information in Exhibit 13.10, evaluate the performance of the QQQ index-based ETF. Specifically, comment on how well it tracks the underlying index and how its performance compares with other similar ETFs.

LG5, p. 531

9. ***Calculating approximate yield on mutual fund.*** About a year ago, Ramon Navarrete bought some shares in the Sapphire Lake Mutual Fund. He bought the fund at $24.50 a share, and it now trades at $26. Last year, the fund paid dividends of 40 cents a share and had capital gains distributions of $1.83 a share. Using the approximate yield formula, what rate of return did Ramon earn on his investment? Repeat the calculation using a handheld financial calculator. What rate of return would he have earned if the stock had risen to $30 a share?

LG5, p. 531

10. ***Calculating mutual fund approximate rate of return.*** A year ago, the Stellar Growth Fund was being quoted at an NAV of $21.50 and an offer price of $23.35; today, it's being quoted at $23.04 (NAV) and $25.04 (offer). Use the approximate yield formula or a handheld financial calculator to find the rate of return on this load fund; it was purchased a year ago, and its dividends and capital gains distributions over the year totaled $1.05 a share. (*Hint:* As an investor, you buy fund shares at the offer price and sell at the NAV.)

11. **Calculating and evaluating mutual fund returns.** Here is the per-share performance record of the Abacus Growth-and-Income fund for 2017 and 2016:

	2017	2016
1. **Net asset value, beginning of period:**	$58.60	$52.92
2. **Income from investment operations:**		
3. Net investment income	$1.39	$1.35
4. Net gains on securities (realized and unrealized)	8.10	9.39
5. Total from investment operations	$9.49	$10.74
6. **Less distributions:**		
7. Dividends from net investment income	($.83)	($1.24)
8. Distributions from realized gains	(2.42)	(3.82)
9. Total distributions	(3.25)	(5.06)
10. **Net asset value, end of period:**	$64.84	$58.60

Use this information to find the rate of return earned on this fund in 2016 and in 2017. What is your assessment of the investment performance of this fund for this time period?

12. **Different ways to invest in real estate.** Assume you've just inherited $100,000 and want to use all or part of it to make a real estate investment.

a. Would you invest directly in real estate, or indirectly through something like a REIT? Explain.
b. Assuming that you decided to invest directly, would you invest in income-producing property or speculative property? Why? Describe the key characteristics of the types of income-producing or speculative property you would seek.
c. What financial and nonfinancial goals would you establish before beginning the search for suitable property?
d. If you decide to invest in real estate indirectly, which type(s) of securities would you buy, and why?

13. **Investing in residential income-producing property.** Mallory Comer is thinking about investing in some residential income-producing property that she can purchase for $200,000. Mallory can either pay cash for the full amount of the property or put up $50,000 of her own money and borrow the remaining $150,000 at 5 percent interest. The property is expected to generate $30,000 per year after all expenses but *before* interest and income taxes. Assume that Mallory is in the 28 percent tax bracket. Calculate her annual profit and return on investment, assuming that she (a) pays the full $200,000 from her own funds or (b) borrows $150,000 at 5 percent. Then discuss the effect, if any, of leverage on her rate of return.

14. **Choosing a REIT.** Choose two REITS from a list available at **https://www.reit.com/investing/investor-resources/reit-directory/reits-sp-indexes.** Using information you can find by clicking on the ticker symbol on this and other Internet sites, prepare a comparison that includes:
a. The type of REIT that each represents (e.g., apartment, office, mortgage).
b. The type and quality of the properties they hold.
c. Each REIT's financial performance and management track record.

Based on your analysis, in which REIT would you invest? Explain why in terms of how it does or does not meet your investment objectives.

15. **Finding real estate stocks.** Using Yahoo! Finance or another investor information Internet site, find three real estate-related stocks. Evaluate them as potential additions to your portfolio. Do you think they provide the same degree of diversification as other forms of real estate investments? Explain.

Applying Personal Finance

The Feeling's Mutual!

Mutual funds offer convenience, diversification, and the services of professional money managers and analysts. Mutual funds can be particularly appealing for small investors who don't have a lot of money and for those who are new to investing. This project will help you learn more about the various types of mutual funds and how to pick the funds that best suit your investment objectives.

Assume that you've just received a windfall of $25,000 and would like to invest it all in mutual funds. There are several ways to classify mutual funds, but for this project, we will consider the following eight categories:

- Growth
- Value
- Equity–income
- Bond
- Balanced
- Index
- Socially responsible
- International

Pick three or four categories that you believe best meet your financial needs and risk tolerance, and then select one fund from each category. You are strongly encouraged to use some of the online sources and other references mentioned in this chapter to help you make your selections. For each fund, find the following information:

a. Name of fund, its ticker symbol, the fund manager, and the tenure of the fund manager.
b. Category and size of the fund—try to find the *Morningstar* style box.
c. Loads, fees, and other charges; minimum investment required.
d. Performance of the fund over the past one, three, and five years. Compare the fund's performance to at least two or three other funds in its category and to an appropriate index over these same periods.
e. How much did the fund pay out last year in dividends and in distributions of short- and long-term capital gains?
f. What was the approximate yield on the fund last year? (You may have to compute this yourself; use the approximate yield formula or a handheld calculator after finding its price one year ago from a source such as **http://finance.yahoo.com.**)
g. What services does the fund offer, such as automatic reinvestment plans or phone switching?
h. Briefly explain why you selected the fund and how it meets your investment objectives.

CRITICAL THINKING CASES

13.1 Damon's Dilemma: Common Stocks, Mutual Funds, or ETFs?

Damon Bellamy has worked in the management services division of Niche Consultants for the past five years. He currently earns an annual salary of about $120,000. At 33, he's still a bachelor and has accumulated about $100,000 in savings over the past few years. He keeps his savings in a money market account, where it earns about 3 percent interest. Damon wants to get "a bigger bang for his buck," so he has considered withdrawing $50,000 from his money market account and investing it in the stock market. He feels that such an investment can easily earn more than 3 percent. Naomi Ladd, a close friend, suggests that he invest in mutual fund shares. Damon has approached you, his broker, for advice.

Critical Thinking Questions

1. Explain to Damon the key reasons for purchasing mutual fund or ETF shares.
2. What special fund features might help Damon achieve his investment objectives?
3. What types of mutual funds or ETFs would you recommend to Damon?
4. What recommendations would you make regarding Damon's dilemma about whether to go into stocks, mutual funds, or ETFs? Explain.
5. Explain to Damon the rationale for choosing ETFs over mutual funds.

13.2 Nichole Ponders Mutual Funds and ETFs

Nichole Whiting is the director of a major charitable organization in Charlotte, North Carolina. A single mother of one young child, she earns what could best be described as a modest income. Because charitable organizations aren't known for their generous retirement programs, Nichole has decided it would be best for her to do a little investing on her own. She'd like to set up a program to supplement her employer's retirement program and, at the same time, provide some funds for her child's college education (which is still 12 years away). Although her income is modest, Nichole believes that with careful planning, she could probably invest about $250 a quarter, and she hopes to increase this amount over time. Nichole now has about $15,000 in a bank savings account, which she's willing to use to start this program. In view of her investment objectives, she isn't interested in taking a lot of risk. Because her knowledge of investments extends no further than savings accounts, series EE bonds, and a little bit about mutual funds and ETFs, she approaches you for some investment advice.

Critical Thinking Questions

1. In view of Nichole's long-term investment goals, do you think mutual funds or ETFs are the more appropriate investment vehicle for her?
2. Do you think that Nichole should use her $15,000 savings to start a mutual fund or an ETF investment program?
3. What type of mutual fund or ETF investment program would you set up for Nichole? In your answer, discuss the types of funds you'd consider, the investment objectives you'd set, and any investment services (such as withdrawal plans) you'd seek. Would taxes be an important consideration in your investment advice? Explain.
4. Do you think some type of real estate investment would make sense for Nichole? If so, what type would you suggest? Explain.

CHAPTER 14

Planning for Retirement

LEARNING GOALS

LG1 Recognize the importance of retirement planning, and identify the three biggest pitfalls to good planning.

LG2 Estimate your income needs in retirement and the level of retirement income you've estimated from various sources.

LG3 Explain the eligibility requirements and benefits of the Social Security program.

LG4 Differentiate among the types of basic and supplemental employer-sponsored pension plans.

LG5 Describe the various types of self-directed retirement plans.

LG6 Choose the right type of annuity for your retirement plan.

How Will This Affect Me?

While almost everyone understands that planning for retirement is important, far too few people actually implement a comprehensive plan, much less set aside enough savings to fund their retirement adequately. This chapter discusses the importance of retirement planning and encourages action by identifying the major pitfalls that you must overcome. In order to make the process more concrete and accessible, the steps for estimating your retirement income needs and the income that your investments will support are explained. Eligibility requirements to receive Social Security benefits and their amounts are detailed, as well as the key aspects of supplemental employer-sponsored pension plans and the potential benefits of self-directed retirement programs like traditional and Roth individual retirement accounts (IRAs). In addition, the usefulness of various annuity products in retirement planning is evaluated. After reading this chapter, you should understand how to develop and implement a financial plan that will help you achieve your long-term retirement objectives.

14-1 AN OVERVIEW OF RETIREMENT PLANNING

LG1, LG2

Do you know your life expectancy? Well, if you're in your late teens or early 20s, you'll probably live another 60 or 70 years. While this prospect may sound delightful, it also brings into focus the need for careful retirement planning. After all, you may work for only about 40 of those years and then spend 20 or more years in retirement. The challenge, of course, is to do it in style, the way you want—and that's where retirement planning comes into the picture! But to enjoy a comfortable retirement, you must *start now.* One of the biggest mistakes people make in retirement planning is waiting too long to begin.

Accumulating adequate retirement funds is a daunting task that takes careful planning. Like budgets, taxes, and investments, retirement planning is vital to your financial well-being and is a critical link in your personal financial plans. Even so, it's difficult for most people under the age of 30 to develop a well-defined set of retirement plans. There are just too many years to go until retirement and too many uncertainties to deal with: inflation, Social Security, family size, the type of pension you'll receive (if any), and how much money you will have when you're ready to retire. Yet it's just this kind of uncertainty that makes retirement planning so important. To cope with uncertainty, you must plan for various outcomes and then monitor and modify your plans as your hopes, abilities, and personal finances change.

14-1a Role of Retirement Planning in Personal Financial Planning

The financial planning process would be incomplete without *retirement planning.* Certainly no financial goal is more important than achieving a comfortable standard of living in retirement. In many respects, retirement planning captures the essence of financial planning. It is forward-looking (perhaps more so than any other aspect of financial planning), affects both your current and future standard of living, and, if successful, can be highly rewarding and contribute significantly to your net worth and quality of life.

As with most aspects of financial planning, you need a goal to get started. That is, the first step in retirement planning is to set *retirement goals* for yourself. Take some time to describe the things you want to do in retirement, the standard of living you hope to maintain, the level of income you'd like to receive, and any special retirement goals you may have (like buying a retirement home in Florida or taking

an around-the-world cruise). Such goals are important because *they give direction to your retirement planning*. Of course, like all goals, they're subject to change over time as the situations and conditions in your life change.

Once you know what you want out of retirement, the next step is to establish the *size of the nest egg* that you're going to need to achieve your retirement goals. In other words, at this point, you'll want to formulate an *investment program* that enables you to build up your required nest egg. This usually involves (1) creating a systematic savings plan in which you put away a certain amount of money each year and (2) identifying the types of investments that will best meet your retirement needs. This phase of your retirement program is closely related to investment and tax planning.

Investments and investment planning (see Chapters 11 through 13) are the vehicles for building up your retirement funds. They're the active, ongoing part of retirement planning in which you invest and manage the funds you've set aside for retirement. It's no coincidence that a major portion of most individual investor portfolios is devoted to building up a pool of funds for retirement. Tax planning (see Chapter 3) is also important because a major objective of sound retirement planning is to legitimately shield as much income as possible from taxes and, in so doing, maximize the accumulation of retirement funds.

14-1b The Three Biggest Pitfalls to Sound Retirement Planning

Human nature being what it is, people often get a little carried away with the amount of money they want to build up for retirement. Having a nest egg of $4 million or $5 million would be great, but it's really beyond the reach of most people. Besides, you don't need that much to live comfortably in retirement. So set a more realistic goal. But when you set that goal, remember: it's not going to happen by itself; you have to do something to bring it about. And this is precisely where things start to fall apart. Why? Because when it comes to retirement planning, people tend to make three big mistakes:

- Starting too late.
- Putting away too little.
- Investing too conservatively.

Many people in their 20s, or even their 30s, find it hard to put money away for retirement. Most often that's because they have other, more pressing financial concerns—such as buying a house, paying off a student loan, or paying for child care. The net result is that they *put off retirement planning until later in life*—in many cases, until they're in their late 30s or 40s. Unfortunately, the longer people put it off, the less they're going to have in retirement. Or they won't be able to retire as early as they'd hoped. Even worse, once people start a retirement program, *they tend to put away too little*. Although this may also be due to pressing financial needs, all too often it boils down to lifestyle choices. They'd rather spend today than save for tomorrow. So they end up putting maybe $1,000 a year into a retirement plan when, with a little more effective financial planning and family budgeting, they could afford to save two or three times that amount easily. So what's enough? While it all depends on your specific goals, start with a default amount of saving at least 15 percent of your pre-tax income and go from there.

On top of all this, many *people tend to be far too conservative* in the way they invest their retirement money. The fact is, they place way too much of their retirement money into *low-yielding*, fixed-income securities such as CDs and

Treasury notes. Although you should *never speculate* with something as important as your retirement plan, there's no need to avoid risk altogether. There's nothing wrong with following an investment program that involves a reasonable amount of risk, provided it results in a correspondingly higher level of expected return. Being overly cautious can be costly in the long run. Indeed, a low rate of return can have an enormous impact on the long-term accumulation of capital and, in many cases, may mean the difference between just getting by or enjoying a comfortable retirement.

Compounding the Errors

All three of these pitfalls become even more important when we introduce *compound interest*. That's because *compounding essentially magnifies the impact of these mistakes*. As an illustration, consider the first variable—starting too late. If you were to start a retirement program at age 35 by putting away $2,000 a year, it would grow to almost $160,000 by the time you're 65 if invested at an average rate of return of 6 percent. Not a bad deal, considering your total out-of-pocket investment over this 30-year period is only $60,000. But look at what you end up with if you start this investment program just 10 years earlier, at age 25: that same $2,000 a year will grow to over $309,000 by the time you're 65. Think of it—for another $20,000 ($2,000 a year for an extra 10 years), you can *nearly double* the terminal value of your investment! Of course, it's not the extra $20,000 that's doubling your money; rather, it's *compound interest* that's doing most of the work.

And the same holds true for the rate of return that you earn on the investments in your retirement account. Take the second situation just described—starting a retirement program at age 25. Earning 6 percent yields a retirement nest egg of over $309,000; increase that rate of return to 8 percent, and your retirement nest egg will be worth just over $518,000! *You're still putting in the same amount of money*, but because your money is working harder, you end up with a much bigger nest egg. Of course, when you seek higher returns (as you would when going from 6 percent to 8 percent), you should expect to take on more risk. But that may not be as much of a problem as it appears, because in retirement planning, *the one thing you have on your side is time* (unless, again, you start your plan later in life). And the more time you have, the easier it is to recover from those temporary market setbacks.

On the other hand, if you cannot tolerate the higher risks that accompany higher returns, then stay away from higher-risk investments. Rather, stick to safer, lower-yielding securities and find some other way to build up your nest egg. For instance, contribute more each year to your plan or extend the length of your investment period. The only other option—and not a particularly appealing one— is to accept the likelihood that you won't be able to build up as big a nest egg as you had thought and therefore will have to accept a lower standard of living in retirement. All else being the same, it should be clear that, the more you sock away each year, the more you're going to have at retirement. By putting away $4,000 a year rather than $2,000, you'll likely end up with at least twice as much money at retirement.

The combined impact of these three variables is seen in Exhibit 14.1. Note that *the combination of these three factors* determines the amount that you'll have at retirement. Consider the trade-offs among these factors. For example, you can offset the effects of earning a lower rate of return on your money by increasing the amount you put in each year or by lengthening the period over which you build up your retirement account—meaning that you start your program earlier in life or work longer and retire later in life. The table shows that *there are several ways of getting to roughly the same result;* that is, knowing the size of the nest egg you'd like to end up with, you can pick the combination of variables (period of accumulation, annual contribution, and rate of return) that you're most comfortable with.

EXHIBIT 14.1   **Building Up Your Retirement Nest Egg**

The size of your retirement nest egg will depend on when you start your program (period of accumulation), how much you contribute each year, and the rate of return that you earn on your investments. As this table shows, you can combine these variables in several ways to end up with a given amount at retirement.

AMOUNT OF ACCUMULATED CAPITAL FROM

Accumulation Period*	Contribution of $2,000/Year at These Average Rates of Return				Contribution of $5,000/Year at These Average Rates of Return			
	4%	6%	8%	10%	4%	6%	8%	10%
10 yrs. (55 yrs. old)	$ 24,010	$ 26,360	$ 28,970	$ 31,870	$ 60,030	$ 65,900	$ 72,440	$ 79,690
20 yrs. (45 yrs. old)	59,560	73,570	91,520	114,550	148,890	183,930	228,810	286,370
25 yrs. (40 yrs. old)	83,290	109,720	146,210	196,690	208,230	274,300	365,530	491,730
30 yrs. (35 yrs. old)	112,170	158,110	226,560	328,980	280,420	395,290	566,410	822,460
35 yrs. (30 yrs. old)	147,300	222,860	344,630	542,040	368,260	557,160	861,570	1,355,090
40 yrs. (25 yrs. old)	190,050	309,520	518,100	885,160	475,120	773,790	1,295,260	2,212,900

*Assumes retirement at age 65, so the age given in parentheses is the age at which the person would start his or her retirement program.

14-1c Estimating Income Needs

Retirement planning would be much simpler if we lived in a static economy. Unfortunately (or perhaps fortunately), we don't, so both your personal budget and the general state of the economy will change over time. This makes accurate forecasting of retirement needs difficult at best. Even so, it's a necessary task, and you can handle it in one of two ways. One strategy is to plan for retirement over *a series of short-run time frames*. A good way to do this is to state your retirement income objectives as a percentage of your present earnings. For example, if you want a retirement income equal to 80 percent of your final take-home pay, then you can determine the amount necessary to fund this need. Then, every 3 to 5 years, you can revise and update your plan.

Alternately, you can follow *a long-term approach* in which you estimate the level of income you'd like to receive in retirement; along with the amount of funds you must amass to achieve that desired standard of living. Rather than addressing the problem in a series of short-run plans, this approach goes 20 or 30 years into the future—to the time when you'll retire—in determining how much saving and investing you must do today in order to achieve your long-run retirement goals. Of course, if conditions or expectations should happen to change dramatically in the future (as they very likely could), then it may be necessary to make corresponding alterations to your long-run retirement goals and strategies. As emphasized in our planning examples below, it's critically important to consider the impact of inflation in implementing your retirement investment strategy.

Determining Future Retirement Needs

To illustrate how future retirement needs and income requirements can be formulated, let's consider the case of Leo and Frances Pendleton. In their mid-30s, they have two children and an annual income of about $80,000 before taxes. Until now, Leo and Frances have given only passing thought to their retirement. But even though it's still some 30 years away, they recognize it's now time to consider their situation seriously to see if they'll be able to pursue a retirement lifestyle that appeals to them.

A worksheet like this one will help you define your income requirements in retirement, the size of your retirement nest egg, and the amount that you must save annually to achieve your retirement goals.

PROJECTING RETIREMENT INCOME AND INVESTMENT NEEDS

Name(s) _Leo & Frances Pendelton_   Date _8/31/2017_

I. Estimated Household Expenditures in Retirement (Note 1):

A. Approximate number of years to retirement   _30_

B. Current level of annual household expenditures, excluding savings $ _56,000_

C. Estimated household expenses in retirement as a *percent* of current expenses   _70%_

D. Estimated annual household expenditures in retirement (B × C) $ _39,200_

II. Estimated Income in Retirement :

E. Social Security, annual income $ _24,000_

F. Company/employer pension plans, annual amounts $ _9,000_

G. Other sources, annual amounts $ _0_

H. Total annual income (E + F + G) $ _33,000_

I. Additional required income, or annual shortfall (D − H) $ _6,200_

III. Inflation Factor :

J. Expected average annual rate of inflation over the period to retirement   _5%_

K. Inflation factor (in Appendix A):   Based on _30_ years to retirement (A) and an expected average annual rate of inflation (J) of _5%_   _4.322_

L. Size of inflation-adjusted annual shortfall (I × K) $ _26,796_

IV. Funding the Shortfall :

M. Anticipated return on assets *after* retirement   _8%_

N. Amount of retirement funds required—size of nest egg (L ÷ M) $ _334,950_

O. Expected rate of return on investments *prior* to retirement   _6%_

P. Compound interest factor (in Appendix B): Based on _30_ years to retirement (A) and an expected rate of return on investments of _6%_   _79.058_

Q. Annual savings required to fund retirement nest egg (N ÷ P) $ _4,237_

Note: Parts I and II are prepared in terms of current (today's) dollars.

Worksheet 14.1 provides the basic steps to follow in determining retirement needs. This worksheet shows how the Pendletons have estimated their retirement income and determined the amount of investment assets they must accumulate to meet their retirement objectives.

Leo and Frances began by determining what their *household expenditures* will likely be in retirement. Their estimate is based on maintaining a "comfortable" standard of living—one that isn't extravagant but still allows them to do the things they'd like to in retirement. A simple way to derive an estimate of expected household expenditures is to base it on the current level of such expenses. Assume that the Pendletons' annual household expenditures (*excluding savings*) currently run about

Behavior Matters

Behavioral Biases in Retirement Planning

Rational investors should be good at forecasting retirement needs by considering expected future lifetime earnings, investment returns, tax rates, family and health situation, and expected longevity. However, research indicates that most people save too little, make questionable investment decisions, and spend their accumulated assets too quickly in retirement. Surveys indicate that about 40 percent of people have not calculated how much they need to retire, 30 percent haven't saved a significant amount, and only 20 percent feel confident they can live comfortably in retirement.

There are some behavioral biases that explain this disturbing lack of preparation for retirement. Recognizing them is more than half of the battle:

- **Self-control.** Most people *intend* to save and plan, but they do not get around to doing so. Commitment approaches like "pay yourself first" and automatic 401(k) deductions are helpful ways to encourage saving and planning follow-through.

- **Choice overload.** Faced with complex retirement investment choices, many people just give up and choose a default option or even decide not to participate in an employer-offered plan. Making the decision to ask for help can make all the difference.

- **Inertia in managing retirement investments.** Many people tend to "anchor" on their *initial* retirement account investment mix and don't revise it enough over their lives. Recognizing this tendency and scheduling periodic investment reviews with an advisor can limit any resulting damage to your retirement accounts.

- **Representativeness and availability biases.** People tend to view recent investment returns as overly representative of long-term returns and consequently tend to overweigh recent experience in their decision-making. For example, just because a mutual fund was a top performer last year does not mean that it will be next year. Similarly, many people tend to rely on the most readily available information in making investment decisions. Just because data are easy to get does not mean that they are sufficient to the task.

- **Overconfidence.** Many retirement investors are overconfident in their choices and consequently do not diversify their investments enough.

Source: Adapted from Olivia S. Mitchell and Stephen P. Utkus, "How Behavior Can Inform Retirement Plan Design," *Journal of Applied Corporate Finance,* Winter 2006, pp. 82–94.

$56,000 a year (this information can be readily obtained by referring to their most recent income and expenditures statement). After making some obvious adjustments for the different lifestyle they'll have in retirement—their children will no longer be living at home, their home will be paid for, and so on—the Pendletons estimate that they should be able to achieve the standard of living they'd like in retirement at an annual level of household expenses equal to about 70 percent of the current amount. Thus, *based on today's dollars*, their estimated household expenditures in retirement will be $56,000 × 0.70 = $39,200. (This process is summarized in steps A through D in Worksheet 14.1.)

Estimating Retirement Income

The next question is: Where will the Pendletons get the money to meet their projected household expenses of $39,200 a year? They've addressed this problem by estimating what their *income* will be in retirement—again *based on today's dollars*. Their two basic sources of retirement income are Social Security and employer-sponsored pension plans. They estimate that they'll receive about $24,000 a year from Social Security (as we'll see later in this chapter, you can obtain an estimate directly from the Social Security Administration of what your future Social Security benefits are likely to be when you retire) and another $9,000 from their employer pension plans, for a total projected annual income of $33,000. When comparing this figure to their projected household expenditures, it's clear the Pendletons will be facing an annual shortfall of $6,200 (see steps E through I in Worksheet 14.1). This is the amount of additional retirement income they must come up with; otherwise, they'll have to reduce their standard of living in retirement.

At this point, we need to introduce the *inflation factor* to our projections in order to put the annual shortfall of $6,200 in terms of retirement dollars. Here, we assume that both income and expenditures will undergo approximately the same average annual rate of inflation, which will cause the shortfall to grow by that rate over time. In essence, 30 years from now, the annual shortfall is going to amount to a lot more than $6,200. How large this number becomes will, of course, depend on what happens to inflation. Assume that the Pendletons expect inflation over the next 30 years to average 5 percent. While that's a bit on the high side by today's standards, the Pendletons are concerned that the ballooning of the federal deficit in response to the financial crisis of 2007–2009 will cause inflation to rise over the long term. Using the compound value table from Appendix A, we find that the *inflation factor* for 5 percent and 30 years is 4.322. Multiplying this inflation factor by the annual shortfall of $6,200 gives the Pendletons an idea of what that figure will be by the time they retire: $6,200 × 4.322 = $26,796 or nearly $27,000 a year (see steps J to L in Worksheet 14.1). Thus, based on their projections, the shortfall should amount to about $26,796 a year when they retire 30 years from now. *This is the amount they'll have to come up with through their own supplemental retirement program.*

EXAMPLE: Effect of Inflation on Future Retirement Needs

Renee expects to retire in 35 years. She's been told it's reasonable to expect long-term inflation to be 4 percent. Renee wants to have annual income of $80,000 in today's dollars. How much will she need in 35 years to have that much?

Using the future value interest factor for 4 percent and 35 years, Renee will need $80,000 × 3.946 = $315,680. While a daunting number, it's good Renee is planning for her retirement so carefully!

Funding a Projected Shortfall

The final two steps in the Pendletons estimation process are to determine (1) *how big their retirement nest egg must be* to cover the projected annual income shortfall, and (2) *how much to save each year* to accumulate the required amount by the time they retire. To find out how much money they need to accumulate by retirement, they must estimate the rate of return they think they'll be able to earn on their investments *after* they retire. This will tell them how big their nest egg will have to be by retirement in order to eliminate the expected annual inflation-adjusted shortfall of $26,796. Let's assume that this rate of return is estimated at 8 percent, in which case the Pendletons should accumulate $334,950 by retirement to cover the projected shortfall. This figure is found by *capitalizing* the estimated shortfall of $26,796 at an 8 percent rate of return: $26,796/0.08 = $334,950 (see steps M and N). Given an 8 percent rate of return, such a nest egg will yield $26,796 a year: $334,950 × 0.08 = $26,796. So long as the capital ($334,950) remains untouched, it will generate the same amount of annual income for as long as the Pendletons live and can eventually become a part of their estate.

Now that the Pendletons know how big their nest egg must be, the final question is: How are they going to accumulate such an amount by the time they retire? For most people, that means setting up a *systematic savings plan* and putting away a certain amount *each* year. To find out how much must be saved each year to achieve a targeted sum in the future, we can use the table of annuity factors in Appendix B. The appropriate interest factor depends on the rate of return one expects to generate and the length of the investment period. In the Pendletons' case, there are 30 years to go until retirement, meaning that the length of their investment period is 30 years. Suppose that they believe they can earn a 6 percent average rate of return on their investments over this 30-year period. From Appendix B, we see that the 6 percent, 30-year interest factor is 79.058. Because the Pendletons must accumulate $334,950 by the time they retire, *the amount they'll have to save each year* (over the next 30 years) can be found by *dividing* the amount they need to accumulate by the appropriate interest factor; that is, $334,950 ÷ 79.058 = $4,237 (see steps O to Q in Worksheet 14.1).

The Pendletons now know what they must do to achieve the kind of retirement that they want: *Put away $4,237 a year and invest it at an average annual rate of 6 percent over the next 30 years.* If they can do that, then they'll have their $334,950 retirement nest egg in 30 years. Of course, they could have been more aggressive in their investing and assumed an average annual rate of 8 percent, in which case they'd either end up with a bigger nest egg at retirement or could get away with saving less than $4,237 a year. How they actually invest their money so as to achieve the desired 6 percent (or 8 percent) rate of return will, of course, depend on the investment vehicles and strategies they use. All the worksheet tells them is how much money they'll need, not how they will get there; it's at this point that investment management enters the picture.

Calculator

INPUTS	FUNCTIONS
30	N
5.0	I/Y
–6200	PV
	CPT
	FV
	SOLUTION
	26,796.04

See Appendix E for details.

Calculator Keystrokes. As you might have suspected, the last few steps in the worksheet can just as easily be done on a handheld financial calculator. For example, consider Part III, *the inflation-adjusted annual projected shortfall*. With the calculator in the *annual mode*, you can determine how big the current annual shortfall of $6,200 will grow to in 30 years (given an average annual inflation rate of 5 percent) by using these keystrokes, where:

N = number of *years* to retirement
I/Y = *expected* annual rate of inflation
PV = additional required annual income (line I in Worksheet 14.1), entered as a *negative number*

Enter CPT (FV) and you should end up with an answer (FV) that is close to $26,796 (see step L in Worksheet 14.1); in this case, it's $26,796.04.

Now take a look at Part IV, *funding the projected shortfall* (step Q in Worksheet 14.1). Again, with the calculator in the *annual mode*, to find the amount that must be put away annually to fund a $334,950 retirement nest egg in 30 years (given an expected return of 6 percent), use the keystrokes shown here, where:

N = number of *years* over which the retirement nest egg is to be accumulated
I/Y = *expected* annual return on invested capital
FV = the size of the targeted nest egg, entered as a *negative number*

Enter CPT (PMT) and a value of 4,236.75 should appear in the display, indicating the amount you must put away annually to reach a target of $334,950 in 30 years.

Calculator

INPUTS	FUNCTIONS
30	N
6.0	I/Y
–334950	FV
	CPT
	PMT
	SOLUTION
	4,236.75

See Appendix E for details.

The procedure outlined here is admittedly a bit simplified, but in light of the uncertainty in the long-range projections being made, it provides a useful estimate of retirement income and investment needs. The procedure is far superior to the alternative of doing nothing! One important simplifying assumption in the procedure, though, is that it ignores the income that can be derived from the *sale of a house*. The sale of a house not only offers some special tax features (see Chapter 3), but also can generate a substantial amount of cash flow. If inflation does occur in the future (and it will!), it's likely to drive up home prices right along with the cost of everything else. Many people sell their homes around the time they retire and either move into smaller houses or decide to rent in order to avoid all the problems of homeownership. Of course, the cash flow from the sale of a house can substantially affect the size of the retirement nest egg. However, rather than trying to factor it into the forecast of retirement income and needs, we suggest that you *recognize* the existence of this cash-flow source in your retirement planning and consider it as a cushion against all the uncertainty inherent in retirement planning projections.

14-1d Online Retirement Planning

Like many other aspects of our lives, retirement planning has become easier with the Internet. Indeed, with the hundreds of sites that offer online retirement planning, the Internet has literally brought retirement planning to our doorsteps! You can find particularly helpful tools at **Quicken.com** and **Bloomberg.com**. At most of these Internet sites, all you do is answer a few key questions about expected inflation, desired rate of return on investments, and current levels of income and expenditures. Then the online app determines the size of any income shortfall, the amount of retirement funds that must be accumulated over time, and different ways to achieve the desired retirement nest egg. *An attractive feature of most of these Internet sites is the ability to run through "what-if" exercises easily.* By just punching a few buttons, you can change one or more key variables to see their effect on the amount of money that you must put away annually. For example, you can find out what would happen if you failed to achieve the desired rate of return on your investments.

14-1e Sources of Retirement Income

As seen in Exhibit 14.2, the principal sources of income for retired people are Social Security, earnings from income-producing assets (such as savings, stocks, and bonds), earnings from full- or part-time jobs, and pension plans. As of 2015, the largest source of income was Social Security, which represented about 38 percent of the average retiree's total income. In recent years, earned income has accounted for a growing amount of total retirement income as more and more people continue to work in retirement as a way to supplement their other sources of income. Keep in mind that these are percentage *sources* of retirement income and not dollar amounts. The *amount* of income retired individuals will receive, of course, will vary from amounts that are barely above the poverty line to six-figure incomes. Obviously, the more individuals make before they retire, the more they'll receive in Social Security benefits (up to a point) and from company-sponsored pension plans—and, very likely, the greater the amount of income-producing assets they'll hold. In this chapter, we examine Social Security and various types of pension plans and retirement programs. We'll also look briefly at an investment vehicle designed especially for retirement income: the *annuity*.

EXHIBIT 14.2 | Sources of Income for the Average Retiree

Social Security is the single largest source of income for the average U.S. retiree. This source alone is larger than the amount the average retiree receives from pension plans and personal wealth/investment assets *combined*.

Income Sources as a Percent of total Income for People Aged 65 and Older

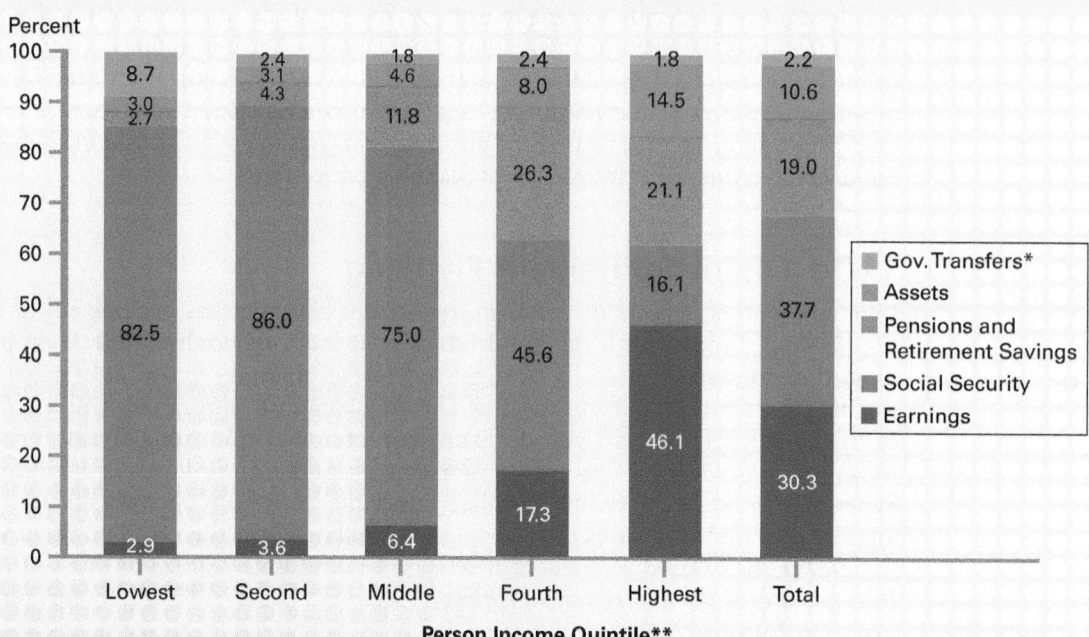

Income Sources as a Percent of total Income for People Aged 65 and Older

Note: Numbers do not sum to 100 percent because other cash income, such as family financial assistance, is not shown.

*Government cash transfers include unemployment compensation, workers' compensation, veterans' benefits, SSI, TANF, and education assistance.

**Income quintiles are based on personal total income. Quintile limits are as follows: $10,080, $16,043, $24,274, and $43,259.

Source: Adapted from Ke Bin Wu, "Sources of Income for Older Americans, 2012," AARP Public Policy Institute, Figure 1, p. 3, based on author tabulation of U.S. Bureau of the Census, March 2013 Current Population Survey, Annual Social and Economic Supplement, http://www.aarp.org/money/low-income-assistance/info-12-2013/sources-of-income-for-older-americans-2012-AARP-ppi-econ-sec.html, accessed September 2015.

TEST YOURSELF

14-1 Discuss the relationship of retirement planning to financial planning. Do investment and tax planning have a role in retirement planning?

14-2 Identify and briefly discuss the three biggest mistakes people tend to make when setting up retirement programs.

14-3 How do income needs fit into the retirement planning process?

14-4 What are the most important sources of retirement income?

14-2 SOCIAL SECURITY

The Social Security Act of 1935 was landmark legislation. It created a basic retirement program for working Americans at all income levels, and it established several other social programs, all administered under the auspices of the *Old Age, Survivor's,*

Disability, and Health Insurance (OASDHI) program. Some of the other services include supplementary security income (SSI), Medicare, unemployment insurance, public assistance, welfare services, and provision for black lung benefits. In this section, we give primary attention to the old age and survivor's portions of the act because they bear directly on retirement planning. We discussed the disability and health/Medicare benefits of Social Security in Chapter 9.

14-2a Coverage

As mandated by Congress, Social Security coverage today extends to nearly all gainfully employed workers. Only two major classes of employees are now exempt from *mandatory* participation in the Social Security system: (1) federal *civilian* employees who were hired before 1984 and are covered under the Civil Service Retirement System; and (2) employees of state and local governments who have chosen not to be covered (although most of these employees are covered through *voluntary participation* in Social Security). Certain employment positions, such as newspaper carriers under age 18 and full-time college students working for a university, are also exempt. By far, the largest group of workers in these excluded classes consists of employees of state and local governments. These people aren't compelled to participate because the federal government is not empowered to impose a tax on state and local governments.

To obtain Social Security benefits, an application must be filed with the Social Security Administration, which then determines the applicant's eligibility for benefits based on whether he or she has had enough quarters (three-month periods) of participation in the system. To qualify for full retirement benefits, nearly all workers today must be employed in a job covered by Social Security for at least 40 quarters, or 10 years. These quarters need not be consecutive. Once this 40-quarter requirement is met, the worker becomes fully insured and remains eligible for retirement payments even if he or she never works again in covered employment.

The surviving spouse and dependent children of a *deceased worker* are also eligible for monthly benefits if the worker was fully insured at the time of death or, in some special cases, if certain other requirements are met. Workers may be considered fully insured if they had 6 quarters of coverage during the three-year period preceding the time of death.

14-2b Social Security Payroll Taxes

The cash benefits provided by Social Security are derived from the payroll (FICA) taxes paid by covered employees and their employers. The tax rate in 2015 for employees was 6.2 percent for Social Security and 1.45 percent for Medicare, or a total of 7.65 percent. Self-employed people are also covered by Social Security; in 2015, they had to pay a Social Security rate of 12.4 percent and a Medicare rate of 2.9 percent for a total of 15.3 percent.

Whether the individual is an employee or self-employed, the indicated tax rate stays in effect only until the employee reaches a maximum *wage base*, which increases each year. For 2015, basic Social Security taxes were paid on the first $118,500 of wages earned or self-employed income. Thus, the maximum Social Security tax paid by an employee in 2015 was about $7,347 ($118,500 × 0.062) and by the *self-employed* was about $14,694 ($118,500 × 0.124). While the Social Security rate is paid up to taxable maximum, the Medicare rate is paid on all earnings. Further, individuals with earned income in excess of $200,000 ($250,000 for married couples filing jointly) pay an addition 0.9 percent in Medicare taxes. Thus, once the Social Security wage base is passed, employees become subject to a Medicare tax rate of 1.45 percent *on all earnings* over $118,500, whereas the added earnings of the self-employed are taxed at the rate of 2.9 percent. And, as previously noted, higher earners must also pay an additional 0.9 percent.

14-2c Social Security Retirement Benefits

Basic Social Security benefits that are important to retired people and their dependents include (1) old-age benefits and (2) survivor's benefits. Both programs provide extended benefits to covered workers and their spouses; in this section, we'll briefly describe the major provisions of each program.

Retirement Benefits

Workers who are fully covered (that is, who have worked the required 40 quarters under Social Security) may receive retirement benefits for life once they reach full retirement age. For anyone born in 1960 or later, the Social Security Administration defines "full retirement age" as age 67. (For our discussions here, we'll use 67 as the full retirement age.) Workers who elect to retire early—at age 62—will receive reduced benefits, currently 70 percent to 80 percent of the full amount (again, depending on when they were born). If the retiree has a spouse age 67 or older, the spouse may be entitled to benefits equal to one-half of the amount received by the retired worker. The spouse may also elect early receipt of reduced benefits at age 62. For retirement planning purposes, it seems reasonable to expect Social Security to provide the average retired wage earner (who is married) with perhaps 40 to 60 percent of the wages he or she was earning in the year before retirement—assuming, of course, that the retiree has had a full career working in covered employment. Social Security, therefore, should be viewed as *a foundation for your retirement income.* By itself, *it's insufficient to enable a worker and spouse to maintain their preretirement standard of living.*

In two-income families, both the husband and wife may be eligible for full Social Security benefits. When they retire, they can choose to receive their benefits in one of two ways: each can (1) take the full benefits to which each is entitled from his or her account or (2) take the husband and wife benefits of the higher-paid spouse. If each takes his or her own full share, there are no spousal benefits. If they take the husband and wife benefits of the higher-paid spouse, they effectively receive 1.5 shares. Obviously, two-income couples should select the option that provides the greater amount of benefits.

Survivor's Benefits

If a covered worker dies, the spouse can receive survivor's benefits from Social Security. These benefits include a small lump-sum payment of several hundred dollars, followed by monthly benefit checks. To be eligible for monthly payments, the surviving spouse generally must be at least 60 years of age or have a dependent and unmarried child of the deceased worker in his or her care. (To qualify for *full* benefits, the surviving spouse must be at least 67 years of age; reduced benefits are payable between ages 60 and 67.) If the children of a deceased worker reach age 16 before the spouse reaches age 60, the monthly benefits cease and do not resume until the spouse turns 60. This period during which survivor's benefits are not paid is sometimes called the *widow's gap.* (As we saw in Chapter 8, Social Security survivor's benefits play a key role in life insurance planning.)

Financial Fact or Fantasy?

In order to receive maximum social security retirement benefits, a worker must retire before his or her 66th birthday. **Fantasy:** To qualify for maximum benefits, a worker must be full retirement age and have career earnings (prior to retirement) that were equal to or greater than the maximum social security tax base for at least 10 years.

14-2d How Much Are Monthly Social Security Benefits?

The amount of Social Security benefits to which an eligible person is entitled is set by law and defined according to a fairly complex formula. But you don't need to worry about doing the math yourself. The Social Security Administration is required by law to provide all covered workers with a *Social Security Statement.* (You can also request a statement by going to the Social Security

FINANCIAL PLANNING TIPS

Should You Depend on Social Security in Retirement Planning?

The old age and disability trust funds supporting Social Security benefits are projected to be unable to pay full benefits by 2034! This is because the birth rate is low, the ratio of workers to beneficiaries is declining, and people are living longer.

While the government will be unable to pay *full* benefits, it should be able to pay *some* benefits. Even if Congress does nothing to fix the problem, resources are expected to be sufficient to pay about 78 percent of the promised benefits. In order to pay full benefits the system

will have to raise the full-retirement age, reduce benefits, increase payroll taxes, or pursue a combination of these options. It's unlikely that any cut in Social Security benefits would be applied uniformly to everyone. They would probably fall disproportionately on the young and higher earners.

How should your retirement planning take these issues into account? A conservative financial plan would reduce the amount of Social Security benefits that you can rely on by at least 20 percent.

Administration's Internet site: **http://www.ssa.gov.**) "Your Social Security Statement" lists the year-by-year Social Security earnings you've been credited with and shows (in today's dollars) what benefits you can expect under three scenarios: (1) if you retire at age 62 and receive 70 percent to 80 percent of the full benefit (depending on your age), (2) the full benefit at age 65 to 67 (depending on your year of birth), and (3) the increased benefit (of up to 8 percent per year) that's available if you delay retirement until age 70. The statement also estimates what your children and surviving spouse would get if you die and how much you'd receive monthly if you became disabled.

Range of Benefits

Using information provided by the Social Security Administration, the *current average level of benefits* (for someone who retired in 2015) is shown in Exhibit 14.3. The average benefits, as of mid-2015, are portrayed for a variety of beneficiaries. Keep in mind that the figures given in the exhibit represent amounts that the beneficiaries will receive in their *first year* of retirement. Those amounts will be adjusted upward each year with subsequent increases in the cost of living.

Note that the average benefits shown in Exhibit 14.3 reflect the fact that they *may be reduced* if the Social Security recipient is *under age 67 and still gainfully employed*—perhaps in a part-time job. In particular, given that full retirement age is now 67, retirees aged 62 through 66 are subject to an *earnings test* that effectively limits the amount of income they can earn before they start losing some (or all) of their Social Security benefits. In 2015, that limit was $15,720 per year (this earnings limit rises annually with wage inflation). The rule states that Social Security recipients aged 62 through 66 will lose $1 in benefits for every $2 they earn above the earnings test amount. So if you earned, say, $18,000 a year at a part-time job, you'd lose $1,140 in annual Social Security benefits—that is, $18,000 − $15,720 = $2,280, which is divided in two to yield $1,140. That's $95 a month you'd lose simply because you hold a job that pays you more than the stipulated maximum. Not a very fair deal! But at least it applies only to early retirees. *Once you reach "full retirement age," the earnings test no longer applies, so you can earn any amount without penalty.* In contrast to earned income, there never have been any limits on so-called unearned income derived from such sources as interest, dividends, rents, or profits

EXHIBIT 14.3 | **Average Monthly Social Security Benefits Paid in 2015**

The Social Security benefits listed here are averages that include a variety of ages at which beneficiaries retired. As time passes, the beneficiary will receive correspondingly higher benefits as the cost of living goes up. However, these average benefits dramatize that you should not rely on such benefits too heavily in your retirement planning.

Type of Beneficiary	Average Monthly Benefit
Retired worker	$1,328
Retired couple	$2,176
Disabled worker	$1,165
Disabled worker with a spouse and child	$1,976
Widow or widower	$1,274
Young widow or widower with two children	$2,680

Source: "Understanding the Benefits," SSA Publication No. 05-10024, ICN 454930, http://www.socialsecurity.gov/pubs/EN-05-10024.pdf#page%031&zoom %03auto,0,576, accessed September 2015.

on securities transactions—a retiree can receive an unlimited amount of such income with no reduction in benefits.

You Can Do It Now

Get a Rough Estimate of Your Future Social Security Benefits

It's easy to get a rough estimate of your future Social Security benefits. While the Quick Calculator doesn't access your actual earnings history, it does provide a useful ballpark estimate: http://www.ssa.gov/oact/quickcalc/. Remember that this estimate does not consider that future Social Security benefits could be reduced somewhat. You can do it now.

Taxes on Benefits

Even though Social Security "contributions" are made in after-tax dollars, you may actually have to pay taxes (again) on at least some of your Social Security benefits. Specifically, as the law now stands, *Social Security retirement benefits are subject to federal income taxes if the beneficiary's annual income exceeds one of the following base amounts:* $25,000 for a single taxpayer, $32,000 for married taxpayers filing jointly, and zero for married taxpayers filing separately. In determining the amount of income that must be counted, the taxpayer starts with his or her *adjusted gross income (AGI)* as defined by current tax law (see Chapter 3) and then adds all nontaxable interest income (such as income from municipal bonds) plus a stipulated portion of the Social Security benefits received. Thus, if for single taxpayers the resulting amount is between $25,000 and $34,000, 50 percent of Social Security benefits are taxable. If income exceeds $34,000, 85 percent of Social Security benefits are subject to income tax for a single taxpayer. If the combined income of married taxpayers filing joint returns is between $32,000 and $44,000, then 50 percent of the Social Security benefits are taxable; the percentage of benefits taxed increases to 85 percent when their combined income exceeds $44,000.

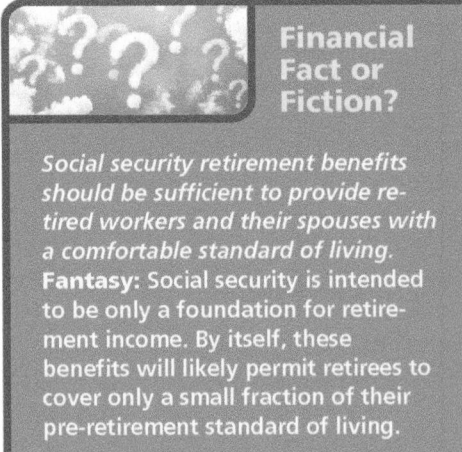

Financial Fact or Fiction?

Social security retirement benefits should be sufficient to provide retired workers and their spouses with a comfortable standard of living.
Fantasy: Social security is intended to be only a foundation for retirement income. By itself, these benefits will likely permit retirees to cover only a small fraction of their pre-retirement standard of living.

TEST YOURSELF

14-5 What benefits are provided under the Social Security Act, and who is covered?

14-6 What is the *earnings test,* and how does it affect Social Security retirement benefits?

14-7 Does Social Security coverage relieve you of the need to do some retirement planning on your own?

14-3 PENSION PLANS AND RETIREMENT PROGRAMS

LG4, LG5

Accompanying the expansion of the Social Security system has been a corresponding growth in employer-sponsored pension and retirement plans. In 1940, when the Social Security program was in its infancy, fewer than 25 percent of the workforce had the benefit of an employer-sponsored plan. Today, around 65 percent of all wage earners and salaried workers (in both the private and public sectors) are covered by some type of employer-sponsored retirement or profit-sharing plan.

Qualified pension plans (discussed later) allow firms to deduct, for tax purposes, their contributions to employee retirement programs. Even better, the employees can also deduct these contributions from their taxable income and can thus build up their own retirement funds on a tax-deferred basis. Of course, when the funds are eventually paid out as benefits, the employees will have to pay taxes on this income.

Employee Retirement Income Security act (ERISA)
A law passed in 1974 to ensure that workers eligible for pensions actually receive such benefits; also permits uncovered workers to establish individual tax-sheltered retirement plans.

Government red tape, however, has taken a toll on pension plans. In particular, the **Employee Retirement Income Security Act (ERISA)** of 1974 (sometimes referred to as **ERISA** or the *Pension Reform Act*), which was established to protect employees participating in private employer retirement plans, has actually led to a reduction in the number of new retirement plans started among firms, especially the smaller ones. Indeed, the percentage of workers covered by company-sponsored plans has fallen dramatically since the late 1970s. It's estimated that today, *in the private sector, only about 40 percent of all full-time workers are covered by company-financed plans—* even worse, only about one-third (or less) of the part-time labor force is covered. In contrast, *there has been a significant increase in salary-reduction forms of retirement plans* (discussed later in this chapter). In addition to ERISA, the widespread availability of Keogh plans, Roth, traditional, and SEP IRAs, and other programs have lessened the urgency for small firms (and bigger ones as well) to offer their own company-financed pension plans.

Pension Protection Act
A federal law passed in 2006 intended to shore up the financial integrity of private traditional (defined benefit) plans and, at the same time, to encourage employees to make greater use of salary reduction (defined contribution) plans.

Now fast-forward some 30 years after ERISA's enactment. In an attempt to curb some of the increasingly serious funding problems occurring in private pension plans, Congress passed, and President George W. Bush signed into law, the **Pension Protection Act** of 2006. One of the major provisions of this Act is that it forces those employers that provide traditional pension plans to their employees (with their defined monthly retirement benefits) to shore up these programs by pumping in tens of billions of dollars in *additional* contributions. At the same time, however, the law encourages employees to make use of various salary reduction (defined contribution) plans, like 401(k)s and IRAs, by setting higher contribution limits and, perhaps what is most important, by making it easier for companies to enroll workers automatically into company-sponsored savings plans (rather than relying on the current system, which leaves the option with the worker). Employees, of course, will still have the right to opt out of the programs if they so wish. This latter measure, which many believe could end up being the most significant part of the legislation, is aimed at substantially raising the participation rate among workers in various types of corporate savings plans. There's still another provision of the law that's intended to help employees manage their retirement accounts by encouraging, rather than limiting, the amount and types of investment advice that mutual funds and other providers can give directly to employees.

14-3a Employer-Sponsored Programs: Basic Plans

Employers can sponsor two types of retirement programs—*basic plans*, in which employees automatically participate after a certain period of employment, and *supplemental plans*, which are mostly voluntary programs that enable employees to increase the amount of funds being set aside for retirement. We'll look first at some key characteristics of basic plans.

Participation Requirements

The vast majority of pension plans require that employees meet certain criteria before becoming eligible for participation. Most common are requirements relating to years of service, minimum age, level of earnings, and employment classification. Years of service and minimum age requirements are often incorporated into retirement plans in the belief that a much higher labor turnover rate applies to both newly hired and younger employees. Therefore, to reduce the administrative costs of the plans, employees in these categories are often excluded—at least initially—from participation. Once these (or any other) participation requirements are met, the employee automatically becomes eligible to participate in the program.

Not everyone who participates in a pension plan will earn *the right to receive retirement benefits*. Pension plans impose certain criteria that must be met before the employee can obtain a nonforfeitable right to a pension, known as vested rights. As the law now stands, *full vesting* rights are required after only three to six years of employment. More specifically, companies must now choose between two vesting schedules. One, the so-called *cliff vesting*, requires full vesting after no more than three years of service—but you obtain no vesting privileges until then. There are no vesting privileges at all for the first three years, and then suddenly you're fully vested. Once vested, you're entitled to everything that's been paid in so far (your contributions *plus* your employer's), as well as everything that will be contributed in the future. Under the alternate procedure, the so-called *graded schedule*, vesting takes place gradually over the first six years of employment. At the minimum, after two years you'd have a nonforfeiture right to at least 20 percent of the benefits, with an additional 20 percent each year thereafter until you're 100 percent vested after six years. Note, however, that these are minimum standards, and employers can grant more favorable vesting terms.

To illustrate the vesting process, assume a medium-sized firm offers a plan in which full vesting of benefits occurs after three years. The plan is contributory, with employees paying 3 percent of their salaries and the employer paying an amount equal to 6 percent of the salaries. Under this plan, employees cannot withdraw the contributions made by the employer until they reach retirement age, usually 65. The plan provides annual benefits in the amount of $11 per year of service for each $100 of an employee's final monthly earnings—the amount earned during the final month in the employ of the firm. Therefore, an employee who worked a minimum of three years for the firm would be eligible for a retirement benefit from that company, even if he or she left the company at, say, age 30.

Because of inflation, the value of the benefit for a worker who leaves the firm long before retirement age is typically very small. Consequently, the employee might be better off simply withdrawing his or her *own* contributions (which always vest immediately) and terminating participation in the plan at the same time he or she leaves the employer. Of course, any worker who leaves the firm before accumulating the required years of service would be entitled only to a return of his or her own contributions to the plan (plus nominal investment earnings). Whenever you terminate

vested rights
Employees' nonforfeitable rights to receive benefits in a pension plan based on their own and their employer's contributions.

noncontributory pension plan
A pension plan in which the employer pays the total cost of the benefits.

contributory pension plan
A pension plan in which the employee bears part of the cost of the benefits.

defined benefit plan
A pension plan in which the formula for computing benefits is stipulated in its provisions.

employment, *resist the urge to spend the money you have built up in your retirement account!* Over time, that can have a devastating effect on your ability to accumulate retirement capital. Instead, *when you take money out of one retirement account, roll it over into another one.*

What's Your Contribution?

Whether you, as an employee, must make payments toward your own pension depends on the type of plan you're in. If you belong to a noncontributory pension plan, then the employer pays the total cost of the benefits—you don't have to pay a thing. Under a contributory pension plan, the employer and the employee share the cost. Today the trend is toward contributory plans. In addition, nearly all plans for employees of federal, state, and local governments require a contribution from the employee. In contributory plans, the employee's share of the costs is often between 3 and 10 percent of annual wages and is typically paid through a payroll deduction. The most common arrangement is for the employer to match the employee's contribution—the employee puts up half the annual contribution and the employer puts up the other half. When employees who've participated in a contributory retirement plan terminate employment before retirement, they're legally entitled to a benefit that is based on the amount of their individual contributions. Usually this benefit is a cash lump sum, but in some cases, it can be taken as a monthly payment at retirement. Whether departing employees receive any benefit from the *employer's* contributions depends on the plan's benefit rights.

Defined Contributions or Defined Benefits

The two most commonly used methods to compute benefits at retirement are the defined contribution plan and the defined benefit plan. A defined contribution plan specifies the amount of contribution that both the employer and employee must make. At retirement, the worker is awarded whatever level of monthly benefits those contributions will purchase. Although such factors as age, income level, and the amount of contributions made to the plan have a great deal to do with the amount of monthly benefits received at retirement, probably no variable is more important than the level of *investment performance* generated on the contributed funds.

A defined contribution plan promises nothing at retirement except the returns the fund managers have been able to obtain. The only thing that's defined is the amount of contribution that the employee and/or employer must make (generally stated as a percentage of the employee's income). The benefits at retirement depend totally on investment results. Thus, the employee bears the risk of funding retirement. Of course, the investment managers follow a certain standard of care, so some protection is provided to the plan participants. Even so, that still leaves a lot of room for variability in returns.

Under a defined benefit plan, it's the formula for computing benefits, not contributions, that is stipulated in the plan provisions. These benefits are paid out regardless of how well (or poorly) the retirement funds are invested. If investment performance falls short, the employer must make up the difference in order to fund the benefits agreed to in the plan. Thus, the employer bears the risk of funding the employee's retirement. This type of plan allows employees to calculate, before retirement, how much their monthly retirement income will be. Often the number of years of service and amount of earnings are prime factors in the formula. For example, workers might be paid 2.5 percent of their final three-year average annual salary for each year of service. Thus, the *annual* benefit to an employee whose final three-year average annual salary was $85,000 and who was with the company for 20 years would be $42,500 (2.5% × $85,000 × 20 years).

Other types of defined benefit plans may simply pay benefits based on (1) a consideration of earnings excluding years of service, (2) a consideration of years of service excluding earnings, or (3) a flat amount with no consideration given to either earnings or years of service. Many defined benefit plans also increase retirement benefits periodically to help retirees keep up with the cost of living. In periods of high inflation, these increases are essential to maintain retirees' standards of living. About 65 percent of all private industry employees have some kind of retirement plan. Of those with retirement plans, about 60 percent of private industry workers have a defined contribution plan, and 20 percent have a defined benefit plan. In addition, most government workers have some kind of defined benefit plan. Even so, while the number of *people covered* by such plans continues to rise, the number of (private-sector) *defined benefit plans in existence* has steadily declined. In fact, there are now more assets held in defined contribution plans than there are in traditional (defined benefit) pension plans. And as noted previously (in discussing the Pension Protection Act of 2006), *it's very likely that this shift to defined contribution plans will only accelerate in the coming years.*

Regardless of the method used to calculate benefits, the employee's key concern should be with the percentage of final take-home pay that the plan is likely to produce

FINANCIAL ROAD SIGN

Be Aware of Potentially Damaging Retirement Planning Myths

Having a well-funded, secure retirement is an important financial goal. While useful information is abundant, there're also some myths that can get in the way of successfully reaching your retirement goals. Here are some of the most common retirement planning myths.

- **I just graduated from college and it's too early to start saving for retirement.** Consider that traditional pension funds are disappearing and future Social Security benefits are far from certain. Saving sooner allows you to gain the most from the compounding of your returns. Starting earlier will also reinforce good financial habits that will guide your financial life well.
- **For planning purposes, I'll need about 80 percent of my current income in retirement.** One size doesn't fit all. What if you want to spend a lot of time traveling in retirement? And what will health care cost when you retire? The future benefit levels of government programs like Medicare are unclear.
- **Social Security will provide no benefits by the time I retire.** As discussed earlier in this chapter, it's unlikely that Social Security will go away completely. However, future benefits may be reduced by 25 percent or so by 2034.
- **I have a lot of financial goals and can't afford to tie up so much money in a retirement plan.** It's true that especially when you're first getting started you're likely saving for emergencies, buying a home, and perhaps going back to school. If you're concerned about retaining access to some of your savings, consider a Roth IRA. As long as the account has been open for at least five years, you can withdraw your contributions any time and for any reason without tax or penalty.
- **I have a retirement plan at work and consequently cannot contribute to an IRA.** While there are income limits for traditional IRA contributions, you can make nondeductible, tax-deferred and possibly Roth IRA contributions.
- **I expect my tax rate to be the same in retirement so tax-deferred plans will provide no benefit.** Even if your *marginal* tax rate remains the same, some of the money in the plan will likely be taxed at lower rates. So the tax deferral feature could provide you with a lower *average* tax rate. And the tax deferral over time will have sheltered your earnings from taxes.

Source: Adapted from Erik Carter, "10 Common Myths That Could Be Hurting Your Retirement Planning," http://www.forbes.com/sites/financialfinesse/2012/08/22/10-common-myths-that-could-be-hurting-your-retirement-planning/, accessed September 2015.

at retirement. A pension is usually thought to be good if, when combined with Social Security, it will result in a monthly income equal to about 70 percent to 80 percent of preretirement net earnings. To reach this goal, however, today's employees must take some responsibility because *there's a growing trend for companies to switch from defined benefit plans to defined contribution programs*. Companies don't like the idea of facing uncertain future pension liabilities. So more and more of them are avoiding these problems altogether by changing to defined contribution plans. And in cases where the firms are sticking with their defined benefit plans, the benefits are often so meager that they don't come close to the desired 70 percent to 80 percent income target. The bottom line is that *the employee is now being forced to assume more responsibility for ensuring the desired level of retirement income*. This means that where you end up in retirement will depend, more than ever, on what *you've* done, rather than on what your employers have done. *Very likely, you're the one who is going to control not only how much goes into the company's retirement programs, but where it goes as well.*

Cash-Balance Plans

cash-balance plan
An employer-sponsored retirement program that combines features of defined contribution and defined benefit plans and is well suited for a mobile workforce.

One of the newest types of employer-sponsored retirement programs is the **cash-balance plan**. A cash-balance plan is much like a traditional defined benefit plan, but it also has features that are similar to those of defined contribution plans. As with traditional pension plans, the company funds the pension (the employee pays nothing into the plan). It also controls the investments and guarantees a benefit payout at retirement. And as with a defined contribution plan, the company contributions are based on a percentage (say, 4 percent or 5 percent) of the employee's current salary. Most important, the company sets up a separate "account" for each employee that shows how much has been accumulated in the account at any given time. In a cash-balance plan, the account is guaranteed by the company to earn a given minimum rate of return, which might be a fixed percentage rate (of perhaps 2 percent or 3 percent) or a variable rate of return that is linked to something like Treasury bills (T-bills). That's it; that's all the company guarantees. So, unlike traditional pension plans, your retirement benefits are in no way linked to the salary you'll be making when you retire. Instead, at retirement, you receive whatever the cash balance of your account happens to be, either in the form of a lump-sum payment or as a stream of fixed annuity payments over time.

Given the low guaranteed earnings rate, there's little doubt that the retirement benefits of cash-balance plans will turn out to be less—and perhaps substantially so—than what would have been paid under traditional plans (where the benefits are linked to how much the employee was making at the time of his or her retirement). But there's a big upside to these plans, particularly for younger employees: *the accounts are portable*. This means that, when employees leave a firm, they can roll their accounts into their new employer's cash-balance plans or into an IRA. Indeed, the portability of cash-balance plans makes them better suited than traditional pension plans to meet the needs of an increasingly mobile workforce.

Qualified Pension Plans

qualified pension plan
A pension plan that meets specified criteria established by the Internal Revenue Code.

The Internal Revenue Code permits a corporate employer making contributions to a **qualified pension plan** to deduct from taxable income its contributions to the plan. As a result, the employees on whose behalf the contributions are made don't have to include these payments as part of their taxable income until the benefits are actually received. Further, in contributory plans, *employees can also shelter their contributions from taxes*. In other words, such contributions aren't counted as part of taxable income in the year that they're made. They consequently act to reduce the amount of taxable income reported to the Internal Revenue Service (IRS) and therefore lead to lower taxes for the employee.

Still another tax advantage of these plans is that any and all investment income is allowed to accumulate tax free. As a result, investment capital can build up more quickly. Yet despite all these tax benefits, many firms still believe that the costs of regulation exceed any benefits that might result and therefore choose to forgo the procedures required for having a plan qualified. Probably the biggest disadvantage of nonqualified pension plans from the employee's perspective is that any contributions made to *contributory* plans are made on an after-tax basis and thus are *not* sheltered from taxes.

14-3b Employer-Sponsored Programs: Supplemental Plans

In addition to basic retirement programs, many employers offer supplemental plans. These plans are often *voluntary* and enable employees not only to increase the amount of funds being held for retirement, but also to enjoy attractive tax benefits. There are three basic types of supplemental plans: profit-sharing, thrift and savings, and salary reduction plans.

Profit-Sharing Plans

profit-sharing plan
An arrangement in which the employees of a firm participate in the company's earnings.

Profit-sharing plans enable employees to participate in the earnings of their employer. A **profit-sharing plan** may be qualified under the IRS and become eligible for essentially the same tax treatment as other types of pension plans. An argument supporting the use of profit-sharing plans is that they encourage employees to work harder because the employees benefit when the firm prospers. From the firm's perspective, a big advantage of profit-sharing plans is that they impose no specific levels of contribution or benefits by the employer. When profits are low, the firm makes smaller contributions to the plan, and when profits are high, it pays more.

Many employers establish minimum and maximum amounts to be paid as contributions to profit-sharing plans, regardless of how low or high corporate earnings are. Contributions to profit-sharing plans are invested in certain types of fixed-interest products, stocks and bonds, and in many cases securities issued by the employing firm itself. Employees who receive the firm's securities may actually benefit twice. When profits are good, larger contributions are made to the profit-sharing plan *and* the price of the shares already owned is likely to increase.

Some major firms offer *voluntary profit-sharing plans* that invest heavily in their own stock. It's common in many of these cases for long-term career employees to accumulate several hundred thousand dollars' worth of the company's stock. And we're not talking about highly paid corporate executives here; rather, these are just average employees who had the discipline to divert a portion of their salary consistently to the company's profit-sharing plan. However, *there is a real and significant downside to this practice:* if the company should hit hard times, then not only could you face salary cuts (or even worse, the loss of your job), but the value of your profit-sharing account will likely tumble as well. Just look at what happened to employees in the tech sector during the 2000–2002 bear market, and to employees in most sectors during the financial crisis of 2007–2009! Certainly, employees should seriously consider taking steps to diversify their pension portfolios more adequately if more than 30 percent to 40 percent of their portfolios is concentrated in their company's stock.

Thrift and Savings Plans

thrift and savings plans
A plan to supplement pension and other fringe benefits; the firm contributes an amount equal to a set proportion of the employee's contribution.

Thrift and savings plans were established to supplement pension and other fringe benefits. Most plans require the employer to make contributions to the savings plan in an amount equal to a set proportion of the amount contributed by the employee. For example, an employer might match an employee's contributions at the rate of 50 cents on the dollar up to, say, 6 percent of salary. Thus, an employee making $40,000 a year could pay $2,400 into the plan annually, and the employer would kick in another $1,200. These contributions are then deposited with a trustee, who invests the money in various types of securities, including stocks and bonds of the employing firm. With IRS-qualified thrift and savings plans, the *employer's* contributions and earnings on the savings aren't included in the *employee's* taxable income until he or she withdraws these sums. Unfortunately, this attractive tax feature doesn't extend to the employee's contributions, so any money put into one of these savings plans is still considered part of the employee's taxable income and subject to regular income taxes.

Thrift and savings plans usually have more liberal vesting and withdrawal privileges than do pension and retirement programs. Often the employee's right to the employer's contributions becomes nonforfeitable immediately upon payment, and the total savings in the plan can be withdrawn by giving proper notice. However, employees who terminate participation in such a plan are frequently prohibited from rejoining it for a specified period, such as one year. An employee who has the option should seriously consider participating in a thrift plan. The returns are usually pretty favorable, especially when you factor in the *employer's* contributions.

Salary Reduction Plans

salary reduction, or 401(k), plan
An agreement by which part of a covered employee's pay is withheld and invested in some form of investment; taxes on the contributions and the account earnings are deferred until the funds are withdrawn.

Another type of supplemental retirement program—and certainly the most popular, judging by employee response—is the salary reduction plan, or the 401(k) plan as it's more commonly known. Our discussion here centers on 401(k) plans, but similar programs are available for employees of public, nonprofit organizations. Known as *403(b) plans* or *457 plans*, they offer many of the same features and tax shelter provisions as 401(k) plans. (Workers at public schools, colleges, universities, nonprofit hospitals, and similar organizations have 403(b) plans; state or local government workers probably have a 457 plan, as do employees at some tax-exempt organizations.) Today, more and more companies are cutting back on their contributions to traditional (defined benefit) retirement plans. They're turning instead to 401(k) plans, a type of defined contribution plan.

According to Fidelity Investments, one of the largest 401(k) providers, the average 401(k) balance was around $91,800 in 2015. And the average balance was about $251,600 for employees having participated in a 401(k) for at least 10 years. Yet these averages are for those who participate in 401(k) programs. According to the National Institute on Retirement Security, more than 45 percent of households do not own any significant retirement account assets. When all households are considered, the median retirement account balance was a mere $3,000 and only $12,000 for those near retirement. Thus, up to 92 percent of households do not meet conservative retirement savings targets for their age and income levels! Thus, a retirement savings crisis is here and growing.

A 401(k) plan basically gives employees the option to divert part of their salary to a company-sponsored, tax-sheltered savings account. In this way, the earnings diverted to the savings plan accumulate tax free. Taxes must be paid eventually, but not until the employee starts drawing down the account at retirement, presumably when he or she is in a lower tax bracket. In 2015, an individual employee could put as much as $18,000 into a tax-deferred 401(k) plan. [Contribution limits for 403(b) and 457 plans are the same as those for 401(k) plans.] And for those over 50 years old, there is a "catch-up" provision that allows them to contribute up to $24,000 in 2015.

EXAMPLE: How Tax-Deferred Plans Work

Gabriela is under 50 years old with taxable income of $75,000 in 2015. She would like to contribute the maximum allowable mount—$18,000—to the 401(k) plan where she works. Doing so reduces her taxable income to $57,000 and, assuming she's in the 25 percent tax bracket, lowers her federal tax bill by $4,500 (i.e., $18,000 × 0.25). Such tax savings will offset a good portion—25 percent—of her contribution to the 401(k) savings plan. In effect, she'll add $18,000 to her retirement program with only $13,500 of her own money. The rest will come from the IRS via a reduced tax bill. What's more, all of the *earnings* on her investment account will accumulate tax free. However, the downside is that if she needs the money before she is 59½ she will have to pay the tax on the withdrawal *plus* a 10 percent penalty to the IRS.

FINANCIAL PLANNING TIPS

Managing Your 401(k) Retirement Account Effectively

A few basic ideas on managing your 401(k) account can take you a long way:

• **A reasonable asset allocation is more important than choosing the "right" funds for your 401(k) account money.** Research shows that over 90 percent of your investment performance will be determined by how much you allocate to cash, bonds, and equity funds. So less than 10 percent of performance is determined by choosing the right funds and by trying to time the market (which is never a good idea anyway). Remember that the conventional wisdom as a starting place: put 100 minus your age as the percentage in equities and the residual in bonds and cash. For example, if you're 30, start out with a plan to put 70 percent in equities and 30 percent in bonds and cash. Then adjust the mix to match your risk tolerance.

• **Invest enough in your 401(k) account.** Invest at least up to your company's matching amount, if you can possibly afford it. For example, if your company matches the first 6 percent of your annual contribution, then you should contribute at least that much or you're just throwing away money. A reasonable overall goal is to contribute at least 15 percent of your annual income to retirement investment accounts, which include 401(k)s, IRAs, and other investment vehicles.

• **Invest in your 401(k) consistently, regardless of its performance.** Some investors panic when their 401(k) accounts lose money and *reduce or even stop* making contributions in an effort to protect themselves from further losses. This is the opposite of what you should do. When you're losing money, it's time to grit your teeth and contribute more to your account, not less! This is because you've got to make up for your losses. If you stop or reduce your contributions, you'll be even less likely to achieve your retirement goal. And keep in mind that when investment values fall, you're buying more shares at lower prices (a principle known as "dollar-cost averaging"). In the long term, this should contribute positively to performance.

These plans are generally viewed as attractive *tax shelters* that offer not only substantial tax savings, but also a way to save for retirement. So long as you can afford to put the money aside, *you should seriously consider joining a 401(k)/403(b)/457 plan if one is offered at your place of employment.* This is especially true when one considers the matching features offered by many of these plans. Most companies that offer 401(k) plans have some type of matching contributions program, often putting up 50 cents (or more) for every dollar contributed by the employee. Such matching plans give both tax and savings incentives to individuals and clearly enhance the appeal of 401(k) plans. (Matching contributions by employers are far less common with 403(b) plans and virtually nonexistent with 457 plans.)

Another kind of 401(k) plan is being offered by a growing number of firms. This retirement savings option, which first became available in 2006, is the so-called *Roth 401(k)*. It's just like a traditional 401(k), except for one important difference: *All contributions to Roth 401(k) plans are made in after-tax dollars.* That means there are no tax savings to be derived from the annual employee contributions; if you earn, say, $75,000 a year and want to put $18,000 into your Roth 401(k), you'll end up paying taxes on the full $75,000. That's the bad news; now the good news. Because all contributions are made in after-tax dollars, *there are no taxes to be paid on plan withdrawals (in other words, they're tax free)*, provided you're at least 59½ and have held the account for five years or more. Like traditional 401(k) plans, Roth 401(k)s also have a contribution cap of $18,000 (in 2015, for those under 50). And that limit applies to *total contributions to both types of 401(k) plans combined,* so you can't put $18,000 into a traditional 401(k) plan and then put another $18,000 into a Roth 401(k). You can also have employer matches with the Roth plans, although those matches will accumulate in a separate account that will be taxed as ordinary income at withdrawal. Essentially, *employer* contributions represent tax-free income to employees, so they'll pay taxes on that income, and on any account earnings, when the funds are withdrawn, as is done with a traditional 401(k). A couple of final points: because of the tax differences in traditional versus Roth 401(k) plans, all earnings generated in the *employee's account* accumulate on a *tax-free basis* in Roth plans; they accumulate on a *tax-deferred basis* in traditional 401(k) plans. And the Roth 401(k) can offer an advantage to high-income individuals who aren't able to contribute to a Roth IRA. There are no income restrictions for using Roth 401(k) plans.

Both Roth and traditional 401(k) plans typically offer their participants various investment options, including equity and fixed-income mutual funds, company stock, and other interest-bearing vehicles such as bank CDs or similar insurance company products. Indeed, the typical 401(k) has about 10 choices, and some plans have as many as 20 or more. Today, the trend is toward giving plan participants more options and providing seminars and other educational tools to help employees make informed retirement plan decisions. As we've discussed throughout the book, behavioral finance research suggests that too many choices overwhelm most consumers.

14-3c Evaluating Employer-Sponsored Pension Plans

When participating in a company-sponsored pension plan, you're entitled to certain benefits in return for meeting certain conditions of membership, which may or may not include making contributions to the plan. Whether your participation is limited to the firm's basic plan or includes one or more of the supplemental programs, *it's vital that you take the time to acquaint yourself with the various benefits and provisions* of these retirement plans. And be sure to familiarize yourself not only with the basic plans (even though participation is mandatory, you ought to know what you're getting for your money) but also with any (voluntary) supplemental plans you may be eligible to join.

So, how should you evaluate these plans? Most experts agree that you can get a good handle on essential plan provisions and retirement benefits by getting answers to questions about the following features:

- Eligibility requirements: Precisely what are they, and if you're not already in the plan, when will you be able to participate?
- Defined benefits or contributions: Which one is defined? If it's the benefits, exactly what formula is used to define them? Pay particular attention to how Social Security benefits are treated in the formula. If it's a defined contribution program, do you have any control over how the money is invested? If so, what are your options? *What you'd like to have:* lots of attractive no-load stock/equity mutual funds to choose from. *What you don't need:* a bunch of low-yielding investment options, such as bank CDs, money market mutual funds, or fixed annuities.
- Vesting procedures: Does the company use a cliff or graded procedure, and precisely when do you become fully vested?
- Contributory or noncontributory: If the plan is contributory, how much comes from you and how much from the company; and what's the total of this contribution as a percentage of your salary? If it's noncontributory, what is the company's contribution as a percentage of your salary?
- Retirement age: What's the normal retirement age, and what provisions are there for *early* retirement? What happens if you leave the company before retirement? Are the pension benefits *portable*—that is, can you take them with you if you change jobs?
- Voluntary supplemental programs: How much of your salary can you put into one or more of these plans, and what—if anything—is matched by the company? Remember, these are like defined contribution plans, so nothing is guaranteed as far as benefits are concerned.

Finding answers to these questions will help you determine where you stand and what improvements are needed in your retirement plans. As part of this evaluation process, try to determine, as best as you can, *a rough estimate of what your benefits are likely to be at retirement*. You'll need to make some projections about future income levels, investment returns, and so on, but it's an exercise well worth taking (before you start cranking out the numbers, check with the people who handle employee benefits at your workplace; they'll often give you the help you need). Then, using a procedure similar to that followed in Worksheet 14.1, you can estimate what portion of your retirement needs will be met from your company's basic pension plan. If there's a shortfall—*and it's likely there will be*—it will indicate the extent to which you need to participate in some type of company-sponsored supplemental program, such as a 401(k) plan, or (alternatively) how much you'll need to rely on your own savings and investments to reach the standard of living you're looking for in retirement. *Such insights will enable you to dovetail more effectively the investment characteristics and retirement benefits of any company-sponsored retirement plans with the savings and investing that you do on your own.*

14-3d Self-Directed Retirement Programs

In addition to participating in company-sponsored retirement programs, individuals can set up their own tax-sheltered retirement plans. There are two basic types of self-directed retirement programs: *Keogh* and *SEP plans*, which are for self-employed individuals, and *IRAs*, which can be set up by almost anyone.

Keogh and SEP Plans

Keogh plan
An account to which self-employed persons may make specified payments that may be deducted from taxable income; earnings also accrue on a tax-deferred basis.

Keogh plans were introduced in 1962 as part of the Self-Employed Individuals Retirement Act, or simply the Keogh Act. Keogh plans allow self-employed individuals to set up tax-deferred retirement plans for themselves and their employees. Like contributions to 401(k) plans, payments to Keogh accounts may be taken as deductions from taxable income. As a result, they reduce the tax bills of self-employed individuals. The maximum contribution to this tax-deferred retirement plan in 2015 was $53,000 per year, or 25 percent of earned income, whichever is less.

Any individual who is self-employed, either full- or part-time, is eligible to set up a Keogh account. These accounts can also be used by individuals who hold full-time jobs and moonlight part-time—for instance, the engineer who has a small consulting business on the side, or the accountant who does tax returns on a freelance basis at night and on weekends. If the engineer, for example, earns $10,000 a year from his part-time consulting business, then he can contribute 25 percent of that income ($2,500) to his Keogh account and thereby reduce both his taxable income and the amount he pays in taxes. Further, he's still eligible to receive full retirement benefits from his full-time job and to have his own IRA (but as we'll see, contributions to his IRA may not qualify as a tax shelter).

Keogh accounts can be opened at banks, insurance companies, brokerage houses, mutual funds, and other financial institutions. Annual contributions must be made at the time the respective tax return is filed or by April 15 of the following calendar year (for example, you have until April 15, 2017, to contribute to your Keogh for 2016). Although a designated financial institution acts as custodian of all the funds held in a Keogh account, *actual investments held in the account are directed completely by the individual contributor*. These are self-directed retirement programs; the *individual* decides which investments to buy and sell (subject to a few basic restrictions).

Income earned from the investments must be reinvested in the account. This income also accrues tax free. All Keogh contributions and investment earnings must remain in the account until the individual turns 59½ unless he or she becomes seriously ill or disabled. Early withdrawals for any other reason are subject to 10 percent tax penalties. However, the individual is not *required* to start withdrawing the funds at age 59½; the funds can stay in the account (and continue earning tax-free income) until the individual is 70½. The individual *must* then begin withdrawing funds from the account, unless he or she continues to be gainfully employed past the age of 70½. Of course, once an individual starts withdrawing funds (upon or after turning 59½), all such withdrawals are treated as ordinary income and subject to normal income taxes. Thus, the taxes on all contributions to and earnings from a Keogh account will eventually have to be paid—a characteristic of any tax-*deferred* (as opposed to tax-*free*) program.

A program that's similar in many ways to the Keogh account is something called a *simplified employee pension plan*—or SEP-IRA for short. It's aimed at small business owners, particularly those with *no employees*, who want a plan that's simple to set up and administer. SEP-IRAs can be used in place of Keoghs and, although simpler to administer, have the same annual contribution caps as a Keogh account: $53,000 per year or 25 percent of earned income (in 2015), whichever is less.

Individual Retirement Account (IRAs)

Some people mistakenly believe that an IRA is a specialized type of investment. It's not. An **individual retirement account (IRA)**, is virtually the same as any other investment account you open with a bank, credit union, stockbroker, mutual fund, or insurance company, except that it's clearly designated as an IRA. That is, you complete a form that designates the account as an IRA and makes the institution its trustee. That's all there is to it. Any gainfully employed person (and spouse) can have an IRA account, although the type of accounts that a person can have and the tax status of those accounts depend on several variables. All IRAs, however, have one thing in common: they're designed to encourage retirement savings for individuals.

Each individual now has three IRA types to choose from, as follows:

individual retirement account (IRA) A retirement plan, open to any working American, to which a person may contribute a specified amount each year.

©DEAN MITCHELL/SHUTTERSTOCK.COM

- **Traditional (deductible) IRA**, which can be opened by anyone without a retirement plan at his or her place of employment, *regardless of income level*, or by couples filing jointly who—even if they are covered by retirement plans at their places of employment—have adjusted gross incomes of less than $98,000 (or single taxpayers with AGIs of less than $61,000). In 2015, individuals who qualify may make tax-deductible contributions of up to $5,500 a year to their accounts (an equal tax deductible amount can be contributed by a nonworking spouse). This maximum annual contribution increases to $6,500 for individuals age 50 or older. All account earnings grow tax free until withdrawn, when ordinary tax rates apply (though a 10 percent penalty normally applies to withdrawals made before age 59½).

- **Nondeductible (after-tax) IRA**, which is open to anyone regardless of their income level or whether they're covered by a retirement plan at their workplace. In 2015, contributions of up to $5,500 a year can be made to this account by those under 50 years of age and up to $6,500 for those over 50, but they're *made with after-tax dollars* (that is, the contributions are not tax deductible). However, *the earnings do accrue tax free and are not subject to tax until they are withdrawn*, after the individual reaches age 59½ (funds withdrawn before age 59½ may be subject to the 10 percent penalty).

- **Roth IRAs** are a lot like *Roth 401(k)s*, which we discussed earlier. Roth IRAs are the newest kid on the block and can be opened by couples filing jointly with adjusted gross incomes of up to $193,000 (singles up to $131,000), whether or not they have other retirement or pension plans. But the best part of the Roth IRA is its tax features—although the annual contributions of up to $6,500 a person in 2015 are made with nondeductible/after-tax dollars, all earnings in the account grow tax free. And *all withdrawals from the account are also tax free*, so long as the account has been open for at least five years and the individual is past the age of 59½. In other words, so long as these conditions are met, you won't have to pay taxes on any withdrawals you make from your Roth IRA!

Key features and provisions of all three of these IRAs are outlined in Exhibit 14.4.

EXAMPLE: Measuring the Benefits of a Roth IRA Over a Taxable Account

Roth IRAs provide no tax deduction for contributions. But all future earnings are sheltered from taxes under current law. So how much would you save over simply investing in a fully taxed fund if you're 25 years old and invested $5,500 a year at 6 percent until retirement at age 66?

Assuming you're in the 25 percent marginal tax bracket and you invested the money at the beginning of each year, you would have $962,228 in a Roth IRA and $648,586 in an unsheltered account at retirement (assuming, for simplicity, that all of your investment returns were taxed at your marginal tax rate). So the tax shelter afforded by the Roth IRA would be worth a whopping $313,642 more than the otherwise comparable but fully taxable account!

You Can Do It Now

Calculating the Value of a Traditional IRA

If you want to estimate the potential value of a traditional IRA at retirement, try the calculator at http://www.bankrate.com/calculators/retirement/traditional-ira-plan-calculator.aspx. You can do it now.

It is possible to convert a traditional IRA to a Roth IRA. If you convert, you will have to pay taxes on any earnings and pretax contributions. So why would you want to do that? It may make sense to convert if you expect your tax rate to remain the same or go up after retirement. Thus, converting to a Roth IRA could allow you to pay a lower amount of taxes on your IRA investments in the long run. However, it's important to be able to pay the taxes using money that doesn't come out of your IRA account. If you make a withdrawal from an IRA account before age 59½, you generally owe a 10 percent penalty on that amount. And you would also give up the opportunity for tax-free Roth IRA compounding on that amount—permanently. It usually makes less sense to convert a traditional IRA to a Roth IRA the older you are. This is because the older you are, the less time you have to make up for what you paid in taxes on the conversion. However, it can still be wise for an older person to convert a traditional to a Roth IRA for estate tax planning purposes. Conversions can be complicated, and it's best to consult a tax advisor.

Regardless of the type and notwithstanding the conditions just described, penalty-free withdrawals are generally allowed from an IRA so long as the funds are being used for first-time home purchases (up to $10,000), qualifying educational costs, certain major medical expenses, or other qualified emergencies. Also, with both the traditional/deductible and nondeductible IRAs, you must start making withdrawals from your account once you reach age 70½—although *this requirement does not apply to Roth IRAs*.

In addition to the three retirement-based IRAs, *Coverdell Education Savings Accounts* (or ESAs) can be set up and used to meet the future education (college) cost

EXHIBIT 14.4   Qualifying for an IRA

Individuals can now select from three types of individual retirement accounts.

Traditional Deductible IRA

- For 2015, if covered by a retirement plan at work, a taxpayer may make an annual contribution of up to $5,500 if under 50 years old and up to $6,500 if 50 years or older. A nonworking spouse can make the fully tax-deductible contribution if the couple's joint income is less than $183,000 and they file a joint return.
- If covered by a retirement plan at work, reduced tax-deductible contributions are available to joint filers with AGIs (in 2015) of $98,000 to $118,000, and to single filers with AGIs (in 2015) of $61,000 to $71,000—essentially, the deductible contribution is reduced at higher levels of AGI and phases out completely at an AGI of $71,000 for single taxpayers and $118,000 for joint returns. If one spouse is covered by a retirement plan at work and the other is not, then the deduction is phased out between AGIs of $183,000 and $193,000.

After-Tax IRA

- Working taxpayers who fail to qualify for deductible IRAs, and their nonworking spouses, each can make annual nondeductible IRA contributions of up to $5,500 (under 50 years old) or $6,500 (50 years or older) in 2015.

Roth IRA

- A working taxpayer with AGI of up to $116,000 on a single return, or $183,000 on a joint return, can make nondeductible contributions of up to $5,500 (younger than 50) or up to $6,500 (50 or older).
- A reduced contribution can be made by joint filers with AGIs (in 2015) of $183,000 to $193,000 and by single filers with AGIs of $116,000 to $131,000.
- A nonworking spouse can make after-tax contributions of up to $5,500 (younger than 50) or $6,500 (50 years or older) per year to a Roth IRA with AGI of $183,000 or less on a joint return.

of a child or grandchild. Specifically, these accounts, which were formerly known as *Education IRAs*, can be opened by couples with AGIs of up to $220,000 (or singles with AGIs up to $110,000) for the benefit of a child under the age of 18. *Nondeductible* annual contributions of up to $2,000 per child are allowed in 2015. As with Roth IRAs, the earnings grow tax free so long as they remain in the account, and all withdrawals (which must be made by the time the beneficiary reaches age 30) are also made tax free and penalty free, provided the funds are used for qualifying education expenses.

Similar to Coverdell ESAs are 529 plans, which are named after Section 529 of the Internal Revenue Code. A 529 plan is an education savings plan operated by a state or educational institution that is designed to help set aside money to fund future college costs. Every state offers at least one 529 plan and the student's chosen school does not have to be in the state in which the 529 plan is based. Savings plans invest your contributions in investments that grow tax deferred. It is also possible to prepay tuition in some states using a 529 plan. The savings plan contributions are not deductible at the federal level, but some states allow an up-front deduction. Distributions to pay for the student's college costs are not taxed. Although Coverdell ESAs and 529 plans are quite similar, they differ significantly in contribution limits, age limits for student use, and the type and level of schooling covered.

Self-Directed Accounts and Their Investment Vehicles

IRAs are like Keogh and SEP plans; they're *self-directed accounts*, which means that you are free to make almost any kind of investment decision you want. An individual can be conservative or aggressive in choosing securities for an IRA (or Keogh), though conventional wisdom favors funding your IRA (and Keogh) with *income-producing assets*. This would also suggest that, if you're looking for capital gains, it's best to do so *outside* your retirement account. The reasons are twofold: (1) growth-oriented securities are by nature *more risky*, and (2) you *cannot write off losses* from the sale of securities held in an IRA (or Keogh) account. This doesn't mean, however, that it would be totally inappropriate to place a good-quality growth stock or mutual fund in a Keogh or IRA. In fact, many advisors contend that growth investments should always have a place in your retirement account because of their often impressive performance and ability to protect against inflation. Such investments may pay off handsomely, as they can appreciate totally free of taxes. In the end, of course, *it's how much you have in your retirement account that matters, not how your earnings were made along the way.*

No matter what type of investment vehicle you use, keep in mind that once you place money in an IRA, it's meant to stay there for the long haul. Like most tax-sheltered retirement programs, there are restrictions on when you can withdraw the funds from an IRA. Specifically, as noted earlier, any funds withdrawn from an IRA prior to age 59½ are subject to a 10 percent tax penalty in addition to the regular tax paid on the withdrawal. (Note, however, that you can avoid the 10 percent tax penalty and still start

Financial Fact or Fantasy?

Your contributions to a traditional IRA account may or may not be tax deductible, depending in part on your level of income. **Fact:** Whether or not your traditional IRA contributions are fully deductible depends to a large extent on your adjusted gross income. And it also depends on whether you and/or a spouse are covered by a retirement plan at work.

withdrawals before age 59½ by setting up a systematic withdrawal program that pays you equal amounts over the rest of your life expectancy. Of course, unless you have a substantial amount of money in your IRA, the annual payments under this program are likely to be pretty small.) Also, when you move your IRA account to a new firm (this is known as a *rollover*), the transfer is subject to a *20 percent withholding tax* if the proceeds from the transfer are paid to you directly. The rule is very clear on this: if you take possession of the funds (even for just a few days), you'll be hit with the withholding tax. So, the best way to handle IRA rollovers is to *arrange for the transfer of funds from one firm to another*.

So, should you contribute to an IRA or not? Obviously, so long as you qualify for either a traditional/tax-deductible IRA or a Roth IRA (see Exhibit 14.4), you should seriously consider making the maximum payments allowable. There are no special record-keeping requirements or forms to file, and the IRA continues to be an excellent vehicle for sheltering income from taxes. Probably the biggest decision you'll have to make is which IRA is right for you—the traditional or the Roth?

TEST YOURSELF

14-8 Which basic features of employer-sponsored pension plans should you be familiar with?

14-9 Under which procedure will you become fully vested most quickly—cliff or graded vesting?

14-10 What is the difference between a profit-sharing plan and a salary reduction, or 401(k), plan?

14-11 Why is it important to evaluate and become familiar with the pension plans and retirement benefits offered by your employer?

14-12 Briefly describe the tax provisions of 401(k) plans and Keogh plans.

14-13 Describe and differentiate between Keogh plans and individual retirement arrangements. What's the difference between a *nondeductible* IRA and a *Roth* IRA?

14-14 Under what circumstances would it make sense to convert your traditional IRA to a Roth IRA?

14-4 ANNUITIES

annuity
An investment product created by life insurance companies that provides a series of payments over time.

accumulation period
The period during which premiums are paid for the purchase of an annuity.

distribution period
The period during which annuity payments are made to an annuitant.

survivorship benefit
On an annuity, the portion of premiums and interest that has not been returned to the annuitant before his or her death.

single premium annuity contract
An annuity contract purchased with a lump-sum payment.

immediate annuity
An annuity in which the annuitant begins receiving monthly benefits immediately.

installment premium annuity contract
An annuity contract purchased through periodic payments made over time.

deferred annuity
An annuity in which benefit payments are deferred for a certain number of years.

An annuity is just the opposite of life insurance. As we pointed out in Chapter 8, life insurance is the systematic accumulation of an estate that is used for protection against financial loss resulting from premature death. In contrast, an **annuity** is the systematic *liquidation* of an estate in such a way that it provides protection against the economic difficulties that could result from outliving personal financial resources. The period during which premiums are paid toward the purchase of an annuity is called the **accumulation period**; correspondingly, the period during which annuity payments are made is called the **distribution period**.

Under a pure life annuity contract, a life insurance company will guarantee regular monthly payments to an individual for as long as he or she lives. These benefits are composed of three parts: principal, interest, and survivorship benefits. The *principal* consists of the premium amounts paid in by the *annuitant* (person buying the annuity) during the accumulation period. *Interest* is the amount earned on these funds between the time they're paid and distributed. The interest earnings on an annuity accrue (that is, accumulate) tax free—but note that, whereas the earnings in an annuity accumulate on a tax-sheltered basis, the amounts paid into an annuity are all made with *after-tax dollars* (that is, no special tax treatment is given to the capital contributions). The portion of the principal and interest that has not been returned to the annuitant before death is the **survivorship benefit**. These funds are available to those members of the annuity group who survive in each subsequent period.

14-4a Classification of Annuities

Annuities may be classified according to several key characteristics, including payment of premiums, disposition of proceeds, inception date of benefits, and method used in calculating benefits. Exhibit 14.5 illustrates this classification system.

Single Premium or Installments

There are two ways to pay the premiums when you purchase an annuity contract: you can make one large (lump-sum) payment up front or pay the premium in installments. The **single premium annuity contract** usually requires a *minimum investment* of anywhere from $2,500 to $10,000, with $5,000 the most common figure. These annuities have become popular primarily because of their attractive tax features. They're often purchased just before retirement as a way of creating a future stream of income. In these circumstances, the individual normally purchases an **immediate annuity**, in which case the stream of monthly benefits begins immediately—the first check arrives a month or so after purchase. Sometimes the cash value of a life insurance policy is used at retirement to acquire a single premium annuity. This is an effective use of a life insurance policy: you get the insurance coverage when you *need* it the most (while you're raising and educating your family) and then a regular stream of income when you can probably *use* it the most (after you've retired).

Although most *group* annuity policies are funded with single premiums, many *individuals* still buy annuities by paying for them in installments. With these **installment premium annuity contracts**, set payments, which can start as low as $100, are made at regular intervals (monthly, quarterly, or annually) over an extended period of time. Sometimes these annuities are set up with a fairly large initial payment (of perhaps several thousand dollars), followed by a series of much smaller installment payments (of, say, $250 a quarter). This approach would be used to purchase a **deferred annuity**, a type of contract in which cash benefits are deferred for several years (note that single premiums can also be used to purchase deferred annuities). A big advantage of *installment premium deferred annuities* is that your savings can build up over time *free of taxes*. With no taxes to pay, you have more money working for you and can build up a bigger retirement nest egg. You'll have to pay taxes on your earnings eventually, of course, but not until you start receiving benefit payments from your annuity.

EXHIBIT 14.5 | **Types of Annuity Contracts**

Annuity contracts vary according to how you pay for the annuity, how the proceeds are disbursed, how earnings accrue, and when you receive the benefits.

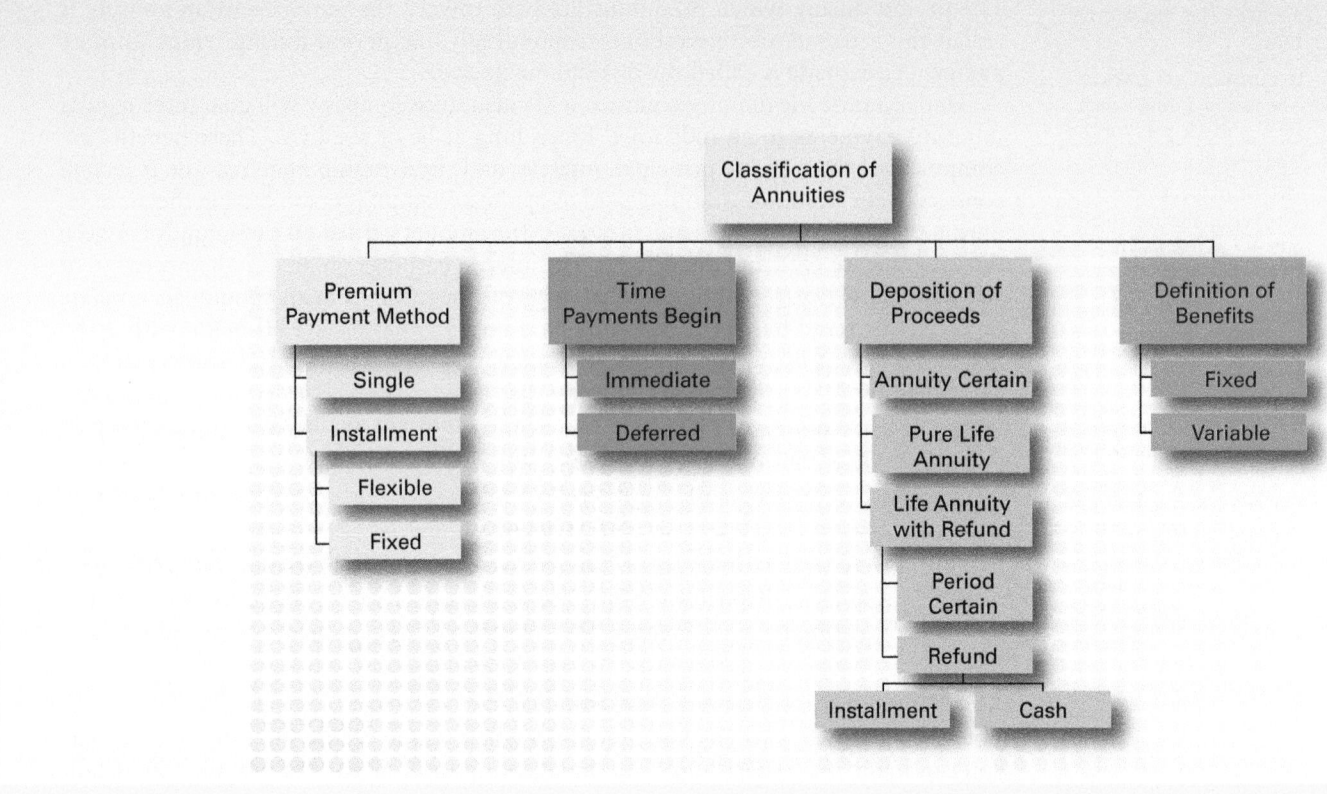

Installment premium contracts also carry an important *life insurance provision*, which stipulates that if an annuitant dies before the distribution period begins, then the annuitant's beneficiaries will receive the market value of the contract or the amount invested, whichever is greater (note that single-premium annuities contain similar life insurance provisions so long as the payout of benefits is deferred to some future date). In addition, the annuitant can terminate an installment premium contract at any time or simply stop paying the periodic installments and take a paid-up annuity for a reduced amount. One potential advantage of purchasing an installment-type annuity relatively early in life is that scheduled benefits are based on mortality rates in effect when the contract was purchased. Even if the mortality rate increases, as it normally does with the passage of time, the annuitant won't be required to pay the higher premium stipulated in contracts issued later.

Disposition of Proceeds

All annuities revolve around the basic concept of "pay now, receive later," so they allow individuals to prepare for future cash needs, such as planning for retirement, while obtaining significant tax benefits. When the annuity is distributed, you can take a lump-sum payment or, as is more often the case, you can *annuitize* the distribution by systematically parceling out the money into regular payments over a defined or open-ended period. Because most people choose to annuitize their proceeds (which is how an annuity is intended to be used), let's look at the most common annuity disbursement options:

- **Life annuity with no refund (pure life).** The annuitant receives a specified amount of income for life, whether the disbursement period turns out to be 1 year or 50 years. The estate or family receives no refunds when the annuitant dies. This results in the largest monthly payments of any of the distribution methods because the issuer (a life insurance company) doesn't have to distribute the principal, if any, to the annuitant's heirs.

- **Guaranteed-minimum annuity (life annuity with refund).** In this type of contract, the benefits (future cash flows) aren't limited to the annuitant only and may extend to named beneficiaries. There are two forms of this annuity. With a **life annuity, period certain**, the annuitant gets a guaranteed monthly income for life, with the added provision that the insurance company will pay the monthly benefits for a minimum number of years (5 or 10, for example). If the annuitant dies soon after the distribution begins, then his or her beneficiaries receive the monthly benefits for the balance of the "period certain." With a **refund annuity**, if the annuitant dies, then the designated beneficiary receives monthly payments (or in some cases a lump-sum cash refund) until the total purchase price of the annuity has been refunded.

- **Annuity certain.** This type of annuity pays a set amount of monthly income for a specified number of years, thereby filling a need for monthly income that will expire after a certain length of time. An annuitant selecting a 10-year annuity certain receives payments for 10 years after retirement, regardless of whether he or she lives for 2 or 20 more years. For example, a widow, age 52, could use a 10-year annuity certain contract to provide income until she reaches age 62 and can apply for Social Security benefits.

Fixed versus Variable Annuity

When you put your money into an annuity, the premium is invested on your behalf by the insurance company, much as a mutual fund invests the money you put into it. How that rate of return is figured on that investment determines whether you own a fixed or variable annuity. In a **fixed-rate annuity**, the insurance company safeguards your principal and agrees to pay a guaranteed minimum rate of interest over the life of the contract—which often amounts to little more than prevailing money market rates existing when you bought the contract. These are conservative, very low-risk annuity products that essentially promise to return *the original investment plus interest* when the money is paid out to the annuitant (or any designated beneficiaries). Unlike bond mutual funds, fixed annuities don't fluctuate in value when interest rates rise or fall; so your principal is always secure. These *interest-earning annuities*, as they're also called, are ideally suited for the cautious investor who likes the secure feeling of knowing what his or her monthly cash flow will be.

Imagine an investment vehicle that lets you move between stocks, bonds, and money funds and, at the same time, accumulate profits tax free. That, in a nutshell, is a variable annuity. With a **variable annuity** contract, the amount that's ultimately paid out to the annuitant varies with the investment results obtained by the insurance company—*nothing is guaranteed, not even the principal!* When you buy a variable annuity, *you decide* where your money will be invested, based on your investment objectives and tolerance for risk; you can usually choose from stocks, bonds, money market securities, real estate, alternative investments, or some combination thereof. As an annuity holder, you can stay put with a single investment for the long haul; or, as with most variable annuities, you can more aggressively play the market by switching from one fund to another. Obviously, when the market goes up, investors in variable annuities do well; but when the market falters, the returns on these policies will likewise be reduced.

Although there's nothing to keep you from staying with market-sensitive variable annuities, in most cases *you can convert to a fixed annuity at distribution*. What you do, in effect, is use the cash value in your variable annuity to buy a paid-up fixed annuity. In this way, you use a *variable annuity during the accumulation period* to build up your capital as much as possible and then switch to a *fixed annuity for the distribution period* to obtain a certain, well-defined stream of future income.

14-4b Sources of Annuities

Annuities are administered by life insurance companies, so it's no surprise that they're also the leading sellers of these financial products. Annuities can also be purchased from stock brokers, mutual fund organizations, banks, and financial planners. When you buy an annuity, the cost will vary with the annuitant's age at issue, the annuitant's age when payments begin, the method used to distribute benefits, the number of lives covered, and the annuitant's gender. There can be substantial differences among the premiums charged by different companies. These differences confirm the need to shop around before making an annuity purchase. The cost to females is higher than the cost to males across all benefit levels because of the lower mortality rates among women.

You Can Do It Now

What Do Annuities Cost?

Want to get a sense of what an annuity costs? Representative quotes based on state, age, and gender can be found at https://www.nylaarp.com/Annuities/Income-Example. You can do it now.

As with mutual funds, there are some annual fees that you should be aware of. In particular, be prepared to pay insurance fees of 1 percent or more—in addition to the annual management fees of perhaps 1 percent to 2 percent paid on variable annuities. That's a total of 2 percent to 3 percent or more taken right off the top, year after year. There is also a *contract charge* (or maintenance fee) that's deducted annually to cover various contract-related expenses; these fees usually run from about $30 to $60 per year. Obviously, these fees can drag down returns and reduce the advantage of tax-deferred income. Finally, most annuities charge hefty *penalties for early withdrawal*. This means that, in order to get out of a poorly performing annuity, you'll have to forfeit a chunk of your money.

14-4c Investment and Income Properties of Annuities

A major attribute of most types of annuities is that they're a source of income that can't be outlived. Although individuals might be able to create a similar arrangement by simply living off the interest or dividends from their investments, they'd find it difficult to liquidate their principal systematically so that the last payment would coincide closely (or exactly) with their death. Another advantage is that the income earned in an annuity is allowed to accumulate tax free, so it's a form of *tax-sheltered investment*. Actually, the income from an annuity is *tax deferred*, meaning that taxes on the earnings will have to be paid when the annuity is liquidated.

Shelter from taxes is an attractive investment attribute, but there's a hitch. You may be faced with a big tax penalty if you close out or withdraw money from an annuity before it's time. Specifically, the IRS treats annuity withdrawals like withdrawals from an IRA: except in cases of serious illness, *anyone who takes money out before reaching age 59½ will incur a 10 percent tax penalty*. So, if you're under age 59½ and in the 28 percent tax bracket, you'll end up paying a 38 percent tax rate on any funds withdrawn from an annuity. (The IRS views withdrawals *as taxable income*

FINANCIAL PLANNING TIPS

Does an Annuity Make Sense for You?

Most of us don't have a traditional defined benefit pension and have to manage with a 401(k) plan, along with careful investing, to fund our retirement. But we still long for the steady income that defined benefit plans provide. Annuities are designed to provide a monthly income for the rest of your life. You enter into an agreement with an insurer that provides that benefit for a predefined time period, after you pay in advance for this service. Annuities are designed to assure that you do not outlive your money.

So when does it make sense to buy an annuity? If you have guaranteed income from several different sources, you may not need an annuity. However, if you don't have a traditional pension plan and want the security of a fixed monthly payment in retirement, you may want to consider using some of your savings to purchase an annuity. Here is some more specific guidance.

A *deferred annuity* is worth considering when:

- You are making the maximum contribution to your employer-sponsored retirement plan and to your IRA (or if you're not eligible for an IRA).

- You don't expect to need the annuity funds until you are at least 59½ years old.

- You have an emergency fund that covers at least six months of living expenses.

An *immediate annuity* may be a good choice when:

- You want to convert part of your retirement savings into income now.

- You are in good health and expect to live at least another 20 years.

- You have sufficient assets to cover large expenses like medical bills.

Source: Adapted, in part, from Phil Taylor, "Do You Need an Annuity?" http://money.usnews.com/money/blogs/on-retirement/2012/01/06/do-you-need-an-annuity, accessed September 2015.

until the account balance falls to the amount of original paid-in principal, after which any further withdrawals are tax free.) Barring some type of serious illness, about the only way to tap your account without penalty before you're 59½ is to *annuitize*. Unfortunately, the annuity payments must be spread out over your estimated remaining life span, which means the size of each monthly payment could be pretty small. All of which only reinforces the notion that *an annuity should always be considered a long-term investment*. Assume that it's a part of your retirement program (after all, that's the way the IRS looks at it), and that you're getting in for the long haul.

From an investment perspective, the returns generated from an annuity can, in some cases, be a bit disappointing. For instance, as we discussed earlier, the returns on *variable annuities* are tied to returns in the money and capital markets; even so, they're still no better than what you can get from other investment vehicles—indeed, they're often lower, in part because of higher annuity fees. Keep in mind that these differential returns aren't due to tax features because in both cases, returns were measured on a before-tax basis. But *returns from annuities are tax sheltered*, so that makes those lower returns a lot more attractive.

If you're considering a variable annuity, go over it much as you would a traditional mutual fund: look for superior past performance, proven management talent/ track record, and the availability of attractive investment alternatives that you can switch in and out of. And *pay particular attention to an annuity's total expense rate*. These products have a reputation for being heavily loaded with fees and charges, but it's possible to find annuities with both above-average performance and relatively low fee structures. That's the combination you're looking for.

One final point: If you're seriously considering buying an annuity, be sure to read the contract carefully and see what the guaranteed rates are, how long the initial rate applies, and if there's a bailout provision. (A *bailout provision* allows you to withdraw your money, free of any surrender fees, if the rate of return on your annuity falls below a specified minimum level. Of course, even if you exercise a bailout provision, you may still have to face a tax penalty for early withdrawal—unless you transfer the funds to another annuity through what's known as a *1035 exchange*.) Just as important, because *the annuity is only as good as the insurance company that stands behind it*, check to see how the company is rated by Best's, Standard & Poor's, or Moody's. It's important to make sure that the insurance company itself is financially sound before buying one of its annuity products. See Chapter 8 for more discussion on these insurance ratings and how they work.

TEST YOURSELF

14-15 What is an *annuity*? Briefly explain how an annuity works and how it differs from a life insurance policy.

14-16 Which one of the annuity distribution procedures will result in the highest monthly benefit payment?

14-17 What is a *fixed-rate* annuity, and how does it differ from a *variable* annuity? Does the type of contract (fixed or variable) have any bearing on the amount of money you'll receive at the time of distribution?

14-18 Which type of contract (fixed or variable) might be most suitable for someone who wants a minimum amount of risk exposure?

14-19 How do variable annuity returns generally compare to mutual fund returns? Can you explain why there would be any difference in returns?

Here are some key considerations for retirement planning in each stage of the life cycle.

Pre-family Independence: 20s	Family Formation/ Career Development: 30–45	Pre-Retirement: 45–65	Retirement: 65 and Beyond
✓ Estimate how much you will need to retire comfortably while taking inflation into account.	✓ Aim to invest between 10 and 15 percent of your income for retirement. The more you invest early on, the better off you'll be at retirement.	✓ Revise your retirement plan in light of recent developments. Try to save even more.	✓ Revise your retirement plan to weight your investments more toward debt and liquid instruments than stocks.
✓ Determine your asset allocation among stocks, bonds, real estate, and cash based on your time horizon and attitude toward risk. Most people are comfortable taking more risk earlier in life.	✓ Review your asset allocation and rebalance it to be more consistent with your goals. Most people are more comfortable reducing the risk of their investments a bit.	✓ Review your asset allocation and rebalance investments within and beyond your employer's retirement plan. Most people reduce the risk of their investments.	✓ Compare your spending rate to your assets and reassess how long your spending rate can be maintained. Consider how the current income produced by your portfolio relates to your day-to-day spending needs.
✓ Match your investments in any employer sponsored 401(k) retirement plan with your overall asset allocation plan.	✓ Gradually increase the amount invested in any employer-sponsored 401(k) retirement plan and re-evaluate how it relates to your asset allocation plan.	✓ Continue to increase the amount you invest in any employer sponsored 401(k) retirement plan gradually, and re-evaluate it periodically to see how it fits into your asset allocation plan.	✓ Integrate your investment asset allocation strategy with estate planning. Keep in mind that the equity in your home can be borrowed against if needed.
✓ Start setting aside money for investment outside your employer's retirement plan. Consider investing in mutual funds and exchange-traded funds (ETFs) under a traditional IRA, a Roth IRA, or both.	✓ Consider increasing your contribution to traditional IRA, a Roth IRA, or both.	✓ Consider increasing your contribution to traditional and Roth IRAs using mutual funds and exchange-traded funds (ETFs). Consider purchasing an annuity to supplement retirement income.	✓ Plan for mandatory withdrawals from tax-sheltered accounts and the associated tax consequences.

Financial Impact of Personal Choices

Carl and Brian's Different Approaches to a Traditional IRA

Carl Rowley and Brian Lyles, both 30 years old, are good friends who work together at a management consulting firm. They both take advantage of their firm's 401(k) plan. But they differ in how they set aside money in a traditional IRA. Carl has just started setting aside $5,500 a year in an IRA that he expects to earn 5 percent per year until he plans to retire at age 66. In contrast, while Brian also expects to retire at age 66, he believes it's too early in his career to bother investing in an IRA because it won't have that much impact in the long-term. He consequently plans to wait five years before following Carl's example.

At age 66 the pre-tax value of Carl's IRA should be about $553,455 while the value of Brian's account should be about $408,644. Carl will have invested $27,000 more than Brian but will end up with $144,811 more in his IRA account! That's because the IRA sheltered the earnings on Carl's investments from taxes and he also benefited handsomely from the compounding of returns on his money. So there's a moral here: invest early, often, and consider the impact of taxes on your investments.

Summary

LG1 **Recognize the importance of retirement planning, and identify the three biggest pitfalls to good planning, p. 557**
Retirement planning plays a vital role in the personal financial planning process. It's based on many of the same principles and concepts of effective financial planning, which include establishing financial goals and strategies, using savings and investment plans, and using certain insurance products such as annuities. The three biggest pitfalls to sound retirement planning are starting too late, not saving enough, and investing too conservatively.

LG2 **Estimate your income needs in retirement and the level of retirement income you've estimated from various sources, p. 557**
Rather than address retirement planning in a series of short-run (3- to 5-year) plans, it's best to take a long-term approach and look 20–30 years into the future to determine how much saving and investing you must do today in order to achieve the retirement goals you've set for tomorrow. Implementing a long-term retirement plan involves determining future retirement needs, estimating retirement income from known sources (such as Social Security and company pension plans), and

deciding how much to save and invest each year to build up a desired nest egg.

LG3 **Explain the eligibility requirements and benefits of the Social Security program, p. 566**
Social Security is the foundation for the retirement programs of most families; except for a few exempt classes (mostly government employees), almost all gainfully employed workers are covered by Social Security. Upon retirement, covered workers are entitled to certain monthly benefits as determined mainly by the employee's earning history and age at retirement.

LG4 **Differentiate among the types of basic and supplemental employer-sponsored pension plans, p. 571**
Employer-sponsored pension and retirement plans provide a vital source of retirement income to many individuals. Such plans can often spell the difference between enjoying a comfortable standard of living in retirement or a bare subsistence. In *basic* retirement programs, all employees participate after a certain period of employment. These plans can be defined contribution or defined benefit plans. There are also several forms of *supplemental* employer-sponsored programs,

including profit-sharing plans, thrift and savings plans, and perhaps most popular, salary reduction plans such as 401(k) plans.

LG5 **Describe the various types of self-directed retirement plans, p. 571**
In addition to company-sponsored retirement programs, individuals can set up their own self-directed tax-sheltered retirement plans; it's through such plans that most individuals can build up the nest eggs they'll need to meet their retirement objectives. The basic types of self-directed retirement programs are Keogh and SEP plans for self-employed individuals as well

as various forms of IRAs, which any salary or wage earner can set up.

LG6 **Choose the right type of annuity for your retirement plan, p. 585**
Annuities are also an important source of income for retired people. An annuity is an investment vehicle that allows investment income to accumulate on a tax-deferred basis; it provides for the systematic liquidation (payout) of all invested capital and earnings over an extended period. There are many types of annuities, including single premium and installment premium, fixed and variable, and immediate and deferred; there are also different payout options.

Key Terms

accumulation period, 585

annuity, 585

annuity certain, 587

cash-balance plan, 575

contributory pension plan, 573

deferred annuity, 585

defined benefit plan, 573

distribution period, 585

employee retirement income security act (ERISA), 571

fixed-rate annuity, 587

guaranteed-minimum annuity (life annuity with refund), 587

immediate annuity, 585

individual retirement account (IRA), 581

installment premium annuity contract, 585

Keogh plan, 580

life annuity, period certain, 587

life annuity with no refund (pure life), 587

noncontributory pension plan, 573

Nondeductible (after-tax) IRA, 581

pension protection act, 571

profit-sharing plan, 576

qualified pension plan, 575

refund annuity, 587

salary reduction, or 401(k), plan, 577

single premium annuity contract, 585

survivorship benefit, 585

thrift and savings plans, 576

Traditional (deductible) IRA, 581

variable annuity, 587

vested rights, 572

Answers to Test Yourself

You can find answers to these questions on this book's companion website. Look for it at *www.cengagebrain.com*. Search for this book by its title, and then add it to your dashboard.

Financial Planning Exercises

LG2, p. 557 1. ***Calculating amount available at retirement.*** Marisa Gale, a 25-year-old personal loan officer at Second National Bank, understands the importance of starting early when it comes to saving for retirement. She has designated $3,000 per year for her retirement fund and assumes that she'll retire at age 65.

a. How much will she have if she invests in CDs and similar money market instruments that earn 4 percent on average?

b. How much will she have if instead she invests in equities and earns 10 percent on average?

c. Marisa is urging her friend, Nolan Ransom, to start his plan right away because he's 35. What would his nest egg amount to if he invested in the same manner as Marisa and he, too, retires at age 65? Comment on your findings.

LG2, p. 557   2.   *Calculating annual investment to meet retirement target.* *Use Worksheet 14.1* to help Andy and Rachel Cutler, who'd like to retire in about 20 years. Both have promising careers, and both make good money. As a result, they're willing to put aside whatever is necessary to achieve a comfortable lifestyle in retirement. Their current level of household expenditures (excluding savings) is around $75,000 a year, and they expect to spend *even more* in retirement; they think they'll need about 125 percent of that amount. (*Note:* 125 percent equals a multiplier factor of 1.25.) They estimate that their Social Security benefits will amount to $20,000 a year in today's dollars and that they'll receive another $35,000 annually from their company pension plans. They feel that future inflation will amount to about 3 percent a year, and they think they'll be able to earn about 6 percent on their investments before retirement and about 4 percent afterward. Use Worksheet 14.1 to find out how big Andy and Rachel's investment nest egg will have to be and how much they'll have to save annually to accumulate the needed amount within the next 20 years.

LG2, p. 557   3.   *Retirement planning.* Use Worksheet 14.1 to assist Tara Easley with her retirement planning needs. She plans to retire in 15 years, and her current household expenditures run about $50,000 per year. Tara estimates that she'll spend 80 percent of that amount in retirement. Her Social Security benefit is estimated at $15,000 per year, and she'll receive $12,000 per year from her employer's pension plan (both in today's dollars). Additional assumptions include an inflation rate of 4 percent and a rate of return on retirement assets of 8 percent a year before retirement and 5 percent afterward. Use Worksheet 14.1 to calculate the required size of Tara's retirement nest egg and the amount that she must save annually over the next 15 years to reach that goal.

LG3, p. 566   4.   *Critical evaluation of Social Security benefits.* Many critics of the Social Security program feel participants are getting a substandard investment return on their money. Discuss why you agree or disagree with this viewpoint.

LG3, p. 566   5.   *Average Social Security benefits and taxes.* Use Exhibit 14.3 to estimate the average Social Security benefits for a retired couple. Assume that one spouse has a part-time job that pays $24,000 a year, and that this person also receives another $47,000 a year from a company pension. Based on current policies, would this couple be liable for any tax on their Social Security income?

LG3, p. 566   6.   *Average Social Security benefits.* Use Exhibit 14.3 to determine the annual Social Security benefit for Bob Lemus, assuming that he is an "average" retiree. Bob is 65 years old and earns $18,000 a year at a part-time job. (Note that Bob is already at "full retirement age," because he was born well before 1960.)

LG3, 4,   7.   *Retirement planning.* At what age would you like to retire? Describe the type of lifestyle you
p. 566, 571   envision—where you want to live, whether you want to work part-time, and so on. Discuss the steps you think you should take to realize this goal.

LG4, p. 571   8.   *Comparing retirement plans.* Ellen Honeycut has just graduated from college and is considering job offers from two companies. Although the salary and insurance benefits are similar, the retirement programs are not. One firm offers a 401(k) plan that matches employee contributions with 25 cents for every dollar contributed by the employee, up to a $10,000 limit. The other firm has a contributory plan that allows employees to contribute up to 10 percent of their annual salary through payroll deduction and matches it dollar for dollar; this plan vests fully after five years. Because Ellen is unfamiliar with these plans, explain the features of each to her so she can make an informed decision.

LG4, p. 571   9.   *After-tax cost of 401(k) contribution.* Brad Shin is an operations manager for a large manufacturer. He earned $72,500 in 2015 and plans to contribute the maximum allowed to the firm's 401(k) plan. Assuming that Brad is in the 25 percent tax bracket, calculate his taxable income and the amount of his tax savings. How much did it actually cost Brad on an after-tax basis to make this retirement plan contribution?

LG4, p. 571 10. **Defined benefit vs. defined contribution pension plans.** Briefly describe the main characteristics of defined contribution and defined benefit pension plans, and discuss how they differ from cash-balance plans. In each of these plans, does the employee or employer bear the risk of poor investment performance?

LG5, p. 571 11. **Nature of different types of IRAs.** Describe the three basic types of IRAs (traditional, Roth, and nondeductible), including their respective tax features and what it takes to qualify for each. Which is most appealing to you personally? Explain.

LG5, p. 571 12. **Deciding between traditional and Roth IRAs.** Clint Crandall is in his early 30s and is thinking about opening an IRA. He can't decide whether to open a traditional/deductible IRA or a Roth IRA, so he turns to you for help.
   a. To support your explanation, you decide to *run some comparative numbers on the two types of accounts;* for starters, use a 25-year period to show Clint what contributions of $4,000 per year will amount to (after 25 years), given that he can earn, say, 10 percent on his money. Will the type of account he opens have any impact on this amount? Explain.
   b. Assuming that Clint is in the 28 percent tax bracket (and will remain there for the next 25 years), determine the annual and total (over 25 years) tax savings that he'll enjoy from the $4,000-a-year contributions to his IRA; contrast the (annual and total) tax savings he'd generate from a traditional IRA with those from a Roth IRA.
   c. Now, fast-forward 25 years. Given the size of Clint's account in 25 years (as computed in part **a**), assume that he takes it all out in one lump sum. If he's still in the 30 percent tax bracket, how much will he have, after taxes, with a traditional IRA, as compared with a Roth IRA? How do the taxes computed here compare with those computed in part **b**? Comment on your findings.
   d. Based on the numbers you have computed as well as any other factors, what kind of IRA would you recommend to Clint? Explain. Would knowing that maximum contributions are scheduled to increase to $7,000 per year make any difference in your analysis? Explain.

LG6, p. 585 13. **Comparing variable annuities and mutual funds.** Explain how buying a variable annuity is much like investing in a mutual fund. Do you, as a buyer, have any control over the amount of investment risk to which you're exposed in a variable annuity contract? Explain.

LG6, p. 585 14. **Tax shelter aspects of annuities.** Briefly explain how annuities are a type of tax-sheltered investment. Do you have to give up anything to obtain this tax-favored treatment? (*Hint:* Age 59½.)

LG6, p. 585 15. **Considerations in annuity purchase.** Why is it important to check an insurance company's financial ratings when buying an annuity? Why should you look at past performance when considering the purchase of a variable annuity?

LG6, p. 585 16. **Fixed vs. variable annuities.** What are the main differences between fixed and variable annuities? Which type is more appropriate for someone who is 60 years old and close to retirement?

Applying Personal Finance

Envisioning Your Ideal Retirement Plan!

Many people have little or no money set aside for their retirement. Those who do may find their retirement funds insufficient for maintaining their desired standard of living during retirement. In this project, you'll contemplate the type and features of a retirement program that would best meet your needs.

Looking back over this chapter, review the features of both employer-sponsored and self-directed retirement programs. Depending on your career, you may actually have both kinds. Develop an outline of your ideal retirement plan or plans (*be realistic*), being sure to consider the following issues:

1. Would the plan be contributory or noncontributory?
2. Stated as a *percentage* of your base salary, how much would be put into your retirement plan each year? Remember that there are certain allowable limits.

3. What would be the eligibility and vesting provisions? Would your plan be portable? Under what conditions?
4. What would be the earliest retirement age? Would there be provisions for early retirement?
5. Would your plan be a defined contribution or a defined benefit plan? You could also have a combination of the two types.
6. Would the plan be qualified?
7. Would you want a voluntary supplemental plan as part of your program? If you could have only one supplemental plan, what would it be?

What would be the advantages and disadvantages of your ideal plan? This research will help you understand the retirement benefits you may have with your current job or as part of the job offers you may receive in the future.

CRITICAL THINKING CASES

LG4, p. 571

14.1 Comparing Pension Plan Features

Linda Calloway and Meredith Perdue are neighbors in Charleston. Linda works as a software engineer for Progressive Apps Corporation, while Meredith works as an executive for Industrial Container Company. Both are married, have two children, and are well paid. Linda and Meredith are interested in better understanding their pension and retirement plans.

Progressive Apps Corporation, the company where Linda works, has a contributory plan in which 5 percent of the employees' annual wages is deducted to meet the cost of the benefits. The firm contributes an amount equal to the employee contribution. The plan uses a five-year graded vesting procedure; it has a normal retirement age of 60 for all employees, and the benefits at retirement are paid according to a defined contribution plan.

Industrial Container, where Meredith works, has a minimum retirement age of 60. Employees (full-time, hourly, or salaried) must meet participation requirements. Further, in contrast to the Progressive Apps plan, the Industrial Container program has a noncontributory feature. Annual retirement benefits are computed according to the following formula: 2 percent of the employee's final annual salary for each year of service with the company is paid upon retirement. The plan vests immediately.

Critical Thinking Questions

1. Discuss and contrast the features of the retirement plans offered by Progressive Apps and Industrial Container.
2. Which plan do you think is more desirable? Consider the features, retirement age, and benefit computations just described. Which plan do you think could be subject to a conversion to a cash-balance plan sometime in the future? Explain. Include in your answer the implications for the employee's future retirement benefits.
3. Explain how you would use each of these plans in developing your own retirement program.
4. What role, if any, could annuities play in these retirement programs? Discuss the pros and cons of using annuities as a part of retirement planning.

LG2, 4, 5, p. 557, 571

14.2 Evaluating Maria Sepulveda's Retirement Prospects

Maria Sepulveda is 57 years old. Never remarried, she has worked full-time since her husband died 13 years ago—in addition to raising her two children, the youngest of whom is now finishing college. After being forced to go back to work in her 40s, Maria's first job was in a fast-food restaurant. Eventually, she upgraded her skills sufficiently to obtain a supervisory position in the personnel department of a major corporation, where she's now earning $58,000 a year.

Although her financial focus for the past 13 years has, of necessity, been on meeting living expenses and getting her kids through college, she feels that now she can turn her attention to her retirement needs. Actually, Maria hasn't done too badly in that area, either. By carefully investing the proceeds from her husband's life insurance policy, Maria has accumulated the following investment assets:

Money market securities, stocks, and bonds	*$72,600*
IRA and 401(k) plans	*$47,400*

Other than the mortgage on her condo, the only other debt she has is $7,000 in college loans.

Maria would like to retire in eight years, and she recently hired a financial planner to help her come up with an effective retirement program. Her planner has estimated that, for her to live comfortably in retirement, she'll need about $37,500 a year (in today's dollars) in retirement income.

Critical Thinking Questions

1. After taking into account the income that Maria will receive from Social Security and her company-sponsored pension plan, the financial planner has estimated that her investment assets will need to provide her with about $15,000 a year to meet the balance of her retirement income needs. Assuming a 6 percent after-tax return on her investments, how big a nest egg will Maria need to earn that kind of income?
2. Suppose she can invest the money market securities, stocks, and bonds (the $72,600) at 5 percent after taxes and can invest the $47,400 accumulated in her tax-sheltered IRA and 401(k) at 7 percent. How much will Maria's investment assets be worth in eight years, when she retires?
3. Maria's employer matches her 401(k) contributions dollar for dollar, up to a maximum of $3,000 a year. If she continues to put $3,000 a year into that program, how much more will she have in eight years, given a 9 percent rate of return?
4. What would you advise Maria about her ability to retire in eight years, as she hopes to?

CHAPTER 15

Preserving Your Estate

LEARNING GOALS

LG1 Describe the role of estate planning in personal financial planning, and identify the seven steps involved in the process.

LG2 Recognize the importance of preparing a will and other documents to protect you and your estate.

LG3 Explain how trusts are used in estate planning.

LG4 Determine whether a gift will be taxable and use planned gifts to reduce estate taxes.

LG5 Calculate federal taxes due on an estate.

LG6 Use effective estate planning techniques to minimize estate taxes.

How Will This Affect Me?

No, you can't take it with you. But there's a next best thing: A carefully designed estate plan will allow your loved ones and family to keep as much of your accumulated wealth as possible. This chapter explains the role of estate planning and the importance of a will. It discusses the use and design of living wills, advance medical directives, and trusts. It also explains how federal estate taxes are calculated. After reading this chapter you should understand the key elements in handling and preserving your estate for your loved ones.

15-1 PRINCIPLES OF ESTATE PLANNING

Like it or not, no one lives forever. Safeguarding the future of the people you care about is one of the most important aspects of financial planning. Unless you develop an estate plan and take steps during your lifetime to accumulate, preserve, and distribute your assets upon your death, chances are that your heirs and beneficiaries will receive only part of your estate. The rest will be consumed (often unnecessarily) by poorly timed sales, sales at less-than-optimum prices, taxes, and various administrative costs. Planning the distribution of your assets to your heirs is necessary to maximize the wealth available to them. To be successful requires knowledge of your property, property law, wills, trusts, and taxes. This overall process is known as *estate planning*.

Understanding these components and their interrelationships will help you minimize estate shrinkage after your death and still allow you to achieve your lifetime personal financial goals. Also, keep in mind that not only wealthy people, but also individuals of modest or moderate means, need to plan their estates. While the amount of money in your estate may be small, planning the transfer of that property will help your heirs at a time of great stress and need.

estate planning
The process of developing a plan to administer and distribute your assets in a manner consistent with your wishes and the needs of your survivors, while minimizing taxes.

Estate planning is the process of developing a plan to administer and distribute your assets in a manner consistent with your wishes and the needs of your survivors. This process occurs over most of your adult life. Planning helps people accumulate enough capital to meet college education costs and other special needs, provide financial security for family members after the death of the head of household, take care of themselves and their family during a long-term disability, and provide for a comfortable retirement. However, estate planning goes beyond financial issues. It also includes plans to manage your affairs if you become disabled, manage your personal wishes for medical care, and make clear how you want your assets to be distributed among your heirs.

As with other financial planning activities, a major objective of estate planning is to legally eliminate or minimize tax exposure. With careful planning, estate taxes may be completely eliminated in most cases. Also, with planning, future income tax on the sale of inherited property may be minimized. Planning for the income and transfer tax increases the amount of your estate that ultimately is passed on to your heirs and beneficiaries. Estate planning also is closely related to insurance and retirement planning. Certainly, the most important reason for buying life insurance is to provide for your family in the event of your premature death. Likewise, a principal challenge of effective retirement planning is to achieve a comfortable standard of living in retirement while preserving as much of your accumulated wealth as possible. This not only

Financial Fact or Fantasy?

Estate planning is one of the key elements of personal financial planning. **Fact:** One of the principal objectives of financial planning is to transfer as much accumulated wealth to your heirs and designated beneficiaries as possible—a goal that is made easier through effective estate planning.

reduces the chances of you (or your spouse) outliving your financial resources but also leaves an estate that can be passed on to your heirs and designated beneficiaries according to your wishes.

Planning should occur in every estate. The estate owner and his or her professional counselors control the plan, but the plan or lack of a plan is subject to federal and state governments that will affect the plan. If an individual fails to plan, then state and federal laws will control the disposition of assets and determine who bears the burden of expenses and taxes. Indeed, the cost of administration and taxes may be higher because of lack of planning. People who wish to plan their estates must systematically uncover problems in several important areas and solve them. Exhibit 15.1 lists the major types of problems and their associated causes or indicators. In later sections, we'll discuss techniques to avoid or minimize these problems.

15-1a Who Needs Estate Planning?

Estate planning should be part of your financial plan, whether you're married or single and have five children or none. For example, married couples who own many assets jointly and have designated beneficiaries for assets such as retirement funds and life insurance policies may think that they don't need wills. However, a will covers many other important details, such as naming an executor to administer the estate and a guardian for children, clarifying how estate taxes will be paid, and distributing property that doesn't go directly to a joint owner.

EXHIBIT 15.1   Potential Estate Planning Problems

Careful estate planning can prevent many problems that arise when settling an estate. The first step toward preventing problems is an awareness and understanding of their major causes or indicators.

Potential Problem	Major Cause or Indicator
• Excessive transfer costs	Taxes and estate administrative expenses higher than necessary
• Lack of liquidity	Insufficient cash; not enough assets that are quickly and inexpensively convertible to cash within a short period of time to meet tax demands and other costs
• Improper disposition of assets	Beneficiaries receive the wrong asset, or the proper asset in the wrong manner or at the wrong time
• Inadequate income at retirement	Capital insufficient or not readily convertible to income-producing status
• Inadequate income, if disabled	High medical costs; capital insufficient or not readily convertible to income-producing status; difficulty in reducing living standards
• Inadequate income for family at estate owner's death	Any of the above causes
• Insufficient capital	Excessive taxes, inflation, improper investment planning
• Special problems	A family member with a serious illness or physical or emotional problem; children of a prior marriage; beneficiaries who have extraordinary medical or financial needs; beneficiaries who can't agree on how to handle various estate matters, business problems, or opportunities

Partners who aren't married and single persons will discover that estate planning is especially important, particularly if they own a home or other assets that they want to leave to specific individuals or to charity. Unmarried couples need to put extra effort into their estate plans. They may need to make special arrangements to be sure they can indeed leave assets to a partner.

The two main areas of estate planning are *people planning* and *asset planning*.

People Planning

People planning means anticipating the psychological and financial needs of those people you love and providing enough income or capital or both to ensure a continuation of their way of life. People planning gives guidance to your heirs who may need help managing assets. People planning also means keeping Mother's cameo brooch in the family and out of the pawnshop, or preserving the business that Great-Granddad started in the early 1900s. People planning is especially important for individuals with children who are minors; children who are exceptionally artistic or intellectually gifted; children or other dependents who are emotionally, mentally, or physically handicapped; and spouses who can't or don't want to handle money, securities, or a business.

Minor children cannot legally handle large sums of money or deal directly with real estate or securities. Custodial accounts, guardianships, or trusts will provide administration, security, financial advice, and the legal capacity to act on behalf of minors. Few children are exceptionally artistic or intellectually gifted, but those who are often need—or should have—special (and often expensive) schooling, travel opportunities, or equipment. Emotionally, mentally, or physically disabled children (and other relatives) may need nursing, medical, or psychiatric care. Outright gifts of money or property to those who can't care for themselves are inappropriate. These individuals may need more (or less) than other children. And an individual who gives all of his or her children equal shares may not be giving them equitable shares.

How many of us have handled hundreds of thousands of dollars? Think of the burden that we place on others when we expect that a spouse who can't—or doesn't want to—handle such large sums of money or securities to do so. This is particularly burdensome when the assets being handled are his or her only assets. Engaging in people planning demonstrates a high degree of caring. People planning also involves talking about estate planning with your loved ones.

Asset Planning

From the standpoint of wealth alone, estate planning is essential for anyone—single, widowed, married, or divorced—with an estate exceeding the "applicable exclusion amount," which is $5,430,000 for an individual in 2015. For a married couple, that number is doubled to $10,860,000. So it is not just about taxes. Your estate plan should match your assets with the people you wish to receive them.

> **You Can Do It Now**
>
> *Estate Planning Conversations*
>
> Talking about the prospect of each other's deaths in a family is never comfortable. But careful estate planning will assure that your intentions are best served in light of the family's needs. A useful perspective on how to have such a conversation may be found at: https://www.fidelity.com/estate-planning-inheritance/estate-planning/talking-estate-planning. The sooner the conversation happens, the more confident you can be that your estate plan will have the intended results. You can do it now.

When an estate involves a closely held business, estate planning is essential to stabilize and maximize its asset and income-producing values, both during the owner's lifetime and at the owner's death or disability. Likewise, estate planning is essential to

Behavior Matters

Recognizing and Overcoming Aversion to Ambiguity in Estate Planning

While many people recognize the need for an estate plan, they often have too little understanding of the process. Thus, too few of us take action at the right time. Why? Estate planning forces us to face and confirm our own mortality, which is hard to do. All too often, therefore, it takes a dramatic and serious health change to push the average American to plan for the worst. Consider how to overcome the *aversion to ambiguity* behavioral barrier so you can establish a timely and effective estate plan.

Estate planning can appear ambiguous to those who do not understand it. And most people dislike this ambiguity but fail to confront it. Two conflicting thoughts create this perceived ambiguity. First, we acknowledge that estate planning is important both for the planner and for the planner's family. Second, we often focus on living long and productive lives—a practice that is wrongly taken to imply that there is no hurry to start the estate planning process. The resulting conflicted feelings draw into question the importance of estate planning. Many, consequently, are paralyzed and do no planning.

So how do we move beyond the aversion to ambiguity and get the estate planning process going? We have to admit that life is too short and that we need to plan for the inevitable. After admitting this, the aversion to ambiguity barrier can be overcome by becoming more familiar with the basics of estate planning. This chapter should go a long way in addressing that issue. In summary, we must face our mortality, familiarize ourselves with the estate planning process, and decisively contact a professional to get the process moving forward.

Source: Adapted from Justin A. Reckers and Robert A. Simon, "Resolving the Aversion to Estate Planning," http://www.morningstar.com/advisor/t/42987539/resolving-the-aversion-to-estate-planning.htm, accessed September 2015.

avoid the special problems that occur when an estate owner holds title to property in more than one state. How you own your property (i.e., who is on the deed or title for the property) will affect your ability to plan for its transfer. The nature of the asset—whether it is cash, real property, cars, collectibles, stocks, or bonds—will also affect your ability to match your assets with the people you want to have them. Careful planning is needed to make sure that your assets will go to the desired beneficiaries.

15-1b Why Does an Estate Break Up?

Quite often, when people die, their estates die with them—not because they've done anything wrong, but because they have done nothing. There are numerous forces that, if unchecked, tend to shrink an estate, reduce the usefulness of its assets, and frustrate the objectives of the person who built it. These include death-related costs, inflation, lack of liquidity, improper use of vehicles of transfer, and disabilities.

1. Death-related costs: When someone dies, the estate incurs certain types of death-related costs. For example, medical bills for a final illness and funeral expenses are good examples of *first-level death-related costs*. *Second-level death-related costs* consist of fees for attorneys, appraisers, and accountants along with probate expenses (so-called administrative costs), federal estate taxes, and state death taxes. Most people also die with some current bills unpaid, outstanding long-term obligations (such as mortgages, business loans, and installment contracts), and unpaid income taxes and property taxes.
2. Inflation: Death-related costs are only the tip of the estate-impairment iceberg. Failure to continuously reappraise and rearrange an estate plan to counter the effects of inflation can impair the ability of assets—liquid, real, and personal property and investments—to provide steady and adequate levels of financial security.

FINANCIAL PLANNING TIPS

Common Excuses for Not Writing a Will

Two out of three people don't have a will! Consider the following common excuses, and why they don't hold up.

- **I'm too young to need a will.** There's a chance you won't live as long as you hope. Without a will, your heirs will have to figure it all out. A will can say who will get everything. Youth is no excuse—a will is needed at all ages.

- **My family knows what to do with my assets.** That may be true, but without a will, the state gets to decide who gets what. For example, even if you want your spouse to inherit all of your assets, your children will likely still be given a piece of your estate.

- **I don't have enough assets to need a will.** It's not just how much you have, it's who gets whatever you own. It's best to provide detailed instructions about who gets what and to update them often.

- **My mother would take care of the kids.** Perhaps she would, but what if your mother-in-law also decides she wants the kids? If there is no will, then a judge will decide who gets your children. So choose guardians carefully and put your choices in a will.

- **Writing a will is too expensive.** Not true. It doesn't cost much to write a will. Many state bar associations make available simple will forms. There's even reasonably priced software to do it.

- **My partner will get all of my assets.** A partner to whom you're not legally married may not get anything. While property and investments would likely go to your spouse or civil partner, without a will personal possessions might not go where you want. And what if you and your partner both die at the same time without a will?

- **I have no kids and I'm single, so there is no one to protect.** Single or married, if you have no will, then the state will leave everything to your relatives. And if you have no relatives, the state gets it all! A will can assure that your friends and favorite charities get something.

3. Lack of liquidity: Insufficient cash to cover death costs and other estate obligations has always been a major factor in estate impairment. Sale of the choicest parcel of farmland or a business that's been in the family for generations, for instance, often has undesirable psychological effects on the heirs. The outcome can be a devastating financial and emotional blow.

4. Improper use of vehicles of transfer: Assets are often put into the hands of beneficiaries who are unwilling or unable to handle them. Improper use of vehicles of transfer may pass property to unintended beneficiaries or to the proper beneficiaries in an improper manner or at an incorrect time. For example, spendthrift spouses or minors may be left large sums of money outright in the form of life insurance, through joint ownership of a savings account, or as the beneficiaries of an employee fringe benefit plan.

5. Disabilities: The prolonged and expensive disability of a family wage earner is often called a *living death*. Loss of income due to disability is often coupled with a massive financial drain caused by the illness itself. The financial situation is further complicated by inadequate management of currently owned assets. This not only threatens the family's financial security but also quickly diminishes the value of the estate.

15-1c What Is Your Estate?

Your estate is your property—whatever you own. Your **probate estate** consists of the real and personal property you own in your own name that can be transferred at death according to the terms of a will or, if you have no valid will, under *intestate* laws. The probate estate is distinct from the gross estate (a tax law term that may encompass a considerably larger amount of property). Your **gross estate** includes all

gross estate
All property that might be subject to federal estate taxes on a person's death.

EXHIBIT 15.2 Steps in the Estate Planning Process

The estate planning process consists of seven important steps, listed here in the order they would be performed.

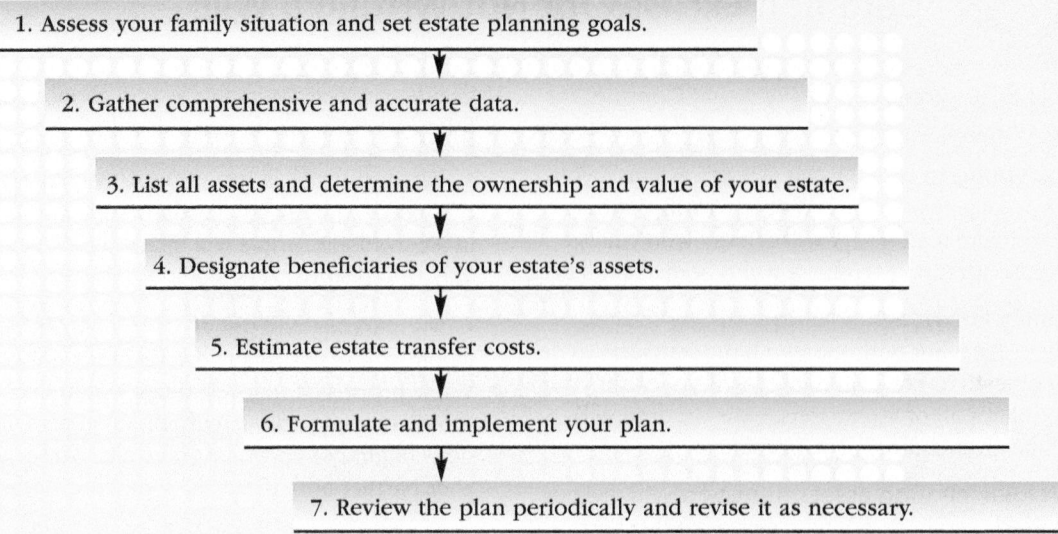

1. Assess your family situation and set estate planning goals.

2. Gather comprehensive and accurate data.

3. List all assets and determine the ownership and value of your estate.

4. Designate beneficiaries of your estate's assets.

5. Estimate estate transfer costs.

6. Formulate and implement your plan.

7. Review the plan periodically and revise it as necessary.

the property—both probate and nonprobate—that might be subject to federal estate taxes at your death. Life insurance, jointly held property with rights of survivorship, and property passing under certain employee benefit plans are common examples of nonprobate assets that might be subject to federal (and state) estate taxes.

You also may provide for property that's not probate property and won't be part of your estate for federal estate tax purposes yet will pass to your family and form part of their financial security program. There are two types of such assets. One is *properly arranged* life insurance. For instance, you could give assets to your daughter to allow her to purchase, pay the premiums for, and be the beneficiary of a policy on your life. At your death, the proceeds normally would not be included as part of your gross estate. The other type of financial asset that falls into this category is *Social Security*. Social Security payments to a surviving spouse and minor children generally are not probate assets and are not subject to any federal (or state) estate taxes. Because of the freedom from administrative costs and taxes, this category of assets provides unique and substantial estate planning opportunities.

15-1d The Estate Planning Process

The estate planning process consists of seven important steps, as summarized in Exhibit 15.2. First, you must assess your family situation, evaluating its strengths and weaknesses, and set estate planning goals. Here is where you focus on "people planning" to set your goals. Next, gather comprehensive and accurate data on all aspects of the family. Exhibit 15.3 summarizes the data that professionals require to prepare detailed estate plans. Most professional estate planners provide forms to help their clients compile this information. Then, you should take inventory and determine the ownership and value of your estate. Next, you must designate beneficiaries of your estate's assets, estimate estate transfer costs, and formulate and implement your plan. The final step is ongoing: review your estate plan periodically—at least every three to five years, and revise it as circumstances dictate.

EXHIBIT 15.3   Data Needed for Estate Planning

The second step in developing an effective estate plan involves gathering comprehensive and accurate data about you and your family. The types of data required by estate planners include the following:

Personal data:	Names, addresses, phone numbers, birth dates, marital status, marital agreements, wills, trusts, custodianships, trust beneficiary, gifts or inheritances, Social Security numbers, and military service
Property:	Classification, title, indebtedness, date and manner of acquisition, value of marketable securities and their locations
Life insurance:	Name of insured, kinds of policies, amounts, insurance companies, agents' names and addresses
Health insurance:	Medical insurance company, policy numbers and benefits; disability income insurance
Business interest:	Name, address, ownership, desired survivorship control; names, addresses, and phone numbers of business attorney and accountant
Employee benefits:	Group insurance plans, pension benefits
Family income:	Income of client, spouse, income tax information
Family finances:	Budget information, investment preferences, capital needs, other objectives
Other data:	Retirement: planned retirement age, potential sources of retirement income; disability: required amount, sources; upon death: expected sources of income for heirs
Liabilities:	Listing of liabilities, creditors, amounts, whether insured or secured
Authorization for information:	Life insurance, executor

The objective of estate plans, of course, is to maximize the usefulness of people's assets during their lives and to achieve their personal objectives after their deaths. Once the plan has been implemented, however, you must reevaluate it regularly. An estate plan is good only so long as it fits the needs, desires, and circumstances of the parties involved. As these elements change, you must modify your estate plan. Key events that should trigger an estate plan review include the death or disability of a spouse or other family member, moving to another state, changing jobs, getting married or divorced, having children, acquiring new assets, and substantial changes in income, health, or living standards. Even if none of these occur, you should automatically review life insurance needs at least once every two years and perform a full estate audit at least once every three to five years (or whenever there has been a major change in the federal or state death-tax laws). Because of the general complexity of the laws relating to estate transfer, it is often necessary to secure the assistance of estate planners, life insurance professionals, Certified Financial Planners® (CFPs®), accountants, and attorneys in the planning and evaluation process. Given the individual nature of estate planning, we cannot include specific guidelines in this chapter. We provide a general framework for considering the key estate planning issues.

TEST YOURSELF

15-1 Discuss the importance and goals of estate planning. Explain why estates often break up. Distinguish between the *probate estate* and the *gross estate*.

15-2 Briefly describe the steps involved in the estate planning process.

15-2 THY WILL BE DONE . . .

will
A written and legally enforceable document expressing how a person's property should be distributed on his or her death.

Having an up-to-date will is an important aspect of personal financial planning and estate planning. Without it, you have no assurance that your assets will be divided according to your desires. A **will** is a written, legally enforceable expression or declaration of a person's wishes concerning the disposition of his or her property on death. Unfortunately, the majority of Americans do not have valid wills. The importance of a valid will becomes very apparent when we examine what happens when someone dies without one.

15-2a Absence of a Valid Will: Intestacy

intestacy
The situation that exists when a person dies without a valid will.

Suppose that Stanley Laughlin died without a valid will, a situation called **intestacy**. State intestacy laws "draw the will the decedent failed to make" in order to determine the disposition of the probate property of persons who have died intestate. These statutes set forth certain preferred classes of survivors. Generally, the decedent's spouse is favored, followed by the children and then other offspring. If the spouse and children or other offspring (e.g., grandchildren or great-grandchildren) survive, then they will divide the estate, and other relatives will receive nothing. If no spouse, children, or other offspring survive, then the deceased's parents, brothers, and sisters will receive a share of the estate.

Exhibit 15.4 gives an example of how a typical intestate estate is distributed. After paying debts and taxes and deducting state-defined family exemptions, that individual's separately owned property would be distributed in the order and percentages shown. Where property goes to the state because there is no will, the property is said to *escheat to the state*. However, if a person without relatives dies with a valid will, then his or her property will go to friends or to charity, as the will directs, rather than to the state.

EXHIBIT 15.4 | **Distribution of a Typical Intestate Estate**

If a person dies intestate (without a valid will), then the estate is distributed according to established state laws of intestate succession. This summary is based on Utah's probate code.

Survivors	Distribution*
Spouse and offspring—children, grandchildren, etc.—not of the surviving spouse	The first $75,000 plus 50 percent of the balance to the surviving spouse and the other 50 percent of the balance to the decedent spouse's offspring by right of representation (the spouse's share is reduced by any nonprobate transfers to him or her)
Spouse and no offspring or decedent's offspring all by the surviving spouse	100 percent to surviving spouse
No spouse but offspring	To decedent's descendants per capita at each generation
No spouse and no offspring, but parent(s)	To parent or parents equally
No spouse, no offspring, no parents, but generation	To parents' descendants per capita at each offspring of parents
No spouse, no offspring, no parents, and no offspring of parents, but grandparents or offspring of grandparents	Divided half to maternal grandparents (or their offspring, if neither survives) and half to paternal grandparents (or their offspring, if neither survives). If one side predeceased and there are no offspring, the other side takes all.
None of the above	The intestate estate passes to the state for the benefit of the state school fund.

*Because intestate laws vary from state to state, the actual distribution of assets may differ from that shown here; however, the Utah probate code is based on the uniform probate code that has been adopted, at least in part, by many states.

Aside from having lost control of the disposition of the property, the person who dies intestate also forfeits the privileges of naming a personal representative to guide the disposition of the estate, naming a guardian for persons and property, and specifying which beneficiaries would bear certain tax burdens. Estate planning and a valid will may also minimize the amount of estate shrinkage through transfer taxes. Having a valid will—regardless of the estate size—is a critical element in the personal financial planning process.

15-2b Preparing the Will

A will allows a person, called a **testator**, to direct the disposition of property at his or her death. The testator can change or revoke a will at any time; on the death of the testator, the will becomes operative.

Will preparation (or drafting) varies in difficulty and cost, depending on individual circumstances. In some cases, a two-page will costing $150 may be adequate; in others, a complex document costing $1,500 or more may be necessary. A will must effectively accomplish the objectives specified for distributing assets, while also taking into consideration income, gift, and estate tax laws. Will preparation also requires knowledge of corporate, trust, real estate, and securities laws. Note that a will, important as it is, may be ineffective or might misinterpret the testator's estate plan if it doesn't consider and coordinate assets passing outside its limits.

A properly prepared will should meet these three important requirements:

- Provide a plan for distributing the testator's assets according to his or her wishes, the beneficiaries' needs, and federal and state dispositive and tax laws
- Consider the changes in family circumstances that might occur after its execution
- Be concise and complete in describing the testator's desires

By following these general guidelines, the testator generally can develop a satisfactory will.

Will drafting, no matter how modest the estate size, should not be attempted by a layperson. The complexity and interrelationships of tax, property, domestic relations, and other laws make the homemade will a potentially dangerous document. Nowhere is the old adage, "He who serves as his own attorney has a fool for a client," more true. Few things may turn out more disastrous in the long run than the do-it-yourself will.

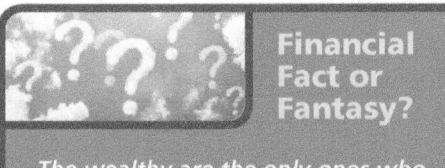

Financial Fact or Fantasy?

The wealthy are the only ones who need to make out wills. **Fantasy:** Nothing could be further from the truth! While the wealthy may have more motivation to do so, anyone who has accumulated an estate—no matter how small—should have a will drawn up that sets out how the estate is to be distributed to heirs and/or beneficiaries.

15-2c Common Features of the Will

There's no absolute format that must be followed when preparing a will, but most wills contain similar distinct sections. Exhibit 15.5, which presents the will of Glenn Alfred Brannon, includes generalized examples of each of these clauses. Refer to the exhibit as you read these descriptions of the clauses. *These clauses must be tailored to individual needs and circumstances by an attorney familiar with the testator's situation.*

LANE V. ERICKSON/SHUTTERSTOCK.COM

EXHIBIT 15.5   A Representative Will for Glenn Alfred Brannon

Glenn Alfred Brannon's will illustrates the eight distinct sections of most wills.

The Last Will and Testament of *Glenn Alfred Brannon*

Section 1 — Introductory Clause

I, Glenn Alfred Brannon, of the city of Chicago, state of Illinois, do, hereby make my last will and revoke all wills and codicils made prior to this will.

Section 2 — Direction of Payments

Article 1: Payment of Debts and Expenses

I direct payment out of my estate of all just debts and the expenses of my last illness and funeral.

Section 3 — Disposition of Property

Article 2: Disposition of Property

I give and bequeath to my wife, Karin Keyes Brannon, all my jewelry, automobiles, books, and photography equipment, as well as all other articles of personal and household use.

I give to the Chicago Historical Society the sum of $100,000.

All the rest, residue, and remainder of my estate, real and personal, wherever located, I give in equal one-half shares to my children, Bryant David and Casey Hanna, their heirs and assigns forever.

Section 4 — Appointment Clause

Article 3: Nomination of Executor and Guardian

I hereby nominate as the Executor of this Will my beloved wife, Karin Keyes Brannon, but if she is unable or unwilling to serve then I nominate my brother, Marshall Drake Brannon. In the event both persons named predecease me, or shall cease or fail to act, then I nominate as Executor in the place of said persons, the Midwestern Trust Bank of Chicago, Illinois.

If my wife does not survive me, I appoint my brother, Byron Franklin Brannon, Guardian of the person and property of my son, Bryant David, during his minority.

Section 5 — Tax Clause

Article 4: Payment of Taxes

I direct that there shall be paid out of my residuary estate (from that portion which does not qualify for the marital deduction) all estate, inheritance, and similar taxes imposed by a government in respect to property includable in my estate for tax purposes, whether the property passes under this will or otherwise.

Section 6 — Simultaneous Death Clause

Article 5: Simultaneous Death

If my wife and I shall die under such circumstances that there is not sufficient evidence to determine the order of our deaths, then it shall be presumed that she survived me. My estate shall be administered and distributed in all respects in accordance with such assumption.

Section 7 — Execution and Attestation Clause

In witness thereof, I have affixed my signature to this, my last will and testament, which consists of five (5) pages, each of which I have initialed, this 15th day of September, 2017.

Glenn Alfred Brannon

Section 8 — Witness Clause

Signed, sealed, and published by Glenn Alfred Brannon, the testator, as his last will, in the presence of us, who, at his request, and in the presence of each other, all being present at the same time, have written our names as witnesses.

(Note: Normally the witness signatures and addresses would follow this clause.)

- **Introductory clause:** An introductory clause, or preamble, normally states the testator's name and residence; this determines the county that will have legal jurisdiction and be considered the testator's domicile for tax purposes. The revocation statement nullifies old and forgotten wills and *codicils*—legally binding modifications of an existing will.
- **Direction of payments:** This clause directs the estate to make certain payments of expenses. As a general rule, however, the rights of creditors are protected by law, and therefore this clause might be left out of a professionally drafted will.

- Disposition of property: Glenn's will has three examples of clauses dealing with disposition of property:
    1. *Disposition of personal effects:* A testator may also make a separate detailed and specific list of personal property and carefully identify each item, and to whom it is to be given, as an informal guide to help the executor divide the property. (This list generally should not appear in the will itself, because it's likely to be changed frequently.)
    2. *Giving money to a specifically named party:* Be sure to use the correct legal title of a charity.
    3. *Distribution of residual assets after specific gifts have been made:* Bequests to close relatives (as defined in the statute) who die before the testator will go to the relative's heirs unless the will includes other directions. Bequests to nonrelatives who predecease the testator will go to the other residual beneficiaries.
- Appointment clause: Appointment clauses name the *executors* (the decedent's personal representatives who administer the estate), guardians for minor children, and trustees and their successors.
- Tax clause: In the absence of a specified provision in the will, the *apportionment statutes* of the testator's state will allocate the burden of taxes among the beneficiaries. The result may be an inappropriate and unintended reduction of certain beneficiaries' shares or other adverse estate tax effects. Earlier statutes tended to charge death taxes on the residual of the estate, but today the trend is toward statutes that charge each beneficiary based on his or her share of the taxable estate. Because the spouse's share and the portion going to a charity are deducted from the gross estate before arriving at the taxable estate, neither is charged with taxes.
- Simultaneous death clause: This clause describes what happens in the event of simultaneous death. The assumption that the spouse survives is used mainly to permit the marital deduction, which offers a tax advantage. Other types of clauses are similarly designed to avoid double probate of the same assets—duplication of administrative and probate costs. Such clauses require that the survivor live for a certain period, such as 30 or 60 days, to be a beneficiary under the will.
- Execution and attestation clause: Every will should be in writing and signed by the testator at its end as a precaution against fraud. Many attorneys suggest that the testator also initial each page after the last line or sign in a corner of each page.
- Witness clause: The final clause helps to affirm that the will in question is really that of the deceased. All states require two witnesses to the testator's signing of the will. Most states require witnesses to sign in the presence of one another after they witness the signing by the testator. Their addresses should be noted on the will. If the testator is unable to sign his or her name for any reason, most states allow the testator to make a mark and to have another person (properly witnessed) sign for him or her.

You Can Do It Now

Importance of Naming Alternative Beneficiaries

When you name beneficiaries on financial accounts or in your will, it's important to name alternate (contingent) beneficiaries as well. This will make clear what happens if your first choice beneficiary doesn't outlive you. See http://www.nolo.com/legal-encyclopedia/why-naming-alternate-beneficiaries-your-will-is-so-important.html for some useful tips on naming beneficiaries and related key issues. You can do it now.

15-2d Requirements of a Valid Will

To be valid, a will must be the product of a person with a sound mind, there must have been no *undue influence* (influence that would remove the testator's freedom of choice), the will itself must have been properly executed, and its execution must be free from fraud.

1. Mental capacity: You must be "of sound mind" to make a valid will. This means that you:

   a. Know what a will is and are aware that you are making and signing one.
   b. Understand your relationship with persons for whom you would normally provide, such as a spouse or children, and who would generally be expected to receive your estate (even though you might not be required to leave anything to them).
   c. Understand what you own.
   d. Are able to decide how to distribute your property.

   Generally, mental capacity is presumed. Setting aside a will requires clear and convincing proof of mental incapacity, and the burden of proof is on the person contesting the will.

2. Freedom of choice: When you prepare and execute your will, you must not be under the undue influence of another person. Threats, misrepresentations, inordinate flattery, or some physical or mental coercion employed to destroy the testator's freedom of choice are all types of undue influence.

3. Proper execution: To be considered properly executed, a will must meet the requirements of the state's wills act or its equivalent. It must also be demonstrable that it is, in fact, the will of the testator. Most states have statutes that spell out who may make a will (generally any person of sound mind, age 18 or older but 14 in Georgia and 16 in Louisiana), the form and execution the will must have (most states require a will to be in writing and to be signed by the testator at the logical end), and requirements for witnesses. Generally, a beneficiary should not serve as a witness. Although the will is otherwise valid, about 60 percent of the states penalize the beneficiary-witness in some way, such as limiting the beneficiary-witness' bequest to the intestate share that he or she would receive.

Most states now provide for a *self-proving will* that indicates in the attestation clause that the correct formalities for will execution were observed. A self-proving will eliminates the need, after the testator's death, to have the witnesses sign a declaration verifying their signatures and that of the testator. This saves time and money and often avoids lots of inconvenience to the executor.

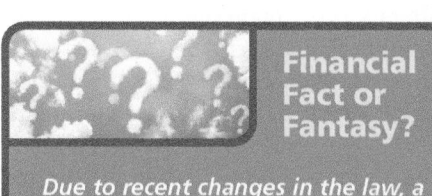

Financial Fact or Fantasy?

Due to recent changes in the law, a person no longer has to be mentally competent in order to draw up a valid will. **Fantasy:** A person still must be mentally competent in order to draw up (or have drawn up) a legally enforceable will.

15-2e Changing or Revoking the Will: Codicils

As life circumstances change, so should your will. Because a will is inoperative until the testator's death, the testator can change it at any time, so long as he or she has the mental capacity. In fact, periodic revisions should occur, especially on these events:

- His or her (or the beneficiaries') health or financial circumstances change significantly.
- Births, deaths, marriages, or divorces alter the operative circumstances.
- The testator moves to a state other than where the will was executed.
- An executor, trustee, or guardian can no longer serve.
- Substantial changes occur in the tax law.

Only the testator can change a will. By reviewing your will regularly, you can be sure that it accurately reflects your current wishes.

FINANCIAL PLANNING TIPS

Choosing a Guardian for Minor Children

Your estate plan will should make careful provisions for any minor children. One key issue is deciding who will take care of your children if you and your spouse die while they are minors. This requires you to choose a guardian or conservator for the children. Below are some important issues that should be considered in making the decision. The best approach is to prioritize these issues in light of what you think is most important and then put together a "pros and cons" list to come up with a list of good guardian prospects. Don't just line up one guardian; make sure you also have a backup plan.

• **Home.** Your children would probably be expected to move in with the guardian. So the size and location of the guardian's home are important considerations. You should be comfortable with both.

• **Religious, political, and moral beliefs.** You should make sure that you know and are comfortable with the potential guardian's religious, political, and moral beliefs. No guardian is likely to be a perfect match, but you should be comfortable with the extent and nature of any mismatches.

• **Parenting skills.** You want to make sure that you understand the potential guardian's parenting skills. What are the prospect's views on child discipline, education, sports, and other school activities? Does the prospect already have children? If so, will adding your children to the mix be too much for the potential guardian to handle?

• **Age of the potential guardian.** An older guardian may have better financial resources and more time to raise your children. On the other hand, an older prospect may not be up to date on current trends in education and parenting. You must also consider what would happen to your children if an older guardian became ill or died while the children were still minors. Alternatively, a younger guardian could be too involved in managing their own career and family to raise your children effectively.

• **Family situation.** It's important to think through the implications of the prospect's family situation. Is the potential guardian married with minor children, married with adult children, a single parent, married without children, or single without children? The potential guardian's family situation is closely related to how well your children would be raised.

• **Financial situation.** It's important to understand how well the potential guardian manages money, the stability of his or her job and that of the spouse, and whether the prospect's resources are sufficient to meet the costs of raising your children.

• **Willingness to serve as guardian.** It's important to ask and confirm explicitly that your prospect is willing to serve as your children's guardian. None of the above criteria matter if the prospect is simply unwilling to perform this critically important task for you. You need to have at least one discussion with this person about what the task would entail.

Source: Adapted from Julie Garber, "How to Choose a Guardian for Your Minor Children," http://wills.about.com/od/planningformino2/tp/howtochooseaguardianforminors.htm, accessed September 2015.

Changing the Will

codicil
A document that legally modifies a will without revoking it.

A **codicil** is a simple, often single-page document that provides a convenient legal means of making minor changes in a will. It reaffirms all the existing provisions in the will except the one to be changed, and it should be executed and witnessed in the same formal manner as a will.

When a will requires substantial changes, a new will is usually preferable to a codicil. In addition, if a gift in the original will is removed, it may be best to make a new will and destroy the old, even if substantial changes aren't required. This avoids offending the omitted beneficiary. Sometimes, however, the prior will should not be destroyed even after the new will has been made and signed. If the new will fails for some reason (because of the testator's mental incapacity, for example), then the prior will may qualify. Also, a prior will could help to prove a "continuity of testamentary purpose"—in other words, that the latest will (which may have provided a substantial gift to charity) continued an earlier intent and wasn't an afterthought or the result of an unduly influenced mind.

Revoking the Will

When he remarried, Stanley Laughlin might have wanted to change his will significantly. In that case, he'd have been better off revoking his old will and writing a new one, rather than doing a codicil. A will may be revoked either by the testator or automatically by the law. A testator can revoke a will in one of four ways:

1. Making a later will that expressly revokes prior wills
2. Making a codicil that expressly revokes all wills before the one being modified
3. Making a later will that is inconsistent with a former will
4. Physically mutilating, burning, tearing, or defacing the will with the intention of revoking it

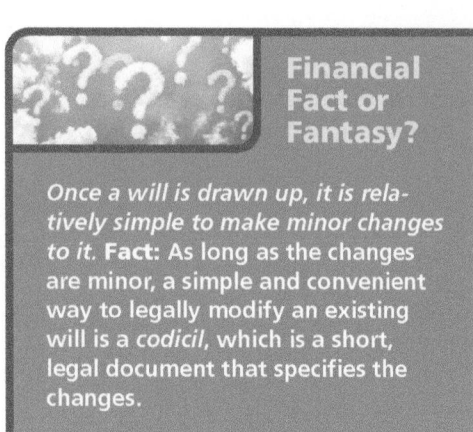

Financial Fact or Fantasy?

Once a will is drawn up, it is relatively simple to make minor changes to it. **Fact:** As long as the changes are minor, a simple and convenient way to legally modify an existing will is a *codicil*, which is a short, legal document that specifies the changes.

The law automatically modifies a will under certain circumstances, which vary from state to state but generally center on divorce, marriage, birth or adoption, and murder. In many states, if a testator becomes divorced after making a will, then all provisions in the will relating to the spouse automatically become ineffective. If a testator marries after making a will, the spouse receives that portion of the estate that would have been received had the testator died without a valid will. If a testator did not provide for a child born or adopted after the will was made (unless it appears that such lack of provision was intentional), then the child receives that share of the estate not passing to the testator's spouse that would have been given to him or her had the deceased not had a will. Finally, almost all states have some type of slayer's statute that forbids a person who commits murder from acquiring property as the result of the deed.

15-2f Safeguarding the Will

In most cases, you should keep your original will in a safe-deposit box, with copies in an accessible and safe place at home and with the attorney who drafted it. Although some authorities and many attorneys recommend leaving the original will with the attorney who drafted it, this may make it awkward for the executor to exercise the right to choose his or her own attorney. Further, it may discourage the estate owner from changing the will or engaging a new attorney, even if he or she moves out of the state in which the will is drawn.

Worksheet 15.1 contains an executor's checklist of documents and information that should be kept in a safe-deposit box. If each spouse has a separate safe-deposit box, then the couple may want to keep their wills in each other's boxes. Some states provide for *lodging* of the will, a mechanism for filing and safekeeping it in the office of the probate court (also called *orphan's* or *surrogate's court*). In those states, this procedure satisfies the need to safeguard the will.

15-2g Letter of Last Instructions

letter of last instructions
An informal memorandum that is separate from a will and contains suggestions or recommendations for carrying out a decedent's wishes.

People often have thoughts they want to convey and instructions they wish others to carry out that aren't appropriate to include in their wills. For example, Stanley Laughlin might have explained why he chose Brenda as his executor rather than choosing her brother. A **letter of last instructions** is the best way to communicate these suggestions or recommendations. It's typically an informal memorandum that is separate from the will. (This letter of last instructions should contain no bequests

This checklist itemizes the various documents and information that the executor may need to carry out the terms of the will effectively. These items should be kept in a safe-deposit box.

CHECKLIST FOR EXECUTORS

Name (Testator) _____   Date _____

_____ 1. Marriage certificates
         (including prior marriages)
_____ 2. Your will and trust agreements
_____ 3. Life insurance policies
         or certificates
_____ 4. Your Social Security number
_____ 5. Military discharge papers

_____ 6. Bonds, stocks, and securities
_____ 7. Real estate deeds
_____ 8. Business agreements
_____ 9. Automobile titles and
         insurance policies
_____ 10. Property insurance policies
_____ 11. Tax information
_____ 12. Letter of last instructions

List all checking and savings account numbers, bank addresses, and locations of safe-deposit boxes:

_____   _____   _____

List names, addresses, and phone numbers of property and life insurance agents:

_____   _____   _____

List names, addresses, and phone numbers of attorney and accountant:

_____   _____   _____

List names, addresses, and phone numbers of (current or last) employer. State retirement date, if applicable. Include employee benefits booklets:

_____   _____   _____

List all debts owed to *and* by you, including names and account numbers:

_____   _____   _____

List the names, addresses, telephone numbers, and birth dates of your children and other beneficiaries (including charities):

_____   _____   _____

Source: Based on Stephan R. Leimberg, Stephen N. Kandell, Ralph Gano Miller, Morey S. Rosenbloom, and Timothy C. Polacek, *The Tools & Techniques of Estate Planning,* 14th ed. (Upper Saddle River, NJ: Prentice Hall, 2006); Metropolitan Life Insurance Company, Taking Legal Action: The Executor's Checklist, http://www.metlife.com/assets/cao/mmi/life-advice/finances/taking-legal-action/executors-check-list.pdf, accessed August 2015.

because it has no legal standing.) It's best to make several copies of the letter, keeping one at home and the others with the estate's executor or attorney, who can deliver it to beneficiaries at the appropriate time.

A letter of last instructions might provide directions regarding such items as:

- Location of the will and other documents
- Funeral and burial instructions (often a will is not opened until after the funeral)
- Suggestions or recommendations as to the continuation, sale, or liquidation of a business (it's easier to freely suggest a course of action in such a letter than in

a will—especially since, in many states, the will is placed in a probate court file that is open to the public)

- Personal matters that the testator might prefer not be made public in the will, such as statements (e.g., comments about a spendthrift spouse or a reckless son) that might sound unkind or inconsiderate but would be valuable to the executor
- Legal and accounting services (executors are free, however, to choose their own counsel—not even testators can bind them in that selection)
- An explanation of the actions taken in the will, which may help avoid litigation (for instance, "I left only $5,000 to my son, James, because . . . " or "I made no provisions for my oldest daughter, Patricia, because . . . ")
- Suggestions on how to divide the personal property

15-2h Administration of an Estate

probate process
The court-supervised disposition of a decedent's estate.

When people die, they usually own property and owe debts. Often, they'll have claims (accounts receivable) against other persons. A process of liquidation called the probate process, similar to that used in dissolving a corporation, might be required. In this process, money owed the decedent is collected, creditors (including tax authorities) are satisfied, and what remains is distributed to the appropriate individuals and organizations. A local court generally supervises the probate process through a person designated as an executor in the decedent's will or, if the decedent died intestate (without a valid will), through a court-appointed administrator.

executor
The personal representative of an estate designated in the decedent's will.

An executor or administrator, sometimes called the *decedent's personal representative,* must collect the decedent's assets, pay debts or provide for payment of debts that aren't currently due, and distribute any remaining assets to the persons entitled to them by will or by the intestate succession law of the appropriate state. Estate administration is important for many reasons. The executor or administrator becomes the decedent's legal representative, taking care of such matters as collecting bank accounts and other contracts, releasing liability, and creating clear title to make real estate marketable. Because of the importance of the estate administration process, you should select executors who are not only familiar with the testator's affairs but also can effectively handle the responsibilities of being an executor.

administrator
The personal representative of the estate appointed by the court if the decedent died intestate.

15-2i Other Important Estate Planning Documents

In addition to your will and the letter of last instructions, you should have several other documents to protect yourself and your family: a durable power of attorney for financial matters, a living will, a durable power of attorney for health care, and an ethical will.

Power of Attorney

durable power of attorney for financial matters
Legal document that authorizes another person to take over someone's financial affairs and act on his or her behalf.

If you're incapacitated by a serious illness, a durable power of attorney for financial matters allows you to name as your agent the person you consider best suited to take over your financial affairs—perhaps a spouse or other relative. Although this is a simple document, it transfers enormous power to your designated appointee, so be sure you can rely on the person you choose to manage your finances responsibly. If you have investments, your power of attorney should include language that covers powers of investment on your behalf. To make it durable—that is, effective even when you are incapacitated—the document must clearly state that your agent's authority to act on your behalf will continue during your incapacity. Just labeling the document a "durable power" is probably insufficient and, without a statement giving your agent authority to act on your behalf while you are incapacitated, his or her authority may cease just when it is needed most. You may want to clear your power of attorney with the brokerage firms and mutual funds where you have accounts.

Living Will

living will
A document that precisely states the treatments a person wants if he or she becomes terminally ill.

Had Stanley Laughlin lingered in a coma, with little or no hope of recovery, his family could have faced difficult decisions regarding his medical care. He hadn't prepared a *living will* or *durable power of attorney for health care* to guide them as to his preferences. These documents address another important aspect of estate planning: determining the medical care you wish to receive, or *not* receive, if you become seriously ill and are unable to give informed consent. The living will states, precisely, the treatments that you want and to what degree you wish them continued. You must be as specific as possible so that your wishes are clear; otherwise, a living will might be put aside because it is too vague. For example, you should define what you mean by "terminal illness." Each state has its own form for a living will, and you can usually complete it yourself.

Durable Power of Attorney for Health Care

durable power of attorney for health care
A written power of attorney authorizing an individual to make health care decisions on behalf of the principal when the principal is unable to make such decisions. Also called *advanced directive for health care.*

Many experts prefer the durable power of attorney for health care, often called *advanced directives for health care,* instead of the living will; some advise having both to reinforce each other. Through the durable power of attorney for health care, you authorize an individual (your *agent*) to make health care decisions for you if you're unable to do so either temporarily or permanently. Unlike the living will, it applies in any case where you cannot communicate your wishes, not just when you're terminally ill. You can limit the scope of the durable power of attorney and include specific instructions for the desired level of medical treatment. You should spend some time making such decisions and then review your ideas and philosophy concerning these matters with your family and the person whom you designate as your agent. These documents, copies of which should be held by your designated agent and your doctor, can make it easier for your family to deal with these difficult issues.

Ethical Wills

ethical wills
A personal statement left for family, friends, and community that shares your values, blessings, life's lessons, and hopes and dreams for the future. Also called *legacy letter.*

Many people today also prepare ethical wills to leave family, friends, and community a personal statement of values, blessings, life's lessons, and hopes and dreams for the future. Sometimes called *legacy letters,* ethical wills are informal documents that are usually added to formal wills and read at the same time. An ethical will is not a legal document and consequently does not distribute your material wealth. An ethical will offers a way to share your morals, ethics, life experiences, family stories and history, and more with future generations. Ethical wills may be in the form of handwritten letters or essays, computer files, videos, or other electronic media.

Writing an ethical will can be a daunting project and may perhaps be even more difficult than writing a regular will. Experts suggest dividing it into smaller steps. You might prepare a list of questions about the impact of certain experiences on shaping your life and values, how you want to be remembered, the lessons that you wish to pass on to your family and friends, and any other important messages.

It's a good idea to review your ethical will with the lawyer who handles your estate planning. An ethical will that can be interpreted in a way that seems to contradict the intentions of the formal will could lead to a challenge of the formal will.

15-2j What about Joint Ownership?

right of survivorship
The right of surviving joint owners of property to receive title to the deceased joint owner's interest in the property.

Many people take title to property jointly, either through a *joint tenancy* or as *tenants by the entirety.* The two forms of joint ownership share the following characteristics:

1. The interest of a decedent passes directly to the surviving joint tenant(s)—that is, to the other joint owner(s)—by operation of the law and is free from the claims of the decedent's creditors, heirs, or personal representatives. This is called the right of survivorship.

joint tenancy
A type of ownership by two or more parties, with the survivor(s) continuing to hold all such property on the death of one or more of the owners.

tenancy by the entirety
A form of ownership by husband and wife, recognized in certain states, in which property automatically passes to the surviving spouse.

2. A joint tenancy may consist of any number of persons. The joint owners need not be related. A tenancy by the entirety, on the other hand, can exist only between husband and wife, and the right of survivorship is always included.

3. In joint tenancy, each joint tenant can unilaterally sever the tenancy. This is not the case with a tenancy by the entirety, which can be severed only by mutual agreement, divorce, or conveyance by both spouses to a third party. In some states, a tenancy by the entirety can exist only with respect to real property; other states don't recognize such tenancies at all.

4. The co-owners must have equal interests.

Joint tenancy with the right of survivorship, the more common form of joint ownership, offers a sense of family security, quick and easy transfer to the spouse at death, exemption of jointly owned property from the claims of the deceased's creditors, and avoidance of delays and publicity in the estate settlement process. The key disadvantage of joint tenancy with the right of survivorship is the inability to control jointly owned property by a will, so that the first joint owner to die cannot control the property's disposition and management on his or her death.

EXAMPLE: Disadvantage of Joint Tenancy with the Right of Survivorship

A father who has two unmarried children—a daughter with whom he has a good relationship and an estranged son—purchases property and places it in his own and his daughter's name as joint tenants. The father has a will that leaves everything he has to his daughter and specifically disinherits his son. The daughter has no estate planning documents. While traveling together, the father is killed outright in a car accident and the daughter is severely injured. She never fully recovers and dies two months later. At her death, intestate, her estate will likely pass to her brother. Had her father held the property in his name only, then he could have stipulated in his will a longer survivorship requirement (say, six months) with a provision that, in the event his daughter did not survive that period, there would be an alternative disposition (e.g., to a charity or to friends).

Creating a joint tenancy might also create a taxable gift. However, unless the donor's cumulative taxable gifts exceed $5,430,000 (the applicable exclusion amount for gifts in 2015), no gift tax must be paid. Yet a gift tax return must be filed if the annual exclusion amount is exceeded. Fortunately, because federal gift tax law doesn't tax most interspousal transfers, the problem won't arise on a federal level when creating a joint tenancy between a married couple (although some states may tax such gifts); the property is transferred to the surviving spouse tax free. Most couples don't have estates large enough to generate an estate tax and so, given that joint holding of major assets such as the home, autos, and bank accounts keeps things simple, joint tenancy is quite commonly used by married couples.

You should also be familiar with two other forms of ownership: *tenancy in common* and *community property*.

Tenancy in Common

tenancy in common
A form of co-ownership under which there is *no right of survivorship* and each co-owner can leave his or her share to whomever he or she desires.

A third common form of co-ownership is called tenancy in common. There is *no right of survivorship*, and each co-owner can leave his or her share to whomever he or she desires. Thus, the decedent owner's will controls the disposition of the decedent's partial interest in the asset. If the decedent dies without a will, then the intestate succession laws of the state where the property is located will determine who inherits the decedent's interest. Unlike joint tenancy, where all interests must be equal, tenancy in common interests can be unequal. Hence a property owned by three co-owners could be apportioned such that their respective shares are 50 percent, 30 percent, and 20 percent of the property.

Community Property

community property
All marital property co-owned equally by both spouses while living in a community property state.

Tenancy by the entirety is a special form of marital property co-ownership that is found only in common-law states (i.e., states that trace their property law to England). In contrast, community property is a form of marital property co-ownership that is based on Roman law and is found primarily in the Southwestern states that had a Spanish or French influence.

Community property is all property acquired by the effort of either or both spouses during marriage while they reside in a community property state. For example, wages and commissions earned and property acquired by either spouse while living in a community property state are automatically owned equally by both spouses, even if only one was directly involved in acquiring the additional wealth. Property acquired before marriage or by gift or inheritance can be maintained as the acquiring spouse's separate property.

By agreement, which typically must be in writing to be enforceable, the couple can change community property into separate property, and vice versa. Each spouse can leave his or her half of the community property to whomever he or she chooses, so there's *no right of survivorship* inherent in this form of ownership.

TEST YOURSELF

15-3 What is a *will*? Why is it important? Describe the consequences of dying *intestate*.

15-4 Describe the basic clauses normally included in a will and the requirements regarding who may make a valid will.

15-5 How can changes in the provisions of a will be made legally? In what four ways can a will be revoked?

15-6 Explain these terms: (a) *intestacy*, (b) *testator*, (c) *codicil*, (d) *letter of last instructions*.

15-7 What is meant by the *probate process*? Who is an *executor*, and what is the executor's role in estate settlement?

15-8 Describe briefly the importance of these documents in estate planning: (a) power of attorney, (b) living will, (c) durable power of attorney for health care, and (d) ethical will.

15-9 Define and differentiate between *joint tenancy* and *tenancy by the entirety*. Discuss the advantages and disadvantages of joint ownership. How does *tenancy in common* differ from joint tenancy?

15-10 What is the right of survivorship? What is community property, and how does it differ from joint tenancy with regard to the right of survivorship?

15-3 TRUSTS

trust
A legal relationship created when one party transfers property to a second party for the benefit of third parties.

Trusts facilitate the transfer of property and the income from that property to another party. Although trusts were once considered estate planning techniques only for the wealthy, today even those of modest means use trusts to their advantage in estate planning. This change is attributed to rising real estate values, bull financial markets, and marketing by estate planning attorneys. Also, as people live longer and are more likely to marry more than once, they need ways to protect and manage assets.

A **trust** is a legal relationship created when one party, the **grantor** (also called the *settlor, trustor,* or *creator*), transfers property to a second party, the trustee (an organization or individual), for the benefit of third parties, the **beneficiaries**, who may or may not include the grantor. The property placed in the trust is called *trust principal* or *res* (pronounced "race"). The trustee holds the legal title to the property in the trust and must use the property and any income it produces solely for the benefit of trust beneficiaries. The trust generally is created by a written document.

The grantor spells out the substantive provisions (such as how to allocate the property in the trust and how to distribute income) and certain administrative provisions. A trust may be *living* (funded during the grantor's life) or *testamentary* (created in a will and funded by the probate process). It may be *revocable* or *irrevocable.* The grantor can regain property placed into a *revocable* trust and alter or amend the terms of the trust. The grantor cannot recover property placed into an *irrevocable* trust during its term.

Let's now look at how trusts solve various estate planning problems.

15-3a Why Use a Trust?

Trusts are designed for various purposes. The most common motives are to manage and conserve property over a long period of time and in some cases, to achieve income and estate tax savings.

Managing and Conserving Property

Minors, spendthrifts, and those who are mentally incompetent need asset management services for obvious reasons. However, busy executives and others who can't or don't want to spend the countless hours necessary to handle large sums of money and other property often use trusts to relieve themselves of those burdens. The trustee assumes the responsibility for managing and conserving the property on behalf of the beneficiaries. In some cases, management by the trustee is held in reserve in case a healthy and vigorous individual is unexpectedly incapacitated and becomes unable or unwilling to manage his or her assets.

Income and Estate Tax Savings

Under certain circumstances, a grantor who is a high-bracket taxpayer can shift the burden of paying taxes on the income produced by securities, real estate, and other investments to a trust or to its beneficiary, both of whom may be subject to lower income tax rates than the grantor is. Impressive *estate tax* savings are possible because the appreciation in the value of property placed into such a trust can be entirely removed from the grantor's estate and possibly benefit several generations of family members without incurring adverse federal estate tax consequences.

15-3b Selecting a Trustee

Five qualities are essential in a trustee. He or she must:

1. Possess sound business knowledge and judgment
2. Have an intimate knowledge of the beneficiary's needs and financial situation
3. Be skilled in investment and trust management
4. Be available to beneficiaries (specifically, this means that the trustee should be young enough to survive the trust term)
5. Be able to make decisions impartially

A corporate trustee, such as a trust company or bank that has been authorized to perform trust duties, may be best able to meet these requirements. A corporate trustee is likely to have investment experience and will not impose the problems created by the death, disability, or absence of the trustee. Unlike a family member, a corporate trustee is impartial and obedient to the directions of the trust instrument. Such objectivity adds value if there are several beneficiaries. On the other hand, a corporate trustee may charge high fees or be overly conservative in investments, be impersonal, or lack familiarity with and understanding of family problems and needs. A compromise often involves appointing one or more individuals and a corporate trustee as co-trustees.

15-3c Common Types and Characteristics of Trusts

Although there are various types of trusts, the most common ones are the *living trust,* the *testamentary trust,* and the *irrevocable life insurance trust,* each of which is described in the following sections. Exhibit 15.6 describes seven other popular trusts.

Living Trusts

living (inter vivos) trust
A trust created and funded during the grantor's lifetime.

A **living (inter vivos) trust** is one created and funded during the grantor's lifetime. It can be either revocable or irrevocable and can last for a limited period or continue long after the grantor's death. Such trusts come in two forms, revocable and irrevocable.

revocable living trust
A trust in which the grantor reserves the right to revoke the trust and regain trust property. The grantor can serve as the initial trustee.

Revocable Living Trust. The grantor reserves the right to revoke the trust and regain trust property in a revocable living trust. For federal income tax purposes, grantors of these trusts are treated as owners of the property in the trust—in other words, just as if they held the property in their own names—and are therefore taxed on any income produced by the trust.

FINANCIAL PLANNING TIPS

Reasons to Set up a Trust

Trusts can be used to achieve various financial objectives. Consider the key reasons that they are so commonly used:

- **Avoid probate.** A trust may be used to avoid the probate process, which can be cost as much as 5 percent of the value of an estate. However, the costs of setting up a trust should be compared with the expected cost of probate. It's important to keep in mind that a probated will is a public document, whereas trusts offer more privacy.

- **Protection in old age and disability.** You can set up a trust, name yourself as beneficiary, and then name yourself and another person as trustees. If you become gravely ill or mentally incapacitated, the other trustee can manage your assets and distribute them as you direct in the trust arrangement.

- **Provide for minors and young adults.** You can use a trust to leave assets to minors and young adults. The trustee will manage the trust until the beneficiary reaches the age that you designate is old enough to handle the assets responsibly.

- **Avoid estate taxes.** You can set up a trust to transfer assets to an irrevocable trust to avoid estate taxes. These assets are not included in your gross estate. However, it's important that the grantor trust is not also a beneficiary or there will be limits on distributions to shield from taxation. The possibility of gift taxes must be considered. And planning must recognize that if a grantor transfers a life insurance policy to an irrevocable trust within three years before the grantor's death, the policy may well be included in the estate.

- **Reduce income taxes.** Certain types of trusts may be used to transfer income to heirs in a lower income tax bracket, which can reduce overall taxes.

- **Benefit charity.** You can transfer assets to a trust, receive income from the trust, and distribute the assets to a charity upon death. Thus, trusts may be used to provide income and estate tax benefits to support your favorite charity.

EXHIBIT 15.6 **Seven Popular Trusts**

Trusts shift assets (and thus appreciation) out of one's estate while retaining some say in the future use of the assets. The drawback is that trusts can be cumbersome and expensive to arrange and administer. Here are brief descriptions of seven popular trusts:

- **Credit shelter trust.** The most common tax-saving trust for estate planning; couples with combined assets worth more than the applicable exclusion amount (AEA) can gain full use of each partner's exclusion by having that amount placed in a bypass trust—that is, one that bypasses the surviving spouse's taxable estate. It's called a *credit shelter trust* because, when one spouse dies, the trust receives assets from the decedent's estate equal in value to the estate AEA. So if the first death occurred in the year 2015, then the trust would be funded with assets worth exactly $5,430,000. This trust does not qualify for the marital deduction, but no tax is due because the tentative tax is equal to the available *unified credit*. The surviving spouse is usually given the right to all the trust income and, in an emergency, even has access to the principal. When the surviving spouse dies, the credit shelter trust is not included in his or her estate regardless of the trust's value, so it avoids having to pay a tax at both deaths. With the addition of the "portability" provision (discussed in this chapter), the need and usefulness of the credit shelter trust is reduced.

- **Qualified terminable interest property (QTIP) trust.** Usually set up in addition to a *credit shelter trust* to ensure that money stays in the family; it receives some or all of the estate assets over the applicable exclusion amount ($5,430,000 in 2015). Assets left outright to a spouse who remarries could be claimed by the new spouse. The survivor receives all income from the property until death, when the assets go to the persons chosen by the first spouse to die. Estate taxes on QTIP trust assets can be delayed until the second spouse dies. It is also useful for couples with children from prior marriages because the QTIP property can be distributed to the children of the grantor-spouse only after the death of the surviving spouse; hence, the survivor benefits from the trust's income, and the deceased spouse's children are assured that they will receive the remainder of the QTIP trust eventually.

- **Special needs trust.** An irrevocable trust established for the benefit of a person with disabilities. It is designed to provide extra help and life enrichment without reducing state and federal government help to the beneficiary.

- **Minor's section 2503(c) trust.** Set up for a minor, often to receive tax-free gifts. However, assets must be distributed to the minor before he or she turns 21.

- **Crummey trust.** Named after the first person to successfully use this trust structure, this is used to make tax-free gifts up to the annual exclusion amounts to children. Unlike a *minor's section 2503(c) trust,* these funds need not be distributed before age 21. However, the beneficiary can withdraw the funds placed into the trust for a limited time (e.g., for up to 30 days), after which the right to make a withdrawal ceases.

- **Charitable lead (or income) trust.** Pays some of or all its income to a charity for a period of time, after which the property is distributed to noncharitable beneficiaries; the grantor receives an immediate income tax deduction based on expected future payout to charity. If the grantor's children are the so-called remaindermen of the trust, then the value of the gift for gift or estate tax purposes is greatly reduced because their possession and enjoyment of the trust assets is delayed until the charitable interest terminates.

- **Charitable remainder trust.** Similar to a *charitable lead trust,* except that income goes to taxable beneficiaries (e.g., the grantor or the grantor's children) and the principal goes to a charity when the trust ends; the grantor gets an immediate income tax deduction based upon the value of the remainder interest that is promised to the charity.

Revocable living trusts have three basic advantages.

1. Management continuity and income flow are ensured even after the grantor's death. No probate is necessary because the trust continues to operate after the death of the grantor just as it did while he or she was alive.
2. The trustee assumes the burdens of investment decisions and management responsibility. For example, an individual may want to control investment decisions and

management policy as long as he is alive and healthy but sets up a trust to provide backup help in case he becomes unable or unwilling to continue managing the assets.

3. The details of the estate plan and the value of assets placed into the trust do not become public knowledge, as they would during the probate process.

The principal disadvantages of these trusts include the fees charged by the trustee for managing the property placed into the trust and the legal fees charged for drafting the trust instruments.

Irrevocable Living Trust. Grantors who establish an irrevocable living trust relinquish title to the property that they place in it and give up the right to revoke or terminate the trust. (The grantor may retain the income from certain types of irrevocable trusts.) Such trusts have all the advantages of revocable trusts plus the potential for reducing taxes. Disadvantages of such a trust relate to the fees charged by trustees for managing assets placed into it, possible gift taxes on assets placed into it, in some cases the grantor's complete loss of the trust property and any income it may produce, and the grantor's forfeiture of the right to alter the terms of the trust as circumstances change.

Living Trusts and Pour-Over Wills. A will can be written so that it "pours over" designated assets into a previously established revocable or irrevocable living trust. The trust may also be named the beneficiary of the grantor's insurance policies. The pour-over will generally contains a provision passing the estate—after debts, expenses, taxes, and specific bequests—to an existing living trust. The pour-over will ensures that the property left out of the living trust, either inadvertently or deliberately, will make its way into the trust (that is, "pour over" into it). The trust contains provisions for administering and distributing those assets (together with insurance proceeds payable to the trust). Such an arrangement provides for easily coordinated and well-administered management of estate assets.

Testamentary Trust

A trust created by a decedent's will is called a testamentary trust. Such a trust comes into existence only after the will is probated. A court order directs the executor to transfer the property to the trustee in order to fund the trust. The revocable living trust and the testamentary trust can have pretty much the same terms and long-range functions—for example, providing for asset management for the trustor's family long after the trustor has died. Indeed, the two main differences are: (1) only the living trust provides for management when and if the trustor becomes incapacitated; and (2) the living trust is funded by transfers to the trustee by assignment or deed during the trustor's life, whereas the funding mechanism for the testamentary trust is a court order distributing the property to the trustee at the end of the probate process.

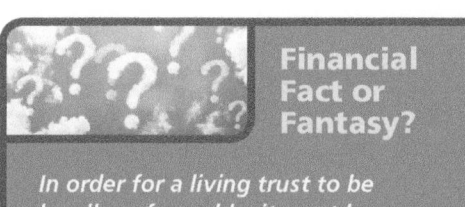

Financial Fact or Fantasy?

In order for a living trust to be legally enforceable, it must be irrevocable. **Fantasy:** A legally enforceable living trust, which is created and exists during the lifetime of the person(s) setting it up, may be either revocable (giving the grantor the right to revoke the trust) or irrevocable (beyond the reach of the grantor).

Irrevocable Life Insurance Trust

A wealthy individual might want to establish an irrevocable life insurance trust in which the major asset of the trust is life insurance on the grantor's life. To avoid having the proceeds of the policy included in the grantor's estate, the independent trustee usually acquires the policy on the life of the wealthy person and names the trustee as the beneficiary. The terms of the trust enable the trustee to use the proceeds to pay the grantor's estate taxes and to take care of the grantor's spouse and children, and probably eventually to distribute the remainder of the proceeds to the children or other beneficiaries as specified in the trust document.

irrevocable living trust
A trust in which the grantor gives up the right to revoke or terminate the trust.

pour-over will
A provision in a will that provides for the passing of the estate—after debts, expenses, taxes, and specific bequests—to an existing living trust.

testamentary trust
A trust created by a decedent's will and funded through the probate process.

irrevocable life insurance trust
An irrevocable trust in which the major asset is life insurance on the grantor's life.

15-4 FEDERAL UNIFIED TRANSFER TAXES

gift tax
A tax levied on the value of certain gifts made during the giver's lifetime.

estate tax
A tax levied on the value of property transferred at the owner's death.

applicable exclusion amount (AEA)
Credit given to each person that can be applied to the amount of federal estate tax owed by that person at death. In 2015 the AEA was $5,430,000 per spouse.

unified rate schedule
A graduated table of rates applied to all taxable transfers; used for *both* federal gift and estate tax purposes.

The federal unified transfer tax is a tax on the right to transfer property from one individual to another. The tax affects two types of transfers: transfer by gift, referred to as the gift tax; and transfers through the estate, referred to as the estate tax. The tax base for both transfers is the fair market value of the property that is transferred. The amount that can pass tax-free, called the applicable exclusion amount (AEA), is $5,430,000 in 2015. In addition, taxable gifts are reduced by an annual exclusion of $14,000 (adjusted for inflation over time) per donee. Thus, combined transfers of $5,430,000 plus the annual gift tax exclusion are not subject to the federal transfer tax. If the taxpayer is married, then the two married taxpayers each have an AEA of $5,430,000, or a total of $10,860,000, before any tax applies. The tax rate for gifts and estates is specified by the unified rate schedule (see the graduated table of rates in Exhibit 15.7). And if one of the spouses dies, then any unused applicable exclusion amount will carry over to the other spouse. This is referred to as the *portability* of the unified transfer tax credit. In order to benefit from the portability provision, it must be elected on the return of the first spouse to die, even if there is no taxable estate. Thus, if there is a chance that the combined estate will exceed $5,430,000, an estate tax return must be filed when the first spouse dies and the portability provision elected.

The applicable exclusion amount is high enough to remove transfer taxes from the concerns of estate planning for the middle-income taxpayer. For the upper-income taxpayer, however, the transfer tax is a major concern. For example, if a couple has a taxable estate of $20,000,000, then the transfer tax due is $3,656,000. That is a significant concern. The remainder of this section addresses these issues.

15-4a Gifts and Taxes

Gifting can be a good way to transfer property to a beneficiary before you die. However, very large transfers might be subject to gift taxes. The transfer tax applies to the fair market value of property transferred to a donee *less* the amount of compensation given to the donor. To determine the taxable gift, this amount is reduced by the annual exclusion ($14,000 in 2015). The annual exclusion applies to each donee who is given gifts. Thus, if the taxpayer gave three people $10,000 each, none of the transfers would be subject to the gift tax because the annual exclusion reduces each taxable gift to $0. The one requirement is that the transfer be a gift of *present interest*, not of a future interest. A typical example of the latter is the transfer of money to a trust with the provision that the trust's beneficiary must be 30 before withdrawing funds from the trust. This beneficiary has only a future interest, not a present interest.

There are two major exceptions to the present interest rule. Transfers to a minor trust—that is, a trust that allows no withdrawals until the minor is 21—qualify for the annual exclusions. A second exception is the Crummey provision, which

EXHIBIT 15.7 Federal Unified Transfer Tax Rates

This *unified rate schedule* defines the amount of federal gift and estate taxes that estates of various sizes would have to pay. It incorporates the rates passed in the *American Taxpayer Relief Act of 2012*, signed into law in 2013. Estates and gifts under the exclusion amount pay no federal tax. The estate exclusion amount increased annually from $2,000,000 in 2006 to $5,430,000 in 2015 (see Exhibit 15.8). From 2009 to 2015, the top tax rates decreased from 45% to 40%.

TAXABLE ESTATE VALUE		TENTATIVE TAX		
More Than	**But Not More Than**	**Base Amount**	**+ Percent**	**On Excess Over**
$ 0	$ 10,000	$ 0	18%	0
10,000	20,000	1,800	20%	$ 10,000
20,000	40,000	3,800	22	20,000
40,000	60,000	8,200	24	40,000
60,000	80,000	13,000	26	60,000
80,000	100,000	18,200	28	80,000
100,000	150,000	23,800	30	100,000
150,000	250,000	38,800	32	150,000
250,000	500,000	70,800	34	250,000
500,000	750,000	155,800	37	500,000
750,000	1,000,000	248,300	39	750,000
1,000,000		345,800	40	1,000,000

Source: Internal Revenue Code, Section 2001.

provides for withdrawal rights to the beneficiary for a specified period (e.g., 30 days). If the beneficiary does not ask for a withdrawal in that time period, the property must remain in the trust until it can be distributed according to the trust terms. Thus, with the Crummey withdrawal rights, transfers to the trust are considered a present interest and will qualify for the annual exclusion interest to the extent of the withdrawal right.

An essential first step to estate planning is making annual gifts to your potential heirs. Giving gifts reduce the taxable estate in two ways. First, any future appreciation of the gifted property is excluded from the estate because the decedent does not own the property on the date of death. Second, if the gift is so large that taxes are due, the money used to pay the tax is also removed from the estate. (There is an exception for gift taxes paid within three years of death.)

Another consideration when making gifts is their impact on the income taxes of the donee. If the gifted property is to be sold by the donee for a gain, it should be noted that property received by gift has a tax basis equal to its basis in the hands of the donor (i.e., a carryover basis). Property that is inherited has a basis equal to the fair market value on the date of death. For example, assume that a taxpayer owns a beach house that was purchased for $100,000 in 1990 and now has a value of $600,000. If the beach house is gifted, the basis to the donee will be $100,000. If passed through the estate, the basis to the heir will be $600,000. So long as the property is not sold or depreciated, the basis really does not matter. However, if it is sold, then there is a difference in income tax of $100,000 (20 percent capital gains rate multiplied by the difference in basis, which is $500,000) between receiving the property by gift rather than through the estate.

On December 17, 2010, the Tax Relief, Unemployment Insurance Reauthorization and Job Creation Act of 2010 was signed into law. The major features of the transfer tax provisions were to reinstate the transfer tax on estates, change the applicable exclusion amount for both gift transfers and estate transfers, and add the portability of the unified transfer tax credit. This table shows the recent history of the applicable exclusion amounts.

Year	Unified Tax Credit—Estates	Applicable Exclusion Amount—Estates	Unified Tax Credit—Gifts	Applicable Exclusion Amount—Gifts
2006	$780,800	$2,000,000	$345,800	$1,000,000
2007	$780,800	$2,000,000	$345,800	$1,000,000
2008	$780,800	$2,000,000	$345,800	$1,000,000
2009	$1,455,800	$3,500,000	$345,800	$1,000,000
2010	Estate tax repealed for 2010		$330,800	$1,000,000
2011	$1,730,800	$5,000,000	$1,730,800	$5,000,000
2012	$1,772,800	$5,120,000	$1,772,800	$5,120,000
2013	$2,045,800	$5,250,000	$2,045,800	$5,250,000
2014	$2,081,800	$5,340,000	$2,081,800	$5,340,000
2015	$2,117,800	$5,430,000	$2,117,800	$5,430,000

15-4b Is It Taxable?

annual exclusions
Under the federal gift tax law, the amount that can be given each year without being subject to gift tax—for example, $14,000 in 2015. This amount is indexed for inflation over time.

gift splitting
A method of reducing gift taxes; a gift given by one spouse, with the consent of the other spouse, can be treated as if each had given one-half of it.

Not everything that's transferred by an individual is subject to a gift tax. **Annual exclusions**, **gift splitting**, charitable deductions, and marital deductions are all means of reducing the total amount for tax purposes.

- Annual exclusions: The gift tax law allows a person to give gifts up to a specified annual amount per calendar year—$14,000 in 2015—to any number of recipients. For example, a person could give gifts of $14,000 each to 30 individuals, for a total of $420,000, without using up any of the recipient's AEA (and, of course, without paying any gift tax). Furthermore, the ability to give tax-free gifts of $14,000 per recipient renews annually. The amount is indexed for inflation over time but rounded down to the nearest thousand. This annual exclusion applies only for gifts given with "no strings attached" and generally only if the recipient is given a "present interest" in the gift, which was discussed previously.
- Gift splitting: Recall that donors may make gifts up to the annual exclusion ($14,000 in 2015) with no tax impact. Thus, a husband and wife may give a total of $28,000 to a single donee and incur no tax. Sometimes it is convenient for only one of the spouses to transfer property to a single donee. If the amount is over the annual exclusion, it may be taxable. In such cases, the donor's spouse may elect to split the donation of a gift. Thus, two annual exclusions apply and each spouse's unified transfer tax credit will apply to the transfer. Because this election by the spouse must be reported, gift tax returns must be filed.
- Charitable deductions: Many estate plans include a provision for charitable contributions. Transfers to charities are not subject to tax because of the deduction for charitable contributions. Once the decision has been made to make charitable contributions, the issue becomes whether to give now (during life) or later (at death) through bequests from the estate. There are many advantages to giving now rather than later. A lifetime gift results in an income tax deduction (namely, a tax savings of 39.6 percent at the top 2015 rate). In addition, such

gifts are removed from the estate and so there is an estate tax saving (40 percent top 2015 rate). Finally, a lifetime gift allows the donor to observe the effect of the gift on the charitable organization and to receive psychic income in the form of gratitude or other recognition. Another consideration is that you should not give so much of your wealth to charity that you no longer have enough to live on. You must provide for yourself and your family before charity. However, many large estates are able and desire to give lifetime charitable gifts.

- Marital deductions: Federal law permits an unlimited deduction for gift tax and estate tax purposes on property given or left to a spouse who is a U.S. citizen. The only qualification is that the property interest must be a nonterminable interest. Thus, an interest that terminates at the death of the spouse is not subject to the marital deduction. Special rules apply for transfers to a spouse who is not a U.S. citizen. These special rules prevent tax avoidance if the noncitizen spouse returns to his or her native country, where the bequest would then escape taxation in the United States.

15-4c Reasons for Making Lifetime Gifts

Estate planners recommend gift giving for the following tax-related reasons:

- Gift tax annual exclusion: As noted earlier, a single individual can give any number of donees up to $14,000 each year, with no tax costs to either the donees or the donor.
- Gift tax exclusion escapes estate tax: Property that qualifies for the annual exclusion is not taxable and thus is free from gift and estate taxes. Estate tax savings from this exclusion can be significant. Regardless of a gift's size—and even if it's made within three years of the donor's death—it's typically not treated as part of the donor's gross estate. However, the taxable portion of lifetime gifts (i.e., the amount above the annual exclusion) are called *adjusted taxable gifts* and these may push the donor's estate into a higher tax bracket.
- Appreciation in value: Generally, a gift's increase in value after it was given is excluded from the donor's estate.

> **EXAMPLE: Excluding Appreciated Value from an Estate**
>
> Suppose that Emilio gives his son, Diego, a gift of stock worth $35,000 in 2015. When Emilio dies two years later, the stock is worth $60,000. The amount subject to transfer taxes in 2015 will be $21,000 ($35,000 – $14,000)—the adjusted taxable gift amount. None of the subsequent appreciation is subject to the gift or estate tax.

- Credit limit: Because of the credit that's used to offset otherwise taxable gifts, gift taxes don't have to be paid on cumulative lifetime gifts up to the applicable gift exclusion amount of $5,430,000. To the extent that the credit is used against lifetime gift taxes, it's not available to offset estate taxes.
- Impact of marital deduction: The transfer tax marital deduction allows one spouse to give the other spouse an unlimited amount of property entirely transfer tax free without reducing the donor-spouse's AEA (i.e., the amount that can be transferred to others tax free). As mentioned before, the unlimited marital deduction is available only if the recipient spouse is a U.S. citizen. Since it is a deduction, a gift tax return is required to be filed.

15-14 What is a gift, and when is a gift made? Describe the following terms as they relate to federal gift taxes: (a) *annual exclusion*, (b) *gift splitting*, (c) *charitable deduction*, and (d) *marital deduction*.

15-15 Discuss the reasons estate planners cite for making lifetime gifts. How can gift giving be used to reduce estate shrinkage?

15-5 CALCULATING ESTATE TAXES

LG5 Estate taxes may be generated when property is transferred at the time of death, so one goal of effective estate planning is to minimize the amount of estate taxes paid. The federal estate tax is levied on the transfer of property at death. The tax base is measured by the fair market value of the property that the deceased transfers (or is deemed to transfer) to others. The phrase "deemed to transfer" is important because the estate tax applies not only to transfers that a deceased actually makes at death but also to certain transfers made during the person's lifetime. In other words, to thwart tax-avoidance schemes, the estate tax is imposed on certain lifetime gifts that essentially are the same as dispositions of property made at death.

Although most gifts made during one's life are not part of the decedent's gross estate, there are some exceptions. A major exception pertains to life insurance if the owner is also the insured. If the owner-insured gives away the policy within three years of his or her death, the proceeds will be included in the insured's gross estate.

TERRY VINE/GETTY IMAGES.

> **EXAMPLE: Use of Life Insurance in an Estate**
>
> In 2015, two years before his death, Neil gave his son, Simon, a $1 million term insurance policy on Neil's life. At the time of the gift, Neil was in good health, and the value of the term insurance policy for gift tax purposes was clearly less than the $14,000 annual exclusion amount. Therefore, Neil did not have to file a gift tax return. But because Neil died within three years of gifting the life insurance policy, the $1 million proceeds amount is included in his gross estate for estate tax purposes. Had Neil outlived the transfer by more than three years, the proceeds would not have been included in his gross estate.

15-5a Computing the Federal Estate Tax

The computation of federal estate taxes involves six steps:

1. Determine the *gross estate*, the fair market value of all property in which the decedent had an interest and that is required to be included in the estate.
2. Find the *adjusted gross estate* by subtracting from the gross estate any allowable funeral and administrative expenses, debts, and other expenses incurred during administration.

3. Calculate the *taxable estate* by subtracting any allowable marital deduction or charitable deduction from the adjusted gross estate.

4. Compute the *estate tax base*. After determining the value of the taxable estate, any "adjusted taxable gifts" (i.e., gifts above the annual exclusion) made after 1976 are added to the taxable estate. The unified tax rate schedule, shown in Exhibit 15.7, is applied to determine a *tentative tax* on the estate tax base.

5. After finding the tentative tax, subtract both the gift taxes the decedent paid on the adjusted taxable gifts and the unified tax credit. The result is total death taxes.

6. Determine the *federal estate tax due*. Some estates will qualify for additional credits—for example, the foreign tax credit (where different portions of the estate are taxed in the United States and in another country) and the prior transfer tax credit (where the decedent's estate includes property inherited from someone who died within the previous 10 years and the earlier estate had to pay an estate tax). These credits are fairly rare, but when available they result in a dollar-for-dollar reduction of the tax. After reducing the total death taxes by any eligible credits, the federal estate tax due is payable by the decedent's executor, generally within nine months of the decedent's death.

unified tax credit
The credit that can be applied against the *tentative tax on estate tax base*.

You can use Worksheet 15.2 to estimate federal estate taxes. The worksheet depicts the computations for a hypothetical situation involving a death in 2015, when the $5,430,000 estate AEA applies. Note that the AEA is not subtracted from the gross estate. The worksheet is useful in following the flow of dollars from the gross estate to the federal estate tax due.

Exhibit 15.8 shows the applicable exclusion amount for estates and the unified credit—the credit that's applied against the tentative tax. The worksheet factors the unified credit for the year 2015 into the calculation on line 9b. The $2,117,800 shown on that line is equal to the tentative tax on an estate tax base of $5,430,000, the AEA. Note the taxpayer is a surviving spouse and his wife elected the portability provision. Thus, the amount of unified transfer tax (UTT) credit is $4,235,600 less the credit used by his wife, the first to die spouse. If the tentative tax shown on line 8 is less than the unified credit available for the decedent's year of death, then no federal estate tax is due.

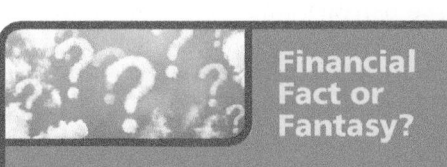

TEST YOURSELF

15-16 Explain the general nature of the federal estate tax. How does the unified tax credit affect the amount of estate tax owed? What is the portability concept?

15-17 Explain the general procedure used to calculate the federal estate tax due.

15-6 ESTATE PLANNING TECHNIQUES

LG6

Estate planning is the process of developing a plan to administer and distribute your estate after your death, in a manner consistent with your wishes and the needs of your survivors, while minimizing taxes. The primary taxes to consider are the income tax, the gift tax, and the estate tax. In developing a plan to distribute your estate, these three taxes must be taken into account. For 2015, the applicable exemption amount is $5,430,000, with a portability feature that allows

This worksheet is useful in determining federal estate tax due. Note that taxes are payable at the marginal tax rate applicable to the estate tax base (line 7), which is the amount that exists before the tax-free exemption is factored in by application of the unified credit.

COMPUTING FEDERAL ESTATE TAX DUE

Name _Peyton Naylor_   Date _9/5/2015_

Line	Computation	Item	Amount	Total Amount
1		*Gross estate*		$ _7,850,000_
2	Subtract sum of:	(a) Funeral expenses	$ _6,800_	
		(b) Administrative expenses	_75,000_	
		(c) Debts	_125,000_	
		(d) Other expenses	_0_	
		Total		(_206,800_)
3	Result:	*Adjusted gross estate*		$ _7,643,200_
4	Subtract sum of:	(a) Marital deduction	_0_	
		(b) Charitable deduction	_180,000_	
		Total		(_180,000_)
5	Result:	*Taxable estate*		$ _7,463,200_
6	Add:	*Adjusted taxable gifts (post-1976)*		$ _0_
7	Result:	*Estate tax base*		$ _7,463,200_
8	Compute:	*Tentative tax on estate tax base*[a]		$ _2,931,080_
9	Subtract sum of:	(a) Gift tax payable on post-1976 gifts	$ _0_	
		(b) Unified tax credit[b]	_2,117,800_	
		Total		($ _2,117,800_)
10	Result:	*Total estate taxes*[c]		_813,280_
10	Subtract:	Other credits		($ _0_)
12	Result:	*Federal estate tax due*		$ _813,280_

[a]Use Exhibit 15.7 to calculate the tentative tax.

[b]Use Exhibit 15.8 to determine the appropriate unified credit.

[c]Note that the amount shown on line 7 is a significant number, because most states use the same estate tax base as is used for the federal tax.

the surviving spouse to use the unified transfer tax credit not used by the deceased spouse. For a married couple, then, there is no transfer tax until $10,860,000 is transferred. In the balance of this section we discuss common estate planning techniques.

15-6a Gift Giving Program

With the annual exclusion of $14,000 and the ability to split gifts, a married couple may transfer $28,000 per year per donee. Giving gifts reduces the transfer tax and gives added joy to the donor. When selecting the property to give, the impact on income tax must be considered. Recall that the basis of gifted property is generally the cost of the property to the donor and that the basis of inherited property is the fair market value reported on the estate tax return. So if the property is expected to be sold, then there will be a higher gain for income tax purposes if the property is gifted (though only at the capital gains tax rate, at a top rate of 20 percent in 2015) than if the property is transferred at death through the estate. If the transfer will result in transfer taxes being paid, then the 40 percent transfer tax will probably be greater than the associated income tax relating to the property. In this case, it would be better to gift the property early, when the value is relatively low, even though the donee will have to pay tax on the gain when the property is sold.

15-6b Use of the Unified Transfer Tax Credit

Prior to 2011, the unified transfer tax (UTT) credit was unique to the individual. Thus, if an individual did not use it, then he or she would lose it. Beginning in 2011, Congress added portability to the credit, which allows the surviving spouse to use the unused deceased spouse's UTT credit. Because it is not certain that the portability feature will remain in the tax law, it is appropriate to take steps to ensure that the combination of the marital deduction and the UTT credit does not result in losing part of the credit. The common tools used are the "credit shelter trust" (also referred to as the *bypass trust*) and the QTIP trust, discussed earlier in this chapter. Property equal in value to the unused applicable exemption amount will be transferred at death to the credit shelter trust, resulting in tax for the first to die. The related unused UTT credit will reduce the estate tax to zero. The property in the credit shelter trust will bypass the surviving spouse's estate. The balance of the estate will be transferred either directly to the surviving spouse or to the QTIP and thereby qualify for the marital deduction resulting in no tax for the first to die. Thus, the full UTT credit has been used by both spouses, and no credit has been lost.

15-6c Life Insurance as an Estate Planning Tool

Life insurance can be a valuable component of your estate plan. A policy can be purchased for an annual premium of from 3 percent to 6 percent of the face (death) value of the policy. If someone other than the insured owns the policy, then the proceeds of such insurance can pass to the decedent's beneficiaries free of income tax, estate tax, inheritance tax, and probate costs. For example, the trustee of an irrevocable life insurance trust applies for and owns the policy. After the insured's death, the trustee uses the insurance proceeds for the benefit of the surviving family members, who in turn might use them to pay death taxes, debts, administrative expenses, or other family expenses such as college costs, mortgage balances, and other major expenditures. What's more, whole life and universal life insurance policies are an attractive form of loan collateral. As we pointed out in Chapters 7 and 8, some lending institutions and other creditors require borrowers to obtain enough life insurance to repay them if borrowers die before fully repaying their loans.

15-6d Charitable Contributions

If the taxpayer desires to make charitable contributions, the question to answer is whether the contribution should be made now (during life) or later (at death). If made now, the taxpayer gets an income tax deduction and the property is out of the estate. The added benefit of the income tax savings tips the charitable contribution timing question in favor of giving during life. Of course, if the funds are needed to support the taxpayer, then no contribution should be made until death. Transfers to charity at death are appropriate in such cases.

15-6e Trusts

One of the many uses of trusts is to split the income among family members and thereby reduce total income tax paid. However, the trust income tax rates are extremely compressed: in 2015, the top rate of 39.6 percent applied to income over $12,300. The trust income tax may be avoided by transferring income property to the beneficiaries. If the beneficiary is a minor, however, such income may be taxed at his or her parents' tax rate.

15-6f Valuation Issues

The tax base for the transfer tax is fair market value. When the estate includes closely held stocks, real estate, or large blocks of listed securities, there are discounts that apply to the value of the property. The following are the most used discounts.

- Minority interest. If the ownership of a closely held company is less than 50 percent of the outstanding stock, then it is a minority interest. Discounts of 25 percent to 30 percent are common. Thus, if the stock is considered to have a value of $100 per share, then a 30 percent minority interest discount will reduce the fair market value for inclusion in the taxable estate to $70 per share.
- Marketability discount. If a large amount of real estate is for sale in one market or area, the value will be reduced solely because of marketability factors. These discounts range from 10 percent to 30 percent.
- Blockage discounts. If a large block of stock of a listed company is sold, the market will react to reduce the price of the stock. For a publicly held company, 1 percent of the stock is a large enough block to reduce the value. So if that amount of stock is in the gross estate, then the value subject to the tax will be reduced by the blockage discount. Discounts of 5 percent to 15 percent are common.

15-6g Future of Estate Taxes

The Congress is always discussing changes to the income and transfer tax. Currently there are proposed laws to eliminate the estate tax, but keep the gift tax. The gift tax is seen as necessary to prevent splitting income among the family in order to minimize the family's income tax. There are proposals to reduce the AEA amount from the 2015 amount of $5,430,000 to $3,500,000. It is not known if any of these proposals will actually be enacted. Thus, when planning an estate, focus on flexibility so you can react when or if the law is changed. Obviously, the tax impact of your estate plan should be reviewed annually to insure the outcome is as you planned.

The transfer tax is a major concern to taxpayers with wealth over $10,680,000 but much less so for less wealthy taxpayers. However, estate planning is a concern to all, and the general issues discussed in this chapter apply to all estates, large and small.

TEST YOURSELF

15-18   Describe and discuss each of the techniques used in estate planning.

Planning Over a Lifetime: *Estate Planning*

Here are some key considerations for estate planning in each stage of the life cycle.

Independent Lifestyle (20s)	Family and Career Development (30s–40s)	Mature Lifestyle (50–60s)	Retirement (65+)
✓ While it might seem unnecessary when you're getting started, a will should be made.	✓ Update your will as your circumstances change. Specify who will care for your children if you and your spouse die prematurely.	✓ Start estate planning and consider trust arrangements for children.	✓ Establish a well-thought out estate plan. Update your will to be as specific as possible about the distribution of all property, especially personal property.
✓ A living will is a good idea as well as a durable power of attorney for health care. Make them available to your family and physicians.	✓ Make sure your will is available to family members.	✓ Revise your will as your children become adults and finish school.	✓ Consider explaining to your children what they will inherit and your rationale.
	✓ Prepare a durable power of attorney for financial matters.	✓ Review and revise as needed your durable power of attorney for financial matters and health care at least every few years.	✓ Make sure that a comprehensive list of your financial accounts is available to your spouse and family.
			✓ You and your spouse should make and fund your funeral arrangements to spare your family this burden.

Financial Impact of Personal Choices
The (Un)intended Effects of Corbin's Beneficiary Designations

Corbin Brenner died suddenly in 2015. He had amassed a significant estate and had an attorney write a will that would distribute his assets among his wife, Vanessa, and two grown daughters, Lydia and Gina, as he wished. Apart from his will, he had heard that it made sense to name beneficiaries on his investment accounts so those assets would go directly to his family and bypass the sometimes long and costly probate process. Corbin had been previously married to Patricia Brenner, who survived him.

Corbin named his wife, Vanessa, as the beneficiary to most of his investment accounts and designated one account to his daughter, Lydia, and one account to his daughter, Gina. He intended for his daughters to get equal amounts. While trying to be careful, Corbin forgot to change the beneficiary on one investment account from Patricia, his prior wife, to his current wife, Vanessa. That account was worth $50,000 at his death.

So what was the effect of Corbin's beneficiary designations? His wife Vanessa received most of the investment accounts as he intended. However, the $50,000 account that had not been updated to name Vanessa as the beneficiary went to Corbin's prior wife, Patricia, which is not what he intended. While it seemed fair to Corbin to designate one investment account to each of his daughters and the accounts had the same initial values, the accounts had grown to different values by the time of his death. Lydia's account had grown to $100,000 while Gina's account had grown to $200,000. Corbin had intended that his daughters receive equal amounts but they did not. Corbin could have achieved his objective by naming *both* of his daughters as beneficiaries on *both* of the accounts. And had Corbin reviewed his beneficiary designations at least once a year, he may well have discovered that he'd forgotten to make an important change.

Summary

LG1 **Describe the role of estate planning in personal financial planning, and identify the seven steps involved in the process, p. 599**
Estate planning involves accumulating, preserving, and distributing an estate in order to most effectively achieve an estate owner's personal goals. The seven major steps to estate planning are (1) assess the family situation and set estate planning goals, (2) gather comprehensive and accurate data, (3) list all assets and determine estate value, (4) designate beneficiaries of the estate's assets, (5) estimate estate transfer costs, (6) formulate and implement a plan, and (7) review the plan periodically and revise it as necessary.

LG2 **Recognize the importance of preparing a will and other documents to protect you and your estate, p. 606**
A person who dies without a valid will forfeits important privileges, including the right to decide how property will be distributed at death and the opportunity to select who will administer the estate and bear the burden of estate taxes and

administrative expenses. The will should provide an explicit and unambiguous expression of the testator's wishes, be flexible enough to encompass possible changes in family circumstances, and give proper regard to minimizing income, gift, and estate taxes. A will is valid only if properly executed by a person of sound mind. Once drawn up, wills can be changed by codicil or be fully revoked. The executor, named in the will, is responsible for collecting the decedent's assets, paying his or her debts and taxes, and distributing any remaining assets to the beneficiaries in the prescribed fashion. In addition to the will, other important estate planning documents include the letter of last instructions, power of attorney, living will, durable power of attorney for health care, and an ethical will.

LG3 **Explain how trusts are used in estate planning, p. 617**
The trust relationship arises when one party, the *grantor* (also called the *trustor* or *settlor*), transfers property to a second party, the *trustee*, for the benefit of a third party, the *beneficiary*. There

are several types of trusts, but each is designed primarily for one or both of these reasons: to manage and conserve property over a long period, and to save income and estate taxes.

LG4 Determine whether a gift will be taxable and use planned gifts to reduce estate taxes, p. 622
Gifts of cash, financial assets, and personal or real property made during the donor's lifetime are subject to federal taxes. A gift, up to the annual exclusion amount, given to each recipient is excluded from the donor's gift tax calculation. Generally, donations to qualified charities and gifts between spouses are also excluded from the gift tax.

LG5 Calculate federal taxes due on an estate, p. 626
Federal estate taxes are a levy on the transfer of assets at death. They are unified (coordinated) with the gift tax—which imposes a graduated tax on the transfer of property during one's lifetime—so that the rates and credits are the same for both. Once federal estate taxes are computed and certain credits are allowed, the resulting amount is payable in full, generally within nine months of the decedent's death.

LG6 Use effective estate planning techniques to minimize estate taxes, p. 627
Well-defined estate plans seek to minimize income, gift, and estate taxes. Common estate planning techniques include gift giving, use of the unified transfer tax (UTT) credit, charitable contributions, life insurance, and trusts that split income among family members.

Key Terms

Answers to Test Yourself

You can find answers to these questions on this book's companion website. Look for it at *www.cengagebrain.com*. Search for this book by its title, and then add it to your dashboard.

LG1, p. 599

1. **Estate planning objectives.** Generate a list of estate planning objectives that apply to your personal family situation. Be sure to consider the size of your potential estate as well as people planning and asset planning. Estate planning is not just about taxes.

LG2, p. 606

2. **Importance of writing a will.** Darrell and Karla Boykin are in their mid-30s and have two children, ages 8 and 5. They have combined annual income of $95,000 and own a house in joint tenancy with a market value of $310,000, on which they have a mortgage of $250,000. Darrell has $100,000 in group term life insurance and an individual universal life policy for $150,000. However, the Boykins haven't prepared their wills. Darrell plans to draw one up soon, but the couple thinks that Karla doesn't need one because the house is jointly owned. Explain why it's important for both Darrell and Karla to draft wills as soon as possible.

LG2, p. 606

3. **Will and last letter preparation.** Prepare a basic will for yourself, using the guidelines presented in the text; also prepare your brief letter of last instructions.

LG2, p. 606

4. **Topics in an ethical will.** State the topics you would cover in your ethical will. Would you consider recording it digitally?

LG2, p. 606

5. **Qualifications of estate executor.** Your best friend has asked you to be executor of his estate. What qualifications do you need, and would you accept the responsibility?

LG2,3,5, p. 606, 617, 626

6. **Trusts in estate planning.** Griffin West, 48 and a widower, and Hailey Burnette, 44 and previously divorced, were married five years ago. There are children from their prior marriages, two children for Griffin and one child for Hailey. The couple's estate is valued at $1.4 million, including a house valued at $475,000, a vacation home at the beach, investments, antique furniture that has been in Hailey's family for many years, and jewelry belonging to Griffin's first wife. Discuss how they could use trusts as part of their estate planning, and suggest some other ideas for them to consider when preparing their wills and related documents.

LG4,5, p. 622, 626

7. **Calculation of estate taxes. Use Worksheet 15.2.** When Jacob Kohler died unmarried in 2015, he left an estate valued at $7,850,000. His trust directed distribution as follows: $20,000 to the local hospital, $160,000 to his alma mater, and the remainder to his three adult children. Death-related costs and expenses were $16,800 for funeral expenses, $40,000 paid to attorneys, $5,000 paid to accountants, and $30,000 paid to the trustee of his living trust. In addition, there were debts of $125,000. Use Worksheet 15.2 and Exhibits 15.7 and 15.8 to calculate the federal estate tax due on his estate.

LG6, p. 627

8. **Recent estate taxes legislation.** Summarize important legislation affecting estate taxes, and briefly describe the impact on estate planning. Explain why getting rid of the estate tax doesn't eliminate the need for estate planning.

Applying Personal Finance

Prepare Your Will!

If you die without a valid will, the laws of your state will determine what happens to your property. That may be fine with people who have few assets, but it's not fine for people who care what happens to their property, and it's certainly not fine for people with dependents. In this project, you'll consider what your current will should contain and what changes you should make to your will based on your future circumstances.

Look back through this chapter and review the common features of a will. Then write your own will, based on the sample clauses and examples of a representative will given in the text. List the property that you currently have, or expect to have in the near future, and name a beneficiary for each. Be sure to name your personal representative, and charge him or her with disposing of your estate according to your wishes. If you have children or expect to have children, or if you have other dependents such as an elderly parent or a disabled sibling, be sure to name a guardian and a backup guardian for them. Also prepare a letter of last instructions to convey any personal thoughts or instructions that you feel cannot be properly included in your will. Remember, this exercise should help you think about the orderly disposition of your estate, which is the final act in implementing your personal financial plans.

CRITICAL THINKING CASES

LG2, p. 606

15.1 A Long-Overdue Will for Carsten

In the late 1980s, Carsten Richter, from Germany, migrated to the United States, where he is now a citizen. A man of many talents and deep foresight, he has built a large fleet of oceangoing oil tankers during his stay in the United States. Now a wealthy man in his 60s, he resides in Aspen, Colorado, with his second wife, Gabriela, age 50. They have two sons, one in junior high and one a high school freshman. For some time, Carsten has considered preparing a will to ensure that his estate will be properly distributed when he dies. A survey of his estate reveals the following:

Ranch in Colorado	$ 1,000,000
Condominium in Santa Barbara	800,000
House in Aspen	1,500,000
Franchise in ice cream stores	2,000,000
Stock in Google	5,000,000
Stock in Wal-Mart	1,000,000
Stock in Silver Mines International	3,000,000
Other assets	200,000
Total assets	$14,500,000

The house and the Silver Mines International shares are held in joint tenancy with his wife, but all other property is in his name alone. He desires that there be a separate fund of $1 million for his sons' education and that the balance of his estate be divided as follows: 40 percent to his sons, 40 percent to his wife, and 20 percent given to other relatives, friends, and charitable institutions. He has scheduled an appointment for drafting his will with his attorney and close friend, Forrest Gauthier. Carsten would like to appoint Forrest, who is 70 years old, and Carsten's 40-year-old cousin, Heinrich Richter (a CPA), as co-executors. If one of them predeceases Carsten, he'd like First National Bank to serve as co-executor.

Critical Thinking Questions

1. Does Carsten really need a will? Explain why or why not. What would happen to his estate if he were to die without a will?
2. Explain to Carsten the common features that need to be incorporated into a will.
3. Might the manner in which titles are held thwart his estate planning desires? What should be done to avoid problems?
4. Is a living trust an appropriate part of his estate plan? How would a living trust change the nature of Carsten's will?
5. How does the age of Carsten's children complicate the estate plan? What special provisions should he consider?
6. What options are available to Carsten if he decides later to change or revoke the will? Is it more difficult to change a living trust?
7. What duties will Forest Gauthier and Heinrich Richter have to perform as co-executors of Carsten's estate? If a trust is created, what should Carsten consider in his selection of a trustee or co-trustees? Might Forrest and Henrich, serving together, be a good choice?

15.2 Estate Taxes on Saul Schwab's Estate

Saul Schwab, of Knoxville, Tennessee, was 65 when he retired in 2010. Camille, his wife of 40 years, passed away the next year. Her will left everything to Saul. Although Camille's estate was valued at $2,250,000, there was no estate tax due because of the 100 percent marital deduction. Their only child, Eli, is married to Kathleen. They have four children, two in college and two in high school. In 2011, Saul made a gift of Apple stock worth $260,000 jointly to Eli and Kathleen. Because of the two $14,000 annual exclusions and the unified credit, no gift taxes were due. When Saul died in 2015, his home was valued at $850,000, his vacation cabin was valued at $485,000, his investments in stocks and bonds were valued at $1,890,000, and his pension funds were worth $645,000 (Eli was named beneficiary). Saul also owned a life insurance policy that paid proceeds of $700,000 to Eli. He left $60,000 to his church and $25,000 to his high school to start a scholarship fund in his wife's name. The rest of the estate was left to Eli. Funeral costs were $15,000. Debts were $90,000 and miscellaneous expenses were $25,000. Attorney and accounting fees came to $36,000. ***Use Worksheet 15.2*** to guide your estate tax calculations as you complete these exercises.

Critical Thinking Questions

1. Compute the value of Saul's *probate estate*.
2. Compute the value of Saul's *gross estate*.
3. Determine the total allowable deductions.
4. Calculate the *estate tax base;* taking into account the gifts given to Eli and Kathleen (remember that the annual exclusions "adjust" the taxable gifts).
5. Use Exhibit 15.7 to determine the *tentative tax on estate tax base*.
6. Subtract the appropriate *unified tax credit* (Exhibit 15.8) for 2015 from the *tentative tax on estate tax base* to arrive at the *federal estate tax due*.
7. Comment on the estate shrinkage experienced by Saul's estate. What might have been done to reduce this shrinkage? Explain.

APPENDIX A

Table of Future Value Factors

Instructions: To use this table, find the future value factor that corresponds to both a given time period (year) and an interest rate. For example, if you want the future value factor for 6 years and 10%, move across from year 6 and down from 10% to the point at which the row and column intersect: 1.772. Other illustrations: for 3 years and 15%, the proper future value factor is 1.521; for 30 years and 8%, it is 10.063.

INTEREST RATE

Period	1%	2%	3%	4%	5%	6%	7%	8%	9%	10%	11%	12%	13%	14%	15%	16%	17%	18%	19%	20%	25%	30%
1	1.010	1.020	1.030	1.040	1.050	1.060	1.070	1.080	1.090	1.100	1.110	1.120	1.130	1.140	1.150	1.160	1.170	1.180	1.190	1.200	1.250	1.300
2	1.020	1.040	1.061	1.082	1.103	1.124	1.145	1.166	1.188	1.210	1.232	1.254	1.277	1.300	1.323	1.346	1.369	1.392	1.416	1.440	1.563	1.690
3	1.030	1.061	1.093	1.125	1.158	1.191	1.225	1.260	1.295	1.331	1.368	1.405	1.443	1.482	1.521	1.561	1.602	1.643	1.685	1.728	1.953	2.197
4	1.041	1.082	1.126	1.170	1.216	1.262	1.311	1.360	1.412	1.464	1.518	1.574	1.630	1.689	1.749	1.811	1.874	1.939	2.005	2.074	2.441	2.856
5	1.051	1.104	1.159	1.217	1.276	1.338	1.403	1.469	1.539	1.611	1.685	1.762	1.842	1.925	2.011	2.100	2.192	2.288	2.386	2.488	3.052	3.713
6	1.062	1.126	1.194	1.265	1.340	1.419	1.501	1.587	1.677	1.772	1.870	1.974	2.082	2.195	2.313	2.436	2.565	2.700	2.840	2.986	3.815	4.827
7	1.072	1.149	1.230	1.316	1.407	1.504	1.606	1.714	1.828	1.949	2.076	2.211	2.353	2.502	2.660	2.826	3.001	3.185	3.379	3.583	4.768	6.275
8	1.083	1.172	1.267	1.369	1.477	1.594	1.718	1.851	1.993	2.144	2.305	2.476	2.658	2.853	3.059	3.278	3.511	3.759	4.021	4.300	5.960	8.157
9	1.094	1.195	1.305	1.423	1.551	1.689	1.838	1.999	2.172	2.358	2.558	2.773	3.004	3.252	3.518	3.803	4.108	4.435	4.785	5.160	7.451	10.604
10	1.105	1.219	1.344	1.480	1.629	1.791	1.967	2.159	2.367	2.594	2.839	3.106	3.395	3.707	4.046	4.411	4.807	5.234	5.695	6.192	9.313	13.786
11	1.116	1.243	1.384	1.539	1.710	1.898	2.105	2.332	2.580	2.853	3.152	3.479	3.836	4.226	4.652	5.117	5.624	6.176	6.777	7.430	11.642	17.922
12	1.127	1.268	1.426	1.601	1.796	2.012	2.252	2.518	2.813	3.138	3.498	3.896	4.335	4.818	5.350	5.936	6.580	7.288	8.064	8.916	14.552	23.298
13	1.138	1.294	1.469	1.665	1.886	2.133	2.410	2.720	3.066	3.452	3.883	4.363	4.898	5.492	6.153	6.886	7.699	8.599	9.596	10.699	18.190	30.288
14	1.149	1.319	1.513	1.732	1.980	2.261	2.579	2.937	3.342	3.797	4.310	4.887	5.535	6.261	7.076	7.988	9.007	10.147	11.420	12.839	22.737	39.374
15	1.161	1.346	1.558	1.801	2.079	2.397	2.759	3.172	3.642	4.177	4.785	5.474	6.254	7.138	8.137	9.266	10.539	11.974	13.590	15.407	28.422	51.186
16	1.173	1.373	1.605	1.873	2.183	2.540	2.952	3.426	3.970	4.595	5.311	6.130	7.067	8.137	9.358	10.748	12.330	14.129	16.172	18.488	35.527	66.542
17	1.184	1.400	1.653	1.948	2.292	2.693	3.159	3.700	4.328	5.054	5.895	6.866	7.986	9.276	10.761	12.468	14.426	16.672	19.244	22.186	44.409	86.504
18	1.196	1.428	1.702	2.026	2.407	2.854	3.380	3.996	4.717	5.560	6.544	7.690	9.024	10.575	12.375	14.463	16.879	19.673	22.901	26.623	55.511	112.455
19	1.208	1.457	1.754	2.107	2.527	3.026	3.617	4.316	5.142	6.116	7.263	8.613	10.197	12.056	14.232	16.777	19.748	23.214	27.252	31.948	69.389	146.192
20	1.220	1.486	1.806	2.191	2.653	3.207	3.870	4.661	5.604	6.727	8.062	9.646	11.523	13.743	16.367	19.461	23.106	27.393	32.429	38.338	86.736	190.050
21	1.232	1.516	1.860	2.279	2.786	3.400	4.141	5.034	6.109	7.400	8.949	10.804	13.021	15.668	18.822	22.574	27.034	32.324	38.591	46.005	108.420	247.065
22	1.245	1.546	1.916	2.370	2.925	3.604	4.430	5.437	6.659	8.140	9.934	12.100	14.714	17.861	21.645	26.186	31.629	38.142	45.923	55.206	135.525	321.184
23	1.257	1.577	1.974	2.465	3.072	3.820	4.741	5.871	7.258	8.954	11.026	13.552	16.627	20.362	24.891	30.376	37.006	45.008	54.649	66.247	169.407	417.539
24	1.270	1.608	2.033	2.563	3.225	4.049	5.072	6.341	7.911	9.850	12.239	15.179	18.788	23.212	28.625	35.236	43.297	53.109	65.032	79.497	211.758	542.801
25	1.282	1.641	2.094	2.666	3.386	4.292	5.427	6.848	8.623	10.835	13.585	17.000	21.231	26.462	32.919	40.874	50.658	62.669	77.388	95.396	264.698	705.641
26	1.295	1.673	2.157	2.772	3.556	4.549	5.807	7.396	9.399	11.918	15.080	19.040	23.991	30.167	37.857	47.414	59.270	73.949	92.092	114.475	330.872	917.333
27	1.308	1.707	2.221	2.883	3.733	4.822	6.214	7.988	10.245	13.110	16.739	21.325	27.109	34.390	43.535	55.000	69.345	87.260	109.589	137.371	413.590	1,192.533
28	1.321	1.741	2.288	2.999	3.920	5.112	6.649	8.627	11.167	14.421	18.580	23.884	30.633	39.204	50.066	63.800	81.134	102.967	130.411	164.845	516.988	1,550.293
29	1.335	1.776	2.357	3.119	4.116	5.418	7.114	9.317	12.172	15.863	20.624	26.750	34.616	44.693	57.575	74.009	94.927	121.501	155.189	197.814	646.235	2,015.381
30	1.348	1.811	2.427	3.243	4.322	5.743	7.612	10.063	13.268	17.449	22.892	29.960	39.116	50.950	66.212	85.850	111.065	143.371	184.675	237.376	807.794	2,619.996
35	1.417	2.000	2.814	3.946	5.516	7.686	10.677	14.785	20.414	28.102	38.575	52.800	72.069	98.100	133.176	180.314	243.503	327.997	440.701	590.668	2,465.190	9,727.860
40	1.489	2.208	3.262	4.801	7.040	10.286	14.974	21.725	31.409	45.259	65.001	93.051	132.782	188.884	267.864	378.721	533.869	750.378	1,051.668	1,469.772	7,523.164	36,118.865

Note: All factors are rounded to the nearest 1/1000 in order to agree with values used in the text.

APPENDIX B

Table of Future Value Annuity Factors

Instructions: To use this table, find the future value of annuity factor that corresponds to both a given time period (year) and an interest rate. For example, if you want the future value of annuity factor for 6 years and 10%, move across from year 6 and down from 10% to the point at which the row and column intersect: 7.716. Other illustrations: for 3 years and 15%, the proper future value of annuity factor is 3.473; for 30 years and 6%, it is 79.058.

INTEREST RATE

Period	1%	2%	3%	4%	5%	6%	7%	8%	9%	10%	11%	12%	13%	14%	15%	16%	17%	18%	19%	20%	25%	30%
1	1.000	1.000	1.000	1.000	1.000	1.000	1.000	1.000	1.000	1.000	1.000	1.000	1.000	1.000	1.000	1.000	1.000	1.000	1.000	1.000	1.000	1.000
2	2.010	2.020	2.030	2.040	2.050	2.060	2.070	2.080	2.090	2.100	2.110	2.120	2.130	2.140	2.150	2.160	2.170	2.180	2.190	2.200	2.250	2.300
3	3.030	3.060	3.091	3.122	3.153	3.184	3.215	3.246	3.278	3.310	3.342	3.374	3.407	3.440	3.473	3.506	3.539	3.572	3.606	3.640	3.813	3.990
4	4.060	4.122	4.184	4.246	4.310	4.375	4.440	4.506	4.573	4.641	4.710	4.779	4.850	4.921	4.993	5.066	5.141	5.215	5.291	5.368	5.766	6.187
5	5.101	5.204	5.309	5.416	5.526	5.637	5.751	5.867	5.985	6.105	6.228	6.353	6.480	6.610	6.742	6.877	7.014	7.154	7.297	7.442	8.207	9.043
6	6.152	6.308	6.468	6.633	6.802	6.975	7.153	7.336	7.523	7.716	7.913	8.115	8.323	8.536	8.754	8.977	9.207	9.442	9.683	9.930	11.259	12.756
7	7.214	7.434	7.662	7.898	8.142	8.394	8.654	8.923	9.200	9.487	9.783	10.089	10.405	10.730	11.067	11.414	11.772	12.142	12.523	12.916	15.073	17.583
8	8.286	8.583	8.892	9.214	9.549	9.897	10.260	10.637	11.028	11.436	11.859	12.300	12.757	13.233	13.727	14.240	14.773	15.327	15.902	16.499	19.842	23.858
9	9.369	9.755	10.159	10.583	11.027	11.491	11.978	12.488	13.021	13.579	14.164	14.776	15.416	16.085	16.786	17.519	18.285	19.086	19.923	20.799	25.802	32.015
10	10.462	10.950	11.464	12.006	12.578	13.181	13.816	14.487	15.193	15.937	16.722	17.549	18.420	19.337	20.304	21.321	22.393	23.521	24.709	25.959	33.253	42.619
11	11.567	12.169	12.808	13.486	14.207	14.972	15.784	16.645	17.560	18.531	19.561	20.655	21.814	23.045	24.349	25.733	27.200	28.755	30.404	32.150	42.566	56.405
12	12.683	13.412	14.192	15.026	15.917	16.870	17.888	18.977	20.141	21.384	22.713	24.133	25.650	27.271	29.002	30.850	32.824	34.931	37.180	39.581	54.208	74.327
13	13.809	14.680	15.618	16.627	17.713	18.882	20.141	21.495	22.953	24.523	26.212	28.029	29.985	32.089	34.352	36.786	39.404	42.219	45.244	48.497	68.760	97.625
14	14.947	15.974	17.086	18.292	19.599	21.015	22.550	24.215	26.019	27.975	30.095	32.393	34.883	37.581	40.505	43.672	47.103	50.818	54.841	59.196	86.949	127.913
15	16.097	17.293	18.599	20.024	21.579	23.276	25.129	27.152	29.361	31.772	34.405	37.280	40.417	43.842	47.580	51.660	56.110	60.965	66.261	72.035	109.687	167.286
16	17.258	18.639	20.157	21.825	23.657	25.673	27.888	30.324	33.003	35.950	39.190	42.753	46.672	50.980	55.717	60.925	66.649	72.939	79.850	87.442	138.109	218.472
17	18.430	20.012	21.762	23.698	25.840	28.213	30.840	33.750	36.974	40.545	44.501	48.884	53.739	59.118	65.075	71.673	78.979	87.068	96.022	105.931	173.636	285.01
18	19.615	21.412	23.414	25.645	28.132	30.906	33.999	37.450	41.301	45.599	50.396	55.750	61.725	68.394	75.836	84.141	93.406	103.74	115.27	128.117	218.045	371.52
19	20.811	22.841	25.117	27.671	30.539	33.760	37.379	41.446	46.018	51.159	56.939	63.440	70.749	78.969	88.212	98.603	110.28	123.41	138.17	154.740	273.556	483.97
20	22.019	24.297	26.870	29.778	33.066	36.786	40.995	45.762	51.160	57.275	64.203	72.052	80.947	91.025	102.444	115.380	130.033	146.628	165.418	186.688	342.945	630.165
21	23.239	25.783	28.676	31.969	35.719	39.993	44.865	50.423	56.765	64.002	72.265	81.699	92.470	104.768	118.810	134.841	153.139	174.021	197.847	225.026	429.681	820.215
22	24.472	27.299	30.537	34.248	38.505	43.392	49.006	55.457	62.873	71.403	81.214	92.503	105.491	120.436	137.632	157.415	180.172	206.345	236.438	271.031	538.101	1,067.280
23	25.716	28.845	32.453	36.618	41.430	46.996	53.436	60.893	69.532	79.543	91.148	104.603	120.205	138.297	159.276	183.601	211.801	244.487	282.362	326.237	673.626	1,388.464
24	26.973	30.422	34.426	39.083	44.502	50.816	58.177	66.765	76.790	88.497	102.174	118.155	136.831	158.659	184.168	213.978	248.808	289.494	337.010	392.484	843.033	1,806.003
25	28.243	32.030	36.459	41.646	47.727	54.865	63.249	73.106	84.701	98.347	114.413	133.334	155.620	181.871	212.793	249.214	292.105	342.603	402.042	471.981	1,054.791	2,348.803
26	29.526	33.671	38.553	44.312	51.113	59.156	68.676	79.954	93.324	109.182	127.999	150.334	176.850	208.333	245.712	290.088	342.763	405.272	479.431	567.377	1,319.489	3,054.444
27	30.821	35.344	40.710	47.084	54.669	63.706	74.484	87.351	102.723	121.100	143.079	169.374	200.841	238.499	283.569	337.502	402.032	479.221	571.522	681.853	1,650.361	3,971.778
28	32.129	37.051	42.931	49.968	58.403	68.528	80.698	95.339	112.968	134.210	159.817	190.699	227.950	272.889	327.104	392.503	471.378	566.481	681.112	819.223	2,063.952	5,164.311
29	33.450	38.792	45.219	52.966	62.323	73.640	87.347	103.966	124.135	148.631	178.397	214.583	258.583	312.094	377.170	456.303	552.512	669.447	811.523	984.068	2,580.939	6,714.604
30	34.785	40.568	47.575	56.085	66.439	79.058	94.461	113.283	136.308	164.494	199.021	241.333	293.199	356.787	434.745	530.312	647.439	790.948	966.712	1,181.882	3,227.174	8,729.985
35	41.660	49.994	60.462	73.652	90.320	111.435	138.237	172.317	215.711	271.024	341.590	431.663	546.681	693.573	881.170	1,120.713	1,426.491	1,816.652	2,314.214	2,948.341	9,856.761	32,422.868
40	48.886	60.402	75.401	95.026	120.800	154.762	199.635	259.057	337.882	442.593	581.826	767.091	1,013.704	1,342.025	1,779.090	2,360.757	3,134.522	4,163.213	5,529.829	7,343.858	30,088.655	120,392.883

Note: All factors are rounded to the nearest 1/1000 in order to agree with values used in the text.

APPENDIX C

Table of Present Value Factors

Instructions: To use this table, find the present value factor that corresponds to both a given time period (year) and an interest rate. For example, if you want the present value factor for 25 years and 7%, move across from year 25 and down from 7% to the point at which the row and column intersect: .184. Other illustrations: for 3 years and 15%, the proper present value factor is .658; for 30 years and 8%, it is .099.

INTEREST RATE

Period	1%	2%	3%	4%	5%	6%	7%	8%	9%	10%	11%	12%	13%	14%	15%	16%	17%	18%	19%	20%	25%	30%
1	0.990	0.980	0.971	0.962	0.952	0.943	0.935	0.926	0.917	0.909	0.901	0.893	0.885	0.877	0.870	0.862	0.855	0.847	0.840	0.833	0.800	0.769
2	0.980	0.961	0.943	0.925	0.907	0.890	0.873	0.857	0.842	0.826	0.812	0.797	0.783	0.769	0.756	0.743	0.731	0.718	0.706	0.694	0.640	0.592
3	0.971	0.942	0.915	0.889	0.864	0.840	0.816	0.794	0.772	0.751	0.731	0.712	0.693	0.675	0.658	0.641	0.624	0.609	0.593	0.579	0.512	0.455
4	0.961	0.924	0.888	0.855	0.823	0.792	0.763	0.735	0.708	0.683	0.659	0.636	0.613	0.592	0.572	0.552	0.534	0.516	0.499	0.482	0.410	0.350
5	0.951	0.906	0.863	0.822	0.784	0.747	0.713	0.681	0.650	0.621	0.593	0.567	0.543	0.519	0.497	0.476	0.456	0.437	0.419	0.402	0.328	0.269
6	0.942	0.888	0.837	0.790	0.746	0.705	0.666	0.630	0.596	0.564	0.535	0.507	0.480	0.456	0.432	0.410	0.390	0.370	0.352	0.335	0.262	0.207
7	0.933	0.871	0.813	0.760	0.711	0.665	0.623	0.583	0.547	0.513	0.482	0.452	0.425	0.400	0.376	0.354	0.333	0.314	0.296	0.279	0.210	0.159
8	0.923	0.853	0.789	0.731	0.677	0.627	0.582	0.540	0.502	0.467	0.434	0.404	0.376	0.351	0.327	0.305	0.285	0.266	0.249	0.233	0.168	0.123
9	0.914	0.837	0.766	0.703	0.645	0.592	0.544	0.500	0.460	0.424	0.391	0.361	0.333	0.308	0.284	0.263	0.243	0.225	0.209	0.194	0.134	0.094
10	0.905	0.820	0.744	0.676	0.614	0.558	0.508	0.463	0.422	0.386	0.352	0.322	0.295	0.270	0.247	0.227	0.208	0.191	0.176	0.162	0.107	0.073
11	0.896	0.804	0.722	0.650	0.585	0.527	0.475	0.429	0.388	0.350	0.317	0.287	0.261	0.237	0.215	0.195	0.178	0.162	0.148	0.135	0.086	0.056
12	0.887	0.788	0.701	0.625	0.557	0.497	0.444	0.397	0.356	0.319	0.286	0.257	0.231	0.208	0.187	0.168	0.152	0.137	0.124	0.112	0.069	0.043
13	0.879	0.773	0.681	0.601	0.530	0.469	0.415	0.368	0.326	0.290	0.258	0.229	0.204	0.182	0.163	0.145	0.130	0.116	0.104	0.093	0.055	0.033
14	0.870	0.758	0.661	0.577	0.505	0.442	0.388	0.340	0.299	0.263	0.232	0.205	0.181	0.160	0.141	0.125	0.111	0.099	0.088	0.078	0.044	0.025
15	0.861	0.743	0.642	0.555	0.481	0.417	0.362	0.315	0.275	0.239	0.209	0.183	0.160	0.140	0.123	0.108	0.095	0.084	0.074	0.065	0.035	0.020
16	0.853	0.728	0.623	0.534	0.458	0.394	0.339	0.292	0.252	0.218	0.188	0.163	0.141	0.123	0.107	0.093	0.081	0.071	0.062	0.054	0.028	0.015
17	0.844	0.714	0.605	0.513	0.436	0.371	0.317	0.270	0.231	0.198	0.170	0.146	0.125	0.108	0.093	0.080	0.069	0.060	0.052	0.045	0.023	0.012
18	0.836	0.700	0.587	0.494	0.416	0.350	0.296	0.250	0.212	0.180	0.153	0.130	0.111	0.095	0.081	0.069	0.059	0.051	0.044	0.038	0.018	0.009
19	0.828	0.686	0.570	0.475	0.396	0.331	0.277	0.232	0.194	0.164	0.138	0.116	0.098	0.083	0.070	0.060	0.051	0.043	0.037	0.031	0.014	0.007
20	0.820	0.673	0.554	0.456	0.377	0.312	0.258	0.215	0.178	0.149	0.124	0.104	0.087	0.073	0.061	0.051	0.043	0.037	0.031	0.026	0.012	0.005
21	0.811	0.660	0.538	0.439	0.359	0.294	0.242	0.199	0.164	0.135	0.112	0.093	0.077	0.064	0.053	0.044	0.037	0.031	0.026	0.022	0.009	0.004
22	0.803	0.647	0.522	0.422	0.342	0.278	0.226	0.184	0.150	0.123	0.101	0.083	0.068	0.056	0.046	0.038	0.032	0.026	0.022	0.018	0.007	0.003
23	0.795	0.634	0.507	0.406	0.326	0.262	0.211	0.170	0.138	0.112	0.091	0.074	0.060	0.049	0.040	0.033	0.027	0.022	0.018	0.015	0.006	0.002
24	0.788	0.622	0.492	0.390	0.310	0.247	0.197	0.158	0.126	0.102	0.082	0.066	0.053	0.043	0.035	0.028	0.023	0.019	0.015	0.013	0.005	0.002
25	0.780	0.610	0.478	0.375	0.295	0.233	0.184	0.146	0.116	0.092	0.074	0.059	0.047	0.038	0.030	0.024	0.020	0.016	0.013	0.010	0.004	0.001
26	0.772	0.598	0.464	0.361	0.281	0.220	0.172	0.135	0.106	0.084	0.066	0.053	0.042	0.033	0.026	0.021	0.017	0.014	0.011	0.009	0.003	0.001
27	0.764	0.586	0.450	0.347	0.268	0.207	0.161	0.125	0.098	0.076	0.060	0.047	0.037	0.029	0.023	0.018	0.014	0.011	0.009	0.007	0.002	0.001
28	0.757	0.574	0.437	0.333	0.255	0.196	0.150	0.116	0.090	0.069	0.054	0.042	0.033	0.026	0.020	0.016	0.012	0.010	0.008	0.006	0.002	0.001
29	0.749	0.563	0.424	0.321	0.243	0.185	0.141	0.107	0.082	0.063	0.048	0.037	0.029	0.022	0.017	0.014	0.011	0.008	0.006	0.005	0.002	*
30	0.742	0.552	0.412	0.308	0.231	0.174	0.131	0.099	0.075	0.057	0.044	0.033	0.026	0.020	0.015	0.012	0.009	0.007	0.005	0.004	0.001	*
35	0.706	0.500	0.355	0.253	0.181	0.130	0.094	0.068	0.049	0.036	0.026	0.019	0.014	0.010	0.008	0.006	0.004	0.003	0.002	0.002	*	*
40	0.672	0.453	0.307	0.208	0.142	0.097	0.067	0.046	0.032	0.022	0.015	0.011	0.008	0.005	0.004	0.003	0.002	0.001	0.001	0.001	*	*

*Present value factor is zero to three decimal places.

Note: All factors are rounded to the nearest 1/1000 in order to agree with values used in the text.

APPENDIX D

Table of Present Value Annuity Factors

Instructions: To use this table, find the present value of annuity factor that corresponds to both a given time period (year) and an interest rate. For example, if you want the present value of annuity factor for 30 years and 7%, move across from year 30 and down from 7% to the point at which the row and column intersect: 12.409. Other illustrations: for 3 years and 15%, the proper present value of annuity factor is 2.283; for 30 years and 8%, it is 11.258.

INTEREST RATE

Period	1%	2%	3%	4%	5%	6%	7%	8%	9%	10%	11%	12%	13%	14%	15%	16%	17%	18%	19%	20%	25%	30%
1	0.990	0.980	0.971	0.962	0.952	0.943	0.935	0.926	0.917	0.909	0.901	0.893	0.885	0.877	0.870	0.862	0.855	0.847	0.840	0.833	0.800	0.769
2	1.970	1.942	1.913	1.886	1.859	1.833	1.808	1.783	1.759	1.736	1.713	1.690	1.668	1.647	1.626	1.605	1.585	1.566	1.547	1.528	1.440	1.361
3	2.941	2.884	2.829	2.775	2.723	2.673	2.624	2.577	2.531	2.487	2.444	2.402	2.361	2.322	2.283	2.246	2.210	2.174	2.140	2.106	1.952	1.816
4	3.902	3.808	3.717	3.630	3.546	3.465	3.387	3.312	3.240	3.170	3.102	3.037	2.974	2.914	2.855	2.798	2.743	2.690	2.639	2.589	2.362	2.166
5	4.853	4.713	4.580	4.452	4.329	4.212	4.100	3.993	3.890	3.791	3.696	3.605	3.517	3.433	3.352	3.274	3.199	3.127	3.058	2.991	2.689	2.436
6	5.795	5.601	5.417	5.242	5.076	4.917	4.767	4.623	4.486	4.355	4.231	4.111	3.998	3.889	3.784	3.685	3.589	3.498	3.410	3.326	2.951	2.643
7	6.728	6.472	6.230	6.002	5.786	5.582	5.389	5.206	5.033	4.868	4.712	4.564	4.423	4.288	4.160	4.039	3.922	3.812	3.706	3.605	3.161	2.802
8	7.652	7.325	7.020	6.733	6.463	6.210	5.971	5.747	5.535	5.335	5.146	4.968	4.799	4.639	4.487	4.344	4.207	4.078	3.954	3.837	3.329	2.925
9	8.566	8.162	7.786	7.435	7.108	6.802	6.515	6.247	5.995	5.759	5.537	5.328	5.132	4.946	4.772	4.607	4.451	4.303	4.163	4.031	3.463	3.019
10	9.471	8.983	8.530	8.111	7.722	7.360	7.024	6.710	6.418	6.145	5.889	5.650	5.426	5.216	5.019	4.833	4.659	4.494	4.339	4.192	3.571	3.092
11	10.368	9.787	9.253	8.760	8.306	7.887	7.499	7.139	6.805	6.495	6.207	5.938	5.687	5.453	5.234	5.029	4.836	4.656	4.486	4.327	3.656	3.147
12	11.255	10.575	9.954	9.385	8.863	8.384	7.943	7.536	7.161	6.814	6.492	6.194	5.918	5.660	5.421	5.197	4.988	4.793	4.611	4.439	3.725	3.190
13	12.134	11.348	10.635	9.986	9.394	8.853	8.358	7.904	7.487	7.103	6.750	6.424	6.122	5.842	5.583	5.342	5.118	4.910	4.715	4.533	3.780	3.223
14	13.004	12.106	11.296	10.563	9.899	9.295	8.745	8.244	7.786	7.367	6.982	6.628	6.302	6.002	5.724	5.468	5.229	5.008	4.802	4.611	3.824	3.249
15	13.865	12.849	11.938	11.118	10.380	9.712	9.108	8.559	8.061	7.606	7.191	6.811	6.462	6.142	5.847	5.575	5.324	5.092	4.876	4.675	3.859	3.268
16	14.718	13.578	12.561	11.652	10.838	10.106	9.447	8.851	8.313	7.824	7.379	6.974	6.604	6.265	5.954	5.668	5.405	5.162	4.938	4.730	3.887	3.283
17	15.562	14.292	13.166	12.166	11.274	10.477	9.763	9.122	8.544	8.022	7.549	7.120	6.729	6.373	6.047	5.749	5.475	5.222	4.990	4.775	3.910	3.295
18	16.398	14.992	13.754	12.659	11.690	10.828	10.059	9.372	8.756	8.201	7.702	7.250	6.840	6.467	6.128	5.818	5.534	5.273	5.033	4.812	3.928	3.304
19	17.226	15.678	14.324	13.134	12.085	11.158	10.336	9.604	8.950	8.365	7.839	7.366	6.938	6.550	6.198	5.877	5.584	5.316	5.070	4.843	3.942	3.311
20	18.046	16.351	14.877	13.590	12.462	11.470	10.594	9.818	9.129	8.514	7.963	7.469	7.025	6.623	6.259	5.929	5.628	5.353	5.101	4.870	3.954	3.316
21	18.857	17.011	15.415	14.029	12.821	11.764	10.836	10.017	9.292	8.649	8.075	7.562	7.102	6.687	6.312	5.973	5.665	5.384	5.127	4.891	3.963	3.320
22	19.660	17.658	15.937	14.451	13.163	12.042	11.061	10.201	9.442	8.772	8.176	7.645	7.170	6.743	6.359	6.011	5.696	5.410	5.149	4.909	3.970	3.323
23	20.456	18.292	16.444	14.857	13.489	12.303	11.272	10.371	9.580	8.883	8.266	7.718	7.230	6.792	6.399	6.044	5.723	5.432	5.167	4.925	3.976	3.325
24	21.243	18.914	16.936	15.247	13.799	12.550	11.469	10.529	9.707	8.985	8.348	7.784	7.283	6.835	6.434	6.073	5.746	5.451	5.182	4.937	3.981	3.327
25	22.023	19.523	17.413	15.622	14.094	12.783	11.654	10.675	9.823	9.077	8.422	7.843	7.330	6.873	6.464	6.097	5.766	5.467	5.195	4.948	3.985	3.329
26	22.795	20.121	17.877	15.983	14.375	13.003	11.826	10.810	9.929	9.161	8.488	7.896	7.372	6.906	6.491	6.118	5.783	5.480	5.206	4.956	3.988	3.330
27	23.560	20.707	18.327	16.330	14.643	13.211	11.987	10.935	10.027	9.237	8.548	7.943	7.409	6.935	6.514	6.136	5.798	5.492	5.215	4.964	3.990	3.331
28	24.316	21.281	18.764	16.663	14.898	13.406	12.137	11.051	10.116	9.307	8.602	7.984	7.441	6.961	6.534	6.152	5.810	5.502	5.223	4.970	3.992	3.331
29	25.066	21.844	19.188	16.984	15.141	13.591	12.278	11.158	10.198	9.370	8.650	8.022	7.470	6.983	6.551	6.166	5.820	5.510	5.229	4.975	3.994	3.332
30	25.808	22.396	19.600	17.292	15.372	13.765	12.409	11.258	10.274	9.427	8.694	8.055	7.496	7.003	6.566	6.177	5.829	5.517	5.235	4.979	3.995	3.332
35	29.409	24.999	21.487	18.665	16.374	14.498	12.948	11.655	10.567	9.644	8.855	8.176	7.586	7.070	6.617	6.215	5.858	5.539	5.251	4.992	3.998	3.333
40	32.835	27.355	23.115	19.793	17.159	15.046	13.332	11.925	10.757	9.779	8.951	8.244	7.634	7.105	6.642	6.233	5.871	5.548	5.258	4.997	3.999	3.333

Note: All factors are rounded to the nearest 1/1000 in order to agree with values used in the text.

APPENDIX E

Using a Financial Calculator

Important Financial Keys on the Typical Financial Calculator

The important financial keys on a typical financial calculator are depicted and defined below. On some calculators the keys may be labeled using lowercase characters for "N" and "I". Also, "I/Y" may be used in place of the "I" key.

CPT — Compute key; used to initiate financial calculation once all values are input
  N — Number of periods
   I — Interest rate per period
 PV — Present value
PMT — Amount of payment; used only for annuities
 FV — Future value

The handheld financial calculator makes it easy to calculate time value. Once you have mastered the time value of money concepts using tables, we suggest you use such a calculator. For one thing, it becomes cumbersome to use tables when calculating anything other than annual compounding. For another, calculators rather than tables are used almost exclusively in the business of personal financial planning.

You don't want to become overly dependent on calculators, however, because you may not be able to recognize a nonsensical answer in the event that you accidentally push the wrong button. The important calculator keys are shown and labeled above. Before using your calculator to make the financial computations described in this text, be aware of the following points.

1. The keystrokes on some of the more sophisticated and expensive calculators are menu-driven: after you select the appropriate routine, the calculator prompts you to input each value; a compute key (CPT) is not needed to obtain a solution.
2. Many calculators allow the user to set the number of payments per year. Most of these calculators are preset for monthly payments, or 12 payments per year. Because we work primarily with *annual* payments—one payment per year—it is important to make sure that your calculator is set for one payment per year. Although most calculators are preset to recognize that all payments occur at the end of the period, it is also important to make sure your calculator is actually in the END mode. Consult the reference guide that accompanies your calculator for instructions on these settings.

3. To avoid including previous data in current calculations, always clear all registers of your calculator before inputting values and making a new computation.
4. The known values can be punched into the calculator in any order; the order specified here and in the text simply reflects the authors' personal preference.

Calculator Keystrokes. Let's go back to the future value calculation on page 64, where we are trying to calculate the future value of $5,000 at the end of 6 years if invested at 5%. Here are the steps for solving the problem with a calculator:

1. Punch in 5000 and press PV.
2. Punch in 6 and press N.
3. Punch in 5 and press I.
4. To calculate the future value, press CPT and then FV. The future value of 6700.48 should appear on the calculator display.

Calculator

INPUTS	FUNCTIONS
5000	PV
6	N
5	I
	CPT
	FV
	SOLUTION
	6700.48

On many calculators, this value will be preceded by a minus sign, which is a way of distinguishing between cash inflows and cash outflows. For our purposes, this sign can be ignored.

To calculate the yearly savings (the amount of an annuity), let's continue with the example on page 64. For this example, the interest rate is 5%, the number of periods is 6, and the future value is $38,300. Your task is to solve the equation for the annuity. The steps using the calculator are:

1. Punch in 6 and press N.
2. Punch in 5 and press I.
3. Punch in 38300 and press FV.
4. To calculate the yearly payment or annuity, press CPT and then PMT.

The annuity of 5,630.77 should appear on the calculator display. Again, a negative sign can be ignored.

Calculator

INPUTS	FUNCTIONS
6	N
5	I
38300	FV
	CPT
	PMT
	SOLUTION
	5630.77

A similar procedure is used to find present value of a future sum or an annuity, except you would first input the FV or PMT before pressing CPT and then PV to calculate the desired result. To find the equal annual future withdrawals from an initial deposit, the PV would be input first; you solve for the PMT by pressing CPT and then PMT.

Index

exhibit = *e*, worksheet = *w*

CALCULUS

THIRD EDITION

Monty J. Strauss

Texas Tech University

Gerald L. Bradley

Claremont McKenna College

Karl J. Smith

Santa Rosa Junior College

Prentice Hall

Prentice Hall, Upper Saddle River, New Jersey 07458

Library of Congress Cataloging in Publication Data

Strauss, Monty J.
  Calculus-3rd ed./Monty J. Strauss, Gerald L. Bradley, Karl J. Smith
  p. cm.
  Rev. ed. of: Calculus, 2nd ed. c1999
  Includes index
  ISBN 0-13-091871-7

  1. Calculus.   I. Smith, Karl J. II. Bradley, Gerald L.,
  III. Strauss, Monty J., Calculus. IV. Title.

QA303.B88218 2002   CIP
515--dc21   20021032734

Acquisition Editor: *George Lobell*
Editor in Chief: *Sally Yagan*
Production Editor: *Lynn Savino Wendel*
Vice President/Director of Production and Manufacturing: *David W. Riccardi*
Senior Managing Editor: *Linda Mihatov Behrens*
Executive Managing Editor: *Kathleen Schiaparelli*
Assistant Managing Editor: *Bayani Mendoza de Leon*
Manufacturing Buyer: *Alan Fischer*
Manufacturing Manager: *Trudy Pisciotti*
Marketing Manager: *Angela Battle*
Assistant Editor of Media: *Vince Jansen*
Marketing Assistant: *Rachel Beckman*
Development Editor: *Irene Nunes*
Editor in Chief, Development: *Carol Trueheart*
Art Director: *Heather Scott*
Assistant to Art Director: *John Christiana*
Creative Director: *Carole Anson*
Director of Creative Services: *Paul Belfanti*
Managing Editor, Audio/Video Assets: *Grace Hazeldine*
Art Editor: *Thomas Benfatti*
Assistant Managing Editor, Math Media Production: *John Matthews*
Interior Designer: *Anne Flanagan*
Editorial Assistant/Supplements Editor: *Melanie Van Benthuysen*
Photo Researcher: *Karen Pugliano*
Photo Editor: *Beth Boyd*
Cover Designer: *Anne Flanagan*
Cover Photo: Inside the Louvre Pyramid (which is shown on back cover) looking upward.
Cover Photo Credits: *Antionio Martinelli*
Historical Quest Portraits: *Steven S. Nau*
Art Studio: Artworks

            Senior Manager: *Patty Burns*
            Production Manager: *Ronda Whitson*
            Manager, Production Technologies: *Matt Haas*
            Project Coordinator: *Jessica Einsig*
            Illustrator: *Mark Landis*

 ©2002, 1999, 1995 by Prentice-Hall, Inc.
Upper Saddle River, New Jersey 07458

Printed in the United States of America

10 9 8 7 6 5 4 3 2 1

ISBN 0-13-091871-7

Pearson Education Ltd.
Pearson Education Australia PTY, Limited
Pearson Education Singapore, Pte. Ltd
Pearson Education North Asia Ltd.
Pearson Education Canada, Ltd.
Pearson Educación de Mexico, S.A. de C.V.
Pearson Education—Japan
Pearson Education Malaysia, Pte. Ltd.

Contents

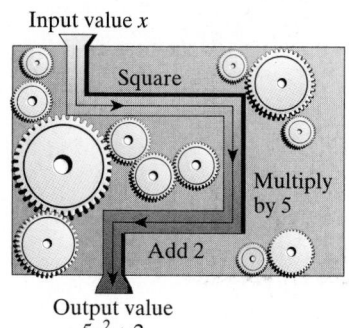
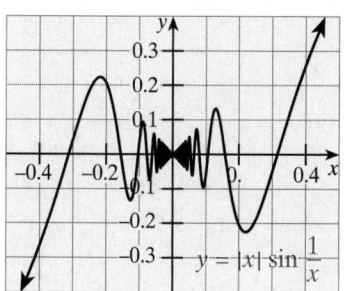

3 Differentiation 97

4 Additional Applications of the Derivative 183

5 Integration 271

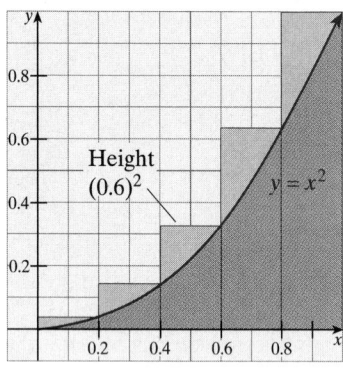

6 Additional Applications of the Integral   **355**

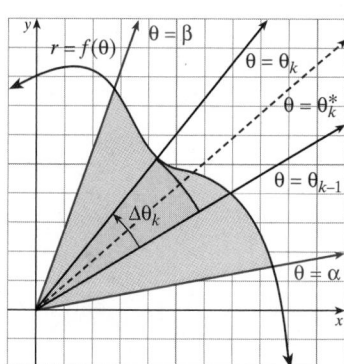

7 Methods of Integration   **425**

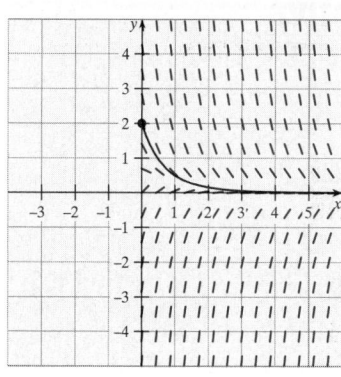

8 Infinite Series   **493**

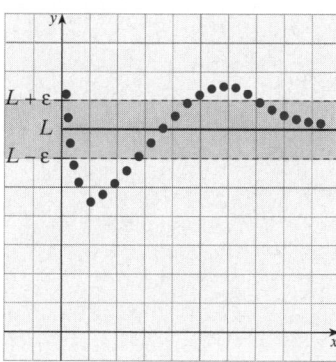

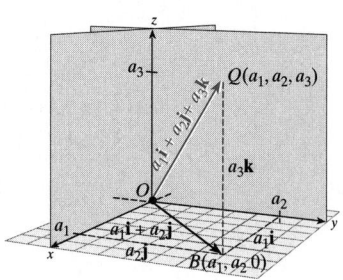

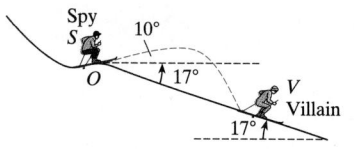

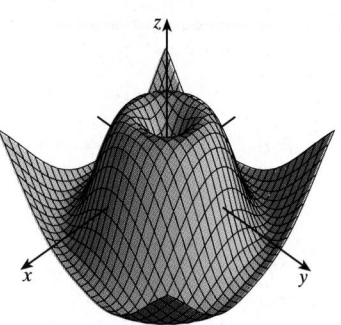

12 Multiple Integration

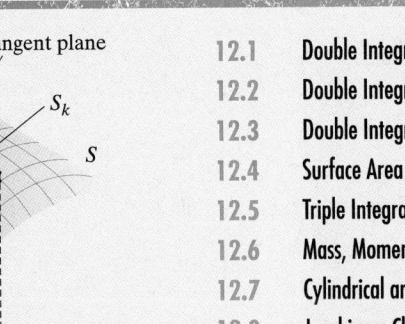

13 Vector Analysis

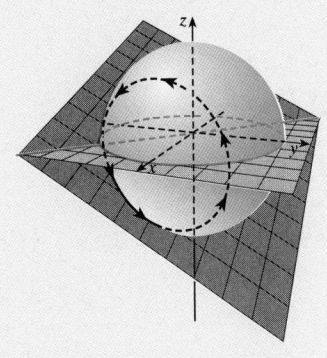

14 Introduction to Differential Equations

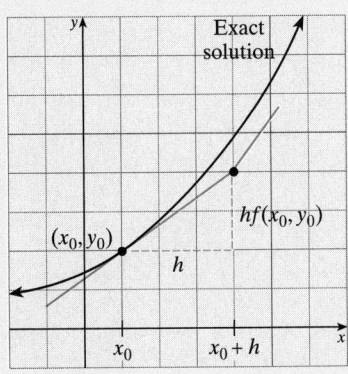

Appendices

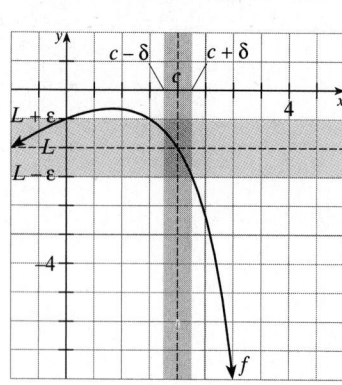

Preface

This text was developed to blend the best aspects of calculus reform with the reasonable goals and methodology of traditional calculus. It achieves this middle ground by providing sound development, stimulating problems, and well-developed pedagogy within a framework of a traditional structure. "Think, then do," is a fair summary of our approach.

New to this Edition

The acceptance and response from our first two editions has been most gratifying. For the third edition, we wanted to take a good book and make it even better. If you are familiar with the previous editions, the first thing you will notice is that we have added a new coauthor, Monty J. Strauss. His added expertise, and his attention to accuracy and detail, as well as his many years of experience teaching calculus, have added a new dimension to our exposition. Here is what is new in the third edition:

Organization

- In this edition we introduce e^x and $\ln x$ in Chapter 2 after we have defined the notion of a limit. This is beneficial because it allows the number e to be properly defined using limits. We also assume a knowledge of the conic sections and their graphs. A free *Student Mathematics Handbook* is available that provides review and reference material on these transcendental functions.
- l'Hôpital's Rule is now covered earlier in Chapter 4. This placement allows instructors to explore more interesting applications like curve sketching.
- A new section covering applications to business, economics, and the life sciences has been added to Chapter 6 on Applications of the Integral. This new material is designed to help students see how calculus relates to and is used in other disciplines.
- The chapter on polar coordinates and parametric forms has been distributed to other chapters in the book. The polar coordinate system and graphing in polar forms is in Chapter 6 in the context of the integration topic of finding areas. Parametric representation of curves now appears in the book where it is first needed, in Chapter 9.
- Modeling continues as a major theme in this edition. Modeling is now introduced in Section 3.4, and then appears in almost every section of the book. These applications are designated MODELING PROBLEMS. Some authors use the words "Modeling Problem" to refer to any applied problem. In the third edition of *Calculus*, we make a distinction between *modeling problems* and *application problems* by defining a modeling problem as follows. A **modeling problem** is a problem that requires that the reader make some assumptions about the real world in order to derive or come up

with the necessary mathematical formula or mathematical information to answer the question. These problems also include real-world examples of modeling by citing the source of the book or journal that shows the modeling process.

Problem Sets

- We have added a new major category of problems, called **counterexample problem**. A *counterexample* is an example that disproves a proposition or theorem, and in mathematics we are often faced with a proposition that is true or false, and our task is to prove the proposition true or to find a counterexample to disprove the proposition. In the third edition of *Calculus*, we attempt to build the student's ability with this type of situation to mean that the student must either find justification that the proposition is true or else find a counterexample. We believe this new form of problem to be important for preparing the student for future work in not only advanced mathematics courses, but also for analytically oriented courses.
- **Exploration Problems** explore concepts which may prove true or false and provide opportunities for innovative thinking.
- **Interpretation Problems** require exposition that requires a line of thinking that is not directly covered in the textbook.

Supplements

- **Interactive CD** (free with every new copy). The new CD-ROM is designed to enhance students' computational and conceptual understanding of calculus. This CD-ROM is not an add-on of extra material to the text but rather an incredibly useful expansion of the text. See the media supplement portion of the Walk-Through for a complete description of each CD.
- **TestGen-EQ.** This easy to use test generator contains all of the questions from the printed Test Item File.
- **Prentice Hall Online Homework Grader.** For more details, see the PH Homework Grader section in the Walk-Through.

Hallmark Features

Some of the distinguishing characteristics of the earlier editions are continued with this edition:

- It is possible to begin the course with either Chapter 1 or Chapter 2 (where the calculus topics begin).
- We believe that students *learn* mathematics by *doing* mathematics. Therefore, the **problems and applications** are perhaps the most important feature of any calculus book. You will find that the problems in this book extend from routine practice to challenging. The problem sets are divided into *A* Problems (routine), *B* Problems (requiring independent thought), and *C* Problems (theory problems). You will find the scope and depth of the problems in this book to be extraordinary while engineering and physics examples and problems play a prominent role, we include applications from a wide variety of fields, such as biology, economics, ecology, psychology, and sociology. In addition, the chapter summaries provide not only topical review, but also many miscellaneous exercises. Although the chapter reviews are typical of examinations, the miscellaneous problems are not presented as graded problems, but rather as a random list of problems loosely tied to the ideas of that chapter. In addition, there are cumulative reviews located at natural subdivision points in the text: Chapters 1–5, Chapters 6–8, Chapters 1–10, and Chapters 11–13. For a full description of each type of problem available, see pages xviii through xxi of Walk-Through.
- We understand that students often struggle with prerequisite material. Further, it is often frustrating for instructors to have to reteach material from previous courses. As

a result, we have created a unique **Student Mathematics Handbook**. This handbook functions as a **"Just-in-Time" Precalculus Review** that provides precalculus drill/review material, a catalog of curves, analytic geometry, and integral tables. Students are guided through the text to this handbook by a SMH symbol located in the text margin. This guide is entirely author-written and offered FREE with every new copy of the text.

(SMH)

- We have taken the introduction of **differential equations** seriously. Students in many allied disciplines need to use differential equations early in their studies and consequently cannot wait for a postcalculus course. We introduce differential equations in a natural and reasonable way. Slope fields are introduced as a geometric view of antidifferentiation in Section 5.1, and then are used to introduce a graphical solution to differential equations in Section 5.6. We consider separable differential equations in Chapter 5 and first-order linear equations in Chapter 7, and demonstrate the use of both modeling a variety of applied situations. Exact and homogeneous differential equations appear in Chapter 14, along with an introduction to second-order linear equations. The "early and often" approach to differential equations is intended to illustrate their value in continuous modeling and to provide a solid foundation for further study.

- **Visualization** is used to help students develop better intuition. Much of this visualization appears in the wide margins to accompany the text. Also, since tough calculus problems are often tough geometry (and algebra) problems, this emphasis on graphs will help students' problem-solving skills. Additional graphs are related to the student problems, including answer art.

- We have included dozens of "Technology Notes" devoted to the use of technology. We strive to keep such references "platform neutral" because specific calculators and computer programs frequently change and are better considered in separate technology manuals. These references are designed to give insight into how technological advances can be used to help understand calculus. Problems requiring a graphing calculator or software and computer also appear in the exercises. On the other hand, problems that are not specially designated may still use technology (for example, to solve a higher-degree equation). Several technology manuals are also available at a discount price. See Instructor/Student Supplement section in the Walk-Through for details.

- **Guest essays** provide alternate viewpoints. The questions that follow are called MATHEMATICAL ESSAYS and are included to encourage individual writing assignments and mathematical exposition. We believe that students will benefit from individual writing and research in mathematics. Another pedagogical feature is the **"What this says:"** box in which we rephrase mathematical ideas in everyday language. In the problem sets we encourage students to summarize procedures and processes or to describe a mathematical result in everyday terms.

- **Group research projects**, each of which appears at the end of a chapter and involves intriguing questions whose mathematical content is tied loosely to the chapter just concluded. These projects have been developed and class-tested by their individual authors, to whom we are greatly indebted. Note that the complexity of these projects increases as we progress through the book and the mathematical maturity of the student is developed.

- We continue to utilize the **humanness** of mathematics. History is not presented as additional material to learn. Rather we have placed history into *problems* that lead the reader from the development of a concept to actually participating in the discovery process. The problems are designated as Historical Quest problems. The problems are not designed to be "add-on or challenge problems," but rather to become an integral part of the assignment. The level of difficulty of Quest problems ranges from easy to difficult. An extensive selection of biographies of noted mathematicians can be found on the internet site accompanying this text (www.prenhall.com/strauss)

> **Accuracy and Error Checking**
>
> Because of careful checking and proofing by several people besides each of the three authors, the authors and publisher believe this book to be substantially error free. For any errors remaining, the authors would be grateful if they were sent to Monty J. Strauss at **M.Strauss@ttu.edu** or Monty J. Strauss, Department of Mathematics and Statistics, Texas Tech University, Lubbock, TX 79409-1042.

Acknowledgments

The writing and publishing of a calculus book is a tremendous undertaking. We take this responsibility very seriously because a calculus book is instrumental in transmitting knowledge from one generation to the next. We would like to thank the many people who helped us in the preparation of this book. First, we thank our editor George Lobell, who led us masterfully through the development and publication of this book. We sincerely appreciate Henri Feiner, who not only worked all of the problems but also read and critiqued each word of the manuscript, and Carol Williams who transcribed our manuscript into TEX. We would like to thank Dennis Kletzing for his work in transforming the manuscript into finished pages. Finally, we would like to thank Lynn Savino Wendel, who led us through the production process.

Of primary concern is the accuracy of the book. We had the assistance of many: Henri Feiner, who read the entire manuscript and offered us many valuable suggestions; and Nancy and Mary Toscano, who were meticulous in their checking of our manuscript. Thanks also to the accuracy checkers of the previous editions, Jerry Alexanderson, Mike Ecker, Ken Sydel, Diana Gerardi, Kurt Norlin, Terri Bittner, Nancy Marsh, and Mary Toscano. We would also like to thank the following readers of the text for the many suggestions for improvement:

REVIEWERS OF THE THIRD EDITION:

Gregory Adams, Bucknell University

Robert Bakula, Ohio State University

J. Caggiano, Arkansas State Univery

James T. Campbell, University of Memphis

Lin Dearing, Clemson University

Stan Dick, George Mason University

Tevian Dray, Oregon State University

Michael W. Ecker, Pennsylvania State University, Wilkes-Barre Campus

Anda Gadidov, Gannon University

Ruth Gornet, Texas Tech University

Julia Hassett, Oakton Community College

Isom H. Herron, Rensselaer Polytechnic Institute

Michael G. Hilgers, University of Missouri–Rolla

Jason P. Huffman, Jacksonville State University

James E. Jamison, University of Memphis

Jeuel G. LaTorre, Clemson University

Ira Wayne Lewis, Texas Tech University

Maura B. Mast, University of Massachusetts–Boston

Mark Naber, Monroe County Community College

Chris Peterson, Colorado State University

Siew-Ching Pye, California State Polytechnic University–Pomona

Joe Rody, Arizona State University

Yongwu Rong, The George Washington University
Eric Rowley, Utah State University
John E. Santomas, Villanova University
Carl Seaquist, Texas Tech University
Dennis Wacker, Saint Louis University
W. Thurmon Whitley, University of New Haven
Teri Woodington, Colorado School of Mines
Cathleen M. Zucco-Teveloff, Trinity College

REVIEWERS OF THE FIRST TWO EDITIONS:

Gerald Alexanderson, Santa Clara University
David Arterburn, New Mexico Tech
Neil Berger, University of Illinois at Chicago
Michael L. Berry, West Virginia Wesleyan College
Linda A. Bolte, Eastern Washington University
Brian Borchers, New Mexico Tech
Barbara H. Briggs, Tennessee Technical University
Robert Broschat, South Dakota State University
Robert D. Brown, University of Kansas
Dan Chiddix, Ricks College
Philip Crooke, Vanderbilt University
Ken Dunn, Dalhousie University
Michael W. Ecker, Pennsylvania State University, Wilkes-Barre Campus
John H. Ellison, Grove City College
Mark Farris, Midwestern State University
Sally Fieschbeck, Rochester Institute of Technology
William P. Francis, Michigan Technological University
Stuart Goldenberg, California Polytechnic State University, San Luis Obispo Campus
Harvey Greenwald, California Polytechnic San Luis Obispo
Richard Hitt, University of South Alabama
Joel W. Irish, University of Southern Maine
Roger Jay, Tomball College
John H. Jenkins, Embry Riddle Aeronautical University
Clement T. Jeske, University of Wisconsin–Platteville
Kathy Kepner, Paducah Community College
Daniel King, Sarah Lawrence College
Lawrence Kratz, Idaho State University
Don Leftwich, Oklahoma Christian University
Sam Lessing, Northeast Missouri University
Estela S. Llinas, University of Pittsburgh at Greensburg
Pauline Lowman, Western Kentucky University
Ching Lu, Southern Illinois University at Edwardsville
William E. Mastrocola, Colgate University
Philip W. McCartney, Northern Kentucky University
E. D. McCune, Stephen F. Austin State University
John C. Michels, Chemeketa Community College

Judith Ann Miller, Delta College

Ann Morlet, Cleveland State University

Dena Jo Perkins, Oklahoma Christian University

Pamela B. Pierce, College of Wooster

Judith Reeves, California Polytechnic State Universty, Pomona Campus

Jim Roznowski, Delta College

Peter Salamon, San Diego State University

Connie Schrock, Emporia State University

Tatiana Shubin, San Jose State University

Jo Smith, Ketering University

Anita E. Solow, DePauw University

Lowell Stultz, Kalamazoo Valley Community College

Tingxiu Wang, Oakton Community College

Monty J. Strauss
Gerald L. Bradley
Karl J. Smith

CALCULUS

HALLMARK FEATURES

Unique Student Mathematics Handbook ▶

(Included on the Student CD-ROM as well as in an optional print supplement)

This "Just-in-Time Precalculus Review" provides precalculus drill/review material, a catalogue of curves, analytic geometry, and integral tables. Students are guided from the text to this handbook by a **SMH** symbol located in the text margin. This guide is entirely text-author written. See the description of the Student CD-ROM for other features.

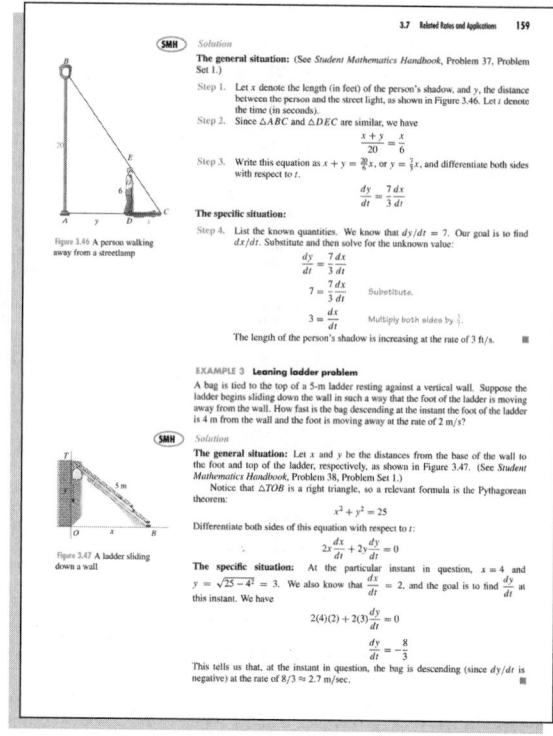

page 159

CD-ROM included free in both the Instructor and Student Editions.

May be shrinkwrapped with any version of the text.

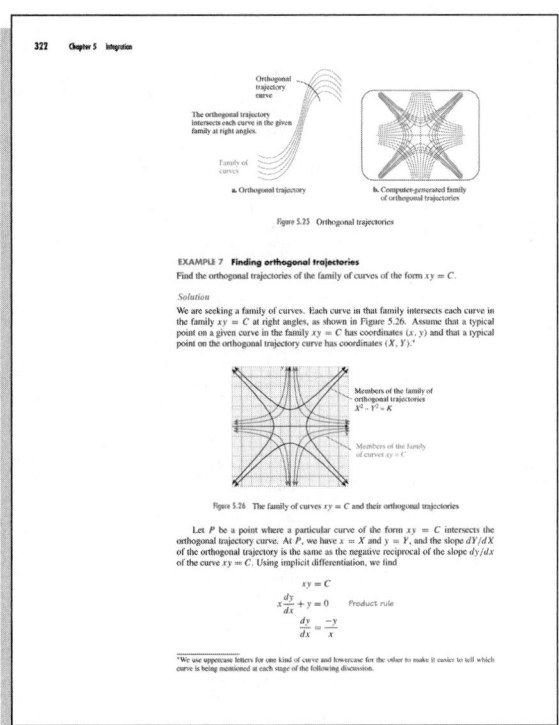

page 322

◀ Emphasis on visualization

Over 1900 graphs and pictures are featured throughout the text. Designed to supplement the text prose, the art program helps student to develop mathematical intuition and problem-solving skills.

Effective use of technology ▶

Graphing calculators and computer algebra systems are carefully integrated throughout the text. The "Technology Notes" feature gives students insight into how technological advances can be used to help understand calculus. Instructors can also encourage students to use technology to complete exercise sets. Laboratory manuals are available at a discount when packaged with the text. See supplements section of a complete list of available technology.

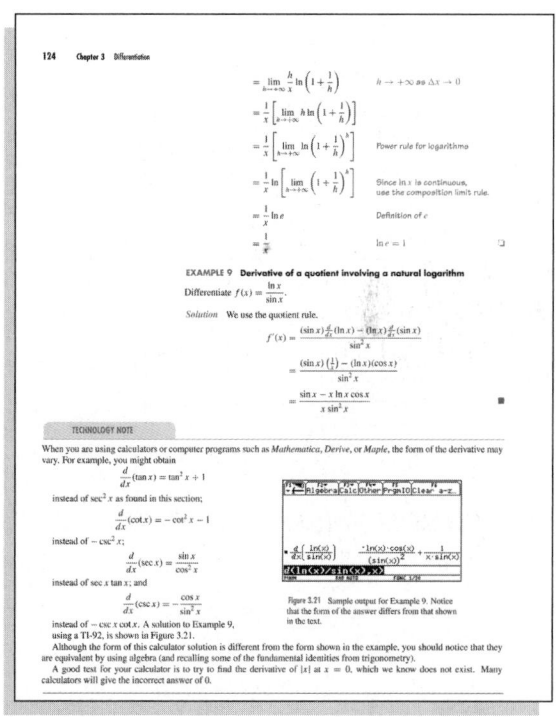

page 124

PROBLEM SETS

"What Does This Say?" Problems ▶

These problems ask students to respond to questions or to rephrase sentences in their own words. Designed to help students develop the essential skill of communicating mathematical ideas.

4.4 PROBLEM SET

Ⓐ **1. WHAT DOES THIS SAY?** Outline a method for curve sketching.

2. WHAT DOES THIS SAY? What are critical numbers? Discuss the importance of critical numbers in curve sketching.

45. The *ideal speed* v for a banked curve on a highway is modeled by the equation

$$v^2 = gr \tan\theta$$

page 227

Interpretation Problems ▶

These problems require exposition that requires a line of thinking that is not directly covered in the textbook. Encourages students to think critically about calculus concepts.

58. Interpretation Problem Evaluate $\lim\limits_{x\to 0}\left[x^2 - \dfrac{\cos x}{1{,}000{,}000{,}000}\right]$. Explain why a calculator solution may lead to an incorrect conclusion about the limit.

page 69

21. $\lim\limits_{x\to 0^+} \dfrac{\sin x}{\sqrt{x}}$

22. $\lim\limits_{x\to 0^+} \dfrac{1-\cos\sqrt{x}}{x}$

23. $\lim\limits_{x\to 0} \dfrac{\sin 2x}{x}$

24. $\lim\limits_{x\to 0} \dfrac{\sin 4x}{9x}$

25. $\lim\limits_{t\to 0} \dfrac{\tan 5t}{\tan 2t}$

26. $\lim\limits_{x\to 0} \dfrac{\cot 3x}{\cot x}$

27. $\lim\limits_{x\to 0} \dfrac{1-\cos x}{\sin x}$

28. $\lim\limits_{x\to 0} \dfrac{\sin^2 x}{2x}$

29. $\lim\limits_{x\to 0} \dfrac{\sin^2 x}{x^2}$

30. $\lim\limits_{x\to 0} \dfrac{x^2\cos 2x}{1-\cos x}$

31. $\lim\limits_{x\to 0} \dfrac{\sec x - 1}{x\sec x}$

32. $\lim\limits_{x\to\pi/4} \dfrac{1-\tan x}{\sin x - \cos x}$

page 69

◀ Computational Problems

Graded exercise sets that are progressively more challenging and grouped into three categories. 'A' problems are routine, 'B' problems require independent thought, and 'C' problems focus on theory. Makes assigning exercises easier and allows students to gain confidence as they progress through the exercises.

20. Modeling Problem Two towns A and B are 12.0 mi apart and are located 5.0 and 3.0 mi, respectively, from a long, straight highway, as shown in Figure 4.62.

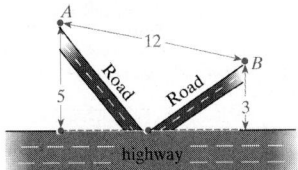

Figure 4.62 Building the shortest road

A construction company has a contract to build a road from A to the highway and then to B. Analyze a model to determine the length (to the nearest tenth of a mile) of the *shortest* road that meets these requirements.

page 246

Counterexample Problems ▶

These problems help students develop the ability to construct counterexamples. Students are asked to formulate an example that satisfies certain conditions.

◀ **Modeling Problems**

Designed to help students see the applications of calculus to multiple disciplines and real-world situations.

67. Counterexample Problem When the line segment $y = x - 2$ between $x = 1$ and $x = 3$ is revolved about the x-axis, it generates part of a cone. The formula obtained in Section 6.4 says that the surface area of the cone is

$$\int_1^3 2\pi(x - 2)\sqrt{2}\,dx$$

but this integral is equal to 0. What is wrong? What is the actual surface area?

page 421

37. Exploration Problem Suppose that $f(t)$ is continuous for all t and that for any number x it is known that the average value of f on $[-1, x]$ is

$$A(x) = \sin x$$

Use this information to deduce the identity of f.

page 333

◀ **Exploration Problems**

These problems explore concepts which may prove true or false and provide opportunities for innovative thinking.

PROBLEM SETS

Spy Problems ▶

A student favorite, these problems which run throughout the text like a movie serial, trace the heroic events of an international spy. His survival requires the students' help by successfully answering calculus questions.

54. Spy problem Just as the Spy is about to catch up with Scélérat (Problem 70 of Chapter 10 Supplementary Problems), the snow gives way and he falls into a cavern. He staggers to his feet and removes his skis. Why is it so warm? Good grief—the cave is a large roasting oven! Fortunately, he is wearing his heat-detector ring, which indicates the direction of greatest temperature decrease. Suppose the bunker is coordinatized so that the temperature at each point (x, y) on the floor of the bunker is given by

$$T(x, y) = 3(x - 6)^2 + 1.5(y - 1)^2 + 41$$

degrees Fahrenheit, where x and y are in feet. The Spy begins at the point $(1, 5)$ and stumbles across the room at the rate of 4 ft/min, always moving in the direction of maximum temperature decrease. But he can last no more than 2 minutes under these conditions! Assuming that there is an escape hole at the point where the temperature is minimal, does he make it or is the Spy toast at last?

page 748

81. HISTORICAL QUEST

Ramanujan was that rarest of mathematicians, an instinctive genius with virtually no formal training. Like his Hindu predecessor, Bhaskara (see the Historical Quest in Problem 55 of Section 4.4), Ramanujan had an uncanny instinct for numerical "truth" and conceived of his results in much the same way that a sculptor "sees" a statue

SRINIVASA RAMANUJAN
1887–1920

in a raw block of stone. In his short life, he initiated new ways of thinking about number theory and made conjectures that are the subject of mathematical inquiry to this day.

A story related by his friend and mentor, the eminent British number theorist G. H. Hardy (1877–1947), serves to illustrate the resonance between Ramanujan's mind and the concept of number. Ramanujan was ill and Hardy came to visit him in the hospital. At a loss for how to begin the conversation, Hardy idly remarked that he had arrived in a taxi with the "dull" number 1729. Ramanujan immediately grew excited and exclaimed, "No, Hardy, it is a very interesting number, for it is the smallest integer that can be expressed as the sum of cubes in two different ways." ($1729 = 1^3 + 12^3 = 9^3 + 10^3$.)

In a letter from Ramanujan to G. H. Hardy at Cambridge University,* Ramanujan stated

$$1 - 5\left(\frac{1}{2}\right)^3 + 9\left(\frac{1 \cdot 3}{2 \cdot 4}\right)^3 - 13\left(\frac{1 \cdot 3 \cdot 5}{2 \cdot 4 \cdot 6}\right)^3 + \cdots = \frac{2}{\pi}$$

Hardy spent a great deal of time wondering how this sum could be equal to $2/\pi$. ■

page 568

◀ **Historical Quest Problems**

These problems help students to place calculus in a historical context, and further encourages them to take part in the mathematical discovery process.

60. Journal Problem *Crux,* problem by John A. Winterink* ■
Prove the validity of the following simple method for finding the center of a conic: For the central conic,

$$\phi(x, y) = ax^2 + 2hxy + by^2 + 2gx + 2fy + c = 0$$

$ab - h^2 \neq 0$, show that the center is the intersection of the lines $\partial\phi/\partial x = 0$ and $\partial\phi/\partial y = 0$.

page 719

◀ **Journal Problems**

Journal problems are reprinted from leading mathematics journals. Citations are provided if students wish to locate additional information. A great resource for further exploration.

END-OF-CHAPTER PROBLEMS

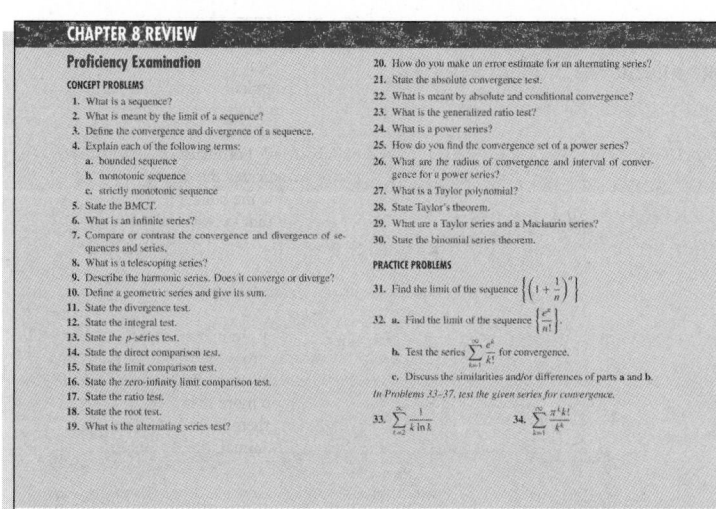

page 566

page 566

◀ Concept Problems

Concept problems are designed to develop students' conceptual understanding of calculus by learning how to think and draw conclusions about calculus topics.

◀ Practice Problems

Practice problems are specifically designed to help students develop their computational skills.

▼ Putnam Examination Problems

These challenging problems are provided to give insight into the types of problems that are asked in mathematical competitions, like the Mathematical Association of America's annual competition.

---

97. Putnam Examination Problem Let f be a real-valued function having partial derivatives defined for $x^2 + y^2 < 1$ that satisfies $|f(x, y)| \leq 1$. Show that there exists a point (x_0, y_0) in the interior of the unit circle such that
$$[f_x(x_0, y_0)]^2 + [f_y(x_0, y_0)]^2 \leq 16.$$

98. Putnam Examination Problem Find the smallest volume bounded by the coordinate planes and a tangent plane to the ellipsoid
$$\frac{x^2}{a^2} + \frac{y^2}{b^2} + \frac{z^2}{c^2} = 1$$

99. Putnam Examination Problem Find the shortest distance between the plane $Ax + By + Cz + 1 = 0$ and the ellipsoid
$$\frac{x^2}{a^2} + \frac{y^2}{b^2} + \frac{z^2}{c^2} \leq 1$$

---

page 774

page 774

Supplementary Problems

Describe the domain of each function given in Problems 1–4.

1. $f(x, y) = \sqrt{16 - x^2 - y^2}$ **2.** $f(x, y) = \dfrac{x^2 - y^2}{x - y}$

3. $f(x, y) = \sin^{-1} x + \cos^{-1} y$ **4.** $f(x, y) = e^{x+y} \tan^{-1}\left(\dfrac{y}{x}\right)$

Find the partial derivatives f_x and f_y for the functions defined in Problems 5–10.

5. $f(x, y) = \dfrac{x^2 - y^2}{x + y}$ **6.** $f(x, y) = x^3 e^{3y/(2x)}$

7. $f(x, y) = x^2 y + \sin \dfrac{y}{x}$ **8.** $f(x, y) = \ln\left(\dfrac{xy}{x + 2y}\right)$

9. $f(x, y) = 2x^3 y + 3xy^2 + \dfrac{y}{x}$ **10.** $f(x, y) = xye^{xy}$

For each function given in Problems 11–15, describe the level curve or level surface $f = c$ for the given values of the constant c.

11. $f(x, y) = x^2 - y;\ c = 2, c = -2$

12. $f(x, y) = 6x + 2y;\ c = 0, c = 1, c = 2$

13. $z = f(x, y) = \begin{cases} \sqrt{x^2 + y^2} & \text{if } z \geq 0 \\ |y| & \text{if } z < 0 \end{cases}$
$c = 0, c = 1, c = -1$

14. $f(x, y, z) = x^2 + y^2 + z^2;\ c = 16, c = 0, c = -25$

15. $f(x, y, z) = x^2 + \dfrac{y^2}{2} + \dfrac{z^2}{9};\ c = 1, c = 2$

Evaluate the limits in Problems 16 and 17, assuming they exist.

16. $\displaystyle\lim_{(x,y)\to(1,1)} \dfrac{xy}{x^2 + y^2}$ **17.** $\displaystyle\lim_{(x,y)\to(0,0)} \dfrac{x + ye^{-x}}{1 + x^2}$

page 771

page 771

▲ Supplemental Problems

Extensive sets of problems (usually about 100) occur at the end of each chapter. These problems are based on randomly selected topics from the complete chapter. Also helps students to check their comprehension of the entire chapter.

MEDIA SUPPLEMENTS

◀ **New Interactive Student CD-ROM**

(free with every new copy)

The new student CD-ROM is designed to enhance students' computational and conceptual understanding of calculus. This CD-ROM is not an add-on of extra material to the text but rather an incredibly useful expansion of the text and includes:

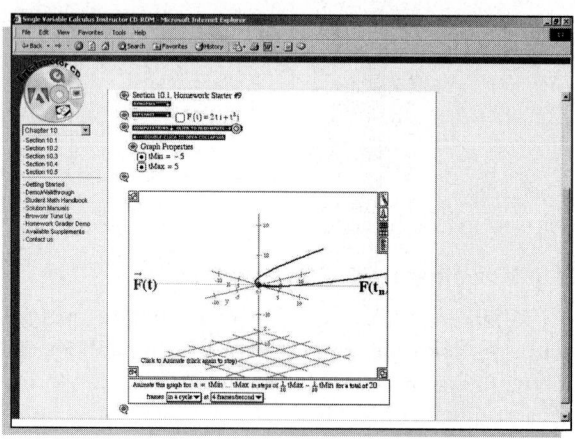

Live Examples

The heart of this CD is the Live Examples powered by Live Math. Nearly every geometric text example is animated. The traditional text environment is enhanced and brought to life with animations and questions exploring what-if scenarios. Algebraic solutions are paired with geometric solutions. There are hundreds of Live Examples to accompany the complete text.

True/False Study Questions

There are 10 T/F questions per text section. These questions focus on the core ideas of calculus. These questions are specifically designed to encourage students to read (not just thumb through the text to find examples matching the questions).

Homework Starters

Each text section includes teaching hints for 3–5 homework problems. These hints often include geometric animations. There are more than 150 Homework Starters.

Unique Student Mathematics Handbook

A unified and complete treatment of prerequisite material, easily referenced and keyed to the textbook. Comes free on the Student CD-ROM. Also available in print format.

MEDIA SUPPLEMENTS

Companion Website ▼

www.prenhall.com/strauss

 This website contains much of what is on the CD-ROM along with other activities better suited to the Internet and includes:

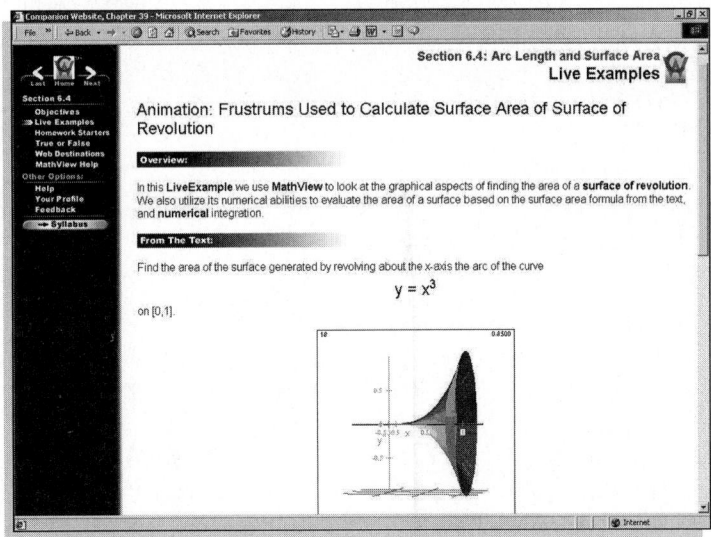

Live Examples

The heart of this website lies in the Live Examples powered by Live Math. Nearly every geometric text example is animated. The traditional text environment is now enhanced and brought to life with animations and questions exploring what-if scenarios. Algebraic solutions are paired with geometric solutions. There are hundreds of Live Examples.

Homework Starters

Each text section includes teaching hints for 3–5 homework problems. These hints often include geometric animations. There are more than 150 Homework Starters.

True/False Study Questions

There are 10 T/F questions per text section. These questions focus on the core ideas of calculus. These questions are specifically designed to encourage students to read (not just thumb through the text to find examples matching the questions).

Links and Destinations

There are roughly five to ten links per text section to other Internet based sites with calculus oriented or related material. For example, one fascinating link is the enormous History Archive Site in St. Andrews, Scotland, which is loaded with hundreds, if not thousands, of biographies and other fascinating historical material.

MEDIA SUPPLEMENTS

Prentice Hall Online Homework Grader ▼

There are over 2000 questions from this calculus text made available in algorithmic form that allows for professors to distribute, collect, grade, and record assignments.

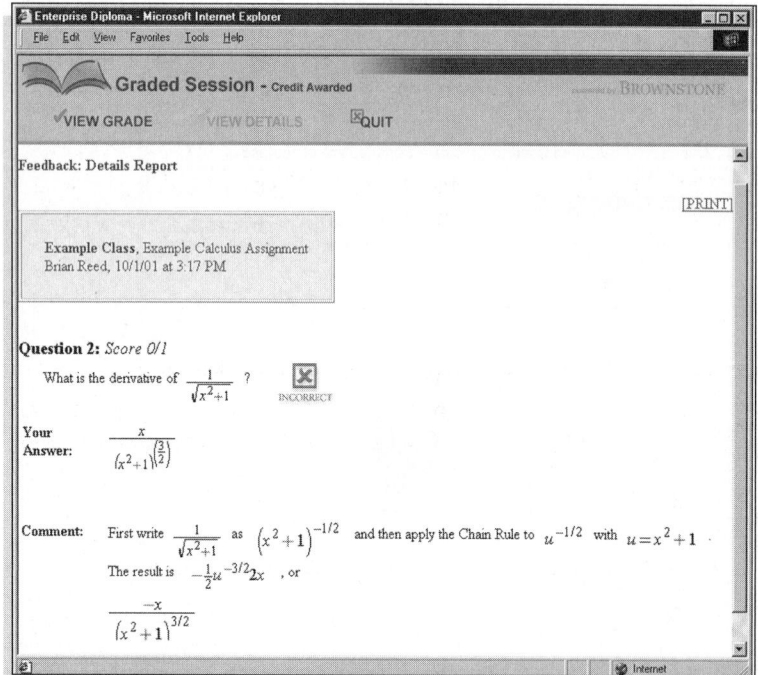

Assessment and Homework Management

This web-based system is designed to help you teach and help your students learn. This system was developed to automate the production and delivery of web-based assignments ranging from both homework and self-paced practice to secure, proctored testing.

For instructors, the system provides a more natural transition from traditional paper-based assignments to time-saving, automatically graded online homework, that improves on the limitations of current course management systems. Students prefer this system because it provides immediate, individualized performance feedback and the opportunity to generate unlimited practice through algorithmic study sessions.

What can you do with the Homework Grader? You can...

■ Easily create self-scoring, web-delivered tests and homework assignments from your own time-tested problem files.
■ Use the 2000 textbook problems already loaded for use.
■ Edit, modify, or expand existing question banks (whether publisher-provided or homegrown).
■ Control the rules and policies surrounding your assignments, including time limitations, ability to retake assignments, feedback content, results reporting, low-stakes or high-stakes forms, and formats.
■ Publish your assignments to your own class-specific website, where your students will log in to complete the work.

For further details go to www.prenhall.com/math

OTHER AVAILABLE SUPPLEMENTS

STUDENT SUPPLEMENTS

Student Survival and Solutions Manual (0-13-067245-9)

Contains carefully worked out solutions to all odd-numbered exercises in the text. Contains helpful hints to bridge the gap between the textbook and a working knowledge of calculus. These hints anticipate the types of errors and difficulties a student may have while taking the course.

Student Mathematics Handbook (0-13-092021-5)

A unified and complete treatment of prerequisite material, easily referenced and keyed to the textbook. Comes free on the Student CD-ROM. Also available in print format.

Student CD-ROM

Comes free packaged with each new text. Contains animations of nearly every text example and 10 True/False questions per section. Also includes Homework Starters, animations, video clips and the complete contents of the Student Math Handbook.

Companion Website

www.prenhall.com/strauss

Provides additional applied examples and problems, animations that explore "what if" scenarios, exciting links to other math sites on the web, True/False quizzes to emphasize key concepts, and a syllabus manager for professors. Contains all the materials from the Student CD-ROM along with a Syllabus Manager and links to other appropriate and helpful math sites on the web.

TECHNOLOGY MANUALS

Available at a discount when packaged with the text.

A MAPLE APPROACH TO CALCULUS, 2E: 0-13-092014-2

A MATHEMATICA APPROACH TO CALCULUS, 2E: 0-13-092015-0

A TI GRAPHIC CALCULATOR APPROACH TO CALCULUS, 2E: 0-13-092017-7

CALCULUS CONCEPTS USING DERIVE: 0-13-085152-3

USING MATLAB IN CALCULUS: 0-13-027268-X

OTHER AVAILABLE SUPPLEMENTS

INSTRUCTOR SUPPLEMENTS

Instructor's Edition (0-13-092010-X)

The Instructor's Edition includes the answers to all odd-numbered exercises and detailed Teaching Notes.

Prentice Hall Homework Grading System

An algorithmically generated on-line homework delivery service that allows professors to distribute, collect, grade and record assignments. Functions both as a homework study device and testing program.
See www.prenhall.com/math

TestGen-EQ (0-13-092018-5)

This easy to use test generator contains all of the questions from the Printed Test Bank.

Printed Test Bank (0-13-062028-9)

The test bank offers a full complement of additional problems that correlate to exercises presented in the text. Computerized versions of the the test bank are also available.

Instructor's Solutions Manual (0-13-062026-2)

Includes solutions to all the exercises in the text.

Instructor's CD-ROM (0-13-067325-0)

Contains the same content of the Student CD-ROM, plus links to an electronic Instructor's Solutions Manual and PowerPoint slides of text art.

Companion Website

www.prenhall.com/strauss

Provides additional applied examples and problems, animations taht explore "what if" scenarios, exciting links to other math sites on the web, True/False quizzes to emphasize key concepts, and a syllabus manager for professors. Contains all the materials from the Student CD-ROM along with a Syllabus Manager and links to other appropriate and helpful math sites on the web.

TECHNOLOGY MANUALS

Available at a discount when packaged with the text.

GRESSER, A MAPLE APPROACH TO CALCULUS, 2E: 0-13-092014-2

GRESSER, A MATHEMATICA APPROACH TO CALCULUS, 2E: 0-13-092015-0

GRESSER, A TI GRAPHIC CALCULATOR APPROACH TO CALCULUS, 2E: 0-13-092017-7

FREESE/STEGEGNA CALCULUS CONCEPTS USING DERIVE: 0-13-085152-3

JENSEN, USING MATLAB IN CALCULUS: 0-13-027268-X

TEXT OPTIONS

Single Variable Calculus, 3e

Includes Chapters 1-10 of the three semester full text. This version is intended for a two-semester course in single variable calculus.

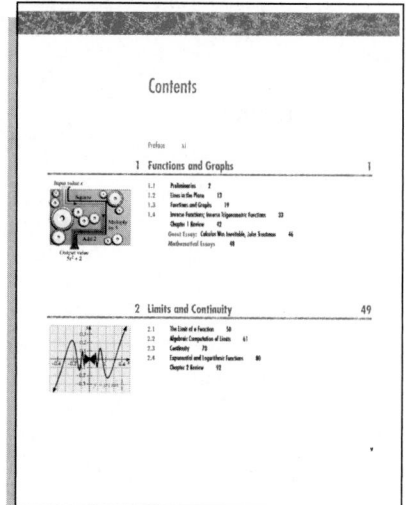 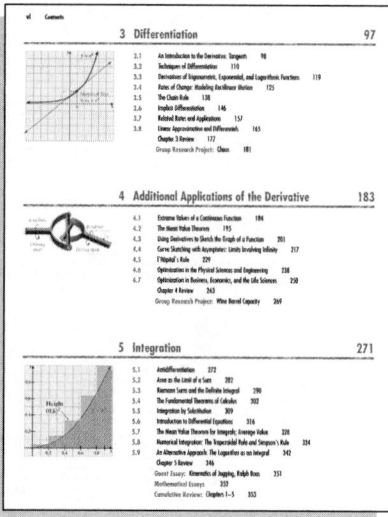 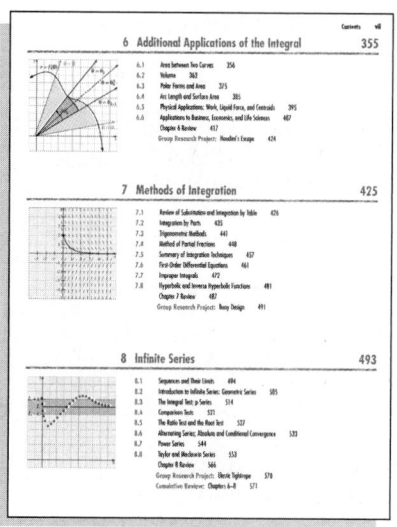

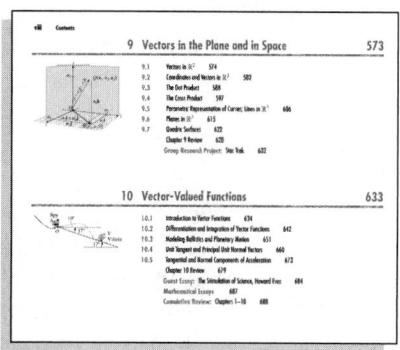

SUPPLEMENTS FOR SINGLE VARIABLE CALCULUS

INSTRUCTOR

Instructor's Edition (0-13-035303-5)
The Instructor's Edition includes the answers to all odd-numbered exercises and detailed Teaching Notes.

TestGen-EQ (0-13-092018-5)
This easy to use test generator contains all of the questions from the Printed Test Bank.

Printed Test Bank (0-13-062028-9)

The test bank offers a full complement of additional problems that correlate to exercises presented in the text. Computerized versions of the the test bank are also available.

Instructor's Solutions Manual (0-13-062026-2)
Includes solutions to all the exercises in the text.

STUDENT

Student Survival and Solutions Manual (0-13-067245-9)
Contains carefully worked out solutions to all odd-numbered exercises in the text. Contains helpful hints to bridge the gap between the textbook and a working knowledge of calculus. These hints anticipate the types of errors and difficulties a student may have while taking the course.

Student Mathematics Handbook (0-13-092021-5)
A unified and complete treatment of prerequisite material, easily referenced and keyed to the textbook. Comes free on the Student CD-ROM. Also available in print format.

Single Variable Text and Student Mathematics Handbook (0-13-074449-2)

Please see Supplement section of this Guide for more complete descriptions.

TEXT OPTIONS

Multivariable Calculus, 3e

Includes Chapters 9-14 of the three-semester full text. This version is intended for a one-semester course in multivariable calculus.

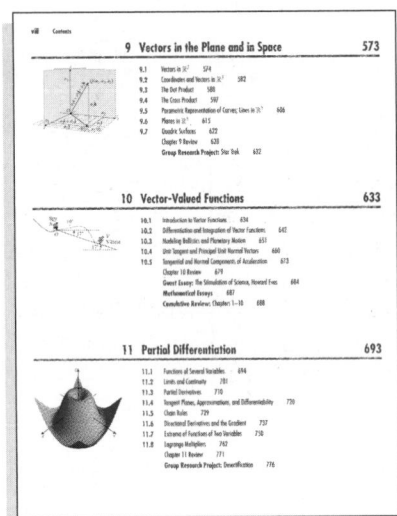

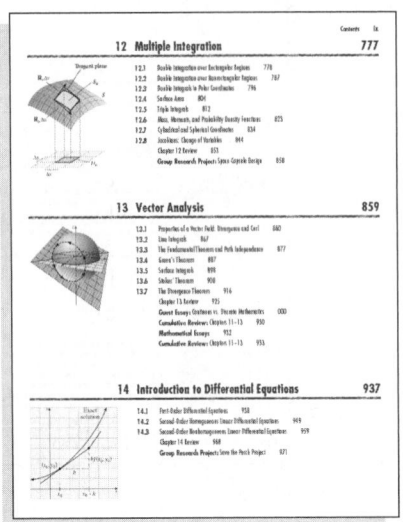

SUPPLEMENTS FOR MULTIVARIABLE CALCULUS

INSTRUCTOR

TestGen-EQ (0-13-092018-5)

This easy to use test generator contains all of the questions from the Printed Test Bank.

Printed Test Bank (0-13-062028-9)

The test bank offers a full complement of additional problems that correlate to exercises presented in the text. Computerized versions of the the test bank are also available.

Instructor's Solutions Manual (0-13-062026-2)

Includes solutions to all the exercises in the text.

STUDENT

Student Survival and Solutions Manual (0-13-067245-9)

Contains carefully worked out solutions to all odd-numbered exercises in the text. Contains helpful hints to bridge the gap between the textbook and a working knowledge of calculus. These hints anticipate the types of errors and difficulties a student may have while taking the course.

Student Mathematics Handbook (0-13-092021-5)

A unified and complete treatment of prerequisite material, easily referenced and keyed to the textbook. Comes free on the Student CD-ROM. Also available in print format.

Multivariable Text and Student Mathematics Handbook
(0-13-074440-9)

Please see Supplement section of this Guide for more complete descriptions.

1

Functions and Graphs

PREVIEW

This chapter uses several topics from algebra and trigonometry that are essential for the study of calculus. The necessary prerequisites for this course are reviewed in a companion book, *Student Mathematics Handbook*, and are briefly discussed in this chapter. This handbook is provided free with new copies of this textbook.

The concept of function is an especially important prerequisite for calculus. Even if you wish to skip most of this initial chapter, you should review the basic notions of functions and inverse functions in Sections 1.3 and 1.4.

PERSPECTIVE

Although modern science requires the use of many different skills and procedures, calculus is the primary mathematical tool for dealing with change. Sir Isaac Newton, one of the discoverers of calculus, once remarked that to accomplish his results, he "stood on the shoulders of giants." Indeed, calculus was not born in a moment of divine inspiration but developed gradually, as a variety of apparently different ideas and methods merged into a coherent pattern. The purpose of this initial chapter is to lay the foundation for the development of calculus.

1.1   Preliminaries

IN THIS SECTION

distance on a number line, absolute value, distance in the plane, trigonometry, solving trigonometric equations

Every mathematical book that is worth reading must be read "backwards and forwards," if I may use the expression. I would modify Lagrange's advice a little and say, "Go on, but often return to strengthen your faith." When you come on a hard and dreary passage, pass it over; come back to it after you have seen its importance or found its importance or found the need for it further on.

———George Chrystal,
Algebra, Part 2 (Edinburgh, 1889)

This section provides a quick review of some fundamental concepts and techniques from precalculus mathematics. If you have recently had a precalculus course, you may skip over this material.

Algebra, geometry, and trigonometry are important ingredients of calculus. Even though we will review many ideas from algebra, geometry, and trigonometry, we will not be able to develop every idea from these courses before we use it in calculus. For example, the law of cosines from trigonometry may be needed to solve a problem in a section that never mentions trigonometry in the exposition. For this reason, we have made available a separate reference manual, *Student Mathematics Handbook*, which includes the background material you will need for this course. We suggest that you keep it close at hand. References to this handbook are indicated by the logo **SMH**

DISTANCE ON A NUMBER LINE

You are probably familiar with the set of **real numbers** and several of its subsets, including the counting or natural numbers, the integers, the rational numbers, and the irrational numbers.

SMH The real numbers, *along with these subsets, are found in Chapter 2 of the Student Mathematics Handbook.*

The real numbers can be visualized most easily by using a **one-dimensional coordinate system** called a **real number line**, as shown in Figure 1.1.

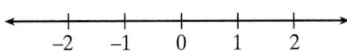

Figure 1.1   Real number line

Notice that a number a is less than a number b if it is to the left of b on a real number line, as shown in Figure 1.2. Similar definitions can be given for $a > b$, $a \le b$, and $a \ge b$.

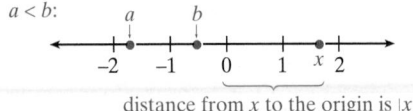

distance from x to the origin is $|x|$

Figure 1.2   Geometric definition of *less than*

The location of the number 0 is chosen arbitrarily, and a unit distance is picked (meters, feet, inches, ...). Numbers are ordered on the real number line according to the following order properties.

Order Properties

For all real numbers a, b, and c

   Trichotomy law: Exactly one of the following is true:
$$a < b, \quad a > b, \quad \text{or} \quad a = b.$$

   Transitive law of inequality: If $a < b$ and $b < c$, then $a < c$.

   Additive law of inequality: If $a < c$ and $b < d$, then $a + b < c + d$.

   Multiplicative law of inequality: If $a < b$, then
$$ac < bc \text{ if } c > 0 \quad \text{and} \quad ac > bc \text{ if } c < 0.$$

ABSOLUTE VALUE

Absolute Value

The **absolute value** of a real number a, denoted by $|a|$, is

$$|a| = \begin{cases} a & \text{if} \quad a \geq 0 \\ -a & \text{if} \quad a < 0 \end{cases}$$

The number x is located $|x|$ units away from 0 — to the right if $x > 0$ and to the left if $x < 0$.

Absolute value is used to describe the distance between points on a number line.

Distance Between Two Points on a Number Line

The **distance** between the numbers x_1 and x_2 on a number line is

$$|x_2 - x_1|$$

WARNING Note that
$|x_2 - x_1| = |x_1 - x_2|$

For example, the distance between 2 and -3 is $|2 - (-3)| = 5$ units, and between -2 and -3 is $|-2 - (-3)| = 1$ unit.

Several properties of absolute value that you will need in this course are summarized in Table 1.1.

TABLE 1.1 Properties of Absolute Value

Let a and b be any real numbers.

Property	Comment
1. $|a| \geq 0$	1. Absolute value is nonnegative.
2. $|-a| = |a|$	2. The absolute value of a number and the absolute value of its opposite are equal.
3. $|a|^2 = a^2$	3. If an absolute value is squared, the absolute value signs can be dropped because both squares are nonnegative.
4. $|ab| = |a|\,|b|$	4. The absolute value of a product is the product of the absolute values.
5. $\left|\dfrac{a}{b}\right| = \dfrac{|a|}{|b|}, \quad b \neq 0$	5. The absolute value of a quotient is the quotient of the absolute values.
6. $-|a| \leq a \leq |a|$	6. This property is true because $|a|$ is either a or $-a$.
7. Let $b \geq 0$; $|a| = b$ if and only if $a = \pm b$	7. This property is useful in solving absolute value equations. See Example 1.
8. Let $b > 0$; $|a| < b$ if and only if $-b < a < b$	8. and 9. These are the main properties used in solving absolute value inequalities. See Example 2.
9. Let $b > 0$; $|a| > b$ if and only if $a > b$ or $a < -b$	
10. $|a + b| \leq |a| + |b|$	10. This property is called the **triangle inequality**. It is used in both theory and numerical computations involving inequalities.

WARNING "p if and only if q" is used to mean that both a statement and its converse are true. That is,

if p, then q, *and*

if q, then p.

For example, property 8 has two parts:

(i) If $|a| < b$, then $-b < a < b$;
(ii) If $-b < a < b$, then $|a| < b$.

Property 7 is sometimes stated for any a or b as $|a| = |b|$ if and only if $a = \pm b$. Since $|b| = \pm b$, it follows that this property is equivalent to property 7. Also, properties 8 and 9 are true for $\leq$ and $\geq$ inequalities. Specifically, if $b \geq 0$, then

$$|a| \leq b \quad \text{if and only if} \quad -b \leq a \leq b$$

and

$$|a| \geq b \quad \text{if and only if} \quad a \geq b \text{ or } a \leq -b$$

A convenient notation for representing intervals on a number line is called **interval notation** and is summarized in the accompanying table. Note that a solid dot (•) at an endpoint of an interval indicates that it is included in the interval, whereas an open dot (○) indicates that it is excluded. An interval is **bounded** if both of its endpoints are real numbers. A bounded interval is **open** if it includes neither of its endpoints, **half-open** if it includes only one endpoint, and **closed** if it includes both endpoints. The symbol "∞" (pronounced *infinity*) is used for intervals that are not limited in one direction or another. In particular, $(-\infty, \infty)$ denotes the entire real number line.

If this notation is new to you, please check the *Handbook* (Section 2.7) for further examples. We will use this interval notation to write the solutions of absolute value equations and absolute value inequality problems.

Name of Interval	Inequality Notation	Interval Notation	Graph
Closed interval	$a \leq x \leq b$	$[a, b]$	
	$a \leq x$	$[a, \infty)$	
	$x \leq b$	$(-\infty, b]$	
Open interval	$a < x < b$	(a, b)	
	$a < x$	(a, ∞)	
	$x < b$	$(-\infty, b)$	
Half-open interval	$a < x \leq b$	$(a, b]$	
	$a \leq x < b$	$[a, b)$	
Real number line	All real numbers	$(-\infty, \infty)$	

Absolute Value Equations   Absolute value property 7 allows us to solve absolute value equations easily. For this reason property 7 is called the **absolute value equation property**.

EXAMPLE 1   Solving an equation with an absolute value on one side

Solve $|2x - 6| = x$.

Solution

If $2x - 6 \geq 0$, then $|2x - 6| = 2x - 6$ so that we solve

$$2x - 6 = x \quad \text{or} \quad x = 6 \qquad \text{Property 7}$$

If $2x - 6 < 0$, then $|2x - 6| = -(2x - 6)$ so that we solve

$$-(2x - 6) = x$$
$$-3x = -6$$
$$x = 2$$

The solutions are $x = 6$ and $x = 2$. ∎

The absolute value expression $|x - a|$ can be interpreted as the distance between x and a on a number line. An equation of the form

$$|x - a| = b$$

is satisfied by two values of x that are a given distance b from a when represented on a number line. For example, $|x - 5| = 3$ states that x is 3 units from 5 on a number line. Thus, x is either 2 or 8.

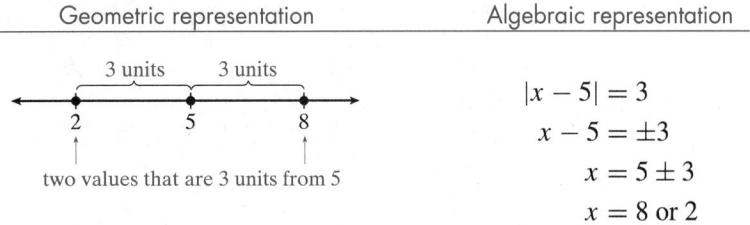

Absolute Value Inequalities   Because $|x - 5| = 3$ states that the distance from x to 5 is 3 units, the inequality $|x - 5| < 3$ states that the distance from x to 5 is less than 3 units, whereas $|x - 5| > 3$ states that the distance from x to 5 is greater than 3 units.

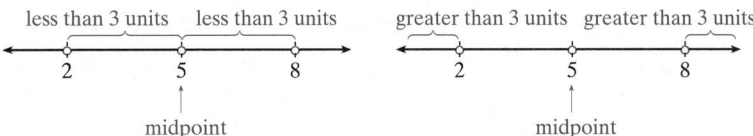

EXAMPLE 2   Solving an absolute value inequality

Solve $|2x - 3| \le 4$.

Solution

Algebraic solution:
$$-4 \le 2x - 3 \le 4 \qquad \text{Property 8}$$
$$-4 + 3 \le 2x - 3 + 3 \le 4 + 3$$
$$-1 \le 2x \le 7$$
$$-\frac{1}{2} \le \frac{2x}{2} \le \frac{7}{2}$$
$$-\frac{1}{2} \le x \le \frac{7}{2}$$

The solution is the interval $[-\frac{1}{2}, \frac{7}{2}]$.

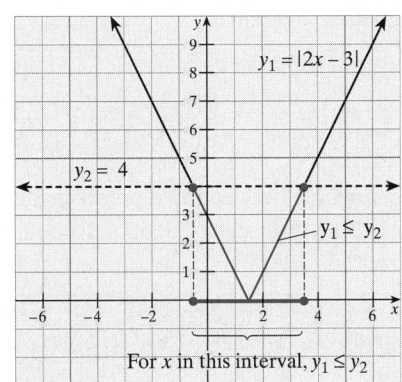

Figure 1.3 Solving an inequality by graphing

Geometric solution: Graph $y_1 = |2x - 3|$ and $y_2 = 4$, as shown in Figure 1.3. Because we are looking for $|2x - 3| \le 4$, we note those x-values on the real number line for which the graph of y_1 is below the graph of y_2. We see that the interval is $[-0.5, 3.5]$ or $[-\frac{1}{2}, \frac{7}{2}]$. ∎

When absolute value is applied to measurement, it is called **tolerance.** Tolerance is an allowable deviation from a standard. For example, a cement bag whose weight w lb is "90 lb plus or minus 2 lb" might be described as having a weight given by $|w - 90| \leq 2$. When considered as a tolerance, the expression $|x - a| \leq b$ may be interpreted as x being compared to a with an **absolute error** of measurement of b units. Consider the following example.

EXAMPLE 3   Absolute value as a tolerance

Suppose you purchase a 90-lb bag of cement. It will not weigh exactly 90 lb. The material must be measured, and the measurement is approximate. Some bags will weigh as much as 2 lb over 90 lb, and some will weigh as much as 2 lb under 90 lb. If so, the bag could weigh as much as 92 lb or as little as 88 lb. State this as an absolute value inequality.

Solution

Let w = weight of the bag of cement in pounds. Then

$$90 - 2 \leq w \leq 90 + 2$$
$$-2 \leq w - 90 \leq 2$$

Equivalently, $|w - 90| \leq 2$.   ■

DISTANCE IN THE PLANE

Absolute value is used to find the distance between two points on a number line. To find the distance between two points in a coordinate plane, we use the *distance formula*, which is derived by using the Pythagorean theorem.

THEOREM 1.1   Distance between two points in the plane

The distance d between the points $P_1(x_1, y_1)$ and $P_2(x_2, y_2)$ in the plane is given by

$$d = \sqrt{(\Delta x)^2 + (\Delta y)^2} = \sqrt{(x_2 - x_1)^2 + (y_2 - y_1)^2}$$

where Δx (read "delta x") is the **horizontal change $x_2 - x_1$** (sometimes called *run*) and Δy (read "delta y") is the **vertical change $y_2 - y_1$** (sometimes called *rise*).

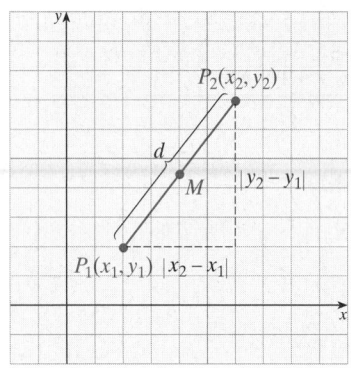

Figure 1.4 Distance formula

Proof   Using the two points, form a right triangle by drawing lines through the given points parallel to the coordinate axes, as shown in Figure 1.4.

The length of the horizontal side of the triangle is $|x_2 - x_1| = |\Delta x|$, and the length of the vertical side is $|y_2 - y_1| = |\Delta y|$. Then

$$d^2 = |\Delta x|^2 + |\Delta y|^2 \qquad \text{Pythagorean theorem}$$
$$d^2 = (\Delta x)^2 + (\Delta y)^2 \qquad \text{Absolute value property 3}$$
$$d = \sqrt{(\Delta x)^2 + (\Delta y)^2} \qquad \text{Solve for } d \qquad \square$$

Midpoint formula   Related to the formula for the distance between two points is the formula for finding the midpoint of a line segment, as shown in Figure 1.4.

Midpoint Formula

> The **midpoint**, M, of the segment with endpoints $P_1(x_1, y_1)$ and $P_2(x_2, y_2)$ has coordinates
> $$M\left(\frac{x_1 + x_2}{2}, \frac{y_1 + y_2}{2}\right)$$

Notice that the coordinates of the midpoint of a segment are found by averaging the first and second components of the coordinates of the endpoints, respectively. You are asked to derive this formula in Problem 74.

Relationship between an equation and a graph   **Analytic geometry** is that branch of geometry that ties together the geometric concept of position with an algebraic representation—namely, coordinates. For example, you remember from algebra that a line can be represented by an equation. Precisely what does this mean? Can we make such a statement that is true for any curve, not just for lines? We answer in the affirmative with the following definition.

Graph of an Equation

> The **graph of an equation** in two variables x and y is the collection of all points $P(x, y)$ whose coordinates (x, y) satisfy the equation.

There are two frequently asked questions in analytic geometry:

1. Given a graph (a geometrical representation), find the corresponding equation.
2. Given an equation (an algebraic representation), find the corresponding graph.

In Example 4, we use the distance formula to derive the equation of a circle. This means that if x and y are numbers that satisfy the equation, then the point (x, y) must lie on the circle. Conversely, the coordinates of any point on the circle will satisfy the equation.

EXAMPLE 4   Using the distance formula to derive an equation of a graph

Find the equation of a circle with center (h, k) and radius r.

Solution

Let (x, y) be any point on a circle. Recall that a circle is the set of all points in the plane a given distance from a given point. The given point (h, k) is the center and the given distance is the radius r.

$$r = \text{DISTANCE FROM } (h, k) \text{ TO } (x, y)$$
$$r = \sqrt{(x - h)^2 + (y - k)^2}$$
$$r^2 = (x - h)^2 + (y - k)^2, \quad \text{or} \quad (x - h)^2 + (y - k)^2 = r^2 \qquad \blacksquare$$

A **unit circle** is a circle of radius 1 and center at the origin, so its equation is $x^2 + y^2 = 1$.

EXAMPLE 5   Finding the equation of a circle

Find the equation of the circle with center $(3, -5)$ that passes through the point $(1, 8)$.

Solution

See Figure 1.5. The radius is the distance from the center to the given point:

$$r = \sqrt{(1 - 3)^2 + [8 - (-5)]^2}$$
$$= \sqrt{4 + 169}$$
$$= \sqrt{173}$$

Thus, the equation of the circle is

$$(x - 3)^2 + [y - (-5)]^2 = (\sqrt{173})^2$$
$$(x - 3)^2 + (y + 5)^2 = 173 \qquad \blacksquare$$

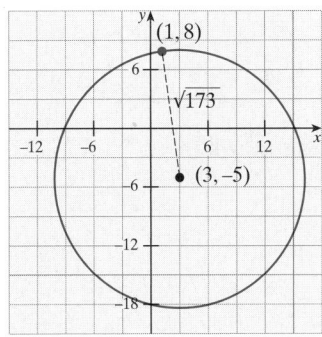

Figure 1.5 Circle with center $(3, -5)$ passing through $(1, 8)$

EXAMPLE 6   Graphing a circle given its equation

Sketch the graph of the circle whose equation is

$$4x^2 + 4y^2 - 4x + 8y - 5 = 0$$

Solution

We need to convert this equation into standard form. To do this we use a process called **completing the square** (see Section 2.6 of the *Student Mathematics Handbook*).

$$4x^2 + 4y^2 - 4x + 8y - 5 = 0$$

$$x^2 + y^2 - x + 2y = \tfrac{5}{4} \qquad \text{Coefficients of squared terms should be 1.}$$

$$(x^2 - x \quad) + (y^2 + 2y \quad) = \tfrac{5}{4} \qquad \text{Associate } x\text{-terms and } y\text{-terms.}$$

$$\left[x^2 - x + (-\tfrac{1}{2})^2\right] + (y^2 + 2y + 1^2) = \tfrac{5}{4} + \tfrac{1}{4} + 1 \qquad \text{Complete the squares by adding } \tfrac{1}{4} \text{ and 1 to both sides.}$$

$$(x - \tfrac{1}{2})^2 + (y + 1)^2 = \tfrac{10}{4} = \tfrac{5}{2}$$

This is a circle with center at $(\tfrac{1}{2}, -1)$ and radius $\sqrt{\tfrac{5}{2}}$. The graph is shown in Figure 1.6. ∎

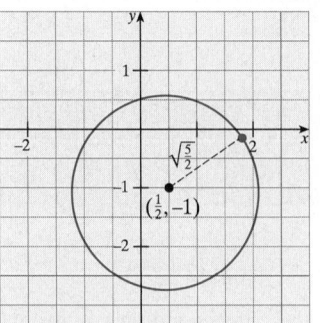

Figure 1.6 Sketch of
$4x^2 + 4y^2 - 4x + 8y - 5 = 0$

TRIGONOMETRY

One of the prerequisites for this book is trigonometry. If you need some review, consult a text on trigonometry or Chapter 4 of the *Student Mathematics Handbook* that accompanies this book. A summary of useful trigonometric formulas is found in Appendix E.

Angles are commonly measured in degrees and radians. A **degree** is defined to be $\tfrac{1}{360}$ revolution and a **radian** $\tfrac{1}{2\pi}$ revolution. Thus, to convert between degree and radian measure use the following formula:

$$\frac{\theta \text{ measured in degrees}}{360} = \frac{\theta \text{ measured in radians}}{2\pi}$$

WARNING
In calculus, angles are usually measured in terms of radians rather than degrees since radian measure often leads to simpler formulas. You may assume that when we write expressions such as $\sin x$, $\cos x$, and $\tan x$, the angle x is in radians unless otherwise specified by a degree symbol.

EXAMPLE 7   Converting degree measure to radian measure

Convert 255° to radian measure.

Solution $\dfrac{255}{360} = \dfrac{\theta}{2\pi}$

$$\theta = \left(\frac{\pi}{180}\right)(255) \approx 4.450589593$$ ∎

EXAMPLE 8   Converting radian measure to degree measure

Express 1 radian in terms of degrees.

Solution $\dfrac{\theta}{360} = \dfrac{1}{2\pi}$

$$\theta = \left(\frac{180}{\pi}\right)(1)$$

$$\approx 57.29577951°$$ ∎

SOLVING TRIGONOMETRIC EQUATIONS

There will be many times in calculus when you will need to solve a trigonometric equation. As you may remember from trigonometry, solving a trigonometric equation is equivalent to evaluating an inverse trigonometric relation. Inverse functions will be introduced in Section 1.4; for now, we will solve trigonometric equations whose solutions involve the values in Table 1.2 (called a **table of exact values**). These exact values from trigonometry are reviewed in the *Student Mathematics Handbook*.

TABLE 1.2   Exact Trigonometric Values

Function \ Angle θ	0	$\dfrac{\pi}{6}$	$\dfrac{\pi}{4}$	$\dfrac{\pi}{3}$	$\dfrac{\pi}{2}$
$\cos \theta$	1	$\dfrac{\sqrt{3}}{2}$	$\dfrac{\sqrt{2}}{2}$	$\dfrac{1}{2}$	0
$\sin \theta$	0	$\dfrac{1}{2}$	$\dfrac{\sqrt{2}}{2}$	$\dfrac{\sqrt{3}}{2}$	1
$\tan \theta$	0	$\dfrac{\sqrt{3}}{3}$	1	$\sqrt{3}$	undefined

It is customary to use the values from Table 1.2 whenever possible. The approximate calculator values will be given only when necessary.

EXAMPLE 9   Evaluating trigonometric functions

Evaluate $\cos \frac{\pi}{3}$; $\sin \frac{5\pi}{6}$; $\tan(-\frac{5\pi}{4})$; $\sec 1.2$; $\csc(-4.5)$; and $\cot 180°$.

Solution

If you use a calculator, make certain it is in the proper mode (radian or degree).

$$\cos \tfrac{\pi}{3} = \tfrac{1}{2} \qquad\qquad \text{Exact value; Quadrant I}$$

$$\sin \tfrac{5\pi}{6} = \tfrac{1}{2} \qquad\qquad \text{Exact value; Quadrant II}$$

$$\tan\left(-\tfrac{5\pi}{4}\right) = -1 \qquad\qquad \text{Exact value; Quadrant II}$$

$$\sec 1.2 \approx 2.759703601 \qquad\qquad \text{Approximate calculator value}$$

$$\csc(-4.5) \approx 1.022986384 \qquad\qquad \text{Approximate calculator value}$$

$$\cot 180° \text{ is not defined.} \qquad\qquad\qquad\qquad\qquad ∎$$

EXAMPLE 10   Solving a trigonometric equation by factoring

Solve $2\cos\theta\sin\theta = \sin\theta$ on $[0, 2\pi)$.

Solution
$$2\cos\theta\sin\theta - \sin\theta = 0$$
$$\sin\theta(2\cos\theta - 1) = 0$$

$$\sin\theta = 0 \qquad 2\cos\theta - 1 = 0$$
$$\theta = 0, \pi \qquad\quad \cos\theta = \tfrac{1}{2}$$
$$\theta = \tfrac{\pi}{3}, \tfrac{5\pi}{3}$$

WARNING   Do not divide both sides by $\sin\theta$, because you might lose a solution. Notice that if $\theta = 0$ or π, then $\sin\theta = 0$. You cannot divide by 0.   ∎

EXAMPLE 11   Solving a trigonometric equation using identities

Solve $\sin x + \sqrt{3}\cos x = 1$ on $[0, 2\pi)$.

Solution

For an algebraic solution,

$$\sqrt{3}\cos x = 1 - \sin x$$

$$3\cos^2 x = 1 - 2\sin x + \sin^2 x \qquad \textit{Square both sides.}$$

$$3(1 - \sin^2 x) = 1 - 2\sin x + \sin^2 x$$

$$2 + 2\sin x - 4\sin^2 x = 0$$

$$2\sin^2 x - \sin x - 1 = 0$$

$$(2\sin x + 1)(\sin x - 1) = 0$$

$$\sin x = -\tfrac{1}{2} \qquad \sin x = 1$$

$$x = \tfrac{7\pi}{6}, \tfrac{11\pi}{6} \qquad x = \tfrac{\pi}{2}$$

However, since we squared both sides, we need to check for extraneous roots by substituting into the *original equation*, since squaring sometimes introduces extraneous solutions (that is, solutions that do not satisfy the given equation). Checking, we see that $x = \tfrac{7\pi}{6}$ is extraneous, and the solution is $x = \tfrac{\pi}{2}, \tfrac{11\pi}{6}$.

It is often worthwhile to check by finding a geometric solution. We graph the left and right sides of the equation on the same axes:

$$y_1 = \sin x + \sqrt{3}\cos x$$

$$y_2 = 1$$

The graphs are shown in Figure 1.7, and for a solution we look to the intersection points.

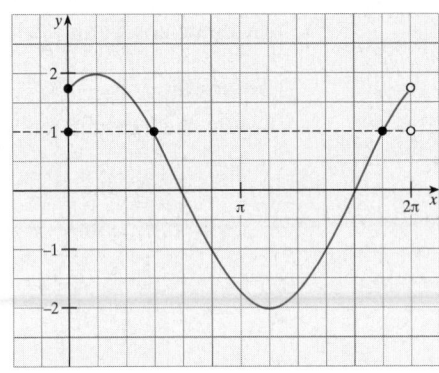

Figure 1.7 There are two intersection points, at $x = \tfrac{\pi}{2}$ and $x = \tfrac{11\pi}{6}$.

1.1 PROBLEM SET

A **1.** Fill in the missing parts in the table.

Inequality Notation	Interval Notation
$-3 < x < 4$	**a.**
b.	$[3, 5]$
c.	$[-2, 1)$
$2 < x \leq 7$	**d.**

2. Fill in the missing parts in the table.

Inequality Notation	Interval Notation
a.	$(-\infty, -2)$
b.	$[\tfrac{\pi}{4}, \sqrt{2}]$
$x > -3$	**c.**
$-1 \leq x \leq 5$	**d.**

3. Represent each of the following on a number line.
   a. $-1 \le x < 4$
   b. $-1 \le x \le 3$
   c. $(0, 2)$
   d. $[-2, 1)$

4. Represent each of the following on a number line.
   a. $x > 2$
   b. $x \le 4$
   c. $(-\infty, 2) \cup (2, \infty)$
   d. $-2 < x \le 3$ or $x \ge 5$

In Problems 5–6, plot the given points P and Q on a Cartesian plane, find the distance between them, and find the coordinates of the midpoint of the line segment $\overline{PQ}$.

5. a. $P(2, 3), Q(-2, 5)$
   b. $P(-2, 3), Q(4, 1)$
6. a. $P(-5, 3), Q(-5, -7)$
   b. $P(-4, 3), Q(3, -4)$

SMH *Solve each equation in Problems 7–24. Assume that a, b, and c are known constants.*

7. $x^2 - x = 0$
8. $2y^2 + y - 3 = 0$
9. $y^2 - 5y + 3 = 17$
10. $x^2 + 5x + a = 0$
11. $3x^2 - bx = c$
12. $4x^2 + 20x + 25 = 0$
13. $|2x + 4| = 16$
14. $|5y + 2| = 12$
15. $|3 - 2w| = 7$
16. $|5 - 3t| = 14$
17. $|3x + 1| = -4$
18. $|1 - 5x| = -2$
19. $\sin x = -\frac{1}{2}$ on $[0, 2\pi)$
20. $(\sin x)(\cos x) = 0$ on $[0, 2\pi)$
21. $(2\cos x + \sqrt{2})(2\cos x - 1) = 0$ on $[0, 2\pi)$
22. $(3\tan x + \sqrt{3})(3\tan x - \sqrt{3}) = 0$ on $[0, 2\pi)$
23. $\cot x + \sqrt{3} = \csc x$ on $[0, 2\pi)$
24. $\sec^2 x - 1 = \sqrt{3}\tan x$ on $[0, 2\pi)$

Solve each inequality in Problems 25–34, and give your answer using interval notation.

25. $3x + 7 < 2$
26. $5(3 - x) > 3x - 1$
27. $-5 < 3x < 0$
28. $-3 < y - 5 \le 2$
29. $3 \le -y < 8$
30. $-5 \le 3 - 2x < 18$
31. $t^2 - 2t \le 3$
32. $s^2 + 3s - 4 > 0$
33. $|x - 8| \le 0.001$
34. $|x - 5| < 0.01$

In Problems 35–38, find an equation of the circle with given center C and radius r.

35. $C(-1, 2); r = 3$
36. $C(3, 0); r = 2$
37. $C(0, 1.5); r = 0.25$
38. $C(-1, -5); r = 4.1$

In Problems 39–42, find the centers and radii of the circles and then graph.

39. $x^2 - 2x + y^2 + 2y + 1 = 0$
40. $4x^2 + 4y^2 + 4y - 15 = 0$
41. $x^2 + y^2 + 2x - 10y + 25 = 0$
42. $2x^2 + 2y^2 + 2x - 6y - 9 = 0$

SMH *Use the sum and difference formulas from trigonometry to find the exact values of the expressions in Problems 43–46. Check by finding a calculator approximation.*

43. $\sin\left(-\frac{\pi}{12}\right)$
44. $\cos\frac{7\pi}{12}$
45. $\tan\frac{\pi}{12}$
46. $\sin 165°$

B 47. **WHAT DOES THIS SAY?*** Describe a process for solving a quadratic equation.

---

*Many problems in this book are labeled **What Does This Say?** Following the question will be a question for you to answer in your own words, or a statement for you to rephrase in your own words. These problems are intended to be similar to the "What This Says" boxes.

48. **WHAT DOES THIS SAY?** Describe a process for solving absolute value equations.

49. **WHAT DOES THIS SAY?** Describe a process for solving absolute value inequalities.

50. **WHAT DOES THIS SAY?** Describe a process for solving trigonometric equations.

SMH *Specify the period for each graph in Problems 51–56. Also graph each curve.*

51. a. $y = \sin x$
    b. $y = \cos x$
    c. $y = \tan x$
52. a. $y = 2\sin 2\pi x$
    b. $y = 3\cos 3\pi x$
    c. $y = 4\tan\left(\frac{\pi x}{5}\right)$
53. $y = \tan(2x - \frac{\pi}{2})$
54. $y = 2\cos(3x + 2\pi) - 2$
55. $y = 4\sin(\frac{1}{2}x + 2) - 1$
56. $y = \tan(\frac{1}{2}x + \frac{\pi}{3})$

57. The current I (in amperes) in a certain circuit (for some convenient unit of time) generates the following set of data points:

Time	Current	Time	Current
0	−60.00000	10	30.00000
1	−58.68886	11	40.14784
2	−54.81273	12	48.54102
3	−48.54102	13	54.81273
4	−40.14784	14	58.68886
5	−30.00000	15	60.00000
6	−18.54102	16	58.68886
7	−6.27171	17	54.81273
8	6.27171	18	48.54102
9	18.54102	19	40.14784
		20	30.00000

Plot the data points and draw a smooth curve passing through these points. Determine possible values of A, B, C, and D so that the graph of these data is approximated by the equation $y - A = B\sin C(x - D)$.

58. Suppose that a point P on a water wheel with a 30-ft radius is d units from the waterline. If the water wheel turns at 6 revolutions per minute, the height of the point P above the waterline is given by the following set of data points:

Time	Height, d	Time	Height, d
0	−1.000	10	−1.000
1	4.729	11	4.729
2	19.729	12	19.729
3	38.271	13	38.270
4	53.271	14	53.270
5	59.000	15	59.000
6	53.271	16	53.271
7	38.271	17	38.271
8	19.729	18	19.730
9	4.729	19	4.730
		20	−1.000

Plot the data points and draw a smooth curve passing through these points. Determine possible values of A, B, C, and D so that the graph of these data is approximated by the equation

$$y - A = B\cos C(x - D)$$

Determine a possible equation of a curve that is generated by this water wheel.

59. The sun and moon tide curves are shown here.* During a new moon, the sun and moon tidal bulges are centered at the same longitude, so their effects are added to produce maximum high tides and minimum low tides. This produces maximum tidal range (the distance between the low and high tides).

NEW MOON (Spring tide)

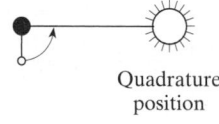

Sun curve   ——————
Moon curve   - - - - - -
Combined curve ——————

Write possible equations for the sun curve, the moon curve, and the combined curve. Assume the tidal range is 10 ft and the period is 12 hours.

60. The sun and moon tide curves are shown in the figure. During the third quarter (neap tide), the sun and moon tidal bulges are at right angles to each other. Thus, the sun tide reduces the effect of the moon tide.

THIRD QUARTER (Neap tide)

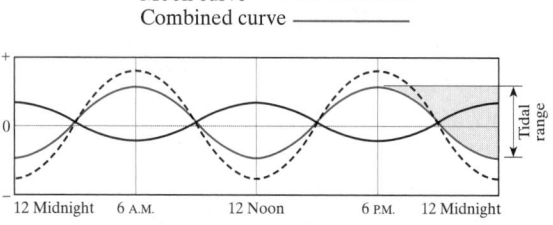

Sun curve   ——————
Moon curve   - - - - - -
Combined curve ——————

Write possible equations for the sun curve, the moon curve, and the combined curve. Assume the tidal range is 4 ft and the period is 12 hours.

61. A person is swimming at a depth of d units beneath the surface of the water. Because the light is refracted by the water, a viewer standing above the waterline sees the swimmer at an apparent depth of s units. (See Figure 1.8.)

---

*From *Introductory Oceanography*, 5th ed., by H. V. Thurman, p. 253. Reprinted with permission of Merrill, an imprint of Macmillan Publishing Company. Copyright ©1988 Merrill Publishing Company, Columbus, Ohio.

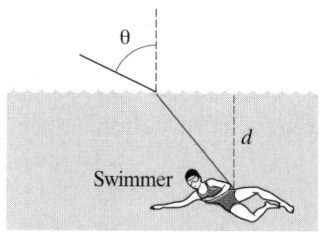

Figure 1.8   Refracted light when viewing an underwater swimmer

In physics,[†] it is shown that if the person is viewed from an angle of incidence θ, then

$$s = \frac{3d \cos \theta}{\sqrt{7 + 9 \cos^2 \theta}}$$

a. If $d = 5.0$ meters and $\theta = 37°$, what is the apparent depth of the swimmer?

b. If the actual depth is $d = 5.0$ meters, what angle of incidence yields an apparent depth of $s = 2.5$ meters?

62. Journal problem   *The Mathematics Student Journal* by Murray Klamkin[‡] ■ Determine all the roots of the quartic equation $x^4 - 4x = 1$.

63. HISTORICAL QUEST   The division of one revolution into 360 equal parts (called degrees) is no doubt due to the sexagesimal (base 60) numeration system used by the Babylonians. Several explanations have been put forward to account for the choice of this number. (For example, see Howard Eves's *In Mathematical Circles*, Boston: Prindle, Weber & Schmidt, 1969.) One possible explanation is put forth by Otto Neugebauer, scholar and authority on early Babylonian mathematics and astronomy. In early Sumerian times, there existed a Babylonian mile, equal to about seven of our miles. Sometime in the first millennium B.C., when Babylonian astronomy reached the stage in which systematic records of the stars were kept, the Babylonian mile was adapted for measuring spans of time. Since a complete day was found to be equal to 12 time-miles, and one complete day is equivalent to one revolution of the sky, a complete circuit was divided into 12 equal parts. Then, for convenience, the Babylonian mile was subdivided into 30 equal parts. One complete circuit therefore has (12)(30) = 360 equal parts. ■

Show that the radius of a circle can be applied exactly six times to its circumference as a chord.

[†]R. A. Serway, *Physics*, 3rd ed., Philadelphia: Saunders, 1992, p. 1007.

[‡]Most mathematics journals have problem sections that solicit interesting problems and solutions for publication. From time to time, we will reprint a problem from a mathematics journal. If you have difficulty solving a journal problem, you may wish to use a library to find the problem and solution as printed in the journal. The title of the journal is included as part of the problem, and we will generally give you a reference as a footnote. This problem is found in the named journal in Volume 28 (1980), issue 3, p. 2.

64. HISTORICAL QUEST The numeration system we use (base 10) evolved over a long period of time. It is often called the *Hindu-Arabic* system because its origins can be traced back to the Hindus in Bactria (now Afghanistan). Later, in A.D. 700, India was invaded by the Arabs who used and modified the Hindu numeration system, and, in turn, introduced it to Western civilization. The Hindu Brahmagupta stated the rules for operations with positive and negative numbers in the seventh century A.D. There are some indications that the Chinese had some knowledge of negative numbers as early as 200 B.C. On the other hand, the Western mathematician Girolamo Cardan (1501–1576) was calling numbers such as (–1) absurd as late as 1545. ∎

Write a paper on the history of the real number system.

C **65.** **Exploration Problem** If $ax + b = 0$, what effect does changing the sign of b have on the solution ($a \neq 0$; keep a fixed)?

66. **Exploration Problem** If $ax^2 + bx + c = 0$, what effect does changing c have on the solution ($a \neq 0$, keep a and b fixed)?

67. **Exploration Problem** If $\sin ax = b$, what effect does changing a have on the solution ($a \neq 0$; keep b fixed)?

68. If $c \geq 0$, show that $|x| \leq c$ if and only if $-c \leq x \leq c$.

69. Show that $-|x| \leq x \leq |x|$ for any number x.

70. Prove that $|a| = |b|$ if and only if $a = b$ or $a = -b$.

71. Prove that if $|a| < b$ and $b > 0$, then $-b < a < b$.

72. Prove the triangle inequality:

$$|x + y| \leq |x| + |y|$$

73. Show that $||x| - |y|| \leq |x - y|$ for all x and y.

74. Derive the **midpoint formula**

$$M\left(\frac{x_1 + x_2}{2}, \frac{y_1 + y_2}{2}\right)$$

for the midpoint of a segment with endpoints $P(x_1, y_1)$ and $Q(x_2, y_2)$.

1.2   Lines in the Plane

IN THIS SECTION   slope of a line, forms for the equation of a line, parallel and perpendicular lines

SLOPE OF A LINE

A distinguishing feature of a line is the fact that its *inclination* with respect to the horizontal is constant. It is common practice to specify inclination by means of a concept called *slope*. A carpenter might describe a roof line that rises 1 ft for every 3 ft of horizontal "run" as having a slope or pitch of 1 to 3.

Let Δx and Δy represent, as before, the amount of change in the variables x and y, respectively. Then a nonvertical line L that rises (or falls) Δy units (measured from bottom to top) for every Δx units of run (measured from left to right) is said to have a *slope* of $m = \Delta y / \Delta x$. (If Δy is negative, then the "rise" is actually a fall; and if Δx is negative, then the run is actually right to left.) In particular, if $P(x_1, y_1)$ and $Q(x_2, y_2)$ are two distinct points on L, then the changes in the variables x and y are given by $\Delta x = x_2 - x_1$ and $\Delta y = y_2 - y_1$, and the slope of L is

$$m = \frac{\Delta y}{\Delta x} = \frac{y_2 - y_1}{x_2 - x_1} \quad \text{for } \Delta x \neq 0 \qquad \textit{See Figure 1.9.}$$

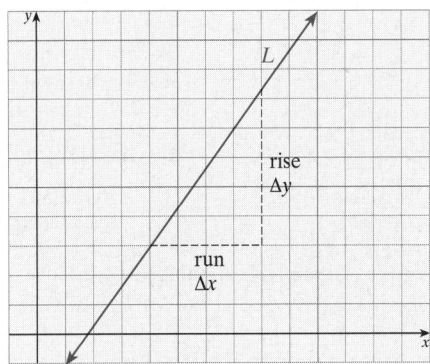

a. The slope of L is $m = \dfrac{\Delta y}{\Delta x}$.

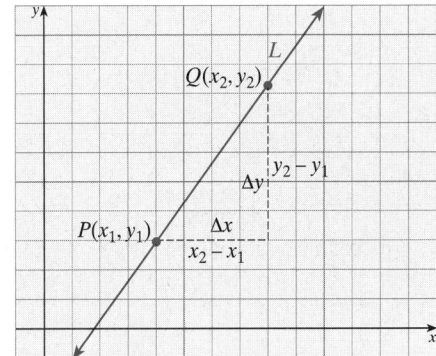

b. The slope is given by $m = \dfrac{y_2 - y_1}{x_2 - x_1}$.

Figure 1.9   The slope of a line

Slope of a Line

A nonvertical line that contains the points $P(x_1, y_1)$ and $Q(x_2, y_2)$ has **slope**

$$m = \frac{\Delta y}{\Delta x} = \frac{y_2 - y_1}{x_2 - x_1}$$

We say that a line with slope m is *rising* (when viewed from left to right) if $m > 0$, *falling* if $m < 0$, and *horizontal* if $m = 0$.

There is a useful trigonometric formulation of slope. The **angle of inclination** of a line L is defined to be the nonnegative angle ϕ ($0 \leq \phi < \pi$) formed between L and the positive x-axis.

Angle of Inclination

WARNING Sometimes we say a vertical line has **infinite slope.**

The **angle of inclination** of a line L is the angle ϕ ($0 \leq \phi < \pi$) between L and the positive x-axis. Then the **slope** of L with inclination ϕ is

$$m = \tan \phi$$

We see that the line L is *rising* if $0 < \phi < \frac{\pi}{2}$ and is *falling* if $\frac{\pi}{2} < \phi < \pi$. The line is *horizontal* if $\phi = 0$ and is *vertical* if $\phi = \frac{\pi}{2}$. Notice that if $\phi = \frac{\pi}{2}$, $\tan \phi$ is not defined; therefore the slope, m, is undefined for a vertical line.

To derive the trigonometric representation for slope we need to find the slope of the line through $P(x_1, y_1)$ and $Q(x_2, y_2)$, where ϕ is the angle of inclination. From the definition of the tangent, we have

$$\tan \phi = \frac{y_2 - y_1}{x_2 - x_1} = \frac{\Delta y}{\Delta x} = m \quad \textit{See Figure 1.10.}$$

Lines with various slopes are shown in Figure 1.11.

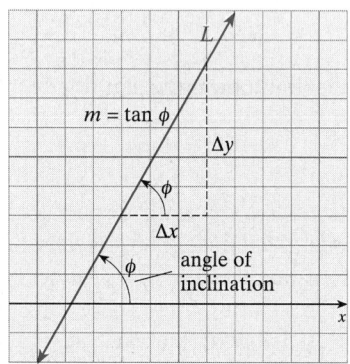

Figure 1.10 Trigonometric form for the slope of a line

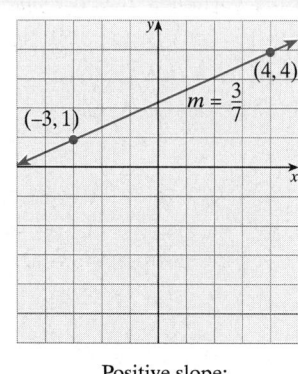

Positive slope;
line rises.

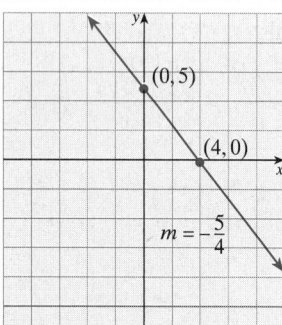

Negative slope;
line falls.

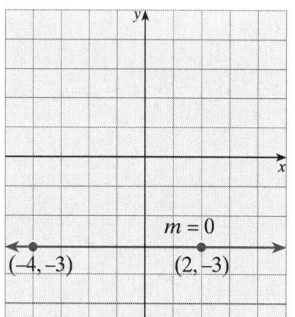

Zero slope ($\Delta y = 0$);
line is horizontal.

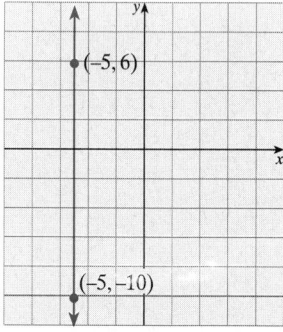

Slope is undefined;
($\Delta x = 0$) line is vertical.

Figure 1.11   Examples of slope

FORMS FOR THE EQUATION OF A LINE

In algebra you studied several forms of the equation of a line. The derivations of some of these are reviewed in the problems. Here is a summary of the forms most frequently used in calculus.

Forms of Linear Equations

Standard Form:	$Ax + By + C = 0$	A, B, C constants
		(A and B not both 0)
Slope-intercept Form:	$y = mx + b$	Slope m, y-intercept $(0, b)$
Point-slope Form:	$y - k = m(x - h)$	Slope m, through point (h, k)
Two-intercept Form:	$\dfrac{x}{a} + \dfrac{y}{b} = 1$	Intercepts $(a, 0)$ and $(0, b)$
Horizontal line:	$y = k$	Slope 0
Vertical line:	$x = h$	Slope undefined

EXAMPLE 1 Deriving the two-intercept form of the equation of a line

Derive the equation of the line with intercepts $(a, 0)$ and $(0, b)$, $a \neq 0$, $b \neq 0$.

Solution

The slope of the equation passing through the given points is

$$m = \frac{b - 0}{0 - a} = -\frac{b}{a}$$

Use the point-slope form with $h = 0$, $k = b$. (You can use either of the given points.)

$$y - b = -\frac{b}{a}(x - 0)$$
$$ay - ab = -bx$$
$$bx + ay = ab$$
$$\frac{x}{a} + \frac{y}{b} = 1 \qquad \text{Divide both sides by } ab. \quad \blacksquare$$

Two quantities x and y that satisfy a linear equation $Ax + By + C = 0$ (A and B not both 0) are said to be *linearly related*. This terminology is illustrated in Example 2.

EXAMPLE 2 Linearly related variables

When a weight is attached to a helical spring, it causes the spring to lengthen. According to Hooke's law, the length d of the spring is linearly related to the weight w.* If $d = 4$ cm when $w = 3$ g and $d = 6$ cm when $w = 6$ g, what is the original length of the spring, and what weight will cause the spring to lengthen to 5 cm?

Solution

Because d is linearly related to w, we know that points (w, d) lie on a line, and the given information tells us that two such points are $(3, 4)$ and $(6, 6)$ as shown in Figure 1.12. We first find the slope of the line and then use the point-slope form to derive its equation.

$$m = \frac{6 - 4}{6 - 3} = \frac{2}{3}$$

Next, substitute into the point-slope form with $h = 3$ and $k = 4$:

$$d - 4 = \tfrac{2}{3}(w - 3)$$
$$d = \tfrac{2}{3}w + 2$$

The original length of the spring is found for $w = 0$:

$$d = \tfrac{2}{3}(0) + 2 = 2$$

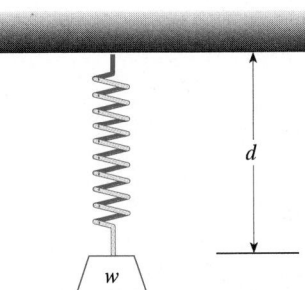

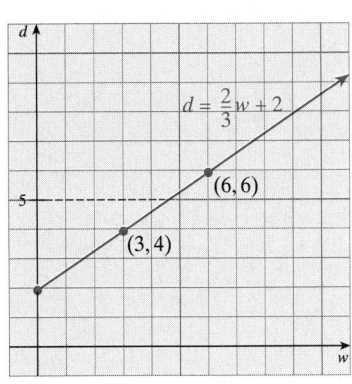

Figure 1.12 The length d of the spring is linearly related to the weight w of the attached object.

---

*Hooke's law is useful for small displacements, but for larger displacements, it may not be a good model.

The original length was 2 cm. To find the weight that corresponds to $d = 5$, we solve the equation

$$5 = \tfrac{2}{3}w + 2$$
$$\tfrac{9}{2} = w$$

Therefore, the weight that corresponds to a length of 5 cm is 4.5 g.   ■

PARALLEL AND PERPENDICULAR LINES

It is often useful to know whether two given lines are either parallel or perpendicular. A vertical line can be parallel only to other vertical lines and perpendicular only to horizontal lines. Cases involving nonvertical lines may be handled by the criteria given in the following box.

Slope Criteria for Parallel and Perpendicular Lines

If L_1 and L_2 are nonvertical lines with slopes m_1 and m_2, then

L_1 and L_2 are **parallel** if and only if $m_1 = m_2$;

L_1 and L_2 are **perpendicular** if and only if $m_1 m_2 = -1$, or $m_1 = -\dfrac{1}{m_2}$.

➡ **What This Says**   Nonvertical and nonhorizontal lines are parallel if and only if their slopes are equal. They are perpendicular if and only if their slopes are negative reciprocals of each other.

The key ideas behind these two slope criteria are displayed in Figure 1.13.

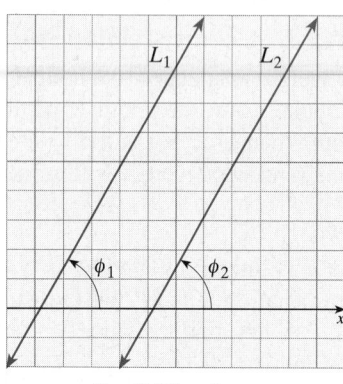

a. Parallel lines have equal slope: $m_1 = m_2$.

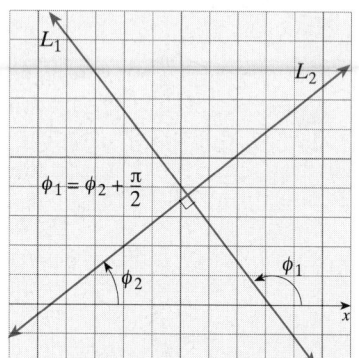

b. Perpendicular lines have negative reciprocal slopes: $m_1 m_2 = -1$.

Figure 1.13

EXAMPLE 3   Finding equations for parallel and perpendicular lines

Let L be the line $3x + 2y = 5$.

a. Find an equation of the line that is parallel to L and passes through $P(4, 7)$.
b. Find an equation of the line that is perpendicular to L and passes through $P(4, 7)$.

Solution

By rewriting the equation of L as $y = -\frac{3}{2}x + \frac{5}{2}$, we see that the slope of L is $m = -\frac{3}{2}$.

a. Any line that is parallel to L must also have slope $m_1 = -\frac{3}{2}$. The required line contains the point $P(4, 7)$. Use the point-slope form to find the equation and write your answer in standard form:

$$y - 7 = -\frac{3}{2}(x - 4)$$
$$2y - 14 = -3x + 12$$
$$3x + 2y - 26 = 0$$

b. Any line perpendicular to L must have slope $m_2 = \frac{2}{3}$ (negative reciprocal of the slope of L). Once again, the required line contains the point $P(4, 7)$, and we find

$$y - 7 = \frac{2}{3}(x - 4)$$
$$3y - 21 = 2x - 8$$
$$2x - 3y + 13 = 0$$

These lines are shown in Figure 1.14. ∎

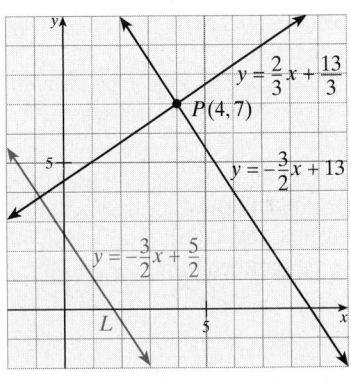

Figure 1.14 Graph of lines parallel and perpendicular to the given line $3x + 2y = 5$

1.2   PROBLEM SET

A **1. WHAT DOES THIS SAY?** Outline a procedure for graphing a linear equation.

In Problems 2–15, find the equation in standard form for the line that satisfies the given requirements.

2. passing through $(1, 4)$ and $(3, 6)$

3. passing through $(-1, 7)$ and $(-2, 9)$

4. horizontal line through $(-2, -5)$

5. passing through the point $(1, \frac{1}{2})$ with slope 0

6. slope 2 and y-intercept $(0, 5)$

7. vertical line through $(-2, -5)$

8. slope -3, x-intercept $(5, 0)$

9. x-intercept $(7, 0)$ and y-intercept $(0, -8)$

10. x-intercept $(4.5, 0)$ and y-intercept $(0, -5.4)$

11. passing through $(-1, 8)$ parallel to $3x + y = 7$

12. passing through $(4, 5)$ parallel to the line passing through $(2, 1)$ and $(5, 9)$

13. passing through $(3, -2)$ perpendicular to $4x - 3y + 2 = 0$

14. passing through $(-1, 6)$ perpendicular to the line through the origin with slope 0.5

15. perpendicular to the line whose equation is $x - 4y + 5 = 0$ where it intersects the line whose equation is $2x + 3y - 1 = 0$

In Problems 16–29, find, if possible, the slope, the y-intercept, and the x-intercept of the line whose equation is given. Sketch the graph of each equation.

16. $y = \frac{2}{3}x - 8$

17. $y = -\frac{5}{7}x + 3$

18. $y - 4 = 4.001(x - 2)$

19. $y - 9 = 6.001(x - 3)$

20. $5x + 3y - 15 = 0$

21. $3x + 5y + 15 = 0$

22. $2x - 3y - 2,550 = 0$

23. $6x - 10y - 3 = 0$

24. $\frac{x}{4} + \frac{y}{6} = 1$

25. $\frac{x}{2} - \frac{y}{3} = 1$

26. $y = 2x$

27. $x = 5y$

28. $y - 5 = 0$

29. $x + 3 = 0$

B **30.** Find an equation for a vertical line(s) L such that a region bounded by L, the x-axis, and the line $2y - 3x = 6$ has area 3.

31. Find an equation for a horizontal line(s) M such that the region bounded by M, the y-axis, and the line $2y - 3x = 6$ has an area of 3.

32. Find the equation of the perpendicular line passing through the midpoint of the line segment connecting $(-3, 7)$ and $(4, -1)$.

33. Three vertices of a parallelogram are $A(1, 3)$, $C(4, 11)$, and $B(3, -2)$. If A and B lie on the same side, what is the fourth vertex?

Use a graphing calculator in Problems 34–45 to solve the systems of equations graphically, and approximate the coordinates of the intersection point. Some calculators have an INTERSECT feature. Check your owner's manual. Then solve the system algebraically and compare the results.

34. $\begin{cases} 2x - 3y = -8 \\ x + y = 6 \end{cases}$

35. $\begin{cases} 2x - 3y = -8 \\ 4x - 6y = 0 \end{cases}$

36. $\begin{cases} 2x - 3y = -8 \\ y = \frac{2}{3}x + \frac{8}{3} \end{cases}$

37. $\begin{cases} 3x - 4y = 16 \\ -x + 2y = -6 \end{cases}$

38. $\begin{cases} y = 3x + 1 \\ x - 2y = 8 \end{cases}$

39. $\begin{cases} 2x + 3y = 12 \\ -4x + 6y = 18 \end{cases}$

40. $\begin{cases} 2x + 3y = 15 \\ y = \frac{2}{3}x - 20 \end{cases}$

41. $\begin{cases} x + y = 12 \\ 0.6y = 0.5(40) \end{cases}$

42. $\begin{cases} x + 3y = \cos^2 \frac{\pi}{3} \\ x + y = -\sin^2 \frac{\pi}{3} \end{cases}$

43. $\begin{cases} x^2 + y^2 = 4 \\ x - y = 0 \end{cases}$

44. $\begin{cases} x^2 + y^2 = 10 \\ (x-3)^2 + y^2 = 9 \end{cases}$ **45.** $\begin{cases} x^2 + y^2 = 15 \\ (x+4)^2 + y^2 = 16 \end{cases}$

46. A life insurance table indicates that a woman who is now A years old can expect to live E years longer. Suppose that A and E are linearly related and that $E = 50$ when $A = 24$ and $E = 20$ when $A = 60$.

   a. At what age may a woman expect to live 30 years longer?

   b. What is the life expectancy of a newborn female child?

   c. At what age is the life expectancy zero?

47. On the Fahrenheit temperature scale, water freezes at $32°$ and boils at $212°$; the corresponding temperatures on the Celsius scale are $0°$ and $100°$. Given that the Fahrenheit and Celsius temperatures are linearly related, first find numbers r and s so that $F = rC + s$, and then answer these questions.

   a. Mercury freezes at $-39°C$. What is the corresponding Fahrenheit temperature?

   b. For what value of C is $F = 0$?

   c. What temperature is the same in both scales?

48. The average SAT mathematics scores of incoming students at an eastern liberal arts college have been declining in recent years. In 1996, the average SAT score was 575; in 2001, it was 545. Assuming the average SAT score varies linearly with time, answer these questions.

   a. Express the average SAT score in terms of time measured from 1996.

   b. If the trend continues, what will the average SAT score of incoming students be in 2014?

   c. When will the average SAT score be 455?

*__49.__ **Spy Problem** An internationally famous spy has escaped from the headquarters of a diamond smuggling ring in the tiny Mediterranean country of Azusa. Our hero, driving a stolen milk truck at 72 km/hr, has a 40-minute head start on his pursuers, who are chasing him in a Ferrari going 168 km/hr. The distance from the smugglers' headquarters in Azusa to freedom in the neighboring country of Duarte is 83.8 km. Is this the end of the Spy, or does he live to return in Chapter 2?

50. A certain car rental agency charges \$40 per day with 100 free miles plus 34¢ per mile after the first 100 miles. First express the cost of renting a car from this agency for one day in terms of the number of miles driven. Then draw the graph and use it to check your answers to these questions.

   a. How much does it cost to rent a car for a 1-day trip of 50 mi?

   b. How many miles were driven if the daily rental cost was \$92.36?

51. A manufacturer buys \$200,000 worth of machinery that depreciates linearly so that its trade-in value after 10 years will be \$10,000. Express the value of the machinery as a function of its age and draw the graph. What is the value of the machinery after 4 years?

52. Show that if the point $P(x, y)$ is equidistant from $A(1, 3)$ and $B(-1, 2)$, its coordinates must satisfy the equation $4x + 2y - 5 = 0$. Sketch the graph of this equation.

53. Let $P_1(2, 6)$, $P_2(-1, 3)$, $P_3(0, -2)$, and $P_4(a, b)$ be points in the plane that are located so that $P_1 P_2 P_3 P_4$ is a parallelogram.

   a. There are three possible choices for P_4. One is $A(3, 1)$. What are the others, which we will call B and C?

   b. The centroid of a triangle is the point where its three medians intersect. Find the centroid of $\triangle ABC$ and of $\triangle P_1 P_2 P_3$. Do you notice anything interesting?

54. **Exploration Problem** Ethyl alcohol is metabolized by the human body at a constant rate (independent of concentration). Suppose the rate is 10 mL per hour.

   a. Express the time t (in hours) required to metabolize the effects of drinking ethyl alcohol in terms of the amount A of ethyl alcohol consumed.

   b. How much time is required to eliminate the effects of a liter of beer containing 3% ethyl alcohol?

   c. Discuss how the function in part **a** can be used to determine a reasonable "cutoff" value for the amount of ethyl alcohol A that each individual may be served at a party.

55. Since the beginning of the month, a local reservoir has been losing water at a constant rate (that is, the amount of water in the reservoir is a linear function of time). On the 12th of the month, the reservoir held 200 million gallons of water; on the 21st, it held only 164 million gallons. How much water was in the reservoir on the 8th of the month?

56. To encourage motorists to form car pools, the transit authority in a certain metropolitan area has been offering a special reduced rate at toll bridges for vehicles containing four or more persons. When the program began 30 days ago, 157 vehicles qualified for the reduced rate during the morning rush hour. Since then, the number of vehicles qualifying has increased at a constant rate (that is, the number is a linear function of time), and 247 vehicles qualified today. If the trend continues, how many vehicles will qualify during the morning rush hour 14 days from now?

57. **Exploration Problem** The value of a certain rare book doubles every 10 years. The book was originally worth \$3.

   a. How much is the book worth when it is 30 years old? When it is 40 years old?

   b. Is the relationship between the value of the book and its age linear? Explain.

58. HISTORICAL QUEST   The region between the Tigris and Euphrates Rivers (present day Iraq) is rightly known as the Cradle of Civilization. During the so-called Babylonian period (roughly 2000–600 B.C.),[†] important mathematical ideas began to germinate in the region, including positional notation for numeration. Unlike their Egyptian contemporaries who usually wrote on fragile papyrus, Babylonian mathematicians recorded their ideas on clay tablets. One of these tablets, in the Yale Collection, shows a system equivalent to

$$\begin{cases} xy = 600 \\ (x+y)^2 - 150(x-y)^2 = 100 \end{cases} \blacksquare$$

Find a positive solution $(x > 0, y > 0)$ for this system correct to the nearest tenth.

---

*Take note: The Spy will accompany us on our journey through this book, if he can survive (which, of course, will require your help).

[†]For an interesting discussion of Mesopotamian mathematics, see *A History of Mathematics*, 2nd ed., by Carl B. Boyer, revised by Uta C. Merzbach, John Wiley and Sons, Inc., New York, 1968, pp. 26-47.

d. F has meaning if and only if $x + 2$ is nonnegative; therefore, the domain is $x \geq -2$, or $[-2, \infty)$.

e. G is defined whenever $5 - \cos x \neq 0$. This imposes no restriction on x since $|\cos x| \leq 1$. Thus, the domain of G is the set of all real numbers; this can be written $(-\infty, \infty)$. ∎

Equality of Functions

> Two functions f and g are **equal** if and only if both
>
> **1.** f and g have the same domain.
> **2.** $f(x) = g(x)$ for all x in the domain.

EXAMPLE 5   Equality of functions

Consider again the functions from Example 4:

$$f(x) = 2x - 1 \qquad g(x) = 2x - 1 \text{ for } x \neq -3 \qquad h(x) = \frac{(2x - 1)(x + 3)}{x + 3}$$

Does $h(x)$ equal $f(x)$ or $g(x)$?

Solution

A common mistake is to "reduce" the function h to obtain the function f:

$$\text{WRONG:} \quad h(x) = \frac{(2x - 1)(x + 3)}{x + 3} = 2x - 1 = f(x)$$

This is wrong because the functions f and h have different domains. In particular, -3 is a valid input for f, but it is not a valid input for h. We say that the function h has a **hole** at $x = -3$. In other words, this WRONG calculation is valid only if $x \neq -3$, so the correct answer is

$$\text{RIGHT:} \quad h(x) = \frac{(2x - 1)(x + 3)}{x + 3} = 2x - 1, \ x \neq -3$$

Therefore, $h(x) = g(x)$. ∎

COMPOSITION OF FUNCTIONS

There are many situations in which a quantity is given as a function of one variable that, in turn, can be written as a function of a second variable. Suppose, for example, that your job is to ship x packages of a product via Federal Express to a variety of addresses. Let x be the number of packages to ship, and let $f(x)$ be the weight of the x objects and $g(w)$ be the cost of shipping a package of weight w. Then

Weight is a function $f(x)$ of the number of objects x.

Cost is a function $g[f(x)]$ of the weight.

So we have expressed cost as a function of the number of packages. This process of evaluating a function of a function is known as *functional composition*.

Composition of Functions

The **composite function** $f \circ g$ is defined by

$$(f \circ g)(x) = f[g(x)]$$

for each x in the domain of g for which $g(x)$ is in the domain of f.

➡ **What This Says**   To visualize how functional composition works, think of $f \circ g$ in terms of an "assembly line" in which g and f are arranged in series, with output $g(x)$ becoming the input of f, as illustrated in Figure 1.18.

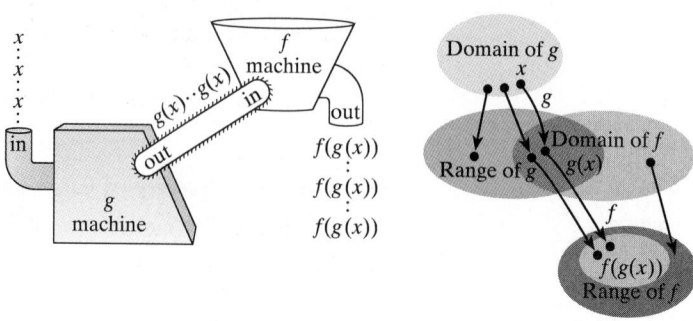

Figure 1.18   Composition of functions

EXAMPLE 6   Finding the composition of functions

If $f(x) = 3x + 5$ and $g(x) = \sqrt{x}$, find the composite functions $f \circ g$ and $g \circ f$.

Solution

The function $f \circ g$ is defined by $f[g(x)]$.

$$(f \circ g)(x) = f[g(x)] = f(\sqrt{x}) = 3\sqrt{x} + 5$$

The function $g \circ f$ is defined by $g[f(x)]$.

$$(g \circ f)(x) = g[f(x)] = g(3x + 5) = \sqrt{3x + 5}$$

WARNING   Example 6 illustrates that functional composition is not commutative.

That is, $f \circ g$ is not, in general, the same as $g \circ f$.

EXAMPLE 7   An application of composite functions

Air pollution is a problem for many metropolitan areas. Suppose a study conducted in a certain city indicates that when the population is p hundred thousand people, then the average daily level of carbon monoxide in the air is given by the formula

$$L(p) = 0.70\sqrt{p^2 + 3}$$

parts per million (ppm). A second study predicts that t years from now, the population will be $p(t) = 1 + 0.02t^3$ hundred thousand people. Assuming these formulas are correct, what level of air pollution should be expected in 4 years?

Solution

The level of pollution is $L(p) = 0.70\sqrt{p^2 + 3}$, where $p(t) = 1 + 0.02t^3$. Thus, the pollution level at time t is given by the composite function

$$(L \circ p)(t) = L[p(t)] = L(1 + 0.02t^3) = 0.70\sqrt{(1 + 0.02t^3)^2 + 3}$$

In particular, when $t = 4$, we have

$$(L \circ p)(4) = 0.70\sqrt{[1 + 0.02(4)^3]^2 + 3} \approx 2.00 \text{ ppm}$$

In calculus, it is frequently necessary to express a function as the composite of two simpler functions. Here is an example that illustrates how this can be done.

EXAMPLE 8   Expressing a given function as a composite of two functions

Express each of the following functions as the composite of two functions u and g so that $f(x) = g[u(x)]$.

a. $f(x) = (x^2 + 5x + 1)^5$ **b.** $f(x) = \cos^3 x$

c. $f(x) = \sin x^3$ **d.** $f(x) = \sqrt{5x^2 - x}$

Solution

There are often many ways to express $f(x)$ as a composite $g[u(x)]$. Perhaps the most natural is to choose u to represent the "inner" portion of f and g as the "outer" portion. Such choices are indicated in the following table.

Given Function $f(x) = g[u(x)]$	Inner Function $u(x)$	Outer Function $g(u)$
a. $f(x) = (x^2 + 5x + 1)^5$	$u(x) = x^2 + 5x + 1$	$g(u) = u^5$
b. $f(x) = \cos^3 x$	$u(x) = \cos x$	$g(u) = u^3$
c. $f(x) = \sin x^3$	$u(x) = x^3$	$g(u) = \sin u$
d. $f(x) = \sqrt{5x^2 - x}$	$u(x) = 5x^2 - x$	$g(u) = \sqrt{u}$

GRAPH OF A FUNCTION

Graphs have visual impact. They also reveal information that may not be evident from verbal or algebraic descriptions. Two graphs depicting practical relationships are shown in Figure 1.19.

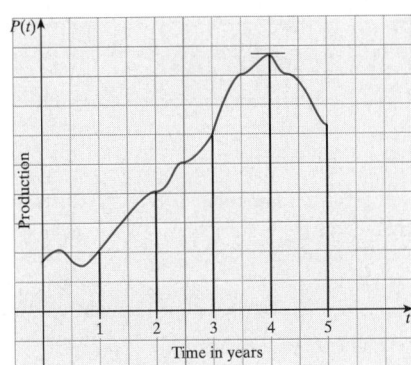

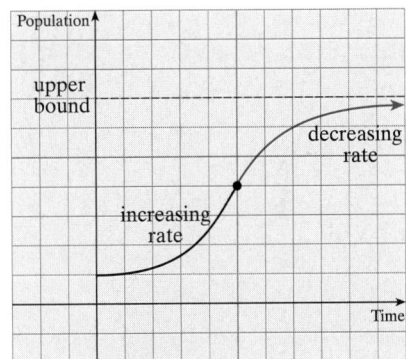

a. A production function

This graph describes the variation in total industrial production in a certain country over a five year time span. The fact that the graph has a peak suggests that production is greatest at the corresponding time.

b. Bounded population growth

This graph represents the growth of a population when environmental factors impose an upper bound on the possible size of the population. It indicates that the rate of population growth increases at first and then decreases as the size of the population gets closer and closer to the upper bound.

Figure 1.19   Two graphs with practical interpretations

To represent a function $y = f(x)$ geometrically as a graph, it is traditional to use a Cartesian coordinate system on which units for the independent variable x are marked on the horizontal axis and units for the dependent variable y on the vertical axis.

Graph of a Function

> The **graph** of a function f consists of points whose coordinates (x, y) satisfy $y = f(x)$, for all x in the domain of f.

In Chapter 4, we will discuss efficient techniques involving calculus that you can use to draw accurate graphs of functions. In algebra you began sketching lines by plotting points, but you quickly discovered that this is not a very efficient way to draw more complicated graphs, especially without the aid of a graphing calculator or computer. Table 1.3 includes a few common graphs you have probably encountered in previous courses. We will assume that you are familiar with their general shape and know how to sketch each of them either by hand or with the assistance of your graphing calculator. There are, however, certain functions, such as $f(x) = \sin\frac{1}{x}$, that are hard to graph even with a calculator or computer. That said, be assured that most functions that appear in this text or in practical applications can be graphed.

Vertical Line Test   By definition of a function, for a given x in the domain there is only one number y in the range. Geometrically, this means that any vertical line $x = a$ crosses the graph of a function at most once. This observation leads to the following useful criterion.

> **The Vertical Line Test**
>
> A curve in the plane is the graph of a function if and only if it intersects no vertical line more than once.

Look at Figure 1.20 for examples of the vertical line test.

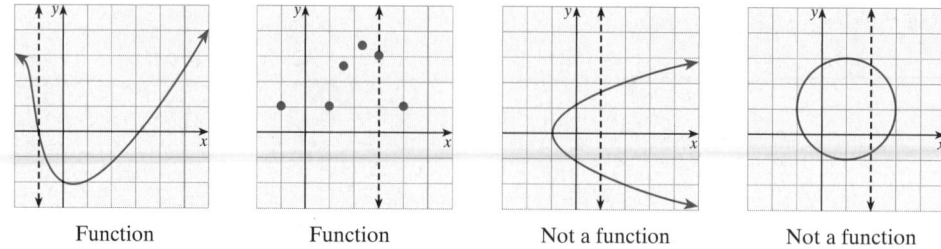

| Function | Function | Not a function | Not a function |

a. The graph of a function: No vertical line intersects the curve more than once.

b. Not the graph of a function: The curve intersects at least one vertical line more than once.

Figure 1.20   The vertical line test

Intercepts   The points where a graph intersects the coordinate axes are called *intercepts*. Here is a definition.

Intercepts

> If the number zero is in the domain of f and $f(0) = b$, then the point $(0, b)$ is called the **y-intercept** of the graph of f. If a is a real number in the domain of f such that $f(a) = 0$, then $(a, 0)$ is an **x-intercept** of f.

> ➡ **What This Says**   To find the x-intercepts, set y equal to 0 and solve for x. To find the y-intercept, set x equal to 0 and solve for y.

TABLE 1.3 Directory of Curves

Identity Function $y = x$	Standard Quadratic Function $y = x^2$	Standard Cubic Function $y = x^3$
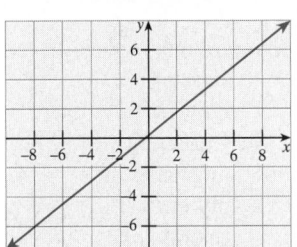	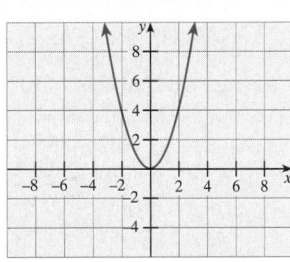	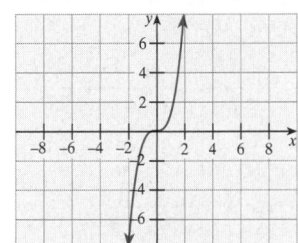

Absolute Value Function $y = |x|$	Square Root Function $y = \sqrt{x}$	Cube Root Function $y = \sqrt[3]{x}$
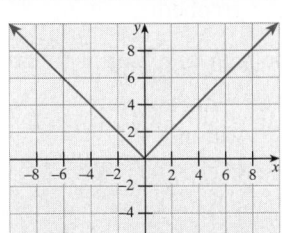	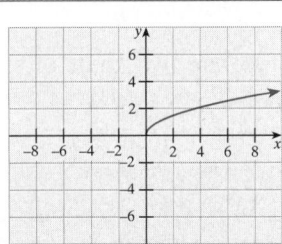	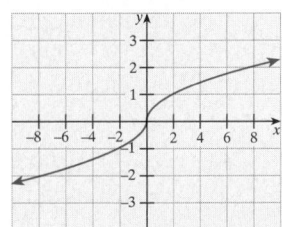

Standard Reciprocal Function $y = \dfrac{1}{x}$	Standard Reciprocal Squared Function $y = \dfrac{1}{x^2}$	Standard Square Root Reciprocal Function $y = \dfrac{1}{\sqrt{x}}$
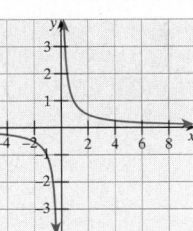	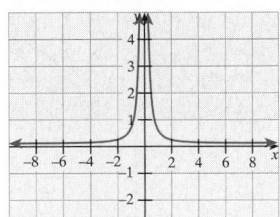	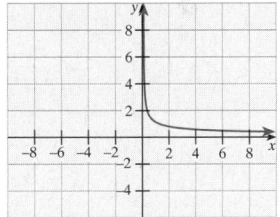

Cosine Function $y = \cos x$	Sine Function $y = \sin x$	Tangent Function $y = \tan x$
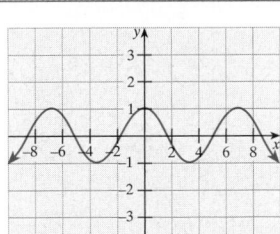	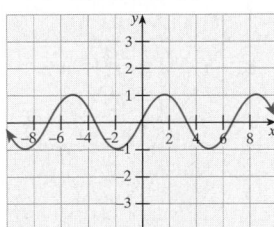	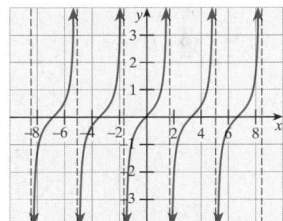

Secant Function $y = \sec x$	Cosecant Function $y = \csc x$	Cotangent Function $y = \cot x$
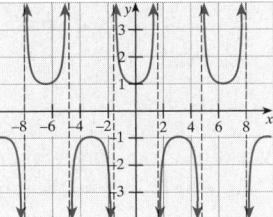	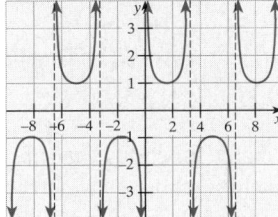	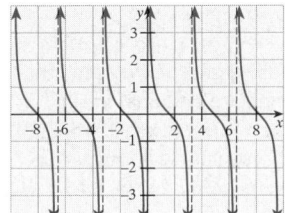

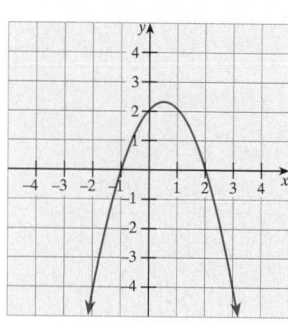

Figure 1.21 Graph of $f(x) = -x^2 + x + 2$ using the intercepts

EXAMPLE 9 **Finding intercepts**

Find all intercepts of the graph of the function $f(x) = -x^2 + x + 2$.

Solution

The y-intercept is $(0, f(0)) = (0, 2)$. To find the x-intercepts, solve the equation $f(x) = 0$. Factoring, we find that

$$-x^2 + x + 2 = 0$$
$$x^2 - x - 2 = 0$$
$$(x + 1)(x - 2) = 0$$
$$x = -1 \text{ or } x = 2$$

Thus, the x-intercepts are $(-1, 0)$ and $(2, 0)$, and the y-intercept is $(0, 2)$. The graph of f is shown in Figure 1.21. ■

Symmetry There are two kinds of symmetry that help in graphing a function, as shown in Figure 1.22 and defined in the following box.

Symmetry

The graph of $y = f(x)$ is **symmetric with respect to the y-axis** if whenever $P(x, y)$ is a point on the graph, so is the point $(-x, y)$ that is the mirror image of P about the y-axis. Thus, y-axis symmetry occurs if and only if $f(-x) = f(x)$ for all x in the domain of f. A function with this property is called an **even function**.

The graph of $y = f(x)$ is **symmetric with respect to the origin** if whenever $P(x, y)$ is on the graph, so is $(-x, -y)$, the mirror image of P about the origin. Symmetry with respect to the origin occurs when $f(-x) = -f(x)$ for all x. A function that satisfies this condition is called an **odd function**.

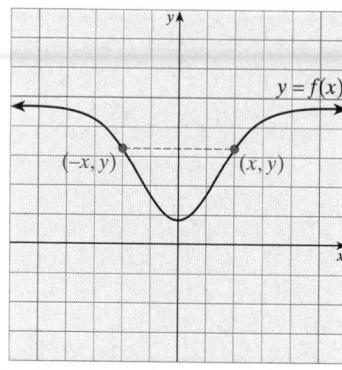
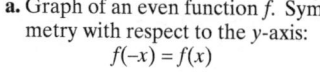
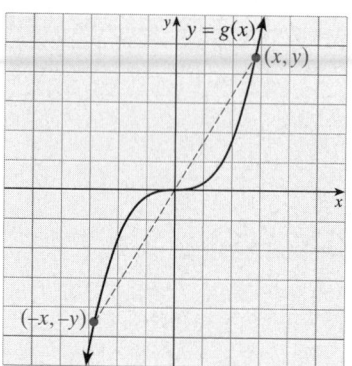

a. Graph of an even function f. Symmetry with respect to the y-axis: $f(-x) = f(x)$

b. Graph of an odd function g. Symmetry with respect to the origin: $g(-x) = -g(x)$

Figure 1.22 Graphs of even and odd functions

WARNING The graph of a nonzero function cannot be symmetric with respect to the x-axis. In other words, if the curve is symmetric with respect to the x-axis, such as the circle, then it will not be a function.

There are many functions that are neither odd nor even. You may wonder why we have said nothing about symmetry with respect to the x-axis, but such symmetry would require $f(x) = -f(x)$, which is precluded by the vertical line test (do you see why?).

EXAMPLE 10 Even and odd functions

Classify the given functions as even, odd, or neither.

a. $f(x) = x^2$ **b.** $g(x) = x^3$ **c.** $h(x) = x^2 + 5x$

Solution

a. $f(x) = x^2$ is *even*, because

$$f(-x) = (-x)^2 = x^2 = f(x)$$

b. $g(x) = x^3$ is *odd*, because

$$g(-x) = (-x)^3 = -x^3 = -g(x)$$

c. $h(x) = x^2 + 5x$ is *neither* even nor odd because

$$h(-x) = (-x)^2 + 5(-x) = x^2 - 5x$$

Note that $h(-x) \neq h(x)$ and $h(-x) \neq -h(x)$.

The graphs of these three functions are shown in Figure 1.23. Note the symmetry in the first two graphs and the lack of symmetry with respect to the axis or the origin in the third.

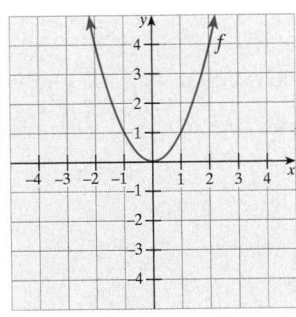 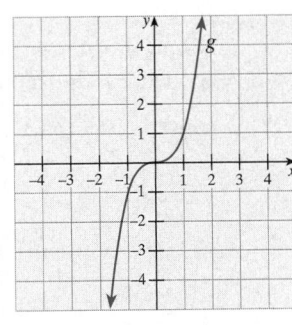 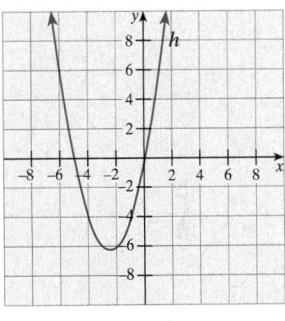

a. $f(x) = x^2$ **b.** $g(x) = x^3$ **c.** $h(x) = x^2 + 5x$

Figure 1.23 Three graphs illustrating the concept of symmetry   ■

CLASSIFICATION OF FUNCTIONS

We will now describe some of the common types of functions used in this text.

Polynomial Function

A **polynomial function** is a function of the form

$$f(x) = a_n x^n + a_{n-1} x^{n-1} + \cdots + a_2 x^2 + a_1 x + a_0$$

where n is a nonnegative integer and $a_n, \ldots, a_2, a_1, a_0$ are constants. If $a_n \neq 0$, the integer n is called the **degree** of the polynomial. The constant a_n is called the **leading coefficient** and the constant a_0 is called the **constant term** of the polynomial function. In particular,

A **constant function** is zero degree: $f(x) = a$
    Example: $f(x) = 5$

A **linear function** is first degree: $f(x) = ax + b$
    Example: $f(x) = 2x - \sqrt{2}$

A **quadratic function** is second degree: $f(x) = ax^2 + bx + c$
    Example: $f(x) = 3x^2 + 5x - \frac{1}{2}$

A **cubic function** is third degree: $f(x) = ax^3 + bx^2 + cx + d$
Example: $f(x) = \sqrt{2}x^3 - \pi x$

A **quartic function** is fourth degree: $f(x) = ax^4 + bx^3 + cx^2 + dx + e$
Example: $f(x) = 3x^4 - \frac{\sqrt{2}}{2}$

Rational Function

A **rational function** is the quotient of two polynomial functions, $p(x)$ and $d(x)$, which can be written in the form

$$f(x) = \frac{p(x)}{d(x)}, \qquad d(x) \neq 0$$

Examples: $f(x) = x^{-1}$; $f(x) = \dfrac{x-5}{x^2 + 2x - 3}$; $f(x) = x^{-3} + \sqrt{2}x$

When we write $d(x) \neq 0$, we mean that all values c for which $d(c) = 0$ are excluded from the domain of d.

If r is any nonzero real number, the function $f(x) = x^r$ is called a **power function** with exponent r. You should be familiar with the following cases:

Integer powers ($r = n$, a positive integer): $f(x) = x^n = \underbrace{x \cdot x \cdot \ldots \cdot x}_{n \text{ factors}}$

Example: $f(x) = x^6$

Reciprocal powers (r is a negative integer): $f(x) = x^{-n} = \dfrac{1}{x^n}$ for $x \neq 0$

Example: $f(x) = x^{-4}$

Roots ($r = \frac{m}{n}$ is a nonzero rational number): $f(x) = x^{m/n} = \sqrt[n]{x^m} = (\sqrt[n]{x})^m$ for all x if n odd, for $x \geq 0$ if n even, $n \neq 0$ ($\frac{m}{n}$ is reduced)

Examples: $f(x) = x^{3/4}$; $f(x) = \sqrt[5]{x^2}$

Power functions can also have irrational exponents (such as $\sqrt{2}$ or π), but such functions must be defined in a special way (see Section 2.4).

A function is called **algebraic** if it can be constructed using a finite number of algebraic operations (such as adding, subtracting, multiplying, dividing, or taking roots) starting with polynomials. Functions that are not algebraic are called **transcendental**. The following are transcendental functions:

Trigonometric functions are the functions sine, cosine, tangent, secant, cosecant, and cotangent. The basic forms of these functions are reviewed in Chapter 4 of the *Student Mathematics Handbook*. You can also review these functions by consulting a trigonometry or precalculus textbook.

SMH

Exponential functions are functions of the form $f(x) = b^x$, where b is a positive constant, $b \neq 1$. We will introduce these functions in Section 2.4.

Logarithmic functions are functions of the form $f(x) = \log_b x$, where b is a positive constant, $b \neq 1$. We will also study these functions in Section 2.4.

1.3 PROBLEM SET

In Problems 1–12, find the domain of f and compute the indicated values or state that the corresponding x-value is not in the domain. Tell whether any of the indicated values are zeros of the function, that is, values of x that cause the functional value to be 0.

Ⓐ 1. $f(x) = 2x + 3$; $f(-2)$, $f(1)$, $f(0)$

2. $f(x) = -x^2 + 2x + 3$; $f(0)$, $f(1)$, $f(-2)$

3. $f(x) = 3x^2 + 5x - 2$; $f(1)$, $f(0)$, $f(-2)$

4. $f(x) = x + \dfrac{1}{x}$; $f(-1)$, $f(1)$, $f(2)$

5. $f(x) = \dfrac{(x+3)(x-2)}{x+3}$; $f(2)$, $f(0)$, $f(-3)$

6. $f(x) = (2x-1)^{-3/2}$; $f(1)$, $f(\frac{1}{2})$, $f(13)$

7. $f(x) = \sqrt{x^2 + 2x}$; $f(-1)$, $f(\frac{1}{2})$, $f(1)$

8. $f(x) = \sqrt{x^2 + 5x + 6}$; $f(0)$, $f(1)$, $f(-2)$

9. $f(x) = \sin(1 - 2x)$; $f(-1)$, $f(\frac{1}{2})$, $f(1)$

10. $f(x) = \sin x - \cos x$; $f(0)$, $f(-\frac{\pi}{2})$, $f(\pi)$

11. $f(x) = \begin{cases} -2x + 4 & \text{if } x \le 1 \\ x + 1 & \text{if } x > 1 \end{cases}$; $f(3)$, $f(1)$, $f(0)$

12. $f(x) = \begin{cases} 3 & \text{if } x < -5 \\ x + 1 & \text{if } -5 \le x \le 5 \\ \sqrt{x} & \text{if } x > 5 \end{cases}$; $f(-6)$, $f(-5)$, $f(16)$

In Problems 13–20, evaluate the difference quotient $\dfrac{f(x+h) - f(x)}{h}$ for the given function.

13. $f(x) = 9x + 3$

14. $f(x) = 5 - 2x$

15. $f(x) = 5x^2$

16. $f(x) = 3x^2 + 2x$

17. $f(x) = |x|$ if $x < -1$ and $0 < h < 1$

18. $f(x) = |x|$ if $x > 1$ and $0 < h < 1$

19. $f(x) = \dfrac{1}{x}$

20. $f(x) = \dfrac{x+1}{x-1}$

State whether the functions f and g in Problems 21–26 are equal.

21. $f(x) = \dfrac{2x^2 + x}{x}$; $g(x) = 2x + 1$

22. $f(x) = \dfrac{2x^2 + x}{x}$; $g(x) = 2x + 1$, $x \ne 0$

23. $f(x) = \dfrac{2x^2 - x - 6}{x - 2}$; $g(x) = 2x + 3$, $x \ne 2$

24. $f(x) = \dfrac{3x^2 - 7x - 6}{x - 3}$; $g(x) = 3x + 2$, $x \ne 3$

25. $f(x) = \dfrac{3x^2 - 5x - 2}{x - 2}$; $g(x) = 3x + 1$

26. $f(x) = \dfrac{(3x+1)(x-2)}{x - 2}$, $x \ne 6$;

$g(x) = \dfrac{(3x+1)(x-6)}{x - 6}$, $x \ne 2$

Classify the functions defined in Problems 27–34 as even, odd, or neither.

27. $f_1(x) = x^2 + 1$

28. $f_2(x) = \sqrt{x^2}$

29. $f_3(x) = \dfrac{1}{3x^3 - 4}$

30. $f_4(x) = x^3 + x$

31. $f_5(x) = \dfrac{1}{(x^3 + 3)^2}$

32. $f_6(x) = \dfrac{1}{(x^3 + x)^2}$

33. $f_7(x) = |x|$

34. $f_8(x) = |x + x^3|$

In Problems 35–40, find the composite functions $f \circ g$ and $g \circ f$.

35. $f(x) = x^2 + 1$ and $g(x) = 2x$

36. $f(x) = \sin x$ and $g(x) = 1 - x^2$

37. $f(t) = \sqrt{t}$ and $g(t) = t^2$

38. $f(u) = \dfrac{u-1}{u+1}$ and $g(u) = \dfrac{u+1}{1-u}$

39. $f(x) = \sin x$ and $g(x) = 2x + 3$

40. $f(x) = \dfrac{1}{x}$ and $g(x) = \tan x$

In Problems 41–50, express f as the composition of two functions u and g such that $f(x) = g(u)$, where u is a function of x.

41. $f(x) = (2x^2 - 1)^4$

42. $f(x) = (x^2 + 1)^3$

43. $f(x) = |2x + 3|$

44. $f(x) = \sqrt{5x - 1}$

45. $f(x) = \tan^2 x$

46. $f(x) = \tan x^2$

47. $f(x) = \sin \sqrt{x}$

48. $f(x) = \sqrt{\sin x}$

49. $f(x) = \sin\left(\dfrac{x+1}{2-x}\right)$

50. $f(x) = \tan\left(\dfrac{2x}{1-x}\right)$

51. If point A in Figure 1.24 has coordinates $(2, f(2))$, what are the coordinates of P and Q?

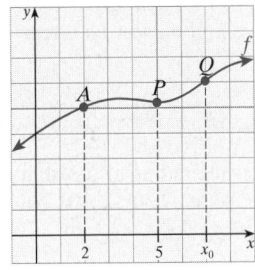
Problem 51

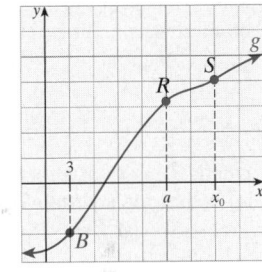
Problem 52

Figure 1.24

52. If point B in Figure 1.24 has coordinates $(3, g(3))$, what are the coordinates of R and S?

Find the x-intercepts, if any, for the functions given in Problems 53–60.

53. $f(x) = 3x^2 - 5x - 2$

54. $f(x) = 6x^2 + 5x - 6$

55. $f(x) = (x - 15)(2x + 25)(3x - 65)(4x + 1)$

56. $f(x) = (x^2 - 10)(x^2 - 12)(x^2 - 20)$

57. $f(x) = 5x^3 - 3x^2 + 2x$

58. $f(x) = x^4 - 41x^2 + 400$

59. $f(x) = \dfrac{x^2 - 1}{x^2 + 2}$

60. $f(x) = \dfrac{x(x^2 - 3)}{x^2 + 5}$

B **61.** Suppose the total cost (in dollars) of manufacturing q units of a certain commodity is given by

$$C(q) = q^3 - 30q^2 + 400q + 500$$

a. Compute the cost of manufacturing 20 units.

b. Compute the cost of manufacturing the 20th unit.

62. An efficiency study of the morning shift at a certain factory indicates that an average worker who arrives on the job at 8:00 A.M. will have assembled

$$f(x) = -x^3 + 6x + 15x^2$$

CD players x hours later ($0 \le x \le 8$).

a. How many players will such a worker have assembled by 10:00 A.M.?

b. How many players will such a worker assemble between 9:00 A.M. and 10:00 A.M.?

63. In physics, a light source of luminous intensity K candles is said to have *illuminance* $I = K/s^2$ on a flat surface s ft away. Suppose a small, unshaded lamp of luminous intensity 30 candles is connected to a rope that allows it to be raised and lowered between the floor and the top of a 10-ft-high ceiling. Assume that the lamp is being raised and lowered in such a way that at time t (in min) it is $s = 6t - t^2$ ft above the floor.

a. Express the illuminance on the floor as a composite function of t for $0 < t < 6$.

b. What is the illuminance when $t = 1$? When $t = 4$?

64. Biologists have found that the speed of blood in an artery is a function of the distance of the blood from the artery's central axis. According to *Poiseuille's law*, the speed (cm³/sec) of blood that is r cm from the central axis of an artery is given by the function

$$S(r) = C \cdot (R^2 - r^2)$$

where C is a constant and R is the radius of the artery.* Suppose that for a certain artery, $C = 1.76 \times 10^5$ cm/sec and $R = 1.2 \times 10^{-2}$ cm. (See Figure 1.25.)

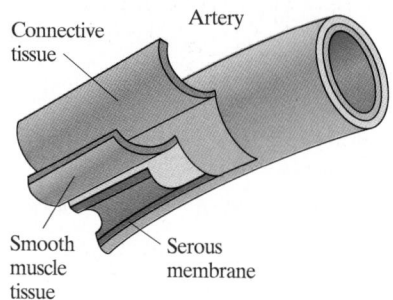

Connective tissue

Artery

Smooth muscle tissue

Serous membrane

Figure 1.25   Artery

a. Compute the speed of the blood at the central axis of this artery.

b. Compute the speed of the blood midway between the artery's wall and central axis.

*The law and the unit *poise*, a unit of viscosity, are both named for the French physician Jean Louis Poiseuille (1799–1869).

65. At a certain factory, the total cost of manufacturing q units during the daily production run is $C(q) = q^2 + q + 900$ dollars. On a typical workday, the number of units manufactured during the first t hours of a production run can be modeled by the function $q(t) = 25t$.

a. Express the total manufacturing cost as a function of t.

b. How much will have been spent on production by the end of the third hour?

c. When will the total manufacturing cost reach $11,000?

66. A ball is thrown directly upward from the edge of a cliff in such a way that t seconds later, it is

$$s = -16t^2 + 96t + 144$$

feet above the ground at the base of the cliff. Sketch the graph of this equation (making the t-axis the horizontal axis) and then answer these questions:

a. How high is the cliff?

b. When (to the nearest tenth of a second) does the ball hit the ground at the base of the cliff?

c. Estimate the time it takes for the ball to reach its maximum height. What is the maximum height?

67. Charles's law for gases states that if the pressure remains constant, then

$$V(T) = V_0 \cdot \left(1 + \frac{T}{273}\right)$$

where V is the volume (in.³), V_0 is the initial volume (in.³), and T is the temperature (in degrees Celsius).

a. Sketch the graph of $V(T)$ for $V_0 = 100$ and $T \ge -273$.

b. What is the temperature needed for the volume to double?

68. To study the rate at which animals learn, a psychology student performed an experiment in which a rat was sent repeatedly through a laboratory maze. Suppose that the time (in minutes) required for the rat to traverse the maze on the nth trial was approximately

$$f(n) = 3 + \frac{12}{n}$$

a. What is the domain of the function $f(x) = 3 + \dfrac{12}{x}$?

b. For what values of n does $f(n)$ have meaning in the context of the psychology experiment?

c. How long did it take the rat to traverse the maze on the third trial?

d. On which trial did the rat first traverse the maze in 4 minutes or less?

e. According to the function f, what will happen to the time required for the rat to traverse the maze as the number of trials increases? Will the rat ever be able to traverse the maze in less than 3 minutes?

69. The trajectory of a cannonball shot from the origin with initial velocity v and angle of inclination α (measured from level ground), is given by the equation

$$y = mx - 16v^{-2}(1 + m^2)x^2$$

where $m = \tan \alpha$. For this problem assume the initial velocity is $v = 200$ ft/s and that the angle of inclination is $42°$.

a. Using a graphing utility of a calculator, determine the maximum height reached by the cannonball.

b. Estimate the point where the cannonball will hit the ground.

c. Which curve in Table 1.3 shows the basic shape of this graph?

70. Draw the path of a cannonball (see Problem 69) for an angle of inclination of 47°. Determine the angle α that will maximize the distance the cannonball will travel.

71. It is estimated that t years from now, the population of a certain suburban community will be

$$P(t) = 20 - \frac{6}{t+1}$$

thousand people.

a. What will the population of the community be nine years from now?

b. By how much will the population increase during the ninth year?

c. What will happen to the size of the population in the "long run"?

C **72. Journal problem:** *The Mathematics Student Journal.** ■ Given that $f(11) = 11$ and

$$f(x+3) = \frac{f(x) - 1}{f(x) + 1}$$

for all x, find $f(2000)$.

---

*Volume 28 (1980), issue 3, p. 2. Note that the journal problem requests $f(1979)$, which, no doubt, was related to the publication date. We have taken the liberty of updating the requested value.

73. HISTORICAL QUEST One of the best known mathematical theorems is the **Pythagorean theorem**, named after the Greek philosopher Pythagoras. Very little is known about the life of Pythagoras, but we do know he was born on the island of Samos. He founded a secret brotherhood called the Pythagoreans that continued for at least 100 years after Pythagoras was murdered for political reasons. Even though the cult was called a "brotherhood," it did admit women. According to Lynn Osen in *Women in Mathematics*,[†] the order was carried on by his wife and daughters after his death. In fact, women were probably more welcome in the centers of learning in ancient Greece than in any other age from that time until now. ■

PYTHAGORAS
ca. 500 B.C.

State and prove the Pythagorean theorem.

[†]MIT Press, Cambridge MA, 1975.

1.4 Inverse Functions; Inverse Trigonometric Functions

IN THIS SECTION inverse functions, criteria for the existence of an inverse f^{-1}, graph of f^{-1}, inverse trigonometric functions, inverse trigonometric identities

INVERSE FUNCTIONS

WARNING The symbol f^{-1} means the inverse of f and does not mean reciprocal, $1/f$.

For a given function f, we write $y_0 = f(x_0)$ to indicate that f maps the number x_0 in its domain into the corresponding number y_0 in its range. If f has an inverse f^{-1}, it is the function that reverses the effect of f in the sense that

$$f^{-1}(y_0) = x_0$$

For example, if

$$f(x) = 2x - 3, \text{ then } f(0) = -3, \ f(1) = -1, \ f(2) = 1,$$

and the inverse f^{-1} reverses f so that

$f(0) = -3$	$\mathbf{f^{-1}(-3) = 0}$	that is, $f^{-1}[f(0)] = 0$
$f(1) = -1$	$\mathbf{f^{-1}(-1) = 1}$	that is, $f^{-1}[f(1)] = 1$
$f(2) = 1$	$\mathbf{f^{-1}(1) = 2}$	that is, $f^{-1}[f(2)] = 2$

In the case where the inverse of a function is itself a function, we have the following definition.

Inverse Function

Let f be a function with domain D and range R. Then the function f^{-1} with domain R and range D is the **inverse of** f if

$$f^{-1}[f(x)] = x \qquad \text{for all } x \text{ in } D$$

and

$$f[f^{-1}(y)] = y \qquad \text{for all } y \text{ in } R$$

➧ **What This Says**   Suppose we consider a function defined by a set of ordered pairs (x, y) where $y = f(x)$. The image of x is y, as shown in Figure 1.26.

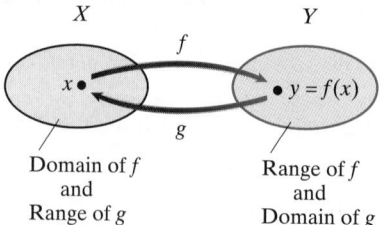

Figure 1.26   Inverse functions f and g

If y is a member of the domain of the function $g = f^{-1}$, then $g(y) = x$. This means that f matches each element of x to exactly one y, and g matches those same elements of y back to the original values of x. If you think of a function as a set of ordered pairs (x, y), the inverse of f is the set of ordered pairs with the components (y, x).

The inverse function f^{-1} reverses the effect of f. This relationship can be illustrated by function "machines," as shown in Figure 1.27. Note that the value input into the first "f machine" is x and the output $f(x)$ from this machine is the input into a second "f^{-1} machine" whose output is the original input value, x.

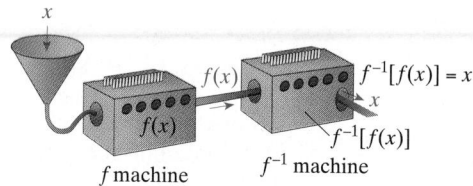

Figure 1.27   Inverse machines

The language of this definition suggests that there is only one inverse function of f. Indeed, it can be shown (see Problem 54) that if f has an inverse, then the inverse is unique.

EXAMPLE 1   Inverse of a given function defined as a set of ordered pairs

Let $f = \{(0, 3), (1, 5), (3, 9), (5, 13)\}$; find f^{-1}, if it exists.

Solution

The inverse simply reverses the ordered pairs:

$$f^{-1} = \{(3, 0), (5, 1), (9, 3), (13, 5)\}$$

■

EXAMPLE 2 Inverse of a given function defined by an equation

Let $f(x) = 2x - 3$; find f^{-1}, if it exists.

Solution

To find f^{-1}, let $y = f(x)$, then interchange the x and y variables, and finally solve for y.

$$\text{Given function:} \quad y = 2x - 3 \qquad \text{Then} \quad x = 2y - 3$$
$$2y = x + 3$$
$$\text{Inverse:} \quad y = \tfrac{1}{2}(x + 3)$$

Thus, we represent the inverse function as $f^{-1}(x) = \tfrac{1}{2}(x + 3)$. To verify that these functions are inverses of each other, we note that

$$f[f^{-1}(x)] = f\left[\tfrac{1}{2}(x + 3)\right] = 2\left[\tfrac{1}{2}(x + 3)\right] - 3 = x + 3 - 3 = x$$

and

$$f^{-1}[f(x)] = f^{-1}(2x - 3) = \tfrac{1}{2}[(2x - 3) + 3] = \tfrac{1}{2}(2x) = x$$

for all x. ■

CRITERIA FOR EXISTENCE OF AN INVERSE f^{-1}

The inverse of a function may not exist. For example, both the functions

$$f = \{(0, 0), (1, 1), (-1, 1), (2, 4), (-2, 4)\} \quad \text{and} \quad g(x) = x^2$$

do not have inverses because if we attempt to find the inverses, we obtain relations that are not functions. In the first case, we find

$$\text{Possible inverse of } f : \{(0, 0), (1, 1), (1, -1), (4, 2), (4, -2)\}$$

This is not a function because not every member of the domain is associated with a single member in the range: $(1, 1)$ and $(1, -1)$, for example.

In the second case, if we interchange the x and y in the equation for the function g where $y = x^2$ and then solve for y, we find

$$x = y^2 \quad \text{or} \quad y = \pm\sqrt{x} \quad \text{for } x \geq 0$$

But this is not a function of x, because for any positive value of x, there are two corresponding values of y, namely, $\sqrt{x}$ and $-\sqrt{x}$.

A function f will have an inverse f^{-1} on the interval I when there is exactly one number in the domain associated with each number in the range. That is, f^{-1} exists if $f(x_1)$ and $f(x_2)$ are equal only when $x_1 = x_2$. A function with this property is said to be **one-to-one**. This is equivalent to the graphical criterion, called the *horizontal line test*, shown in Figure 1.28.

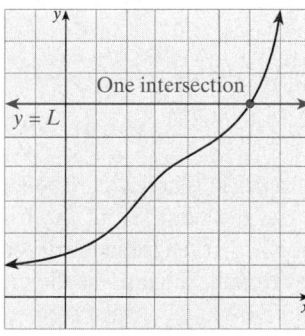

a. A function that has an inverse

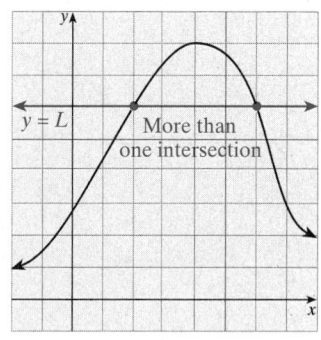

b. A function that does not have an inverse

Figure 1.28 Horizontal line test

A function is said to be **strictly increasing** on an interval I if its graph is always rising on I, and **strictly decreasing** on I if the graph always falls on I. It is called **strictly monotonic** on I if it is either strictly increasing or strictly decreasing throughout that interval. A strictly monotonic function must be one-to-one and hence must have an inverse. For example, if f is strictly increasing on the interval I, we know that

$$x_1 > x_2 \quad \text{implies} \quad f(x_1) > f(x_2)$$

so there is no way to have $f(x_1) = f(x_2)$ unless $x_1 = x_2$. This observation is formalized in the following theorem.

THEOREM 1.2   A strictly monotonic function has an inverse

Let f be a function that is strictly monotonic on an interval I. Then f^{-1} exists and is monotonic on I (increasing if f is increasing and decreasing if f is decreasing).

Proof   We have already commented on why f^{-1} exists. To show that f^{-1} is strictly increasing whenever f is increasing, let y_1 and y_2 be numbers in the range of f, with $y_2 > y_1$. We will show that $f^{-1}(y_2) > f^{-1}(y_1)$. Because y_1, y_2 are in the range of f, there exist numbers x_1, x_2 in the domain I such that $y_1 = f(x_1)$ and $y_2 = f(x_2)$. Because $y_2 > y_1$, it follows that $f(x_2) > f(x_1)$, and because f is strictly increasing, we must have $x_2 > x_1$. Thus, $f^{-1}(y_2) > f^{-1}(y_1)$, and f^{-1} is strictly increasing. Similarly, if f is strictly decreasing, then so is f^{-1}. (The details are left for the reader.)   ❑

GRAPH OF f^{-1}

The graphs of f and its inverse f^{-1} are closely related. In particular, if (a, b) is a point on the graph of f, then $b = f(a)$ and $a = f^{-1}(b)$, so (b, a) is on the graph of f^{-1}. It can be shown that (a, b) and (b, a) are reflections of one another in the line $y = x$. (See Figure 1.29.) These observations yield the following procedure for sketching the graph of an inverse function.

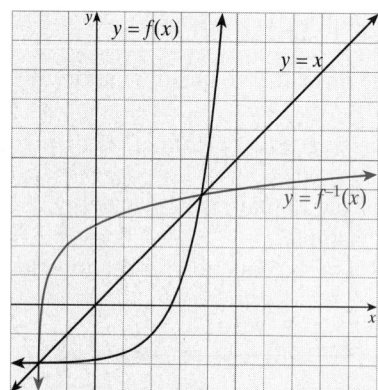

Figure 1.29 The graphs of f and f^{-1} are reflections in the line $y = x$

Procedure for Obtaining the Graph of f^{-1}

If f^{-1} exists, its graph may be obtained by reflecting the graph of f in the line $y = x$.

INVERSE TRIGONOMETRIC FUNCTIONS

The trigonometric functions are not one-to-one, so their inverses do not exist. However, if we restrict the domains of the trigonometric functions, then the inverses exist on those domains. In trigonometry you probably distinguished between the sine curve with unrestricted domain and the sine curve with restricted domain by writing $y = \sin x$ and $y = \operatorname{Sin} x$, respectively. In calculus, it is not customary to make such a distinction by using a capital letter.

Let us consider the sine function first. We know that the sine function is strictly increasing on the closed interval $[-\frac{\pi}{2}, \frac{\pi}{2}]$, and if we restrict $\sin x$ to this interval, it does have an inverse, as shown in Figure 1.30.

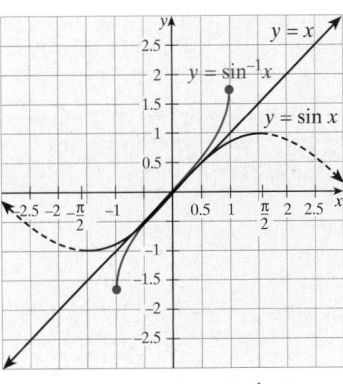

a. The graph of $y = \sin^{-1} x$ is obtained by reflecting the part of the sine on $\left[-\frac{\pi}{2}, \frac{\pi}{2}\right]$ about $y = x$.

b. The graph of the inverse sine function, $y = \sin^{-1} x$.

Figure 1.30 Inverse sine function

Inverse Sine Function

$$y = \sin^{-1} x \quad \text{if and only if} \quad x = \sin y \quad \text{and} -\frac{\pi}{2} \leq y \leq \frac{\pi}{2}$$

The function $\sin^{-1} x$ is sometimes written $\arcsin x$.

WARNING The function $\sin^{-1} x$ is NOT the reciprocal of $\sin x$. To denote the reciprocal, write $(\sin x)^{-1}$. In other words, $\sin^{-1} x \neq \dfrac{1}{\sin x}$, whereas $(\sin x)^{-1} = \dfrac{1}{\sin x}$.

Inverses of the other five trigonometric functions may be constructed in a similar manner. For example, by restricting $\tan x$ to the open interval $\left(-\frac{\pi}{2}, \frac{\pi}{2}\right)$ where it is one-to-one, we can define the inverse tangent function as follows.

Inverse Tangent Function

$$y = \tan^{-1} x \quad \text{if and only if} \quad x = \tan y \quad \text{and} \quad -\frac{\pi}{2} < y < \frac{\pi}{2}$$

The function $\tan^{-1} x$ is sometimes written $\arctan x$.

The graph of $y = \tan^{-1} x$ is shown in Figure 1.31.

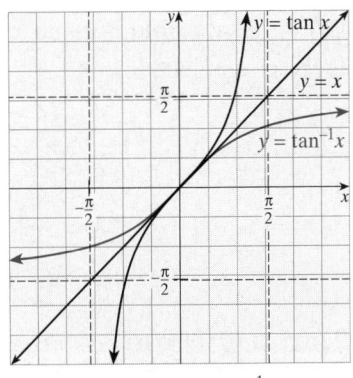
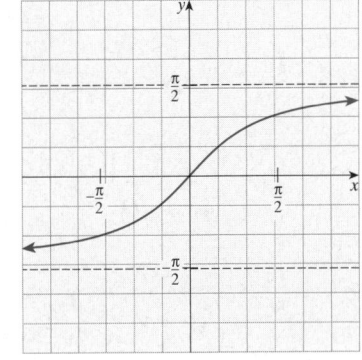

a. The graph of $y = \tan^{-1} x$ is obtained by reflecting the part of the tangent graph on $\left(-\frac{\pi}{2}, \frac{\pi}{2}\right)$ about the line $y = x$.

b. The graph of $y = \tan^{-1} x$

Figure 1.31 Graph of the inverse tangent function

Definitions and graphs of four other fundamental inverse trigonometric functions are given in Table 1.4 and Figure 1.32, respectively.

WARNING It is easier to remember the restrictions on the domain and range if you do so in terms of quadrants, as shown in Table 1.4.

TABLE 1.4 Definition of Inverse Trigonometric Functions

Inverse Function	Domain	Range
$y = \sin^{-1} x$	$-1 \leq x \leq 1$	$-\frac{\pi}{2} \leq y \leq \frac{\pi}{2}$ Quadrants I and IV
$y = \cos^{-1} x$	$-1 \leq x \leq 1$	$0 \leq y \leq \pi$ Quadrants I and II
$y = \tan^{-1} x$	$-\infty < x < +\infty$	$-\frac{\pi}{2} < y < \frac{\pi}{2}$ Quadrants I and IV
$y = \csc^{-1} x$	$x \geq 1$ or $x \leq -1$	$-\frac{\pi}{2} \leq y \leq \frac{\pi}{2}, \; y \neq 0$ Quadrants I and IV
$y = \sec^{-1} x$	$x \geq 1$ or $x \leq -1$	$0 \leq y \leq \pi, \; y \neq \frac{\pi}{2}$ Quadrants I and II
$y = \cot^{-1} x$	$-\infty < x < +\infty$	$0 < y < \pi$ Quadrants I and II

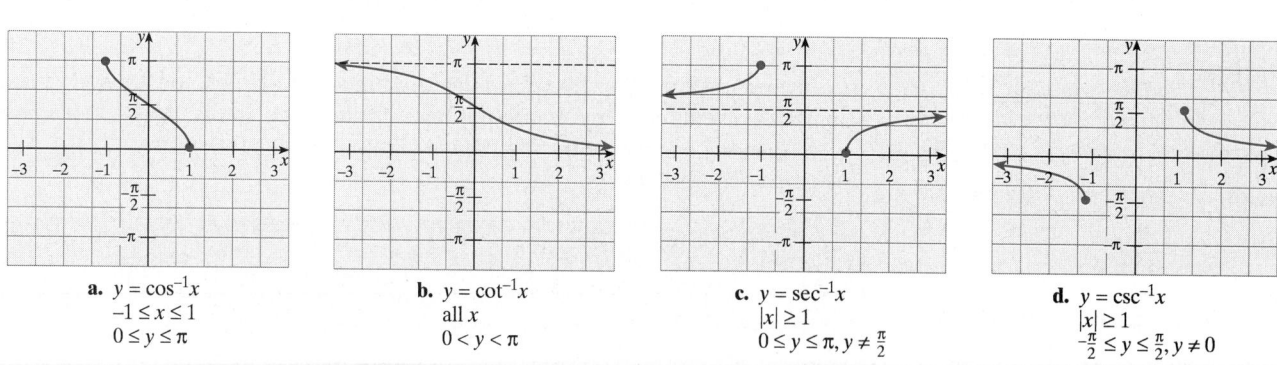

a. $y = \cos^{-1} x$
$-1 \leq x \leq 1$
$0 \leq y \leq \pi$

b. $y = \cot^{-1} x$
all x
$0 < y < \pi$

c. $y = \sec^{-1} x$
$|x| \geq 1$
$0 \leq y \leq \pi, y \neq \frac{\pi}{2}$

d. $y = \csc^{-1} x$
$|x| \geq 1$
$-\frac{\pi}{2} \leq y \leq \frac{\pi}{2}, y \neq 0$

Figure 1.32 Graphs of four inverse trigonometric functions

EXAMPLE 3 Evaluating inverse trigonometric functions

Evaluate the given functions.

a. $\sin^{-1}(\frac{-\sqrt{2}}{2})$ **b.** $\sin^{-1} 0.21$ **c.** $\cos^{-1} 0$ **d.** $\tan^{-1}(\frac{1}{\sqrt{3}})$

Solution

a. $\sin^{-1}(\frac{-\sqrt{2}}{2}) = -\frac{\pi}{4}$ Think: $x = \frac{-\sqrt{2}}{2}$ is negative, so y is in Quadrant IV; the reference angle is the angle whose sine is $\frac{\sqrt{2}}{2}$; it is $\frac{\pi}{4}$, so in Quadrant IV the angle is $-\frac{\pi}{4}$.

b. $\sin^{-1} 0.21 \approx 0.2115750$ By calculator; be sure to use radian mode and inverse sine (not reciprocal).

c. $\cos^{-1} 0 = \frac{\pi}{2}$ Memorized exact value.

d. $\tan^{-1}(\frac{1}{\sqrt{3}}) = \frac{\pi}{6}$ Think: $x = \frac{1}{\sqrt{3}}$ is positive, so y is in Quadrant I; the reference angle is the same as the value of the inverse tangent in Quadrant I. ∎

INVERSE TRIGONOMETRIC IDENTITIES

The definition of inverse functions yields four formulas, which we call the inversion formulas for sine and tangent.

Inversion Formulas

$$\sin(\sin^{-1} x) = x \qquad \text{for } -1 \le x \le 1$$

$$\sin^{-1}(\sin y) = y \qquad \text{for } -\tfrac{\pi}{2} \le y \le \tfrac{\pi}{2}$$

$$\tan(\tan^{-1} x) = x \qquad \text{for all } x$$

$$\tan^{-1}(\tan y) = y \qquad \text{for } -\tfrac{\pi}{2} < y < \tfrac{\pi}{2}$$

EXAMPLE 4   Inversion formula for x inside and outside domain

Evaluate the given functions.

a. $\sin(\sin^{-1} 0.5)$ **b.** $\sin(\sin^{-1} 2)$ **c.** $\sin^{-1}(\sin 0.5)$ **d.** $\sin^{-1}(\sin 2)$

Solution

a. $\sin(\sin^{-1} 0.5) = 0.5$, because $-1 \le 0.5 \le 1$.
b. $\sin(\sin^{-1} 2)$ does not exist, because 2 is not between -1 and 1.
c. $\sin^{-1}(\sin 0.5) = 0.5$, because $-\tfrac{\pi}{2} \le 0.5 \le \tfrac{\pi}{2}$.
d. $\sin^{-1}(\sin 2) = 1.1415927$, by calculator.
   For exact values, notice that

$$\sin 2 = \sin(\pi - 2) \quad (\text{and } -\tfrac{\pi}{2} \le \pi - 2 \le \tfrac{\pi}{2})$$

so that we have $\sin^{-1}(\sin 2) = \sin^{-1}[\sin(\pi - 2)] = \pi - 2$. ∎

Some trigonometric identities correspond to inverse trigonometric identities, but others do not. For example,

$$\sin(-x) = -\sin x \quad \text{and} \quad \cos(-x) = \cos x$$

It is true that

$$\sin^{-1}(-x) = -\sin^{-1}(x)$$

but in general,

$$\cos^{-1}(-x) \ne \cos^{-1} x$$

(For a counterexample, try $x = 1$: $\cos^{-1}(-1) = \pi$; and $\cos^{-1} 1 = 0$.)

EXAMPLE 5   Proving inverse trigonometric identities

For $-1 \le x \le 1$, show that

a. $\sin^{-1}(-x) = -\sin^{-1} x$ **b.** $\cos(\sin^{-1} x) = \sqrt{1 - x^2}$

Solution

a. Let
$$y = \sin^{-1}(-x)$$
$$\sin y = -x \qquad\qquad \textit{Definition of inverse sine}$$
$$-\sin y = x$$
$$\sin(-y) = x \qquad\qquad \textit{Opposite angle identity}$$
$$-y = \sin^{-1} x \qquad\qquad \textit{Definition of inverse sine}$$
$$y = -\sin^{-1} x$$

Thus, $\sin^{-1}(-x) = -\sin^{-1} x$.

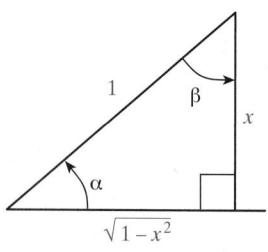

Figure 1.33 A reference triangle

b. Let $\alpha = \sin^{-1} x$, so $\sin \alpha = x$, where $-\frac{\pi}{2} \leq \alpha \leq \frac{\pi}{2}$. Here we consider the case where $0 \leq \alpha \leq \frac{\pi}{2}$, and the other case where $-\frac{\pi}{2} \leq \alpha < 0$ is handled similarly. Construct a right triangle with an acute angle α and hypotenuse 1, as shown in Figure 1.33. We call this triangle a **reference triangle**.

The side opposite α is x (since $\sin \alpha = x$), and by the Pythagorean theorem, the adjacent side is $\sqrt{1 - x^2}$. Thus, we have

$$\cos(\sin^{-1} x) = \cos \alpha$$
$$= \frac{\pm\sqrt{1 - x^2}}{1}$$
$$= \sqrt{1 - x^2} \quad \text{Substitute } \cos \alpha = x \text{ and choose the positive value for the radical because } \alpha \text{ is in Quadrant I.} \quad \blacksquare$$

Reference triangles, such as the one shown in Figure 1.33, are extremely useful devices for obtaining inverse trigonometric identities. For instance, let α and β be angles of a right triangle with hypotenuse 1. If the side opposite α is x (so that $\sin \alpha = x$), then $\alpha = \sin^{-1} x$ and $\beta = \cos^{-1} x$ so that

$$\sin^{-1} x + \cos^{-1} x = \alpha + \beta = \frac{\pi}{2} \quad \text{for } 0 \leq x \leq 1$$

since the acute angles of a right triangle must sum to $\pi/2$. The same reasoning can also be used to show that

$$\tan^{-1} x + \cot^{-1} x = \frac{\pi}{2}$$

and

$$\sec^{-1} x + \csc^{-1} x = \frac{\pi}{2}$$

Identities involving inverse trigonometric functions have a variety of uses. For instance, most calculators have keys for evaluating $\sin^{-1} x$, $\cos^{-1} x$, and $\tan^{-1} x$, but what about the other three inverse trigonometric functions? The answer is given by the following theorem, which allows us to compute $\sec^{-1} x$, $\csc^{-1} x$, and $\cot^{-1} x$ using reciprocal identities involving the three inverse trigonometric functions the calculator does have.

THEOREM 1.3   Reciprocal identities for inverse trigonometric functions

$$\sec^{-1} x = \cos^{-1} \frac{1}{x} \quad \text{if } |x| \geq 1$$
$$\csc^{-1} x = \sin^{-1} \frac{1}{x} \quad \text{if } |x| \geq 1$$
$$\cot^{-1} x = \frac{\pi}{2} - \tan^{-1} x$$

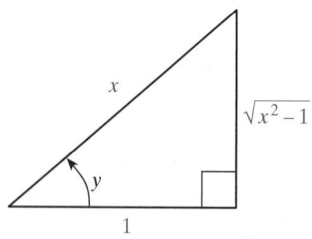

Figure 1.34 Reference triangle

Proof We will prove that $\sec^{-1} x = \cos^{-1} \frac{1}{x}$ and leave the other two parts as an exercise. Let $y = \sec^{-1} x$. Then $\sec y = x$ and by using the reference triangle in Figure 1.34, we see that $\cos y = \frac{1}{x}$ so that

$$y = \sec^{-1} x = \cos^{-1} \frac{1}{x}$$

Note that the reference triangle is valid only if $|x| \geq 1$.   ❏

EXAMPLE 6   Evaluating inverse reciprocal functions

Evaluate the given inverse functions using the inverse identities and a calculator.

    a. $\sec^{-1}(-3)$ **b.** $\csc^{-1} 7.5$ **c.** $\cot^{-1} 2.4747$

Solution

    a. $\sec^{-1}(-3) = \cos^{-1}(-\frac{1}{3}) \approx 1.910633236$

    b. $\csc^{-1} 7.5 = \sin^{-1}(\frac{1}{7.5}) \approx 0.1337315894$

    c. $\cot^{-1} 2.4747 = \frac{\pi}{2} - \tan^{-1} 2.4747 \approx 0.3840267299$ ■

1.4   PROBLEM SET

A **1. Exploration Problem**   Discuss the restrictions on the domain and range in the definition of the inverse trigonometric functions.

2. Exploration Problem   Discuss the use of reference triangles with respect to the inverse trigonometric functions.

Determine which pairs of functions defined by the equations in Problems 3–8 are inverses of each other.

3. $f(x) = 5x + 3$; $g(x) = \dfrac{x-3}{5}$

4. $f(x) = \frac{2}{3}x + 2$; $g(x) = \frac{3}{2}x + 3$

5. $f(x) = \frac{4}{5}x + 4$; $g(x) = \frac{5}{4}x + 3$

6. $f(x) = \dfrac{1}{x}, x \neq 0$; $g(x) = \dfrac{1}{x}, x \neq 0$

7. $f(x) = x^2, x < 0$; $g(x) = \sqrt{x}, x > 0$

8. $f(x) = x^2, x \geq 0$; $g(x) = \sqrt{x}, x \geq 0$

Find the inverse (if it exists) of each function given in Problems 9–18.

9. $f = \{(4, 5), (6, 3), (7, 1), (2, 4)\}$

10. $g = \{(3, 9), (-3, 9), (4, 16), (-4, 16)\}$

11. $f(x) = 2x + 3$ **12.** $g(x) = -3x + 2$

13. $f(x) = x^2 - 5, x \geq 0$ **14.** $g(x) = x^2 - 5, x < 0$

15. $F(x) = \sqrt{x} + 5$ **16.** $G(x) = 10 - \sqrt{x}$

17. $h(x) = \dfrac{2x - 6}{3x + 3}$ **18.** $h(x) = \dfrac{2x + 1}{x}$

Give the exact values for functions in Problems 19–30.

19. a. $\cos^{-1} \frac{1}{2}$ **b.** $\sin^{-1}(-\frac{\sqrt{3}}{2})$

20. a. $\sin^{-1}(-\frac{1}{2})$ **b.** $\cos^{-1}(-\frac{1}{2})$

21. a. $\tan^{-1}(-1)$ **b.** $\cot^{-1}(-\sqrt{3})$

22. a. $\sec^{-1}(-\sqrt{2})$ **b.** $\csc^{-1}(-\sqrt{2})$

23. a. $\sin^{-1}(-\frac{\sqrt{3}}{2})$ **b.** $\sec^{-1}(-1)$

24. a. $\sec^{-1}(\frac{2}{\sqrt{3}})$ **b.** $\cot^{-1}(-1)$

25. $\cos(\sin^{-1} \frac{1}{2})$ **26.** $\sin(\cos^{-1} \frac{1}{\sqrt{2}})$

27. $\cot(\tan^{-1} \frac{1}{3})$ **28.** $\tan(\sin^{-1} \frac{1}{3})$

29. $\cos(\sin^{-1} \frac{1}{5} + 2\cos^{-1} \frac{1}{5})$

    SMH   *Hint:* Use the addition law for $\cos(\alpha + \beta)$.

30. $\sin(\sin^{-1} \frac{1}{5} + \cos^{-1} \frac{1}{4})$

    SMH   *Hint:* Use the addition law for $\sin(\alpha + \beta)$.

31. Suppose that α is an acute angle of a right triangle where

$$\sin \alpha = \frac{s^2 - t^2}{s^2 + t^2} \quad (s > t > 0)$$

Show that $\alpha = \tan^{-1}\left(\dfrac{s^2 - t^2}{2st}\right)$.

32. If $\sin \alpha + \cos \alpha = s$ and $\sin \alpha - \cos \alpha = t$, show that

$$\alpha = \tan^{-1}\left(\frac{s + t}{s - t}\right)$$

B *Sketch the graph of f in Problems 33–38 and then use the horizontal line test to determine whether f has an inverse. If f^{-1} exists, sketch its graph.*

33. $f(x) = x^2$, for all x **34.** $f(x) = x^2, x \leq 0$

35. $f(x) = \sqrt{1 - x^2}$, on $(-1, 1)$

36. $f(x) = x(x - 1)(x - 2)$, on $[1, 2]$

37. $f(x) = \cos x$, on $[0, \pi]$

38. $f(x) = \tan x$, on $(-\frac{\pi}{2}, \frac{\pi}{2})$

Simplify each expression in Problems 39–44.

39. $\sin(2 \tan^{-1} x)$ **40.** $\tan(2 \tan^{-1} x)$

41. $\tan(\cos^{-1} x)$ **42.** $\cos(2 \sin^{-1} x)$

43. $\sin(\sin^{-1} x + \cos^{-1} x)$ **44.** $\cos 2(\sin^{-1} x + \cos^{-1} x)$

45. Use reference triangles, if necessary, to justify each of the following identities.

    a. $\cot^{-1} x = \frac{\pi}{2} - \tan^{-1} x$ for all x

    b. $\csc^{-1} x = \sin^{-1}\left(\dfrac{1}{x}\right)$ for all $|x| \geq 1$

46. Use the identities in Theorem 1.3 to evaluate each function rounded to four decimal places.

    a. $\cot^{-1} 0.67$ **b.** $\sec^{-1} 1.34$

    c. $\csc^{-1} 2.59$ **d.** $\cot^{-1}(-1.54)$

47. Use the identities in Theorem 1.3 to evaluate each function rounded to four decimal places.

    a. $\cot^{-1} 1.5$ **b.** $\cot^{-1}(-1.5)$

    c. $\sec^{-1}(-1.7)$ **d.** $\csc^{-1}(-1.84)$

48. A painting 3 ft high is hung on a wall in such a way that its lower edge is 7 ft above the floor. An observer whose eyes are 5 ft above the floor stands x ft away from the wall. Express the angle θ subtended by the painting as a function of x.

49. To determine the height of a building (see Figure 1.35), select a point P and find the angle of elevation to be α. Then move out a distance of x units (on a level plane) to point Q and find that the angle of elevation is now β. Find the height h of the building, as a function of x.

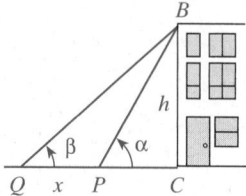

Figure 1.35   Determining height

(C) 50. a. Find $\tan^{-1} 1 + \tan^{-1} 2 + \tan^{-1} 3$ using a calculator. Make a conjecture about the exact value. Prove your conjecture using reference triangles.
b. Prove the conjecture from part **a** using trigonometric identities. *Hint:* Find $\tan(\tan^{-1} 1 + \tan^{-1} 2 + \tan^{-1} 3)$.

51. Prove the conjecture from Problem 50a using right triangles as follows. You may use the figure shown in Figure 1.36; assume that $\triangle ABC$, $\triangle ABD$, and $\triangle DEF$ are all right triangles with lengths of sides as shown in the figure.

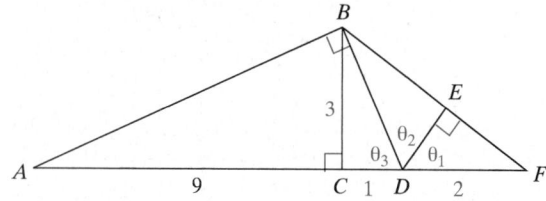

Figure 1.36 $\theta_1 + \theta_2 + \theta_3 = \pi$

52. We proved the identity

$$\csc^{-1} x = \sin^{-1}\left(\frac{1}{x}\right) \text{ for all } |x| \geq 1$$

By examining the graph of $y = \csc^{-1} x$, conjecture an identity of the form

$$\csc^{-1}(-x) = A + B \csc^{-1} x \text{ for } x > 1$$

Prove this identity, and then use it to evaluate $\csc^{-1}(-9.38)$.

53. Counterexample Problem   In Theorem 1.3 we proved the identity

$$\sec^{-1} x = \cos^{-1}\left(\frac{1}{x}\right) \text{ for all } x \geq 1$$

The graph of $y = \sec^{-1} x$ suggests that

$$\sec^{-1}(-x) = \pi + \sec^{-1} x \text{ for } x > 1$$

Either prove this identity or find a counterexample.

54. Show that if f^{-1} exists, it is unique. *Hint:* If g_1 and g_2 both satisfy

$$g_1[f(x)] = x = f[g_1(x)]$$
$$g_2[f(x)] = x = f[g_2(x)]$$

then $g_1(x) = g_2(x)$.

55. Suppose that $\triangle ABC$ is *not* a right triangle but has an obtuse angle γ. Draw $\overline{BD}$ perpendicular to $\overline{AC}$, forming right triangles $\triangle ABD$ and $\triangle BDC$ (with right angles at D). Show that

$$\frac{\sin \alpha}{a} = \frac{\sin \gamma}{c}$$

CHAPTER 1 REVIEW

Proficiency Examination

CONCEPT PROBLEMS

1. Characterize the following sets of numbers: natural numbers ($\mathbb{N}$), whole numbers ($\mathbb{W}$), integers ($\mathbb{Z}$), rational numbers ($\mathbb{Q}$), irrational numbers ($\mathbb{Q}'$), and real numbers ($\mathbb{R}$).

2. Define absolute value.

3. State the triangle inequality.

4. State the distance formula for points $P(x_1, y_1)$ and $Q(x_2, y_2)$.

5. Define slope in terms of angle of inclination.

6. List the following forms of the equation of a line:
a. standard form
b. slope-intercept form
c. point-slope form
d. horizontal line
e. vertical line

7. State the slope criteria for parallel and for perpendicular lines.

8. Define function.

9. Define the composition of functions.

10. What is meant by the graph of a function?

11. Draw a quick sketch of an example of each of the following functions.
a. identity function
b. standard quadratic function
c. standard cubic function
d. absolute value function
e. cube root function
f. standard reciprocal function
g. standard reciprocal squared function
h. cosine function
i. sine function
j. tangent function
k. secant function
l. cosecant function
m. cotangent function
n. inverse cosine function

o. inverse sine function

p. inverse tangent function

q. inverse secant function

r. inverse cosecant function

s. inverse cotangent function

12. What is a polynomial function?

13. What is a rational function?

14. a. Define an inverse function.

   b. What is the procedure for graphing the inverse of a given function?

15. What is the horizontal line test?

16. State the inversion formulas for sine and tangent.

17. State the reciprocal inverse trigonometric identities.

PRACTICE PROBLEMS

18. Find an equation for the lines satisfying the given conditions:

   a. through $(-\frac{1}{2}, 5)$ with slope $m = -\frac{3}{4}$

   b. through $(-3, 5)$ and $(7, 2)$

   c. with x-intercept $(4, 0)$ and y-intercept $(0, -\frac{3}{7})$

   d. through $(-\frac{1}{2}, 5)$ and parallel to the line $2x + 5y - 11 = 0$

   e. the perpendicular bisector of the line segment joining $P(-3, 7)$ and $Q(5, 1)$

Sketch the graph of each of the equations in Problems 19–26.

19. $3x + 2y - 12 = 0$

20. $y - 3 = |x + 1|$

21. $y - 3 = -2(x - 1)^2$

22. $y = x^2 - 4x - 10$

23. $y = 2\cos(x - 1)$

24. $y + 1 = \tan(2x + 3)$

25. $y = \sin^{-1}(2x)$

26. $y = \tan^{-1} x^2$

27. If $f(x) = \dfrac{1}{x + 1}$, what value(s) of x satisfy

$$f\left(\frac{1}{x+1}\right) = f\left(\frac{2x+1}{2x+4}\right)?$$

28. If $f(x) = \sqrt{\dfrac{x}{x-1}}$ and $g(x) = \dfrac{\sqrt{x}}{\sqrt{x-1}}$, does $f = g$? Why or why not?

29. If $f(x) = \sin x$ and $g(x) = \sqrt{1 - x^2}$, find the composite functions $f \circ g$ and $g \circ f$.

30. An open box with a square base is to be built for $96. The sides of the box will cost \$3/ft^2 and the base will cost \$8/ft^2. Express the volume of the box as a function of the length of its base.

Supplementary Problems*

In Problems 1–3, find the perimeter and area of the given figure.

1. the right triangle with vertices $(-1, 3)$, $(-1, 8)$, and $(11, 8)$

2. the triangle bounded by the lines $y = 5$, $3y - 4x = 11$, and $12x + 5y = 25$

3. the trapezoid with vertices $A(-3, 0)$, $B(5, 0)$, $C(2, 8)$, and $D(0, 8)$

In Problems 4–7, find an equation for the indicated line or circle.

4. the vertical line through the point where the line $y = 2x - 7$ intersects the parabola $y = x^2 + 6x - 3$

5. the circle that is tangent to the x-axis and is centered at $(5, 4)$

---

*The supplementary problems are presented in a somewhat random order, not necessarily in order of difficulty.

6. the circle with center on the y-axis that passes through the origin and is tangent to the line $3x + 4y - 40 = 0$

7. the line through the two points where the circles $x^2 + y^2 - 5x + 7y = 3$ and $x^2 + y^2 + 4y = 0$ intersect

8. Find constants A and B so that $\tan\left(x + \dfrac{\pi}{3}\right) = \dfrac{A + \tan x}{1 + B\tan x}$.

9. Find constants A and B so that $\sin^3 x = A\sin 3x + B\sin x$.

10. In a triangle, the perpendicular segment drawn from a given vertex to the opposite side is called the *altitude* on that side. Consider the triangle with vertices $(-2, 1)$, $(5, 6)$, and $(3, -2)$. Find an equation for each line containing an altitude of this triangle.

11. Show that the three lines found in Problem 10 intersect at the same point. Find the coordinates of this point. Is this the same point where the three medians meet?

12. Let $f(x) = x^2 + 5x - 9$. For what values of x is it true that $f(2x) = f(3x)$?

13. If an object is shot upward from the ground with an initial velocity of 256 ft/sec, its distance in feet above the ground at the end of t seconds is given by $s(t) = 256t - 16t^2$ (neglecting air resistance). What is the highest point for this projectile?

14. It is estimated that t years from now, the population of a certain suburban community will be

$$P(t) = \frac{11t + 12}{2t + 3}$$

thousand people. What is the current population of the community? What will the population be in 6 years? When will there be 5,000 people in the community?

15. Evaluate each of the given numbers (calculator approximations).

   a. $\tan^{-1} 2$ **b.** $\cot^{-1} 2$ **c.** $\sec^{-1}(-3.1)$

16. Evaluate each of the given numbers (exact values).

   a. $\sin(\cos^{-1}\frac{\sqrt{5}}{4})$ **b.** $\sin(2\tan^{-1} 3)$

   c. $\sin\left(\cos^{-1}\frac{3}{5} + \sin^{-1}\frac{5}{13}\right)$

17. Solve $\sqrt{x} = \cos^{-1} 0.317 + \sin^{-1} 0.317$

In Problems 18–21, find f^{-1} if it exists.

18. $f(x) = 2x^3 - 7$

19. $f(x) = \sqrt[7]{2x + 1},\ x \geq -\frac{1}{2}$

20. $f(x) = \sqrt{\sin x},\ 0 < x < \frac{\pi}{2}$

21. $f(x) = \dfrac{x + 5}{x - 7},\ x \neq 7$

22. Show that for any constant $a \neq 1$, the function $f(x) = \dfrac{x + a}{x - 1}$ is its own inverse.

23. Let $f(x) = \dfrac{ax + b}{cx + d}$, for constants $a, b, c,$ and d. Find $f^{-1}(x)$ in terms of $a, b, c,$ and d.

24. Find $f^{-1}(x)$ if $f(x) = \dfrac{x + 1}{x - 1}$. What is the domain of f^{-1}?

25. First show that $\tan^{-1} x + \tan^{-1} y = \tan^{-1}\left(\dfrac{x + y}{1 - xy}\right)$ for $xy \neq 1$ whenever $-\dfrac{\pi}{2} < \tan^{-1}\left(\dfrac{x + y}{1 - xy}\right) < \dfrac{\pi}{2}$. Then establish the following equations.

   a. $\tan^{-1}\frac{1}{2} + \tan^{-1}\frac{1}{3} = \frac{\pi}{4}$ **b.** $2\tan^{-1}\frac{1}{3} + \tan^{-1}\frac{1}{7} = \frac{\pi}{4}$

   c. $4\tan^{-1}\frac{1}{5} - \tan^{-1}\frac{1}{239} = \frac{\pi}{4}$

Note: The identity in part **c** will be used in Chapter 8 to estimate the value of π.

26. Counterexample Problem Each of the following equations may be either true or false. In each case, either show that the equation is generally true or find a counterexample.

a. $\tan^{-1} x = \dfrac{\sin^{-1} x}{\cos^{-1} x}$ **b.** $\tan^{-1} x = \dfrac{1}{\tan x}$

c. $\cot^{-1} x = \dfrac{\pi}{2} - \tan^{-1} x$ **d.** $\cos(\sin^{-1} x) = \sqrt{1 - x^2}$

e. $\sec^{-1}\left(\dfrac{1}{x}\right) = \cos^{-1} x$

27. Many materials, such as brick, steel, aluminum, and concrete, expand with increases in temperature. This is why spaces are placed between the cement slabs in sidewalks. Suppose you have a 100-ft length of material securely fastened at both ends, and assume that the buckle is linear. (It is not, but this assumption will serve as a worthwhile approximation.) If the height of the buckle is x ft and the percentage of swelling is y, then x and y are related as shown in Figure 1.37. Find the amount of buckling (to the nearest inch) for the following materials:

a. brick; $y = 0.03$ [This means $(0.03\%)(100 \text{ ft}) = 0.03$ ft, which is y in Figure 1.37.]

b. steel; $y = 0.06$

c. aluminum; $y = 0.12$ **d.** concrete; $y = 0.05$

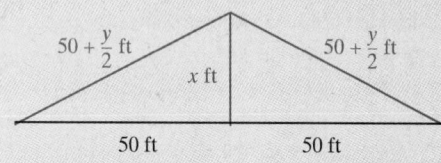

Figure 1.37 Buckling of a given material

28. A ball has been dropped from the top of a building. Its height (in feet) after t seconds is given by the function

$$h(t) = -16t^2 + 256$$

a. How high will the ball be after 2 sec?

b. How far will the ball travel during the third second?

c. How tall is the building?

d. When will the ball hit the ground?

29. Suppose the number of worker-hours required to distribute new telephone books to x percent of the households in a certain rural community is given by the function

$$f(x) = \frac{600x}{300 - x}$$

a. What is the domain of the function f?

b. For what values of x does $f(x)$ have a practical interpretation in this context?

c. How many worker-hours were required to distribute new telephone books to the first 50% of the households?

d. How many worker-hours were required to distribute new telephone books to the entire community?

e. What percentage of the households in the community had received new telephone books by the time 150 worker-hours had been expended?

30. Find the area of each of the following plane figures:

a. the circle with $P(0, 0)$ and $Q(2, 3)$ endpoints of a diameter

b. the trapezoid with vertices $A(0, 0)$, $B(4, 0)$, $C(1, 3)$, and $D(2, 3)$

31. Find the volume and the surface area of each of the following solid figures:

a. a sphere with radius 4

b. a rectangular parallelepiped (box) with sides of length 2, 3, and 5

c. a right circular cylinder (including top and bottom) with height 4 and radius 2

d. an inverted cone with height 5 and top radius 3 (lateral surface only)

32. Consider the triangle with vertices $A(-1, 4)$, $B(3, 2)$, and $C(3, -6)$. Determine the midpoints M_1 and M_2 of sides $\overline{AB}$ and $\overline{AC}$, respectively, and show that the line segment $\overline{M_1 M_2}$ is parallel to side $\overline{BC}$ with half its length.

33. Generalize the procedure of Problem 32 to show that the line segment joining the midpoints of any two sides of a given triangle is parallel to the third side and has half its length.

34. Let $ABCD$ be a quadrilateral in the plane, and let P, Q, R, and S be the midpoints of sides $\overline{AB}$, $\overline{BC}$, $\overline{CD}$, and $\overline{DA}$, as shown in Figure 1.38. Show that $PQRS$ is a parallelogram.

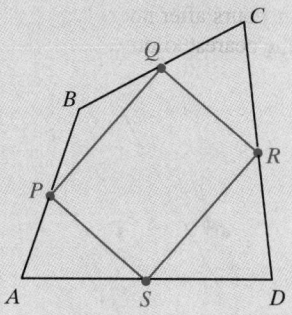

Figure 1.38 Problem 34

35. Find a constant c that guarantees that the graph of the equation

$$x^2 + xy + cy = 4$$

will have a y-intercept of $(0, -5)$. What are the x-intercepts of the graph?

36. A bus charter company offers a travel club the following arrangements: If no more than 100 people go on a certain tour, the cost will be $500 per person, but the cost per person will be reduced by $4 for each person in excess of 100 who takes the tour.

a. Express the total revenue R obtained by the charter company as a function of the number of people who go on the tour.

b. Sketch the graph of R. Estimate the number of people that results in the greatest total revenue for the charter company.

37. A mural 7 feet high is hung on a wall in such a way that its lower edge is 5 feet higher than the eye of an observer standing 12 feet from the wall. (See Figure 1.39.) Find the angle θ subtended by the mural at the observer's eye.

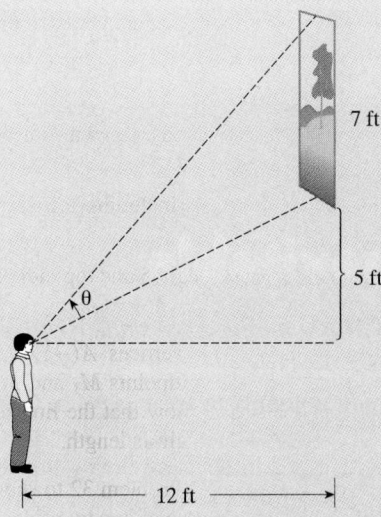

7 ft

5 ft

θ

|← 12 ft →|

Figure 1.39 Problem 37

38. In Figure 1.40, ship A is at point P at noon and sails due east at 9 km/hr. Ship B arrives at point P at 1:00 P.M. and sails at 7 km/hr along a course that forms an angle of 60° with the course of ship A. Find a formula for the distance $s(t)$ separating the ships t hours after noon ($t \geq 1$). Approximately how far apart (to the nearest kilometer) are the ships at 4:00 P.M.?

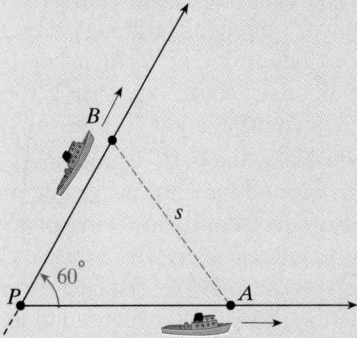

B

s

60°

P A

Figure 1.40 Problem 38

39. A manufacturer estimates that when the price for each unit is p dollars, the profit will be $N = -p^2 + 14p - 48$ thousand dollars. Sketch the graph of the profit function and answer these questions.

a. For what values of p is this a profitable operation? (That is, when is $N > 0$?)

b. What price results in maximum profit? What is the maximum profit?

40. Two jets bound for Los Angeles leave New York 30 minutes apart. The first travels 550 mph, and the second flies at 650 mph. How long will it take the second plane to pass the first?

41. To raise money, a service club has been collecting used bottles that it plans to deliver to a local glass company for recycling. Since the project began 8 days ago, the club has collected 2,400 pounds of glass, for which the glass company currently offers 15¢ per pound. However, since bottles are accumulating faster than they can be recycled, the company plans to reduce the price it pays by 1¢ per pound each day until the price reaches 0¢ fifteen days from now. Assuming that the club can continue to collect bottles at the same rate and that transportation costs make more than one trip to the glass company unfeasible, express the club's revenue from its recycling project as a function of the number of additional days the project runs. Draw the graph and estimate when the club should conclude the project and deliver the bottles in order to maximize its revenue.

42. An open box with a square base is to be built for $48. The sides of the box will cost $3/ft^2 and the base will cost $4/ft^2. Express the volume of the box as a function of the length of its base.

43. A closed box with a square base is to have a volume of 250 cubic feet. The material for the top and bottom of the box costs $2/ft^2, and the material for the sides costs $1/ft^2. Express the construction cost of the box as a function of the length of its base.

44. The famous author John Uptight must decide between two publishers who are vying for the rights to his new book, *Zen and the Art of Taxidermy*. Publisher A offers royalties of 1% of net proceeds on the first 30,000 copies sold and 3.5% on all copies in excess of that figure, and expects to net $2 on each copy sold. Publisher B will pay no royalties on the first 4,000 copies sold but will pay 2% on the net proceeds of all copies sold in excess of 4,000 copies, and expects to net $3 on each copy sold.

a. Express the revenue John should expect if he signs with Publisher A (as a function P_A of the number of books sold, x). Likewise, find the revenue function P_B associated with Publisher B.

b. Sketch the graphs of $P_A(x)$ and $P_B(x)$ on the same coordinate axes.

c. For what value(s) of x are the two offers equivalent?

d. With whom should he sign if he expects to sell 5,000 copies? 100,000 copies? 200,000 copies?

e. State a simple criterion for determining which publisher he should choose if he expects to sell N copies.

*45. Putnam Examination Problem If f and g are real-valued functions of one real variable, show that there exist numbers x, y such that

$$0 \leq x \leq 1, \ 0 \leq y \leq 1, \ \text{and} \ |xy - f(x) - g(y)| \geq \tfrac{1}{4}$$

*46. Putnam Examination Problem Consider a polynomial $f(x)$ with real coefficients having the property $f(g(x)) = g(f(x))$ for every polynomial $g(x)$ with real coefficients. What is $f(x)$?

---

*The Putnam Examination is a national annual examination given under the auspices of the Mathematical Association of America and is designed to recognize mathematically talented college and university students. We include Putnam examination problems, which should be considered optional, to encourage students to consider taking the examination. Putnam problems used by permission of the Mathematical Association of America. Solutions to Putnam Examinations generally appear in *The American Mathematical Monthly,* approximately one year after the examination.

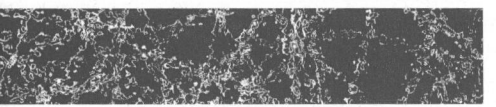

Calculus Was Inevitable

By John L. Troutman, Professor of Mathematics at Syracuse University

The invention of calculus is now credited jointly to Isaac Newton (1642–1727) and Gottfried W. Leibniz (1646–1716), when they produced their separate publications. However (around 1685) there was a bitter controversy throughout Europe as to whose work had been done first. Part of the explanation for this is the fact that each had done his actual work earlier (Newton in 1669; Leibniz, a little later); some can be attributed to the rivalry between scientists in England who championed Newton and those in Europe who supported Leibniz; but much simply reflects how ripe the intellectual climate was for the blooming of calculus. Indeed, even if neither of these great mathematicians had existed, it seems almost certain that the principles of calculus—including the fundamental theorem (introduced in Chapter 5)—would have been announced by the end of the seventeenth century.

Emergence of calculus was effectively demanded by the philosophical spirit of the times. Natural philosophers had long believed that the universe was constructed according to understandable mathematical principles, although they disagreed about just what these principles were and how they might be formulated. For example, the Pythagorean school (ca. 600 B.C.) maintained that everything consisted of (whole) numbers and their ratios; hence their consternation upon discovering that different entities such as $\sqrt{2}$ could be constructed. Next, the early astronomers announced that heavenly bodies move in circular orbits around the earth as center, and later that the earth itself must be a perfect sphere to reflect the divine hand of its Creator. Both of these assertions are now known to be false, and by 1612, Kepler had already explained why. Galileo (1564–1642) announced that the distance traveled by a heavy body falling from rest is proportional to the square of the elapsed time, and Fermat asserted (in 1657) that light moves along those paths that minimize the time of travel (we will discuss this principle in Chapter 4). The question was whether such laws could be formulated and justified mathematically, and what kind of mathematics would be appropriate to describe these phenomena.

For already from antiquity there was the warning of Zeno (ca. 450 B.C.), in the form of paradoxes, against unwise speculation about phenomena whose analysis involved infinite processes. In particular, he "proved" that motion was impossible if time consisted of individual "instants," and conversely, that covering a given distance was impossible if length was capable of infinite subdivision (see Chapter 8). Thus, although seventeenth-century scientists and philosophers might propose such principles, it was evident that there must be underlying subtleties in the mathematics required to support them (that, in fact, required another two centuries for satisfactory clarification).

To understand better how the mathematics developed, we must examine some of the previous attempts to solve the twin problems of classical origin that motivated the emergence of the calculus—those of finding the tangent line to a given planar geometrical curve and finding the area under the curve. Newton himself acknowledged that his greater vision resulted from his "standing on the shoulders of giants." Who were these giants, and what had they contributed? First, there were the efforts of the Greek mathematicians, principally Eudoxus, Euclid, and Archimedes, who had originated the geometric concepts of tangency and area between 400 B.C. and 200 B.C., together with examples of each, such as the construction of tangent lines to a circle and the area under a parabolic curve. The Hindu and Arabic mathematicians had extended the number system and the formal language of algebra with certain of its laws by 1300 A.D., but it was not until Newton's own era that the methods of algebra and geometry were combined satisfactorily in the analytic geometry of René Descartes (1596–1650) to produce the recognition that a geometrical curve could be regarded as the locus of points whose coordinates satisfied an algebraic equation. This provided potential numerical exactitude to geometric constructions as well as the possibility of giving geometric proofs for limiting algebraic arguments. Since Euclidian geometry was then generally regarded as the only reliable mathematics, it was the latter direction that was most frequently taken. And it was this direction that was taken in the seventeenth century by de Roberval, Fermat, Cavalieri, Huygens, Wallis, and others, not the least of whom was Newton's own teacher at Cambridge, Isaac Barrow (1630–1677). These giants, as Newton called them, obtained equations for tangent lines to, and the (correct) areas under, polynomial curves with equations $y = x^n$ for $n = 1, 2, 3, \ldots, 9$, and certain other geometrically defined curves such as the spiral and the cycloid.

In his analysis of tangency, Barrow incorporated the approximating infinitesimal triangle with sides Δx, Δy, Δs that is now standard in expositions of calculus, and Cavalieri attempted to "count" an indefinite number of parallel equidistant lines to obtain areas. It was known that in specific cases these problems were related, and that they were equivalent, respectively, to the kinematic problems of characterizing velocity and distance traveled during a motion, problems which directly confronted the paradoxes of Zeno.

All that remained was for some mathematicians to sense the generality underlying these specific constructions and to devise a usable notation for presenting the results. This was accomplished essentially independently by Newton (who, justly mistrusting the required limiting arguments, suppressed his own contributions until he could validate them geometrically) and by the only slightly less cautious Leibniz. However, as we have argued, by this time (about 1670), it was almost inevitable that someone should do so.

What calculus has provided is a mathematical language that, by means of the derivative, can describe the rates of change used to characterize various physical processes (such as velocity) and, by means of the integral, can show how macroscopic entities (such as area or distance) can emerge from properly assembled microscopic elements. Moreover, the fundamental theorem, which states that these are inverse operations, supplies an exact method for passing between these types of description. Finally, the ability to relate the results of limiting arguments by simple algebraic formulas permits the correct use of calculus while retaining skepticism regarding its foundations. This has enabled applications to go forward while mathematicians have sought an appropriate axiomatic basis.

Our present technological age attests to the success of this endeavor, and to the value of calculus.

Mathematical Essays

Use a library or references other than this textbook to research the information necessary to answer the questions in Problems 1–10.

1. HISTORICAL QUEST Sir Isaac Newton was one of the greatest mathematicians of all time. He was a genius of the highest order but was often absent-minded. One story about Newton is that, when he was a boy, he was sent to cut a hole in the bottom of the barn door for the cats to go in and out. He cut two holes, a large one for the cat and a small one for the kittens.

ISAAC NEWTON
1642–1727

   Newton considered himself a theologian rather than a mathematician or a physicist. He spent years searching for clues about the end of the world and the geography of hell. One of Newton's quotations about himself is, "I seem to have been only like a boy playing on the seashore and diverting myself in now and then finding a smoother pebble or prettier shell than ordinary, whilst the great ocean of truth lay all undiscovered before me." ■

   Write an essay about Isaac Newton and his discovery of calculus. This essay should be at least 500 words.

2. HISTORICAL QUEST At the age of 14, Gottfried Leibniz attempted to reform Aristotelian logic. He wanted to create a general method of reasoning by calculation. At the age of 20, he applied for his doctorate at the university in Leipzig and was refused (because, officials said, he was too young). He received his doctorate the next year at the University of Altdorf, where he made

GOTTFRIED LEIBNIZ
1646–1716

   such a favorable impression that he was offered a professorship, which he declined, saying he had very different things in view. Leibniz went on to invent calculus, but not without a bitter controversy developing between Leibniz and Newton. Most historians agree that the bitterness over who invented calculus materially affected the history of mathematics. J. S. Mill characterized Leibniz by saying, "It would be difficult to name a man more remarkable for the greatness and universality of his intellectual powers than Leibniz." ■

   Write a 500-word essay about Gottfried Leibniz and his discovery of calculus.

3. HISTORICAL QUEST Write a 500-word essay about the controversy surrounding the discovery of calculus by Newton and Leibniz.

4. The Greek mathematicians mentioned in this guest essay include Eudoxus, Euclid, and Archimedes. Write a short paper about contributions they made that might have been used by Newton.

5. What is the definition of elementary functions as given by Joseph Liouville?

6. The guest essay mentions the contributions of de Roberval, Fermat, Cavalieri, Huygens, Wallis, and Barrow toward the invention of calculus. Write a short paper about these contributions.

7. In this guest essay, Troutman argues that the invention of calculus was inevitable, and even if Newton and Leibniz had not invented it, someone else would have. Write a 500-word essay either defending or refuting this thesis.

8. HISTORICAL QUEST Sophie Germain was one of the first women to publish original mathematical research in number theory. In her time, women were not admitted to first-rate universities and were not, for the most part, taken seriously, so she wrote at first under the pseudonym LeBlanc. The situation is not too different from that portrayed by Barbra Streisand in the movie *Yentl*. Even

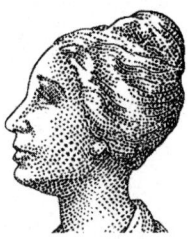

SOPHIE GERMAIN
1776–1831

though Germain's most important research was in number theory, she was awarded the prize of the French Academy for a paper entitled "Memoir on the Vibrations of Elastic Plates." ■

   As we progress through this book we will profile many mathematicians in the history of mathematics, and you will notice that most of them are white males. Why? Write a paper on the history of women mathematicians and their achievements. Your paper should include a list of many prominent women mathematicians and their primary contributions. It should also include a lengthy profile of at least one woman mathematician.

9. HISTORICAL QUEST The Navajo are a Native American people who, despite considerable interchange and assimilation with the surrounding dominant culture, maintain a world view that remains vital and distinctive. The Navajo believe in a dynamic universe. Rather than consisting of objects and situations, the universe is made up of processes. Central to our Western mode of thought is the idea that things are separable entities that can be subdivided into smaller discrete units. For us, things that change through time do so by going from one specific state to another specific state. While we believe time to be continuous, we often even break it into discrete units or freeze it and talk about an instant or point in time. Among the Navajo, where the focus is on process, change is ever present; interrelationship and motion are of primary significance. These incorporate and subsume space and time.

   There are, in every culture, groups or individuals who think more about some ideas than do others. For other cultures, we know about the ideas of some professional groups or some ideas of the culture at large. We know little, however, about the mathematical thoughts of individuals in those cultures who are specially inclined toward mathematical ideas. In Western culture, on the other hand, we focus on, and record much about, those special individuals while including little about everyone else. Realization of this difference should make us particularly wary of any comparisons across cultures. Even more important, it should encourage finding out more about the ideas of mathematically oriented innovators in other cultures and, simultaneously, encourage expanding the scope of Western history to recognize and include mathematical ideas held by different groups within our culture or by our culture as a whole.* ■

   Write a paper discussing this quotation.

10. **Book Report** "Ethnomathematics, as it is being addressed here, has the goal of broadening the history of mathematics to one that has a multicultural, global perspective." Read the book *Ethnomathematics* by Marcia Ascher (Pacific Grove: Brooks/Cole, 1991), and prepare a book report.

---

*From *Ethnomathematics* by Marcia Ascher, pp. 128–129 and 188–189.

2

Limits and Continuity

PREVIEW

Calculus is the mathematics of motion and change, while algebra, geometry, and trigonometry are more static in nature. The development of calculus in the seventeenth century by Newton, Leibniz, and others grew out of attempts by these and earlier mathematicians to answer certain fundamental questions about dynamic real-world situations. These investigations led to two fundamental procedures, *differentiation* and *integration*, which can be formulated in terms of a concept called the *limit*. We will introduce the limit in this chapter and study its basic properties. In addition, we will continue the investigation of functions begun in Chapter 1 by exploring the concept of functional continuity, and using limits to introduce exponential and logarithmic functions.

PERSPECTIVE

The limit is a mathematical tool for studying the tendency of a function as its independent variable approaches some value. For instance, in the guest essay at the end of Chapter 1, John Troutman mentions Zeno's paradoxes, which involve infinite processes. One such paradox can be stated as follows:

> Archilles fires an arrow, but it can never reach its target. Why? Because if the arrow takes T seconds to travel half the distance to the target, it will take $T/2$ seconds to finish half the rest, and so on for each half. No matter how close the arrow is to the target, it will take finite time to travel half the distance that remains, so the arrow will never reach its destination.

Common sense tells that the arrow will strike home in $2T$ seconds, so where is the error in reasoning? If we measure the total time of the arrow's flight by the "half, then half of that, and so on," approach of the paradox, it will take

$$T + \frac{T}{2} + \frac{T}{4} + \cdots$$

seconds for the arrow to strike the target; that is, an infinite sum of finite time intervals. The Greeks of Zeno's time assumed that such a sum would have to be infinite. However, the limit process can be used to show that this particular sum is not only finite, but equals $2T$, as common sense would suggest. We will study infinite sums in Chapter 8, but first it is necessary to introduce and explore a different kind of limit, the *limit of a function*, and that is the goal of this chapter.

In a very real sense, the concept of limit is the threshold to modern mathematics. You are about to cross that threshold, and beyond lies the fascinating world of calculus.

2.1   The Limit of a Function

IN THIS SECTION   informal computation of limits, one-sided limits, limits that do not exist, formal definition of a limit

The goal of this section is to define and explore what is meant by the *limit of a function*. We will begin with an informal discussion of the limit concept, emphasizing graphical and numerical computations. Then in Section 2.2, we will develop algebraic techniques for computing limits more systematically.

The development of the limit concept was a major breakthrough in the history of mathematics, and you should not be surprised or disappointed if certain aspects of this concept seem difficult to comprehend or apply. Be patient and this crucial concept will soon become part of your mathematical toolkit.

INFORMAL COMPUTATION OF LIMITS

The limit of a function f is a tool for investigating the behavior of $f(x)$ as x gets closer and closer to a particular number c. That is, the limit concerns the *tendency* of $f(x)$ for x near c rather than the *value* of f at $x = c$. The following example illustrates how such a tendency can be used to compute velocity.

EXAMPLE 1   Computing velocity as a limit

A freely falling body experiencing no air resistance falls $s(t) = 16t^2$ feet in t seconds. Express the body's velocity at time $t = 2$ as a limit.

Solution

What we want is the *instantaneous velocity* after 2 seconds, which can be thought of as the "speedometer reading" of the falling body at $t = 2$. To approximate the instantaneous velocity, we compute the average velocity of the body over smaller and smaller time intervals, either ending with or beginning with $t = 2$. For instance, over the time interval $1.9 \leq t \leq 2$, the average velocity, $\overline{v}(t)$, is

$$\overline{v}(t) = \frac{\text{DISTANCE TRAVELED}}{\text{ELAPSED TIME}} \qquad \text{Where distance is in ft and time is in seconds}$$

$$= \frac{s(2) - s(1.9)}{2 - 1.9}$$

$$= \frac{16(2)^2 - 16(1.9)^2}{0.1}$$

$$= 62.4 \text{ ft/s}$$

Similar computations of average velocity over short time intervals ending or beginning with time $t = 2$ are contained in the following table:

Time interval	$1.8 \leq t \leq 2$	$1.9 \leq t \leq 2$	$1.99 \leq t \leq 2$	$1.999 \leq t \leq 2$	$2 \leq t \leq 2.0001$	$2 \leq t \leq 2.001$	$2 \leq t \leq 2.01$
Interval length (sec)	0.2	0.1	0.01	0.001	0.0001	0.001	0.01
Average velocity (ft/s)	60.8	62.4	63.84	63.98	64.0016	64.016	64.16

Examining the bottom row of this table, we see that the average velocity seems to be approaching the value 64 as the time intervals become smaller and smaller. Thus, it is reasonable to expect the velocity at the instant when $t = 2$ to be 64 ft/s.

In symbols, the average velocity of the falling body over the time interval $2 \leq t \leq 2 + h$ is given by

$$\frac{s(2 + h) - s(2)}{(2 + h) - 2} = \frac{16(2 + h)^2 - 16(2)^2}{h}$$

We say that the average velocity has a limiting value of 64 as the length h of the time interval tends to zero (gets smaller and smaller), and we denote this tendency by writing

$$\lim_{h \to 0} \frac{16(2+h)^2 - 16(2)^2}{h} = 64$$ ∎

Here is a general, though informal, definition of the limit of a function.

Limit of a Function (Informal Definition)

The notation

$$\lim_{x \to c} f(x) = L$$

is read "the limit of $f(x)$ as x approaches c is L" and means that the functional values $f(x)$ can be made arbitrarily close to a unique number L by choosing x sufficiently close to c (but not equal to c).

➡ **What This Says** If $f(x)$ becomes arbitrarily close to a single number L as x approaches c from either side, then we say that L is the limit of $f(x)$ as x approaches c. It means that the functional values of f "home in" on the number L as x gets closer and closer to c. The values of x can approach c from either side, but $x = c$ itself is excluded.

Notation: Sometimes we will find it convenient to represent the limit statement

$$\lim_{x \to c} f(x) = L$$

by writing $f(x) \to L$ as $x \to c$.

This informal definition of limit cannot be used in proofs until we give precise meaning to terms such as "arbitrarily close to L" and "sufficiently close to c." This will be done at the end of this section. For now, we will use this informal definition to explore a few basic features of the limiting process.

EXAMPLE 2 Informal computation of a limit

Use a table to guess the value of

$$L = \lim_{x \to -2} \frac{x^2 + x - 2}{x + 2}$$

Solution

It would be nice if we could simply substitute $x = -2$ into the formula for

$$f(x) = \frac{x^2 + x - 2}{x + 2}$$

but note that $f(-2)$ is not defined. This is of no consequence since the limit process is concerned only when x *approaches* -2 and has nothing to do with the value of f at $x = -2$. We form a table of values of $f(x)$ for x near -2:

x	-2.3	-2.1	-2.05	-2.001	-2	-1.9997	-1.995
$f(x)$	-3.3	-3.1	-3.05	-3.001	undefined	-2.9997	-2.995

The numbers on the bottom row of this table suggest that $f(x) \to -3$ as $x \to -2$; that is,

$$L = \lim_{x \to -2} \frac{x^2 + x - 2}{x + 2} = -3$$

The graph of f is shown in Figure 2.1. Notice that the graph is a line with a "hole" at the point $(-2, -3)$. ∎

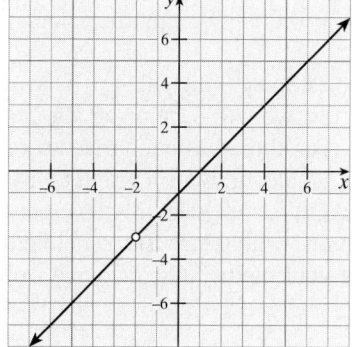

Figure 2.1 Graph of
$$f(x) = \frac{x^2 + x - 2}{x + 2}$$

EXAMPLE 3   Finding limits of trigonometric functions

Evaluate $\lim_{x \to 0} \sin x$ and $\lim_{x \to 0} \cos x$.

Solution

We can evaluate these limits by table.

x	1	0.5	0.1	0.01	-0.01	-0.1	-0.5
$\sin x$	0.84	0.48	0.0998	0.0099998	-0.0099998	-0.0998	-0.48
$\cos x$	0.54	0.88	0.9950	0.9999500	0.99995	0.9950	0.88

The pattern of numbers in the table suggests that

$$\lim_{x \to 0} \sin x = 0 = \sin 0 \qquad \text{and} \qquad \lim_{x \to 0} \cos x = 1 = \cos 0 \qquad \blacksquare$$

EXAMPLE 4   A computational dilemma

Use a table to guess the value of

$$L = \lim_{x \to 0} \frac{2\sqrt{x+1} - x - 2}{x^2}$$

Solution

Form a table of values of

$$f(x) = \frac{2\sqrt{x+1} - x - 2}{x^2}$$

for x near 0:

x	-0.5	-0.1	-0.01	-0.001	0	0.001	0.005
$f(x)$	-0.3431	-0.2633	-0.2513	-0.2501	undefined	-0.2499	-0.2494

The numbers on the bottom line suggest that the limit is $L = -0.25$. $\blacksquare$

In Example 4, note that if you decide to try $x = 0.0000001$ just to make sure you have taken numbers close enough to 0, you may find that the calculator gives the value 0. Does this mean the limit is actually 0 instead of -0.25? No, the problem is that the numerator $2\sqrt{x+1} - x - 2$ is so close to 0 when $x = 0.0000001$ that the calculator gives a false value for f.

The point is this: When you use your calculator to estimate limits, always be aware that this method can introduce errors. In the next section, we will develop an algebraic approach for computing limits that is more reliable. The three basic approaches (examining appropriate data by using a calculator and/or a table, drawing a graph to find a limit, or using algebraic rules) each has its virtues and faults. As you study this section and the next, you need to learn all three approaches, along with their virtues and faults, and this knowledge will serve you well for the rest of your mathematical course work.

ONE-SIDED LIMITS

Sometimes we will be interested in the limiting behavior of a function from only one side; that is, the limit as x approaches a number c from the left or the analogous limit from the right.

One-Sided Limits

> **Right-hand limit**   We write $\lim\limits_{x \to c^+} f(x) = L$ if we can make the number $f(x)$ as close to L as we please by choosing x sufficiently close to c on a small interval (c, b) *immediately to the right of c.*
>
> **Left-hand limit**   We write $\lim\limits_{x \to c^-} f(x) = L$ if we can make the number $f(x)$ as close to L as we please by choosing x sufficiently close to c on a small interval (a, c) *immediately to the left of c.*

For instance, note that the graph in Figure 2.2 is "broken" at $x = 3$. The limit as x approaches 3 from the left is 1, while the limit from the right at the same point is -1.

Observe that the "two-sided" limit, $\lim\limits_{x \to 3} h(x)$, defined earlier in this section, does not exist since $h(x)$ does not tend toward a single limiting value L as x approaches $c = 3$ from either side. It should be clear that, in general, a two-sided limit cannot exist if the corresponding pair of one-sided limits are different. Conversely, it can be shown that if the two one-sided limits of a given function f as $x \to c^-$ and $x \to c^+$ both exist and are equal, then the two-sided limit $\lim\limits_{x \to c} f(x)$ must also exist. These observations are so important that we state them in the form of a theorem.

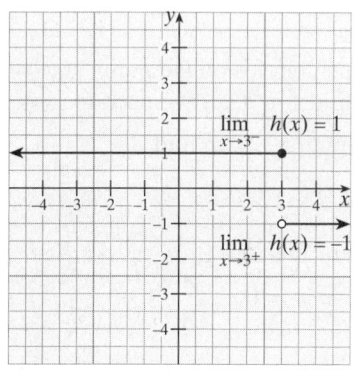

Figure 2.2 Graph of
$$h(x) = \begin{cases} 1 & \text{if } x \le 3 \\ -1 & \text{if } x > 3, \end{cases}$$
a graph illustrating one-sided limits

THEOREM 2.1   One-sided limit theorem

The two-sided limit $\lim\limits_{x \to c} f(x)$ exists if and only if the two one-sided limits $\lim\limits_{x \to c^-} f(x) = L$ and $\lim\limits_{x \to c^+} f(x)$ both exist and are equal. Furthermore, if $\lim\limits_{x \to c^-} f(x) = L = \lim\limits_{x \to c^+} f(x)$, then $\lim\limits_{x \to c} f(x) = L$.   ❑

One-sided and two-sided limits are illustrated in Figure 2.3.

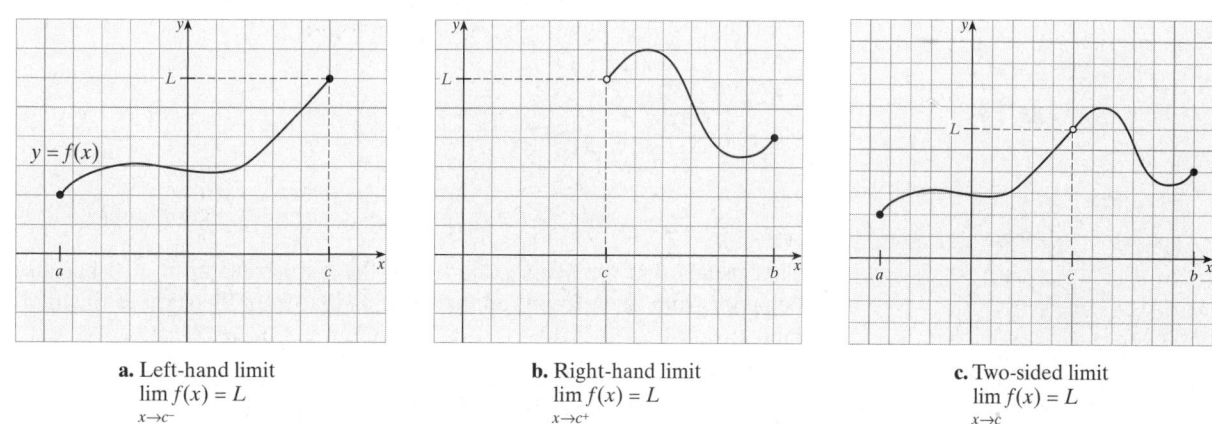

a. Left-hand limit
$\lim\limits_{x \to c^-} f(x) = L$

b. Right-hand limit
$\lim\limits_{x \to c^+} f(x) = L$

c. Two-sided limit
$\lim\limits_{x \to c} f(x) = L$

Figure 2.3   We say that $\lim\limits_{x \to c} f(x) = L$ if and only if $\lim\limits_{x \to c^-} f(x) = \lim\limits_{x \to c^+} f(x) = L$.

EXAMPLE 5   Estimating limits by graphing

Given the functions defined by the graphs in Figure 2.4, find the requested limits by inspection, if they exist.

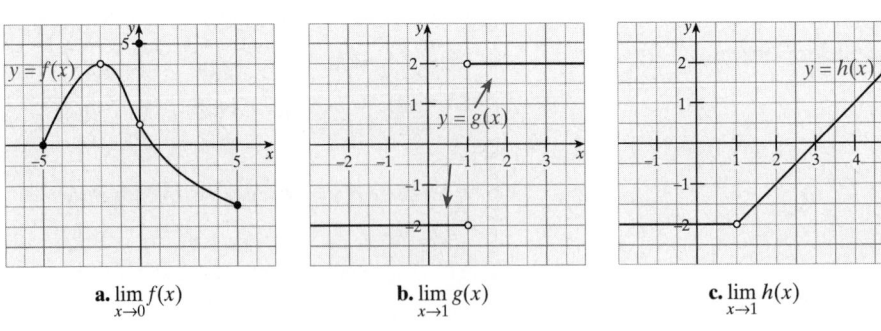

a. $\lim_{x\to 0} f(x)$ **b.** $\lim_{x\to 1} g(x)$ **c.** $\lim_{x\to 1} h(x)$

Figure 2.4   Limits from a graph

Solution

a. Take a good look at the given graph; notice the open circles on the graph at $x = 0$ and $x = -2$ and also notice that $f(0) = 5$. To find $\lim_{x\to 0} f(x)$ we need to look at both the left-hand and right-hand limits. Look at Figure 2.4a to find

$$\lim_{x\to 0^-} f(x) = 1 \quad \text{and} \quad \lim_{x\to 0^+} f(x) = 1$$

so $\lim_{x\to 0} f(x)$ exists and $\lim_{x\to 0} f(x) = 1$. Notice here that *the value of the limit as $x \to 0$ is not the same as the value of the function at $x = 0$.*

b. Look at Figure 2.4b to find

$$\lim_{x\to 1^-} g(x) = -2 \quad \text{and} \quad \lim_{x\to 1^+} g(x) = 2$$

so the *limit as $x \to 1$ does not exist.*

c. Look at Figure 2.4c to find

$$\lim_{x\to 1^-} h(x) = -2 \quad \text{and} \quad \lim_{x\to 1^+} h(x) = -2$$

so $\lim_{x\to 1} h(x) = -2$.   ∎

EXAMPLE 6   Evaluating a trigonometric limit using a table

Evaluate $\lim_{x\to 0} \dfrac{\sin x}{x}$.

Solution

$f(x) = \dfrac{\sin x}{x}$ is an even function because

$$f(-x) = \frac{\sin(-x)}{-x} = \frac{-\sin x}{-x} = \frac{\sin x}{x} = f(x)$$

This means that we need to find only the right-hand limit at 0 because the limiting behavior from the left will be the same as that from the right. Consider the following table.

x	0.1 $\dashrightarrow$	0.05 $\dashrightarrow$	0.01 $\dashrightarrow$	0.001 $\dashrightarrow$	0
$f(x)$	0.998334	0.999583	0.9999833	0.999999833	Undefined

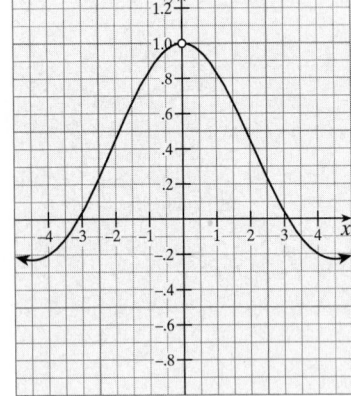

Figure 2.5 Graph of $f(x) = \dfrac{\sin x}{x}$

The table suggests that $\lim_{x\to 0^+} \dfrac{\sin x}{x} = 1$ and hence that $\lim_{x\to 0} \dfrac{\sin x}{x} = 1$. We will revisit this limit in Section 2.2. The graph of $f(x) = \dfrac{\sin x}{x}$ is shown in Figure 2.5.   ∎

LIMITS THAT DO NOT EXIST

It may happen that a function f does not have a (finite) limit as $x \to c$. When $\lim\limits_{x \to c} f(x)$ fails to exist, the functional values $f(x)$ are said to **diverge** as $x \to c$.

EXAMPLE 7   A function that diverges

Evaluate $\lim\limits_{x \to 0} \dfrac{1}{x^2}$.

Solution

As $x \to 0$, the corresponding functional values of $f(x) = \dfrac{1}{x^2}$ grow arbitrarily large, as indicated in the following table.

	x approaches 0 from the left; $x \to 0^-$.				x approaches 0 from the right; $x \to 0^+$.		
x	$-0.1 \dashrightarrow$	$-0.05 \dashrightarrow$	$-0.001 \dashrightarrow$	0	$\leftarrow$-- 0.001	$\leftarrow$-- 0.005	$\leftarrow$-- 0.01
$f(x) = \dfrac{1}{x^2}$	100	400	1×10^6	undefined	1×10^6	4×10^4	1×10^4

The graph of f is shown in Figure 2.6.

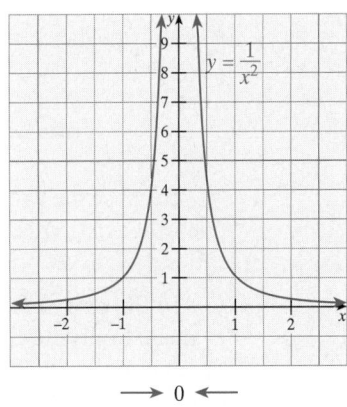

$\longrightarrow 0 \longleftarrow$

Figure 2.6 $\lim\limits_{x \to 0} \dfrac{1}{x^2}$ does not exist, and the graph illustrates that f rises without bound.

Geometrically, the graph of $y = f(x)$ rises without bound as $x \to 0$. Thus, $\lim\limits_{x \to 0} \dfrac{1}{x^2}$ does not exist.   ■

Infinite Limits

WARNING   It is important to remember that ∞ is *not* a number, but is merely a symbol denoting unrestricted growth in the magnitude of the function.

A function f that increases or decreases without bound as x approaches c is said to **tend to infinity** (∞) at c. We indicate this behavior by writing

$$\lim_{x \to c} f(x) = +\infty \qquad \text{if } f \text{ increases without bound}$$

and by

$$\lim_{x \to c} f(x) = -\infty \qquad \text{if } f \text{ decreases without bound}$$

Using this notation, we can rewrite the answer to Example 7 as

$$\lim_{x \to 0} \frac{1}{x^2} = +\infty$$

EXAMPLE 8 **A function that diverges by oscillation**

Evaluate $\lim\limits_{x\to 0} \sin\dfrac{1}{x}$.

Solution

Note this is not the same as $\lim\limits_{x\to 0} \dfrac{\sin x}{x}$. The values of $f(x) = \sin\dfrac{1}{x}$ oscillate infinitely often between 1 and -1 as x approaches 0. For example, $f(x) = 1$ for $x = \dfrac{2}{\pi}, \dfrac{2}{5\pi}, \dfrac{2}{9\pi}, \ldots$, and $f(x) = -1$ for $x = \dfrac{2}{3\pi}, \dfrac{2}{7\pi}, \dfrac{2}{11\pi}, \ldots$. The graph of $f(x)$ is shown in Figure 2.7.

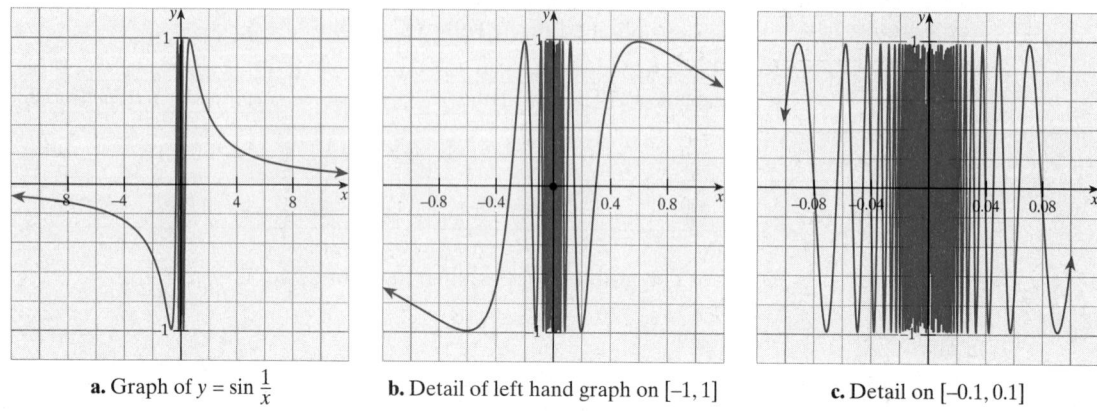

a. Graph of $y = \sin\dfrac{1}{x}$ **b.** Detail of left hand graph on $[-1, 1]$ **c.** Detail on $[-0.1, 0.1]$

Figure 2.7 $\sin\dfrac{1}{x}$ diverges by oscillation as $x \to 0$.

Because the values of $f(x)$ do not approach a unique number L as $x \to 0$, the limit does not exist. This kind of limiting behavior is called **divergence by oscillation**. ∎

In the next section, we will introduce some properties of limits that will help us evaluate limits efficiently. In the following problem set remember that the emphasis is on an intuitive understanding of limits, including their evaluation by graphing and by table.

FORMAL DEFINITION OF A LIMIT

Our informal definition of the limit provides valuable intuition and allows you to develop a working knowledge of this fundamental concept. For theoretical work, however, the intuitive definition will not suffice, because it gives no precise, quantifiable meaning to the terms "arbitrarily close to L" and "sufficiently close to c." In the nineteenth century, leading mathematicians, including Augustin-Louis Cauchy (1789–1857) and Karl Weierstrass (1815–1897), sought to put calculus on a sound logical foundation by giving precise definitions for the foundational ideas of calculus. The following definition, derived from the work of Cauchy and Weierstrass, gives precision to the limit notion.

Limit of a Function
(Formal definition)

The limit statement

$$\lim_{x\to c} f(x) = L$$

means that for each number $\epsilon > 0$, there corresponds a number $\delta > 0$ with the property that

$$|f(x) - L| < \epsilon \quad \text{whenever} \quad 0 < |x - c| < \delta$$

We show this definition graphically in Figure 2.8.

For each ε > 0	**there is a δ > 0**	**such that**	**if 0 < |x − c| < δ,**	**then |f(x) − L| < ε.**
This forms an interval around L on the y-axis.	This forms an interval around c on the x-axis.		This says that if x is in the δ-interval on the x-axis...	...then f(x) is in the ε-interval on the y-axis.

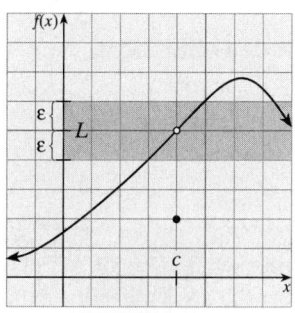 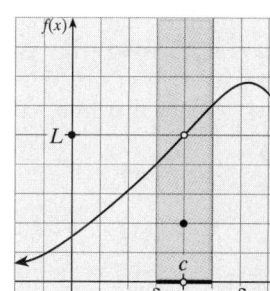 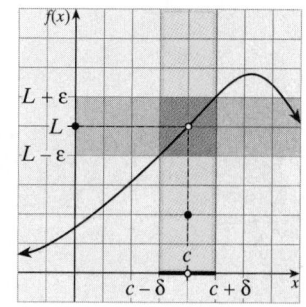

Figure 2.8 Formal definition of limit: $\lim_{x \to c} f(x) = L$

Because the Greek letters ϵ (epsilon) and δ (delta) are traditionally used in this context, the formal definition of limit is sometimes called the **epsilon-delta** definition of the limit. The goal of this section is to show how this formal definition embodies our intuitive understanding of the limit process and how it can be used rigorously to establish a variety of results.

Do not be discouraged if this material seems difficult—it is. Probably your best course of action is to read this section carefully and examine the details of a few examples closely. Then, using the examples as models, try some of the exercises. This material often takes several attempts, but if you persevere, you should come away with an appreciation of the epsilon-delta process—and with it, a better understanding of calculus.

Behind the formal language is a fairly straightforward idea. In particular, to establish a specific limit, say $\lim_{x \to c} f(x) = L$, a number $\epsilon > 0$ is chosen first to establish a desired degree of proximity to L, and then a number $\delta > 0$ is found that determines how close x must be to c to ensure that $f(x)$ is within ϵ units of L.

The situation is summarized in Figure 2.9, which shows a function that satisfies the conditions of the definition. Notice that whenever x is within δ units of c (but not equal to c), the point $(x, f(x))$ on the graph of f must lie in the rectangle (shaded region) formed by the intersection of the horizontal band of width 2ϵ centered at L and the vertical band of width 2δ centered at c. The smaller the ϵ-interval around the proposed limit L, generally the smaller the δ-interval will need to be for $f(x)$ to lie in the ϵ-interval. If such a δ can be found no matter how small ϵ is, then $f(x)$ and L are arbitrarily close, so L must be the limit. The following examples illustrate epsilon-delta proofs, one in which the limit exists and one in which it does not.

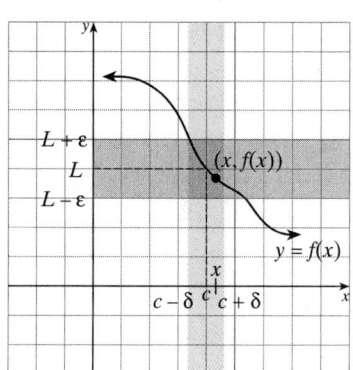

Figure 2.9 The epsilon-delta definition of limit

EXAMPLE 9   An epsilon-delta proof of a limit statement

Show that $\lim_{x \to 2}(4x - 3) = 5$.

Solution

From the graph of $f(x) = 4x - 3$ (see Figure 2.10), we guess that the limit as $x \to 2$ is 5. The object of this example is to *prove* that the limit is 5. We have

$$|f(x) - L| = |4x - 3 - 5|$$
$$= |4x - 8|$$
$$= \underbrace{4|x - 2|}$$

This must be less than ϵ whenever $|x - 2| < \delta$.

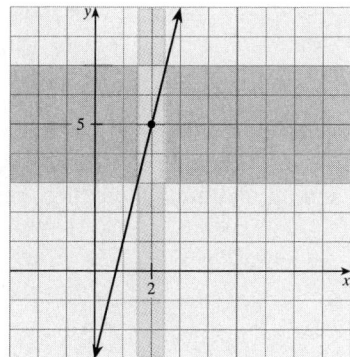

Figure 2.10 $\lim_{x \to 2}(4x - 3) = 5$

For a given $\epsilon > 0$, choose $\delta = \dfrac{\epsilon}{4}$; then

$$|f(x) - L| = 4\,|x - 2| < 4\delta = 4\left(\frac{\epsilon}{4}\right) = \epsilon \qquad \blacksquare$$

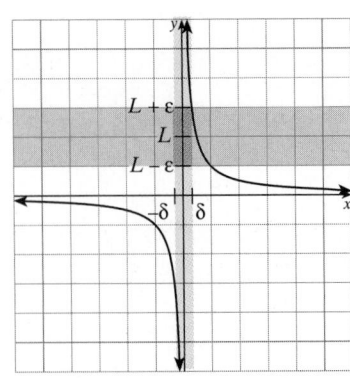

Figure 2.11 $\displaystyle\lim_{x \to 0} \frac{1}{x}$

EXAMPLE 10   An epsilon-delta proof that a limit does not exist

Show that $\displaystyle\lim_{x \to 0} \frac{1}{x}$ does not exist.

Solution

Let $f(x) = \dfrac{1}{x}$ and L be any number. Suppose that $\displaystyle\lim_{x \to 0} f(x) = L$. Look at the graph of f, as shown in Figure 2.11. It would seem that no matter what value of ϵ is chosen, it would be impossible to find a corresponding δ. Consider the absolute value expression required by the definition of limit: If

$$|f(x) - L| < \epsilon, \quad \text{or, for this example,} \quad \left|\frac{1}{x} - L\right| < \epsilon$$

then

$$-\epsilon < \frac{1}{x} - L < \epsilon \qquad \text{\textit{Property of absolute value}} \\ \text{\textit{(Table 1.1, p. 3)}}$$

and

$$L - \epsilon < \frac{1}{x} < L + \epsilon$$

If $\epsilon = 1$ (not a particularly small ϵ), then

$$\left|\frac{1}{x}\right| < |L| + 1$$

$$|x| > \frac{1}{|L| + 1}$$

If $\epsilon = 1$ (not a particularly small ϵ), then

$$\left|\frac{1}{x}\right| < |L| + 1$$

$$|x| > \frac{1}{|L| + 1}$$

In general, given any $\epsilon > 0$, then no matter how $\delta > 0$ is chosen, there will always be numbers x in the interval $0 < |x - 0| < \delta$ such that $\dfrac{1}{|x|} > L + \epsilon$. Since L was chosen arbitrarily, it follows that the limit does not exist. $\qquad \blacksquare$

Appendix B gives many of the important proofs in calculus, and if you look there, you will see many of them are given in ϵ-δ form. In the following problem set, remember that the emphasis is on an intuitive understanding of limits, including their evaluation by graphing and by table.

2.1 PROBLEM SET

Ⓐ *Given the functions defined by the graphs in Figure 2.12, find the limits in Problems 1–6.*

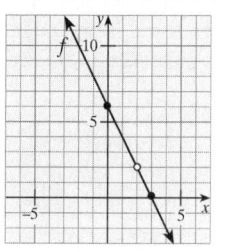
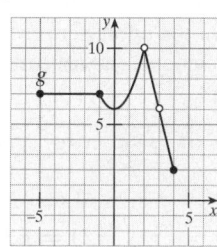
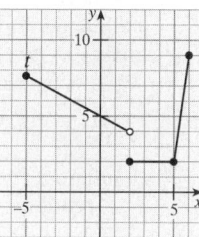

Graph of f Graph of g Graph of t

Figure 2.12 Graphs of the functions f, g, and t

1. a. $\lim\limits_{x \to 3} f(x)$ **b.** $\lim\limits_{x \to 2} f(x)$ **c.** $\lim\limits_{x \to 0} f(x)$

2. a. $\lim\limits_{x \to -3} g(x)$ **b.** $\lim\limits_{x \to -1} g(x)$ **c.** $\lim\limits_{x \to 4^-} g(x)$

3. a. $\lim\limits_{x \to 4} t(x)$ **b.** $\lim\limits_{x \to -4} t(x)$ **c.** $\lim\limits_{x \to -5^+} t(x)$

4. a. $\lim\limits_{x \to 2^-} f(x)$ **b.** $\lim\limits_{x \to 2^+} f(x)$ **c.** $\lim\limits_{x \to 2} f(x)$

5. a. $\lim\limits_{x \to 3^-} g(x)$ **b.** $\lim\limits_{x \to 3^+} g(x)$ **c.** $\lim\limits_{x \to 3} g(x)$

6. a. $\lim\limits_{x \to 2^-} t(x)$ **b.** $\lim\limits_{x \to 2^+} t(x)$ **c.** $\lim\limits_{x \to 2} t(x)$

Find the limits by filling in the appropriate values in the tables in Problems 7–9.

7. $\lim\limits_{x \to 5^-} f(x)$, where $f(x) = 4x - 5$

$x \to 5^-$					
x	2	3	4	4.5	4.9	4.99
$f(x)$	3					

$f(x) \to \ ?$

8. $\lim\limits_{x \to 2^-} g(x)$, where $g(x) = \dfrac{x^3 - 8}{x^2 + 2x + 4}$

$x \to 2^-$					
x	1	1.5	1.9	1.99	1.999	1.9999
$g(x)$	-1					

$g(x) \to \ ?$

9. $\lim\limits_{x \to 2} h(x)$, where $h(x) = \dfrac{3x^2 - 2x - 8}{x - 2}$

$x \to 2^-$				$2^+ \leftarrow x$			
x	1	1.9	1.99	1.999	2.001	2.1	2.5	3
$h(x)$	7							

$h(x) \to \ ? \leftarrow h(x)$

10. Find $\lim\limits_{x \to 0} \dfrac{\tan 2x}{\tan 3x}$ using the following procedure based on the fact that $f(x) = \tan x$ is an odd function.

If $f(x) = \dfrac{\tan 2x}{\tan 3x}$, then

$$f(-x) = \frac{\tan(-2x)}{\tan(-3x)} = \frac{-\tan 2x}{-\tan 3x} = f(x).$$

Thus, we simply need to check for $x \to 0^+$. Find the limit by completing the following table.

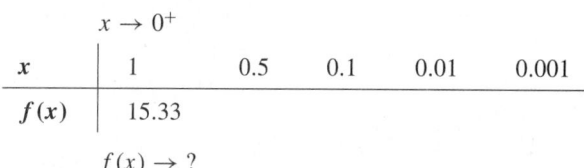

	$x \to 0^+$				
x	1	0.5	0.1	0.01	0.001
$f(x)$	15.33				

$f(x) \to \ ?$

Describe each illustration in Problems 11–16 using a limit statement.

11. 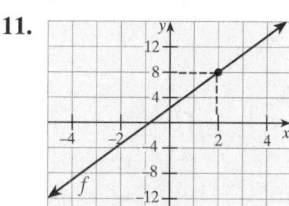   **12.**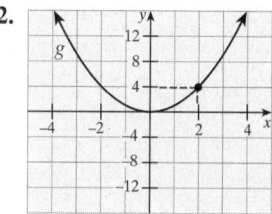

13. 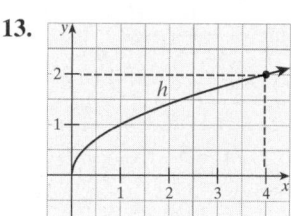   **14.**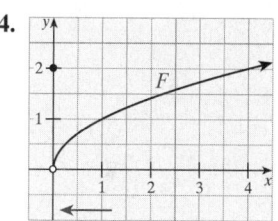

15. 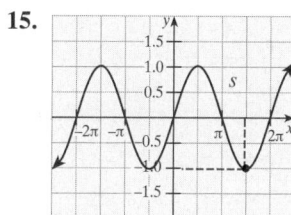   **16.**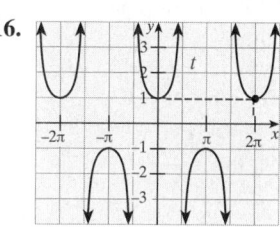

Ⓑ **17. WHAT DOES THIS SAY?**[*] Explain a process for finding a limit.

Evaluate the limits in Problems 18–44 to two decimal places by graphing or by using a table of values, and check your answer using a calculator. If the limit does not exist, explain why.

18. $\lim\limits_{x \to 0^+} x^4$ **19.** $\lim\limits_{x \to 0^+} \cos x$

20. $\lim\limits_{x \to 2^-} (x^2 - 4)$ **21.** $\lim\limits_{x \to 3^-} (x^2 - 4)$

22. $\lim\limits_{x \to 1^+} \dfrac{1}{x - 3}$ **23.** $\lim\limits_{x \to -3^+} \dfrac{1}{x - 3}$

24. $\lim\limits_{x \to 3} \dfrac{1}{x - 3}$ **25.** $\lim\limits_{x \to \pi/2} \tan x$

---

[*]Many problems in this book are labeled What Does This Say? Following the question will be a question for you to answer in your own words, or a statement for you to rephrase in your own words. These problems are intended to be similar to the "What This Says" boxes.

26. a. $\lim\limits_{x \to 0} \dfrac{\cos x}{x}$

b. $\lim\limits_{x \to \pi} \dfrac{\cos x}{x}$

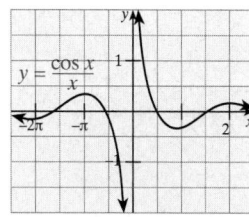

27. a. $\lim\limits_{x \to 0} \dfrac{1 - \cos x}{x}$

b. $\lim\limits_{x \to \pi} \dfrac{1 - \cos x}{x}$

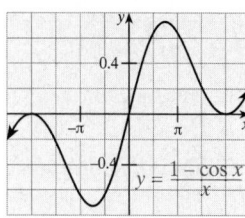

28. a. $\lim\limits_{x \to 0.4} |x| \sin \dfrac{1}{x}$

b. $\lim\limits_{x \to 0} |x| \sin \dfrac{1}{x}$

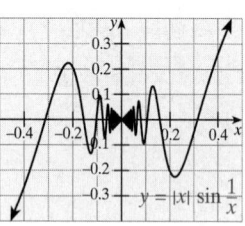

29. $\lim\limits_{x \to 3} \dfrac{x^2 + 3x - 10}{x - 2}$

30. $\lim\limits_{x \to 3} \dfrac{x^2 + 3x - 10}{x - 3}$

31. $\lim\limits_{x \to \pi/2} \dfrac{2x - \pi}{\cos x}$

32. $\lim\limits_{x \to 1} \dfrac{\sin \frac{\pi}{x}}{x - 1}$

33. $\lim\limits_{x \to 9} \dfrac{\sqrt{x} - 3}{x - 9}$

34. $\lim\limits_{x \to 9} \dfrac{\sqrt{x} - 3}{x - 3}$

35. $\lim\limits_{x \to 2} \dfrac{\sqrt{x + 2} - 2}{x - 2}$

36. $\lim\limits_{x \to 1} \dfrac{\sqrt[3]{x} - 1}{\sqrt{x} - 1}$

37. $\lim\limits_{x \to 3^+} \dfrac{\sqrt{x - 3} + x}{3 - x}$

38. $\lim\limits_{x \to 4^+} \dfrac{\frac{1}{\sqrt{x}} - \frac{1}{2}}{x - 4}$

39. $\lim\limits_{x \to 0} \dfrac{\sin 2x}{x}$

40. $\lim\limits_{x \to 0} \dfrac{\sin 3x}{x}$

41. $\lim\limits_{x \to 0} \dfrac{1 - \frac{1}{x + 1}}{x}$

42. $\lim\limits_{x \to 1} \dfrac{1 - \frac{1}{x}}{x - 1}$

43. $\lim\limits_{x \to 0} \cos \dfrac{1}{x}$

44. $\lim\limits_{x \to 0} \tan \dfrac{1}{x}$

45. A ball is thrown directly upward from the edge of a cliff and travels in such a way that t seconds later, its height (in feet) above the ground at the base of the cliff is

$$s(t) = -16t^2 + 40t + 24$$

a. Compute the limit

$$v(t) = \lim_{x \to t} \dfrac{s(x) - s(t)}{x - t}$$

to find the instantaneous velocity of the ball at time t.

b. What is the ball's initial velocity?

c. When does the ball hit the ground, and what is its impact velocity at time $t = 0$?

d. When does the ball have velocity 0? What physical interpretation should be given to this time?

46. Tom and Sue are driving along a straight, level road in a car whose speedometer needle is broken but that has a trip odometer that can measure the distance traveled from an arbitrary starting point in tenths of a mile. At 2:50 P.M., Tom says he would like to know how fast they are traveling at 3:00 P.M., so Sue takes down the odometer readings listed in the table, makes a few calculations, and announces the desired velocity. What is her result?

time t	2:50	2:55	2:59	3:00	3:01	3:03	3:06
odometer reading	33.9	38.2	41.5	42.4	43.2	44.9	47.4

In Problems 47–48, estimate the limits by plotting points or by using tables.

47. $\lim\limits_{x \to 13} \dfrac{x^3 - 9x^2 - 45x - 91}{x - 13}$

48. $\lim\limits_{x \to 13} \dfrac{x^3 - 9x^2 - 39x - 86}{x - 13}$

49. HISTORICAL QUEST   By the second half of the 1700s, it was generally accepted that without logical underpinnings, calculus would be limited. Augustin-Louis Cauchy developed an acceptable theory of limits, and in doing so removed much doubt about the logical validity of calculus. Cauchy is described by the historian Howard Eves not only as a first-rate mathematician with tremendous mathematical productivity but also as a lawyer (he practiced law for 14 years), a mountain climber, and a painter (he worked in watercolors). Among other characteristics that distinguished him from his contemporaries, he advocated respect for the environment.

AUGUSTIN–LOUIS CAUCHY 1789–1857

Cauchy wrote a treatise on integrals in 1814 that is considered a classic, and in 1816 his paper on wave propagation in liquids won a prize from the French Academy. It has been said that with his work the modern era of analysis began. In all, he wrote over 700 papers, which are, today, considered no less than brilliant. ∎

Cauchy did not formulate the ϵ-δ definition of limit that we use today, but formulated instead a purely arithmetical definition. Consult some history of mathematics books to find a translation of Cauchy's definition, which appeared in his monumental treatise, *Cours d'Analyse de l'Ecole Royale Polytechnique* (1821). As part of your research, find when and where the ϵ-δ definition of limit was first used.

© *In Problems 50–55, use the formal definition of the limit to prove or disprove the given limit statement.*

50. $\lim\limits_{x \to 2} (x + 3) = 5$

51. $\lim\limits_{t \to 0} (3t - 1) = 0$

52. $\lim\limits_{x \to -2} (3x + 7) = 1$

53. $\lim\limits_{x \to 1} (2x - 5) = -3$

54. $\lim\limits_{x \to 2} (x^2 + 2) = 6$

55. $\lim\limits_{x \to 2} \dfrac{1}{x} = \dfrac{1}{2}$

56. The tabular approach is a convenient device for discussing limits informally, but if it is not used very carefully, it can be misleading. For example, for $x \neq 0$, let

$$f(x) = \sin \dfrac{1}{x}$$

a. Construct a table showing the values of $f(x)$ for $x = \frac{-2}{\pi}, \frac{-2}{9\pi}, \frac{-2}{13\pi}, \frac{2}{19\pi}, \frac{2}{7\pi}, \frac{2}{3\pi}$. Based on this table, what would you say about $\lim\limits_{x \to 0} f(x)$?

b. Construct a second table, this time showing the values of

$f(x)$ for $x = \frac{-1}{2\pi}, \frac{-1}{11\pi}, \frac{-1}{20\pi}, \frac{1}{50\pi}, \frac{1}{30\pi}, \frac{1}{5\pi}$. Now what would you say about $\lim\limits_{x \to 0} f(x)$?

c. Based on the results in parts **a** and **b**, what do you conclude about $\lim\limits_{x \to 0} \sin \frac{1}{x}$?

2.2   Algebraic Computation of Limits

IN THIS SECTION   computations with limits, using algebra to find limits, two special trigonometric limits, limits of piecewise-defined functions

COMPUTATIONS WITH LIMITS

In Section 2.1, we observed that finding limits by tables or by graphing is risky. In this section, we will explore a more exact way of computing limits that is based on the following properties.

Basic Properties and Rules for Limits

For any real number c, suppose the functions f and g both have limits at $x = c$.

Constant rule $\lim\limits_{x \to c} k = k$ for any constant k

Limit of x rule $\lim\limits_{x \to c} x = c$

Multiple rule $\lim\limits_{x \to c} [kf(x)] = k \lim\limits_{x \to c} f(x)$ for any constant k

The limit of a constant times a function is the constant times the limit of the function.

Sum rule $\lim\limits_{x \to c} [f(x) + g(x)] = \lim\limits_{x \to c} f(x) + \lim\limits_{x \to c} g(x)$

The limit of a sum is the sum of the limits.

Difference rule $\lim\limits_{x \to c} [f(x) - g(x)] = \lim\limits_{x \to c} f(x) - \lim\limits_{x \to c} g(x)$

The limit of a difference is the difference of the limits.

Product rule $\lim\limits_{x \to c} [f(x)g(x)] = \left[\lim\limits_{x \to c} f(x)\right]\left[\lim\limits_{x \to c} g(x)\right]$

The limit of a product is the product of the limits.

Quotient rule $\lim\limits_{x \to c} \dfrac{f(x)}{g(x)} = \dfrac{\lim\limits_{x \to c} f(x)}{\lim\limits_{x \to c} g(x)}$ if $\lim\limits_{x \to c} g(x) \neq 0$

The limit of a quotient is the quotient of the limits, as long as the limit of the denominator is not zero.

Power rule $\lim\limits_{x \to c} [f(x)]^n = \left[\lim\limits_{x \to c} f(x)\right]^n$ n is a rational number and the limit on the right exists.

The limit of a power is the power of the limit.

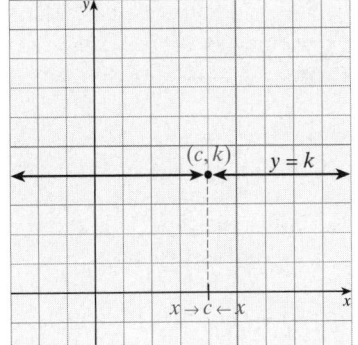

a. Limit of a constant: $\lim\limits_{x \to c} k = k$

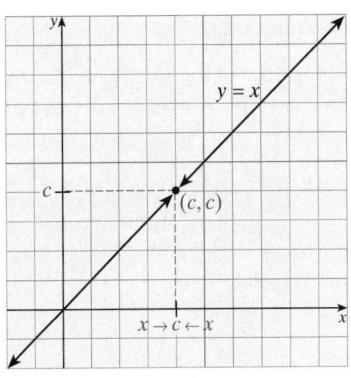

b. Limit of x: $\lim\limits_{x \to c} x = c$

Figure 2.13 Two basic limits

It is fairly easy to justify graphically the rules for the limit of a constant and the limit of x, as shown in Figure 2.13. All of these properties of limits (including the two basic limits shown in Figure 2.13) can be proved using the formal definition of limit.

EXAMPLE 1   Finding the limit of a polynomial function

Evaluate $\lim\limits_{x \to 2} (2x^5 - 9x^3 + 3x^2 - 11)$.

Solution

$$\lim_{x \to 2}(2x^5 - 9x^3 + 3x^2 - 11) = \lim_{x \to 2}(2x^5) - \lim_{x \to 2}(9x^3) + \lim_{x \to 2}(3x^2) - \lim_{x \to 2}(11)$$

Sum and difference rules

$$= 2\left[\lim_{x \to 2} x^5\right] - 9\left[\lim_{x \to 2} x^3\right] + 3\left[\lim_{x \to 2} x^2\right] - 11$$

Multiple and constant rules

$$= 2\left[\lim_{x \to 2} x\right]^5 - 9\left[\lim_{x \to 2} x\right]^3 + 3\left[\lim_{x \to 2} x\right]^2 - 11$$

Power rule

$$= 2(2)^5 - 9(2)^3 + 3(2)^2 - 11 = -7$$

Limit of x rule   ∎

Comment: If you consider Example 1 carefully, it is easy to see that if P is any polynomial, then the limit at $x = c$ can be found by substituting $x = c$ into the formula for $P(x)$.

Limit of a Polynomial Function

If P is a polynomial function, then

$$\lim_{x \to c} P(x) = P(c)$$

EXAMPLE 2   Finding the limit of a rational function

Evaluate $\lim\limits_{z \to -1} \dfrac{z^3 - 3z + 7}{5z^2 + 9z + 6}$.

Solution

$$\lim_{z \to -1} \frac{z^3 - 3z + 7}{5z^2 + 9z + 6} = \frac{\lim\limits_{z \to -1}(z^3 - 3z + 7)}{\lim\limits_{z \to -1}(5z^2 + 9z + 6)}$$

Quotient rule

$$= \frac{(-1)^3 - 3(-1) + 7}{5(-1)^2 + 9(-1) + 6}$$

$$= \frac{9}{2}$$ Both numerator and denominator are polynomial functions.   ∎

Notice that if the denominator of the rational function is not zero, the limit can be found by substitution. If the limit of the denominator is zero, we find ourselves dividing by zero, an illegal operation.

Limit of a Rational Function

If Q is a rational function defined by $Q(x) = \dfrac{P(x)}{D(x)}$, then

$$\lim_{x \to c} Q(x) = \frac{P(c)}{D(c)}$$

provided $\lim\limits_{x \to c} D(x) \neq 0$.

EXAMPLE 3   Finding the limit of a power (or root) function

Evaluate $\lim\limits_{x \to -2} \sqrt[3]{x^2 - 3x - 2}$.

Solution $\lim\limits_{x \to -2} \sqrt[3]{x^2 - 3x - 2} = \lim\limits_{x \to -2} (x^2 - 3x - 2)^{1/3}$

$$= \left[\lim\limits_{x \to -2} (x^2 - 3x - 2) \right]^{1/3} \qquad \text{Power rule}$$

$$= [(-2)^2 - 3(-2) - 2]^{1/3} = 8^{1/3} = 2 \qquad \blacksquare$$

Once again, for values of the function for which $f(c)$ is defined, the limit can be found by substitution.

In the previous section we used a table to find that $\lim\limits_{x \to 0} \sin x = 0$ and $\lim\limits_{x \to 0} \cos x = 1$. In the following example we use this information, along with the properties of limits, to find other trigonometric limits.

EXAMPLE 4   Finding trigonometric limits algebraically

Given that $\lim\limits_{x \to 0} \sin x = 0$ and $\lim\limits_{x \to 0} \cos x = 1$, evaluate:

a. $\lim\limits_{x \to 0} \sin^2 x$ **b.** $\lim\limits_{x \to 0} (1 - \cos x)$

Solution

a. $\lim\limits_{x \to 0} \sin^2 x = \left[\lim\limits_{x \to 0} \sin x \right]^2 \qquad \text{Power rule}$

$$= 0^2 \qquad\qquad \lim\limits_{x \to 0} \sin x = 0$$

$$= 0$$

b. $\lim\limits_{x \to 0} (1 - \cos x) = \lim\limits_{x \to 0} 1 - \lim\limits_{x \to 0} \cos x \qquad \text{Difference rule}$

$$= 1 - 1 \qquad\qquad \text{Constant rule and} \lim\limits_{x \to 0} \cos x = 1$$

$$= 0 \qquad\qquad\qquad\qquad\qquad\qquad\qquad \blacksquare$$

The following theorem states that we can find limits of trigonometric functions by direct substitution, as long as the number that x is approaching is in the domain of the given function. Proofs of several parts are outlined in the problem set, and in fact an examination of the graphs of the functions indicates why they are true.

THEOREM 2.2   Limits of trigonometric functions

If c is any number in the domain of the given function, then

$$\lim\limits_{x \to c} \cos x = \cos c \qquad \lim\limits_{x \to c} \sin x = \sin c \qquad \lim\limits_{x \to c} \tan x = \tan c$$

$$\lim\limits_{x \to c} \sec x = \sec c \qquad \lim\limits_{x \to c} \csc x = \csc c \qquad \lim\limits_{x \to c} \cot x = \cot c$$

Proof   We will show that $\lim\limits_{x \to c} \sin x = \sin c$. The other limit formulas may be proved in a similar fashion (see Problems 63–64). Let $h = x - c$. Then $x = h + c$, so $x \to c$ as $h \to 0$. Thus,

$$\lim\limits_{x \to c} \sin x = \lim\limits_{h \to 0} \sin(h + c)$$

Using the trigonometric identity

$$\sin(A + B) = \sin A \cos B + \cos A \sin B$$

and the limit formulas for sums and products, we find that

$$\lim_{x \to c} \sin x = \lim_{h \to 0} \sin(h + c)$$

$$= \lim_{h \to 0} [\sin h \cos c + \cos h \sin c]$$

$$= \lim_{h \to 0} \sin h \cdot \lim_{h \to 0} \cos c + \lim_{h \to 0} \cos h \cdot \lim_{h \to 0} \sin c$$

$$= 0 \cdot \cos c + 1 \cdot \sin c \qquad \lim_{h \to 0} \sin h = 0 \text{ and } \lim_{h \to 0} \cos h = 1$$

$$= \sin c$$

Note that $\sin c$ and $\cos c$ do not change as $h \to 0$ because these are constants with respect to h. ❑

EXAMPLE 5   **Finding limits of trigonometric functions**

Evaluate the following limits:

a. $\lim\limits_{x \to 1} (x^2 \cos \pi x)$ **b.** $\lim\limits_{x \to 0} \dfrac{x}{\cos x}$

Solution

a. $\lim\limits_{x \to 1} (x^2 \cos \pi x) = \left[\lim\limits_{x \to 1} x \right]^2 \cdot \left[\lim\limits_{x \to 1} \cos \pi x \right] = 1^2 \cos \pi = -1$

b. $\lim\limits_{x \to 0} \dfrac{x}{\cos x} = \dfrac{\lim\limits_{x \to 0} x}{\lim\limits_{x \to 0} \cos x} = \dfrac{0}{1} = 0$ ■

USING ALGEBRA TO FIND LIMITS

Sometimes the limit of $f(x)$ as $x \to c$ *cannot* be evaluated by direct substitution. In such a case, we look for another function that agrees with f for all values of x *except at the troublesome value $x = c$*. We illustrate this procedure with some examples.

EXAMPLE 6   **Evaluating a limit using fractional reduction**

Evaluate $\lim\limits_{x \to 2} \dfrac{x^2 + x - 6}{x - 2}$.

Solution

If you try substitution on this limit, you will obtain

If $x = 2$, then $x^2 + x - 6 = 0$.

$$\downarrow$$

$$\lim_{x \to 2} \frac{x^2 + x - 6}{x - 2} = \frac{0}{0}$$

$$\uparrow$$

If $x = 2$, then $x - 2 = 0$.

The form $\frac{0}{0}$ is called an **indeterminate form** because the value of the limit cannot be determined without further analysis.

If the expression is a rational expression, the next step is to try to simplify the function by factoring and checking to see if the reduced form is a polynomial.

$$\lim_{x \to 2} \frac{x^2 + x - 6}{x - 2} = \lim_{x \to 2} \frac{(x + 3)(x - 2)}{x - 2} = \lim_{x \to 2} (x + 3)$$

This simplification is valid only if $x \neq 2$. Now complete the evaluation of the reduced function by direct substitution. This is not a problem, because the limit is concerned with values *as x approaches* 2, not the value where $x = 2$. In the preceding expression

$$\lim_{x \to 2} \frac{x^2 + x - 6}{x - 2} = \lim_{x \to 2} (x + 3) = 5$$ ■

Another algebraic technique for finding limits is to rationalize either the numerator or the denominator to obtain an algebraic form that is not indeterminate.

EXAMPLE 7   Evaluating a limit by rationalizing

Evaluate $\lim\limits_{x\to 4} \dfrac{\sqrt{x}-2}{x-4}$.

Solution

Once again, notice that both the numerator and denominator of this rational expression are 0 when $x = 4$, so we cannot evaluate the limit by direct substitution. Instead, rationalize the numerator:

$$\lim_{x\to 4}\frac{\sqrt{x}-2}{x-4} = \lim_{x\to 4}\frac{\sqrt{x}-2}{x-4}\cdot\frac{\sqrt{x}+2}{\sqrt{x}+2} \qquad \text{Multiply by 1.}$$
$$= \lim_{x\to 4}\frac{\cancel{x-4}}{\cancel{(x-4)}(\sqrt{x}+2)}$$
$$= \lim_{x\to 4}\frac{1}{\sqrt{x}+2}$$
$$= \frac{1}{\sqrt{4}+2}=\frac{1}{4}$$

WARNING   This method will work only if the resulting numerator allows the fraction to be simplified. Pay close attention to this example because it illustrates a procedure we will use over and over.

LIMITS OF PIECEWISE-DEFINED FUNCTIONS

In Section 1.3 we discussed *piecewise-defined functions*. To evaluate $\lim\limits_{x\to c} f(x)$ where the domain of f is divided into pieces, we first look to see whether c is a value separating two of the pieces. If so, we need to consider one-sided limits, as illustrated by the following examples.

EXAMPLE 8   Limit of a piecewise-defined function

Find $\lim\limits_{x\to 0} f(x)$, where $f(x) = \begin{cases} x+5 & \text{if } x > 0 \\ x & \text{if } x < 0 \end{cases}$.

Solution

Notice that $f(0)$ is not defined, and that it is necessary to consider left- and right-hand limits because $f(x)$ is defined differently on each side of $x = 0$. We have

$$\lim_{x\to 0^-} f(x) = \lim_{x\to 0^-} x \qquad\qquad f(x) = x \text{ to the left of } 0.$$
$$= 0$$
$$\lim_{x\to 0^+} f(x) = \lim_{x\to 0^+} (x+5) \qquad f(x) = x+5 \text{ to the right of } 0.$$
$$= 5$$

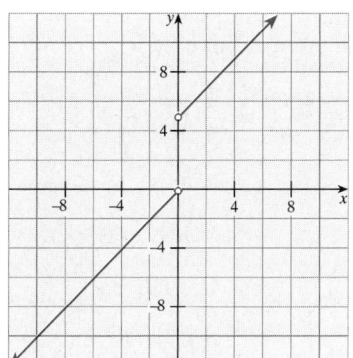

Figure 2.14 Graph of f

Because the left- and right-hand limits are not the same, we conclude that $\lim\limits_{x\to 0} f(x)$ does not exist. If we look at the graph, as shown in Figure 2.14, it is easy to see that the left- and right-hand limits are not the same.

EXAMPLE 9   Limit of a piecewise-defined function

Find $\lim\limits_{x\to 0} g(x)$, where $g(x) = \begin{cases} x+1 & \text{if } x > 0 \\ x^2+1 & \text{if } x < 0 \end{cases}$.

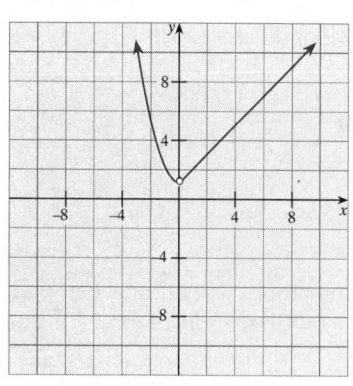

Figure 2.15 Graph of g

Solution

$$\lim_{x \to 0^-} g(x) = \lim_{x \to 0^-} (x^2 + 1) = 1$$

$$\lim_{x \to 0^+} g(x) = \lim_{x \to 0^+} (x + 1) = 1$$

Because the left- and right-hand limits are equal, we conclude that $\lim_{x \to 0} g(x) = 1$. This time, by looking at the graph in Figure 2.15, we see that the left- and right-hand limits are the same (even though the function is not defined at $x = 0$). Compare this graph with the graph in Example 8. ∎

TWO SPECIAL TRIGONOMETRIC LIMITS

The following theorem contains two additional limits that play an important role in calculus. We evaluated the first of these limits by table and graphically in Example 6 of Section 2.1.

THEOREM 2.3   Special limits involving sine and cosine

$$\lim_{h \to 0} \frac{\sin h}{h} = 1 \qquad \lim_{h \to 0} \frac{\cos h - 1}{h} = 0$$

Proof   A geometric argument justifying these rules is given at the end of this section. ❑

For now, let us concentrate on illustrating how these rules can be used.

EXAMPLE 10   Evaluation of trigonometric and inverse trigonometric limits

Find each of the following limits.

a. $\lim\limits_{x \to 0} \dfrac{\sin 3x}{5x}$ **b.** $\lim\limits_{x \to 0} \dfrac{\sin^{-1} x}{x}$ **c.** $\lim\limits_{h \to 0} \dfrac{\cos h - 1}{h^2}$

Solution

a. We prepare the limit for evaluation by Theorem 2.3 by writing

$$\frac{\sin 3x}{5x} = \frac{3}{5} \left(\frac{\sin 3x}{3x} \right) \qquad \text{WARNING} \qquad \sin 3x \neq 3 \sin x$$

Since $3x \to 0$ as $x \to 0$, we can set $h = 3x$ in Theorem 2.3 to obtain

$$\lim_{x \to 0} \frac{\sin 3x}{5x} = \lim_{x \to 0} \frac{3}{5} \left(\frac{\sin 3x}{3x} \right) = \frac{3}{5} \lim_{h \to 0} \frac{\sin h}{h} = \frac{3}{5}(1) = \frac{3}{5}$$

b. Let $u = \sin^{-1} x$, so $\sin u = x$. Thus $u \to 0$ as $x \to 0$, and

$$\lim_{x \to 0} \frac{\sin^{-1} x}{x} = \lim_{u \to 0} \frac{u}{\sin u} = 1$$

c. We begin by writing

$$\begin{aligned} \frac{\cos h - 1}{h^2} &= \frac{(\cos h - 1)(\cos h + 1)}{h^2(\cos h + 1)} \\ &= \frac{\cos^2 h - 1}{h^2(\cos h + 1)} \\ &= \frac{-\sin^2 h}{h^2(\cos h + 1)} \qquad \text{Since } \sin^2 h + \cos^2 h = 1 \end{aligned}$$

Thus, we have

$$\lim_{h \to 0} \frac{\cos h - 1}{h^2} = \lim_{h \to 0} \frac{-\sin^2 h}{h^2(\cos h + 1)}$$

$$= -\left[\lim_{h \to 0} \frac{\sin^2 h}{h^2}\right]\left[\lim_{h \to 0} \frac{1}{\cos h + 1}\right]$$

$$= -\left[\lim_{h \to 0} \frac{\sin h}{h}\right]^2 \left[\lim_{h \to 0} \frac{1}{\cos h + 1}\right]$$

$$= -(1)^2 \left(\frac{1}{1 + 1}\right)$$

$$= -\frac{1}{2} \qquad \blacksquare$$

We conclude this section with a justification of Theorem 2.3. Our argument is based on the following useful property that is proved in Appendix A.

Squeeze Rule*

If $g(x) \leq f(x) \leq h(x)$ on an open interval containing c, and if

$$\lim_{x \to c} g(x) = \lim_{x \to c} h(x) = L, \text{ then } \lim_{x \to c} f(x) = L$$

➡ **What This Says** If a function can be squeezed between two functions whose limits at a particular point c have the same value L, then that function must also have limit L at $x = c$.

With this squeeze rule in our toolkit, we are now ready to justify Theorem 2.3.

Proof Proof that $\lim\limits_{h \to 0} \dfrac{\sin h}{h} = 1$.

To prove the sine limit theorem requires some principles that are not entirely obvious. However, we can demonstrate its plausibility by considering Figure 2.16, in which AOC is a sector of a circle of radius 1 with angle h measured in radians. The line segments $\overline{AD}$ and $\overline{BC}$ are drawn perpendicular to segment $\overline{OC}$.

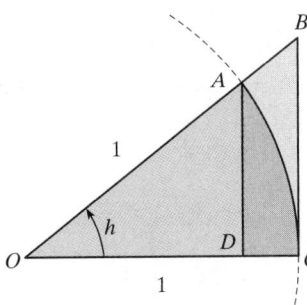

Assume $0 < h < \frac{\pi}{2}$; that is, h is in Quadrant I.

$$\left|\widehat{AC}\right| = h$$

$$\left|\overline{AD}\right| = \sin h$$

$$\left|\overline{BC}\right| = \tan h = \frac{\sin h}{\cos h}$$

$$\left|\overline{OD}\right| = \cos h$$

Figure 2.16 Trigonometric relationships in the proof that $\lim\limits_{h \to 0} \dfrac{\sin h}{h} = 1$

---

*This rule is sometimes known as the **sandwich rule**.

Now, compare the area of the sector AOC with those of $\triangle AOD$ and $\triangle BOC$. In particular, since the area of the circular sector of radius r and central angle θ is $\frac{1}{2}r^2\theta$ (see the *Student Mathematics Handbook*), sector AOC must have area

SMH

$$\tfrac{1}{2}(1)^2 h = \tfrac{1}{2}h$$

We also find that $\triangle AOD$ has area

$$\tfrac{1}{2}\left|\overline{OD}\right|\left|\overline{AD}\right| = \tfrac{1}{2}\cos h \sin h,$$

and $\triangle BOC$ has area

$$\tfrac{1}{2}\left|\overline{BC}\right|\left|\overline{OC}\right| = \tfrac{1}{2}\left|\overline{BC}\right|(1) = \frac{1}{2}\frac{\sin h}{\cos h}$$

By comparing areas (see Figure 2.16), we have

$\underbrace{\text{AREA OF } \triangle AOD}$		$\underbrace{\text{AREA OF SECTOR } AOC}$		$\underbrace{\text{AREA OF } \triangle BOC}$	
$\frac{1}{2}\cos h \sin h$	$\leq$	$\frac{1}{2}h$	$\leq$	$\dfrac{\sin h}{2\cos h}$	
$\cos h$	$\leq$	$\dfrac{h}{\sin h}$	$\leq$	$\dfrac{1}{\cos h}$	Divide by $\frac{1}{2}\sin h$.
$\dfrac{1}{\cos h}$	$\geq$	$\dfrac{\sin h}{h}$	$\geq$	$\cos h$	Take reciprocals (reverse order).
$\cos h$	$\leq$	$\dfrac{\sin h}{h}$	$\leq$	$\dfrac{1}{\cos h}$	Interchange left and right sides (reverse order again).

This same inequality holds in the interval $(-\frac{\pi}{2}, 0)$, which is Quadrant IV for the angle h. This can be shown by using the trigonometric identities $\cos(-h) = \cos h$ and $\sin(-h) = -\sin h$. Finally, we take the limit of all parts as $h \to 0$ to find

$$\lim_{h\to 0}\cos h \leq \lim_{h\to 0}\frac{\sin h}{h} \leq \lim_{h\to 0}\frac{1}{\cos h}$$

By Theorem 2.2, $\lim\limits_{h\to 0}\cos h = \cos 0 = 1$. Thus,

$$1 \leq \lim_{h\to 0}\frac{\sin h}{h} \leq \frac{1}{1}$$

From the squeeze rule, we conclude that $\lim\limits_{h\to 0}\dfrac{\sin h}{h} = 1$.

You are asked to prove the second part of this theorem in Problem 59.   ❑

2.2 PROBLEM SET

A *In Problems 1–32, evaluate each limit.*

1. $\lim\limits_{x\to -2}(x^2 + 3x - 7)$

2. $\lim\limits_{t\to 0}(t^3 - 5t^2 + 4)$

3. $\lim\limits_{x\to 3}(x + 5)(2x - 7)$

4. $\lim\limits_{x\to 0}\dfrac{\sin^{-1}x}{x - 1}$

5. $\lim\limits_{z\to 1}\dfrac{z^2 + z - 3}{z + 1}$

6. $\lim\limits_{x\to 3}\dfrac{x^2 + 3x - 10}{3x^2 + 5x - 7}$

7. $\lim\limits_{x\to \pi/3}\sec x$

8. $\lim\limits_{x\to \pi/4}\dfrac{1 + \tan x}{\csc x + 2}$

9. $\lim\limits_{x\to 1/3}\dfrac{x\sin \pi x}{1 + \cos \pi x}$

10. $\lim\limits_{x\to 6}\dfrac{\tan(\pi/x)}{x - 1}$

11. $\lim\limits_{u\to -2}\dfrac{4 - u^2}{2 + u}$

12. $\lim\limits_{x\to 2}\dfrac{x^2 - 4x + 4}{x^2 - x - 2}$

13. $\lim\limits_{x \to 1} \dfrac{\frac{1}{x} - 1}{x - 1}$

14. $\lim\limits_{x \to 0} \dfrac{(x + 1)^2 - 1}{x}$

15. $\lim\limits_{x \to 1} \left(\dfrac{x^2 - 3x + 2}{x^2 + x - 2} \right)^2$

16. $\lim\limits_{x \to 3} \sqrt{\dfrac{x^2 - 2x - 3}{x - 3}}$

17. $\lim\limits_{x \to 1} \dfrac{\sqrt{x} - 1}{x - 1}$

18. $\lim\limits_{y \to 2} \dfrac{\sqrt{y + 2} - 2}{y - 2}$

19. $\lim\limits_{x \to 0} \dfrac{\sqrt{x + 1} - 1}{x}$

20. $\lim\limits_{x \to 0} \dfrac{\sqrt{x^2 + 4} - 2}{x}$

21. $\lim\limits_{x \to 0^+} \dfrac{\sin x}{\sqrt{x}}$

22. $\lim\limits_{x \to 0^+} \dfrac{1 - \cos \sqrt{x}}{x}$

23. $\lim\limits_{x \to 0} \dfrac{\sin 2x}{x}$

24. $\lim\limits_{x \to 0} \dfrac{\sin 4x}{9x}$

25. $\lim\limits_{t \to 0} \dfrac{\tan 5t}{\tan 2t}$

26. $\lim\limits_{x \to 0} \dfrac{\cot 3x}{\cot x}$

27. $\lim\limits_{x \to 0} \dfrac{1 - \cos x}{\sin x}$

28. $\lim\limits_{x \to 0} \dfrac{\sin^2 x}{2x}$

29. $\lim\limits_{x \to 0} \dfrac{\sin^2 x}{x^2}$

30. $\lim\limits_{x \to 0} \dfrac{x^2 \cos 2x}{1 - \cos x}$

31. $\lim\limits_{x \to 0} \dfrac{\sec x - 1}{x \sec x}$

32. $\lim\limits_{x \to \pi/4} \dfrac{1 - \tan x}{\sin x - \cos x}$

33. WHAT DOES THIS SAY? How do you find the limit of a polynomial function?

34. WHAT DOES THIS SAY? How do you find the limit of a rational function?

35. WHAT DOES THIS SAY? How do you find

$$\lim\limits_{x \to 0} \dfrac{\sin ax}{x}$$

for $a \ne 0$?

B *In Problems 36–43, compute the one-sided limit or use one-sided limits to find the given limit, if it exists.*

36. $\lim\limits_{x \to 2^-} (x^2 - 2x)$

37. $\lim\limits_{x \to 1^+} \dfrac{\sqrt{x - 1} + x}{1 - 2x}$

38. $\lim\limits_{x \to 2} |x - 2|$

39. $\lim\limits_{x \to 3} |3 - x|$

40. $\lim\limits_{x \to 0} \dfrac{|x|}{x}$

41. $\lim\limits_{x \to -2} \dfrac{|x + 2|}{x + 2}$

42. $\lim\limits_{x \to 2} f(x)$, where $f(x) = \begin{cases} 3 - 2x & \text{if } x \le 2 \\ x^2 - 5 & \text{if } x > 2 \end{cases}$

43. $\lim\limits_{s \to 1} g(s)$, where $g(s) = \begin{cases} \dfrac{s^2 - s}{s - 1} & \text{if } s > 1 \\ \sqrt{1 - s} & \text{if } s \le 1 \end{cases}$

WHAT DOES THIS SAY? *In Problems 44–51, explain why the given limit does not exist.*

44. $\lim\limits_{x \to 1} \dfrac{1}{x - 1}$

45. $\lim\limits_{x \to 2^+} \dfrac{1}{\sqrt{x - 2}}$

46. $\lim\limits_{t \to 2} \dfrac{t^2 - 4}{t^2 - 4t + 4}$

47. $\lim\limits_{x \to 3} \dfrac{x^2 + 4x + 3}{x - 3}$

48. $\lim\limits_{x \to 1} f(x)$, where $f(x) = \begin{cases} 2 & \text{if } x \ge 1 \\ -5 & \text{if } x < 1 \end{cases}$

49. $\lim\limits_{t \to -1} g(t)$, where $g(t) = \begin{cases} 2t + 1 & \text{if } t \ge -1 \\ 5t^2 & \text{if } t < -1 \end{cases}$

50. $\lim\limits_{x \to \pi/2} \tan x$

51. $\lim\limits_{x \to 1} \csc \pi x$

In Problems 52–57, either evaluate the limit or explain why it does not exist.

52. $\lim\limits_{x \to 1} \dfrac{\frac{1}{x} - 1}{\sqrt{x} - 1}$

53. $\lim\limits_{x \to 0} \left(\dfrac{1}{x} - \dfrac{1}{x^2} \right)$

54. $\lim\limits_{x \to 5} f(x)$, where $f(x) = \begin{cases} x + 3 & \text{if } x \ne 5 \\ 4 & \text{if } x = 5 \end{cases}$

55. $\lim\limits_{x \to 2} g(t)$, where $g(t) = \begin{cases} t^2 & \text{if } -1 \le t < 2 \\ 3t - 2 & \text{if } t \ge 2 \end{cases}$

56. $\lim\limits_{x \to 2} f(x)$, where $f(x) = \begin{cases} 2(x + 1) & \text{if } x < 3 \\ 4 & \text{if } x = 3 \\ x^2 - 1 & \text{if } x > 3 \end{cases}$

57. $\lim\limits_{x \to 3} f(x)$, where $f(x) = \begin{cases} 2(x + 1) & \text{if } x < 3 \\ 4 & \text{if } x = 3 \\ x^2 - 1 & \text{if } x > 3 \end{cases}$

58. Interpretation Problem Evaluate $\lim\limits_{x \to 0} \left[x^2 - \dfrac{\cos x}{1{,}000{,}000{,}000} \right]$. Explain why a calculator solution may lead to an incorrect conclusion about the limit.

C **59.** Prove the second part of Theorem 2.3: $\lim\limits_{h \to 0} \dfrac{\cos h - 1}{h} = 0$.

60. Counterexample Problem Give an example for which neither $\lim\limits_{x \to c} f(x)$ nor $\lim\limits_{x \to c} g(x)$ exists, but $\lim\limits_{x \to c} [f(x) + g(x)]$ does exist.

61. Let $f(x) = \dfrac{1}{x^2}$ with $x \ne 0$, and let L be any fixed positive integer. Show that

$$f(x) > 100L \text{ if } |x| < \dfrac{1}{10\sqrt{L}}$$

What does this imply about $\lim\limits_{x \to 0} f(x)$?

62. Use the sum rule to show that if $\lim\limits_{x \to c} [f(x) + g(x)]$ and $\lim\limits_{x \to c} f(x)$ both exist, then so does $\lim\limits_{x \to c} g(x)$.

63. Show that $\lim\limits_{x \to x_0} \cos x = \cos x_0$. *Hint:* You will need to use the trigonometric identity $\cos(A + B) = \cos A \cos B - \sin A \sin B$.

64. Show that $\lim\limits_{x \to x_0} \tan x = \tan x_0$ whenever $\cos x_0 \ne 0$.

2.3   Continuity

IN THIS SECTION   intuitive notion of continuity, definition of continuity, continuity theorems, continuity on an interval, the intermediate value theorem

INTUITIVE NOTION OF CONTINUITY

$\lim_{x \to c} f(x)$ exists and is equal to $f(c)$.

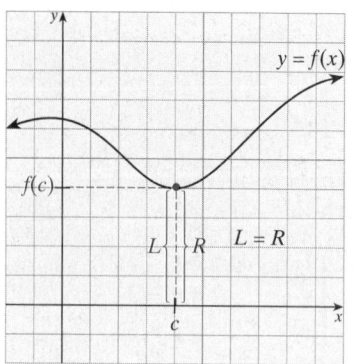

Figure 2.17 A function continuous at a point $x = c$

The idea of *continuity* may be thought of informally as the quality of having parts that are in immediate connection with one another, as shown in Figure 2.17. The idea evolved from the vague or intuitive notion of a curve "without breaks or jumps" to a rigorous definition first given toward the end of the nineteenth century (see Historical Quest Problem 45).

We begin with a discussion of *continuity at a point*. It may seem strange to talk about continuity *at a point*, but it should seem natural to talk about a curve being "discontinuous at a point." A few such discontinuities are illustrated by Figure 2.18.

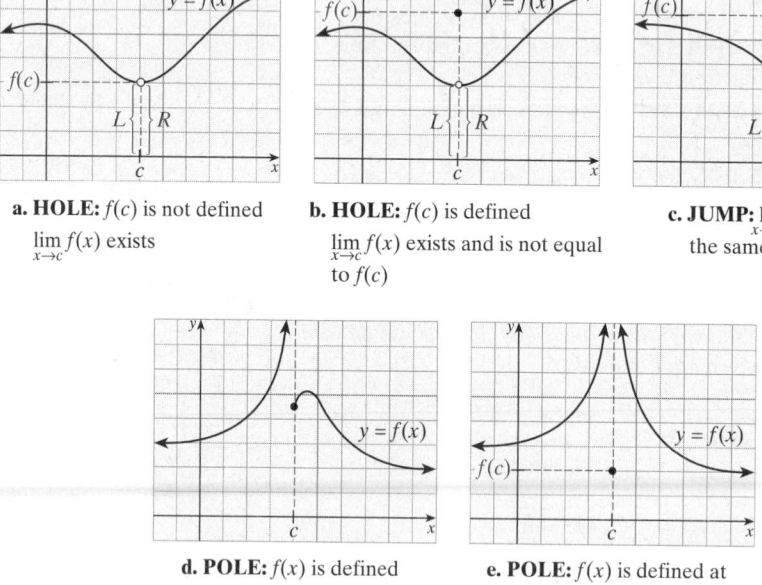

a. HOLE: $f(c)$ is not defined
$\lim_{x \to c} f(x)$ exists

b. HOLE: $f(c)$ is defined
$\lim_{x \to c} f(x)$ exists and is not equal
to $f(c)$

c. JUMP: $\lim_{x \to c^-} f(c)$ is not
the same as $\lim_{x \to c^+} f(x)$

d. POLE: $f(x)$ is defined
at $x = c$; $\lim_{x \to c^-} f(x) = +\infty$

e. POLE: $f(x)$ is defined at
$x = c$; $\lim_{x \to c^-} f(x) = +\infty$ and
$\lim_{x \to c^+} f(x) = +\infty$

Figure 2.18   Types of discontinuity: holes, poles, and jumps

DEFINITION OF CONTINUITY

Let us consider the conditions that must be satisfied for a function f to be continuous at a point c. First, $f(c)$ must be defined or we have a "hole" in the graph, as shown in Figure 2.18a. (An open dot indicates an excluded point.) In Figure 2.18b, there is a "hole" even though $f(c)$ is defined. If $\lim_{x \to c} f(x)$ has one value as $x \to c^-$ and another as $x \to c^+$, then $\lim_{x \to c} f(x)$ does not exist and there will be a "jump" in the graph of f, as shown in Figure 2.18c. Finally, if one or both of the one-sided limits at c are infinite ($+\infty$ or $-\infty$), there will be a "pole" at $x = c$, as shown in Figures 2.18d and e.

Continuity of a Function at a Point

A function f is **continuous at a point** $x = c$ if the following three conditions are satisfied:

1. $f(c)$ is defined;
2. $\lim\limits_{x \to c} f(x)$ exists;
3. $\lim\limits_{x \to c} f(x) = f(c)$.

A function that is not continuous at c is said to have a **discontinuity** at that point.

➡ **What This Says**   The third condition $\lim\limits_{x \to c} f(x) = f(c)$ summarizes the idea behind continuity. It says that if x is close to c, then $f(x)$ must be close to $f(c)$.

If f is continuous at c, the points $(x, f(x))$ converge to $(c, f(c))$ as $x \to c$.

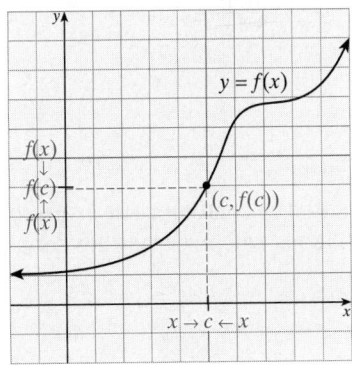

Figure 2.19 The geometric interpretation of continuity

WARNING   Do not rely on graphing calculators to test for continuity. For example, the graph of $y = \dfrac{x-2}{x-2}$ looks like a constant function when done with a calculator; it does not show the discontinuity at $x = 2$.

If f is continuous at $x = c$, the difference between $f(x)$ and $f(c)$ is small whenever x is close to c because $\lim\limits_{x \to c} f(x) = f(c)$. Geometrically, this means that the points $(x, f(x))$ on the graph of f converge to the point $(c, f(c))$ as $x \to c$, and this is what guarantees that the graph is unbroken at $(c, f(c))$ with no "gap" or "hole," as shown in Figure 2.19.

We should note that not every continuous function can be graphed (for example, see Example 2e later in this section), so you cannot test continuity by graphing, even though graphing can help for many functions.

EXAMPLE 1   Testing continuity

Test the continuity of each of the following functions at $x = 1$. If the given function is not continuous at $x = 1$, explain.

a. $f(x) = \dfrac{x^2 + 2x - 3}{x - 1}$

b. $g(x) = \dfrac{x^2 + 2x - 3}{x - 1}$ if $x \neq 1$ and $g(x) = 6$ if $x = 1$

c. $h(x) = \dfrac{x^2 + 2x - 3}{x - 1}$ if $x \neq 1$ and $h(x) = 4$ if $x = 1$

d. $F(x) = \dfrac{x + 3}{x - 1}$ if $x \neq 1$ and $F(x) = 4$ if $x = 1$

e. $G(x) = 7x^3 + 3x^2 - 2$

f. $H(x) = 2 \sin x - \tan x$

Solution

a. The function f is not continuous at $x = 1$ [hole; $f(1)$ not defined] because it is not defined at this point.

b. 1. $g(1)$ is defined; $g(1) = 6$.

   2. $\lim\limits_{x \to 1} g(x) = \lim\limits_{x \to 1} \dfrac{x^2 + 2x - 3}{x - 1}$

   $= \lim\limits_{x \to 1} \dfrac{(x - 1)(x + 3)}{x - 1}$

   $= \lim\limits_{x \to 1} (x + 3) = 4$

   3. $\lim\limits_{x \to 1} g(x) \neq g(1)$, so g is not continuous at $x = 1$ [hole; $g(1)$ defined].

c. Compare h with g of part **b.** We see that all three conditions of continuity are satisfied, so h is continuous at $x = 1$.

d. 1. $F(1)$ is defined; $F(1) = 4$.

2. $\lim\limits_{x \to 1} F(x) = \lim\limits_{x \to 1} \dfrac{x + 3}{x - 1}$; the limit does not exist.

The function F is not continuous at $x = 1$ (pole).

e. 1. $G(1)$ is defined; $G(1) = 8$.

2. $\lim\limits_{x \to 1} G(x) = 7 \left(\lim\limits_{x \to 1} x \right)^3 + 3 \left(\lim\limits_{x \to 1} x \right)^2 - \lim\limits_{x \to 1} 2 = 8$.

3. $\lim\limits_{x \to 1} G(x) = G(1)$.

Because the three conditions of continuity are satisfied, G is continuous at $x = 1$.

f. 1. $H(1)$ is defined; $H(1) = 2 \sin 1 - \tan 1$.

2. $\lim\limits_{x \to 1} H(x) = 2 \lim\limits_{x \to 1} \sin x - \lim\limits_{x \to 1} \tan x = 2 \sin 1 - \tan 1$.

3. $\lim\limits_{x \to 1} H(x) = H(1)$.

Because the three conditions of continuity are satisfied, H is continuous at $x = 1$.

■

CONTINUITY THEOREMS

It is often difficult to determine whether a given function is continuous at a specified number. However, many common functions are continuous wherever they are defined.

THEOREM 2.4 Continuity theorem

If f is a polynomial or a rational function, a power function, a trigonometric function, or an inverse trigonometric function, then f is continuous at any number $x = c$ for which $f(c)$ is defined.

Proof The proof of the continuity theorem is based on the limit properties stated in the previous section. For instance, a polynomial is a function of the form

$$P(x) = a_n x^n + a_{n-1} x^{n-1} + \cdots + a_1 x + a_0$$

where $a_0, a_1, \ldots, a_n$ are constants. We know that $\lim\limits_{x \to c} a_0 = a_0$ and that $\lim\limits_{x \to c} x^m = c^m$ for $m = 1, 2, \ldots, n$. This is precisely the statement that the function $g(x) = a x^m$ is continuous at any number $x = c$, or simply continuous. Because P is a sum of functions of this form and a constant function, it follows from the limit properties that P is continuous.

The proofs of the other parts follow similarly. ❑

The limit properties of the previous section can also be used to prove a second continuity theorem. This theorem tells us that continuous functions may be combined in various ways *without creating a discontinuity.*

THEOREM 2.5   Properties of continuous functions

If f and g are functions that are continuous at $x = c$, then the following functions are also continuous at $x = c$.

Scalar multiple	sf	for any constant s (called a *scalar*)
Sum and difference	$f + g$ and $f - g$	
Product	fg	
Quotient	$\dfrac{f}{g}$	provided $g(c) \neq 0$
Composition	$f \circ g$	provided g is continuous at c and f is continuous at $g(c)$

Proof   The first four properties in this theorem follow directly from the basic limit rules given in Section 2.2. For instance, to prove the product property, note that since f and g are given to be continuous at $x = c$, we have

$$\lim_{x \to c} f(x) = f(c) \quad \text{and} \quad \lim_{x \to c} g(x) = g(c)$$

If $P(x) = (fg)(x) = f(x)g(x)$, then

$$\begin{aligned} \lim_{x \to c} P(x) &= \lim_{x \to c} f(x)g(x) \\ &= \left[\lim_{x \to c} f(x) \right] \left[\lim_{x \to c} g(x) \right] \\ &= f(c)g(c) = P(c) \end{aligned}$$

so $P(x)$ is continuous at $x = c$, as required.   ❑

The continuous composition property is proved in a similar fashion, but requires the following limit rule, which we state without proof.

Composition Limit Rule

If $\lim_{x \to c} g(x) = L$ and f is a function continuous at L, then $\lim_{x \to c} f[g(x)] = f(L)$. That is,

$$\lim_{x \to c} f[g(x)] = f(L) = f\left(\lim_{x \to c} g(x) \right)$$

This property applies in the same way to other kinds of limits, in particular to one-sided limits.

Now we can prove the continuous composition property of Theorem 2.5. Let $h(x) = (f \circ g)(x)$. Then we have

$$\begin{aligned} \lim_{x \to c} (f \circ g)(x) &= \lim_{x \to c} f[g(x)] & &\text{\textit{Definition of composition}} \\ &= f\left[\lim_{x \to c} g(x) \right] & &\text{\textit{Composition limit rule}} \\ &= f[g(c)] & &\text{\textit{g is continuous at $x = c$.}} \\ &= (f \circ g)(c) & &\text{\textit{Definition of composition}} \quad ❑ \end{aligned}$$

➡ **What This Says**   The limit of a continuous function is the function of the limiting value. The continuous composition property says that a continuous function of a continuous function is continuous.

We need to talk about a function being continuous on an interval. To do so, we must first know how to handle continuity at the endpoints of the interval, which leads to the following definition.

One-Sided Continuity

The function f is **continuous from the right at a** if and only if

$$\lim_{x \to a^+} f(x) = f(a)$$

and it is **continuous from the left at b** if and only if

$$\lim_{x \to b^-} f(x) = f(b)$$

CONTINUITY ON AN INTERVAL

The function f is said to be **continuous on the open interval (a, b)** if it is continuous at each number in this interval. Also note that the endpoints are not part of open intervals. If f is also continuous from the right at a, we say it is **continuous on the half-open interval $[a, b)$**. Similarly, f is **continuous on the half-open interval $(a, b]$** if it is continuous at each number between a and b and is continuous from the left at the endpoint b. Finally, f is **continuous on the closed interval $[a, b]$** if it is continuous at each number between a and b and is both continuous from the right at a and continuous from the left at b.

EXAMPLE 2   Testing for continuity on an interval

Find the intervals on which each of the given functions is continuous.

a. $f_1(x) = \dfrac{x^2 - 1}{x^2 - 4}$ **b.** $f_2(x) = |x^2 - 4|$ **c.** $f_3(x) = \csc x$

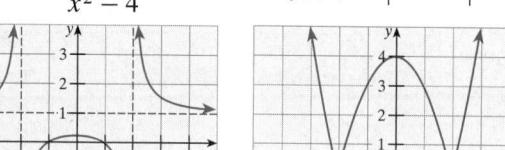 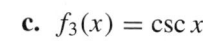 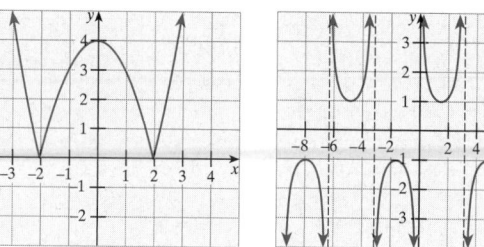

d. $f_4(x) = \sin \dfrac{1}{x}$ **e.** $f_5(x) = \begin{cases} x \sin \frac{1}{x} & \text{if } x \neq 0 \\ 0 & \text{if } x = 0 \end{cases}$

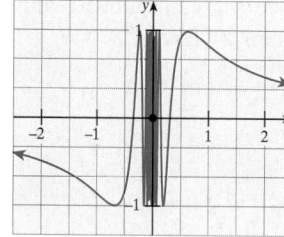 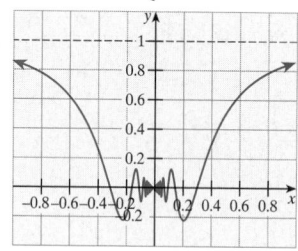

Solution

a. Function f_1 is not defined when $x^2 - 4 = 0$; that is, when $x = 2$ or $x = -2$. The function is continuous on $(-\infty, -2) \cup (-2, 2) \cup (2, \infty)$.

b. Function f_2 is continuous on $(-\infty, \infty)$.

c. The cosecant function is not defined at $x = n\pi$, n an integer. At all other points it is continuous.

d. Because $1/x$ is continuous except at $x = 0$ and the sine function is continuous everywhere, we need only check continuity at $x = 0$

$$\lim_{x \to 0} \sin \frac{1}{x} \quad \text{does not exist}$$

Therefore, $f(x) = \sin \frac{1}{x}$ is continuous on $(-\infty, 0) \cup (0, \infty)$.

e. It can be shown that since

$$-1 \le \sin \frac{1}{x} \le 1$$

then

$$-|x| \le x \sin \frac{1}{x} \le |x|, \quad x \ne 0$$

We can now use the squeeze rule. Because $\lim_{x \to 0} |x| = 0$ and $\lim_{x \to 0} (-|x|) = 0$, it follows that $\lim_{x \to 0} x \sin \frac{1}{x} = 0$. Because $f_5(0) = 0$ we see that f is continuous at $x = 0$ and therefore is continuous on $(-\infty, \infty)$. ■

Usually there are only a few points in the domain of a given function f where a discontinuity can occur. We use the term **suspicious point** for a number c where either

1. The defining rule for f changes.
2. Substitution of $x = c$ causes division by 0 in the function.

For Example 2, the suspicious points can be listed:

a. $\dfrac{x^2 - 1}{x^2 - 4}$ has suspicious points for division by zero when $x = 2$ and $x = -2$.

b. $|x^2 - 4| = x^2 - 4$ when $x^2 - 4 \ge 0$ and $|x^2 - 4| = 4 - x^2$ when $x^2 - 4 < 0$. This means the definition of the function changes when $x^2 - 4 = 0$, namely, when $x = 2$ and $x = -2$.

c. There are no suspicious points; we know the function cannot be continuous at places where the function is not defined.

d. $\sin \frac{1}{x}$ has a suspicious point when $x = 0$ (division by 0).

e. $x \sin \frac{1}{x}$ has a suspicious point when $x = 0$ (division by 0).

EXAMPLE 3 Checking continuity at suspicious points

Let $f(x) = \begin{cases} 3 - x & \text{if } -5 \le x < 2 \\ x - 2 & \text{if } 2 \le x < 5 \end{cases}$ and $g(x) = \begin{cases} 2 - x & \text{if } -5 \le x < 2 \\ x - 2 & \text{if } 2 \le x < 5 \end{cases}$.

Find the intervals on which f and g are continuous.

Solution

We find that the domain for both functions is $[-5, 5)$; the continuity theorem tells us both functions are continuous everywhere on that interval except possibly at the suspicious points. Consider the graphs of f and g as shown in Figure 2.20. Examining f, we see

$$\lim_{x \to 2^-} f(x) = \lim_{x \to 2^-} (3 - x) = 1 \quad \text{and} \quad \lim_{x \to 2^+} f(x) = \lim_{x \to 2^+} (x - 2) = 0$$

so $\lim_{x \to 2} f(x)$ does not exist and f is discontinuous at $x = 2$. Thus, f is continuous for $-5 \le x < 2$ and for $2 < x < 5$.

For g, the domain is also $-5 \le x < 5$, and again, the only suspicious point is $x = 2$. We have $g(2) = 0$ and

$$\lim_{x \to 2^-} g(x) = \lim_{x \to 2^-} (2 - x) = 0 \quad \text{and} \quad \lim_{x \to 2^+} g(x) = \lim_{x \to 2^+} (x - 2) = 0$$

Therefore, $\lim_{x \to 2} g(x) = 0 = g(2)$, and g is continuous at $x = 2$. Hence, g is continuous throughout the interval $[-5, 5)$. ■

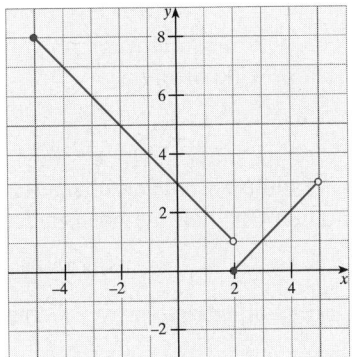

Although a graph is not part of the derivation, it can often be helpful in finding suspicious points. This is the graph of the function f.

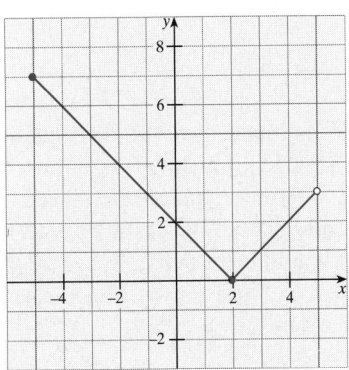

This is the graph of g. Does the graph reinforce our conclusions?

Figure 2.20 Graphs of f and g

THE INTERMEDIATE VALUE THEOREM

Intuitively, if f is continuous throughout an entire interval, its graph on that interval may be drawn "without the pencil leaving the paper." That is, if $f(x)$ varies continuously from $f(a)$ to $f(b)$ as x increases from a to b, then it must hit every number L between $f(a)$ and $f(b)$, as shown in Figure 2.21.

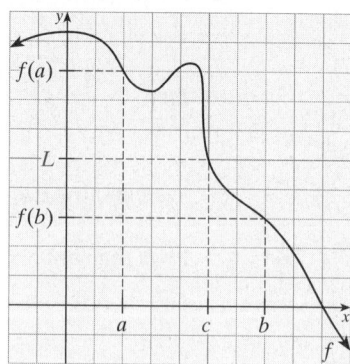

Figure 2.21   If L lies between $f(a)$ and $f(b)$, then $f(c) = L$ for some c between a and b.

To illustrate the property shown in Figure 2.21, suppose f is a function defined as the weight of a person at age x. If we assume that weight varies continuously with time, a person who weighs 50 pounds at age 6 and 120 pounds at age 15 must weigh 100 pounds at some time between ages 6 and 15.

This feature of continuous functions is known as the *intermediate value property*. A formal statement of this property is contained in the following theorem.

THEOREM 2.6   The intermediate value theorem

If f is a continuous function on the closed interval $[a, b]$ and L is some number strictly between $f(a)$ and $f(b)$, then there exists at least one number c on the open interval (a, b) such that $f(c) = L$.

Proof   This theorem is intuitively obvious, but it is not at all easy to prove. A proof may be found in most advanced calculus textbooks.   ❏

> ➡ **What This Says**   If f is a continuous function (with emphasis on the word *continuous*) on some *closed* interval $[a, b]$, then $f(x)$ must take on all values between $f(a)$ and $f(b)$.

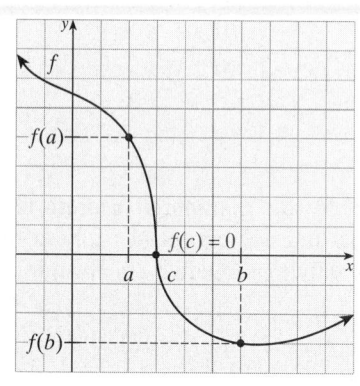

Figure 2.22   Because $f(a) > 0$ and $f(b) < 0$, then $f(c) = 0$ for some c between a and b.

The intermediate value theorem can be used to estimate roots of the equation $f(x) = 0$. Suppose $f(a) > 0$ and $f(b) < 0$, so the graph of f is above the x-axis at $x = a$ and below for $x = b$. Then, if f is continuous on the closed interval $[a, b]$, there must be a point $x = c$ between a and b where the graph crosses the x-axis, that is, where $f(c) = 0$. The same conclusion would be drawn if $f(a) < 0$ and $f(b) > 0$. The key is that $f(x)$ changes sign between $x = a$ and $x = b$. This is shown in Figure 2.22 and is summarized in the following theorem.

THEOREM 2.7   Root location theorem

If f is continuous on the closed interval $[a, b]$ and if $f(a)$ and $f(b)$ have opposite algebraic signs (one positive and the other negative), then $f(c) = 0$ for at least one number c on the open interval (a, b).

Proof   This follows directly from the intermediate value theorem (see Figure 2.22). The details of this proof are left as a problem.   ❏

EXAMPLE 4   Using the root location theorem

Show that $\cos x = x^3 - x$ has at least one solution on the interval $[\frac{\pi}{4}, \frac{\pi}{2}]$.

Solution

We can use a graphing utility to estimate the point of intersection, as shown in Figure 2.23.

We will now use the root location theorem to confirm the intersection point shown in Figure 2.23. By calculator, we estimate $c \approx 1.16$.

Notice that the function $f(x) = \cos x - x^3 + x$ is continuous on $[\frac{\pi}{4}, \frac{\pi}{2}]$. We find that

$$f(\tfrac{\pi}{4}) = \cos \tfrac{\pi}{4} - \left(\tfrac{\pi}{4}\right)^3 + \tfrac{\pi}{4} \approx 1.008$$

$$f(\tfrac{\pi}{2}) = \cos \tfrac{\pi}{2} - \left(\tfrac{\pi}{2}\right)^3 + \tfrac{\pi}{2} \approx -2.305$$

Therefore, by the root location theorem there is at least one number c on $(\frac{\pi}{4}, \frac{\pi}{2})$ for which $f(c) = 0$, and it follows that $\cos c = c^3 - c$.   ■

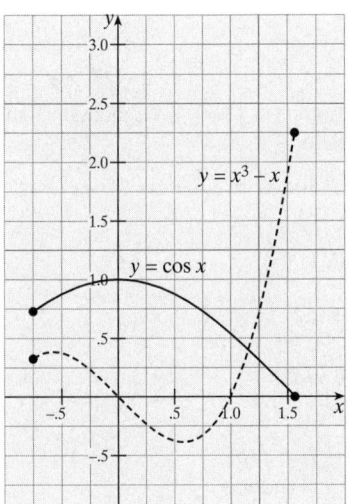

Figure 2.23 Estimate the point of intersection to be $x \approx 1.16$.

Since the definition of continuity involves the limit, formal proofs of continuity theorems can be given in terms of the ϵ-δ definition of limit. Here is an example.

EXAMPLE 5   Formal proof of the sum rule for continuity

Show that if f and g are continuous at $x = x_0$, then $f + g$ is also continuous at $x = x_0$.

Solution

The continuity of f and g at $x = x_0$ says that

$$\lim_{x \to x_0} f(x) = f(x_0) \quad \text{and} \quad \lim_{x \to x_0} g(x) = g(x_0)$$

This means that if $\epsilon > 0$ is given, there exist numbers δ_1 and δ_2 such that

$$|f(x) - f(x_0)| < \frac{\epsilon}{2} \quad \text{whenever} \quad 0 < |x - x_0| < \delta_1$$

and

$$|g(x) - g(x_0)| < \frac{\epsilon}{2} \quad \text{whenever} \quad 0 < |x - x_0| < \delta_2$$

Let δ be the smaller of δ_1 and δ_2; that is, $\delta = \min(\delta_1, \delta_2)$. Then

$$0 < |x - x_0| < \delta_1 \quad \text{and} \quad 0 < |x - x_0| < \delta_2$$

must both be true whenever $0 < |x - x_0| < \delta$ so that (by the triangle inequality)

$$\begin{aligned}
|[f(x) + g(x)] - [f(x_0) + g(x_0)]| &= |[f(x) - f(x_0)] + [g(x) - g(x_0)]| \\
&\leq |f(x) - f(x_0)| + |g(x) - g(x_0)| \\
&< \frac{\epsilon}{2} + \frac{\epsilon}{2} = \epsilon
\end{aligned}$$

Thus, $|(f + g)(x) - (f + g)(x_0)| < \epsilon$ whenever $0 < |x - x_0| < \delta$, and it follows from the definition of limit that

$$\lim_{x \to x_0} [f(x) + g(x)] = f(x_0) + g(x_0)$$

In other words, $f + g$ is continuous at $x = x_0$, as claimed.   ■

2.3 PROBLEM SET

Ⓐ *Which of the functions described in Problems 1–4 represent continuous functions? State the domain, if possible, for each example.*

1. the temperature on a specific day at a given location considered as a function of time

2. the humidity on a specific day at a given location considered as a function of time

3. the charges for a taxi ride across town considered as a function of mileage

4. the charges to mail a package as a function of its weight

Identify all suspicious points and determine all points of discontinuity in Problems 5–14.

5. $f(x) = x^3 - 7x + 3$

6. $f(x) = \dfrac{3x + 5}{2x - 1}$

7. $f(x) = \dfrac{3x}{x^2 - x}$

8. $f(t) = 3 - (5 + 2t)^3$

9. $h(x) = \sqrt{x} + \dfrac{3}{x}$

10. $f(u) = \sqrt[3]{u^2 - 1}$

11. $f(x) = \begin{cases} x^2 - 2 & \text{if } x > 1 \\ 2x - 3 & \text{if } x \le 1 \end{cases}$

12. $g(t) = \begin{cases} 3t + 2 & \text{if } t \le 1 \\ 5 & \text{if } 1 < t \le 3 \\ 3t^2 - 1 & \text{if } t > 3 \end{cases}$

13. $f(x) = 3\tan x - 5\sin x \cos x$

14. $g(x) = \dfrac{\cot x}{\sin x - \cos x}$

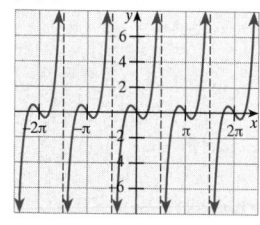 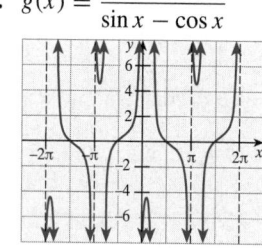

In Problems 15–20, the given function is defined for all $x > 0$, except at $x = 2$. In each case, find the value that should be assigned to $f(2)$, if any, to guarantee that f will be continuous at 2.

15. $f(x) = \dfrac{x^2 - x - 2}{x - 2}$

16. $f(x) = \sqrt{\dfrac{x^2 - 4}{x - 2}}$

17. $f(x) = \dfrac{\sin(\pi x)}{x - 2}$

18. $f(x) = \dfrac{\cos \frac{\pi}{x}}{x - 2}$

19. $f(x) = \begin{cases} 2x + 5 & \text{if } x > 2 \\ 15 - x^2 & \text{if } x < 2 \end{cases}$

20. $f(x) = \dfrac{\frac{1}{x} - 1}{x - 2}$

In Problems 21–25, determine whether or not the given function is continuous on the prescribed interval.

21. **a.** $f(x) = \dfrac{1}{x}$ on $[1, 2]$ **b.** $f(x) = \dfrac{1}{x}$ on $[0, 1]$

22. $f(x) = \begin{cases} x^2 & \text{if } 0 \le x < 2 \\ 3x + 1 & \text{if } 2 \le x < 5 \end{cases}$

23. $g(t) = \begin{cases} 15 - t^2 & \text{if } -3 < t \le 0 \\ 2t & \text{if } 0 < t \le 1 \end{cases}$

24. $f(x) = x \sin x$ on $(0, \pi)$

25. $f(x) = \dfrac{\cos x - 1}{x}$ on $[-\pi, \pi]$

Ⓑ 26. Let $f(x) = \begin{cases} x & \text{if } x \ne 0 \\ 2 & \text{if } x = 0 \end{cases}$ and $g(x) = \begin{cases} 3x & \text{if } x \ne 0 \\ -2 & \text{if } x = 0 \end{cases}$

Show that $f + g$ is continuous at $x = 0$ even though f and g are both discontinuous there.

In Problems 27–32, show that the given equation has at least one solution on the indicated interval.

27. $\sqrt[3]{x} = x^2 + 2x - 1$ on $(0, 1)$

28. $\dfrac{1}{x + 1} = x^2 - x - 1$ on $(1, 2)$

29. $\sqrt[3]{x - 8} + 9x^{2/3} = 29$ on $(0, 8)$

30. $\tan x = 2x^2 - 1$ on $\left(-\frac{\pi}{4}, 0\right)$

31. $\cos x - \sin x = x$ on $\left(0, \frac{\pi}{2}\right)$

32. $\cos x = x^2 - 1$ on $(0, \pi)$

33. Let $f(x) = \begin{cases} x^2 & \text{if } x > 2 \\ x + 1 & \text{if } x \le 2 \end{cases}$

Show that f is continuous from the left at 2, but not from the right.

34. Find constants a and b such that $f(2) + 3 = f(0)$ and f is continuous at $x = 1$.

$$f(x) = \begin{cases} ax + b & \text{if } x > 1 \\ 3 & \text{if } x = 1 \\ x^2 - 4x + b + 3 & \text{if } x < 1 \end{cases}$$

35. **Interpretation Problem** Use the intermediate value theorem to explain why the hands of a clock coincide at least once every hour.

36. **Interpretation Problem** The graph shown in Figure 2.24 models how the growth rate of a bacterial colony changes with temperature.*

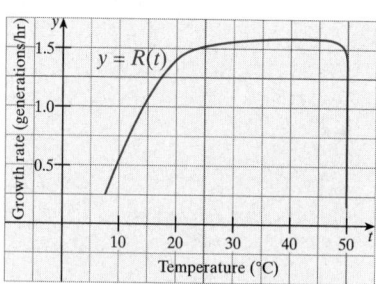

Figure 2.24 Growth rate of a bacterial colony

---

*Michael D. La Grega, Philip L. Buckingham, and Jeffery C. Evans, *Hazardous Waste Management*, New York: McGraw-Hill, 1994, pp. 565–566.

What happens when the temperature reaches 45°C? Does it make sense to compute $\lim_{t \to 50} R(t)$? Write a paragraph describing how temperature affects the growth rate of a species.

37. A fish swims upstream at a constant speed v relative to the water, which in turn flows at a constant speed v_w $(v_w < v)$ relative to the ground. The energy expended by the fish in traveling to a point upstream is given by

$$E(v) = \frac{Cv^k}{v - v_w}$$

where $C > 0$ is a physical constant and $k > 0$ is a number that depends on the type of fish.*

a. Compute $\lim_{v \to v_w} E(v)$. Interpret your result in words.

b. What happens to $E(v)$ as $v \to +\infty$? Interpret your result in words.

38. The population (in thousands) of a colony of bacteria t minutes after the introduction of a toxin is given by the function

$$P(t) = \begin{cases} t^2 + 1 & \text{if } 0 \leq t < 5 \\ -8t + 66 & \text{if } t \geq 5 \end{cases}$$

a. When does the colony die out?

b. Show that at some time between $t = 2$ and $t = 7$, the population is 9,000.

In Problems 39–44, find constants a and b so that the given function will be continuous for all x.

39. $f(x) = \begin{cases} ax + 3 & \text{if } x > 5 \\ 8 & \text{if } x = 5 \\ x^2 + bx + 1 & \text{if } x < 5 \end{cases}$

40. $f(x) = \begin{cases} \dfrac{ax - 4}{x - 2} & \text{if } x \neq 2 \\ b & \text{if } x = 2 \end{cases}$

41. $f(x) = \begin{cases} \dfrac{\sqrt{x} - a}{x - 1} & \text{if } x > 1 \\ b & \text{if } x \leq 1 \end{cases}$

42. $f(x) = \begin{cases} 2\sin(a\cos^{-1} x) & \text{if } x > 0 \\ \sqrt{3} & \text{if } x = 0 \\ ax + b & \text{if } x < 0 \end{cases}$

43. $g(x) = \begin{cases} \dfrac{\sin ax}{x} & \text{if } x < 0 \\ 5 & \text{if } x = 0 \\ x + b & \text{if } x > 0 \end{cases}$

44. $f(x) = \begin{cases} \dfrac{\tan ax}{\tan bx} & \text{if } x < 0 \\ 4 & \text{if } x = 0 \\ ax + b & \text{if } x > 0 \end{cases}$

45. HISTORICAL QUEST The first modern formulation of the notion of continuity appeared in a pamphlet published by Bernard Bolzano, a Czechoslovakian priest whose mathematical work was, for the most part, overlooked by his contemporaries. In explaining the concept of continuity, Bolzano said that one must understand the phrase, "A function $f(x)$ (that) varies according to the law of continuity for all values of x which lie inside or outside certain limits, is nothing other than this: If x is any such value, the difference

BERNARD BOLZANO
1781–1848

$$f(x + \omega) - f(x)$$

can be made smaller than any given quantity, if one makes ω as small as one wishes."

In his book, *Cours d'Analyse*, Cauchy (see Historical Quest Problem 49, Section 2.1) introduces the concept of continuity for a function defined on an interval in essentially the same way as Bolzano. In this book Cauchy points out that the continuity of many functions is easily verified. As an example, he argues that $\sin x$ is continuous on every interval because "the numerical value of $\sin \frac{1}{2}\alpha$, and consequently that of the difference

$$\sin(x + \alpha) - \sin x = 2\sin\tfrac{1}{2}\alpha \cos(x + \tfrac{1}{2}\alpha)$$

decreases indefinitely with that of α."[†]

Show that $\sin x$ is continuous, and also show that the given expression decreases as claimed by Cauchy.

We conclude this Historical Quest by noting that the formal ϵ-δ definition of limits and continuity that we use today was first done by Karl Weierstrass (1815–1897), a German secondary school teacher who did his research at night. The historian David Burton describes Weierstrass as "the world's greatest analyst during the last third of the nineteenth century—the father of modern analysis."

46. Let f be a continuous function and suppose that $f(a)$ and $f(b)$ have opposite signs. The root location theorem tells us that at least one root of $f(x) = 0$ lies between $x = a$ and $x = b$.

a. Let $c = (a + b)/2$ be the midpoint of the interval $[a, b]$. Explain how the root location theorem can be used to determine whether the root lies in $[a, c]$ or in $[c, b]$. Does anything special have to be said about the case where the interval $[a, b]$ contains more than one root?

b. Based on your observation in part **a**, describe a procedure for approximating a root of $f(x) = 0$ more and more accurately. This is called the *bisection method* for root location.

c. Apply the bisection method to locate at least one root of $x^3 + x - 1 = 0$ on $[0, 1]$. Check your answer using your calculator.

47. Apply the bisection method (see Problem 46) to locate at least one root of each of the given equations, and then check your answer using your calculator.

a. $\sin x + \cos x = x$ on $[0, \frac{\pi}{2}]$

b. $\cos(x + 1) = \sin(x - 1)$ on $[0, 1]$

---

*E. Batschelet, *Introduction to Mathematics for Life Scientists*, 2nd ed., New York: Springer-Verlag, 1976, p. 280.

[†]A. L. Cauchy, *Cours d'Analyse de l'Ecole Royale Polytechnique, Oeuvres*, Ser. 2, Vol. 3. Paris: Gauthier-Villars, 1897, p. 44.

48. Counterexample Problem Find functions f and g such that f is discontinuous at $x = 1$ but fg is continuous there.

49. Counterexample Problem Give an example of a function defined for all real numbers that is continuous at only one point.

50. Prove the root location theorem, assuming the intermediate value theorem.

51. Show that f is continuous at c if and only if it is both continuous from the right and continuous from the left at c.

52. Show that if f and g are both continuous at $x = c$ and $g(c) \neq 0$, then f/g must also be continuous there.

53. Let $u(x) = x$ and $f(x) = \begin{cases} 0 & \text{if } x \neq 0 \\ 1 & \text{if } x = 0 \end{cases}$.

Show that $\lim_{x \to 0} f[u(x)] \neq f\left[\lim_{x \to 0} u(x)\right]$.

2.4   Exponential and Logarithmic Functions

IN THIS SECTION   exponential functions, logarithmic functions, natural exponential and logarithmic functions, continuous compounding of interest

In Chapter 1, we introduced polynomial and rational functions, power functions, trigonometric functions, and inverse trigonometric functions. In this section, we will complete our list of the elementary functions typically used in calculus by using limits to introduce exponential functions and their inverses, the logarithmic functions.

EXPONENTIAL FUNCTIONS

Recall that if n is a natural number, then

$$b^n = \underbrace{b \cdot b \cdot b \cdot \cdots \cdot b}_{n \text{ factors}}$$

If $b \neq 0$, then $b^0 = 1$, $b^{-n} = \dfrac{1}{b^n}$, and furthermore, if $b > 0$, then $b^{1/n} = \sqrt[n]{b}$. Also, if m and n are any integers, and m/n is a reduced fraction, then

$$b^{m/n} = (b^{1/n})^m$$

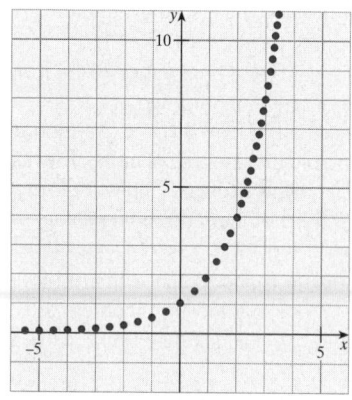

Figure 2.25 Graph of $y = 2^x$ for rational exponents

This definition tells us what b^x means for rational values of x. However, we now wish to enlarge the domain of x to include all real numbers. To get a feeling for what is involved in this problem, let us examine the special case where $b = 2$. In Figure 2.25, we have plotted several points with coordinates $(r, 2^r)$, where r is a rational number. We must now attach meaning to b^x if x is not a rational number by filling those holes or spaces to make the graph continuous for all x. We use the following fundamental fact about the real number system, called the **completeness property**.

For any real number x, there exist rational numbers r_n such that

$$x = \lim_{n \to \infty} r_n$$

which means that for any number $\epsilon > 0$, there exists a number N such that $|x - r_n| < \epsilon$ whenever $n > N$.

Another way of expressing the completeness property is to say that *each real number x can be approximated to any degree of accuracy by a rational number.* Using the completeness property, we can now define an exponential function.

Exponential Function

> Let x be a real number, and let r_n be a sequence of rational numbers such that $x = \lim\limits_{n \to \infty} r_n$. Then the **exponential function** with base $b > 0$ $(b \neq 1)$ is given by
>
> $$b^x = \lim_{n \to \infty} b^{r_n}$$

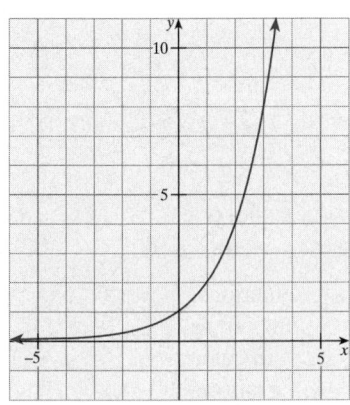

Figure 2.26 Graph of $y = 2^x$

For example, the number $\sqrt{3}$ has an infinite decimal representation

$$\sqrt{3} \approx 1.732050808 \cdots$$

which means that $\sqrt{3}$ can be approximated to any desired degree of accuracy by members of the sequence of rational numbers

$$r_1 = 1, \ r_2 = 1.7, \ r_3 = 1.73, \ r_4 = 1.732, \ r_5 = 1.7320, \ r_6 = 1.73205, \ \ldots$$

Therefore, the exponential number $2^{\sqrt{3}}$ is given by the limit of the sequence of numbers

$$2^1, \ 2^{1.7}, \ 2^{1.73}, \ 2^{1.732}, \ 2^{1.7320}, \ 2^{1.73205}, \ldots$$

In this fashion, we can fill the holes and gaps shown in Figure 2.25 to obtain the continuous graph of $y = 2^x$, as shown in Figure 2.26.

The shape of the graph of $y = b^x$ for any $b > 1$ is essentially the same as that of $y = 2^x$. The graph of $y = b^x$ for a typical base $b > 1$ is shown in Figure 2.27a and is rising (when viewed from left to right). For a base b where $0 < b < 1$ the graph is falling, as shown in Figure 2.27b.

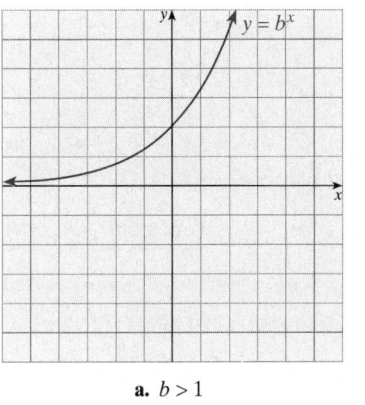
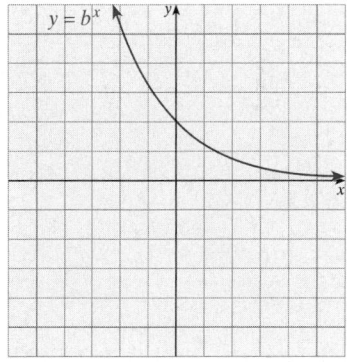

a. $b > 1$ **b.** $0 < b < 1$

Figure 2.27 Graph of $y = b^x$

We summarize the basic properties of exponential functions with the following theorem. Many of these properties for bases with rational exponents should be familiar from previous courses.

THEOREM 2.8 Properties of exponential functions

Let x, y be real numbers, a and b positive real numbers.

Equality rule	If $b \neq 1$, then $b^x = b^y$ if and only if $x = y$.
Inequality rules	If $x > y$ and $b > 1$, then $b^x > b^y$.
	If $x > y$ and $0 < b < 1$, then $b^x < b^y$.
Product rule	$b^x b^y = b^{x+y}$
Quotient rule	$\dfrac{b^x}{b^y} = b^{x-y}$
Power rules	$(b^x)^y = b^{xy}$; $(ab)^x = a^x b^x$; $\left(\dfrac{a}{b}\right)^x = \dfrac{a^x}{b^x}$

Graphical Properties

The function $y = b^x$ is continuous for all x. Furthermore, its graph is always above the x-axis ($b^x > 0$), and is always rising for $b > 1$ and always falling for $0 < b < 1$.

Several parts of this theorem are used in the following example.

EXAMPLE 1   Exponential equations

Solve each of the following exponential equations.

a. $2^{x^2+3} = 16$ **b.** $2^x 3^{x+1} = 108$ **c.** $(\sqrt{2})^{x^2} = \dfrac{8^x}{4}$

Solution

a. $2^{x^2+3} = 16$

$2^{x^2+3} = 2^4$ Write 16 as 2^4 so that the equality rule can be used.

$x^2 + 3 = 4$,   or $x = \pm 1$

b. $2^x 3^{x+1} = 108$

$2^x 3^x 3 = 3 \cdot 36$ Product rule

$(2 \cdot 3)^x = 36$ Divide both sides by 3 and then use the power rule.

$6^x = 6^2$

$x = 2$ Equality rule

c. $(\sqrt{2})^{x^2} = \dfrac{8^x}{4}$

$(2^{1/2})^{x^2} = \dfrac{(2^3)^x}{2^2}$

$2^{x^2/2} = 2^{3x-2}$

$\dfrac{x^2}{2} = 3x - 2$ Equality rule

$x^2 - 6x + 4 = 0$

$x = \dfrac{6 \pm \sqrt{36 - 4(1)(4)}}{2} = 3 \pm \sqrt{5}$ ∎

LOGARITHMIC FUNCTIONS

Since the exponential function $y = b^x$ for $b > 0$, $b \neq 1$ is monotonic (its graph is either always rising for all x or always falling), it must have an inverse that is itself monotonic. This inverse function is called the **logarithm of x to the base b**. Here is a definition, with some notation.

Logarithmic Function

If $b > 0$ and $b \neq 1$, the **logarithm of x to the base b** is the function $y = \log_b x$ that satisfies $b^y = x$; that is,

$$y = \log_b x \quad \text{means} \quad b^y = x$$

➧ **What This Says**   It is useful to think of a logarithm as an exponent. That is, consider the following sequence of interpretations:

$$y = \log_b x$$

y is the logarithm to the base b of x.

y is the **exponent to the base b** that gives x.

$$b^y = x$$

Notice that $y = \log_b x$ is defined only for $x > 0$ because $b^y > 0$ for all y. We have sketched the graph of $y = \log_b x$ for $b > 1$ in Figure 2.28 by reflecting the graph of $y = b^x$ in the line $y = x$.

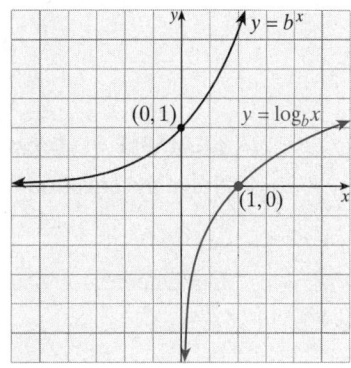

Figure 2.28 The graph of $y = \log_b x$ for $b > 1$

Because $y = b^x$ is a continuous, increasing function that satisfies $b^x > 0$ for all x, $\log_b x$ must also be continuous and increasing, and its graph must lie entirely to the right of the y-axis.

Also, because $b^0 = 1$ and $b^1 = b$, we have

$$\log_b 1 = 0 \quad \text{and} \quad \log_b b = 1$$

so $(1, 0)$ and $(b, 1)$ lie on the logarithmic curve.

Theorem 2.9 lists several general properties of logarithms.

WARNING Remember that $\log_b x$ is defined only for $x > 0$. Any undefined values for $\log_b x$ are excluded.

THEOREM 2.9 Basic properties of logarithmic functions

Assume $b > 0$ and $b \neq 1$.

Equality rule	$\log_b x = \log_b y$ if and only if $x = y$.
Inequality rules	If $x > y$ and $b > 1$, then $\log_b x > \log_b y$.
	If $x > y$ and $0 < b < 1$, then $\log_b x < \log_b y$.
Product rule	$\log_b(xy) = \log_b x + \log_b y$
Quotient rule	$\log_b\left(\dfrac{x}{y}\right) = \log_b x - \log_b y$
Power rule	$\log_b x^p = p \log_b x$ for any real number p
Inversion rules	$b^{\log_b x} = x$ and $\log_b b^x = x$
Special values	$\log_b b = 1$ and $\log_b 1 = 0$

Proof Each part of this theorem can be derived by using the definition of the logarithm in conjunction with a suitable property of exponentials. (See Problems 73–75.) ❑

EXAMPLE 2 Evaluating a logarithmic expression

Evaluate $\log_2\left(\frac{1}{8}\right) + \log_2 128$.

Solution

Using Theorem 2.9, we find that

$$\log_2\left(\tfrac{1}{8}\right) + \log_2 128 = \log_2(2)^{-3} + \log_2 2^7$$
$$= \log_2[2^{-3}(2^7)] = \log_2 2^4 = 4\log_2 2 = 4(1) = 4$$

What we have shown here is longer than what you would do in your work, which would probably be shortened as follows:

$$\log_2 \left(\tfrac{1}{8}\right) + \log_2 128 = \log_2 16 \qquad \text{Because } \left(\tfrac{1}{8}\right)(128) = 16$$
$$= 4 \qquad \text{Because 4 is the exponent on 2 that yields 16}$$

■

EXAMPLE 3 Logarithmic equation

Solve the equation $\log_3(2x + 1) - 2\log_3(x - 3) = 2$.

Solution

Use Theorem 2.9, and remember that both $2x + 1 > 0$ and $x - 3 > 0$.

$$\log_3(2x + 1) - 2\log_3(x - 3) = 2$$
$$\log_3(2x + 1) - \log_3(x - 3)^2 = 2$$
$$\log_3 \frac{2x + 1}{(x - 3)^2} = 2$$
$$3^2 = \frac{2x + 1}{(x - 3)^2}$$
$$9(x - 3)^2 = 2x + 1$$
$$9x^2 - 56x + 80 = 0$$
$$(x - 4)(9x - 20) = 0$$
$$x = 4, \tfrac{20}{9}$$

Notice that $x - 3 < 0$ if $x = \tfrac{20}{9}$. The given logarithmic equation has only $x = 4$ as a solution because we cannot take the logarithm of a negative number. ■

NATURAL EXPONENTIAL AND LOGARITHMIC FUNCTIONS

In elementary algebra you probably studied logarithms to base 10 or possibly to base 2, but in calculus, it turns out to be convenient to use the number e defined by the limit*

$$e = \lim_{n \to \infty} \left(1 + \frac{1}{n}\right)^n$$

which can be thought of as the number approached by expressions of the form $(1 + \frac{1}{n})^n$ as n grows large without bound.

"But wait," you may be thinking, "as n grows large without bound, the expression $1 + 1/n$ tends toward 1 and since $1^n = 1$ for all n, no matter how large the number n, e must equal 1." However, the limit process does not work that way, and as you can see from Table 2.1, e is a number slightly less than 3. In fact, to twelve decimal places,

$$e \approx 2.71828182845 \cdots$$

The letter e was chosen to represent this number in honor of the great Swiss mathematician Leonhard Euler (1707–1783), who discovered many of its special properties and investigated applications in which e plays a vital role.

The number e is called the **natural exponential base** because many formulas in calculus assume an especially simple or "natural" form when expressed in terms of exponentials or logarithms to the base e. For this reason, e^x is called the **natural exponential function,** and $\log_e x$ is the **natural logarithm.** We will have more to say about what makes these functions "natural" in Chapter 3. Here is some special notation and terminology associated with these functions.

WARNING You must be careful when using software to reach conclusions in calculus. For example, on most software or calculators, if you input

$$\left(1 + \frac{1}{10^{20}}\right)^{10^{20}}$$

the output is 1 (which, of course, is incorrect). We know (from the definition of e) that $\lim_{n \to \infty}(1 + \frac{1}{n})^n = e > 1$.

```
Y₁ ⊟ (1+1/X)^X
```

X	Y₁
1	2
2	2.25
3	2.3704
4	2.4414
5	2.4883
10	2.5937
50	2.6916
100	2.7048
1000	2.7169
5000	2.718
10000	2.7181
1E6	2.7183
X=1E7	2.7183

TABLE 2.1 Calculator approximations of e

---

*Limits such as $n \to \infty$ are called "limits at infinity" and will be discussed in detail in Chapter 4.

EXP NOTATION

The natural exponential function e^x is sometimes denoted by $\exp(x)$.

COMMON LOGARITHM

The **common logarithm**, $\log_{10} x$, is denoted by $\log x$.

NATURAL LOGARITHM

The **natural logarithm**, $\log_e x$, is denoted by $\ln x$.
($\ln x$ is pronounced "ell n x" or "lawn x.")

The "exp" notation for the natural exponential function is especially useful for representing composite functions. For instance, the awkward expression

$$e^{3x^2 - 2\sin x + 8}$$

can be expressed more compactly as

$$\exp(3x^2 - 2\sin x + 8)$$

The following theorem summarizes the key properties of natural exponential and logarithmic functions.

THEOREM 2.10   Basic properties of the natural logarithm

a. $\ln 1 = 0$ **b.** $\ln e = 1$

c. $e^{\ln x} = x$ for all $x > 0$ **d.** $\ln e^y = y$ for all y

e. $b^x = e^{x \ln b}$ for any $b > 0$ $(b \neq 1)$

Proof   Parts **a** and **b** follow immediately from the definitions of $\ln x$ and e^x. Parts **c** and **d** are just the inversion rules for base e.

We show the proof of part **e**.

$$e^{x \ln b} = e^{\ln b^x} \qquad \text{Power rule (Theorem 2.9)}$$

$$= b^x \qquad\qquad \text{Property of natural log (Theorem 2.10c)} \qquad \square$$

WARNING   If you are using a software package such as *Mathematica*, *Derive*, or *Maple*, sometimes referred to as CAS (Computer Algebra System), be careful about the notation. Some versions do not distinguish between $\log x$ (common logarithm) and $\ln x$ (natural logarithm). All logarithms on these versions are assumed to be natural logarithms, so to evaluate a common logarithm requires using the change-of-base theorem.

On calculators, there are usually two logarithm keys, $\boxed{\text{LOG}}$ and $\boxed{\text{LN}}$. For other logarithms, you will need the useful conversion formula contained in the following theorem.

THEOREM 2.11   Change-of-base theorem

$$\log_b x = \frac{\ln x}{\ln b} \quad \text{for any } b > 0 \; (b \neq 1)$$

Proof   Let $y = \log_b x$. Then

$$b^y = x \qquad\qquad \text{Definition of logarithm}$$

$$\ln b^y = \ln x \qquad\quad \text{Equality rule of logarithms}$$

$$y \ln b = \ln x \qquad\quad \text{Power rule of logarithms}$$

$$y = \frac{\ln x}{\ln b} \qquad\quad \text{Divide both sides by } \ln b. \qquad \square$$

EXAMPLE 4   Solving an exponential equation using the change-of-base theorem

Solve $6^x = 200$.

Solution

$$6^x = 200$$

$$x = \log_6 200 \qquad \textit{Definition of exponent}$$

$$= \frac{\ln 200}{\ln 6} \qquad \textit{Change-of-base theorem}$$

$$\approx 2.957047225 \qquad \textit{Approximate with a calculator.}$$ ■

EXAMPLE 5   Finding a velocity

An object moves along a straight line in such a way that after t seconds, its velocity is given by

$$v(t) = 10 \log_5 t + 3 \log_2 t$$

ft/s. How long will it take for the velocity to reach 20 ft/s?

Solution

We want to solve the equation

$$10 \log_5 t + 3 \log_2 t = 20$$

$$10 \frac{\ln t}{\ln 5} + 3 \frac{\ln t}{\ln 2} = 20 \qquad \textit{Change-of-base formula}$$

$$\left(\frac{10}{\ln 5} + \frac{3}{\ln 2} \right) \ln t = 20 \qquad \textit{Factor.}$$

$$\ln t = 20 \left(\frac{10}{\ln 5} + \frac{3}{\ln 2} \right)^{-1} \approx 1.89727$$

$$t \approx e^{1.89727} \approx 6.6677$$

Thus, it takes about 6.67 seconds for the velocity to reach 20 ft/s.   ■

EXAMPLE 6   Changing an exponential from base b to base e

Change 10^{2x} to an exponential to the natural base.

Solution

We wish to find N for

$$10^{2x} = e^N$$

$$\ln 10^{2x} = \ln e^N \qquad \textit{Log of both sides}$$

$$2x \ln 10 = N \ln e \qquad \textit{Power rule of logarithms}$$

$$2x \ln 10 = N \qquad \textit{ln } e = 1$$

Thus, $10^{2x} = e^{2x \ln 10}$.   ■

EXAMPLE 7   Solving an exponential equation with base e

Solve $\frac{1}{2} = e^{-0.000425t}$.

Solution

We have

$$\frac{1}{2} = e^{-0.000425t}$$

$$-0.000425t = \ln 0.5 \qquad \begin{array}{l} \textit{Remember that } -0.000425t \textit{ is the} \\ \textit{exponent on base } e \textit{ that equals } \frac{1}{2} = 0.5 \end{array}$$

$$t = \frac{\ln 0.5}{-0.000425} \approx 1630.934542$$ ■

EXAMPLE 8   Exponential growth

A biological colony grows in such a way that at time t (in minutes), the population is

$$P(t) = P_0 e^{kt}$$

where P_0 is the initial population and k is a positive constant. Suppose the colony begins with 5,000 individuals and contains a population of 7,000 after 20 min. Find k and determine the population (rounded to the nearest hundred individuals) after 30 min.

Solution

Because $P_0 = 5,000$, the population after t minutes will be

$$P(t) = 5,000 e^{kt}$$

In particular, because the population is 7,000 after 20 min,

$$P(20) = 5,000 e^{k(20)}$$
$$7,000 = 5,000 e^{20k}$$
$$\tfrac{7}{5} = e^{20k}$$
$$20k = \ln(\tfrac{7}{5})$$
$$k = \tfrac{1}{20} \ln(\tfrac{7}{5})$$
$$\approx 0.0168236$$

Finally, to determine the population after 30 min, substitute this value for k to find

$$P(30) = 5,000 e^{30k}$$
$$\approx 8,282.5117$$

The expected population is approximately $8,300$.   ∎

CONTINUOUS COMPOUNDING OF INTEREST

One reason e is called the "natural" exponential base is that many natural growth phenomena can be described in terms of e^x. As an illustration of this fact, we close this section by showing how e^x can be used to describe the accounting procedure called *continuous compounding of interest*.

Suppose a sum of money is invested and the interest is compounded once during a particular period. If P is the initial investment (the **present value** or **principal**) and i is the **interest rate** during the period, then the **future value** (in dollars), A, after the interest is added will be

$$A = \underset{\uparrow}{P} + \underset{\uparrow}{Pi} = P(1 + i)$$
$$\text{principal} \quad \text{interest}$$

Thus, to compute the balance at the end of an interest period, we multiply the balance at the beginning of the period by the expression $1 + i$.

Interest is usually compounded more than once a year. The interest added to the account during one period will itself earn interest during subsequent periods. If the annual interest rate is r and the interest is compounded n times per year, then the year is divided into n equal interest periods and the interest rate during each such period is $i = \frac{r}{n}$. To compute the balance at the end of any period, you multiply the balance at the beginning of that period by the expression $1 + \frac{r}{n}$, so the balance at the end of the first period is

$$A_1 = P\left(1 + \frac{r}{n}\right)$$

At the end of the second period, the balance is

$$A_2 = A_1\left(1 + \frac{r}{n}\right) = \left[P\left(1 + \frac{r}{n}\right)\right]\left(1 + \frac{r}{n}\right) = P\left(1 + \frac{r}{n}\right)^2$$

At the end of the third period, the balance is

$$A_3 = A_2\left(1 + \frac{r}{n}\right) = \left[P\left(1 + \frac{r}{n}\right)^2\right]\left(1 + \frac{r}{n}\right) = P\left(1 + \frac{r}{n}\right)^3$$

and so on. At the end of t years, the interest has been compounded nt times, and the future value is

$$A(t) = P\left(1 + \frac{r}{n}\right)^{nt}$$

The first two graphs in Figure 2.29 show how an amount of money in an account over a one-year period of time grows, first with quarterly compounding and then with monthly compounding. Notice that these are "step" graphs, with jumps occurring at the end of each compounding period.

a. Quarterly compounding   **b.** Monthly compounding   **c.** Continuous compounding

Figure 2.29   The growth of an account over a one-year period with different compounding frequencies

With continuous compounding, we compound interest not quarterly, or monthly, or daily, or even every second, but *instantaneously*, so that the future amount of money A in the account grows continuously, as shown in Figure 2.29c. In other words, for a one-year period we compute A as the limiting value of

$$P\left(1 + \frac{r}{n}\right)^n$$

as the number of compounding periods n grows without bound. We denote by $A(t)$, the future value after t years, as with the definition of e, by the limit notation $n \to \infty$:

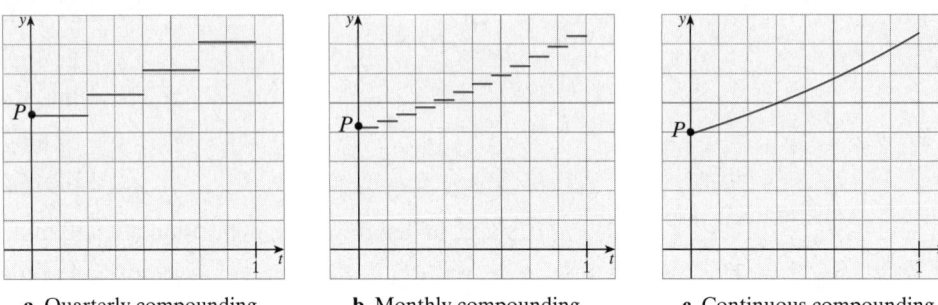

$$A(t) = \lim_{n \to \infty} P\left(1 + \frac{r}{n}\right)^{nt} \qquad \text{Let } k = \frac{n}{r}, \text{ so that } krt = nt \text{ and } \frac{r}{n} = \frac{1}{k};$$
$$\text{also } k \to \infty \text{ as } n \to \infty.$$

$$= \lim_{k \to \infty} P\left(1 + \frac{1}{k}\right)^{krt}$$

$$= \lim_{k \to \infty} P\left[\left(1 + \frac{1}{k}\right)^k\right]^{rt}$$

$$= P\left[\lim_{k \to \infty}\left(1 + \frac{1}{k}\right)^k\right]^{rt} \qquad \text{Scalar rule for limits}$$

$$= Pe^{rt} \qquad \text{Definition of } e$$

These observations are now summarized.

> **Future Value**
>
> If P dollars are compounded n times per year at an annual rate r, then the future value after t years is given by
>
> $$A(t) = P\left(1 + \frac{r}{n}\right)^{nt}$$
>
> and if the compounding is continuous, the future value is
>
> $$A(t) = Pe^{rt}$$

EXAMPLE 9 Continuous compounding of interest

If $12,000 is invested for 5 years at 18%, find the future value at the end of 5 years if interest is compounded

a. monthly.   **b.** continuously.

c. If the interest is compounded continuously, how long will it take for the money to double?

Solution

$P = \$12,000$; $t = 5$; and $r = 18\% = 0.18$ are given.

a. $n = 12$; $A = P\left(1 + \frac{r}{n}\right)^{nt} = \$12,000\left(1 + \frac{0.18}{12}\right)^{12.5} \approx \$29,318.64$

b. $A = \$12,000e^{0.18(5)} \approx \$29,515.24$

c. The account doubles when $A(t) = 2P = \$24,000$; that is, when

$$12,000e^{0.18t} = 24,000$$

$$e^{0.18t} = 2$$

$$0.18t = \ln 2 \qquad \text{Definition of logarithm}$$

$$t = \frac{\ln 2}{0.18} \approx 3.851$$

This is about 3 years and 10 months. ∎

2.4 PROBLEM SET

A *Sketch the graph of the functions in Problems 1–4.*

1. $y = 3^x$

2. $y = 4^{-x}$

3. $y = -e^{-x}$

4. $y = -e^x$

Evaluate the expressions (with calculator accuracy) in Problems 5–12.

5. $32^{2/5} + 9^{3/2}$

6. $(1 + 4^{3/2})^{-1/2}$

7. $e^3 e^{2.3}$

8. $\dfrac{(e^{1.3})^2}{e^{1.3} + \sqrt{e^{-1.4}}}$

9. $5,000\left(1 + \frac{0.135}{12}\right)^{12(5)}$

10. $145,000\left(1 + \frac{0.073}{365}\right)^{-365(5)}$

11. $2,589e^{0.45(6)}$

12. $850,000e^{-0.04(10)}$

Evaluate the expressions given in Problems 13–22.

13. $\log_2 4 + \log_3 \frac{1}{9}$

14. $2^{\log_2 3 - \log_2 5}$

15. $5\log_3 9 - 2\log_2 16$

16. $\left(\log_2 \frac{1}{8}\right)(\log_3 27)$

17. $(3^{\log_7 1})(\log_5 0.04)$

18. $e^{5\ln 2}$

19. $\log_3 3^4 - \ln e^{0.5}$

20. $\ln(\log 10^e)$

21. $\exp(\ln 3 - \ln 10)$

22. $\exp(\log_{e^2} 25)$

Solve the logarithmic and exponential equations to calculator accuracy in Problems 23–40.

23. $\log_x 16 = 2$

24. $\log x = 5.1$

25. $e^{-3x} = 0.5$

26. $\ln x^2 = 9$

27. $7^{-x} = 15$

28. $e^{2x} = \ln(4 + e)$

29. $\frac{1}{2}\log_3 x = \log_2 8$

30. $\log_2(x^{\log_2 x}) = 4$

31. $3^{x^2 - x} = 9$

32. $4^{x^2 + x} = 16$

33. $2^x 5^{x+2} = 25,000$

34. $3^x 4^{x+(1/2)} = 3,456$

35. $(\sqrt[3]{2})^{x+10} = 2^{x^2}$

36. $(\sqrt[3]{5})^{x+2} = 5^{x^2}$

37. $e^{2x+3} = 1$

38. $\dfrac{e^{x^2}}{e^{x+6}} = 1$

39. $\log_3 x + \log_3(2x + 1) = 1$

40. $\ln\left(\dfrac{x^2}{1-x}\right) = \ln x + \ln\left(\dfrac{2x}{1+x}\right)$

In Problems 41–46, evaluate the given limits.

41. a. $\lim\limits_{x \to 0^+} x^2 e^{-x}$ **b.** $\lim\limits_{x \to 1} x^2 e^{-x}$

42. a. $\lim\limits_{x \to 0} e^{-x^3}$ **b.** $\lim\limits_{x \to 1} e^{-x^3}$

43. a. $\lim\limits_{x \to 0^+} (1+x)^{1/x}$ **b.** $\lim\limits_{x \to 1}(1+x)^{1/x}$

44. a. $\lim\limits_{x \to 0^-} e^{1/x}$ **b.** $\lim\limits_{x \to 0^+} \ln x$

45. $\lim\limits_{x \to e} x \ln x^2$ **46.** $\lim\limits_{x \to e} \dfrac{\ln \sqrt{x}}{x}$

Ⓑ 47. If $\log_b 1{,}296 = 4$, what is $\left(\frac{3}{2}b\right)^{3/2}$?

48. If $\log_{\sqrt{b}} 106 = 2$, what is $\sqrt{b - 25}$?

49. Solve $\log_2 x + \log_5 (2x+1) = \ln x$ correct to the nearest tenth.

50. Solve $\log_x 2 = \log_3 x$ correct to the nearest tenth.

Data points with a curve fit to those points are shown in Problems 51–54. Decide whether the data are better modeled by an exponential or a logarithmic function.

51.

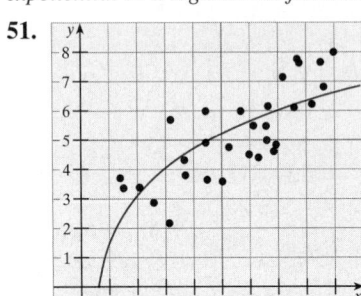

52.

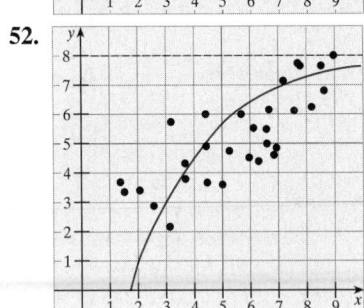

53.

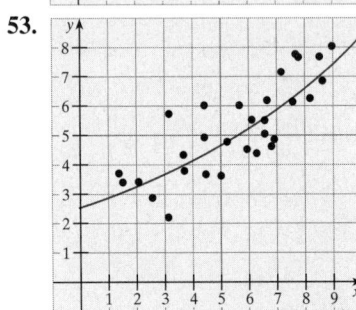

54.

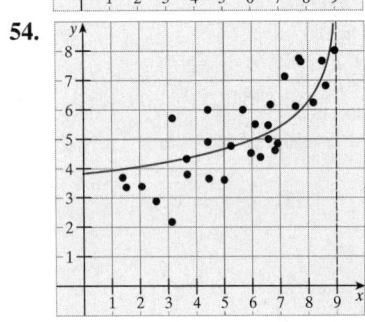

55. According to the *Bouguer–Lambert law*, a beam of light that strikes the surface of a body of water with intensity I_0 will have intensity I at a depth of x meters, where

$$I = I_0 e^{kx}, \qquad k > 0$$

The constant k, called the *absorption coefficient*, depends on such things as the wavelength of the beam of light and the purity of the water. Suppose a given beam of light is only 5% as intense at a depth of 2 meters as it is at the surface. Find k and determine at what depth (to the nearest meter) the intensity is 1% of the intensity at the surface. (This explains why plant life exists only in the top 10 m of a lake or sea.)

56. A certain bank pays 6% interest compounded continuously. How long will it take for $835 to double?

57. If an amount of money is compounded continuously at an annual rate r, how long will it take for that amount of money to double?

58. First National Bank pays 7% interest compounded monthly, and World Savings pays 6.95% interest compounded continuously. Which bank offers a better deal?

59. A person invests $8,500 in a bank that compounds interest continuously. If the investment doubles in 10 years, what is the (annual) rate of interest (correct to the nearest hundredth percent)?

60. In 1626, Peter Minuit traded trinkets worth $24 for land on Manhattan Island. Assume that in 2000 the same land was worth $43.9 billion. Find the annual rate of interest compounded continuously at which the $24 would have had to be invested during this time to yield the same amount.

61. Biologists estimate that the population of a bacterial colony is

$$P(t) = P_0 2^{kt}$$

at time t (in minutes). Suppose the population is found to be 1,000 after 20 minutes and that it doubles every hour.

a. Find P_0 and k.

b. When (to the nearest minute) will the population be 5,000?

62. Spy Problem Having escaped from the smugglers (Problem 49, Section 1.2), the Spy receives an e-mail message that his best friend, Sigmund ("Siggy") Leiter, has been found murdered, the body stuffed unceremoniously in a freezer. Fighting back tears of grief, he remembers that t hours after death, a body has temperature

$$T = A + (B - A)e^{-0.03t}$$

where A is the air temperature and B is the temperature of the body at the time of death. The police inform the Spy that at the time of discovery, 1:00 P.M. on Thursday, the corpse had temperature $40°$F, and the freezer $10°$F. The Spy knows the deed was done by either Coldfinger or André Scélérat. If Coldfinger was in jail from Monday until Wednesday noon and Scélérat was at a villains' convention in Las Vegas from noon on Wednesday until Friday, who "iced" Siggy and when? (By the way, one of the few normal things about Siggy was his body temperature, $98.6°$F.)

63. The *Richter scale* measures the intensity of earthquakes. Specifically, if E is the energy (watt/cm^3) released by a quake, then it is said to have *magnitude M*, where

$$M = \frac{\log E - 11.4}{1.5}$$

a. Express E in terms of M.

b. How much more energy is released in an $M = 8.5$ earthquake (such as the devastating Alaska quake of 1964) than in an average quake of magnitude $M = 6.5$ (the Los Angeles quake of 1994)?

64. Exploration Problem   In the definition of the exponential function $f(x) = b^x$, we require that b be a positive constant. What happens if $b < 0$, for example, if $b = -2$? For what values of x is f defined? Describe the graph of f in this case.

65. Let $E(x) = 2^{x^2-2x}$.

a. Use a calculator to sketch $E(x)$.

b. Where does the graph cross the y-axis? What happens to the graph as $x \to +\infty$ and as $x \to -\infty$?

c. Use a calculator utility to find the value of x that minimizes $E(x)$. What is the minimum value?

66. A manufacturer of car batteries estimates that p percent of the batteries will work for at least t months, where

$$p(t) = 100e^{-0.03t}$$

a. What percent of the batteries can be expected to last at least 40 months?

b. What percent can be expected to *fail* before 50 months?

c. What percent can be expected to *fail* between the 40th and 50th months?

67. If \$3,600 is invested at 15% compounded daily, how much money will there be in 7 years?

a. Use a 365-day year; this is known as *exact interest*.

b. Use a 360-day year; this is known as *ordinary interest*.

68. If P dollars are borrowed for a total of N months compounded monthly at an annual interest rate of r, then the monthly payment is found by the formula

$$m = \frac{P\left(\frac{r}{12}\right)}{1 - \left(1 + \frac{r}{12}\right)^{-N}}$$

a. Use this formula to determine the monthly car payment for a new car costing \$17,487 with a down payment of \$7,487. The car is financed for 4 years at 12%.

b. A home loan is made for \$210,000 at 8% interest for 30 years. What is the monthly payment with a 20% down payment?

69. A cool drink is removed from a refrigerator and is placed in a room where the temperature is $70°$F. According to a result in physics known as *Newton's law of cooling*, the temperature of the drink in t minutes will be

$$F(t) = 70 - Ae^{-kt}$$

where A and k are positive constants. Suppose the temperature of the drink was $35°$F when it left the refrigerator, and 30 minutes later, it was $50°$F [that is, $F(0) = 35$ and $F(30) = 50$].

a. Find A and e^{-30k}.

b. What will the temperature of the drink be after one hour (to the nearest degree)?

c. What would you expect to happen to the temperature as $t \to +\infty$?

70. HISTORICAL QUEST   John Napier was a Scottish landowner who was the Isaac Asimov of his day, having envisioned the tank, the machine gun, and the submarine. He also predicted that the end of the world would occur between 1688 and 1700. He is best known today as the inventor of logarithms, which until the advent of the calculator were used extensively with complicated calculations.

JOHN NAPIER
1550–1617

Napier's logarithms are not identical to the logarithms we use today. Napier chose to use $1 - 10^{-7}$ as his given number, and then he multiplied by 10^7. That is, if

$$N = 10^7 \left(1 - \frac{1}{10^7}\right)^L$$

then L is Napier's logarithm of the number N; that is, $L = \text{nog } N$ means $N = 10^7(1 - 10^{-7})^L$. ∎

One difference between Napier's logarithms (which for clarity we will call a nog) and modern logarithms is apparent when stating the product, quotient, and power rules for logarithms.

a. Show that if $L_1 = \text{nog } N_1$ and $L_2 = \text{nog } N_2$, then

$$\text{nog } N_1 + \text{nog } N_2 = \text{nog }\left(\frac{N_1 N_2}{10^7}\right).$$

b. State and prove similar results for a quotient rule and a power rule for Napier logarithms.

c. What is nog 10^7?

d. If nog $N = 10^7$, then $N \approx e^r$ for some rational number r. What is r?

e. Fortunately, Napier's 1614 paper on logarithms was read by a true mathematician, Henry Briggs (1561–1630), and together they decided that base 10 made a lot more sense. In the year Napier died, Briggs published a table of common logarithms (base 10) that at the time was a major accomplishment. In this paper he used the words "mantissa" and "characteristic." What is the meaning that Briggs gave to these words?

f. Who was the first person to publish a table of natural logarithms (base e)?

Ⓒ 71. For $b > 0$ and all positive integers m and n, show that

a. $b^m b^n = b^{m+n}$ **b.** $\dfrac{b^m}{b^n} = b^{m-n}$

72. For $b > 0$ and all positive integers m and n, show that

a. $(b^m)^n = b^{mn}$ **b.** $(\sqrt[n]{b})^m = \sqrt[n]{b^m}$

73. Prove:

a. $\log_b x + \log_b y = \log_b(xy)$

b. $\log_b x - \log_b y = \log_b \dfrac{x}{y}$

74. Let b be any positive number other than 1. Show that

$$x^x = b^{x \log_b x}$$

75. Let a and b be any positive numbers other than 1. Show that

a. $\log_a x = \dfrac{\log_b x}{\log_b a}$ **b.** $(\log_a b)(\log_b a) = 1$

CHAPTER 2 REVIEW

Proficiency Examination

CONCEPT PROBLEMS

1. State the informal definition of a limit of a function. Discuss this informal definition.
2. State the formal definition of a limit.
3. State the following basic rules for limits:
   a. limit of a constant
   b. multiple rule
   c. sum rule
   d. difference rule
   e. product rule
   f. quotient rule
   g. power rule
   h. limit of a polynomial function
   i. limit of a rational function
   j. limit of a transcendental function
4. State the squeeze rule.
5. What are the values of the given limits?
   a. $\lim\limits_{x \to 0} \dfrac{\sin x}{x}$
   b. $\lim\limits_{x \to 0} \dfrac{\cos x - 1}{x}$
6. Define the continuity of a function at a point and discuss.
7. State the continuity theorem.
8. State the composition limit rule.
9. State the intermediate value theorem.
10. State the root location theorem.
11. State the completeness property.
12. a. What is an exponential function?
    b. How is such a function related to a logarithmic function?
13. Define e.
14. a. What is a logarithmic function?
    b. What is a common logarithm?
    c. What is a natural logarithm?
15. Draw a quick sketch of:
    a. An exponential function b^x for $b > 1$
    b. An exponential function b^x for $0 < b < 1$
16. Draw a quick sketch of:
    a. A logarithmic function $\log_b x$ for $b > 1$.
    b. A logarithmic function $\log_b x$ for $0 < b < 1$.
17. State each of the following exponential properties:
    a. Equality rule
    b. Inequality rules
    c. Product rule
    d. Quotient rule
    e. Power rules
18. Complete the statement of each of the following natural logarithm properties:
    a. $\ln 1 = $ _____
    b. $\ln e = $ _____
    c. $e^{\ln x} = $ _____
    d. $\ln e^y = $ _____
    e. $b^x = $ _____ (write as a power of e)

PRACTICE PROBLEMS

Evaluate the limits in Problems 19–24.

19. $\lim\limits_{x \to 3} \dfrac{x^2 - 4x + 9}{x^2 + x - 8}$
20. $\lim\limits_{x \to 4} \dfrac{\sqrt{x} - 2}{x - 4}$
21. $\lim\limits_{x \to 2} \dfrac{x^2 - 5x + 6}{x^2 - 4}$
22. $\lim\limits_{x \to 0} \dfrac{1 - \cos x}{2 \tan x}$
23. $\lim\limits_{x \to 0} \dfrac{\sin 9x}{\sin 5x}$
24. $\lim\limits_{x \to \frac{1}{2}^-} \dfrac{|2x - 1|}{2x - 1}$

25. Decide whether each of the curves is exponential or logarithmic.

   a.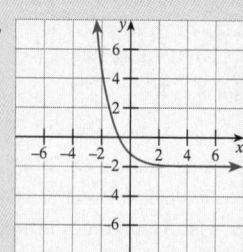
   b.
   c.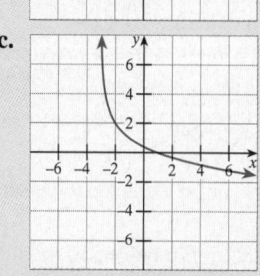
   d.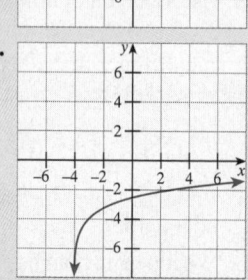

Determine whether the functions given in Problems 26–27 are continuous on the interval $[-5, 5]$.

26. $f(t) = \dfrac{1}{t} - \dfrac{3}{t + 1}$
27. $g(x) = \dfrac{x^2 - 1}{x^2 + x - 2}$

28. How quickly will \$2,000 grow to \$5,000 when invested at an annual rate of 8% if interest is compounded:
    a. quarterly?
    b. monthly?
    c. continuously?

29. Find constants A and B such that f is continuous for all x:
$$f(x) = \begin{cases} Ax + 3 & \text{if } x < 1 \\ 2 & \text{if } x = 1 \\ x^2 + B & \text{if } x > 1 \end{cases}$$

30. Show that the equation
$$x + \sin x = \frac{1}{\sqrt{x} + 3}$$
has at least one solution on the interval $(0, \pi)$.

Supplementary Problems*

1. Evaluate each of the given numbers (calculator approximations for parts **a** and **b**).
   a. $\ln 4.5$
   b. $e^{2.8}$
   c. $e^{\ln \pi}$
   d. $\ln e^{\sqrt{2}}$

Solve each equation in Problems 2–8 for x.

2. $4^{x-1} = 8$
3. $2^{x^2 + 4x} = \frac{1}{16}$
4. $\log_2 2^{x^2} = 4$
5. $\log_4 \sqrt{x(x - 15)} = 1$
6. $\log_2 x + \log_2(x - 15) = 4$
7. $3^{2x-1} = 6^x 3^{1-x}$
8. $\ln(x - 1) + \ln(x + 1) = 2 \ln \sqrt{12}$

*The supplementary problems are presented in a somewhat random order, not necessarily in order of difficulty.

In Problems 9–28, evaluate the given limit.

9. $\lim\limits_{x\to 2} \dfrac{3x^2 - 7x + 2}{x - 2}$

10. $\lim\limits_{x\to -3} \dfrac{4x^2 + 11x - 3}{x^2 - x - 12}$

11. $\lim\limits_{x\to 1^+} \sqrt{\dfrac{x^2 - x}{x - 1}}$

12. $\lim\limits_{x\to 1} \dfrac{x^3 - 1}{x^2 - 1}$

13. $\lim\limits_{x\to 4} |4 - x|$

14. $\lim\limits_{x\to 0^-} \dfrac{|x|}{x}$

15. $\lim\limits_{x\to 1} \dfrac{x^2 - 3x + 2}{x^2 - 1}$

16. $\lim\limits_{x\to 1/\pi} \dfrac{1 + \cos \frac{1}{x}}{\pi x - 1}$

17. $\lim\limits_{x\to 0^+} (1 + x)^{4/x}$

18. $\lim\limits_{x\to 0^+} (1 + 2x)^{1/x}$

19. $\lim\limits_{x\to 1} \dfrac{x^5 - 1}{x - 1}$

20. $\lim\limits_{x\to e^2} \dfrac{(\ln x)^3 - 8}{\ln x - 2}$

21. $\lim\limits_{x\to 0} \dfrac{\sin 3x}{\sin 2x}$

22. $\lim\limits_{t\to 0} \dfrac{\tan^{-1} t}{\sin^{-1} t}$

23. $\lim\limits_{x\to 0} \dfrac{\sin(\cos x)}{\sec x}$

24. $\lim\limits_{x\to 0} \tan 2x \cot x$

25. $\lim\limits_{x\to 0} \dfrac{1 - \sin x}{\cos^2 x}$

26. $\lim\limits_{x\to 0} \dfrac{1 - 2\cos x}{\sqrt{3} - 2\sin x}$

27. $\lim\limits_{x\to 0} \dfrac{e^{3x} - 1}{e^x - 1}$

28. $\lim\limits_{x\to 3} \dfrac{\frac{1}{x} - \frac{1}{3}}{x - 3}$

Evaluate $\lim\limits_{\Delta x \to 0} \dfrac{f(x + \Delta x) - f(x)}{\Delta x}$ *for the function* f *in Problems 29–36.*

29. $f(x) = 7$

30. $f(x) = 3x + 5$

31. $f(x) = \sqrt{2x}$

32. $f(x) = x(x + 1)$

33. $f(x) = \dfrac{4}{x}$

34. $f(x) = \sin x$

35. $f(x) = e^x$

36. $f(x) = \ln x$

Decide whether the functions in Problems 37–40 are continuous on the given intervals. If not, define or redefine the function at one point to make it continuous everywhere on the given interval, or else explain why that cannot be done.

37. $f(x) = \dfrac{x + 4}{x - 8}$ on $[-5, 5]$

38. $f(x) = \dfrac{x + 4}{x - 8}$ on $[0, 10]$

39. $f(x) = \dfrac{\sqrt{x} - 8}{x - 64}$ on $\mathbb{R}$

40. $f(x) = \dfrac{\sqrt{x} - 6}{x - 36}$ on $[-5, 5]$

Decide whether the functions in Problems 41–44 are continuous on the given intervals. Check all of the suspicious points.

41. $r(x) = \begin{cases} 1 & \text{if } x \text{ is rational} \\ -1 & \text{if } x \text{ is irrational} \end{cases}$

42. $f(x) = |x - 2|$ on $[-5, 5]$

43. a. $f(x) = \dfrac{x^2 - x - 6}{x + 2}$ on $[0, 5]$

b. $f(x) = \dfrac{x^2 - x - 6}{x + 2}$ on $[-5, 5]$

c. $f(x) = \begin{cases} \dfrac{x^2 - x - 6}{x + 2} & \text{on } [-5, 5], x \neq -2 \\ -4 & \text{for } x = -2 \end{cases}$

d. $f(x) = \begin{cases} \dfrac{x^2 - x - 6}{x + 2} & \text{on } [-5, 5], x \neq -2 \\ -5 & \text{for } x = -2 \end{cases}$

44. a. $g(x) = \dfrac{x^2 - 3x - 10}{x + 2}$ on $[0, 5]$

b. $g(x) = \dfrac{x^2 - 3x - 10}{x + 2}$ on $[-5, 5]$

c. $g(x) = \begin{cases} \dfrac{x^2 - 3x - 10}{x + 2} & \text{for } -5 \leq x < -2 \\ -7 & \text{for } x = -2 \\ x - 5 & \text{for } -2 < x \leq 5 \end{cases}$

*The **greatest integer function** $f(x) = [\![x]\!]$ is the largest integer that is less than or equal to x. This definition is used in Problems 45–47.*

45. a. Graph $f(x) = [\![x]\!]$ on $[-3, 6]$.

b. Find $\lim\limits_{x\to 3} f(x)$.

c. For what values of a does $\lim\limits_{x\to a} f(x)$ exist?

46. Repeat Problem 45 for $f(x) = [\![\frac{x}{2}]\!]$.

47. Let $f(x) = [\![x^2 + 1]\!]^{[\![x + 1]\!]}$; find $\lim\limits_{x\to 1} f(x)$.

48. Find constants A and B such that f is continuous for all x:

$$f(x) = \begin{cases} Ax + 3 & \text{if } x < 1 \\ 5 & \text{if } x = 1 \\ x^2 + B & \text{if } x > 1 \end{cases}$$

49. Find numbers a and b so that

$$\lim\limits_{x\to 0} \dfrac{\sqrt{ax + b} - 1}{x} = 1$$

50. Find a number c so that

$$\lim\limits_{x\to 3} \dfrac{x^3 + cx^2 + 5x + 12}{x^2 - 7x + 12}$$

exists. Then find the corresponding limit.

51. A manufacturer of lightbulbs estimates that the fraction $F(t)$ of bulbs that remain burning after t weeks is given by

$$F(t) = e^{-kt}$$

where k is a positive constant. Suppose twice as many bulbs are burning after 5 weeks as after 9 weeks.

a. Find k and determine the fraction of bulbs still burning after 7 weeks.

b. What fraction of the bulbs burn out before 10 weeks?

c. What fraction of the bulbs can be expected to burn out between the 4th and 5th weeks?

52. How much should you invest now at an annual interest rate of 6.25% so that your balance 10 years from now will be $2,000 if interest is compounded

a. quarterly?   **b.** continuously?

53. A *decibel* (named for Alexander Graham Bell) is the smallest increase of the loudness of a sound that is detectable by the human ear. In physics, it is shown that when two sounds of intensity I_1 and I_2 (watts/cm^3) occur, the difference in loudness is D decibels, where

$$D = 10 \log \left(\dfrac{I_1}{I_2} \right)$$

When sound is rated in relation to the threshold of human hearing ($I_0 = 10^{-16}$), the level of normal conversation is 50 decibels, whereas that of a rock concert is 110 decibels. Show that a rock concert is 60 times as loud as normal conversation but a million times as intense.

54. If a function f is not continuous at $x = c$, but can be made continuous at c by being given a new value at the point, it is said to have a *removable discontinuity* at $x = c$. Which of the following functions has a removable discontinuity at $x = c$?

    a. $f(x) = \dfrac{2x^2 + x - 15}{x + 3}$ at $c = -3$

    b. $f(x) = \dfrac{x - 2}{|x - 2|}$ at $c = 2$

    c. $f(x) = \dfrac{2 - \sqrt{x}}{4 - x}$ at $c = 4$

55. If $f(x) = x^3 - x^2 + x + 1$, show that there is a number c such that $f(c) = 0$.

56. Prove that $\sqrt{x + 3} = e^x$ has at least one real root, and then use a graphing utility to find the root correct to the nearest tenth.

57. Show that the tangent line to the circle $x^2 + y^2 = r^2$ at the point (x_0, y_0) has the equation $y_0 y + x_0 x = r^2$. *Hint:* Recall that the tangent line at a point P on a circle with center C is the line that passes through P and is perpendicular to the line segment $\overline{CP}$.

58. **Counterexample Problem**   It is not necessarily true that $\lim_{x \to c} f(x)$ and $\lim_{x \to c} g(x)$ exist whenever $\lim_{x \to c}[f(x) \cdot g(x)]$ exists. Find functions f and g such that $\lim_{x \to c}[f(x) \cdot g(x)]$ exists and $\lim_{x \to c} g(x) = 0$, but $\lim_{x \to c} f(x)$ does not exist.

59. **Counterexample Problem**   It is not necessarily true that $\lim_{x \to c} f(x)$ and $\lim_{x \to c} g(x)$ exist whenever $\lim_{x \to c} \dfrac{f(x)}{g(x)}$ exists. Find functions f and g such that $\lim_{x \to 0} \dfrac{f(x)}{g(x)}$ exists, but neither $\lim_{x \to 0} f(x)$ nor $\lim_{x \to 0} g(x)$ exists.

60. When analyzing experimental data involving two variables, a useful procedure is to pass a smooth curve through a number of plotted data points and then perform computations as if the curve were the graph of an equation relating the variables. Suppose the following data are gathered as a result of a physiological experiment in which skin tissue is subjected to external heat for t seconds, and a measurement is made of the change in temperature ΔT required to cause a change of $2.5°C$ at a depth of 0.5 mm in the skin:

t (sec)	1	2	3	4	10	20	25	30
ΔT (°C)	12.5	7.5	5.8	5.0	4.5	3.5	2.9	2.8

    Plot the data points in a coordinate plane and then answer these questions.

    a. What temperature difference ΔT would be expected if the exposure time is 2.2 sec?

    b. Approximately what exposure time t corresponds to a temperature difference $\Delta T = 8.0°C$?

61. **Journal Problem**   The theorem

    $$\lim_{h \to 0} \frac{\sin h}{h} = 1$$

    stated in this chapter has been the subject of much discussion in mathematical journals:

W. B. Gearhart and H. S. Schultz, "The Function $\sin x / x$," *College Mathematics Journal* (1990): 90–99.

L. Gillman, "π and the Limit of $(\sin \alpha)/\alpha$," *American Mathematical Monthly* (1991): 345–348.

F. Richman, "A Circular Argument," *College Mathematics Journal* (1993): 160–162.

D. A. Rose, "The Differentiability of $\sin x$," *College Mathematics Journal* (1991): 139–142.

P. Ungar, "Reviews," *American Mathematical Monthly* (1986): 221–230.

Some of these articles argue that the demonstration shown in the text is circular, since we use the fact that the area of a circle is πr^2. How do we know the area of a circle? The answer, of course, is that we learned it in elementary school, but that does not constitute a proof. On the other hand, some of these articles argue that the reasoning is not necessarily circular. Read one or more of these journal articles and write a report.

62. **a.** Show that $\sin x < x$ if $0 < x < \frac{\pi}{2}$. Refer to Figure 2.30. *Hint:* Compare the area of an appropriate triangle and sector.

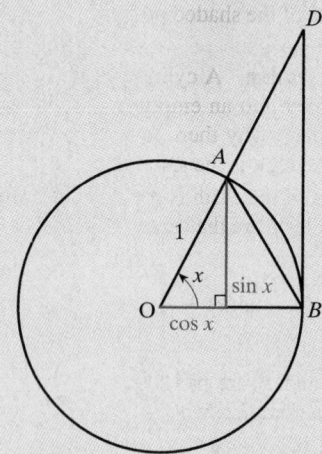

Figure 2.30   Figure for Problems 62 and 63

   b. Show that $|\sin x| < |x|$ if $0 < |x| < \frac{\pi}{2}$.

   c. Use the definition of continuity to show that $\sin x$ is continuous at $x = 0$.

   d. Use the formula

   $$\sin(\alpha + \beta) = \sin \alpha \cos \beta + \cos \alpha \sin \beta$$

   to show that $\sin x$ is continuous for all real x.

63. Follow the procedure outlined in Problem 62 to show that $\cos x$ is continuous for all x. *Hint:* After showing that

   $$\lim_{x \to 0} \cos x = 1$$

   you may need the identity

   $$\cos(\alpha + \beta) = \cos \alpha \cos \beta - \sin \alpha \sin \beta$$

   to show that $\cos x$ is continuous for $x \neq 0$.

64. A regular polygon of n sides is inscribed in a circle of radius R, as shown in Figure 2.31.

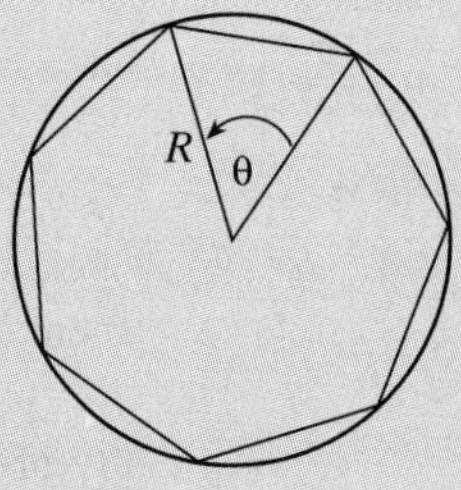

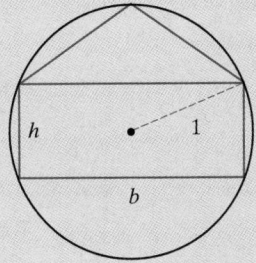

Figure 2.31 A regular polygon of seven sides with central angle θ (Problem 64)

a. Show that the perimeter of the polygon is given by $P(\theta) = \dfrac{4\pi R}{\theta}\sin\dfrac{\theta}{2}$, where $\theta = \dfrac{2\pi}{n}$ is the central angle subtended by one side of the polygon.

b. Use the formula in part **a** together with the fact that $\displaystyle\lim_{x\to 0}\frac{\sin x}{x}=1$ to show that a circle of radius R has circumference $2\pi R$.

c. Modify the approach suggested in parts **a** and **b** to show that a circle of radius R has area πR^2. *Hint*: First express the area of the shaded polygon in Figure 2.31 as a function of θ.

65. **Exploration Problem** A cylindrical tank containing 50 L of water is drained into an empty rectangular trough that can hold 75 L. Explain why there must be a time when the height of water in the tank is the same as that in the trough.

66. The radius of the earth is roughly 4,000 mi, and an object located x miles from the center of the earth weighs w lb, where

$$w(x) = \begin{cases} Ax & \text{if } x \le 4{,}000 \\ \dfrac{B}{x^2} & \text{if } x > 4{,}000 \end{cases}$$

where A and B are positive constants. Assuming that w is continuous for all x, what must be true about A and B?

67. The windchill temperature in degrees is a function of the air temperature T (in degrees Fahrenheit) and the wind speed v (in mi/h).* If we hold T constant and consider the windchill as a function of v, we have

$$W(v) = \begin{cases} T & \text{if } 0 \le v \le 4 \\ 91.4 + (91.4 - T)(0.0203v - 0.304\sqrt{v} - 0.474) \\ \qquad\qquad \text{if } 4 < v < 45 \\ 1.6T - 55 & \text{if } v \ge 45 \end{cases}$$

a. If $T = 30$, what is the windchill for $v = 20$? What is it for $v = 50$?

b. For $T = 30$, what wind speed corresponds to a windchill temperature of $0°$ Fahrenheit?

c. For what value of T is the windchill function continuous at $v = 4$? At $v = 45$?

68. Based on the estimate that there are 10 billion acres of arable land on the earth and that each acre can produce enough food to feed 4 people, some demographers believe that the earth can support a population of no more than 40 billion people.

The population of the earth reached approximately 5 billion in 1986 and 6 billion in 1999. If the population of the earth were growing according to the formula

$$P(t) = P_0 e^{rt}$$

where t is the time after the population is P_0 and r is the growth rate, when would the population reach the theoretical limit of 40 billion?

69. A function f is said to satisfy a *Lipschitz condition* (named for the nineteenth century mathematician Rudolf Lipschitz, 1832–1903) on a given interval if there is a positive constant M such that

$$|f(x) - f(y)| < M\,|x - y|$$

for all x and y in the interval (with $x \ne y$). Suppose f satisfies a Lipschitz condition on an interval and let c be a fixed number chosen arbitrarily from the interval. Use the formal definition of limit to prove that f is continuous at c.

70. A population model employed at one time by the U.S. Census Bureau uses the formula

$$P(t) = \frac{202.31}{1 + e^{3.98 - 0.314t}}$$

to estimate the population of the United States (in millions) for every tenth year from the base year of 1790. For example, if $t = 0$, then the year is 1790, and if $t = 20$, the year is 1990.

a. Draw the graph using this population model and predict the population in the year 2000.

b. Consult an almanac or some other source to find the actual population figures for the years from 1790 to present.

c. What happens to the population P "in the long run," that is, as t increases without bound?

*71. **Putnam Examination Problem** Evaluate

$$\lim_{x \to +\infty}\left[\frac{1}{x} \cdot \frac{a^x - 1}{a - 1}\right]^{1/x} \qquad \text{where } a > 0, a \ne 1$$

*72. **Putnam Examination Problem** Figure 2.32 shows a rectangle of base b and height h inscribed in a circle of radius 1, surmounted by an isosceles triangle. Find $\displaystyle\lim_{h\to 2/5}\frac{A(h)}{bh}$.

Figure 2.32 Putnam problem

*From William Bosch and L. G. Cobb, "Windchill," *UMAP Module No. 658*, (1984), pp. 244–247.

*The Putnam Examination is a national annual examination given under the auspices of the Mathematical Association of America and is designed to recognize mathematically talented college and university students. We include Putnam examination problems, which should be considered optional, to encourage students to consider taking the examination. Putnam problems used by permission of the American Mathematical Association. Solutions to Putnam Examinations generally appear in *The American Mathematical Monthly*, approximately one year after the examination.

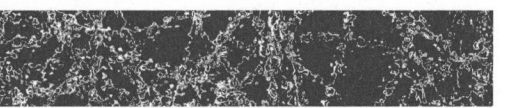

3

Differentiation

PREVIEW

In this chapter, we develop the main ideas of differential calculus. We begin by defining the *derivative*, which is the central concept of differential calculus. Then we develop a list of rules and formulas for finding the derivative of a variety of expressions involving polynomials, rational and root functions, and trigonometric, logarithmic, and inverse trigonometric functions. Along the way, we will see how the derivative can be used to find slopes of tangent lines and rates of change.

PERSPECTIVE

A *calculus* is a body of calculation or reasoning associated with a certain concept. For *differential calculus*, that concept is the *derivative*, one of the fundamental ideas in all mathematics and, arguably, a cornerstone of modern scientific thought. The basic ideas of what we now call calculus had been fermenting in intellectual circles throughout much of the seventeenth century. The genius of Newton and Leibniz (see the guest essay at the end of Chapter 1) centered not so much on the discovery of those ideas as on their systematization.

In this chapter, we will consider various ways of efficiently computing derivatives. We will also see how the derivative can be used to find rates of change and to measure the direction (slope) at each point on a graph. Falling body problems in physics and marginal analysis from economics are examples of applied topics to be discussed, and we will also explore several topics involving basic concepts. It is fair to say that your success with differential calculus hinges on understanding this material.

3.1 An Introduction to the Derivative: Tangents

IN THIS SECTION tangent lines, the derivative, relationship between the graphs of f and f', existence of derivatives, continuity and differentiability, derivative notation

TANGENT LINES

Since classical times, mathematicians have known that the tangent line at a given point on a circle has the property that it is the only line that intersects the circle exactly once, but the same principle cannot be applied to finding tangent lines to more general curves. Indeed, as shown in Figure 3.1, the line we may intuitively think of as being tangent to the graph of $y = f(x)$ at point P can intersect the curve at other points, and for that matter, there may be many lines that intersect the curve only at P, but are clearly not tangent lines.

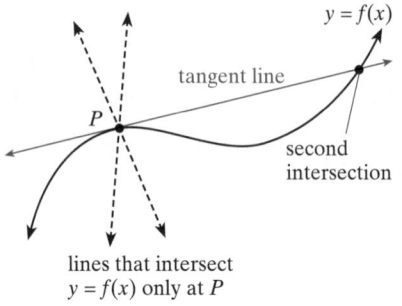

Figure 3.1 Tangent line at P

We begin this section by computing the slope of a tangent line as a limit, using a procedure originally developed by the French mathematician Pierre de Fermat (1601–1665). Fermat's use of the "dynamic" limit process rather than the "static" procedures of classical geometry and algebra was a breakthrough in thinking that eventually led to the development of differential calculus by Isaac Newton (1642–1727) and Gottfried Leibniz (1646–1716) in the latter half of the seventeenth century. Following in the footsteps of these giants, we, too, will use what we discover about tangent lines as a springboard for introducing the derivative and studying its basic properties.

Suppose we wish to find the slope of the tangent line to $y = f(x)$ at the point $P(x_0, f(x_0))$. The strategy is to approximate the tangent line by other lines whose slopes can be computed directly. In particular, consider the line joining the given point P to the neighboring point Q on the graph of f, as shown in Figure 3.2. This line is called a **secant line.** Compare the secant lines shown in Figure 3.2.

WARNING Do not confuse *secant line* (a line that intersects a curve in two or more points) with the *secant function* of trigonometry.

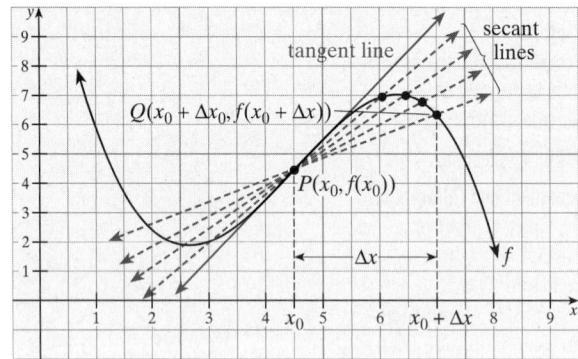

Figure 3.2 The secant line $\overline{PQ}$

Notice that a secant line is a good approximation to the tangent line at point P as long as Q is close to P.

To compute the slope of a secant line, first label the coordinates of the neighboring point Q, as indicated in Figure 3.2. In particular, let Δx denote the change in the x-coordinate between the given point $P(x_0, f(x_0))$ and the neighboring point $Q(x_0 + \Delta x, f(x_0 + \Delta x))$.

The slope of this secant line, m_{sec}, is easy to calculate:

$$m_{\text{sec}} = \frac{\Delta y}{\Delta x} = \frac{f(x_0 + \Delta x) - f(x_0)}{\Delta x}$$

To bring the secant line closer to the tangent line, let Q approach P *on the graph of f* by letting Δx approach 0. As this happens, the slope of the secant line should approach the slope of the tangent line at P. We denote the slope of the tangent line by m_{tan} to distinguish it from the slope of a secant line. These observations suggest the following definition.

Slope of a Line Tangent to a Graph at a Point

At the point $P(x_0, f(x_0))$, the tangent line to the graph of f has **slope** given by the formula

$$m_{\text{tan}} = \lim_{\Delta x \to 0} \frac{f(x_0 + \Delta x) - f(x_0)}{\Delta x}$$

provided this limit exists.

EXAMPLE 1   Slope of a tangent line at a particular point

Find the slope of the tangent line to the graph of $f(x) = x^2$ at the point $P(-1, 1)$.

Solution

Figure 3.3 shows the tangent line to f at $x = -1$. The slope of the tangent line is given by

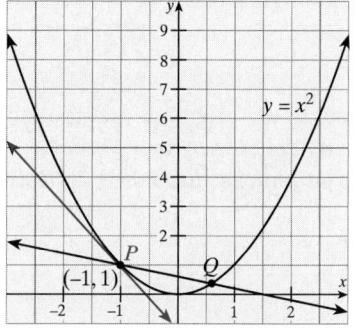

Tangent line at $(-1, 1)$

Figure 3.3 Tangent line to the graph of $y = x^2$ at $(-1, 1)$

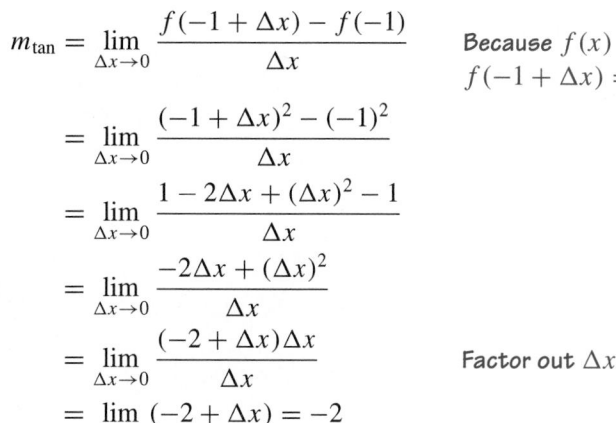

$$
\begin{aligned}
m_{\text{tan}} &= \lim_{\Delta x \to 0} \frac{f(-1 + \Delta x) - f(-1)}{\Delta x} && \text{Because } f(x) = x^2, \\
&&& f(-1 + \Delta x) = (-1 + \Delta x)^2. \\
&= \lim_{\Delta x \to 0} \frac{(-1 + \Delta x)^2 - (-1)^2}{\Delta x} \\
&= \lim_{\Delta x \to 0} \frac{1 - 2\Delta x + (\Delta x)^2 - 1}{\Delta x} \\
&= \lim_{\Delta x \to 0} \frac{-2\Delta x + (\Delta x)^2}{\Delta x} \\
&= \lim_{\Delta x \to 0} \frac{(-2 + \Delta x)\Delta x}{\Delta x} && \text{Factor out } \Delta x \text{ and reduce.} \\
&= \lim_{\Delta x \to 0} (-2 + \Delta x) = -2 \qquad \blacksquare
\end{aligned}
$$

In Example 1, we found the slope of the tangent line to the graph of $y = x^2$ at the point $(-1, 1)$. In Example 2, we perform the same calculation again, this time representing the given point algebraically as (x, x^2). This is the situation shown in Figure 3.4 for the slope of the tangent line to $y = x^2$ at *any* point (x, x^2).

EXAMPLE 2   Slope of a tangent line at an arbitrary point

Derive a formula for the slope of the tangent line to the graph of $f(x) = x^2$, and then use the formula to compute the slope at $(4, 16)$.

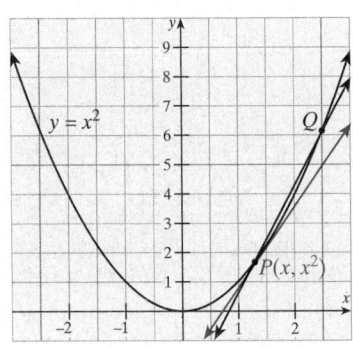

Tangent line at (x, x^2)

Figure 3.4 Tangent line to the graph of $y = x^2$ at (x, x^2)

Solution

Figure 3.4 shows a tangent line at an arbitrary point $P(x, x^2)$ on the curve. From the definition of slope of the tangent line,

$$m_{\tan} = \lim_{\Delta x \to 0} \frac{f(x + \Delta x) - f(x)}{\Delta x} \qquad \text{\textit{Because }} f(x) = x^2,$$
$$f(x + \Delta x) = (x + \Delta x)^2.$$

$$= \lim_{\Delta x \to 0} \frac{(x + \Delta x)^2 - x^2}{\Delta x}$$

$$= \lim_{\Delta x \to 0} \frac{x^2 + 2x\,\Delta x + (\Delta x)^2 - x^2}{\Delta x}$$

$$= \lim_{\Delta x \to 0} \frac{2x\,\Delta x + (\Delta x)^2}{\Delta x}$$

$$= \lim_{\Delta x \to 0} \frac{(2x + \Delta x)\,\Delta x}{\Delta x} \qquad \text{\textit{Factor and reduce.}}$$

$$= \lim_{\Delta x \to 0} (2x + \Delta x) = 2x$$

At the point $(4, 16)$, $x = 4$, so $m_{\tan} = 2(4) = 8$. ∎

The result of Example 2 gives a general formula for the slope of a line tangent to the graph of $f(x) = x^2$, namely, $m_{\tan} = 2x$. The answer from Example 1 can now be verified using this formula; if $x = -1$, then $m_{\tan} = 2(-1) = -2$.

THE DERIVATIVE

The expression

$$\frac{f(x + \Delta x) - f(x)}{\Delta x}$$

which gives a formula for the slope of a secant line to the graph of a function f, is called the **difference quotient** of f. The limit of the difference quotient

$$\lim_{\Delta x \to 0} \frac{f(x + \Delta x) - f(x)}{\Delta x}$$

which gives a formula for the slope of the tangent line to the graph of f at the point $(x, f(x))$, is called the **derivative** of f and is frequently denoted by the symbol $f'(x)$ (read "eff prime of x"). To **differentiate** a function f at x means to find its derivative at the point $(x, f(x))$.

Derivative

> The **derivative** of f at x is given by
>
> $$f'(x) = \lim_{\Delta x \to 0} \frac{f(x + \Delta x) - f(x)}{\Delta x}$$
>
> provided this limit exists.

Alternatively, we can write

$$f'(x) = \lim_{t \to x} \frac{f(t) - f(x)}{t - x}$$

where $t = x + \Delta x$. Occasionally, this form is easier to use in computations.

The derivative is one of the fundamental concepts in calculus, and it is important to make some observations regarding this definition.

1. If the limit for the difference quotient exists, then we say that the function f is **differentiable at** x.

2. The value of a derivative depends only on the limit process and not on the symbols used in that process. In Example 2, we found that if $f(x) = x^2$, then $f'(x) = 2x$. This means that we also know

$$\text{If } g(t) = t^2, \text{ then } g'(t) = 2t.$$
$$\text{If } h(u) = u^2, \text{ then } h'(u) = 2u.$$
$$\vdots$$

3. Notice that the derivative of a function is itself a function.

Finding the slope of a tangent line is just one of several applications of the derivative that we will discuss in this chapter. In Section 3.4, we will examine rectilinear motion and other rates of change, and in Section 3.8, marginal analysis from economics. In Chapter 4 we will examine more complex applications such as curve sketching and optimization.

EXAMPLE 3   Derivative using the definition

Differentiate $f(t) = \sqrt{t}$.

WARNING   Notice that $f(t) = \sqrt{t}$ is defined for all $t \geq 0$, whereas its derivative $f'(t) = 1/(2\sqrt{t})$ is defined for all $t > 0$. This shows that a function need not be differentiable throughout its entire domain.

Solution

$$\begin{aligned} f'(t) &= \lim_{\Delta t \to 0} \frac{f(t + \Delta t) - f(t)}{\Delta t} \\ &= \lim_{\Delta t \to 0} \frac{\sqrt{t + \Delta t} - \sqrt{t}}{\Delta t} \\ &= \lim_{\Delta t \to 0} \frac{\sqrt{t + \Delta t} - \sqrt{t}}{\Delta t} \left(\frac{\sqrt{t + \Delta t} + \sqrt{t}}{\sqrt{t + \Delta t} + \sqrt{t}} \right) & \text{Rationalize numerator.} \\ &= \lim_{\Delta t \to 0} \frac{(t + \Delta t) - t}{\Delta t (\sqrt{t + \Delta t} + \sqrt{t})} \\ &= \lim_{\Delta t \to 0} \frac{\Delta t}{\Delta t (\sqrt{t + \Delta t} + \sqrt{t})} \\ &= \lim_{\Delta t \to 0} \frac{1}{\sqrt{t + \Delta t} + \sqrt{t}} & \text{Reduce fraction.} \\ &= \frac{1}{2\sqrt{t}} & \text{For } t > 0 \quad \blacksquare \end{aligned}$$

Δx	$\dfrac{\pi}{6} + \Delta x$	Difference quotient $\dfrac{\Delta y}{\Delta x}$
1	1.523598776	−0.81885
0.5	1.023598776	−0.69146
0.125	0.648598776	−0.55276
0.0625	0.586098776	−0.52673
0.015625	0.539223776	−0.50675
0.00195313	0.525551906	−0.50085
0.00012207	0.523720846	−0.50005
0.000007629	0.523606405	−0.50001
$\downarrow$	$\downarrow$	$\downarrow$
0	$\frac{\pi}{6} \approx$	$-\frac{1}{2}$
0	0.5235987756	$-\frac{1}{2}$

EXAMPLE 4   Estimating a derivative using a table

Estimate the derivative of $f(x) = \cos x$ at $x = \frac{\pi}{6}$ by evaluating the difference quotient

$$\frac{\Delta y}{\Delta x} = \frac{f(x + \Delta x) - f(x)}{\Delta x}$$

near the point $x = \frac{\pi}{6}$.

Solution $\dfrac{\Delta y}{\Delta x} = \dfrac{\cos(\frac{\pi}{6} + \Delta x) - \cos \frac{\pi}{6}}{\Delta x}$

Choose a sequence of values for $\Delta x \to 0$: say $1, \frac{1}{2}, \frac{1}{4}, \frac{1}{8}, \ldots$ and use a calculator (or a computer) to estimate the difference quotient by table. We show selected elements from this sequence of calculations:

A similar table for negative values of Δx should also be considered. From the table, we would guess that $f'(\frac{\pi}{6}) = -0.5$. $\blacksquare$

THEOREM 3.1   Equation of a line tangent to a curve at a point

If f is a differentiable function at x_0, the graph of $y = f(x)$ has a tangent line at the point $P(x_0, f(x_0))$ with slope $f'(x_0)$ and equation

$$y = f'(x_0)(x - x_0) + f(x_0)$$

Proof   To find the equation of the tangent line to the curve $y = f(x)$ at the point $P(x_0, y_0)$, we use the fact that the slope of the tangent line is the derivative $f'(x_0)$ and apply the point-slope formula for the equation of a line:

$$y - k = m(x - h) \qquad \text{Point-slope formula}$$
$$y - y_0 = m(x - x_0) \qquad \text{Given point } (x_0, y_0)$$
$$y - f(x_0) = f'(x_0)(x - x_0) \qquad y_0 = f(x_0) \text{ and } m_{\tan} = f'(x_0)$$
$$y = f'(x_0)(x - x_0) + f(x_0) \qquad \text{Add } f(x_0) \text{ to both sides.} \qquad ❏$$

EXAMPLE 5   Finding the equation of a tangent line

Find an equation for the tangent line to the graph of $f(x) = \frac{1}{x}$ at the point where $x = 2$.

Solution

The graph of the function $y = \frac{1}{x}$, the point where $x = 2$, and the tangent line at the point are shown in Figure 3.5. First, find $f'(x)$:

$$f'(x) = \lim_{\Delta x \to 0} \frac{f(x + \Delta x) - f(x)}{\Delta x} \qquad \text{Definition of derivative}$$

$$= \lim_{\Delta x \to 0} \frac{\dfrac{1}{x + \Delta x} - \dfrac{1}{x}}{\Delta x} \qquad f(x) = \frac{1}{x}; f(x + \Delta x) = \frac{1}{x + \Delta x}$$

$$= \lim_{\Delta x \to 0} \frac{x - (x + \Delta x)}{x \Delta x (x + \Delta x)} \qquad \text{Simplify the fraction.}$$

$$= \lim_{\Delta x \to 0} \frac{-1}{x(x + \Delta x)}$$

$$= \frac{-1}{x^2}$$

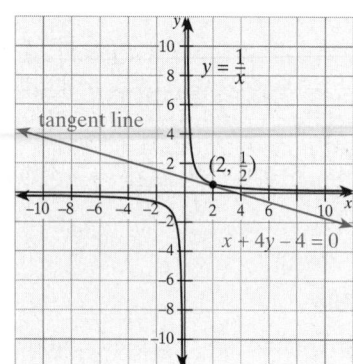

Figure 3.5 Tangent line to $y = \frac{1}{x}$ at $(2, \frac{1}{2})$

WARNING   The slope of f at x_0 is not the derivative f' but the value of the derivative at x_0. In Example 5 the function is defined by $f(x) = 1/x$, the derivative is $f'(x) = -1/x^2$, and the slope at $x = 2$ is the number $f'(2) = -\frac{1}{4}$.

Next, find the slope of the tangent line at $x = 2$: $m_{\tan} = f'(2) = -\frac{1}{4}$. Since $f(2) = \frac{1}{2}$, the equation of the tangent line can now be found by using Theorem 3.1:

$$y = -\frac{1}{4}(x - 2) + \frac{1}{2}, \quad \text{or in standard form,} \quad x + 4y - 4 = 0 \qquad ∎$$

EXAMPLE 6   Finding a line that is perpendicular to a tangent line

Find the equation of the line that is perpendicular to the tangent line to $f(x) = \frac{1}{x}$ at $x = 2$ and intersects it at the point of tangency.

Solution

In Example 5, we found that the slope of the tangent line is $f'(2) = -\frac{1}{4}$ and that the point of tangency is $(2, \frac{1}{2})$. In Section 1.2, we saw that two lines are perpendicular if and only if their slopes are negative reciprocals of each other. Thus, the perpendicular line we seek has slope 4 (the negative reciprocal of $m = -\frac{1}{4}$). The desired equation is

$$y - \tfrac{1}{2} = 4(x - 2) \qquad \text{Point-slope formula}$$

In standard form, $4x - y - \frac{15}{2} = 0$; compare the coefficients of the variables in the tangent and perpendicular lines. ∎

The perpendicular line we found in Example 6 has a name.

Normal Line to a Graph

> The **normal line** to the graph of f at the point P is the line that is perpendicular to the tangent line to the graph at P.

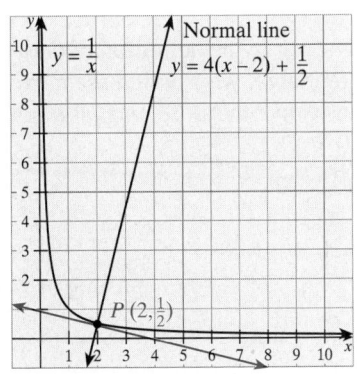

Figure 3.6 Graph of $y = \frac{1}{x}$ along with its normal $y = 4(x - 2) + \frac{1}{2}$

Figure 3.6 shows the graph of the function from Example 6, along with the graph of its normal line.

RELATIONSHIP BETWEEN THE GRAPHS OF f AND f'

It is important to take some time to study the relationship between the graph of a function and its derivative. Since slope is measured by f', it follows that at points x where $f'(x) > 0$, the tangent line must be tilted upward, and the graph is rising. Similarly, where $f'(x) < 0$, the tangent line is tilted downward, and the graph is falling. If $f'(x) = 0$, the tangent line is horizontal at x, so the graph "flattens." These observations are illustrated in Figure 3.7.

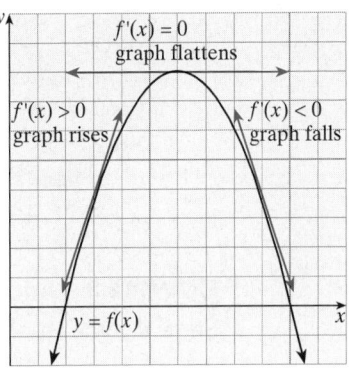

Figure 3.7 How the sign of f determines whether the tangent line slants up, down, or is horizontal

EXAMPLE 7 Sketching the graph of f', given the graph of f

The graph of a function f is shown in Figure 3.8. Sketch a possible graph for the derivative f'.

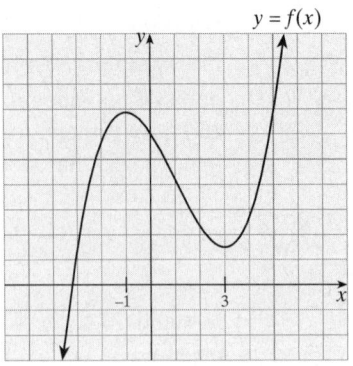

Figure 3.8 Graph of a function f

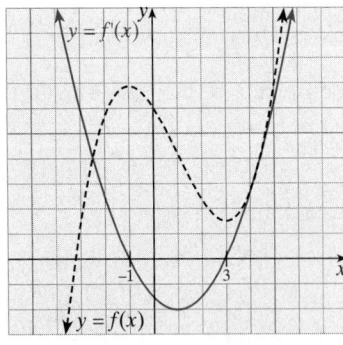

Figure 3.9 A possible graph for the derivative of the function whose graph is given in Figure 3.8

Solution

Notice that the graph of f is rising for $x < -1$ and for $x > 3$; it is falling for $-1 < x < 3$; and it has horizontal tangent lines at $x = -1$ and $x = 3$. Thus, the graph of f' is above the x-axis ($f'(x) > 0$) for $x < -1$ and $x > 3$, below the axis for $-1 < x < 3$ ($f'(x) < 0$), and crosses the axis at $x = -1$ and at $x = 3$. One possible graph with these features is shown in Figure 3.9. ∎

EXISTENCE OF DERIVATIVES

We observed that a function is differentiable only if *the limit* in the definition of derivative exists. At points where a function f is not differentiable, we say that *the derivative of f does not exist*. Three common ways for a derivative to fail to exist at a point $(c, f(c))$ in the domain of f are shown in Figure 3.10.

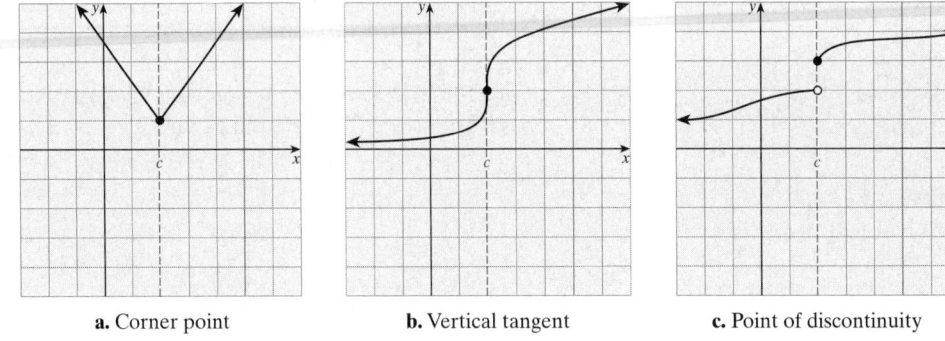

a. Corner point   **b.** Vertical tangent   **c.** Point of discontinuity

Figure 3.10 Common examples where a derivative does not exist

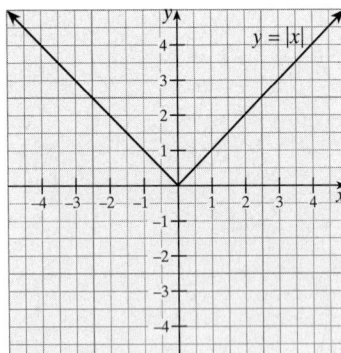

Figure 3.11 $f(x) = |x|$ is not differentiable at $x = 0$ because the slope from the left does not equal the slope from the right

EXAMPLE 8 A function that does not have a derivative because of a corner

Show that the absolute value function $f(x) = |x|$ is not differentiable at $x = 0$.

Solution

The graph of $f(x) = |x|$ is shown in Figure 3.11. Note that because the slope "from the left" at $x = 0$ is -1 while the slope "from the right" is $+1$, the graph has a corner at the origin, which prevents a unique tangent line from being drawn there.

We can show this algebraically by using the definition of derivative:

$$f'(0) = \lim_{\Delta x \to 0} \frac{f(0 + \Delta x) - f(0)}{\Delta x}$$

$$= \lim_{\Delta x \to 0} \frac{f(\Delta x) - f(0)}{\Delta x}$$

$$= \lim_{\Delta x \to 0} \frac{|\Delta x|}{\Delta x}$$

We must now consider one-sided limits, because

$$|\Delta x| = \Delta x \text{ when } \Delta x > 0, \text{ and } |\Delta x| = -\Delta x \text{ when } \Delta x < 0$$

$$\lim_{\Delta x \to 0^-} \frac{|\Delta x|}{\Delta x} = \lim_{\Delta x \to 0^-} \frac{-\Delta x}{\Delta x} = -1 \qquad \text{Derivative from the left}$$

$$\lim_{\Delta x \to 0^+} \frac{|\Delta x|}{\Delta x} = \lim_{\Delta x \to 0^+} \frac{\Delta x}{\Delta x} = 1 \qquad \text{Derivative from the right}$$

The left- and right-hand limits are not the same; therefore, the limit does not exist. This means that the derivative does not exist at $x = 0$. ∎

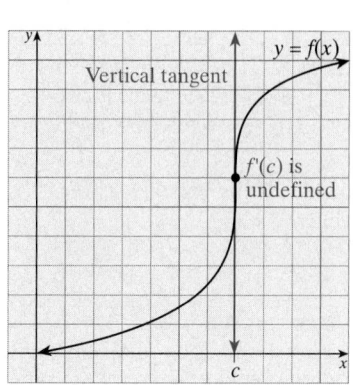

Figure 3.12 Vertical tangent line at $x = c$

The continuous function $f(x) = |x|$ in Example 8 failed to be differentiable at $x = 0$ because the one-sided limits of its difference quotient were unequal. A continuous function may also fail to be differentiable at $x = c$ if its difference quotient diverges to infinity. In this case, the function is said to have a *vertical tangent line* at $x = c$, as illustrated in Figure 3.12. We will have more to say about such functions when we discuss curve sketching with derivatives in Chapter 4.

CONTINUITY AND DIFFERENTIABILITY

If the graph of a function has a tangent line at a point, we would expect to be able to draw the graph continuously (without the pencil leaving the paper). In other words, we expect the following theorem to be true.

THEOREM 3.2   Differentiability implies continuity

If a function f is differentiable at c, then it is also continuous at c.

Proof   Recall that for f to be continuous at $x = c$: (1) $f(c)$ must be defined; (2) $\lim_{x \to c} f(x)$ exists; and (3) $\lim_{x \to c} f(x) = f(c)$. Thus, continuity can be established by showing that $\lim_{\Delta x \to 0} f(c + \Delta x) = f(c)$ or, equivalently,

$$\lim_{\Delta x \to 0} [f(c + \Delta x) - f(c)] = 0$$

Because f is a differentiable function at $x = c$, $f'(c)$ exists and

$$\lim_{\Delta x \to 0} \frac{f(c + \Delta x) - f(c)}{\Delta x} = f'(c)$$

Therefore, by applying the product rule for limits, we find that

$$\lim_{\Delta x \to 0} [f(c + \Delta x) - f(c)] = \lim_{\Delta x \to 0} \left[\frac{f(c + \Delta x) - f(c)}{\Delta x} \cdot \Delta x \right]$$

$$= \left[\lim_{\Delta x \to 0} \frac{f(c + \Delta x) - f(c)}{\Delta x} \right] \left[\lim_{\Delta x \to 0} \Delta x \right]$$

$$= f'(c) \cdot 0 = 0$$

Thus, $\lim_{x \to c} f(x) = f(c)$, and we see that the conditions for continuity are satisfied.   ❑

WARNING   Be sure you understand what we have just shown with Example 8 and Theorem 3.2: If a function is differentiable at $x = c$, then it must be continuous at that point. The converse is not true: If a function is continuous at $x = c$, then it may or may not be differentiable at that point. Finally, if a function is discontinuous at $x = c$, then it cannot possibly have a derivative at that point. (See Figure 3.13c.)

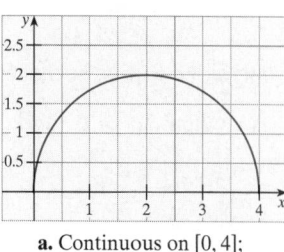

a. Continuous on $[0, 4]$; differentiable on $(0, 4)$

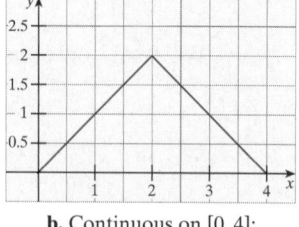

b. Continuous on $[0, 4]$; not differentiable at $x = 2$

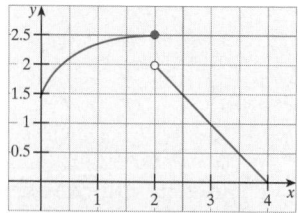

c. Discontinuous at $x = 2$; cannot be differentiable at $x = 2$

Figure 3.13   A function continuous at $x = 2$ may or may not be differentiable at $x = 2$. A function discontinuous at $x = 2$ cannot be differentiable at $x = 2$.

DERIVATIVE NOTATION

In certain situations, it is convenient or suggestive to denote the derivative of $y = f(x)$ by $\dfrac{dy}{dx}$ instead of $f'(x)$. This notation is called the *Leibniz notation* because Leibniz was the first to use it.

For example, if $y = x^2$, the derivative is $y' = 2x$ or, using Leibniz notation, $\dfrac{dy}{dx} = 2x$. The symbol $\dfrac{dy}{dx}$ is read "the derivative of y with respect to x." When we wish to denote the value of the derivative at c in the Leibniz notation, we will write

$$\frac{dy}{dx}\bigg|_{x=c}$$

For instance, we would evaluate $\dfrac{dy}{dx} = 4x^2$ at $x = 3$ by writing

$$\frac{dy}{dx}\bigg|_{x=3} = 4x^2\big|_{x=3} = 4(3)^2 = 36$$

Another notation omits reference to y and f altogether, and we can write

$$\frac{d}{dx}(x^2) = 2x$$

which is read "the derivative of x^2 with respect to x is $2x$."

WARNING   Despite its appearance, $\frac{dy}{dx}$ is a single symbol and is *not a fraction*. In Section 3.8, we introduce a concept called a *differential* that will provide independent meaning to symbols like dy and dx, but for now, these symbols have meaning only in connection with the Leibniz derivative symbol $\frac{dy}{dx}$.

EXAMPLE 9   Derivative at a point with Leibniz notation

Find $\dfrac{dy}{dx}\bigg|_{x=-1}$ if $y = x^3$.

Solution

$$\frac{dy}{dx} = \frac{d}{dx}(x^3)$$

$$= \lim_{\Delta x \to 0} \frac{(x + \Delta x)^3 - x^3}{\Delta x}$$

$$= \lim_{\Delta x \to 0} \frac{[x^3 + 3x^2 \Delta x + 3x(\Delta x)^2 + (\Delta x)^3] - x^3}{\Delta x}$$

$$= \lim_{\Delta x \to 0} [3x^2 + 3x(\Delta x) + (\Delta x)^2]$$

$$= 3x^2$$

At $x = -1$, $\left.\dfrac{dy}{dx}\right|_{x=-1} = 3x^2\big|_{x=-1} = 3$.   ■

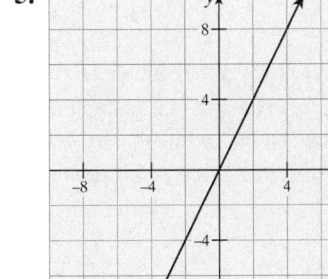

Figure 3.14 Typical calculator output for $\left.\frac{dy}{dx}\right|_{x=-1}$, where $y = x^3$

If you are using technology to find derivatives, most formats require that you input not only the function, but the variable in the expression and the value at which you wish to find the derivative. The usual format is nDeriv(*expression, variable, value*). The symbol "nDeriv" depends on the calculator or software, and sometimes is "nDer" (TI-85/86), "d" (TI-92), "diff" (Maple V), or "Dif" (Derive). This notation is used in Figure 3.14. Some software and calculators will find the exact value of a derivative, whereas some will do a numerical evaluation (as shown in Figure 3.14).

3.1   PROBLEM SET

Ⓐ 1. **WHAT DOES THIS SAY?** Describe the process of finding a derivative using the definition.

2. **WHAT DOES THIS SAY?** What is the definition of a derivative?

3. **WHAT DOES THIS SAY?** Discuss the truth or falsity of the following statements:

If a function f is continuous on (a, b), then it is differentiable on (a, b).
If a function f is differentiable on (a, b), then it is continuous on (a, b).

4. **WHAT DOES THIS SAY?** Discuss the relationship between the derivative of a function f at a point $x = x_0$ and the tangent line at that same point.

In each of Problems 5–10, the graph of a function f is given. Sketch a graph of f'.

5.

6.
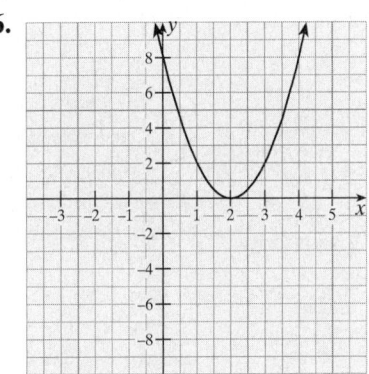

7.
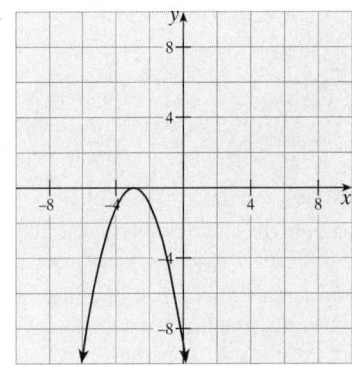

8. 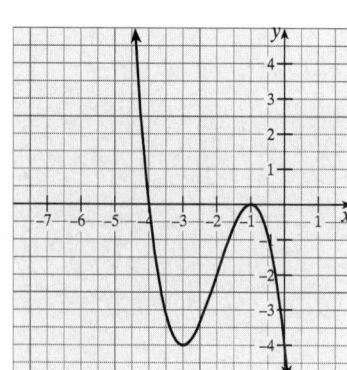   **9.** 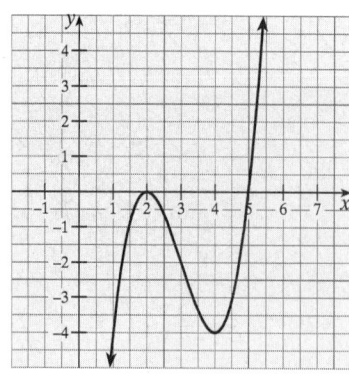   **10.**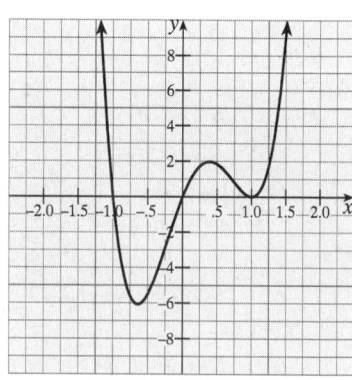

In each of Problems 11–16, a function f is given along with a number c in its domain.

a. *Find the difference quotient of f.*

b. *Find $f'(c)$ by computing the limit of the difference quotient.*

11. $f(x) = 3$ at $c = -5$ **12.** $f(x) = x$ at $c = 2$

13. $f(x) = 2x$ at $c = 1$ **14.** $f(x) = 2x^2$ at $c = 1$

15. $f(x) = 2 - x^2$ at $c = 0$ **16.** $f(x) = -x^2$ at $c = 2$

Use the definition to differentiate the functions given in Problems 17–28, and then describe the set of all numbers for which the function is differentiable.

17. $f(x) = 5$ **18.** $g(x) = 3x$

19. $f(x) = 3x - 7$ **20.** $g(x) = 4 - 5x$

21. $g(x) = 3x^2$ **22.** $h(x) = 2x^2 + 3$

23. $f(x) = x^2 - x$ **24.** $g(t) = 4 - t^2$

25. $f(s) = (s - 1)^2$ **26.** $f(x) = \dfrac{1}{2x}$

27. $f(x) = \sqrt{5x}$ **28.** $f(x) = \sqrt{x + 1}$

Find an equation for the tangent line to the graph of the function at the specified point in Problems 29–34.

29. $f(x) = 3x - 7$ at $(3, 2)$ **30.** $g(x) = 3x^2$ at $(-2, 12)$

31. $f(s) = s^3$ at $s = -\frac{1}{2}$ **32.** $g(t) = 4 - t^2$ at $t = 0$

33. $f(x) = \dfrac{1}{x + 3}$ at $x = 2$ **34.** $g(x) = \sqrt{x - 5}$ at $x = 9$

Find an equation of the normal line to the graph of the function at the specified point in Problems 35–38.

35. $f(x) = 3x - 7$ at $(3, 2)$ **36.** $g(x) = 4 - 5x$ at $(0, 4)$

37. $f(x) = \dfrac{1}{x + 3}$ at $x = 3$ **38.** $f(x) = \sqrt{5x}$ at $x = 5$

Find $\left.\dfrac{dy}{dx}\right|_{x=c}$ for the functions and values of c given in Problems 39–42.

39. $y = 2x$, $c = -1$ **40.** $y = 4 - x$, $c = 2$

41. $y = 1 - x^2$, $c = 0$ **42.** $y = \dfrac{4}{x}$, $c = 1$

ⓑ 43. Suppose $f(x) = x^2$.

a. Compute the slope of the secant line joining the points on the graph of f whose x-coordinates are -2 and -1.9.

b. Use calculus to compute the slope of the line that is tangent to the graph when $x = -2$ and compare this slope with your answer in part **a.**

44. Suppose $f(x) = x^3$.

a. Compute the slope of the secant line joining the points on the graph of f whose x-coordinates are 1 and 1.1.

b. Use calculus to compute the slope of the line that is tangent to the graph when $x = 1$ and compare this slope to your answer from part **a.**

45. Sketch the graph of the function $y = x^2 - x$. Determine the value(s) of x for which the derivative is 0. What happens to the graph at the corresponding point(s)?

46. a. Find the derivative of $f(x) = x^2 - 3x$.

b. Show that the parabola whose equation is $y = x^2 - 3x$ has one horizontal tangent line. Find the equation of this line.

c. Find a point on the graph of f where the tangent line is parallel to the line $3x + y = 11$.

d. Sketch the graph of the parabola whose equation is $y = x^2 - 3x$. Display the horizontal tangent line and the tangent line found in part **c.**

47. a. Find the derivative of $f(x) = 4 - 2x^2$.

b. The graph of f has one horizontal tangent line. What is its equation?

c. At what point on the graph of f is the tangent line parallel to the line $8x + 3y = 4$?

48. Show that the function $f(x) = |x - 2|$ is not differentiable at $x = 2$.

49. Is the function $f(x) = 2|x + 1|$ differentiable at $x = 1$?

50. Let $f(x) = \begin{cases} -x^2 & \text{if } x < 0 \\ x^2 & \text{if } x \geq 0 \end{cases}$.

Does $f'(0)$ exist? *Hint:* Find the difference quotient and take the limit as $\Delta x \to 0$ from the left and from the right.

51. Let $f(x) = \begin{cases} -2x & \text{if } x < 1 \\ \sqrt{x} - 3 & \text{if } x \geq 1 \end{cases}$.

a. Sketch the graph of f.

b. Show that f is continuous but not differentiable at $x = 1$.

52. Counterexample Problem   Give an example of a function that is continuous on $(-\infty, \infty)$ but is not differentiable at $x = 5$.

Estimate the derivative $f'(c)$ in Problems 53–58 by evaluating the difference quotient

$$\frac{\Delta y}{\Delta x} = \frac{f(c + \Delta x) - f(c)}{\Delta x}$$

at a succession of numbers near c.

53. $f(x) = (2x - 1)^2$ for $c = 1$ **54.** $f(x) = \dfrac{1}{x + 1}$ for $c = 2$

55. $f(x) = \sin x$ for $c = \frac{\pi}{3}$ **56.** $f(x) = \cos x$ for $c = \frac{\pi}{3}$

57. $f(x) = \sqrt{x}$ for $c = 4$ **58.** $f(x) = \sqrt[3]{x}$ for $c = 8$

59. Show that the tangent line to the parabola $y = Ax^2$ (for $A \neq 0$) at the point where $x = c$ will intersect the x-axis at the point $(\frac{c}{2}, 0)$. Where does it intersect the y-axis?

60. Find the point(s) on the graph of $f(x) = -x^2$ such that the tangent line at that point passes through the point $(0, -9)$.

61. Interpretation Problem

    a. Find the derivatives of the functions $y = x^2$ and $y = x^2 - 3$ and account geometrically for their similarity.

    b. Without further computation, find the derivative of $y = x^2 + 5$.

62. Interpretation Problem

    a. Find the derivative of $f(x) = x^2 + 3x$.

    b. Find the derivatives of the functions $g(x) = x^2$ and $h(x) = 3x$ separately. How are these derivatives related to the derivative in part **a**?

    c. In general, if $f(x) = g(x) + h(x)$, what would you guess is the relationship between the derivative of f and the derivatives of g and h?

63. Consider a graph of the function defined by $f(x) = x^{2/3}$.

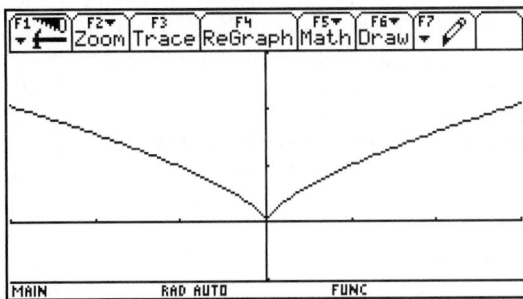

There is a tangent utility on many calculators that will draw tangent lines at a given point. Use this utility or use the preceding simulated graph to draw tangent lines as $x \to 0^-$. Next, draw tangent lines as $x \to 0^+$. Describe what happens, and use this description to support the conclusion that there is no tangent line at $x = 0$.

64. Consider the function

$$f(x) = (x - 2)^{2/3} + 2x^3$$

which gives trouble in seeking the tangent line at $(2, f(2))$. Attempt to compute $f'(2)$, either "by hand" or using a calculator. Describe what happens; in particular, do you see why the tangent line there is meaningless?

65. Compute the difference quotient for the function defined by

$$f(x) = \begin{cases} \dfrac{\sin x}{x} & \text{if } x \neq 0 \\ 1 & \text{if } x = 0 \end{cases}$$

Do you think $f(x)$ is differentiable at $x = 0$? If so, what is the equation of the tangent line at $x = 0$?

66. HISTORICAL QUEST In the guest essay at the end of Chapter 1, it was noted that Isaac Newton, who invented calculus at the same time as Leibniz, considered Fermat as "one of the giants" on whose shoulders he stood. Fermat was a lawyer by profession, but he liked to do mathematics in his spare time. He wrote well over 3,000 mathematical papers and notes. Fermat developed a general procedure for finding tangent lines that is a precursor to the methods of Newton and Leibniz. ∎

PIERRE DE FERMAT
1601–1665

We will explore this procedure by finding a tangent line to the curve

$$x^3 + y^3 - 2xy = 0$$

A graph is shown in Figure 3.15.

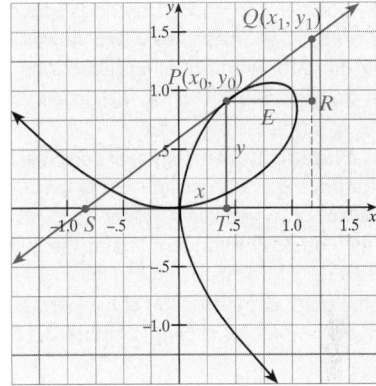

Figure 3.15 Fermat's method of subtangents

    a. Let $P(x_0, y_0)$ be a given point on the curve, and let S be the x-axis intercept of the tangent line at P. Let $Q(x_1, y_1)$ be another point on the tangent line and let T and R be located so $\triangle STP$ and $\triangle PRQ$ are right triangles. Finally, let $A = \left| \overline{ST} \right|$ and $E = \left| \overline{PR} \right|$. Express x_1 and y_1 in terms of x_0, y_0, A, and E.

    b. Fermat reasoned that if E were very small, then Q would "almost" be on the curve. Substitute the values for x_1 and y_1 you found in part **a** into the equation

$$x^3 + y^3 - 2xy = 0$$

That is, substitute the (x, y) values you found in part **a** into this equation.

    c. With the answer from part **b**, you can follow the steps of Fermat by dividing both sides of the equation by E. Fermat reasoned that since E was close to 0, this step should be permitted. Now, after doing this, Fermat further reasoned that since E was close to 0, he could now set $E = 0$ and solve for A. Carry out these steps to write A in terms of x_0 and y_0.

    d. Fermat then constructed the tangent line at P by joining P to S. Draw the tangent line for the given curve at the point $(0.5, 0.93)$ by plotting the point corresponding to the calculated value of A. Find an equation for the tangent line to the curve

$$x^3 + y^3 - 2xy = 0$$

at the point $P(0.5, 0.93)$.

67. HISTORICAL QUEST The groundwork for much of the mathematics we do today, and certainly a necessity for calculus, is the development of analytic geometry by Descartes and Pierre de Fermat (see Problem 66). Descartes' ideas for analytic geometry were published in 1637 as one of three appendices to his *Discourse on the Method* (of Reasoning Well and Seeking Truth in the Sciences). In that same

RENÉ DESCARTES
1596–1650

year, Fermat sent an essay entitled *Introduction to Plane and Solid Loci* to Paris, and in this essay he laid the foundation for analytic geometry. Fermat's paper was more complete and systematic, but Descartes' was published first. Descartes is generally credited with the discovery of analytic geometry, and we speak today of the Cartesian coordinate system and Cartesian geometry to honor Descartes' discovery. Today we describe analytic geometry from two viewpoints: (1) Given a curve, describe it by an equation (Descartes' viewpoint); and (2) given an equation, describe it by a curve (Fermat's viewpoint).

In this Historical Quest we will describe Descartes' circle method for finding a tangent line to a given curve. This method uses algebra and geometry rather than limits. Descartes' method for finding the tangent line to the curve $y = f(x)$ at the point $P(x_0, f(x_0))$ involved first finding the point $Q(x_1, 0)$, which is the point of intersection of the normal line to the curve at P with the x-axis, as shown in Figure 3.16.

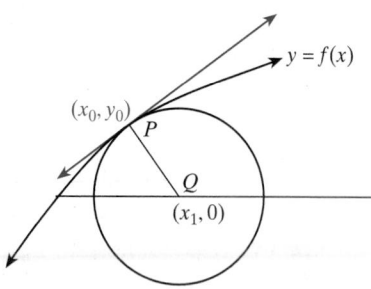

Figure 3.16 Descartes' circle method for finding tangent lines

Descartes then wrote the equation of the circle with center Q passing through P:

$$(x - x_1)^2 + y^2 = (x_0 - x_1)^2 + y_0^2$$

Descartes' next step was to use the equation of the given curve $y = f(x)$ (actually any equation involving two variables) to eliminate one of the variables (usually y) from the equation of the circle. Descartes reasoned that the circle will cut the given curve in two places except when $\overline{PQ}$ is normal, in which case the two intersection points will coincide and the circle will be tangent line to the curve at P. That is, Descartes imposed the condition that the resulting equation (after substitution) has only one root to solve for x_1. The point Q is thus found and the normal line was then known to Descartes. The tangent line can be taken as the perpendicular through P to the normal line. ∎

Carry out Descartes circle method for the parabola $y^2 = 4x$ at the point (4, 4).

68. HISTORICAL QUEST Pierre de Fermat (see Problem 66) also obtained the first method for differentiating polynomials, but his real love was number theory. His most famous problem has come to be known as Fermat's last theorem. He wrote in the margin of a text: *"To divide a cube into two cubes, a fourth power, or in general, any power whatever above the second, into powers of the same denominations, is impossible, and I have assuredly found an admirable proof of this, but the margin is too narrow to contain it."* ∎

In 1993 an imaginative, but lengthy, proof was constructed by Andrew Wiles, and in 1997 Wiles was awarded the Wolfskehl Prize for proving this theorem. An engaging book, *Fermat's Enigma*, shows how a great mathematical puzzle of our age was solved: Lock yourself in a room and emerge seven years later. Write a paper on the history of Fermat's last theorem, including some discussion of the current status of its proof. [You might begin with "Fermat's Last Theorem, The Four Color Conjecture, and Bill Clinton for April Fools' Day," by Edward B. Burger and Frank Morgan, *American Mathematical Monthly*, March 1997, pp. 246–250. Next, see the NOVA film, *The Proof*, which was shown in 1997 on many PBS stations (check with your library or PBS Online). Finally, see "Fermat's Last Stand" by Simon Singh and Kenneth A. Ribet, *Scientific American*, November 1997, pp. 68–73.]

○ 69. If $f'(c) \neq 0$, what is the equation of the normal line to $y = f(x)$ at the point $P(c, f(c))$? What is the equation if $f'(c) = 0$?

70. Suppose a parabola is given in the plane along with its axis of symmetry. Explain how you could construct the tangent line at a given point P on the parabola using only compass and straightedge methods. *Hint:* You may assume that the parabola has an equation of the form $y = Ax^2$ in which the y-axis is the axis of symmetry and the vertex of the parabola is at the origin. Then use the result of Problem 59.

3.2 Techniques of Differentiation

IN THIS SECTION derivative of a constant function, derivative of a power function, procedural rules for finding derivatives, higher-order derivatives

If we had to compute the limit of a difference quotient every time we wished to find a derivative, differentiation would not be the valuable tool that it is. Fortunately, there is a better way, and in this section, we will derive several formulas that will enable us to compute derivatives indirectly, without evaluating any limits.

DERIVATIVE OF A CONSTANT FUNCTION

We begin by proving that the derivative of any constant function is zero. Notice that this is plausible because the graph of the constant function $f(x) = k$ is a horizontal line, and its slope is zero. Thus, for example, if $f(x) = 5$, then $f'(x) = 0$.

THEOREM 3.3 Constant rule

A constant function $f(x) = k$ has derivative $f'(x) = 0$; in Leibniz notation,

$$\frac{d}{dx}(k) = 0$$

Proof Note that if $f(x) = k$, then $f(x + \Delta x) = k$ for all Δx. Therefore, the difference quotient is

$$\frac{f(x + \Delta x) - f(x)}{\Delta x} = \frac{k - k}{\Delta x} = 0$$

and

$$f'(x) = \lim_{\Delta x \to 0} \frac{f(x + \Delta x) - f(x)}{\Delta x} = \lim_{\Delta x \to 0} 0 = 0$$

as claimed. ❑

WARNING Remember $\Delta x \neq 0$ even though $\Delta x \to 0$.

DERIVATIVE OF A POWER FUNCTION

Recall that a **power function** is a function of the form $f(x) = x^n$, where n is a real number. For example, $f(x) = x^2$, $g(x) = x^{-3}$, $h(x) = x^{1/2}$ are all power functions. So are

$$F(x) = \frac{1}{x^2} = x^{-2} \quad \text{and} \quad G(x) = \sqrt[3]{x^2} = x^{2/3}$$

Here is a simple rule for finding the derivative of any power function.

THEOREM 3.4 Power rule

For any real number n, the power function $f(x) = x^n$ has the derivative $f'(x) = nx^{n-1}$; in Leibniz notation,

$$\frac{d}{dx}(x^n) = nx^{n-1}$$

Proof If the exponent n is a positive integer, we can prove the power rule by using the binomial theorem with the definition of derivative. Begin with the difference quotient:

$$\frac{f(x + \Delta x) - f(x)}{\Delta x} = \frac{(x + \Delta x)^n - x^n}{\Delta x}$$

$$= \frac{\left[x^n + nx^{n-1}\Delta x + \frac{n(n-1)}{2}x^{n-2}(\Delta x)^2 + \cdots + (\Delta x)^n \right] - x^n}{\Delta x}$$

$$= \frac{nx^{n-1}\Delta x + \frac{n(n-1)}{2}x^{n-2}(\Delta x)^2 + \cdots + (\Delta x)^n}{\Delta x}$$

$$= nx^{n-1} + \frac{n(n-1)}{2}x^{n-2}\Delta x + \cdots + (\Delta x)^{n-1}$$

Note that Δx is a factor of every term in this expression except the first. Hence, as $\Delta x \to 0$, we have

$$f'(x) = \lim_{\Delta x \to 0} \frac{f(x + \Delta x) - f(x)}{\Delta x}$$

$$= \lim_{\Delta x \to 0} \left[nx^{n-1} + \frac{n(n-1)}{2}x^{n-2}\Delta x + \cdots + (\Delta x)^{n-1} \right]$$

$$= nx^{n-1}$$

If $n = 0$, then $f(x) = x^0 = 1$, so $f'(x) = 0$. We will prove the power rule for negative integer exponents later in this section, and we will deal with the case in which the exponent is any real number in Section 3.6. Note, however, that we have already verified the power rule for $n = 3$ in Example 9 of Section 3.1 and for the rational exponent $\frac{1}{2}$ in Example 3 of Section 3.1, when we showed that the derivative of $f(t) = \sqrt{t} = t^{1/2}$ is

$$f'(t) = \frac{1}{2}t^{-1/2} = \frac{1}{2\sqrt{t}} \quad \text{for } t > 0$$

For the following examples, and the problems at the end of this section, you may assume that the power rule is valid when the exponent n is any real number. ❑

EXAMPLE 1   Using the power rule to find a derivative

Differentiate each of the following functions.

a. $f(x) = x^8$ **b.** $g(x) = x^{3/2}$ **c.** $h(x) = \dfrac{\sqrt[3]{x}}{x^2}$

Solution

a. Applying the power rule with $n = 8$, we find that

$$\frac{d}{dx}(x^8) = 8x^{8-1} = 8x^7$$

b. Applying the power rule with $n = \frac{3}{2}$, we get

$$\frac{d}{dx}(x^{3/2}) = \tfrac{3}{2}x^{3/2-1} = \tfrac{3}{2}x^{1/2} = \tfrac{3}{2}\sqrt{x}$$

c. For this part you need to recognize that $h(x) = \dfrac{x^{1/3}}{x^2} = x^{-5/3}$. Applying the power rule with $n = -\frac{5}{3}$, we find that

$$\frac{d}{dx}(x^{-5/3}) = -\tfrac{5}{3}x^{-5/3-1} = -\tfrac{5}{3}x^{-8/3}$$ ∎

PROCEDURAL RULES FOR FINDING DERIVATIVES

The next theorem expands the class of functions that we can differentiate easily by giving rules for differentiating certain combinations of functions, such as sums, differences, products, and quotients. We will see that the derivative of a sum (difference) is the sum (difference) of derivatives, but the derivative of a product (or quotient) does not have such a simple form. For example, to convince yourself that the derivative of a product is not the product of the separate derivatives, consider the power functions

$$f(x) = x \quad \text{and} \quad g(x) = x^2$$

and their product

$$p(x) = f(x)g(x) = x^3$$

WARNING   Note the derivative of a product is not the product of derivatives. A similar warning applies to the derivative of a quotient. (See Theorem 3.5.)

Because $f'(x) = 1$ and $g'(x) = 2x$, the product of the derivatives is

$$f'(x)g'(x) = (1)(2x) = 2x$$

whereas the actual derivative of $p(x) = x^3$ is $p'(x) = 3x^2$. The product rule tells us how to find the derivative of a product.

THEOREM 3.5   Basic rules for combining derivatives—Procedural forms

If f and g are differentiable functions at all x, and a, b, and c are any real numbers, then the functions cf, $f + g$, fg, and f/g (for $g(x) \neq 0$) are also differentiable, and their derivatives satisfy the following formulas:

Name of Rule	Function Notation	Leibniz Notation
Constant multiple	$[cf(x)]' = cf'(x)$	$\dfrac{d}{dx}(cf) = c\dfrac{df}{dx}$
Sum rule	$[f(x) + g(x)]' = f'(x) + g'(x)$	$\dfrac{d}{dy}(f + g) = \dfrac{df}{dx} + \dfrac{dg}{dx}$
Difference rule	$[f(x) - g(x)]' = f'(x) - g'(x)$	$\dfrac{d}{dx}(f - g) = \dfrac{df}{dx} - \dfrac{dg}{dx}$

The constant multiple, sum, and difference rules can be combined into a single rule, which is called the *linearity rule*.

Linearity rule	$[af(x) + bg(x)]' = af'(x) + bg'(x)$	$\dfrac{d}{dx}(af + bg) = a\dfrac{df}{dx} + b\dfrac{dg}{dx}$
Product rule	$[f(x)g(x)]' = f(x)g'(x) + f'(x)g(x)$	$\dfrac{d}{dx}(fg) = f\dfrac{dg}{dx} + g\dfrac{df}{dx}$
Quotient rule	$\left[\dfrac{f(x)}{g(x)}\right]' = \dfrac{g(x)f'(x) - f(x)g'(x)}{[g(x)]^2}$	$\dfrac{d}{dx}\left(\dfrac{f}{g}\right) = \dfrac{g\dfrac{df}{dx} - f\dfrac{dg}{dx}}{g^2}$

WARNING   Note that the order of terms in the quotient rule matters because

$$gf' - fg' \neq fg' - gf'$$

Proof   We will prove the product rule in detail, leaving the other rules as problems.

Let $f(x)$ and $g(x)$ be differentiable functions of x and let $p(x) = f(x)g(x)$. We will add and subtract the term $f(x + \Delta x)g(x)$ to the numerator of the difference quotient for $p(x)$ to create difference quotients for $f(x)$ and $g(x)$. Thus,

$$p'(x) = \frac{dp}{dx} = \lim_{\Delta x \to 0} \frac{p(x + \Delta x) - p(x)}{\Delta x}$$

$$= \lim_{\Delta x \to 0} \frac{f(x + \Delta x)g(x + \Delta x) - f(x)g(x)}{\Delta x}$$

$$= \lim_{\Delta x \to 0} \frac{f(x + \Delta x)g(x + \Delta x) - f(x + \Delta x)g(x) + f(x + \Delta x)g(x) - f(x)g(x)}{\Delta x}$$

$$= \lim_{\Delta x \to 0} \left[f(x + \Delta x)\left[\frac{g(x + \Delta x) - g(x)}{\Delta x}\right] + g(x)\left[\frac{f(x + \Delta x) - f(x)}{\Delta x}\right] \right]$$

$$= \lim_{\Delta x \to 0} f(x + \Delta x) \underbrace{\lim_{\Delta x \to 0} \left[\frac{g(x + \Delta x) - g(x)}{\Delta x}\right]}_{\text{This is the derivative of } g.} + \lim_{\Delta x \to 0} g(x) \underbrace{\lim_{\Delta x \to 0} \left[\frac{f(x + \Delta x) - f(x)}{\Delta x}\right]}_{\text{This is the derivative of } f.}$$

$$= f(x)g'(x) + g(x)f'(x) \qquad \lim_{\Delta x \to 0} f(x + \Delta x) = f(x) \text{ because } f \text{ is continuous.} \qquad \square$$

Note that in each part of Theorem 3.5, we prove the differentiability of the appropriate functional combination at the same time we are establishing the differentiation formula.

EXAMPLE 2 Using the basic rules to find derivatives

Differentiate each of the following functions.

a. $f(x) = 2x^2 - 5\sqrt{x}$ **b.** $p(x) = (3x^2 - 1)(7 + 2x^3)$

c. $q(x) = \dfrac{4x - 7}{3 - x^2}$ **d.** $g(x) = (4x + 3)^2$

e. $F(x) = \dfrac{2}{3x^2} - \dfrac{x}{3} + \dfrac{4}{5} + \dfrac{x + 1}{x}$

Solution

a. Apply the linearity rule (constant multiple, sum, and difference) and power rules:

$$f'(x) = 2(x^2)' - 5(x^{1/2})' = 2(2x) - 5\left(\tfrac{1}{2}\right)(x^{-1/2}) = 4x - \tfrac{5}{2}x^{-1/2}$$

b. Apply the product rule; then apply the linearity and power rules:

$$\begin{aligned}
p'(x) &= (3x^2 - 1)(7 + 2x^3)' + (3x^2 - 1)'(7 + 2x^3) \\
&= (3x^2 - 1)[0 + 2(3x^2)] + [3(2x) - 0](7 + 2x^3) \\
&= (3x^2 - 1)(6x^2) + (6x)(7 + 2x^3) \\
&= 6x(5x^3 - x + 7)
\end{aligned}$$

c. Apply the quotient rule, then the linearity and power rules:

$$\begin{aligned}
q'(x) &= \frac{(3 - x^2)(4x - 7)' - (4x - 7)(3 - x^2)'}{(3 - x^2)^2} \\
&= \frac{(3 - x^2)(4 - 0) - (4x - 7)(0 - 2x)}{(3 - x^2)^2} \\
&= \frac{12 - 4x^2 + 8x^2 - 14x}{(3 - x^2)^2} = \frac{4x^2 - 14x + 12}{(3 - x^2)^2}
\end{aligned}$$

d. Apply the product rule:

$$\begin{aligned}
g'(x) &= (4x + 3)(4x + 3)' + (4x + 3)'(4x + 3) \\
&= (4x + 3)(4) + (4)(4x + 3) = 8(4x + 3)
\end{aligned}$$

Sometimes when the exponent is 2, it is easier to expand before differentiating:

$$g(x) = (4x + 3)^2 = 16x^2 + 24x + 9$$
$$g'(x) = 32x + 24$$

e. Write the function using negative exponents for reciprocal powers:

$$F(x) = \tfrac{2}{3}x^{-2} - \tfrac{1}{3}x + \tfrac{4}{5} + 1 + x^{-1}$$

Then apply the power rule term by term to obtain

$$\begin{aligned}
F'(x) &= \tfrac{2}{3}(-2x^{-3}) - \tfrac{1}{3} + 0 + 0 + (-1)x^{-2} \\
&= -\tfrac{4}{3}x^{-3} - \tfrac{1}{3} - x^{-2}
\end{aligned}$$

    In applying the power rule term by term in Example 2e, we really used the following generalization of the linearity rule.

COROLLARY TO THEOREM 3.5 The extended linearity rule

If $f_1, f_2, \ldots, f_n$ are differentiable functions and $a_1, a_2, \ldots, a_n$ are constants, then

$$\frac{d}{dx}[a_1 f_1 + a_2 f_2 + \cdots + a_n f_n] = a_1 \frac{df_1}{dx} + a_2 \frac{df_2}{dx} + \cdots + a_n \frac{df_n}{dx}$$

Proof   The proof is a straightforward extension (using mathematical induction) of the proof of the linearity rule of Theorem 3.5.

Example 3 illustrates how the extended linearity rule can be used to differentiate a polynomial.

EXAMPLE 3   Derivative of a polynomial function

Differentiate the polynomial function $p(x) = 2x^5 - 3x^2 + 8x - 5$.

Solution

$$\begin{aligned}
p'(x) &= \frac{d}{dx}[2x^5 - 3x^2 + 8x - 5] \\
&= 2\frac{d}{dx}(x^5) - 3\frac{d}{dx}(x^2) + 8\frac{d}{dx}(x) - \frac{d}{dx}(5) &&\text{Extended linearity rule} \\
&= 2(5x^4) - 3(2x) + 8(1) - 0 &&\text{Power rule; constant rule} \\
&= 10x^4 - 6x + 8
\end{aligned}$$

  ■

EXAMPLE 4   Derivative of a product of polynomials

Differentiate $p(x) = (x^3 - 4x + 7)(3x^5 - x^2 + 6x)$.

Solution

We could expand the product function $p(x)$ as a polynomial and proceed as in Example 3, but it is easier to use the product rule.

$$\begin{aligned}
p'(x) &= (x^3 - 4x + 7)(3x^5 - x^2 + 6x)' + (x^3 - 4x + 7)'(3x^5 - x^2 + 6x) \\
&= (x^3 - 4x + 7)(15x^4 - 2x + 6) + (3x^2 - 4)(3x^5 - x^2 + 6x)
\end{aligned}$$

This form is an acceptable answer, but if you are using software or an algebraic calculator, more than likely you will obtain the expanded formula

$$p'(x) = 24x^7 - 72x^5 + 100x^4 + 24x^3 + 12x^2 - 62x + 42$$

  ■

EXAMPLE 5   Equation of a tangent line

Find the standard form equation for the line tangent to the graph of

$$f(x) = \frac{3x^2 + 5}{2x^2 + x - 3}$$

at the point where $x = -1$.

Solution

Evaluating $f(x)$ at $x = -1$, we find that $f(-1) = -4$ (verify); therefore, the point of tangency is $(-1, -4)$. The slope of the tangent line at $(-1, -4)$ is $f'(-1)$. Find $f'(x)$ by applying the quotient rule:

$$\begin{aligned}
f'(x) &= \frac{(2x^2 + x - 3)(3x^2 + 5)' - (3x^2 + 5)(2x^2 + x - 3)'}{(2x^2 + x - 3)^2} \\
&= \frac{(2x^2 + x - 3)(6x) - (3x^2 + 5)(4x + 1)}{(2x^2 + x - 3)^2}
\end{aligned}$$

The slope of the tangent line is

$$f'(-1) = \frac{(2 - 1 - 3)(-6) - (3 + 5)(-4 + 1)}{(2 - 1 - 3)^2} = \frac{(-2)(-6) - (8)(-3)}{(-2)^2} = 9$$

From the formula (Theorem 3.1) $y = f'(x_0)(x - x_0) + f(x_0)$, we find that an equation for the tangent line at $(-1, -4)$ is

$$y = 9(x + 1) + (-4)$$

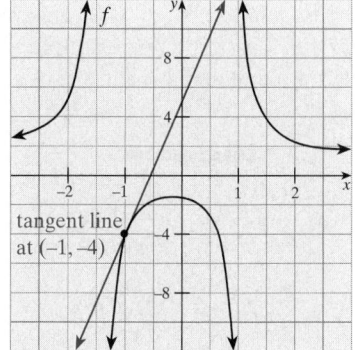

Figure 3.17 Graph of f and the tangent line at the point $(-1, -4)$

or in standard form $9x - y + 5 = 0$. The graphs of both f and its tangent line at $(-1, -4)$ are shown in Figure 3.17.

  ■

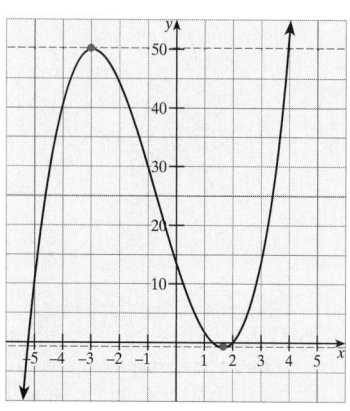

Figure 3.18 Graph of curve and the horizontal tangent lines

EXAMPLE 6 **Finding horizontal tangent lines**

Let $y = (x - 2)(x^2 + 4x - 7)$. Find all points on this curve where the tangent line is horizontal.

Solution

The tangent line will be horizontal when $dy/dx = 0$, because the derivative dy/dx measures the slope and a horizontal line has slope 0 (see Figure 3.18). Applying the product rule, we find

$$\frac{dy}{dx} = (x - 2)(x^2 + 4x - 7)' + (x - 2)'(x^2 + 4x - 7)$$
$$= (x - 2)(2x + 4) + (1)(x^2 + 4x - 7)$$
$$= 2x^2 - 8 + x^2 + 4x - 7$$
$$= 3x^2 + 4x - 15 = (3x - 5)(x + 3)$$

Thus, $\dfrac{dy}{dx} = 0$ when $x = \frac{5}{3}$ or $x = -3$. The corresponding points $(\frac{5}{3}, -\frac{22}{27})$ and $(-3, 50)$ are the points on the curve at which the tangent line is horizontal. ∎

In the following example, we use the quotient rule to extend the proof of the power rule to the case in which the exponent n is a negative integer.

EXAMPLE 7 **Proof of the power rule for negative exponents**

Show that $\dfrac{d}{dx}(x^n) = nx^{n-1}$ if $n = -m$, where m is a positive integer.

Solution

We have $f(x) = x^n = x^{-m} = 1/x^m$, so apply the quotient rule:

$$\frac{d}{dx}(x^n) = \frac{d}{dx}\left(\frac{1}{x^m}\right) = \frac{x^m(1)' - (1)(x^m)'}{(x^m)^2} = \frac{x^m(0) - mx^{m-1}}{x^{2m}}$$
$$= -mx^{(m-1)-2m} = -mx^{-m-1} = nx^{n-1} \qquad \text{Substitute } -m = n. \quad ∎$$

HIGHER-ORDER DERIVATIVES

Occasionally, it is useful to differentiate the derivative of a function. In this context, we will refer to f' as the **first derivative** of f and to the derivative of f' as the **second derivative** of f. We could denote the second derivative by $(f')'$, but for simplicity we write f''. Other higher-order derivatives are defined and denoted similarly. Thus, the **third derivative** of f is the derivative of f'' and is denoted by f'''. In general, for $n > 3$, the **nth derivative** of f is denoted by $f^{(n)}$; $f^{(4)}$ or $f^{(5)}$, for example. In Leibniz notation, higher-order derivatives for $y = f(x)$ are denoted as follows:

			Leibniz notation	
First derivative:	y'	$f'(x)$	$\dfrac{dy}{dx}$	**or** $\dfrac{d}{dx}f(x)$
Second derivative:	y''	$f''(x)$	$\dfrac{d}{dx}\left(\dfrac{dy}{dx}\right) = \dfrac{d^2y}{dx^2}$	**or** $\dfrac{d^2}{dx^2}f(x)$
Third derivative:	y'''	$f'''(x)$	$\dfrac{d}{dx}\left(\dfrac{d^2y}{dx^2}\right) = \dfrac{d^3y}{dx^3}$	**or** $\dfrac{d^3}{dx^3}f(x)$

Leibniz notation

Fourth derivative: $y^{(4)}$ $f^{(4)}(x)$ $\dfrac{d^4 y}{dx^4}$ or $\dfrac{d^4}{dx^4}f(x)$

$\vdots$ $\qquad$ $\vdots$ $\quad$ $\vdots$ $\qquad$ $\vdots$ $\qquad\quad$ $\vdots$

nth derivative $\quad$ $y^{(n)}$ $\quad$ $f^{(n)}(x)$ $\quad$ $\dfrac{d^n y}{dx^n}$ or $\dfrac{d^n}{dx^n}f(x)$

▶ **What This Says** Because the derivative of a function is a function, differentiation can be applied over and over, as long as the derivative itself is a differentiable function. That is, we can take derivatives of derivatives.

Notice also that for derivatives of higher order than the third, the parentheses distinguish a derivative from a power. For example, $f^4 \neq f^{(4)}$.

You should note that all higher-order derivatives of a polynomial $p(x)$ will also be polynomials, and if p has degree n, then $p^{(k)}(x) = 0$ for $k \geq n + 1$, as illustrated in the following example.

EXAMPLE 8 Higher-order derivatives for a polynomial function

Find the derivatives of all orders of

$$p(x) = -2x^4 + 9x^3 - 5x^2 + 7$$

Solution

$$p'(x) = -8x^3 + 27x^2 - 10x; \quad p''(x) = -24x^2 + 54x - 10;$$

$$p'''(x) = -48x + 54; \quad p^{(4)}(x) = -48; \quad p^{(5)}(x) = 0; \ldots \quad p^{(k)}(x) = 0 \ (k \geq 5)$$

■

3.2 PROBLEM SET

A *To demonstrate the power of the theorems of this section, Problems 1–4 ask you to go back and rework some problems in Section 3.1, using the material of this section instead of the definition of derivative.*

1. Find the derivatives of the functions given in Problems 11–16 of Problem Set 3.1.
2. Find the derivatives of the functions given in Problems 17–22 of Problem Set 3.1.
3. Find the derivatives of the functions given in Problems 23–27 of Problem Set 3.1.
4. Find the derivatives of the functions given in Problems 39–42 of Problem Set 3.1.

Differentiate the functions given in Problems 5–20. Assume that C is a constant.

5. **a.** $f(x) = 3x^4 - 9$ $\qquad$ **b.** $g(x) = 3(9)^4 - x$
6. **a.** $f(x) = 5x^2 + x$ $\qquad$ **b.** $g(x) = \pi^3$
7. **a.** $f(x) = x^3 + C$ $\qquad$ **b.** $g(x) = C^2 + x$
8. **a.** $f(t) = 10t^{-1}$ $\qquad$ **b.** $g(t) = \dfrac{7}{t}$
9. $r(t) = t^2 - \dfrac{1}{t^2} + \dfrac{5}{t^4}$ $\qquad$ 10. $f(x) = \pi^3 - 3\pi^2$

11. $f(x) = \dfrac{7}{x^2} + x^{2/3} + C$ $\qquad$ 12. $g(x) = \dfrac{1}{2\sqrt{x}} + \dfrac{x^2}{4} + C$

13. $f(x) = \dfrac{x^3 + x^2 + x - 7}{x^2}$ $\qquad$ 14. $g(x) = \dfrac{2x^5 - 3x^2 + 11}{x^3}$

15. $f(x) = (2x + 1)(1 - 4x^3)$ $\qquad$ 16. $g(x) = (x + 2)(2\sqrt{x} + x^2)$

17. $f(x) = \dfrac{3x + 5}{x + 9}$ $\qquad$ 18. $f(x) = \dfrac{x^2 + 3}{x^2 + 5}$

19. $g(x) = x^2(x + 2)^2$ $\qquad$ 20. $f(x) = x^2(2x + 1)^2$

In Problems 21–24, find f', f'', f''', and $f^{(4)}$.

21. $f(x) = x^5 - 5x^3 + x + 12$
22. $f(x) = \frac{1}{4}x^8 - \frac{1}{2}x^6 - x^2 + 2$

23. $f(x) = \dfrac{-2}{x^2}$ $\qquad$ 24. $f(x) = \dfrac{4}{\sqrt{x}}$

25. Find $\dfrac{d^2 y}{dx^2}$, where $y = 3x^3 - 7x^2 + 2x - 3$.

26. Find $\dfrac{d^2 y}{dx^2}$, where $y = (x^2 + 4)(1 - 3x^3)$.

In Problems 27–32, find the standard form equation for the tangent line to $y = f(x)$ at the specified point.

27. $f(x) = x^2 - 3x - 5$, where $x = -2$

28. $f(x) = x^5 - 3x^3 - 5x + 2$, where $x = 1$

29. $f(x) = (x^2 + 1)(1 - x^3)$, where $x = 1$

30. $f(x) = \dfrac{x+1}{x-1}$, where $x = 0$

31. $f(x) = \dfrac{x^2+5}{x+5}$, where $x = 1$

32. $f(x) = 1 - \dfrac{1}{x} + \dfrac{2}{\sqrt{x}}$, where $x = 4$

Find the coordinates of each point on the graph of the given function where the tangent line is horizontal in Problems 33–39.

33. $f(x) = 2x^3 - 7x^2 + 8x - 3$

34. $f(t) = t^4 + 4t^3 - 8t^2 + 3$ **35.** $g(x) = (3x - 5)(x - 8)$

36. $f(t) = \dfrac{1}{t^2} - \dfrac{1}{t^3}$ **37.** $f(x) = \sqrt{x}(x - 3)$

38. $h(u) = \dfrac{1}{\sqrt{u}}(u + 9)$ **39.** $h(x) = \dfrac{4x^2 + 12x + 9}{2x + 3}$

B 40. a. Differentiate the function $f(x) = 2x^2 - 5x - 3$.

    b. Factor the function in part **a** and differentiate by using the product rule. Show that the two answers are the same.

41. a. Use the quotient rule to differentiate $f(x) = \dfrac{2x - 3}{x^3}$.

    b. Rewrite the function in part **a** as $f(x) = x^{-3}(2x - 3)$ and differentiate by using the product rule.

    c. Rewrite the function in part **a** as $f(x) = 2x^{-2} - 3x^{-3}$ and differentiate.

    d. Show that the answers to parts **a**, **b**, and **c** are all the same.

42. Find numbers a, b, and c that guarantee that the graph of the function $f(x) = ax^2 + bx + c$ will have x-intercepts at $(0, 0)$ and $(5, 0)$ and a tangent line with slope 1 where $x = 2$.

43. Find the equation for the tangent line to the curve with equation $y = x^4 - 2x + 1$ that is parallel to the line $2x - y - 3 = 0$.

44. Find equations for two tangent lines to the graph of $f(x) = \dfrac{3x + 5}{1 + x}$ that are perpendicular to the line $2x - y = 1$.

45. Let $f(x) = (x^3 - 2x^2)(x + 2)$.

    a. Find an equation for the tangent line to the graph of f at the point where $x = 1$.

    b. Find an equation for the normal line to the graph of f at the point where $x = 0$.

46. Find an equation for a normal line to the graph of $f(x) = (x^3 - 2x^2)(x + 2)$ that is parallel to the line $x - 16y + 17 = 0$.

47. Find all points (x, y) on the graph of $y = 4x^2$ with the property that the tangent line at (x, y) passes through the point $(2, 0)$.

48. Find the equations of all the tangent lines to the graph of the function $f(x) = x^2 - 4x + 25$ that pass through the origin.

Determine which (if any) of the functions $y = f(x)$ given in Problems 49–52 satisfy the equation

$$y''' + y'' + y' = x + 1$$

49. $f(x) = x^2 + 2x - 3$ **50.** $f(x) = x^3 + x^2 + x$

51. $f(x) = \frac{1}{2}x^2 + 3$ **52.** $f(x) = 2x^2 + x$

53. HISTORICAL QUEST   When working with rational expressions, we need to be careful about division by zero. One of the earliest recorded treatments of division by zero is attributed to the Hindu mathematician Āryabhata (476–550), in whose honor the first Indian satellite was named. He also gave rules for approximations of square roots and sums of arithmetic progressions as well as rules for basic algebraic manipulations. One example of his work is the following calculation for π: "Add four to one hundred, multiply by eight and add again sixty-two thousand; the result is the approximate value of the circumference of a circle whose diameter is twenty-thousand."

    Follow the steps of Āryabhata's approximation for π. After you have completed this demonstration, discuss the procedure and technology you used and contrast it with the tools that Āryabhata must have had available.

C 54. What is the relationship between the degree of a polynomial function P and the value of k for which $P^{(k)}(x)$ is first equal to 0?

55. Prove the constant multiple rule $(cf)' = cf'$.

56. Prove the sum rule $(f + g)' = f' + g'$.

57. Use the definition of the derivative to find the derivative of f^2, given that f is a differentiable function.

58. Prove the product rule by using the result of Problem 57 and the identity

$$fg = \tfrac{1}{2}\left[(f + g)^2 - f^2 - g^2\right]$$

59. Prove the quotient rule

$$\left(\frac{f}{g}\right)' = \frac{gf' - fg'}{g^2}$$

where $g(x) \neq 0$. *Hint*: First show that the difference quotient for f/g can be expressed as

$$\frac{\frac{f}{g}(x + \Delta x) - \frac{f}{g}(x)}{\Delta x} = \frac{f(x + \Delta x)g(x) - f(x)g(x + \Delta x)}{(\Delta x)g(x + \Delta x)g(x)}$$

and then subtract and add the term $g(x)f(x)$ in the numerator.

60. Show that the reciprocal function $r(x) = 1/f(x)$ has the derivative $r'(x) = -f'(x)/[f(x)]^2$ at each point x where f is differentiable and $f(x) \neq 0$.

61. If f, g, and h are differentiable functions, show that the product fgh is also differentiable and

$$(fgh)' = fgh' + fg'h + f'gh$$

62. Let f be a function that is differentiable at x.

    a. If $g(x) = [f(x)]^3$, show that $g'(x) = 3[f(x)]^2 f'(x)$.
    Hint: Write $g(x) = [f(x)]^2 f(x)$ and use the product rule.

    b. Show that $p(x) = [f(x)]^4$ has the derivative

$$p'(x) = 4[f(x)]^3 f'(x).$$

63. Find constants A, B, and C so that $y = Ax^3 + Bx + C$ satisfies the equation

$$y''' + 2y'' - 3y' + y = x$$

3.3 Derivatives of Trigonometric, Exponential, and Logarithmic Functions

IN THIS SECTION derivatives of the sine and cosine functions, differentiation of the other trigonometric functions, derivatives of exponential and logarithmic functions

DERIVATIVES OF THE SINE AND COSINE FUNCTIONS

In calculus we assume that the trigonometric functions are functions of real numbers or of angles measured in radians.

We make this assumption because the trigonometric differentiation formulas rely on limit formulas that become complicated if degree measurement is used instead of radian measure.

Before stating the theorem for the derivatives of the sine and cosine functions, suppose we look at the graph of the difference quotient. Consider $f(x) = \sin x$. Then

$$\frac{\sin(x + \Delta x) - \sin x}{\Delta x} = \frac{\sin(x + 0.01) - \sin x}{0.01}$$

is the difference quotient for $\Delta x = 0.01$. To graph this difference quotient, shown in Figure 3.19, we input to a calculator as

$$Y1=(SIN(X+.01)-SIN\ X)/.01$$

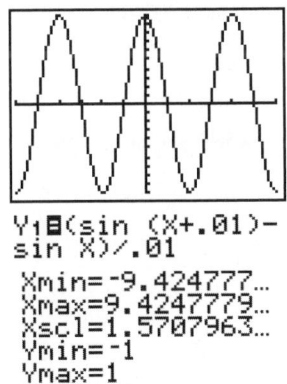

Y₁◘(sin (X+.01)-
sin X)/.01

Xmin=-9.424777…
Xmax=9.4247779…
Xscl=1.5707963…
Ymin=-1
Ymax=1
Yscl=.1

Figure 3.19 Calculator graph of the difference quotient for $y = \sin x$

From the graph of this difference quotient, it appears that the derivative of $f(x) = \sin x$ is $f'(x) = \cos x$. We now verify this with the following theorem, which uses the following limits established earlier in Theorem 2.3:

$$\lim_{h \to 0} \frac{\sin h}{h} = 1 \qquad \lim_{h \to 0} \frac{\cos h - 1}{h} = 0$$

THEOREM 3.6 Derivatives of the sine and cosine functions

The functions $\sin x$ and $\cos x$ are differentiable for all x and

$$\frac{d}{dx} \sin x = \cos x \qquad \frac{d}{dx} \cos x = -\sin x$$

Proof   The proofs of these two formulas are similar. We will prove the first using the trigonometric identity

$$\sin(\alpha + \beta) = \sin \alpha \cos \beta + \cos \alpha \sin \beta$$

and leave the proof of the second formula as a problem. From the definition of the derivative

$$\frac{d}{dx} \sin x = \lim_{\Delta x \to 0} \frac{\sin(x + \Delta x) - \sin x}{\Delta x}$$

$$= \lim_{\Delta x \to 0} \frac{\sin x \cos \Delta x + \cos x \sin \Delta x - \sin x}{\Delta x}$$

$$= \lim_{\Delta x \to 0} \left[\sin x \left(\frac{\cos \Delta x}{\Delta x} \right) + \cos x \left(\frac{\sin \Delta x}{\Delta x} \right) - \frac{\sin x}{\Delta x} \right]$$

$$= (\sin x) \lim_{\Delta x \to 0} \left(\frac{\cos \Delta x - 1}{\Delta x} \right) + (\cos x) \lim_{\Delta x \to 0} \frac{\sin \Delta x}{\Delta x}$$

$$= (\sin x)(0) + (\cos x)(1)$$

$$= \cos x \qquad\qquad ❑$$

EXAMPLE 1   Derivative involving a trigonometric function

Differentiate $f(x) = 2x^4 + 3 \cos x + \sin a$, for constant a.

Solution

$$f'(x) = \frac{d}{dx}(2x^4 + 3\cos x + \sin a)$$

$$= 2\frac{d}{dx}(x^4) + 3\frac{d}{dx}(\cos x) + \frac{d}{dx}(\sin a) \quad \text{Extended linearity rule}$$

$$= 2(4x^3) + 3(-\sin x) + 0 \quad \text{Power rule, derivative of cosine, and derivative of a constant}$$

$$= 8x^3 - 3\sin x$$

EXAMPLE 2   Derivative of a trigonometric function with product rule

Differentiate $f(x) = x^2 \sin x$.

Solution

$$f'(x) = \frac{d}{dx}(x^2 \sin x)$$

$$= x^2\frac{d}{dx}(\sin x) + \sin x\frac{d}{dx}(x^2) \quad \text{Product rule}$$

$$= x^2 \cos x + 2x \sin x \quad \text{Power rule and derivative of sine}$$

EXAMPLE 3   Derivative of a trigonometric function with quotient rule

Differentiate $h(t) = \dfrac{\sqrt{t}}{\cos t}$.

Solution

Write $\sqrt{t}$ as $t^{1/2}$. Then

$$h'(t) = \frac{d}{dt}\left[\frac{t^{1/2}}{\cos t}\right]$$

$$= \frac{\cos t\dfrac{d}{dt}(t^{1/2}) - t^{1/2}\dfrac{d}{dt}\cos t}{\cos^2 t} \quad \text{Quotient rule}$$

$$= \frac{\frac{1}{2}t^{-1/2}\cos t - t^{1/2}(-\sin t)}{\cos^2 t} \quad \text{Power rule and derivative of sine}$$

$$= \frac{\frac{1}{2}t^{-1/2}(\cos t + 2t \sin t)}{\cos^2 t} \quad \text{Common factor } \frac{1}{2}t^{-1/2}$$

$$= \frac{\cos t + 2t \sin t}{2\sqrt{t}\cos^2 t}$$

DIFFERENTIATION OF THE OTHER TRIGONOMETRIC FUNCTIONS

You will need to be able to differentiate not only the sine and cosine functions, but also the other trigonometric functions. To find the derivatives of these functions you will need the following identities, which are given in the *Student Mathematics Handbook* and Appendix E.

$$\tan x = \frac{\sin x}{\cos x} \qquad \cot x = \frac{\cos x}{\sin x}$$

$$\sec x = \frac{1}{\cos x} \qquad \csc x = \frac{1}{\sin x}$$

You will also need the following identities:

$$\cos^2 x + \sin^2 x = 1, \quad 1 + \tan^2 x = \sec^2 x, \quad \cot^2 x + 1 = \csc^2 x$$

THEOREM 3.7   Derivatives of the trigonometric functions

The six basic trigonometric functions $\sin x$, $\cos x$, $\tan x$, $\csc x$, $\sec x$, and $\cot x$ are all differentiable wherever they are defined, and

$$\frac{d}{dx}\sin x = \cos x \qquad\qquad \frac{d}{dx}\cos x = -\sin x$$

$$\frac{d}{dx}\tan x = \sec^2 x \qquad\qquad \frac{d}{dx}\cot x = -\csc^2 x$$

$$\frac{d}{dx}\sec x = \sec x \tan x \qquad\qquad \frac{d}{dx}\csc x = -\csc x \cot x$$

Proof   The derivatives for the sine and cosine functions were given in Theorem 3.6. All the other derivatives in this theorem are proved by using the quotient rule along with formulas for the derivatives of the sine and cosine functions. We will obtain the derivative of the tangent function and leave the rest as problems (see Problems 56–59).

$$\frac{d}{dx}\tan x = \frac{d}{dx}\frac{\sin x}{\cos x} \qquad\qquad \text{Trigonometric identity}$$

$$= \frac{\cos x \dfrac{d}{dx}\sin x - \sin x \dfrac{d}{dx}\cos x}{\cos^2 x} \qquad\qquad \text{Quotient rule}$$

$$= \frac{\cos x(\cos x) - \sin x(-\sin x)}{\cos^2 x} \qquad\qquad \text{Derivative of } \sin x \text{ and } \cos x$$

$$= \frac{\cos^2 x + \sin^2 x}{\cos^2 x}$$

$$= \frac{1}{\cos^2 x} \qquad\qquad \cos^2 x + \sin^2 x = 1$$

$$= \sec^2 x \qquad\qquad 1/\cos^2 x = \sec^2 x \qquad \square$$

EXAMPLE 4   Derivative of a trigonometric function with the product rule

Differentiate $f(\theta) = 3\theta \sec \theta$.

Solution
$$f'(\theta) = \frac{d}{d\theta}(3\theta \sec \theta)$$
$$= 3\theta\frac{d}{d\theta}\sec \theta + \sec \theta \frac{d}{d\theta}(3\theta) \qquad \text{Product rule}$$
$$= 3\theta \sec \theta \tan \theta + 3 \sec \theta \qquad \blacksquare$$

EXAMPLE 5   Derivative of a product of trigonometric functions

Differentiate $f(x) = \sec x \tan x$.

Solution
$$f'(x) = \frac{d}{dx}(\sec x \tan x)$$
$$= \sec x \frac{d}{dx}\tan x + \tan x \frac{d}{dx}\sec x \qquad \text{Product rule}$$
$$= \sec x(\sec^2 x) + \tan x(\sec x \tan x)$$
$$= \sec^3 x + \sec x \tan^2 x \qquad \blacksquare$$

EXAMPLE 6   Equation of a tangent line involving a trigonometric function

Find the equation of the tangent line to the curve $y = \cot x - 2\csc x$ at the point where $x = \frac{2\pi}{3}$.

Solution

When $x = \frac{2\pi}{3}$, we have

$$\cot \frac{2\pi}{3} - 2 \csc \frac{2\pi}{3} = \frac{-\sqrt{3}}{3} - 2\left(\frac{2\sqrt{3}}{3}\right) = \frac{-5\sqrt{3}}{3}$$

so the point of tangency is $P\left(\frac{2\pi}{3}, \frac{-5\sqrt{3}}{3}\right)$. To find the slope of the tangent line at P, we first compute the derivative $\frac{dy}{dx}$:

$$
\begin{aligned}
\frac{dy}{dx} &= \frac{d}{dx}(\cot x - 2 \csc x) \\
&= \frac{d}{dx} \cot x - 2 \frac{d}{dx} \csc x \qquad \text{Linearity rule} \\
&= -\csc^2 x - 2(-\csc x \cot x) \\
&= 2 \csc x \cot x - \csc^2 x
\end{aligned}
$$

Then the slope of the tangent line is given by

$$
\begin{aligned}
\left.\frac{dy}{dx}\right|_{x=2\pi/3} &= 2 \csc \frac{2\pi}{3} \cot \frac{2\pi}{3} - \csc^2 \frac{2\pi}{3} \\
&= 2\left(\frac{2}{\sqrt{3}}\right)\left(\frac{-1}{\sqrt{3}}\right) - \left(\frac{2}{\sqrt{3}}\right)^2 \\
&= \frac{-8}{3}
\end{aligned}
$$

so the tangent line at $\left(\frac{2\pi}{3}, \frac{-5\sqrt{3}}{3}\right)$ with slope $-\frac{8}{3}$ is

$$y + \frac{5\sqrt{3}}{3} = -\frac{8}{3}\left(x - \frac{2\pi}{3}\right)$$

$$24x + 9y + 15\sqrt{3} - 16\pi = 0 \qquad \blacksquare$$

DERIVATIVES OF EXPONENTIAL AND LOGARITHMIC FUNCTIONS

The next theorem, which is easy to prove and remember, is one of the most important results in all of differential calculus.

THEOREM 3.8   Derivative rule for the natural exponential

The natural exponential function e^x is differentiable for all x, with derivative

$$\frac{d}{dx}(e^x) = e^x$$

Proof   We will proceed informally. Recall the definition of e:

$$\lim_{n \to \infty}\left(1 + \frac{1}{n}\right)^n = e$$

Let $n = \frac{1}{\Delta x}$, so that $\lim\limits_{\Delta x \to 0}(1 + \Delta x)^{1/\Delta x} = e$. This means that for Δx very small, $e \approx (1 + \Delta x)^{1/\Delta x}$ or $e^{\Delta x} \approx 1 + \Delta x$, so that $e^{\Delta x} - 1 \approx \Delta x$. Thus, $\lim\limits_{\Delta x \to 0} \dfrac{e^{\Delta x} - 1}{\Delta x} = 1$. Finally, using the limit in the definition of derivative for e^x, we obtain

$$
\begin{aligned}
\frac{d}{dx}(e^x) &= \lim_{\Delta x \to 0} \frac{e^{(x+\Delta x)} - e^x}{\Delta x} \\
&= \lim_{\Delta x \to 0} \frac{e^x(e^{\Delta x} - 1)}{\Delta x} \\
&= e^x \lim_{\Delta x \to 0} \frac{e^{\Delta x} - 1}{\Delta x} \\
&= e^x(1) = e^x \qquad \qquad \square
\end{aligned}
$$

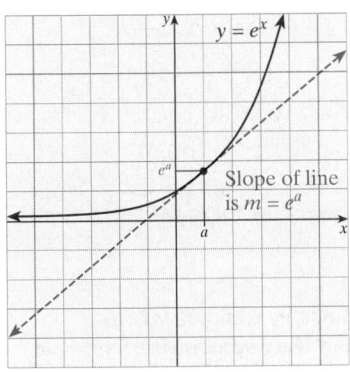

Figure 3.20 The slope of $y = e^x$ at each point (a, e^a) is $m = e^a$.

Note: An easier proof of the derivative formula in Theorem 3.8 is given in Example 6 of Section 3.6 using methods developed in that section.

The fact that $\dfrac{d}{dx}(e^x) = e^x$ means that the slope of the graph of $y = e^x$ at any point (a, e^a) is $m = e^a$, the y-coordinate of the point, as shown in Figure 3.20. This is one of the features of the exponential function $y = e^x$ that makes it "natural."

EXAMPLE 7   A derivative involving e^x

Differentiate $f(x) = x^2 e^x$. For what values of x does $f'(x) = 0$?

Solution

Using the product rule, we find

$$
f'(x) = \frac{d}{dx}(x^2 e^x)
$$

$$
= x^2 \left[\frac{d}{dx} e^x \right] + \left[\frac{d}{dx} x^2 \right] e^x
$$

$$
= x^2 e^x + 2x e^x \qquad \text{Exponential and power rules}
$$

To find where $f'(x) = 0$, we solve

$$
x^2 e^x + 2x e^x = 0
$$

$$
x(x + 2)e^x = 0
$$

$$
x(x + 2) = 0 \qquad \text{Since } e^x \neq 0 \text{ for all } x
$$

$$
x = 0,\ -2
$$

∎

EXAMPLE 8   A second derivative involving e^x

For $f(x) = e^x \sin x$, find $f'(x)$ and $f''(x)$.

Solution

Apply the product rule twice:

$$
f'(x) = e^x (\sin x)' + (e^x)' \sin x
$$

$$
= e^x (\cos x) + e^x (\sin x)
$$

$$
= e^x (\cos x + \sin x)
$$

$$
f''(x) = e^x (\cos x + \sin x)' + (e^x)'(\cos x + \sin x)
$$

$$
= e^x (-\sin x + \cos x) + e^x (\cos x + \sin x)
$$

$$
= 2e^x \cos x
$$

∎

THEOREM 3.9   Derivative rule for the natural logarithmic function

The natural logarithmic function $\ln x$ is differentiable for all $x > 0$, with derivative

$$
\frac{d}{dx}(\ln x) = \frac{1}{x}
$$

Proof   According to the definition of the derivative, we have

$$
\frac{d}{dx}(\ln x) = \lim_{\Delta x \to 0} \frac{\ln(x + \Delta x) - \ln x}{\Delta x}
$$

$$
= \lim_{\Delta x \to 0} \frac{1}{\Delta x} \ln \left(\frac{x + \Delta x}{x} \right)
$$

$$
= \lim_{\Delta x \to 0} \frac{1}{\Delta x} \ln \left(1 + \frac{\Delta x}{x} \right) \qquad \text{Let } h = \frac{x}{\Delta x}, \text{ so } \Delta x = \frac{x}{h}.
$$

$$= \lim_{h \to +\infty} \frac{h}{x} \ln\left(1 + \frac{1}{h}\right) \qquad\qquad h \to +\infty \text{ as } \Delta x \to 0$$

$$= \frac{1}{x}\left[\lim_{h \to +\infty} h \ln\left(1 + \frac{1}{h}\right)\right]$$

$$= \frac{1}{x}\left[\lim_{h \to +\infty} \ln\left(1 + \frac{1}{h}\right)^h\right] \qquad \text{Power rule for logarithms}$$

$$= \frac{1}{x} \ln\left[\lim_{h \to +\infty}\left(1 + \frac{1}{h}\right)^h\right] \qquad \begin{array}{l}\text{Since } \ln x \text{ is continuous,}\\ \text{use the composition limit rule.}\end{array}$$

$$= \frac{1}{x} \ln e \qquad\qquad\qquad \text{Definition of } e$$

$$= \frac{1}{x} \qquad\qquad\qquad \ln e = 1 \qquad\qquad \square$$

EXAMPLE 9 **Derivative of a quotient involving a natural logarithm**

Differentiate $f(x) = \dfrac{\ln x}{\sin x}$.

Solution We use the quotient rule.

$$f'(x) = \frac{(\sin x)\frac{d}{dx}(\ln x) - (\ln x)\frac{d}{dx}(\sin x)}{\sin^2 x}$$

$$= \frac{(\sin x)\left(\frac{1}{x}\right) - (\ln x)(\cos x)}{\sin^2 x}$$

$$= \frac{\sin x - x \ln x \cos x}{x \sin^2 x} \qquad\qquad\qquad\qquad \blacksquare$$

TECHNOLOGY NOTE

When you are using calculators or computer programs such as *Mathematica*, *Derive*, or *Maple*, the form of the derivative may vary. For example, you might obtain

$$\frac{d}{dx}(\tan x) = \tan^2 x + 1$$

instead of $\sec^2 x$ as found in this section;

$$\frac{d}{dx}(\cot x) = -\cot^2 x - 1$$

instead of $-\csc^2 x$;

$$\frac{d}{dx}(\sec x) = \frac{\sin x}{\cos^2 x}$$

instead of $\sec x \tan x$; and

$$\frac{d}{dx}(\csc x) = -\frac{\cos x}{\sin^2 x}$$

instead of $-\csc x \cot x$. A solution to Example 9, using a TI-92, is shown in Figure 3.21.

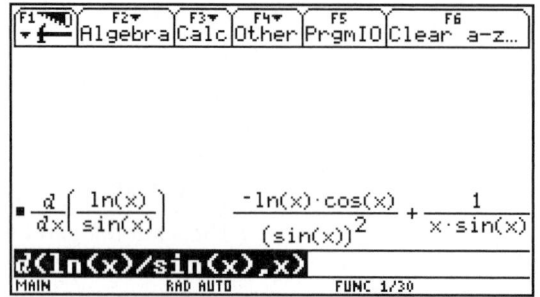

Figure 3.21 Sample output for Example 9. Notice that the form of the answer differs from that shown in the text.

Although the form of this calculator solution is different from the form shown in the example, you should notice that they are equivalent by using algebra (and recalling some of the fundamental identities from trigonometry).

A good test for your calculator is to try to find the derivative of $|x|$ at $x = 0$, which we know does not exist. Many calculators will give the incorrect answer of 0.

3.3 PROBLEM SET

Ⓐ *Differentiate the functions given in Problems 1–32.*

1. $f(x) = \sin x + \cos x$

2. $f(x) = 2 \sin x + \tan x$

3. $g(t) = t^2 + \cos t + \cos \frac{\pi}{4}$

4. $g(t) = 2 \sec t + 3 \tan t - \tan \frac{\pi}{3}$

5. $f(t) = \sin^2 t$ *Hint*: Use the product rule.

6. $g(x) = \cos^2 x$ *Hint*: Use the product rule.

7. $f(x) = \sqrt{x} \cos x + x \cot x$ **8.** $f(x) = 2x^3 \sin x - 3x \cos x$

9. $p(x) = x^2 \cos x$ **10.** $p(t) = (t^2 + 2) \sin t$

11. $q(x) = \dfrac{\sin x}{x}$ **12.** $r(x) = \dfrac{e^x}{\sin x}$

13. $h(t) = e^t \csc t$ **14.** $f(\theta) = \dfrac{\sec \theta}{2 - \cos \theta}$

15. $f(x) = x^2 \ln x$ **16.** $g(x) = \dfrac{\ln x}{x^2}$

17. $h(x) = e^{2x}(\sin x - \cos x)$ **18.** $f(x) = \dfrac{\ln x}{x}$

19. $f(x) = \dfrac{\sin x}{e^x}$ **20.** $g(x) = \dfrac{x \cos x}{e^x}$

21. $f(x) = \dfrac{\tan x}{1 - 2x}$ **22.** $g(t) = \dfrac{1 + \sin t}{\sqrt{t}}$

23. $f(t) = \dfrac{2 + \sin t}{t + 2}$ **24.** $f(\theta) = \dfrac{\theta - 1}{2 + \cos \theta}$

25. $f(x) = \dfrac{\sin x}{1 - \cos x}$ **26.** $f(x) = \dfrac{x}{1 - \sin x}$

27. $f(x) = \dfrac{1 + \sin x}{2 - \cos x}$ **28.** $g(x) = \dfrac{\cos x}{1 + \cos x}$

29. $f(x) = \dfrac{\sin x + \cos x}{\sin x - \cos x}$ **30.** $f(x) = \dfrac{x^2 + \tan x}{3x + 2 \tan x}$

31. $g(x) = \sec^2 x - \tan^2 x + \cos x$

32. $g(x) = \cos^2 x + \sin^2 x + \sin x$

Find the second derivative of each function given in Problems 33–44.

33. $f(\theta) = \sin \theta$ **34.** $f(\theta) = \cos \theta$

35. $f(\theta) = \tan \theta$ **36.** $f(\theta) = \cot \theta$

37. $f(\theta) = \sec \theta$ **38.** $f(\theta) = \csc \theta$

39. $f(x) = \sin x + \cos x$ **40.** $f(x) = x \sin x$

41. $f(x) = e^x \cos x$ **42.** $g(t) = t^3 e^t$

43. $h(t) = \sqrt{t} \ln t$ **44.** $f(t) = \dfrac{\ln t}{t}$

Ⓑ *Find an equation for the tangent line at the prescribed point for each function in Problems 45–52.*

45. $f(\theta) = \tan \theta$ at $(\frac{\pi}{4}, 1)$ **46.** $f(\theta) = \sec \theta$ at $(\frac{\pi}{3}, 2)$

47. $f(x) = \sin x$, where $x = \frac{\pi}{6}$

48. $f(x) = \cos x$, where $x = \frac{\pi}{3}$

49. $y = x + \sin x$, where $x = 0$

50. $y = x \sec x$, where $x = 0$

51. $y = e^x \cos x$, where $x = 0$

52. $y = x \ln x$, where $x = 1$

53. Which of the following functions satisfy $y'' + y = 0$?

    a. $y_1 = 2 \sin x + 3 \cos x$ **b.** $y_2 = 4 \sin x - \pi \cos x$

    c. $y_3 = x \sin x$ **d.** $y_4 = e^x \cos x$

54. For what values of A and B does $y = A \cos x + B \sin x$ satisfy $y'' + 2y' + 3y = 2 \sin x$?

55. For what values of A and B does $y = Ax \cos x + Bx \sin x$ satisfy $y'' + y = -3 \cos x$?

Ⓒ **56.** Complete the proof of Theorem 3.6 by showing that $\dfrac{d}{dx} \cos x = -\sin x$. *Hint*: You will need to use the identity $\cos(\alpha + \beta) = \cos \alpha \cos \beta - \sin \alpha \sin \beta$.

Prove the requested parts of Theorem 3.7 in Problems 57–59.

57. $\dfrac{d}{dx} \cot x = -\csc^2 x$

58. $\dfrac{d}{dx} \sec x = \sec x \tan x$

59. $\dfrac{d}{dx} \csc x = -\csc x \cot x$

60. Use the limit of a difference quotient to prove that

$$\frac{d}{dx} \tan x = \sec^2 x$$

61. **Exploration Problem**   Write a short paper on the difficulties of differentiating trigonometric functions measured in degrees.*

---

*See, for example, "Fallacies, Flaws, and Flimflam," *The College Mathematics Journal*, Vol. 23, No. 3, May 1992, and Vol. 24, No. 4, September 1993. Another very understandable article, "Why Use Radians in Calculus?", by Carl E. Crockett, can be found in *The AMATYC Review*, Vol.19, No. 2, Spring 1998, pp. 44–47.

3.4   Rates of Change: Modeling Rectilinear Motion

IN THIS SECTION   average and instantaneous rate of change, introduction to mathematical modeling, rectilinear motion (modeling in physics), falling body problems

The speed of a car or airplane; interest rates; the growth rate of a population; the drip rate of an intravenous injection—these are examples of the many situations in which rates of change are an important consideration in practical problems. In this section, we begin by showing how rates of change can be computed using differentiation. Then we discuss the general notion of mathematical modeling and conclude by demonstrating modeling principles in a variety of practical problems involving motion along a line.

AVERAGE AND INSTANTANEOUS RATE OF CHANGE

The graph of a linear function $f(x) = ax + b$ is the line $y = ax + b$, whose slope $m = a$ can be thought of as the rate at which y is changing with respect to x (see Figure 3.22a). However, for another function g that is *not* linear, the average (and instantaneous) rate of change of $y = g(x)$ with respect to x varies from point to point, as shown in Figure 3.22b.

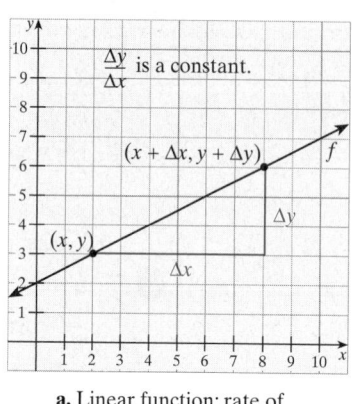

a. Linear function: rate of change $\Delta y/\Delta x$ is constant.

b. Nonlinear function: rate of change $\Delta y/\Delta x$ depends on chosen points.

Figure 3.22   Rate of change is measured by the slope of a tangent line

Because the slope of the tangent line is given by the derivative of the function, the preceding geometric observations suggest that the rate of change of a function is measured by its derivative. This connection will be made more precise in the following discussion.

Suppose y is a function of x, say $y = f(x)$. Corresponding to a change from x to $x + \Delta x$ the variable y changes from $f(x)$ to $f(x + \Delta x)$. The change in y is $\Delta y = f(x + \Delta x) - f(x)$, and the **average rate of change of y with respect to x** is

$$\text{AVERAGE RATE OF CHANGE} = \frac{\text{CHANGE IN } y}{\text{CHANGE IN } x} = \frac{\Delta y}{\Delta x} = \frac{f(x + \Delta x) - f(x)}{\Delta x}$$

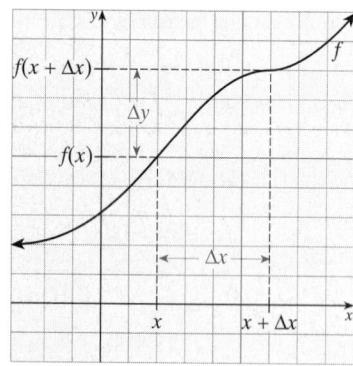

Figure 3.23 A change in Δy corresponding to a change Δx

WARNING   This formula for the change in y is important. Find Δy in Figure 3.23.

As the interval over which we are averaging becomes shorter (that is, as $\Delta x \to 0$), the average rate of change approaches what we would intuitively call the **instantaneous rate of change of y with respect to x**, and the difference quotient approaches the derivative $\dfrac{dy}{dx}$. Thus, we have

$$\begin{array}{c}\text{INSTANTANEOUS} \\ \text{RATE OF CHANGE}\end{array} = \lim_{\Delta x \to 0} \frac{\Delta y}{\Delta x} = \lim_{\Delta x \to 0} \frac{f(x + \Delta x) - f(x)}{\Delta x} = f'(x)$$

To summarize,

Instantaneous Rate of Change

Suppose $f(x)$ is differentiable at $x = x_0$. Then the **instantaneous rate of change** of $y = f(x)$ with respect to x at x_0 is the value of the derivative of f at x_0. That is,

$$\text{INSTANTANEOUS RATE OF CHANGE} = f'(x_0) = \frac{dy}{dx}\bigg|_{x=x_0}$$

EXAMPLE 1   Instantaneous rate of change

Find the rate at which the function $y = x^2 \sin x$ is changing with respect to x when $x = \pi$.

Solution

For any x, the instantaneous rate of change is the derivative,

$$\frac{dy}{dx} = 2x \sin x + x^2 \cos x$$

Thus, the rate when $x = \pi$ is

$$\frac{dy}{dx}\bigg|_{x=\pi} = 2\pi \sin \pi + \pi^2 \cos \pi = 2\pi(0) + \pi^2(-1) = -\pi^2$$

The negative sign indicates that when $x = \pi$, the function is *decreasing* at the rate of $\pi^2 \approx 9.9$ units of y for each one-unit increase in x. ■

Let us consider an example comparing the average rate of change with the instantaneous rate of change.

EXAMPLE 2   Comparison between average rate and instantaneous rate of change

Let $f(x) = x^2 - 4x + 7$.

a. Find the average rate of change of f with respect to x between $x = 3$ and 5.
b. Find the instantaneous rate of change of f at $x = 3$.

Solution

a. The (average) rate of change from $x = 3$ to $x = 5$ is found by dividing the change in f by the change in x. The change in f from $x = 3$ to $x = 5$ is

$$f(5) - f(3) = [5^2 - 4(5) + 7] - [3^2 - 4(3) + 7] = 8$$

Thus, the average rate of change is

$$\frac{f(5) - f(3)}{5 - 3} = \frac{8}{2} = 4$$

The slope of the secant line is 4, as shown in Figure 3.24.

b. The derivative of the function is

$$f'(x) = 2x - 4$$

Thus, the instantaneous rate of change of f at $x = 3$ is

$$f'(3) = 2(3) - 4 = 2$$

The tangent line at $x = 3$ has slope 2, as shown in Figure 3.24. ■

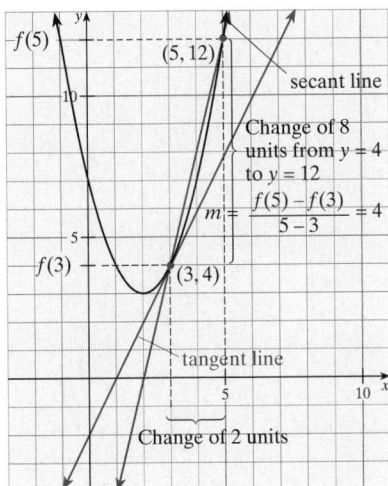

Figure 3.24 Comparison of the instantaneous rate of change and the average rate of change from 3 to 5

Often we are not as interested in the instantaneous rate of change of a quantity as its relative rate of change, defined as follows:

$$\text{RELATIVE RATE} = \frac{\text{INSTANTANEOUS RATE OF CHANGE}}{\text{SIZE OF QUANTITY}}$$

For instance, if you are earning \$15,000/yr and receive a \$3,000 raise, you would probably be very pleased. However, that \$3,000 raise might be much less meaningful if you were earning \$100,000/yr. In both cases, the change is the quantity \$3,000, but in the first case the relative rate of change is $3,000/15,000 = 20\%$, whereas in the second, it is a much smaller $3,000/100,000 = 3\%$.

In terms of the derivative, the relative rate of change may be defined as follows:

Relative Rate of Change

The **relative rate of change** of $y = f(x)$ at $x = x_0$ is given by the ratio

$$\text{RELATIVE RATE OF CHANGE} = \frac{f'(x_0)}{f(x_0)}$$

EXAMPLE 3   Relative rate of change

The aerobic rate is the rate of a person's oxygen consumption and is sometimes modeled by the function A defined by

$$A(x) = 110 \left[\frac{\ln x - 2}{x} \right]$$

where x is the person's age. What is the relative rate of change of the aerobic rating of a 20-year-old person? A 50-year-old person?

Solution

Applying the quotient rule, we obtain the derivative of $A(x)$:

$$A'(x) = 110 \left[\frac{x(1/x) - (\ln x - 2)(1)}{x^2} \right] = 110 \left[\frac{3 - \ln x}{x^2} \right]$$

Thus, the relative rate of change of A at age x is

$$\text{RELATIVE RATE} = \frac{A'(x)}{A(x)} = \frac{110 \left[\dfrac{3 - \ln x}{x^2} \right]}{110 \left[\dfrac{\ln x - 2}{x} \right]} = \frac{3 - \ln x}{(\ln x - 2)x}$$

In particular, when $x = 20$, the relative rate is

$$\frac{A'(20)}{A(20)} = \frac{3 - \ln 20}{(\ln 20 - 2)20} \approx 0.0002143$$

In other words, at age 20, the person's aerobic rating is increasing at the rate of 0.02%/yr. However, at age 50, the relative rate is

$$\frac{A'(50)}{A(50)} = \frac{3 - \ln 50}{(\ln 50 - 2)50} \approx -0.0095399$$

and the person's aerobic rating is *decreasing* (because of the negative sign) at the relative rate of 0.95%/yr. ■

INTRODUCTION TO MATHEMATICAL MODELING

A real-life situation is usually far too complicated to be precisely and mathematically defined. When confronted with a problem in the real world, therefore, it is usually necessary to develop a mathematical framework based on certain assumptions about the real world. This framework can then be used to find a solution to the real-world problem. The process of developing this body of mathematics is referred to as **mathematical modeling**.

Some mathematical models are quite accurate, particularly many used in the physical sciences. For example, one of the models we will consider in calculus is a model for the path of a projectile. Other rather precise models predict such things as the time of sunrise and sunset, or the distance which an object falls in a vacuum. Some mathematical models, however, are less accurate, especially those that involve examples from the life sciences and social sciences. Only recently has modeling in these disciplines become precise enough to be expressed in terms of calculus.

What, exactly, is a mathematical model? Sometimes, mathematical modeling can mean nothing more than a textbook word problem. But mathematical modeling can also mean choosing appropriate mathematics to solve a problem that has previously been unsolved. In this book, we use the term "mathematical modeling" to mean something between these two extremes. That is, it is a process we will apply to some real-life problem that does not have an obvious solution. It usually cannot be solved by applying a single formula.

Learning to use modeling techniques is an important part of your mathematical education. The first step in the modeling process involves *abstraction*, in which certain assumptions about a given practical problem are made in order to formulate a version of the problem in abstract terms. Next, the abstract version of the problem is *analyzed* using appropriate mathematical methods such as calculus, and finally, results derived from the abstract analysis are *interpreted* in terms of the original problem. The results obtained from the model often lead to predictions about the "real-world" situations related to the given problem. Data can be gathered to check the accuracy of these predictions and to modify the initial assumptions of the model to make it more precise. The process continues until a model is obtained that fits "reality" with acceptable accuracy. The steps in the modeling process are demonstrated in Figure 3.25. You may also find it interesting to read the article on modeling weather from *Scientific American* quoted in the margin.

HOW GLOBAL CLIMATE IS MODELED

We find a good example of mathematical modeling by looking at the work being done with weather prediction. In theory, if the correct assumptions could be programmed into a computer, along with appropriate mathematical statements of the ways global climate conditions operate, we would have a model to predict the weather throughout the world. In the global climate model, a system of equations calculates time-dependent changes in wind as well as temperature and moisture changes in the atmosphere and on the land. The model may also predict alterations in the temperature of the ocean's surface. At the National Center for Atmospheric Research, a CRAY supercomputer is used to do this modeling.

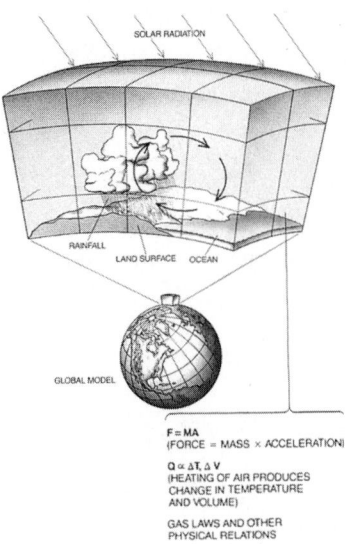

From *Scientific American*,
March 1991

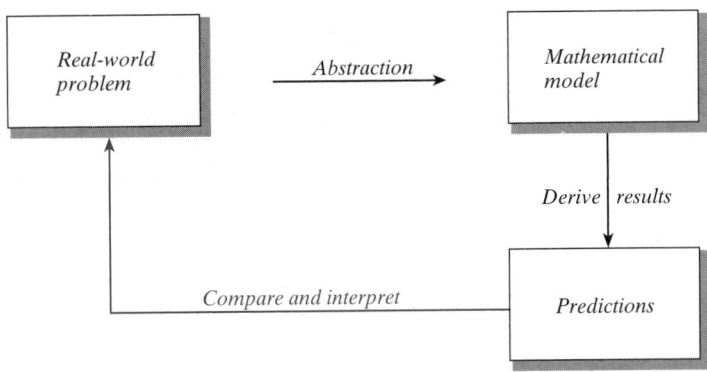

Figure 3.25 Mathematical modeling

EXAMPLE 4   Identifying models

It is common to gather data when studying most phenomena. Classifying the data by comparing with known models is an important mathematical skill. Identify each of the data sets as an example of a linear model, a quadratic model, a cubic model, a logarithmic model, an exponential model, or a sinusoidal model.

a.

x	y
−4	2.00
−3	1.28
−2	0.72
−1	0.32
0	0.08
1	0.00
2	0.08
3	0.32
4	0.72

b.

x	y
−4	−20.7
−3	−16.5
−2	−12.3
−1	−8.2
0	−3.8
1	0.4
2	4.7
3	8.9
4	13.12

c.

x	y
0.0	0.0
1.0	1.7
1.5	2.0
2.5	1.2
3.5	−0.7
4.5	−1.9
5.5	−1.4
6.0	−0.6
6.5	0.4

d.

x	y
−4	0.27
−3	0.30
−2	0.33
−1	0.36
0	0.40
1	0.44
2	0.49
3	0.52
4	0.60

e.

x	y
3	0.00
4	0.69
5	1.10
6	1.39
7	1.61
8	1.79
9	1.95
10	2.08
11	2.20
12	2.30

Solution

Sketch each graph and observe the pattern (if any) of the graphs.

a. Quadratic model

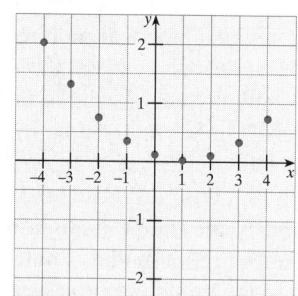

b. Linear model

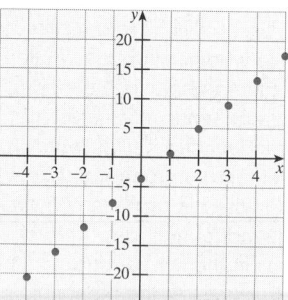

c. The data points seem to form a pattern, and we hypothesize that the data points are periodic, namely a sinusoidal model.

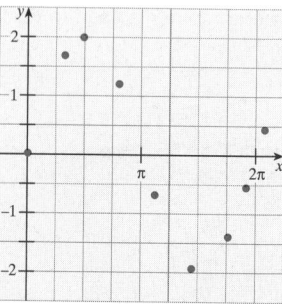

d. The data points look almost linear (but not quite), so we hypothesize that the data points may indicate an exponential model.

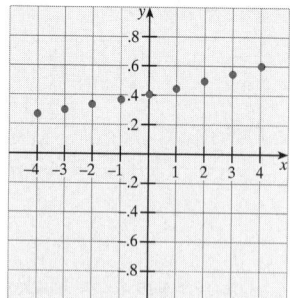

e. The data points seem to indicate a logarithmic model.

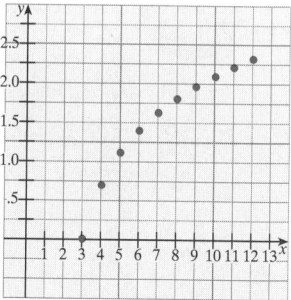

Mathematical models will appear in both examples and exercises throughout this text. In the next subsection, we begin our work with modeling by studying rectilinear motion, an important topic from physics.

RECTILINEAR MOTION (MODELING IN PHYSICS)

Rectilinear motion is motion along a straight line. For example, the up and down motion of a yo-yo may be regarded as rectilinear, as may the motion of a rocket early in its flight.

When studying rectilinear motion, we may assume that the object is moving along a coordinate line. The *position* of the object on the line is a function of time t and is often expressed as $s(t)$. The rate of change of $s(t)$ with respect to time is the object's **velocity** $v(t)$, and the rate of change of the velocity with respect to t is its **acceleration** $a(t)$. The absolute value of the velocity is called **speed**. Thus,

$$\text{Velocity is } v(t) = \frac{ds}{dt}$$

$$\text{Speed is } |v(t)| = \left|\frac{ds}{dt}\right|$$

$$\text{Acceleration is } a(t) = \frac{dv}{dt} = \frac{d^2s}{dt^2}$$

If $v(t) > 0$, we say that the object is *advancing*, and if $v(t) < 0$, it is *retreating*. If $v(t) = 0$, the object is neither advancing nor retreating, and we say it is *stationary*. The object is *accelerating* when $a(t) > 0$ and is *decelerating* when $a(t) < 0$. The significance of the acceleration is that it gives the rate at which the velocity is changing. When you are riding in a car, you do not feel the velocity, but you do feel the acceleration. That is, you feel *changes* in the velocity.

These ideas are summarized in the following box.

Rectilinear Motion

An object that moves along a straight line with *position* $s(t)$ has *velocity* $v(t) = \dfrac{ds}{dt}$ and *acceleration* $a(t) = \dfrac{dv}{dt} = \dfrac{d^2s}{dt^2}$ when these derivatives exist. The *speed* of the object is $|v(t)|$.

WARNING Rectilinear motion involves *position, velocity,* and *acceleration.* Sometimes there is confusion between the words "speed" and "velocity." Because speed is the absolute value of the velocity, it indicates how fast an object is moving, whereas velocity indicates both speed and direction (relative to a given coordinate system).

Notational comment: If distance is measured in meters and time in seconds, then velocity is measured in meters per second (m/s). Acceleration is recorded in meters per second per second (m/s/s). The notation m/s/s is awkward, so m/s^2 is more commonly used. Similarly, if distance is measured in feet, then velocity is measured in feet per second (ft/s) and acceleration in feet per second per second (ft/s^2).

EXAMPLE 5 **The position, velocity, and acceleration of a moving object**

Assume that the position at time t of an object moving along a line is given by

$$s(t) = 3t^3 - 40.5t^2 + 162t$$

for t on $[0, 8]$. Find the initial position, velocity, and acceleration for the object and discuss the motion. Compute the total distance traveled.

Solution

The position at time t is given by the function s. The initial position occurs at time $t = 0$, so

$$s(0) = 0 \qquad \textit{The object starts at the origin.}$$

The velocity is determined by finding the derivative of the position function.

$$v(t) = s'(t) = 9t^2 - 81t + 162$$
$$= 9(t^2 - 9t + 18)$$
$$= 9(t - 3)(t - 6) \qquad \textit{The initial velocity is } v(0) = 162.$$

When $t = 3$ and when $t = 6$, the velocity v is 0, which means the *object is stationary* at those times. Furthermore,

$$v(t) > 0 \quad \text{on} \quad [0, 3) \qquad \textit{Object is advancing.}$$
$$v(t) < 0 \quad \text{on} \quad (3, 6) \qquad \textit{Object is retreating.}$$
$$v(t) > 0 \quad \text{on} \quad (6, 8] \qquad \textit{Object is advancing.}$$

For the acceleration,

$$a(t) = s''(t) = v'(t) = 18t - 81$$
$$= 18(t - 4.5) \qquad \textit{The initial acceleration is } a(0) = -81.$$

We see that

$$a(t) < 0 \quad \text{on} \quad [0, 4.5] \qquad \textit{Velocity is decreasing;}$$
$$\textit{that is, the object is decelerating.}$$

$$a(t) = 0 \quad \text{at} \quad t = 4.5 \qquad \textit{Velocity is not changing.}$$
$$a(t) > 0 \quad \text{on} \quad (4.5, 8] \qquad \textit{Velocity is increasing;}$$
$$\textit{so the object is accelerating.}$$

The table in the margin gives certain values for s, v, and a. We use these values to plot a few points, as shown in Figure 3.26. The actual path of the object is back and forth on the axis and the figure is for clarification only.

t	s	v	a
0	0	162	−81
1	124.5	90	−63
2	186	36	−45
3	202.5	0	−27
4	192	−18	−9
4.5	182.25	−20.25	0
5	172.5	−18	9
6	162	0	27
7	178.5	36	45
8	240	90	63

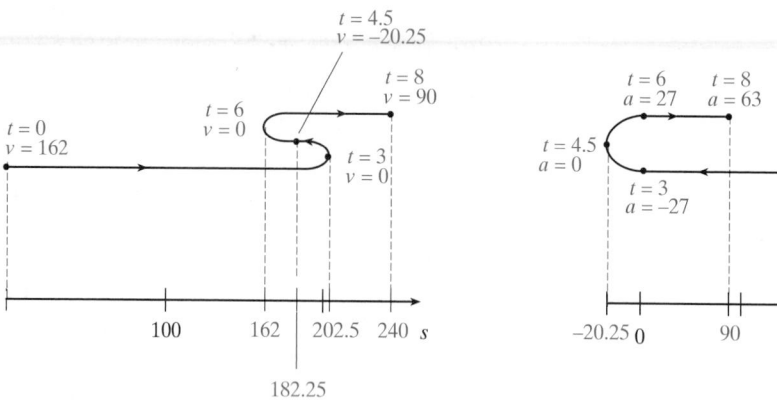

a. Position of the object: when $v > 0$, the object advances, and when $v < 0$, the object retreats.

b. Velocity of the object: when $a > 0$, the velocity increases, and when $a < 0$, the velocity decreases.

Figure 3.26 Analysis of rectilinear motion

Recall that the *speed* of the object is the absolute value of its velocity. The speed decreases from 162 to 0 between $t = 0$ and $t = 3$ and increases from 0 to 20.25 as the velocity becomes negative between $t = 3$ and $t = 4.5$. Then for $4.5 < t < 6$, the object slows down again, from 20.25 to 0, after which it speeds up.

The total distance traveled is

$$|s(3) - s(0)| + |s(6) - s(3)| + |s(8) - s(6)| = 202.5 + 40.5 + 78 = 321 \qquad \blacksquare$$

A common mistake is to think that a particle moving on a straight line speeds up when its acceleration is positive and slows down when the acceleration is negative, but this is not quite correct. Instead, the following is generally true:

The speed *increases* (particle speeds up) when the velocity and acceleration have the same signs.

The speed *decreases* (particle slows down) when the velocity and acceleration have opposite signs.

FALLING BODY PROBLEMS

As a second example of rectilinear motion, we will consider a *falling body problem*. In such a problem, it is assumed that an object is projected (that is, thrown, fired, dropped, etc.) vertically in such a way that the only acceleration acting on the object is the constant downward acceleration g due to gravity, which on the earth near sea level is approximately 32 ft/s^2 or 9.8 m/s^2.* Thus, we disregard air resistance. At time t, the height of the projectile is given by the following formula:

Formula for the height of a projectile

v_0 is the initial velocity.
$$\downarrow$$
$$h(t) = -\tfrac{1}{2}gt^2 + v_0 t + s_0 \;\; \leftarrow s_0 \text{ is the initial height.}$$
$$\uparrow$$
g is the acceleration due to gravity.

where s_0 and v_0 are the projectile's initial height and velocity, respectively. You are asked to derive this formula for earth's gravity and a particular initial velocity and a particular initial position in a problem in Section 5.1.

EXAMPLE 6   Position, velocity, and acceleration of a falling object

Suppose a person standing at the top of the Tower of Pisa (176 ft high) throws a ball directly upward with an initial speed of 96 ft/s.

a. Find the ball's height, its velocity, and acceleration at time t.
b. When does the ball hit the ground, and what is its impact velocity?
c. How far does the ball travel during its flight?

Solution

First, draw a picture such as the one shown in Figure 3.27 to help you understand the problem.

a. Substitute the known values into the formula for the height of an object:

$v_0 = 96$ ft/s: Initial velocity
$$\downarrow$$
$$h(t) = -\tfrac{1}{2}(32)t^2 + 96t + 176 \;\; \leftarrow h_0 = 176 \text{ ft is the height of tower}$$
$$\uparrow$$
$g = 32$ ft/s^2: Constant downward gravitational acceleration

$$h(t) = -16t^2 + 96t + 176 \qquad \text{This is the position function.}$$
It gives the height of the ball.

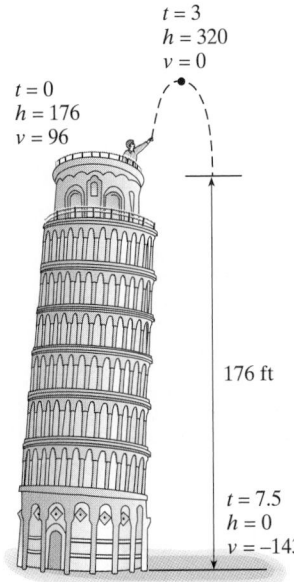

$t = 3$
$h = 320$
$v = 0$

$t = 0$
$h = 176$
$v = 96$

176 ft

$t = 7.5$
$h = 0$
$v = -143$

Figure 3.27 The motion of a ball thrown upward from the Tower of Pisa

*Although 32 ft/s^2 is the particular number we will use in this text, engineers in earthbound vehicular activity use 32.174 ft/s^2 as a better approximation for gravity.

The velocity at time t is the derivative:

$$v(t) = \frac{dh}{dt} = -32t + 96$$

The acceleration is the derivative of the velocity function:

$$a(t) = \frac{dv}{dt} = \frac{d^2h}{dt^2} = -32$$

This means that the acceleration of the ball is always decreasing at the rate of 32 ft/s^2.

b. The ball hits the ground when $h(t) = 0$. Solve the equation

$$-16t^2 + 96t + 176 = 0$$

to find that this occurs when $t \approx -1.47$ and $t \approx 7.47$. Disregarding the negative value, we see that impact occurs at $t \approx 7.47$ sec. The impact velocity is

$$v(7.47) \approx -143 \text{ ft/s}$$

The negative sign here means the ball is coming down at the moment of impact.

c. The ball travels upward for some time and then falls downward to the ground, as shown in Figure 3.27. We need to find the distance it travels upward plus the distance it falls to the ground. The turning point at the top (the highest point) occurs when the velocity is zero. Solve the equation

$$-32t + 96 = 0$$

to find that this occurs when $t = 3$. The ball starts at $h(0) = 176$ ft and rises to a maximum height when $t = 3$. Thus, the maximum height is

$$h(3) = -16(3)^2 + 96(3) + 176 = 320$$

and the total distance traveled is

$$\underbrace{(320 - 176)}_{\underset{\text{Initial height}}{\uparrow}} + \underbrace{320}_{\text{Downward distance}} = 464$$

Upward distance   Downward distance

The total distance traveled is 464 ft.   ■

3.4   PROBLEM SET

Ⓐ **1. WHAT DOES THIS SAY?**   What is a mathematical model?

2. Interpretation Problem   Why are mathematical models necessary or useful?

For each function f given in Problems 3–16, find the rate of change with respect to x at $x = x_0$.

3. $f(x) = x^2 - 3x + 5$ when $x_0 = 2$

4. $f(x) = 14 + x - x^2$ when $x_0 = 1$

5. $f(x) = -2x^2 + x + 4$ for $x_0 = 1$

6. $f(x) = \dfrac{-2}{x+1}$ for $x_0 = 1$

7. $f(x) = \dfrac{2x-1}{3x+5}$ when $x_0 = -1$

8. $f(x) = (x^2 + 2)(x + \sqrt{x})$ when $x_0 = 4$

9. $f(x) = x \cos x$ when $x_0 = \pi$

10. $f(x) = (x+1) \sin x$ when $x_0 = \frac{\pi}{2}$

11. $f(x) = x \ln \sqrt{x}$ when $x_0 = 1$

12. $f(x) = \dfrac{x^2}{e^x}$ when $x_0 = 0$

13. $f(x) = \sin x \cos x$ when $x_0 = \frac{\pi}{2}$

14. $f(x) = \dfrac{x^2}{x^2 + 1}$ when $x_0 = 1$

15. $f(x) = \left(x - \dfrac{2}{x}\right)^2$ when $x_0 = 1$

16. $f(x) = \sin^2 x$ when $x_0 = \frac{\pi}{4}$

The function $s(t)$ in Problems 17–24 gives the position of an object moving along a line. In each case,

a. *Find the velocity at time t.*

b. *Find the acceleration at time t.*

c. Describe the motion of the object; that is, tell when it is advancing and when it is retreating. Compute the total distance traveled by the object during the indicated time interval.

d. Tell when the object is accelerating and when it is decelerating.

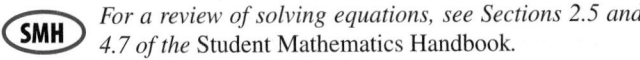 *For a review of solving equations, see Sections 2.5 and 4.7 of the* Student Mathematics Handbook.

17. $s(t) = t^2 - 2t + 6$ on $[0, 2]$

18. $s(t) = 3t^2 + 2t - 5$ on $[0, 1]$

19. $s(t) = t^3 - 9t^2 + 15t + 25$ on $[0, 6]$

20. $s(t) = t^4 - 4t^3 + 8t$ on $[0, 4]$

21. $s(t) = \dfrac{2t + 1}{t^2}$ for $1 \le t \le 3$

22. $s(t) = t^2 + t \ln t$ for $1 \le t \le e$

23. $s(t) = 3 \cos t$ for $0 \le t \le 2\pi$

24. $s(t) = 1 + \sec t$ for $0 \le t \le \frac{\pi}{4}$

Modeling Problems Identify each of the data sets in Problems 25–34 as an example of a linear model, a quadratic model, a cubic model, a logarithmic model, an exponential model, or a sinusoidal model.

25.

x	y
−4	−140
−3	−96
−2	−60
−1	−32
0	−12
1	0
2	4
3	0
4	−12

26.

x	y
−4	−10.2
−3	−8.0
−2	−5.8
−1	−3.6
0	−1.4
1	0.8
2	3.0
3	5.2
4	7.4

27.

x	y
−4	−0.019531
−3	−0.078125
−2	−0.3125
−1	−1.25
0	−5
1	−20
2	−80
3	−320
4	−1280

28.

x	y
−4	−0.0003
−3	−0.0009
−2	−0.0027
−1	−0.0082
0	−0.0247
1	−0.0741
2	−0.2222
3	−0.6667
4	−2.0000

29.

x	y
−4	238
−3	173
−2	118
−1	73
0	38
1	13
2	−2
3	−7
4	−2

30.

x	y
−4	4.84
−3	2.46
−2	−1.41
−1	−4.42
0	−4.76
1	−2.20
2	1.68
3	4.55
4	4.66

31.

x	y
−2.0	−28.0
−1.5	−8.5
−1.0	1.0
−0.5	3.5
0.0	2.0
0.5	−0.5
1.0	−1.0
1.5	3.5
2.0	16.0

32.

x	y
−4	−3.5
−3	−2.4
−2	−1.3
−1	−0.2
0	0.9
1	2.0
2	3.1
3	4.2
4	5.3

33.

x	y
2	0.0
3	−1.2
4	−1.9
5	−2.4
6	−2.8
7	−3.1
8	−3.4
9	−3.6
10	−3.8

34.

x	y
1	4.2
2	5.6
3	6.4
4	7.0
5	7.4
6	7.8
7	8.1
8	8.4
9	8.6

Ⓑ 35. It is estimated that x years from now, $0 \le x \le 10$, the average SAT score of the incoming students at a certain eastern liberal arts college will be

$$f(x) = -6x + 1,082$$

a. Derive an expression for the rate at which the average SAT score will be changing with respect to time x years from now.

b. What is the significance of the fact that the expression in part **a** is a negative constant?

36. A particle moving on the x-axis has position

$$x(t) = 2t^3 + 3t^2 - 36t + 40$$

after an elapsed time of t seconds.

a. Find the velocity of the particle at time t.

b. Find the acceleration at time t.

c. What is the total distance traveled by the particle during the first 3 seconds?

37. An object moving on the x-axis has position

$$x(t) = t^3 - 9t^2 + 24t + 20$$

after t seconds. What is the total distance traveled by the object during the first 8 seconds?

38. A car has position

$$s(t) = 50t \ln t + 80$$

ft after t seconds of motion. What is its acceleration (to the nearest hundredth ft/s^2) after 10 seconds?

39. An object moves along a straight line so that after t minutes, its position relative to its starting point (in meters) is

$$s(t) = 10t + \frac{t}{e^t}$$

a. At what speed (to the nearest thousandth m/min) is the object moving at the end of 4 min?

b. How far (to the nearest thousandth m) does the object actually travel during the fifth minute?

40. A bucket containing 5 gal of water has a leak. After t seconds, there are

$$Q(t) = 5\left(1 - \frac{t}{25}\right)^2$$

gallons of water in the bucket.

a. At what rate (to the nearest hundredth gal) is water leaking from the bucket after 2 seconds?

b. How long does it take for all the water to leak out of the bucket?

c. At what rate is the water leaking when the last drop leaks out?

Modeling Problems   *In Problems 41–48, set up and solve an appropriate model to answer the given question. Be sure to state your assumptions.*

41. A person standing at the edge of a cliff throws a rock directly upward. It is observed that 2 seconds later the rock is at its maximum height (in ft) and that 5 seconds after that, it hits the ground at the base of the cliff.

a. What is the initial velocity of the rock?

b. How high is the cliff?

c. What is the velocity of the rock at time t?

d. With what velocity does the rock hit the ground?

42. A projectile is shot upward from the earth with an initial velocity of 320 ft/s.

a. What is its velocity after 5 seconds?

b. What is its acceleration after 3 seconds?

43. A rock is dropped from a height of 90 ft. One second later another rock is dropped from height H. What is H (to the nearest foot) if the two rocks hit the ground at the same time?

44. A ball is thrown vertically upward from the ground with an initial velocity of 160 ft/s.

a. When will the ball hit the ground?

b. With what velocity will the ball hit the ground?

c. When will the ball reach its maximum height?

45. An object is dropped (initial velocity $v_0 = 0$) from the top of a building and falls 3 seconds before hitting the pavement below. Determine the height of the building in ft.

46. An astronaut standing at the edge of a cliff on the moon throws a rock directly upward and observes that it passes her on the way down exactly 4 seconds later. Three seconds after that, the rock hits the ground at the base of the cliff. Use this information to determine the initial velocity v_0 and the height of the cliff. *Note:* $g = 5.5$ ft/s^2 on the moon.

47. Answer the question in Problem 46 assuming the astronaut is on Mars, where $g = 12$ ft/s^2.

48. A car is traveling at 88 ft/s (60 mi/h) when the driver applies the brakes to avoid hitting a child. After t seconds, the car is $s(t) = 88t - 8t^2$ feet from the point where the brakes were first applied. How long does it take for the car to come to a stop, and how far does it travel before stopping?

49. It is estimated that t years from now, the circulation of a local newspaper can be modeled by the formula

$$C(t) = 100t^2 + 400t + 50t \ln t$$

a. Find an expression for the rate at which the circulation will be changing with respect to time t years from now.

b. At what rate will the circulation be changing with respect to time 5 years from now?

c. By how much will the circulation actually change during the sixth year?

50. An efficiency study of the morning shift at a certain factory indicates that an average worker who arrives on the job at 8:00 A.M. will have assembled

$$f(x) = -\tfrac{1}{3}x^3 + \tfrac{1}{2}x^2 + 50x$$

units x hours later.

a. Find a formula for the rate at which the worker will be assembling the units after x hours.

b. At what rate will the worker be assembling units at 9:00 A.M.?

c. How many units will the worker actually assemble between 9:00 A.M. and 10:00 A.M.?

51. An environmental study of a certain suburban community suggests that t years from now, the average level of carbon monoxide in the air can be modeled by the formula

$$q(t) = 0.05t^2 + 0.1t + 3.4$$

parts per million.

a. At what rate will the carbon monoxide level be changing with respect to time one year from now?

b. By how much will the carbon monoxide level change in the first year?

c. By how much will the carbon monoxide level change over the next (second) year?

52. According to *Newton's law of universal gravitation*, if an object of mass M is separated by a distance r from a second object of mass m, then the two objects are attracted to one another by a force that acts along the line joining them and has magnitude

$$F = \frac{GmM}{r^2}$$

where G is a positive constant. Show that the rate of change of F with respect to r is inversely proportional to r^3.

53. The population of a bacterial colony is approximately

$$P(t) = P_0 + 61t + 3t^2$$

thousand t hours after observation begins, where P_0 is the initial population. Find the rate at which the colony is growing after 5 hours.

54. The gross domestic product (GDP) of a certain country is

$$g(t) = t^2 + 5t + 106$$

billion dollars t years after 2001.

a. At what rate does the GDP change in 2003?

b. At what percentage rate does the GDP change in 2003?

55. It is projected that x months from now, the population of a certain town will be

$$P(x) = 2x + 4x^{3/2} + 5{,}000$$

a. At what rate will the population be changing with respect to time 9 months from now?

b. At what percentage rate will the population be changing with respect to time 9 months from now?

56. Assume that your starting salary is $30,000 and you get a raise of $3,000 each year.

a. Express the percentage rate of change of your salary as a function of time.

b. At what percentage rate will your salary be increasing after one year?

c. What will happen to the percentage rate of change of your salary in the long run?

57. The GDP of a certain country is growing at a constant rate. In 1999 the GDP was 125 billion dollars, and in 2001 it was 155 billion dollars. At what percentage rate did the GDP grow in 2000?

58. If y is a linear function of x, what will happen to the percentage rate of change of y with respect to x as x increases without bound?

59. According to Debye's formula in physical chemistry, the orientation polarization P of a gas satisfies

$$P = \frac{4}{3}\pi N \left(\frac{\mu^2}{3kT} \right)$$

where μ, k, and N are constants and T is the temperature of the gas. Find the rate of change of P with respect to T.

60. A disease is spreading in such a way that after t weeks, for $0 \le t \le 6$, it has affected

$$N(t) = 5 - t^2(t - 6)$$

hundred people. Health officials declare that this disease will reach epidemic proportions when the percentage rate of increase of $N(t)$ at the start of a particular week is at least 30% per week. The epidemic designation level is dropped when the percentage rate falls below this level.

a. Find the percentage rate of change of $N(t)$ at time t.

b. Between what weeks is the disease at the epidemic level?

61. An object attached to a helical spring is pulled down from its equilibrium position and then released, as shown in Figure 3.28.

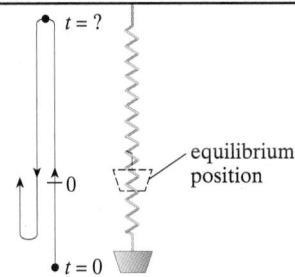

Figure 3.28 Helical spring

Suppose that t seconds later, its position (in centimeters, measured relative to the equilibrium position) is modeled by

$$s(t) = 7 \cos t$$

a. Find the velocity and acceleration of the object at time t.

b. Find the length of time required for one complete oscillation. This is called the *period* of the motion.

c. What is the distance between the highest point reached by the object and the lowest point? Half of this distance is called the *amplitude* of the motion.

62. Two cars leave a town at the same time and travel at constant speeds along straight roads that meet at an angle of 60° in the town. If one car travels twice as fast as the other and the distance between them increases at the rate of 45 mi/h, how fast is the slower car traveling?

63. **Spy Problem** In an attempt to divert the Spy from seeking revenge for the death of his friend Siggy (Problem 62, Section 2.4), his superior, Lord Newton Fleming (affectionately known as the "Flamer"), assigns him to a mission in space. However, an encounter with an enemy agent leaves him with a mild concussion that causes him to forget where he is. Fortunately, he remembers the values of g for various heavenly bodies (32 ft/s² on earth, 5.5 ft/s² on the moon, 12 ft/s² on Mars, and 28 ft/s² on Venus). To deduce his whereabouts, he throws a rock directly upward (from ground level) and notes that it reaches a maximum height of 37.5 ft and hits the ground 5 s after leaving his hand. Where is he?

C 64. Find the rate of change of the volume of a cube with respect to the length of one of its edges. How is this rate related to the surface area of the cube?

65. Show that the rate of change of the volume of a sphere with respect to its radius is equal to its surface area.

66. Van der Waal's equation states that a gas that occupies a volume V at temperature T (Kelvin) exerts pressure P, where

$$\left(P + \frac{A}{V^2} \right)(V - B) = kT$$

and A, B, and k are physical constants. Find the rate of change of pressure with respect to volume, assuming fixed temperature.

3.5 The Chain Rule

IN THIS SECTION introduction to the chain rule, extended derivative formulas, justification of the chain rule

INTRODUCTION TO THE CHAIN RULE

Suppose it is known that the carbon monoxide pollution in the air is changing at the rate of 0.02 ppm (parts per million) for each person in a town whose population is growing at the rate of 1,000 people per year. To find the rate at which the level of pollution is increasing with respect to time, we form the product

$$(0.02 \text{ ppm/person}) \, (1,000 \text{ people/year}) = 20 \text{ ppm/year}$$

In this example, the level of pollution L is a function of the population P, which is itself a function of time t. Thus, L is a composite function of t, and

$$\begin{bmatrix} \text{RATE OF CHANGE OF } L \\ \text{WITH RESPECT TO } t \end{bmatrix} = \begin{bmatrix} \text{RATE OF CHANGE OF } L \\ \text{WITH RESPECT TO } P \end{bmatrix} \begin{bmatrix} \text{RATE OF CHANGE OF } P \\ \text{WITH RESPECT TO } t \end{bmatrix}$$

Expressing each of these rates in terms of an appropriate derivative in Leibniz form, we obtain the following equation:

$$\frac{dL}{dt} = \frac{dL}{dP}\frac{dP}{dt}$$

These observations anticipate the following important theorem.

THEOREM 3.10 Chain rule

If $y = f(u)$ is a differentiable function of u and u in turn is a differentiable function of x, then $y = f(u(x))$ is a differentiable function of x and its derivative is given by the product

$$\frac{dy}{dx} = \frac{dy}{du}\frac{du}{dx}$$

Proof   A rigorous proof involves a few details that make it inappropriate to include at this point in the text. A justification (partial proof) is given at the end of this section, and a full proof of the chain rule is included in Appendix B.

WARNING   Recall our earlier warning in Section 3.1 against thinking of $\frac{dy}{dx}$ as a fraction. That said, there are certain times when this incorrect reasoning can be used as a mnemonic device. For instance, "canceling du," as indicated below, makes it easy to remember the chain rule:

$$\frac{dy}{dx} = \frac{dy\,\cancel{du}}{\cancel{du}\,dx}$$

❑

EXAMPLE 1   The chain rule

Find $\dfrac{dy}{dx}$ if $y = u^3 - 3u^2 + 1$ and $u = x^2 + 2$.

Solution

Because $\dfrac{dy}{du} = 3u^2 - 6u$ and $\dfrac{du}{dx} = 2x$, it follows from the chain rule that

$$\frac{dy}{dx} = \frac{dy}{du}\frac{du}{dx} = (3u^2 - 6u)(2x)$$

Notice that this derivative is expressed in terms of the variables x and u. To express dy/dx in terms of x alone, we substitute $u = x^2 + 2$ as follows:

$$\frac{dy}{dx} = [3(x^2 + 2)^2 - 6(x^2 + 2)](2x) = 6x^3(x^2 + 2)$$

■

The chain rule is actually a rule for differentiating composite functions. In particular, if $y = f(u)$ and $u = u(x)$, then y is the composite function $y = (f \circ u)(x) = f[u(x)]$, and the chain rule can be rewritten as follows:

THEOREM 3.10a   The chain rule (alternate form)

If u is differentiable at x and f is differentiable at $u(x)$, then the composite function $f \circ u$ is differentiable at x and

$$\frac{d}{dx} f[u(x)] = \frac{d}{du} f(u) \frac{du}{dx}$$

or

$$(f \circ u)'(x) = f'[u(x)]u'(x)$$

> ➡ **What This Says**   In Section 1.3 when we introduced composite functions, we talked about the "inner" and "outer" functions. With this terminology, the chain rule says that the derivative of the composite function $f[u(x)]$ is equal to the derivative of the inner function u times the derivative of the outer function f evaluated at the inner function.

❑

EXAMPLE 2   The chain rule applied to a power

Differentiate $y = (3x^4 - 7x + 5)^3$.

Solution

Here, the "inner" function is $u(x) = 3x^4 - 7x + 5$ and the "outer" function is u^3, so we have

$$\begin{aligned} y' &= (u^3)'[u(x)]' \\ &= (3u^2)(12x^3 - 7) \\ &= 3(3x^4 - 7x + 5)^2(12x^3 - 7) \end{aligned}$$ ∎

With a lot of work, you could have found the derivative in Example 2 without using the chain rule either by expanding the polynomial or by using the product rule. The answer would be the same but would involve much more algebra. The chain rule allows us to find derivatives that would otherwise be very difficult to handle.

EXAMPLE 3   Differentiation with quotient rule inside the chain rule

Differentiate $g(x) = \sqrt[4]{\dfrac{x}{1 - 3x}}$.

Solution

Write $g(x) = \left(\dfrac{x}{1 - 3x}\right)^{1/4} = u^{1/4}$, where $u = \dfrac{x}{1 - 3x}$ is the inner function and $u^{1/4}$ is the outer function. Then

$$g'(x) = (u^{1/4})'u'(x) = \tfrac{1}{4}u^{-3/4}u'(x)$$

and we have

$$\begin{aligned} g'(x) &= \frac{1}{4}\left(\frac{x}{1 - 3x}\right)^{-3/4}\left(\frac{x}{1 - 3x}\right)' \\ &= \frac{1}{4}\left(\frac{x}{1 - 3x}\right)^{-3/4}\left[\frac{(1 - 3x)(1) - x(-3)}{(1 - 3x)^2}\right] \quad \textit{Quotient rule} \end{aligned}$$

$$= \frac{1}{4} \left(\frac{x}{1 - 3x} \right)^{-3/4} \left[\frac{1}{(1 - 3x)^2} \right]$$

$$= \frac{1}{4x^{3/4}(1 - 3x)^{5/4}} \qquad \blacksquare$$

EXTENDED DERIVATIVE FORMULAS

The chain rule can be used to obtain generalized differentiation formulas for the standard functions, as displayed in the following box.

If u is a differentiable function of x, then

Extended Power Rule

$$\frac{d}{dx} u^n = nu^{n-1} \frac{du}{dx}$$

Extended Trigonometric Rules

$$\frac{d}{dx} \sin u = \cos u \frac{du}{dx} \qquad \qquad \frac{d}{dx} \cos u = -\sin u \frac{du}{dx}$$

$$\frac{d}{dx} \tan u = \sec^2 u \frac{du}{dx} \qquad \qquad \frac{d}{dx} \cot u = -\csc^2 u \frac{du}{dx}$$

$$\frac{d}{dx} \sec u = \sec u \tan u \frac{du}{dx} \qquad \frac{d}{dx} \csc u = -\csc u \cot u \frac{du}{dx}$$

Extended Exponential and Logarithmic Rules

$$\frac{d}{dx} e^u = e^u \frac{du}{dx} \qquad \qquad \frac{d}{dx} \ln u = \frac{1}{u} \frac{du}{dx}$$

EXAMPLE 4   Chain rule with a trigonometric function

Differentiate $f(x) = \sin(3x^2 + 5x - 7)$.

Solution

Think of this as $f(u) = \sin u$, where $u = 3x^2 + 5x - 7$, and apply the chain rule:

$$f'(x) = \cos(3x^2 + 5x - 7) \cdot (3x^2 + 5x - 7)'$$

$$= (6x + 5) \cos(3x^2 + 5x - 7) \qquad \blacksquare$$

EXAMPLE 5   Chain rule with other rules

Differentiate $g(x) = \cos x^2 + 5\left(\frac{3}{x} + 4\right)^6$.

Solution
$$\frac{dg}{dx} = \frac{d}{dx} \cos x^2 + 5 \frac{d}{dx} (3x^{-1} + 4)^6$$

$$= -\sin x^2 \frac{d}{dx}(x^2) + 5 \left[6(3x^{-1} + 4)^5 \frac{d}{dx}(3x^{-1} + 4) \right]$$

$$= (-\sin x^2)(2x) + 30(3x^{-1} + 4)^5(-3x^{-2})$$

$$= -2x \sin x^2 - 90x^{-2}(3x^{-1} + 4)^5 \qquad \blacksquare$$

EXAMPLE 6   Extended power and cosine rules

Differentiate $y = \cos^4(3x + 1)^2$.

Solution

$$\frac{dy}{dx} = 4\cos^3(3x+1)^2 \frac{d}{dx}\cos(3x+1)^2 \qquad \text{Extended power rule}$$

$$= 4\cos^3(3x+1)^2 \cdot [-\sin(3x+1)^2] \cdot \frac{d}{dx}(3x+1)^2 \qquad \text{Extended cosine rule}$$

$$= -4\cos^3(3x+1)^2\sin(3x+1)^2 \cdot 2(3x+1)(3) \qquad \text{Extended power rule}$$

$$= -24(3x+1)\cos^3(3x+1)^2\sin(3x+1)^2 \qquad \blacksquare$$

EXAMPLE 7   Extended power rule inside quotient rule

Differentiate $p(x) = \dfrac{\tan 7x}{(1-4x)^5}$.

Solution

$$\frac{dp}{dx} = \frac{(1-4x)^5\left[\dfrac{d}{dx}\tan 7x\right] - \tan 7x\left[\dfrac{d}{dx}(1-4x)^5\right]}{[(1-4x)^5]^2}$$

$$= \frac{(1-4x)^5(\sec^2 7x)\dfrac{d}{dx}(7x) - (\tan 7x)[5(1-4x)^4\dfrac{d}{dx}(1-4x)]}{(1-4x)^{10}}$$

$$= \frac{(1-4x)^5(\sec^2 7x)(7) - (\tan 7x)(5)(1-4x)^4(-4)}{(1-4x)^{10}}$$

$$= \frac{(1-4x)^4[7(1-4x)\sec^2 7x + 20\tan 7x]}{(1-4x)^{10}}$$

$$= \frac{7(1-4x)\sec^2 7x + 20\tan 7x}{(1-4x)^6} \qquad \blacksquare$$

EXAMPLE 8   Extended exponential rule within product rule

Differentiate $e^{-3x}\sin x$.

Solution

Use the product rule:

$$\frac{d}{dx}[e^{-3x}\sin x] = e^{-3x}\left[\frac{d}{dx}(\sin x)\right] + \left[\frac{d}{dx}(e^{-3x})\right]\sin x \qquad \text{Product rule}$$

$$= e^{-3x}(\cos x) + [e^{-3x}(-3)]\sin x$$

$$= e^{-3x}(\cos x - 3\sin x) \qquad \blacksquare$$

EXAMPLE 9   Finding a horizontal tangent line

Find the x-coordinate of each point on the graph of

$$f(x) = x^2(4x+5)^3$$

where the tangent line is horizontal.

Solution

Because horizontal tangent lines have zero slope, we need to solve the equation $f'(x) = 0$. We find that

$$f'(x) = [x^2(4x+5)^3]'$$

$$= [x^2]'(4x+5)^3 + x^2[(4x+5)^3]' \qquad \text{Product rule}$$

$$= [2x](4x+5)^3 + x^2[3(4x+5)^2(4)] \quad \text{Extended power rule}$$
$$= 2x(4x+5)^2[4x+5+6x] \quad \text{Common factor}$$
$$= 2x(4x+5)^2(10x+5)$$
$$= 10x(4x+5)^2(2x+1)$$

From the factored form of the derivative, we see that $f'(x) = 0$ when $x = 0$, $x = -\frac{5}{4}$, and $x = -\frac{1}{2}$, so these are the x-coordinates of the points on the graph of f where horizontal tangent lines occur. ∎

EXAMPLE 10 A modeling problem using the chain rule

An environmental study of a certain suburban community suggests that the average daily level of carbon monoxide in the air may be modeled by the formula

$$C(p) = \sqrt{0.5p^2 + 17}$$

parts per million when the population is p thousand. It is estimated that t years from now, the population of the community will be

$$p(t) = 3.1 + 0.1t^2$$

thousand. At what rate will the carbon monoxide level be changing with respect to time 3 years from now?

Solution

$$\frac{dC}{dt} = \frac{dC}{dp}\frac{dp}{dt} = \left[\frac{1}{2}(0.5p^2+17)^{-1/2}(0.5)(2p)\right][0.2t]$$

When $t = 3$, $p(3) = 3.1 + 0.1(3)^2 = 4$, so

$$\left.\frac{dC}{dt}\right|_{t=3} = \left[\frac{1}{2}(0.5\cdot 4^2 + 17)^{-1/2}(4)\right][0.2(3)] = 0.24$$

The carbon monoxide level will be changing at the rate of 0.24 parts per million. It will be increasing because the sign of dC/dt is positive. ∎

JUSTIFICATION OF THE CHAIN RULE

To get a better feel for why the chain rule is true, suppose x is changed by a small amount Δx. This will cause u to change by an amount Δu, which, in turn, will cause y to change by an amount Δy. *If Δu is not zero*, we can write

$$\frac{\Delta y}{\Delta x} = \frac{\Delta y}{\Delta u}\frac{\Delta u}{\Delta x}$$

By letting $\Delta x \to 0$, we force Δu to approach zero as well, since

$$\Delta u = \left(\frac{\Delta u}{\Delta x}\right)\Delta x \quad \text{so} \quad \lim_{\Delta x \to 0}\Delta u = \left(\frac{du}{dx}\right)(0) = 0$$

It follows that

$$\lim_{\Delta x \to 0}\frac{\Delta y}{\Delta x} = \left(\lim_{\Delta u \to 0}\frac{\Delta y}{\Delta u}\right)\left(\lim_{\Delta x \to 0}\frac{\Delta u}{\Delta x}\right)$$

or, equivalently,

$$\frac{dy}{dx} = \frac{dy}{du}\frac{du}{dx}$$

Unfortunately, there is a flaw in this "proof" of the chain rule. At the beginning we assumed that $\Delta u \neq 0$. However, it is theoretically possible for a small change in x to produce no change in u so that $\Delta u = 0$. This is the case that we consider in the proof in Appendix B.

Historical Note

A calculus book written by the famous mathematician G. H. Hardy (1877–1947) contained essentially this "incorrect" proof rather than the one given in Appendix B. It is even more remarkable that the error was not noticed until the fourth edition.

3.5 PROBLEM SET

A 1. **WHAT DOES THIS SAY?** What is the chain rule?

2. **WHAT DOES THIS SAY?** When do you need to use the chain rule?

In Problems 3–8, use the chain rule to compute the derivative dy/dx and write your answer in terms of x only.

3. $y = u^2 + 1; u = 3x - 2$

4. $y = 2u^2 - u + 5; u = 1 - x^2$

5. $y = \dfrac{2}{u^2}; u = x^2 - 9$

6. $y = \cos u; u = x^2 + 7$

7. $y = u \tan u; u = 3x + \dfrac{6}{x}$

8. $y = u^2; u = \ln x$

Differentiate each function in Problems 9–12 with respect to the given variable of the function.

9. **a.** $g(u) = u^3$ **b.** $u(x) = x^2 + 1$
c. $f(x) = (x^2 + 1)^3$

10. **a.** $g(u) = u^5$ **b.** $u(x) = 3x - 1$
c. $f(x) = (3x - 1)^5$

11. **a.** $g(u) = u^7$ **b.** $u(x) = 5 - 8x - 12x^2$
c. $f(x) = (5 - 8x - 12x^2)^7$

12. **a.** $g(u) = u^{15}$ **b.** $u(x) = 3x^2 + 5x - 7$
c. $f(x) = (3x^2 + 5x - 7)^{15}$

In Problems 13–40, find the derivative of the given function.

13. $f(x) = (5x - 2)^5$

14. $f(x) = (x^4 - 7x)^{15}$

15. $f(x) = (3x^2 - 2x + 1)^4$

16. $f(x) = (3 - x^2 - x^4)^{11}$

17. $s(\theta) = \sin(4\theta + 2)$

18. $c(\theta) = \cos(5 - 3\theta)$

19. $f(x) = e^{-x^2 + 3x}$

20. $y = e^{x^3 - \pi}$

21. $y = e^{\sec x}$

22. $g(x) = e^{\sin x}$

23. $f(t) = \exp(t^2 + t + 5)$

24. $g(t) = t^2 e^{-t} + (\ln t)^2$

25. $g(x) = x \sin 5x$

26. $h(x) = \dfrac{\tan 3x}{x^2}$

27. $f(x) = \left(\dfrac{1}{1 - 2x}\right)^3$

28. $f(x) = \sqrt[3]{\dfrac{1}{2 - 3x}}$

29. $f(x) = xe^{1 - 2x}$

30. $g(x) = \ln(3x^4 + 5x)$

31. $p(x) = \sin x^2 \cos x^2$

32. $f(x) = \csc^2(\sqrt{x})$

33. $f(x) = x^3(2 - 3x)^2$

34. $f(x) = x^4(2 - x - x^2)^3$

35. $f(x) = \sqrt{\dfrac{x^2 + 3}{x^2 - 5}}$

36. $f(x) = \sqrt{\dfrac{2x^2 - 1}{3x^2 + 2}}$

37. $f(x) = \sqrt[3]{x + \sqrt{2x}}$

38. $g(x) = \ln(\ln x)$

39. $f(x) = \ln(\sin x + \cos x)$

40. $T(x) = \ln(\sec x + \tan x)$

Find the x-coordinate of each point in Problems 41–46 where the graph of the given function has a horizontal tangent line.

41. $f(x) = x\sqrt{1 - 3x}$

42. $g(x) = x^2(2x + 3)^2$

43. $q(x) = \dfrac{(x - 1)^2}{(x + 2)^3}$

44. $f(x) = (2x^2 - 7)^3$

45. $T(x) = x^2 e^{1 - 3x}$

46. $V(x) = \dfrac{\ln \sqrt{x}}{x^2}$

B 47. The graphs of $u = g(x)$ and $y = f(u)$ are shown in Figure 3.29.

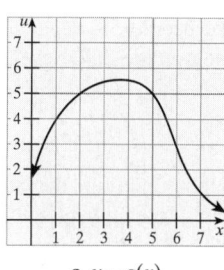
a. $u = g(x)$

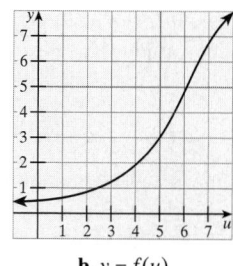
b. $y = f(u)$

Figure 3.29 Find the slope of $y = f[g(x)]$.

a. Find the approximate value of u at $x = 2$. What is the slope of the tangent line at that point?

b. Find the approximate value of y at $x = 5$. What is the slope of the tangent line at that point?

c. Find the slope of $y = f[g(x)]$ at $x = 2$.

48. The graphs of $y = f(x)$ and $y = g(x)$ are shown in Figure 3.30.

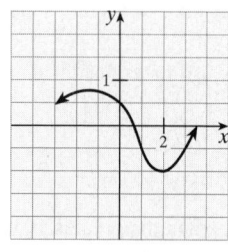
a. $y = f(x)$

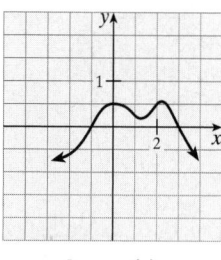
b. $y = g(x)$

Figure 3.30 Problem 48

Let $h(x) = f[g(x)]$.
a. Estimate $h'(-1)$ **b.** $h'(1)$ **c.** $h'(3)$

49. Repeat Problem 48 for $h(x) = g[f(x)]$.

50. If $g(x) = f[f(x)]$, use the table to find the value of $g'(2)$.

x	0.0	1.0	2.0	3.0	4.0	5.0
$f(x)$	18.5	9.4	4.0	2.6	8.3	14.0

51. If $h(x) = f[g(x)]$, use the table to find the value of $h'(1)$.

x	0.0	1.0	2.0	3.0	4.0	5.0
$f(x)$	6.9	4.3	3.1	2.8	2.2	2.0
$g(x)$	0.8	2.0	2.5	1.8	0.9	0.4

52. Assume that a spherical snowball melts in such a way that its radius decreases at a constant rate (that is, the radius is a linear function of time). Suppose it begins as a sphere with radius 10 cm and takes 2 hours to disappear.

a. What is the rate of change of its volume after 1 hour? (Recall $V = \frac{4}{3}\pi r^3$.)

b. At what rate is its surface area changing after 1 hour? (Recall $S = 4\pi r^2$.)

53. It is estimated that t years from now, the population of a certain suburban community is modeled by the formula

$$p(t) = 20 - \frac{6}{t+1}$$

where $p(t)$ is in thousands of people. A separate environmental study indicates that the average daily level of carbon monoxide in the air will be

$$L(p) = 0.5\sqrt{p^2 + p + 58}$$

ppm when the population is p thousand. Find the rate at which the level of carbon monoxide will be changing with respect to time two years from now.

54. At a certain factory, the total cost of manufacturing q units during the daily production run is

$$C(q) = 0.2q^2 + q + 900$$

dollars. From experience, it has been determined that approximately

$$q(t) = t^2 + 100t$$

units are manufactured during the first t hours of a production run. Compute the rate at which the total manufacturing cost is changing with respect to time one hour after production begins.

55. An importer of Brazilian coffee estimates that local consumers will buy approximately

$$D(p) = \frac{4,374}{p^2}$$

pounds of the coffee per week when the price is p dollars per pound. It is estimated that t weeks from now, the price of Brazilian coffee will be

$$p(t) = 0.02t^2 + 0.1t + 6$$

dollars per pound. At what rate will the weekly demand for the coffee be changing with respect to time 10 weeks from now? Will the demand be increasing or decreasing?

56. When electric blenders are sold for p dollars apiece, local consumers will buy

$$D(p) = \frac{8,000}{p}$$

blenders per month. It is estimated that t months from now, the price of the blenders will be

$$p(t) = 0.04t^{3/2} + 15$$

dollars. Compute the rate at which the monthly demand for the blenders will be changing with respect to time 25 months from now. Will the demand be increasing or decreasing?

When a point source of light of luminous intensity K (candles) shines directly on a point on a surface s meters away, the illuminance on the surface is given by the formula $I = Ks^{-2}$. Use this formula to answer the questions in Problems 57–58. (Note that 1 lux = 1 candle/m^2.)

57. Suppose a person carrying a 20-candlepower light walks toward a wall in such a way that at time t (seconds) the distance to the wall is $s(t) = 28 - t^2$ meters.

a. How fast is the illuminance on the wall increasing when the person is 19 m from the wall?

b. How far is the person from the wall when the illuminance is changing at the rate of 1 lux/s?

58. A lamp of luminous intensity 40 candles is 20 m above the floor of a room and is being lowered at the constant rate of 2 m/s. At what rate will the illuminance at the point on the floor directly under the lamp be increasing when the lamp is 15 m above the floor? Your answer should be in lux/s rounded to the nearest hundredth.

59. To form a *simple pendulum*, a weight is attached to a rod that is then suspended by one end in such a way that it can swing freely in a vertical plane. Let θ be the angular displacement of the rod from the vertical, as shown in Figure 3.31.

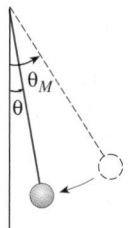

Figure 3.31   Problem 59

It can be shown that as long as the maximum displacement θ_M is small, it is reasonable to assume that $\theta = \theta_M \sin kt$ at time t, where k is a constant that depends on the length of the rod and θ_M is a constant. Show that

$$\frac{d^2\theta}{dt^2} + k^2\theta = 0$$

60. A lighthouse is located 2 km directly across the sea from a point O on the shoreline, as shown in Figure 3.32.

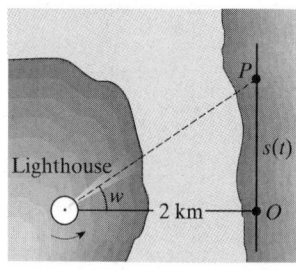

Figure 3.32   Problem 60

A beacon in the lighthouse makes 3 complete revolutions (that is, 6π radians) each minute, and during part of each revolution, the light sweeps across the face of a row of cliffs lining the shore.

a. Show that t minutes after it passes point O, the beam of light is at a point P located $s(t) = 2 \tan(6\pi t)$ km from O.

b. How fast is the beam of light moving at the time it passes a point on the cliff that is 4 km from the lighthouse?

61. The average Fahrenheit temperature t hours after midnight in a certain city is modeled by the formula

$$T(t) = 58 + 17\sin\left(\frac{\pi t}{10} - \frac{5}{6}\right)$$

At what rate is the temperature changing with respect to time at 2 A.M.? Is it getting hotter or colder at that time?

62. In physics, it is shown that when an object is viewed at depth d under water from an angle of incidence θ, then refraction causes the apparent depth of the object to be

$$s(\theta) = \frac{3d\cos\theta}{\sqrt{7 + 9\cos^2\theta}}$$

(see Figure 3.33). At what rate is the apparent depth changing with respect to θ when $d = 2$ m and $\theta = \frac{\pi}{6}$?

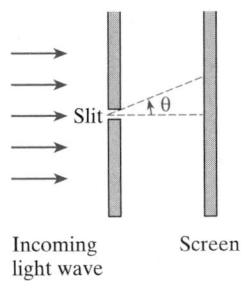

Figure 3.33 Light refraction

63. In the study of Frauenhofer diffraction in optics, a light beam of intensity I_0 from a source L passes through a narrow slit and is diffracted onto a screen (see Figure 3.34.)

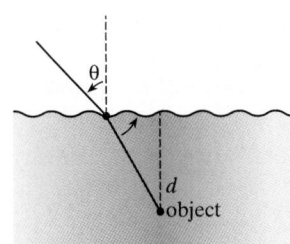

Incoming light wave   Screen

Figure 3.34 Optical diffraction

Experiments indicate that the intensity $I(\theta)$ of light on the screen depends on the diffraction angle θ shown in Figure 3.34 in such a way that

$$I(\beta) = I_0\left(\frac{\sin\beta}{\beta}\right)^2$$

where $\beta = \pi a \sin(\theta/\lambda)$, λ is the wavelength of the light, and a is a constant related to the width of the screen. Use the chain rule to find $dI/d\theta$, the rate of change of intensity with respect to θ.

64. A worker pushes a heavy crate across a warehouse floor at a constant velocity. If the crate weighs W pounds and the worker applies a force F at an angle θ, as shown in Figure 3.35, then

$$F(\theta) = \frac{\mu W \sec\theta}{1 + \mu\tan\theta}$$

where μ is a constant (the coefficient of friction). For the case where $W = 100$ lb and $\mu = 0.25$, find $\dfrac{dF}{d\theta}$ when $\theta = 27°$.

Figure 3.35 Pushing a crate with variable force

C 65. Using only the formula

$$\frac{d}{dx}\sin u = \cos u \frac{du}{dx}$$

and the identities $\cos x = \sin(\frac{\pi}{2} - x)$ and $\sin x = \cos(\frac{\pi}{2} - x)$, show that

$$\frac{d}{dx}\cos u = -\sin u \frac{du}{dx}$$

66. Let $g(x) = f[u(x)]$, where $u(-3) = 5$, $u'(-3) = 2$, $f(5) = 3$, and $f'(5) = -3$. Find an equation for the tangent line to the graph of g at the point where $x = -3$.

67. Let f be a function for which

$$f'(x) = \frac{1}{x^2 + 1}$$

a. If $g(x) = f(3x - 1)$, what is $g'(x)$?

b. If $h(x) = f\left(\dfrac{1}{x}\right)$, what is $h'(x)$?

68. Let f be a function for which $f(2) = -3$ and $f'(x) = \sqrt{x^2 + 5}$. If $g(x) = x^2 f\left(\dfrac{x}{x - 1}\right)$, what is $g'(2)$?

69. a. If $F(x) = \ln|\cos x|$, show that $F'(x) = -\tan x$.

b. If $F(x) = \ln|\sec x + \tan x|$, show that $F'(x) = \sec x$.

70. If $\dfrac{df}{dx} = \dfrac{\sin x}{x}$ and $u(x) = \cot x$, what is $\dfrac{df}{du}$?

71. Use the chain rule to find

$$\frac{d}{dx}f'[f(x)] \quad \text{and} \quad \frac{d}{dx}f[f'(x)]$$

assuming these derivatives exist.

72. Show that if a particle moves along a straight line with position $s(t)$ and velocity $v(t)$, then its acceleration satisfies

$$a(t) = v(t)\frac{dv}{ds}$$

Use this formula to find $\dfrac{dv}{ds}$ in the case where

$$s(t) = -2t^3 + 4t^2 + t - 3$$

3.6 Implicit Differentiation

IN THIS SECTION general procedure for implicit differentiation, derivative formulas for the inverse trigonometric functions, logarithmic differentiation

GENERAL PROCEDURE FOR IMPLICIT DIFFERENTIATION

The equation $y = \sqrt{1 - x^2}$ **explicitly** defines $y = f(x) = \sqrt{1 - x^2}$ as a function of x for $-1 \leq x \leq 1$, but the same function can also be defined **implicitly** by the equation $x^2 + y^2 = 1$, as long as we restrict y by $0 \leq y \leq 1$ so that the vertical line test is satisfied. To find the derivative of the explicit form, we use the chain rule:

$$\frac{d}{dx}\sqrt{1-x^2} = \frac{d}{dx}(1-x^2)^{1/2} = \frac{1}{2}(1-x^2)^{-1/2}(-2x) = \frac{-x}{\sqrt{1-x^2}}$$

To obtain the derivative of the same function in its implicit form, we simply differentiate across the equation $x^2 + y^2 = 1$, remembering that y is a function of x:

$$\frac{d}{dx}(x^2 + y^2) = \frac{d}{dx}(1) \qquad \text{Derivative of both sides}$$

$$2x + 2y\frac{dy}{dx} = 0 \qquad \text{Chain rule for the derivative of } y$$

$$\frac{dy}{dx} = -\frac{x}{y} \qquad \text{Solve for } \frac{dy}{dx}.$$

$$= -\frac{x}{\sqrt{1-x^2}} \qquad \text{Write as a function of } x, \text{ if desired.}$$

The procedure we have just illustrated is called **implicit differentiation**. Our illustrative example was simple, but consider a differentiable function $y = f(x)$ defined by the equation

$$x^2y^3 - 6 = 5y^3 + x$$

Implicit differentiation tells us that

$$x^2\frac{d}{dx}(y^3) + y^3\frac{d}{dx}(x^2) - \frac{d}{dx}(6) = 5\frac{d}{dx}(y^3) + \frac{d}{dx}(x)$$

$$x^2\left(3y^2\frac{dy}{dx}\right) + y^3(2x) - 0 = 5\left(3y^2\frac{dy}{dx}\right) + 1$$

$$(3x^2y^3 - 15y^2)\frac{dy}{dx} = 1 - 2xy^3$$

$$\frac{dy}{dx} = \frac{1 - 2xy^3}{3x^2y^2 - 15y^2}$$

You may think that we are not finished since the derivative involves both x and y, but for many applications, that is enough as we may know both x and y simultaneously at a point. In this example, we could have found y as an explicit function of x, namely

$$y = \left(\frac{x+6}{x^2-5}\right)^{1/3}$$

and then found dy/dx by the chain rule.

Now consider a differentiable function $y = f(x)$ defined by the equation

$$x^2y + 2y^3 = 3x + 2y$$

Finding y as an explicit function of x is very difficult in this case, and it is not at all hard to imagine similar situations where solving for y in terms of x would be impossible or at least not worth the effort. We begin our work with implicit differentiation by using it to find the slope of a tangent line at a point on a circle.

EXAMPLE 1 Slope of a tangent line using implicit differentiation

Find the slope of the tangent line to the circle $x^2 + y^2 = 10$ at the point $P(-1, 3)$.

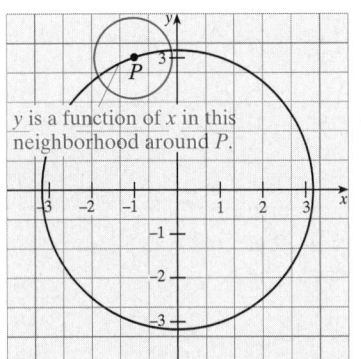

y is a function of *x* in this neighborhood around *P*.

Figure 3.36 Graph of $x^2 + y^2 = 10$ showing a neighborhood about $P(-1, 3)$

Solution

We recognize the graph of $x^2 + y^2 = 10$ as not being the graph of a function. However, if we look at a small neighborhood around the point $(-1, 3)$, as shown in Figure 3.36, we see that this part of the graph *does pass the vertical line test* for functions. Thus, the required slope can be found by evaluating the derivative dy/dx at $(-1, 3)$. Instead of solving for y and finding the derivative, we *take the derivative of both sides of the equation*:

$$x^2 + y^2 = 10 \qquad \text{Given equation}$$

$$\frac{d}{dx}(x^2 + y^2) = \frac{d}{dx}(10) \qquad \text{Derivative of both sides}$$

$$2x + 2y\frac{dy}{dx} = 0 \qquad \text{Do not forget that } y \text{ is a function of } x.$$

$$\frac{dy}{dx} = -\frac{x}{y} \qquad \text{Solve the equation for } \frac{dy}{dx}.$$

The slope of the tangent line at $P(-1, 3)$ is

$$\left.\frac{dy}{dx}\right|_P = -\left.\frac{x}{y}\right|_{(-1,3)} = -\frac{-1}{3} = \frac{1}{3} \qquad \blacksquare$$

Here is a general description of the procedure for implicit differentiation.

Procedure for Implicit Differentiation

Suppose an equation defines y implicitly as a differentiable function of x. To find $\dfrac{dy}{dx}$:

Step 1. Differentiate both sides of the equation with respect to x. Remember that y is really a function of x for part of the curve and use the chain rule when differentiating terms containing y.

Step 2. Solve the differentiated equation algebraically for $\dfrac{dy}{dx}$. $\qquad \blacksquare$

EXAMPLE 2 Implicit differentiation

If $y = f(x)$ is a differentiable function of x such that

$$x^2 y + 2y^3 = 3x + 2y$$

find $\dfrac{dy}{dx}$.

Solution

The process is to differentiate both sides of the given equation with respect to x. To help remember that y is a function of x, replace y by the symbol $y(x)$:

$$x^2 y(x) + 2[y(x)]^3 = 3x + 2y(x)$$

Differentiate both sides of this equation term by term with respect to x:

$$\frac{d}{dx}\{x^2 y(x) + 2[y(x)]^3\} = \frac{d}{dx}\{3x + 2y(x)\}$$

$$\frac{d}{dx}[x^2 y(x)] + 2\frac{d}{dx}[y(x)]^3 = 3\frac{d}{dx}x + 2\frac{d}{dx}y(x)$$

$$\underbrace{x^2\frac{d}{dx}y(x) + y(x)\frac{d}{dx}x^2}_{\text{Product rule}} + 2\underbrace{\left\{3[y(x)]^2\frac{d}{dx}y(x)\right\}}_{\text{Extended power rule}} = 3 + 2\frac{d}{dx}y(x)$$

$$x^2\frac{d}{dx}y(x) + 2xy(x) + 6[y(x)]^2\frac{d}{dx}y(x) = 3 + 2\frac{d}{dx}y(x)$$

Now replace $y(x)$ by y and $\frac{d}{dx}y(x)$ by $\frac{dy}{dx}$ and rewrite the equation:

$$x^2\frac{dy}{dx} + 2xy + 6y^2\frac{dy}{dx} = 3 + 2\frac{dy}{dx}$$

Finally, solve this equation for $\frac{dy}{dx}$:

$$x^2\frac{dy}{dx} + 6y^2\frac{dy}{dx} - 2\frac{dy}{dx} = 3 - 2xy$$

$$(x^2 + 6y^2 - 2)\frac{dy}{dx} = 3 - 2xy$$

$$\frac{dy}{dx} = \frac{3 - 2xy}{x^2 + 6y^2 - 2}$$

Notice that the formula for dy/dx contains both the independent variable x and the dependent variable y. This is usual when derivatives are computed implicitly.   ■

WARNING   It is important to realize that implicit differentiation is a technique for finding dy/dx that is valid only if y is a differentiable function of x, and careless application of the technique can lead to errors. For example, there is clearly no real-valued function $y = f(x)$ that satisfies the equation $x^2 + y^2 = -1$, yet formal application of implicit differentiation yields the "derivative" $dy/dx = -x/y$. To be able to evaluate this "derivative," we must find some values of x and y for which $x^2 + y^2 = -1$. Because no such values exist, the derivative does not exist.

In Example 2 it was suggested that you temporarily replace y by $y(x)$, so you would not forget to use the chain rule when first learning implicit differentiation. In the following example, we eliminate this unnecessary step and differentiate the given equation directly. Just keep in mind that y is really a function of x and remember to use the chain rule (or extended power rule) when it is appropriate.

EXAMPLE 3   Implicit differentiation; simplified notation

Find $\dfrac{dy}{dx}$ if y is a differentiable function of x that satisfies

$$\sin(x^2 + y) = y^2(3x + 1)$$

Solution

There is no obvious way to solve the given equation explicitly for y. Differentiate implicitly to obtain

$$\frac{d}{dx}[\sin(x^2 + y)] = \frac{d}{dx}[y^2(3x + 1)]$$

$$\underbrace{\cos(x^2 + y)\frac{d}{dx}(x^2 + y)}_{\text{Chain rule}} = \underbrace{y^2\frac{d}{dx}(3x + 1) + (3x + 1)\frac{d}{dx}y^2}_{\text{Product rule}}$$

$$\cos(x^2 + y)\left(2x + \frac{dy}{dx}\right) = y^2(3) + (3x + 1)\left(2y\frac{dy}{dx}\right)$$

Finally, solve for $\dfrac{dy}{dx}$:

$$2x\cos(x^2 + y) + \cos(x^2 + y)\frac{dy}{dx} = 3y^2 + 2y(3x + 1)\frac{dy}{dx}$$

$$[\cos(x^2 + y) - 2y(3x + 1)]\frac{dy}{dx} = 3y^2 - 2x\cos(x^2 + y)$$

$$\frac{dy}{dx} = \frac{3y^2 - 2x\cos(x^2 + y)}{\cos(x^2 + y) - 2y(3x + 1)}$$ ∎

EXAMPLE 4 Slope of a tangent line using implicit differentiation

Find the slope of a line tangent to the circle $x^2 + y^2 = 5x + 4y$ at the point $P(5, 4)$.

Solution

The slope of a curve $y = f(x)$ is $\dfrac{dy}{dx}$, which we find implicitly.

$$x^2 + y^2 = 5x + 4y$$

$$\frac{d}{dx}(x^2 + y^2) = \frac{d}{dx}(5x + 4y)$$

$$2x + 2y\frac{dy}{dx} = 5 + 4\frac{dy}{dx}$$

$$2y\frac{dy}{dx} - 4\frac{dy}{dx} = 5 - 2x$$

$$(2y - 4)\frac{dy}{dx} = 5 - 2x$$

$$\frac{dy}{dx} = \frac{5 - 2x}{2y - 4}$$

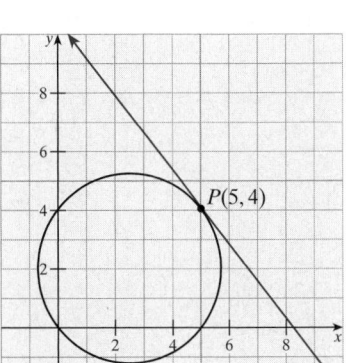

Figure 3.37 Graph of circle and tangent line

At $(5, 4)$, the slope of the tangent line is

$$\frac{dy}{dx}\bigg|_{(5,4)} = \frac{5 - 2x}{2y - 4}\bigg|_{(5,4)} = \frac{5 - 2(5)}{2(4) - 4} = -\frac{5}{4}$$

Note that the expression is undefined at $y = 2$; this makes sense when you see that the tangent line is vertical there. Look at the graph in Figure 3.37 and see whether you should exclude any other values. ∎

EXAMPLE 5 Second derivative by implicit differentiation

Find $\dfrac{d^2y}{dx^2}$ if $x^2 + y^2 = 10$.

Solution

In Example 1 we found (implicitly) that $\dfrac{dy}{dx} = -\dfrac{x}{y}$. Thus,

$$\frac{d^2y}{dx^2} = \frac{d}{dx}\left(\frac{-x}{y}\right) = \underbrace{\frac{y\frac{d}{dx}(-x) - (-x)\frac{d}{dx}y}{y^2}}_{\text{Quotient rule}} = \frac{-y + x\frac{dy}{dx}}{y^2}$$

Note that the expression for the second derivative contains the first derivative dy/dx. To simplify the answer, substitute the algebraic expression previously found for dy/dx:

$$\frac{-y + x\dfrac{dy}{dx}}{y^2} = \frac{-y + x\left(\dfrac{-x}{y}\right)}{y^2} \qquad \text{Substitute } \frac{dy}{dx} = -\frac{x}{y}.$$

$$= \frac{-y^2 - x^2}{y^3}$$

$$= \frac{-(x^2 + y^2)}{y^3}$$

$$= \frac{-10}{y^3} \qquad \text{Substitute } x^2 + y^2 = 10.$$

Thus, $\dfrac{d^2y}{dx^2} = \dfrac{-10}{y^3}$. ■

In Section 3.3, we found the derivative of $f(x) = e^x$ (Theorem 3.8). This derivative is more easily found using implicit differentiation, as shown in the following example.

EXAMPLE 6 Derivative rule for the natural exponential

Show that

$$\frac{d}{dx}(e^x) = e^x$$

Solution

Let $v = e^x$, so that $x = \ln v$. Then

$$\frac{d}{dx}(x) = \frac{d}{dx}(\ln v) \qquad \text{Derivative of both sides of } x = \ln v$$

$$1 = \frac{1}{v}\frac{dv}{dx} \qquad \text{Implicit differentiation}$$

$$v = \frac{dv}{dx}$$

$$e^x = \frac{dv}{dx} = \frac{d}{dx}(e^x) \qquad \text{Because } v = e^x$$ ■

Implicit differentiation is a valuable theoretical tool. For example, in Section 3.2 we proved the power rule for the case where the exponent is an integer. Implicit differentiation now allows us to extend the proof for all real exponents.

EXAMPLE 7 Proof of power rule for real (rational and irrational) exponents

Prove that $\dfrac{d}{dx}(x^r) = rx^{r-1}$ holds for all real numbers r if $x > 0$.

Solution

If $y = x^r$, then $y = e^{r \ln x}$, so that

$$\ln y = r \ln x \qquad \text{Definition of exponent}$$

$$\frac{1}{y} \frac{dy}{dx} = r \left(\frac{1}{x} \right) \qquad \text{Implicit differentiation}$$

$$\frac{dy}{dx} = y \left(\frac{r}{x} \right) \qquad \text{Solve for } \frac{dy}{dx}.$$

$$= x^r \left(\frac{r}{x} \right) \qquad \text{Substitute } y = x^r.$$

$$= rx^{r-1} \qquad \text{Property of exponents} \qquad \blacksquare$$

Notice in Example 7 that $y = x^r = e^{r \ln x}$ is differentiable because it is defined as the composition of the differentiable functions $y = e^u$ and $u = r \ln x$.

DERIVATIVE FORMULAS FOR THE INVERSE TRIGONOMETRIC FUNCTIONS

Next, we will use implicit differentiation to obtain differentiation formulas for the six inverse trigonometric functions. Note that these derivatives are not inverse trigonometric functions or even trigonometric functions, but are instead rational functions or roots of rational functions. In fact, the usefulness of inverse trigonometric functions in many areas is related to the simplicity of their derivatives.

THEOREM 3.11 Differentiation formulas for six inverse trigonometric functions

If u is a differentiable function of x, then

$$\frac{d}{dx}(\sin^{-1} u) = \frac{1}{\sqrt{1 - u^2}} \frac{du}{dx} \qquad\qquad \frac{d}{dx}(\cos^{-1} u) = -\frac{1}{\sqrt{1 - u^2}} \frac{du}{dx}$$

$$\frac{d}{dx}(\tan^{-1} u) = \frac{1}{1 + u^2} \frac{du}{dx} \qquad\qquad \frac{d}{dx}(\cot^{-1} u) = \frac{-1}{1 + u^2} \frac{du}{dx}$$

$$\frac{d}{dx}(\sec^{-1} u) = \frac{1}{|u| \sqrt{u^2 - 1}} \frac{du}{dx} \qquad\qquad \frac{d}{dx}(\csc^{-1} u) = \frac{-1}{|u| \sqrt{u^2 - 1}} \frac{du}{dx}$$

WARNING   Note that the derivative of each inverse trigonometric function $y = \cos^{-1} x$, $y = \cot^{-1} x$, and $y = \csc^{-1} x$ is the opposite of the derivative of the corresponding inverse cofunction $y = \sin^{-1} x$, $y = \tan^{-1} x$, and $y = \sec^{-1} x$.

Proof   We will prove the first formula and leave the others as problems. Let $\alpha = \sin^{-1} x$, so $x = \sin \alpha$. Because the sine function is one-to-one and differentiable on $[-\pi/2, \pi/2]$, the inverse sine function is also differentiable. To find its derivative, we proceed implicitly:

$$\sin \alpha = x$$

$$\frac{d}{dx}(\sin \alpha) = \frac{d}{dx}(x)$$

$$\cos \alpha \frac{d\alpha}{dx} = 1$$

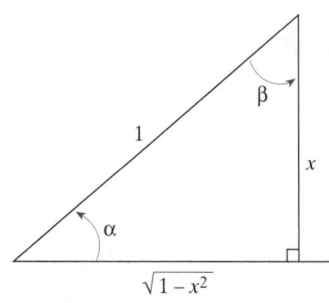

Figure 3.38 $\sin \alpha = x$ and $\cos \alpha = \sqrt{1 - x^2}$

Since $-\frac{\pi}{2} \le \alpha \le \frac{\pi}{2}$, $\cos \alpha \ge 0$, so

$$\frac{d\alpha}{dx} = \frac{1}{\cos \alpha} = \frac{1}{\sqrt{1 - \sin^2 \alpha}} = \frac{1}{\sqrt{1 - x^2}}$$ Note the reference triangle in Figure 3.38.

If u is a differentiable function of x, then the chain rule gives

$$\frac{d}{dx}(\sin^{-1} u) = \frac{d}{dx}(\sin^{-1} u)\frac{du}{dx} = \frac{1}{\sqrt{1 - u^2}}\frac{du}{dx}$$ ❑

EXAMPLE 8   **Derivatives involving inverse trigonometric functions**

Differentiate each of the following functions.

a. $f(x) = \tan^{-1} \sqrt{x}$ **b.** $g(t) = \sin^{-1}(1 - t)$ **c.** $h(x) = \sec^{-1} e^{2x}$

Solution

a. Let $u = \sqrt{x}$ in the formula for $\frac{d}{dx}(\tan^{-1} u)$:

$$f'(x) = \frac{d}{dx}(\tan^{-1} \sqrt{x})$$

$$= \frac{1}{1 + (\sqrt{x})^2}\frac{d}{dx}(\sqrt{x}) = \frac{1}{1 + x}\left(\frac{1}{2}\frac{1}{\sqrt{x}}\right) = \frac{1}{2\sqrt{x}(1 + x)}$$

b. Let $u = (1 - t)$:

$$g'(t) = \frac{d}{dt}\left[\sin^{-1}(1 - t)\right]$$

$$= \frac{1}{\sqrt{1 - (1 - t)^2}}\frac{d}{dt}(1 - t) = \frac{-1}{\sqrt{1 - (1 - t)^2}} = \frac{-1}{\sqrt{2t - t^2}}$$

c. Let $u = e^{2x}$:

$$h'(x) = \frac{d}{dx}\left[\sec^{-1} e^{2x}\right] = \frac{1}{\left|e^{2x}\right|\sqrt{(e^{2x})^2 - 1}}\frac{d}{dx}(e^{2x})$$

$$= \frac{1}{e^{2x}\sqrt{e^{4x} - 1}}(2e^{2x}) = \frac{2}{\sqrt{e^{4x} - 1}}$$ ∎

The derivatives of b^u and $\log_b u$ for a differentiable function $u = u(x)$ and a base b other than e can be obtained using the chain rule and the change-of-base formulas from Chapter 2. We summarize the results in the following theorem.

THEOREM 3.12   **Derivatives of exponential and logarithmic functions with base b**

Let u be a differentiable function of x and b be a positive number (other than 1). Then

$$\frac{d}{dx}b^u = (\ln b)b^u\frac{du}{dx}$$

$$\frac{d}{dx}(\log_b u) = \frac{1}{\ln b} \cdot \frac{1}{u}\frac{du}{dx}$$

WARNING $\frac{d}{dx}b^u \ne ub^{u-1}\frac{du}{dx}$ since b^u is a constant to a variable power, not a variable to a constant power.

Proof   Because $b^u = e^{u \ln b}$, we can apply the chain rule as follows:

$$\frac{d}{dx}b^u = \frac{d}{dx}(e^{u \ln b}) = e^{u \ln b}\frac{d}{dx}(u \ln b) = e^{u \ln b}\left(\ln b\frac{du}{dx}\right) = (\ln b)b^u\frac{du}{dx}$$

To differentiate the logarithm, recall the change-of-base formula $\log_b u = \frac{\ln u}{\ln b}$ so that

$$\frac{d}{dx}\log_b u = \frac{d}{dx}\left(\frac{\ln u}{\ln b}\right) = \frac{1}{\ln b} \cdot \frac{1}{u}\frac{du}{dx}$$ ❑

> ➡ **What This Says** The derivatives of b^x and $\log_b x$ are the same as the derivatives of e^x and $\ln x$, respectively, except for a factor of $\ln b$ that appears as a multiplier in the formula
>
> $$\frac{d}{dx}(b^x) = (\ln b)b^x$$
>
> and as a divisor in the formula
>
> $$\frac{d}{dx}(\log_b x) = \frac{1}{(\ln b)x}$$

EXAMPLE 9 Derivative of an exponential function with base $b \neq e$

Differentiate $f(x) = x(2^{1-x})$.

Solution

Apply the product rule:

$$f'(x) = \frac{d}{dx}(x2^{1-x}) = x\frac{d}{dx}(2^{1-x}) + 2^{1-x}\frac{d}{dx}(x)$$
$$= x(\ln 2)(2^{1-x})(-1) + 2^{1-x}(1) = 2^{1-x}(1 - x\ln 2) \qquad ■$$

The following theorem will prove useful in Chapter 5.

THEOREM 3.13 Derivative of $\ln|u|$

If $f(x) = \ln|x|$, $x \neq 0$, then $f'(x) = \frac{1}{x}$. Also, if u is a differentiable function of x, then

$$\frac{d}{dx}\ln|u| = \frac{1}{u}\frac{du}{dx}$$

Proof Using the definition of absolute value,

$$f(x) = \begin{cases} \ln x & \text{if } x > 0 \\ \ln(-x) & \text{if } x < 0 \end{cases}$$

so

$$f'(x) = \begin{cases} \dfrac{1}{x} & \text{if } x > 0 \\ \dfrac{1}{-x}(-1) = \dfrac{1}{x} & \text{if } x < 0 \end{cases}$$

Thus, $f'(x) = \frac{1}{x}$ for all $x \neq 0$.

The second part of the theorem (for u, a differentiable function of x) follows from the chain rule. ❑

LOGARITHMIC DIFFERENTIATION

Logarithmic differentiation is a procedure in which logarithms are used to trade the task of differentiating products and quotients for that of differentiating sums and differences. It is especially valuable as a means for handling complicated product or quotient functions and exponential functions where variables appear in both the base and the exponent.

EXAMPLE 10   Logarithmic differentiation

Find the derivative of $y = \dfrac{e^{2x}(2x-1)^6}{(x^3+5)^2(4-7x)}$ if $y > 0$.

Solution

The procedure called logarithmic differentiation requires that we first take the logarithm of both sides and then apply properties of logarithms before attempting to take the derivative.

$$y = \frac{e^{2x}(2x-1)^6}{(x^3+5)^2(4-7x)}$$

$$\ln y = \ln\left[\frac{e^{2x}(2x-1)^6}{(x^3+5)^2(4-7x)}\right]$$

$$= \ln e^{2x} + \ln(2x-1)^6 - \ln(x^3+5)^2 - \ln(4-7x)$$

$$= 2x + 6\ln(2x-1) - 2\ln(x^3+5) - \ln(4-7x)$$

Next, differentiate both sides with respect to x and then solve for $\dfrac{dy}{dx}$:

$$\frac{1}{y}\frac{dy}{dx} = 2 + 6\left[\frac{1}{2x-1}(2)\right] - 2\left[\frac{1}{x^3+5}(3x^2)\right] - \left[\frac{1}{4-7x}(-7)\right]$$

$$\frac{dy}{dx} = y\left[2 + \frac{12}{2x-1} - \frac{6x^2}{x^3+5} + \frac{7}{4-7x}\right]$$

This is the derivative in terms of x and y. If we want the derivative in terms of x alone, we can substitute the expression for y:

$$\frac{dy}{dx} = \frac{e^{2x}(2x-1)^6}{(x^3+5)^2(4-7x)}\left[2 + \frac{12}{2x-1} - \frac{6x^2}{x^3+5} + \frac{7}{4-7x}\right] \qquad \blacksquare$$

EXAMPLE 11   Derivative with variables in both the base and the exponent

Find $\dfrac{dy}{dx}$, where $y = (x+1)^{2x}$.

Solution
$$y = (x+1)^{2x}$$

$$\ln y = \ln\left[(x+1)^{2x}\right] = 2x\ln(x+1)$$

Differentiate both sides of this equation:

$$\frac{1}{y}\frac{dy}{dx} = 2x\left\{\frac{d}{dx}[\ln(x+1)]\right\} + \left[\frac{d}{dx}(2x)\right]\ln(x+1) \qquad \text{Product rule}$$

$$= 2x\left[\frac{1}{x+1}(1)\right] + 2\ln(x+1)$$

$$= \frac{2x}{x+1} + 2\ln(x+1)$$

Finally, multiply both sides by $y = (x+1)^{2x}$:

$$\frac{dy}{dx} = \left[\frac{2x}{x+1} + 2\ln(x+1)\right](x+1)^{2x} \qquad \blacksquare$$

3.6 PROBLEM SET

Ⓐ *Find $\dfrac{dy}{dx}$ by implicit differentiation in Problems 1–14.*

1. $x^2 + y^2 = 25$ **2.** $x^2 + y = x^3 + y^3$

3. $xy = 25$ **4.** $xy(2x + 3y) = 2$

5. $x^2 + 3xy + y^2 = 15$ **6.** $x^3 + y^3 = x + y$

7. $\dfrac{1}{y} + \dfrac{1}{x} = 1$ **8.** $(2x + 3y)^2 = 10$

9. $\sin(x + y) = x - y$ **10.** $\tan \dfrac{x}{y} = y$

11. $\cos xy = 1 - x^2$ **12.** $e^{xy} + 1 = x^2$

13. $\ln(xy) = e^{2x}$ **14.** $e^{xy} + \ln y^2 = x$

In Problems 15–18, find $\dfrac{dy}{dx}$ in two ways:

a. *By implicit differentiation of the equation*

b. *By differentiating an explicit formula for y*

15. $x^2 + y^3 = 12$ **16.** $xy + 2y = x^2$

17. $x + \dfrac{1}{y} = 5$ **18.** $xy - x = y + 2$

Find the derivative $\dfrac{dy}{dx}$ in Problems 19–32.

19. $y = \sin^{-1}(2x + 1)$ **20.** $y = \cos^{-1}(4x + 3)$

21. $y = \tan^{-1}\sqrt{x^2 + 1}$ **22.** $y = \cot^{-1} x^2$

23. $y = (\sin^{-1} 2x)^3$ **24.** $y = (\tan^{-1} x^2)^4$

25. $y = \sec^{-1}(e^{-x})$ **26.** $y = \ln\left|\sin^{-1} x\right|$

27. $y = \tan^{-1}\left(\dfrac{1}{x}\right)$ **28.** $y = \cos^{-1}(\sin x),\ \sin x \geq 0$

29. $y = \sin^{-1}(\cos x),\ \cos x \geq 0$ **30.** $y = \ln[\sin^{-1}(e^x)]$

31. $x\sin^{-1} y + y\tan^{-1} x = x$ **32.** $\sin^{-1} y + y = 2xy$

In Problems 33–38, find an equation of the tangent line to the graph of each equation at the prescribed point.

33. $x^2 + y^2 = 13$ at $(-2, 3)$

34. $x^3 + y^3 = y + 21$ at $(3, -2)$

35. $\sin(x - y) = xy$ at $(0, \pi)$

36. $3^x + \log_2(xy) = 10$ at $(2, 1)$

37. $x\tan^{-1} y = x^2 + y$ at $(0, 0)$

38. $\sin^{-1}(xy) + \dfrac{\pi}{2} = \cos^{-1} y$ at $(1, 0)$

Find the slope of the tangent line to the graph at the points indicated in Problems 39–42.

39. bifolium:
$(x^2 + y^2)^2 = 4x^2 y$
at $(1, 1)$

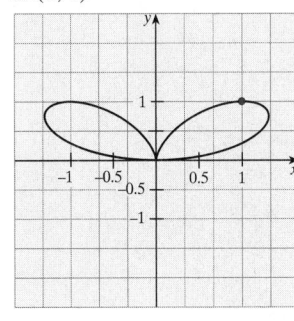

40. lemniscate of Bernoulli:
$(x^2 + y^2)^2 = \frac{25}{3}(x^2 - y^2)$
at $(2, 1)$

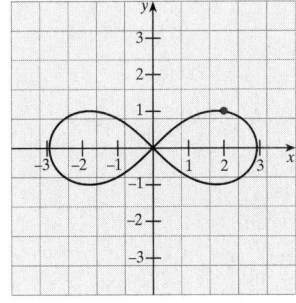

41. folium of Descartes:
$x^3 + y^3 - \frac{9}{2}xy = 0$
at $(2, 1)$

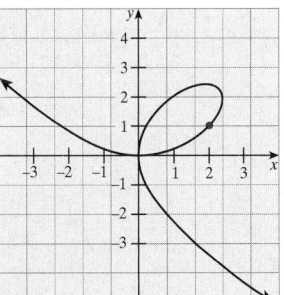

42. cissoid of Diocles:
$y^2(6 - x) = x^3$ at $(3, 3)$

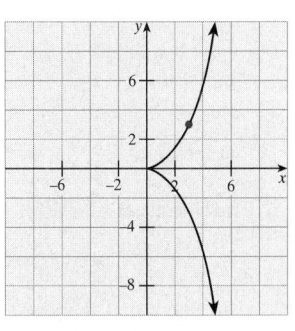

43. Find an equation of the normal line to the curve $x^2 + 2xy = y^3$ at $(1, -1)$.

44. Find an equation of the normal line to the curve $x^2\sqrt{y - 2} = y^2 - 3x - 5$ at $(1, 3)$.

Use implicit differentiation to find the second derivative y'' of the functions given in Problems 45–46.

45. $7x + 5y^2 = 1$ **46.** $x^2 + 2y^3 = 4$

Ⓑ **47. Interpretation Problem** Compare and contrast the derivatives of the following functions:

  a. $y = x^2$ **b.** $y = 2^x$ **c.** $y = e^x$ **d.** $y = x^e$

48. Interpretation Problem Compare and contrast the derivatives of the following functions:

  a. $y = \log x$ **b.** $y = \ln x$

49. Interpretation Problem Discuss logarithmic differentiation.

Use logarithmic differentiation in Problems 50–55 to find dy/dx. You may express your answer in terms of both x and y, and you do not need to simplify the resulting rational expressions.

50. $y = \sqrt[18]{(x^{10} + 1)^3(x^7 - 3)^8}$

51. $y = \dfrac{(2x - 1)^5}{\sqrt{x - 9}(x + 3)^2}$

52. $y = \dfrac{e^{2x}}{(x^2 - 3)^2 \ln\sqrt{x}}$

53. $y = \dfrac{e^{3x^2}}{(x^3 + 1)^2(4x - 7)^{-2}}$

54. $y = x^x$ **55.** $y = x^{\ln\sqrt{x}}$

56. Let $\dfrac{u^2}{a^2} + \dfrac{v^2}{b^2} = 1$, where a and b are nonzero constants. Find

  a. $\dfrac{du}{dv}$ **b.** $\dfrac{dv}{du}$

57. Show that the tangent line at the point (a, b) on the curve whose equation is $2x^2 + 3xy + y^2 = -2$ is horizontal if $4a + 3b = 0$. Find two such points on the curve.

58. Find two points on the curve whose equation is $x^2 - 3xy + 2y^2 = -2$, where the tangent line is vertical.

59. Let g be a differentiable function of x that satisfies $g(x) < 0$ and $x^2 + g^2(x) = 10$ for all x.

  a. Use implicit differentiation to show that $\dfrac{dg}{dx} = \dfrac{-x}{g(x)}$.

b. Show that $g(x) = -\sqrt{10 - x^2}$ satisfies the given requirements. Then use the chain rule to verify that

$$\frac{dg}{dx} = \frac{-x}{g(x)}$$

60. Find the equation of the tangent line and the normal line to the curve

$$x^3 + y^3 = 2Axy$$

at the point (A, A), where A is a nonzero constant.

61. Counterexample Problem

a. If $x^2 + y^2 = 6y - 10$ and $\dfrac{dy}{dx}$ exists, show that $\dfrac{dy}{dx} = \dfrac{x}{3 - y}$.

b. Show that there are no real numbers x, y that satisfy the equation $x^2 + y^2 = 6y - 10$.

c. What can you conclude from the result found in part **a** in light of the observation in part **b**?

62. Find all points on the lemniscate

$$(x^2 + y^2)^2 = 4(x^2 - y^2)$$

where the tangent line is horizontal. (See Figure 3.39.)

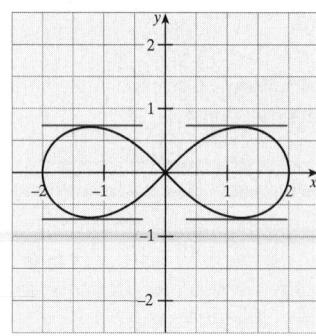

Figure 3.39   Lemniscate $(x^2 + y^2)^2 = 4(x^2 - y^2)$

63. Find all points on the cardioid

$$x^2 + y^2 = \sqrt{x^2 + y^2} + x$$

where the tangent line is vertical. (See Figure 3.40)

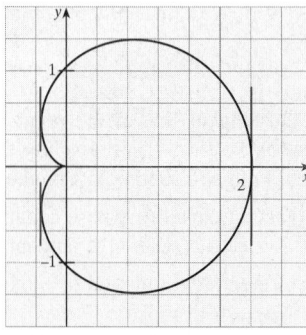

Figure 3.40   Cardioid $x^2 + y^2 = \sqrt{x^2 + y^2} + x$

64. The tangent line to the curve $x^{2/3} + y^{2/3} = 8$ at the point $(8, 8)$ and the coordinate axes form a triangle, as shown in Figure 3.41. What is the area of this triangle?

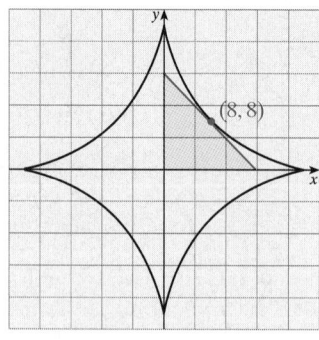

Figure 3.41   Graph of $x^{2/3} + y^{2/3} = 8$

65. Modeling Problem   A worker stands 4 m from a hoist being raised at the rate of 2 m/s, as shown in Figure 3.42. Model the worker's angle of sight θ using an inverse trigonometric function, and then determine how fast θ is changing at the instant when the hoist is 1.5 m above eye level.

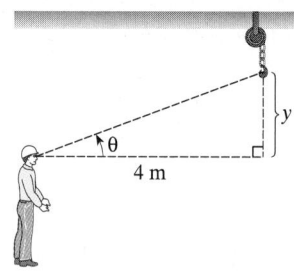

Figure 3.42   Modeling an angle of elevation

C **66.** Find two differentiable functions f that satisfy the equation

$$x - [f(x)]^2 = 9$$

Give the explicit form of each function, and sketch its graph.

67. Show that the tangent line to the ellipse

$$\frac{x^2}{a^2} + \frac{y^2}{b^2} = 1$$

at the point (x_0, y_0) is

$$\frac{x_0 x}{a^2} + \frac{y_0 y}{b^2} = 1$$

(See Figure 3.43.)

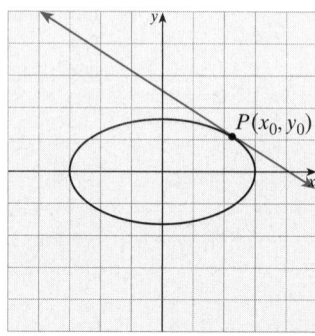

Figure 3.43   Ellipse $\dfrac{x^2}{a^2} + \dfrac{y^2}{b^2} = 1$

68. Find an equation of the tangent line to the hyperbola $\dfrac{x^2}{a^2} - \dfrac{y^2}{b^2} = 1$ at the point (x_0, y_0). (See Figure 3.44.)

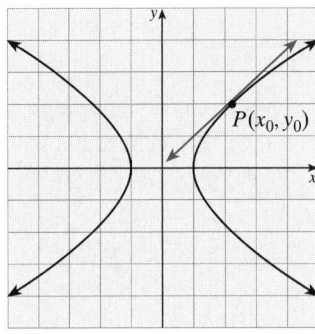

Figure 3.44 Hyperbola $\dfrac{x^2}{a^2} - \dfrac{y^2}{b^2} = 1$

69. Use implicit differentiation to find the second derivative y'', where y is a differentiable function of x that satisfies $ax^2 + by^2 = c$ (a, b, and c are constants).

70. Show that the sum of the x-intercept and the y-intercept of any tangent line to the curve $\sqrt{x} + \sqrt{y} = C$ is equal to C^2.

*The **angle between curves C_1 and C_2** at the point of intersection P is defined as the angle $0 \le \theta \le \frac{\pi}{2}$ between the tangent lines at P. Specifically, the angle between C_1 and C_2 is the angle between the tangent line to C_1 at P and the tangent line to C_2 at P as shown in Figure 3.45.*

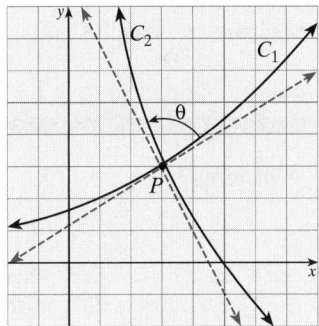

Figure 3.45 The angle θ between C_1 and C_2 at P

Use this information for Problems 71–72.

71. If θ is the angle between curve C_1 and curve C_2 at P and the tangent lines to C_1 and C_2 at P have slopes m_1 and m_2, respectively, show that

$$\tan \theta = \frac{|m_2 - m_1|}{1 + m_1 m_2}$$

72. Find the angle between the circle $x^2 + y^2 = 1$ and the circle $x^2 + (y - 1)^2 = 1$ at each of the two points of intersection.

73. **Journal Problem** *The Pi Mu Epsilon Journal* by Bruce W. King* : ∎ When a professor asked the calculus class to find the derivative of y^2 with respect to x^2 for the function $y = x^2 - x$, one student found

$$\frac{dy}{dx} \cdot \frac{y}{x}$$

Was this answer correct? Suppose

$$y = x^3 - 3x^2 + \frac{7}{x}$$

What is the derivative of y^2 with respect to x^2 for this function?

74. Use implicit differentiation to obtain the differentiation formulas for $y = \tan^{-1} u$ and $y = \sec^{-1} u$.

75. Use the identity $\sin^{-1} u + \cos^{-1} u = \frac{\pi}{2}$ to obtain the differentiation formula for $y = \cos^{-1} u$. Similar identities can be used to obtain differentiation formulas for $y = \cot^{-1} u$ and $y = \csc^{-1} u$.

3.7 Related Rates and Applications

Certain practical problems involve a functional relationship $y = f(x)$ in which both x and y are themselves functions of another variable, such as time t. Implicit differentiation is then used to relate the rate of change dy/dt to the rate dx/dt. In this section, we will examine a variety of such **related rate problems**.

When working a related rate problem, you must distinguish between the general situation and the specific situation. The *general situation* comprises properties that are true at *every* instant of time, whereas the *specific situation* refers to those properties that are guaranteed to be true only at the *particular* instant of time that the problem investigates. Here is an example.

EXAMPLE 1   An application involving related rates

A spherical balloon is being filled with a gas in such a way that when the radius is 2 ft, the radius is increasing at the rate of 1/6 ft/min. How fast is the volume changing at this time?

Solution

The general situation: Let V denote the volume and r the radius, both of which are functions of time t (minutes). Since the container is a sphere, its volume is given by

$$V = \tfrac{4}{3}\pi r^3$$

Differentiating both sides implicitly with respect to time t yields

$$\frac{dV}{dt} = \frac{d}{dt}\left(\frac{4}{3}\pi r^3\right)$$

$$= 4\pi r^2 \frac{dr}{dt} \qquad \text{Do not forget to use the chain rule because } r \text{ is also a function of time.}$$

The specific situation: Our goal is to find $\dfrac{dV}{dt}$ at the time when $r = 2$ ft and $\dfrac{dr}{dt} = \dfrac{1}{6}$.

$$\left.\frac{dV}{dt}\right|_{r=2} = 4\pi(2)^2\left(\frac{1}{6}\right) = \frac{8\pi}{3}$$

This means that the volume of the container is increasing at about 8.38 ft³/min when the radius is 2 ft.   ∎

Although each related rate problem has its own "personality," many can be handled by the following summary:

Procedure for Solving Related Rate Problems

The General Situation

Step 1.   *Draw a figure, if appropriate, and assign variables to the quantities that vary.* Be careful not to label a quantity with a number unless it *never* changes in the problem.

Step 2.   *Find a formula or equation that relates the variables.* Eliminate unnecessary variables; some of these "extra" variables may be constants, but others may be eliminated because of given relationships among the variables.

Step 3.   *Differentiate the equations.* You will usually differentiate implicitly with respect to time.

The Specific Situation

Step 4.   *Substitute specific numerical values and solve algebraically for any required rate.* List the known quantities; list as unknown the quantity you wish to find. Substitute all values into the formula. The only remaining variable should be the unknown, which may be a variable or a rate. Solve for the unknown.

EXAMPLE 2   Moving shadow problem

A person 6 ft tall is walking away from a streetlight 20 ft high at the rate of 7 ft/s. At what rate is the length of the person's shadow increasing?

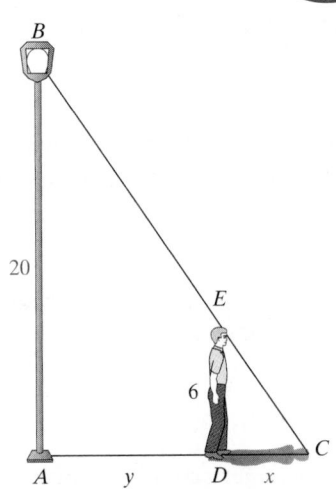

Figure 3.46 A person walking away from a streetlamp

Solution

The general situation: (See *Student Mathematics Handbook*, Problem 37, Problem Set 1.)

Step 1. Let x denote the length (in feet) of the person's shadow, and y, the distance between the person and the street light, as shown in Figure 3.46. Let t denote the time (in seconds).

Step 2. Since $\triangle ABC$ and $\triangle DEC$ are similar, we have

$$\frac{x+y}{20} = \frac{x}{6}$$

Step 3. Write this equation as $x + y = \frac{20}{6}x$, or $y = \frac{7}{3}x$, and differentiate both sides with respect to t.

$$\frac{dy}{dt} = \frac{7}{3}\frac{dx}{dt}$$

The specific situation:

Step 4. List the known quantities. We know that $dy/dt = 7$. Our goal is to find dx/dt. Substitute and then solve for the unknown value:

$$\frac{dy}{dt} = \frac{7}{3}\frac{dx}{dt}$$

$$7 = \frac{7}{3}\frac{dx}{dt} \qquad \text{Substitute.}$$

$$3 = \frac{dx}{dt} \qquad \text{Multiply both sides by } \tfrac{3}{7}.$$

The length of the person's shadow is increasing at the rate of 3 ft/s. ∎

EXAMPLE 3 Leaning ladder problem

A bag is tied to the top of a 5-m ladder resting against a vertical wall. Suppose the ladder begins sliding down the wall in such a way that the foot of the ladder is moving away from the wall. How fast is the bag descending at the instant the foot of the ladder is 4 m from the wall and the foot is moving away at the rate of 2 m/s?

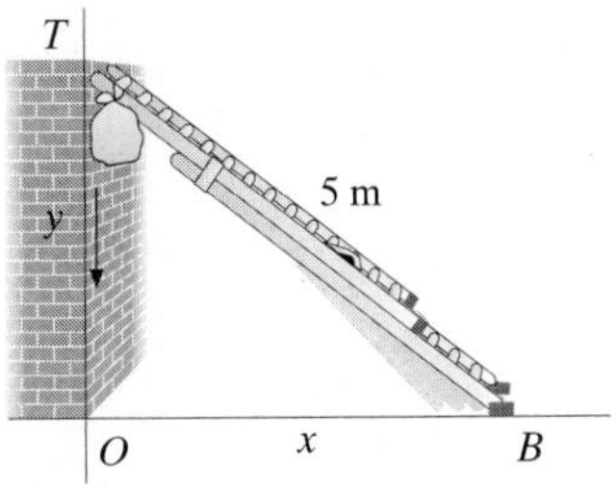

Figure 3.47 A ladder sliding down a wall

Solution

The general situation: Let x and y be the distances from the base of the wall to the foot and top of the ladder, respectively, as shown in Figure 3.47. (See *Student Mathematics Handbook*, Problem 38, Problem Set 1.)

Notice that $\triangle TOB$ is a right triangle, so a relevant formula is the Pythagorean theorem:

$$x^2 + y^2 = 25$$

Differentiate both sides of this equation with respect to t:

$$2x\frac{dx}{dt} + 2y\frac{dy}{dt} = 0$$

The specific situation: At the particular instant in question, $x = 4$ and $y = \sqrt{25 - 4^2} = 3$. We also know that $\frac{dx}{dt} = 2$, and the goal is to find $\frac{dy}{dt}$ at this instant. We have

$$2(4)(2) + 2(3)\frac{dy}{dt} = 0$$

$$\frac{dy}{dt} = -\frac{8}{3}$$

This tells us that, at the instant in question, the bag is descending (since dy/dt is negative) at the rate of $8/3 \approx 2.7$ m/sec. ∎

EXAMPLE 4   Modeling a physical application involving related rates

When air expands *adiabatically* (that is, with no change in heat), the pressure P and the volume V satisfy the relationship

$$PV^{1.4} = C$$

where C is a constant. At a certain instant, the pressure is 20 lb/in.^{2} and the volume is 280 in.^{3}. If the volume is decreasing at the rate of 5 in.^{3}/s at this instant, what is the rate of change of the pressure?

Solution

The general situation: The required equation was given, so we begin by differentiating both sides with respect to t. Remember, because C is a constant, its derivative with respect to t is zero.

$$1.4PV^{0.4}\frac{dV}{dt} + V^{1.4}\frac{dP}{dt} = 0 \qquad \text{Product rule}$$

The specific situation: At the instant in question, $P = 20$, $V = 280$, and $dV/dt = -5$ (negative because the volume is decreasing). The goal is to find dP/dt. First substitute to obtain

$$(20)(1.4)(280)^{0.4}(-5) + (280)^{1.4}\frac{dP}{dt} = 0$$

Now, solve for $\dfrac{dP}{dt}$:

$$\frac{dP}{dt} = \frac{5(20)(1.4)(280)^{0.4}}{(280)^{1.4}} = 0.5$$

Thus, at the instant in question, the pressure is increasing (because its derivative is positive) at the rate of 0.5 lb/in.^{2} per second. ∎

EXAMPLE 5   The water level in a cone-shaped tank

A tank filled with water is in the shape of an inverted cone 20 ft high with a circular base (on top) whose radius is 5 ft. Water is running out of the bottom of the tank at the constant rate of 2 ft^3/min. How fast is the water level falling when the water is 8 ft deep?

Solution

The general situation: Consider a conical tank with height 20 ft and circular base of radius 5 ft, as shown in Figure 3.48. Suppose that the water level is h ft and that the radius of the surface of the water is r.

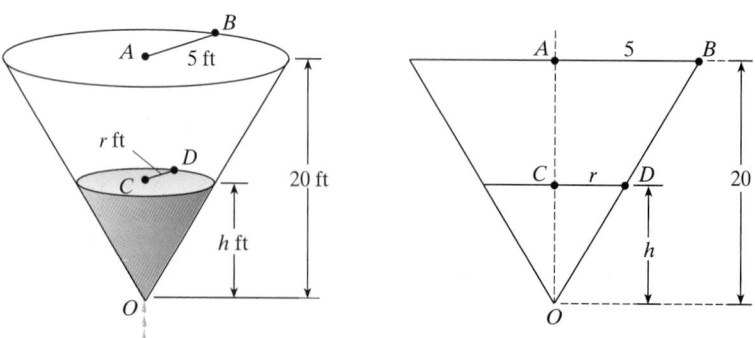

Figure 3.48   A conical water tank

Let V denote the volume of water in the tank after t minutes. We know that

$$V = \tfrac{1}{3}\pi r^2 h$$

(See *Student Mathematics Handbook*, Problem 39, Problem Set 1.) Once again, we use similar triangles (see Figure 3.48) to write $\frac{5}{20} = \frac{r}{h}$, or $r = \frac{h}{4}$. We substitute this into the formula to obtain

$$V = \frac{1}{3}\pi \left(\frac{h}{4}\right)^2 h = \frac{1}{48}\pi h^3$$

and then differentiate both sides of this equation with respect to t.

$$\frac{dV}{dt} = \frac{\pi}{16}h^2 \frac{dh}{dt}$$

WARNING A common error in solving related rate problems is to substitute numerical values too soon or, equivalently, to use relationships that apply only at a particular moment in time. This is the reason we have separated related rate problems into two distinct parts. Be careful to work with general relationships among the variables and substitute specific numerical values only after you have found general rate relationships by differentiation.

The specific situation: Begin with the known quantities: We know that $dV/dt = -2$ (negative, because the volume is decreasing). The goal is to find dh/dt. At the particular instant in question, $h = 8$; we substitute to find

$$-2 = \frac{\pi}{16}(8)^2 \frac{dh}{dt}$$

$$\frac{-1}{2\pi} = \frac{dh}{dt}$$

At the instant when the water is 8 ft deep, the water level is falling (since dh/dt is negative) at a rate of $\frac{1}{2\pi} \approx 0.16$ ft/min ≈ 2 in./min. ∎

EXAMPLE 6 Modeling with an angle of elevation

Every day, a flight to Los Angeles flies directly over my home at a constant altitude of 4 mi. If I assume that the plane is flying at a constant speed of 400 mi/h, at what rate is the angle of elevation of my line of sight changing with respect to time when the horizontal distance between the approaching plane and my location is exactly 3 mi?

Solution

The general situation: Let x denote the horizontal distance between the plane and the observer, as shown in Figure 3.49. The height of the observer is insignificant when compared to the height of the plane.

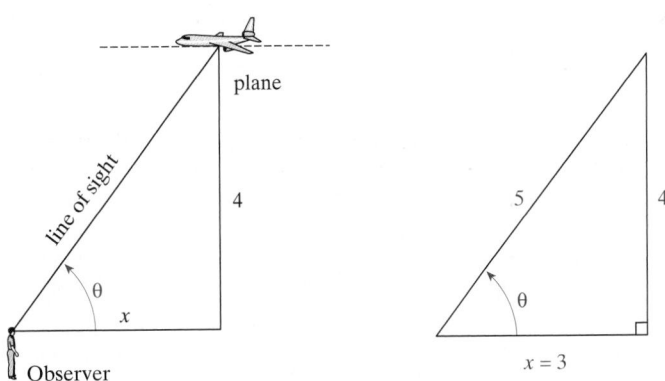

a. Observer of an approaching plane **b.** Triangle for computing $\sin\theta$ when $x = 3$

Figure 3.49 Angle of elevation problem

Then the angle of observation θ can be modeled by

$$\cot\theta = \frac{x}{4} \qquad \text{or} \qquad \theta = \cot^{-1}\left(\frac{x}{4}\right)$$

Differentiate both sides of this last equation with respect to t to obtain

$$\frac{d\theta}{dt} = \frac{-1}{1 + (\frac{x}{4})^2}\left(\frac{1}{4}\right)\frac{dx}{dt} = \frac{-4}{16 + x^2}\frac{dx}{dt}$$

The specific situation: At the instant when $x = 3$, we are given that $\dfrac{dx}{dt} = -400$ (negative because the distance is decreasing). Thus, the angle of elevation is changing at the rate of

$$\frac{d\theta}{dt} = \frac{-4}{16 + 3^2}(-400) = 64 \text{ rad/hr}$$

The angle of elevation is changing at the rate of 64 radians per hour or, equivalently,

$$(64 \text{ rad/hr})\left(\frac{360 \text{ deg}}{2\pi \text{ rad}}\right)\left(\frac{1 \text{ hr}}{3{,}600 \text{ s}}\right) \approx 1.02 \text{ deg/sec} \qquad \blacksquare$$

3.7 PROBLEM SET

A *Find the indicated rate in Problems 1–9, given the other information. Assume $x > 0$ and $y > 0$.*

1. If $x^2 + y^2 = 25$ and $\dfrac{dx}{dt} = 4$, find $\dfrac{dy}{dt}$ when $x = 3$.

2. If $x^2 + y^2 = 25$ and $\dfrac{dy}{dt} = 2$, find $\dfrac{dx}{dt}$ when $x = 4$.

3. If $5x^2 - y = 100$ and $\dfrac{dx}{dt} = 10$, find $\dfrac{dy}{dt}$ when $x = 10$.

4. If $4x^2 - y = 100$ and $\dfrac{dy}{dt} = -6$, find $\dfrac{dx}{dt}$ when $x = 1$.

5. If $y = 2\sqrt{x} - 9$ and $\dfrac{dy}{dt} = 5$, find $\dfrac{dx}{dt}$ when $x = 9$.

6. If $y = 5\sqrt{x + 9}$ and $\dfrac{dx}{dt} = 2$, find $\dfrac{dy}{dt}$ when $x = 7$.

7. If $xy = 10$, and $\dfrac{dx}{dt} = -2$, find $\dfrac{dy}{dt}$ when $x = 5$.

8. If $5xy = 10$, and $\dfrac{dx}{dt} = -2$, find $\dfrac{dy}{dt}$ when $x = 1$.

9. If $x^2 + xy - y^2 = 11$ and $\dfrac{dy}{dt} = 5$, find $\dfrac{dx}{dt}$ when $x = 4$ and $y > 0$.

In physics, Hooke's law says that when a spring is stretched x units beyond its natural length, the elastic force $F(x)$ exerted by the spring is $F(x) = -kx$, where k is a constant that depends on the spring. Assume $k = 12$ in Problems 10 and 11.

10. If a spring is stretched at the constant rate of $\frac{1}{4}$ in./s, how fast is the force $F(x)$ changing when $x = 2$ in.?

11. If a spring is stretched at the constant rate of $\frac{1}{4}$ in./s, how fast is the force $F(x)$ changing when $x = 3$ in.?

12. A particle moves along the parabolic path given by $y^2 = 4x$ in such a way that when it is at the point $(1, -2)$, its horizontal velocity (in the direction of the x-axis) is 3 ft/s. What is its vertical velocity (in the direction of the y-axis) at this instant?

13. A particle moves along the elliptical path given by $4x^2 + y^2 = 4$ in such a way that when it is at the point $(\sqrt{3}/2, 1)$, its x-coordinate is increasing at the rate of 5 units per second. How fast is the y-coordinate changing at that instant?

14. A rock is dropped into a lake and an expanding circular ripple results. When the radius of the ripple is 8 in., the radius is increasing at a rate of 3 in./s. At what rate is the area enclosed by the ripple changing at this time?

15. A pebble dropped into a pond causes a circular ripple. Find the rate at which the radius of the ripple is changing at a time when the radius is one foot and the area enclosed by the ripple is increasing at the rate of 4 ft^2/s.

16. An environmental study of a certain community indicates that there will be $Q(p) = p^2 + 3p + 1{,}200$ units of a harmful pollutant in the air when the population is p thousand. The population is currently 30,000 and is increasing at a rate of 2,000 per year. At what rate is the level of air pollution increasing currently?

17. It is estimated that the annual advertising revenue received by a certain newspaper will be $R(x) = 0.5x^2 + 3x + 160$ thousand dollars when its circulation is x thousand. The circulation of the paper is currently 10,000 and is increasing at a rate of 2,000 per year. At what rate will the annual advertising revenue be increasing with respect to time 2 years from now?

18. Hospital officials estimate that approximately $N(p) = p^2 + 5p + 900$ people will seek treatment in the emergency room each year if the population of the community is p thousand. The population is currently 20,000 and is growing at the rate of 1,200 per year. At what rate is the number of people seeking emergency room treatment increasing?

19. Boyle's law states that when gas is compressed at constant temperature, the pressure P of a given sample satisfies the equation $PV = C$, where V is the volume of the sample and C is a constant. Suppose that at a certain time the volume is 30 in.^{3}, the pressure is 90 lb/in.^{2}, and the volume is increasing at the rate of 10 in.^{3}/s. How fast is the pressure changing at this instant? Is it increasing or decreasing?

B 20. **Interpretation Problem** What do we mean by a related rate problem?

21. **Interpretation Problem** Outline a procedure for solving related-rate problems.

22. The volume of a spherical balloon is increasing at a constant rate of 3 in.^{3}/s. At what rate is the radius of the balloon increasing when the radius is 2 in.?

23. The surface area of a sphere is decreasing at the constant rate of 3π cm^2/s. At what rate is the volume of the sphere decreasing at the instant its radius is 2 cm?

24. A person 6 ft tall walks away from a streetlight at the rate of 5 ft/s. If the light is 18 ft above ground level, how fast is the person's shadow lengthening?

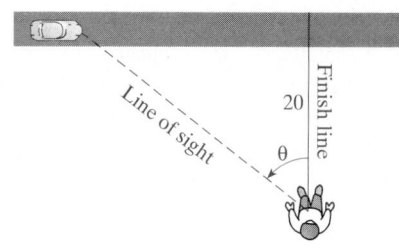

Figure 3.52 Problem 31

25. A ladder 13 ft long rests against a vertical wall and is sliding down the wall at the rate of 3 ft/s at the instant the foot of the ladder is 5 ft from the base of the wall. At this instant, how fast is the foot of the ladder moving away from the wall?

26. A car traveling north at 40 mi/h and a truck traveling east at 30 mi/h leave an intersection at the same time. At what rate will the distance between them be changing 3 hours later?

27. A person is standing at the end of a pier 12 ft above the water and is pulling in a rope attached to a rowboat at the waterline at the rate of 6 ft of rope per minute, as shown in Figure 3.50. How fast is the boat moving in the water when it is 16 ft from the pier?

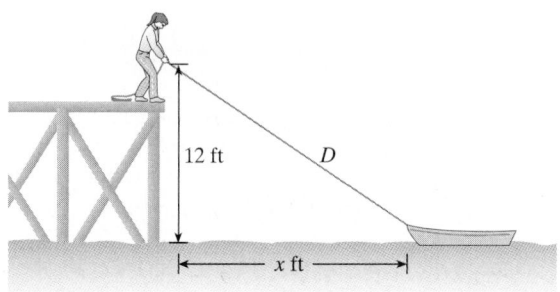

Figure 3.50 Problem 27

28. One end of a rope is fastened to a boat and the other end is wound around a windlass located on a dock at a point 4 m above the level of the boat. If the boat is drifting away from the dock at the rate of 2 m/min, how fast is the rope unwinding at the instant when the length of the rope is 5 m?

29. A ball is dropped from a height of 160 ft. A light is located at the same level, 10 ft away from the initial position of the ball. How fast is the ball's shadow moving along the ground one second after the ball is dropped?

30. A person 6 ft tall stands 10 ft from point P directly beneath a lantern hanging 30 ft above the ground, as shown in Figure 3.51.

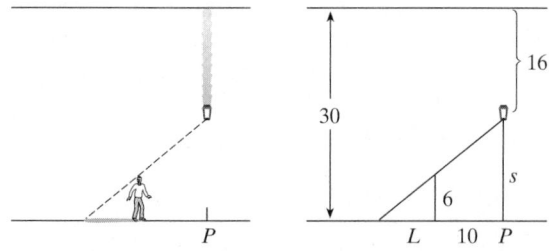

Figure 3.51 Problem 30

The lantern starts to fall, thus causing the person's shadow to lengthen. Given that the lantern falls $16t^2$ ft in t seconds, how fast will the shadow be lengthening when $t = 1$?

31. A race official is watching a race car approach the finish line at the rate of 200 km/h. Suppose the official is sitting at the finish line, 20 m from the point where the car will cross, and let θ be the angle between the finish line and the official's line of sight to the car, as shown as Figure 3.52. At what rate is θ changing when the car crosses the finish line? Give your answer in terms of rad/s.

Modeling Problems: *In Problems 32–35, set up and solve an appropriate model to answer the given question. Be sure to state your assumptions.*

32. Consider a piece of ice in the shape of a sphere that is melting at the rate of 5 in.^{3}/min. Model the volume of ice by a function of the radius r. How fast is the radius changing at the instant when the radius is 4 in.? How fast is the surface area of the sphere changing at the same instant?

33. A certain medical procedure requires that a balloon be inserted into the stomach and then inflated. Model the shape of the balloon by a sphere of radius r. If r is increasing at the rate of 0.3 cm/min, how fast is the volume changing when the radius is 4 cm?

34. Model a water tank by a cone 40 ft high with a circular base of radius 20 ft at the top. Water is flowing into the tank at a constant rate of 80 ft^3/min. How fast is the water level rising when the water is 12 ft deep? Give your answer to the nearest hundredth of a foot per minute.

35. In Problem 34, suppose that water is also flowing out the bottom of the tank. At what rate should the water be allowed to flow out so that the water level will be rising at a rate of only 0.05 ft/min when the water is 12 ft deep? Give your answer to the nearest tenth of a cubic foot per minute.

36. The air pressure $p(s)$ at a height of s meters above sea level is modeled by the formula $p(s) = e^{-0.000125s}$ atmospheres. An instrument box carrying a device for measuring pressure is dropped into the ocean from a plane and falls in such a way that after t seconds it is

$$s(t) = 3,000 - 49t - 245(e^{-t/5} - 1)$$

meters above the ocean's surface.

a. Find ds/dt and then use the chain rule to find dp/dt. How fast is the air pressure changing 2 seconds after the box begins to fall?

b. When (to the nearest second) does the box hit the water? How fast is the air pressure changing at the time of impact?

What assumptions are you making in this model?

37. At noon on a certain day, a truck is 250 mi due east of a car. The truck is traveling west at a constant speed of 25 mi/h, while the car is traveling north at 50 mi/h.

a. At what rate is the distance between them changing at time t?

b. At what time is the distance between the car and the truck neither increasing nor decreasing?

c. What is the minimal distance between the car and the truck? *Hint:* This distance must occur at the time found in part b. Do you see why?

38. A weather balloon is rising vertically at the rate of 10 ft/s. An observer is standing on the ground 500 ft horizontally from the point where the balloon was released. At what rate is the distance between the observer and the balloon changing when the balloon is 400 ft high?

39. An observer watches a plane approach at a speed of 500 mi/h and an altitude of 3 mi. At what rate is the angle of elevation of the observer's line of sight changing with respect to time when the horizontal distance between the plane and the observer is 4 mi? Give your answer in radians per minute.

40. A person 6 ft tall is watching a streetlight 18 ft high while walking toward it at a speed of 5 ft/s, as shown in Figure 3.53. At what rate is the angle of elevation of the person's line of sight changing with respect to time when the person is 9 ft from the base of the light?

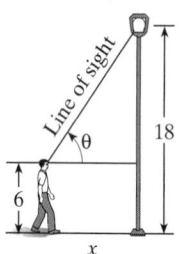

Figure 3.53 Streetlight problem

41. A revolving searchlight in a lighthouse 2 mi offshore is following a beachcomber along the shore, as shown in Figure 3.54.

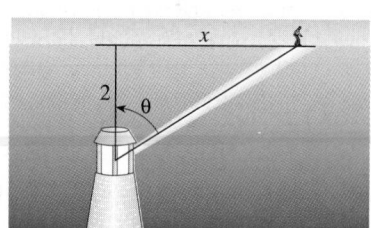

Figure 3.54 Problem 41

When the beachcomber is 1 mi from the point on the shore that is closest to the lighthouse, the searchlight is turning at the rate of 0.25 rev/h. How fast is the beachcomber walking at that moment? *Hint:* Note that 0.25 rev/h is the same as $\frac{\pi}{2}$ rad/h.

42. A water trough is 2 ft deep and 10 ft long. It has a trapezoidal cross section with base lengths 2 ft and 5 ft, as shown in Figure 3.55.

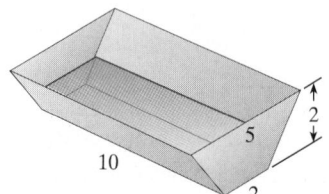

Figure 3.55 Water trough

a. Find a relationship between the volume of water in the trough at any given time and the depth of the water at that time.

b. If water enters the trough at the rate of 10 ft³/min, how fast is the water level rising (to the nearest $\frac{1}{2}$ in./min) when the water is 1 ft deep?

43. At noon, a ship sails due north from a point P at 8 knots (nautical miles per hour). Another ship, sailing at 12 knots, leaves the same point 1 h later on a course 60° east of north. How fast is the distance between the ships increasing at 2 P.M.? At 5 P.M.? *Hint:* Use the law of cosines.

44. A swimming pool is 60 ft long and 25 ft wide. Its depth varies uniformly from 3 ft at the shallow end to 15 ft at the deep end, as shown in Figure 3.56.

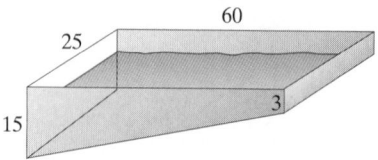

Figure 3.56 Swimming pool

Suppose the pool is being filled with water at the rate of 800 ft³/min. At what rate is the depth of water increasing at the deep end when it is 5 ft deep at that end?

45. Suppose a water bucket is modeled by the frustum of a cone with height 1 ft and upper and lower radii of 1 ft and 9 in., respectively, as shown in Figure 3.57.

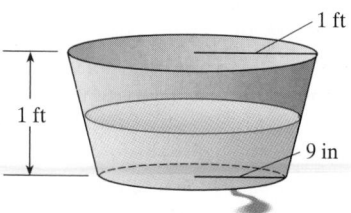

Figure 3.57 Water bucket

If water is leaking from the bottom of the bucket at the rate of 8 in.³/min, at what rate is the water level falling when the depth of water in the bucket is 6 in.? *Hint:* The volume of the frustum of a cone with height h and base radii r and R is

$$V = \frac{\pi h}{3}(R^2 + rR + r^2).$$

46. A lighthouse is located 2 km directly across the sea from a point S on the shoreline. A beacon in the lighthouse makes 3 complete revolutions (6π radians) each minute, and during part of each revolution, the light sweeps across the face of a row of cliffs lining the shore.

a. Show that t minutes after it passes point S, the beam of light is at a point P located $s(t) = 2 \tan 6\pi t$ km from S.

b. How fast is the beam of light moving at the time it passes a point on the cliff located 4 km from the lighthouse?

47. Modeling Problem A car is traveling at the rate of 40 ft/s along a straight, level road that parallels the seashore. A rock with a family of seals is located 50 yd offshore.

a. Model the angle θ between the road and the driver's line of sight as a function of the distance x to the point P directly opposite the rock.

b. As the distance x in Figure 3.58 approaches 0, what happens to $d\theta/dt$?

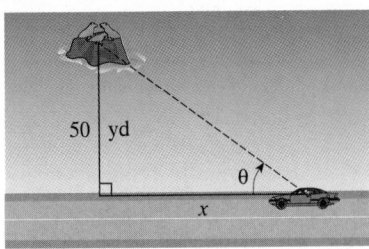

Figure 3.58   Problem 47

c. Suppose the car is traveling at v ft/s. Now what happens to $d\theta/dt$ as $x \to 0$? What effect does this have on a passenger looking at the seals if the car is traveling at a high rate of speed?

3.8   Linear Approximation and Differentials

IN THIS SECTION   tangent line approximation, the differential, error propagation, marginal analysis in economics, the Newton–Raphson method for approximating roots

TANGENT LINE APPROXIMATION

If $f(x)$ is differentiable at $x = a$, the tangent line at a point $P(a, f(a))$ on the graph of $y = f(x)$ has slope $m = f'(a)$ and equation

$$\frac{y - f(a)}{x - a} = f'(a) \quad \text{or} \quad y = f(a) + f'(a)(x - a)$$

In the immediate vicinity of P, the tangent line closely approximates the shape of the curve $y = f(x)$. For instance, if $f(x) = x^3 - 2x + 5$, the tangent line at $P(1, 4)$ has slope $f'(1) = 3(1)^2 - 2 = 1$ and equation

$$y = 4 + (1)(x - 1) = x + 3$$

The graph of $y = f(x)$, the tangent line at $P(1, 4)$, and two enlargements showing how the tangent line approximates the graph of f near P are shown in Figure 3.59.

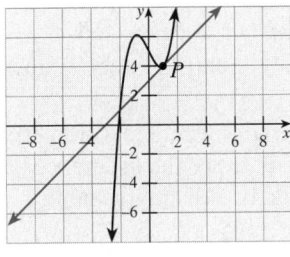
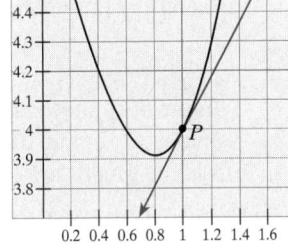
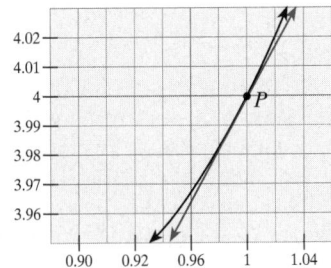

Figure 3.59   Tangent line approximation of $f(x) = x^3 - 2x + 5$ at $P(1, 4)$

Our observation about tangent lines suggests that if x_1 is near a, then $f(x_1)$ must be close to the point on the tangent line to $y = f(x)$ at $x = x_1$. That is,

$$f(x_1) \approx f(a) + f'(a)(x_1 - a)$$

We refer to this as a *linear approximation* of $f(x)$ at $x = a$, and the function

$$L(x) = f(a) + f'(a)(x - a)$$

is called a **linearization** of the function at a point $x = a$. We can use this line as an approximation of f as long as the line remains close to the graph of f, as shown in Figure 3.60.

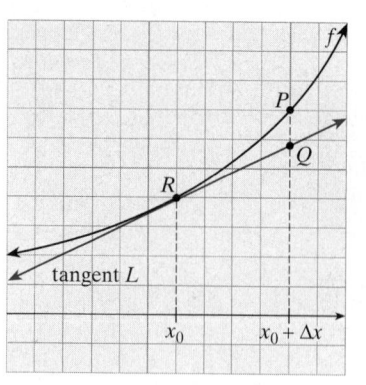
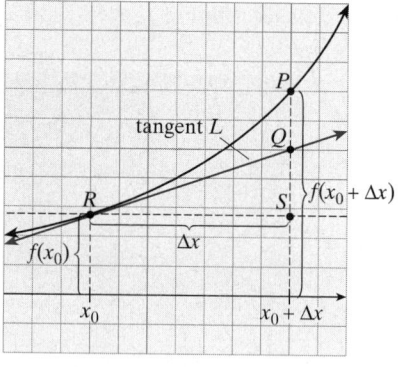

a. Tangent line to f at R **b.** Tangent line approximation

Figure 3.60   Tangent line approximation

Recall from Section 1.1, that for a line, we used the notation Δx for the horizontal change and Δy for the vertical change. Then, the linear approximation formula measures the vertical change from point R to point Q even though we really want the vertical change from the point R to the point P. If the distance Δx is small, then these two vertical distances should be approximately equal. This version of linear approximation is sometimes called the *incremental approximation formula*.

$$f(x_1) - f(a) \approx f'(a)(x_1 - a)$$
$$\Delta y \approx f'(a)\Delta x$$

EXAMPLE 1   Incremental approximation

Show that if $f(x) = \sin x$, the function $\dfrac{\Delta f}{\Delta x}$ approximates the function $f'(x) = \cos x$ for small values of Δx.

Solution

The approximation formula $\Delta f = f(x_0 + \Delta x) - f(x_0) \approx f'(x_0)\Delta x$ implies that
$$\frac{\Delta f}{\Delta x} = \frac{f(x_0 + \Delta x) - f(x_0)}{\Delta x} \approx f'(x_0)$$
Because $f(x) = \sin x$, $f'(x) = \cos x$, and
$$\frac{\sin(x + \Delta x) - \sin x}{\Delta x} \approx \cos x$$
Figure 3.61 shows the graphs for three different choices of Δx. Notice as Δx becomes smaller, it is more difficult to see the difference between f and g; in fact, for very small Δx, the graphs are virtually indistinguishable.

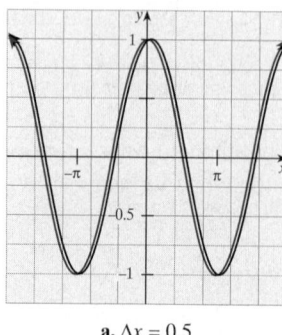
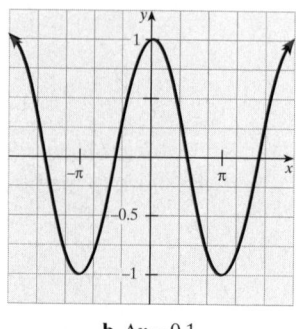
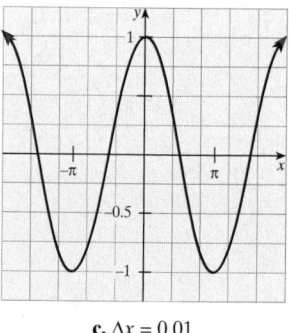

a. $\Delta x = 0.5$ **b.** $\Delta x = 0.1$ **c.** $\Delta x = 0.01$

Figure 3.61   Graphs of $f'(x) = \cos x$ and $g(x) = \dfrac{f(x + \Delta x) - f(x)}{\Delta x}$

THE DIFFERENTIAL

We have already observed that writing the derivative of $f(x)$ in the Leibniz notation df/dx suggests that the derivative may be incorrectly regarded as a quotient of "df" by "dx." It is a tribute to the genius of Leibniz that this erroneous interpretation of his notation often turns out to make good sense.

To give dx and dy meaning as separate quantities, let x be fixed and define dx to be an independent variable equal to Δx, the change in x. That is, define dx, called the **differential of x**, to be an independent variable equal to Δx, the change in x. Then, if f is differentiable at x, we define dy, called the **differential of y**, by the formula

$$dy = f'(x)\,dx \quad \text{or, equivalently,} \quad df = f'(x)\,dx$$

If we relate differentials to Figure 3.62, we see that $dx = \Delta x$ and that Δy is the rise of f that occurs for a change of Δx, whereas dy is the rise of a tangent line relative to the same change in x (Δy and dy are not the same thing). This is shown in Figure 3.62.

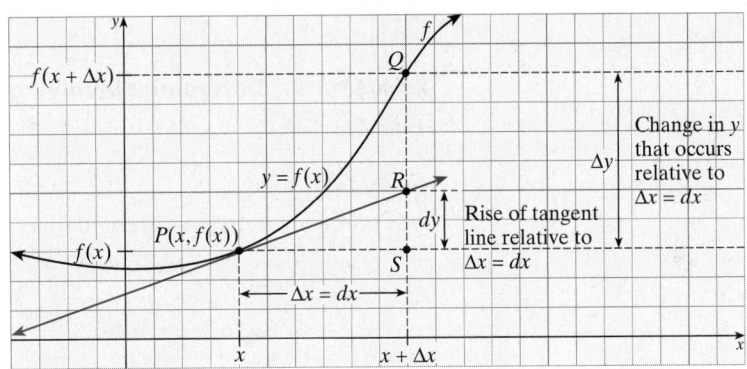

Figure 3.62 Geometrical definition of dx and dy

We now restate the standard rules and formulas for differentiation in terms of differentials. Remember that a and b are constants, while f and g are functions.

Differential rules

Linearity rule $\qquad d(af + bg) = a\,df + b\,dg$

Product rule $\qquad d(fg) = f\,dg + g\,df$

Quotient rule $\qquad d\left(\dfrac{f}{g}\right) = \dfrac{g\,df - f\,dg}{g^2} \qquad (g \neq 0)$

Power rule $\qquad d(x^n) = nx^{n-1}\,dx$

Trigonometric rules

$$d(\sin x) = \cos x\,dx \qquad\qquad d(\cos x) = -\sin x\,dx$$
$$d(\tan x) = \sec^2 x\,dx \qquad\qquad d(\cot x) = -\csc^2 x\,dx$$
$$d(\sec x) = \sec x \tan x\,dx \qquad\quad d(\csc x) = -\csc x \cot x\,dx$$

Exponential and logarithmic rules

$$d(e^x) = e^x\,dx \qquad\qquad d(\ln x) = \frac{1}{x}\,dx$$

Differential rules (Continued)

Inverse trigonometric rules

$$d(\sin^{-1} x) = \frac{dx}{\sqrt{1 - x^2}} \qquad d(\cos^{-1} x) = \frac{-dx}{\sqrt{1 - x^2}}$$

$$d(\tan^{-1} x) = \frac{dx}{1 + x^2} \qquad d(\cot^{-1} x) = \frac{-dx}{1 + x^2}$$

$$d(\sec^{-1} x) = \frac{dx}{|x| \sqrt{x^2 - 1}} \qquad d(\csc^{-1} x) = \frac{-dx}{|x| \sqrt{x^2 - 1}}$$

Note that each of the above differential formulas resembles the earlier derivative formula, and they can be remembered by "multiplying through" the corresponding derivative formula by "dx."

EXAMPLE 2   Differential involving a product and a trigonometric function

Find $d(x^2 \sin x)$.

Solution

You can work with the differential, as follows:

$$d(x^2 \sin x) = x^2 \, d(\sin x) + \sin x \, d(x^2)$$
$$= x^2 (\cos x \, dx) + \sin x (2x \, dx)$$
$$= (x^2 \cos x + 2x \sin x) \, dx$$

Or, you can work with the derivative, as shown:

$$\frac{d}{dx}(x^2 \sin x) = x^2 \cos x + 2x \sin x$$

so

$$d(x^2 \sin x) = (x^2 \cos x + 2x \sin x) \, dx \qquad \blacksquare$$

We can use differentials to approximate functional values, as shown in the following example.

EXAMPLE 3   Comparing differential and calculator approximations

Approximate $\frac{1}{3.98}$ using differentials, and compare with a calculator approximation.

Solution

Let $f(x) = \frac{1}{x} = x^{-1}$, so $f'(x) = -x^{-2}$. We know

$$f(x_0 + \Delta x) \approx f(x_0) + f'(x_0) \, dx$$

so we let $x_0 = 4$ and $\Delta x = dx = -0.02$ to find

$$\frac{1}{3.98} = \frac{1}{4 + (-0.02)}$$
$$\approx f(4) + f'(4)(-0.02)$$
$$= \frac{1}{4} + \frac{-1}{16}(-0.02)$$
$$= 0.25 + 0.00125$$
$$= 0.25125$$

By calculator, we find $\frac{1}{3.98} \approx 0.2512562814$. $\qquad \blacksquare$

ERROR PROPAGATION

In the next example, the approximation formula is used to study **propagation of error**, which is the term used to describe error that accumulates from other errors in an approximation. In particular, in the next example, the derivative is used to estimate the maximum error in a calculation that is based on figures obtained by imperfect measurement.

EXAMPLE 4   Propagation of error in a volume measurement

You measure the side of a cube and find it to be 10 cm long. From this you conclude that the volume of the cube is $10^3 = 1,000$ cm^3. If your original measurement of the side is accurate to within 2%, approximately how accurate is your calculation of the volume?

Solution

The volume of the cube is $V(x) = x^3$, where x is the length of a side. If you take the length of a side to be 10 when it is really $10 + \Delta x$, your error is Δx; and your corresponding error when computing the volume will be ΔV, given by

$$\Delta V = V(10 + \Delta x) - V(10) \approx V'(10)\Delta x$$

Now, $V'(x) = 3x^2$, so $V'(10) = 300$. Also, your measurement of the side can be off by as much as 2%—that is, by as much as $0.02(10) = 0.2$ cm in either direction. Substituting $\Delta x = \pm 0.2$ in the incremental approximation formula for ΔV, we get

$$\Delta V = 3(10)^2(\pm 0.2) \approx \pm 60$$

Thus, the propagated error in computing the volume is approximately ± 60 cm^3. Hence the maximum error in your measurement of the side is $|\Delta x| = 0.2$ and the corresponding maximum error in your calculation for the volume is

$$|\Delta V| \approx V'(10)\,|\Delta x| = 300(0.2) = 60$$

This says that, at worst, your calculation of the volume as $1,000$ cm^3 is off by 60 cm^3, or 6% of the calculated volume, when your maximum error in measuring the side is 2%. ∎

Error Propagation

If x_0 represents the measured value of a variable and $x_0 + \Delta x$ represents the exact value, then Δx is the **error in measurement**. The difference between $f(x + \Delta x)$ and $f(x)$ is called the **propagated error** at x and is defined by

$$\Delta f = f(x + \Delta x) - f(x)$$

Relative Error

The **relative error** is $\dfrac{\Delta f}{f} \approx \dfrac{df}{f}$.

Percentage Error

The **percentage error** is $100\left(\dfrac{\Delta f}{f}\right)$%.

In Example 4, the approximate propagated error in measuring volume is ± 60, and the approximate relative error is $\Delta V/V = \pm 60/10^3 = \pm 0.06$.

EXAMPLE 5   Estimating relative error and percentage error

A certain container is modeled by a right circular cylinder whose height is twice the radius of the base. The radius is measured to be 17.3 cm, with a maximum measurement error of 0.02 cm. Estimate the corresponding propagated error, the relative error, and the percentage error when calculating the surface area S.

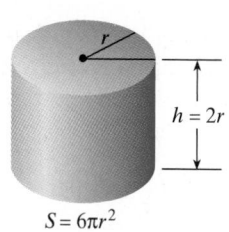

$S = 6\pi r^2$

Figure 3.63 Surface area of a right circular cylinder

Solution

Figure 3.63 shows the container. We have

$$S = \underbrace{2\pi r}_{\substack{\text{Circumference}}} \underbrace{2r}_{} + \underbrace{\pi r^2}_{\text{Top}} + \underbrace{\pi r^2}_{\text{Bottom}} = 6\pi r^2$$

$$\underbrace{\qquad\qquad}_{\text{Lateral side}}$$

Height

where r is the radius of the cylinder's base. Then the approximate *propagated error* is

$$\Delta S \approx S'(r)\Delta r = 12\pi r\, \Delta r = 12\pi(17.3)(\pm 0.02) \approx \pm 13.0438927$$

Thus, the maximum error in the measurement of the surface area is about 13.04 cm². Is this a large or a small error? The *relative error* is found by computing the ratio

$$\frac{\Delta S}{S} = \frac{12\pi r\, \Delta r}{6\pi r^2} = 2r^{-1}\Delta r = 2(17.3)^{-1}(\pm 0.02) \approx \pm 0.0023121$$

This tells us that the maximum error of approximately 13.04 is fairly small relative to the surface area S. The corresponding *percentage error* is found by

$$100\left(\frac{\Delta S}{S}\right)\% = 100(\pm 0.0023121387)\% = \pm 0.23121387\%$$

This means that the percentage error is about $\pm 0.23\%$. ∎

MARGINAL ANALYSIS IN ECONOMICS

Marginal analysis is an area of economics concerned with estimating the effect on quantities such as cost, revenue, and profit when the level of production is changed by a unit amount. For example, if $C(x)$ is the cost of producing x units of a certain commodity, then the **marginal cost**, $MC(x)$, is the additional cost of producing one more unit and is given by the difference $MC(x) = C(x + 1) - C(x)$. Using the linear approximation formula with $\Delta x = 1$, we see that

$$MC(x) = C(x + 1) - C(x) \approx C'(x)(1)$$

and for this reason, we will compute marginal cost by the derivative $C'(x)$.

Similarly, if $R(x)$ is the revenue obtained from producing x units of a commodity, then the **marginal revenue**, $MR(x)$, is the additional revenue obtained from producing one more unit, and we compute MR by the derivative $R'(x)$. To summarize:

Marginal Cost And Marginal Revenue

The marginal cost of producing x units of a commodity is computed by the derivative $MC(x) = C'(x)$ and the marginal revenue of producing x units is computed by $MR(x) = R'(x)$.

EXAMPLE 6 Modeling change in cost and revenue

A manufacturer models the total cost (in dollars) of a particular commodity by the function

$$C(x) = \tfrac{1}{8}x^2 + 3x + 98$$

and the price per item (in dollars) by

$$p(x) = \tfrac{1}{3}(75 - x)$$

where x is the number of items produced ($0 \le x \le 50$). The function p is called the **demand function** which is the market price per unit when x units are produced.

a. Find the marginal cost and the marginal revenue.

b. Use marginal cost to estimate the cost of producing the 9th unit. What is the actual cost of producing the 9th unit?

c. Use marginal revenue to estimate the revenue derived from producing the 9th unit. What is the actual revenue derived from producing the 9th unit?

Solution

You can compare the values on [0, 50] using a calculator in order to get a sense of the meaning of the problem.

No.	Total cost; Avg. cost	Price per item
0	$98.00	$25.00
5	$116.13; $23.23	$23.33
10	$140.50; $14.05	$21.67
15	$171.13; $11.41	$20.00
20	$208.00; $10.40	$18.33
25	$251.13; $10.05	$16.67
30	$300.50; $10.02	$15.00
35	$356.13; $10.18	$13.33
40	$418.00; $10.45	$11.67
45	$486.13; $10.80	$10.00
50	$560.50; $11.21	$8.33

a. The marginal cost is

$$C'(x) = \tfrac{1}{4}x + 3$$

To find the marginal revenue, we must first find the revenue function:

$$R(x) = xp(x) = x\left(\tfrac{1}{3}\right)(75 - x) = -\tfrac{1}{3}x^2 + 25x$$

Thus, the marginal revenue is

$$R'(x) = -\tfrac{2}{3}x + 25$$

b. The cost of producing the 9th unit is the change in cost as x increases from 8 to 9 and is estimated by

$$C'(8) = \tfrac{1}{4}(8) + 3 = 5$$

We estimate the cost of producing the 9th unit to be $5. The actual cost is

$$\Delta C = C(9) - C(8) = \left[\tfrac{1}{8}(9)^2 + 3(9) + 98\right] - \left[\tfrac{1}{8}(8)^2 + 3(8) + 98\right]$$
$$= 5\tfrac{1}{8} = 5.125 \quad \text{(that is, \$5.13)}$$

WARNING Remember that the marginal revenue from the sale of the 9th item is not the revenue derived from selling 9 items. Rather, it is the additional revenue the company has earned by selling the 9th item—that is, the total revenue of 9 items minus the total revenue of 8 items.

c. The revenue (to the nearest cent) obtained from the sale of the 9th unit is approximated by the marginal revenue:

$$R'(8) = -\tfrac{2}{3}(8) + 25 = \tfrac{59}{3} \approx 19.67 \quad \text{(that is, \$19.67)}$$

The actual revenue (to the nearest cent) obtained from the sale of the 9th unit is

$$\Delta R = R(9) - R(8) = \tfrac{58}{3} \approx 19.33 \quad \text{(that is, \$19.33)} \qquad \blacksquare$$

THE NEWTON-RAPHSON METHOD FOR APPROXIMATING ROOTS

The Newton–Raphson method is a different kind of tangent line approximation, one that uses tangent lines as a means for estimating roots of equations. The basic idea behind the procedure is illustrated in Figure 3.64. In this figure, r is a root of the equation $f(x) = 0$, x_0 is an approximation to r, and x_1 is a better approximation obtained by taking the x-intercept of the line that is tangent to the graph of f at $(x_0, f(x_0))$.

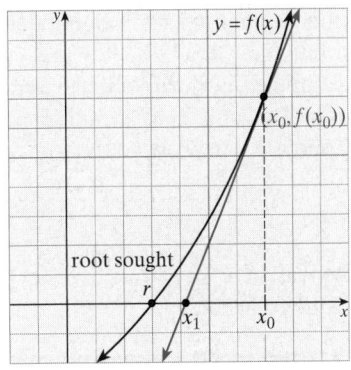
a. Estimating a root, r, of $y = f(x)$

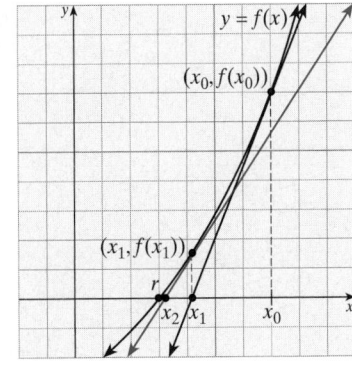
b. First, second, and third estimates ($x_0, x_1,$ and x_2, respectively)

Figure 3.64 The Newton–Raphson method

THEOREM 3.14   The Newton–Raphson method

To approximate a root of the equation $f(x) = 0$, start with a preliminary estimate x_0 and generate a sequence $x_1, x_2, x_3, \ldots$ using the formula

$$x_{n+1} = x_n - \frac{f(x_n)}{f'(x_n)} \qquad f'(x_n) \neq 0$$

Either this sequence of approximations will approach a limit that is a root of the equation or else the sequence does not have a limit.

Proof   Rather than present a formal proof, we will present a geometric description of the procedure to help you understand what is happening. Let x_0 be an initial approximation such that $f'(x_0) \neq 0$. To find a formula for the improved approximation x_1, recall that the slope of the tangent line through $(x_0, f(x_0))$ is the derivative $f'(x_0)$. Therefore (see Figure 3.64b),

$$\underbrace{f'(x_0)}_{\text{Slope of the tangent line through } (x_0,\, f(x_0))} = \frac{\Delta y}{\Delta x} = \frac{f(x_0) - 0}{x_0 - x_1}$$

or, equivalently (by solving the equation for x_1),

$$x_1 = x_0 - \frac{f(x_0)}{f'(x_0)} \qquad f'(x_0) \neq 0$$

If this procedure is repeated using x_1 as the initial approximation, an even better approximation may often be obtained (see Figure 3.64b). This approximation, x_2, is related to x_1 as x_1 was related to x_0. That is,

$$x_2 = x_1 - \frac{f(x_1)}{f'(x_1)} \qquad f'(x_1) \neq 0$$

If this process produces a limit, it can be continued until the desired degree of accuracy is obtained. In general, the nth approximation x_n is related to the $(n-1)$st by the formula

$$x_n = x_{n-1} - \frac{f(x_{n-1})}{f'(x_{n-1})} \qquad f'(x_{n-1}) \neq 0 \qquad \square$$

Here is a step-by-step procedure for applying the Newton–Raphson method. A flowchart for the method appears in Figure 3.65.

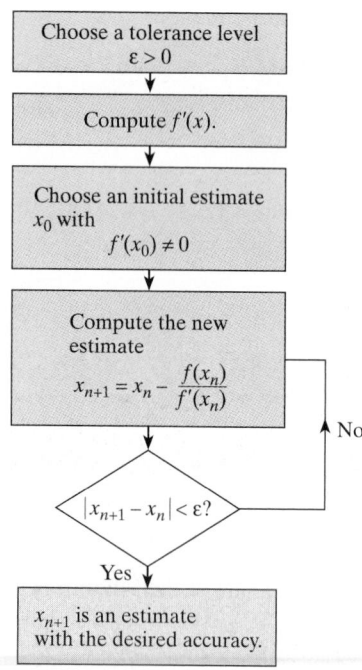

Choose a tolerance level
$\varepsilon > 0$

Compute $f'(x)$.

Choose an initial estimate
x_0 with
$f'(x_0) \neq 0$

Compute the new
estimate
$x_{n+1} = x_n - \dfrac{f(x_n)}{f'(x_n)}$

$|x_{n+1} - x_n| < \varepsilon$?   No

Yes

x_{n+1} is an estimate
with the desired accuracy.

Figure 3.65 Flowchart for the Newton–Raphson method

Procedure for Applying the Newton–Raphson Method to Solve the Equation $f(x) = 0$

1. Choose a number $\epsilon > 0$ that determines the allowable tolerance for estimated solutions.
2. Compute $f'(x)$ and choose a number x_0 (with $f'(x_0) \neq 0$) "close" to a solution of $f(x) = 0$ as an initial estimate.
3. Compute a new approximation with the formula

$$x_{n+1} = x_n - \frac{f(x_n)}{f'(x_n)} \qquad f'(x_n) \neq 0$$

4. Repeat step 3 until $|x_{n+1} - x_n| < \epsilon$. The estimate $\overline{x} = x_{n+1}$ then has the required accuracy.

EXAMPLE 7   Estimating a root with the Newton–Raphson method

Approximate a real root of the equation $x^3 + x + 1 = 0$ on $[-2, 2]$.

Solution

Let $f(x) = x^3 + x + 1$. Our goal is to find a root of the equation $f(x) = 0$. The derivative of f is $f'(x) = 3x^2 + 1$, and so

$$x - \frac{f(x)}{f'(x)} = x - \frac{x^3 + x + 1}{3x^2 + 1} = \frac{2x^3 - 1}{3x^2 + 1}$$

Thus, for $n = 0, 1, 2, 3, \ldots,$

$$x_{n+1} = x_n - \frac{f(x_n)}{f'(x_n)} = \frac{2x_n^3 - 1}{3x_n^2 + 1}$$

A convenient choice for the preliminary estimate is $x_0 = -1$. Then

$$x_1 = \frac{2x_0^3 - 1}{3x_0^2 + 1} = -0.75 \qquad \text{You will need a calculator or a spreadsheet to help you with these calculations.}$$

$$x_2 = \frac{2x_1^3 - 1}{3x_1^2 + 1} \approx -0.6860465$$

$$x_3 = \frac{2x_2^3 - 1}{3x_2^2 + 1} \approx -0.6823396$$

So, to two decimal places, the root seems to be approximately $x_n \approx -0.68$. ∎

In general, we will stop finding new estimates when successive approximations x_n and x_{n+1} are within a desired tolerance of each other. Specifically, if we wish to have the solutions to be within ϵ ($\epsilon > 0$) of each other, we compute approximations until $|x_{n+1} - x_n| < \epsilon$ is satisfied. Using the Newton–Raphson method (Theorem 3.14), we see that this condition is equivalent to

$$|x_{n+1} - x_n| = \left| \frac{-f(x_n)}{f'(x_n)} \right| < \epsilon$$

3.8 PROBLEM SET

Ⓐ *Find the differentials indicated in Problems 1–16.*

1. $d(2x^3)$

2. $d(3 - 5x^2)$

3. $d(2\sqrt{x})$

4. $d(x^5 + \sqrt{x^2 + 5})$

5. $d(x \cos x)$

6. $d(x \sin 2x)$

7. $d\left(\dfrac{\tan 3x}{2x} \right)$

8. $d(xe^{-2x})$

9. $d(\ln |\sin x|)$

10. $d(x \tan^{-1} x)$

11. $d(e^x \ln x)$

12. $d\left(\dfrac{\sin^{-1} x}{e} \right)$

13. $d\left(\dfrac{x^2 \sec x}{x - 3} \right)$

14. $d(x\sqrt{x^2 - 1})$

15. $d\left(\dfrac{x - 5}{\sqrt{x + 4}} \right)$

16. $d\left(\dfrac{\ln \sqrt{x}}{x} \right)$

17. **WHAT DOES THIS SAY?**   What is a differential?

18. **Interpretation Problem**   Discuss error propagation, including relative error, and percentage error.

Ⓑ *Use differentials to approximate the requested values in Problems 19–22 and then determine the error as compared to the calculator value.*

19. $\sqrt{0.99}$

20. $\cos(\frac{\pi}{2} + 0.01)$

21. $(3.01)^5 - 2(3.01)^3 + 3(3.01)^2 - 2$

22. $\sqrt[4]{4,100} + \sqrt[3]{4,100} + 3\sqrt{4,100}$

23. You measure the radius of a circle to be 12 cm and use the formula $A = \pi r^2$ to calculate the area. If your measurement of the radius is accurate to within 3%, approximately how accurate (to the nearest percent) is your calculation of the area?

24. **Exploration Problem**   Suppose a 12-oz can of Coke® has a height of 4.5 in. If your measurement of the radius has an accuracy to within 1%, how accurate is your measurement for volume? Check your answer by examining a Coke can.

25. You measure the radius of a sphere to be 6 in. Use the formula $V = \frac{4}{3}\pi r^3$ to calculate the volume. If your measurement of the radius is accurate to within 1%, approximately how accurate (to the nearest percent) is your calculation of the volume?

26. It is projected that t years from now the circulation of a local newspaper will be

$$C(t) = 100t^2 + 400t + 5,000$$

Estimate the amount by which the circulation will increase during the next 6 months.

27. An environmental study suggests that t years from now, the average level of carbon monoxide in the air will be

$$Q(t) = 0.05t^2 + 0.1t + 3.4$$

parts per million (ppm). By approximately how much will the carbon monoxide level change during the next 6 months?

28. A manufacturer's total cost (in dollars) is

$$C(q) = 0.1q^3 - 0.5q^2 + 500q + 200$$

when the level of production is q units. The current level of production is 4 units, and the manufacturer is planning to decrease this to 3.9 units. Estimate how the total cost will change as a result.

29. At a certain factory, the daily output is

$$Q(L) = 60,000L^{1/3}$$

units, where L denotes the size of the labor force measured in worker-hours. Currently 1,000 worker-hours of labor are used each day. Estimate the effect on output that will be produced if the labor force is cut to 940 worker-hours.

30. Modeling Problem   In a model developed by John Helms, the water evaporation $E(T)$ for a ponderosa pine is modeled by

$$E(T) = 4.6e^{17.3T/(T+237)}$$

where T (degrees Celsius) is the surrounding air temperature.[*] If the temperature is increased by 5% from 30°C, use differentials to estimate the corresponding percentage change in $E(T)$.

31. A soccer ball made of leather $\frac{1}{8}$ in. thick has an inner diameter of $8\frac{1}{2}$ in. Model the ball as a hollow sphere and estimate the volume of its leather shell.

32. A cubical box is to be constructed from three kinds of building materials. The material used in the four sides of the box costs 2¢/in.^{2}, the material in the bottom costs 3¢/in.^{2}, and the material used for the lid costs 4¢/in.^{2}. Estimate the additional total cost of all the building materials if the length of a side is increased from 20 in. to 21 in.

33. In a healthy person of height x in., the average pulse rate in beats per minute is modeled by the formula

$$P(x) = \frac{596}{\sqrt{x}} \qquad 30 \le x \le 100$$

Estimate the change in pulse rate that corresponds to a height change from 59 to 60 in.

34. A drug is injected into a patient's bloodstream. The concentration of the drug in the bloodstream t hours after the drug is injected is modeled by the formula

$$C(t) = \frac{0.12t}{t^2 + t + 1}$$

milligrams per cubic centimeter. Estimate the change in concentration over the time period from 30 to 35 minutes after injection.

35. Modeling Problem   According to Poiseuille's law, the speed of blood flowing along the central axis of an artery of radius R is modeled by the formula $S(R) = cR^2$, where c is a constant.[†] What percentage error (rounded to the nearest percent) will you make in the calculation of $S(R)$ from this formula if you make a 1% error in the measurement of R?

36. Modeling Problem   One of the laws attributed to Poiseuille models the volume of a fluid flowing through a small tube in unit time under fixed pressure by the formula $V = kR^4$, where k is a positive constant and R is the radius of the tube. This formula is used in medicine to determine how wide a clogged artery must be opened to restore a healthy flow of blood. Suppose the radius of a certain artery is increased by 5%. Approximately what effect does this have on the volume of the blood flowing through the artery?[‡]

37. Modeling Problem   A certain cell is modeled as a sphere. If the formulas $S = 4\pi r^2$ and $V = \frac{4}{3}\pi r^3$ are used to compute the surface area and volume of the sphere, respectively, estimate the effect on S and V produced by a 1% increase in the radius r.

38. The period of a pendulum is given by the formula

$$T = 2\pi\sqrt{\frac{L}{g}}$$

where L is the length of the pendulum in feet, $g = 32$ ft/s^2 is the acceleration due to gravity, and T is time in seconds. If the pendulum has been heated enough to increase its length by 0.4%, what is the approximate percentage change in its period?

39. The *thermal expansion coefficient* of an object is defined to be

$$\sigma = \frac{L'(T)}{L(T)}$$

where $L(T)$ is the length of the object when the temperature is T. Suppose a 75-ft span of a bridge is built with steel with $\sigma = 1.4 \times 10^{-5}$ per degree Celsius. Approximately how much will the length change during a year when the temperature varies from $-10°$C in winter to 40°C in summer?

40. The radius R of a spherical ball is measured as 14 in.

   a. Use differentials to estimate the maximum propagated error in computing volume V if R is measured with a maximum error of $\frac{1}{8}$ inch.

   b. With what accuracy must the radius R be measured to guarantee an error of at most 2 in.^{3} in the calculated volume?

41. A thin horizontal beam of alpha particles strikes a thin vertical foil, and the scattered alpha particles will travel along a cone of vertex angle θ, as shown in Figure 3.66.

[*]John A. Helms, "Environmental Control of Net Photosynthesis in Naturally Grown Pinus Ponderosa Nets," *Ecology* (Winter 1972), p. 92.

[†]See *Introduction to Mathematics for Life Scientists*, 2nd edition. New York: Springer-Verlag (1976), pp. 102–103.

[‡]Ibid.

Time 1: Stream is focused.

Time 2: Stream hits foil.

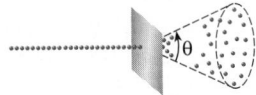

Time 3: Stream is scattered after colliding with foil and disperses in the shape of a cone.

Figure 3.66 Paths of alpha particles

A vertical screen is placed at a fixed distance from the point of scattering. Physical theory predicts that the number N of alpha particles falling on a unit area of the screen is inversely proportional to $\sin^4\left(\frac{\theta}{2}\right)$. Suppose N is modeled by the formula

$$N = \frac{1}{\sin^4\left(\frac{\theta}{2}\right)}$$

Estimate the change in the number of alpha particles per unit area of the screen if θ changes from 1 to 1.1.

42. Suppose the total cost of manufacturing q units is

$$C(q) = 3q^2 + q + 500$$

dollars.

   a. Use marginal analysis to estimate the cost of manufacturing the 41st unit.

   b. Compute the actual cost of manufacturing the 41st unit.

43. A manufacturer's total cost is

$$C(q) = 0.1q^3 - 5q^2 + 500q + 200$$

dollars, where q is the number of units produced.

   a. Use marginal analysis to estimate the cost of manufacturing the 4th unit.

   b. Compute the actual cost of manufacturing the 4th unit.

44. Suppose the total cost of producing x units of a particular commodity is modeled by

$$C(x) = \tfrac{1}{7}x^2 + 4x + 100$$

and that each unit of the commodity can be sold for

$$p(x) = \tfrac{1}{4}(80 - x)$$

dollars.

   a. What is the marginal cost?

   b. What is the price when the marginal cost is 10?

   c. Estimate the cost of producing the 11th unit.

   d. Find the actual cost of producing the 11th unit.

45. At a certain factory, the daily output is modeled by the formula

$$Q(L) = 360L^{1/3}$$

units, where L is the size of the labor force measured in worker-hours. Currently, 1,000 worker-hours of labor are used each day. Use differentials to estimate the effect that one additional worker-hour will have on the daily output.

46. Approximate $\sqrt{2}$ to four decimal places by using the Newton–Raphson method.

47. Approximate $-\sqrt{2}$ to four decimal places by using the Newton–Raphson method.

48. Use the Newton–Raphson method to estimate a root of the equation $\cos x = x$. You may start with $x_0 = 1$.

49. Use the Newton–Raphson method to estimate a root of the equation $e^{-x} = x$. You may start with $x_0 = 1$.

50. Use the Newton–Raphson method to estimate a root of the equation

$$x^6 - x^5 + x^3 = 3$$

51. Let $f(x) = -2x^4 + 3x^2 + \frac{11}{8}$.

   a. Show that the equation $f(x) = 0$ has at least two solutions. *Hint*: Use the intermediate value theorem.

   b. Use $x_0 = 2$ in the Newton–Raphson method to find a root of the equation $f(x) = 0$.

   c. Show that the Newton–Raphson method fails if you choose $x_0 = \frac{1}{2}$ as the initial estimate. *Hint*: You should obtain $x_1 = -x_0, x_2 = x_0, \dots$.

52. It can be shown that the volume of a spherical segment is given by

$$V = \frac{\pi}{3}H^2(3R - H)$$

where R is the radius of the sphere and H is the height of the segment, as shown in Figure 3.67.

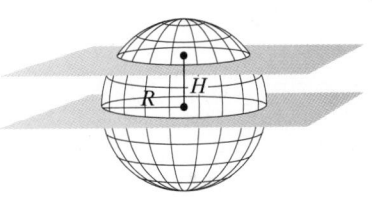

Figure 3.67 Problem 52

If $V = 8$ and $R = 2$, use the Newton–Raphson method to estimate the corresponding H.

53. HISTORICAL QUEST The Greek geometer Archimedes (see Essay Question 4 in Chapter 1) is acknowledged to be one of the greatest mathematicians of all time. Ten treatises of Archimedes have survived the rigors of time (as well as traces of some lost works) and are masterpieces of mathematical exposition. In one of these works, *On the Sphere and Cylinder*, Archimedes asks where a sphere should be cut in order to divide it into two pieces whose volumes have a given ratio. ∎

ARCHIMEDES
287–212 B.C.

Show that if a plane at distance x_c from the center of a sphere with $R = 1$ divides the sphere into two parts, one with volume twice that of the other, then

$$3x_c^3 - 9x_c^2 + 2 = 0$$

Use the Newton–Raphson method to estimate x_c.

54. Suppose the plane described in Problem 53 is located so that it divides the sphere in the ratio 1:3. Find an equation for x_c, and estimate the value of x_c by the Newton–Raphson method. *Hint*: You may need the result of Problem 52.

C 55. Show that if h is sufficiently small, then
   a. $\sqrt{1+h}$ is approximately equal to $1 + \frac{h}{2}$.
   b. $\dfrac{1}{1+h}$ is approximately equal to $1 - h$.

56. If h is sufficiently small, find an approximate value for $\sqrt[n]{A^n + h}$ for constant A.

57. Tangent line approximations are useful only if Δx is small. Illustrate this fact by trying to approximate $\sqrt{97}$ by regarding 97 as being near 81 (instead of 100).

58. Let $f(x) = -x^4 + x^2 + A$ for constant A. What value of A should be chosen that guarantees that if $x_0 = \frac{1}{3}$ is chosen as the initial estimate, the Newton–Raphson method produces $x_1 = -x_0, x_2 = x_0, x_3 = -x_0, \ldots$?

59. Suppose that when x units of a certain commodity are produced, the total cost is $C(x)$ and the total revenue is $R(x)$. Let $P(x) = R(x) - C(x)$ denote the total profit, and let

$$A(x) = \frac{C(x)}{x}$$

be the average cost.
   a. Show that $P'(x) = 0$ when marginal revenue equals marginal cost.
   b. Show that $A'(x) = 0$ when average cost equals marginal cost.

60. Can you solve the equation $\sqrt{x} = 0$ using the Newton–Raphson method with the initial estimate $x_0 = 0.05$? Does it make any difference if we choose another initial estimate (other than $x_0 = 0$)?

61. Interpretation Problem Suppose that when we try to use the Newton–Raphson method to approximate a solution of $f(x) = 0$, we find that $f(x_n) = 0$ but $f'(x_n) \neq 0$ for some x_n. What does this imply about $x_{n+1}, x_{n+2}, \ldots$? Explain.

62. HISTORICAL QUEST   Among the peoples of the region between the Tigris and Euphrates rivers (at different times) during the period 2000–600 B.C. were Sumerians, Akkadians, Chaldeans, and Assyrians. Since the middle half of the nineteenth century, archeologists have found well over 50,000 clay tablets describing these great civilizations. Records show that they had highly developed religion, history, science (including alchemy, astronomy, botany, chemistry, mathematics, and zoology). ■

Mesopotamian culture had iterative formulas for computing algebraic quantities such as roots. In particular, they approximated $\sqrt{N}$ by repeatedly applying the formula

$$x_{n+1} = \frac{1}{2}\left(x_n + \frac{N}{x_n}\right) \quad \text{for } n = 0, 1, 2, 3, \ldots$$

   a. Apply the Newton–Raphson method to $f(x) = x^2 - N$ to justify this formula.
   b. Apply the formula to estimate $\sqrt{1{,}265}$ correct to five decimal places.

CHAPTER 3 REVIEW

Proficiency Examination

CONCEPT PROBLEMS

1. What is the slope of a tangent line? How does this compare to the slope of a secant line?
2. Define the derivative of a function.
3. What is a normal line to a graph?
4. What is the relationship between continuity and differentiability?
5. List and explain some of the notations for derivative.
6. State the following procedural rules for finding derivatives:
   a. constant multiple   b. sum rule
   c. difference rule   d. linearity rule
   e. product rule   f. quotient rule
   g. State each of these rules again, this time in differential form.
7. State the following derivative rules:
   a. constant rule   b. power rule
   c. trigonometric rules   d. exponential rule
   e. logarithmic rule   f. inverse trigonometric rules
8. What is a higher-order derivative? List some of the different notations for higher-order derivatives.
9. What is meant by rate of change? Distinguish between average and instantaneous rate of change.
10. What is relative rate of change?
11. How do you find the velocity and the acceleration for an object with position $s(t)$? What is speed?
12. State the chain rule.
13. Outline a procedure for logarithmic differentiation.
14. Outline a procedure for implicit differentiation.
15. Outline a procedure for solving related rate problems.
16. What is meant by tangent line approximation?
17. Define the differential of x and the differential of y for a function $y = f(x)$. Draw a sketch showing Δx, Δy, dx, and dy.
18. Define the terms propagated error, relative error, and percentage error.
19. What is meant by marginal analysis?
20. What is the Newton–Raphson method?

PRACTICE PROBLEMS

Find $\dfrac{dy}{dx}$ in Problems 21–30.

21. $x^3 + x\sqrt{x} + \cos 2x$
22. $y = \sqrt{3x} + \dfrac{3}{x^2}$
23. $y = \sqrt{\sin(3 - x^2)}$
24. $xy + y^3 = 10$
25. $y = x^2 e^{-\sqrt{x}}$
26. $y = \dfrac{\ln 2x}{\ln 3x}$
27. $y = \sin^{-1}(3x + 2)$
28. $y = \tan^{-1} 2x$
29. $y = \sin^2(x^{10} + \sqrt{x}) + \cos^2(x^{10} + \sqrt{x})$
30. $y = \dfrac{\ln(x^2 - 1)}{\sqrt[3]{x}(1 - 3x)^3}$
31. Find $\dfrac{d^2 y}{dx^2}$, the second derivative of $y = x^2(2x - 3)^3$.

32. Use the definition of the derivative to find $\frac{d}{dx}(x - 3x^2)$.
33. Find the equation of the tangent line to the graph of
$$y = (x^2 + 3x - 2)(7 - 3x)$$
at the point where $x = 1$.
34. Let $f(x) = \sin^2\left(\dfrac{\pi x}{4}\right)$. Find equations of the tangent line and the normal line to the graph of f at $x = 1$.
35. A rock tossed into a stream causes a circular ripple of water whose radius increases at a constant rate of 0.5 ft/s. How fast is the area contained inside of the ripple changing when the radius is 2 ft?

Supplementary Problems

Find dy/dx in Problems 1–36.

1. $y = x^4 + 3x^2 - 7x + 5$
2. $y = x^5 + 3x^3 - 11$
3. $y = \sqrt{\dfrac{x^2 - 1}{x^2 - 5}}$
4. $y = \dfrac{\cos x}{x + \sin x}$
5. $2x^2 - xy + 2y = 5$
6. $y = (x^2 + 3x - 5)^7$
7. $y = (x^3 + x)^{10}$
8. $y = \sqrt{x}(x^2 + 5)^{10}$
9. $y = \sqrt[3]{x}(x^3 + 1)^5$
10. $y = (x^2 + 3)^5 (x^3 - 5)^8$
11. $y = (x^4 - 1)^{10}(2x^4 + 3)^7$
12. $y = \sqrt{\sin 5x}$
13. $y = \sqrt{\cos \sqrt{x}}$
14. $y = (\sin x + \cos x)^3$
15. $y = (\sqrt{x} + \sqrt[3]{x})^5$
16. $y = \sqrt{\dfrac{x^3 - x}{4 - x^2}}$
17. $y = \exp(2x^2 + 5x - 3)$
18. $y = \ln(x^2 - 1)$
19. $y = x3^{2-x}$
20. $y = \log_3(x^2 - 1)$
21. $e^{xy} + 2 = \ln\dfrac{y}{x}$
22. $y = \sqrt{x}\sin^{-1}(3x + 2)$
23. $y = e^{\sin x}$
24. $y = 2^x \log_2 x$
25. $y = e^{-x}\log_5 3x$
26. $x2^y + y2^x = 3$
27. $\ln(x + y^2) = x^2 + 2y$
28. $y = e^{-x}\sqrt{\ln 2x}$
29. $y = \sin(\sin x)$
30. $y = \cos(\sin x)$
31. $x^{1/2} + y^{1/2} = x$
32. $4x^2 - 16y^2 = 64$
33. $\sin xy = y + x$
34. $\sin(x + y) + \cos(x - y) = xy$
35. $y = \dfrac{x}{\sin^{-1} x} + \dfrac{\tan^{-1} x}{x}$
36. $y = (\sin x)(\sin^{-1} x) + x\cot^{-1} x$

Find $d^2 y/dx^2$ in Problems 37–41.

37. $y = x^5 - 5x^4 + 7x^3 - 3x^2 + 17$
38. $y = \dfrac{x - 5}{2x + 3} + (3x - 1)^2$
39. $x^2 + y^3 = 10$
40. $x^2 + \sin y = 2$
41. $x^2 + \tan^{-1} y = 2$

In Problems 42–54, find an equation of the tangent line to the curve at the indicated point.

42. $y = x^4 - 7x^3 + x^2 - 3$ at $(0, -3)$
43. $y = (3x^2 + 5x - 7)^3$, where $x = 1$
44. $y = (x^3 - 3x^2 + 3)^3$, where $x = -1$
45. $y = x\cos x$, where $x = \frac{\pi}{2}$

46. $y = (\cos x)^2$, where $x = \pi$

47. $xy^2 + x^2 y = 2$ at $(1, 1)$

48. $y = x \ln(ex)$, where $x = 1$

49. $y = xe^{2x-1}$, where $x = \frac{1}{2}$

50. $e^{xy} = x - y$ at $(1, 0)$

51. $y = (1 - x)^x$, where $x = 0$

52. $y = 2^x - \log_2 x$, where $x = 1$

53. $y = \dfrac{3x - 4}{3x^2 + x - 5}$, where $x = 1$

54. $x^{2/3} + y^{2/3} = 2$ at $(1, 1)$

55. Let $f(x) = (x^3 - x^2 + 2x - 1)^4$. Find equations of the tangent and normal lines to the graph of f at $x = 1$.

56. Find equations for the tangent and normal lines to the graph of $y = \left(2x + \dfrac{1}{x}\right)^3$ at the point $(1, 27)$.

57. Use the chain rule to find $\dfrac{dy}{dt}$ when $y = x^3 - 7x$ and $x = t \sin t$.

58. Find $f''(x)$ if $f(x) = x^2 \sin x^2$.

59. Find $f^{(4)}(x)$ if $f(x) = x^4 - \dfrac{1}{x^4}$.

60. Find $f'''(x)$ if $f(x) = x(x^2 + 1)^{7/2}$.

61. Let $f(x) = \sqrt[3]{\dfrac{x^4 + 1}{x^4 - 2}}$. Find $f'(x)$ by implicitly differentiating $[f(x)]^3$.

62. Find y' if $x^3 y^3 + x - y = 1$. Leave your answer in terms of x and y.

63. Find y' and y'' if $x^2 + 4xy - y^2 = 8$. Your answer may involve x and y, but not y'.

64. Find the derivative of $f(x) = \begin{cases} x^2 + 5x + 4 & \text{for } x \leq 0 \\ 5x + 4 & \text{for } 0 < x < 6 \\ x^2 - 2 & \text{for } x \geq 6 \end{cases}$.

65. **Advanced Placement Question** *The following problem is found on the 1982 BC AP Exam.* Let f be the function defined by

$$f(x) = \begin{cases} x^2 \sin \dfrac{1}{x} & \text{for } x \neq 0 \\ 0 & \text{for } x = 0 \end{cases}$$

a. Using the definition of the derivative, prove that f is differentiable at $x = 0$.

b. Find $f'(x)$ for $x \neq 0$.

c. Show that f' is not continuous at $x = 0$.

66. Use differentials to approximate $(16.01)^{3/2} + 2\sqrt{16.01}$.

67. Use differentials to approximate $\cos \frac{101\pi}{600}$.

68. Use differentials to estimate the change in the volume of a cone if the height of the cone is increased from 10 cm to 10.01 cm while the radius of the base stays fixed at 2 cm.

69. On New Year's Eve, a network TV camera is focusing on the descent of a lighted ball from the top of a building that is 600 ft away. The ball is falling at the rate of 20 ft/min. At what rate is the angle of elevation of the camera's line of sight changing with respect to time when the ball is 800 ft from the ground?

70. Suppose f is a differentiable function whose derivative satisfies $f'(x) = 2x^2 + 3$. Find $\dfrac{d}{dx} f(x^3 - 1)$.

71. Suppose f is a differentiable function such that $f'(x) = x^2 + x$. Find $\dfrac{d}{dx} f(x^2 + x)$.

72. Let $f(x) = 3x^2 + 1$ for all x. Use the chain rule to find $\dfrac{d}{dx}(f \circ f)(x)$.

73. Let $f(x) = \sin 2x + \cos 3x$ and $g(x) = x^2$. Use the chain rule to find $\dfrac{d}{dx}(f \circ g)(x)$.

74. Let $f(x) = \begin{cases} x \sin \dfrac{1}{x} & \text{if } x \neq 0 \\ 0 & \text{if } x = 0 \end{cases}$. Use the definition of the derivative to find $f'(0)$, if it exists.

75. A car and a truck leave an intersection at the same time. The car travels north at 60 mi/h and the truck travels east at 45 mi/h. How fast is the distance between them changing after 45 minutes?

76. A spherical balloon is being filled with air in such a way that its radius is increasing at a constant rate of 2 cm/s. At what rate is the volume of the balloon increasing at the instant when its surface has area 4π cm^2?

77. Suppose the total cost of producing x units of a particular commodity is

$$C(x) = \tfrac{2}{5}x^2 + 3x + 10$$

and that each unit of the commodity can be sold for

$$p(x) = \tfrac{1}{5}(45 - x)$$

dollars.

a. What is the marginal cost?

b. What is the price when the marginal cost is 23?

c. Estimate the cost of producing the 11th unit.

d. Find the actual cost of producing the 11th unit.

78. A block of ice in the shape of a cube originally having volume 1,000 cm^3 is melting in such a way that the length of each of its edges is decreasing at the rate of 1 cm/hr. At what rate is its surface area decreasing at the time its volume is 27 cm^3? Assume that the block of ice maintains its cubical shape.

79. Show that the rate of change of the area of a circle with respect to its radius is equal to the circumference.

80. A charged particle is projected into a linear accelerator. The particle undergoes a constant acceleration that changes its velocity from 1,200 m/s to 6,000 m/s in 2×10^{-3} seconds. Find the acceleration of the particle.

81. A rocket is launched vertically from a point on level ground that is 3,000 feet from an observer with binoculars. If the rocket is rising vertically at the rate of 750 ft/s at the instant it is 4,000 ft above the ground, how fast must the observer change the angle of elevation of her line of sight in order to keep the rocket in sight at that instant?

82. **Modeling Problem** Assume that a certain artery in the body is modeled by a circular tube whose cross section has radius 1.2 mm. Fat deposits are observed to build up uniformly on the inside wall of the artery. Find the rate at which the cross-sectional area of the artery is decreasing relative to the thickness of the fat deposit at the instant when the deposit is 0.3 mm thick.

83. A processor who sells a certain raw material has analyzed the market and determined that the unit price should be modeled by the formula

$$p(x) = 60 - x^2$$

(thousand dollars) for x tons ($0 \le x \le 7$) produced. Estimate the change in the unit price that accompanies each change in sales:

a. from 2 tons to 2.05 tons

b. from 1 ton to 1.1 tons

c. from 3 tons to 2.95 tons

84. A company sends out a truck to deliver its products. To estimate costs, the manager models gas consumption by the formula

$$G(x) = \frac{1}{300}\left(\frac{1,500}{x} + x\right)$$

gal/mi, under the assumption that the truck travels at a constant rate of x mi/h ($x \ge 5$). The driver is paid \$16 per hour to drive the truck 300 mi. Gasoline costs \$2 per gallon.

a. Find an expression for the total cost $C(x)$ of the trip.

b. Use differentials to estimate the additional cost if the truck is driven at 57 mi/h instead of 55 mi/h.

85. A viewer standing at ground level and 30 ft from a platform watches a balloon rise from that platform (at the same height as the viewer's eyes) at the constant rate of 3 ft/s. (See Figure 3.68) How fast is the angle of sight between the viewer and the object changing at the instant when $\theta = \frac{\pi}{4}$?

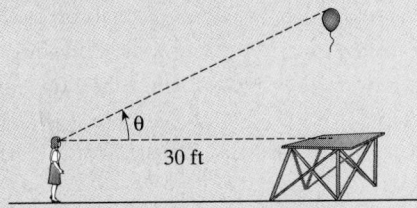

Figure 3.68   Problem 85

86. A lighthouse is 4,000 ft from a straight shore. Watching the beam on the shore from the point P on the shore that is closest to the lighthouse, an observer notes that the light is moving at the rate of 3 ft/s when it is 1,000 ft from P. How fast is the light revolving at this instant (in radians per second)?

87. A light is 4 miles from a straight shoreline. The light revolves at the rate of 2 rev/min. Find the speed of the spot of light along the shore when the light spot is 2 miles past the point on the shore closest to the source of light.

88. A particle of mass m moves along the x-axis. The velocity $v = \dfrac{dx}{dt}$ and position $x = x(t)$ satisfy the equation

$$m(v^2 - v_0^2) = k(x_0^2 - x^2)$$

where k, x_0, and v_0 are positive constants. The force F acting on the object is defined by $F = ma$, where a is the object's acceleration. Show that $F = -kx$.

89. The equation $\dfrac{d^2s}{dt^2} + ks = 0$ is called a **differential equation of simple harmonic motion.** Let A be any number. Show that the function $s(t) = A \sin 2t$ satisfies the equation

$$\frac{d^2s}{dt^2} + 4s = 0$$

90. Suppose $L(x)$ is a function with the property that $L'(x) = x^{-1}$. Use the chain rule to find the derivatives of the following functions.

a. $f(x) = L(x^2)$ **b.** $f(x) = L\left(\dfrac{1}{x}\right)$

c. $f(x) = L\left(\dfrac{2}{3\sqrt{x}}\right)$ **d.** $f(x) = L\left(\dfrac{2x+1}{1-x}\right)$

91. Let f and g be differentiable functions such that $f[g(x)] = x$ and $g[f(x)] = x$ for all x (that is, f and g are inverses). Show that

$$\frac{dg}{dx} = \frac{1}{\dfrac{df}{dx}}$$

92. A baseball player is stealing second base, as shown in Figure 3.69.

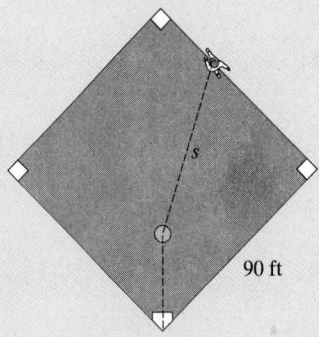

Figure 3.69   Baseball diamond

He runs at 30 ft/s and when he is 25 ft from second base, the catcher, while standing at home plate, throws the ball toward the base at a speed of 120 ft/s. At what rate is the distance between the ball and the player changing at the time the ball is thrown?

93. A connection rod $\overline{OA}$ 2 m long is rotating counterclockwise in a plane about O at the rate of 3 rev/s, as shown in Figure 3.70.

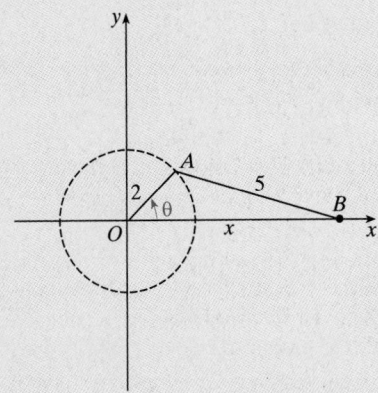

Figure 3.70   Connection rod

The rod $\overline{AB}$ is attached to $\overline{OA}$ at A, and the end B slides along the x-axis. Suppose $\overline{AB}$ is 5 meters long. What are the velocity and the acceleration of the motion of the point B along the x-axis?

94. The ideal gas law states that for an ideal gas, pressure P is given by the formula $P = kT/V$, where V is the volume, T is the temperature, and k is a constant. Suppose the temperature is kept fixed at $100°C$, and the pressure decreases at the rate of 7 lb/in.^{2} per min. At what rate is the volume changing at the instant the pressure is 25 lb/in.^{2} and the volume is 30 in.^{3}?

95. **Putnam Examination Problem**   Suppose $f(x) = ax^2 + bx + c$, where a, b, and c are real numbers and $|f(x)| \leq 1$ for $x \leq 1$.

Show that $|f'(x)| \leq 4$ for $|x| \leq 1$.

96. **Putnam Examination Problem**   A point P is taken on the curve $y = x^3$. The tangent line at P meets the curve again at Q. Prove that the slope of the curve at Q is four times the slope at P.

97. **Putnam Examination Problem**   A particle of unit mass moves on a straight line under the action of a force that is a function $f(v)$ of the velocity v of the particle, but the form of this function is not known. A motion is observed, and the distance x covered in time t is found to be related to t by the formula $x = at + bt^2 + ct^3$, where a, b, and c have numerical values determined by observation of the motion. Find the function $f(v)$ for the range of v covered by this experiment.

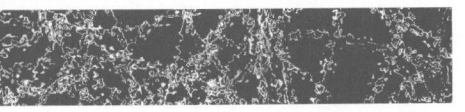
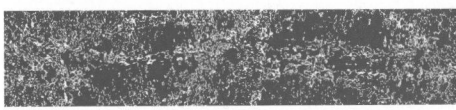

Group Research Project

Chaos

This fractal image is an example of what is called mathematical chaos.

An exciting new topic in mathematics attempts to bring order to the universe by considering disorder. This topic is called **chaos theory**, and it shows how structures of incredible complexity and disorder really exhibit beauty and order.

Water flowing through a pipe offers one of the simplest physical models of chaos. Pressure is applied to the end of the pipe and the water flows in straight lines. More pressure increases the speed of the laminar flow until the pressure reaches a critical value, and a radically new situation evolves—turbulence. A simple laminar flow suddenly changes to a flow of beautiful complexity consisting of swirls within swirls. Before turbulence, the path of any particle was quite predictable. After a minute change in the pressure, turbulence occurs and predictability is lost. **Chaos** is concerned with systems in which minute changes suddenly transform predictability into unpredictability.*

For this research project begin with

$$f(x) = x^3 - x = x(x-1)(x+1)$$

Use the Newton–Raphson method to investigate what happens as you change the starting value, x_0, to solve $f(x) = 0$. What would you select as a starting value? Two important x-values in our study are

$$s_3 = \frac{1}{\sqrt{3}} \qquad \text{and} \qquad s_5 = \frac{1}{\sqrt{5}}$$

One would not want to pick x_0 as either $\pm s_3$. Why not? Also, what happens if one picks $x_0 = s_5$? That is, what are $x_1, x_2, \ldots$?

Generate a good plot of $f(x)$ on $[-2, 2]$. Explain from the plots why you would *expect* that an initial value $x_0 > s_3$ would lead to $\lim_{n \to +\infty} x_n = 1$. (Also, by symmetry, $x_0 < -s_3$ leads to $\lim_{n \to +\infty} x_n = -1$.)

Explain why if $|x_0| < s_5$, you would expect $x_n \to 0$. Numerically verify your assertions. Now to see the "chaos," use the following x_0 values and take 6 to 10 iterations, until convergence occurs, and report what happens: 0.448955; 0.447503; 0.447262; 0.447222; 0.4472215; 0.4472213. Write a paper telling what you see and why.

Extended paper for further study Attempt to define chaos. Your paper should include, but not be limited to, answers to the questions on this page. Some references (to get you started) are listed:

Chaos: Making a New Science, James Gleick, Penguin Books, 1988.

Chaos and Fractals: New Frontiers of Science, H. O. Peitgen, H. Jürgens, and D. Saupe, Springer-Verlag, 1992.

Newton's Method and Fractal Patterns, Phillip D. Straffin, Jr., UMAP Module 716, COMAP, 1991.

*Thanks to Jack Wadhams of Golden West College for this paragraph.

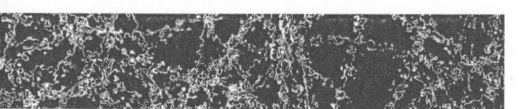

4

Additional Applications
of the Derivative

PREVIEW

In Chapter 3, we used the derivative to find tangent lines and to compute rates of change. The primary goal of this chapter is to examine the use of calculus in curve sketching, optimization, and other applications.

PERSPECTIVE

Homing pigeons and certain other birds are known to avoid flying over large bodies of water whenever possible. The reason for this behavior is not entirely known. However, it is reasonable to speculate that it may have something to do with minimizing the energy expended in flight, because the air over a lake is often "heavier" than that over land. Suppose a pigeon is released from a boat at point B on the lake shown in the accompanying figure.* It will fly to its loft at point L on the lakeshore by heading across water to a point P on the shore and then flying directly from P to L along the shore. If the pigeon expends e_ω units of energy per mile over water and e_L units over land, where should P be located to minimize the total energy expended in flight?†

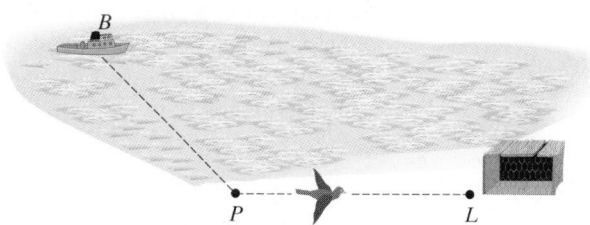

Optimization (finding the maximum or minimum values) is one of the most important applications we will study in calculus, from maximizing profit and minimizing cost to maximizing the strength of a structure and minimizing the distance traveled. Optimization problems are considered in depth in Sections 4.6 and 4.7.

---

*Edward Batschelet, *Introduction to Mathematics for Life Scientists*, 2nd ed. (New York: Springer-Verlag, 1979), pp. 276–277.

†See Problem 32, Section 4.7.

4.1 Extreme Values of a Continuous Function

IN THIS SECTION extreme value theorem, relative extrema, absolute extrema, optimization

EXTREME VALUE THEOREM

One of the principal goals of calculus is to investigate the behavior of various functions. As part of this investigation, we will be laying the groundwork for solving a large class of problems that involve finding the maximum or minimum value of a function, if one exists. Such problems are called **optimization problems**. We begin by introducing some useful terminology.

Absolute Maximum and Minimum

> Let f be a function defined on an interval I that contains the number c. Then
>
> $f(c)$ is an **absolute maximum** of f on I if $f(c) \geq f(x)$ for all x in I
>
> $f(c)$ is an **absolute minimum** of f on I if $f(c) \leq f(x)$ for all x in I

Sometimes we just use the terms *maximum* and/or *minimum* if the context is clear. Together, the absolute maximum and minimum of f on the interval I are called the **extreme values**, or the **absolute extrema,** of f on I. A function does not necessarily have extreme values on a given interval. For instance, the continuous function $g(x) = x$ has neither a maximum nor a minimum on the open interval $(0, 1)$, as shown in Figure 4.1a.

The discontinuous function defined by

$$h(x) = \begin{cases} x^2 & \text{for } x \neq 0 \\ 1 & \text{for } x = 0 \end{cases}$$

has a maximum which is on the closed interval $[-1, 1]$, but no minimum, as shown in Figure 4.1b. Incidentally, this graph also illustrates the fact that a function may assume an absolute extremum at more than one point. In this case, the maximum occurs at the points $(-1, 1)$, $(0, 1)$, and $(1, 1)$. If a function f is continuous and the interval I is closed and bounded, it can be shown that both an absolute maximum and an absolute minimum *must* occur. This result, called the **extreme value theorem**, plays an important role in our work.

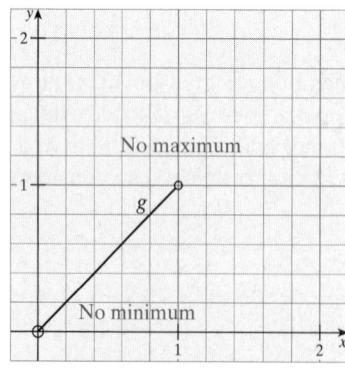

a. The continuous function $g(x) = x$ has no extrema on the open interval $(0, 1)$.

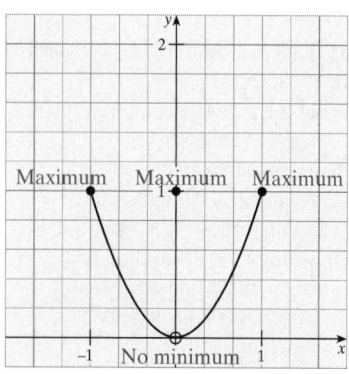

b. The discontinuous function h has a maximum, but not a minimum on the closed interval $[-1, 1]$.

Figure 4.1 Functions that lack one or both extreme values

THEOREM 4.1   The extreme value theorem

A function f has both an absolute maximum and an absolute minimum on any closed, bounded interval $[a, b]$ where it is continuous.

Proof   Even though this result may seem quite reasonable (see Figure 4.2), its proof requires concepts beyond the scope of this text and will be omitted.

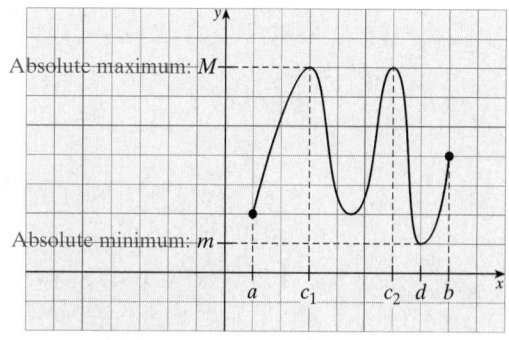

Absolute maximum at $x = c_1$ and $x = c_2$
Absolute minimum at $x = d$

Figure 4.2   Extreme value theorem   ❏

If f is discontinuous or the interval is not both closed and bounded, you cannot conclude that f has both a largest and smallest value. You will be asked for appropriate counterexamples in the problem set. Sometimes there are extreme values even when the conditions of the theorem are not satisfied, but if the conditions hold, the extreme values are guaranteed.

Note that the maximum of a function occurs at the highest point on its graph and the minimum occurs at the lowest point. These properties are illustrated in Example 1.

EXAMPLE 1   Extreme values of a continuous function

The graph of a function f is shown in Figure 4.3. Locate the extreme values of f defined on the closed interval $[a, b]$.

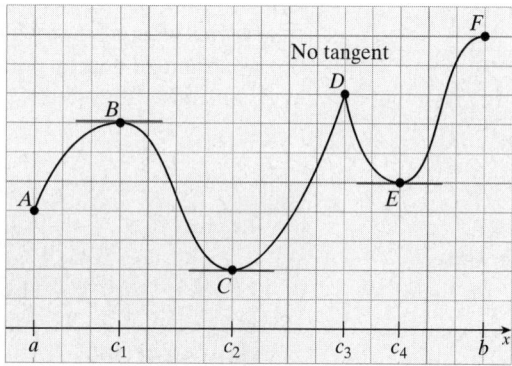

Figure 4.3   A continuous function on a closed interval $[a, b]$

Solution

The highest point on the graph occurs at the right endpoint F, and the lowest point occurs at C. Thus, the absolute maximum is $f(b)$, and the absolute minimum is $f(c_2)$.

■

In Example 1, the existence of maxima and minima as required by the extreme value theorem may seem obvious, but there are times when it seems that the extreme value theorem fails. If this occurs, you need to see which of the conditions of the extreme value theorem are not satisfied. Consider Example 2.

EXAMPLE 2   Conditions of the extreme value theorem

In each case, explain why the given function does not contradict the extreme value theorem:

a. $f(x) = \begin{cases} 2x & \text{if } 0 \le x < 1 \\ 1 & \text{if } 1 \le x \le 2 \end{cases}$ **b.** $g(x) = x^2$ on $0 < x \le 2$

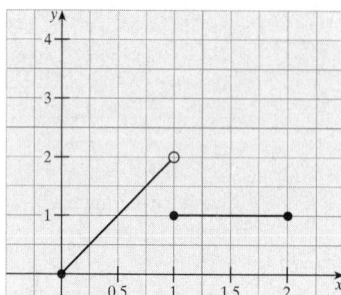

Does not have a maximum value.

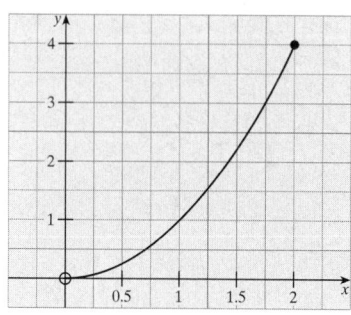

g does not have a minimum value
(but it does have a maximum value).

Solution

a. The function f has no maximum. It takes on all values less than, but arbitrarily close to, 2. However, it never reaches the value 2. This function does not contradict the extreme value theorem because f is not continuous on $[0, 2]$.

b. Although the functional values of $g(x)$ become arbitrarily small as x approaches 0, $g(x)$ never reaches the value 0 so g has no minimum. The function g is continuous on the interval $(0, 2]$, but the extreme value theorem is not contradicted because the interval is not closed. ■

RELATIVE EXTREMA

Typically, the extrema of a continuous function occur either at endpoints of the interval or at points where the graph has a "peak" or a "valley" (points where the graph is higher or lower than all nearby points). For example, the function f in Figure 4.3 has "peaks" at B, D, and "valleys" at C, E. Peaks and valleys are what we call *relative extrema*.

Relative Maximum and Relative Minimum

> The function f is said to have a **relative maximum** at the point c if $f(c) \ge f(x)$ for all x in an open interval containing c. Likewise, f is said to have a **relative minimum** at d if $f(d) \le f(x)$ for all x in an open interval containing d. Collectively, relative maxima and relative minima are called **relative extrema**.

WARNING   Note that an extremum at an endpoint is, by definition, not a relative extremum, since there is not an open interval around the endpoint entirely contained in the domain of the function.

Next we will formulate a procedure for finding relative extrema. By looking at Figure 4.3, we see that there are horizontal tangents at B, C, and E, while no tangent can be defined at the point D. This suggests that the relative extrema of f occur either where the derivative is zero (horizontal tangent) or where the derivative does not exist (no tangent). This notion leads us to the following definition.

Critical Numbers and Critical Points

> Suppose f is defined at c and either $f'(c) = 0$ or $f'(c)$ does not exist. Then the number c is called a **critical number** of f, and the point $P(c, f(c))$ on the graph of f is called a **critical point**.

WARNING   Note that if $f(c)$ is not defined, then c **cannot** be a critical number.

EXAMPLE 3   Finding critical numbers

Find the critical numbers for the given functions.

a. $f(x) = 4x^3 - 5x^2 - 8x + 20$

b. $f(x) = \dfrac{e^x}{x - 2}$ Note that $x \neq 2$.

c. $f(x) = 2\sqrt{x}(6 - x)$ Note that $x \geq 0$.

Solution

a. $f'(x) = 12x^2 - 10x - 8$ is defined for all values of x. Solve

$$12x^2 - 10x - 8 = 0$$

$$2(3x - 4)(2x + 1) = 0$$

$$x = \tfrac{4}{3}, \ -\tfrac{1}{2} \qquad \textit{These are the critical numbers.}$$

b. $f'(x) = \dfrac{(x - 2)e^x - e^x(1)}{(x - 2)^2} = \dfrac{e^x(x - 3)}{(x - 2)^2}$ Note that $x \neq 2$.

The derivative is not defined at $x = 2$, but f is not defined at 2 either, so $x = 2$ is not a critical number. The actual critical numbers are found by solving $f'(x) = 0$:

$$\dfrac{e^x(x - 3)}{(x - 2)^2} = 0$$

$$x = 3 \quad \textit{This is the only critical number since } e^x > 0.$$

c. Write $f(x) = 12x^{1/2} - 2x^{3/2}$ so $f'(x) = 6x^{-1/2} - 3x^{1/2}$. The derivative is not defined at $x = 0$. We have $f(0) = 12(0)^{1/2} - 2(0)^{3/2} = 0$, so we see that f is defined at $x = 0$, which means that $x = 0$ is a critical number. For other critical numbers, solve $f'(x) = 0$:

$$6x^{-1/2} - 3x^{1/2} = 0$$

$$3x^{-1/2}(2 - x) = 0$$

$$x = 2$$

The critical numbers are $x = 0, 2$. ∎

EXAMPLE 4   Critical numbers and critical points

Find the critical numbers and the critical points for the function

$$f(x) = (x - 1)^2(x + 2)$$

Solution

Because the function f is a polynomial, we know that it is continuous and that its derivative exists for all x. Thus, we find the critical numbers by using the product rule and extended power rule to solve the equation $f'(x) = 0$:

$$f'(x) = (x - 1)^2(1) + 2(x - 1)(1)(x + 2)$$

$$= (x - 1)[(x - 1) + 2(x + 2)]$$

$$= 3(x - 1)(x + 1)$$

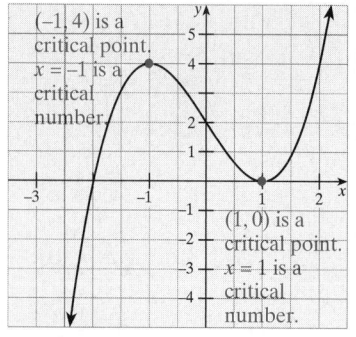

Figure 4.4 The graph of
$f(x) = (x-1)^2(x+2)$

The critical numbers are $x = \pm 1$. To find the critical points, we need to find the y-coordinate for each critical number.

$$f(1) = (1-1)^2(1+2) = 0$$
$$f(-1) = (-1-1)^2(-1+2) = 4$$

Thus, the critical points are $(1, 0)$ and $(-1, 4)$. The graph of $f(x) = (x-1)^2(x+2)$ is shown in Figure 4.4. ∎

Note how the relative extrema occur at the critical points. Our observation that the relative extrema occur only at points on a graph where there is either a horizontal tangent line or no tangent at all is equivalent to the following result.

THEOREM 4.2   Critical number theorem

If a continuous function f has a relative extremum at c, then c must be a critical number of f.

> ➡ **What This Says**   If a point is a relative maximum or a relative minimum value for a function, then either the derivative is 0 or the derivative does not exist at that point. We do not claim the converse.

Proof   Since f has a relative extremum at c, $f(c)$ is defined. If $f'(c)$ does not exist, then c is a critical number by definition. We will show that if $f'(c)$ exists and a relative maximum occurs at c, then $f'(c) = 0$. Our approach will be to examine the difference quotient. (The case where $f'(c)$ exists and a relative minimum occurs at c is handled similarly in Problem 61.)

Because a relative maximum occurs at c, we have $f(c) \geq f(x)$ for every number x in an open interval (a, b) containing c. Therefore, if Δx not equal to zero is small enough so $c + \Delta x$ is in (a, b), then

$$f(c) \geq f(c + \Delta x) \qquad \text{Because a relative maximum occurs at } c$$

$$f(c) - f(c + \Delta x) \geq 0$$
$$f(c + \Delta x) - f(c) \leq 0 \qquad \text{Multiply both sides by } -1, \text{ reversing the inequality.}$$

For the next step we want to divide both sides by Δx (to write the left side as a difference quotient). However, as this is an inequality, we need to consider two possibilities:

1. Suppose $\Delta x > 0$ (the inequality does not reverse):

$$\frac{f(c + \Delta x) - f(c)}{\Delta x} \leq 0 \qquad \text{Divide both sides by } \Delta x.$$

Now we take the limit of both sides as Δx approaches 0 from the right (because Δx is positive).

$$\underbrace{\lim_{\Delta x \to 0^+} \frac{f(c + \Delta x) - f(c)}{\Delta x}}_{f'(c)} \leq \underbrace{\lim_{\Delta x \to 0^+} 0}_{0}$$

$$f'(c) \leq 0$$

2. Next, suppose $\Delta x < 0$ (the inequality reverses). Then

$$\frac{f(c + \Delta x) - f(c)}{\Delta x} \geq 0$$

This time we take the limit of both sides as Δx approaches 0 from the left (because Δx is negative).

$$\lim_{\Delta x \to 0^-} \frac{f(c + \Delta x) - f(c)}{\Delta x} \geq \lim_{\Delta x \to 0^-} 0$$
$$f'(c) \geq 0$$

Because we have shown that $f'(c) \leq 0$ and $f'(c) \geq 0$, it follows that $f'(c) = 0$. ❏

WARNING Theorem 4.2 tells us that a relative extremum of a continuous function f can occur *only* at a critical number, but it does not say that a relative extremum must occur at each critical number.

For example, if $f(x) = x^3$, then $f'(x) = 3x^2$ and $f'(0) = 0$, so 0 is a critical number. But there is no relative extremum at $c = 0$ on the graph of f because the graph is rising for $x < 0$ and also for $x > 0$, as shown in Figure 4.5a. It is also quite possible for a continuous function g to have no relative extremum at a point c where $g'(x)$ does not exist (see Figure 4.5b).

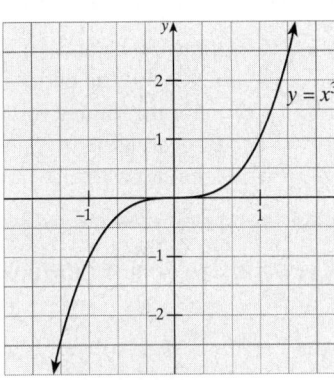 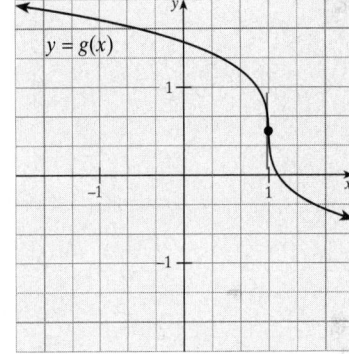

a. The graph of $f(x) = x^3$ No relative extremum occurs at $c = 0$ even though $f'(0) = 0$.

b. Although $g'(1)$ does not exist, no relative extremum occurs at $c = 1$.

Figure 4.5 A relative extremum may not occur at each critical number.

EXAMPLE 5 Critical numbers where the derivative does not exist

Find the critical numbers for $f(x) = |x + 1|$ on $[-5, 5]$. The graph is shown in Figure 4.6.

Solution

If $x > -1$, then $f(x) = x + 1$ and $f'(x) = 1$. However, if $x < -1$, then $f(x) = -x - 1$ and $f'(x) = -1$. We need to check what happens at $x = -1$.

$$f'(-1) = \lim_{\Delta x \to 0} \frac{f(-1 + \Delta x + 1) - f(-1 + 1)}{\Delta x}$$
$$= \lim_{\Delta x \to 0} \frac{|\Delta x| - |0|}{\Delta x}$$
$$= \lim_{\Delta x \to 0} \frac{|\Delta x|}{\Delta x}$$

Figure 4.6 Graph of $f(x) = |x + 1|$ on $[-5, 5]$

We consider the left and right limits:

$$\lim_{\Delta x \to 0^+} \frac{|\Delta x|}{\Delta x} = \lim_{\Delta x \to 0^+} \frac{\Delta x}{\Delta x} = 1$$

and

$$\lim_{\Delta x \to 0^-} \frac{|\Delta x|}{\Delta x} = \lim_{\Delta x \to 0^-} \frac{-\Delta x}{\Delta x} = -1$$

Because these are not the same, this limit does not exist and thus the function $f(x) = |x + 1|$ is not differentiable at $x = -1$. Because $f(-1)$ is defined, it follows that -1 is the only critical number.   ∎

ABSOLUTE EXTREMA

Suppose we are looking for the absolute extrema of a continuous function f on the closed, bounded interval $[a, b]$. Theorem 4.1 tells us that these extrema exist and Theorem 4.2 enables us to narrow the list of "candidates" for points where extrema can occur from the entire interval $[a, b]$ to just the endpoints $x = a$, $x = b$, and the critical numbers between a and b. This suggests the following procedure.

Procedure for Finding Absolute Extrema

To find the absolute extrema of a continuous function f on $[a, b]$:

Step 1.   Compute $f'(x)$ and find all critical numbers of f on $[a, b]$.
Step 2.   Evaluate f at the endpoints a and b and at each critical number c.
Step 3.   Compare the values in step 2.
            The largest value of f is the absolute maximum of f on $[a, b]$.
            The smallest value of f is the absolute minimum of f on $[a, b]$.

Figure 4.7 shows some of the possibilities in the application of this procedure.

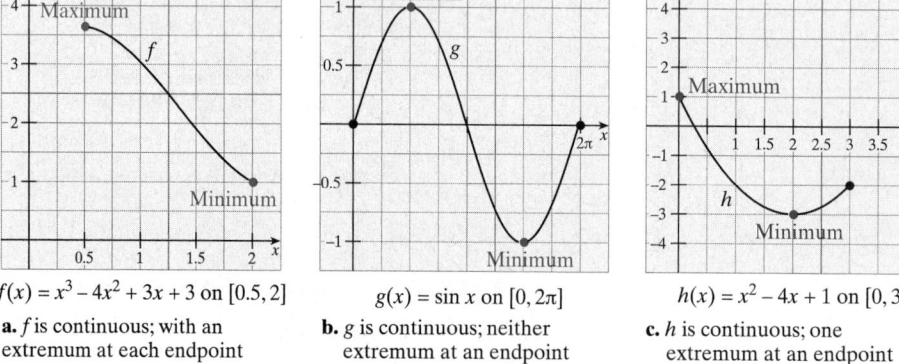

$f(x) = x^3 - 4x^2 + 3x + 3$ on $[0.5, 2]$

a. f is continuous; with an extremum at each endpoint

$g(x) = \sin x$ on $[0, 2\pi]$

b. g is continuous; neither extremum at an endpoint

$h(x) = x^2 - 4x + 1$ on $[0, 3]$

c. h is continuous; one extremum at an endpoint

Figure 4.7   Absolute extrema

EXAMPLE 6   Absolute extrema of a polynomial function

Find the absolute extrema of the function defined by the equation $f(x) = x^4 - 2x^2 + 3$ on the closed interval $[-1, 2]$.

Solution

Because f is a polynomial function, it is continuous on the closed interval $[-1, 2]$. Theorem 4.1 tells us that there must be an absolute maximum and an absolute minimum on the interval.

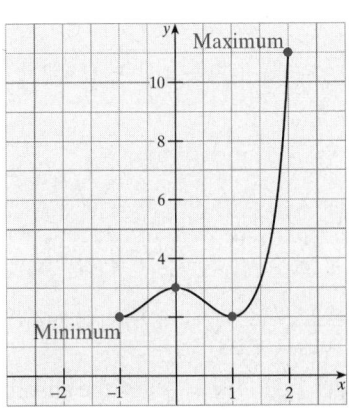

Figure 4.8 The graph of $f(x) = x^4 - 2x^2 + 3$ on $[-1, 2]$

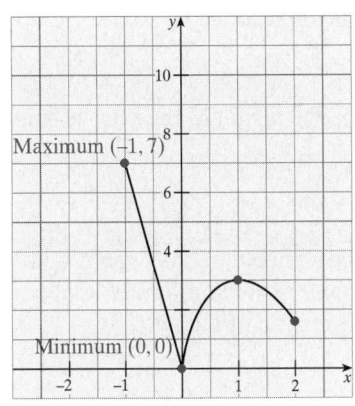

Figure 4.9 Graph of $f(x) = 5x^{2/3} - 2x^{5/3}$ on $[-1, 2]$

Step 1. $f'(x) = 4x^3 - 2(2x)$
$$= 4x(x^2 - 1)$$
$$= 4x(x - 1)(x + 1)$$
The critical numbers are $x = 0, 1$, and -1.

Step 2. Values at endpoints: $f(-1) = 2$
$$f(2) = 11$$
Critical numbers: $f(0) = 3$
$$f(1) = 2$$

Step 3. The absolute maximum of f occurs at $x = 2$ and is $f(2) = 11$; the absolute minimum of f occurs at $x = 1$ and $x = -1$ and are $f(1) = f(-1) = 2$. The graph of f is shown in Figure 4.8. ∎

EXAMPLE 7   Absolute extrema when the derivative does not exist

Find the absolute extrema of $f(x) = x^{2/3}(5 - 2x)$ on the interval $[-1, 2]$.

Solution

Step 1. To find the derivative, rewrite the given function as $f(x) = 5x^{2/3} - 2x^{5/3}$. Then
$$f'(x) = \tfrac{10}{3}x^{-1/3} - \tfrac{10}{3}x^{2/3} = \tfrac{10}{3}x^{-1/3}(1 - x)$$
Critical numbers are found by solving $f'(x) = 0$ and by locating the places where the derivative does not exist. First,
$$f'(x) = 0 \quad \text{when} \quad x = 1$$
Even though $f(0)$ exists, we note that $f'(x)$ does not exist at $x = 0$ (notice the division by zero when $x = 0$). Thus, the critical numbers are $x = 0$ and $x = 1$.

Step 2. Values at endpoints: $f(-1) = 7$
$$f(2) = 2^{2/3} \approx 1.587401052$$
Critical numbers: $f(0) = 0$
$$f(1) = 3$$

Step 3. The absolute maximum of f occurs at $x = -1$ and is $f(-1) = 7$; the absolute minimum of f occurs at $x = 0$ and is $f(0) = 0$. The graph of f is shown in Figure 4.9. ∎

EXAMPLE 8   Absolute extrema for a trigonometric function

Find the absolute extrema of the continuous function
$$T(x) = \tfrac{1}{2}(\sin^2 x + \cos x) + 2\sin x - x$$
on the interval $[0, \tfrac{\pi}{2}]$.

Solution

Step 1. To find where $T'(x) = 0$, we begin by finding $T'(x)$:
$$T'(x) = \tfrac{1}{2}(2\sin x \cos x - \sin x) + 2\cos x - 1$$
$$= \tfrac{1}{2}(2\sin x \cos x - \sin x + 4\cos x - 2)$$
$$= \tfrac{1}{2}[2(\cos x)(\sin x + 2) - (\sin x + 2)]$$
$$= \tfrac{1}{2}[(\sin x + 2)(2\cos x - 1)]$$
Since the factor $(\sin x + 2)$ is never zero, it follows that $T'(x) = 0$ only when $2\cos x - 1 = 0$; that is, when $x = \tfrac{\pi}{3}$. This is the only critical number in $[0, \tfrac{\pi}{2}]$.

Step 2.   Evaluate the function at the endpoints:

$$T(0) = \tfrac{1}{2}(\sin^2 0 + \cos 0) + 2\sin 0 - 0 = \tfrac{1}{2}(0 + 1) + 2(0) - 0 = 0.5$$

$$T\left(\tfrac{\pi}{2}\right) = \tfrac{1}{2}\left(\sin^2 \tfrac{\pi}{2} + \cos \tfrac{\pi}{2}\right) + 2\sin \tfrac{\pi}{2} - \tfrac{\pi}{2}$$

$$= \tfrac{1}{2}(1 + 0) + 2(1) - \tfrac{\pi}{2} = \tfrac{5}{2} - \tfrac{\pi}{2} \approx 0.9292036732$$

Evaluate the function at the critical number:

$$T\left(\tfrac{\pi}{3}\right) = \tfrac{1}{2}\left(\sin^2 \tfrac{\pi}{3} + \cos \tfrac{\pi}{3}\right) + 2\sin \tfrac{\pi}{3} - \tfrac{\pi}{3}$$

$$= \tfrac{1}{2}\left(\tfrac{3}{4} + \tfrac{1}{2}\right) + 2\left(\tfrac{\sqrt{3}}{2}\right) - \tfrac{\pi}{3} = \tfrac{5}{8} + \sqrt{3} - \tfrac{\pi}{3} \approx 1.309853256$$

Step 3.   The absolute maximum of T is approximately 1.31 at $x = \tfrac{\pi}{3}$ and the absolute minimum of T is 0.5 at $x = 0$.   ■

OPTIMIZATION

In our next two examples, we examine applications involving optimization. Such problems are investigated in more depth in Sections 4.6 and 4.7.

EXAMPLE 9   An applied maximum value problem

A box with a square base is constructed so that the length of one side of the base plus the height is 10 in. What is the largest possible volume of such a box?

Solution

We let b be the length of one side of the base and h be the height of the box, as shown in Figure 4.10. The volume, V, is

$$V = b^2 h$$

Because our methods apply only to functions of one variable, it may seem that we cannot deal with V as a function of two variables. However, we know that $b + h = 10$; therefore, $h = 10 - b$, and we can now write V as a function of b alone:

$$V(b) = b^2(10 - b)$$

The domain is not stated, but for physical reasons we must have $b \geq 0$ and $10 - b = h \geq 0$, so that $0 \leq b \leq 10$. Figure 4.10 shows the volume for various choices of b.

Now, find the value of b that produces the maximum volume. First, we find the critical numbers. Note that V is a polynomial function, so the derivative exists everywhere in the domain. Write $V(b) = 10b^2 - b^3$ and find $V'(b) = 20b - 3b^2$. Then

$$V'(b) = 0$$
$$20b - 3b^2 = 0$$
$$b(20 - 3b) = 0$$
$$b = 0, \ \tfrac{20}{3}$$

Checking the endpoints and the critical numbers, we have

$$V(0) = 0$$
$$V(10) = 10^2(10 - 10) = 0$$
$$V\left(\tfrac{20}{3}\right) = \left(\tfrac{20}{3}\right)^2\left(10 - \tfrac{20}{3}\right) = \tfrac{4,000}{27}$$

Thus, the largest value for the volume V is $\tfrac{4,000}{27} \approx 148.1$ in.^{3}. It occurs when the square base has a side of length $\tfrac{20}{3}$ in. and the height is $h = 10 - \tfrac{20}{3} = \tfrac{10}{3}$ in.   ■

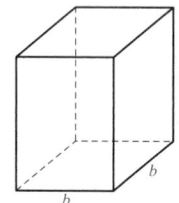

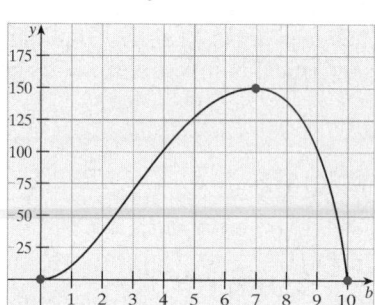

Figure 4.10   Volume of a box

Alternatively, we could have solved the problem with V as a function of h:
$V(h) = (10 - h)^2 h, 0 \leq h \leq 10$, with the same result. We must write V as a function of one variable so that we can find its derivative.

EXAMPLE 10   Maximum and minimum velocity of a moving particle

A particle moves along the s-axis with position

$$s(t) = t^4 - 8t^3 + 18t^2 + 60t - 8$$

Find the largest and smallest values of its velocity for $1 \leq t \leq 5$.

Solution

The velocity is

$$v(t) = s'(t) = 4t^3 - 24t^2 + 36t + 60$$

(**Note**: v is a polynomial function, so it has a derivative for all t.) To find the largest value of $v(t)$, we compute the derivative of v:

$$v'(t) = 12t^2 - 48t + 36$$
$$= 12(t-1)(t-3)$$

Setting $v'(t) = 0$, we find that the critical numbers of $v(t)$ are $t = 1, 3$. Now we evaluate v at the critical numbers and endpoints.

$t = 1$ is both a critical number and an endpoint:

$$v(1) = 4(1)^3 - 24(1)^2 + 36(1) + 60 = 76$$

$t = 5$ is an endpoint:

$$v(5) = 4(5)^3 - 24(5)^2 + 36(5) + 60 = 140$$

$t = 3$ is a critical number:

$$v(3) = 4(3)^3 - 24(3)^2 + 36(3) + 60 = 60$$

The largest value of the velocity is 140 at the endpoint where $t = 5$, and the smallest value is 60 when $t = 3$.   ∎

4.1   PROBLEM SET

Ⓐ *In Problems 1–14, find the critical numbers for each continuous function on the given closed, bounded interval, and then tell whether each yields a minimum, maximum, or neither.*

1. $f(x) = 5 + 10x - x^2$ on $[-3, 3]$
2. $f(x) = 10 + 6x - x^2$ on $[-4, 4]$
3. $f(x) = x^3 - 3x^2$ on $[-1, 3]$
4. $f(t) = t^4 - 8t^2$ on $[-3, 3]$
5. $f(x) = x^3$ on $\left[-\frac{1}{2}, 1\right]$
6. $g(x) = x^3 - 3x$ on $[-2, 2]$
7. $f(x) = x^5 - x^4$ on $[-1, 1]$
8. $g(t) = 3t^5 - 20t^3$ on $[-1, 2]$
9. $h(t) = te^{-t}$ on $[0, 2]$
10. $s(x) = \dfrac{\ln \sqrt{x}}{x}$ on $[1, 3]$
11. $f(x) = |x|$ on $[-1, 1]$
12. $f(x) = |x - 3|$ on $[-4, 4]$
13. $f(u) = \sin^2 u + \cos u$ on $[0, 2]$
14. $g(u) = \sin u - \cos u$ on $[0, \pi]$
15. **WHAT DOES THIS SAY?**   Outline a procedure for finding the absolute extrema of a continuous function on a closed, bounded interval. Include in your outline a discussion of what is meant by critical numbers.

16. **Exploration Problem**   Why is it important to check endpoints when finding an optimum value?

17. In Example 7, we found that the maximum value of $f(x) = x^{2/3}(5 - 2x)$ on $[-1, 2]$ is 7 and occurs at $x = -1$. The graph of this function on a leading brand of graphing calculator is shown:

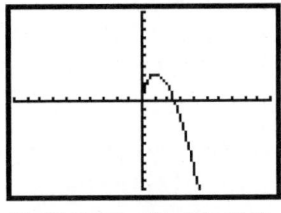

```
Y₁BX^(2/3)(5-2X)
Xmin=-10 Ymin=-10
Xmax=10  Ymax=10
Xscl=1   Yscl=1
```

This graph is not correct. Can you explain the discrepancy? It is not our intent to "make up" problems to use with a calculator, but *whenever* you use a calculator or computer to assist you with calculus, you must understand the nature of the functions with which you are working, and not rely only on the calculator or computer output.

In Problems 18–29, find the absolute maximum and absolute minimum (largest and smallest values, respectively) of each continuous function on the closed, bounded interval. If the function is not continuous on the interval, then the extreme value theorem does not apply; if this is the case, so state.

18. $f(u) = 1 - u^{2/3}$ on $[-1, 1]$

19. $g(t) = (50 + t)^{2/3}$ on $[-50, 14]$

20. $g(x) = 2x^3 - 3x^2 - 36x + 4$ on $[-4, 4]$

21. $g(x) = x^3 + 3x^2 - 24x - 4$ on $[-4, 4]$

22. $f(x) = \frac{8}{3}x^3 - 5x^2 + 8x - 5$ on $[-4, 4]$

23. $f(x) = \frac{1}{6}(x^3 - 6x^2 + 9x + 1)$ on $[0, 2]$

24. $h(x) = \tan x + \sec x$ on $[0, 2\pi]$

25. $s(t) = t \cos t - \sin t$ on $[0, 2\pi]$

26. $f(x) = e^{-x} \sin x$ on $[0, 2\pi]$

27. $g(x) = \cot^{-1}\left(\frac{x}{9}\right) - \cot^{-1}\left(\frac{x}{5}\right)$ on $[0, 10]$

28. $f(x) = \begin{cases} 9 - 4x & \text{if } x < 1 \\ -x^2 + 6x & \text{if } x \geq 1 \end{cases}$ on $[0, 4]$

29. $f(x) = \begin{cases} 8 - 3x & \text{if } x < 2 \\ -x^2 + 3x & \text{if } x \geq 2 \end{cases}$ on $[-1, 4]$

Find the required extremum in Problems 30–35, or explain why it does not exist.

30. the smallest value of $f(x) = \dfrac{1}{x(x+1)}$ on $[-0.5, 0)$

31. the smallest value of $g(x) = \dfrac{9}{x} + x - 3$ on $[1, 9]$

32. the smallest value of $g(x) = \dfrac{x^2 - 1}{x^2 + 1}$ on $[-1, 1]$

33. the largest value of $f(t) = \begin{cases} -t^2 - t + 2 & \text{if } t < 1 \\ 3 - t & \text{if } t \geq 1 \end{cases}$
on $[-2, 3]$

34. the smallest value of $f(x) = e^x + e^{-x} - x$ on $[0, 2]$

35. the largest value of $g(x) = \dfrac{\ln x}{\cos x}$ on $[2, 3]$ correct to the nearest tenth.

B *In Problems 36–43, find the extrema (that is, the absolute maxima and minima).*

36. $f(\theta) = \cos^3 \theta - 4\cos^2 \theta$ on $[-0.1, \pi + 0.1]$

37. $g(\theta) = \theta \sin \theta$ on $[-2, 2]$

38. $f(x) = 20 \sin(378\pi x)$ on $[-1, 1]$

39. $g(u) = 98u^3 - 4u^2 + 72u$ on $[0, 4]$

40. $f(w) = \sqrt{w}(w - 5)^{1/3}$ on $[0, 4]$

41. $h(x) = \sqrt[3]{x}\sqrt[3]{(x - 3)^2}$ on $[-1, 4]$

42. $h(x) = \cos^{-1} x \tan^{-1} x$ on $[0, 1]$

43. $f(x) = e^{-x}(\cos x + \sin x)$ on $[0, 2\pi]$

In Problems 44–47, find functions that satisfy the stated conditions and each of the following side conditions, if possible:

a. *a minimum but no maximum*

b. *a maximum but no minimum*

c. *both a maximum and a minimum*

d. *neither a maximum nor a minimum*

Note that in each problem, there may be a different solution function for each side condition.

44. Counterexample Problem For each of the four given conditions, find a function that is discontinuous and defined on an open interval.

45. Counterexample Problem For each of the four given conditions, find a function that is discontinuous and defined on a closed interval.

46. Counterexample Problem For each of the four given conditions, find a function that is continuous and defined on an open interval.

47. Counterexample Problem For each of the four given conditions, find a function that is continuous and defined on a closed interval.

48. Counterexample Problem Give a counterexample to show that the extreme value theorem does not necessarily apply if one disregards the condition that f be continuous.

49. Counterexample Problem Give a counterexample to show that the extreme value theorem does not necessarily apply if one disregards the condition that f be defined on a closed interval.

50. An object moves along the s-axis with position

$$s(t) = t^3 - 6t^2 - 15t + 11$$

Find the largest value of its velocity on $[0, 4]$.

51. An object moves along the s-axis with position

$$s(t) = t^4 - 2t^3 - 12t^2 + 60t - 10$$

Find the largest value of its velocity on $[0, 3]$.

52. Find two nonnegative numbers whose sum is 8 and the product of whose squares is as large as possible.

53. Find two nonnegative numbers such that the sum of one and twice the other is 12 if it is required that their product be as large as possible.

54. Under the condition that $3x + y = 80$, maximize xy^3 when $x \geq 0$, $y \geq 0$.

55. Under the condition that $3x + y = 126$, maximize xy when $x \geq 0$ and $y \geq 0$.

56. Under the condition that $2x - 5y = 18$, minimize $x^2 y$ when $x \geq 0$ and $y \leq 0$.

57. Show that if a rectangle with fixed perimeter P is to enclose the greatest area, it must be a square.

58. Find all points on the circle $x^2 + y^2 = a^2$ ($a \geq 0$) such that the product of the x-coordinate and the y-coordinate is as large as possible.

C **59. a.** Show that $\frac{1}{2}$ is the number that is greater than or equal to its own square by the greatest amount.

b. Which nonnegative number is greater than or equal to its own cube by the greatest amount?

c. Which nonnegative number is greater than or equal to its nth power ($n > 0$) by the greatest amount?

60. Given the constants $a_1, a_2, \ldots, a_n$, find the value of x that guarantees that the sum

$$S(x) = (a_1 - x)^2 + (a_2 - x)^2 + \cdots + (a_n - x)^2$$

will be as small as possible.

61. Without using Theorem 4.2, show that if $f'(c)$ exists and a

relative minimum occurs at c, then $f'(x) = 0$.

62. Explain why the function

$$f(\theta) = \frac{8}{\sin \theta} + \frac{27}{\cos \theta}$$

must attain a minimum in the open interval $(0, \frac{\pi}{2})$.

4.2 The Mean Value Theorem

IN THIS SECTION Rolle's theorem, statement and proof of the mean value theorem, the zero-derivative theorem

If a car travels smoothly down a straight, level road with average velocity 60 mi/h, we would expect the speedometer reading to be exactly 60 mi/h at least once during the trip. After all, if the car's velocity were always above 60 mi/h, the average velocity would also be above that level, and the same reasoning applies if the velocity were always below 60 mi/h. More generally, if $s(t)$ is the car's position at time t during a trip over the time interval $a \leq t \leq b$, then there should be a time $t = c$ when the velocity $s'(c)$ equals the average velocity between times $t = a$ and $t = b$. That is, for some c with $a < c < b$,

$$\underbrace{\frac{s(b) - s(a)}{b - a}}_{\text{Average velocity}} = \underbrace{s'(c)}_{\text{Instantaneous velocity}}$$

This example illustrates a result called the mean value theorem for derivatives (abbreviated MVT) that is fundamental in the study of calculus. Our proof of the MVT is based on the following special case, which is named for the French mathematician, Michel Rolle (1652–1719), who gave a version of the result in an algebra text published in 1690.*

ROLLE'S THEOREM

The key to the proof of the mean value theorem is the following result, which is really just the MVT in the special case where $f(a) = f(b)$. In terms of our car example, Rolle's theorem says that if a moving car begins and ends at the same place, then somewhere during its journey, it must reverse direction, since $\dfrac{f(b) - f(a)}{b - a} = 0$ for $f(a) = f(b)$.

THEOREM 4.3 Rolle's theorem

Suppose f is continuous on the closed interval $[a, b]$ and differentiable on the open interval (a, b). If $f(a) = f(b)$, then there exists at least one number c between a and b such that $f'(c) = 0$.

Proof To construct a formal proof, note that since f is continuous on the closed interval $[a, b]$, it follows from the extreme value theorem (Theorem 4.1) that f must have both a largest value and a smallest value on $[a, b]$. The case where f is constant on $[a, b]$ is easy since then $f'(x) = 0$ for all x in the interval (see Figure 4.11a).

---

*Incidentally, Rolle was a number theorist at heart and thoroughly distrusted the methods of calculus, which he regarded as a "collection of ingenious fallacies."

In the case where f is not constant throughout $[a, b]$, the largest and smallest values cannot be the same, and since $f(a) = f(b)$, we can conclude that at least one extreme value occurs at a number c that is not an endpoint; that is, $a < c < b$. Finally, since c is in the open interval (a, b) throughout which $f'(x)$ exists, it follows from the critical number theorem (Theorem 4.2) that $f'(c) = 0$. A graph illustrating this case is shown in Figure 4.11b.

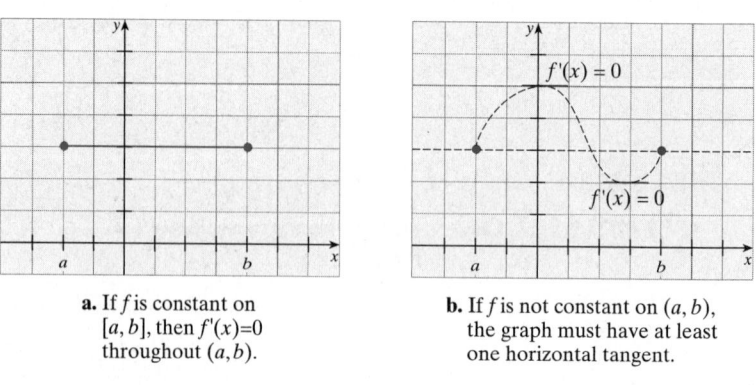

a. If f is constant on
$[a, b]$, then $f'(x)=0$
throughout (a, b).

b. If f is not constant on (a, b),
the graph must have at least
one horizontal tangent.

Figure 4.11   A geometrical interpretation of Rolle's theorem

Note: Rolle's theorem asserts only that at least one number c exists between a and b such that $f'(c) = 0$. As illustrated in Figure 4.11b, there may be more than one such number.

STATEMENT AND PROOF OF THE MEAN VALUE THEOREM

Rolle's theorem can be interpreted as saying that there is at least one number c between a and b such that the tangent line to the graph of f at the point $(c, f(c))$ is parallel to the horizontal line through the points $(a, f(a))$ and $(b, f(b))$. It is reasonable to expect a similar result to hold if the endpoints of the graph are not necessarily at the same level of the graph; that is, if the graph in Figure 4.12a is tilted as shown in Figure 4.12b. This "tilted" version can be interpreted as showing that the line segment joining points $(a, f(a))$ and $(b, f(b))$ on the graph of a differentiable function $y = f(x)$ has the same slope as the tangent line to the graph at some point c between a and b. This observation leads to the following statement of the mean value theorem.

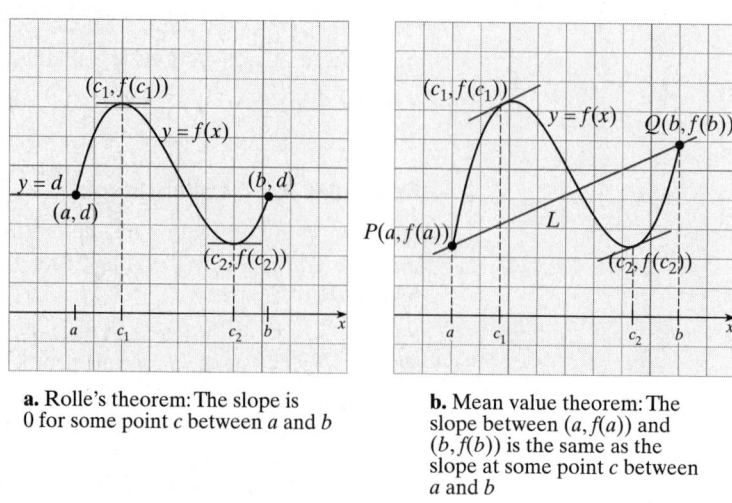

a. Rolle's theorem: The slope is
0 for some point c between a and b

b. Mean value theorem: The
slope between $(a, f(a))$ and
$(b, f(b))$ is the same as the
slope at some point c between
a and b

Figure 4.12   A geometrical comparison of Rolle's theorem with the mean value theorem

THEOREM 4.4 **The mean value theorem for derivatives (MVT)**

If f is continuous on the closed interval $[a, b]$ and differentiable on the open interval (a, b), then there exists in (a, b) at least one number c such that

$$\frac{f(b) - f(a)}{b - a} = f'(c)$$

Proof Our strategy will be to apply Rolle's theorem to a function g related to f; namely the function

$$g(x) = \frac{f(b) - f(a)}{b - a}(x - a) + f(a) - f(x)$$

for $a \leq x \leq b$. Because f satisfies the hypotheses of the MVT, the function g is also continuous on the closed interval $[a, b]$ and differentiable on the open interval (a, b). In addition, we find that

$$g(a) = \left[\frac{f(b) - f(a)}{b - a}\right](a - a) + f(a) - f(a) = 0$$

$$g(b) = \left[\frac{f(b) - f(a)}{b - a}\right](b - a) + f(a) - f(b)$$

$$= [f(b) - f(a)] + f(a) - f(b) = 0$$

Thus, g satisfies the hypotheses of Rolle's theorem, so there exists at least one number c between a and b for which $g'(c) = 0$. Differentiating the function g, we find that

$$g'(x) = \frac{f(b) - f(a)}{b - a} - f'(x)$$

Because $g'(c) = 0$, we have

$$0 = g'(c) = \frac{f(b) - f(a)}{b - a} - f'(c)$$

This means that

$$f'(c) = \frac{f(b) - f(a)}{b - a}$$

as required. ❏

The MVT asserts the existence of a number, c, but does not tell us how to find it. The following example illustrates one method for finding such a number c.

EXAMPLE 1 **Finding the number c specified by the MVT**

Show that the function $f(x) = x^3 + x^2$ satisfies the hypotheses of the MVT on the closed interval $[1, 2]$, and find a number c between 1 and 2 so that

$$f'(c) = \frac{f(2) - f(1)}{2 - 1}$$

Solution

Because f is a polynomial function, it is differentiable and also continuous on the entire interval $[1, 2]$. Thus, the hypotheses of the MVT are satisfied.

By differentiating f, we find that

$$f'(x) = 3x^2 + 2x$$

for all x. Therefore, we have $f'(c) = 3c^2 + 2c$, and the MVT equation

$$f'(c) = \frac{f(2) - f(1)}{2 - 1}$$

is satisfied when

$$3c^2 + 2c = \frac{f(2) - f(1)}{2 - 1} = \frac{12 - 2}{1} = 10$$

Solving the resulting equation $3c^2 + 2c - 10 = 0$ by the quadratic formula, we obtain

$$c = \frac{-1 \pm \sqrt{31}}{3}$$

The negative value is not in the open interval $(1, 2)$, but the positive value

$$c = \frac{-1 + \sqrt{31}}{3} \approx 1.522588121$$

satisfies the requirements of the MVT.   ∎

EXAMPLE 2   Using the MVT to prove a trigonometric inequality

Show that $|\sin x - \sin y| \leq |x - y|$ for all numbers x and y by applying the mean value theorem.

Solution

The inequality is true if $x = y$. Suppose $x \neq y$; then $f(\theta) = \sin \theta$ is differentiable and hence continuous for all θ, with $f'(\theta) = \cos \theta$. By applying the MVT to f on the closed interval with endpoints x and y, we see that

$$\frac{f(x) - f(y)}{x - y} = f'(c)$$

for some c between x and y. Because $f'(c) = \cos c$ and

$$f(x) - f(y) = \sin x - \sin y$$

it follows that

$$\frac{\sin x - \sin y}{x - y} = \cos c$$

Finally, we take the absolute value of the expression on each side, remembering that $|\cos c| \leq 1$ for any number c:

$$\left| \frac{\sin x - \sin y}{x - y} \right| = |\cos c| \leq 1$$

Thus, $|\sin x - \sin y| \leq |x - y|$, as claimed.   ∎

THE ZERO-DERIVATIVE THEOREM

The primary use of the MVT is as a tool for proving certain key theoretical results of calculus. For example, we know that the derivative of a constant is 0, and in Theorem 4.5, we prove a partial converse of this result by showing that a function whose derivative is 0 throughout the interval must be constant on that interval. This apparently simple result and its corollary (Theorem 4.6) turn out to be crucial to our development of integration in Chapter 5.

THEOREM 4.5   Zero-derivative theorem

Suppose f is a continuous function on the closed interval $[a, b]$ and is differentiable on the open interval (a, b), with $f'(x) = 0$ for all x on (a, b). Then the function f is constant on $[a, b]$.

Proof Let x_1 and x_2 be two distinct numbers ($x_1 \neq x_2$) chosen arbitrarily from the closed interval $[a, b]$. The function f satisfies the requirements of the MVT on the interval with endpoints x_1 and x_2, which means that there exists a number c between x_1 and x_2 such that

$$\frac{f(x_2) - f(x_1)}{x_2 - x_1} = f'(c)$$

By hypothesis, $f'(x) = 0$ throughout the open interval (a, b), and because c lies within this interval, we have $f'(c) = 0$. Thus, by substitution, we have

$$\frac{f(x_2) - f(x_1)}{x_2 - x_1} = 0$$
$$f(x_2) = f(x_1)$$

Because x_1 and x_2 were chosen arbitrarily from $[a, b]$, we conclude that $f(x) = k$, a constant, for all x, as required. $\square$

THEOREM 4.6 Constant difference theorem

Suppose the functions f and g are continuous on the closed interval $[a, b]$ and differentiable on the open interval (a, b). Then if $f'(x) = g'(x)$ for all x in (a, b), there exists a constant C such that

$$f(x) = g(x) + C$$

for all x on $[a, b]$.

Proof Let $h(x) = f(x) - g(x)$; then
$$h'(x) = f'(x) - g'(x)$$
$$= 0 \qquad \text{Because } f'(x) = g'(x)$$

Thus, by Theorem 4.5, $h(x) = C$ for some constant C and all x on $[a, b]$, and because $h(x) = f(x) - g(x)$, it follows that

$$f(x) - g(x) = C$$
$$f(x) = g(x) + C \qquad \text{Add } g(x) \text{ to both sides.} \qquad \square$$

➡ **What This Says** Two functions with equal derivatives on an open interval differ by a constant on that interval.

4.2 PROBLEM SET

A 1. **Exploration Problem** What does Rolle's theorem say, and why is it important?

2. **Exploration Problem** State the hypotheses used in the proof of the MVT. How are the hypotheses used in the proof? Can the conclusion of the MVT be true if any or all of the hypotheses are not satisfied?

In Problems 3–20, verify that the given function f satisfies the hypotheses of the MVT on the given interval $[a, b]$. Then find all numbers c between a and b for which

$$\frac{f(b) - f(a)}{b - a} = f'(c)$$

3. $f(x) = 2x^2 + 1$ on $[0, 2]$ 4. $f(x) = -x^2 + 4$ on $[-1, 0]$
5. $f(x) = x^3 + x$ on $[1, 2]$ 6. $f(x) = 2x^3 - x^2$ on $[0, 2]$
7. $f(x) = x^4 + 2$ on $[-1, 2]$ 8. $f(x) = x^5 + 3$ on $[2, 4]$
9. $f(x) = \sqrt{x}$ on $[1, 4]$ 10. $f(x) = \dfrac{1}{\sqrt{x}}$ on $[1, 4]$
11. $f(x) = \dfrac{1}{x+1}$ on $[0, 2]$ 12. $f(x) = 1 + \dfrac{1}{x}$ on $[1, 4]$

13. $f(x) = \cos x$ on $[0, \frac{\pi}{2}]$

14. $f(x) = \sin x + \cos x$ on $[0, 2\pi]$

15. $f(x) = e^x$ on $[0, 1]$

16. $f(x) = \frac{1}{2}(e^x + e^{-x})$ on $[0, 1]$

17. $f(x) = \ln x$ on $[\frac{1}{2}, 2]$ 18. $f(x) = \dfrac{\ln \sqrt{x}}{x}$ on $[1, 3]$

19. $f(x) = \tan^{-1} x$ on $[0, 1]$ 20. $f(x) = x \sin^{-1} x$ on $[0, 1]$

Decide whether Rolle's theorem can be applied to f on the interval indicated in Problems 21–30.

21. $f(x) = |x - 2|$ on $[0, 4]$ 22. $f(x) = \tan x$ on $[0, 2\pi]$

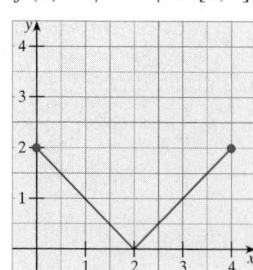 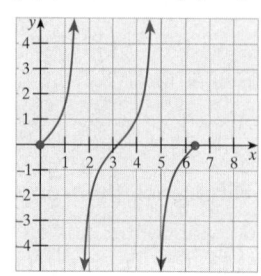

23. $f(x) = \sin x$ on $[0, 2\pi]$ 24. $f(x) = |x| - 2$ on $[0, 4]$

25. $f(x) = \sqrt[3]{x} - 1$ on $[-8, 8]$ 26. $f(x) = \dfrac{1}{x - 2}$ on $[-1, 1]$

27. $f(x) = \dfrac{1}{x - 2}$ on $[1, 2]$

28. $f(x) = 3x + \sec x$ on $[-\pi, \pi]$

29. $f(x) = \sin^2 x$ on $[-\frac{\pi}{2}, \frac{\pi}{2}]$

30. $f(x) = \sqrt{\ln x}$ on $[1, 2]$

31. Let $g(x) = 8x^3 - 6x + 8$. Find a function f with $f'(x) = g'(x)$ and $f(1) = 12$.

32. Let $g(x) = \sqrt{x^2 + 5}$. Find a function f with $f'(x) = g'(x)$ and $f(2) = 1$.

33. Show that $f(x) = \dfrac{x + 4}{5 - x}$ and $g(x) = \dfrac{-9}{x - 5}$ differ by a constant. Are the conditions of the constant difference theorem satisfied? Does $f'(x) = g'(x)$?

34. Let $f(x) = (x - 2)^3$ and $g(x) = (x^2 + 12)(x - 6)$. Use f and g to demonstrate the constant difference theorem.

35. Let $f(x) = (x - 1)^3$ and $g(x) = (x^2 + 3)(x - 3)$. Use f and g to demonstrate the constant difference theorem.

36. Let f be defined as shown in Figure 4.13.

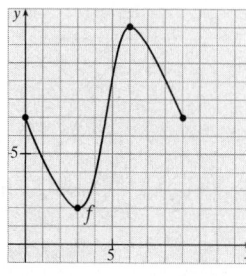

Figure 4.13   Function f on $[0, 9]$

Use the graph of f to estimate the values of c that satisfy the conclusion of Rolle's theorem on $[0, 9]$. What theorem would apply for the interval $[0, 5]$?

37. Let g be defined as shown in Figure 4.14.

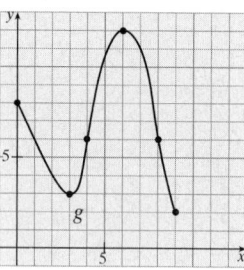

Figure 4.14   Function g on $[0, 9]$

Use the graph of g to estimate the values of c that satisfy the conclusion of the mean value theorem on $[0, 9]$. What theorem would apply for the interval $[4, 8]$?

B 38. **Alternative form of the mean value theorem:** If f is continuous on $[a, b]$ and differentiable on (a, b), then there exists a number c in (a, b) such that

$$f(b) = f(a) + (b - a)f'(c)$$

Prove this alternative form of the MVT.

39. Let u and v be any two numbers between $-\frac{\pi}{2}$ and $\frac{\pi}{2}$. Use the MVT to show that

$$|\tan u - \tan v| \geq |u - v|$$

40. If $f(x) = \dfrac{1}{x}$ on $[-1, 1]$, does the mean value theorem apply? Why or why not?

41. If $g(x) = |x|$ on $[-2, 2]$, does the mean value theorem apply? Why or why not?

42. **Counterexample Problem**   Is it true that

$$|\cos x - \cos y| \leq |x - y|$$

for all x and y? Either prove that the inequality is always valid or find a counterexample.

43. **Counterexample Problem**   Consider

$$f(x) = \begin{cases} 1 & \text{if } x \geq 0 \\ -1 & \text{if } x < 0 \end{cases}$$

$f'(x) = 0$ for all x in the domain, but f is not a constant. Does this example contradict the zero-derivative theorem? Why or why not?

44. **a.** Let n be a positive integer. Show that there is a number c between 0 and x for which

$$\frac{(1 + x)^n - 1}{x} = n(1 + c)^{n-1}$$

     b. Use part **a** to evaluate

$$\lim_{x \to 0} \frac{(1 + x)^n - 1}{x}$$

45. **a.** Show that there is a number w between 0 and x for which

$$\frac{\cos x - 1}{x} = -\sin w$$

     b. Use part **a** to evaluate

$$\lim_{x \to 0} \frac{\cos x - 1}{x}$$

46. Use the MVT to evaluate

$$\lim_{x \to \pi^+} \frac{\cos x + 1}{x - \pi}$$

47. Let $f(x) = 1 + \dfrac{1}{x}$. If a and b are constants such that $a < 0$ and $b > 0$, show that there is no number w between a and b for which

$$f(b) - f(a) = f'(w)(b - a)$$

48. Show that for any $x > 4$, there is a number w between 4 and x such that

$$\frac{\sqrt{x} - 2}{x - 4} = \frac{1}{2\sqrt{w}}$$

Use this fact to show that if $x > 4$, then

$$\sqrt{x} < 1 + \frac{x}{4}$$

49. Show that if an object moves along a straight line in such a way that its velocity is the same at two different times (that is, for a differentiable function v, we are given $v(t_1) = v(t_2)$ for $t_1 \neq t_2$), then there is some intermediate time when the acceleration is zero.

50. Modeling Problem Two radar patrol cars are located at fixed positions 6 mi apart on a long, straight road where the speed limit is 55 mi/h. A sports car passes the first patrol car traveling at 53 mi/h, and then 5 min later, it passes the second patrol car going 48 mi/h. Analyze a model of this situation to show that at some time between the two clockings, the sports car exceeded the speed limit. *Hint*: Use the MVT.

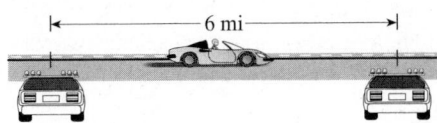

51. Modeling Problem Suppose two race cars begin at the same time and finish at the same time. Analyze a model to show that at some point in the race they had the same speed.

52. Use Rolle's theorem with

$$f(x) = (x - 1)\sin x$$

to show that the equation $\tan x = 1 - x$ has at least one solution for $0 < x < 1$.

53. Use the MVT to show that

$$\sqrt{1 + x} - 4 < \tfrac{1}{8}(x - 15)$$

if $x > 15$. *Hint*: Let $f(x) = \sqrt{1 + x}$.

54. Use the MVT to show that

$$\frac{1}{2x + 1} > \frac{1}{5} + \frac{2}{25}(2 - x)$$

if $0 \leq x \leq 2$.

C 55. Let $f(x) = \tan x$. Note that

$$f(\pi) = f(0) = 0$$

Show that there is no number w between 0 and π for which $f'(w) = 0$. Why does this fact not contradict the MVT?

56. Use Rolle's theorem or the MVT to show that there is no number a for which the equation

$$x^3 - 3x + a = 0$$

has *two* distinct solutions in the interval $[-1, 1]$.

57. If $a > 0$ is a constant, show that the equation

$$x^3 + ax - 1 = 0$$

has exactly one real solution. *Hint*: Let $f(x) = x^3 + ax - 1$ and use the intermediate value theorem to show that there is at least one root. Then assume there are two roots, and use Rolle's theorem to obtain a contradiction.

58. For constants a and b, $a > 0$, and n a positive integer, use Rolle's theorem or the MVT to show that the polynomial

$$p(x) = x^{2n+1} + ax + b$$

can have at most one real root.

59. Show that if $f''(x) = 0$ for all x, then f is a linear function. (That is, $f(x) = Ax + B$ for constants $A \neq 0$ and B.)

60. Show that if $f'(x) = Ax + B$ for constants $A \neq 0$ and B, then $f(x)$ is a quadratic function. (That is, $f(x) = ax^2 + bx + c$ for constants a, b, and c, where $a \neq 0$.)

4.3 Using Derivatives to Sketch the Graph of a Function

IN THIS SECTION increasing and decreasing functions, the first-derivative test, concavity and inflection points, the second-derivative test, curve sketching using the first and second derivatives

Our next goal is to see how information about the derivative f' and the second derivative f'' can be used to determine the shape of the graph of f. We begin by showing how the sign of f' is related to whether the graph of f is rising or falling.

INCREASING AND DECREASING FUNCTIONS

Suppose an ecologist has modeled the size of a population of a certain species as a function f of time t (months). If it turns out that the population is increasing until the end of the first year and is decreasing thereafter, it is reasonable to expect the population to be maximized at time $t = 12$ months and for the population curve to have a high point at $t = 12$, as shown in Figure 4.15. If the graph of a function f, such as this population curve, is rising throughout the interval $0 < x < 12$, we say that f is *strictly increasing* on that interval. Similarly, the graph of the function in Figure 4.15 is *strictly decreasing* on the interval $12 < t < 20$. These terms may be defined more formally as follows:

Strictly Increasing and Strictly Decreasing Functions

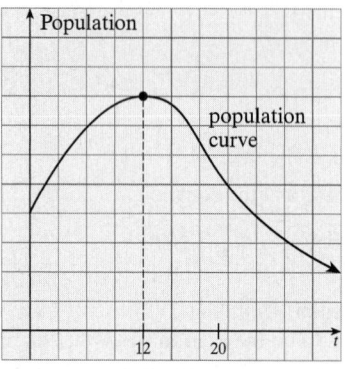

Figure 4.15 A population curve

The function f is **strictly increasing** on an interval I if

$$f(x_1) < f(x_2) \quad \text{whenever} \quad x_1 < x_2$$

for x_1 and x_2 on I. Likewise, f is **strictly decreasing** on I if

$$f(x_1) > f(x_2) \quad \text{whenever} \quad x_1 < x_2$$

for x_1 and x_2 on I. (See Figure 4.16.)

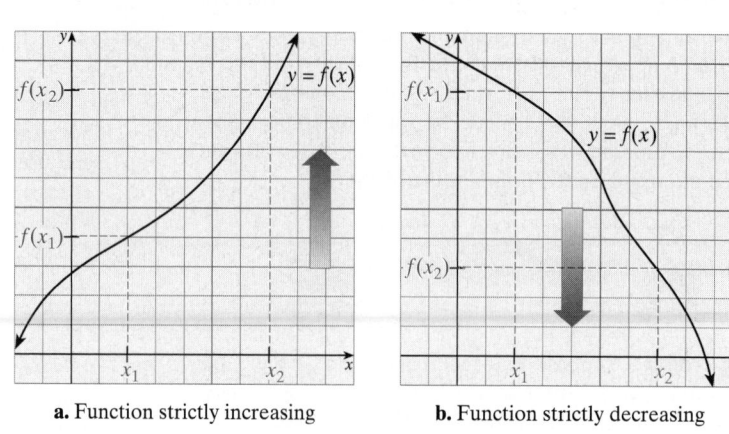

a. Function strictly increasing

b. Function strictly decreasing

Figure 4.16 Increasing and decreasing functions

Note that we do not use the word "strictly" every time we talk about a strictly monotonic function, or a strictly increasing function, or a strictly decreasing function.

A function f is said to be (strictly) **monotonic** on an interval I if it is either strictly increasing on all of I or strictly decreasing on all of I. The monotonic behavior is closely related to the sign of the derivative $f'(x)$. In particular, if the graph of a function has tangent lines with positive slope on I, the graph will be inclined upward and f will be increasing on I (see Figure 4.17). Since the slope of the tangent at each

WARNING A note on usage: We say that functions are **increasing** and that graphs are **rising**. For example, if $f(x) = x^2$, we say that the function f is increasing for $x > 0$ and that the graph is rising for $x > 0$.

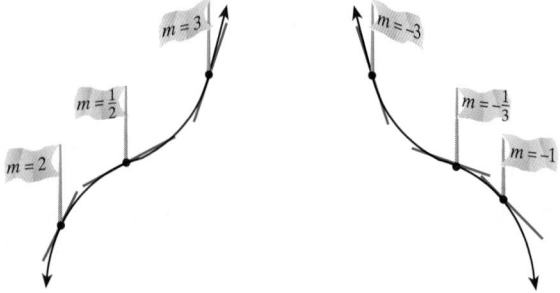

Figure 4.17 The graph is rising where $f' > 0$ and falling where $f' < 0$. Notice that the small flags indicate the slope at various points on the graph.

point on the graph is measured by the derivative f', it is reasonable to expect f to be increasing on intervals where $f' > 0$. Similarly, it is reasonable to expect f to be decreasing on an interval when $f' < 0$. These observations are established formally in Theorem 4.7.

THEOREM 4.7   Monotone function theorem

Let f be differentiable on the open interval (a, b).

If $f'(x) > 0$ on (a, b), then f is strictly increasing on (a, b).

If $f'(x) < 0$ on (a, b), then f is strictly decreasing on (a, b).

Proof   We will prove that f is strictly increasing on (a, b) if $f'(x) > 0$ throughout the interval. The strictly decreasing case is similar and is left as an exercise for the reader.

Suppose $f'(x) > 0$ throughout the interval (a, b), and let x_1 and x_2 be two numbers chosen arbitrarily from this interval, with $x_1 < x_2$. The MVT tells us that

$$\frac{f(x_2) - f(x_1)}{x_2 - x_1} = f'(c) \qquad \text{or} \qquad f(x_2) - f(x_1) = f'(c)(x_2 - x_1)$$

for some number c between x_1 and x_2. Because both $f'(c) > 0$ and $x_2 - x_1 > 0$, it follows that $f'(c)(x_2 - x_1) > 0$, and therefore

$$f(x_2) - f(x_1) > 0 \qquad \text{or} \qquad f(x_2) > f(x_1)$$

That is, if x_1 and x_2 are any two numbers in (a, b) such that $x_1 < x_2$, then $f(x_1) < f(x_2)$, which means that f is strictly increasing on (a, b).   ❑

To determine where a function f is increasing or decreasing, we begin by finding the critical numbers (where the derivative is zero or does not exist). These numbers divide the x-axis into intervals, and we test the sign of $f'(x)$ in each of these intervals. If $f'(x) > 0$ in an interval, then f is increasing in that same interval, and if $f'(x) < 0$ in an interval, then f is decreasing in that same interval.

To indicate where a given function f is increasing and where it is decreasing, we will mark the critical values on a number line and use an up arrow ($\uparrow$) to indicate an interval where f is increasing and a down arrow ($\downarrow$) to indicate an interval where f is decreasing. Sometimes, when the full graph of f is displayed, we indicate the sign of f' on an interval bounded by critical numbers with a string of $+$ signs if f is increasing on the interval or a string of $-$ signs if f is decreasing there. This notation is illustrated in the following example.

EXAMPLE 1   Finding intervals of increase and decrease

Determine where the function defined by $f(x) = x^3 - 3x^2 - 9x + 1$ is strictly increasing and where it is strictly decreasing.

Solution

First, we find the derivative:

$$f'(x) = 3x^2 - 6x - 9 = 3(x + 1)(x - 3)$$

Next, we determine the critical numbers: $f'(x)$ exists for all x and $f'(x) = 0$ at $x = -1$ and $x = 3$. These critical numbers divide the x-axis into three parts, as shown in Figure 4.18a, and we select any arbitrary number from each of these intervals. For example, we select -2, 0, and 4, evaluate the derivative at these numbers, and mark each interval as increasing ($\uparrow$) or decreasing ($\downarrow$), according to whether the derivative is positive or negative, respectively. This is shown in Figure 4.18b. The function f is increasing for $x < -1$ and for $x > 3$; f is decreasing for $-1 < x < 3$.   ■

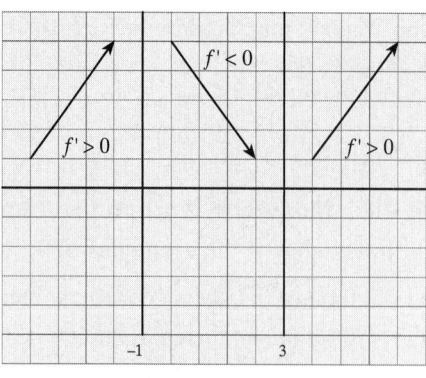

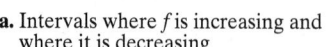

a. Intervals where f is increasing and where it is decreasing

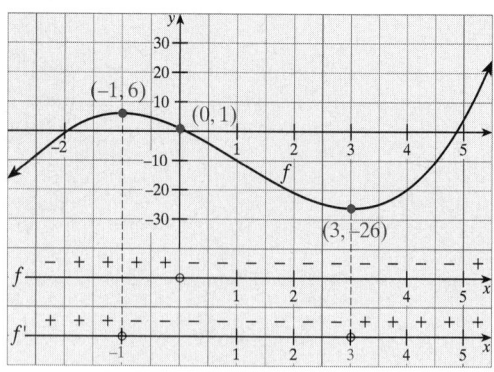

b. The graph of f along with the sign graphs for f and f'

Figure 4.18 $f(x) = x^3 - 3x^2 - 9x + 1$

EXAMPLE 2 Comparing the graphs of a function and its derivative

Graph $f(x) = x^3 - 3x^2 - 9x + 1$ and $f'(x) = 3x^2 - 6x - 9$ and compare.

a. When $f' > 0$, what can be said about the graph of f?
b. When the graph of f is falling, what can be said about the graph of f'?
c. Where do the critical numbers of f appear on the graph of f?

Solution

The graphs of f and f' are shown in Figure 4.19.

a. When $f'(x) > 0$, the graph of f is rising. This occurs when $x < -1$ and when $x > 3$.
b. When the graph of f is falling (for $-1 < x < 3$), we have $f'(x) < 0$, so the graph of f' is below the x-axis.
c. The critical numbers of f are where $f'(x) = 0$; that is, at $x = -1$ and $x = 3$, so they are the x-intercepts of the graph of f'. ∎

THE FIRST-DERIVATIVE TEST

Every relative extremum is a critical point. However, as we saw in Section 4.1, not every critical point of a continuous function is necessarily a relative extremum. If the derivative is positive to the immediate left of a critical number and negative to its immediate right, the graph changes from increasing to decreasing and the critical point must be a relative maximum, as shown in Figure 4.20a. If the derivative is negative to the immediate left of a critical number and positive to its immediate right, the graph changes from decreasing to increasing and the critical point is a relative minimum (Figure 4.20b). However, if the sign of the derivative is the same on both immediate sides of the critical number, then it is neither a relative maximum nor a relative minimum (Figure 4.20c). These observations are summarized in a procedure called the *first-derivative test for relative extrema*.

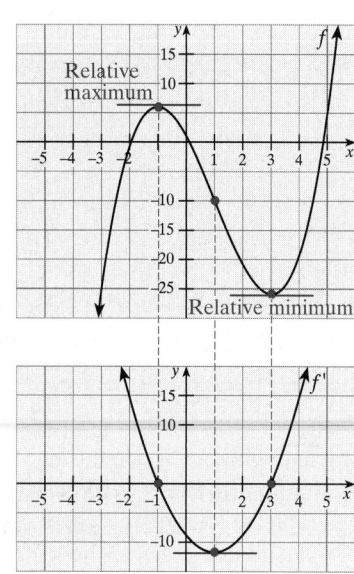

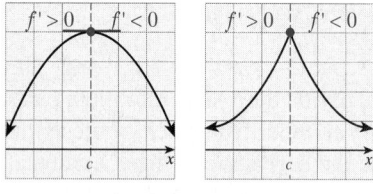

Figure 4.19 Graphs of f and f'

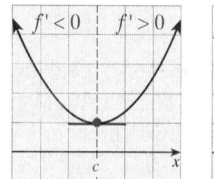

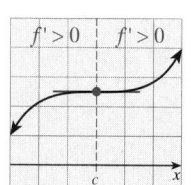

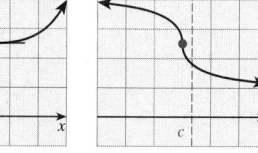

a. A relative maximum   **b.** A relative minimum   **c.** No extremum

Figure 4.20 Three patterns of behavior near a critical number

The First-Derivative Test for Relative Extrema

Step 1. Find all critical numbers of a continuous function f. That is, find all numbers c such that $f(c)$ is defined and either $f'(c) = 0$ or $f'(c)$ does not exist.

Step 2. Classify each critical point $(c, f(c))$ as follows:

a. The point $(c, f(c))$ is a **relative maximum** if

$f'(x) > 0$ (graph rising) for all x in an open interval (a, c) to the left of c, and

$f'(x) < 0$ (graph falling) for all x in an open interval (c, b) to the right of c.

b. The point $(c, f(c))$ is a **relative minimum** if

$f'(x) < 0$ (graph falling) for all x in an open interval (a, c) to the left of c, and

$f'(x) > 0$ (graph rising) for all x in an open interval (c, b) to the right of c.

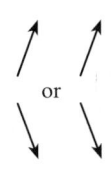
or
c. The point $(c, f(c))$ is **not an extremum** if the derivative $f'(x)$ has the same sign for all x in open intervals (a, c) and (c, b) on each side of c.

Suppose we apply this first-derivative test to the polynomial $f(x) = x^3 - 3x^2 - 9x + 1$ In Example 2 we found that this function has the critical numbers -1 and 3 and that f is increasing when $x < -1$ and $x > 3$ and decreasing when $-1 < x < 3$ (see the arrow pattern above). The first-derivative test tells us there is a relative maximum at -1 ($\uparrow \downarrow$ pattern) and a relative minimum at 3 ($\downarrow \uparrow$ pattern).

EXAMPLE 3   Relative extrema using the first-derivative test

Find all critical numbers of $g(t) = t - 2 \sin t$ for $0 \leq t \leq 2\pi$, and determine whether each corresponds to a relative maximum, a relative minimum, or neither. Sketch the graph of g.

Solution Because $g'(t) = 1 - 2 \cos t$ exists for all t, the only critical numbers occur when $g'(t) = 0$; that is, when $\cos t = \frac{1}{2}$. Solving, we find that the critical numbers for $g(t)$ on the interval $[0, 2\pi]$ are $\frac{\pi}{3}$ and $\frac{5\pi}{3}$.

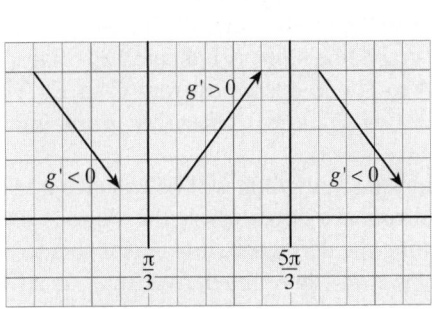

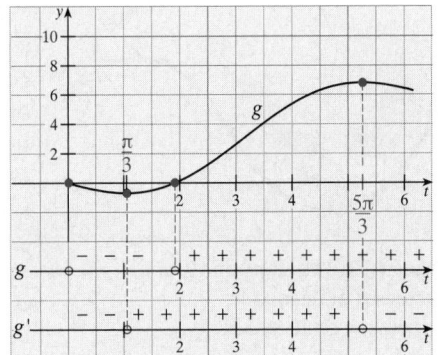

a. Intervals where $g(t) = t - 2 \sin t$ is increasing or decreasing

b. The graph of $g(t) = t - 2 \sin t$ for $0 \leq t \leq 2\pi$

Figure 4.21   The first-derivative test for $g(t) = t - 2 \sin t$

Next, we examine the sign of $g'(t)$. Thanks to the intermediate value theorem, because $g'(t)$ is continuous, it is enough to check the sign of $g'(t)$ at convenient numbers on each side of the critical numbers, as shown in Figure 4.21a. Notice that the arrows show the increasing and decreasing pattern for g. According to the first-derivative test, there is a relative minimum at $\frac{\pi}{3}$ and a relative maximum at $\frac{5\pi}{3}$. The graph of g is shown in Figure 4.21b. ∎

CONCAVITY AND INFLECTION POINTS

Knowing where a given graph is rising and falling gives only a partial picture of the graph. For example, suppose we wish to sketch the graph of $f(x) = x^3 + 3x + 1$. The derivative $f'(x) = 3x^2 + 3$ is positive for all x so the graph is always rising. But in what *way* is it rising? Each of the graphs in Figure 4.22 is a possible graph of f, but they are quite different from one another.

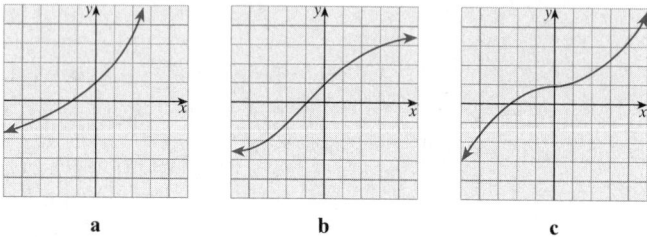

a   b   c

Figure 4.22 Which curve is the graph of $f(x) = x^3 + 3x + 1$?

Figure 4.22 shows three possibilities for the graph of f. All three are always rising, but they differ in the way they "bend" as they rise. The "bending" of a curve is measured by its *concavity*. If a curve lies above its tangent lines on some interval (a, b), then we say the curve is *concave up*, and if the curve lies below its tangent lines, we say it is *concave down* on (a, b). We will examine concavity, and then return in Example 4 to determine which of the three candidates in Figure 4.22 is indeed the graph of $f(x) = x^3 + 3x + 1$.

Concavity

> If the graph of a function f lies above all of its tangents on an interval I, then it is said to be **concave up** on I. If the graph of f lies below all of its tangents on I, it is said to be **concave down**.

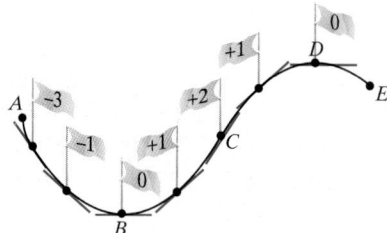

Figure 4.23 The slope of a graph increases or decreases, depending on its concavity.

To be specific, a portion of a graph that is cupped upward is called *concave up*, and a portion that is cupped downward is *concave down*. Figure 4.23 shows a graph that is concave up between A and C and concave down between C and E. At various points on the graph, the slope is indicated by "flags," and we observe that the slope increases from A to C and decreases from C to E. This is no accident! *The slope of a graph increases on an interval where the graph is concave up and decreases where the graph is concave down.*

Conversely, a graph will be concave up on any interval where the slope is increasing and concave down where the slope is decreasing. Because the slope is found by computing the derivative, it is reasonable to expect the graph of a given function f to be concave up where the derivative f' is strictly increasing. According to the monotone function theorem (Theorem 4.7), this occurs when $(f')' > 0$, which means that the graph of f is concave up where the *second derivative* f'' satisfies $f'' > 0$. Similarly, the graph is concave down where $f'' < 0$. We use this observation to characterize concavity.

Derivative Characterization of Concavity

The graph of a function f is **concave up** on any open interval I where $f''(x) > 0$, and it is **concave down** where $f''(x) < 0$.

When discussing the concavity of a function f, we will display a diagram in which a "cup" symbol ($\cup$) above an interval indicates that f is concave up on the interval and a "cap" symbol ($\cap$) indicates that f is concave down there. This convention is illustrated in the following example.

EXAMPLE 4   Concavity for a polynomial function

Find where the graph of $f(x) = x^3 + 3x + 1$ is concave up and where it is concave down.

Solution

We find that $f'(x) = 3x^2 + 3$ and $f''(x) = 6x$. Therefore, $f''(x) < 0$ if $x < 0$ and $f''(x) > 0$ if $x > 0$, so the graph of f is concave down for $x < 0$ and concave up for $x > 0$, as indicated in Figure 4.24. Returning to Figure 4.22c, the graph is concave down to the left of $x = 0$ and concave up to the right. Hence, this is the graph of $f(x)$. ∎

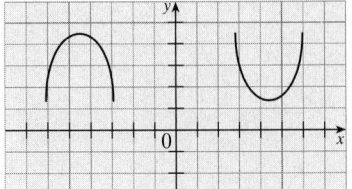

Figure 4.24 Intervals of concavity

In Figure 4.23, notice that the graph changes from concave up to concave down at the point C. It will be convenient to have a special name for such transition points.

A point $P(c, f(c))$ on a curve is called an **inflection point** if the graph is concave up on one side of P and concave down on the other side.

Inflection Point

WARNING   An inflection point must be on the graph, meaning $f(c)$ must be defined if there is an inflection point at $x = c$.

Returning to Example 4, notice that the graph of $f(x) = x^3 + 3x + 1$ has exactly one inflection point, at $(0, 1)$, where the concavity changes from down to up.

Various kinds of graphical behavior are illustrated in Figure 4.25. Note that the graph is rising on the interval $[a, c_1]$, falling on $[c_1, c_2]$, rising on $[c_2, c_3]$, falling on $[c_3, c_4]$, rising on $[c_4, c_5]$, and falling on $[c_5, b]$. The concavity is up on $[p_1, p_2]$, and down otherwise. In this figure, and elsewhere, when the graph of f is displayed, we will indicate the sign of f'' on an interval by a string of $+$ signs if $f'' > 0$ on the interval, and a string of $-$ signs if $f'' < 0$ there.

The graph has relative maxima at c_1, c_3, and c_5, and relative minima at c_2 and c_4. There are horizontal tangents ($f'(x) = 0$) at all of these points except at c_1 and c_3, where there are sharp points, called *corners* ($f'(c_1)$ and $f'(c_3)$ do not exist). There is a horizontal tangent at p_1; that is, $f'(p_1) = 0$, but no relative extremum appears there. Instead, we have points of inflection at p_1 and p_2, because the concavity changes direction at each of these points.

In general, the concavity of the graph of f will change only at points where $f''(x) = 0$ or $f''(x)$ does not exist—that is, at critical numbers of the derivative $f'(x)$. We will call the number c a **second-order critical number** if $f''(c) = 0$ or $f''(c)$ does not exist, and in this context an "ordinary" critical number (where $f'(c) = 0$ or $f'(c)$ does not exist) will be referred to as a **first-order critical number.** If we do not specify otherwise, a critical number is always a first-order critical number. Inflection points correspond to second-order critical numbers and must actually be on the graph

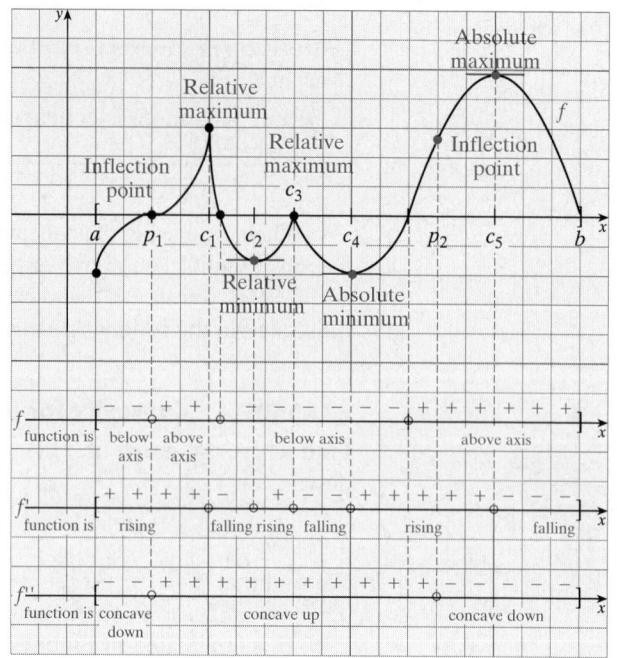

Figure 4.25   A graph of a function showing critical points and inflection points

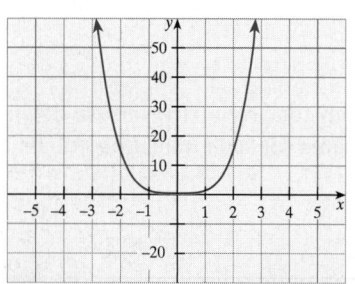

Figure 4.26 The graph of $f(x) = x^4$ has no inflection point at $(0, 0)$ even though $f''(0) = 0$.

WARNING   A continuous function f need not have an inflection point at every number c where $f''(c) = 0$. For instance, if $f(x) = x^4$, we have $f''(0) = 0$, but the graph of f is always concave up (see Figure 4.26).

of f. Specifically, a number c such that $f''(c)$ is not defined and the concavity of f changes at c will correspond to an inflection point if and only if $f(c)$ is defined.

Here is an example of one way inflection points may appear in applications.

EXAMPLE 5   Peak worker efficiency

An efficiency study of the morning shift at a factory indicates that the number of units produced by an average worker t hours after 8:00 A.M. may be modeled by the formula $Q(t) = -t^3 + 9t^2 + 12t$. At what time in the morning is the worker performing most efficiently?

Solution

We assume that the morning shift runs from 8:00 A.M. until noon and that worker efficiency is maximized when the rate of production

$$R(t) = Q'(t) = -3t^2 + 18t + 12$$

is as large as possible for $0 \leq t \leq 4$. The derivative of R is

$$R'(t) = Q''(t) = -6t + 18$$

which is zero when $t = 3$; this is the critical number. Using the optimization criterion of Section 4.1, we know that the extrema of $R(t)$ on the closed interval $[0, 4]$ must occur at either the interior critical number 3 or at one (or both) of the endpoints (which are 0 and 4). We find that

$$R(0) = 12 \quad R(3) = 39 \quad R(4) = 36$$

so the rate of production $R(t)$ is greatest and the worker is performing most efficiently when $t = 3$; that is, at 11:00 A.M. The graphs of the production function Q and its derivative, the rate-of-production function R, are shown in Figure 4.27. Notice that the production curve is steepest and the rate of production is greatest when $t = 3$.

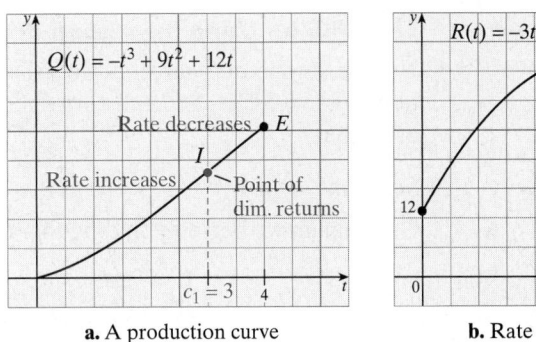

a. A production curve

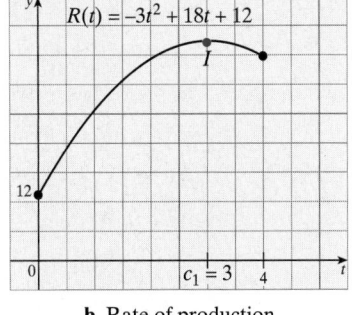

b. Rate of production

Figure 4.27   Graph of a production curve showing the point of diminishing returns   ■

In Example 5, note how the rate of production, as measured by the slope of the graph of the average worker's output, increases from 0 to the inflection point I and then decreases from I to E, as shown in Figure 4.27a. Because the point I marks the point where the rate of production "peaks out," it is natural to refer to I as a point of **diminishing returns.** It is also an inflection point on the graph of Q. Knowing that this point occurs at 11:00 A.M., the manager of the factory might be able to increase the overall output of the labor force by scheduling a break near this time, since the production rate changes from increasing to decreasing at this time.

THE SECOND-DERIVATIVE TEST

It is often possible to classify a critical point $P(c, f(c))$ on the graph of f by examining the sign of $f''(c)$. Specifically, suppose $f'(c) = 0$ and $f''(c) > 0$. Then there is a horizontal tangent line at P and the graph of f is concave up in the neighborhood of P. This means that the graph of f is cupped upward from the horizontal tangent at P, and it is reasonable to expect P to be a relative minimum, as shown in Figure 4.28a. Similarly, we expect P to be a relative maximum if $f'(c) = 0$ and $f''(c) < 0$, because the graph is cupped down beneath the critical point P, as shown in Figure 4.28b.

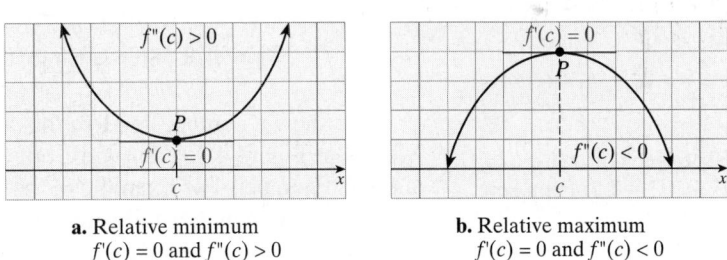

a. Relative minimum
$f'(c) = 0$ and $f''(c) > 0$

b. Relative maximum
$f'(c) = 0$ and $f''(c) < 0$

Figure 4.28   Second-derivative test for relative extrema

These observations lead to the *second-derivative test* for relative extrema.

The Second-Derivative Test for Relative Extrema

Let f be a function such that $f'(c) = 0$ and the second derivative exists on an open interval containing c.

If $f''(c) > 0$, there is a **relative minimum** at $x = c$.

If $f''(c) < 0$, there is a **relative maximum** at $x = c$.

If $f''(c) = 0$, then the second-derivative test **fails** (either a maximum, or a minimum, or neither may occur).

EXAMPLE 6 Using the second-derivative test

Use the second-derivative test to determine whether each critical number of the function $f(x) = 3x^5 - 5x^3 + 2$ corresponds to a relative maximum, a relative minimum, or neither.

Solution

Once again, we begin by finding the first and second derivatives:

$$f'(x) = 15x^4 - 15x^2 = 15x^2(x-1)(x+1)$$
$$f''(x) = 60x^3 - 30x = 30x(2x^2 - 1)$$

Solving $f'(x) = 0$, we find that the critical numbers are $x = 0$, $x = 1$, and $x = -1$. We plot these points on a number line, as shown in Figure 4.29. To apply the second-derivative test, we evaluate $f''(x)$ at each critical number.

$f''(0) = 0$; test fails at $x = 0$.

$f''(1) = 30 > 0$; positive, so the test tells us that there is a relative minimum at $x = 1$.

$f''(-1) = -30 < 0$; negative, so the test tells us that there is a relative maximum at $x = -1$. ∎

When the second-derivative test fails, as at $x = 0$ in Example 6, the critical point can often be classified using the first-derivative test. For instance, the first derivative in Example 6 is

$$f'(x) = 15x^2(x-1)(x+1)$$

We see $f'(x) = 0$ at $x = -1$, 0, and 1. We can plot these points on a number line, shown in Figure 4.29, and then evaluate $f'(x)$ at test numbers just to the left and just to the right of each critical number.

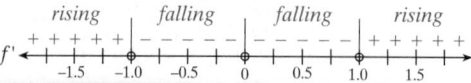

Figure 4.29 Sign graph for the derivative of $f(x) = 3x^5 - 5x^3 + 2$

We show a number line like this as part of the graph of many of our examples (as we did in Figure 4.25), but most often we show the derivative to the right and left of a critical number. For Example 6, the derivative is negative both to the immediate left and right of 0, which we illustrate as shown in Figure 4.30. Neither kind of extremum occurs at $x = 0$ ($\downarrow \downarrow$ pattern).

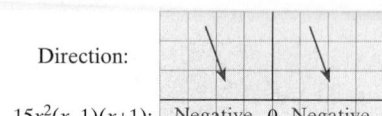

Figure 4.30 The graph of $f(x) = 3x^5 - 5x^3 + 2$ is falling on both sides of $x = 0$.

EXAMPLE 7 Finding inflection points

Find the inflection points for the function $f(x) = 3x^5 - 5x^3 + 2$, given in Example 6.

Solution

We begin with the second derivative (from Example 6):

$$f''(x) = 30x(2x^2 - 1)$$

To find the inflection points, we look at the second-order critical numbers, namely, where $f''(x) = 0$; that is, at $x = 0$ and $x = \pm\sqrt{\frac{1}{2}} = \pm\frac{\sqrt{2}}{2}$. We can show these on a sign graph of the second derivative, as in Figure 4.31. Notice that the inflection points occur where the sign of the second derivative changes.

The graph of f is shown in Figure 4.32, along with the sign graphs for both the first and second derivatives. Spend some time studying this figure to see how the signs of the first derivative indicate where the graph is rising and where it is falling, as well

concave down | concave up | concave down | concave up

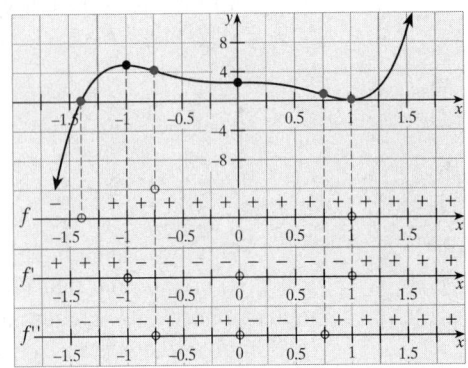

Figure 4.31 Sign graph for the second derivative of $f(x) = 3x^5 - 5x^3 + 2$

as how the signs of the second derivative show the concavity. For completeness, the figure also shows the sign graph for the function itself: The graph is above the x-axis where f is positive, below the x-axis where f is negative, and crosses the x-axis where $f(x) = 0$.

Figure 4.32 Graph of $f(x) = 3x^5 - 5x^3 + 2$ ∎

Example 7 demonstrates both the strength and the weakness of the second-derivative test. In particular, when it is relatively easy to find the second derivative (as with a polynomial) and if the zeros of this function are easy to find, then the second-derivative test provides a quick means for classifying the critical points. However, if it is difficult to compute $f''(c)$ or if $f''(c) = 0$, it may be easier, or even necessary, to apply the first-derivative test.

CURVE SKETCHING USING THE FIRST AND SECOND DERIVATIVES

Now, we are ready to develop a procedure for curve sketching. The key ideas appear in Example 8.

EXAMPLE 8 Sketching the graph of a polynomial function

Determine where the function $f(x) = x^4 - 4x^3 + 10$ is increasing, where it is decreasing, where its graph is concave up, and where its graph is concave down. Find the relative extrema and inflection points, and sketch the graph of f.

Solution

The first derivative,
$$f'(x) = 4x^3 - 12x^2 = 4x^2(x - 3)$$
is zero when $x = 0$ and when $x = 3$. Because $4x^2 > 0$ for $x \neq 0$, we have $f'(x) < 0$ for $x < 3$ (except for $x = 0$) and $f'(x) > 0$ for $x > 3$. The pattern showing where f is increasing and where it is decreasing is displayed in Figure 4.33a.

Next, to determine the concavity of the graph we compute
$$f''(x) = 12x^2 - 24x = 12x(x - 2)$$
If $x < 0$ or $x > 2$, then $f''(x) > 0$ and the graph is concave up. It is concave down when $0 < x < 2$, because $f''(x) < 0$ on this interval. The concavity of the graph of f is shown in Figure 4.33b.

Direction:

$4x^2(x-3)$: | Negative | 0 | Negative | 3 | Positive |

a. First derivative signs.

Shape:

$12x(x-2)$: | Positive | 0 | Negative | 2 | Positive |

b. Second derivative signs.

Figure 4.33 Intervals of increase and decrease and concavity for $f(x) = x^4 - 4x^3 + 10$

The two diagrams in Figure 4.33 tell us that there is a relative minimum at $x = 3$ and inflection points at $x = 0$ and $x = 2$ (because the second derivative changes sign at these points).

To find the y-values of the critical points and the inflection points, evaluate f at $x = 0, 2$, and 3:

$$f(0) = (0)^4 - 4(0)^3 + 10 = 10$$
$$f(2) = (2)^4 - 4(2)^3 + 10 = -6$$
$$f(3) = (3)^4 - 4(3)^3 + 10 = -17$$

Finally, to sketch the graph of f, we first place a "cup" ($\cup$) at the minimum point $(3, -17)$ and note that $(0, 10)$ and $(2, -6)$ are inflection points. Remember there is also a horizontal tangent at $(0, 10)$. The preliminary graph is shown in Figure 4.34a. Complete the sketch by passing a smooth curve through these points, using the two diagrams in Figure 4.33 as a guide for determining where the graph is rising and falling and where it is concave up and down. The completed graph is shown in Figure 4.34b.

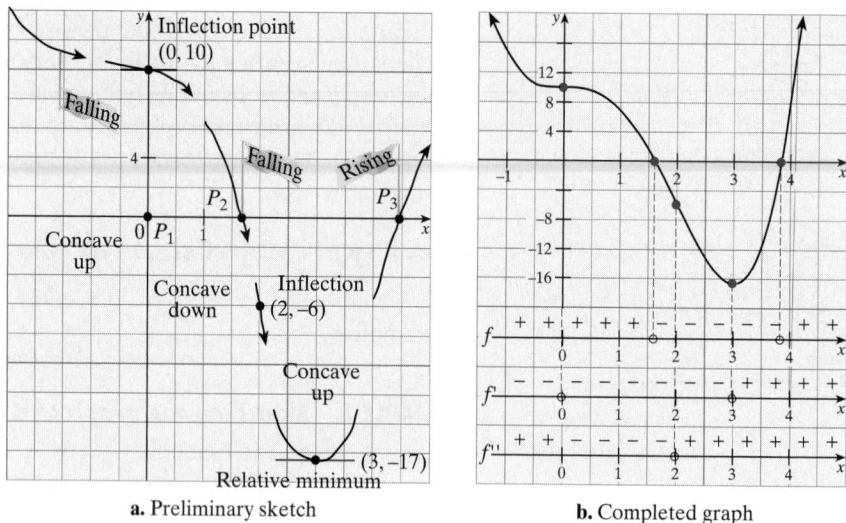

a. Preliminary sketch

b. Completed graph

Figure 4.34 Graphing $f(x) = x^4 - 4x^3 + 10$ ∎

EXAMPLE 9 Sketching the graph of an exponential function

Determine where the function

$$f(x) = \frac{1}{\sqrt{2\pi}} e^{-x^2/2}$$

is increasing, decreasing, concave up, and concave down. Find the relative extrema and inflection points and sketch the graph. This function plays an important role in statistics, where it is called the *standard normal density function*.

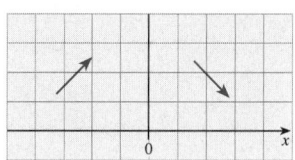

a. Intervals of increase and decrease for $f(x)$

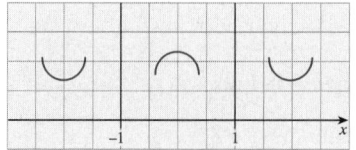

b. Concavity for $f(x)$

Figure 4.35 Intervals of increase, decrease, and concavity for $f(x) = \dfrac{1}{\sqrt{2\pi}}e^{-x^2/2}$

Solution

The first derivative is

$$f'(x) = \frac{-x}{\sqrt{2\pi}}e^{-x^2/2}$$

Because $e^{-x^2/2}$ is always positive, $f'(x) = 0$ if and only if $x = 0$. Hence, the corresponding point

$$\left(0, \frac{1}{\sqrt{2\pi}}\right) \approx (0, 0.4)$$

is the only critical point. Checking the sign of f' on each side of 0, we find that f is increasing for $x < 0$ and decreasing for $x > 0$, so there is a relative maximum at $x = 0$, as indicated in Figure 4.35a.

We find that the second derivative of f is

$$f''(x) = \frac{x^2}{\sqrt{2\pi}}e^{-x^2/2} - \frac{1}{\sqrt{2\pi}}e^{-x^2/2} = \frac{1}{\sqrt{2\pi}}(x^2 - 1)e^{-x^2/2}$$

which is zero when $x = \pm 1$. We find that $f(1) = f(-1) \approx 0.24$, and that the concavity of the graph of f is as indicated in Figure 4.35b.

Finally, we draw a smooth curve through the known points, as shown in Figure 4.36. The graph of f rises to the high point at approximately $(0, 0.4)$ and then falls indefinitely, approaching the x-axis arbitrarily closely because $e^{-x^2/2}$ approaches 0 as $|x|$ increases without bound. Note that the graph has no x-intercepts, because $e^{-x^2/2}$ is always positive.

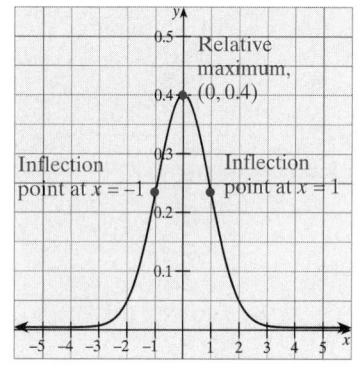

Figure 4.36 Graph of $f(x) = \dfrac{1}{\sqrt{2\pi}}e^{-x^2/2}$

■

EXAMPLE 10   Sketching the graph of a trigonometric function

Sketch the graph of $T(x) = \sin x + \cos x$ on $[0, 2\pi]$.

Solution

You probably graphed this function in trigonometry by adding ordinates. However, with this example we wish to illustrate the power of calculus to draw the graph. Thus, we begin by finding the first and second derivatives.

$$T'(x) = \cos x - \sin x \qquad\qquad T''(x) = -\sin x - \cos x$$

We find the critical numbers (both T' and T'' are defined for all values of x):

$T'(x) = 0$ when $\cos x = \sin x$; thus, $x = \frac{\pi}{4}$ and $x = \frac{5\pi}{4}$.

$T''(x) = 0$ when $\cos x = -\sin x$; thus, $x = \frac{3\pi}{4}$ and $x = \frac{7\pi}{4}$.

The intervals of increase and decrease as well as the concavity pattern are shown in Figure 4.37.

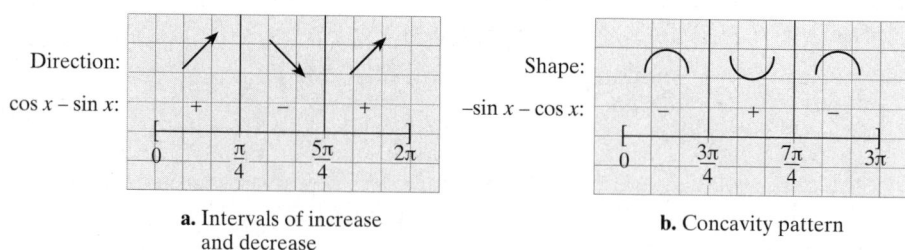

Direction:

$\cos x - \sin x$:   + − +

a. Intervals of increase and decrease

Shape:

$-\sin x - \cos x$:   − + −

b. Concavity pattern

Figure 4.37   Preliminary work for sketching $T(x) = \sin x + \cos x$

Find the critical points, the points of inflection, and the endpoints:

Relative maximum: $T\left(\frac{\pi}{4}\right) = \sqrt{2}$; the critical point is $\left(\frac{\pi}{4}, \sqrt{2}\right)$.

Relative minimum: $T\left(\frac{5\pi}{4}\right) = -\sqrt{2}$; the critical point is $\left(\frac{5\pi}{4}, -\sqrt{2}\right)$.

Inflection: $T\left(\frac{3\pi}{4}\right) = 0$; the inflection point is $\left(\frac{3\pi}{4}, 0\right)$.
$T\left(\frac{7\pi}{4}\right) = 0$; the inflection point is $\left(\frac{7\pi}{4}, 0\right)$.

Endpoints: $T(0) = 1$ and $T(2\pi) = 1$.

Finally, pass a smooth curve through these key points as indicated in the preliminary sketch in Figure 4.38a to obtain the completed graph shown in Figure 4.38b.

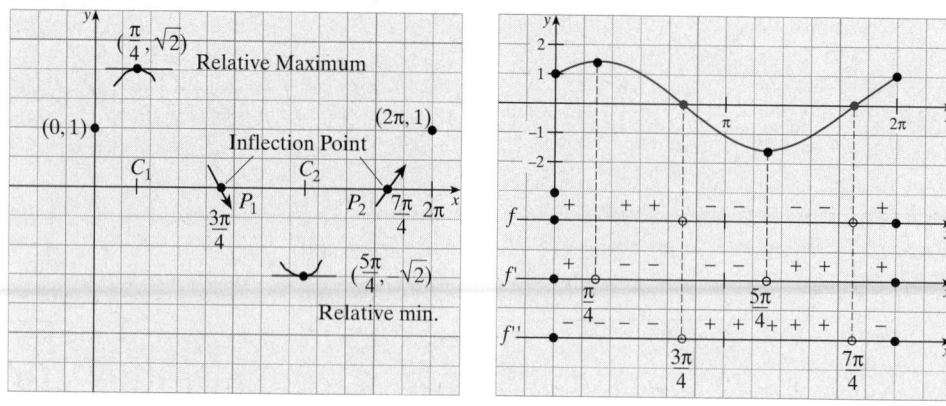

a. Preliminary sketch

b. Completed sketch

Figure 4.38   Graph of $T(x) = \sin x + \cos x$ on $[0, 2\pi]$ ∎

4.3   PROBLEM SET

A   1. **WHAT DOES THIS SAY?**   What is the first-derivative test?
2. **Exploration Problem**   What is the relationship between the graph of a function and the graph of its derivative?
3. **WHAT DOES THIS SAY?**   What is the second-derivative test?
4. **WHAT DOES THIS SAY?**   What is the relationship between concavity, points of inflection, and the second derivative?
5. **Exploration Problem**   The cartoon on page 209 exclaims, "Our prices are rising slower than any place in town." Restate using calculus.

In Problems 6–7, identify which curve represents a function f and which curve represents its derivative f′.

6.

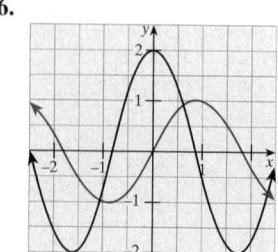

7.

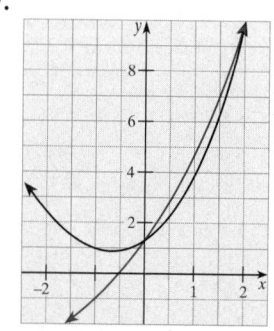

Draw a curve that represents the derivative of the function defined by the curves shown in Problems 8–11.

8.

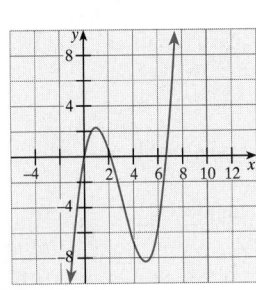

9.

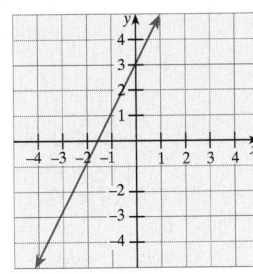

10.

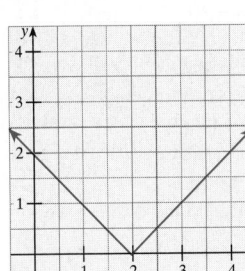

11.

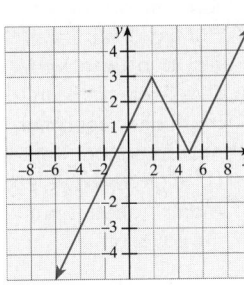

For the functions in Problems 12–19,

  a. *Find all critical numbers.*

  b. *Find where the function is increasing and decreasing.*

  c. *Find the critical points and identify each as a relative maximum, relative minimum, or neither.*

  d. *Find the second-order critical numbers and tell where the graph is concave up and where it is concave down.*

  e. *Sketch the graph.*

12. $f(x) = \frac{1}{3}x^3 - 9x + 2$ **13.** $f(x) = x^3 + 3x^2 + 1$

14. $f(x) = x^5 + 5x^4 - 550x^3 - 2{,}000x^2 + 60{,}000x$

15. $f(x) = x^3 + 35x^2 - 125x - 9{,}375$

16. $f(x) = x + \dfrac{1}{x}$ **17.** $f(x) = \dfrac{x-1}{x^2+3}$

18. $f(x) = x \ln x$ **19.** $f(t) = (t+1)^2(t-5)$

In Problems 20–35, determine the intervals of increase and decrease and concavity for the given function, and then use those intervals to help you sketch its graph.

20. $f(x) = (x-12)^4 - 2(x-12)^3$

21. $f(x) = 1 + 2x + 18/x$

22. $f(u) = 3u^4 - 2u^3 - 12u^2 + 18u - 5$

23. $g(u) = u^4 + 6u^3 - 24u^2 + 26$

24. $f(x) = \sqrt{x^2+1}$ **25.** $g(t) = (t^3+t)^2$

26. $f(t) = (t^3+3t^2)^3$ **27.** $f(x) = \dfrac{x}{x^2+1}$

28. $f(t) = t - \ln t$ **29.** $f(t) = t^2 e^{-3t}$

30. $f(x) = e^x + e^{-x}$ **31.** $f(x) = (\ln x)^2$

32. $t(\theta) = \sin\theta - 2\cos\theta$ for $0 \le \theta \le 2\pi$

33. $t(\theta) = \theta + \cos 2\theta$ for $0 \le \theta \le \pi$

34. $f(x) = 2x - \sin^{-1} x$ for $-1 \le x \le 1$

35. $f(x) = x^3 + \sin x$ on $\left[-\frac{\pi}{2}, \frac{\pi}{2}\right]$

In Problems 36–39, use the first-derivative test to classify each of the given critical numbers as a relative minimum, a relative maximum, or neither.

36. $f(x) = (x^3 - 3x + 1)^7$ at $x = 1, x = -1$

37. $f(x) = \dfrac{e^{-x^2}}{3 - 2x}$ at $x = 1, x = \frac{1}{2}$

38. $f(x) = (x^2 - 4)^4(x^2 - 1)^3$ at $x = 1, x = 2$

39. $f(x) = \sqrt[3]{x^3 - 48x}$ at $x = 4$

In Problems 40–43, use the second-derivative test to classify each of the given critical numbers as a relative minimum, a relative maximum, or neither.

40. $f(x) = 2x^3 + 3x^2 - 12x + 11$ at $x = 1, x = -2$

41. $f(x) = \dfrac{x^2 - x + 5}{x + 4}$ at $x = -9, x = 1$

42. $f(x) = (x^2 - 3x + 1)e^{-x}$ at $x = 1, x = 4$

43. $f(x) = \sin x + \frac{1}{2}\cos 2x$ at $x = \frac{\pi}{6}, x = \frac{\pi}{2}$

Ⓑ 44. Exploration Problem   Sketch the graph of a function with the following properties:

$$
\begin{aligned}
f'(x) &> 0 \quad \text{when} \quad x < -1 \\
f'(x) &> 0 \quad \text{when} \quad x > 3 \\
f'(x) &< 0 \quad \text{when} \quad -1 < x < 3 \\
f''(x) &< 0 \quad \text{when} \quad x < 2 \\
f''(x) &> 0 \quad \text{when} \quad x > 2
\end{aligned}
$$

45. Exploration Problem   Sketch the graph of a function with the following properties:

$$
\begin{aligned}
f'(x) &> 0 \quad \text{when} \quad x < 2 \quad \text{and when} \quad 2 < x < 5 \\
f'(x) &< 0 \quad \text{when} \quad x > 5 \\
f'(2) &= 0 \\
f''(x) &< 0 \quad \text{when} \quad x < 2 \quad \text{and when} \quad 4 < x < 7 \\
f''(x) &> 0 \quad \text{when} \quad 2 < x < 4 \quad \text{and when} \quad x > 7
\end{aligned}
$$

46. Exploration Problem   Sketch the graph of a function with the following properties:

$$
\begin{aligned}
f'(x) &> 0 \quad \text{when} \quad x < 1 \\
f'(x) &< 0 \quad \text{when} \quad x > 1 \\
f''(x) &> 0 \quad \text{when} \quad x < 1 \\
f''(x) &> 0 \quad \text{when} \quad x > 1
\end{aligned}
$$

What can you say about the derivative of f when $x = 1$?

47. Sketch the graph of a function with the following properties: There are relative extrema at $(-1, 7)$ and $(3, 2)$. There is an inflection point at $(1, 4)$. The graph is concave down only when $x < 1$. The x-intercept is $(-4, 0)$ and the y-intercept is $(0, 5)$.

48. Sketch a graph of a function f that satisfies the following conditions:

  (i) $f'(x) > 0$ when $x < -5$ and when $x > 1$.

  (ii) $f'(x) < 0$ when $-5 < x < 1$.

  (iii) $f(-5) = 4$ and $f(1) = -1$.

49. Sketch a graph of a function f that satisfies the following conditions:

  (i) $f'(x) < 0$ when $x < -1$.

  (ii) $f'(x) > 0$ when $-1 < x < 3$ and when $x > 3$.

  (iii) $f'(-1) = 0$ and $f'(3) = 0$.

50. In physics, the formula

$$I(\theta) = I_0 \left(\frac{\sin\theta}{\theta}\right)^2 \quad \text{where} \quad I(0) = \lim_{\theta \to 0} I(\theta)$$

and I_0 is a constant, is used to model light intensity in the study of Fraunhofer diffraction.

a. Show that $I(0) = I_0$.

b. Sketch the graph for $[-3\pi, 3\pi]$. What are the critical points on this interval?

51. At a temperature of T (in degrees Celsius), the speed of sound in air is modeled by the formula

$$v = v_0 \sqrt{1 + \frac{1}{273}T}$$

where v_0 is the speed at $0°C$. Sketch the graph of v for $T > 0$, and use calculus to check for critical points.

Modeling Problems: *In Problems 52–53, set up an appropriate model to answer the given question. Be sure to state your assumptions.*

52. At noon on a certain day, Frank sets out to assemble five stereo sets. His rate of assembly increases steadily throughout the afternoon until 4:00 P.M., at which time he has completed three sets. After that, he assembles sets at a slower and slower rate until he finally completes the fifth set at 8:00 P.M. Sketch a rough graph of a function that represents the number of sets Frank has completed after t hours of work.

53. An industrial psychologist conducts two efficiency studies at the Chilco appliance factory. The first study indicates that the average worker who arrives on the job at 8:00 A.M. will have assembled

$$-t^3 + 6t^2 + 13t$$

blenders in t hours (without a break), for $0 \le t \le 4$. The second study suggests that after a 15-minute coffee break, the average worker can assemble

$$-\frac{1}{3}t^3 + \frac{1}{2}t^2 + 25t$$

blenders in t hours after the break for $0 < t \le 4$. *Note:* The 15-minute break is not part of the work time.

a. Verify that if the coffee break occurs at 10:00 A.M., the average worker will assemble 42 blenders before the break and $49\frac{1}{3}$ blenders for the two hours after the break.

b. Suppose the coffee break is scheduled to begin x hours after 8:00 A.M. Find an expression for the total number of blenders $N(x)$ assembled by the average worker during the morning shift (8 A.M. to 12:15 P.M.).

c. At what time should the coffee break be scheduled so that the average worker will produce the maximum number of blenders during the morning shift? How is this optimum time related to the point of diminishing returns?

54. Research indicates that the power P required by a bird to maintain flight is given by the formula

$$P = \frac{w^2}{2\rho S v} + \frac{1}{2}\rho A v^3$$

where v is the relative speed of the bird, w is its weight, ρ is the density of air, and S and A are constants associated

with the bird's size and shape.* What speed will minimize the power? You may assume that v, w, ρ, S, and A are all positive.

55. The deflection of a hardwood beam of length is given by

$$D(x) = \frac{9}{4}x^4 - 7\ell x^3 + 5\ell^2 x^2$$

where x is the distance from one end of the beam. What value of x yields the maximum deflection?

56. HISTORICAL QUEST One of the most famous women in the history of mathematics is Maria Gaëtana Agnesi (pronounced än yā´zē). She was born in Milan, the first of 21 children. Her first publication was at age 9, when she wrote a Latin discourse defending higher education for women. Her most important work was a now-classic calculus textbook published in 1748. Maria Agnesi is primarily remembered for a curve defined by the equation

MARIA AGNESI
1718–1799

$$y = \frac{a^3}{x^2 + a^2}, \quad a \text{ a positive constant}$$

The curve was named *versiera* (from the Italian verb *to turn*) by Agnesi, but John Colson, an Englishman who translated her work, confused the word *versiera* with the word *avversiera*, which means "wife of the devil" in Italian; the curve has ever since been called the "witch of Agnesi." This was particularly unfortunate because Colson wanted Agnesi's work to serve as a model for budding young mathematicians, especially young women. ■

Graph this curve and find the critical numbers, extrema, and points of inflection.

57. Journal Problem: *Mathematics Magazine*[†] ■ Give an elementary proof that

$$f(x) = \frac{1}{\sin x} - \frac{1}{x}, \quad 0 < x \le \frac{\pi}{2}$$

is positive and increasing.

58. An important formula in physical chemistry is *van der Waals' equation*, which says that

$$\left(P + \frac{a}{V^2}\right)(V - b) = nRT$$

where P, V, and T are the pressure, volume, and temperature, respectively, of a gas, and a, b, n, and R are positive constants. The *critical temperature* T_C of the gas is the highest temperature at which the gaseous and liquid phases can exist as separate states.

a. When $T = T_C$, the pressure P can be expressed as a function $P(V)$ of V alone. Show how this can be done, and then find $P'(V)$ and $P''(V)$.

---

*C. J. Pennycuick, "The Mechanics of Bird Migration," *Ibis* III (1969), pp. 525–556.

[†]Volume 55 (1982), p. 300. "Elementary proof" in the question means that you should use only techniques from beginning calculus. For our purposes, you simply need to give a reasonable argument to justify the conclusion.

b. The *critical volume* V_C is the volume that satisfies $P'(V_C) = 0$ and $P''(V_C) = 0$. Find V_C.

c. Find T_C, the point where $P''(V) = 0$, using the V_C from part **b** to write it in terms of a, b, n, and R. Finally, find the *critical pressure* $P_C = P(V_C)$ in terms of a, b, n, and R.

d. Sketch P as a function of V.

59. Prove or disprove that if the graphs of the functions f and g are both concave up on an interval, then the graph of their sum $f + g$ is also concave up on that interval.

60. Use calculus to prove that for constants a, b, and c, the vertex (relative extremum) of the quadratic function

$$y = ax^2 + bx + c \qquad (a \neq 0)$$

occurs at $x = -b/(2a)$.

61. Find constants A, B, and C that guarantee that the function

$$f(x) = Ax^3 + Bx^2 + C$$

will have a relative extremum at $(2, 11)$ and an inflection point at $(1, 5)$. Sketch the graph of f.

62. Find constants a, b, and c that guarantee that the graph of

$$f(x) = x^3 + ax^2 + bx + c$$

will have a relative maximum at $(-3, 18)$ and a relative minimum at $(1, -14)$.

63. Exploration Problem Consider the graph of $y = x^3 + bx^2 + cx + d$ for constants b, c, and d. What happens to the graph as b changes?

64. Find constants A, B, C, and D that guarantee that the graph of

$$f(x) = 3x^4 + Ax^3 + Bx^2 + Cx + D$$

will have horizontal tangents at $(2, -3)$ and $(0, 7)$. There is a third point that has a horizontal tangent. Find this point. Then, for all three points, determine whether each corresponds to a relative maximum, a relative minimum, or neither.

4.4 Curve Sketching with Asymptotes: Limits Involving Infinity

IN THIS SECTION limits to infinity, infinite limits, graphs with asymptotes, vertical tangents and cusps, a general graphing strategy

LIMITS TO INFINITY

In applications, we are often concerned with "long run" behavior of a function. To indicate such behavior, we write

$$\lim_{x \to +\infty} f(x) = L$$

to indicate that $f(x)$ approaches the number L as x increases without bound. Similarly, we write

$$\lim_{x \to -\infty} f(x) = M$$

to indicate that $f(x)$ approaches the number M as x decreases without bound. Here are the formal definitions of these *limits to infinity*.

Limits to Infinity

WARNING Even though the symbols ∞ and $+\infty$ mean the same thing, for the time being we use $+\infty$ to help distinguish between $+\infty$ and $-\infty$.

The limit statement $\lim_{x \to +\infty} f(x) = L$ means that for any number $\epsilon > 0$, there exists a number N_1 such that

$$|f(x) - L| < \epsilon \quad \text{whenever} \quad x > N_1$$

for x in the domain of f. Similarly, $\lim_{x \to -\infty} f(x) = M$ means that for any $\epsilon > 0$, there exists a number N_2 such that

$$|f(x) - M| < \epsilon \quad \text{whenever} \quad x < N_2$$

This definition can be illustrated graphically, as shown in Figure 4.39.

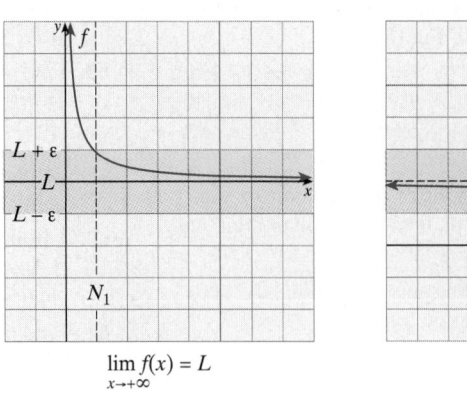

Figure 4.39 Graphical representation of limits to infinity

With this formal definition, we can show that all the rules for limits established in Chapter 2 also apply to $\lim\limits_{x \to +\infty} f(x)$ and $\lim\limits_{x \to -\infty} f(x)$.

Limit Rules

If $\lim\limits_{x \to +\infty} f(x)$ and $\lim\limits_{x \to +\infty} g(x)$ exist, then for constants a and b:

Power rule: $\quad \lim\limits_{x \to +\infty} [f(x)]^n = \left[\lim\limits_{x \to +\infty} f(x) \right]^n$

Linearity rule: $\quad \lim\limits_{x \to +\infty} [af(x) + bg(x)] = a \lim\limits_{x \to +\infty} f(x) + b \lim\limits_{x \to +\infty} g(x)$

Product rule: $\quad \lim\limits_{x \to +\infty} [f(x)g(x)] = \left[\lim\limits_{x \to +\infty} f(x) \right] \left[\lim\limits_{x \to +\infty} g(x) \right]$

Quotient rule: $\quad \lim\limits_{x \to +\infty} \dfrac{f(x)}{g(x)} = \dfrac{\lim\limits_{x \to +\infty} f(x)}{\lim\limits_{x \to +\infty} g(x)}$ if $\lim\limits_{x \to +\infty} g(x) \neq 0$

Analogous results hold for $\lim\limits_{x \to -\infty} f(x)$, if it exists.

The following theorem will allow us to evaluate certain limits to infinity with ease.

THEOREM 4.8 Special limits to infinity

If A is any real number and r is a positive rational number, then

$$\lim_{x \to +\infty} \frac{A}{x^r} = 0$$

Furthermore, if r is such that x^r is defined for $x < 0$, then

$$\lim_{x \to -\infty} \frac{A}{x^r} = 0$$

Proof We begin by proving that $\lim\limits_{x \to +\infty} \dfrac{1}{x} = 0$. For $\epsilon > 0$, let $N = \dfrac{1}{\epsilon}$. Then for $x > N$ we have

$$x > N = \frac{1}{\epsilon} \qquad \text{so that} \qquad \frac{1}{x} < \epsilon$$

This means that $\left|\dfrac{1}{x} - 0\right| < \epsilon$, so that, from the definition of limit we have $\displaystyle\lim_{x \to +\infty} \dfrac{1}{x} = 0$.

Now let r be a rational number, say $r = p/q$. Then

$$\lim_{x \to +\infty} \frac{A}{x^r} = \lim_{x \to +\infty} \frac{A}{x^{p/q}} = A \lim_{x \to +\infty} \left[\frac{1}{\sqrt[q]{x}}\right]^p$$

$$= A \left[\sqrt[q]{\lim_{x \to +\infty} \frac{1}{x}}\right]^p = A\left[\sqrt[q]{0}\right]^p = A \cdot 0 = 0$$

The proof for the analogous limit as $x \to -\infty$ follows similarly. ❏

When evaluating a limit of the form

$$\lim_{x \to +\infty} \frac{p(x)}{d(x)} \qquad \text{or} \qquad \lim_{x \to -\infty} \frac{p(x)}{d(x)}$$

where $p(x)$ and $d(x)$ are polynomials, it is often useful to divide both $p(x)$ and $d(x)$ by the highest power of x that occurs in either. The limit can then be found by applying Theorem 4.8. This process is illustrated by the following examples.

EXAMPLE 1 Evaluating a limit to infinity

Evaluate $\displaystyle\lim_{x \to +\infty} \dfrac{3x^3 - 5x + 9}{5x^3 + 2x^2 - 7}$.

Solution

We may assume that $x \neq 0$, because we are interested only in very large values of x. Dividing both the numerator and denominator of the given expressions by x^3, the highest power of x appearing in the fraction, we find

$$\frac{3x^3 - 5x + 9}{5x^3 + 2x^2 - 7} = \frac{3x^3 - 5x + 9}{5x^3 + 2x^2 - 7} \cdot \frac{\dfrac{1}{x^3}}{\dfrac{1}{x^3}} = \frac{3 - \dfrac{5}{x^2} + \dfrac{9}{x^3}}{5 + \dfrac{2}{x} - \dfrac{7}{x^3}}$$

Thus,

$$\lim_{x \to +\infty} \frac{3x^3 - 5x + 9}{5x^3 + 2x^2 - 7} = \lim_{x \to +\infty} \frac{3 - \dfrac{5}{x^2} + \dfrac{9}{x^3}}{5 + \dfrac{2}{x} - \dfrac{7}{x^3}}$$

$$= \frac{\displaystyle\lim_{x \to +\infty}\left(3 - \frac{5}{x^2} + \frac{9}{x^3}\right)}{\displaystyle\lim_{x \to +\infty}\left(5 + \frac{2}{x} - \frac{7}{x^3}\right)}$$

$$= \frac{3 - 0 + 0}{5 + 0 - 0} = \frac{3}{5}$$

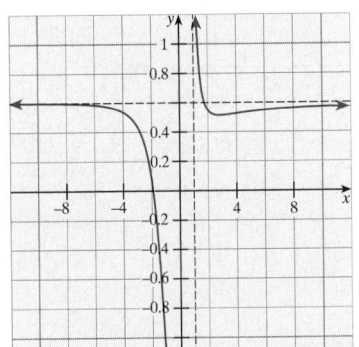

Figure 4.40 Graph of
$$y = \frac{3x^3 - 5x + 9}{5x^3 + 2x^2 - 7}$$

The graph of the given rational function is shown in Figure 4.40. Notice how the curve seems to approach $y = \frac{3}{5}$ as $x \to +\infty$ and as $x \to -\infty$. ∎

Example 2 illustrates how Theorem 4.8 can be used along with the other limit properties to evaluate limits to infinity.

EXAMPLE 2 Evaluating limits to infinity

Evaluate

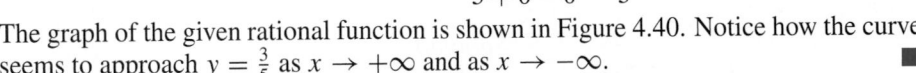

$$\lim_{x \to +\infty} \sqrt{\frac{3x - 5}{x - 2}} \qquad \text{and} \qquad \lim_{x \to -\infty} \left(\frac{3x - 5}{x - 2}\right)^3$$

Solution

Notice that for $x \neq 0$,

$$\frac{3x - 5}{x - 2} = \frac{x\left(3 - \dfrac{5}{x}\right)}{x\left(1 - \dfrac{2}{x}\right)} = \frac{3 - \dfrac{5}{x}}{1 - \dfrac{2}{x}}$$

Also, according to Theorem 4.8, we know that

$$\lim_{x \to +\infty} \frac{5}{x} = 0 \qquad \text{and} \qquad \lim_{x \to +\infty} \frac{2}{x} = 0$$

We now find the limits using the quotient rule, the power rule, and Theorem 4.8:

$$\lim_{x \to +\infty} \sqrt{\frac{3x - 5}{x - 2}} = \lim_{x \to +\infty} \left(\frac{3x - 5}{x - 2}\right)^{1/2} = \left(\lim_{x \to +\infty} \frac{3x - 5}{x - 2}\right)^{1/2}$$

$$= \left(\frac{\displaystyle\lim_{x \to +\infty} \left(3 - \frac{5}{x}\right)}{\displaystyle\lim_{x \to +\infty} \left(1 - \frac{2}{x}\right)}\right)^{1/2} = \left(\frac{3 - 0}{1 - 0}\right)^{1/2} = \sqrt{3}$$

Similarly,

$$\lim_{x \to -\infty} \left(\frac{3x - 5}{x - 2}\right)^{3} = 3^{3} = 27 \qquad \blacksquare$$

EXAMPLE 3   Evaluating a limit to negative infinity

Evaluate $\displaystyle\lim_{x \to -\infty} \frac{95x^3 + 57x + 30}{x^5 - 1{,}000}$.

Solution

Dividing the numerator and the denominator by the highest power, x^5, we find that

$$\lim_{x \to -\infty} \frac{95x^3 + 57x + 30}{x^5 - 1{,}000} = \lim_{x \to -\infty} \frac{95x^3 + 57x + 30}{x^5 - 1{,}000} \cdot \frac{\dfrac{1}{x^5}}{\dfrac{1}{x^5}}$$

$$= \lim_{x \to -\infty} \frac{\dfrac{95}{x^2} + \dfrac{57}{x^4} + \dfrac{30}{x^5}}{1 - \dfrac{1{,}000}{x^5}}$$

$$= \frac{0 + 0 + 0}{1 - 0}$$

$$= 0$$

The graph of the rational function is shown in Figure 4.41. $\blacksquare$

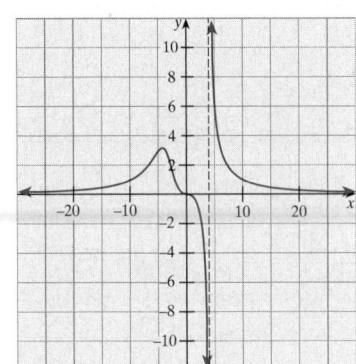

Figure 4.41 Graph of
$$y = \frac{95x^3 + 57x + 30}{x^5 - 1{,}000}$$

EXAMPLE 4   Evaluating a limit to infinity involving e^x

Find $\displaystyle\lim_{x \to +\infty} e^{-x} \cos x$.

Solution

We cannot use the product rule for limits since $\displaystyle\lim_{x \to +\infty} \cos x$ does not exist (it diverges by oscillation—do you see why?). Note, however, that the magnitude of

$$e^{-x} \cos x = \frac{\cos x}{e^x}$$

must become smaller and smaller as $x \to +\infty$ since the numerator $\cos x$ is bounded between -1 and 1, while the denominator e^x grows relentlessly larger with x. Thus by the squeeze rule,

$$\lim_{x \to +\infty} e^{-x} \cos x = 0$$

The graph of $y = e^{-x} \cos x$ is shown in Figure 4.42. $\blacksquare$

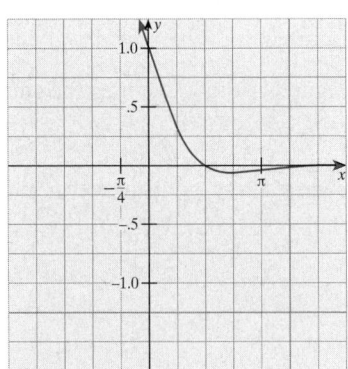

Figure 4.42 Graph of $y = e^{-x} \cos x$

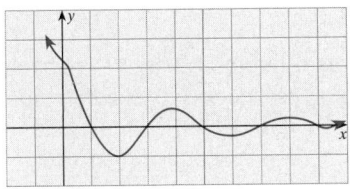

Try drawing the graph of $y = e^{-x} \cos x$ on your calculator, or other graphing software, and you will see that what you get does not properly illustrate the oscillatory behavior of this graph. This demonstrates the importance of *not* relying on technology for graphing. In fact, the accompanying graph (without scale) shows more clearly the behavior of the graph of the function $y = e^{-x} \cos x$ for large, positive values of x.

INFINITE LIMITS

In mathematics, the symbol ∞ is not a number, but is used to describe either the process of unrestricted growth or the result of such growth. Thus, a limit statement such as

$$\lim_{x \to c} f(x) = +\infty$$

means that the function f increases without bound as x approaches c from either side, while

$$\lim_{x \to c} g(x) = -\infty$$

means that g decreases without bound as x approaches c. Such limits may be defined formally as follows.

Infinite Limits

> We write $\lim_{x \to c} f(x) = +\infty$ if for any number $N > 0$ (no matter how large), it is possible to find a number $\delta > 0$ such that $f(x) > N$ whenever $0 < |x - c| < \delta$. Similarly, $\lim_{x \to c} f(x) = -\infty$ if for any $N > 0$, it is possible to find a number $\delta > 0$ so that $f(x) < -N$ when $0 < |x - c| < \delta$.

> ➡ **What This Says**   Remember, ∞ *is **not** a number*, so an infinite limit does not exist in the sense that limits were defined in Chapter 2. However, there are several ways for a limit not to exist (for example, $\lim_{x \to \infty} \cos x$ fails to exist by oscillation), so saying that $\lim_{x \to c} f(x) = +\infty$ or $\lim_{x \to c} f(x) = -\infty$ conveys more information than simply observing that the limit does not exist.

EXAMPLE 5   Infinite limits

Find $\lim\limits_{x \to 2^-} \dfrac{3x - 5}{x - 2}$ and $\lim\limits_{x \to 2^+} \dfrac{3x - 5}{x - 2}$.

Solution

Notice that $\dfrac{1}{x - 2}$ increases without bound as x approaches 2 from the right and $\dfrac{1}{x - 2}$ decreases without bound as x approaches 2 from the left. That is,

$$\lim_{x \to 2^+} \frac{1}{x - 2} = +\infty \qquad \text{and} \qquad \lim_{x \to 2^-} \frac{1}{x - 2} = -\infty$$

We also have $\lim\limits_{x \to 2}(3x - 5) = 1$, and it follows that

$$\lim_{x \to 2^+} \frac{3x - 5}{x - 2} = +\infty \qquad \text{and} \qquad \lim_{x \to 2^-} \frac{3x - 5}{x - 2} = -\infty \qquad \blacksquare$$

GRAPHS WITH ASYMPTOTES

Figure 4.43 shows a graph that approaches the horizontal line $y = 2$ as $x \to +\infty$ and $y = -1$ as $x \to -\infty$, and the vertical line $x = 3$ as x approaches 3 from either side.

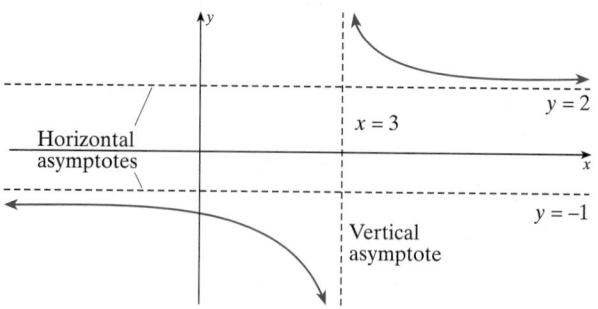

Figure 4.43   A typical graph with asymptotes

Vertical and Horizontal Asymptotes

The line $x = c$ is a **vertical asymptote** of the graph of f if either of the one-sided limits

$$\lim_{x \to c^-} f(x) \qquad \text{or} \qquad \lim_{x \to c^+} f(x)$$

is infinite. The line $y = L$ is a **horizontal asymptote** of the graph of f if

$$\lim_{x \to +\infty} f(x) = L \qquad \text{or} \qquad \lim_{x \to -\infty} f(x) = L$$

EXAMPLE 6   Graphing a rational function with asymptotes

Sketch the graph of $f(x) = \dfrac{3x - 5}{x - 2}$.

Solution

Vertical Asymptotes   First, make sure the rational function is written in simplified (reduced) form. Because vertical asymptotes for $f(x) = \dfrac{3x - 5}{x - 2}$ occur at values of c for which $\lim\limits_{x \to c^-} f(x)$ or $\lim\limits_{x \to c^+} f(x)$ is infinite, we look for values that cause the denominator to be zero (and the numerator not to be zero); that is, we solve $d(c) = 0$, where $d(x)$ is the denominator of $f(x)$, and then evaluate $\lim\limits_{x \to c^-} f(x)$ and $\lim\limits_{x \to c^+} f(x)$ to ascertain the behavior of the function at $x = c$. For this example, $x = 2$ is a value that causes division by zero, so we find

$$\lim_{x \to 2^+} \frac{3x - 5}{x - 2} = +\infty \qquad \text{and} \qquad \lim_{x \to 2^-} \frac{3x - 5}{x - 2} = -\infty$$

(We found these limits in Example 5.) This means that $x = 2$ is a vertical asymptote and that the graph is moving downward as $x \to 2$ from the left and upward as $x \to 2$ from the right. This information is recorded on the preliminary graph shown in Figure 4.44a by a dashed vertical line with upward ($\uparrow$) and downward ($\downarrow$) arrows.

Horizontal Asymptotes   To find the horizontal asymptotes we compute

$$\lim_{x \to +\infty} \frac{3x - 5}{x - 2} = \lim_{x \to +\infty} \frac{3x - 5}{x - 2} \cdot \frac{\frac{1}{x}}{\frac{1}{x}} = \lim_{x \to +\infty} \frac{3 - \frac{5}{x}}{1 - \frac{2}{x}} = \frac{3 - 0}{1 - 0} = 3$$

and

$$\lim_{x \to -\infty} \frac{3x - 5}{x - 2} = 3 \qquad \text{(The steps here are the same as for } x \to +\infty.\text{)}$$

This means that $y = 3$ is a horizontal asymptote. This information is recorded on the preliminary graph shown in Figure 4.44a by a dashed horizontal line with outbound arrows $(\leftarrow, \rightarrow)$.

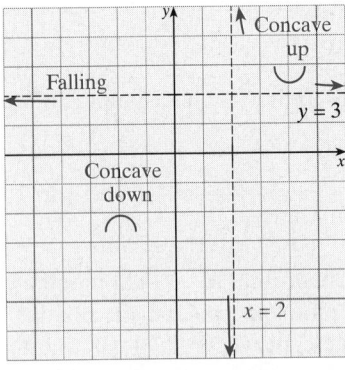

a. Preliminary sketch

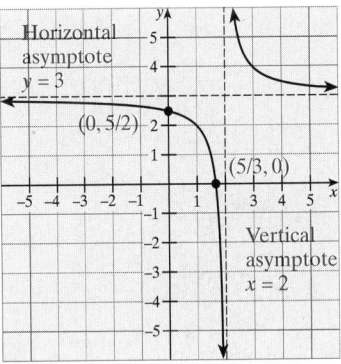

b. Completed sketch

Figure 4.44 Graph of $f(x) = \dfrac{3x - 5}{x - 2}$

The preliminary sketch gives us some valuable information about the graph, but it does not present the entire picture. Next, we use calculus to find where the function is increasing and decreasing (first derivative) and where it is concave up and concave down (second derivative):

$$f'(x) = \frac{-1}{(x - 2)^2} \qquad \text{and} \qquad f''(x) = \frac{2}{(x - 2)^3}$$

Neither derivative is ever zero, and both are undefined at $x = 2$. Checking the signs of the first and second derivatives, we find that the graph is always falling and that it is concave up for $x > 2$ and concave down for $x < 2$. However, it does not have a point of inflection (the function is not defined at $x = 2$). This information is added to the preliminary sketch shown in Figure 4.44a. The completed graph is shown in Figure 4.44b, which also shows the x- and y-intercepts at $(\frac{5}{3}, 0)$ and $(0, \frac{5}{2})$. ∎

EXAMPLE 7   Sketching a curve with asymptotes

Discuss and sketch the graph of $f(x) = \dfrac{x^2 - x - 2}{x - 3}$.

Solution   We find that

$$f'(x) = \frac{x^2 - 6x + 5}{(x - 3)^2} \qquad \text{and} \qquad f''(x) = \frac{8}{(x - 3)^3}$$

Solving $f'(x) = 0$, we see that the critical numbers are $x = 1$ and $x = 5$. Testing on each side of the critical numbers and $x = 3$, where $f(x)$ is not defined, we obtain the intervals of increase and decrease and concavity shown in Figure 4.45.

Note that there is a relative maximum at $x = 1$ and a relative minimum at $x = 5$. The concavity changes (from ↓ to ↑) at $x = 3$, but this does not correspond to an inflection point since $f(3)$ is not defined. We look for vertical asymptotes where $f(x)$ (in reduced form) is not defined; in this case, at $x = 3$. Testing with limits, we find that

$$\lim_{x \to 3^-} \frac{x^2 - x - 2}{x - 3} = -\infty \qquad \text{and} \qquad \lim_{x \to 3^+} \frac{x^2 - x - 2}{x - 3} = +\infty$$

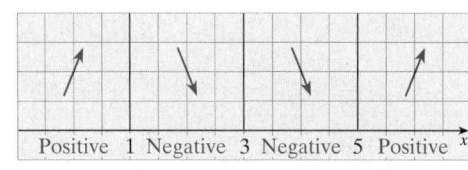

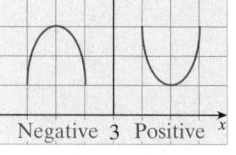

a. Intervals of increase and decrease

b. Intervals of concavity

Figure 4.45 Intervals of increase and decrease and concavity for $f(x) = \dfrac{x^2 - x - 2}{x - 3}$

To check for horizontal asymptotes, we compute

$$\lim_{x \to +\infty} \frac{x^2 - x - 2}{x - 3} = +\infty \qquad \text{and} \qquad \lim_{x \to -\infty} \frac{x^2 - x - 2}{x - 3} = -\infty$$

Since neither limit of $f(x)$ at infinity is finite, there are no horizontal asymptotes.

We plot some points: the relative maximum $(1, 1)$; the relative minimum $(5, 9)$; the x-intercepts $(2, 0)$, $(-1, 0)$; and the y-intercept $(0, \frac{2}{3})$. We also show the vertical asymptote $x = 3$, and, using the intervals of increase and decrease and concavity indicated in Figure 4.45, we obtain the graph shown in Figure 4.46. ∎

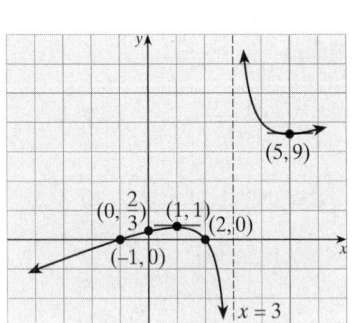

Figure 4.46 Graph of $f(x) = \dfrac{x^2 - x - 2}{x - 3}$

VERTICAL TANGENTS AND CUSPS

Suppose the function f is continuous at the point P where $x = c$ and that $f'(x)$ becomes infinite as x approaches c. Then the graph of f has a *vertical tangent* at P if the graph turns smoothly through P and a *cusp* at P if the graph changes direction abruptly there. These graphical features can be defined in terms of limits, as follows:

Vertical Tangents and Cusps

> Suppose the function f is continuous at the point $P(c, f(c))$. Then the graph of f has
>
> a **vertical tangent** at P if $\lim\limits_{x \to c^-} f'(x)$ and $\lim\limits_{x \to c^+} f'(x)$ are either both $+\infty$ or both $-\infty$;
>
> a **cusp** at P if $\lim\limits_{x \to c^-} f'(x)$ and $\lim\limits_{x \to c^+} f'(x)$ are both infinite with opposite signs (one $+\infty$ and the other $-\infty$).

These possibilities are shown in Figure 4.47.

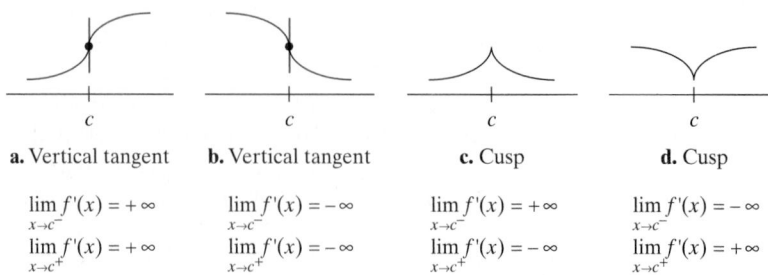

a. Vertical tangent	**b.** Vertical tangent	**c.** Cusp	**d.** Cusp
$\lim\limits_{x \to c^-} f'(x) = +\infty$	$\lim\limits_{x \to c^-} f'(x) = -\infty$	$\lim\limits_{x \to c^-} f'(x) = +\infty$	$\lim\limits_{x \to c^-} f'(x) = -\infty$
$\lim\limits_{x \to c^+} f'(x) = +\infty$	$\lim\limits_{x \to c^+} f'(x) = -\infty$	$\lim\limits_{x \to c^+} f'(x) = -\infty$	$\lim\limits_{x \to c^+} f'(x) = +\infty$

Figure 4.47 Vertical tangents and cusps

EXAMPLE 8   Identifying vertical tangents and cusps

In each of the following cases, determine whether the graph of the given function has a vertical tangent or a cusp:

a. $f(x) = x^{2/3}(2x + 5)$ **b.** $g(x) = x^{1/3}(x + 4)$

Solution

a. Writing $f(x) = 2x^{5/3} + 5x^{2/3}$, we find that

$$f'(x) = \tfrac{10}{3}x^{2/3} + \tfrac{10}{3}x^{-1/3} = \tfrac{10}{3}x^{-1/3}(x + 1)$$

so $f'(x)$ becomes infinite only at $x = 0$. Since

$$\lim_{x \to 0^-} f'(x) = \lim_{x \to 0^-} \tfrac{10}{3}x^{-1/3}(x + 1) = -\infty$$

and

$$\lim_{x \to 0^+} f'(x) = \lim_{x \to 0^+} \tfrac{10}{3}x^{-1/3}(x + 1) = +\infty$$

it follows that there is a cusp on the graph of f at $(0, 0)$. The graph is shown in Figure 4.48a.

b. The derivative

$$g'(x) = \tfrac{4}{3}x^{-2/3}(x + 1)$$

becomes infinite only when $x = 0$. We find that

$$\lim_{x \to 0^-} g'(x) = \lim_{x \to 0^-} \tfrac{4}{3}x^{-2/3}(x + 1) = +\infty$$

and

$$\lim_{x \to 0^+} g'(x) = \lim_{x \to 0^+} \tfrac{4}{3}x^{-2/3}(x + 1) = +\infty$$

Since the limit approaches $+\infty$ as x approaches zero from both the left and the right, we conclude that a vertical tangent occurs at the origin $(0, 0)$. The graph is shown in Figure 4.48b.

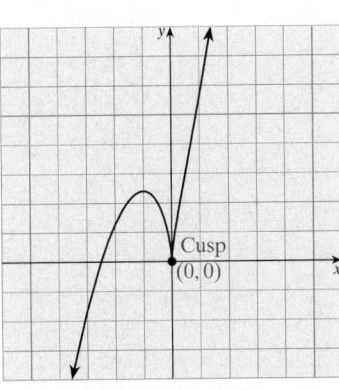
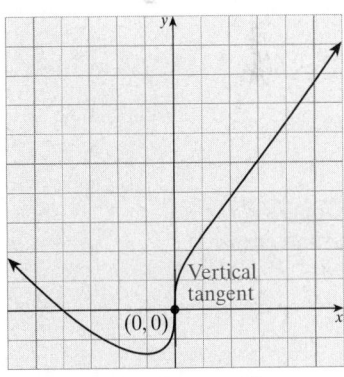

a. The graph of $f(x) = x^{2/3}(2x + 5)$ **b.** The graph of $g(x) = x^{1/3}(x + 4)$

Figure 4.48   A graph with a cusp and another with a vertical tangent

A GENERAL GRAPHING STRATEGY

It is worthwhile to combine the techniques of curve sketching from calculus with those techniques studied in precalculus courses. You may be familiar with **extent** (finding the domain and the range of the function) and **symmetry** (with respect to the x-axis, y-axis, or origin). These features are reviewed in Chapter 8 of the *Student Mathematics Handbook*. We now have all the tools we need to describe a general procedure for curve sketching, and this procedure is summarized in Table 4.1.

TABLE 4.1 Graphing Strategy for a Function Defined by $y = f(x)$

Step	Procedure
Simplify.	If possible, simplify algebraically the function you wish to graph. For example, if $f(x) = \dfrac{(x-2)(x+3)}{x-2}$, you must write this as $f(x) = x + 3$, $x \neq 2$ before beginning the procedure listed here.
Find derivatives and critical numbers.	Compute the first and second derivatives; set each equal to zero and solve (by factoring, if possible), and find the first- and second-order critical numbers.
Determine intervals of increase and decrease.	Use the first-order critical numbers of f: $f'(x) > 0$, curve rising (indicate these regions by ↑) $f'(x) < 0$, curve falling (indicate these regions by ↓)
Apply the second-derivative test.	Use the second-derivative test to find the relative maxima or minima: Substitute the first-order critical numbers, c_1, with the following test: $f''(x) > 0$, relative minimum $f''(x) < 0$, relative maximum $f''(x) = 0$, test fails; use first-derivative test
Determine concavity and points of inflection.	Find the points of inflection. These are located where the concavity changes from up to down or down to up, and are found by checking the intervals on either side of the second-order critical numbers.
Apply the first-derivative test.	Use the first-derivative test if the second-derivative test fails or is too complicated. 1. Let c_1 be a first-order critical number of a continuous function f. 2. **a.** $(c_1, f(c_1))$ is a relative maximum if $f'(x) > 0$ for all x in an open interval (a, c_1) to the left of c_1 $f'(x) < 0$ for all x in an open interval (c_1, b) to the right of c_1. Maximum **b.** $(c_1, f(c_1))$ is a relative minimum if $f'(x) < 0$ for all x in an open interval (a, c_1) to the left of c_1 $f'(x) > 0$ for all x in an open interval (c_1, b) to the right of c_1. Minimum **c.** $(c_1, f(c_1))$ is not an extremum if $f'(x)$ has the same sign in open intervals (a, c_1) and (c_1, b) on both sides of c_1.
Find asymptotes, vertical tangents, and cusps.	1. *Vertical asymptotes*—Vertical asymptotes, if any exist, will occur at values $x = c$ for which f is not defined. Use the limits $\lim\limits_{x \to c^-} f(x)$ and $\lim\limits_{x \to c^+} f(x)$ to determine the behavior of the graph near $x = c$. Show this behavior with arrows (↑↓). 2. *Horizontal asymptotes*—Compute $\lim\limits_{x \to +\infty} f(x)$ and $\lim\limits_{x \to -\infty} f(x)$. If either is finite, plot the associated horizontal asymptote. 3. *Vertical tangents* and *cusps*—Find the vertical tangents and cusps; the graph has a vertical tangent at P if $\lim\limits_{x \to c^-} f'(x)$ and $\lim\limits_{x \to c^+} f'(x)$ are either both $+\infty$ or both $-\infty$. It has a cusp at P if $\lim\limits_{x \to c^-} f'(x)$ and $\lim\limits_{x \to c^+} f'(x)$ are both infinite with opposite signs.
Plot points.	1. If $f(c)$ is a relative maximum, relative minimum, or inflection point, plot $(c, f(c))$. Show the relative maximum points by using a "cap" (∩) and relative minimum points by using a "cup" (∪). 2. x-intercepts: Set $y = 0$ and if $x = a$ is a solution, plot $(a, 0)$. y-intercepts: Set $x = 0$ and if $y = b$ is a solution, plot $(0, b)$; a function will have, at most, one y-intercept.
Sketch the curve.	Draw a curve using the above information.

4.4 PROBLEM SET

A 1. **WHAT DOES THIS SAY?**   Outline a method for curve sketching.

2. **WHAT DOES THIS SAY?**   What are critical numbers? Discuss the importance of critical numbers in curve sketching.

3. **Exploration Problem**   Discuss the importance of concavity and points of inflection in curve sketching.

4. **Exploration Problem**   Discuss the importance of asymptotes in curve sketching.

Evaluate the limits in Problems 5–24.

5. $\lim\limits_{x \to +\infty} \dfrac{2{,}000}{x+1}$

6. $\lim\limits_{x \to +\infty} \dfrac{7{,}000}{\sqrt{x}+1}$

7. $\lim\limits_{x \to +\infty} \dfrac{3x+5}{x-2}$

8. $\lim\limits_{x \to +\infty} \dfrac{x+2}{3x-5}$

9. $\lim\limits_{t \to +\infty} \dfrac{9t^5 + 50t^2 + 800}{t^5 - 1{,}000}$

10. $\lim\limits_{x \to -\infty} \dfrac{(2x+5)(x-3)}{(7x-2)(4x+1)}$

11. $\lim\limits_{x \to +\infty} \dfrac{x}{\sqrt{x^2 + 1{,}000}}$

12. $\lim\limits_{x \to -\infty} \dfrac{3x}{\sqrt{4x^2 + 10}}$

13. $\lim\limits_{x \to +\infty} \dfrac{x^{5.916}+1}{x^{\sqrt{35}}}$

14. $\lim\limits_{x \to +\infty} \dfrac{x^{6.083}+1}{x^{\sqrt{37}}}$

15. $\lim\limits_{x \to 1^-} \dfrac{x-1}{|x^2 - 1|}$

16. $\lim\limits_{x \to 3^+} \dfrac{x^2 - 4x + 3}{x^2 - 6x + 9}$

17. $\lim\limits_{x \to 0^+} \dfrac{x^2 - x + 1}{x - \sin x}$

18. $\lim\limits_{x \to (\pi/4)^+} \dfrac{\sec x}{\tan x - 1}$

19. $\lim\limits_{x \to +\infty} \left(x \sin \dfrac{1}{x} \right)$

20. $\lim\limits_{x \to 0^+} \dfrac{x^2}{1 - \cos x}$

21. $\lim\limits_{x \to 0^+} \dfrac{\ln \sqrt[3]{x}}{\sin x}$

22. $\lim\limits_{x \to +\infty} \dfrac{\ln \sqrt[3]{x}}{\sin x}$

23. $\lim\limits_{x \to -\infty} e^x \sin x$

24. $\lim\limits_{x \to +\infty} \dfrac{\tan^{-1} x}{e^{0.1x}}$

B *Find all vertical and horizontal asymptotes of the graph of each function given in Problems 25–44. Find where each graph is rising and where it is falling, determine concavity, and locate all critical points and points of inflection. Finally, sketch the graph. Be sure to show any special features, such as cusps or vertical tangents.*

25. $f(x) = \dfrac{3x+5}{7-x}$

26. $g(x) = \dfrac{15}{x+4}$

27. $f(x) = 4 + \dfrac{2x}{x-3}$

28. $g(x) = 1 - \dfrac{x}{4-x}$

29. $f(x) = \dfrac{x^3 + 1}{x^3 - 8}$

30. $f(x) = \dfrac{2x^2 - 5x + 7}{x^2 - 9}$

31. $g(x) = \dfrac{8}{x-1} + \dfrac{27}{x+4}$

32. $f(x) = \dfrac{1}{x+1} + \dfrac{1}{x-1}$

33. $g(t) = (t^3 + t)^2$

34. $g(t) = t^{-1/2} + \frac{1}{3}t^{3/2}$

35. $f(x) = (x^2 - 9)^2$

36. $g(x) = x(x^2 - 12)$

37. $f(x) = x^{1/3}(x - 4)$

38. $f(u) = u^{2/3}(u - 7)$

39. $f(x) = \tan^{-1} x^2$

40. $f(x) = \ln(4 - x^2)$

41. $t(\theta) = \sin \theta - \cos \theta$ for $0 \le \theta \le 2\pi$

42. $f(x) = x - \sin 2x$ for $0 \le x \le \pi$

43. $f(x) = \sin^2 x - 2\sin x + 1$ for $0 \le x \le \pi$

44. $T(\theta) = \tan^{-1} \theta - \tan^{-1} \dfrac{\theta}{3}$

45. The *ideal speed v* for a banked curve on a highway is modeled by the equation

$$v^2 = gr \tan \theta$$

where g is the constant acceleration due to gravity, r is the radius of the curve, and θ is the angle of the bank. Assuming that r is constant, sketch the graph of v as a function of θ for $0 \le \theta \le \frac{\pi}{2}$.*

46. According to Einstein's special theory of relativity, the mass of a body is modeled by the expression

$$m = \dfrac{m_0}{\sqrt{1 - \dfrac{v^2}{c^2}}}$$

where m_0 is the mass of the body at rest in relation to the observer, m is the mass of the body when it moves with speed v in relation to the observer, and c is the speed of light. Sketch the graph of m as a function of v. What happens as $v \to c^-$?

47. Sketch a graph of a function f with all the following properties: The graph has $y = 1$ and $x = 3$ as asymptotes; f is increasing for $x < 3$ and $3 < x < 5$ and is decreasing elsewhere; the graph is concave up for $x < 3$ and for $x > 7$ and concave down for $3 < x < 7$; $f(0) = 4 = f(5)$ and $f(7) = 2$.

48. Sketch a graph of a function g with all of the following properties:

(i) g is increasing for $x < -1$ and $-1 < x < 1$ and decreasing for $1 < x < 3$ and $x > 3$;

(ii)   The graph has only one critical point $(1, -1)$, no inflection points;

(iii) $\lim\limits_{x \to -\infty} g(x) = -1$; $\lim\limits_{x \to +\infty} g(x) = 2$;

$$\lim\limits_{x \to -1^+} g(x) = \lim\limits_{x \to 3^-} g(x) = -\infty.$$

49. **Exploration Problem**   Frank Kornerkutter has put off doing his math homework until the last minute, and he is now trying to evaluate

$$\lim\limits_{x \to 0^+} \left(\dfrac{1}{x^2} - \dfrac{1}{x} \right)$$

At first he is stumped, but suddenly he has an idea: Because

$$\lim\limits_{x \to 0^+} \dfrac{1}{x^2} = +\infty \quad \text{and} \quad \lim\limits_{x \to 0^+} \dfrac{1}{x} = +\infty$$

it must surely be true that the limit in question has the value $+\infty - (+\infty) = 0$. Having thus "solved" his problem, he celebrates by taking a nap. Is he right, and, if not, what is wrong with his argument?

---

*In physics it is shown that if one travels around the curve at the ideal speed, no frictional force is required to prevent slipping. This greatly reduces wear on tires and contributes to safety.

50. In an experiment, a biologist introduces a toxin into a bacterial colony and then measures the effect on the population of the colony. Suppose that at time t (in minutes) the population is

$$P(t) = 5 + e^{-0.04t}(t + 1)$$

thousand. At what time will the population be the largest? What happens to the population in the long run (as $t \to +\infty$)? Find where the graph of P has an inflection point, and interpret this point in terms of the population. Sketch the graph of P.

51. Let $P(x) = a_n x^n + a_{n-1}x^{n-1} + \cdots + a_1 x + a_0$ be a polynomial with $a_n \neq 0$ and let $L = \lim_{x \to -\infty} P(x)$ and $M = \lim_{x \to +\infty} P(x)$. Fill in the missing entries in the following table:

Sign of a_n	n	L	M
+	even	a.	$+\infty$
+	odd	$-\infty$	b.
−	even	c.	d.
−	odd	e.	$-\infty$

52. **a.** Show that, in general, the graph of the function

$$f(x) = \frac{ax^2 + bx + c}{rx^2 + sx + t}$$

will have $y = \dfrac{a}{r}$ as a horizontal asymptote and that when $br \neq as$, the graph will cross this asymptote at the point where

$$x = \frac{at - cr}{br - as}$$

b. Sketch the graph of each of the following functions:

$$g(x) = \frac{x^2 - 4x - 5}{2x^2 + x - 10} \qquad h(x) = \frac{3x^2 - x - 7}{-12x^2 + 4x + 8}$$

53. Find constants a and b that guarantee that the graph of the function defined by

$$f(x) = \frac{ax + 5}{3 - bx}$$

will have a vertical asymptote at $x = 5$ and a horizontal asymptote at $y = -3$.

54. **Journal Problem:** *Parabola.** ■ Draw a careful sketch of the curve $y = \dfrac{x^2}{x^2 - 1}$, indicating clearly any vertical or horizontal asymptotes, turning points, or points of inflection.

55. HISTORICAL QUEST   The possibility of division by zero is a fact that causes special concern to mathematicians. One of the first recorded observations of division by zero comes from the twelfth-century Hindu mathematician Bhaskaracharya (also known as Bhaskara), who made the following observation: "The fraction whose denominator is zero is termed an infinite quantity." Bhaskaracharya then went on to give a very beautiful conception of infinity that involved his view of God

and creation. Bhaskaracharya gave a solution for the so-called Pell equation

$$x^2 = 1 + py^2 \qquad x, y \text{ both nonnegative}$$

which is related to the problem of cutting a given sphere so the volumes of the two parts have a specified ratio.

Solve this equation for $p = 2/3$ and write this Pell equation as $y = f(x)$.[†] Find $\lim_{x \to +\infty} f(x)$.

Ⓒ *Counterexample Problems*   In Problems 56–59, either show that the statement is generally true or find a counterexample.

56. If f is concave up and g is concave down on an interval I, then fg is neither concave up nor concave down on I.

57. If f and g are concave up on the interval I, then so is $f + g$.

58. If $f(x) > 0$ and $g(x) > 0$ for all x on I and if f and g are concave up on I, then fg is also concave up on I.

59. If $f(x) < 0$ and $f''(x) > 0$ for all x on I, then the function $g = f^2$ is concave up on I.

60. **Exploration Problem**   State what you think should be the formal definition of each of the following limit statements:

   a. $\lim_{x \to c^+} f(x) = -\infty$ **b.** $\lim_{x \to c^-} f(x) = +\infty$

61. Consider the rational function

$$f(x) = \frac{a_n x^x + a_{n-1}x^{n-1} + \cdots + a_1 x + a_0}{b_m x^m + b_{m-1}x^{m-1} + \cdots + b_1 x + b_0}$$

   a. If $m > n$ and $b_m \neq 0$, show that the x-axis is the only horizontal asymptote of the graph of f.

   b. If $m = n$, show that the line $y = a_n/b_m$ is the only horizontal asymptote of the graph of f.

   c. If $m < n$, is it possible for the graph to have a horizontal asymptote? Explain.

62. Prove the following limit rule.   If $\lim_{x \to c} f(x) = +\infty$ and $\lim_{x \to c} g(x) = A$ $(A > 0)$, then

$$\lim_{x \to c} [f(x)g(x)] = +\infty$$

Hint: Notice that because $\lim_{x \to c} g(x) = A$, the function $g(x)$ is near A when x is near c. Therefore, because $\lim_{x \to +\infty} f(x) = +\infty$, the product $f(x)g(x)$ is large if x is near c. Formalize these observations for the proof.

63. Prove that if $\lim_{x \to +\infty} f(x)$ and $\lim_{x \to +\infty} g(x)$ both exist, so do $\lim_{x \to +\infty} [f(x) + g(x)]$ and

$$\lim_{x \to +\infty} [f(x) + g(x)] = \lim_{x \to +\infty} f(x) + \lim_{x \to +\infty} g(x)$$

Hint: The key is to show that if $|f(x) - L| < \dfrac{\epsilon}{2}$ for $x > N_1$ and $|g(x) - M| < \dfrac{\epsilon}{2}$ for $x > N_2$, then whenever $x > N$ for some number N,

$$|[f(x) + g(x)] - (L + M)| < \epsilon$$

You should also show that N relates to N_1 and N_2.

---

*Volume 20, Issue 1 (1984).

[†]From "Mathematics in India in the Middle Ages," by Chandra B. Sharma, *Mathematical Spectrum*, Volume 14(1), pp. 6–8, 1982.

4.5 l'Hôpital's Rule

IN THIS SECTION a rule to evaluate indeterminate forms, indeterminate forms 0/0 and ∞/∞, other indeterminate forms, special limits involving e^x and $\ln x$

A RULE TO EVALUATE INDETERMINATE FORMS

In curve sketching, optimization, and other applications, it is often necessary to evaluate a limit of the form $\lim\limits_{x \to c} \dfrac{f(x)}{g(x)}$, where $\lim\limits_{x \to c} f(x)$ and $\lim\limits_{x \to c} g(x)$ are either both 0 or both ∞. Such limits are called 0/0 *indeterminate forms* and ∞/∞ *indeterminate forms*, respectively, because their value cannot be determined without further analysis. There is a rule to evaluate such indeterminate forms, known as *l'Hôpital's rule*, which relates the evaluation to a computation of $\lim\limits_{x \to c} \dfrac{f'(x)}{g'(x)}$, the limit of the ratio of the derivatives of f and g. Here is a precise statement of the rule.

WARNING First check the hypotheses (make sure it is of the form 0/0 or ∞/∞), and then take f'/g', not $(f/g)'$.

THEOREM 4.9   l'Hôpital's Rule

Let f and g be differentiable functions with $g'(x) \neq 0$ on an open interval containing c (except possibly at c itself). Suppose $\lim\limits_{x \to c} \dfrac{f(x)}{g(x)}$ produces an indeterminate form $\frac{0}{0}$ or $\frac{\infty}{\infty}$ and that

$$\lim_{x \to c} \frac{f'(x)}{g'(x)} = L$$

where L is either a finite number, $+\infty$, or $-\infty$. Then

$$\lim_{x \to c} \frac{f(x)}{g(x)} = L$$

The theorem also applies to one-sided limits and to limits at infinity (where $x \to +\infty$ and $x \to -\infty$).

Proof   The proof of an important special case is given in Appendix B. However, we can obtain a sense of why it is true in the following argument. Suppose $f(x)$ and $g(x)$ are differentiable functions such that $f(a) = g(a) = 0$. Then, using the linearization formula for a differentiable function F

$$F(x) \approx F(a) + F'(a)(x - a) \qquad \textit{See Section 3.8.}$$

we can write

$$\frac{f(x)}{g(x)} \approx \frac{f(a) + f'(a)(x - a)}{g(a) + g'(a)(x - a)} = \frac{0 + f'(a)(x - a)}{0 + g'(a)(x - a)} = \frac{f'(a)}{g'(a)}$$

so

$$\lim_{x \to a} \frac{f(x)}{g(x)} = \frac{f'(a)}{g'(a)} \qquad \qquad \square$$

l'Hôpital's rule is named after Guillaume François Antoine de l'Hôpital (1661–1704), the author of the first textbook on differential calculus, published in 1696. However, the result that bears l'Hôpital's name was actually due to Johann Bernoulli (see the Historical Quest in Problem 58).

INDETERMINATE FORMS 0/0 and ∞/∞

We now consider a variety of problems involving indeterminate forms. We begin with a limit first computed in Chapter 2, but instead of using a geometric argument together with the squeeze rule of limits, we use l'Hôpital's rule.

EXAMPLE 1   Using l'Hôpital's rule to compute a familiar trigonometric limit

Evaluate $\lim\limits_{x \to 0} \dfrac{\sin x}{x}$.

Solution

Note that this is an indeterminate form because $\sin x$ and x both approach 0 as $x \to 0$. This means that l'Hôpital's rule applies:

$$\lim_{x \to 0} \frac{\sin x}{x} = \lim_{x \to 0} \frac{\cos x}{1} = 1 \qquad \blacksquare$$

EXAMPLE 2   l'Hôpital's rule with a 0/0 form

Evaluate $\lim\limits_{x \to 2} \dfrac{x^7 - 128}{x^3 - 8}$.

Solution

For this example, $f(x) = x^7 - 128$ and $g(x) = x^3 - 8$, and the form is 0/0.

$$\lim_{x \to 2} \frac{x^7 - 128}{x^3 - 8} = \lim_{x \to 2} \frac{7x^6}{3x^2} \qquad \text{l'Hôpital's rule}$$

$$= \lim_{x \to 2} \frac{7x^4}{3} \qquad \text{Simplify.}$$

$$= \frac{7(2)^4}{3} = \frac{112}{3} \qquad \text{Limit of a quotient} \qquad \blacksquare$$

EXAMPLE 3   Limit is not an indeterminate form

Evaluate $\lim\limits_{x \to 0} \dfrac{1 - \cos x}{\sec x}$.

Solution

You must always remember to check that you have an indeterminate form before applying l'Hôpital's rule. The limit is

$$\lim_{x \to 0} \frac{1 - \cos x}{\sec x} = \frac{\lim\limits_{x \to 0}(1 - \cos x)}{\lim\limits_{x \to 0} \sec x} = \frac{0}{1} = 0 \qquad \blacksquare$$

WARNING   If you blindly apply l'Hôpital's rule in Example 3, you obtain the WRONG answer:

$$\lim_{x \to 0} \frac{1 - \cos x}{\sec x} = \lim_{x \to 0} \frac{\sin x}{\sec x \tan x} \qquad \text{This is NOT correct.}$$

$$= \lim_{x \to 0} \frac{\cos x}{\sec x} = \frac{1}{1} = 1$$

This answer is blatantly WRONG, as you can see by looking at the Technology Note.

You can use a graphing calculator to help find many indeterminate-form limits. For instance, the limit in Example 3 can easily be checked by looking at the graph. If you have a graphing calculator, you can see that as $x \to 0$ from either the left or the right, the limit looks the same, namely, 0.

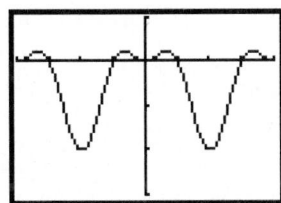

```
Y₁◻(1-cos X)cos
X
Xmin=-6.283185…
Xmax=6.2831853…
Xscl=1.5707963…
Ymin=-3
Ymax=1
Yscl=1
```

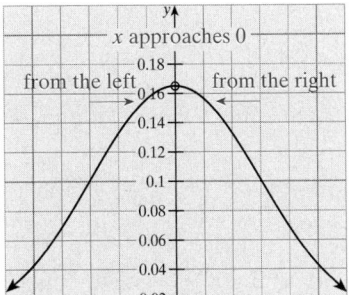

By looking at the graph, you can reinforce the result obtained using l'Hôpital's rule.

EXAMPLE 4   l'Hôpital's rule applied more than once

Evaluate $\displaystyle\lim_{x \to 0} \frac{x - \sin x}{x^3}$.

Solution

This is a 0/0 indeterminate form, and we find that

$$\lim_{x \to 0} \frac{x - \sin x}{x^3} = \lim_{x \to 0} \frac{1 - \cos x}{3x^2}$$

This is still the indeterminate form 0/0, so l'Hôpital's rule can be applied once again:

$$\lim_{x \to 0} \frac{1 - \cos x}{3x^2} = \lim_{x \to 0} \frac{-(-\sin x)}{6x} = \frac{1}{6} \lim_{x \to 0} \frac{\sin x}{x} = \frac{1}{6}(1) = \frac{1}{6} \quad\blacksquare$$

EXAMPLE 5   l'Hôpital's rule with an ∞/∞ form

Evaluate $\displaystyle\lim_{x \to +\infty} \frac{2x^2 - 3x + 1}{3x^2 + 5x - 2}$.

Solution

Using the methods of Section 2.2, we could compute this limit by multiplying by $(1/x^2)/(1/x^2)$. Instead, we note that this is of the form ∞/∞ and apply l'Hôpital's rule:

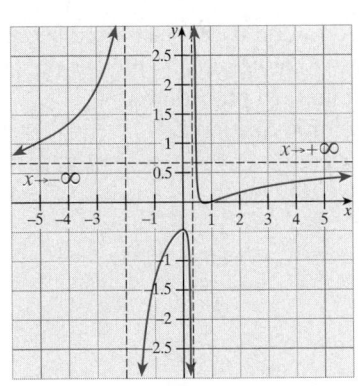

$$\lim_{x \to +\infty} \frac{2x^2 - 3x + 1}{3x^2 + 5x - 2} = \lim_{x \to +\infty} \frac{4x - 3}{6x + 5} \qquad \text{Apply l'Hôpital's rule again.}$$

$$= \lim_{x \to +\infty} \frac{4}{6} = \frac{2}{3} \quad\blacksquare$$

It may happen that even when l'Hôpital's rule applies to a limit, it is not the best way to proceed, as illustrated by the following example.

EXAMPLE 6   Using l'Hôpital's rule with other limit properties

Evaluate $\displaystyle\lim_{x \to 0} \frac{(1 - \cos x) \sin 4x}{x^3 \cos x}$.

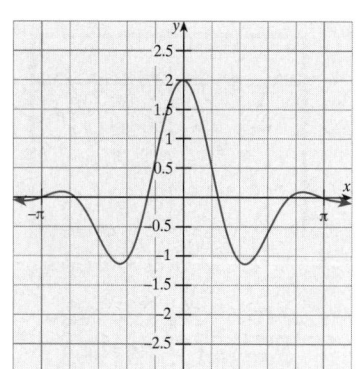

Solution

This limit has the form 0/0, but direct application of l'Hôpital's rule leads to a real mess (try it!). Instead, we compute the given limit by using the product rule for limits first, followed by two simple applications of l'Hôpital's rule. Specifically, using the product rule for limits (assuming the limits exist), we have

$$\lim_{x \to 0} \frac{(1 - \cos x) \sin 4x}{x^3 \cos x} = \left[\lim_{x \to 0} \frac{1 - \cos x}{x^2}\right] \left[\lim_{x \to 0} \frac{\sin 4x}{x}\right] \left[\lim_{x \to 0} \frac{1}{\cos x}\right]$$

$$= \left[\lim_{x \to 0} \frac{\sin x}{2x}\right] \left[\lim_{x \to 0} \frac{4 \cos 4x}{1}\right] \left[\lim_{x \to 0} \frac{1}{\cos x}\right]$$

$$= \left(\frac{1}{2}\right)(4)(1) = 2 \qquad \blacksquare$$

EXAMPLE 7   Hypotheses of l'Hôpital's rule are not satisfied

Evaluate $\displaystyle\lim_{x \to +\infty} \frac{x + \sin x}{x - \cos x}$.

Solution

This limit has the indeterminate form ∞/∞. If you try to apply l'Hôpital's rule, you find

$$\lim_{x \to +\infty} \frac{x + \sin x}{x - \cos x} = \lim_{x \to +\infty} \frac{1 + \cos x}{1 + \sin x}$$

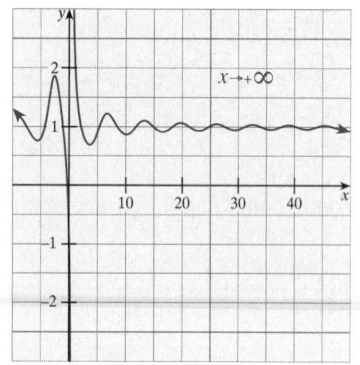

The limit on the right does not exist, because both $\sin x$ and $\cos x$ oscillate between -1 and 1 as $x \to +\infty$. Recall that l'Hôpital's rule applies only if $\displaystyle\lim_{x \to c} \frac{f'(x)}{g'(x)} = L$ or is $\pm\infty$. This does not mean that the limit of the original expression does not exist or that we cannot find it; it simply means that we cannot apply l'Hôpital's rule. To find this limit, factor out an x from the numerator and denominator and proceed as follows:

$$\lim_{x \to +\infty} \frac{x + \sin x}{x - \cos x} = \lim_{x \to +\infty} \frac{x(1 + \frac{\sin x}{x})}{x(1 - \frac{\cos x}{x})} = \lim_{x \to +\infty} \frac{1 + \frac{\sin x}{x}}{1 - \frac{\cos x}{x}} = \frac{1 + 0}{1 - 0} = 1 \qquad \blacksquare$$

OTHER INDETERMINATE FORMS

WARNING   l'Hôpital's rule itself applies only to the indeterminate form 0/0 and ∞/∞.

Other indeterminate forms, such as 1^∞, 0^0, ∞^0, $\infty - \infty$, and $0 \cdot \infty$, can often be manipulated algebraically into one of the standard forms 0/0 or ∞/∞ and then evaluated using l'Hôpital's rule. The following examples illustrate such procedures.

We begin by deriving a formula given without proof in Section 2.4.

EXAMPLE 8   Limit of the form 1^∞

Show that $\displaystyle\lim_{x \to +\infty} \left(1 + \frac{1}{x}\right)^x = e$.

Solution

Note that this limit is indeed of the indeterminate form 1^∞. Let

$$L = \lim_{x \to +\infty} \left(1 + \frac{1}{x}\right)^x$$

Take the logarithm of both sides:

$$\ln L = \ln \left[\lim_{x \to +\infty} \left(1 + \frac{1}{x} \right)^x \right]$$

$$= \lim_{x \to +\infty} \ln \left(1 + \frac{1}{x} \right)^x \qquad \text{ln } x \text{ is continuous}$$

$$= \lim_{x \to +\infty} x \ln \left(1 + \frac{1}{x} \right) \qquad \text{Property of logarithms}$$

$$= \lim_{x \to +\infty} \frac{\ln \left(1 + \dfrac{1}{x} \right)}{\dfrac{1}{x}} \qquad \text{Form } \frac{0}{0}$$

$$= \lim_{x \to +\infty} \frac{\dfrac{1}{1 + 1/x} \left(-\dfrac{1}{x^2} \right)}{-\dfrac{1}{x^2}} \qquad \text{l'Hôpital's rule}$$

$$= \lim_{x \to +\infty} \frac{1}{1 + \dfrac{1}{x}} \qquad \text{Simplify}$$

$$= \frac{1}{1 + 0}$$

$$= 1$$

Thus, $\ln L = 1$ and $L = e^1 = e$. ∎

EXAMPLE 9   l'Hôpital's rule with the form $0 \cdot \infty$

Evaluate $\displaystyle\lim_{x \to \pi/2^-} \left(x - \frac{\pi}{2} \right) \tan x$.

Solution

This limit has the form $0 \cdot \infty$, because

$$\lim_{x \to \pi/2^-} \left(x - \frac{\pi}{2} \right) = 0 \qquad \text{and} \qquad \lim_{x \to \pi/2^-} \tan x = +\infty$$

Write $\tan x = \dfrac{1}{\cot x}$ to obtain

$$\lim_{x \to \pi/2^-} \left(x - \frac{\pi}{2} \right) \tan x = \lim_{x \to \pi/2^-} \frac{x - \frac{\pi}{2}}{\cot x} \qquad \text{Form } \frac{0}{0}$$

$$= \lim_{x \to \pi/2^-} \frac{1}{-\csc^2 x} \qquad \text{l'Hôpital's rule}$$

$$= \lim_{x \to \pi/2^-} (-\sin^2 x) = -1 \qquad \blacksquare$$

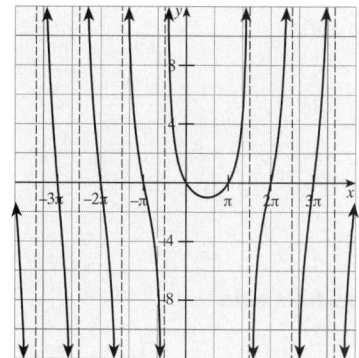

Look at the graph as $x \to \frac{\pi}{2}$ from both the left and the right.

EXAMPLE 10   Limit of the form 0^0

Find $\displaystyle\lim_{x \to 0^+} x^{\sin x}$.

Solution

This is a 0^0 indeterminate form. From the graph shown in Figure 4.49, it looks as though the desired limit is 1. We can verify this conjecture analytically.

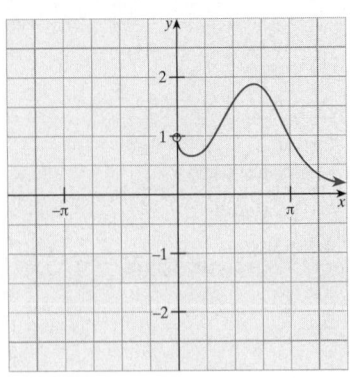

Figure 4.49 Graph of $x^{\sin x}$

As in Example 8, we begin by using properties of logarithms.

$$L = \lim_{x \to 0^+} x^{\sin x}$$

$$\ln L = \ln \lim_{x \to 0^+} x^{\sin x}$$

$$= \lim_{x \to 0^+} \ln x^{\sin x} \qquad \text{ln is continuous}$$

$$= \lim_{x \to 0^+} (\sin x) \ln x \qquad \text{This is } 0 \cdot \infty \text{ form.}$$

$$= \lim_{x \to 0^+} \frac{\ln x}{\csc x} \qquad \text{This is } \frac{\infty}{\infty} \text{ form.}$$

$$= \lim_{x \to 0^+} \frac{1/x}{-\csc x \cot x} \qquad \text{l'Hôpital's rule}$$

$$= \lim_{x \to 0^+} \frac{-\sin^2 x}{x \cos x}$$

$$= \lim_{x \to 0^+} \left(\frac{\sin x}{x} \right) \left(\frac{-\sin x}{\cos x} \right)$$

$$= (1)(0) = 0$$

Thus, $L = e^0 = 1$. ∎

EXAMPLE 11   Limit of the form ∞^0

Find $\displaystyle \lim_{x \to +\infty} x^{1/x}$.

Solution

This is a limit of the indeterminate form ∞^0.

If $L = \displaystyle \lim_{x \to +\infty} x^{1/x}$, then

$$\ln L = \ln \lim_{x \to +\infty} x^{1/x}$$

$$= \lim_{x \to +\infty} \ln x^{1/x} \qquad \text{The limit of a log is the log of the limit.}$$

$$= \lim_{x \to +\infty} \frac{1}{x} \ln x$$

$$= \lim_{x \to +\infty} \frac{\ln x}{x} \qquad \text{This is } \frac{\infty}{\infty} \text{ form.}$$

$$= \lim_{x \to +\infty} \frac{\frac{1}{x}}{1} \qquad \text{l'Hôpital's rule}$$

$$= 0$$

Thus, we have $\ln L = 0$; therefore, $L = e^0 = 1$. ∎

EXAMPLE 12   Horizontal asymptotes with l'Hôpital's rule

Find all horizontal asymptotes of the graph of $y = xe^{-2x}$.

Solution

To test for horizontal asymptotes, we compute

$$\lim_{x \to -\infty} xe^{-2x} \qquad \text{and} \qquad \lim_{x \to +\infty} xe^{-2x}$$

For the first limit, we find

$$\lim_{x \to -\infty} xe^{-2x} = -\infty$$

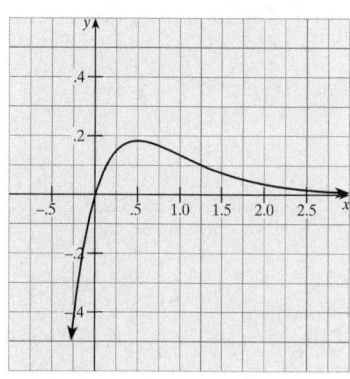

Figure 4.50 Graph of $y = xe^{-2x}$ showing the x-axis as a horizontal asymptote

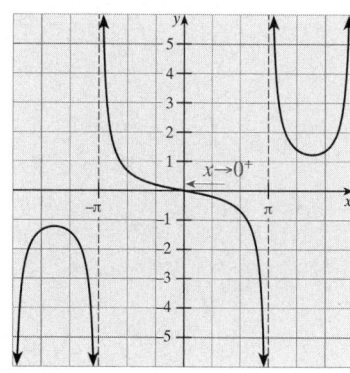

and for the second,

$$
\begin{aligned}
\lim_{x \to +\infty} xe^{-2x} &= \lim_{x \to +\infty} \frac{x}{e^{2x}} & \frac{\infty}{\infty} \text{ form}\\
&= \lim_{x \to +\infty} \frac{1}{2e^{2x}} & \text{l'Hôpital's rule}\\
&= 0
\end{aligned}
$$

Thus, $y = 0$ (the x-axis) is a horizontal asymptote. The graph of $y = xe^{-2x}$ is shown in Figure 4.50. ■

EXAMPLE 13 l'Hôpital's rule with the form $\infty - \infty$

Evaluate $\displaystyle\lim_{x \to 0^+} \left(\frac{1}{x} - \frac{1}{\sin x} \right)$.

Solution

As it stands, this has the form $\infty - \infty$, because $\dfrac{1}{x} \to +\infty$ and $\dfrac{1}{\sin x} \to +\infty$ as $x \to 0$ from the right. However, using a little algebra, we find

$$
\lim_{x \to 0^+} \left(\frac{1}{x} - \frac{1}{\sin x} \right) = \lim_{x \to 0^+} \frac{\sin x - x}{x \sin x}
$$

This limit is now of the form $0/0$, so the hypotheses of l'Hôpital's rule are satisfied. Thus,

$$
\begin{aligned}
\lim_{x \to 0^+} \frac{\sin x - x}{x \sin x} &= \lim_{x \to 0^+} \frac{\cos x - 1}{\sin x + x \cos x} & \text{Again, the form } \frac{0}{0}\\
&= \lim_{x \to 0^+} \frac{-\sin x}{\cos x + x(-\sin x) + \cos x} = \frac{0}{2} = 0 \quad ■
\end{aligned}
$$

WARNING Not all limits that appear indeterminate actually are indeterminate. For example,

$$
\lim_{x \to 0^+} (\sin x)^{1/x} = 0 \qquad 0^{\infty} \text{ form}
$$

$$
\lim_{x \to 0^+} (\csc x - \ln x) = +\infty \qquad +\infty - (-\infty) \text{ form}
$$

$$
\lim_{x \to 0^+} \frac{\tan x}{\ln x} = 0 \qquad \frac{0}{\infty} \text{ form}
$$

Other such "false indeterminate forms" include $+\infty + (+\infty)$, $\infty/0$, and $\infty \cdot \infty$, which are all actually infinite.

SPECIAL LIMITS INVOLVING e^x AND $\ln x$

We close this section with a theorem that summarizes the behavior of certain important special functions involving e^x and $\ln x$ near 0 and at $\pm\infty$.

THEOREM 4.10 Limits involving natural logarithms and exponentials

If k and n are positive numbers, then

$$
\lim_{x \to 0^+} \frac{\ln x}{x^n} = -\infty \qquad\qquad \lim_{x \to +\infty} \frac{\ln x}{x^n} = 0
$$

$$
\lim_{x \to +\infty} \frac{e^{kx}}{x^n} = +\infty \qquad\qquad \lim_{x \to +\infty} x^n e^{-kx} = 0
$$

Proof   These can all be verified directly or by applying l'Hôpital's rule. For example,

$$\lim_{x\to+\infty} \frac{\ln x}{x^n} = \lim_{x\to+\infty} \frac{\frac{1}{x}}{nx^{n-1}} = \lim_{x\to+\infty} \frac{1}{nx^n} = 0$$

The other parts are left for you to verify.   ❑

→ **What This Says**   The limit statements

$$\lim_{x\to+\infty} \frac{e^{kx}}{x^n} = +\infty \qquad \text{and} \qquad \lim_{x\to+\infty} \frac{\ln x}{x^n} = 0$$

are especially important. They tell us that, in the long run, any exponential e^{kx} dominates any power x^n, for k and n positive, which, in turn, dominates any logarithm.

4.5 PROBLEM SET

Ⓐ **1.** An incorrect use of l'Hôpital's rule is illustrated in the following limit computations. In each case, explain what is wrong and find the correct value of the limit.

   a. $\lim_{x\to\pi} \frac{1-\cos x}{x} = \lim_{x\to\pi} \frac{\sin x}{1} = 0$

   b. $\lim_{x\to\pi/2} \frac{\sin x}{x} = \lim_{x\to\pi/2} \frac{\cos x}{1} = 0$

2. Exploration Problem   Sometimes l'Hôpital's rule leads to faulty computations. For example, observe what happens when the rule is applied to

$$\lim_{x\to+\infty} \frac{x}{\sqrt{x^2-1}}$$

Use any method you wish to evaluate this limit.

Find each of the limits in Problems 3–36.

3. $\lim_{x\to1} \dfrac{x^3-1}{x^2-1}$

4. $\lim_{x\to2} \dfrac{x^3-27}{x^2-9}$

5. $\lim_{x\to1} \dfrac{x^{10}-1}{x-1}$

6. $\lim_{x\to-1} \dfrac{x^{10}-1}{x+1}$

7. $\lim_{x\to0} \dfrac{1-\cos^2 x}{\sin^3 x}$

8. $\lim_{x\to0} \dfrac{1-\cos^2 x}{3\sin x}$

9. $\lim_{x\to\pi} \dfrac{\cos\frac{x}{2}}{\pi-x}$

10. $\lim_{x\to0} \dfrac{1-\cos x}{x^2}$

11. $\lim_{x\to0} \dfrac{\sin ax}{\cos bx}, ab\neq0$

12. $\lim_{x\to0} \dfrac{\tan 3x}{\sin 5x}$

13. $\lim_{x\to0} \dfrac{x-\sin x}{\tan x - x}$

14. $\lim_{x\to0} \dfrac{1-\cos^2 x}{x\tan x}$

15. $\lim_{x\to\pi/2} \dfrac{3\sec x}{2+\tan x}$

16. $\lim_{x\to0} \dfrac{x+\sin^3 x}{x^2+2x}$

17. $\lim_{x\to0} \dfrac{\sin 3x \sin 2x}{x\sin 4x}$

18. $\lim_{x\to\pi/2} \dfrac{\sin 2x \cos x}{x\sin 4x}$

19. $\lim_{x\to0} \dfrac{x^2+\sin x^2}{x^2+x^3}$

20. $\lim_{x\to0} x^2\sin\dfrac{1}{x}$

21. $\lim_{x\to+\infty} x^{3/2}\sin\dfrac{1}{x}$

22. $\lim_{x\to0} \left(\cot x - \dfrac{1}{x}\right)$

23. $\lim_{x\to1} \dfrac{(x-1)\sin(x-1)}{1-\cos(x-1)}$

24. $\lim_{\theta\to0} \dfrac{\theta-1+\cos^2\theta}{\theta^2+5\theta}$

25. $\lim_{x\to0} \dfrac{x+\sin(x^2+x)}{3x+\sin x}$

26. $\lim_{x\to\pi/2^-} \sec 3x\cos 9x$

27. $\lim_{x\to0} \left(\dfrac{1}{\sin 2x} - \dfrac{1}{2x}\right)$

28. $\lim_{x\to+\infty} x^{-5}\ln x$

29. $\lim_{x\to0^+} x^{-5}\ln x$

30. $\lim_{x\to0^+} (\sin x)\ln x$

31. $\lim_{x\to+\infty} \dfrac{\ln(\ln x)}{x}$

32. $\lim_{x\to-\infty} \left(1-\dfrac{3}{x}\right)^{2x}$

33. $\lim_{x\to+\infty} \left(1+\dfrac{1}{2x}\right)^{3x}$

34. $\lim_{x\to+\infty} (\ln x)^{1/x}$

35. $\lim_{x\to0^+} (e^x+x)^{1/x}$

36. $\lim_{x\to0^+} (\sin x)^{1/\ln\sqrt{x}}$

Ⓑ *Find each of the limits in Problems 37–51.*

37. $\lim_{x\to(\pi/2)^-} \left(\dfrac{1}{\pi-2x}+\tan x\right)$

38. $\lim_{x\to+\infty} \left(\sqrt{x^2-x}-x\right)$

39. $\lim_{x\to+\infty} [x-\ln(x^3-1)]$ *Hint:* $\ln e^x = x$

40. $\lim_{x\to+\infty} [x-\ln(e^x+e^{-x})]$ *Hint:* $\ln e^x = x$

41. $\lim_{x\to0^+} \left(\dfrac{1}{x^2}-\ln\sqrt{x}\right)$

42. $\lim_{x\to0} (e^x-1-x)^x$

43. $\lim_{x\to0^+} (\ln x)(\cot x)$

44. $\lim_{x\to0^+} (e^x-1)^{1/\ln x}$

45. $\lim_{x\to+\infty} \dfrac{x+\sin 3x}{x}$

46. $\lim_{x\to+\infty} \dfrac{x(\pi+\sin x)}{x^2+1}$

47. $\lim_{x\to0^+} \left(\dfrac{2\cos x}{\sin 2x}-\dfrac{1}{x}\right)$

48. $\lim_{x\to+\infty} \left(\dfrac{x^3}{x^2-x+1}-\dfrac{x^3}{x^2+x-1}\right)$

49. $\lim_{x\to0} \dfrac{(2-x)(e^x-x-2)}{x^3}$

50. $\lim\limits_{x \to 0} \dfrac{\tan^{-1}(3x) - 3\tan^{-1} x}{x^3}$

51. $\lim\limits_{x \to +\infty} x^5 \left[\sin\left(\dfrac{1}{x}\right) - \dfrac{1}{x} + \dfrac{1}{6x^3} \right]$

52. Find A so that $\lim\limits_{x \to +\infty} \left(\dfrac{x + A}{x - 2A} \right)^x = 5$.

In Problems 53–56, use l'Hôpital's rule to determine all horizontal asymptotes to the graph of the given function. You are NOT required to sketch the graph.

53. $f(x) = x^3 e^{-0.01x}$

54. $f(x) = \dfrac{\ln x^5}{x^{0.02}}$

55. $f(x) = (\ln \sqrt{x})^{2/x}$

56. $f(x) = \left(\dfrac{x + 3}{x + 2} \right)^{2x}$

57. Exploration Problem Write a paper on using technology to evaluate limits.

58. HISTORICAL QUEST The French mathematician Guillaume de l'Hôpital is best known today for the rule that bears his name, but the rule was discovered by l'Hôpital's teacher, Johann Bernoulli. Not only did l'Hôpital neglect to cite his sources in his book, but there is also evidence that he paid Bernoulli for his results and for keeping their arrangements for payment confidential. In a letter dated March 17, 1694, he asked Bernoulli "to communicate to me your discoveries ..."—with the request not to mention them to others—"... it would not please me if they were made public." L'Hôpital's argument, which was originally given without using functional notation, can easily be reproduced*:

$$\begin{aligned} \frac{f(a + dx)}{g(a + dx)} &= \frac{f(a) + f'(a)\,dx}{g(a) + g'(a)\,dx} \\ &= \frac{f'(a)\,dx}{g'(a)\,dx} \\ &= \frac{f'(a)}{g'(a)} \quad \blacksquare \end{aligned}$$

Supply reasons for this argument, and give necessary conditions for the functions f and g.

59. HISTORICAL QUEST The remarkable Bernoulli family of Switzerland produced at least eight noted mathematicians over three generations. Two brothers, Jacob (1654–1705) and Johann (1667–1748), were bitter rivals. These brothers were extremely influential advocates of the newly born calculus. Johann was the most prolific of the clan and was responsible for the discovery of l'Hôpital's rule (see Problem 58), Bernoulli numbers, Bernoulli polynomials, the lemniscate of Bernoulli, the Bernoulli equation, the Bernoulli theorem, and the Bernoulli

*D. J. Struik, *A Source Book in Mathematics*, 1200–1800. Cambridge, MA: Harvard University Press, 1969, pp. 313–316.

distribution. He did a great deal of work with differential equations. Johann was jealous and cantankerous; he tossed a son (Daniel) out of the house for winning an award he had expected to win himself. ∎

Write a report on the Bernoulli family.

C *Find the limits in Problems 60–62 using the following methods.*

  a. *graphically*   **b.** *analytically*   **c.** *numerically*

Compare, contrast, and reconcile the three methods.

60. $\lim\limits_{x \to 0^+} x^x$

61. $\lim\limits_{x \to 0^+} (x^x)^x$

62. $\lim\limits_{x \to +\infty} \left[x \sin^{-1}\left(\dfrac{1}{x} \right) \right]^{x^2}$

63. Find constants a and b so that

$$\lim\limits_{x \to 0} \left(\frac{\sin 2x}{x^3} + \frac{a}{x^2} + b \right) = 1$$

64. Find all values of A and B so that

$$\lim\limits_{x \to 0} \frac{\sin Ax + Bx}{x^3} = 36$$

65. For a certain value of C, the limit

$$\lim\limits_{x \to +\infty} (x^4 + 5x^3 + 3)^C - x$$

is finite and nonzero. Find C and then compute the limit.

66. For which values of constants D and E is it true that

$$\lim\limits_{x \to 0} (x^{-3} \sin 7x + Dx^{-2} + E) = -2?$$

67. A weight hanging by a spring is made to vibrate by applying a sinusoidal force, and the displacement at time t is given by

$$f(t) = \frac{C}{\beta^2 - \alpha^2} (\sin \alpha t - \sin \beta t)$$

where C, α, and β are constants such that $\alpha \neq \beta$. What happens to the displacement as $\beta \to \alpha$? You may assume that α is fixed.

68. For F and G positive constants, define

$$f(x) = (e^x + Fx)^{G/x}$$

  a. Compute $L_1 = \lim\limits_{x \to 0} f(x)$ and $L_2 = \lim\limits_{x \to +\infty} f(x)$.

  b. What is the largest value of F for which the equation $L_1 = GL_2$ has a solution? What are L_1 and L_2 in this case?

4.6   Optimization in the Physical Sciences and Engineering

IN THIS SECTION   optimization procedure, Fermat's principle of optics and Snell's law

We introduced the process of mathematical modeling in Chapter 3, and now that we have developed the necessary calculus skills, we will use mathematical modeling and calculus to solve optimization problems.

OPTIMIZATION PROCEDURE

NOTHING TAKES PLACE in the world whose meaning is not that of some maximum or minimum.

——Leonhard Euler

When light travels from one medium to another—say, from air into water—which path does it follow? In a mechanical system involving pulleys, which arrangement results in minimal potential energy? At what temperature does a given mass of water occupy the least volume (the answer is not 0°C)? These are typical *optimization problems* from the physical sciences and engineering and will be examined in the examples and exercises of this section. The process of finding the maximum or minimum of a function is called **optimization**. Then, in the next section, we will explore optimization involving applications to business, economics, and the social and life sciences. We begin by outlining a general optimization procedure based on ideas originally suggested by George Pólya (1887–1985), one of the great problem solvers of twentieth-century mathematics (see the Historical Quest in Problem 61 of Section 7.4).

Optimization Procedure

Step 1.   Draw a figure (if appropriate) and label all quantities relevant to the problem.

Step 2.   Focus on the quantity to be optimized. Name it. Find a formula for the quantity to be maximized or minimized.

Step 3.   Use conditions in the problem to eliminate variables in order to express the quantity to be maximized or minimized in terms of a single variable.

Step 4.   Find the practical domain for the variables in Step 3; that is, the interval of possible values determined from the physical restrictions in the problem.

Step 5.   If possible, use the methods of calculus to obtain the required optimum value.

EXAMPLE 1   Maximizing a constrained area

You need to fence a rectangular play zone for children. What is the maximum area for this play zone if it is to fit into a right-triangular plot with sides measuring 4 m and 12 m?

Solution

A picture of the play zone is shown in Figure 4.51. Let x and y denote the length and width of the inscribed rectangle. The appropriate formula for the area is

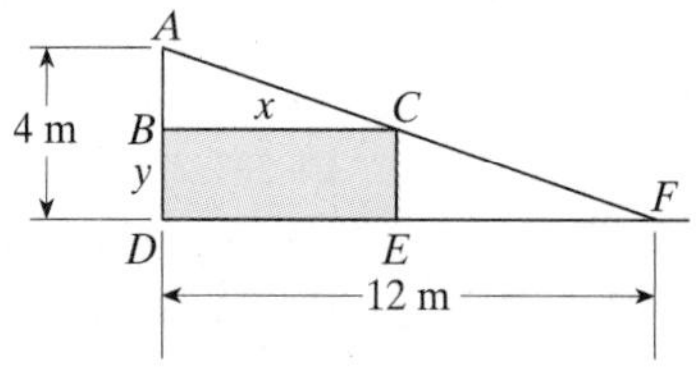

$$A = (\text{LENGTH})(\text{WIDTH}) = xy$$

We wish to maximize A, where $A = xy$, but first we must express A as a function of a single variable. To do this, note that, because $\triangle ABC$ is similar to $\triangle ADF$, the corresponding sides of these triangles are proportional,

$$\frac{4-y}{4} = \frac{x}{12}$$
$$y = 4 - \tfrac{1}{3}x$$

Figure 4.51 Children's play zone

 SMH   See Section 1.5 of the *Student Mathematics Handbook* for similar triangles.

We can now write A as a function of x alone:

$$A(x) = x(4 - \tfrac{1}{3}x) = 4x - \tfrac{1}{3}x^2$$

The domain for A is $0 \le x \le 12$. The critical numbers for A are values such that $A'(x) = 0$ (since $A'(x)$ exists for all x). Since

$$A'(x) = 4 - \tfrac{2}{3}x$$

the only critical number is $x = 6$. Evaluate $A(x)$ at the endpoints and the critical number:

$$A(6) = 4(6) - \tfrac{1}{3}(6)^2 = 12; \quad A(0) = 0; \quad A(12) = 0$$

The maximum area occurs when $x = 6$. This means that

$$y = 4 - \tfrac{1}{3}(6) = 2$$

Thus, the largest rectangular play zone that can be built in the triangular plot is a rectangle 6 m long and 2 m wide.   ∎

EXAMPLE 2   Maximizing a volume

A carpenter wants to make an open-topped box out of a rectangular sheet of tin 24 in. wide and 45 in. long. The carpenter plans to cut congruent squares out of each corner of the sheet and then bend and solder the edges of the sheet upward to form the sides of the box, as shown in Figure 4.52.

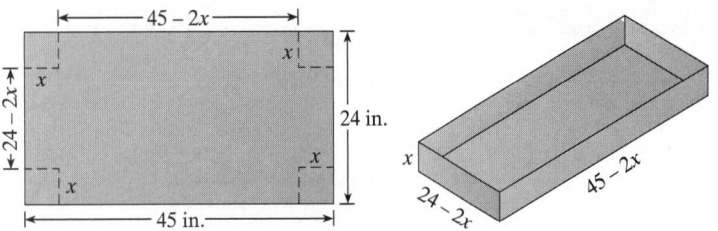

Figure 4.52   A box cut from a 24 in. by 45 in. piece of tin

For what dimensions does the box have the greatest possible volume?

Solution

If each square corner cut out has side x, the box will be x inches deep, $45 - 2x$ inches long, and $24 - 2x$ inches wide. The volume of the box shown in Figure 4.52 is

$$V(x) = x(45 - 2x)(24 - 2x) = 4x^3 - 138x^2 + 1{,}080x$$

and this is the quantity to be maximized. To find the domain, we note that the dimensions must all be nonnegative; therefore, $x \ge 0$, $45 - 2x \ge 0$ (or $x \le 22.5$), and $24 - 2x \ge 0$ (or $x \le 12$). This implies that the domain is $[0, 12]$.

To find the critical numbers (the derivative is defined everywhere in the domain), we find values for which the derivative is 0:

$$V'(x) = 12x^2 - 276x + 1{,}080 = 12(x - 18)(x - 5)$$

The critical numbers are $x = 5$ and $x = 18$, but $x = 18$ is not in the domain, so the only relevant critical number is $x = 5$. Evaluating $V(x)$ at the critical number $x = 5$ and the endpoints $x = 0$, $x = 12$, we find

$$V(5) = 5(45 - 10)(24 - 10) = 2{,}450; \quad V(0) = 0; \quad V(12) = 0$$

Thus, the box with the largest volume is found when $x = 5$. Such a box has dimensions 5 in. × 14 in. × 35 in.   ∎

You will note in Example 2 we did not have to test whether the critical point was a maximum or a minimum, but knew that it was a maximum because the continuous function V is nonnegative on the interval $[0, 12]$ and is indeed zero at the endpoints. Since there is only one critical number $x = 5$, that must yield the maximum. Similar reasoning can be used in many examples, allowing us to forgo having to test for a maximum or minimum with the first- or second-derivative test. We summarize this procedure with the following definition.

EVT Convention

> If the hypotheses of the extreme value theorem apply to a particular problem, we can often avoid testing a candidate to see whether it is a maximum or a minimum. Suppose we have three candidates and two are obviously minima—the third *must be a maximum*. We will refer to this principle of not testing a candidate as the **EVT convention** because it is shorthand for using the extreme value theorem.

EXAMPLE 3   Maximizing illumination

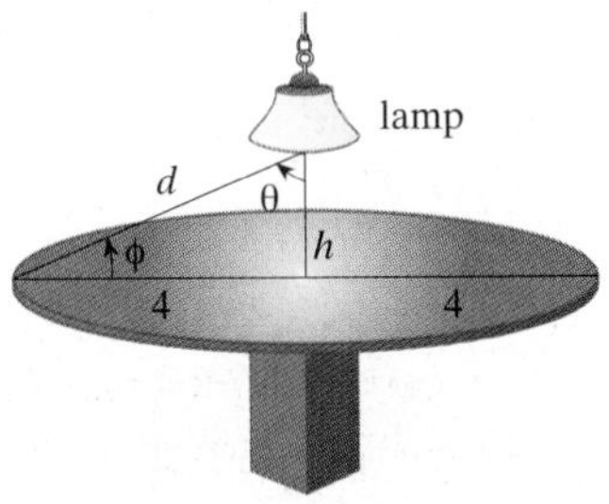

Figure 4.53 Illumination on a kitchen table

A lamp with adjustable height hangs directly above the center of a circular kitchen table that is 8 ft in diameter. Model the illumination I at the edge of the table to be directly proportional to the cosine of the angle θ and inversely proportional to the square of the distance d, where θ and d are as shown in Figure 4.53. How close to the table should the lamp be lowered to maximize the illumination at the edge of the table?

Solution

We note that

$$I(\theta) = \frac{k \cos \theta}{d^2}$$

where k is a (positive) constant of proportionality. Moreover, from the right triangle shown in Figure 4.53,

$$\sin \theta = \frac{4}{d} \quad \text{or} \quad d = \frac{4}{\sin \theta}$$

Hence,

$$I(\theta) = k \cos \theta \left[\frac{1}{(4/\sin \theta)^2} \right]$$

$$= \frac{k}{16} \cos \theta \sin^2 \theta$$

Only values of θ between 0 and $\frac{\pi}{2}$ are meaningful in the context of this problem. Hence, the goal is to find the absolute maximum of the function $I(\theta)$ on $[0, \frac{\pi}{2}]$.

Using the product rule and the chain rule to differentiate $I(\theta)$, we obtain

$$I'(\theta) = \frac{k}{16} [\cos \theta (2 \sin \theta \cos \theta) + \sin^2 \theta (-\sin \theta)]$$

$$= \frac{k}{16} (2 \cos^2 \theta \sin \theta - \sin^3 \theta)$$

$$= \frac{k}{16} \sin \theta (2 \cos^2 \theta - \sin^2 \theta)$$

This is zero when $\theta = 0$ (since $\sin 0 = 0$) and when

$$2 \cos^2 \theta - \sin^2 \theta = 0$$

$$\frac{\sin^2 \theta}{\cos^2 \theta} = 2$$

$$\tan^2 \theta = 2$$

$$\theta = \tan^{-1} \sqrt{2}$$

Evaluating $I(\theta)$ at the endpoints, $\theta = 0$ and $\theta = \frac{\pi}{2}$, and at the interior critical number $\tan^{-1}\sqrt{2} \approx 0.9553$, we find that

$$I(0) = \frac{k}{16}(\cos 0)(\sin^2 0) = 0$$

$$I\left(\frac{\pi}{2}\right) = \frac{k}{16}\left(\cos\frac{\pi}{2}\right)\left(\sin^2\frac{\pi}{2}\right) = 0$$

$$I(\tan^{-1}\sqrt{2}) \approx I(0.9553) \approx \frac{k}{16}(\cos 0.9553)(\sin^2 0.9553) \approx 0.0241k$$

Finally, to find the height h that maximizes the illumination I, observe from Figure 4.53 that

$$\tan\theta = \frac{4}{h}$$

Since $\tan\theta = \sqrt{2}$ when I is maximized, it follows that

$$h = \frac{4}{\tan\theta} = \frac{4}{\sqrt{2}} \approx 2.83$$

To maximize the illumination, the lamp should be placed about 2.8 ft (2 ft 10 in.) above the table. ■

EXAMPLE 4   Minimizing time of travel

A dune buggy is on the desert at a point A located 40 km from a point B, which lies on a long, straight road, as shown in Figure 4.54. The driver can travel at 45 km/h on the desert and 75 km/h on the road. The driver will win a prize if she arrives at the finish line at point D, 50 km from B, in 84 min or less. What route should she travel to minimize the time of travel? Does she win the prize?

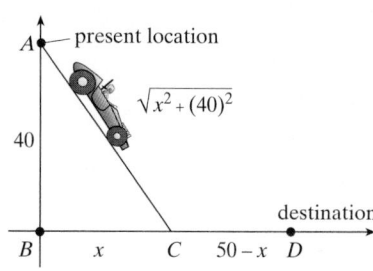

Figure 4.54 A path traveled by a dune buggy

Solution

Suppose the driver heads for a point C located x km down the road from B toward her destination, as shown in Figure 4.54. We want to minimize the time. We will need to remember the formula $d = rt$, or in terms of time, $t = \frac{d}{r}$.

$$\text{TIME} = \text{TIME FROM } A \text{ TO } C + \text{TIME FROM } C \text{ TO } D$$

$$= \frac{\text{DISTANCE FROM } A \text{ TO } C}{\text{RATE FROM } A \text{ TO } C} + \frac{\text{DISTANCE FROM } C \text{ TO } D}{\text{RATE FROM } C \text{ TO } D}$$

$$T(x) = \frac{\sqrt{x^2 + 1{,}600}}{45} + \frac{50 - x}{75}$$

The domain of T is $[0, 50]$. Next, find the derivative of time T with respect to x:

$$T'(x) = \frac{1}{45}\left[\frac{1}{2}(x^2 + 1{,}600)^{-1/2}(2x)\right] + \frac{1}{75}(-1)$$

$$= \frac{x}{45\sqrt{x^2 + 1{,}600}} - \frac{1}{75}$$

$$= \frac{5x - 3\sqrt{x^2 + 1{,}600}}{225\sqrt{x^2 + 1{,}600}}$$

The derivative exists for all x and is zero when

$$5x - 3\sqrt{x^2 + 1{,}600} = 0$$

Solving this equation, we find $x = 30$ (-30 is extraneous). Evaluating $T(x)$ here and at the endpoints, we find that

$$T(30) = \frac{\sqrt{30^2 + 1{,}600}}{45} + \frac{50 - 30}{75} \approx 1.3778 \text{ hr} \approx 83 \text{ min}$$

$$T(0) = \frac{\sqrt{0^2 + 1{,}600}}{45} + \frac{50 - 0}{75} \approx 1.5556 \text{ hr} \approx 93 \text{ min}$$

$$T(50) = \frac{\sqrt{50^2 + 1{,}600}}{45} + \frac{50 - 50}{75} \approx 1.4229 \text{ hr} \approx 85 \text{ min}$$

The driver can minimize the total driving time by heading for a point that is 30 miles from the point B and then traveling on the road to point D. She wins the prize because this minimal route requires only 83 minutes. ∎

EXAMPLE 5   Optimizing a constrained area

A wire of length L is to be cut into two pieces, one of which will be bent to form a circle and the other to form a square. Determine how the wire should be cut to

a. maximize the sum of the areas enclosed by the two pieces.
b. minimize the sum of the areas enclosed by the two pieces.

Solution

To understand the problem we draw a sketch, as shown in Figure 4.55, and label the radius of the circle r and the side of the square s.

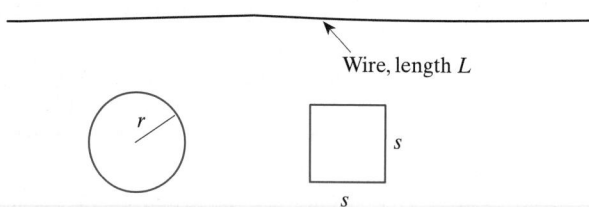

Figure 4.55   Forming a circle and a square from a wire with length L

We find that the combined area is

$$\text{AREA} = \text{AREA OF CIRCLE} + \text{AREA OF SQUARE} = \pi r^2 + s^2$$

We need to write the radius r and the side s in terms of the length of wire, L.

$$L = \text{CIRCUMFERENCE OF CIRCLE} + \text{PERIMETER OF SQUARE}$$
$$= 2\pi r + 4s$$

so $s = \frac{1}{4}(L - 2\pi r)$. (We could just as easily have solved for r.) By substitution,

$$A(r) = \pi r^2 + \left[\tfrac{1}{4}(L - 2\pi r)\right]^2 = \pi r^2 + \tfrac{1}{16}(L - 2\pi r)^2$$

To find the domain, we note that $r \geq 0$ and that $L - 2\pi r \geq 0$, so the domain is $0 \leq r \leq \dfrac{L}{2\pi}$. Note when $r = 0$ there is no circle, and when $r = \dfrac{L}{2\pi}$ there is no square. The derivative of $A(r)$ is

$$A'(r) = 2\pi r + \tfrac{1}{8}(L - 2\pi r)(-2\pi)$$
$$= 2\pi r - \tfrac{\pi}{4}(L - 2\pi r)$$
$$= \tfrac{\pi}{4}(8r - L + 2\pi r)$$

Solve $A'(r) = 0$ to find $r = \dfrac{L}{2(\pi + 4)}$.

Thus, the extreme values of the area function on $\left[0, \dfrac{L}{2\pi}\right]$ must occur either at the endpoints or at the critical number $\dfrac{L}{2\pi + 8}$. Evaluating $A(r)$ at each of these numbers, we find

$$A(0) = \pi (0)^2 + \frac{1}{16}[L - 2\pi (0)]^2 = \frac{L^2}{16}$$

$$A\left(\frac{L}{2\pi}\right) = \pi \left(\frac{L}{2\pi}\right)^2 + \frac{1}{16}\left[L - 2\pi \left(\frac{L}{2\pi}\right)\right]^2 = \frac{L^2}{4\pi}$$

$$A\left(\frac{L}{2\pi + 8}\right) = \pi \left(\frac{L}{2\pi + 8}\right)^2 + \frac{1}{16}\left[L - 2\pi \left(\frac{L}{2\pi + 8}\right)\right]^2 = \frac{L^2}{4(\pi + 4)}$$

Comparing these values, we see that the smallest area occurs at $r = \dfrac{L}{2\pi + 8}$ and the largest area occurs at $x = L/(2\pi)$. To summarize,

1. To maximize the sum of the areas, do not cut the wire at all. Bend the wire to form a circle of radius $r = \dfrac{L}{2\pi}$.

2. To minimize the sum of the areas, cut the wire at the point located $2\pi r = \dfrac{2\pi L}{2\pi + 8}$

$= \dfrac{\pi L}{\pi + 4}$ units from one end, and form the circular part with resulting radius $r = \dfrac{L}{2\pi + 8}$.

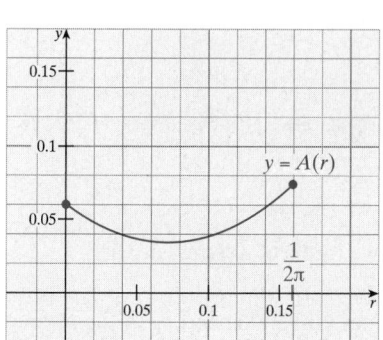

Figure 4.56 Graph of $A(r) = \pi r^2 + \frac{1}{16}(1 - 2\pi r)^2$

If you use a graphing calculator or a computer, you can verify this result (for $L = 1$) by looking at the graph of the area function, as shown in Figure 4.56. ∎

EXAMPLE 6 Optimizing an angle of observation

A painting is hung on a wall in such a way that its upper and lower edges are 10 ft and 7 ft above the floor, respectively. An observer whose eyes are 5 ft above the floor stands x feet from the wall, as shown in Figure 4.57. How far away from the wall should the observer stand to maximize the angle subtended by the painting?

Solution

In Figure 4.57, θ is the angle whose vertex occurs at the observer's eyes at a point O located x feet from the wall. Note that α is the angle between the line $\overline{OA}$ drawn horizontally from the observer's eyes to the wall and the line $\overline{OB}$ from the eyes to the bottom edge of the painting. In $\triangle OAB$, the angle at O is α, with $\cot \alpha = \frac{x}{2}$. In $\triangle OAC$, the angle at O is $(\alpha + \theta)$, and $\cot(\alpha + \theta) = \frac{x}{5}$. By using the definition of inverse cotangent, we have

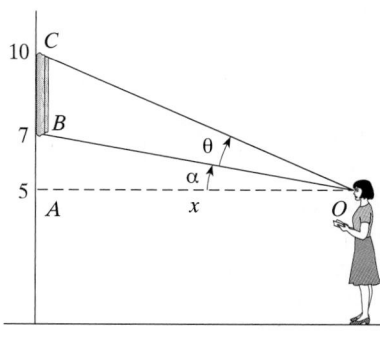

Figure 4.57 The angle θ is subtended by the observer's eye

$$\theta = (\alpha + \theta) - \alpha = \cot^{-1}\left(\frac{x}{5}\right) - \cot^{-1}\left(\frac{x}{2}\right)$$

To maximize θ, we first compute the derivative:

$$\frac{d\theta}{dx} = \frac{-1}{\left[1 + \left(\frac{x}{5}\right)^2\right]}\left(\frac{1}{5}\right) - \frac{-1}{\left[1 + \left(\frac{x}{2}\right)^2\right]}\left(\frac{1}{2}\right) = \frac{-5}{25 + x^2} + \frac{2}{4 + x^2}$$

Solving the equation $\dfrac{d\theta}{dx} = 0$ yields

$$-5(4 + x^2) + 2(25 + x^2) = 0$$

$$-3x^2 + 30 = 0$$

$$x = \pm\sqrt{10}$$

Because distance must be nonnegative, we reject the negative value. We apply the first-derivative test to show that the positive critical number $\sqrt{10}$ corresponds to a relative maximum (verify). Thus, the angle θ is maximized when the observer stands $\sqrt{10}$ ft away from the wall. ∎

FERMAT'S PRINCIPLE OF OPTICS AND SNELL'S LAW

Light travels at different rates in different media; the more optically dense the medium, the slower the speed of transit. Consider the situation shown in Figure 4.58, in which a beam of light originates at a point A in one medium, then strikes the upper surface of a second, denser medium at a point P, and is refracted to a point B in the second medium.

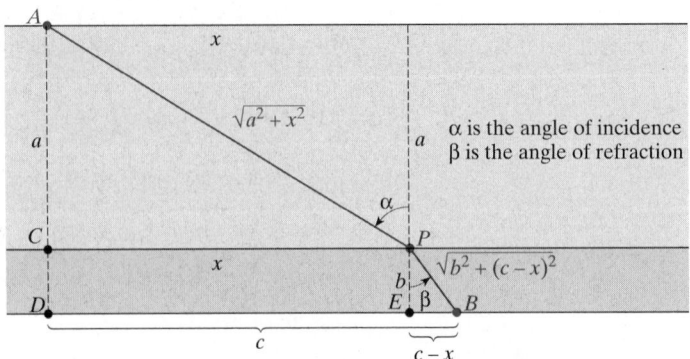

Figure 4.58 The path of a light beam through two media of different density

Suppose light travels with speed v_1 in the first medium and speed v_2 in the second. What can be said about the path followed by the beam of light?

Our method of investigating this question is based on the following optical property.

Fermat's Principle of Optics

Light travels between two points in such a way as to minimize the time of transit.

This problem is very similar to the dune buggy problem of Example 4: Light minimizes the time, and determining minimum time was the goal of that example. In Figure 4.58, let $a = \left|\overline{AC}\right|$, $b = \left|\overline{CD}\right|$, and $c = \left|\overline{DB}\right|$, and let x denote the distance from C to P. Because A and B are fixed points, the path APB is determined by the location of P, which, in turn, is determined by x. Because v_1 is a given constant, the time required for the light to travel from A to P is given by

$$T_1 = \frac{\left|\overline{AP}\right|}{v_1} = \frac{\sqrt{a^2 + x^2}}{v_1}$$

and the time required for the light to go from P to B is

$$T_2 = \frac{\left|\overline{PB}\right|}{v_2} = \frac{\sqrt{b^2 + (c - x)^2}}{v_2}$$

for another given constant v_2. Therefore, the total time of transit is

$$T = T_1 + T_2 = \frac{\sqrt{a^2 + x^2}}{v_1} + \frac{\sqrt{b^2 + (c - x)^2}}{v_2}$$

where it is clear that $0 \le x \le c$. According to Fermat's principle, the path followed by the beam of light is the one that corresponds to the smallest possible value of T; that is, we want to minimize T as a function of x.

Toward this end, we begin by finding $\dfrac{dT}{dx}$.

$$\frac{dT}{dx} = \frac{x}{v_1\sqrt{a^2 + x^2}} - \frac{c - x}{v_2\sqrt{b^2 + (c - x)^2}}$$

Note from Figure 4.58 that if α is the angle of incidence of the beam of light and β is the angle of refraction, then (from the definition of sine)

$$\sin \alpha = \frac{x}{\sqrt{a^2 + x^2}} \quad \text{and} \quad \sin \beta = \frac{c - x}{\sqrt{b^2 + (c - x)^2}}$$

Therefore (by substitution), we see the derivative of T can be expressed as

$$\frac{dT}{dx} = \frac{\sin \alpha}{v_1} - \frac{\sin \beta}{v_2}$$

and it follows that the only critical number occurs when

$$\frac{\sin \alpha}{\sin \beta} = \frac{v_1}{v_2}$$

By using the first-derivative test, it can be shown that this critical number corresponds to an absolute minimum. The corresponding value of x enables us to locate P and hence to determine the path followed by the beam of light. We have established the following law of optics.

Snell's Law of Refraction

If a beam of light strikes the boundary between two media with angle of incidence α and is refracted through an angle β, then

$$\frac{\sin \alpha}{\sin \beta} = \frac{v_1}{v_2}$$

where v_1 and v_2 are the rates at which light travels through the first and second medium, respectively. The constant ratio

$$n = \frac{\sin \alpha}{\sin \beta}$$

is called the **relative index of refraction** of the two media.

4.6 PROBLEM SET

A **1. WHAT DOES THIS SAY?** Describe an optimization procedure.

2. WHAT DOES THIS SAY? What is Fermat's principle of optics?

B **3.** A woman plans to fence off a rectangular garden whose area is 64 ft². What should be the dimensions of the garden if she wants to minimize the amount of fencing used?

4. The highway department is planning to build a rectangular picnic area for motorists along a major highway. It is to have an area of 5,000 yd² and is to be fenced off on the three sides not adjacent to the highway. What is the least amount of fencing that will be needed to complete the job?

5. Exploration Problem Pull out a sheet of $8\frac{1}{2}$-in. by 11-in. engineering or binder paper. Cut squares from the corners and fold the sides up to form a container. Show that the maximum volume of such a container is about 1 liter.

6. Journal Problem: *Parabola.** ■ Farmer Jones has to build a fence to enclose a 1,200 m² rectangular area $ABCD$. Fencing

costs \$3 per meter, but Farmer Smith has agreed to pay half the cost of fencing $\overline{CD}$, which borders the property. Given x is the length of side $\overline{CD}$, what is the minimum amount (to the nearest cent) Jones has to pay?

7. Find the rectangle of largest area that can be inscribed in a semicircle of radius R, assuming that one side of the rectangle lies on the diameter of the semicircle.

8. A cylindrical container with no top is to be constructed to hold a fixed volume V_0 of liquid. The cost of the material used for the bottom is 50¢/in.², and the cost of the material used for the curved lateral side is 30¢/in.² Use calculus to find the radius (in terms of V_0) of the least expensive container.

9. Find the dimensions of the right circular cylinder of largest volume that can be inscribed in a sphere of radius R.

10. Given a sphere of radius R, find the radius r and altitude $2h$ of the right circular cylinder with largest lateral surface area that can be inscribed in the sphere.

11. Each edge of a square has length L, as shown in Figure 4.59.

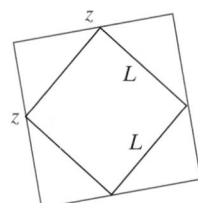

Figure 4.59   Square in a square

Determine the edge of the square of largest area that can be circumscribed about the given square.

12. Find the dimensions of the right circular cylinder of largest volume that can be inscribed in a right circular cone of radius R and altitude H. *Hint*: Begin with Figure 4.60.

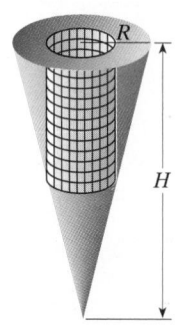

Figure 4.60   Cylinder in a cone

13. A truck is 250 mi due east of a sports car and is traveling west at a constant speed of 60 mi/h. Meanwhile, the sports car is going north at 80 mi/h. When will the truck and the car be closest to each other? What is the minimum distance between them? *Hint*: Minimize the square of the distance.

14. Show that of all rectangles with a given perimeter, the square has the largest area.

15. Show that of all rectangles with a given area, the square has the smallest perimeter.

16. A closed box with square base is to be built to house an ant colony. The bottom of the box and all four sides are to be made of material costing $1/ft^2$, and the top is to be constructed of glass costing $5/ft^2$. What are the dimensions of the box of greatest volume that can be constructed for $72?

17. According to postal regulations, the girth plus the length of a parcel sent by fourth-class mail may not exceed 108 in. What is the largest possible volume of a rectangular parcel with two square sides that can be sent by fourth-class mail?

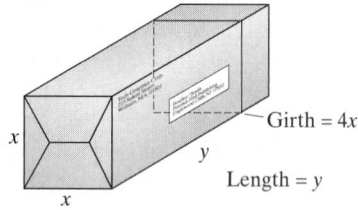

Girth $= 4x$

Length $= y$

18. The bottom of an 8-ft-high mural painted on a vertical wall is 13 ft above the ground. The lens of a camera fixed to a tripod is 4 ft above the ground. How far from the wall should

the camera be placed to photograph the mural with the largest possible angle?

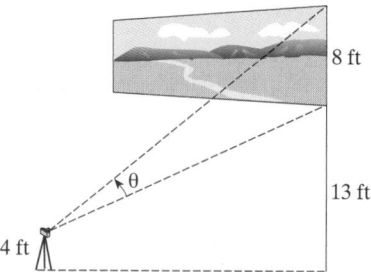

19. Missy Smith is at a point A on the north bank of a long, straight river 6 mi wide. Directly across from her on the south bank is a point B, and she wishes to reach a cabin C located s mi down the river from B, as shown in Figure 4.61.

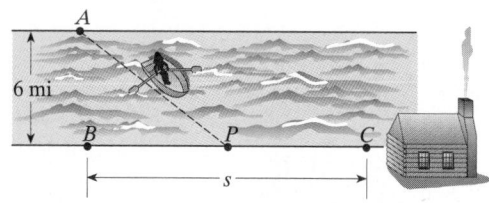

Figure 4.61   Getting Missy home

Given that Missy can row at 6 mi/h (including the effect of the current) and run at 10 mi/h, what is the minimum time (to the nearest minute) required for her to travel from A to C in each case?

a. $s = 4$ **b.** $s = 6$

20. **Modeling Problem**   Two towns A and B are 12.0 mi apart and are located 5.0 and 3.0 mi, respectively, from a long, straight highway, as shown in Figure 4.62.

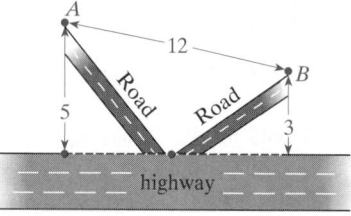

Figure 4.62   Building the shortest road

A construction company has a contract to build a road from A to the highway and then to B. Analyze a model to determine the length (to the nearest tenth of a mile) of the *shortest* road that meets these requirements.

21. A poster is to contain 108 cm² of printed matter, with margins of 6 cm each at top and bottom and 2 cm on the sides. What is the minimum cost of the poster if it is to be made of material costing 20 ¢/cm²?

22. An isosceles trapezoid has a base of 14 cm and slant sides of 6 cm, as shown in Figure 4.63. What is the largest area of such a trapezoid?

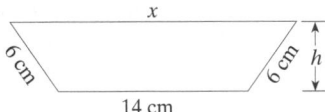

Figure 4.63   Area of a trapezoid

23. **Spy Problem**   It is noon. The Spy has returned from space (Problem 63 of Section 3.4) and is driving a jeep through the sandy desert in the tiny principality of Alta Loma. He is 32 km from the nearest point on a straight, paved road. Down the road 16 km is a power plant in which a band of international terrorists has placed a time bomb set to explode at 12:50 P.M. The jeep can travel at 48 km/h on the sand and at 80 km/h on the paved road. If he arrives at the power plant in the shortest possible time, how long will our hero have to defuse the bomb?

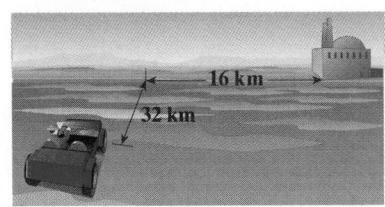

24. A storage bin is to be constructed by removing a sector with central angle θ from a circular piece of tin of radius 10 ft and folding the remainder of the tin to form a cone, as shown in Figure 4.64. What is the maximum volume of a storage bin formed in this fashion?

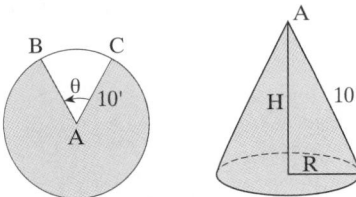

Figure 4.64   Fabricating a cone from a sheet of tin

25. **Exploration Problem**   Use the fact that 12 oz $\approx$ 355 mL = 355 cm^3 to find the dimensions of the 12-oz Coke® can that can be constructed by using the least amount of metal. Compare these dimensions with a Coke from your refrigerator. What do you think accounts for the difference? An interesting article that discusses a similar question regarding tuna fish cans and the resulting responses is "What Manufacturers Say about a Max/Min Application," by Robert F. Cunningham, Trenton State College, *The Mathematics Teacher*, March 1994, pp. 172–175.

26. A stained glass window in the form of an equilateral triangle is built on top of a rectangular window, as shown in Figure 4.65.

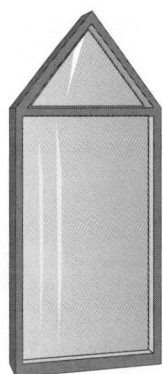

Figure 4.65   Maximizing the amount of light

The rectangular part of the window is of clear glass and transmits twice as much light per square foot as the triangular part, which is made of stained glass. If the entire window has a perimeter of 20 ft, find the dimensions (to the nearest ft) of the window that will admit the most light.

27. Figure 4.66 shows a thin lens located p cm from an object AB and q cm from the image RS.

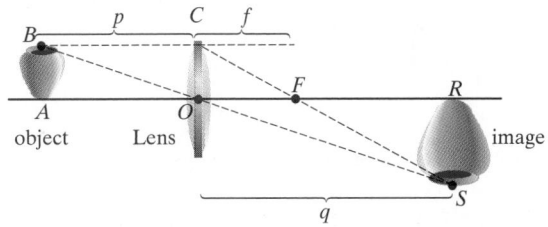

Figure 4.66   Image from a lens

The distance f from the center O of the lens to the point labeled F is called the focal length of the lens.

a. Using similar triangles, show that

$$\frac{1}{p} + \frac{1}{q} = \frac{1}{f}$$

b. Suppose a lens maker wishes to have $p + q = 24$. What is the largest value of f for which this condition can be satisfied?

28. One end of a cantilever beam of length L is built into a wall and the other end is supported by a single post. The deflection, or "sag," of the beam at a point located x units from the built-in end is modeled by the formula

$$D = k(2x^4 - 5Lx^3 + 3L^2x^2)$$

where k is a positive constant. Where does the maximum deflection occur on the beam?

29. When a mechanical system is at rest in an equilibrium position, its potential energy is minimized with respect to any small change in its position. Figure 4.67 shows a system involving a pulley, two small weights of mass m, and a larger weight of mass M.

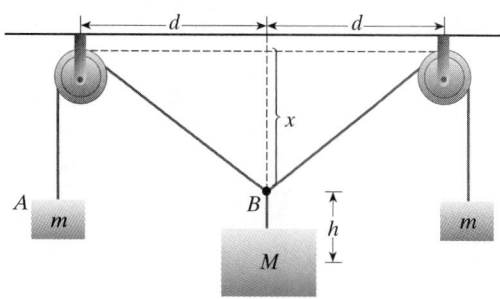

Figure 4.67   A pulley system

In physics, the total potential energy of the system is modeled by

$$E = -Mg(x + h) - 2mg(L - \sqrt{x^2 + d^2})$$

where x, h, and d are the distances shown in Figure 4.67, L is the length of the cord from A around one pulley to B, and g is the constant acceleration due to gravity. All the other symbols represent constants. Use this information to find the critical value(s) for E.

30. A resistor of R ohms is connected across a battery of E volts whose internal resistance is r ohms. According to the principles of electricity, the formula

$$I = \frac{E}{R + r}$$

gives the current (amperes) in the circuit, while

$$P = I^2 R$$

gives the power (watts) in the external resistor. Assuming that E and r are constant, what value of R will result in maximum power in the external resistor?

31. Modeling Problem   One model of a computer disk storage system uses the function

$$T(x) = N\left(k + \frac{c}{x}\right) p^{-x}$$

for the average time needed to send a file correctly by modem (including all retransmission of messages in which errors are detected), where x is the number of information bits, p is the (fixed) probability that any particular file will be received correctly, and N, k, and c are positive constants.[*]

a. Find $T'(x)$.

b. For what value of x is $T(x)$ minimized?

c. Sketch the graph of T.

32. Modeling Problem   In crystallography, a fundamental problem is the determination of the *packing fraction* of a crystal lattice, which is defined as the fraction of space occupied by the atoms in the lattice, assuming the atoms are hard spheres. When the

lattice contains exactly two different kinds of atoms, the packing fraction is modeled by the formula

$$F(x) = \frac{K(1 + c^2 x^3)}{(1 + x)^3}$$

where $x = r/R$ is the ratio of the radii of the two kinds of atoms in the lattice and c and K are positive constants.[†]

a. The function F has exactly one critical number. Find it and use the second-derivative test to determine whether it corresponds to a relative maximum or a relative minimum.

b. The numbers c and K and the domain of F depend on the cell structure in the lattice. For ordinary rock salt, it turns out that $c = 1$, $K = 2\pi/3$, and the domain is $[\sqrt{2} - 1, 1]$. Find the largest and smallest values of F on this domain.

c. Repeat part **b** for β-cristobalite, for which $c = \sqrt{2}$, $K = \sqrt{3}\pi/6$, and the domain is $[0, 1]$.

33. If air resistance is neglected, it can be shown that the stream of water emitted by a fire hose will have height

$$y = -16(1 + m^2)(x/v)^2 + mx$$

above a point located x ft from the nozzle, where m is the slope of the nozzle, and v is the velocity of the stream of water as it leaves the nozzle. (See Figure 4.68.) Assume v is constant.

a. For fixed m, determine the distance x that results in maximum height.

b. If m is allowed to vary but the firefighter must stand $x = x_0$ ft from the base of a burning building, what is the highest point on the building that the firefighter can reach with the water from her hose?

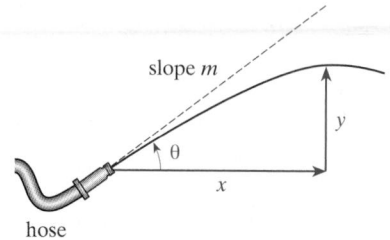

Figure 4.68   Stream of water from a fire hose

34. A telecommunications satellite is located

$$r(t) = \frac{4{,}831}{1 + 0.15 \cos 0.06t}$$

miles above the center of the earth t minutes after achieving orbit.

a. Sketch the graph of $r(t)$.

b. What are the lowest and highest points on the satellite's orbit? These are called the *perigee* and *apogee* positions, respectively.

[*]Paul J. Campbell, "Calculus Optimization in Information Technology," *UMAP module 1991: Tools for Teaching.* Lexington, MA: CUPM Inc., 1992; pp. 175–199.

[†]John C. Lewis and Peter P. Gillis, "Packing Factors in Diatomic Crystals," *American Journal of Physics*, Vol. 61, No. 5 (1993), pp. 434–438.

35. According to relativity theory, a particle's energy is related to its rest mass m_0, and its wavelength λ by the formula

$$E = \sqrt{\left(\frac{hc}{\lambda}\right)^2 + m_0^2 c^4}$$

where m_0 is the rest mass of the particle and h is a constant (Planck's constant). This equation is used mostly in atomic, nuclear, and particle physics where the masses are not very large. Sketch the graph of $E(\lambda)$. What happens to E as $\lambda \to +\infty$?

36. The theory of relativity models the Doppler shift s of an object traveling at a velocity v:

$$s = \sqrt{\frac{c+v}{c-v}} - 1$$

where c is the speed of light and $v < c$.

a. Express v as a function of s and sketch the graph of $v(s)$.

b. Certain stellar objects called quasars appear to be moving away at velocities approaching c. The fastest one has a redshift of $s = 3.78$. What is its velocity in relation to c?

c. How fast is the velocity changing with respect to s when $s = 3.78$?

C **37.** The lower right-hand corner of a piece of paper is folded over to reach the leftmost edge, as shown in Figure 4.69.

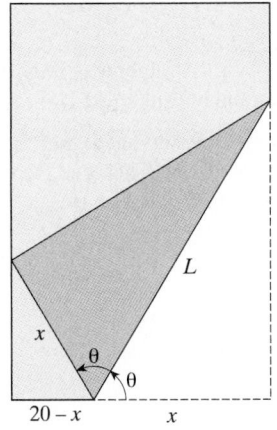

Figure 4.69 Paper folding problem

If the page is 20 cm wide and 30 cm long, what is the length L of the shortest possible crease? *Hint*: First express $\cos\theta$ and $\cos 2\theta$ in terms of x and then use the trigonometric identity

$$\cos 2\theta = 2\cos^2\theta - 1$$

to eliminate θ and express L in terms of x alone.

38. Find the length of the longest pipe that can be carried horizontally around a corner joining two corridors that are $2\sqrt{2}$ ft wide. *Hint*: Show that the length L can be written as

$$L(\theta) = \frac{2\sqrt{2}}{\sin\theta} + \frac{2\sqrt{2}}{\cos\theta}$$

and find the absolute minimum of $L(\theta)$ on an appropriate interval, as shown in Figure 4.70.

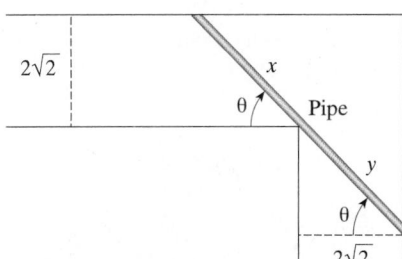

Figure 4.70 Corner problem

39. It is known that water expands and contracts according to its temperature. Physical experiments suggest that an amount of water that occupies 1 liter at $0°C$ will occupy

$$V(T) = 1 - 6.42 \times 10^{-5} T$$
$$+ 8.51 \times 10^{-6} T^2 - 6.79 \times 10^{-8} T^3$$

liters when the temperature is $T°C$. At what temperature is $V(T)$ minimized? How is this result related to the fact that ice forms only at the upper levels of a lake during winter?

40. Modeling Problem Light emanating from a source A is reflected by a mirror to a point B, as shown in Figure 4.71. Use Fermat's principle of optics to show that the angle of incidence α equals the angle of reflection β.

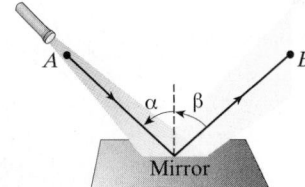

Figure 4.71 Angle of incidence is equal to the angle of reflection

41. Congruent triangles are cut out of a square piece of paper 20 cm on a side, leaving a starlike figure that can be folded to form a pyramid, as indicated in Figure 4.72.

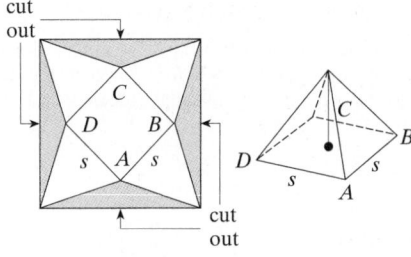

Figure 4.72 Constructing a pyramid

What is the largest volume of the pyramid that can be formed in this manner?

42. Modeling Problem A universal joint is a coupling used in cars and other mechanical systems to join rotating shafts together at an angle. In a model designed to explore the mechanics of the universal joint mechanism, the angular velocity $\beta(t)$ of the output (driven) shaft is modeled by the formula

$$\beta(t) = \frac{\alpha \cos\gamma}{1 - \sin^2\gamma \sin^2(\alpha t)}$$

where α (in rad/s) is the angular velocity of the input (driving) shaft, and γ is the angle between the two shafts, as shown in Figure 4.73.*

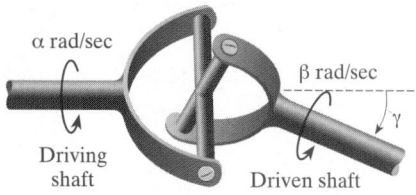

Figure 4.73   Universal joint

a. Sketch the graph of $\beta(t)$ for the case where α and γ are both positive constants.

b. What are the largest and smallest values of $\beta(t)$?

43. Modeling Problem   Rainbows are formed when sunlight traveling through the air is both reflected and refracted by raindrops.† Figure 4.74 shows a raindrop, which we assume to be a sphere for simplicity. An incoming beam of sunlight strikes the raindrop at point A with angle of incidence α, and some of the light is refracted through the angle β to point B. The process is then reversed, as indicated in the figure, and the light finally exits the drop at point C.

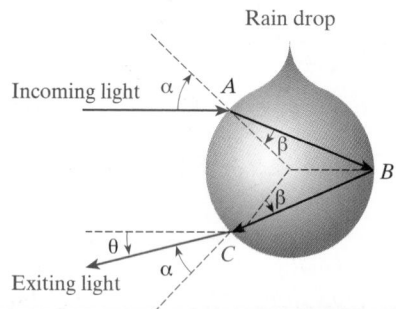

Figure 4.74   Light passing through a raindrop

---

*Thomas O'Neil, "A Mathematical Model of a Universal Joint," *UMAP Modules 1982: Tools for Teaching*. Lexington, MA: Consortium for Mathematics and Its Applications, Inc., 1983, pp. 393–405.

†This problem is based on an article by Steve Janke, "Somewhere Within the Rainbow," *UMAP Modules 1992: Tools for Teaching*. Lexington, MA: Consortium for Mathematics and Its Applications, Inc., 1993.

a. At the interface points, A, B, and C, the light beam is deflected (from a straight line path) and loses intensity. For instance, at A, the incoming beam is deflected through a clockwise rotation of $(\alpha - \beta)$ radians. Show that the total deflection (at all three interfaces) is

$$D = \pi + 2\alpha - 4\beta$$

b. For raindrops falling through the air, Snell's law of refraction has the form $\sin \alpha = 1.33 \sin \beta$. Use this fact to express the derivative $D'(\alpha)$ in terms of α and β.

c. The intensity of rainbow light reaching the eye of an observer will be greatest when the total deflection $D(\alpha)$ is minimized. If the minimum deflection occurs when $\alpha = \alpha_0$, the corresponding angle of observation $\theta = \pi - D(\alpha_0)$ is called the *rainbow angle* because the rainbow is brightest when viewed in that direction (see Figure 4.75).

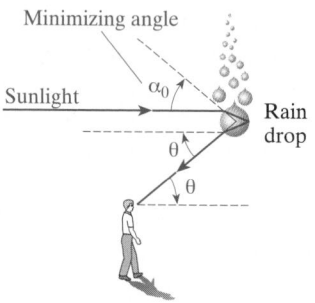

Figure 4.75   A rainbow is brightest when viewed at the rainbow angle

Solve $D'(\alpha) = 0$ and show that the critical number you find minimizes $D(\alpha)$. Then find the rainbow angle θ. *Hint:* You may assume $0 \le \alpha - \beta \le \frac{\pi}{2}$.

4.7   Optimization in Business, Economics, and the Life Sciences

IN THIS SECTION   **economics**: maximizing profit and marginal analysis, **business management**: an inventory model and optimal holding time, **physiology**: concentration of a drug in the bloodstream and optimal angle for vascular branching

In the previous section, we saw how differentiation can be used to solve optimization problems in the physical sciences and engineering. The methods of calculus are also used in business and economics and are becoming increasingly prominent in the social and life sciences. We will examine a selection of such applications, and we begin with two modeling problems involving maximization of profit.

ECONOMICS

Maximizing Profit

EXAMPLE 1 Maximizing profits

A manufacturer can produce a pair of earrings at a cost of $3. The earrings have been selling for $5 per pair and at this price, consumers have been buying 4,000 pairs per month. The manufacturer is planning to raise the price of the earrings and estimates that for each $1 increase in the price, 400 fewer pairs of earrings will be sold each month. At what price should the manufacturer sell the earrings to maximize profit?

Solution

Let x denote the number of $1 price increases, and let $P(x)$ represent the corresponding profit.

$$\text{PROFIT} = \text{REVENUE} - \text{COST}$$
$$= (\text{NUMBER SOLD})(\text{PRICE PER PAIR}) - (\text{NUMBER SOLD})(\text{COST PER PAIR})$$
$$= (\text{NUMBER SOLD})(\text{PRICE PER PAIR} - \text{COST PER PAIR})$$

Recall that 4,000 pairs of earrings are sold each month when the price is $5 per pair and 400 fewer pairs will be sold each month for each added dollar in the price. Thus,

$$\text{NUMBER OF PAIRS SOLD} = 4,000 - 400(\text{NUMBER OF \$1 INCREASES})$$
$$= 4,000 - 400x$$

Knowing that the price per pair is $5 + x$, we can now write the profit as a function of x:

$$P(x) = (\text{NUMBER SOLD})(\text{PRICE PER PAIR} - \text{COST PER PAIR})$$
$$= (4,000 - 400x)[(5 + x) - 3]$$
$$= 400(10 - x)(2 + x)$$

To find the domain, we note that $x \geq 0$. And $400(10 - x)$, the number of pairs sold, should be nonnegative, so $x \leq 10$. Thus, the domain is [0, 10].

The critical numbers are found when the derivative is 0 (P is a polynomial function, so there are no values for which the derivative is not defined):

$$P'(x) = 400(10 - x)(1) + 400(-1)(2 + x)$$
$$= 400(8 - 2x) = 800(4 - x)$$

The critical number is $x = 4$ and the endpoints are $x = 0$ and $x = 10$. Checking for the maximum profit,

$$P(4) = 400(10 - 4)(2 + 4) = 14,400; \quad P(0) = 8,000; \quad P(10) = 0$$

The maximum possible profit is $14,400, which will be generated if the earrings are sold for $5.00 + $4.00 = $9.00 per pair. The graph of the profit function is shown in Figure 4.76. ∎

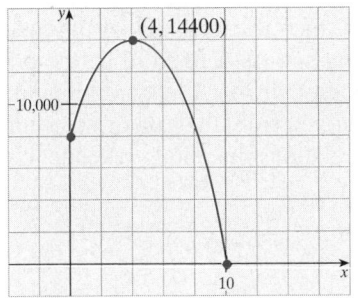

Figure 4.76 The profit function $P(x)$

Sometimes the function to be optimized has practical meaning only when its independent variable is a positive integer. Such functions are said to have a discrete domain and are called **discrete functions**. Technically, the methods of calculus cannot be applied to discrete functions because the theorems we have developed apply only to continuous functions. However, useful information about a discrete function $f(n)$ can often be obtained by analyzing the related continuous function $f(x)$ obtained by replacing the discrete variable n by a real variable x. Here is an example that illustrates the general procedure.

EXAMPLE 2   Maximizing a discrete revenue function

A travel company plans to sponsor a special tour to Africa. There will be accommodations for no more than 40 people, and the tour will be canceled if no more than 10 people book reservations. Based on past experience, the manager determines that if n people book the tour, the profit (in dollars) may be modeled by the function

$$P(n) = -n^3 + 27.6n^2 + 970.2n - 4{,}235$$

For what size tour group is profit maximized?

Solution

The domain of $P(n)$ is the set of integers n between 10 and 40. To optimize this function, we apply the methods developed in this chapter to the related continuous function

$$P(x) = -x^3 + 27.6x^2 + 970.2x - 4{,}235$$

where x is a real variable defined on the interval $10 \le x \le 40$. To determine the critical numbers of $P(x)$, we solve

$$P'(x) = -3x^2 + 55.2x + 970.2 = 0$$

and obtain $x = 29.4$ and $x = -11$. Only $x = 29.4$ is in the domain, and by testing the sign of $P'(x)$ on each side of this critical number, we find that the continuous function $P(x)$ is increasing for $0 < x < 29.4$ and decreasing for $29.4 < x < 40$. Therefore, the original discrete function $P(n)$ is maximized either at $n = 29$ or at $n = 30$. Since

$$P(29) = 22{,}723.4 \quad \text{and} \quad P(30) = 22{,}711$$

we conclude that the maximum profit is $\$22{,}723.40$, and occurs when 29 people book the tour. The graphs of $P(n)$ and the related continuous function $P(x)$ are shown in Figure 4.77.   ■

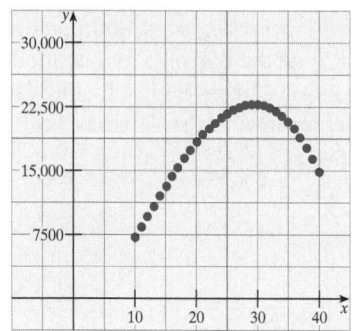

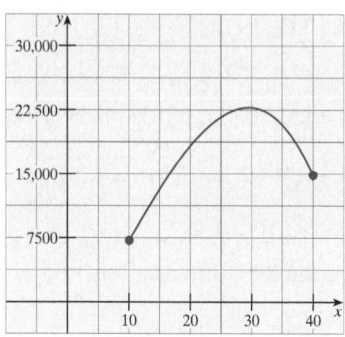

Figure 4.77 Discrete and continuous graphs of the profit function P

Marginal Analysis   In Section 3.8, we described *marginal analysis* as that branch of economics that is concerned with the way quantities such as price, cost, revenue, and profit vary with small changes in the level of production. Specifically, recall that if x is the number of units produced and brought to market, then the total cost of producing the units is denoted by $C(x)$. The **demand** function $p(x)$ is defined to be the price that consumers will pay for each unit of the commodity when x units are brought to market. Then $R(x) = xp(x)$ is the **total revenue** derived from the sale of the x units and $P(x) = R(x) - C(x)$ is the **total profit**. The relationship among revenue, cost, and profit is shown in Figure 4.78.

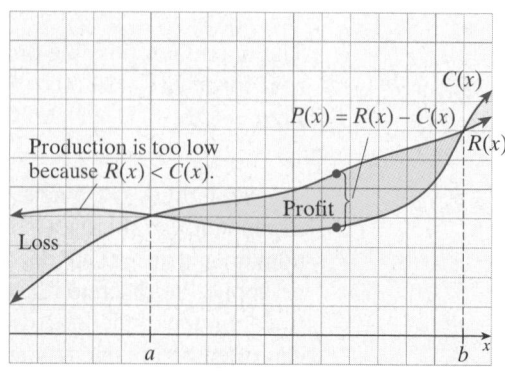

Figure 4.78   Cost, revenue, and profit functions

In Section 3.8, we worked with marginal quantities and their role as rates of change, namely, $C'(x)$, the *marginal cost*, and $R'(x)$, the *marginal revenue*.*

We will now consider these functions in optimization problems. For example, the manufacturer certainly would like to know what level of production results in maximum profit. To solve this problem, we want to maximize the profit function

$$P(x) = R(x) - C(x)$$

We differentiate with respect to x and find that

$$P'(x) = R'(x) - C'(x)$$

Thus, $P'(x) = 0$ when $R'(x) = C'(x)$, and by using economic arguments we can show that a maximum occurs at the corresponding critical point.

Maximum Profit

Profit is maximized when marginal revenue equals marginal cost.

EXAMPLE 3   Using marginal analysis to maximize profit

A manufacturer estimates that when x units of a particular commodity are produced each month, the total cost (in dollars) will be

$$C(x) = \tfrac{1}{8}x^2 + 4x + 200$$

and all units can be sold at a price of $p(x) = 49 - x$ dollars per unit. Determine the price that corresponds to the maximum profit.

Solution

The marginal cost is $C'(x) = \tfrac{1}{4}x + 4$. The revenue is

$$\begin{aligned}
R(x) &= xp(x) \\
&= x(49 - x) \\
&= 49x - x^2
\end{aligned}$$

The marginal revenue is $R'(x) = 49 - 2x$. The profit is maximized when $R'(x) = C'(x)$:

$$\begin{aligned}
R'(x) &= C'(x) \\
49 - 2x &= \tfrac{1}{4}x + 4 \\
x &= 20
\end{aligned}$$

Thus, the price that corresponds to the maximum profit is $p(20) = 49 - 20 = 29$ dollars/unit. ■

A second general principle of economics involves the following relationship between marginal cost and the *average cost* $A(x) = \dfrac{C(x)}{x}$.

Minimum Average Cost

Average cost is minimized at the level of production where the marginal cost equals the average cost.

---

*Recall (from Section 3.8) that marginal cost is the instantaneous rate of change of production cost C with respect to the number of units x_0 produced and the marginal revenue is the instantaneous rate of change of revenue with respect to the number of units x_0 produced.

To justify this second business principle, find the derivative of the average cost function:

$$A'(x) = \frac{xC'(x) - C(x)}{x^2} = \frac{C'(x) - \dfrac{C(x)}{x}}{x} = \frac{C'(x) - A(x)}{x}$$

Thus, $A'(x) = 0$ when $C'(x) = A(x)$. Once again, economic theory can be used to justify this result as a minimum.

EXAMPLE 4   Using marginal analysis to minimize average cost

A manufacturer estimates that when x units of a particular commodity are produced each month, the total cost (in dollars) will be

$$C(x) = \tfrac{1}{8}x^2 + 4x + 200$$

and they can all be sold at a price of $p(x) = 49 - x$ dollars per unit. Determine the level of production at which the average cost is minimized.

Solution

The average cost is $A(x) = \dfrac{C(x)}{x} = \dfrac{1}{8}x + 4 + 200x^{-1}$ and $A(x)$ is minimized when $C'(x) = A(x)$. Thus,

$$\tfrac{1}{4}x + 4 = \tfrac{1}{8}x + 4 + 200x^{-1}$$
$$x^2 = 1600 \qquad \text{Multiply both sides by } 8x \text{ and simplify.}$$

If we disregard the negative solution, it follows that the minimal average cost occurs when $x = 40$ units.

You might have noticed that we did not need the information $p(x) = 49 - x$ in arriving at the solution to this example. When doing real-world modeling, you must often make a choice about which parts of the available information are necessary to solve the problem. ∎

BUSINESS MANAGEMENT

Sometimes mathematical methods can be used to assist managers in making certain business decisions. As an illustration, we will show how calculus can be applied to a problem involving inventory control.

An Inventory Model   For each shipment of raw materials, a manufacturer must pay an ordering fee to cover handling and transportation. When the raw materials arrive, they must be stored until needed and storage costs result. If each shipment of raw materials is large, few shipments will be needed and ordering costs will be low, but storage costs will be high. If each shipment is small, ordering costs will be high because many shipments will be needed, but storage cost will be low. Managers want to determine the shipment size that will minimize the total cost. Here is an example of how such a problem may be solved using calculus.

EXAMPLE 5   Modeling Problem: Managing inventory to minimize cost

A retailer buys 6,000 calculator batteries a year from a distributor and is trying to decide how often to order the batteries. The ordering fee is $20 per shipment, the storage cost is $0.96 per battery per year, and each battery costs the retailer $0.25. Suppose that the batteries are sold at a constant rate throughout the year and that each shipment arrives uniformly throughout the year just as the preceding shipment has been used up. How many batteries should the retailer order each time to minimize the total cost?

Solution

We begin by writing the cost function:

TOTAL COST = STORAGE COST + ORDERING COST + COST OF BATTERIES

We need to find an expression for each of these unknowns. Assume that the same number of batteries must be ordered each time an order is placed; denote this number by x so that $C(x)$ is the corresponding total cost. The average number of batteries in storage during the year is half of a given order (that is, $x/2$), and we assume that the total yearly storage cost is the same as if the $x/2$ batteries were kept in storage for the entire year. This situation is shown in Figure 4.79.

$$\text{STORAGE COST} = \left(\begin{matrix}\text{AVERAGE NUMBER} \\ \text{IN STORAGE PER YR}\end{matrix}\right)\left(\begin{matrix}\text{COST OF STORING 1} \\ \text{BATTERY FOR 1 YR}\end{matrix}\right)$$

$$= \left(\frac{x}{2}\right)(0.96)$$

$$= 0.48x$$

To find the total ordering cost, we can multiply the ordering cost per shipment by the number of shipments. We also note that because 6,000 batteries are ordered during the year and because each shipment contains x batteries, the number of shipments is $6,000/x$.

$$\text{ORDERING COST} = \left(\begin{matrix}\text{ORDERING COST} \\ \text{PER SHIPMENT}\end{matrix}\right)\left(\begin{matrix}\text{NUMBER OF} \\ \text{SHIPMENTS}\end{matrix}\right)$$

$$= (20)\left(\frac{6,000}{x}\right) = \frac{120,000}{x}$$

Finally, we must also include the cost of purchasing the batteries:

$$\text{COST OF BATTERIES} = \left(\begin{matrix}\text{TOTAL NUMBER} \\ \text{OF BATTERIES}\end{matrix}\right)\left(\begin{matrix}\text{COST PER} \\ \text{BATTERY}\end{matrix}\right)$$

$$= 6,000(0.25) = 1,500$$

Thus, we model the total cost by the function

$$C(x) = 0.48x + \frac{120,000}{x} + 1,500$$

The goal is to minimize $C(x)$ on $(0, 6000]$. To obtain the critical numbers, we find the derivative

$$C'(x) = 0.48 - 120,000x^{-2}$$

and then solve $C'(x) = 0$:

$$0.48 - 120,000x^{-2} = 0$$
$$0.48x^2 = 120,000$$
$$x = \pm 500$$

The root $x = -500$ does not lie in the interval $(0, 6000]$. It is easy to check that C is decreasing on $(0, 500)$ and increasing on $(500, 6000]$, as shown in Figure 4.80. Thus, the absolute minimum of C on the interval $(0, 6000]$ occurs when $x = 500$, and we conclude that to minimize cost, the manufacturer should order the batteries in lots of 500. ∎

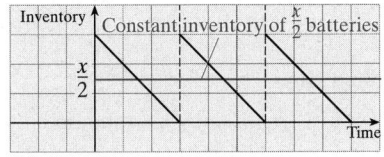

Figure 4.79 Inventory graph

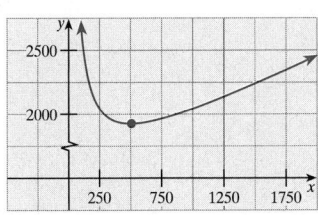

Figure 4.80 The total cost function $C(x) = 0.48x + 120,000x^{-1} + 1,500$

Optimal Holding Time   Even with an asset that increases in value, there often comes a time when continuing to hold the asset is less advantageous than selling it and investing the proceeds of the sale. How should the investor decide when to sell? One way is to hold the asset until the time its present value at the current prevailing rate of interest is maximized. In other words, hold until today's dollar equivalent of the selling price is as large as possible, and then sell. Here is an example that illustrates this strategy.

EXAMPLE 6   Modeling Problem: Optimal holding time

Suppose you own an asset whose market price t years from now is modeled by $V(t) = 10{,}000e^{\sqrt{t}}$ dollars. If the prevailing rate of interest is 8% compounded continuously, when should the asset be sold?

Solution

The present value of the asset in t years is modeled by the function $P(t) = V(t)e^{-rt}$, where r is the annual interest rate and t is the time in years. Thus,

$$P(t) = 10{,}000e^{\sqrt{t}}e^{-0.08t}$$
$$= 10{,}000\exp(\sqrt{t} - 0.08t)$$

To maximize P, find $P'(t)$ and solve $P'(t) = 0$:

$$P'(t) = 10{,}000\exp(\sqrt{t} - 0.08t)\left(\frac{1}{2} \cdot \frac{1}{\sqrt{t}} - 0.08\right)$$

$P'(t) = 0$ when $\dfrac{1}{2\sqrt{t}} - 0.08 = 0$ or $t \approx 39.06$ years. Thus, the asset should be held for 39 years and then sold.   ∎

PHYSIOLOGY

Calculus can be used to model a variety of situations in the biological and life sciences. We will consider two examples from physiology. In the first, we use a model for the concentration of a drug in the bloodstream of a patient to determine when the maximum concentration occurs.

Concentration of a Drug in the Bloodstream

EXAMPLE 7   Modeling Problem: Maximum concentration of a drug

Let $C(t)$ denote the concentration in the blood at time t of a drug injected into the body intramuscularly. In a classic paper by E. Heinz, it was observed that the concentration may be modeled by

$$C(t) = \frac{k}{b - a}(e^{-at} - e^{-bt}) \qquad t \geq 0$$

where a, b (with $b > a$), and k are positive constants that depend on the drug.* At what time does the largest concentration occur? What happens to the concentration as $t \to +\infty$?

Solution

To locate the extrema, we solve $C'(t) = 0$.

$$C'(t) = \frac{d}{dt}\left[\frac{k}{b - a}(e^{-at} - e^{-bt})\right]$$
$$= \frac{k}{b - a}[(-a)e^{-at} - (-b)e^{-bt}] = \frac{k}{b - a}(be^{-bt} - ae^{-at})$$

---

*E. Heinz, "Probleme bei der Diffusion kleiner Substanzmengen innerhalb des menschlichen Körpers," *Biochem.*, Vol. 319 (1949), pp. 482–492.

We see that $C'(t) = 0$ when

$$be^{-bt} = ae^{-at}$$

$$\frac{b}{a} = e^{bt}e^{-at} = e^{bt-at}$$

$$bt - at = \ln \frac{b}{a} \qquad \text{Definition of logarithm}$$

$$t = \frac{1}{b-a} \ln \frac{b}{a}$$

The second-derivative test can be used to show that the largest value of $C(t)$ occurs at this t (see Problem 49).

To see what happens to the concentration as $t \to +\infty$, we compute the limit

$$\lim_{t \to +\infty} C(t) = \lim_{t \to +\infty} \frac{k}{b-a}[e^{-at} - e^{-bt}]$$

$$= \frac{k}{b-a}\left[\lim_{t \to +\infty} \frac{1}{e^{at}} - \lim_{t \to +\infty} \frac{1}{e^{bt}}\right]$$

$$= \frac{k}{b-a}[0 - 0]$$

$$= 0$$

This tells us that the longer the drug is in the blood, the closer the concentration is to 0. The graph of C is shown in Figure 4.81.

Intuitively, we would expect the Heinz concentration function to begin at 0, increase to a maximum, and then gradually drop off to 0 in a finite amount of time. Figure 4.81 indicates that $C(t)$ does not have these characteristics, because it does not quite get back to 0 in finite time. This suggests that the Heinz model may apply most reliably to the period of time right after the drug has been injected. ∎

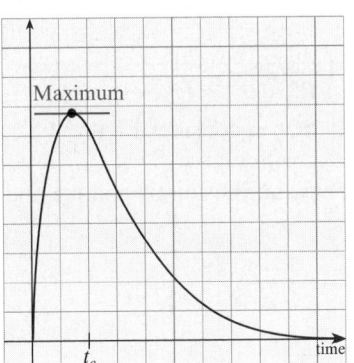

Figure 4.81 Graph of $C(t) = \dfrac{k}{b-a}(e^{-at} - e^{-bt})$

Optimal Angle for Vascular Branching The blood vascular system operates in such a way that the circulation of blood—from the heart, through the organs of the body, and back to the heart—is accomplished with as little expenditure of energy as possible. Thus, it is reasonable to expect that when an artery branches, the angle between the "parent" artery and its "daughter" should minimize the total resistance to the flow of blood. Figure 4.82 shows a small artery of radius r branching from a larger artery of radius R. Blood flows in the direction of the arrows from point A to the branch at B and then to points C and D. For simplicity, we assume that C and D are located in such a way that $\overline{CD}$ is perpendicular to the main line through A, B, and D. We wish to find the value of the branching angle θ that minimizes the total resistance to the flow of blood as it moves from A to B and then to point C, which is located a fixed perpendicular distance h from the line through A and B.* (See Figure 4.82.)

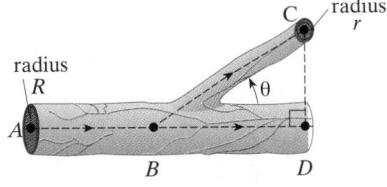

Figure 4.82 Vascular branching

> **Poiseuille's Resistance To Flow Law**
>
> The resistance to the flow of blood in an artery is directly proportional to the artery's length and inversely proportional to the fourth power of its radius.

---

*The key to solving this problem is a result due to work of the nineteenth-century French physiologist Jean Louis Poiseuille (1789–1869). Our discussion of vascular branching is adapted from *Introduction to Mathematics for Life Scientists*, 2nd edition, by Edward Batschelet (New York: Springer-Verlag, 1976, pp. 278–280). In this excellent little book, Batschelet develops a number of interesting applications of calculus, several of which appear in the problem set.

According to Poiseuille's law, the resistance to flow, f_1, from A to B is

$$f_1 = \frac{ks_1}{R^4}$$

where R is the radius of the larger artery, and the resistance to flow, f_2, from B to C is

$$f_2 = \frac{ks_2}{r^4}$$

where r is the radius of the smaller artery, k is a viscosity constant, $s_1 = |\overline{AB}|$, and $s_2 = |\overline{BC}|$. Thus, the total resistance to flow may be modeled by the sum

$$f = f_1 + f_2 = \frac{ks_1}{R^4} + \frac{ks_2}{r^4} = k\left(\frac{s_1}{R^4} + \frac{s_2}{r^4}\right)$$

The next task is to write f as a function of θ. To do this, reconsider Figure 4.82 by labeling s_1, s_2, h, and ℓ as shown in Figure 4.83.

We want to find equations for s_1 and s_2 in terms of h and θ; to this end we notice that

$$\sin\theta = \frac{h}{s_2} \qquad\qquad \tan\theta = \frac{h}{\ell - s_1}$$

$$s_2 = \frac{h}{\sin\theta} \qquad\qquad \ell - s_1 = \frac{h}{\tan\theta}$$

$$= h\csc\theta \qquad\qquad s_1 = \ell - \frac{h}{\tan\theta}$$

$$= \ell - h\cot\theta$$

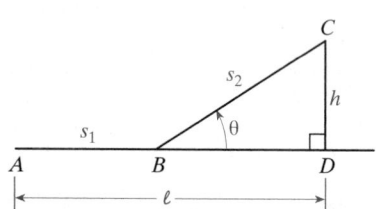

Figure 4.83 Minimizing the resistance to blood flow

We can now write f as a function of θ:

$$f(\theta) = k\left(\frac{s_1}{R^4} + \frac{s_2}{r^4}\right) = k\left(\frac{\ell - h\cot\theta}{R^4} + \frac{h\csc\theta}{r^4}\right)$$

To minimize f, we need to find the critical numbers (remember that h and k are positive constants):

$$\frac{df}{d\theta} = k\left[\frac{-h(-\csc^2\theta)}{R^4} + \frac{h(-\csc\theta\cot\theta)}{r^4}\right]$$

$$= kh\csc\theta\left(\frac{\csc\theta}{R^4} - \frac{\cot\theta}{r^4}\right)$$

$$\left(\frac{\csc\theta}{R^4} - \frac{\cot\theta}{r^4}\right) = 0$$

$$\frac{\csc\theta}{R^4} = \frac{\cot\theta}{r^4}$$

$$\frac{1}{R^4\sin\theta} = \frac{\cos\theta}{r^4\sin\theta}$$

$$\frac{r^4}{R^4} = \cos\theta$$

By finding the second derivative and noting that both r and R are positive, we can show that any value θ_m that satisfies this equation yields a value $f(\theta_m)$ that is a minimum. Thus, the required optimal angle is $\theta_m = \cos^{-1}(r^4/R^4)$.

4.7 PROBLEM SET

Ⓐ *In Problems 1–3, we give the cost C of producing x units of a particular commodity and the selling price p when x units are produced. In each case, determine the level of production that maximizes profit.*

1. $C(x) = \frac{1}{8}x^2 + 5x + 98$ and $p(x) = \frac{1}{2}(75 - x)$

2. $C(x) = \frac{2}{5}x^2 + 3x + 10$ and $p(x) = \frac{1}{5}(45 - x)$

3. $C(x) = \frac{1}{5}(x + 30)$ and $p(x) = \dfrac{70 - x}{x + 30}$

4. Suppose the total cost of producing x units of a certain commodity is

$$C(x) = 2x^4 - 10x^3 - 18x^2 + x + 5$$

   Determine the largest and smallest values of the marginal cost for $0 \le x \le 5$.

5. Suppose the total cost of manufacturing x units of a certain commodity is

$$C(x) = 3x^2 + x + 48$$

   dollars. Determine the minimum average cost.

6. A toy manufacturer produces an inexpensive doll (Flopsy) and an expensive doll (Mopsy) in units of x hundreds and y hundreds, respectively. Suppose it is possible to produce the dolls in such a way that

$$y = \frac{82 - 10x}{10 - x} \qquad 0 \le x \le 8$$

   and that the company receives *twice* as much for selling a Mopsy doll as for selling a Flopsy doll. Find the level of production for both x and y for which the total revenue derived from selling these dolls is maximized. What vital assumption must be made about sales in this model?

7. A business manager estimates that when p dollars are charged for every unit of a product, the sales will be $x = 380 - 20p$ units. At this level of production, the average cost is modeled by

$$A(x) = 5 + \frac{x}{50}$$

   a. Find the total revenue and total cost functions, and express the profit as a function of x.

   b. What price should the manufacturer charge to maximize profit? What is the maximum profit?

8. Suppose a manufacturer estimates that, when the market price of a certain product is p, the number of units sold will be

$$x = -6\ln\left(\frac{p}{40}\right)$$

   It is also estimated that the cost of producing these x units will be

$$C(x) = 4xe^{-x/6} + 30$$

   a. Find the average cost, the marginal cost, and the marginal revenue for this production process.

   b. What level of production x corresponds to maximum profit?

9. A manufacturer can produce shoes at a cost of \$50 a pair and estimates that if they are sold for x dollars a pair, consumers will buy approximately

$$s(x) = 1,000e^{-0.1x}$$

   pairs of shoes per week. At what price should the manufacturer sell the shoes to maximize profit?

10. A certain industrial machine depreciates in such a way that its value (in dollars) after t years is

$$Q(t) = 20,000e^{-0.4t}$$

   a. At what rate is the value of the machine changing with respect to time after 5 years?

   b. At what percentage rate is the value of the machine changing with respect to time after t years?

11. It is projected that t years from now, the population of a certain country will be $P(t) = 50e^{0.02t}$ million.

   a. At what rate will the population be changing with respect to time 10 years from now?

   b. At what percentage rate will the population be changing with respect to time t years from now?

12. Some psychologists model a child's ability to memorize by a function of the form

$$g(t) = \begin{cases} t\ln t + 1 & \text{if } 0 < t \le 4 \\ 1 & \text{if } t = 0 \end{cases}$$

   where t is time, measured in years. Determine when the largest and smallest values of g occur.

13. It is estimated that t years from now the population of a certain country will be

$$p(t) = \frac{160}{1 + 8e^{-0.01t}}$$

   million. When will the population be growing most rapidly?

Ⓑ 14. **Modeling Problem** The owner of the Pill Boxx drugstore expects to sell 600 bottles of hair spray each year. Each bottle costs \$4, and the ordering fee is \$30 per shipment. In addition, it costs 90¢ per year to store each bottle. Assuming that the hair spray sells at a uniform rate throughout the year and that each shipment arrives just as the last bottle from the previous shipment is sold, how frequently should shipments of hair spray be ordered to minimize the total cost?

15. **Modeling Problem** An electronics firm uses 18,000 cases of connectors each year. The cost of storing one case for a year is \$4.50, and the ordering fee is \$20 per shipment. Assume that the connectors are used at a constant rate throughout the year and that each shipment arrives just as the preceding shipment has been used up. How many cases should the firm order each time to keep total cost to a minimum?

16. Suppose the total cost (in dollars) of manufacturing x units of a certain commodity is

$$C(x) = 3x^2 + 5x + 75$$

   a. At what level of production is the average cost per unit the smallest?

   b. At what level of production is the average cost per unit equal to the marginal cost?

   c. Graph the average cost and the marginal cost functions on the same set of axes, for $x > 0$.

17. Suppose the total revenue (in dollars) from the sale of x units of a certain commodity is

$$R(x) = -2x^2 + 68x - 128$$

   a. At what level of sales is the average revenue per unit equal to the marginal revenue?

   b. Verify that the average revenue is increasing if the level of sales is less than the level in part **a** and decreasing if the level of sales is greater than the level in part **a**.

   c. On the same set of axes, graph the relevant portions of the average and marginal revenue functions.

18. A manufacturer finds that the demand function for a certain product is

$$x(p) = \frac{73}{\sqrt{p}}$$

   Should the price p be raised or lowered to increase consumer expenditure? Explain your answer.

19. Suppose you own a rare book whose value t years from now is modeled as $300e^{\sqrt{3t}}$. If the prevailing rate of interest remains constant at 8% compounded continuously, when will be the most advantageous time to sell?

20. Suppose you own a parcel of land whose value t years from now is modeled as

$$P(t) = 200 \ln \sqrt{2t}$$

   thousand dollars. If the prevailing rate of interest is 10% compounded continuously, when will be the most advantageous time to sell?

21. A store has been selling skateboards at the price of $40 per board, and at this price skaters have been buying 45 boards a month. The owner of the store wishes to raise the price and estimates that for each $1 increase in price, 3 fewer boards will be sold each month. If each board costs the store $29, at which price should the store sell the boards to maximize profit?

22. **Modeling Problem** As more and more industrial areas are constructed, there is a growing need for standards ensuring control of the pollutants released into the air. Suppose that the pollution at a particular location is based on the distance from the source of the pollution according to the principle that for distances greater than or equal to 1 mi, the concentration of particulate matter (in parts per million, ppm) decreases as the reciprocal of the distance from the source. This means that if you live 3 mi from a plant emitting 60 ppm, the pollution at your home is $\frac{60}{3} = 20$ ppm. On the other hand, if you live 10 mi from the plant, the pollution at your home is $\frac{60}{10} = 6$ ppm. Suppose that two plants 10 mi apart are releasing 60 and 240 ppm, respectively. At what point between the plants is the pollution a minimum? Where is it a maximum?

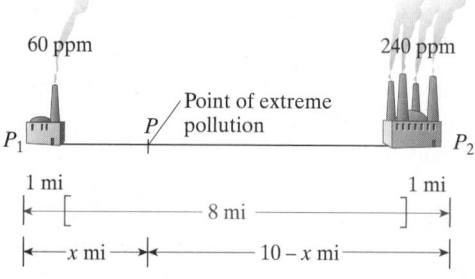

23. A tour agency is booking a tour and has 100 people signed up. The price of a ticket is $2,000 per person. The agency has booked a plane seating 150 people at a cost of $125,000. Additional costs to the agency are incidental fees of $500 per person. For each $10 that the price is lowered, a new person will sign up. How much should the price be lowered for all participants to maximize the profit to the tour agency?

24. A bookstore can obtain the best-seller *20,000 Leagues Under the Majors* from the publisher at a cost of $6 per book. The store has been offering the book at a price of $30 per copy and has been selling 200 copies per month at this price. The bookstore is planning to lower its price to stimulate sales and estimates that for each $2 reduction in the price, 20 more books will be sold per month. At what price should the bookstore sell the book to generate the greatest possible profit?

25. A Florida citrus grower estimates that if 60 orange trees are planted, the average yield per tree will be 400 oranges. The average yield will decrease by 4 oranges for each additional tree planted on the same acreage. How many trees should the grower plant to maximize the total yield?

26. Farmers can get $2 per bushel for their potatoes on July 1, and after that the price drops 2¢ per bushel per day. On July 1, a farmer has 80 bushels of potatoes in the field and estimates that the crop is increasing at the rate of 1 bushel per day. When should the farmer harvest the potatoes to maximize revenue?

27. A viticulturist estimates that if 50 grapevines are planted per acre, each grapevine will produce 150 lb of grapes. Each additional grapevine planted per acre (up to 20) reduces the average yield per vine by 2 lb. How many grapevines should be planted to maximize the yield per acre?

28. A commuter train carries 600 passengers each day from a suburb to a city. It now costs $5 per person to ride the train. A study shows that 50 additional people will ride the train for each 25¢ reduction in fare. What fare should be charged to maximize total revenue?

29. **Modeling Problem** To raise money, a service club has been collecting used bottles, which it plans to deliver to a local glass company for recycling. Since the project began 80 days ago, the club has collected 24,000 pounds of glass, for which the glass company offers 1¢ per pound. However, because bottles are accumulating faster than they can be recycled, the company plans to reduce the price it will pay by 1¢ per 100 pounds of used glass.

   a. What is the most advantageous time for the club to conclude its project and deliver all the bottles?

   b. What assumptions must be made in part **a** to solve the problem with the given information?

30. Suppose that the demand function for a certain commodity is expressed as

$$p(x) = \sqrt{\frac{120 - x}{0.1}} \quad \text{for} \quad 0 \le x \le 120$$

   where x is the number of items sold.

   a. Find the total revenue function explicitly and use its first derivative to determine the price at which revenue is maximized.

   b. Graph the relevant portions of the demand and revenue functions.

31. Suppose the demand function for a certain commodity is linear, that is,

$$p(x) = \frac{b - x}{a} \quad \text{for} \quad 0 \le x \le b$$

where a and b are positive constants.

a. Find the total revenue function explicitly and use its first derivative to determine its intervals of increase and decrease.

b. Graph the relevant portions of the demand and revenue functions.

32. Modeling Problem Homing pigeons will rarely fly over large bodies of water unless forced to do so, presumably because it requires more energy to maintain altitude in flight over the cool water. Suppose a pigeon is released from a boat floating on a lake 3 mi from a point A on the shore and 10 mi away from the pigeon's loft, as shown in Figure 4.84.

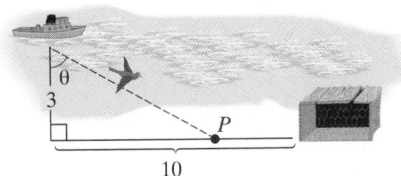

Figure 4.84 Flight path for a pigeon

Assuming the pigeon requires twice as much energy to fly over water as over land and it follows a path that minimizes total energy, find the angle θ of its heading as it leaves the boat. (This is the situation in the Perspective section of the chapter introduction.)

33. Modeling Problem In an experiment, a fish swims s meters upstream at a constant velocity v m/sec relative to the water, which itself has velocity v_1 relative to the ground. The results of the experiment suggest that if the fish takes t seconds to reach its goal (that is, to swim s meters), the energy it expends may be modeled by

$$E = cv^k t$$

where $c > 0$ and $k > 2$ are physical constants. Assuming v_1 is known, what velocity v minimizes the energy?

34. In a learning model, two responses (A and B) are possible for each of a series of observations. If there is a probability p of getting response A in any observation, the probability of getting a response A exactly n times in a series of M observations is

$$F(p) = p^n (1 - p)^{M - n}$$

The *maximum likelihood estimate* is the value of p that maximizes $F(p)$ on $[0, 1]$. For what value of p does this occur?

35. Modeling Problem The production of blood cells plays an important role in medical research involving leukemia and other so-called *dynamical diseases*. In 1977, a mathematical model was developed by A. Lasota that involved the cell production function

$$P(x) = Ax^s e^{-sx/r}$$

where A, s, and r are positive constants and x is the number of granulocytes (a type of white blood cell) present.[*]

a. Find the granulocyte level x that maximizes the production function P. How do you know it is a maximum?

b. If $s > 1$, show that the graph of P has two inflection points. Sketch the graph of P and give a brief interpretation of the inflection points.

c. Sketch the graph for the case where $0 < s < 1$. What is different about this case?

36. Modeling Problem During a cough, the diameter of the trachea decreases. The velocity v of air in the trachea during a cough may be modeled by the formula

$$v = Ar^2 (r_0 - r)$$

where A is a constant, r is the radius of the trachea during the cough, and r_0 is the radius of the trachea in a relaxed state. Find the radius of the trachea when the velocity is greatest, and find the maximum velocity of air. (Notice that $0 \le r \le r_0$.)

37. Modeling Problem The work of V. A. Tucker and K. Schmidt-Koenig[†] models the energy expended in flight by a certain kind of bird by the function

$$E = \frac{1}{v} [a(v - b)^2 + c]$$

where a, b, and c are positive constants, v is the velocity of the bird, and the domain of v is $[16, 60]$. Which value of v will minimize the energy expenditure in the case where $a = 0.04$, $b = 36$, and $c = 9$?

38. Modeling Problem A plastics firm has received an order from the city recreation department to manufacture 8,000 special styrofoam kickboards for its summer swimming program. The firm owns 10 machines, each of which can produce 50 kickboards per hour. The cost of setting up the machines to produce the kickboards is $800 per machine. Once the machines have been set up, the operation is fully automated and can be overseen by a single production supervisor earning $35 per hour.

a. How many machines should be used to minimize the cost of production?

b. How much will the supervisor earn during the production run if the optimal number of machines is used?

39. Modeling Problem After hatching, the larva of the codling moth goes looking for food. The period between hatching and finding food is called the *searching period*. According to a model developed by P. L. Shaffer and H. J. Gold[‡] the length (in days) of the searching period is given by

$$S(T) = (-0.03T^2 + 1.67T - 13.67)^{-1}$$

[*]See "A Blood Cell Population Model, Dynamical Diseases, and Chaos," by W. B. Gearhart and M. Martelli, *UMAP Modules 1990: Tools for Teaching*. Arlington, MA: Consortium for Mathematics and Its Applications (CUPM) Inc., 1991.

[†]V. A. Tucker and K. Schmidt-Koenig, "Flight of Birds in Relation to Energetics and Wind Directions," *The Auk*, Vol. 88 (1971), pp. 97–107.

[‡]P. L. Shaffer and H. J. Gold, "A Simulation Model of Population Dynamics of the Codling Moth *Cydia Pomonella*," *Ecological Modeling*, Vol. 30 (1985) pp. 247–274.

where T (°C) is the air temperature ($20 \le T \le 30$), and the percentage of larvae that survive the searching period is

$$N(T) = -0.85T^2 + 45.45T - 547$$

a. Sketch the graph of N and find the largest and smallest survival percentages for the allowable range of temperatures, $20 \le T \le 30$.

b. Find $S'(T)$ and solve $S'(T) = 0$. Sketch the graph of S for $20 \le T \le 30$.

c. The percentage of codling moth eggs that hatch at a given temperature T is given by

$$H(T) = -0.53T^2 + 25T - 209$$

for $20 \le T \le 30$. Sketch the graph of H and determine the temperatures at which the largest and smallest hatching percentages occur.

40. According to a certain logistic model, the world's population (in billions) t years after 1960 is modeled by the function

$$P(t) = \frac{40}{1 + 12e^{-0.08t}}$$

a. If this model is correct, at what rate will the world's population be increasing with respect to time in the year 2010? At what percentage rate will it be increasing at this time?

b. Sketch the graph of P. What feature on the graph corresponds to the time when the population is growing most rapidly? What happens to $P(t)$ as $t \to +\infty$ (that is, "in the long run")?

C 41. **Modeling Problem**   Generalize Problem 38. Specifically, a manufacturing firm received an order for Q units of a certain commodity. Each of the firm's machines can produce n units per hour. The setup cost is S dollars per machine, and the operating cost is p dollars per hour.

a. Derive a formula for the number of machines that should be used to minimize the total cost of filling the order.

b. Show that when the total cost is minimal, the setup cost is equal to the cost of operating the machines.

42. **Modeling Problem**   (Continuation of Problem 39) Suppose you have 10,000 codling moth eggs. Find a function F for the number of moths that hatch and survive to have their first meal when the temperature is T. For what temperature T on [20, 30] is the number of dining moths the greatest? How large is the optimum dining party and how long did it take to find its meal?

43. An epidemic spreads through a community in such a way that t weeks after its outbreak, the number of residents who have been infected is modeled by a function of the form

$$f(t) = \frac{A}{1 + Ce^{-kt}}$$

where A is the total number of susceptible residents. Show that the epidemic is spreading most rapidly when half the susceptible residents have been infected.

44. In certain tissues, cells exist in the shape of circular cylinders. Suppose such a cylinder has radius r and height h. If the volume is fixed (say, at v_0), find the value of r that minimizes the total surface area ($S = 2\pi rh + 2\pi r^2$) of the cell.

45. **Modeling Problem**   A store owner expects to sell Q units of a certain commodity each year. It costs S dollars to order each new shipment of x units; and it costs t dollars to store each unit for a year. Assuming that the commodity is used at a constant rate throughout the year and that each shipment arrives just as the preceding shipment has been used up, show that the total cost of maintaining inventory is minimized when the ordering cost equals the storage cost.

46. **Modeling Problem**   Sometimes investment managers determine the optimal holding time of an asset worth $V(t)$ dollars by finding when the relative rate of change $V'(t)/V(t)$ equals the prevailing rate of interest r. Show that the optimal time determined by this criterion is the same as that found by maximizing the present value of $V(t)$.

47. An important quantity in economic analysis is *elasticity of demand*, defined by

$$E(x) = \frac{p}{x}\frac{dx}{dp}$$

where x is the number of units of a commodity demanded when the price is p dollars per unit.* Show that

$$\frac{dR}{dx} = \frac{R}{x}\left[1 + \frac{1}{E(x)}\right]$$

That is, marginal revenue is $[1 + 1/E(x)]$ times average revenue.

48. **Modeling Problem**   There are alternatives to the inventory model analyzed in Example 5. Suppose a company must supply N units/month at a uniform rate. Assume the storage cost/unit is S_1 dollars/month and that the setup cost is S_2 dollars. Further assume that production is at a uniform rate of m units/month (with no units left over in inventory at the end of the month). Let x be the number of items produced in each run.

a. Explain why the total average cost per month may be modeled by

$$C(x) = \frac{S_1 x}{2}\left(1 - \frac{N}{m}\right) + \frac{S_2 N}{x}$$

b. Find an expression for the number of items that should be produced in each run in order to minimize the total average cost C.

Economists refer to the optimum found in this inventory model as the *economic production quantity* (EPQ), whereas the optimum found in the model analyzed in Example 5 is called the *economic order quantity* (EOQ).

49. In this section we showed that the Heinz concentration function,

$$C(t) = \frac{k}{b - a}(e^{-at} - e^{-bt})$$

for $b > a$ has exactly one critical number, namely,

$$t_c = \frac{1}{b - a}\ln\left(\frac{b}{a}\right)$$

Find $C''(t)$ and use the second-derivative test to show that a relative maximum for the concentration $C(t)$ occurs at time $t = t_c$.

---

*See the module with the intriguing title, "Price Elasticity of Demand: Gambling, Heroin, Marijuana, Prostitution, and Fish," by Yves Nievergelt, *UMAP Modules 1987: Tools for Teaching*. Arlington, MA: CUPM Inc., 1988, pp. 153–181.

50. Let $f(\theta)$ be the resistance to blood flow obtained on page 257, namely

$$f(\theta) = k\left(\frac{\ell - h\cot\theta}{R^4} + \frac{h\csc\theta}{r^4}\right)$$

We found that $\theta_m = \cos^{-1}(r^4/R^4)$ is a critical number of f. Find $f''(\theta)$ and use the second-derivative test to verify that a relative minimum occurs at $\theta = \theta_m$. Explain why this must be an *absolute* minimum.

51. Beehives are formed by packing together cells that may be modeled as regular hexagonal prisms open at one end, as shown in Figure 4.85. It can be shown that a cell with hexagonal side of length s and prism height h has surface area

$$S(\theta) = 6sh + 1.5s^2(-\cot\theta + \sqrt{3}\csc\theta)$$

for $0 < \theta < \frac{\pi}{2}$. What is the angle θ (to the nearest degree) that

minimizes the surface area of the cell (assuming that s and h are fixed)?

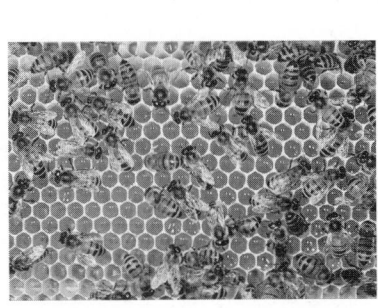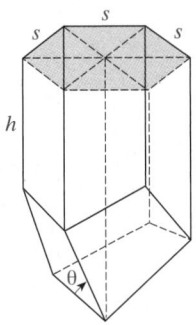

Figure 4.85   Beehive (left) and beehive cell (right)

CHAPTER 4 REVIEW

Proficiency Examination

CONCEPT PROBLEMS

1. What is the difference between absolute and relative extrema of a function?

2. State the extreme value theorem.

3. What are the critical numbers of a function? What is the difference between critical numbers and critical points?

4. Outline a procedure for finding the absolute extrema of a continuous function on a closed interval $[a, b]$.

5. State both Rolle's theorem and the mean value theorem, and discuss the relationship between them.

6. What is the zero-derivative theorem?

7. State the first-derivative and second-derivative tests, and discuss when and in which order you would use them.

8. What is a vertical asymptote? A horizontal asymptote?

9. How would you identify a cusp? A vertical tangent?

10. State l'Hôpital's rule.

11. Define $\lim_{x\to+\infty} f(x) = L$ and $\lim_{x\to c} f(x) = +\infty$.

12. Outline a graphing strategy for a function defined by $y = f(x)$.

13. What do we mean by optimization? Outline an optimization procedure.

14. What is Fermat's principle of optics?

15. What is Snell's law of refraction?

16. When is the profit maximized in terms of marginal revenue and marginal cost? When is the average cost minimized?

17. What is Poiseuille's law of resistance to flow?

PRACTICE PROBLEMS

Evaluate the limits in Problems 18–21.

18. $\lim_{x\to\pi/2} \dfrac{\sin 2x}{\cos x}$

19. $\lim_{x\to 1} \dfrac{1 - \sqrt{x}}{x - 1}$

20. $\lim_{x\to+\infty} \left(\dfrac{1}{x} - \dfrac{1}{\sqrt{x}}\right)$

21. $\lim_{x\to+\infty} \left(1 + \dfrac{2}{x}\right)^{3x}$

Sketch the graph of each function in Problems 22–27. Include all key features, such as relative extrema, inflection points, asymptotes, intercepts, cusps, and vertical tangents.

22. $f(x) = x^3 + 3x^2 - 9x + 2$

23. $f(x) = x^{1/3}(27 - x)$

24. $f(x) = \dfrac{x^2 - 1}{x^2 - 4}$

25. $f(x) = (x^2 - 3)e^{-x}$

26. $f(x) = x + \tan^{-1} x$

27. $f(x) = \sin^2 x - 2\cos x$ on $[0, 2\pi]$

28. Determine the largest and smallest values of

$$f(x) = x^4 - 2x^5 + 5$$

on the closed interval $[0, 1]$.

29. A box is to have a square base, an open top, and volume of 2 ft^3. Find the dimensions of the box (to the nearest inch) that uses the least amount of material.

30. The personnel manager of a department store estimates that if N temporary salespersons are hired for the holiday season, the total net revenue derived (in hundreds of dollars) from their efforts may be modeled by the function

$$R(N) = -3N^4 + 50N^3 - 261N^2 + 540N$$

for $0 \le N \le 9$. How many salespersons should be hired to maximize total net revenue?

Supplementary Problems

Sketch the graph of each function in Problems 1–20. Use as many as possible of the key features such as domain, relative extrema, inflection points, concavity, asymptotes, intercepts, cusps, and vertical tangents.

1. $f(x) = x^3 + 6x^2 + 9x - 1$ 2. $f(x) = x^4 + 4x^3 + 4x^2 + 1$

3. $f(x) = 3x^4 - 4x^3 + 1$ 4. $f(x) = 3x^4 - 4x^2 + 1$

5. $f(x) = 6x^5 - 15x^4 + 10x^3$

6. $f(x) = 3x^5 - 10x^3 + 15x + 1$

7. $f(x) = \dfrac{9 - x^2}{3 + x^2}$ **8.** $f(x) = \dfrac{x}{1 - x}$

9. $f(x) = \sin 2x - \sin x$ on $[-\pi, \pi]$

10. $f(x) = \sin x \sin 2x$ on $[-\pi, \pi]$

11. $f(x) = \dfrac{x^2 - 4}{x^2}$ **12.** $f(x) = \dfrac{x^2 + 2x - 3}{x^2 - 3x + 2}$

13. $f(x) = \dfrac{3x - 2}{(x + 1)^2(x - 2)}$ **14.** $f(x) = \dfrac{x^3 + 3}{x(x + 1)(x + 2)}$

15. $f(x) = x^2 \ln \sqrt{x}$ **16.** $f(x) = \sin^{-1} x + \cos^{-1} x$

17. $f(x) = x(e^{-2x} + e^{-x})$ **18.** $f(x) = \ln\left(\dfrac{x - 1}{x + 1}\right)$

19. $f(x) = \dfrac{5}{1 + e^{-x}}$ **20.** $f(x) = xe^{1/x}$

In Problems 21–24, the graph of the given function $f(x)$ for $x > 0$ is one of the six curves shown in Figure 4.86. In each case, match the function to a graph.

21. $f(x) = x2^{-x}$ **22.** $f(x) = \dfrac{\ln \sqrt{x}}{x}$

23. $f(x) = \dfrac{e^x}{x}$ **24.** $f(x) = e^{-x} \sin x$

a.   b.

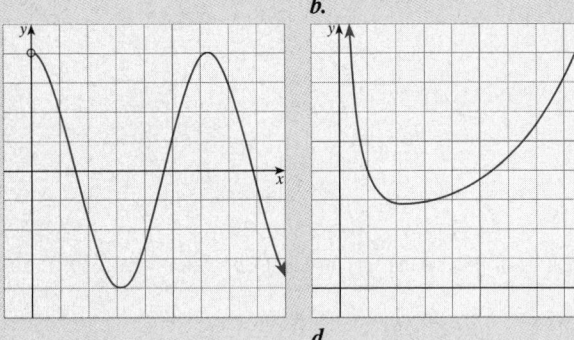

c.   d.

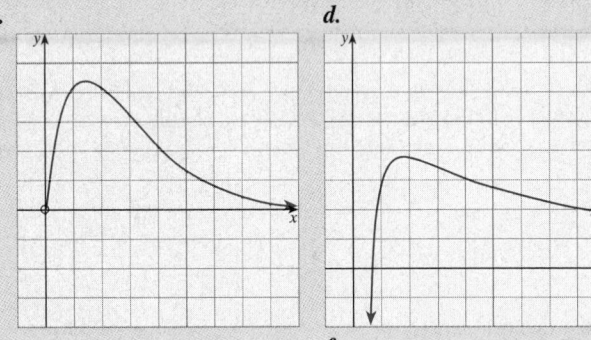

e.   f.

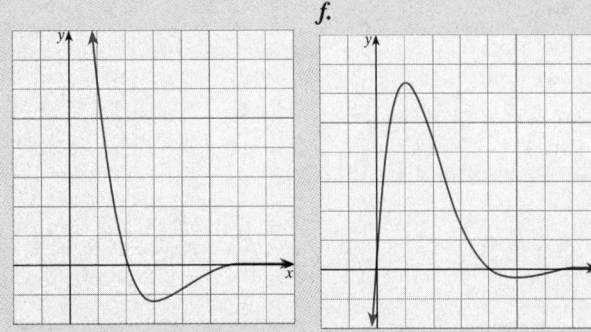

Figure 4.86   Problems 21–24

Determine the absolute maximum and absolute minimum value of each function on the interval given in Problems 25–28.

25. $f(x) = x^4 - 8x^2 + 12$ on $[-1, 2]$

26. $f(x) = \sqrt{x}(x - 5)^{1/3}$ on $[0, 6]$

27. $f(x) = 2x - \sin^{-1} x$ on $[0, 1]$

28. $f(x) = e^{-x} \ln x$ on $\left[\frac{1}{2}, 2\right]$

Evaluate the limits in Problems 29–50.

29. $\displaystyle\lim_{x \to +\infty} \dfrac{x \sin^2 x}{x^2 + 1}$ **30.** $\displaystyle\lim_{x \to +\infty} \dfrac{2x^4 - 7}{6x^4 + 7}$

31. $\displaystyle\lim_{x \to +\infty} (\sqrt{x^2 - x} - x)$ **32.** $\displaystyle\lim_{x \to +\infty} [\sqrt{x(x + b)} - x]$

33. $\displaystyle\lim_{x \to 0} \dfrac{x \sin x}{x + \sin^3 x}$ **34.** $\displaystyle\lim_{x \to 0} \dfrac{x \sin x}{x^2 - \sin^3 x}$

35. $\displaystyle\lim_{x \to 0} \dfrac{x \sin^2 x}{x^2 - \sin^2 x}$ **36.** $\displaystyle\lim_{x \to 0} \dfrac{x - \sin x}{\tan^3 x}$

37. $\displaystyle\lim_{x \to 0} \dfrac{\sin^2 x}{\sin x^2}$ **38.** $\displaystyle\lim_{x \to 0} \left(\dfrac{1}{x^2} - \dfrac{1}{x^2 \sec x}\right)$

39. $\displaystyle\lim_{x \to \pi/2^-} \dfrac{\sec^2 x}{\sec^2 3x}$ **40.** $\displaystyle\lim_{x \to \pi/2^-} (1 - \sin x) \tan x$

41. $\displaystyle\lim_{x \to \pi/2^-} (\sec x - \tan x)$

42. $\displaystyle\lim_{x \to +\infty} \left(\sqrt{x^2 + 4} - \sqrt{x^2 - 4}\right)$

43. $\displaystyle\lim_{x \to 0^+} (1 + x)^{4/x}$ **44.** $\displaystyle\lim_{x \to 1^-} \left(\dfrac{1}{1 - x}\right)^x$

45. $\displaystyle\lim_{x \to 0^+} x^{\tan x}$ **46.** $\displaystyle\lim_{x \to 0} \dfrac{5^x - 1}{x}$

47. $\displaystyle\lim_{x \to 0} \dfrac{\ln(x^2 + 1)}{x}$ **48.** $\displaystyle\lim_{x \to +\infty} \left(\dfrac{1}{x}\right)^x$

49. $\displaystyle\lim_{x \to +\infty} \left(4 - \dfrac{1}{x}\right)^x$ **50.** $\displaystyle\lim_{x \to +\infty} \dfrac{e^x \cos x - 1}{x}$

51. Journal Problem *Mathematics Teacher.** ■ Which of the graphs in Figure 4.87 is the derivative and which is the function?

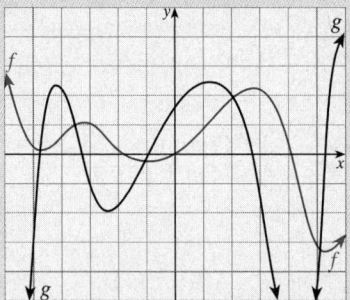

Figure 4.87   A function and its derivative

52. Determine a, b, and c such that the graph of $f(x) = ax^3 + bx^2 + c$ has an inflection point and slope 1 at $(-1, 2)$.

53. Exploration Problem   Explain why the graph of a quadratic polynomial cannot have a point of inflection. How many inflection points does the graph of a cubic polynomial have?

54. Find the points on the hyperbola $x^2 - y^2 = 4$ that are closest to the point $(0, 1)$.

*December 1990, p. 718.

55. Find numbers A, B, C, and D that guarantee that the function

$$f(x) = Ax^3 + Bx^2 + Cx + D$$

will have a relative maximum at $(-1, 1)$ and a relative minimum at $(1, -1)$.

56. A Norman window consists of a rectangle with a semicircle surmounted on the top. What are the dimensions of the Norman window of largest area with a fixed perimeter of P_0 meters?

57. An apartment complex has 200 units. When the monthly rent for each unit is $600, all units are occupied. Experience indicates that for each $20-per-month increase in rent, 5 units will become vacant. Each rented apartment costs the owners of the complex $80 per month to maintain. What monthly rent should be charged to maximize the owner's profit? What is maximum profit? How many units are rented when profit is a maximum?

58. A farmer wishes to enclose a rectangular pasture with 320 ft of fence. Find the dimensions that give the maximum area in these situations:

a. The fence is on all four sides of the pasture.

b. The fence is on three sides of the pasture and the fourth side is bounded by a wall.

59. A peach grower has determined that if 30 trees are planted per acre, each tree will average 200 lb of peaches per season. However, for each tree grown in addition to the 30 trees, the average yield for each of the trees in the grove drops by 5 lb per tree. How many peach trees should be planted on each acre in order to maximize the yield of peaches per acre? What is the maximum yield?

60. Modeling Problem To obtain the maximum price, a shipment of fruit should reach the market as early as possible after the fruit has been picked. If a grower picks the fruit immediately for shipment, 100 cases can be shipped at a profit of $10 per case. By waiting, the grower estimates that the crop will yield an additional 25 cases per week, but because the competitor's yield will also increase, the grower's profit will decrease by $1 per case per week. Use calculus to determine when the grower should ship the fruit to maximize profit. What will be the maximum profit?

61. Modeling Problem Oil from an offshore rig located 3 mi from the shore is to be pumped to a location on the edge of the shore that is 8 mi east of the rig. The cost of constructing a pipe in the ocean from the rig to the shore is 1.5 times as expensive as the cost of construction on land. Set up and analyze a model to determine how the pipe should be laid to minimize cost.

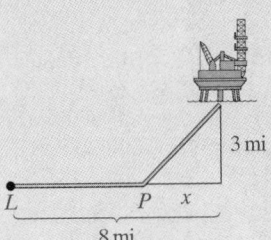

62. The owner of a novelty store can obtain joy buzzers from the manufacturer for 40¢ apiece. It is estimated that 60 buzzers will be sold when the price is $1.20 per buzzer and that 10 more buzzers will be sold for every 10¢ decrease in price. What price should be charged to maximize profit?

63. Journal Problem *AMATYC Review*[*] ■ You are to build a rectangular enclosure with front side made of material costing $10 per foot and with the other three sides (back, left, right) of material costing $5 per foot. If the enclosure is to contain exactly 600 square feet and to be built at minimum total cost, how long should the side be and what is the total cost?

Answer: $600.

Here is the real question: By coincidence, the answer matches the constrained area (both 600, aside from units, of course). *Question*: Characterize when this happens more generally, and thus describe the relationship that exists in such problems in which the resultant minimum cost matches the given area (all in appropriate units).

64. Journal Problem *Quantum*[†] ■ Two students are pondering the following problem: A tin can takes the form of a right circular cylinder with radius R and height H. An ant is sitting on the border circle of one of its bases (point A in Figure 4.88). It wants to crawl to the most distant point B at the border circle of the other base (symmetric to A with respect to the center of the tin). Find the shortest path for the ant.

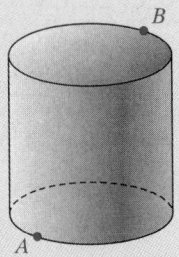

Figure 4.88 Shortest path from A to B?

a. What is the length of the shortest path?

b. *After* finding a solution, compare your solution with that of the first student as follows: "It's a simple problem!" the first student says confidently. "We just have to consider the planar development of the tin. Let's say, for the sake of definiteness, that the ant first crawls along the side surface and then across the upper base (of course, it's possible that the ant takes the symmetric route: first crawling across the lower base, then along the side surface; but the length of this route is the same)."

c. Compare your solution with that of the second student, as follows: "Wait a second," the other student replies. "One can very comfortably develop the tin can in a different way! Just throw away the lids and spread the side surface on the plane so that we get a rectangle. Then the shortest path will be the segment connecting points A and B, where the image of the ant's route on the tin can will be part of a corkscrew line."

d. Either your solution matched one of the students' solutions or it did not. Which of the two (or possibly three) solutions provides the minimum? Before you answer, find out the conditions whereby the lengths of both of the students' routes are the equal. Critique the solutions given by the two students.

[*] Spring 1995, pp. 67–68.

[†] September/October, 1997, Vol. 7, No. 4, pp. 50–53.

65. Westel Corporation manufactures telephones and has developed a new cellular phone. Production analysis shows that its price must not be less than \$50; if x units are sold, then the price per unit is given by the formula $p(x) = 150 - x$. The total cost of producing x units is given by the formula $C(x) = 2,500 + 30x$. Find the maximum profit, and determine the price that should be charged to maximize the profit.

66. Modeling Problem A manufacturer receives an order for 5,000 items. There are 12 machines available, each of which can produce 25 items per hour. The cost of setting up a machine for a production run is \$50. Once the machines are in operation, the procedure is fully automated and can be supervised by a single worker earning \$20 per hour. Set up and analyze a model to determine the number of machines that should be used to minimize the total cost of filling the order. State any assumptions that must be made.

67. Show that the graph of a polynomial of degree n, with $n > 2$, has at most $n - 2$ inflection points.

68. Show that the graph of the function $f(x) = x^n$ with $n > 1$ has either one or no inflection points, depending on whether n is odd or even.

69. Each tangent line to the circle $x^2 + y^2 = 1$ at a point in the first quadrant will intersect the coordinate axes at points $(x_1, 0)$ and $(0, y_1)$. Determine the line for which $x_1 + y_1$ is a minimum.

70. An accelerated particle moving at speed close to the speed of light emits power P in the direction θ given by

$$P(\theta) = \frac{a \sin \theta}{(1 - b \cos \theta)^5} \quad \text{for} \quad 0 < b < 1 \quad \text{and} \quad a > 0$$

Find the value of θ ($0 \le \theta \le \pi$) for which P has the greatest value.

71. Suppose that f is a continuous function defined on the closed interval $[a, b]$ and that $f'(x) = c$ on the open interval (a, b) for some constant c. Use the MVT to show that

$$f(x) = c(x - a) + f(a)$$

for all x in the interval $[a, b]$.

72. Find the point of inflection of the curve

$$y = (x + 1) \tan^{-1} x$$

73. Find the critical numbers for the function

$$f(x) = \tan^{-1}\left(\frac{x}{a}\right) - \tan^{-1}\left(\frac{x}{b}\right), \qquad a > b$$

Classify each as corresponding to a relative maximum, a relative minimum, or neither.

74. Suppose that $f''(x)$ exists for all x and that $f''(x) + c^2 f(x) = 0$ for some number c with $f'(0) = 1$. Show that for any $x = x_0$, there is a number w between 0 and x_0 for which $f'(x_0) + c^2 f(w)x_0 = 1$.

75. Modeling Problem According to the *Mortality and Morbidity Report* of the U.S. Centers for Disease Control, the following table gives the number of annual deaths from acquired immune deficiency syndrome (AIDS) in the United States for the years 1982–1991.*

---

*For an interesting discussion of how mathematical modeling can be applied to a problem of great public and personal interest, see "Modeling the AIDS Epidemic," by Allyn Jackson, *Notices of the American Mathematical Society*, Vol. 36, No. 8 (October 1989), pp. 981–983.

Year	Deaths	Year	Deaths
1982	400	1987	13,900
1983	1,400	1988	17,300
1984	3,200	1989	32,000
1985	6,200	1990	39,000
1986	10,660	1991	45,000

a. To model the number of annual AIDS deaths, a data analysis program produced the cubic polynomial

$$N(x) = -8.58197x^3 + 732.727x^2 - 3,189.9x + 4,375.09$$

Sketch the graph of N and determine the time when its highest point occurs for $0 \le x \le 20$, where $x = 0$ represents 1982.

b. The same report gives the number of cases of reported AIDS for the period 1984–1991:

Year	Deaths	Year	Deaths
1984	4,445	1988	31,001
1985	8,249	1989	33,722
1986	12,932	1990	41,595
1987	21,070	1991	43,672

The same data analysis program used in part **a** yields

$$C(x) = -171.247x^3 + 3,770.90x^2 - 19,965.1x + 34,893.9$$

as a modeling polynomial for the number of cases as a function of time x. When does this model predict the number of reported cases will be the largest? When does it predict the number of reported cases will drop to 0?

c. When the data in part **b** are modeled exponentially, the data analysis program produces the function

$$y = 1,676e^{0.3256x}$$

Sketch the cubic modeling formula $y = C(x)$ from part **b** and this exponential formula on the same set of coordinate axes along with the data points from the table in part **b**. Which formula do you think does a better job of fitting the data?

d. Explore other modeling formulas for the data given in part **a**.

e. Call the Centers for Disease Control or check the World Wide Web (www.cdc.gov) for the most recent updates for the data in parts **a** and **b**. Do the formulas in this problem correctly model the current information? Explain the discrepancies.

f. Based on the information you obtained in part **e**, find new models for the information in parts **a** and **b** using all the data you have available.

Using the graphing and differentiation programs of your computer or calculator, graph $f(x)$, $f'(x)$, $f''(x)$ for each function in Problems 76–79. Print out a copy, if possible. On each graph, indicate where

a. $f'(x) > 0$ **b.** $f'(x) < 0$ **c.** $f''(x) > 0$
d. $f''(x) < 0$ **e.** $f'(x) = 0$ **f.** $f'(x)$ does not exist
g. $f''(x) = 0$

Describe how these inequalities qualitatively determine the shape of the graph of the functions over the given interval.

76. $f(x) = \sin 2x$ on $[-\pi, \pi]$

77. $f(x) = x^3 - x^2 - x + 1$ on $\left[-\frac{3}{2}, 2\right]$

78. $f(x) = x^4 - 2x^2$ on $[-2, 2]$

79. $f(x) = x^3 - x + \dfrac{1}{x} + 1$ on $[-2, 2]$

80. Consider a string 60 in. long that is formed into a rectangle. Using a graphing calculator or a graphing program, graph the area $A(x)$ enclosed by the string as a function of the length x of a given side ($0 < x < 30$). From the graph, deduce that the maximum area is enclosed when the rectangle is a square. What is the minimum area enclosed? Compare this problem to the exact solution. What conclusions do you draw about the desirability of analytical solutions and the role of the computer?

81. Modeling Problem The beach of a lake follows contours that are approximated by the curve $4x^2 + y^2 = 1$, and a nearby road lies along the curve $y = 1/x$ for $x > 0$. Using your graphing calculator or computer software, determine the closest approach of the road to the lake in the north-south direction. Take the positive y-axis as pointing north.

82. Using your graphing and differentiation programs, locate and identify all the relative extrema for the function defined by

$$f(x) = \tfrac{1}{5}x^5 - \tfrac{5}{4}x^4 + 2x^2$$

This may require judicious choices of the window settings.

83. Modeling Problem Suppose you are a manager of a fleet of delivery trucks. Each truck is driven at a constant speed of x mi/h ($15 \le x \le 55$), and gas consumption (gal/mi) is modeled by the function

$$\frac{1}{250}\left(\frac{750}{x} + x\right)$$

Using a graphing and differentiation program (and/or root-solving program on your computer or calculator), answer the following questions:

a. If gas costs $1.70/gal, estimate the steady speed that will minimize the cost of fuel for a 500-mi trip.

b. Estimate the steady speed that minimizes the cost if the driver is paid $28 per hour and the price of gasoline remains constant at $1.70/gal.

84. HISTORICAL QUEST   Leonhard Euler is one of the giants in the history of mathematics. His name is attached to almost every branch of mathematics. He was the most prolific writer on the subject of mathematics, and his mathematical textbooks were masterfully written. His writing was not at all slowed down by his total blindness for the last 17 years of his life. He possessed a phenomenal memory, had

LEONHARD EULER
1707–1783

almost total recall, and could mentally calculate long and complicated problems. The basis for the historical development of calculus, as well as modern-day analysis, is the notion of a function. Euler's book *Introductio in analysin infinitorum* (1784) first used the function concept as the basic idea. It was the identification of functions, rather than curves, as the principal object of study, that permitted the advancement of mathematics in general, and calculus in particular. In Chapter 2, we noted that the number e is named in honor of Euler. Euler did not use the definition we use today, namely,

$$e = \lim_{n \to +\infty}\left(1 + \frac{1}{n}\right)^n$$

Instead, Euler used series in his work (which we will study in Chapter 8). ∎

   In this Historical Quest problem we will lay the groundwork for a Historical Quest in Chapter 8. Euler introduced $\log_a x$ (which he wrote as ℓx) as that exponent y such that $a^y = x$. This was done in 1748, which makes it the first appearance of a logarithm interpreted explicitly as an exponent. He does not define $a^0 = 1$, but instead writes

$$a^\epsilon = 1 + k\epsilon$$

for an infinitely small number ϵ. In other words,

$$k = \lim_{\epsilon \to 0} \frac{a^\epsilon - 1}{\epsilon}$$

Explain why $k = \ln a$.

   When Euler was 13, he registered at the University of Basel and was introduced to another famous mathematician, Johann Bernoulli, who was an instructor there at the time (see Historical Quest, Section 4.5, Problems 58–59). If Bernoulli thought that a student was promising, he would provide, sometimes gratis, private instruction. Here is Euler's own account of this first encounter with Bernoulli

I soon found an opportunity to gain introduction to the famous professor Johann Bernoulli, whose good pleasure it was to advance me further in the mathematical sciences. True, because of his business he flatly refused me private lessons, but he gave me much wiser advice, namely, to get some more difficult mathematical books and work through them with all industry, and wherever I should find some check or difficulties, he gave me free access to him every Saturday afternoon and was so kind as to elucidate all difficulties, which happened with such greatly desired advantage that whenever he had obviated one check for me, because of that ten others disappeared right away, which is certainly the way to make a happy advance in the mathematical sciences.*

**From *Elements of Algebra* by Leonhard Euler, 1840. London: Longman, Orme, and Co. Reprinted by Springer-Verlag.

85. **Putnam Examination Problem**   Given the parabola $y^2 = 2mx$, what is the length of the shortest chord that is normal to the curve at one end? *Hint*: If $\overline{AB}$ is normal to the parabola, where A and B are the points $(2mt^2, 2mt)$ and $(2ms^2, 2ms)$, show that the slope of the tangent at A is $1/(2t)$.

86. **Putnam Examination Problem**   Prove that the polynomial

$$(a - x)^6 - 3a(a - x)^5 + \tfrac{5}{2}a^2(a - x)^4 - \tfrac{1}{2}a^4(a - x)^2$$

has only negative values for $0 < x < a$. *Hint*: Show that if $x = g(1 - y)$, the polynomial becomes $a^6 y^2 g(y)$, where

$$g(y) = y^4 - 3y^3 + \tfrac{5}{2}y^2 - \tfrac{1}{2}$$

and then prove that $g(y) < 0$ for $0 < y < 1$.

87. **Putnam Examination Problem**   Find the maximum value of $f(x) = x^3 - 3x$ on the set of all real numbers x satisfying $x^4 + 36 \le 13x^2$.

88. **Putnam Examination Problem**   Let T be an acute triangle. Inscribe a pair R and S of rectangles in T, as shown in Figure 4.89. Let $A(X)$ denote the area of polygon X. Find the maximum value, or show that no maximum exists, of the ratio

$$\frac{A(R) + A(S)}{A(T)}$$

where T ranges over all triangles, and R and S range over all rectangles as shown in Figure 4.89.

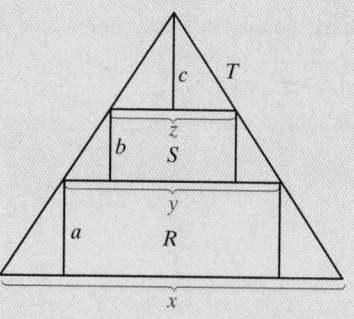

Figure 4.89   Problem 88

89. **Putnam Examination Problem**   Which is greater

$$(\sqrt{n})^{\sqrt{n+1}} \qquad \text{or} \qquad (\sqrt{n+1})^{\sqrt{n}}$$

where $n > 8$? *Hint*: Use the function $f(x) = \dfrac{\ln x}{x}$, and show that $x^y > y^x$ when $e \le x < y$.

90. **Putnam Examination Problem**   The graph of the equation $x^y = y^x$ for $x > 0$, $y > 0$ consists of a straight line and a curve. Find the coordinates of the point where the line and the curve intersect.

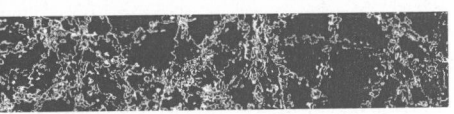

Group Research Project*

Wine Barrel Capacity*

This project is to be done in groups of three or four students. Each group will submit a single written report.

A wine barrel has a hole in the middle of its side called a **bung hole**. To determine the volume of wine in the barrel, a **bung rod** is inserted in the hole until it hits the lower seam. Determine how to calibrate such a rod so that it will measure the volume of the wine in the barrel. You should make the following assumptions:

1. The barrel is cylindrical.
2. The distance from the bung hole to the corner is λ.
3. The ratio of the height to the diameter of the barrel is t. This ratio should be chosen so that for a given λ value, the volume of the barrel is maximal.

Your paper is not limited to the following questions, but it should include these concerns: You should show that the volume of the cylindrical barrel is

$$V = 2\pi\lambda^3 t(4 + t^2)^{-3/2}$$

and you should find the approximate ideal value for t. Johannes Kepler was the first person to show mathematically why coopers were guided in their construction of wine barrels by one rule: *make the staves* (the boards that make up the sides of the barrel) *one and one-half times as long as the diameter.* (This is the approximate t-value.) You should provide dimensions for the barrel as well as for the bung rod.

JOHANNES KEPLER (1571–1630) is usually remembered for his work in astronomy, in particular for his three laws of planetary motion. Tycho Brahe (1546-1601) was working for Rodolf II, Holy Roman Emperor in Prague in 1599, and he asked Kepler to work with him. The historian Burton describes this as a fortunate alliance. "Tycho was a splendid observer but a poor mathematician, while Kepler was a splendid mathematician but a poor observer." Because Kepler was a Protestant during a time when most intellectuals were required to be Catholic, Kepler had trouble supporting himself, and consequently worked for many benefactors. While serving the Austrian emperor Matthew I, Kepler observed with admiration the ability of a young vintner to declare quickly and easily the capacities of a number of different wine casks. He describes how this can be done in his book *The New Stereometry of Wine Barrels, Mostly Austrian.*

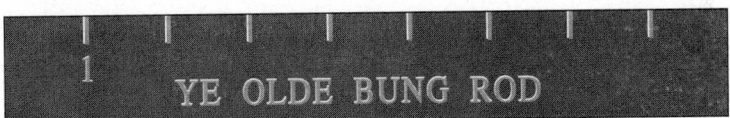

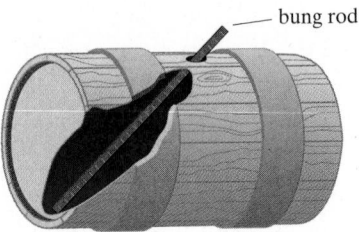

bung rod

*The idea for this group research project comes from research done at Iowa State University as part of a National Science Foundation grant. Our thanks to Elgin Johnston of Iowa State University.

5

Integration

PREVIEW

A traveler, driving a car down a straight, level road at 40 mi/h, applies the brakes, which decelerate the car at the rate of 21 ft/s^2. How far does the car travel before coming to a full stop? An ecologist measures the width of an oil spill at intervals of 5 ft along its length. What is the approximate area of the spill? On Christmas day, it starts snowing at a steady rate. A snowplow starts out at noon, going 2 mi during the first hour and 1 mi during the second hour. When did it start to snow?

We will examine questions such as these in the examples and problems of this chapter, as we study **integral calculus**, the companion to the **differential calculus** developed in Chapters 3 and 4.

PERSPECTIVE

The key concept in integral calculus is *integration*, a procedure that involves computing a special kind of limit of sums called the *definite integral*. We will find that such limits can often be computed by reversing the process of differentiation; that is, given a function f, we find a function F such that $F' = f$. This is called *indefinite integration*, and the equation $F' = f$ is an example of a *differential equation*.

Finding integrals and solving differential equations are extremely important processes in calculus. We begin our study of these topics by defining definite and indefinite integration and showing how they are connected by a remarkable result called the *fundamental theorem of calculus*. Then we examine several techniques of integration and show how area, average value, and other quantities can be set up and analyzed by integration. Our study of differential equations begins in this chapter and will continue in appropriate sections throughout this text. We also establish a mean value theorem for integrals and develop numerical procedures for estimating the value of a definite integral.

5.1 Antidifferentiation

IN THIS SECTION reversing differentiation, antiderivative notation, antidifferentiation formulas, applications, area as an antiderivative

REVERSING DIFFERENTIATION

A physicist who knows the acceleration of a particle may want to determine its velocity or its position at a particular time. An ecologist who knows the rate at which a certain pollutant is being absorbed by a particular species of fish might want to know the actual amount of pollutant in the fish's system at a given time. In each of these cases, a derivative f' is given and the problem is that of finding the corresponding function f. Toward this end, we make the following definition.

Antiderivative

> A function F is called an **antiderivative** of a given function f on an interval I if
> $$F'(x) = f(x)$$
> for all x in I.

Suppose we know $f(x) = 3x^2$. We wish to find a function $F(x)$ such that $F'(x) = 3x^2$. It is not difficult to use the power rule in reverse to discover that $F(x) = x^3$ is such a function. However, that is not the only possibility:

Given: $F(x) = x^3$ $\qquad G(x) = x^3 - 5$ $\qquad H(x) = x^3 + \pi^2$

Find: $F'(x) = 3x^2$ $\qquad G'(x) = 3x^2$ $\qquad H'(x) = 3x^2$

In fact, if F is an antiderivative of f, then so is $F + C$ for any constant C, because

$$[F(x) + C]' = F'(x) + 0 = f(x)$$

In the following theorem, we use the constant difference theorem of Section 4.2 to show that *any* antiderivative of f can be expressed in this form.

THEOREM 5.1 **Antiderivatives of the same function differ by a constant**

If F is an antiderivative of the continuous function f, then any other antiderivative, G, of f must have the form

$$G(x) = F(x) + C$$

> ➨ **What This Says** Two antiderivatives of the same function differ by a constant.

Proof If F and G are both antiderivatives of f, then $F' = f$ and $G' = f$ and Theorem 4.6 (the constant difference theorem) tells us that

$$G(x) - F(x) = C$$

so $G(x) = F(x) + C$. ❏

EXAMPLE 1 Finding antiderivatives

Find general antiderivatives for the given functions.

a. $f(x) = x^5$ **b.** $s(x) = \sin x$ **c.** $y'(x) = \dfrac{1}{x}$

Solution

a. If $F(x) = x^6$, then $F'(x) = 6x^5$, so we see that a particular antiderivative of f is $F(x) = \dfrac{x^6}{6}$ to obtain $F'(x) = \dfrac{6x^5}{6} = x^5$. By Theorem 5.1, the most general antiderivative is $G(x) = \dfrac{x^6}{6} + C$.

b. If $S(x) = -\cos x$, then $S'(x) = \sin x$, so $G(x) = -\cos x + C$.

c. If $y(x) = \ln|x|$, then $y'(x) = \dfrac{1}{x}$, so $G(x) = \ln|x| + C$. ■

Recall that the slope of a function $y = f(x)$ at any point (x, y) on its graph is given by the derivative $f'(x)$. We can exploit this fact to obtain a "picture" of the graph of f. Reconsider Example 1c where $y' = 1/x$. There is an antiderivative $F(x)$ of $1/x$ such that the slope of F at each point $(x, F(x))$ is $1/x$ for each nonzero value of x. Let us draw a graph of these slopes:

If $x = 1$, then the slope is $\frac{1}{1} = 1$. Draw short line segments at $x = 1$, each with slope 1, for different y-values as shown in Figure 5.1a.

If $x = -3$, then the slope is $-1/3$, so draw short line segments at $x = -3$, each with slope $-1/3$, also shown in Figure 5.1a.

If we continue to plot these slope points for different values of x, we obtain many little slope lines. The resulting graph shown in Figure 5.1c is known as a **slope field** for the equation $y' = 1/x$. Beginning in Section 5.6 slope fields are also called *direction fields*.

Finally, notice the relationship between the slope field for $y' = 1/x$ and its antiderivative $y = \ln|x| + C$ (found in Example 1c). If we choose particular values for C, say $C = 0$, $C = -\ln 2$, or $C = 2$, and draw these particular antiderivatives in Figure 5.1c, we notice that these particular solutions are anticipated by the slope field drawn in part b. That is, the slope field shows the entire family of antiderivatives of the original equation.

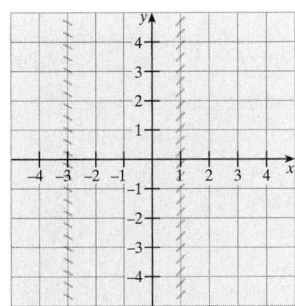

a. Slopes for $x = 1$ and $x = -3$

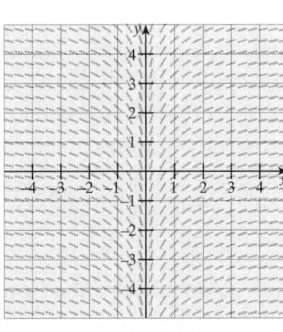

b. Slope field

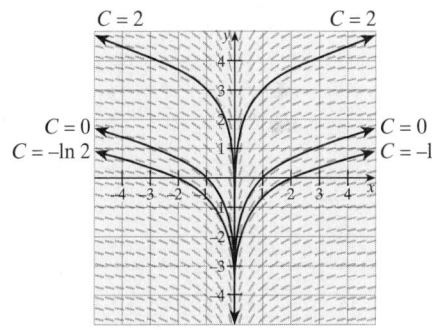

c. Sample antiderivatives

Figure 5.1 Slope field for the equation $y' = \dfrac{1}{x}$

Slope fields will be discussed in more detail in Section 5.6. In general, slope fields, and antiderivatives obtained by using slope fields, are usually generated using technology in computers and calculators.

Here is an example in which the antiderivatives cannot be obtained as elementary functions.

EXAMPLE 2   Finding an antiderivative using a slope field

Consider the slope field for $y' = e^{x^2}$, which is shown in Figure 5.2. Draw a possible graph of the antiderivative of e^{x^2} that passes through the point $(0, 0)$.

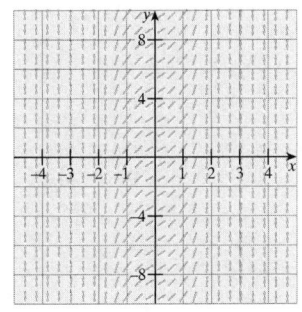

Figure 5.2 Slope field for $y' = e^{x^2}$

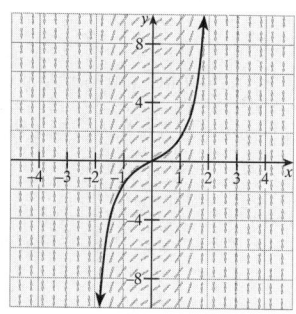

Figure 5.3 Antiderivative of $y' = e^{x^2}$ passing through $(0, 0)$

Indefinite Integral

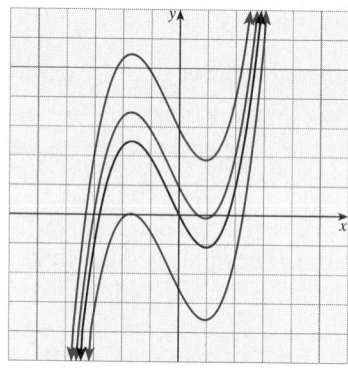

Figure 5.4 Several members of the family of curves $y = F(x) + C$

Solution

Each little segment represents the slope of e^{x^2} for a particular x value. For example, if $x = 0$, the slope is 1, if $x = 1$, the slope is e, and if $x = 2$, the slope is e^4 (quite steep). However, to draw the antiderivative, step back and take a large view of the graph, and "go with the flow." We sketch the apparent graph that passes through $(0, 0)$, as shown in Figure 5.3.   ∎

ANTIDERIVATIVE NOTATION

It is worthwhile to define a notation to indicate the operation of antidifferentiation.

The notation

$$\int f(x)\,dx = F(x) + C$$

where C is an arbitrary constant means that F is an antiderivative of f. It is called the **indefinite integral of** f and satisfies the condition that $F'(x) = f(x)$ for all x in the domain of f.

➡ **What This Says**   This is nothing more than the definition of the antiderivative, along with a convenient notation. We also agree that in the context of antidifferentiation, C is an arbitrary constant.

The graph of $F(x) + C$ for different values of C is called **a family of functions** (see Figure 5.4).

WARNING   It is important to remember that $\int f(x)\,dx$ represents a family of functions, not just a single function.

Because each member of the family $y = F(x) + C$ has the same derivative at x, the slope of the graph at x is the same. This means that the graph of all functions of the form $y = F(x) + C$ is a collection of parallel curves, as shown in Figure 5.4.

The process of finding indefinite integrals is called **indefinite integration**. Notice that this process amounts to finding an antiderivative of f and adding an arbitrary constant C, which is called the **constant of integration**.

EXAMPLE 3   Antidifferentiation

Find each of the following indefinite integrals.

a. $\int 5x^3\,dx$ **b.** $\int \sec^2 x\,dx$ **c.** $\int e^x\,dx$

Solution

a. Since $\dfrac{d}{dx}(x^4) = 4x^3$, it follows that $\dfrac{d}{dx}\left(\dfrac{5x^4}{4}\right) = 5x^3$. Thus,

$$\int 5x^3\,dx = \frac{5x^4}{4} + C$$

b. Because $\dfrac{d}{dx}(\tan x) = \sec^2 x$, we have $\int \sec^2 x\,dx = \tan x + C$.

c. Since $\dfrac{d}{dx}(e^x) = e^x$, we have $\int e^x\,dx = e^x + C$.   ∎

ANTIDIFFERENTIATION FORMULAS

Example 3 leads us to state formulas for antidifferentiation. Theorem 5.2 summarizes several fundamental properties of indefinite integrals, each of which can be derived by reversing an appropriate differentiation formula. Assume that f and g are functions; u is a variable; a, b, c are given constants; and C is an arbitrary constant.

THEOREM 5.2   **Basic integration rules**

Differentiation Formulas   *Integration Formulas*

PROCEDURAL RULES

Constant multiple: $\dfrac{d}{du}(cf) = c\dfrac{df}{du}$ $\displaystyle\int cf(u)\,du = c\int f(u)\,du$

Sum rule: $\dfrac{d}{du}(f+g) = \dfrac{df}{du} + \dfrac{dg}{du}$ $\displaystyle\int [f(u) + g(u)]\,du = \int f(u)\,du + \int g(u)\,du$

Difference rule: $\dfrac{d}{du}(f-g) = \dfrac{df}{du} - \dfrac{dg}{du}$ $\displaystyle\int [f(u) - g(u)]\,du = \int f(u)\,du - \int g(u)\,du$

Linearity rule: $\dfrac{d}{du}(af+bg) = a\dfrac{df}{du} + b\dfrac{dg}{du}$ $\displaystyle\int [af(u) + bg(u)]\,du = a\int f(u)\,du + b\int g(u)\,du$

BASIC FORMULAS

Constant rule: $\dfrac{d}{du}(c) = 0$ $\displaystyle\int 0\,du = 0 + C$

Exponential rule: $\dfrac{d}{du}(e^u) = e^u$ $\displaystyle\int e^u\,du = e^u + C$

Power rule: $\dfrac{d}{du}(u^n) = nu^{n-1}$ $\displaystyle\int u^n\,du = \begin{cases} \dfrac{u^{n+1}}{n+1} + C; & n \neq -1 \\ \ln|u| + C; & n = -1 \end{cases}$

Logarithmic rule:[*] $\dfrac{d}{du}(\ln|u|) = \dfrac{1}{u}$

Trigonometric rules: $\dfrac{d}{du}(\cos u) = -\sin u$ $\displaystyle\int \sin u\,du = -\cos u + C$

$\dfrac{d}{du}(\sin u) = \cos u$ $\displaystyle\int \cos u\,du = \sin u + C$

$\dfrac{d}{du}(\tan u) = \sec^2 u$ $\displaystyle\int \sec^2 u\,du = \tan u + C$

$\dfrac{d}{du}(\sec u) = \sec u \tan u$ $\displaystyle\int \sec u \tan u\,du = \sec u + C$

$\dfrac{d}{du}(\csc u) = -\csc u \cot u$ $\displaystyle\int \csc u \cot u\,du = -\csc u + C$

$\dfrac{d}{du}(\cot u) = -\csc^2 u$ $\displaystyle\int \csc^2 u\,du = -\cot u + C$

---

[*]Note the absolute value. This is the result of reversing Theorem 3.13, Section 3.6.

Inverse trigonometric rules:

$$\frac{d}{du}(\sin^{-1} u) = \frac{1}{\sqrt{1 - u^2}} \qquad \int \frac{du}{\sqrt{1 - u^2}} = \sin^{-1} u + C$$

The other three inverse trigonometric rules are not needed since, for example, $\sin^{-1} u + \cos^{-1} u = \dfrac{\pi}{2}$, so that

$$\frac{d}{du}(\tan^{-1} u) = \frac{1}{1 + u^2} \qquad \int \frac{du}{1 + u^2} = \tan^{-1} u + C$$

$$\frac{d}{du}(\sec^{-1} u) = \frac{1}{|u|\sqrt{u^2 - 1}} \qquad \int \frac{du}{|u|\sqrt{u^2 - 1}} = \sec^{-1} u + C$$

$$\int \frac{du}{\sqrt{1 - u^2}} = \frac{\pi}{2} - \cos^{-1} u + C_1$$

$$= -\cos^{-1} u + C$$

Proof Each of these parts can be derived by reversing the accompanying derivative formula. For example, to obtain the power rule, note that if n is any number other than -1, then

$$\frac{d}{du}\left[\frac{1}{n + 1}u^{n+1}\right] = \frac{1}{n + 1}\left[(n + 1)u^n\right] = u^n$$

so that $\dfrac{1}{n + 1}u^{n+1}$ is an antiderivative of u^n and

$$\int u^n \, du = \frac{1}{n + 1}u^{n+1} + C \quad \text{for} \quad n \neq -1 \qquad \Box$$

Now we will use these rules to compute a number of indefinite integrals.

EXAMPLE 4   Indefinite integral of a polynomial function

Evaluate $\displaystyle\int (x^5 - 3x^2 - 7)\,dx$.

Solution

The first two steps are usually done mentally:

$$\int (x^5 - 3x^2 - 7)\,dx = \int x^5\,dx - \int 3x^2\,dx - \int 7\,dx \quad \text{Sum and difference rules}$$

$$= \int x^5\,dx - 3\int x^2\,dx - 7\int dx \quad \text{Constant multiple}$$

$$= \frac{x^{5+1}}{5 + 1} - 3\frac{x^{2+1}}{2 + 1} - 7x + C \qquad \text{Power rule}$$

$$= \tfrac{1}{6}x^6 - x^3 - 7x + C \qquad \blacksquare$$

EXAMPLE 5   Indefinite integral with a mixture of forms

Evaluate $\displaystyle\int (5\sqrt{x} + 4\sin x)\,dx$.

Solution

$$\int (5\sqrt{x} + 4\sin x)\,dx = 5\int x^{1/2}\,dx + 4\int \sin x\,dx \qquad \text{Sum and constant rules}$$

$$= 5\frac{x^{3/2}}{\frac{3}{2}} + 4(-\cos x) + C \qquad \text{Power and trig rules}$$

$$= \tfrac{10}{3}x^{3/2} - 4\cos x + C \qquad \blacksquare$$

Antiderivatives will be used extensively in integration in connection with a marvelous result called the fundamental theorem of calculus (Section 5.4).

APPLICATIONS

In Chapter 3, we used differentiation to compute the slope at each point on the graph of a function. Example 6 shows how this procedure can be reversed.

EXAMPLE 6   Finding the function with a given slope through a particular point

The graph of a certain function F has slope $4x^3 - 5$ at each point (x, y) and contains the point $(1, 2)$. Find the function F.

Solution

We will work this problem twice; first we find an analytic solution and the second time we approximate the solution using technology, which is often sufficient.

Analytic solution: Because the slope of the tangent at each point (x, y) is given by $F'(x)$, we have

$$F'(x) = 4x^3 - 5$$

and it follows that

$$\int F'(x)\, dx = \int (4x^3 - 5)\, dx$$

$$F(x) = 4\left(\frac{x^4}{4}\right) - 5x + C$$

$$= x^4 - 5x + C$$

The family of curves is $y = x^4 - 5x + C$. To find the one that passes through $(1, 2)$, substitute:

$$2 = 1^4 - 5(1) + C$$

$$6 = C$$

The curve is $y = x^4 - 5x + 6$.

Technology solution: Begin by drawing the slope field, as shown in Figure 5.5a. We are interested in drawing the particular solution passing through $(1, 2)$. Remember to "go with the flow," as shown in Figure 5.5b. If we compare the analytic solution and the graphical solution, we see that the graph of the equation in the analytic solution is the same as the one found by technology.

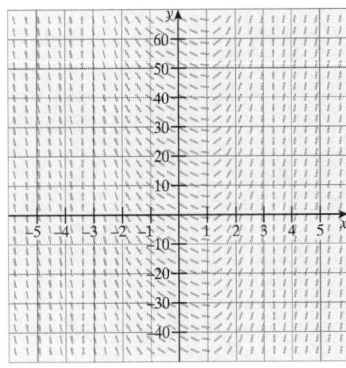

a. Slope field

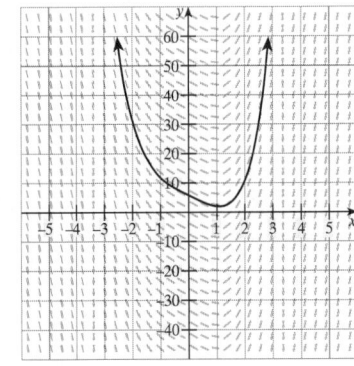

b. Particular solution

Figure 5.5   Slope field for $F'(x) = 4x^3 - 5$

In Section 3.4, we observed that an object moving along a straight line with position $s(t)$ has velocity $v(t) = \dfrac{ds}{dt}$ and acceleration $a(t) = \dfrac{dv}{dt}$. Thus, we have

$$v(t) = \int a(t)\,dt \qquad \text{and} \qquad s(t) = \int v(t)\,dt$$

These formulas are used in Examples 7 and 8.

EXAMPLE 7 Modeling Problem: The motion of a particle

A particle moves along a coordinate axis in such a way that its acceleration is modeled by $a(t) = 2t^{-2}$ for time $t > 0$. If the particle is at $s = 5$ when $t = 1$ and has velocity $v = -3$ at this time, where is it (to four decimal places) when $t = 4$?

Solution

Because $a(t) = v'(t)$, it follows that

$$v(t) = \int a(t)\,dt = \int 2t^{-2}\,dt = -2t^{-1} + C_1$$

and since $v(1) = -3$, we have

$$-3 = v(1) = \frac{-2}{1} + C_1 \qquad \text{so} \qquad C_1 = -3 + 2 = -1$$

We also know $v(t) = s'(t)$, so

$$s(t) = \int v(t)\,dt = \int (-2t^{-1} - 1)\,dt = -2\ln|t| - t + C_2$$

Since $s(1) = 5$, we have

$$5 = s(1) = -2\ln|1| - 1 + C_2 \qquad \text{or} \qquad C_2 = 6$$

Thus, $s(t) = -2\ln|t| - t + 6$ so that $s(4) \approx -0.7726$. The particle is at -0.7726 when $t = 4$. ∎

EXAMPLE 8 Stopping distance for an automobile

The brakes of a certain automobile produce a constant deceleration of 22 ft/s². If the car is traveling at 60 mi/h (88 ft/s) when the brakes are applied, how far will it travel before coming to a complete stop?

Solution

Let $a(t)$, $v(t)$, and $s(t)$ denote the acceleration, velocity, and position of the car t seconds after the brakes are applied. We will assume that s is measured from the point where the brakes are applied, so that $s(0) = 0$.

$$
\begin{aligned}
v(t) &= \int a(t)\,dt \\[4pt]
&= \int (-22)\,dt \qquad &\text{Negative because the car is decelerating} \\[4pt]
&= -22t + C_1 \qquad &v(0) = -22(0) + C_1 = 88, \text{ so that } C_1 = 88 \\
& &\text{Starting velocity is } 88. \\[4pt]
&= -22t + 88
\end{aligned}
$$

Similarly,

$$
\begin{aligned}
s(t) &= \int v(t)\,dt \\[4pt]
&= \int (-22t + 88)\,dt \\[4pt]
&= -11t^2 + 88t + C_2 \qquad &s(0) = -11(0)^2 + 88(0) + C_2 = 0 \\
& &\text{so that } C_2 = 0 \\[4pt]
&= -11t^2 + 88t \qquad &\text{Starting distance is } 0.
\end{aligned}
$$

Finally, the car comes to rest when its velocity is 0, so we need to solve $v(t) = 0$ for t:

$$-22t + 88 = 0$$
$$t = 4$$

This means that the car decelerates for 4 sec before coming to rest, and in that time it travels

$$s(4) = -11(4)^2 + 88(4) = 176 \text{ ft}$$ ∎

Indefinite integration also has applications in business and economics. Recall from Section 4.7 that the *demand function* for a particular commodity is the function $p(x)$, which gives the price p that consumers will pay for each unit of the commodity when x units are brought to market. Then the total revenue is $R(x) = xp(x)$, and the marginal revenue is $R'(x)$. The next example shows how the demand function can be determined from the marginal revenue.

EXAMPLE 9 Finding the demand function given the marginal revenue

A manufacturer estimates that the marginal revenue of a certain commodity is $R'(x) = 240 + 0.1x$ when x units are produced. Find the demand function $p(x)$.

Solution

$$R(x) = \int R'(x)\, dx$$
$$= \int (240 + 0.1x)\, dx$$
$$= 240x + 0.1 \left(\tfrac{1}{2}x^2\right) + C$$
$$= 240x + 0.05x^2 + C$$

Because $R(x) = xp(x)$, where $p(x)$ is the demand function, we must have $R(0) = 0$ so that

$$240(0) + 0.05(0)^2 + C = 0 \quad \text{or} \quad C = 0$$

Thus, $R(x) = 240x + 0.05x^2$. It follows that the demand function is

$$p(x) = \frac{R(x)}{x} = \frac{240x + 0.05x^2}{x} = 240 + 0.05x$$ ∎

AREA AS AN ANTIDERIVATIVE

In the next section, we will consider area as the limit of a sum, and we conclude this section by showing how area can be computed by antidifferentiation. The connection between area as a limit and area as an antiderivative is then made by a result called the fundamental theorem of calculus (see Section 5.4).

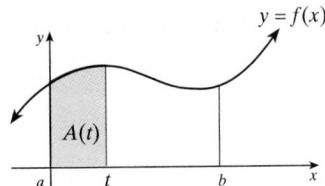

Figure 5.6 Area function $A(t)$

THEOREM 5.3   Area as an antiderivative

If f is a continuous function such that $f(x) \geq 0$ for all x on the closed interval $[a, b]$, then the area bounded by the curve $y = f(x)$, the x-axis, and the vertical lines $x = a$, $x = t$, viewed as a function of t, is an antiderivative of $f(t)$ on $[a, b]$.

Proof   Define an **area function**, $A(t)$, as the area of the region bounded by the curve $y = f(x)$, the x-axis, and the vertical lines $x = a$, $x = t$ for $a \leq t \leq b$, as shown in Figure 5.6. We need to show that $A(t)$ is an antiderivative of f on the interval $[a, b]$; that is, we need to show that $A'(t) = f(t)$.

Let $h > 0$ be small enough so that $t + h < b$ and consider the numerator of the difference quotient for $A(t)$, namely, the difference $A(t + h) - A(t)$. Geometrically this difference is the area under the curve $y = f(x)$ between $x = t$ and $x = t + h$, as shown in Figure 5.7a.

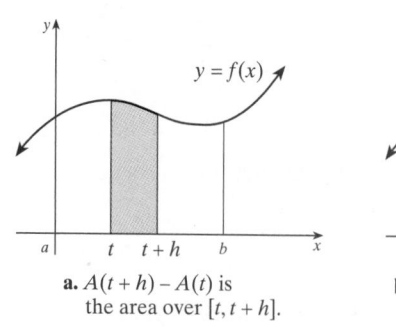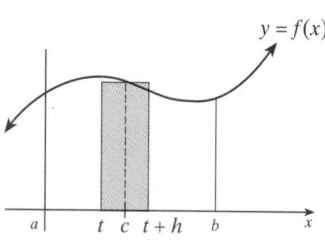

a. $A(t + h) - A(t)$ is the area over $[t, t + h]$.

b. $A(t + h) - A(t)$ is approximated by the area of a rectangle.

Figure 5.7   The area under the curve $y = f(x)$

If h is small enough, this area is approximately the same as the area of a rectangle with base h and height $f(c)$, where c is the midpoint of the interval $[t, t + h]$, as shown in Figure 5.7b. Thus, we have

$$\underbrace{A(t + h) - A(t)}_{\text{Area under the curve on } [t, t + h]} \approx \underbrace{hf(c)}_{\text{Area of rectangle}}$$

The difference quotient for $A(t)$ satisfies

$$\frac{A(t + h) - A(t)}{h} \approx f(c)$$

Finally, by taking the limit as $h \to 0^+$, we find the derivative of the area function $A(t)$ satisfies

$$\lim_{h \to 0^+} \frac{A(t + h) - A(t)}{h} = \lim_{h \to 0^+} f(c)$$

$$A'(t) = f(t)$$

The limit on the left is the definition of derivative, and on the right we see that since f is continuous and c is the midpoint of the interval $[t, t + h]$, c must approach t as $h \to 0^+$. A similar argument works as $h \to 0^-$. Thus, $A(t)$ is an antiderivative of $f(t)$. ❏

EXAMPLE 10   Area as an antiderivative

Find the area under the parabola $y = x^2$ over the interval $[0, 1]$. This area is shown in Figure 5.8.

Solution

Let $A(t)$ be the area function for this example—namely, the area under $y = x^2$ on $[0, t]$. Since f is continuous and $f(x) \geq 0$ on $[0, 1]$, Theorem 5.3 tells us that $A(t)$ is an antiderivative of $f(t) = t^2$ on $[0, 1]$. That is,

$$A(t) = \int t^2 \, dt = \tfrac{1}{3}t^3 + C$$

for all t in the interval $[0, 1]$. Clearly, $A(0) = 0$, so

$$A(0) = \tfrac{1}{3}(0)^3 + C \quad \text{or} \quad C = 0$$

and the area under the curve is

$$A(1) = \tfrac{1}{3}(1)^3 + 0 = \tfrac{1}{3}$$ ∎

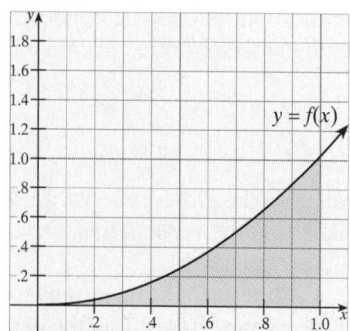

Figure 5.8 Area of $y = f(x)$ over $[0, 1]$

5.1 PROBLEM SET

A *Find the indefinite integral in Problems 1–30.*

1. $\int 2\,dx$

2. $\int -4\,dx$

3. $\int (2x + 3)\,dx$

4. $\int (4 - 5x)\,dx$

5. $\int (4t^3 + 3t^2)\,dt$

6. $\int (-8t^3 + 15t^5)\,dt$

7. $\int \dfrac{dx}{2x}$

8. $\int 14e^x\,dx$

9. $\int (6u^2 - 3\cos u)\,du$

10. $\int (5t^3 - \sqrt{t})\,dt$

11. $\int \sec^2 \theta\,d\theta$

12. $\int \sec \theta \tan \theta\,d\theta$

13. $\int 2 \sin \theta\,d\theta$

14. $\int \dfrac{\cos \theta}{3}\,d\theta$

15. $\int \dfrac{5}{\sqrt{1 - y^2}}\,dy$

16. $\int \dfrac{dx}{10(1 + x^2)}$

17. $\int (u^{3/2} - u^{1/2} + u^{-10})\,du$

18. $\int (x^3 - 3x + \sqrt[4]{x} - 5)\,dx$

19. $\int x(x + \sqrt{x})\,dx$

20. $\int y(y^2 - 3y)\,dy$

21. $\int \left(\dfrac{1}{t^2} - \dfrac{1}{t^3} + \dfrac{1}{t^4} \right) dt$

22. $\int \dfrac{1}{t} \left(\dfrac{2}{t^2} - \dfrac{3}{t^3} \right) dt$

23. $\int (2x^2 + 5)^2\,dx$

24. $\int (3 - 4x^3)^2\,dx$

25. $\int \left(\dfrac{x^2 + 3x - 1}{x^4} \right) dx$

26. $\int \dfrac{x^2 + \sqrt{x} + 1}{x^2}\,dx$

27. $\int \dfrac{x^2 + x - 2}{x^2}\,dx$

28. $\int \left(1 + \dfrac{1}{x} \right)\left(1 - \dfrac{4}{x^2} \right) dx$

29. $\int \dfrac{\sqrt{1 - x^2} - 1}{\sqrt{1 - x^2}}\,dx$

30. $\int \dfrac{x^2}{x^2 + 1}\,dx$

The slope $F'(x)$ at each point on a graph is given in Problems 31–38 along with one point (x_0, y_0) on the graph. Use this information to find F both graphically and analytically.

31. $F'(x) = x^2 + 3x$
with point $(0, 0)$

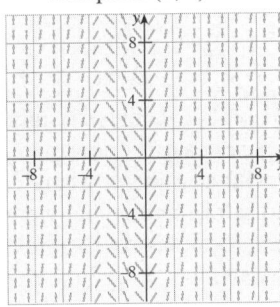

32. $F'(x) = (2x - 1)^2$
with point $(1, 3)$

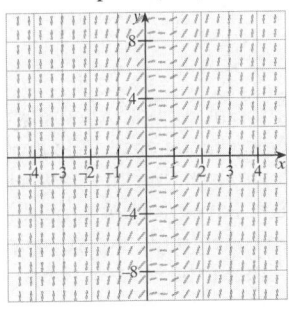

33. $F'(x) = (\sqrt{x} + 3)^2$
with point $(4, 36)$

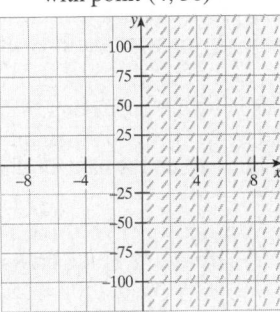

34. $F'(x) = 3 - 2 \sin x$
with point $(0, 0)$

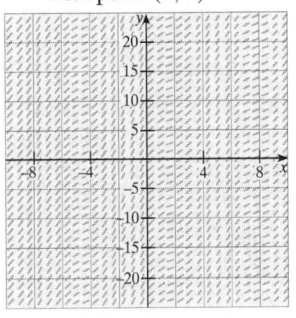

35. slope $\dfrac{x + 1}{x^2}$
with point $(1, -2)$

36. slope $\dfrac{2}{x\sqrt{x^2 - 1}}$
with point $(4, 1)$

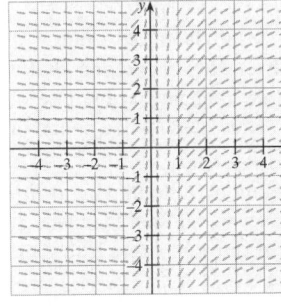

37. slope $x + e^x$
with point $(0, 2)$

38. slope $\dfrac{x^2 - 1}{x^2 + 1}$
with point $(0, 0)$

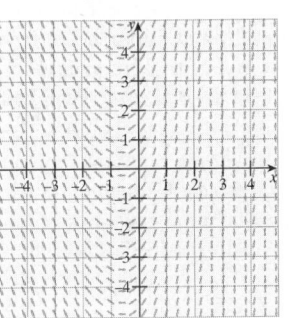

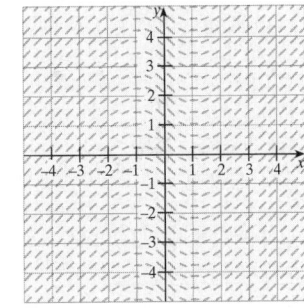

B **39. a.** If $F(x) = \int \left(\dfrac{1}{\sqrt{x}} - 4 \right) dx$, find F so that $F(1) = 0$.

b. Sketch the graphs of $y = F(x)$, $y = F(x) + 3$, and $y = F(x) - 1$.

c. Find a constant C_0 so that the largest value of $G(x) = F(x) + C_0$ is 0.

40. A ball is thrown directly upward from ground level with an initial velocity of 96 ft/s. Assuming that the ball's only acceleration is that due to gravity (that is, $a(t) = -32$ ft/s^2), determine the maximum height reached by the ball and the time it takes to return to ground level.

41. The marginal cost of a certain commodity is $C'(x) = 6x^2 - 2x + 5$, where x is the level of production. If it costs \$5 to produce 1 unit, what is the total cost of producing 5 units?

42. The marginal revenue of a certain commodity is $R'(x) = -3x^2 + 4x + 32$, where x is the level of production (in thousands). Assume $R(0) = 0$.

   a. Find the demand function $p(x)$.

   b. Find the level of production that results in maximum revenue. What is the market price per unit at this level of production?

43. It is estimated that t months from now, the population of a certain town will be changing at the rate of $4 + 5t^{2/3}$ people per month. If the current population is 10,000, what will the population be 8 months from now?

44. A particle travels along the x-axis in such a way that its acceleration at time t is $a(t) = \sqrt{t} + t^2$. If it starts at the origin with an initial velocity of 2 (that is, $s(0) = 0$ and $v(0) = 2$), determine its position and velocity when $t = 4$.

45. An automobile starts from rest (that is, $v(0) = 0$) and travels with constant acceleration $a(t) = k$ in such a way that 6 sec after it begins to move, it has traveled 360 ft from its starting point. What is k?

46. The price of bacon is currently $1.80/lb in Styxville. A consumer service has conducted a study predicting that t months from now, the price will be changing at the rate of $0.084 + 0.012\sqrt{t}$ cents per month. How much will a pound of bacon cost 4 months from now?

47. An airplane has a constant acceleration while moving down the runway from rest. What is the acceleration of the plane at liftoff if the plane requires 900 ft of runway before lifting off at 88 ft/s (60 mi/h)?

48. After its brakes are applied, a certain sports car decelerates at a constant rate of 28 ft/s². Compute the stopping distance if the car is going 60 mi/h (88 ft/s) when the brakes are applied.

49. The brakes of a certain automobile produce a constant deceleration of k ft/s². The car is traveling at 60 mi/h (88 ft/s) when the driver is forced to hit the brakes, and it comes to rest at a point 121 ft from the point where the brakes were applied. What is k?

50. Spy Problem   The Spy, having defused the bomb in Problem 23, Section 4.6, is driving the sports car in Problem 48 at a speed of 60 mi/h on Highway 1 in the remote republic of San Dimas. Suddenly he sees a camel in the road 199 ft in front of

the car. After a reaction time of 00.7 seconds, he steps on the brakes. Will he stop before hitting the camel?

51. A particle moves along the x-axis in such a way that at time $t > 0$, its velocity (in ft/s) is

$$v(t) = t^{-1} + t$$

How far does it move between times $t = 1$ and $t = e^2$?

52. A manufacturer estimates that the marginal cost in a certain production process is

$$C'(x) = 0.1e^x + 21\sqrt{x}$$

when x units are produced. If the cost of producing 1 unit is $100, what does it cost (to the nearest cent) to produce 4 units?

In Problems 53–58, find the area under the curve defined by the given equation, above the x-axis, and over the given interval.

53. $y = x^2$ over $[1, 4]$ **54.** $y = \sqrt{x}$ over $[1, 4]$

55. $y = e^x - x$ over $[0, 2]$ **56.** $y = \dfrac{x+1}{x}$ over $[1, 2]$

57. $y = \cos x$ over $\left[0, \frac{\pi}{2}\right]$ **58.** $y = (1 - x^2)^{-1/2}$ over $\left[0, \frac{1}{2}\right]$

59. Evaluate $\displaystyle\int \frac{dy}{2y\sqrt{y^2 - 1}}$ using the indicated methods.

   a. Use an inverse trigonometric differentiation rule.

   b. Use technology (TI-92, *Maple*, *Mathematica*, or *Derive*) to evaluate this integral.

   c. Reconcile your answers for parts **a** and **b**.

C 60. If a, b, and c are constants, use the linearity rule twice to show that

$$\int [af(x) + bg(x) + ch(x)]\,dx$$

$$= a\int f(x)\,dx + b\int g(x)\,dx + c\int h(x)\,dx$$

61. Use the area as an antiderivative theorem (Theorem 5.3) to find the area under the line $y = mx + b$ over the interval $[c, d]$, where $m > 0$ and $mc + b > 0$. Check your result by using geometry to find the area of a trapezoid.

5.2   Area as the Limit of a Sum

IN THIS SECTION   area as the limit of a sum, the general approximation scheme, summation notation, area using summation formulas

AREA AS THE LIMIT OF A SUM

Computing area has been a problem of both theoretical and practical interest since ancient times, but except for a few special cases, the problem is not easy. For example, you may know the formulas for computing the area of a rectangle, square, triangle, circle, and even a trapezoid. You have probably found the areas of regions that were more complicated but could be broken up into parts using these formulas. In Example 10 of the previous section we found the area between the parabola $y = x^2$ and the *x*-axis on the interval [0, 1] (see Figure 5.9a). We revisit this example to demonstrate a general procedure for computing area.

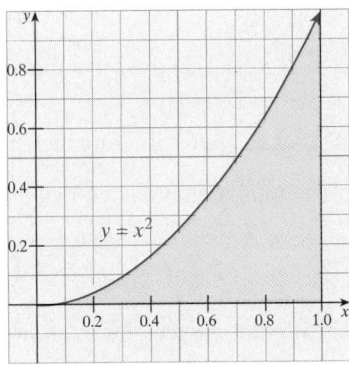

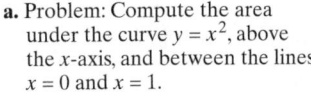

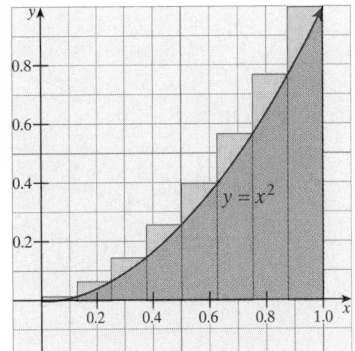

a. Problem: Compute the area under the curve $y = x^2$, above the *x*-axis, and between the lines $x = 0$ and $x = 1$.

b. The required area is approximately the same as the total area bounded by the shaded rectangles.

Figure 5.9 Example of the area problem

EXAMPLE 1 Estimating an area using rectangles and right endpoints

Estimate the area under the parabola $y = x^2$ on the interval [0, 1].

Solution

In the previous section we found this area using the area function. In this example, we will *estimate* the area by adding the areas of approximating rectangles constructed on subintervals of [0, 1], as shown in Figure 5.9b. To simplify computations, we will require all approximating rectangles to have the same width and will take the height of each rectangle to be the *y*-coordinate of the parabola above the *right endpoint* of the subinterval on which it is based.[*]

For the first estimate, we divide the interval [0, 1] into 5 subintervals, as shown in Figure 5.10a. Because the approximating rectangles all have the same width, the right endpoints are $x_1 = 0.2$, $x_2 = 0.4$, $x_3 = 0.6$, $x_4 = 0.8$, and $x_5 = 1$. This subdivision is called a *partition* of the interval. The width of each subdivision is denoted by Δx and is found by dividing the length of the interval by the number of subintervals:

$$\Delta x = \frac{1 - 0}{5} = \frac{1}{5} = 0.2$$

Let S_n be the total area of n rectangles. For the case where $n = 5$,

$$
\begin{aligned}
S_5 &= f(x_1)\Delta x + f(x_2)\Delta x + f(x_3)\Delta x + f(x_4)\Delta x + f(x_5)\Delta x \\
&= [f(x_1) + f(x_2) + f(x_3) + f(x_4) + f(x_5)]\Delta x \\
&= [f(0.2) + f(0.4) + f(0.6) + f(0.8) + f(1)](0.2) \\
&= [0.2^2 + 0.4^2 + 0.6^2 + 0.8^2 + 1^2](0.2) \\
&= 0.44
\end{aligned}
$$

■

Even though $S_5 = 0.44$ serves as a reasonable approximation of the area, we see from Figure 5.10b that this approximation seems too large. Let us rework Example

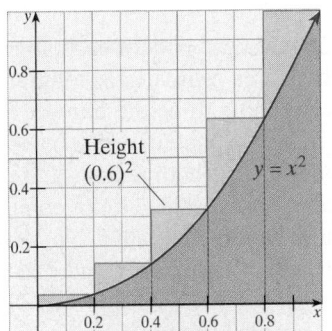

a. Partition into 5 subdivisions

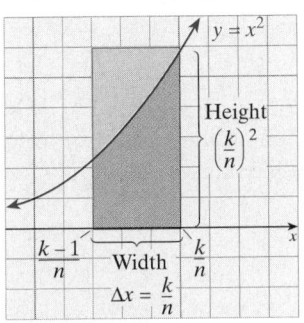

b. Detail showing one rectangle

Figure 5.10 Partitioning of Figure 5.8a into 5 subdivisions

---

[*]Actually, there is nothing special about right endpoints, and we could just as easily have used any other point in the base subinterval—say, the left endpoint or the midpoint.

1 using a general scheme rather than a specified number of rectangles. Partition the interval $[0, 1]$ into n equal parts, each with width

$$\Delta x = \frac{1 - 0}{n} = \frac{1}{n}$$

For $k = 1, 2, 3, \ldots, n$, the kth subinterval is $\left[\dfrac{k-1}{n}, \dfrac{k}{n}\right]$, and on this subinterval we then construct an approximating rectangle with width $\Delta x = \dfrac{1}{n}$ and height $\left(\dfrac{k}{n}\right)^2$, since $y = x^2$. The total area bounded by all n rectangles is

$$S_n = \left[\left(\frac{1}{n}\right)^2 + \left(\frac{2}{n}\right)^2 + \cdots + \left(\frac{n}{n}\right)^2\right]\left(\frac{1}{n}\right)$$

Consider different choices for n, as shown in Figure 5.11.

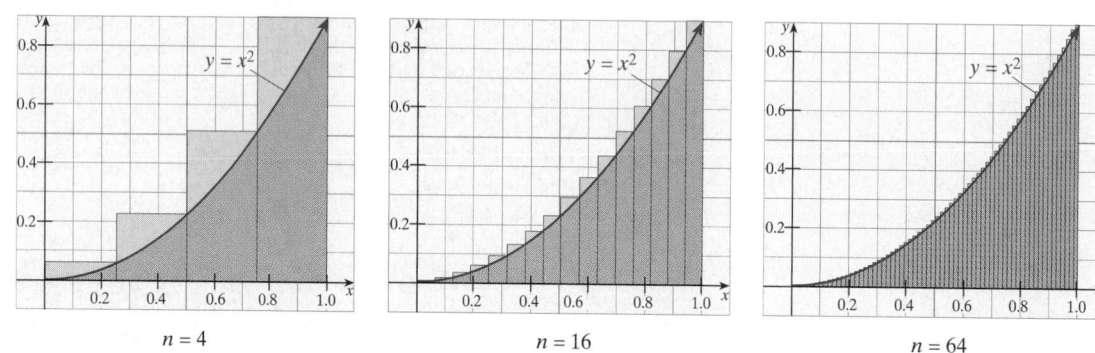

$$n = 4 \qquad n = 16 \qquad n = 64$$

Figure 5.11 The area estimate is improved by taking more rectangles.

n	S_n	
5	0.440	(Example 1 result)
4	0.469	(Figure 5.11a result)
16	0.365	(Figure 5.11b result)
64	0.341	(Figure 5.11c result)
100	0.338	
1,000	0.334	
5,000	0.333	

If we increase the number of subdivisions n, the width $\Delta x = \frac{1}{n}$ of each approximating rectangle will decrease, and we would expect the area estimates S_n to improve. Thus, it is reasonable to *define* the area A under the parabola to be the *limit* of S_n as $\Delta x \to 0$ or, equivalently, as $n \to +\infty$. We can attempt to predict its value by seeing what happens to the sum as n grows large without bound. It is both tedious and difficult to evaluate such sums by hand, but fortunately we can use a calculator or computer to obtain some (rounded) values for S_n, as shown in the following table. Notice that for $n = 5$, the value 0.44 corresponds to the calculation in Example 1 and that as n increases, S_n appears to approach $1/3$.

Figure 5.12 displays some computer-generated drawings showing the area under the curve $y = x^2$ on $[1, 5]$ as approximated by rectangles using left endpoints (as contrasted with right endpoints in Example 1). The sums in these outputs are called *Riemann sums*, which we will discuss in the next section.

THE GENERAL APPROXIMATION SCHEME

We now compute the area under any curve $y = f(x)$ on an interval $[a, b]$, where f is a nonnegative continuous function. We first partition the interval $[a, b]$ into n equal subintervals, each of width

$$\Delta x = \frac{b - a}{n}$$

For $k = 1, 2, 3, \ldots, n$ the kth subinterval is $[a + (k - 1)\Delta x, a + k\Delta x]$, and the kth approximating rectangle is constructed with width Δx and height $f(a + k\Delta x)$ equal to the height of the curve $y = f(x)$ above the right endpoint of the subinterval. Adding the areas of these n rectangles, we obtain

$$S_n = \overbrace{f(a + \Delta x)\Delta x}^{\text{Area of first rectangle}} + \overbrace{f(a + 2\Delta x)\Delta x}^{\text{Area of second rectangle}} + \cdots + \overbrace{f(a + n\Delta x)\Delta x}^{\text{Area of } n\text{th rectangle}}$$

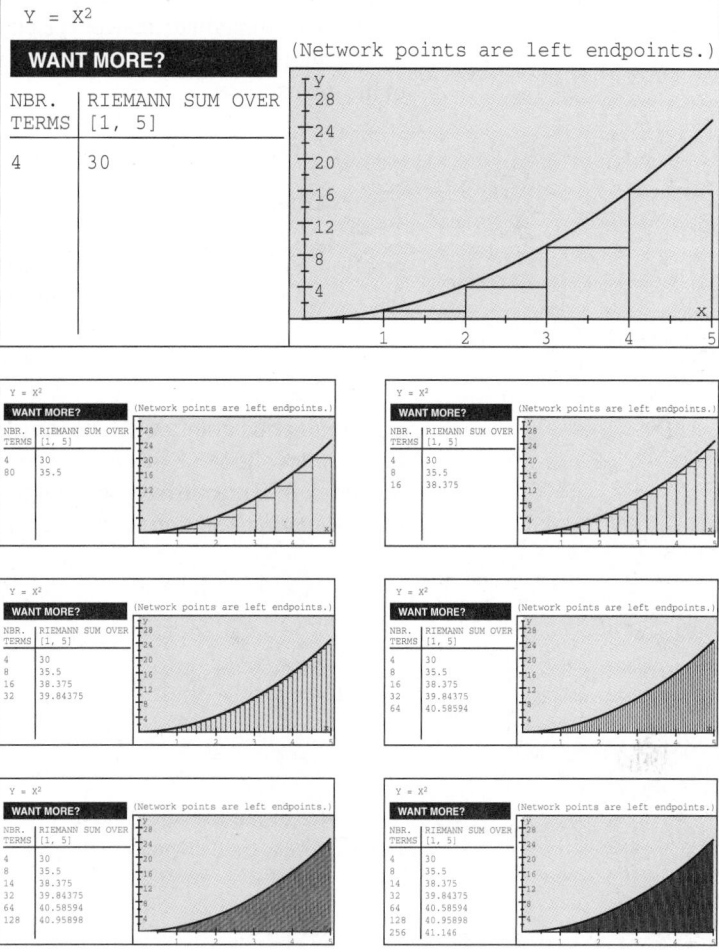

Figure 5.12 Sample of finding successive rectangular approximations

as an estimate of the area under the curve. In advanced calculus, it is shown that the continuity of f guarantees the existence of $\lim\limits_{\Delta x \to 0} S_n$, and we use this limit to define the required area, as shown in the following box.

Area as the Limit of a Sum

Suppose f is continuous and $f(x) \geq 0$ throughout the interval $[a, b]$. Then the **area** of the region under the curve $y = f(x)$ over this interval is

$$A = \lim_{\Delta x \to 0} [f(a + \Delta x) + f(a + 2\Delta x) + \cdots + f(a + n\Delta x)]\Delta x$$

where $\Delta x = \dfrac{b - a}{n}$.

The definition of area as a limit of a sum is consistent with the area concept introduced in plane geometry, and with the area function defined in Section 5.1. For example, it would not be difficult to use this formula to show that a rectangle has area $A = \ell w$ or that a triangle has area $A = \frac{1}{2}bh$. You will also note that we maintained everyday usage in saying that the *formula* for the area of a rectangle is $A = \ell w$ or the *area* of the region under the curve $y = f(x)$ is a limit, but what we are really doing is *defining* area as a limit.

The problem we now face is how to implement this definition of area as the limit of a sum. The immediate answer (discussed in this section) is to use summation formulas and technology. The long-range goal is to develop integral calculus, which is discussed in the next section.

SUMMATION NOTATION

The expanded form of the sum for the definition of area makes it awkward to use. Therefore, we will digress to introduce a more compact notation for sums, and that notation will motivate integral notation. Using this **summation notation**, we express the sum $a_1 + a_2 + \cdots + a_n$ as follows:

$$a_1 + a_2 + \cdots + a_n = \sum_{k=1}^{n} a_k$$

The summation notation is sometimes called the **sigma notation** because the uppercase Greek letter sigma (Σ) is used to denote the summation process. The **index** k is called the **index of summation** (or *running index*). The terminology used in connection with the summation notation is shown:

Upper limit of summation

General term

$$\sum_{k=1}^{n} \overbrace{a_k}^{}$$

Index of summation

Lower limit of summation

Note that in the summation process, the choice of summation index is immaterial. For example, the following sums are all exactly the same:

$$\sum_{k=3}^{7} k^2 = \sum_{j=3}^{7} j^2 = \sum_{i=3}^{7} i^2 = \sum_{\lambda=3}^{7} \lambda^2$$

In general, an index (k, j, i, or λ) that represents a process in which it has no direct effect on the result is called a **dummy variable**.

Several useful properties of sums and sum formulas are listed in Theorem 5.4. We will use the summation notation throughout the rest of this text, especially in this chapter, Chapter 6, and Chapter 8.

THEOREM 5.4   Basic rules for sums

For any numbers c and d and positive integers m and n,

1. **Constant term rule** $\displaystyle\sum_{k=1}^{n} c = \underbrace{c + c + \cdots + c}_{n \text{ terms}} = nc$

2. **Sum rule** $\displaystyle\sum_{k=1}^{n} (a_k + b_k) = \sum_{k=1}^{n} a_k + \sum_{k=1}^{n} b_k$

3. **Scalar multiple rule** $\displaystyle\sum_{k=1}^{n} ca_k = c \sum_{k=1}^{n} a_k = \left(\sum_{k=1}^{n} a_k \right) c$

4. **Linearity rule** $\displaystyle\sum_{k=1}^{n} (ca_k + db_k) = c \sum_{k=1}^{n} a_k + d \sum_{k=1}^{n} b_k$

5. **Subtotal rule**   If $1 < m < n$, then $\displaystyle\sum_{k=1}^{n} a_k = \sum_{k=1}^{m} a_k + \sum_{k=m+1}^{n} a_k$

6. **Dominance rule**   If $a_k \le b_k$ for $k = 1, 2, \ldots, n$, then $\displaystyle\sum_{k=1}^{n} a_k \le \sum_{k=1}^{n} b_k$

Proof   These properties can all be established by applying well-known algebraic rules (see Problem 50). ❑

AREA USING SUMMATION FORMULAS

Using summation notation, we can streamline the symbolism in the formula for the area under the curve $y = f(x)$, $f(x) \geq 0$ on the interval $[a, b]$. In particular, note that the approximating sum S_n is

$$S_n = [f(a + \Delta x) + f(a + 2\Delta x) + \cdots + f(a + n\Delta x)]\Delta x$$

$$= \sum_{k=1}^{n} f(a + k\Delta x)\Delta x$$

where $\Delta x = \dfrac{b - a}{n}$. Thus, the formula for the definition of area is shown:

Area under $y = f(x)$ above the x-axis between $x = a$ and $x = b$

n is the number of approximating rectangles

Width of each rectangle

$$A = \lim_{n \to +\infty} S_n = \lim_{\Delta x \to 0} \sum_{k=1}^{n} f(a + k\Delta x) \; \Delta x$$

Height of the kth rectangle

From algebra we recall certain summation formulas (which can be proved using mathematical induction) that we will need in order to find areas using the limit definition.

Summation Formulas

$$\sum_{k=1}^{n} 1 = n$$

$$\sum_{k=1}^{n} k = 1 + 2 + 3 + \cdots + n = \frac{n(n + 1)}{2}$$

$$\sum_{k=1}^{n} k^2 = 1^2 + 2^2 + 3^2 + \cdots + n^2 = \frac{n(n + 1)(2n + 1)}{6}$$

$$\sum_{k=1}^{n} k^3 = 1^3 + 2^3 + 3^3 + \cdots + n^3 = \frac{n^2(n + 1)^2}{4}$$

EXAMPLE 2   Area using the definition and summation formulas

Use the summation definition of area to find the area under the parabola $y = x^2$ on the interval $[0, 1]$. You estimated this area in Example 1.

Solution

Partition the interval $[0, 1]$ into n subintervals with width $\Delta x = \dfrac{1 - 0}{n}$. The right endpoint of the kth subinterval is $a + k\Delta x = \dfrac{k}{n}$ and $f\left(\dfrac{k}{n}\right) = \dfrac{k^2}{n^2}$. Thus, from the definition of area we have

$$A = \lim_{\Delta x \to 0} \sum_{k=1}^{n} f(a + k\Delta x)\Delta x$$

$$= \lim_{n \to +\infty} \sum_{k=1}^{n} \left(\frac{k^2}{n^2}\right)\left(\frac{1}{n}\right)$$

$$= \lim_{n \to +\infty} \sum_{k=1}^{n} \frac{k^2}{n^3} \qquad \text{Note that } 1/n^3 \text{ is independent of the index of summation, } k.$$

$$= \lim_{n \to +\infty} \frac{1}{n^3} \sum_{k=1}^{n} k^2 \qquad \text{Scalar multiple rule}$$

$$= \lim_{n \to +\infty} \frac{1}{n^3} \left[\frac{n(n+1)(2n+1)}{6}\right] \qquad \text{Summation formula for squares}$$

$$= \lim_{n \to +\infty} \frac{1}{6} \left[2 + \frac{3}{n} + \frac{1}{n^2}\right] = \frac{1}{3}$$

This is the same as the answer found by antidifferentiation in Example 10 of Section 5.1 and is consistent with the table on page 284. ■

EXAMPLE 3 Tabular approach for finding area

Use a computer to estimate the area under the curve $y = \sin x$ on the interval $\left[0, \frac{\pi}{2}\right]$.

Solution

We see $a = 0$ and $b = \frac{\pi}{2}$, so $\Delta x = \frac{\frac{\pi}{2} - 0}{n} = \frac{\pi}{2n}$. The right endpoints are

$$a + \Delta x = 0 + \left(\frac{\pi}{2n}\right) = \frac{\pi}{2n}; a + 2\Delta x = \frac{2\pi}{2n} = \frac{\pi}{n}; a + 3\Delta x = \frac{3\pi}{2n}; \dots$$

$$a + n\Delta x = \frac{n\pi}{2n} = \frac{\pi}{2} = b$$

Thus, $S_n = \sum_{k=1}^{n} f\left(0 + \frac{k\pi}{2n}\right)\left(\frac{\pi}{2n}\right) = \sum_{k=1}^{n} \left[\sin\left(\frac{k\pi}{2n}\right)\right]\left(\frac{\pi}{2n}\right)$. Now we know from the definition that the actual area is

$$S = \lim_{n \to +\infty} \sum_{k=1}^{n} \left[\sin\left(\frac{k\pi}{2n}\right)\right]\left(\frac{\pi}{2n}\right) = \frac{\pi}{2} \lim_{n \to +\infty} \sum_{k=1}^{n} \frac{1}{n} \sin\left(\frac{k\pi}{2n}\right)$$

n	S_n
10	1.07648
20	1.03876
50	1.01563
100	1.00783
500	1.00157

which we can estimate by computing S_n for successively large values of n, as summarized in the table in this margin. Note that the table suggests that

$$\lim_{\Delta x \to 0} S_n = \lim_{n \to +\infty} S_n = 1$$

Thus, we expect the actual area under the curve to be 1 square unit. ■

5.2 PROBLEM SET

Ⓐ *Evaluate the sums in Problems 1–8 by using the summation formulas.*

1. $\sum_{k=1}^{6} 1$

2. $\sum_{k=1}^{250} 2$

3. $\sum_{k=1}^{15} k$

4. $\sum_{k=1}^{10} (k+1)$

5. $\sum_{k=1}^{5} k^3$

6. $\sum_{k=1}^{7} k^2$

7. $\sum_{k=1}^{100} (2k-3)$

8. $\sum_{k=1}^{100} (k-1)^2$

Use the properties of summation notation in Problems 9–12 to evaluate the given limits.

9. $\displaystyle\lim_{n\to+\infty}\sum_{k=1}^{n}\frac{k}{n^2}$

10. $\displaystyle\lim_{n\to+\infty}\sum_{k=1}^{n}\frac{k^3}{n^4}$

11. $\displaystyle\lim_{n\to+\infty}\sum_{k=1}^{n}\left(1+\frac{k}{n}\right)\left(\frac{2}{n}\right)$

12. $\displaystyle\lim_{n\to+\infty}\sum_{k=1}^{n}\left(1+\frac{2k}{n}\right)^2\left(\frac{2}{n}\right)$

First sketch the region under the graph of $y = f(x)$ on the interval $[a, b]$ in Problems 13–21. Then approximate the area of each region by using right endpoints and the formula

$$S_n = \sum_{k=1}^{n} f(a + k\Delta x)\Delta x$$

for $\Delta x = \dfrac{b-a}{n}$ and the indicated values of n.

13. $f(x) = 4x + 1$ on $[0, 1]$ for

    a. $n = 4$ **b.** $n = 8$

14. $f(x) = 3 - 2x$ on $[0, 1]$ for

    a. $n = 3$ **b.** $n = 6$

15. $f(x) = x^2$ on $[1, 2]$ for

    a. $n = 4$ **b.** $n = 6$

16. $f(x) = \cos x$ on $\left[-\frac{\pi}{2}, 0\right]$ for $n = 4$

17. $f(x) = x + \sin x$ on $\left[0, \frac{\pi}{4}\right]$ for $n = 3$

18. $f(x) = \dfrac{1}{x^2}$ on $[1, 2]$ for $n = 4$

19. $f(x) = \dfrac{2}{x}$ on $[1, 2]$ for $n = 4$

20. $f(x) = \sqrt{x}$ on $[1, 4]$ for $n = 4$

21. $f(x) = \sqrt{1 + x^2}$ on $[0, 1]$ for $n = 4$

B *Find the exact area under the given curve on the interval prescribed in Problems 22–27 by using area as the limit of a sum and the summation formulas.*

22. $y = 4x^3 + 2x$ on $[0, 2]$

23. $y = 4x^3 + 2x$ on $[1, 2]$

24. $y = 6x^2 + 2x + 4$ on $[0, 3]$

25. $y = 6x^2 + 2x + 4$ on $[1, 3]$

26. $y = 3x^2 + 2x + 1$ on $[0, 1]$

27. $y = 4x^3 + 3x^2$ on $[0, 1]$

Counterexample Problems *Show that each statement about area in Problems 28–33 is generally true or provide a counterexample. It will probably help to sketch the indicated region for each problem.*

28. If $C > 0$ is a constant, the region under the line $y = C$ on the interval $[a, b]$ has area $A = C(b - a)$.

29. If $C > 0$ is a constant and $b > a \geq 0$, the region under the line $y = Cx$ on the interval $[a, b]$ has area $A = \frac{1}{2}C(b - a)$.

30. The region under the parabola $y = x^2$ on the interval $[a, b]$ has area less than $\frac{1}{2}(b^2 + a^2)(b - a)$.

31. The region under the curve $y = \sqrt{1 - x^2}$ on the interval $[-1, 1]$ has area $A = \frac{\pi}{2}$.

32. Let f be a function that satisfies $f(x) \geq 0$ for x in the interval $[a, b]$. Then the area under the curve $y = f^2(x)$ on the interval $[a, b]$ must always be greater than the area under $y = f(x)$ on the same interval.

33. Recall that a function f is said to be **even** if $f(-x) = f(x)$ for all x. If f is even and $f(x) \geq 0$ throughout the interval $[-a, a]$, then the area under the curve $y = f(x)$ on this interval is *twice* the area under $y = f(x)$ on $[0, a]$.

34. Show that the region under the curve $y = x^3$ on the interval $[0, 1]$ has area $\frac{1}{4}$ square units.

35. Use the definition of area to show that the area of a rectangle equals the product of its length ℓ and its width w.

36. Show that the triangle with vertices $(0, 0)$, $(0, h)$, and $(b, 0)$ has area $A = \frac{1}{2}bh$ using the area as the limit of a sum.

37. a. Compute the area under the parabola $y = 2x^2$ on the interval $[1, 2]$ as the limit of a sum.

    b. Let $f(x) = 2x^2$ and note that $g(x) = \frac{2}{3}x^3$ defines a function that satisfies $g'(x) = f(x)$ on the interval $[1, 2]$. Verify that the area computed in part **a** satisfies $A = g(2) - g(1)$.

    c. The function defined by

$$h(x) = \tfrac{2}{3}x^3 + C$$

    for any constant C also satisfies $h'(x) = f(x)$. Is it true that the area in part **a** satisfies $A = h(2) - h(1)$?

Use a tabular approach to compute the area under the curve $y = f(x)$ on each interval given in Problems 38–44 as the limit of a sum of terms.

38. $f(x) = 4x$ on $[0, 1]$

39. $f(x) = x^2$ on $[0, 4]$

40. $f(x) = \cos x$ on $\left[-\frac{\pi}{2}, 0\right]$ (Compare with Problem 16.)

41. $f(x) = x + \sin x$ on $\left[0, \frac{\pi}{4}\right]$ (Compare with Problem 17.)

42. $f(x) = \ln(x^2 + 1)$ on $[0, 3]$

43. $f(x) = e^{-3x^2}$ on $[0, 1]$

44. $f(x) = \cos^{-1}(x + 1)$ on $[-1, 0]$

45. a. Use the tabular approach to compute the area under the curve $y = \sin x + \cos x$ on the interval $[0, \frac{\pi}{2}]$ as the limit of a sum.

    b. Let $f(x) = \sin x + \cos x$ and note that $g(x) = -\cos x + \sin x$ satisfies $g'(x) = f(x)$ on the interval $[0, \frac{\pi}{2}]$. Verify that the area computed in part **a** satisfies $A = g(\frac{\pi}{2}) - g(0)$.

    c. The function $h(x) = -\cos x + \sin x + C$ for constant C also satisfies $h'(x) = f(x)$. Is it true that the area in part **a** satisfies $A = h(\frac{\pi}{2}) - h(0)$?

C 46. Derive the formula

$$\sum_{k=1}^{n} k = 1 + 2 + 3 + \cdots + n = \frac{n(n+1)}{2}$$

by completing these steps:

    a. Use the basic rules for sums to show that

$$\sum_{k=1}^{n} k = \frac{1}{2}\sum_{k=1}^{n}[k^2 - (k-1)^2] + \frac{1}{2}\sum_{k=1}^{n} 1$$

$$= \frac{1}{2}\sum_{k=1}^{n}[k^2 - (k-1)^2] + \frac{1}{2}n$$

    b. Show that

$$\sum_{k=1}^{n}[k^2 - (k-1)^2] = n^2$$

    Hint: Expand the sum by writing out a few terms. Note the internal cancellation.

c. Combine parts **a** and **b** to show that

$$\sum_{k=1}^{n} k = \frac{n(n+1)}{2}$$

47. a. First find constants a, b, c, and d such that

$$k^3 = a[k^4 - (k-1)^4] + bk^2 + ck + d$$

b. Modify the approach outlined in Problem 46 to establish the formula

$$\sum_{k=1}^{n} k^2 = \frac{n(n+1)(2n+1)}{6}$$

48. The purpose of this problem is to verify the results shown in Figure 5.11. Specifically, we will find the area A under the parabola $y = x^2$ on the interval $[0, 1]$ using approximating rectangles with heights taken at the *left* endpoints.

Verify that

$$\lim_{n \to +\infty} \sum_{k=1}^{n} \left(\frac{k-1}{n} \right)^2 \left(\frac{1}{n} \right) = \frac{1}{3}$$

Compare this with the procedure outlined in Example 1. Note that when the interval $[0, 1]$ is subdivided into n equal parts, the kth subinterval is

$$\left[\frac{k-1}{n}, \frac{k}{n} \right]$$

49. Develop a formula for area based on approximating rectangles with heights taken at the *midpoints* of subintervals.

50. Use the properties of real numbers to establish the summation formulas in Theorem 5.4. For example, to prove the linearity rule, use the associative, commutative, and distributive properties of real numbers to note that

$$\sum_{k=1}^{n} (ca_k + db_k)$$
$$= (ca_1 + db_1) + (ca_2 + db_2) + \cdots + (ca_n + db_n)$$
$$= (ca_1 + ca_2 + \cdots + ca_n) + (db_1 + db_2 + \cdots + db_n)$$
$$= c(a_1 + a_2 + \cdots + a_n) + d(b_1 + b_2 + \cdots + b_n)$$
$$= c \sum_{k=1}^{n} a_k + d \sum_{k=1}^{n} b_k$$

5.3   Riemann Sums and the Definite Integral

IN THIS SECTION   Riemann sums, the definite integral, area as an integral, properties of the definite integral, distance as an integral

We will soon discover that not just area, but other useful quantities such as distance, volume, mass, and work, can be first approximated by sums and then obtained exactly by taking a limit involving the approximating sums. The special kind of limit of a sum that appears in this context is called the *definite integral*, and the process of finding integrals is called *definite integration* or *Riemann integration* in honor of the German mathematician Georg Bernhard Riemann (1826–1866), who pioneered the modern approach to integration theory. We begin by introducing some special notation and terminology.

RIEMANN SUMS

Recall from Section 5.2 that to find the area under the graph of the function $y = f(x)$ on the closed interval $[a, b]$ using sums where f is continuous and $f(x) \geq 0$, we proceed as follows:

1. Partition the interval into n subintervals of equal width $\Delta x = \dfrac{b-a}{n}$.

2. Evaluate f at the right endpoint $a + k\Delta x$ of the kth subinterval for $k = 1, 2, \ldots, n$.

3. Form the approximating sum of the areas of the n rectangles, which we denote by

$$S_n = \sum_{k=1}^{n} f(a + k\Delta x)\Delta x.$$

4. Because we expect the estimates S_n to improve as Δx decreases, we *define* the area A under the curve, above the x-axis, and bounded by the lines $x = a$ and $x = b$, to be the limit of S_n as $\Delta x \to 0$. Thus, we write

$$A = \lim_{n \to +\infty} \sum_{k=1}^{n} f(a + k\Delta x)\Delta x$$

if this limit exists. This means that A can be estimated to any desired degree of accuracy by approximating the sum S_n with Δx sufficiently small (or, equivalently, n sufficiently large).

This approach to the area problem contains the essentials of integration, but there is no compelling reason for the partition points to be evenly spaced or to insist on evaluating f at right endpoints. These conventions are for convenience of computation, but to accommodate easily as many applications as possible, it is useful to consider a more general type of approximating sum and to specify what is meant by the limit of such sums. The approximating sums that occur in integration problems are called **Riemann sums**, and the following definition contains a step-by-step description of how such sums are formed.

Riemann Sum

Suppose a bounded function f is given along with a closed interval $[a, b]$ on which f is defined. Then

Step 1.   Partition the interval $[a, b]$ into n subintervals by choosing points $\{x_0, x_1, \ldots, x_n\}$ arranged in such a way that

$$a = x_0 < x_1 < x_2 < \cdots < x_{n-1} < x_n = b$$

Call this partition P. For $k = 1, 2, \ldots, n$, the kth subinterval width is $\Delta x_k = x_k - x_{k-1}$. The largest of these widths is called the **norm** of the partition P and is denoted by $\|P\|$; that is,

$$\|P\| = \max_{k=1,2,\ldots,n} \{\Delta x_k\}$$

Step 2.   Choose a number arbitrarily from each subinterval. For $k = 1, 2, \ldots, n$, the number x_k^* chosen from the kth subinterval $[x_{k-1}, x_k]$ is called the *kth subinterval representative* of the partition P.

Step 3.   Form the sum

$$R_n = f(x_1^*)\Delta x_1 + f(x_2^*)\Delta x_2 + \cdots + f(x_n^*)\Delta x_n = \sum_{k=1}^{n} f(x_k^*)\Delta x_k$$

This is the **Riemann sum** associated with f, the given partition P, and the chosen subinterval representatives $x_1^*, x_2^*, \ldots, x_n^*$.

➡ **What This Says**   We will express quantities from geometry, physics, economics, and other applications in terms of a Riemann sum

$$\sum_{k=1}^{n} f(x_k^*)\Delta x_k$$

Riemann sums are generally used to model a quantity for a particular application. Note that the Riemann sum *does not* require that the function f be nonnegative, nor does it require that all the intervals must be the same length. In addition, x_k^* is *any* point in the kth subinterval and does not need to be something "nice" like the left or right endpoint, or the midpoint.

EXAMPLE 1   Formation of the Riemann sum for a given function

Suppose the interval $[-2, 1]$ is partitioned into 6 subintervals with subdivision points $a = x_0 = -2$, $x_1 = -1.6$, $x_2 = -0.93$, $x_3 = -0.21$, $x_4 = 0.35$, $x_5 = 0.82$, and

$x_6 = 1 = b$. Find the norm of this partition P and the Riemann sum associated with the function $f(x) = 2x$, the given partition, and the subinterval representatives $x_1^* = -1.81$, $x_2^* = -1.12$, $x_3^* = -0.55$, $x_4^* = -0.17$, $x_5^* = 0.43$, and $x_6^* = 0.94$.

Solution

Before we can find the norm of the partition or the required Riemann sum, we must compute the subinterval width Δx_k and evaluate f at each subinterval representative x_k^*. These values and computations are shown in Figure 5.13.

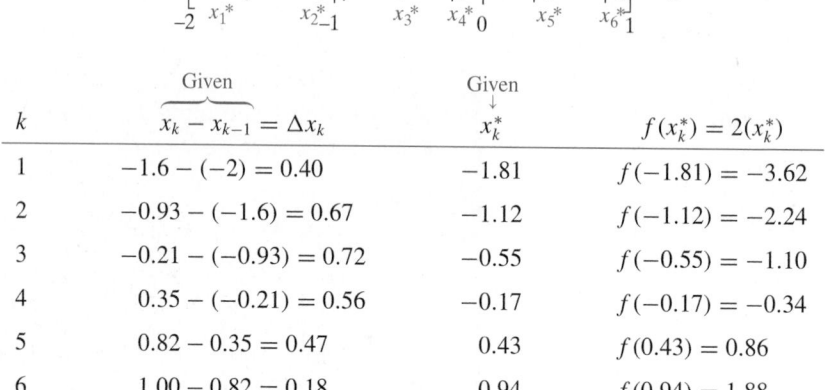

k	$x_k - x_{k-1} = \Delta x_k$ (Given)	x_k^* (Given)	$f(x_k^*) = 2(x_k^*)$
1	$-1.6 - (-2) = 0.40$	-1.81	$f(-1.81) = -3.62$
2	$-0.93 - (-1.6) = 0.67$	-1.12	$f(-1.12) = -2.24$
3	$-0.21 - (-0.93) = 0.72$	-0.55	$f(-0.55) = -1.10$
4	$0.35 - (-0.21) = 0.56$	-0.17	$f(-0.17) = -0.34$
5	$0.82 - 0.35 = 0.47$	0.43	$f(0.43) = 0.86$
6	$1.00 - 0.82 = 0.18$	0.94	$f(0.94) = 1.88$

Figure 5.13 Riemann sum

WARNING   Notice from Example 1 that the Riemann sum does not necessarily represent an area. The sum found is negative (and area must be nonnegative).

From the table, we see that the largest subinterval width is $\Delta x_3 = 0.72$, so the partition has norm $\|P\| = 0.72$. Finally, by using the definition, we compute the Riemann sum:

$$R_6 = (-3.62)(0.40) + (-2.24)(0.67) + (-1.10)(0.72) + (-0.34)(0.56)$$
$$+ (0.86)(0.47) + (1.88)(0.18)$$
$$\approx -3.1886 \approx -3.19$$

$\blacksquare$

THE DEFINITE INTEGRAL

By comparing the formula for the Riemann sum with that of area in the previous section, we recognize that the sum S_n used to approximate area is actually a special kind of Riemann sum that has

$$\Delta x_k = \Delta x = \frac{b-a}{n} \quad \text{and} \quad x_k^* = a + k\Delta x$$

for $k = 1, 2, \ldots, n$. Because the subintervals in the partition P associated with S_n are equally spaced, it is called a **regular partition**. When we express the area under the curve $y = f(x)$ as $A = \lim_{\Delta x \to 0} S_n$, we are actually saying that A can be estimated to any desired accuracy by finding a Riemann sum of the form S_n with norm

$$\|P\| = \frac{b-a}{n}$$

sufficiently small. We use this interpretation as a model for the following definition.

Definite Integral

If f is defined on the closed interval $[a, b]$, we say f is **integrable on $[a, b]$** if

$$I = \lim_{\|P\| \to 0} \sum_{k=1}^{n} f(x_k^*) \Delta x_k$$

exists. This limit is called the **definite integral** of f from a to b. The definite integral is denoted by

$$I = \int_a^b f(x)\, dx$$

→ **What This Says**   To say that f is *integrable* with definite integral I means the number I can be approximated to any prescribed degree of accuracy by *any* Riemann sum of f with norm sufficiently small. As long as the conditions of this definition are satisfied (that is, f is defined on $[a, b]$ and the Riemann sum exists), we can write

$$\int_a^b f(x)\, dx = \lim_{\|P\| \to 0} \sum_{k=1}^{n} f(x_k^*) \Delta x_k$$

Formally, I is the definite integral of f on $[a, b]$ if for each number $\epsilon > 0$, there exists a number $\delta > 0$ such that if

$$\sum_{k=1}^{n} f(x_k^*) \Delta x_k$$

is any Riemann sum of f whose norm satisfies $\|P\| < \delta$, then

$$\left| I - \sum_{k=1}^{n} f(x_k^*) \Delta x_k \right| < \epsilon$$

In advanced calculus, it is shown that when this limit exists, it is unique. Moreover, its value is independent of the particular way in which the partitions of $[a, b]$ and the subinterval representatives x_k^* are chosen.

WARNING   Take a few minutes to make sure you understand the integral notation and terminology.

$$\int_a^b \overbrace{f(x)}^{\text{integrand}} dx$$
↓ upper limit of integration
↑ lower limit of integration

The "dx" indicates the variable of integration.

The function f that is being integrated is called the **integrand**; the interval $[a, b]$ is the **interval of integration**; and the endpoints a and b are called, respectively, the **lower and upper limits of integration**.

In the special case where $a = b$, the interval of integration $[a, b]$ is really just a point, and the integral of any function on this "interval" is defined to be 0; that is,

$$\int_a^a f(x)\, dx = 0 \qquad \text{Why does this makes sense?}$$

Also, at times, we will consider integrals in which the lower limit of integration is a larger number than the upper limit. To handle this case, we specify that the integral from b to a is the negative of the integral from a to b:

$$\int_b^a f(x)\, dx = -\int_a^b f(x)\, dx$$

To summarize,

Definite Integral at a Point

$$\int_a^a f(x)\, dx = 0$$

Interchanging the Limits of a Definite Integral

$$\int_b^a f(x)\, dx = -\int_a^b f(x)\, dx$$

At first, the definition of the definite integral may seem rather imposing. How are we to tell whether a given function f is integrable on an interval $[a, b]$? If f is integrable, how are we supposed to actually compute the definite integral? Answering these questions is not easy, but in advanced calculus, it is shown that f is integrable on a closed interval $[a, b]$ if it is continuous on the interval except at a finite number of points and if it is bounded on the interval (that is, there is a number $A > 0$ such that $|f(x)| < A$ for all x in the interval). We will state a special case of this result as a theorem.

THEOREM 5.5 Integrability of a continuous function

If f is continuous on an interval $[a, b]$, then f is integrable on $[a, b]$.

Proof The proof requires the methods of advanced calculus and is omitted here. ❑

Our next example illustrates how to use the definition to find a definite integral.

EXAMPLE 2 Evaluating a definite integral using the definition

Evaluate $\displaystyle\int_{-2}^{1} 4x\, dx$.

Solution

The integral exists because $f(x) = 4x$ is continuous on $[-2, 1]$. Because the integral can be computed by any partition whose norm approaches 0 (that is, the integral is independent of the sequence of partitions *and* the subinterval representatives), we will simplify matters by choosing a partition in which the points are evenly spaced. Specifically, we divide the interval $[-2, 1]$ into n subintervals, each of width

$$\Delta x = \frac{1 - (-2)}{n} = \frac{3}{n}$$

For each k, we choose the kth subinterval representative to be the right endpoint of the kth subinterval; that is,

$$x_k^* = -2 + k\Delta x = -2 + k\left(\frac{3}{n}\right)$$

Finally, we form the Riemann sum

$$\int_{-2}^{1} 4x\, dx = \lim_{\|P\| \to 0} \sum_{k=1}^{n} f(x_k^*)\Delta x$$

$$= \lim_{n \to +\infty} \sum_{k=1}^{n} 4\left(-2 + \frac{3k}{n}\right)\left(\frac{3}{n}\right) \qquad n \to +\infty \text{ as } \|P\| \to 0$$

$$= \lim_{n \to +\infty} \frac{12}{n^2} \sum_{k=1}^{n} (-2n + 3k)$$

$$= \lim_{n \to +\infty} \frac{12}{n^2} \left(\sum_{k=1}^{n} (-2n) + \sum_{k=1}^{n} 3k \right)$$

$$= \lim_{n \to +\infty} \frac{12}{n^2} \left((-2n)n + 3 \left[\frac{n(n+1)}{2} \right] \right) \quad \text{Summation formulas}$$

$$= \lim_{n \to +\infty} \frac{12}{n^2} \left(\frac{-4n^2 + 3n^2 + 3n}{2} \right)$$

$$= \lim_{n \to +\infty} \frac{-6n^2 + 18n}{n^2} = -6 \qquad \blacksquare$$

AREA AS AN INTEGRAL

Because we have used the development of area in Section 5.2 as the model for our definition of the definite integral, it is no surprise to discover that the area under a curve can be expressed as a definite integral. However, integrals can be positive, zero, or negative (as in Example 2), and we certainly would not expect the area under a curve to be a negative number! The actual relationship between integrals and area under a curve is contained in the following observation, which follows from the definition of area as the limit of a sum, along with Theorem 5.5.

WARNING We will find areas using a definite integral, but not every definite integral can be interpreted as an area.

> **Area as an Integral**
> Suppose f is continuous and $f(x) \geq 0$ on the closed interval $[a, b]$. Then the area under the curve $y = f(x)$ on $[a, b]$ is given by the definite integral of f on $[a, b]$. That is,
> $$\text{AREA} = \int_a^b f(x)\, dx$$

Usually we find area by evaluating a definite integral, but sometimes area can be used to help us evaluate the integral. At this stage of our study, it is not easy to evaluate Riemann sums, so if you happen to recognize that the integral represents the area of some common geometric figure, you can use the known formula instead of the definite integral, as shown in Example 3.

EXAMPLE 3 Evaluating an integral using an area formula

Evaluate $\displaystyle\int_{-3}^{3} \sqrt{9 - x^2}\, dx$.

Solution

Let $f(x) = \sqrt{9 - x^2}$. The curve $y = \sqrt{9 - x^2}$ is a semicircle centered at the origin of radius 3, as shown in Figure 5.14. The given integral can be interpreted as the area under the semicircle on the interval $[-3, 3]$. From geometry, we know the area of the circle is $A = \pi r^2 = \pi(3)^2 = 9\pi$. Thus, the area of the semicircle is $\frac{9\pi}{2}$, and we conclude that

$$\int_{-3}^{3} \sqrt{9 - x^2}\, dx = \frac{9\pi}{2} \qquad \blacksquare$$

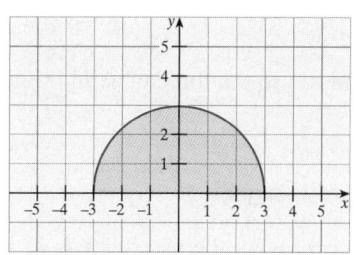

Figure 5.14 The curve $y = \sqrt{9 - x^2}$ is a semicircle of radius 3.

If f is continuous and $f(x) \leq 0$ on the closed interval $[a, b]$, then the area between the curve $y = f(x)$ and the x-axis on $[a, b]$ is the opposite of the definite integral of f on $[a, b]$, since $-f(x) \geq 0$. That is,

$$\text{AREA} = -\int_a^b f(x)\, dx$$

More generally, as illustrated in Figure 5.15, if a continuous function f is sometimes positive and sometimes negative, then

$$\int_a^b f(x)\, dx = A_1 - A_2$$

where

A_1 is the sum of all areas of the region above the x-axis and below the graph of f (that is, where $f(x) \geq 0$).

A_2 is the sum of all areas of the region below the x-axis and above the graph of f (that is, where $f(x) \leq 0$).

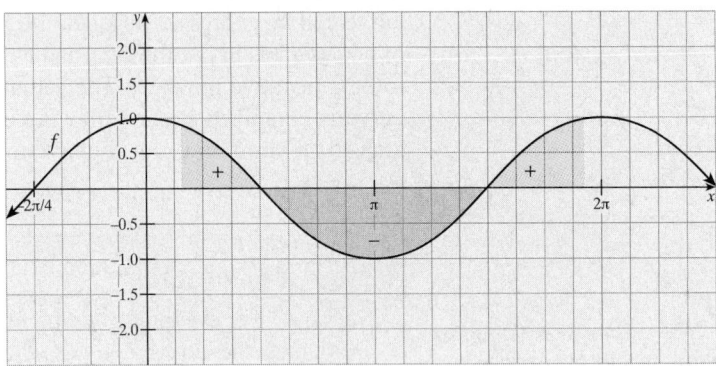

Figure 5.15 A_1 is the sum of the areas marked "$+$" and A_2 is the sum of the areas marked "$-$".

We just worked Example 2 (see Figure 5.16) using a Riemann sum, and it is easy to see from our knowledge of areas of triangles that the area of Triangle I (above the x-axis) is

$$A_1 = \tfrac{1}{2}bh = \tfrac{1}{2}(4)(1) = 2$$

and the area of Triangle II (below the x-axis) is

$$A_2 = \tfrac{1}{2}bh = \tfrac{1}{2}(8)(2) = 8$$

and we see that

$$A_1 - A_2 = 2 - 8 = -6$$

is the same as the value of the integral.

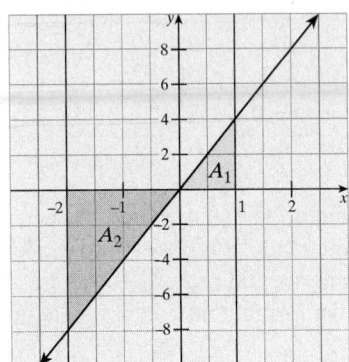

Figure 5.16 Area interpretation of Example 2

PROPERTIES OF THE DEFINITE INTEGRAL

In computations involving integrals, it is often helpful to use the three general properties listed in the following theorem.

THEOREM 5.6   General Properties of the Definite Integral

Linearity rule   If f and g are integrable on $[a, b]$, then so is $rf + sg$ for constants r, s, and

$$\int_a^b [rf(x) + sg(x)]\, dx = r\int_a^b f(x)\, dx + s\int_a^b g(x)\, dx$$

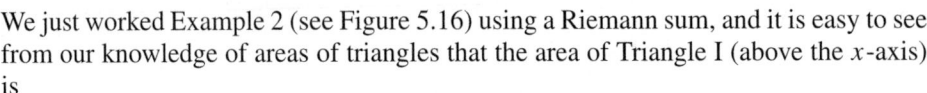

Dominance rule   If f and g are integrable on $[a, b]$ and $f(x) \leq g(x)$ throughout this interval, then

$$\int_a^b f(x)\,dx \leq \int_a^b g(x)\,dx$$

Subdivision rule   For any number c such that $a < c < b$,

$$\int_a^b f(x)\,dx = \int_a^c f(x)\,dx + \int_c^b f(x)\,dx$$

assuming all three integrals exist.

Proof   Each of these rules can be established by using a familiar property of sums or limits with the definition of the definite integral. For example, to derive the linearity rule, we note that any Riemann sum of the function $rf + sg$ can be expressed as

$$\sum_{k=1}^n [rf(x_k^*) + sg(x_k^*)]\Delta x_k = r\left[\sum_{k=1}^n f(x_k^*)\Delta x_k\right] + s\left[\sum_{k=1}^n g(x_k^*)\Delta x_k\right]$$

and the linearity rule then follows by taking the limit on each side of this equation as the norm of the partition tends to 0.   ❑

The dominance rule and the subdivision rule are interpreted geometrically for non-negative functions in Figure 5.17.

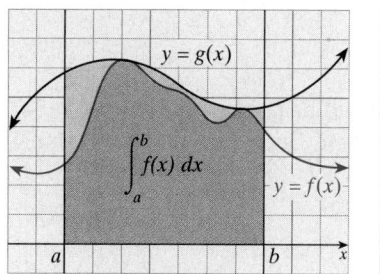
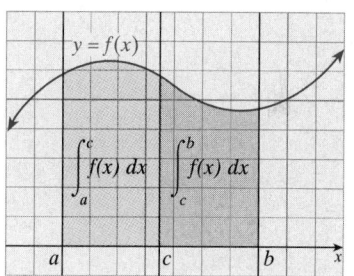

a. The dominance rule
If $g(x) \geq f(x)$, the area under $y = g(x)$ can be no less than the area under $y = f(x)$.

b. The subdivision rule
The area under $y = f(x)$ on $[a, b]$ equals the sum of the areas on $[a, c]$ and $[c, b]$.

Figure 5.17   The dominance and subdivision rules

Notice that if $g(x) \geq f(x) \geq 0$, the curve $y = g(x)$ is always above (or touching) the curve $y = f(x)$, as shown in Figure 5.17a. The dominance rule expresses the fact that the area under the upper curve $y = g(x)$ cannot be less than the area under $y = f(x)$. The subdivision rule says that the area under $y = f(x)$ above $[a, b]$ is the sum of the area on $[a, c]$ and the area on $[c, b]$, as shown in Figure 5.17b. The following example illustrates one way of using the subdivision rule.

EXAMPLE 4   Subdivision rule

If $\int_{-2}^1 f(x)\,dx = 3$ and $\int_{-2}^7 f(x)\,dx = -5$, what is $\int_1^7 f(x)\,dx$?

Solution

According to the subdivision rule, we have

$$\int_{-2}^7 f(x)\,dx = \int_{-2}^1 f(x)\,dx + \int_1^7 f(x)\,dx$$

Therefore,

$$\int_1^7 f(x)\,dx = \int_{-2}^7 f(x)\,dx - \int_{-2}^1 f(x)\,dx = (-5) - 3 = -8 \qquad ■$$

DISTANCE AS AN INTEGRAL

Many quantities other than area can be computed as the limit of a sum. For example, suppose an object moving along a line is known to have continuous velocity $v(t)$ for each time t between $t = a$ and $t = b$, and we wish to compute the total distance traveled by the object during this time period.

Let the interval $[a, b]$ be partitioned into n equal subintervals, each of length $\Delta t = \dfrac{b - a}{n}$ as shown in Figure 5.18.

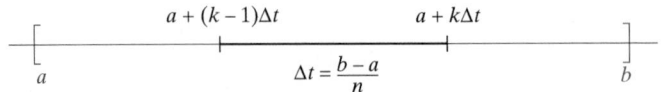

Figure 5.18   The distance traveled during the kth time subinterval

The kth subinterval is $[a + (k - 1)\Delta t, a + k\Delta t]$, and if Δt is small enough, the velocity $v(t)$ will not change much over the subinterval so it is reasonable to approximate $v(t)$ by the constant velocity of $v[a + (k - 1)\Delta t]$ throughout the entire subinterval.

The corresponding change in the object's position will be approximated by the product

$$v[a + (k - 1)\Delta t]\Delta t$$

and will be positive if $v[a + (k - 1)\Delta t]$ is positive and negative if $v[a + (k - 1)\Delta t]$ is negative. Both cases may be summarized by the formula

$$|v[a + (k - 1)\Delta t]|\, \Delta t$$

and the total distance traveled by the object as t varies from $t = a$ to $t = b$ is given by the sum

$$S_n = \sum_{k=1}^{n} |v[a + (k - 1)\Delta t]|\, \Delta t$$

which we recognize as a Riemann sum. We can make the approximation more precise by taking more refined partitions (that is, shorter and shorter time intervals Δt). Therefore, it is reasonable to *define* the exact distance S traveled as the *limit* of the sum S_n as $\Delta t \to 0$ or, equivalently, as $n \to +\infty$, so that

$$S = \lim_{n \to +\infty} \sum_{k=1}^{n} |v[a + (k - 1)\Delta t]|\, \Delta t = \int_{a}^{b} |v(t)|\, dt$$

The reason that we use $|v|$ is that if we travel 300 miles east and then 300 miles west, for example, the *net* distance traveled is $300 - 300 = 0$ miles, but we are usually interested in the total distance traveled, $300 + 300 = 600$ miles.

Distance

> The **total distance traveled** by an object with continuous velocity $v(t)$ along a straight line from time $t = a$ to $t = b$ is
>
> $$S = \int_{a}^{b} |v(t)|\, dt$$

Note: There is a difference between the *total distance* traveled by an object over a given time interval $[a, b]$, and the **net distance** or **displacement** of the object over the same interval, which is defined as the difference between the object's final and initial positions. It is easy to see that displacement is given by

$$D = \int_a^b v(t)\, dt$$

EXAMPLE 5   Distance traveled by an object whose velocity is known

An object moves along a straight line with velocity $v(t) = t^2$ for $t > 0$. How far does the object travel between times $t = 1$ and $t = 2$?

Solution

We have $a = 1$, $b = 2$, and $\Delta t = \dfrac{2-1}{n} = \dfrac{1}{n}$; therefore, the required distance is

$$S = \int_1^2 |v(t)|\, dt$$

$$= \lim_{n\to+\infty} \sum_{k=1}^n \left| v\left[1 + (k-1)\left(\frac{1}{n}\right)\right]\right| \left(\frac{1}{n}\right)$$

$$= \lim_{n\to+\infty} \sum_{k=1}^n \left| v\left(\frac{n+k-1}{n}\right)\right| \left(\frac{1}{n}\right)$$

$$= \lim_{n\to+\infty} \sum_{k=1}^n \frac{(n+k-1)^2}{n^2}\left(\frac{1}{n}\right)$$

$$= \lim_{n\to+\infty} \frac{1}{n^3} \sum_{k=1}^n [(n^2 - 2n + 1) + k^2 + 2(n-1)k]$$

$$= \lim_{n\to+\infty} \frac{1}{n^3}\left[(n^2 - 2n + 1)\sum_{k=1}^n 1 + \sum_{k=1}^n k^2 + 2(n-1)\sum_{k=1}^n k\right]$$

$$= \lim_{n\to+\infty} \frac{1}{n^3}\left[(n^2 - 2n + 1)n + \frac{n(n+1)(2n+1)}{6} + 2(n-1)\frac{n(n+1)}{2}\right]$$

$$= \lim_{n\to+\infty} \frac{14n^3 - 9n^2 + n}{6n^3} = \frac{14}{6} = \frac{7}{3}$$

Thus, we expect the object to travel $\frac{7}{3}$ units during the time interval $[1, 2]$.   ∎

By considering the distance as an integral, we see again that zero or negative values of a definite integral can also be interpreted geometrically. When $v(t) > 0$ on a time interval $[a, b]$, then the total distance S traveled by the object between times $t = a$ and $t = b$ is the same as the area under the graph of $v(t)$ on $[a, b]$.

When $v(t) > 0$, the object moves forward (to the right), but when $v(t) < 0$, it reverses direction and moves backward (to the left). In the general case, where $v(t)$ changes sign on the time interval $[a, b]$, the integral

$$\int_a^b v(t)\, dt$$

measures the net distance or displacement of the object, taking into account both forward ($v > 0$) and backward ($v < 0$) motion. For instance, an object that moves forward 2 units and back 3 on a given time interval has moved a total distance of 5 units, but its displacement is -1 because it ends up 1 unit to the left of its initial position.

For example, for the velocity function $v(t)$ graphed in Figure 5.19a, the net displacement is 0 because the area above the t-axis is the same as the area below, but in Figure 5.19b, there is more area below the t-axis, which means the net displacement is negative, and the object ends up "behind" (to the left of) its starting position.

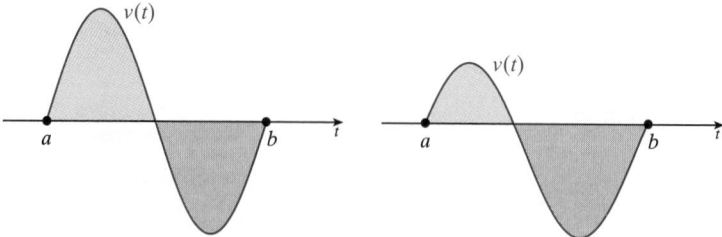

a. Net displacement of 0
There is as much area under the positive part of the velocity curve as there is above the negative part.

b. Negative net displacement
There is more area above the negative part of the velocity curve than there is under the positive part.

Figure 5.19   Definite integral in terms of displacement

PREVIEW

Students often become discouraged at this point, thinking they will have to compute all definite integrals using the limit of a Riemann sum definition, so we offer an encouraging word. Recall the definition of derivative in Chapter 3. It was difficult to find derivatives using the definition, but we soon proved some theorems to make it easier to find and evaluate derivatives. The same is true of integration. It is difficult to apply the definition of a definite integral, but you will soon discover that computing most definite integrals is no harder than finding an antiderivative.

As a preview of this result, consider an object moving along a straight line. We assume that its position is given by $s(t)$ and that its velocity $v(t) = s'(t)$ is positive ($v(t) > 0$) so that it is always moving forward. The total distance traveled by such an object between times $t = a$ and $t = b$ is clearly $S = s(b) - s(a)$, but earlier in this section, we showed that this distance is also given by the definite integral of $v(t)$ over the interval $[a, b]$. Thus we have

$$\text{TOTAL DISTANCE} = \int_a^b v(t)\, dt = s(b) - s(a)$$

where $s(t)$ is an antiderivative of $v(t)$.

This observation anticipates the *fundamental theorem of calculus*, which provides a vital link between differential and integral calculus. We will formally introduce the fundamental theorem in the next section. To illustrate, notice how our observation applies to Example 5, where $v(t) = t^2$ and the interval is $[1, 2]$. Since an antiderivative of $v(t)$ is $s(t) = \frac{1}{3}t^3$, we have

$$S = \int_1^2 t^2\, dt = s(2) - s(1) = \left[\frac{1}{3}(2)^3 - \frac{1}{3}(1)^3\right] = \frac{7}{3}$$

which coincides with the result found numerically in Example 5.

5.3   PROBLEM SET

A *In Problems 1–10, estimate (using right endpoints) the given integral* $\int_a^b f(x)\,dx$ *by using a Riemann sum*

$$S_n = \sum_{k=1}^n f(a + k\Delta x)\Delta x \text{ for } n = 4.$$

1. $\int_0^1 (2x + 1)\,dx$ **2.** $\int_0^1 (4x^2 + 2)\,dx$

3. $\int_1^3 x^2\,dx$ **4.** $\int_0^2 x^3\,dx$

5. $\int_0^1 (1 - 3x)\,dx$ **6.** $\int_1^3 (x^2 - x^3)\,dx$

7. $\int_{-\pi/2}^0 \cos x\,dx$ **8.** $\int_0^{\pi/4} (x + \sin x)\,dx$

9. $\int_0^1 e^x\,dx$ **10.** $\int_1^2 \frac{dx}{x}$

In Problems 11–16, $v(t)$ is the velocity of an object moving along a straight line. Use the formula

$$S_n = \sum_{k=1}^n |v(a + k\Delta t)|\,\Delta t$$

where $\Delta t = \dfrac{b - a}{n}$ *to estimate (using right endpoints) the total distance traveled by the object during the time interval $[a, b]$. Let $n = 4$.*

11. $v(t) = 3t + 1$ on $[1, 4]$ **12.** $v(t) = 1 + 2t$ on $[1, 2]$

13. $v(t) = \sin t$ on $[0, \pi]$ **14.** $v(t) = \cos t$ on $[0, \frac{\pi}{2}]$

15. $v(t) = e^{-t}$ on $[0, 1]$ **16.** $v(t) = \dfrac{1}{t + 1}$ on $[0, 1]$

Evaluate each of the integrals in Problems 17–22 by using the following information together with the linearity and subdivision properties:

$$\int_{-1}^2 x^2\,dx = 3; \quad \int_{-1}^0 x^2\,dx = \frac{1}{3}; \quad \int_{-1}^2 x\,dx = \frac{3}{2}; \quad \int_0^2 x\,dx = 2$$

17. $\int_0^{-1} x^2\,dx$ **18.** $\int_{-1}^2 (x^2 + x)\,dx$

19. $\int_{-1}^2 (2x^2 - 3x)\,dx$ **20.** $\int_0^2 x^2\,dx$

21. $\int_{-1}^0 x\,dx$ **22.** $\int_{-1}^0 (3x^2 - 5x)\,dx$

Use the dominance property of integrals to establish the given inequality in Problems 23–24.

23. $\int_0^1 x^3\,dx \le \dfrac{1}{2}$ *Hint: Note that $x^3 \le x$ on $[0, 1]$.*

24. $\int_0^\pi \sin x\,dx \le \pi$ *Hint: $\sin x \le 1$ for all x.*

B **25.** Given $\int_{-2}^4 [5f(x) + 2g(x)]\,dx = 7$ and $\int_{-2}^4 [3f(x) + g(x)]\,dx = 4$, find

$$\int_{-2}^4 f(x)\,dx \quad \text{and} \quad \int_{-2}^4 g(x)\,dx$$

26. Suppose $\int_0^2 f(x)\,dx = 3$, $\int_0^2 g(x)\,dx = -1$, and $\int_0^2 h(x)\,dx = 3$.

a. Evaluate $\int_0^2 [2f(x) + 5g(x) - 7h(x)]\,dx$.

b. Find a constant s such that

$$\int_0^2 [5f(x) + sg(x) - 6h(x)]\,dx = 0$$

27. Evaluate $\int_{-1}^2 f(x)\,dx$ given that

$$\int_{-1}^1 f(x)\,dx = 3; \quad \int_2^3 f(x)\,dx = -2; \quad \int_1^3 f(x)\,dx = 5$$

28. Let $f(x) = \begin{cases} 2 & \text{for } -1 \le x \le 1 \\ 3 - x & \text{for } 1 < x < 4 \\ 2x - 9 & \text{for } 4 \le x \le 5 \end{cases}$

Sketch the graph of f on the interval $[-1, 5]$ and show that f is continuous on this interval. Then use Theorem 5.6 to evaluate

$$\int_{-1}^5 f(x)\,dx$$

29. Let $f(x) = \begin{cases} 5 & \text{for } -3 \le x \le -1 \\ 4 - x & \text{for } -1 < x < 2 \\ 2x - 2 & \text{for } 2 \le x \le 5 \end{cases}$

Sketch the graph of f on the interval $[-3, 5]$ and show that f is continuous on this interval. Then use Theorem 5.6 to evaluate

$$\int_{-3}^5 f(x)\,dx$$

30. HISTORICAL QUEST
During the eighteenth century, integrals were considered simply as antiderivatives. That is, there were no underpinnings for the concept of an integral until Cauchy formulated the definition of the integral in 1823 (see Historical Quest 49, Problem Set 2.1). This formulation was later completed by Georg Friedrich Riemann. In this section, we see that

GEORG FRIEDRICH RIEMANN
1826–1866

history honored Riemann by naming the process after him. In his personal life he was frail, bashful, and timid, but in his professional life he was one of the giants in mathematical history. Riemann used what are called topological methods in his theory of functions and in his work with surfaces and spaces. Riemann is remembered for his work in geometry (Riemann surfaces) and analysis. In his book *Space Through the Ages*, Cornelius Lanczos wrote, "Although Riemann's collected papers fill only one single volume of 538 pages, this volume weighs tons if measured intellectually. Every one of his many discoveries was destined to change the course of mathematical science." ∎

For this Historical Quest, investigate the Königsberg bridge problem, and its solution.

This famous problem was formulated by Leonhard Euler (1707–1783). The branch of mathematics known today as *topology* began with Euler's work on the bridge problem and other related questions and was extended in the nineteenth century by Riemann and others.

31. Generalize the subdivision property by showing that for $a \leq c \leq d \leq b$

$$\int_a^b f(x)\, dx = \int_a^c f(x)\, dx + \int_c^d f(x)\, dx + \int_d^b f(x)\, dx$$

whenever all these integrals exist.

32. If $Cx + D \geq 0$ for $a \leq x \leq b$, show that

$$\int_a^b (Cx + D)\, dx = (b - a)\left[\frac{C}{2}(b + a) + D\right]$$

Hint: Sketch the region under the line $y = Cx + D$, and express the integral as an area.

33. For $b > a > 0$, show that

$$\int_a^b x^2\, dx = \frac{1}{3}(b^3 - a^3)$$

In Problems 34–36, use the partition $P = \{-1, -0.2, 0.9, 1.3, 1.7, 2\}$ *on the interval* $[-1, 2]$.

34. Find the subinterval widths

$$\Delta x_k = x_k - x_{k-1}$$

for $k = 1, 2, \ldots, 5$. What is the norm of P?

35. Compute the Riemann sum on $[-1, 2]$ associated with $f(x) = 4 - 5x$; the partition P with $\Delta x_1 = 0.8$, $\Delta x_2 = 1.1$, $\Delta x_3 = 0.4$, $\Delta x_4 = 0.4$, and $\Delta x_5 = 0.3$; and the subinterval representatives $x_1^* = -0.5$, $x_2^* = 0.8$, $x_3^* = 1$, $x_4^* = 1.3$, $x_5^* = 1.8$. What is the norm of P?

36. Compute the Riemann sum on $[-1, 2]$ associated with $f(x) = x^3$; the partition P with $\Delta x_1 = 0.8$, $\Delta x_2 = 1.1$, $\Delta x_3 = 0.4$, $\Delta x_4 = 0.4$, and $\Delta x_5 = 0.3$; and subinterval representatives $x_1^* = -1$, $x_2^* = 0$, $x_3^* = 1$, $x_4^* = \frac{128}{81}$, and $x_5^* = \frac{125}{64}$. What is the norm of P?

37. If the numbers a_k and b_k satisfy $a_k \leq b_k$ for $k = 1, 2, \ldots, n$, then $\displaystyle\sum_{k=1}^n a_k \leq \sum_{k=1}^n b_k$. Use this dominance property of sums to establish the dominance property of integrals.

38. Counterexample Problem Either prove that the following result is generally true or find a counterexample: If f and g are continuous on $[a, b]$, then

$$\int_a^b f(x)g(x)\, dx = \left[\int_a^b f(x)\, dx\right]\left[\int_a^b g(x)\, dx\right]$$

39. Counterexample Problem Either prove that the following result is generally true or find a counterexample: There exists a nonzero continuous function f defined on $[a, b]$ with a nonzero area between the x-axis and the function f on the interval such that

$$\int_a^b f(x)\, dx = 0$$

40. Recall that a function f is **odd** if $f(-x) = -f(x)$ for all x. If f is odd, show that

$$\int_{-a}^a f(x)\, dx = 0$$

for all a. This problem is analogous to Problem 33 of the previous section.

41. Prove the *bounding rule* for definite integrals: If f is integrable on the closed interval $[a, b]$ and $m \leq f(x) \leq M$ for constants m, M, and all x in the closed interval, then

$$m(b - a) \leq \int_a^b f(x)\, dx \leq M(b - a)$$

42. Use the definition of the definite integral to prove that

$$\int_a^b C\, dx = C(b - a)$$

5.4   The Fundamental Theorems of Calculus

IN THIS SECTION   the first fundamental theorem of calculus, the second fundamental theorem of calculus

THE FIRST FUNDAMENTAL THEOREM OF CALCULUS

In the previous section we observed that if $v(t)$ is the velocity of an object at time t as it moves along a straight line, then

$$\int_a^b v(t)\, dt = s(b) - s(a)$$

where $s(t)$ is the displacement of the object and satisfies $s'(t) = v(t)$. This result is an application of the following general theorem which was discovered by the English mathematician Isaac Barrow (1630–1677), Newton's mentor at Cambridge.

THEOREM 5.7   The first fundamental theorem of calculus

If f is continuous on the interval $[a, b]$ and F is any function that satisfies $F'(x) = f(x)$ throughout this interval, then

$$\int_a^b f(x)\,dx = F(b) - F(a)$$

Proof   Let $P = \{x_0, x_1, x_2, \ldots, x_n\}$ be a regular partition of the interval, with subinterval widths $\Delta x = \dfrac{b - a}{n}$. Note that F satisfies the hypotheses of the mean value theorem (Theorem 4.4, Section 4.2) on each of the closed subintervals $[x_{k-1}, x_k]$. Thus, the MVT tells us that there is a point x_k^* in each open subinterval (x_{k-1}, x_k) for which

$$\frac{F(x_k) - F(x_{k-1})}{x_k - x_{k-1}} = F'(x_k^*)$$

$$F(x_k) - F(x_{k-1}) = F'(x_k^*)(x_k - x_{k-1})$$

Because $F'(x_k^*) = f(x_k^*)$ and $x_k - x_{k-1} = \Delta x = \dfrac{b - a}{n}$, we can write $F(x_k) - F(x_{k-1}) = f(x_k^*)\Delta x$, so that

$$F(x_1) - F(x_0) = f(x_1^*)\Delta x$$

$$F(x_2) - F(x_1) = f(x_2^*)\Delta x$$

$$\vdots$$

$$F(x_n) - F(x_{n-1}) = f(x_n^*)\Delta x$$

Thus, by adding both sides of all the equations, we obtain

$$\sum_{k=1}^n f(x_k^*)\Delta x = f(x_1^*)\Delta x + f(x_2^*)\Delta x + \cdots + f(x_n^*)\Delta x$$

$$= [F(x_1) - F(x_0)] + [F(x_2) - F(x_1)] + \cdots + [F(x_n) - F(x_{n-1})]$$

$$= F(x_n) - F(x_0)$$

Because $x_0 = a$ and $x_n = b$, we have

$$\sum_{k=1}^n f(x_k^*)\Delta x = F(b) - F(a)$$

Finally, we take the limit of the left side as $\|P\| \to 0$ (i.e., $n \to +\infty$), and because $F(b) - F(a)$ is a constant, we have

$$\int_a^b f(x)\,dx = F(b) - F(a)$$ ❑

→ **What This Says**   The definite integral $\displaystyle\int_a^b f(x)\,dx$ can be computed by finding an antiderivative on the interval $[a, b]$ and evaluating it at the limits of integration a and b. It is a consequence of the first fundamental theorem of calculus that our two definitions of area between the graph of $y = f(x)$ for $y \geq 0$ and the x-axis from the first two sections of this chapter agree. Also notice that this theorem does not say *how* to find the antiderivative, nor does it say that an antiderivative F *exists*. The existence of an antiderivative is asserted by the second fundamental theorem of calculus, which is examined later in this section (page 306).

To give you some insight into why this theorem is important enough to be named *the fundamental theorem of calculus*, we repeat Example 2 from Section 5.3 on the left and then work the same example using the fundamental theorem, on the right.

EXAMPLE 1   Evaluating a definite integral

Evaluate $\int_{-2}^{1} 4x \, dx$ using the definition of the definite integral and also using the fundamental theorem.

Solution

Solution from Section 5.3 using Riemann sums:

$$\int_{-2}^{1} 4x \, dx = \lim_{\|P\|\to 0} \sum_{k=1}^{n} f(x_k^*)\Delta x$$

$$= \lim_{n\to+\infty} \sum_{k=1}^{n} 4\left(-2 + \frac{3k}{n}\right)\left(\frac{3}{n}\right)$$

$$= \lim_{n\to+\infty} \frac{12}{n^2} \sum_{k=1}^{n}(-2n + 3k)$$

$$= \lim_{n\to+\infty} \frac{12}{n^2}\left(\sum_{k=1}^{n}(-2n) + \sum_{k=1}^{n} 3k\right)$$

$$= \lim_{n\to+\infty} \frac{12}{n^2}\left((-2n)n + 3\left[\frac{n(n+1)}{2}\right]\right)$$

$$= \lim_{n\to+\infty} \frac{12}{n^2}\left(\frac{-4n^2 + 3n^2 + 3n}{2}\right)$$

$$= \lim_{n\to+\infty} \frac{-6n^2 + 18n}{n^2}$$

$$= -6$$

Solution using the fundamental theorem of calculus:

If $F(x) = 2x^2$, then $F'(x) = 4x$, so F is an antiderivative of f. Thus,

$$\int_{-2}^{1} 4x \, dx = F(1) - F(-2)$$

$$= 2(1)^2 - 2(-2)^2 = -6$$

Note that if we choose a *different* antiderivative, say $G(x) = 2x^2 + 3$, then $G(1) - G(-2) = -6$, as well.

■

The variable used in a definite integral is a **dummy variable** in the sense that it can be replaced by any other variable with no effect on the value of the integral. For instance, we have just found that

$$\int_{-2}^{1} 4x \, dx = -6$$

and without further computation, it follows that

$$\int_{-2}^{1} 4t \, dt = -6 \qquad \int_{-2}^{1} 4u \, du = -6 \qquad \int_{-2}^{1} 4N \, dN = -6$$

Henceforth, when evaluating an integral by the fundamental theorem, we will denote the difference

$$F(b) - F(a) \quad \text{by} \quad F(x)\big|_a^b$$

Sometimes we also write $[F(x)]_a^b$, where $F'(x) = f(x)$ on $[a, b]$. This notation is illustrated in Example 2.

EXAMPLE 2   Finding the area under a curve using the fundamental theorem of calculus

Find the area under the curve $y = \cos x$ on $\left[-\frac{\pi}{2}, \frac{\pi}{2}\right]$.

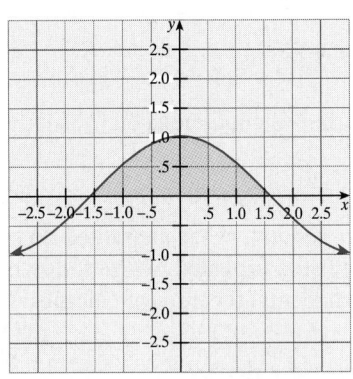

If you look at the graph of $f(x) = \cos x$ on $\left[-\frac{\pi}{2}, \frac{\pi}{2}\right]$, you can see that an area of 2 seems reasonable.

Figure 5.20 Graph to estimate area

Solution

Note that $f(x) = \cos x$ is continuous and $f(x) \geq 0$ on $\left[-\frac{\pi}{2}, \frac{\pi}{2}\right]$, as shown in Figure 5.20. Because the derivative of $\sin x$ is $\cos x$, it follows (from the definition of the antiderivative) that $\sin x$ is an antiderivative of $\cos x$. Thus, the required area is given by the integral

$$A = \int_{-\pi/2}^{\pi/2} \cos x \, dx = \sin x \big|_{-\pi/2}^{\pi/2} = \sin \tfrac{\pi}{2} - \sin\left(-\tfrac{\pi}{2}\right) = 1 - (-1) = 2$$

The region has area $A = 2$ square units.

WARNING It is important to remember that, for fixed numerical values of a and b, the definite integral $\int_a^b f(x) \, dx$ is a number, whereas the indefinite integral $\int f(x) \, dx$ is a family of functions. The relationship between the indefinite and definite integral is given by

$$\int_a^b f(x) \, dx = \left[\int f(x) \, dx \right] \Big|_a^b \qquad \blacksquare$$

EXAMPLE 3 Evaluating an integral using the fundamental theorem

Evaluate

a. $\displaystyle\int_{-3}^5 (-10) \, dx$ **b.** $\displaystyle\int_4^9 \left[\frac{1}{\sqrt{x}} + x \right] dx$ **c.** $\displaystyle\int_{-2}^2 |x| \, dx$

Solution

a. $\displaystyle\int_{-3}^5 (-10) \, dx = -10x \big|_{-3}^5 = -10(5 + 3) = -80$

b. $\displaystyle\int_4^9 \left[\frac{1}{\sqrt{x}} + x \right] dx = \int_4^9 \left[x^{-1/2} + x \right] dx = \left[\left(\frac{x^{1/2}}{\frac{1}{2}} \right) + \frac{x^2}{2} \right] \Bigg|_4^9$

$$= \left(6 + \tfrac{81}{2} \right) - \left(4 + \tfrac{16}{2} \right) = 34\tfrac{1}{2}$$

c. $\displaystyle\int_{-2}^2 |x| \, dx = \int_{-2}^0 |x| \, dx + \int_0^2 |x| \, dx$ Subdivision rule

$$= \int_{-2}^0 (-x) \, dx + \int_0^2 x \, dx \qquad \text{Recall,} \quad \begin{matrix} |x| = x & \text{if } x \geq 0 \\ |x| = -x & \text{if } x < 0 \end{matrix}$$

$$= -\frac{x^2}{2} \Big|_{-2}^0 + \frac{x^2}{2} \Big|_0^2 = -\left(0 - \frac{4}{2} \right) + \left(\frac{4}{2} + 0 \right) = 4$$

Note that we must use the subdivision rule because we do not know an antiderivative of the function $|x|$, where x is defined on an interval containing zero. $\blacksquare$

THE SECOND FUNDAMENTAL THEOREM OF CALCULUS

In certain circumstances, it is useful to consider an integral of the form

$$\int_a^x f(t) \, dt$$

where the upper limit of integration is a variable instead of a constant. As x varies, so does the value of the integral, and

$$F(x) = \int_a^x f(t) \, dt$$

is a function of the variable x. (Note that the integrand does not contain x.) For instance,

$$F(x) = \int_2^x t^2\, dt = \tfrac{1}{3}x^3 - \tfrac{1}{3}(2)^3 = \tfrac{1}{3}x^3 - \tfrac{8}{3}$$

The first fundamental theorem of calculus tells us that if f is continuous on $[a, b]$, then

$$\int_a^b f(x)\, dx = F(b) - F(a)$$

where F is an antiderivative of f on $[a, b]$. But in general, what guarantee do we have that such an antiderivative even exists? The answer is provided by the following theorem, which is often referred to as the second fundamental theorem of calculus.

THEOREM 5.8   The second fundamental theorem of calculus

Let $f(t)$ be continuous on the interval $[a, b]$ and define the function G by the integral equation

$$G(x) = \int_a^x f(t)\, dt$$

for $a \le x \le b$. Then G is an antiderivative of f on $[a, b]$; that is,

$$G'(x) = \frac{d}{dx}\left[\int_a^x f(t)\, dt \right] = f(x)$$

on $[a, b]$.

Proof   Apply the definition of the derivative to G:

$$G'(x) = \lim_{\Delta x \to 0} \frac{G(x + \Delta x) - G(x)}{\Delta x} \qquad \text{x is fixed, only Δx changes}$$

$$= \lim_{\Delta x \to 0} \frac{1}{\Delta x}[G(x + \Delta x) - G(x)]$$

$$= \lim_{\Delta x \to 0} \frac{1}{\Delta x}\left[\int_a^{x+\Delta x} f(t)\, dt - \int_a^x f(t)\, dt \right]$$

$$= \lim_{\Delta x \to 0} \frac{1}{\Delta x}\left[\int_a^{x+\Delta x} f(t)\, dt + \int_x^a f(t)\, dt \right]$$

$$= \lim_{\Delta x \to 0} \frac{1}{\Delta x}\left[\int_x^{x+\Delta x} f(t)\, dt \right] \qquad \text{Subdivision rule}$$

Since f is continuous on $[a, b]$, it is continuous on $[x, x + \Delta x]$ for any x in $[a, b]$. Let $m(x)$ and $M(x)$ be the smallest and largest values, respectively, for $f(t)$ on $[x, x+\Delta x]$. (*Note*: In general, m and M depend on x and Δx but are constants as far as t-integration is concerned.) Since $m(x) \le f(t) \le M(x)$, we have (by the dominance rule)

$$\int_x^{x+\Delta x} m(x)\, dt \le \int_x^{x+\Delta x} f(t)\, dt \le \int_x^{x+\Delta x} M(x)\, dt$$

so

$$m(x)[(x + \Delta x) - x] \le \int_x^{x+\Delta x} f(t)\, dt \le M(x)[(x + \Delta x) - x]$$

or

$$m(x) \le \frac{1}{\Delta x}\int_x^{x+\Delta x} f(t)\, dt \le M(x)$$

Since

$$m(x) \le f(x) \le M(x)$$

on $[x, x + \Delta x]$, it follows that $m(x)$ and $M(x)$ are both "squeezed" toward $f(x)$ as $\Delta x \to 0$ and we have

$$G'(x) = \lim_{\Delta x \to 0} \frac{1}{\Delta x}\int_x^{x+\Delta x} f(t)\, dt = f(x) \qquad \Box$$

We also note that the function G is continuous, since it is differentiable. If F is *any* antiderivative of f on the interval $[a, b]$, then the antiderivative

$$G(x) = \int_a^x f(t)\, dt$$

found in Theorem 5.8 satisfies $G(x) = F(x) + C$ for some constant C and all x on the interval $[a, b]$. In particular, when $x = a$, we have

$$0 = \int_a^a f(t)\, dt = G(a) = F(a) + C$$

so that $C = -F(a)$. Finally, by letting $x = b$, we find that

$$\int_a^b f(t)\, dt = G(b) = F(b) + C = F(b) + [-F(a)] = F(b) - F(a)$$

as claimed by the first fundamental theorem.

EXAMPLE 4   Using the second fundamental theorem

Differentiate $F(x) = \displaystyle\int_7^x (2t - 3)\, dt$.

Solution

From the second fundamental theorem, we can obtain $F'(x)$ by simply replacing t with x in the integrand $f(t) = 2t - 3$. Thus,

$$F'(x) = \frac{d}{dx}\left[\int_7^x (2t - 3)\, dt \right] = 2x - 3 \qquad \blacksquare$$

The second fundamental theorem of calculus can also be applied to an integral function with a variable *lower* limit of integration. For example, to differentiate

$$G(z) = \int_z^5 \frac{\sin u}{u}\, du$$

reverse the order of integration and apply the second fundamental theorem of calculus as before:

$$G'(z) = \frac{d}{dz}\left[\int_z^5 \frac{\sin u}{u}\, du \right] = \frac{d}{dz}\left[-\int_5^z \frac{\sin u}{u}\, du \right] = -\frac{d}{dz}\left[\int_5^z \frac{\sin u}{u}\, du \right] = -\frac{\sin z}{z}$$

EXAMPLE 5   Second fundamental theorem with the chain rule

Find the derivative of $F(x) = \displaystyle\int_0^{x^2} t^2\, dt$.

Solution

$$
\begin{aligned}
F'(x) &= \frac{d}{dx}\left[\int_0^{x^2} t^2\, dt \right] = \frac{d}{du}\left[\int_0^u t^2\, dt \right]\frac{du}{dx} \qquad \text{Chain rule; } u = x^2 \\
&= u^2 \frac{du}{dx} \qquad \text{Second fundamental theorem of calculus} \\
&= \left(x^2 \right)^2 (2x) \\
&= 2x^5 \qquad\qquad\qquad\qquad\qquad\qquad\qquad\qquad\qquad\quad \blacksquare
\end{aligned}
$$

5.4   PROBLEM SET

Ⓐ *In Problems 1–30, evaluate the definite integral.*

1. $\int_{-10}^{10} 7\,dx$

2. $\int_{-5}^{7} (-3)\,dx$

3. $\int_{-3}^{5} (2x + a)\,dx$

4. $\int_{-2}^{2} (b - x)\,dx$

5. $\int_{-1}^{2} ax^3\,dx$

6. $\int_{-1}^{1} (x^3 + bx^2)\,dx$

7. $\int_{1}^{2} \frac{c}{x^3}\,dx$

8. $\int_{-2}^{-1} \frac{p}{x^2}\,dx$

9. $\int_{0}^{9} \sqrt{x}\,dx$

10. $\int_{0}^{27} \sqrt[3]{x}\,dx$

11. $\int_{0}^{1} (5u^7 + \pi^2)\,du$

12. $\int_{0}^{1} (7x^8 + \sqrt{\pi})\,dx$

13. $\int_{1}^{2} x^{2a}\,dx,\ a \neq -\frac{1}{2}$

14. $\int_{1}^{2} (2x)^{\pi}\,dx$

15. $\int_{\ln 2}^{\ln 5} 5e^x\,dx$

16. $\int_{e^{-2}}^{e} \frac{dx}{x}$

17. $\int_{0}^{4} \sqrt{x}(x + 1)\,dx$

18. $\int_{0}^{1} \sqrt{t}(t - \sqrt{t})\,dt$

19. $\int_{1}^{2} \frac{x^3 + 1}{x^2}\,dx$

20. $\int_{1}^{4} \frac{x^2 + x - 1}{\sqrt{x}}\,dx$

21. $\int_{1}^{\sqrt{3}} \frac{6a}{1 + x^2}\,dx$

22. $\int_{0}^{0.5} \frac{b\,dx}{\sqrt{1 - x^2}}$

23. $\int_{-2}^{3} (\sin^2 x + \cos^2 x)\,dx$

24. $\int_{0}^{\pi/4} (\sec^2 x - \tan^2 x)\,dx$

25. $\int_{0}^{1} (1 - e^t)\,dt$

26. $\int_{1}^{2} \frac{x^3 + 1}{x}\,dx$

27. $\int_{0}^{1} \frac{x^2 - 4}{x - 2}\,dx$

28. $\int_{0}^{1} \frac{x^2 - 1}{x^2 + 1}\,dx$

29. $\int_{-1}^{2} (x + |x|)\,dx$

30. $\int_{0}^{2} (x - |x - 1|)\,dx$

In Problems 31–38, find the area of the region under the given curve over the prescribed interval.

31. $y = x^2 + 1$ on $[-1, 1]$

32. $y = \sqrt{t}$ on $[0, 1]$

33. $y = \sec^2 x$ on $\left[0, \frac{\pi}{4}\right]$

34. $y = \sin x + \cos x$ on $\left[0, \frac{\pi}{2}\right]$

35. $y = e^t - t$ on $[0, 1]$

36. $y = (x^2 + x + 1)\sqrt{x}$ on $[1, 4]$

37. $y = \dfrac{x^2 - 2x + 3}{x}$ on $[1, 2]$

38. $y = \dfrac{2}{1 + t^2}$ on $[0, 1]$

In Problems 39–44, find the derivative of the given function.

39. $F(x) = \int_{0}^{x} \frac{t^2 - 1}{\sqrt{t + 1}}\,dt$

40. $F(x) = \int_{-2}^{x} (t + 1)\sqrt[3]{t}\,dt$

41. $F(t) = \int_{1}^{t} \frac{\sin x}{x}\,dx$

42. $F(t) = \int_{t}^{2} \frac{e^x}{x}\,dx$

43. $F(x) = \int_{x}^{1} \frac{dt}{\sqrt{1 + 3t^2}}$

44. $F(x) = \int_{\pi/3}^{x} \sec^2 t \tan t\,dt$

Ⓑ *The formulas in Problems 45–50 are taken from a table of integrals. In each case, use differentiation to verify that the formula is correct.*

45. $\int \cos^2 au\,du = \dfrac{u}{2} + \dfrac{\sin 2au}{4a} + C$

46. $\int u \cos^2 au\,du = \dfrac{u^2}{4} + \dfrac{u \sin 2au}{4a} + \dfrac{\cos 2au}{8a^2} + C$

47. $\int \dfrac{u\,du}{(a^2 - u^2)^{3/2}} = \dfrac{1}{\sqrt{a^2 - u^2}} + C$

48. $\int \dfrac{du}{u^2 - a^2} = \dfrac{1}{2a} \ln\left|\dfrac{u - a}{u + a}\right| + C$

49. $\int \dfrac{u\,du}{\sqrt{a^2 - u^2}} = -\sqrt{a^2 - u^2} + C$

50. $\int (\ln |u|)^2\,du = u(\ln |u|)^2 - 2u \ln |u| + 2u + C$

51. Exploration Problem   What is the relationship between finding an area and evaluating an integral?

52. Journal Problem   *FOCUS** ■ The area of the shaded region in Figure 5.21a is 8 times the area of the shaded region in Figure 5.21b. What is c in terms of a?

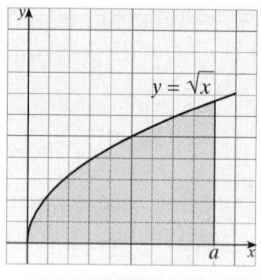
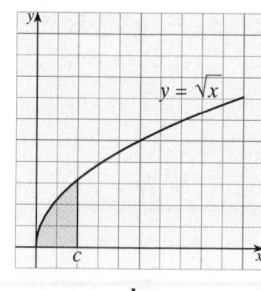

a.   b.

Figure 5.21   Comparing areas

53. Exploration Problem   If you use the first fundamental theorem for the following integral, you find

$$\int_{-1}^{1} \frac{dx}{x^2} = \left[-\frac{1}{x}\right]\Big|_{-1}^{1} = -1 - 1 = -2$$

But the function $y = \dfrac{1}{x^2}$ is never negative. What's wrong with this "evaluation"?

54. Evaluate

$$\int_{0}^{2} f(x)\,dx \quad \text{where} \quad f(x) = \begin{cases} x^3 & \text{if } 0 \leq x < 1 \\ x^4 & \text{if } 1 \leq x \leq 2 \end{cases}$$

55. Evaluate

$$\int_{0}^{\pi} f(x)\,dx \quad \text{where} \quad f(x) = \begin{cases} \cos x & \text{if } 0 \leq x < \pi/2 \\ x & \text{if } \pi/2 \leq x \leq \pi \end{cases}$$

---

*February 1995, p. 15.

56. a. If $F(x) = \int \left(\dfrac{1}{\sqrt{x}} - 4 \right) dx$, find F so that $F(1) = 0$.

b. Sketch the graphs of $y = F(x)$, $y = F(x) + 3$, and $y = F(x) - 1$.

c. Find a constant K such that the largest value of $G(x) = F(x) + K$ is 0.

57. Let $g(x) = \displaystyle\int_0^x f(t)\,dt$, where f is the function defined by the following graph. Note that f crosses the x-axis at 3 points on $[0, 2]$; label these (from left to right), $x = a$, $x = b$, and $x = c$.

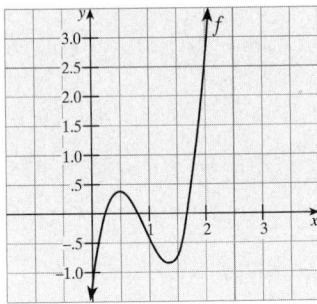

a. What can you say about $g(a)$?

b. Estimate $g(1)$.

c. Where does g have a maximum value on $[0, 2]$?

d. Sketch a rough graph of g.

58. Let $g(x) = \displaystyle\int_0^x f(t)\,dt$, where f is the function defined by the following graph.

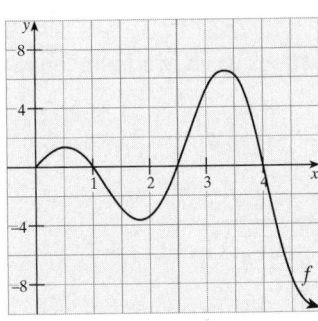

a. Where does g have a relative minimum on $[0, 5]$?

b. Where does g have a relative maximum value on $[0, 5]$?

c. If $g(1) = 1$, $g(2.5) = -2.5$, and $g(4) = 4$, sketch a rough graph of g.

C 59. Counterexample Problem The purpose of this problem is to provide a counterexample showing that the integral of a product (or quotient) is not necessarily equal to the product (quotient) of the respective integrals.

a. Show that $\int x\sqrt{x}\,dx \neq (\int x\,dx)(\int \sqrt{x}\,dx)$.

b. Show that $\displaystyle\int \dfrac{\sqrt{x}}{x}\,dx \neq \dfrac{\int \sqrt{x}\,dx}{\int x\,dx}$.

60. Suppose f is a function with the property that $f'(x) = f(x)$ for all x.

a. Show that $\displaystyle\int_a^b f(x)\,dx = f(b) - f(a)$.

b. Show that $\displaystyle\int_a^b [f(x)]^2\,dx = \dfrac{1}{2}\{[f(b)]^2 - [f(a)]^2\}$.

61. Find $\dfrac{d}{dx}\displaystyle\int_0^{x^4}(2t - 3)\,dt$ using the second fundamental theorem of calculus. Check your work by evaluating the integral directly and then taking the derivative of your answer.

62. Find $\dfrac{d}{dx}\displaystyle\int_0^{x^2}\sin t\,dt$ using the second fundamental theorem of calculus. Check your work by evaluating the integral directly and then taking the derivative of your answer.

63. Find an equation for the tangent line to the curve $y = F(x)$ at the point P where $x = 1$ and

$$F(x) = \int_1^{\sqrt{x}} \frac{2t + 1}{t + 2}\,dt$$

64. Find an equation for the tangent line to the curve $y = F(x)$ at the point P where $x = 1$ and

$$F(x) = \int_1^{x^3} \frac{t^2 + 1}{t - 2}\,dt$$

65. Suppose $F(x)$ is the integral function $F(x) = \displaystyle\int_{u(x)}^{v(x)} f(t)\,dt$. What is $F'(x)$? This result is called *Leibniz' rule*.

66. Suppose $F(x) = \displaystyle\int_{-x}^{x} e^t\,dt$. Find $F'(x)$.

5.5 Integration by Substitution

IN THIS SECTION substitution with indefinite integration, substitution with definite integration

SUBSTITUTION WITH INDEFINITE INTEGRATION

Recall that according to the chain rule, the derivative of $(x^2 + 3x + 5)^9$ is

$$\frac{d}{dx}(x^2 + 3x + 5)^9 = 9(x^2 + 3x + 5)^8(2x + 3)$$

Thus,

$$\int 9(x^2 + 3x + 5)^8(2x + 3)\,dx = (x^2 + 3x + 5)^9 + C$$

Note that the product is of the form $g(u)\dfrac{du}{dx}$ where, in this case, $g(u) = 9u^8$ and $u = x^2 + 3x + 5$. The following theorem generalizes this procedure by showing how products of the form $g(u)\dfrac{du}{dx}$ can be integrated by reversing the chain rule.

THEOREM 5.9   Integration by substitution

Let f, g, and u be differentiable functions of x such that

$$f(x) = g(u)\frac{du}{dx}$$

Then

$$\int f(x)\, dx = \int g(u)\frac{du}{dx}\, dx = \int g(u)\, du = G(u) + C$$

where G is an antiderivative of g.

Proof   If G is an antiderivative of g, then $G'(u) = g(u)$ and, by the chain rule,

$$f(x) = \frac{d}{dx}[G(u)] = G'(u)\frac{du}{dx} = g(u)\frac{du}{dx}$$

Integrating both sides of this equation, we obtain

$$\int f(x)\, dx = \int \left[g(u)\frac{du}{dx} \right] dx = \int \left[\frac{d}{dx}G(u) \right] dx = G(u) + C$$

as required.   ❑

EXAMPLE 1   Indefinite integral by substitution

Find $\displaystyle\int 9(x^2 + 3x + 5)^8(2x + 3)\, dx$.

Solution

Look at the integral and make the observations as shown in the boxes:

If $u = x^2 + 3x + 5$,
$\boxed{\text{Let } u = x^2 + 3x + 5.}$ ← then $du = (2x + 3)\, dx$.

$$\int 9\underbrace{(x^2 + 3x + 5)^8}_{\boxed{\text{This is } g(u).}} \underbrace{(2x + 3)\, dx}_{\boxed{\text{This is } du.}} = \int 9u^8\, du$$

Now complete the integration of $g(u)$ and, when you are finished, back-substitute to express u in terms of x:

$$\int 9u^8\, du = 9\left(\frac{u^9}{9} \right) + C = (x^2 + 3x + 5)^9 + C \qquad ■$$

EXAMPLE 2   Finding an integral by substitution

Find $\displaystyle\int (2x + 7)^5\, dx$.

Solution

$$\int (2x + 7)^5\, dx = \int u^5 \left(\tfrac{1}{2}\, du \right) \qquad \text{Note: If } du = 2\, dx \text{, then } dx = \tfrac{1}{2}\, du.$$

$\boxed{\text{Let } u = 2x + 7 \text{, so } du = 2\, dx.}$

$$= \tfrac{1}{2}\left[\tfrac{1}{6}u^6 \right] + C \qquad \text{Power rule for integrals}$$

$$= \tfrac{1}{12}(2x + 7)^6 + C \qquad \text{Replace } u = 2x + 7. \qquad ■$$

When choosing a substitution to evaluate $\int f(x)\,dx$, where $f(x)$ is a composite function $f(x) = g(u(x))$, it is usually a good idea to pick the "inner" function $u = u(x)$. In Example 2, we chose $u = 2x + 7$, **NOT** the entire power $(2x + 7)^5$.

When making a substitution $u = u(x)$, remember that $du = u'(x)\,dx$, so you cannot simply replace dx by du in the transformed integral. For example, when you use the substitution $u = \sin x$, you have $du = \cos x\,dx$ and then replace the entire expression $\cos x\,dx$ by du in the transformed integral, as shown in the following example.

EXAMPLE 3   Substitution with a trigonometric function

Find $\int (4 - 2\cos\theta)^3 \sin\theta\,d\theta$.

Solution

Let $u = 4 - 2\cos\theta$, so $\dfrac{du}{d\theta} = -2(-\sin\theta) = 2\sin\theta$ and $d\theta = \dfrac{du}{2\sin\theta}$; substitute:

$$\int (4 - 2\cos\theta)^3 \sin\theta\,d\theta = \int u^3 \sin\theta \frac{du}{2\sin\theta} = \frac{1}{2}\int u^3\,du$$

$$= \frac{1}{2}\left(\frac{u^4}{4}\right) + C = \frac{1}{8}(4 - 2\cos\theta)^4 + C \qquad \blacksquare$$

Note: We will use a shorthand notation for substitution by placing a "box" under the integrand as follows:

$$\int (4 - 2\cos\theta)^3 \sin\theta\,d\theta = \int u^3 \sin\theta \frac{d\theta}{2\sin\theta}$$
$$\boxed{u = 4 - 2\cos\theta;\ du = -2(-\sin\theta)\,d\theta}$$

This notation is used in the following example.

EXAMPLE 4   Substitution in an exponential integral

Evaluate $\int xe^{4-x^2}\,dx$.

Solution

$$\int xe^{4-x^2}\,dx = \int e^u\left(-\tfrac{1}{2}\,du\right)$$
$$\boxed{u = 4 - x^2;\ du = -2x\,dx}$$
$$= -\tfrac{1}{2}e^u + C$$
$$= -\tfrac{1}{2}e^{4-x^2} + C \qquad \blacksquare$$

WARNING   When using the method of substitution, all terms involving x in the original integral $\int f(x)\,dx$ must be converted into terms involving u in the transformed integral $\int g(u)\,du$. That is, after you have made your substitution and simplified, there should be no "leftover" x-values in the integrand.

EXAMPLE 5   Substitution with leftover x-values

Find $\int x(4x - 5)^3\,dx$.

Solution

$$\int x(4x-5)^3\,dx = \int xu^3 \left(\frac{du}{4}\right) = \frac{1}{4}\int xu^3\,du$$

$$\boxed{u = 4x-5;\ du = 4\,dx}$$
$$\text{There is a leftover } x\text{-value.}$$

We are not ready to integrate until the leftover x-term has been eliminated. Because $u = 4x - 5$, we can solve for x:

$$x = \frac{u+5}{4}$$

so

$$\frac{1}{4}\int xu^3\,du = \frac{1}{4}\int \left(\frac{u+5}{4}\right)u^3\,du = \frac{1}{16}\int (u^4 + 5u^3)\,du$$

$$= \frac{1}{16}\left(\frac{u^5}{5} + 5\frac{u^4}{4}\right) + C = \frac{1}{80}(4x-5)^5 + \frac{5}{64}(4x-5)^4 + C \quad \blacksquare$$

Note: Always introduce the constant of integration immediately after the last integration.

The next example derives formulas that will be used many times throughout the text, often enough, in fact, that you should remember them or mark them for future reference.

EXAMPLE 6   Integral formulas for the tangent and cotangent functions

Show that $\int \tan x\,dx = -\ln|\cos x| + C$ and $\int \cot x\,dx = \ln|\sin x| + C$.

Solution

$$\int \tan x\,dx = \int \frac{\sin x}{\cos x}\,dx \qquad \text{Trigonometric identity } \tan x = \frac{\sin x}{\cos x}$$

$$= \int \left(\frac{1}{\cos x}\right)(\sin x\,dx) \qquad \text{Let } u = \cos x,\, du = -\sin x\,dx.$$

$$= -\int \frac{du}{u}$$

$$= -\ln|u| + C$$

$$= -\ln|\cos x| + C$$

This can also be written as $\ln\left|(\cos x)^{-1}\right| + C = \ln|\sec x| + C$. Similarly,

$$\int \cot x\,dx = \int \frac{\cos x}{\sin x}\,dx = \ln|\sin x| + C. \qquad \blacksquare$$

Here is a problem in which the rate of change of a quantity is known and we use the method of substitution to find an expression for the quantity itself.

EXAMPLE 7   Find the volume when the rate of flow is known

Water is flowing into a tank at the rate of $\sqrt{3t+1}$ ft³/min. If the tank is empty when $t = 0$, how much water does it contain 5 min later?

Solution

Because the rate at which the volume V is changing is dV/dt,

$$\frac{dV}{dt} = \sqrt{3t+1}$$

$$V = \int \sqrt{3t+1}\, dt = \int \sqrt{u}\,\frac{du}{3}$$

$$\boxed{u = 3t+1;\, du = 3\, dt}$$

$$V = \frac{1}{3} \int u^{1/2}\, du$$

$$= \frac{1}{3} \cdot \frac{2}{3} u^{3/2} + C$$

$$V = \tfrac{2}{9}(3t+1)^{3/2} + C$$

$$V(0) = \tfrac{2}{9}(3\cdot 0+1)^{3/2} + C = 0 \quad \text{so that} \quad C = -\tfrac{2}{9} \qquad \text{The initial volume is } 0.$$

$$V(t) = \tfrac{2}{9}(3t+1)^{3/2} - \tfrac{2}{9} \quad \text{and} \quad V(5) = \tfrac{2}{9}(16)^{3/2} - \tfrac{2}{9} = 14$$

The tank contains 14 ft^3 of water after 5 minutes. ■

SUBSTITUTION WITH DEFINITE INTEGRATION

Example 7 could be considered as a definite integral:

$$\int_0^5 \sqrt{3t+1}\, dt = \frac{2}{9}(3t+1)^{3/2}\Big|_0^5 = \tfrac{2}{9}(16)^{3/2} - \tfrac{2}{9}(1)^{3/2} = 14$$

Notice that the definite integral eliminates the need for finding C. Furthermore, the following theorem eliminates the need for returning to the original variable (even though sometimes it is more convenient to do so).

THEOREM 5.10 Substitution with the definite integral

If $f(u)$ is a continuous function of u and $u(x)$ is a differentiable function of x, then

$$\int_a^b f[u(x)]u'(x)\, dx = \int_{u(a)}^{u(b)} f(u)\, du$$

Proof Let $F(u) = \int f(u)\, du$ be an antiderivative of $f(u)$. Then the first fundamental theorem of calculus tells us that

$$\int_a^b f[u(x)]u'(x)\, dx = F[u(x)]\big|_{x=a}^{x=b} = F[u(b)] - F[u(a)]$$

But since $F(u)$ is an antiderivative of $f(u)$, it also follows that

$$\int_{u(a)}^{u(b)} f(u)\, du = F(u)\big|_{u=u(a)}^{u=u(b)} = F[u(b)] - F[u(a)]$$

Thus,

$$\int_a^b f[u(x)]u'(x)\, dx = \int_{u(a)}^{u(b)} f(u)\, du \qquad \qquad \square$$

We now have two valid methods for evaluating a definite integral of the form $\int_a^b f[u(x)]u'(x)\,dx$:

1. Use substitution to evaluate the indefinite integral and then evaluate it between the limits of integration $x = a$ and $x = b$.
2. Change the limits of integration to conform with the change of variable $u = u(x)$ and evaluate the transformed definite integral between the limits of integration $u = u(a)$ and $u = u(b)$.

These two methods are illustrated in Example 8.

EXAMPLE 8 Substitution with the definite integral

Evaluate $\int_1^2 (4x - 5)^3\,dx$.

Solution

Method I: We first use a substitution with an indefinite integral.

$$\int (4x - 5)^3\,dx = \int u^3 \left(\frac{1}{4}\,du\right) = \frac{1}{4}\left(\frac{u^4}{4}\right) + C = \frac{1}{16}(4x - 5)^4 + C$$

$$\boxed{\text{Let } u = 4x - 5;\, du = 4\,dx}$$

Now evaluate the definite integral of $f(x)$ between $x = 1$ and $x = 2$ by using the fundamental theorem of calculus:

$$\int_1^2 (4x - 5)^3\,dx = \frac{1}{16}(4x - 5)^4 \Big|_{x=1}^{x=2}$$

$$= \frac{1}{16}[4(2) - 5]^4 - \frac{1}{16}[4(1) - 5]^4$$

$$= \frac{1}{16}(81) - \frac{1}{16}(1)$$

$$= 5$$

Method II: This is similar to method I, except that as part of the integration process, we change the limits of integration when we are doing the substitution.

$$\boxed{\text{Let } u = 4x - 5;\, du = 4\,dx.}$$

If $x = 2$, then $u = 4(2) - 5 = 3$.

$$\downarrow \qquad\qquad \downarrow$$

$$\int_1^2 (4x - 5)^3\,dx = \int_{-1}^3 u^3\,\frac{du}{4}$$

$$\uparrow \qquad\qquad \uparrow$$

If $x = 1$, then $u = 4(1) - 5 = -1$.

WARNING You cannot change variables and keep the orginal limits of integration because the limits of integration are expressed in terms of the variable of integration.

$$= \frac{1}{4} \cdot \frac{u^4}{4} \Big|_{-1}^3$$

$$= \frac{1}{16}(81 - 1) = 5$$

∎

5.5 PROBLEM SET

A *Problems 1–8 present pairs of integration problems, one of which will require substitution and one of which will not. As you are working these problems, think about when substitution may be appropriate.*

1. a. $\int_0^4 (2t+4)\,dt$ **b.** $\int_0^4 (2t+4)^{-1/2}\,dt$

2. a. $\int_0^{\pi/2} \sin\theta\,d\theta$ **b.** $\int_0^{\pi/2} \sin 2\theta\,d\theta$

3. a. $\int_0^{\pi} \cos t\,dt$ **b.** $\int_0^{\sqrt{\pi}} t\cos t^2\,dt$

4. a. $\int_0^4 \sqrt{x}\,dx$ **b.** $\int_{-4}^0 \sqrt{-x}\,dx$

5. a. $\int_0^{16} \sqrt[4]{x}\,dx$ **b.** $\int_{-16}^0 \sqrt[4]{-x}\,dx$

6. a. $\int x(3x^2-5)\,dx$ **b.** $\int x(3x^2-5)^{50}\,dx$

7. a. $\int x^2\sqrt{2x^3}\,dx$ **b.** $\int x^2\sqrt{2x^3-5}\,dx$

8. a. $\int \dfrac{dx}{\sqrt{1-x^2}}$ **b.** $\int \dfrac{x\,dx}{\sqrt{1-x^2}}$

Use substitution to evaluate the indefinite integrals in Problems 9–34.

9. $\int (2x+3)^4\,dx$ **10.** $\int \sqrt{3t-5}\,dt$

11. $\int [\tan(x^2+5x+3)(2x+5)]\,dx$ **12.** $\int (11-2x)^{-4/5}\,dx$

13. $\int (x^2-\cos 3x)\,dx$ **14.** $\int \csc^2 5t\,dt$

15. $\int \sin(4-x)\,dx$ **16.** $\int \cot[\ln(x^2+1)]\dfrac{2x\,dx}{x^2+1}$

17. $\int \sqrt{t}(t^{3/2}+5)^3\,dt$ **18.** $\int \dfrac{(6x-9)\,dx}{(x^2-3x+5)^3}$

19. $\int x\sin(3+x^2)\,dx$ **20.** $\int \sin^3 t\cos t\,dt$

21. $\int \dfrac{x\,dx}{2x^2+3}$ **22.** $\int \dfrac{x^2\,dx}{x^3+1}$

23. $\int x\sqrt{2x^2+1}\,dx$ **24.** $\int \dfrac{4x\,dx}{2x+1}$

25. $\int \sqrt{x}e^{x\sqrt{x}}\,dx$ **26.** $\int \dfrac{e^{\sqrt[3]{x}}\,dx}{x^{2/3}}$

27. $\int x(x^2+4)^{1/2}\,dx$ **28.** $\int x^3(x^2+4)^{1/2}\,dx$

29. $\int \dfrac{\ln x}{x}\,dx$ **30.** $\int \dfrac{\ln(x+1)}{x+1}\,dx$

31. $\int \dfrac{dx}{\sqrt{x}(\sqrt{x}+7)}$ **32.** $\int \dfrac{dx}{x^{2/3}(\sqrt[3]{x}+1)}$

33. $\int \dfrac{e^t\,dt}{e^t+1}$ **34.** $\int \dfrac{e^{\sqrt{t}}\,dt}{\sqrt{t}(e^{\sqrt{t}}+1)}$

Evaluate the definite integrals given in Problems 35–44. Approximate the answers to Problems 43 and 44 to two significant digits.

35. $\int_0^1 \dfrac{5x^2\,dx}{2x^3+1}$ **36.** $\int_1^4 \dfrac{e^{-\sqrt{x}}\,dx}{\sqrt{x}}$

37. $\int_{-\ln 2}^{\ln 2} \dfrac{1}{2}(e^x-e^{-x})\,dx$ **38.** $\int_0^2 (e^x-e^{-x})^2\,dx$

39. $\int_1^2 \dfrac{e^{1/x}}{x^2}\,dx$ **40.** $\int_0^2 x\sqrt{2x+1}\,dx$

41. $\int_0^{\pi/6} \tan 2x\,dx$ **42.** $\int_0^1 x^2(x^3+9)^{1/2}\,dx$

43. $\int_0^5 \dfrac{0.58}{1+e^{-0.2x}}\,dx$ **44.** $\int_0^{12} \dfrac{5,000}{1+10e^{-t/5}}\,dt$

45. HISTORICAL QUEST   Johann Peter Gustav Lejeune Dirichlet was a professor of mathematics at the University of Berlin and is known for his role in formulating a rigorous foundation for calculus. He was not known as a good teacher. His nephew wrote that the mathematics instruction he received from Dirichlet was the most dreadful experience of his life. Howard Eves tells of the time Dirichlet was to deliver a lecture on definite integrals, but because of illness he posted the following note:

LEJEUNE DIRICHLET
1805–1859

> *Because of illness I cannot lecture today*
>
> *Dirichlet*

The students then doctored the note to read as follows:

> *Michaelmas*
> $\int$ *Because of illness I cannot lecture today*   *d (1 Frdor)*
> *Easter*
>
> *Dirichlet*

Michaelmas and Easter were school holidays, and 1 Frdor (Friedrichsd'or) was the customary honorarium for a semester's worth of lectures. ∎

a. What is the answer when you integrate the student-doctored note?

b. The so-called *Dirichlet function* is often used for counterexamples in calculus. Look up the definition of this function. What special property does it have?

B *Find the area of the region under the curves given in Problems 46–49.*

46. $y=t\sqrt{t^2+9}$ on $[0,4]$ **47.** $y=\dfrac{1}{t^2}\sqrt{5-\dfrac{1}{t}}$ on $[\frac{1}{5},1]$

48. $y = x(x-1)^{1/3}$ on $[2, 9]$ **49.** $y = \dfrac{x}{\sqrt{x^2+1}}$ on $[1, 3]$

50. a. In Section 5.3 (Problem 40), you were asked to prove that if f is continuous and **odd** [that is, $f(-x) = -f(x)$] on the interval $[-a, a]$, then

$$\int_{-a}^{a} f(x)\,dx = 0$$

b. In Section 5.2 (Problem 33), you were asked to find a counterexample or informally show that if f is continuous and **even** [$f(-x) = f(x)$] on the interval $[-a, a]$, then

$$\int_{-a}^{a} f(x)\,dx = 2\int_{0}^{a} f(x)\,dx = 2\int_{-a}^{0} f(x)\,dx$$

For this problem, use the properties of integrals to prove each of these statements.

Use the results of Problem 50 to evaluate the integrals given in Problems 51–54.

51. $\displaystyle\int_{-\pi}^{\pi} \sin x\,dx$ **52.** $\displaystyle\int_{-\pi/2}^{\pi/2} \cos x\,dx$

53. $\displaystyle\int_{-3}^{3} x\sqrt{x^4+1}\,dx$ **54.** $\displaystyle\int_{-1}^{1} \dfrac{\sin x\,dx}{x^2+1}$

55. In each of the following cases, determine whether the given relationship is true or false.

a. $\displaystyle\int_{-175}^{175} (7x^{1001} + 14x^{99})\,dx = 0$

b. $\displaystyle\int_{0}^{\pi} \sin^2 x\,dx = \int_{0}^{\pi} \cos^2 x\,dx$

c. $\displaystyle\int_{-\pi/2}^{\pi/2} \cos x\,dx = \int_{-\pi}^{0} \sin x\,dx$

56. The slope at each point (x, y) on the graph of $y = F(x)$ is given by $x(x^2-1)^{1/3}$, and the graph passes through the point $(3, 1)$. Use this information to find F. Sketch the graph of F.

57. The slope at each point (x, y) on the graph of $y = F(x)$ is given by $\dfrac{2x}{1-3x^2}$. What is $F(x)$ if the graph passes through $(0, 5)$?

58. A particle moves along the t-axis in such a way that at time t, its velocity is $v(t) = t^2(t^3-8)^{1/3}$.

a. At what time does the particle turn around?

b. If the particle starts at a position which we denote as 1, where does it turn around?

59. A rectangular storage tank has a square base 10 ft on a side. Water is flowing into the tank at the rate modeled by the function

$$R(t) = t(3t^2+1)^{-1/2} \quad \text{ft}^3/\text{s}$$

at time t seconds. If the tank is empty at time $t = 0$, how much water does it contain 4 sec later? What is the depth of the water (to the nearest quarter inch) at that time?

60. Journal Problem   *College Mathematics Journal.*[*]   ■ Evaluate

$$\int [(x^2-1)(x+1)]^{-2/3}\,dx$$

61. Modeling Problem   A group of environmentalists model the rate at which the ozone level is changing in a suburb of Los Angeles by the function

$$L'(t) = \dfrac{0.24 - 0.03t}{\sqrt{36 + 16t - t^2}}$$

parts per million per hour (ppm/h) t hours after 7:00 A.M.

a. Express the ozone level $L(t)$ as a function of t if L is 4 ppm at 7:00 A.M.

b. Use the graphing utility of your calculator to find the time between 7:00 A.M. and 7:00 P.M. when the highest level of ozone occurs. What is the highest level?

c. Use your graphing utility or another utility of your calculator to determine a second time during the day when the ozone level is the same as it is at 11:00 A.M.

●62. A *logistic* function is one of the form $Q(t) = \dfrac{B}{1 + Ae^{-rt}}$.

Evaluate $\displaystyle\int Q(t)\,dt$.

*Vol. 20, No. 4, Sept. 1989, p. 343. Problem by Murray Klamkin.

5.6   Introduction to Differential Equations

IN THIS SECTION   introduction and terminology, direction fields, separable differential equations, modeling exponential growth and decay, orthogonal trajectories, modeling fluid flow through an orifice, modeling the motion of a projectile: escape velocity

The study of differential equations is as old as calculus itself. Today, it would be virtually impossible to make a serious study of physics, astronomy, chemistry, or engineering without encountering physical models based on differential equations. In addition, differential equations are beginning to appear more frequently in the biological and social sciences, especially in economics. We begin by introducing some basic terminology and examining a few modeling procedures.

INTRODUCTION AND TERMINOLOGY

Any equation that contains a derivative or differential is called a **differential equation**. For example, the equations

$$\frac{dy}{dx} = 3x^3 + 5, \quad \frac{dP}{dt} = kP^2, \quad \left(\frac{dy}{dx}\right)^2 + 3\frac{dy}{dx} + 2y = xy, \quad \frac{d^2x}{dt^2} + 2\frac{dx}{dt} + 5t = \sin t$$

are all differential equations.

Many practical situations, especially those involving rates, can be described mathematically by differential equations. For example, the assumption that population P grows at a rate proportional to its size can be expressed by the differential equation

$$\frac{dP}{dt} = kP$$

where t is time and k is the constant of proportionality.

A **solution** of a given differential equation is a function that satisfies the equation. A **general solution** is a characterization of all possible solutions of the equation. We say that the differential equation is **solved** when we find a general solution.

For example, $y = x^2$ is a solution of the differential equation

$$\frac{dy}{dx} = 2x$$

because

$$\frac{dy}{dx} = \frac{d}{dx}(y) = \frac{d}{dx}(x^2) = 2x$$

Moreover, because any solution of this equation must be an indefinite integral of $2x$, it follows that

$$y = \int 2x\,dx = x^2 + C$$

is the general solution of the differential equation.

EXAMPLE 1 Verifying that a given function is a solution to a differential equation

If $4x - 3y^2 = 10$, verify that $\dfrac{dy}{dx} = \dfrac{2}{3y}$.

Solution

$$4x - 3y^2 = 10$$

$$\frac{d}{dx}(4x - 3y^2) = \frac{d}{dx}(10) \qquad \text{Take the derivative of both sides.}$$

$$4 - 6y\frac{dy}{dx} = 0 \qquad \text{Don't forget the chain rule, since } y \text{ is a function of } x.$$

$$\frac{dy}{dx} = \frac{4}{6y} = \frac{2}{3y} \qquad \text{Solve for } \frac{dy}{dx}. \qquad \blacksquare$$

EXAMPLE 2 Finding future revenue

An oil well that yields 300 barrels of crude oil a day will run dry in 3 years. It is estimated that t days from now the price of the crude oil will be $p(t) = 30 + 0.3\sqrt{t}$ dollars per barrel. If the oil is sold as soon as it is extracted from the ground, what will be the total future revenue from the well?

Solution

Let $R(t)$ denote the total revenue up to time t. Then the rate of change of revenue is $\dfrac{dR}{dt}$, the number of dollars received per barrel is $p(t) = 30 + 0.3\sqrt{t}$, and the number of barrels sold per day is 300. Thus, we have

$$\begin{bmatrix} \text{RATE OF CHANGE} \\ \text{OF TOTAL REVENUE} \end{bmatrix} = \begin{bmatrix} \text{NUMBER OF DOLLARS} \\ \text{PER BARREL} \end{bmatrix}\begin{bmatrix} \text{NUMBER OF BARRELS} \\ \text{SOLD PER DAY} \end{bmatrix}$$

$$\frac{dR}{dt} = (30 + 0.3\sqrt{t})(300)$$

$$= 9{,}000 + 90\sqrt{t}$$

This is actually a statement of the chain rule: $\dfrac{dR}{dt} = \dfrac{dR}{dB} \cdot \dfrac{dB}{dt}$, where B denotes the number of barrels extracted and R denotes the revenue. It is often helpful to use the chain rule in this way when setting up differential equations.

We solve this differential equation by integration:

$$R = \int \frac{dR}{dt}\, dt = \int (9{,}000 + 90\sqrt{t})\, dt$$

$$R(t) = 9{,}000t + 60t^{3/2} + C$$

Since $R(0) = 0$, it follows that $C = 0$. We also are given that the well will run dry in 3 years or 1,095 days, so that the total revenue obtained during the life of the well is

$$R(1{,}095) = 9{,}000(1{,}095) + 60(1{,}095)^{3/2}$$

$$\approx 12{,}029{,}064.52$$

The total future revenue is approximately \$12 million. ∎

DIRECTION FIELDS

We can use slope fields to help with a visualization of a differential equation. In Section 5.1 we looked at small segments with slope defined by the derivative of some function. The collection of all such line segments is called the *slope field* or **direction field** of the differential equation. Today, with the assistance of computers, we can sometimes draw the direction field in order to obtain a particular solution (or a family of solutions) as shown in the following example.

EXAMPLE 3 Finding a solution, given the direction field

The direction field for the differential equation

$$\frac{dy}{dx} = y - x^2$$

is shown in Figure 5.22.

a. Sketch a solution to the initial value problem passing through $(2, 1)$.
b. Sketch a solution to the initial value problem passing through $(0, 1)$.

Solution

a. The initial value $y(2) = 1$ means the solution passes through $(2, 1)$ and is shown in Figure 5.23a.
b. Since $y(0) = 1$, the solution passes through $(0, 1)$, as shown in Figure 5.23b.

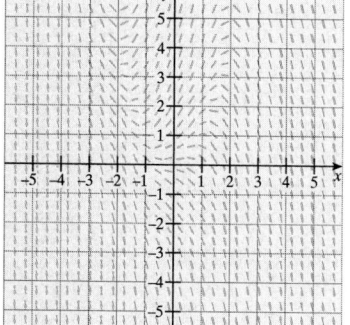

Figure 5.22 Direction field for $y' = y - x^2$

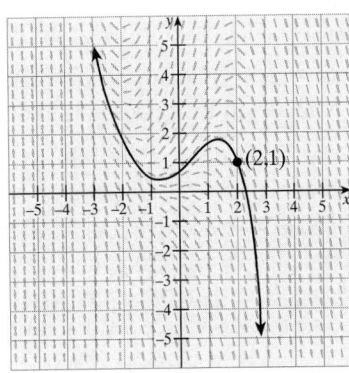 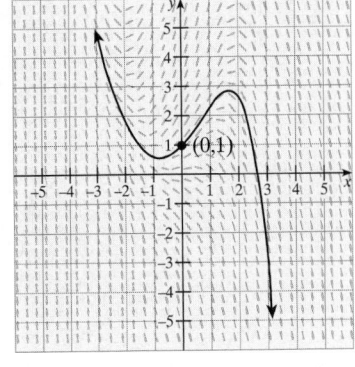

a. Solution passes through $(2, 1)$ **b.** Solution passes through $(0, 1)$

Figure 5.23   Particular solutions from a given direction field   ■

SEPARABLE DIFFERENTIAL EQUATIONS

Solving a differential equation is often a complicated process. However, many important equations can be expressed in the form

$$\frac{dy}{dx} = \frac{g(x)}{f(y)}$$

To solve such an equation, first separate the variables into the differential form

$$f(y)\,dy = g(x)\,dx$$

and then integrate both sides separately to obtain

$$\int f(y)\,dy = \int g(x)\,dx$$

A differential equation expressible in the form $dy/dx = g(x)/f(y)$ is said to be **separable**. This procedure is illustrated in Example 4.

EXAMPLE 4   Solving a separable differential equation

Solve $\dfrac{dy}{dx} = \dfrac{x}{y}$.

Solution
$$\frac{dy}{dx} = \frac{x}{y}$$
$$y\,dy = x\,dx$$
$$\int y\,dy = \int x\,dx$$
$$\tfrac{1}{2}y^2 + C_1 = \tfrac{1}{2}x^2 + C_2$$
$$x^2 - y^2 = C \qquad \text{where } C = 2(C_1 - C_2).$$
■

Notice the treatment of constants in Example 4. Because all constants can be combined into a single constant, it is customary not to write $2(C_1 - C_2)$ but rather to simply replace all the arbitrary constants in the problem by a single arbitrary constant, C, immediately after the last integral is found.

The remainder of this section is devoted to selected applications involving separable differential equations.

MODELING EXPONENTIAL GROWTH AND DECAY

A process is said to undergo **exponential change** if the relative rate of change of the process is modeled by a constant; in other words,

$$\frac{Q'(t)}{Q(t)} = k \quad \text{or} \quad \frac{dQ}{dt} = kQ(t)$$

If the constant k is positive, the exponential change is called **growth**, and if k is negative, it is called **decay**. Exponential growth occurs in certain populations, and exponential decay occurs in the disintegration of radioactive substances.

To solve the growth/decay equation, separate the variables and integrate both sides.

$$\frac{dQ}{dt} = kQ$$

$$\int \frac{dQ}{Q} = \int k \, dt$$

$$\ln|Q| = kt + C_1$$

$$e^{kt+C_1} = Q \qquad \textit{Definition of natural logarithm}$$

$$e^{kt}e^{C_1} = Q$$

Thus, $Q = Ce^{kt}$, where $C = e^{C_1}$. Finally, if we let Q_0 be the initial amount (that is, when $t = 0$), we see that

$$Q_0 = Ce^0 \quad \text{or} \quad C = Q_0, \quad \text{so} \quad Q(t) = Q_0 e^{kt}$$

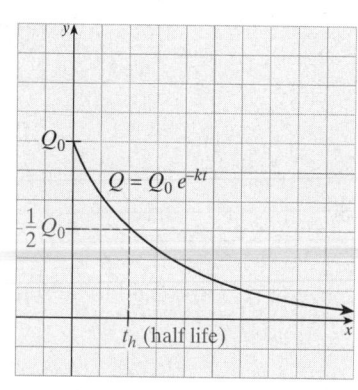

Figure 5.24 The decay curve for a radioactive substance

Growth/Decay Equation

The **growth/decay equation** of a substance is

$$Q(t) = Q_0 e^{kt}$$

where $Q(t)$ is the amount of the substance present at time t, Q_0 is the initial amount of the substance, and k is a constant that depends on the substance. If $k > 0$, it is a *growth* equation; if $k < 0$, it is a *decay* equation.

The graph of $Q = Q_0 e^{kt}$ for $k < 0$ is shown in Figure 5.24. In Figure 5.24 we have also indicated the time t_h required for half of a given substance to disintegrate. The time t_h is called the **half-life** of the substance, and it provides a measure of the substance's rate of disintegration.

EXAMPLE 5   Amount of a radioactive substance present

A particular radioactive substance has a half-life of 600 yr. Find k for this substance and determine how much of a 50-g sample will remain after 125 yr.

Solution

From the decay equation,

$$Q(t) = Q_0 e^{kt}$$

$$\frac{Q(t)}{Q_0} = e^{kt}$$

$$\frac{1}{2} = e^{k(600)} \qquad \textit{Half-life is 600 years.}$$

$$k(600) = \ln \frac{1}{2} \qquad \textit{Definition of logarithm}$$

$$k = \frac{\ln \frac{1}{2}}{600} \approx -0.0011552453$$

Next, to see how much of a 50-g sample will remain after 125 yr, substitute $Q_0 = 50$, $k = -0.0011552453$, and $t = 125$ into the decay equation:

$$Q(125) \approx 50e^{-0.0011552453(125)} \approx 43.27682805$$

There will be about 43 g present. ■

One of the more interesting applications of radioactive decay is a technique known as **carbon dating**, which is used by geologists, anthropologists, and archaeologists to estimate the age of various specimens.* The technique is based on the fact that all animal and vegetable systems (whether living or dead) contain both stable carbon ^{12}C and a radioactive isotope ^{14}C. Scientists assume that the ratio of ^{14}C to ^{12}C in the air has remained approximately constant throughout history. Living systems absorb carbon dioxide from the air, so the ratio of ^{14}C to ^{12}C in a living system is the same as that in the air itself. When a living system dies, the absorption of carbon dioxide ceases. The ^{12}C already in the system remains while the ^{14}C decays, and the ratio of ^{14}C to ^{12}C decreases exponentially. The half-life of ^{14}C is approximately 5,730 years. The ratio of ^{14}C to ^{12}C in a specimen t years after it was alive is approximately

$$R = R_0 e^{kt}$$

where $k = \dfrac{\ln(1/2)}{5,730}$ and R_0 is the ratio of ^{14}C to ^{12}C in the atmosphere. By comparing $R(t)$ with R_0, scientists can estimate the age of the object. Here is an example.

EXAMPLE 6 Modeling Problem: Carbon dating

An archaeologist has found a specimen in which the ratio of ^{14}C to ^{12}C is 20% the ratio found in the atmosphere. Approximately how old is the specimen?

Solution

The age of the specimen is the value of t for which $R(t) = 0.20R_0$:

$$0.20R_0 = R_0 e^{kt}$$
$$0.20 = e^{kt}$$
$$kt = \ln 0.20$$
$$t = \frac{1}{k}\ln 0.2 \qquad k = \frac{\ln(1/2)}{5,730}$$
$$\approx 13{,}304.64798$$

The specimen is approximately 13,000 yr old. ■

ORTHOGONAL TRAJECTORIES

A curve that intersects each member of a given family of curves at right angles is called an **orthogonal trajectory** of that family and is shown in Figure 5.25. Orthogonal families arise in many applications. For example, in thermodynamics, the heat flow across a planar surface is orthogonal to the curves of constant temperature, called *isotherms*. In the theory of fluid flow, the flow lines are orthogonal trajectories of *velocity potential curves*. The basic procedure for finding orthogonal trajectories involves differential equations and is demonstrated in Example 7.

---

*Carbon dating is used primarily for estimating the age of relatively "recent" specimens. For example, it was used (along with other methods) to determine that the Dead Sea Scrolls were written and deposited in the Caves of Qumran approximately 2,000 years ago. For dating older specimens, it is better to use techniques based on radioactive substances with longer half-lives. In particular, potassium 40 is often used as a "clock" for events that occurred between 5 and 15 million years ago. Paleoanthropologists find this substance especially valuable because it often occurs in volcanic deposits and can be used to date specimens trapped in such deposits. See Mathematical Essay 5 on page 352.

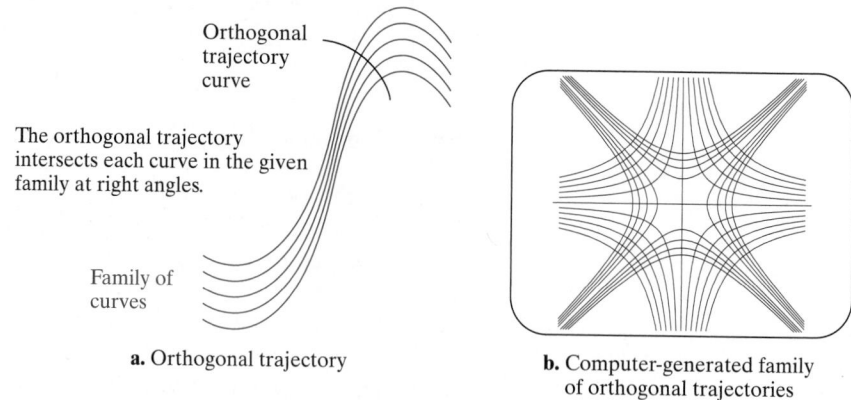

a. Orthogonal trajectory

b. Computer-generated family
of orthogonal trajectories

Figure 5.25   Orthogonal trajectories

EXAMPLE 7   Finding orthogonal trajectories

Find the orthogonal trajectories of the family of curves of the form $xy = C$.

Solution

We are seeking a family of curves. Each curve in that family intersects each curve in
the family $xy = C$ at right angles, as shown in Figure 5.26. Assume that a typical
point on a given curve in the family $xy = C$ has coordinates (x, y) and that a typical
point on the orthogonal trajectory curve has coordinates (X, Y).*

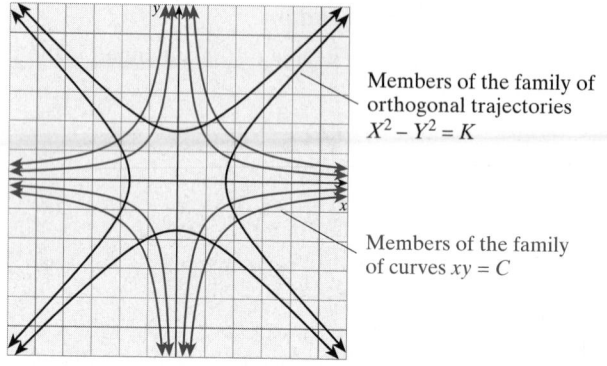

Members of the family of
orthogonal trajectories
$X^2 - Y^2 = K$

Members of the family
of curves $xy = C$

Figure 5.26   The family of curves $xy = C$ and their orthogonal trajectories

Let P be a point where a particular curve of the form $xy = C$ intersects the
orthogonal trajectory curve. At P, we have $x = X$ and $y = Y$, and the slope dY/dX
of the orthogonal trajectory is the same as the negative reciprocal of the slope dy/dx
of the curve $xy = C$. Using implicit differentiation, we find

$$xy = C$$

$$x\frac{dy}{dx} + y = 0 \qquad \text{Product rule}$$

$$\frac{dy}{dx} = \frac{-y}{x}$$

---

*We use uppercase letters for one kind of curve and lowercase for the other to make it easier to tell which
curve is being mentioned at each stage of the following discussion.

Thus, at the point of intersection P, the slope $\dfrac{dY}{dX}$ of the orthogonal trajectory is

$$\frac{dY}{dX} = -\frac{1}{\dfrac{dy}{dx}} = -\frac{1}{\dfrac{-y}{x}} = \frac{x}{y} = \frac{X}{Y}$$

According to this equation, the coordinates (X, Y) of the orthogonal trajectory curve satisfy the separable differential equation

$$\frac{dY}{dX} = \frac{X}{Y}$$

discussed in Example 4. Using the result of that example, we see that the orthogonal trajectories of the family $xy = C$ are the curves in the family

$$X^2 - Y^2 = K$$

where K is a constant. The given family of curves $xy = C$ and the family of orthogonal trajectory curves $X^2 - Y^2 = K$ are shown in Figure 5.26. ■

MODELING FLUID FLOW THROUGH AN ORIFICE

Fluid has height h above a hole of area A_0.

Figure 5.27 The flow of a fluid through an orifice

Consider a tank that is filled with a fluid being slowly drained through a small, sharp-edged hole in its base, as shown in Figure 5.27. By using a principle of physics known as Torricelli's law,[†] we can show that the rate of discharge dV/dt at time t is proportional to the square root of the depth h at that time. Specifically, if all dimensions are given in terms of feet, the drain hole has area A_0, and the height above the hole is h at time t (seconds), then

$$\frac{dV}{dt} = -4.8 A_0 \sqrt{h}$$

is the rate of flow of water in cubic feet per second. This formula is used in Example 8.

EXAMPLE 8 Fluid flow through an orifice

A cylindrical tank (with a circular base) is filled with a liquid that is draining through a small circular hole in its base. If the tank is 9 ft high with radius 4 ft and the drain hole has radius 1 in., how long does it take for the tank to empty?

Solution

Because the drain hole is a circle of radius $\frac{1}{12}$ ft (= 1 in.), its area is $\pi r^2 = \pi \left(\frac{1}{12}\right)^2$, and the rate of flow is

$$\frac{dV}{dt} = -4.8 \left(\frac{\pi}{144}\right) \sqrt{h}$$

Because the tank is cylindrical, the amount of fluid in the tank at any particular time will form a cylinder of radius 4 ft and height h. Also, because we are using $g = 32$ ft/s^2, it is implied that the time, t, is measured in seconds. The volume of such a liquid cylinder is

$$V = \pi r^2 h = \pi (4)^2 h = 16 \pi h$$

[†]Torricelli's law says that the stream of liquid through the orifice has velocity $\sqrt{2gh}$, where $g = 32$ ft/s^2 is the acceleration due to gravity and h is the height of the liquid above the orifice. The factor 4.8 that appears in the rate of flow equation is required to compensate for the effect of friction.

and by differentiating both sides of this equation with respect to t, we obtain

$$\frac{dV}{dt} = 16\pi \frac{dh}{dt}$$

$$-4.8\left(\frac{\pi}{144}\right)\sqrt{h} = 16\pi\frac{dh}{dt} \qquad \text{Torricelli's law}$$

$$\frac{dh}{dt} = \frac{-4.8\sqrt{h}}{144(16)} \approx -0.0021\sqrt{h}$$

$$\frac{1}{\sqrt{h}}dh = -0.0021\,dt \qquad \text{Separate the variables.}$$

$$\int h^{-1/2}dh = \int(-0.0021)\,dt \qquad \text{Integrate both sides.}$$

$$2h^{1/2} + C_1 = -0.0021t + C_2$$

$$2\sqrt{h} = -0.0021t + C$$

To evaluate C, recall that the tank is full at time $t = 0$. Thus, $h = 9$ when $t = 0$, so

$$2\sqrt{9} = -0.0021(0) + C, \quad \text{or} \quad C = 6$$

and the general formula is

$$2\sqrt{h} = -0.0021t + 6$$

where time t is in seconds (because g is 32 ft/s^2).

Now we can find the depth of the fluid at any given time or the time at which a prescribed depth occurs. In particular, the tank is empty at the time t_e when $h = 0$. By substituting $h = 0$ into this formula we find

$$2\sqrt{0} = -0.0021t_e + 6 \quad \text{so that} \quad t_e \approx 2,880 \text{ sec}$$

Thus, roughly 48 min are required to drain the tank.   ∎

MODELING THE MOTION OF A PROJECTILE: ESCAPE VELOCITY

Consider a projectile that is launched with initial velocity v_0 from a planet's surface along a direct line through the center of the planet, as shown in Figure 5.28. We will find a general formula for the velocity of the projectile and the minimal value of v_0 required to guarantee that the projectile will escape the planet's gravitational attraction.

We assume that the only force acting on the projectile is that due to gravity, although in practice, factors such as air resistance must also be considered. With this assumption, Newton's law of gravitation can be used to show that when the projectile is at a distance s from the center of the planet, its acceleration is given by the formula

$$a = \frac{-gR^2}{s^2}$$

where R is the radius of the planet and g is the acceleration due to gravity at the planet's surface (see Problem 69).*

Our first goal is to express the velocity v of the projectile in terms of the height s. Because the projectile travels along a straight line, we know that

$$a = \frac{dv}{dt} \quad \text{and} \quad v = \frac{ds}{dt}$$

and by applying the chain rule, we see that

$$a = \frac{dv}{dt} = \frac{dv}{ds} \cdot \frac{ds}{dt} = \frac{dv}{ds}v$$

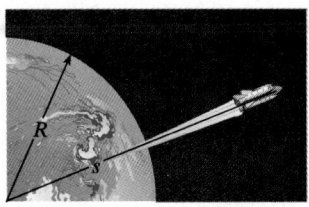

Figure 5.28 A projectile launched from the surface of a planet

---

*According to Newton's law of gravitation, the force of gravity acting on a projectile of mass m has magnitude $F = mk/s^2$, where k is constant. If this is the only force acting on the projectile, then $F = ma$, and we have $ma = F = mk/s^2$. By canceling the m's on each side of the equation, we obtain $a = k/s^2$.

Therefore, by substitution for a we have

$$\frac{dv}{ds}v = \frac{-gR^2}{s^2}$$

$$v\,dv = -gR^2 s^{-2}\,ds$$

$$\int v\,dv = \int -gR^2 s^{-2}\,ds$$

$$\tfrac{1}{2}v^2 + C_1 = gR^2 s^{-1} + C_2$$

$$v^2 = 2gR^2 s^{-1} + C$$

To evaluate the constant C, recall that the projectile was fired from the planet's surface with initial velocity v_0. Thus, $v = v_0$ when $s = R$, and by substitution

$$v_0^2 = 2gR^2 R^{-1} + C, \quad \text{which implies} \quad C = v_0^2 - 2gR$$

so

$$v^2 = 2gR^2 s^{-1} + v_0^2 - 2gR$$

Because the projectile is launched in a direction away from the center of the planet, we would expect it to keep moving in that direction until it stops. In other words, *the projectile will keep moving away from the planet until it reaches a point where $v = 0$.* Because $2gR^2 s^{-1} > 0$ for all $s > 0$, v^2 will always be positive if $v_0^2 - 2gR \geq 0$. On the other hand, if $v_0^2 - 2gR < 0$, then sooner or later v will become 0 and the projectile will eventually fall back to the surface of the planet.

Therefore, we conclude that the projectile will escape from the planet's gravitational attraction if $v_0^2 \geq 2gR$; that is, $v_0 \geq \sqrt{2gR}$. For this reason, the minimum speed for which this can occur, namely,

$$v_0 = \sqrt{2gR}$$

is called the **escape velocity** of the planet. In particular, for the earth, $R = 3{,}956$ mi and $g = 32$ ft/s$^2 = 0.00606$ mi/s^2, and the escape velocity is

$$v_0 = \sqrt{2gR} \approx \sqrt{2(0.00606)(3{,}956)} \approx 6.924357$$

The escape velocity for the earth is 6.92 mi/s.

5.6 PROBLEM SET

Ⓐ *Verify in Problems 1–8 that if y satisfies the prescribed relationship with x, then it will be a solution of the given differential equation.*

1. If $x^2 + y^2 = 7$, then $\dfrac{dy}{dx} = -\dfrac{x}{y}$.

2. If $5x^2 - 2y^2 = 3$, then $\dfrac{dy}{dx} = \dfrac{5x}{2y}$.

3. If $xy = C$, then $\dfrac{dy}{dx} = \dfrac{-y}{x}$.

4. If $x^2 - 3xy + y^2 = 5$, then $(2x - 3y)\,dx + (2y - 3x)\,dy = 0$.

5. If $y = \sin(Ax + B)$, then $\dfrac{d^2y}{dx^2} + A^2 y = 0$.

6. If $y = \dfrac{x^4}{20} - \dfrac{A}{x} + B$, then $x\dfrac{d^2y}{dx^2} + 2\dfrac{dy}{dx} = x^3$.

7. If $y = 2e^{-x} + 3e^{2x}$, then $y'' - y' - 2y = 0$.

8. If $y = Ae^x + Be^x \ln x$, then $xy'' + (1 - 2x)y' - (1 - x)y = 0$.

Find the particular solution of the first-order linear differential equations in Problems 9–14. A graphical solution within its direction field is shown.

9. $\dfrac{dy}{dx} = -\dfrac{x}{y}$
passing through (2, 2)

10. $\dfrac{dy}{dx} - y = 10$
passing through $(-2, -9)$

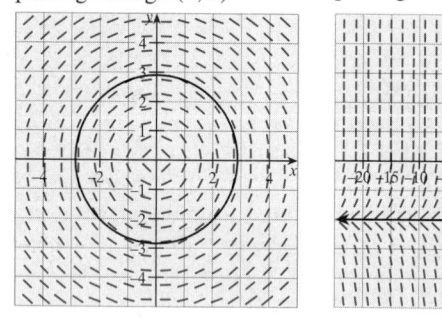

11. $\dfrac{dy}{dx} - y^2 = 1$
passing through $(\pi, 1)$

12. $\dfrac{dy}{dx} = e^{x+y}$
passing through (0, 0)

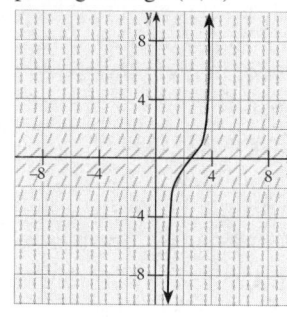 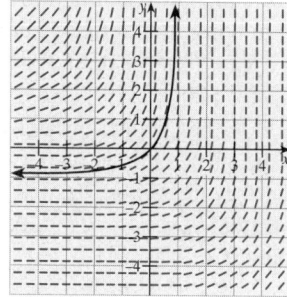

13. $\dfrac{dy}{dx} = \sqrt{\dfrac{x}{y}}$
passing through (4, 1)

14. $\dfrac{dy}{dx} = y^2\sqrt{x}$
passing through $\left(9, -\dfrac{1}{18}\right)$

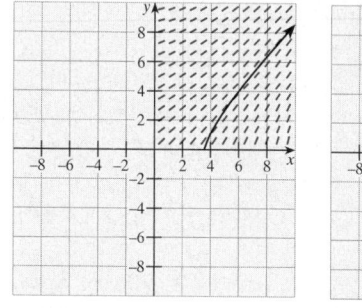 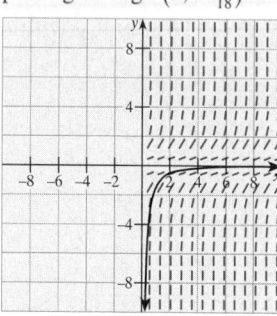

In each of Problems 15–20, sketch the particular solution passing through the given point for the differential equation whose direction field is given.

15. (0, 1) **16.** (0, 1)

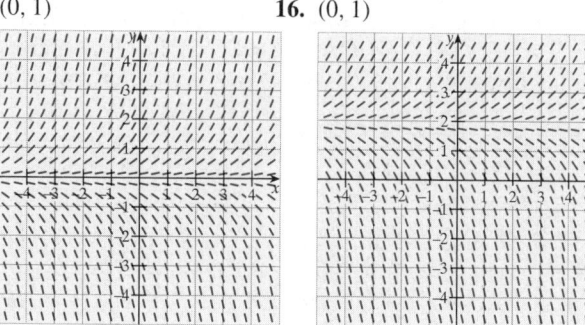

17. (0, 0) **18.** (3, 3)

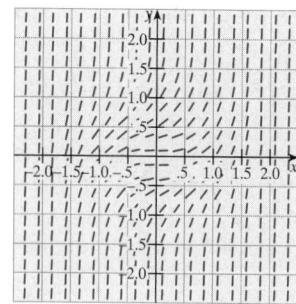 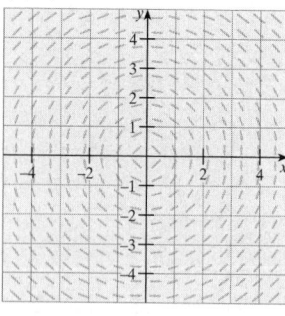

19. (1, 0) **20.** (0, 0)

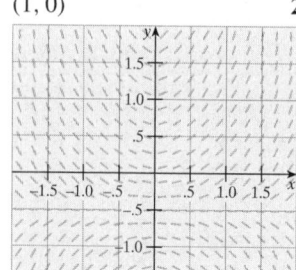 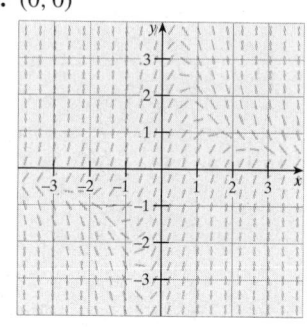

Find the general solution of the separable differential equations given in Problems 21–30. Note that for some problems, the general solution will be a relationship between x and y, rather than $y = f(x)$.

21. $\dfrac{dy}{dx} = 3xy$

22. $\dfrac{dy}{dx} = \sqrt{\dfrac{y}{x}}$

23. $\dfrac{dy}{dx} = \dfrac{x}{y}\sqrt{1 - x^2}$

24. $\dfrac{dy}{dx} = (y - 4)^2$

25. $xy\,dx + \sqrt{xy}\,dy = 0$

26. $\dfrac{dy}{dx} = \dfrac{y}{\sqrt{1 - 2x^2}}$

27. $\dfrac{dy}{dx} = \dfrac{\sin x}{\cos y}$

28. $x^2\,dy + \sec y\,dx = 0$

29. $xy\dfrac{dy}{dx} = \dfrac{\ln x}{\sqrt{1 - y^2}}$

30. $\dfrac{dy}{dx} = e^{y-x}$

In Problems 31–34, find the general solution of the given differential equation by using either the product or the quotient rule.

31. $x\,dy + y\,dx = 0$

32. $\dfrac{x\,dy - y\,dx}{x^2} = 0$

33. $y\,dx = x\,dy, x > 0, y > 0$ **34.** $x^2y\,dy + xy^2\,dx = 0$

B *Find the orthogonal trajectories of the family of curves given in Problems 35–42. In each case, sketch several members of the given family of curves and several members of the family of orthogonal trajectories on the same coordinate axes.*

35. the lines $2x - 3y = C$ **36.** the lines $y = x + C$

37. the cubic curves $y = x^3 + C$

38. the curves $y = x^4 + C$

39. the curves $xy^2 = C$ **40.** the parabolas $y^2 = 4kx$

41. the circles $x^2 + y^2 = r^2$

42. the exponential curves $y = Ce^{-x}$

Modeling Problems *Write a differential equation to model the situation given in each of Problems 43–48. Be sure to define your unknown function first. Do not solve.*

43. The number of bacteria in a culture grows at a rate that is proportional to the number present.

44. A sample of radium decays at a rate that is proportional to the amount of radium present in the sample.

45. The rate at which the temperature of an object changes is proportional to the difference between its own temperature and the temperature of the surrounding medium.

46. When a person is asked to recall a set of facts, the rate at which the facts are recalled is proportional to the number of relevant facts in the person's memory that have not yet been recalled. *Hint:* Let Q denote the number of facts recalled and N the total number of relevant facts in the person's memory.

47. The rate at which an epidemic spreads through a community of P susceptible people is proportional to the product of the number of people who have caught the disease and the number who have not.

48. The rate at which people are implicated in a government scandal is proportional to the product of the number of people already implicated and the number of people involved who have not yet been implicated.

49. What do you think the orthogonal trajectories of the family of curves $x^2 - y^2 = C$ will be? Verify your conjecture. *Hint*: Take another look at Example 7.

50. The following is a list of six families of curves. Sketch several members of each family and then determine which pairs are orthogonal trajectories of one another.
   a. the circles $x^2 + y^2 = A$ b. the ellipses $2x^2 + y^2 = B^2$
   c. the ellipses $x^2 + 2y^2 = C$ d. the lines $y = Cx$
   e. the parabolas $y^2 = Cx$ f. the parabolas $y = Cx^2$

51. The Dead Sea Scrolls were written on parchment in about 100 B.C. What percentage of ^{14}C originally contained in the parchment remained when the scrolls were discovered in 1947?

52. Tests of an artifact discovered at the Debert site in Nova Scotia show that 28% of the original ^{14}C is still present. What is the probable age of the artifact?

53. HISTORICAL QUEST The Shroud of Turin is a rectangular linen cloth kept in the Chapel of the Holy Shroud in the cathedral of St. John the Baptist in Turin, Italy. It shows the image of a man whose wounds correspond with the biblical accounts of the crucifixion.

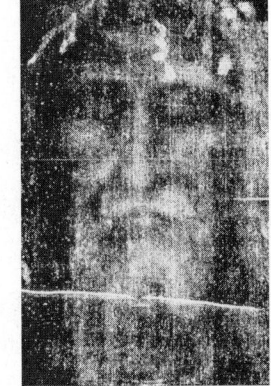

   In 1389, Pierre d'Arcis, the Bishop of Troyes, wrote a memo to the Pope, accusing a colleague of passing off "a certain cloth, cunningly painted" as the burial shroud of Jesus Christ. Despite this early testimony of forgery, this so-called Shroud of Turin has survived as a famous relic. In 1988, a small sample of the Shroud of Turin was taken and scientists from Oxford University, the University of Arizona, and the Swiss Federal Institute of Technology were permitted to test it. It was found that the cloth contained 92.3% of the original ^{14}C. ∎

   According to this information, how old is the Shroud?

54. A cylindrical tank of radius 3 ft is filled with water to a depth of 5 ft. Determine how long (to the nearest minute) it takes to drain the tank through a sharp-edged circular hole in the bottom with radius 2 in.

55. Rework Problem 54 for a tank with a sharp-edged drain hole that is square with side of length 1.5 in.

56. **Experiment** A rectangular tank has a square base 2 ft on a side that is filled with water to a depth of 4 ft. It is being drained from the bottom of the tank through a sharp-edged square hole that is 2 in. on a side.
   a. Show that at time t, the depth h satisfies the differential equation
$$\frac{dh}{dt} = -\frac{1}{30}\sqrt{h}$$
   b. How long will it take to empty the tank?
   c. Construct this tank and then drain it out of the 4 in.^{2} hole. Is the time that it takes consistent with your answer to part **b**?

57. A toy rocket is launched from the surface of the earth with initial velocity $v_0 = 150$ ft/s. (The radius of the earth is roughly 3,956 mi, and $g = 32$ ft/s^2.)
   a. Determine the velocity (to the nearest ft/s) of the rocket when it is first 200 feet above the ground. (Remember, this is not the same as 200 ft from the center of the earth.)
   b. What is s when $v = 0$? Determine the maximum height above the ground that is attained by the rocket.

58. Determine the escape velocity of each of the following heavenly bodies:
   a. moon ($R = 1,080$ mi; $g = 5.5$ ft/s^2)
   b. Mars ($R = 2,050$ mi; $g = 12$ ft/s^2)
   c. Venus ($R = 3,800$ mi; $g = 28$ ft/s^2)

59. Population statistics indicate that t years after 1990, a certain city was growing at a rate of approximately $1,500t^{-1/2}$ people per year. In 1994, the population of the city was 39,000.
   a. What was the population in 1990?
   b. If this pattern continued, how many people were living in the city in the year 1999?

60. The radius of planet X is one-fourth that of planet Y, and the acceleration due to gravity at the surface of X is eight-ninths that at the surface of Y. If the escape velocity of planet X is 6 ft/s, what is the escape velocity of planet Y?

61. A survey indicates that the population of a certain town is growing in such a way that the rate of growth at time t is proportional to the square root of the population P at the time. If the population was 4,000 ten years ago and is observed to be 9,000 now, how long will it take before 16,000 people live in the town?

62. A scientist has discovered a radioactive substance that disintegrates in such a way that at time t, the rate of disintegration is proportional to the *square* of the amount present.
   a. If a 100-g sample of the substance dwindles to only 80 g in 1 day, how much will be left after 6 days?
   b. When will only 10 g be left?

63. The shape of a tank is such that when it is filled to a depth of h feet, it contains $V = 9\pi h^3$ ft^3 of water. The tank is being drained through a sharp-edged circular hole of radius 1 in. If the tank is originally filled to a depth of 4 ft, how long does it take for the tank to empty?

64. A rectangular tank has a square base 4 ft on a side and is 10 ft high. Originally, it was filled with water to a depth of 6 feet, but now is being drained from the bottom of the tank through a sharp-edged square hole 1 in. on a side.

a. Find an equation involving the rate dh/dt.

b. How long will it take to drain the tank?

65. The radioactive substance neptunium-139 decays to 73.36% of its original amount after 24 hours. How long would it take for 43% of the original neptunium to be present? What is the half-life of neptunium-139?

66. A certain artifact is tested by carbon dating and found to contain 73% of its original carbon-14. As a cross-check, it is also dated using radium and is found to contain 32% of the original amount. Assuming the dating procedures are accurate, what is the half-life of radium?

67. The radioactive isotope gallium-67 (symbol ^{67}Ga) used in the diagnosis of malignant tumors has a half-life of 46.5 hours. If we start with 100 mg of ^{67}Ga, what percent is lost between the 30th and 35th hours? Is this the same as the percent lost over any other 5-hour period?

C **68. Modeling Problem** A projectile is launched from the surface of a planet whose radius is R and where the acceleration due to gravity at the surface is g.

a. If the initial velocity v_0 of the projectile satisfies $v_0 < \sqrt{2gR}$, show that the maximum height above the surface of the planet reached by the projectile is

$$h = \frac{v_0^2 R}{2gR - v_0^2}$$

b. On a certain planet, it is known that $g = 25$ ft/s^2. A projectile is fired with an initial velocity of $v_0 = 2$ mi/s and attains a maximum height of 450 mi. What is the radius of the planet?

69. A projectile is launched from the surface of a planet whose radius is R and where the constant acceleration due to gravity

is g. According to Newton's law of gravitation, the force of gravity acting on a projectile of mass m has magnitude

$$F = \frac{mk}{s^2}$$

where k is a constant. If this is the only force acting on the projectile, then $F = ma$, where a is the acceleration of the projectile. Show that

$$a = \frac{-gR^2}{s^2}$$

70. Modeling Problem In physics, it is shown that the amount of heat Q (calories) that flows through an object by conduction will satisfy the differential equation

$$\frac{dQ}{dt} = -kA\frac{dT}{ds}$$

where t (seconds) is the time of flow, k is a physical constant (the *thermal conductivity* of the object), A is the surface area of the object measured at right angles to the direction of flow, and T is the temperature at a point s centimeters within the object, measured in the direction of the flow, as shown in Figure 5.29.

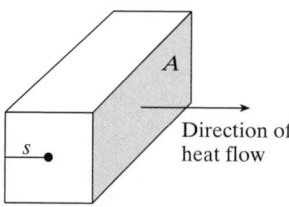

Figure 5.29 Heat conduction through an object

Under certain conditions (equilibrium), the rate of heat flow dQ/dt will be constant. Assuming these conditions exist, find the number of calories that will flow each second across the face of a square pane of glass 2 cm thick and 50 cm on a side if the temperature on one side of the pane is 5°C and on the other side is 60°C. The thermal conductivity of glass is approximately $k = 0.0025$.

5.7   The Mean Value Theorem for Integrals; Average Value

IN THIS SECTION   mean value theorem for integrals, modeling average value of a function

MEAN VALUE THEOREM FOR INTEGRALS

In Section 4.2 we established a very useful theoretical tool called the mean value theorem, which said that under reasonable conditions, there is at least one number c in the interval (a, b) such that

$$\frac{f(b) - f(a)}{b - a} = f'(c)$$

The mean value theorem for integrals is similar, and in the special case where $f(x) \geq 0$ it has a geometric interpretation that makes the theorem easy to understand.

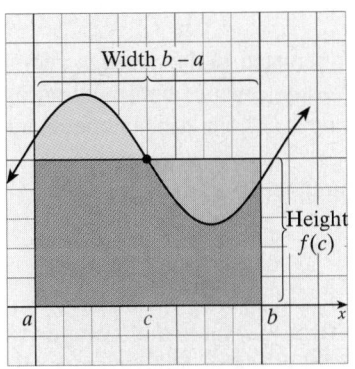

Width $b - a$

Height $f(c)$

The shaded rectangle has the same area as the region under the curve $y = f(x)$ on $[a, b]$.

Figure 5.30 Geometric interpretation of the mean value theorem for integrals

In particular, the theorem says that it is possible to find at least one number c on the interval (a, b) such that the area of the rectangle with height $f(c)$ and width $(b - a)$ has exactly the same area as the region under the curve $y = f(x)$ on $[a, b]$. This is illustrated in Figure 5.30.

THEOREM 5.11   Mean value theorem for integrals

If f is continuous on the interval $[a, b]$, then there is at least one number c between a and b such that

$$\int_a^b f(x)\,dx = f(c)(b - a)$$

Proof   Suppose M and m are the absolute maximum and the absolute minimum of f, respectively, on $[a, b]$. This means that

$$m \leq \quad f(x) \quad \leq M \quad \text{when } a \leq x \leq b$$

$$\int_a^b m\,dx \leq \quad \int_a^b f(x)\,dx \quad \leq \int_a^b M\,dx \qquad \text{Dominance rule}$$

$$m(b - a) \leq \quad \int_a^b f(x)\,dx \quad \leq M(b - a)$$

$$m \leq \frac{1}{b - a}\int_a^b f(x)\,dx \leq M$$

Because f is continuous on the closed interval $[a, b]$ and because the number

$$I = \frac{1}{b - a}\int_a^b f(x)\,dx$$

lies between m and M, the intermediate value theorem (Theorem 2.6 of Section 2.3) says that there exists a number c between a and b for which $f(c) = I$; that is,

$$\frac{1}{b - a}\int_a^b f(x)\,dx = f(c)$$

$$\int_a^b f(x)\,dx = f(c)(b - a) \qquad \square$$

The mean value theorem for integrals does not specify how to determine c. It simply guarantees the existence of at least one number c in the interval. However, Example 1 shows how to find a value of c guaranteed by this theorem for a particular function and interval.

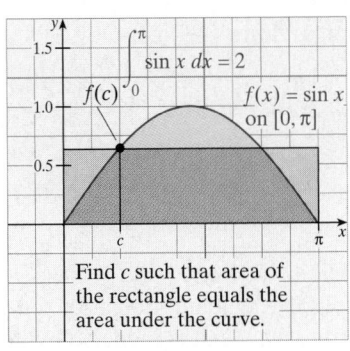

$\int_0^\pi \sin x\,dx = 2$

$f(c)$

$f(x) = \sin x$ on $[0, \pi]$

Find c such that area of the rectangle equals the area under the curve.

Figure 5.31 Graph of $f(x) = \sin x$ illustrating the mean value theorem on $[0, \pi]$

EXAMPLE 1   Finding c using the mean value theorem for integrals

Find a value of c guaranteed by the mean value theorem for integrals for $f(x) = \sin x$ on $[0, \pi]$.

Solution

$$\int_0^\pi \sin x\,dx = -\cos x\big|_0^\pi = -\cos\pi + \cos 0 = -(-1) + 1 = 2$$

The region bounded by f and the x-axis on $[0, \pi]$ is shaded in Figure 5.31.

The mean value theorem for integrals asserts the existence of a number c on $[0, \pi]$ such that $f(c)(b - a) = 2$. We can solve this equation to find this value:

$$f(c)(b - a) = 2$$
$$(\sin c)(\pi - 0) = 2$$
$$\sin c = \frac{2}{\pi}$$
$$c \approx 0.690107 \quad \text{or} \quad 2.451486$$

Because each choice of c is between 0 and π, we have found two values of c guaranteed by the mean value theorem for integrals. ∎

MODELING AVERAGE VALUE OF A FUNCTION

There are many practical situations in which one is interested in the *average value* of a continuous function on an interval, such as the average level of air pollution over a 24-hour period, the average speed of a truck during a 3-hour trip, or the average productivity of a worker during a production run.

You probably know that the average value of n numbers $x_1, x_2, \ldots, x_n$ is

$$\frac{x_1 + x_2 + \cdots + x_n}{n}$$

but what if there are infinitely many numbers? Specifically, what is the average value of $f(x)$ on the interval $a \le x \le b$? To see how the definition of finite average value can be used, imagine that the interval $[a, b]$ is divided into n equal subintervals, each of width

$$\Delta x = \frac{b - a}{n}$$

For $k = 1, 2, \ldots, n$, let x_k^* be a number chosen arbitrarily from the kth subinterval. Then the average value AV of f on $[a, b]$ is estimated by the sum

$$S_n = \frac{f(x_1^*) + f(x_2^*) + \cdots + f(x_n^*)}{n} = \frac{1}{n} \sum_{k=1}^{n} f(x_k^*)$$

Because $\Delta x = \dfrac{b - a}{n}$, we know that $\dfrac{1}{n} = \dfrac{1}{b - a} \Delta x$ and

$$S_n = \frac{1}{n} \sum_{k=1}^{n} f(x_k^*) = \left[\frac{1}{b - a} \Delta x \right] \sum_{k=1}^{n} f(x_k^*) = \frac{1}{b - a} \sum_{k=1}^{n} f(x_k^*) \Delta x$$

The sum on the right is a Riemann sum with norm $\| P \| = \dfrac{b - a}{n}$. It is reasonable to expect the estimating average S_n to approach the "true" average value AV of $f(x)$ on $[a, b]$ as $n \to +\infty$. Thus, we model average value by

$$AV = \lim_{n \to +\infty} \frac{1}{b - a} \sum_{k=1}^{n} f(x_k^*) \Delta x = \frac{1}{b - a} \int_a^b f(x)\, dx$$

We use this integral as the definition of average value.

Average Value

> If f is continuous on the interval $[a, b]$, the **average value** (AV) of f on this interval is given by the integral
>
> $$AV = \frac{1}{b - a} \int_a^b f(x)\, dx$$

EXAMPLE 2   Modeling average speed of traffic

Suppose a study suggests that between the hours of 1:00 P.M. and 4:00 P.M. on a normal weekday the speed of the traffic at a certain expressway exit is modeled by the formula

$$S(t) = 2t^3 - 21t^2 + 60t + 20$$

kilometers per hour, where t is the number of hours past noon. Compute the average speed of the traffic between the hours of 1:00 P.M. and 4:00 P.M.

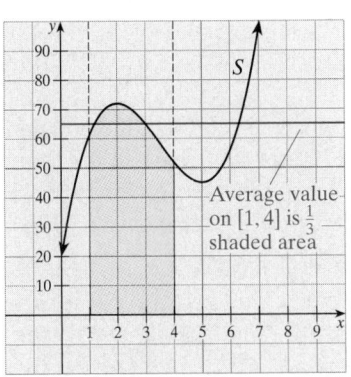

Figure 5.32 Graph of S and the average value

Solution

Our goal is to find the average value of $S(t)$ on the interval $[1, 4]$. The average speed is

$$\frac{1}{4-1}\int_1^4 (2t^3 - 21t^2 + 60t + 20)\,dt = \frac{1}{3}\left[\frac{1}{2}t^4 - 7t^3 + 30t^2 + 20t\right]_1^4$$
$$= \frac{1}{3}(240 - 43.5) = 65.5$$

The function, as well as the average value, is shown in Figure 5.32. ∎

According to the mean value theorem for integrals, we have

$$\frac{1}{b-a}\int_a^b f(x)\,dx = f(c)$$

which says that the *average value of a continuous function f on $[a, b]$ equals the value of f for at least one number c between a and b.* This is quite reasonable since the intermediate value theorem for continuous functions assures us that a continuous function f assumes every value between its maximum M and minimum m, and we would expect the average value to be between these two extremes. Example 3 illustrates one way of using these ideas.

EXAMPLE 3   Modeling average temperature

Suppose that during a typical winter day in Minneapolis, the temperature (in degrees Celsius) x hours after midnight is modeled by the formula

$$T(x) = 2 - \tfrac{1}{7}(x - 13)^2$$

A graph of this formula is shown in Figure 5.33. Find the average temperature over the time period from 2:00 A.M. to 2:00 P.M., and find a time when the average temperature actually occurs.

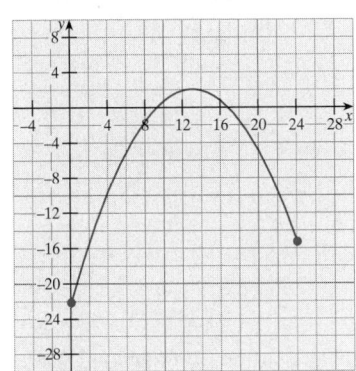

Figure 5.33 Graph of temperatures in Minneapolis over a 24-hour period

Solution

We wish to find the average temperature T on the interval $[2, 14]$ (because 2 P.M. is 14 hours after midnight). The average value is

$$T = \frac{1}{14-2}\int_2^{14}\left[2 - \frac{1}{7}(x-13)^2\right]dx = \frac{1}{12}\left[2x - \frac{1}{7}\cdot\frac{1}{3}(x-13)^3\right]\Big|_2^{14}$$
$$= \frac{1}{12}\left[\frac{587}{21} - \frac{1{,}415}{21}\right] \approx -3.2857143$$

Thus, the average temperature on the given time period is approximately $3.3°C$ below zero. To determine when this temperature actually occurs, solve the equation

$$\text{AVERAGE TEMPERATURE} = \text{TEMPERATURE AT TIME } x$$
$$-3.2857143 = 2 - \tfrac{1}{7}(x - 13)^2$$
$$37 = (x - 13)^2$$
$$x = 13 \pm \sqrt{37} \approx 19.082763 \quad \text{or} \quad 6.9172375$$

The first value is to be rejected because it is not in the interval $[2, 14]$, so we find that the average temperature occurs 6.917 hr after midnight, or at approximately 6:55 A.M. ∎

EXAMPLE 4   Modeling average population

The logistic formula

$$P(t) = \frac{202.31}{1 + e^{3.938 - 0.314t}}$$

was developed by the United States Bureau of the Census to represent the population of the United States (in millions) during the period 1790–1990. Time t in the formula is the number of decades after 1790. Thus, $t = 0$ for 1790, $t = 20$ for 1990. Use this formula to compute the average population of the United States between 1790 and 1990. When did the average population actually occur?

Solution

The average population is given by the integral

$$A = \frac{1}{20 - 0} \int_0^{20} \frac{202.31 \, dt}{1 + e^{3.938 - 0.314t}} \qquad \text{Multiply by } \frac{e^{0.314t}}{e^{0.314t}}.$$

$$= \frac{1}{20} \int_0^{20} \frac{202.31 e^{0.314t}}{e^{0.314t} + e^{3.938}} \, dt \qquad \begin{array}{l} \text{Let } u = e^{0.314t} + e^{3.938}; \\ du = 0.314 e^{0.314t} \, dt. \end{array}$$

$$= \frac{1}{20} \left(\frac{202.31}{0.314} \right) \int_{t=0}^{t=20} \frac{du}{u}$$

$$= \frac{1}{20} \left(\frac{202.31}{0.314} \right) \ln \left| e^{0.314t} + e^{3.938} \right| \Big|_0^{20} \approx 77.7827445296$$

To find when the average population of 77.7827 million actually occurred, solve $P(t) = 77.7827$:

$$\frac{202.31}{1 + e^{3.938 - 0.314t}} = 77.7827$$

$$e^{3.938 - 0.314t} = \frac{202.31}{77.7827} - 1$$

$$3.938 - 0.314t = \ln \left(\frac{202.31}{77.7827} - 1 \right)$$

$$t \approx 11.043$$

The average population occurred approximately 11 decades after 1790, around the year 1900. ∎

5.7   PROBLEM SET

A *In Problems 1–10, find c such that*

$$\int_a^b f(x) \, dx = f(c)(b - a)$$

as guaranteed by the mean value theorem for integrals. If you cannot find such a value, explain why the theorem does not apply.

1. $f(x) = 4x^3$ on $[1, 2]$ **2.** $f(x) = x^2 + 4x + 1$ on $[0, 2]$
3. $f(x) = 15x^{-2}$ on $[1, 5]$ **4.** $f(x) = 12x^{-3}$ on $[-3, 3]$
5. $f(x) = 2 \csc^2 x$ on $\left[-\frac{\pi}{3}, \frac{\pi}{3}\right]$ **6.** $f(x) = \cos x$ on $\left[-\frac{\pi}{2}, \frac{\pi}{2}\right]$
7. $f(x) = e^{2x}$ on $\left[-\frac{1}{2}, \frac{1}{2}\right]$ **8.** $f(x) = \dfrac{x}{1 + x}$ on $[0, 1]$
9. $f(x) = \dfrac{x + 1}{1 + x^2}$ on $[-1, 1]$ **10.** $f(x) = \tan x$ on $[0, 2]$

Determine the area of the indicated region in Problems 11–16 and then draw a rectangle with base $(b - a)$ and height $f(c)$ for some c on $[a, b]$ so that the area of the rectangle is equal to the area of the given region.

11. $y = \frac{1}{2}x$ on $[0, 10]$

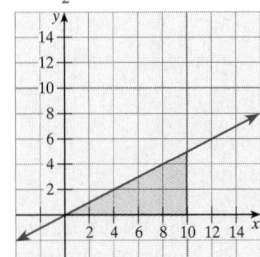

12. $y = x^2$ on $[0, 3]$

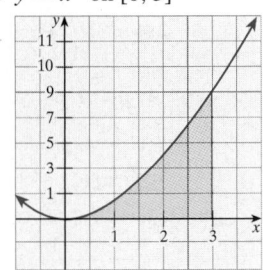

13. $y = x^2 + 2x + 3$ on $[0, 2]$ **14.** $y = \dfrac{1}{x^2}$ on $[0.5, 2]$

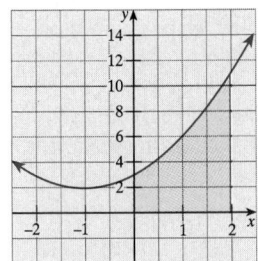 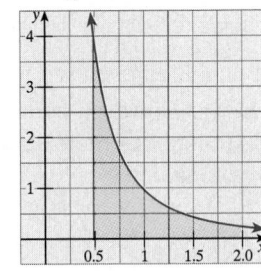

15. $y = \cos x$ on $[-1, 1.5]$ **16.** $y = x + \sin x$ on $[0, 10]$

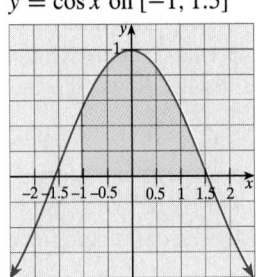 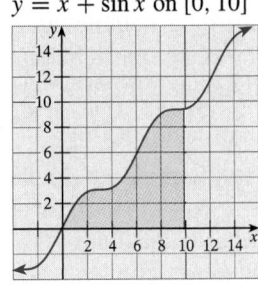

Find the average value of the function given in Problems 17–30 on the prescribed interval.

17. $f(x) = x^2 - x + 1$ on $[-1, 2]$

18. $f(x) = x^3 - 3x^2$ on $[-2, 1]$

19. $f(x) = e^x - e^{-x}$ on $[-1, 1]$

20. $f(x) = \dfrac{x}{2x + 3}$ on $[0, 1]$

21. $f(x) = \sin x$ on $\left[0, \frac{\pi}{4}\right]$

22. $f(x) = 2 \sin x - \cos x$ on $\left[0, \frac{\pi}{2}\right]$

23. $f(x) = \sqrt{4 - x}$ on $[0, 4]$

24. $f(x) = \sqrt[3]{1 - x}$ on $[-7, 0]$

25. $f(x) = (2x - 3)^3$ on $[0, 1]$

26. $f(x) = x\sqrt{2x^2 + 7}$ on $[0, 1]$

27. $f(x) = x(x^2 + 1)^3$ on $[-2, 1]$

28. $f(x) = \dfrac{x}{\sqrt{x^2 + 1}}$ on $[0, 3]$

29. $f(x) = \sqrt{9 - x^2}$ on $[-3, 3]$ *Hint: The integral can be evaluated as the area of part of a circle.*

30. $f(x) = \sqrt{2x - x^2}$ on $[0, 2]$ *Hint: The integral can be evaluated as the area of part of a circle.*

B 31. If an object is propelled upward from ground level with an initial velocity v_0, then its height at time t is given by

$$s = -\tfrac{1}{2}gt^2 + v_0 t$$

where g is the constant acceleration due to gravity. Show that between times t_0 and t_1, the average height of the object is

$$s = -\tfrac{1}{6}g[t_1^2 + t_1 t_0 + t_0^2] + \tfrac{1}{2}v_0(t_1 + t_0)$$

32. What is the average velocity for the object described in Problem 31 during the same time period?

33. Records indicate that t hours past midnight, the temperature at the local airport was

$$f(t) = -0.1t^2 + t + 50$$

degrees Fahrenheit. What was the average temperature at the airport between 9:00 A.M. and noon?

34. Suppose a study indicates that t years from now, the level of carbon dioxide in the air of a certain city will be

$$L(t) = te^{-0.01t^2}$$

parts per million (ppm) for $0 \le t \le 20$.

a. What is the average level of carbon dioxide in the first 3 years?

b. At what time (or times) does the average level of carbon dioxide actually occur? Answer to the nearest month.

35. The number of bacteria (in thousands) present in a certain culture after t minutes is modeled by

$$Q(t) = \frac{2{,}000}{1 + 0.3e^{-0.276t}}$$

a. What was the average population during the *second* ten minutes ($10 \le t \le 20$)?

b. At what time during the period $10 \le t \le 20$ is the average population actually attained?

C 36. Let $f(t)$ be a function that is continuous and satisfies $f(t) \ge 0$ on the interval $\left[0, \frac{\pi}{2}\right]$. Suppose it is known that for any number x between 0 and $\frac{\pi}{2}$, the region under the graph of f on $[0, x]$ has area $A(x) = \tan x$.

a. Explain why $\displaystyle\int_0^x f(t)\,dt = \tan x$ for $0 \le x \le \frac{\pi}{2}$.

b. Differentiate both sides of the equation in part **a** and deduce the identity of f.

37. Exploration Problem Suppose that $f(t)$ is continuous for all t and that for any number x it is known that the average value of f on $[-1, x]$ is

$$A(x) = \sin x$$

Use this information to deduce the identity of f.

38. Modeling Problem In Example 7 of Section 4.7, we gave the Heinz function

$$f(t) = \frac{k}{b - a}(e^{-at} - e^{-bt}) \qquad t \ge 0$$

where $f(t)$ is the concentration of a drug in a person's bloodstream t hours after an intramuscular injection. The coefficients a and b ($b > a$) are characteristics of the drug and the patient's metabolism and are called the absorption and diffusion rates, respectively.

a. Show that for each fixed t, $f(t)$ can be thought of as the average value of a function of the form

$$g(\lambda) = (At^2 + Bt + C)e^{-\lambda t}$$

over the interval $a \le \lambda \le b$. Find A, B, and C.

b. Exploration Problem So what? In particular, can you see any value in the interpretation of the Heinz concentration function as an average value? Explain.

5.8 Numerical Integration: The Trapezoidal Rule and Simpson's Rule

IN THIS SECTION approximation by rectangles, trapezoidal rule, Simpson's rule, error estimation

The fundamental theorem of calculus can be used to evaluate an integral whenever an appropriate antiderivative is known. However, certain functions, such as $f(x) = e^{x^2}$, have no simple antiderivatives. To find a definite integral of such a function, it is often necessary to use numerical approximation.

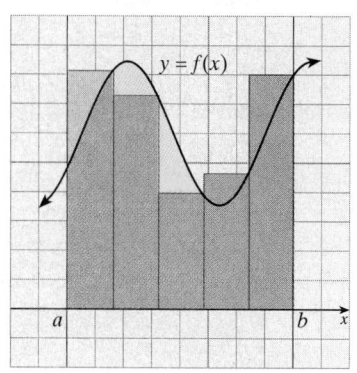

Figure 5.34 Approximation by rectangles

APPROXIMATION BY RECTANGLES

If $f(x) \geq 0$ on the interval $[a, b]$, the definite integral $\int_a^b f(x)\, dx$ is equal to the area under the graph of f on $[a, b]$. As we saw in Section 5.2, one way to approximate this area is to use n rectangles, as shown in Figure 5.34. In particular, divide the interval $[a, b]$ into n subintervals, each of width $\Delta x = \dfrac{b - a}{n}$, and let x_k^* denote the right endpoint of the kth subinterval. The base of the kth rectangle is the kth subinterval, and its height is $f(x_k^*)$. Hence, the area of the kth rectangle is $f(x_k^*)\Delta x$. The sum of the areas of all n rectangles is an approximation for the area under the curve and hence an approximation for the corresponding definite integral. Thus,

$$\int_a^b f(x)\, dx \approx f(x_1^*)\Delta x + f(x_2^*)\Delta x + \cdots + f(x_n^*)\Delta x$$

This approximation improves as the number of rectangles increases, and we can estimate the integral to any desired degree of accuracy by taking n large enough. However, because fairly large values of n are usually required to achieve reasonable accuracy, approximation by rectangles is rarely used in practice.

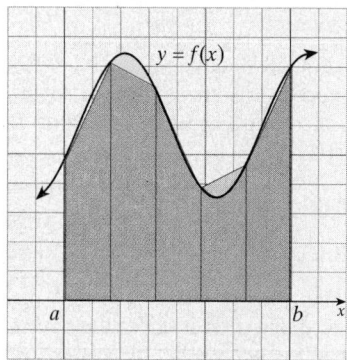

Figure 5.35 Approximation by trapezoids

TRAPEZOIDAL RULE

The accuracy of the approximation generally improves significantly if trapezoids are used instead of rectangles. Figure 5.35 shows the area from Figure 5.34 approximated by n trapezoids instead of rectangles. Even from these rough illustrations you can see how much better the approximation is in this case.

Suppose the interval $[a, b]$ is partitioned into n equal parts by the subdivision points $x_0, x_1, \ldots, x_n$, where $x_0 = a$ and $x_n = b$. The kth trapezoid is shown in greater detail in Figure 5.36. Recall the formula for the area of a trapezoid:

$$A = \tfrac{1}{2}(b_1 + b_2)h$$

If we let T_n denote the sum of the areas of n trapezoids, we see that

$$T_n = \tfrac{1}{2}[f(x_0) + f(x_1)]\Delta x + \tfrac{1}{2}[f(x_1) + f(x_2)]\Delta x + \cdots + \tfrac{1}{2}[f(x_{n-1}) + f(x_n)]\Delta x$$
$$= \tfrac{1}{2}[f(x_0) + 2f(x_1) + 2f(x_2) + \cdots + 2f(x_{n-1}) + f(x_n)]\Delta x$$

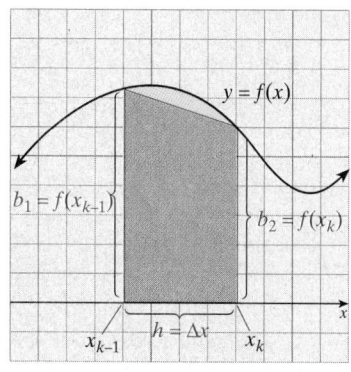

Figure 5.36 The kth trapezoid has area $\tfrac{1}{2}[f(x_{k-1}) + f(x_k)]\Delta x$.

The sum T_n estimates the total area under the curve $y = f(x)$ on the interval $[a, b]$ and hence also estimates the integral

$$\int_a^b f(x)\, dx$$

This approximation formula is known as the *trapezoidal rule* and applies as a means of approximating the integral, even if the function f is not positive.

> **Trapezoidal Rule**
>
> Let f be continuous on $[a, b]$. The **trapezoidal rule** is
>
> $$\int_a^b f(x)\,dx \approx \tfrac{1}{2}[f(x_0) + 2f(x_1) + 2f(x_2) + \cdots + 2f(x_{n-1}) + f(x_n)]\Delta x$$
>
> where $\Delta x = \dfrac{b-a}{n}$ and, for the kth subinterval, $x_k = a + k\Delta x$. Moreover, the larger the value for n, the better the approximation.

Our first example uses the trapezoidal rule to estimate the value of an integral that we can compute exactly by using the fundamental theorem.

EXAMPLE 1   Trapezoidal rule approximation

Use the trapezoidal rule with $n = 4$ to estimate $\displaystyle\int_{-1}^2 x^2\,dx$.

Solution

The interval is $[a, b] = [-1, 2]$, so $a = -1$ and $b = 2$. Then
$$\Delta x = \frac{2 - (-1)}{4} = \frac{3}{4} = 0.75. \text{ Thus,}$$

$$
\begin{aligned}
x_0 &= a = -1 & f(x_0) &= f(-1) = (-1)^2 = 1 \\
x_1 &= a + 1 \cdot \Delta x = -1 + \tfrac{3}{4} = -\tfrac{1}{4} & 2f(x_1) &= 2\left(-\tfrac{1}{4}\right)^2 = \tfrac{1}{8} = 0.125 \\
x_2 &= a + 2 \cdot \Delta x = -1 + \tfrac{6}{4} = \tfrac{1}{2} & 2f(x_2) &= 2\left(\tfrac{1}{2}\right)^2 = \tfrac{1}{2} = 0.5 \\
x_3 &= a + 3 \cdot \Delta x = -1 + \tfrac{9}{4} = \tfrac{5}{4} & 2f(x_3) &= 2\left(\tfrac{5}{4}\right)^2 = \tfrac{25}{8} = 3.125 \\
x_4 &= a + 4 \cdot \Delta x = b = 2 & f(x_4) &= 2^2 = 4 \\
\end{aligned}
$$

$$T_4 = \tfrac{1}{2}[1 + 0.125 + 0.5 + 3.125 + 4](0.75) = 3.28125 \qquad \blacksquare$$

The exact value of the integral in Example 1 is

$$\int_{-1}^2 x^2\,dx = \frac{x^3}{3}\bigg|_{-1}^2 = \frac{8}{3} - \frac{-1}{3} = 3$$

Therefore, the trapezoidal estimate T_4 involves an error, which we denote by E_4. We find that

$$E_4 = \int_{-1}^2 x^2\,dx - T_4 = 3 - 3.28125 = -0.28125$$

The negative sign indicates that the trapezoidal formula *overestimated* the true value of the integral in Example 1.

Software for numerical evaluation of integrals is common (see the *Technology Manual*). The output for Example 1 is shown in the margin.

Trapezoidal Rule to calculate estimate		
Type of estimate	# of sub- intervals	Estimate over [-1, 2]
Trapezoid	4	3.28125
Trapezoid	10	3.045
Trapezoid	100	3.00045
Trapezoid	1000	3.000005

SIMPSON'S RULE

Roughly speaking, the accuracy of a procedure for estimating the area under a curve depends on how well the upper boundary of each approximating area fits the shape of the given curve. Trapezoidal strips often result in a better approximation than rectangular strips, and it is reasonable to expect even greater accuracy to occur if the approximating regions have curved upper boundaries, as shown in Figure 5.37.

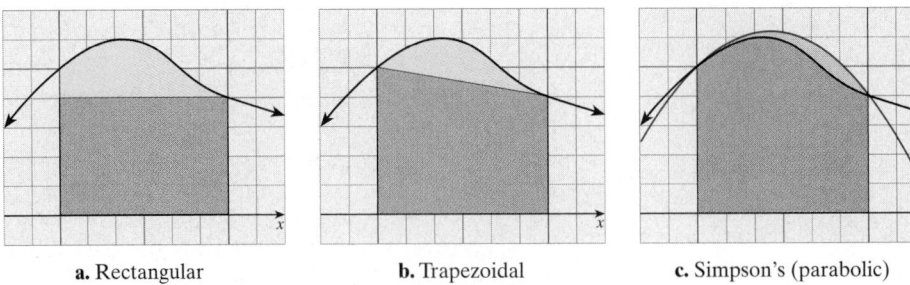

a. Rectangular   **b.** Trapezoidal   **c.** Simpson's (parabolic)

Figure 5.37 A comparison of approximation methods

The name given to the procedure in which the approximating strip has a parabolic arc for its upper boundary is called **Simpson's rule**.*

As with the trapezoidal rule, we will derive Simpson's rule as a means for approximating the area under the curve $y = f(x)$ on the interval $[a, b]$, where f is continuous and satisfies $f(x) \geq 0$. First, we partition the given interval into a number of equal subintervals, but this time, we require the number of subdivisions to be an *even* number (because this requirement will simplify the formula associated with the final result).

If $x_0, x_1, \ldots, x_n$ are the subdivision points in our partition (with $x_0 = a$ and $x_n = b$), we pass a parabolic arc through the points, three at a time (the points with x-coordinates x_0, x_1, x_2, then those with x_2, x_3, x_4, and so on). It can be shown (see Problem 42) that the region under the parabolic curve $y = f(x)$ on the interval $[x_{2k-2}, x_{2k}]$ has area

$$\tfrac{1}{3}[f(x_{2k-2}) + 4f(x_{2k-1}) + f(x_{2k})]\Delta x$$

where $\Delta x = \dfrac{b - a}{n}$. This procedure is illustrated in Figure 5.38.

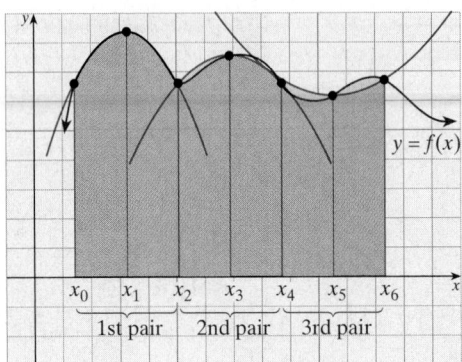

Figure 5.38 Approximation using parabolas

By adding the area of the approximating parabolic strips and combining terms, we obtain the sum S_n of n parabolic regions:

$$S_n = \tfrac{1}{3}[f(x_0) + 4f(x_1) + f(x_2)]\Delta x + \tfrac{1}{3}[f(x_2) + 4f(x_3) + f(x_4)]\Delta x$$
$$+ \cdots + \tfrac{1}{3}[f(x_{n-2}) + 4f(x_{n-1}) + f(x_n)]\Delta x$$
$$= \tfrac{1}{3}[f(x_0) + 4f(x_1) + 2f(x_2) + 4f(x_3) + \cdots + 4f(x_{n-1}) + f(x_n)]\Delta x$$

These observations are summarized in the following box:

---

*This rule is named for Thomas Simpson (1710–1761), an English mathematician who, curiously, neither discovered nor made any special use of the formula that bears his name.

Simpson's Rule

Let f be continuous on $[a, b]$. **Simpson's rule** is

$$\int_a^b f(x)\,dx \approx \tfrac{1}{3}[f(x_0) + 4f(x_1) + 2f(x_2) + 4f(x_3) + 2f(x_4) + \cdots$$
$$+ 4f(x_{n-1}) + f(x_n)]\Delta x$$

where $\Delta x = \dfrac{b - a}{n}$, $x_k = a + k\Delta x$, k an integer and n an even integer. Moreover, the larger the value for n, the better the approximation.

EXAMPLE 2   Approximation by Simpson's rule

Use Simpson's rule with $n = 10$ to approximate $\displaystyle\int_1^2 \frac{dx}{x}$.

Solution

We have $\Delta x = \dfrac{2 - 1}{10} = 0.1$, and $x_0 = a = 1$, $x_1 = 1.1$, $x_2 = 1.2, \ldots, x_9 = 1.9$, $x_{10} = b = 2$.

$$\int_1^2 \frac{1}{x}\,dx \approx S_{10}$$

$$= \frac{1}{3}\left(\frac{1}{1} + \frac{4}{1.1} + \frac{2}{1.2} + \frac{4}{1.3} + \frac{2}{1.4} + \frac{4}{1.5} + \frac{2}{1.6} + \frac{4}{1.7} + \frac{2}{1.8} + \frac{4}{1.9} + \frac{1}{2}\right)(0.1)$$

$$\approx 0.6931502$$

This estimate compares well with the value found directly by applying the fundamental theorem of calculus:

$$\int_1^2 \frac{dx}{x} = \ln 2 - \ln 1 \approx 0.6931472$$

An example of the output of a computer program for this type of problem is shown in the margin.   ∎

Comparison of Simpson's and trapezoidal rules		
Type of estimate	# of sub-intervals	Estimate over [1, 2]
Trapezoid	10	.693771403175
Simpson	10	.693150230689
Trapezoid	100	.693153430482
Simpson	100	.693147180872
Trapezoid	1000	.693147243060
Simpson	1000	.693147100560

Comparison of Simpson's and trapezoidal rules

ERROR ESTIMATION

The difference between the value of an integral and its estimated value is called its error. Since this error is a function of n we denote it by E_n.

THEOREM 5.12   Error in the trapezoidal rule and Simpson's rule

If f has a continuous second derivative on $[a, b]$, then the error E_n in approximating $\int_a^b f(x)\,dx$ by the trapezoidal rule satisfies the following:

Trapezoidal error: $|E_n| \le \dfrac{(b - a)^3}{12n^2} M$, where M is the maximum value of $|f''(x)|$ on $[a, b]$.

Moreover, if f has a continuous fourth derivative on $[a, b]$, then the error E_n (n even) in approximating $\int_a^b f(x)\,dx$ by Simpson's rule satisfies the following:

Simpson's error: $|E_n| \le \dfrac{(b - a)^5}{180n^4} K$, where K is the maximum value of $|f^{(4)}(x)|$ on $[a, b]$.

Proof   The proofs of these error estimates are beyond the scope of this book and can be found in many advanced calculus textbooks and in most numerical analysis books.   ❑

EXAMPLE 3 Estimate of error when using Simpson's rule

Estimate the accuracy of the approximation of $\int_1^2 \dfrac{dx}{x}$ by Simpson's rule with $n = 10$ in Example 2.

Solution

If $f(x) = \dfrac{1}{x}$, we find that $f^{(4)}(x) = 24x^{-5}$. The maximum value of this function will occur at a critical number (there is none on $[1, 2]$) or at an endpoint. Thus, the largest value of $\left| f^{(4)}(x) \right|$ on $[1, 2]$ is $\left| f^{(4)}(1) \right| = 24$. Now, apply the error formula with $K = 24$, $a = 1$, $b = 2$, and $n = 10$ to obtain

$$|E_{10}| \leq \frac{k(b-a)^5}{180n^4} = \frac{24(2-1)^5}{180(10)^4} \approx 0.0000133$$

That is, the error in the approximation in Example 2 is guaranteed to be no greater than 0.0000133. ∎

With the aid of the error estimates, we can decide in advance how many subintervals to use to achieve a desired degree of accuracy.

EXAMPLE 4 Choosing the number of subintervals to guarantee given accuracy

How many subintervals are required to guarantee that the error will be correct to four decimal places in the approximation of

$$\int_1^2 \frac{dx}{x}$$

on $[1, 2]$ using the trapezoidal rule?

Solution

To be correct to four decimal places means that $|E_n| < 0.00005$. Because $f(x) = x^{-1}$, we have $f''(x) = 2x^{-3}$. On $[1, 2]$ the largest value of $\left| f''(x) \right|$ is $\left| f''(1) \right| = 2$, so $M = 2$, $a = 1$, $b = 2$, and

$$|E_n| \leq \frac{2(2-1)^3}{12n^2} = \frac{1}{6n^2}$$

The goal is to find the smallest positive integer n for which

$$\frac{1}{6n^2} < 0.00005$$

$$10{,}000 < 3n^2 \qquad \textit{Multiply by the positive number } 60{,}000n^2.$$

$$10{,}000 - 3n^2 < 0$$

$$(100 - \sqrt{3}n)(100 + \sqrt{3}n) < 0$$

$$n < -\frac{100}{\sqrt{3}} \quad \text{or} \quad n > \frac{100}{\sqrt{3}} \approx 57.735$$

The smallest positive integer that satisfies this condition is $n = 58$; therefore, 58 subintervals are required to ensure the desired accuracy. ∎

If f is the linear function $f(x) = Ax + B$, then $f''(x) = 0$ and we can take $M = 0$ as the error estimate. In this case, the error in applying the trapezoidal rule satisfies $|E_n| \leq 0$. That is, the trapezoidal rule is exact for a linear function, which is what we would expect, because the region under a line on an interval is a trapezoid.

In discussing the accuracy of the trapezoidal rule as a means of estimating the value of the definite integral

$$I = \int_a^b f(x)\, dx$$

we have focused attention on the "error term," but this only measures the error that comes from estimating I by the trapezoidal or Simpson approximation sum. There are other kinds of errors that must be considered in this or any other method of approximation. In particular, each time we cut off digits from a decimal, we incur what is known as a round-off error. For example, a round-off error occurs when we use 0.66666667 in place of $\frac{2}{3}$ or 3.1415927 for the number π. Round-off errors occur even in large computers and can accumulate to cause real problems. Specialized methods for dealing with these and other errors are studied in numerical analysis.

The examples of numerical integration examined in this section are intended as illustrations and thus involve relatively simple computations, whereas in practice, such computations often involve hundreds of terms and can be quite tedious. Fortunately, these computations are extremely well suited to automatic computing, and the reader who is interested in pursuing computer methods in numerical integration will find an introduction to this topic in the *Technology Manual*.

5.8 PROBLEM SET

A *Approximate the integrals in Problems 1–2 using the trapezoidal rule and Simpson's rule with the specified number of subintervals and then compare your answers with the exact value of the definite integral.*

1. $\int_1^2 x^2 \, dx$ with $n = 4$ **2.** $\int_0^4 \sqrt{x} \, dx$ with $n = 6$

Approximate the integrals given in Problems 3–8 with the specified number of subintervals using

   a. *the trapezoidal rule*   **b.** *Simpson's rule*

3. $\int_0^1 \dfrac{dx}{1 + x^2}$ with $n = 4$

4. $\int_{-1}^0 \sqrt{1 + x^2} \, dx$ with $n = 4$

5. $\int_2^4 \sqrt{1 + \sin x} \, dx$ with $n = 4$

6. $\int_0^2 x \cos x \, dx$ with $n = 6$

7. $\int_0^2 x e^{-x} \, dx$ with $n = 6$

8. $\int_1^2 \ln x \, dx$ with $n = 6$

B   **9. WHAT DOES THIS SAY?**   Describe the trapezoidal rule.

10. WHAT DOES THIS SAY?   Describe Simpson's rule.

Estimate the value of the integrals in Problems 11–18 to within the prescribed accuracy.

11. $\int_0^1 \dfrac{dx}{x^2 + 1}$ with error less than 0.05. Use the trapezoidal rule.

12. $\int_{-1}^2 \sqrt{1 + x^2} \, dx$ with error less than 0.05. Use Simpson's rule.

13. $\int_0^1 \cos 2x \, dx$ accurate to three decimal places. Use Simpson's rule.

14. $\int_1^2 x^{-1} \, dx$ accurate to three decimal places. Use Simpson's rule.

15. $\int_0^2 x\sqrt{4 - x} \, dx$ with error less than 0.01. Use the trapezoidal rule.

16. $\int_0^\pi \theta \cos^2 \theta \, d\theta$ with error less than 0.01. Use Simpson's rule.

17. $\int_0^1 \tan^{-1} x \, dx$ with error less than 0.01. Use Simpson's rule.

18. $\int_0^\pi e^{-x} \sin x \, dx$ to three decimal places. Use Simpson's rule.

In Problems 19–23, determine how many subintervals are required to guarantee accuracy to within 0.00005 using

   a. *the trapezoidal rule*   **b.** *Simpson's rule*

19. $\int_1^3 x^{-1} \, dx$ **20.** $\int_{-1}^4 (x^3 + 2x^2 + 1) \, dx$

21. $\int_1^4 \dfrac{dx}{\sqrt{x}}$ **22.** $\int_0^2 \cos x \, dx$

23. $\int_1^2 \ln \sqrt{x} \, dx$ **24.** $\int_0^1 e^{-2x} \, dx$

25. A quarter-circle of radius 1 has the equation $y = \sqrt{1 - x^2}$ for $0 \le x \le 1$, which implies that

$$\int_0^1 \sqrt{1 - x^2} \, dx = \frac{\pi}{4}$$

   a. Estimate π correct to one decimal place by applying the trapezoidal rule to this integral.

   b. Estimate π correct to one decimal place by applying Simpson's rule to this integral.

26. Find the smallest value of n for which the trapezoidal rule estimates the value of the integral

$$\int_1^2 x^{-1} \, dx$$

with six-decimal-place accuracy.

27. The width of an irregularly shaped dam is measured at 5-m intervals, with the results indicated in Figure 5.39. Use the trapezoidal rule to estimate the area of the face of the dam.

Figure 5.39 Area of the face of a dam

28. Jack and Jill are traveling in a car with a broken odometer. In order to determine the distance they traveled between noon and 1:00 P.M., Jack (the passenger) takes a speedometer reading every 5 minutes.

Minutes (after noon)	0	5	10	15	20
Speedometer reading	54	57	50	51	55

Minutes	25	30	35	40	45	50	55	60
Speedometer	60	49	53	47	39	42	48	53

Use the trapezoidal rule to estimate the total distance traveled by the couple from noon to 1:00 P.M.

29. An industrial plant spills pollutant into a lake. The pollutant spread out to form the pattern shown in Figure 5.40. All distances are in feet.

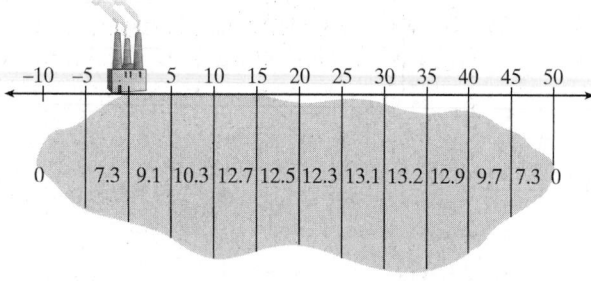

Figure 5.40 Pollutant spill

Use Simpson's rule to estimate the area of the spill.

30. Apply the trapezoidal rule to estimate $\int_0^3 f(x)\,dx$, where the values for f are found on the following spreadsheet (table):

	A	B
1	x	$f(x)$
2	0	3.7
3	0.3	3.9
4	0.6	4.1
5	0.9	4.1
6	1.2	4.2
7	1.5	4.4
8	1.8	4.6
9	2.1	4.9
10	2.4	5.2
11	2.7	5.5
12	3	6

31. Apply Simpson's rule to estimate $\int_0^5 f(x)\,dx$, where the values for f are found on the following spreadsheet (table):

	A	B
1	x	$f(x)$
2	0	10
3	0.5	9.75
4	1	10
5	1.5	10.75
6	2	12
7	2.5	13.75
8	3	16
9	3.5	18.75
10	4	22
11	4.5	25.75
12	5	30

32. In this problem, we explore the "order of convergence" of three numerical integration methods. A method is said to have "order of convergence n^k" if $E_n \cdot n^k = C$, where n is the number of intervals in the approximation and k is a constant power. In other words, the error $E_n \to 0$ as $C/n^k \to 0$. In each of the following cases, use the fact that

$$I = \int_0^\pi \sin x\,dx = -\cos x\,\big|_0^\pi = 2$$

   a. Use the trapezoidal rule to estimate I for $n = 10, 20, 40$, and 80. Compute the error E_n in each case and compute $E_n \cdot n^k$ for $k = 1, 2, 3, 4$. Based on your results, you should be able to conclude that the order of convergence of the trapezoidal approximation is n^2.

   b. Repeat part **a** using Simpson's rule. Based on your results, what is the order of convergence for Simpson's rule?

   c. Repeat part **a** using a rectangular approximation with right endpoints. What is the order of convergence for this method?

33. Let $I = \int_0^\pi (9x - x^3)\,dx$.

   a. Estimate I using rectangles, the trapezoidal rule, and Simpson's rule, for $n = 10, 20, 40, 80$. Something interesting happens with Simpson's rule. Explain.

   b. **Simpson struggles!** In contrast to part **a**, here is an example where Simpson's rule does not live up to expectations. For $n = 10, 20, 40$, and 80, use Simpson's rule and the rectangular rule (select midpoints) for this integral and make a table of errors. Then try to explain Simpson's poor performance. *Hint:* Look at the formula for the error.

$$\int_0^2 \sqrt{4 - x^2}\,dx = \pi$$

34. HISTORICAL QUEST   The mathematician Seki Kōwa was born in Fujioka, Japan, the son of a samurai, but was adopted by a patriarch of the Seki family. Seki invented and used an early form of determinants for solving systems of equations, and he also invented a method for approximating areas that is very similar to the rectangular

TAKAKAZU SEKI KŌWA
1642–1708

method introduced in this section. This method, known as the yenri (circle principle), found the area of a circle by dividing the circle into small rectangles, as shown in Figure 5.41.

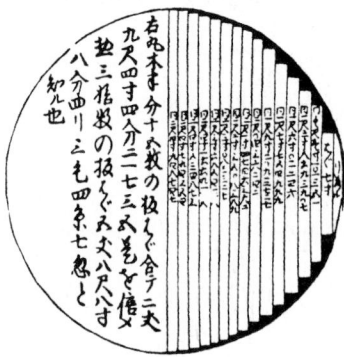

Figure 5.41 Early Asian calculus

The sample shown in Figure 5.41 was drawn by a student of Seki Kōwa. ∎

For this quest, draw a circle with radius 10 cm. Draw vertical chords through each centimeter on a diameter (you should have 18 rectangles). Measure the heights of the rectangles and approximate the area of the circle by adding the areas of the rectangles. Compare this with the formula for the area of this circle.

35. HISTORICAL QUEST   In 1670, a predecessor of Seki Kōwa (see Problem 34), Kazuyuki Sawaguchi wrote seven volumes that concluded with fifteen problems that he believed were unsolvable. In 1674, Seki Kōwa published solutions to all fifteen of Kazuyuki's unsolvable problems. One of the "unsolvable" problems was the following: Three circles are inscribed in a circle, each tangent to the other two and to the original circle. All three cover all but 120 square units of the circumscribing circle. The diameters of the two smaller inscribed circles are equal, and each is five units less than the diameter of the larger inscribed circle. Find the diameters of the three inscribed circles.

The solution to this "impossible" problem is beyond the scope of this course (it involves solving a 6th degree equation with a horrendous amount of computation), but we can replace it with a simpler problem: Consider two circles inscribed in a circle, each tangent to the other and to the original circle. The diameter of the smaller circle is five units less than the diameter of the larger inscribed circle. The sum of the areas of the larger circle and twice the smaller circle cover all but 120 square units of the circumscribing circles. Find the diameters of the two inscribed circles.

36. HISTORICAL QUEST   Isaac Newton (see Historical Quest essay at the end of Chapter 1 on page 48) invented a preliminary version of Simpson's rule. In 1779, Newton wrote an article to an addendum to *Methodus Differentials* (1711) in which he gave the following example: If there are four ordinates at equal intervals, let A be the sum of the first and fourth, B the sum of the second and third, and R the interval

ROGER COTES
1682–1716

between the first and fourth; then . . . the area between the first and fourth ordinates is approximated by $\frac{1}{8}(A + 3B)R$. This is known today as the "Newton-Cotes three-eighths rule," which can be expressed in the form

$$\int_{x_0}^{x_3} f(x)\,dx \approx \tfrac{3}{8}(y_0 + 3y_1 + 3y_2 + y_3)\Delta x$$

Roger Cotes and James Stirling (1692–1770) both knew this formula, as well as what we called in this section Simpson's rule. In 1743, this rule was rediscovered by Thomas Simpson (1710–1761). ∎

Estimate the integral

$$\int_0^3 \tan^{-1} x\,dx$$

using the Newton-Cotes three-eighths rule, and then compare with approximation using left endpoints (rectangles) and trapezoids with $n = 4$. Which of the three rules gives the most accurate estimate?

37. Show that if $p(x)$ is any polynomial of degree less than or equal to 3, then

$$\int_a^b p(x)\,dx = \frac{b-a}{6}\left[p(a) + 4p\left(\frac{a+b}{2}\right) + p(b)\right]$$

This result is often called the *prismoidal rule*.

38. Use the prismoidal rule (Problem 37) to evaluate

$$\int_{-1}^2 (x^3 - 3x + 4)\,dx$$

39. Use the prismoidal rule (Problem 37) to evaluate

$$\int_{-1}^3 (x^3 + 2x^2 - 7)\,dx$$

40. Let $p(x)$ be a polynomial of degree at most 3.
   a. Find a number c between 0 and 1 such that

   $$\int_{-1}^1 p(x)\,dx = p(c) + p(-c)$$

   b. Find a number c between $-\frac{1}{2}$ and $\frac{1}{2}$ such that

   $$\int_{-1/2}^{1/2} p(x)\,dx = \tfrac{1}{3}[p(-c) + p(0) + p(c)]$$

41. Let $p(x) = Ax^3 + Bx^2 + Cx + D$ be a cubic polynomial. Show that Simpson's rule gives the exact value for

$$\int_a^b p(x)\,dx$$

42. The object of this exercise is to prove Simpson's rule for the special case involving three points.
   a. Let $P_1(-h, f(-h))$, $P_2(0, f(0))$, $P_3(h, f(h))$. Find the equation of the form $y = Ax^2 + Bx + C$ for the parabola through the points P_1, P_2, and P_3.

b. If $y = p(x)$ is the quadratic function found in part **a**, show that

$$\int_{-h}^{h} p(x)\,dx = \frac{h}{3}[p(-h) + 4p(0) + p(h)]$$

c. Let $Q_1(x_1, f(x_1))$, $Q_2(x_2, f(x_2))$, $Q_3(x_3, f(x_3))$ be points with $x_2 = x_1 + h$, and $x_3 = x_1 + 2h$. Explain why

$$\int_{x_1}^{x_3} p(x)\,dx = \frac{h}{3}[p(x_1) + 4p(x_2) + p(x_3)]$$

5.9 An Alternative Approach: The Logarithm as an Integral

IN THIS SECTION natural logarithm as an integral, geometric interpretation, the natural exponential function

NATURAL LOGARITHM AS AN INTEGRAL

You may have noticed in Section 2.4 that we did not prove the properties of exponential functions for all real number exponents. To treat exponentials and logarithms *rigorously*, we use the alternative approach provided in this section. Specifically, we use a definite integral to introduce the *natural logarithmic function* and then use this function to *define* the *natural exponential function*.

"When I use a word," Humpty Dumpty said, "it means just what I choose it to mean—nothing more or less."
——Lewis Carroll (1832–1898)

Natural Logarithm

> The **natural logarithm** is the function defined by
>
> $$\ln x = \int_{1}^{x} \frac{dt}{t} \qquad x > 0$$

At first glance, it appears there is nothing "natural" about this definition, but if this integral function has the properties of a logarithm, why should we not call it a logarithm? We begin with a theorem that shows that $\ln x$ does indeed have the properties we would expect of a logarithm.

THEOREM 5.13 **Properties of a logarithm as defined by** $\ln x = \int_{1}^{x} \frac{dt}{t}$

Let $x > 0$ and $y > 0$ be positive numbers. Then

a. $\ln 1 = 0$ **b.** $\ln xy = \ln x + \ln y$

c. $\ln \dfrac{x}{y} = \ln x - \ln y$ **d.** $\ln x^p = p \ln x$ for all rational numbers p

Proof

a. Let $x = 1$. Then $\displaystyle\int_{1}^{1} \frac{dt}{t} = 0$.

b. For fixed positive numbers x and y, we use the additive property of integrals as follows:

$$\ln(xy) = \int_{1}^{xy} \frac{dt}{t} = \int_{1}^{x} \frac{dt}{t} + \int_{x}^{xy} \frac{dt}{t}$$

$$= \ln x + \int_{1}^{y} \frac{x\,du}{ux}$$

$$= \ln x + \int_{1}^{y} \frac{du}{u}$$

$$= \ln x + \ln y$$

> Let $u = \dfrac{t}{x}$, so $t = ux$;
>
> $dt = x\,du$.
> If $t = x$, then $u = 1$;
> if $t = xy$, then $u = y$.

c. and **d.** The proofs are outlined in the problem set. ❑

GEOMETRIC INTERPRETATION

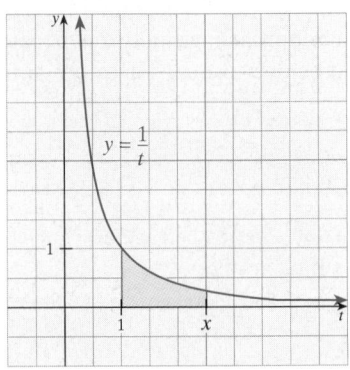

Figure 5.42 If $x > 1$, $\ln x = \int_1^x \dfrac{dt}{t}$ is the area under $y = \dfrac{1}{t}$ on $[1, x]$.

An advantage of defining the logarithm by the integral formula is that calculus can be used to study the properties of $\ln x$ from the beginning. For example, note that if $x > 1$, the integral

$$\ln x = \int_1^x \frac{dt}{t}$$

may be interpreted geometrically as the area under the graph of $y = \dfrac{1}{t}$ from $t = 1$ to $t = x$, as shown in Figure 5.42. If $x > 1$, then $\ln x > 0$. On the other hand, if $0 < x < 1$, then

$$\ln x = \int_1^x \frac{dt}{t} = -\int_x^1 \frac{dt}{t} < 0$$

so that

$$\ln x > 0 \quad \text{if } x > 1$$
$$\ln 1 = 0$$
$$\ln x < 0 \quad \text{if } 0 < x < 1$$

The definition $\ln x = \int_1^x \dfrac{dt}{t}$ makes it easy to differentiate $\ln x$. Recall from Section 5.4 that according to the second fundamental theorem of calculus, if f is continuous on $[a, b]$, then

$$F(x) = \int_a^x f(t)\,dt$$

is a differentiable function of x with derivative $\dfrac{dF}{dx} = f(x)$ on any interval $[a, x]$. Therefore, because $\dfrac{1}{t}$ is continuous for all $t > 0$, it follows that $\ln x = \int_1^x \dfrac{dt}{t}$ is differentiable for all $x > 0$ with derivative $\dfrac{d}{dx}(\ln x) = \dfrac{1}{x}$. By applying the chain rule, we also find that

$$\frac{d}{dx}(\ln u) = \frac{1}{u}\frac{du}{dx}$$

for any differentiable function u of x with $u > 0$.

To analyze the graph of $f(x) = \ln x$, we use the curve-sketching methods of Chapter 4:

a. $\ln x$ is continuous for all $x > 0$ (because it is differentiable), so its graph is "unbroken."

b. The graph of $\ln x$ is always *rising*, because the derivative

$$\frac{d}{dx}(\ln x) = \frac{1}{x}$$

is positive for $x > 0$. (Recall that the natural logarithm is defined only for $x > 0$.)

c. The graph of $\ln x$ is *concave down*, because the second derivative

$$\frac{d^2}{dx^2}(\ln x) = \frac{d}{dx}\left(\frac{1}{x}\right) = \frac{-1}{x^2}$$

is negative for all $x > 0$.

d. Note that $\ln 2 > 0$ (because $\int_1^2 \frac{dt}{t} > 0$) and because $\ln 2^p = p \ln 2$, it follows that $\lim\limits_{p \to +\infty} \ln 2^p = +\infty$. But the graph of $f(x) = \ln x$ is always rising, and thus $\lim\limits_{x \to +\infty} \ln x = +\infty$. Similarly, it can be shown that $\lim\limits_{x \to 0^+} \ln x = -\infty$.

e. If b is any positive number, there is exactly one number a such that $\ln a = b$ (because the graph of $\ln x$ is always rising for $x > 0$). In particular, we define $x = e$ as the unique number that satisfies $\ln x = 1$.

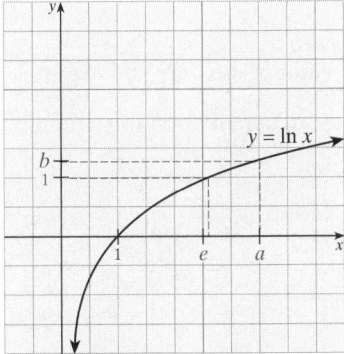

Figure 5.43 The graph of the natural logarithm function, $\ln x$

These features are shown in Figure 5.43.

THE NATURAL EXPONENTIAL FUNCTION

Originally, we introduced the natural exponential function e^x and then defined the natural logarithm $\ln x$ as the inverse of e^x. In this alternative approach, we note that because the natural logarithm is an increasing function, it must be one-to-one. Therefore, it has an inverse function, which we denote by $E(x)$.

Because $\ln x$ and $E(x)$ are inverses, we have

$$E(x) = y \quad \text{if and only if} \quad \ln y = x$$

From the definition of inverse formulas we have

$$E(\ln x) = x \quad \text{and} \quad \ln[E(x)] = x$$

We call these formulas the **inversion formulas**. Therefore,

$$
\begin{aligned}
E(0) &= E(\ln 1) && \text{Because } \ln 1 = 0 \\
&= 1 && \text{Because } E(\ln x) = x
\end{aligned}
$$

and

$$
\begin{aligned}
E(1) &= E(\ln e) && \text{Because } \ln e = 1 \\
&= e && \text{Because } E(\ln e) = e
\end{aligned}
$$

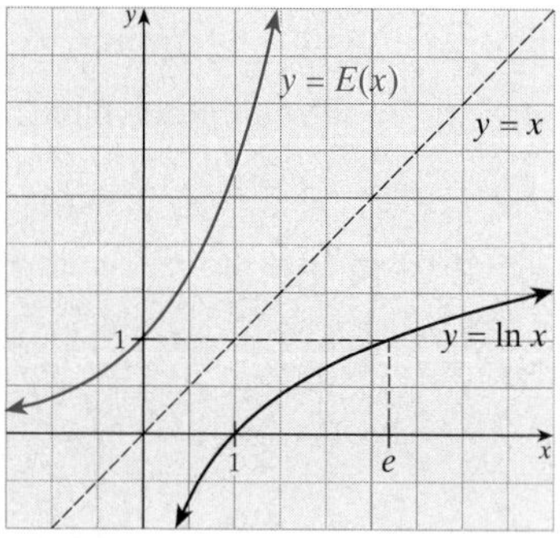

To obtain the graph of $E(x)$, we reflect the graph of $y = \ln x$ in the line $y = x$. The graph is shown in Figure 5.44. Notice that $\ln x = 1$ has the unique solution $x = e$.

The following algebraic properties of the natural exponential function can be obtained by using the properties of the natural logarithm given in Theorem 5.13 along with the inversion formulas.

Figure 5.44 The graph of $E(x)$ is the reflection of the graph of $\ln x$ in the line $y = x$.

THEOREM 5.14 Properties of the exponential as defined by $E(x)$

For any numbers x and y,

a. $E(0) = 1$

b. $E(x + y) = E(x)E(y)$

c. $E(x - y) = \dfrac{E(x)}{E(y)}$

d. $[E(x)]^p = E(px)$

Proof

a. Proved above (inversion formula).

b. We use the fact that $\ln AB = \ln A + \ln B$ to show that

$$
\begin{aligned}
\ln[E(x)E(y)] &= \ln E(x) + \ln E(y) && \text{Property of logarithms} \\
&= x + y && \text{Inversion formula} \\
&= \ln E(x + y) && \text{Inversion formula}
\end{aligned}
$$

Because $\ln x$ is a one-to-one function, we conclude that

$$E(x)E(y) = E(x + y)$$

c. and **d.** The proofs are similar and are left as exercises. ❑

Next, we use implicit differentiation along with the differentiation formula

$$\frac{d}{dx}(\ln x) = \frac{1}{x}$$

to obtain a differentiation formula for $E(x)$.

THEOREM 5.15 Derivative of $E(x)$

The function defined by $E(x)$ is differentiable and

$$\frac{dE}{dx} = E(x)$$

Proof It can be shown that the inverse of any differentiable function is also differentiable so long as the derivative is never zero (see Appendix B). Since $\ln x$ is differentiable, it follows that its inverse $E(x)$ is also differentiable, and using implicit differentiation, we find that

$$\ln y = \ln[E(x)] \qquad y = E(x)$$

$$\ln y = x \qquad \text{Inversion formula}$$

$$\frac{1}{y}\frac{dy}{dx} = 1 \qquad \text{Differentiate implicitly.}$$

$$\frac{dy}{dx} = y$$

$$\frac{dE}{dx} = E(x) \qquad \text{Because } \frac{dy}{dx} = \frac{dE}{dx} \text{ and } E(x) = y \qquad \square$$

Finally, we observe that if r is a rational number, then

$$\ln(e^r) = r \ln e = r$$

so that

$$E(r) = e^r$$

This means that $E(x) = e^x$ when x is a rational number, and we **define** $E(x)$ to be e^x for irrational x as well. In particular, we now have an alternative definition for e: $E(1) = e^1 = e$.

5.9 PROBLEM SET

Ⓒ 1. Use the integral definition

$$\ln x = \int_1^x \frac{dt}{t}$$

to show that $\ln x \to -\infty$ as $x \to 0^+$. *Hint*: What happens to $\ln(2^{-N})$ as N grows large without bound?

2. Use Simpson's rule with $n = 8$ subintervals to estimate

$$\ln 3 = \int_1^3 \frac{dt}{t}$$

Compare your estimate with the value of $\ln 3$ obtained from your calculator.

3. Use the error estimate for Simpson's rule to determine the accuracy of the estimate in Problem 2. How many subintervals should be used in Simpson's rule to estimate $\ln 3$ with an error not greater than 0.00005?

4. Prove the quotient rule for logarithms,

$$\ln\left(\frac{x}{y}\right) = \ln x - \ln y$$

for all $x > 0$, $y > 0$. *Hint*: Use the product rule for logarithms.

5. Show that $\ln(x^p) = p \ln x$ for $x > 0$ and all rational exponents p by completing the following steps.

a. Let $F(x) = \ln(x^p)$ and $G(x) = p \ln x$. Show that $F'(x) = G'(x)$ for $x > 0$. Conclude that $F(x) = G(x) + C$.

b. Let $x = 1$ and conclude that $F(x) = G(x)$. That is, $\ln(x^p) = p \ln x$.

6. Use Rolle's theorem to show that

$$\ln M = \ln N$$

if and only if $M = N$. *Hint*: Show that if $M \neq N$, Rolle's theorem implies that

$$\frac{d}{dx}(\ln x) = 0$$

for some number c between M and N. Why is this impossible?

7. The product rule for logarithms states

$$\log_b(MN) = \log_b M + \log_b N$$

For this reason, we want the natural logarithm function $\ln x$ to satisfy the functional equation

$$f(xy) = f(x) + f(y)$$

Suppose $f(x)$ is a function that satisfies this equation throughout its domain D.

a. Show that if $f(1)$ is defined, then $f(1) = 0$.

b. Show that if $f(-1)$ is defined, then $f(-1) = 0$.

c. Show that $f(-x) = f(x)$ for all x in D.

d. If $f'(x)$ is defined for each $x \neq 0$, show that

$$f'(x) = \frac{f'(1)}{x}$$

Then show that

$$f(x) = f'(1) \int_1^x \frac{dt}{t} \quad \text{for} \quad x > 0$$

e. Conclude that any solution of

$$f(xy) = f(x) + f(y)$$

that is not identically 0 and has a derivative for all $x \neq 0$ must be a multiple of

$$L(x) = \int_1^{|x|} \frac{dt}{t} \quad \text{for } x \neq 0$$

8. Show that for each number A, there is only one number x for which $\ln x = A$. *Hint*: If not, then $\ln x = \ln y = A$ for $x \neq y$. Why is this impossible?

9. a. Use an area argument to show that $\ln 2 < 1$.

b. Show that $\ln 3 > 1$, and then explain why $2 < e < 3$.

10. Prove $E(x - y) = \dfrac{E(x)}{E(y)}$.

11. Prove $E(x)^p = E(px)$.

Proficiency Examination

CONCEPT PROBLEMS

1. What is an antiderivative?
2. State the integration rule for powers.
3. State the exponential rule for integration.
4. State the integration rules we have learned for the trigonometric functions.
5. State the integration rules for the inverse trigonometric functions.
6. What is an area function? What do we mean by area as an antiderivative? What conditions are necessary for an integral to represent an area?
7. What is the formula for area as the limit of a sum?
8. What is a Riemann sum?
9. Define a definite integral.
10. Complete these statements summarizing the general properties of the definite integral.

   a. Definite integral at a point: $\displaystyle\int_a^a f(x)\,dx = $ _____

   b. Switching limits of a definite integral: $\displaystyle\int_b^a f(x)\,dx = $ ____

11. How can distance traveled by an object be expressed as an integral?
12. State the first fundamental theorem of calculus.
13. State the second fundamental theorem of calculus.
14. Describe in your own words the process of integration by substitution.
15. What is a differential equation?
16. What is a separable differential equation? How do you solve such an equation?
17. What is the growth/decay equation? Describe carbon dating.
18. What is an orthogonal trajectory?
19. State the mean value theorem for integrals.
20. What is the formula for the average value of a continuous function?
21. State the following approximation rules:
   a. rectangular approximation
   b. trapezoidal rule
   c. Simpson's rule

PRACTICE PROBLEMS

22. Given that $\displaystyle\int_0^1 [f(x)]^4\,dx = \frac{1}{5}$ and $\displaystyle\int_0^1 [f(x)]^2\,dx = \frac{1}{3}$, find

$$\int_0^1 [f(x)]^2\{2[f(x)]^2 - 3\}\,dx$$

23. Find $F'(x)$ if $F(x) = \displaystyle\int_3^x t^5\sqrt{\cos(2t+1)}\,dt$.

Evaluate the integrals in Problems 24–29.

24. $\displaystyle\int \frac{dx}{1+4x^2}$

25. $\displaystyle\int xe^{-x^2}\,dx$

26. $\displaystyle\int_1^4 (\sqrt{x} + x^{-3/2})\,dx$

27. $\displaystyle\int_0^1 (2x-6)(x^2-6x+2)^2\,dx$

28. $\displaystyle\int_0^{\pi/2} \frac{\sin x\,dx}{(1+\cos x)^2}$

29. $\displaystyle\int_{-2}^1 (2x+1)\sqrt{2x^2+2x+5}\,dx$

30. Find the area under the curve $f(x) = 3x^2 + 2$ over $[-1, 3]$.

31. Approximate the area under the curve $g(x) = e^{x^2}$ over $[1, 2]$.*

32. Find the average value of $y = \cos 2x$ on the interval $\left[0, \frac{\pi}{2}\right]$.

33. **Modeling Problem** In 1995, a team of archaeologists led by Michel Brunet of the University of Poitiers announced the identification in Chad of *Australopithecus* specimens believed to be about 3.5 Myr (million years) old.[†] Using the exponential decay equation, explain why the archaeologists were reluctant to use carbon-14 to date their find.

---

*There is an interesting discussion of this integral in the May 1999 issue of *The American Mathematical Monthly* in an article entitled, "What Is a Closed-Form Number?" The function $\int e^{x^2}$ is an example of a function that is **not** an elementary function (that we mentioned in Section 1.3).

[†]"Early Hominid Fossils from Africa," by Meave Leakey and Alan Walker, *Scientific American*, June 1997, p. 79.

34. A slope field for the differential equation

$$y' = x + y$$

is given in Figure 5.45.

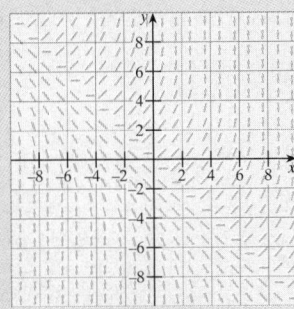

Figure 5.45 Direction field

Draw the particular solutions passing through the points requested in parts **a–d**.

a. $(0, -4)$ **b.** $(0, 2)$ **c.** $(4, 0)$ **d.** $(-4, 0)$

e. All of the curves you have drawn in parts **a–d** seem to have a common asymptote. From the slope field, write the equation for this asymptote.

35. a. Find the necessary n to estimate the value of $\displaystyle\int_0^{\pi/2} \cos x \, dx$ to within 0.0005 of its correct value using the trapezoidal rule.

b. What is n if Simpson's rule is used?

Supplementary Problems

Find the definite integrals of the functions in Problems 1–3.

1. Given that $\displaystyle\int_{-1}^0 f(x)\,dx = 3,\quad \int_0^1 f(x)\,dx = -1,$ and $\displaystyle\int_{-1}^1 g(x)\,dx = 7,$ find $\displaystyle\int_{-1}^1 [3g(x) + 2f(x)]\,dx.$

2. Use the definition of the definite integral to find $\displaystyle\int_0^1 (3x^2 + 2x - 1)\,dx.$

3. Use the definition of the definite integral to find $\displaystyle\int_0^1 (4x^3 + 6x^2 + 3)\,dx.$

Find the definite and indefinite integrals in Problems 4–31. If you do not have a technique for finding a closed (exact) answer, approximate the integral using numerical integration.

4. $\displaystyle\int_0^1 (5x^4 - 8x^3 + 1)\,dx$

5. $\displaystyle\int_{-1}^2 30(5x - 2)^2\,dx$

6. $\displaystyle\int_0^1 (x\sqrt{x} + 2)^2\,dx$

7. $\displaystyle\int_1^2 \frac{x^2\,dx}{\sqrt{x^3 + 1}}$

8. $\displaystyle\int_2^2 (x + \sin x)^3\,dx$

9. $\displaystyle\int_{-1}^0 \frac{dx}{\sqrt{1 - 2x}}$

10. $\displaystyle\int_1^2 \frac{dx}{\sqrt{3x - 1}}$

11. $\displaystyle\int_{-1}^0 \frac{dx}{\sqrt[3]{1 - 2x}}$

12. $\displaystyle\int \frac{1}{x^3}\,dx$

13. $\displaystyle\int \frac{5x^2 - 2x + 1}{\sqrt{x}}\,dx$

14. $\displaystyle\int \frac{x + 1}{2x}\,dx$

15. $\displaystyle\int \frac{3 - x}{\sqrt{1 - x^2}}\,dx$

16. $\displaystyle\int (e^{-x} + 1)e^x\,dx$

17. $\displaystyle\int \frac{\sin x - \cos x}{\sin x + \cos x}\,dx$

18. $\displaystyle\int \sqrt{x}(x^2 + \sqrt{x} + 1)\,dx$

19. $\displaystyle\int (x - 1)^2\,dx$

20. $\displaystyle\int \frac{x^2 + 1}{x^2}\,dx$

21. $\displaystyle\int (\sin^2 x + \cos^2 x)\,dx$

22. $\displaystyle\int x(x + 4)\sqrt{x^3 + 6x^2 + 2}\,dx$

23. $\displaystyle\int x(2x^2 + 1)\sqrt{x^4 + x^2}\,dx$

24. $\displaystyle\int \frac{dx}{\sqrt{x}(\sqrt{x} + 1)^2}$

25. $\displaystyle\int x\sqrt{1 - 5x^2}\,dx$

26. $\displaystyle\int \sqrt{\sin x - \cos x}(\sin x + \cos x)\,dx$

27. $\displaystyle\int x^3 \cos(\tan^{-1} x)\,dx$

28. $\displaystyle\int (\cos^{11} x \sin^9 x - \cos^9 x \sin^{11} x)\,dx$

29. $\displaystyle\int \frac{\ln x}{x}\sqrt{1 + \ln(2x)}\,dx$

30. $\displaystyle\int_{-10}^{10} [3 + 7x^{73} - 100x^{101}]\,dx$

31. $\displaystyle\int_{-\pi/4}^{\pi/4} [\sin(4x) + 2\cos(4x)]\,dx$

In Problems 32–35, draw the indicated particular solution for the differential equations whose direction fields are given.

32. $y(4) = 0$

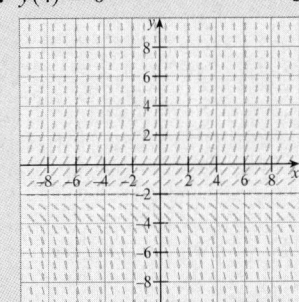

33. $y(10) = 1$

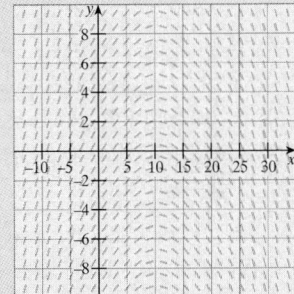

34. $y(0) = 2$

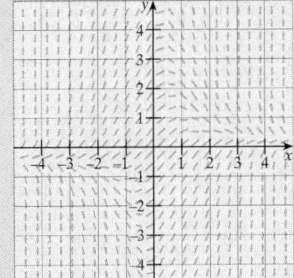

35. $y(0) = 0$

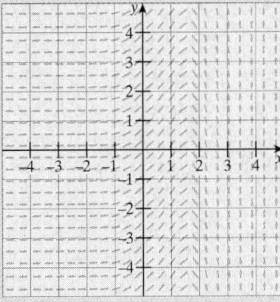

36. Find $F'(x)$, where $F(x) = \displaystyle\int_5^x t^2 \cos^4 t \, dt$

37. Find the area under $f(x) = x^{-1}$ on $[1, 4]$.

38. Find the area under $f(x) = 2 + x - x^2$ on $[-1, 1]$.

39. Find the area under $f(x) = e^{4x}$ on $[0, 2]$.

40. Find the area bounded by the curve $y = x\sqrt{x^2 + 5}$, the x-axis, and the vertical lines $x = -1$ and $x = 2$.

41. Find $f(t)$ if $f''(t) = \sin 4t - \cos 2t$ and $f\left(\frac{\pi}{2}\right) = f'\left(\frac{\pi}{2}\right) = 1$.

42. Find $f(x)$ if $f'''(x) = 2x^3 + x^2$, given that $f''(1) = 2$, $f'(1) = 1$, and $f(1) = 0$.

Solve the differential equations in Problems 43–50.

43. $\dfrac{dy}{dx} = (1 - y)^2$ **44.** $\dfrac{dy}{dx} = \dfrac{\cos 4x}{y}$

45. $\dfrac{dy}{dx} = \left(\dfrac{\cos y}{\sin x}\right)^2$ **46.** $\dfrac{dy}{dx} = \dfrac{x}{y}$

47. $\dfrac{dy}{dx} = y(x^2 + 1)$ **48.** $\dfrac{dy}{dx} = \dfrac{x}{y}\sqrt{\dfrac{y^2 + 2}{x^2 + 1}}$

49. $\dfrac{dy}{dx} = \dfrac{\cos^2 y}{\cot x}$ **50.** $\dfrac{dy}{dx} = \sqrt{\dfrac{x}{y}}$

51. Find the average value of $f(x) = \dfrac{\sin x}{\cos^2 x}$ on the interval $\left[0, \frac{\pi}{4}\right]$.

52. Find the average value of $f(x) = \sin x$
   a. on $[0, \pi]$ **b.** on $[0, 2\pi]$

53. Use the trapezoidal rule with $n = 6$ to approximate $\displaystyle\int_0^\pi \sin x \, dx$. Compare your result with the exact value of this integral.

54. Estimate $\displaystyle\int_0^1 \sqrt{1 + x^3} \, dx$ using the trapezoidal rule with $n = 6$.

55. Estimate $\displaystyle\int_0^1 \dfrac{dx}{\sqrt{1 + x^3}}$ using the trapezoidal rule with $n = 8$.

56. Estimate $\displaystyle\int_0^1 \sqrt{1 + x^3} \, dx$ using Simpson's rule with $n = 6$.

57. Use the trapezoidal rule to approximate $\displaystyle\int_0^1 \dfrac{x^2 \, dx}{1 + x^2}$ with an error no greater than 0.005.

58. Use the trapezoidal rule to estimate to within 0.00005 the value of the integral

$$\int_1^2 \sqrt{x + \frac{1}{x}} \, dx$$

59. HISTORICAL QUEST Karl Gauss is considered to be one of the four greatest mathematicians of all time, along with Archimedes (Historical Quest, Problem 53, Section 3.8), Newton (Historical Quest, Problem 1, Mathematical Essays of Chapter 1, p. 48), and Euler (Historical Quest, Chapter 4 supplementary Problem 84). Gauss graduated from college at the age of 15 and  KARL GAUSS 1777–1855 proved what was to become the fundamental theorem of algebra for his doctoral thesis at the age of 22. He published only a small portion of the ideas that seemed to storm his mind, because he believed that each published result had to be complete, concise, polished, and convincing. His motto was "Few, but ripe." Carl B. Boyer, in *A History of Mathematics*, describes Gauss as the last mathematician to know everything in his subject, and we could relate Gauss to nearly every topic of this book. Such a generalization is bound to be inexact, but it does emphasize the breadth of interest Gauss displayed.

A **prime number**, p, is a counting number that has exactly two divisors. **The prime number theorem**, conjectured by Gauss in 1793, says that the number of primes $\pi(x)$ less than a real number x is a function that behaves like $x/\ln x$ as $x \to \infty$; that is,

$$\lim_{x \to +\infty} \frac{\pi(x)}{x/\ln x} = 1$$

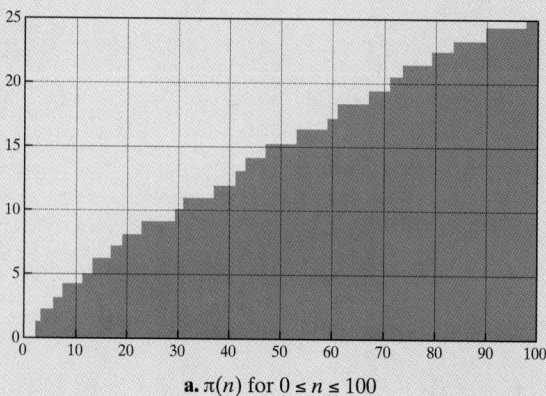
a. $\pi(n)$ for $0 \le n \le 100$

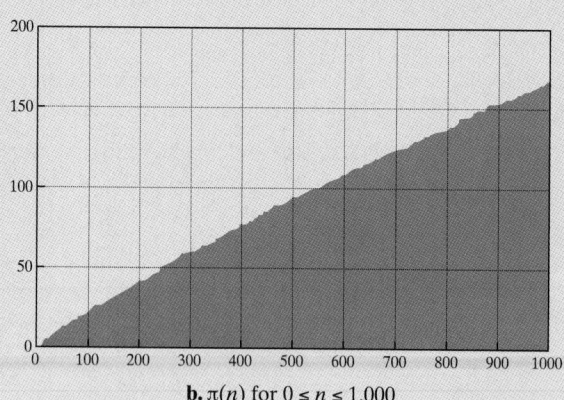
b. $\pi(n)$ for $0 \le n \le 1{,}000$

Figure 5.46 Graphs of $\pi(n)$

Gauss estimated the prime distribution function $\pi(x)$ by the integral

$$G(x) = \int_2^x \frac{dt}{\ln t}$$

known as the *integral logarithm* function. History records many who constructed tables for $\pi(n)$, and Figure 5.46 shows values for $\pi(n)$ for various choices of n. ∎

Your Quest is to examine this estimate by using the trapezoidal rule to approximate $G(x)$ for $x = 100$, $1{,}000$, and $10{,}000$. The actual value of $\pi(x)$ for selected values of x are as follows:

n	$\pi(n)$
10^3	168
10^4	1,229
10^5	9,592
10^6	78,498
10^{10}	455,052,511

60. HISTORICAL QUEST There are many ways to estimate the prime distribution function $\pi(x)$ defined in Problem 59 other than by the integral function $G(x)$ used by Gauss. Adrien-Marie Legendre is best known for his work with elliptic integrals and mathematical physics. In 1794, he proved that π was an irrational number and formulated a conjecture that is equivalent to the prime number theorem. He made his estimate using the function

ADRIEN-MARIE
LEGENDRE
1752–1833

$$\pi(x) \approx L(x) = \frac{x}{\ln x - 1.08366} \quad \blacksquare$$

For this Quest, use $L(x)$ to estimate $\pi(x)$ for $x = 100$, 1,000, and 10,000, and then compare with the results found using $G(x)$ in Problem 59.

61. Approximate the average value of the function defined by

$$f(x) = \frac{\cos x}{1 - \dfrac{x^2}{2}}$$

on $[0, 1]$. *Hint*: Use the trapezoidal rule with $n = 6$.

62. The brakes of a certain automobile produce a constant deceleration of k m/s^2. The car is traveling at 25 m/s when the driver is forced to hit the brakes. If it comes to rest at a point 50 m from the point where the brakes are applied, what is k?

63. A particle moves along the t-axis in such a way that $a(t) = -4s(t)$, where $s(t)$ and $a(t)$ are its position and acceleration, respectively, at time t. The particle starts from rest at $s = 5$.

  a. Show that $v^2 + 4s^2 = 100$, where $v(t)$ is the velocity of the particle. *Hint*: First use the chain rule to show that $a(t) = v(dv/ds)$.

  b. What is the velocity when the particle first reaches $s = 3$? *Note*: At the time in question, the sign of v is determined by the direction the particle is moving.

64. An object experiences linear acceleration given by

$$a(t) = 2t + 1 \quad \text{ft/s}^2$$

Find the velocity and position of the object, given that it starts its motion (at $t = 0$) at $s = 4$ with initial velocity 2 ft/s.

65. When it is x years old, a certain industrial machine generates revenue at the rate of $R'(x) = 1{,}575 - 5x^2$ thousand dollars per year. Find a function that measures the amount of revenue, and find the revenue for the first five years.

66. A manufacturer estimates marginal revenue to be $100x^{-1/3}$ dollars per unit when the level of production is x units. The corresponding marginal cost is found to be $0.4x$ dollars per unit. Suppose the manufacturer's profit is $520 when the level of production is 16 units. What is the manufacturer's profit when the level of production is 25 units?

67. A tree has been transplanted and after t years is growing at a rate of

$$1 + \frac{1}{(t+1)^2}$$

feet per year. After 2 years it has reached a height of 5 ft. How tall was the tree when it was transplanted?

68. A manufacturer estimates that the marginal revenue of a certain commodity is

$$R'(x) = \sqrt{x}(x^{3/2} + 1)^{-1/2}$$

dollars per unit when x units are produced. Assuming no revenue is obtained when $x = 0$, how much revenue is obtained from producing $x = 4$ units?

69. Find a function whose tangent has slope $x\sqrt{x^2 + 5}$ for each value of x and whose graph passes through the point $(2, 10)$.

70. A particle moves along the x-axis in such a way that after t seconds its acceleration is $a(t) = 12(2t + 1)^{-3/2}$. If it starts at rest at $x = 3$, where will it be 4 seconds later?

71. An environmental study of a certain community suggests that t years from now, the level of carbon monoxide in the air will be changing at the rate of $0.1t + 0.2$ parts per million per year. If the current level of carbon monoxide in the air is 3.4 parts per million, what will the level be 3 years from now?

72. A woman, driving on a straight, level road at the constant speed v_0, is forced to apply her brakes to avoid hitting a cow. The car comes to a stop 3 seconds later, s_0 ft from the point where the brakes were applied. Continuing on her way, she increases her speed by 20 ft/s to make up time but is again forced to hit the brakes, and this time it takes her 5 seconds and s_1 feet to come to a full stop. Assuming that her brakes supplied a constant deceleration k ft/s^2 each time they were used, find k and determine v_0, s_0, and s_1.

73. A study indicates that x months from now the population of a certain town will be increasing at the rate of $10 + 2\sqrt{x}$ people per month. By how much will the population of the town increase over the next 9 months?

74. It is estimated that t days from now a farmer's crop will be increasing at the rate of $0.3t^2 + 0.6t + 1$ bushels per day. By how much will the value of the crop increase during the next 6 days if the market price remains fixed at $2 per bushel?

75. Records indicate that t months after the beginning of the year, the price of turkey in local supermarkets was

$$P(t) = 0.06t^2 - 0.2t + 1.2$$

dollars per pound. What was the average price of turkey during the first 6 months of the year?

76. Modeling Problem V. A. Tucker and K. Schmidt-Koenig have investigated the relationship between the velocity v (km/h) of a bird in flight and the energy $E(v)$ expended by the bird.[*] Their study showed that for a certain kind of parakeet, the rate of change of the energy expended with respect to velocity is modeled (for $v > 0$) by

$$\frac{dE}{dv} = \frac{0.074v^2 - 112.65}{v^2}$$

  a. What is the most economical velocity for the parakeet? That is, find the velocity v_0 that minimizes the energy.

  b. Suppose it is known that $E = E_0$ when $v = v_0$. Express E in terms of v_0 and E_0.

  c. Express the average energy expended as the parakeet's velocity ranges from $v = \frac{1}{2}v_0$ to $v = v_0$ in terms of E_0.

[*]Adapted from "Flight Speeds of Birds in Relation to Energies and Wind Directions," by V. A. Tucker and K. Schmidt-Koenig. *The Auk*, Vol. 88 (1971), pp. 97–107.

77. Modeling Problem A toxin is introduced into a bacterial culture, and t hours later, the population $P(t)$ of the culture is found to be changing at the rate

$$\frac{dP}{dt} = -(\ln 2)2^{5-t}$$

If there were 1 million bacteria in the culture when the toxin was introduced, when will the culture die out?

78. Modeling Problem *The Snowplow Problem of R. P. Agnew** ■ (This problem was mentioned in the preview for this chapter.) One day it starts snowing at a steady rate sometime before noon. At noon, a snowplow starts to clear a straight, level section of road. If the plow clears 1 mile of road during the first hour but requires 2 hr to clear the second mile, at what time did it start snowing? Answer this question by completing the following steps:

a. Let t be the time (in hours) from noon. Let h be the depth of the snow at time t, and let s be the distance moved by the plow. If the plow has width w and clears snow at the constant rate p, explain why $wh\dfrac{ds}{dt} = p$.

b. Suppose it started snowing t_0 hours before noon. Let r denote the (constant) rate of snowfall. Explain why

$$h(t) = r(t + t_0)$$

By combining this equation with the differential equation in part **a**, note that

$$wr(t + t_0)\frac{ds}{dt} = p$$

Solve this differential equation (with appropriate conditions) to obtain t_0 and answer the question posed in the problem.

79. a. If f is continuous on $[a, b]$, show that

$$\left| \int_a^b f(x)\,dx \right| \le \int_a^b |f(x)|\,dx$$

b. Show that $\left| \displaystyle\int_1^4 \frac{\sin x}{x}\,dx \right| \le \dfrac{3}{2}$.

80. A company plans to hire additional advertising personnel. Suppose it is estimated that if x new people are hired, they will bring in additional revenue of $R(x) = \sqrt{2x}$ thousand dollars and that the cost of adding these x people will be $C(x) = \frac{1}{3}x$ thousand dollars. How many new people should be hired? How much total net revenue (that is, revenue minus cost) is gained by hiring these people?

81. The half-life of the radioactive isotope cobalt-60 is 5.25 years.

a. What percentage of a given sample of cobalt-60 remains after 5 years?

b. How long will it take for 90% of a given sample to disintegrate?

82. The rate at which salt dissolves in water is directly proportional to the amount that remains undissolved. If 8 lb of salt is placed in a container of water and 2 lb dissolves in 30 min, how long will it take for 1 lb to dissolve?

83. Scientists are observing a species of insect in a certain swamp region. The insect population is estimated to be 10 million and is expected to grow at the rate of 2% per year. Assuming that the growth is exponential and stays that way for a period of years, what will the insect population be in 10 yr? How long will it take to double?

84. Solve the system of differential equations

$$\begin{cases} 2\dfrac{dx}{dt} + 5\dfrac{dy}{dt} = t \\[2mm] \dfrac{dx}{dt} + 3\dfrac{dy}{dt} = 7\cos t \end{cases}$$

Hint: Solve for $\dfrac{dx}{dt}$ and $\dfrac{dy}{dt}$ algebraically, and then integrate.

85. Spy Problem While lunching on cassoulet de chameau at his favorite restaurant in San Dimas (recall Problem 50, Section 5.1), the Spy finds a message from his esteemed superior, Lord Newton Fleming, spelled out in his alphabet soup, "The average of the temperature $F(t) = at^3 + bt^2 + ct + d$ over the time period from 9 A.M. to 3 P.M. is the average temperature between two fixed times t_1 and t_2. Mother waits at the well."

The Spy knows that "Mother" is the codename of Lord Newton himself, and "the well" is a sleazy bar at the edge of town. He decides that time t is measured from noon because the soup was served at that time. The cryptic nature of the message suggests that t_1 and t_2 are independent of a, b, c, and d and that one of them is the rendezvous time. When should he arrive for the meeting? (Remember, it's not wise to go to the well too often.)

86. Putnam Examination Problem Where on the parabola $4ay = x^2$ ($a > 0$) should a chord be drawn so that it will be normal to the parabola and cut off a parabolic sector of minimum area? That is, find P so that the shaded area in Figure 5.47 is as small as possible.

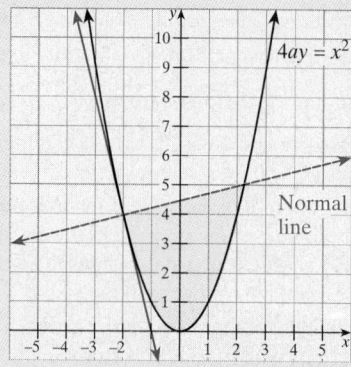

Figure 5.47 Minimum area problem

87. Putnam Examination Problem If $a_0, a_1, \ldots, a_n$ are real numbers that satisfy

$$\frac{a_0}{1} + \frac{a_1}{2} + \cdots + \frac{a_n}{n+1} = 0$$

show that the equation $a_0 + a_1 x + a_2 x^2 + \cdots + a_n x^n = 0$ has at least one real root. *Hint*: Use the mean value theorem for integrals.

---

*There is an interesting discussion of this problem, along with a BASIC computer simulation, in the November 1995 (Vol. 26, No. 5) issue of *The College Mathematics Journal* in the article "The Meeting of the Plows: A Simulation" by Jerome Lewis (pp. 395–400).

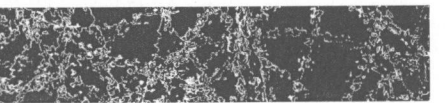

Guest Essay

Kinematics of Jogging

Ralph Boas (1912–1992), who was a professor of mathematics at Northwestern University, wrote this guest essay. Professor Boas was well known for his many papers and professional activities. In addition to his work in real and complex analysis, he wrote many expository articles, such as this guest essay, about teaching or using mathematics.

NATURE HERSELF EXHIBITS to us measurable and observable quantities in definite mathematical dependence; the conception of a function is suggested by all the processes of nature where we observe natural phenomena varying according to distance or to time. Nearly all the "known" functions have presented themselves in the attempt to solve geometrical, mechanical, or physical problems.

———J. T. Mertz
A History of European Thought in the Nineteenth Century
(Edinburgh and London, 1903), p. 696.

Some people think that calculus is dull, but it did not seem so three centuries ago, when it was invented. Then, it produced unexpected results; and, now and then, it still does. This essay is about such a result.

You have learned about the intermediate value theorem (see Section 2.3), which tells you, for instance, that if you jog at 8 min per mile, there must be some instant when your speed is exactly $\frac{1}{8}$ mi per minute—assuming, as is only natural in a course in calculus, that your elapsed time is a continuous function of the distance covered. This principle is very intuitive and was recognized before calculus was invented: Galileo was aware of it in 1638, and thought that it had been known to Plato. On the other hand, there is a question with a much less intuitive answer that was noticed only recently (and, as happens more often than mathematicians like to admit, by a physicist). Suppose that you average 8 min/mi; must you cover some one continuous mile (such as a "measured mile" on a highway) in exactly 8 min? The answer is not intuitive at all: It depends on whether or not your total distance was an integral number of miles. More precisely, if you cover an integral number of miles, then you cover exactly one mile in some 8 min. However, if you cover a nonintegral number of miles, there is not necessarily any one continuous mile that you cover in 8 min.

To prove this, let x be the distance (in miles) covered at any point during your trip, and suppose that when you stop you have covered an integral number of n miles. Let $f(x)$ be the time (in minutes) that it took to cover the first x miles; we will suppose that f is a continuous function. If you averaged 8 min/mi, then $f(x) - 8x = 0$ when $x = 0$ and when $x = n$. Now suppose that you never did cover any consecutive mile in 8 min; in mathematical terms,

$$f(x+1) - f(x) \neq 8$$

Because

$$f(x+1) - f(x) - 8$$

is continuous and never 0, it must either always be positive, or else always negative; let us suppose the former. Write the corresponding facts for $x = 0, 1, \ldots, n$:

$$f(1) - f(0) > 8$$
$$f(2) - f(1) > 8$$
$$\vdots$$
$$f(n) - f(n-1) > 8$$

If we add these inequalities, we obtain

$$f(n) - f(0) > 8n$$

But we started with the assumption that $f(n) = 8n$ and $f(0) = 0$, so assuming that $f(x+1) - f(x)$ is never 8 leads to a contradiction.

351

It is somewhat harder to show that only integral values of n will work. Suppose you jog so that your time to cover x miles is

$$J(x) = k \sin^2 \frac{\pi x}{n} + 8x$$

where n is not an integer and k is a small number. This is a legitimate assumption, because J is an increasing function (as a time has to be), if k is small enough. To be sure of this, we calculate $J'(x)$—and here we actually have to use some calculus (or have a calculator that will do it for us). We find

$$J'(x) = \frac{k\pi}{n} \sin \frac{2\pi x}{n} + 8$$

If k is small enough ($k < \frac{8n}{\pi}$), then $J'(x) > 0$. This shows not only that J increases but also that

$$J(x + 1) - J(x)$$

cannot be eight. Because $J(x + 1) - J(x)$ is never negative, if you jog so that your time is $J(x)$, you will never cover a whole mile in less than 8 min.

Mathematical Essays

Use the Internet, a library, or references other than this textbook to research the information necessary to answer questions in Problems 1–11

1. HISTORICAL QUEST   The derivative is one of the great ideas of calculus. Write an essay of at least 500 words about some application of the derivative that is not discussed in this text.

2. HISTORICAL QUEST   The concept of the integral is one of the great ideas of calculus. Write an essay of at least 500 words about the relationship of integration and differentiation as it relates to the history of calculus.

3. HISTORICAL QUEST   Write a report on Georg Riemann. (See Historical Quest in Section 5.3.) Include the 1984 development in the solution of the Riemann hypothesis.

4. HISTORICAL QUEST   As we saw in a Historical Quest in Section 5.8, the mathematician Seki Kōwa was doing a form of integration at about the same time that Newton and Leibniz were inventing the calculus. Write a paper on the history of calculus from the Eastern viewpoint.

5. "Lucy," the famous prehuman whose skeleton was discovered in East Africa, has been found to be approximately 3.8 million years old. About what percentage of ^{14}C would you expect to find if you tried to "date" Lucy by the usual carbon dating procedure? The answer you get to this question illustrates why it is reasonable to use carbon dating only on more recent artifacts, usually less than 50,000 years old (roughly the time since the last major ice age). Read an article on alternative dating procedures such as potassium-argon and rubidium-strontium dating. Write a paper comparing and contrasting such methods.

6. In the guest essay it was assumed that the time to cover x miles is

$$J(x) = k \sin^2 \frac{\pi x}{n} + 8x$$

Suppose that $n = 5$. What choices for k seem reasonable?

7. Suppose that the time to cover x miles is given by

$$J(x) = \sin^2 \frac{\pi x}{5} + 8x$$

Graph this function on $[0, 8]$.

8. Use calculus to find how small k (from the guest essay) needs to be in the expression

$$J(x) = k \sin^2 \frac{\pi x}{n} + 8x$$

so that $J'(x) > 0$.

9. **a.** Find a number x, $x \neq 0$, that, when divided by 2, gives a display of 0 on your calculator. Write a paper describing your work as well as the processes on your calculator.

   b. Calculate $\sqrt{2}$ using a calculator. Next, repeatedly subtract the integer part of the displayed number and multiply the result by 10. Describe the outcome, and then devise a method for finding $\sqrt{2}$ using calculus. Write a paper comparing these answers.

10. Book Report   Eli Maor, a native of Israel, has a long-standing interest in the relations between mathematics and the arts. Read the fascinating book *To Infinity and Beyond, A Cultural History of the Infinite* (Boston: Birkhäuser, 1987), and prepare a book report.

11. Book Report   In Section 3.1, we told the story of Fermat's last theorem. The book *Fermat's Enigma* by Simon Singh (New York: Walker & Company, 1997) tells the story of how Andrew Wiles solved the greatest mathematical puzzle of our age: He locked himself in a room and emerged seven years later. Read this book and prepare a book report.

12. Make up a word problem involving an application of the integral. Send your problem and solution to

   Strauss, Bradley, and Smith
   Prentice Hall Publishing Company
   1 Lake Street
   Upper Saddle River, NJ 07458

   The best one submitted will appear in the next edition (along with credit to the problem poser).

CHAPTERS 1–5 Cumulative Review

1. **WHAT DOES THIS SAY?** Define limit. Explain what this definition is saying using your own words.

2. **WHAT DOES THIS SAY?** Define derivative. Explain what this definition is saying using your own words.

3. **WHAT DOES THIS SAY?** Define a definite integral. Explain what this definition is saying using your own words.

4. **WHAT DOES THIS SAY?** Define a differential equation, and in your own words describe the procedure for solving a separable differential equation.

Evaluate the limits in Problems 5–13.

5. $\displaystyle\lim_{x\to2}\frac{3x^2-5x-2}{3x^2-7x+2}$

6. $\displaystyle\lim_{x\to+\infty}\frac{3x^2+7x+2}{5x^2-3x+3}$

7. $\displaystyle\lim_{x\to+\infty}(\sqrt{x^2+x}-x)$

8. $\displaystyle\lim_{x\to\pi/2}\frac{\cos^2 x}{\cos x^2}$

9. $\displaystyle\lim_{x\to0}\frac{x\sin x}{x+\sin^2 x}$

10. $\displaystyle\lim_{x\to0}\frac{\sin 3x}{x}$

11. $\displaystyle\lim_{x\to+\infty}(1+x)^{2/x}$

12. $\displaystyle\lim_{x\to0}\frac{\tan^{-1}x-x}{x^3}$

13. $\displaystyle\lim_{x\to0^+}x^{\sin x}$

Find the derivatives in Problems 14–22.

14. $y=6x^3-4x+2$

15. $y=(x^2+1)^3(3x-4)^2$

16. $y=\dfrac{x^2-4}{3x+1}$

17. $y=\dfrac{x}{x+\cos x}$

18. $x^2+3xy+y^2=0$

19. $y=\sec^2 3x$

20. $y=e^{5x-4}$

21. $y=\ln(5x^2+3x-2)$

22. $y=\tan^{-1}(x^2-3)$

Find the integrals in Problems 23–28.

23. $\displaystyle\int_4^9 d\theta$

24. $\displaystyle\int_{-1}^1 50(2x-5)^3\,dx$

25. $\displaystyle\int_0^1 \frac{x\,dx}{\sqrt{9+x^2}}$

26. $\displaystyle\int \csc 3\theta\cot 3\theta\,d\theta$

27. $\displaystyle\int \frac{e^x\,dx}{e^x+2}$

28. $\displaystyle\int \frac{x^3+2x-5}{x}\,dx$

29. Approximate $\displaystyle\int_0^4 \frac{dx}{\sqrt{1+x^3}}$ using Simpson's rule with $n=6$.

30. Sketch the graph of $y=x^3-5x^2+2x+8$.

31. Sketch the graph of $y=\dfrac{4+x^2}{4-x^2}$.

32. Find the largest value of $f(x)=\frac{1}{3}x^3-2x^2+3x-10$ on $[0,6]$.

Solve the differential equations in Problems 33–34.

33. $\dfrac{dy}{dx}=x^2y^2\sqrt{4-x^3}$

34. $(1+x^2)\,dy=(x+1)y\,dx$

Find the particular solution of the differential equations in Problems 35–36.

35. $\dfrac{dy}{dx}=2(5-y);\ y=3$ when $x=0$

36. $\dfrac{dy}{dx}=e^y\sin x;\ y=5$ when $x=0$

37. The graph of a function f consists of a semicircle of radius 3 and two line segments as shown in Figure 5.48. Let F be the function defined by

$$F(x)=\int_0^x f(t)\,dt$$

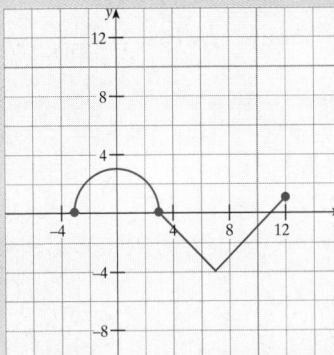

Figure 5.48 Graph of f

a. Find $F(7)$.

b. Find all values on the interval $(-3,12)$ at which F has a relative maximum.

c. Write an equation for the line tangent to the graph of F at $x=7$.

d. Find the x-coordinate of each point of inflection of the graph of F on the interval $(-3,12)$.

38. An electric charge Q_0 is distributed uniformly over a ring of radius R. The electric field intensity at any point x along the axis of the ring is given by

$$E(x)=\frac{Q_0 x}{(x^2+R^2)^{3/2}}$$

At what point on the axis is $E(x)$ maximized?

39. A rocket is launched vertically from a point on the ground 5,000 ft from a TV camera. If the rocket is rising vertically at the rate of 850 ft/s at the instant the rocket is 4,000 ft above the ground, how fast must the TV camera change the angle of elevation to keep the rocket in the picture?

40. A particle moves along the x-axis so that its velocity at any time $t\ge0$ is given by $v(t)=6t^2-2t-4$. It is known that the particle is at position $x=6$ for $t=2$.

a. Find the position of the particle at any time $t\ge0$.

b. For what value(s) of t, $0\le t\le3$, is the particle's instantaneous velocity the same as its average velocity over the interval $[0,3]$.

c. Find the total distance traveled by the particle from time $t=0$ to $t=3$.

41. Let f be the function defined by $f(x)=2\cos x$. Let $P(0,2)$ and $Q\left(\frac{\pi}{2},0\right)$ be the points where f crosses the y-axis and x-axis, respectively.

a. Write an equation for the secant line passing through points P and Q.

b. Write an equation for the tangent line of f at point Q.

c. Find the x-coordinate of the point on the graph of f, between point P and Q, at which the line tangent to the graph of f is parallel to $\overline{PQ}$. Cite a theorem or result that assures the existence of such a tangent.

42. Let f be the function defined by $f(x) = \sqrt{x-2}$.

   a. Sketch f and shade the region R enclosed by the graph of f, the x-axis, and the vertical line $x = 5$.

   b. Find the area of R.

43. Let f be the function defined by $f(x) = x^3 - 6x^2 + k$ for k an arbitrary constant.

   a. Find the relative maximum and minimum of f in terms of k.

   b. For which values of k does f have three distinct roots?

   c. Find the values of k for which the average value of f over $[-1, 2]$ is 2.

44. An object is thrown directly downward with velocity 5 ft/s from an airplane, and t seconds later is falling with acceleration

$$a(t) = 32 - 0.08v$$

where $v(t)$ is the object's velocity at time t.

   a. Find an expression for v in terms of t.

   b. If the terminal velocity is defined as $\lim\limits_{t \to +\infty} v(t)$, find the terminal velocity of the object (to the nearest ft/s).

   c. The object can land safely if the impact velocity is no greater than 60 ft/s. What is the maximum altitude the airplane can fly to guarantee a safe landing for the object?

45. Solve the differential equation $\dfrac{dy}{dx} = y^2 \sin 3x$.

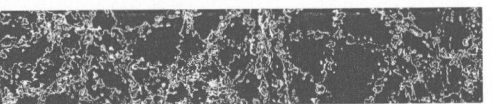

6

Additional Applications of the Integral

PREVIEW

In Chapter 5, we found that area and average value can be expressed in terms of the definite integral. The goal of this chapter is to consider various other applications of integration, such as computing volume, arc length, surface area, work, hydrostatic force, centroids of planar regions, and applications to business, economics, and life sciences.

PERSPECTIVE

What is the volume of the material that remains when a hole of radius of $0.5R$ is drilled into a sphere of radius R? The "center" of a rectangle is the point where its diagonals intersect, but what is the center of a quarter circle? If a reservoir is filled to the top of a dam shaped like a parabola, what is the total force of the water on the face of the dam? If a worker is carrying a bag of sand up a ladder and the bag is leaking sand through a hole in such a way that all the sand is gone when the worker reaches the top, how much work is done by the worker? An investor asks a question seeking the future value of an income flow, or a physician asks how to measure the flow of blood through an artery. These questions are typical of the kind we will answer in this chapter.

6.1 Area Between Two Curves

IN THIS SECTION area between curves, area using vertical strips, area using horizontal strips

AREA BETWEEN CURVES

In some practical problems, you may have to compute the area between two curves. Suppose f and g are functions such that $f(x) \geq g(x)$ on the interval $[a, b]$, as shown in Figure 6.1. We do not insist that both f and g be nonnegative functions, but we begin by showing that case in Figure 6.1.

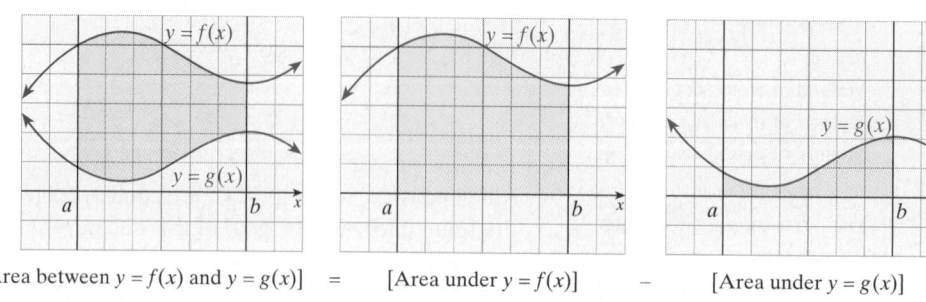

[Area between $y = f(x)$ and $y = g(x)$] = [Area under $y = f(x)$] − [Area under $y = g(x)$]

Figure 6.1 Area between two curves

To find the area of the region R between the curves defined by $y = f(x)$ and $y = g(x)$ from $x = a$ to $x = b$, we subtract the area between the lower curve $y = g(x)$ and the x-axis from the area between the upper curve $y = f(x)$ and the x-axis; that is,

$$\text{AREA OF } R = \int_a^b f(x)\,dx - \int_a^b g(x)\,dx = \int_a^b [f(x) - g(x)]\,dx$$

This formula seems obvious in the situation where both $f(x) \geq 0$ and $g(x) \geq 0$, as shown in Figure 6.1. However, the following derivation requires only that f and g be continuous and satisfy $f(x) \geq g(x)$ on the interval $[a, b]$. We wish to find the area between the curves $y = f(x)$ and $y = g(x)$ on this interval. Choose a partition

$$\{x_0 = a, x_1, x_2, \ldots, x_n = b\}$$

of the interval $[a, b]$ and a representative number x_k^* from each subinterval $[x_{k-1}, x_k]$. Next, for each index k, with $k = 1, 2, \ldots, n$, construct a rectangle of width

$$\Delta x_k = x_k - x_{k-1}$$

and height

$$f(x_k^*) - g(x_k^*)$$

equal to the vertical distance between the two curves at $x = x_k^*$. A typical approximating rectangle is shown in Figure 6.2b. We refer to this approximating rectangle as a **vertical strip**.

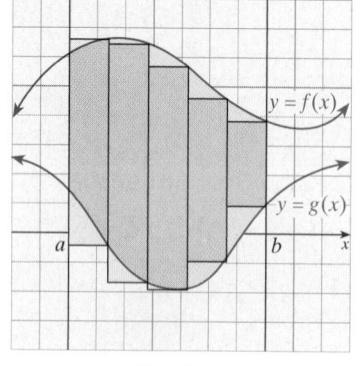
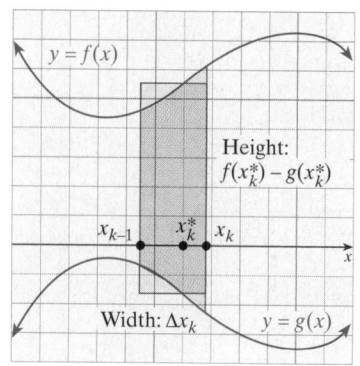

a. Approximating rectangles   **b.** A typical vertical strip

Figure 6.2 Using Riemann sums to find the area between two curves

The representative rectangle has area

$$\Delta A_k = [f(x_k^*) - g(x_k^*)]\Delta x_k$$

and the total area between the curves $y = f(x)$ and $y = g(x)$ can be estimated by the Riemann sum

$$A_n = \sum_{k=1}^{n} [f(x_k^*) - g(x_k^*)]\Delta x_k$$

It is reasonable to expect this estimate to improve if we increase the number of subdivision points in the partition P in such a way that the norm $\|P\|$ approaches 0. Thus, the region between the two curves has area

$$A = \lim_{\|P\| \to 0} \sum_{k=1}^{n} [f(x_k^*) - g(x_k^*)]\Delta x_k$$

which we recognize as the integral of the function $f(x) - g(x)$ over the interval $[a, b]$. These observations may be used to define the area between the curves.

Area Between Two Curves

If f and g are continuous and satisfy $f(x) \geq g(x)$ on the closed interval $[a, b]$, then the **area between the two curves** $y = f(x)$ and $y = g(x)$ is given by

$$A = \int_a^b [f(x) - g(x)]\, dx$$

➔ **What This Says** To find the area between two curves on a given closed interval $[a, b]$ use the formula

$$A = \int_a^b [\text{TOP CURVE} - \text{BOTTOM CURVE}]\, dx$$

It is no longer necessary to require either curve to be above the x-axis. In fact, we will see later in this section that the curves might cross somewhere in the domain so that one curve is on top for part of the interval and the other curve is on top for the rest.

EXAMPLE 1   Area between two curves

Find the area of the region between the curves $y = x^3$ and $y = x^2 - x$ on the interval $[0, 1]$.

Solution

The region is shown in Figure 6.3. We need to know which curve is the *top curve* on $[0, 1]$. Solve

$$x^3 = x^2 - x \quad \text{or} \quad x(x^2 - x + 1) = 0$$

to find the points of intersection. The only real root is $x = 0$ ($x^2 - x + 1 = 0$ has no real roots). Thus, by the intermediate value theorem, the same curve is on top throughout the interval $[0, 1]$. To see which curve is on top, take some representative value in $[0, 1]$, such as $x = 0.5$, and note that because $(0.5)^3 > 0.5^2 - 0.5$, the curve $y = x^3$ must be above $y = x^2 - x$. Thus, the required area is given by

$$A = \int_0^1 [\underbrace{x^3}_{\text{Top curve}} - \underbrace{(x^2 - x)}_{\text{Bottom curve}}]\, dx = \left(\tfrac{1}{4}x^4 - \tfrac{1}{3}x^3 + \tfrac{1}{2}x^2\right)\Big|_0^1 = \tfrac{5}{12} \qquad \blacksquare$$

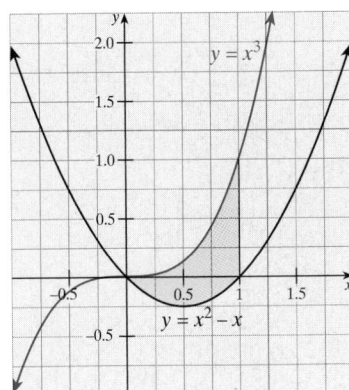

Figure 6.3 The area between the curves $y = x^3$ and $y = x^2 - x$ on $[0, 1]$

In Section 5.1, we defined area for a continuous function f with the restriction that $f(x) \geq 0$. Example 1 shows us that when considering the area between two curves, we need to be concerned no longer with the nonnegative restriction but only with whether $f(x) \geq g(x)$. We now use this idea to find the area for a function that is negative.

EXAMPLE 2   Area with a negative function

Find the area of the region bounded by the curve $y = e^{2x} - 3e^x + 2$ and the x-axis.

Solution

We find the points of intersection of the curve and the x-axis:

$$e^{2x} - 3e^x + 2 = 0 \qquad \textit{The curve intersects the x-axis where } y = 0.$$
$$(e^x - 1)(e^x - 2) = 0 \qquad \textit{so that} \quad x = 0, \ln 2$$

The graph of $f(x) = e^{2x} - 3e^x + 2$ is shown in Figure 6.4. We see that on the interval $[0, \ln 2]$, $f(x) \leq 0$, but we can find the area of the given region by considering the area between the curves defined by equations $y = 0$ and $y = e^{2x} - 3e^x + 2$.

$$A = \int_0^{\ln 2} [\underbrace{0}_{\text{Top curve}} - \underbrace{(e^{2x} - 3e^x + 2)}_{\text{Bottom curve}}]\, dx = \left(-\frac{e^{2x}}{2} + 3e^x - 2x \right)\Bigg|_0^{\ln 2}$$

$$= \frac{3}{2} - 2\ln 2 \approx 0.114 \qquad\blacksquare$$

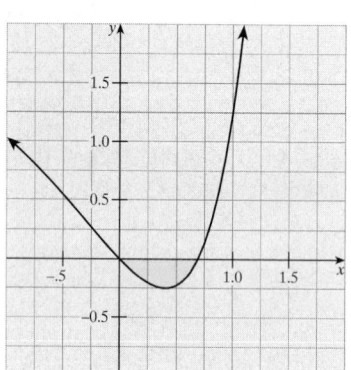

Figure 6.4 Area of region

AREA USING VERTICAL STRIPS

Although the only mathematically correct way to establish a formula involving integrals is to form Riemann sums and take the limit according to the definition of the definite integral, we can simulate this procedure with approximating strips. This simplification is especially useful for finding the area of a complicated region formed when two curves intersect one or more times, as shown in Figure 6.5. Note that the vertical strip has height $f(x) - g(x)$ if $y = f(x)$ is above $y = g(x)$, and height $g(x) - f(x)$ if $y = g(x)$ is above $y = f(x)$. In either case, the height can be represented by $|f(x) - g(x)|$, and the area of the vertical strip is

$$\Delta A = |f(x) - g(x)|\, \Delta x = |f(x) - g(x)|\, dx$$

Thus, we have a new integration formula for area; namely,

$$A = \int_a^b |f(x) - g(x)|\, dx$$

WARNING   You cannot use the formula $A = \int [f - g]\, dx$ directly here because the hypothesis $f \geq g$ is not satisfied. In order to use $A = \int |f - g|\, dx$ over the entire interval, you must remember that $|f - g|$ might be $f - g$ over part of the interval and $g - f$ over another part (see Figure 6.5b). Make sure you check to see which curve is on top. Because the curves cross in Example 3, the interval must be subdivided accordingly.

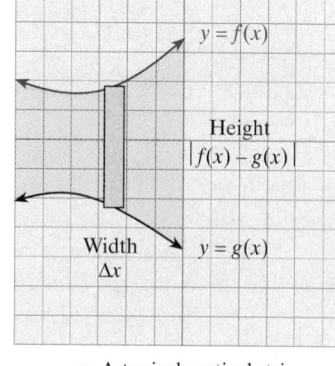

a. A typical vertical strip

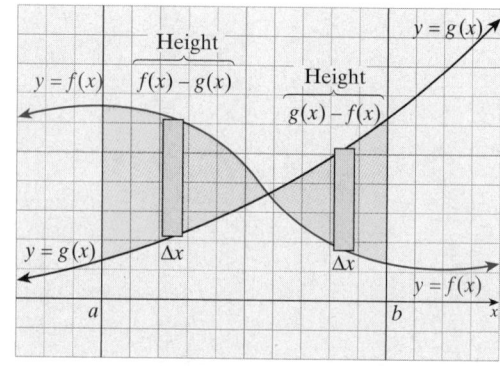

b. Approximation by strips

Figure 6.5   Area by vertical strips

EXAMPLE 3   Area using vertical strips

Find the area of the region bounded by the line $y = 3x$ and the curve $y = x^3 + 2x^2$.

Solution

The region between the curve and the line is the shaded portion of Figure 6.6. Part of the process of graphing these curves is to find which is the top curve and which is the bottom. To do this we need to find where the curves intersect:

$$x^3 + 2x^2 = 3x \quad \text{or} \quad x(x+3)(x-1) = 0$$

The points of intersection occur at $x = -3, 0,$ and 1. In the subinterval $[-3, 0]$, labeled A_1 in Figure 6.6, the curve $y = x^3 + 2x^2$ is on top (test a typical point in the subinterval, such as $x = -1$), and on $[0, 1]$, the region labeled A_2, curve $y = 3x$ is on top. The representative vertical strips are shown in Figure 6.6, and the area between the curve and the line is given by the sum

$$A = \int_{-3}^{0} [(x^3 + 2x^2) - (3x)]\, dx + \int_{0}^{1} [(3x) - (x^3 + 2x^2)]\, dx$$

$$= \left(\tfrac{1}{4}x^4 + \tfrac{2}{3}x^3 - \tfrac{3}{2}x^2\right)\Big|_{-3}^{0} + \left(\tfrac{3}{2}x^2 - \tfrac{1}{4}x^4 - \tfrac{2}{3}x^3\right)\Big|_{0}^{1}$$

$$= 0 - \left(\tfrac{81}{4} - \tfrac{54}{3} - \tfrac{27}{2}\right) + \left(\tfrac{3}{2} - \tfrac{1}{4} - \tfrac{2}{3}\right) - 0$$

$$= \frac{71}{6}$$ ∎

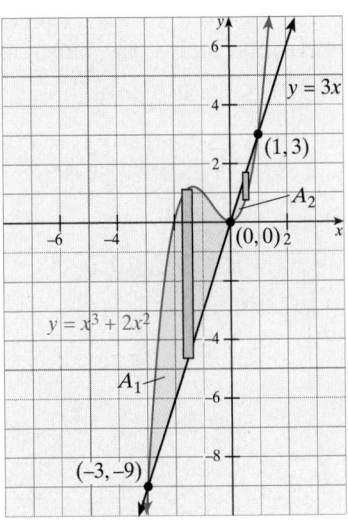

Figure 6.6 The area between the curve $y = x^3 + 2x^2$ and the line $y = 3x$

EXAMPLE 4   Area using symmetry

Find the area bounded by the curve $y = \sin x$ and the x-axis between $x = -\pi/2$ and $x = \pi/2$.

Solution

We sketch the region as shown in Figure 6.7. The area we seek is found by

$$\int_{-\pi/2}^{0} (0 - \sin x)\, dx + \int_{0}^{\pi/2} (\sin x - 0)\, dx = \cos x\big|_{-\pi/2}^{0} + (-\cos x)\big|_{0}^{\pi/2}$$

$$= (1 - 0) + (0 + 1) = 2$$

There is an easier procedure using symmetry of the curve $y = \sin x$ with respect to the origin. Symmetry uses the fact that the area bounded by the lines $x = -\pi/2$ and $x = 0$ is the same as the area bounded by the lines $x = 0$ and $x = \pi/2$. As a result, we often work this type of problem as shown here:

$$A = 2\int_{0}^{\pi/2} (\sin x - 0)\, dx \qquad \text{By symmetry}$$

$$= 2(-\cos x)\big|_{0}^{\pi/2}$$

$$= 2(0 + 1)$$

$$= 2$$ ∎

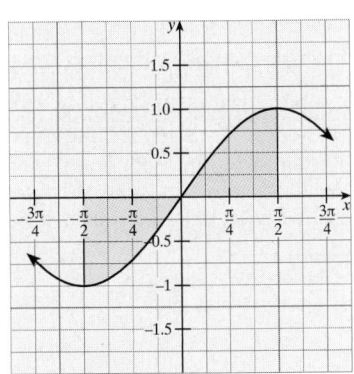

Figure 6.7 Area bounded by $y = \sin x$, $y = 0$, $x = -\pi/2$ and $x = \pi/2$

WARNING   A common mistake is to work this problem by evaluating the integral

$$\int_{-\pi/2}^{\pi/2} \sin x\, dx = (-\cos x)\big|_{-\pi/2}^{\pi/2} = -0 + 0 = 0$$

forgetting that the integral does not give the area unless the function is nonnegative.

AREA USING HORIZONTAL STRIPS

For many regions, it is easier to form horizontal strips rather than vertical strips. The procedure for horizontal strips duplicates the procedure for vertical strips. If we want to find the area between two curves of the form $x = F(y)$ and $x = G(y)$ on the interval $[c, d]$ on the y-axis, we form horizontal strips. In Figure 6.8, such a region and its typical horizontal approximating rectangles, or **horizontal strips**, are illustrated. Note that the width of the horizontal strip is denoted by Δy.

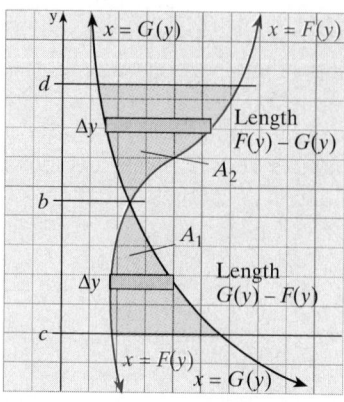
a. Approximation by horizontal strips of width Δy

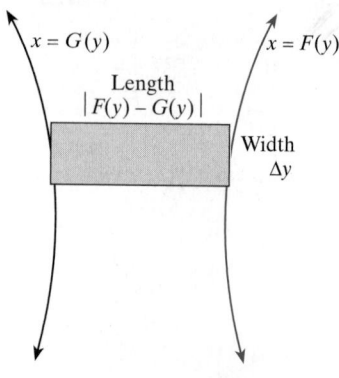
b. A typical horizontal strip

Figure 6.8 Area by horizontal strips

Regardless of which curve is "ahead" or "behind," the horizontal strip has length $|F(y) - G(y)|$ and area

$$\Delta A = |F(y) - G(y)|\, \Delta y$$

However, in practice, you must make sure to find the points of intersection of the curves and divide the integrals so that in each region one curve is the *leading curve* ("right curve") and the other is the *trailing curve* ("left curve"). Suppose the curves intersect where $y = b$ for b on the interval $[c, d]$, as shown in Figure 6.8. Then

$$A = \int_c^b \underbrace{[G(y) - F(y)]}_{G \text{ leading } F}\, dy + \int_b^d \underbrace{[F(y) - G(y)]}_{F \text{ leading } G}\, dy$$

EXAMPLE 5 Area using horizontal strips

Find the area of the region between the parabola $x = 4y - y^2$ and the line $x = 2y - 3$.

Solution

Figure 6.9 shows the region between the parabola and the line, together with a typical horizontal strip. To find where the line and the parabola intersect, solve

$$4y - y^2 = 2y - 3 \quad \text{to obtain} \quad y = -1 \text{ and } y = 3$$

Throughout the interval $[-1, 3]$ the parabola is to the right of the line (test a typical point between -1 and 3, such as $y = 0$). Thus, the horizontal strip has area

$$\Delta A = [\underbrace{(4y - y^2)}_{\text{Right curve}} - \underbrace{(2y - 3)}_{\text{Left curve}}]\Delta y$$

and the area between the parabola and the line is given by

$$A = \int_{-1}^3 [(4y - y^2) - (2y - 3)]\, dy = \int_{-1}^3 (3 + 2y - y^2)\, dy$$
$$= \left(3y + y^2 - \tfrac{1}{3}y^3\right)\Big|_{-1}^3 = (9 + 9 - 9) - \left(-3 + 1 + \tfrac{1}{3}\right) = \tfrac{32}{3} \qquad \blacksquare$$

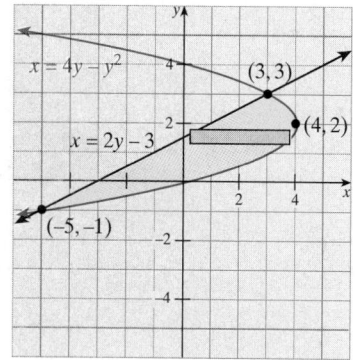

Figure 6.9 The area between the curves $x = 4y - y^2$ and $x = 2y - 3$ using horizontal strips

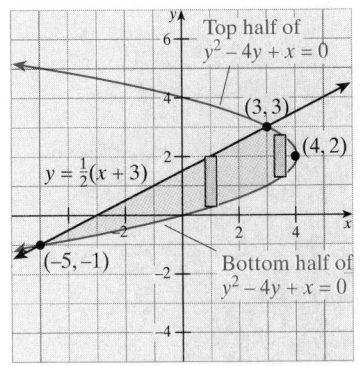

In Example 5, the area can also be found by using vertical strips, but the procedure is more complicated. Note in Figure 6.10 that on the interval $[-5, 3]$, a representative vertical strip would extend from the bottom half of the parabola $y^2 - 4y + x = 0$ to the line $y = \frac{1}{2}(x + 3)$, whereas on the interval $[3, 4]$, a typical vertical strip would extend from the bottom half of the parabola $y^2 - 4y + x = 0$ to the top half. Thus, the area is given by the sum of two integrals, the second of which requires solving the equation $y^2 - 4y + x = 0$ for y using the quadratic formula. With some effort, it can be shown that the computation of area by vertical strips gives the same result as that found by horizontal strips in Example 5.

Figure 6.10 The area between the curves $x = 4y - y^2$ and $x = 2y - 3$ using vertical strips

6.1 PROBLEM SET

Ⓐ *Sketch a representative vertical or horizontal strip and find the area of the given regions bounded by the specified curves in Problems 1–6.*

1. $y = -x^2 + 6x - 5$,
$y = \frac{3}{2}x - \frac{3}{2}$

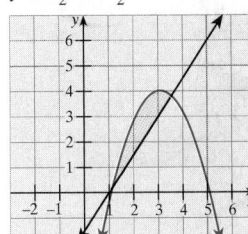

2. $y = x^2 - 8x$,
$y = 0$

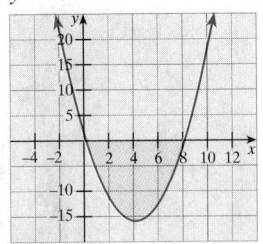

3. $y = \sin 2x$ on $[0, \pi]$,
$y = 0$

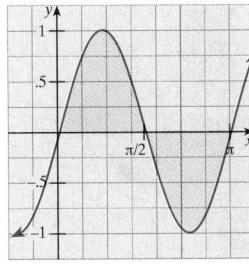

4. $y = (x - 1)^3$,
$y = x - 1$

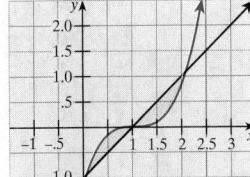

5. $x = y^2 - 5y$,
$x = 0$

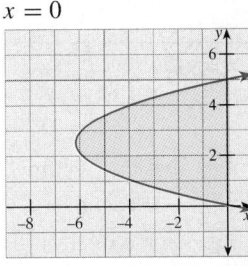

6. $x = y^2 - 6y$,
$x = -y$

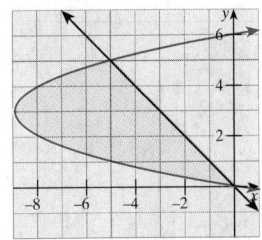

Sketch the region bounded between the given curves and then find the area of each region in Problems 7–25.

7. $y = x^2$, $y = x$, $x = -1$, $x = 1$

8. $y = x^3$, $y = x$, $x = -1$, $x = 1$

9. $y = x^2$, $y = x^3$

10. $y = x^2$, $y = \sqrt[3]{x}$

11. $y = x^2 - 1$, $x = -1$, $x = 2$, $y = 0$

12. $y = 4x^2 - 9$, $x = 3$, $x = 0$, $y = 0$

13. $y = x^4 - 3x^2$, $y = 6x^2$

14. $x = 8 - y^2$, $x = y^2$

15. $x = 2 - y^2$, $x = y$

16. $y = x^2 + 3x - 5$, $y = -x^2 + x + 7$

17. $y = 2x^3 + x^2 - x - 1$, $y = x^3 + 2x^2 + 5x - 1$

18. $y = \sin x$, $y = \cos x$, $x = 0$, $x = \frac{\pi}{4}$

19. $y = \sin x$, $y = \sin 2x$, $x = 0$, $x = \pi$

20. $y = |x|$, $y = x^2 - 6$

21. $y = |4x - 1|$, $y = x^2 - 5$, $x = 0$, $x = 4$

22. x-axis, $y = x^3 - 2x^2 - x + 2$

23. y-axis, $x = y^3 - 3y^2 - 4y + 12$

24. $y = e^x$, $y = \frac{1}{2}e^x + \frac{1}{2}$, $x = -2$, $x = 2$

25. $y = \dfrac{1}{\sqrt{1 - x^2}}$, $y = \dfrac{2}{x + 1}$, y-axis

Ⓑ **26. WHAT DOES THIS SAY?** When finding the area between two curves, discuss criteria for deciding between vertical and horizontal strips.

27. Find the number k (correct to two decimal places) so that the line $y = k$ bisects the area under the curve $y = \sin^{-1} x$ for $0 \le x \le 1$.

28. Find the area of the region that contains the origin and is bounded by the lines $2y = 11 - x$ and $y = 7x + 13$ and the curve $y = x^2 - 5$.

29. Show that the region defined by the inequalities $x^2 + y^2 \le 8$, $x \ge y$, and $y \ge 0$ has area π.

30. Find the area of the region bounded by the curve $\sqrt{x} + \sqrt{y} = 1$ and the coordinate axes.

C 31. **Modeling Problem**   Imagine a cylindrical fuel tank of length L lying on its side; the ends are circular with radius b. Determine the amount of fuel in the tank for a given level by completing these steps:

a. Explain why the volume of the tank may be modeled by

$$V = 2L \int_{-b}^{b} \sqrt{b^2 - y^2}\, dy$$

b. Explain why the volume of fuel at level h $(-b \le h \le b)$

may be modeled by

$$V(h) = 2L \int_{-b}^{h} \sqrt{b^2 - y^2}\, dy$$

c. Finally, for $b = 4$ and $L = 20$, numerically compute $V(h)$ for $h = -3, -2, \ldots, 4$. *Note*: $V(0)$ and $V(4)$ will serve as a check on your work.

32. The curve with the equation $(x^2 + y^2)^3 = x^2$ has a loop for $0 \le x \le 1$. Find the area of the loop. *Hint*: Use the substitution $u = x^{1/3}$ in the area integral.

6.2   Volume

IN THIS SECTION   method of cross sections, method of disks and washers, method of cylindrical shells

The methods used in Section 6.1 to compute area by integration can be modified to compute the volume of a solid region. We will develop methods for computing volume of several kinds of solids in this section, beginning with the case where the solid has a known cross section.

METHOD OF CROSS SECTIONS

Let S be a solid and suppose that for $a \le x \le b$, the cross section of S that is perpendicular to the x-axis at x has area $A(x)$. Think of cutting the solid with a knife at $x = x_k^*$ and removing a very thin slab whose face has area $A(x_k^*)$ and whose thickness is Δx_k, as shown in Figure 6.11.

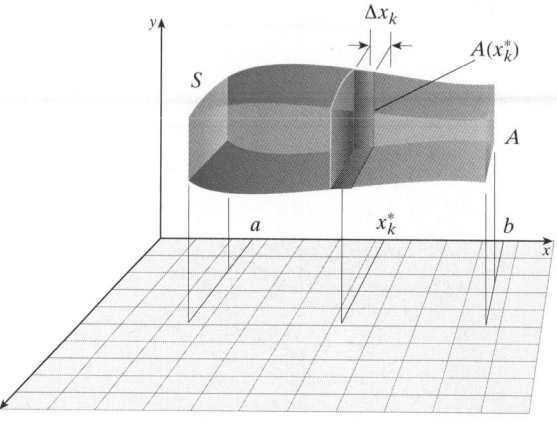

Figure 6.11   Volumes of solids with known cross sections

To find the volume of S, we first take a partition $x_0 = a, x_1, x_2, \ldots, x_n = b$ of the interval $[a, b]$ and choose a representative number x_k^* in each subinterval $[x_{k-1}, x_k]$. Next, we consider a slab with width

$$\Delta x_k = x_k - x_{k-1}$$

and cross-sectional area $A(x_k^*)$, as indicated in Figure 6.11. This slab has volume

$$\Delta V_k = A(x_k^*)\Delta x_k$$

and by adding up the volumes of all such slabs, we obtain an approximation to the volume of the solid S:

$$V_n = \sum_{k=1}^{n} A(x_k^*)\Delta x_k$$

The approximation improves as the number of partition points increases, and it is reasonable to *define* the volume V of the solid S as the limit of V_n as the norm of the partition $\|P\|$ tends to 0. That is,

$$V = \lim_{\|P\| \to 0} \sum_{k=1}^{n} A(x_k^*)\Delta x_k$$

which we recognize as the definite integral $\int_a^b A(x)\,dx$. To summarize:

Volume of a Solid with Known Cross-Sectional Area

> A solid S with cross-sectional area $A(x)$ perpendicular to the x-axis at each point on the interval $[a, b]$ has **volume**
>
> $$V = \int_a^b A(x)\,dx$$

EXAMPLE 1 Volume of a solid using square cross sections

The base of a solid is the region in the xy-plane bounded by the y-axis and the lines $y = 1 - x$, $y = 2x + 5$, and $x = 3$. Each cross section perpendicular to the x-axis is a square. Find the volume of the solid.

Solution

The solid resembles a tapered brick, and it may be constructed by "gluing" together a number of thin slabs with square cross sections, like the one shown in Figure 6.12c. We begin by drawing the base in two dimensions and then find the volume of the kth slice.

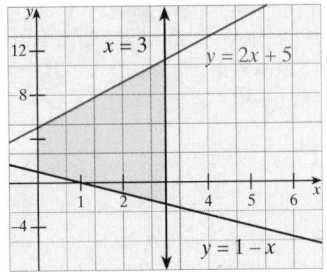

a. Two-dimensional graph of the given base

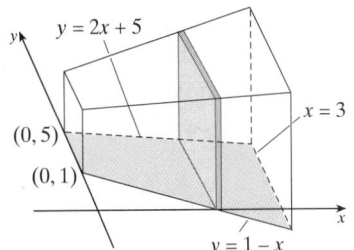

b. Three-dimensional solid

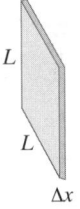

c. Cross-sectional representative element: $\Delta V = L^2\,\Delta x$

Figure 6.12 A solid with a square cross section

To model this construction mathematically, we subdivide the interval $[0, 3]$, form a vertical approximating rectangle on each resulting subinterval, and then construct a slab with square cross section on each approximating rectangle. If we choose the thickness of a typical slab to be Δx and the height and width to be L, the slab will have volume ΔV, where

$$\begin{aligned}
\Delta V &= L^2 \Delta x \\
&= L^2(x)\Delta x \\
&= [(2x + 5) - (1 - x)]^2 \Delta x \\
&= (3x + 4)^2 \Delta x
\end{aligned}$$

The volume of the entire solid is obtained by integrating to "add up" all the volumes ΔV, and we find that the volume of the solid is

$$
\begin{aligned}
V &= \int_0^3 (3x + 4)^2 \, dx \\
&= \int_0^3 (9x^2 + 24x + 16) \, dx \\
&= (3x^3 + 12x^2 + 16x)\big|_0^3 = 237
\end{aligned}
$$ ∎

EXAMPLE 2   Volume of a regular pyramid with a square base

SMH See Example 1.7, Section 1.5, of the *Student Mathematics Handbook*.

A regular pyramid has a square base of side L and its apex located H units above the center of its base. Derive the formula $V = \frac{1}{3}HL^2$.

Solution

The pyramid is shown in Figure 6.13.

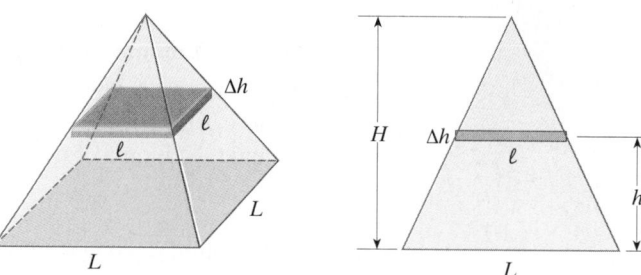

Figure 6.13   The volume of a pyramid

This pyramid can be constructed by stacking a number of thin square slabs. Suppose that a representative slab has side ℓ and thickness Δh, and that it is located h units above the base of the pyramid as shown in Figure 6.13. By creating a proportion from corresponding parts of similar triangles, we see that

$$
\frac{\ell}{L} = \frac{H - h}{H} \quad \text{so that} \quad \ell = \left(1 - \frac{h}{H}\right)L
$$

Therefore, the volume of the representative slab is

$$
\begin{aligned}
\Delta V &= \ell^2 \Delta h \\
&= \left(1 - \frac{h}{H}\right)^2 L^2 \Delta h
\end{aligned}
$$

To compute the volume V of the entire pyramid, we integrate with respect to h from the base of the pyramid ($h = 0$) to the apex ($h = H$). Thus,

$$
\begin{aligned}
V &= \int_0^H \left(1 - \frac{h}{H}\right)^2 L^2 \, dh = L^2 \int_0^H \left[1 - \frac{2}{H}h + \frac{1}{H^2}h^2\right] dh \\
&= L^2 \left(h - \frac{h^2}{H} + \frac{h^3}{3H^2}\right)\Big|_0^H = L^2 \left(H - \frac{H^2}{H} + \frac{H^3}{3H^2}\right) = \frac{1}{3}HL^2
\end{aligned}
$$ ∎

Other volume formulas can be found in a similar fashion (see Problems 61 and 62).

METHOD OF DISKS AND WASHERS

A **solid of revolution** is a solid figure S obtained by revolving a region R in the xy-plane about a line L (called the **axis of revolution**) that lies outside or on the boundary of R. Note that such a solid S may be thought of as having circular cross sections in the direction perpendicular to L.

Suppose the function f is continuous and satisfies $f(x) \geq 0$ on the interval $[a, b]$, and suppose we wish to find the volume of the solid S generated when the region R under the curve $y = f(x)$ on $[a, b]$ is revolved about the x-axis. That is, *the axis of revolution is horizontal and it is a boundary of the region R.* Our strategy will be to form vertical strips and revolve them about the x-axis, generating what are called **disks** (that is, thin right circular cylinders) that approximate a portion of the solid of revolution S, as shown in Figure 6.14.

Now we can compute the total volume of S by using integration to sum the volumes of all the approximating disks. Recall that the formula for the volume of a cylinder of height h and cross-sectional area A is Ah. Figure 6.14a shows a typical vertical strip with height $f(x_k)$ and width Δx_k. You might notice that the width of the strip is the same as the thickness of the disk. The solid of revolution can be thought of as having cross sections perpendicular to the x-axis that are circular disks of volume

$$\Delta V_k(x) = \underbrace{\pi [f(x_k)]^2}_{\text{Area of circular cross section}} \Delta x_k$$

The total volume may be found by integration:

$$V = \int_a^b \overbrace{A(x)}^{\text{Area of cross section}} \ \overbrace{dx}^{\text{Thickness}} = \int_a^b \pi [f(x)]^2 \, dx$$

This procedure may be summarized as follows:

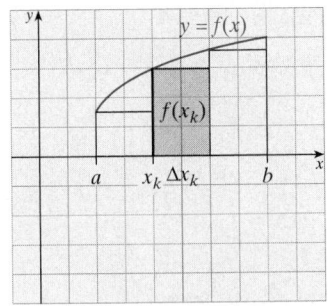

a. A representative vertical strip has height $f(x_k)$ and width Δx_k.

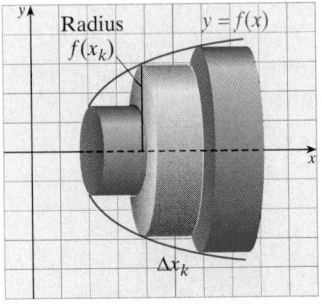

b. The representative disk is formed by revolving the representative strip about the x-axis. This disk has radius $f(x_k)$ and thickness Δx_k.

Figure 6.14 The disk method

The Disk Method

The **disk method** is used to find a volume generated when a region R is revolved about an axis L that is *perpendicular* to a typical approximating strip in R. Suppose R is the region bounded by the curve $y = f(x)$, the x-axis, and the vertical lines $x = a$ and $x = b$. Then if R is revolved about the x-axis, it generates a solid with volume

$$V = \int_a^b \pi y^2 \, dx = \int_a^b \pi [f(x)]^2 \, dx$$

➡ **What This Says** The following diagram may help you remember the key ideas behind the disk method.

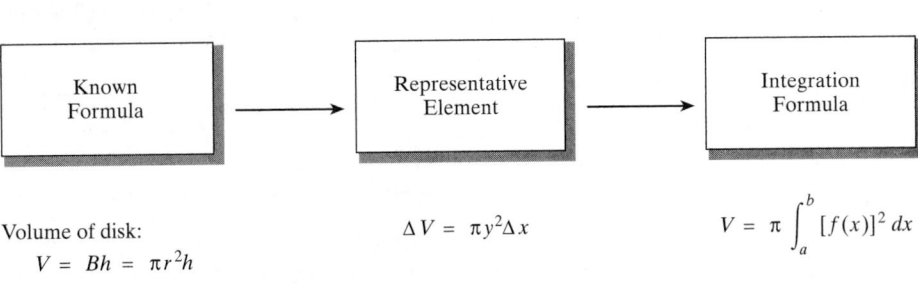

Known Formula	Representative Element	Integration Formula

Volume of disk:
$V = Bh = \pi r^2 h$

$\Delta V = \pi y^2 \Delta x$

$V = \pi \int_a^b [f(x)]^2 \, dx$

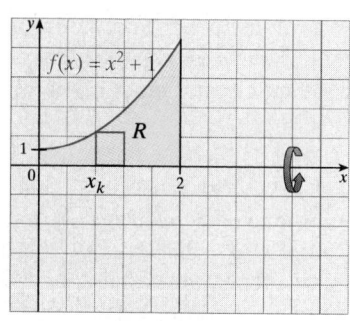

a. The region under
$y = x^2 + 1$ on $[0, 2]$

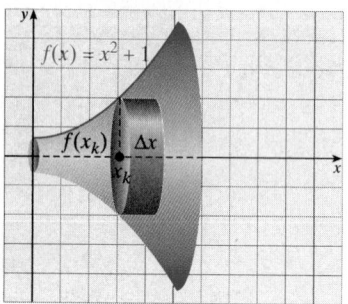

b. The solid of revolution

Figure 6.15 Volume of a solid of revolution: Disk method

EXAMPLE 3   **Volume by disks**

Find the volume of the solid S formed by revolving the region under the curve $y = x^2 + 1$ on the interval $[0, 2]$ about the x-axis.

Solution

The region is shown in Figure 6.15.

$$V = \pi \int_0^2 (x^2 + 1)^2\, dx = \pi \int_0^2 (x^4 + 2x^2 + 1)\, dx$$

$$= \pi \left(\frac{1}{5}x^5 + \frac{2}{3}x^3 + x \right)\Bigg|_0^2 = \frac{206}{15}\pi \approx 43.14453911 \qquad \blacksquare$$

With a small modification of the disk method, we can find the volume of a solid figure generated by revolving about the x-axis the region between two curves $y = f(x)$ and $y = g(x)$, where $f(x) \geq g(x)$ for $a \leq x \leq b$. When a typical vertical strip is revolved about the x-axis, a "washer" with cross-sectional area $\pi([f(x)]^2 - [g(x)]^2)$ is formed, as shown in Figure 6.16. This can be remembered by $\pi R^2 - \pi r^2$, where R is the outer radius and r is the inner radius.

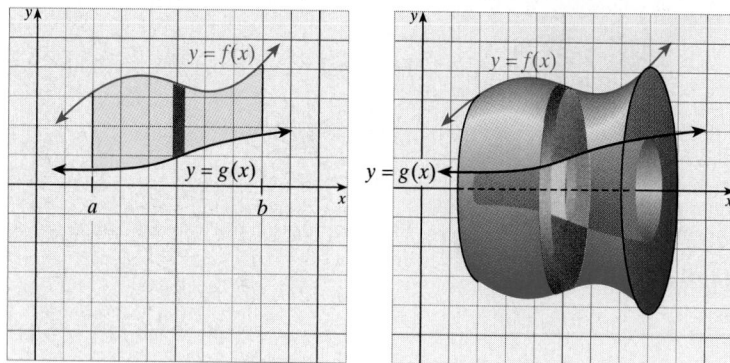

Figure 6.16   The washer method

The volume of the solid of revolution is found by the formula given in the following box.

The Washer Method

The **washer method** is used to find volume when a region between two curves is revolved about an external axis perpendicular to the approximating strip. In particular, suppose f and g are continuous functions on $[a, b]$ with $f(x) \geq g(x) \geq 0$. If R is the radius of the (outer) curve $y = f(x)$ and r is the radius of the (inner) curve $y = g(x)$, and the region bounded by $y = f(x)$, $y = g(x)$, $x = a$, and $x = b$ is revolved about the x-axis, then the volume thus formed is

$$V = \int_a^b \pi \left(\underbrace{[f(x)]^2}_{\text{Outer radius}} - \underbrace{[g(x)]^2}_{\text{Inner radius}} \right) dx$$

WARNING $f^2 - g^2 \neq (f - g)^2$

The disk method and the washer method also apply when the axis of revolution is a line other than the x-axis. In Example 4, we consider what happens when a particular region R is revolved not only about the x-axis, but also about other axes.

EXAMPLE 4   Volume by washers

Let D be the solid region bounded by the parabola $y = x^2$ and the line $y = x$. Find the volume of the solid generated when D is revolved about the

a. x-axis   **b.** y-axis   **c.** line $y = 2$

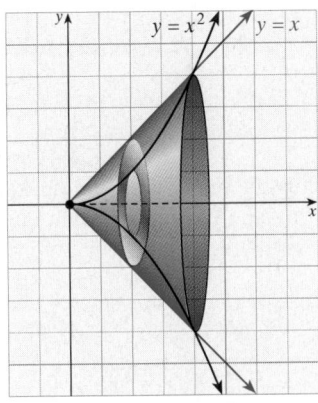
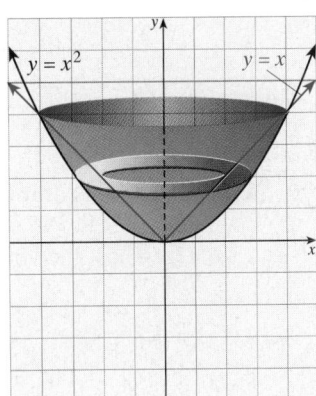
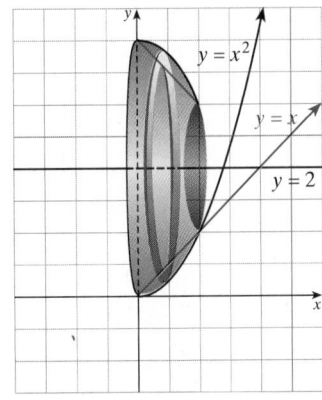

Solution

The region D to be rotated is shown in Figure 6.17. Note that since $x = x^2$ at $x = 0$ and at $x = 1$, the line and parabola intersect at the origin and at $(1, 1)$.

a. The line is always above the parabola on the interval $[0, 1]$, so when we form a washer to approximate the volume of revolution, the outer radius is $R = x$ and the inner radius is $r = x^2$, as shown in Figure 6.17a. Thus, the required volume is

$$V = \pi \int_0^1 [x^2 - (x^2)^2]\, dx$$

$$= \pi \int_0^1 (x^2 - x^4)\, dx$$

$$= \pi \left(\tfrac{1}{3} x^3 - \tfrac{1}{5} x^5 \right)\Big|_0^1 = \frac{2\pi}{15}$$

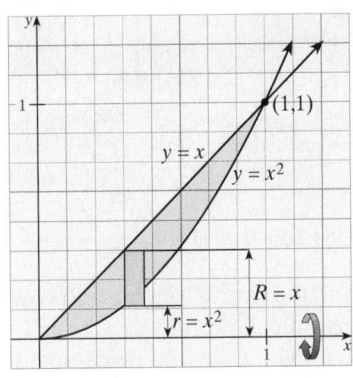

a. The vertical strip is
rotated about the x-axis

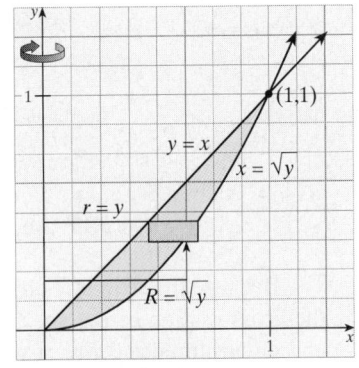

b. The horizontal strip is
rotated about the y-axis

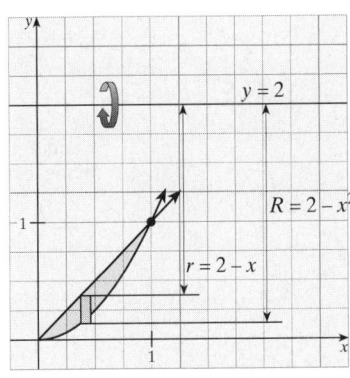

c. The vertical strip is
rotated about the line $y = 2$

Figure 6.17   Volume obtained by revolving a region about different lines

b. Because we are revolving R about the y-axis, we use *horizontal* strips to approximate the solid of revolution, as shown in Figure 6.17b. Note that the parabola $x = \sqrt{y}$ is to the right of the line $x = y$ on the interval $[0, 1]$, so the approximating washer has outer radius $R = \sqrt{y}$ and inner radius $r = y$; thus,

$$V = \pi \int_0^1 [(\sqrt{y})^2 - (y)^2] \, dy$$

$$= \pi \int_0^1 (y - y^2) \, dy$$

$$= \pi \left[\frac{y^2}{2} - \frac{y^3}{3} \right]\Big|_0^1 = \frac{\pi}{6}$$

c. Since the axis of rotation is the line $y = 2$, the outer radius of a typical approximating washer is $R = 2 - x^2$, and the inner radius is $r = 2 - x$, as shown in Figure 6.17c. Thus, the volume of revolution is

$$V = \pi \int_0^1 [(2 - x^2)^2 - (2 - x)^2] \, dx$$

$$= \pi \int_0^1 (x^4 - 5x^2 + 4x) \, dx$$

$$= \pi \left[\frac{x^5}{5} - \frac{5x^3}{3} + \frac{4x^2}{2} \right]\Big|_0^1 = \frac{8\pi}{15} \qquad \blacksquare$$

METHOD OF CYLINDRICAL SHELLS

Sometimes it is easier (or even necessary) to compute a volume by taking the approximating strip parallel to the axis of rotation instead of perpendicular to the axis as in the disk and washer methods. Figure 6.18a shows a region R under the curve $y = f(x)$ on the interval $[a, b]$, together with a representative vertical strip. When this strip is revolved about the y-axis, it forms a solid called a **cylindrical shell** of height $f(x)$ and thickness Δx, as shown in Figure 6.18b.

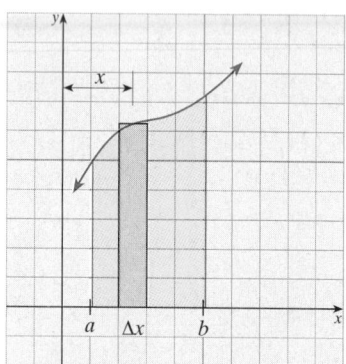

a. A vertical strip in the region R under the curve $y = f(x)$ on the interval $[a, b]$

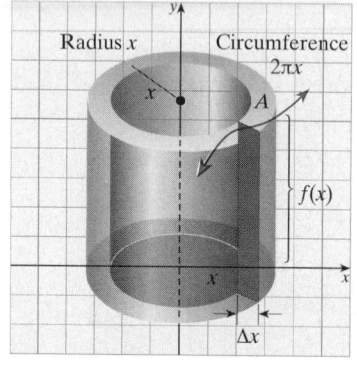

b. When the strip is revolved about the y-axis, a shell is generated.

c. The unwrapped "flattened" shell has volume $\Delta V = 2\pi x f(x) \Delta x$.

Figure 6.18 Method of cylindrical shells

Because the strip is x units from the axis of rotation and is assumed to be very thin, the cross section of the shell (perpendicular to the y-axis) will be a circle of radius x and circumference $2\pi x$. If we imagine the shell to be cut and flattened out, it is seen to be a rectangular slab of volume

$$\Delta V = \underbrace{2\pi x f(x)}_{\text{Area of the rectangular slab}} \overbrace{\Delta x}^{\text{Thickness}}$$

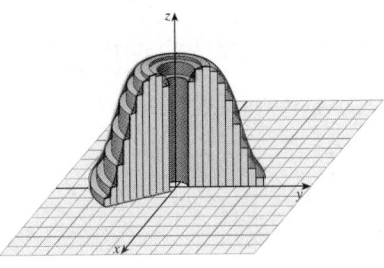

Figure 6.19 Approximating a solid of revolution by cylindrical shells

(See Figure 6.18c.) Thus, the total volume of the solid is given by the integral

$$V = \int_a^b 2\pi x f(x)\, dx$$

The approximating shells are shown in Figure 6.19 and the formula is repeated in the following box.

Method Of Cylindrical Shells

The **shell method** is used to find a volume generated when a region R is revolved about an axis L *parallel* to a typical approximating strip in R. In particular, if R is the region, as shown in Figure 6.20, bounded by the curve $y = f(x)$, the x-axis, and the vertical lines $x = a$ and $x = b$, where $0 \le a \le b$, then the solid generated by revolving R about the y-axis has volume

$$V = \int_a^b 2\pi x f(x)\, dx$$

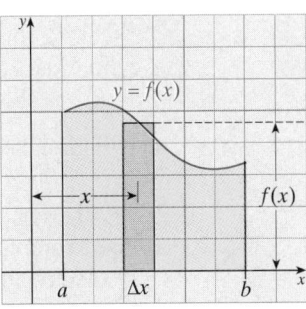

Figure 6.20 Shell Method

EXAMPLE 5 Volume using cylindrical shells

Find the volume of the solid formed by revolving the region bounded by the x-axis and the graphs of $y = x^3 + x^2 + 1$, $x = 1$, and $x = 3$ about the y-axis.

Solution

The region to be rotated is shown in Figure 6.21, along with a typical vertical strip of height $f(x) = x^3 + x^2 + 1$ and width Δx. The volume, by the method of shells, is

$$V = 2\pi \int_1^3 x(x^3 + x^2 + 1)\, dx = 2\pi \int_1^3 (x^4 + x^3 + x)\, dx$$

$$= 2\pi \left(\tfrac{1}{5}x^5 + \tfrac{1}{4}x^4 + \tfrac{1}{2}x^2 \right)\Big|_1^3 = 144.8\pi \approx 454.9 \qquad \blacksquare$$

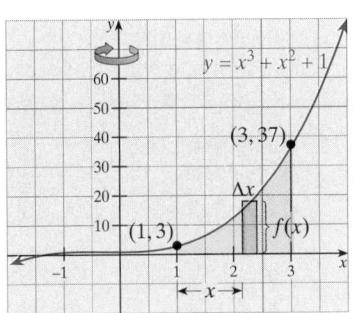

Figure 6.21 A volume of revolution by the shell method

When the axis of rotation is a line $x = L$ parallel to the y-axis, the distance of a typical vertical strip from the axis will no longer be x. Here is an example that illustrates how to compute volume of revolution in such a case.

EXAMPLE 6 Volume of revolution about a horizontal or vertical line

Find the volume of the solid formed by revolving the region R bounded by the curve $y = x^{-2}$ and the x-axis for $1 \le x \le 2$ about the line $x = -1$.

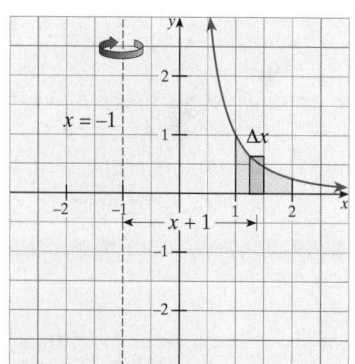

Figure 6.22 Volume by shells (rotating about $x = -1$)

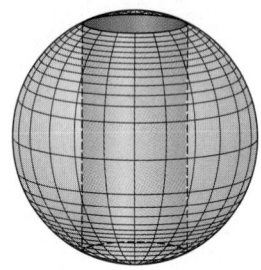

Figure 6.23 Drill a hole in a sphere

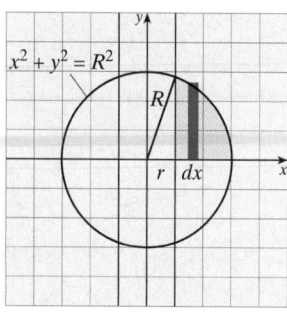

Figure 6.24 Volume of solid by cylindrical shells; strip parallel to axis of rotation

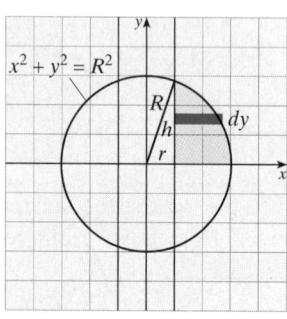

Figure 6.25 Volume of solid by washer method; strip perpendicular to axis of rotation

Solution

The region R is shown in Figure 6.22, along with a typical vertical strip of height $f(x) = x^{-2}$. If we were revolving this strip about the y-axis, the distance from the axis to the strip would be $L = x$, but since the axis of rotation is $x = -1$, the distance is $L = x + 1$.

$$V = 2\pi \int_1^2 [x - (-1)] \left(\frac{1}{x^2}\right) dx$$
$$= 2\pi \int_1^2 (x^{-1} + x^{-2})\, dx$$
$$= 2\pi \left[\ln x - x^{-1}\right]\Big|_1^2$$
$$= 2\pi \left[\ln 2 + \tfrac{1}{2}\right]$$
$$\approx 7.4968 \qquad \blacksquare$$

Sometimes you have a choice between using shells or washers to compute a volume of revolution. The decision as to which method to use often comes down to which leads to the easier integration. Which method would you choose in the following example?

EXAMPLE 7   Comparing the methods of shells and washers

A cylindrical hole of radius r is bored through the center of a solid sphere of radius R ($r < R$), as shown in Figure 6.23. Find the volume of the solid that remains by using

a. cylindrical shells   **b.** washers

Solution

a. The required volume can be thought of as twice the volume generated when the shaded region of Figure 6.24 is revolved about the y-axis.

If we use vertical strips, a typical strip has height $y = \sqrt{R^2 - x^2}$ and is x units from the axis of rotation. The volume is given by

$$V = 2 \int_r^R 2\pi x y\, dx = 4\pi \int_r^R x\sqrt{R^2 - x^2}\, dx$$
$$= 4\pi \left[-\frac{1}{3}(R^2 - x^2)^{3/2}\right]\Big|_r^R = \frac{4\pi}{3}(R^2 - r^2)^{3/2}$$

where we have used the substitution $u = R^2 - x^2$ to evaluate the integral.

b. For the washer method, we use horizontal strips and note that a typical washer has outer radius $x = \sqrt{R^2 - y^2}$ and inner radius r (see Figure 6.25). We integrate from 0 to h, where $h = \sqrt{R^2 - r^2}$, so the volume (again by symmetry) is given by

$$V = 2 \int_0^h \pi \left[\left(\sqrt{R^2 - y^2}\right)^2 - r^2\right] dy$$
$$= 2\pi \int_0^{\sqrt{R^2 - r^2}} \left[(R^2 - y^2) - r^2\right] dy$$
$$= 2\pi \left[(R^2 - r^2)y - \frac{y^3}{3}\right]\Big|_0^{\sqrt{R^2 - r^2}}$$
$$= 2\pi \left[(R^2 - r^2)^{3/2} - \frac{1}{3}(R^2 - r^2)^{3/2}\right]$$
$$= \frac{4\pi}{3}(R^2 - r^2)^{3/2} \qquad \blacksquare$$

Table 6.1 compares and contrasts the disk, washer, and shell methods for computing volume.

TABLE 6.1   Volumes of revolution when the axis of revolution is either the *x*-axis or the *y*-axis.

Summary

a. Disk method: A representative rectangle is **perpendicular** to the axis of revolution. The axis of revolution is a boundary of the region.

b. Washer method: A representative rectangle is **perpendicular** to the axis of revolution. The axis of revolution is *not* part of the boundary.

Horizontal axis of revolution	Vertical axis of revolution	Horizontal axis of revolution	Vertical axis of revolution
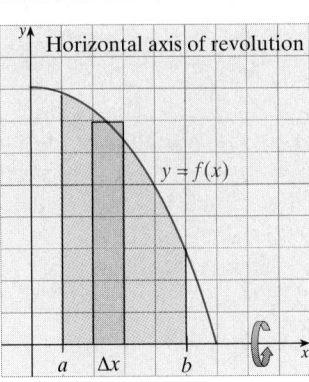	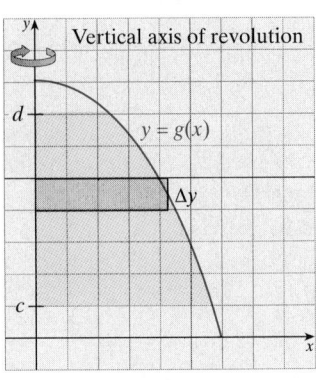	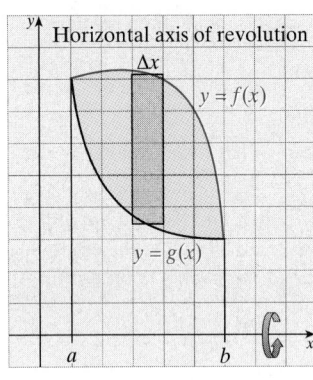	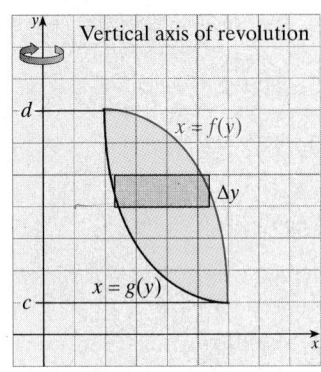

Width of rectangle is Δx.

$$V = \pi \int_a^b \underbrace{[f(x)]^2}_{\text{Length of rectangle}} \overbrace{dx}$$

Width of rectangle is Δy.

$$V = \pi \int_c^d \underbrace{[g(y)]^2}_{\text{Length of rectangle}} \overbrace{dy}$$

Top curve

$$V = \pi \int_a^b \left([f(x)]^2 - [g(x)]^2\right) \overbrace{dx}^{\text{Width}}$$

Bottom curve

Right curve

$$V = \pi \int_c^d \left([f(y)]^2 - [g(y)]^2\right) \overbrace{dy}^{\text{Width}}$$

Left curve

c. Shell method: A representative rectangle is **parallel** to the axis of revolution.

Horizontal axis of revolution	Vertical axis of revolution
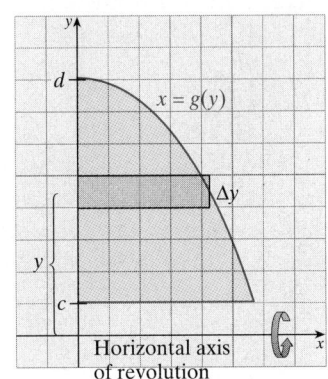	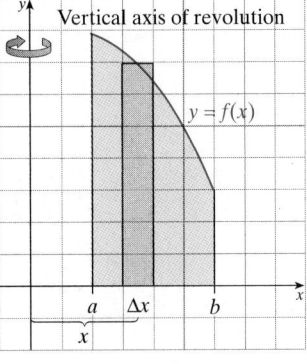

$$V = 2\pi \int_c^d \underset{\uparrow \text{Length}}{y} \underbrace{[g(y)]}\ \overbrace{dy}^{\text{Width}}$$

Distance to axis

$$V = 2\pi \int_a^b \underset{\uparrow \text{Length}}{x} \underbrace{[f(x)]}\ \overbrace{dx}^{\text{Width}}$$

Distance to axis

6.2 PROBLEM SET

Ⓐ *In Problems 1–4, sketch the given region and then find the volume of the solid whose base is the given region and which has the property that each cross section perpendicular to the x-axis is a square.*

1. the triangular region bounded by the coordinate axes and the line $y = 3 - x$

2. the region bounded by the x-axis and the semicircle $y = \sqrt{16 - x^2}$

3. the region bounded by the line $y = x + 1$ and the curve $y = x^2 - 2x + 3$

4. the region bounded above by $y = \sqrt{\sin x}$ and below by the x-axis on the interval $[0, \pi]$

In Problems 5–8, sketch the region and then find the volume of the solid whose base is the given region and which has the property that each cross section perpendicular to the x-axis is an equilateral triangle.

5. the region bounded by the circle $x^2 + y^2 = 9$

6. the region bounded by the curves $y = x^3$ and $y = x^2$

7. the region bounded above by $y = \sqrt{\cos x}$ and below by the x-axis on the interval $\left[-\frac{\pi}{2}, \frac{\pi}{2}\right]$

8. the triangular region with vertices $A(1, 1)$, $B(3, 5)$, and $C(3, -2)$

In Problems 9–12, sketch the region and then find the volume of the solid where the base is the given region and which has the property that each cross section perpendicular to the x-axis is a semicircle.

9. the region bounded by the y-axis, the parabola $y = x^2$, and the line $2x + y - 3 = 0$

10. the region bounded above by $y = \cos x$, below by $y = \sin x$, and on the left by the y-axis

11. the region bounded above by the curve $y = \tan x$ and below by the x-axis, on the interval $\left[0, \frac{\pi}{4}\right]$

12. the region bounded by the x-axis and the curve $y = e^x$ between $x = 1$ and $x = 3$

In Problems 13–20, find the volume of the solid formed when the region described is revolved about the x-axis using washers or disks.

13. the region under the curve $y = \sqrt{x}$ on the interval $0 \le x \le 1$

14. the region under the curve $y = \sqrt[3]{x}$ on the interval $0 \le x \le 8$

15. the region bounded by the lines $y = x$, $y = 2x$, and $x = 1$

16. the region bounded by the lines $x = 0$, $x = 1$, $y = x + 1$, and $y = x + 2$

17. the region under the curve $y = x^2 + x^3$ on the interval $0 \le x \le \pi$; approximate your answer to the nearest unit

18. the region under the curve $y = \sqrt{2 \sin x}$ on the interval $0 \le x \le \pi$

19. the region between $y = \sin x$ and $y = \cos x$ on $0 \le x \le \pi/4$

20. the region bounded by the curves $y = e^x$ and $y = e^{-x}$ on $[0, 2]$

In Problems 21–26, use shells to find the volume of the solid formed by revolving the given region about the y-axis.

21. the region bounded by the lines $y = 2x$, the y-axis, and $y = 1$

22. the region bounded by the curve $y = \sqrt{x}$, the y-axis, and the line $y = 1$

23. the region bounded by the parabola $y = 1 - x^2$, the y-axis, and the positive x-axis

24. the region bounded by the parabolas $y = x^2$, $y = 1 - x^2$, and the y-axis for $x \ge 0$

25. the region bounded by the curve $y = e^{-x^2}$, the y-axis, and the line $y = \frac{1}{2}$

26. the region inside the ellipse $2(x - 3)^2 + 3(y - 2)^2 = 6$ about the y-axis

In Problems 27–34, set up but do not evaluate an integral using the shaded strips for the volume generated when the given region is revolved about:

a. the x-axis

b. the y-axis

c. the line $y = -1$

d. the line $x = -2$

27. $y = 4 - x, 0 \le x \le 4$

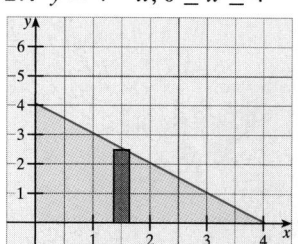

28. $y = 4 - x^2, 0 \le x \le 2$

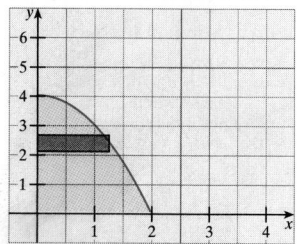

29. $y = \sqrt{4 - x^2}, 0 \le x \le 2$

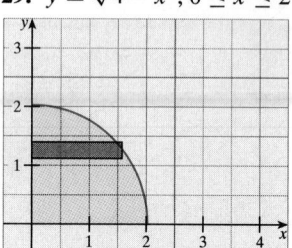

30. $y = \sqrt{4 - x^2}, 0 \le x \le 2$

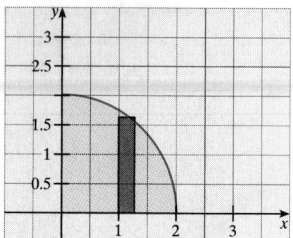

31. $y = e^{-x}, 0 \le x \le 1$

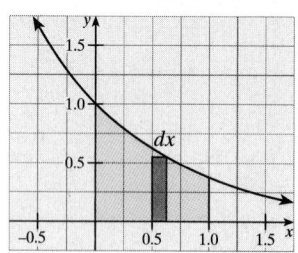

32. $y = \dfrac{x}{x + 1}, 0 \le x \le 1$

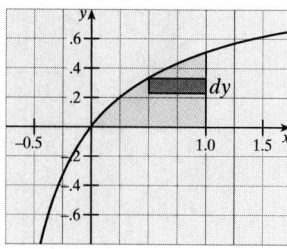

33. $y = \sin^{-1} x, 0 \le x \le 1$

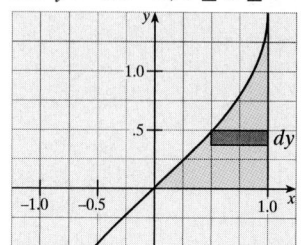

34. $y = \ln x, 1 \le x \le 2$

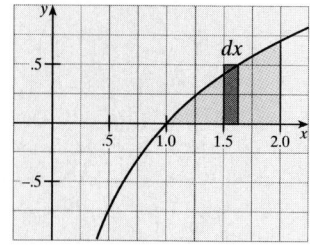

In Problems 35–40, draw a representative strip and set up an integral for the volume of the solid formed by revolving the given region:

a. *about the x-axis*   **b.** *about the y-axis*

Set up the integral only; DO NOT EVALUATE.

35. the region bounded by
$x = y^2$ and $y = x^2$

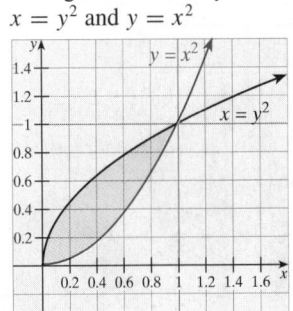

36. the region bounded by
$y = \frac{1}{3}x$ and $x = y^2$

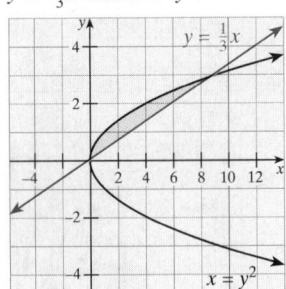

37. the region bounded by the
lines $y = 1$, $x = 2$, and the
curve $y = x^2 + 1$

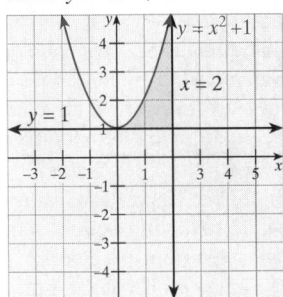

38. the region bounded by the
curves $y = x^2$ and
$y = -x^2 - 4x$

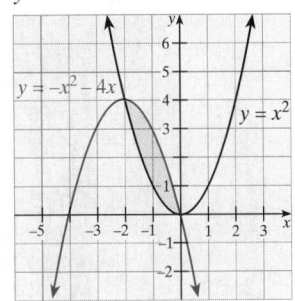

39. the region bounded by
$y = 0.1x^2$ and $y = \ln x$

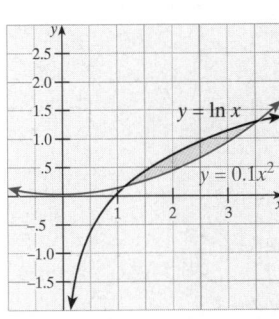

40. the region bounded by
$y = e^x - 1$, $y = 2e^{-x}$, and
$x = 0$

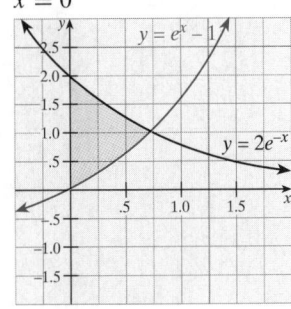

B *In each of Problems 41–44, find the volume by the*

a. *disk/washer method*   **b.** *shell method*

41. Revolve the region bounded by $y = x^2$ and $y = x^3$ about the
x-axis.

42. Revolve the region bounded by $y = x^2$ and $y = x^3$ about the
y-axis.

43. Revolve the region bounded by $y = x$, $y = 2x$, and $y = 1$
about the x-axis.

44. Revolve the region bounded by $y = x$, $y = 2x$, and $y = 1$
about the y-axis.

45. Derive the formula for the volume of a sphere of radius r by
revolving the region bounded by the semicircle $y = \sqrt{r^2 - x^2}$
about the x-axis.

*In Problems 46–49, find the volume of the solid whose base is
bounded by the circle $x^2 + y^2 = 9$ with the indicated cross sections
taken perpendicular to the x-axis.*

46. squares

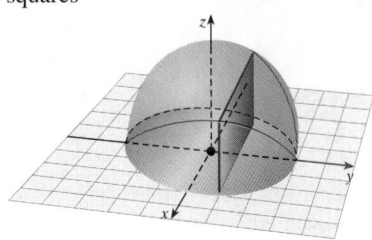

47. equilateral triangles

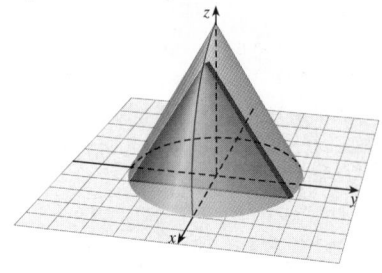

48. isosceles right triangles

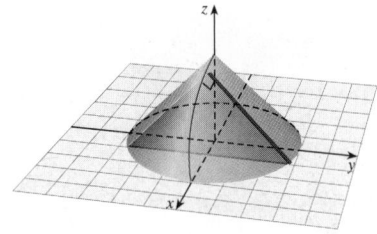

49. semicircles

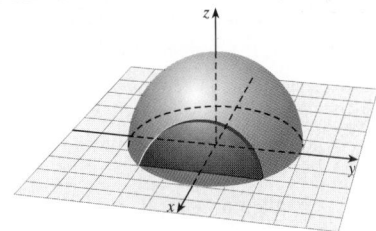

*In Problems 50–51, find the volume V of the solid with the given
information regarding its cross section.*

50. The base of the solid is the hyperbola

$$\frac{x^2}{4} - \frac{y^2}{9} = 1$$

for $2 \leq x \leq 5$, and the cross sections perpendicular to the
x-axis are squares.

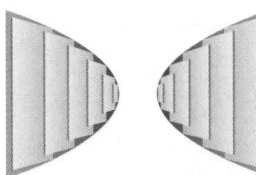

51. The base of the solid is an equilateral triangle, each side of which has length 4. The cross sections perpendicular to a given altitude of the triangle are squares.

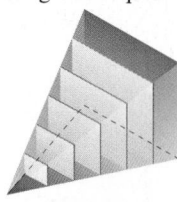

52. The base of the solid is an isosceles right triangle whose legs are each 4 units long. Each cross section perpendicular to a side is a semicircle.

53. The great pyramid of Cheops is approximately 480 ft tall and 750 ft square at the base. Find the volume of this pyramid by using the cross section method.

54. When viewed from above, a swimming pool has the shape of the ellipse

$$\frac{x^2}{900} + \frac{y^2}{400} = 1$$

The cross sections of the pool perpendicular to the ground and parallel to the y-axis are squares. If the units are in feet, what is the volume of the pool?

55. Find the volume of the solid generated when the region $y = x^{-1/2}$ on the interval [1, 4] is revolved about
    a. the x-axis   **b.** the y-axis   **c.** the line $y = -2$

56. Let R be the region in the first quadrant bounded by the curve $y = kx$ and the line $x = k, k > 0$. Find the volume when R is revolved about
    a. the y-axis   **b.** the line $x = 2k$

57. The portion on the ellipse $\dfrac{x^2}{9} + \dfrac{y^2}{4} = 1$ with $x \geq 0$ is rotated about the y-axis to form a solid S. A hole of radius 1 is drilled through the center of S, along the y-axis. Find the volume of the part of S that remains.

58. Cross-sectional areas are measured at 1-foot intervals along the length of an irregularly shaped object, with the results listed in the following table (x in ft and A in ft^2):

x	0	1	2	3	4	5
A	1.12	1.09	1.05	1.03	0.99	1.01

x	6	7	8	9	10
A	0.98	0.99	0.96	0.93	0.91

Estimate the volume (correct to the nearest hundredth) by using the trapezoidal rule.

59. Cross-sectional areas are measured at 2-meter intervals along the length of an irregularly shaped object, with the results listed in the following table (x in meters and A in m^2):

x	0	2	4	6	8	10
A	1.12	1.09	1.05	1.03	0.99	1.01

x	12	14	16	18	20
A	0.98	0.99	0.96	0.93	0.91

Estimate the volume (correct to the nearest hundredth) by using Simpson's rule.

60. HISTORICAL QUEST   Johannes Kepler is usually remembered for his work in astronomy (see Section 10.3, and Historical Quests at the end of Chapter 10). Kepler also made interesting mathematical discoveries. In fact, he has been described as "number-intoxicated." He was looking for mathematical harmonies in the physical universe. He is quoted in *The World of Mathematics*[*]: "Nothing holds me; I will indulge my sacred fury; I will triumph over mankind by the honest confession that I have stolen the golden vases of the Egyptians to build up a tabernacle for my God far away from the confines of Egypt." ■

JOHANNES KEPLER
1571–1630

In this Historical Quest we look at Kepler's derivation for the volume of a torus, generated by revolving a circle of radius a around a vertical axis at a distance b from its center ($b \geq a$). He found $V = (\pi a^2)(2\pi b) = 2\pi^2 a^2 b$. He derived this formula by dissecting a torus into infinitely many thin vertical circular slices by considering planes perpendicular to the axis of revolution, as shown in Figure 6.26.

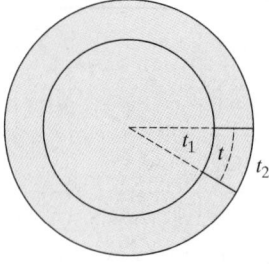

Figure 6.26   Torus cross section

Note that each slice is thinner (t_1) on the inside (nearer the axis) and thicker (t_2) on the outside. Kepler assumed that the volume of each slice is $\pi a^2 t$, where $t = \frac{1}{2}(t_1 + t_2)$. Because t is the average of its minimum and maximum thickness, it must be the thickness of the slice at its center. Use washers or shells to verify Kepler's formula for the volume of a torus.

61. A hemisphere of radius r may be regarded as a solid whose base is the region bounded by the circle $x^2 + y^2 = r^2$ and with the property that each cross section perpendicular to the x-axis is a semicircle with a diameter in the base. Use this characterization and the method of cross sections to show that a sphere of radius r has volume $V = \frac{4}{3}\pi r^3$.

*Vol. I, James R. Newman (New York: Simon & Schuster, 1956), p. 220.

62. Use the method of cross sections to show that the volume of a regular tetrahedron of side a is $\frac{1}{12}\sqrt{2}a^3$.

63. A student, Frank Kornercutter, conjectures that a tetrahedron is nothing more than a solid figure with an equilateral triangular base and cross sections perpendicular to that base that are also equilateral triangles. Is Frank correct this time? Either prove that he is or show that his conjecture must be false.

64. Find the volume of the football-shaped solid (called an *ellipsoid*) formed by revolving the ellipse

$$\frac{x^2}{a^2} + \frac{y^2}{b^2} = 1$$

about the x-axis. What is the volume if the ellipse is revolved about the y-axis?

65. A "cap" is formed by truncating a sphere of radius R at a point h units from the center, as shown in Figure 6.27. Find the volume of the cap.

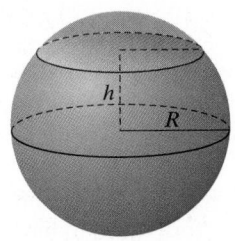

Figure 6.27 Volume of the cap of a sphere

66. The *frustum of a cone* is the solid region bounded by a cone and two parallel planes, as shown in Figure 6.28. Suppose the planes are h units apart and intersect the cone in plane regions of area A_1 and A_2, respectively. Use integration to show that the frustum has volume

$$V = \frac{h}{3}\left(A_1 + \sqrt{A_1 A_2} + A_2\right)$$

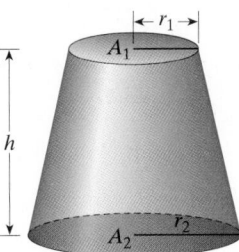

Figure 6.28 Volume of the frustum of a cone

6.3 Polar Forms and Area

IN THIS SECTION the polar coordinate system, polar graphs, intersection of polar-form curves, polar area

THE POLAR COORDINATE SYSTEM

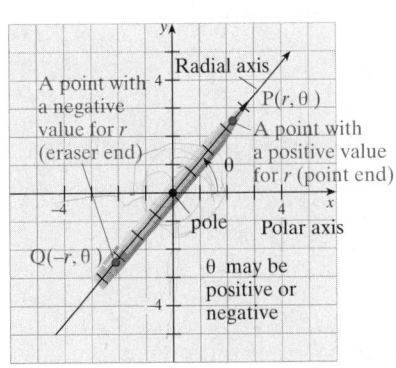

Figure 6.29 Polar-form points

SMH For a more complete discussion of the polar coordinate system, see Chapter 5 of the *Student Mathematics Handbook*.

In the **polar coordinate system**, points are plotted in relation to a fixed point O, called the origin or **pole** and a fixed ray emanating from the origin called the **polar axis**. We then associate with each point P in the plane an ordered pair of numbers $P(r, \theta)$, where r is the distance from O to P and θ is the angle measured from the polar axis to the ray OP, as shown in Figure 6.29. The number r is called the **radial coordinate** of P, and θ is the **polar angle**. The polar angle is regarded as positive if measured counterclockwise up from the polar axis, and negative if measured clockwise. The origin O has radial coordinate 0, and it is convenient to say that O has polar coordinates $(0, \theta)$, for all angles θ.

If the point P has polar coordinates (r, θ), we say that the point Q obtained by reflecting P in the origin O has coordinates $(-r, \theta)$. Thus, if you think of a pencil lying along the directed line segment $\overline{OP}$, with its midpoint at O and tip at $P(r, \theta)$, then the eraser will be at $Q(-r, \theta)$, as illustrated in Figure 6.29.

While each point in the plane is associated with exactly one pair of rectangular coordinates, a given point in polar coordinates has an infinite number of representations. For example, $\left(5, \frac{3\pi}{2}\right)$, $\left(-5, \frac{\pi}{2}\right)$, and $\left(5, -\frac{\pi}{2}\right)$ all represent the same point in polar coordinates. The nonuniqueness of representation in the polar coordinate system causes some difficulties, but they can be handled by exercising a little care. We will point out situations in our examples where the multiplicity of polar representation must be taken into account.

There is a simple trigonometric relationship linking polar and rectangular coordinates. Specifically, if we assume that the origin of the rectangular coordinate system is the pole and the positive x-axis is the polar axis, then the rectangular coordinates (x, y) of each point are related to the polar coordinates (r, θ) of the same point by the formulas summarized in the following box.

Relationship between Rectangular and Polar Coordinates

1. To change *from polar to rectangular*:

$$x = r \cos \theta \qquad y = r \sin \theta$$

2. To change *from rectangular to polar*:

$$r = \sqrt{x^2 + y^2}$$

$$\tan \theta = \frac{y}{x} \quad \text{if } x \neq 0$$

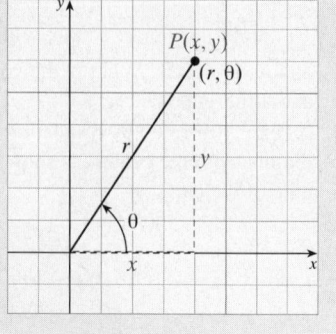

Note that the preceding formula gives r as the distance from the pole to the point. This does not mean that ordered pairs in polar form need to have positive first components. For example $\left(1, \frac{3\pi}{2}\right)$ is the same point as $\left(-1, \frac{\pi}{2}\right)$.

EXAMPLE 1   Converting from polar to rectangular coordinates

Change the polar coordinates $\left(-3, \frac{5\pi}{4}\right)$ to rectangular coordinates.

Solution

$$x = -3 \cos \frac{5\pi}{4} = -3\left(-\frac{\sqrt{2}}{2}\right) = \frac{3\sqrt{2}}{2}$$

$$y = -3 \sin \frac{5\pi}{4} = -3\left(-\frac{\sqrt{2}}{2}\right) = \frac{3\sqrt{2}}{2}$$

The rectangular coordinates are $\left(\dfrac{3\sqrt{2}}{2}, \dfrac{3\sqrt{2}}{2}\right)$.   ∎

EXAMPLE 2   Converting from rectangular coordinates to polar coordinates

Write polar-form coordinates for the point with rectangular coordinates $\left(\dfrac{5\sqrt{3}}{2}, -\dfrac{5}{2}\right)$.

Solution $r = \sqrt{\left(\dfrac{5\sqrt{3}}{2}\right)^2 + \left(-\dfrac{5}{2}\right)^2} = \sqrt{\dfrac{75}{4} + \dfrac{25}{4}} = 5$

Note that θ is in Quadrant IV because x is positive and y is negative.

$$\bar{\theta} = \tan^{-1}\left|\frac{-\frac{5}{2}}{\frac{5\sqrt{3}}{2}}\right| = \tan^{-1}\left(\frac{1}{\sqrt{3}}\right) = \frac{\pi}{6}; \quad \text{thus,} \quad \theta = \frac{11\pi}{6} \qquad \text{(Quadrant IV)}$$

Polar-form coordinates are $\left(5, \frac{11\pi}{6}\right)$. A representation with a negative r is $\left(-5, \frac{5\pi}{6}\right)$.   ∎

POLAR GRAPHS

The **graph** of an equation in polar coordinates is the set of all points P whose polar coordinates (r, θ) satisfy the given equation. Circles, lines through the origin, and rays emanating from the origin have particularly simple equations in polar coordinates.*

EXAMPLE 3   Graphing circles, lines, and rays

Graph

a. $r = 6$ **b.** $\theta = \frac{\pi}{6}$

Solution

a. The graph is the set of all points (r, θ) such that the first component is 6 for any angle θ. This is a circle with radius 6 centered at the origin, as shown in Figure 6.30a.

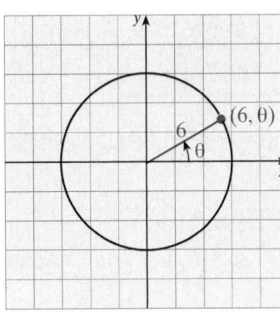 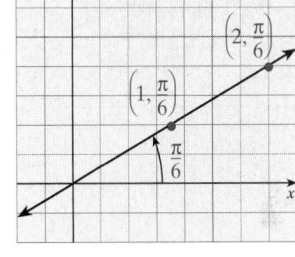

a. The circle r = 6

b. The line θ = $\frac{\pi}{6}$

Figure 6.30   Two polar graphs

b. The graph is the set of all polar points (r, θ) with polar angle $\theta = \frac{\pi}{6}$. This is a line through the origin (pole) that makes an angle $\pi/6$ with the positive x-axis, as shown in Figure 6.30b. If we further require that $r \geq 0$, then the graph is a *ray* (sometimes called a *half-line*). ∎

EXAMPLE 4   Graphing a polar curve by converting to rectangular coordinates

Graph $r = 4 \cos \theta$ by first converting the polar form to rectangular form.

Solution $r = 4 \cos \theta$	*Given*
$r^2 = 4r \cos \theta$	*Multiply both sides by r.*
$x^2 + y^2 = 4x$	$r^2 = x^2 + y^2$ *and* $x = r \cos \theta$
$x^2 - 4x + y^2 = 0$	
$(x - 2)^2 + y^2 = 2^2$	*Complete the square; add 2^2 to both sides.*

This is a circle with center at $(2, 0)$ and radius 2, as shown in Figure 6.31. ∎

In our next example, we sketch a more complicated polar graph by plotting points in a polar coordinate plane. The graph is called a **cardioid** because of its heart-like shape.

Figure 6.31 Graph of $r = 4 \cos \theta$

---

*Many books use what is called **polar graph paper**, but such paper is not really necessary. It also obscures the fact that polar curves and rectangular curves are both plotted as ordered pairs, only with a different meaning attached to the ordered pairs. You can estimate the angles as necessary without polar graph paper.

EXAMPLE 5 Graphing a polar curve by plotting points

Graph $r = 2(1 - \cos\theta)$.

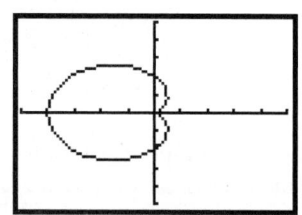
Solution

Construct a table of values by choosing values for θ and approximating the corresponding values for r.

θ	r
0	0
1	0.9193954
2	2.832294
3	3.979985
4	3.307287
5	1.432676
6	0.079659

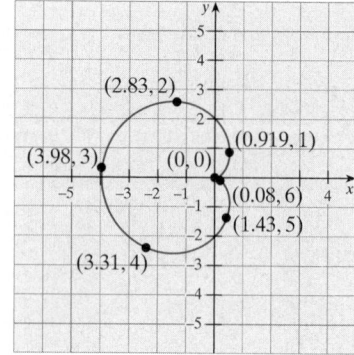

The points are connected as shown in Figure 6.32.

Figure 6.32 Graph of $r = 2(1 - \cos\theta)$

The graph of any polar equation of the general form

$$r = b \pm a\cos\theta \quad \text{or} \quad r = b \pm a\sin\theta$$

is called a **limaçon** (derived from the Latin word *limax*, which means "slug"; in French, it is the word for *snail*). The special case where $a = b$ is the *cardioid*. Figure 6.33 shows four different kinds of limaçons that can occur. Note how the appearance of the graph depends on the ratio b/a.

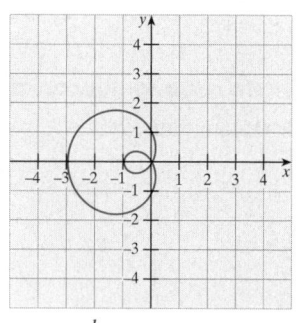

a. $\frac{b}{a} < 1$; inner loop
Case I
($r = 1 - 2\cos\theta$)

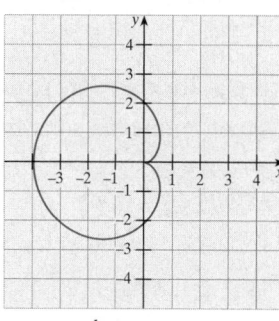

b. $\frac{b}{a} = 1$; cardioid
Case II
($r = 2 - 2\cos\theta$)

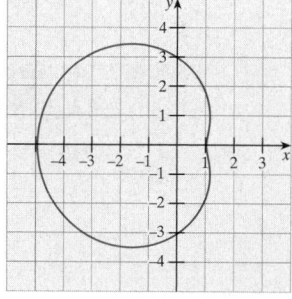

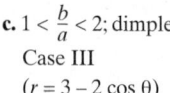

c. $1 < \frac{b}{a} < 2$; dimple
Case III
($r = 3 - 2\cos\theta$)

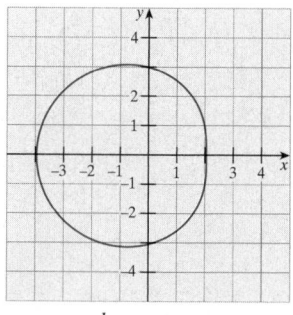

d. $\frac{b}{a} \geq 2$; convex
Case IV
($r = 3 - \cos\theta$)

Figure 6.33 Limaçons: $r = b \pm a\cos\theta$

Summary of Polar-Form Curves There are several polar-form curves which you can graph by plotting points or by using a graphing calculator (be sure to convert to polar form). Table 6.2 gives you the names of some of the special types of polar-form curves you will encounter. There are many others, some of which are represented in the problems. Others may be found in Chapter 5 of the *Student Mathematics Handbook*.

TABLE 6.2   Directory of Polar-Form Curves

Limaçons $r = b \pm a \cos\theta$ **or** $r = b \pm a \sin\theta$

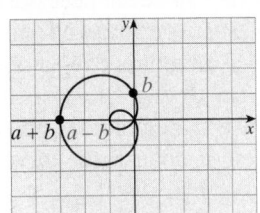

$r = b - a\cos\theta, \frac{b}{a} < 1$
standard form
with inner loop

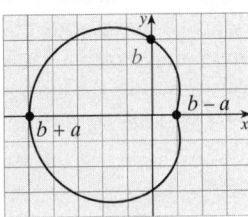

$r = b - a\cos\theta, 1 < \frac{b}{a} < 2$
standard form
with a dimple

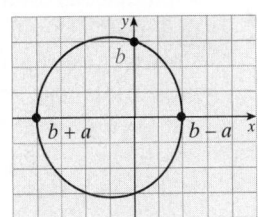

$r = b - a\cos\theta, \frac{b}{a} \geq 2$
standard form,
convex

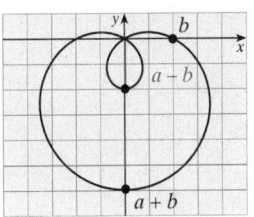

$r = b - a\sin\theta, \frac{b}{a} < 1$
$\frac{\pi}{2}$ rotation
with inner loop

Cardioids $r = a(1 \pm \cos\theta)$ **or** $r = a(1 \pm \sin\theta)$

Limaçons in which $a = b$

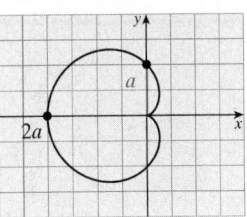

$r = a - a\cos\theta$
standard form

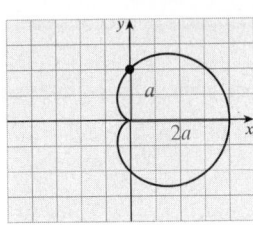

$r = a + a\cos\theta$
π rotation

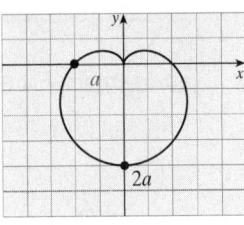

$r = a - a\sin\theta$
$\frac{\pi}{2}$ rotation

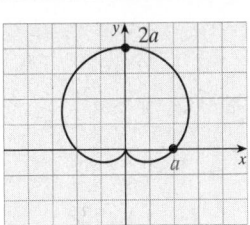

$r = a + a\sin\theta$
$\frac{3\pi}{2}$ rotation

Rose Curves

$r = a\cos n\theta$ **or** $r = a\sin n\theta$

If n is odd, the rose has n petals (leaves); if n is even, it has $2n$ petals.

Lemniscates

$r^2 = a^2\cos 2\theta$ **or** $r^2 = a^2\sin 2\theta$

Two loops

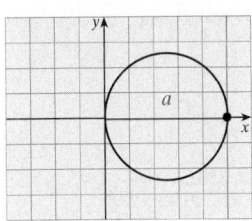

$r = a\cos\theta$
standard form
one (circular) petal

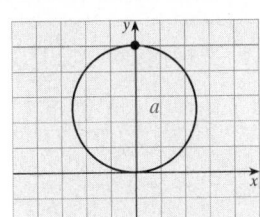

$r = a\sin\theta$
$\frac{\pi}{2}$ rotation,
one (circular) petal

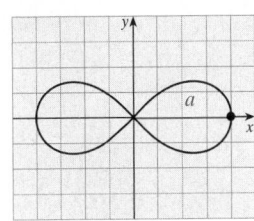

$r^2 = a^2\cos 2\theta$
standard form

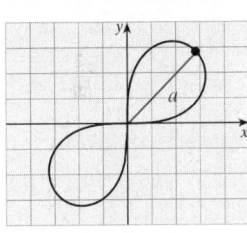

$r^2 = a^2\sin 2\theta$
$\frac{\pi}{4}$ rotation

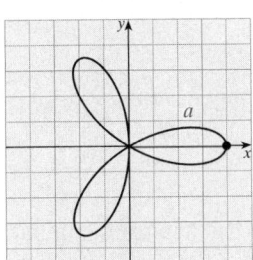

$r = a\cos 3\theta$
standard form,
three petals

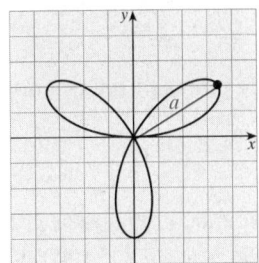

$r = a\sin 3\theta$
$\frac{\pi}{6}$ rotation,
three petals

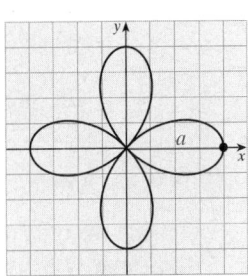

$r = a\cos 2\theta$
standard form,
four petals

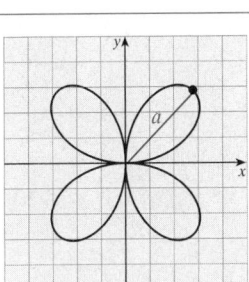

$r = a\sin 2\theta$
$\frac{\pi}{4}$ rotation,
four petals

INTERSECTION OF POLAR-FORM CURVES

To find the points of intersection of graphs in rectangular form, you need only find the simultaneous solution of the equations that define those graphs. It is not even necessary to draw the graphs, because there is a one-to-one correspondence between ordered pairs satisfying an equation and points on its graph. However, in polar form, this one-to-one property is lost, so that without drawing the graphs you may fail to find all points of intersection. For example, $(-1, \pi)$ and $(1, 0)$ both represent the same point, in polar coordinates. Therefore, our method for finding the intersection of polar-form curves will include sketching the graphs.

Graphical Solution of the Intersection of Polar Curves

Step 1.   Find all simultaneous solutions of the given system of equations.
Step 2.   Determine whether the pole lies on the two graphs.
Step 3.   Graph the curves to look for other points of intersection.

EXAMPLE 6   Intersection of polar-form curves

Find the points of intersection of the curves $r = \frac{3}{2} - \cos\theta$ and $\theta = \frac{2\pi}{3}$.

Solution

Step 1.   Solve the system by substitution:
$$r = \tfrac{3}{2} - \cos\tfrac{2\pi}{3} = \tfrac{3}{2} - \left(-\tfrac{1}{2}\right) = 2$$
The solution is $\left(2, \frac{2\pi}{3}\right)$.

Step 2.   If $r = 0$, the first equation has no solution because
$$0 = \tfrac{3}{2} - \cos\theta \quad \text{or} \quad \cos\theta = \tfrac{3}{2}$$
and a cosine cannot be larger than 1.

Step 3.   Now look at the graphs, as shown in Figure 6.34. We see that $\left(-1, \frac{2\pi}{3}\right)$ may also be a point of intersection. It satisfies the equation $\theta = \frac{2\pi}{3}$, but what about $r = \frac{3}{2} - \cos\theta$? Check $\left(-1, \frac{2\pi}{3}\right)$:
$$-1 \overset{?}{=} \tfrac{3}{2} - \cos\left(\tfrac{2\pi}{3}\right)$$
$$= \tfrac{3}{2} - \left(-\tfrac{1}{2}\right)$$
$$= 2 \qquad \text{Not satisfied}$$

However, if you check an alternative representation of $\left(-1, \frac{2\pi}{3}\right)$, namely $\left(1, \frac{5\pi}{3}\right)$:
$$1 \overset{?}{=} \tfrac{3}{2} - \cos\left(\tfrac{5\pi}{3}\right)$$
$$= \tfrac{3}{2} - \tfrac{1}{2}$$
$$= 1 \qquad \text{Satisfied}$$

Be sure to check for points of intersection that you may have missed.   ■

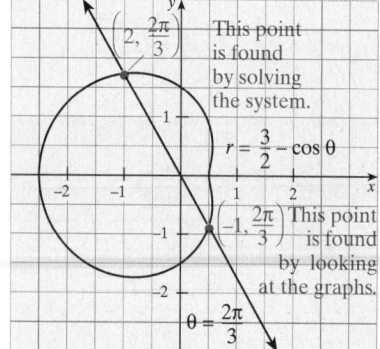

Figure 6.34 Graphs of $r = \frac{3}{2} - \cos\theta$ and $\theta = \frac{2\pi}{3}$

In the figure: $\left(2, \frac{2\pi}{3}\right)$ This point is found by solving the system. $r = \frac{3}{2} - \cos\theta$. $\left(-1, \frac{2\pi}{3}\right)$ This point is found by looking at the graphs. $\theta = \frac{2\pi}{3}$

POLAR AREA

To find the area of a region bounded by a polar graph, we use Riemann sums in much the same way as when we developed the integral formula for the area of a region described in rectangular form. However, instead of using rectangular areas as the basic units being summed, in polar form, we sum areas of *circular sectors*. A typical circular sector is shown in Figure 6.35. Recall the formula for the area of such a sector from trigonometry.

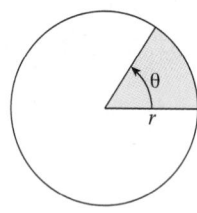

Figure 6.35 Sector of a circle

Area of a Sector

The area of a circular sector of radius r is given by

$$A = \tfrac{1}{2}r^2\theta$$

where θ is the central angle of the sector measured in radians.

Using this formula for the area of a sector, we now state a theorem that gives us a formula for finding the area enclosed by a polar curve. If $r = f(\theta)$, then we call r a **polar function** of θ.

THEOREM 6.1 Area in polar coordinates

Let $r = f(\theta)$ define a polar curve, where f is continuous and $f(\theta) \geq 0$ on the closed interval $\alpha \leq \theta \leq \beta$ for $0 \leq \beta - \alpha \leq 2\pi$. Then the region bounded by the curve $r = f(\theta)$ and the rays $\theta = \alpha$ and $\theta = \beta$ has area

$$A = \frac{1}{2}\int_\alpha^\beta r^2\, d\theta = \frac{1}{2}\int_\alpha^\beta [f(\theta)]^2\, d\theta$$

Proof   The region is shown in Figure 6.36. To find the area bounded by the graphs of the polar functions, partition the region between $\theta = \alpha$ and $\theta = \beta$ by a collection of rays, say $\theta_0, \theta_1, \ldots, \theta_n$. Let $\alpha = \theta_0$ and $\beta = \theta_n$.

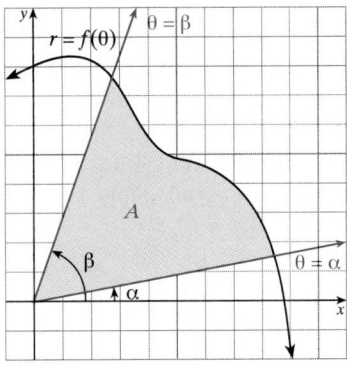
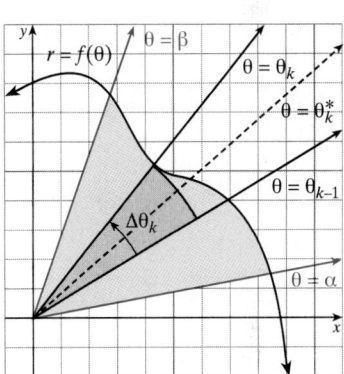

a. The region bounded by the polar curve $r = f(\theta)$ and the rays $\theta = a$ and $\theta = b$

b. The area A can be estimated by adding the area of "small" (gray) circular sectors.

Figure 6.36   Area in polar form

Pick any ray $\theta = \theta_k^*$, with $\theta_{k-1} \leq \theta_k^* \leq \theta_k$. Then the area ΔA_k of the circular sector is approximately the same as the area of the region bounded by the graph of f and the lines $\theta = \theta_{k-1}$ and $\theta = \theta_k$. Because this circular sector has radius $f(\theta_k^*)$ and central angle $\Delta\theta_k$, its area is

$$\Delta A_k \approx \tfrac{1}{2}(\text{radius})^2(\text{central angle}) = \tfrac{1}{2}\left[f(\theta_k^*)\right]^2 \Delta\theta_k$$

The sum $\displaystyle\sum_{k=1}^{n}\Delta A_k$ is an approximation to the total area A bounded by the polar curve, and by taking the limit as $n \to \infty$, we obtain

$$A = \lim_{n\to\infty}\sum_{k=1}^{n}\Delta A_k = \lim_{n\to\infty}\frac{1}{2}\sum_{k=1}^{n}\left[f(\theta_k^*)\right]^2 \Delta\theta_k \qquad \text{Riemann sum}$$

$$= \frac{1}{2}\int_\alpha^\beta [f(\theta)]^2\, d\theta \qquad\qquad\qquad\qquad\qquad\quad \square$$

You will probably find that the most difficult part of the problem is deciding on the limits of integration. A sketch of the region will help with this.

EXAMPLE 7 Finding area of part of a cardioid

Find the area of the top half ($0 \leq \theta \leq \pi$) of the cardioid $r = 1 + \cos\theta$.

Solution

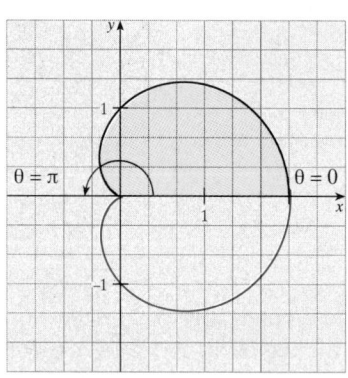

Figure 6.37 Area of the top half of the cardioid $r = 1 + \cos\theta$

The cardioid is shown in Figure 6.37. Note that the top half of the graph lies between the rays $\theta = 0$ and $\theta = \pi$. Hence the required area is given by

$$A = \frac{1}{2}\int_0^\pi (1 + \cos\theta)^2 \, d\theta = \frac{1}{2}\int_0^\pi (1 + 2\cos\theta + \cos^2\theta) \, d\theta$$

$$= \frac{1}{2}\left[\theta + 2\sin\theta + \frac{\theta}{2} + \frac{\sin 2\theta}{4}\right]\Big|_0^\pi \qquad \text{Integration table, formula 317}$$

$$= \frac{1}{2}\left[\pi + 2(0) + \frac{\pi}{2} + \frac{0}{4} - 0\right] = \frac{3\pi}{4} \qquad \blacksquare$$

EXAMPLE 8 Finding area enclosed by a four-leaved rose

Find the area enclosed by the four-leaved rose $r = \cos 2\theta$.

Solution

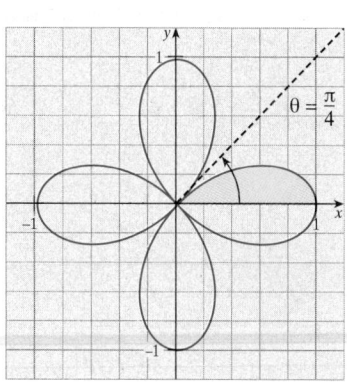

Figure 6.38 Area enclosed by the four-leaved rose $r = \cos 2\theta$

The rose curve is shown in Figure 6.38. We will find the area of the top half of the right loop (shaded portion) to make sure $f(\theta) \geq 0$. We see that this corresponds to angles with measures from $\theta = 0$ to $\theta = \pi/4$. If you have a calculator, the easiest way to see this is to plot the graph and then use the *trace* feature to find the θ-values for the top half of the first leaf. By symmetry, the entire area enclosed by the four-leaved rose is 8 times the shaded region. Thus, the required area is given by

$$A = 8\left[\frac{1}{2}\int_0^{\pi/4} \cos^2 2\theta \, d\theta\right]$$

$$= 4\left[\frac{\theta}{2} + \frac{\sin 4\theta}{8}\right]\Big|_0^{\pi/4} \qquad \text{Integration table, formula 317}$$

$$= 4\left[\frac{\pi}{8} + 0 - 0\right]$$

$$= \frac{\pi}{2} \qquad \blacksquare$$

EXAMPLE 9 Finding the area of a region between two polar curves

Find the area of the region common to the circles $r = a\cos\theta$ and $r = a\sin\theta$.

Solution

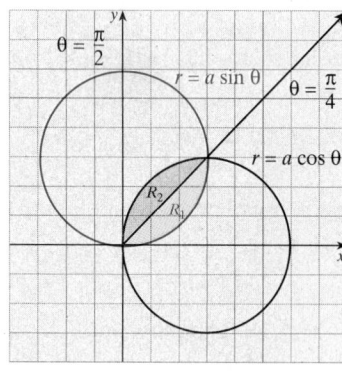

Figure 6.39 Area bounded by $r = a\cos\theta$ and $r = a\sin\theta$

The circles are shown in Figure 6.39. Solve $a\cos\theta = a\sin\theta$ to find that the circles intersect at $\theta = \pi/4$ and at the pole. To set up the integrals properly, remember to think in terms of polar coordinates and not in terms of rectangular coordinates. Specifically, we must **scan radially**. This means that we need to find the area of intersection by adding the areas of the regions marked R_1 and R_2. Region R_1 is bounded by the circle $r = a\sin\theta$ and the rays $\theta = 0$, $\theta = \frac{\pi}{4}$. Region R_2 is bounded by the circle $r = a\cos\theta$ and $\theta = \frac{\pi}{4}$, $\theta = \frac{\pi}{2}$. Note that the rays $\theta = 0$ and $\theta = \frac{\pi}{2}$ are not necessary as geometric boundaries for R_1 and R_2, but they are necessary to describe which part of each circle is being calculated.

$$A = \text{AREA OF } R_1 + \text{AREA OF } R_2$$

$$= \frac{1}{2}\int_0^{\pi/4} a^2 \sin^2\theta \, d\theta + \frac{1}{2}\int_{\pi/4}^{\pi/2} a^2 \cos^2\theta \, d\theta$$

$$= \frac{a^2}{2}\left[\frac{\theta}{2} - \frac{\sin 2\theta}{4}\right]\Big|_0^{\pi/4} + \frac{a^2}{2}\left[\frac{\theta}{2} + \frac{\sin 2\theta}{4}\right]\Big|_{\pi/4}^{\pi/2}$$
Integration table, formulas 348 and 317

$$= \frac{a^2}{2}\left[\frac{\pi}{8} - \frac{1}{4} - 0\right] + \frac{a^2}{2}\left[\frac{\pi}{4} + 0 - \frac{\pi}{8} - \frac{1}{4}\right] = \frac{a^2}{2}\left[\frac{\pi}{4} - \frac{1}{2}\right]$$

$$= \frac{1}{8}a^2(\pi - 2)$$ ∎

EXAMPLE 10   Finding the area between a circle and a limaçon

Find the area between the circle $r = 5\cos\theta$ and the limaçon $r = 2 + \cos\theta$. Round your answer to the nearest hundredth of a square unit.

Solution

As usual, begin by drawing the graphs, as shown in Figure 6.40. Note that both the limaçon and circle are symmetric with respect to the x-axis, so we can find the area in the first quadrant and multiply by 2.

Next, we need to find the points of intersection. We see that the curves do not intersect at the pole. Now solve

$$5\cos\theta = 2 + \cos\theta$$

$$\cos\theta = \frac{1}{2}$$

$$\theta = \frac{\pi}{3} \qquad \text{Solution in the first quadrant}$$

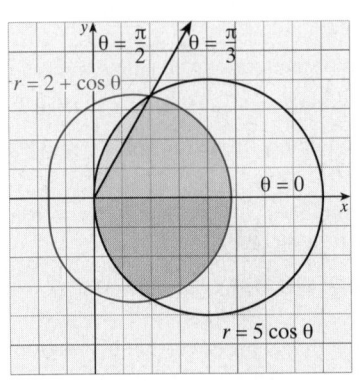

Figure 6.40 Area between $r = 5\cos\theta$ and $r = 2 + \cos\theta$

To find the area, divide the region into two parts, along the ray $\theta = \pi/3$. The right part (gray region above the x-axis) is bounded by the limaçon $r = 2 + \cos\theta$ and the rays $\theta = 0$ and $\theta = \pi/3$. The left part (shaded region shown in color above the x-axis) is bounded by the circle $r = 5\cos\theta$ and the rays $\theta = \pi/3$ and $\theta = \pi/2$. Using this preliminary information, we can now set up and evaluate a sum of integrals for the required area

$$A = 2[\text{AREA OF RIGHT PART} + \text{AREA OF LEFT PART}]$$

$$= 2\left[\frac{1}{2}\int_0^{\pi/3}(2 + \cos\theta)^2 \, d\theta + \frac{1}{2}\int_{\pi/3}^{\pi/2}(5\cos\theta)^2 \, d\theta\right]$$

$$= \int_0^{\pi/3}(4 + 4\cos\theta + \cos^2\theta) \, d\theta + \int_{\pi/3}^{\pi/2} 25\cos^2\theta \, d\theta$$

$$= \left[4\theta + 4\sin\theta + \frac{\theta}{2} + \frac{\sin 2\theta}{4}\right]\Big|_0^{\pi/3} + 25\left[\frac{\theta}{2} + \frac{\sin 2\theta}{4}\right]\Big|_{\pi/3}^{\pi/2}$$

$$= \left[\frac{4\pi}{3} + \frac{4\sqrt{3}}{2} + \frac{\pi}{6} + \frac{\sqrt{3}}{8} - 0\right] + 25\left[\frac{\pi}{4} + 0 - \frac{\pi}{6} - \frac{\sqrt{3}}{8}\right]$$

$$= \frac{43\pi}{12} - \sqrt{3} \approx 9.53$$ ∎

6.3　PROBLEM SET

Ⓐ 1. WHAT DOES THIS SAY?　Discuss a procedure for finding the intersection of polar-form curves.

2. WHAT DOES THIS SAY?　Discuss a procedure for finding the area enclosed by a polar curve.

3. Identify each of the curves as a cardioid, rose curve (state number of petals), lemniscate, limaçon, circle, line, or none of the above.

　a. $r^2 = 9\cos 2\theta$　　　　**b.** $r = 2\sin\frac{\pi}{6}$

　c. $r = 3\sin 3\theta$　　　　**d.** $r = 3\theta$

　e. $r = 2 - 2\cos\theta$　　　**f.** $\theta = \frac{\pi}{6}$

　g. $r^2 = \sin 2\theta$　　　　**h.** $r - 2 = 4\cos\theta$

4. Identify each of the curves as a cardioid, rose curve (state number of petals), lemniscate, limaçon, circle, line, or none of the above.

　a. $r = 2\sin 2\theta$　　　　**b.** $r^2 = 2\cos 2\theta$

　c. $r = 5\cos 60°$　　　　　**d.** $r = 5\sin 8\theta$

　e. $r\theta = 3$　　　　　　　**f.** $r^2 = 9\cos(2\theta - \frac{\pi}{4})$

　g. $r = \sin 3(\theta + \frac{\pi}{6})$　　**h.** $\cos\theta = 1 - r$

5. Identify each of the curves as a cardioid, rose curve (state number of petals), lemniscate, limaçon, circle, line, or none of the above.

　a. $r = 2\cos 2\theta$　　　　**b.** $r = 4\sin 30°$

　c. $r + 2 = 3\sin\theta$　　　**d.** $r + 3 = 3\sin\theta$

　e. $\theta = 4$　　　　　　　**f.** $\theta = \tan\frac{\pi}{4}$

　g. $r = 3\cos 5\theta$　　　　**h.** $r\cos\theta = 2$

Graph the polar-form curves given in Problems 6–21.

6. $r = 3, 0 \le \theta \le \frac{\pi}{2}$　　　**7.** $\theta = -\frac{\pi}{2}, 0 \le r \le 3$

8. $r = \theta + 1, 0 \le \theta \le \pi$　　**9.** $r = 2\theta, \theta \ge 0$

10. $r = 2\cos 2\theta$　　　　　**11.** $r = 5\sin 3\theta$

12. $r^2 = 16\cos 2\theta$　　　　**13.** $r = 3\cos 3(\theta - \frac{\pi}{3})$

14. $r = 5\cos 3(\theta - \frac{\pi}{4})$　　**15.** $r = \sin(2\theta + \frac{\pi}{3})$

16. $r^2 = 16\cos 2(\theta - \frac{\pi}{6})$　　**17.** $r = 2 + \cos\theta$

18. $r = 1 + \sin\theta$　　　　　**19.** $r\cos\theta = 2$

20. $r = 1 + 3\cos\theta$　　　　**21.** $r = -2\sin\theta$

Find the points of intersection of the curves given in Problems 22–29.

22. $\begin{cases} r = 4\cos\theta \\ r = 4\sin\theta \end{cases}$　　**23.** $\begin{cases} r = 4\sin\theta \\ r = 2 \end{cases}$

24. $\begin{cases} r^2 = 9\cos 2\theta \\ r = 3 \end{cases}$　　**25.** $\begin{cases} r = 2(1 + \sin\theta) \\ r = 2(1 - \sin\theta) \end{cases}$

26. $\begin{cases} r = 3\theta \\ \theta = \frac{\pi}{3} \end{cases}$　　**27.** $\begin{cases} r^2 = \sin 2\theta \\ r = \sqrt{2}\sin\theta \end{cases}$

28. $\begin{cases} r = 2(1 - \cos\theta) \\ r = 4\sin\theta \end{cases}$　　**29.** $\begin{cases} r = \dfrac{4}{1 - \cos\theta} \\ r = 2\cos\theta \end{cases}$

Ⓑ *Find the area of each polar region enclosed by $f(\theta)$ for $a \le \theta \le b$ in Problems 30–37.*

30. $f(\theta) = \sin\theta, 0 \le \theta \le \frac{\pi}{6}$　　**31.** $f(\theta) = \cos\theta, 0 \le \theta \le \frac{\pi}{6}$

32. $f(\theta) = \sec\theta, -\frac{\pi}{4} \le \theta \le \frac{\pi}{4}$　**33.** $f(\theta) = \sqrt{\sin\theta}, \frac{\pi}{6} \le \theta \le \frac{\pi}{2}$

34. $f(\theta) = e^{\theta/2}, 0 \le \theta \le 2\pi$

35. $f(\theta) = \sin\theta + \cos\theta, 0 \le \theta \le \frac{\pi}{4}$

36. $f(\theta) = \dfrac{\theta}{\pi}, 0 \le \theta \le 2\pi$　　**37.** $f(\theta) = \dfrac{\theta^2}{\pi}, 0 \le \theta \le 2\pi$

38. **Spirals** are interesting mathematical curves. There are three special types of spirals:

　a. A **spiral of Archimedes** has the form $r = a\theta$. Graph $r = 2\theta$.

　b. A **hyperbolic spiral** has the form $r\theta = a$. Graph $r\theta = 2$.

　c. A **logarithmic spiral** has the form $r = a^{k\theta}$. Graph $r = 2^\theta$.

39. The **strophoid** is a curve of the form $r = a\cos 2\theta\sec\theta$. Graph this curve for $a = 2$.

40. The **bifolium** has the form $r = a\sin\theta\cos^2\theta$. Graph this curve for $a = 1$.

41. The **folium of Descartes** has the form $r = \dfrac{3a\sin\theta\cos\theta}{\sin^3\theta + \cos^3\theta}$. Graph this curve for $a = 2$.

42. Find the area of one loop of the four-leaved rose $r = 2\sin 2\theta$.

43. Find the area enclosed by the three-leaved rose $r = a\sin 3\theta$.

44. Find the area of the region that is inside the circle $r = 4\cos\theta$ and outside the circle $r = 2$.

45. Find the area of the region that is inside the circle $r = a$ and outside the cardioid $r = a(1 - \cos\theta)$.

46. Find the area of the region that is inside the circle $r = \sin\theta$ and outside the cardioid $r = 1 - \cos\theta$.

47. Find the area of the region that is inside the circle $r = 6\cos\theta$ and outside the cardioid $r = 2(1 + \cos\theta)$.

48. Find the area of the portion of the lemniscate $r^2 = 8\cos 2\theta$ that lies in the region $r \ge 2$.

49. Find the area between the inner and outer loops of the limaçon $r = 2 - 4\sin\theta$.

50. Find the area to the right of the line $r\cos\theta = 1$ and inside the lemniscate $r^2 = 2\cos 2\theta$.

51. Find the area to the right of the line $r\cos\theta = 1$ and inside the lemniscate $r^2 = 2\sin 2\theta$.

52. Find the maximum value of the y-coordinate of points on the limaçon $r = 2 + 3\cos\theta$.

53. Find the maximum value of the x-coordinate of points on the cardioid $r = 3 + 3\sin\theta$.

Ⓒ 54. a. Show that if the polar curve $r = f(\theta)$ is rotated about the pole through an angle α, the equation for the new curve is $r = f(\theta - \alpha)$.

　b. Use a rotation to sketch $r = 2\sec(\theta - \frac{\pi}{3})$.

55. The **ovals of Cassini** have the polar form $r^4 + b^4 - 2b^2r^2\cos 2\theta = k^4$. Graph the curve where $b = 2$, $k = 3$.

56. Sketch the graph of

$$r = \frac{\theta}{\cos\theta} \quad \text{for} \quad 0 \le \theta \le \frac{\pi}{2}$$

In particular, show that the graph has a vertical asymptote at $x = \frac{\pi}{2}$.

57. If f is a differentiable function of θ, then show that the tangent line to the polar curve $r = f(\theta)$ at the point $P(r, \theta)$ has slope

$$m = \frac{f(\theta)\cos\theta + f'(\theta)\sin\theta}{-f(\theta)\sin\theta + f'(\theta)\cos\theta}$$

whenever the denominator is not zero. *Hint*: $\dfrac{dy}{dx} = \dfrac{dy/d\theta}{dx/d\theta}$.

58. Because the formula for the slope in polar form is complicated (see Problem 57), it is more convenient to measure the inclination of the tangent line to a polar curve in terms of the angle α extended from the radial line to the tangent line, as shown in Figure 6.41.

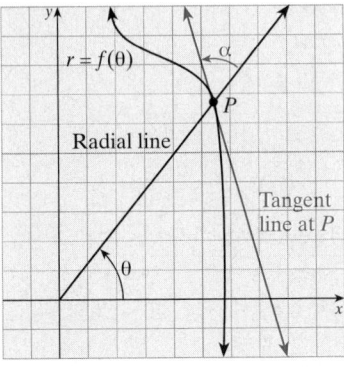

Figure 6.41   Problem 58

Let P be a point on the polar curve $r = f(\theta)$, and let α be the angle extending from the radial line to the tangent line, as shown in Figure 6.41. Assuming that $f'(\theta) \neq 0$, show that

$$\tan\alpha = \frac{f(\theta)}{f'(\theta)}$$

Hint: Use the formula $\tan\alpha = \tan(\phi - \theta) = \dfrac{\tan\phi - \tan\theta}{1 + \tan\phi\tan\theta}$.

59. Use the formula in Problem 58 to find $\tan\alpha$ for each of the following:
   a. the circle $r = a\cos\theta$
   b. the cardioid $r = 2(1 - \cos\theta)$
   c. the logarithmic spiral $r = 2e^{3\theta}$

60. Journal Problem*   *School Science and Mathematics* ■ Graph the polar curve $r = 4 + 2\sin\dfrac{5\theta}{2}$ and find the total area interior to this curve. Then find the area of the "star."

*Problem 3949 by V. C. Bailey, Vol. 83, 1983, p. 356.

6.4   Arc Length and Surface Area

IN THIS SECTION   the arc length of a curve, the area of a surface of revolution, polar arc length and surface area

THE ARC LENGTH OF A CURVE

If a function f has a derivative that is continuous on some interval, then f is said to be **continuously differentiable** on the interval. The portion of the graph of a continuously differentiable function f that lies between $x = a$ and $x = b$ is called the **arc** of the graph on the interval $[a, b]$. To find, and define, the length of this arc, let P be a partition of the interval $[a, b]$, with subdivision points $x_0, x_1, \ldots, x_n$, where $x_0 = a$ and $x_n = b$. Let P_k denote the point (x_k, y_k) on the graph, where $y_k = f(x_k)$. By joining the points $P_0, P_1, \ldots, P_n$, we obtain a polygonal path whose length approximates that of the arc. Figure 6.42 demonstrates the labeling for the case where $n = 6$.

   The length of the polygonal path connecting the points $P_0, P_1, \ldots, P_n$ on the graph of f is the sum

$$\sum_{k=1}^{n} \Delta s_k$$

where Δs_k is the length of the segment joining P_{k-1} to P_k. By applying the distance formula and rearranging terms with $\Delta x_k = x_k - x_{k-1}$ and $\Delta y_k = y_k - y_{k-1}$, we find

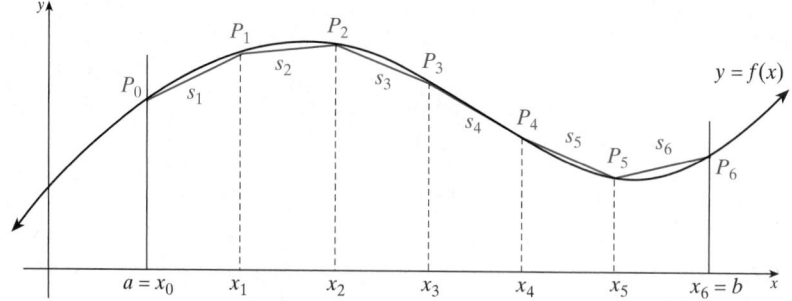

Figure 6.42 A polygonal path approximating an arc of a curve

that

$$\Delta s_k = \sqrt{(x_k - x_{k-1})^2 + (y_k - y_{k-1})^2}$$
$$= \sqrt{(\Delta x_k)^2 + (\Delta y_k)^2}$$
$$= \sqrt{\frac{(\Delta x_k)^2 + (\Delta y_k)^2}{(\Delta x_k)^2}} \, \Delta x_k$$
$$= \sqrt{1 + \left(\frac{\Delta y_k}{\Delta x_k}\right)^2} \, \Delta x_k$$

It is reasonable to expect a connection between the ratio $\Delta y_k / \Delta x_k$ and the derivative $dy/dx = f'(x)$. Indeed, it can be shown (see Problem 42) that

$$\Delta s_k = \sqrt{1 + [f'(x_k^*)]^2} \, \Delta x_k$$

for some number x_k^* between x_{k-1} and x_k. Therefore, the arc length of the graph of f on the interval $[a, b]$ may be estimated by the Riemann sum

$$\sum_{k=1}^{n} \sqrt{1 + [f'(x_k^*)]^2} \, \Delta x_k$$

This estimate may be improved by increasing the number of subdivision points in the partition P of the interval $[a, b]$ in such a way that the subinterval lengths tend to zero. Thus, it is reasonable to define the actual arc length to be the limit

$$\lim_{\|P\| \to 0} \sum_{k=1}^{n} \sqrt{1 + [f'(x_k^*)]^2} \, \Delta x_k$$

Notice that if f' is continuous on the interval $[a, b]$, then so is $\sqrt{1 + [f'(x)]^2}$. Thus, this limit exists and is the integral of $\sqrt{1 + [f'(x)]^2}$ with respect to x on the interval $[a, b]$. These observations lead us to the following definition.*

---

*We have used integration to obtain a meaningful definition of arc length for a function $f(x)$ with a continuous derivative $f'(x)$. It is possible to define arc length for certain curves $y = f(x)$ when $f(x)$ does not have a continuous derivative, but we will not pursue this more general topic.

Arc Length

Let f be a function whose derivative f' is continuous on the interval $[a, b]$ and differentiable on (a, b). Then the **arc length**, s, of the graph of $y = f(x)$ between $x = a$ and $x = b$ is given by the integral

$$s = \int_a^b \sqrt{1 + [f'(x)]^2}\, dx$$

Similarly, for the graph of $x = g(y)$, where g' is continuous on the interval $[c, d]$, the arc length from $y = c$ to $y = d$ is

$$s = \int_c^d \sqrt{1 + [g'(y)]^2}\, dy$$

EXAMPLE 1   Arc length of a curve

Find the arc length (rounded to two decimal places) of the curve $y = x^{3/2}$ on the interval $[0, 4]$.

Solution

The graph is shown in Figure 6.43. Let $f(x) = x^{3/2}$; therefore, $f'(x) = \frac{3}{2}x^{1/2}$.

$$s = \int_0^4 \sqrt{1 + \left[\frac{3}{2}x^{1/2}\right]^2}\, dx$$

$$= \int_0^4 \sqrt{1 + \frac{9}{4}x}\, dx = \left[\frac{4}{9} \cdot \frac{2}{3}\left(1 + \frac{9}{4}x\right)^{3/2}\right]\Big|_0^4$$

$$= \frac{8}{27}\left[(10)^{3/2} - (1)^{3/2}\right] \approx 9.07 \qquad \blacksquare$$

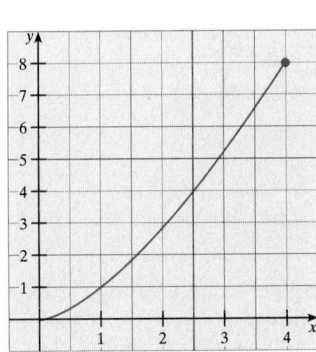

Figure 6.43 What is the length of this curve?

EXAMPLE 2   Arc length of a curve $x = g(y)$

Find the arc length of the curve $x = \frac{1}{3}y^3 + \frac{1}{4}y^{-1}$ from $y = 1$ to $y = 3$.

Solution

Because $g(y) = \frac{1}{3}y^3 + \frac{1}{4}y^{-1}$, we have $g'(y) = y^2 - \frac{1}{4}y^{-2} = \dfrac{4y^4 - 1}{4y^2}$, which is continuous throughout the interval from $y = 1$ to $y = 3$. Therefore, the arc length is

$$\int_1^3 \sqrt{1 + [g'(y)]^2}\, dy = \int_1^3 \sqrt{1 + \left(\frac{4y^4 - 1}{4y^2}\right)^2}\, dy$$

$$= \int_1^3 \sqrt{1 + \frac{16y^8 - 8y^4 + 1}{16y^4}}\, dy$$

$$= \int_1^3 \sqrt{\frac{16y^4 + 16y^8 - 8y^4 + 1}{16y^4}}\, dy$$

$$= \int_1^3 \sqrt{\frac{(4y^4 + 1)^2}{(4y^2)^2}}\, dy$$

$$= \int_1^3 \frac{4y^4 + 1}{4y^2}\, dy$$

$$= \int_1^3 \left(y^2 + \frac{1}{4}y^{-2}\right) dy$$

$$= \left(\frac{1}{3}y^3 + \frac{1}{4}\cdot\frac{y^{-1}}{-1}\right)\Big|_1^3 = \frac{53}{6} \qquad \blacksquare$$

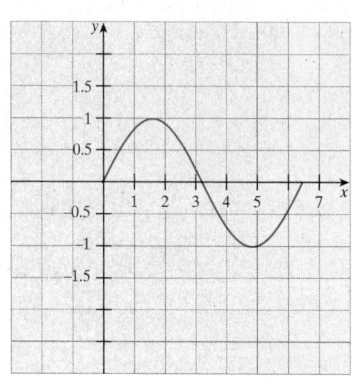

Figure 6.44 Finding the length of an arc

EXAMPLE 3   Estimating arc length using numerical integration

Find the length of the curve defined by $y = \sin x$ on $[0, 2\pi]$.

Solution

The region is shown in Figure 6.44. Because $y' = \cos x$, we have, from the arc length formula,

$$s = \int_0^{2\pi} \sqrt{1 + \cos^2 x}\, dx$$

We do not have techniques to allow us to evaluate this integral, so we turn to numerical integration. If we consider four rectangles, we find, by various methods:

Method ($n = 4$)	Approximation
Rectangles	
Left endpoints	7.584476
Right endpoints	7.584476
Midpoints	7.695299
Trapezoidal rule	7.584476
Simpson's rule	7.150712
Calculator (n not specified)	7.640396

In practice, you would choose just *one* of the methods whose approximate values are given. You might also note that, for this example, Simpson's rule performs worse than the trapezoidal, midpoint, or even the left- and right-endpoint methods. For more accurate results, you might wish to use a computer program. A simple output is shown in Figure 6.45.

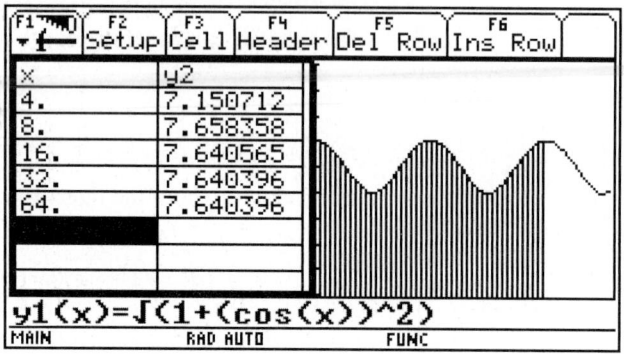

Figure 6.45   Using technology to find an arc length

The actual arc length (rounded to six places) computed as an area is 7.640396.   ∎

THE AREA OF A SURFACE OF REVOLUTION

When the arc of a curve is revolved about a line L, it generates a surface called a **surface of revolution**, as shown in Figure 6.46a. In particular, if the generating arc is a line segment, the frustum of a cone is generated (Figure 6.46b).

We will obtain a formula for the lateral area of the frustum of a cone, which will then be used as part of an approximation scheme for the area of a general surface of revolution. Accordingly, first note that a cone with slant height s and base radius r has lateral surface area $A = \pi r s$. To see this, cut the cone along a dashed line as shown in Figure 6.47a and flatten it out as shown in Figure 6.47b. The angle θ is determined by noting that the circumference of the circular base of the cone is $2\pi r$, which is the

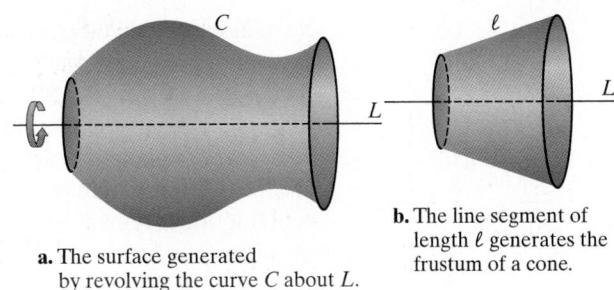

a. The surface generated by revolving the curve C about L.

b. The line segment of length ℓ generates the frustum of a cone.

Figure 6.46 Surfaces of revolution

same as the arclength $s\theta$ after the cone is flattened. Thus, $2\pi r = s\theta$ and $\theta = \dfrac{2\pi r}{s}$. The lateral surface area of the cone is the area of sector COD; namely,

$$A = \frac{1}{2}s^2\theta = \frac{1}{2}s^2\left(\frac{2\pi r}{s}\right) = \pi r s$$

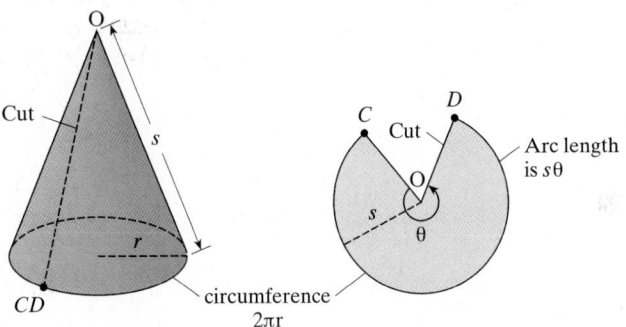

a. A cone with base radius r and slant height s is cut along CD.

b. The flattened cone is a sector with central angle θ in a circle of radius s.

Figure 6.47 A cone with slant height s and base radius r has area $A = \pi r s$

Finally, the frustum of the cone shown in Figure 6.48 has slant height ℓ, top radius r_1 and bottom radius r_2 and can be formed by removing a small cone of base radius r_1 and slant height ℓ_1 from the larger cone of base radius r_2 and slant height $\ell_2 = \ell_1 + \ell$. Thus, the lateral surface area F of the frustum can be found by subtracting the area of the smaller cone from that of the larger:

$$F = \pi r_2 \ell_2 - \pi r_1 \ell_1$$
$$= \pi r_2(\ell_1 + \ell) - \pi r_1 \ell_1$$
$$= \pi[(r_2 - r_1)\ell_1 + r_2\ell]$$

Using similar triangles, we see that

$$\frac{\ell_1}{r_1} = \frac{\ell_1 + \ell}{r_2} \qquad \text{or} \qquad r_1\ell = (r_2 - r_1)\ell_1$$

so that

$$F = \pi[(r_2 - r_1)\ell_1 + r_2\ell]$$
$$= \pi[r_1\ell + r_2\ell]$$
$$= 2\pi\left(\frac{r_1 + r_2}{2}\right)\ell$$

where $\frac{1}{2}(r_1 + r_2)$ is the average of the radii of the frustum.

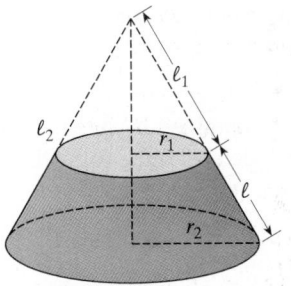

Figure 6.48 Frustum of cone

Next, assuming that the function $f(x)$ is continuous with $f(x) \geq 0$ on the interval $[a, b]$, we will derive a formula for the area of the surface generated by revolving the curve $y = f(x)$ about the x-axis. Rather than argue formally with Riemann sums, we will proceed heuristically. Figure 6.49a shows an approximating line segment with length Δs, whose endpoints are, respectively, distances r_1 and r_2 above the x-axis. Let $f(x)$ be the average height of the segment above the x-axis; that is, $f(x) = \frac{1}{2}(r_1 + r_2)$. By revolving this segment about the x-axis, we generate the frustum of a cone, with surface area

$$\Delta S = 2\pi \left(\frac{r_1 + r_2}{2} \right) \Delta s = 2\pi f(x)\sqrt{1 + [f'(x)]^2}\, \Delta x$$

where Δx is the projection of the line segment on the x-axis.

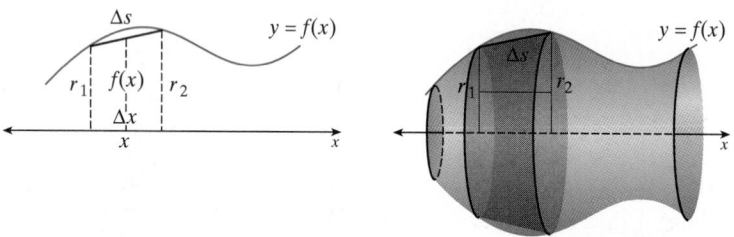

a. The approximating line segment of length Δs is at average height $f(x) = \frac{1}{2}(r_1 + r_2)$ above the x-axis.

b. Revolving the segment about the x-axis generates the frustum of a cone.

Figure 6.49   Approximating the area of a surface of revolution by the area of the frustum of a cone.

The area of the entire surface of revolution S can be obtained by integrating this expression over the interval $[a, b]$. These considerations lead us to the following definition.

Surface Area

> Suppose f' is continuous on the interval $[a, b]$ and differentiable on (a, b). Then the surface generated by revolving about the x-axis the arc of the curve $y = f(x)$ on $[a, b]$ has **surface area**
>
> $$S = 2\pi \int_a^b f(x)\sqrt{1 + [f'(x)]^2}\, dx$$

WARNING An easy-to-remember form for surface area is $S = 2\pi \int y\, ds$ since $ds = \sqrt{1 + [f'(x)]^2}\, dx$.

You may find it instructive to derive this formula by the more rigorous approach outlined in Problem 43. We close with two examples that illustrate the use of the surface area formula.

EXAMPLE 4   Area of a surface of revolution

Find the area of the surface generated by revolving about the x-axis the arc of the curve $y = x^3$ on $[0, 1]$.

Solution

The graph is shown in Figure 6.50. Because $f(x) = x^3$, we have $f'(x) = 3x^2$, which is certainly continuous on the interval [0, 1].

$$S = 2\pi \int_0^1 x^3 \sqrt{1 + (3x^2)^2}\, dx = 2\pi \int_0^1 x^3 \sqrt{1 + 9x^4}\, dx = 2\pi \int_1^{10} u^{1/2} \left(\frac{du}{36}\right)$$

> Let $u = 1 + 9x^4$; $du = 36x^3\, dx$.
> If $x = 1$, then $u = 10$.
> If $x = 0$, then $u = 1$.

$$= \frac{\pi}{18}\left(\frac{2}{3}u^{3/2}\right)\Big|_1^{10} = \frac{\pi}{27}[10\sqrt{10} - 1] \approx 3.5631 \qquad \blacksquare$$

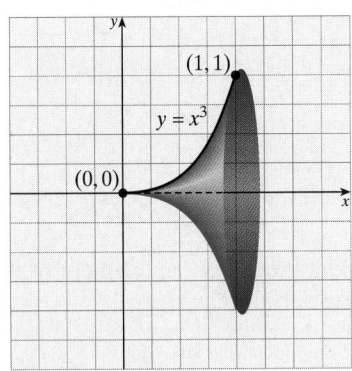

Figure 6.50 Graph of surface of revolution

EXAMPLE 5 Derive the formula for the surface area of a sphere

Find a formula for the surface area of a sphere of radius r.

Solution

We can generate the surface of the sphere by revolving the semicircle $y = \sqrt{r^2 - x^2}$ about the x-axis (see Figure 6.51). We find that

$$y' = -x(r^2 - x^2)^{-1/2} = \frac{-x}{\sqrt{r^2 - x^2}}$$

Because the semicircle intersects the x-axis at $x = r$ and $x = -r$, the interval of integration will be $[-r, r]$. Finally, by applying the formula for the surface area, we find

$$S = 2\pi \int_{-r}^{r} \sqrt{r^2 - x^2} \sqrt{1 + \left(\frac{-x}{\sqrt{r^2 - x^2}}\right)^2}\, dx$$

$$= 2\pi \int_{-r}^{r} \sqrt{(r^2 - x^2)\left(\frac{r^2 - x^2 + x^2}{r^2 - x^2}\right)}\, dx$$

$$= 2\pi \int_{-r}^{r} r\, dx = 2\pi r(2r) = 4\pi r^2 \qquad \blacksquare$$

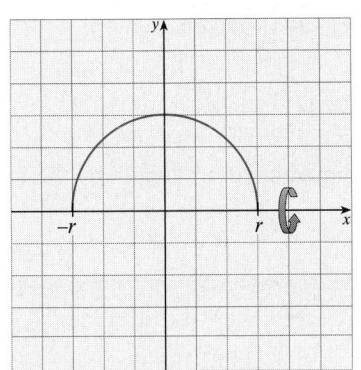

Figure 6.51 Graph of semicircle

To generalize the formula for surface area to apply to any vertical or horizontal axis of revolution, suppose that an axis of revolution is $R(x)$ units from a typical element of arc on the graph of $y = f(x)$, as shown in Figure 6.52.

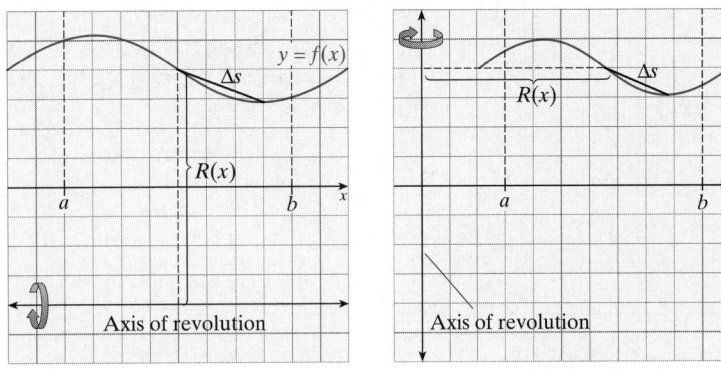

Figure 6.52 Surface of revolution about a general vertical or horizontal axis

Then $2\pi R(x)$ is the circumference of a circle of radius $R(x)$, and it can be shown that an element of surface area is

$$\Delta S = 2\pi R(x)\Delta s = 2\pi R(x)\sqrt{1 + [f'(x)]^2}\, \Delta x$$

Thus, the surface of revolution on the interval $[a, b]$ has area

$$S = 2\pi \int_a^b R(x)\sqrt{1 + [f'(x)]^2}\, dx$$

In particular, if the graph of $y = f(x)$ is revolved about the y-axis, an element of the arc is $R(x) = x$ units from the y-axis, and the resulting surface has area

$$S = 2\pi \int_a^b x\sqrt{1 + [f'(x)]^2}\, dx$$

POLAR ARC LENGTH AND SURFACE AREA

Sometimes we wish to find arc length and surface area in polar form. Figure 6.53 shows the portion of a polar curve subtended by a central angle $\Delta\theta$. If $\Delta\theta$ is small, the corresponding arc length Δs may be thought of as the hypotenuse of a right triangle with sides Δr and $r\,\Delta\theta$, the length of the circular arc AB with radius r. We have,

$$\Delta s = \sqrt{(r\,\Delta\theta)^2 + (\Delta r)^2} \qquad \text{Pythagorean theorem}$$

$$= \sqrt{r^2 + \left(\frac{\Delta r}{\Delta\theta}\right)^2}\, \Delta\theta$$

By formalizing these observations, we are led to compute polar arc length by the following formula.

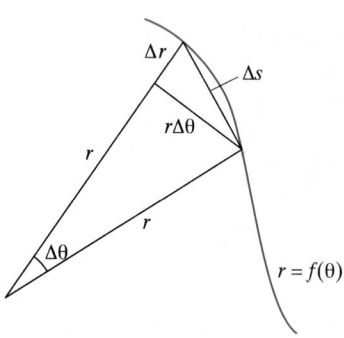

Figure 6.53 Polar arc length

Arc Length in Polar Coordinates

The length of a polar curve $r = f(\theta)$ for $\alpha \le \theta \le \beta$ is given by the integral

$$s = \int_\alpha^\beta \sqrt{r^2 + \left(\frac{dr}{d\theta}\right)^2}\, d\theta$$

EXAMPLE 6 Computing polar arc length

Find the length of the circle $r = 2\sin\theta$.

Solution

This circle is shown in Figure 6.54, and since this is a unit circle, we know the circumference to be 2π. We will verify this conclusion using the arc length formula. Note that $0 \le \theta \le \pi$.

$$s = \int_0^\pi \sqrt{r^2 + \left(\frac{dr}{d\theta}\right)^2}\, d\theta \qquad \text{Arc length formula} \\ \text{where } \alpha = 0 \text{ and } \beta = \pi$$

$$= \int_0^\pi \sqrt{(2\sin\theta)^2 + (2\cos\theta)^2}\, d\theta \qquad r = 2\sin\theta;\ \frac{dr}{d\theta} = 2\cos\theta$$

$$= \int_0^\pi 2\, d\theta \qquad \sin^2\theta + \cos^2\theta = 1$$

$$= 2\pi$$

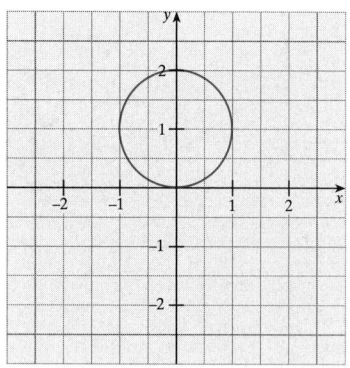

Figure 6.54 Circle $r = 2\sin\theta$

If a polar curve $r = f(\theta)$ between $\theta = \alpha$ and $\theta = \beta$ is revolved about the x-axis, it generates a surface of area

$$A = \int_{\alpha}^{\beta} 2\pi y \, ds$$

$$= 2\pi \int_{\alpha}^{\beta} (r \sin \theta) \sqrt{r^2 + \left(\frac{dr}{d\theta}\right)^2} \, d\theta$$

We conclude this section with an example showing the use of this formula.

EXAMPLE 7   Computing surface area in polar coordinates

Find the area of the surface generated by revolving about the x-axis the top half of the cardioid $r = 1 + \cos \theta$ (that is, for $0 \leq \theta \leq \pi$).

Solution

The cardioid is shown in Figure 6.55. Since $r = 1 + \cos \theta$ and $r' = -\sin \theta$, the surface area is given by

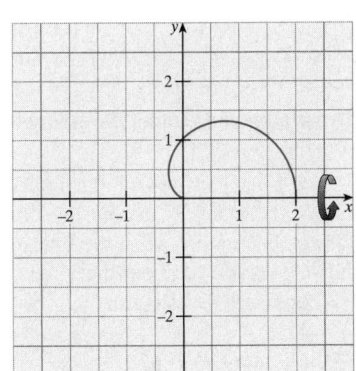

$$A = 2\pi \int_0^\pi (r \sin \theta) \sqrt{r^2 + \left(\frac{dr}{d\theta}\right)^2} \, d\theta$$

$$= 2\pi \int_0^\pi (1 + \cos \theta) \sin \theta \sqrt{(1 + \cos \theta)^2 + (-\sin \theta)^2} \, d\theta$$

$$= 2\pi \int_0^\pi (1 + \cos \theta) \sin \theta \sqrt{1 + 2\cos \theta + \cos^2 \theta + \sin^2 \theta} \, d\theta$$

$$= 2\pi \int_0^\pi \sqrt{2}(1 + \cos \theta)^{3/2} \sin \theta \, d\theta \qquad \text{Since } \sin^2 \theta + \cos^2 \theta = 1$$

$$= 2\sqrt{2}\pi \left[-\frac{2}{5}(1 + \cos \theta)^{5/2} \right]\Big|_0^\pi \qquad \text{Substitute using } u = 1 + \cos \theta$$

$$= \frac{32\pi}{5} \qquad\qquad\qquad \blacksquare$$

Figure 6.55 Cardioid
$r = 1 + \cos \theta$ for $0 \leq \theta \leq \pi$

6.4   PROBLEM SET

A *Find the length of the arc of the curve $y = f(x)$ on the intervals given in Problems 1–10.*

1. $f(x) = 3x + 2$ on $[-1, 2]$

2. $f(x) = 5 - 4x$ on $[-2, 0]$

3. $f(x) = 1 - 2x$ on $[1, 3]$

4. $f(x) = x^{3/2}$ on $[0, 4]$

5. $f(x) = \frac{2}{3}x^{3/2} + 1$ on $[0, 4]$

6. $f(x) = \frac{1}{3}(2 + x^2)^{3/2}$ on $[0, 3]$

7. $f(x) = \frac{1}{12}x^5 + \frac{1}{5}x^{-3}$ on $[1, 2]$

8. $f(x) = \frac{1}{3}x^3 + \frac{1}{4}x^{-1}$ on $[1, 4]$

9. $f(x) = \frac{1}{4}x^4 + \frac{1}{8}x^{-2}$ on $[1, 2]$

10. $f(x) = \sqrt{e^{2x} - 1} - \sec^{-1}(e^x)$ on $[0, \ln 2]$

11. Find the length of the curve defined by $9x^2 = 4y^3$ between the points $(0, 0)$ and $(2\sqrt{3}, 3)$.

12. Find the length of the curve defined by $(y + 1)^2 = 4x^3$ between the points $(0, -1)$ and $(1, 1)$.

Find the surface area generated when the graph of each function given in Problems 13–16 on the prescribed interval is revolved about the x-axis. Give your answer to the nearest hundredth.

13. $f(x) = 2x + 1$ on $[0, 2]$

14. $f(x) = \sqrt{x}$ on $[2, 6]$

15. $f(x) = \frac{1}{3}x^3 + \frac{1}{4}x^{-1}$ on $[1, 2]$

16. $f(x) = \frac{1}{4}x^4 + \frac{1}{8}x^{-2}$ on $[1, 2]$

Find the length of the polar curves given in Problems 17–22.

17. $r = \cos \theta$

18. $r = \sin \theta + \cos \theta$

19. $r = e^{3\theta}, 0 \leq \theta \leq \frac{\pi}{2}$

20. $r = e^{1-\theta}, 0 \leq \theta \leq 1$

21. $r = \theta^2, 0 \leq \theta \leq 1$

22. $r = \sin^2 \frac{\theta}{2}$

In Problems 23–26, find the surface area generated when the given polar curve is revolved about the x-axis.

23. $r = 5, 0 \leq \theta \leq \frac{\pi}{3}$

24. $r = 1 - \cos \theta, 0 \leq \theta \leq \pi$

25. $r = \csc \theta, \frac{\pi}{4} \leq \theta \leq \frac{\pi}{3}$

26. $r = \cos^2 \frac{\theta}{2}, 0 \leq \theta \leq \pi$

B *In Problems 27 and 28, use numerical integration to find the arc length.*

27. $f(x) = \sin x$ on $[0, \pi]$ **28.** $f(x) = \tan x$ on $[0, 1]$

29. Find the area of the surface generated when the arc of the curve

$$y = \tfrac{1}{3}x^3 + (4x)^{-1}$$

between $x = 1$ and $x = 3$ is revolved about:

a. the x-axis   **b.** the y-axis

30. Find the area of the surface generated when the arc of the curve

$$x = \tfrac{3}{5}y^{5/3} - \tfrac{3}{4}y^{1/3}$$

between $y = 0$ and $y = 1$ is revolved about:

a. the y-axis   **b.** the x-axis   **c.** the line $y = -1$

Find the surface area generated when the graph of each function given in Problems 31–34 on the prescribed interval is revolved about the y-axis. Give your answers to the nearest hundredth.

31. $f(x) = \tfrac{1}{3}(12 - x)$ on $[0, 3]$ **32.** $f(x) = \tfrac{2}{3}x^{3/2}$ on $[0, 3]$

33. $f(x) = \tfrac{1}{3}\sqrt{x}(3 - x)$ on $[1, 3]$ **34.** $f(x) = 2\sqrt{4 - x}$ on $[1, 3]$

35. The graph of the equation $x^{2/3} + y^{2/3} = 1$ is an **astroid**.

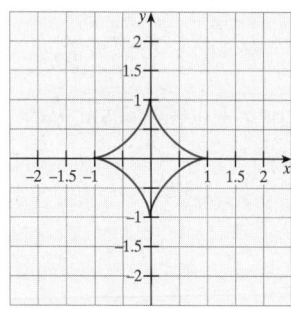

Find the length of this particular astroid by finding the length of the first quadrant portion, $y = (1 - x^{2/3})^{3/2}$ on $[0, 1]$. By symmetry, the length of the entire curve is four times the length of the arc in the first quadrant.

36. Find the area of the surface generated by revolving the portion of the astroid with $y \geq 0$ (see Problem 35) $x^{2/3} + y^{2/3} = 1$ on $[-1, 1]$ about the x-axis.

37. Estimate the area of the surface obtained by revolving $y = \tan x$ about the x-axis on the interval $[0, 1]$.

38. The following table gives the slope $f'(x_k)$ for points x_k located at 0.3-unit intervals on a certain curve defined by $y = f(x)$. Use the trapezoidal rule to estimate the arc length of $y = f(x)$ over the interval $[0, 3]$.

x_k	$f'(x_k)$	x_k	$f'(x_k)$
0.0	3.7	1.8	4.6
0.3	3.9	2.1	4.9
0.6	4.1	2.4	5.2
0.9	4.1	2.7	5.5
1.2	4.2	3.0	6.0
1.5	4.4		

39. Use the table in Problem 38 to estimate the surface area generated when $y = f(x)$ is revolved about the y-axis over the interval $[0, 3]$.

40. Show that a cone of radius r and height h has lateral surface area

$$S = \pi r \sqrt{r^2 + h^2}$$

Hint: Revolve part of the line $hy = rx$ about the x-axis.

C **41.** Show that when the arc of the graph of $f(x)$ between $x = a$ and $x = b$ is revolved about the y-axis, the surface generated has area

$$S = 2\pi \int_a^b x\sqrt{1 + [f'(x)]^2}\,dx$$

42. If $f'(x)$ exists throughout the interval $[x_{k-1}, x_k]$, show that there exists a number x_k^* in this interval for which

$$\sqrt{(\Delta x_k)^2 + (\Delta y_k)^2} = \sqrt{1 + [f'(x_k^*)]^2}\,\Delta x_k$$

where $\Delta x_k = x_k - x_{k-1}$ and $\Delta y_k = f(x_k) - f(x_{k-1})$. *Hint*: Use the mean value theorem.

43. Verify the surface area formula by completing the following steps (see Figure 6.56).

a. Let $P = \{x_0, x_1, \ldots, x_n\}$ be a partition of the interval $[a, b]$, and for $k = 0, 1, \ldots, n$, let P_k denote the point (x_k, y_k), where $y_k = f(x_k)$. Show that when the line segment between P_{k-1} and P_k is revolved about the x-axis, it generates a frustum of a cone with surface area

$$\pi(y_{k-1} + y_k)\ell_k$$

where ℓ_k is the distance between P_{k-1} and P_k.

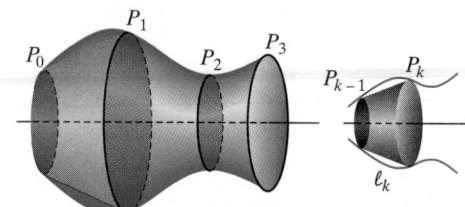

Figure 6.56   Surface area formula

b. Notice that $\tfrac{1}{2}(y_{k-1} + y_k)$ is a number between y_{k-1} and y_k. Use the intermediate value theorem (Section 2.3) to show that

$$y_{k-1} + y_k = 2f(c_k)$$

for some number c_k between x_{k-1} and x_k.

c. Explain why the surface generated when the arc of the graph of f between $x = a$ and $x = b$ is revolved about the x-axis has area

$$\lim_{\|P\| \to 0} \sum_{k=1}^{n} 2\pi f(c_k)\sqrt{1 + [f'(x_k^*)]^2}\,\Delta x_k$$

d. Notice that as $\|P\| \to 0$, the numbers c_k and x_k^* are "squeezed" together. Use this observation to show that the surface area is given by the integral

$$S = 2\pi \int_a^b f(x)\sqrt{1 + [f'(x)]^2}\,dx$$

44. The center of a circle of radius r is located at $(R, 0)$, where $R > r$. When the circle is revolved about the y-axis, it generates a *torus* (a doughnut-shaped solid). What is the surface area of the torus?

45. Let n be a positive integer and C, D be constants such that

$$n(n - 1) = \frac{1}{16CD}$$

Find the length of the curve

$$y = Cx^{2n} + Dx^{2(1-n)}$$

from $x = a$ to $x = b$.

46. Find the length of

$$y = \frac{x^3}{24} + \frac{2}{x}$$

from $x = 2$ to $x = 3$. Find a general formula for the length of the curve

$$y = Cx^n + Dx^{2-n}$$

from $x = a$ to $x = b$ for

$$n(n - 2) = \frac{1}{4CD}$$

47. Suppose it is known that the arc length of the curve $y = f(t)$ on the interval $0 \leq t \leq x$ is

$$L(x) = \ln(\sec x + \tan x)$$

for every x on $0 \leq x \leq 1$. If the curve $y = f(x)$ passes through the origin, what is $f(x)$?

6.5   Physical Applications: Work, Liquid Force, and Centroids

IN THIS SECTION   work, modeling fluid pressure and force, modeling the centroid of a plane region, volume theorem of Pappus

WORK

In physics, "force" is an influence that tends to cause motion in a body. When a constant force of magnitude F is applied to an object through a distance d, it performs **work** measured by the product $W = Fd$.

Work Done by a Constant Force

TABLE 6.3   Common Units of Work and Force

Mass	Dist.	Force	Work
kg	m	newton (N)	joule
g	cm	dyne (dyn)	erg
slug	ft	pound	ft-lb

If there is no movement, there is no work!

> If a body moves a distance d in the direction of an applied constant force F, the **work** W done is
> $$W = Fd$$

For example, the work done in lifting a 90-lb bag of concrete 3 ft is $W = Fd = (90 \text{ lb})(3 \text{ ft}) = 270$ ft·lb. Notice that this definition does not conform to everyday use of the word *work*. If you work at lifting the concrete all day, but you are not able to move the sack of concrete, then no work has been done. Table 6.3 shows some common units of work and force.

To find the work done in moving an object against a variable force, calculus is required. Suppose F is a continuous function and $F(x)$ is a variable force that acts on an object moving along the x-axis from $x = a$ to $x = b$. We will heuristically define the work done by this force. Partition the interval $[a, b]$ into n subintervals, and let Δx_k be the length of the kth subinterval I_k. If Δx_k is sufficiently small, we can expect the force to be essentially constant on I_k, equal, for instance, to $F(x_k^*)$, where x_k^* is a point chosen arbitrarily from the interval I_k. It is reasonable to expect that the work ΔW_k required to move the object on the interval I_k is approximately $\Delta W_k = F(x_k^*)\Delta x_k$, and the total work is estimated by the sum

$$\sum_{k=1}^{n} F(x_k^*)\Delta x_k$$

as indicated in Figure 6.57.

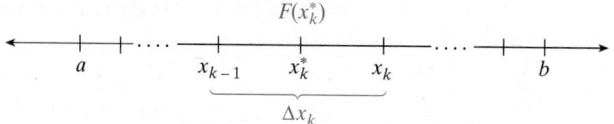

Figure 6.57   Work performed by a variable force

By taking the limit as the norm of the partition approaches 0, we find that the total work may be modeled by

$$W = \lim_{\|P\| \to 0} \sum_{k=1}^{n} F(x_k^*) \Delta x_k = \int_a^b F(x) \, dx$$

Work Done by a Variable Force

The work done by the variable force $F(x)$ in moving an object along the x-axis from $x = a$ to $x = b$ is given by

$$W = \int_a^b F(x) \, dx$$

EXAMPLE 1   Work done by a variable force

An object located x ft from a fixed starting position is moved along a straight road by a force of $F(x) = (3x^2 + 5)$ lb. What work is done by the force to move the object

a. through the first 4 ft?   **b.** from 1 ft to 4 ft?

Solution

a. $W = \displaystyle\int_0^4 (3x^2 + 5) \, dx = (x^3 + 5x)\Big|_0^4 = 84$ ft-lb

b. $W = \displaystyle\int_1^4 (3x^2 + 5) \, dx = (x^3 + 5x)\Big|_1^4 = 78$ ft-lb ∎

   Hooke's law, named for the English physicist Robert Hooke (1635–1703), states that *when a spring is pulled x units past its equilibrium (rest) position, there is a restoring force F(x) = kx that pulls the spring back toward equilibrium.** (See Figure 6.58.) The constant k in this formula is called the **spring constant**.

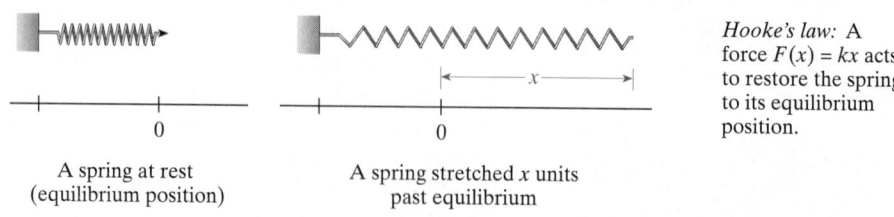

Hooke's law: A force $F(x) = kx$ acts to restore the spring to its equilibrium position.

A spring at rest (equilibrium position)   A spring stretched x units past equilibrium

Figure 6.58   Hooke's law

---

*Actually, Hooke's law applies only in ideal circumstances, and a spring for which the law applies is sometimes called an ideal (or linear) spring.

EXAMPLE 2   Modeling work using Hooke's formula

The natural length of a certain spring is 10 cm. If it requires 2 ergs of work to stretch the spring to a total length of 18 cm, how much work will be performed in stretching the spring to a total length of 20 cm? (See Figure 6.59.)

Solution

Assume that the point of equilibrium is at 0 on a number line, and let x be the length the free end of the spring is extended past equilibrium. Because the stretching force of the spring is $F(x) = kx$, the work done in stretching the spring b cm beyond equilibrium is

$$W = \int_0^b F(x)\, dx = \int_0^b kx\, dx = \tfrac{1}{2}kb^2$$

We are given that $W = 2$ when $b = 8$ (since 18 cm is 8 cm beyond equilibrium), so

$$2 = \tfrac{1}{2}k(8)^2 \quad \text{implying} \quad k = \tfrac{1}{16}$$

Thus, the work done in stretching the spring b cm beyond equilibrium is

$$W = \tfrac{1}{2}\left(\tfrac{1}{16}\right)b^2 = \tfrac{1}{32}b^2 \text{ ergs}$$

In particular, when the total length of the spring is 20 cm, it is extended $b = 10$ cm, and the required work is

$$W = \tfrac{1}{32}(10)^2 = \tfrac{25}{8} = 3.125 \text{ ergs} \qquad \blacksquare$$

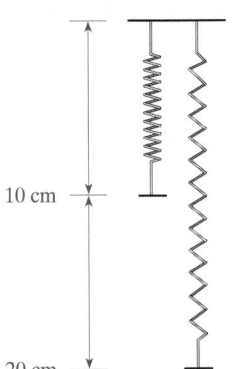

Figure 6.59 Stretching a spring

EXAMPLE 3   Modeling the work performed in pumping water out of a tank

A tank in the shape of a right circular cone of height 12 ft and radius 3 ft is inserted into the ground with its vertex pointing down and its top at ground level, as shown in Figure 6.60a. If the tank is filled with water (density $\rho = 62.4$ lb/ft^3) to a depth of 6 ft, how much work is performed in pumping all the water in the tank to ground level? What changes if the water is pumped to a height of 3 ft above ground level?

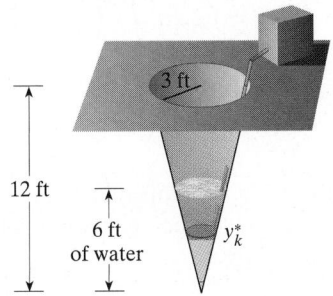

a. A conical water tank

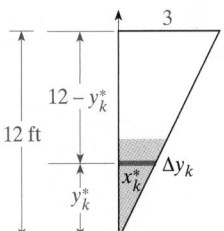

b. A disk of water is $12 - y_k^*$ units from the top.

Figure 6.60   Work in pumping water

Solution

Set up a coordinate system with the origin at the vertex of the cone and the y-axis as the axis of symmetry (Figure 6.60b). Partition the interval $0 \le y \le 6$ (remember, the water only comes up 6 ft). Choose a representative point y_k^* in the kth subinterval, and construct a thin disklike slab of water y_k^* units above the vertex of the cone. Our plan is to think of the water in the tank as a collection of these slabs of water piled on top of each other. We will find the work done to raise a typical water disk and then compute the total work by using integration to add the contributions of all such slabs.

Note that the force required to lift the slab is equal to the weight of the slab, which equals its volume multiplied by the weight per cubic foot of water. Let x_k^* be the radius of the kth slab. By similar triangles (Figure 6.60b), we have

$$\frac{x_k^*}{y_k^*} = \frac{3}{12}, \quad \text{which implies} \quad x_k^* = \frac{y_k^*}{4}$$

Hence, the volume of the cylindrical slab is

$$\Delta V = \pi x_k^{*2} \Delta y_k = \pi \underbrace{\left(\frac{y_k^*}{4}\right)^2}_{\text{Radius}} \overbrace{\Delta y_k}^{\text{Thickness}}$$

so that the weight of the kth slab is modeled by

$$62.4\pi \left(\frac{y_k^*}{4}\right)^2 \Delta y_k \text{ lb}$$

From Figure 6.60b, we see that the slab of water must be raised $12 - y_k^*$ feet, which means that the work ΔW required to raise this kth slab is

$$\Delta W = \underbrace{62.4\pi \left(\frac{y_k^*}{4}\right)^2 \Delta y_k}_{\text{Weight (force)}} \underbrace{(12 - y_k^*)}_{\text{Distance}} = 62.4\pi \left(\frac{y_k^*}{4}\right)^2 (12 - y_k^*)\Delta y_k$$

Finally, to compute the total work, we add the work required to lift each thin slab and take the limit of the sum as the norm of the partition approaches 0.

$$W = \lim_{n \to \infty} 62.4\pi \sum_{k=1}^{n} \left(\frac{y_k^*}{4}\right)^2 (12 - y_k^*)\Delta y_k$$

$$= 62.4\pi \int_0^6 \left(\frac{y}{4}\right)^2 (12 - y)\, dy = \frac{62.4}{16}\pi \int_0^6 (12y^2 - y^3)\, dy$$

$$= 3.9\pi \left(4y^3 - \frac{1}{4}y^4\right)\Big|_0^6 = 2{,}106\pi \approx 6{,}616 \text{ ft-lb}$$

If the water is pumped to a height of 3 ft above ground level, all that changes is the distance moved by the kth slab of water. It becomes $12 + 3 - y_k^* = 15 - y_k^*$, and the work is given by

$$W = 62.4\pi \int_0^6 \left(\frac{y}{4}\right)^2 (15 - y)\, dy \approx 9{,}263 \text{ ft-lb} \qquad \blacksquare$$

MODELING FLUID PRESSURE AND FORCE

Anyone who has dived into water has probably noticed that the pressure (that is, the force per unit area) due to the water's weight increases with depth. Careful observations show that the water pressure at any given point is directly proportional to the depth at that point. The same principle applies to other fluids.

In physics, **Pascal's principle** (named for Blaise Pascal, 1623–1662, a French mathematician and scientist) states that fluid pressure is the same in all directions (see Figure 6.61). This means that the pressure must be the same at all points on a surface submerged horizontally, and in this case, the fluid force on the surface is given by the formula in the following box.

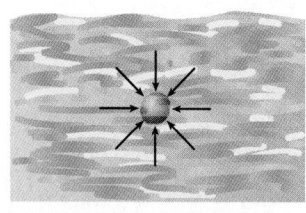

Figure 6.61 Pascal's principle: In an equilibrium state, the fluid pressure is the same in all directions.

Fluid Force

> If a surface of area A is submerged horizontally at a depth h in a fluid, the weight of the fluid exerts a force of
>
> $$F = (\text{PRESSURE})(\text{AREA}) = \rho h A$$
>
> on the surface, where ρ is the fluid density (weight per unit volume). This is called **fluid force** or **hydrostatic force**.

TABLE 6.4 Weight-density, ρ (lb/ft³)

Water	62.4
Seawater	64.0
Gasoline	42.0
Kerosene	51.2
Milk	64.5
Mercury	849.0

Table 6.4 shows the fluid density for some common fluids. It turns out that this fluid force does not depend on the shape of the container or its size. For instance, each of the containers in Figure 6.62 has the same pressure on its base because the fluid depth h and the base area A are the same in each case.

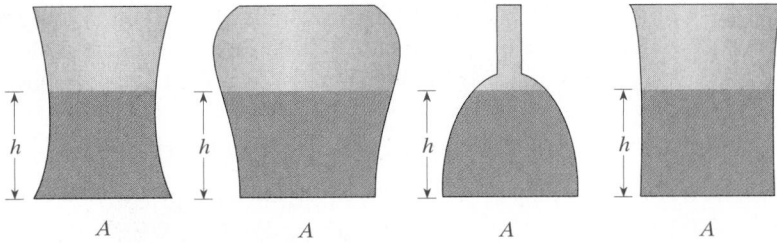

Figure 6.62 The fluid force $F = \rho h A$ does not depend on the shape or size of the container

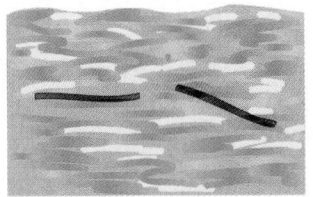

Figure 6.63 Pressure on a submerged object

When the surface is submerged vertically or at an angle, however, this simple formula does not apply because different parts of the surface are at different depths, as shown in Figure 6.63. We will use integration to compute the fluid force in such cases. Consider a plate that is submerged vertically in a fluid of density ρ as shown in Figure 6.64a. We set up a coordinate system with the horizontal axis on the surface of the fluid and the positive h-axis (depth) pointing down. Thus, greater depths correspond to larger values of h (see Figure 6.64b). For simplicity, we assume the plate is oriented so its top and bottom are located a units and b units below the surface, respectively.

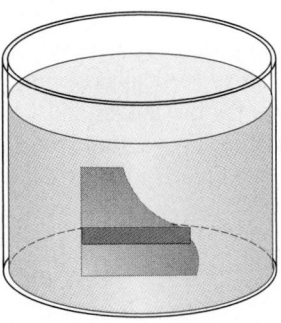 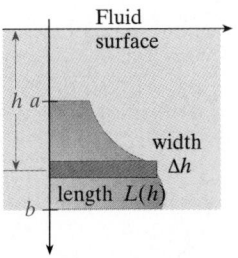

a. A plate submerged vertically in a fluid of density ρ

b. A typical slab has area $A = L(h)\Delta h$.

Figure 6.64 Hydrostatic force

Our strategy will be to think of the plate as a pile of subplates or slabs, each so thin that we may regard it as being at a constant depth below the surface. A typical slab (a horizontal strip) is shown in Figure 6.64b. Note that it has thickness Δh and length $L = L(h)$, so that its area is $\Delta A = L \Delta h$. Because the slab is at a constant depth h below the surface, the fluid force on its surface is

$$\Delta F = (\text{PRESSURE})(\text{AREA}) = \rho h \Delta A = \rho h L(h) \Delta h$$

and by integrating as h varies from a to b, we can model the total force on the plate.

Fluid (Hydrostatic) Force

Suppose a flat surface (a plate) is submerged vertically in a fluid of weight density ρ (lb/ft^3) and that the submerged portion of the plate extends from $h = a$ to $h = b$ on a vertical axis. Then the total force F exerted by the fluid is given by

$$F = \int_a^b \rho h L(h) \, dh$$

where h is the depth and $L(h)$ is the corresponding length of a typical horizontal approximating strip.

EXAMPLE 4   Fluid force on a vertical surface

The cross sections of a certain trough are inverted isosceles triangles with height 6 ft and base 4 ft, as shown in Figure 6.65. Suppose the trough contains water to a depth of 3 ft. Find the total fluid force on one end.

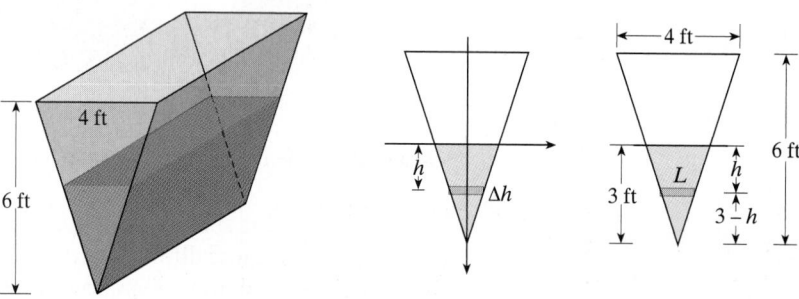

a. A trough with half-filled triangular cross sections

b. Side view of trough

c. Use similar triangles to find $\dfrac{L}{4} = \dfrac{3 - h}{6}$.

Figure 6.65   Fluid force

Solution

First, we set up a coordinate system in which the horizontal axis lies at the fluid surface and the positive vertical axis (the h-axis) points down (see Figure 6.65b). *Next*, we find expressions for the length and depth of a typical thin slab (horizontal strip) in terms of the variables. We assume the slab has thickness Δh and length L. Then by similar triangles (see Figure 6.65c) we have

$$\frac{L}{4} = \frac{3 - h}{6} \quad \text{so that} \quad L = \frac{2}{3}(3 - h)$$

We see that the approximating slab has area $\Delta A = L \Delta h = \frac{2}{3}(3 - h)\Delta h$. *Finally*, we multiply the product of the fluid's weight-density at a given depth (ρh) and the area of the approximating slab (ΔA) and integrate on the interval of depths occupied by the vertical plate.

$$F = \int_0^3 \underbrace{\tfrac{2}{3}\rho h(3 - h) \, dh}_{\Delta F \,=\, \text{force on a typical slab}}$$

$\quad$ *Note:* (density)(depth)(area of strip)

$$\qquad\qquad\qquad \rho \qquad h \qquad \tfrac{2}{3}(3 - h)\Delta h$$

$$= \tfrac{2}{3}(62.4)\int_0^3 (3h - h^2) \, dh \qquad \rho = 62.4 \text{ lb/ft}^3 \text{ for water}$$

$$= 41.6\left(\tfrac{3}{2}h^2 - \tfrac{1}{3}h^3\right)\Big|_0^3 = 187.2 \text{ lb} \qquad\blacksquare$$

EXAMPLE 5   Modeling the force on one face of a dam

A reservoir is filled with water to the top of a dam. If the dam is in the shape of a parabola 40 ft high and 20 ft wide at the top, as shown in Figure 6.66, what is the total fluid force on the face of the dam?

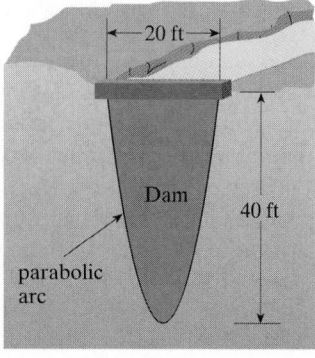

a. Cross section of a dam

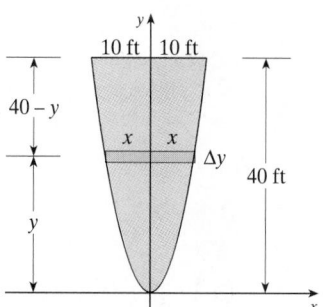

b. A typical horizontal strip is $40 - y$ ft below the water surface.

Figure 6.66   Force on one face of a dam

Solution

Instead of putting the x-axis on the surface of the water (at the top of the dam), we place the origin at the vertex of the parabola and the positive y-axis along the parabola's axis of symmetry (Figure 6.66b). The advantage of this choice of axes is that the parabola can be represented by an equation of the form $y = cx^2$. Because we know that $y = 40$ when $x = 10$, it follows that

$$40 = c(10)^2 \quad \text{so that} \quad c = \tfrac{2}{5} \quad \text{and thus} \quad y = \tfrac{2}{5}x^2$$

The typical horizontal strip on the face of the dam is located y feet above the x-axis, which means it is $h = 40 - y$ feet below the surface of the water. The strip is Δy feet wide and $L = 2x$ feet long. Write L as a function of y:

$$y = \tfrac{2}{5}x^2 \quad \text{so that} \quad x = \sqrt{\tfrac{5}{2}y}$$

and

$$L(y) = 2x = 2\left(\sqrt{\tfrac{5}{2}y}\right) = \sqrt{10y}$$

Therefore,

$$\Delta A = L\,\Delta y = \sqrt{10y}\,\Delta y$$

and the total force may be modeled by the integral

$$F = \int_0^{40} \rho h \underbrace{L(y)\,dy}_{\substack{\text{Area of the strip}}} = \int_0^{40} (62.4)(40 - y)\sqrt{10y}\,dy$$

Depth below water: $h = 40 - y$

Density of water $= 62.4$

$$= 62.4\sqrt{10} \int_0^{40} (40y^{1/2} - y^{3/2})\,dy$$

$$= 62.4\sqrt{10}\left(\frac{80}{3}y^{3/2} - \frac{2}{5}y^{5/2}\right)\Bigg|_0^{40}$$

$$= 62.4\sqrt{10}\left(y^{3/2}\right)\left(\frac{80}{3} - \frac{2}{5}y\right)\Bigg|_0^{40}$$

$$= 532{,}480 \text{ lb}$$

MODELING THE CENTROID OF A PLANE REGION

In mechanics, its often important to determine the point where an irregularly shaped plate will balance. The **moment of a force** measures its tendency to produce rotation in an object and depends on the magnitude of the force and the point on the object where it is applied. Since the time of Archimedes (287–212 B.C.), it has been known that the balance point of an object occurs where all its moments cancel out (so there is no rotation).

The **mass** of an object is a measure of its **inertia**; that is, its propensity to maintain a state of rest or uniform motion. A thin plate whose material is distributed uniformly, so that its density ρ (mass per unit area) is constant, is called a **homogeneous lamina**. The balance point of such a lamina is called its **centroid** and may be thought of as its geometrical center. We will see how centroids can be computed by integration in this section, and will examine the topic even further in Section 12.6.

Consider a homogeneous lamina that covers a region R bounded by the curves $y = f(x)$ and $y = g(x)$ on the interval $[a, b]$, and consider a thin, vertical approximating strip within R, as shown in Figure 6.67. The mass of the strip is given by

$$\Delta m = \rho \underbrace{[f(x) - g(x)]\Delta x}_{\text{Area of strip}}$$

$\uparrow$ Density

and the total mass of the lamina may be found by integration:

$$m = \rho \int_a^b [f(x) - g(x)]\,dx$$

Note that $m = \text{AREA}$ if $\rho = 1$.

The centroid (geometrical center) of the approximating strip is $(\tilde{x}, \tilde{y})$, where $\tilde{x} = x$ and $\tilde{y} = \frac{1}{2}[f(x) + g(x)]$. The **moment of the approximating strip about the y-axis** is defined to be the product

$$\Delta M_y = \tilde{x}\underbrace{\Delta m}_{\text{Mass of strip}} = \tilde{x}\{\rho[f(x) - g(x)]\Delta x\}$$

Distance of the
strip from y-axis

This product provides a measure of the tendency of the strip to rotate about the y-axis. Similarly, the **moment of the strip about the x-axis** is defined to be the product

$$\Delta M_x = \tilde{y}\Delta m = \underbrace{\tfrac{1}{2}[f(x) + g(x)]}_{\text{Average distance of the strip from x-axis}}\{\rho[f(x) - g(x)]\Delta x\}$$

$$= \tfrac{1}{2}\rho\{[f(x)]^2 - [g(x)]^2\}\Delta x$$

This product provides a measure of the tendency of the strip to rotate about the x-axis.

Integrating on $[a, b]$, we find the moments of the entire lamina R about the y-axis and x-axis may be modeled by

$$M_y = \rho \int_a^b x[f(x) - g(x)]\,dx \quad \text{and} \quad M_x = \tfrac{1}{2}\rho \int_a^b \{[f(x)]^2 - [g(x)]^2\}\,dx$$

If the entire mass m of the lamina R were located at the point $(\bar{x}, \bar{y})$, then its moments about the x-axis and y-axis would be $m\bar{y}$ and $m\bar{x}$, respectively. Thus, we have $m\bar{x} = M_y$ and $m\bar{y} = M_x$, so that

$$\bar{x} = \frac{M_y}{m} = \frac{\rho \int_a^b x[f(x) - g(x)]\,dx}{\rho \int_a^b [f(x) - g(x)]\,dx} \quad \text{and} \quad \bar{y} = \frac{M_x}{m} = \frac{\tfrac{1}{2}\rho \int_a^b \{[f(x)]^2 - [g(x)]^2\}\,dx}{\rho \int_a^b [f(x) - g(x)]\,dx}$$

We can now summarize these results.

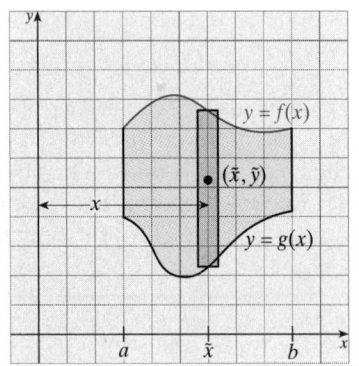

Centroid

Theoretically, the lamina should balance on a point placed at its centroid.

Figure 6.67 Homogeneous lamina with a vertical approximating strip

Let f and g be continuous and satisfy $f(x) \geq g(x)$ on the interval $[a, b]$, and consider a thin plate (lamina) of uniform density ρ that covers the region R between the graphs of $y = f(x)$ and $y = g(x)$ on the interval $[a, b]$. Then

MASS

The **mass** of R is $\quad m = \rho \int_a^b [f(x) - g(x)] \, dx$

CENTROID

The **centroid** of R is the point $(\bar{x}, \bar{y})$ such that

$$\bar{x} = \frac{M_y}{m} = \frac{\displaystyle\int_a^b x[f(x) - g(x)] \, dx}{\displaystyle\int_a^b [f(x) - g(x)] \, dx}$$

and

$$\bar{y} = \frac{M_x}{m} = \frac{\frac{1}{2}\displaystyle\int_a^b \{[f(x)]^2 - [g(x)]^2\} \, dx}{\displaystyle\int_a^b [f(x) - g(x)] \, dx}$$

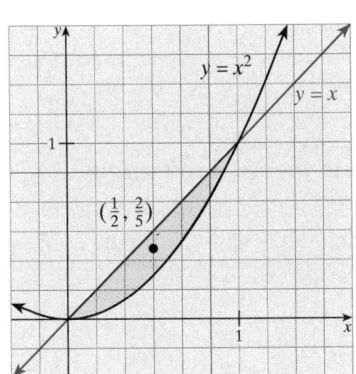

Figure 6.68 The centroid of a planar region

EXAMPLE 6   Centroid of a thin plate

A homogeneous lamina R has constant density $\rho = 1$ and is bounded by the parabola $y = x^2$ and the line $y = x$. Find the mass and the centroid of R.

Solution

We see that the line and the parabola intersect at the origin and at the point $(1, 1)$, as shown in Figure 6.68. Because $\rho = 1$, the mass is the same as the area of the region R. That is,

$$m = A = \int_0^1 (x - x^2) \, dx = \left(\frac{x^2}{2} - \frac{x^3}{3} \right)\Big|_0^1 = \frac{1}{6}$$

and we find that the region has moments M_y and M_x about the y-axis and x-axis, respectively, where

$$M_y = \int_0^1 x(x - x^2) \, dx = \left(\frac{x^3}{3} - \frac{x^4}{4} \right)\Big|_0^1 = \frac{1}{12}$$

and

$$M_x = \frac{1}{2} \int_0^1 (x + x^2)(x - x^2) \, dx = \frac{1}{2} \int_0^1 (x^2 - x^4) \, dx$$

$$= \frac{1}{2} \left(\frac{x^3}{3} - \frac{x^5}{5} \right)\Big|_0^1 = \frac{1}{2}\left(\frac{1}{3} - \frac{1}{5} \right) = \frac{1}{15}$$

Thus, the centroid of the region R has coordinates

$$\bar{x} = \frac{M_y}{m} = \frac{\frac{1}{12}}{\frac{1}{6}} = \frac{1}{2} \quad \text{and} \quad \bar{y} = \frac{M_x}{m} = \frac{\frac{1}{15}}{\frac{1}{6}} = \frac{2}{5} \qquad \blacksquare$$

VOLUME THEOREM OF PAPPUS

There is a remarkable result attributed to Pappus of Alexandria (ca. 300 A.D.), whom many regard as the last great Greek geometer, which gives a connection between centroids and volumes of revolution.

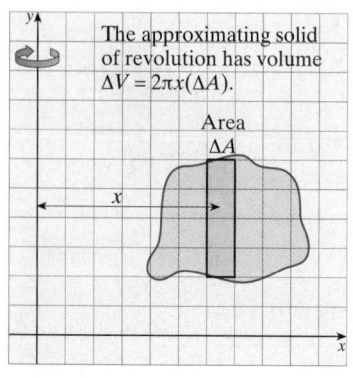

The approximating solid of revolution has volume $\Delta V = 2\pi x(\Delta A)$.

Area ΔA

Figure 6.69 The volume theorem of Pappus

THEOREM 6.2   Volume theorem of Pappus

The solid generated by revolving a region R about a line outside its boundary (but in the same plane) has volume $V = As$, where A is the area of R and s is the distance traveled by the centroid of R.

Proof   First, choose a coordinate system in which the y-axis coincides with the axis of revolution. Figure 6.69 shows a typical region R together with a vertical approximating rectangle. We will assume that this rectangle has area ΔA and that it is located x units from the y-axis.

Notice that when the rectangle is revolved about the y-axis, it generates a shell of volume $\Delta V = 2\pi x \Delta A$. Thus, by partitioning the region R into a number of rectangles and taking the limit of the sum of the volumes of all the related approximating shells as the norm of the partition approaches 0, we find that

$$V = \lim_{\|P\| \to 0} \sum_{k=1}^{n} 2\pi x_k \Delta A_k = \int 2\pi x \, dA = 2\pi \int x \, dA$$

$$= 2\pi \bar{x} \int dA \quad \text{Because } \bar{x} = \frac{\int x \, dA}{\int dA}$$

$$= 2\pi \bar{x} A \quad \text{Because } \int dA = A$$

$$= As \quad \text{Where } s = 2\pi \bar{x} \text{ is the distance traveled by the centroid (the circumference of a circle of radius } \bar{x})$$ ❑

We close this section with an example that illustrates the use of the volume theorem of Pappus.

EXAMPLE 7   Volume of a torus using the volume theorem of Pappus

When a circle of radius r is revolved about a line in the plane of the circle located R units from its center ($R > r$), the solid figure so generated is called a **torus**, as shown in Figure 6.70. Show that the torus has volume $V = 2\pi^2 r^2 R$.

Axis of revolution

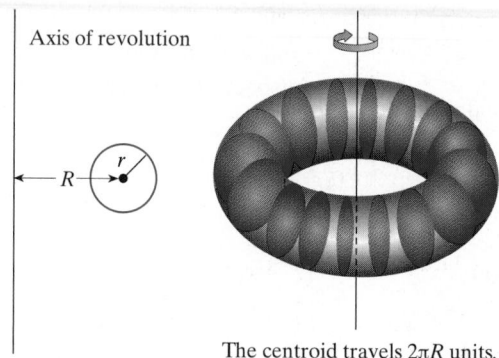

The centroid travels $2\pi R$ units.

Figure 6.70   The volume of a torus

Solution

The circle has area $A = \pi r^2$ and its center (which is its centroid) travels $2\pi R$ units. Comparing this example to the volume theorem of Pappus, we see $s = 2\pi R$. Therefore, the torus has volume

$$V = (2\pi R)A = 2\pi R(\pi r^2) = 2\pi^2 r^2 R$$ ∎

Incidentally, the volume found in Example 7 using the theorem of Pappus was worked in Problem 60 of Section 6.2 by using washers.

6.5 PROBLEM SET

A **1. WHAT DOES THIS SAY?** Discuss work and how to find it. (*Hint*: The answer is *not* to apply at the unemployment office!)

2. WHAT DOES THIS SAY? Discuss fluid force and how to find it.

3. WHAT DOES THIS SAY? What is meant by a centroid? Outline a procedure for finding both the mass and the centroid.

4. What is the work done in lifting a 50-lb bag of salt 5 ft?

5. What is the work done in lifting an 850-lb billiard table 15 ft?

6. Suppose it takes 4 erg of work to stretch a spring 10 cm beyond its natural length. How much more work is needed to stretch it 4 cm further?

7. A bucket weighing 75 lb when filled and 10 lb when empty is pulled up the side of a 100-ft building. How much more work is done in pulling up the full bucket than the empty bucket?

8. A spring whose natural length is 10 cm exerts a force of 30 m/s when stretched to a length of 15 cm. (*Note*: 15 cm − 10 cm = 5 cm = 0.05 m.) Find the spring constant, and then determine the work done in stretching the spring 7 cm (= 0.07 m) beyond its natural length.

9. A 5-lb force will stretch a spring 9 in. (= 0.75 ft) beyond its natural length. How much work is required to stretch it 1 ft beyond its natural length?

10. A 30-ft rope weighing 0.4 lb/ft hangs over the edge of a building 100 ft high. How much work is done in pulling the rope to the top of the building? Assume that the top of the rope is flush with the top of the building and the lower end of the rope is swinging freely.

11. A 30-lb ball hangs at the bottom of a cable that is 50 ft long and weighs 20 lb. The entire length of cable hangs over a cliff. Find the work done to raise the cable and get the ball to the top of the cliff.

12. An object moving along the x-axis is acted upon by a force $F(x) = x^4 + 2x^2$. Find the total work done by the force in moving the object from $x = 1$ cm to $x = 2$ cm. *Note*: Distance is in cm, so force is in dynes.

13. An object moving along the x-axis is acted upon by a force $F(x) = |\sin x|$. Find the total work done by the force in moving the object from $x = 0$ cm to $x = 2\pi$ cm. *Note*: Distance is in cm, so force is in dynes.

In Problems 14–17, the given figure is the vertical cross section of a tank containing the indicated fluid. Find the fluid force against the end of the tank. The weight densities are given in Table 6.4 on page 399.

14. water
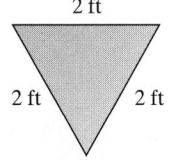

15. seawater
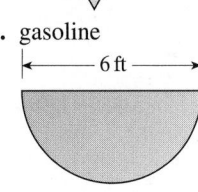

16. gasoline

17. kerosene
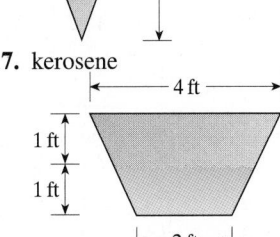

In Problems 18–21, set up, but do not evaluate, an integral for the fluid force against the indicated vertical plate.

18. water
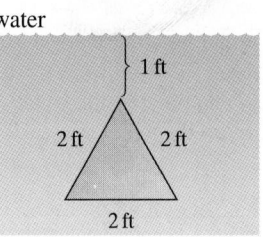

19. milk (half cookie)
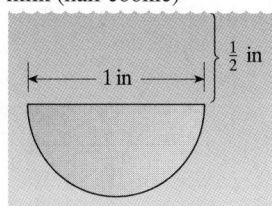

20. mercury
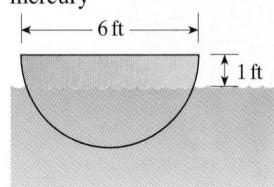

21. kerosene
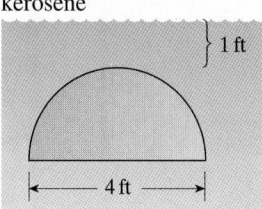

Find the centroid ($\rho = 1$) of each planar region in Problems 22–27.

22. the region in the first quadrant bounded by the curves $y = x^3$ and $y = \sqrt[3]{x}$

23. the region bounded by the parabola $y = x^2 - 9$ and the x-axis

24. the region bounded by the parabola $y = 4 - x^2$ and the line $y = x + 2$

25. the region bounded by the curve $y = x^{-1}$, the x-axis, and the lines $x = 1$ and $x = 2$

26. the region bounded by the curve $y = x^{-1}$ and the line $2x + 2y = 5$

27. the region bounded by $y = \dfrac{1}{\sqrt{x}}$ and the x-axis on [1, 4]

Use the theorem of Pappus to compute the volume of the solids generated by revolving the regions given in Problems 28–31 about the prescribed axes.

28. the region bounded by the parabola $y = \sqrt{x}$, the x-axis, and the line $x = 4$ about the line $x = -1$

29. the triangular region with vertices $(-3, 0)$, $(0, 5)$, and $(2, 0)$, about the line $y = -1$

30. the semicircular region $y = \sqrt{1 - x^2}$, about the line $y = -1$

31. the semicircular region $x = \sqrt{4 - y^2}$, about the line $x = -2$

B **32.** The centroid of any triangle lies at the intersection of the medians, two-thirds the distance from each vertex to the midpoint of the opposite side. Locate the centroid of the triangle with vertices $(0, 0)$, $(7, 3)$, and $(7, -2)$ using this method, and then check your result by calculus.

33. A tank in the shape of an inverted right circular cone of height 6 ft and top radius 3 ft is filled to a depth of 3 ft.

  a. How much work is performed in pumping all the water over the top edge of the tank?

  b. How much work is performed in draining all the water from the tank through a hole at the tip?

34. A tank is formed by rotating the curve $y = x^2$ about the y-axis for $0 \le x \le 4$, where x is in feet. If the tank is filled with water to a depth of 12 feet, how much work is performed in pumping all the water to a height of 3 ft above the top of the tank?

35. A hemispherical bowl with radius 10 ft is filled with water to a level of 6 ft. Find the work done to the nearest ft-lb to pump all the water to the top of the bowl.

36. A holding tank has the shape of a rectangular parallelepiped 20 ft by 30 ft by 10 ft.

    a. How much work is done in pumping all the water to the top of the tank?

    b. How much work is done in pumping all the water out of the tank to a height of 2 ft above the top of the tank?

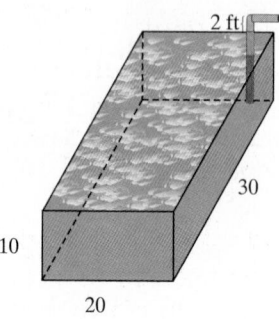

37. A cylindrical tank of radius 3 ft and height 10 ft is filled to a depth of 2 ft with a liquid of density $\rho = 40$ lb/ft³. Find the work done in pumping all the liquid to a height of 2 ft above the top of the tank.

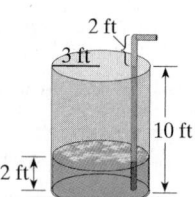

38. An oil can in the shape of a rectangular parallelepiped is filled with oil of density 0.87 g/cm³. What is the total force on a side of the can if it is 20 cm high and has a square base 15 cm on a side?

39. A swimming pool 20 ft by 15 ft by 10 ft deep is filled with water. A cube 1 ft on a side lies on the bottom of the pool. Find the total fluid force on the five exposed faces of the cube.

40. Suppose a log of radius 1 ft lies at the bottom of the pool in Problem 39. What is the total fluid force on one end of the log?

41. An object weighing 800 lb on the surface of the earth is propelled to a height of 200 mi above the earth. How much work is done against gravity? *Hint*: Assume the radius of the earth is 4,000 mi, and use Newton's law, $F = -k/x^2$, for the force on an object x miles from the center of the earth.

42. A dam is in the shape of an isosceles trapezoid 200 ft at the top, 100 ft at the bottom, and 75 ft high. When water is up to the top of the dam, what is the force on its face?

43. **Modeling Problem**   According to Coulomb's law in physics, two similarly charged particles repel each other with a force inversely proportional to the square of the distance between them. Suppose the force is 12 dynes when they are 5 cm apart.

    a. How much work is done in moving one particle from a distance of 10 cm to a distance of 8 cm from the other?

    b. Set up and analyze a model to determine the amount of work performed in moving one particle from an "infinite" distance to a distance of 8 cm from the other. State any assumptions that you must make.

44. **Modeling Problem**   Figure 6.71 shows a dam whose face against the water is an inclined rectangle.

    a. Set up and analyze a model for determining the fluid force against the face of the dam when the water is level with the top.

    b. What would the fluid force be if the face of the dam were a vertical rectangle (not inclined)?

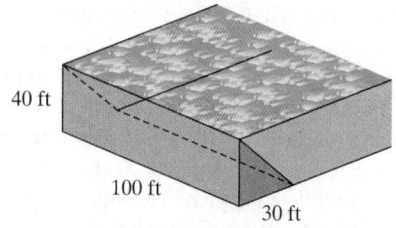

Figure 6.71   Dam with face at an inclined rectangle

45. **Modeling Problem**   Figure 6.72 shows a swimming pool, part of whose bottom is an inclined plane. Set up and analyze a model for determining the fluid force on the bottom when the pool is filled to the top with water.

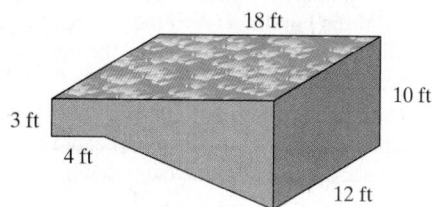

Figure 6.72   Swimming pool dimensions

46. An irregular plate is measured at 0.2-ft intervals from top to bottom, and the corresponding widths noted. The plate is then submerged vertically in water with its top 1 ft below the surface. Use Simpson's rule to estimate the total force on the face of the plate.

Depth, x_k	Width, L_k
1.0	0.0
1.2	3.3
1.4	3.6
1.6	3.7
1.8	3.7
2.0	3.6
2.2	3.4
2.4	2.9
2.6	0.0

*A region R with uniform density is said to have **moments of inertia** I_x about the x-axis and I_y about the y-axis, where*

$$I_x = \int y^2 \, dA \quad and \quad I_y = \int x^2 \, dA$$

The d A represents the area of an approximating strip. In Problems 47–48, find I_x and I_y for the given region.

47. the region bounded by the parabola $y = \sqrt{x}$, the x-axis, and the line $x = 4$

48. the region bounded by the curve $y = \sqrt[3]{1 - x^3}$ and the coordinate axes

49. Modeling Problem If a region has area A and moment of inertia I_y about the y-axis, then it is said to have a **radius of gyration**

$$\rho_y = \sqrt{\frac{I_y}{A}}$$

with respect to the y-axis. Set up and analyze a model to determine the radius of gyration for the triangular region bounded by the line $y = 4 - x$ and the positive coordinate axes.

C 50. Show that the centroid of a rectangle is the point of intersection of its diagonals.

51. A right circular cone is generated when the region bounded by the line $y = x$ and the vertical lines $x = 0$ and $x = r$ is revolved about the x-axis. Use Pappus' theorem to show that the volume of this cone is $V = \frac{1}{3}\pi r^3$.

52. Let R be the triangular region bounded by the line $y = x$, the x-axis, and the vertical line $x = r$. When R is rotated about the x-axis, it generates a cone of volume $V = \frac{1}{3}\pi r^3$. Use Pappus' theorem to determine $\bar{y}$, the y-coordinate of the centroid of R. Then use similar reasoning to find $\bar{x}$.

53. Find the volume of the solid figure generated when a square of side L is revolved about a line that is outside the square, parallel to two of its sides, and located s units from the closer side.

54. Find the volume of the solid figure generated by revolving an equilateral triangle of side L about one of its sides.

55. Let R be a region in the plane, and suppose that R can be partitioned into two subregions R_1 and R_2. Let $(\bar{x}_1, \bar{y}_1)$ and $(\bar{x}_2, \bar{y}_2)$ be the centroids of R_1 and R_2, respectively, and let A_1 and A_2 be the areas of the subregions. Show that $(\bar{x}, \bar{y})$ is the centroid of R, where

$$\bar{x} = \frac{A_1 x_1 + A_2 x_2}{A_1 + A_2} \quad \text{and} \quad \bar{y} = \frac{A_1 y_1 + A_2 y_2}{A_1 + A_2}$$

6.6 Applications to Business, Economics, and Life Sciences

IN THIS SECTION future and present value of a flow of income; cumulative change: net earnings; consumer's and producer's surplus; survival and renewal; flow of blood through an artery

In Section 6.5, we saw how integration can be applied to the physical sciences. The goal of this section is to explore applications to a variety of other areas, especially business, economics, and the life sciences.

FUTURE AND PRESENT VALUE OF A FLOW OF INCOME

Recall from Chapter 2 that when P_0 dollars are invested at the continuous compounding annual rate r, then after t years, the account is worth $A = P_0 e^{rt}$ dollars. The amount A is called the *future value* of the initial value P_0 dollars, but what is the future value if the money were not deposited just once, in a lump sum P_0, but continuously over the entire time period? The difficulty is that at any given time, the "old" money deposited earlier in the time period has been accumulating interest longer than "new" money deposited more recently. To compute future value, in this case, our strategy will be to approximate the continuous income flow by a sequence of discrete deposits called an **annuity**. Then, the amount of the approximating annuity is a sum whose limit is a definite integral that gives the future value of the income flow. The general procedure is illustrated in Example 1.

EXAMPLE 1 Computing future value of a continuous income flow

Money is transferred into an account continuously at the rate of $1,500$ dollars/yr. If the account earns interest at the rate of 7% compounded continuously, what is the future value of the account 5 years from now?

Solution

To approximate the future value of the income flow, divide the 5-yr time period $0 \le t \le 5$ into n intervals, each of length $\Delta_n t = (5 - 0)/n$, and for $k = 1, 2, \ldots, n$, let t_{k-1} denote the beginning of the kth subinterval $[t_{k-1}, t_k]$. The amount of money deposited during the kth subinterval is $1,500\Delta_n t$. Therefore, if as an approximation, we assume that all this money is deposited at time t_{k-1}, then since $5 - t_{k-1}$ years remain in the 5-yr investment period, it follows that this money would grow to $(1,500\Delta_n t)e^{0.07(5-t_{k-1})}$ dollars; that is,

$$\begin{bmatrix} \text{FUTURE VALUE OF MONEY DEPOSITED} \\ \text{DURING THE } k\text{TH SUBINTERVAL} \end{bmatrix} = 1,500e^{0.07(5-t_{k-1})}\Delta_n t$$

This approximation is illustrated in Figure 6.73.

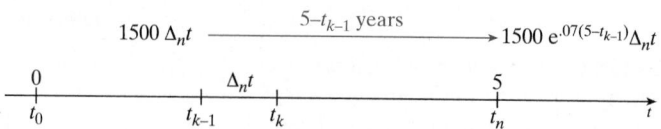

Figure 6.73   Approximate future value of money deposited during the kth subinterval

The future value of the entire income stream can be approximated by the sum of the future values of the money deposited during all n time subintervals. Hence, we have

$$[\text{FUTURE VALUE OF INCOME FLOW}] \approx \sum_{k=1}^{n} 1,500e^{0.07(5-t_{k-1})}\Delta_n t$$

As n increases without bound, the length of each subinterval tends toward zero, and there is less and less error in our assumption that all the money in the kth subinterval is deposited at time $t = t_{k-1}$. Therefore, it is reasonable to compute the total future value of the income flow by taking the limit of the approximating sum as $n \to +\infty$. We recognize this sum as a Riemann sum, and the limit as the definite integral. That is

$$\begin{aligned}
[\text{FUTURE VALUE OF INCOME FLOW}] &= \lim_{n \to +\infty} \sum_{k=1}^{n} 1,500e^{0.07(5-t_{k-1})}\Delta_n t \\
&= \int_0^5 1,500e^{0.07(5-t)}\, dt \\
&= 1,500e^{0.35} \int_0^5 e^{-0.07t}\, dt \\
&= 1,500e^{0.35} \left[\frac{e^{-0.07t}}{-0.07} \right]\bigg|_0^5 \\
&= 8,980.02 \qquad\blacksquare
\end{aligned}$$

Recall from Chapter 2, that the *present value*, PV, of A dollars invested at the annual interest rate r compounded continuously for a term T years is the amount of money $PV = Ae^{-rt}$ that must be deposited today at the prevailing interest rate to generate A dollars at the end of the term. Likewise, the present value of an income stream $f(t)$ generated continuously at a certain rate over a specified term is the amount of money that would have to be deposited at the beginning of the term at the prevailing interest rate to generate the income stream over the entire term. As with future value, the strategy is to approximate the continuous income stream by a sequence of discrete payments; that is, by an annuity. The present value of the approximating annuity is a sum, and by taking the limit of that sum, we obtain an integral

$$\int_0^T f(t)e^{-rt}\, dt$$

that represents the present value of the entire income flow. The details of this approximation scheme are outlined in the problem set. Here is a summary of the formulas to be used for computing future and present value of an income flow.

Future Value and Present Value of an Income Flow

Let $f(t)$ be the amount of money deposited at time t over the time period $[0, T]$ in an account that earns interest at the annual rate r compounded continuously. Then the **future value** of the income flow over the time period is given by

$$FV = \int_0^T f(t)e^{rt}\, dt$$

and the **present value** of the same income flow over the time period is

$$PV = \int_0^T f(t)e^{-rt}\, dt$$

CUMULATIVE CHANGE: NET EARNINGS

In certain applications, we are given the rate of change $Q'(x)$ of a quantity $Q(x)$ and are required to find the net change $Q(b) - Q(a)$ in $Q(x)$ as x varies from $x = a$ to $x = b$. But because $Q(x)$ is an antiderivative of $Q'(x)$, the fundamental theorem of calculus tells us that the net change is given by the definite integral

$$Q(b) - Q(a) = \int_a^b Q'(x)\, dx$$

Since the definite integral on the right "adds" all the instantaneous changes in $Q(x)$ over the time period $[a, b]$, the integral can also be thought of as **cumulative change**. For example, if $N(t)$ is the population of a certain species that is growing at the rate $N'(t)$ at time t, then the cumulative change in population over the time period $[t_1, t_2]$ is given by the integral

$$N(t_2) - N(t_1) = \int_{t_1}^{t_2} N'(t)\, dt$$

A business application involves the **net earnings** of an industrial process. Suppose $C(x)$ represents the total cost of producing x units and $R(x)$ represents the revenue generated by the sale of those units. Then $E(x) = R(x) - C(x)$ represents earnings, and if the marginal cost $C'(x)$ and marginal revenue $R'(x)$ are known, the net earnings for the production range $a \leq x \leq b$ are given by the definite integral

$$E(b) - E(a) = \int_a^b E'(x)\, dx$$
$$= \int_a^b [R'(x) - C'(x)]\, dx$$

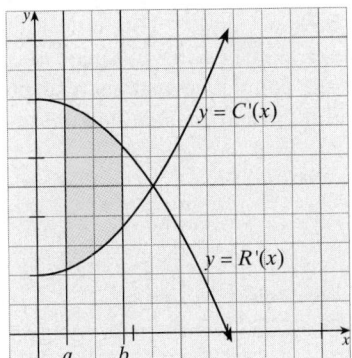

Figure 6.74 Net earnings as an area

Net earnings can be interpreted geometrically as an area between the marginal revenue and marginal cost curves as shown in Figure 6.74. These ideas are illustrated in Example 2.

EXAMPLE 2   Computing net earnings

For a certain industrial process, the marginal cost and marginal revenue (in thousands of dollars) associated with producing x units are

$$C'(x) = 0.1x^2 + 4x + 10 \quad \text{and} \quad R'(x) = 70 - x$$

respectively. What are the net earnings of the process as x ranges from $x = 0$ to $x = x_m$, where x_m is the level of production at which marginal cost equals marginal revenue?

Solution

First, note that marginal cost equals marginal revenue when

$$0.1x^2 + 4x + 10 = 70 - x$$
$$0.1x^2 + 5x - 60 = 0$$
$$x^2 + 50x - 600 = 0$$
$$(x + 60)(x - 10) = 0$$
$$x = 10, -60$$

Reject the negative value, giving the solution $x_m = 10$, so that the net earnings as x ranges from $x = 0$ to $x = 10$ are given by

$$E(10) - E(0) = \int_0^{10} [R'(x) - C'(x)]\,dx$$
$$= \int_0^{10} [70 - x - (0.1x^2 + 4x + 10)]\,dx$$
$$= \int_0^{10} [-0.1x^2 - 5x + 60]\,dx = \frac{950}{3} = 316.\bar{6}$$

That is, the net earnings are $316,667, and are shown as the area between the marginal cost and marginal revenue curves in Figure 6.75. ∎

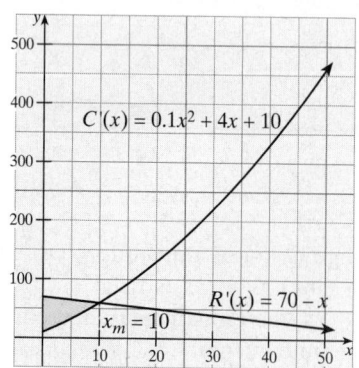

Figure 6.75 Net earnings for the marginal cost and marginal revenue

CONSUMER'S AND PRODUCER'S SURPLUS

In a competitive economy, the total amount that consumers actually spend on a commodity is usually less than the total amount they would have been willing to spend. The difference between the two amounts can be thought of as a savings realized by consumers and is known in economics as the **consumer's surplus**.

To get a better feel for the concept of consumer's surplus, consider an example of a couple who are willing to spend $500 for their first TV set, $300 for a second set, and only $50 for a third set. If the market price is $300, then the couple would buy only two sets and would spend a total of $2 \times \$300 = \$600$. This is less than the $\$500 + \$300 = \$800$ that the couple would have been willing to spend to get the two sets. The savings of $\$800 - \$600 = \$200$ is the couple's consumer's surplus. Consumer's surplus has a simple geometric interpretation, which is illustrated in Figure 6.76.

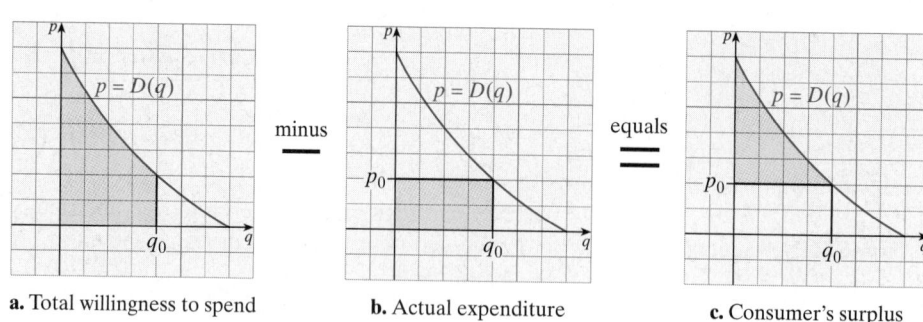

a. Total willingness to spend   **b.** Actual expenditure   **c.** Consumer's surplus

Figure 6.76 Geometric interpretation of consumer's surplus

Note that p and q denote the market price and the corresponding demand, respectively. Figure 6.76a shows the region under the demand curve $p = D(q)$ from $q = 0$ to $q = q_0$, and the area of this region represents the total amount that consumers are willing to spend to get q_0 units of the commodity. The rectangle in Figure 6.76b has an area of $p_0 q_0$ and represents the actual consumer expenditure for q_0 units at p_0 dollars per unit. The difference between these two areas (Figure 6.76c) represents the consumer's surplus. That is, consumer's surplus is the area of the region between the demand curve $p = D(q)$ and the horizontal line $p = p_0$ so that

$$\int_0^{q_0} [D(q) - p_0] \, dq = \int_0^{q_0} D(q) \, dq - \int_0^{q_0} p_0 \, dq = \int_0^{q_0} D(q) \, dq - p_0 q_0$$

Consumer's Surplus

If q_0 units of a commodity are sold at a price of p_0 dollars per unit, and if $p = D(q)$ is the consumer's demand function for the commodity, then

$$\begin{bmatrix} \text{CONSUMER'S} \\ \text{SURPLUS} \end{bmatrix} = \begin{bmatrix} \text{TOTAL AMOUNT} \\ \text{CONSUMERS ARE} \\ \text{WILLING TO SPEND} \\ \text{FOR } q_0 \text{ UNITS} \end{bmatrix} - \begin{bmatrix} \text{ACTUAL CONSUMER} \\ \text{EXPENDITURE FOR} \\ q_0 \text{ UNITS} \end{bmatrix}$$

$$CS = \int_0^{q_0} D(q) \, dq - p_0 q_0$$

Producer's surplus is the other side of the coin from consumer's surplus. In particular, a supply function $p = S(q)$ gives the price per unit that producers are willing to accept in order to supply q units to the marketplace. However, any producer who is willing to accept less than $p_0 = S(q_0)$ dollars for q_0 units gains from the fact that the price is actually p_0. Then **producer's surplus** is the difference between what producers would be willing to accept for supplying q units and the price they actually receive. Reasoning as we did with consumer's surplus, we obtain the following formula for producer's surplus.

Producer's Surplus

If q_0 units of a commodity are sold at a price of p_0 dollars per unit, and if $p = S(q)$ is the producer's supply function for the commodity, then

$$\begin{bmatrix} \text{PRODUCER'S} \\ \text{SURPLUS} \end{bmatrix} = \begin{bmatrix} \text{ACTUAL CONSUMER} \\ \text{EXPENDITURE FOR} \\ q_0 \text{ UNITS} \end{bmatrix} - \begin{bmatrix} \text{TOTAL AMOUNT} \\ \text{PRODUCERS RECEIVE} \\ \text{WHEN } q_0 \text{ UNITS} \\ \text{ARE SUPPLIED} \end{bmatrix}$$

$$PS = p_0 q_0 - \int_0^{q_0} S(q) \, dq$$

EXAMPLE 3   Computing consumer's and producer's surplus

A tire manufacturer estimates that q (thousand) radial tires will be purchased (that is, demanded) by wholesalers when the price is

$$p = D(q) = -0.1q^2 + 90$$

dollars/tire, and the same number of tires will be supplied when the price is

$$p = S(q) = 0.2q^2 + q + 50$$

dollars/tire.

a. Find the equilibrium price (that is, where supply equals demand) and the quantity supplied and demanded at that price.

b. Determine the consumer's and producer's surplus at the equilibrium price.

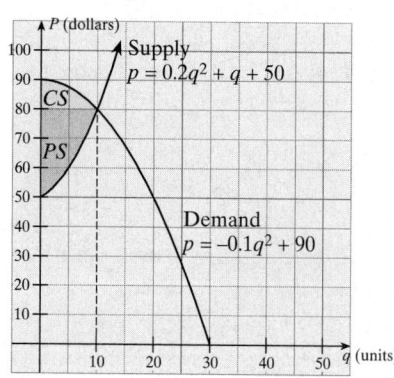

Figure 6.77 Consumer's and producer's surplus at equilibrium for the given supply and demand functions

Solution

a. The supply and demand curves are shown in Figure 6.77. Supply equals demand when

$$0.2q^2 + q + 50 = -0.1q^2 + 90$$
$$0.3q^2 + q - 40 = 0$$
$$q = 10 \qquad (\text{reject } q = -\tfrac{40}{3})$$

and $p = S(10) = D(10) = 80$. Thus, equilibrium occurs at a price of $80/tire, when 10,000 tires are supplied and demanded.

b. Using $p_0 = 80$ and $q_0 = 10$, we find that the consumer's surplus is

$$\int_0^{10} (-0.1q^2 + 90)\, dq - (80)(10) = \left[-0.1\left(\frac{q^3}{3}\right) + 90q\right]\Big|_0^{10} - (80)(10)$$
$$= \frac{2,600}{3} - (80)(10)$$
$$= \frac{200}{3} = 66.\bar{6}$$

The producer's surplus is

$$(80)(10) - \int_0^{10} (0.2q^2 + q + 50)\, dq = (80)(10) - \left[0.2\left(\frac{q^3}{3}\right) + \left(\frac{q^2}{2}\right) + 50q\right]\Big|_0^{10}$$
$$= (80)(10) - \frac{1,850}{3}$$
$$= 183.\bar{3}$$

Since q is in thousands, the consumer's surplus is about $66,667, and the producer's surplus is $183,333. The consumer's surplus and producer's surplus are the regions labeled CS and PS, respectively, in Figure 6.77. ■

SURVIVAL AND RENEWAL

There is an important category of problems in which a survival function gives the fraction of individuals in a group of population that can be expected to remain in the group and a renewal function gives the rate at which new members can be expected to join the group. Such **survival and renewal** problems arise in many fields, including sociology, ecology, demography, and even finance, where the "population" is the number of dollars in an investment account and "survival and renewal" refers to results of an investment strategy. The following example illustrates the general procedure for modeling with survival and renewal functions.

EXAMPLE 4   Modeling enrollment using survival and renewal

A new county mental health clinic has just opened. Statistics from similar facilities suggest that the fraction of patients who will still be receiving treatment at the clinic t months after their initial visit is given by the function $f(t) = e^{-t/20}$. The clinic initially accepts 300 people for treatment and plans to accept new patients at the rate of 10 per month. Approximately how many people will be receiving treatment at the clinic 15 months from now?

Solution

Since $f(15)$ is the fraction of patients whose treatment continues at least 15 months, it follows that of the current 300 patients, only $300 f(15)$ will still be receiving treatment 15 months from now.

To approximate the number of *new* patients who will be receiving treatment 15 months from now, divide the 15-month time interval $0 \le t \le 15$ into n equal subintervals of length Δt months and let t_{j-1} denote the beginning of the jth subinterval. Since new patients are accepted at the rate of 10/mo, the number of new patients accepted during the jth subinterval is $10\Delta t$. Fifteen months from now, approximately $15 - t_{j-1}$ months will have elapsed since these $10\Delta t$ new patients had their initial visits, and so approximately $(10\Delta t)f(15 - t_{j-1})$ of them will still be receiving treatment at that time (see Figure 6.78).

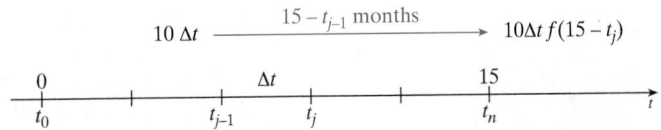

Figure 6.78   New members arriving during the jth subinterval

It follows that the total number of new patients still receiving treatment 15 months from now can be approximated by the sum

$$\sum_{j=1}^{n} 10 f(15 - t_{j-1})\Delta t$$

Adding this to the number of current patients who will still be receiving treatment in 15 months, we obtain

$$P \approx 300 f(15) + \sum_{j=1}^{n} 10 f(15 - t_{j-1})\Delta t$$

where P is the total number of patients who will be receiving treatment 15 months from now. As n increases without bound, the approximation improves and approaches the true value of P. That is,

$$P = 300 f(15) + \lim_{n \to +\infty} \sum_{j=1}^{n} 10 f(15 - t_{j-1})\Delta t$$

$$= 300 f(15) + \int_{0}^{15} 10 f(15 - t)\, dt$$

Since $f(t) = e^{-t/20}$, we have $f(15) = e^{-3/4}$ and $f(15 - t) = e^{-(15-t)/20} = e^{-3/4}e^{t/20}$. Thus,

$$P = 300 e^{-3/4} + 10 e^{-3/4} \int_{0}^{15} e^{t/20}\, dt$$

$$= 300 e^{-3/4} + 200 e^{-3/4} e^{t/20} \Big|_{0}^{15}$$

$$= 300 e^{-3/4} + 200(1 - e^{-3/4})$$

$$\approx 247.24$$

That is, 15 months from now, the clinic will be treating approximately 247 patients.   ■

THE FLOW OF BLOOD THROUGH AN ARTERY

In biology, Poiseuille's law of flow* asserts that the speed of blood in an artery is a function of the distance of the blood from the artery's central axis. That is, the speed (in cm/s) of blood that is r centimeters from the central axis of the artery may be modeled by

$$S(r) = k(R^2 - r^2)$$

where R is the radius of the artery and k is a constant. In the following example, you will see how to use this information to compute the rate (in cm^3/s) at which blood flows through the artery.

*The law of flow is named for the same French physician, Jean Louis Poiseuille (1799–1869), responsible for the resistance to flow law cited in Section 4.7.

EXAMPLE 5 Modeling blood flow

Find an expression for the volume rate (in cm^3/s) at which blood flows through an artery of radius R if the speed of the blood r cm from the central axis is $S(r) = k(R^2 - r^2)$, where k is a constant.

Solution

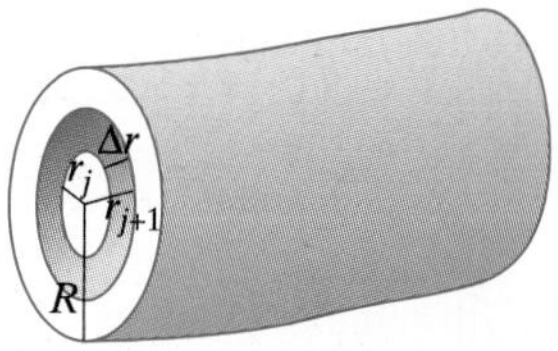

To find the approximate volume of blood that flows through a cross section of the artery each second, divide the interval $0 \leq r \leq R$ into n equal subintervals of width Δr cm and let r_j denote the beginning of the jth subinterval. These subintervals determine n concentric rings, as illustrated in Figure 6.79.

Figure 6.79 Subdividing a cross section of an artery into concentric rings

If Δr is small, the area of the jth ring is approximately the area of a rectangle whose length is the circumference of the (inner) boundary of the ring and whose width is Δr. That is,

$$\text{AREA OF THE } j\text{TH RING} \approx 2\pi r_j \Delta r$$

If we multiply the area of the jth ring (cm^2) by the speed (cm/s) of the blood flowing through this ring, we obtain the volume rate (cm^3/s) at which blood flows through the jth ring. Since the speed of blood flowing through the jth ring is approximately $S(r_j)$ cm/s, it follows that

$$\begin{pmatrix} \text{VOLUME RATE OF FLOW} \\ \text{THROUGH THE } j\text{TH RING} \end{pmatrix} \approx (\text{AREA OF } j\text{TH RING}) \begin{pmatrix} \text{SPEED OF BLOOD} \\ \text{THROUGH THE } j\text{TH RING} \end{pmatrix}$$

$$= (2\pi r_j \Delta r) S(r_j)$$

$$= (2\pi r_j \Delta r) \left[k(R^2 - r_j^2) \right]$$

$$= 2\pi k(R^2 r_j - r_j^3) \Delta r$$

The volume rate of flow of blood through the entire cross section is the sum of n such terms, one for each of the n concentric rings. That is,

$$\text{VOLUME RATE OF FLOW} \approx \sum_{j=1}^{n} 2\pi k(R^2 r_j - r_j^3) \Delta r$$

As n increases without bound, this approximation approaches the true value of the volume rate of flow. That is,

$$\text{VOLUME RATE OF FLOW} = \lim_{n \to +\infty} \sum_{j=1}^{n} 2\pi k(R^2 r_j - r_j^3) \Delta r$$

$$= \int_0^R 2\pi k(R^2 r - r^3) \, dr$$

$$= 2\pi k \left(\frac{R^2}{2} r^2 - \frac{1}{4} r^4 \right) \Big|_0^R$$

$$= \frac{\pi k R^4}{2} \quad \text{in } cm^3/s \qquad \blacksquare$$

6.6 PROBLEM SET

A 1. **WHAT DOES THIS SAY?** What is cumulative change for a quantity $Q(x)$?

2. **WHAT DOES THIS SAY?** What are the future and present values of an income flow?

3. **WHAT DOES THIS SAY?** What are consumer's and producer's surplus?

Find the consumer's surplus for the given demand function defined by $D(q)$ at the point that corresponds to the sales level q as given in Problems 4–7.

4. $D(q) = 3.5 - 0.5q$
   a. $q_0 = 1$ b. $q_0 = 1.5$

5. $D(q) = 2.5 - 1.5q$
   a. $q_0 = 1$ b. $q_0 = 0$

6. $D(q) = 100 - 8q$
   a. $q_0 = 4$ b. $q_0 = 10$

7. $D(q) = 150 - 6q$
   a. $q_0 = 5$ b. $q_0 = 12$

In Problems 8–11, $p = D(q)$ is the price (in dollars/unit) at which q units of a particular commodity will be demanded by the market (that is, all q units will be sold at this price), and q_0 is a specified level of production. In each case, find the price $p_0 = D(q_0)$ at which q_0 units will be demanded and compute the corresponding consumer's surplus. Sketch the demand curve $y = D(q)$ and shade the region whose area represents the consumer's surplus.

8. $D(q) = 2(64 - q^2); q_0 = 3$ units

9. $D(q) = 150 - 2q - 3q^2; q_0 = 6$ units

10. $D(q) = 40e^{-0.05q}; q_0 = 5$ units

11. $D(q) = 75e^{-0.04q}; q_0 = 3$ units

In Problems 12–15, $p = S(q)$ is the price (in dollars/unit) at which q units of a particular commodity will be supplied to the market by producers, and q_0 is a specified level of production. In each case, find the price $p_0 = S(q_0)$ at which q_0 units will be supplied and compute the corresponding producer's surplus. Sketch the supply curve $y = S(q)$ and shade the region whose area represents the producer's surplus.

12. $S(q) = 0.3q^2 + 30; q_0 = 4$ units

13. $S(q) = 0.5q + 15; q_0 = 5$ units

14. $S(q) = 10 + 15e^{0.03q}; q_0 = 3$ units

15. $S(q) = 17 + 11e^{0.01q}; q_0 = 7$ units

B *In Problems 16–19, find the consumer's surplus at the point of market equilibrium (the level of production where supply $S(q)$ equals demand $D(q)$).*

Demand function	Supply function
16. $D(q) = 14 - q^2$	$S(q) = 2q^2 + 2$
17. $D(q) = 25 - q^2$	$S(q) = 5q^2 + 1$
18. $D(q) = 32 - 2q^2$	$S(q) = \frac{1}{3}q^2 + 2q + 5$
19. $D(q) = 27 - q^2$	$S(q) = \frac{1}{4}q^2 + \frac{1}{2}q + 5$

20. A manufacturer has determined that when q units of a particular commodity are produced, the price at which all the units can be sold is $p = D(q)$ dollars per unit, where D is the demand function given by

$$D(q) = \frac{300}{(0.1q + 1)^2}$$

a. How many units can the manufacturer expect to sell if the commodity is priced at $p_0 = \$12$/unit?

b. Find the consumer's surplus that corresponds to the level of production q_0 found in part **a**.

21. Money is transferred continuously into an account at the constant rate of $3,000/yr. The account earns interest at the annual rate of 8% compounded continuously.

a. What is the future value of the income flow in three years?

b. What is the present value of the income flow over a three-year term?

22. The management of a small firm expects to generate income at the rate of $f(t) = 2,000e^{0.03t}$ dollars/yr. The prevailing rate of interest is 7% compounded continuously.

a. What is the future value for the firm over a five-year term?

b. What is the present value for the firm over the same five-year term?

23. Suppose an industrial machine that is x years old generates revenue at the rate of

$$R'(x) = 6,025 - 10x^2$$

dollars per year and costs accumulate at the rate of

$$C'(x) = 4,000 + 15x^2$$

dollars per year for operation and maintenance.

a. The machine will be sold when earnings $E(x) = R(x) - C(x)$ are maximized. When does this occur?

b. What are the net earnings generated by the machine between now and when it is sold? Interpret this amount as the area between two curves.

24. After t hours on the job, Joan is producing units at the rate of

$$Q_1'(t) = 60 - 2(t - 1)^2$$

units per hour, and Jill is producing at the rate of

$$Q_2'(t) = 50 - 5t$$

units per hour. If both arrive on the job at 8:00 A.M., how many more units (to the nearest unit) will Joan have produced by noon than Jill? Interpret your answer as the area between two curves.

25. Suppose that x years from now, one investment plan will be generating profit at the rate of

$$P_1'(x) = 100 + x^2$$

dollars per year, whereas a second plan will be generating profit at the rate of

$$P_2'(x) = 190 + 2x$$

dollars per year. Neither plan generates a profit in the beginning; that is, $P_1(0) = P_2(0) = 0$.

a. For how many years will the second plan be more profitable?

b. How much more total profit will you earn if you invest in the second plan instead of the first for the period of time in part **a**? Interpret the extra profit as the area between two curves.

26. Parts for a piece of heavy machinery are sold in units of 1,000. The demand for the parts (in dollars) is given by $p(x) = 110 - x$. The total cost is given by $C(x) = x^3 - 25x^2 + 2x + 30$ (dollars).

a. For what value of x is the profit

$$P(x) = xp(x) - C(x)$$

maximized?

b. Find the consumer's surplus with respect to the price that corresponds to maximum profit.

27. Repeat Problem 26 with $p(x) = 124 - 2x$ and $C(x) = 2x^3 - 59x^2 + 4x + 76$.

28. Suppose when q units of a commodity are produced, the demand is $p(q) = 45 - q^2$ dollars per unit, and the marginal cost is

$$\frac{dC}{dq} = 6 + \frac{1}{4}q^2$$

Assume there is no overhead (so $C(0) = 0$).

a. Find the total revenue and the marginal revenue.

b. Find the value of q (to the nearest unit) that maximizes profit.

c. Find the consumer's surplus at the value of q where profit is maximized. (Use the exact value of q.)

29. Repeat Problem 28 with

$$p(q) = \tfrac{1}{4}(10 - q)^2 \qquad \text{and} \qquad \frac{dC}{dq} = \tfrac{3}{4}q^2 + 5$$

30. A company plans to hire additional personnel. Suppose it is estimated that as x new people are hired, it will cost $C(x) = 0.2x$ thousand dollars and that these x people will bring in $R(x) = \sqrt{3x}$ thousand dollars in additional revenue. How many new people would be hired to maximize the profit? How much net revenue would the company gain by hiring these people?

31. Suppose that the demand function for a certain commodity is $D(q) = 20 - 4q^2$, and that the marginal cost is $C'(q) = 2q + 6$, where q is the number of units produced. Find the consumer's surplus at the sales level q_0 where profit is maximized.

32. The resale value of a certain industrial machine decreases over a ten-year period at a rate that changes with time. When the machine is x years old, its value is decreasing at the rate of $220(x - 10)$ dollars/yr. By how much does the machine depreciate during the second year?

33. The promoters of a country fair estimate that t hours after the gates open at 9:00 A.M. visitors will be entering the fair at the rate of $-4(t + 2)^3 + 54(t + 2)^2$ people/hr. How many people will enter the fair between 10:00 A.M. and noon?

34. At a certain factory, the marginal cost is $6(q - 5)^2$ dollars/unit when the level of production is q units. By how much will the total manufacturing cost increase if the level of production is raised from 10 to 13 units?

35. A certain oil well that yields 400 barrels of crude oil a month will run dry in two years. The price of crude oil is currently \$18/barrel and is expected to rise at a constant rate of \$0.03 per barrel per month. If the oil is sold as soon as it is extracted from the ground, what will be the total future revenue from the well?

36. It is estimated that t days from now a farmer's crop (in bushels) will be increasing at the rate of $0.3t^2 + 0.6t + 1$ bu/day. By how much will the value of the crop increase during the next five days if the market price remains fixed at \$3/bu?

37. It is estimated that the demand for a manufacturer's product is increased exponentially at the rate of 2%/yr. If the current demand is 5,000 units/yr and if the price remains fixed at \$400/unit, how much revenue will the manufacturer receive from the sale of the product over the next two years?

38. After t hours on the job, a factory worker can produce $100(2 + \sin t)$ units/hr. How many units does a worker who arrives on the job at 8:00 A.M. produce between 10:00 A.M. and noon?

39. Suppose that t years from now, one investment plan will be generating profit at the rate of $P_1'(t) = 100 + t^2$ hundred dollars per year, while a second investment will be generating profit at the rate of $P_2'(t) = 220 + 2t$ hundred dollars per year.

a. For how many years does the rate of profitability of the second investment exceed that of the first?

b. Compute the net excess profit assuming that you invest in the second plan for the time period determined in part **a**.

c. Sketch the rate of profitability curves $y = P_1'(t)$ and $y = P_2'(t)$ and shade the region whose area represents the net excess profit computed in part **b**.

40. Answer the questions in Problem 39 for two investments with respective rates of profitability $P_1'(t) = 130 + t^2$ hundred dollars per year and $P_2'(t) = 306 + 5t$ hundred dollars per year.

41. Answer the questions in Problem 39 for two investments with respective rates of profitability $P_1'(t) = 60e^{0.12t}$ thousand dollars per year and $P_2'(t) = 160e^{0.08t}$ thousand dollars per year.

42. Answer the questions in Problem 39 for two investments with respective rates of profitability $P_1'(t) = 90e^{0.1t}$ thousand dollars per year and $P_2'(t) = 140e^{0.07t}$ thousand dollars per year.

43. Suppose that when it is t years old, a particular industrial machine generates revenue at the rate $R'(t) = 6{,}025 - 8t^2$ dollars/yr and that operating and servicing costs accumulate at the rate of $C'(t) = 4{,}681 + 13t^2$ dollars/yr.

a. How many years pass before the profitability of the machine begins to decline?

b. Compute the net earnings generated by the machine over the time period determined in part **a**.

c. Sketch the revenue rate curve $y = R'(t)$ and the cost rate curve $y = C'(t)$ and shade the region whose area represents the net earnings computed in part **b**.

44. Answer the questions in Problem 43 for a machine that generates revenue at the rate $R'(t) = 7{,}250 - 18t^2$ dollars/yr and for which costs accumulate at the rate $C'(t) = 3{,}620 + 12t^2$ dollars/yr.

45. After t hours on the job, one factory worker is producing $Q_1'(t) = 60 - 2(t - 1)^2$ units/hr, while a second worker is producing $Q_2'(t) = 50 - 5t$ units/hr.

a. If both arrive on the job at 8:00 A.M., how many more units will the first worker have produced by noon than the second worker?

b. Interpret the answer in part **a** as the area between two curves.

46. A national consumers' association has compiled statistics suggesting that the fraction of its members who are still active t months after joining is given by the function $f(t) = e^{-0.2t}$. A new local chapter has 200 charter members and expects to attract new members at the rate of 10/mo. How many members can the chapter expect to have at the end of 8 months?

47. The population density r miles from the center of a certain city is $D(r) = 25{,}000e^{-0.05r^2}$ people/mi². How many people live between 1 and 2 miles from the city center?

48. The population density r miles from the center of a certain city is $D(r) = 5{,}000e^{-0.1r^2}$ people/mi². How many people live within 3 miles from the city center?

49. Calculate the volume rate (in cm³/s) at which blood flows through an artery of radius 0.1 cm if the speed of the blood r cm from the central axis is $8(1 - 100r^2)$ cm/s.

50. **Modeling Problem** Blood flows through an artery of radius R. At a distance r cm from the central axis of the artery, the speed of the blood is given by $S(r) = k(R^2 - r^2)$. Show that the average speed of the blood is one-half the maximum speed.

51. A study indicates that x months from now the population of a certain town will be increasing at the rate of $5 + 3x^{2/3}$

people/mo. By how much will the population of the town increase over the next 8 months?

52. An object is moving so that its speed after t minutes is $5 + 2t + 3t^2$ m/min. How far does the object travel during the second minute?

53. It is estimated that the demand for oil is increasing exponentially at the rate of 10%/yr. If the demand for oil is currently 30 billion barrels per year, how much oil will be consumed during the next 10 years?

54. It is estimated that t weeks from now, contributions in response to a fund-raising campaign will be coming in at the rate of $R'(t) = 5,000e^{-0.2t}$ dollars/wk, while campaign expenses are expected to accumulate at the constant rate of $676/wk.

   a. For how many weeks does the rate of revenue exceed the rate of cost?

   b. What net earnings will be generated by the campaign during the period of time determined in part **a**.

   c. Interpret the net earnings in part **b** as an area between two curves.

55. Spy Problem   The Spy arrives at the sleazy bar at the appointed time for his meeting with his superior (recall Supplementary Problem 85, Chapter 5), but, as usual, his peerless leader is fashionably late. While waiting, the Spy reflects on the dangerous life he leads. Ten years ago he took his spying oath, followed on the same day by 6 friends from college. On average, 30 new people join each year, and he estimates that the fraction of spies still alive after t years of service is $F(t) = e^{-t/20}$. Approximately how many people who joined the service after the Spy are still alive?

C 56. The administrators of a town estimate that the fraction of people who will still be residing in the town t years after they arrive is given by the function $f(t) = e^{-0.04t}$. If the current population is 20,000 people and new townspeople arrive at the rate of 500/yr, what will the population be ten years from now? *Hint*: Divide the interval $0 \le t \le 10$ into n equal subintervals and form a Riemann sum.

57. The operators of a new computer dating service estimate that the fraction of people who will retain their membership in the service for at least t months is given by the function $f(t) = e^{-t/10}$. There are 8,000 charter members, and the operators expect to attract 200 new members/mo. How many

members will the service have ten months from now? *Hint*: Divide the interval $0 \le t \le 10$ into n equal subintervals and form a Riemann sum.

58. Modeling Problem   A certain nuclear power plant produces radioactive waste in the form of strontium-90 at the constant rate of 500 pounds/yr. The waste decays exponentially with a half-life of 28 years. How much of the radioactive waste from the nuclear plant will be present after 140 years. *Hint*: Think of this as a survival and renewal problem and form a Riemann sum.

59. Modeling Problem   A certain investment generates income continuously over a period of N years. After t years, the investment will be generating income at the rate of $f(t)$ dollars/yr. The prevailing annual rate of interest, compounded continuously, is r. Derive the formula

$$\int_0^N f(t)e^{-rt}\, dt$$

for the present value of the income flow by completing these steps.

   a. Subdivide the time interval $[0, N]$ into n equal subintervals, the kth of which is $[t_{k-1}, t_k]$ for $k = 1, 2, \ldots, n$. Assuming that the income generated during the entire kth subinterval is $f(t_k)$, what is the present value of this income?

   b. Approximate the present value of the total income flow by an appropriate sum.

   c. Note that the sum in part **b** is a Riemann sum. Make the approximation precise by taking a limit to obtain the required integral formula for present value.

60. Modeling Problem   A manufacturer receives N units of a certain raw material that are initially placed in storage and then withdrawn and used at a constant rate until the supply is exhausted one year later. Suppose storage costs remain fixed at p dollars per unit per year. Use definite integration to find an expression for the total storage costs the manufacturer will pay during the year. *Hint*: Let $Q(t)$ denote the number of units in storage after t years and find an expression for $Q(t)$. Then subdivide the interval $0 \le t \le 1$ into n equal subintervals and express the total storage cost as the limit of a sum.

CHAPTER 6 REVIEW

Proficiency Examination

CONCEPT PROBLEMS

1. Describe the process for finding the area between two curves.

2. Describe the process for finding volumes of solids with a known cross-sectional area.

3. Compare and contrast the methods of finding volumes by disks, washers, and shells.

4. What are the formulas for changing from polar to rectangular form? From rectangular to polar form?

5. Draw one example of each of the given polar-form curves.

   a. cardioid   **b.** limaçon   **c.** lemniscate

   b. rose curve with three petals

6. Identify and then sketch each of the given curves.

   a. $r = 2\cos\theta$ **b.** $r = \cos\theta - 1$

   c. $r = \theta, r \ge 0$ **d.** $r^2 = \cos 2\theta$

7. What is the procedure for finding the intersection of polar-form curves?

8. Outline a procedure for finding the area bounded by a polar graph.

9. What is the formula for arc length of a graph?

10. What is the formula for area of a surface of revolution?

11. How do you find the work done by a variable force?

12. How do you find the force exerted by a liquid on an object submerged vertically?

13. What are the formulas for the mass and centroid of a homogeneous lamina?

14. State the volume theorem of Pappus.

15. What formulas are used to compute future value and present value of an income flow?

16. How do you find the net change of a function f whose derivative f' is given?

17. Describe the process for finding consumer's and producer's surplus.

18. Describe a typical survival and renewal problem.

19. What formula is used for computing the flow of blood through an artery?

PRACTICE PROBLEMS

20. **Journal Problem** *Mathematics Teacher** ■ *Use the integrals A–G to answer the given questions.*

A. $\pi \displaystyle\int_a^b [f(x)]^2 \, dx$ B. $\pi \displaystyle\int_c^d [f(y)]^2 \, dy$

C. $\displaystyle\int_a^b A(x) \, dx$ D. $\displaystyle\int_c^d A(y) \, dy$

E. $\pi \displaystyle\int_a^b [f(x) - g(x)] \, dx$

F. $\pi \displaystyle\int_a^b \{[f(x)]^2 - [g(x)]^2\} \, dx$

G. $\pi \displaystyle\int_c^d \{[f(y)]^2 - [g(y)]^2\} \, dy$

   a. Which formula does not seem to belong to this list?
   b. Which expressions represent volumes of solids of revolution?
   c. Which expressions represent volumes of solids containing holes?
   d. Which expressions represent volumes of a solid with cross sections that are perpendicular to an axis?
   e. Which expressions represent volumes of solids of revolution revolved about the x-axis?
   f. Which expressions represent volumes of solids of revolution revolved about the y-axis?

21. Find the area above the curve $f(x) = 3x^2 - 6$ and below the x-axis.

22. Find the area between the curves $y = x^2$ and $y^3 = x$.

23. The base of a solid in the xy-plane is the circular region given by $x^2 + y^2 = 4$. Every cross section perpendicular to the x-axis is a rectangle whose height is twice the length of the side that lies in the xy-plane. Find the volume of this solid.

24. Let R be a region bounded by the graphs of the equations $y = (x - 2)^2$ and $y = 4$.
   a. Sketch the graph of R and find its area.
   b. Find the volume of a solid of revolution of R about the x-axis.
   c. Find the volume of a solid of revolution of R about the y-axis.

25. Find the area of the intersection of the circles $r = 2a \cos \theta$ and $r = 2a \sin \theta$, where $a > 0$ is constant.

*Vol. 83, No. 9, December 1990, p. 695.

26. Find the arc length of the curve $y = 2 - x^{3/2}$ from $(0, 2)$ to $(1, 1)$. Give the exact value.

27. Find the surface area obtained by revolving the parabolic arc $y^2 = x$ from $(0, 0)$ to $(1, 1)$ about the x-axis. Give the answer to the nearest hundredth unit.

28. Find the centroid of the homogeneous region between $y = x^2 - x$ and $y = x - x^3$ on $[0, 1]$.

29. An observation porthole on a ship is circular with diameter of 2 feet and is located so its center is 3 feet below the waterline. Find the fluid force on the porthole, assuming that the boat is in seawater (density is 64 lb/ft^3). Set up the integral only.

30. Money is transferred continuously into an account at the constant rate of $1,200/yr. The account earns interest at the annual rate of 8% compounded continuously. How much money will be in the account at the end of 5 years?

Supplementary Problems

Name and sketch the curves whose equations are given in Problems 1–8.

1. $r = 2 \sin \theta - 3 \cos \theta$ 2. $r = -2\theta, \theta \geq 0$
3. $r = -\csc \theta$ 4. $r = \sin 3\theta$
5. $r = \cos(\theta - \frac{\pi}{3})$ 6. $r^2 = 3 \cos 2\theta$
7. $r = \dfrac{4}{1 - \cos \theta}$ 8. $r = \dfrac{5}{2 + 3 \sin \theta}$

Find the points of intersection of the polar-form curves in Problems 9–12.

9. $\begin{cases} r = 2 \cos \theta \\ r = 1 + \cos \theta \end{cases}$ 10. $\begin{cases} r = 1 + \sin \theta \\ r = 1 + \cos \theta \end{cases}$

11. $\begin{cases} r \cos \theta + 2r \sin \theta = 4 \\ r = 2 \sec \theta \end{cases}$ 12. $\begin{cases} r = 2 \sin 2\theta \\ r = 1 \text{ for } 0 \leq \theta \leq \frac{\pi}{2} \end{cases}$

Find the area of the regions bounded by the curves and lines in Problems 13–21.

13. $4y^2 = x$ and $2y = x - 2$ 14. $y = x^3, y = x^4$

15. $x = y^{2/3}, x = y^2$

16. $y = \sqrt{3} \sin x$, $y = \cos x$, and the vertical lines $x = 0$ and $x = \pi/2$

17. the region bounded by the polar curve $r = 4 \cos 2\theta$

18. the region inside both the circles $r = 1$ and $r = 2 \sin \theta$

19. the region inside one loop of the lemniscate $r^2 = \cos 2\theta$

20. the region inside one petal of the rose curve $r = \sin 2\theta$

21. the region inside the circle $r = 2a \sin \theta$ and outside the circle $r = a$

Find the volume of a solid of revolution obtained by revolving the region R about the indicated axis in Problems 22–25.

22. R is bounded by $y = \sqrt{x}, x = 9, y = 0$; about the x-axis

23. R is bounded by $y = x^2, y = 9 - x^2$, and $x = 0$; about the y-axis

24. R is bounded by $y = x^2$ and $y = x^4$; about the x-axis

25. R is bounded by $y = \sqrt{\cos x}, x = \frac{\pi}{4}, x = \frac{\pi}{3}$, and $y = 0$; about the x-axis.

26. The base of a solid is the region in the xy-plane that is bounded by the curve $y = 4 - x^2$ and the x-axis. Every cross section of the solid perpendicular to the y-axis is a rectangle whose height is twice the length of the side that lies in the xy-plane. Find the volume of the solid.

27. The base of a solid is the region R in the xy-plane bounded by the curve $y^2 = x$ and the line $y = x$. Find the volume of the solid if each cross section perpendicular to the x-axis is a semicircle with a diameter in the xy-plane.

28. Find the centroid of a homogeneous lamina covering the region R that is bounded by the parabola $y = 2 - x^2$ and the line $y = x$.

29. A force of 100 lb is required to compress a spring from its natural length of 10 in. to a length of 8 in. Find the work required to compress it to a length of 7 in. from its natural length.

30. A bowl is formed by revolving the region bounded by the curve $y = 2x^2$ and the lines $x = 0$ and $y = 1$ about the y-axis (units are in ft). The bowl is filled with water to a height of 9 in.

    a. How much work is done in pumping the water to the top of the bowl?

    b. How much work is done in pumping the water to a point 0.5 ft above the top of the bowl?

31. Two solids S_1 and S_2 have as their base the region in the xy-plane bounded by the parabola $y = x^2$ and the line $y = 1$. For solid S_1, each cross section perpendicular to the x-axis is a square, and for S_2, each cross section perpendicular to the y-axis is a square. Which solid has the greater volume?

32. Use calculus to find the lateral surface area of a right circular cylinder with radius r and height h.

33. Use calculus to find the surface area of a right circular cone with (top) radius r and height h.

34. A 20-lb bucket in a well is attached to the end of a 60-ft chain that weighs 16 lb. If the bucket is filled with 50 lb of water, how much work is done in lifting the bucket and chain to the top of the well?

35. A swimming pool is 3 ft deep at one end and 8 ft deep at the other, as shown in Figure 6.80. The pool is 30 ft long and 25 ft wide with vertical sides. Set up and analyze a model to find the fluid force against one of the 30-ft sides.

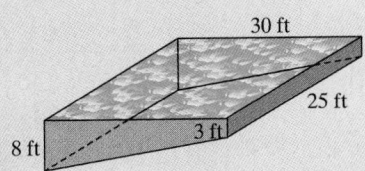

Figure 6.80 Cross section of a swimming pool

36. The ends of a container filled with water have the shape of the region R bounded by the curve $y = x^4$ and the line $y = 16$. Find the fluid force (to two decimal places) exerted by the water on one end of the container.

37. A conical tank whose vertex points down is 12 ft high with (top) diameter 6 ft. The tank is filled with a fluid of density $\rho = 22$ lb/ft^3. If the tank is filled to a depth of 6 ft, find the work required to pump all the fluid to a height of 2 ft above the top of the tank.

38. Each end of a container filled with water has the shape of an isosceles triangle, as shown in Figure 6.81. Find the force exerted by the water on an end of the container.

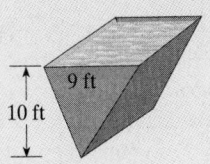

Figure 6.81 Water pressure in a tank

39. A container has the shape of the solid formed by rotating the region bounded by the curve $y = x^3$ and the lines $x = 0$ and $y = 1$ about the y-axis, where x and y are measured in feet. If the container is filled with water, how much work is required to pump all the water out of the container?

40. A gate in a water main has the shape of a circle with diameter 10 ft. If water stands 2 ft high in the main, what is the force exerted by the water on the gate?

*Suppose a particle of mass m moves along a number line under the influence of a variable force F which always acts in a direction parallel to the line of motion. At a given time the particle is said to have **kinetic energy***

$$K = \tfrac{1}{2}mv^2$$

*where v is the particle's velocity, and it has **potential energy***

$$P = -\int_{s_0}^{s} F \, dx$$

relative to the point s on the line of motion. Use these definitions in Problems 41–42.

41. A spring at rest has potential energy $P = 0$. If the spring constant is 30 lb/ft, how far must the spring be stretched so that its potential energy is 20 ft-lb?

42. A particle with mass m falls freely near the earth's surface. At time $t = 0$, the particle is s_0 units above the ground and is falling with velocity v_0.

    a. Find the potential energy P of the particle in terms of position, s, if the potential energy is 0 when $s = s_0$.

    b. Find the potential energy P and the kinetic energy K of the particle in terms of time t.

43. An object weighs $w = 1,000r^{-2}$ grams, where r is the object's distance from the center of the earth. What work is required to lift the object from the surface of the earth ($r = 6,400$ km) to a point 3,600 km above the surface of the earth?

44. **Modeling Problem** A certain species has population $P(t)$ at time t whose growth rate is affected by seasonal variations in the food supply. Suppose the population may be modeled by the differential equation

$$\frac{dP}{dt} = k(P - A)\cos t$$

where k and A are physical constants. Solve the differential equation and express $P(t)$ in terms of k, A, and P_0, the initial population.

45. Find the center of mass of a thin plate of constant density if the plate occupies the region bounded by the lines $2y = x$, $x + 3y = 5$, and the x-axis.

46. The portion of the ellipse (Figure 6.82)

$$\frac{x^2}{a^2} + \frac{y^2}{b^2} = 1$$

that lies in the first quadrant between $x = r$ and $x = a$, for $0 < r < a$, is revolved about the x-axis to form a solid S. Find the volume of S.

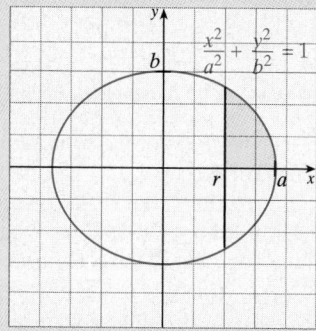

Figure 6.82   Ellipse

47. What is the present value of an investment that will generate income continuously at a constant rate of $1,000/yr for 10 years if the prevailing annual interest rate remains fixed at 7% compounded continuously?

48. In a certain community the fraction of the homes placed on the market that remain unsold for at least t weeks is approximately $f(t) = e^{-0.2t}$. If 200 homes are currently on the market and if additional homes are placed on the market at the rate of 8 per week, approximately how many homes will be on the market 10 weeks from now?

49. The population density r miles from the center of a certain city is $D(r) = 5,000e^{-0.02r^2}$ people/mi^2. How many people live within 5 miles of the center of the city?

50. A certain oil well that yields 900 barrels of crude oil per month will run dry in 3 years. The price of crude oil is currently $16/barrel and is expected to rise at the constant rate of 8¢ per barrel per month. If the oil is sold as soon as it is extracted from the ground, what will be the total future revenue from the well?

51. Suppose that the consumer's demand function for a certain commodity is $D(q) = 50 - 3q - q^2$ dollars per unit.
   a. Find the number of units that will be bought if the market price is $32/unit.
   b. Compute the consumer's surplus when the market price is $32/unit.
   c. Graph the demand curve and interpret the consumer's surplus as an area in relation to this curve.

52. Let R be the part of the ellipse
$$\frac{x^2}{a^2} + \frac{y^2}{b^2} = 1$$
that lies in the first quadrant. Use the theorem of Pappus to find the coordinates of the centroid of R. You may use the facts that R has area $A = \frac{1}{4}\pi ab$, and the semiellipsoid it generates when it is revolved about the x-axis has volume $V = \frac{2}{3}\pi ab^2$.

53. Modeling Problem   A container of a certain fluid is raised from the ground on a pulley. While resting on the ground, the container and fluid together weigh 200 lb. However, as the container is raised, fluid leaks out in such a way that at height x feet above the ground, the total weight of the container and fluid is $200 - 0.5x$ lb. Set up and analyze a model to find the work done in raising the container 100 ft.

54. A bag of sand is being lifted vertically upward at the rate of 31 ft/min. If the bag originally weighed 40 lb and leaks at the rate of 0.2 lb/s, how much work is done in raising it until it is empty?

55. The vertical end of a trough is an equilateral triangle, 3 ft on a side. Assuming the trough is filled with a fluid of density $\rho = 40$ lb/ft^3, find the force on the end of the trough.

56. The radius of a circular water main is 2 ft. Assuming the main is half full of water, find the total force exerted by the water on a gate that crosses the main at one end (see Figure 6.83).

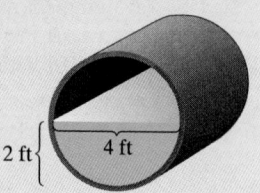

Figure 6.83   Problem 56

57. The force acting on an object moving along a straight line is known to be a linear function of its position. Find the force function F if it is known that 13 ft-lb of work is required to move the object 6 ft and 44 ft-lb of work is required to move it 12 ft.

58. A tank has the shape of a rectangular parallelepiped with length 10 ft, width 6 ft, and height 8 ft. The tank contains a liquid of density $\rho = 20$ lb/ft^3. Find the level of the liquid in the tank if it will require 2,400 ft-lb of work to move all the liquid in the tank to the top.

59. A tank is constructed by placing a right circular cylinder of height 10 ft and radius 2 ft on top of a hemisphere with the same radius (see Figure 6.84).

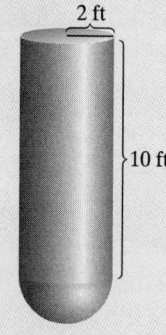

Figure 6.84   Problem 59

If the tank is filled with a fluid of density $\rho = 24$ lb/ft^3, how much work is done in bringing all the fluid to the top of the tank?

60. Modeling Problem   A piston in a cylinder causes a gas either to expand or to contract. Assume the pressure P and the volume of gas V in the cylinder satisfy the adiabatic law (no exchange of heat)
$$P(V^{1.4}) = C$$
where C is a constant.

a. If the gas goes from volume V_1 to volume V_2, show that the work done may be modeled by

$$W = \int_{V_1}^{V_2} CV^{-1.4} \, dV$$

b. How much work is done if 0.6 m³ of steam at a pressure of 2,500 newtons/m² expands 50%?

61. A thin sheet of tin is in the shape of a square, 16 cm on a side. A rectangular corner of area 156 cm² is cut from the square, and the centroid of the portion that remains is found to be 4.88 cm from one side of the original square, as shown in Figure 6.85. How far is it from the other three sides?

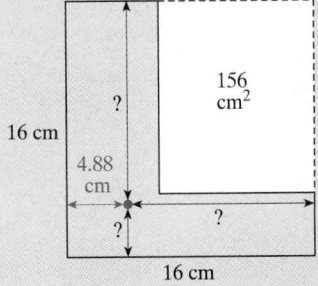

Figure 6.85 Centroid of a region

62. Let R be the region bounded by the semicircle $y = \sqrt{4 - x^2}$ and the x-axis, and let S be the solid with base R and trapezoidal cross sections perpendicular to the x-axis. Assume that the two slant sides and the shorter parallel side are all half the length that lies in the base, as shown in Figure 6.86. Set up and evaluate an integral for the volume of S.

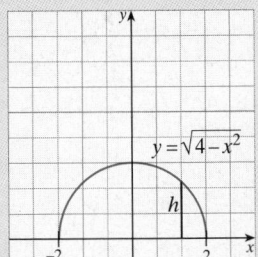 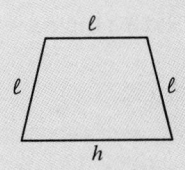

Figure 6.86 Volume of a region S

63. A child is building a sand structure at the beach.

a. Find the work done if the density of the sand is $\rho = 140$ lb/ft³ and the structure is a cone of height 1 ft and diameter 2 ft.

b. What if the structure is a tower (cylinder) of height 1 ft and radius 4 in.?

64. Let S be the solid generated by revolving about the x-axis the region bounded by the parabola $y = x^2$ and the line $y = x$. Find the number A so that the plane perpendicular to the x-axis at $x = A$ divides S in half. That is, the volume on one side of A equals the volume on the other side.

65. A plate in the shape of an isosceles triangle is submerged vertically in water, as shown in Figure 6.87.

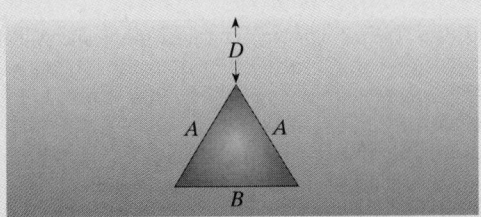

Figure 6.87 Hydrostatic force

a. Find the force on one side of the plate if the two equal sides have length 3, the third side has length 5, and the top vertex of the triangle is 4 units below the surface.

b. Find the fluid force for the general case where the triangle has equal sides of length A, the third side has length B, and the top vertex is D units below the surface.

66. Find the arc length of the curve

$$y = Ax^3 + \frac{B}{x}$$

on the interval $[a, b]$, where A and B are positive constants with $AB = 1/12$.

67. **Counterexample Problem** When the line segment $y = x - 2$ between $x = 1$ and $x = 3$ is revolved about the x-axis, it generates part of a cone. The formula obtained in Section 6.4 says that the surface area of the cone is

$$\int_1^3 2\pi(x - 2)\sqrt{2} \, dx$$

but this integral is equal to 0. What is wrong? What is the actual surface area?

68. HISTORICAL QUEST
Emmy Noether has been called the greatest woman mathematician in the history of mathematics. Once again, we see a woman overcoming great obstacles in achieving her education. At the time she received her Ph.D. at the University of Erlangen (in 1907), the Academic Senate declared that the admission of women students would "overthrow all academic order." Emmy Noether is famous for her work in physics and mathematics. In mathematics, she opened up entire areas for study in the theory of ideals, and in 1921 she published a paper on rings, which have since been called Noetherian rings. Rings and ideals are objects of study in modern algebra. She was not only a renowned mathematician but also an excellent teacher. It has been reported that she often lectured by "working it out as she went." Nevertheless, her students flocked around her "as if following the Pied Piper." In the fall of 1934, pressure from the Nazi regime forced her to immigrate to Bryn Mawr College in Pennsylvania. In the years that followed, there were mass dismissals of "racially undesirable" professors, and many noted European Jewish mathematicians immigrated to American universities. ∎

AMALIE ("EMMY") NOETHER
1882–1935

For this Historical Quest compile a list of notable mathematicians who immigrated to the United States from 1933 to 1940.

69. Modeling Problem An object below the surface of the earth is attracted by a gravitational force that is directly proportional to the square of the distance from the object to the center of the earth. Set up and analyze a model to find the work done in lifting an object weighing P lb from a depth of s feet (below the surface) to the surface. (Assume the earth's radius is 4,000 mi.)

In Problems 70–71, consider a continuous curve $y = f(x)$ that passes through $(-1, 4)$, $(0, 3)$, $(1, 4)$, $(2, 6)$, $(3, 5)$, $(4, 6)$, $(5, 7)$, $(6, 6)$, $(7, 4)$, $(8, 3)$ and $(9, 4)$.

70. Use Simpson's rule to estimate the volume of the solid formed by revolving this curve about the x-axis for $[-1, 9]$. Assume the curve passes through $(9, 4)$.

71. Use the trapezoidal rule to estimate the volume of the solid formed by revolving this curve about the line $y = -1$ on $[-1, 9]$.

72. Modeling Problem In this computational problem we revisit a problem similar to the group research project at the end of Chapter 4, but add a couple of complications. Imagine a cylindrical fuel tank of length L lying on its side; its ends are elliptically shaped and are defined by the equation

$$\left(\frac{x}{a}\right)^2 + \left(\frac{y}{b}\right)^2 = 1$$

We are concerned with the amount of fuel in the tank for a given level.

a. Explain why the area of an end of the tank can be modeled by

$$A = 2a \int_{-b}^{b} \sqrt{1 - \left(\frac{y}{b}\right)^2} \, dy$$

b. By making the right substitution in the integral in part **a**, we can obtain an integral representing half the area inside the circle (with unit radius). Do this and show that the area inside the above ellipse is πab.

c. Explain why the volume of the fuel at level h ($-b \le h \le b$) may be modeled by

$$V(h) = 2La \int_{-b}^{h} \sqrt{1 - \left(\frac{y}{b}\right)^2} \, dy$$

d. For $a = 5$, $b = 4$, and $L = 20$, numerically compute $V(h)$ for $h = -3, -2, \ldots, 3, 4$. *Note:* $V(0)$ and $V(4)$ will serve as a check on your work.

73. We think of the last part of Problem 72 as the "direct" problem: Given a value of h, compute $V(h)$ by a formula. Now we turn to the "inverse" problem: For a set value of V, say V_0, find h such that $V(h) = V_0$. Typically, the inverse problem is more difficult than the direct problem and requires some sort of iterative method to approximate the solution (for example, the Newton-Raphson method). For example, if $V_0 = 500$ ft^3, we could define $f(h) = V(h) - 500$ and seek the relevant zero of f. Set up the necessary computer program to do this and find the h values, to two-decimal-place accuracy, corresponding to these values of V:

a. 500   **b.** 800

Hint: A key to this problem is thinking about $V'(h)$, where $V(h)$ is expressed in Problem 72**c**. Also, for starting values h_0, refer to your work in Problem 72**d**.

74. Find the centroid of a right triangle whose legs have lengths a and b. *Hint:* Use the volume theorem of Pappus.

75. The largest of the pyramids at Giza in Egypt is roughly 480 ft high and has a square base 750 ft on a side. How much work was required to lift the stones to build this pyramid if we assume that the rock in the pyramid had an average density of 160 lb/ft^3?

76. Find the length of the curve $y = e^x$ on the interval $[0, 1]$.

77. Find the volume of the solid generated when the region under the curve

$$y = \frac{1}{\sqrt{9 - x^2}}$$

on the interval $[0, 2]$ is revolved about the y-axis.

78. Find the volume of the solid formed by revolving about the x-axis the region bounded by the curve

$$y = \frac{2}{\sqrt{3x - 2}}$$

the x-axis, and the lines $x = 1$ and $x = 2$.

79. Find the area between the curves $y = \tan^2 x$ and $y = \sec^2 x$ on the interval $\left[0, \frac{\pi}{4}\right]$.

80. Find the surface area of the solid generated by revolving the region bounded by the x-axis and the curve

$$y = e^x + \tfrac{1}{4}e^{-x}$$

on $[0, 1]$ about the x-axis.

81. Find the volume of the solid whose base is the region R bounded by the curve $y = e^x$ and the lines $y = 0$, $x = 0$, $x = 1$, if cross sections perpendicular to the x-axis are equilateral triangles.

82. Find the length of the curve

$$x = \frac{ay^2}{b^2} - \frac{b^2}{8a} \ln \frac{y}{b}$$

between $y = b$ and $y = 2b$.

83. Putnam Examination Problem Find the length of the curve $y^2 = x^3$ from the origin to the point where the tangent makes an angle of $45°$ with the x-axis.

84. Putnam Examination Problem A solid is bounded by two bases in the horizontal planes $z = h/2$ and $z = -h/2$, and by a surface with the property that every horizontal cross section has area given by an expression of the form

$$A = a_0 z^3 + a_1 z^2 + a_2 z + a_3$$

a. Show that the solid has volume $V = \tfrac{1}{6}h(B_1 + B_2 + 4M)$, where B_1 and B_2 are the area of the bases and M is the area of the middle horizontal cross section.

b. Show that the formulas for the volume of a cone and a sphere can be obtained from the formula in part **a** for certain special choices of a_0, a_1, a_2, and a_3.

85. **Putnam Examination Problem** The horizontal line $y = c$ intersects the curve $y = 2x - 3x^3$ in the first quadrant as shown in Figure 6.88. Find c so that the areas of the two shaded regions are equal.

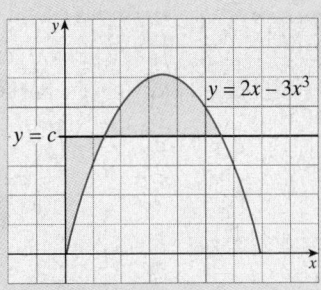

Figure 6.88 Putnam Examination Problem

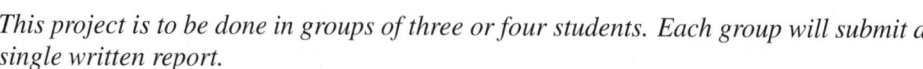

"Houdini's Escape"

This project is to be done in groups of three or four students. Each group will submit a single written report.

Harry Houdini (born Ehrich Weiss) (1874–1926)

Harry Houdini was a famous escape artist. In this project we relive a trick of his that challenged his mathematical prowess, as well as his skill and bravery. It may challenge these qualities in you as well.

Houdini had his feet shackled to the top of a concrete block which was placed on the bottom of a giant laboratory flask. The cross-sectional radius of the flask, measured in feet, was given as a function of height z from the ground by the formula $r(z) = 10z^{-1/2}$, with the bottom of the flask at $z = 1$ ft. The flask was then filled with water at a steady rate of 22π ft^3/min. Houdini's job was to escape the shackles before he was drowned by the rising water in the flask.

Now Houdini knew it would take him exactly 10 minutes to escape the shackles. For dramatic impact, he wanted to time his escape so it was completed precisely at the moment the water level reached the top of his head. Houdini was exactly 6 ft tall. In the design of the apparatus, he was allowed to specify only one thing: the height of the concrete block he stood on.

Your paper is not limited to the following questions but should include these concerns: How high should the block be? (You can neglect Houdini's volume and the volume of the block.) How fast is the water level changing when the flask first starts to fill? How fast is the water level changing at the instant when the water reaches the top of his head? You might also help Houdini with any size flask by generalizing the derivation: Consider a flask with cross-sectional radius $r(z)$, an arbitrary function of z with a constant inflow rate of $dV/dt = A$. Can you find dh/dt as a function of $h(t)$?

MATHEMATICS is the gate and key of the sciences. ... Neglect of mathematics works injury to all knowledge, since he who is ignorant of it cannot know the other sciences or the things of this world. And what is worse, those who are thus ignorant are unable to perceive their own ignorance and so do not seek a remedy.

——Roger Bacon
Opus Majus, Part 4,
Distinctia Prima, cap. 1.

IT SEEMS TO BE EXPECTED of every pilgrim up the slopes of the mathematical Parnassus, that he will at some point or other of his journey sit down and invent a definite integral or two towards the increase of the common stock.

——J. J. Sylvester
"Notes to the Meditation
on Poncelet's Theorem,"
Mathematical Papers,
Vol. 2, p. 214.

[*]*MAA Notes* 17 (1991), "Priming the Calculus Pump: Innovations and Resources," by Marcus S. Cohen, Edward D. Gaughan, R. Arthur Knoebel, Douglas S. Kurtz, and David J. Pengelley.

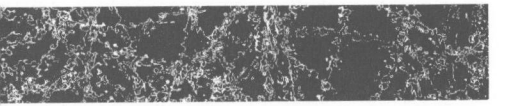

7

Methods of Integration

PREVIEW

In this chapter we increase the number of techniques and procedures for integrating a function. One of the most important techniques, substitution, is reviewed in the first section and is then expanded in several different contexts. Other important integration procedures include using tables, integrating by parts, and using partial fractions. In addition, improper integrals, hyperbolic functions, and inverse hyperbolic functions are discussed, along with first-order differential equations.

PERSPECTIVE

It is possible to differentiate most functions that arise in practice by applying a fairly short list of rules and formulas, but integration is a more complicated process. The purpose of this chapter is to increase your ability to integrate a variety of different functions. Learning to integrate is like learning to play a musical instrument: At first, it may seem impossibly complicated, but if you persevere, after a while music starts to happen. It should be noted that as more powerful technology becomes available, *techniques* become less important and *ideas* become more important. If you have such technology available, you might wish to consult the *Technology Manual*.

7.1   Review of Substitution and Integration by Table

IN THIS SECTION   review of substitution, using tables of integrals

In Chapter 5, we derived a number of integration formulas and examined various algebraic procedures for reducing a given integral to a form that can be handled by these formulas. In this section, we review those formulas as well as the important method of integration by substitution. Today's technology has greatly enhanced the ability of professional mathematicians and scientists in techniques of integration, thereby minimizing the need for spending hours learning rarely used integration techniques. Along with this new technology, the use of integral tables has increased in importance. Most mathematical handbooks contain extensive integral tables, and we have included such an integration table in the accompanying *Student Mathematics Handbook.* For your convenience, we have also included a short table of integrals in Appendix D and will refer to these integrals by number throughout the rest of the book.

For easy reference, the most important integration rules and formulas are listed inside the back cover. Notice that the first four integration formulas are the procedural rules, which allow us to break up integrals into simpler forms, whereas those on the remainder of the page form the building blocks of integration.

REVIEW OF SUBSTITUTION

Remember that when doing substitution you must choose u, calculate du, and then substitute to make the form you are integrating look *exactly like* one of the known integration formulas. We will review substitution by looking at different situations and special substitutions that prove useful.

EXAMPLE 1   Integration by substitution

Find $\displaystyle\int \frac{x^2\,dx}{(x^3-2)^5}$.

Solution

Let u be the value in parentheses; that is, let $u = x^3 - 2$. Then $du = 3x^2\,dx$, so by substitution,

$$\int \frac{x^2\,dx}{(x^3-2)^5} = \int \frac{\frac{du}{3}}{u^5} = \frac{1}{3}\int u^{-5}\,du \qquad \text{All } x\text{'s must be eliminated.}$$

$$= \frac{1}{3}\frac{u^{-4}}{-4} + C = -\frac{1}{12}(x^3-2)^{-4} + C$$

You can check your work by finding the derivative of your answer to see if you obtain the integrand. For this example,

$$\frac{d}{dx}\left[-\frac{1}{12}(x^3-2)^{-4} + C\right] = -\frac{1}{12}\left[-4(x^3-2)^{-5}(3x^2) + 0\right]$$

$$= \frac{x^2}{(x^3-2)^5} \qquad\blacksquare$$

EXAMPLE 2   Fitting the form of a known integration formula by substitution

Find $\displaystyle\int \frac{t\,dt}{\sqrt{1-t^4}}$.

Solution

We notice the similarity between this and the formula for inverse sine if we let $a = 1$ and $u = t^2$. Then $du = 2t\,dt$ and

Formula 22, Appendix D (inverse sine):

$$\int \frac{du}{\sqrt{a^2 - u^2}} = \sin^{-1} \frac{u}{a}$$

$$\int \frac{t\,dt}{\sqrt{1 - t^4}} = \int \frac{\frac{du}{2}}{\sqrt{1 - u^2}}$$

> If $u = t^2$, then $du = 2t\,dt$, $t\,dt = \dfrac{du}{2}$, and $\sqrt{1 - t^4} = \sqrt{1 - (t^2)^2} = \sqrt{1 - u^2}$.

$$= \frac{1}{2} \int \frac{du}{\sqrt{1 - u^2}} \qquad \text{\textit{Don't forget the factor} } \tfrac{1}{2}.$$

$$= \tfrac{1}{2} \sin^{-1} u + C = \tfrac{1}{2} \sin^{-1} t^2 + C \qquad \blacksquare$$

The method of substitution (Section 5.5) is very important, because many of the techniques developed in this chapter will be used in conjunction with substitution. Examples 3 and 4 illustrate additional ways substitution can be used in integration problems.

EXAMPLE 3   Multiplication by 1 to derive an integration formula

Find $\displaystyle\int \sec x\,dx$.

Solution

Multiply the integrand $\sec x$ by $\sec x + \tan x$ and divide by the same quantity:

$$\int \sec x\,dx = \int \frac{\sec x(\sec x + \tan x)}{\sec x + \tan x}\,dx = \int \frac{\sec^2 x + \sec x \tan x}{\sec x + \tan x}\,dx$$

The advantage of this rearrangement is that the numerator is now the derivative of the denominator. That is, using the substitution

$$\boxed{\begin{aligned} u &= \tan x + \sec x \\ du &= (\sec^2 x + \sec x \tan x)\,dx \end{aligned}}$$

we find

$$\int \frac{\sec^2 x + \sec x \tan x}{\sec x + \tan x}\,dx = \int \frac{du}{u} = \ln|u| + C = \ln|\sec x + \tan x| + C \qquad \blacksquare$$

You may wonder why anyone would think to multiply and divide the integrand $\sec x$ in Example 3 by $\sec x + \tan x$. To say that we do it "because it works" is probably not a very satisfying answer. However, techniques like this are passed on from generation to generation, and it should be noted that multiplication by 1 is a common method in mathematics for changing the form of an expression to one that can be manipulated more easily.

EXAMPLE 4   Substitution after an algebraic manipulation and polynomial division

Find $\displaystyle\int \frac{dx}{1 + e^x}$.

Solution

The straightforward substitution $u = 1 + e^x$ does not work:

$$\int \frac{dx}{1 + e^x} = \int \frac{\frac{du}{e^x}}{u} = \int \frac{du}{e^x u} \qquad \text{\textit{This is not an appropriate form because }} x \text{ \textit{has not been eliminated.}}$$

$$\boxed{u = 1 + e^x; \quad du = e^x\,dx}$$

Instead rewrite the integrand as follows:

$$\frac{1}{1 + e^x} = \frac{e^{-x}}{e^{-x}} \left(\frac{1}{1 + e^x} \right) = \frac{e^{-x}}{e^{-x} + 1}; \quad \text{then make the substitution}$$

$$u = e^{-x} + 1; \quad du = -e^{-x}\, dx$$

$$\int \frac{dx}{1 + e^x} = \int \frac{e^{-x}\, dx}{e^{-x} + 1} = \int \frac{-du}{u} = -\ln|u| + C = -\ln(e^{-x} + 1) + C$$

Remember, $e^{-x} + 1 > 0$ for all x, so $\ln\left|e^{-x} + 1\right| = \ln(e^{-x} + 1)$. ∎

When the integrand involves terms with fractional exponents, it is usually a good idea to choose the substitution $x = u^n$, where n is the smallest integer that is divisible by all the denominators of the exponents (that is, the least common multiple of the denominators). For example, if the integrand involves terms such as $x^{1/4}, x^{2/3}$, and $x^{1/6}$, then the substitution $x = u^{12}$ is suggested, because 12 is the smallest integer divisible by the exponential denominators $4, 3$, and 6. The advantage of this policy is that it guarantees that each fractional power of x becomes an integral power of u. Thus,

$$x^{1/6} = (u^{12})^{1/6} = u^2, \quad x^{1/4} = (u^{12})^{1/4} = u^3, \quad x^{2/3} = (u^{12})^{2/3} = u^8$$

EXAMPLE 5 Substitution with fractional exponents

Find $\displaystyle\int \frac{dx}{x^{1/3} + x^{1/2}}$.

Solution

Because 6 is the smallest integer divisible by the denominators 2 and 3, we set $u = x^{1/6}$, so that $u^6 = x$ and $6u^5\, du = dx$. We now use substitution

$$\int \frac{dx}{x^{1/3} + x^{1/2}} = \int \frac{6u^5\, du}{(u^6)^{1/3} + (u^6)^{1/2}} \qquad \text{Let } x = u^6.$$

$$= \int \frac{6u^5\, du}{u^2 + u^3} = \int \frac{6u^5\, du}{u^2(1 + u)} = \int \frac{6u^3\, du}{1 + u}$$

Substitution does not guarantee an obvious integrable form. When the degree of the numerator is greater than or equal to the degree of the denominator, division is often helpful. By long division

$$\frac{6u^3}{1 + u} = 6u^2 - 6u + 6 + \frac{-6}{1 + u}$$

$$\int \frac{6u^3\, du}{1 + u} = \int \left(6u^2 - 6u + 6 + \frac{-6}{1 + u} \right) du$$

$$= 2u^3 - 3u^2 + 6u - 6\ln|1 + u| + C$$

$$= 2(x^{1/6})^3 - 3(x^{1/6})^2 + 6x^{1/6} - 6\ln\left|1 + x^{1/6}\right| + C \quad \text{Because } u = x^{1/6}$$

$$= 2x^{1/2} - 3x^{1/3} + 6x^{1/6} - 6\ln(1 + x^{1/6}) + C \qquad \text{Note: } 1 + x^{1/6} > 0$$

∎

USING TABLES OF INTEGRALS

Example 5 (especially the part involving long division) seems particularly lengthy. When faced with the necessity of integrating a function such as

$$\int \frac{6u^3\, du}{1 + u}$$

most people would turn to a computer, calculator, or a table of integrals. If you look, for example, at the short integration table (Appendix D), you will find (Formula 37)

$$\int \frac{u^3 \, du}{au + b} = \frac{(au + b)^3}{3a^4} - \frac{3b(au + b)^2}{2a^4} + \frac{3b^2(au + b)}{a^4} - \frac{b^3}{a^4} \ln |au + b|$$

If we let $a = 1$ and $b = 1$, we find

$$\int \frac{6u^3 \, du}{1 + u} = 6 \left[\frac{(u + 1)^3}{3} - \frac{3(u + 1)^2}{2} + \frac{3(u + 1)}{1} - \ln |u + 1| \right] + C$$
$$= 2(u + 1)^3 - 9(u + 1)^2 + 18(u + 1) - 6 \ln |u + 1| + C$$

When using integration tables, we note that the algebraic form does not always match the form we obtain by direct integration. You might wish to show algebraically that the form we have just found and the form

$$2u^3 - 3u^2 + 6u - 6 \ln |1 + u| + C$$

from Example 5 differ by a constant and hence are equivalent.

To use an integral table, first classify the integral by form. To facilitate substitution of forms, we use u as the variable of integration, and let a, b, c, m, and n represent constants. The forms listed in the table of integrals included in the *Student Mathematics Handbook* are as follows:

Elementary forms (Formulas 1–29; these were developed in the text)

Linear and quadratic forms (Formulas 30–134)
   Forms involving $au + b$; $u^2 + a^2$; $u^2 - a^2$; $a^2 - u^2$; $au + b$ and $pu + q$; $au^2 + bu + c$

Radical forms (Formulas 135–270)
   Forms involving $\sqrt{au + b}$; both $\sqrt{au + b}$ and $pu + q$; both $\sqrt{au + b}$ and $\sqrt{pu + q}$; $\sqrt{u^2 + a^2}$; $\sqrt{u^2 - a^2}$; $\sqrt{a^2 - u^2}$; $\sqrt{au^2 + bu + c}$

Higher degree binomials (Formulas 271–310)
   Forms involving $u^3 + a^3$; $u^4 \pm a^4$, $u^n \pm a^n$

Trigonometric forms (Formulas 311–444)
   Forms involving $\cos au$; $\sin au$; both $\sin au$ and $\cos au$; $\tan au$; $\cot au$; $\sec au$; $\csc au$

Inverse trigonometric forms (Formulas 445–482)

Exponential and logarithmic forms (Formulas 483–513)
   Forms involving e^{au}; $\ln |u|$

Hyperbolic forms (Formulas 514–619; we study these in Section 7.8)
   Forms involving $\cosh au$; $\sinh au$; $\sinh au$ and $\cosh au$; $\tanh au$; $\coth au$; $\text{sech } au$; $\text{csch } au$

Inverse hyperbolic forms (Formulas 620–650; Section 7.8)

A condensed version of this table is provided in Appendix D.

There is a common misconception that integration will be easy if a table is provided, but even with a table available there can be a considerable amount of work. After deciding which form applies, match the individual type with the problem at hand by making appropriate choices for the arbitrary constants. More than one form may apply, but the results derived by using different formulas will be the same (except for the constants) even though they may look quite different. We will not include the constants in the table listing, but you should remember to include them with your answers when using the table for integration.

SMH

Take a few moments to look at the integration table in the *Student Mathematics Handbook* (or Appendix D). Notice that the table has two basic types of integration formulas. The first gives a formula that is the antiderivative, whereas the second, called a *reduction formula*, simply rewrites the integral in another form. The following illustration demonstrates each of these forms.

Table of Integrals

Integrals Involving $au + b$

30. $\displaystyle \int (au + b)^n \, du = \frac{(au + b)^{n+1}}{(n + 1)a}$

31. $\displaystyle \int u(au + b)^n \, du = \frac{(au + b)^{n+2}}{(n + 2)a^2} - \frac{b(au + b)^{n+1}}{(n + 1)a^2}$

32. $\displaystyle \int u^2(au + b)^n \, du = \frac{(au + b)^{n+3}}{(n + 3)a^3} - \frac{2b(au + b)^{n+2}}{(n + 2)a^3} + \frac{b^2(au + b)^{n+1}}{(n + 1)a^3}$

33. $\displaystyle \int u^m(au + b)^n \, du = \begin{cases} \dfrac{u^{m+1}(au + b)^n}{m + n + 1} + \dfrac{nb}{m + n + 1} \displaystyle\int u^m(au + b)^{n-1} \, du \\[3ex] \dfrac{u^m(au + b)^{n+1}}{(m + n + 1)a} - \dfrac{mb}{(m + n + 1)a} \displaystyle\int u^{m-1}(au + b)^n \, du \\[3ex] \dfrac{-u^{m+1}(au + b)^{n+1}}{(n + 1)b} - \dfrac{m + n + 2}{(n + 1)b} \displaystyle\int u^m(au + b)^{n+1} \, du \end{cases}$

34. $\displaystyle \int \frac{du}{au + b} = \frac{1}{a} \ln|au + b|$

EXAMPLE 6 Integration using a table of integrals

Find $\displaystyle \int x^2(3 - x)^5 \, dx$.

Solution

We can evaluate this integral using substitution:

$$\int x^2(3 - x)^5 \, dx = \int (3 - u)^2 u^5 \, (-du)$$

$$\boxed{u = 3 - x; \, du = -dx}$$

$$= \int (-u^7 + 6u^6 - 9u^5) \, du$$

$$= -\frac{u^8}{8} + \frac{6u^7}{7} - \frac{9u^6}{6} + C$$

$$= -\tfrac{1}{8}(3 - x)^8 + \tfrac{6}{7}(3 - x)^7 - \tfrac{3}{2}(3 - x)^6 + C$$

Even though this was not too difficult, it is a bit tedious, so we might think to evaluate this integral by using a table of integrals. This is an integral involving an expression of the form $au + b$; we find that this is Formula 32, where $u = x$, $a = -1$, $b = 3$, and $n = 5$.

$$\int x^2(3 - x)^5 \, dx = \frac{(3 - x)^{5+3}}{(5 + 3)(-1)^3} - \frac{2(3)(3 - x)^{5+2}}{(5 + 2)(-1)^3} + \frac{3^2(3 - x)^{5+1}}{(5 + 1)(-1)^3} + C$$

$$= -\tfrac{1}{8}(3 - x)^8 + \tfrac{6}{7}(3 - x)^7 - \tfrac{3}{2}(3 - x)^6 + C$$

One of the difficult considerations when using tables or computer software to carry out integration is recognizing the variety of different forms for acceptable answers. Note that it is not easy to show that these forms are algebraically equivalent. If we use computer software for this evaluation, we find yet another algebraically equivalent form:

$$\int x^2(3-x)^5 \, dx = -\frac{x^8}{8} + \frac{15x^7}{7} - 15x^6 + 54x^5 - \frac{405x^4}{4} + 81x^3$$

Once again, remember that you must add the $+C$ to the computer software form. ∎

EXAMPLE 7   Integration using a reduction formula from a table of integrals

Find $\int (\ln x)^4 \, dx$ for $x > 0$.

Solution

The integrand is in logarithmic form; from the table of integrals we see that Formula 501 applies, where $u = x$ and $n = 4$. Take a close look at Formulas 499–502, and note that Formula 501 gives another integral as part of the result.

Integrals Involving ln $|u|$
499. $\displaystyle\int \ln|u| \, du = u \ln|u| - u$
500. $\displaystyle\int (\ln|u|)^2 \, du = u\,(\ln|u|)^2 - 2u \ln|u| + 2u$
501. $\displaystyle\int (\ln|u|)^n \, du = u\,(\ln|u|)^n - n \int (\ln|u|)^{n-1} \, du$
502. $\displaystyle\int u \ln|u| \, du = \frac{u^2}{2}\left(\ln|u| - \frac{1}{2}\right)$

This is called a **reduction formula** because it enables us to compute the given integral in terms of an integral of a similar type, only with a lower power in the integral.

$$\int (\ln x)^4 \, dx = x(\ln x)^4 - 4 \int (\ln x)^{4-1} \, dx \qquad \text{Formula 501}$$

$$= x(\ln x)^4 - 4\left[x(\ln x)^3 - 3 \int (\ln x)^{3-1} \, dx\right] \qquad \text{Formula 501 again}$$

$$= x(\ln x)^4 - 4x(\ln x)^3 + 12 \int (\ln x)^2 \, dx$$

$$= x(\ln x)^4 - 4x(\ln x)^3 + 12\left[x(\ln x)^2 - 2x \ln x + 2x\right] + C$$

$$\qquad \qquad \qquad \qquad \qquad \text{This is Formula 500.}$$

$$= x(\ln x)^4 - 4x(\ln x)^3 + 12x(\ln x)^2 - 24x \ln x + 24x + C \qquad ∎$$

Reduction formulas in a table of integrals, such as the one illustrated in Example 7, are usually obtained using substitution and integration by parts (which we will do in Section 7.2).

Note from the previous example that we follow the convention of adding the constant C only after eliminating the last integral sign (rather than being technically correct and writing $C_1, C_2, \ldots$ for *each* integral). The reason we can do this is that $C_1 + C_2 + \cdots = C$, for arbitrary constants.

It is often necessary to make substitutions before using one of the integration formulas, as shown in the following example.

EXAMPLE 8   Using an integral table after substitution

Find $\displaystyle\int \frac{x\,dx}{\sqrt{8-5x^2}}$.

Solution

(SMH)   This is an integral of the form $\sqrt{a^2-u^2}$, but it does not exactly match any of the formulas.

Integrals Involving $\sqrt{a^2-u^2}$
224. $\displaystyle\int \frac{du}{\sqrt{a^2-u^2}} = \sin^{-1}\frac{u}{a}$
225. $\displaystyle\int \frac{u\,du}{\sqrt{a^2-u^2}} = -\sqrt{a^2-u^2}$
226. $\displaystyle\int \frac{u^2\,du}{\sqrt{a^2-u^2}} = -\frac{u\sqrt{a^2-u^2}}{2} + \frac{a^2}{2}\sin^{-1}\frac{u}{a}$

Note, however, that except for the coefficient of 5, it is like Formula 225. Let $u = \sqrt{5}\,x$ (so $u^2 = 5x^2$); then $du = \sqrt{5}\,dx$:

$$\int \frac{x\,dx}{\sqrt{8-5x^2}} = \int \frac{\frac{u}{\sqrt{5}}\cdot\frac{du}{\sqrt{5}}}{\sqrt{8-u^2}}$$

> Let $u = \sqrt{5}\,x$ so that $x = \dfrac{u}{\sqrt{5}}$;
>
> $du = \sqrt{5}\,dx$ so that $dx = \dfrac{du}{\sqrt{5}}$

$$= \frac{1}{5}\int \frac{u\,du}{\sqrt{8-u^2}}$$

Now apply Formula 225, where $a^2 = 8$:

$$\frac{1}{5}\int \frac{u\,du}{\sqrt{8-u^2}} = \frac{1}{5}\left(-\sqrt{8-u^2}\right) + C = -\frac{1}{5}\sqrt{8-5x^2} + C \qquad \blacksquare$$

As you can see from Example 8, using an integral table is not a trivial task. In fact, other methods of integration may be preferable. For Example 8, you can let $u = 8-5x^2$ and integrate by substitution:

> Let $u = 8 - 5x^2$; $du = -10x\,dx$

$$\int \frac{x\,dx}{\sqrt{8-5x^2}} = \int \frac{x\left(\dfrac{du}{-10x}\right)}{\sqrt{u}} = -\frac{1}{10}\int u^{-1/2}\,du$$

$$= -\frac{1}{10}(2u^{1/2}) + C = -\frac{1}{5}\sqrt{8-5x^2} + C$$

Of course, this answer is the same as the one we obtained in Example 8. The point of this calculation is to emphasize that you should try simple methods of integration before turning to the table of integrals.

EXAMPLE 9   Integration by table (multiple forms with substitution)

Find $\displaystyle\int 5x^2\sqrt{3x^2+1}\,dx$.

Solution

This is similar to Formula 170, but you must take care of the 5 (constant multiple) and the 3 (by making a substitution).

Integrals Involving $\sqrt{u^2 + a^2}$
168. $\displaystyle\int \sqrt{u^2 + a^2}\, du = \dfrac{u\sqrt{u^2 + a^2}}{2} + \dfrac{a^2}{2}\ln\left|u + \sqrt{u^2 + a^2}\right|$
169. $\displaystyle\int u\sqrt{u^2 + a^2}\, du = \dfrac{(u^2 + a^2)^{3/2}}{3}$
170. $\displaystyle\int u^2\sqrt{u^2 + a^2}\, du = \dfrac{u(u^2 + a^2)^{3/2}}{4} - \dfrac{a^2 u\sqrt{u^2 + a^2}}{8} - \dfrac{a^4}{8}\ln\left|u + \sqrt{u^2 + a^2}\right|$

$$\boxed{\text{Let } u = \sqrt{3}\,x;\; du = \sqrt{3}\,dx}$$

$$\int 5x^2\sqrt{3x^2 + 1}\, dx = 5\int \left(\frac{u^2}{3}\right)\sqrt{u^2 + 1}\,\frac{du}{\sqrt{3}}$$

$$u^2 = 3x^2 \text{ so that } x^2 = \frac{u^2}{3}$$

$$= \frac{5}{3\sqrt{3}}\int u^2\sqrt{u^2 + 1}\, du \qquad \text{Use Formula 170, where } a = 1.$$

$$= \frac{5}{3\sqrt{3}}\left[\frac{u(u^2 + 1)^{3/2}}{4} - \frac{u\sqrt{u^2 + 1}}{8} - \frac{1}{8}\ln\left|u + \sqrt{u^2 + 1}\right|\right] + C$$

$$= \frac{5}{24\sqrt{3}}\left[2\sqrt{3}\,x(3x^2 + 1)^{3/2} - \sqrt{3}\,x\sqrt{3x^2 + 1} - \ln\left|\sqrt{3}\,x + \sqrt{3x^2 + 1}\right|\right] + C$$

$$= \frac{5}{24}\left[2x(3x^2 + 1)^{3/2} - x\sqrt{3x^2 + 1} - \frac{1}{\sqrt{3}}\ln\left(\sqrt{3}\,x + \sqrt{3x^2 + 1}\right)\right] + C$$

You might want to show that $u + \sqrt{u^2 + 1} > 0$.

If you use a calculator or computer, you will probably obtain an alternate, but equivalent, form:

$$-\frac{5\sqrt{3}\ln\left|\sqrt{3x^2 + 1} + \sqrt{3}\,x\right|}{72} - \frac{5x\sqrt{3x^2 + 1}\,(6x^2 + 1)}{24}$$

■

7.1 PROBLEM SET

A *Find each integral in Problems 1–12.*

1. $\displaystyle\int \frac{2x + 5}{\sqrt{x^2 + 5x}}\, dx$

2. $\displaystyle\int \frac{\ln x}{x}\, dx$

3. $\displaystyle\int \frac{dx}{x\ln x}$

4. $\displaystyle\int \cos x\, e^{\sin x}\, dx$

5. $\displaystyle\int \frac{x\, dx}{4 + x^4}$

6. $\displaystyle\int \frac{t^2\, dt}{9 + t^6}$

7. $\displaystyle\int (1 + \cot x)^4 \csc^2 x\, dx$

8. $\displaystyle\int \frac{4x^3 - 4x}{x^4 - 2x^2 + 3}\, dx$

9. $\displaystyle\int \frac{x^3 - x}{(x^4 - 2x^2 + 3)^2}\, dx$

10. $\displaystyle\int \frac{2x + 4}{x^2 + 4x + 3}\, dx$

11. $\displaystyle\int \frac{2x + 1}{x^2 + x + 1}\, dx$

12. $\displaystyle\int \frac{2x - 1}{(4x^2 - 4x)^2}\, dx$

Integrate the expressions in Problems 13–24 using the short table of integrals given in Appendix D.

13. $\displaystyle\int \frac{dx}{x^2\sqrt{x^2 - a^2}}$

14. $\displaystyle\int \frac{dx}{x^2\sqrt{a^2 - x^2}}$

15. $\displaystyle\int x\ln x\, dx$

16. $\displaystyle\int \ln x\, dx$

17. $\displaystyle\int xe^{ax}\, dx$

18. $\displaystyle\int \frac{dx}{a + be^{2x}}$

19. $\displaystyle\int \frac{x^2\,dx}{\sqrt{x^2+1}}$

20. $\displaystyle\int \frac{dx}{x^2\sqrt{x^2+16}}$

21. $\displaystyle\int \frac{x\,dx}{\sqrt{4x^2+1}}$

22. $\displaystyle\int \frac{dx}{x\sqrt{1-9x^2}}$

23. $\displaystyle\int e^{-4x}\sin 5x\,dx$

24. $\displaystyle\int x\sin^{-1}x\,dx$

Evaluate the integrals in Problems 25–33. If you use the integral table, state the number of the formula used, and if you use substitution, show each step. If you use an alternative table of integrals, then cite the source as well as the formula.

25. $\displaystyle\int (1+bx)^{-1}\,dx$

26. $\displaystyle\int \frac{x\,dx}{\sqrt{a^2-x^2}}$

27. $\displaystyle\int x(1+x)^3\,dx$

28. $\displaystyle\int x\sqrt{1+x}\,dx$

29. $\displaystyle\int xe^{4x}\,dx$

30. $\displaystyle\int x\ln 2x\,dx$

31. $\displaystyle\int \frac{dx}{1+e^{2x}}$

32. $\displaystyle\int \ln^3 x\,dx$

33. $\displaystyle\int \frac{x^3\,dx}{\sqrt{4x^4+1}}$

B   *Use the Student Mathematics Handbook or other available integration tables to find the integrals given in Problems 34–39. Cite the formula number or source you are using.*

(SMH)

34. $\displaystyle\int \frac{\sqrt{4x^2+1}}{x}\,dx$

35. $\displaystyle\int \sec^3\left(\frac{x}{2}\right)dx$

36. $\displaystyle\int \sin^6 x\,dx$

37. $\displaystyle\int \frac{dx}{9x^2+6x+1}$

38. $\displaystyle\int (9-x^2)^{3/2}\,dx$

39. $\displaystyle\int \frac{\sin^2 x}{\cos x}\,dx$

40. Derive the **sine squared formula** shown on the inside back cover (Formula 348):

$$\int \sin^2 x\,dx = \tfrac{1}{2}x - \tfrac{1}{4}\sin 2x + C$$

Hint: Use the identity $\sin^2 x = \dfrac{1-\cos 2x}{2}$.

41. Derive the **cosine squared formula** shown on the inside back cover (Formula 317):

$$\int \cos^2 x\,dx = \tfrac{1}{2}x + \tfrac{1}{4}\sin 2x + C$$

Hint: Use the identity $\cos^2 x = \dfrac{1+\cos 2x}{2}$.

Problems 42–44 use substitution to integrate certain powers of sine and cosine.

42. $\displaystyle\int \sin^4 x\cos x\,dx$ *Hint:* Let $u=\sin x$.

43. $\displaystyle\int \sin^3 x\cos^4 x\,dx$ *Hint:* Let $u=\cos x$.

44. $\displaystyle\int \sin^2 x\cos^2 x\,dx$ *Hint:* Use the identities shown in Problems 40 and 41.

45. Exploration Problem   Using Problems 42–44 formulate a procedure for integrals of the form

$$\int \sin^m x\,\cos^n x\,dx$$

Find each integral in Problems 46–51.

46. $\displaystyle\int \frac{e^x\,dx}{1+e^{x/2}}$

47. $\displaystyle\int \frac{dx}{x^{1/2}+x^{1/4}}$

48. $\displaystyle\int \frac{4\,dx}{x^{1/3}+2x^{1/2}}$

49. $\displaystyle\int \frac{18\tan^2 t\sec^2 t}{(2+\tan^3 t)^2}\,dt$

50. $\displaystyle\int \frac{dx}{\left(x+\frac{1}{2}\right)\sqrt{4x^2+4x}}$

51. $\displaystyle\int \frac{e^{-x}-e^x}{e^{2x}+e^{-2x}+2}\,dx$

52. Find the area of the region bounded by the graphs of $y=\dfrac{2x}{\sqrt{x^2+9}}$ and $y=0$ from $x=0$ to $x=4$.

53. Find the volume of the solid generated when the region under the curve

$$y=\frac{x^{3/2}}{\sqrt{x^2+9}}$$

between $x=0$ and $x=9$ is revolved about the x-axis.

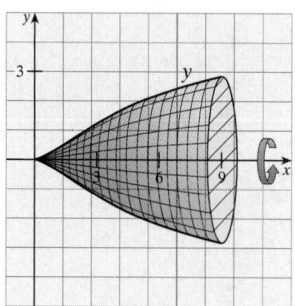

54. Find the volume of the solid generated when the curve $y=x(1-x^2)^{1/4}$ from $x=0$ to $x=1$ is revolved about the x-axis.

55. Find the volume of the solid generated when the curve

$$y=\frac{1}{\sqrt{x}}(1+\sqrt{x})^{1/3}$$

between $x=1$ and $x=4$ is revolved about the y-axis.

56. Find the volume of the solid generated when the curve $x=\sqrt[4]{4-y^2}$ between $y=1$ and $y=2$ is revolved about the y-axis.

57. Let $y=f(x)$ be a function that satisfies the differential equation

$$xy'=\sqrt{(\ln x)^2-x^2}$$

Find the arc length of $y=f(x)$ between $x=\frac{1}{4}$ and $x=\frac{1}{2}$.

58. Find the arc length of the curve $y=\ln(\cos x)$ on the interval $[0,\pi/4]$.

59. Find the area of the surface generated when the curve $y=x^2$ on the interval $[0,1]$ is revolved about the x-axis.

60. Find the area of the surface generated when the curve $y=x^2$ on the interval $[0,1]$ is revolved about the y-axis.

61. Show that $\displaystyle\int \csc x\,dx = -\ln|\csc x+\cot x|+C.$

Hint: Multiply the integrand by $\dfrac{\csc x+\cot x}{\csc x+\cot x}$.

62. Find $\displaystyle\int 2\sin x\cos x\,dx$ by using the indicated substitution.

a. Let $u=\cos x$.

b. Let $u = \sin x$.

c. Write $2 \sin x \cos x = \sin 2x$ and carry out the integration.

d. Show that the answers you obtained for parts **a–c** are the same.

C **63.** Derive the formula

$$\int_0^\pi x f(\sin x)\,dx = \frac{\pi}{2} \int_0^\pi f(\sin x)\,dx$$

64. Find the surface area of the torus generated when the circle

$$x^2 + (y - b)^2 = 1, \qquad b > 1$$

is revolved about the x-axis.

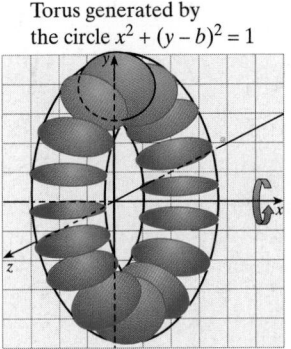

Torus generated by
the circle $x^2 + (y - b)^2 = 1$

7.2   Integration by Parts

IN THIS SECTION integration by parts formula, repeated use of integration by parts, definite integration by parts

Integration by parts is a procedure based on reversing the product rule for differentiation. We present this section not only as a technique of integration but also as a procedure that is necessary in a variety of useful applications.

INTEGRATION BY PARTS FORMULA

Recall the formula for differentiation of a product. If u and v are differentiable functions, then

$$d(uv) = u\,dv + v\,du$$

Integrate both sides of this equation to find the formula for integration by parts:

$$\int d(uv) = \int u\,dv + \int v\,du$$

$$uv = \int u\,dv + \int v\,du$$

If we rewrite this last equation, we obtain the formula summarized in the following box.

Formula for Integration by Parts

$$\int u\,dv = uv - \int v\,du$$

EXAMPLE 1   Integration by parts

Find $\int x e^x\,dx$.

Solution

To use integration by parts, we must choose u and dv so that the new integral is easier to integrate than the original.

$$\int \underbrace{x}_{u} \underbrace{e^x \, dx}_{dv}$$

> Let $u = x$ and $dv = e^x \, dx$
> $du = dx$ $v = \int e^x \, dx = e^x$

$$\int xe^x \, dx = \underbrace{x}_{u} \underbrace{e^x}_{v} - \int \underbrace{e^x}_{v} \underbrace{dx}_{du} = xe^x - e^x + C$$

You can check your work with integration by parts by differentiating, using software, or using the integration table found in Appendix D or the *Student Mathematics Handbook* (Formula 484, with $a = 1$). ∎

Note: You may wonder why an arbitrary constant (call it K) was not included when performing the integration associated with $\int dv$ in integration by parts. The reason is that when applying integration by parts, we need just *one* function v whose derivative is dv, so we take the simplest one—the one with $K = 0$. You may find it instructive to see that taking $v = e^x + K$ gives the same result.

Integration by parts is often difficult the first time you try to do it because there is no absolute choice for u and dv. In Example 1, you might have chosen

$$u = e^x \qquad \text{and} \quad dv = x \, dx$$
$$du = e^x \, dx \qquad v = \int x \, dx = \frac{x^2}{2}$$

Then

$$\int xe^x \, dx = \underbrace{e^x}_{u} \underbrace{\frac{x^2}{2}}_{v} - \int \underbrace{\frac{x^2}{2}}_{v} \underbrace{e^x \, dx}_{du}$$

$$= \frac{1}{2}x^2 e^x - \frac{1}{2} \int x^2 e^x \, dx$$

Note, however, that this choice of u and dv leads to a more complicated form than the original. In general, when you are integrating by parts, if you make a choice for u and dv that leads to a more complicated form than when you started, consider going back and making another choice for u and dv.

Generally, you want to choose dv to be as difficult as possible (and still be something you can integrate), with the remainder being left for the u-factor.

EXAMPLE 2   When the differentiable part is the entire integrand

Find $\int \ln x \, dx$ for $x > 0$.

Solution

> Let $u = \ln x$ and $dv = dx$
> $du = \dfrac{1}{x} \, dx$ $v = x$

$$\int \ln x \, dx = (\ln x)x - \int x\frac{1}{x} \, dx = x \ln x - \int dx = x \ln x - x + C$$

Check with Formula 499 (Appendix D), where $a = 1$, which we worked as Problem 16 of Problem Set 7.1. ∎

REPEATED USE OF INTEGRATION BY PARTS

Sometimes integration by parts must be applied several times to evaluate a given integral.

EXAMPLE 3   Repeated integration by parts

Find $\int x^2 e^{-x}\, dx$.

Solution

$$
\boxed{\begin{array}{ll} \text{Let } u = x^2 & \text{and } dv = e^{-x}\, dx \\ \quad du = 2x\, dx & \qquad v = -e^{-x} \end{array}}
$$

$$
\int x^2 e^{-x}\, dx = x^2(-e^{-x}) - \int (-e^{-x})(2x\, dx)
$$

$$
= -x^2 e^{-x} + 2 \int x e^{-x}\, dx
$$

$$
\boxed{\begin{array}{ll} \text{Let } u = x & \text{and } dv = e^{-x}\, dx \\ \quad du = dx & \qquad v = -e^{-x} \end{array}}
$$

$$
= -x^2 e^{-x} + 2\left[x(-e^{-x}) - \int (-e^{-x})\, dx \right]
$$

Do not forget the grouping symbols here.

$$
= -x^2 e^{-x} - 2x e^{-x} - 2e^{-x} + C
$$

$$
= -e^{-x}(x^2 + 2x + 2) + C
$$

Check with Formula 485, where $a = -1$.   ∎

In the following example, it is necessary to apply integration by parts more than once, but as you will see, when we do so a second time we return to the original integral. Note carefully how this situation can be handled algebraically.

EXAMPLE 4   Repeated integration by parts with algebraic manipulation

Find $\int e^{2x} \sin x\, dx$.

Solution   For this problem you will see that it will be useful to call the original integral I. That is, we let

$$
I = \int e^{2x} \sin x\, dx
$$

$$
\boxed{\begin{array}{ll} \text{Let } u = e^{2x} & \text{and } dv = \sin x\, dx \\ \quad du = 2e^{2x}\, dx & \qquad v = -\cos x \end{array}}
$$

$$
I = \int e^{2x} \sin x\, dx = e^{2x}(-\cos x) - \int (-\cos x)(2e^{2x}\, dx)
$$

$$
= -e^{2x} \cos x + 2 \int e^{2x} \cos x\, dx
$$

$$
\boxed{\begin{array}{ll} u = e^{2x} & \text{and } dv = \cos x\, dx \\ \quad du = 2e^{2x}\, dx & \qquad v = \sin x \end{array}}
$$

$$= -e^{2x} \cos x + 2\left[e^{2x}(\sin x) - \int \sin x (2e^{2x}\, dx) \right]$$

$$= -e^{2x} \cos x + 2e^{2x} \sin x - 4 \int e^{2x} \sin x\, dx$$

Notice that this last integral is I. Thus, we have

$$I = -e^{2x} \cos x + 2e^{2x} \sin x - 4I \qquad \text{Solve this equation for } I.$$

$$5I = -e^{2x} \cos x + 2e^{2x} \sin x \qquad \text{Add } 4I \text{ to both sides.}$$

$$I = \tfrac{1}{5}e^{2x}(2 \sin x - \cos x)$$

Thus, $\displaystyle\int e^{2x} \sin x\, dx = \tfrac{1}{5}e^{2x}(2 \sin x - \cos x) + C.$

Check with the integration table (Formula 492, where $a = 2$ and $b = 1$), or by taking the derivative. ∎

DEFINITE INTEGRATION BY PARTS

The integration by parts formula can be used for definite integrals, as summarized in the following box.

Integration by Parts for Definite Integrals

$$\int_a^b u\, dv = uv\Big|_a^b - \int_a^b v\, du$$

You should recognize that this formula for definite integrals is the same as the formula for indefinite integrals, where the first term after the equal sign has been evaluated at the appropriate limits of integration. This is illustrated by the following example.

EXAMPLE 5 Integration by parts with a definite integral

Evaluate $\displaystyle\int_0^1 xe^{2x}\, dx.$

Solution

| Let $u = x$ and $dv = e^{2x}\, dx$ |
| $du = dx$ $\qquad v = \tfrac{1}{2}e^{2x}$ |

$$\int_0^1 xe^{2x}\, dx = \frac{1}{2}xe^{2x}\bigg|_0^1 - \frac{1}{2}\int_0^1 e^{2x}\, dx$$

It is sometimes easier to simplify the algebra and then do one evaluation here at the end of the integration part of the problem.
↓

$$= \left(\frac{1}{2}xe^{2x} - \frac{1}{4}e^{2x} \right)\bigg|_0^1 = \frac{1}{4}e^2 + \frac{1}{4}$$

Check in Appendix D (Formula 484, with $a = 2$). ∎

TECHNOLOGY NOTE

You can use computer software or many calculators to evaluate definite integrals. Some calculators give the exact form just shown, while others only give a decimal approximation such as 2.097264025.

EXAMPLE 6 Integration by parts followed by substitution

Evaluate $\displaystyle\int_0^{\pi/4} \tan^{-1} x\, dx.$

Solution

$$\text{Let}\quad u = \tan^{-1} x \quad \text{and} \quad dv = dx$$
$$du = \frac{dx}{1 + x^2} \qquad\qquad v = x$$

$$\int_0^{\pi/4} \underbrace{\tan^{-1} x}_{u} \underbrace{dx}_{dv} = \underbrace{(\tan^{-1} x)}_{u} \underbrace{x}_{v} \bigg|_0^{\pi/4} - \int_0^{\pi/4} \underbrace{\frac{x \, dx}{1 + x^2}}_{v \, du}$$

$$= \left[x \tan^{-1} x - \frac{1}{2} \ln(1 + x^2) \right] \bigg|_0^{\pi/4}$$

Use substitution where $w = 1 + x^2$ and $dw = 2x \, dx$.

$$\int \frac{x \, dx}{1 + x^2} = \int \frac{dw}{2w} = \frac{1}{2} \ln w = \frac{1}{2} \ln(1 + x^2)$$

$$= \left[\frac{\pi}{4} \left(\tan^{-1} \frac{\pi}{4} \right) - \frac{1}{2} \ln \left(1 + \frac{\pi^2}{16} \right) \right] - \left[0 - \frac{1}{2} \ln 1 \right]$$

$$= \frac{\pi}{4} \tan^{-1} \frac{\pi}{4} - \frac{1}{2} \ln \left(1 + \frac{\pi^2}{16} \right) \approx 0.2827$$

Check with an integration table (Formula 457, for example, with $a = 1$). ∎

7.2 PROBLEM SET

Ⓐ *Find each integral in Problems 1–16.*

1. $\int x e^{-2x} \, dx$

2. $\int x \sin x \, dx$

3. $\int x \ln x \, dx$

4. $\int x \tan^{-1} x \, dx$

5. $\int \sin^{-1} x \, dx$

6. $\int x^2 \sin x \, dx$

7. $\int e^{-3x} \cos 4x \, dx$

8. $\int e^{2x} \sin 3x \, dx$

9. $\int x^2 \ln x \, dx$

10. $\int (x + \sin x)^2 \, dx$

11. $\int \sin(\ln x) \, dx$

12. $\int x \sin x \cos x \, dx$

13. $\int \ln(x^2 + 1) \, dx$

14. $\int \sin \sqrt{x} \, dx$

15. $\int \frac{x e^{-x}}{(x - 1)^2} \, dx$

16. $\int \frac{\ln(\sin x) \, dx}{\tan x}$

Find the exact value of the definite integrals in Problems 17–22 using integration by parts, and then check by using a calculator to find an approximate answer correct to four decimal places.

17. $\int_1^4 \sqrt{x} \, \ln x \, dx$

18. $\int_1^e x^3 \ln x \, dx$

19. $\int_1^e (\ln x)^2 \, dx$

20. $\int_{1/3}^e 3(\ln 3x)^2 \, dx$

21. $\int_0^\pi e^{2x} \cos 2x \, dx$

22. $\int_0^\pi x(\sin x + \cos x) \, dx$

Ⓑ 23. WHAT DOES THIS SAY? Describe the process known as *integration by parts*.

In Problems 24–27, first use an appropriate substitution and then integrate by parts to evaluate the integral. Remember to give your answers in terms of x.

24. $\int \frac{\ln x \sin(\ln x)}{x} \, dx$

25. $\int [\sin 2x \ln(\cos x)] \, dx$

26. $\int e^{2x} \sin e^x \, dx$

27. $\int [\sin x \ln(2 + \cos x)] \, dx$

28. a. Evaluate $\int \frac{x^3}{x^2 - 1} \, dx$ using integration by parts.

b. Evaluate the integral in part **a** by first dividing the integrand.

29. Evaluate $\int \cos^2 x \, dx$.

30. Evaluate $\int \frac{x \, dx}{\sqrt{x^2 + 1}}$.

31. Use Problem 29 to evaluate $\int x \cos^2 x \, dx$ using integration by parts.

32. Use Problem 30 to evaluate $\int \frac{x^3 \, dx}{\sqrt{x^2 + 1}}$ using integration by parts.

33. Find $\int x^n \ln x \, dx$, where n is any positive real number.

34. After t seconds, an object is moving along a line with velocity of $te^{-t/2}$ meters per second. Express the position of the moving object as a function of time.

35. After t hours on the job, a factory worker can produce $100te^{-0.5t}$ units per hour. How many units does the worker produce during the first 3 hours?

36. After t weeks, contributions in response to a local fund-raising campaign were coming in at the rate of $2{,}000te^{-0.2t}$ dollars per week. How much money was raised during the first 5 weeks?

37. Find the volume of the solid generated when the region under the curve $y = e^{-x}$ on the interval $[0, 2]$ is revolved about the y-axis.

38. Find the volume of the solid generated when the region under the curve $y = \sin x + \cos x$ on the interval $[0, \frac{\pi}{4}]$ is revolved about the y-axis.

39. Find the volume of the solid generated when the region under the curve $y = \ln x$ on the interval $[1, e]$ is revolved about the indicated axis:

    a. x-axis   **b.** y-axis

40. Find the centroid (with coordinates rounded to the nearest hundredth) of the region in the first quadrant bounded by the curves $y = \sin x$ and $y = \cos x$ and the y-axis.

41. Find the centroid (with coordinates rounded to the nearest hundredth) of the region bounded by the curves $y = e^x$, $y = e^{-x}$, and the line $x = 1$.

In Problems 42–43, solve the given separable differential equations.

42. $\dfrac{dy}{dx} = xe^{y-x}$ **43.** $\dfrac{dy}{dx} = \sqrt{xy} \ln x$

44. Find a function $y = f(x)$ whose graph passes through $(1, 1)$ and has the property that at each point (x, y) on the graph, the slope of the tangent line is $y \tan^{-1} x$.

45. Find a function $y = f(x)$ whose graph passes through $(0, 1)$ and has the property that the normal line at each point (x, y) on the graph has slope $\dfrac{\sec x}{xy}$.

46. Suppose it is known that $f(0) = 3$ and

$$\int_0^\pi [f(x) + f''(x)] \sin x \, dx = 0$$

What is $f(\pi)$?

47. Because a rocket burns fuel in flight, its mass decreases with time, and this in turn affects its velocity. It can be shown that the velocity $v(t)$ of the rocket at time t in its flight is given by

$$v(t) = -r \ln \frac{w - kt}{w} - gt$$

where w is the initial weight of the rocket (including its fuel) and r and k are, respectively, the expulsion speed and the rate of consumption of the fuel, which are assumed to be constant. As usual, $g = 32$ ft/s^2 is the constant acceleration due to gravity. Suppose $w = 30{,}000$ lb, $r = 8{,}000$ ft/s, and $k = 200$ lb/sec. What is the height of the rocket after 2 minutes (120 seconds)?

48. In physics, it is known that loudness L of a sound is related to its intensity I by the equation

$$L = 10 \log \frac{I}{I_0}$$

decibels, where $I_0 = 10^{-12}$ watt/m^2 is the threshold of audibility (the lowest intensity that can be heard). What is the average value of L as the intensity of a TV show ranges between I_0 and $I_1 = 3 \cdot 10^{-5}$ watt/m^2?

49. The displacement from equilibrium of a mass oscillating at the end of a spring hanging from the ceiling is given by

$$y = 2.3e^{-0.25t} \cos 5t$$

feet. What is the average displacement (rounded to the nearest hundredth) of the mass between times $t = 0$ and $t = \pi/5$ seconds?

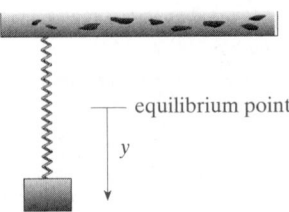

50. A photographer is taking a picture of a clever sign on the back of a truck. The sign is 5 ft high and its lower edge is 1 ft above the lens of the camera. At first the truck is 4 ft away from the photographer, but then it begins to move away. What is the average value of the angle θ (correct to two decimal places) subtended by the camera lens as the truck moves from 4 ft to 20 ft away from the photographer?

51. If n moles of an ideal gas expand at constant temperature T, then its pressure p and volume V satisfy the equation $pV = nRT$, for constant R. It can be shown that the work done by the gas in expanding from volume V_1 to V is

$$W = nRT \ln \frac{V}{V_1}$$

What is the average work done as V increases from V_1 to $V_2 = 10V_1$?

52. Evaluate $\displaystyle\int \frac{(2x - 1)}{x^2} e^{2x} \, dx$.

53. Derive the reduction formula

$$\int x^n e^x \, dx = x^n e^x - n \int x^{n-1} e^x \, dx$$

(This is Formula 486, with $a = 1$.)

54. Derive the reduction formula

$$\int (\ln x)^n \, dx = x(\ln x)^n - n \int (\ln x)^{n-1} \, dx$$

(This is Formula 501.)

C **55. Wallis's formula** If n is an even positive integer, use reduction formulas to show

$$\int_0^{\pi/2} \sin^n x \, dx = \int_0^{\pi/2} \cos^n x \, dx$$

$$= \left[\frac{1 \cdot 3 \cdot 5 \cdot \cdots \cdot (n-1)}{2 \cdot 4 \cdot 6 \cdot \cdots \cdot n} \right] \frac{\pi}{2}$$

56. Exploration Problem State and prove a result similar to the one in Problem 55 for the case where n is an odd positive integer.

7.3 Trigonometric Methods

IN THIS SECTION powers of sine and cosine, powers of secant and tangent, trigonometric substitutions, quadratic-form integrals

POWERS OF SINE AND COSINE

Problems 40–45 of Problem Set 7.1 anticipated the results of this section. We begin by considering a product of powers of sine and cosine, which we represent in the form

$$\int \sin^m x \cos^n x \, dx$$

There are essentially two cases that must be considered, depending on whether the powers m and n are both even or not. We will state the general strategy for handling each case and then illustrate the procedure with an example.

Case I: Either m or n is odd (or both)
General strategy: Suppose, for simplicity, that m is odd. Separate a factor of $\sin x$ from the rest of the integrand, so the remaining power of $\sin x$ is even; use the identity $\sin^2 x = 1 - \cos^2 x$ to express everything but the term $(\sin x \, dx)$ in terms of $\cos x$. Substitute $u = \cos x$, $du = -\sin x \, dx$ to convert the integral into a polynomial in u and integrate using the power rule. The case where n is odd is handled in analogous fashion, as shown in the following example by reversing the roles of $\sin x$ and $\cos x$.

EXAMPLE 1 Power of cosine is odd

Evaluate $\displaystyle\int \sin^4 x \cos^3 x \, dx$.

Solution
Since $n = 3$ is odd, peel off a factor of $\cos x$ and use $\cos^2 x = 1 - \sin^2 x$ to express the integral as a polynomial in $\sin x$.

$$\int \sin^4 x \cos^3 x \, dx = \int \sin^4 x \cos^2 x (\cos x \, dx)$$

$$= \int \sin^4 x (1 - \sin^2 x)(\cos x \, dx)$$

$$= \int u^4 (1 - u^2) \, du \quad \boxed{u = \sin x; \quad du = \cos x \, dx}$$

$$= \tfrac{1}{5} u^5 - \tfrac{1}{7} u^7 + C$$

$$= \tfrac{1}{5} \sin^5 x - \tfrac{1}{7} \sin^7 x + C$$

■

Case II: Neither m nor n is odd

General strategy: Convert this into Case I by using the identities $\sin^2 x = \frac{1}{2}(1 - \cos 2x)$ and $\cos^2 x = \frac{1}{2}(1 + \cos 2x)$. These are sometimes called *half-angle identities.*

EXAMPLE 2   All powers are even

Evaluate $\displaystyle\int \sin^2 x \cos^4 x \, dx$.

Solution

$$\int \sin^2 x \cos^4 x \, dx = \int \tfrac{1}{2}(1 - \cos 2x)\left(\tfrac{1}{4}\right)(1 + \cos 2x)^2 \, dx$$

$$= \tfrac{1}{8} \int (1 + \cos 2x - \cos^2 2x - \cos^3 2x) \, dx$$

Half-angle identities

$$= \tfrac{1}{8} \int \left[1 + \cos 2x - \tfrac{1}{2}(1 + \cos 4x) - (1 - \sin^2 2x)(\cos 2x)\right] dx$$

Half-angle identities again

$$= \tfrac{1}{8} \int \left[1 + \cos 2x - \tfrac{1}{2} - \tfrac{1}{2}\cos 4x - \cos 2x + (\sin^2 2x) \cos 2x\right] dx$$

$$= \tfrac{1}{8} \int \left(\tfrac{1}{2} - \tfrac{1}{2}\cos 4x\right) dx + \tfrac{1}{8} \int \sin^2 2x(\cos 2x) \, dx$$

$$\boxed{u = \sin 2x; \quad du = 2\cos 2x \, dx}$$

$$= \tfrac{1}{16}x - \tfrac{1}{64}\sin 4x + \tfrac{1}{48}\sin^3 2x + C \qquad \blacksquare$$

TECHNOLOGY NOTE

One computer algebra system applied to this example yields

$$\int \sin^2 x \cos^4 x \, dx = -\tfrac{1}{6}\sin x \cos^5 x + \tfrac{1}{24}\sin x \cos^3 x + \tfrac{1}{16}\sin x \cos x + \tfrac{1}{16}x$$

(Recall, technology does not show the "$+C$" term.) Both answers are correct. They are related by trigonometric identities, and it can be shown that they differ by a constant.

POWERS OF SECANT AND TANGENT

The simplest integrals of this form are

$$\int \tan x \, dx = \ln|\sec x| + C$$

$$\int \sec x \, dx = \ln|\sec x + \tan x| + C$$

For the more general situation, which we write as

$$\int \tan^m x \sec^n x \, dx,$$

there are three essentially different cases to consider.

Case I: *n* is even

General strategy: Peel off a factor of $\sec^2 x$ from the integrand and use the identity $\sec^2 x = \tan^2 x + 1$ to express the integrand in powers of $\tan x$ except for $(\sec^2 x \, dx)$; substitute $u = \tan x$, $du = \sec^2 x \, dx$, and integrate by using the power rule.

EXAMPLE 3   Power of the secant is even

Evaluate $\displaystyle\int \tan^2 x \sec^4 x \, dx$.

Solution

$$\int \tan^2 x \sec^4 x \, dx = \int \tan^2 x \sec^2 x (\sec^2 x \, dx)$$

$$= \int \tan^2 x (\tan^2 x + 1) \sec^2 x \, dx$$

$$= \int u^2 (u^2 + 1) \, du \quad \boxed{u = \tan x; \quad du = \sec^2 x \, dx}$$

$$= \tfrac{1}{5} u^5 + \tfrac{1}{3} u^3 + C$$

$$= \tfrac{1}{5} \tan^5 x + \tfrac{1}{3} \tan^3 x + C \qquad \blacksquare$$

Case II: *m* is odd

General strategy: Peel off a factor of $\sec x \tan x$ from the integrand and use the identity $\tan^2 x = \sec^2 x - 1$ to express the integrand in powers of $\sec x$, except for $(\sec x \tan x \, dx)$; substitute $u = \sec x$, $du = \sec x \tan x \, dx$, and integrate using the power rule.

EXAMPLE 4   Power of the tangent is odd

Evaluate $\displaystyle\int \tan x \sec^6 x \, dx$.

Solution

$$\int \tan x \sec^6 x \, dx = \int \sec^5 x (\sec x \tan x \, dx)$$

$$= \int u^5 \, du \quad \boxed{u = \sec x; \quad du = \sec x \tan x \, dx}$$

$$= \tfrac{1}{6} \sec^6 x + C \qquad \blacksquare$$

Case III: *m* is even and *n* is odd

General strategy: Use the identity $\tan^2 x = \sec^2 x - 1$ to express the integrand in terms of powers of $\sec x$; then use the reduction Formula 428:

$$\int \sec^n x \, dx = \frac{\sec^{n-2} x \tan x}{n-1} + \frac{n-2}{n-1} \int \sec^{n-2} x \, dx$$

EXAMPLE 5   Power of the tangent is even and power of the secant is odd

Evaluate $\displaystyle\int \tan^2 x \sec^3 x \, dx$.

Solution

$$\int \tan^2 x \sec^3 x \, dx = \int (\sec^2 x - 1) \sec^3 x \, dx$$

$$= \int \sec^5 x \, dx - \int \sec^3 x \, dx$$

$$= \left[\frac{\sec^3 x \tan x}{4} + \frac{3}{4} \int \sec^3 x \, dx \right] - \int \sec^3 x \, dx$$

$$= \frac{\sec^3 x \tan x}{4} - \frac{1}{4} \int \sec^3 x \, dx$$

$$= \frac{\sec^3 x \tan x}{4} - \frac{1}{4} \left[\frac{\sec x \tan x}{2} + \frac{1}{2} \int \sec x \, dx \right]$$

$$= \frac{\sec^3 x \tan x}{4} - \frac{\sec x \tan x}{8} - \frac{1}{8} \ln |\sec x + \tan x| + C \quad \blacksquare$$

TRIGONOMETRIC SUBSTITUTIONS

Trigonometric substitutions can also be useful. For instance, suppose an integrand contains the term $\sqrt{a^2 - u^2}$, where $a > 0$. Then by setting $u = a \sin \theta$ for an acute angle θ, and using the identity $\cos^2 \theta = 1 - \sin^2 \theta$, we obtain

$$\sqrt{a^2 - u^2} = \sqrt{a^2 - a^2 \sin^2 \theta} = a \sqrt{1 - \sin^2 \theta} = a \cos \theta$$

Thus, the substitution $u = a \sin \theta$, $du = a \cos \theta \, d\theta$ eliminates the square root and may convert the given integral into one involving only sine and cosine. This substitution can best be remembered by setting up a reference triangle. This process is illustrated in the following example.

EXAMPLE 6 Trigonometric substitution with form $\sqrt{a^2 - u^2}$

Find $\int \sqrt{4 - x^2} \, dx$.

Solution

First, using a table of integration, we find (Formula 231; $a = 2$)

$$\int \sqrt{4 - x^2} \, dx = \frac{x \sqrt{4 - x^2}}{2} + 2 \sin^{-1} \left(\frac{x}{2} \right) + C$$

Our goal with this example is to show how we might obtain this formula with a trigonometric substitution. Refer to the triangle shown in Figure 7.1.

Let $x = 2 \sin \theta$, so $dx = 2 \cos \theta \, d\theta$. Then,

$$\int \sqrt{4 - x^2} \, dx = \int \sqrt{4 - 4 \sin^2 \theta} \, (2 \cos \theta \, d\theta)$$

$$= 4 \int \cos^2 \theta \, d\theta \qquad \text{Since } \sqrt{1 - \sin^2 \theta} = \cos \theta$$

$$= 4 \int \frac{1 + \cos 2\theta}{2} \, d\theta \qquad \text{Half-angle identity}$$

$$= 2\theta + \sin 2\theta + C$$

$$= 2\theta + 2 \sin \theta \cos \theta + C$$

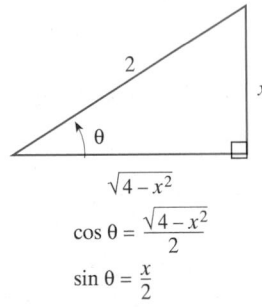

$$\cos \theta = \frac{\sqrt{4 - x^2}}{2}$$

$$\sin \theta = \frac{x}{2}$$

Figure 7.1 Reference triangle with form $\sqrt{a^2 - u^2}$

The final step is to convert this answer back to terms involving x. Using the reference triangle in Figure 7.1, we find that

$$\sin \theta = \frac{x}{2} \quad \text{and} \quad \cos \theta = \frac{1}{2}\sqrt{4 - x^2}$$

Thus, we have $\theta = \sin^{-1} \dfrac{x}{2}$

$$\int \sqrt{4 - x^2}\, dx = 2 \sin^{-1}\left(\frac{x}{2}\right) + 2\left(\frac{x}{2}\right)\left(\frac{\sqrt{4 - x^2}}{2}\right) + C$$

$$= 2 \sin^{-1}\left(\frac{x}{2}\right) + \frac{x}{2}\sqrt{4 - x^2} + C \qquad \blacksquare$$

Similar methods can be used to convert integrals that involve terms of the form $\sqrt{a^2 + u^2}$ or $\sqrt{u^2 - a^2}$ into trigonometric integrals, as shown in Table 7.1. For this table, we require $0 \le \theta < \frac{\pi}{2}$.

TABLE 7.1 Trigonometric substitution for integrands involving a radical form

If the integrand involves ...	substitute ...	to obtain ...
$\sqrt{a^2 - u^2}$	$u = a \sin \theta$	$\sqrt{a^2 - u^2} = a \cos \theta$
$\sqrt{a^2 + u^2}$	$u = a \tan \theta$	$\sqrt{a^2 + u^2} = a \sec \theta$
$\sqrt{u^2 - a^2}$	$u = a \sec \theta$	$\sqrt{u^2 - a^2} = a \tan \theta$

EXAMPLE 7 Trigonometric substitution with form $\sqrt{a^2 + u^2}$

Evaluate $\displaystyle\int x^2\sqrt{9 + x^2}\, dx$.

Solution

Let $x = 3 \tan \theta$, $dx = 3 \sec^2 \theta\, d\theta$; then

$$\int x^2\sqrt{9 + x^2}\, dx = \int (3 \tan \theta)^2 \sqrt{9 + 9 \tan^2 \theta}\, (3 \sec^2 \theta\, d\theta)$$

$$= \int (9 \tan^2 \theta)(3 \sec \theta)(3 \sec^2 \theta\, d\theta) \quad 1 + \tan^2 \theta = \sec^2 \theta$$

$$= 81 \int \tan^2 \theta \sec^3 \theta\, d\theta$$

This integration can now be completed by looking at Example 5. In order to express the antiderivative in terms of the original variable x, you can use the reference triangle in Figure 7.2.

Since $\tan \theta = x/3$, we have $\sec \theta = (\sqrt{9 + x^2})/3$, and by substituting into the solution shown in Example 5, we find

$$\int x^2\sqrt{9 + x^2}\, dx = 81\left[\frac{\sec^3 \theta \tan \theta}{4} - \frac{\sec \theta \tan \theta}{8} - \frac{1}{8}\ln|\sec \theta + \tan \theta|\right] + C$$

$$= \frac{81}{4}\left(\frac{\sqrt{9 + x^2}}{3}\right)^3\left(\frac{x}{3}\right) - \frac{81}{8}\left(\frac{\sqrt{9 + x^2}}{3}\right)\left(\frac{x}{3}\right) - \frac{81}{8}\ln\left|\frac{\sqrt{9 + x^2}}{3} + \frac{x}{3}\right| + C$$

$$= \frac{x}{4}(9 + x^2)^{3/2} - \frac{9x}{8}(9 + x^2)^{1/2} - \frac{81}{8}\ln\left|\frac{(9 + x^2)^{1/2}}{3} + \frac{x}{3}\right| + C \qquad \blacksquare$$

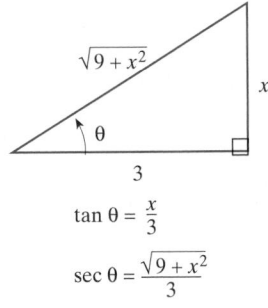

$\tan \theta = \dfrac{x}{3}$

$\sec \theta = \dfrac{\sqrt{9 + x^2}}{3}$

Figure 7.2 Reference triangle with form $\sqrt{a^2 + u^2}$

EXAMPLE 8 Trigonometric substitution with form $\sqrt{u^2 - a^2}$

Evaluate $\displaystyle\int x^3 \sqrt{x^2 - 1}\, dx$.

Solution

Let $x = \sec\theta$, $dx = \sec\theta\tan\theta\, d\theta$; we use the reference triangle shown in Figure 7.3.

$$\int x^3 \sqrt{x^2 - 1}\, dx = \int \sec^3\theta \sqrt{\sec^2\theta - 1}\,(\sec\theta\tan\theta\, d\theta)$$

$$= \int \sec^4\theta \tan^2\theta\, d\theta \qquad \tan^2\theta = \sec^2\theta - 1$$

$$= \int \sec^2\theta \tan^2\theta (\sec^2\theta\, d\theta)$$

$$= \int (\tan^2\theta + 1)\tan^2\theta (\sec^2\theta\, d\theta)$$

$$= \int (\tan^4\theta + \tan^2\theta)(\sec^2\theta\, d\theta)$$

$$= \int (u^4 + u^2)\, du \qquad \text{Where } u = \tan\theta$$

$$= \tfrac{1}{5}u^5 + \tfrac{1}{3}u^3 + C$$

$$= \tfrac{1}{5}\tan^5\theta + \tfrac{1}{3}\tan^3\theta + C$$

$$= \tfrac{1}{5}(x^2 - 1)^{5/2} + \tfrac{1}{3}(x^2 - 1)^{3/2} + C \qquad ■$$

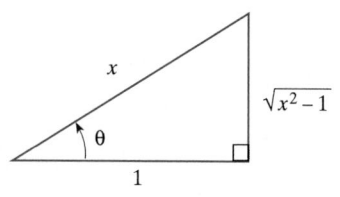

$\sec\theta = x$, $\tan\theta = \sqrt{x^2 - 1}$

Figure 7.3 Reference triangle with form $\sqrt{x^2 - a^2}$

QUADRATIC-FORM INTEGRALS

An integral involving an expression of the form $Ax^2 + Bx + C$, with $A \neq 0$, $B \neq 0$, can often be evaluated by completing the square and making an appropriate substitution to convert it to one of the forms we have previously analyzed.

EXAMPLE 9 Integration by completing the square

Evaluate $\displaystyle\int \sqrt{16x - 2x^2 - 23}\, dx$.

Solution

Complete the square within the radicand:

$$16x - 2x^2 - 23 = -2(x^2 - 8x \qquad) - 23$$

$$= -2(x^2 - 8x + 4^2) + 2 \cdot 4^2 - 23$$

$$= -2(x - 4)^2 + 9$$

Thus,

$$\int \sqrt{16x - 2x^2 - 23}\, dx = \int \sqrt{9 - 2(x - 4)^2}\, dx$$

$$= \int \sqrt{9 - u^2}\left(\frac{du}{\sqrt{2}}\right) \qquad \text{Where } u = \sqrt{2}(x - 4)$$

$$= \int \sqrt{9 - (3\sin\theta)^2}\left(\frac{3}{\sqrt{2}}\cos\theta\, d\theta\right) \qquad \text{Where } u = 3\sin\theta$$

$$= \frac{3}{\sqrt{2}}\int 3\sqrt{1 - \sin^2\theta}\,\cos\theta\, d\theta$$

$$= \frac{9}{\sqrt{2}}\int \cos^2\theta\, d\theta$$

$$= \frac{9}{2\sqrt{2}}\left[\theta + \frac{\sin 2\theta}{2}\right] + C \qquad \text{Half-angle identity}$$

$$= \frac{9}{2\sqrt{2}} \sin^{-1} \left[\frac{\sqrt{2}}{3}(x-4) \right] + \frac{x-4}{2} \sqrt{16x - 2x^2 - 23} + C$$

This last step requires back-substituting from θ to u and then from u to x. Details are left as an exercise. ∎

7.3 PROBLEM SET

Ⓐ **1. WHAT DOES THIS SAY?** Explain how to integrate $\int \sin^m x \cos^n x \, dx$ when m and n are both even.

2. WHAT DOES THIS SAY? Explain how to integrate $\int \tan^m x \sec^n x \, dx$ when n is even.

3. WHAT DOES THIS SAY? Explain the process of using a trigonometric substitution on integrals of the form $\sqrt{a^2 + u^2}$.

4. WHAT DOES THIS SAY? Explain the process of using a trigonometric substitution on integrals of the form $\sqrt{a^2 - u^2}$. How is this different from handling an integral involving $\sqrt{u^2 - a^2}$?

Evaluate the integrals in Problems 5–50.

5. $\int \cos^3 x \, dx$

6. $\int \sin^5 x \, dx$

7. $\int \sin^2 x \cos^3 x \, dx$

8. $\int \sin^3 x \cos^3 x \, dx$

9. $\int \sqrt{\cos t} \, \sin t \, dt$

10. $\int \frac{\cos x \, dx}{1 + 3 \sin x}$

11. $\int e^{\cos x} \sin x \, dx$

12. $\int \cos^2(2t) \, dt$

13. $\int \sin^2 x \cos^2 x \, dx$

14. $\int \frac{\sin x \, dx}{\cos^5 x}$

15. $\int \tan 2\theta \, d\theta$

16. $\int \sec \left(\frac{x}{2} \right) dx$

17. $\int \tan^3 x \sec^4 x \, dx$

18. $\int \sec^5 x \tan x \, dx$

19. $\int (\tan^2 x + \sec^2 x) \, dx$

20. $\int (\sin x + \cos x)^2 \, dx$

21. $\int \tan^2 u \sec u \, du$

22. $\int \sec^4 x \, dx$

23. $\int \sqrt[3]{\tan x} \, \sec^2 x \, dx$

24. $\int e^x \sec(e^x) \, dx$

25. $\int x \sin x^2 \cos x^2 \, dx$

26. $\int x \sec^2 x \, dx$

27. $\int \tan^4 t \sec t \, dt$

28. $\int \csc(2\theta) \, d\theta$

29. $\int \csc^3 x \cot x \, dx$

30. $\int \csc^2 x \cot^2 x \, dx$

31. $\int \csc^2 x \cos x \, dx$

32. $\int \tan x \csc^3 x \, dx$

33. $\int \sqrt{4 - t^2} \, dt$

34. $\int \frac{dx}{\sqrt{9 - x^2}}$

35. $\int \frac{x + 1}{\sqrt{4 + x^2}} \, dx$

36. $\int \sqrt{9 + x^2} \, dx$

37. $\int \frac{dx}{\sqrt{x^2 - 7}}$

38. $\int \frac{dx}{5 + 2x^2}$

39. $\int \frac{dx}{\sqrt{5 - x^2}}$

40. $\int \frac{dx}{x \sqrt{7x^2 - 4}}$

41. $\int \frac{dx}{x^2 \sqrt{4 - x^2}}$

42. $\int \frac{dx}{x \sqrt{x^2 + 9}}$

43. $\int \frac{\sqrt{x^2 - 4}}{x} \, dx$

44. $\int \frac{dx}{(x - 1)^2 + 4}$

45. $\int \frac{x \, dx}{9 - (x + 1)^2}$

46. $\int \sqrt{2x - x^2} \, dx$

47. $\int \frac{dx}{\sqrt{x^2 - 2x + 6}}$

48. $\int \frac{dx}{\sqrt{x^2 + 8x + 3}}$

49. $\int \frac{\sin^3 u \, du}{\cos^5 u}$ *tan/sec'*

50. $\int \frac{\sec^2 x \, dx}{\tan^2 x + \sec^2 x}$

Ⓑ **51.** Find the average value of $f(x) = \sin^2 x$ over the interval $[0, \pi]$.

52. Find the centroid of the region (correct to two decimal places) bounded by the curve $y = \cos^2 x$, the x-axis, and the vertical lines $x = \frac{\pi}{4}$ and $x = \frac{\pi}{3}$.

53. Find the volume (correct to four decimal places) of the solid generated when the region bounded by the curve $y = \sin^2 x$ and the x-axis is revolved about the y-axis $0 \le x \le \pi$.

54. A particle moves along the x-axis in such a way that the acceleration at time t is $a(t) = \sin^2 t$. What is the total distance traveled by the particle over the time interval $[0, \pi]$ if its initial velocity is $v(0) = 2$ units per second?

55. Evaluate $\int \sqrt{1 + \cos x} \, dx$.

Hint: Use the identity $\cos x = 2 \cos^2 \frac{x}{2} - 1$.

In Problems 56–59, use the following identities:

$$\sin A \cos B = \tfrac{1}{2} [\sin(A - B) + \sin(A + B)]$$
$$\longrightarrow \sin A \sin B = \tfrac{1}{2} [\cos(A - B) - \cos(A + B)]$$
$$\cos A \cos B = \tfrac{1}{2} [\cos(A - B) + \cos(A + B)]$$

56. $\int \sin 3x \sin 5x \, dx$

57. $\int \cos \frac{x}{2} \sin 2x \, dx$

58. $\int \cos 7x \cos(-3x) \sin 4x \, dx$

59. $\int \sin^2 3x \cos 4x \, dx$

60. Let f be a twice differentiable function that satisfies the initial value problem

$$f''(x) = \tfrac{1}{2}(\tan x) f'(x) \qquad f'(0) = f(0) = 1$$

on the interval $\left[0, \frac{\pi}{2} \right]$. Find the arc length of the curve $y = f(x)$ over this interval.

Ⓒ **61.** Evaluate $\int \frac{x \, dx}{9 - x^2 - \sqrt{9 - x^2}}$.

7.4 Method of Partial Fractions

IN THIS SECTION partial fraction decomposition, integrating rational functions, rational functions of sine and cosine

PARTIAL FRACTION DECOMPOSITION

You are familiar with the algebraic procedure of adding a string of rational expressions to form a combined rational function with a common denominator. For example,

$$\frac{2}{x+1} + \frac{-3}{x+2} = \frac{2(x+2) + (-3)(x+1)}{(x+1)(x+2)} = \frac{-x+1}{x^2+3x+2}$$

In **partial fraction decomposition**, we do just the opposite: We start with the reduced fraction

$$\frac{-x+1}{x^2+3x+2}$$

and write it as the sum of fractions

$$\frac{2}{x+1} + \frac{-3}{x+2}$$

This procedure has great value for integration because the terms $\dfrac{2}{x+1}$ and $\dfrac{-3}{x+2}$ are easy to integrate. In particular,

$$\int \frac{-x+1}{x^2+3x+2}\, dx = \int \frac{2}{x+1}\, dx + \int \frac{-3}{x+2}\, dx$$
$$= 2\ln|x+1| - 3\ln|x+2| + C$$

In the following discussion, we will consider rational functions

$$f(x) = \frac{P(x)}{D(x)}$$

that are reduced in the sense that $P(x)$ and $D(x)$ are polynomials in x which have no common factors and the degree of P is less than the degree of D. In algebra, it is shown that if $P(x)/D(x)$ is such an expression, then

$$\frac{P(x)}{D(x)} = F_1(x) + F_2(x) + \cdots + F_N(x)$$

where the $F_k(x)$ are expressions of the form

$$\frac{A}{(x-r)^n} \quad \text{or} \quad \frac{Ax+B}{(x^2+sx+t)^m}$$

If $\dfrac{P(x)}{D(x)}$ is not reduced, then we simply divide until a reduced form is obtained. For example ($x \neq 1$),

TECHNOLOGY NOTE

Software programs will decompose rational expressions quite handily using the direction "expand."

$$\frac{(2x^3 + 7x^2 + 6x + 3)(x-1)}{(x-1)(x^2+3x+2)} = 2x + 1 + \frac{-x+1}{x^2+3x+2}$$
$$= 2x + 1 + \frac{2}{x+1} + \frac{-3}{x+2}$$

We will examine a nonreduced rational expression in Example 5.

We begin by focusing on the case where $D(x)$ can be expressed as a product of linear powers.

> **Partial Fraction Decomposition: A Single Linear Power**
>
> Let $f(x) = P(x)/(x-r)^n$, where $P(x)$ is a polynomial of degree less than n and $P(r) \neq 0$. Then $f(x)$ can be **decomposed** into partial fractions in the following "cascading form"
>
> $$\frac{A_1}{x-r} + \frac{A_2}{(x-r)^2} + \cdots + \frac{A_n}{(x-r)^n}$$

EXAMPLE 1   Partial fraction decomposition with a single linear power

Decompose $\dfrac{x^2 - 6x + 3}{(x-2)^3}$ into a sum of partial fractions.

Solution $\dfrac{x^2 - 6x + 3}{(x-2)^3} = \dfrac{A_1}{x-2} + \dfrac{A_2}{(x-2)^2} + \dfrac{A_3}{(x-2)^3}$

Multiply both sides by $(x-2)^3$ to obtain

$$x^2 - 6x + 3 = A_1(x-2)^2 + A_2(x-2) + A_3$$

$$\text{Let } x = 2: \quad 2^2 - 6(2) + 3 = A_1(0) + A_2(0) + A_3$$
$$-5 = A_3$$

Substitute $A_3 = -5$ and expand the right side to obtain

$$x^2 - 6x + 3 = A_1 x^2 + (-4A_1 + A_2)x + (4A_1 - 2A_2 - 5)$$

This implies (by equating the coefficients of the similar terms) that

$$
\begin{array}{ll}
1 = A_1 & x^2 \text{ terms} \\
-6 = -4A_1 + A_2 & x \text{ terms} \\
3 = 4A_1 - 2A_2 - 5 & \text{Constants}
\end{array}
$$

Because $A_1 = 1$, we find $A_2 = -2$, so the decomposition is

$$\frac{x^2 - 6x + 3}{(x-2)^3} = \frac{1}{x-2} + \frac{-2}{(x-2)^2} + \frac{-5}{(x-2)^3} \qquad \blacksquare$$

If there are two or more linear factors in the factorization of $D(x)$, there must be a separate cascade for each power. In particular, if $D(x)$ can be expressed as the product of n distinct linear factors, then

$$\frac{P(x)}{(x-r_1)(x-r_2)\cdots(x-r_n)}$$

is decomposed into separate terms

$$\frac{A_1}{x-r_1} + \frac{A_2}{x-r_2} + \cdots + \frac{A_n}{x-r_n}$$

This process is illustrated with the following example.

EXAMPLE 2   Partial fraction decomposition with distinct linear factors

Decompose $\dfrac{8x - 1}{x^2 - x - 2}$.

Solution

$$\frac{8x-1}{x^2-x-2} = \frac{8x-1}{(x-2)(x+1)}$$ First factor the denominator.

$$= \frac{A_1}{x-2} + \frac{A_2}{x+1}$$ Break up the fraction into parts, each with a linear denominator. The task is to find A_1 and A_2.

$$= \frac{A_1(x+1) + A_2(x-2)}{(x-2)(x+1)}$$ Obtain the least common denominator on the right.

WARNING Note that the degree of the denominator is the same number as the number of arbitrary constants, A_1 and A_2. This provides a quick intermediate check on the correct procedure.

Now, multiply both sides of this equation by the least common denominator, which is $(x-2)(x+1)$ for this example.

$$8x - 1 = A_1(x+1) + A_2(x-2)$$

Substitute, one at a time, the values that cause each of the factors in the least common denominator to be zero.

Let $x = -1$:

$$8x - 1 = A_1(x+1) + A_2(x-2)$$
$$8(-1) - 1 = A_1(-1+1) + A_2(-1-2)$$
$$-9 = -3A_2$$
$$3 = A_2$$

Let $x = 2$:

$$8x - 1 = A_1(x+1) + A_2(x-2)$$
$$8(2) - 1 = A_1(2+1) + A_2(2-2)$$
$$15 = 3A_1$$
$$5 = A_1$$

Thus, $\dfrac{8x-1}{x^2-x-2} = \dfrac{5}{x-2} + \dfrac{3}{x+1}$. ∎

If there is a mixture of distinct and repeated linear factors, we combine the procedures illustrated in the preceding examples. For example,

$$\frac{5x^2 + 21x + 4}{(x+1)^3(x-3)} \quad \text{is decomposed as} \quad \frac{A_1}{x+1} + \frac{A_2}{(x+1)^2} + \frac{A_3}{(x+1)^3} + \frac{A_4}{x-3}$$

Note that the degree of the denominator is 4, so we use four constants.

If the denominator $D(x)$ in the rational expression $P(x)/D(x)$ contains an irreducible quadratic power, the partial fraction decomposition contains a different kind of cascading sum.

Partial Fraction Decomposition: A Single Irreducible Quadratic Factor

Let $f(x) = P(x)/(x^2 + sx + t)^m$, where $P(x)$ is a polynomial of degree less than $2m$. Then $f(x)$ can be decomposed into partial fractions in the following "cascading form":

$$\frac{A_1 x + B_1}{x^2 + sx + t} + \frac{A_2 x + B_2}{(x^2 + sx + t)^2} + \cdots + \frac{A_m x + B_m}{(x^2 + sx + t)^m}$$

Because the degree of the denominator is $2m$, we have $2m$ arbitrary constants, namely, $A_1, A_2, \ldots, A_m, B_1, B_2, \ldots, B_m$.

WARNING Note that the numerator in each term of a linear cascade is a constant A_k, while each numerator in a quadratic cascade is a linear term of the form $A_k x + B_k$.

EXAMPLE 3   Partial fraction decomposition with a single quadratic power

Decompose $\dfrac{-3x^3 - x}{(x^2 + 1)^2}$.

Solution

The decomposition gives

$$\frac{-3x^3 - x}{(x^2 + 1)^2} = \frac{A_1 x + B_1}{x^2 + 1} + \frac{A_2 x + B_2}{(x^2 + 1)^2}$$

Multiply both sides of this equation by $(x^2 + 1)^2$, and simplify algebraically.

$$-3x^3 - x = (A_1 x + B_1)(x^2 + 1) + (A_2 x + B_2)$$
$$= A_1 x^3 + B_1 x^2 + (A_1 + A_2)x + (B_1 + B_2)$$

Next, equate the corresponding coefficients on each side of this equation and solve the resulting system of equations to find $A_1 = -3$, $A_2 = 2$, $B_1 = 0$, and $B_2 = 0$. This means that

$$\frac{-3x^3 - x}{(x^2 + 1)^2} = \frac{-3x}{x^2 + 1} + \frac{2x}{(x^2 + 1)^2} \qquad \blacksquare$$

Many of the examples we encounter will offer a mixture of linear and quadratic factors. For example,

$$\frac{x^2 + 4x - 23}{(x^2 + 4)(x + 3)^2} \quad \text{is decomposed as} \quad \frac{A_1 x + B_1}{x^2 + 4} + \frac{A_2}{x + 3} + \frac{A_3}{(x + 3)^2}$$

The degree of the denominator is four, and there are four constants.

In algebra, the theory of equations tells us that any polynomial P with real coefficients can be expressed as a product of linear and irreducible quadratic powers, some of which may be repeated. This fact can be used to justify the following general procedure for obtaining the partial fraction decomposition of a rational function.

Partial Fraction Decomposition of the Rational Function $P(x)/D(x)$

Let $f(x) = \dfrac{P(x)}{D(x)}$, where $P(x)$ and $D(x)$ are polynomials with no common factors and $D(x) \neq 0$.

Step 1. If the degree of P is greater than or equal to the degree of D, use long (or synthetic) division to express $\dfrac{P(x)}{D(x)}$ as the sum of a polynomial and a fraction $\dfrac{R(x)}{D(x)}$ in which the degree of the remainder polynomial $R(x)$ is less than the degree of the denominator polynomial $D(x)$.

Step 2. Factor the denominator $D(x)$ into the product of linear and irreducible quadratic powers.

Step 3. Express $\dfrac{P(x)}{D(x)}$ as a cascading sum of partial fractions of the form

$$\frac{A_i}{(x - r)^n} \quad \text{and} \quad \frac{A_k x + B_k}{(x^2 + sx + t)^m}.$$

INTEGRATING RATIONAL FUNCTIONS

We will now apply the procedure of partial fraction decomposition to integration.

EXAMPLE 4   Integrating a rational function with a repeated linear factor

Find $\displaystyle\int \frac{x^2 - 6x + 3}{(x - 2)^3}\, dx.$

Solution

From Example 1, we have

$$\int \frac{x^2 - 6x + 3}{(x-2)^3}\, dx = \int \left[\frac{1}{x-2} + \frac{-2}{(x-2)^2} + \frac{-5}{(x-2)^3} \right] dx$$

$$= \int (x-2)^{-1}\, dx - 2 \int (x-2)^{-2}\, dx - 5 \int (x-2)^{-3}\, dx$$

$$= \ln|x-2| + \frac{2}{x-2} + \frac{5}{2(x-2)^2} + C \qquad \blacksquare$$

EXAMPLE 5 **Integrating a rational expression with distinct linear factors**

Find $\displaystyle\int \frac{x^4 + 2x^3 - 4x^2 + x - 3}{x^2 - x - 2}\, dx$.

Solution

We have $P(x) = x^4 + 2x^3 - 4x^2 + x - 3$ and $D(x) = x^2 - x - 2$; because the degree of P is greater than the degree of D, we carry out the long division and write

$$\int \frac{x^4 + 2x^3 - 4x^2 + x - 3}{x^2 - x - 2}\, dx = \int \left(x^2 + 3x + 1 + \frac{8x - 1}{x^2 - x - 2} \right) dx$$

The polynomial part is easy to integrate. The rational expression was decomposed into partial fractions in Example 2.

$$\int \frac{x^4 + 2x^3 - 4x^2 + x - 3}{x^2 - x - 2}\, dx = \int \left(x^2 + 3x + 1 + \frac{8x - 1}{x^2 - x - 2} \right) dx$$

$$= \int \left(x^2 + 3x + 1 + \frac{5}{x-2} + \frac{3}{x+1} \right) dx$$

$$= \int x^2\, dx + 3 \int x\, dx + \int dx + 5 \int (x-2)^{-1}\, dx + 3 \int (x+1)^{-1}\, dx$$

$$= \frac{x^3}{3} + \frac{3x^2}{2} + x + 5 \ln|x-2| + 3 \ln|x+1| + C \qquad \blacksquare$$

EXAMPLE 6 **Integrating a rational function with repeated quadratic factors**

Find $\displaystyle\int \frac{-3x^3 - x}{(x^2 + 1)^2}\, dx$.

Solution

From Example 3,

$$\int \frac{-3x^3 - x}{(x^2 + 1)^2}\, dx = \int \frac{2x}{(x^2 + 1)^2}\, dx + \int \frac{-3x}{x^2 + 1}\, dx$$

$$\boxed{u = x^2 + 1;\ du = 2x\, dx}$$

$$= \int u^{-2}\, du - \frac{3}{2} \int u^{-1}\, du$$

$$= -u^{-1} - \frac{3}{2} \ln|u| + C$$

$$= \frac{-1}{x^2 + 1} - \frac{3}{2} \ln(x^2 + 1) + C \qquad \blacksquare$$

EXAMPLE 7 **Repeated linear factors**

Find $\displaystyle\int \frac{5x^2 + 21x + 4}{(x+1)^2(x-3)}\,dx$.

Solution

The partial fraction decomposition of the integrand is

$$\frac{5x^2 + 21x + 4}{(x+1)^2(x-3)} = \frac{A_1}{(x+1)^2} + \frac{A_2}{x+1} + \frac{A_3}{x-3}$$

Multiply both sides by $(x+1)^2(x-3)$:

$$5x^2 + 21x + 4 = A_1(x-3) + A_2(x+1)(x-3) + A_3(x+1)^2$$

As in Example 2, we substitute $x = -1$ and $x = 3$ on both sides of the equation to obtain $A_1 = 3$ and $A_3 = 7$, but A_2 cannot be obtained in this fashion. To find A_2, multiply out the polynomial on the right:

$$5x^2 + 21x + 4 = (A_2 + A_3)x^2 + (A_1 - 2A_2 + 2A_3)x + (-3A_1 - 3A_2 + A_3)$$

Equate the coefficients of x^2, x, and 1 (the constant term) on each side of the equation:

$$\begin{aligned} 5 &= A_2 + A_3 && x^2 \text{ terms} \\ 21 &= A_1 - 2A_2 + 2A_3 && x \text{ terms} \\ 4 &= -3A_1 - 3A_2 + A_3 && \text{Constants} \end{aligned}$$

Because we already know that $A_1 = 3$ and $A_3 = 7$, we use the equation $5 = A_2 + A_3$ to obtain $A_2 = -2$. We now turn to the integration:

$$\int \frac{5x^2 + 21x + 4}{(x+1)^2(x-3)}\,dx = \int \frac{3\,dx}{(x+1)^2} + \int \frac{-2\,dx}{x+1} + \int \frac{7\,dx}{x-3}$$

$$= -3(x+1)^{-1} - 2\ln|x+1| + 7\ln|x-3| + C \qquad \blacksquare$$

EXAMPLE 8 **Distinct linear and quadratic factors**

Find $\displaystyle\int \frac{x^2 + 4x - 23}{(x^2 + 4)(x+3)}\,dx$.

Solution

The partial fraction decomposition of the integrand has the form

$$\frac{x^2 + 4x - 23}{(x^2 + 4)(x+3)} = \frac{A_1 x + B_1}{x^2 + 4} + \frac{A_2}{x+3}$$

Multiply both sides by $(x^2 + 4)(x+3)$ and then combine the terms on the right:

$$x^2 + 4x - 23 = (A_1 x + B_1)(x+3) + A_2(x^2 + 4)$$

$$= (A_1 + A_2)x^2 + (3A_1 + B_1)x + (3B_1 + 4A_2)$$

Equate the coefficients to set up the following system of equations:

$$\begin{cases} A_1 + A_2 = 1 & x^2 \text{ terms} \\ 3A_1 + B_1 = 4 & x \text{ terms} \\ 3B_1 + 4A_2 = -23 & \text{Constants} \end{cases}$$

Solve this system (the details are not shown) to find $A_1 = 3$, $B_1 = -5$, and $A_2 = -2$. We now turn to the integration:

$$\int \frac{x^2 + 4x - 23}{(x^2 + 4)(x+3)}\,dx = \int \frac{3x - 5}{x^2 + 4}\,dx + \int \frac{-2\,dx}{x+3}$$

$$= 3 \underbrace{\int \frac{x\,dx}{x^2+4}}_{\uparrow} - 5 \int \frac{dx}{x^2+4} - 2 \int \frac{dx}{x+3}$$

$$\boxed{u = x^2 + 4;\ du = 2x\,dx}$$

$$= 3 \left[\frac{1}{2} \ln(x^2 + 4) \right] - 5 \left[\frac{1}{2} \tan^{-1} \left(\frac{x}{2} \right) \right] - 2 \ln|x + 3| + C \qquad \blacksquare$$

RATIONAL FUNCTIONS OF SINE AND COSINE

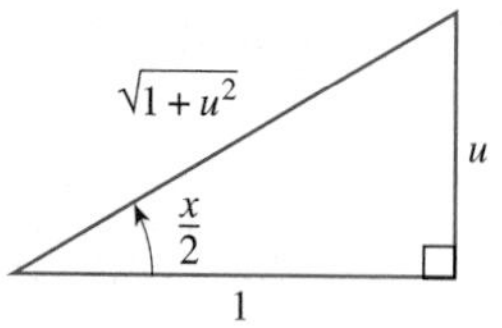

The German mathematician Karl Weierstrass (1815–1897) noticed that the substitution

$$u = \tan \frac{x}{2} \qquad -\pi < x < \pi$$

will convert any rational function of $\sin x$ and $\cos x$ into a rational function of x. To see why this is true, we use the double-angle identities for sine and cosine (see Figure 7.4):

$\tan \frac{x}{2} = u$

$\cos \frac{x}{2} = \frac{1}{\sqrt{1+u^2}}$

$\sin \frac{x}{2} = \frac{u}{\sqrt{1+u^2}}$

Figure 7.4 Weierstrass substitution

$$\sin x = 2 \sin \frac{x}{2} \cos \frac{x}{2} \qquad \text{and} \qquad \cos x = \cos^2 \frac{x}{2} - \sin^2 \frac{x}{2}$$

$$= 2 \left(\frac{u}{\sqrt{1+u^2}} \right) \left(\frac{1}{\sqrt{1+u^2}} \right) \qquad\qquad = \left(\frac{1}{\sqrt{1+u^2}} \right)^2 - \left(\frac{u}{\sqrt{1+u^2}} \right)^2$$

$$= \frac{2u}{1+u^2} \qquad\qquad\qquad\qquad\qquad = \frac{1-u^2}{1+u^2}$$

Finally, because $u = \tan \frac{x}{2}$, we have $x = 2 \tan^{-1} u$, so $dx = \frac{2}{1+u^2}\,du$.

Weierstrass Substitution

> For $-\pi < x < \pi$, let $u = \tan \dfrac{x}{2}$ so that
>
> $$\sin x = \frac{2u}{1+u^2}, \qquad \cos x = \frac{1-u^2}{1+u^2}, \qquad \text{and} \qquad dx = \frac{2}{1+u^2}\,du$$
>
> This is called the **Weierstrass substitution**.

The following example illustrates how this substitution can be used along with partial fractions to integrate a rational trigonometric function.

EXAMPLE 9   Integrating a rational trigonometric function

Find $\displaystyle \int \frac{dx}{3 \cos x - 4 \sin x}$.

Solution

Use the Weierstrass substitution—that is, let $u = \tan \dfrac{x}{2}$. Remember, $dx = \dfrac{2\,du}{1+u^2}$; $\cos x = \dfrac{1-u^2}{1+u^2}$; and $\sin x = \dfrac{2u}{1+u^2}$.

$$\int \frac{dx}{3 \cos x - 4 \sin x} = \int \frac{\dfrac{2\,du}{1+u^2}}{3 \left(\dfrac{1-u^2}{1+u^2} \right) - 4 \left(\dfrac{2u}{1+u^2} \right)} \qquad \text{Simplify.}$$

$$= \int \frac{-2\,du}{3u^2 + 8u - 3} = \int \frac{-2\,du}{(3u-1)(u+3)}$$

This integral can be handled by the method of partial fractions.

$$\frac{-2}{(3u-1)(u+3)} = \frac{A_1}{3u-1} + \frac{A_2}{u+3}$$

Solve this to find $A_1 = -\frac{3}{5}$ and $A_2 = \frac{1}{5}$. We continue with the integration.

$$\begin{aligned}
\int \frac{dx}{3\cos x - 4\sin x} &= \int \frac{-2\,du}{(3u-1)(u+3)} \\
&= \int \frac{-\frac{3}{5}\,du}{3u-1} + \int \frac{\frac{1}{5}\,du}{u+3} \\
&= -\frac{3}{5}\cdot\frac{1}{3}\ln|3u-1| + \frac{1}{5}\cdot\ln|u+3| + C \\
&= -\frac{1}{5}\ln\left|3\tan\frac{x}{2}-1\right| + \frac{1}{5}\ln\left|\tan\frac{x}{2}+3\right| + C
\end{aligned}$$ ∎

Once again, observe that when carrying out integration, you may obtain very different forms for the result. For Example 9, you might use an integration table (Formula 393 in the *Student Mathematics Handbook*, for example) to find

SMH

$$\int \frac{du}{p\sin au + q\cos au} = \frac{1}{a\sqrt{p^2+q^2}}\ln\left|\tan\left(\frac{au + \tan^{-1}\left(\frac{q}{p}\right)}{2}\right)\right|$$

Let $p = -4$, $q = 3$, $a = 1$, so that

$$\int \frac{dx}{3\cos x - 4\sin x} = \frac{1}{5}\ln\left|\tan\left(\frac{x + \tan^{-1}\left(-\frac{3}{4}\right)}{2}\right)\right| + C$$

Problem 67 asks you to derive the formula

$$\int \sec x\,dx = \ln|\sec x + \tan x| + C$$

from scratch. You might recall that we derived this formula using an unusual algebraic step in Example 3 of Section 7.1. You can now derive it by using a Weierstrass substitution.

7.4 PROBLEM SET

A *Write each rational function given in Problems 1–14 as a sum of partial fractions.*

1. $\dfrac{1}{x(x-3)}$

2. $\dfrac{3x-1}{x^2-1}$

3. $\dfrac{3x^2+2x-1}{x(x+1)}$

4. $\dfrac{2x^2+5x-1}{x(x^2-1)}$

5. $\dfrac{4}{2x^2+x}$

6. $\dfrac{x^2-x+3}{x^2(x-1)}$

7. $\dfrac{4x^3+4x^2+x-1}{x^2(x+1)^2}$

8. $\dfrac{x^2-5x-4}{(x^2+1)(x-3)}$

9. $\dfrac{x^3+3x^2+3x-4}{x^2(x+3)^2}$

10. $\dfrac{1}{x^3-1}$

11. $\dfrac{1}{1-x^4}$

12. $\dfrac{x^4-x^2+2}{x^2(x-1)}$

13. $\dfrac{x^2+x-1}{x(x+1)(2x-1)}$

14. $\dfrac{x^3-2x^2+x-5}{x(x^2-1)(3x+5)}$

Compute the integrals given in Problems 15–20. Notice that in each case, the integrand is a rational function decomposed into partial fractions in Problems 1–6.

15. $\displaystyle\int \frac{dx}{x(x-3)}$

16. $\displaystyle\int \frac{3x-1}{x^2-1}\,dx$

17. $\displaystyle\int \frac{3x^2+2x-1}{x(x+1)}\,dx$

18. $\displaystyle\int \frac{2x^2+5x-1}{x(x^2-1)}\,dx$

19. $\displaystyle\int \frac{4\,dx}{2x^2+x}$

20. $\displaystyle\int \frac{x^2-x+3}{x^2(x-1)}\,dx$

Find the indicated integrals in Problems 21–36.

21. $\int \dfrac{2x^3 + 9x - 1}{x^2(x^2 - 1)}\, dx$

22. $\int \dfrac{x^4 - x^2 + 2}{x^2(x - 1)}\, dx$

23. $\int \dfrac{x^2 + 1}{x^2 + x - 2}\, dx$

24. $\int \dfrac{dx}{x^3 - 8}$

25. $\int \dfrac{x^4 + 1}{x^4 - 1}\, dx$

26. $\int \dfrac{x^3 + 1}{x^3 - 1}\, dx$

27. $\int \dfrac{x\, dx}{(x + 1)^2}$

28. $\int \dfrac{2x\, dx}{(x - 2)^2}$

29. $\int \dfrac{dx}{x(x + 1)(x - 2)}$

30. $\int \dfrac{x + 2}{x(x - 1)^2}\, dx$

31. $\int \dfrac{x\, dx}{(x + 1)(x + 2)^2}$

32. $\int \dfrac{x + 1}{x(x^2 + 2)}\, dx$

33. $\int \dfrac{5x + 7}{x^2 + 2x - 3}\, dx$

34. $\int \dfrac{5x\, dx}{x^2 - 6x + 9}$

35. $\int \dfrac{3x^2 - 2x + 4}{x^3 - x^2 + 4x - 4}\, dx$

36. $\int \dfrac{3x^2 + 4x + 1}{x^3 + 2x^2 + x - 2}\, dx$

Ⓑ **37. WHAT DOES THIS SAY?** Describe the process of partial fraction decomposition.

Find the indicated integrals in Problems 38–55.

38. $\int \dfrac{\cos x\, dx}{\sin^2 x - \sin x - 2}$

39. $\int \dfrac{e^x\, dx}{2e^{2x} - 5e^x - 3}$

40. $\int \dfrac{e^x\, dx}{e^{2x} - 1}$

41. $\int \dfrac{\sin x\, dx}{(1 + \cos x)^2}$

42. $\int \dfrac{\tan x\, dx}{\sec^2 x + 4}$

43. $\int \dfrac{\sec^2 x\, dx}{\tan x + 4}$

44. $\int \dfrac{dx}{x^{1/4} - x}$

45. $\int \dfrac{dx}{x^{2/3} - x^{1/2}}$

46. $\int \dfrac{dx}{\sin x - \cos x}$

47. $\int \dfrac{dx}{3\cos x + 4\sin x}$

48. $\int \dfrac{dx}{5\sin x + 4}$

49. $\int \dfrac{\sin x - \cos x}{\sin x + \cos x}\, dx$

50. $\int \dfrac{dx}{4\cos x + 5}$

51. $\int \dfrac{dx}{\sec x - \tan x}$

52. $\int \dfrac{dx}{3\sin x + 4\cos x + 5}$

53. $\int \dfrac{dx}{4\sin x - 3\cos x - 5}$

54. $\int \dfrac{dx}{2\csc x - \cot x + 2}$

55. $\int \dfrac{dx}{x(3 - \ln x)(1 - \ln x)}$

56. Find the area under the curve $y = \dfrac{1}{x^2 + 5x + 4}$ between $x = 0$ and $x = 3$.

57. Find the area of the region bounded by the curve $y = \dfrac{1}{6 - 5x + x^2}$ and the lines $x = \frac{4}{3}$, $x = \frac{7}{4}$, and $y = 0$.

58. Find the volume (to four decimal places) of the solid generated when the curve

$$y = \frac{1}{x^2 + 5x + 4}, \qquad 0 \le x \le 1$$

is revolved about

    a. the y-axis   **b.** the x-axis   **c.** the line $x = -1$

59. Find the volume (to four decimal places) of the solid generated when the region under the curve

$$y = \frac{1}{\sqrt{x^2 + 4x + 3}}$$

on the interval $[0, 3]$ is revolved about

    a. the x-axis   **b.** the y-axis

60. Find both the exact and approximate volume of the solid generated when the region under the curve $y^2 = x^2\left(\dfrac{4 - x}{4 + x}\right)$ on the interval $[0, 4]$ is revolved about the x-axis.

61. HISTORICAL QUEST   George Pólya was born in Hungary and attended universities in Budapest, Vienna, Göttingen, and Paris. He was a professor of mathematics at Stanford University. Pólya's research and winning personality earned him a place of honor not only among mathematicians, but among students and teachers as well. His discoveries spanned an impressive range of mathematics,

GEORGE PÓLYA
1887–1985

including real and complex analysis, probability, combinatorics, number theory, and geometry. Pólya's book, *How to Solve It*, has been translated into 20 languages. His books have a clarity and elegance seldom seen in mathematics, making them a joy to read. For example, here is his explanation of why he was a mathematician: "It is a little shortened but not quite wrong to say: I thought I am not good enough for physics and I am too good for philosophy. Mathematics is in between." ∎

A story told by Pólya provides our next Quest. "A number of years ago," Pólya related with his lovable accent, "I deliberately put the problem

$$\int \frac{x\, dx}{x^2 - 9}$$

as the first problem on a test of techniques of integration, to give my students a boost as they began the exam. With the substitution $u = x^2 - 9$, which I expected the students to use, you can knock the problem off in just a few seconds. Half of the students did this, and got off to a good start. But a fourth of them used the correct but time-consuming procedure of partial fractions—and because they spent so much time on the problem, they did poorly on the exam. Half of the rest used the trig substitution $x = 3\sin\theta$—also correct but so time-consuming that they wound up very far behind and bombed the exam. It is interesting that the students who used the harder techniques showed they knew 'more,' or at least more difficult mathematics than the ones who used the easy technique. But they showed that 'it's not just what you know; it's how and when you use it.' It's nice when what you do is right, but it's much better when it's also *appropriate*."* Carry out all three methods of solution of the given integral Pólya described in this quotation.

---

*"Pólya, Problem Solving, and Education," by Alan H. Schoenfeld, *Mathematics Magazine*, Vol. 60, No. 5, December 1987, p. 290.

62. Spy Problem After waiting hours at the sleazy bar for his superior, Lord Newton Fleming (recall Problem 55, Section 6.6), the Spy is about to leave when a courier arrives with shocking news—Lord Newton has been kidnapped by Ernst Stavro Blohardt! The Spy hurries to the village outside the thug's château disguised as an old duck plucker. On the day he arrives, his true identity is known only to the Redselig twins, Hans and Franz, but the next day, Hans' girlfriend, Blabba, finds out. Soon, word begins to circulate among the 60 citizens of the village as to the Spy's true identity. He determines that the rate at which the rumor concerning his identity will spread is jointly proportional to the product of the number N of those who already know and the number $60 - N$ of those who do not, so that

$$\frac{dN}{dt} = kN(60 - N)$$

for a constant k. He needs a week to get the information to break into the château to free Lord Newton, but figures that as soon as 20 or more villagers know his identity, Blohardt is sure to find out, too. Does he complete his mission, or is he about to be a dead duck plucker?

63. Two substances, A and B, are being converted into a single compound C. In the laboratory, it is shown that the time rate of change of the amount x of compound C is proportional to the product of the amount of unconverted substances A and B. Thus,

$$\frac{dx}{dt} = k(a - x)(b - x)$$

for initial concentrations a and b of A and B, respectively.

a. Solve this differential equation to express x in terms of time t. What happens to $x(t)$ as $t \to +\infty$ if $b > a$? What if $a > b$?

b. Suppose $a = b$. What is $x(t)$? What happens to $x(t)$ as $t \to +\infty$ in this case?

64. Use partial fractions to derive the integration formula

$$\int \frac{dx}{a^2 - x^2} = \frac{1}{2a} \ln \left| \frac{a + x}{a - x} \right| + C$$

65. Use partial fractions to derive the integration formula

$$\int \frac{dx}{x(ax + b)} = \frac{1}{b} \ln \left| \frac{x}{ax + b} \right| + C$$

66. Exploration Problem Consider the integral $\int \sqrt{1 - \cos x}\, dx$.

a. If you have access to a CAS, report on your attempts to find this integral.

b. Use a Weierstrass substitution to find this integral.

c. Can you think of an even more clever way to perform the integration?

C 67. Derive the formula

$$\int \sec x\, dx = \ln |\sec x + \tan x| + C$$

using a Weierstrass substitution.

68. Derive the formula

$$\int \csc x\, dx = -\ln |\csc x + \cot x| + C$$

using a Weierstrass substitution.

7.5 Summary of Integration Techniques

IN THIS SECTION integration strategy

We conclude our study of integration techniques with a table summarizing integration techniques.

TABLE 7.2 Integration Strategy

Step 1. Simplify.	Simplify the integrand, if possible, and use one of the procedural rules (see the inside back cover or the table of integrals).
Step 2. Use basic formulas. SMH	Use the basic integration formulas (1–29 in the integration table in Appendix D and the *Student Mathematics Handbook*). These are the fundamental building blocks for integration. Almost every integration will involve some basic formulas somewhere in the process, which means that you should memorize these formulas.
Step 3. Substitute.	Make any substitution that will transform the integral into one of the basic forms.
Step 4. Classify.	Classify the integrand according to form in order to use a table of integrals. You may need to use substitution to transform the integrand into a form contained in the integration table. Some special types of substitution are contained in the following list:

TABLE 7.2 Integration Strategy (Continued)

I. Integration by parts

   A. Forms $\int x^n e^{ax}\,dx$, $\int x^n \sin ax\,dx$, $\int x^n \cos ax\,dx$
     Let $u = x^n$.
   B. Forms $\int x^n \ln x\,dx$, $\int x^n \sin^{-1} ax\,dx$, $\int x^n \tan^{-1} ax\,dx$
     Let $dv = x^n\,dx$.
   C. Forms $\int e^{ax} \sin bx\,dx$, $\int e^{ax} \cos bx\,dx$
     Let $dv = e^{ax}\,dx$.

II. Trigonometric forms

   A. $\int \sin^m x \cos^n x\,dx$
     m odd: Peel off a factor of $(\sin x\,dx)$ and **let $u = \cos x$.**
     n odd: Peel off a factor of $(\cos x\,dx)$ and **let $u = \sin x$.**
     m and n both even: **Use half-angle identities:**

$$\cos^2 x = \tfrac{1}{2}(1 + \cos 2x) \quad \text{and} \quad \sin^2 x = \tfrac{1}{2}(1 - \cos 2x)$$

   B. $\int \tan^m x \sec^n x\,dx$
     n even: Peel off a factor of $(\sec^2 x\,dx)$ and **let $u = \tan x$.**
     m odd: Peel off a factor of $(\sec x \tan x\,dx)$ and **let $u = \sec x$.**
     m even, n odd: Write using powers of secant and **use a reduction formula** (Formula 428 in the integration tables).
   C. For a rational trigonometric integral, try the Weierstrass substitution.
     Let $u = \tan \frac{x}{2}$, so that $\sin x = \dfrac{2u}{1 + u^2}$, $\cos x = \dfrac{1 - u^2}{1 + u^2}$, and $dx = \dfrac{2}{1 + u^2}\,du$.

III. Radical forms; try a trigonometric substitution.

   A. Form $\sqrt{a^2 - u^2}$: **Let $u = a \sin \theta$.**
   B. Form $\sqrt{a^2 + u^2}$: **Let $u = a \tan \theta$.**
   C. Form $\sqrt{u^2 - a^2}$: **Let $u = a \sec \theta$.**

IV. Rational forms; try partial fraction decomposition.

Step 5. Try again.   **Still stuck?**

1. Manipulate the integrand:
   Multiply by 1 (clever choice of numerator or denominator).
   Rationalize the numerator.
   Rationalize the denominator.
2. Relate the problem to a previously worked problem.
3. Look at another table of integrals or consult computer software that does integration.
4. Some integrals do not have simple antiderivatives, so all these methods may fail. We will look at some of these forms later in the text.
5. If dealing with a definite integral, an approximation may suffice. It may be appropriate to use a calculator, computer, or the techniques introduced in Section 5.8.

EXAMPLE 1 **Deciding on an integration procedure**

Indicate a procedure to set up each integral. It is not necessary to carry out the integration.

a. $\displaystyle\int \frac{\sin \sqrt{x}}{\sqrt{x}}\,dx$ **b.** $\displaystyle\int (1 + \tan^2 \theta)\,d\theta$ **c.** $\displaystyle\int \sin^3 x \cos^2 x\,dx$

d. $\displaystyle\int 4x^2 \cos 3x\,dx$ **e.** $\displaystyle\int \frac{x\,dx}{\sqrt{9 - x^2}}$ **f.** $\displaystyle\int \frac{x^2\,dx}{\sqrt{9 - x^2}}$

g. $\displaystyle\int e^{3x} \sin 2x\,dx$ **h.** $\displaystyle\int \frac{\cos^4 x\,dx}{1 - \sin^2 x}$

Solution

Keep in mind that there may be several correct approaches, and the way you proceed from problem to solution is often a matter of personal preference. However, to give you some practice, we will present several hints and suggestions in the context of this example.

a. $\displaystyle\int \frac{\sin \sqrt{x}}{\sqrt{x}}\, dx$

The integrand is simplified and is not a fundamental type. Substitution will work well for this problem if you let $u = \sqrt{x}$. After you make this substitution you can integrate using a basic formula.

b. $\displaystyle\int (1 + \tan^2 \theta)\, d\theta$

The integrand can be simplified using a trigonometric identity $(1 + \tan^2 \theta = \sec^2 \theta)$, so that it can now be integrated using a basic formula.

c. $\displaystyle\int \sin^3 x \cos^2 x\, dx$

The integrand is simplified, it is not a basic formula, and there does not seem to be an easy substitution. Next, try to classify the integrand. We see that it involves powers of trigonometric functions of the type $\int \sin^m x \cos^n x\, dx$, where $m = 3$ (odd) and $n = 2$ (even), so we make the substitution $u = \cos x$.

d. $\displaystyle\int 4x^2 \cos 3x\, dx$

The integrand is simplified (you can bring the 4 out in front of the integral, if you wish), it is not a basic formula, and there is no easy substitution. You might try integration by parts (several steps) or you can check the table of integrals and find it to be Formula 313.

e. $\displaystyle\int \frac{x\, dx}{\sqrt{9 - x^2}}$

The integrand is simplified and is not a basic formula. However, we might try the substitution $u = 9 - x^2$. It looks like this will work because the degree of the numerator is one less than the degree of the denominator.

f. $\displaystyle\int \frac{x^2\, dx}{\sqrt{9 - x^2}}$

The integrand is simplified, it is not a basic formula, and it looks as though an algebraic substitution will not work because of the degree of the numerator. Since the integrand involves $\sqrt{9 - x^2}$, we use the trigonometric substitution $x = 3 \sin \theta$, $dx = 3 \cos \theta\, d\theta$. If the integral had been $\displaystyle\int \frac{x^2\, dx}{\sqrt{x^2 - 9}}$, you would have used the substitution $x = 3 \sec \theta$, $dx = 3 \tan \theta \sec \theta\, d\theta$.

g. $\displaystyle\int e^{3x} \sin 2x\, dx$

The integrand is simplified and it is not a basic formula. If we try to classify the integrand, we see that integration by parts will work with $u = \sin 2x$ and $dv = e^{3x}\, dx$. We also find that this form is Formula 492 in the integration table.

h. $\displaystyle\int \frac{\cos^4 x \, dx}{1 - \sin^2 x}$

The integration can be simplified by writing $1 - \sin^2 x = \cos^2 x$. After doing this substitution, you will obtain

$$\int \frac{\cos^4 x \, dx}{1 - \sin^2 x} = \int \frac{\cos^4 x \, dx}{\cos^2 x} = \int \cos^2 x \, dx$$

This form can be integrated by using a half-angle identity or Formula 317 in the table of integrals. It can also be integrated by parts. ∎

7.5 PROBLEM SET

Ⓐ *Find each integral in Problems 1–54.*

1. $\displaystyle\int \frac{2x - 1}{(x - x^2)^3} \, dx$

2. $\displaystyle\int \frac{2x + 3}{\sqrt{x^2 + 3x}} \, dx$

3. $\displaystyle\int (x \sec 2x^2) \, dx$

4. $\displaystyle\int (x^2 \csc^2 2x^3) \, dx$

5. $\displaystyle\int (e^x \cot e^x) \, dx$

6. $\displaystyle\int \frac{\tan \sqrt{x} \, dx}{\sqrt{x}}$

7. $\displaystyle\int \frac{\tan(\ln x) \, dx}{x}$

8. $\displaystyle\int \sqrt{\cot x} \, \csc^2 x \, dx$

9. $\displaystyle\int \frac{(3 + 2 \sin t)}{\cos t} \, dt$

10. $\displaystyle\int \frac{2 + \cos x}{\sin x} \, dx$

11. $\displaystyle\int \frac{e^{2t} \, dt}{1 + e^{4t}}$

12. $\displaystyle\int \frac{\sin 2x \, dx}{1 + \sin^4 x}$

13. $\displaystyle\int \frac{x^2 + x + 1}{x^2 + 9} \, dx$

14. $\displaystyle\int \frac{3x + 2}{\sqrt{4 - x^2}} \, dx$

15. $\displaystyle\int \frac{1 + e^x}{1 - e^x} \, dx$

16. $\displaystyle\int \frac{e^{1 - \sqrt{x}} \, dx}{\sqrt{x}}$

17. $\displaystyle\int \frac{2t^2 \, dt}{\sqrt{1 - t^6}}$

18. $\displaystyle\int \frac{t^3 \, dt}{2^8 + t^8}$

19. $\displaystyle\int \frac{dx}{1 + e^{2x}}$

20. $\displaystyle\int \frac{dx}{4 - e^{-x}}$

21. $\displaystyle\int \frac{dx}{x^2 + 2x + 2}$

22. $\displaystyle\int \frac{dx}{x^2 + x + 4}$

23. $\displaystyle\int \frac{dx}{x^2 + x + 1}$

24. $\displaystyle\int \frac{dx}{x^2 - x + 1}$

25. $\displaystyle\int \tan^{-1} x \, dx$

26. $\displaystyle\int x^3 \sin x^2 \, dx$

27. $\displaystyle\int e^{-x} \cos x \, dx$

28. $\displaystyle\int e^{2x} \sin 3x \, dx$

29. $\displaystyle\int \cos^{-1}(-x) \, dx$

30. $\displaystyle\int x \sec^{-1} x \, dx, x > 0$

31. $\displaystyle\int \sin^3 x \, dx$

32. $\displaystyle\int \cos^5 x \, dx$

33. $\displaystyle\int \sin^3 x \cos^2 x \, dx$

34. $\displaystyle\int \sin^3 x \cos^3 x \, dx$

35. $\displaystyle\int \sin^2 x \cos^4 x \, dx$

36. $\displaystyle\int \sin^2 x \cos^5 x \, dx$

37. $\displaystyle\int \sin^5 x \cos^4 x \, dx$

38. $\displaystyle\int \sin^4 x \cos^2 x \, dx$

39. $\displaystyle\int \tan^5 x \sec^4 x \, dx$

40. $\displaystyle\int \tan^4 x \sec^4 x \, dx$

41. $\displaystyle\int \frac{\sqrt{1 - x^2}}{x} \, dx$

42. $\displaystyle\int \frac{dx}{\sqrt{x^2 - 16}}$

43. $\displaystyle\int \frac{2x + 3}{\sqrt{2x^2 - 1}} \, dx$

44. $\displaystyle\int \frac{dx}{x\sqrt{x^2 - 1}}$

45. $\displaystyle\int \frac{dx}{x\sqrt{x^2 + 1}}$

46. $\displaystyle\int x\sqrt{x^2 + 1} \, dx$

47. $\displaystyle\int \frac{(2x + 1) \, dx}{\sqrt{4x - x^2 - 2}}$

48. $\displaystyle\int \sqrt{3 + 4x - 4x^2} \, dx$

49. $\displaystyle\int \frac{\cos x \, dx}{\sqrt{1 + \sin^2 x}}$

50. $\displaystyle\int \frac{\sec^2 x \, dx}{\sqrt{\sec^2 x - 2}}$

51. $\displaystyle\int \sin^5 x \, dx$

52. $\displaystyle\int \cos^6 x \, dx$

53. $\displaystyle\int \tan^4 x \, dx$

54. $\displaystyle\int \sec^4 x \, dx$

Find the exact value of the definite integrals in Problems 55–62.

55. $\displaystyle\int_0^2 \sqrt{4 - x^2} \, dx$

56. $\displaystyle\int_0^1 \frac{dx}{\sqrt{9 - x^2}}$

57. $\displaystyle\int_0^{\ln 2} e^t \sqrt{1 + e^{2t}} \, dt$

58. $\displaystyle\int_0^1 \frac{dt}{4t^2 + 4t + 5}$

59. $\displaystyle\int_1^2 \frac{dx}{x^4 \sqrt{x^2 + 3}}$

60. $\displaystyle\int_0^2 \frac{x^3}{(3 + x^2)^{3/2}} \, dx$

61. $\displaystyle\int_{-2}^{2\sqrt{3}} x^3 \sqrt{x^2 + 4} \, dx$

62. $\displaystyle\int_0^{\sqrt{5}} x^2 \sqrt{5 - x^2} \, dx$

Ⓑ *Find each integral in Problems 63–72.*

63. $\displaystyle\int \frac{e^x \, dx}{\sqrt{1 + e^{2x}}}$

64. $\displaystyle\int \frac{(2x + 1) \, dx}{\sqrt{4x^2 + 4x + 2}}$

65. $\displaystyle\int \frac{x^2 + 4x + 3}{x^3 + x^2 + x} \, dx$

66. $\displaystyle\int \frac{5x^2 + 3x - 2}{x^3 + 2x^2} \, dx$

67. $\displaystyle\int \frac{5x^2 + 18x + 34}{(x - 7)(x + 2)^2} \, dx$

68. $\displaystyle\int \frac{-3x^2 + 9x + 21}{(x + 2)^2(2x + 1)} \, dx$

69. $\displaystyle\int \frac{3x + 5}{x^2 + 2x + 1} \, dx$

70. $\displaystyle\int \frac{3x^2 + 2x + 1}{x^3 + x^2 + x} \, dx$

71. $\displaystyle\int \frac{x \, dx}{(x + 1)(x + 2)(x + 3)}$

72. $\displaystyle\int \frac{5x^2 - 4x + 9}{x^3 - x^2 + 4x - 4} \, dx$

73. Find the average value (to the nearest hundredth) of the function $f(x) = x \sin^3 x^2$ between $x = 0$ and $x = 1$.

74. An object moves along the x-axis in such a way that its velocity at time t is $v(t) = \sin t + \sin^2 t \cos^3 t$. Find the distance moved by the object between times $t = 0$ and $t = \frac{\pi}{3}$.

75. Exploration Problem Integrals of the general form

$$\int \cot^m x \csc^n x \, dx$$

are handled in much the same way as those of the form

$$\int \tan^m x \sec^n x \, dx$$

a. What substitution would you use in the case where m is odd?

b. What substitution would you use if n is even?

c. What would you do if n is odd and m is even?

76. Find the arc length (correct to four decimal places) of the curve $y = \ln x$ from $x = 2$ to $x = 3$.

77. Find the arc length (correct to four decimal places) of the curve $y = x^2$ from $x = -1$ to $x = 1$.

78. Find the volume of the solid generated when the region under the curve $y = \cos x$ between $x = 0$ and $x = \frac{\pi}{2}$ is revolved about the x-axis.

79. Find the area of the region bounded by the graphs of $y = \dfrac{2x}{\sqrt{x^2 + 9}}$, $y = 0$, $x = 0$, and $x = 4$.

80. What is the volume of the solid obtained when the region bounded by $y = \sqrt{x}e^{-x^2}$, $y = 0$, $x = 0$, and $x = 2$ is revolved about the x-axis?

81. What is the volume of the solid obtained when the region bounded by $y = x\sqrt{9 - x^2}$ and $y = 0$ is revolved about the x-axis?

82. Find the length of the curve $y = \ln(\sec x)$ from $x = 0$ to $x = \frac{\pi}{4}$.

83. Find the centroid (to the nearest hundredth) of the region bounded by the curve $y = x^2 e^{-x}$ and the x-axis, between $x = 0$ and $x = 1$.

84. Generalize the result of Example 4, Section 7.2 by showing that

$$\int e^{ax} \sin bx \, dx = \frac{(a \sin bx - b \cos bx)e^{ax}}{a^2 + b^2} + C$$

for constants a and b. (This is Formula 492.)

85. Let f'' be continuous on the closed interval $[a, b]$. Use integration by parts to show that

$$\int_a^b x f''(x) \, dx = bf'(b) - f(b) + f(a) - af'(a)$$

86. Derive the reduction formula

$$\int x^m (\ln x)^n \, dx = \frac{x^{m+1}(\ln x)^n}{m + 1} - \frac{n}{m + 1} \int x^m (\ln x)^{n-1} \, dx$$

where m and n are positive integers. (This is Formula 510 in the *Student Mathematics Handbook*.) Use the formula to find

$$\int x^2 (\ln x)^3 \, dx$$

87. Derive the reduction formula

$$\int \sin^n Ax \, dx = \frac{-\sin^{n-1} Ax \cos Ax}{An} + \frac{n - 1}{n} \int \sin^{n-2} Ax \, dx$$

(This is Formula 352 in the *Student Mathematics Handbook*.) Use this formula to evaluate

$$\int \sin^4 4x \, dx$$

7.6 First-Order Differential Equations

IN THIS SECTION first-order linear differential equations, applications of first-order equations

FIRST-ORDER LINEAR DIFFERENTIAL EQUATIONS

We introduced separable differential equations in Section 5.6, but not all first-order differential equations have the separable form

$$\frac{dy}{dx} = \frac{f(x)}{g(y)}$$

The goal of this section is to examine a second class of differential equations, called **first-order linear**, that have the general form

$$\frac{dy}{dx} + P(x)y = Q(x)$$

For example, the differential equation

$$\frac{dy}{dx} - \frac{y}{x} = e^{-x}$$

is first-order linear, with $P(x) = -\dfrac{1}{x}$ and $Q(x) = e^{-x}$, and

$$x^2 \frac{dy}{dx} - (x^2 + 2)y = x^5$$

can be put into this form by dividing by x^2, the coefficient of $\dfrac{dy}{dx}$, to obtain

$$\frac{dy}{dx} - \left(\frac{x^2 + 2}{x^2} \right) y = \frac{x^5}{x^2}$$

(Note that $P(x) = -\left(\dfrac{x^2 + 2}{x^2} \right) = -1 - 2x^{-2}$ and $Q(x) = \dfrac{x^5}{x^2} = x^3$.)

First-order linear equations can be used to model a variety of important situations in the physical, social, and life sciences. We will examine a few such models as well as additional models involving separable equations later in this section, but first we need to know how first-order linear differential equations may be solved.

THEOREM 7.1 **General solution of a first-order linear differential equation**

The general solution of the first-order linear differential equation

$$\frac{dy}{dx} + P(x)y = Q(x)$$

is given by

$$y = \frac{1}{I(x)} \left[\int Q(x)I(x)\,dx + C \right]$$

where $I(x) = e^{\int P(x)\,dx}$, and C is an arbitrary constant.

WARNING Coefficient of $\dfrac{dy}{dx}$ must be 1. The $\int P(x)\,dx$ that appears in the exponent of $I(x)$ is any antiderivative of $P(x)$.

Proof First, note that

$$\frac{dI(x)}{dx} = e^{\int P(x)\,dx} \left[\frac{d}{dx} \int P(x)\,dx \right] = e^{\int P(x)\,dx} P(x) = I(x)P(x)$$

because $\dfrac{d}{dx} e^u = e^u \dfrac{du}{dx}$. Thus,

$$\frac{d}{dx}[I(x)y] = I(x)\frac{dy}{dx} + y\frac{d}{dx}I(x) = I(x)\frac{dy}{dx} + yI(x)P(x) \quad \text{Product rule}$$

We use this computation as the third step in the following.

$$\frac{dy}{dx} + P(x)y = Q(x) \qquad\qquad \text{Given}$$

$$I(x)\left[\frac{dy}{dx} + P(x)y \right] = I(x)Q(x) \qquad\qquad \text{Multiply both sides by } I(x).$$

$$I(x)\frac{dy}{dx} + I(x)P(x)y = I(x)Q(x)$$

$$\frac{d}{dx}[I(x)y] = I(x)Q(x) \qquad\qquad \text{Substitute.}$$

$$\int \frac{d}{dx}[I(x)y]\,dx = \int I(x)Q(x)\,dx \qquad\qquad \text{Integrate both sides.}$$

$$I(x)y = \int I(x)Q(x)\,dx + C$$

As usual, the constant of integration C is added after the last integration.

$$y = \frac{1}{I(x)} \left[\int I(x)Q(x)\,dx + C \right]$$

Because multiplying both sides of the differential equation

$$\frac{dy}{dx} + P(x)y = Q(x)$$

by $I(x)$ makes the left side an exact derivative, the function $I(x)$ is called an **integrating factor** of the differential equation.

A first-order **initial value problem** involves a first-order equation and the value of y at a particular value $x = x_0$. Here is an example of such a problem.

EXAMPLE 1 First-order linear initial value problem

Solve $\dfrac{dy}{dx} = e^{-x} - 2y$, $x \geq 0$, subject to the initial condition $y = 2$ when $x = 0$.

Solution

A graphical solution (using technology) is found by looking at the direction field as shown in Figure 7.5.

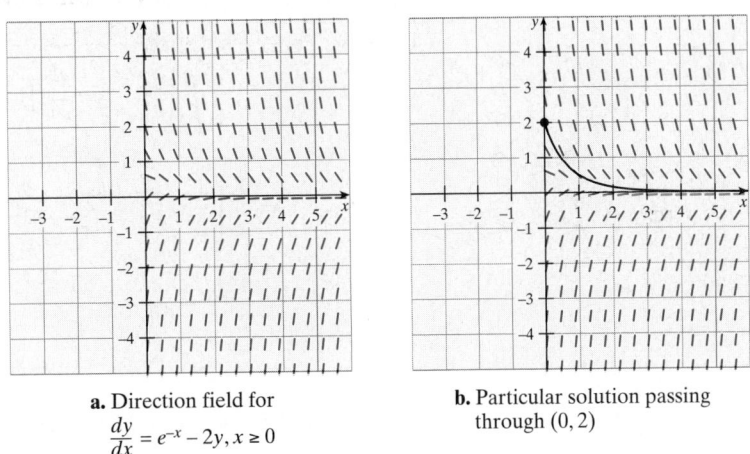

a. Direction field for
$\frac{dy}{dx} = e^{-x} - 2y, x \geq 0$

b. Particular solution passing through $(0, 2)$

Figure 7.5 Graphical solution using a direction field

To find an analytic solution, we use Theorem 7.1. The differential equation can be expressed in first-order linear form by adding $2y$ to both sides:

$$\frac{dy}{dx} + 2y = e^{-x} \qquad \text{for} \quad x \geq 0$$

We have $P(x) = 2$ and $Q(x) = e^{-x}$. Both $P(x)$ and $Q(x)$ are continuous in the domain $x \geq 0$. An integrating factor is given by

$$I(x) = e^{\int P(x)\, dx} = e^{\int 2\, dx} = e^{2x} \qquad \text{for} \quad x \geq 0$$

We now use the first-order linear differential equation theorem, where $I(x) = e^{2x}$ and $Q(x) = e^{-x}$, to find y.

$$y = \frac{1}{e^{2x}} \left[\int e^{2x} e^{-x}\, dx + C \right]$$

$$= \frac{1}{e^{2x}} \left[e^{x} + C \right] = e^{-x} + Ce^{-2x} \qquad \text{for} \quad x \geq 0$$

To find C, note that because $y = 2$ when $x = 0$, it follows that $1 = C$. Thus, $y = e^{-x} + e^{-2x}$, $x \geq 0$.

You might wish to compare the analytic and graphical solutions by noting that the graph of the equation matches the solution shown in Figure 7.5b. ■

Integration by parts is often used in solving first-order linear differential equations. Here is an example.

EXAMPLE 2   First-order linear differential equation

Find the general solution of the differential equation

$$x\frac{dy}{dx} + y = xe^{2x}, \qquad x > 0$$

Solution

As a first step, divide each term in the given equation by x so that we can use integrating factors, as in Theorem 7.1.

$$\frac{dy}{dx} + \frac{y}{x} = e^{2x}$$

For this equation, $P(x) = \frac{1}{x}$ and $Q(x) = e^{2x}$. The integrating factor is

$$I(x) = e^{\int (1/x)\,dx} = e^{\ln x} = x$$

Thus, the general solution is

$$y = \frac{1}{x}\left[\int xe^{2x}\,dx + C\right] \qquad \text{Integrate } \int xe^{2x}\,dx \text{ by parts.}$$

$$= \frac{1}{x}\left[\frac{1}{2}xe^{2x} - \frac{1}{4}e^{2x} + C\right] \qquad \text{See Example 5, Section 7.2.}$$

$$= \frac{1}{2}e^{2x} - \frac{e^{2x}}{4x} + \frac{C}{x} \qquad\blacksquare$$

APPLICATIONS OF FIRST-ORDER LINEAR EQUATIONS

Modeling Logistic Growth   When the population $Q(t)$ of a colony of living organisms (humans, bacteria, etc.) is small, it is reasonable to expect the relative rate of change of the population to be constant. In other words,

$$\frac{\frac{dQ}{dt}}{Q} = k \quad \text{or} \quad \frac{dQ}{dt} = kQ$$

where k is a constant (the **unrestricted growth rate**). This is called **exponential growth**. As long as the colony has plenty of food and living space, its population will obey this unrestricted growth rate formula and $Q(t)$ will grow exponentially.

However, in practice, there often comes a time when environmental factors begin to restrict the further expansion of the colony, and at this point, the growth ceases to be purely exponential in nature. To construct a population model that takes into account the effect of diminishing resources and crowding, we assume that the population of the species has a "cap" B, called the **carrying capacity** of the species. We further assume that the relative rate of change in population is jointly proportional to the current population $Q(t)$ and the difference $B - Q$, which can be thought of as the potential unborn population of the species. That is,

$$\frac{\frac{dQ}{dt}}{Q} = k(B - Q) \quad \text{or} \quad \frac{dQ}{dt} = kQ(B - Q)$$

This is called a **logistic equation**, and it arises not only in connection with population models, but also in a variety of other situations. The following example illustrates one way such an equation can arise.

EXAMPLE 3   Logistic equation for the spread of an epidemic

The rate at which an epidemic spreads through a community is proportional to the product of the number of residents who have been infected and the number of susceptible uninfected residents. Express the number of residents who have been infected as a function of time.

Solution

Let $Q(t)$ denote the number of residents who have been infected by time t and B the total number of susceptible residents. Then the number of susceptible residents who have not been infected is $B - Q$, and the differential equation describing the spread of the epidemic is

$$\frac{dQ}{dt} = kQ(B - Q) \qquad k \text{ is the constant of proportionality.}$$

$$\frac{dQ}{Q(B - Q)} = k \, dt \qquad \text{Use separation of variables.}$$

$$\int \frac{dQ}{Q(B - Q)} = \int k \, dt$$

The integral on the right causes no difficulty, but the integral on the left requires partial fractions:

$$\frac{1}{Q(B - Q)} = \frac{1}{B}\left[\frac{1}{Q} + \frac{1}{B - Q}\right]$$

We now substitute the form on the left into the equation and complete the integration:

$$\frac{1}{B}\int \frac{dQ}{Q} + \frac{1}{B}\int \frac{dQ}{B - Q} = \int k \, dt$$

$$\frac{1}{B}\ln|Q| - \frac{1}{B}\ln|B - Q| = kt + C \qquad \text{Integrate each term.}$$

$$\frac{1}{B}\ln\left|\frac{Q}{B - Q}\right| = kt + C \qquad \text{Division property of logs}$$

$$\ln\left(\frac{Q}{B - Q}\right) = Bkt + BC \qquad \begin{array}{l}\text{Multiply both sides by } B\\ \text{(note that } Q > 0,\ B > Q\text{).}\end{array}$$

$$\frac{Q}{B - Q} = e^{Bkt + BC} \qquad \text{Definition of ln}$$

$$Q = (B - Q)e^{Bkt}e^{BC} \qquad \begin{array}{l}\text{Because } e^{BC} \text{ is a constant,}\\ \text{we can let } A_1 = e^{BC}.\end{array}$$

$$Q = A_1 B e^{Bkt} - A_1 Q e^{Bkt}$$

$$Q + A_1 Q e^{Bkt} = A_1 B e^{Bkt}$$

$$Q = \frac{A_1 B e^{Bkt}}{1 + A_1 e^{Bkt}}$$

To simplify the equation, we make another substitution; let $A = \dfrac{1}{A_1}$, so that (after several simplification steps) we have

$$Q = \frac{\dfrac{B e^{Bkt}}{A}}{1 + \dfrac{e^{Bkt}}{A}} = \frac{B}{1 + A e^{-Bkt}}$$

The graph of $Q(t)$ is shown in Figure 7.6. Note that the curve has an inflection point where

$$Q(t) = \frac{B}{2}$$

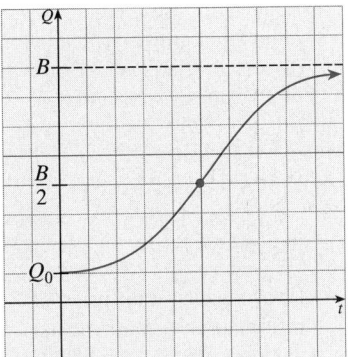

Figure 7.6 A logistic curve:
$$Q(t) = \frac{B}{1 + A e^{-Bkt}}$$

since

$$\frac{d^2 Q}{dt^2} = kQ(-1) + k(B - Q)$$

$$= k(B - 2Q)$$

$$= 0 \quad \text{when } Q = \frac{B}{2}.$$

This corresponds to the fact that the epidemic is spreading most rapidly when half the susceptible residents have been infected.

Note also in Example 3 that $y = Q(t)$ approaches the line $y = B$ asymptotically as $t \to +\infty$. Thus, the number of infected people approaches the number of those susceptible in the long run. ∎

A summary of growth models is given in Table 7.3.

TABLE 7.3 Summary of Growth Models

Graph	Growth Model	Equation and Solution	Sample Applications

$Q(t)$ is the population at time t, Q_0 is the initial population, and k is a constant of proportionality. If $Q(t)$ has a limiting value, let it be denoted by B.

Graph	Growth Model	Equation and Solution	Sample Applications
J-curve 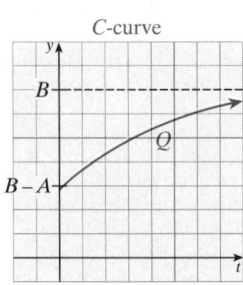	**Uninhibited growth** $(k > 0)$ Rate is proportional to the amount present.	$\dfrac{dQ}{dt} = kQ$ *Solution*: $Q = Q_0 e^{kt}$	Exponential growth; interest compounded continuously; inflation; price/supply curves
L-curve	**Uninhibited decay** $(k < 0)$ Rate is proportional to the amount present.	$\dfrac{dQ}{dt} = kQ$ *Solution*: $Q = Q_0 e^{kt}$	Radioactive decay; depletion of natural resources; price/demand curves; electric condenser discharge
S-curve	**Inhibited (logistic) growth** Rate is jointly proportional to the amount present and to the difference between the amount present and the maximum amount possible B (called the carrying capacity).	$\dfrac{dQ}{dt} = kQ(B - Q)$ *Solution*: $Q = \dfrac{B}{1 + Ae^{-Bkt}}$ where A is an arbitrary constant	Long-term restricted population growth; spread of a disease in a population; growth of a business; spread of a rumor
C-curve	**Limited growth** $(k > 0)$ Rate is proportional to the difference between the amount present and a fixed limiting value B.	$\dfrac{dQ}{dt} = k(B - Q)$ *Solution*: $Q = B - Ae^{-kt}$ where A is an arbitrary constant.	Learning curve; diffusion of information by mass media; amount of drug retained after intravenous injection; Newton's law of cooling; sales of new products; growth of a business

Compartmental Analysis: Modeling Dilution

EXAMPLE 4   A dilution problem

A tank contains 20 lb of salt dissolved in 50 gal of water. Suppose 3 gal of brine containing 2 lb of dissolved salt per gallon runs into the tank every minute and that the mixture (kept uniform by stirring) runs out of the tank at the rate of 2 gal/min. Find the amount of salt in the tank at any time t. How much salt is in the tank at the end of one hour?

Solution

Let $S(t)$ denote the amount of salt in the tank at the end of t minutes. Because 3 gal of brine flows into the tank each minute and each gallon contains 2 lb of salt, it follows that $(3)(2) = 6$ lb of salt flows into the tank each minute (see Figure 7.7). This is the inflow rate.

For the outflow, note that at time t, there are $S(t)$ lb of salt and $50+(3-2)t$ gallons of solution (because solution flows in at 3 gal/min and out at 2 gal/min). Thus, the concentration of salt in the solution at time t is

$$\frac{S(t)}{50+t} \text{ lb/gal}$$

and the outflow rate of salt is

$$\left[\frac{S(t)}{50+t} \text{ lb/gal}\right]\left[2 \text{ gal/min}\right] = \frac{2S(t)}{50+t} \text{ lb/min}$$

Combining these observations, we see that the net rate of change of salt dS/dt is given by

$$\frac{dS}{dt} = \underbrace{6}_{\substack{\uparrow \\ \text{Inflow}}} - \underbrace{\frac{2S}{50+t}}_{\text{Outflow}}$$

or

$$\frac{dS}{dt} + \frac{2S}{50+t} = 6$$

which we recognize as a first-order linear differential equation with

$$P(t) = \frac{2}{50+t}$$

and $Q(t) = 6$. An integrating factor is

$$I(t) = e^{\int P(t)\,dt} = e^{\int (2\,dt)/(50+t)} = e^{2\ln|50+t|} = (50+t)^2$$

and the general solution is

$$S(t) = \frac{1}{(50+t)^2}\left[\int 6(50+t)^2\,dt + C\right]$$

$$= \frac{1}{(50+t)^2}\left[2(50+t)^3 + C\right]$$

$$= 2(50+t) + \frac{C}{(50+t)^2}$$

To evaluate C, we recall that there are 20 lb of salt initially in the solution. This means $S(0) = 20$, so that

$$S(0) = 2(50+0) + \frac{C}{(50+0)^2}$$

$$20 = 100 + \frac{C}{50^2}$$

$$-80(50^2) = C$$

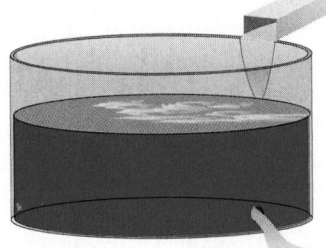

Inflow rate of salt: 6 lb/min

Outflow rate of salt: $\dfrac{S(t)}{50+t}$ lb / min

Figure 7.7 Rate of flow equals inflow rate minus outflow rate.

Thus, the solution to the given differential equation, subject to the initial condition $S(0) = 20$, is

$$S(t) = 2(50 + t) - \frac{80(50)^2}{(50 + t)^2}$$

Specifically, at the end of 1 hour (60 min), the tank contains

$$S(60) = 2(50 + 60) - \frac{80(50)^2}{(50 + 60)^2} \approx 203.4710744$$

The tank contains about 200 lb of salt. ■

Modeling *RL* Circuits Another application of first-order linear differential equations involves the current in an *RL* electric circuit. An *RL* circuit is one with a constant resistance, R, and a constant inductance, L. Figure 7.8 shows an electric circuit with an electromotive force (EMF), a resistor, and an inductor connected in series.

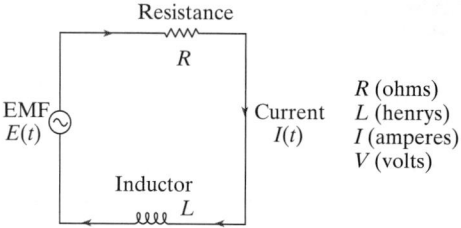

Figure 7.8 An *RL* circuit diagram

The EMF source, which is usually a battery or generator, supplies voltage that causes a current to flow in the circuit. According to Kirchhoff's second law, if the circuit is closed at time $t = 0$, then the applied electromotive force is equal to the sum of the voltage drops in the rest of the circuit. It can be shown that this implies that the current $I(t)$ that flows in the circuit at time t must satisfy the first-order linear differential equation

$$L\frac{dI}{dt} + RI = E$$

where L (the inductance) and R (the resistance) are positive constants.* Write

$$\frac{dI}{dt} + \frac{R}{L}I = \frac{E}{L}$$

to see that $P(t) = \dfrac{R}{L}$ (a constant) and $Q(t) = \dfrac{E}{L}$. In the case where E is a constant, we have

$$\begin{aligned}
I(t) &= e^{-\int (R/L)\, dt}\left[\int \frac{E}{L}e^{\int (R/L)\, dt}\, dt + C\right] \\
&= e^{-(R/L)t}\left[\frac{E}{L}\int e^{(R/L)t}\, dt + C\right] \\
&= e^{-(R/L)t}\left[\frac{E}{L}\cdot\frac{L}{R}e^{(R/L)t} + C\right] \\
&= \frac{E}{R} + Ce^{-(R/L)t}
\end{aligned}$$

---

*It is common practice in physics and applied mathematics to use I as the symbol for current. Of course, this has nothing to do with the concept of integrating factor introduced earlier in this section.

It is reasonable to assume that no current flows when $t = 0$. That is, $I = 0$ when $t = 0$, so we have $0 = E/R + C$ or $C = -E/R$. The solution of the initial value problem is

$$I = \frac{E}{R}\left(1 - e^{-Rt/L}\right)$$

Notice that because $e^{-(Rt/L)} \to 0$ as $t \to +\infty$, we have

$$\lim_{t \to +\infty} I(t) = \lim_{t \to +\infty} \frac{E}{R}\left(1 - e^{-Rt/L}\right)$$
$$= \frac{E}{R}(1 - 0)$$
$$= \frac{E}{R}$$

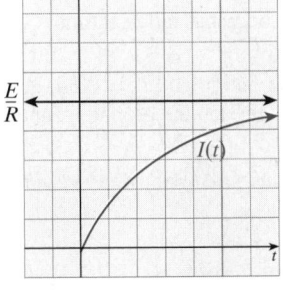

This means that, in the long run, the current I must approach $\dfrac{E}{R}$. The solution of the differential equation consists of two parts, which are given special names:

$$\frac{E}{R} \text{ is the } \textbf{steady-state current}.$$

$$-\frac{E}{R}e^{-Rt/L} \text{ is the } \textbf{transient current.}$$

Figure 7.9 The current in an RL circuit with constant EMF

Figure 7.9 shows how the current $I(t)$ varies with time t.

7.6 PROBLEM SET

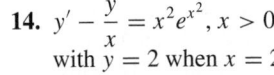

A *Solve the differential equations in Problems 1–10.*

1. $\dfrac{dy}{dx} + \dfrac{3y}{x} = x$

2. $\dfrac{dy}{dx} - \dfrac{2y}{x} = \sqrt{x} + 1$

3. $x^4\dfrac{dy}{dx} + 2x^3y = 5$

4. $x^2\dfrac{dy}{dx} + xy = 2$

5. $x\dfrac{dy}{dx} + 2y = xe^{x^3}$

6. $\dfrac{dy}{dx} + \left(\dfrac{2x+1}{x}\right)y = e^{-2x}$

7. $\dfrac{dy}{dx} + \dfrac{y}{x} = \tan^{-1}x$

8. $\dfrac{dy}{dx} + \dfrac{2y}{x} = \dfrac{\ln x}{x}$

9. $\dfrac{dy}{dx} + (\tan x)y = \sin x$

10. $\dfrac{dy}{dx} + (\sec x)y = \sin 2x$

In Problems 11–14, solve the initial value problems. A graphical solution is shown as a check for your work.

11. $\dfrac{dy}{dx} + \dfrac{xy}{1+x} = x(1+x)$
with $y = -1$ when $x = 0$

12. $\dfrac{dy}{dx} + \dfrac{2xy}{1+x^2} = \sin x$
with $y = 1$ when $x = 0$

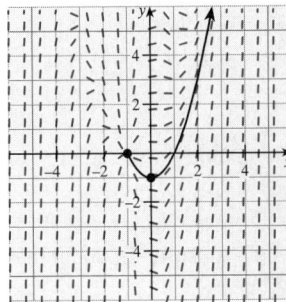

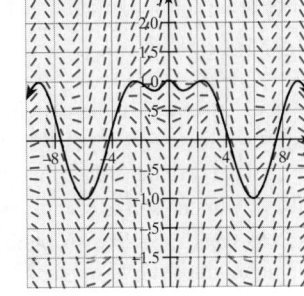

13. $x\dfrac{dy}{dx} - 2y = 2x^3$, $x > 0$
with $y = 0$ when $x = 3$

14. $y' - \dfrac{y}{x} = x^2e^{x^2}$, $x > 0$
with $y = 2$ when $x = 2$

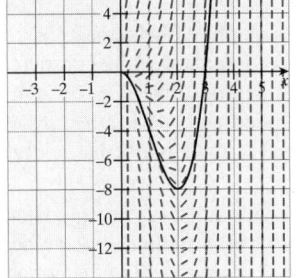

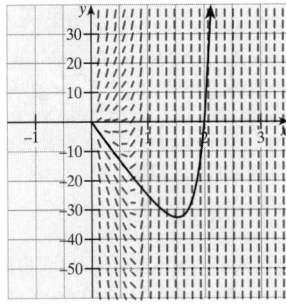

B *In Problems 15–18, find the orthogonal trajectories of the given family of curves. Recall from Section 5.6 that a curve is an orthogonal trajectory of a given family if it intersects each member of that family at right angles.*

15. the family of parabolas $y^2 = 4kx$
16. the family of hyperbolas $xy = c$
17. the family of circles $x^2 + y^2 = r^2$
18. the family of exponential curves $y = Ce^{-x}$

Modeling Problems. *In Problems 19–30, set up and solve an appropriate model to answer the given question. Be sure to state your assumptions.*

19. In 2000 the gross domestic product (GDP) of the United States was \$9,382 billion (in constant 1996 dollars). Suppose the growth rate from 1999 to 2000 was 6.42%. Predict the GDP in 2010.

20. In 1992 the gross domestic product (GDP) of the United States in constant 1996 dollars was \$6,803 billion. Suppose the growth rate from 1992 to 2000 was 4.0% per year. Predict the GDP in 2002. Consult an almanac to see if this prediction is correct.

21. According to the Department of Health and Human Services, the divorce rate in 1990 in the United States was 4.7% and there were 1,175,000 divorces that year. How many divorces will there be in 2005 if the divorce rate is constant?

22. According to the Department of Health and Human Services, the marriage rate in 1990 in the United States was 9.8% and there were 2,448,000 marriages that year. How many marriages will there be in 2005 if the marriage rate is constant?

23. A tank contains 10 lb of salt dissolved in 30 gal of water. Suppose 2 gal of brine containing 1 lb of dissolved salt per gallon runs into the tank every minute and that the mixture (kept uniform by stirring) runs out at the same rate.

   a. Find the amount of salt in the tank at time t.

   b. How long does it take (to the nearest second) for the tank to contain 15 lb of salt?

24. In Problem 23, suppose the tank has a capacity of 100 gal and that the mixture flows out at the rate of 1 gal/min (instead of 2 gal/min).

   a. How long will it take for the tank to fill?

   b. How much salt will be in the tank when it is full?

25. The rate at which a drug is absorbed into the blood system is given by

$$\frac{db}{dt} = \alpha - \beta b$$

where $b(t)$ is the concentration of the drug in the bloodstream at time t. What does $b(t)$ approach in the long run (that is, as $t \to +\infty$)? At what time is $b(t)$ equal to half this limiting value? Assume that $b(0) = 0$.

26. An RL circuit has a resistance of R ohms, inductance of L henries, and EMF of E volts, where R, L, and E are constant. Suppose no current flows in the circuit at time $t = 0$. If L is doubled and E and R are held constant, what effect does this have on the "long run" current in the circuit (that is, the current as $t \to +\infty$)?

27. The 1990 census recorded a population of 16.1 million Hispanics, while in 2000 the figure was 32.8 million. Assuming that the rate of population growth is proportional to the population, predict the Hispanic population in the year 2005.

28. A population of animals on Catalina Island is limited by the amount of food available. Studies show there were 1,800 animals present in 1980 and 2,000 in 1986 and suggest that 5,000 animals can be supported by the conditions present on the island. Use a logistic model to predict the animal population in the year 2005.

29. In 1986 the Chernobyl nuclear disaster in the Soviet Union contaminated the atmosphere. The buildup of radioactive material in the atmosphere satisfies the differential equation

$$\frac{dM}{dt} = r\left(\frac{k}{r} - M\right), \qquad M = 0 \text{ when } t = 0$$

where M = mass of radioactive material in the atmosphere after time t (in years); k is the rate at which the radioactive material is introduced into the atmosphere; r is the annual decay rate of the radioactive material. Find the solution, $M(t)$, of this differential equation in terms of k and r.

30. **The Motion of a Body Falling through a Resisting Medium** A body of mass m is dropped from a great height and falls in a straight line. Assume that the only forces acting on the body are the earth's gravitational attraction mg and air resistance kv. (Recall $g = -32$ ft/s^2.)

   a. According to Newton's second law,

$$m\frac{dv}{dt} = mg - kv$$

   Solve this equation, assuming the object has velocity $v_0 = 0$ at time $t = 0$.

   b. Find the distance $s(t)$ the body has fallen at time t. Assume $s = 0$ at time $t = 0$.

   c. If the body weighs $W = 100$ lb and $k = 0.35$, how long does it take for the body to reach the ground from a height of 10,000 ft?

Recall from Section 5.6 that a tank filled with water drains at the rate

$$\frac{dV}{dt} = -4.8A_0\sqrt{h}$$

where h is the height of water at time t (in seconds) and A_0 is the area (in ft^2) of the drain hole. This formula, called Torricelli's law, is used in Problems 31 and 32.

31. A full tank of water has a drain with area 0.07 ft^2. If the tank has a constant cross-sectional area of $A = 5$ ft^2 and height of $h_0 = 4$ ft, how long does it take to empty?

32. A full tank of water of height 5 ft and constant cross-sectional area $A = 3$ ft^2 has two drains, both of area 0.02 ft^2. One drain is at the bottom and the other at height 2 ft. How long does it take for the tank to drain?

33. **The Euler Beam Model** For a rigid beam with uniform loading, the deflection $y(x)$ is modeled by the differential equation $y^{(4)} = -k$, where $k > 0$ is a constant and x measures the distance along the beam from one of its ends. Assume that $y(0) = y(L) = 0$, where L is the length of the beam, and that $y''(0) = y''(L) = 0$.

   a. Solve the beam equation to find $y(x)$.

   b. Where does the maximum deflection occur? What is the maximum deflection?

   c. Suppose the beam is cantilevered, so that $y(0) = y(L) = 0$ and $y''(0) = y'(L) = 0$. Now where does the maximum deflection occur? Is the maximum deflection greater or less than the case considered in part **b**? Would you expect the graph of the deflection $y = y(x)$ to be concave up or concave down on $[0, L]$? Prove your conjecture.

34. **Modeling Problem** A tank initially contains 5 lb of salt in 50 ft^3 of solution. At time $t = 0$, brine begins to enter the tank at the rate of 2 ft^3/h, and the mixed solution drains at the same rate. The brine coming into the tank has concentration

$$C(t) = 1 - e^{-0.2t} \text{ lb/ft}^3$$

t hours after the dilution begins.

   a. Set up and solve a differential equation for the amount of salt $S(t)$ in the solution at time t.

   b. How much salt is eventually in the tank (as $t \to +\infty$)?

   c. At what time is $S(t)$ minimized? What is the minimum amount of salt in the tank?

35. Modeling Problem Two 100-gallon tanks initially contain pure water. Brine containing 2 lb of salt per gallon enters the first tank at the rate of 1 gal/min, and the mixed solution drains into the second tank at the same rate. There, it is again thoroughly mixed and drains at the same rate, 1 gal/min.

a. Set up and solve a differential equation of the amount of salt $S_1(t)$ in the first tank at time t (minutes).

b. Set up and solve a second differential equation for the amount of salt $S_2(t)$ in the second tank at time t.

c. Let $S(t) = S_1 - S_2$. Intuitively, $S(t) \geq 0$ for all t. At what time is the excess $S(t)$ maximized? What is the maximum excess?

36. Modeling Problem A chemical in a solution diffuses from a compartment with known concentration $C_1(t)$ across a membrane to a second compartment whose concentration $C_2(t)$ changes at a rate proportional to the difference $C_1 - C_2$. Set up and solve the differential equation for $C_2(t)$ in the following cases:

a. $C_1(t) = 5e^{-2t}$; $k = 1.7$; $C_2(0) = 0$

b. $k = 4$; $C_2(0) = 3$, and

$$C_1(t) = \begin{cases} 4 & \text{if } 0 \leq t \leq 3 \\ 5 & \text{if } t > 3 \end{cases}$$

37. The Gompertz equation for a population $P(t)$ is

$$\frac{dP}{dt} = kP(B - \ln P)$$

where k and B are positive constants. If the initial population is $P(0) = P_0$, and the ultimate population is

$$\lim_{t \to +\infty} P(t) = P_\infty$$

find $P(t)$.

38. Modeling Problem Uranium-234 (half-life 2.48×10^5 yr) decays to Thorium-230 (half-life 80,000 yr).

a. If $U(t)$ and $T(t)$ are the amounts of uranium and thorium at time t, then

$$\frac{dU}{dt} = -k_1 U, \quad \frac{dT}{dt} = -k_2 T + k_1 U$$

Solve this system of differential equations to obtain $U(t)$ and $T(t)$.

b. If we start with 100 g of pure U-234, how much Th-230 will there be after $t = 5,000$ yr?

39. Solve the differential equation

$$\frac{dy}{dx} = \frac{1+y}{xy + e^y(1+y)}$$

by regarding y as the independent variable (i.e., reverse the roles of x and y).

40. Certain biological processes occur periodically over the 24 hours of a day. Suppose a patient's metabolic exertion rate is modeled by

$$R(t) = \frac{1}{4} - \frac{1}{8} \cos \frac{\pi}{12}(t - 6)$$

and the rate of intake is $I(t)$ for $0 \leq t \leq 24$. The patient's body contains 200 g of the substance when $t = 0$.

a. If $I(t) = 0$ (the patient intakes only water), the amount of substance $Q(t)$ in the patient's body at time t satisfies

$$\frac{dQ}{dt} = 0 - R(t)$$

Solve this equation for $Q(t)$.

b. Suppose the patient intakes the substance at a constant rate for part of the day. Specifically,

$$I(t) = \begin{cases} 0.4 \text{ g/h} & \text{for } 10 \leq t \leq 20 \\ 0 & \text{otherwise} \end{cases}$$

Set up and solve a differential equation for the amount of substance $Q(t)$ in the patient's body at time t. When is $Q(t)$ maximized?

41. An RL circuit has a resistance of $R = 10$ ohms and an inductance of $L = 5$ henries. Find the current $I(t)$ in the circuit at time t if $I(0) = 0$ and the electromotive force (EMF) is:

a. $E = 15$ volts **b.** $E = 5e^{-2t} \sin t$

42. An RL circuit has an inductance of $L = 3$ henries and a resistance $R = 6$ ohms in series with an EMF of $E = 50 \sin 30t$. Assume $I(0) = 0$.

a. What is the current $I(t)$ at time t?

b. What is the transient current? The steady-state current?

43. Modeling Problem A lake has a volume of 6 billion ft³, and its initial pollutant content is 0.22%. A river whose waters contain only 0.06% pollutants flows into the lake at the rate of 350 million ft³/day, and another river flows out of the lake also carrying 350 million ft³/day. Assume that the water in the two rivers and the lake is always well mixed. How long does it take for the pollutant content to be reduced to 0.15%?

Ⓒ 44. A Bernoulli equation is a differential equation of the form

$$y' + P(x)y = Q(x)y^n$$

where n is a real number, $n \neq 0$, $n \neq 1$.

a. Show that the change of variable $u = y^{1-n}$ transforms such an equation into one of the form

$$u'(x) + (1-n)P(x)u(x) = (1-n)Q(x)$$

This transformed equation is a first-order linear differential equation in u and can be solved by the methods of this section, yielding a solution to the given Bernoulli equation.

b. Use the change of variable suggested to solve the Bernoulli equation

$$y' + \frac{y}{x} = 2y^2$$

45. HISTORICAL QUEST Daniel Bernoulli was a member of the famous Bernoulli family (see Historical Quest Problem 59, Section 4.5). Between 1725 and 1749 he won ten prizes for his work in astronomy, gravity, tides, magnetism, ocean currents, and the behavior of ships at sea. While modeling the effects of a smallpox epidemic, he obtained the differential equation

DANIEL BERNOULLI
1700–1782

$$\frac{dS}{dt} = -pS + \left(\frac{S}{N}\right)\frac{dN}{dt} + \frac{pS^2}{mN}$$

In this equation $S(t)$ is the number of people at age t that are susceptible to smallpox; $N(t)$ is the number of people at age t who survive; p is the probability of a susceptible person getting the disease, and $1/m$ is the proportion of those who die from the disease. ∎

Let $y = S/N$, and solve the resulting equation for $y(t)$. Then write N as a function of S. (*Hint:* You will need the result of Problem 44.)

46. Consider a curve with the property that when horizontal and vertical lines are drawn from each point $P(x, y)$ on the curve to the coordinate axes, the area A_1 under the curve is twice the area A_2 above the curve, as shown in Figure 7.10.

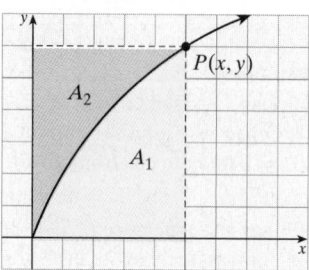

Figure 7.10   Problem 46

Show that x and y satisfy the differential equation

$$\frac{dy}{dx} = \frac{y}{2x}$$

Solve the equation and characterize the family of all curves that satisfy the given geometric condition.

47. An object of mass m is projected upward from ground level with initial velocity v_0 against air resistance proportional to its velocity $v(t)$. Thus,

$$m\frac{dv}{dt} = -mg - kv$$

a. Solve this equation for $v(t)$, and then find $s(t)$, the height of the object above the ground at time t.

b. When does the object reach its maximum height? What is the maximum height?

c. Suppose $k = \frac{3}{4}$. For an object weighing 20 lb with initial velocity $v_0 = 150$ ft/s, what is the maximum height? When does the object hit the ground?

d. Suppose the same object as in part **c** is launched with the same initial velocity but in a vacuum, where there is no air resistance ($k = 0$). Would you expect the object to hit the ground sooner or later than the object in part **c**? Prove your conjecture.

48. A body of mass m falls from a height of s_0 ft against air resistance modeled to be proportional to the *square* of its velocity v, so that

$$m\frac{dv}{dt} = mg - kv^2$$

a. Solve this differential equation to find $v(t)$. Then find the height $s(t)$ of the object at time t (in seconds).

b. If the object weighs 1,000 lb, $s_0 = 100$ ft, and $k = 0.01$, how long does it take for the object to hit the ground? Interpret this result.

7.7   Improper Integrals

IN THIS SECTION   improper integrals with infinite limits of integration, improper integrals with unbounded integrands

We have defined the definite integral $\displaystyle\int_a^b f(x)\,dx$ on a closed bounded interval $[a, b]$ where the integrand $f(x)$ is bounded. In this section, we extend the concept of integral to the case where the interval of integration is infinite and also to the case where f is unbounded at a finite number of points on the interval of integration. Collectively, these are called **improper integrals**.

IMPROPER INTEGRALS WITH INFINITE LIMITS OF INTEGRATION

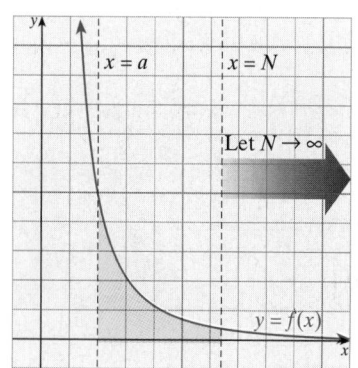

Figure 7.11 Finding the area under a curve on an unbounded region

In physics, economics, probability and statistics, and other applied areas, it is useful to have a concept of an integral that is defined on the entire real line or on half-lines of the form $x \geq a$ or $x \leq a$. If $f(x) \geq 0$, the integral of f on the interval $x \geq a$ can be thought of as the area under the curve $y = f(x)$ on this unbounded interval, as shown in Figure 7.11. A reasonable strategy for finding this area is first to use a definite integral to compute the area from $x = a$ to some finite number $x = N$ and then to let N approach infinity in the resulting expression. Here is a definition.

Improper Integrals (First Type)

Let a be a fixed number and assume $\int_a^N f(x)\,dx$ exists for all $N \geq a$. Then if $\lim\limits_{N \to +\infty} \int_a^N f(x)\,dx$ exists, we define the **improper integral** $\int_a^{+\infty} f(x)\,dx$ by

$$\int_a^{+\infty} f(x)\,dx = \lim_{N \to +\infty} \int_a^N f(x)\,dx$$

The improper integral is said to **converge** if this limit is a finite number and to **diverge** otherwise.

EXAMPLE 1   Convergent improper integral

Evaluate $\displaystyle\int_1^{+\infty} \frac{dx}{x^2}$.

Solution

The region under the curve $y = 1/x^2$ for $x \geq 1$ is shown in Figure 7.12. This region is unbounded, so it might seem reasonable to conclude that the area is also infinite. Begin by computing the integral from 1 to N:

$$\int_1^N \frac{dx}{x^2} = -\frac{1}{x}\Big|_1^N = -\frac{1}{N} + 1$$

Let us consider the situation more carefully, as shown in Figure 7.13.

Figure 7.12 Graph of $y = \dfrac{1}{x^2}$

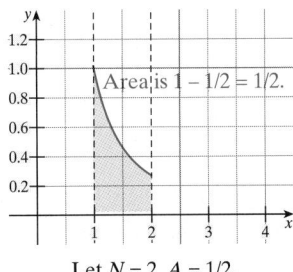

Let $N = 2, A = 1/2.$

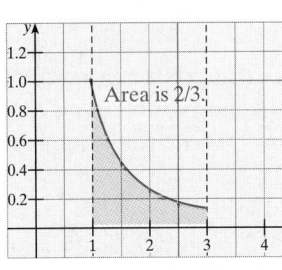

Let $N = 3, A = 2/3.$

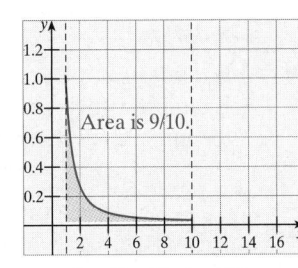

Let $N = 10, A = 9/10.$

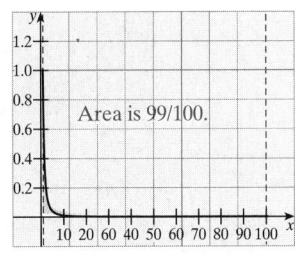

Let $N = 100, A = 99/100.$

Figure 7.13   Area enclosed by $y = \dfrac{1}{x^2}$, the x-axis, $x = 1$, and $y = N$

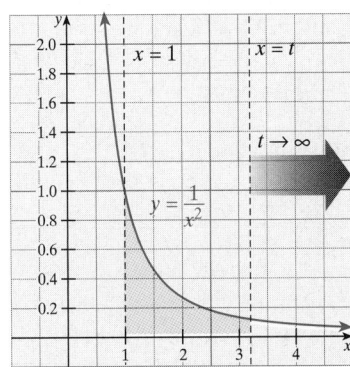

Figure 7.14 The region to the right of $x = 1$, bounded by the curve $y = 1/x^2$ and the x-axis, has area 1.

For $N = 2, 3, 10$, or 100, this integral has values $\frac{1}{2}$, $\frac{2}{3}$, $\frac{9}{10}$, and $\frac{99}{100}$, respectively, suggesting that the region under $y = 1/x^2$ for $x \geq 1$ actually has finite area approaching 1 as N gets larger and larger.

To find this area analytically, we take the limit as $N \to +\infty$, as shown in Figure 7.14.

$$\int_1^{+\infty} \frac{dx}{x^2} = \lim_{N \to +\infty} \int_1^N \frac{dx}{x^2}$$
$$= \lim_{N \to +\infty} \left[-x^{-1}\right]\Big|_1^N$$
$$= \lim_{N \to +\infty} \left[-N^{-1} + 1\right]$$
$$= 1$$

Thus, the improper integral converges and has the value 1. ∎

EXAMPLE 2 A divergent improper integral

Evaluate $\int_1^{+\infty} \dfrac{dx}{x}$.

Solution

The graph of $y = 1/x$, shown in Figure 7.15, looks very much like the graph of $y = 1/x^2$ in Figure 7.14. We compute the integral from 1 to N and then let N go to infinity.

$$\int_1^{+\infty} \frac{dx}{x} = \lim_{N \to +\infty} \int_1^N \frac{dx}{x}$$
$$= \lim_{N \to +\infty} \ln|x|\,\big|\big|_1^N$$
$$= \lim_{N \to +\infty} \ln N = +\infty$$

The limit is not a finite number, which means the improper integral diverges. ∎

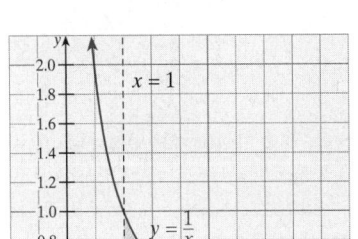

Figure 7.15 The area to the right of the line $x = 1$ bounded by the curve $y = 1/x$ and the x-axis is infinite.

We have shown that the improper integral $\int_1^{+\infty} \dfrac{dx}{x^2}$ converges and that the improper integral $\int_1^{+\infty} \dfrac{dx}{x}$ diverges. In geometric terms, this says that the area to the right of $x = 1$ under the curve $y = 1/x^2$ is finite, whereas the corresponding area under the curve $y = 1/x$ is infinite. The reason for the difference is that as x increases, $1/x^2$ approaches zero more quickly than does $1/x$, as shown in Figure 7.16.

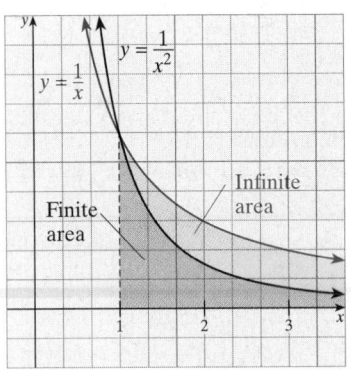

Figure 7.16 An unbounded region may have either a finite or an infinite area.

EXAMPLE 3 Determine convergence of an improper integral

Show that the improper integral $\int_1^{+\infty} \dfrac{dx}{x^p}$ converges only for constant $p > 1$.

Solution

For this example, remember that p is a constant and x is the variable. We have seen in Example 1 that the integral converges for $p = 2$. We also know from Example 2 that the integral diverges for $p = 1$, so we can assume $p \neq 1$ in the following computation:

$$\int_1^{+\infty} \frac{dx}{x^p} = \lim_{N \to +\infty} \int_1^N \frac{dx}{x^p} = \lim_{N \to +\infty} \left[\frac{x^{-p+1}}{-p+1}\right]\Big|_1^N = \lim_{N \to +\infty} \frac{1}{1-p}\left[N^{1-p} - 1\right]$$

If $p > 1$, then $1 - p < 0$, so $N^{1-p} \to 0$ as $N \to +\infty$, and

$$\int_1^{+\infty} \frac{dx}{x^p} = \lim_{N \to +\infty} \frac{1}{1-p}\left[N^{1-p} - 1\right] = \frac{1}{1-p}[-1] = \frac{1}{p-1}$$

If $p < 1$, then $1 - p > 0$, so $N^{1-p} \to +\infty$ as $N \to +\infty$, and

$$\int_1^{+\infty} \frac{dx}{x^p} = \lim_{N \to +\infty} \frac{1}{1-p}\left[N^{1-p} - 1\right] = +\infty$$

Thus, the improper integral diverges for $p \leq 1$ and converges for $p > 1$. ∎

➡ **What This Says** The improper integral

$$\int_1^{+\infty} \frac{dx}{x^p} = \begin{cases} \dfrac{1}{p-1} & \text{if } p > 1 \\[2mm] \infty & \text{if } p \leq 1 \end{cases}$$

EXAMPLE 4   **Improper integral using l'Hôpital's rule and integration by parts**

Evaluate $\displaystyle\int_0^{+\infty} xe^{-2x}\,dx$.

Solution

$$\int_0^{+\infty} xe^{-2x}\,dx = \lim_{N\to+\infty}\int_0^N \underbrace{x}_{u}\,\underbrace{e^{-2x}\,dx}_{dv}$$

> By parts:
> Let $u = x$ and $dv = e^{-2x}\,dx$
> $du = dx$ $v = \frac{1}{-2}e^{-2x}$

$$= \lim_{N\to+\infty}\left[\left(\underbrace{\frac{x}{-2}}_{u}\,\underbrace{e^{-2x}}_{v}\right)\Bigg|_0^N - \int_0^N \underbrace{\frac{1}{-2}e^{-2x}}_{v}\,\underbrace{dx}_{du}\right]$$

$$= \lim_{N\to+\infty}\left[\frac{-xe^{-2x}}{2} - \frac{e^{-2x}}{4}\right]\Bigg|_0^N$$

$$= \lim_{N\to+\infty}\left[-\frac{1}{2}Ne^{-2N} - \frac{1}{4}e^{-2N} + 0 + \frac{1}{4}\right]$$

$$= -\frac{1}{2}\lim_{N\to+\infty}\left(\frac{N}{e^{2N}}\right) + \frac{1}{4}$$

$$= -\frac{1}{2}\lim_{N\to+\infty}\left(\frac{1}{2e^{2N}}\right) + \frac{1}{4}\qquad\text{l'Hôpital's rule}$$

$$= \frac{1}{4}\qquad\blacksquare$$

EXAMPLE 5   **Gabriel's horn: a solid with a finite volume but infinite surface area**

Gabriel's horn is the name given to the solid formed by revolving about the x-axis the unbounded region under the curve $y = \frac{1}{x}$ for $x \geq 1$. Show that this solid has finite volume but infinite surface area.

Solution

We will find the volume, V, by using disks, as shown in Figure 7.17.

$$V = \pi\int_1^{+\infty}(x^{-1})^2\,dx = \pi\lim_{N\to+\infty}\int_1^N x^{-2}\,dx = \pi\lim_{N\to+\infty}\left(-\frac{1}{N}+1\right) = \pi$$

We also find the surface area, S:

$$S = 2\pi\int_1^{+\infty} f(x)\sqrt{1+[f'(x)]^2}\,dx = 2\pi\int_1^{+\infty}\frac{1}{x}\sqrt{1+\frac{1}{x^4}}\,dx$$

$$= 2\pi\int_1^{+\infty}\frac{1}{x}\sqrt{\frac{x^4+1}{x^4}}\,dx = 2\pi\int_1^{+\infty}\frac{\sqrt{x^4+1}}{x^3}\,dx$$

> Let $u = x^2$
> $du = 2x\,dx$

$$= 2\pi\int_1^{+\infty}\frac{\sqrt{u^2+1}}{2u^2}\,du = \pi\lim_{N\to+\infty}\int_1^N \frac{\sqrt{u^2+1}}{u^2}\,du$$

$$= \pi\lim_{N\to+\infty}\left[\frac{-\sqrt{u^2+1}}{u} + \ln\left|u+\sqrt{u^2+1}\right|\right]\Bigg|_1^N \qquad\text{Formula 180}$$

$$= +\infty\qquad\text{(The details are left for the reader.)}\qquad\blacksquare$$

We can also define an improper integral on an interval that is unbounded to the left or on the entire real number line.

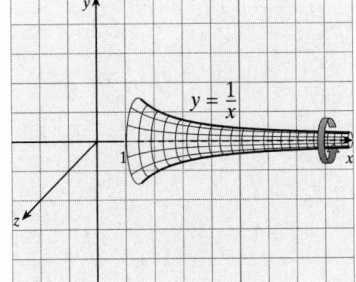

Figure 7.17 Gabriel's horn

You can fill Gabriel's horn with a finite amount of paint, but it takes an infinite amount of paint to color its inside surface!

**Improper Integrals
(First Type, Extended)**

Let b be a fixed number and assume $\int_t^b f(x)\,dx$ exists for all $t < b$. Then if

$\lim\limits_{t \to -\infty} \int_t^b f(x)\,dx$ exists, we define the **improper integral**

$$\int_{-\infty}^b f(x)\,dx = \lim_{t \to -\infty} \int_t^b f(x)\,dx$$

The improper integral $\int_{-\infty}^b f(x)\,dx$ is said to **converge** if this limit is a finite number and to **diverge** otherwise. If both

$$\int_a^{+\infty} f(x)\,dx \quad \text{and} \quad \int_{-\infty}^a f(x)\,dx$$

converge for some number a, the improper integral of $f(x)$ on the entire x-axis is defined by

$$\int_{-\infty}^{+\infty} f(x)\,dx = \int_{-\infty}^a f(x)\,dx + \int_a^{+\infty} f(x)\,dx$$

EXAMPLE 6 **Improper integral to negative infinity**

a. Evaluate $\displaystyle\int_{-\infty}^0 \frac{dx}{1+x^2}$.

b. How would you expect the value of $\displaystyle\int_{-\infty}^\infty \frac{dx}{1+x^2}$ to be related to the improper integral in **a**? Verify your conjecture by evaluating this integral.

Solution

a.
$$\int_{-\infty}^0 \frac{dx}{1+x^2} = \lim_{t \to -\infty} \int_t^0 \frac{dx}{1+x^2}$$
$$= \lim_{t \to -\infty} \tan^{-1} x \Big|_t^0$$
$$= \lim_{t \to -\infty} \left[\tan^{-1} 0 - \tan^{-1} t \right]$$
$$= 0 - \left(-\frac{\pi}{2} \right)$$
$$= \frac{\pi}{2}$$

b. Since $y(x) = y(-x)$, we see that $y = \dfrac{1}{1+x^2}$ is symmetric about the y-axis, and it is reasonable to conjecture that the integral in part **b** is twice the integral in part **a**. We have

$$\int_{-\infty}^{+\infty} \frac{dx}{1+x^2} = \lim_{s \to -\infty} \int_s^0 \frac{dx}{1+x^2} + \lim_{N \to +\infty} \int_0^N \frac{dx}{1+x^2}$$
$$= \frac{\pi}{2} + \lim_{N \to +\infty} (\tan^{-1} N - \tan^{-1} 0)$$
$$= \frac{\pi}{2} + \left(\frac{\pi}{2} - 0 \right)$$
$$= \pi$$

We see this integral is indeed twice that in part **a**, as conjectured. ∎

EXAMPLE 7   An improper polar integral

Evaluate $\displaystyle\int_0^{+\infty} \frac{1}{2} e^{-2\theta} \, d\theta$.

Solution
$$\int_0^{+\infty} \frac{1}{2} e^{-2\theta} \, d\theta = \lim_{M \to +\infty} \int_0^M \frac{1}{2} e^{-2\theta} \, d\theta$$
$$= \lim_{M \to +\infty} -\frac{1}{4} e^{-2\theta} \Big|_0^M$$
$$= \lim_{M \to +\infty} \left[-\frac{1}{4} e^{-2M} - \left(-\frac{1}{4} \right) \right]$$
$$= \frac{1}{4} \qquad\blacksquare$$

IMPROPER INTEGRALS WITH UNBOUNDED INTEGRANDS

A function f is **unbounded** at c if it has arbitrarily large values near c. Geometrically, this occurs when the line $x = c$ is a vertical asymptote to the graph of f at c, as shown in Figure 7.18.

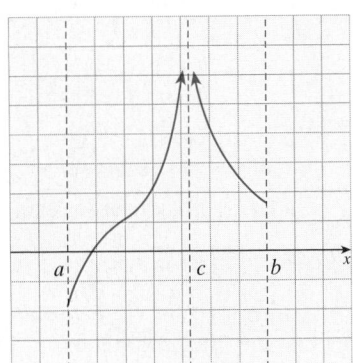 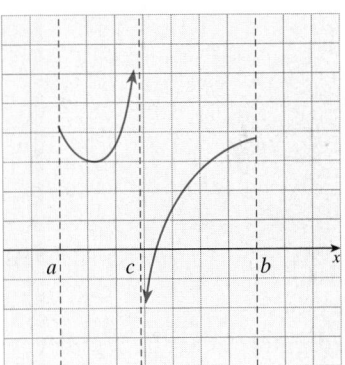

Figure 7.18   Two functions that are unbounded at c

If f is unbounded at c and $a \le c \le b$, the Riemann integral $\int_a^b f(x) \, dx$ is not even defined (only bounded functions are Riemann integrable). However, it may still be possible to define $\int_a^b f(x) \, dx$ as an improper integral in certain cases.

Let us examine a specific problem. Suppose

$$f(x) = \frac{1}{\sqrt{x}} \quad \text{for} \quad 0 < x \le 1$$

Then f is unbounded at $x = 0$ and $\int_0^1 f(x) \, dx$ is not defined. However,

$$f(x) = \frac{1}{\sqrt{x}}$$

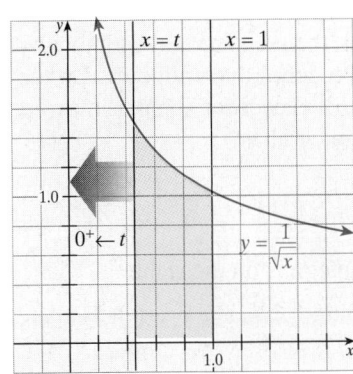

Figure 7.19 Graph of $y = \dfrac{1}{\sqrt{x}}$

is continuous on every interval $[t, 1]$ for $t > 0$, as shown in Figure 7.19. For any such interval $[t, 1]$, we have

$$\int_t^1 \frac{dx}{\sqrt{x}} = \int_t^1 x^{-1/2} \, dx = 2\sqrt{x} \Big|_t^1 = 2 - 2\sqrt{t}$$

If we let $t \to 0$ through positive values, we see that

$$\lim_{t \to 0^+} \int_t^1 \frac{dx}{\sqrt{x}} = \lim_{t \to 0^+} (2 - 2\sqrt{t}) = 2$$

This is called a **convergent improper integral** with value 2, and it seems reasonable to say

$$\int_0^1 \frac{dx}{\sqrt{x}} = \lim_{t \to 0^+} \int_t^1 \frac{dx}{\sqrt{x}} = 2$$

In this example, f is unbounded at the left endpoint of the interval of integration, but similar reasoning would apply if it were unbounded at the right endpoint or at an interior point. Here is a definition of this kind of improper integral.

Improper Integral (Second Type)

If f is unbounded at a and $\int_t^b f(x)\,dx$ exists for all t such that $a < t \le b$, then

$$\int_a^b f(x)\,dx = \lim_{t \to a^+} \int_t^b f(x)\,dx$$

If the limit exists (as a finite number), we say that the improper integral **converges**; otherwise, the improper integral **diverges**. Similarly, if f is unbounded at b and $\int_a^t f(x)\,dx$ exists for all t such that $a \le t < b$, then

$$\int_a^b f(x)\,dx = \lim_{t \to b^-} \int_a^t f(x)\,dx$$

If f is unbounded at c, where $a < c < b$, and the improper integrals $\int_a^c f(x)\,dx$ and $\int_c^b f(x)\,dx$ both converge, then

$$\int_a^b f(x)\,dx = \int_a^c f(x)\,dx + \int_c^b f(x)\,dx$$

We say that the integral on the left diverges if *either* (or both) of the integrals on the right diverges.

➤ **What This Says** If a function is continuous on the open interval (a, b) but is unbounded at one of its endpoints of the interval, then replace that endpoint by t, evaluate the integral, and take the limit as t approaches that endpoint. On the other hand, if f is continuous on the interval $[a, b]$, except for some c in (a, b) where f has an infinite discontinuity, rewrite the integral as

$$\int_a^b f(x)\,dx = \int_a^c f(x)\,dx + \int_c^b f(x)\,dx$$

You will then need limits to evaluate each of the integrals on the right.

EXAMPLE 8 Improper integral at a right endpoint

Find $\displaystyle\int_0^1 \frac{dx}{(x-1)^{2/3}}$.

Solution

$f(x) = (x-1)^{-2/3}$ is unbounded at the right endpoint of the interval of integration and is continuous on $[0, t]$ for any t with $0 \le t < 1$. We find that

$$\int_0^1 \frac{dx}{(x-1)^{2/3}} = \lim_{t \to 1^-} \int_0^t \frac{dx}{(x-1)^{2/3}} = \lim_{t \to 1^-} [3(x-1)^{1/3}]\Big|_0^t$$

$$= 3 \lim_{t \to 1^-} [(t - 1)^{1/3} - (-1)] = 3$$

That is, the improper integral converges and has the value 3. ∎

EXAMPLE 9 Improper integral at a left endpoint

Find $\displaystyle\int_{\pi/2}^{\pi} \sec x \, dx$.

Solution

Because $\sec x$ is unbounded at the left endpoint $\frac{\pi}{2}$ of the interval of integration and is continuous on $[t, \pi]$ for any t with $\frac{\pi}{2} < t \leq \pi$, we find that

$$\int_{\pi/2}^{\pi} \sec x \, dx = \lim_{t \to (\pi/2)^+} \int_{t}^{\pi} \sec x \, dx = \lim_{t \to (\pi/2)^+} \ln|\sec x + \tan x||_{t}^{\pi}$$

$$= \lim_{t \to (\pi/2)^+} [\ln|-1 + 0| - \ln|\sec t + \tan t|] = -\infty$$

Thus, the integral diverges. ∎

EXAMPLE 10 Improper integral at an interior point

Find $\displaystyle\int_{0}^{3} (x - 2)^{-1} \, dx$.

Solution

WARNING A common mistake is to fail to notice the discontinuity at $x = 2$. It is WRONG to write

$$\int_{0}^{3} (x - 2)^{-1} \, dx = \ln|x - 2||_{0}^{3}$$
$$= \ln 1 - \ln 2$$
$$= -\ln 2$$

Notice that this mistake leads to the conclusion that the integral converges, which, as you can see, is incorrect. You must also be cautious in using computer software with improper integrals, because it may not detect that the integral is improper.

The integral is improper because the integrand is unbounded at $x = 2$. If the improper integral converges, we have

$$\int_{0}^{3} (x - 2)^{-1} \, dx = \int_{0}^{2} (x - 2)^{-1} \, dx + \int_{2}^{3} (x - 2)^{-1} \, dx$$

$$= \lim_{t \to 2^-} \int_{0}^{t} (x - 2)^{-1} \, dx + \lim_{t \to 2^+} \int_{t}^{3} (x - 2)^{-1} \, dx$$

If either of these limits fails to exist, then the original integral diverges. Because

$$\lim_{t \to 2^-} \int_{0}^{t} (x - 2)^{-1} \, dx = \lim_{t \to 2^-} \ln|x - 2||_{0}^{t}$$

$$= \lim_{t \to 2^-} [\ln|t - 2| - \ln 2]$$

$$= -\infty$$

we find that the original integral diverges. ∎

7.7 PROBLEM SET

A **1. WHAT DOES THIS SAY?** What is an improper integral?

2. WHAT DOES THIS SAY? Discuss the different types of improper integrals.

In Problems 3–46, either show that the improper integral con-

verges and find its value, or show that it diverges.

3. $\displaystyle\int_{1}^{+\infty} \frac{dx}{x^3}$

4. $\displaystyle\int_{1}^{+\infty} \frac{dx}{\sqrt[3]{x}}$

5. $\displaystyle\int_{1}^{+\infty} \frac{dx}{x^{0.99}}$

6. $\displaystyle\int_{1}^{+\infty} \frac{dx}{\sqrt{x}}$

7. $\displaystyle\int_{1}^{+\infty} \frac{dx}{x^{1.1}}$

8. $\displaystyle\int_{1}^{+\infty} x^{-2/3} \, dx$

9. $\displaystyle\int_{3}^{+\infty} \frac{dx}{2x - 1}$

10. $\displaystyle\int_{3}^{+\infty} \frac{dx}{\sqrt[3]{2x - 1}}$

11. $\displaystyle\int_{3}^{+\infty} \frac{dx}{(2x - 1)^2}$

12. $\displaystyle\int_{0}^{+\infty} e^{-x} \, dx$

13. $\displaystyle\int_{0}^{+\infty} 5e^{-2x} \, dx$

14. $\displaystyle\int_{1}^{+\infty} e^{1-x} \, dx$

15. $\displaystyle\int_{1}^{+\infty} \frac{x^2\,dx}{(x^3+2)^2}$

16. $\displaystyle\int_{1}^{+\infty} \frac{x^2\,dx}{x^3+2}$

17. $\displaystyle\int_{1}^{+\infty} \frac{x^2\,dx}{\sqrt{x^3+2}}$

18. $\displaystyle\int_{0}^{+\infty} xe^{-x^2}\,dx$

19. $\displaystyle\int_{1}^{+\infty} \frac{e^{-\sqrt{x}}}{\sqrt{x}}\,dx$

20. $\displaystyle\int_{0}^{+\infty} xe^{-x}\,dx$

21. $\displaystyle\int_{0}^{+\infty} 5xe^{10-x}\,dx$

22. $\displaystyle\int_{1}^{+\infty} \frac{\ln x\,dx}{x}$

23. $\displaystyle\int_{2}^{+\infty} \frac{dx}{x\ln x}$

24. $\displaystyle\int_{2}^{+\infty} \frac{dx}{x\sqrt{\ln x}}$

25. $\displaystyle\int_{0}^{+\infty} x^2 e^{-x}\,dx$

26. $\displaystyle\int_{0}^{+\infty} x^3 e^{-x^2}\,dx$

27. $\displaystyle\int_{-\infty}^{0} \frac{2x\,dx}{x^2+1}$

28. $\displaystyle\int_{1}^{+\infty} \frac{x\,dx}{(1+x^2)^2}$

29. $\displaystyle\int_{-\infty}^{0} \frac{dx}{\sqrt{2-x}}$

30. $\displaystyle\int_{-\infty}^{4} \frac{dx}{(5-x)^2}$

31. $\displaystyle\int_{-\infty}^{+\infty} xe^{-|x|}\,dx$

32. $\displaystyle\int_{-\infty}^{+\infty} \frac{dx}{x^2+1}$

33. $\displaystyle\int_{0}^{1} \frac{dx}{x^{1/5}}$

34. $\displaystyle\int_{0}^{4} \frac{dx}{x\sqrt{x}}$

35. $\displaystyle\int_{0}^{1} \frac{dx}{(1-x)^{1/2}}$

36. $\displaystyle\int_{0}^{2} \frac{dx}{(1-x)^2}$

37. $\displaystyle\int_{-1}^{1} \frac{e^x}{\sqrt[3]{1-e^x}}\,dx$

38. $\displaystyle\int_{-\infty}^{+\infty} \frac{3x\,dx}{(3x^2+2)^3}$

39. $\displaystyle\int_{0}^{1} \ln x\,dx$

40. $\displaystyle\int_{1}^{+\infty} \ln x\,dx$

41. $\displaystyle\int_{e}^{+\infty} \frac{dx}{x(\ln x)^2}$

42. $\displaystyle\int_{0}^{1} \frac{x\,dx}{1-x^2}$

43. $\displaystyle\int_{0}^{1} e^{-(1/2)\ln x}\,dx$

44. $\displaystyle\int_{0}^{+\infty} \frac{dx}{e^x+e^{-x}}$

45. $\displaystyle\int_{0}^{\pi/3} \frac{\sec^2 x\,dx}{1-\tan x}$

46. $\displaystyle\int_{0}^{\pi/2} \frac{\sin x\,dx}{\sqrt[3]{1-2\cos x}}$

Ⓑ 47. Find the area of the unbounded region between the x-axis and the curve

$$y = \frac{2}{(x-4)^3} \quad \text{for } x \geq 6$$

48. Find the area of the unbounded region between the x-axis and the curve

$$y = \frac{2}{(x-4)^3} \quad \text{for } x \leq 2$$

49. The total amount of radioactive material present in the atmosphere at time T is modeled by

$$A = \int_{0}^{T} Pe^{-rt}\,dt$$

where P is a constant and t is the number of years. Suppose a recent United Nations publication indicates that, at the present time, $r = 0.002$ and $P = 200$ millirads. Estimate the total future buildup of radioactive material in the atmosphere if these values remain constant.

50. Suppose that an oil well produces $P(t)$ thousand barrels of crude oil per month according to the formula

$$P(t) = 100e^{-0.02t} - 100e^{-0.1t}$$

where t is the number of months the well has been in production. What is the total amount of oil produced by the oil well?

51. Let $f(x) = \begin{cases} \dfrac{1}{x^2} & \text{for } x \geq 1 \\ 1 & \text{for } -1 < x < 1 \\ e^{x+1} & \text{for } x \leq -1 \end{cases}$

Sketch the graph of f and evaluate

$$\int_{-\infty}^{+\infty} f(x)\,dx$$

52. Find all values of p for which $\displaystyle\int_{2}^{+\infty} \frac{dx}{x(\ln x)^p}$ converges, and find the value of the integral when it exists.

53. Find all values of p for which $\displaystyle\int_{0}^{1} \frac{dx}{x^p}$ converges, and find the value of the integral when it exists.

54. Find all values of p for which $\displaystyle\int_{0}^{1/2} \frac{dx}{x(\ln x)^p}$ converges, and find the value of the integral when it exists.

55. Counterexample Problem Discuss the calculation

$$\int_{-1}^{1} \frac{dx}{x^2} = \left.\frac{-1}{x}\right|_{-1}^{1} = -[1-(-1)] = -2$$

Is the calculation correct? Explain.

56. Journal Problem *College Mathematics Journal*[*] ∎ Peter Lindstrom of North Lake College in Irving, Texas, had a student who handled an ∞/∞ form as follows:

$$\int_{1}^{+\infty} (x-1)e^{-x}\,dx = \int_{1}^{+\infty} \frac{x-1}{e^x}\,dx$$
$$= \int_{1}^{+\infty} \frac{1}{e^x} \qquad \text{l'Hôpital's rule}$$
$$= \frac{1}{e}$$

What is wrong, if anything, with this student's solution?

57. Find $\displaystyle\int_{0}^{2} f(x)\,dx$, where

$$f(x) = \begin{cases} \dfrac{1}{\sqrt[4]{x^3}} & \text{for } 0 < x \leq 1 \\ \dfrac{1}{\sqrt[4]{(x-1)^3}} & \text{for } 1 < x < 2 \end{cases}$$

58. Evaluate the improper polar integral $\displaystyle\int_{0}^{+\infty} \theta e^{-\theta}\,d\theta$.

59. Find the total area between the spirals $r = e^{-2\theta}$ and $r = e^{-5\theta}$ for $\theta \geq 0$.

---

[*]Vol. 24, No. 4, September 1993, p. 343.

c *The **Laplace transform** of the function f is defined by the improper integral*

$$F(s) = \mathcal{L}\{f(t)\} = \int_0^{+\infty} e^{-st} f(t)\, dt$$

where s is a constant. This notation is used in Problems 60–67.

60. Show that for constant a (with $s - a > 0$)

    a. $\mathcal{L}\{e^{at}\} = \dfrac{1}{s-a}$ **b.** $\mathcal{L}\{a\} = \dfrac{a}{s}$

    c. $\mathcal{L}(t) = \dfrac{1}{s^2}$ **d.** $\mathcal{L}(t^n) = \dfrac{n!}{s^{n+1}}$

    e. $\mathcal{L}\{\cos at\} = \dfrac{s}{s^2 + a^2}$ **f.** $\mathcal{L}\{\sin at\} = \dfrac{a}{s^2 + a^2}$

61. Show that $\mathcal{L}\{af + bg\} = a\mathcal{L}\{f\} + b\mathcal{L}\{g\}$.

62. Let $\mathcal{L}^{-1}\{F(s)\}$ denote the inverse Laplace transform of $F(s)$; that is, the function $f(t)$ such that $\mathcal{L}\{f(t)\} = F(s)$. Find the following inverse Laplace transformations (Problems 60 and 61 may help).

    a. $\mathcal{L}^{-1}\left\{\dfrac{5}{s}\right\}$ **b.** $\mathcal{L}^{-1}\left\{\dfrac{s+2}{s^2+4}\right\}$

    c. $\mathcal{L}^{-1}\left\{\dfrac{2s^2 - 3s + 3}{s^2(s-1)}\right\}$

    Hint: Use partial fraction decomposition.

    d. $\mathcal{L}^{-1}\left\{\dfrac{3s^3 + 2s^2 - 3s - 17}{(s^2+4)(s^2-1)}\right\}$

63. If $F(s) = \mathcal{L}\{f(t)\}$, show that $\mathcal{L}\{e^{at} f(t)\} = F(s-a)$.

64. Use the result in Problem 63, along with those of Problem 60, to find the following Laplace transforms and inverse transforms.

    a. $\mathcal{L}\{t^3 e^{-2t}\}$ **b.** $\mathcal{L}\{e^{-3t}\cos 2t\}$

    c. $\mathcal{L}^{-1}\left\{\dfrac{5}{(s-1)^2}\right\}$

    d. $\mathcal{L}^{-1}\left\{\dfrac{4s}{s^2 + 4s + 5}\right\}$

    Hint: Complete the square.

65. a. If $F(s) = \mathcal{L}\{f(t)\}$, show that $\mathcal{L}\{tf(t)\} = -F'(s)$. You may assume that

$$\frac{d}{ds}\int_0^{+\infty} e^{-st} f(t)\, dt = \int_0^{+\infty} \frac{d}{ds}[e^{-st} f(t)\, dt]$$

    b. Use the result to find $\mathcal{L}\{t\cos 2t\}$.

66. What is $\mathcal{L}\{t^2 f(t)\}$? What about $\mathcal{L}\{t^n f(t)\}$?

67. Let $\mathcal{L}\{f\} = F(s)$. Suppose that f is continuous on $[0, \infty)$ and that f' is piecewise continuous on $[0, k]$ for every positive number k. Further suppose that $\lim_{k\to\infty} e^{-sk} f(k) = 0$ if $s > 0$.

    a. Show that $\mathcal{L}\{f'\} = sF(s) - f(0)$. *Hint*: Use integration by parts.

    b. Apply the result in part **a** to find $\mathcal{L}\{y\}$, where y satisfies the initial value problem

$$y' + 3y = \sin 2t$$

    with $y(0) = 2$.

    c. Solve the initial value problem in part **b** by using inverse Laplace transforms to obtain y.

7.8   Hyperbolic and Inverse Hyperbolic Functions

IN THIS SECTION   hyperbolic functions, derivatives and integrals involving hyperbolic functions, inverse hyperbolic functions

HYPERBOLIC FUNCTIONS

In physics, it is shown that a heavy, flexible cable (for example, a power line) that is suspended between two points at the same height assumes the shape of a curve called a **catenary** (see Figure 7.20), with an equation of the form

$$y = \frac{a}{2}\left(e^{x/a} + e^{-x/a}\right)$$

This is one of several important applications that involve sums of exponential functions. The goal of this section is to study such sums and their inverses.

    In certain ways, the functions we will study are analogous to the trigonometric functions, and they have essentially the same relationship to the hyperbola that the trigonometric functions have to the circle. For this reason, these functions are called **hyperbolic functions**. Three basic hyperbolic functions are the **hyperbolic sine** (denoted $\sinh x$ and pronounced "cinch"), the **hyperbolic cosine** ($\cosh x$; pronounced "kosh"), and the **hyperbolic tangent** ($\tanh x$; pronounced "tansh"). They are defined as follows.

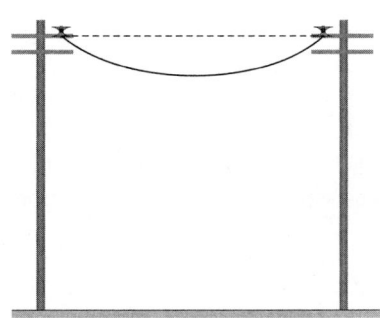

Figure 7.20 The hanging cable problem

Hyperbolic Functions

$$\sinh x = \frac{e^x - e^{-x}}{2} \qquad \text{for all } x$$

$$\cosh x = \frac{e^x + e^{-x}}{2} \qquad \text{for all } x$$

$$\tanh x = \frac{\sinh x}{\cosh x} = \frac{e^x - e^{-x}}{e^x + e^{-x}} \qquad \text{for all } x$$

Graphs of the three basic hyperbolic functions are shown in Figure 7.21.

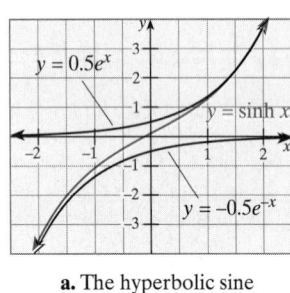
a. The hyperbolic sine
$y = \sinh x$

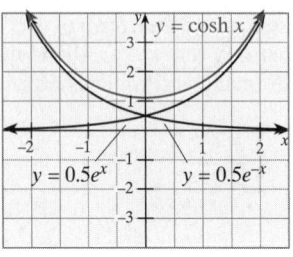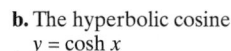
b. The hyperbolic cosine
$y = \cosh x$

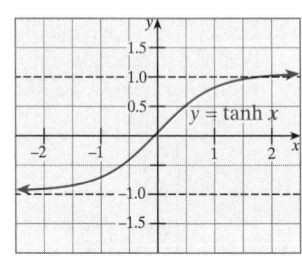
c. The hyperbolic tangent
$y = \tanh x$

Figure 7.21   Graphs of the three basic hyperbolic functions

The list of properties in the following theorem suggests that the basic hyperbolic functions are analogous to the trigonometric functions.

THEOREM 7.2   **Properties of the basic hyperbolic functions**

$$\cosh^2 x - \sinh^2 x = 1$$
$$\sinh(-x) = -\sinh x \qquad (\sinh x \text{ is odd})$$
$$\cosh(-x) = \cosh x \qquad (\cosh x \text{ is even})$$
$$\tanh(-x) = -\tanh x \qquad (\tanh x \text{ is odd})$$
$$\sinh(x + y) = \sinh x \cosh y + \cosh x \sinh y$$
$$\cosh(x + y) = \cosh x \cosh y + \sinh x \sinh y$$

WARNING   A major difference between the trigonometric and hyperbolic functions is that the trigonometric functions are periodic, but the hyperbolic functions are not.

Proof   We will verify the first identity and leave the others for the reader.

$$\cosh^2 x - \sinh^2 x = \left(\frac{e^x + e^{-x}}{2}\right)^2 - \left(\frac{e^x - e^{-x}}{2}\right)^2$$

$$= \frac{e^{2x} + 2 + e^{-2x}}{4} - \frac{e^{2x} - 2 + e^{-2x}}{4} = 1 \qquad \square$$

TECHNOLOGY NOTE

Some of the software packages show these in simplified form as:

$$\coth x = \frac{e^{2x} + 1}{e^{2x} - 1}$$

$$\text{sech } x = \frac{2e^x}{e^{2x} + 1}$$

$$\text{csch } x = \frac{2e^x}{e^{2x} - 1}$$

There are three additional hyperbolic functions: the **hyperbolic cotangent** (coth x), the **hyperbolic secant** (sech x), and the **hyperbolic cosecant** (csch x). These functions are defined as follows:

$$\coth x = \frac{1}{\tanh x} = \frac{e^x + e^{-x}}{e^x - e^{-x}}$$

$$\text{sech } x = \frac{1}{\cosh x} = \frac{2}{e^x + e^{-x}}$$

$$\text{csch } x = \frac{1}{\sinh x} = \frac{2}{e^x - e^{-x}}$$

Two identities involving these functions are

$$\text{sech}^2 x = 1 - \tanh^2 x \quad \text{and} \quad \text{csch}^2 x = \coth^2 x - 1$$

You will be asked to verify these identities in the problems.

DERIVATIVES AND INTEGRALS INVOLVING HYPERBOLIC FUNCTIONS

Rules for differentiating the hyperbolic functions are listed in Theorem 7.3.

THEOREM 7.3   Rules for differentiating hyperbolic functions

Let u be a differentiable function of x. Then

$$\frac{d}{dx}(\sinh u) = \cosh u \frac{du}{dx} \qquad \frac{d}{dx}(\cosh u) = \sinh u \frac{du}{dx}$$

$$\frac{d}{dx}(\tanh u) = \text{sech}^2 u \frac{du}{dx} \qquad \frac{d}{dx}(\coth u) = -\text{csch}^2 u \frac{du}{dx}$$

$$\frac{d}{dx}(\text{sech}\, u) = -\text{sech}\, u \tanh u \frac{du}{dx} \qquad \frac{d}{dx}(\text{csch}\, u) = -\text{csch}\, u \coth u \frac{du}{dx}$$

Proof   Each of these rules can be obtained by differentiating the exponential functions that make up the appropriate hyperbolic function. For example, to differentiate $\sinh x$, we use the definition of $\sinh x$:

$$\frac{d}{dx}(\sinh x) = \frac{d}{dx}\left(\frac{e^x - e^{-x}}{2}\right)$$

$$= \tfrac{1}{2}e^x - \tfrac{1}{2}e^{-x}(-1) = \tfrac{1}{2}(e^x + e^{-x}) = \cosh x$$

The proofs for the other derivatives can be handled similarly.   ☐

EXAMPLE 1   Derivatives involving hyperbolic functions

Find $\dfrac{dy}{dx}$ for each of the following functions:

a. $y = \cosh Ax$ (A is constant)   **b.** $y = \tanh(x^2 + 1)$ **c.** $y = \ln(\sinh x)$

Solution

a. We have

$$\frac{d}{dx}(\cosh Ax) = \sinh(Ax)\frac{d}{dx}(Ax) = A \sinh Ax$$

b. We find that

$$\frac{d}{dx}[\tanh(x^2 + 1)] = \text{sech}^2(x^2 + 1)\frac{d}{dx}(x^2 + 1) = 2x \,\text{sech}^2(x^2 + 1)$$

c. Using the chain rule, with $u = \sinh x$, we obtain

$$\frac{d}{dx}[\ln(\sinh x)] = \frac{1}{\sinh x}\frac{d}{dx}(\sinh x) = \frac{1}{\sinh x}(\cosh x) = \coth x \qquad ■$$

Each differentiation formula for hyperbolic functions corresponds to an integration formula. These formulas are listed in the following theorem.

THEOREM 7.4   Integration formulas involving the hyperbolic functions

$$\int \sinh x \, dx = \cosh x + C \qquad \int \cosh x \, dx = \sinh x + C$$

$$\int \text{sech}^2 x \, dx = \tanh x + C \qquad \int \text{csch}^2 x \, dx = -\coth x + C$$

$$\int \text{sech}\, x \tanh x \, dx = -\text{sech}\, x + C \qquad \int \text{csch}\, x \coth x \, dx = -\text{csch}\, x + C$$

Proof The proof of each of these formulas follows directly from the corresponding derivative formula. ❏

EXAMPLE 2 Integration involving hyperbolic forms

Find each of the following integrals:

a. $\displaystyle\int \cosh^3 x \sinh x \, dx$ **b.** $\displaystyle\int x \operatorname{sech}^2(x^2) \, dx$ **c.** $\displaystyle\int \tanh x \, dx$

Solution

a. $\displaystyle\int \cosh^3 x \sinh x \, dx = \int u^3 \, du = \frac{u^4}{4} + C = \frac{1}{4}\cosh^4 x + C$

$\boxed{\text{Let } u = \cosh x; \, du = \sinh x \, dx}$

b. $\displaystyle\int x \operatorname{sech}^2(x^2) \, dx = \int \operatorname{sech}^2(x^2)(x \, dx)$

$\boxed{\text{Let } u = x^2; \, du = 2x \, dx}$

$\displaystyle = \int \operatorname{sech}^2 u \left(\frac{1}{2} \, du\right)$

$\displaystyle = \tfrac{1}{2}\tanh u + C$

$\displaystyle = \tfrac{1}{2}\tanh x^2 + C$

c. $\displaystyle\int \tanh x \, dx = \int \frac{\sinh x \, dx}{\cosh x}$

$\boxed{\text{Let } u = \cosh x; \, du = \sinh x \, dx}$

$\displaystyle = \int \frac{du}{u} = \ln|u| + C = \ln(\cosh x) + C$ ∎

INVERSE HYPERBOLIC FUNCTIONS

Inverse hyperbolic functions are also of interest, mainly because they enable us to express certain integrals in simple terms.

Because $\sinh x$ is continuous and strictly monotonic (increasing), it is one-to-one and has an inverse, which is defined by

$$y = \sinh^{-1} x \quad \text{if and only if} \quad x = \sinh y$$

for all x and y. This is called the **inverse hyperbolic sine** function, and its graph is obtained by reflecting the graph of $y = \sinh x$ in the line $y = x$, as shown in Figure 7.22. Other inverse hyperbolic functions are defined similarly (see Problem 60).

Because the hyperbolic functions are defined in terms of exponential functions, we may expect to be able to express the inverse hyperbolic functions in terms of logarithmic functions. We summarize these relationships in the following theorem.

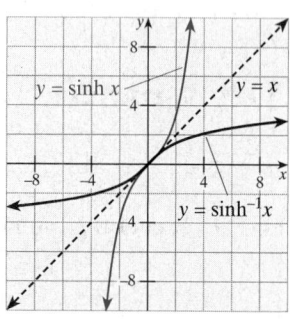

The graph of $y = \sinh^{-1}x$ is obtained by reflecting $y = \sinh x$ in the line $y = x$.

Figure 7.22 The graph of $y = \sinh^{-1} x$

THEOREM 7.5 Logarithmic formulas for inverse hyperbolic functions

$$\sinh^{-1} x = \ln(x + \sqrt{x^2 + 1}), \text{ all } x \qquad \operatorname{csch}^{-1} x = \ln\left(\frac{1}{x} + \frac{\sqrt{1 + x^2}}{|x|}\right), x \neq 0$$

$$\cosh^{-1} x = \ln(x + \sqrt{x^2 - 1}), x \geq 1 \qquad \operatorname{sech}^{-1} x = \ln\left(\frac{1 + \sqrt{1 - x^2}}{x}\right), 0 < x \leq 1$$

$$\tanh^{-1} x = \frac{1}{2}\ln\frac{1 + x}{1 - x}, |x| < 1 \qquad \coth^{-1} x = \frac{1}{2}\ln\frac{x + 1}{x - 1}, |x| > 1$$

Proof   We will prove the first formula and leave the next two formulas for you to verify (see Problem 61). The other formulas are proved similarly. Let $y = \sinh^{-1} x$; then its inverse is

$$x = \sinh y$$
$$= \tfrac{1}{2}(e^y - e^{-y})$$
$$2x = e^y - \frac{1}{e^y}$$

$$e^{2y} - 2xe^y - 1 = 0 \qquad \text{Quadratic formula with } a = 1, b = -2x, c = -1$$

$$e^y = \frac{2x \pm \sqrt{4x^2 + 4}}{2}$$
$$= x \pm \sqrt{x^2 + 1}$$

Because $e^y > 0$ for all y, the only solution is $e^y = x + \sqrt{x^2 + 1}$, and from the definition of logarithms,

$$y = \ln(x + \sqrt{x^2 + 1}) \qquad \square$$

Differentiation and integration formulas involving inverse hyperbolic functions are listed in Theorem 7.6.

THEOREM 7.6   Differentiation and integration formulas involving the inverse hyperbolic functions

$$\frac{d}{dx}(\sinh^{-1} u) = \frac{1}{\sqrt{1 + u^2}}\frac{du}{dx} \qquad \int \frac{du}{\sqrt{1 + u^2}} = \sinh^{-1} u + C$$

$$\frac{d}{dx}(\cosh^{-1} u) = \frac{1}{\sqrt{u^2 - 1}}\frac{du}{dx} \qquad \int \frac{du}{\sqrt{u^2 - 1}} = \cosh^{-1} u + C$$

$$\frac{d}{dx}(\tanh^{-1} u) = \frac{1}{1 - u^2}\frac{du}{dx} \qquad \int \frac{du}{1 - u^2} = \tanh^{-1} u + C$$

$$\frac{d}{dx}(\operatorname{csch}^{-1} u) = \frac{-1}{|u|\sqrt{1 + u^2}}\frac{du}{dx} \qquad \int \frac{du}{u\sqrt{1 + u^2}} = -\operatorname{csch}^{-1}|u| + C$$

$$\frac{d}{dx}(\operatorname{sech}^{-1} u) = \frac{-1}{u\sqrt{1 - u^2}}\frac{du}{dx} \qquad \int \frac{du}{u\sqrt{1 - u^2}} = -\operatorname{sech}^{-1}|u| + C$$

$$\frac{d}{dx}(\coth^{-1} u) = \frac{1}{1 - u^2}\frac{du}{dx} \qquad \int \frac{du}{1 - u^2} = \coth^{-1} u + C$$

Proof   The derivative of each inverse hyperbolic function can be found either by differentiating the appropriate logarithmic function or by using the definition in terms of hyperbolic functions. We will show how this is done for $y = \sinh^{-1} x$ and then leave it for you to apply the chain rule for u, a differentiable function of x. By definition of inverse, we see

$$x = \sinh y \quad \text{and} \quad \frac{dx}{dy} = \cosh y$$

Thus,

$$\frac{d}{dx}(\sinh^{-1} x) = \frac{dy}{dx} = \frac{1}{\dfrac{dx}{dy}} = \frac{1}{\cosh y} = \frac{1}{\sqrt{1 + \sinh^2 y}} = \frac{1}{\sqrt{1 + x^2}}$$

since $\cosh^2 y - \sinh^2 y = 1$ and $\sinh y = x$. The integration formula that corresponds to this differentiation formula is

$$\int \frac{dx}{\sqrt{1 + x^2}} = \sinh^{-1} x + C$$

The other differentiation and integration formulas follow similarly. $\square$

EXAMPLE 3 **Derivatives involving inverse hyperbolic functions**

Find $\dfrac{dy}{dx}$ for   **a.** $y = \sinh^{-1}(ax + b)$ **b.** $y = \cosh^{-1}(\sec x), 0 \le x < \dfrac{\pi}{2}$

Solution

a. $\dfrac{d}{dx}\left[\sinh^{-1}(ax + b)\right] = \dfrac{1}{\sqrt{1 + (ax + b)^2}}\dfrac{d}{dx}(ax + b)$

$= \dfrac{a}{\sqrt{1 + (ax + b)^2}}$

b. $\dfrac{d}{dx}\left[\cosh^{-1}(\sec x)\right] = \dfrac{1}{\sqrt{\sec^2 x - 1}}\dfrac{d}{dx}(\sec x)$

$= \dfrac{\sec x \tan x}{\sqrt{\tan^2 x}} = \sec x$ ∎

The result of Example 3b implies

Recall that the formula

$$\int \sec x \, dx = \ln|\sec x + \tan x| + C$$

was derived using algebraic procedures in Section 7.1.

$$\int \sec x \, dx = \cosh^{-1}(\sec x) + C$$

$$= \ln(\sec x + \sqrt{\sec^2 x - 1}) + C$$

$$= \ln(\sec x + \tan x) + C$$

Notice that we do not need absolute values because $0 \le x < \frac{\pi}{2}$.

EXAMPLE 4 **Integral involving an inverse hyperbolic function**

Evaluate $\displaystyle\int_0^1 \dfrac{dx}{\sqrt{1 + x^2}}$.

Solution

$$\int_0^1 \dfrac{dx}{\sqrt{1 + x^2}} = \left[\sinh^{-1} x\right]\Big|_0^1$$

$$= \ln(x + \sqrt{x^2 + 1})\Big|_0^1$$

$$= \ln(1 + \sqrt{2}) - \ln(1)$$

$$= \ln(1 + \sqrt{2})$$

It may be a worthwhile exercise to evaluate this integral using a trigonometric substitution to obtain the same result. ∎

7.8 PROBLEM SET

A *Evaluate (correct to four decimal places) the indicated hyperbolic or inverse hyperbolic functions in Problems 1–12.*

1. $\sinh 2$

2. $\cosh 3$

3. $\tanh(-1)$

4. $\sinh^{-1} 0$

5. $\coth 1.2$

6. $\tanh^{-1} 0$

7. $\cosh^{-1} 1.5$

8. $\sinh(\ln 2)$

9. $\cosh(\ln 3)$

10. $\operatorname{sech}^{-1} 0.2$

11. $\operatorname{sech} 1$

12. $\coth^{-1}(-3)$

Find $\dfrac{dy}{dx}$ in Problems 13–29.

13. $y = \sinh 3x$

14. $y = \cosh(1 - 2x^2)$

15. $y = \cosh(2x^2 + 3x)$

16. $y = \sinh\sqrt{x}$

17. $y = \sinh x^{-1}$

18. $y = \cosh^{-1}(x^2)$

19. $y = \sinh^{-1}(x^3)$

20. $y = x\tanh^{-1}(3x)$

21. $y = \sinh^{-1}(\tan x)$

22. $y = \cosh^{-1}(\sec x)$

23. $y = \tanh^{-1}(\sin x)$

24. $y = \operatorname{sech}\left(\dfrac{1 - x}{1 + x}\right)$

25. $y = \dfrac{\sinh^{-1} x}{x}$

26. $y = \sinh^{-1} x - \sqrt{1 + x^2}$

27. $y = x\cosh^{-1} x - \sqrt{x^2 - 1}$ **28.** $x\cosh y = y\sinh x + 5$

29. $e^x \sinh^{-1} x + e^{-x}\cosh^{-1} y = 1$

Compute the integrals in Problems 30–45.

30. $\displaystyle\int x\cosh(1 - x^2)\,dx$

31. $\displaystyle\int \dfrac{\sinh\frac{1}{x}\,dx}{x^2}$

32. $\int \dfrac{\mathrm{sech}^2(\ln x)\,dx}{x}$

33. $\int \coth x\,dx$

34. $\int \dfrac{dx}{\sqrt{4x^2+16}}$

35. $\int \dfrac{dt}{\sqrt{9t^2-16}}$

36. $\int \dfrac{dt}{36-16t^2}$

37. $\int \dfrac{\cos x\,dx}{\sqrt{1+\sin^2 x}}$

38. $\int \dfrac{x\,dx}{\sqrt{1+x^4}}$

39. $\int \dfrac{x^2\,dx}{1-x^6}$

40. $\int_0^{1/2} \dfrac{dx}{1-x^2}$

41. $\int_2^3 \dfrac{dx}{1-x^2}$

42. $\int_0^1 \dfrac{t^5\,dt}{\sqrt{1+t^{12}}}$

43. $\int_1^2 \dfrac{e^x\,dx}{\sqrt{e^{2x}-1}}$

44. $\int_0^{\ln 2} \sinh 3x\,dx$

45. $\int_0^1 x\,\mathrm{sech}^2 x^2\,dx$

B **46.** Show that

  a. $\tanh(x+y)=\dfrac{\tanh x+\tanh y}{1+\tanh x\tanh y}$

  b. $\sinh 2x = 2\sinh x\cosh x$

  c. $\cosh 2x = \cosh^2 x + \sinh^2 x$

47. Evaluate $\displaystyle\lim_{x\to+\infty}\dfrac{\sinh^{-1}x}{\cosh^{-1}x}$

48. Show that

  a. $-1<\tanh x<1$ for all x

  b. $\displaystyle\lim_{x\to+\infty}\tanh x = 1$ and $\displaystyle\lim_{x\to-\infty}\tanh x = -1$

49. Determine where the graph of $y=\tanh x$ is rising and falling and where it is concave up and concave down. Sketch the graph and compare with Figure 7.21c.

50. Sketch the graph of $y=\coth x$. Be sure to show key features such as intercepts, high and low points, and points of inflection.

51. First show that $\cosh x+\sinh x = e^x$, and then use this result to prove that $(\sinh x+\cosh x)^n = \cosh nx + \sinh nx$ for positive integers n.

52. If $x=a\cosh t$ and $y=b\sinh t$ where a,b are positive constants and t is any number, show that
$$\dfrac{x^2}{a^2}-\dfrac{y^2}{b^2}=1$$

53. a. Verify that $y=a\cosh cx+b\sinh cx$ satisfies the differential equation
$$y''-c^2 y = 0$$

  b. Use part **a** to find a solution of the differential equation
$$y''-4y=0$$
subject to the initial conditions $y(0)=1$, $y'(0)=2$.

54. Find the volume V generated when the region bounded by the curves $y=\sinh x$, $y=\cosh x$, the y-axis, and the line $x=c$ ($c>0$) is revolved about the x-axis. For what value of c does $V=1$?

55. Find the length of the catenary $y=a\cosh\dfrac{x}{a}$ between $x=-a$ and $x=a$.

56. Find the volume of the solid formed by revolving the region bounded by the curve $y=\tanh x$ on the interval $[0,1]$ about the x-axis.

57. Find the surface area of the solid generated by revolving the curve $y=\cosh x$ on the interval $[-1,1]$ about the x-axis.

C **58.** Prove the following formulas

  a. $\mathrm{sech}^2 x + \tanh^2 x = 1$ **b.** $\coth^2 x - \mathrm{csch}^2 x = 1$

59. Derive the differentiation formulas for $\cosh u$, $\tanh u$, and $\mathrm{sech}\,u$, where u is a differentiable function of x.

60. First give definitions for $\cosh^{-1}x$, $\tanh^{-1}x$, and $\mathrm{sech}^{-1}x$, and then derive the differentiation formulas for these functions by using these definitions.

61. Prove

  a. $\cosh^{-1}x = \ln(x+\sqrt{x^2-1})$, $x\ge 1$

  b. $\tanh^{-1}x = \dfrac{1}{2}\ln\dfrac{1+x}{1-x}$, $|x|<1$

62. Show that
$$\int \dfrac{dx}{\sqrt{x^2+a^2}} = \sinh^{-1}\dfrac{x}{a}+C$$
for constant $a>0$. State and prove a similar formula for
$$\int \dfrac{dx}{\sqrt{x^2-a^2}}$$
with $x>a>0$.

CHAPTER 7 REVIEW

Proficiency Examination

CONCEPT PROBLEMS

1. Discuss the method of integration by substitution for both indefinite and definite integrals.

2. a. What is the formula for integration by parts?

  b. What is a reduction formula for integration?

3. a. When should you consider a trigonometric substitution?

  b. What are the substitutions to use when integrating rational trigonometric integrals?

4. When should you consider the method of partial fractions?

5. Outline a strategy for integration.

6. What is a first-order linear differential equation? Outline a procedure for solving such an equation.

7. What is an improper integral?

8. Define the hyperbolic sine, hyperbolic cosine, and hyperbolic tangent.

9. State the rules for differentiating and integrating the hyperbolic functions.

10. What are the logarithmic formulas for the inverse hyperbolic formulas?

11. State the differentiation and integration formulas for the inverse hyperbolic functions.

PRACTICE PROBLEMS

12. Evaluate each of the given numbers.

    a. $\tanh^{-1}(0.5)$ **b.** $\sinh(\ln 3)$ **c.** $\coth^{-1}(2)$

Find the integrals in Problem 13–18.

13. $\displaystyle\int \frac{2x+3}{\sqrt{x^2+1}}\,dx$ **14.** $\displaystyle\int x\sin 2x\,dx$

15. $\displaystyle\int \sinh(1-2x)\,dx$ **16.** $\displaystyle\int \frac{dx}{\sqrt{4-x^2}}$

17. $\displaystyle\int \frac{x^2\,dx}{(x^2+1)(x-1)}$ **18.** $\displaystyle\int \frac{x^3\,dx}{x^2-1}$

Evaluate the definite integrals in Problems 19–22.

19. $\displaystyle\int_1^2 x\ln x^3\,dx$ **20.** $\displaystyle\int_2^3 \frac{dx}{(x-1)^2(x+2)}$

21. $\displaystyle\int_3^4 \frac{dx}{2x-x^2}$ **22.** $\displaystyle\int_0^{\pi/4} \sec^3 x\tan x\,dx$

Determine whether each improper integral in Problems 23–26 converges, and if it does, find its value.

23. $\displaystyle\int_0^{+\infty} xe^{-2x}\,dx$ **24.** $\displaystyle\int_0^{\pi/4} \frac{\sec^2 x\,dx}{\sqrt{\tan x}}$

25. $\displaystyle\int_0^1 \frac{2x+3}{x^2(x-2)}\,dx$ **26.** $\displaystyle\int_0^{+\infty} e^{-x}\sin x\,dx$

27. Find $\dfrac{dy}{dx}$ for $y = \sqrt{\tanh^{-1} 2x}$.

28. Find the volume of the solid generated when the region under the curve

$$y = \frac{1}{\sqrt{9-x^2}}$$

    on the interval $[0, 2]$ is revolved about the y-axis.

29. Solve the first-order linear differential equation

$$\frac{dy}{dx} + \frac{xy}{x+1} = e^{-x}$$

    subject to the condition $y = 1$ when $x = 0$.

30. A tank contains 200 gal of saturated brine with 2 lb of salt per gallon. A salt solution containing 1.3 lb of salt per gallon flows in at the rate of 5 gal/min, and the uniform mixture flows out at 3 gal/min. Find the amount of salt in the tank after 1 hour.

Supplementary Problems

Find the derivative $\dfrac{dy}{dx}$ in Problems 1–5.

1. $y = \tanh^{-1}\dfrac{1}{x}$ **2.** $y = x\cosh^{-1}(3x+1)$

3. $y = \dfrac{\sinh x}{e^x}$ **4.** $y = \sinh x\cosh x$

5. $y = x\sinh x + \sinh(e^x + e^{-x})$

Find the integrals in Problems 6–43.

6. $\displaystyle\int \cos^{-1} x\,dx$ **7.** $\displaystyle\int \frac{x^2\,dx}{\sqrt{4-x^2}}$

8. $\displaystyle\int \frac{x\,dx}{x^2-2x+5}$ **9.** $\displaystyle\int \frac{3x-2}{x^3-2x^2}\,dx$

10. $\displaystyle\int \frac{dx}{(x^2+x+1)^{3/2}}$ **11.** $\displaystyle\int \frac{dx}{\sqrt{x}(1+\sqrt[4]{x})}$

12. $\displaystyle\int \frac{\sqrt{9x^2-1}\,dx}{x}$ **13.** $\displaystyle\int x^2\tan^{-1} x\,dx$

14. $\displaystyle\int \frac{dx}{\sin x+\tan x}$ **15.** $\displaystyle\int e^x\sqrt{4-e^{2x}}\,dx$

16. $\displaystyle\int \cos\frac{x}{2}\sin\frac{x}{3}\,dx$ **17.** $\displaystyle\int \frac{\sqrt{1+1/x^2}}{x^5}\,dx$

18. $\displaystyle\int \frac{\sin x\,dx}{\cos^5 x}$ **19.** $\displaystyle\int \sqrt{1+\sin x}\,dx$

20. $\displaystyle\int \cos x\ln(\sin x)\,dx$ **21.** $\displaystyle\int \sin(\ln x)\,dx$

22. $\displaystyle\int e^{2x}\operatorname{sech}(e^{2x})\,dx$ **23.** $\displaystyle\int \frac{\sinh x\,dx}{2+\cosh x}$

24. $\displaystyle\int \frac{\tanh^{-1} x\,dx}{1-x^2}$ **25.** $\displaystyle\int x^2\cot^{-1} x\,dx$

26. $\displaystyle\int x(1+x)^{1/3}\,dx$ **27.** $\displaystyle\int \frac{x^2+2}{x^3+6x+1}\,dx$

28. $\displaystyle\int \frac{\sin x-\cos x}{(\sin x+\cos x)^{1/4}}\,dx$ **29.** $\displaystyle\int \cos(\sqrt{x+2})\,dx$

30. $\displaystyle\int \sqrt{5+2\sin^2 x}\,\sin 2x\,dx$ **31.** $\displaystyle\int \frac{x^3+2x}{x^4+4x^2+3}\,dx$

32. $\displaystyle\int \frac{x\,dx}{\sqrt{5-x^2}}$ **33.** $\displaystyle\int \frac{\sqrt{5-x^2}\,dx}{x}$

34. $\displaystyle\int \frac{\sqrt{x^2+x}\,dx}{x}$ **35.** $\displaystyle\int x^3(x^2+4)^{-1/2}\,dx$

36. $\displaystyle\int \sin^2\left(\frac{x}{2}\right)\cos^2\left(\frac{x}{2}\right)\,dx$ **37.** $\displaystyle\int \sec^3 x\tan x\,dx$

38. $\displaystyle\int \sec^5 x\tan^2 x\,dx$ **39.** $\displaystyle\int \frac{x^{1/3}\,dx}{x^{1/2}+x^{2/3}}$

40. $\displaystyle\int \frac{\sin x\,dx}{\sin x+\cos x}$ **41.** $\displaystyle\int \frac{\cos x+\sin x}{1+\cos x-\sin x}\,dx$

42. $\displaystyle\int \frac{dx}{x^{1/4}+1}$ **43.** $\displaystyle\int \frac{e^x\,dx}{e^{x/3}-e^{x/2}}$

In Problems 44–48, solve the given differential equations.

44. $\dfrac{dy}{dx} = \sqrt{\dfrac{x^2-1}{y^2+1}}$ **45.** $\dfrac{dy}{dx} = \dfrac{1-y}{1+x}$

46. $\dfrac{dy}{dx} - \dfrac{y}{2x} = \dfrac{1}{x^{1/2}+1}$ **47.** $y' + (\tan x)y = \sec^3 x$

48. $(\cos^3 x)y' = \sin^3 x\cos y$

Determine whether the improper integral in Problems 49–52 converges, and if it does, find its value.

49. $\displaystyle\int_0^{\pi/2} \frac{\cos x\,dx}{\sqrt{\sin x}}$ **50.** $\displaystyle\int_{-\infty}^{+\infty} \frac{dx}{4+x^2}$

51. $\displaystyle\int_{-1}^1 \frac{dx}{(2x+1)^{1/3}}$ **52.** $\displaystyle\int_1^{+\infty} \frac{dx}{x^4+x^2}$

53. If n is a positive integer and a is a positive number, find

$$\int_0^{+\infty} x^n e^{-ax}\,dx$$

54. Find $\displaystyle\int \frac{\sin x\,dx}{\sqrt{\cos 2x}}$.

55. Show that $\int_0^1 x^m(1-x)^n \, dx = \int_0^1 x^n(1-x)^m \, dx$ for positive integers m, n.

56. **Counterexample Problem**   Each of the following equations may be either true or false. In each case, either show that the equation is generally true or find a number x for which it fails.

   a. $\tanh\left(\frac{1}{2}\ln x\right) = \frac{x-1}{x+1}, x > 0$

   b. $\sinh^{-1}(\tan x) = \tanh^{-1}(\sin x)$ for $-\frac{\pi}{2} < x < \frac{\pi}{2}$

57. Compute $\int_0^1 xf''(3x) \, dx$, given that $f'(0)$ is defined, $f(0) = 1$, $f(3) = 4$, and $f'(3) = -2$.

58. What is $\int_0^{\pi/2} [f(x) + f''(x)]\cos x \, dx$ if $f(0)$ is defined, $f(\frac{\pi}{2}) = 5$, and $f'(0) = -1$?

59. **Newton's law of cooling** says that the temperature T of a body satisfies

$$\frac{dT}{dt} = k(T - T_0)$$

   where T_0 is the temperature of the surrounding medium. Solve this equation for T.

60. **Modeling Problem**   The psychologist L. L. Thurstone investigated the way people learn using the differential equation

$$\frac{dS}{dt} = \frac{2k}{\sqrt{m}}[S(1-S)]^{3/2}$$

   where $S(t)$ is the state of the learner at time t, and k and m are positive constants depending on the learner and the nature of the task.* Solve this equation.

61. If $s > 0$, the integral function defined by

$$\Gamma(s) = \int_0^{+\infty} e^{-t}t^{s-1} \, dt$$

   is called the **gamma function**. It was introduced by Leonhard Euler in 1729 and has some useful properties.

   a. Show that $\Gamma(s)$ converges for all $s > 0$.

   b. Show that $\Gamma(s+1) = s\Gamma(s)$.

   c. Show that $\Gamma(n+1) = n!$ for any positive integer n.

62. Find the centroid of a thin plate of constant density that occupies the region bounded by the graph of $y = \sin x + \cos x$, the coordinate axes, and the line $x = \pi/4$.

63. Repeat Problem 62 for a plate that occupies the region bounded by $y = \sec^2 x$, the coordinate axes, and the line $x = \pi/3$.

64. Find the volume obtained by revolving about the y-axis the region bounded by the curve $y = \sinh x$, the x-axis, and the line $x = 1$.

65. Find the volume obtained by revolving about the y-axis the region bounded by the curve $y = \cosh x$, the y-axis, and the line $y = 2$.

66. The region bounded by the graph of $y = \sin x$ and the x-axis between $x = 0$ and $x = \pi$ is revolved about the x-axis to generate a solid. Find the volume of the solid and its surface area.

*L. L. Thurstone, "The Learning Function," *J. of General Psychology* 3 (1930), pp. 469–493.

67. Find the length of the arc of the curve $y = \frac{4}{5}x^{5/4}$ that lies between $x = 0$ and $x = 1$.

68. Find the volume of the solid obtained by revolving about the x-axis the region bounded by the curve $y = (9 - x^2)^{1/4}$ and the x-axis.

69. Find the volume of the solid formed by revolving about the y-axis the region bounded by the curve

$$y = \frac{1}{1 + x^4}$$

   between $x = 0$ and $x = 4$.

70. Find the volume of the solid formed by revolving about the x-axis the region bounded by the curve

$$y = \frac{2}{\sqrt{3x - 2}}$$

   the x-axis, and the lines $x = 1$ and $x = 2$.

71. Find the surface area of the solid generated by revolving the region bounded by the curve

$$y = e^x + \frac{1}{4}e^{-x}$$

   on $[0, 1]$ about the x-axis.

72. Find the volume of the solid whose base is the region R bounded by the curve $y = e^x$ and the lines $y = 0$, $x = 0$, $x = 1$, if cross sections perpendicular to the x-axis are equilateral triangles.

73. Show that the area under $y = \frac{1}{x}$ on the interval $[1, a]$ equals the area under the same curve on $[k, ka]$ for any number $k > 0$.

74. Find the length of the curve $y = \ln(\csc x)$ on the interval $[\frac{\pi}{3}, \frac{\pi}{2}]$.

75. Find the length of the curve

$$x = \frac{ay^2}{b^2} - \frac{b^2}{8a}\ln\frac{y}{b}$$

   between $y = b$ and $y = 2b$.

76. Derive the reduction formula

$$\int (a^2 - x^2)^n \, dx = \frac{x(a^2 - x^2)^n}{2n+1} + \frac{2a^2n}{2n+1}\int (a^2 - x^2)^{n-1} \, dx$$

   Use this formula to find $\int (9 - x^2)^{5/2} \, dx$.

77. Derive the reduction formula

$$\int \frac{\sin^n x \, dx}{\cos^m x} = \frac{1}{m-1}\frac{\sin^{n-1} x}{\cos^{m-1} x} - \frac{n-1}{m-1}\int \frac{\sin^{n-2} x \, dx}{\cos^{m-2} x}$$

78. Derive a reduction formula for $\int \frac{\cos^n x \, dx}{\sin^m x}$.

79. Derive a reduction formula for $\int x^n(x^2 + a^2)^{-1/2} \, dx$.

80. Derive the reduction formula

$$\int \frac{dx}{x^n\sqrt{ax+b}} = \frac{-\sqrt{ax+b}}{(n-1)bx^{n-1}} - \frac{(2n-3)a}{(2n-2)b}\int \frac{dx}{x^{n-1}\sqrt{ax+b}}$$

81. The improper integral $\displaystyle\int_{1}^{+\infty}\left[\frac{2Ax^3}{x^4+1}-\frac{1}{x+1}\right]dx$ converges for exactly one value of the constant A. Find A and then compute the value of the integral.

82. Evaluate $\displaystyle\int_{0}^{+\infty}\frac{\sqrt{x}\ln x\,dx}{(x+1)(x^2+x+1)}$ if it exists. *Hint:* Let $u=\dfrac{1}{x}$.

83. Spectroscopic measurements based on the *Doppler effect* yield an observed mass m_0 for a certain type of binary star. The true mass m is then estimated by $m=m_0/I$, where

$$I=\int_{0}^{\pi/2}\sin^4 x\,dx$$

Determine the number I.

84. **Modeling Problem** The residents of a certain community have voted to discontinue the fluoridation of their water supply. The local reservoir currently holds 200 million gallons of fluoridated water containing 1,600 lb of fluoride. The fluoridated water flows out of the reservoir at the rate of 4 million gallons per day and is replaced by unfluoridated water at the same rate. At all times, the remaining fluoride in the reservoir is evenly distributed. Set up and solve a differential equation for the amount $F(t)$ of fluoride in the reservoir at time t. When will 90% of the fluoride be replaced?

85. **Modeling Problem** The Nuclear Regulatory Commission puts atomic waste into sealed containers and dumps them into the ocean. It is important to dump the containers in water shallow enough to ensure they do not break when they hit bottom. Suppose $s(t)$ is the depth of the container at time t and let W and B denote the container's weight and the constant buoyancy force, respectively. Assume there is a "drag force" proportional to velocity v.

   a. Explain why the motion of the containers may be modeled by the differential equation

   $$\frac{W}{g}\frac{dv}{dt}=W-B-kv$$

   where g is the constant acceleration due to gravity. Solve this equation to express $v(t)$ in terms of W, k, B, and g.

   b. Integrate the expression for $v(t)$ in part **a** to find $s(t)$.

   c. Suppose $W=1,125$ newtons (about 250 lb), $B=1,100$ newtons, and $k=0.64$ kg/s. If the container breaks when the impact speed exceeds 10 m/s, what is the maximum depth for safe dumping?

86. **The Evans price-adjustment model** assumes that if there is an excess demand D over supply S in any time period, the price p changes at a rate proportional to the excess, $D-S$; that is,

$$\frac{dp}{dt}=k(D-S)$$

Suppose for a certain commodity, demand is linear,

$$D(p)=c-pd$$

and supply is cyclical

$$S(t)=a\sin(bt)$$

Solve the differential equation to express price $p(t)$ in terms of a, b, c, and d. What happens to $p(t)$ "in the long run" (as $t\to+\infty$)? Use $p_0=p(0)$.

87. **Modeling Problem** A country has 5 billion dollars of paper currency. Each day about 10 million dollars comes into banks and 12 million is paid out. The government decides to issue new currency, and whenever an "old" bill comes into the bank, it is replaced by a "new" bill. Set up and solve a differential equation to model the currency replacement. How long will it take for 95% of the currency in circulation to be "new" style bills? How much total currency will be in circulation at this time?

88. **Putnam Examination Problem** Show that

$$\frac{22}{7}-\pi=\int_{0}^{1}\frac{x^4(1-x)^4\,dx}{1+x^2}$$

89. **Putnam Examination Problem** Evaluate

$$\int_{0}^{\pi/2}\frac{dx}{1+(\tan x)^{\sqrt{2}}}$$

90. **Putnam Examination Problem** Evaluate

$$\int_{0}^{+\infty}t^{-1/2}\exp\left[-1985\left(t+\frac{1}{t}\right)\right]dt$$

You may assume that $\displaystyle\int_{-\infty}^{+\infty}e^{-x^2}\,dx=\sqrt{\pi}$.

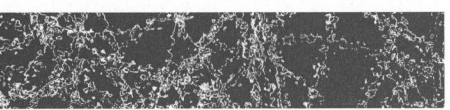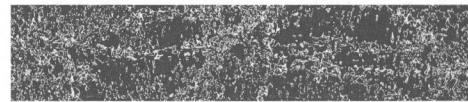
Buoy Design

This project is to be done in groups of three or four students. Each group will submit a single written report.

You have been hired as a special consultant by the U.S. Coast Guard to evaluate some proposed new designs for navigational aids (buoys).

The buoys are floating cans that need to be visible from some distance away, without rising too far out of the water. Each buoy has a circular cross section and will be fitted with a superstructure that carries equipment such as lights and batteries.

To be acceptable, a fully equipped buoy must float with not less than 1.5 ft nor more than 3 ft of freeboard. (Freeboard is the distance from the water level to the top of the device.)

You should make the following assumptions:

a. A floating object will displace a volume of water whose weight equals the weight of the floating object. (This is Archimedes' principle.)
b. Your devices will be floating in salt water, which weighs 65.5500 lb/ft^3.
c. The buoys will be constructed of $\frac{1}{2}$ in.-thick sheet metal that weighs 490 lb/ft^3.
d. You can estimate an additional 20% in weight attributable to welds, bolts, and the like.
e. Each buoy will be fitted with a superstructure and equipment weighing a total of 2,000 lb.
f. Each design you are given to evaluate will be presented to you in the form of a curve $x = f(y)$, to be revolved about the y-axis.

---

*This project is adapted from a computer project used at the U.S. Coast Guard Academy.

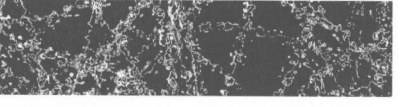

8

Infinite Series

PREVIEW

Is it possible for the sum of infinitely many nonzero numbers to be finite? This concept, which may seem paradoxical at first, plays a central role in mathematics and has a variety of important applications. The goal of this chapter is to examine the theory and applications of infinite sums, which will be referred to as *infinite series*. Geometric series, introduced in Section 8.2, are among the simplest infinite series we will encounter and, in some ways, the most important. In Sections 8.3–8.6, we will develop *convergence tests*, which provide ways of determining quickly whether or not certain infinite series have a finite sum. Next, we will turn our attention to series in which the individual terms are functions instead of numbers. We will be especially interested in the properties of *power series*, which may be thought of as polynomials of infinite degree, although some of their properties are quite different from those of polynomials. We will find that many common functions, such as e^x, $\ln(x + 1)$, $\sin x$, $\cos x$, and $\tan^{-1} x$, can be represented as power series, and we will discuss some important theoretical and computational aspects of this kind of representation.

PERSPECTIVE

Series, or sums, arise in many different ways. For example, suppose it is known that a certain pollutant is released into the atmosphere at weekly intervals and is dissipated at the rate of 2% per week. If m grams of pollutant are released each week, then at the beginning of the first week, there will be $S_1 = m$ grams in the atmosphere, and at the beginning of the second, there will be $0.98m$ grams of "old" pollutant left plus m grams of "new" pollutant, to yield a total of $S_2 = m + 0.98m$ grams. Continuing, at the beginning of the nth week there will be

$$S_n = m + 0.98m + (0.98)^2 m + \cdots + (0.98)^{n-1} m$$

grams. It is natural to wonder how much pollutant will accumulate in the "long run" (as $n \to +\infty$), and the answer is given by the infinite sum

$$S_{+\infty} = m + 0.98m + (0.98)^2 m + \cdots$$

But just exactly what do we mean by such a sum, and if the total is a finite number, how can we compute its value? We seek answers to these questions in this chapter.

8.1 Sequences and Their Limits

IN THIS SECTION sequences; limits of sequences; bounded, monotonic sequences

The making of a motion picture is a complex process, and editing all the film into a movie requires that all the frames of the action be labeled in chronological order. For example, R21-435 might signify the 435th frame of the 21st reel. A mathematician might refer to the movie editor's labeling procedure by saying the frames are arranged in a *sequence*.

SEQUENCES

A sequence is a succession of numbers that are listed according to a given prescription or rule. Specifically, if n is a positive integer, the sequence whose nth term is the number a_n can be written as

$$a_1, a_2, \ldots, a_n, \ldots$$

or, more simply,

$$\{a_n\}$$

The number a_n is called the **general term** of the sequence. We will deal only with infinite sequences, so each term a_n has a **successor** a_{n+1} and for $n > 1$, a **predecessor** a_{n-1}. For example, by associating each positive integer n with its reciprocal $\dfrac{1}{n}$, we obtain the sequence denoted by

$$\left\{\frac{1}{n}\right\}, \text{ which represents the succession of numbers } 1, \frac{1}{2}, \frac{1}{3}, \cdots, \frac{1}{n}, \cdots$$

The general term is denoted by $a_n = \dfrac{1}{n}$.

The following examples illustrate the notation and terminology used in connection with sequences.

These consecutive frames from a 16-mm movie film show a golfer from the moment he is at the top of his backswing until he hits the ball. If this film were projected at a rate of 24 frames per second, the viewer would have the illusion of seeing the golfer in action as he makes his downswing.

It is sometimes useful to start a sequence with a_0 instead of a_1.

EXAMPLE 1 **Given the general term, find particular terms of a sequence**

Find the 1st, 2nd, and 15th terms of the sequence $\{a_n\}$, where the general term is

$$a_n = \left(\frac{1}{2}\right)^{n-1}$$

Solution

If $n = 1$, then $a_1 = \left(\frac{1}{2}\right)^{1-1} = 1$. Similarly,

$$a_2 = \left(\frac{1}{2}\right)^{2-1} = \frac{1}{2}$$

$$a_{15} = \left(\frac{1}{2}\right)^{15-1} = \left(\frac{1}{2}\right)^{14} = 2^{-14}$$

The reverse question, that of finding a general term given certain terms of a sequence, is a more difficult task, and even if we find a general term, we have no assurance that the general term is unique. For example, consider the sequence

$$2, 4, 6, 8, \ldots$$

This seems to have a general term $a_n = 2n$. However, the general term

$$a_n = (n-1)(n-2)(n-3)(n-4) + 2n$$

has the same first four terms, but $a_5 = 34$ (not 10, as we would expect from the sequence $2, 4, 6, 8$).

So far, we have been discussing the concept of a sequence informally, without a definition. We have observed that a sequence $\{a_n\}$ associates the number a_n with the positive integer n. Hence, a sequence is really a special kind of function, one whose domain is the set of all positive (or possibly, nonnegative) integers.

Sequence

A **sequence** $\{a_n\}$ is a function whose domain is a set of nonnegative integers and whose range is a subset of the real numbers. The functional values $a_1, a_2, a_3, \ldots$ are called the **terms** of the sequence, and a_n is called the **nth term,** or **general term**, of the sequence.

LIMITS OF SEQUENCES

It is often desirable to examine the behavior of a given sequence $\{a_n\}$ as n gets arbitrarily large. For example, consider the sequence

$$a_n = \frac{n}{n + 1}$$

WARNING Even though we write a_n, remember this is a function, $f(n) = \dfrac{n}{n + 1}$, where the domain is the set of nonnegative integers.

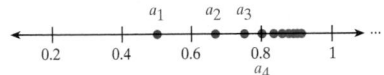

a_1 a_2 a_3

0.2   0.4   0.6   0.8   1
                 a_4

a. Graphing a sequence in one dimension

Because $a_1 = \frac{1}{2}, a_2 = \frac{2}{3}, a_3 = \frac{3}{4}, \cdots$, we can plot the terms of this sequence on a number line, as shown in Figure 8.1a, or the sequence can be plotted in two dimensions, as shown in Figure 8.1b.

By looking at either graph in Figure 8.1, we see that it appears the terms of the sequence are approaching 1. In general, if the terms of the sequence approach the number L as n increases without bound, we say that the sequence *converges to the limit L* and write

$$L = \lim_{n \to \infty} a_n$$

(Note that for simplicity, the limiting behavior is denoted by $n \to \infty$ instead of the usual $n \to +\infty$.) For instance, in our example we would expect

$$\lim_{n \to \infty} \frac{n}{n + 1} = 1$$

This limiting behavior is analogous to the continuous case (discussed in Section 4.4), and may be defined formally as follows.

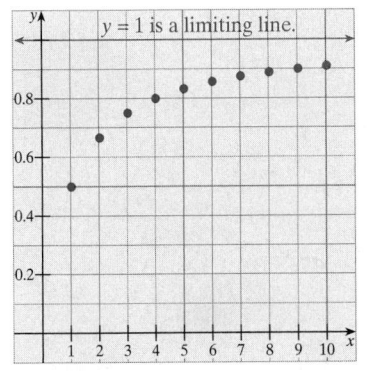

b. Graphing a sequence in two dimensions

Figure 8.1 Graphing the sequence $a_n = \dfrac{n}{n + 1}$

Convergent Sequence

The sequence $\{a_n\}$ **converges** to the number L, and we write

$$L = \lim_{n \to \infty} a_n$$

if for every $\epsilon > 0$, there is an integer N such that

$$|a_n - L| < \epsilon \quad \text{whenever} \quad n > N$$

Otherwise, the sequence **diverges**.

➡ **What This Says** The notation $L = \lim\limits_{n \to \infty} a_n$ means that eventually the terms of the sequence $\{a_n\}$ can be made as close to L as may be desired by taking n sufficiently large.

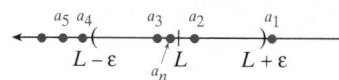

a. one dimension

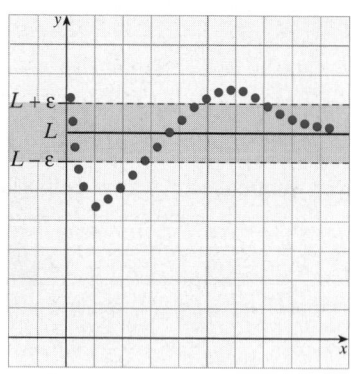

b. two dimensions

Figure 8.2 Geometric interpretation of a converging sequence

A geometric interpretation of this definition is shown in Figure 8.2. Note that the numbers a_n may be practically anywhere at first (that is, for "small" n), but eventually, the a_n must "cluster" near the limiting value L.

The theorem on limits of functions carries over to sequences. We have the following useful result.

THEOREM 8.1   Limit theorem for sequences

If $\lim\limits_{n\to\infty} a_n = L$ and $\lim\limits_{n\to\infty} b_n = M$, then

Linearity rule for sequences $\qquad \lim\limits_{n\to\infty} (ra_n + sb_n) = rL + sM$

Product rule for sequences $\qquad \lim\limits_{n\to\infty} (a_n b_n) = LM$

Quotient rule for sequences $\qquad \lim\limits_{n\to\infty} \dfrac{a_n}{b_n} = \dfrac{L}{M}$ provided $M \neq 0$

Root rule for sequences $\qquad \lim\limits_{n\to\infty} \sqrt[m]{a_n} = \sqrt[m]{L}$ provided $\sqrt[m]{a_n}$ is defined for all n and $\sqrt[m]{L}$ exists

Proof   The proof of these rules is similar to the limit rules that were stated in Section 4.4.   ❏

EXAMPLE 2   Convergent sequences

Find the limit of each of these convergent sequences:

a. $\left\{ \dfrac{100}{n} \right\}$ **b.** $\left\{ \dfrac{2n^2 + 5n - 7}{n^3} \right\}$

c. $\left\{ \dfrac{3n^4 + n - 1}{5n^4 + 2n^2 + 1} \right\}$

Solution

a. As n grows arbitrarily large, $100/n$ gets smaller and smaller. Thus,

$$\lim_{n\to\infty} \frac{100}{n} = 0$$

A graphical representation is shown in Figure 8.3.

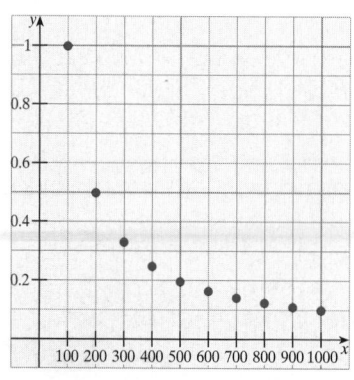

Figure 8.3 Graphical representation of $a_n = 100/n$

b. We cannot use the quotient rule of Theorem 8.1 because neither the limit in the numerator nor the one in the denominator exists. However,

$$\frac{2n^2 + 5n - 7}{n^3} = \frac{2}{n} + \frac{5}{n^2} - \frac{7}{n^3}$$

and by using the linearity rule, we find that

$$\lim_{n\to\infty} \frac{2n^2 + 5n - 7}{n^3} = \lim_{n\to\infty} \frac{2}{n} + 5 \lim_{n\to\infty} \frac{1}{n^2} - 7 \lim_{n\to\infty} \frac{1}{n^3}$$
$$= 0 + 0 + 0$$
$$= 0$$

A graph is shown in Figure 8.4.

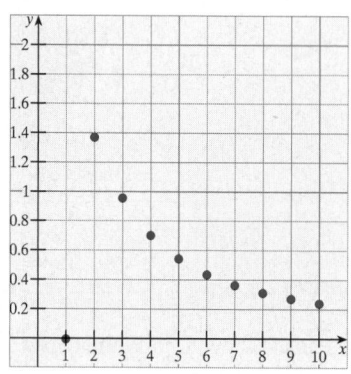

Figure 8.4 Graph of
$a_n = \dfrac{2n^2 + 5n - 7}{n^3}$

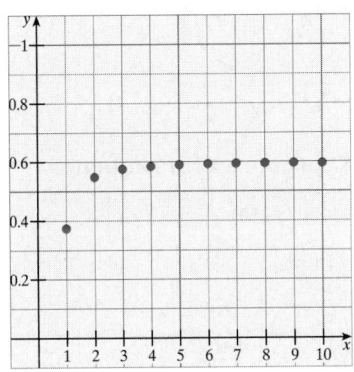

Figure 8.5 Graph of
$$a_n = \frac{3n^4 + n - 1}{5n^4 + 2n^2 + 1}$$

c. Divide the numerator and denominator by n^4, the highest power of n that occurs in the expression, to obtain

$$\lim_{n\to\infty} \frac{3n^4 + n - 1}{5n^4 + 2n^2 + 1} = \lim_{n\to\infty} \frac{3 + \dfrac{1}{n^3} - \dfrac{1}{n^4}}{5 + \dfrac{2}{n^2} + \dfrac{1}{n^4}} = \frac{3}{5}$$

Note that this procedure is very similar to the one we used in Section 4.4 when we evaluated limits of functions to infinity. A graph of this sequence is shown in Figure 8.5. ∎

EXAMPLE 3   Divergent sequences

Show that the following sequences diverge:

a. $\{(-1)^n\}$ **b.** $\left\{ \dfrac{n^5 + n^3 + 2}{7n^4 + n^2 + 3} \right\}$

Solution

a. The sequence defined by $\{(-1)^n\}$ is $-1, 1, -1, 1, \ldots$, and this sequence diverges by oscillation because the nth term is always either 1 or -1. Thus a_n cannot approach one specific number L as n grows large. The graph is shown in Figure 8.6a.

b. $\lim_{n\to\infty} \dfrac{n^5 + n^3 + 2}{7n^4 + n^2 + 3} = \lim_{n\to\infty} \dfrac{1 + \dfrac{1}{n^2} + \dfrac{2}{n^5}}{\dfrac{7}{n} + \dfrac{1}{n^3} + \dfrac{3}{n^5}}$

The numerator tends toward 1 as $n \to \infty$, and the denominator approaches 0. Hence the quotient increases without bound, and the sequence must diverge. The graph is shown in Figure 8.6b.

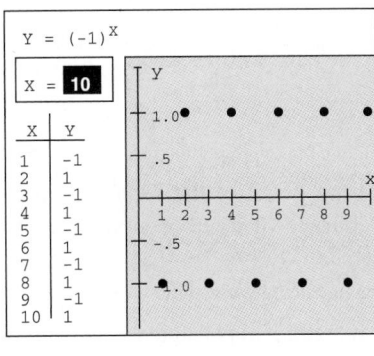

a. $a_n = (-1)^n$

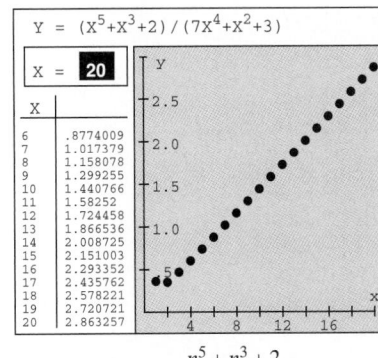

b. $a_n = \dfrac{n^5 + n^3 + 2}{7n^4 + n^2 + 3}$

Figure 8.6   Graphs and values for two divergent sequences ∎

If $\lim_{n\to\infty} a_n$ does not exist because the numbers a_n become arbitrarily large as $n \to \infty$, we write $\lim_{n\to\infty} a_n = \infty$. We summarize this more precisely in the following box.

Limit Notation

$\lim\limits_{n\to\infty} a_n = \infty$	means that for any real number A, we have $a_n > A$ for all sufficiently large n.
$\lim\limits_{n\to\infty} b_n = -\infty$	means that for any real number B, we have $b_n < B$ for all sufficiently large n.

Rewriting the answer to Example 3b in this notation,

$$\lim_{n \to \infty} \frac{n^5 + n^3 + 2}{7n^4 + n^2 + 3} = \infty$$

EXAMPLE 4   Determining the convergence or divergence of a sequence

Determine the convergence or divergence of the sequence $\left\{ \sqrt{n^2 + 3n} - n \right\}$.

Solution

Consider

$$\lim_{n \to \infty} (\sqrt{n^2 + 3n} - n)$$

It would not be correct to apply the linearity property for sequences (because neither $\lim_{n \to \infty} \sqrt{n^2 + 3n}$ nor $\lim_{n \to \infty} n$ exists). It is also not correct to use this as a reason to say that the limit does not exist. You might even try some values of n (shown in Figure 8.7) to guess that there is some limit. To find the limit, however, we will rewrite the general term algebraically as follows:

$$\sqrt{n^2 + 3n} - n = (\sqrt{n^2 + 3n} - n)\frac{\sqrt{n^2 + 3n} + n}{\sqrt{n^2 + 3n} + n}$$

$$= \frac{n^2 + 3n - n^2}{\sqrt{n^2 + 3n} + n} \frac{\dfrac{1}{n}}{\dfrac{1}{n}}$$

$$= \frac{3}{\dfrac{\sqrt{n^2 + 3n}}{n} + 1} = \frac{3}{\sqrt{\dfrac{n^2 + 3n}{n^2}} + 1} = \frac{3}{\sqrt{1 + \dfrac{3}{n}} + 1}$$

Hence,

$$\lim_{n \to \infty} (\sqrt{n^2 + 3n} - n) = \lim_{n \to \infty} \frac{3}{\sqrt{1 + \dfrac{3}{n}} + 1} = \frac{3}{2} \qquad \blacksquare$$

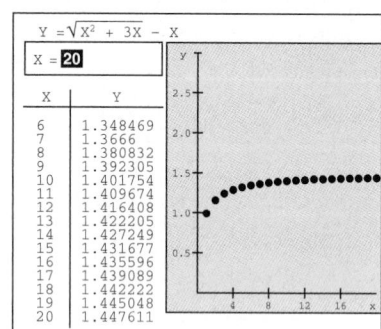

Figure 8.7 Graph of $a_n = \sqrt{n^2 + 3n} - n$; convergent or divergent?

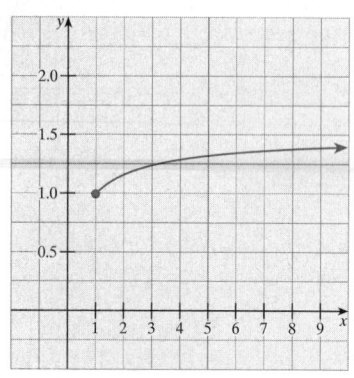

Figure 8.8 Graph of $f(x) = \sqrt{x^2 + 3x} - x, x \geq 1$

Note the graph of the sequence in Example 4 in Figure 8.7. The graph of a sequence consists of a succession of isolated points. This can be compared with the graph of $y = \sqrt{x^2 + 3x} - x, x \geq 1$, which is a continuous curve (shown in Figure 8.8). The only difference between $\lim_{n \to \infty} a_n = L$ and $\lim_{x \to \infty} f(x) = L$ is that n is required to be an integer. This is stated in the hypothesis of the following theorem.

THEOREM 8.2   Limit of a sequence from the limit of a continuous function

Given the sequence $\{a_n\}$, let f be a continuous function such that $a_n = f(n)$ for $n = 1, 2, \ldots$. If $\lim_{x \to \infty} f(x)$ exists and $\lim_{x \to \infty} f(x) = L$, the sequence $\{a_n\}$ converges and $\lim_{n \to \infty} a_n = L$.

Proof   Let $\epsilon > 0$ be given. Because $\lim_{x \to \infty} f(x) = L$, there exists a number $N > 0$ such that

$$|f(x) - L| < \epsilon \quad \text{whenever } x > N$$

In particular, if $n > N$, it follows that $|f(n) - L| = |a_n - L| < \epsilon$. $\qquad \square$

Be sure you read this theorem correctly. In particular, note that it *does not* say that if $\lim_{n \to \infty} a_n = L$, then $\lim_{x \to \infty} f(x) = L$ (see Figure 8.9b).

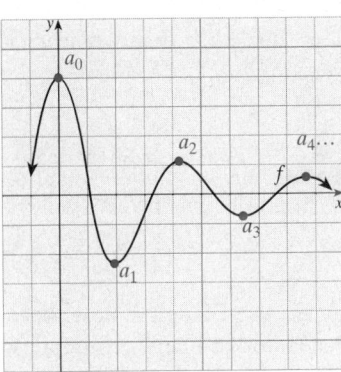

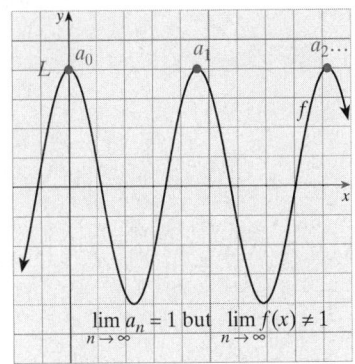

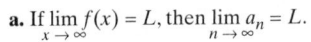

a. If $\lim\limits_{x \to \infty} f(x) = L$, then $\lim\limits_{n \to \infty} a_n = L$.

b. WARNING ➤ If $\lim\limits_{n \to \infty} a_n = L$, then $\lim\limits_{x \to \infty} f(x)$ does NOT necessarily equal L. ◄

Figure 8.9 Graphical comparison of $\lim\limits_{n \to \infty} a_n$ and $\lim\limits_{x \to \infty} f(x)$, where $f(n) = a_n$ for $n = 1, 2, \ldots$.

EXAMPLE 5   Evaluating a limit using l'Hôpital's rule

Given that the sequence $\left\{ \dfrac{n^2}{1 - e^n} \right\}$ converges, evaluate $\lim\limits_{n \to \infty} \dfrac{n^2}{1 - e^n}$.

Solution

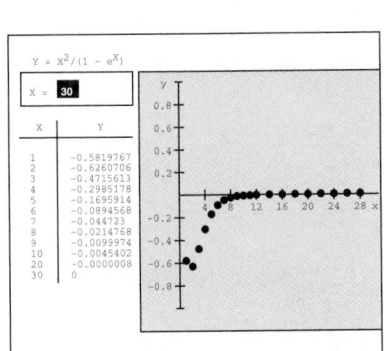

Figure 8.10 From the graph, it looks like $\lim\limits_{n \to \infty} a_n = 0$.

Let $L = \lim\limits_{x \to \infty} f(x)$, where $f(x) = \dfrac{x^2}{1 - e^x}$. Because $f(n) = a_n$ for $n = 1, 2, \ldots$, Theorem 8.2 tells us that $\lim\limits_{n \to \infty} \dfrac{n^2}{1 - e^n}$ is the same as $\lim\limits_{n \to \infty} f(x)$, provided this latter limit exists. Since the function f is continuous for all $x \neq 0$, we use l'Hôpital's rule.

$$\lim_{x \to \infty} \frac{x^2}{1 - e^x} = \lim_{x \to \infty} \frac{2x}{-e^x} \qquad \text{l'Hôpital's rule}$$

$$= \lim_{x \to \infty} \frac{2}{-e^x} \qquad \text{l'Hôpital's rule again}$$

$$= 0$$

Thus, by Theorem 8.2, $\lim\limits_{n \to \infty} \dfrac{n^2}{1 - e^n} = \lim\limits_{x \to \infty} f(x) = L = 0$. This conclusion is confirmed geometrically, as shown in Figure 8.10. ■

The squeeze rule (Section 2.2) can be reformulated in terms of sequences.

THEOREM 8.3   Squeeze rule for sequences

If $a_n \le b_n \le c_n$ for all $n > N$, and $\lim\limits_{n \to \infty} a_n = \lim\limits_{n \to \infty} c_n = L$, then $\lim\limits_{n \to \infty} b_n = L$.

Proof   The proof of this theorem follows the same steps as the proof of the squeeze rule given in Appendix A. ❑

EXAMPLE 6   Using l'Hôpital's rule and the squeeze rule

Show that the following sequences converge, and find their limits.

a. $\lim\limits_{n \to \infty} n^{1/n}$ **b.** $\lim\limits_{n \to \infty} \dfrac{n!}{n^n}$

Solution

a. Let $L = \lim_{n \to \infty} n^{1/n}$; then we let $f(x) = x^{1/x}$. The function f is continuous for all $x > 0$, so we can apply l'Hôpital's rule.

$$\ln L = \lim_{n \to \infty} \frac{\ln n}{n} = \lim_{x \to \infty} \frac{\ln x}{x} = \lim_{x \to \infty} \frac{\frac{1}{x}}{1} \qquad \text{l'Hôpital's rule}$$
$$= 0$$

Thus, $L = e^0 = 1$.

b. We cannot use l'Hôpital's rule because $x!$ is not defined as an elementary function when x is not an integer. Instead, we use the squeeze rule for sequences. Accordingly, note that if we let $a_n = 0$ and $c_n = \dfrac{1}{n}$, for all n, we have

$$\overbrace{0}^{a_n} \leq \overbrace{\frac{n!}{n^n}}^{b_n} \leq \overbrace{\frac{1}{n}}^{c_n}$$

The right inequality is true because

$$\frac{n!}{n^n} = \frac{n(n-1)(n-2)\cdots 1}{n \cdot n \cdot n \cdot \cdots \cdot n}$$
$$= \left(\frac{n}{n}\right)\left(\frac{n-1}{n}\right)\left(\frac{n-2}{n}\right)\cdots\left(\frac{1}{n}\right)$$
$$< (1)\left(\frac{n}{n}\right)\left(\frac{n}{n}\right)\cdots\left(\frac{n}{n}\right)\left(\frac{1}{n}\right) = \frac{1}{n}$$

Because $\lim_{n \to \infty} a_n = 0$ and $\lim_{n \to \infty} c_n = 0$, it follows from the squeeze rule that $\lim_{n \to \infty} \dfrac{n!}{n^n} = 0$. ∎

BOUNDED, MONOTONIC SEQUENCES

We introduce, along with a simple example, some terminology associated with sequences $\{a_n\}$.

Name	Condition	Example
Strictly increasing	$a_1 < a_2 < \cdots < a_{k-1} < a_k < \cdots$	$1, 2, 3, 4, 5, \ldots$
Increasing	$a_1 \leq a_2 \leq \cdots \leq a_{k-1} \leq a_k \leq \cdots$	$1, 1, 2, 2, 3, 3, \ldots$
Strictly decreasing	$a_1 > a_2 > \cdots > a_{k-1} > a_k > \cdots$	$1, \frac{1}{2}, \frac{1}{3}, \frac{1}{4}, \ldots$
Decreasing	$a_1 \geq a_2 \geq \cdots \geq a_{k-1} \geq a_k \geq \cdots$	$1, 1, \frac{1}{2}, \frac{1}{2}, \frac{1}{3}, \frac{1}{3}, \ldots$
Bounded above by M	$a_n \leq M$ for $n = 1, 2, 3, \ldots$	$M = 1$ for $1, \frac{1}{2}, \frac{1}{3}, \frac{1}{4}, \ldots$. $M = 2$, $M = 3$, are other choices for M.
Bounded below by m	$m \leq a_n$ for $n = 1, 2, 3, \ldots$	$m = 1$ for $1, 2, 3, 4, \ldots$ $m = 0$, $m = -1$, are other choices for m.
Bounded	if it is bounded both above and below	$1, \frac{1}{2}, \frac{1}{3}, \frac{1}{4}, \ldots$ $m = 0$ and $M = 1$, so sequence is bounded.

We also say that a series is **monotonic** if it is increasing or decreasing or **strictly monotonic** if it is strictly increasing or strictly decreasing. In general, it is difficult to tell whether a given sequence converges or diverges, but because of the following theorem, it is easy to make this determination if we know the sequence is monotonic.

THEOREM 8.4 BMCT: The bounded, monotonic, convergence theorem

A monotonic sequence $\{a_n\}$ converges if it is bounded and diverges otherwise.

Proof A formal proof of the BMCT is outlined in Problem 53. For the following informal argument, we will assume that $\{a_n\}$ is an increasing sequence. You might wish to see whether you can give a similar informal argument for the decreasing case. Because the terms of the sequence satisfy $a_1 \leq a_2 \leq a_3 \leq \cdots$, we know that the sequence is bounded from below by a_1 and that the graph of the corresponding points (n, a_n) will be rising in the plane. Two cases can occur, as shown in Figure 8.11.

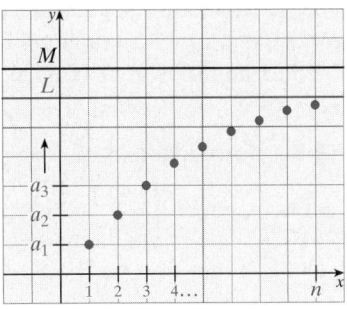   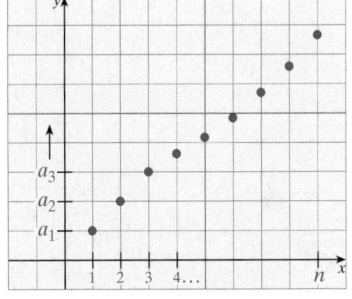

a. If $a_n < M$ for $n = 1, 2, \ldots$, the graph of the points (n, a_n) will approach a horizontal "barrier" line $y = L$.

b. If $\{a_n\}$ is not bounded from above, the graph rises indefinitely.

Figure 8.11 Graphical possibilities for the BMCT theorem

Suppose the sequence $\{a_n\}$ is also bounded from above by a number M, so that $a_1 \leq a_n \leq M$ for $n = 1, 2, \ldots$. Then the graph of the points (n, a_n) must continually rise (because the sequence is monotonic) and yet it must stay below the line $y = M$. The only way this can happen is for the graph to approach a "barrier" line $y = L$ (where $L \leq M$), and we have $\lim_{n \to \infty} a_n = L$, as shown in Figure 8.11a. However, if the sequence is not bounded from above, the graph will rise indefinitely (Figure 8.11b), and the terms in the sequence $\{a_n\}$ cannot approach any finite number L. ❑

EXAMPLE 7 Convergence using the BMCT

Show that the sequence $\left\{ \dfrac{1 \cdot 3 \cdot 5 \cdot \cdots \cdot (2n - 1)}{2 \cdot 4 \cdot 6 \cdot \cdots \cdot (2n)} \right\}$ converges.

Solution

The first few terms of this sequence are

$$a_1 = \frac{1}{2} \qquad a_2 = \frac{1 \cdot 3}{2 \cdot 4} = \frac{3}{8} \qquad a_3 = \frac{1 \cdot 3 \cdot 5}{2 \cdot 4 \cdot 6} = \frac{5}{16}$$

Because $\dfrac{1}{2} > \dfrac{3}{8} > \dfrac{5}{16}$, it appears that the sequence is decreasing (that is, it is monotonic). We can prove this by showing that $a_{n+1} < a_n$ for all $n > 0$, or equivalently,

$\dfrac{a_{n+1}}{a_n} < 1$. (Note that $a_n \neq 0$ for all n.)

$$\frac{a_{n+1}}{a_n} = \frac{\dfrac{1 \cdot 3 \cdot 5 \cdots [2(n+1)-1]}{2 \cdot 4 \cdot 6 \cdots [2(n+1)]}}{\dfrac{1 \cdot 3 \cdot 5 \cdots (2n-1)}{2 \cdot 4 \cdot 6 \cdots (2n)}}$$

$$= \frac{1 \cdot 3 \cdot 5 \cdots (2n+1)}{2 \cdot 4 \cdot 6 \cdots (2n+2)} \cdot \frac{2 \cdot 4 \cdot 6 \cdots (2n)}{1 \cdot 3 \cdot 5 \cdots (2n-1)}$$

$$= \frac{2n+1}{2n+2} < 1$$

for any $n > 0$. Hence $a_{n+1} < a_n$ for all n, and $\{a_n\}$ is a decreasing sequence. Because $a_n > 0$ for all n, it follows that $\{a_n\}$ is bounded below by 0. Applying the BMCT, we see that $\{a_n\}$ converges, but the BMCT tells us nothing about the limit. ∎

The BMCT also applies to sequences whose terms are *eventually* monotonic. That is, it can be shown that the sequence $\{a_n\}$ converges if it is bounded and there exists an integer N such that $\{a_n\}$ is monotonic for all $n > N$. This modified form of the BMCT is illustrated in the following example.

EXAMPLE 8 Convergence of a sequence that is eventually monotonic

Show that the sequence $\left\{ \dfrac{\ln n}{\sqrt{n}} \right\}$ converges.

Solution

We will apply the BMCT. A few values are shown in Figure 8.12. The succession of numbers suggests that the sequence increases at first and then gradually begins to decrease. To verify this behavior, we let

$$f(x) = \frac{\ln x}{\sqrt{x}}$$

and find that

$$f'(x) = \frac{\sqrt{x}\left(\frac{1}{x}\right) - (\ln x)\left(\frac{1}{2}x^{-1/2}\right)}{x} = \frac{2\sqrt{x} - \sqrt{x}\ln x}{2x^2}$$

Find the critical values:

$$\frac{2\sqrt{x} - \sqrt{x}\ln x}{2x^2} = 0$$

$$2\sqrt{x} = \sqrt{x}\ln x$$

$$\ln x = 2$$

$$e^2 = x$$

Thus, $x = e^2$ is the only critical value, and you can show that $f'(x) < 0$ for $x > e^2$. This means that f is a decreasing function for $x > e^2$. Thus, the sequence $\left\{ \dfrac{\ln n}{\sqrt{n}} \right\}$ must be decreasing for $n > 8$ (because e^2 is between 7 and 8). We see that the sequence $\left\{ \dfrac{\ln n}{\sqrt{n}} \right\}$ is bounded from below because

$$0 < \frac{\ln n}{\sqrt{n}} \quad \text{for all } n \geq 2$$

Therefore, the given sequence is bounded from below and is eventually decreasing, so it must converge. ∎

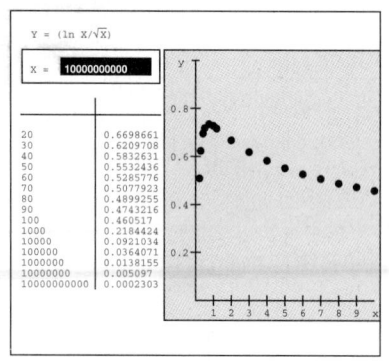

20	0.6698661
30	0.6209708
40	0.5832631
50	0.5532436
60	0.5285776
70	0.5077923
80	0.4899255
90	0.4743216
100	0.460517
1000	0.2184424
10000	0.0921034
100000	0.0364071
1000000	0.0138155
10000000	0.005097
10000000000	0.0002303

$Y = (\ln x / \sqrt{x})$

$x = 10000000000$

Figure 8.12 $a_n = \dfrac{\ln n}{\sqrt{n}}$

The BMCT is an extremely valuable theoretical tool. For example, in Section 2.4, we defined the number e by the limit

$$\lim_{n \to \infty} \left(1 + \frac{1}{n}\right)^n = e$$

but to do so we assumed that this limit exists. We can now show this assumption is warranted, because it turns out that the sequence $\left\{(1 + \frac{1}{n})^n\right\}$ is increasing and bounded from above by 3 (see Problem 80 in the Supplementary Problems). Thus, the BMCT assures us that the sequence converges, and this in turn guarantees the existence of the limit. We end this section with a result that will be useful in our subsequent work. The proof makes use of the formal definition of BMCT.

THEOREM 8.5 Convergence of a power sequence

If r is a fixed number such that $|r| < 1$, then $\lim\limits_{n \to \infty} r^n = 0$.

Proof   The case where $r = 0$ is trivial. We will prove the theorem for the case $0 < r < 1$ and leave the case $-1 < r < 0$ as an exercise.

$$0 \le r^{n+1} = r^n r < r^n$$

The sequence $\{r^n\}$ is monotonic and bounded, so the limit exists. Either $\lim\limits_{n \to \infty} r^n = 0$ or $\lim\limits_{n \to \infty} r^n = L > 0$. Suppose

$$\lim_{n \to \infty} r^n = L$$

$$r \lim_{n \to \infty} r^n = rL \qquad \text{Multiply both sides by } r.$$

$$\lim_{n \to \infty} r r^n = rL$$

$$\lim_{n \to \infty} r^{n+1} = rL < L \qquad \text{Since } 0 < r < 1 \text{ and } L > 0$$

But $\lim\limits_{n \to \infty} r^{n+1} = \lim\limits_{n \to \infty} r^n = L$ by the definition of limit. Hence $L = rL < L$, which is impossible, so $\lim\limits_{n \to \infty} r^n = 0$. ❑

8.1 PROBLEM SET

A **1. WHAT DOES THIS SAY?**   What do we mean by the limit of a sequence?

2. WHAT DOES THIS SAY?   What is meant by the bounded, monotonic, convergence theorem?

Write out the first five terms (beginning with $n = 1$) of the sequences given in Problems 3–11.

3. $\{1 + (-1)^n\}$

4. $\left\{\left(\dfrac{-1}{2}\right)^{n+2}\right\}$

5. $\left\{\dfrac{\cos 2n\pi}{n}\right\}$

6. $\left\{n \sin \dfrac{n\pi}{2}\right\}$

7. $\left\{\dfrac{3n+1}{n+2}\right\}$

8. $\left\{\dfrac{n^2 - n}{n^2 + n}\right\}$

9. $\{a_n\}$ where $a_1 = 256$ and $a_n = \sqrt{a_{n-1}}$ for $n \ge 2$

10. $\{a_n\}$ where $a_1 = -1$ and $a_n = n + a_{n-1}$ for $n \ge 2$

11. $\{a_n\}$ where $a_1 = 1$ and $a_n = (a_{n-1})^2 + a_{n-1} + 1$ for $n \ge 2$

Compute the limit of the convergent sequences in Problems 12–35.

12. $\left\{\dfrac{5n+8}{n}\right\}$

13. $\left\{\dfrac{5n}{n+7}\right\}$

14. $\left\{\dfrac{2n+1}{3n-4}\right\}$

15. $\left\{\dfrac{4-7n}{8+n}\right\}$

16. $\left\{\dfrac{8n^2 + 800n + 5{,}000}{2n^2 - 1{,}000n + 2}\right\}$

17. $\left\{\dfrac{100n + 7{,}000}{n^2 - n - 1}\right\}$

18. $\left\{\dfrac{8n^2 + 6n + 4{,}000}{n^3 + 1}\right\}$

19. $\left\{\dfrac{n^3 - 6n^2 + 85}{2n^3 - 5n + 170}\right\}$

20. $\left\{\dfrac{2n}{n + 7\sqrt{n}}\right\}$

21. $\left\{\dfrac{8n - 500\sqrt{n}}{2n + 800\sqrt{n}}\right\}$

22. $\left\{\dfrac{3\sqrt{n}}{5\sqrt{n} + \sqrt[4]{n}}\right\}$

23. $\left\{\dfrac{\ln n}{n^2}\right\}$

24. $\{2^{5/n}\}$

25. $\{n^{3/n}\}$

26. $\left\{\left(1 + \dfrac{3}{n}\right)^n\right\}$

27. $\{(n+4)^{1/n}\}$

28. $\left\{n^{1/(n+2)}\right\}$

29. $\left\{(\ln n)^{1/n}\right\}$

30. $\left\{\int_0^\infty e^{-nx}\,dx\right\}$

31. $\left\{\sqrt{n^2+n}-n\right\}$

32. $\left\{\sqrt{n+5\sqrt{n}}-\sqrt{n}\right\}$

33. $\left\{\sqrt[n]{n}\right\}$

34. $\{\ln n - \ln(n+1)\}$

35. $\left\{(an+b)^{1/n}\right\}$, a and b positive constants

B *Show that each sequence given in Problems 36–41 converges either by showing it is increasing with an upper bound or decreasing with a lower bound.*

36. $\left\{\dfrac{n}{2^n}\right\}$

37. $\left\{\ln\left(\dfrac{n+1}{n}\right)\right\}$

38. $\left\{\dfrac{3n-2}{n}\right\}$

39. $\left\{\dfrac{4n+5}{n}\right\}$

40. $\left\{\dfrac{3n-7}{2^n}\right\}$

41. $\left\{\sqrt[n]{n}\right\}$

Explain why each sequence in Problems 42–45 diverges.

42. $\{1+(-1)^n\}$

43. $\{\cos n\pi\}$

44. $\left\{\dfrac{n^3-7n+5}{100n^2+219}\right\}$

45. $\{\sqrt{n}\}$

46. Suppose that a particle of mass m moves back and forth along a line segment of length $|a|$. In classical mechanics, the particle can move at any speed, and thus its energy can be any positive number. However, quantum mechanics replaces this continuous model of the particle's behavior with one in which the particle's energy level can have only certain discrete values, say, $E_1, E_2, \dots$. Specifically, it can be shown that the nth term in this quantum sequence has the value

$$E_n = \frac{n^2 h^2}{8ma^2} \qquad n=1,2,\dots$$

where h is a physical constant known as *Planck's constant* ($h \approx 6.6254 \times 10^{-34}$ Js). List the first four values of E_n for a particle with mass $m = 0.008$ g moving along a segment of length $a = 1$ m.

47. Modeling Problem A drug is administered into the body. At the end of each hour, the amount of drug present is half what it was at the end of the previous hour. What percent of the drug is present at the end of 4 hours? At the end of n hours?

48. HISTORICAL QUEST Leonardo de Pisa, also known as Fibonacci, was one of the best mathematicians of the Middle Ages. He played an important role in reviving ancient mathematics and introduced the Hindu-Arabic place-value decimal system to Europe. His book, Liber Abaci, published in 1202, introduced the Arabic numerals, as well as the famous **rabbit problem**, for which Fibonacci is best remembered today. ∎

FIBONACCI
1170–1250

To describe Fibonacci's rabbit problem, we consider a sequence whose nth term is defined by a *recursion formula*—that is, a formula in which the nth term is given in terms of previous terms in the sequence. Suppose rabbits breed in such a way that each pair of adult rabbits produces a pair of baby rabbits each month.

Number of Months	Number of Pairs	Pairs of Rabbits (the blue rabbits are ready to reproduce)
Start		
1	1	
2	2	
3	3	
4	5	
5	8	
⋮	⋮	

Same pair
(rabbits never die)

The first month after birth, the rabbits are adolescents and produce no offspring. However, beginning with the second month the rabbits are adults, and each pair produces a pair of offspring every month. The sequence of numbers describing the number of rabbits is called the *Fibonacci sequence*, and it has applications in many areas, including biology and botany.

In this Quest you are to examine some properties of the Fibonacci sequence. Let a_n denote the number of pairs of rabbits in the "colony" at the end of n months.

a. Explain why $a_1 = 1$, $a_2 = 1$, $a_3 = 2$, $a_4 = 3$, and, in general, $a_{n+1} = a_n + a_{n-1}$ for $n = 2, 3, 4, \dots$. The equation $a_{n+1} = a_n + a_{n-1}$ that specifies each term of the sequence $\{a_n\}$ for $n = 2, 3, \dots$ is called a *recursion formula* because it defines later terms from those that precede them.

b. The *growth rate* of the colony during the $(n+1)$th month is

$$r_n = \frac{a_{n+1}}{a_n}$$

Compute r_n for $n = 1, 2, 3, \dots, 10$.

c. Assume that the growth rate sequence $\{r_n\}$ defined in part **b** converges. Find

$$L = \lim_{n\to\infty} r_n$$

Hint: Use the recursion formula in part **a**.

C **49.** The claim is made that $\lim\limits_{n\to\infty} \dfrac{n}{n+1} = 1$. If $\epsilon = 0.01$ is chosen, find N so that $\left|\dfrac{n}{n+1} - 1\right| < 0.01$ if $n > N$.

50. The claim is made that $\lim\limits_{n\to\infty} \dfrac{2n+1}{n+3} = 2$. If $\epsilon = 0.01$ is chosen, find N so that $\left|\dfrac{2n+1}{n+3} - 2\right| < 0.01$ if $n > N$.

51. The claim is made that $\lim\limits_{n\to\infty} \dfrac{n^2+1}{n^3} = 0$. If $\epsilon = 0.001$ is chosen, find N so that $\left|\dfrac{n^2+1}{n^3}\right| < 0.001$ if $n > N$.

52. The claim is made that $\lim\limits_{n\to\infty} e^{-n} = 0$. If $\epsilon = 0.001$ is chosen, find N so that $\dfrac{1}{e^n} < 0.001$ if $n > N$.

53. Proof of the BMCT Suppose there exist a number M and a positive integer N so that $a_n \leq a_{n+1} \leq M$ for all $n > N$.

a. It is a fundamental property of the real numbers that a sequence with an upper bound must have a *least* upper bound; that is, there must be a number A with the property that $a_n \leq A$ for all n but if c is a number such that $c < A$, then $a_m > c$ for at least one m. Use this property to show that if $\epsilon > 0$ is given, there exists a positive integer N so that

$$A - \epsilon < a_n < A$$

for all $n > N$.

b. Show that $|a_n - A| < \epsilon$ for all $n > N$ and conclude that $\lim_{n \to \infty} a_n = A$.

8.2 Introduction to Infinite Series; Geometric Series

IN THIS SECTION definition of infinite series, general properties of infinite series, geometric series, applications of geometric series

DEFINITION OF INFINITE SERIES

One way to add a list of numbers is to form subtotals until the end of the list is reached. Similarly, to give meaning to the infinite sum

$$S = a_1 + a_2 + a_3 + a_4 + \cdots$$

it is natural to examine the "partial sums"

$$a_1, \quad a_1 + a_2, \quad a_1 + a_2 + a_3, \quad a_1 + a_2 + a_3 + a_4, \ldots$$

If it is possible to attach a numerical value to the infinite sum, we would expect the partial sums $S_n = a_1 + a_2 + \cdots + a_n$ to approach that value as n increases without bound. These ideas lead us to the following definition.

Infinite Series

An **infinite series** is an expression of the form

$$a_1 + a_2 + a_3 + \cdots = \sum_{k=1}^{\infty} a_k$$

and the **nth partial sum** of the series is

$$S_n = a_1 + a_2 + \cdots + a_n = \sum_{k=1}^{n} a_k$$

The series is said to **converge with sum S** if the *sequence* of partial sums $\{S_n\}$ converges to S. In this case, we write

$$\sum_{k=1}^{\infty} a_k = \lim_{n \to \infty} S_n = S$$

If the sequence $\{S_n\}$ does not converge, the series

$$\sum_{k=1}^{\infty} a_k$$

diverges and has no sum.

➡ **What This Says** An infinite series converges if its sequence of partial sums converges and diverges otherwise. If it converges, its sum is defined to be the limit of the sequence of partial sums.

REMARK: We will use the symbol $\sum_{k=1}^{\infty} a_k$ to denote the series $a_1 + a_2 + a_3 + \cdots$ regardless of whether this series converges or diverges. If the sequence of partial sums $\{S_n\}$ converges, then

$$\sum_{k=1}^{\infty} a_k = \lim_{n \to \infty} \left(\sum_{k=1}^{n} a_k \right)$$

and the symbol $\sum_{k=1}^{\infty} a_k$ is used to represent *both* the series and its sum.

We will also consider certain series in which the starting point is not 1; for example, the series

$$\frac{1}{3} + \frac{1}{4} + \frac{1}{5} + \cdots \quad \text{can be denoted by} \quad \sum_{k=3}^{\infty} \frac{1}{k} \quad \text{or} \quad \sum_{k=2}^{\infty} \frac{1}{k+1}$$

EXAMPLE 1 Convergent series

Show that the series $\sum_{k=1}^{\infty} \frac{1}{2^k}$ converges.

Solution

This series has the following partial sums.

$$S_1 = \frac{1}{2} \qquad\qquad \text{Note:} \quad 1 - \frac{1}{2^1} = \frac{1}{2}$$

$$S_2 = \frac{1}{2} + \frac{1}{4} = \frac{3}{4} \qquad\qquad 1 - \frac{1}{2^2} = \frac{3}{4}$$

$$S_3 = \frac{1}{2} + \frac{1}{4} + \frac{1}{8} = \frac{7}{8} \qquad\qquad 1 - \frac{1}{2^3} = \frac{7}{8}$$

$$\vdots$$

$$S_n = \frac{1}{2} + \frac{1}{4} + \cdots + \frac{1}{2^n}$$

The sequence of partial sums is $\frac{1}{2}, \frac{3}{4}, \frac{7}{8}, \frac{15}{16}, \frac{31}{32}, \frac{63}{64}, \frac{127}{128}, \cdots$, and in general (by mathematical induction)

$$S_n = 1 - \frac{1}{2^n}$$

Because $\lim_{n \to \infty} \left(1 - \frac{1}{2^n} \right) = 1$, we conclude that the series converges and its sum is $S = 1$. ∎

EXAMPLE 2 Divergent series

Show that the series $\sum_{k=1}^{\infty} (-1)^k$ diverges.

Solution

The series can be **expanded** (written out) as

$$\sum_{k=1}^{\infty} (-1)^k = -1 + 1 - 1 + 1 - 1 + 1 - \cdots$$

and we see that the nth partial sum is

$$S_n = \begin{cases} -1 & \text{if } n \text{ is odd} \\ 0 & \text{if } n \text{ is even} \end{cases}$$

Because the sequence $\{S_n\}$ has no limit, the given series must diverge. ∎

A series is called a **telescoping series** (or collapsing series) if there is internal cancellation in the partial sums, as illustrated by the following example.

EXAMPLE 3 A telescoping series

Show that the series $\displaystyle\sum_{k=1}^{\infty} \frac{1}{k^2 + k}$ converges and find its sum.

Solution

Using partial fractions, we find that

$$\frac{1}{k^2 + k} = \frac{1}{k(k + 1)} = \frac{1}{k} + \frac{-1}{k + 1}$$

Thus, the nth partial sum of the given series can be represented as follows:

$$S_n = \sum_{k=1}^{n} \frac{1}{k^2 + k} = \sum_{k=1}^{n} \left[\frac{1}{k} - \frac{1}{k + 1} \right]$$

$$= \left(1 - \frac{1}{2} \right) + \left(\frac{1}{2} - \frac{1}{3} \right) + \left(\frac{1}{3} - \frac{1}{4} \right) + \cdots + \left(\frac{1}{n} - \frac{1}{n + 1} \right)$$

$$= 1 + \left(-\frac{1}{2} + \frac{1}{2} \right) + \left(-\frac{1}{3} + \frac{1}{3} \right) + \cdots + \left(-\frac{1}{n} + \frac{1}{n} \right) - \frac{1}{n + 1}$$

$$= 1 - \frac{1}{n + 1}$$

The limit of the sequence of partial sums is

$$\lim_{n \to \infty} S_n = \lim_{n \to \infty} \left[1 - \frac{1}{n + 1} \right] = 1$$

so the series converges, with sum $S = 1$. ∎

GENERAL PROPERTIES OF INFINITE SERIES

Next, we will examine two general properties of infinite series. Here and elsewhere, *when the starting point of a series is not important, we may denote the series by writing*

$$\sum a_k \quad \text{instead of} \quad \sum_{k=1}^{\infty} a_k$$

THEOREM 8.6 Linearity of infinite series

If Σa_k and Σb_k are convergent series, then so is $\Sigma(ca_k + db_k)$ for constants c, d, and

$$\sum(ca_k + db_k) = c\sum a_k + d\sum b_k$$

Proof Compare this with the linearity property in Theorem 5.4. In Chapter 5, the limit properties are for finite sums, and this theorem is for infinite sums. The proof of this theorem is similar to the proof of Theorem 5.4, but in this case it follows from the linearity rule for sequences (Theorem 8.1). The details are left as a problem. ❑

EXAMPLE 4 Linearity used to establish convergence

Show that the series $\displaystyle\sum_{k=1}^{\infty} \left[\frac{4}{k^2 + k} - \frac{6}{2^k} \right]$ converges, and find its sum.

Solution

Because we know from Examples 1 and 3 that $\displaystyle\sum_{k=1}^{\infty}\frac{1}{k^2+k}$ and $\displaystyle\sum_{k=1}^{\infty}\frac{1}{2^k}$ both converge with sum 1, the linearity property allows us to write the given series as

$$4\sum_{k=1}^{\infty}\frac{1}{k^2+k} - 6\sum_{k=1}^{\infty}\frac{1}{2^k}$$

We can now conclude that the series converges and that the sum is

$$4\sum_{k=1}^{\infty}\frac{1}{k^2+k} - 6\sum_{k=1}^{\infty}\frac{1}{2^k} = 4(1) - 6(1) = -2 \qquad \blacksquare$$

The linearity property also provides useful information about a series of the form $\Sigma(ca_k + db_k)$ when exactly one of Σa_k or Σb_k diverges; that is, one converges and the other diverges.

THEOREM 8.7   Divergence of the sum of a convergent and a divergent series

If either Σa_k or Σb_k diverges and the other converges, then the series $\Sigma(a_k + b_k)$ must diverge.

Proof   Suppose Σa_k diverges and Σb_k converges. Then if the series $\Sigma(a_k + b_k)$ also converges, the linearity property tells us that the series

$$\sum[(a_k + b_k) - b_k] = \sum a_k$$

must converge, contrary to hypotheses. It follows that the series $\Sigma(a_k + b_k)$ diverges.
❏

This theorem tells us, for example, that $\displaystyle\sum_{k=1}^{\infty}\left[\frac{1}{k^2+k} + (-1)^k\right]$ must diverge because even though $\displaystyle\sum_{k=1}^{\infty}\frac{1}{k^2+k}$ converges (Example 3), the series $\displaystyle\sum_{k=1}^{\infty}(-1)^k$ diverges (Example 2).

GEOMETRIC SERIES

We are still very limited in the available techniques for determining whether a given series is convergent or divergent. In fact, the purpose of a great part of this chapter is to develop efficient techniques for making this determination. We begin this quest by considering an important special kind of series.

Geometric Series

> A **geometric series** is an infinite series in which the ratio of successive terms in the series is constant. If this constant ratio is r, then the series has the form
>
> $$\sum_{k=0}^{\infty} ar^k = a + ar + ar^2 + ar^3 + \cdots + ar^n + \cdots \qquad a \neq 0$$

For example, $3 + \frac{3}{2} + \frac{3}{4} + \frac{3}{8} + \cdots$ is a geometric series because each term is one-half the preceding term. The ratio of a geometric series may be positive or negative. For example,

$$\sum_{k=0}^{\infty}\frac{2}{(-3)^k} = 2 - \frac{2}{3} + \frac{2}{9} - \frac{2}{27} + \cdots$$

is a geometric series with $r = -\frac{1}{3}$. The following theorem tells us how to determine whether a given geometric series converges or diverges and, if it does converge, what its sum must be.

THEOREM 8.8 Geometric series theorem

The geometric series $\sum_{k=0}^{\infty} ar^k$ with $a \neq 0$ diverges if $|r| \geq 1$ and converges if $|r| < 1$ with sum

$$\sum_{k=0}^{\infty} ar^k = \frac{a}{1-r}$$

Proof Note that the nth partial sum of the geometric series is

$$S_n = a + ar + ar^2 + \cdots + ar^{n-1}$$

Thus,

$$rS_n = ar + ar^2 + ar^3 + \cdots + ar^n \qquad \text{Multiply both sides by } r.$$

$$rS_n - S_n = (ar + ar^2 + ar^3 + \cdots + ar^n) - (a + ar + ar^2 + \cdots + ar^{n-1})$$

$$(r-1)S_n = ar^n - a$$

$$S_n = \frac{a(r^n - 1)}{r - 1} \qquad \text{if } r \neq 1$$

If $|r| > 1$, the sequence of partial sums $\{S_n\}$ has no limit since r^n is unbounded in this case, so the geometric series must diverge. However, if $|r| < 1$, Theorem 8.5 tells us that $r^n \to 0$ as $n \to \infty$, so we have

$$\sum_{k=0}^{\infty} ar^k = \lim_{n \to \infty} S_n = \lim_{n \to \infty} a\left(\frac{r^n - 1}{r - 1}\right) = \frac{a(0-1)}{r-1} = \frac{a}{1-r}$$

To complete the proof, it must be shown that the geometric series diverges when $|r| = 1$, and we leave this final step as a problem. ❑

EXAMPLE 5 Testing for convergence in a geometric series

Determine whether each of the following geometric series converges or diverges. If the series converges, find its sum.

a. $\displaystyle\sum_{k=0}^{\infty} \frac{1}{7}\left(\frac{3}{2}\right)^k$ **b.** $\displaystyle\sum_{k=2}^{\infty} 3\left(-\frac{1}{5}\right)^k$

Solution

a. Because $r = \frac{3}{2}$ satisfies $|r| \geq 1$, the series diverges.

b. We have $r = -\frac{1}{5}$ so $|r| < 1$, and the geometric series converges. The first value of k is 2 (not 0), so the value a (the first value) is $a = 3\left(-\frac{1}{5}\right)^2 = \frac{3}{25}$, and

$$\sum_{k=2}^{\infty} 3\left(-\frac{1}{5}\right)^k = \frac{a}{1-r} = \frac{\frac{3}{25}}{1-(-\frac{1}{5})} = \frac{1}{10} \qquad \blacksquare$$

APPLICATIONS OF GEOMETRIC SERIES

Geometric series can be used in many different ways. Our next three examples illustrate several applications involving geometric series.

Recall that a rational number r is one that can be written as $r = p/q$ for integer p and nonzero integer q. It can be shown that any such number has a decimal representation in which a pattern of numbers repeats. For instance,

$$\frac{5}{10} = 0.5 = 0.5\overline{0} \qquad\qquad \frac{5}{11} = 0.454545\cdots = 0.\overline{45}$$

where the bar indicates that the pattern repeats indefinitely. Example 6 shows how geometric series can be used to reverse this process by writing a given repeating decimal as a rational number.

EXAMPLE 6 **Expressing a repeating decimal as a rational number**

Write $15.4\overline{23}$ as a rational number $\dfrac{p}{q}$.

Solution

The bar over the 23 indicates that this block of digits is to be repeated, that is, $15.4\overline{23} = 15.423232323\ldots$. The repeating part of the decimal can be written as a geometric series as follows.

$$
\begin{aligned}
15.4\overline{23} &= 15 + \frac{4}{10} + \frac{23}{10^3} + \frac{23}{10^5} + \frac{23}{10^7} + \cdots \\[2mm]
&= 15 + \frac{4}{10} + \frac{23}{10^3}\left[1 + \frac{1}{10^2} + \frac{1}{10^4} + \cdots\right] \\[2mm]
&= 15 + \frac{4}{10} + \frac{23}{10^3}\left[\frac{1}{1 - \frac{1}{100}}\right] \qquad \textit{Sum of a geometric series} \\
&\qquad\qquad\qquad\qquad\qquad\qquad\quad \textit{with } a = 1 \textit{ and } r = 1/100 \\[2mm]
&= 15 + \frac{4}{10} + \frac{23}{10^3}\left[\frac{100}{99}\right] \\[2mm]
&= 15 + \frac{4}{10} + \frac{23}{990} \\[2mm]
&= \frac{15{,}269}{990}
\end{aligned}
$$
■

A tax rebate that returns a certain amount of money to taxpayers can result in spending that is many times this amount. This phenomenon is known in economics as the *multiplier effect*. It occurs because the portion of the rebate that is spent by one individual becomes income for one or more others, who, in turn, spend some of it again, creating income for yet other individuals to spend. If the fraction of income that is saved remains constant as this process continues indefinitely, the total amount spent as a result of the rebate is the sum of a geometric series.*

EXAMPLE 7 **Modeling Problem: Multiplier effect in economics**

Suppose that nationwide approximately 90% of all income is spent and 10% is saved. How much total spending will be generated by a \$40 billion tax rebate if savings habits do not change?

Solution

The amount (in billions) spent by original recipients of the rebate is 40. This becomes new income, of which 90%, or 0.9(40), is spent. This, in turn, generates additional spending of 0.9[0.9(40)], and so on. The total amount spent if this process continues indefinitely is

$$
\begin{aligned}
40 + 0.9(40) + 0.9^2(40) + 0.9^3(40) + \cdots &= 40[1 + 0.9 + 0.9^2 + \cdots] \\[2mm]
&= 40\sum_{k=0}^{\infty} 0.9^k \qquad \textit{Geometric series} \\
&\qquad\qquad\qquad\quad \textit{with } a = 1, r = 0.9 \\[2mm]
&= 40\left(\frac{1}{1 - 0.9}\right) \\[2mm]
&= 400 \text{ (billion)}
\end{aligned}
$$
■

---

*The fraction s of income that is saved is called the *marginal propensity to save* and $c = 1 - s$ is the *marginal propensity to consume*. In Example 7, we have $s = 0.1$ and $c = 0.9$.

EXAMPLE 8 Modeling Problem: Accumulation of medication in a body

A patient is given an injection of 10 units of a certain drug every 24 hours. The drug is eliminated exponentially so that the proportion that remains in the patient's body after t days is $f(t) = e^{-t/5}$. If the treatment is continued indefinitely, approximately how many units of the drug will eventually be in the patient's body just prior to an injection?

Solution

Of the original dose of 10 units, only $10e^{-1/5}$ are left in the patient's body after the first day (just prior to the second injection). That is,

$$S_1 = 10e^{-1/5}$$

The medication in the patient's body after 2 days consists of what remains from the first two doses. Of the original dose, only $10e^{-2/5}$ units are left (because 2 days have elapsed), and of the second dose, $10e^{-1/5}$ units remain:

$$S_2 = 10e^{-1/5} + 10e^{-2/5}$$

Similarly, for n days,

$$S_n = 10e^{-1/5} + 10e^{-2/5} + \cdots + 10e^{-n/5} = \sum_{k=1}^{n} 10e^{-k/5}$$

The amount S of medication in the patient's body in the long run is the limit of S_n as $n \to \infty$. That is,

$$S = \lim_{n \to \infty} S_n$$

$$= \sum_{k=1}^{\infty} 10e^{-k/5} \qquad \text{\textit{Geometric series with}}\ a = 10e^{-1/5}\ \text{\textit{and}}\ r = e^{-1/5}$$

$$= \frac{10e^{-1/5}}{1 - e^{-1/5}}$$

$$\approx 45.166556$$

We see that about 45 units remain in the patient's body. ∎

WARNING As a final note, remember that a sequence is a succession of terms, whereas a series is a sum of such terms. Do not confuse the two concepts because they have very different properties. For example, a sequence of terms may converge, but the series of the same terms may diverge:

$$\left\{ 1 + \frac{1}{2^n} \right\} \text{ is the sequence } \frac{3}{2}, \frac{5}{4}, \frac{9}{8}, \frac{17}{16}, \ldots, \text{ which converges to 1.}$$

$$\sum_{n=1}^{\infty} \left(1 + \frac{1}{2^n} \right) \text{ is the series } \frac{3}{2} + \frac{5}{4} + \frac{9}{8} + \cdots, \text{ which diverges.}$$

8.2 PROBLEM SET

A **1. WHAT DOES THIS SAY?** Explain the difference between sequences and series.

2. WHAT DOES THIS SAY? What is a geometric series?

Determine whether the geometric series given in Problems 3–22 converges or diverges, and find the sum of each convergent series.

3. $\displaystyle\sum_{k=0}^{\infty} \left(\frac{4}{5} \right)^k$

4. $\displaystyle\sum_{k=0}^{\infty} \left(-\frac{4}{5} \right)^k$

5. $\displaystyle\sum_{k=0}^{\infty} \frac{2}{3^k}$

6. $\displaystyle\sum_{k=0}^{\infty} \frac{2}{(-3)^k}$

7. $\displaystyle\sum_{k=1}^{\infty} \left(\frac{3}{2} \right)^k$

8. $\displaystyle\sum_{k=1}^{\infty} \frac{3}{2^k}$

9. $\displaystyle\sum_{k=0}^{\infty} \frac{(-2)^k}{5^{2k+1}}$

10. $\displaystyle\sum_{k=1}^{\infty} 5(0.9)^k$

11. $\displaystyle\sum_{k=1}^{\infty} e^{-0.2k}$

12. $\displaystyle\sum_{k=1}^{\infty} \frac{3^k}{4^{k+2}}$

13. $\displaystyle\sum_{k=2}^{\infty} \frac{(-2)^{k-1}}{3^{k+1}}$

14. $\displaystyle\sum_{k=2}^{\infty} (-1)^k \frac{2^{k+1}}{3^{k-3}}$

15. $\dfrac{1}{2} - \dfrac{1}{2^2} + \dfrac{1}{2^3} - \dfrac{1}{2^4} + \cdots$

16. $1 + \pi + \pi^2 + \pi^3 + \cdots$

17. $\dfrac{1}{4} + \left(\dfrac{1}{4}\right)^4 + \left(\dfrac{1}{4}\right)^7 + \left(\dfrac{1}{4}\right)^{10} + \cdots$

18. $\dfrac{2}{3} - \left(\dfrac{2}{3}\right)^3 + \left(\dfrac{2}{3}\right)^5 - \left(\dfrac{2}{3}\right)^7 + \cdots$

19. $2 + \sqrt{2} + 1 + \frac{1}{\sqrt{2}} + \cdots$

20. $3 - \sqrt{3} + 1 - \frac{1}{\sqrt{3}} + \cdots$

21. $(1 + \sqrt{2}) + 1 + (-1 + \sqrt{2}) + (3 - 2\sqrt{2}) + \cdots$

22. $(\sqrt{2} - 1) + 1 + (\sqrt{2} + 1) + (2\sqrt{2} + 3) + \cdots$

In Problems 23–30, each series telescopes. In each case, express the nth partial sum S_n in terms of n and determine whether the series converges or diverges by examining $\lim_{n\to\infty} S_n$. Notice that some of these problems may require partial fraction decomposition.

23. $\displaystyle\sum_{k=1}^{\infty} \left[\frac{1}{k^{0.1}} - \frac{1}{(k+1)^{0.1}} \right]$

24. $\displaystyle\sum_{k=1}^{\infty} \left[\frac{1}{2k+1} - \frac{1}{2k+3} \right]$

25. $\displaystyle\sum_{k=0}^{\infty} \frac{1}{(k+1)(k+2)}$

26. $\displaystyle\sum_{k=2}^{\infty} \frac{1}{k(k+1)}$

27. $\displaystyle\sum_{k=1}^{\infty} \ln\left(1 + \frac{1}{k}\right)$

28. $\displaystyle\sum_{k=1}^{\infty} \frac{1}{(2k-1)(2k+1)}$

29. $\displaystyle\sum_{k=1}^{\infty} \frac{2k+1}{k^2(k+1)^2}$

30. $\displaystyle\sum_{k=1}^{\infty} \frac{\sqrt{k+1} - \sqrt{k}}{\sqrt{k^2+k}}$. *Hint: Note that $\sqrt{k^2 + k} = \sqrt{k}\sqrt{k+1}$.*

Express each repeating decimal given in Problems 31–34 as a common (reduced) fraction.

31. $0.\overline{01}$

32. $2.23\overline{1}$

33. $1.\overline{405}$

34. $41.\overline{2010}$

B **35. a.** Find numbers A and B such that

$$\frac{k-1}{2^{k+1}} = \frac{Ak}{2^k} - \frac{B(k+1)}{2^{k+1}}$$

b. Evaluate $\displaystyle\sum_{k=1}^{\infty} \frac{k-1}{2^{k+1}}$ as a telescoping series.

36. Evaluate $\displaystyle\sum_{k=1}^{\infty} \frac{2k-1}{3^{k+1}}$. *Hint: Follow the procedure in Problem 35.*

37. Evaluate $\displaystyle\sum_{n=1}^{\infty} \frac{\ln\left(\dfrac{n^{n+1}}{(n+1)^n}\right)}{n(n+1)}$. *Hint: Use the properties of logarithms to show that the series telescopes.*

38. Evaluate $\displaystyle\sum_{n=1}^{\infty} \frac{n}{(n+1)!}$. *Hint: Express as a telescoping series.*

39. Find $\displaystyle\sum_{k=0}^{\infty} (2a_k + 2^{-k})$ given that $\displaystyle\sum_{k=0}^{\infty} a_k = 3.57$.

40. Find $\displaystyle\sum_{k=0}^{\infty} \frac{b_k - 3^{-k}}{2}$ given that $\displaystyle\sum_{k=0}^{\infty} b_k = 0.54$.

41. Evaluate $\displaystyle\sum_{k=0}^{\infty} \left(\frac{1}{2^k} + \frac{1}{3^k} \right)^2$.

42. Evaluate $\displaystyle\sum_{k=0}^{\infty} \left[\left(\frac{2}{3}\right)^k + \left(\frac{3}{4}\right)^k \right]^2$.

43. Show that $\displaystyle\sum_{k=0}^{\infty} \frac{1}{(a+k)(a+k+1)} = \frac{1}{a}$ if $a > 0$.

44. Evaluate $\displaystyle\sum_{k=0}^{\infty} \frac{1}{(2+k)^2 + 2 + k}$.

45. If $\displaystyle\sum_{k=0}^{\infty} a_k^2 = \sum_{k=0}^{\infty} b_k^2 = 4$ and $\displaystyle\sum_{k=0}^{\infty} a_k b_k = 3$, what is

$$\sum_{k=0}^{\infty} (a_k - b_k)^2?$$

Modeling Problems *In Problems 46–56, set up an appropriate model to answer the given question.*

46. A pendulum is released through an arc of length 20 cm from a vertical position and is allowed to swing freely until it eventually comes to rest. Each subsequent swing of the bob of the pendulum is 90% as far as the preceding swing. How far will the bob travel before coming to rest?

47. A flywheel rotates at 500 rpm and slows in such a way that during each minute it revolves at two-thirds the rate of the preceding minute. How many total revolutions does the flywheel make before coming to rest?

48. A ball is dropped from a height of 10 ft. Each time the ball bounces, it rises 0.6 the distance it had previously fallen. What is the total distance traveled by the ball?

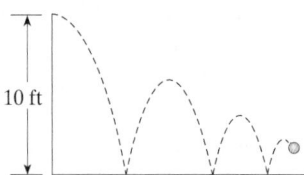

49. Suppose the ball in Problem 48 is dropped from a height of h feet and on each bounce rises 75% of the distance it had previously fallen. If it travels a total distance of 21 ft, what is h?

50. Suppose that nationwide approximately 92% of all income is spent and 8% is saved. How much total spending will be generated by a $50 billion tax cut if savings habits do not change?

51. Suppose that a piece of machinery costing $10,000 depreciates 20% of its current value each year. That is, the first year $10,000(0.20) = $2,000 is depreciated. The second year's depreciation is $8,000(0.20) = $1,600, because the value for the second year is $10,000 − $2,000 = $8,000. If the depreciation is calculated this way indefinitely, what is the total depreciation?

52. Winnie Winner wins $100 in a pie-baking contest run by the Hi-Do Pie Co. The company gives Winnie the $100. However, the tax collector wants 20% of the $100. Winnie pays the tax. But then she realizes that she didn't really win a $100 prize and tells her story to the Hi-Do Co. The friendly Hi-Do Co. gives Winnie the $20 she paid in taxes. Unfortunately, the tax collector now wants 20% of the $20. She pays the tax again and then goes back to the Hi-Do Co. with her story. Assume that this can go on indefinitely. How much money does the Hi-Do Co. have to give Winnie so that she will really win $100? How much does she pay in taxes?

53. A patient is given an injection of 20 units of a certain drug every 24 hr. The drug is eliminated exponentially, so the part that remains in the patient's body after t days is $f(t) = e^{-t/2}$. If the treatment is to continue indefinitely, approximately how many units of the drug will eventually be in the patient's body just before an injection?

54. A certain drug is injected into a body. It is known that the amount of drug in the body at the end of a given hour is $\frac{1}{4}$ the amount that was present at the end of the previous hour. One unit is injected initially, and to keep the concentration up, an additional unit is injected at the end of each subsequent hour. What is the highest possible amount of the drug that can ever be present in the body?

55. Each January 1, the administration of a certain private college adds six new members to its board of trustees. If the fraction of trustees who remain active for at least t years is $f(t) = e^{-0.2t}$, approximately how many active trustees will the college have in the long run? Assume that there were six members on the board on January 1 of the present year.

56. How much should you invest today at an annual interest rate of 15% compounded continuously so that, starting next year, you can make annual withdrawals of $2,000 forever?

57. HISTORICAL QUEST The Greek philosopher Zeno of Elea (495–435 B.C.) presented a number of paradoxes that caused a great deal of concern to the mathematicians of his period. These paradoxes were important in the development of the notion of infinitesimals. Perhaps the most famous is the *racecourse paradox*, which can be stated as follows:

A runner can never reach the end of a race: As he runs the track, he must first run $\frac{1}{2}$ the length of the track, then $\frac{1}{2}$ the remaining distance, so that at this point he has run $\frac{1}{2} + \frac{1}{4} = \frac{3}{4}$ of the length of the track, and $\frac{1}{4}$ remains to be run. After running half this distance, he finds he still has $\frac{1}{8}$ of the track to run, and so on, indefinitely.

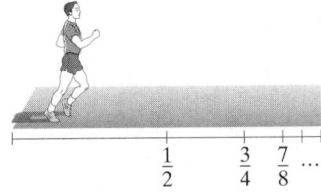

Suppose the runner runs at a constant pace and that it takes him T minutes to run the first half of the track. Set up an infinite series that gives the total time required to run the track, and verify that the total time is $2T$, as intuition would lead us to expect.

58. HISTORICAL QUEST A professor of mathematics at the University of Warsaw, Waclaw Sierpinski was the first person to give a lecture course devoted entirely to set theory. He became interested in set theory in 1907 when he came across a theorem which stated that points in the plane could be specified with a single coordinate. He wrote to a friend and asked how such a result could be possible, and he received a one word reply: "Cantor." Georg Cantor (1845–1918) wrote a series of eight papers that provided the basis for what we today call set theory. ∎

WACLAW SIERPINSKI
1882–1969

For this quest, we investigate an interesting geometrical figure named after Sierpinski, namely the *Sierpinski gasket*, shown in Figure 8.13.

Figure 8.13 Sierpinski gasket

To form the gasket, begin by drawing an equilateral triangle, T, with sides of length 1. Remove the middle triangle formed by joining the midpoints of the sides of T, as shown in Figure 8.14a. This leaves three equal triangular regions, and the next step is to remove the middle triangle from each of these, as shown in Figure 8.14b. If you continue this process indefinitely, what remains is the Sierpinski gasket. Show that the Sierpinski gasket has area 0. *Hint:* What is the sum of the areas of the regions removed?

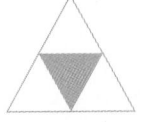 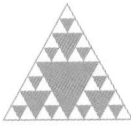 

a. First step   **b.** Second step   **c.** Third step   **d.** Fourth step

Figure 8.14 Construction of a Sierpinski gasket

59. HISTORICAL QUEST John von Neumann was one of the original six mathematics professors at the Institute for Advanced Study in Princeton, the other five also being world-class mathematicians or Nobel laureates: J. W. Alexander, Albert Einstein, Marston Morse, Oswald Veblen, and Hermann Weyl. Von Neumann, a pioneer in computer science, received two Presidential Awards, the Medal for Merit, and the Medal for Freedom. The fact that he had a brilliant mind is an

JOHN VON NEUMANN
1903–1957

understatement, as illustrated in the following anecdote, stated in the form of a quest problem. ∎

Two trains, each traveling at 10 mph approach each other on the same straight track. When the trains are 5 miles apart, a fly begins flying back and forth from train to train at the rate of 16 mi/h. Between the time the fly starts and the time the trains collide, how far does the fly fly?

a. Find the fly's total distance traveled by determining how long the fly flies.

b. When von Neumann gave the correct answer almost immediately, the poser of the problem was convinced he had used the "trick" suggested in part **a**. "What trick?" asked von Neumann. "I summed the series." Follow von Neumann's lead by summing an infinite series whose terms are the distances traveled by the fly as it flies between the trains.

C **60. a.** Let $\displaystyle\sum_{k=1}^{n} a_k = S_n$ be the nth partial sum of an infinite series. Show that $S_n - S_{n-1} = a_n$.

b. Use part **a** to find the nth term of the infinite series whose nth partial sum is $S_n = \dfrac{n}{2n + 3}$.

61. Prove that if $\Sigma a_k = A$ and $\Sigma b_k = B$, then $\Sigma(a_k + b_k) = A + B$.

62. Show that if Σa_k converges and Σb_k diverges, then $\Sigma(a_k - b_k)$ diverges. *Hint*: Note that $b_k = a_k - (a_k - b_k)$.

63. Counterexample Problem Either prove or disprove (by finding a counterexample) each of the following statements:

a. If Σa_k and Σb_k are both divergent series, then $\Sigma(a_k + b_k)$ is also divergent.

b. If Σa_k and Σb_k are both convergent series, then $\Sigma(a_k + b_k)$ is also convergent.

64. Show that $\displaystyle\sum_{k=0}^{\infty} ar^k$ diverges if $|r| \geq 1$.

65. a. Show that $\displaystyle\sum_{k=1}^{n}(a_k - a_{k+2}) = (a_1 + a_2) - (a_{n+1} + a_{n+2})$.

b. Use part **a** to show that if

$$\lim_{k\to\infty} a_k = A, \quad \text{then} \quad \sum_{k=1}^{\infty}(a_k - a_{k+2}) = a_1 + a_2 - 2A$$

c. Use part **b** to evaluate $\displaystyle\sum_{k=1}^{\infty}\left[k^{1/k} - (k+2)^{1/(k+2)}\right]$.

d. Evaluate $\displaystyle\sum_{k=2}^{\infty}\dfrac{1}{k^2 - 1}$.

66. Square $ABCD$ has sides of length 1. Square $EFGH$ is formed by connecting the midpoints of the sides of the first square, as shown in Figure 8.15. Assume that the pattern of shaded regions in the square is continued indefinitely. What is the total area of the shaded regions?

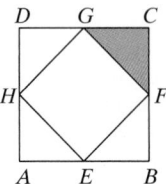

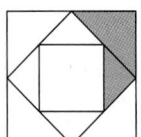 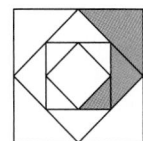 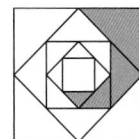

Figure 8.15   Find the area of the shaded regions.

67. Evaluate $\displaystyle\sum_{k=1}^{\infty}\dfrac{12^k}{(4^k - 3^k)(4^{k+1} - 3^{k+1})}$.

Hint: Find A and B so that

$$\frac{3^k A}{4^k - 3^k} + \frac{3^k B}{4^{k+1} - 3^{k+1}} = \frac{12^k}{(4^k - 3^k)(4^{k+1} - 3^{k+1})}$$

8.3   The Integral Test; p-Series

IN THIS SECTION   divergence test, series of nonnegative numbers, the integral test, p-series

The convergence or divergence of an infinite series is determined by the behavior of its nth partial sum, S_n, as $n \to \infty$. In Section 8.2, we saw how algebraic methods can sometimes be used to find formulas for the nth partial sum of a series. Unfortunately, it is often difficult or even impossible to find a usable formula for the nth partial sum S_n of a series, and other techniques must be used to determine convergence or divergence.

DIVERGENCE TEST

When investigating the infinite series Σa_k, it is easy to confuse the sequence of *general terms* $\{a_k\}$ with the sequence of *partial sums* $\{S_n\}$, where

$$S_n = \sum_{k=1}^{n} a_k$$

Because the sequence $\{a_k\}$ is usually more accessible than $\{S_n\}$, it would be convenient if the convergence of $\{S_n\}$ could be settled by examining

$$\lim_{k \to \infty} a_k$$

Even though we do not have one simple, definitive test for convergence, the following theorem tells us that if certain conditions are not met, the series must diverge.

THEOREM 8.9 The divergence test

WARNING Theorem 8.9 gives a necessary but not a sufficient condition for convergence. For example, clouds are necessary for rain; clouds are not sufficient for rain.

If $\lim_{k \to \infty} a_k \neq 0$, then the series Σa_k must diverge.

Proof Suppose the sequence of partial sums $\{S_n\}$ converges with sum L, so that $\lim_{n \to \infty} S_n = L$. Then we also have

$$\lim_{n \to \infty} S_{n-1} = L$$

Because $S_k - S_{k-1} = a_k$, it follows that

$$\lim_{k \to \infty} a_k = \lim_{k \to \infty} (S_k - S_{k-1}) = \lim_{k \to \infty} S_k - \lim_{k \to \infty} S_{k-1} = L - L = 0$$

If the series $\sum a_k$ converges, then $\lim_{k \to \infty} a_k = 0$. Thus, if $\lim_{k \to \infty} a_k \neq 0$, the series Σa_k must diverge. ❏

➤ **What This Says** The divergence test can only tell us that Σa_k diverges if $\lim_{k \to \infty} a_k \neq 0$, **but it *cannot* be used to show convergence of a series.** In Example 2, we show that the series $\Sigma \frac{1}{k}$ *diverges* even though $\lim_{k \to \infty} \frac{1}{k} = 0$.

EXAMPLE 1 Divergence test to show divergence

Show that the series $\displaystyle\sum_{k=0}^{\infty} \frac{k - 300}{4k + 750}$ diverges.

Solution

Taking the limit of the *k*th term as $k \to \infty$, we find

$$\lim_{k \to \infty} \frac{k - 300}{4k + 750} = \frac{1}{4}$$

Because this limit is not 0, the divergence test tells us that the series must diverge. ∎

SERIES OF NONNEGATIVE NUMBERS, THE INTEGRAL TEST

Series whose terms are all nonnegative numbers play an important role in the general theory of infinite series and in applications. Our next goal is to develop methods for investigating the convergence of nonnegative-term series, and we begin by establishing the following general principle.

THEOREM 8.10 Convergence criterion for series with nonnegative terms

A series Σa_k with $a_k \geq 0$ for all k converges if its sequence of partial sums is bounded from above and diverges otherwise.

Proof   Suppose Σa_k is a series of nonnegative terms, and let S_n denote its nth partial sum; that is

$$S_n = \sum_{k=1}^{n} a_k = a_1 + a_2 + \cdots + a_n$$

Because $S_{n+1} = S_n + a_{n+1}$ and because $a_k \geq 0$ for all k, it follows that

$$S_{n+1} \geq S_n$$

for all n, so that $\{S_n\}$ is an increasing sequence. According to the BMCT, the increasing sequence $\{S_n\}$ converges if it is bounded from above and diverges otherwise. Hence, because the series Σa_k represents the limit of the sequence $\{S_n\}$, the series Σa_k converges if the sequence $\{S_n\}$ is bounded from above and diverges if it is unbounded.   ❏

This convergence criterion is often difficult to apply because it is not easy to determine whether the sequence of partial sums $\{S_n\}$ is bounded from above. Our next goal in this section and in Sections 8.4–8.6 is to examine various "tests for convergence." These are procedures that allow us to determine indirectly whether a given series converges or diverges without actually having to compute the limit of the partial sums. We begin with a convergence test that relates the convergence of a series to that of an improper integral.

THEOREM 8.11   The integral test

If $a_k = f(k)$ for $k = 1, 2, \ldots$, where f is a positive, continuous, and decreasing function of x for $x \geq 1$, then

$$\sum_{k=1}^{\infty} a_k \quad \text{and} \quad \int_{1}^{\infty} f(x)\, dx$$

either both converge or both diverge.

WARNING   When applying the integral test, the function f need not be decreasing for all $x \geq 1$, only for all $x \geq N$ for some number N. That is, f must be decreasing "in the long run."

Proof   We will use a geometric argument to show that the sequence of partial sums $\{S_n\}$ of the series $\displaystyle\sum_{k=1}^{\infty} a_k$ is bounded from above if the improper integral $\displaystyle\int_{1}^{\infty} f(x)\, dx$ converges and that it is unbounded if the integral diverges. Accordingly, Figures 8.16a and 8.16b show the graph of a continuous decreasing function f that satisfies $f(k) = a_k$ for $k = 1, 2, 3, \ldots$. Rectangles have been constructed at unit intervals in both figures, but in Figure 8.16a the kth rectangle has height $f(k+1) = a_{k+1}$, whereas in Figure 8.16b, the comparable rectangle has height $f(k) = a_k$. Notice that in Figure 8.16a, the rectangles are inscribed so that

AREA OF THE FIRST $n - 1$ RECTANGLES $<$ AREA UNDER $y = f(x)$ OVER $[1, n]$

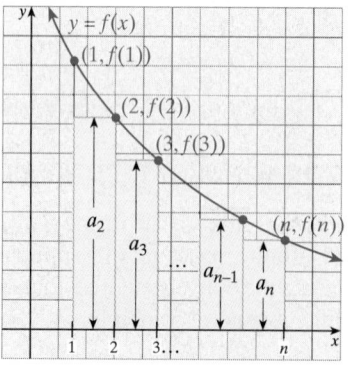

a. The kth rectangle has height $f(k+1) = a_{k+1}$.

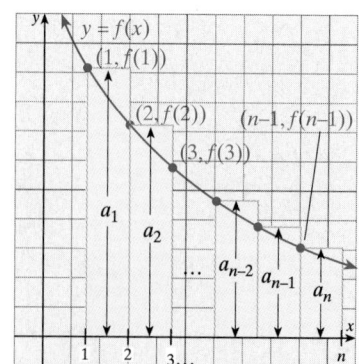

b. The kth rectangle has height $f(k) = a_k$.

Figure 8.16   Integral test

$$a_2 + a_3 + \cdots + a_n < \int_1^n f(x)\,dx$$

$$a_1 + a_2 + a_3 + \cdots + a_n < a_1 + \int_1^n f(x)\,dx \qquad \text{Add } a_1 \text{ to both sides.}$$

Similarly, in Figure 8.16b, the rectangles are circumscribed so that

AREA UNDER $y = f(x)$ OVER $[1, n+1]$ < AREA OF THE FIRST n RECTANGLES

$$\int_1^{n+1} f(x)\,dx < a_1 + a_2 + a_3 + \cdots + a_n$$

Let $S_n = a_1 + a_2 + a_3 + \cdots + a_n$ be the nth partial sum of the series so that

$$\int_1^{n+1} f(x)\,dx < S_n < a_1 + \int_1^n f(x)\,dx$$

Now, suppose the improper integral $\int_1^\infty f(x)\,dx$ converges and has the value I; that is, $\int_1^\infty f(x)\,dx = I$. Then

$$S_n < a_1 + \int_1^n f(x)\,dx < a_1 + \int_1^\infty f(x)\,dx = a_1 + I$$

It follows that the sequence of partial sums is bounded from above (by $a_1 + I$), and the convergence criterion for nonnegative term series tells us that the series $\sum_{k=1}^\infty a_k$ must converge.

On the other hand, if the improper integral $\int_1^\infty f(x)\,dx$ diverges, then

$$\lim_{n \to \infty} \int_1^{n+1} f(x)\,dx = \infty$$

It follows that $\lim_{n \to \infty} S_n = \infty$ also because $\int_1^{n+1} f(x)\,dx < S_n$. This means that the series must diverge. Thus, the series and the improper integral either both converge or both diverge, as claimed. ❏

A series that arises in connection with overtones produced by a vibrating string is

$$\sum_{k=1}^\infty \frac{1}{k} = 1 + \frac{1}{2} + \frac{1}{3} + \frac{1}{4} + \cdots$$

This is called the **harmonic series**, and in the next example, we use the integral test to show that this series diverges.

EXAMPLE 2 Harmonic series diverges

Test the series $\sum_{k=1}^\infty \frac{1}{k}$ for convergence.

Solution

Because $f(x) = \dfrac{1}{x}$ is positive, continuous, and decreasing for $x \geq 1$, the conditions of the integral test are satisfied.

$$\int_1^\infty \frac{1}{x}\,dx = \lim_{b \to \infty} \int_1^b \frac{1}{x}\,dx = \lim_{b \to \infty} [\ln b - \ln 1] = \infty$$

The integral diverges, so the harmonic series diverges. ∎

EXAMPLE 3   Integral test for convergence

Test the series $\displaystyle\sum_{k=1}^{\infty} \frac{k}{e^{k/5}}$ for convergence.

Solution

The function $f(x) = \dfrac{x}{e^{x/5}} = xe^{-x/5}$ is positive and continuous for all $x > 0$. We find that

$$f'(x) = x\left(-\frac{1}{5}e^{-x/5}\right) + e^{-x/5} = \left(1 - \frac{x}{5}\right)e^{-x/5}$$

The critical number is found when $f'(x) = 0$, so we solve

$$\left(1 - \frac{x}{5}\right)e^{-x/5} = 0$$

$$1 - \frac{x}{5} = 0 \qquad \text{Since } e^{-x/5} \neq 0$$

$$x = 5$$

We see that $f'(x) < 0$ for $x > 5$, so it follows that f is decreasing for $x > 5$. Thus, the conditions for the integral test have been established, and the given series and the improper integral either both converge or both diverge. Computing the improper integral, we find

$$\int_5^{\infty} xe^{-x/5}\,dx = \lim_{b\to\infty} \int_5^b xe^{-x/5}\,dx$$

$$\boxed{\begin{array}{ll} \text{Let } u = x & dv = e^{-x/5}\,dx \\ du = dx & v = -5e^{-x/5} \end{array}}$$

$$= \lim_{b\to\infty}\left[-5xe^{-x/5}\Big|_5^b - \int_5^b (-5e^{-x/5})\,dx \right]$$

$$= \lim_{b\to\infty}\left[-5xe^{-x/5} - 25e^{-x/5} \right]\Big|_5^b$$

$$= \lim_{b\to\infty}\left[-5be^{-b/5} - 25e^{-b/5} + 25e^{-1} + 25e^{-1} \right]$$

$$= -5\lim_{b\to\infty} \frac{b+5}{e^{b/5}} + \lim_{b\to\infty} 50e^{-1}$$

$$= -5\lim_{b\to\infty} \frac{1}{\left(\frac{1}{5}\right)e^{b/5}} + 50e^{-1} \qquad \text{l'Hôpital's rule}$$

$$= 50e^{-1} \qquad\qquad\qquad \lim_{b\to\infty}\frac{1}{e^{b/5}} = 0$$

Thus, the improper integral converges, which in turn assures the convergence of the given series. ∎

WARNING   Note that the series converges because the integral converges to a finite number $50e^{-1}$, but this does not mean that the series

$$\sum_{k=1}^{\infty} \frac{k}{e^{k/5}}$$

converges to the same number $50e^{-1}$.

p-SERIES

The harmonic series $\Sigma 1/k$ is a special case of a more general series form called a *p*-series.

p-Series

A series of the form

$$\sum_{k=1}^{\infty} \frac{1}{k^p} = \frac{1}{1^p} + \frac{1}{2^p} + \frac{1}{3^p} + \cdots$$

where p is a positive constant is called a **p-series.** The harmonic series (Example 2) is the case where $p = 1$.

The following theorem shows how the convergence of a p-series depends on the value of p.

THEOREM 8.12 The p-series test

The p-series $\displaystyle\sum_{k=1}^{\infty} \frac{1}{k^p}$ converges if $p > 1$ and diverges if $p \leq 1$.

Proof We leave it for the reader to verify that $f(x) = \dfrac{1}{x^p}$ is continuous, positive, and decreasing for $x \geq 1$ and $p > 0$. We know the harmonic series ($p = 1$) diverges. For $p > 0$, $p \neq 1$, we have

$$\int_1^{\infty} \frac{dx}{x^p} = \lim_{b \to \infty} \int_1^b x^{-p} \, dx = \lim_{b \to \infty} \frac{b^{1-p} - 1}{1 - p} = \begin{cases} \dfrac{1}{p-1} & \text{if } p > 1 \\ \infty & \text{if } 0 < p < 1 \end{cases}$$

That is, this improper integral converges if $p > 1$ and diverges if $0 < p < 1$. For $p = 0$, the series becomes

$$\sum_{k=1}^{\infty} \frac{1}{k^0} = \frac{1}{1} + \frac{1}{1} + \frac{1}{1} + \cdots$$

and if $p < 0$, we have $\displaystyle\lim_{k \to \infty} \frac{1}{k^p} = \infty$, so the series diverges by the divergence test (Theorem 8.9). Thus, a p-series converges only when $p > 1$. ❑

➡ **What This Says** It should be clear that all functions of the form $y = 1/x^p$ with $p > 0$ are decreasing, but why should the series $\Sigma \frac{1}{k^p}$ converge only for $p > 1$? The answer lies in the rate of decrease for $y = 1/x^p$. If $p > 1$, the curve $y = 1/x^p$ falls fast enough to guarantee that the area under the curve for $p > 1$ is finite (see Figure 8.17a), while if $p \leq 1$, the curve $1/x^p$ falls more gradually, and the area under the curve is infinite (Figure 8.17b).

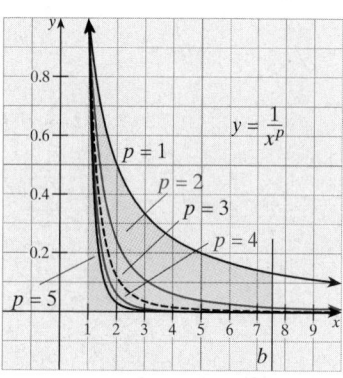

Areas are bounded.

a. $\displaystyle\int_1^{\infty} \frac{dx}{x^p} = \lim_{b \to \infty} \int_1^b \frac{dx}{x^p}$
converges if $p > 1$

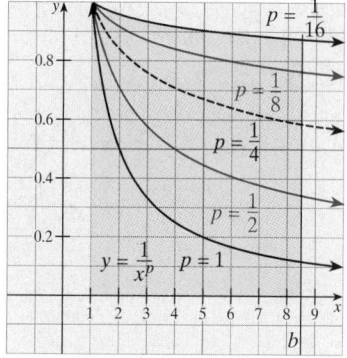

Areas are not bounded.

b. $\displaystyle\int_1^{\infty} \frac{dx}{x^p} = \lim_{b \to \infty} \int_1^b \frac{dx}{x^p}$
diverges if $p \leq 1$

Figure 8.17 Graphs for the p-series test

EXAMPLE 4 *p*-series test

Test each of the following series for convergence.

a. $\displaystyle\sum_{k=1}^{\infty} \frac{1}{\sqrt{k^3}}$ b. $\displaystyle\sum_{k=1}^{\infty}\left(\frac{1}{e^k} - \frac{1}{\sqrt{k}}\right)$

Solution

a. Here $\sqrt{k^3} = k^{3/2}$, so $p = \frac{3}{2} > 1$, and the series converges.

b. $\displaystyle\sum_{k=1}^{\infty}\left(\frac{1}{e^k} - \frac{1}{\sqrt{k}}\right)$; We note that

$$\sum_{k=1}^{\infty} \frac{1}{e^k} \quad \text{converges, because it is geometric with } |r| = \frac{1}{e} < 1$$

and

$$\sum_{k=1}^{\infty} \frac{1}{\sqrt{k}} \quad \text{diverges, because it is a } p\text{-series with } p = \frac{1}{2} < 1$$

Because one series in the difference converges and the other diverges, the given series must diverge (Theorem 8.7). ∎

8.3 PROBLEM SET

Ⓐ **1. WHAT DOES THIS SAY?** What is a *p*-series?

2. WHAT DOES THIS SAY? What is the integral test?

For the p-series given in Problems 3–6, specify the value of p and tell whether the series converges or diverges.

3. $\displaystyle\sum_{k=1}^{\infty} \frac{1}{k^3}$

4. $\displaystyle\sum_{k=1}^{\infty} \frac{100}{\sqrt{k}}$

5. $\displaystyle\sum_{k=1}^{\infty} \frac{1}{\sqrt[3]{k}}$

6. $\displaystyle\sum_{k=1}^{\infty} \frac{1}{2k\sqrt{k}}$

Show that the function f determined by the nth term of each series given in Problems 7–12 satisfies the hypotheses of the integral test. Then use the integral test to determine whether the series converges or diverges.

7. $\displaystyle\sum_{k=1}^{\infty} \frac{1}{(2+3k)^2}$

8. $\displaystyle\sum_{k=1}^{\infty} (2+k)^{-3/2}$

9. $\displaystyle\sum_{k=2}^{\infty} \frac{\ln k}{k}$

10. $\displaystyle\sum_{k=2}^{\infty} \frac{1}{k(\ln k)^2}$

11. $\displaystyle\sum_{k=1}^{\infty} \frac{(\tan^{-1} k)^2}{1+k^2}$

12. $\displaystyle\sum_{k=1}^{\infty} k e^{-k^2}$

In Problems 13–18, either use the divergence test to show that the given series diverges or show that the divergence test does not apply.

13. $\displaystyle\sum_{k=1}^{\infty} \frac{k}{k+1}$

14. $\displaystyle\sum_{k=1}^{\infty}\left(1+\frac{1}{k}\right)^{-k}$

15. $\displaystyle\sum_{k=2}^{\infty} \frac{k}{\sqrt{k^2-1}}$

16. $\displaystyle\sum_{k=1}^{\infty} e^{-1/k}$

17. $\displaystyle\sum_{k=0}^{\infty} \cos(k\pi)$

18. $\displaystyle\sum_{k=1}^{\infty} k e^{-k}$

Test the series in Problems 19–42 for convergence.

19. $\displaystyle\sum_{k=1}^{\infty} \frac{\ln k}{k^2}$

20. $\displaystyle\sum_{k=1}^{\infty} e^{-k}$

21. $\displaystyle\sum_{k=1}^{\infty}\left(2+\frac{3}{k}\right)^k$

22. $\displaystyle\sum_{k=1}^{\infty}\left(1+\frac{2}{k}\right)^k$

23. $\displaystyle\sum_{k=1}^{\infty} \frac{1}{k^4}$

24. $\displaystyle\sum_{k=1}^{\infty} \frac{5}{\sqrt{k}}$

25. $\displaystyle\sum_{k=1}^{\infty} k^{-3/4}$

26. $\displaystyle\sum_{k=1}^{\infty} k^{-4/3}$

27. $\displaystyle\sum_{k=1}^{\infty} \frac{k}{k^2+1}$

28. $\displaystyle\sum_{k=1}^{\infty} \frac{k^2}{\sqrt{k^3+2}}$

29. $\displaystyle\sum_{k=1}^{\infty} k e^{-k^2}$

30. $\displaystyle\sum_{k=1}^{\infty} \frac{1}{(0.25)^k}$

31. $\displaystyle\sum_{k=2}^{\infty} \frac{\ln \sqrt{k}}{\sqrt{k}}$

32. $\displaystyle\sum_{k=2}^{\infty} \frac{1}{k\sqrt{\ln k}}$

33. $\displaystyle\sum_{k=1}^{\infty} \frac{k}{e^k}$

34. $\displaystyle\sum_{k=1}^{\infty} \frac{k^2}{e^k}$

35. $\displaystyle\sum_{k=1}^{\infty} \frac{\tan^{-1} k}{1+k^2}$

36. $\displaystyle\sum_{k=1}^{\infty} \cot^{-1} k$

37. $\displaystyle\sum_{k=1}^{\infty} \tan^{-1} k$

38. $\displaystyle\sum_{k=1}^{\infty} \frac{1}{e^k + e^{-k}}$

39. $\displaystyle\sum_{k=1}^{\infty} \frac{k - \sin k}{3k + 2\sin k}$

40. $\displaystyle\sum_{k=1}^{\infty}\left(\sqrt{k^2+k} - k\right)$

41. $\displaystyle\sum_{k=1}^{\infty} k \sin \frac{1}{k}$

42. $\displaystyle\sum_{k=4}^{\infty} \ln\left(\frac{k}{k-3}\right)$

Use the divergence test and the p-series test to determine which of the series in Problems 43–54 converge. Write "inconclusive" if there is not yet enough information to settle convergence.

43. $\displaystyle\sum_{k=1}^{\infty} \frac{k-1}{k+1}$

44. $\displaystyle\sum_{k=1}^{\infty} \frac{k^2+1}{k+5}$

45. $\displaystyle\sum_{k=1}^{\infty} \frac{k^2+1}{k^3}$

46. $\displaystyle\sum_{k=1}^{\infty} \frac{2k^4+3}{k^5}$

47. $\displaystyle\sum_{k=1}^{\infty} \frac{1}{k^2}$

48. $\displaystyle\sum_{k=1}^{\infty} \frac{-k^5+k^2+1}{k^5+2}$

49. $\displaystyle\sum_{k=1}^{\infty} \frac{k^{\sqrt{3}}+1}{k^{2.7321}}$

50. $\displaystyle\sum_{k=1}^{\infty} \frac{k^{\sqrt{5}}+1}{k^{2.236}}$

51. $\displaystyle\sum_{k=1}^{\infty} \left[\frac{1}{k}+\frac{k+1}{k+2}\right]$

52. $\displaystyle\sum_{k=1}^{\infty} \left[\frac{1}{2k}+\left(\frac{3}{2}\right)^k\right]$

53. $\displaystyle\sum_{k=1}^{\infty} \left[\frac{1}{2^k}+\frac{2k+3}{3k+4}\right]$

54. $\displaystyle\sum_{k=1}^{\infty} \left[\frac{1}{2^k}-\frac{1}{k}\right]$

B *Find all values of p for which each series given in Problems 55–60 converges.*

55. $\displaystyle\sum_{k=2}^{\infty} \frac{k}{(k^2-1)^p}$

56. $\displaystyle\sum_{k=1}^{\infty} \frac{k^2}{(k^2+4)^p}$

57. $\displaystyle\sum_{k=3}^{\infty} \frac{1}{k^p \ln k}$

58. $\displaystyle\sum_{k=2}^{\infty} \frac{\ln k}{k^p}$

59. $\displaystyle\sum_{k=3}^{\infty} \frac{1}{k \ln k[\ln(\ln k)]^p}$

60. $\displaystyle\sum_{k=2}^{\infty} \frac{1}{k(\ln k)^p}$

61. Counterexample Problem If Σa_k converges, Σb_k diverges, and $\displaystyle\lim_{k\to\infty} b_k = 0$, then $\Sigma a_k b_k$ must diverge. Either prove this statement or provide a counterexample to show it is not generally true.

62. Counterexample Problem If $\displaystyle\lim_{k\to\infty} a_k = 0$, $\displaystyle\lim_{k\to\infty} b_k = 0$, and Σa_k and Σb_k both diverge, then $\Sigma a_k b_k$ must also diverge. Either prove this statement or provide a counterexample to show it is not generally true.

C 63. Let $f(x)$ be a positive, continuous, decreasing function for $x \geq 1$, and let $a_k = f(k)$ for $k = 1, 2, \ldots$. If Σa_k converges, show that

$$\int_1^{\infty} f(x)\, dx \leq \sum_{k=1}^{\infty} a_k \leq a_1 + \int_1^{\infty} f(x)\, dx$$

64. Getting a feeling for a series by examining its graph is a good idea, but you should be careful because you cannot always obtain a graph. Decide whether

$$\sum \left(1 - \frac{100}{n}\right)^n$$

converges or diverges, and then see if you can verify your result graphically.

8.4 Comparison Tests

IN THIS SECTION direct comparison test, limit comparison tests

DIRECT COMPARISON TEST

THEOREM 8.13 Direct comparison test

Suppose $0 \leq a_k \leq c_k$ for all $k \geq N$ for some N.

If $\displaystyle\sum_{k=1}^{\infty} c_k$ converges, then $\displaystyle\sum_{k=1}^{\infty} a_k$ also converges.

Let $0 \leq d_k \leq a_k$ for all $k \geq N$ for some N.

If $\displaystyle\sum_{k=1}^{\infty} d_k$ diverges, then $\displaystyle\sum_{k=1}^{\infty} a_k$ also diverges.

Proof Suppose Σa_k is a given nonnegative term series that is **dominated by** a convergent series Σc_k in the sense that for sufficiently large k, $0 \leq a_k \leq c_k$ for all k. Then, because the series Σc_k converges, its sequence of partial sums is bounded from above (say, by M), and we have

$$\sum_{k=1}^{n} a_k \leq \sum_{k=1}^{n} c_k < M \qquad \text{for all } n$$

Thus, the sequence of partial sums of the dominated series Σa_k is also bounded from above by M, and it, too, must converge.

On the other hand, suppose the given series Σa_k **dominates** a divergent series Σd_k so that $0 \le d_k \le a_k$. Then because the sequence of partial sums of Σd_k is unbounded, the same must be true for the partial sums of the dominating series Σa_k, and Σa_k must also diverge. $\square$

➡ **What This Says**   Let Σa_k, Σc_k and Σd_k be series with positive terms. The series Σa_k *converges* if it is "smaller" than (dominated by) a known convergent series Σc_k and *diverges* if it is "larger" than (dominates) a known divergent series Σd_k. That is, "smaller than convergent is convergent," and "bigger than divergent is divergent."

EXAMPLE 1   Convergence using the direct comparison test

Test the series $\displaystyle\sum_{k=1}^{\infty} \frac{1}{3^k + 1}$ for convergence.

Solution

For $k \ge 0$, we have $3^k + 1 > 3^k > 0$, and $0 < \dfrac{1}{3^k + 1} < \dfrac{1}{3^k}$. Thus, the given series is *dominated by* the convergent geometric series $\displaystyle\sum_{k=1}^{\infty} \frac{1}{3^k}$ (convergent because $r = \frac{1}{3}$). The direct comparison test tells us the given series must converge.   ■

EXAMPLE 2   Divergence using the direct comparison test

Test the series $\displaystyle\sum_{k=2}^{\infty} \frac{1}{\sqrt{k} - 1}$ for convergence.

Solution

For $k \ge 2$, we have

$$\frac{1}{\sqrt{k} - 1} > \frac{1}{\sqrt{k}} > 0,$$

so the given series *dominates* the divergent p-series $\displaystyle\sum_{k=2}^{\infty} \frac{1}{k^{1/2}}$ (divergent because $p = \frac{1}{2} < 1$). The direct comparison test tells us the given series must diverge.   ■

EXAMPLE 3   Applying the direct comparison test

Test the series $\displaystyle\sum_{k=1}^{\infty} \frac{1}{k!}$ for convergence.

Solution

We will compare the given series with a geometric series. Specifically, note that if $k \ge 2$, then $1/k! > 0$ and

$$k! = k(k-1)(k-2) \cdots 3 \cdot 2 \cdot 1 \ge \underbrace{2 \cdot 2 \cdot 2 \cdots 2 \cdot 2}_{k-1 \text{ terms}} \cdot 1 = 2^{k-1}$$

Therefore, we have $0 < \dfrac{1}{k!} \le \dfrac{1}{2^{k-1}}$, and because the given series is *dominated by* the convergent geometric series $\displaystyle\sum_{k=1}^{\infty} \frac{1}{2^{k-1}}$ (with $r = \frac{1}{2}$), it must also converge.   ■

LIMIT COMPARISON TESTS

It is not always easy or even possible to make a suitable direct comparison between two similar series. For example, we would expect the series $\Sigma 1/(2^k - 5)$ to converge because it is so much like the convergent geometric series $\Sigma 1/2^k$. To compare the series, we must first note that $\dfrac{1}{2^k - 5}$ is negative for $k = 1$ and $k = 2$ and positive for $k \geq 3$. Thus, if $k \geq 3$,

$$0 \leq \frac{1}{2^k} < \frac{1}{2^k - 5}$$

That is, $\Sigma 1/(2^k - 5)$ *dominates* the convergent series $\Sigma 1/2^k$, which means the comparison test cannot be used to determine the convergence of $\Sigma 1/(2^k - 5)$ by comparing with $\Sigma 1/2^k$. In such situations, the following test is often useful.

THEOREM 8.14 Limit comparison test

Suppose $a_k > 0$ and $b_k > 0$ for all sufficiently large k and that

$$\lim_{k \to \infty} \frac{a_k}{b_k} = L$$

where L is finite and positive ($0 < L < \infty$). Then

$$\Sigma a_k \text{ and } \Sigma b_k \text{ either both converge or both diverge.}$$

Proof The limit comparison test is proved by using the direct comparison test. Details of the proof are given in Appendix B. ❑

➡ **What This Says** We have the following procedure for testing the convergence of Σa_k.

Step 1. Find a series Σb_k whose convergence properties are known and whose general term b_k is "essentially the same" as a_k.

Step 2. Verify that $\lim\limits_{k \to \infty} \dfrac{a_k}{b_k}$ exists and is positive.

Step 3. Determine whether Σb_k converges or diverges. Then the limit comparison test tells us that Σa_k does the same.

EXAMPLE 4 Convergence using the limit comparison test

Test the series $\displaystyle\sum_{k=1}^{\infty} \frac{1}{2^k - 5}$ for convergence.

Solution

Because the given series has the same general appearance as the convergent geometric series $\Sigma 1/2^k$, compute the limit

$$\lim_{k \to \infty} \frac{\dfrac{1}{2^k - 5}}{\dfrac{1}{2^k}} = \lim_{k \to \infty} \frac{2^k}{2^k - 5} = 1$$

This limit is finite and positive, so the limit comparison test tells us that the given series will have the same convergence properties as $\Sigma 1/2^k$. Thus, the given series converges. ∎

EXAMPLE 5   Divergence using the limit comparison test

Test the series $\displaystyle\sum_{k=1}^{\infty} \frac{3k+2}{\sqrt{k}(3k-5)}$ for convergence.

Solution

For large values of k, the general term of the given series

$$a_k = \frac{3k+2}{\sqrt{k}(3k-5)}$$

seems to be similar to

$$b_k = \frac{3k}{\sqrt{k}(3k)} = \frac{1}{\sqrt{k}}$$

To apply the limit comparison test, we first compute the limit

$$\lim_{k\to\infty} \frac{a_k}{b_k} = \lim_{k\to\infty} \frac{\dfrac{3k+2}{\sqrt{k}(3k-5)}}{\dfrac{1}{\sqrt{k}}} = \lim_{k\to\infty} \frac{3k+2}{3k-5} = 1$$

Because the limit is finite and positive, it follows that the given series behaves like the series $\Sigma 1/\sqrt{k}$, which is a divergent p-series ($p = \frac{1}{2}$). We conclude that the given series diverges.   ∎

EXAMPLE 6   Applying the limit comparison test

Test the series $\displaystyle\sum_{k=1}^{\infty} \frac{7k+100}{e^{k/5}-70}$ for convergence.

Solution

For large k,

$$a_k = \frac{7k+100}{e^{k/5}-70} \quad \text{seems to behave like} \quad b_k = \frac{k}{e^{k/5}}$$

and indeed, we find that

$$\lim_{k\to\infty} \frac{\dfrac{7k+100}{e^{k/5}-70}}{\dfrac{k}{e^{k/5}}} = \lim_{k\to\infty} \frac{e^{k/5}(7k+100)}{k(e^{k/5}-70)} = 7$$

In Example 3, Section 8.3, we showed that the series $\Sigma k/e^{k/5}$ converges, and therefore the limit comparison test tells us that the given series also converges.   ∎

Occasionally, two series Σa_k and Σb_k appear to have similar convergence properties, but it turns out that

$$\lim_{k\to\infty} \frac{a_k}{b_k}$$

is either 0 or ∞, and the limit comparison test therefore does not apply. In such cases, it is often useful to have the following generalization of the limit comparison test.

THEOREM 8.15   The zero-infinity limit comparison test

Suppose $a_k > 0$ and $b_k > 0$ for all sufficiently large k.

$$\text{If } \lim_{k \to \infty} \frac{a_k}{b_k} = 0 \text{ and } \Sigma b_k \text{ converges, then the series } \Sigma a_k \text{ converges.}$$

$$\text{If } \lim_{k \to \infty} \frac{a_k}{b_k} = \infty \text{ and } \Sigma b_k \text{ diverges, then the series } \Sigma a_k \text{ diverges.}$$

Proof   The first part of the proof is outlined in Problem 61; the second part follows similarly.   ❏

EXAMPLE 7   Convergence of the q-log series

Show that the series $\displaystyle\sum_{k=1}^{\infty} \frac{\ln k}{k^q}$ converges if $q > 1$ and diverges if $q \leq 1$. We call this the **q-log** series.

Solution

We will carry out this proof in three parts:

Case I: $(q > 1)$
Let p be a number that satisfies $1 < p < q$, and let

$$a_k = \frac{\ln k}{k^q} \quad \text{and} \quad b_k = \frac{1}{k^p}$$

Then

$$\lim_{k \to \infty} \frac{a_k}{b_k} = \lim_{k \to \infty} \frac{\dfrac{\ln k}{k^q}}{\dfrac{1}{k^p}}$$

$$= \lim_{k \to \infty} \frac{\ln k}{k^{q-p}} \qquad \text{This is the indeterminate form } \infty/\infty \text{ because } q - p > 0.$$

$$= \lim_{k \to \infty} \frac{\dfrac{1}{k}}{(q-p)k^{q-p-1}} \qquad \text{l'Hôpital's rule}$$

$$= \lim_{k \to \infty} \frac{1}{(q-p)k^{q-p}} = 0 \qquad \text{Because } q - p > 0$$

Because $\Sigma 1/k^p$ converges (p-series with $p > 1$), the series converges by the zero-infinity limit comparison test.

Case II: $(q < 1)$
Now, let p satisfy $q < p < 1$. Then with a_k and b_k defined as in case I, we have

$$\lim_{k \to \infty} \frac{a_k}{b_k} = \lim_{k \to \infty} \frac{\ln k}{k^{q-p}} = \lim_{k \to \infty} \left[(\ln k)k^{p-q}\right] = \infty$$

Because $\displaystyle\sum_{k=1}^{\infty} b_k = \sum_{k=1}^{\infty} \frac{1}{k^p}$ diverges (we know $p < 1$), it follows from the zero-infinity comparison test that $\displaystyle\sum_{k=1}^{\infty} \frac{\ln k}{k^q}$ diverges when $q < 1$.

Case III: $(q = 1)$

Here, the series is $\displaystyle\sum_{k=1}^{\infty} \frac{\ln k}{k}$, which diverges by the integral test:

$$\int_1^{\infty} \frac{\ln x}{x}\, dx = \lim_{b \to \infty} \left[\frac{\ln^2 x}{2} \right]\Bigg|_1^b = \infty$$

$$\boxed{\text{Let } u = \ln x;\, du = \frac{1}{x}\, dx}$$

8.4 PROBLEM SET

Ⓐ *The most common series used for comparison are given in Problems 1 and 2. Tell when each converges and when it diverges.*

1. geometric series: $\displaystyle\sum_{k=0}^{\infty} r^k$ **2.** p-series: $\displaystyle\sum_{k=1}^{\infty} \frac{1}{k^p}$

Each series in Problems 3–12 can be compared to the geometric series or p-series given in Problems 1 and 2. State which, and then determine whether it converges or diverges.

3. $\displaystyle\sum_{k=1}^{\infty} \cos^k\left(\frac{\pi}{6}\right)$ **4.** $\displaystyle\sum_{k=0}^{\infty} 0.5^k$

5. $\displaystyle\sum_{k=0}^{\infty} 1.5^k$ **6.** $\displaystyle\sum_{k=0}^{\infty} 2^{k/2}$

7. $\displaystyle\sum_{k=1}^{\infty} \frac{1}{k}$ **8.** $\displaystyle\sum_{k=1}^{\infty} \frac{1}{k^{0.5}}$

9. $\displaystyle\sum_{k=1}^{\infty} \frac{1}{k^{3/2}}$ **10.** $\displaystyle\sum_{k=1}^{\infty} \sqrt{\frac{2}{k}}$

11. $\displaystyle\sum_{k=0}^{\infty} 1^k$ **12.** $\displaystyle\sum_{k=1}^{\infty} e^k$

Test the series in Problems 13–44 for convergence.

13. $\displaystyle\sum_{k=1}^{\infty} \frac{1}{k^2 + k}$ **14.** $\displaystyle\sum_{k=1}^{\infty} \frac{1}{k^2 + 3k + 2}$

15. $\displaystyle\sum_{k=1}^{\infty} \frac{1}{\sqrt{k}}$ **16.** $\displaystyle\sum_{k=1}^{\infty} \frac{1}{k\sqrt{k}}$

17. $\displaystyle\sum_{k=1}^{\infty} \frac{1}{\sqrt{2k + 3}}$ **18.** $\displaystyle\sum_{k=1}^{\infty} \frac{1}{\sqrt{k(k + 1)}}$

19. $\displaystyle\sum_{k=1}^{\infty} \frac{1}{\sqrt{k^3 + 2}}$ **20.** $\displaystyle\sum_{k=1}^{\infty} \frac{1}{\sqrt{k^2 + 1}}$

21. $\displaystyle\sum_{k=1}^{\infty} \frac{2k^2}{k^4 - 4}$ **22.** $\displaystyle\sum_{k=1}^{\infty} \frac{k + 1}{k^2 + 1}$

23. $\displaystyle\sum_{k=1}^{\infty} \frac{(k + 2)(k + 3)}{k^{7/2}}$ **24.** $\displaystyle\sum_{k=1}^{\infty} \frac{(k + 1)^3}{k^{9/2}}$

25. $\displaystyle\sum_{k=1}^{\infty} \frac{2k + 3}{k^2 + 3k + 2}$ **26.** $\displaystyle\sum_{k=1}^{\infty} \frac{3k^2 + 2}{k^2 + 3k + 2}$

27. $\displaystyle\sum_{k=1}^{\infty} \frac{k}{(k + 2)2^k}$ **28.** $\displaystyle\sum_{k=1}^{\infty} \frac{5}{4^k + 3}$

29. $\displaystyle\sum_{k=1}^{\infty} \frac{1}{k(k + 2)}$ **30.** $\displaystyle\sum_{k=1}^{\infty} \frac{1}{(k + 2)(k + 3)}$

31. $\displaystyle\sum_{k=1}^{\infty} \frac{1}{\sqrt{k}\, 2^k}$ **32.** $\displaystyle\sum_{k=1}^{\infty} \frac{1,000}{\sqrt{k}\, 3^k}$

33. $\displaystyle\sum_{k=1}^{\infty} \frac{|\sin(k!)|}{k^2}$ **34.** $\displaystyle\sum_{k=2}^{\infty} \frac{1}{\sqrt{k}\, \ln k}$

35. $\displaystyle\sum_{k=1}^{\infty} \frac{2k^3 + k + 1}{k^3 + k^2 + 1}$ **36.** $\displaystyle\sum_{k=1}^{\infty} \frac{6k^3 - k - 4}{k^3 - k^2 - 3}$

37. $\displaystyle\sum_{k=1}^{\infty} \frac{k}{4k^3 - 5}$ **38.** $\displaystyle\sum_{k=1}^{\infty} \frac{\ln k}{\sqrt{2k + 3}}$

39. $\displaystyle\sum_{k=1}^{\infty} \frac{k^2 + 1}{(k^2 + 2)k^2}$ **40.** $\displaystyle\sum_{k=1}^{\infty} \sin\frac{1}{k}$

41. $\displaystyle\sum_{k=1}^{\infty} \frac{6k^2 + 2k + 1}{k^{1.1}(4k^2 + k + 4)}$ **42.** $\displaystyle\sum_{k=1}^{\infty} \frac{6k^2 + 2k + 1}{k^{0.9}(4k^2 + k + 4)}$

43. $\displaystyle\sum_{k=1}^{\infty} \frac{\sqrt[6]{k}}{\sqrt[4]{k^3} + 2\sqrt[8]{k}}$ **44.** $\displaystyle\sum_{k=1}^{\infty} \frac{\sqrt{k}}{\sqrt[3]{k^3} + 1\sqrt[6]{k^5}}$

Ⓑ *Test the series given in Problems 45–52 for convergence.*

45. $\displaystyle\sum_{k=1}^{\infty} \frac{1}{k^3 + 4}$ **46.** $\displaystyle\sum_{k=2}^{\infty} \frac{\ln k}{k - 1}$

47. $\displaystyle\sum_{k=1}^{\infty} \frac{\ln(k + 1)}{(k + 1)^3}$ **48.** $\displaystyle\sum_{k=1}^{\infty} \frac{\ln k}{k^2}$

49. $\displaystyle\sum_{k=2}^{\infty} \frac{1}{(k + 3)(\ln k)^{1.1}}$ **50.** $\displaystyle\sum_{k=2}^{\infty} \frac{1}{(k + 3)(\ln k)^{0.9}}$

51. $\displaystyle\sum_{k=1}^{\infty} k^{(1-k)/k}$ **52.** $\displaystyle\sum_{k=1}^{\infty} k^{(1+k)/k}$

53. Show that the series

$$\sum_{k=1}^{\infty} \frac{k^2}{(k + 3)!} = \frac{1}{4!} + \frac{4}{5!} + \frac{9}{6!} + \cdots$$

converges by using the limit comparison test.

54. Show that the series

$$1 + \frac{1}{1 \cdot 3} + \frac{1}{1 \cdot 3 \cdot 5} + \frac{1}{1 \cdot 3 \cdot 5 \cdot 7} + \cdots + \frac{2^k k!}{(2k + 1)!} + \cdots$$

converges. *Hint:* Compare with the convergent series $\sum 1/k!$.

55. Use a comparison test to show that

$$\sum_{k=2}^{\infty} \frac{1}{(\ln k)^{\ln k}}$$

converges. *Hint*: Use the fact that $\ln k > e^2$ for sufficiently large k.

56. a. Let $\{a_n\}$ be a positive sequence such that

$$\lim_{k \to \infty} k^p a_k$$

exists. Use the limit comparison test to show that Σa_k converges if $p > 1$.

b. Show that Σe^{-k^2} converges. *Hint*: Show that $\lim_{k \to \infty} k^2 e^{-k^2}$ exists and use part **a**.

57. Let Σa_k be a series of positive terms and let $\{b_k\}$ be a sequence of positive numbers that converge to a positive number. Show that Σa_k converges if and only if $\Sigma a_k b_k$ converges. *Hint*: Use the limit comparison test.

58. Suppose $0 \le a_k \le A$ for some number A and $b_k \ge k^2$. Show that $\Sigma \dfrac{a_k}{b_k}$ converges.

59. Suppose $a_k > 0$ for all k and that Σa_k converges. Show that $\Sigma \dfrac{1}{a_k}$ diverges.

60. Counterexample Problem Suppose that $0 < a_k < 1$ for every k, and that Σa_k converges. Use a comparison test to show that Σa_k^2 converges. Find a counterexample where Σa_k^2 converges, but Σa_k diverges.

61. Show that if $a_k > 0$, $b_k > 0$, and

$$\lim_{k \to \infty} \frac{a_k}{b_k} = 0$$

then Σa_k converges whenever Σb_k converges. *Hint*: Show that there is an integer N such that $a_k < b_k$ if $k > N$. Then use a comparison test.

62. Show that $\displaystyle\sum_{k=2}^{\infty} \frac{1}{k(\ln k)^q}$ converges if and only if $q > 1$.

8.5 The Ratio Test and the Root Test

IN THIS SECTION ratio test, root test

RATIO TEST

Intuitively, a series of positive terms Σa_k converges if and only if the sequence $\{a_k\}$ decreases rapidly toward 0. One way to measure the rate at which the sequence $\{a_k\}$ is decreasing is to examine the ratio a_{k+1}/a_k as k grows large. This approach leads to the following result.

THEOREM 8.16   The ratio test

Given the series Σa_k with $a_k > 0$, suppose that

$$\lim_{k \to \infty} \frac{a_{k+1}}{a_k} = L$$

The **ratio test** states the following:

If $L < 1$, then Σa_k converges.

If $L > 1$ or if L is infinite, then Σa_k diverges.

If $L = 1$, the test is inconclusive.

Proof In a sense, the ratio test is a limit comparison test in which Σa_k is compared to itself. We will use the direct comparison test to show that Σa_k converges if $L < 1$. Choose R such that $0 < L < R < 1$. Then there exists some $N > 0$ such that

$$\frac{a_{k+1}}{a_k} < R \quad \text{for all } k > N; \qquad \text{\small Since the ratios } a_{k+1}/a_k \text{\small{ are eventually very close to } } L$$

Therefore,

$$a_{N+1} < a_N R$$

$$a_{N+2} < a_{N+1} R < a_N R^2$$

$$a_{N+3} < a_{N+2} R < a_{N+1} R^2 < a_N R^3$$

$$\vdots$$

The geometric series

$$\sum_{k=1}^{\infty} a_N R^k = a_N R + a_N R^2 + \cdots + a_N R^n + \cdots$$

converges because $0 < R < 1$, which means the "smaller" series

$$\sum_{k=1}^{\infty} a_{N+k} = a_{N+1} + a_{N+2} + \cdots + a_{N+n} + \cdots$$

also converges by the direct comparison test. Thus, Σa_k converges, because we can discard a finite number of terms ($k \le N$).

The proof of the second part is similar, except now we choose R such that

$$\lim_{k \to \infty} \frac{a_{k+1}}{a_k} = L > R > 1$$

and show there exists some $M > 0$ so that $a_{M+k} > a_M R^k$.

To prove that the ratio test is inconclusive if $L = 1$, it is enough to note that the harmonic series

$$\sum_{k=1}^{\infty} \frac{1}{k} \quad \text{diverges} \quad \text{with} \quad \lim_{k \to \infty} \frac{a_{k+1}}{a_k} = \lim_{k \to \infty} \frac{\dfrac{1}{k+1}}{\dfrac{1}{k}} = 1$$

while the p-series

$$\sum_{k=1}^{\infty} \frac{1}{k^2} \quad \text{converges} \quad \text{with} \quad \lim_{k \to \infty} \frac{a_{k+1}}{a_k} = \lim_{k \to \infty} \frac{\dfrac{1}{(k+1)^2}}{\dfrac{1}{k^2}} = 1 \qquad \square$$

EXAMPLE 1   Convergence using the ratio test

WARNING   You will find the ratio test most useful with series involving factorials or exponentials.

Test the series $\displaystyle\sum_{k=1}^{\infty} \frac{2^k}{k!}$ for convergence.

Solution

Let $a_k = \dfrac{2^k}{k!}$ and note that

$$L = \lim_{k \to \infty} \frac{a_{k+1}}{a_k} = \lim_{k \to \infty} \frac{\dfrac{2^{k+1}}{(k+1)!}}{\dfrac{2^k}{k!}} = \lim_{k \to \infty} \frac{k! 2^{k+1}}{(k+1)! 2^k} = \lim_{k \to \infty} \frac{2}{k+1} = 0$$

Thus $L < 1$, and the ratio test tells us that the given series converges.   ∎

EXAMPLE 2   Divergence using the ratio test

Test the series $\displaystyle\sum_{k=1}^{\infty} \frac{k^k}{k!}$ for convergence.

Solution

Let $a_k = \dfrac{k^k}{k!}$ and note that

$$L = \lim_{k \to \infty} \frac{a_{k+1}}{a_k} = \lim_{k \to \infty} \frac{\dfrac{(k+1)^{k+1}}{(k+1)!}}{\dfrac{k^k}{k!}} = \lim_{k \to \infty} \frac{k!(k+1)^{k+1}}{k^k(k+1)!}$$

$$= \lim_{k \to \infty} \frac{(k+1)^k}{k^k} = \lim_{k \to \infty} \left(1 + \frac{1}{k}\right)^k = e > 1$$

Because $L > 1$, the given series diverges.   ∎

TECHNOLOGY NOTE

It is instructive to compare and contrast two different ways you can use technology to help you with problems such as Example 2. First, as you have seen, you can use a calculator or a computer to calculate the partial sums directly. This table is shown below at the left.

A second procedure is to use the ratio test for Example 2. In this case, we are interested in

$$\lim_{k\to\infty} \frac{a_{k+1}}{a_k} = \lim_{k\to\infty} \frac{\dfrac{(k+1)^{k+1}}{(k+1)!}}{\dfrac{k^k}{k!}} = \lim_{k\to\infty} \left(1 + \frac{1}{k}\right)^k$$

We can look at terms of the sequence $a_k = \left(1 + \dfrac{1}{k}\right)^k$ to see whether this limit is greater than, less than, or equal to 1. This is shown below at the right.

By table:

$$\sum_{k=1}^{\infty} \frac{k^k}{k!}$$

N	F(1)+...+F(N)
1	1
2	3
3	7.5
4	18.16667
5	44.20833
6	109.0083
7	272.4097
8	688.5113
9	1756.138
10	4511.87
11	11659.53
12	30273.46
13	78912.3
14	206375.3
15	541239.9

By graph:

$$\lim_{k\to\infty} \left(1 + \frac{1}{k}\right)^k$$

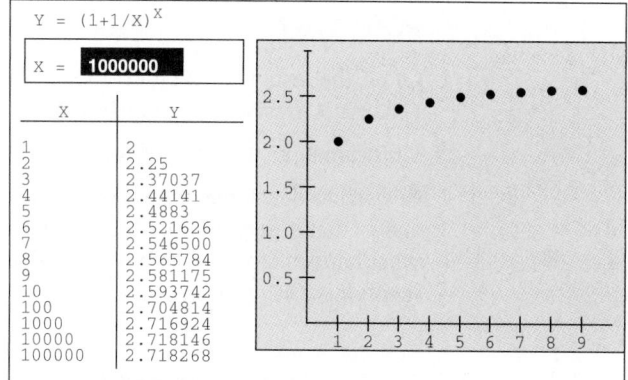

The partial sums seem to diverge.   We see that the ratio test gives a limit greater than 1.

Finally, you might test this using a calculator to verify that it diverges.

EXAMPLE 3   Ratio test fails

Test the series $\displaystyle\sum_{k=2}^{\infty} \frac{1}{2k-3}$ for convergence.

Solution

Let $a_k = \dfrac{1}{2k-3}$ and find

$$L = \lim_{k\to\infty} \frac{\dfrac{1}{2(k+1)-3}}{\dfrac{1}{2k-3}} = \lim_{k\to\infty} \frac{2k-3}{2k-1} = 1$$

The ratio test is inconclusive. We can use the integral test or the limit comparison test to determine convergence. Note that

$$\sum_{k=2}^{\infty} \frac{1}{2k-3} \quad \text{is similar to the known divergent series} \quad \sum_{k=2}^{\infty} \frac{1}{2k}$$

so we conclude the given series is divergent.   ∎

EXAMPLE 4   Convergence of a series of power functions

Find all numbers $x > 0$ for which the series

$$\sum_{k=1}^{\infty} k^3 x^k = x + 2^3 x^2 + 3^3 x^3 + \cdots$$

converges. This is called a *power series*, and it will be discussed in more detail in Sections 8.7 and 8.8.

Solution

Viewing x as fixed (that is, as a constant), we apply the ratio test:

$$L = \lim_{k \to \infty} \frac{(k+1)^3 x^{k+1}}{k^3 x^k} = \lim_{k \to \infty} \left(\frac{k+1}{k}\right)^3 x = x$$

Thus, the series converges if $L = x < 1$ and diverges if $x > 1$. When $x = 1$, the series becomes $\sum_{k=1}^{\infty} k^3$, which diverges by the divergence test.   ■

ROOT TEST

Of all the tests we have developed, the divergence test is perhaps the easiest to apply, because it involves simply computing $\lim_{k \to \infty} a_k$ and observing whether that limit is zero. Unfortunately, most "interesting" series have $\lim_{k \to \infty} a_k = 0$, so the divergence test cannot be used to determine whether they converge or diverge. However, the following result shows that it may be possible to say more about the convergence of Σa_k by examining what happens to $\sqrt[k]{a_k}$ as $k \to \infty$. This test will prove particularly useful with a series involving a kth power.

THEOREM 8.17   The root test

Given the series Σa_k with $a_k \geq 0$, suppose that $\lim_{k \to \infty} \sqrt[k]{a_k} = L$. The **root test** states the following:

> If $L < 1$, then $\sum a_k$ converges.
> If $L > 1$ or if L is infinite, then $\sum a_k$ diverges.
> If $L = 1$, the root test is inconclusive.

Proof   The proof of this theorem is similar to that of the ratio test and is outlined in Problem 57.   ❑

EXAMPLE 5   Convergence with the root test

Test the series $\sum_{k=2}^{\infty} \frac{1}{(\ln k)^k}$ for convergence.

Solution

Let $a_k = \frac{1}{(\ln k)^k}$ and note that

$$L = \lim_{k \to \infty} \sqrt[k]{a_k} = \lim_{k \to \infty} \sqrt[k]{(\ln k)^{-k}} = \lim_{k \to \infty} \frac{1}{\ln k} = 0$$

Because $L < 1$, the root test tells us that the given series converges.   ■

EXAMPLE 6   Divergence with the root test

Test the series $\displaystyle\sum_{k=1}^{\infty} \left(1 + \frac{1}{k}\right)^{k^2}$ for convergence.

Solution

$$L = \lim_{k \to \infty} \left[\left(1 + \frac{1}{k}\right)^{k^2}\right]^{1/k} \qquad \text{Root test}$$

$$= \lim_{k \to \infty} \left(1 + \frac{1}{k}\right)^{k}$$

$$= e > 1$$

Since $L > 1$, the series diverges.   ■

We have seen that the ratio test is especially useful for series Σa_k for which the general term a_k involves factorials or powers, and the root test applies naturally if a_k involves a power of k. However, both the ratio test and the root test fail with certain very simple series such as the p-series $\Sigma \frac{1}{k^p}$ since

$$\lim_{k \to \infty} \frac{\dfrac{1}{(k+1)^p}}{\dfrac{1}{k^p}} = \lim_{k \to \infty} \left(\frac{k}{k+1}\right)^p = 1^p = 1 \qquad \text{Inconclusive ratio test}$$

$$\lim_{k \to \infty} \sqrt[k]{\frac{1}{k^p}} = \left[\lim_{k \to \infty} k^{1/k}\right]^{-p} = 1^{-p} = 1 \qquad \begin{array}{l}\text{Inconclusive root test}\\ \text{where l'Hôpital's rule}\\ \text{is used to evaluate the limit.}\\ \text{See Example 11 of Section 4.5.}\end{array}$$

EXAMPLE 7   Testing for convergence

Test the following series for convergence:

$$\sum_{k=0}^{\infty} \frac{k!}{1 \cdot 4 \cdot 7 \cdots (3k+1)} = 1 + \frac{1!}{1 \cdot 4} + \frac{2!}{1 \cdot 4 \cdot 7} + \frac{3!}{1 \cdot 4 \cdot 7 \cdot 10} + \cdots$$

Solution

Let $a_k = \dfrac{k!}{1 \cdot 4 \cdot 7 \cdots (3k+1)}$. Because a_k involves $k!$, we try the ratio test.

$$\frac{a_{k+1}}{a_k} = \frac{\dfrac{(k+1)!}{1 \cdot 4 \cdot 7 \cdots [3(k+1)+1]}}{\dfrac{k!}{1 \cdot 4 \cdot 7 \cdots (3k+1)}} = \frac{(k+1)! \cdot [1 \cdot 4 \cdot 7 \cdots (3k+1)]}{k! \cdot [1 \cdot 4 \cdot 7 \cdots (3k+4)]}$$

$$= \frac{k+1}{3k+4}$$

Thus,

$$L = \lim_{k \to \infty} \frac{a_{k+1}}{a_k} = \lim_{k \to \infty} \frac{k+1}{3k+4} = \frac{1}{3}$$

Because $L < 1$, the given series converges.   ■

EXAMPLE 8   Testing for convergence

Test the series $\displaystyle\sum_{k=1}^{\infty} \frac{k!}{k^k}$ for convergence.

Solution

The general term $a_k = \dfrac{k!}{k^k}$ involves a kth power, which suggests using the root test, but the presence of the factorial $k!$ makes using the ratio test much more reasonable.

$$L = \lim_{k\to\infty} \frac{\dfrac{(k+1)!}{(k+1)^{k+1}}}{\dfrac{k!}{k^k}} = \lim_{k\to\infty} \frac{(k+1)!\,k^k}{k!(k+1)^{k+1}} = \lim_{k\to\infty} \frac{(k+1)k^k}{(k+1)^{k+1}}$$

$$= \lim_{k\to\infty} \left(\frac{k}{k+1}\right)^k = \lim_{k\to\infty} \frac{1}{\left(1+\dfrac{1}{k}\right)^k} = \frac{1}{e} < 1$$

Since $L < 1$, the series converges. ∎

8.5 PROBLEM SET

A 1. **WHAT DOES THIS SAY?** Describe the ratio test.

2. **WHAT DOES THIS SAY?** Describe the root test.

Use either the ratio test or the root test to determine the convergence of the series given in Problems 3–26.

3. $\displaystyle\sum_{k=1}^{\infty} \frac{1}{k!}$

4. $\displaystyle\sum_{k=1}^{\infty} \frac{k!}{2^k}$

5. $\displaystyle\sum_{k=1}^{\infty} \frac{k!}{2^{3k}}$

6. $\displaystyle\sum_{k=1}^{\infty} \frac{3^k}{k!}$

7. $\displaystyle\sum_{k=1}^{\infty} \frac{k}{2^k}$

8. $\displaystyle\sum_{k=1}^{\infty} \frac{2^k}{k^2}$

9. $\displaystyle\sum_{k=1}^{\infty} \frac{k^{100}}{e^k}$

10. $\displaystyle\sum_{k=1}^{\infty} ke^{-k}$

11. $\displaystyle\sum_{k=1}^{\infty} k\left(\frac{4}{3}\right)^k$

12. $\displaystyle\sum_{k=1}^{\infty} k\left(\frac{3}{4}\right)^k$

13. $\displaystyle\sum_{k=1}^{\infty} \left(\frac{2}{k}\right)^k$

14. $\displaystyle\sum_{k=1}^{\infty} \frac{k^{10}2^k}{k!}$

15. $\displaystyle\sum_{k=1}^{\infty} \frac{k^5}{10^k}$

16. $\displaystyle\sum_{k=1}^{\infty} \frac{3^k}{k^2}$

17. $\displaystyle\sum_{k=1}^{\infty} \left(\frac{k}{3k+1}\right)^k$

18. $\displaystyle\sum_{k=1}^{\infty} \frac{3k+1}{2^k}$

19. $\displaystyle\sum_{k=1}^{\infty} \frac{k!}{(k+2)^4}$

20. $\displaystyle\sum_{k=1}^{\infty} \frac{k^5+100}{k!}$

21. $\displaystyle\sum_{k=1}^{\infty} \frac{(k!)^2}{(2k)!}$

22. $\displaystyle\sum_{k=1}^{\infty} \frac{(k!)^2}{[(2k)!]^2}$

23. $\displaystyle\sum_{k=1}^{\infty} k^2 2^{-k}$

24. $\displaystyle\sum_{k=1}^{\infty} k^4 3^{-k}$

25. $\displaystyle\sum_{k=1}^{\infty} \left(\frac{k-2}{k}\right)^{k^2}$

26. $\displaystyle\sum_{k=1}^{\infty} \left(\frac{k}{2k+1}\right)^k$

Test the series in Problems 27–44 for convergence. Justify your answers (that is, state explicitly which test you are using).

27. $\displaystyle\sum_{k=1}^{\infty} \frac{1,000}{k}$

28. $\displaystyle\sum_{k=1}^{\infty} \frac{5,000}{k\sqrt{k}}$

29. $\displaystyle\sum_{k=1}^{\infty} \frac{5k+2}{k2^k}$

30. $\displaystyle\sum_{k=1}^{\infty} \frac{(k!)^2}{k^k}$

31. $\displaystyle\sum_{k=1}^{\infty} \frac{\sqrt{k!}}{2^k}$

32. $\displaystyle\sum_{k=1}^{\infty} \frac{3k+5}{k3^k}$

33. $\displaystyle\sum_{k=1}^{\infty} \frac{2^k k!}{k^k}$

34. $\displaystyle\sum_{k=1}^{\infty} \frac{2^{2k} k!}{k^k}$

35. $\displaystyle\sum_{k=1}^{\infty} \frac{\sqrt{k+1}}{k^{k+0.5}}$

36. $\displaystyle\sum_{k=1}^{\infty} \frac{1}{k^k}$

37. $\displaystyle\sum_{k=1}^{\infty} \frac{k!}{(k+1)!}$

38. $\displaystyle\sum_{k=1}^{\infty} \frac{2^{1,000k}}{k^{k/2}}$

39. $\displaystyle\sum_{k=1}^{\infty} \left(1+\frac{1}{k}\right)^{-k^2}$

40. $\displaystyle\sum_{k=1}^{\infty} \left(\frac{k+2}{k}\right)^{-k^2}$

41. $\displaystyle\sum_{k=1}^{\infty} \left|\frac{\cos k}{2^k}\right|$

42. $\displaystyle\sum_{k=1}^{\infty} \left|\frac{\sin k}{3^k}\right|$

43. $\displaystyle\sum_{k=2}^{\infty} \left(\frac{\ln k}{k}\right)^k$

44. $\displaystyle\sum_{k=2}^{\infty} \frac{1}{(\ln k)^k}$

B *In Problems 45–52, assume $x > 0$ and find all x for which the given series converges.*

45. $\displaystyle\sum_{k=1}^{\infty} k^2 x^k$

46. $\displaystyle\sum_{k=1}^{\infty} kx^k$

47. $\displaystyle\sum_{k=1}^{\infty} \frac{(x+0.5)^k}{k\sqrt{k}}$

48. $\displaystyle\sum_{k=1}^{\infty} \frac{(3x-0.4)^k}{k^2}$

49. $\displaystyle\sum_{k=1}^{\infty} \frac{x^k}{k!}$

50. $\displaystyle\sum_{k=1}^{\infty} \frac{x^{2k}}{k}$

51. $\displaystyle\sum_{k=1}^{\infty}(ax)^k$ for $a > 0$ **52.** $\displaystyle\sum_{k=1}^{\infty}kx^{2k}$

53. Use the root test to show that $\Sigma k^p e^{-k}$ converges for any fixed positive real number p. What does this imply about the following improper integral?

$$\int_1^{\infty} x^p e^{-x}\, dx$$

54. Consider the series $\displaystyle\sum_{k=1}^{\infty}2^{-k+(-1)^k}$. What can you conclude about the convergence of this series if you use each of the following?

   a. the ratio test   **b.** the root test

55. Let $\{a_k\}$ be a sequence of positive numbers and suppose that $\displaystyle\lim_{k\to\infty}\frac{a_{k+1}}{a_k} = L$, where $0 < L < 1$.

   a. Show that $\displaystyle\lim_{k\to\infty}a_k = 0$. *Hint*: Note that Σa_k converges.

   b. Show that $\displaystyle\lim_{k\to\infty}\frac{x^k}{k!} = 0$ for any $x > 0$.

56. Consider the series

$$1 + \frac{1}{2} + \frac{1}{2} + \frac{1}{4} + \frac{1}{4} + \frac{1}{8} + \frac{1}{8} + \frac{1}{16} + \cdots$$

   a. Show that the ratio test fails.

   b. What is the result of applying the root test?

57. Prove the root test by completing the steps in the following outline:

   a. Let $\displaystyle\lim_{n\to\infty}\sqrt[n]{a_n} = R$. If $R < 1$, choose x so $R < x < 1$. Explain why there is an N such that

$$0 \le \sqrt[n]{a_n} \le x$$

   for all $n \ge N$. Then use the direct comparison test to show that Σa_n converges.

   b. If $R > 1$, explain why $a_n > 1$ for all but a finite number of n. Use the divergence test to show Σa_n diverges.

   c. Find two series Σa_n and Σb_n with $R = 1$, so that Σa_n converges but Σb_n diverges.

58. **Exploration Problem**   Recall from Problem 48, Section 8.1, that the Fibonacci sequence $\{a_n\}$ is

$$1, 1, 2, 3, 5, 8, 13, 21, \ldots$$

where $a_1 = 1$, $a_2 = 1$, and the rest of the terms are defined recursively by the formula $a_{n+1} = a_n + a_{n-1}$ for $n = 2, 3, \ldots$. Determine whether the series of reciprocal Fibonacci numbers

$$\sum_{k=1}^{\infty}\frac{1}{a_k} = 1 + 1 + \frac{1}{2} + \frac{1}{3} + \frac{1}{5} + \cdots$$

converges or diverges.

8.6   Alternating Series; Absolute and Conditional Convergence

IN THIS SECTION   alternating series test, error estimates for alternating series, absolute and conditional convergence, summary of convergence tests for series, rearrangement of terms in an absolutely convergent series

There are two classes of series for which the successive terms alternate in sign, and each of these series is appropriately called an **alternating series**:

$$\text{odd-indexed terms are negative:} \quad \sum_{k=1}^{\infty}(-1)^k a_k = -a_1 + a_2 - a_3 + \cdots$$

$$\text{even-indexed terms are negative:} \quad \sum_{k=1}^{\infty}(-1)^{k+1} a_k = a_1 - a_2 + a_3 - \cdots$$

where in both cases $a_k > 0$.

ALTERNATING SERIES TEST

In general, just knowing that $\displaystyle\lim_{k\to\infty}a_k = 0$ tells us very little about the convergence properties of the series Σa_k, but it turns out that an alternating series must converge if the absolute value of its terms decreases monotonically toward zero. This result, first established by Leibniz in the 17th century, may be stated as shown in the following theorem.

THEOREM 8.18 Alternating series test

An alternating series

$$\sum_{k=1}^{\infty}(-1)^k a_k \quad \text{or} \quad \sum_{k=1}^{\infty}(-1)^{k+1} a_k \qquad \text{where } a_k > 0 \text{ for all } k$$

converges if both of the following two conditions are satisfied:

1. $\displaystyle\lim_{k\to\infty} a_k = 0$
2. $\{a_k\}$ is a decreasing sequence; that is, $a_{k+1} \le a_k$ for all k.

Proof We will show that when an alternating series of the form

$$\sum_{k=1}^{\infty}(-1)^{k+1} a_k$$

satisfies the two required properties, it converges. The steps for the other type of alternating series are similar. For this proof we are given that

$$\lim_{k\to\infty} a_k = 0 \quad \text{and} \quad a_{k+1} \le a_k \quad \text{for all } k$$

We need to prove that the sequence of partial sums $\{S_n\}$ converges, where

$$S_n = \sum_{k=1}^{n}(-1)^{k+1} a_k = a_1 - a_2 + a_3 - a_4 + \cdots + (-1)^{n+1} a_n$$

Our strategy will be to show first that the sequence of *even*-indexed partial sums $\{S_{2n}\}$ is *increasing* and converges to a certain limit L. Then we will show that the sequence of odd-indexed partial sums $\{S_{2n-1}\}$ also converges to L.

To understand why we would think to break up S_n into even- and odd-indexed partial sums, consider Figure 8.18. Start at the origin. Because $a_1 > 0$, S_1 will be somewhere to the right of 0 as shown in Figure 8.18a. We know that $a_2 \le a_1$ (decreasing sequence) so S_2 is to the left of S_1 but to the right of 0, as shown in Figure 8.18b. As you continue this process you can see that the partial sums oscillate back and forth. Because $a_n \to 0$, the successive steps are getting smaller and smaller, as shown in Figure 8.18c.

Note that the even partial sums of the alternating series satisfy

$$S_2 = a_1 - a_2$$
$$S_4 = (a_1 - a_2) + (a_3 - a_4)$$
$$\vdots$$
$$S_{2n} = (a_1 - a_2) + (a_3 - a_4) + \cdots + (a_{2n-1} - a_{2n})$$

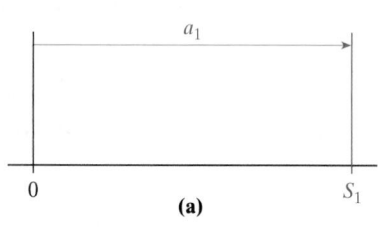

(a)

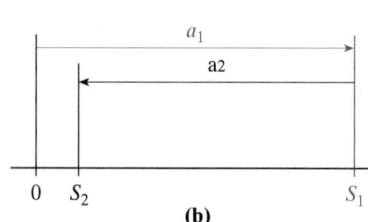

(b)

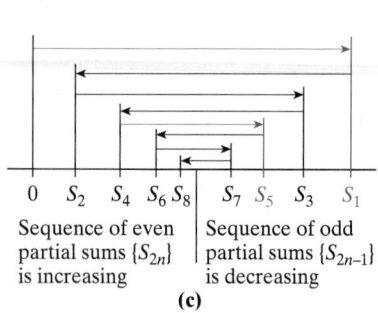

Sequence of even partial sums $\{S_{2n}\}$ is increasing | Sequence of odd partial sums $\{S_{2n-1}\}$ is decreasing

(c)

Figure 8.18 Alternating series test

Because $\{a_k\}$ is a decreasing sequence, each of the quantities in parentheses $(a_{2j-1} - a_{2j})$ is nonnegative, and it follows that $\{S_{2n}\}$ is an increasing sequence:

$$S_2 \le S_4 \le S_6 \le \cdots$$

Moreover, because

$$S_2 = a_1 - a_2 \le a_1$$
$$S_4 = a_1 - (a_2 - a_3) - a_4 \le a_1$$
$$\vdots$$
$$S_{2n} = a_1 - (a_2 - a_3) - (a_4 - a_5) - \cdots - (a_{2n-2} - a_{2n-1}) - a_{2n} \le a_1$$

the sequence of even partial sums $\{S_{2n}\}$ is bounded above by a_1, and because it is also an increasing sequence, the BMCT tells us that this sequence must converge, say, to L; that is,

$$\lim_{n\to\infty} S_{2n} = L$$

Next, consider $\{S_{2n-1}\}$, the sequence of odd partial sums. Because $S_{2n} - S_{2n-1} = a_{2n}$ and $\lim_{n\to\infty} a_n = 0$, it follows that $S_{2n-1} = S_{2n} - a_{2n}$ and

$$\lim_{n\to\infty} S_{2n-1} = \lim_{n\to\infty} S_{2n} - \lim_{n\to\infty} a_{2n} = L - 0 = L$$

Since the sequence of even partial sums and the sequence of odd partial sums both converge to L, it follows that $\{S_n\}$ converges to L, and the alternating series must converge (in fact, to L). ❑

REMARK: When you are testing the alternating series $\Sigma(-1)^{k+1}a_k$ for convergence, it is wise to begin by computing $\lim_{k\to\infty} a_k$. If $\lim_{k\to\infty} a_k \neq 0$, you know immediately that the series diverges (by the divergence test), and no further computation is necessary. However, if this limit is 0, you can show that the alternating series converges by verifying that $\{a_k\}$ is a decreasing sequence.

EXAMPLE 1 Convergence using the alternating series test

Test the series $\displaystyle\sum_{k=1}^{\infty} \frac{(-1)^k}{k}$ for convergence. This series is called the **alternating harmonic series.**

Solution

The series can be expressed as $\Sigma(-1)^k a_k$, where $a_k = \dfrac{1}{k}$. We have $\lim_{k\to\infty} \dfrac{1}{k} = 0$ and because

$$\frac{1}{k+1} < \frac{1}{k}$$

for all $k > 0$, the sequence $\{a_k\}$ is decreasing. Thus, the alternating series test tells us that the given series must converge. ∎

EXAMPLE 2 Using l'Hôpital's rule with the alternating series test

Test the series $\displaystyle\sum_{k=1}^{\infty} \frac{(-1)^{k+1}\ln k}{k}$ for convergence.

Solution

Express the series in the form $\Sigma(-1)^{k+1}a_k$, where $a_k = \dfrac{\ln k}{k}$ (note that $a_k > 0$ for $k > 1$). The graph of $y = (\ln x)/x$ is shown in Figure 8.19. By applying l'Hôpital's rule, we find that

$$\lim_{x\to\infty} \frac{\ln x}{x} = \lim_{x\to\infty} \frac{\frac{1}{x}}{1} = 0$$

It remains to show that the sequence $\{a_k\}$ is decreasing. We can do this by setting $f(x) = \dfrac{\ln x}{x}$ and noting that the derivative

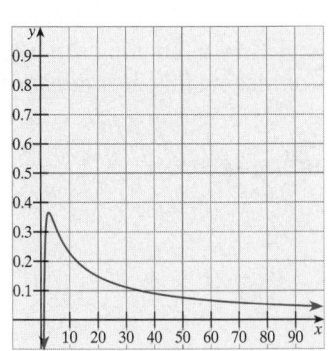

Figure 8.19 Graph of $y = \dfrac{\ln x}{x}$

$$f'(x) = \frac{1 - \ln x}{x^2}$$

satisfies $f'(x) < 0$ for all $x > e$. Thus, the sequence $\{a_k\}$ is (eventually) decreasing for all $k > 3 > e$. The conditions of the alternating series test are satisfied, and the given alternating series must converge. ∎

EXAMPLE 3   Divergence of an alternating series

Test the series $\displaystyle\sum_{k=1}^{\infty}(-1)^{k+1}e^{1/k}$ for convergence.

Solution

Since

$$\lim_{k\to\infty} e^{1/k} = \exp\left(\lim_{k\to\infty}\frac{1}{k}\right) = e^0 = 1 \neq 0$$

the series diverges by the divergence test.   ■

Alternating p-Series

> The series $\displaystyle\sum_{k=1}^{\infty}\frac{(-1)^{k+1}}{k^p}$ is called the **alternating p-series**.

The following example shows that the alternating p-series converges for all $p > 0$.

EXAMPLE 4   Alternating p-series

Prove that the alternating p-series $\displaystyle\sum_{k=1}^{\infty}\frac{(-1)^{k+1}}{k^p}$ converges for $p > 0$.

Solution

If $a_k = \dfrac{1}{k^p}$, then $\displaystyle\lim_{k\to\infty} a_k = 0$ for $p > 0$. To show that the sequence $\{a_k\}$ is decreasing, we note that

$$\frac{a_{k+1}}{a_k} = \frac{\dfrac{1}{(k+1)^p}}{\dfrac{1}{k^p}} = \frac{k^p}{(k+1)^p} < 1$$

so $a_k > a_{k+1}$. Thus, the alternating p-series converges for all $p > 0$.   ■

ERROR ESTIMATES FOR ALTERNATING SERIES

For any convergent series with sum L, the nth partial sum is an approximation to L that we expect to improve as n increases. In general, it is difficult to know how large an n to pick in order to ensure that the approximation will have a desired degree of accuracy. However, if the series in question satisfies the conditions of the alternating series test, the following theorem provides a convenient criterion for making this determination.

THEOREM 8.19   The error estimate for an alternating series

Suppose an alternating series

$$\sum_{k=1}^{\infty}(-1)^k a_k \quad \text{or} \quad \sum_{k=1}^{\infty}(-1)^{k+1}a_k$$

satisfies the conditions of the alternating series test; namely,

$$\lim_{k\to\infty} a_k = 0 \quad \text{and} \quad \{a_k\} \text{ is a decreasing sequence } (a_{k+1} \le a_k)$$

If the series has sum S, then

$$|S - S_n| \le a_{n+1}$$

where S_n is the nth partial sum of the series.

Proof   We will prove the result for the second form of the alternating series and leave the first form for the reader. That is, let

$$S = \sum_{k=1}^{\infty}(-1)^{k+1}a_k \quad \text{and} \quad S_n = \sum_{k=1}^{n}(-1)^{k+1}a_k$$

Begin with $S - S_n$:

$$S - S_n = \sum_{k=1}^{\infty}(-1)^{k+1}a_k - \sum_{k=1}^{n}(-1)^{k+1}a_k$$

$$= \sum_{k=n+1}^{\infty}(-1)^{k+1}a_k$$

$$= (-1)^{n+2}a_{n+1} + (-1)^{n+3}a_{n+2} + (-1)^{n+4}a_{n+3} + \cdots$$

$$= (-1)^n(-1)^2a_{n+1} + (-1)^n(-1)^3a_{n+2} + (-1)^n(-1)^4a_{n+3} + \cdots$$

$$= (-1)^n[a_{n+1} - a_{n+2} + a_{n+3} - a_{n+4} + \cdots]$$

$$= (-1)^n[a_{n+1} - (a_{n+2} - a_{n+3}) - (a_{n+4} - a_{n+5}) - \cdots]$$

Because the sequence $\{a_n\}$ is decreasing, we have $a_k - a_{k+1} \geq 0$ for all k, and it follows that

$$|S - S_n| = |a_{n+1} - (a_{n+2} - a_{n+3}) - (a_{n+4} - a_{n+5}) - \cdots| \leq a_{n+1}$$

since every quantity in parentheses is positive.   ❏

→ **What This Says**   If an alternating series satisfies the conditions of the alternating series test, you can approximate the sum of the series by using the nth partial sum (S_n), and your error will have an absolute value no greater than the first term left off (namely, a_{n+1}).

EXAMPLE 5   Error estimate for an alternating series

Consider the convergent alternating series $\displaystyle\sum_{k=1}^{\infty}\frac{(-1)^{k+1}}{k^4}$.

a. Estimate the sum of the series by taking the sum of the first four terms. How accurate is this estimate?

b. How many terms of the series are necessary to estimate its sum with three-decimal-place accuracy? What is this estimate?

Solution

a. Let $a_k = \dfrac{1}{k^4}$ and let S denote the actual sum of the series. The error estimate tells us that

$$|S - S_4| = a_5$$

where S_4 is the sum of the first four terms of the series. Using a calculator, we find

$$S_4 = \frac{1}{1^4} - \frac{1}{2^4} + \frac{1}{3^4} - \frac{1}{4^4} \approx 0.9459394$$

and $a_5 = \dfrac{1}{5^4} = 0.0016$. Thus, if we estimate S by $S_4 \approx 0.9459$, we incur an error of about 0.0016, which means that

$$|S - S_4| \leq 0.0016$$

$$0.9459394 - 0.0016 \leq S \leq 0.9459394 + 0.0016$$

$$0.9443394 \leq S \leq 0.9475394$$

b. Because we want to approximate S by a partial sum S_n with three-decimal-place accuracy, we can allow an error of no more than 0.0005. According to Theorem 8.19, we want to find an index n such that $a_{n+1} \leq 0.0005$; that is,

$$\frac{1}{(n+1)^4} \leq 0.0005$$

$$\frac{1}{0.0005} \leq (n+1)^4$$

$$\sqrt[4]{2,000} \leq n+1$$

$$6.687403 - 1 \leq n$$

Thus, $n \geq 5.687403$, so we need at least 6 terms to achieve the required accuracy. We find that

$$S_6 = \frac{1}{1^4} - \frac{1}{2^4} + \frac{1}{3^4} - \frac{1}{4^4} + \frac{1}{5^4} - \frac{1}{6^4} \approx 0.94677$$

The first term left off (namely $\frac{1}{7^4} \approx 0.00042$) is positive, so

$$0.94677 < S < 0.94677 + 0.00042$$

$$0.94677 < S < 0.94719$$

Both bounds round to 0.947, so $S \approx 0.947$, with three-decimal-place accuracy. ∎

ABSOLUTE AND CONDITIONAL CONVERGENCE

The convergence tests we have developed cannot be applied to a series that has mixed terms or does not strictly alternate. In such cases, it is often useful to apply the following result.

THEOREM 8.20   The absolute convergence test

A series of real numbers Σa_k must converge if the related absolute value series $\Sigma |a_k|$ converges.

Proof   Assume $\Sigma |a_k|$ converges and let $b_k = a_k + |a_k|$ for all k. Note that

$$b_k = \begin{cases} 2|a_k| & \text{if } a_k > 0 \\ 0 & \text{if } a_k \leq 0 \end{cases}$$

Thus, we have $0 \leq b_k \leq 2|a_k|$ for all k. Because the series $\Sigma |a_k|$ converges and both Σb_k and $\Sigma |a_k|$ are series of nonnegative terms, the direct comparison test tells us that the dominated series Σb_k also converges. Finally, because

$$a_k = b_k - |a_k|$$

and both Σb_k and $\Sigma |a_k|$ converge, it follows that Σa_k must also converge. ❑

EXAMPLE 6   Convergence using the absolute convergence test

Test the series $1 + \frac{1}{4} + \frac{1}{9} - \frac{1}{16} - \frac{1}{25} + \frac{1}{36} + \frac{1}{49} + \frac{1}{64} - \frac{1}{81} - \frac{1}{100} \cdots$ for convergence. This is the series in which the absolute value of the general term is $\dfrac{1}{k^2}$ and the pattern of the signs is $+ + + - - + + + - - \cdots$.

Solution

This is not a series of positive terms, nor is it strictly alternating. However, we find that the corresponding series of absolute values is the convergent p-series

$$1 + \frac{1}{4} + \frac{1}{9} + \frac{1}{16} + \cdots = \sum_{k=1}^{\infty} \frac{1}{k^2}$$

Because the absolute value series converges, the absolute convergence test assures us that the given series also converges. ∎

EXAMPLE 7   Convergence of a trigonometric series

Test the series $\displaystyle\sum_{k=1}^{\infty} \frac{\sin k}{2^k}$ for convergence.

Solution

Because $\sin k$ takes on both positive and negative values, the series cannot be analyzed by methods that apply only to series of positive terms. Moreover, note that the series is not strictly alternating:

$$\sum_{k=1}^{\infty} \frac{\sin k}{2^k} = 0.421 + 0.227 + 0.018 - 0.047 - 0.030 - 0.004 + 0.005 + \cdots$$

The corresponding series of absolute values is

$$\sum_{k=1}^{\infty} \left| \frac{\sin k}{2^k} \right|$$

which is dominated by the convergent geometric series $\Sigma \frac{1}{2^k}$ because $|\sin k| \le 1$ for all k; that is,

$$0 \le \left| \frac{\sin k}{2^k} \right| \le \frac{1}{2^k} \quad \text{for all } k$$

Therefore, the absolute convergence test assures us that the given series converges. The graph of the related continuous function $y = (\sin x)/(2^x)$ is shown in Figure 8.20. ∎

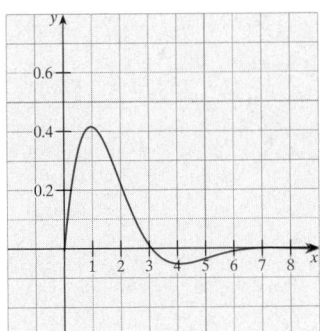

Figure 8.20 Graph of $y = \dfrac{\sin x}{2^x}$

If Σa_k converges, then $\Sigma |a_k|$ may either converge or diverge. The two cases that can occur are given the following special names.

Absolutely And Conditionally Convergent Series

WARNING   Note that a convergent series is either absolutely convergent or conditionally convergent, but it cannot be both.

> The series Σa_k is **absolutely convergent** (or converges absolutely) if the related series $\Sigma |a_k|$ converges. The series Σa_k is **conditionally convergent** (or converges conditionally) if it converges but $\Sigma |a_k|$ diverges.

For example, the series in Examples 6 and 7 are both absolutely convergent, but the alternating harmonic series

$$\sum_{k=1}^{\infty} \frac{(-1)^{k+1}}{k}$$

is conditionally convergent because it converges (see Example 1), whereas the related series of absolute value terms $\Sigma 1/k$ (the harmonic series) diverges.

The ratio test and the root test for positive-term series can be generalized to apply to arbitrary series. The following is a statement and proof of the generalized ratio test.

THEOREM 8.21   The generalized ratio test

For the series $\sum a_k$, suppose $a_k \ne 0$ for $k \ge 1$ and that

$$\lim_{k \to \infty} \left| \frac{a_{k+1}}{a_k} \right| = L$$

where L is a real number or ∞. Then

If $L < 1$, the series Σa_k converges absolutely and hence converges.

If $L > 1$ or if L is infinite, the series Σa_k diverges.

If $L = 1$, the test is inconclusive.

Proof   Assume $L < 1$; then the positive series $\Sigma\,|a_k|$ converges by the ratio test, and hence Σa_k converges absolutely. Assume $L > 1$; then the sequence $\{|a_k|\}$ is eventually increasing, which means that $\{a_k\}$ cannot converge to 0 as $k \to \infty$, so Σa_k diverges by the divergence test. Assume $L = 1$; see Problem 61 for this part of the proof.   ❏

EXAMPLE 8   Convergence and divergence using the generalized ratio test

Find all values of x for which the series $\Sigma k x^k$ converges.

Solution

Let $a_k = k x^k$.

$$L = \lim_{k\to\infty}\left|\frac{a_{k+1}}{a_k}\right|$$

$$= \lim_{k\to\infty}\left|\frac{(k+1)x^{k+1}}{kx^k}\right|$$

$$= \lim_{k\to\infty}\left(\frac{k+1}{k}\right)\left|\frac{x^{k+1}}{x^k}\right|$$

$$= \lim_{k\to\infty}\left(1+\frac{1}{k}\right)|x|$$

$$= |x|$$

Thus, by the generalized ratio test, since $L = |x|$ the series converges for $|x| < 1$ and diverges if $|x| > 1$. If $x = 1$, the series is $\Sigma k(1)^k$, which clearly diverges by the divergence test. Similarly, if $x = -1$, $\Sigma k(-1)^k$ diverges by the divergence test. Thus, the series converges for $|x| < 1$ and diverges for $|x| \geq 1$.   ■

The statement and proof of the generalized root test is left to the problems (see Problem 60).

SUMMARY OF CONVERGENCE TESTS FOR SERIES

This concludes our basic study of convergence tests. There are no firm rules for deciding how to test the convergence of a given series Σa_k, but we can offer a few guidelines (Table 8.1).

TABLE 8.1   Guidelines for Determining Convergence of the Series Σa_k

Series with known convergence properties	
Geometric series, $\displaystyle\sum_{k=0}^{\infty} ar^k$	diverges if $|r| \geq 1$, and converges if $|r| < 1$ with sum $S = \dfrac{a}{1-r}$
p-series, $\displaystyle\sum_{k=1}^{\infty}\frac{1}{k^p}$	converges if $p > 1$ and diverges if $p \leq 1$
Harmonic series, $\displaystyle\sum_{k=1}^{\infty}\frac{1}{k}$	special case, $p = 1$, of a p-series (diverges)
q-log series $\displaystyle\sum_{k=1}^{\infty}\frac{\ln k}{k^q}$	converges if $q > 1$ and diverges if $q \leq 1$

TABLE 8.1   (continued)

Series with known convergence properties	Review of Convergence Tests
Divergence test	Compute $\lim\limits_{k \to \infty} a_k$. If this limit is anything but 0, the series diverges.
Tests for Series Σa_k with $a_k > 0$	
Limit comparison test	Check to see whether Σa_k is similar in appearance to a series Σb_k whose convergence properties are known, and apply the limit comparison test. If $\lim\limits_{k \to \infty} a_k/b_k = L$, where L is finite and positive, then Σa_k and Σb_k either both converge or both diverge.
Ratio test	If a_k involves $k!$, k^p, or c^k, try the ratio test, $\lim\limits_{k \to \infty} \dfrac{a_{k+1}}{a_k} = L$. Converges if $L < 1$, diverges if $L > 1$, test is inconclusive if $L = 1$.
Root test	If it is easy to find $\lim\limits_{k \to \infty} \sqrt[k]{a_k} = L$, try the root test. Converges if $L < 1$, diverges if $L > 1$, test is inconclusive if $L = 1$.
Integral test	If f is continuous, positive, and decreasing, and if $a_k = f(k)$ for all k, then $\sum\limits_{k=1}^{\infty} a_k$ and the improper integral $\int_{1}^{\infty} f(x)\,dx$ either both converge or both diverge. Consider using this test when f is easy to integrate or if a_k involves a logarithm, a trigonometric function, or an inverse trigonometric function.
Direct comparison test	If $0 \le a_k \le c_k$ and $\sum\limits_{k=1}^{\infty} c_k$ converges, then $\sum\limits_{k=1}^{\infty} a_k$ converges. If $0 \le d_k \le a_k$ and $\sum\limits_{k=1}^{\infty} d_k$ diverges, then $\sum\limits_{k=1}^{\infty} a_k$ diverges.
Zero-infinity limit comparison test	If $\lim\limits_{k \to \infty} \dfrac{a_k}{b_k} = 0$ and Σb_k converges, then the series Σa_k converges. If $\lim\limits_{k \to \infty} \dfrac{a_k}{b_k} = \infty$ and Σb_k diverges, then the series Σa_k diverges.
Tests for Series Σa_k that do not require $a_k > 0$	
Absolute convergence test	Take the absolute value of each term and proceed to test for convergence of positive series, as summarized previously. 1. If $\Sigma \lvert a_k \rvert$ *converges*, then $\sum a_k$ converges. 2. If $\Sigma \lvert a_k \rvert$ diverges, then the series is *not absolutely convergent*; but may still converge *conditionally*.
Alternating series test (conditional convergence)	The alternating series $\Sigma(-1)^k a_k$ or $\Sigma(-1)^{k+1} a_k$ with $a_k > 0$ converges if $a_{k+1} \le a_k$ for $k = 1, 2, \ldots$ and $\lim\limits_{k \to \infty} a_k = 0$.

REARRANGEMENT OF TERMS IN AN ABSOLUTELY CONVERGENT SERIES

You may be surprised to learn that if the terms in a conditionally convergent series are rearranged (that is, the order of the summands is changed), the new series may not converge or it may converge to a different sum from that of the original series! For example, we know that the alternating harmonic series

$$\sum_{k=1}^{\infty} \frac{(-1)^{k+1}}{k}$$

converges conditionally, and it can be shown (see Problem 52) that

$$1 - \frac{1}{2} + \frac{1}{3} - \frac{1}{4} + \frac{1}{5} - \frac{1}{6} + \frac{1}{7} - \frac{1}{8} + \frac{1}{9} - \cdots = \ln 2$$

If we rearrange this series by placing two successive subtracted terms after each added term, we obtain

$$1 - \frac{1}{2} - \frac{1}{4} + \frac{1}{3} - \frac{1}{6} - \frac{1}{8} + \frac{1}{5} - \cdots = \left(1 - \frac{1}{2}\right) - \frac{1}{4} + \left(\frac{1}{3} - \frac{1}{6}\right) - \frac{1}{8} + \cdots$$
$$= \frac{1}{2} - \frac{1}{4} + \frac{1}{6} - \frac{1}{8} + \cdots$$
$$= \frac{1}{2}\left(1 - \frac{1}{2} + \frac{1}{3} - \frac{1}{4} + \cdots\right)$$
$$= \frac{1}{2}\ln 2$$

In general, it can be shown that if Σa_k is conditionally convergent, there is a rearrangement of the terms of Σa_k so that the sum is equal to any specified finite number. In Problem 53, for example, you are asked to rearrange the terms of the series

$$\sum_{k=1}^{\infty} \frac{(-1)^{k+1}}{k}$$

so that the sum is $\frac{3}{2}\ln 2$.

This information may be somewhat unsettling, because it is reasonable to expect a sum to be unaffected by the order in which the summands are taken. Absolutely convergent series behave more in the way we would expect. In fact, if the series Σa_k converges absolutely with sum S, then **any** rearrangement of the terms also converges absolutely to S. A detailed discussion of rearrangement of terms of a series requires the techniques of advanced calculus.

8.6   PROBLEM SET

Ⓐ 1. **WHAT DOES THIS SAY?** Discuss absolute versus conditional convergence.

2. **WHAT DOES THIS SAY?** Discuss the convergence of the alternating p-series.

3. **WHAT DOES THIS SAY?** Outline a procedure for determining the convergence of Σa_k for $a_k > 0$.

Determine whether each series in Problems 4–31 converges absolutely, converges conditionally, or diverges.

4. $\displaystyle\sum_{k=1}^{\infty} \frac{(-1)^{k+1}k}{k^2 + 1}$

5. $\displaystyle\sum_{k=1}^{\infty} \frac{(-1)^{k+1}k^2}{k^3 + 1}$

6. $\displaystyle\sum_{k=1}^{\infty} \frac{(-1)^{k+1}k}{2k + 1}$

7. $\displaystyle\sum_{k=1}^{\infty} \frac{(-1)^{k+1}k^2}{k^2 + 1}$

8. $\displaystyle\sum_{k=1}^{\infty} \frac{(-1)^{k+1}}{k^{3/2}}$

9. $\displaystyle\sum_{k=1}^{\infty} \frac{(-1)^{k+1}k}{2^k}$

10. $\displaystyle\sum_{k=1}^{\infty} (-1)^{k+1}\frac{k^2}{e^k}$

11. $\displaystyle\sum_{k=1}^{\infty} \frac{(-1)^k}{\sqrt{k}}$

12. $\displaystyle\sum_{k=1}^{\infty} (-1)^k\frac{(1 + k^2)}{k^3}$

13. $\displaystyle\sum_{k=1}^{\infty} \frac{(-1)^{k+1}k!}{k^k}$

14. $\displaystyle\sum_{k=2}^{\infty} (-1)^k\frac{k!}{\ln k}$

15. $\displaystyle\sum_{k=1}^{\infty} \frac{(-1)^k(2k)!}{k^k}$

16. $\displaystyle\sum_{k=1}^{\infty} (-1)^{k+1}\frac{2^k}{k!}$

17. $\displaystyle\sum_{k=1}^{\infty} \frac{(-3)^k(k + 1)}{k!}$

18. $\displaystyle\sum_{k=1}^{\infty} (-1)^{k+1}\frac{2^{2k+1}}{k!}$

19. $\displaystyle\sum_{k=2}^{\infty} \frac{(-1)^{k+1}}{\ln k}$

20. $\displaystyle\sum_{k=1}^{\infty} \frac{(-1)^{k+1}k}{(k + 1)(k + 2)}$

21. $\displaystyle\sum_{k=2}^{\infty} \frac{(-1)^{k+1}}{(\ln k)^4}$

22. $\displaystyle\sum_{k=2}^{\infty} \frac{(-1)^{k+1}}{\ln(\ln k)}$

23. $\displaystyle\sum_{k=2}^{\infty} \frac{(-1)^{k+1}}{k\ln k}$

24. $\displaystyle\sum_{k=1}^{\infty} \frac{(-1)^{k+1}\ln k}{k}$

25. $\displaystyle\sum_{k=2}^{\infty} \frac{(-1)^{k+1}k}{\ln k}$

26. $\displaystyle\sum_{k=1}^{\infty} (-1)^{k+1}\frac{\ln k}{k^2}$

27. $\displaystyle\sum_{k=1}^{\infty} \frac{(-1)^{k+1}k}{(k + 2)^2}$

28. $\displaystyle\sum_{k=1}^{\infty} (-1)^{k+1}\left(\frac{k}{k + 1}\right)^k$

29. $\displaystyle\sum_{k=2}^{\infty} (-1)^{k+1}\frac{\ln(\ln k)}{k\ln k}$

30. $\displaystyle\sum_{k=1}^{\infty} (-1)^{k+1}\left(\frac{1}{k}\right)^{1/k}$

31. $\displaystyle\sum_{k=1}^{\infty} (-1)^{k+1}\frac{k^5 5^{k+2}}{2^{3k}}$

Ⓑ *Given the series in Problems 32–37,*

  a. *Estimate the sum of the series by taking the sum of the first four terms. How accurate is this estimate?*

  b. *How many terms of the series are necessary to estimate its sum with three-place accuracy? What is this estimate?*

32. $\displaystyle\sum_{k=1}^{\infty} \frac{(-1)^{k+1}}{2^{2k-2}}$

33. $\displaystyle\sum_{k=1}^{\infty} \frac{(-1)^{k+1}}{k!}$

34. $\displaystyle\sum_{k=1}^{\infty} \frac{(-1)^k}{k^2}$

35. $\displaystyle\sum_{k=1}^{\infty} \left(\frac{-1}{3}\right)^{k+1}$

36. $\displaystyle\sum_{k=1}^{\infty} \frac{(-1)^{k+1}}{k^3}$

37. $\displaystyle\sum_{k=1}^{\infty} \left(\frac{-1}{5}\right)^k$

Use the generalized ratio test in Problems 38–43 to find all numbers x for which the given series converges.

38. $\displaystyle\sum_{k=1}^{\infty} \frac{x^k}{k}$

39. $\displaystyle\sum_{k=1}^{\infty} \frac{(2x)^k}{\sqrt{k}}$

40. $\displaystyle\sum_{k=1}^{\infty} \frac{2^k x^k}{k!}$

41. $\displaystyle\sum_{k=1}^{\infty} \frac{(k+2)x^k}{k^2(k+3)}$

42. $\displaystyle\sum_{k=1}^{\infty} (-1)^{k+1}\left(\frac{x}{k}\right)^k$

43. $\displaystyle\sum_{k=1}^{\infty} (-1)^k k^p x^k$, for $p > 0$

44. Find an upper bound for the error if the convergent alternating series $\displaystyle\sum_{k=1}^{\infty} \frac{(-1)^{k+1}}{k}$ is approximated by the partial sum

$$S_5 = 1 - \frac{1}{2} + \frac{1}{3} - \frac{1}{4} + \frac{1}{5}$$

45. Find an upper bound for the error if the convergent alternating series $\displaystyle\sum_{k=1}^{\infty} \frac{(-1)^{k+1}}{k^2}$ is approximated by the partial sum

$$S_5 = 1 - \frac{1}{2^2} + \frac{1}{3^2} - \frac{1}{4^2} + \frac{1}{5^2}$$

46. Find an upper bound for the error if the convergent alternating series $\displaystyle\sum_{k=2}^{\infty} \frac{(-1)^k}{\ln k}$ is approximated by the partial sum

$$S_7 = \frac{1}{\ln 2} - \frac{1}{\ln 3} + \frac{1}{\ln 4} - \frac{1}{\ln 5} + \frac{1}{\ln 6} - \frac{1}{\ln 7}$$

47. Find an upper bound for the error if the convergent alternating series $\displaystyle\sum_{k=1}^{\infty} \frac{(-1)^{k+1}k}{2^k}$ is approximated by the partial sum

$$S_6 = \frac{1}{2} - \frac{2}{2^2} + \frac{3}{2^3} - \frac{4}{2^4} + \frac{5}{2^5} - \frac{6}{2^6}$$

48. For what numbers p does the alternating series $\displaystyle\sum_{k=2}^{\infty} \frac{(-1)^{k+1}}{k(\ln k)^p}$ converge? For what numbers p does it converge absolutely?

49. Test the series $\displaystyle\sum_{k=1}^{\infty} \frac{\sin \sqrt[k]{2}}{k^2}$ for convergence.

50. Use series methods to evaluate $\displaystyle\lim_{k\to\infty} \frac{x^k}{k!}$ where x is a real number.

C **51.** Show that the sequence $\{a_n\}$ converges, where

$$a_n = \frac{1}{1} + \frac{1}{2} + \frac{1}{3} + \cdots + \frac{1}{n} - \ln n$$

52. Show that $\displaystyle\sum_{k=1}^{\infty} \frac{(-1)^{k+1}}{k} = \ln 2$ by completing the following steps.

a. Let $S_m = \displaystyle\sum_{k=1}^{m} \frac{(-1)^{k+1}}{k}$ and let $H_m = \displaystyle\sum_{k=1}^{m} \frac{1}{k}$. Show that $S_{2m} = H_{2m} - H_m$.

b. It can be shown (see Problem 50)

$$\lim_{m\to\infty}\left(1 + \frac{1}{2} + \cdots + \frac{1}{m} - \ln m\right)$$

exists. The value of this limit is a number $\gamma \approx 0.57722$, called **Euler's constant.** Use this fact, along with the relationship in part **a**, to show that $\lim_{h\to\infty} S_n = \ln 2$. *Hint*: Note that

$$S_{2m} = H_{2m} - H_m$$
$$= [H_{2m} - \ln(2m)] - [H_m - \ln m] + \ln(2m) - \ln m$$

53. Consider the following rearrangement of the conditionally convergent alternating harmonic series $\displaystyle\sum_{k=1}^{\infty} \frac{(-1)^{k+1}}{k}$:

$$1 + \frac{1}{3} - \frac{1}{2} + \frac{1}{5} + \frac{1}{7} - \frac{1}{4} + \frac{1}{9} + \frac{1}{11} - \frac{1}{6} + \cdots$$

a. Let S_n and H_n denote the nth partial sum of the given rearranged series and the harmonic series $\displaystyle\sum_{k=1}^{\infty} \frac{1}{k}$, respectively. Show that if n is a multiple of 3, say $n = 3m$, then

$$S_{3m} = H_{4m} - \frac{1}{2} H_{2m} - \frac{1}{2} H_m$$

b. Show that $\displaystyle\lim_{n\to\infty} S_n = \frac{3}{2} \ln 2$. *Hint*: You many find it helpful to use

$$\lim_{n\to\infty}\left(1 + \frac{1}{2} + \cdots + \frac{1}{n} - \ln n\right) = \gamma$$

given in Problem 52**b**.

54. **Journal Problem** *School Science and Mathematics* by Michael Brozinsky* ∎ Show that the series

$$1 + \frac{1}{2} + \frac{1}{3} - \frac{1}{4} - \frac{1}{5} - \frac{1}{6} + \frac{1}{7} + \frac{1}{8} + \frac{1}{9} - - - + + + \cdots$$

converges and find its sum.

55. **Exploration Problem** What (if anything) is wrong with the following computation?

$$1 - \frac{1}{2} + \frac{1}{3} - \frac{1}{4} + \frac{1}{5} - \frac{1}{6} + \cdots$$

$$= 1 + \left(\frac{1}{2} - 1\right) + \frac{1}{3} + \left(\frac{1}{4} - \frac{1}{2}\right) + \frac{1}{5} + \left(\frac{1}{6} - \frac{1}{3}\right) + \cdots$$

$$= \left(1 + \frac{1}{2} + \frac{1}{3} + \frac{1}{4} + \cdots\right) - 1 - \frac{1}{2} - \frac{1}{3} - \frac{1}{4} - \cdots$$

$$= \left(1 + \frac{1}{2} + \frac{1}{3} + \cdots\right) - \left(1 + \frac{1}{2} + \frac{1}{3} + \cdots\right)$$

$$= 0$$

56. Suppose $\{a_k\}$ is a sequence with the property that $|a_n| < A^n$ for some positive number A and all positive integers n. Show that the series $\Sigma a_k x^k$ converges absolutely for $|x| \leq 1/A$.

57. **Counterexample Problem** Let Σa_k^2 be a series that converges. Either prove that Σa_k must diverge or find a counterexample.

58. **Counterexample Problem** Let Σa_k^2 be a series that converges. Either prove that Σa_k must also converge or find a counterexample.

59. **Counterexample Problem** Let Σa_k be a series that converges. Either prove that Σa_k^2 must also converge or find a counterexample.

*Volume 82, 1982, p. 175.

60. Prove the generalized root test, which may be stated as follows: Suppose that $\lim_{k \to \infty} \sqrt[k]{|a_k|} = L$. Then

If $L < 1$, the series Σa_k converges absolutely.

If $L > 1$, the series Σa_k diverges.

If $L = 1$, the test is inconclusive.

61. Show that if

$$L = \lim_{k \to \infty} \left| \frac{a_{k+1}}{a_k} \right| = 1$$

the series Σa_k can either converge or diverge. *Hint*: Find a convergent series with $L = 1$ and a divergent series that satisfies the same condition.

62. Let $\Sigma(-1)^{k+1} a_k$ be an alternating series such that $\{a_k\}$ is decreasing and

$$\lim_{k \to \infty} a_k = 0$$

Show that the sequence of odd partial sums $\{S_{2n-1}\}$ is decreasing.

63. Exploration Problem Construct a divergent alternating series
$$\sum_{k=1}^{\infty}(-1)^{k+1} a_k$$
such that $\lim_{k \to \infty} a_k = 0$, but $\{a_k\}$ is not decreasing.

8.7 Power Series

IN THIS SECTION convergence of a power series, term-by-term differentiation and integration of power series

An infinite series of the form

$$\sum_{k=0}^{\infty} a_k(x - c)^k = a_0 + a_1(x - c) + a_2(x - c)^2 + \cdots$$

is called a **power series** in $(x - c)$. The numbers $a_0, a_1, a_2, \ldots$ are the *coefficients* of the power series. If $c = 0$, the series has the form

$$\sum_{k=0}^{\infty} a_k x^k = a_0 + a_1 x + a_2 x^2 + a_3 x^3 + \cdots$$

A power series in x may be considered as an extension of a polynomial in x.

CONVERGENCE OF A POWER SERIES

For what numbers x does a given power series converge? The following theorem answers this question for the case where $c = 0$.

THEOREM 8.22 Convergence of a power series

For a power series $\sum_{k=0}^{\infty} a_k x^k$, exactly one of the following is true:

1. The series converges for all x.
2. The series converges only for $x = 0$.
3. The series **converges absolutely** for all x in an open interval $(-R, R)$ and **diverges** for $|x| > R$. It may either converge or diverge at the endpoints of the interval, $x = R$ and $x = -R$.

Proof   The proof is found in most advanced calculus textbooks.   ❑

The set of values for which a series converges is called the **convergence set** for the series. The following three examples show each of these possibilities.

EXAMPLE 1 When the convergence set is the entire x-axis

Show that the power series $\sum_{k=1}^{\infty} \dfrac{x^k}{k!}$ converges for all x.

Solution

If $x = 0$, then the series is trivial and converges. For $x \neq 0$, we use the generalized ratio test to find

$$L = \lim_{k \to \infty} \left| \frac{\dfrac{x^{k+1}}{(k+1)!}}{\dfrac{x^k}{k!}} \right| = \lim_{k \to \infty} \left| \frac{x^{k+1}k!}{(k+1)!x^k} \right| = \lim_{k \to \infty} \frac{|x|}{k+1} = 0$$

Because $L = 0$ and thus $L < 1$, the series converges for all x. ∎

EXAMPLE 2   Convergence only at the point $x = 0$

Show that the power series $\displaystyle\sum_{k=1}^{\infty} k! x^k$ converges only when $x = 0$.

Solution

We use the generalized ratio test to find

$$L = \lim_{k \to \infty} \left| \frac{(k+1)!x^{k+1}}{k!x^k} \right| = \lim_{k \to \infty} (k+1)\,|x|$$

For any x other than 0, we have $L = \infty$. Hence, the power series converges only when $x = 0$. ∎

EXAMPLE 3   Convergence set is a bounded interval

Find the convergence set for the power series

$$\sum_{k=1}^{\infty} \frac{x^k}{\sqrt{k}}$$

Solution

Using the generalized ratio test, we find

$$L = \lim_{k \to \infty} \left| \frac{\dfrac{x^{k+1}}{\sqrt{k+1}}}{\dfrac{x^k}{\sqrt{k}}} \right| = \lim_{k \to \infty} \left| \frac{\sqrt{k}}{\sqrt{k+1}} \right| |x| = |x|$$

The power series converges absolutely if $|x| < 1$, and diverges if $|x| > 1$. We must also check the endpoints of the interval $|x| < 1$, namely $x = -1$ and $x = 1$:

$$x = -1: \quad \sum_{k=1}^{\infty} \frac{(-1)^k}{\sqrt{k}} \quad \textit{converges} \text{ by the alternating series test}$$

$$\left(\frac{1}{\sqrt{k+1}} < \frac{1}{\sqrt{k}} \quad \text{and} \quad \lim_{k \to \infty} \frac{1}{\sqrt{k}} = 0 \right)$$

$$x = 1: \quad \sum_{k=1}^{\infty} \frac{(1)^k}{\sqrt{k}} \quad \textit{diverges} \ (p\text{-series with } p = \tfrac{1}{2} < 1)$$

Thus, the given power series converges for $-1 \leq x < 1$ and diverges otherwise. ∎

According to Theorem 8.22, the set of numbers for which the power series $\Sigma a_k x^k$ converges is an interval centered at $x = 0$. We call this the **interval of convergence** of the power series. If this interval has length $2R$, then R is called the **radius of convergence** of the series, as shown in Figure 8.21. If the series converges only for $x = 0$, the series has radius of convergence $R = 0$, and if it converges for all x, we say that $R = \infty$.

May converge or diverge at endpoints

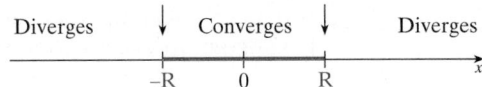

Diverges   ↓   Converges   ↓   Diverges

−R   0   R

Figure 8.21   The interval of convergence of a power series

In Example 1, we found that $\Sigma x^k/k!$ converges for all x, so $R = \infty$ and the interval of convergence is the entire real line. In Example 2, we found that the power series $\Sigma k! x^k$ has radius of convergence 0. In Example 3, we found that $\Sigma x^k/\sqrt{k}$ converges on $[-1, 1)$, so $R = 1$.

The procedure for determining the convergence set of a power series is further illustrated in the following examples.

EXAMPLE 4   Finding the interval of convergence for a power series

Find the interval of convergence for the power series $\displaystyle\sum_{k=1}^{\infty} \frac{2^k x^k}{k}$. What is the radius of convergence?

Solution

We apply the generalized ratio test to find

$$L = \lim_{k \to \infty} \left| \frac{\dfrac{2^{k+1} x^{k+1}}{k+1}}{\dfrac{2^k x^k}{k}} \right| = \lim_{k \to \infty} \left| \frac{2k}{k+1} \right| |x| = 2 |x|$$

Thus, the series converges absolutely for $2 |x| < 1$; that is, for $-\frac{1}{2} < x < \frac{1}{2}$. The radius of convergence is $R = \frac{1}{2}$. Checking the endpoints, we find

WARNING   Do not forget to check the endpoints.

$$x = \frac{1}{2}: \quad \sum_{k=1}^{\infty} \frac{2^k}{k} \left(\frac{1}{2} \right)^k = \sum_{k=1}^{\infty} \frac{1}{k} \text{ diverges} \qquad \text{Harmonic series}$$

$$x = -\frac{1}{2}: \quad \sum_{k=1}^{\infty} \frac{2^k}{k} \left(-\frac{1}{2} \right)^k = \sum_{k=1}^{\infty} \frac{(-1)^k}{k} \text{ converges} \qquad \text{Alternating harmonic series}$$

The interval of convergence is $-\frac{1}{2} \leq x < \frac{1}{2}$.   ∎

EXAMPLE 5   Finding an interval of convergence

Find the radius of convergence and the interval of convergence for the power series

$$\sum_{k=1}^{\infty} \frac{2^k x^k}{k!}$$

Solution

Applying the generalized ratio test, we find

$$L = \lim_{k \to \infty} \left| \frac{\dfrac{2^{k+1} x^{k+1}}{(k+1)!}}{\dfrac{2^k x^k}{k!}} \right| = \lim_{k \to \infty} \left| \frac{2}{k+1} \right| |x| = 0$$

Thus, the power series converges absolutely for x, and the radius of convergence is infinite.   ∎

EXAMPLE 6   Radius of convergence using the root test

Find the radius of convergence of the power series $\displaystyle\sum_{k=1}^{\infty} \left(\frac{k+1}{k}\right)^{k^2} x^k$.

Solution

Using the root test to examine absolute convergence, we find that

$$L = \lim_{k\to\infty} \sqrt[k]{\left|\left(\frac{k+1}{k}\right)^{k^2} x^k\right|} = \lim_{k\to\infty} \left|\left(\frac{k+1}{k}\right)^{k^2} x^k\right|^{1/k}$$

$$= \lim_{k\to\infty} \left(1 + \frac{1}{k}\right)^k |x| = e\,|x|$$

Thus, the power series converges absolutely for $e\,|x| < 1$; that is, for $-e^{-1} < x < e^{-1}$. It follows that the radius of convergence is $R = e^{-1}$. We do not need to test the endpoints because we are not finding the interval of convergence. ■

In some applications, we will encounter power series of the form

$$\sum_{k=0}^{\infty} a_k(x-c)^k = a_0 + a_1(x-c) + a_2(x-c)^2 + \cdots$$

in which each term is a constant times a power of $x - c$, where c is a constant. The intervals of convergence are intervals of the form $-R < x - c < R$, including possibly one or both of the endpoints $x = c - R$ and $x = c + R$. The procedure for determining the interval of convergence of such power series is illustrated in the following example.

EXAMPLE 7   Power series in $(x - c)$

Find the interval of convergence of the power series

$$\sum_{k=0}^{\infty} \frac{(x+1)^k}{3^k}$$

Solution

Applying the generalized ratio rest, we obtain

$$L = \lim_{k\to\infty} \left|\frac{\dfrac{(x+1)^{k+1}}{3^{k+1}}}{\dfrac{(x+1)^k}{3^k}}\right| = \lim_{k\to\infty} \left|\frac{3^k}{3^{k+1}}\right| |x+1| = \lim_{k\to\infty} \frac{1}{3} |x+1|$$

Thus, the power series converges absolutely for

$$\tfrac{1}{3}|x+1| < 1$$
$$|x+1| < 3$$
$$-3 < x+1 < 3$$
$$-4 < x < 2$$

Checking the endpoints, we find

$$x = -4: \quad \sum_{k=0}^{\infty} \frac{(-4+1)^k}{3^k} = \sum_{k=0}^{\infty}(-1)^k \text{ diverges (by oscillation)}$$

$$x = 2: \quad \sum_{k=0}^{\infty} \frac{(2+1)^k}{3^k} = \sum_{k=0}^{\infty} 1^k \text{ diverges (by divergence test)}$$

The interval of convergence is $(-4, 2)$. ■

TERM-BY-TERM DIFFERENTIATION AND INTEGRATION OF POWER SERIES

The power series $\sum_{k=0}^{\infty} a_k x^k$ can be thought of as a function defined on its interval of convergence. It is reasonable to ask if this function is differentiable and if it is integrable and, if so, what are its derivative and integral. This is useful because we can form new series using differentiation or integration of known series. If we regard a power series as an "infinite polynomial," we would expect to be able to differentiate and integrate it term by term. The following theorem shows that this procedure is legitimate on the interval of absolute convergence.

THEOREM 8.23 **Term-by-term differentiation and integration of a power series**

A power series $\sum_{k=0}^{\infty} a_k x^k$ with radius of convergence $R > 0$ can be differentiated or integrated term by term on its interval of absolute convergence $-R < x < R$. More specifically, if $f(x) = \sum_{k=0}^{\infty} a_k x^k$ for $|x| < R$, then for $|x| < R$ we have

$$f'(x) = \sum_{k=1}^{\infty} k a_k x^{k-1} = a_1 + 2a_2 x + 3a_3 x^2 + 4a_4 x^3 + \cdots$$

and

$$\int f(x)\, dx = \int \left(\sum_{k=0}^{\infty} a_k x^k \right) dx = \sum_{k=0}^{\infty} \left(\int a_k x^k\, dx \right) = \sum_{k=0}^{\infty} \frac{a_k}{k+1} x^{k+1} + C$$

Proof A proof can be found in most advanced calculus texts. ❑

> ➦ **What This Says** In many ways, a function defined by a power series behaves like a polynomial. It is differentiable, hence continuous, inside its interval of absolute convergence, and its derivative and integral can be determined by differentiating and integrating term by term, respectively.

EXAMPLE 8 **Term-by-term differentiation of a power series**

Let f be a function defined by the power series

$$f(x) = \sum_{k=0}^{\infty} \frac{x^k}{k!} \qquad \text{for all } x$$

Show that $f'(x) = f(x)$ for all x, and deduce that $f(x) = e^x$.

Solution

The given power series converges for all x (by the generalized ratio test—see Example 1), and Theorem 8.23 tells us that it is differentiable for all x. Differentiating term by term, we find

$$f'(x) = \frac{d}{dx}\left[1 + x + \frac{x^2}{2!} + \frac{x^3}{3!} + \frac{x^4}{4!} + \cdots\right]$$

$$= 0 + 1 + \frac{2x}{2!} + \frac{3x^2}{3!} + \frac{4x^3}{4!} + \cdots$$

$$= 1 + x + \frac{x^2}{2!} + \frac{x^3}{3!} + \cdots$$

$$= f(x)$$

In Chapter 5, we found that the differential equation $f'(x) = f(x)$ has the general solution $f(x) = Ce^x$. Substituting $x = 0$ into the power series for $f(x)$, we obtain

$$f(0) = 1 + 0 + \frac{0^2}{2!} + \frac{0^3}{3!} + \cdots = 1$$

and by solving the equation $1 = Ce^0$ for C, we find $C = 1$; therefore, $f(x) = e^x$. ∎

A power series can be differentiated term by term—not just once, but infinitely often in its interval of absolute convergence. The key to this fact lies in showing that if f satisfies

$$f(x) = \sum_{k=0}^{\infty} a_k x^k$$

and R is the radius of convergence of the power series on the right, then the derivative series

$$f'(x) = \sum_{k=1}^{\infty} k a_k x^{k-1}$$

also has the radius of convergence R. (You are asked to show this in Problem 44.) Therefore, Theorem 8.23 can be applied to the derivative series to obtain the second derivative

$$f''(x) = \sum_{k=2}^{\infty} k(k-1) a_k x^{k-2}$$

for $|x| < R$. Continuing in this fashion, we can apply Theorem 8.23 to $f'''(x)$, $f^{(4)}$, and all other higher derivatives of f.

For example, we know that the geometric series

$$\sum_{k=0}^{\infty} x^k \quad \text{converges absolutely to} \quad f(x) = \frac{1}{1-x} \quad \text{for } |x| < 1$$

Thus, the term-by-term derivative

$$\frac{d}{dx}\left[\sum_{k=0}^{\infty} x^k\right] = \sum_{k=1}^{\infty} k x^{k-1} = 1 + 2x + 3x^2 + \cdots$$

converges to $f'(x) = \dfrac{1}{(1-x)^2}$ for $|x| < 1$, and the term-by-term *second derivative*

$$\frac{d^2}{dx^2}\left[\sum_{k=0}^{\infty} x^k\right] = \frac{d}{dx}\left[\sum_{k=1}^{\infty} k x^{k-1}\right] = \sum_{k=2}^{\infty} k(k-1) x^{k-2}$$

converges to $f''(x) = \dfrac{2}{(1-x)^3}$, and so on. These ideas are illustrated in our next example.

EXAMPLE 9   Second derivative of a power series

Let f be the function defined by the power series

$$f(x) = \sum_{k=0}^{\infty} \frac{(-1)^k x^{2k}}{(2k)!}$$

for all x. Show that $f''(x) = -f(x)$ for all x.

Solution

First, we use the ratio test to verify that the given power series converges absolutely for all x.

$$L = \lim_{k \to \infty} \left| \frac{\dfrac{(-1)^{k+1} x^{2(k+1)}}{[2(k+1)]!}}{\dfrac{(-1)^k x^{2k}}{(2k)!}} \right| = \lim_{k \to \infty} \frac{x^{2k+2}}{[2(k+1)]!} \cdot \frac{(2k)!}{x^{2k}} = \lim_{k \to \infty} \frac{x^2}{(2k+2)(2k+1)} = 0$$

Because $L < 1$, the series converges for all x. Next, differentiate the series term by term:

$$f'(x) = \frac{d}{dx}\left[1 - \frac{x^2}{2!} + \frac{x^4}{4!} - \frac{x^6}{6!} + \cdots \right] = -\frac{2x}{2!} + \frac{4x^3}{4!} - \frac{6x^5}{6!} + \cdots$$

$$= -\frac{x}{1!} + \frac{x^3}{3!} - \frac{x^5}{5!} + \cdots$$

Finally, by differentiating term by term again, we obtain

$$f''(x) = \frac{d}{dx}\left[-\frac{x}{1!} + \frac{x^3}{3!} - \frac{x^5}{5!} + \cdots \right] = -1 + \frac{3x^2}{3!} - \frac{5x^4}{5!} + \cdots$$

$$= -\left[1 - \frac{x^2}{2!} + \frac{x^4}{4!} - \cdots \right] = -f(x) \qquad \blacksquare$$

EXAMPLE 10   Term-by-term integration of a power series

By integrating an appropriate geometric series term by term, show that

$$\sum_{k=0}^{\infty} \frac{x^{k+1}}{k+1} = -\ln(1-x) \quad \text{for } -1 < x < 1$$

Solution

Integrating the geometric series $\displaystyle\sum_{k=0}^{\infty} u^k = \frac{1}{1-u}$ term by term in the interval $-1 < u < 1$, we obtain

$$\int_0^x \frac{1}{1-u}\, du = \int_0^x \left[\sum_{k=0}^{\infty} u^k \right] du = \int_0^x [1 + u + u^2 + u^3 + \cdots]\, du$$

$$= x + \frac{x^2}{2} + \frac{x^3}{3} + \cdots = \sum_{k=0}^{\infty} \frac{x^{k+1}}{k+1} \quad \text{for } -1 < x < 1$$

We also know

$$\int_0^x \frac{du}{1-u} = -\ln(1-x) \qquad \text{for } -1 < x < 1$$

Thus,

$$-\ln(1-x) = \int_0^x \frac{du}{1-u} = \sum_{k=0}^{\infty} \frac{x^{k+1}}{k+1} \qquad \text{for } -1 < x < 1$$

If we check endpoints, we find the series actually converges for $-1 \le x < 1$. $\qquad \blacksquare$

EXAMPLE 11   Term-by-term integration of a power series

Find a power series for $\tan^{-1} x$.

Solution

We will use the fact that $\tan^{-1} x = \int_0^x \frac{dt}{1+t^2}$. Consider the integrand as a geometric series:

$$\frac{1}{1+t^2} = 1 - t^2 + t^4 - t^6 + \cdots = \sum_{k=0}^{\infty} (-1)^k t^{2k}$$

Thus,

$$\begin{aligned}
\tan^{-1} x &= \int_0^x \frac{1}{1+t^2}\, dt \\
&= \int_0^x \left[1 - t^2 + t^4 - t^6 + \cdots \right] dt \\
&= \sum_{k=0}^{\infty} \int_0^x (-1)^k t^{2k}\, dt \\
&= \sum_{k=0}^{\infty} (-1)^k \frac{t^{2k+1}}{2k+1} \Big|_0^x \\
&= x - \frac{x^3}{3} + \frac{x^5}{5} - \frac{x^7}{7} + \cdots \\
&= \sum_{k=0}^{\infty} \frac{(-1)^k x^{2k+1}}{2k+1} \quad \text{for } |x| < 1
\end{aligned}$$

If we check the endpoints, we find the series converges for $|x| \le 1$. ∎

This series for $\tan^{-1} x$ is called **Gregory's series** after the British mathematician James Gregory (1638–1675), who developed it in 1671 (see Figure 8.22). Because it converges at $x = 1$ and $x = -1$, it can be used to represent $\tan^{-1} x$ on $[-1, 1]$. For example, at $x = 1$

$$\frac{\pi}{4} = \tan^{-1} 1 = 1 - \frac{1}{3} + \frac{1}{5} - \frac{1}{7} + \frac{1}{9} - \cdots$$

$$\pi = 4\left[1 - \frac{1}{3} + \frac{1}{5} - \frac{1}{7} + \frac{1}{9} - \cdots \right]$$

This is the *Leibniz formula* for π. Unfortunately, as a means of estimating the actual value of π, it has a serious drawback—the convergence is very slow. Look at the partial sums for the 49th and 50th terms, and note that these are not very close to the limit (which is $\pi \approx 3.14159265359\cdots$).

In 1706, the mathematician John Machin discovered another series that converges much faster. The identity

$$\tan(\alpha + \beta) = \frac{\tan\alpha + \tan\beta}{1 - \tan\alpha \tan\beta}$$

can be used to show that

$$\tan^{-1} 1 = 4\tan^{-1}\tfrac{1}{5} - \tan^{-1}\tfrac{1}{239}$$

$$\frac{\pi}{4} = 4\left[\tfrac{1}{5} - \tfrac{1}{3}\left(\tfrac{1}{5}\right)^3 + \tfrac{1}{5}\left(\tfrac{1}{5}\right)^5 - \cdots \right]$$
$$- \left[\tfrac{1}{239} - \tfrac{1}{3}\left(\tfrac{1}{239}\right)^3 + \tfrac{1}{5}\left(\tfrac{1}{239}\right)^5 - \cdots \right]$$

No. of terms	Gregory's Series term	partial sum
0	4	
1	−1.33333333333333	2.666666667
2	0.8	3.466666667
3	−0.57142857142857	2.895238095
4	0.44444444444444	3.33968254
5	−0.36363636363636	2.976046176
6	0.30769230769231	3.283738484
7	−0.26666666666667	3.017071817
8	0.23529411764706	3.252365935
9	−0.21052631578947	3.041839619
10	0.19047619047619	3.232315809
11	−0.17391304347826	3.058402766
12	0.16	3.218402766
13	−0.14814814814815	3.070254618
14	0.13793103448276	3.208185652
15	−0.12903225806452	3.079153394
16	0.12121212121212	3.200365515
17	−0.11428571428571	3.086079801
18	0.10810810810811	3.194187909
19	−0.1025641025641	3.091623807
20	0.09560975609756	3.189184782
21	−0.09302325581395	3.096161526
22	0.088888888888889	3.185050415
23	−0.08510638297872	3.099944032
24	0.081632653061224	3.181576685
25	−0.07843137254902	3.103145313
26	0.075471698113208	3.178617011
27	−0.07272727272727	3.105889738
28	0.070175438596491	3.176065177
29	−0.06779661016949	3.108268567
30	0.065573770491803	3.173842337
31	−0.06349206349206	3.110350274
32	0.061538461538462	3.171888735
33	−0.05970149253731	3.112187243
34	0.057971014492754	3.170158257
35	−0.05633802816901	3.113820229
36	0.054794520547945	3.16861475
37	−0.05333333333333	3.115281416
38	0.051948051948052	3.167229468
39	−0.05063291139241	3.116596557
40	0.049382716049383	3.165979273
41	−0.048192771084344	3.117786502
42	0.047058823529412	3.164845325
43	−0.04597701149425	3.118868314
44	0.044943820224719	3.163812134
45	−0.04395604395604	3.11985609
46	0.043010752688172	3.162866843
47	−0.04210526315789	3.12076158
48	0.041237113402062	3.161998693
49	−0.04040404040404	3.121594653
50	0.03960396039604	3.161198613

Figure 8.22 Approximation of π using Gregory's series

No. of terms	Machin's Series term	partial sum
0	3.1832635983264	
1	−0.0426665690003	3.140597029
2	0.0010239999998974	3.141621029
3	−2.9257142857E−05	3.141591772
4	9.10222222222E−07	3.141592682
5	−2.9789090909E−08	3.141592653
6	1.00824615385E−09	3.141592654
7	−3.4952533333E−11	3.141592654

If we multiply both sides by 4, we find another series for π:

$$\pi = 16\left[\tfrac{1}{5} - \tfrac{1}{3}\left(\tfrac{1}{5}\right)^3 + \tfrac{1}{5}\left(\tfrac{1}{5}\right)^5 - \cdots\right]$$
$$-4\left[\tfrac{1}{239} - \tfrac{1}{3}\left(\tfrac{1}{239}\right)^3 + \tfrac{1}{5}\left(\tfrac{1}{239}\right)^5 - \cdots\right]$$

By comparing the spreadsheet in the margin with the one in Figure 8.22, we see that Machin's formula for π converges much more rapidly than the Leibniz formula. Indeed, the sum of the first seven terms $M_7 = 3.141592654$ already coincides with π for the first eight decimal places.

8.7   PROBLEM SET

A *Find the convergence set for the power series given in Problems 1–28.*

1. $\displaystyle\sum_{k=1}^{\infty} \frac{kx^k}{k+1}$

2. $\displaystyle\sum_{k=1}^{\infty} \frac{k^2 x^k}{k+1}$

3. $\displaystyle\sum_{k=1}^{\infty} \frac{k(k+1)x^k}{k+2}$

4. $\displaystyle\sum_{k=1}^{\infty} \sqrt{k-1}\, x^k$

5. $\displaystyle\sum_{k=1}^{\infty} k^2 3^k (x-3)^k$

6. $\displaystyle\sum_{k=1}^{\infty} \frac{k^2(x-2)^k}{3^k}$

7. $\displaystyle\sum_{k=0}^{\infty} \frac{3^k(x+3)^k}{4^k}$

8. $\displaystyle\sum_{k=0}^{\infty} \frac{4^k(x+1)^k}{3^k}$

9. $\displaystyle\sum_{k=0}^{\infty} \frac{k!(x-1)^k}{5^k}$

10. $\displaystyle\sum_{k=0}^{\infty} \frac{(x-15)^k}{\ln(k+1)}$

11. $\displaystyle\sum_{k=1}^{\infty} \frac{k^2}{2^k}(x-1)^k$

12. $\displaystyle\sum_{k=1}^{\infty} \frac{2^k(x-3)^k}{k(k+1)}$

13. $\displaystyle\sum_{k=1}^{\infty} \frac{k(3x-4)^k}{(k+1)^2}$

14. $\displaystyle\sum_{k=0}^{\infty} \frac{(2x+3)^k}{4^k}$

15. $\displaystyle\sum_{k=1}^{\infty} \frac{kx^k}{7^k}$

16. $\displaystyle\sum_{k=0}^{\infty} \frac{(2k)!x^k}{(3k)!}$

17. $\displaystyle\sum_{k=1}^{\infty} \frac{(k!)^2 x^k}{k^k}$

18. $\displaystyle\sum_{k=1}^{\infty} \frac{(-1)^k kx^k}{\ln(k+2)}$

19. $\displaystyle\sum_{k=2}^{\infty} \frac{(-1)^k x^k}{k(\ln k)^2}$

20. $\displaystyle\sum_{k=0}^{\infty} \frac{(3x)^k}{2^{k+1}}$

21. $\displaystyle\sum_{k=0}^{\infty} \frac{(2x)^{2k}}{k!}$

22. $\displaystyle\sum_{k=0}^{\infty} \frac{(x+2)^{2k}}{3^k}$

23. $\displaystyle\sum_{k=0}^{\infty} \frac{k!}{2^k}(3x)^{3k}$

24. $\displaystyle\sum_{k=1}^{\infty} \frac{(3x)^{3k}}{\sqrt{k}}$

25. $\displaystyle\sum_{k=0}^{\infty} \frac{2^k}{k!}(2x-1)^{2k}$

26. $\displaystyle\sum_{k=0}^{\infty} 2^k (3x)^{3k}$

27. $\displaystyle\sum_{k=1}^{\infty} \frac{x^k}{k\sqrt{k}}$

28. $\displaystyle\sum_{k=1}^{\infty} \frac{(\ln k)x^k}{k}$

B *Find the radius of convergence R in Problems 29–34.*

29. $\displaystyle\sum_{k=1}^{\infty} k^2(x+1)^{2k+1}$

30. $\displaystyle\sum_{k=1}^{\infty} 2^{\sqrt{k}}(x-1)^k$

31. $\displaystyle\sum_{k=1}^{\infty} \frac{k!x^k}{k^k}$

32. $\displaystyle\sum_{k=1}^{\infty} \frac{(k!)^2 x^k}{(2k)!}$

33. $\displaystyle\sum_{k=1}^{\infty} k(ax)^k$ for constant a

34. $\displaystyle\sum_{k=1}^{\infty} (a^2 x)^k$ for constant a

In Problems 35–38, find the derivative $f'(x)$ by differentiating term by term.

35. $f(x) = \displaystyle\sum_{k=0}^{\infty} \left(\frac{x}{2}\right)^k$

36. $f(x) = \displaystyle\sum_{k=1}^{\infty} \frac{x^k}{k}$

37. $f(x) = \displaystyle\sum_{k=0}^{\infty} (k+2)x^k$

38. $f(x) = \displaystyle\sum_{k=0}^{\infty} kx^k$

In Problems 39–42, find $\displaystyle\int_0^x f(u)\,du$ by integrating term by term.

39. $f(x) = \displaystyle\sum_{k=0}^{\infty} \left(\frac{x}{2}\right)^k$

40. $f(x) = \displaystyle\sum_{k=1}^{\infty} \frac{x^k}{k}$

41. $f(x) = \displaystyle\sum_{k=0}^{\infty} (k+2)x^k$

42. $f(x) = \displaystyle\sum_{k=1}^{\infty} kx^k$

43. Counterexample Problem   Show that the series

$$S = \sum_{k=1}^{\infty} \frac{\sin(k!x)}{k^2}$$

converges for all x. Differentiate term by term to obtain the series

$$T = \sum_{k=1}^{\infty} \frac{k!\cos(k!x)}{k^2}$$

Show that this series diverges for all x. Why does this not violate Theorem 8.23?

C 44. Suppose $\{a_k\}$ is a sequence for which

$$\lim_{k\to\infty} \sqrt[k]{|a_k|} = \frac{1}{R}$$

Show that the power series

$$\sum_{k=1}^{\infty} ka_k x^{k-1}$$

has radius of convergence R.

45. Show that if $f(x) = \sum\limits_{k=1}^{\infty} a_k x^k$ has radius of convergence $R > 0$, then the series

$$\sum_{k=1}^{\infty} a_k x^{kp}$$

where p is a positive integer, has radius of convergence $R^{1/p}$.

46. For what values of x does the series $\sum\limits_{k=1}^{\infty} \dfrac{x}{k+x}$ converge?

Note: This is not a power series.

47. For what values of x does the series $\sum\limits_{k=1}^{\infty} \dfrac{k}{x^k}$ converge?

Note: This is not a power series.

48. For what values of x does the series $\sum\limits_{k=1}^{\infty} \dfrac{1}{kx^k}$ converge?

Note: This is not a power series.

49. Use term-by-term differentiation of a geometric series to find a power series for

$$f(x) = \frac{1}{(1-x)^3}$$

For what values of x does this power series converge?

50. Find the radius of convergence for $\sum\limits_{k=1}^{\infty} \dfrac{(k+3)! \, x^k}{k!(k+4)!}$.

51. Find the radius of convergence for $\sum\limits_{k=1}^{\infty} \dfrac{1 \cdot 2 \cdot 3 \cdots k(-x)^{2k-1}}{1 \cdot 3 \cdot 5 \cdots (2k-1)}$.

52. Let f be the function defined by the power series $f(x) = \sum\limits_{k=0}^{\infty} \dfrac{(-1)^k x^{2k+1}}{(2k+1)!}$ for all x. Show that $f''(x) = -f(x)$ for all x.

53. Let f be the function defined by the power series $f(x) = \sum\limits_{k=0}^{\infty} \dfrac{x^{2k}}{(2k)!}$ for all x. Show that $f''(x) = f(x)$ for all x.

54. Find the radius of convergence for the power series $\sum\limits_{k=0}^{\infty} \dfrac{(qk)!}{(k!)^q} x^k$, where q is a positive integer.

8.8 Taylor and Maclaurin Series

IN THIS SECTION Taylor and Maclaurin polynomials, Taylor's theorem, Taylor and Maclaurin series, operations with Taylor and Maclaurin series

TAYLOR AND MACLAURIN POLYNOMIALS

Consider a function f that can be differentiated n times on some interval I. Our goal is to find a polynomial function that approximates f at a number c in its domain. For simplicity, we begin by considering an important special case where $c = 0$. For example, consider the function $f(x) = e^x$ at the point $x = 0$, as shown in Figure 8.23. To approximate f by a polynomial function $M(x)$, we begin by making sure that both the polynomial function and f pass through the same point. That is, $M(0) = f(0)$. We say that the polynomial is **expanded about $c = 0$** or that it is **centered at 0**.

There are many polynomial functions that we could choose to approximate f at $x = 0$, and we proceed by making sure that both f and M have the same slope at $x = 0$. That is,

$$M'(0) = f'(0)$$

The graph in Figure 8.23 shows that we have $f(x) = e^x$, so $f'(x) = e^x$ and $f'(0) = f'(0) = 1$. To find M, we let

$$M_1(x) = a_0 + a_1 x \qquad M_1'(x) = a_1$$

and require $M_1(0) = 1$ and $M_1'(0) = 1$. Because $M_1(0) = a_1 = 1$ and $M_1'(0) = a_0 = 1$, we find that

$$M_1(x) = 1 + x$$

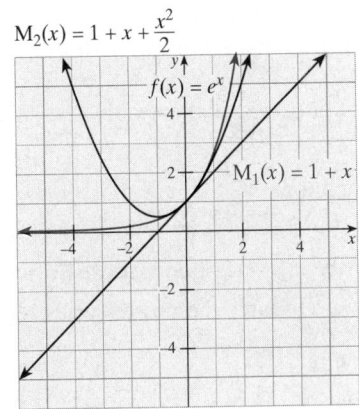

Figure 8.23 Graph of $f(x) = e^x$ and approximating polynomials $M_1(x)$ and $M_2(x)$

We see from Figure 8.23 that close to $x = c$ the approximation of f by M_1 is good, but as we move away from $(0, 1)$, M_1 no longer serves as a good approximation. To improve the approximation, we impose the requirement that the values of the second derivatives of M and f agree at $x = 0$. Using this criterion, we find

$$M_2(x) = a_0 + a_1 x + a_2 x^2$$

so that

$$M_2'(x) = a_1 + 2a_2x \quad \text{and} \quad M_2''(x) = 2a_2$$

Because $f''(x) = e^x$ and $f''(0) = 1$, we want

$$2a_2 = 1 \quad \text{or} \quad a_2 = \tfrac{1}{2}$$

Thus,

$$M_2(x) = 1 + x + \tfrac{1}{2}x^2$$

To improve the approximation even further, we can require that the values of the approximating polynomials $M_3, M_4, \cdots, M_n$ at $x = 0$ have derivatives that match those of f at $x = 0$. We find that

$$M_3(x) = 1 + x + \tfrac{1}{2}x^2 + \tfrac{1}{6}x^3$$

$$M_4(x) = 1 + x + \tfrac{1}{2}x^2 + \tfrac{1}{6}x^3 + \tfrac{1}{24}x^4$$

$$M_5(x) = 1 + x + \tfrac{1}{2}x^2 + \tfrac{1}{6}x^3 + \tfrac{1}{24}x^4 + \tfrac{1}{120}x^5$$

$$M_n(x) = 1 + \frac{x}{1!} + \frac{x^2}{2!} + \frac{x^3}{3!} + \cdots + \frac{x^n}{n!}$$

This nth-degree polynomial approximation of f at $x = 0$ is called the **nth-degree Maclaurin polynomial for f.** If we repeat the steps for $x = c$ rather than for $x = 0$, we find

$$T_n(x) = e^c + \frac{(x-c)}{1!}e^c + \frac{(x-c)^2}{2!}e^c + \frac{(x-c)^3}{3!}e^c + \cdots + \frac{(x-c)^n}{n!}e^c$$

which is called the **nth-degree Taylor polynomial** of the function $f(x) = e^x$ at $x = c$.

TAYLOR'S THEOREM

Instead of stopping at the nth term, we will now approximate a function f by an infinite series. A function f is said to be represented by the power series

$$\sum_{k=0}^{\infty} a_k(x - c)^k$$

on an interval I if $f(x) = \displaystyle\sum_{k=0}^{\infty} a_k(x - c)^k$ for all x in I. Power series representation of functions are extremely useful, but before we can deal effectively with such representations, we must answer two questions.

1. **Existence:** Under what conditions does a given function have a power series representation?
2. **Uniqueness:** When f can be represented by a power series, is there only one such series, and, if so, what is it?

The uniqueness issue is addressed in the following theorem.

THEOREM 8.24   The uniqueness theorem for power series representation

Suppose an infinitely differentiable function f is known to have the power series representation

$$f(x) = \sum_{k=0}^{\infty} a_k(x - c)^k$$

for $-R < x-c < R$. Then there is exactly one such representation, and the coefficients a_k must satisfy

$$a_k = \frac{f^{(k)}(c)}{k!} \quad \text{for } k = 0, 1, 2, \ldots$$

Proof   The uniqueness theorem may be established by differentiating the given power series term by term and evaluating successive derivatives at c. We start with

$$f(x) = \sum_{k=0}^{\infty} a_k (x - c)^k$$

and substitute $x = c$ to obtain

$$f(c) = a_0 + a_1(c - c) + a_2(c - c)^2 + \cdots = a_0$$

Next, differentiate the original series, term by term, to get

$$f'(x) = a_1 + 2a_2(x - c) + 3a_3(x - c)^2 + \cdots$$

and thus, $f'(c) = a_1 + 2a_2(0) + 3a_3(0)^2 + \cdots = a_1$. Differentiating once again and substituting $x = c$, we find

$$f''(c) = 2a_2 \quad \text{so that} \quad a_2 = \frac{f''(c)}{2}$$

In general, the kth derivative of f at $x = c$ is given by

$$f^{(k)}(c) = k! a_k \quad \text{so that} \quad a_k = \frac{f^{(k)}(c)}{k!}$$

The question of existence—that is, under what conditions a given function has a power series representation—is answered by considering what is called the **Taylor remainder function**:

$$R_n(x) = f(x) - T_n(x)$$

We see that f is represented by its Taylor series in I if and only if

$$\lim_{n \to \infty} R_n(x) = 0 \quad \text{for all } x \text{ in } I$$

This relationship among f, its Taylor polynomial $T_n(x)$, and the Taylor remainder function $R_n(x)$ is summarized in the following theorem.

THEOREM 8.25   Taylor's theorem

If f and all its derivatives exist in an open interval I containing c, then for each x in I,

$$f(x) = f(c) + \frac{f'(c)}{1!}(x - c) + \frac{f''(c)}{2!}(x - c)^2 + \cdots + \frac{f^{(n)}(c)}{n!}(x - c)^n + R_n(x)$$

where the remainder function $R_n(x)$ is given by

$$R_n(x) = \frac{f^{(n+1)}(z_n)}{(n + 1)!}(x - c)^{n+1}$$

for some z_n that depends on x and lies between c and x.

Proof   The proof of this theorem is given in Appendix B.

The formula for $R_n(x)$ is called the *Lagrange form* of the Taylor remainder function, after the French/Italian mathematician Joseph Lagrange (1736–1813). There are other forms for the remainder, principally one developed by Cauchy (see the HISTORICAL QUEST in Problem 49 of Section 2.1), but we will consider only the Lagrange form in this text.

When applying Taylor's theorem, we do not expect to be able to find the exact value of z_n. However, we can often determine an upper bound for $|R_n(x)|$ in an open interval. We will illustrate this situation later in this section.

TAYLOR AND MACLAURIN SERIES

The uniqueness theorem tells us that if f has a power series representation at c, it must be the series

$$f(c) + \frac{f'(c)}{1!}(x-c) + \frac{f''(c)}{2!}(x-c)^2 + \frac{f'''(c)}{3!}(x-c)^3 + \cdots$$

and Taylor's theorem says that $f(x)$ is represented by such a series precisely where the remainder term $R_n(x) \to 0$ as $n \to \infty$. It is convenient to have the following terminology.

Taylor And Maclaurin Series

WARNING The uniqueness theorem may be summarized by saying that the Taylor series of f at c is the only power series of the form $\Sigma a_k(x-c)^k$ that can possibly represent f on I. But it does not say that f is equal to the power series on I. All we really know is that if f has a power series representation at c, then that representation must be its Taylor series.

Suppose there is an open interval I containing c throughout which the function f and all its derivatives exist. Then the power series

$$f(c) + \frac{f'(c)}{1!}(x-c) + \frac{f''(c)}{2!}(x-c)^2 + \frac{f'''(c)}{3!}(x-c)^3 + \cdots$$

is called the **Taylor series of f at c.** The special case where $c = 0$ is called the **Maclaurin series of f:**

$$f(0) + \frac{f'(0)}{1!}x + \frac{f''(0)}{2!}x^2 + \frac{f'''(0)}{3!}x^3 + \cdots$$

EXAMPLE 1   Maclaurin series

Find the Maclaurin series for $f(x) = \cos x$.

Solution

First, note that f is infinitely differentiable at $x = 0$. We find

$$
\begin{array}{ll}
f(x) = \cos x & f(0) = 1 \\
f'(x) = -\sin x & f'(0) = 0 \\
f''(x) = -\cos x & f''(0) = -1 \\
f'''(x) = \sin x & f'''(0) = 0 \\
f^{(4)}(x) = \cos x & f^{(4)}(0) = 1 \\
\quad \vdots & \quad \vdots
\end{array}
$$

Thus, by using the definition of a Maclaurin series, we have

$$\cos x = 1 - \frac{x^2}{2!} + \frac{x^4}{4!} - \frac{x^6}{6!} + \cdots = \sum_{k=0}^{\infty} \frac{(-1)^k x^{2k}}{(2k)!} \qquad \blacksquare$$

You might ask about the relationship between a Maclaurin series and a Maclaurin polynomial. Figure 8.24 shows the function $f(x) = \cos x$ from Example 1 along with some successive Maclaurin polynomials. We use the notation $M_n(x)$ to represent the first $n + 1$ terms of the corresponding Maclaurin series. Note that the polynomials are quite close to the function near $x = 0$, but that they become very different as x moves away from the origin.

EXAMPLE 2   Maximum error when using a Maclaurin polynomial approximation

Find the Maclaurin polynomial $M_5(x)$ for the function $f(x) = e^x$ and use this polynomial to approximate e. Use Taylor's theorem to determine the accuracy of this approximation.

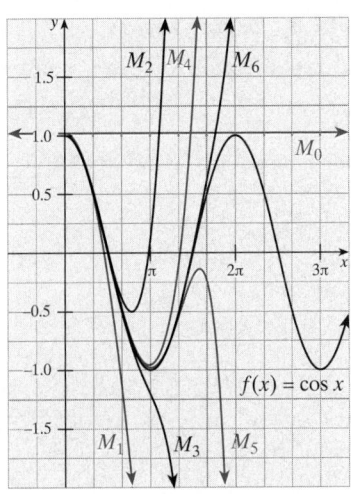

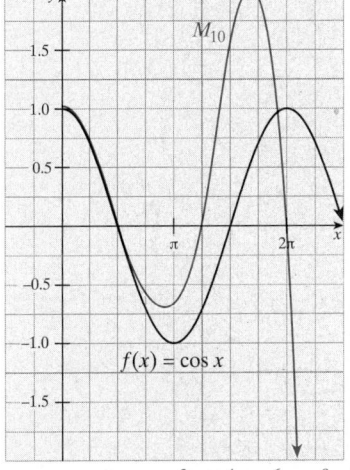

a. $M_0(x) = 1,\ M_1(x) = 1 - \dfrac{x^2}{2!}$,

$\quad M_2(x) = 1 - \dfrac{x^2}{2!} + \dfrac{x^4}{4!}$,

$\quad M_3(x) = 1 - \dfrac{x^2}{2!} + \dfrac{x^4}{4!} - \dfrac{x^6}{6!}$

b. $M_{10}(x) = 1 - \dfrac{x^2}{2!} + \dfrac{x^4}{4!} - \dfrac{x^6}{6!} + \dfrac{x^8}{8!}$

$\quad - \dfrac{x^{10}}{10!} + \dfrac{x^{12}}{12!} - \dfrac{x^{14}}{14!} + \dfrac{x^{16}}{16!} - \dfrac{x^{18}}{18!}$

$\quad + \dfrac{x^{20}}{20!}$

Figure 8.24 Comparison of $\cos x$ and its Maclaurin polynomials

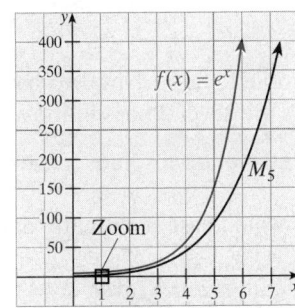

a. Comparison of f and M_5 shown on domain $[0, 7]$

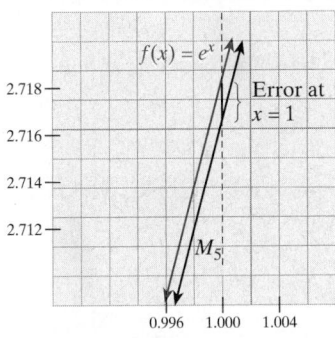

b. Zoom showing the error at $x = 1$

Figure 8.25 Comparison of $f(x) = e^x$ and $M_5(x) = 1 + x + \dfrac{x^2}{2} + \dfrac{x^3}{6} + \dfrac{x^4}{24} + \dfrac{x^5}{120}$

Solution

First find the Maclaurin series for $f(x) = e^x$.

$$f(x) = e^x \qquad\qquad f(0) = 1$$
$$f'(x) = e^x \qquad\qquad f'(0) = 1$$
$$\vdots \qquad\qquad\qquad \vdots$$

The Maclaurin series for e^x is

$$e^x = 1 + \frac{1}{1!}x + \frac{1}{2!}x^2 + \frac{1}{3!}x^3 + \cdots = \sum_{k=0}^{\infty} \frac{x^k}{k!}$$

Then find $M_5(x)$:

$$M_5(x) = 1 + x + \frac{x^2}{2} + \frac{x^3}{6} + \frac{x^4}{24} + \frac{x^5}{120} \approx e^x$$

A comparison of f and $M_5(x)$ is shown in Figure 8.25. Notice from the graphs of these functions that the error seems to increase as x moves away from the origin.

To determine the accuracy, we use Taylor's theorem

$$e = 1 + 1 + \frac{1}{2} + \frac{1}{6} + \frac{1}{24} + \frac{1}{120} + R_5(1)$$
$$= 2.71\overline{6} + R_5(1)$$

The remainder term is given by

$$R_5(1) = \frac{e^{z_5}}{(5+1)!}(1)^{5+1}$$

for some z_5 between 0 and 1. Because $0 < z_5 < 1$, we have $e^{z_5} < e$, and since $e < 3$, it follows that

$$R_5(1) < \frac{e}{6!} < \frac{3}{6!} \approx 0.004167$$

Thus, the number e satisfies

$$2.716667 - 0.004167 < e < 2.716667 + 0.004167$$
$$2.712500 < e < 2.720834 \qquad\blacksquare$$

EXAMPLE 3 Taylor series

Find the Taylor series for $f(x) = \ln x$ at $c = 1$.

Solution

Note that f is infinitely differentiable at $x = 1$. We find

$$f(x) = \ln x \qquad\qquad\qquad f(1) = 0$$

$$f'(x) = \frac{1}{x} \qquad\qquad\qquad f'(1) = 1$$

$$f''(x) = \frac{-1}{x^2} \qquad\qquad\qquad f''(1) = -1$$

$$f'''(x) = \frac{2}{x^3} \qquad\qquad\qquad f'''(1) = 2$$

$$f^{(4)}(x) = \frac{-6}{x^4} \qquad\qquad\qquad f^{(4)}(1) = -6$$

$$\vdots \qquad\qquad\qquad\qquad \vdots$$

$$f^{(k)}(x) = \frac{(-1)^{k+1}(k-1)!}{x^k} \qquad\qquad f^{(k)}(1) = (-1)^{k+1}(k-1)!$$

Then, use the definition of a Taylor series to write

$$\ln x = 0 + \frac{1}{1!}(x-1) - \frac{1}{2!}(x-1)^2 + \frac{2}{3!}(x-1)^3 - \frac{6}{4!}(x-1)^4 + \cdots$$

$$= (x-1) - \frac{1}{2}(x-1)^2 + \frac{1}{3}(x-1)^3 - \frac{1}{4}(x-1)^4 + \cdots$$

$$= \sum_{k=1}^{\infty} \frac{(-1)^{k+1}(x-1)^k}{k} \qquad \blacksquare$$

Suppose f is a function that is infinitely differentiable at c. Now we have two mathematical quantities, f and its Taylor series. There are several possibilities:

1. The Taylor series of f may converge to f on the interval of absolute convergence, $-R < x - c < R$ (that is, $|x - c| < R$).
2. The Taylor series may converge only at $x = c$, in which case it certainly does not represent f on any interval containing c.
3. The Taylor series of f may have a positive radius of convergence (even $R = \infty$), but it may converge to a function g that does not equal f on the interval $|x - c| < R$.

EXAMPLE 4 A function defined at points where its Taylor series does not converge

Show that the function $\ln x$ is defined at points for which its Taylor series at $c = 1$ does not converge.

Solution

We know that $\ln x$ is defined for all $x > 0$. From the previous example, we know the Taylor series for $\ln x$ at $c = 1$ is

$$\sum_{k=1}^{\infty} \frac{(-1)^{k-1}(x-1)^k}{k}$$

We find the interval of convergence for this series centered at $c = 1$ by computing

$$L = \lim_{k \to \infty} \left| \frac{\dfrac{(-1)^k(x-1)^{k+1}}{k+1}}{\dfrac{(-1)^{k-1}(x-1)^k}{k}} \right| = \lim_{k \to \infty} \left| \frac{\dfrac{(-1)^k}{k+1}}{\dfrac{(-1)^{k-1}}{k}} \right| |x - 1|$$

$$= \lim_{k \to \infty} \left(\frac{k}{k+1} \right) |x - 1| = |x - 1|$$

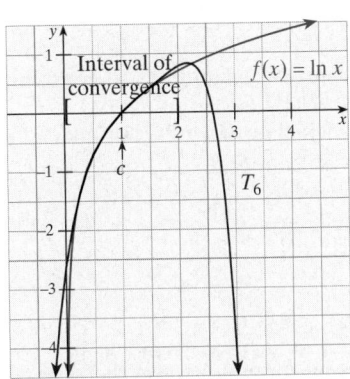

Figure 8.26 The graphs of $f(x) = \ln x$ and the Taylor polynomial

$$T_6(x) = \sum_{k=1}^{6} \frac{(-1)^{k-1}}{k}(x-1)$$

are very close near 1.

This means that the power series converges absolutely for

$$|x - 1| < 1$$
$$0 < x < 2$$

Test the endpoints:

$$x = 0: \quad \sum_{k=1}^{\infty} \frac{(-1)^{k-1}(0-1)^k}{k} = \sum_{k=1}^{\infty} \frac{-1}{k} \text{ diverges} \qquad \textit{Opposite of harmonic series}$$

$$x = 2: \sum_{k=1}^{\infty} \frac{(-1)^{k-1}(2-1)^k}{k} = \sum_{k=1}^{\infty} \frac{(-1)^{k-1}}{k} \text{ converges} \qquad \textit{Alternating harmonic series}$$

Thus, the series converges only on $(0, 2]$, but the function $\ln x$ is defined for all $x > 0$. The function is compared with the sixth degree Taylor approximation in Figure 8.26. ∎

The next example introduces a function whose Maclaurin series does not represent that function on *any* interval.

EXAMPLE 5   A function represented by its Maclaurin series at a single point

Let f be the function defined by

$$f(x) = \begin{cases} 0 & \text{if } x = 0 \\ e^{-1/x^2} & \text{if } x \neq 0 \end{cases}$$

Show that f is represented by its Maclaurin series only at $x = 0$.

Solution

It can be shown that f is infinitely differentiable at 0 and that $f^{(k)}(0) = 0$ for all k. Therefore, f has the Maclaurin series

$$0 + \frac{0}{1!}x + \frac{0}{2!}x^2 + \frac{0}{3!}x^3 + \cdots$$

which converges to the zero function for all x and thus represents $f(x)$ only at $x = 0$. The graph of f and the Maclaurin series are shown in Figure 8.27. ∎

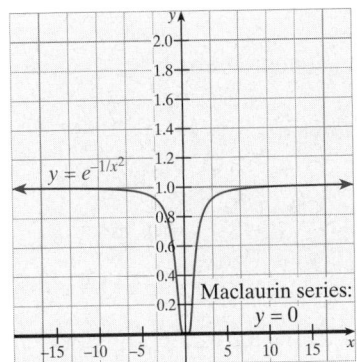

Figure 8.27 Graph of f and its Maclaurin series $y = 0$

OPERATIONS WITH TAYLOR AND MACLAURIN SERIES

According to the uniqueness theorem, the Taylor series for f at c is the only power series in $x - c$ that can satisfy $f(x) = \sum_{k=0}^{\infty} a_k(x - c)^k$ for all x in some interval containing c. The coefficients in this series can always be found by substituting into the formula $a_k = \frac{f^{(k)}(c)}{k!}$, but occasionally they can also be found by algebraic manipulation. In several of the examples that follow, we will use the geometric series equation

$$\frac{1}{1-u} = \sum_{k=0}^{\infty} u^k \qquad \text{for } |u| < 1$$

to obtain Maclaurin series for rational functions. The general procedure is illustrated in Example 6.

EXAMPLE 6   Maclaurin series using substitution in a geometric series

Find the Maclaurin series for $\dfrac{1}{1 + x^2}$.

Solution

We want a series of the form $\sum_{k=0}^{\infty} a_k u^k$ that represents $\dfrac{1}{1+x^2}$ on an interval containing 0. We could proceed directly using the definition of a Maclaurin series, but instead we will modify a known series. We know that if $|u| < 1$ we can write

$$\frac{1}{1-u} = 1 + u + u^2 + \cdots$$

so by substitution ($u = -x^2$) we have

$$\frac{1}{1+x^2} = \frac{1}{1-(-x^2)} = 1 - x^2 + x^4 - x^6 + \cdots$$

provided $\left| -x^2 \right| < 1$; that is, $-1 < x < 1$. Hence, by the uniqueness theorem, the desired representation is

$$\frac{1}{1+x^2} = \sum_{k=0}^{\infty} (-1)^k x^{2k} \quad \text{for } -1 < x < 1 \qquad \blacksquare$$

EXAMPLE 7 Maclaurin series by modifying a geometric series

Find the Maclaurin series for $f(x) = \dfrac{5-2x}{3+2x}$ and determine the interval of convergence of this series.

Solution

Our strategy is to rewrite $f(x)$ in the form $\dfrac{1}{1-u}$ of a geometric series:

$$
\begin{aligned}
\frac{5-2x}{3+2x} &= -1 + \frac{8}{3+2x} && \text{Long division} \\[2mm]
&= -1 + \frac{\frac{8}{3}}{1-\left(-\frac{2}{3}x\right)} && \text{Writing in the form } \frac{1}{1-u} \\[2mm]
&= -1 + \sum_{k=0}^{\infty} \frac{8}{3}\left[-\frac{2}{3}x\right]^k \\[2mm]
&= -1 + \frac{8}{3} - \frac{16}{9}x + \frac{32}{27}x^2 - \frac{64}{81}x^3 + \cdots
\end{aligned}
$$

The convergence set for $f(x)$ is the same as for the series $\sum_{k=1}^{\infty}\left(-\dfrac{2}{3}x\right)^k$; namely,

$$\left| -\frac{2}{3}x \right| < 1$$
$$-\frac{3}{2} < x < \frac{3}{2} \qquad \blacksquare$$

EXAMPLE 8 Using a trigonometric identity with a known series

Find the Maclaurin series for

a. $\cos x^2$ **b.** $\cos^2 x$

Solution

a. In Example 1 we found that

$$\cos u = 1 - \frac{u^2}{2!} + \frac{u^4}{4!} - \frac{u^6}{6!} + \cdots \qquad \text{for all } u$$

Therefore, by substituting $u = x^2$, we obtain

$$
\begin{aligned}
\cos x^2 &= 1 - \frac{(x^2)^2}{2!} + \frac{(x^2)^4}{4!} - \frac{(x^2)^6}{6!} + \cdots \\[2mm]
&= 1 - \frac{x^4}{2!} + \frac{x^8}{4!} - \frac{x^{12}}{6!} + \cdots \qquad \text{for all } x
\end{aligned}
$$

b. For $\cos^2 x$ we could use the definition of a Maclaurin series, but instead we will use a double-angle trigonometric identity.

$$\cos^2 x = \frac{1}{2} + \frac{1}{2}\cos 2x$$

$$= \frac{1}{2} + \frac{1}{2}\left[1 - \frac{(2x)^2}{2!} + \frac{(2x)^4}{4!} - \frac{(2x)^6}{6!} + \cdots\right] \qquad \text{Let } u = 2x.$$

$$= \frac{1}{2} + \frac{1}{2} - \frac{2x^2}{2!} + \frac{2^3 x^4}{4!} - \frac{2^5 x^6}{6!} + \cdots$$

$$= 1 - x^2 + \frac{1}{3}x^4 - \frac{2}{45}x^6 + \cdots \qquad \text{for all } x \qquad \blacksquare$$

EXAMPLE 9 Maclaurin series using substitution

Find the Maclaurin series for $f(x) = \ln\left(\dfrac{1+x}{1-x}\right)$ and use this series to compute $\ln 2$ correct to five decimal places.

Solution

For this function, we first use a property of logarithms:

$$f(x) = \ln\left(\frac{1+x}{1-x}\right) = \ln(1+x) - \ln(1-x)$$

From Example 3, we know

$$\ln x = (x - 1) - \tfrac{1}{2}(x - 1)^2 + \tfrac{1}{3}(x - 1)^3 - \cdots$$

so that

$$\ln(1 + x) = [1 + x - 1] - \tfrac{1}{2}[1 + x - 1]^2 + \tfrac{1}{3}[1 + x - 1]^3 - \cdots$$

$$= x - \frac{x^2}{2} + \frac{x^3}{3} - \frac{x^4}{4} + \cdots$$

$$\ln(1 - x) = [1 - x - 1] - \tfrac{1}{2}[1 - x - 1]^2 + \tfrac{1}{3}[1 - x - 1]^3 - \cdots$$

$$= (-x) - \frac{(-x)^2}{2} + \frac{(-x)^3}{3} - \frac{(-x)^4}{4} + \cdots$$

$$= -x - \frac{x^2}{2} - \frac{x^3}{3} - \frac{x^4}{4} - \cdots$$

By subtracting series, we find

$$f(x) = \ln(1 + x) - \ln(1 - x)$$

$$= \left[x - \frac{x^2}{2} + \frac{x^3}{3} - \frac{x^4}{4} + \cdots\right] - \left[-x - \frac{x^2}{2} - \frac{x^3}{3} - \frac{x^4}{4} - \cdots\right]$$

$$= 2\left[x + \frac{x^3}{3} + \frac{x^5}{5} + \cdots\right]$$

Next, by solving the equation $\dfrac{1+x}{1-x} = 2$, we find $x = \tfrac{1}{3}$, so we are looking for $\ln\left(\dfrac{1+x}{1-x}\right)$ where $x = \tfrac{1}{3}$. It follows that

$$\ln 2 = 2\left[\frac{1}{3} + \frac{\left(\frac{1}{3}\right)^3}{3} + \frac{\left(\frac{1}{3}\right)^5}{5} + \cdots\right] = 2\left[\frac{1}{3} + \frac{1}{3}\left(\frac{1}{3}\right)^3 + \frac{1}{5}\left(\frac{1}{3}\right)^5 + \cdots\right]$$

According to Taylor's theorem, we find

$$\ln 2 = \frac{2}{3} + \frac{2}{3}\left(\frac{1}{3}\right)^3 + \frac{2}{5}\left(\frac{1}{3}\right)^5 + \cdots + \frac{2}{2n+1}\left(\frac{1}{3}\right)^{2n+1} + R_n\left(\frac{1}{3}\right)$$

where $R_n\left(\frac{1}{3}\right)$ is the remainder term. To estimate the remainder, we note that $R_n\left(\frac{1}{3}\right)$ is the tail of the infinite series for $\ln 2$. Thus,

$$\left|R_n\left(\frac{1}{3}\right)\right| = \frac{2}{2n+3}\left(\frac{1}{3}\right)^{2n+3} + \frac{2}{2n+5}\left(\frac{1}{3}\right)^{2n+5} + \frac{2}{2n+7}\left(\frac{1}{3}\right)^{2n+7} + \cdots$$

$$< \frac{2}{2n+3}\left(\frac{1}{3}\right)^{2n+3} + \frac{2}{2n+3}\left(\frac{1}{9}\right)\left(\frac{1}{3}\right)^{2n+3} + \cdots$$

$$= \frac{2}{2n+3}\left(\frac{1}{3}\right)^{2n+3}\left[1 + \frac{1}{9} + \frac{1}{81} + \cdots\right]$$

Because the geometric series in brackets converges to $\dfrac{1}{1-\frac{1}{9}} = \dfrac{9}{8}$, we find that

$$\left|R_n\left(\frac{1}{3}\right)\right| < \frac{2}{2n+3}\left(\frac{9}{8}\right)\left(\frac{1}{3}\right)^{2n+3}$$

In particular, to achieve five-place accuracy, we must make sure the term on the right is less than 0.000005 (six places to account for round-off error). With a calculator we can see that if $n = 4$, we have

$$\frac{2}{2(4)+3}\left(\frac{9}{8}\right)\left(\frac{1}{3}\right)^{11} = 0.0000012$$

Thus, we approximate $\ln 2$ with $n = 4$:

$$\ln 2 \approx T_4\left(\frac{1}{3}\right) = \frac{2}{3} + \frac{2}{3}\left(\frac{1}{3}\right)^3 + \frac{2}{5}\left(\frac{1}{3}\right)^5 + \frac{2}{7}\left(\frac{1}{3}\right)^7 + \frac{2}{9}\left(\frac{1}{3}\right)^9 \approx 0.6931460$$

which is correct with an error of no more than 0.0000012; therefore,

$$0.6931460 - 0.0000012 < \ln 2 < 0.6931460 + 0.0000012$$

$$0.6931448 < \ln 2 < 0.6931472$$

Rounded to five-place accuracy, $\ln 2 = 0.69315$. We can check with calculator accuracy: $\ln 2 \approx 0.6931471806$. ∎

Some of the more common power series that we have derived are given in Table 8.2. For a more complete list, see the *Student Mathematics Handbook*. Before we present this table, there is one last result we should consider. It is a generalization of the binomial theorem that was discovered by Isaac Newton while he was still a student at Cambridge University.

THEOREM 8.26 Binomial series

If p is any real number and $-1 < x < 1$, then

$$(1+x)^p = 1 + px + \frac{p(p-1)}{2!}x^2 + \frac{p(p-1)(p-2)}{3!}x^3 + \cdots = \sum_{k=0}^{\infty}\binom{p}{k}x^k$$

where $\binom{p}{k} = \dfrac{p!}{k!(p-k)!}$ for $k = 1, 2, \ldots$.

Proof We begin by showing how the Maclaurin series is found. Let $f(x) = (1+x)^p$.

$$f(x) = (1+x)^p \qquad\qquad\qquad f(0) = 1$$

$$f'(x) = p(1+x)^{p-1} \qquad\qquad\qquad f'(0) = p$$

$$f''(x) = p(p-1)(1+x)^{p-2} \qquad\qquad f''(0) = p(p-1)$$

$$f'''(x) = p(p-1)(p-2)(1+x)^{p-3} \qquad f'''(0) = p(p-1)(p-2)$$

$$\vdots \qquad\qquad\qquad\qquad\qquad \vdots$$

$$f^{(n)}(x) = p(p-1)\cdots(p-n+1)(1+x)^{p-n} \qquad f^{(n)}(0) = p(p-1)\cdots(p-n+1)$$

TABLE 8.2   Power Series for Elementary Functions

Name	Series	Interval of Convergence
	Taylor series at $x = c$ follows the Maclaurin series for each function.	
Exponential series	$e^u = 1 + u + \dfrac{u^2}{2!} + \dfrac{u^3}{3!} + \dfrac{u^4}{4!} + \cdots + \dfrac{u^k}{k!} + \cdots$	$(-\infty, \infty)$
	$e^x = e^c + e^c(x - c) + \dfrac{e^c(x - c)^2}{2!} + \dfrac{e^c(x - c)^3}{3!} + \cdots + \dfrac{e^c(x - c)^k}{k!} + \cdots$	$(-\infty, \infty)$
Cosine series	$\cos u = 1 - \dfrac{u^2}{2!} + \dfrac{u^4}{4!} - \dfrac{u^6}{6!} + \cdots + \dfrac{(-1)^k u^{2k}}{(2k)!} + \cdots$	$(-\infty, \infty)$
	$\cos x = \cos c - (x - c)\sin c - \dfrac{(x - c)^2}{2!}\cos c + \dfrac{(x - c)^3}{3!}\sin c + \cdots$	$(-\infty, \infty)$
Sine series	$\sin u = u - \dfrac{u^3}{3!} + \dfrac{u^5}{5!} - \dfrac{u^7}{7!} + \cdots + \dfrac{(-1)^k u^{2k+1}}{(2k+1)!} + \cdots$	$(-\infty, \infty)$
	$\sin x = \sin c + (x - c)\cos c - \dfrac{(x - c)^2}{2!}\sin c - \dfrac{(x - c)^3}{3!}\cos c + \cdots$	$(-\infty, \infty)$
Geometric series	$\dfrac{1}{1 - u} = 1 + u + u^2 + u^3 + \cdots + u^k + \cdots$	$(-1, 1)$
Reciprocal series	$\dfrac{1}{u} = 1 - (u - 1) + (u - 1)^2 - (u - 1)^3 + (u - 1)^4 - \cdots$	$(0, 2)$
Logarithmic series	$\ln u = (u - 1) - \dfrac{(u - 1)^2}{2} + \dfrac{(u - 1)^3}{3} - \cdots + \dfrac{(-1)^{k-1}(u - 1)^k}{k} + \cdots$	$(0, 2]$
	$\ln(1 + x) = x - \dfrac{1}{2}x^2 + \dfrac{1}{3}x^3 - \dfrac{1}{4}x^4 + \cdots + \dfrac{(-1)^n x^{n+1}}{n + 1} + \cdots$	$(-1, 1]$
	$\ln x = \ln c + \dfrac{x - c}{c} - \dfrac{(x - c)^2}{2c^2} + \dfrac{(x - c)^3}{3c^3} - \cdots + \dfrac{(-1)^{k-1}(x - c)^k}{kc^k} + \cdots$	$(0, 2c]$
Inverse tangent series	$\tan^{-1} u = u - \dfrac{u^3}{3} + \dfrac{u^5}{5} - \dfrac{u^7}{7} + \cdots + \dfrac{(-1)^k u^{2k+1}}{2k + 1} + \cdots$	$[-1, 1]$
Inverse sine series	$\sin^{-1} u = u + \dfrac{u^3}{2 \cdot 3} + \dfrac{1 \cdot 3 u^5}{2 \cdot 4 \cdot 5} + \dfrac{1 \cdot 3 \cdot 5 u^7}{2 \cdot 4 \cdot 6 \cdot 7} + \cdots + \dfrac{1 \cdot 3 \cdot 5 \cdots (2k - 3)u^{2k-1}}{2 \cdot 4 \cdot 6 \cdots (2k - 2)(2k - 1)} + \cdots$	$[-1, 1]$
Binomial series	$(1 + u)^p = 1 + pu + \dfrac{p(p - 1)}{2!}u^2 + \dfrac{p(p - 1)(p - 2)}{3!}u^3 + \cdots + \binom{p}{q}u^q + \cdots$	

which produces the Maclaurin series. We could use the ratio test to show that this series converges on the interval $(-1, 1)$, but to show that it converges to $(1 + x)^p$ requires advanced calculus. ❑

The binomial series converges on the open interval $-1 < x < 1$, but convergence at the endpoints $x = -1$ and $x = 1$ of this interval depends on the exponent p. In particular, it can be shown that

if $-1 < p < 0$, the series converges at $x = 1$;

if $p \geq 0$, the series converges at both $x = 1$ and $x = -1$.

Moreover, if p is a nonnegative integer, the series terminates after only a finite number of terms (since $\binom{p}{k} = 0$ for $k > p$) and thus reduces to the ordinary binomial expansion, which, of course, converges for all x. The next example illustrates how the binomial series theorem can be used.

EXAMPLE 10   Using the binomial series theorem to obtain a Maclaurin series expansion

Determine the Maclaurin series for $f(x) = \sqrt{9+x}$ and find its interval of convergence.

Solution

Write $f(x) = \sqrt{9+x} = (9+x)^{1/2} = 3\left(1+\dfrac{x}{9}\right)^{1/2}$. Thus,

$$\sqrt{9+x} = 3\left(1+\frac{x}{9}\right)^{1/2}$$

$$= 3\left[1 + \frac{1}{2}\left(\frac{x}{9}\right) + \frac{\frac{1}{2}\left(\frac{1}{2}-1\right)}{2!}\left(\frac{x}{9}\right)^2 + \frac{\frac{1}{2}\left(\frac{1}{2}-1\right)\left(\frac{1}{2}-2\right)}{3!}\left(\frac{x}{9}\right)^3 + \cdots\right]$$

$$= 3\left[1 + \frac{1}{18}x - \frac{1}{648}x^2 + \frac{1}{11,664}x^3 - \cdots\right]$$

$$= 3 + \frac{1}{6}x - \frac{1}{216}x^2 + \frac{1}{3,888}x^3 - \cdots$$

Since the exponent $p = \frac{1}{2}$ satisfies $p > 0$, p not an integer, it follows from Theorem 8.26 that the series converges for $\left|\dfrac{x}{9}\right| \le 1$, that is, for $|x| \le 9$. ∎

8.8 PROBLEM SET

A 1. WHAT DOES THIS SAY? Compare and contrast Maclaurin and Taylor series.

2. WHAT DOES THIS SAY? Discuss the binomial series theorem.

Find the Maclaurin series for the functions given in Problems 3–30. Assume that a is any constant, and that all the derivatives of all orders exist at $x = 0$.

3. e^{2x}

4. e^{-x}

5. e^{x^2}

6. e^{ax}

7. $\sin x^2$

8. $\sin^2 x$

9. $\sin ax$

10. $\cos ax$

11. $\cos 2x^2$

12. $\cos x^3$

13. $x^2 \cos x$

14. $\sin \dfrac{x}{2}$

15. $x^2 + 2x + 1$

16. $x^3 - 2x^2 + x - 5$

17. xe^x

18. $e^{-x} + e^{2x}$

19. $e^x + \sin x$

20. $\sin x + \cos x$

21. $\dfrac{1}{1+4x}$

22. $\dfrac{1}{1-ax}, a \ne 0$

23. $\dfrac{1}{a+x}, a \ne 0$

24. $\dfrac{1}{a^2+x^2}, a \ne 0$

25. $\ln(3+x)$

26. $\log(1+x)$

27. $\tan^{-1}(2x)$

28. $\sqrt{1-x}$

29. e^{-x^2}

30. $f(x) = \begin{cases} \dfrac{\sin x}{x} & \text{if } x \ne 0 \\ 1 & \text{if } x = 0 \end{cases}$

Find the first four terms of the Taylor series of the functions in Problems 31–42 at the given value of c.

31. $f(x) = e^x$ at $c = 1$

32. $f(x) = \ln x$ at $c = 3$

33. $f(x) = \cos x$ at $c = \frac{\pi}{3}$

34. $f(x) = \sin x$ at $c = \frac{\pi}{4}$

35. $f(x) = \tan x$ at $c = 0$

36. $f(x) = x^2 + 2x + 1$ at $c = 200$

37. $f(x) = x^3 - 2x^2 + x - 5$ at $c = 2$

38. $f(x) = \sqrt{x}$ at $c = 9$

39. $f(x) = \dfrac{1}{2-x}$ at $c = 5$

40. $f(x) = \dfrac{1}{4-x}$ at $c = -2$

41. $f(x) = \dfrac{3}{2x-1}$ at $c = 2$

42. $f(x) = \dfrac{5}{3x+2}$ at $c = 2$

Expand each function in Problems 43–48 as a binomial series. Give the interval of convergence of the series.

43. $f(x) = \sqrt{1+x}$

44. $f(x) = \dfrac{1}{\sqrt{1+x^2}}$

45. $f(x) = (1+x)^{2/3}$

46. $f(x) = (4+x)^{-1/3}$

47. $f(x) = \dfrac{x}{\sqrt{1-x^2}}$

48. $f(x) = \sqrt[4]{2-x}$

B 49. Use term-by-term integration to show that

$$\ln(1+x) = \sum_{k=1}^{\infty} \frac{(-1)^{k-1}x^k}{k} \quad \text{for } |x| < 1$$

50. Use the Maclaurin series for e^x and e^{-x} to find the Maclaurin series for

$$\cosh x = \frac{e^x + e^{-x}}{2}$$

51. Use the Maclaurin series for e^x and e^{-x} to find the Maclaurin series for

$$\sinh x = \frac{e^x - e^{-x}}{2}$$

52. Use the Maclaurin series expansion of e^x to estimate $\sqrt{e}$ with three-decimal-place accuracy? How many terms are needed?

53. Use the Maclaurin series expansion of e^x to estimate $\sqrt[3]{e}$ with three-decimal-place accuracy. How many terms are needed?

Find the Maclaurin series for the functions given in Problems 54–56. Hint: Begin by expressing each function as a sum of partial fractions.

54. $f(x) = \dfrac{2x}{x^2 - 1}$ **55.** $f(x) = \dfrac{1}{x^2 - 3x + 2}$

56. $f(x) = \dfrac{x^2}{(x + 2)(x^2 - 1)}$

57. Use an appropriate identity to find the Maclaurin series for $f(x) = \sin x \cos x$.

58. a. It can be shown that $\cos 3x = 4\cos^3 x - 3\cos x$. Use this identity to find the Maclaurin series for $\cos^3 x$.

  b. Find the Maclaurin series for $\sin^3 x$.

59. Use the identity $2\cos\alpha\cos\beta = \cos(\alpha + \beta) + \cos(\alpha - \beta)$ to find the Maclaurin series for

$$f(x) = \left(\cos\frac{3x}{2}\right)\left(\cos\frac{x}{2}\right)$$

60. Find the Maclaurin series for $\ln[(1 + 2x)(1 + 3x)]$.

61. Find the Maclaurin series for $\ln\left[\dfrac{1 + 2x}{1 - 3x + 2x^2}\right]$.

62. Find the Maclaurin series for $f(x) = x + \sin x$ and then use this series to find $\lim\limits_{x\to 0} \dfrac{x + \sin x}{x}$.

63. Find the Maclaurin series for $g(x) = e^x - 1$ and then use this series to find $\lim\limits_{x\to 0} \dfrac{e^x - 1}{x}$.

In Problems 64–66, the Maclaurin series of a function appears with its remainder. Verify that the remainder satisfies the given inequality.

64. $e^x = \sum\limits_{k=0}^{\infty} \dfrac{x^k}{k!};\ |R_n(x)| \le \dfrac{e^p |x|^{n+1}}{(n+1)!}$, where p is some constant such that $0 < p < x$.

65. $\cos x = \sum\limits_{k=0}^{\infty} \dfrac{(-1)^k x^{2k}}{(2k)!};\ |R_n(x)| \le \dfrac{|x|^{n+1}}{(n+1)!}$

66. $\ln(x + 1) = \sum\limits_{k=0}^{\infty} \dfrac{(-1)^k x^{k+1}}{k + 1}$ for $0 \le x < 1;\ |R_n(x)| \le \dfrac{|x|^{n+1}}{n + 1}$

67. HISTORICAL QUEST The two mathematicians most closely associated with power series are Brook Taylor and Colin Maclaurin. The result stated in this section, called Taylor's theorem, was published by Taylor in 1712, but the result itself was discovered by the Scottish mathematician James Gregory (1638–1675) in 1670 and was obtained by Taylor in 1688, after Gregory's death.

BROOK TAYLOR
1685–1731

James Gregory was a Scottish mathematician who apparently anticipated some of the key calculus discoveries, but died prematurely and never received proper recognition for his work. In 1694, Johann Bernoulli (see Historical Quests 58 and 59, Section 4.5) published a series that was very similar to what we call Taylor's series. In fact, after Taylor published his work in 1714, Bernoulli accused him of plagiarism. ∎

In this Quest we seek to duplicate Bernoulli's work. He started by writing

$$n\,dx = n\,dx + \left(x\,dn - x\frac{dn}{dx}\,dx\right)$$

$$= n\,dx + \left(x\,dn - x\frac{dn}{dx}\,dx\right) - \left(\frac{x^2}{2!}\frac{d^2n}{dx^2}\,dx - \frac{x^2}{2!}\frac{d^2n}{dx^2}\,dx\right)$$

$$= n\,dx + \left(x\,dn - x\frac{dn}{dx}\,dx\right) - \left(\frac{x^2}{2!}\frac{d^2n}{dx^2}\,dx - \frac{x^2}{2!}\frac{d^2n}{dx^2}\,dx\right)$$

$$+ \left(\frac{x^3}{3!}\frac{d^3n}{dx^3}\,dx - \frac{x^3}{3!}\frac{d^3n}{dx^3}\,dx\right) - \cdots$$

$$= (n\,dx + x\,dn) - \left(x\frac{dn}{dx} + \frac{x^2}{2!}\frac{d^2n}{dx^2}\right)dx$$

$$+ \left(\frac{x^2}{2!}\frac{d^2n}{dx^2} + \frac{x^3}{3!}\frac{d^3n}{dx^3}\right)dx - \cdots$$

$$= d(nx) - d\left(\frac{x^2}{2!}\frac{dn}{dx}\right) + d\left(\frac{x^3}{3!}\frac{d^2n}{dx^2}\right) - \cdots$$

Integrate termwise to obtain what is known as Bernoulli's series. Next, see if you can show what angered Bernoulli by deriving Taylor's series from Bernoulli's series.

Incidentally, Bernoulli's assertion was not founded. The first known explicit statement of the general Taylor series was in *De Quadrature* (1691) by Isaac Newton.

68. HISTORICAL QUEST Colin Maclaurin was a mathematical prodigy. He entered the University of Glasgow at the age of 11. At 15 he took his master's degree and gave a remarkable public defense of his thesis on gravitational attraction. At 19 he was elected to the chair of mathematics at the Marischal College in Aberdeen and at 21 published his first important work, *Geometrica organica*. At 27 he became deputy, or assistant, to the professor of mathematics at the University of Edinburgh. There was some difficulty in obtaining a salary to cover his assistantship, and Newton offered to bear the cost personally so that the university could secure the services of such an outstanding young man. In time Maclaurin succeeded Newton and at the age of 44, published the first systematic exposition of Newton's work. In his work, Maclaurin uses what were called at the time fluxions, rather than derivatives. Here is what he concluded:

COLIN MACLAURIN
1698–1746

"If the first fluxion of the ordinate, with its fluxions of several subsequent orders vanish, the ordinate is a minimum or maximum, when the number of all those fluxions that vanish is 1, 3, 5, or any odd number. The ordinate is a *minimum*, when the fluxion next to those that vanish is positive; but a *maximum* when the fluxion is negative . . . . But if the number of all the fluxions of the first and successive orders that vanish be an even number, the ordinate is then neither a *maximum* nor *minimum*."[*] ∎

What is Maclaurin saying in this quotation?

---

[*]*The Historical Development of the Calculus* by C. H. Edwards, Jr., Springer-Verlag, 1979, p. 292.

69. Use series methods to approximate $\displaystyle\int_0^{1/2} \dfrac{dx}{1+x^7}$ correct to six decimal places.

70. Express $\displaystyle\int_0^1 x^{0.2} e^x \, dx$ as an infinite series.

71. The functions $J_0(x)$ and $J_1(x)$ are defined as the following power series:

$$J_0(x) = \sum_{k=0}^{\infty} \frac{(-1)^k x^{2k}}{(k!)^2 2^{2k}} \quad \text{and} \quad J_1(x) = \sum_{k=0}^{\infty} \frac{(-1)^k x^{2k+1}}{k!(k+1)! 2^{2k+1}}$$

a. Show that $J_0(x)$ and $J_1(x)$ both converge for all x.

b. Show that $J_0'(x) = -J_1(x)$.

These functions are called **Bessel functions of the first kind.** Bessel functions were first used in analyzing Kepler's laws of planetary motion. These functions play an important role in physics and engineering.

72. Show that J_0, the Bessel function of the first kind defined in Problem 71, satisfies the differential equation $x^2 J_0''(x) + x J_0'(x) + x^2 J_0(x) = 0$.

73. For x in the open interval $(-1, 1)$, let

$$f(x) = x + \frac{x^2}{2} + \frac{x^3}{3} + \cdots + \frac{x^k}{k} + \cdots$$

Show that f is a logarithmic function. *Hint:* Find f' and then retrieve f by integrating f'.

74. Given that

$$\frac{1}{(1-x)(1-2x)} = \sum a_n x^n$$

and

$$\frac{1+2x}{(1-x)(1-2x)(1-4x)} = \sum b_n x^n$$

show that $b_n = a_n^2$ for all n. *Hint:* Use a partial fraction decomposition.

75. Journal Problem   *The Pi Mu Epsilon Journal* by Robert C. Gebhardt* ■ For what x does $\displaystyle\sum_{n=0}^{\infty} \frac{x^n}{(2n)!}$ converge, and what is the sum?

---

*Volume 8, 1984, Problem 586.

Proficiency Examination

CONCEPT PROBLEMS

1. What is a sequence?

2. What is meant by the limit of a sequence?

3. Define the convergence and divergence of a sequence.

4. Explain each of the following terms:
a. bounded sequence
b. monotonic sequence
c. strictly monotonic sequence

5. State the BMCT.

6. What is an infinite series?

7. Compare or contrast the convergence and divergence of sequences and series.

8. What is a telescoping series?

9. Describe the harmonic series. Does it converge or diverge?

10. Define a geometric series and give its sum.

11. State the divergence test.

12. State the integral test.

13. State the p-series test.

14. State the direct comparison test.

15. State the limit comparison test.

16. State the zero-infinity limit comparison test.

17. State the ratio test.

18. State the root test.

19. What is the alternating series test?

20. How do you make an error estimate for an alternating series?

21. State the absolute convergence test.

22. What is meant by absolute and conditional convergence?

23. What is the generalized ratio test?

24. What is a power series?

25. How do you find the convergence set of a power series?

26. What are the radius of convergence and interval of convergence for a power series?

27. What is a Taylor polynomial?

28. State Taylor's theorem.

29. What are a Taylor series and a Maclaurin series?

30. State the binomial series theorem.

PRACTICE PROBLEMS

31. Find the limit of the sequence $\left\{ \left(1 + \dfrac{1}{n} \right)^n \right\}$

32. a. Find the limit of the sequence $\left\{ \dfrac{e^n}{n!} \right\}$.

b. Test the series $\displaystyle\sum_{k=1}^{\infty} \frac{e^k}{k!}$ for convergence.

c. Discuss the similarities and/or differences of parts **a** and **b**.

In Problems 33–37, test the given series for convergence.

33. $\displaystyle\sum_{k=2}^{\infty} \frac{1}{k \ln k}$

34. $\displaystyle\sum_{k=1}^{\infty} \frac{\pi^k k!}{k^k}$

35. $\displaystyle\sum_{k=2}^{\infty} \frac{1}{(\ln k)^{1/k}}$

36. $\displaystyle\sum_{k=1}^{\infty} \frac{3k^2 - k + 1}{(1 - 2k)k}$

37. $1 - \dfrac{1}{4} + \dfrac{1}{9} - \dfrac{1}{16} + \dfrac{1}{25} - \dfrac{1}{36} + \dfrac{1}{49} - \dfrac{1}{64} + \cdots + \dfrac{(-1)^{n+1}}{n^2} + \cdots$

38. Find the convergence set for the series

$$1 - 2u + 3u^2 - 4u^3 + \cdots$$

39. Find the Maclaurin series for $f(x) = \sin 2x$.

40. Find the Taylor series for $f(x) = \dfrac{1}{x - 3}$ at $c = \frac{1}{2}$.

Supplementary Problems

Determine whether each sequence in Problems 1–16 converges or diverges. If it converges, find its limit.

1. $\left\{ \dfrac{(-2)^n}{n^2 + 1} \right\}$

2. $\left\{ \dfrac{(\ln n)^2}{\sqrt{n}} \right\}$

3. $\left\{ \left(1 - \dfrac{2}{n}\right)^n \right\}$

4. $\left\{ \dfrac{e^{0.1n}}{n^5 - 3n + 1} \right\}$

5. $\left\{ \dfrac{n + (-1)^n}{n} \right\}$

6. $\left\{ \dfrac{3^n}{3^n + 2^n} \right\}$

7. $\left\{ \dfrac{5n^4 - n^2 - 700}{3n^4 - 10n^2 + 1} \right\}$

8. $\left\{ \left(1 + \dfrac{e}{n}\right)^{2n} \right\}$

9. $\left\{ \sqrt{n+1} - \sqrt{n} \right\}$

10. $\left\{ \sqrt{n^4 + 2n^2} - n^2 \right\}$

11. $\left\{ \dfrac{\ln n}{n} \right\}$

12. $\{ 1 + (-1)^n \}$

13. $\left\{ \left(1 + \dfrac{4}{n}\right)^n \right\}$

14. $\{ 5^{2/n} \}$

15. $\left\{ \dfrac{n^{3/4} \sin n^2}{n + 4} \right\}$

16. $\left\{ \displaystyle\sum_{k=1}^{n} \dfrac{n}{n^2 + k^2} \right\}$ *Hint:* This sequence is related to an integral.

17. Find the sum $\displaystyle\sum_{k=-123,456,788}^{123,456,789} \dfrac{k}{370,370,367}$

Find the sum of the given convergent geometric or telescoping series in Problems 18–27.

18. $\displaystyle\sum_{k=1}^{\infty} 4\left(\dfrac{2}{3}\right)^k$

19. $\displaystyle\sum_{k=1}^{\infty} \left(\dfrac{e}{3}\right)^k$

20. $\displaystyle\sum_{k=2}^{\infty} \dfrac{1}{k^2 - 1}$

21. $\displaystyle\sum_{k=1}^{\infty} \dfrac{1}{4k^2 - 1}$

22. $\displaystyle\sum_{k=0}^{\infty} \left[\left(\dfrac{-3}{8}\right)^k + \left(\dfrac{3}{4}\right)^{2k} \right]$

23. $\displaystyle\sum_{k=0}^{\infty} \dfrac{e^k + 3^{k-1}}{6^{k+1}}$

24. $\displaystyle\sum_{k=1}^{\infty} (-1)^{k+1}\left(\dfrac{1}{k} + \dfrac{1}{k+1}\right)$

25. $\displaystyle\sum_{k=2}^{\infty} \left[\dfrac{1}{\ln(k+1)} - \dfrac{1}{\ln k} \right]$

26. $\displaystyle\sum_{k=0}^{\infty} \left[3\left(\dfrac{2}{3}\right)^{2k} - \left(\dfrac{-1}{3}\right)^{4k} \right]$

27. $\displaystyle\sum_{k=1}^{\infty} \dfrac{k}{(k+1)(k+2)(k+3)}$

Test the series in Problems 28–45 for convergence.

28. $\displaystyle\sum_{k=1}^{\infty} \dfrac{5^k k!}{k^k}$

29. $\displaystyle\sum_{k=1}^{\infty} \dfrac{1}{\sqrt{k^2 + 4}}$

30. $\displaystyle\sum_{k=0}^{\infty} \dfrac{k!}{2^k}$

31. $\displaystyle\sum_{k=1}^{\infty} \dfrac{1}{2k - 1}$

32. $\displaystyle\sum_{k=0}^{\infty} ke^{-k}$

33. $\displaystyle\sum_{k=0}^{\infty} \dfrac{k^3}{k!}$

34. $\displaystyle\sum_{k=1}^{\infty} \dfrac{7^k}{k^2}$

35. $\displaystyle\sum_{k=1}^{\infty} \dfrac{k}{(2k - 1)!}$

36. $\displaystyle\sum_{k=0}^{\infty} \dfrac{k^2}{(k^3 + 1)^2}$

37. $\displaystyle\sum_{k=0}^{\infty} \dfrac{k^2}{3^k}$

38. $\displaystyle\sum_{k=2}^{\infty} \dfrac{1}{k(\ln k)^{1.1}}$

39. $\displaystyle\sum_{k=2}^{\infty} \dfrac{1}{k(\ln k)^2}$

40. $\displaystyle\sum_{k=0}^{\infty} (\sqrt{k^3 + 1} - \sqrt{k^3})$

41. $\displaystyle\sum_{k=1}^{\infty} \dfrac{1}{\sqrt{k(k+1)}}$

42. $\displaystyle\sum_{k=1}^{\infty} \dfrac{k - 1}{k2^k}$

43. $\displaystyle\sum_{k=1}^{\infty} \dfrac{k!}{k^2(k+1)^2}$

44. $\displaystyle\sum_{k=0}^{\infty} \dfrac{1}{1 + \sqrt{k}}$

45. $\displaystyle\sum_{k=1}^{\infty} \dfrac{k^2 3^k}{k!}$

Determine whether each series given in Problems 46–55 converges conditionally, converges absolutely, or diverges.

46. $\dfrac{1}{1 \cdot 2} - \dfrac{1}{3 \cdot 2} + \dfrac{1}{5 \cdot 2} - \dfrac{1}{7 \cdot 2} + \cdots$

47. $\dfrac{1}{1 \cdot 2} - \dfrac{1}{2 \cdot 3} + \dfrac{1}{3 \cdot 4} - \dfrac{1}{4 \cdot 5} + \cdots$

48. $\dfrac{3}{2} - \dfrac{4}{3} + \dfrac{5}{4} - \dfrac{6}{5} + \cdots$

49. $1 - \dfrac{1}{3} + \dfrac{1}{9} - \dfrac{1}{27} + \dfrac{1}{81} - \cdots$

50. $\dfrac{1}{5} - \dfrac{1}{7} + \dfrac{1}{9} - \dfrac{1}{11} + \cdots$

51. $-1 + \dfrac{1}{\sqrt{2}} - \dfrac{1}{\sqrt[3]{3}} + \dfrac{1}{\sqrt[4]{4}} - \cdots$

52. $\displaystyle\sum_{k=1}^{\infty} \dfrac{(-1)^k}{k[\ln(k + 1)]^2}$

53. $\displaystyle\sum_{k=1}^{\infty} (-1)^k \left(\dfrac{3k + 85}{4k + 1}\right)^k$

54. $\displaystyle\sum_{k=1}^{\infty} (-1)^k \tan^{-1}\left(\dfrac{1}{2k + 1}\right)$

55. $\displaystyle\sum_{k=1}^{\infty} \dfrac{(-1)^{k(k+1)/2}}{2^k}$

Find the interval of convergence for each power series in Problems 56–67.

56. $\displaystyle\sum_{k=1}^{\infty} \dfrac{kx^k}{3^k}$

57. $\displaystyle\sum_{k=1}^{\infty} k(x - 1)^k$

58. $\displaystyle\sum_{k=1}^{\infty} \dfrac{x^k}{k(k + 1)}$

59. $\displaystyle\sum_{k=1}^{\infty} \dfrac{\ln k(x^2)^k}{\sqrt{k}}$

60. $\displaystyle\sum_{k=1}^{\infty} \dfrac{k^2(x + 1)^{2k}}{2^k}$

61. $\displaystyle\sum_{k=1}^{\infty} \dfrac{(-1)^k x^k}{k^k}$

62. $\displaystyle\sum_{k=1}^{\infty} \dfrac{(-1)^k(2x - 1)^k}{k^2}$

63. $\displaystyle\sum_{k=1}^{\infty} \dfrac{(x + 2)^k}{k \ln(k + 1)}$

64. $\displaystyle\sum_{k=1}^{\infty} \frac{k(x-3)^k}{(k+3)!}$

65. $\displaystyle\sum_{n=1}^{\infty} \frac{(3n)!}{n!}x^n$

66. $\displaystyle\sum_{n=1}^{\infty} \frac{(-1)^n x^n}{9n^2-1}$

67. $x - \dfrac{x^3}{3!} + \dfrac{x^5}{5!} - \dfrac{x^7}{7!} + \cdots + \dfrac{(-1)^{k+1}x^{2k-1}}{(2k-1)!} + \cdots$

Find the Maclaurin series for each function given in Problems 68–73.

68. $f(x) = x^2 e^{-3x}$

69. $f(x) = x^3 \sin x$

70. $f(x) = 3^x$

71. $f(x) = x^2 + \tan^{-1} x$

72. $f(x) = \dfrac{5+7x}{1+2x-3x^2}$

73. $f(x) = \dfrac{11x-1}{2+x-3x^2}$

74. Compute the sum of the series

$$1 - \frac{1}{2} + \frac{1}{2!}\left(\frac{1}{2}\right)^2 - \frac{1}{3!}\left(\frac{1}{2}\right)^3 + \cdots$$

correct to three decimal places.

75. Find a bound on the error incurred by approximating the sum of the series

$$1 - \frac{1}{2!} + \frac{2}{3!} - \frac{3}{4!} + \cdots$$

by the sum of the first eight terms.

76. Use geometric series to write $12.342\overline{132}$ as a rational number.

77. A ball is dropped from a height of A feet. Each time it drops h feet, it rebounds $0.8h$ feet. If it travels a total distance of 20 feet before coming to a stop, what is A?

78. Find the first three nonzero terms of the Maclaurin series for $\tan x$ and then use term-by-term integration to find the first three nonzero terms of the Maclaurin series for $\ln |\cos x|$.

79. **Spy Problem** The Spy, who is smarter than he looks, aborts his mission to the village after six days of duck plucking (recall Problem 62, Section 7.4). As he races away, he is confronted by four of Blohardt's thugs and soon finds himself in a gun battle using a revolver he managed to steal from Blabba. While dodging bullets, he recalls from his math class at Spy Academy that if the probability of a bullet being "good" is p, then on average, the number of bullets fired before a bad one jams the gun is given by the series $\displaystyle\sum_{n=0}^{\infty} np^{n-1}(1-p)$. If he takes five shots to dispose of each villain, what is the smallest value of p that will guarantee he gets off enough rounds to dispatch all four foes before a "bad" bullet gets him into another jam?

80. **Convergence of the sequence** $\left\{\left(1+\dfrac{1}{n}\right)^n\right\}$

   a. Suppose n is a positive integer. Use the binomial theorem to show that

$$\left(1+\frac{1}{n}\right)^n = 1 + 1 + \frac{1}{2!}\left(1-\frac{1}{n}\right)$$
$$+ \frac{1}{3!}\left(1-\frac{1}{n}\right)\left(1-\frac{2}{n}\right) + \cdots$$
$$+ \frac{1}{n!}\left(1-\frac{1}{n}\right)\left(1-\frac{2}{n}\right)\cdots\left(1-\frac{n-1}{n}\right)$$

   b. Use part **a** to show that $\left(1+\dfrac{1}{n}\right)^n < 3$ for all n.

   c. Use part **a** to show that $\left\{\left(1+\dfrac{1}{n}\right)^n\right\}$ is an increasing sequence. Then use the BMCT to show that this sequence converges.

81. HISTORICAL QUEST
Ramanujan was that rarest of mathematicians, an instinctive genius with virtually no formal training. Like his Hindu predecessor, Bhaskara (see the Historical Quest in Problem 55 of Section 4.4), Ramanujan had an uncanny instinct for numerical "truth" and conceived of his results in much the same way that a sculptor "sees" a statue

SRINIVASA RAMANUJAN
1887–1920

in a raw block of stone. In his short life, he initiated new ways of thinking about number theory and made conjectures that are the subject of mathematical inquiry to this day.

A story related by his friend and mentor, the eminent British number theorist G. H. Hardy (1877–1947), serves to illustrate the resonance between Ramanujan's mind and the concept of number. Ramanujan was ill and Hardy came to visit him in the hospital. At a loss for how to begin the conversation, Hardy idly remarked that he had arrived in a taxi with the "dull" number 1729. Ramanujan immediately grew excited and exclaimed, "No, Hardy, it is a very interesting number, for it is the smallest integer that can be expressed as the sum of cubes in two different ways." ($1729 = 1^3 + 12^3 = 9^3 + 10^3$.)

In a letter from Ramanujan to G. H. Hardy at Cambridge University,* Ramanujan stated

$$1 - 5\left(\frac{1}{2}\right)^3 + 9\left(\frac{1\cdot 3}{2\cdot 4}\right)^3 - 13\left(\frac{1\cdot 3\cdot 5}{2\cdot 4\cdot 6}\right)^3 + \cdots = \frac{2}{\pi}$$

Hardy spent a great deal of time wondering how this sum could be equal to $2/\pi$. ∎

   a. Find a_k so this sum can be expressed as $\displaystyle\sum_{k=1}^{\infty} a_k$.

   b. There is no elementary way to prove this identity. Use technology to check that this formula is valid.

82. HISTORICAL QUEST Leonhard Euler (1707–1783) was introduced in Chapter 4 Supplementary Problem 84, where we saw that Euler writes $a^\epsilon = 1 + k\epsilon$ for an "infinitely small" number ϵ. In this Historical Quest we will see why we define

$$\lim_{n\to+\infty}\left(1+\frac{1}{n}\right)^n = e$$

by asking you to reconstruct the steps of Euler's work.

Let x be a (finite) number. Euler introduced the "infinitely large" number $N = x/\epsilon$. Explain each step.

---

*Quantum, March/April 1998.

$$a^x = a^{N\epsilon} = (a^\epsilon)^N$$

$$= (1 + k\epsilon)^N$$

$$= \left(1 + \frac{kx}{N}\right)^N$$

$$= 1 + N\left(\frac{kx}{N}\right) + \frac{N(N-1)}{2!}\left(\frac{kx}{N}\right)^2$$

$$+ \frac{N(N-1)(N-2)}{3!}\left(\frac{kx}{N}\right)^3 + \cdots$$

$$= 1 + kx + \frac{1}{2!}\frac{N(N-1)}{N^2}k^2x^2$$

$$+ \frac{1}{3!}\frac{N(N-1)(N-2)}{N^3}k^3x^3 + \cdots$$

Because N is infinitely large, Euler assumed that

$$1 = \frac{N-1}{N} = \frac{N-2}{N} = \cdots$$

Substitute these values into the given derivation and also substitute e for a to obtain

$$e = 1 + \frac{1}{1!} + \frac{1}{2!} + \frac{1}{3!} + \cdots$$

Euler calculated e to 26 places:

$$e \approx 2.71828182845904523536028$$

Show that Euler's derivation is equivalent to $\displaystyle\lim_{n \to +\infty}\left(1 + \frac{1}{n}\right)^n$.

83. Show that

$$\cos x = \cos c - (\sin c)(x-c) - (\cos c)\frac{(x-c)^2}{2!}$$

$$+ (\sin c)\frac{(x-c)^3}{3!} + \cdots$$

84. Show that

$$e^x = e^c + e^c(x-c) + e^c\frac{(x-c)^2}{2!} + \cdots + e^c\frac{(x-c)^k}{k!} + \cdots$$

85. Express the integral $\displaystyle\int \sqrt{x^3 + 1}\, dx$ as an infinite series by writing the first four nonzero terms. *Hint*: Use the binomial theorem and then integrate term by term.

86. Estimate the value of the integral

$$\int_0^{0.4} \frac{dx}{\sqrt{1 + x^3}}$$

with five-decimal-place accuracy.

87. Show that if $a > 0$, $a \neq 1$,

$$a^x = \sum_{k=0}^{\infty} \frac{(\ln a)^k}{k!}x^k \qquad \text{for all } x$$

88. Show that for $0 < x < 2c$,

$$\frac{1}{x} = \frac{1}{c} - \frac{1}{c^2}(x-c) + \frac{1}{c^3}(x-c)^2 - \frac{1}{c^4}(x-c)^3 + \cdots$$

89. Use series to find $\sin 0.2$ correct to five decimal places.

90. Use series to find $\ln 1.05$ correct to five decimal places.

91. Use a Maclaurin series to find a cubic polynomial that approximates e^{2x} for $|x| < 0.001$. Find an upper bound for the error in this approximation.

92. For what values of x can $\sin x$ be replaced by $x - \dfrac{x^3}{6}$ if the allowable error is 0.0005?

93. For what values of x can $\cos x$ be replaced by $1 - \dfrac{x^2}{2}$ if the allowable error is 0.00005?

94. Find the Maclaurin series for $f(x) = \dfrac{2\tan x}{1 + \tan^2 x}$.

95. Modeling Problem When we studied carbon dating in Section 5.6, it was pointed out that radiocarbon methods apply only to objects that are not too "old" (roughly 40,000 years). To date older objects, radioactive isotopes other than ^{14}C are often employed. Regardless of the radioactive substance used, it can be shown that the ratio of stable isotope to radioactive isotope at any given time may be modeled by

$$\frac{S(t) - S(0)}{R(t)} + 1 = e^{(\ln 2)t/\lambda}$$

where $R(t)$ is the number of atoms of radioactive material at time t, $S(t)$ is the number of atoms of the stable product of radioactive decay, $S(0)$ is the number of atoms of stable product initially present (at $t = 0$), and λ is the half-life of the radioactive isotope.*

a. Use the first two terms of the Maclaurin series for e^x to approximate $e^{(\ln 2)t/\lambda}$, and then solve the modeling equation for t.

b. Suppose a piece of mica is analyzed, and it is found that 5% of the atoms in the rock are radioactive rubidium-87 and 0.04% of the atoms are strontium-87. Assuming that the strontium was produced by decay of the rubidium-87 originally in the rock, what is the approximate age of the sample? Use the result in part **a**, with $\lambda = 4.86 \times 10^9$ years as the half-life of rubidium-87.

96. Putnam Examination Problem Express

$$\sum_{k=1}^{\infty} \frac{6^k}{(3^{k+1} - 2^{k+1})(3^k - 2^k)}$$

as a rational number.

97. Putnam Examination Problem Find the sum of the convergent alternating series $\displaystyle\sum_{n=0}^{\infty} \frac{(-1)^{n+1}}{3n - 2}$.

98. Putnam Examination Problem For positive real x, let

$$B_n(x) = 1^x + 2^x + 3^x + \cdots + n^x$$

Test for convergence of the series

$$\sum_{k=2}^{\infty} \frac{B_k(\log_k 2)}{(k \log_2 k)^2}$$

*This model is discussed in detail in the article, "How Old Is the Earth?" by Paul J. Campbell, *UMAP Modules 1992: Tools for Teaching*, Lexington, MA: Consortium for Mathematics and Its Applications, Inc., 1993, pp. 105–137.

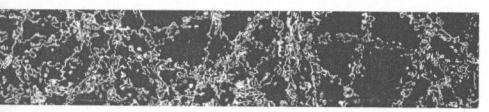
Elastic Tightrope

THE INFINITE! No other question has ever moved so profoundly the spirit of man; no other idea has so fruitfully stimulated his intellect; yet no other concept stands in greater need of clarification than that of the infinite.

——David Hilbert
To Infinity and Beyond
by Eli Maor
(Birkhäuser, 1987), p. vii.

THERE IS NOTHING now which ever gives me any thought or care in algebra except divergent series, which I cannot follow the French in rejecting.

——Augustus De Morgan
Graves' Life of W.R. Hamilton
(New York: 1882–1889), p. 249

This project is to be done in groups of three or four students. Each group will submit a single written report.

Suppose a cockroach starts at one end of a 100-m tightrope and runs toward the other end at a speed of 1 m/s. At the end of every minute, the tightrope stretches uniformly and instantaneously, increasing its length by 100 meters each time. Thus, after the first minute, the roach has traveled 60 meters and the length of the tightrope is 200 m. After the second minute, the roach has traveled another 60 meters and the tightrope has become 300 m long, and so on.

Does the roach ever reach the other end? If so, how long does it take?

Your paper is not limited to the following questions but should include these concerns. Suppose it is you standing on the elastic rope b meters from one end and c meters from the other end. Then suppose the entire rope stretches uniformly, increasing its length by d meters. Only the tightrope stretches; units of length and time remain constant. How far are you from each end? You might also try to generalize the roach problem.

*This group project is courtesy of David Pengelley, New Mexico State University, Las Cruces.

CHAPTERS 6–8   Cumulative Review

1. **WHAT DOES THIS SAY?**   Describe a procedure for using integration to compute
   a. work done by a variable force
   b. fluid (or hydrostatic) force
2. **WHAT DOES THIS SAY?**   Describe integration by parts.
3. **WHAT DOES THIS SAY?**   Describe a geometric series. For what values does such a series converge? What is the sum of a convergent geometric series?
4. **WHAT DOES THIS SAY?**   Describe a procedure for determining the convergence set of the power series $\Sigma a_k x^k$.

Evaluate each of the integrals in Problems 5–10.

5. $\displaystyle\int \ln \sqrt{x}\, dx$

6. $\displaystyle\int \sin^2 x \cos^3 x\, dx$

7. $\displaystyle\int \frac{\tan^{-1} x}{1 + x^2}\, dx$

8. $\displaystyle\int \sec^{3/2} x \tan x\, dx$

9. $\displaystyle\int \sqrt{4 - x^2}\, dx$

10. $\displaystyle\int \frac{1 - x^2}{1 + x^2}\, dx$

11. Let $f(x) = \dfrac{x^2 + 17x - 8}{(2x + 3)(x - 1)^2}$

    a. Express $f(x)$ as a partial fraction sum.

    b. Find $\displaystyle\int f(x)\, dx$.

    c. Either evaluate the improper integral $\displaystyle\int_2^\infty f(x)\, dx$ or show that it diverges.

12. In each of the following cases, either evaluate the given improper integral or show that it diverges.

    a. $\displaystyle\int_0^\infty x e^{-2x}\, dx$

    b. $\displaystyle\int_0^{\pi/2} \sec x\, dx$

In Problems 13–18, test the given series for convergence.

13. $\displaystyle\sum_{k=0}^\infty \frac{k^2 3^{k+1}}{4^k}$

14. $\displaystyle\sum_{k=1}^\infty \frac{k + 3k^{3/2}}{5k^2 - k + 3}$

15. $\displaystyle\sum_{k=1}^\infty \frac{(-1)^{k+1} k}{k + 1}$

16. $\displaystyle\sum_{k=1}^\infty \left(\frac{2k + 5}{3k - 2}\right)^k$

17. $\displaystyle\sum_{k=1}^\infty k e^{-k^2}$

18. $\displaystyle\sum_{k=1}^\infty \frac{k^2}{k!}$

In Problems 19 and 20, find the sum of the given convergent series.

19. $\displaystyle\sum_{k=1}^\infty 5\left(\frac{-2}{3}\right)^{2k-1}$

20. $\displaystyle\sum_{k=1}^\infty \frac{2}{(k + 1)(k + 3)}$

In Problems 21 and 22, find the convergence set of the given power series.

21. $\displaystyle\sum_{k=1}^\infty \frac{x^k}{k^3}$

22. $\displaystyle\sum_{k=1}^\infty \frac{(-x)^k}{k + 1}$

23. A tank has the shape of a circular cone with height 10 ft and top radius 4 ft. If the tank is filled with water ($\rho = 62.4$ lb/ft^3) to a depth of 6 ft, how much work is done (rounded to the nearest ft-lb) in pumping all the water in the tank to a height 2 ft above the top?

24. A triangular plate is submerged in oil ($\rho = 50$ lb/ft^3) to a depth of 2 ft, as shown in Figure 8.28. Find the fluid force on the plate.

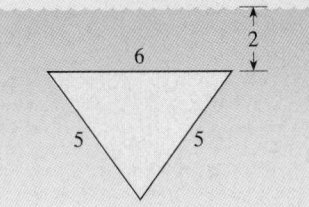

Figure 8.28   Submerged plate

25. Find the arc length of the curve $y = \frac{3}{2} x^{2/3}$ on the interval $\left[\frac{1}{8}, 8\right]$.

26. Let R be the region bounded by the x-axis, the curve $y = \dfrac{1}{\sqrt{x + 1}}$, and the lines $x = 3$ and $x = 8$. Find the volume of the solid generated when R is revolved about

    a. the x-axis   b. the y-axis   c. the line $y = -1$

27. Solve each of the given first-order linear differential equations.

    a. $y' - \dfrac{y}{x} = \dfrac{x}{1 + x^2}$

    b. $y' + (\tan x)y = \tan x$, where $y = 3$ when $x = 0$

28. A ball is dropped from a height of 20 ft. Each time it bounces, it rises to $\frac{3}{4}$ of its previous height. What is the total distance traveled by the ball?

29. Find the Maclaurin series for each of the following functions.

    a. $f(x) = \sin x^2$

    b. $f(x) = \sqrt{e^x}$

    c. $f(x) = \dfrac{3x - 2}{5 + 2x}$

30. A tank contains 15 lb of salt dissolved in 70 gallons of water. Suppose four gallons of brine containing 3 lb/gal of salt run into the tank every minute and the mixture (kept uniform by stirring) runs out of the tank at the rate of 2 gal/min.

    a. Set up and solve a differential equation for the amount of salt $S(t)$ in the tank at time t.

    b. Suppose the capacity of the tank is 100 gal. How much salt is in the tank at the time it just begins to overflow?

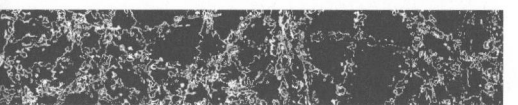

9

Vectors in the Plane and in Space

PREVIEW

In this chapter, we focus on various algebraic and geometric aspects of vector representations. Then in Chapter 10, we see how vectors can be combined with calculus to study motion in space and other applications.

PERSPECTIVE

Suppose a person is pulling a block of ice across the floor. The effect of this effort on the block of ice is dependent on the direction it is pulled, as well as the magnitude of the force that is applied when pulling. In this chapter, we consider the concept of a *vector*, which is defined as a quantity with both direction and magnitude. In Problem 43 in Section 9.3 we consider the amount of work done by dragging a large block of ice, which we compute using vectors and vector operations.

In general, a *scalar* quantity is one that can be described in terms of magnitude alone, whereas a *vector* quantity requires both magnitude and direction. Force, velocity, and acceleration are common vector quantities, and an important goal of this chapter is to develop methods for dealing with such quantities.

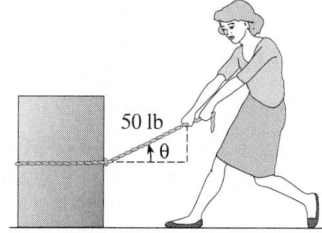

Finding the amount of work to pull a box across the floor can be formulated as a vector calculation.

9.1 Vectors in $\mathbb{R}^2$

IN THIS SECTION introduction to vectors, vectors in component form, standard representation of vectors in the plane

INTRODUCTION TO VECTORS

A **vector** is a quantity (such as velocity or force) that has both magnitude and direction. We sometimes represent a vector as a directed line segment, an "arrow" with **initial point** P and **terminal point** Q. The direction of the vector is that of the arrow, and its magnitude is represented by the arrow's length, as shown in Figure 9.1. We will indicate such a vector by writing **PQ** in boldface type, but in your work you may write an arrow over the designated points: $\overrightarrow{PQ}$. The order of letters you write down is important: **PQ** means that the vector is from P to Q, but **QP** means that the vector is from Q to P. The first letter is the initial point and the second letter is the terminal point.

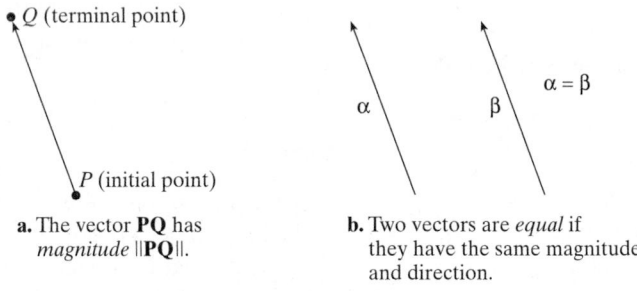

a. The vector **PQ** has *magnitude* ‖**PQ**‖.

b. Two vectors are *equal* if they have the same magnitude and direction.

Figure 9.1 Magnitude and equality of vectors

We will denote the **magnitude** (length) of a vector **PQ** by ‖**PQ**‖. Two vectors are regarded as **equal** (or **equivalent**) if they have the same magnitude and the same direction, even if they are in different locations. Thus, the initial point of a given vector may be moved to any convenient location by translating the vector parallel to its original position.

A vector with magnitude 0 is called the **zero** (or **null**) **vector** and is denoted by **0**. The **0** vector has no specific direction, and we will adopt the convention of assigning it any direction that may be convenient in a particular problem.

Vectors can be multiplied by scalars and added to one another according to the rules originally developed in physics. A **scalar** quantity is one that has only magnitude and, in the context of vectors, is used to describe a real number. A scalar multiple $s\mathbf{v}$ of **v** is parallel to **v** with magnitude $|s|\,\|\mathbf{v}\|$ and points in the same direction as **v** if $s > 0$, and in the opposite direction if $s < 0$, as shown in Figure 9.2. If $s = 0$ or $\mathbf{v} = \mathbf{0}$, then $s\mathbf{v} = \mathbf{0}$.

Physical experiments indicate that force and velocity vectors can be added according to a **triangle rule** displayed in Figure 9.3a, and we use this rule as our definition

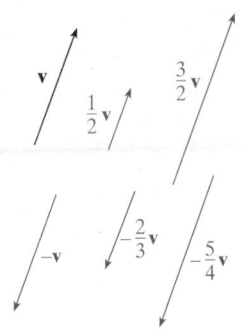

Figure 9.2 Some multiples of the vector **v**

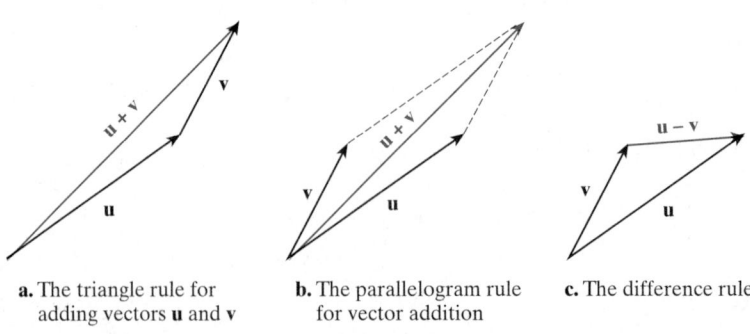

a. The triangle rule for adding vectors **u** and **v**

b. The parallelogram rule for vector addition

c. The difference rule

Figure 9.3 Vector addition and subtraction

of vector addition. In particular, to add the vector **v** to the vector **u**, we place the initial point of **v** at the tip (terminal point) of **u** and define the **sum**, also called the **resultant** **u** + **v**, to be the vector that extends from the initial point of **u** to the terminal point of **v**.

Equivalently, **u** + **v** is the diagonal of the parallelogram formed with sides **u** and **v**, as shown in Figure 9.3b. The **difference u** − **v** is just the vector **w** that satisfies **v** + **w** = **u**, and it may be found by placing the initial points of **u** and **v** together and extending a vector from the terminal point of **v** to the terminal point of **u** (see Figure 9.3c). Note that **u** + **v** = **v** + **u**. The vector **v** − **u** may be found similarly and has the same magnitude, but points in the opposite direction to **u** − **v**.

VECTORS IN COMPONENT FORM

Many issues involving vectors can be simplified by introducing a rectangular coordinate system. Suppose the vector **v** is positioned in a rectangular coordinate plane with its initial point at the origin $(0, 0)$ and its terminal point at (v_1, v_2), as shown in Figure 9.4. Then v_1 and v_2 are called the **standard components** of **v**, and we write **v** = $\langle v_1, v_2 \rangle$. The "dart" parentheses "$\langle \quad \rangle$" are used to distinguish the **component form** $\langle v_1, v_2 \rangle$ of **v** from the point (v_1, v_2) in $\mathbb{R}^2$.

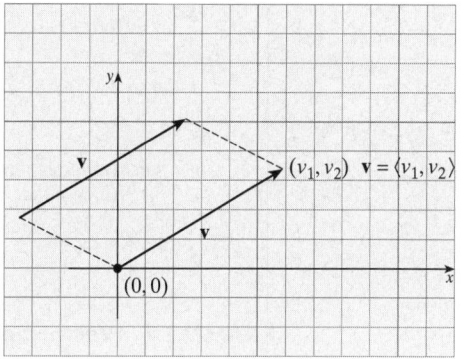

Figure 9.4   The standard component form of a vector **v**

Using the geometric relationships shown in Figure 9.5, the vector **PQ** with initial point $P(a, b)$ and terminal point $Q(c, d)$ equals the vector **OR**, where $O(0, 0)$ is the origin and R is the point with coordinates $(c - a, d - b)$.

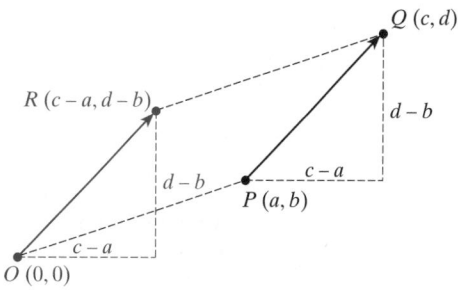

Figure 9.5   Given $P(a, b)$ and $Q(c, d)$, the vector **PQ** is $\langle c - a, d - b \rangle$.

Thus, we can make the following general statement.

Standard Components of a Vector in the Plane

If $P(a, b)$ and $Q(c, d)$ are points in a coordinate plane, then the vector **PQ** has the unique standard component form **PQ** = $\langle c - a, d - b \rangle$.

Vector properties are easily represented when vectors are given in component form. In particular, we have

$$\langle a_1, b_1 \rangle = \langle a_2, b_2 \rangle \qquad \text{if and only if } a_1 = a_2 \text{ and } b_1 = b_2$$
$$k \langle a, b \rangle = \langle ka, kb \rangle \qquad \text{for constant } k$$
$$\langle a, b \rangle + \langle c, d \rangle = \langle a + c, b + d \rangle$$
$$\langle a, b \rangle - \langle c, d \rangle = \langle a - c, b - d \rangle$$

These formulas may be verified geometrically. For instance, the rule for multiplication by a scalar can be obtained by using the relationships in Figure 9.6a, and Figure 9.6b illustrates the rule for vector addition.

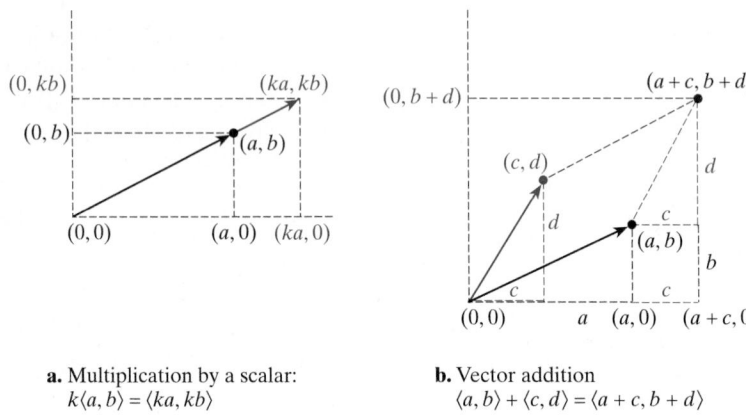

a. Multiplication by a scalar:
$k\langle a, b \rangle = \langle ka, kb \rangle$

b. Vector addition
$\langle a, b \rangle + \langle c, d \rangle = \langle a + c, b + d \rangle$

Figure 9.6   Vector operations

EXAMPLE 1   Vector operations

For the vectors $\mathbf{u} = \langle 2, -3 \rangle$ and $\mathbf{v} = \langle -1, 7 \rangle$, find

a. $\mathbf{u} + \mathbf{v}$ **b.** $\frac{3}{4}\mathbf{u}$ **c.** $3\mathbf{u} - \frac{1}{2}\mathbf{v}$

Solution

a. $\mathbf{u} + \mathbf{v} = \langle 2, -3 \rangle + \langle -1, 7 \rangle = \langle 2 + (-1), -3 + 7 \rangle = \langle 1, 4 \rangle$

b. $\frac{3}{4}\mathbf{u} = \frac{3}{4} \langle 2, -3 \rangle = \left\langle \frac{3}{4}(2), \frac{3}{4}(-3) \right\rangle = \left\langle \frac{3}{2}, \frac{-9}{4} \right\rangle$

c. $3\mathbf{u} - \frac{1}{2}\mathbf{v} = 3 \langle 2, -3 \rangle - \frac{1}{2} \langle -1, 7 \rangle$

$= \langle 6, -9 \rangle + \left\langle \frac{1}{2}, -\frac{7}{2} \right\rangle$ Scalar multiplication

$= \left\langle 6 + \frac{1}{2}, -9 - \frac{7}{2} \right\rangle$ Vector addition

$= \left\langle \frac{13}{2}, -\frac{25}{2} \right\rangle$ Simplify

An expression of the form $a\mathbf{u} + b\mathbf{v}$ is called a **linear combination** of the vectors $\mathbf{u}$ and $\mathbf{v}$ and scalars a and b. Note that if $\mathbf{u} = \langle u_1, u_2 \rangle$ and $\mathbf{v} = \langle v_1, v_2 \rangle$, then

$$a\mathbf{u} + b\mathbf{v} = a\langle u_1, u_2 \rangle + b\langle v_1, v_2 \rangle = \langle au_1 + bv_1, au_2 + bv_2 \rangle$$

Vector addition and multiplication of a vector by a scalar inherit many properties of ordinary addition and multiplication. The following theorem lists several useful properties of these operations.

THEOREM 9.1   Properties of vector operations

For any vectors $\mathbf{u}$, $\mathbf{v}$, and $\mathbf{w}$ in the plane and scalars s and t:

Commutativity of vector addition $\mathbf{u} + \mathbf{v} = \mathbf{v} + \mathbf{u}$

Associativity of vector addition $(\mathbf{u} + \mathbf{v}) + \mathbf{w} = \mathbf{u} + (\mathbf{v} + \mathbf{w})$

Associativity of scalar multiplication	$(st)\mathbf{u} = s(t\mathbf{u})$
Identity for addition	$\mathbf{u} + \mathbf{0} = \mathbf{u}$
Inverse property for addition	$\mathbf{u} + (-\mathbf{u}) = \mathbf{0}$
Distributive laws	$(s + t)\mathbf{u} = s\mathbf{u} + t\mathbf{u}$
	$s(\mathbf{u} + \mathbf{v}) = s\mathbf{u} + s\mathbf{v}$

Proof Each vector property can be established by using a corresponding property of real numbers. For example, to prove associativity of vector addition, let $\mathbf{u} = \langle u_1, u_2 \rangle$, $\mathbf{v} = \langle v_1, v_2 \rangle$ and $\mathbf{w} = \langle w_1, w_2 \rangle$. Then

$$(\mathbf{u} + \mathbf{v}) + \mathbf{w} = (\langle u_1, u_2 \rangle + \langle v_1, v_2 \rangle) + \langle w_1, w_2 \rangle$$
$$= \langle u_1 + v_1, u_2 + v_2 \rangle + \langle w_1, w_2 \rangle$$
$$= \langle (u_1 + v_1) + w_1, (u_2 + v_2) + w_2 \rangle$$
$$= \langle u_1 + (v_1 + w_1), u_2 + (v_2 + w_2) \rangle$$

Associativity of addition for the real numbers

$$= \langle u_1, u_2 \rangle + (\langle v_1, v_2 \rangle + \langle w_1, w_2 \rangle)$$
$$= \mathbf{u} + (\mathbf{v} + \mathbf{w})$$

You are asked to prove other of these properties in the problem set. ❏

Many results from geometry can be proved easily by using vector notation and vector properties. An illustration of this procedure is proved in Example 2.

EXAMPLE 2 Vector proof of a geometric property

Show that the line segment joining the midpoints of two sides of a triangle is parallel to the third side and has half its length.

Solution

Consider $\triangle ABC$, and let P and Q be the midpoints of sides $\overline{AC}$ and $\overline{BC}$, respectively, as shown in Figure 9.7.

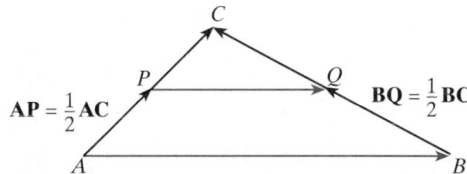

Figure 9.7 Vector proof of a geometric property

We have $\mathbf{AP} = \frac{1}{2}\mathbf{AC}$ and $\mathbf{BQ} = \frac{1}{2}\mathbf{BC}$, and we wish to show that $\mathbf{PQ}$ is parallel to $\mathbf{AB}$ with $\|\mathbf{PQ}\| = \frac{1}{2}\|\mathbf{AB}\|$. Equivalently, we will show that $\mathbf{PQ} = \frac{1}{2}\mathbf{AB}$. Toward this end, we begin by noting that $\mathbf{AB}$ can be expressed as the following vector sum:

$$\mathbf{AB} = \mathbf{AP} + \mathbf{PQ} + \mathbf{QB}$$
$$= \tfrac{1}{2}\mathbf{AC} + \mathbf{PQ} - \mathbf{BQ} \qquad\qquad \text{$\mathbf{AP} = \tfrac{1}{2}\mathbf{AC}$ and $\mathbf{QB} = -\mathbf{BQ}$}$$
$$= \tfrac{1}{2}(\mathbf{AB} + \mathbf{BC}) + \mathbf{PQ} - \tfrac{1}{2}\mathbf{BC} \qquad \text{$\mathbf{AC} = (\mathbf{AB} + \mathbf{BC})$ and $\mathbf{BQ} = \tfrac{1}{2}\mathbf{BC}$}$$
$$= \tfrac{1}{2}\mathbf{AB} + \tfrac{1}{2}\mathbf{BC} + \mathbf{PQ} - \tfrac{1}{2}\mathbf{BC}$$
$$= \tfrac{1}{2}\mathbf{AB} + \mathbf{PQ}$$
$$\tfrac{1}{2}\mathbf{AB} = \mathbf{PQ} \qquad\qquad\qquad\qquad \text{Subtract $\tfrac{1}{2}\mathbf{AB}$ from both sides.} \qquad ∎$$

When a vector $\mathbf{u}$ is represented in component form $\mathbf{u} = \langle u_1, u_2 \rangle$, its length is given by the formula

$$\|\mathbf{u}\| = \sqrt{u_1^2 + u_2^2}$$

This is a simple application of the Pythagorean theorem as shown in Figure 9.8a. Another important relationship involving the length of vectors is the *triangle inequality*

$$\|\mathbf{u} + \mathbf{v}\| \leq \|\mathbf{u}\| + \|\mathbf{v}\|$$

for any vectors **u** and **v**. Equality will occur precisely when **u** and **v** are nonnegative multiples of one another (that is, when **u** and **v** have the same direction). To establish the inequality, we observe that if **u** and **v** are positioned as two sides of a triangle in the plane, then the third side, **u** + **v**, has length $\|\mathbf{u} + \mathbf{v}\|$ and is "shorter" than the sum $\|\mathbf{u}\| + \|\mathbf{v}\|$ of the lengths of the other two sides, as shown in Figure 9.8b.

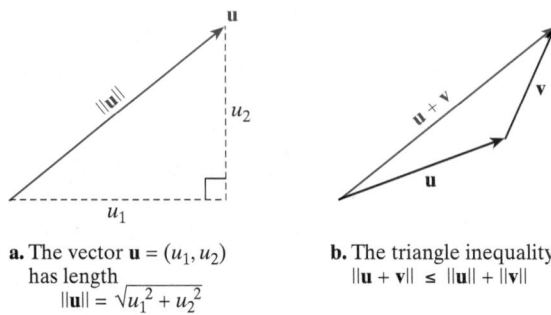

a. The vector $\mathbf{u} = (u_1, u_2)$ has length $\|\mathbf{u}\| = \sqrt{u_1^2 + u_2^2}$

b. The triangle inequality $\|\mathbf{u} + \mathbf{v}\| \leq \|\mathbf{u}\| + \|\mathbf{v}\|$

Figure 9.8   Geometric representation of two vector properties

EXAMPLE 3   Speed and heading of a motorboat

A river 4 mi wide flows south with a current of 5 mi/h. What speed and heading should a motorboat assume to travel directly across the river from east to west in 20 min?

Solution

Begin by drawing a diagram, like the one shown in Figure 9.9.

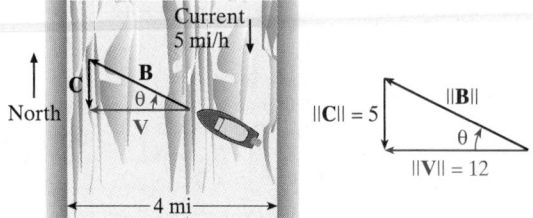

Figure 9.9   A velocity problem

Let **B** be the velocity vector of the boat in the direction of the angle θ. If the river's current has velocity **C**, the given information tells us that $\|\mathbf{C}\| = 5$ mi/h and that **C** points directly south. Moreover, because the boat is to cross the river from east to west in 20 min (that is, $\frac{1}{3}$ hr), its *effective velocity* after compensating for the current is a vector **V** that points west and has magnitude

$$\|\mathbf{V}\| = \frac{\text{WIDTH OF THE RIVER}}{\text{TIME OF CROSSING}} = \frac{4 \text{ mi}}{\frac{1}{3} \text{ h}} = 12 \text{ mi/h} \qquad \textit{Since } d = rt$$

The effective velocity **V** is the resultant of **B** and **C**; that is, $\mathbf{V} = \mathbf{B} + \mathbf{C}$. Because **V** and **C** act in perpendicular directions, we can determine **B** by referring to the right triangle with sides $\|\mathbf{V}\| = 12$ and $\|\mathbf{C}\| = 5$ and hypotenuse $\|\mathbf{B}\|$. We find that

$$\|\mathbf{B}\| = \sqrt{\|\mathbf{V}\|^2 + \|\mathbf{C}\|^2} = \sqrt{12^2 + 5^2} = 13$$

The direction of the velocity vector **V** is given by the angle θ in Figure 9.9, and we find that

$$\tan \theta = \tfrac{5}{12} \quad \text{so that} \quad \theta = \tan^{-1}\left(\tfrac{5}{12}\right) \approx 0.3948$$

Thus, the boat should travel at 13 mi/h in a direction of approximately 0.3948 radian. In navigation, it is common to specify direction in degrees rather than radians ($0.3948 \approx 22.6°$) and to measure the direction as an angle from either north or south. In this case, it is $90° - 22.6° = 57.4°$, or N57.4°W (that is, 57.4° west of north). ∎

A **unit vector** is a vector with length 1, and a **direction vector** for a given nonzero vector **v** is a unit vector **u** that points in the same direction as **v**. Such a vector can be found by dividing **v** by its length $\|\mathbf{v}\|$; that is,

$$\mathbf{u} = \frac{\mathbf{v}}{\|\mathbf{v}\|}$$

EXAMPLE 4 Finding a direction vector

Find a direction vector for the vector $\mathbf{v} = \langle 2, -3 \rangle$.

Solution

The vector **v** has length (magnitude) $\|\mathbf{v}\| = \sqrt{2^2 + (-3)^2} = \sqrt{13}$. Thus, the required direction vector is the unit vector

$$\mathbf{u} = \frac{\mathbf{v}}{\|\mathbf{v}\|} = \frac{\langle 2, -3 \rangle}{\sqrt{13}} = \frac{1}{\sqrt{13}}\langle 2, -3 \rangle = \left\langle \frac{2}{\sqrt{13}}, \frac{-3}{\sqrt{13}} \right\rangle$$ ∎

STANDARD REPRESENTATION OF VECTORS IN THE PLANE

The unit vectors $\mathbf{i} = \langle 1, 0 \rangle$ and $\mathbf{j} = \langle 0, 1 \rangle$ point in the directions of the positive x- and y-axes, respectively, and are called **standard basis vectors**. Any vector $\mathbf{v} = \langle v_1, v_2 \rangle$ in the plane can be expressed as a linear combination of the vectors **i** and **j**, because

$$\mathbf{v} = \langle v_1, v_2 \rangle = v_1 \langle 1, 0 \rangle + v_2 \langle 0, 1 \rangle = v_1 \mathbf{i} + v_2 \mathbf{j}$$

This is called the **standard representation** of the vector **v**, and it can be shown that the representation is unique in the sense that if $\mathbf{v} = a\mathbf{i} + b\mathbf{j}$, then $a = v_1$ and $b = v_2$. In this context, the scalars v_1 and v_2 are called the **horizontal and vertical components** of **v**, respectively. See Figure 9.10.

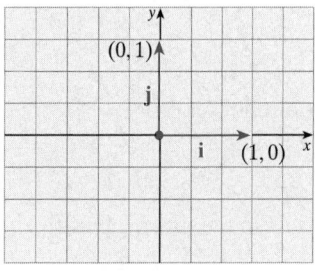
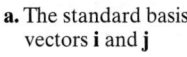
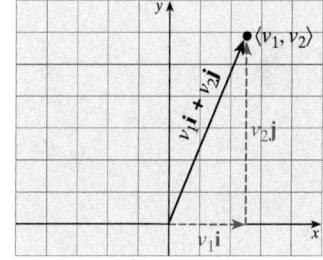

a. The standard basis vectors **i** and **j**

b. Any vector $\mathbf{v} = \langle v_1, v_2 \rangle$ can be expressed uniquely as $\mathbf{v} = v_1 \mathbf{i} + v_2 \mathbf{j}$

Figure 9.10 Standard representation of vectors in the plane

EXAMPLE 5 Finding the standard representation of a vector

If $\mathbf{u} = 3\mathbf{i} + 2\mathbf{j}$, $\mathbf{v} = -2\mathbf{i} + 5\mathbf{j}$, and $\mathbf{w} = \mathbf{i} - 4\mathbf{j}$, what is the standard representation of the vector $2\mathbf{u} + 5\mathbf{v} - \mathbf{w}$?

Solution

Using Theorem 9.1, we find that

$$\begin{aligned}
2\mathbf{u} + 5\mathbf{v} - \mathbf{w} &= 2(3\mathbf{i} + 2\mathbf{j}) + 5(-2\mathbf{i} + 5\mathbf{j}) - (\mathbf{i} - 4\mathbf{j}) \\
&= [2(3) + 5(-2) - 1]\mathbf{i} + [2(2) + 5(5) - (-4)]\mathbf{j} \\
&= -5\mathbf{i} + 33\mathbf{j}
\end{aligned}$$ ∎

EXAMPLE 6 **Finding the standard representation of a vector connecting two points**

Find the standard representation of the vector **PQ** for the points $P(3, -4)$ and $Q(-2, 6)$.

Solution

The component form of **PQ** is

$$\mathbf{PQ} = \langle (-2) - 3, 6 - (-4) \rangle = \langle -5, 10 \rangle$$

This means that **PQ** has the standard representation $\mathbf{PQ} = -5\mathbf{i} + 10\mathbf{j}$. ∎

EXAMPLE 7 **Computing a compensating force**

Two forces $\mathbf{F}_1$ and $\mathbf{F}_2$ act on the same body. It is known that $\mathbf{F}_1$ has magnitude 3 newtons and acts in the direction of $-\mathbf{i}$, whereas $\mathbf{F}_2$ has magnitude 2 newtons and acts in the direction of the unit vector

$$\mathbf{u} = \tfrac{3}{5}\mathbf{i} - \tfrac{4}{5}\mathbf{j}$$

Find the magnitude and direction of the additional force $\mathbf{F}_3$ that must be applied to keep the body at rest.

Solution

According to the given information, we have

$$\mathbf{F}_1 = 3(-\mathbf{i}) = -3\mathbf{i} \quad \text{and} \quad \mathbf{F}_2 = 2\left(\tfrac{3}{5}\mathbf{i} - \tfrac{4}{5}\mathbf{j}\right) = \tfrac{6}{5}\mathbf{i} - \tfrac{8}{5}\mathbf{j}$$

and we want to find $\mathbf{F}_3 = a\mathbf{i} + b\mathbf{j}$ so that $\mathbf{F}_1 + \mathbf{F}_2 + \mathbf{F}_3 = \mathbf{0}$ (see Figure 9.11). Substituting into this vector equation, we obtain

$$(-3\mathbf{i}) + \left(\tfrac{6}{5}\mathbf{i} - \tfrac{8}{5}\mathbf{j}\right) + (a\mathbf{i} + b\mathbf{j}) = 0\mathbf{i} + 0\mathbf{j}$$

By combining terms on the left, we find that

$$\left(-3 + \tfrac{6}{5} + a\right)\mathbf{i} + \left(-\tfrac{8}{5} + b\right)\mathbf{j} = 0\mathbf{i} + 0\mathbf{j}$$

Because the standard representation is unique, we must have

$$-3 + \tfrac{6}{5} + a = 0 \quad \text{and} \quad -\tfrac{8}{5} + b = 0$$
$$a = \tfrac{9}{5} \qquad\qquad b = \tfrac{8}{5}$$

The required force is $\mathbf{F}_3 = \tfrac{9}{5}\mathbf{i} + \tfrac{8}{5}\mathbf{j}$. This is a force of magnitude

$$\|\mathbf{F}_3\| = \sqrt{\left(\tfrac{9}{5}\right)^2 + \left(\tfrac{8}{5}\right)^2} = \tfrac{1}{5}\sqrt{145} \quad \text{newtons}$$

which acts in the direction of the unit vector

$$\mathbf{v} = \frac{\mathbf{F}_3}{\|\mathbf{F}_3\|} = \frac{5}{\sqrt{145}}\left(\tfrac{9}{5}\mathbf{i} + \tfrac{8}{5}\mathbf{j}\right) = \frac{9}{\sqrt{145}}\mathbf{i} + \frac{8}{\sqrt{145}}\mathbf{j}$$ ∎

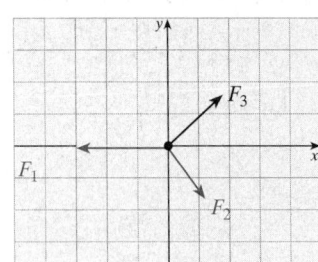

Figure 9.11 Find $\mathbf{F}_3$ so $\mathbf{F}_1 + \mathbf{F}_2 + \mathbf{F}_3 = \mathbf{0}$

9.1 PROBLEM SET

A *Sketch each vector given in Problems 1–4 assuming that its initial point is at the origin.*

1. $3\mathbf{i} - 4\mathbf{j}$ **2.** $-2\mathbf{i} - 3\mathbf{j}$

3. $-\tfrac{1}{2}\mathbf{i} + \tfrac{5}{2}\mathbf{j}$ **4.** $-2(-\mathbf{i} + 2\mathbf{j})$

The initial point **P** *and terminal point* **Q** *of a vector are given in Problems 5–8. Sketch each vector, write it in standard component form, and find* $\|\mathbf{PQ}\|$.

5. $P(3, -1), Q(7, 2)$ **6.** $P(5, -2), Q(5, 8)$

7. $P(3, 4), Q(-2, 4)$ **8.** $P\left(\tfrac{1}{2}, 6\right), Q(-3, -2)$

Find the standard representation and the length of each vector **PQ** *in Problems 9–12.*

9. $P(-1, -2), Q(1, -2)$ **10.** $P(5, 7), Q(6, 8)$

11. $P(-4, -3), Q(0, -1)$ **12.** $P(3, -5), Q(2, 8)$

Find a unit vector that points in the direction of each of the vectors given in Problems 13–16.

13. $\mathbf{i} + \mathbf{j}$ **14.** $\tfrac{1}{2}\mathbf{i} + \tfrac{1}{4}\mathbf{j}$ **15.** $3\mathbf{i} - 4\mathbf{j}$ **16.** $-4\mathbf{i} + 7\mathbf{j}$

Let $\mathbf{u} = \langle -3, 4 \rangle$ *and* $\mathbf{v} = \langle 1, -1 \rangle$. *Find scalars s and t so that the given equation in Problems 17–20 is satisfied.*

17. $s\mathbf{u} + t\mathbf{v} = \langle 6, 0 \rangle$ **18.** $s\langle 0, -3 \rangle + t\mathbf{u} = \mathbf{v}$
19. $s\mathbf{v} + t\langle -2, 1 \rangle = \mathbf{u}$ **20.** $s\mathbf{u} + \langle 8, 11 \rangle = t\mathbf{v}$

Suppose $\mathbf{u} = 3\mathbf{i} - 4\mathbf{j}$, $\mathbf{v} = 4\mathbf{i} - 3\mathbf{j}$, *and* $\mathbf{w} = \mathbf{i} + \mathbf{j}$. *Represent each of the expressions in Problems 21–24 in standard form.*

21. $2\mathbf{u} + 3\mathbf{v} - \mathbf{w}$ **22.** $\frac{1}{2}(\mathbf{u} + \mathbf{v}) - \frac{1}{4}\mathbf{w}$
23. $\|\mathbf{v}\|\mathbf{u} + \|\mathbf{u}\|\mathbf{v}$ **24.** $\|\mathbf{u}\| \|\mathbf{v}\| \mathbf{w}$

Find all real numbers x and y that satisfy the vector equations given in Problems 25–28.

25. $(x - y - 1)\mathbf{i} + (2x + 3y - 12)\mathbf{j} = \mathbf{0}$
26. $x\mathbf{i} - 4y^2\mathbf{j} = (5 - 3y)\mathbf{i} + (10 - 7x)\mathbf{j}$
27. $(x^2 + y^2)\mathbf{i} + y\mathbf{j} = 20\mathbf{i} + (x + 2)\mathbf{j}$
28. $(y - 1)\mathbf{i} + y\mathbf{j} = (\log x)\mathbf{i} + [\log 2 + \log(x + 4)]\mathbf{j}$

In Problems 29–32, find a unit vector $\mathbf{u}$ *with the given characteristics.*

29. $\mathbf{u}$ makes an angle of $30°$ measured from the positive x-axis.
30. $\mathbf{u}$ has the same direction as the vector $2\mathbf{i} - 3\mathbf{j}$.
31. $\mathbf{u}$ has the opposite direction of the vector $-4\mathbf{i} + \mathbf{j}$.
32. $\mathbf{u}$ has the direction of the vector from $P(-1, 5)$ to $Q(7, -3)$.

In Problems 33–34, let $\mathbf{u} = 4\mathbf{i} - \mathbf{j}$, $\mathbf{v} = \mathbf{i} + 2\mathbf{j}$, *and* $\mathbf{w} = -3\mathbf{i} + 4\mathbf{j}$.

33. Find a unit vector in the same direction as $\mathbf{u} + \mathbf{v}$.
34. Find a vector of length 3 with the same direction as $\mathbf{u} - 2\mathbf{v} + 2\mathbf{w}$.
35. Find the terminal point of the vector $5\mathbf{i} + 7\mathbf{j}$ if the initial point is $(-2, 3)$.
36. Find the initial point of the vector $-\mathbf{i} + 2\mathbf{j}$ if the terminal point is $(-1, -2)$.
37. a. Find the vector from the point P to the midpoint of the line segment joining the points $P(-3, -8)$ and $Q(9, -2)$.
   b. What is the vector from P to the point which is located $\frac{5}{6}$ of the distance from P to Q?
38. If $\|\mathbf{v}\| = 3$ and $-3 \le r \le 1$, what are the possible values of $r\|\mathbf{v}\|$?
39. Show that $\mathbf{v} = (\cos\theta)\mathbf{i} + (\sin\theta)\mathbf{j}$ is a unit vector for any angle θ.
B 40. If $\mathbf{u}$ and $\mathbf{v}$ are nonzero vectors and $r = \dfrac{\|\mathbf{u}\|}{\|\mathbf{v}\|}$, what is $\|r\mathbf{v}\|$?
41. If $\mathbf{u}$ and $\mathbf{v}$ are nonzero vectors with $\|\mathbf{u}\| = \|\mathbf{v}\|$, does it follow that $\mathbf{u} = \mathbf{v}$? Explain.
42. If $\mathbf{u} = 2\mathbf{i} - 3\mathbf{j}$ and $\mathbf{v} = x\mathbf{i} + y\mathbf{j}$, describe the set of points in the plane whose coordinates (x, y) satisfy $\|\mathbf{v} - \mathbf{u}\| \le 2$.
43. Let $\mathbf{u}_0 = x_0\mathbf{i} + y_0\mathbf{j}$ for constants x_0 and y_0, and let $\mathbf{u} = x\mathbf{i} + y\mathbf{j}$. Describe the set of all points in the plane whose coordinates satisfy
   a. $\|\mathbf{u} - \mathbf{u}_0\| = 1$ **b.** $\|\mathbf{u} - \mathbf{u}_0\| \le r$
44. Let $\mathbf{u} = 3\mathbf{i} - \mathbf{j}$ and $\mathbf{v} = -6\mathbf{i} + 2\mathbf{j}$. Show that there are no numbers a, b for which $a\mathbf{u} + b\mathbf{v} = 2\mathbf{i} + 5\mathbf{j}$.
45. Suppose $\mathbf{u}$ and $\mathbf{v}$ are a pair of nonzero, nonparallel vectors. Find all numbers a, b, c such that $a\mathbf{u} + b(\mathbf{u} - \mathbf{v}) + c(\mathbf{u} + \mathbf{v}) = \mathbf{0}$.
46. Let $\mathbf{u} = \langle 2, 1 \rangle$ and $\mathbf{v} = \langle -3, 4 \rangle$.
   a. Sketch the vector $c\mathbf{u} + (1 - c)\mathbf{v}$ for the cases where $c = 0$, $c = \frac{1}{4}$, $c = \frac{1}{2}$, $c = \frac{3}{4}$, and $c = 1$.
   b. In general, if the initial point of $c\mathbf{u} + (1 - c)\mathbf{v}$ for $0 \le c \le 1$ is at the origin, where is its terminal point (x, y)?

47. Two forces $\mathbf{F}_1 = 3\mathbf{i} + 4\mathbf{j}$ and $\mathbf{F}_2 = 3\mathbf{i} - 7\mathbf{j}$ act on an object. What additional force should be applied to keep the body at rest?
48. Three forces $\mathbf{F}_1 = \mathbf{i} - 2\mathbf{j}$, $\mathbf{F}_2 = 3\mathbf{i} - 7\mathbf{j}$, and $\mathbf{F}_3 = \mathbf{i} + \mathbf{j}$ act on an object. What additional force $\mathbf{F}_4$ should be applied to keep the body at rest?
49. A river 2.1 mi wide flows south with a current of 3.1 mi/h. What speed and heading should a motorboat assume to travel across the river from east to west in 30 min?
50. Four forces act on an object: $\mathbf{F}_1$ has magnitude 10 lb and acts at an angle of $\frac{\pi}{6}$ measured counterclockwise from the positive x-axis; $\mathbf{F}_2$ has magnitude 8 lb and acts in the direction of the vector $\mathbf{j}$; $\mathbf{F}_3$ has magnitude 5 lb and acts at an angle of $4\pi/3$ measured counterclockwise from the positive x-axis. What must the fourth force $\mathbf{F}_4$ be to keep the object at rest?
C 51. Use vector methods to show that the diagonals of a parallelogram bisect each other.
52. In a triangle, let $\mathbf{u}$, $\mathbf{v}$, and $\mathbf{w}$ be the vectors from each vertex to the midpoint of the opposite side. Use vector methods to show that $\mathbf{u} + \mathbf{v} + \mathbf{w} = \mathbf{0}$.
53. Prove that the medians of a triangle (see Figure 9.12) intersect at a single point by completing the following argument.

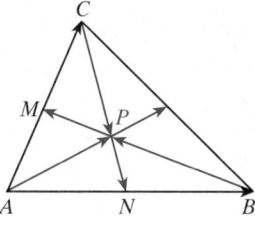

Figure 9.12 $\triangle ABC$

   a. Let M and N be the midpoints of sides $\overline{AC}$ and $\overline{AB}$, respectively. Show that
$$\mathbf{CN} = \tfrac{1}{2}\mathbf{AB} - \mathbf{AC} \quad \text{and} \quad \mathbf{BM} = \tfrac{1}{2}\mathbf{AC} - \mathbf{AB}$$
   b. Let P be the point where medians $\overline{BM}$ and $\overline{CN}$ intersect, and let r, s be constants such that
$$\mathbf{CP} = r(\mathbf{CN}) \quad \text{and} \quad \mathbf{BP} = s(\mathbf{BM})$$
   Note that $\mathbf{CP} + \mathbf{PB} = \mathbf{CB}$. Use this relationship to prove that $r = s = \frac{2}{3}$. Explain why this shows that any pair of medians meet at a point located $\frac{2}{3}$ the distance from each vertex to the midpoint of the opposite side. Why does this show that *all three* medians meet at a single point?
   c. The *centroid* of a triangle is the point where the medians meet. Show that a triangle with vertices $A(x_1, y_1)$, $B(x_2, y_2)$, $C(x_3, y_3)$ has centroid with coordinates
$$\left(\frac{x_1 + x_2 + x_3}{3}, \frac{y_1 + y_2 + y_3}{3} \right)$$

54. Prove the following parts of Theorem 9.1.
   a. Commutativity
   b. Identity
   c. Inverse property of addition
   d. The distributive law $s(\mathbf{u} + \mathbf{v}) = s\mathbf{u} + s\mathbf{v}$

55. Let A, B, C, and D be any four points in the plane. If M and N are midpoints of $\overline{AC}$ and $\overline{BD}$, show that

$$\mathbf{MN} = \tfrac{1}{4}(\mathbf{AB} + \mathbf{AD} + \mathbf{CB} + \mathbf{CD})$$

56. Let A, B, C, and D be vertices of a quadrilateral, and let M, N, P, and Q, be the midpoints of the sides $\overline{AB}$, $\overline{BC}$, $\overline{CD}$, and $\overline{AD}$, respectively, as shown in Figure 9.13. Use vector methods to show that $MNPQ$ is a parallelogram.

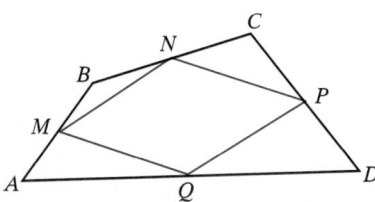

Figure 9.13 Quadrilateral $ABCD$

9.2 Coordinates and Vectors in $\mathbb{R}^3$

IN THIS SECTION coordinates in $\mathbb{R}^3$; graphs in $\mathbb{R}^3$: spheres and cylinders; vectors in $\mathbb{R}^3$

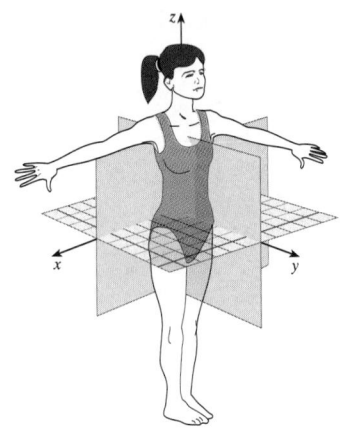

Figure 9.14 A "right-handed" rectangular coordinate system for $\mathbb{R}^3$

COORDINATES IN $\mathbb{R}^3$

We have already considered ordered pairs in $\mathbb{R}^2$, and because we exist in a *three-dimensional* world, it is also important to consider a three-dimensional system. We call this *three-space* and denote it by $\mathbb{R}^3$. We introduce a coordinate system to three-space by choosing three mutually perpendicular axes to serve as a frame of reference. The orientation of our reference system will be *right-handed* in the sense that if you stand at the origin with your right arm along the positive x-axis and your left arm along the positive y-axis, as shown in Figure 9.14, your head will then point in the direction of the positive z-axis.

To orient yourself to a three-dimensional coordinate system, think of the x-axis and y-axis as lying in the plane of the floor and the z-axis as a line perpendicular to the floor. All the graphs that we have drawn in the first eight chapters of this book would now be drawn on the floor. If you orient yourself in a room as shown in Figure 9.15, you may notice some important planes. Assume that the room is 25 ft × 30 ft × 8 ft and fix the origin at a front corner (where the board hangs).

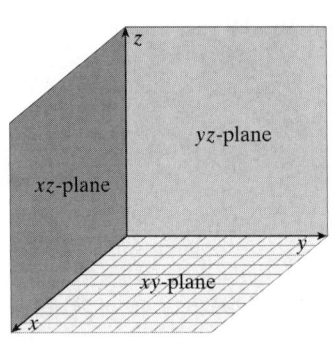

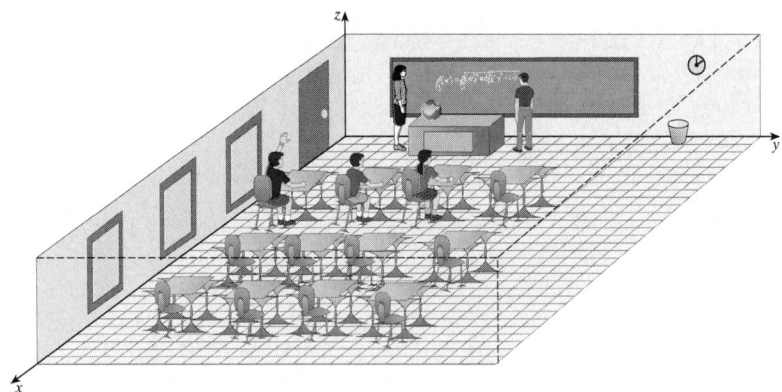

Figure 9.15 A typical classroom; assume the dimensions are 25 ft by 30 ft with an 8-foot ceiling

Floor:	**xy-plane**; equation is $z = 0$.
Ceiling:	plane parallel to the xy-plane; equation is $z = 8$.
Front wall:	**yz-plane**; equation is $x = 0$.
Back wall:	plane parallel to the yz-plane; equation is $x = 30$.
Left wall:	**xz-plane**; equation is $y = 0$.
Right wall:	plane parallel to the xz-plane; equation is $y = 25$.

The xy-, xz-, and yz-planes are called the **coordinate planes**. We will obtain equations for planes in space after we discuss vectors in $\mathbb{R}^3$. However, in beginning to visualize objects in $\mathbb{R}^3$, we do not want to ignore planes, because they are so common (for example, the walls, ceiling, and floor in Figure 9.15). We will show that the graph of $Ax + By + Cz = D$ is a plane if A, B, C, and D are real numbers (not all zero). Points in $\mathbb{R}^3$ are located by their position in relation to the three coordinate planes and are given appropriate coordinates. Specifically, the point P is assigned coordinates (a, b, c) to indicate that it is a, b, and c units, respectively, from the yz-, xz-, and xy-planes.

EXAMPLE 1 Points in three dimensions

Graph the following ordered triples:

a. $(10, 20, 10)$ **b.** $(-12, 6, 12)$ **c.** $(-12, -18, 6)$ **d.** $(20, -10, 18)$

Solution

The points are plotted as shown in Figure 9.16.

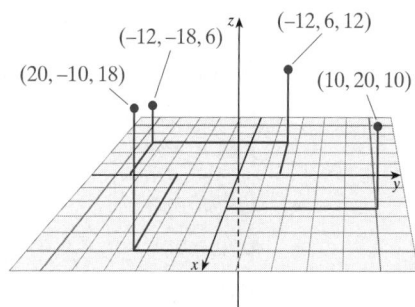

Figure 9.16 Plotting points in $\mathbb{R}^3$ ■

In $\mathbb{R}^2$, the distance from the origin $(0, 0)$ to the point (a, b) is $d = \sqrt{a^2 + b^2}$, and in $\mathbb{R}^3$, the distance from $(0, 0, 0)$ to (a, b, c) is $d = \sqrt{a^2 + b^2 + c^2}$, as shown in Figure 9.17. We can now summarize.

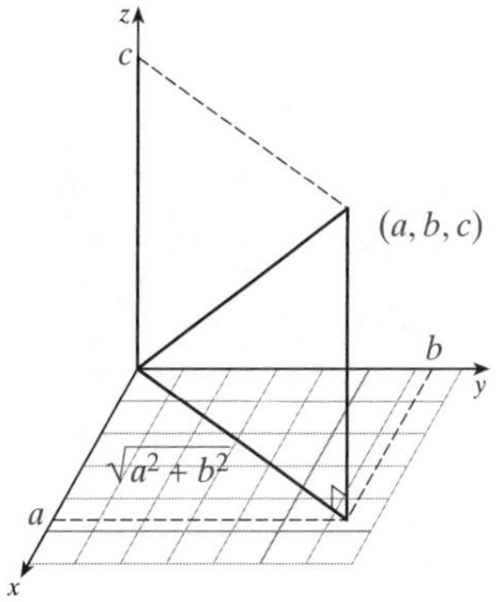

Distance Formula

The distance $|P_1 P_2|$ between $P_1(x_1, y_1, z_1)$ and $P_2(x_2, y_2, z_2)$ is

$$|P_1 P_2| = \sqrt{(x_2 - x_1)^2 + (y_2 - y_1)^2 + (z_2 - z_1)^2}$$

Figure 9.17 Distance from the origin $(0, 0, 0)$ to the point (a, b, c) is

$$d = \sqrt{\left(\sqrt{a^2 + b^2}\right)^2 + c^2}$$
$$= \sqrt{a^2 + b^2 + c^2}$$

EXAMPLE 2 Finding the distance between points in $\mathbb{R}^3$

Find the distance between $(10, 20, 10)$ and $(-12, 6, 12)$.

Solution
$$d = \sqrt{(-12 - 10)^2 + (6 - 20)^2 + (12 - 10)^2}$$
$$= \sqrt{684}$$
$$= 6\sqrt{19}$$ ■

GRAPHS IN $\mathbb{R}^3$: SPHERES AND CYLINDERS

In $\mathbb{R}^3$, the collection of all points (x, y, z) whose coordinates satisfy a given equation is called the **graph of an equation**. Geometrically, the graph of an equation in x, y, z is a **surface** in $\mathbb{R}^3$. In this section, we will examine two kinds of surfaces, spheres and cylinders. Later in the chapter, we will examine a variety of other surfaces.

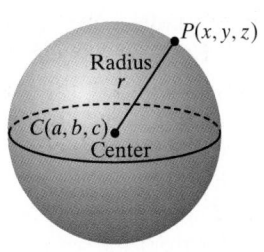

Figure 9.18 Graph of a sphere with center (a, b, c), radius r

Equation of a Sphere

Spheres A **sphere** (see Figure 9.18) is defined as the collection of all points located a fixed distance (the **radius**) from a fixed point (the **center**).

In particular, if $P(x, y, z)$ is a point on the sphere with radius r and center $C(a, b, c)$, then the distance from C to P is r. Thus,

$$r = \sqrt{(x - a)^2 + (y - b)^2 + (z - c)^2}$$

If you square both sides of this equation, you can see that it is equivalent to the equation of a sphere displayed in the following box. Conversely, if the point (x, y, z) satisfies an equation of this form, it must lie on a sphere with center (a, b, c) and radius r.

> The graph of the equation
>
> $$(x - a)^2 + (y - b)^2 + (z - c)^2 = r^2$$
>
> is a sphere with center (a, b, c) and radius r, and any sphere has an equation of this form. This is called the **standard form of the equation of a sphere** (or simply *standard-form sphere*).

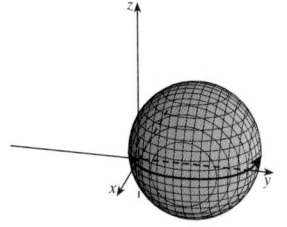

Figure 9.19 Graph of a sphere

EXAMPLE 3 Center and radius of a sphere from a given equation

Show that the graph of the equation $x^2 + y^2 + z^2 + 4x - 6y - 3 = 0$ is a sphere, and find its center and radius.

Solution

By completing the square in both variables x and y, we have

$$(x^2 + 4x) + (y^2 - 6y) + z^2 = 3$$
$$(x^2 + 4x + 2^2) + [y^2 - 6y + (-3)^2] + z^2 = 3 + 4 + 9$$
$$(x + 2)^2 + (y - 3)^2 + z^2 = 16$$

Comparing this equation with the standard form, we see that it is the equation of a sphere with center $(-2, 3, 0)$ and radius 4, as shown in Figure 9.19. ∎

Cylinders A **cross section** of a surface in $\mathbb{R}^3$ is a curve obtained by intersecting the surface with a plane. If parallel planes intersect a given surface in congruent cross-sectional curves, the surface is called a **cylinder**. We define a cylinder with *principal cross sections C and generating line L* to be the surface obtained by moving lines parallel to L along the boundary of the curve C, as shown in Figure 9.20. In this context, the curve C is called a **directrix** of the cylinder, and L is the **generatrix**.

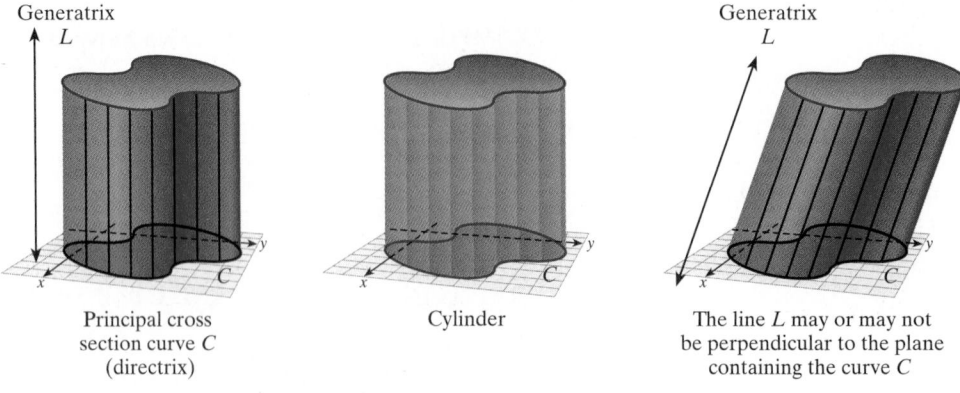

Generatrix L

Principal cross section curve C (directrix)

Cylinder

Generatrix L

The line L may or may not be perpendicular to the plane containing the curve C

Figure 9.20 A cylinder with directrix C and generatrix L

We will deal primarily with cylinders in which the directrix is a conic section and the generatrix L is one of the coordinate axes. Such a cylinder is often named for the type of conic section in its principal cross sections and is described by an equation involving only two of the variables x, y, z. In this case, the generating line L is parallel to the coordinate axis of the missing variable. Thus,

$$x^2 + y^2 = 5 \qquad \text{is a \textbf{circular cylinder} with } L \text{ parallel to the } z\text{-axis}$$

$$y^2 - z^2 = 9 \qquad \text{is a \textbf{hyperbolic cylinder} with } L \text{ parallel to the } x\text{-axis}$$

$$x^2 + 2z^2 = 25 \qquad \text{is an \textbf{elliptic cylinder} with } L \text{ parallel to the } y\text{-axis.}$$

The graphs of these cylinders are shown in Figure 9.21.

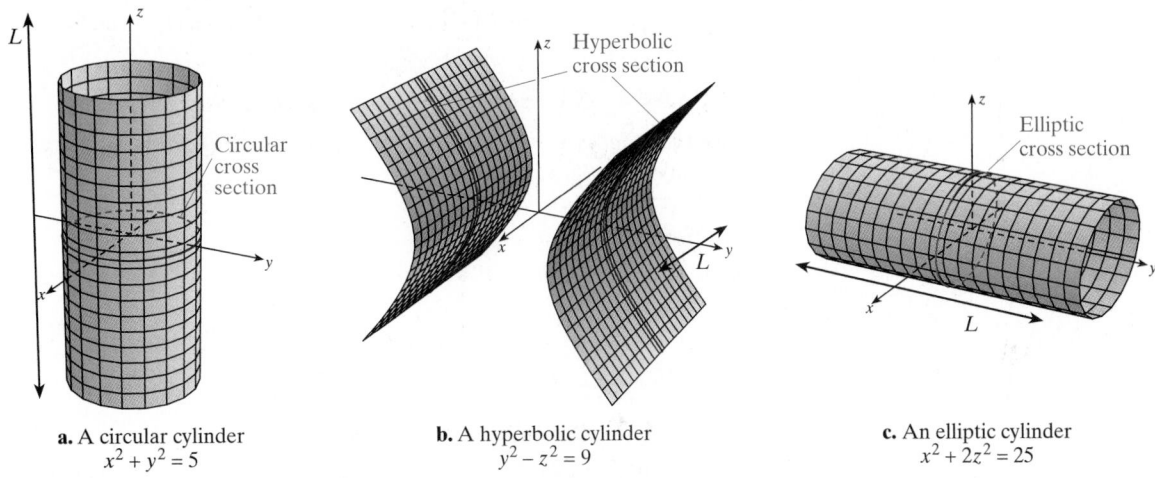

a. A circular cylinder
$x^2 + y^2 = 5$

b. A hyperbolic cylinder
$y^2 - z^2 = 9$

c. An elliptic cylinder
$x^2 + 2z^2 = 25$

Figure 9.21   Cylinders

VECTORS IN $\mathbb{R}^3$

A vector in $\mathbb{R}^3$ is a directed line segment (an "arrow") in space. The vector $\mathbf{P_1P_2}$ with initial point $P_1(x_1, y_1, z_1)$ and terminal point $P_2(x_2, y_2, z_2)$ has the component form analogous to the $\mathbb{R}^2$ case

$$\mathbf{P_1P_2} = \langle x_2 - x_1, y_2 - y_1, z_2 - z_1 \rangle$$

Vector addition and multiplication of a vector by a scalar are defined for vectors in $\mathbb{R}^3$ in the same way as these operations were defined for vectors in $\mathbb{R}^2$. In addition, the properties of vector algebra listed in Theorem 9.1 of Section 9.1 apply to vectors in $\mathbb{R}^3$ as well as to those in $\mathbb{R}^2$.

For example, we observed that each vector in $\mathbb{R}^2$ can be expressed as a unique linear combination of the standard basis vectors $\mathbf{i}$ and $\mathbf{j}$. This representation can be extended to vectors in $\mathbb{R}^3$ by adding a vector $\mathbf{k}$ defined to be the unit vector in the direction of the positive z-axis. In component form, we have in $\mathbb{R}^3$,

$$\mathbf{i} = \langle 1, 0, 0 \rangle \qquad \mathbf{j} = \langle 0, 1, 0 \rangle \qquad \mathbf{k} = \langle 0, 0, 1 \rangle$$

We call these the **standard basis vectors** in $\mathbb{R}^3$ (shown in Figure 9.22a). The **standard representation** of the vector with initial point at the origin O and terminal point $Q(a_1, a_2, a_3)$ is $\mathbf{OQ} = a_1\mathbf{i} + a_2\mathbf{j} + a_3\mathbf{k}$ as shown in Figure 9.22b. More generally, the vector $\mathbf{P_1P_2}$ with initial point $P_1(x_1, y_1, z_1)$ and terminal point $P_2(x_2, y_2, z_2)$ has the standard representation

$$\mathbf{P_1P_2} = (x_2 - x_1)\mathbf{i} + (y_2 - y_1)\mathbf{j} + (z_2 - z_1)\mathbf{k}$$

with magnitude

$$\|\mathbf{P_1P_2}\| = \sqrt{(x_2 - x_1)^2 + (y_2 - y_1)^2 + (z_2 - z_1)^2}$$

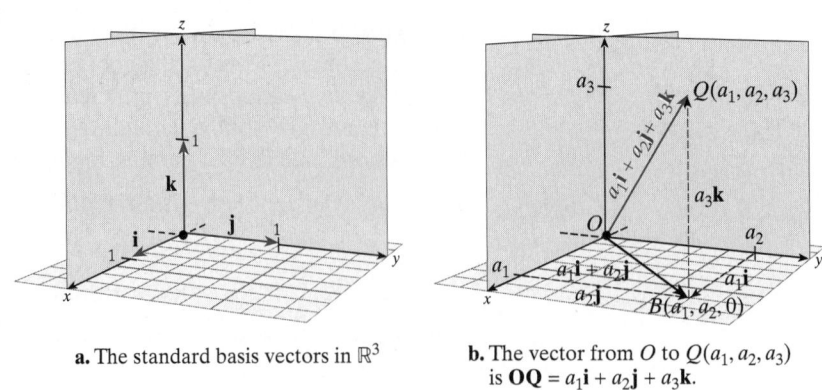

a. The standard basis vectors in $\mathbb{R}^3$

b. The vector from O to $Q(a_1, a_2, a_3)$ is $\mathbf{OQ} = a_1\mathbf{i} + a_2\mathbf{j} + a_3\mathbf{k}$.

Figure 9.22   Standard representation of vectors in $\mathbb{R}^3$

EXAMPLE 4   Standard representation of a vector in $\mathbb{R}^3$

Find the standard representation of the vector **PQ** with initial point $P(-1, 2, 2)$ and terminal point $Q(3, -2, 4)$.

Solution

We have

$$\mathbf{PQ} = [3 - (-1)]\mathbf{i} + [-2 - 2]\mathbf{j} + [4 - 2]k = 4\mathbf{i} - 4\mathbf{j} + 2\mathbf{k} \qquad \blacksquare$$

EXAMPLE 5   Magnitude of a vector in $\mathbb{R}^3$

Find the magnitude of the vector $\mathbf{v} = 2\mathbf{i} - 3\mathbf{j} + 5\mathbf{k}$ and the distance between the points $A(1, -1, -4)$ and $B(-2, 3, 8)$.

Solution $\|\mathbf{v}\| = \sqrt{2^2 + (-3)^2 + 5^2} = \sqrt{38}$ and

$$\|\overline{AB}\| = \sqrt{(-2 - 1)^2 + [3 - (-1)]^2 + [8 - (-4)]^2} = 13 \qquad \blacksquare$$

As in $\mathbb{R}^2$, if **v** is a given nonzero vector in $\mathbb{R}^3$, then the unit vector **u** that points in the same direction as **v** is

$$\mathbf{u} = \frac{\mathbf{v}}{\|\mathbf{v}\|}$$

EXAMPLE 6   Finding a direction vector

Find the unit vector that points in the direction of the vector **PQ** from $P(-1, 2, 5)$ to $Q(0, -3, 7)$.

Solution $\mathbf{PQ} = [0 - (-1)]\mathbf{i} + [-3 - 2]\mathbf{j} + [7 - 5]\mathbf{k} = \mathbf{i} - 5\mathbf{j} + 2\mathbf{k}$

$\|\mathbf{PQ}\| = \sqrt{1^2 + (-5)^2 + 2^2} = \sqrt{30}$

Thus,

$$\mathbf{u} = \frac{\mathbf{PQ}}{\|\mathbf{PQ}\|} = \frac{\mathbf{i} - 5\mathbf{j} + 2\mathbf{k}}{\sqrt{30}} = \frac{1}{\sqrt{30}}\mathbf{i} - \frac{5}{\sqrt{30}}\mathbf{j} + \frac{2}{\sqrt{30}}\mathbf{k} \qquad \blacksquare$$

As in $\mathbb{R}^2$, two vectors in $\mathbb{R}^3$ are **parallel** if they are scalar multiples of one another. Similarly, nonzero vectors **u** and **v** are parallel if and only if $\mathbf{u} = s\mathbf{v}$ for some nonzero scalar s.

EXAMPLE 7   Parallel vectors

A vector **PQ** has initial point $P(1, 0, -3)$ and length 3. Find **Q** so that **PQ** is parallel to $\mathbf{v} = 2\mathbf{i} - 3\mathbf{j} + 6\mathbf{k}$.

Solution

Let **Q** have coordinates (a_1, a_2, a_3). Then

$$\mathbf{PQ} = [a_1 - 1]\mathbf{i} + [a_2 - 0]\mathbf{j} + [a_3 - (-3)]\mathbf{k}$$
$$= (a_1 - 1)\mathbf{i} + a_2\mathbf{j} + (a_3 + 3)\mathbf{k}$$

Because **PQ** is parallel to **v**, we have $\mathbf{PQ} = s\mathbf{v}$ for some scalar s, that is,

$$(a_1 - 1)\mathbf{i} + a_2\mathbf{j} + (a_3 + 3)\mathbf{k} = s(2\mathbf{i} - 3\mathbf{j} + 6\mathbf{k})$$

Since the standard representation is unique, this implies that

$$a_1 - 1 = 2s \qquad a_2 = -3s \qquad a_3 + 3 = 6s$$
$$a_1 = 2s + 1 \qquad\qquad\qquad a_3 = 6s - 3$$

Because **PQ** has length 3, we have

$$3 = \sqrt{(a_1 - 1)^2 + a_2^2 + (a_3 + 3)^2}$$
$$= \sqrt{[(2s + 1) - 1]^2 + (-3s)^2 + [(6s - 3) + 3]^2}$$
$$= \sqrt{4s^2 + 9s^2 + 36s^2} = \sqrt{49s^2} = 7\,|s|$$

Thus, $s = \pm\frac{3}{7}$ and for the two cases, we have

$$s = \tfrac{3}{7}: \qquad a_1 = 2(\tfrac{3}{7}) + 1 = \tfrac{13}{7} \qquad a_2 = -3(\tfrac{3}{7}) = -\tfrac{9}{7} \qquad a_3 = 6(\tfrac{3}{7}) - 3 = -\tfrac{3}{7}$$
$$s = -\tfrac{3}{7}: \qquad a_1 = 2(-\tfrac{3}{7}) + 1 \qquad a_2 = -3(-\tfrac{3}{7}) \qquad a_3 = 6(-\tfrac{3}{7}) - 3$$
$$\qquad\qquad a_1 = \tfrac{1}{7} \qquad\qquad a_2 = \tfrac{9}{7} \qquad\qquad a_3 = -\tfrac{39}{7}$$

There are two points that satisfy the conditions for the required terminal point Q: $\left(\tfrac{13}{7}, -\tfrac{9}{7}, -\tfrac{3}{7}\right)$ and $\left(\tfrac{1}{7}, \tfrac{9}{7}, -\tfrac{39}{7}\right)$. ∎

9.2   PROBLEM SET

A *For the given vectors in Problems 1–4, find*

   a. $\mathbf{u} + \mathbf{v}$ *b.* $\mathbf{u} - \mathbf{v}$ *c.* $\frac{5}{2}\mathbf{u}$ *d.* $2\mathbf{u} + 3\mathbf{v}$

   1. $\mathbf{u} = \langle 4, -3, 1 \rangle$, $\mathbf{v} = \langle -2, 5, 3 \rangle$
   2. $\mathbf{u} = \langle 2, -1, 0 \rangle$, $\mathbf{v} = \langle 5, -3, 4 \rangle$
   3. $\mathbf{u} = \langle 1, -2, 5 \rangle$, $\mathbf{v} = \langle 0, -1, 3 \rangle$
   4. $\mathbf{u} = \langle 0, 3, -1 \rangle$, $\mathbf{v} = \langle 4, -2, 0 \rangle$

In Problems 5–8, plot the points P and Q in $\mathbb{R}^3$, and find $\|\mathbf{PQ}\|$.

   5. $P(3, -4, 5)$, $Q(1, 5, -3)$ **6.** $P(3, 0, 0)$, $Q(-2, 5, 7)$
   7. $P(-3, -5, 8)$, $Q(3, 6, -7)$ **8.** $P(0, 5, -3)$, $Q(2, -1, 0)$

In Problems 9–12, find the standard form equation of the sphere with the given center C and radius r.

   9. $C(0, 0, 0)$, $r = 1$ **10.** $C(-3, 5, 7)$, $r = 2$
   11. $C(0, 4, -5)$, $r = 3$ **12.** $C(-2, 3, -1)$, $r = \sqrt{5}$

Find the center and radius of each sphere whose equations are given in Problems 13–16.

   13. $x^2 + y^2 + z^2 - 2y + 2z - 2 = 0$
   14. $x^2 + y^2 + z^2 + 4x - 2z - 8 = 0$
   15. $x^2 + y^2 + z^2 - 6x + 2y - 2z + 10 = 0$

   16. $x^2 + y^2 + z^2 - 2x - 4y + 8z + 17 = 0$

*Find the standard representation of the vector **PQ**, and then find $\|\mathbf{PQ}\|$ in Problems 17–20.*

   17. $P(1, -1, 3)$, $Q(-1, 1, 4)$ **18.** $P(0, 2, 3)$, $Q(2, 3, 0)$
   19. $P(1, 1, 1)$, $Q(-3, -3, -3)$ **20.** $P(3, 0, -4)$, $Q(0, -4, 3)$

In Problems 21–24, perform the indicated operations.

$$\mathbf{u} = 2\mathbf{i} - \mathbf{j} + 3\mathbf{k} \qquad \mathbf{v} = \mathbf{i} + \mathbf{j} - 5\mathbf{k} \qquad \mathbf{w} = 5\mathbf{i} + 7\mathbf{k}$$

   21. $\mathbf{u} + \mathbf{v} - 2\mathbf{w}$ **22.** $2\mathbf{u} - \mathbf{v} + 3\mathbf{w}$
   23. $4\mathbf{u} + \mathbf{w}$ **24.** $3\mathbf{u} - \mathbf{v} - 5\mathbf{w}$

*In Problems 25–28, find a unit vector that points in the same direction as the given vector **v**.*

   25. $\mathbf{v} = \langle 3, -2, 1 \rangle$ **26.** $\mathbf{v} = \langle -1, 1, \sqrt{2} \rangle$
   27. $\mathbf{v} = \langle -5, 3, 4 \rangle$ **28.** $\mathbf{v} = \langle 1, \sqrt{2}, 7 \rangle$

Sketch the cylindrical surfaces given in Problems 29–32.

   29. $x^2 + y^2 = 4$ **30.** $z = 9 - x^2$
   31. $y = 3z^2$ **32.** $z = \sin x$

33. Find an equation for a sphere, given that the endpoints of a diameter of the sphere are $(1, 2, -3)$ and $(-2, 3, 3)$.

Evaluate the expressions given in Problems 34–37.

34. $\|\mathbf{i} + \mathbf{j} + \mathbf{k}\|$

35. $\|\mathbf{i} - \mathbf{j} + \mathbf{k}\|$

36. $\|2\mathbf{i} + \mathbf{j} - 3\mathbf{k}\|^2$

37. $\|2(\mathbf{i} - \mathbf{j} + \mathbf{k}) - 3(2\mathbf{i} + \mathbf{j} - \mathbf{k})\|^2$

Let $\mathbf{v} = \mathbf{i} - 2\mathbf{j} + 2\mathbf{k}$ and $\mathbf{w} = 2\mathbf{i} + 4\mathbf{j} - \mathbf{k}$; find the vector or scalar requested in Problems 38–41.

38. $2\|\mathbf{v}\| - 3\|\mathbf{w}\|$

39. $\|\mathbf{v}\|\mathbf{w}$

40. $\|2\mathbf{v} - 3\mathbf{w}\|$

41. $\|\mathbf{v} - \mathbf{w}\|(\mathbf{v} + \mathbf{w})$

Determine whether each vector in Problems 42–45 is parallel to $\mathbf{u} = 2\mathbf{i} - 3\mathbf{j} + 5\mathbf{k}$.

42. $\mathbf{v} = \langle 4, -6, 10 \rangle$

43. $\mathbf{v} = \langle -2, 6, -10 \rangle$

44. $\mathbf{v} = \langle 1, -\frac{3}{2}, 2 \rangle$

45. $\mathbf{v} = \langle -1, \frac{3}{2}, -\frac{5}{2} \rangle$

Ⓑ *The vertices A, B, and C of a triangle in $\mathbb{R}^3$ are given in Problems 46–49. Find the lengths of the sides of the triangle and determine whether it is a right triangle, an isosceles triangle, both, or neither.*

46. $A(3, -1, 0)$, $B(7, 1, 4)$, $C(1, 3, 4)$

47. $A(1, 1, 1)$, $B(3, 3, 2)$, $C(3, -3, 5)$

48. $A(1, 2, 3)$, $B(-3, 2, 4)$, $C(1, -4, 3)$

49. $A(2, 4, 3)$, $B(-3, 2, -4)$, $C(-6, 8, -10)$

50. Let $\mathbf{u} = \langle -1, 1, 2 \rangle$, $\mathbf{v} = \langle 0, 2, -3 \rangle$, and $\mathbf{w} = \langle 5, -1, 0 \rangle$. Find a vector $\mathbf{q}$ so that $2\mathbf{u} - \mathbf{v} + 5\mathbf{q} = 3\mathbf{w}$.

In Problems 51 and 52, determine whether the given points are collinear (that is, lie on the same line). Note: For three points A, B, and C to be collinear, $\mathbf{AC}$ must be a multiple of $\mathbf{AB}$.

51. $(2, 3, 2)$, $(-1, 4, 0)$, $(-4, 5, -2)$

52. $(3, 0, 3)$, $(2, -3, 5)$, $(4, 3, 1)$

53. A 150-lb tennis official is sitting on a three-legged judge's stool. Suppose a coordinate system is chosen with the official at point $P(0, 0, 6)$ and the feet of the stool's legs at $A(0, -2, 0)$, $B(-\sqrt{3}, 1, 0)$, and $C(\sqrt{3}, 1, 0)$, as shown in Figure 9.23. Find the force exerted on each of the three legs.

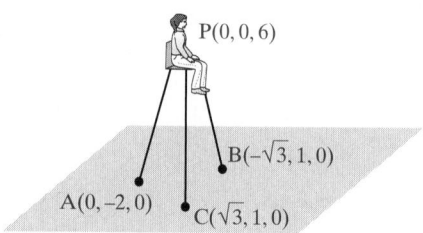

Figure 9.23   Tennis judge

Ⓒ **54.** Let $P(3, 2, -1)$, $Q(-2, 1, c)$, and $R(c, 1, 0)$ be points in $\mathbb{R}^3$. For what values of c (if any) is PQR a right triangle?

55. Find the point P that lies $\frac{2}{3}$ of the distance from the point $A(-1, 3, 9)$ to the midpoint of the line segment joining points $B(-2, 3, 7)$ and $C(4, 1, -3)$.

9.3   The Dot Product

IN THIS SECTION   definition and basic properties of the dot product, angle between vectors, direction cosines, projections, work as a dot product

DEFINITION AND BASIC PROPERTIES OF THE DOT PRODUCT

In the first two sections of this chapter, you have learned how to add vectors and multiply a vector by a scalar. We now turn our attention to the product of two vectors. The **dot (scalar) product** and the **cross (vector) product** are two important vector operations. We will examine the dot product in this section and the cross product in the next section. The dot product is also known as a *scalar product* because it is a product of vectors that gives a scalar (that is, real number) as a result. Sometimes the dot product is called the *inner product*.

Dot Product

> The **dot product** of vectors $\mathbf{v} = a_1\mathbf{i} + a_2\mathbf{j} + a_3\mathbf{k}$ and $\mathbf{w} = b_1\mathbf{i} + b_2\mathbf{j} + b_3\mathbf{k}$ is the scalar denoted by $\mathbf{v} \cdot \mathbf{w}$ and defined by
>
> $$\mathbf{v} \cdot \mathbf{w} = a_1b_1 + a_2b_2 + a_3b_3$$

The dot product of two vectors $\mathbf{v} = a_1\mathbf{i} + a_2\mathbf{j}$ and $\mathbf{w} = b_1\mathbf{i} + b_2\mathbf{j}$ in a plane is given by a similar formula with $a_3 = b_3 = 0$, namely,

$$\mathbf{v} \cdot \mathbf{w} = a_1b_1 + a_2b_2$$

EXAMPLE 1 Dot product

Find the dot product of $\mathbf{v} = -3\mathbf{i} + 2\mathbf{j} + \mathbf{k}$ and $\mathbf{w} = 4\mathbf{i} - \mathbf{j} + 2\mathbf{k}$.

Solution $\mathbf{v} \cdot \mathbf{w} = -3(4) + 2(-1) + 1(2) = -12$ ∎

EXAMPLE 2 Dot product of vectors in component form

If $\mathbf{v} = \langle 4, -1, 3 \rangle$ and $\mathbf{w} = \langle -1, -2, 5 \rangle$, find the dot product, $\mathbf{v} \cdot \mathbf{w}$.

Solution $\mathbf{v} \cdot \mathbf{w} = 4(-1) + (-1)(-2) + 3(5) = 13$ ∎

Before we can apply the dot product to geometric and physical problems, we need to know how it behaves algebraically. A number of important general properties of the dot product are listed in the following theorem.

THEOREM 9.2 Properties of the dot product

If $\mathbf{u}$, $\mathbf{v}$, and $\mathbf{w}$ are vectors in $\mathbb{R}^2$ or $\mathbb{R}^3$ and c is a scalar, then

Magnitude of a vector	$\mathbf{v} \cdot \mathbf{v} = \|\mathbf{v}\|^2$
Zero product	$\mathbf{0} \cdot \mathbf{v} = 0$
Commutativity	$\mathbf{v} \cdot \mathbf{w} = \mathbf{w} \cdot \mathbf{v}$
Multiple of a dot product	$c(\mathbf{v} \cdot \mathbf{w}) = (c\mathbf{v}) \cdot \mathbf{w} = \mathbf{v} \cdot (c\mathbf{w})$
Distributivity	$\mathbf{u} \cdot (\mathbf{v} + \mathbf{w}) = \mathbf{u} \cdot \mathbf{v} + \mathbf{u} \cdot \mathbf{w}$

Proof Let $\mathbf{u} = a_1\mathbf{i} + a_2\mathbf{j} + a_3\mathbf{k}$, $\mathbf{v} = b_1\mathbf{i} + b_2\mathbf{j} + b_3\mathbf{k}$, and $\mathbf{w} = c_1\mathbf{i} + c_2\mathbf{j} + c_3\mathbf{k}$.

Magnitude of a vector

$$\|\mathbf{v}\|^2 = \left(\sqrt{a_1^2 + a_2^2 + a_3^2} \right)^2 = a_1^2 + a_2^2 + a_3^2 = \mathbf{v} \cdot \mathbf{v}$$

Zero product, commutativity, and **multiple of a dot product** can be established in a similar fashion.

Distributivity

$$\mathbf{u} \cdot (\mathbf{v} + \mathbf{w})$$
$$= (a_1\mathbf{i} + a_2\mathbf{j} + a_3\mathbf{k}) \cdot [(b_1 + c_1)\mathbf{i} + (b_2 + c_2)\mathbf{j} + (b_3 + c_3)\mathbf{k}]$$
$$= a_1(b_1 + c_1) + a_2(b_2 + c_2) + a_3(b_3 + c_3)$$
$$= a_1b_1 + a_1c_1 + a_2b_2 + a_2c_2 + a_3b_3 + a_3c_3$$

and

$$\mathbf{u} \cdot \mathbf{v} + \mathbf{u} \cdot \mathbf{w} = (a_1b_1 + a_2b_2 + a_3b_3) + (a_1c_1 + a_2c_2 + a_3c_3)$$
$$= a_1b_1 + a_1c_1 + a_2b_2 + a_2c_2 + a_3b_3 + a_3c_3$$

Thus, $\mathbf{u} \cdot (\mathbf{v} + \mathbf{w}) = \mathbf{u} \cdot \mathbf{v} + \mathbf{u} \cdot \mathbf{w}$. ❑

ANGLE BETWEEN VECTORS

The angle between two nonzero vectors $\mathbf{v}$ and $\mathbf{w}$ in $\mathbb{R}^2$ or $\mathbb{R}^3$ is defined to be the angle θ with $0 \le \theta \le \pi$ that is formed when the vectors are in standard position (initial points at the origin), as shown in Figure 9.24.

The angle between two vectors plays an important role in certain applications and may be computed by using the following formula involving the dot product.

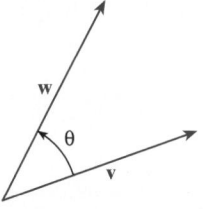

Figure 9.24 The angle between two vectors

THEOREM 9.3   Angle between two vectors

If θ is the angle between the nonzero vectors $\mathbf{v}$ and $\mathbf{w}$, then

$$\cos\theta = \frac{\mathbf{v}\cdot\mathbf{w}}{\|\mathbf{v}\|\|\mathbf{w}\|}$$

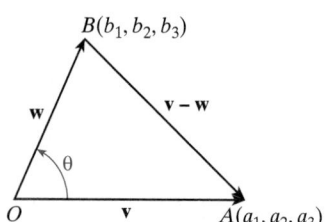

Figure 9.25 Finding an angle between two vectors

Proof   Suppose $\mathbf{v} = a_1\mathbf{i} + a_2\mathbf{j} + a_3\mathbf{k}$ and $\mathbf{w} = b_1\mathbf{i} + b_2\mathbf{j} + b_3\mathbf{k}$, and consider $\triangle AOB$ with vertices at the origin O and the points $A(a_1, a_2, a_3)$ and $B(b_1, b_2, b_3)$, as shown in Figure 9.25.

Note that sides $\overline{OA}$ and $\overline{OB}$ have lengths

$$\|\mathbf{v}\| = \sqrt{a_1^2 + a_2^2 + a_3^2} \quad \text{and} \quad \|\mathbf{w}\| = \sqrt{b_1^2 + b_2^2 + b_3^2}$$

respectively, and that side $\overline{AB}$ has length

$$\|\mathbf{v} - \mathbf{w}\| = \sqrt{(a_1 - b_1)^2 + (a_2 - b_2)^2 + (a_3 - b_3)^2}$$

Next, we apply the law of cosines to the sides $\overline{OA}$ and $\overline{OB}$:

$$\|\mathbf{v} - \mathbf{w}\|^2 = \|\mathbf{v}\|^2 + \|\mathbf{w}\|^2 - 2\|\mathbf{v}\|\|\mathbf{w}\|\cos\theta \qquad \text{Law of cosines}$$

$$\cos\theta = \frac{\|\mathbf{v}\|^2 + \|\mathbf{w}\|^2 - \|\mathbf{v} - \mathbf{w}\|^2}{2\|\mathbf{v}\|\|\mathbf{w}\|} \qquad \text{Solve for } \cos\theta.$$

$$= \frac{a_1^2 + a_2^2 + a_3^2 + b_1^2 + b_2^2 + b_3^2 - [(a_1 - b_1)^2 + (a_2 - b_2)^2 + (a_3 - b_3)^2]}{2\|\mathbf{v}\|\|\mathbf{w}\|}$$

$$= \frac{2a_1b_1 + 2a_2b_2 + 2a_3b_3}{2\|\mathbf{v}\|\|\mathbf{w}\|} = \frac{\mathbf{v}\cdot\mathbf{w}}{\|\mathbf{v}\|\|\mathbf{w}\|} \qquad \square$$

EXAMPLE 3   Angle between two given vectors

Let $\triangle ABC$ be the triangle with vertices $A(1, 1, 8)$, $B(4, -3, -4)$, and $C(-3, 1, 5)$. Find the angle formed at A (to two-place accuracy).

Solution

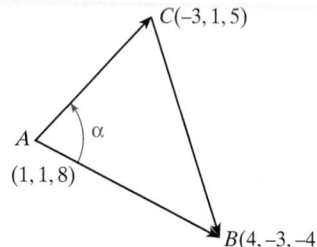

Figure 9.26 Find an angle of a triangle

Draw $\triangle ABC$ and label the angle formed at A as α, as shown in Figure 9.26. The angle α is the angle between vectors $\mathbf{AB}$ and $\mathbf{AC}$, where

$$\mathbf{AB} = (4 - 1)\mathbf{i} + (-3 - 1)\mathbf{j} + (-4 - 8)\mathbf{k} = 3\mathbf{i} - 4\mathbf{j} - 12\mathbf{k}$$
$$\mathbf{AC} = (-3 - 1)\mathbf{i} + (1 - 1)\mathbf{j} + (5 - 8)\mathbf{k} = -4\mathbf{i} - 3\mathbf{k}$$

Thus,

$$\cos\alpha = \frac{\mathbf{AB}\cdot\mathbf{AC}}{\|\mathbf{AB}\|\|\mathbf{AC}\|} = \frac{3(-4) + (-4)(0) + (-12)(-3)}{\sqrt{3^2 + (-4)^2 + (-12)^2}\sqrt{(-4)^2 + (-3)^2}}$$

$$= \frac{24}{\sqrt{169}\sqrt{25}} = \frac{24}{65}$$

and the required angle is $\alpha = \cos^{-1}\left(\frac{24}{65}\right) \approx 1.19$.   ■

The formula for the angle between vectors is often used in conjunction with the dot product. If we multiply both sides of the formula by $\|\mathbf{v}\|\|\mathbf{w}\|$, we obtain the following alternate form for the dot product formula.

Geometric Formula for the Dot Product

$$\mathbf{v}\cdot\mathbf{w} = \|\mathbf{v}\|\|\mathbf{w}\|\cos\theta$$

where θ is the angle $(0 \le \theta \le \pi)$ between the vectors $\mathbf{v}$ and $\mathbf{w}$.

Two vectors are said to be **perpendicular**, or **orthogonal**, if the angle between them is $\theta = \pi/2$. The following theorem provides a useful criterion for orthogonality.

THEOREM 9.4 The orthogonal vector theorem

Nonzero vectors **v** and **w** are **orthogonal** if and only if

$$\mathbf{v} \cdot \mathbf{w} = 0$$

Proof If the vectors are orthogonal, then the angle between them is $\frac{\pi}{2}$; therefore,

$$\mathbf{v} \cdot \mathbf{w} = \|\mathbf{v}\|\|\mathbf{w}\| \cos \frac{\pi}{2} = 0$$

Conversely, if $\mathbf{v} \cdot \mathbf{w} = 0$, and **v** and **w** are nonzero vectors, then $\cos \theta = 0$, so that $\theta = \frac{\pi}{2}$ (since $0 \leq \theta \leq \pi$) and the vectors are orthogonal. ❑

➡ **What This Says** The orthogonal vector theorem allows you to show that two vectors are orthogonal by finding the dot product of the vectors and showing this dot product is 0. On the other hand, if you know the vectors are orthogonal, then it follows that the dot product of the vectors is 0. In particular, $\mathbf{i} \cdot \mathbf{j} = \mathbf{j} \cdot \mathbf{k} = \mathbf{k} \cdot \mathbf{i} = 0$.

EXAMPLE 4 Orthogonal vectors

Determine which (if any) pairs of the following vectors are orthogonal:

$$\mathbf{u} = 3\mathbf{i} + 7\mathbf{j} - 2\mathbf{k} \qquad \mathbf{v} = 5\mathbf{i} - 3\mathbf{j} - 3\mathbf{k} \qquad \mathbf{w} = \mathbf{j} - \mathbf{k}$$

Solution

$$\mathbf{u} \cdot \mathbf{v} = 3(5) + 7(-3) + (-2)(-3) = 0; \ \mathbf{u} \text{ and } \mathbf{v} \text{ are orthogonal.}$$
$$\mathbf{u} \cdot \mathbf{w} = 3(0) + 7(1) + (-2)(-1) = 9; \ \mathbf{u} \text{ and } \mathbf{w} \text{ are not orthogonal.}$$
$$\mathbf{v} \cdot \mathbf{w} = 5(0) + (-3)(1) + (-3)(-1) = 0; \ \mathbf{v} \text{ and } \mathbf{w} \text{ are orthogonal.}$$ ∎

DIRECTION COSINES

The direction of a vector in $\mathbb{R}^2$ positioned with its initial point at the origin may be specified by determining its angle of inclination; that is, the angle ϕ is the smallest positive angle the vector makes with the positive x-axis, as shown in Figure 9.27a. In $\mathbb{R}^3$, it is common practice to measure the direction of a nonzero vector **v** in terms of angles α, β, and γ between **v** and the positive coordinate axes as shown in Figure 9.27b. These angles are called the **direction angles** of **v**, and their cosines are the **direction cosines** of **v**.

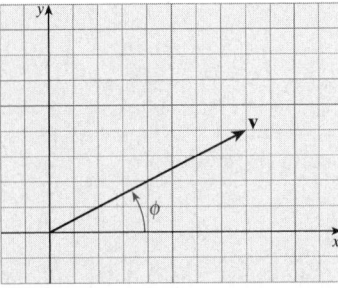

a. In $\mathbb{R}^2$, the direction of **v** is given by the angle of inclination ϕ

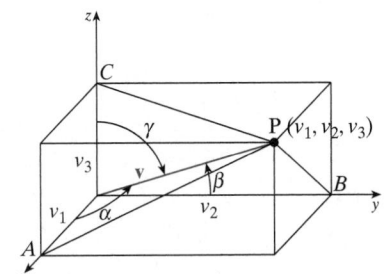

b. In $\mathbb{R}^3$, the direction of **v** is given by the angles α, β, and γ

Figure 9.27 The direction angles of a vector **v**

The direction cosines of $\mathbf{v} = \langle v_1, v_2, v_3 \rangle$ can be computed by taking the dot product of $\mathbf{v}$ with the three standard basis vectors, $\mathbf{i} = \langle 1, 0, 0 \rangle$, $\mathbf{j} = \langle 0, 1, 0 \rangle$, and $\mathbf{k} = \langle 0, 0, 1 \rangle$. For example, to find $\cos \alpha$, note that

$$\mathbf{v} = \mathbf{v} \cdot \mathbf{i} = \|\mathbf{v}\| \|\mathbf{i}\| \cos \alpha, \quad \text{so that} \quad \cos \alpha = \frac{v_1}{\|\mathbf{v}\|}$$

and, similarly,

$$\cos \beta = \frac{v_2}{\|\mathbf{v}\|} \quad \text{and} \quad \cos \gamma = \frac{v_3}{\|\mathbf{v}\|}$$

It can be shown (Problem 53) that

$$\cos^2 \alpha + \cos^2 \beta + \cos^2 \gamma = 1$$

This identity can be used to check whether you have computed the direction cosines correctly.

EXAMPLE 5   Direction cosines and direction angles

Find the direction cosines and direction angles (to the nearest degree) of the vector $\mathbf{v} = -2\mathbf{i} + 3\mathbf{j} + 5\mathbf{k}$, and verify the formula $\cos^2 \alpha + \cos^2 \beta + \cos^2 \gamma = 1$.

Solution

We find $\|\mathbf{v}\| = \sqrt{(-2)^2 + 3^2 + 5^2} = \sqrt{38}$. Therefore,

$$\cos \alpha = \frac{v_1}{\|\mathbf{v}\|} = \frac{-2}{\sqrt{38}} \approx -0.3244428 \qquad \alpha \approx \cos^{-1}(-0.324428) \approx 109°$$

$$\cos \beta = \frac{v_2}{\|\mathbf{v}\|} = \frac{3}{\sqrt{38}} \approx 0.4866642 \qquad \beta \approx \cos^{-1}(0.4866642) \approx 61°$$

$$\cos \gamma = \frac{v_3}{\|\mathbf{v}\|} = \frac{5}{\sqrt{38}} \approx 0.8111071 \qquad \gamma \approx \cos^{-1}(0.8111071) \approx 36°$$

and

$$\cos^2 \alpha + \cos^2 \beta + \cos^2 \gamma = \left(\frac{-2}{\sqrt{38}}\right)^2 + \left(\frac{3}{\sqrt{38}}\right)^2 + \left(\frac{5}{\sqrt{38}}\right)^2 = 1$$

These direction angles are shown in Figure 9.28.

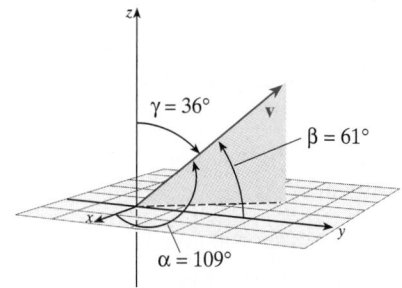

Figure 9.28 The vector $\mathbf{v} = -2\mathbf{i} + 3\mathbf{j} + 5\mathbf{k}$ forms the angles 109°, 61°, and 36° with the coordinate axes

PROJECTIONS

Let $\mathbf{v}$ and $\mathbf{w}$ be two vectors in $\mathbb{R}^3$ drawn so that they have a common initial point, as shown in Figure 9.29. If we drop a perpendicular from the tip of $\mathbf{v}$ to the line determined by $\mathbf{w}$, we determine a vector called the **vector projection of v onto w,** which we have labeled $\mathbf{u}$ in Figure 9.29. To find a formula for the vector projection, note that $\mathbf{u} = t\mathbf{w}$ for some scalar t and that $\mathbf{v} - t\mathbf{w}$ is orthogonal to $\mathbf{w}$. Thus,

$$(\mathbf{v} - t\mathbf{w}) \cdot \mathbf{w} = 0$$
$$\mathbf{v} \cdot \mathbf{w} = t(\mathbf{w} \cdot \mathbf{w})$$
$$t = \frac{\mathbf{v} \cdot \mathbf{w}}{\mathbf{w} \cdot \mathbf{w}}$$

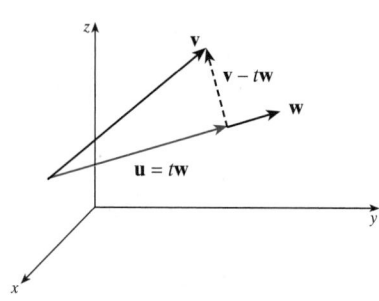

Figure 9.29 The vector $\mathbf{u}$ is the projection of $\mathbf{v}$ onto $\mathbf{w}$.

and the vector projection is

$$\mathbf{u} = \left(\frac{\mathbf{v} \cdot \mathbf{w}}{\mathbf{w} \cdot \mathbf{w}}\right) \mathbf{w}$$

We sometimes denote the vector projection of $\mathbf{v}$ onto $\mathbf{w}$ by $\text{proj}_{\mathbf{w}} \mathbf{v}$. Since $\mathbf{w} \cdot \mathbf{w} = \|\mathbf{w}\|^2$, we see that

$$\text{proj}_{\mathbf{w}} \mathbf{v} = \left(\frac{\mathbf{v} \cdot \mathbf{w}}{\|\mathbf{w}\|^2}\right) \mathbf{w}$$

Notice that $\text{proj}_\mathbf{w}\,\mathbf{v}$ can also be written

$$\text{proj}_\mathbf{w}\,\mathbf{v} = \left(\frac{\mathbf{v}\cdot\mathbf{w}}{\|\mathbf{w}\|}\right)\frac{\mathbf{w}}{\|\mathbf{w}\|}$$

where $\dfrac{\mathbf{w}}{\|\mathbf{w}\|}$ is the direction vector for $\mathbf{w}$. The scalar $\left(\dfrac{\mathbf{v}\cdot\mathbf{w}}{\|\mathbf{w}\|}\right)$ is called the **scalar projection** of $\mathbf{v}$ onto $\mathbf{w}$, or the **component** of $\mathbf{v}$ in the direction of $\mathbf{w}$, and is denoted by $\text{comp}_\mathbf{w}\,\mathbf{v}$. Thus,

$$\text{comp}_\mathbf{w}\,\mathbf{v} = \frac{\mathbf{v}\cdot\mathbf{w}}{\|\mathbf{w}\|} = \|\mathbf{v}\|\cos\theta \qquad \text{Since } \mathbf{v}\cdot\mathbf{w} = \|\mathbf{v}\|\|\mathbf{w}\|\cos\theta$$

so $\text{comp}_\mathbf{w}\,\mathbf{v} > 0$ when $0 < \theta < \frac{\pi}{2}$ and $\text{comp}_\mathbf{w}\,\mathbf{v} < 0$ when $\frac{\pi}{2} < \theta < \pi$.

To summarize

WARNING   Note that $\left(\dfrac{\mathbf{v}\cdot\mathbf{w}}{\mathbf{w}\cdot\mathbf{w}}\right)\mathbf{w}$ is not the same as $\left(\dfrac{\mathbf{v}}{\mathbf{w}}\right)\mathbf{w}$; you cannot "cancel" the vector $\mathbf{w}$. Remember, $\mathbf{v}\cdot\mathbf{w}$ and $\mathbf{w}\cdot\mathbf{w}$ are numbers, whereas $\mathbf{v}/\mathbf{w}$ is not defined.

Vector and Scalar Projections of $\mathbf{v}$ onto $\mathbf{w}$

If $\mathbf{v}$ and $\mathbf{w}$ are nonzero vectors,

then the **vector projection** of $\mathbf{v}$ onto $\mathbf{w}$ is the vector:

$$\text{proj}_\mathbf{w}\,\mathbf{v} = \left(\frac{\mathbf{v}\cdot\mathbf{w}}{\mathbf{w}\cdot\mathbf{w}}\right)\mathbf{w}$$

the **scalar projection** of $\mathbf{v}$ onto $\mathbf{w}$ is the number:

$$\text{comp}_\mathbf{w}\,\mathbf{v} = \frac{\mathbf{v}\cdot\mathbf{w}}{\|\mathbf{w}\|}$$

It is important to note that the $\mathbf{i}$, $\mathbf{j}$, and $\mathbf{k}$ components of any vector $\mathbf{v}$ are the scalar projections of $\mathbf{v}$ onto the appropriate basis vectors, as shown in Figure 9.30.

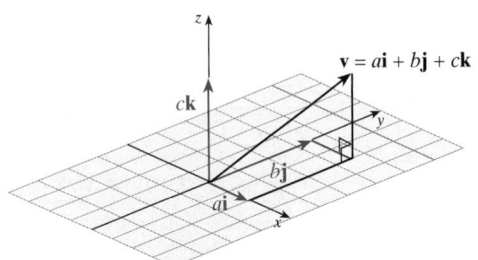

Figure 9.30   The $\mathbf{i}$, $\mathbf{j}$, and $\mathbf{k}$ components of $\mathbf{v} = a\mathbf{i} + b\mathbf{j} + c\mathbf{k}$ are scalar projections of $\mathbf{v}$ onto $\mathbf{i}$, $\mathbf{j}$, and $\mathbf{k}$.

EXAMPLE 6   Vector and scalar projections

Find the vector and scalar projections of $\mathbf{v} = 2\mathbf{i} + 3\mathbf{j} + 5\mathbf{k}$ onto $\mathbf{w} = 2\mathbf{i} - 2\mathbf{j} - \mathbf{k}$.

Solution

The vector projection of $\mathbf{v}$ onto $\mathbf{w}$ is

$$\text{proj}_\mathbf{w}\,\mathbf{v} = \left(\frac{\mathbf{v}\cdot\mathbf{w}}{\mathbf{w}\cdot\mathbf{w}}\right)\mathbf{w} = \left(\frac{2(2) + (3)(-2) + 5(-1)}{2^2 + (-2)^2 + (-1)^2}\right)(2\mathbf{i} - 2\mathbf{j} - \mathbf{k})$$

$$= -\tfrac{7}{9}(2\mathbf{i} - 2\mathbf{j} - \mathbf{k}) = -\tfrac{14}{9}\mathbf{i} + \tfrac{14}{9}\mathbf{j} + \tfrac{7}{9}\mathbf{k}$$

To find the scalar projection, we use the scalar projection formula:

$$\text{comp}_\mathbf{w}\,\mathbf{v} = \frac{\mathbf{v}\cdot\mathbf{w}}{\|\mathbf{w}\|} = \frac{2\cdot 2 + 3\cdot(-2) + 5\cdot(-1)}{\sqrt{2^2 + (-2)^2 + (-1)^2}} = \frac{-7}{3}$$

WORK AS A DOT PRODUCT

In Section 6.5, we noted that when a constant force **F** acts in the direction of motion of an object moving from P to Q along a straight line, it produces work, W, given by

$$W = (\text{MAGNITUDE OF } \mathbf{F})(\text{DISTANCE MOVED}) = \|\mathbf{F}\|\,\|\mathbf{PQ}\|$$

where **PQ** is the displacement vector of the object's motion.

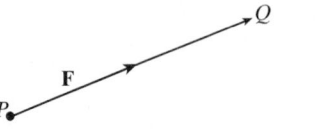
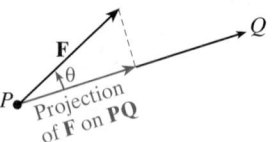

a. If the force **F** acts along the line of motion, then $W = \|\mathbf{F}\|\,\|\mathbf{PQ}\|$.

b. If **F** acts at a nonzero angle with the line of motion, then $W = \|\text{proj. of } \mathbf{F} \text{ onto } \mathbf{PQ}\|\,\|\mathbf{PQ}\|$.

Figure 9.31 The work performed

More generally, if the force **F** remains constant but points in a direction that makes an angle θ with the direction of motion (see Figure 9.31b), then the work W done by **F** in moving the object along the line from P to Q is given by the product of the *component* of **F** on the displacement vector **PQ** times the distance moved; that is,

$$W = (\text{SCALAR COMPONENT OF } \mathbf{F} \text{ ALONG } \mathbf{PQ})(\text{DISTANCE MOVED})$$
$$= (\text{comp}_{\mathbf{PQ}}\,\mathbf{F})(\|\mathbf{PQ}\|)$$
$$= (\|\mathbf{F}\|\cos\theta)\|\mathbf{PQ}\|$$
$$= \mathbf{F} \cdot \mathbf{PQ}$$

Work As a Dot Product

The work W done by a constant force **F** on an object moving along the line from point P to point Q is given by

$$W = \mathbf{F} \cdot \mathbf{PQ}$$

where **PQ** is the displacement vector of the object's motion.

Note that this formula also gives the work in the case where $\theta = 0$.

EXAMPLE 7 Work performed by a constant force

A boat sails north aided by a wind blowing in a direction of N30°E (30° east of north) with magnitude 500 lb. How much work is performed by the wind as the boat moves 100 ft?

Solution

The wind force is $\|\mathbf{F}\| = 500$ lb, acting in a direction $\theta = 30°$, as shown in Figure 9.32. The displacement vector is $\mathbf{PQ} = 100\mathbf{j}$, so $\|\mathbf{PQ}\| = 100$ ft. Thus, $\mathbf{F} = 500\cos 60°\,\mathbf{i} + 500\sin 60°\,\mathbf{j} = 250\mathbf{i} + 250\sqrt{3}\,\mathbf{j}$. The work performed is

$$W = \mathbf{F} \cdot \mathbf{PQ} = 100(250\sqrt{3}) = 25{,}000\sqrt{3}$$

Therefore, the work is approximately 43,300 ft-lb. ∎

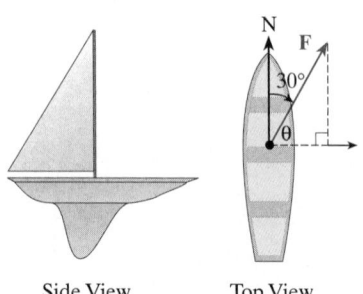

Side View   Top View

Figure 9.32 Work performed on a sail

9.3 PROBLEM SET

A 1. **WHAT DOES THIS SAY?** Discuss how to find a dot product, and describe an application of dot product.

2. **WHAT DOES THIS SAY?** What does it mean for vectors to be orthogonal? What is meant by the vector and scalar projections of a vector **v** onto another vector **w**.

Find the dot product **v** · **w** *in Problems 3–6.*

3. $\mathbf{v} = \langle 3, -2, 4 \rangle$; $\mathbf{w} = \langle 2, -1, -6 \rangle$
4. $\mathbf{v} = \langle 2, -6, 0 \rangle$; $\mathbf{w} = \langle 0, -3, 7 \rangle$
5. $\mathbf{v} = 2\mathbf{i} + 3\mathbf{j} - \mathbf{k}$; $\mathbf{w} = -3\mathbf{i} + 5\mathbf{j} + 4\mathbf{k}$
6. $\mathbf{v} = 3\mathbf{i} - \mathbf{j}$; $\mathbf{w} = 2\mathbf{i} + 5\mathbf{j}$

State whether the given pairs of vectors in Problems 7–10 are orthogonal.

7. $\mathbf{v} = \mathbf{i}$; $\mathbf{w} = \mathbf{k}$ 8. $\mathbf{v} = \mathbf{j}$; $\mathbf{w} = -\mathbf{k}$
9. $\mathbf{v} = 3\mathbf{i} - 2\mathbf{j}$; $\mathbf{w} = 6\mathbf{i} + 9\mathbf{j}$
10. $\mathbf{v} = 4\mathbf{i} - 5\mathbf{j} + \mathbf{k}$; $\mathbf{w} = 8\mathbf{i} + 10\mathbf{j} - 2\mathbf{k}$

Let $\mathbf{v} = 3\mathbf{i} - 2\mathbf{j} + \mathbf{k}$ *and* $\mathbf{w} = \mathbf{i} + \mathbf{j} - \mathbf{k}$. *Evaluate the expressions in Problems 11–14.*

11. $(\mathbf{v} + \mathbf{w}) \cdot (\mathbf{v} - \mathbf{w})$ 12. $(\mathbf{v} \cdot \mathbf{w})\mathbf{w}$
13. $(\|\mathbf{v}\|\mathbf{w}) \cdot (\|\mathbf{w}\|\mathbf{v})$ 14. $\dfrac{2\mathbf{v} + 3\mathbf{w}}{\|3\mathbf{v} + 2\mathbf{w}\|}$

Find the angle between the vectors given in Problems 15–18. Round to the nearest degree.

15. $\mathbf{v} = \mathbf{i} + \mathbf{j} + \mathbf{k}$; $\mathbf{w} = \mathbf{i} - \mathbf{j} + \mathbf{k}$
16. $\mathbf{v} = 2\mathbf{i} + \mathbf{k}$; $\mathbf{w} = \mathbf{j} - 3\mathbf{k}$
17. $\mathbf{v} = 2\mathbf{j} + \mathbf{k}$; $\mathbf{w} = \mathbf{i} - 2\mathbf{k}$
18. $\mathbf{v} = 4\mathbf{i} - \mathbf{j} + \mathbf{k}$; $\mathbf{w} = 2\mathbf{i} + 3\mathbf{j} + 5\mathbf{k}$

Find the scalar and vector projections of **v** *onto* **w** *in Problems 19–22.*

19. $\mathbf{v} = \mathbf{i} + \mathbf{j} + \mathbf{k}$; $\mathbf{w} = 2\mathbf{k}$ 20. $\mathbf{v} = 2\mathbf{i} - 3\mathbf{j}$; $\mathbf{w} = 2\mathbf{j} - 3\mathbf{k}$
21. $\mathbf{v} = \mathbf{i} + 2\mathbf{k}$; $\mathbf{w} = -3\mathbf{j}$ 22. $\mathbf{v} = \mathbf{i} + \mathbf{j} - 2\mathbf{k}$; $\mathbf{w} = \mathbf{i} + \mathbf{j} + \mathbf{k}$

23. Find two distinct unit vectors orthogonal to both $\mathbf{v} = \mathbf{i} + \mathbf{j} - \mathbf{k}$ and $\mathbf{w} = -\mathbf{i} + \mathbf{j} + \mathbf{k}$.

24. Find two distinct unit vectors orthogonal to both $\mathbf{v} = 2\mathbf{i} + \mathbf{j} + 2\mathbf{k}$ and $\mathbf{w} = -\mathbf{i} + 2\mathbf{j} - \mathbf{k}$.

25. Find a unit vector that points in the direction opposite to $\mathbf{v} = 2\mathbf{i} + 3\mathbf{j} - 2\mathbf{k}$.

26. Find a vector that points in the same direction as $\mathbf{v} = \mathbf{i} + 2\mathbf{j} - \mathbf{k}$ and has one-third its length.

27. Find x, y, and z that solve
    $x(\mathbf{i} + \mathbf{j} + \mathbf{k}) + y(\mathbf{i} - \mathbf{j} + 2\mathbf{k}) + z(\mathbf{i} + \mathbf{k}) = 2\mathbf{i} + \mathbf{k}$.

28. Find x, y, and z that solve $x(\mathbf{i} - \mathbf{k}) + y(\mathbf{j} + \mathbf{k}) + z(\mathbf{i} - \mathbf{j}) = 5\mathbf{i} - \mathbf{k}$.

29. Find a number a that guarantees that the vectors $3\mathbf{i} - 2\mathbf{j} + \mathbf{k}$ and $2\mathbf{i} + a\mathbf{j} - 2a\mathbf{k}$ will be orthogonal.

30. Find x if the vectors $\mathbf{v} = 3\mathbf{i} - x\mathbf{j} + 2\mathbf{k}$ and $\mathbf{w} = x\mathbf{i} + \mathbf{j} - 2\mathbf{k}$ are to be orthogonal.

Find the direction cosines and the direction angles for the vectors given in Problems 31–34.

31. $\mathbf{v} = 2\mathbf{i} - 3\mathbf{j} - 5\mathbf{k}$ 32. $\mathbf{v} = 3\mathbf{i} - 2\mathbf{k}$
33. $\mathbf{v} = 5\mathbf{i} - 4\mathbf{j} + 3\mathbf{k}$ 34. $\mathbf{v} = \mathbf{j} - 5\mathbf{k}$

35. Find the cosine of the angle between the vectors $\mathbf{v} = \mathbf{i} - \mathbf{j} + 2\mathbf{k}$ and $\mathbf{w} = 2\mathbf{i} + \mathbf{j} - \mathbf{k}$. Then find the vector projection of **v** onto **w**.

36. Let $\mathbf{v} = 4\mathbf{i} - \mathbf{j} + \mathbf{k}$ and $\mathbf{w} = 2\mathbf{i} + 3\mathbf{j} - \mathbf{k}$. Find
    a. $\mathbf{v} \cdot \mathbf{w}$
    b. $\cos \theta$, where θ is the angle between **v** and **w**
    c. a scalar s such that **v** is orthogonal to $\mathbf{v} - s\mathbf{w}$
    d. a scalar s such that $s\mathbf{v} + \mathbf{w}$ is orthogonal to **w**

37. Let $\mathbf{v} = 2\mathbf{i} - 3\mathbf{j} + 6\mathbf{k}$ and $\mathbf{w} = 4\mathbf{i} + 3\mathbf{k}$. Find
    a. $\mathbf{v} \cdot \mathbf{w}$
    b. $\cos \theta$, where θ is the angle between **v** and **w**
    c. a scalar s such that **v** is orthogonal to $\mathbf{v} - s\mathbf{w}$
    d. a scalar t such that $\mathbf{v} + t\mathbf{w}$ is orthogonal to **w**

38. Find the scalar projection of the force $\mathbf{F} = 4\mathbf{i} - 2\mathbf{j} + 3\mathbf{k}$ in the direction of the vector $\mathbf{v} = \mathbf{i} - \mathbf{j} + 2\mathbf{k}$.

39. Find the work done by the constant force $\mathbf{F} = 2\mathbf{i} + 3\mathbf{j} + \mathbf{k}$ when it moves a particle along the line from $P(1, 0, -1)$ to $Q(3, 1, 2)$.

40. Find the work performed when a force $\mathbf{F} = \frac{6}{7}\mathbf{i} - \frac{2}{7}\mathbf{j} + \frac{6}{7}\mathbf{k}$ is applied to an object moving along the line from $P(-3, -5, 4)$ to $Q(4, 9, 11)$.

B 41. Fred and his friend Sam are pulling a heavy log along flat horizontal ground by ropes attached to the front of the log. The ropes are 8 ft long. Fred holds his rope 2 ft above the log and 1 ft to the side, and Sam holds his end 1 ft above the log and 1 ft to the opposite side, as shown in Figure 9.33.

Side View   Top View

Figure 9.33 Problem 40

If Fred exerts a force of 30 lb and Sam exerts a force of 20 lb, what is the resultant force on the log?

42. Find the force required to keep a 5,000-lb van from rolling downhill if it is parked on a 10° slope (see Figure 9.34).

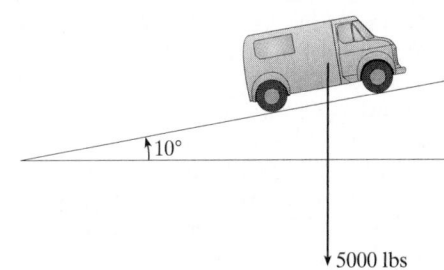

Figure 9.34 Problem 42

43. A block of ice is dragged 20 ft across a floor, using a force of 50 lb, as shown in Figure 9.35. Find the work done if the direction of the force is inclined θ to the horizontal, where

    a. $\theta = \frac{\pi}{3}$ **b.** $\theta = \frac{\pi}{4}$

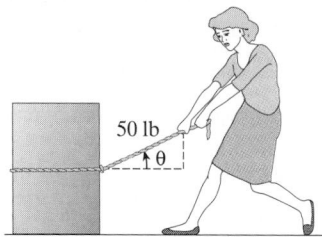

Figure 9.35   Problem 43

44. Suppose that the wind is blowing with a 1,000-lb magnitude force **F** in the direction of N60°W behind a boat's sail. How much work does the wind perform in moving the boat in a northerly direction a distance of 50 ft? Give your answer in foot-pounds.

Orthogonality of functions   *One of the big discoveries in modern mathematics was that it is very fruitful to extend some of the geometric notions of this chapter to functions—for example, taking the dot product of two functions or asking whether two functions are orthogonal, or attempting to project a function onto a second function (or onto a "plane" of functions). You are introduced to these important concepts in Problems 45 and 46.*

45. We say that two functions f and g are **orthogonal** on $[a, b]$ if

$$\int_a^b f(x)g(x)\,dx = 0$$

    a. Show that the two functions x^2 and $x^3 - 5x$ are orthogonal on $[-b, b]$ for any positive b.

    b. For distinct positive integers k and n, show that $\sin kx$ and $\sin nx$ are orthogonal on the interval $[-\pi, \pi]$. That is, the *family* of functions $\sin x, \sin 2x, \cdots$ are *mutually* orthogonal on $[-\pi, \pi]$. You may need the product-to-sum identity (trigonometric identity 28 from the *Student Mathematics Handbook*):

$$2 \sin \alpha \sin \beta = \cos(\alpha - \beta) - \cos(\alpha + \beta)$$

46. HISTORICAL QUEST   Jean Baptiste Joseph Fourier began his studies by training for the priesthood. In spite of this first calling, his interest in mathematics remained intense, and in 1789 he wrote, "Yesterday was my 21st birthday, and at that age Newton and Pascal had already acquired many claims to immortality." He did not take his religious vows but continued his mathematical research while teaching. Fourier was renowned as an outstanding teacher, but it was not until around 1804–1807 that he did his important mathematical work on the theory of heat. ∎

JEAN FOURIER
1768–1830

    During that time, he expanded on an idea of Daniel Bernoulli by showing how many functions, both continuous and discontinuous, can be represented by trigonometric series of the general form

$$\tfrac{1}{2}a_0 + a_1 \cos x + a_2 \cos 2x + a_3 \cos 3x + \cdots$$
$$+ b_1 \sin x + b_2 \sin 2x + b_3 \sin 3x + \cdots$$

The study of such series, called **Fourier series**, is of fundamental importance in both theoretical and applied mathematics, and they are used for modeling phenomena in engineering and physics as well as in areas such as computer science and medical research.

    The issue of whether a given function f can be represented by a Fourier series is a matter for a more advanced course. For this Quest, assume that $f(x)$ is such a function and that

$$f(x) = \tfrac{1}{2}a_0 + \sum_{k=1}^{\infty} a_k \cos kx + \sum_{k=1}^{\infty} b_k \sin kx$$

on the interval $[-\pi, \pi]$. In particular, if f is a continuous odd function (that is, $f(-x) = -f(x)$) on $[-\pi, \pi]$, it can be shown that $a_k = 0$ for $k = 0, 1, 2, \ldots$, and that

$$b_k = \frac{1}{\pi} \int_{-\pi}^{\pi} f(x) \sin kx\,dx$$
$$= \frac{2}{\pi} \int_0^{\pi} f(x) \sin kx\,dx \quad \text{for } k = 1, 2, \ldots$$

    a. Using this result, show that the function $f(x) = x$ on $[-\pi, \pi]$ has the Fourier series representation

$$f(x) = 2 \sum_{k=1}^{\infty} \frac{(-1)^{k+1}}{k} \sin(kx)$$

    b. Use the Fourier series in part **a** to evaluate the convergent alternating series

$$\sum_{k=1}^{\infty} \frac{(-1)^{k+1}}{2k - 1} = 1 - \frac{1}{3} + \frac{1}{5} - \frac{1}{7} + \frac{1}{9} - \cdots$$

⊙ 47. Let $\mathbf{u_0} = a\mathbf{i} + b\mathbf{j} + c\mathbf{k}$ and let $\mathbf{u} = x\mathbf{i} + y\mathbf{j} + z\mathbf{k}$. Describe the set of points in $\mathbb{R}^3$ defined by

$$\|\mathbf{u_0} - \mathbf{u}\| < r$$

where $r > 0$ and a, b, c are constants.

48. Find the angle (to the nearest degree) between the diagonal of a cube and a diagonal of one of its faces. Assume both diagonals have the same initial point.

49. Show that the vector $\mathbf{B} = \|\mathbf{v}\|\mathbf{u} + \|\mathbf{u}\|\mathbf{v}$ bisects the angle θ between the two nonzero vectors $\mathbf{u}$ and $\mathbf{v}$.

50. Use vector methods to prove that an angle inscribed in a semicircle must be a right angle.

51.   **a.** Show that $(\mathbf{v} + \mathbf{w}) \cdot (\mathbf{v} + \mathbf{w}) = \|\mathbf{v}\|^2 + \|\mathbf{w}\|^2 + 2(\mathbf{v} \cdot \mathbf{w})$.

    b. Use part **a** to prove the **triangle inequality:**

$$\|\mathbf{v} + \mathbf{w}\| \le \|\mathbf{v}\| + \|\mathbf{w}\|$$

    Hint: Note that

$$\|\mathbf{v} + \mathbf{w}\|^2 = (\mathbf{v} + \mathbf{w}) \cdot (\mathbf{v} + \mathbf{w})$$

52. The **Cauchy-Schwarz** inequality in $\mathbb{R}^3$ states that for any vectors **v** and **w**

$$|\mathbf{v} \cdot \mathbf{w}| \le \|\mathbf{v}\|\|\mathbf{w}\|$$

a. Prove the Cauchy-Schwarz inequality. *Hint*: Use the formula for the angle between vectors.

b. Show that equality $|\mathbf{v} \cdot \mathbf{w}| = \|\mathbf{v}\|\|\mathbf{w}\|$ occurs if and only if $\mathbf{v} = t\mathbf{w}$ for some scalar t.

c. Use the Cauchy-Schwarz inequality to prove the **triangle**

inequality:

$$\|\mathbf{v} + \mathbf{w}\| \leq \|\mathbf{v}\| + \|\mathbf{w}\|$$

53. Show that $\cos^2 \alpha + \cos^2 \alpha + \cos^2 \gamma = 1$, where α, β, and γ are the direction angles of a triangle $\triangle ABC$.

9.4 The Cross Product

IN THIS SECTION definition and basic properties of the cross product; geometric interpretation of the cross product; applications of the cross product: area and torque; the scalar triple product

DEFINITION AND BASIC PROPERTIES OF THE CROSS PRODUCT

The dot product is not the only way to multiply vectors, In this section, we will study a second product involving vectors, called the *cross product*, *vector product*, or sometimes the *outer product*. Unlike the dot product, in which two vectors are multiplied to produce a scalar, the cross product produces a vector. Here is the definition.

Cross Product

> If $\mathbf{v} = a_1\mathbf{i} + a_2\mathbf{j} + a_3\mathbf{k}$ and $\mathbf{w} = b_1\mathbf{i} + b_2\mathbf{j} + b_3\mathbf{k}$, the **cross product** of the vector $\mathbf{v}$ with the vector $\mathbf{w}$, written $\mathbf{v} \times \mathbf{w}$, is the vector
>
> $$\mathbf{v} \times \mathbf{w} = (a_2b_3 - a_3b_2)\mathbf{i} + (a_3b_1 - a_1b_3)\mathbf{j} + (a_1b_2 - a_2b_1)\mathbf{k}$$

SMH Determinants are reviewed in Section 2.8 of the Student Mathematics Handbook.

The form of the cross product may seem odd to you, but you will soon discover that the cross product has a variety of useful properties.

A convenient way of remembering the cross product is the following determinant form:

$$\mathbf{v} \times \mathbf{w} = \begin{vmatrix} \mathbf{i} & \mathbf{j} & \mathbf{k} \\ a_1 & a_2 & a_3 \\ b_1 & b_2 & b_3 \end{vmatrix}$$

To verify the determinant formula for the cross product, we expand about the first row.

$$\mathbf{v} \times \mathbf{w} = \begin{vmatrix} \mathbf{i} & \mathbf{j} & \mathbf{k} \\ a_1 & a_2 & a_3 \\ b_1 & b_2 & b_3 \end{vmatrix} = \begin{vmatrix} a_2 & a_3 \\ b_2 & b_3 \end{vmatrix}\mathbf{i} - \begin{vmatrix} a_1 & a_3 \\ b_1 & b_3 \end{vmatrix}\mathbf{j} + \begin{vmatrix} a_1 & a_2 \\ b_1 & b_2 \end{vmatrix}\mathbf{k}$$

j is in row 1, column 2, so do not forget the negative sign here.

$$= (a_2b_3 - a_3b_2)\mathbf{i} - (a_1b_3 - a_3b_1)\mathbf{j} + (a_1b_2 - a_2b_1)\mathbf{k}$$
$$= (a_2b_3 - a_3b_2)\mathbf{i} + (a_3b_1 - a_1b_3)\mathbf{j} + (a_1b_2 - a_2b_1)\mathbf{k}$$

EXAMPLE 1 Cross product

Find $\mathbf{v} \times \mathbf{w}$, where $\mathbf{v} = 2\mathbf{i} - \mathbf{j} + 3\mathbf{k}$ and $\mathbf{w} = 7\mathbf{j} - 4\mathbf{k}$.

Solution

$$\mathbf{v} \times \mathbf{w} = \begin{vmatrix} \mathbf{i} & \mathbf{j} & \mathbf{k} \\ 2 & -1 & 3 \\ 0 & 7 & -4 \end{vmatrix}$$

Do not forget minus here (**j** is in the negative position).
↓

$$= [(-1)(-4) - 3(7)]\mathbf{i} - [2(-4) - 0(3)]\mathbf{j} + [2(7) - 0(-1)]\mathbf{k}$$
$$= -17\mathbf{i} + 8\mathbf{j} + 14\mathbf{k}$$ ∎

SMH

See Example 2.31 and Problem 66 of Problem Set 2 of the Student Mathematics Handbook.

TECHNOLOGY NOTE

Mathematical programs such as *Mathematica*, *Maple*, *Derive*, and *Matlab* all do vector operations, including dot and cross products. Many CAS programs and calculators use brackets to input vectors, with the components separated by commas, as in $[a, b, c]$.

The graphic in Figure 9.36 shows the dot product and the cross product of the vectors in Example 1.

Notice that the output shows a number, -19, for the dot product, and a vector, $[-17, 8, 14]$, for the cross product. In vector notation,

$$[-17, 8, 14] = -17\mathbf{i} + 8\mathbf{j} + 14\mathbf{k}$$

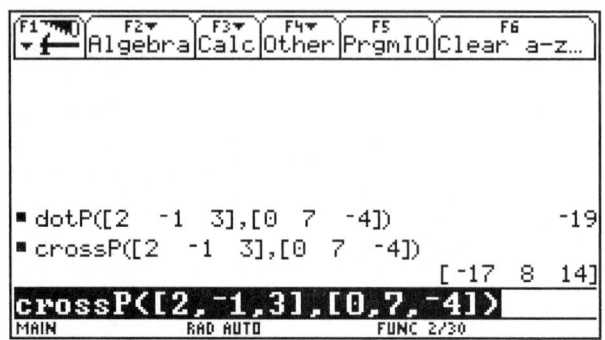

Figure 9.36 Example 1 using a calculator

Properties of determinants can also be used to establish properties of the cross product. For instance, the following computation shows that the cross product is not commutative. This property is sometimes called **anticommutativity**.

$$\mathbf{v} \times \mathbf{w} = \begin{vmatrix} \mathbf{i} & \mathbf{j} & \mathbf{k} \\ a_1 & a_2 & a_3 \\ b_1 & b_2 & b_3 \end{vmatrix} = - \begin{vmatrix} \mathbf{i} & \mathbf{j} & \mathbf{k} \\ b_1 & b_2 & b_3 \\ a_1 & a_2 & a_3 \end{vmatrix} = -(\mathbf{w} \times \mathbf{v})$$

This and other properties are listed in the following theorem.

THEOREM 9.5 Properties of the cross product

If $\mathbf{u}$, $\mathbf{v}$, $\mathbf{w}$, $\mathbf{a}$, $\mathbf{b}$, and $\mathbf{c}$ are vectors in $\mathbb{R}^3$ and s and t are scalars, then

Scalar distributivity $(s\mathbf{v}) \times (t\mathbf{w}) = st(\mathbf{v} \times \mathbf{w})$

Distributivity for cross product over addition

$$\mathbf{u} \times (\mathbf{v} + \mathbf{w}) = (\mathbf{u} \times \mathbf{v}) + (\mathbf{u} \times \mathbf{w})$$
$$(\mathbf{u} + \mathbf{v}) \times \mathbf{w} = (\mathbf{u} \times \mathbf{w}) + (\mathbf{v} \times \mathbf{w})$$

Anticommutativity $\mathbf{v} \times \mathbf{w} = -(\mathbf{w} \times \mathbf{v})$

Product of a multiple $\mathbf{v} \times s\mathbf{v} = \mathbf{0}$; in particular, $\mathbf{v} \times \mathbf{v} = \mathbf{0}$

Zero product $\mathbf{v} \times \mathbf{0} = \mathbf{0} \times \mathbf{v} = \mathbf{0}$

Lagrange's identity $\|\mathbf{v} \times \mathbf{w}\|^2 = \|\mathbf{v}\|^2 \|\mathbf{w}\|^2 - (\mathbf{v} \cdot \mathbf{w})^2$

cab-bac formula $\mathbf{a} \times (\mathbf{b} \times \mathbf{c}) = (\mathbf{c} \cdot \mathbf{a})\mathbf{b} - (\mathbf{b} \cdot \mathbf{a})\mathbf{c}$

Proof   Let $\mathbf{u} = a_1\mathbf{i} + a_2\mathbf{j} + a_3\mathbf{k}$, $\mathbf{v} = b_1\mathbf{i} + b_2\mathbf{j} + b_3\mathbf{k}$, and $\mathbf{w} = c_1\mathbf{i} + c_2\mathbf{j} + c_3\mathbf{k}$.

Scalar distributivity and *vector distributivity* are proved by using the definition of cross product and the corresponding properties of real numbers.

Anticommutativity was proved in the paragraph preceding this theorem.

Product of a multiple

$$\mathbf{v} \times s\mathbf{v} = \begin{vmatrix} \mathbf{i} & \mathbf{j} & \mathbf{k} \\ b_1 & b_2 & b_3 \\ sb_1 & sb_2 & sb_3 \end{vmatrix} = s\begin{vmatrix} \mathbf{i} & \mathbf{j} & \mathbf{k} \\ b_1 & b_2 & b_3 \\ b_1 & b_2 & b_3 \end{vmatrix} = \mathbf{0} \quad \text{A determinant with two identical rows is } 0.$$

Zero product is obvious.

Lagrange's identity

$$\begin{aligned} \|\mathbf{v} \times \mathbf{w}\|^2 &= (b_2c_3 - b_3c_2)^2 + (b_3c_1 - b_1c_3)^2 + (b_1c_2 - b_2c_1)^2 \\ &= (b_1^2 + b_2^2 + b_3^2)(c_1^2 + c_2^2 + c_3^2) - (b_1c_1 + b_2c_2 + b_3c_3)^2 \\ &= \|\mathbf{v}\|^2\|\mathbf{w}\|^2 - (\mathbf{v} \cdot \mathbf{w})^2 \end{aligned}$$

You are asked to prove the *cab-bac formula* in Problem 55.   ❑

WARNING   You are accustomed to dealing with products in which the order does not matter, but the order of the terms in the cross product $\mathbf{v} \times \mathbf{w}$ matters very much, since $\mathbf{w} \times \mathbf{v} = -(\mathbf{v} \times \mathbf{w})$.

Cross products involving the basic vectors $\mathbf{i}$, $\mathbf{j}$, and $\mathbf{k}$ occur so frequently in computations that it is useful to have the following list:

$$\begin{array}{lll} \mathbf{i} \times \mathbf{i} = \mathbf{0} & \mathbf{i} \times \mathbf{j} = \mathbf{k} & \mathbf{i} \times \mathbf{k} = -\mathbf{j} \\ \mathbf{j} \times \mathbf{i} = -\mathbf{k} & \mathbf{j} \times \mathbf{j} = \mathbf{0} & \mathbf{j} \times \mathbf{k} = \mathbf{i} \\ \mathbf{k} \times \mathbf{i} = \mathbf{j} & \mathbf{k} \times \mathbf{j} = -\mathbf{i} & \mathbf{k} \times \mathbf{k} = \mathbf{0} \end{array}$$

These nine rules can be established by using the definition of cross product, or by using the determinant form. For example,

$$\mathbf{j} \times \mathbf{i} = \begin{vmatrix} \mathbf{i} & \mathbf{j} & \mathbf{k} \\ 0 & 1 & 0 \\ 1 & 0 & 0 \end{vmatrix} = -\mathbf{k}$$

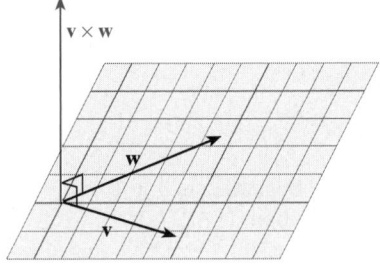

Figure 9.37 $\mathbf{v} \times \mathbf{w}$ is orthogonal to both $\mathbf{v}$ and $\mathbf{w}$

GEOMETRIC INTERPRETATION OF THE CROSS PRODUCT

The cross product is frequently used for geometric purposes, such as determining a vector that is orthogonal to two given vectors. The following theorem lists one of the most important geometric properties of the cross product. It says that for any two nonzero vectors $\mathbf{v}$ and $\mathbf{w}$, the cross product is a vector orthogonal to the plane determined by the vectors $\mathbf{v}$ and $\mathbf{w}$, as shown in Figure 9.37.

THEOREM 9.6   Orthogonality property of the cross product

If $\mathbf{v}$ and $\mathbf{w}$ are nonzero vectors in $\mathbb{R}^3$ that are not multiples of one another, then $\mathbf{v} \times \mathbf{w}$ is orthogonal to both $\mathbf{v}$ and $\mathbf{w}$.

Proof   The theorem is illustrated in Figure 9.37. We will show that $(\mathbf{v} \times \mathbf{w})$ is orthogonal to $\mathbf{v}$ and leave the proof that $\mathbf{v} \times \mathbf{w}$ is orthogonal to $\mathbf{w}$ as an exercise. Let $\mathbf{v} = a_1\mathbf{i} + a_2\mathbf{j} + a_3\mathbf{k}$ and $\mathbf{w} = b_1\mathbf{i} + b_2\mathbf{j} + b_3\mathbf{k}$. Then

$$\mathbf{v} \times \mathbf{w} = \begin{vmatrix} \mathbf{i} & \mathbf{j} & \mathbf{k} \\ a_1 & a_2 & a_3 \\ b_1 & b_2 & b_3 \end{vmatrix} = (a_2b_3 - a_3b_2)\mathbf{i} - (a_1b_3 - a_3b_1)\mathbf{j} + (a_1b_2 - a_2b_1)\mathbf{k}$$

so that

$$\mathbf{v} \cdot (\mathbf{v} \times \mathbf{w}) = a_1(a_2 b_3 - a_3 b_2) - a_2(a_1 b_3 - a_3 b_1) + a_3(a_1 b_2 - a_2 b_1)$$
$$= a_1 a_2 b_3 - a_1 a_3 b_2 - a_1 a_2 b_3 + a_2 a_3 b_1 + a_1 a_3 b_2 - a_2 a_3 b_1 = 0$$

Thus, according to Theorem 9.4, $\mathbf{v} \times \mathbf{w}$ is orthogonal to $\mathbf{v}$. ❏

EXAMPLE 2 A vector orthogonal to two given vectors

Find a nonzero vector that is orthogonal to both $\mathbf{v} = -2\mathbf{i} + 3\mathbf{j} - 7\mathbf{k}$ and $\mathbf{w} = 5\mathbf{i} + 9\mathbf{k}$.

Solution

The cross product $\mathbf{v} \times \mathbf{w}$ is orthogonal to both $\mathbf{v}$ and $\mathbf{w}$.

$$\mathbf{v} \times \mathbf{w} = \begin{vmatrix} \mathbf{i} & \mathbf{j} & \mathbf{k} \\ -2 & 3 & -7 \\ 5 & 0 & 9 \end{vmatrix} = (27 + 0)\mathbf{i} - (-18 + 35)\mathbf{j} + (0 - 15)\mathbf{k}$$

$$= 27\mathbf{i} - 17\mathbf{j} - 15\mathbf{k}$$

■

In Section 9.3, we showed that the dot product satisfies $\mathbf{v} \cdot \mathbf{w} = \|\mathbf{v}\| \|\mathbf{w}\| \cos \theta$, where θ is the angle between $\mathbf{v}$ and $\mathbf{w}$. The following theorem establishes a similar result for the cross product.

THEOREM 9.7 Magnitude of the cross product

If $\mathbf{v}$ and $\mathbf{w}$ are nonzero vectors in $\mathbb{R}^3$ with θ the angle between $\mathbf{v}$ and $\mathbf{w}$ $(0 \leq \theta \leq \pi)$, then

$$\|\mathbf{v} \times \mathbf{w}\| = \|\mathbf{v}\| \|\mathbf{w}\| \sin \theta$$

Proof We will use Lagrange's identity from Theorem 9.5.

$$\|\mathbf{v} \times \mathbf{w}\|^2 = \|\mathbf{v}\|^2 \|\mathbf{w}\|^2 - [\|\mathbf{v}\| \|\mathbf{w}\| \cos \theta]^2 \qquad \textit{Lagrange's identity}$$
$$= \|\mathbf{v}\|^2 \|\mathbf{w}\|^2 - \|\mathbf{v}\|^2 \|\mathbf{w}\|^2 \cos^2 \theta$$
$$= \|\mathbf{v}\|^2 \|\mathbf{w}\|^2 (1 - \cos^2 \theta)$$
$$= \|\mathbf{v}\|^2 \|\mathbf{w}\|^2 \sin^2 \theta$$

Thus,

$$\|\mathbf{v} \times \mathbf{w}\| = \|\mathbf{v}\| \|\mathbf{w}\| |\sin \theta| = \|\mathbf{v}\| \|\mathbf{w}\| \sin \theta \qquad \textit{Because } \sin \theta \geq 0$$
$$\textit{when } 0 \leq \theta \leq \pi \qquad ❏$$

From Theorem 9.7, we know the magnitude of the cross product $\mathbf{v} \times \mathbf{w}$, but what is its direction? It turns out that this direction can be described by the following rule:

The Right-Hand Rule

With **v** and **w** positioned so that their initial points coincide, place the little finger of your right hand along the vector **v** with the tip of your little finger pointing toward the tip of **v**, and curl your fingers toward **w**. Then your thumb points in the direction of **v** × **w**, as shown in Figure 9.38, so that

$$\mathbf{v} \times \mathbf{w} = \|\mathbf{v}\|\|\mathbf{w}\| \sin\theta \, \mathbf{n}$$

where **n** is a unit vector determined by the right-hand rule.

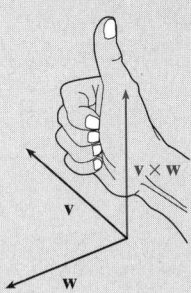

Figure 9.38 The right-hand rule: If you place the little finger of your right hand along **v** and curl your fingers toward **w** to cover the smaller angle between **v** and **w**, then your thumb points in the direction of **v** × **w**.

➧ **What This Says** Theorem 9.7 provides a *coordinate-free way* of computing the cross product in the sense that it depends only on the geometry of the vectors involved and not on any particular choice of representation. This is important to physicists and engineers because it enables them to choose whichever coordinate system is most convenient to compute cross products that arise in applications.

APPLICATIONS OF THE CROSS PRODUCT: AREA AND TORQUE

The cross product can be used in a variety of ways in geometry and physics. For example, using Theorem 9.7, it can be shown that the parallelogram having **v** and **w** as adjacent sides has area $\|\mathbf{v} \times \mathbf{w}\|$ (see Figure 9.39). To see this, note that the height of the parallelogram is $h = \|\mathbf{w}\| \sin\theta$, so that the area is given by

$$\text{AREA} = (\text{BASE})(\text{HEIGHT}) = \|\mathbf{v}\|(\|\mathbf{w}\| \sin\theta) = \|\mathbf{v} \times \mathbf{w}\|$$

From this formula, it follows immediately that the area of a triangle in $\mathbb{R}^3$ is half the area of the corresponding parallelogram. For future reference, we let **v** be defined by the points A and B, and **w** by the points A and C, and summarize these formulas for area in the following box.

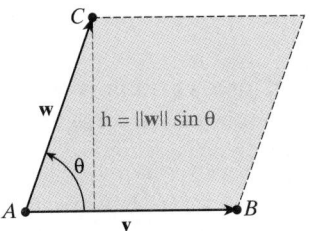

Figure 9.39 A geometric interpretation of $\|\mathbf{v} \times \mathbf{w}\|$

The parallelogram with adjacent sides $\overline{AB}$ and $\overline{AC}$ has

$$\text{AREA} = \|\mathbf{AB} \times \mathbf{AC}\|$$

Let A, B, and C be points in $\mathbb{R}^3$. Then the triangle with vertices A, B, and C has

$$\text{AREA} = \tfrac{1}{2}\|\mathbf{AB} \times \mathbf{AC}\|$$

EXAMPLE 3   Area of a triangle

Find the area of the triangle with vertices $P(-2, 4, 5)$, $Q(0, 7, -4)$, and $R(-1, 5, 0)$.

Solution

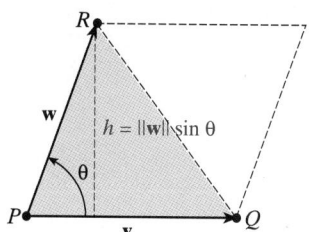

Figure 9.40 Area of a triangle by cross product

Draw this triangle as shown in Figure 9.40. Then $\triangle PQR$ has half the area of the parallelogram determined by the vectors **PQ** and **PR**; that is, the triangle has area

$$A = \tfrac{1}{2}\|\mathbf{PQ} \times \mathbf{PR}\|$$

First find

$$\mathbf{PQ} = (0 + 2)\mathbf{i} + (7 - 4)\mathbf{j} + (-4 - 5)\mathbf{k} = 2\mathbf{i} + 3\mathbf{j} - 9\mathbf{k}$$

$$\mathbf{PR} = (-1 + 2)\mathbf{i} + (5 - 4)\mathbf{j} + (0 - 5)\mathbf{k} = \mathbf{i} + \mathbf{j} - 5\mathbf{k}$$

and compute the cross product:

$$\mathbf{PQ} \times \mathbf{PR} = \begin{vmatrix} \mathbf{i} & \mathbf{j} & \mathbf{k} \\ 2 & 3 & -9 \\ 1 & 1 & -5 \end{vmatrix}$$

$$= (-15 + 9)\mathbf{i} - (-10 + 9)\mathbf{j} + (2 - 3)\mathbf{k}$$

$$= -6\mathbf{i} + \mathbf{j} - \mathbf{k}$$

Thus, the triangle has area

$$A = \tfrac{1}{2}\|\mathbf{PQ} \times \mathbf{PR}\|$$

$$= \tfrac{1}{2}\sqrt{(-6)^2 + 1^2 + (-1)^2}$$

$$= \tfrac{1}{2}\sqrt{38} \qquad \blacksquare$$

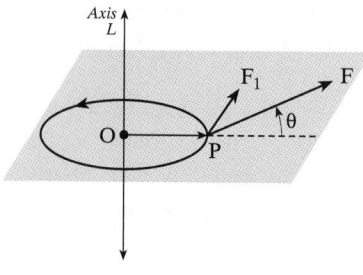

Figure 9.41 The torque of F about a point O

An important application of the cross product to physics involves computing the tendency of an object to rotate about an axis. Figure 9.41 shows an object at point P rotating about an axis L. A force **F** operates on the object to produce rotation and $\mathbf{F}_1$ is the component of **F** in the direction of motion (orthogonal to **OP**). Experience suggests that the tendency to rotate depends both on the magnitude of the component force $\mathbf{F}_1$ and on the distance $\|\mathbf{OP}\|$ of the rotating object from the axis of rotation. We have $\mathbf{F}_1 = \|\mathbf{F}\| \sin\theta$, where θ is the angle between **F** and **OP**, so the tendency to rotate can be measured by the product

$$\|\mathbf{OP}\|\|\mathbf{F}_1\| = \|\mathbf{OP}\|\|\mathbf{F}\| \sin\theta$$

$$= \|\mathbf{OP} \times \mathbf{F}\|$$

The cross product $\mathbf{OP} \times \mathbf{F}$ is called the **torque of F about O**. The magnitude of the torque measures the tendency to rotate, and the direction of the torque vector is the direction of the axis of rotation.

EXAMPLE 4   Torque on the hinge of a door

Figure 9.42 shows a half-open door that is 3 ft wide. A force of 30 lb is applied in a horizontal direction at the edge of the door. Find the torque of the force about the hinges on the door.

Solution

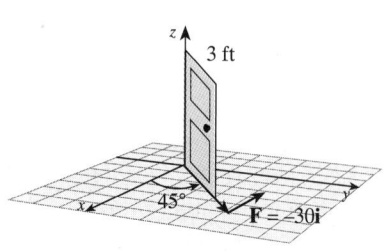

Figure 9.42 The torque of a force applied at the edge of a door about the hinges

We represent the force by $\mathbf{F} = -30\mathbf{i}$ (see Figure 9.42). Because the door is half open, it makes an angle of $\frac{\pi}{4}$ with the positive x-axis, and we can represent the "arm" **PQ** by the vector

$$\mathbf{PQ} = 3\left(\cos\tfrac{\pi}{4}\mathbf{i} + \sin\tfrac{\pi}{4}\mathbf{j}\right) = 3\left(\frac{\sqrt{2}}{2}\mathbf{i} + \frac{\sqrt{2}}{2}\mathbf{j}\right) = \frac{3\sqrt{2}}{2}\mathbf{i} + \frac{3\sqrt{2}}{2}\mathbf{j}$$

The torque can now be found:

$$\mathbf{T} = \mathbf{PQ} \times \mathbf{F} = \begin{vmatrix} \mathbf{i} & \mathbf{j} & \mathbf{k} \\ \frac{3\sqrt{2}}{2} & \frac{3\sqrt{2}}{2} & 0 \\ -30 & 0 & 0 \end{vmatrix} = 45\sqrt{2}\,\mathbf{k}$$

The magnitude of the torque ($45\sqrt{2}$ lb-ft) is a measure of the tendency of the door to rotate about its hinges. $\qquad \blacksquare$

THE SCALAR TRIPLE PRODUCT

The cross product can also be used to compute the volume of a parallelepiped in $\mathbb{R}^3$. Consider the parallelepiped determined by three nonzero vectors **u**, **v**, and **w** that do not all lie in the same plane, as shown in Figure 9.43.

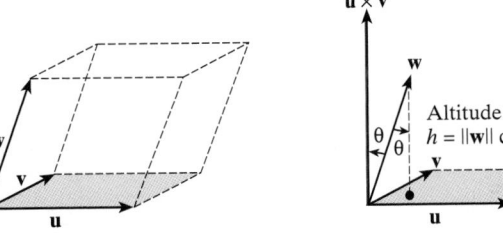

a. The parallelepiped determined by **u**, **v**, and **w**

b. The parallelepiped has volume $V = Ah = |(\mathbf{u} \times \mathbf{v}) \cdot \mathbf{w}|$.

Figure 9.43 Computing volume with the scalar triple product

It is known from solid geometry that this parallelepiped has volume $V = Ah$, where A is the area of the face determined by **u** and **v** and h is the altitude from the tip of **w** to this face (see Figure 9.43b).

The face determined by **u** and **v** is a parallelogram with area $A = \|\mathbf{u} \times \mathbf{v}\|$, and we know that the cross-product vector $\mathbf{u} \times \mathbf{v}$ is perpendicular to both **u** and **v** and hence to the face determined by **u** and **v**. From the geometric formula for the dot product, we have

$$(\mathbf{u} \times \mathbf{v}) \cdot \mathbf{w} = \|\mathbf{u} \times \mathbf{v}\| \|\mathbf{w}\| \cos \theta$$

where θ is the angle between $\mathbf{u} \times \mathbf{v}$ and **w**. Since the parallelepiped has altitude

$$h = |\|\mathbf{w}\| \cos \theta| = \left| \frac{(\mathbf{u} \times \mathbf{v}) \cdot \mathbf{w}}{\|\mathbf{u} \times \mathbf{v}\|} \right|$$

the volume is given by

$$V = Ah = \|\mathbf{u} \times \mathbf{v}\| \left| \frac{(\mathbf{u} \times \mathbf{v}) \cdot \mathbf{w}}{\|\mathbf{u} \times \mathbf{v}\|} \right| = |(\mathbf{u} \times \mathbf{v}) \cdot \mathbf{w}|$$

The combined operation $(\mathbf{u} \times \mathbf{v}) \cdot \mathbf{w}$ is called the **scalar triple product** of **u**, **v**, and **w**. These observations are summarized in the following box.

Volume Interpretation of the Scalar Triple Product

Let **u**, **v**, and **w** be nonzero vectors that do not all lie in the same plane. Then the parallelepiped determined by these vectors has volume

$$V = |(\mathbf{u} \times \mathbf{v}) \cdot \mathbf{w}|$$

EXAMPLE 5 Volume of a parallelepiped

Find the volume of the parallelepiped determined by the vectors

$$\mathbf{u} = \mathbf{i} - 2\mathbf{j} + 3\mathbf{k} \qquad \mathbf{v} = -4\mathbf{i} + 7\mathbf{j} - 11\mathbf{k} \qquad \mathbf{w} = 5\mathbf{i} + 9\mathbf{j} - \mathbf{k}$$

Solution

We first find the cross product

$$\mathbf{u} \times \mathbf{v} = \begin{vmatrix} \mathbf{i} & \mathbf{j} & \mathbf{k} \\ 1 & -2 & 3 \\ -4 & 7 & -11 \end{vmatrix}$$

$$= (22 - 21)\mathbf{i} - (-11 + 12)\mathbf{j} + (7 - 8)\mathbf{k}$$

$$= \mathbf{i} - \mathbf{j} - \mathbf{k}$$

Thus,

$$V = |(\mathbf{u} \times \mathbf{v}) \cdot \mathbf{w}| = |(\mathbf{i} - \mathbf{j} - \mathbf{k}) \cdot (5\mathbf{i} + 9\mathbf{j} - \mathbf{k})| = |5 - 9 + 1| = 3$$

The volume of the parallelepiped is 3 cubic units.   ∎

THEOREM 9.8   Determinant form for a scalar triple product

If $\mathbf{u} = a_1\mathbf{i} + a_2\mathbf{j} + a_3\mathbf{k}$, $\mathbf{v} = b_1\mathbf{i} + b_2\mathbf{j} + b_3\mathbf{k}$, and $\mathbf{w} = c_1\mathbf{i} + c_2\mathbf{j} + c_3\mathbf{k}$, then the scalar triple product can be found by evaluating the determinant

$$(\mathbf{u} \times \mathbf{v}) \cdot \mathbf{w} = \begin{vmatrix} a_1 & a_2 & a_3 \\ b_1 & b_2 & b_3 \\ c_1 & c_2 & c_3 \end{vmatrix} \begin{matrix} \leftarrow \text{ components of } \mathbf{u} \\ \leftarrow \text{ components of } \mathbf{v} \\ \leftarrow \text{ components of } \mathbf{w} \end{matrix}$$

Proof   The proof follows by expanding the determinant (see Problem 49).   ❏

We can use Theorem 9.8 to rework Example 5:

$$(\mathbf{u} \times \mathbf{v}) \cdot \mathbf{w} = \begin{vmatrix} 1 & -2 & 3 \\ -4 & 7 & -11 \\ 5 & 9 & -1 \end{vmatrix} = -3$$

(SMH)   *See Problem 65 of Problem Set 2 of the Student Mathematics Handbook.*
Thus, the volume is $|-3| = 3$, as computed directly in Example 5.

WARNING   In the problem set, we have included several exercises involving the scalar triple product and the triple vector product $\mathbf{u} \times \mathbf{v} \times \mathbf{w}$. In case you wonder why we neglect the product $(\mathbf{u} \cdot \mathbf{v}) \times \mathbf{w}$, notice that such a product makes no sense, because $\mathbf{u} \cdot \mathbf{v}$ is a scalar and the cross product is an operation involving only vectors. Thus, the product $\mathbf{u} \cdot \mathbf{v} \times \mathbf{w}$ must mean $\mathbf{u} \cdot (\mathbf{v} \times \mathbf{w})$.

9.4   PROBLEM SET

 Find $\mathbf{v} \times \mathbf{w}$ *for the vectors given in Problems 1–10.*

1. $\mathbf{v} = \mathbf{i}$; $\mathbf{w} = \mathbf{j}$ **2.** $\mathbf{v} = \mathbf{k}$; $\mathbf{w} = \mathbf{k}$

3. $\mathbf{v} = 3\mathbf{i} + 2\mathbf{k}$; $\mathbf{w} = 2\mathbf{i} + \mathbf{j}$ **4.** $\mathbf{v} = \mathbf{i} - 3\mathbf{j}$; $\mathbf{w} = \mathbf{i} + 5\mathbf{k}$

5. $\mathbf{v} = 3\mathbf{i} - 2\mathbf{j} + 4\mathbf{k}$; $\mathbf{w} = \mathbf{i} + 4\mathbf{j} - 7\mathbf{k}$

6. $\mathbf{v} = 5\mathbf{i} - \mathbf{j} + 2\mathbf{k}$; $\mathbf{w} = 2\mathbf{i} + \mathbf{j} - 3\mathbf{k}$

7. $\mathbf{v} = 3\mathbf{i} - \mathbf{j} + 2\mathbf{k}$; $\mathbf{w} = 2\mathbf{i} + 3\mathbf{j} - 4\mathbf{k}$

8. $\mathbf{v} = -\mathbf{j} + 4\mathbf{k}$; $\mathbf{w} = 5\mathbf{i} + 6\mathbf{k}$

9. $\mathbf{v} = \mathbf{i} - 6\mathbf{j} + 10\mathbf{k}$; $\mathbf{w} = -\mathbf{i} + 5\mathbf{j} - 6\mathbf{k}$

10. $\mathbf{v} = \cos\theta\mathbf{i} + \sin\theta\mathbf{j}$; $\mathbf{w} = -\sin\theta\mathbf{i} + \cos\theta\mathbf{j}$ for any angle θ

Use the cross product to find $\sin\theta$ *where* θ *is the angle between* $\mathbf{v}$ *and* $\mathbf{w}$ *in Problems 11–14.*

11. $\mathbf{v} = \mathbf{i} + \mathbf{k}$; $\mathbf{w} = \mathbf{i} + \mathbf{j}$ **12.** $\mathbf{v} = \mathbf{i} + \mathbf{j}$; $\mathbf{w} = \mathbf{i} + \mathbf{j} + \mathbf{k}$

13. $\mathbf{v} = \mathbf{j} + \mathbf{k}$; $\mathbf{w} = \mathbf{i} + \mathbf{k}$ **14.** $\mathbf{v} = \mathbf{i} + \mathbf{j}$; $\mathbf{w} = \mathbf{j} + \mathbf{k}$

Find a unit vector that is orthogonal to both $\mathbf{v}$ *and* $\mathbf{w}$ *in Problems 15–18.*

15. $\mathbf{v} = 2\mathbf{i} + \mathbf{k}$; $\mathbf{w} = \mathbf{i} - \mathbf{j} - \mathbf{k}$

16. $\mathbf{v} = \mathbf{j} - 3\mathbf{k}$; $\mathbf{w} = -\mathbf{i} + \mathbf{j} + \mathbf{k}$

17. $\mathbf{v} = \mathbf{i} + \mathbf{j} + \mathbf{k}$; $\mathbf{w} = 3\mathbf{i} + 12\mathbf{j} - 4\mathbf{k}$

18. $\mathbf{v} = 2\mathbf{i} - 2\mathbf{j} + \mathbf{k}$; $\mathbf{w} = 4\mathbf{i} + 2\mathbf{j} - 3\mathbf{k}$

Find the area of the parallelogram determined by the vectors in Problems 19–22.

19. $\mathbf{v} = 3\mathbf{i} + 4\mathbf{j}$ and $\mathbf{w} = \mathbf{i} + \mathbf{j} - \mathbf{k}$

20. $\mathbf{v} = 2\mathbf{i} - \mathbf{j} + 2\mathbf{k}$ and $\mathbf{w} = 4\mathbf{i} - 3\mathbf{j}$

21. $\mathbf{v} = 4\mathbf{i} - \mathbf{j} + \mathbf{k}$ and $\mathbf{w} = 2\mathbf{i} + 3\mathbf{j} - \mathbf{k}$

22. $\mathbf{v} = 2\mathbf{i} + 3\mathbf{k}$ and $\mathbf{w} = 2\mathbf{j} - 3\mathbf{k}$

Find the area of △PQR in Problems 23–26.

23. $P(0, 1, 1)$, $Q(1, 1, 0)$, $R(1, 0, 1)$

24. $P(1, 0, 0)$, $Q(2, 1, -1)$, $R(0, 1, -2)$

25. $P(1, 2, 3)$, $Q(2, 3, 1)$, $R(3, 1, 2)$

26. $P(-1, -1, -1)$, $Q(1, -1, -1)$, $R(-1, 1, -1)$

Determine whether each product in Problems 27–29 is a scalar or a vector or does not exist. Explain your reasoning.

27. **a.** $\mathbf{u} \times (\mathbf{v} \cdot \mathbf{w})$ **b.** $\mathbf{u} \cdot (\mathbf{v} \times \mathbf{w})$

28. **a.** $\mathbf{u} \times (\mathbf{v} \times \mathbf{w})$ **b.** $\mathbf{u} \cdot (\mathbf{v} \cdot \mathbf{w})$

29. **a.** $(\mathbf{u} \times \mathbf{v}) \cdot (\mathbf{u} \times \mathbf{w})$ **b.** $(\mathbf{u} \times \mathbf{v}) \times (\mathbf{u} \times \mathbf{w})$

In Problems 30–33, find the volume of the parallelepiped determined by vectors **u,** **v,** *and* **w.**

30. $\mathbf{u} = \mathbf{i} + \mathbf{j}$; $\mathbf{v} = \mathbf{j} + 2\mathbf{k}$; $\mathbf{w} = 3\mathbf{k}$

31. $\mathbf{u} = \mathbf{j} + \mathbf{k}$; $\mathbf{v} = 2\mathbf{i} + \mathbf{j} + 2\mathbf{k}$; $\mathbf{w} = 5\mathbf{i}$

32. $\mathbf{u} = \mathbf{i} + \mathbf{j} + \mathbf{k}$; $\mathbf{v} = \mathbf{i} - \mathbf{j} - \mathbf{k}$; $\mathbf{w} = 2\mathbf{i} + 3\mathbf{k}$

33. $\mathbf{u} = 2\mathbf{i} + \mathbf{j} - \mathbf{k}$; $\mathbf{v} = 3\mathbf{i} + \mathbf{k}$; $\mathbf{w} = \mathbf{j} + \mathbf{k}$

B **34.** **WHAT DOES THIS SAY?** Contrast dot and cross products of vectors, including a discussion of some of their properties.

35. **WHAT DOES THIS SAY?** What is the right-hand rule?

36. **Counterexample Problem**

a. If $\mathbf{u} \times \mathbf{w} = \mathbf{v} \times \mathbf{w}$, does it follow that $\mathbf{u} = \mathbf{v}$?

b. If $\mathbf{u} \cdot \mathbf{w} = \mathbf{v} \cdot \mathbf{w}$, does it follow that $\mathbf{u} = \mathbf{v}$?

37. Find a number s that guarantees that the vectors $\mathbf{i}$, $\mathbf{i} + \mathbf{j} + \mathbf{k}$, and $\mathbf{i} + 2\mathbf{j} + s\mathbf{k}$ will all be coplanar (in the same plane).

38. Find a number t that guarantees the vectors $\mathbf{i} + \mathbf{j}$, $2\mathbf{i} - \mathbf{j} + \mathbf{k}$, and $\mathbf{i} + \mathbf{j} + t\mathbf{k}$ will all be coplanar (in the same plane).

39. Let $\mathbf{u} = \mathbf{i} + \mathbf{j}$, $\mathbf{v} = 2\mathbf{i} - \mathbf{j} + \mathbf{k}$, and $\mathbf{w} = 3\mathbf{i}$. Compute $(\mathbf{u} \times \mathbf{v}) \times \mathbf{w}$ and $\mathbf{u} \times (\mathbf{v} \times \mathbf{w})$. What does this say about the associativity of the cross product?

40. Show that $(a\mathbf{u}) \times (b\mathbf{v}) = ab(\mathbf{u} \times \mathbf{v})$ for any scalars a and b.

41. For a given vector $\mathbf{v}$ in $\mathbb{R}^3$, find all vectors $\mathbf{w}$ such that $\mathbf{v} \times \mathbf{w} = \mathbf{w}$.

42. What can be said about nonzero vectors $\mathbf{v}$ and $\mathbf{w}$ if $\mathbf{v} \cdot \mathbf{w} = 0$? What can be said if $\mathbf{v} \times \mathbf{w} = \mathbf{0}$?

43. One end of a 2-ft lever pivots about the origin in the yz-plane, as shown in Figure 9.44.

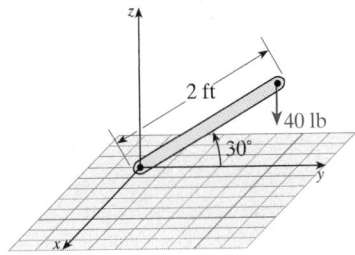

Figure 9.44 Finding the torque

If a vertical force of 40 lb is applied at the end of the lever, what is the torque of the lever about the pivot point (the origin) when the lever makes an angle of 30° with the xy-plane?

44. A 40-lb child sits on a seesaw, 3 ft from the fulcrum, as shown in Figure 9.45. What torque is exerted when the child is 2 ft above the horizontal?

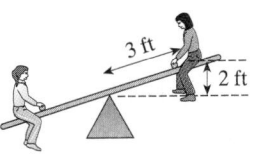

Figure 9.45 Seesaw torque

45. Find the angle between the vector $2\mathbf{i} - \mathbf{j} + \mathbf{k}$ and the plane determined by the points $P(1, -2, 3)$, $Q(-1, 2, 3)$, and $R(1, 2, -3)$.

46. **a.** Show that the vectors $\mathbf{u}$, $\mathbf{v}$, and $\mathbf{w}$ are coplanar (all in the same plane) if

$$\mathbf{u} \cdot (\mathbf{v} \times \mathbf{w}) = 0 \quad \text{or} \quad (\mathbf{u} \times \mathbf{v}) \cdot \mathbf{w} = 0$$

b. Are the vectors $\mathbf{u} = \mathbf{i} + 3\mathbf{j} + \mathbf{k}$, $\mathbf{v} = 2\mathbf{i} - \mathbf{j} - \mathbf{k}$, and $\mathbf{w} = 7\mathbf{j} + 3\mathbf{k}$ coplanar?

47. Show that the triangle with vertices (x_1, y_1), (x_2, y_2), (x_3, y_3) has area $A = \frac{1}{2}|D|$, where

$$D = \begin{vmatrix} x_1 & y_1 & 1 \\ x_2 & y_2 & 1 \\ x_3 & y_3 & 1 \end{vmatrix}$$

48. Using the properties of determinants, show that

$$\mathbf{u} \cdot (\mathbf{v} \times \mathbf{w}) = (\mathbf{u} \times \mathbf{v}) \cdot \mathbf{w}$$

for any vectors $\mathbf{u}$, $\mathbf{v}$, and $\mathbf{w}$.

C **49.** Prove the determinant formula for evaluating a scalar triple product.

50. Let A, B, C, and D be four points that do not lie in the same plane; see Figure 9.46, for example. It can be shown that the volume of the tetrahedron with vertices A, B, C, and D satisfies

$$\begin{bmatrix} \text{VOLUME OF} \\ \text{TETRAHEDRON} \\ ABCD \end{bmatrix} = \frac{1}{3} \begin{pmatrix} \text{AREA OF} \\ \triangle ABC \end{pmatrix} \begin{pmatrix} \text{ALTITUDE} \\ \text{FROM } D \\ \text{TO } \triangle ABC \end{pmatrix}$$

Show that the volume is given by

$$V = \tfrac{1}{6}|(\mathbf{AB} \times \mathbf{AC}) \cdot \mathbf{AD}|$$

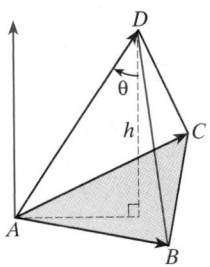

Figure 9.46 Problem 50

51. Show that if $\mathbf{u}$, $\mathbf{v}$, and $\mathbf{w}$ are vectors in $\mathbb{R}^3$ with $\mathbf{u} + \mathbf{v} + \mathbf{w} = \mathbf{0}$, then

$$\mathbf{u} \times \mathbf{v} = \mathbf{v} \times \mathbf{w} = \mathbf{w} \times \mathbf{u}$$

52. Suppose $\mathbf{u}$, $\mathbf{v}$, and $\mathbf{w}$ are nonzero vectors in $\mathbb{R}^3$ with $\mathbf{u} \times \mathbf{v} = \mathbf{w}$ and $\mathbf{u} \cdot \mathbf{v} = 0$. Show that

$$\mathbf{v} = s(\mathbf{w} \times \mathbf{u}) \quad \text{and} \quad \mathbf{u} = t(\mathbf{v} \times \mathbf{w})$$

for scalars s and t.

53. Show that

$$\tan\theta = \frac{\|\mathbf{v} \times \mathbf{w}\|}{\mathbf{v} \cdot \mathbf{w}}$$

where θ $(0 \leq \theta < \frac{\pi}{2})$ is the angle between $\mathbf{v}$ and $\mathbf{w}$.

54. Let $\mathbf{u}$, $\mathbf{v}$, and $\mathbf{w}$ be nonzero vectors in $\mathbb{R}^3$ that do not all lie in the same plane. Show that

$$|\mathbf{u} \cdot (\mathbf{v} \times \mathbf{w})| = |\mathbf{v} \cdot (\mathbf{u} \times \mathbf{w})|$$

What other scalar triple products involving $\mathbf{u}$, $\mathbf{v}$, and $\mathbf{w}$ have the same absolute values?

55. Let $\mathbf{a}$, $\mathbf{b}$, and $\mathbf{c}$ be vectors in space. Prove the "cab - bac" formula.

$$\mathbf{a} \times (\mathbf{b} \times \mathbf{c}) = (\mathbf{c} \cdot \mathbf{a})\mathbf{b} - (\mathbf{b} \cdot \mathbf{a})\mathbf{c}$$

Establish the validity of the equations in Problems 56–59 for arbitrary vectors $\mathbf{u}$, $\mathbf{v}$, $\mathbf{w}$, and $\mathbf{z}$ in $\mathbb{R}^3$. You may use the result of Problem 55.

56. $(\mathbf{u} \times \mathbf{v}) \times (\mathbf{w} \times \mathbf{z}) = (\mathbf{u} \cdot \mathbf{w} \times \mathbf{z})\mathbf{v} - (\mathbf{v} \cdot \mathbf{w} \times \mathbf{z})\mathbf{u}$

57. $\mathbf{u} \times (\mathbf{v} \times \mathbf{w}) + \mathbf{v} \times (\mathbf{w} \times \mathbf{u}) + \mathbf{w} \times (\mathbf{u} \times \mathbf{v}) = \mathbf{0}$

58. $\mathbf{u} \times \mathbf{v} = (\mathbf{u} \cdot \mathbf{v} \times \mathbf{i})\mathbf{i} + (\mathbf{u} \cdot \mathbf{v} \times \mathbf{j})\mathbf{j} + (\mathbf{u} \cdot \mathbf{v} \times \mathbf{k})\mathbf{k}$

59. $\mathbf{u} \times [\mathbf{u} \times (\mathbf{u} \times \mathbf{v})] \cdot \mathbf{w} = -\|\mathbf{u}\|^2 \mathbf{u} \cdot \mathbf{v} \times \mathbf{w}$

60. Show that if vectors $\mathbf{OP}$, $\mathbf{OQ}$, $\mathbf{OR}$, and $\mathbf{OS}$ lie in the same plane, then

$$(\mathbf{OP} \times \mathbf{OQ}) \times (\mathbf{OR} \times \mathbf{OS}) = \mathbf{0}$$

9.5 Parametric Representation of Curves; Lines in $\mathbb{R}^3$

IN THIS SECTION parametric equations, parameterizing a curve, lines in $\mathbb{R}^3$

PARAMETRIC EQUATIONS

Until now, most of the curves we have considered have been graphs of functions of the form $y = f(x)$. This form of representation is limited by the requirements of the vertical line test, which precludes closed curves such as circles or any curve with a self-intersection. However, such restrictions are often not necessary for curves where the coordinates x and y of each point $P(x, y)$ on the curve are themselves functions of a third variable, called a *parameter*. We will begin by examining parametric representations in $\mathbb{R}^2$, and then extend our results to $\mathbb{R}^3$.

Parametric Representation for a Curve in $\mathbb{R}^2$

> Let f and g be continuous functions of t on an interval I; then the equations
>
> $$x = f(t) \quad \text{and} \quad y = g(t)$$
>
> are called **parametric equations** with **parameter** t. As t varies over the **parametric set** I, the points $(x, y) = (f(t), g(t))$ trace out a **parametric curve**.

Note: The letter "t" used for the parameter does not necessarily denote time, although in many applications, time is a suitable parameter. Indeed, any letter or symbol may be used to denote a parameter.

EXAMPLE 1 **Sketching the path of a parametric curve**

Sketch the path of the curve $x = t^2 - 9$, $y = \frac{1}{3}t$ for $-3 \leq t \leq 2$.

Solution

Values of x and y corresponding to various choices of the parameter t are shown in the following table:

t	x	y	
-3	0	-1	(Starting or **initial** point)
-2	-5	$-\frac{2}{3}$	
-1	-8	$-\frac{1}{3}$	
0	-9	0	
1	-8	$\frac{1}{3}$	
2	-5	$\frac{2}{3}$	(Ending or **terminal** point)

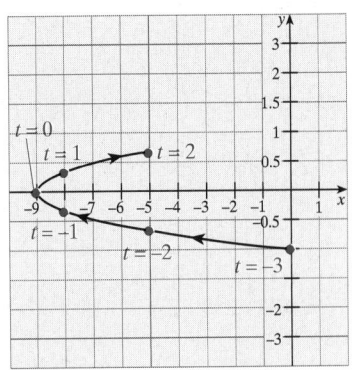

Figure 9.47 Graph of $x = t^2 - 9$, $y = \frac{1}{3}t$, for $-3 \leq t \leq 2$. Notice how the arrows show the orientation as t increases from -3 to 2.

The graph is shown in Figure 9.47. ∎

If you are using a computer or a graphing calculator, plotting points can be an effective way of sketching a parametric curve. Sometimes, however, we wish to eliminate the parameter to obtain a Cartesian equation. For instance, in Example 1, we have $y = \frac{1}{3}t$, so $t = 3y$, and by substituting into the equation $x = t^2 - 9$, we obtain

$$x = (3y)^2 - 9 = 9y^2 - 9$$

which is the Cartesian equation for a parabola that opens to the right. Because of the domain of the parameter t, we see that the parametric curve in Figure 9.47 is a subset of the set of points that satisfy the equation $x = 9y^2 - 9$.

Parameterizations are not unique. For example, the curve with parametric equations

$$x = 9(9t^2 - 1), \quad y = 3t \quad \text{for } -\frac{1}{3} \leq t \leq \frac{2}{9}$$

is the same as the curve in Figure 9.47.

EXAMPLE 2   Sketching the path of a parametric curve by eliminating the parameter

Describe the path $x = \sin \pi t$, $y = \cos 2\pi t$ for $0 \leq t \leq 0.5$.

Solution

Using a double angle identity, we find

$$\cos 2\pi t = 1 - 2\sin^2 \pi t$$

so that

$$y = 1 - 2x^2$$

We recognize this as a Cartesian equation for a parabola. Because $y' = -4x$, we can find the critical number $x = 0$, which locates the vertex of the parabola at $(0, 1)$. The parabola is the curve shown in color as the dashed curve in Figure 9.48.

Because t is restricted to the interval $0 \leq t \leq 0.5$, the parametric representation involves only part of the right side of the parabola $y = 1 - 2x^2$. The curve is oriented from the point $(0, 1)$, where $t = 0$, to the point $(1, -1)$, where $t = 0.5$, and is the portion of the parabola shown in black in Figure 9.48. ∎

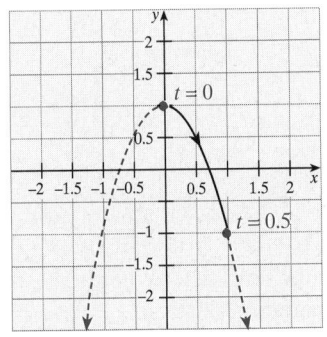

Figure 9.48 The parabolic arc $x = \sin \pi t$, $y = \cos 2\pi t$ for $0 \leq t \leq 0.5$

When it is difficult to eliminate the parameter from a given parametric representation, we can sometimes get a good picture of the parametric curve by plotting points.

EXAMPLE 3 **Describing a spiraling path**

Discuss the path of the curve described by the parametric equations

$$x = e^{-t}\cos t, \qquad y = e^{-t}\sin t \qquad \text{for } t \geq 0$$

Solution

We have no convenient way of eliminating the parameter so we write out a table of values (x, y) that correspond to various values of t. The curve is obtained by plotting these points in a Cartesian plane and passing a smooth curve through the plotted points, as shown in Figure 9.49.

t	x	y
0	1	0
$\frac{\pi}{4}$	0.32	0.32
1	0.20	0.31
$\frac{\pi}{2}$	0	0.21
2	-0.06	0.12
π	-0.04	0
$\frac{3\pi}{2}$	0	-0.01
2π	0.00	0

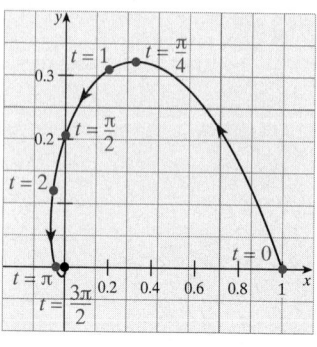

Figure 9.49 Graph of $x = e^{-t}\cos t$, $y = e^{-t}\sin t$ for $t \geq 0$

Note that for each value of t, the distance from $P(x, y)$ on the curve to the origin is

$$\sqrt{x^2 + y^2} = \sqrt{(e^{-t}\cos t)^2 + (e^{-t}\sin t)^2} = \sqrt{e^{-2t}(1)} = e^{-t}$$

Because e^{-t} decreases as t increases, it follows that P gets closer and closer to the origin as t increases. However, because $\cos t$ and $\sin t$ vary between -1 and $+1$, the approach is not direct but takes place along a spiral. ∎

PARAMETERIZING A CURVE

So far, our examples have dealt with sketching a parametric curve given the parametric equations. In general, this process may be tedious, but generally can be done easily using technology. However, the reverse process, finding a suitable set of parametric equations for a given curve, is an art for which there is no simple procedure. Indeed, a given curve can have many different parameterizations and there are curves for which no simple parameterization can be given. The following two examples illustrate various methods for parameterizing a given curve.

EXAMPLE 4 **Parameterizing two curves**

In each of the following cases, parameterize the given curve:

a. $y = 9x^2$ **b.** $r = 5\cos^3\theta$ in polar coordinates

Solution

a. The usual parameterization for a parabola is to let the parameter t be the variable that is squared: $x = t$, $y = 9t^2$. However, another parameterization is to let $t = 3x$ so that $x = \frac{1}{3}t$ and $y = t^2$.

b. In polar coordinates we have $x = r\cos\theta$, $y = r\sin\theta$, so we can parameterize x and y in terms of the parameter θ:

$$\begin{aligned} x &= r\cos\theta & y &= r\sin\theta \\ &= (5\cos^3\theta)\cos\theta & &= (5\cos^3\theta)\sin\theta \\ &= 5\cos^4\theta \end{aligned}$$

EXAMPLE 5   Modeling Problem: Finding parametric equations for a trochoid

A bicycle wheel has radius a and a reflector is attached at a point P on a spoke of the bicycle wheel at a fixed distance d from the center. Find parametric equations for the curve described by P as the wheel rolls along a straight line without slipping. Such a curve is called a **trochoid**, and is shown in Figure 9.50.

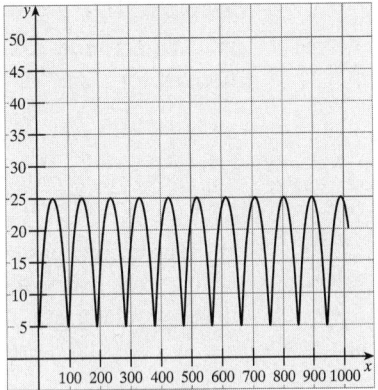

Figure 9.50   The path of a reflector placed 5 in. from the tire on the wheel of a bike with 30-in. wheel. This is an example of a trochoid.

Solution

Assume that the wheel rolls along the x-axis and that the center C of the wheel begins at $(0, a)$ on the y-axis. Further assume that P also starts on the y-axis, d units below C. Figure 9.51 shows the initial position of the wheel and its position after turning through an angle θ (radians).

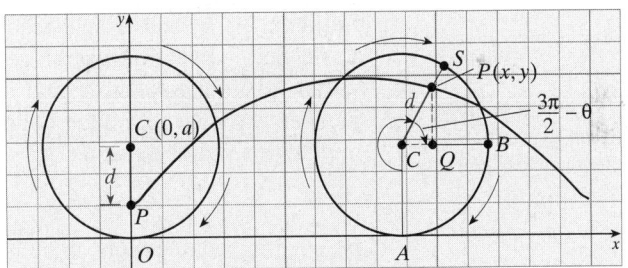

Figure 9.51   The path of a reflector on a bicycle

We begin by labeling some points: The point A is on the x-axis directly beneath C, whereas B is the point where the horizontal line through C meets the rim of the wheel. Finally, Q is the point on BC directly beneath P, and S is the point where the line through C and P intersects the rim. Let P have coordinates (x, y).

We need to find representations (in terms of a, d, and θ) for x and y.

$$x = |\overline{OA}| + |\overline{CQ}|$$
$$= a\theta + |\overline{CQ}|$$

Because the wheel rolls along the x-axis without slipping, $|\overline{OA}|$ is the same as the arc length from A to S, so $|\overline{OA}| = a\theta$.

$$y = |\overline{AC}| + |\overline{QP}|$$
$$= a + |\overline{QP}|$$

To complete our evaluation of x and y, we need to compute $\left|\overline{CQ}\right|$ and $\left|\overline{QP}\right|$. These are sides of $\triangle PCQ$. Note that $\angle PCQ = \frac{3\pi}{2} - \theta$; therefore, by the definitions of cosine and sine, we have

$$\cos\left(\frac{3\pi}{2} - \theta\right) = \frac{\left|\overline{CQ}\right|}{d} \quad \text{so} \quad \left|\overline{CQ}\right| = d\cos\left(\frac{3\pi}{2} - \theta\right) = -d\sin\theta$$

Similarly, $\left|\overline{QP}\right| = d\sin\left(\frac{3\pi}{2} - \theta\right) = -d\cos\theta$.

We can now substitute these values for $\left|\overline{CQ}\right|$ and $\left|\overline{QP}\right|$ into the equations we derived for x and y.

$$x = a\theta + \left|\overline{CQ}\right| = a\theta - d\sin\theta$$
$$y = a + \left|\overline{QP}\right| = a - d\cos\theta \qquad \blacksquare$$

The special case where P is on the rim of the wheel in Example 5 (when $d = a$) is a curve called a **cycloid**. There are several problems involving these and similar curves in the problem set.

If f, g, and h are continuous functions of a variable t on an interval I, then

$$x = f(t) \qquad y = g(t) \qquad z = h(t)$$

are parametric equations with parameter t, and as t varies over I, the points $(x, y, z) = (f(t), g(t), h(t))$ trace out a parametric curve in $\mathbb{R}^3$. The rest of this section is devoted to examining lines in $\mathbb{R}^3$, which we will represent in parametric form. More general curves in $\mathbb{R}^3$ will be studied in Chapter 10.

LINES IN $\mathbb{R}^3$

As in the plane, a line in $\mathbb{R}^3$ is completely determined once we know one of its points and its direction. We used the concept of slope to measure the direction of a line in the plane, but in space, it is more convenient to specify direction with vectors.

Suppose L is a line in $\mathbb{R}^3$ that is parallel to the vector $\mathbf{v} = A\mathbf{i} + B\mathbf{j} + C\mathbf{k}$ and also contains $Q(x_0, y_0, z_0)$, as shown in Figure 9.52. We say that the line has **direction numbers** A, B, and C and denote these direction numbers by $[A, B, C]$. The vector $\mathbf{v}$ is called a **direction vector** of the line L. If $P(x, y, z)$ is any point on L, then the vector $\mathbf{QP}$ is parallel to $\mathbf{v}$ and must satisfy the vector equation $\mathbf{QP} = t\mathbf{v}$ for some number t. If we introduce coordinates and use the standard representation, we can rewrite this vector equation as

$$(x - x_0)\mathbf{i} + (y - y_0)\mathbf{j} + (z - z_0)\mathbf{k} = t(A\mathbf{i} + B\mathbf{j} + C\mathbf{k})$$

By equating components on both sides of this equation, we find that the coordinates of P must satisfy the linear system

$$x - x_0 = tA \qquad y - y_0 = tB \qquad z - z_0 = tC$$

where t is a real number. Note that each point on L corresponds to exactly one value of the parameter t.

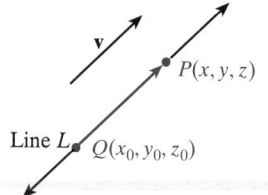

Figure 9.52 If L is parallel to $\mathbf{v}$ and contains Q, then P is on L whenever $QP = t\mathbf{v}$.

Parametric Form of a Line in $\mathbb{R}^3$

If L is a line that contains the point (x_0, y_0, z_0) and is parallel to the vector $\mathbf{v} = A\mathbf{i} + B\mathbf{j} + C\mathbf{k}$, then L has parametric form

$$x = x_0 + tA \qquad y = y_0 + tB \qquad z = z_0 + tC$$

Conversely, the set of all points (x, y, z) that satisfy such a set of equations is a line that passes through the point (x_0, y_0, z_0) and is parallel to a vector with direction numbers $[A, B, C]$.

EXAMPLE 6   **Parametric equations of a line in $\mathbb{R}^3$**

Find parametric equations for the line that contains the point $(3, 1, 4)$ and is parallel to the vector $\mathbf{v} = -\mathbf{i} + \mathbf{j} - 2\mathbf{k}$. Find where this line passes through the coordinate planes and sketch the line.

Solution

The direction numbers are $[-1, 1, -2]$ and $x_0 = 3$, $y_0 = 1$, $z_0 = 4$, so the line has the parametric form

$$x = 3 - t \qquad y = 1 + t \qquad z = 4 - 2t$$

This line will intersect the xy-plane when $z = 0$;

$$0 = 4 - 2t \quad \text{implies} \quad t = 2$$

If $t = 2$, then $x = 3 - 2 = 1$ and $y = 1 + 2 = 3$. This is the point $(1, 3, 0)$. Similarly, the line intersects the xz-plane at $(4, 0, 6)$ and the yz-plane at $(0, 4, -2)$. Plot these points and draw the line, as shown in Figure 9.53.   ∎

In the special case where none of the direction numbers A, B, or C is 0, we can solve each of the parametric-form equations for t to obtain the following **symmetric equations** for a line.

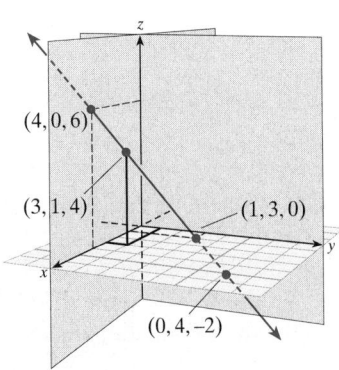

Figure 9.53 Graph of the line $x = 3 - t$, $y = 1 + t$, $z = 4 - 2t$

Symmetric Form of a Line in $\mathbb{R}^3$

If L is a line that contains the point (x_0, y_0, z_0) and is parallel to the vector $\mathbf{v} = A\mathbf{i} + B\mathbf{j} + C\mathbf{k}$ (A, B, and C nonzero numbers), then the point (x, y, z) is on L if and only if its coordinates satisfy

$$\frac{x - x_0}{A} = \frac{y - y_0}{B} = \frac{z - z_0}{C}$$

EXAMPLE 7   **Symmetric form of the equation of a line in $\mathbb{R}^3$**

Find symmetric equations for the line L through the points $P(-1, 3, 7)$ and $Q(4, 2, -1)$. Find the points of intersection with the coordinate planes and sketch the line.

Solution

The required line passes through P and is parallel to the vector

$$\mathbf{PQ} = [4 - (-1)]\mathbf{i} + [2 - 3]\mathbf{j} + [-1 - 7]\mathbf{k} = 5\mathbf{i} - \mathbf{j} - 8\mathbf{k}$$

Thus, the direction numbers of the line are $[5, -1, -8]$, and we can choose either P or Q as (x_0, y_0, z_0). Choosing P, we obtain

$$\frac{x + 1}{5} = \frac{y - 3}{-1} = \frac{z - 7}{-8}$$

Next, we find points of intersection with the coordinate planes. For the xy-plane ($z = 0$), we have

$$\frac{x + 1}{5} = \frac{0 - 7}{-8} \qquad \text{and} \qquad \frac{y - 3}{-1} = \frac{0 - 7}{-8}$$

$$x = \frac{27}{8} \qquad\qquad\qquad y = \frac{17}{8}$$

The point of intersection of the line with the xy-plane is $\left(\frac{27}{8}, \frac{17}{8}, 0\right)$. Similarly, the other points of intersections are

$$xz\text{-plane:} \quad (14, 0, -17) \qquad yz\text{-plane:} \quad \left(0, \frac{14}{5}, \frac{27}{5}\right)$$

The graph is shown in Figure 9.54.   ∎

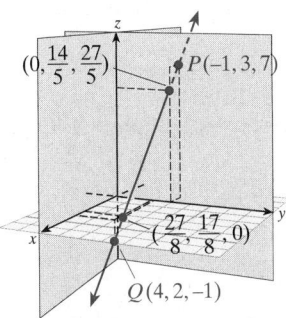

Figure 9.54 Graph of $\dfrac{x + 1}{5} = \dfrac{y - 3}{-1} = \dfrac{z - 7}{-8}$

If one or more of the direction numbers $[A, B, C]$ of a line L in $\mathbb{R}^3$ is zero, then L is parallel to at least one coordinate plane. For example, the line

$$x = 3 + 2t, \quad y = 5, \quad z = 4 - t$$

has direction numbers $[2, 0, -1]$ and lies in the plane $y = 5$, parallel to the xz-plane. The symmetric form for this line is

$$\frac{x - 3}{2} = \frac{z - 4}{-1}; \quad y = 5$$

Turning things around, the line with symmetric form

$$\frac{y + 1}{4} = \frac{z - 3}{-2}; \quad x = 7$$

lies in the plane $x = 7$, parallel to the yz-plane and has direction numbers $[0, 4, -2]$.

Recall that two lines in $\mathbb{R}^2$ must intersect if their slopes are different (because they cannot be parallel). However, two lines in $\mathbb{R}^3$ may have different direction numbers and still not intersect. In this case, the lines are said to be **skew.** The three different situations that can occur (ignoring the trivial case where the lines coincide) are shown in Figure 9.55.

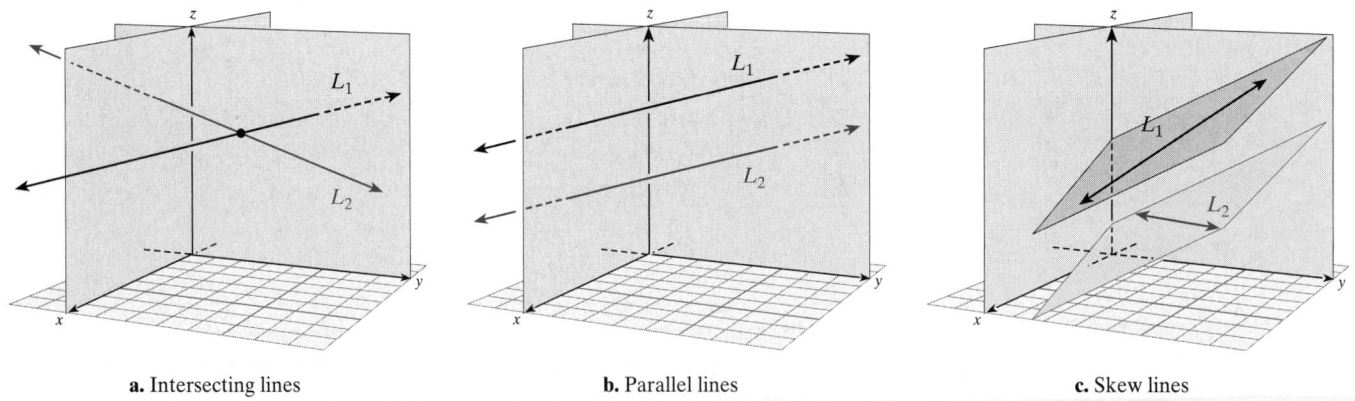

a. Intersecting lines   **b.** Parallel lines   **c.** Skew lines

Figure 9.55 Lines in space may intersect, be parallel, or skew.

EXAMPLE 8   Intersecting lines in $\mathbb{R}^3$

Show that the lines

$$L_1 : \frac{x - 1}{2} = \frac{y + 1}{1} = \frac{z - 2}{4} \quad \text{and} \quad L_2 : \frac{x + 2}{4} = \frac{y}{-3} = \frac{z - \frac{1}{2}}{-1}$$

intersect and find the point of intersection.

Solution

L_1 has direction numbers $[2, 1, 4]$ and L_2 has direction numbers $[4, -3, -1]$. Because there is no t for which $[2, 1, 4] = t[4, -3, -1]$, the lines are not parallel. Express the lines in parametric form:

$$L_1 : x = 1 + 2s \qquad y = -1 + s \qquad z = 2 + 4s$$
$$L_2 : x = -2 + 4t \qquad y = -3t \qquad z = \tfrac{1}{2} - t$$

At an intersection point we must have

$$1 + 2s = -2 + 4t \qquad \text{or} \qquad 2s - 4t = -3$$
$$-1 + s = -3t \qquad \text{or} \qquad s + 3t = 1$$
$$2 + 4s = \tfrac{1}{2} - t \qquad \text{or} \qquad 4s + t = -\tfrac{3}{2}$$

Solving the first two equations simultaneously, we find $s = -\frac{1}{2}$, $t = \frac{1}{2}$. This solution satisfies the third equation, namely,

$$4\left(-\tfrac{1}{2}\right) + \tfrac{1}{2} = -\tfrac{3}{2}$$

If the solution did not satisfy the third equation, the lines would be skew. To find the coordinates of the point of intersection, substitute $s = -\frac{1}{2}$ into the parametric-form equations for L_1 (or substitute $t = \frac{1}{2}$ into L_2) to obtain

$$x_0 = 1 + 2\left(-\tfrac{1}{2}\right) = 0$$
$$y_0 = -1 + \left(-\tfrac{1}{2}\right) = -\tfrac{3}{2}$$
$$z_0 = 2 + 4\left(-\tfrac{1}{2}\right) = 0$$

WARNING   Notice that we used two parameters (s and t) for the lines in Example 8. This is because it is quite possible for two lines to intersect at "different times" (that is, different values of the parameter). In Example 8, we have $s = -\frac{1}{2}$ and $t = \frac{1}{2}$ at the point of intersection, rather than $s = t$.

Thus, the lines intersect at $P\left(0, -\frac{3}{2}, 0\right)$.   ∎

EXAMPLE 9   Skew lines in $\mathbb{R}^3$

Determine whether the following lines intersect, are parallel, or are skew.

$$L_1 : \frac{x-1}{2} = \frac{y+1}{1} = \frac{z-2}{4} \quad \text{and} \quad L_2 : \frac{x+2}{4} = \frac{y}{-3} = \frac{z+1}{1}$$

Solution

Note that L_1 has direction numbers $[2, 1, 4]$; that is, L_1 is parallel to $(2\mathbf{i} + \mathbf{j} + 4\mathbf{k})$ and L_2 has direction numbers $[4, -3, 1]$. If we try to solve

$$\langle 2, 1, 4 \rangle = t \langle 4, -3, 1 \rangle$$

for t, we find no possible solution for any value of t. This implies that the lines are not parallel.

Next we determine whether the lines intersect or are skew. Note that $S(1, -1, 2)$ lies on L_1 and $T(-2, 0, -1)$ lies on L_2. The lines intersect if and only if there is a point P that lies on both lines. To determine this, we write the equations of the lines in parametric form:

$$L_1 : x = 1 + 2s \qquad y = -1 + s \qquad z = 2 + 4s$$
$$L_2 : x = -2 + 4t \qquad y = -3t \qquad z = -1 + t$$

The lines intersect if there are numbers s and t for which

$$x = 1 + 2s = -2 + 4t \qquad \text{or} \qquad 2s - 4t = -3$$
$$y = -1 + s = -3t \qquad \text{or} \qquad s + 3t = 1$$
$$z = 2 + 4s = -1 + t \qquad \text{or} \qquad 4s - t = -3$$

This is equivalent to the system of linear equations

$$\begin{cases} 2s - 4t = -3 \\ s + 3t = 1 \\ 4s - t = -3 \end{cases}$$

Any solution of this system must correspond to a point of intersection of L_1 and L_2, and if no solution exists, then L_1 and L_2 are skew. Because this is a system of three equations with two unknowns, we first solve the first two equations simultaneously to find $s = -\frac{1}{2}$, $t = \frac{1}{2}$. However, $(s, t) = \left(-\frac{1}{2}, \frac{1}{2}\right)$ does not satisfy the third equation, so it follows that L_1 and L_2 do not intersect and they must be skew.   ∎

9.5 PROBLEM SET

A   1. **WHAT DOES THIS SAY?**   What is a parameter?

2. **WHAT DOES THIS SAY?**   Contrast the parametric and symmetric forms of the equation of a line.

Find an explicit relationship between x and y in Problems 3–16 by eliminating the parameter. In each case, sketch the path described by the parametric equations over the prescribed interval.

3. $x = t + 1, y = t - 1, 0 \le t \le 2$

4. $x = -t, y = 3 - 2t, 0 \le t \le 1$

5. $x = 60t, y = 80t - 16t^2, 0 \le t \le 3$

6. $x = 30t, y = 60t - 9t^2, -1 \le t \le 2$

7. $x = t^3, y = t^2, t \ge 0$

8. $x = t^4, y = t^2, -1 \le t \le \sqrt{2}$

9. $x = 3\cos\theta, y = 3\sin\theta, 0 \le \theta \le 2\pi$

10. $x = 2\sin\theta, y = 2\cos\theta, 0 \le \theta \le 2\pi$

11. $x = 1 + \sin t, y = -2 + \cos t, 0 \le t \le 2\pi$

12. $x = 1 + \sin^2 t, y = -2 + \cos t, 0 \le t \le \pi$

13. $x = 4\tan 2t, y = 3\sec 2t, 0 \le t \le \pi$

14. $x = 4\sec 2t, y = 2\tan 2t, 0 \le t \le \pi$

15. $x = t^3, y = 3\ln t, t > 0$

16. $x = e^t, y = e^{-t}, (-\infty, \infty)$

Find the parametric and symmetric equations for the line(s) passing through the given points with the properties described in Problems 17–25.

17. $(1, -1, -2)$; parallel to $3\mathbf{i} - 2\mathbf{j} + 5\mathbf{k}$

18. $(1, 0, -1)$; parallel to $3\mathbf{i} + 4\mathbf{j}$

19. $(1, -1, 2)$; through $(2, 1, 3)$

20. $(2, 2, 3)$; through $(1, 3, -1)$

21. $(1, -3, 6)$; parallel to $\dfrac{x-5}{1} = \dfrac{y+2}{-3} = \dfrac{z}{-5}$

22. $(1, -1, 2)$; parallel to $\dfrac{x+3}{4} = \dfrac{y-2}{5} = \dfrac{z+5}{1}$

23. $(0, 4, -3)$; parallel to $\dfrac{x-1}{22} = \dfrac{y+2}{-6} = \dfrac{z-1}{10}$

24. $(1, 0, -4)$; parallel to $x = -2 + 3t, y = 4 + t, z = 2 + 2t$

25. $(-1, 1, 6)$; perpendicular to $3x + y - 2z = 5$

26. Find the parametric form of the equation of the line passing through $(3, -1, 0)$ parallel to both the xy- and yz-planes.

Find the points of intersection of each line in Problems 27–30 with each of the coordinate planes.

27. $\dfrac{x-4}{4} = \dfrac{y+3}{3} = \dfrac{z+2}{1}$

28. $\dfrac{x+1}{1} = \dfrac{y+2}{2} = \dfrac{z-6}{3}$

29. $x = 6 - 2t, y = 1 + t, z = 3t$

30. $x = 6 + 3t, y = 2 - t, z = 2t$

In Problems 31–36, tell whether the two lines intersect, are parallel, are skew, or coincide. If they intersect, give the point of intersection.

31. $\dfrac{x-4}{2} = \dfrac{y-6}{-3} = \dfrac{z+2}{5}; \dfrac{x}{4} = \dfrac{y+2}{-6} = \dfrac{z-3}{10}$

32. $x = 4 - 2t, y = 6t, z = 7 - 4t;$
$x = 5 + t, y = 1 - 3t, z = -3 + 2t$

33. $x = 3 + 3t, y = 1 - 4t, z = -4 - 7t;$
$x = 2 + 3t, y = 5 - 4t, z = 3 - 7t$

34. $x = 2 - 4t, y = 1 + t, z = \frac{1}{2} + 5t;$
$x = 3t, y = -2 - t, z = 4 - 2t$

35. $\dfrac{x-3}{2} = \dfrac{y-1}{-1} = \dfrac{z-4}{1}; \dfrac{x+2}{3} = \dfrac{y-3}{-1} = \dfrac{z-2}{1}$

36. $\dfrac{x+1}{2} = \dfrac{y-3}{-1} = \dfrac{z-2}{1}; \dfrac{x+1}{2} = \dfrac{y+1}{3} = \dfrac{z-3}{-4}$

37. Find two unit vectors parallel to the line

$$\frac{x-3}{4} = \frac{y-1}{2} = \frac{z+1}{1}$$

38. Find two unit vectors parallel to the line

$$\frac{x-1}{2} = \frac{y+2}{4} = \frac{z+5}{1}$$

B   *Find the parametric equations for each of the curves in Problems 39–44.*

39. A circle of radius 3, centered at the origin, oriented counterclockwise.

40. A circle of radius 2 centered at the origin, oriented clockwise.

41. The ellipse $\dfrac{x^2}{9} + \dfrac{y^2}{4} = 1$, oriented counterclockwise.

42. The parabola $y^2 = 4x + 9$, oriented from $(4, -5)$ to $(0, 3)$.

43. The hyperbola $\dfrac{x^2}{16} - \dfrac{y^2}{9} = 1$.

44. The ellipse $\dfrac{(x-2)^2}{3} + \dfrac{(y+3)^2}{5} = 1$.

45. Describe the path of the curve described by $x = \sin \pi t$, $y = \cos 2\pi t$ for $0 \le t < 1$.

46. Let $x = 4a\sin t, y = b\cos^2 t$. Express y as a function of x.

47. Show that the vector $\mathbf{v} = 3\mathbf{i} - 4\mathbf{j} + \mathbf{k}$ is orthogonal to the line that passes through the points $P(0, 0, 1)$ and $Q(2, 1, -1)$.

48. Show that the vector $\mathbf{v} = 7\mathbf{i} + 4\mathbf{j} + 3\mathbf{k}$ is orthogonal to the line passing through the points $P(-2, 2, 7)$ and $Q(3, -3, 2)$.

49. Find constants a and b so that the following lines coincide:

$$L_1 : \frac{x-a}{2} = \frac{y-1}{4} = \frac{z+2}{1}$$

and

$$L_2 : \frac{x-2}{-4} = \frac{y-b}{-8} = \frac{z+1}{-2}$$

50. Consider the lines

$$L_1 : x = -1 + 2t, \quad y = 3 - t, \quad z = 2 + 2t$$
$$L_2 : x = -2 - t, \quad y = 5 + 2t, \quad z = -2t$$

Show that L_1 and L_2 intersect and find the acute angle θ (to the nearest degree) between them.

51. Find an equation for the line L_1 that contains the point $P(-1, 3, 1)$ and is orthogonal to the line

$$L_1 : \quad x = 2 - t, \quad y = 1 - 2t, \quad z = 5 + t$$

C 52. What can be said about the lines

$$\frac{x - x_0}{a_1} = \frac{y - y_0}{b_1} = \frac{z - z_0}{c_1}$$

and

$$\frac{x - x_0}{a_2} = \frac{y - y_0}{b_2} = \frac{z - z_0}{c_2}$$

in the case where $a_1 a_2 + b_1 b_2 + c_1 c_2 = 0$?

53. Spy Problem Our friend, the internationally famous Spy, is on a mission to save his superior, Lord Newton Fleming, known as the "Flamer." Having escaped from the minions of his abductor, the archfiend Ernst Stavro Blohardt (Supplementary Problem 79 of Chapter 8), the Spy finds himself in the desert, where Blohardt has just taken off in a helicopter! Suppose the desert and the air space above are coordinatized (units in thousands of feet) and that two observation posts are located at points $A(7, 0, 0)$ and $B(0, 4, 0)$. At noon, Blohardt's helicopter is observed from A in the direction of the vector $\langle -4, 2, 5 \rangle$ and simultaneously from B in the direction of $\langle 3, -2, 5 \rangle$. One minute later, it is observed from A and B in the directions of $\langle 6, 7, 5.005 \rangle$ and $\langle 13, 3, 5.005 \rangle$, respectively. The Spy is notified and at 12:10 P.M. is flying at the point $Q(0, 0, 1)$ in an attack helicopter traveling at 150 mph. Assuming that Blohardt does not change his direction or rate, in what direction from Q should the Spy fly in order to intercept the villain?

54. Modeling Problem A circle of radius R rolls without slipping on the *outside* of a fixed circle of radius a. Assume the fixed circle is centered at the origin and that the moving point begins at $(a, 0)$. Let t be the angle measured from the positive x-axis to the ray from the origin to the center of the rolling circle.

Show that this *epicycloid* may be modeled by the parametric equations

$$x = (a + R)\cos t - R\cos\left(\frac{a + R}{R}\right)t,$$

$$y = (a + R)\sin t - R\sin\left(\frac{a + R}{R}\right)t$$

55. Modeling Problem A circle of radius R rolls without slipping on the inside of a fixed circle of radius a. Find parametric equations to model the curve traced out by a point P on the circumference of the rolling circle of radius R. Let t be the angle measured from the positive x-axis to the ray that passes through the center of the rolling circle, and assume that the point P begins on the x-axis (that is, P has coordinates $(a, 0)$ when $t = 0$). Show that this *hypocycloid* has parametric equations

$$x = (a - R)\cos t + R\cos\left(\frac{a - R}{R}\right)t,$$

$$y = (a - R)\sin t - R\sin\left(\frac{a - R}{R}\right)t$$

56. Journal Problem *The MATYC Journal*[*] ■ A rectangle is "rolled" along a straight line by rotations of 90° about each vertex in turn. One vertex traces out a series of arches where each arch is the union of three circular arcs. Show that the area of the region bounded by the straight line and one arch equals the area of the rectangle plus twice the area of the circumscribed circle.

---

[*]Problem 148 by Frank Kocher, Vol. 14, 1980, p. 155.

9.6 Planes in $\mathbb{R}^3$

IN THIS SECTION   forms for the equation of a plane in $\mathbb{R}^3$, vector methods for measuring distances in $\mathbb{R}^3$

FORMS FOR THE EQUATION OF A PLANE IN $\mathbb{R}^3$

Planes in space can also be characterized by vector methods. In particular, any plane is completely determined once we know one of its points and its orientation; that is, the "direction" it faces. A common way to specify the direction of a plane is by means of a vector $\mathbf{N}$ that is orthogonal to every vector in the plane, as shown in Figure 9.56. Such a vector is called a **normal** to the plane.

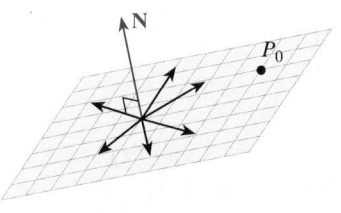

Figure 9.56 A plane may be described by specifying one of its points and a normal vector $\mathbf{N}$.

EXAMPLE 1   Finding an equation for a plane

Find an equation for the plane that contains the point $Q(3, -7, 2)$ and is normal to the vector $\mathbf{N} = 2\mathbf{i} + \mathbf{j} - 3\mathbf{k}$.

Solution

The normal vector $\mathbf{N}$ is orthogonal to every vector in the plane. In particular, if $P(x, y, z)$ is any point in the plane, then $\mathbf{N}$ must be orthogonal to the vector

$$\mathbf{QP} = (x - 3)\mathbf{i} + (y + 7)\mathbf{j} + (z - 2)\mathbf{k}$$

Because the dot (or scalar) product of two orthogonal vectors is 0, we have

$$\mathbf{N} \cdot \mathbf{QP} = 2(x - 3) + (1)(y + 7) + (-3)(z - 2) = 0$$
$$2x - 6 + y + 7 - 3z + 6 = 0$$
$$2x + y - 3z + 7 = 0$$

Therefore, $2x + y - 3z + 7 = 0$ is the equation of the plane. ■

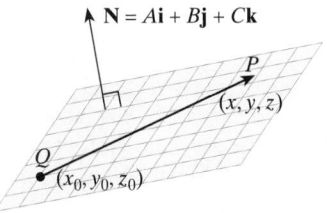

Figure 9.57 The graph of a plane with attitude numbers $[A, B, C]$

By generalizing the approach illustrated in Example 1, we can show that the plane that contains the point (x_0, y_0, z_0) and has normal vector $\mathbf{N} = A\mathbf{i} + B\mathbf{j} + C\mathbf{k}$ must have the Cartesian equation

$$A(x - x_0) + B(y - y_0) + C(z - z_0) = 0$$

This is called the **point-normal form** of the equation of a plane. By rearranging terms, we can rewrite this equation in the form $Ax + By + Cz + D = 0$. This is called the **standard form** of the equation of a plane. The numbers $[A, B, C]$ are called **attitude numbers** of the plane (see Figure 9.57).

Notice from Figure 9.57 that *attitude numbers of a plane are the same as direction numbers of a normal vector.* This means that you can find normal vectors to a plane *by inspecting the equation of the plane.*

EXAMPLE 2 Relationship between normal vectors and planes

Find normal vectors to the planes

a. $5x + 7y - 3z = 0$ **b.** $3x - 7z = 10$

Solution

a. A normal to the plane $5x + 7y - 3z = 0$ is $\mathbf{N} = 5\mathbf{i} + 7\mathbf{j} - 3\mathbf{k}$.
b. For $3x - 7z = 10$ a normal is $\mathbf{N} = 3\mathbf{i} - 7\mathbf{k}$. ■

Forms for the Equation of a Plane

An equation for the plane with normal $\mathbf{N} = A\mathbf{i} + B\mathbf{j} + C\mathbf{k}$ that contains the point (x_0, y_0, z_0) has the following forms:

Point-normal form: $A(x - x_0) + B(y - y_0) + C(z - z_0) = 0$
Standard form: $Ax + By + Cz + D = 0$

Conversely, a normal vector to the plane $Ax + By + Cz + D = 0$ is

$$\mathbf{N} = A\mathbf{i} + B\mathbf{j} + C\mathbf{k}$$

EXAMPLE 3 Equation of a plane containing three given points

Find the standard form equation of a plane containing $P(-1, 2, 1)$, $Q(0, -3, 2)$, and $R(1, 1, -4)$.

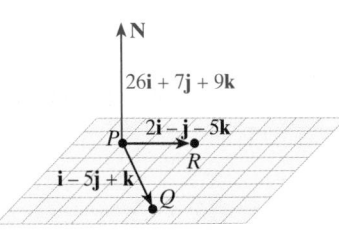

Figure 9.58 A plane passing through three given points

Solution

Because a normal $\mathbf{N}$ to the required plane is orthogonal to the vectors $\mathbf{PQ}$ and $\mathbf{PR}$, we find $\mathbf{N}$ by computing the cross product $\mathbf{N} = \mathbf{PR} \times \mathbf{PQ}$. The situation is illustrated in Figure 9.58.

$$\mathbf{PQ} = (0 + 1)\mathbf{i} + (-3 - 2)\mathbf{j} + (2 - 1)\mathbf{k} = \mathbf{i} - 5\mathbf{j} + \mathbf{k}$$
$$\mathbf{PR} = (1 + 1)\mathbf{i} + (1 - 2)\mathbf{j} + (-4 - 1)\mathbf{k} = 2\mathbf{i} - \mathbf{j} - 5\mathbf{k}$$

$$\mathbf{N} = \mathbf{PQ} \times \mathbf{PR} = \begin{vmatrix} \mathbf{i} & \mathbf{j} & \mathbf{k} \\ 1 & -5 & 1 \\ 2 & -1 & -5 \end{vmatrix}$$

$$= 26\mathbf{i} + 7\mathbf{j} + 9\mathbf{k}$$

We can now find the equation of the plane using this normal vector and any point in the plane. We will use the point P:

Attitude numbers of the plane—from $\mathbf{N} = 26\mathbf{i} + 7\mathbf{j} + 9\mathbf{k}$

$$26(x + 1) + 7(y - 2) + 9(z - 1) = 0$$

Point on the plane; we are using $P(-1, 2, 1)$.

Thus, the equation of the plane is

$$26x + 26 + 7y - 14 + 9z - 9 = 0$$
$$26x + 7y + 9z + 3 = 0$$

∎

EXAMPLE 4   Equation of a line orthogonal to a given plane

Find an equation of the line that passes through the point $Q(2, -1, 3)$ and is orthogonal to the plane $3x - 7y + 5z + 55 = 0$. Where does the line intersect the plane?

Solution

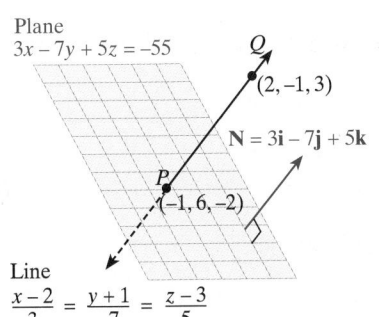

Plane
$3x - 7y + 5z = -55$

$\mathbf{N} = 3\mathbf{i} - 7\mathbf{j} + 5\mathbf{k}$

Line
$\dfrac{x-2}{3} = \dfrac{y+1}{-7} = \dfrac{z-3}{5}$

Figure 9.59 Intersection of a line and a plane

By inspection of the equation of the plane we see that $\mathbf{N} = 3\mathbf{i} - 7\mathbf{j} + 5\mathbf{k}$ is a normal vector. Because the required line is also orthogonal to the plane, it must be parallel to $\mathbf{N}$ (see Figure 9.59). Thus, the line contains the point $Q(2, -1, 3)$ and has direction numbers $[3, -7, 5]$, so its parametric form is

$$x = 2 + 3t, \quad y = -1 - 7t, \quad \text{and} \quad z = 3 + 5t$$

Now, substitute into the equation of the plane:

$$3(2 + 3t) - 7(-1 - 7t) + 5(3 + 5t) = -55$$
$$6 + 9t + 7 + 49t + 15 + 25t = -55$$
$$t = -1$$

Then, the point of intersection is found by substituting $t = -1$ for x, y, and z:

$$x = 2 + 3(-1) = -1$$
$$y = -1 - 7(-1) = 6$$
$$z = 3 + 5(-1) = -2$$

The point of intersection is $(-1, 6, -2)$.

∎

EXAMPLE 5   Equation of a line parallel to the intersection of two given planes

Find the equation of a line passing through $(-1, 2, 3)$ that is parallel to the line of intersection of the planes $3x - 2y + z = 4$ and $x + 2y + 3z = 5$.

Solution

By inspection, we see that normals to the given planes are $\mathbf{N}_1 = 3\mathbf{i} - 2\mathbf{j} + \mathbf{k}$ and $\mathbf{N}_2 = \mathbf{i} + 2\mathbf{j} + 3\mathbf{k}$. The desired line is perpendicular to both of these normals, so a vector parallel to the line is found by computing the cross product:

$$\mathbf{N}_1 \times \mathbf{N}_2 = \begin{vmatrix} \mathbf{i} & \mathbf{j} & \mathbf{k} \\ 3 & -2 & 1 \\ 1 & 2 & 3 \end{vmatrix} = (-6 - 2)\mathbf{i} - (9 - 1)\mathbf{j} + (6 + 2)\mathbf{k}$$

$$= -8\mathbf{i} - 8\mathbf{j} + 8\mathbf{k}$$
$$= -8(\mathbf{i} + \mathbf{j} - \mathbf{k})$$

Thus, the required line passes through $(-1, 2, 3)$ and is parallel to the vector $\langle 1, 1, -1 \rangle$ so it has parametric form

$$x = -1 + t, \quad y = 2 + t, \quad z = 3 - t$$

∎

An equation for the line of intersection of two planes can be found by determining a point P in the intersection, and then proceeding as in Example 5 (using P instead of the point $(-1, 2, 3)$). In Example 6, we turn things around by finding the equation of a plane containing two given intersecting lines.

EXAMPLE 6   Equation of a plane containing two intersecting lines

Find the standard-form equation of the plane determined by the intersecting lines
$$\frac{x-2}{3} = \frac{y+5}{-2} = \frac{z+1}{4} \quad \text{and} \quad \frac{x+1}{2} = \frac{y}{-1} = \frac{z-16}{5}$$

Solution

The given lines, respectively, have direction numbers $[3, -2, 4]$ and $[2, -1, 5]$. A vector orthogonal to both $\mathbf{v}_1$ and $\mathbf{v}_2$ and hence to the required planes determined by the intersecting lines is given by the cross product:

$$\mathbf{v}_1 \times \mathbf{v}_2 = \begin{vmatrix} \mathbf{i} & \mathbf{j} & \mathbf{k} \\ 3 & -2 & 4 \\ 2 & -1 & 5 \end{vmatrix} = (-10 + 4)\mathbf{i} - (15 - 8)\mathbf{j} + (-3 + 4)\mathbf{k}$$

$$= -6\mathbf{i} - 7\mathbf{j} + \mathbf{k}$$

The points $(2, -5, -1)$ and $(-1, 0, 16)$ are both in the required plane. We use $(2, -5, -1)$ to obtain

$$-6(x - 2) - 7(y + 5) + 1(z + 1) = 0$$
$$6x + 7y - z + 22 = 0$$

as the equation for the plane.

VECTOR METHODS FOR MEASURING DISTANCES IN $\mathbb{R}^3$

Vector methods can also be used for measuring distances in $\mathbb{R}^3$, between points, lines, and planes. We begin by deriving the following formula for the distance from a point to a plane.

THEOREM 9.9   Distance from a point to a plane in $\mathbb{R}^3$

The distance from the point $P(x_0, y_0, z_0)$ to the plane $Ax + By + Cz + D = 0$ is given by

$$d = \frac{|\mathbf{QP} \cdot \mathbf{N}|}{\|\mathbf{N}\|} = \frac{|Ax_0 + By_0 + Cz_0 + D|}{\sqrt{A^2 + B^2 + C^2}}$$

where Q is any point in the given plane and $\mathbf{N}$ is a normal to the given plane.

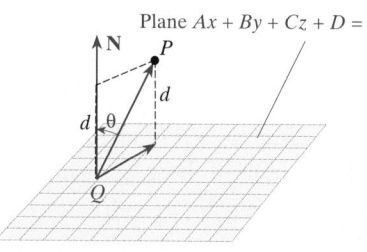

Plane $Ax + By + Cz + D = 0$

Figure 9.60 The distance from a point to a plane in $\mathbb{R}^3$

Proof   The required distance is found by projecting the vector $\mathbf{QP}$ onto the normal $\mathbf{N}$. Thus, the distance from the point to the plane is given by

$$d = \|\mathbf{QP}\| \, |\cos \theta| = \frac{\|\mathbf{QP}\| \|\mathbf{N}\| \, |\cos \theta|}{\|\mathbf{N}\|} = \frac{|\mathbf{QP} \cdot \mathbf{N}|}{\|\mathbf{N}\|}$$

where θ is the angle between $\mathbf{QP}$ and $\mathbf{N}$ (see Figure 9.60). Suppose $Q(x_1, y_1, z_1)$ is any particular point in the plane, so that

$$\mathbf{QP} = (x_0 - x_1)\mathbf{i} + (y_0 - y_1)\mathbf{j} + (z_0 - z_1)\mathbf{k}$$

The dot product of $\mathbf{QP}$ with $\mathbf{N} = A\mathbf{i} + B\mathbf{j} + C\mathbf{k}$ is given by

$$\mathbf{QP} \cdot \mathbf{N} = (x_0 - x_1)A + (y_0 - y_1)B + (z_0 - z_1)C$$
$$= (Ax_0 + By_0 + Cz_0) - (Ax_1 + By_1 + Cz_1)$$
$$= Ax_0 + By_0 + Cz_0 - (-D) \qquad \text{Since } Ax_1 + By_1 + Cz_1 + D = 0$$

Because the normal vector has length $\|\mathbf{N}\| = \sqrt{A^2 + B^2 + C^2}$, we can substitute into the formula for d to obtain

$$d = \frac{|\mathbf{QP} \cdot \mathbf{N}|}{\|\mathbf{N}\|} = \frac{|Ax_0 + By_0 + Cz_0 + D|}{\sqrt{A^2 + B^2 + C^2}} \qquad \square$$

EXAMPLE 7   Finding an equation for a sphere tangent to a given plane

Find an equation for the sphere with center $C(-3, 1, 5)$ that is tangent to the plane $6x - 2y + 3z = 9$.

Solution

The radius r of the sphere is the distance from the center C to the given plane, as shown in Figure 9.61; namely,

$$r = \left| \frac{6(-3) + (-2)(1) + 3(5) - 9}{\sqrt{6^2 + (-2)^2 + 3^2}} \right| = \left| \frac{-14}{7} \right| = 2$$

Therefore, an equation of the sphere is

$$(x + 3)^2 + (y - 1)^2 + (z - 5)^2 = 2^2 \qquad \blacksquare$$

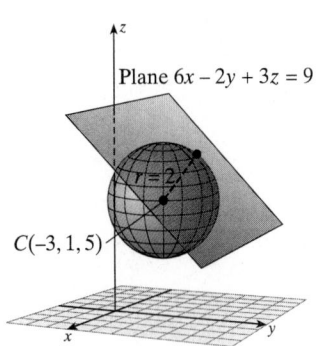

Figure 9.61 The sphere with center $C(-3, 1, 5)$ and radius 2 is tangent to the plane $6x - 2y + 3z = 9$.

Vector methods can also be used to derive a formula for the distance between two skew lines L_1 and L_2 in $\mathbb{R}^3$.

EXAMPLE 8   Computing the distance between skew lines

Find the distance between the skew lines

$$L_1 : x = 1 + 2s \qquad y = -1 + s \qquad z = 2 + 4s$$
$$L_2 : x = -2 + 4t \qquad y = -3t \qquad z = -1 + t$$

Solution

Recall from Section 9.5 that skew lines do not intersect and are not parallel, but do lie in parallel planes. Thus, the distance d between the lines L_1 and L_2 is the same as the distance between the parallel planes p_1 and p_2 that contain them (see Figure 9.62). Our strategy for finding the distance d is to find the distance from a point Q on p_1 to the plane p_2.

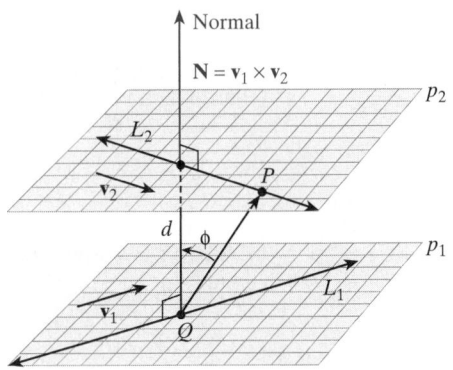

Figure 9.62   Distance between skew lines

First, find a point Q on p_1 by setting $s = 0$ in the parametric equations for L_1. Then $x = 1$, $y = -1$, and $z = 2$, so $Q(1, -1, 2)$ is such a point. Next, vectors $\mathbf{v}_1 = \langle 2, 1, 4 \rangle$ and $\mathbf{v}_2 = \langle 4, -3, 1 \rangle$ are parallel to L_1 and L_2, respectively, and the cross product $\mathbf{N} = \mathbf{v}_1 \times \mathbf{v}_2$ is normal to both p_1 and p_2. We find that

$$\mathbf{N} = \begin{vmatrix} \mathbf{i} & \mathbf{j} & \mathbf{k} \\ 2 & 1 & 4 \\ 4 & -3 & 1 \end{vmatrix} = 13\mathbf{i} + 14\mathbf{j} - 10\mathbf{k}$$

Setting $t = 0$, we see that the point $P(-2, 0, -1)$ is on p_2, so an equation for p_2 is

$$13(x + 2) + 14(y - 0) - 10(z + 1) = 0$$
$$13x + 14y - 10z + 16 = 0$$

The distance d between the lines L_1 and L_2 is the same as the distance from the point $Q(1, -1, 2)$ to the plane p_2. Thus

$$d = \frac{|13(1) + 14(-1) - 10(2) + 16|}{\sqrt{13^2 + 14^2 + (-10)^2}} = \frac{5}{\sqrt{465}} \approx 0.2319 \qquad \blacksquare$$

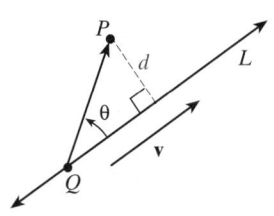

Figure 9.63 The distance from a point to a line in $\mathbb{R}^3$

In the final example of this section, we find the distance from a point P to a line L in $\mathbb{R}^3$. Let Q be a point on L and let $\mathbf{v}$ be a vector parallel to L. Then, as shown in Figure 9.63, the distance from P to L is given by

$$d = \|\mathbf{QP}\| \, |\sin\theta|$$

where θ is the angle between $\mathbf{v}$ and the vector $\mathbf{QP}$. This reminds us of the cross product $\mathbf{v} \times \mathbf{QP}$, and because

$$\|\mathbf{v} \times \mathbf{QP}\| = \|\mathbf{v}\|\|\mathbf{QP}\| \sin\theta$$

we have

$$d = \|\mathbf{QP}\| \sin\theta = \frac{\|\mathbf{v} \times \mathbf{QP}\|}{\|\mathbf{v}\|}$$

These observations are summarized in the following theorem.

THEOREM 9.10   **Distance from a point to a line**

The distance from point P to the line L is given by the formula

$$d = \frac{\|\mathbf{v} \times \mathbf{QP}\|}{\|\mathbf{v}\|}$$

where $\mathbf{v}$ is a vector parallel to L and Q is any point on L.

Proof   A sketch of the proof precedes the statement of the theorem.   ❏

EXAMPLE 9   **Distance from a point to a line**

Find the distance from the point $P(3, -8, 1)$ to the line

$$\frac{x - 3}{3} = \frac{y + 7}{-1} = \frac{z + 2}{5}$$

Solution

We need to find a point Q on the line. We see that $Q(3, -7, -2)$ is on the line and that $\mathbf{QP} = \langle 0, -1, 3 \rangle$. A vector parallel to L is $\mathbf{v} = \langle 3, -1, 5 \rangle$, so that

$$\mathbf{v} \times \mathbf{QP} = \begin{vmatrix} \mathbf{i} & \mathbf{j} & \mathbf{k} \\ 3 & -1 & 5 \\ 0 & -1 & 3 \end{vmatrix} = 2\mathbf{i} - 9\mathbf{j} - 3\mathbf{k}$$

Thus,

$$d = \frac{\|\mathbf{v} \times \mathbf{QP}\|}{\|\mathbf{v}\|} = \frac{\sqrt{(2)^2 + (-9)^2 + (-3)^2}}{\sqrt{3^2 + (-1)^2 + 5^2}} = \frac{\sqrt{94}}{\sqrt{35}} \approx 1.64 \qquad \blacksquare$$

9.6   PROBLEM SET

A 1. **WHAT DOES THIS SAY?**   Describe the relationship between normal vectors and planes.

2. **WHAT DOES THIS SAY?**   Describe a procedure for finding the distance from a point to a plane.

3. **WHAT DOES THIS SAY?**   Describe a procedure for finding the distance from a point to a line in $\mathbb{R}^3$.

Write each equation for a plane given in Problems 4–7 in standard form.

4. $4(x + 1) - 2(y + 1) + 6(z - 2) = 0$
5. $5(x - 2) - 3(y + 2) + 4(z + 3) = 0$
6. $-3(x - 4) + 2(y + 1) - 2(z + 1) = 0$
7. $-2(x + 1) + 4(y - 3) - 8z = 0$

Find an equation for the plane that contains the point P and has the normal vector $\mathbf{N}$ given in Problems 8–13.

8. $P(-1, 3, 5); \mathbf{N} = 2\mathbf{i} + 4\mathbf{j} - 3\mathbf{k}$
9. $P(0, -7, 1); \mathbf{N} = -\mathbf{i} + \mathbf{k}$
10. $P(0, -3, 0); \mathbf{N} = -2\mathbf{j} + 3\mathbf{k}$
11. $P(1, 1, -1); \mathbf{N} = -\mathbf{i} - 2\mathbf{j} + 3\mathbf{k}$
12. $P(0, 0, 0); \mathbf{N} = \mathbf{k}$ 13. $P(0, 0, 0); \mathbf{N} = \mathbf{i}$
14. Find two unit vectors perpendicular to the plane $2x + 4y - 3z = 4$.
15. Find two unit vectors perpendicular to the plane $5x - 3y + 2z = 15$.

Find the distance between the point and the plane given in Problems 16–21.

16. $P(1, 0, -1); x + y - z = 1$
17. $P(0, 0, 0); 2x - 3y + 5z = 10$
18. $P(1, 1, -1); x - y + 2z = 4$
19. $P(2, 1, -2); 3x - 4y + z = -1$
20. $P(a, -a, 2a); 2ax - y + az = 4a, a \neq 0$
21. $P(a, 2a, 3a); 3x - 2y + z = -1/a, a \neq 0$

Find the distance from the point $(-1, 2, 1)$ to each plane given in Problems 22–25.

22. the plane through the points $(0, 0, 0)$, $(1, 2, 4)$, and $(-2, -1, 1)$
23. the plane through the points $(-1, 1, 1)$, $(4, 3, 7)$, and $(3, -1, 0)$
24. the plane through the point $(-3, 5, 1)$ with normal vector $3\mathbf{i} + \mathbf{j} + 5\mathbf{k}$
25. the plane through the point $(1, 0, 1)$ with normal vector $2\mathbf{i} - \mathbf{j} + 2\mathbf{k}$

Find the distance from the point P to the line L in Problems 26–31.

26. $P(4, 5); 3x - 4y + 8 = 0$
27. $P(9, -3); 3x - 4y + 8 = 0$
28. $P(4, -3); 12x + 5y - 2 = 0$
29. $P(1, 0, -1); \dfrac{x - 2}{3} = \dfrac{y + 1}{1} = \dfrac{z - 1}{2}$
30. $P(1, 0, 1); \dfrac{x}{3} = \dfrac{y - 1}{2} = \dfrac{z}{1}$
31. $P(1, -2, 2); \dfrac{x}{1} = \dfrac{2y}{1} = \dfrac{z}{-1}$

Find the distance between the lines given in Problems 32–35.

32. $\dfrac{x + 1}{3} = \dfrac{y - 2}{-2} = \dfrac{z - 1}{1}$ and $\dfrac{x - 2}{5} = \dfrac{y + 1}{1} = \dfrac{z}{3}$
33. $x = 2 - t, y = 5 + 2t, z = 3t$ and $x = 2t, y = -1 - t, z = 1 + 2t$
34. $\dfrac{x + 1}{1} = \dfrac{y - 3}{2} = \dfrac{z + 2}{3}$ and the line passing through $(1, 3, -2)$ and $(0, 1, -1)$
35. $x = -1 + t, y = -2t, z = 3$ and the line passing through $(0, -1, 2)$ and $(1, -2, 3)$
36. Find the equation of the sphere with center $C(-2, 3, 7)$ that is tangent to the plane $2x + 3y - 6z = 5$.

B 37. **a.** Show that the line
$$\frac{x - 1}{3} = \frac{y}{-2} = \frac{z + 1}{1}$$
   is parallel to the plane $x + 2y + z = 1$.
   b. Find the distance from the line to the plane in part **a**.

38. Three of the four vertices of a parallelogram $QRTS$ in $\mathbb{R}^3$ are $Q(-1, 3, 5)$, $R(6, -3, 2)$, and $S(2, 4, -3)$. (Note that the fourth vertex of the parallelogram may be located in one of several locations.) What is the area of the parallelogram?

39. Find an equation for the set of all points $P(x, y, z)$ such that the distance from P to the point $P_0(-1, 2, 4)$ is the same as the distance from P to the plane $2x - 5y + 3z = 7$. (Do not expand binomials.)

40. Find an equation for the set of all points $P(x, y, z)$ such that the distance from P to the line
$$\frac{x - 1}{4} = \frac{y + 1}{-1} = \frac{z}{3}$$
is 5. (Do not expand.)

41. In Figure 9.64, $\mathbf{N}$ is normal to the plane P and L is a line that intersects p. Assume $\mathbf{N} = a\mathbf{i} + b\mathbf{j} + c\mathbf{k}$ and that L is given by $x = x_0 + At, y = y_0 + Bt, z = z_0 + Ct$
   a. Find $\cos \theta$ for the angle θ between L and the plane p.
   b. Find the angle between the plane $x + y + z = 10$ and the line
$$\frac{x - 1}{2} = \frac{y + 3}{3} = \frac{z - 2}{-1}$$

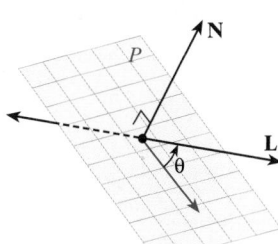

Figure 9.64   Problem 41

42. Find an equation for the line that passes through the point $P(0, 1, -1)$ and is parallel to the line of intersection of the planes $2x + y - 2z = 5$ and $3x - 6y - 2z = 7$.

43. Find a vector that is parallel to the line of intersection of the planes $2x + 3y = 0$ and $3x - y + z = 1$.

44. Find an equation for the line of intersection of the planes $2x - y + z = 8$ and $x + y - z = 5$.

45. Find the direction cosines of a vector determined by the line of intersection of the planes $x + y + z = 3$ and $2x + 3y - z = 4$.

46. Find an equation for the plane that passes through $P(1, -1, 2)$ and is normal to $\mathbf{PQ}$ where Q is $Q(2, 1, 3)$.

47. Find an equation for the line that passes through the point $(1, -5, 3)$ and is orthogonal to the plane $2x - 3y + z = 1$.

48. Find two unit vectors that are parallel to the line of intersection of the planes $x + y = 1$ and $x - 2z = 3$.

49. Find two unit vectors that are parallel to the line of intersection of the planes $x + y + z = 3$ and $x - y + z = 1$.

50. Find an equation for the plane that contains the point $(2, 1, -1)$ and is orthogonal to the line
$$\frac{x-3}{3} = \frac{y+1}{5} = \frac{z}{2}$$

51. Find a plane that passes through the point $(1, 2, -1)$ and is parallel to the plane $2x - y + 3z = 1$.

52. Show that the line
$$\frac{x-1}{2} = \frac{y+1}{3} = \frac{z-2}{4}$$
is parallel to the plane $x - 2y + z = 6$.

53. Find the point where the line
$$\frac{x-1}{2} = \frac{y+1}{-1} = \frac{z}{3}$$
intersects the plane $3x + 2y - z = 5$.

54. The *angle between two planes* is defined to be the acute angle between their normal vectors. Find the angle between the planes $2x + y - 4z = 3$ and $x - y + z = 2$, rounded to the nearest degree.

55. Find an equation for the line that passes through the point $P(2, 3, 1)$ and is parallel to the line of intersection of the planes $x + 2y - 3z = 4$ and $x - 2y + z = 0$.

Ⓒ 56. The planes $Ax + By + Cz = D_1$ and $Ax + By + Cz = D_2$ are parallel.

a. Is the distance between the planes $|D_1 - D_2|$? If not, what is the correct formula?

b. Find the distance between the parallel planes $x + y + 2z = 2$ and $x + y + 2z = 4$.

57. Show that the angle between the planes
$$A_1 x + B_1 y + C_1 z + D_1 = 0$$
and
$$A_2 x + B_2 y + C_2 z + D_2 = 0$$
is $\pi/2$ if and only if
$$A_1 A_2 + B_1 B_2 + C_1 C_2 = 0$$

58. Show that a plane with x-intercept a, y-intercept b, and z-intercept c has the equation
$$\frac{x}{a} + \frac{y}{b} + \frac{z}{c} = 1$$
assuming a, b, and c are all nonzero.

59. Suppose planes p_1 and p_2 intersect. If $\mathbf{v}_1$ and $\mathbf{w}_1$ are nonzero vectors on p_1 and $\mathbf{v}_2$ and $\mathbf{w}_2$ are nonzero vectors on plane p_2, then show that
$$(\mathbf{v}_1 \times \mathbf{w}_1) \times (\mathbf{v}_2 \times \mathbf{w}_2)$$
is parallel to the line of intersection of the planes.

60. Let L_1 and L_2 be skew lines that contain the points P_1 and P_2, respectively, and are parallel to the vectors $\mathbf{v}_1$ and $\mathbf{v}_2$. Show that the distance between the lines is given by
$$d = \left| \frac{(\mathbf{v}_1 \times \mathbf{v}_2) \cdot \mathbf{P}_1\mathbf{P}_2}{\|\mathbf{v}_1 \times \mathbf{v}_2\|} \right|$$

9.7 Quadric Surfaces

IN THIS SECTION methods for graphing quadric surfaces; a catalog of quadric surfaces:

You might want to review graphs whose equations are of the form
$$Ax^2 + Bxy + Cy^2 + Dx + Ey + F = 0$$

which are called **conic sections** (see Chapters 6 and 7 of the *Student Mathematics Handbook*). Conic sections are graphs in $\mathbb{R}^2$ that can be represented by a second-degree equation in two variables, and quadric surfaces are graphs in $\mathbb{R}^3$ which can be represented by a second-degree equation in three variables.

SMH

METHODS FOR GRAPHING QUADRIC SURFACES

Spheres, and elliptic, parabolic, and hyperbolic cylinders are examples of **quadric surfaces.** In general, such a surface is the graph of an equation of the form
$$Ax^2 + By^2 + Cz^2 + Dxy + Exz + Fyz + Gx + Hy + Iz + J = 0$$

where A, B, C, D, E, F, G, H, I, and J are constants. By using rotations and translations, it can be shown that any such equation can be expressed in one of the following standard forms:

$$z = Mx^2 + Ny^2 \quad \text{or} \quad Px^2 + Qy^2 + Rz^2 = S$$

We will concentrate on examining graphs of the standard forms.

The intersection of a surface with a plane is called the **trace** of the surface in that plane. The quadric surfaces are three-dimensional analogues of the conic sections in the sense that the traces of each quadric surface with respect to planes parallel to the coordinate planes are conic sections. The following three examples show how traces can be used to determine the appearance of a quadric surface.

EXAMPLE 1 Using traces to sketch the graph of an ellipsoid

Sketch the graph of the quadric surface given by

$$\frac{x^2}{4} + \frac{y^2}{5} + \frac{z^2}{9} = 1$$

Solution

Consider the trace of the given surface in the plane $z = 0$. We substitute $z = 0$ into the equation to obtain

$$\frac{x^2}{4} + \frac{y^2}{5} = 1$$

which we recognize as an ellipse. More generally, the trace in the plane $z = k$ is, by substitution,

$$\frac{x^2}{4} + \frac{y^2}{5} + \frac{k^2}{9} = 1 \quad \text{or} \quad \frac{x^2}{4} + \frac{y^2}{5} = 1 - \frac{k^2}{9}$$

which is also an ellipse for $k^2 \leq 9$, since the right-hand side is a constant. Similarly, the trace of the surface in a plane of the form $y = k$ is

$$\frac{x^2}{4} + \frac{k^2}{5} + \frac{z^2}{9} = 1 \quad \text{or} \quad \frac{x^2}{4} + \frac{z^2}{9} = 1 - \frac{k^2}{5}$$

which is an ellipse for $k^2 \leq 5$, as is the trace in the plane $x = k$ (for $k^2 \leq 4$):

$$\frac{k^2}{4} + \frac{y^2}{5} + \frac{z^2}{9} = 1 \quad \text{or} \quad \frac{y^2}{5} + \frac{z^2}{9} = 1 - \frac{k^2}{4}$$

Sketch these traces in $\mathbb{R}^3$ as shown in Figure 9.65. Since the traces in all three principal directions are ellipses, we call this surface an **ellipsoid**. ∎

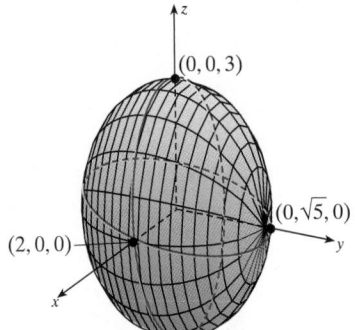

Figure 9.65 Graph of the ellipsoid
$$\frac{x^2}{4} + \frac{y^2}{5} + \frac{z^2}{9} = 1$$

EXAMPLE 2 Using traces to sketch the graph of a hyperboloid

Sketch the graph of the surface $9x^2 + 36y^2 - 4z^2 + 36 = 0$.

Solution

We begin by setting $z = k$, to obtain

$$9x^2 + 36y^2 = 4k^2 - 36$$

which is impossible for $k^2 < 9$, and represents an ellipse for $k^2 \geq 9$.

For $x = k$, we have

$$4z^2 - 36y^2 = 36 + 9k^2$$

and for $y = k$

$$4z^2 - 9x^2 = 36 + 36k^2$$

both of which represent hyperbolas for all k.

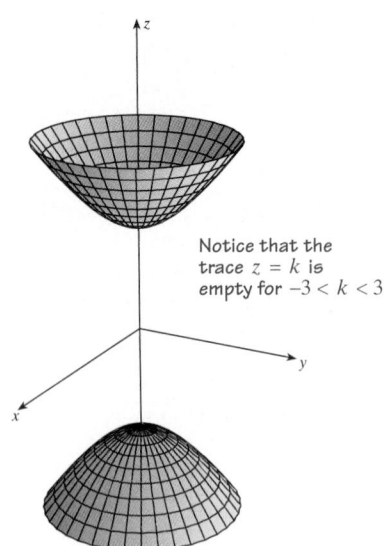

Notice that the trace $z = k$ is empty for $-3 < k < 3$.

Figure 9.66 The hyperboloid of two sheets $9x^2 + 36y^2 - 4z^2 + 36 = 0$

To summarize, the surface has hyperbolic traces for planes parallel to the yz-plane and the xz-plane and elliptical traces for planes parallel to the xy-plane, except for a "gap" corresponding to the planes of the form $z = k$ with $|k| < 3$. This surface is called a **hyperboloid of two sheets.** The graph is shown in Figure 9.66.

EXAMPLE 3   Using traces to sketch a hyperbolic paraboloid

Sketch the graph of the surface

$$z = \frac{y^2}{9} - \frac{x^2}{16}$$

Solution

For $z = 0$, we have

$$0 = \frac{y^2}{9} - \frac{x^2}{16}$$

$$y = \pm\frac{3}{4}x$$

which is a pair of intersecting lines, as shown in Figure 9.67a.

For $z = k$,

$$k = \frac{y^2}{9} - \frac{x^2}{16}$$

and the corresponding trace is a hyperbola (along the y-axis if $k > 0$, and along the x-axis if $k < 0$). These traces are also shown in Figure 9.67a.

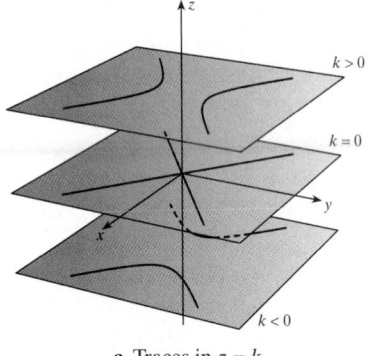

a. Traces in $z = k$

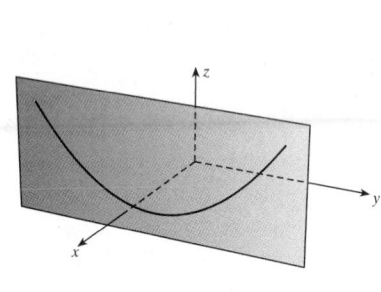

b. Traces in $x = k$

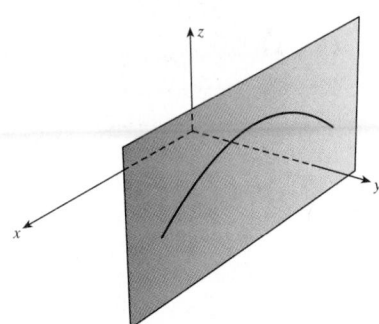

c. Traces in $y = k$

Figure 9.67   Traces in the surface $z = \dfrac{y^2}{9} - \dfrac{x^2}{16}$

If $x = k$, we have

$$z = \frac{y^2}{9} - \frac{k^2}{16}$$

and the trace is a parabola that opens up (Figure 9.67b), while if $y = k$, the corresponding equation

$$z = \frac{k^2}{9} - \frac{x^2}{16}$$

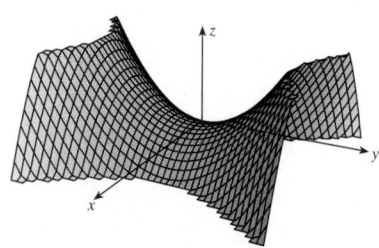

Figure 9.68 The hyperbolic paraboloid (saddle surface) $z = \dfrac{y^2}{9} - \dfrac{x^2}{16}$

is a parabola opening down (Figure 9.67c).   This surface is called a **hyperbolic paraboloid**, but is more commonly referred to as a **saddle surface** because its shape near the origin resembles that of a saddle, as shown in Figure 9.68.   ∎

A CATALOG OF QUADRIC SURFACES

A catalog of quadric surfaces is shown in Table 9.1, where x, y, and z are variables and a, b, and c are constants.

TABLE 9.1 Quadric Surfaces

Surface	Description	Surface	Description
Elliptic cone	The trace in the xy-plane is a point; in planes parallel to the xy-plane, it is an ellipse. Traces in the xz- and yz-planes are intersecting lines; in planes parallel to these, they are hyperbolas: $$z^2 = \frac{x^2}{a^2} + \frac{y^2}{b^2}$$	*Elliptic paraboloid*	The trace in the xy-plane is a point; in planes parallel to the xy-plane, it is an ellipse. Traces in the xz- and yz-planes are parabolas: $$z = \frac{x^2}{a^2} + \frac{y^2}{b^2}$$
Hyperboloid of one sheet 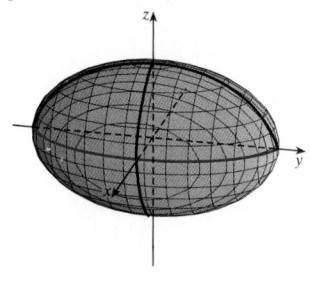	The trace in the xy-plane is an ellipse; in the xz- and yz-planes, the traces are hyperbolas: $$\frac{x^2}{a^2} + \frac{y^2}{b^2} - \frac{z^2}{c^2} = 1$$	*Hyperboloid of two sheets* 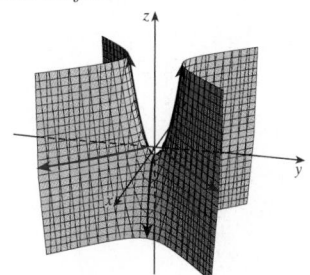	There is no trace in the xy-plane. In planes parallel to the xy-plane that intersect the surface, the traces are ellipses. Traces in the xz- and yz-planes are hyperbolas: $$\frac{x^2}{a^2} + \frac{y^2}{b^2} - \frac{z^2}{c^2} = -1$$
Ellipsoid	The traces in the coordinate planes are ellipses: $$\frac{x^2}{a^2} + \frac{y^2}{b^2} + \frac{z^2}{c^2} = 1$$	*Hyperbolic paraboloid*, also called a *saddle surface*	The trace in the xy-plane is two intersecting lines; in planes parallel to the xy-plane, the traces are hyperbolas. Traces in the xz- and yz-planes are parabolas: $$z = \frac{y^2}{b^2} - \frac{x^2}{a^2}$$
Sphere 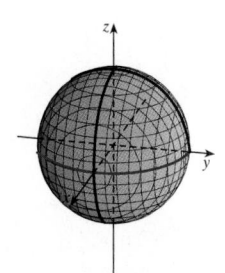	The sphere is a special kind of ellipsoid for which $a = b = c = r$: $$x^2 + y^2 + z^2 = r^2$$		

EXAMPLE 4   Identifying a quadric surface

Describe the given surfaces.

a. $7x^2 + 4y^2 - 28z^2 = 0$ **b.** $3x^2 + 5y^2 - 15z = 0$

Solution

a. We rewrite the equation in one of the two standard forms:

$$z^2 = \frac{x^2}{4} + \frac{y^2}{7}$$

We see this is an elliptic cone.

b. Rewrite as

$$z = \frac{x^2}{5} + \frac{y^2}{3}$$

We see that the surface is an elliptic paraboloid.   ■

9.7   PROBLEM SET

A **1. WHAT DOES THIS SAY?**   What is a quadric surface?

2. WHAT DOES THIS SAY?   What is the trace of a surface?

In Problems 3–12, match the equation with its graph (A–L).

3. $x^2 = z^2 + y^2$

4. $z^2 = \dfrac{x^2}{4} + \dfrac{y^2}{9}$

5. $\dfrac{x^2}{2} - \dfrac{y^2}{4} + \dfrac{z^2}{9} = 1$

6. $\dfrac{x^2}{9} + \dfrac{y^2}{16} - \dfrac{z^2}{4} = 1$

7. $x^2 + y^2 + z^2 = 9$

8. $y = x^2 + z^2$

9. $x = \dfrac{y^2}{25} + \dfrac{z^2}{16}$

10. $y = \dfrac{z^2}{4} - \dfrac{x^2}{9}$

11. $y^2 + z^2 - x^2 = -1$

12. $\dfrac{x^2}{4} - \dfrac{y^2}{9} + \dfrac{z^2}{9} = -1$

E.
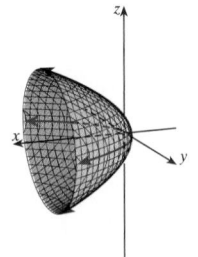

F.
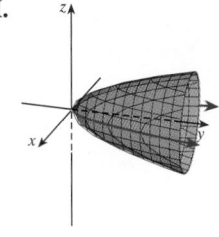

G.
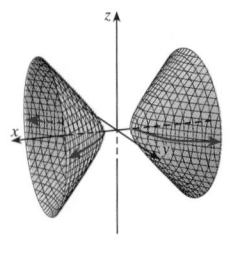

H.
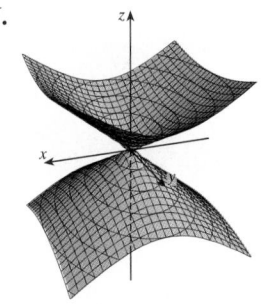

A.
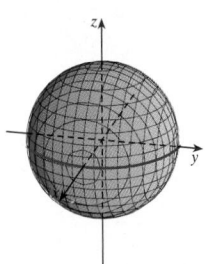

B.
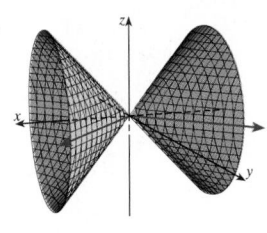

C.
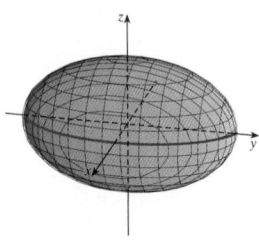

D.
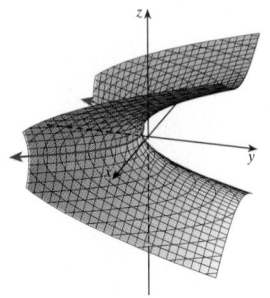

I.

J.

K.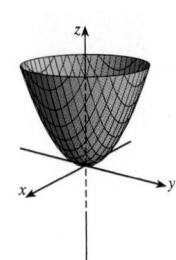

L.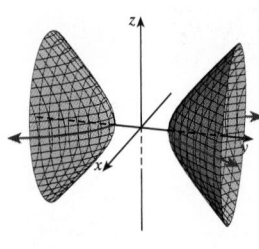

In Problems 13–20, identify the quadric surface and describe the traces in planes parallel to the coordinate planes. Sketch the graph.

13. $9x^2 + 4y^2 + z^2 = 1$

14. $\dfrac{x^2}{4} + y^2 + \dfrac{z^2}{9} = 1$

15. $\dfrac{x^2}{4} + \dfrac{y^2}{9} - z^2 = 1$

16. $\dfrac{x^2}{9} - y^2 - z^2 = 1$

17. $z = x^2 + \dfrac{y^2}{4}$

18. $z = \dfrac{x^2}{9} - \dfrac{y^2}{16}$

19. $x^2 + 2y^2 = 9z^2$

20. $z^2 = 1 + \dfrac{x^2}{9} + \dfrac{y^2}{4}$

The equations given in Problems 21–24 represent quadric surfaces whose axis of symmetry is either the x-axis or the y-axis. Identify and sketch the surface.

21. $y - x^2 - 9z^2 = 0$

22. $x = \dfrac{y^2}{4} - \dfrac{z^2}{9}$

23. $y^2 = x^2 + 3z^2$

24. $y^2 - x^2 + z^2 = 1$

Describe each of the translated quadric surfaces in Problems 25–30.

25. $\dfrac{(x-1)^2}{4} + (y+2)^2 + \dfrac{(z-3)^2}{9} = 1$

26. $z = (2x+1)^2 + \dfrac{(y-1)^2}{9} + 3$

27. $7x^2 + y^2 + 3z^2 - 9x + 4y + 7z = 1$

28. $z^2 = x^2 - y^2 + 2x + y - z + 5$

29. $y = x^2 - x + z^2 + z + 5$

30. $\dfrac{(x-1)^2}{2} - \dfrac{(y+1)^2}{4} - \dfrac{z^2}{9} = 1$

B Describe the curve of intersection of the quadric surfaces in Problems 31 and 32.

31. $\dfrac{x^2}{9} + \dfrac{y^2}{4} + \dfrac{z^2}{5} = 1$ and $z^2 = \dfrac{x^2}{3} + \dfrac{y^2}{2}$

32. $z = \dfrac{y^2}{9} - \dfrac{x^2}{16}$ and $\dfrac{x^2}{16} + \dfrac{y^2}{2} - \dfrac{z^2}{3} = 1$

33. Use the method of cross-sections (Section 6.2) to show that the ellipsoid

$$\frac{x^2}{a^2} + \frac{y^2}{b^2} + \frac{z^2}{c^2} = 1$$

has volume $V = \frac{4}{3}\pi abc$. *Hint:* You may assume that the ellipse $\dfrac{x^2}{A^2} + \dfrac{y^2}{B^2} = 1$ has area πAB.

34. Use the methods of Section 6.2 to find the volume bounded by the plane $z = 5$ and the paraboloid $9z = x^2 + y^2$.

35. What is the intersection of the surfaces $z = x^2 + y^2$ and $z = 1 - y^2$?

36. What is the intersection of the surfaces $z = x^2 + y^2$ and $z = y$?

37. Rotational forces cause the earth to flatten at the poles so its shape is really an ellipsoid rather than a true sphere. Assume that the equatorial radius of the earth is 6,378.2 km and that its polar radius is 6,356.5 km.

a. Assuming that the earth is an ellipsoid with the general equation

$$\frac{x^2}{a^2} + \frac{y^2}{a^2} + \frac{z^2}{b^2} = 1$$

find a and b.

b. Use the formula in Problem 33 to find the volume of the earth.

C **38.** The line

$$x = 1 - t, \qquad y = 2 + t, \qquad z = 3t$$

intersects the hyperboloid

$$\frac{z^2}{9} - \frac{x^2}{1} + \frac{y^2}{4} = 1$$

in two points P and Q. Find the distance between P and Q.

39. Find an equation for the surface S comprised of all points (x, y, z) the sum of whose distances from the points $A(1, 0, 0)$ and $B(-1, 0, 0)$ is 3. Is S a quadric surface?

40. Find an equation for the surface S comprised of all points (x, y, z) whose distance from the origin is the same as their distance from the plane $x + y + z = 5$. Is S a quadric surface?

CHAPTER 9 REVIEW

Proficiency Examination

CONCEPT PROBLEMS

1. What is a vector and what is a scalar?
2. Give both an algebraic and a geometric interpretation of multiplication of a vector by a scalar.
3. What is the parallelogram rule for vector sums?
4. State each of the following properties of vector operations:
   a. commutativity of vector addition
   b. associativity of vector addition
   c. identity for vector addition
   d. inverse property for vector addition
   e. magnitude of a vector for dot product
   f. commutativity for dot product
   g. multiple of a dot product
   h. distributivity for dot product over addition
   i. cross product of a zero vector
   j. anticommutativity for cross product
   k. distributivity for cross product over addition
5. If **u** and **v** are parallel vectors, what can be said about **u** × **v**?
6. How do you find the length of a vector? What is a unit vector?
7. State the triangle inequality.
8. What are the standard basis vectors in $\mathbb{R}^3$?
9. What is the standard-form equation of a sphere?
10. What is a cylinder?
11. What is the distance between two points in $\mathbb{R}^3$?
12. How do you find a unit vector **u** in the direction of a given vector **v**?
13. What is Lagrange's identity?
14. Define dot product.
15. What is the formula for the angle between two vectors?
16. What is meant by orthogonal vectors? What is the algebraic condition for orthogonality?
17. What is a vector projection? Give a formula for finding the vector projection of **v** onto **w**.
18. What is a scalar projection? Give a formula for finding the scalar projection of **v** onto **w**.
19. What is the vector formula for work?
20. Define cross product.
21. What is the right-hand rule for a coordinate system?
22. a. Give a geometric interpretation of cross product.
    b. What is the formula for the magnitude of a cross product?
23. What is the determinant form for the scalar triple product?
24. How do you find the volume of a parallelepiped?
25. a. What is the parametric form of a line in $\mathbb{R}^3$?
    b. What is the symmetric form of a line in $\mathbb{R}^3$?
26. What are the direction cosines of a vector in $\mathbb{R}^3$?
27. What is the normal vector of a plane in $\mathbb{R}^3$?
28. What is the point-normal form of a plane in $\mathbb{R}^3$?
29. What is the standard form of a plane in $\mathbb{R}^3$?
30. What is the formula for the distance from a point to a plane?
31. What is the formula for the distance from a point to a line?
32. What is a quadric surface?

PRACTICE PROBLEMS

33. Given $\mathbf{v} = 2\mathbf{i} - 3\mathbf{j} + \mathbf{k}$, $\mathbf{w} = 3\mathbf{i} - 2\mathbf{j}$. Find each of the following vectors or scalars.
    a. $2\mathbf{v} + 3\mathbf{w}$ b. $\|\mathbf{v}\|^2 - \|\mathbf{w}\|^2$
    c. $\mathbf{v} \cdot \mathbf{w}$ d. $\mathbf{v} \times \mathbf{w}$
    e. vector projection of **v** onto **w**
    f. scalar projection of **w** onto **v**
34. Given $\mathbf{u} = 2\mathbf{i} - 3\mathbf{j} + \mathbf{k}$, $\mathbf{v} = \mathbf{i} + \mathbf{j} - 2\mathbf{k}$, and $\mathbf{w} = 3\mathbf{i} + 5\mathbf{k}$. In each of the following cases, either perform the indicated computation or explain why it is not defined.
    a. $(\mathbf{u} \times \mathbf{v}) \cdot \mathbf{w}$ b. $(\mathbf{u} \cdot \mathbf{v}) \times \mathbf{w}$
    c. $(\mathbf{u} \times \mathbf{v}) \times \mathbf{w}$ d. $(\mathbf{u} \cdot \mathbf{v}) \cdot \mathbf{w}$

Find the equations for the lines and planes in Problems 35–38.

35. the line through the points $P(-1, 4, -3)$ and $Q(0, -2, 1)$
36. the plane that contains the point $P(1, 1, 3)$ and is normal to the vector $\mathbf{v} = 2\mathbf{i} + 3\mathbf{k}$
37. the line of intersection of the planes $2x + 3y + z = 2$ and $y - 3z = 5$
38. the plane that contains the points $P(0, 2, -1)$, $Q(1, -3, 5)$, and $R(3, 0, -2)$
39. Find the direction cosines and the direction angles of the vector $\mathbf{u} = -2\mathbf{i} + 3\mathbf{j} + \mathbf{k}$. Round to the nearest degree.
40. In each case, determine whether the lines intersect, are parallel, or are skew. If they intersect, find the point of intersection.
    a. $x = 2t - 3$, $y = 4 - t$, $z = 2t$ and $\dfrac{x+2}{3} = \dfrac{y-3}{5}$; $z = 3$
    b. $\dfrac{x-7}{5} = \dfrac{y-6}{4} = \dfrac{z-8}{5}$ and $\dfrac{x-8}{6} = \dfrac{y-6}{4} = \dfrac{z-9}{6}$
41. Let $\mathbf{u} = 2\mathbf{i} + \mathbf{j}$, $\mathbf{v} = \mathbf{i} - \mathbf{j} - \mathbf{k}$, and $\mathbf{w} = 3\mathbf{i} + \mathbf{k}$.
    a. Find the volume of the parallelepiped determined by these vectors.
    b. Find a positive number A that guarantees that the tetrahedron determined by $A\mathbf{u}$, $A\mathbf{v}$, and **w** has volume that is twice the volume of the original tetrahedron. *Hint:* See Problem 50, Section 9.4.
42. Find the distance from $P(-1, 1, 4)$ to $2x + 5y - z = 3$.
43. Find the distance between the skew lines $x = t$, $y = 2t$, $z = 3t - 1$ and $x = 1 - t$, $y = t + 2$, $z = t$.
44. Find the distance from the point $P(4, 5, 0)$ to the line
$$\frac{x-2}{3} = \frac{y}{5} = \frac{z+1}{-1}$$
45. An airplane flies at 200 mi/h parallel to the ground at an altitude of 10,000 ft. If the plane flies due south and the wind is blowing toward the northeast at 50 mi/h, what is the ground speed of the plane (that is, effective speed)?
46. A girl pulls a sled 50 ft on level ground with a rope inclined at an angle of 30° with the horizontal (the ground). If she applies 3 lb of tension to the rope, how much work is performed on the sled?

47. Sketch the graph of $x = 2^t$, $y = 2^{t+1}$ for $t > 0$ by

   a. using the parametric form   **b.** eliminating the parameter

48. Graph the line $\dfrac{x}{4} = -\dfrac{y}{9}$

   a. using the rectangular form   **b.** by parameterizing

49. Graph the line $\dfrac{x}{4} = -\dfrac{y}{9} = \dfrac{z}{1}$

   a. using the symmetric form   **b.** by parameterizing

50. Identify the graph of each given equation.

   a. $x^2 = z^2 + y^2$ **b.** $x^2 = z + y^2$

   c. $\dfrac{x^2}{2} - \dfrac{y^2}{4} - \dfrac{z^2}{9} = 1$ **d.** $\dfrac{x^2}{2} + \dfrac{y^2}{4} - \dfrac{z^2}{9} = 1$

   e. $\dfrac{x}{2} - \dfrac{y}{4} - \dfrac{z}{9} = 1$ **f.** $\dfrac{x}{2} = \dfrac{y}{4} = \dfrac{z}{9}$

   g. $x^2 + y^2 + z^2 = 9$ **h.** $y = x^2 + z^2$

   i. $y^2 + z^2 - x^2 = -1$ **j.** $x^2 - y^2 + z^2 = -1$

Supplementary Problems

1. A triangle in $\mathbb{R}^3$ has vertices $A(0, 2, -1)$, $B(1, 1, 3)$, and $C(1, 0, -4)$.

   a. Find the perimeter of the triangle.

   b. Find the area of the triangle.

   c. Find the three vertex angles of the triangle. (Round to the nearest degree.)

   d. Find a number p such that the points A, B, C, and $D(p, p, 0)$ form a tetrahedron of volume $v = 100$ cubic units. *Hint*: See Problem 50, Section 9.4.

Find equations, in both parametric and symmetric forms, of the lines described in Problems 2–3. Find two additional points on each line.

2. passing through $A(1, -2, 3)$, $B(4, -1, 2)$

3. passing through $P(1, 4, 0)$ with direction numbers $[2, 0, 1]$

4. Find an equation for the line passing through $P(3, 4, -1)$ and parallel to the line of intersection of the planes $x + 2y + 2z + 5 = 0$ and $2x + y - 3z - 6 = 0$.

Find an equation for the plane satisfying the conditions given in Problems 5–12.

5. the xy-plane

6. the plane parallel to the xz-plane passing through $(4, 3, 7)$

7. the plane through $(1, -3, 4)$ with attitude numbers $[3, 4, -1]$

8. the plane through $(-1, 4, 5)$ and orthogonal to a line with direction numbers $[4, 4, -3]$

9. the plane through $(4, -3, 2)$ and parallel to the plane $5x - 2y + 3z - 10 = 0$

10. the plane containing

$$\frac{x-3}{4} = \frac{z-1}{2}; \; y = -2; \quad \text{and} \quad \frac{x-3}{3} = \frac{y+2}{1} = \frac{z-1}{-2}$$

11. the plane passing through $P(4, 1, 3)$, $Q(-4, 2, 1)$, and $R(1, 0, 2)$

12. the plane passing through $(4, -1, 2)$ and parallel to the lines

$$\frac{x+2}{3} = \frac{y-2}{-1} = \frac{z+1}{2} \quad \text{and} \quad \frac{x-2}{1} = \frac{y-3}{2} = \frac{z-4}{3}$$

13. If $\mathbf{u}$ and $\mathbf{v}$ are orthogonal unit vectors, show that $(\mathbf{u} \times \mathbf{v}) \times \mathbf{u} = \mathbf{v}$. What is $(\mathbf{u} \times \mathbf{v}) \times \mathbf{v}$?

14. Show that three planes whose normals $\mathbf{u}$, $\mathbf{v}$, $\mathbf{w}$ satisfy $\mathbf{u} \times \mathbf{v} \cdot \mathbf{w} \neq 0$ intersect in exactly one point.

15. Show that $\mathbf{u} \times (\mathbf{v} \times \mathbf{w}) = (\mathbf{u} \times \mathbf{v}) \times \mathbf{w}$ if and only if $\mathbf{v} \times (\mathbf{w} \times \mathbf{u}) = \mathbf{0}$.

16. Given the vectors $\mathbf{v} = 3\mathbf{i} - 2\mathbf{j} + \mathbf{k}$ and $\mathbf{w} = 4\mathbf{i} + \mathbf{j} - 3\mathbf{k}$, find $\|\mathbf{v}\|$, $\mathbf{v} - \mathbf{w}$, and $2\mathbf{v} + 3\mathbf{w}$.

17. Given $\mathbf{u} = \mathbf{i} - \mathbf{j} + \mathbf{k}$, $\mathbf{v} = 3\mathbf{i} - 2\mathbf{j} + 5\mathbf{k}$, and $\mathbf{w} = \mathbf{i} + \mathbf{j} - \mathbf{k}$, find $(\mathbf{u} - \mathbf{v}) \cdot \mathbf{w}$ and $(2\mathbf{u} + \mathbf{v}) \times (\mathbf{u} - \mathbf{w})$.

18. Given the vectors $\mathbf{v} = 4\mathbf{i} + 2\mathbf{j} + \mathbf{k}$, $\mathbf{w} = 2\mathbf{i} + \mathbf{j} - 5\mathbf{k}$. Find

   a. $5\mathbf{v} - 3\mathbf{w}$ **b.** $\|2\mathbf{v} - \mathbf{w}\|$

   c. vector projection of $\mathbf{v}$ onto $\mathbf{w}$

   d. scalar projection of $\mathbf{w}$ onto $\mathbf{v}$

19. Find the direction cosines for $\mathbf{v} = (2\mathbf{i} + \mathbf{j}) \times (\mathbf{i} + \mathbf{j} - 3\mathbf{k})$.

20. Find two unit vectors that are parallel to the line

$$\frac{x}{6} = \frac{y}{2} = \frac{z-1}{6}$$

21. Find the (acute) angle, rounded to the nearest degree, between the intersecting lines

$$\frac{x-1}{3} = \frac{y-3}{-1} = \frac{z+5}{2} \quad \text{and} \quad \frac{x-1}{2} = \frac{y-3}{-1} = \frac{z+5}{-2}$$

22. Find the area of the parallelogram determined by $3\mathbf{i} - 4\mathbf{j}$ and $-\mathbf{i} - \mathbf{j} + \mathbf{k}$.

23. Find the center and the radius of the sphere

$$4x^2 + 4y^2 + 4z^2 + 12y - 4z + 1 = 0$$

24. Find the points of intersection of the line $x = 6 + 3t$, $y = 10 - 2t$, $z = 5t$ with each of the coordinate planes.

25. Find the point of intersection of the planes $3x - y + 4z = 15$, $2x + y - 3z = 1$, and $x + 3y + 5z = 2$

26. Find the equation of the plane determined by the intersecting lines

$$\frac{x+3}{3} = \frac{y}{-2} = \frac{z-7}{6} \quad \text{and} \quad \frac{x+6}{1} = \frac{y+5}{-3} = \frac{z-1}{2}$$

27. Find an equation for the set of all points that are equidistant from the planes $3x - 4y + 12z = 6$ and $4x + 3z = 7$.

28. Graph the planes defined by the given equations.

   a. $x + 3y + 2z = 6$ **b.** $y + z = 5$ **c.** $x = 4$

29. Graph the curve defined by the functions $x = 2\cos t$, $y = 2\sin t$ for $0 \leq t < 2\pi$.

30. Vertices B and C of $\triangle ABC$ lie along the line

$$\frac{x+2}{2} = \frac{y-1}{1} = \frac{z}{4}$$

Find the area of the triangle given that A has coordinates $(1, -1, 2)$ and line segment $\overline{BC}$ has length 5.

31. Find the work done by the constant force $\mathbf{F} = 5\mathbf{i} + 4\mathbf{j} + \mathbf{k}$ in moving a particle along the line from $P(2, 1, -1)$ to $Q(4, 1, 2)$.

32. How much work does it take to move a container 25 m along a horizontal loading platform onto a truck using a constant force of 100 newtons at an angle of $\frac{\pi}{6}$ from the horizontal?

33. Find a formula for the surface area of the tetrahedron determined by vectors $\mathbf{u}$, $\mathbf{v}$, and $\mathbf{w}$. Assume the vectors do not all lie in the same plane.

34. Suppose $\mathbf{v}$ and $\mathbf{w}$ are nonzero vectors. Show that $\|\mathbf{v}\|\mathbf{w} + \|\mathbf{w}\|\mathbf{v}$ and $\|\mathbf{v}\|\mathbf{w} - \|\mathbf{w}\|\mathbf{v}$ are orthogonal vectors.

35. Let $\mathbf{v} = \cos\theta\,\mathbf{i} + \sin\theta\,\mathbf{j}$ and $\mathbf{w} = \cos\phi\,\mathbf{i} + \sin\phi\,\mathbf{j}$. Find $\mathbf{v} \times \mathbf{w}$. Interpret this cross product geometrically, and use it to derive a well-known trigonometric identity.

36. Find the three vertex angles (rounded to the nearest degree) of the triangle whose vertices are $(1, -2, 3)$, $(-1, 2, -3)$, and $(2, 1, -3)$.

37. Find a relationship between the numbers a_1, b_1, and c_1 so that the angle between the vectors $\mathbf{v} = a_1\mathbf{i} + b_1\mathbf{j} + c_1\mathbf{k}$ and $\mathbf{w}_1 = \mathbf{i} - 2\mathbf{j}$ is the same as the angle between $\mathbf{v}$ and $\mathbf{w}_2 = 2\mathbf{i} + \mathbf{k}$.

38. Find an equation of the plane that passes through $(a, 0, 0)$, $(0, a, 0)$, and $(0, 0, a)$.

39. Find the area of the triangle with vertices $A(0, -1, 2)$, $B(1, 2, -1)$, and $C(3, -1, 2)$.

40. Find an equation for the surface comprised of all points equidistant from $D(0, 0, 6)$ and the xy-plane. Is this a quadric surface?

41. Find the area of the triangle determined by the vectors $\mathbf{v} = \mathbf{i} - \mathbf{j} + \mathbf{k}$ and $\mathbf{w} = 2\mathbf{i} + \mathbf{j} - 2\mathbf{k}$.

42. Find an equation for the plane that passes through the origin and is parallel to the vectors $\mathbf{v} = \mathbf{i} - 2\mathbf{j} - 3\mathbf{k}$ and $\mathbf{w} = -\mathbf{i} + \mathbf{j} + 2\mathbf{k}$.

43. Find an equation for the plane that passes through the origin and whose normal vector is parallel to the line of intersection of the planes $2x - y + z = 4$ and $x + 3y - z = 2$.

44. Find a number A such that the angle between the planes $2Ax + 3y + z = 1$ and $x - Ay + 3z = 5$ is $\pi/2$.

45. The lines L_1 and L_2 are parallel to the vectors $\mathbf{v}_1 = \mathbf{i} - \mathbf{j}$ and $\mathbf{v}_2 = \mathbf{i} - \mathbf{j} + 2\mathbf{k}$, respectively. Find an equation for the line L that passes through the point $(-1, 2, 0)$ and is orthogonal to both L_1 and L_2.

46. A parallelepiped is determined by the vectors $\mathbf{u} = \mathbf{i} - \mathbf{j} + \mathbf{k}$, $\mathbf{v} = \mathbf{i} + 2\mathbf{j} - \mathbf{k}$, and $\mathbf{w} = 2\mathbf{i} + \mathbf{j} + \mathbf{k}$. Find the altitude from the tip of $\mathbf{w}$ to the side determined by $\mathbf{u}$ and $\mathbf{v}$.

47. In Chapter 10, we will show that $\mathbf{T} = \mathbf{i} + 2x\mathbf{j}$ is a vector in the direction of the tangent line at each point $P(x, x^2)$ on the parabola $y = x^2$. Find a unit vector normal to the parabola at the point $(3, 9)$.

48. For nonzero vectors $\mathbf{u}$, $\mathbf{v}$, and $\mathbf{w}$, show that the vector $(\mathbf{u} \times \mathbf{v}) \times (\mathbf{u} \times \mathbf{w})$ is parallel to $\mathbf{u}$.

49. Let $\mathbf{v} = a\mathbf{i} + b\mathbf{j} + c\mathbf{k}$ and $\mathbf{w} = A\mathbf{i} + B\mathbf{j} + C\mathbf{k}$, where a, b, c, A, B, and C are constants. Describe the set of vectors $\mathbf{v} + t\mathbf{w}$, where t is any scalar.

50. Use vectors to show that the sum of the squares of the lengths of the sides of a parallelogram equals the sum of the squares of the lengths of the diagonals.

51. The vectors $\mathbf{u}$, $\mathbf{v}$, and $\mathbf{w}$ are said to be *linearly independent* in $\mathbb{R}^3$ if the only solution to the equation $a\mathbf{u} + b\mathbf{v} + c\mathbf{w} = \mathbf{0}$ is $a = b = c = 0$. Otherwise, the vectors are *linearly dependent*. The simplest example of a set of linearly independent vectors is $\mathbf{i}$, $\mathbf{j}$, and $\mathbf{k}$. Determine whether the vectors $\mathbf{u} = -\mathbf{i} + 2\mathbf{k}$, $\mathbf{v} = 2\mathbf{i} - \mathbf{j} + 3\mathbf{k}$, $\mathbf{w} = \mathbf{i} + 3\mathbf{j} - 2\mathbf{k}$ are linearly independent or dependent.

52. Figure 9.69 shows a parallelogram $ABCD$. If M is the midpoint of side $\overline{AB}$, show that line $\overline{CM}$ intersects diagonal $\overline{BD}$ at a point P located one-third of the distance from B to D by completing the following steps.

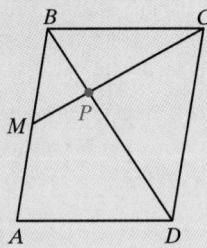

Figure 9.69 Parallelogram $ABCD$

a. Let a and b be scalars such that $\mathbf{MP} = a\mathbf{MC}$ and $\mathbf{BP} = b\mathbf{BD}$. Show that

$$\tfrac{1}{2}\mathbf{AB} + b(\mathbf{AD} - \mathbf{AB}) = a\left(\mathbf{AD} + \tfrac{1}{2}\mathbf{AB}\right)$$

b. Two vectors $\mathbf{u}$ and $\mathbf{v}$ in $\mathbb{R}^2$ are *linearly independent* if the only solution to $a\mathbf{u} + b\mathbf{v} = \mathbf{0}$ is $a = b = 0$, and it can be shown that this is equivalent to saying that the two vectors are not parallel to each other. Use the fact that $\mathbf{AB}$ and $\mathbf{AD}$ are linearly independent to show that

$$\tfrac{1}{2} - b - \tfrac{1}{2}a = 0 \quad \text{and} \quad a - b = 0$$

Solve this system of equations to show that P has the required location.

53. Show that $\mathbf{u} = a_1\mathbf{i} + a_2\mathbf{j} + a_3\mathbf{k}$, $\mathbf{v} = b_1\mathbf{i} + b_2\mathbf{j} + b_3\mathbf{k}$ and $\mathbf{w} = c_1\mathbf{i} + c_2\mathbf{j} + c_3\mathbf{k}$ are linearly dependent (see Problem 51), if and only if

$$\begin{vmatrix} a_1 & a_2 & a_3 \\ b_1 & b_2 & b_3 \\ c_1 & c_2 & c_3 \end{vmatrix} = 0$$

54. Show that

$$\begin{vmatrix} \mathbf{u}_1 \cdot \mathbf{v}_1 & \mathbf{u}_1 \cdot \mathbf{v}_2 \\ \mathbf{u}_2 \cdot \mathbf{v}_1 & \mathbf{u}_2 \cdot \mathbf{v}_2 \end{vmatrix} = (\mathbf{u}_1 \times \mathbf{u}_2) \cdot (\mathbf{v}_1 \times \mathbf{v}_2)$$

55. Let $A(-2, 3, 7)$, $B(1, 5, -3)$, and $C(2, 8, -1)$ be the vertices of a triangle in $\mathbb{R}^3$. What are the coordinates of the point M where the medians of the triangle meet (the centroid)?

56. The medians of a triangle meet at a point (the centroid) located two-thirds of the distance from each vertex to the midpoint of the opposite side. Generalize this result by showing that the four lines that join each vertex of a tetrahedron to the centroid of the opposite face meet at a point located three-fourths of the distance from the vertex to the centroid.

57. Spy Problem The Spy forces Blohardt's helicopter to land (see Problem 53, Section 9.5), but when he and his men approach, they discover no occupants—the helicopter is remote controlled! There is, however, a note attached to the control panel. There are map coordinates, a crude drawing, and these words: "From the snowman, pace off the distance to the woodpile, turn left, pace off an equal distance and drive a stake. From the snowman again, pace off the distance to the flagpole, turn right, pace off an equal distance and drive a second stake. Dig halfway between the stakes." A bloody letter "*F*" marks the spot on the map between the stakes.

"Flamer!" gasps the Spy. Gripped by trepidation, he arrives at the location indicated by the map coordinates. There is a woodpile and a flagpole, but the snowman has melted. How can the Spy know where to dig?

58. A triangle in $\mathbb{R}^3$ is determined by the vectors $\mathbf{v}$ and $\mathbf{w}$ as shown in Figure 9.70.

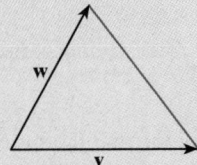

Figure 9.70   Area of a triangle

Show that the triangle has area

$$A = \tfrac{1}{2}\sqrt{\|\mathbf{v}\|^2\|\mathbf{w}\|^2 - (\mathbf{v}\cdot\mathbf{w})^2}$$

59. Exploration Problem   In Figure 9.71, $\triangle ABC$ is equilateral and the points M, N, and O are located so that

$$\mathbf{AM} = \tfrac{1}{3}\mathbf{AB} \qquad \mathbf{BN} = \tfrac{1}{3}\mathbf{BC} \qquad \mathbf{CO} = \tfrac{1}{3}\mathbf{CA}$$

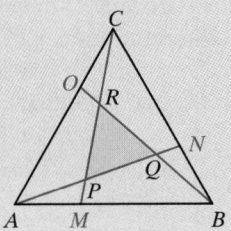

Figure 9.71   Problem 59

It can be shown that $\triangle PQR$ is also equilateral, and $\|\mathbf{PM}\| = \|\mathbf{QN}\| = \|\mathbf{RO}\|$ and $\|\mathbf{AP}\| = \|\mathbf{BQ}\| = \|\mathbf{CR}\|$.

a. Show that $\mathbf{PQ} = \tfrac{3}{7}\mathbf{AN}$, then show that $\|\mathbf{AN}\|^2 = \tfrac{7}{9}\|\mathbf{AB}\|^2$. *Hint:* Use the law of cosines.

b. Show that $\triangle PQR$ has area $\tfrac{1}{7}$ that of $\triangle ABC$.

c. Do you think the same result would hold if $\triangle ABC$ were not equilateral? Investigate your conjecture.

60. Gram-Schmidt orthogonalization process   Let $\mathbf{u}$, $\mathbf{v}$, and $\mathbf{w}$ be nonzero vectors in $\mathbb{R}^3$ that do not lie on the same plane. Define vectors α and β as follows:

$$\alpha = \mathbf{v} - \left[\frac{\mathbf{v}\cdot\mathbf{u}}{\|\mathbf{u}\|^2}\right]\mathbf{u} \quad \text{and} \quad \beta = \mathbf{w} - \left[\frac{\mathbf{w}\cdot\mathbf{u}}{\|\mathbf{u}\|^2}\right]\mathbf{u} - \left[\frac{\mathbf{w}\cdot\alpha}{\|\alpha\|^2}\right]\alpha$$

a. Show that $\mathbf{u}$, α, β are mutually orthogonal (any pair is orthogonal).

b. If γ is any vector in $\mathbb{R}^3$, show that

$$\gamma = \left[\frac{\gamma\cdot\mathbf{u}}{\|\mathbf{u}\|^2}\right]\mathbf{u} + \left[\frac{\gamma\cdot\alpha}{\|\alpha\|^2}\right]\alpha + \left[\frac{\gamma\cdot\beta}{\|\beta\|^2}\right]\beta$$

61. Exploration Problem

a. In Figure 9.72, $ABCD$ is a rectangle, with M the midpoint of side $\overline{CD}$ and $\mathbf{AR}_k = \dfrac{1}{2k+1}\mathbf{AB}$. If P is the intersection of $\overline{AM}$ and $\overline{CR}_k$, and R_{k+1} is the foot of the perpendicular drawn from P to $\overline{AB}$, show that

$$\mathbf{AR}_{k+1} = \frac{1}{2k+3}\mathbf{AB}$$

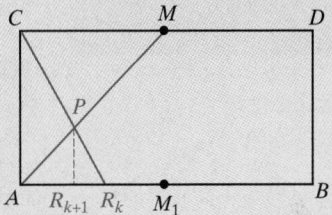

Figure 9.72   Problem 61

b. It is easy to subdivide a line segment $\overline{AB}$ in half, or fourths, or eighths, etc. However, dividing it into thirds or fifths, … is more difficult. Use the result obtained in part **a** to describe a procedure for subdividing $\overline{AB}$ into an odd number of equal parts.

62. Putnam Examination Problem   Find the equations of two straight lines, each of which cuts all four of the following lines:

$$\begin{aligned}
L_1: &\quad x = 1, \quad y = 0 \\
L_2: &\quad y = 1, \quad z = 0 \\
L_3: &\quad z = 1, \quad x = 0 \\
L_4: &\quad x = y = -6z
\end{aligned}$$

63. Putnam Examination Problem   Find the equation of the smallest sphere that is tangent to both the lines

$$L_1: \quad x = t+1, \ y = 2t+4, \ z = -3t+5 \text{ and}$$
$$L_2: \quad x = 4t-12, \ y = t+8, \ z = t+17$$

64. Putnam Examination Problem   The hands of an accurate clock have lengths 3 cm and 4 cm. Find the distance between the tips of the hands when the distance is increasing most rapidly.

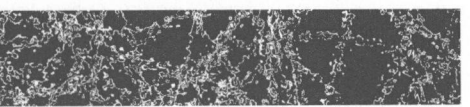

Group Research Project[*]

Star Trek

This project is to be done in groups of three or four students. Each group will submit a single written report.

The starship *Enterprise* has been captured by the evil Romulans and is being held in orbit by a Romulan tractor beam. The orbit is elliptical with the planet Romulus at one focus of the ellipse. Repeated efforts to escape have been futile and have almost exhausted the fuel supplies. Morale is low and food reserves are dwindling.

In searching the ship's log, Lieutenant Commander Data discovers that the Enterprise had been captured long ago by a Romulan tractor beam and had escaped. The key to that escape was to fire the ship's thrusters at exactly the right position in the orbit. Captain Picard gives the command to feed the required information into the computer to find that position. But, alas, a Romulan virus has rendered the computer useless for this task. Everyone turns to you and asks for your help in solving the problem.

Here is what Data discovered. If F represents the focus of the ellipse and P is the position of the ship on the ellipse, then the vector $\mathbf{FP}$ can be written as a sum $\mathbf{T} + \mathbf{N}$ where $\mathbf{T}$ is tangent to the ellipse and $\mathbf{N}$ is normal to the ellipse (not necessarily unit vectors). The thrusters must be fired when the ratio $\|\mathbf{T}\|/\|\mathbf{N}\|$ is equal to the eccentricity of the ellipse.

Your mission is to save the starship from the evil Romulans.

Even though quaternions are not particularly important today, they preceded the modern concept of a vector. Our use of **i**, **j**, *and* **k** *derives from Hamilton's quaternions.*

---

[*]*MAA Notes:* 17 (1991) "Priming the Calculus Pump: Innovations and Resources," by Marcus S. Cohen, Edward D. Gaughan, R. Arthur Knoebel, Douglas S. Kurtz, and David J. Pengelley.

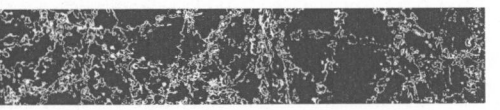

10

Vector-Valued Functions

PREVIEW

The marriage of calculus and vector methods forms what is called *vector calculus*. The key to using vector calculus is the concept of a *vector-valued function*. In this chapter, we introduce such functions and examine some of their properties. We will see that vector-valued functions behave much like the *scalar-valued functions* studied earlier in this text.

PERSPECTIVE

A car travels down a curved road at a constant speed of 55 mi/h. What additional information do we need about the car to determine whether it will stay on the road or skid off as it rounds a particular curve? Can we modify the road (say, by banking) so an average-sized car can travel at moderate speeds without skidding? A soldier fires a howitzer whose muzzle speed and angle of elevation are known. If the shell overshoots its target by 40 yd, how should the angle of elevation be changed to ensure a hit on the next shot? If a satellite is in orbit above the earth, how fast must it travel to remain stationary above a particular point on the equator? These and other similar questions can be answered using vector calculus.

10.1 Introduction to Vector Functions

IN THIS SECTION vector-valued functions, operations with vector-valued functions, limits and continuity of vector functions

VECTOR-VALUED FUNCTIONS

In Section 9.5, we described a *plane curve* using parametric equations

$$x = f(t) \quad \text{and} \quad y = g(t)$$

where f and g are functions of t on some interval. We extend this definition to three dimensions. A **curve in $\mathbb{R}^3$** is the set of all ordered triples $(f_1(t), f_2(t), f_3(t))$ satisfying the parametric equations $x = f_1(t), y = f_2(t), z = f_3(t)$, where $f_1, f_2,$ and f_3 are functions of t on some domain D, which lies in $\mathbb{R}$.

The concept of a vector-valued function is fundamental to the ideas we plan to explore. Here is a definition.

Vector-Valued Function

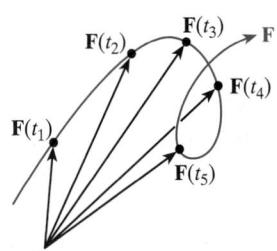

A **vector-valued function** (or, simply, a **vector function**) $\mathbf{F}$ of a real variable with *domain D* assigns to each number t in the set D a unique vector $\mathbf{F}(t)$. The set of all vectors $\mathbf{v}$ of the form $\mathbf{v} = \mathbf{F}(t)$ for t in D is the *range* of $\mathbf{F}$. That is,

$$\mathbf{F}(t) = f_1(t)\mathbf{i} + f_2(t)\mathbf{j} \qquad \text{Plane } (\mathbb{R}^2)$$

$$\mathbf{F}(t) = f_1(t)\mathbf{i} + f_2(t)\mathbf{j} + f_3(t)\mathbf{k} \qquad \text{Three-Space } (\mathbb{R}^3)$$

where $f_1, f_2,$ and f_3 are real-valued (**scalar-valued**) functions of the real number t defined on the domain set D. In this context, $f_1, f_2,$ and f_3 are called the **components** of $\mathbf{F}$. A vector function may also be denoted by $\mathbf{F}(t) = \langle f_1(t), f_2(t) \rangle$ or $\mathbf{F}(t) = \langle f_1(t), f_2(t), f_3(t) \rangle$.

Figure 10.1 The graph of the vector function $\mathbf{F}(t)$ is traced out by the terminal point of $\mathbf{F}(t)$ as t varies over the domain D.

Let $\mathbf{F}$ be a vector function, and suppose the initial point of the vector $\mathbf{F}(t)$ is at the origin. The graph of $\mathbf{F}$ is the curve traced out by the terminal point of the vector $\mathbf{F}(t)$ as t varies over the domain set D, as shown in Figure 10.1. In this context, $\mathbf{F}(t)$ is called the **position vector** at t for the point $P(f_1(t), f_2(t), f_3(t))$ on C.

EXAMPLE 1 Graph of a vector function

Sketch the graph of the vector function

$$\mathbf{F}(t) = (3 - t)\mathbf{i} + (2t)\mathbf{j} + (3t - 4)\mathbf{k}$$

for all t.

Solution

The graph is the collection of all points (x, y, z) with

$$x = 3 - t \qquad y = 2t \qquad z = -4 + 3t$$

for all t. We recognize these as the parametric equations for the line in $\mathbb{R}^3$ that contains the point $P_0(3, 0, -4)$ and is parallel to the vector

$$\mathbf{v} = -\mathbf{i} + 2\mathbf{j} + 3\mathbf{k}$$

as shown in Figure 10.2. ∎

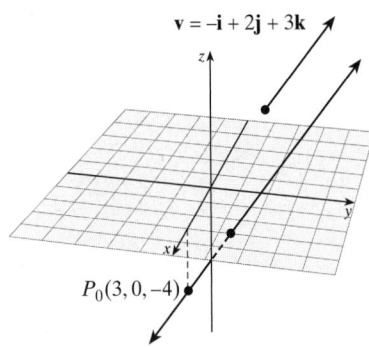

Figure 10.2 The graph of $\mathbf{F}(t) = (3 - t)\mathbf{i} + (2t)\mathbf{j} + (3t - 4)\mathbf{k}$

EXAMPLE 2 Graph of a circular helix

Sketch the graph of the vector function

$$\mathbf{F}(t) = (2 \sin t)\mathbf{i} - (2 \cos t)\mathbf{j} + (3t)\mathbf{k}$$

Solution

The graph of **F** is the collection of all points (x, y, z) in $\mathbb{R}^3$ whose coordinates satisfy

$$x = 2\sin t \qquad y = -2\cos t \qquad z = 3t \qquad \text{for all } t$$

The first two components satisfy

$$x^2 + y^2 = (2\sin t)^2 + (-2\cos t)^2 = 4(\sin^2 t + \cos^2 t) = 4$$

which means that the graph lies on the surface of the circular cylinder with radius 2 as shown in Figure 10.3.

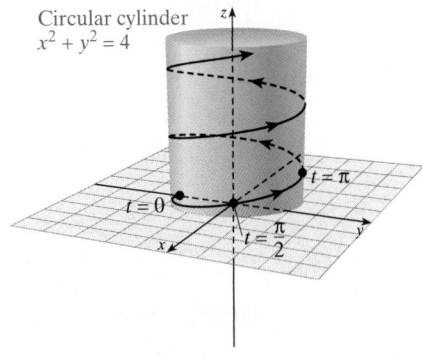

Figure 10.3 The graph of $\mathbf{F}(t) = (2\sin t)\mathbf{i} - (2\cos t)\mathbf{j} + (3t)\mathbf{k}$

Next notice the axis of symmetry for the graph in Figure 10.3 is the z-axis. We also know that as t increases, the z-coordinate of the point $P(x, y, z)$ on the graph of **F** increases according to the formula $z = 3t$, which means that the point (x, y, z) on the graph rises in a spiral on the surface of the cylinder $x^2 + y^2 = 4$. The point on the graph of **F** that corresponds to $t = 0$ is $(0, -2, 0)$, and the points that correspond to $t = \frac{\pi}{2}$ and $t = \pi$ are $(2, 0, \frac{3\pi}{2})$ and $(0, 2, 3\pi)$, respectively. Thus, the graph spirals upward counterclockwise (as viewed from above). The graph, known as a **right circular helix**, is shown in Figure 10.3. ∎

A well-known example of a helix is the DNA (deoxyribonucleic acid) molecule, which has a structure consisting of two intertwined helixes, as shown in Figure 10.4. Some other computer-generated helixes are also shown.

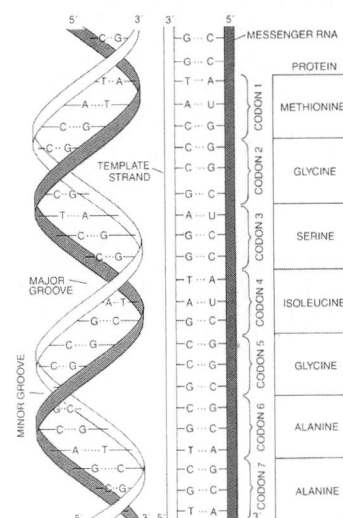

a. DNA molecule

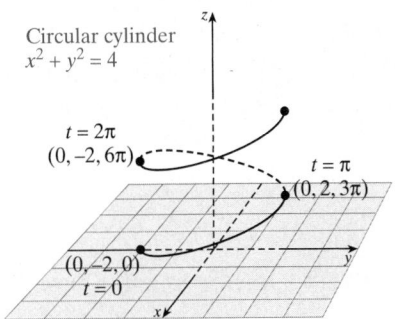

b. A computer-generated image of the helix in Example 2: $\mathbf{F}(t) = (2\sin t)\mathbf{i} - (2\cos t)\mathbf{j} + 3t\mathbf{k}$

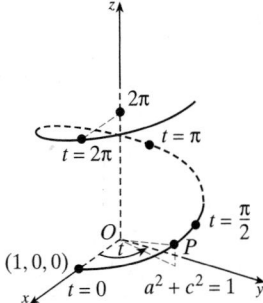

c. A computer-generated image of the helix: $\mathbf{F}(t) = (\cos 2t)\mathbf{i} + (\sin 2t)\mathbf{j} + 0.2t\mathbf{k}$

Figure 10.4 Examples of helixes

Examples 1 and 2 illustrate how the graph of a vector function

$$\mathbf{F}(t) = f_1(t)\mathbf{i} + f_2(t)\mathbf{j} + f_3(t)\mathbf{k}$$

can be obtained by examining the parametric equations

$$x = f_1(t) \qquad y = f_2(t) \qquad z = f_3(t)$$

In Example 3, we turn things around and find a vector function whose graph is a given curve.

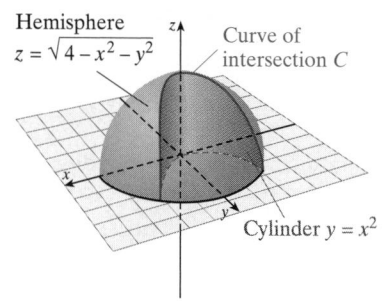

Hemisphere
$z = \sqrt{4 - x^2 - y^2}$

Curve of
intersection C

Cylinder $y = x^2$

Figure 10.5 The curve of intersection of the hemisphere and the cylinder

EXAMPLE 3   Find a vector function

Find a vector function **F** whose graph is the curve of intersection of the hemisphere $z = \sqrt{4 - x^2 - y^2}$ and the parabolic cylinder $y = x^2$, as shown in Figure 10.5.

Solution

Finding a parametric representation is sometimes called **parameterizing the curve**. There are several ways this can be done, but one choice is to let $x = t$. Then $y = t^2$ (from the equation of the parabolic cylinder), and by substituting into the equation for the hemisphere, we find

$$z = \sqrt{4 - x^2 - y^2} = \sqrt{4 - (t)^2 - (t^2)^2} = \sqrt{4 - t^2 - t^4}$$

We can now state a formula for a vector-valued function of the given graph:

$$\mathbf{F}(t) = t\mathbf{i} + t^2\mathbf{j} + \sqrt{4 - t^2 - t^4}\,\mathbf{k} \qquad \blacksquare$$

OPERATIONS WITH VECTOR FUNCTIONS

It follows from the definition of vector operations that vector functions can be added, subtracted, multiplied by a scalar function, and multiplied together. We summarize these operations in the following box.

Vector Function Operations

> Let **F** and **G** be vector functions of the real variable t, and let $f(t)$ be a scalar function. Then, $\mathbf{F} + \mathbf{G}$, $\mathbf{F} - \mathbf{G}$, $f\mathbf{F}$, and $\mathbf{F} \times \mathbf{G}$ are vector functions, and $\mathbf{F} \cdot \mathbf{G}$ is a scalar function. These operations are defined as follows:
>
> Vector functions:
>
> $$(\mathbf{F} + \mathbf{G})(t) = \mathbf{F}(t) + \mathbf{G}(t) \qquad (\mathbf{F} - \mathbf{G})(t) = \mathbf{F}(t) - \mathbf{G}(t)$$
> $$(f\mathbf{F})(t) = f(t)\mathbf{F}(t) \qquad (\mathbf{F} \times \mathbf{G})(t) = \mathbf{F}(t) \times \mathbf{G}(t)$$
>
> Scalar function:
>
> $$(\mathbf{F} \cdot \mathbf{G})(t) = \mathbf{F}(t) \cdot \mathbf{G}(t)$$
>
> These operations are defined on the intersection of the domain of the vector and scalar functions that occur in their definitions.

WARNING $(\mathbf{F} \times \mathbf{G})(t)$ is a vector and $(\mathbf{F} \cdot \mathbf{G})(t)$ is a scalar.

EXAMPLE 4   Vector function operations

Let $\mathbf{F}(t) = t^2\mathbf{i} + t\mathbf{j} - (\sin t)\mathbf{k}$ and $\mathbf{G}(t) = t\mathbf{i} + \dfrac{1}{t}\mathbf{j} + 5\mathbf{k}$. Find

a. $(\mathbf{F} + \mathbf{G})(t)$ **b.** $(e^t\mathbf{F})(t)$ **c.** $(\mathbf{F} \times \mathbf{G})(t)$ **d.** $(\mathbf{F} \cdot \mathbf{G})(t)$

Solution

a. $(\mathbf{F} + \mathbf{G})(t) = \mathbf{F}(t) + \mathbf{G}(t)$

$$= [t^2\mathbf{i} + t\mathbf{j} - (\sin t)\mathbf{k}] + \left[t\mathbf{i} + \frac{1}{t}\mathbf{j} + 5\mathbf{k}\right]$$

$$= (t^2 + t)\mathbf{i} + \left(t + \frac{1}{t}\right)\mathbf{j} + (5 - \sin t)\mathbf{k}$$

b. $(e^t \mathbf{F})(t) = e^t \mathbf{F}(t) = e^t t^2 \mathbf{i} + e^t t \mathbf{j} - (e^t \sin t)\mathbf{k}$

c. $(\mathbf{F} \times \mathbf{G})(t) = \mathbf{F}(t) \times \mathbf{G}(t)$

$$= [t^2 \mathbf{i} + t\mathbf{j} - (\sin t)\mathbf{k}] \times \left[t\mathbf{i} + \frac{1}{t}\mathbf{j} + 5\mathbf{k} \right]$$

$$= \begin{vmatrix} \mathbf{i} & \mathbf{j} & \mathbf{k} \\ t^2 & t & -\sin t \\ t & \dfrac{1}{t} & 5 \end{vmatrix}$$

$$= \left[5t + \frac{\sin t}{t} \right]\mathbf{i} - [5t^2 + t\sin t]\mathbf{j} + [t - t^2]\mathbf{k}$$

d. $(\mathbf{F} \cdot \mathbf{G})(t) = \mathbf{F}(t) \cdot \mathbf{G}(t)$

$$= [t^2 \mathbf{i} + t\mathbf{j} - (\sin t)\mathbf{k}] \cdot \left[t\mathbf{i} + \frac{1}{t}\mathbf{j} + 5\mathbf{k} \right]$$

$$= t^3 + 1 - 5\sin t$$

■

TECHNOLOGY NOTE

Representing a vector function using technology is generally the same whether using a calculator or a software package. Square brackets are often used to denote vector functions. For Example 4, we denote $\mathbf{F}$ as the function $y1(x)$, and $\mathbf{G}$ as $y2(x)$:

$$y1(x) = [x^2, x, -\sin x]$$
$$y2(x) = [x, 1/x, 5]$$

A sample of these input values is shown in Figure 10.6a. Next, we work through each of the parts of Example 4, as shown in Figure 10.6b. Notice that if the answer is a vector, it is shown in brackets (as in parts **a**, **b**, and **c**). If the answer is a scalar (as in part **d**), the answer is not shown in brackets.

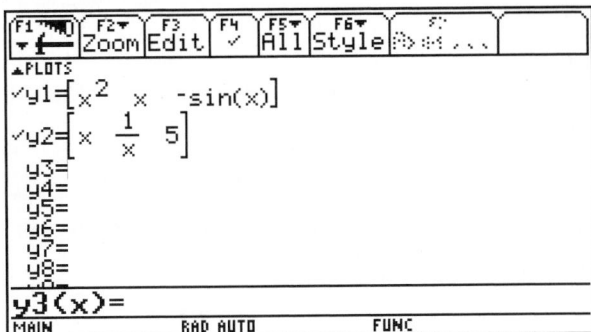

a. Input vector functions for Example 4

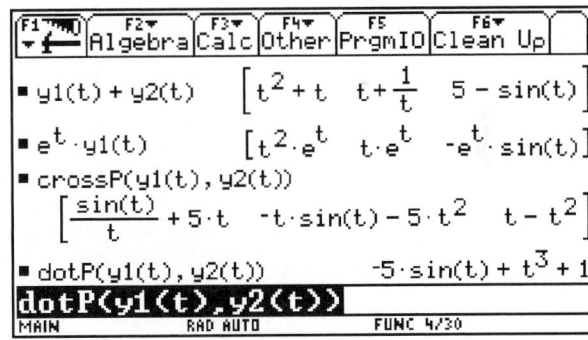

b. Technology solution for Example 4

Figure 10.6 Using technology with vector functions

LIMITS AND CONTINUITY OF VECTOR FUNCTIONS

Limit of a Vector Function

Suppose the components f_1, f_2, f_3 of the vector function

$$\mathbf{F}(t) = f_1(t)\mathbf{i} + f_2(t)\mathbf{j} + f_3(t)\mathbf{k}$$

all have finite limits as $t \to t_0$, where t_0 is any number or $\pm\infty$. Then the **limit** of $\mathbf{F}(t)$ as $t \to t_0$ is the vector

$$\lim_{t \to t_0} \mathbf{F}(t) = \left[\lim_{t \to t_0} f_1(t) \right]\mathbf{i} + \left[\lim_{t \to t_0} f_2(t) \right]\mathbf{j} + \left[\lim_{t \to t_0} f_3(t) \right]\mathbf{k}$$

EXAMPLE 5   Limit of a vector function

Find $\lim\limits_{t \to 2} \mathbf{F}(t)$, where $\mathbf{F}(t) = (t^2 - 3)\mathbf{i} + e^t\mathbf{i} + (\sin \pi t)\mathbf{k}$.

Solution

$$
\begin{aligned}
\lim_{t \to 2} \mathbf{F}(t) &= \left[\lim_{t \to 2}(t^2 - 3)\right]\mathbf{i} + \left[\lim_{t \to 2}(e^t)\right]\mathbf{j} + \left[\lim_{t \to 2}(\sin \pi t)\right]\mathbf{k} \\
&= 1\mathbf{i} + e^2\mathbf{j} + (\sin 2\pi)\mathbf{k} \\
&= \mathbf{i} + e^2\mathbf{j}
\end{aligned}
$$

∎

Vector limits behave like scalar limits. The following theorem contains some useful general properties of such limits.

THEOREM 10.1   Rules for Vector Limits

If the vector functions $\mathbf{F}$ and $\mathbf{G}$ are functions of a real variable t and $h(t)$ is a scalar function such that all three functions have finite limits as $t \to t_0$, then

Limit of a sum	$\lim\limits_{t \to t_0}[\mathbf{F}(t) + \mathbf{G}(t)] = \lim\limits_{t \to t_0} \mathbf{F}(t) + \lim\limits_{t \to t_0} \mathbf{G}(t)$
Limit of a difference	$\lim\limits_{t \to t_0}[\mathbf{F}(t) - \mathbf{G}(t)] = \lim\limits_{t \to t_0} \mathbf{F}(t) - \lim\limits_{t \to t_0} \mathbf{G}(t)$
Limit of a scalar multiple	$\lim\limits_{t \to t_0}[h(t)\mathbf{F}(t)] = \left[\lim\limits_{t \to t_0} h(t)\right]\left[\lim\limits_{t \to t_0} \mathbf{F}(t)\right]$
Limit of a dot product	$\lim\limits_{t \to t_0}[\mathbf{F}(t) \cdot \mathbf{G}(t)] = \left[\lim\limits_{t \to t_0} \mathbf{F}(t)\right] \cdot \left[\lim\limits_{t \to t_0} \mathbf{G}(t)\right]$
Limit of a cross product	$\lim\limits_{t \to t_0}[\mathbf{F}(t) \times \mathbf{G}(t)] = \left[\lim\limits_{t \to t_0} \mathbf{F}(t)\right] \times \left[\lim\limits_{t \to t_0} \mathbf{G}(t)\right]$

These limit formulas are also valid as $t \to +\infty$ or as $t \to -\infty$, assuming all expressions have finite limits.

Proof   We will establish the formula for the limit of a dot product and leave the rest of the proof as an exercise. Let

$$\mathbf{F}(t) = f_1(t)\mathbf{i} + f_2(t)\mathbf{j} + f_3(t)\mathbf{k} \quad \text{and} \quad \mathbf{G}(t) = g_1(t)\mathbf{i} + g_2(t)\mathbf{j} + g_3(t)\mathbf{k}$$

Apply the limit of a vector function along with the sum rule and product rule for scalar limits to write

$$
\begin{aligned}
\lim_{t \to t_0}[\mathbf{F}(t) \cdot \mathbf{G}(t)] &= \lim_{t \to t_0}[f_1(t)g_1(t) + f_2(t)g_2(t) + f_3(t)g_3(t)] \\
&= \left[\lim_{t \to t_0} f_1(t)\right]\left[\lim_{t \to t_0} g_1(t)\right] + \left[\lim_{t \to t_0} f_2(t)\right]\left[\lim_{t \to t_0} g_2(t)\right] + \left[\lim_{t \to t_0} f_3(t)\right]\left[\lim_{t \to t_0} g_3(t)\right] \\
&= \left(\left[\lim_{t \to t_0} f_1(t)\right]\mathbf{i} + \left[\lim_{t \to t_0} f_2(t)\right]\mathbf{j} + \left[\lim_{t \to t_0} f_3(t)\right]\mathbf{k}\right) \cdot \left(\left[\lim_{t \to t_0} g_1(t)\right]\mathbf{i} + \left[\lim_{t \to t_0} g_2(t)\right]\mathbf{j} + \left[\lim_{t \to t_0} g_3(t)\right]\mathbf{k}\right) \\
&= \left[\lim_{t \to t_0} \mathbf{F}(t)\right] \cdot \left[\lim_{t \to t_0} \mathbf{G}(t)\right]
\end{aligned}
$$

∎

EXAMPLE 6   Limit of a cross product of vector functions

Show that $\lim\limits_{t \to 1}[\mathbf{F}(t) \times \mathbf{G}(t)] = \left[\lim\limits_{t \to 1} \mathbf{F}(t)\right] \times \left[\lim\limits_{t \to 1} \mathbf{G}(t)\right]$ for the vector functions

$$\mathbf{F}(t) = t\mathbf{i} + (1 - t)\mathbf{j} + t^2\mathbf{k} \quad \text{and} \quad \mathbf{G}(t) = e^t\mathbf{i} - (3 + e^t)\mathbf{k}$$

Solution

$$\mathbf{F}(t) \times \mathbf{G}(t) = \begin{vmatrix} \mathbf{i} & \mathbf{j} & \mathbf{k} \\ t & 1-t & t^2 \\ e^t & 0 & -(3+e^t) \end{vmatrix}$$

$$= [(1-t)(-3-e^t) - 0]\mathbf{i} - [-t(3+e^t) - t^2 e^t]\mathbf{j} + [0 - e^t(1-t)]\mathbf{k}$$

$$= (te^t + 3t - e^t - 3)\mathbf{i} + (t^2 e^t + te^t + 3t)\mathbf{j} + (te^t - e^t)\mathbf{k}$$

Thus, the limit of the cross product is

$$\lim_{t\to 1}[\mathbf{F}(t) \times \mathbf{G}(t)] = \lim_{t\to 1}[te^t + 3t - e^t - 3]\mathbf{i} + \lim_{t\to 1}[t^2 e^t + te^t + 3t]\mathbf{j} + \lim_{t\to 1}[te^t - e^t]\mathbf{k}$$

$$= (e + 3 - e - 3)\mathbf{i} + (e + e + 3)\mathbf{j} + (e - e)\mathbf{k} = (2e + 3)\mathbf{j}$$

Now we find the cross product of the limits.

$$\lim_{t\to 1} \mathbf{F}(t) = \left[\lim_{t\to 1} t\right]\mathbf{i} + \left[\lim_{t\to 1}(1-t)\right]\mathbf{j} + \left[\lim_{t\to 1} t^2\right]\mathbf{k} = \mathbf{i} + \mathbf{k}$$

$$\lim_{t\to 1} \mathbf{G}(t) = \left[\lim_{t\to 1} e^t\right]\mathbf{i} + \left[\lim_{t\to 1}(-3 - e^t)\right]\mathbf{k} = e\mathbf{i} + (-3 - e)\mathbf{k}$$

Thus,

$$\left[\lim_{t\to 1} \mathbf{F}(t)\right] \times \left[\lim_{t\to 1} \mathbf{G}(t)\right] = \begin{vmatrix} \mathbf{i} & \mathbf{j} & \mathbf{k} \\ 1 & 0 & 1 \\ e & 0 & -3-e \end{vmatrix}$$

$$= (0 - 0)\mathbf{i} - (-3 - e - e)\mathbf{j} + (0 - 0)\mathbf{k} = (3 + 2e)\mathbf{j}$$

We see $\lim_{t\to 1}[\mathbf{F}(t) \times \mathbf{G}(t)] = \left[\lim_{t\to 1} \mathbf{F}(t)\right] \times \left[\lim_{t\to 1} \mathbf{G}(t)\right]$. ∎

Continuity of a Vector Function

> A vector function $\mathbf{F}(t)$ is said to be **continuous** at t_0 if t_0 is in the domain of $\mathbf{F}$ and $\lim_{t\to t_0} \mathbf{F}(t) = \mathbf{F}(t_0)$.

> ➡ **What This Says** This is the same as requiring each component of $\mathbf{F}(t)$ to be continuous at t_0. That is,
>
> $$\mathbf{F}(t) = f_1(t)\mathbf{i} + f_2(t)\mathbf{j} + f_3(t)\mathbf{k}$$
>
> is continuous at t_0 when t_0 is in the domain of the component functions $f_1(t)$, $f_2(t)$, and $f_3(t)$ and
>
> $$\lim_{t\to t_0} f_1(t) = f_1(t_0) \qquad \lim_{t\to t_0} f_2(t) = f_2(t_0) \qquad \lim_{t\to t_0} f_3(t) = f_3(t_0)$$

The rules for vector limits listed in Theorem 10.1 can be used to derive general properties of vector function continuity.

EXAMPLE 7   Continuity of a vector function

For what values of t is $\mathbf{F}(t) = (\sin t)\mathbf{i} + (1-t)^{-1}\mathbf{j} + (\ln t)\mathbf{k}$ continuous?

Solution

The vector function $\mathbf{F}$ is continuous where its component functions

$$f_1(t) = \sin t \qquad f_2(t) = (1-t)^{-1} \qquad f_3(t) = \ln t$$

are continuous. The function f_1 is continuous for all t; f_2 is continuous whenever $1 - t \neq 0$ (that is, when $t \neq 1$); f_3 is continuous for $t > 0$. Thus, $\mathbf{F}$ is continuous when t is a positive number other than 1; that is, $t > 0$, $t \neq 1$. ∎

10.1   PROBLEM SET

Ⓐ *Find the domain of the vector functions given in Problems 1–8.*

1. $\mathbf{F}(t) = 2t\mathbf{i} - 3t\mathbf{j} + \dfrac{1}{t}\mathbf{k}$

2. $\mathbf{F}(t) = (1 - t)\mathbf{i} + \sqrt{t}\,\mathbf{j} - \dfrac{1}{t - 2}\mathbf{k}$

3. $\mathbf{F}(t) = (\sin t)\mathbf{i} + (\cos t)\mathbf{j} + (\tan t)\mathbf{k}$

4. $\mathbf{F}(t) = (\cos t)\mathbf{i} - (\cot t)\mathbf{j} + (\csc t)\mathbf{k}$

5. $h(t)\mathbf{F}(t)$, where $h(t) = \sin t$ and

$$\mathbf{F}(t) = \frac{1}{\cos t}\mathbf{i} + \frac{1}{\sin t}\mathbf{j} + \frac{1}{\tan t}\mathbf{k}$$

6. $\mathbf{F}(t) + \mathbf{G}(t)$, where $\mathbf{F}(t) = 3t\mathbf{j} + t^{-1}\mathbf{k}$ and
$\mathbf{G}(t) = 5t\mathbf{i} + \sqrt{10 - t}\,\mathbf{j}$

7. $\mathbf{F}(t) - \mathbf{G}(t)$, where $\mathbf{F}(t) = (\ln t)\mathbf{i} + 3t\mathbf{j} - t^2\mathbf{k}$ and
$\mathbf{G}(t) = \mathbf{i} + 5t\mathbf{j} - t^2\mathbf{k}$

8. $\mathbf{F}(t) \times \mathbf{G}(t)$ where $\mathbf{F}(t) = t^2\mathbf{i} - t\mathbf{j} + 2t\mathbf{k}$ and
$\mathbf{G}(t) = \dfrac{1}{t + 2}\mathbf{i} + (t + 4)\mathbf{j} - \sqrt{-t}\,\mathbf{k}$

Describe the graph of the vector functions given in Problems 9–20 or sketch a graph in $\mathbb{R}^3$. A graph in $\mathbb{R}^2$ may help with your description.

9. $\mathbf{F}(t) = 2t\mathbf{i} + t^2\mathbf{j}$ **10.** $\mathbf{G}(t) = (1 - t)\mathbf{i} + \dfrac{1}{t}\mathbf{j}$

11. $\mathbf{G}(t) = (\sin t)\mathbf{i} - (\cos t)\mathbf{j}$ **12.** $\mathbf{F}(t) = (2\cos t)\mathbf{i} + (\sin t)\mathbf{j}$

13. $\mathbf{F}(t) = t\mathbf{i} - 4\mathbf{k}$ **14.** $\mathbf{G}(t) = e^t\mathbf{j} + t\mathbf{k}$

15. $\mathbf{F}(t) = (\cos t)\mathbf{i} + (\sin t)\mathbf{j} + t\mathbf{k}$

16. $\mathbf{F}(t) = e^t\mathbf{i} + e^t\mathbf{j} + e^{-t}\mathbf{k}$

17. $\mathbf{G}(t) = (1 - t)\mathbf{i} + t^2\mathbf{j} + t\mathbf{k}$

18. $\mathbf{F}(t) = \left(\dfrac{\sqrt{2}}{2}\sin t\right)\mathbf{i} + \left(\dfrac{\sqrt{2}}{2}\sin t\right)\mathbf{j} + (\cos^2 t)\mathbf{k}$

19. $\mathbf{F}(t) = t\mathbf{i} + (t^2 + 1)\mathbf{j} + t^2\mathbf{k}$

20. $\mathbf{G}(t) = (2\sin t)\mathbf{i} + (2\cos t)\mathbf{j} + 3\mathbf{k}$

Perform the operations indicated in Problems 21–32 with

$$\mathbf{F}(t) = 2t\mathbf{i} - 5\mathbf{j} + t^2\mathbf{k},$$

$$\mathbf{G}(t) = (1 - t)\mathbf{i} + \frac{1}{t}\mathbf{k},$$

$$\mathbf{H}(t) = (\sin t)\mathbf{i} + e^t\mathbf{j}$$

21. $2\mathbf{F}(t) - 3\mathbf{G}(t)$ **22.** $t^2\mathbf{F}(t) - 3\mathbf{H}(t)$

23. $\mathbf{F}(t) \cdot \mathbf{G}(t)$ **24.** $\mathbf{F}(t) \cdot \mathbf{H}(t)$

25. $\mathbf{G}(t) \cdot \mathbf{H}(t)$ **26.** $\mathbf{F}(t) \times \mathbf{G}(t)$

27. $\mathbf{F}(t) \times \mathbf{H}(t)$ **28.** $\mathbf{G}(t) \times \mathbf{H}(t)$

29. $2e^t\mathbf{F}(t) + t\mathbf{G}(t) + 10\mathbf{H}(t)$ **30.** $\mathbf{F}(t) \cdot [\mathbf{H}(t) \times \mathbf{G}(t)]$

31. $\mathbf{G}(t) \cdot [\mathbf{H}(t) \times \mathbf{F}(t)]$ **32.** $\mathbf{H}(t) \cdot [\mathbf{G}(t) \times \mathbf{F}(t)]$

Ⓑ **33. WHAT DOES THIS SAY?** Discuss the concept of a vector-valued function.

34. WHAT DOES THIS SAY? Discuss the concept of the limit of a vector-valued function.

35. Show that the curve given by
$\mathbf{R}(t) = (2\sin t)\mathbf{i} + (2\sin t)\mathbf{j} + (\sqrt{8}\cos t)\mathbf{k}$
lies on a sphere centered at the origin.

36. Sketch the graph of the curve given by
$\mathbf{R}(t) = (2\cos t)\mathbf{i} + (\sin t)\mathbf{j} - 2t\mathbf{k}$.

Find a vector function $\mathbf{F}$ whose graph is the curve given in Problems 37–42.

37. $y = x^2$; $z = 2$

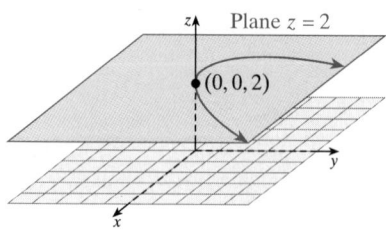

38. $x^2 + y^2 = 4$; $z = -1$

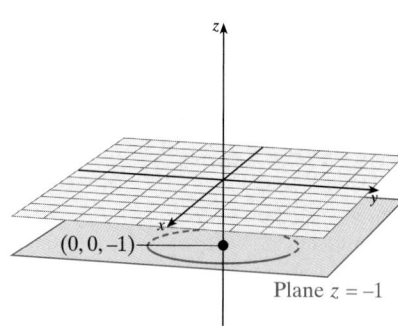

39. $x = 2t$, $y = 1 - t$, $z = \sin t$

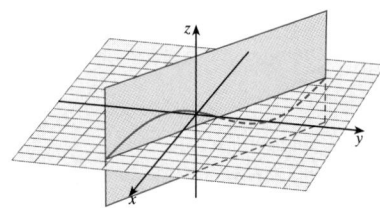

40. $\dfrac{x - 2}{3} = \dfrac{y - 1}{2} = \dfrac{z}{4}$

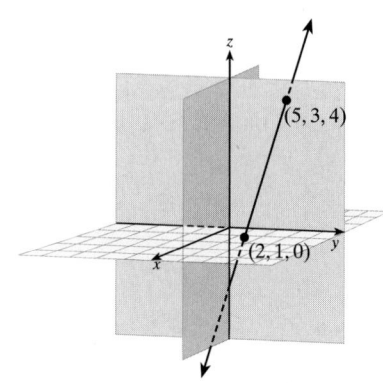

41. The curve of intersection of the hemisphere $z = \sqrt{9 - x^2 - y^2}$ and the parabolic cylinder $x = y^2$

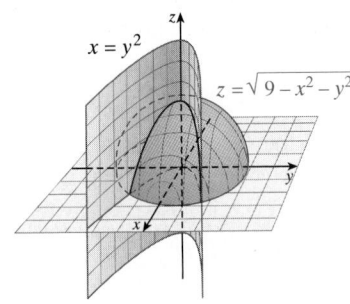

42. The line of intersection of the planes $2x + y + 3z = 6$ and $x - y - z = 1$

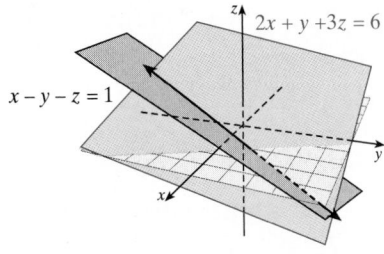

43. Which of the following curves lies on the surface $z = x^2 + y^2$?

a. $x = \sin t, \ y = \cos t, \ z = t$

b. $x = e^{-t} \cos t, \ y = e^{-t} \sin t, \ z = e^{-2t}$

c. $x = 1 + \dfrac{1}{t}, \ y = 1 - \dfrac{1}{t}, \ z = 2 + \dfrac{2}{t^2}$

44. Find parametric equations for the curve of intersection of the elliptical cylinder $x^2 + 3y^2 = 1$ and the parabolic cylinder $z = 2x^2 - 1$.

Find each limit indicated in Problems 45–52.

45. $\lim\limits_{t \to 1} \left[2t\mathbf{i} - 3\mathbf{j} + e^t\mathbf{k} \right]$

46. $\lim\limits_{t \to 1} [3t\mathbf{i} + e^{2t}\mathbf{j} + (\sin \pi t)\mathbf{k}]$

47. $\lim\limits_{t \to 0} \left[\dfrac{(\sin t)\mathbf{i} - t\mathbf{k}}{t^2 + t - 1} \right]$

48. $\lim\limits_{t \to 1} \left[\dfrac{t^3 - 1}{t - 1}\mathbf{i} + \dfrac{t^2 - 3t + 2}{t^2 + t - 2}\mathbf{j} + (t^2 + 1)e^{t-1}\mathbf{k} \right]$

49. $\lim\limits_{t \to 0} \left[\dfrac{te^t}{1 - e^t}\mathbf{i} + \dfrac{e^{t-1}}{\cos t}\mathbf{j} \right]$

50. $\lim\limits_{t \to 0} \left[\dfrac{\sin t}{t}\mathbf{i} + \dfrac{1 - \cos t}{t}\mathbf{j} + e^{1-t}\mathbf{k} \right]$

51. $\lim\limits_{t \to 0^+} \left[\dfrac{\sin 3t}{\sin 2t}\mathbf{i} + \dfrac{\ln(\sin t)}{\ln(\tan t)}\mathbf{j} + (t \ln t)\mathbf{k} \right]$

52. $\lim\limits_{t \to 2} \left[(2\mathbf{i} - t\mathbf{j} + e^t\mathbf{k}) \times (t^2\mathbf{i} + 4 \sin t\mathbf{j}) \right]$

Determine all values of t for which the vector function given in Problems 53–58 is continuous.

53. $\mathbf{F}(t) = t\mathbf{i} + 3\mathbf{j} - (1 - t)\mathbf{k}$ **54.** $\mathbf{G}(t) = t\mathbf{i} - \dfrac{1}{t}\mathbf{k}$

55. $\mathbf{G}(t) = \dfrac{\mathbf{i} + 2\mathbf{j}}{t^2 + t}$

56. $\mathbf{F}(t) = (e^t \sin t)\mathbf{i} + (e^t \cos t)\mathbf{k}$

57. $\mathbf{F}(t) = e^t \left[t\mathbf{i} + \dfrac{1}{t}\mathbf{j} + 3\mathbf{k} \right]$

58. $\mathbf{G}(t) = \dfrac{\mathbf{u}}{\|\mathbf{u}\|}$, where $\mathbf{u} = t\mathbf{i} + \sqrt{t}\,\mathbf{j}$

59. The graph of

$$\mathbf{R}(t) = t\mathbf{i} + \left(\frac{1 - t}{t} \right)\mathbf{j} + \left(\frac{1 - t^2}{t} \right)\mathbf{k}$$

lies in a plane. What is the equation of this plane?

60. How many revolutions are made by the circular helix

$$\mathbf{R}(t) = (2 \sin t)\mathbf{i} + (2 \cos t)\mathbf{j} + \tfrac{5}{8}t\mathbf{k}$$

in a vertical distance of 8 units?

61. Given the vector functions $\mathbf{F}(t) = t\mathbf{i} + t^2\mathbf{j} + t^3\mathbf{k}$ and $\mathbf{G}(t) = \frac{1}{t}\mathbf{i} - e^t\mathbf{j}$, directly verify each of the following limit formulas (that is, without using Theorem 10.1).

a. $\lim\limits_{t \to 0} e^t \mathbf{F}(t) = \left[\lim\limits_{t \to 0} e^t \right]\left[\lim\limits_{t \to 0} \mathbf{F}(t) \right]$

b. $\lim\limits_{t \to 1} \mathbf{F}(t) \cdot \mathbf{G}(t) = \left[\lim\limits_{t \to 1} \mathbf{F}(t) \right] \cdot \left[\lim\limits_{t \to 1} \mathbf{G}(t) \right]$

c. $\lim\limits_{t \to 1} [\mathbf{F}(t) \times \mathbf{G}(t)] = \left[\lim\limits_{t \to 1} \mathbf{F}(t) \right] \times \left[\lim\limits_{t \to 1} \mathbf{G}(t) \right]$

Ⓒ 62. If $\mathbf{H}(t)$ is a vector function, we define the **difference operator** $\Delta\mathbf{H}$ by the formula

$$\Delta\mathbf{H} = \mathbf{H}(t + \Delta t) - \mathbf{H}(t)$$

where Δt is a change in the parameter t. (*Note:* Usually, $|\Delta t|$ is a small number.) If $\mathbf{F}(t)$ and $\mathbf{G}(t)$ are vector functions, show that $\Delta(\mathbf{F} \times \mathbf{G})(t) = \mathbf{F}(t + \Delta t) \times \Delta\mathbf{G}(t) + \Delta\mathbf{F}(t) \times \mathbf{G}(t)$. *Hint:* Observe that

$$\Delta(\mathbf{F} \times \mathbf{G})(t) = \mathbf{F}(t + \Delta t) \times \mathbf{G}(t + \Delta t)$$
$$- \mathbf{F}(t + \Delta t) \times \mathbf{G}(t) + \mathbf{F}(t + \Delta t) \times \mathbf{G}(t)$$
$$- \mathbf{F}(t) \times \mathbf{G}(t)$$

63. Prove the limit of a sum rule of Theorem 10.1. (The difference rule is proved similarly.)

64. a. Prove the limit of a scalar multiple rule of Theorem 10.1.

b. Prove the limit of a cross product rule of Theorem 10.1.

65. Counterexample Problem Let $\mathbf{F}(t)$ and $\mathbf{G}(t)$ be vector functions that are continuous at t_0, and let $h(t)$ be a scalar function continuous at t_0. In each of the following cases, either show that the given function is continuous at t_0 or provide a counterexample to show that it is not continuous.

a. $3\mathbf{F}(t) + 5\mathbf{G}(t)$ **b.** $\mathbf{F}(t) \cdot \mathbf{G}(t)$

c. $(h(t))^{-1}\mathbf{F}(t)$ **d.** $\mathbf{F}(t) \times \mathbf{G}(t)$

66. Counterexample Problem Find a vector function $\mathbf{F}(t) = \langle f_1(t), f_2(t), f_3(t) \rangle$ such that $\|\mathbf{F}(t)\|$ is continuous at $t = 0$ but $\mathbf{F}(t)$ is not continuous at $t = 0$.

10.2 Differentiation and Integration of Vector Functions

IN THIS SECTION vector derivatives, tangent vectors, properties of vector derivatives, modeling the motion of an object in $\mathbb{R}^3$, vector integrals

VECTOR DERIVATIVES

In Chapter 3, we defined the derivative of the (scalar) function f to be the limit as $\Delta x \to 0$ of the difference quotient $\Delta f / \Delta x$. The **difference quotient of a vector function F** is the vector expression

$$\frac{\Delta \mathbf{F}}{\Delta t} = \frac{\mathbf{F}(t + \Delta t) - \mathbf{F}(t)}{\Delta t}$$

and we define the derivative of $\mathbf{F}$ as follows.

Derivative of a Vector Function

The **derivative** of the vector function $\mathbf{F}$ is the vector function $\mathbf{F}'$ determined by the limit

$$\mathbf{F}'(t) = \lim_{\Delta t \to 0} \frac{\Delta \mathbf{F}}{\Delta t} = \lim_{\Delta t \to 0} \frac{\mathbf{F}(t + \Delta t) - \mathbf{F}(t)}{\Delta t}$$

wherever this limit exists. In the Leibniz notation, the derivative of $\mathbf{F}$ is denoted by $\dfrac{d\mathbf{F}}{dt}$. We say that the vector function $\mathbf{F}$ is **differentiable** at $t = t_0$ if $\mathbf{F}'(t)$ is defined at t_0.

The following theorem establishes a convenient method for computing the derivative of a vector function.

THEOREM 10.2 Derivative of a vector function

The vector function $\mathbf{F}(t) = f_1(t)\mathbf{i} + f_2(t)\mathbf{j} + f_3(t)\mathbf{k}$ is differentiable whenever the component functions f_1, f_2, and f_3 are each differentiable, and in this case

$$\mathbf{F}'(t) = f_1'(t)\mathbf{i} + f_2'(t)\mathbf{j} + f_3'(t)\mathbf{k}$$

Proof We use the definition of the derivative, along with rules of vector limits (Theorem 10.1), and the fact that the scalar derivatives $f_1'(t)$, $f_2'(t)$, and $f_3'(t)$ all exist.

$$\mathbf{F}'(t) = \lim_{\Delta t \to 0} \frac{\mathbf{F}(t + \Delta t) - \mathbf{F}(t)}{\Delta t}$$

$$= \lim_{\Delta t \to 0} \frac{[f_1(t + \Delta t)\mathbf{i} + f_2(t + \Delta t)\mathbf{j} + f_3(t + \Delta t)\mathbf{k}] - [f_1(t)\mathbf{i} + f_2(t)\mathbf{j} + f_3(t)\mathbf{k}]}{\Delta t}$$

$$= \left[\lim_{\Delta t \to 0} \frac{f_1(t + \Delta t) - f_1(t)}{\Delta t} \right]\mathbf{i} + \left[\lim_{\Delta t \to 0} \frac{f_2(t + \Delta t) - f_2(t)}{\Delta t} \right]\mathbf{j} + \left[\lim_{\Delta t \to 0} \frac{f_3(t + \Delta t) - f_3(t)}{\Delta t} \right]\mathbf{k}$$

$$= f_1'(t)\mathbf{i} + f_2'(t)\mathbf{j} + f_3'(t)\mathbf{k} \qquad \square$$

EXAMPLE 1 Differentiability of a vector function

For what values of t is $\mathbf{G}(t) = |t|\,\mathbf{i} + (\cos t)\mathbf{j} + (t - 5)\mathbf{k}$ differentiable?

Solution

The component functions $\cos t$ and $t - 5$ are differentiable for all t, but $|t|$ is not differentiable at $t = 0$. Thus, the vector function $\mathbf{G}$ is differentiable for all $t \neq 0$. ∎

EXAMPLE 2 **Derivative of a vector function**

Find the derivative of the vector function

$$\mathbf{F}(t) = e^t\mathbf{i} + (\sin t)\mathbf{j} + (t^3 + 5t)\mathbf{k}$$

Solution

Differentiating each component separately, we find that

$$\mathbf{F}'(t) = (e^t)'\mathbf{i} + (\sin t)'\mathbf{j} + (t^3 + 5t)'\mathbf{k} = e^t\mathbf{i} + (\cos t)\mathbf{j} + (3t^2 + 5)\mathbf{k} \qquad \blacksquare$$

TANGENT VECTORS

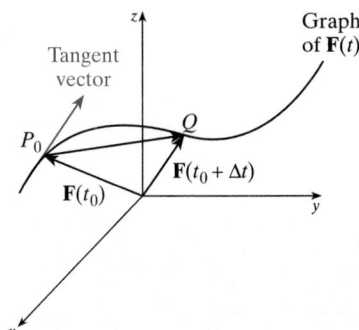

Figure 10.7 The difference quotient is a multiple of the secant line vector.

Recall that the scalar derivative $f'(x_0)$ gives the slope of the tangent line to the graph of f at the point where $x = x_0$ and thus provides a measure of the graph's direction at that point. Our first goal is to extend this interpretation by showing how the vector derivative can be used to find tangent vectors to curves in space. Let t be a number in the domain of the vector function $\mathbf{F}(t)$, and let P_0 be the point on the graph of $\mathbf{F}$ that corresponds to t_0, as shown in Figure 10.7. Then for any positive number Δt, the difference quotient

$$\frac{\Delta\mathbf{F}}{\Delta t} = \frac{\mathbf{F}(t_0 + \Delta t) - \mathbf{F}(t_0)}{\Delta t}$$

is a vector that points in the same direction as the secant vector

$$\mathbf{P_0Q} = \mathbf{F}(t_0 + \Delta t) - \mathbf{F}(t_0),$$

where Q is the point on the graph of $\mathbf{F}$ that corresponds to $t = t_0 + \Delta t$ (see Figure 10.7). If we choose $\Delta t < 0$, the difference quotient $\Delta\mathbf{F}/\Delta t$ points in the *opposite* direction to that of the secant vector $\mathbf{P_0Q}$.

Suppose the difference quotient $\Delta\mathbf{F}/\Delta t$ has a limit as $\Delta t \to 0$ and that

$$\lim_{\Delta t \to 0} \frac{\Delta\mathbf{F}}{\Delta t} \neq \mathbf{0}$$

Then, as $\Delta t \to 0$, the direction of the secant vector, $\mathbf{P_0Q}$, and hence that of the difference quotient $\Delta\mathbf{F}/\Delta t$, will approach the direction of the tangent vector at P_0, as shown in Figure 10.8. Thus, we expect the tangent vector at P_0 to be the limit vector

$$\lim_{\Delta t \to 0} \frac{\Delta\mathbf{F}}{\Delta t}$$

Figure 10.8 As $\Delta t \to 0$, the vector $\mathbf{P_0Q}$ and hence the difference quotient $\Delta\mathbf{F}/\Delta t$ approaches the tangent vector at P_0.

which we recognize as the vector derivative $\mathbf{F}'(t_0)$. These observations lead to the following interpretation.

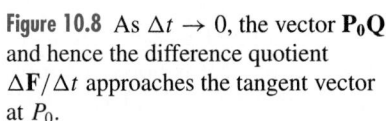

Tangent Vector

> Suppose $\mathbf{F}(t)$ is differentiable at t_0 and that $\mathbf{F}'(t_0) \neq 0$. Then $\mathbf{F}'(t_0)$ is a **tangent vector** to the graph of $\mathbf{F}(t)$ at the point where $t = t_0$ and points in the direction of increasing t.

EXAMPLE 3 **Finding a tangent vector**

Find a tangent vector at the point P_0 where $t = 0.2$ on the graph of the vector function

$$\mathbf{F}(t) = e^{2t}\mathbf{i} + (t^2 - t)\mathbf{j} + (\ln t)\mathbf{k}$$

What is an equation for the tangent line at P_0?

Solution

The derivative of $\mathbf{F}(t)$ is

$$\mathbf{F}'(t) = 2e^{2t}\mathbf{i} + (2t-1)\mathbf{j} + t^{-1}\mathbf{k}$$

so a tangent vector at the point where $t = 0.2$ is

$$\mathbf{F}'(0.2) = 2e^{0.4}\mathbf{i} - 0.6\mathbf{j} + 5\mathbf{k}$$

The tangent line to the graph of $\mathbf{F}(t)$ at P_0 is the line that passes through P_0 and is parallel to the vector $\mathbf{F}(0.2)$. Since

$$\mathbf{F}(0.2) = e^{0.4}\mathbf{i} - 0.16\mathbf{j} + (\ln 0.2)\mathbf{k}$$

the point of tangency is $(e^{0.4}, -0.16, \ln 0.2)$. Thus, the tangent line has parametric equations

$$x = e^{0.4} + 2e^{0.4}t, \qquad y = -0.16 - 0.6t, \qquad z = \ln 0.2 + 5t \qquad \blacksquare$$

If $\mathbf{F}'(t_0) \neq \mathbf{0}$ and we also require the derivative $\mathbf{F}'$ to be continuous at t_0, then the tangent vector at each point of the graph of $\mathbf{F}$ near P_0 will be close to the tangent vector at P_0. In this case, the graph is said to be *smooth* at P_0.

Smooth Curve

> The graph of the vector function defined by $\mathbf{F}(t)$ is **smooth** on any interval of t where $\mathbf{F}'$ is continuous and $\mathbf{F}'(t) \neq \mathbf{0}$. The graph is **piecewise smooth** on an interval that can be subdivided into a finite number of subintervals on which $\mathbf{F}$ is smooth.

EXAMPLE 4   Determining whether a curve is smooth

Determine whether the graph of the vector function

$$\mathbf{F}(t) = \langle t^2 + 1, \cos t, e^t + e^{-t} \rangle$$

is smooth for all t.

Solution

The derivative

$$\mathbf{F}'(t) = \langle 2t, -\sin t, e^t - e^{-t} \rangle$$

is continuous for all t, but $\mathbf{F}'(0) = \langle 0, 0, 1 - 1 \rangle = \mathbf{0}$. Thus, the graph is not smooth for all t, but it is smooth on any interval not containing $t = 0$. $\qquad \blacksquare$

A graph will not be smooth on any interval containing a point where there is an abrupt change in direction. For example, the graph in Figure 10.9 is not smooth on any interval containing the point corresponding to the sharp corner P_0. In Example 4, such a point occurs when $t = 0$, namely $P_0(1, 1, 2)$. However, this curve is piecewise smooth because it consists of a finite number of smooth pieces.

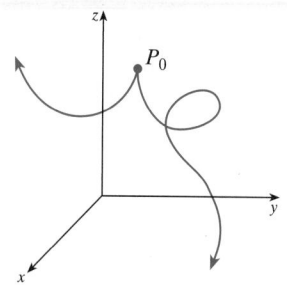

Figure 10.9 A curve that is not smooth

PROPERTIES OF VECTOR DERIVATIVES

Higher-order derivatives of a vector function $\mathbf{F}$ are obtained by successively differentiating the components of $\mathbf{F}(t) = f_1(t)\mathbf{i} + f_2(t)\mathbf{j} + f_3(t)\mathbf{k}$. For instance, the **second derivative** of $\mathbf{F}$ is the vector function

$$\mathbf{F}''(t) = [\mathbf{F}'(t)]' = f_1''(t)\mathbf{i} + f_2''(t)\mathbf{j} + f_3''(t)\mathbf{k}$$

whereas the **third derivative** $\mathbf{F}'''(t)$ is the derivative of $\mathbf{F}''(t)$, and so on. In the Leibniz notation, the second vector derivative of $\mathbf{F}$ with respect to t is denoted by $\dfrac{d^2\mathbf{F}}{dt^2}$, and the third derivative, by $\dfrac{d^3\mathbf{F}}{dt^3}$.

EXAMPLE 5 **Higher-order derivatives of a vector function**

Find the second and third derivatives of the vector function

$$\mathbf{F}(t) = e^{2t}\mathbf{i} + (1 - t^2)\mathbf{j} + (\cos 2t)\mathbf{k}$$

Solution

$$\mathbf{F}'(t) = 2e^{2t}\mathbf{i} + (-2t)\mathbf{j} + (-2\sin 2t)\mathbf{k}$$
$$\mathbf{F}''(t) = 4e^{2t}\mathbf{i} - 2\mathbf{j} - (4\cos 2t)\mathbf{k}$$
$$\mathbf{F}'''(t) = 8e^{2t}\mathbf{i} + (8\sin 2t)\mathbf{k}$$

■

Several rules for computing derivatives of vector functions are listed in the following theorem.

THEOREM 10.3 **Rules for differentiating vector functions**

If the vector functions **F** and **G** and the scalar function h are differentiable at t, and if a and b are constants, then $a\mathbf{F} + b\mathbf{G}$, $h\mathbf{F}$, $\mathbf{F} \cdot \mathbf{G}$, and $\mathbf{F} \times \mathbf{G}$ are also differentiable at t, and

Linearity rule	$(a\mathbf{F} + b\mathbf{G})'(t) = a\mathbf{F}'(t) + b\mathbf{G}'(t)$
Scalar multiple rule	$(h\mathbf{F})'(t) = h'(t)\mathbf{F}(t) + h(t)\mathbf{F}'(t)$
Dot product rule	$(\mathbf{F} \cdot \mathbf{G})'(t) = (\mathbf{F}' \cdot \mathbf{G})(t) + (\mathbf{F} \cdot \mathbf{G}')(t)$
Cross product rule	$(\mathbf{F} \times \mathbf{G})'(t) = (\mathbf{F}' \times \mathbf{G})(t) + (\mathbf{F} \times \mathbf{G}')(t)$
Chain rule	$[\mathbf{F}(h(t))]' = h'(t)\mathbf{F}'(h(t))$

WARNING The order of the factors is important in the cross product rule, because the cross product of vectors is not commutative.

Proof We will prove the linearity rule and leave the rest of the proof as exercises. Note that if **F** and **G** are vector functions differentiable at t, and a and b are constants, then the linear combination $a\mathbf{F} + b\mathbf{G}$ has the difference quotient

$$\frac{\Delta(a\mathbf{F} + b\mathbf{G})}{\Delta t} = \frac{a\Delta\mathbf{F}}{\Delta t} + \frac{b\Delta\mathbf{G}}{\Delta t}$$

We can now find the derivative:

$$(a\mathbf{F} + b\mathbf{G})'(t) = \lim_{\Delta t \to 0} \left[\frac{\Delta(a\mathbf{F} + b\mathbf{G})}{\Delta t} \right]$$
$$= \lim_{\Delta t \to 0} \left[\frac{a\Delta\mathbf{F}}{\Delta t} + \frac{b\Delta\mathbf{G}}{\Delta t} \right]$$
$$= a \lim_{\Delta t \to 0} \frac{\Delta\mathbf{F}}{\Delta t} + b \lim_{\Delta t \to 0} \frac{\Delta\mathbf{G}}{\Delta t}$$
$$= a\mathbf{F}'(t) + b\mathbf{G}'(t)$$

❑

EXAMPLE 6 **Derivative of a cross product**

Let $\mathbf{F}(t) = \mathbf{i} + t\mathbf{j} + t^2\mathbf{k}$ and $\mathbf{G}(t) = t\mathbf{i} + e^t\mathbf{j} + 3\mathbf{k}$. Verify that

$$(\mathbf{F} \times \mathbf{G})'(t) = (\mathbf{F}' \times \mathbf{G})(t) + (\mathbf{F} \times \mathbf{G}')(t)$$

Solution

First find the derivative of the cross product:

$$(\mathbf{F} \times \mathbf{G})(t) = \begin{vmatrix} \mathbf{i} & \mathbf{j} & \mathbf{k} \\ 1 & t & t^2 \\ t & e^t & 3 \end{vmatrix} = (3t - t^2 e^t)\mathbf{i} - (3 - t^3)\mathbf{j} + (e^t - t^2)\mathbf{k}$$

so that $(\mathbf{F} \times \mathbf{G})'(t) = (3 - 2te^t - t^2 e^t)\mathbf{i} + (3t^2)\mathbf{j} + (e^t - 2t)\mathbf{k}$.

Next, find $(\mathbf{F}' \times \mathbf{G})(t) + (\mathbf{F} \times \mathbf{G}')(t)$ by first finding the derivatives of $\mathbf{F}$ and $\mathbf{G}$ and then the appropriate cross products.

$$\mathbf{F}'(t) = \mathbf{j} + 2t\mathbf{k} \qquad \text{and} \qquad \mathbf{G}'(t) = \mathbf{i} + e^t\mathbf{j}$$

$$(\mathbf{F}' \times \mathbf{G})(t) = \begin{vmatrix} \mathbf{i} & \mathbf{j} & \mathbf{k} \\ 0 & 1 & 2t \\ t & e^t & 3 \end{vmatrix} = (3 - 2te^t)\mathbf{i} - (-2t^2)\mathbf{j} + (-t)\mathbf{k}$$

$$(\mathbf{F} \times \mathbf{G}')(t) = \begin{vmatrix} \mathbf{i} & \mathbf{j} & \mathbf{k} \\ 1 & t & t^2 \\ 1 & e^t & 0 \end{vmatrix} = (-t^2 e^t)\mathbf{i} - (-t^2)\mathbf{j} + (e^t - t)\mathbf{k}$$

Finally, add these vector functions:

$$(\mathbf{F}' \times \mathbf{G})(t) + (\mathbf{F} \times \mathbf{G}')(t) = [(3 - 2te^t) - t^2 e^t]\mathbf{i} + [2t^2 + t^2]\mathbf{j} + [-t + e^t - t]\mathbf{k}$$
$$= (3 - 2te^t - t^2 e^t)\mathbf{i} + (3t^2)\mathbf{j} + (e^t - 2t)\mathbf{k}$$

Thus, $(\mathbf{F} \times \mathbf{G})' = (\mathbf{F}' \times \mathbf{G}) + (\mathbf{F} \times \mathbf{G}')$. ∎

EXAMPLE 7   Derivatives of vector function expressions

Let $\mathbf{F}(t) = \mathbf{i} + e^t\mathbf{j} + t^2\mathbf{k}$ and $\mathbf{G}(t) = 3t^2\mathbf{i} + e^{-t}\mathbf{j} - 2t\mathbf{k}$. Find

a. $\dfrac{d}{dt}[2\mathbf{F}(t) + t^3\mathbf{G}(t)]$ **b.** $\dfrac{d}{dt}[\mathbf{F}(t) \cdot \mathbf{G}(t)]$

Solution

Begin by finding $\dfrac{d\mathbf{F}}{dt}$ and $\dfrac{d\mathbf{G}}{dt}$:

$$\frac{d\mathbf{F}}{dt} = e^t\mathbf{j} + 2t\mathbf{k} \quad \text{and} \quad \frac{d\mathbf{G}}{dt} = 6t\mathbf{i} - e^{-t}\mathbf{j} - 2\mathbf{k}$$

a. $\dfrac{d}{dt}[2\mathbf{F}(t) + t^3\mathbf{G}(t)] = 2\dfrac{d\mathbf{F}}{dt} + \left[t^3\dfrac{d\mathbf{G}}{dt} + \dfrac{d}{dt}(t^3)\mathbf{G}(t)\right]$

$= 2(e^t\mathbf{j} + 2t\mathbf{k}) + t^3(6t\mathbf{i} - e^{-t}\mathbf{j} - 2\mathbf{k}) + 3t^2(3t^2\mathbf{i} + e^{-t}\mathbf{j} - 2t\mathbf{k})$

$= (6t^4 + 9t^4)\mathbf{i} + (2e^t - t^3 e^{-t} + 3t^2 e^{-t})\mathbf{j} + (4t - 2t^3 - 6t^3)\mathbf{k}$

$= 15t^4\mathbf{i} + [2e^t + e^{-t}t^2(3 - t)]\mathbf{j} - 4t(2t^2 - 1)\mathbf{k}$

b. $\dfrac{d}{dt}[\mathbf{F}(t) \cdot \mathbf{G}(t)] = \dfrac{d\mathbf{F}}{dt} \cdot \mathbf{G}(t) + \mathbf{F}(t) \cdot \dfrac{d\mathbf{G}}{dt}$

$= (e^t\mathbf{j} + 2t\mathbf{k}) \cdot (3t^2\mathbf{i} + e^{-t}\mathbf{j} - 2t\mathbf{k}) + (\mathbf{i} + e^t\mathbf{j} + t^2\mathbf{k}) \cdot (6t\mathbf{i} - e^{-t}\mathbf{j} - 2\mathbf{k})$

$= [0(3t^2) + e^t(e^{-t}) + 2t(-2t)] + [1(6t) + e^t(-e^{-t}) + t^2(-2)]$

$= (1 - 4t^2) + (6t - 1 - 2t^2)$

$= -6t^2 + 6t$ ∎

We will use Theorem 10.3 in both applied and theoretical problems. In the following theorem, we establish an important geometric property of vector functions.

THEOREM 10.4   Orthogonality of a function of constant length and its derivative

If the nonzero vector function $\mathbf{F}(t)$ is differentiable and has constant length, then $\mathbf{F}(t)$ is orthogonal to the derivative vector $\mathbf{F}'(t)$.

Proof We are given that $\|\mathbf{F}(t)\| = r$ for some constant r and all t. To prove that $\mathbf{F}$ and $\mathbf{F}'$ are orthogonal, we will show that $\mathbf{F}(t) \cdot \mathbf{F}'(t) = 0$ for all t. First, note that

$$r^2 = \|\mathbf{F}(t)\|^2 = \mathbf{F}(t) \cdot \mathbf{F}(t)$$

for all t. We take the derivative of both sides (remember that the derivative of r^2 is zero because it is a constant).

$$[r^2]' = [\mathbf{F}(t) \cdot \mathbf{F}(t)]'$$
$$0 = \mathbf{F}'(t) \cdot \mathbf{F}(t) + \mathbf{F}(t) \cdot \mathbf{F}'(t)$$
$$0 = 2\mathbf{F}(t) \cdot \mathbf{F}'(t)$$
$$0 = \mathbf{F}(t) \cdot \mathbf{F}'(t)$$

Thus, $\mathbf{F}$ and $\mathbf{F}'$ are orthogonal. ❏

In plane geometry, it is shown that a tangent line to a circle is always perpendicular to the radial line from the center of a circle to the point of tangency. Theorem 10.4 can be used to extend this property to spheres in $\mathbb{R}^3$.

Suppose $\mathbf{R}(t) = \langle f(t), g(t), h(t) \rangle$ is a vector function whose graph lies entirely on the sphere $x^2 + y^2 + z^2 = r^2$ and let P_0 be the point on the graph that corresponds to $t = t_0$, as shown in Figure 10.10. Then $\mathbf{R}(t_0)$ is the vector from the center O to P_0, and $\mathbf{R}'(t_0)$ is a tangent vector to the graph of $\mathbf{R}(t)$ at P_0. Thus $\mathbf{R}'(t_0)$ is also tangent to the sphere at P_0, and since $\mathbf{R}(t)$ has constant length,

$$\|\mathbf{R}(t)\| = \sqrt{x^2(t) + y^2(t) + z^2(t)} = r \quad \text{for all } t$$

it follows from Theorem 10.4 that $\mathbf{R}$ is orthogonal to $\mathbf{R}'$. That is, the tangent vector $\mathbf{R}'(t_0)$ at P_0 is orthogonal to the vector $\mathbf{R}(t_0)$ from the center of the sphere to the point of tangency.

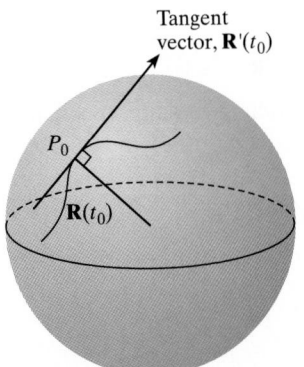

Figure 10.10 The tangent $\mathbf{R}'(t_0)$ at P_0 is orthogonal to the radius vector $\mathbf{R}(t_0)$ from the center of the sphere to P_0.

MODELING THE MOTION OF AN OBJECT IN $\mathbb{R}^3$

Recall from Chapter 3 that the derivative of an object's position with respect to time is the velocity, and the derivative of the velocity is the acceleration. We frequently know the acceleration and can use integration to find the velocity and the position. We will now express these concepts in terms of vector functions.

Vector Motion

An object that moves in such a way that its position at time t is given by the vector function $\mathbf{R}(t)$. Then

Velocity vector V is $\dfrac{d\mathbf{R}}{dt}$

Speed $\|\mathbf{V}\|$ is the magnitude of the velocity,

Direction of motion is the unit vector $\dfrac{\mathbf{V}}{\|\mathbf{V}\|}$

Acceleration vector is the derivative of the velocity:

$$\mathbf{A} = \frac{d\mathbf{V}}{dt} = \frac{d^2\mathbf{R}}{dt^2}$$

Figure 10.11 The velocity vector is tangent to the trajectory of the moving object

The graph of the position vector $\mathbf{R}(t)$ is called the **trajectory** of the moving object. According to the results obtained earlier in this section, the velocity $\mathbf{V}(t) = \mathbf{R}'(t)$ is a tangent vector to the trajectory at any point where $\mathbf{V}(t)$ exists and $\mathbf{V}(t) \neq \mathbf{0}$ (see Figure 10.11). When $\mathbf{V}(t) = \mathbf{0}$, the object is **stationary**. The *direction of motion* is given by the unit vector $\mathbf{V}/\|\mathbf{V}\|$, so the velocity satisfies

$$\mathbf{V} = \|\mathbf{V}\| \left(\frac{\mathbf{V}}{\|\mathbf{V}\|} \right) = (\text{SPEED})(\text{DIRECTION})$$

In practice, the position vector is often represented in the form

$$\mathbf{R}(t) = f_1(t)\mathbf{i} + f_2(t)\mathbf{j} + f_3(t)\mathbf{k}$$

and in this case, the velocity and the acceleration vectors are given by

$$\mathbf{V}(t) = \mathbf{R}'(t) = f_1'(t)\mathbf{i} + f_2'(t)\mathbf{j} + f_3'(t)\mathbf{k}$$

and

$$\mathbf{A}(t) = \mathbf{V}'(t) = \mathbf{R}''(t) = f_1''(t)\mathbf{i} + f_2''(t)\mathbf{j} + f_3''(t)\mathbf{k}$$

EXAMPLE 8   Speed and direction of a particle

A particle's position at time t is determined by the vector

$$\mathbf{R}(t) = (\cos t)\mathbf{i} + (\sin t)\mathbf{j} + t^3\mathbf{k}$$

Analyze the particle's motion. In particular, find the particle's velocity, speed, acceleration, and direction of motion at time $t = 2$.

Solution
$$\mathbf{V} = \frac{d\mathbf{R}}{dt} = (-\sin t)\mathbf{i} + (\cos t)\mathbf{j} + 3t^2\mathbf{k}$$

$$\mathbf{A} = \frac{d\mathbf{V}}{dt} = (-\cos t)\mathbf{i} - (\sin t)\mathbf{j} + 6t\mathbf{k}$$

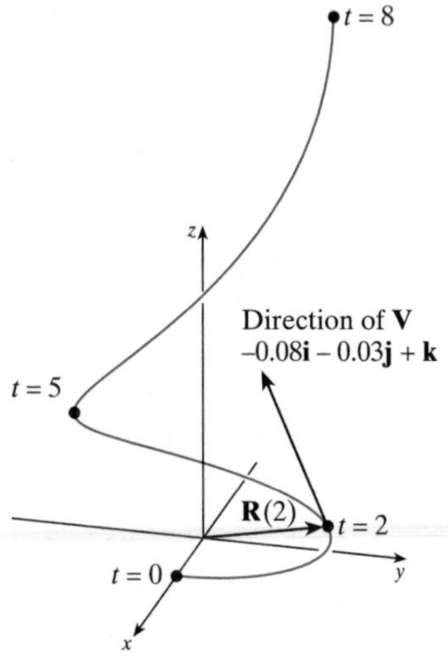

The velocity at time $t = 2$ is $\mathbf{V}(2)$:

$$(-\sin 2)\mathbf{i} + (\cos 2)\mathbf{j} + 3(2)^2\mathbf{k} \approx -0.91\mathbf{i} - 0.42\mathbf{j} + 12\mathbf{k}$$

The acceleration at $t = 2$ is

$$(-\cos 2)\mathbf{i} - (\sin 2)\mathbf{j} + 6(2)\mathbf{k} \approx 0.42\mathbf{i} - 0.91\mathbf{j} + 12\mathbf{k}$$

The speed is

$$\|\mathbf{V}\| = \sqrt{(-\sin t)^2 + (\cos t)^2 + (3t^2)^2}$$
$$= \sqrt{1 + 9t^4}$$

At time $t = 2$, the speed is $\|\mathbf{V}(2)\| = \sqrt{1 + 144} \approx 12.04$. The direction of motion is

$$\frac{\mathbf{V}}{\|\mathbf{V}\|} = \frac{1}{\sqrt{145}}[(-\sin t)\mathbf{i} + (\cos t)\mathbf{j} + 3t^2\mathbf{k}]$$

At time $t = 2$, the direction is $\mathbf{V}(2)/\|\mathbf{V}(2)\|$:

$$\frac{1}{\sqrt{145}}[(-\sin 2)\mathbf{i} + (\cos 2)\mathbf{j} + 12\mathbf{k}] \approx -0.08\mathbf{i} - 0.03\mathbf{j} + \mathbf{k}$$

The geometry of this example is shown in Figure 10.12. ∎

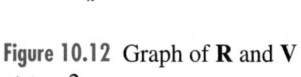

Figure 10.12 Graph of $\mathbf{R}$ and $\mathbf{V}$ at $t = 2$

VECTOR INTEGRALS

Like vector limits and derivatives, vector integration is performed in a componentwise fashion.

Vector Integrals

> Let $\mathbf{F}(t) = f_1(t)\mathbf{i} + f_2(t)\mathbf{j} + f_3(t)\mathbf{k}$, where f_1, f_2, and f_3 are continuous on the closed interval $a \leq t \leq b$. Then the **indefinite integral** of $\mathbf{F}(t)$ is the vector function
>
> $$\int \mathbf{F}(t)\, dt = \left[\int f_1(t)\, dt\right]\mathbf{i} + \left[\int f_2(t)\, dt\right]\mathbf{j} + \left[\int f_3(t)\, dt\right]\mathbf{k} + \mathbf{C}$$
>
> where $\mathbf{C} = C_1\mathbf{i} + C_2\mathbf{j} + C_3\mathbf{k}$ is an arbitrary constant vector. The **definite integral** of $\mathbf{F}(t)$ on $a \leq t \leq b$ is the vector
>
> $$\int_a^b \mathbf{F}(t)\, dt = \left[\int_a^b f_1(t)\, dt\right]\mathbf{i} + \left[\int_a^b f_2(t)\, dt\right]\mathbf{j} + \left[\int_a^b f_3(t)\, dt\right]\mathbf{k}$$

EXAMPLE 9 **Integral of a vector function**

Find $\int_0^\pi [t\mathbf{i} + 3\mathbf{j} - (\sin t)\mathbf{k}] \, dt$.

Solution

$$\int_0^\pi [t\mathbf{i} + 3\mathbf{j} - (\sin t)\mathbf{k}] \, dt = \left[\int_0^\pi t \, dt\right]\mathbf{i} + \left[\int_0^\pi 3 \, dt\right]\mathbf{j} - \left[\int_0^\pi \sin t \, dt\right]\mathbf{k}$$
$$= \left(\frac{t^2}{2}\right)\Big|_0^\pi \mathbf{i} + (3t)|_0^\pi \, \mathbf{j} - (-\cos t)|_0^\pi \, \mathbf{k}$$
$$= \tfrac{1}{2}\pi^2\mathbf{i} + 3\pi\mathbf{j} + (\cos\pi - \cos 0)]\mathbf{k}$$
$$= \tfrac{1}{2}\pi^2\mathbf{i} + 3\pi\mathbf{j} - 2\mathbf{k} \qquad\blacksquare$$

EXAMPLE 10 **Position of a particle given its velocity**

The velocity of a particle moving in space is

$$\mathbf{V}(t) = e^t\mathbf{i} + t^2\mathbf{j} + (\cos 2t)\mathbf{k}$$

Find the particle's position as a function of t if the position at time $t = 0$ is $\mathbf{R}(0) = 2\mathbf{i} + \mathbf{j} - \mathbf{k}$.

Solution

We need to solve the initial value problem that consists of

The differential equation $\mathbf{V}(t) = \dfrac{d\mathbf{R}}{dt} = e^t\mathbf{i} + t^2\mathbf{j} + (\cos 2t)\mathbf{k}$

The initial condition $\mathbf{R}(0) = 2\mathbf{i} + \mathbf{j} - \mathbf{k}$

We integrate both sides of the differential equation with respect to t:

$$\int d\mathbf{R} = \left[\int e^t \, dt\right]\mathbf{i} + \left[\int t^2 \, dt\right]\mathbf{j} + \left[\int \cos 2t \, dt\right]\mathbf{k}$$
$$\mathbf{R}(t) = (e^t + C_1)\mathbf{i} + \left(\tfrac{1}{3}t^3 + C_2\right)\mathbf{j} + \left(\tfrac{1}{2}\sin 2t + C_3\right)\mathbf{k}$$
$$= e^t\mathbf{i} + \tfrac{1}{3}t^3\mathbf{j} + \left(\tfrac{1}{2}\sin 2t\right)\mathbf{k} + \underbrace{C_1\mathbf{i} + C_2\mathbf{j} + C_3\mathbf{k}}_{\mathbf{C}}$$

Now use the initial condition to find $\mathbf{C}$:

$$\underbrace{2\mathbf{i} + \mathbf{j} - \mathbf{k}}_{\mathbf{R}(0)} = e^0\mathbf{i} + \tfrac{1}{3}(0)^3\mathbf{j} + \left(\tfrac{1}{2}\sin 0\right)\mathbf{k} + \mathbf{C} = \mathbf{i} + \mathbf{C}$$

We solve three separate equations:

$$2\mathbf{i} = \mathbf{i} + C_1\mathbf{i} \qquad \mathbf{j} = C_2\mathbf{j} \qquad -\mathbf{k} = C_3\mathbf{k}$$

so

$$C_1 = 1, \qquad C_2 = 1, \qquad C_3 = -1$$

and

$$\mathbf{i} + \mathbf{j} - \mathbf{k} = \mathbf{C}$$

Thus, the particle's position at any time t is

$$\mathbf{R}(t) = e^t\mathbf{i} + \tfrac{1}{3}t^3\mathbf{j} + \left(\tfrac{1}{2}\sin 2t\right)\mathbf{k} + \mathbf{i} + \mathbf{j} - \mathbf{k}$$
$$= (e^t + 1)\mathbf{i} + \left(\tfrac{1}{3}t^3 + 1\right)\mathbf{j} + \left(\tfrac{1}{2}\sin 2t - 1\right)\mathbf{k} \qquad\blacksquare$$

10.2 PROBLEM SET

A *Find the vector derivative **F**′ in Problems 1–4.*

1. $\mathbf{F}(t) = t\mathbf{i} + t^2\mathbf{j} + (t + t^3)\mathbf{k}$
2. $\mathbf{F}(s) = (s\mathbf{i} + s^2\mathbf{j} + s^2\mathbf{k}) + (2s^2\mathbf{i} - s\mathbf{j} + 3\mathbf{k})$
3. $\mathbf{F}(s) = (\ln s)[s\mathbf{i} + 5\mathbf{j} - e^s\mathbf{k}]$
4. $\mathbf{F}(\theta) = (\cos \theta)[\mathbf{i} + (\tan \theta)\mathbf{j} + 3\mathbf{k}]$

*Find **F**′ and **F**″ for the vector functions given in Problems 5–8.*

5. $\mathbf{F}(t) = t^2\mathbf{i} + t^{-1}\mathbf{j} + e^{2t}\mathbf{k}$
6. $\mathbf{F}(s) = (1 - 2s^2)\mathbf{i} + (s \cos s)\mathbf{j} - s\mathbf{k}$
7. $\mathbf{F}(s) = (\sin s)\mathbf{i} + (\cos s)\mathbf{j} + s^2\mathbf{k}$
8. $\mathbf{F}(\theta) = (\sin^2 \theta)\mathbf{i} + (\cos 2\theta)\mathbf{j} + \theta^2\mathbf{k}$

Differentiate the scalar functions in Problems 9–12.

9. $f(x) = [x\mathbf{i} + (x + 1)\mathbf{j}] \cdot [(2x)\mathbf{i} - (3x^2)\mathbf{j}]$
10. $f(x) = \langle \cos x, x, -x \rangle \cdot \langle \sec x, -x^2, 2x \rangle$
11. $g(x) = \| \langle \sin x, -2x, \cos x \rangle \|$
12. $f(x) = \| [x\mathbf{i} + x^2\mathbf{j} - 2\mathbf{k}] + [(1 - x)\mathbf{i} - e^x\mathbf{j}] \|$

*In Problems 13–18, **R** is the position vector for a particle in space at time t. Find the particle's velocity and acceleration vectors and then find the speed and direction of motion for the given value of t.*

13. $\mathbf{R}(t) = t\mathbf{i} + t^2\mathbf{j} + 2t\mathbf{k}$ at $t = 1$
14. $\mathbf{R}(t) = (1 - 2t)\mathbf{i} - t^2\mathbf{j} + e^t\mathbf{k}$ at $t = 0$
15. $\mathbf{R}(t) = (\cos t)\mathbf{i} + (\sin t)\mathbf{j} + 3t\mathbf{k}$ at $t = \frac{\pi}{4}$
16. $\mathbf{R}(t) = (2 \cos t)\mathbf{i} + t^2\mathbf{j} + (2 \sin t)\mathbf{k}$ at $t = \frac{\pi}{2}$
17. $\mathbf{R}(t) = e^t\mathbf{i} + e^{-t}\mathbf{j} + e^{2t}\mathbf{k}$ at $t = \ln 2$
18. $\mathbf{R}(t) = (\ln t)\mathbf{i} + \frac{1}{2}t^3\mathbf{j} - t\mathbf{k}$ at $t = 1$

*Find the tangent vector to the graph of the given vector function **F** at the points indicated in Problems 19–22.*

19. $\mathbf{F}(t) = t^2\mathbf{i} + 2t\mathbf{j} + (t^3 + t^2)\mathbf{k}$; $t = 0, t = 1, t = -1$
20. $\mathbf{F}(t) = \dfrac{t\mathbf{i} + t^2\mathbf{j} + t^3\mathbf{k}}{1 + 2t}$; $t = 0, t = 2$
21. $\mathbf{F}(t) = t^2\mathbf{i} + (\cos t)\mathbf{j} + (t^2 \cos t)\mathbf{k}$; $t = 0, t = \frac{\pi}{2}$
22. $\mathbf{F}(t) = (e^t \sin \pi t)\mathbf{i} + (e^t \cos \pi t)\mathbf{j} + (\sin \pi t + \cos \pi t)\mathbf{k}$; $t = 0, t = 1, t = 2$

*In Problems 23–24, find parametric equations for the tangent line to the graph of the given vector function **F**(t) at the point P_0 corresponding to t_0.*

23. $\mathbf{F}(t) = \langle t^{-3}, t^{-2}, t^{-1} \rangle$; $t_0 = -1$
24. $\mathbf{F}(t) = \langle \sin t, \cos t, 3t \rangle$; $t_0 = 0$

Find the indefinite vector integrals in Problems 25–30.

25. $\displaystyle\int \langle t, -e^{3t}, 3 \rangle \, dt$
26. $\displaystyle\int \langle \cos t, \sin t, -2t \rangle \, dt$
27. $\displaystyle\int \langle \ln t, -t, 3 \rangle \, dt$
28. $\displaystyle\int e^{-t} \langle 3, t, \sin t \rangle \, dt$
29. $\displaystyle\int \langle t \ln t, -\sin(1 - t), t \rangle \, dt$
30. $\displaystyle\int \langle \sinh t, -3, \cosh t \rangle \, dt$

*Find the position vector **R**(t), given the velocity **V**(t) and the initial position **R**(0) in Problems 31–34.*

31. $\mathbf{V}(t) = t^2\mathbf{i} - e^{2t}\mathbf{j} + \sqrt{t}\,\mathbf{k}$; $\mathbf{R}(0) = \mathbf{i} + 4\mathbf{j} - \mathbf{k}$
32. $\mathbf{V}(t) = t\mathbf{i} - \sqrt[3]{t}\,\mathbf{j} + e^t\mathbf{k}$; $\mathbf{R}(0) = \mathbf{i} - 2\mathbf{j} + \mathbf{k}$
33. $\mathbf{V}(t) = 2\sqrt{t}\,\mathbf{i} + (\cos t)\mathbf{j}$; $\mathbf{R}(0) = \mathbf{i} + \mathbf{j}$
34. $\mathbf{V}(t) = -3t\mathbf{i} + (\sin^2 t)\mathbf{j} + (\cos^2 t)\mathbf{k}$; $\mathbf{R}(0) = \mathbf{j}$

*Find the position vector **R**(t) and velocity vector **V**(t), given the acceleration **A**(t) and initial position and velocity vectors **R**(0) and **V**(0), respectively, in Problems 35–36.*

35. $\mathbf{A}(t) = (\cos t)\mathbf{i} - (t \sin t)\mathbf{k}$; $\mathbf{R}(0) = \mathbf{i} - 2\mathbf{j} + \mathbf{k}$; $\mathbf{V}(0) = 2\mathbf{i} + 3\mathbf{k}$
36. $\mathbf{A}(t) = t^2\mathbf{i} - 2\sqrt{t}\,\mathbf{j} + e^{3t}\mathbf{k}$; $\mathbf{R}(0) = 2\mathbf{i} + \mathbf{j} - \mathbf{k}$; $\mathbf{V}(0) = \mathbf{i} - \mathbf{j} - 2\mathbf{k}$

37. The velocity of a particle moving in space is $\mathbf{V}(t) = e^t\mathbf{i} + t^2\mathbf{j}$. Find the particle's position as a function of t if $\mathbf{R}(0) = \mathbf{i} - \mathbf{j}$.

38. The velocity of a moving particle is $\mathbf{V}(t) = (t \cos t)\mathbf{i} + e^{2t}\mathbf{k}$. Find the particle's position as a function of t if $\mathbf{R}(0) = \mathbf{i} + 2\mathbf{k}$.

39. The acceleration of a moving particle is $\mathbf{A}(t) = 24t^2\mathbf{i} + 4\mathbf{j}$. Find the particle's position as a function of t if $\mathbf{R}(0) = \mathbf{i} + 2\mathbf{j}$ and $\mathbf{V}(0) = \mathbf{0}$.

B 40. **WHAT DOES THIS SAY?** Describe the concept of a smooth curve.

41. **WHAT DOES THIS SAY?** Compare or contrast the notions of speed and velocity of a moving object.

Let $\mathbf{v} = 2\mathbf{i} - \mathbf{j} + 5\mathbf{k}$ and $\mathbf{w} = \mathbf{i} + 2\mathbf{j} - 3\mathbf{k}$. Find the derivatives in Problems 42–45.

42. $\dfrac{d}{dt}(\mathbf{v} + t\mathbf{w})$
43. $\dfrac{d^2}{dt^2}(\mathbf{v} \cdot t^4\mathbf{w})$
44. $\dfrac{d^2}{dt^2}(t\|\mathbf{v}\| + t^2\|\mathbf{w}\|)$
45. $\dfrac{d}{dt}(t\mathbf{v} \times t^2\mathbf{w})$

In Problems 46–47, verify the indicated equations for the vector functions

$$\mathbf{F}(t) = (3 + t^2)\mathbf{i} - (\cos 3t)\mathbf{j} + t^{-1}\mathbf{k} \quad \text{and}$$
$$\mathbf{G}(t) = \sin(2 - t)\mathbf{i} - e^{2t}\mathbf{k}$$

46. $(3\mathbf{F} - 2\mathbf{G})'(t) = 3\mathbf{F}'(t) - 2\mathbf{G}'(t)$
47. $(\mathbf{F} \cdot \mathbf{G})'(t) = (\mathbf{F}' \cdot \mathbf{G})(t) + (\mathbf{F} \cdot \mathbf{G}')(t)$

In Problems 48–49, find a value of a that satisfies the given equation.

48. $\displaystyle\int_0^a \left[\left(t\sqrt{1 + t^2} \right)\mathbf{i} + \left(\frac{1}{1 + t^2} \right)\mathbf{j} \right] dt = \frac{1}{3}(2\sqrt{2} - 1)\mathbf{i} + \frac{\pi}{4}\mathbf{j}$

49. $\displaystyle\int_0^{2a} [(\cos t)\mathbf{i} + (\sin t)\mathbf{j} + (\sin t \cos t)\mathbf{k}] \, dt = \mathbf{i} + \mathbf{j} + \frac{1}{2}\mathbf{k}$

*In Problems 50–51, show that **F**(t) and **F**″(t) are parallel for all t if k is constant.*

50. $\mathbf{F}(t) = e^{kt}\mathbf{i} + e^{-kt}\mathbf{j}$
51. $\mathbf{F}(t) = (\cos kt)\mathbf{i} + (\sin kt)\mathbf{j}$

*Determine whether the given vector function **F**(t) in Problems 52–53 is smooth over the interval I.*

52. $\mathbf{F}(t) = \langle t^2 - t, \cos t, \sin t^2 \rangle$ over $[-\pi, \pi]$
53. $\mathbf{F}(t) = \langle e^t - t, t^{3/2}, \cos t \rangle$ over $[-1, 2]$

C 54. Let $\mathbf{F}(t) = u(t)\mathbf{i} + v(t)\mathbf{j} + w(t)\mathbf{k}$, where u, v, and w are differentiable scalar functions of t. Show that

$$\mathbf{F}(t) \cdot \mathbf{F}'(t) = \|\mathbf{F}(t)\| \, (\|\mathbf{F}(t)\|)'$$

55. Let $\mathbf{F}(t)$ be a differentiable vector function and let $h(t)$ be a differentiable scalar function of t. Show that

$$[h(t)\mathbf{F}(t)]' = h(t)\mathbf{F}'(t) + h'(t)\mathbf{F}(t)$$

56. If **F** and **G** are differentiable vector functions of t, prove

$$(\mathbf{F} \cdot \mathbf{G})'(t) = (\mathbf{F} \cdot \mathbf{G}')(t) + (\mathbf{F}' \cdot \mathbf{G})(t)$$

57. If $\mathbf{F}$ and $\mathbf{G}$ are differentiable vector functions of t, prove

$$(\mathbf{F} \times \mathbf{G})'(t) = (\mathbf{F}' \times \mathbf{G})(t) + (\mathbf{F} \times \mathbf{G}')(t)$$

58. If $\mathbf{F}$ is a differentiable vector function such that $\mathbf{F}(t) \neq \mathbf{0}$, show that

$$\frac{d}{dt}\left(\frac{\mathbf{F}(t)}{\|\mathbf{F}(t)\|}\right) = \frac{\mathbf{F}'(t)}{\|\mathbf{F}(t)\|} - \frac{[\mathbf{F}(t) \cdot \mathbf{F}'(t)]\mathbf{F}(t)}{\|\mathbf{F}(t)\|^3}$$

59. Show that $\dfrac{d}{dt}\|\mathbf{R}(t)\| = \dfrac{1}{\|\mathbf{R}\|}\mathbf{R} \cdot \dfrac{d\mathbf{R}}{dt}$.

60. Verify that

$$\frac{d}{dt}[\mathbf{F} \cdot (\mathbf{G} \times \mathbf{H})] = \mathbf{F}' \cdot (\mathbf{G} \times \mathbf{H}) + \mathbf{F} \cdot (\mathbf{G}' \times \mathbf{H}) + \mathbf{F} \cdot (\mathbf{G} \times \mathbf{H}')$$

61. Verify that $\dfrac{d}{dt}[\mathbf{F} \times (\mathbf{G} \times \mathbf{H})] = [(\mathbf{H} \cdot \mathbf{F})\mathbf{G}]' - [(\mathbf{G} \cdot \mathbf{F})\mathbf{H}]'$.

62. If $\mathbf{G} = \mathbf{F} \cdot (\mathbf{F}' \times \mathbf{F}'')$, what is $\mathbf{G}'$?

63. Counterexample Problem Is it true that whenever the vector functions $\mathbf{F}(t)$ and $\mathbf{G}(t)$ are smooth over the interval $[a, b]$, then $\mathbf{F}(t) + \mathbf{G}(t)$ is also smooth over the same interval? Either prove that this statement is generally true, or find a counterexample.

10.3 Modeling Ballistics and Planetary Motion

IN THIS SECTION modeling the motion of a projectile in a vacuum, Kepler's second law

MODELING THE MOTION OF A PROJECTILE IN A VACUUM

In general, it can be quite difficult to analyze the motion of a projectile, but the problem becomes manageable if we assume that the acceleration due to gravity is constant and that the projectile travels in a vacuum, so we will make this assumption. A model of the motion in the real world (with air resistance, for example) based on these assumptions is fairly realistic as long as the projectile is reasonably heavy, travels at relatively low speed, and stays close to the surface of the earth.

Figure 10.13 shows a projectile that is fired from a point P and travels in a vertical plane coordinatized so that P is directly above the origin O and the impact point I is on the x-axis at ground level. We let s_0 be the height of P above O, v_0 be the initial speed of the projectile (the **muzzle speed**), and α be the angle of elevation (the angle at which the projectile is launched).

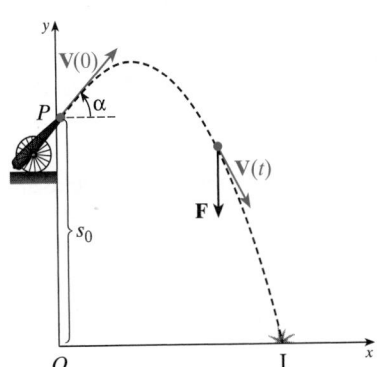

Figure 10.13 The motion of a projectile

Because the projectile is to travel in a vacuum, we will assume that the only force acting on the projectile at any given time is the force due to gravity. This force $\mathbf{F}$ is directed downward. The magnitude of this force is the projectile's weight. If m is the mass of the projectile and g is the "free-fall" acceleration due to gravity (g is approximately 32 ft/s^2 or 9.8 m/s^2), then the magnitude of $\mathbf{F}$ is mg. Also, according to **Newton's second law of motion**, the sum of all the forces acting on the projectile must equal $m\mathbf{A}(t)$, where $\mathbf{A}(t)$ is the acceleration of the projectile at time t. Because $\mathbf{F} = -mg\mathbf{j}$ is the only force acting on the projectile, it follows that

$$-mg\mathbf{j} = \mathbf{F} = m\mathbf{A}(t)$$
$$\mathbf{A}(t) = -g\mathbf{j} \qquad \text{for all } t \geq 0$$

The velocity $\mathbf{V}(t)$ of the projectile can now be obtained by integrating $\mathbf{A}(t)$. Specifically, we have

$$\mathbf{V}(t) = \int \mathbf{A}(t)\,dt = \int (-g\mathbf{j})\,dt = -gt\mathbf{j} + \mathbf{C}_1$$

where $\mathbf{C}_1 = \mathbf{V}(0)$ is the velocity when $t = 0$ (that is, the *initial velocity*). Because the projectile is fired with initial speed $v_0 = \|\mathbf{V}(0)\|$ at an angle of elevation α, the initial velocity must be

$$\mathbf{C}_1 = \mathbf{V}(0) = (v_0 \cos \alpha)\mathbf{i} + (v_0 \sin \alpha)\mathbf{j}$$

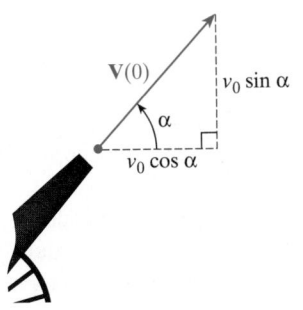

Figure 10.14 Components of the initial velocity vector $\mathbf{V}(0)$

(as shown in Figure 10.14),

and by substitution we find

$$\mathbf{V}(t) = -gt\mathbf{j} + (v_0 \cos\alpha)\mathbf{i} + (v_0 \sin\alpha)\mathbf{j}$$
$$= (v_0 \cos\alpha)\mathbf{i} + (v_0 \sin\alpha - gt)\mathbf{j}$$

Next, by integrating $\mathbf{V}$ with respect to t, we find that the position vector of the projectile is

$$\mathbf{R}(t) = \int \mathbf{V}(t)\,dt = \int [(v_0 \cos\alpha)\mathbf{i} + (v_0 \sin\alpha - gt)\mathbf{j}]\,dt$$
$$= (v_0 \cos\alpha)t\mathbf{i} + \left[(v_0 \sin\alpha)t - \tfrac{1}{2}gt^2\right]\mathbf{j} + \mathbf{C}_2$$

where $\mathbf{C}_2 = \mathbf{R}(0)$ is the position at time $t = 0$. Because the projectile begins its flight at P, the initial position is $\mathbf{R}(0) = s_0\mathbf{j}$, and by substituting this expression for $\mathbf{C}_2$, we find that the position at time t is

$$\mathbf{R}(t) = [(v_0 \cos\alpha)t]\mathbf{i} + \left[(v_0 \sin\alpha)t - \tfrac{1}{2}gt^2 + s_0\right]\mathbf{j}$$

Specifically, $\mathbf{R}(t)$ gives the position of the projectile at any time t after it is fired and before it hits the ground. If we let $x(t)$ and $y(t)$ denote the horizontal and vertical components of $\mathbf{R}(t)$, respectively, we can make the following statement.

Motion of a Projectile in a Vacuum

Consider a projectile that travels in a vacuum in a coordinate plane, with the x-axis along level ground. If the projectile is fired from a height of s_0 with initial speed v_0 and angle of elevation α, then at time t ($t \geq 0$) it will be at the point $(x(t), y(t))$, where

$$x(t) = (v_0 \cos\alpha)t \quad \text{and} \quad y(t) = -\tfrac{1}{2}gt^2 + (v_0 \sin\alpha)t + s_0$$

The parametric equations for the motion of a projectile in a vacuum provide useful general information about a projectile's motion. For instance, note that if $\alpha \neq 90°$, we can eliminate the parameter t by solving the first equation, obtaining

$$t = \frac{x}{v_0 \cos\alpha}$$

By substituting into the second equation, we find

$$y = -\frac{1}{2}g\left[\frac{x}{v_0 \cos\alpha}\right]^2 + (v_0 \sin\alpha)\left[\frac{x}{v_0 \cos\alpha}\right] + s_0$$
$$= \left[\frac{-g}{2(v_0 \cos\alpha)^2}\right]x^2 + (\tan\alpha)x + s_0$$

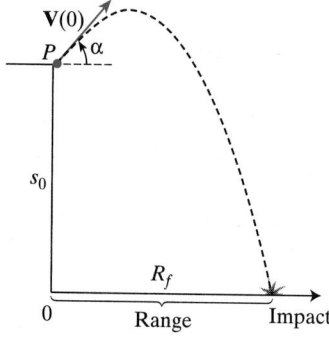

$\mathbf{V}(0)$
P α
s_0
R_f
0 Range   Impact

Figure 10.15 The motion of a projectile. The trajectory is part of a parabolic arc.

This is the Cartesian equation for the trajectory of the projectile, and because the equation has the general form $y = ax^2 + bx + c$, with $a < 0$, the trajectory must be part of a downward-opening parabola. That is, *if a projectile is not fired vertically (so that* $\tan\alpha$ *is defined), its trajectory will be part of a downward-opening parabolic arc,* as shown in Figure 10.15.

The *time of flight* T_f of a projectile is the elapsed time between launch and impact, and the *range* is the total horizontal distance R_f traveled by the projectile during its flight. Because $y = 0$ at impact, it follows that T_f must satisfy the quadratic equation

$$-\tfrac{1}{2}gT_f^2 + (v_0 \sin\alpha)T_f + s_0 = 0$$

Then, because the flight begins at $x = 0$ when $t = 0$ and ends at $x = R_f$ when $t = T_f$, the range R_f can be computed by evaluating $x(t)$ at $t = T_f$. That is,

$$R_f = (v_0 \cos\alpha)T_f$$

EXAMPLE 1   Modeling the path of a projectile

A boy standing at the edge of a cliff throws a ball upward at a 30° angle with an initial speed of 64 ft/s. Suppose that when the ball leaves the boy's hand, it is 48 ft above the ground at the base of the cliff.

a. What are the time of flight of the ball and its range?
b. What are the velocity of the ball and its speed at impact?
c. What is the highest point reached by the ball during its flight?

Solution

We know that $g = 32$ ft/s^2, and we are given $s_0 = 48$ ft, $v_0 = 64$ ft/s, and $\alpha = 30°$, so the ball's trajectory has parametric equations

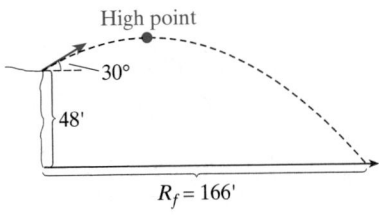

High point

30°

48'

$R_f = 166'$

$$x(t) = (v_0 \cos\alpha)t = (64\cos 30°)t = 32\sqrt{3}\,t$$

$$y(t) = -\tfrac{1}{2}gt^2 + (v_0 \sin\alpha)t + s_0$$

$$= -\tfrac{1}{2}(32)t^2 + (64\sin 30°)t + 48$$

$$= -16t^2 + 32t + 48$$

a. The ball hits the ground when $y = 0$, and by solving the equation $-16t^2 + 32t + 48 = 0$ for $t \geq 0$, we find that $t = 3$, so the time of flight is $T_f = 3$ seconds. The range is

$$x(3) = 32\sqrt{3}\,(3) \approx 166.27688$$

That is, the ball hits the ground about 166 ft from the base of the cliff.

b. We find that $x'(t) = 32\sqrt{3}$ and $y'(t) = -32t + 32$, so the velocity at time t is

$$\mathbf{V}(t) = 32\sqrt{3}\,\mathbf{i} + (-32t + 32)\mathbf{j}$$

Thus, at impact (when $t = 3$), the velocity is $\mathbf{V}(3) = 32\sqrt{3}\,\mathbf{i} - 64\mathbf{j}$, and its speed is

$$\|\mathbf{V}(3)\| = \sqrt{(32\sqrt{3})^2 + (-64)^2} \approx 84.664042$$

That is, the speed at impact is about 85 ft/s.

c. The ball attains its maximum height when the upward (vertical) component of its velocity $\mathbf{V}(t)$ is 0—that is, when $y'(t) = 0$. Solving the equation $-32t + 32 = 0$, we find that this occurs when $t = 1$. Therefore, the maximum height attained by the ball is

$$y_m = y(1) = -16(1)^2 + 32(1) + 48 = 64$$

$$x_m = x(1) = 32\sqrt{3}\,(1) \approx 55.425626$$

and the highest point reached by the ball has coordinates (rounded to the nearest foot) of $(55, 64)$. ■

In general, if the projectile is fired from ground level (so $s_0 = 0$), the time of flight T_f satisfies

$$-\tfrac{1}{2}gT_f^2 + (v_0 \sin\alpha)T_f = 0$$

$$T_f = \frac{2}{g}v_0 \sin\alpha$$

Thus, the range R_f is

$$R_f = x(T_f) = (v_0 \cos\alpha)\left(\frac{2v_0 \sin\alpha}{g}\right) = \frac{v_0^2}{g}(2\sin\alpha\cos\alpha) = \frac{v_0^2}{g}\sin 2\alpha$$

Notice that for a given initial speed v_0, the range assumes its largest value when $\sin 2\alpha = 1$; that is, when $\alpha = 45° = \tfrac{\pi}{4}$. To summarize,

---

Time of Flight and Range of a Projectile Fired from Ground Level

A projectile fired from *ground level* has **time of flight** T_f and **range** R_f given by the equations

$$T_f = \frac{2}{g}v_0 \sin\alpha \quad \text{and} \quad R_f = \frac{v_0^2}{g}\sin 2\alpha$$

The maximal range is $R_m = \dfrac{v_0^2}{g}$, and it occurs when $\alpha = \frac{\pi}{4}$.

EXAMPLE 2   Time of flight and range for the motion of a projectile

A projectile is fired from ground level at an angle of 40° with muzzle speed 110 ft/s. Find the time of flight and the range.

Solution

With $g = 32$ ft/s^2, we see that the flight time T_f is

$$T_f = \frac{2}{g}v_0 \sin\alpha = \frac{2}{32}(110)(\sin 40°) \approx 4.4191648$$

The range R_f is

$$R_f = \frac{v_0^2}{g}\sin 2\alpha = \frac{(110)^2}{32}(\sin 80°) \approx 372.38043$$

That is, the projectile travels about 372 ft horizontally before it hits the ground, and the flight takes a little more than 4 seconds. ■

KEPLER'S SECOND LAW

In the seventeenth century, the German astronomer Johannes Kepler (1571–1630) formulated three useful laws for describing planetary motion. The guest essay at the end of this chapter discusses the discovery of these laws.

Kepler's Laws

1. The planets move about the sun in elliptical orbits, with the sun at one focus.
2. The radius vector joining a planet to the sun sweeps out equal areas in equal intervals of time.
3. The square of the time of one complete revolution of a planet about its orbit is proportional to the cube of the length of the semimajor axis of its orbit.

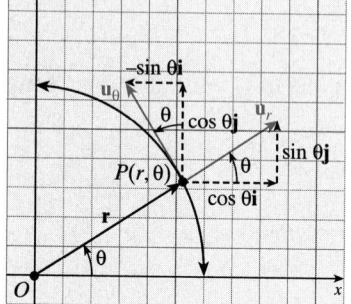

Figure 10.16 Description of the motion of a particle along a curve

Kepler's approach was empirical, but his three laws were proved eighty years later by Isaac Newton, in the *Principia Mathematica* (1687). We will prove the second law using vector methods. The other two laws can be established similarly.

We begin by introducing some useful notation involving polar coordinates. Let $\mathbf{u}_r$ and $\mathbf{u}_\theta$ denote unit vectors along the radial axis and orthogonal to that axis, respectively, as shown in Figure 10.16. Then, in terms of the unit Cartesian vectors $\mathbf{i}$ and $\mathbf{j}$, we have

$$\mathbf{u}_r = (\cos\theta)\mathbf{i} + (\sin\theta)\mathbf{j} \quad \text{and} \quad \mathbf{u}_\theta = (-\sin\theta)\mathbf{i} + (\cos\theta)\mathbf{j}$$

The derivatives $\dfrac{d\mathbf{u}_r}{d\theta}$ and $\dfrac{d\mathbf{u}_\theta}{d\theta}$ satisfy

$$\frac{d\mathbf{u}_r}{d\theta} = (-\sin\theta)\mathbf{i} + (\cos\theta)\mathbf{j} = \mathbf{u}_\theta$$

$$\frac{d\mathbf{u}_\theta}{d\theta} = (-\cos\theta)\mathbf{i} + (-\sin\theta)\mathbf{j} = -\mathbf{u}_r$$

Now, suppose the sun S is at the origin (pole) of a polar coordinate system, and consider the motion of a body B (planet, comet, artificial satellite) about S. The radial vector $\mathbf{R} = \mathbf{SB}$ can be expressed as

$$\mathbf{R} = r\mathbf{u}_r = (r\cos\theta)\mathbf{i} + (r\sin\theta)\mathbf{j}$$

where $r = \|\mathbf{R}\|$, and the velocity $\mathbf{V}$ satisfies

$$\mathbf{V} = \frac{d\mathbf{R}}{dt} = \frac{dr}{dt}\mathbf{u}_r + r\frac{d\mathbf{u}_r}{dt} \qquad \textit{Derivative of a scalar multiple}$$

$$= \frac{dr}{dt}\mathbf{u}_r + r\frac{d\mathbf{u}_r}{d\theta}\frac{d\theta}{dt} \qquad \textit{Chain rule}$$

$$= \frac{dr}{dt}\mathbf{u}_r + r\frac{d\theta}{dt}\mathbf{u}_\theta$$

A similar formula for acceleration can be derived (see Problem 41). We summarize these formulas in the following box.

Polar Formulas for Velocity and Acceleration

$$\mathbf{V}(t) = \frac{dr}{dt}\mathbf{u}_r + r\frac{d\theta}{dt}\mathbf{u}_\theta$$

$$\mathbf{A}(t) = \frac{d\mathbf{V}(t)}{dt} = \frac{d^2\mathbf{R}}{dt^2} = \left[\frac{d^2r}{dt^2} - r\left(\frac{d\theta}{dt}\right)^2\right]\mathbf{u}_r + \left[r\frac{d^2\theta}{dt^2} + 2\frac{dr}{dt}\frac{d\theta}{dt}\right]\mathbf{u}_\theta$$

EXAMPLE 3   Velocity of a moving body using polar unit vectors

The position vector of a moving body is $\mathbf{R}(t) = 2t\mathbf{i} - t^2\mathbf{j}$ for $t \geq 0$. Express $\mathbf{R}$ and the velocity vector $\mathbf{V}(t)$ in terms of $\mathbf{u}_r$ and $\mathbf{u}_\theta$.

Solution

We note that on the trajectory, $x = 2t$, $y = -t^2$, so $\mathbf{R}$ has length

$$r = \|\mathbf{R}(t)\| = \sqrt{(2t)^2 + (-t^2)^2} = \sqrt{4t^2 + t^4} = t\sqrt{t^2 + 4}$$

and $\mathbf{R} = r\mathbf{u}_r = t\sqrt{t^2 + 4}\,\mathbf{u}_r$. Because $\mathbf{V}(t) = \dfrac{dr}{dt}\mathbf{u}_r + r\dfrac{d\theta}{dt}\mathbf{u}_\theta$, we need $\dfrac{dr}{dt}$ and $\dfrac{d\theta}{dt}$. We find that

$$\frac{dr}{dt} = \sqrt{t^2 + 4} + t\left(\tfrac{1}{2}\right)(t^2 + 4)^{-1/2}(2t) = \frac{2t^2 + 4}{\sqrt{t^2 + 4}}$$

and because the polar angle satisfies $\theta = \tan^{-1}\left(\dfrac{y}{x}\right)$ for all points (x, y) on the curve (except where $x = 0$), we have

$$\theta = \tan^{-1}\left(\frac{-t^2}{2t}\right) = \tan^{-1}\left(-\frac{t}{2}\right)$$

$$\frac{d\theta}{dt} = \frac{1}{1 + \left(-\frac{t}{2}\right)^2}\left(-\frac{1}{2}\right) = \frac{-2}{t^2 + 4}$$

Thus,

$$\mathbf{V}(t) = \frac{2t^2 + 4}{\sqrt{t^2 + 4}}\mathbf{u}_r + t\sqrt{t^2 + 4}\left(\frac{-2}{t^2 + 4}\right)\mathbf{u}_\theta = \frac{(2t^2 + 4)\mathbf{u}_r - 2t\mathbf{u}_\theta}{\sqrt{t^2 + 4}} \qquad\blacksquare$$

We now have the tools we need to establish Kepler's second law.

THEOREM 10.5   Kepler's second law

The radius vector from the sun to a planet in its orbit sweeps out equal areas in equal intervals of time.

Proof   The situation described by Kepler's second law is illustrated in Figure 10.17. We will assume that the only force acting on a planet is the gravitational attraction of the sun. According to the universal law of gravitation, the force of attraction is given by

$$\mathbf{F} = -G\frac{mM}{r^2}\mathbf{u}_r$$

where G is a physical constant, and m and M are the masses of the planet and the sun, respectively. Because this is the only force acting on the planet, Newton's second law of motion tells us that $\mathbf{F} = m\mathbf{A}$, where $\mathbf{A}$ is the acceleration of the planet in its orbit. By equating these two expressions for the force $\mathbf{F}$ we find

$$m\mathbf{A} = -G\frac{mM}{r^2}\mathbf{u}_r$$

$$\mathbf{A} = \frac{-GM}{r^2}\mathbf{u}_r$$

This says that *the acceleration of a planet in its orbit has only a radial component.* Note how this conclusion depends on our assumption that the only force on the planet is the sun's gravitational attraction, which acts along radial lines from the sun to the planet.

This means that the $\mathbf{u}_\theta$ component of the planet's acceleration is 0, and by examining the polar formula for acceleration, we see that this condition is equivalent to the differential equation

$$r\frac{d^2\theta}{dt^2} + 2\frac{dr}{dt}\frac{d\theta}{dt} = 0$$

If we set $w = \dfrac{d\theta}{dt}$, we obtain $\dfrac{d^2\theta}{dt^2} = \dfrac{dw}{dt}$, so that

$$r\frac{dw}{dt} + 2w\frac{dr}{dt} = 0 \qquad\qquad \textit{Separation of variables}$$

$$w^{-1}\frac{dw}{dt} = -2r^{-1}\frac{dr}{dt}$$

$$\int w^{-1}\,dw = \int(-2r^{-1})\,dr$$

$$\ln|w| + C_1 = -2\ln|r| + C_2$$

$$\ln w = \ln(Cr^{-2}) \qquad\qquad \textit{Since } r > 0 \text{ and } w > 0$$

$$w = Cr^{-2}$$

$$\frac{d\theta}{dt} = Cr^{-2}$$

$$r^2\frac{d\theta}{dt} = C$$

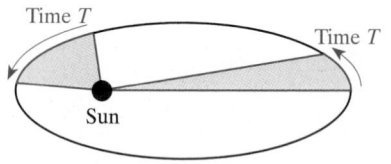

Figure 10.17 The radial line sweeps out equal area in equal time

Time T

Time T

Sun

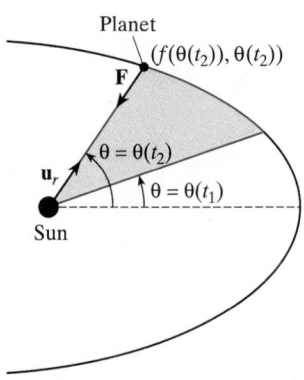

Figure 10.18 The radial line sweeps out area at the rate $\dfrac{dA}{dt} = \dfrac{1}{2} r^2 \dfrac{d\theta}{dt}$.

Now, let $[t_1, t_2]$ and $[t_3, t_4]$ be two time intervals of equal length, so $t_2 - t_1 = t_4 - t_3$. According to Theorem 6.1, the area swept out in the time period $[t_1, t_2]$ (see Figure 10.18) is

$$S_1 = \int_{t_1}^{t_2} \frac{1}{2} r^2 \, d\theta = \int_{t_1}^{t_2} \frac{1}{2} \left[r^2 \frac{d\theta}{dt} \right] dt = \int_{t_1}^{t_2} \frac{1}{2} C \, dt \qquad \text{Since } r^2 \frac{d\theta}{dt} = C$$

Thus, $S_1 = \frac{1}{2} C (t_2 - t_1)$. Similarly, the area swept out in time period $[t_3, t_4]$ is $S_2 = \frac{1}{2} C (t_4 - t_3)$, and we have

$$S_1 = \frac{1}{2} C (t_2 - t_1) = \frac{1}{2} C (t_4 - t_3) = S_2$$

so equal area is swept out in equal time, as claimed by Kepler. ❏

An object is said to move in a **central force field** if it is subject to a single force that is always directed toward a particular point. Our derivation of Kepler's second law is based on the assumption that planetary motion occurs in a central force field. In particular, the formula

$$\mathbf{A} = \frac{-GM}{r^2} \mathbf{u}_r$$

shows that a planet's acceleration has only a radial component, and this turns out to be true for an object moving in a plane in any central force field.

Much of what we know about the motion of the planets is derived from Kepler's laws. Some of these data are listed in Table 10.1.

TABLE 10.1 Data on Planetary Orbits

Planet	Mean Orbit (in millions of miles)	Eccentricity	Period (in days)	Comparative Mass (Earth = 1.00)
Mercury	36.0	0.2056	88.0	0.06
Venus	67.3	0.0068	224.7	0.81
Earth	**93.0**	**0.0167**	**365.256**	**1.00**
Mars	141.7	0.0934	687.0	0.1074
Jupiter	484.0	0.0484	4,332.589	317.83
Saturn	887.0	0.0543	10,759.22	95.16
Uranus	1,787.0	0.0460	30,685.4	14.5
Neptune	2,797.0	0.0082	60,189.0	17.2
Pluto	3,675.0	0.2481	90,465.0	0.00215

10.3 PROBLEM SET

Ⓐ *In Problems 1–8, find the time of flight T_f (to the nearest tenth second) and the range R_f (to the nearest unit) of a projectile fired (in a vacuum) from ground level at the given angle α with the indicated initial speed v_0. Assume that $g = 32$ ft/s^2 or $g = 9.8$ m/s^2.*

1. $\alpha = 35°$, $v_0 = 128$ ft/s **2.** $\alpha = 45°$, $v_0 = 80$ ft/s

3. $\alpha = 48.5°$, $v_0 = 850$ m/s **4.** $\alpha = 43.5°$, $v_0 = 185$ m/s

5. $\alpha = 23.74°$, $v_0 = 23.3$ m/s **6.** $\alpha = 31.04°$, $v_0 = 38.14$ m/s

7. $\alpha = 14.11°$, $v_0 = 100$ ft/s **8.** $\alpha = 78.09°$, $v_0 = 88$ ft/s

In Problems 9–14, an object moves along the given curve in the plane (described in either polar or parametric form). Find its velocity and acceleration in terms of the unit polar vectors $\mathbf{u}_r$ and $\mathbf{u}_\theta$.

9. $x = 2t$, $y = t$ **10.** $x = \sin t$, $y = \cos t$

11. $r = \sin \theta$, $\theta = 2t$ **12.** $r = e^{-\theta}$, $\theta = 1 - t$

13. $r = 5(1 + \cos \theta)$, $\theta = 2t + 1$

14. $r = \dfrac{1}{1 - \cos \theta}$, $\theta = t$

Ⓑ **15.** A shell fired from ground level at an angle of 45° hits the ground 2000 m away. What is the muzzle speed of the shell?

16. A gun at ground level has muzzle speed of 300 ft/s. What angle of elevation (to the nearest tenth of a degree) should be used to hit an object 1,500 ft away?

17. At what angle (to the nearest tenth of a degree) should a projectile be fired from ground level if its muzzle speed is 167.1 ft/s and the desired range is 600 ft?

18. A shell is fired at ground level with a muzzle speed of 280 ft/s and at an elevation of 45° from ground level.

   a. Find the maximum height attained by the shell.

   b. Find the time of flight and the range of the shell.

   c. Find the velocity and speed of the shell at impact.

19. Derek Jeter hits a baseball at a 30° angle with a speed of 144 ft/s. If the ball is 4 ft above ground level when it is hit, what is the maximum height reached by the ball? How far will it travel from home plate before it lands? If it just barely clears a 5-foot wall in the outfield (see Figure 10.19), how far (to the nearest foot) is the wall from home plate?

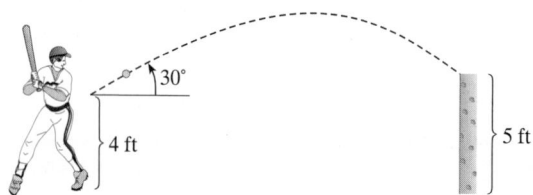

Figure 10.19 Home run distance

20. A baseball hit at a 24° angle from 3 ft above the ground just goes over the 9-ft fence 400 ft from home plate. About how fast was the ball traveling, and how long did it take the ball to reach the wall?

21. A nozzle discharges a stream of water with an initial velocity $v_0 = 50$ ft/s into the end of a horizontal pipe of inside diameter $d = 5$ ft (see Figure 10.20). What is the maximum horizontal distance that the stream can reach?

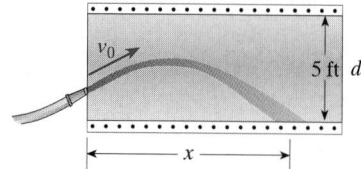

Figure 10.20 Problem 21

22. If a shotputter throws a shot from a height of 5 ft with an angle of 46° and initial speed of 25 ft/s, what is the horizontal distance of the throw?

23. Modeling Problem In 1974, Evel Knievel attempted a skycycle ride across the Snake River (see Figure 10.21), and at the time there was a great deal of hype about "will he make it?" If the angle of the launching ramp was 45° and if the horizontal distance the skycycle needed to travel was 4,700 ft, at what speed did Evel have to leave the ramp to make it across the Snake River Canyon?

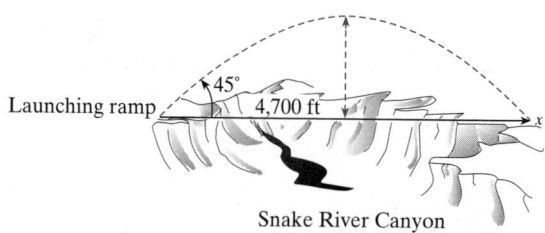

Figure 10.21 Evel Knievel's jump

Assume that the opposite edges of the canyon are at the same height and neglect wind resistance.

24. Payton Manning, a quarterback for the Indianapolis Colts, throws a pass at a 45° angle from a height of 6.5 ft with a speed of 50 ft/s (see Figure 10.22). A receiver races straight downfield on a fly pattern at a constant speed of 32 ft/s and catches the ball at a height of 6 ft. If Manning and the receiver both line up on the 50 yard line at the start of the play, how far does Manning fade back (retreat) from the line of scrimmage before he releases the ball?

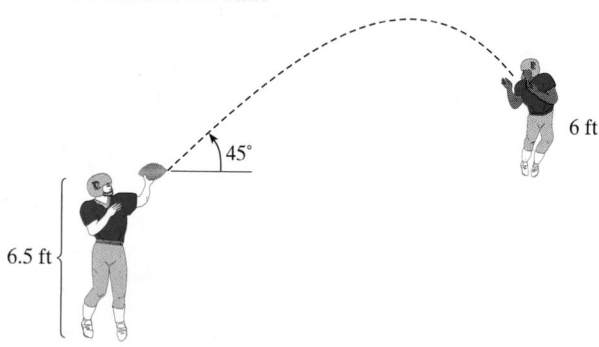

Figure 10.22 Downfield pass

25. A golf ball is hit from the tee to a green with an initial speed of 125 ft/s at an angle of elevation of 45°. How long will it take for the ball to hit the green?

26. Modeling Problem A 3-oz paddleball attached to a string is swung in a circular path with a 1-ft radius, as shown in Figure 10.23. If the string will break under a force of 2 lb, find the maximum speed the ball can attain without breaking the string. *Hint:* 3 oz is 3/16 lb.

Figure 10.23 Paddleball path

27. Spy Problem The Spy figures out where to dig (Supplementary Problem 57 of Chapter 9) and unearths a human-size box. With shaking hands, he opens the lid, and to his relief, finds not the body of Lord Fleming, but his favorite pipe and a ringing cell phone. He picks up the phone and hears the cold, calculating voice of Ernst Stavro Blohardt. "Do what you're told or the next box will be heavier!" he threatens. "You're going to help me eliminate my competition, starting with Scélérat." The Spy is still peeved with Scélérat for icing his friend, Siggy Leiter (Problem 62, Section 2.4), so he agrees. He's told that the Frenchman and his gang are holed up in a bunker on the side of a hill inclined at an angle of 15° to the horizontal, as shown in Figure 10.24. The Spy returns to his helicopter and flies toward the bunker traveling at 200 ft/s at an altitude of 10,000 ft. Just as the helicopter flies over the base of the hill, the Spy sights a ventilation hole in the top of the bunker at an angle of 20°. He decides to drop a canister of knockout gas into the bunker through the hole. How long should he wait before releasing the canister?

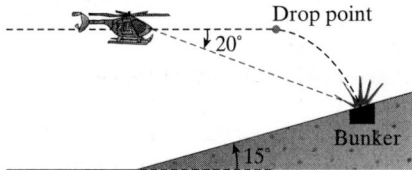

Figure 10.24 Spy and the bunker target

28. A child, running along level ground at the top of a 30-ft-high vertical cliff at a speed of 15 ft/s, throws a rock over the cliff into the sea below, as shown in Figure 10.25. Suppose the child's arm is 3 ft above the ground and her arm speed is 25 ft/s. If the rock is released 10 ft from the edge of the cliff at an angle of 30°, how long does it take for the rock to hit the water? How far from the base of the cliff does it hit?

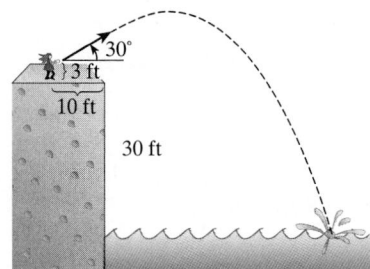

Figure 10.25 Tossing an object off a cliff

29. **Modeling Problem** A calculus text (other than the one you are now reading) is hurled downward from the top of a 120-ft high building at an angle of 30° from the horizontal, as shown in Figure 10.26. Assume that the initial speed of the book is 8 ft/s. How far from the base of the building will the text land?

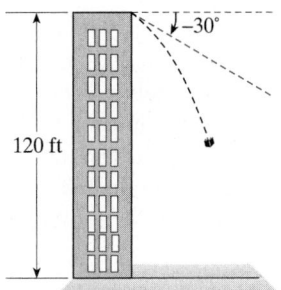

Figure 10.26 Path of an object thrown from a building

30. A particle moves along the polar path (r, θ), where $r(t) = 3 + 2 \sin t$, $\theta(t) = t^3$. Find $\mathbf{V}(t)$ and $\mathbf{A}(t)$ in terms of $\mathbf{u}_r$ and $\mathbf{u}_\theta$.

In Problems 31–34, consider a particle moving on a circular path of radius a described by the equation

$\mathbf{R}(t) = (a \cos \omega t)\mathbf{i} + (a \sin \omega t)\mathbf{j}$, *where* $\omega = \dfrac{d\theta}{dt}$ *is the constant angular velocity.*

31. Find the velocity vector and show that it is orthogonal to $\mathbf{R}(t)$.

32. Find the speed of the particle.

33. Find the acceleration vector and show that its direction is always toward the center of the circle.

34. Find the magnitude of the acceleration vector.

35. A mortar is placed at the top of a hill sloping downward at a 20° angle, as shown in Figure 10.27.

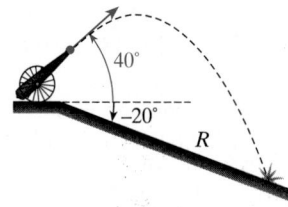

Figure 10.27 Path of a projectile fired from a sloping surface

A shell is fired with muzzle speed of $v_0 = 100$ m/s at an angle of 40° relative to the horizontal.

a. How far down the slope does the shell land?

b. What is the impact speed of the shell?

36. Find two angles of elevation α_1 and α_2 (to the nearest degree) so that a shell fired at ground level with muzzle speed of 650 ft/s will hit a target 6,000 ft away (also at ground level).

37. A gun is fired with muzzle speed $v_0 = 550$ ft/s at an angle of $\alpha = 22.0°$. The shell overshoots the target by 50 ft. At what angle should a second shot be fired with the same muzzle speed to hit the target?

38. A gun is fired with muzzle speed $v_0 = 700$ ft/s at an angle of $\alpha = 25°$. It overshoots the target by 60 ft. The target moves away from the gun at a constant speed of 10 ft/s. If the gunner takes 30 seconds to reload, at what angle should a second shot be fired with the same muzzle speed to hit the target?

39. A shell is fired from ground level with muzzle speed of 750 ft/s at an angle of 25°. An enemy gun 20,000 ft away fires a shot 2 seconds later and the shells collide 50 ft above the ground at the same speed. What are the muzzle speed v_0 and angle of elevation α of the second gun?

C 40. Suppose a shell is fired with muzzle speed v_0 at an angle α from a height s_0 above level ground.

a. Show that the range R_f must satisfy

$$g(\sec^2 \alpha)R_f^2 - 2v_0^2(\tan \alpha)R_f - 2v_0^2 s_0 = 0$$

b. Show that the maximum range R_m occurs at angle α_m, where $R_m \tan \alpha_m = \dfrac{v_0^2}{g}$.

c. Show that

$$R_{\max} = \frac{v_0}{g}\sqrt{v_0^2 + 2gs_0} \quad \text{and} \quad \alpha_m = \tan^{-1}\left(\frac{v_0}{\sqrt{v_0^2 + 2gs_0}}\right)$$

41. Use the formula

$$\mathbf{V}(t) = \frac{dr}{dt}\mathbf{u}_r + r\frac{d\theta}{dt}\mathbf{u}_\theta$$

to derive the formula for polar acceleration:

$$\mathbf{A}(t) = \left[\frac{d^2r}{dt^2} - r\left(\frac{d\theta}{dt}\right)^2\right]\mathbf{u}_r + \left[r\frac{d^2\theta}{dt^2} + 2\frac{dr}{dt}\frac{d\theta}{dt}\right]\mathbf{u}_\theta$$

Hint: Begin by using the chain rule to show

$$\frac{d\mathbf{u}_r}{dt} = \mathbf{u}_\theta\frac{d\theta}{dt} \quad \text{and} \quad \frac{d\mathbf{u}_\theta}{dt} = -\mathbf{u}_r\frac{d\theta}{dt}$$

42. Use the results of Problem 41 to show that the force $\mathbf{F}(t)$ acting on an object moving with acceleration $\mathbf{A}(t)$ acts only in a radial direction (parallel to $\mathbf{u}_r$) if and only if

$$mr^2\frac{d\theta}{dt} = C$$

where C is a constant. Under what conditions will $\mathbf{F}(t)$ act only in a direction orthogonal to $\mathbf{u}_r$?

43. Modeling Problem A cannon is placed at the top of a downward-sloping hill as in Problem 35. A shell is fired with muzzle speed v_0 at an angle of elevation α with respect to the horizontal. Assume the hill is sloped at an angle β with the horizontal, as shown in Figure 10.28.

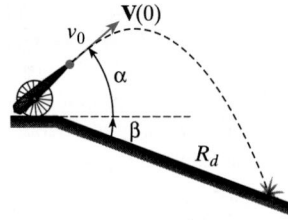

Figure 10.28   Projectile fired on a sloping hill

a. Derive a formula for the time of flight T_f of the shell and the downhill range R_d (measured along the slope).

b. What should α be in order to maximize the downhill range R_d?

10.4   Unit Tangent and Principal Unit Normal Vectors; Curvature

IN THIS SECTION   unit tangent and principal unit normal vectors, arc length as a parameter, curvature

UNIT TANGENT AND PRINCIPAL UNIT NORMAL VECTORS

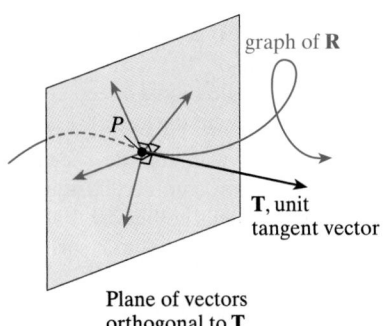

Figure 10.29 Unit tangent vector **T** and vectors orthogonal to **T** on a given curve

In Section 10.2, we observed that if $\mathbf{R}(t)$ is a vector function whose graph is a smooth curve C, then the nonzero derivative $\mathbf{R}'(t)$ is tangent to C at the point P that corresponds to t. Since the curve C is smooth, we have $\mathbf{R}'(t) \neq \mathbf{0}$ and a **unit tangent vector T** to C can be obtained by dividing $\mathbf{R}'(t)$ by its length, that is,

$$\mathbf{T}(t) = \frac{\mathbf{R}'(t)}{\|\mathbf{R}'(t)\|}$$

Figure 10.29 shows a smooth curve C and the unit tangent **T** at a particular point P.

According to Theorem 10.4 (orthogonality of a function of constant length and its derivative), since $\mathbf{T}(t)$ has constant magnitude (namely $\|\mathbf{T}(t)\| = 1$), it follows that its derivative $\mathbf{T}'(t)$ is orthogonal to $\mathbf{T}(t)$ and hence is normal to the curve C at P. As indicated in Figure 10.29, there are infinitely many vectors that are orthogonal to **T** and thus deserve to be called normal vectors. To distinguish $\mathbf{T}'(t)$ from the others, we normalize it by dividing by its length and refer to it as the **principal unit normal N**(t), so

$$\mathbf{N}(t) = \frac{\mathbf{T}'(t)}{\|\mathbf{T}'(t)\|}$$

To summarize,

Unit Tangent and Principal Unit Normal Vectors

If $\mathbf{R}(t)$ is a vector function that defines a smooth graph, then at each point a **unit tangent vector** is

$$\mathbf{T}(t) = \frac{\mathbf{R}'(t)}{\|\mathbf{R}'(t)\|}$$

and the **principal unit normal** vector is

$$\mathbf{N}(t) = \frac{\mathbf{T}'(t)}{\|\mathbf{T}'(t)\|}$$

Note these are pairs of unit vectors that change direction depending on where you are on the curve.

EXAMPLE 1   Unit tangent and principal unit normal

Find the unit tangent vector $\mathbf{T}(t)$ and the principal unit normal vector $\mathbf{N}(t)$ at each point on the graph of the vector function

$$\mathbf{R}(t) = \langle 3\sin t, 4t, 3\cos t\rangle$$

Solution

We have $\mathbf{R}'(t) = \langle 3\cos t, 4, -3\sin t\rangle$, so

$$\begin{aligned}
\|\mathbf{R}'(t)\| &= \sqrt{(3\cos t)^2 + 4^2 + (-3\sin t)^2} \\
&= \sqrt{9\cos^2 t + 16 + 9\sin^2 t} \\
&= \sqrt{9 + 16} \qquad \text{Since } \sin^2 t + \cos^2 t = 1 \\
&= 5
\end{aligned}$$

Thus, the unit tangent vector is

$$\begin{aligned}
\mathbf{T}(t) &= \frac{\mathbf{R}'(t)}{\|\mathbf{R}'(t)\|} = \tfrac{1}{5}\langle 3\cos t, 4, -3\sin t\rangle \\
&= \left\langle \tfrac{3}{5}\cos t, \tfrac{4}{5}, -\tfrac{3}{5}\sin t\right\rangle
\end{aligned}$$

To find the principal unit normal $\mathbf{N}$, we first find $\mathbf{T}'(t)$ and then its magnitude:

$$\mathbf{T}'(t) = \langle -\tfrac{3}{5}\sin t, 0, -\tfrac{3}{5}\cos t\rangle$$

$$\begin{aligned}
\|\mathbf{T}'(t)\| &= \sqrt{\left(-\tfrac{3}{5}\sin t\right)^2 + 0 + \left(-\tfrac{3}{5}\cos t\right)^2} \\
&= \sqrt{\tfrac{9}{25}(\sin^2 t + \cos^2 t)} \\
&= \tfrac{3}{5}
\end{aligned}$$

So, the unit normal is

$$\begin{aligned}
\mathbf{N}(t) &= \frac{\mathbf{T}'(t)}{\|\mathbf{T}'(t)\|} = \frac{\langle -\tfrac{3}{5}\sin t, 0, -\tfrac{3}{5}\cos t\rangle}{\tfrac{3}{5}} \\
&= \langle -\sin t, 0, -\cos t\rangle \qquad\qquad\blacksquare
\end{aligned}$$

Suppose an object moves along the graph C of a vector function $\mathbf{R}(t)$ in the direction of increasing t. Then at each point P on the trajectory C, the unit tangent $\mathbf{T}(t)$ points in the direction of motion, while the principal unit normal $\mathbf{N}(t)$ points in the direction the object is turning, as shown in Figure 10.30a. For a trajectory in a plane, this means that $\mathbf{N}(t)$ points toward the concave side of the trajectory (Figure 10.30b).

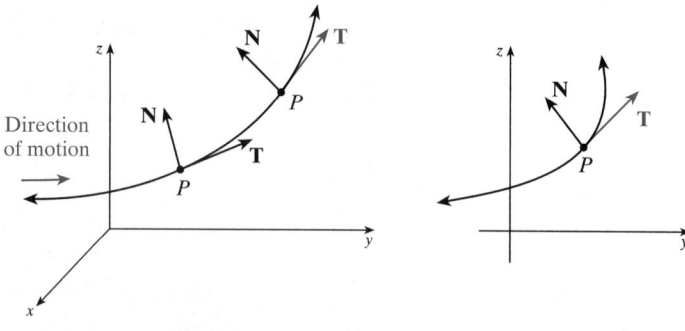

a. $\mathbf{T}$ points in the direction of motion while $\mathbf{N}$ points in the direction the moving object is turning

b. In the plane, $\mathbf{N}$ points toward the concave side of the trajectory

Figure 10.30   Unit tangent $\mathbf{T}$ and principal unit normal $\mathbf{N}$ at each point on the trajectory of a moving object

ARC LENGTH AS A PARAMETER

Recall from Section 6.4 that the arc length of the graph of $y = F(x)$ on the interval $[a, b]$ is given by the integral

$$s = \int_a^b \sqrt{1 + \left(\frac{dy}{dx}\right)^2}\, dx$$

If the graph is described by parametric equations $x = x(t)$ and $y = y(t)$, then by the chain rule $\dfrac{dy}{dt} = \dfrac{dy}{dx}\dfrac{dx}{dt}$, so we have

$$\frac{dy}{dx} = \frac{\dfrac{dy}{dt}}{\dfrac{dx}{dt}} \qquad \text{for } \frac{dx}{dt} \neq 0,$$

Thus, if the graph is traced out exactly once over the parameter interval $t_1 \leq t \leq t_2$, its arc length is given by

$$s = \int_a^b \sqrt{1 + \left(\frac{dy/dt}{dx/dt}\right)^2}\, dx$$

$$= \int_{t_1}^{t_2} \sqrt{\frac{\left(\frac{dx}{dt}\right)^2 + \left(\frac{dy}{dt}\right)^2}{\left(\frac{dx}{dt}\right)^2}} \left(\frac{dx}{dt}\right) dt$$

$$= \int_{t_1}^{t_2} \sqrt{\left(\frac{dx}{dt}\right)^2 + \left(\frac{dy}{dt}\right)^2}\, dt$$

Similarly, if $x = x(t)$, $y = y(t)$, $z = z(t)$ are parametric equations for a smooth curve C in $\mathbb{R}^3$ that is traced out exactly once over the parameter interval $t_1 \leq t \leq t_2$, then the arc length of C is given by the integral

$$s = \int_{t_1}^{t_2} \sqrt{\left(\frac{dx}{dt}\right)^2 + \left(\frac{dy}{dt}\right)^2 + \left(\frac{dz}{dt}\right)^2}\, dt$$

Often, however, we want a formula for arc length that does not depend on t or any other particular parameter used in its computation. It can be shown that the following definition of the arc length function is, indeed, independent of parameterization.

Arc Length Function

Let C be a piecewise-smooth curve that is the graph of the vector described parameterically by $\mathbf{R}(t) = x(t)\mathbf{i} + y(t)\mathbf{j} + z(t)\mathbf{k}$, and let $P_0 = P(t_0)$ be a particular point on C (called the **base point**). Then the length of C from the base point P_0 to the variable point $P(t)$ is given by the **arc length function** $s(t)$ defined by

$$s(t) = \int_{t_0}^{t} \sqrt{\left(\frac{dx}{du}\right)^2 + \left(\frac{dy}{du}\right)^2 + \left(\frac{dz}{du}\right)^2}\, du$$

➡ **What This Says** The arc length function $s(t)$ measures the distance along the curve C from $P(t_0)$ to $P(t)$ if $t > t_0$ and the opposite of that distance if $t < t_0$ (see Figure 10.31). Since the length along C is a geometric property, it does not depend on the fact that we have used t as a parameter for describing $\mathbf{R}(t)$.

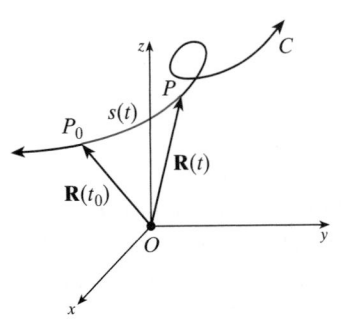

Figure 10.31 $s(t)$ is the length of the curve C from the point $P(t_0)$ to $P(t)$ if $t > t_0$.

This definition allows us to use arc length $s(t)$ as a parameter for describing a curve. While time is a natural parameter for studying motion in space, it is usually more fruitful to use the arc length parameter for describing a curve's geometric features.

EXAMPLE 2 Finding the arc length of a curve defined by parametric equations

Find the arc length of the curve defined by $\mathbf{R}(t) = \langle 12t, 5\cos t, 3 - 5\sin t \rangle$ from $t = 0$ to $t = 2$.

Solution

We find that

$$\frac{dx}{dt} = 12, \frac{dy}{dt} = -5\sin t, \frac{dz}{dt} = -5\cos t$$

Thus,

$$s = \int_0^2 \sqrt{\left(\frac{dx}{dt}\right)^2 + \left(\frac{dy}{dt}\right)^2 + \left(\frac{dz}{dt}\right)^2}\, dt$$

$$= \int_0^2 \sqrt{12^2 + (-5\sin t)^2 + (-5\cos t)^2}\, dt$$

$$= \int_0^2 13\, dt$$

$$= 26$$

The formula for arc length can be used to obtain the following useful formula for the speed of an object moving in space.

THEOREM 10.6 **Speed as the derivative of arc length**

Suppose an object moves along a smooth curve C that is the graph of the position function $\mathbf{R}(t) = \langle x(t), y(t), z(t) \rangle$, where $\mathbf{R}'(t)$ is continuous on the interval $[t_1, t_2]$. Then the object has speed

$$\frac{ds}{dt} = \|\mathbf{V}(t)\| = \|\mathbf{R}'(t)\| \qquad \text{for } t_1 \leq t \leq t_2$$

Proof Apply the second fundamental theorem of calculus to the arc length formula (where we use u as the variable of integration to distinguish it from t):

$$s = \int_{t_1}^{t} \sqrt{\left(\frac{dx}{du}\right)^2 + \left(\frac{dy}{du}\right)^2 + \left(\frac{dz}{du}\right)^2}\, du$$

$$\frac{ds}{dt} = \sqrt{\left(\frac{dx}{dt}\right)^2 + \left(\frac{dy}{dt}\right)^2 + \left(\frac{dz}{dt}\right)^2}$$

$$= \|\mathbf{R}'(t)\| \qquad\qquad \square$$

EXAMPLE 3 **Speed and distance traveled by an object moving in space**

The position vector of a moving object is $\mathbf{R}(t) = \langle e^t, \sqrt{2t+3}, e^{-t} \rangle$. Find the speed of the object at time t and compute the distance the object travels between times $t = 0$ and $t = 1$.

Solution

By differentiating $\mathbf{R}(t)$ with respect to t, we find the velocity:

$$\mathbf{V}(t) = \mathbf{R}'(t) = \langle e^t, \sqrt{2}, -e^{-t} \rangle$$

Therefore, the speed at time t is

$$\frac{ds}{dt} = \|\mathbf{R}'(t)\| = \sqrt{(e^t)^2 + (\sqrt{2})^2 + (-e^{-t})^2}$$

$$= \sqrt{e^{2t} + 2 + e^{-2t}} = \sqrt{(e^t + e^{-t})^2} = e^t + e^{-t}$$

The distance traveled by the object between times $t = 0$ and $t = 1$ is the arc length and is given by

$$s = \int_0^1 (e^t + e^{-t})\, dt = \left[e^t - e^{-t} \right]_0^1 = e - e^{-1} - 1 + 1 \approx 2.3504024 \qquad \blacksquare$$

To change a given parameterization from a given form, say $\mathbf{R}(t)$, to a form involving the parameter s, we first find $s(t)$ using the arc length formula (as in the proof of Theorem 10.6), and then solve for t as a function of s. The graph of $\mathbf{R}(t)$ can then be parameterized in terms of s by substituting $t = t(s)$. The general procedure is illustrated in the following example.

EXAMPLE 4 **Using arc length to parameterize a curve**

Express the helix $\mathbf{R}(t) = \langle \sin t, \cos t, 2t \rangle$ in terms of arc length measured from the point $P_0(0, 1, 0)$ in the direction of increasing t.

Solution

The point P_0 corresponds to $t = 0$, so arc length $s(t)$ is given by the integral

$$s(t) = \int_0^t \sqrt{\left(\frac{dx}{du}\right)^2 + \left(\frac{dy}{du}\right)^2 + \left(\frac{dz}{du}\right)^2}\, du$$

$$= \int_0^t \sqrt{(\cos u)^2 + (-\sin u)^2 + 2^2}\, du$$

$$= \int_0^t \sqrt{5}\, du$$

$$= \sqrt{5}\, t$$

Solving $s = \sqrt{5}\, t$ for t, we obtain $t = \dfrac{1}{\sqrt{5}} s$, and the required reparameterization is

$$x = \sin\left(\frac{s}{\sqrt{5}}\right), \quad y = \cos\left(\frac{s}{\sqrt{5}}\right), \quad z = \frac{2s}{\sqrt{5}} \qquad \blacksquare$$

Expressing a given position vector $\mathbf{R}$ in terms of the arc length parameter s often leads to complicated computation. However, once we have such a parameterization, the corresponding unit tangent vector $\mathbf{T}$ and principal unit normal vector $\mathbf{N}$ can be expressed in the relatively simple forms shown in the following theorem.

THEOREM 10.7   Formulas for T and N in terms of arc length s

If $\mathbf{R}(t)$ has a piecewise-smooth graph and is represented as $\mathbf{R}(s)$ in terms of the arc length parameter s, then the unit tangent vector $\mathbf{T}$ and the principal unit normal vector $\mathbf{N}$ satisfy

$$\mathbf{T} = \frac{d\mathbf{R}}{ds} \quad \text{and} \quad \mathbf{N} = \frac{1}{\kappa}\frac{d\mathbf{T}}{ds}$$

where $\kappa = \left\|\dfrac{d\mathbf{T}}{ds}\right\|$ is a scalar function of s.

Proof   By the chain rule, we have $\dfrac{d\mathbf{R}}{dt} = \dfrac{d\mathbf{R}}{ds}\dfrac{ds}{dt}$, and since $\dfrac{ds}{dt} = \|\mathbf{R}'(t)\|$, it follows that

$$\frac{d\mathbf{R}}{ds} = \frac{\dfrac{d\mathbf{R}}{dt}}{\dfrac{ds}{dt}} = \frac{\mathbf{R}'(t)}{\|\mathbf{R}'(t)\|} = \mathbf{T}$$

Next, to obtain the formula for the principal unit normal vector

$$\mathbf{N} = \frac{\mathbf{T}'(t)}{\|\mathbf{T}'(t)\|}$$

in terms of the arc length parameter s, we first note that

$$\mathbf{T}'(t) = \frac{d\mathbf{T}}{dt} = \frac{d\mathbf{T}}{ds}\frac{ds}{dt} \qquad \text{Chain rule}$$

Because $\dfrac{ds}{dt} > 0$, it follows that the vector derivatives $\dfrac{d\mathbf{T}}{dt}$ and $\dfrac{d\mathbf{T}}{ds}$ point in the same direction, and $\mathbf{N}$ can be computed by finding $\dfrac{d\mathbf{T}}{ds}$ and dividing by its length; that is,

$$\mathbf{N} = \frac{\dfrac{d\mathbf{T}}{ds}}{\left\|\dfrac{d\mathbf{T}}{ds}\right\|} = \frac{1}{\kappa}\frac{d\mathbf{T}}{ds}$$

as claimed.   ❑

CURVATURE

Let C be a smooth curve that is the graph of a vector function $\mathbf{R}(s)$ parameterized in terms of arc length s. Since the unit tangent $\mathbf{T}(s)$ is a unit vector, only its direction changes with s and the rate of change of that direction may be measured by the magnitude of the derivative $\dfrac{d\mathbf{T}}{ds}$. As shown in Figure 10.32a, if the curve is a line, then the direction remains constant so that $\dfrac{d\mathbf{T}}{ds} = \mathbf{0}$, but if the curve is bent sharply, the direction of $\mathbf{T}$ changes rapidly so $\dfrac{d\mathbf{T}}{ds}$ is relatively large in magnitude (Figure 10.32b). The magnitude of $\dfrac{d\mathbf{T}}{ds}$ is called the *curvature* of C.

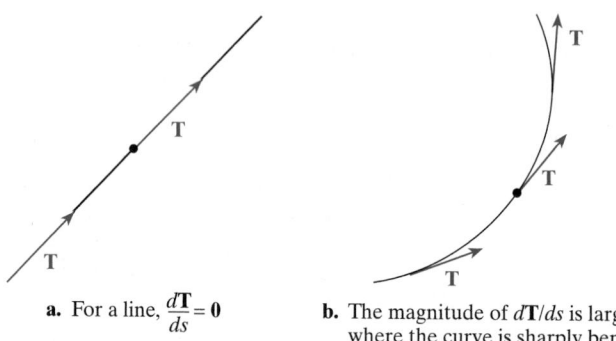

a. For a line, $\dfrac{d\mathbf{T}}{ds} = \mathbf{0}$ **b.** The magnitude of $d\mathbf{T}/ds$ is large where the curve is sharply bent.

Figure 10.32   The sharpness of a curve C is related to the magnitude of $\dfrac{d\mathbf{T}}{ds}$.

Curvature

> Suppose the smooth curve C is the graph of the vector function $\mathbf{R}(s)$, parameterized in terms of the arc length s. Then the **curvature** of C is the function
>
> $$\kappa(s) = \left\| \frac{d\mathbf{T}}{ds} \right\|$$
>
> where $\mathbf{T}(s)$ is the unit tangent vector.

First, notice that κ in Theorem 10.7 is the curvature of $\mathbf{R}(s)$. Since a vector function $\mathbf{R}$ is often represented in terms of a parameter other than arc length s, it may not be especially convenient to compute the curvature using the formula $\kappa = \left\| \dfrac{d\mathbf{T}}{ds} \right\|$. For instance, if the parameter is t, then according to the chain rule, we have

$$\frac{d\mathbf{T}}{dt} = \frac{d\mathbf{T}}{ds}\frac{ds}{dt}$$

so that

$$\left\| \frac{d\mathbf{T}}{ds} \right\| = \frac{\left\| \dfrac{dT}{dt} \right\|}{\dfrac{ds}{dt}}$$

(Remember, s increases in the same direction as t, so $\dfrac{ds}{dt} > 0$.) Since $\dfrac{ds}{dt} = \|\mathbf{R}'(t)\|$, it follows that

$$\kappa = \frac{\|\mathbf{T}'(t)\|}{\|\mathbf{R}'(t)\|}$$

which we will refer to as the **two derivatives form** of the curvature. This form is often used in practice to compute κ because it involves only the magnitudes of $\mathbf{R}'(t)$ and $\mathbf{T}'(t)$, both of which are usually easier to compute than $\left\|\dfrac{d\mathbf{T}}{ds}\right\|$. In Example 5, we illustrate the use of the two derivatives form by computing the curvature of a circle.

EXAMPLE 5 **Finding the curvature of a circle**

Show that the circle with radius r

$$\mathbf{R}(t) = \langle r\cos t, r\sin t\rangle$$

has curvature equal to the reciprocal of its radius; that is, $\kappa = \dfrac{1}{r}$.

Solution

Since $\mathbf{R}'(t) = \langle -r\sin t, r\cos t\rangle$, we have

$$\|\mathbf{R}'(t)\| = \sqrt{(-r\sin t)^2 + (r\cos t)^2} = r$$

Then

$$\mathbf{T}(t) = \frac{\mathbf{R}'(t)}{\|\mathbf{R}'(t)\|} = \frac{\langle -r\sin t, r\cos t\rangle}{r} = \langle -\sin t, \cos t\rangle$$

and

$$\mathbf{T}'(t) = \langle -\cos t, -\sin t\rangle$$

Since

$$\|\mathbf{T}'(t)\| = \sqrt{(-\cos t)^2 + (-\sin t)^2} = 1$$

the curvature is

$$\kappa = \frac{\|\mathbf{T}'(t)\|}{\|\mathbf{R}'(t)\|} = \frac{1}{r} \qquad \blacksquare$$

The definition of curvature, $\kappa = \dfrac{\|\mathbf{T}'(t)\|}{\|\mathbf{R}'(t)\|}$, can lead to difficult computations when $\|\mathbf{R}'(t)\|$ is not a constant. The formula for curvature derived in the following theorem may then be easier to apply.

THEOREM 10.8 **The cross derivative formula for curvature**

Suppose the smooth curve C is the graph of the vector function $\mathbf{R}(t)$. Then the curvature is given by

$$\kappa = \frac{\|\mathbf{R}' \times \mathbf{R}''\|}{\|\mathbf{R}'\|^3}$$

Proof Since $\|\mathbf{R}'\| = \dfrac{ds}{dt}$, we have

$$\mathbf{R}' = \|\mathbf{R}'\|\mathbf{T} = \left(\frac{ds}{dt}\right)\mathbf{T}$$

$$\mathbf{R}'' = \frac{d}{dt}\left(\frac{ds}{dt}\right)\mathbf{T} + \frac{ds}{dt}\frac{d\mathbf{T}}{dt}$$

$$= \frac{d^2s}{dt^2}\mathbf{T} + \frac{ds}{dt}\mathbf{T}'$$

Therefore, we have

$$\mathbf{R}' \times \mathbf{R}'' = \left(\frac{ds}{dt}\mathbf{T}\right) \times \left(\frac{d^2s}{dt^2}\mathbf{T} + \frac{ds}{dt}\mathbf{T}'\right)$$

$$= \left(\frac{ds}{dt}\right)\left(\frac{d^2s}{dt^2}\right)(\mathbf{T} \times \mathbf{T}) + \left(\frac{ds}{dt}\right)^2(\mathbf{T} \times \mathbf{T}')$$

$$= \left(\frac{ds}{dt}\right)^2(\mathbf{T} \times \mathbf{T}') \qquad \text{Since } \mathbf{T} \times \mathbf{T} = \mathbf{0}$$

Since $\|\mathbf{T}\| = 1$, it follows from the orthogonality of a function of constant length and its derivative (Theorem 10.4) that $\mathbf{T} \cdot \mathbf{T}' = 0$, so the angle between $\mathbf{T}$ and $\mathbf{T}'$ is $\theta = \frac{\pi}{2}$. Thus,

$$\|\mathbf{R}' \times \mathbf{R}''\| = \left(\frac{ds}{dt}\right)^2 \|\mathbf{T} \times \mathbf{T}'\|$$

$$= \left(\frac{ds}{dt}\right)^2 \|\mathbf{T}\|\|\mathbf{T}'\| \sin\theta$$

$$= \left(\frac{ds}{dt}\right)^2 \|\mathbf{T}\|\|\mathbf{T}'\| \qquad \text{Since } \sin\frac{\pi}{2} = 1$$

$$= \left(\frac{ds}{dt}\right)^2 \|\mathbf{T}'\| \qquad \text{Since } \|\mathbf{T}\| = 1$$

$$= \|\mathbf{R}'\|^2 \|\mathbf{T}'\|$$

The curvature is given by

$$\kappa = \frac{\|\mathbf{T}'\|}{\|\mathbf{R}'\|}$$

$$= \frac{\dfrac{\|\mathbf{R}' \times \mathbf{R}''\|}{\|\mathbf{R}'\|^2}}{\|\mathbf{R}'\|}$$

$$= \frac{\|\mathbf{R}' \times \mathbf{R}''\|}{\|\mathbf{R}'\|^3} \qquad \qquad \square$$

EXAMPLE 6 Curvature of a helix

Given that a and b are both nonnegative, express the curvature κ of $\mathbf{R}(t) = (a\cos t)\mathbf{i} + (a\sin t)\mathbf{j} + bt\mathbf{k}$ in terms of a and b. The curve defined by $\mathbf{R}$ is shown in Figure 10.33.

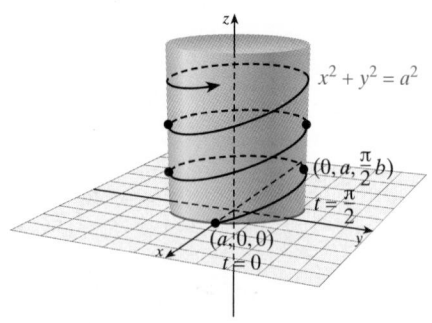

Figure 10.33 Graph of $\mathbf{R}(t) = (a\cos t)\mathbf{i} + (a\sin t)\mathbf{j} + bt\mathbf{k}$

Solution

$$\mathbf{R}'(t) = (-a\sin t)\mathbf{i} + (a\cos t)\mathbf{j} + b\mathbf{k}$$

$$\mathbf{R}''(t) = (-a\cos t)\mathbf{i} + (-a\sin t)\mathbf{j}$$

$$\mathbf{R}' \times \mathbf{R}'' = \begin{vmatrix} \mathbf{i} & \mathbf{j} & \mathbf{k} \\ -a\sin t & a\cos t & b \\ -a\cos t & -a\sin t & 0 \end{vmatrix} = (ab\sin t)\mathbf{i} - (ab\cos t)\mathbf{j} + a^2\mathbf{k}$$

We now need to find the magnitude of this vector, as well as that of $\mathbf{R}'$:

$$\|\mathbf{R}' \times \mathbf{R}''\| = \sqrt{(ab\sin t)^2 + (ab\cos t)^2 + a^4}$$

$$= \sqrt{a^2b^2(\sin^2 t + \cos^2 t) + a^4}$$

$$= \sqrt{a^2b^2 + a^4}$$

$$= a\sqrt{a^2 + b^2} \qquad a > 0 \text{ is given}$$

and

$$\|\mathbf{R}'\| = \sqrt{a^2\cos^2 t + a^2\sin^2 t + b^2} = \sqrt{a^2 + b^2}$$

Then we have

$$\kappa = \frac{\|\mathbf{R}' \times \mathbf{R}''\|}{\|\mathbf{R}'\|^3} = \frac{a\sqrt{a^2 + b^2}}{(\sqrt{a^2 + b^2})^3} = \frac{a\sqrt{a^2 + b^2}}{(a^2 + b^2)\sqrt{a^2 + b^2}} = \frac{a}{a^2 + b^2} \qquad ■$$

In the special case where C is a curve in the plane with the equation $y = f(x)$, the curvature has the form given in the following theorem.

THEOREM 10.9   Curvature of a planar curve using $y = f(x)$

The graph C of the function $y = f(x)$ has curvature

$$\kappa = \frac{|f''(x)|}{\left(1 + [f'(x)]^2\right)^{3/2}}$$

wherever $f(x)$ and its derivatives $f'(x)$ and $f''(x)$ all exist.

Proof   Using x as a parameter, we can regard the curve C as the graph of the vector function $\mathbf{R}(x) = x\mathbf{i} + f(x)\mathbf{j}$. Then, $\mathbf{R}' = \mathbf{i} + f'(x)\mathbf{j}$ and $\mathbf{R}'' = f''(x)\mathbf{j}$, so

$$\mathbf{R}' \times \mathbf{R}'' = \begin{vmatrix} \mathbf{i} & \mathbf{j} & \mathbf{k} \\ 1 & f'(x) & 0 \\ 0 & f''(x) & 0 \end{vmatrix} = f''(x)\mathbf{k}$$

Therefore, since $\|\mathbf{R}'\| = \sqrt{1 + [f'(x)]^2}$, the curvature of C is given by

$$\kappa = \frac{\|\mathbf{R}' \times \mathbf{R}''\|}{\|\mathbf{R}'\|^3}$$

$$= \frac{|f''(x)|}{\left(\sqrt{1 + [f'(x)]^2}\right)^3}$$

$$= \frac{|f''(x)|}{\left(1 + [f'(x)]^2\right)^{3/2}} \qquad ❏$$

EXAMPLE 7   Maximizing the curvature of a planar curve

Find the curvature of $y = x^{-1}$ for $x > 0$. For what value of x is the curvature the largest?

Solution

For $f(x) = x^{-1}$, we have $f'(x) = -x^{-2}$ and $f''(x) = 2x^{-3}$, so the curvature is

$$\kappa = \frac{|f''(x)|}{\left(1 + [f'(x)]^2\right)^{3/2}}$$

$$= \frac{2x^{-3}}{\left(1 + [-x^{-2}]^2\right)^{3/2}}$$

$$= \frac{2x^3}{(x^4 + 1)^{3/2}}$$

To find the largest value of κ, we compute the derivative of $\kappa(x)$ and solve the equation $\kappa'(x) = 0$:

$$\kappa'(x) = \frac{6x^2(1 - x^4)}{(x^4 + 1)^{5/2}}$$

Now $\kappa'(x) = 0$ when

$$6x^2(1 - x^4) = 0$$
$$6x^2(1 - x)(1 + x)(1 + x^2) = 0$$
$$x = 0, 1, -1 \quad \text{The 0 and } -1 \text{ are not in the domain.}$$

Since $\kappa'(x) > 0$ for $x < 1$ and $\kappa'(x) < 0$ for $x > 1$, it follows that the largest value of the curvature must occur at $x = 1$. ∎

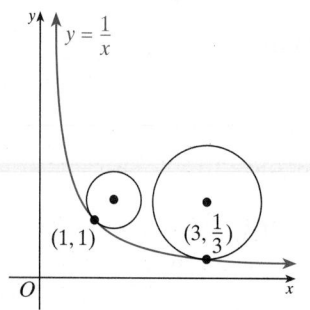

Figure 10.34 Osculating circles to the curve $y = x^{-1}$ at the points $(1, 1)$ and $\left(3, \frac{1}{3}\right)$

Suppose a curve C in the plane has curvature $\kappa \neq 0$ at a point P. Then the circle of radius $\rho = \dfrac{1}{\kappa}$ that is centered on the concave side of the curve and shares a common tangent with C at P is called the **osculating** (kissing) **circle** at P. The radius ρ of the osculating circle is called the **radius of curvature** and the center of the circle is called the **center of curvature**. The osculating circle and the curve C are tangent and have the same curvature at P, and in this sense, the osculating circle is the circle that best approximates the curve C at P.

Figure 10.34 shows the curve $y = x^{-1}$ for $x > 0$ whose curvature we found in Example 7, along with the osculating circle at the point $P(1, 1)$ that corresponds to $x = 1$. Note that the curvature at P is

$$\kappa(1) = \frac{2(1)^3}{\left(1^4 + 1\right)^{3/2}} = \frac{1}{\sqrt{2}}$$

so the radius of curvature is

$$\rho(1) = \frac{1}{\kappa(1)} = \sqrt{2}$$

In Problem 56, you are asked to show that the osculating circle at P has the equation

$$(x - 2)^2 + (y - 2)^2 = 2$$

We conclude this section by providing a summary of various formulas for computing curvature (Table 10.2).

TABLE 10.2 Curvature Formulas

Type	Given Information	Formula to Use	Where Derived
Arc length parameter	$\mathbf{R}(s)$	$\left\|\dfrac{d\mathbf{T}}{ds}\right\|$	Definition
Two derivatives form	$\mathbf{R}(t)$	$\dfrac{\|\mathbf{T}'(t)\|}{\|\mathbf{R}'(t)\|}$	Pages 666–667
Cross derivative form	$\mathbf{R}(t)$	$\dfrac{\|\mathbf{R}' \times \mathbf{R}''\|}{\|\mathbf{R}'\|^3}$	Theorem 10.8
Functional form	$y = f(x)$	$\dfrac{\|f''(x)\|}{(1 + [f'(x)]^2)^{3/2}}$	Theorem 10.9
Parametric form	$x = x(t),\ y = y(t)$	$\dfrac{\|x'y'' - y'x''\|}{[(x')^2 + (y')^2]^{3/2}}$	Problem 46
Polar form	$r = f(\theta)$	$\dfrac{\left\|r^2 + 2r'^2 - rr''\right\|}{(r^2 + r'^2)^{3/2}}$	Problem 47

10.4 PROBLEM SET

A *In Problems 1–8, find the unit tangent vector* $\mathbf{T}(t)$ *and the principal unit normal vector* $\mathbf{N}(t)$ *for the curve given by* $\mathbf{R}(t)$.

1. $\mathbf{R}(t) = t^2\mathbf{i} + t^3\mathbf{j},\ t \neq 0$ **2.** $\mathbf{R}(t) = t^2\mathbf{i} + \sqrt{t}\,\mathbf{j},\ t > 0$

3. $\mathbf{R}(t) = (e^t \cos t)\mathbf{i} + (e^t \sin t)\mathbf{j}$

4. $\mathbf{R}(t) = (t \cos t)\mathbf{i} + (t \sin t)\mathbf{j}$

5. $\mathbf{R}(t) = (\cos t)\mathbf{i} + (\sin t)\mathbf{j} + t\mathbf{k}$

6. $\mathbf{R}(t) = (\sin t)\mathbf{i} - (\cos t)\mathbf{j} + t\mathbf{k}$

7. $\mathbf{R}(t) = (\ln t)\mathbf{i} + t^2\mathbf{k}$

8. $\mathbf{R}(t) = (e^{-t} \sin t)\mathbf{i} + e^{-t}\mathbf{j} + (e^{-t} \cos t)\mathbf{k}$

In Problems 9–14, find the length of the given curve over the given interval.

9. $\mathbf{R}(t) = 2t\mathbf{i} + t\mathbf{j}$, over $[0, 4]$

10. $\mathbf{R}(t) = t\mathbf{i} + 3t\mathbf{j}$, over $[0, 4]$

11. $\mathbf{R}(t) = 3t\mathbf{i} + (3 \cos t)\mathbf{j} + (3 \sin t)\mathbf{k}$, over $[0, \frac{\pi}{2}]$

12. $\mathbf{R}(t) = t\mathbf{i} + 2t\mathbf{j} + 3t\mathbf{k}$, over $[0, 2]$

13. $\mathbf{R}(t) = (4 \cos t)\mathbf{i} + (4 \sin t)\mathbf{j} + 5t\mathbf{k}$, over $[0, \pi]$

14. $\mathbf{R}(t) = (\cos^3 t)\mathbf{i} + (\cos^2 t)\mathbf{k}$, over $[0, \frac{\pi}{2}]$

Find the curvature of the plane curves at the points indicated in Problems 15–20.

15. $y = 4x - 2$ at $x = 2$ **16.** $y = x - \frac{1}{9}x^2$ at $x = 3$

17. $y = x + \dfrac{1}{x}$ at $x = 1$ **18.** $y = \sin x$ at $x = \frac{\pi}{2}$

19. $y = \ln x$ at $x = 1$ **20.** $y = e^x$ at $x = 0$

Express the vector function $\mathbf{R}(t)$ *in Problems 21–24 in terms of the arc length parameter s measured from the point where* $t = 0$ *in the direction of increasing t.*

21. $\mathbf{R}(t) = \langle e^{-t}, 1 - e^{-t} \rangle$ **22.** $\mathbf{R}(t) = \langle \sin t, \cos t \rangle$

23. $\mathbf{R}(t) = \langle 2 - 3t, 1 + t, -4t \rangle$

24. $\mathbf{R}(t) = \langle 3 \cos t + 3t \sin t, 2t^2, 3 \sin t - 3t \cos t \rangle$

25. Let $\mathbf{u}$ and $\mathbf{v}$ be constant, nonzero vectors. Show that the line given by $\mathbf{R}(t) = \mathbf{u} + t\mathbf{v}$ has curvature 0 at each point.

26. Find the unit tangent $\mathbf{T}$ for $\mathbf{R}(t) = (\cosh t)\mathbf{i} + (\sinh t)\mathbf{j}$ at the point where $t = 0$.

27. Find the unit tangent $\mathbf{T}$ for $\mathbf{R}(t) = [\ln(\sin t)]\mathbf{i} + [\ln(\cos t)]\mathbf{j}$ at the point where $t = \frac{\pi}{3}$.

B 28. A curve C in the plane is given parameterically by $x = 32t$, $y = 16t^2 - 4$.

     a. Sketch the graph of the curve.

     b. Find the unit tangent vector when $t = 3$.

     c. Find the radius of curvature of the point P on C where $t = 3$.

29. For the curve given by $\mathbf{R}(t) = (\sin t)\mathbf{i} + (\cos t)\mathbf{j} + t\mathbf{k}$,

     a. Find a unit tangent vector $\mathbf{T}$ at the point on the curve where $t = \pi$.

     b. Find the curvature when $t = \pi$.

     c. Find the length of the curve from $t = 0$ to $t = \pi$.

30. Let C be the curve given by
$\mathbf{R}(t) = (t - \sin t)\mathbf{i} + (1 - \cos t)\mathbf{j} + \left(4 \sin \frac{1}{2}t\right)\mathbf{k}$.

     a. Find the unit tangent vector $\mathbf{T}(t)$ to C.

     b. Find $\dfrac{d\mathbf{T}}{ds}$ and the curvature $\kappa(t)$.

31. Find the point (or points) where the ellipse $9x^2 + 4y^2 = 36$ has maximum curvature.

32. Find the maximum curvature on the curve $y = e^{2x}$.

33. Find the radius of curvature at each relative extremum of the graph of $y = x^6 - 3x^2$.

34. Find the curvature of the graph defined by $x = t - \sin t$, $y = 1 - \cos t$. Sketch the curve for $0 \leq t \leq 2\pi$ and sketch the osculating circle at the point where $t = \frac{\pi}{2}$.

There are several different formulas for finding curvature, as summarized in Table 10.2. In Problems 35–42, find the curvature of each of the given curves using the indicated formula.

35. $\mathbf{R}(t) = t\mathbf{i} + t^2\mathbf{j} + t^3\mathbf{k}$; cross derivative form

36. $\mathbf{R}(t) = (t - \cos t)\mathbf{i} + (\sin t)\mathbf{j} + 3\mathbf{k}$; cross derivative form

37. $y = x^2$; functional form

38. $y = x^3$; functional form

39. $y = x^{-2}$; functional form

40. $y = \sin x$; functional form

41. the spiral $r = e^\theta$; polar form

42. the cardioid $r = 1 + \cos\theta$, for $0 \le \theta \le 2\pi$; polar form

43. A *pestus houseflyus* is observed to zip around a room in such a way that at time t its position with respect to the nose of an observer is given by the vector function

$$\mathbf{R}(t) = t\mathbf{u} + t^2\mathbf{v} + 2\left(\tfrac{2}{3}t\right)^{3/2}(\mathbf{u} \times \mathbf{v})$$

where $\mathbf{u}$ and $\mathbf{v}$ are unit vectors separated by an angle of 60°. Compute the fly's speed and find how long it takes to move a distance of 20 units along its path (starting from the nose), as shown in Figure 10.35.

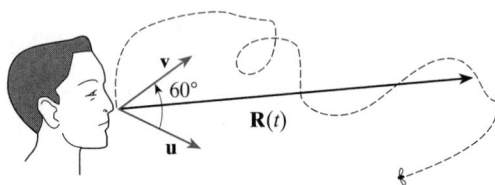

Figure 10.35 Path of a *pestus houseflyus*

44. **WHAT DOES THIS SAY?** Describe what is meant by using arc length as a parameter.

45. **WHAT DOES THIS SAY?** Discuss the various curvature formulas given in Table 10.2.

46. Let C be a smooth curve in $\mathbb{R}^2$ described by the parametric equations $x = x(t)$ and $y = y(t)$.

   a. Show that the curvature of C is given by

   $$\kappa = \frac{|x'y'' - y'x''|}{[(x')^2 + (y')^2]^{3/2}}$$

   b. Find the curvature of the curve described by $x = 1 - \cos t$, $y = 2 + \sin t$.

47. Let f be a twice differentiable function in $\mathbb{R}^2$ described by the polar function $r = f(\theta)$. Show that the curvature is

   $$\kappa(\theta) = \frac{|r^2 + 2r'^2 - rr''|}{(r^2 + r'^2)^{3/2}}$$

   Hint: Use the formula in Problem 46 with $x = f(\theta)\cos\theta$, $y = f(\theta)\sin\theta$.

48. Use the formula in Problem 47 to find the curvature of the graphs with the given equations.

   a. the cardioid $r = 1 + \cos\theta$

   b. the spiral $r = \theta$

   c. the circle $r = \sin\theta$

49. Show that the formula for polar curvature in Problem 47 reduces to $\kappa = \dfrac{2}{|r'|}$ at the pole (where $r = 0$).

50. Let $P(a, b)$ be a point on the graph C of the vector function $\mathbf{R}(t)$.

   a. Describe a general procedure for finding an equation for the osculating circle to C at P.

   b. Find an equation for the osculating circle at the point $P(32, 12)$ on the curve C defined by $x = 32t$, $y = 16t^2 - 4$.

51. The *Cornu spiral* is a parametric curve described by the equations

   $$x = \int_0^t \cos\left(\frac{\pi u^2}{2}\right) du \qquad y = \int_0^t \sin\left(\frac{\pi u^2}{2}\right) du$$

   It is used in optics to study amplitudes of light waves, and in the design of highway off ramps. It also has interesting mathematical properties.

   a. Show that the arc length of the spiral measured from the origin $(0, 0)$ satisfies $s = t$.

   b. Show that the curvature of the spiral satisfies $\kappa(s) = \pi|s|$. Thus, for $s \ge 0$, the curvature increases at a constant rate.

   c. What happens to the curvature, κ, as $s \to +\infty$? That is, evaluate $\lim\limits_{s \to +\infty} \kappa(s)$.

52. If $\mathbf{T}$ and $\mathbf{N}$ are the unit tangent and normal vectors, respectively, on the trajectory of a moving body, then the cross product vector $\mathbf{B} = \mathbf{T} \times \mathbf{N}$ is called the unit **binormal** of the trajectory. Three planes determined by $\mathbf{T}$, $\mathbf{N}$, and $\mathbf{B}$ are shown in Figure 10.36.

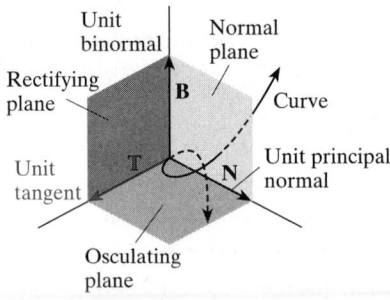

Figure 10.36 Three planes determined by $\mathbf{T}$, $\mathbf{N}$, and $\mathbf{B}$

   a. Show that $\mathbf{T}$ is orthogonal to $\dfrac{d\mathbf{B}}{ds}$. *Hint:* Differentiate $\mathbf{B} \cdot \mathbf{T}$.

   b. Show that $\mathbf{B}$ is orthogonal to $\dfrac{d\mathbf{B}}{ds}$. *Hint:* Differentiate $\mathbf{B} \cdot \mathbf{B}$.

   c. Show that $\dfrac{d\mathbf{B}}{ds} = -\tau\mathbf{N}$ for some constant τ. *Note:* τ is called the **torsion** of the trajectory.

53. Prove the Frenet-Serret formulas:

   $$\frac{d\mathbf{T}}{ds} = \kappa\mathbf{N} \qquad \frac{d\mathbf{N}}{ds} = -\kappa\mathbf{T} + \tau\mathbf{B} \qquad \frac{d\mathbf{B}}{ds} = -\tau\mathbf{N}$$

   where κ is the curvature and $\tau = \tau(s)$ is a scalar function called the torsion, which provides a measure of the amount of twisting at each point on the trajectory.

54. Show that the torsion may be computed by the formula

   $$\tau = \frac{[\mathbf{R}'(t) \times \mathbf{R}''(t)] \cdot \mathbf{R}'''(t)}{\|\mathbf{R}'(t) \times \mathbf{R}''(t)\|^2}$$

55. A highway has an exit ramp that begins at the origin and follows the curve $y = \frac{1}{32}x^{5/2}$ to the point $(4, 1)$. Then it follows the shape of the osculating circle at $(4, 1)$ until the point where $y = 3$. What is the total length of the exit ramp?

56. Show that the osculating circle at the point $(1, 1)$ on the curve $y = x^{-1}$ has the equation
$$(x - 2)^2 + (y - 2)^2 = 2$$

57. Find the curvature of the cycloid with parametric equations
$$x = t - \sin t, \quad y = 1 - \cos t$$

What are the largest and smallest values of the curvature $\kappa(t)$?

58. Counterexample Problem Let f be a function that is twice differentiable. Either prove that the largest curvature of the curve $y = f(x)$ occurs at a relative extremum of f or find a counterexample.

10.5 Tangential and Normal Components of Acceleration

IN THIS SECTION components of acceleration, applications

COMPONENTS OF ACCELERATION

When a body is caused to accelerate or brakes are applied, it is of interest to know how much of the acceleration acts in the direction of the body's motion, as indicated by the unit tangent vector **T** and how much in the direction of the principal unit normal **N**. This question is answered by the following theorem.

THEOREM 10.10 Tangential and normal components of acceleration

An object moving along a smooth curve (with $\mathbf{T}' \neq \mathbf{0}$) has velocity **V** and acceleration **A**, where

$$\mathbf{V} = \left(\frac{ds}{dt}\right)\mathbf{T} \quad \text{and} \quad \mathbf{A} = \left(\frac{d^2s}{dt^2}\right)\mathbf{T} + \kappa\left(\frac{ds}{dt}\right)^2\mathbf{N}$$

and s is the arc length along the trajectory.

Proof The formula for **V** follows from the fact that the velocity vector has magnitude $\|\mathbf{V}\| = \dfrac{ds}{dt}$ from Theorem 10.6 and points in the direction of the unit tangent. To establish the formula for **A**, first note that

$$\frac{d\mathbf{T}}{ds} = \left\|\frac{d\mathbf{T}}{ds}\right\|\mathbf{N} = \kappa\mathbf{N}$$

since the derivative of $\mathbf{T}(s)$ points in a direction orthogonal to **T**. Using this formula, we find

$$\mathbf{A} = \frac{d\mathbf{V}}{dt} \qquad\qquad \text{Definition of } \mathbf{A}$$

$$= \frac{d}{dt}\left[\mathbf{T}\frac{ds}{dt}\right] \qquad\qquad \mathbf{V} = \left(\frac{ds}{dt}\right)\mathbf{T}$$

$$= \frac{d^2s}{dt^2}\mathbf{T} + \frac{ds}{dt}\frac{d\mathbf{T}}{dt} \qquad\qquad \text{Product rule}$$

$$= \frac{d^2s}{dt^2}\mathbf{T} + \frac{ds}{dt}\left[\frac{d\mathbf{T}}{ds}\frac{ds}{dt}\right] \qquad\qquad \text{Chain rule}$$

$$= \frac{d^2s}{dt^2}\mathbf{T} + \left(\frac{ds}{dt}\right)^2\frac{d\mathbf{T}}{ds}$$

$$= \frac{d^2s}{dt^2}\mathbf{T} + \left(\frac{ds}{dt}\right)^2(\kappa\mathbf{N}) \qquad\qquad \kappa\mathbf{N} = \frac{d\mathbf{T}}{ds} \qquad \square$$

→ **What This Says**   At each point on the trajectory of a moving object, the velocity **V** points in the direction of the unit tangent **T**, but the acceleration **A** may have both a tangential and normal component. The trajectory may twist and turn, but the acceleration is always in the plane determined by **T** and the unit normal **N**.

Tangential and Normal Components of Acceleration

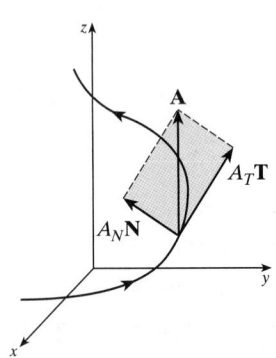

Figure 10.37 Components of acceleration $A = A_T\mathbf{T} + A_N\mathbf{N}$

The acceleration **A** of a moving object can be written as

$$\mathbf{A} = A_T\mathbf{T} + A_N\mathbf{N}$$

where

$$A_T = \frac{d^2s}{dt^2}   \text{is the \textbf{tangential component}.}$$

$$A_N = \kappa\left(\frac{ds}{dt}\right)^2   \text{is the \textbf{normal component}.}$$

The tangential and normal components are shown in Figure 10.37.

The formulas $A_T = \dfrac{d^2s}{dt^2}$ and $A_N = \kappa\left(\dfrac{ds}{dt}\right)^2$ provide useful information about the way a moving object travels along its trajectory, but they are often not the most convenient computational forms. The following theorem provides alternative formulas for A_T and A_N that use only the derivatives $\mathbf{R}'$ and $\mathbf{R}''$ of the position vector $\mathbf{R}(t)$.

THEOREM 10.11   Formulas for the components of acceleration

Let $\mathbf{R}(t)$ be the position vector for an object moving along a smooth curve C. Then the tangential and normal components of the object's acceleration are given by

$$A_T = \frac{\mathbf{R}'\cdot\mathbf{R}''}{\|\mathbf{R}'\|}   \text{and}   A_N = \frac{\|\mathbf{R}'\times\mathbf{R}''\|}{\|\mathbf{R}'\|}$$

Proof   Let θ be the angle between $\mathbf{R}'$ and $\mathbf{R}''$. Then, since the acceleration is given by $\mathbf{A} = \mathbf{R}''$, we have

$$A_T = \|\mathbf{A}\|\cos\theta = \frac{\|\mathbf{R}'\|\|\mathbf{A}\|\cos\theta}{\|\mathbf{R}'\|} = \frac{\mathbf{R}'\cdot\mathbf{R}''}{\|\mathbf{R}'\|}$$

and

$$A_N = \|\mathbf{A}\|\sin\theta = \frac{\|\mathbf{R}'\|\|\mathbf{A}\|\sin\theta}{\|\mathbf{R}'\|} = \frac{\|\mathbf{R}'\times\mathbf{R}''\|}{\|\mathbf{R}'\|}$$ ◻

EXAMPLE 1   Finding tangential and normal components of acceleration

Find the tangential and normal components of the acceleration of an object that moves with position vector $\mathbf{R}(t) = \langle t^3, t^2, t\rangle$.

Solution

Since $\mathbf{R}'(t) = \mathbf{V}(t) = \langle 3t^2, 2t, 1\rangle$ and $\mathbf{R}''(t) = \mathbf{A}(t) = \langle 6t, 2, 0\rangle$, we have

$$\mathbf{R}'\cdot\mathbf{R}'' = \mathbf{V}\cdot\mathbf{A} = (3t^2)(6t) + (2t)(2) = 18t^3 + 4t$$

and

$$\mathbf{R}' \times \mathbf{R}'' = \mathbf{V} \times \mathbf{A} = \begin{vmatrix} \mathbf{i} & \mathbf{j} & \mathbf{k} \\ 3t^2 & 2t & 1 \\ 6t & 2 & 0 \end{vmatrix} = -2\mathbf{i} + 6t\mathbf{j} - 6t^2\mathbf{k}$$

Therefore, the components of acceleration are

$$A_T = \frac{\mathbf{R}' \cdot \mathbf{R}''}{\|\mathbf{R}'\|} = \frac{\mathbf{V} \cdot \mathbf{A}}{\|\mathbf{V}\|} = \frac{18t^3 + 4t}{\sqrt{(3t^2)^2 + (2t)^2 + 1}} = \frac{18t^3 + 4t}{\sqrt{9t^4 + 4t^2 + 1}}$$

$$A_N = \frac{\|\mathbf{R}' \times \mathbf{R}''\|}{\|\mathbf{R}'\|} = \frac{\|\mathbf{V} \times \mathbf{A}\|}{\|\mathbf{V}\|} = \frac{\sqrt{(-2)^2 + (6t)^2 + (-6t^2)^2}}{\sqrt{9t^4 + 4t^2 + 1}} = 2\sqrt{\frac{9t^4 + 9t^2 + 1}{9t^4 + 4t^2 + 1}}$$

∎

Note in Figure 10.37 that $\|\mathbf{A}\|$ is the hypotenuse of a right triangle whose other two sides have lengths $\|A_T \mathbf{T}\| = |A_T|$ and $\|A_N \mathbf{N}\| = A_N$. Therefore, by the Pythagorean theorem, we have

$$\|\mathbf{A}\|^2 = A_T^2 + A_N^2$$

$$A_N = \sqrt{\|\mathbf{A}\|^2 - A_T^2}$$

This formula is used to compute A_N in the following example.

EXAMPLE 2   Finding components of acceleration on a helix

An object moves with position vector $\mathbf{R}(t) = \langle \cos t, \sin t, t \rangle$. Find the tangential and normal components of acceleration.

Solution

The trajectory is a helix, and we find

$$\mathbf{V} = \frac{d\mathbf{R}}{dt} = \langle -\sin t, \cos t, 1 \rangle \quad \text{and} \quad \mathbf{A} = \frac{d\mathbf{V}}{dt} = \langle -\cos t, -\sin t, 0 \rangle$$

$$\frac{ds}{dt} = \|\mathbf{V}\| = \sqrt{\sin^2 t + \cos^2 t + 1} = \sqrt{2} \quad \text{and} \quad A_T = \frac{d^2 s}{dt^2} = 0$$

$$A_N = \sqrt{\|\mathbf{A}\|^2 - A_T^2} = \sqrt{\left(\sqrt{\cos^2 t + \sin^2 t}\right)^2 - 0^2} = 1$$

The tangential and normal components of acceleration are 0 and 1, respectively. This means that the acceleration satisfies

$$\mathbf{A} = A_T \mathbf{T} + A_N \mathbf{N} = (0)\mathbf{T} + (1)\mathbf{N} = \mathbf{N}$$

That is, the acceleration vector is the principal unit normal $\mathbf{N}$, and the acceleration is always normal to the helical trajectory. ∎

APPLICATIONS

Now that we know how to compute the tangential and normal components of acceleration, A_T and A_N, we will examine some applications. First, according to Newton's second law of motion, the total force acting on a moving object of mass m satisfies $\mathbf{F} = m\mathbf{A}$, where $\mathbf{A}$ is the acceleration of the object. Because $\mathbf{A} = A_T \mathbf{T} + A_N \mathbf{N}$, we have

$$\mathbf{F} = m\mathbf{A} = (mA_T)\mathbf{T} + (mA_N)\mathbf{N} = F_T \mathbf{T} + F_N \mathbf{N}$$

where

$$F_T = m\frac{d^2 s}{dt^2} \quad \text{and} \quad F_N = m\kappa \left(\frac{ds}{dt}\right)^2$$

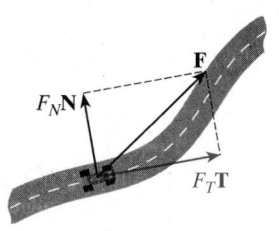

Figure 10.38 Tendency to skid

For instance, experience leads us to expect a car to skid if it makes a sharp turn at moderate speed or even a gradual turn at high speed. Mathematically, a "sharp turn" occurs when the radius of curvature $\rho = 1/\kappa$ is small (that is, when κ is large), and "high speed" means that ds/dt is large. In either case,

$$F_N = m\kappa \left(\frac{ds}{dt}\right)^2$$

will be relatively large, and the car will stay on the road (its trajectory) only if (assuming no banking) there is a correspondingly large frictional force between the tires of the car and the surface of the road (see Figure 10.38).

When forces, masses, and accelerations are involved, it is customary to express the mass m in slugs of an object whose weight W has been given in pounds.* From the definition of weight,

$$m = \frac{W}{g}$$

where g is the acceleration of gravity ($g \approx 32$ ft/s^2).

EXAMPLE 3 Modeling Application: Tendency of a vehicle to skid

A car weighing 2,700 lb makes a turn on a flat road while traveling at 56 ft/s (about 38 mi/h). If the radius of the turn is 70 ft, how much frictional force is required to keep the car from skidding?

Solution

The force tending to push the car off the road is $F_N = m\kappa \left(\dfrac{ds}{dt}\right)^2$, where m is the mass of the car and κ is the curvature of the road. This is the force that must be compensated for by friction if the car is not to skid. We know that $\dfrac{ds}{dt} = 56$ ft/s, and because the car weighs $W = 2,700$ lb, its mass is $m = \dfrac{W}{g} = \dfrac{2,700}{32} \approx 84.38$ slugs. Because the turn radius is 70 ft, we have $\kappa = \frac{1}{70}$, so that

$$F_N = \left(\frac{2,700}{32}\text{ slugs}\right)\left(\frac{1}{70\text{ ft}}\right)\left(56\frac{\text{ft}}{\text{s}}\right)^2 = 3,780\frac{\text{lb}\cdot\text{s}^2}{\text{ft}}\frac{1}{\text{ft}}\frac{\text{ft}^2}{\text{s}^2} = 3,780\text{ lb} \qquad\blacksquare$$

There are certain important applications in which an object moves along its trajectory with constant speed ds/dt, and when this occurs, the acceleration $\mathbf{A}$ can have only a normal component, because $d^2s/dt^2 = 0$.

THEOREM 10.12 Acceleration of an object with constant speed

The acceleration of an object moving with constant speed is always orthogonal to the direction of motion.

Proof Notice that we really do not need to know anything about components of acceleration to prove this result. Saying that the object has constant speed means that $\|\mathbf{R}'(t)\|$ is constant, and by Theorem 10.4, we conclude that $\mathbf{R}'(t)$ is orthogonal to its derivative $\mathbf{R}''(t) = \mathbf{A}(t)$. But $\mathbf{R}'(t)$ points in the direction of the object's motion along its trajectory, which means that the acceleration $\mathbf{A}$ is orthogonal to the direction of motion. ❑

---

*A slug is a unit of measurement defined as the unit of mass that receives an acceleration of 1 ft/s^2 when a force of 1 lb is applied to it. That is, 1 slug $= \dfrac{1\text{ lb}}{1\text{ ft/s}^2} = \dfrac{\text{lb s}^2}{\text{ft}}$

As an application of this result, note that when an object moves with constant speed v_0 along a circular path of radius R (so that $\kappa = 1/R$), its acceleration is directed toward the center of the path and has magnitude

$$A_N = \kappa \left(\frac{ds}{dt} \right)^2 = \frac{1}{R} v_0^2$$

(See Figure 10.39.)

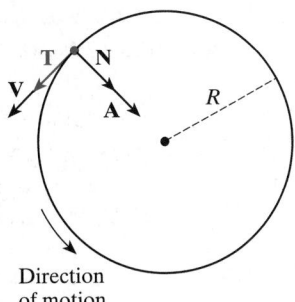

If the constant speed is v_0 and the path has radius R, the acceleration is

$$\mathbf{A} = \frac{v_0^2}{R} \mathbf{N}$$

Direction of motion

Figure 10.39   An object moving with constant speed on a circular path

EXAMPLE 4   Modeling Application: Period of a satellite

An artificial satellite travels at constant speed in a stable circular orbit 20,000 km above the earth's surface. How long does it take for the satellite to make one complete circuit of the earth?

Solution

Let m denote the satellite's mass and v denote its speed. We will assume that the earth is a sphere of radius 6,440 km, so the curvature of the path is $\kappa = 1/R$, where

$$R = \underbrace{6{,}440}_{\text{Radius of earth}} + \overbrace{20{,}000}^{\text{Height}} = 26{,}440 \text{ km}$$

is the distance of the satellite from the center of the earth. The satellite maintains a stable orbit when the magnitude of the force $\mathbf{F}_c = mv^2/R$ produced by the rate of change of tangential velocity, called *centripetal* (center directed) *acceleration*, equals the magnitude of the force $\mathbf{F}_g$ due to gravity but is opposite in direction. (See Figure 10.40.)

According to Newton's law of universal gravitation, $\|\mathbf{F}_g\| = GmM/R^2$, where M is the mass of the earth and G is the *gravitational constant*. Thus, for stability we must have

$$\frac{mv^2}{R} = \frac{GmM}{R^2}$$

so $v = \sqrt{GM/R}$. Experiments indicate that $GM = 398{,}600 \text{ km}^3/\text{s}^2$, and by substituting $R = 26{,}440$, we obtain

$$v = \sqrt{\frac{GM}{R}} = \sqrt{\frac{398{,}600}{26{,}440}} \approx 3.88273653$$

For this example, we see that the speed of the satellite is approximately 3.883 km/s.

Finally, suppose T is the time required for the satellite to make one complete circuit of the earth (called the **period** of the satellite). In each period, the satellite travels a distance equal to the circumference of a circle of radius $R = 26{,}440$ km, and because it travels at v km/s, we must have $vT = 2\pi R$, so that

$$T = \frac{2\pi R}{v} \approx \frac{2\pi (26{,}440)}{3.88273653} \approx 42{,}786.16852 \text{ seconds}$$

or approximately 713 minutes (11 hr 53 min). ■

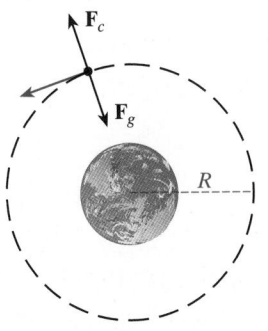

Figure 10.40 A satellite in a stable orbit; magnitude of centripetal force $\mathbf{F}_c$ equals the magnitude of the force $\mathbf{F}_g$ due to gravity, but points in the opposite direction.

10.5 PROBLEM SET

A *In Problems 1–8,* $\mathbf{R}(t)$ *is the position vector of a moving object. Find the tangential and normal components of the object's acceleration.*

1. $\mathbf{R}(t) = t\mathbf{i} + t^2\mathbf{j}$
2. $\mathbf{R}(t) = t\mathbf{i} + e^t\mathbf{j}$
3. $\mathbf{R}(t) = \langle t\sin t, t\cos t\rangle$
4. $\mathbf{R}(t) = \langle 3\cos t, 2\sin t\rangle$
5. $\mathbf{R}(t) = \langle t, t^2, t\rangle$
6. $\mathbf{R}(t) = \langle 4\cos t, 0, \sin t\rangle$
7. $\mathbf{R}(t) = (\sin t)\mathbf{i} + (\cos t)\mathbf{j} + (\sin t)\mathbf{k}$
8. $\mathbf{R}(t) = \left(\frac{5}{13}\cos t\right)\mathbf{i} + \frac{12}{13}(1 - \cos t)\mathbf{j} + \sin t\,\mathbf{k}$

In Problems 9–12, the velocity $\mathbf{V}$ *and acceleration* $\mathbf{A}$ *of a moving object are given at a certain instant. Find* A_T *and* A_N *at this instant.*

9. $\mathbf{V}_0 = \langle 1, -3\rangle$; $\mathbf{A}_0 = \langle 2, 5\rangle$
10. $\mathbf{V}_0 = -\mathbf{i} + 7\mathbf{j}$; $\mathbf{A}_0 = 4\mathbf{i} + \mathbf{j}$
11. $\mathbf{V}_0 = 2\mathbf{i} + 3\mathbf{j} - \mathbf{k}$; $\mathbf{A}_0 = -\mathbf{i} - 5\mathbf{j} + 2\mathbf{k}$
12. $\mathbf{V}_0 = \langle 5, -1, 2\rangle$; $\mathbf{A}_0 = \langle 1, 0, -7\rangle$

In Problems 13–16, the speed $\|\mathbf{V}\|$ *of a moving object is given. Find* A_T, *the tangential component of acceleration, at the indicated time.*

13. $\|\mathbf{V}\| = \sqrt{5t^2 + 3}$; $t = 1$
14. $\|\mathbf{V}\| = \sqrt{t^2 + t + 1}$; $t = 3$
15. $\|\mathbf{V}\| = \sqrt{\sin^2 t + \cos(2t)}$; $t = 0$
16. $\|\mathbf{V}\| = \sqrt{e^{-t} + t^4}$; $t = 0$

17. Find the maximum and minimum speeds of a particle whose position vector is

$$\mathbf{R}(t) = (4\sin 2t)\mathbf{i} - (3\cos 2t)\mathbf{j}$$

18. Where on the trajectory of

$$\mathbf{R}(t) = (2t^2 - 5t)\mathbf{i} + (5t + 2)\mathbf{j} + 4t^2\mathbf{k}$$

is the speed minimized? What is the minimum speed?

19. The position of an object at time t is (x, y), where $x = 1 + \cos 2t$, $y = \sin 2t$. Find the velocity, the acceleration, and the normal and tangential components of acceleration of the object at time t.

20. An object moves with constant angular velocity ω around the circle $x^2 + y^2 = r^2$ in the xy-plane. Find a parameterization for the circle and compute the tangential and normal components of acceleration for the moving object.

B 21. Find the tangential and normal components of the acceleration of an object that moves along the parabolic path $y = 4x^2$ at the instant the speed is $ds/dt = 20$.

Modeling Problems *In Problems 22–25, set up an appropriate model to answer the given question. Be sure to state your assumptions.*

22. A pail attached to a rope 1 yd long is swung at the rate of 1 rev/s. Find the tangential and normal components of the pail's acceleration. Assume the rope is swung in a level plane.

23. A boy holds onto a pail of water weighing 2 lb and swings it in a vertical circle with a radius of 3 ft. If the pail travels at ω rpm, what is the force of the water on the bottom of the pail at the highest and lowest points of the swing? What is the *smallest* value of ω required to keep the water from spilling from the pail? Assume the pail is held by a handle so that its bottom is straight up when it is at its highest point.

24. A car weighing 2,700 lb moves along the elliptic path $900x^2 + 400y^2 = 1$, where x and y are measured in miles. If the car travels at the constant speed of 45 mi/h, how much frictional force is required to keep it from skidding as it turns the "corner" at $\left(\frac{1}{30}, 0\right)$? What about the corner $\left(0, \frac{1}{20}\right)$?

25. Curved sections of road such as expressway off ramps are often banked to protect against skidding. Consider a road with a circular curve of radius 150 feet, as shown in Figure 10.41, and assume the magnitude of the force of static friction $\mathbf{F}_s$ (the force resisting the tendency to skid) is proportional to the car's weight; that is $\|\mathbf{F}_s\| = \mu W$, where μ is a constant called the *coefficient of static friction*. For this problem, we assume $\mu = 0.47$.

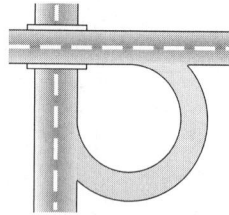

Figure 10.41 A road with a circular arc

a. First, suppose the road is not banked. What is the largest speed v_m that a 3,500 lb car can travel around the curve without skidding? Would the answer be different for a smaller car, say one weighing 2,000 lb?

b. Now suppose the curve is banked at 17° and answer the questions in part **a**.

c. Suppose the highway engineers want the maximum safe speed at 50 mi/h. At what angle should the road be banked?

26. What is the smallest radius that should be used for a circular highway exchange as shown in Figure 10.42 if the normal component of the acceleration of a car traveling at 45 mi/h is not to exceed 2.4 ft/s²?

Figure 10.42 Highway exchange

27. A Ferris wheel (see Figure 10.43) with radius 15 ft rotates in a vertical plane at ω rpm. What is the maximum value of ω for a Ferris wheel carrying a person of weight W? (That is, the largest ω so the passenger is not "thrown off.")

Figure 10.43 Ferris wheel

Use the formulas in Theorem 10.11 to find A_T and A_N for the given position vector $\mathbf{R}(t)$ in Problems 28–31.

28. $\mathbf{R}(t) = t^3\mathbf{i} + t^2\mathbf{j} + t\mathbf{k}$ **29.** $\mathbf{R}(t) = t\mathbf{i} + 2t\mathbf{j} + t^2\mathbf{k}$

30. $\mathbf{R}(t) = (\cos t)\mathbf{i} + (\sin t)\mathbf{j} + \mathbf{k}$

31. $\mathbf{R}(t) = (e^t \cos t)\mathbf{i} + (e^t \sin t)\mathbf{j} + e^t\mathbf{k}$

32. Modeling Problem An amusement park ride consists of a large (25-ft radius), flat, horizontal wheel. Customers board the wheel while it is stationary and try to stay on as long as possible as it begins to rotate. The purpose of this problem is to discover how fast the wheel can rotate without losing its passengers.

   a. Suppose the wheel rotates at ω revolutions per minute and that a volunteer weighing W lb sits 15 feet from the center of the wheel, as shown Figure 10.44. Find $\mathbf{F}_N = m\mathbf{A}_N$, where $m = W/g$ is the volunteer's mass. This is the force tending to push the volunteer off the wheel.

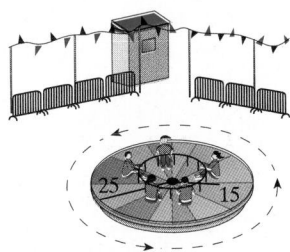

Figure 10.44 Carnival fun ride

   b. If the frictional force of the volunteer in part **a** to stay on the wheel is $0.12W$, find the largest value of ω that will allow the volunteer to stay in place. Wait, we did not tell you the volunteer's weight. Does it matter?

33. Modeling Problem A curve in a railroad track has the shape of the parabola $x = y^2/120$. If a train is loaded so that its scalar normal component of acceleration cannot exceed 30 units/s^2, what is its maximum possible speed as it rounds the curve at $(0, 0)$?

C 34. Let $\mathbf{T}$ be the unit tangent vector, $\mathbf{N}$ the principal unit normal, and $\mathbf{B}$ the unit binormal vector (see Problem 52, Section 10.4) to a given curve C. Show that

$$\frac{d\mathbf{B}}{ds} = \mathbf{T} \times \frac{d\mathbf{N}}{ds}$$

35. Suppose an object moves in the plane along the curve $y = f(x)$. Use the formulas obtained in Theorem 10.11 to

show that

$$A_T = \frac{f'(x)f''(x)}{\sqrt{1 + [f'(x)]^2}}; \quad A_N = \frac{|f''(x)|}{\sqrt{1 + [f'(x)]^2}}$$

36. If the graph of the function f has an inflection point at $x = a$ and $f''(a)$ exists, show that the graph of f has curvature 0 at $(a, f(a))$.

37. A projectile is fired from ground level with an angle of elevation α and muzzle speed v_0. Find formulas for the tangential and normal components of the projectile's acceleration at time t. What are A_T and A_N at the time the projectile is at its maximum height?

38. An object connected to a string of length r is spun counterclockwise in a circular path in a horizontal plane. Let ω be the constant angular velocity of the object.

   a. Show that the position vector of the object is $\mathbf{R}(t) = (r \cos \omega t)\mathbf{i} + (r \sin \omega t)\mathbf{j}$.

   b. Find the normal component of the object's acceleration.

   c. If the angular velocity ω is doubled, what is the effect on the normal component of acceleration? What is the effect on $\mathbf{A}$ if ω is unchanged but the length of the string is doubled? What happens to A_N if ω is doubled and r is halved?

39. An artificial satellite travels at constant speed in a stable circular orbit R km above the earth's surface (as in Example 4).

   a. Show that the satellite's period is given by the formula

$$T = 2\pi \frac{(R + R_e)^{3/2}}{\sqrt{GM}}$$

   where R_e is the radius of the earth.

   b. A satellite is said to be in **geosynchronous orbit** if it completes one orbit every sidereal day (23 hours, 56 minutes). How high above the earth should the satellite be to achieve such an orbit? Assume the radius of the earth is approximately 6,440 miles.

   c. What is the speed of a satellite in geosynchronous orbit?

40. Modeling Problem For Mars the following facts are known (all in relation to Earth):

diameter	0.533
length of day	1.029
mass	0.1074
gravity (g)	0.3776

Use these facts to determine how high above the surface of Mars a satellite must be to achieve Mars synchronous orbit. How fast would such a satellite be traveling?

CHAPTER 10 REVIEW

Proficiency Examination

CONCEPT PROBLEMS

   1. What is a vector-valued function?

   2. What are the components of a vector function?

   3. Describe what is meant by the graph of a vector function.

   4. Define the limit of a vector function.

   5. Define the derivative of a vector function.

   6. Define the integral of a vector function.

   7. What is a smooth curve?

8. State the following rules for differentiating vector functions:
   a. Linearity rule   b. Scalar multiple rule
   c. Dot product rule   d. Cross product rule
   e. Chain rule

9. State the theorem about the orthogonality of a vector function of constant length and its derivative.

10. What are the position, velocity, and acceleration vectors?

11. What is the speed of a particle moving on a curve C?

12. What are the formulas for the motion of a projectile in a vacuum?

13. What are the formulas for time of flight and range of a projectile?

14. State Kepler's laws.

15. What are the unit polar vectors, $\mathbf{u}_r$ and $\mathbf{u}_\theta$?

16. What are the unit tangent and principal unit normal vectors?

17. What is speed in terms of arc length?

18. Give a formula for the arc length of a curve in $\mathbb{R}^3$.

19. What is the curvature of a graph?

20. What is a formula for curvature in terms of the velocity and acceleration vectors?

21. What are the formulas for unit tangent and principal unit normal in terms of the arc length parameter?

22. What is the radius of curvature?

23. What are the tangential and normal components of acceleration?

PRACTICE PROBLEMS

24. Sketch the graph of $\mathbf{R}(t) = (3\cos t)\mathbf{i} + (3\sin t)\mathbf{j} + t\mathbf{k}$, and find the length of this curve from $t = 0$ to $t = 2\pi$.

25. If $\mathbf{F}(t) = \dfrac{t}{1+t}\mathbf{i} + \dfrac{\sin t}{t}\mathbf{j} + (\cos t)\mathbf{k}$, find $\mathbf{F}'(t)$ and $\mathbf{F}''(t)$.

26. Evaluate $\displaystyle\int_1^2 \langle 3t, 0, 3\rangle \times \langle 0, \ln t, -t^2\rangle \, dt$.

27. Find a vector function $\mathbf{F}$ such that $\mathbf{F}''(t) = \langle e^t, -t^2, 3\rangle$ and $\mathbf{F}(0) = \langle 1, -2, 0\rangle$, $\mathbf{F}'(0) = \langle 0, 0, 3\rangle$.

28. Find the velocity $\mathbf{V}$, the speed $\dfrac{ds}{dt}$, and the acceleration $\mathbf{A}$ for the body with position vector $\mathbf{R}(t) = t\mathbf{i} + 2t\mathbf{j} + te^t\mathbf{k}$.

29. Find $\mathbf{T}$, $\mathbf{N}$, A_T and A_N (the tangential and normal components of acceleration), and κ (curvature) for an object with position vector $\mathbf{R}(t) = t^2\mathbf{i} + 3t\mathbf{j} - 3t\mathbf{k}$.

30. A projectile is fired from ground level with muzzle speed 50 ft/s at an angle of elevation of $\alpha = 30°$.
   a. What is the maximum height reached by the projectile?
   b. What are the time of flight and the range?

Supplementary Problems

Find the vector limits in Problems 1–6.

1. $\displaystyle\lim_{t \to 0}\left[t^2\mathbf{i} - 3te^t\mathbf{j} + \dfrac{\sin 2t}{t}\mathbf{k}\right]$

2. $\displaystyle\lim_{t \to 0}\left[\dfrac{\mathbf{i} + t\mathbf{j} - e^{-t}\mathbf{k}}{1 - t}\right]$

3. $\displaystyle\lim_{t \to 0}\langle t, 0, 5\rangle \cdot \langle \sin t, 3t, -(1-t)\rangle$

4. $\displaystyle\lim_{t \to \pi}\langle 1 + t, -3, 0\rangle \times \langle 0, t^2, \cos t\rangle$

5. $\displaystyle\lim_{t \to 0^+}\left[\left(1 + \dfrac{1}{t}\right)^t \mathbf{i} - \left(\dfrac{\sin t}{t}\right)\mathbf{j} - t\mathbf{k}\right]$

6. $\displaystyle\lim_{t \to \infty}\left[\left(\dfrac{1 - \cos t}{t}\right)\mathbf{i} + 4\mathbf{j} + \left(1 + \dfrac{3}{t}\right)^t\mathbf{k}\right]$

Find $\mathbf{F}'(t)$ and $\mathbf{F}''(t)$ for the vector functions in Problems 7–12.

7. $\mathbf{F}(t) = te^t\mathbf{i} + t^2\mathbf{j}$ 8. $\mathbf{F}(t) = (t\ln 2t)\mathbf{i} + t^{3/2}\mathbf{k}$

9. $\mathbf{F}(t) = \langle 2t^{-1}, -2t, te^{-t}\rangle$

10. $\mathbf{F}(t) = \langle t, -(1-t), 0\rangle \times \langle 0, t^2, e^{-t}\rangle$

11. $\mathbf{F}(t) = (t^2 + e^{at})\mathbf{i} + (te^{-at})\mathbf{j} + (e^{at+1})\mathbf{k}$, a constant

12. $\mathbf{F}(t) = (1-t)^{-1}\mathbf{i} + (\sin 2t)\mathbf{j} + (\cos^2 t)\mathbf{k}$

Sketch the graph of the vector functions in Problems 13–15.

13. $\mathbf{F}(t) = te^t\mathbf{i} + t^2\mathbf{j}$ 14. $\mathbf{F}(t) = t^2\mathbf{i} - 3t\mathbf{j}$

15. $\mathbf{F}(t) = (1 - \cos t)\mathbf{i} + (\sin t)\mathbf{k}$

Sketch the graph of the vector functions in Problems 16–18.

16. $\mathbf{F}(t) = \langle 3\cos t, 3\sin t, t\rangle$ 17. $\mathbf{F}(t) = \langle 2\sin t, 2\cos t, 5t\rangle$

18. $\mathbf{F}(t) = 2t^2\mathbf{i} + (1-t)\mathbf{j} + 3\mathbf{k}$

Find the indicated derivative in terms of $\mathbf{F}$ and $\mathbf{F}'$ in Problems 19–24.

19. $\dfrac{d}{dt}[\mathbf{F}(t) \cdot \mathbf{F}(t)]$ 20. $\dfrac{d}{dt}[\|\mathbf{F}(t)\|\mathbf{F}(t)]$

21. $\dfrac{d}{dt}\left[\dfrac{\mathbf{F}(t)}{\|\mathbf{F}(t)\|}\right]$ 22. $\dfrac{d}{dt}\|\mathbf{F}(t)\|$

23. $\dfrac{d}{dt}[\mathbf{F}(t) \times \mathbf{F}(t)]$ 24. $\dfrac{d}{dt}\mathbf{F}(e^t)$

Evaluate the definite and indefinite vector integrals in Problems 25–30.

25. $\displaystyle\int_{-1}^1 (e^{-t}\mathbf{i} + t^3\mathbf{j} + 3\mathbf{k})\, dt$

26. $\displaystyle\int_1^2 [(1-t)\mathbf{i} - t^{-1}\mathbf{j} + e^t\mathbf{k}]\, dt$

27. $\displaystyle\int [te^t\mathbf{i} - (\sin 2t)\mathbf{j} + t^2\mathbf{k}]\, dt$

28. $\displaystyle\int e^{2t}[2\mathbf{i} - t\mathbf{j} + (\sin t)\mathbf{k}]\, dt$

29. $\displaystyle\int t[e^t\mathbf{i} + (\ln t)\mathbf{j} + 3\mathbf{k}]\, dt$

30. $\displaystyle\int [e^t\mathbf{i} + 2\mathbf{j} - t\mathbf{k}] \cdot [e^{-t}\mathbf{i} - t\mathbf{j}]\, dt$

In Problems 31–34, $\mathbf{R}$ is the position vector of a moving body. Find the velocity $\mathbf{V}$, the speed ds/dt, and the acceleration $\mathbf{A}$.

31. $\mathbf{R}(t) = t\mathbf{i} + (3-t)\mathbf{j} + 2\mathbf{k}$

32. $\mathbf{R}(t) = (\sin 2t)\mathbf{i} + 2\mathbf{j} - (\cos 2t)\mathbf{k}$

33. $\mathbf{R}(t) = \langle t\sin t, te^{-t}, -(1-t)\rangle$

34. $\mathbf{R}(t) = \langle \ln t, e^t, -\tan t\rangle$

Find $\mathbf{T}$ and $\mathbf{N}$ for the vector functions given in Problems 35–38.

35. $\mathbf{R}(t) = t\mathbf{i} - t^2\mathbf{j}$

36. $\mathbf{R}(t) = (3\cos t)\mathbf{i} - (3\sin t)\mathbf{j}$

37. $\mathbf{R}(t) = \langle 4\cos t, -3t, 4\sin t\rangle$

38. $\mathbf{R}(t) = \langle e^t\sin t, e^t, e^t\cos t\rangle$

In Problems 39–42, find the tangential and normal components of acceleration, and the curvature of a moving object with position vector $\mathbf{R}(t)$.

39. $\mathbf{R}(t) = t^2\mathbf{i} + 2t\mathbf{j} + e^t\mathbf{k}$

40. $\mathbf{R}(t) = t^2\mathbf{i} - 2t\mathbf{j} + (t^2 - t)\mathbf{k}$

41. $\mathbf{R}(t) = (4 \sin t)\mathbf{i} + (4 \cos t)\mathbf{j} + 4t\mathbf{k}$

42. $\mathbf{R}(t) = (a \sin 3t)\mathbf{i} + (a + a \cos 3t)\mathbf{j} + (3a \sin t)\mathbf{k}$,
for constant $a > 0$

A polar curve C is given by $r = f(\theta)$. If $f''(\theta)$ exists, then the curvature can be found by the formula

$$\kappa = \frac{|r^2 + 2r'^2 - rr''|}{(r^2 + r'^2)^{3/2}}$$

(see Problem 47, Section 10.4). Find the curvature at the given point on each of the polar curves given in Problems 43–48.

43. $r = 4 \cos \theta$, where $\theta = \frac{\pi}{3}$ **44.** $r = \theta^2$, where $\theta = 2$

45. $r = e^{-\theta}$, where $\theta = 1$

46. $r = 1 + \cos \theta$, where $\theta = \frac{\pi}{2}$

47. $r = 4 \cos 3\theta$, where $\theta = \frac{\pi}{6}$

48. $r = 1 - 2 \sin \theta$, where $\theta = \frac{\pi}{4}$

49. For what values of t is the following vector function continuous?

$$\mathbf{F}(t) = (2t - 1)\mathbf{i} + \left(\frac{t^2 - 1}{t - 1}\right)\mathbf{j} + 4\mathbf{k}$$

50. Find the length of the graph of the vector function

$$\mathbf{R}(t) = \left(\frac{t^2 - 2}{2}\right)\mathbf{i} + \frac{(2t + 1)^{3/2}}{3}\mathbf{j}$$

from $t = 0$ to $t = 6$.

51. Find a vector function $\mathbf{F}$ such that $\mathbf{F}(0) = \mathbf{F}'(0) = \mathbf{i}$, $\mathbf{F}''(0) = 2\mathbf{j} + \mathbf{k}$, and

$$\mathbf{F}'''(t) = (\cos t)\mathbf{i} + (\sin t)\mathbf{j} + \frac{t}{\pi}\mathbf{k}$$

52. Find parametric equations for the tangent line to the graph of

$$\mathbf{R}(t) = te^{-t}\mathbf{i} + t^2\mathbf{j} + te^{-2t}\mathbf{k}$$

at the highest point on the graph (that is, where z has the largest value).

53. Let $\mathbf{R}(t) = t\mathbf{i} + t\mathbf{j} + t^3\mathbf{k}$.

a. Find parametric equations for the tangent line to the graph of $\mathbf{R}$ at the point where $x = 1$.

b. The tangent line in part **a** intersects the graph of $\mathbf{R}(t)$ in a second point. Find the coordinates of this point.

54. An object moves in space with acceleration $\mathbf{A}(t) = \langle -t, 2, 2 - t \rangle$. When $t = 0$, it is known that the object is at the point $(1, 0, 0)$ and that it has velocity $\mathbf{V}(0) = \langle 2, -4, 0 \rangle$.

a. Find the velocity $\mathbf{V}(t)$ and the position vector $\mathbf{R}(t)$.

b. What are the speed and location of the object when $t = 1$?

c. When is the object stationary and what is its position at that time?

55. The position vector for a curve is given in terms of arc length s by $\mathbf{R}(s) = \left\langle a \cos \frac{s}{a}, a \sin \frac{s}{a}, 2s \right\rangle$ for $0 \le s \le 2\pi a$, $a \neq 0$. Find the unit tangent vector $\mathbf{T}(s)$ and the principal unit normal $\mathbf{N}(s)$.

56. Find the radius of curvature of the curve given by $y = 1 + \sin x$ at the points where x is

a. $\frac{\pi}{6}$ b. $\frac{\pi}{4}$ c. $\frac{3\pi}{2}$

57. Find the radius of curvature of the ellipse given by $\mathbf{R}(t) = \langle a \cos t, b \sin t \rangle$, where $a > 0$, $b > 0$, $a \neq b$, and $0 \le t \le 2\pi$, at the points where $t = 0$ and $\pi/2$.

58. Modeling Problem   A stunt pilot flying horizontally at an altitude of 4,000 ft with a speed of 180 mi/hr drops a weighted marker, attempting to hit a target on the ground below, as shown in Figure 10.45. How far away from the target (measured horizontally) should the pilot be when she releases the marker? You may neglect air resistance.

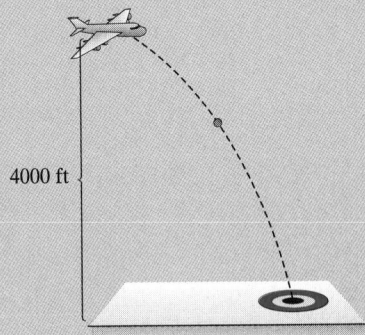

Figure 10.45   Problem 58

59. The position of an object moving in space is given by

$$\mathbf{R}(t) = (e^{-t} \cos t)\mathbf{i} + (e^{-t} \sin t)\mathbf{j} + e^{-t}\mathbf{k}$$

a. Find the velocity, speed, and acceleration of the object at arbitrary time t.

b. Determine the curvature of the trajectory at time t.

60. Find the point or points on the curve $y = e^{ax}$ $(a > 0)$ where the curvature is maximized.

61. Modeling Problem   A car weighing 3,000 lb travels at a constant speed of 60 mi/h on a flat road and then makes a circular turn on an interchange (see Figure 10.46). If the radius of the turn is 160 ft, what frictional force is needed to keep the car from skidding?

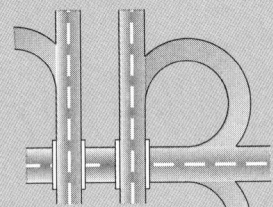

Figure 10.46   Problem 61

62. The position vector of an object in space is

$$\mathbf{R}(t) = (a \cos \omega t)\mathbf{i} + (a \sin \omega t)\mathbf{j} + \omega^2 t\mathbf{k}$$

Find $\omega \neq 0$ so that the sum of the object's tangential and normal components of acceleration equals half its speed.

63. A particle moves along a path given in parametric form where $r(t) = 1 + \cos at$ and $\theta(t) = e^{-at}$ (for positive constant a). Find the velocity and acceleration of the particle in terms of the unit polar vectors $\mathbf{u}_r$ and $\mathbf{u}_\theta$.

64. Basketball player Kobe Bryant attempts a shot while standing 20 ft from the basket, as shown in Figure 10.47. If Bryant shoots from a height of 7 ft and the ball reaches a maximum height of 12 ft before passing through the 10-ft-high basket, what is the initial speed of the ball?

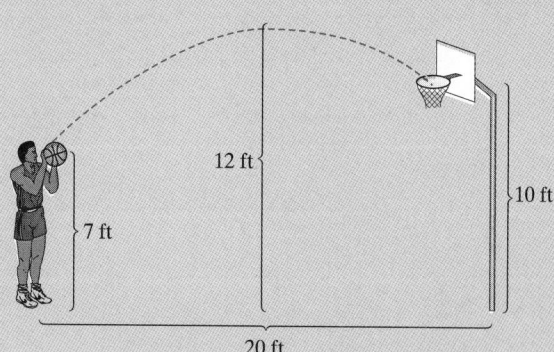

Figure 10.47 Basketball shot

65. Sketch the graph of the vector function

$$\mathbf{R}(t) = \left(\frac{3t}{1+t^3}\right)\mathbf{i} + \left(\frac{3t^2}{1+t^3}\right)\mathbf{j}$$

then find parametric equations for the tangent line at the point where $t = 2$. This curve is called the *folium of Descartes*.

66. Modeling Problem A fireman stands 5.5 m from the front of a burning building 15 m high. His fire hose discharges water at a speed of v_0 m/s from a height of 1.2 m at an angle of 62°, as shown in Figure 10.48.

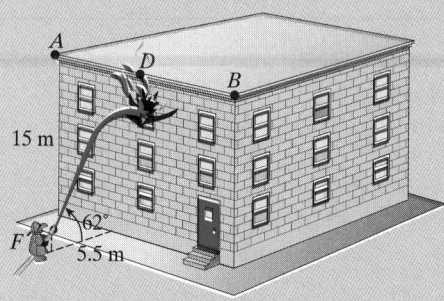

Figure 10.48 Problem 66

a. What is the smallest value of v_0 that will allow water from the hose to reach a window 11 m above the ground?

b. Suppose $v_0 = 50$ m/s. At what angle should the hose be held so the water can be directed onto a fire on the roof of the building (at a height of 15 m)?

67. A DNA molecule has the shape of a double helix (see Figure 10.4a). The radius of each helix is about 10^{-8} μm. Each helix rises about 3×10^{-8} μm during each complete turn and there are about 3×10^8 complete turns. Estimate the length of each helix.

68. Show that the tangential component of acceleration of a moving object is 0 if the object has constant speed. Is the converse statement also true? That is, if $A_T = 0$, can we conclude that the speed is constant?

69. The path of a particle P is an Archimedean spiral described in polar coordinates by $r = 10t$ and $\theta = 2\pi t$, where r is expressed in inches and t is in seconds. Determine the velocity of the particle (in terms of $\mathbf{u}_r$ and $\mathbf{u}_\theta$) when

a. $t = 0$ **b.** $t = 0.25$ sec

70. Spy Problem After dropping the knockout gas into Scélérat's bunker (Problem 27, Section 10.3), the Spy lands and, as expected, enters a bunker full of sleeping thugs—but no Scélérat! He races through the back door of the bunker and finds himself in a ski resort. By the time he locates Scélérat, the French fiend is skiing down the mountain. The Spy grabs a pair of skis and runs over to a conveniently located ski jump. His keen mind quickly determines that the slope of the mountain is 17° and the angle at the lip of the jump is 10°, as shown in Figure 10.49.

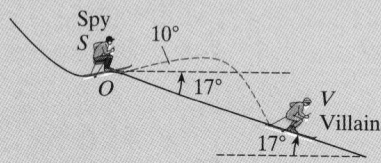

Figure 10.49 Spy scene

Suppose Scélérat is 150 ft down the mountainside skiing at 75 ft/s when the Spy launches himself from the end of the ski jump with a speed of 85 ft/s. How close will he be to Scélérat when he lands?

In Problems 71–72, find $\mathbf{F}'(x)$.

71. $\mathbf{F}(x) = \int_1^x [(\sin t)\mathbf{i} - (\cos 2t)\mathbf{j} + e^{-t}\mathbf{k}]\,dt$

72. $\mathbf{F}(x) = \int_1^{2x} [t^2\mathbf{i} + (\sec e^{-t})\mathbf{j} - (\tan e^{2t})\mathbf{k}]\,dt$

In Problems 73–76, solve the initial value problems for $\mathbf{F}$ *as a vector function of* t.

73. differential equation: $\mathbf{F}'(t) = t\mathbf{i} + t\mathbf{j} - t\mathbf{k}$;
initial condition: $\mathbf{F}(0) = \mathbf{i} + 2\mathbf{j} - 3\mathbf{k}$

74. differential equation: $\mathbf{F}'(t) = \frac{3}{2}\sqrt{t+1}\,\mathbf{i} + (t+1)^{-1}\mathbf{j} + e^t\mathbf{k}$;
initial condition: $\mathbf{F}(0) = \mathbf{j} + 2\mathbf{k}$

75. differential equation:

$$\mathbf{F}'(t) = (\sin 2t)\mathbf{i} + (e^t\cos t)\mathbf{j} - \left(\frac{3}{t+1}\right)\mathbf{k};$$

initial condition: $\mathbf{F}(0) = \mathbf{i} - 3\mathbf{k}$

76. differential equation: $\dfrac{d^2\mathbf{F}}{dt^2} = -32\mathbf{j}$;

initial conditions: $\mathbf{F} = 50\mathbf{j}$ and $\dfrac{d\mathbf{F}}{dt} = 5\mathbf{i} + 5\mathbf{k}$ at $t = 0$

77. Putnam Examination Problem A shell strikes an airplane flying at a height h above the ground. It is known that the shell was fired from a gun on the ground with muzzle speed v_0, but the position of the gun and its angle of elevation are both unknown. Deduce that the gun is situated within a circle whose center lies directly below the airplane and whose radius is

$$\frac{v_0}{g}\sqrt{v_0^2 - 2gh}$$

Neglect resistance of the atmosphere.

78. **Putnam Examination Problem**   A coast artillery gun can fire at any angle of elevation between 0° and 90° in a fixed vertical plane. If air resistance is neglected and the muzzle speed is constant $(v = v_0)$, determine the set H of points in the plane that can be hit. Consider only those points above the horizontal.

79. **Putnam Examination Problem**   A particle moves on a circle with center O, starting from rest at a point P and coming to rest again at a point Q, without coming to rest at any intermediate point. Prove that the acceleration vector of the particle does not vanish at any point between P and Q, and that, at some point R between P and Q, the acceleration vector points in along the radius $\overline{RO}$.

The Stimulation of Science

Howard Eves was born in Paterson, New Jersey, in 1911 and is professor emeritus of mathematics at the University of Maine. This guest essay first appeared in Great Moments in Mathematics Before 1650.* Professor Eves reminds us, "It must be remembered that a moment in history is sometimes an inspired flash and sometimes an evolution extending over a long period of time." Howard Eves's lectures (from which this guest essay was taken) are so renowned that each college and university at which he taught awarded him, at one time or another, every available honor for distinguished teaching. Howard Eves is a prolific and successful textbook author with a real love for the history of mathematics. He now lives with his wife at the retirement retreat in Lubec, Maine.

THE DIE IS CAST; I have written my book; it will be read either in the present age or by posterity, it matters not which; it may well await a reader, since God has waited six thousand years for an interpreter of his words.

———Johannes Kepler

From James R. Newman, *The World of Mathematics, Volume I*, (New York: Simon and Schuster, 1956), p. 220.

The mighty Antaeus was the giant son of Neptune (god of the sea) and Ge (goddess of the earth), and his strength was invincible so long as he remained in contact with his Mother Earth. Strangers who came to his country were forced to wrestle to the death with him, and so it chanced one day that Hercules and Antaeus came to grips with one another. But Hercules, aware of the source of Antaeus' great strength, lifted and held the giant from the earth and crushed him in the air.

There is a parable here for mathematicians. For just as Antaeus was born of and nurtured by his Mother Earth, history has shown us that all significant and lasting mathematics is born of and nurtured by the real world. As in the case of Antaeus, so long as mathematics maintains its contact with the real world, it will remain powerful. But should it be lifted too long from the solid ground of its birth into the filmy air of pure abstraction, it runs the risk of weakening. It must of necessity return, at least occasionally, to the real world for renewed strength.

Such a rejuvenation of mathematics occurred in the seventeenth century, following discoveries made by two eminent mathematicians-scientists—Galileo Galilei (1564–1642) and Johannes Kepler (1571–1630). Galileo, through a sequence of experiments started before his 25th birthday, discovered a number of basic facts concerning the motion of bodies in the earth's gravitational field, and Kepler, by 1619, had deduced all three of his famous laws of planetary motion. These achievements proved to be so influential on the development of so much of subsequent mathematics that they must be ranked as two of the GREAT MOMENTS IN MATHEMATICS. Galileo's discoveries led to the creation of the modern science of dynamics and Kepler's to the creation of modern celestial mechanics; and each of these studies, in turn, required, for their development, the creation of a new mathematical tool—the calculus—capable of dealing with change, flux, and motion.

Galileo was born in Pisa in 1564 as the son of an impoverished Florentine nobleman. After a disinterested start as a medical student, Galileo obtained parental permission to change his studies to science and mathematics, fields in which he possessed a strong natural talent. While still a medical student at the University of Pisa, he made his historically famous observation that the great pendulous lamp in the cathedral there

---

*©1980 Published by Mathematical Association of America, Washington, DC.

oscillated to and fro with a period independent of the size of the arc of oscillation.[†] Later, he showed that the period of a pendulum is also independent of the weight of the pendulum's bob. When he was 25, he accepted an appointment as professor of mathematics at the University of Pisa. It was during this appointment that he is alleged to have performed experiments from the leaning tower of Pisa, showing that, contrary to the teaching of Aristotle, heavy bodies do not fall faster than light ones. By rolling balls down inclined planes, he arrived at the law that the distance a body falls is proportional to the square of the time of falling, in accordance with the now familiar formula $s = \frac{1}{2}gt^2$.

Unpleasant local controversies caused Galileo to resign his chair at Pisa in 1591, and the following year he accepted a professorship in mathematics at the University of Padua, where there reigned an atmosphere more friendly to scientific pursuits. Here at Padua, for nearly 18 years, Galileo continued his experiments and his teaching, achieving a widespread fame. While at Padua, he heard of the discovery, in about 1607, of the telescope by the Dutch lens-grinder Johann Lipersheim, and he set about making instruments of his own, producing a telescope with a magnifying power of more than 30 diameters. With this telescope he observed sunspots (contradicting Aristotle's assertion that the sun is without blemish), saw mountains on the moon, and noticed the phases of Venus, Saturn's rings, and the four bright satellites of Jupiter (all three of these lending credence to the Copernican theory of the solar system). Galileo's discoveries roused the opposition of the Church, and finally, in the year 1633, he was summoned to appear before the Inquisition, and there forced to recant his scientific findings. Not many years later the great scientist became blind. He died, a prisoner in his own home, in 1642, the year Isaac Newton was born.

Johannes Kepler was born near Stuttgart, Germany in 1571 and commenced his studies at the University of Tübingen with the intention of becoming a Lutheran minister. Like Galileo, he found his first choice of an occupation far less congenial than his deep interest in science, particularly astronomy, and he accordingly changed his plans. In 1594, when in his early twenties, he accepted a lectureship at the University of Gräz in Austria. Five years later he became assistant to the famous Danish-Swedish astronomer Tycho Brahe, who had moved to Prague to serve as the court astronomer to Kaiser Rudolph II. Shortly after, in 1601, Brahe suddenly died, and Kepler inherited both his master's position and his vast collection of very accurate data on the positions of the planets as they moved about the sky. With amazing perseverance, Kepler set out to find, from Brahe's enormous mass of observational data, just how the planets move in space.

It has often been remarked that almost any problem can be solved if one but continuously worries over it and works at it a sufficiently long time. As Thomas Edison said, genius is 1% inspiration and 99% perspiration. Perhaps nowhere in the history of science is this more clearly demonstrated than in Kepler's incredible pertinacity in solving the problem of the motion of the planets about the sun. Thoroughly convinced of the Copernican theory that the planets revolve in orbits about the central sun, Kepler strenuously sought to determine the nature and position of those orbits and the manner in which the planets travel in their orbits. With Brahe's great set of observational recordings at hand, the problem became this: to obtain a pattern of motion of the planets that would exactly agree with Brahe's observations. So dependable were Brahe's recordings that any solution that should differ from Brahe's observed positions by even as little as a quarter of the moon's apparent diameter must be discarded as incorrect. Kepler had, then, first to guess with his *imagination* some plausible solution and then, with painful *perseverance*, to endure the mountain of tedious calculations needed to confirm or reject his guess. He made hundreds of fruitless attempts and performed reams and reams of calculations, laboring with undiminished zeal and patience for many years. Finally he solved his problem, in the form of his three famous laws of

---

[†]This is only approximately true, the approximation being very close in the case of small amplitudes of oscillation.

planetary motion, the first two around 1609 and the third one 10 years later in 1619:

 I. The planets move about the sun in elliptical orbits with the sun at one focus.
 II. The radius vector joining a planet to the sun sweeps over equal areas in equal intervals of time.
 III. The square of the time of one complete revolution of a planet about its orbit is proportional to the cube of the orbit's semimajor axis.

The empirical discovery of these laws from Brahe's mass of data constitutes one of the most remarkable inductions ever made in science. With justifiable pride, Kepler prefaced his *Harmony of the Worlds* of 1619 with the following outburst:

> I am writing a book for my contemporaries or--it does not matter--for posterity. It may be that my book will wait for a hundred years for a reader. Has not God waited 6000 years for an observer?

Kepler's laws of planetary motion are landmarks in the history of astronomy and mathematics, for in the effort to justify them, Isaac Newton was led to create modern celestial mechanics. It is very interesting that 1800 years after the Greeks had developed the properties of the conic sections there should occur such an illuminating practical application of them. *One never knows when a piece of pure mathematics may receive an unexpected application.*

In order to compute the areas involved in his second law, Kepler had to resort to a crude form of the integral calculus, making him one of the precursors of that calculus. Also, in his *Stereometria doliorum vinorum* (*Solid Geometry of Wine Barrels*, 1615), he applied crude integration procedures to the finding of the volumes of 93 different solids obtained by revolving arcs of conic sections about axes in their planes. Among these solids were the torus and two that he called *the apple* and *the lemon*, these latter being obtained by revolving a major and a minor arc, respectively, of a circle about the arc's chord as an axis. Kepler's interest in these matters arose when he observed some of the poor methods in use by the wine gaugers of the time. (See Group Research Project, page 269.)

It was Kepler who introduced the word *focus* (Latin for "hearth") into the geometry of conic sections. He approximated the perimeter of an ellipse of semiaxes a and b by the formula $\pi(a + b)$. He also laid down a so-called *principle of continuity*, which postulates the existence in a plane of certain ideal points and an ideal line having many of the properties of ordinary points and lines, lying at infinity. Thus he explained that a straight line can be considered as closed at infinity and that a parabola may be regarded as the limiting case of either an ellipse or a hyperbola in which one of the foci has retreated to infinity. The ideas were extended by later geometers.

Kepler was a confirmed Pythagorean, with the result that his work is often a blend of the fancifully mystical and the carefully scientific. It is sad that his personal life was made almost unendurable by a multiplicity of worldly misfortunes. An infection from smallpox when he was four years old left his eyesight much impaired. In addition to his general lifelong weakness, he spent a joyless youth; his marriage was a constant source of unhappiness; his favorite child died of smallpox; his wife went mad and died; he was expelled from his lectureship at the University of Gräz when the city fell to the Catholics; his mother was charged and imprisoned for witchcraft, and for almost a year he desperately tried to save her from the torture chamber; he himself very narrowly escaped condemnation for heterodoxy; and his stipend was always in arrears. One report says that his second marriage was even less fortunate than his first, although he took the precaution to analyze carefully the merits and demerits of 11 women before choosing the wrong one. He was forced to augment his income by casting horoscopes, and he died of a fever in 1630 at the age of 59 while on a journey to try to collect some of his long overdue salary.

Mathematical Essays

1. Write a 500-word essay on the life and mathematics of Galileo Galilei.

2. HISTORICAL QUEST

For this Quest, explain the remark in Galileo's *Discorsi e dimonstrazioni matematiche intorno à due nuove scienze* of 1638 that "neither is the number of squares less than the totality of all numbers, nor the latter greater than the former."

GALILEO GALILEI
1564–1642

3. HISTORICAL QUEST In 1638, Galileo published his ideas about dynamics in his book *Discorsi e dimonstrazioni matematiche intorno à due nuove scienze*. In this book, he considers the following problem:

Suppose the larger circle of Figure 10.50 has made one revolution in rolling along the straight line from A to B, so that $|\overline{AB}|$ is equal to the circumference of the large circle. Then the small circle, fixed to the large one, has also made one revolution, so that $|\overline{CD}|$ is equal to the circumference of the small circle. It follows that the *two circles have equal circumferences*.

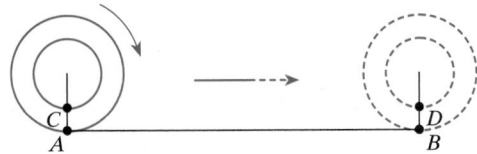

Figure 10.50 Aristotle's wheel

This paradox had been earlier described by Aristotle and is therefore sometimes referred to as *Aristotle's wheel*. Can you explain what is going on?

4. HISTORICAL QUEST In a previous Historical Quest (#60, Section 6.2), we outlined a procedure by Johannes Kepler for finding the volume of a torus.

This Quest asks you to use Kepler's reasoning to find the area of an ellipse.

a. Kepler divided a circle of radius r and circumference C into a large number of very thin sectors. By regarding each sector as a thin isosce-

JOHANNES KEPLER
1571–1630

les triangle of altitude r and base equal to the arc of the sector, he heuristically arrived at the formula $A = \frac{1}{2}rC$ for the area of a circle. Show how this was done.

b. Use Kepler's reasoning to obtain a volume V of a sphere of radius r and surface area S as $V = \frac{1}{3}rS$.

c. Use Kepler's reasoning to show that an ellipse of semimajor axis a and semiminor axis b has area $A = \pi ab$.

5. Prove Kepler's first law. You may search the literature or the internet for help with this proof.

6. Prove Kepler's third law. You may search the literature or the internet for help with this proof.

7. Where is a planet in its orbit when its speed is the greatest? Support your response.

8. Two hypothetical planets are moving about the sun in elliptical orbits having equal major axes. The minor axis of one, however, is half that of the other. How do the periods of the two planets compare? Support your response.

9. HISTORICAL QUEST The three laws of Kepler described in this section forever changed the way we view the universe, but it was not Kepler who correctly proved these laws. Isaac Newton (Historical Quest #1, Chapter 1 mathematical essays) proved these laws from the inverse-square law of gravitation.

In Section 10.3 we proved Kepler's second law. Write a 500-word essay on the life and mathematics of Johannes Kepler, and include, as part of your essay, where Kepler made his mistake in his proof of his second law.

10. **Book Report** "Science is that body of knowledge that describes, defines, and where possible, explains the universe . . . we think of the history of science as a history of men. . . . [History] is the story of thousands of people who contributed to the knowledge and theories that constituted the science of their eras and made the 'great leaps' possible. Many of these people were women." So begins a history of women in science entitled *Hypatia's Heritage* by Margaret Alic (Boston: Beacon Press, 1986). Read this book and write a book report.

11. Make up a word problem involving the calculus of vector-valued functions. Send your problem and its solution to

Strauss, Bradley, and Smith
Prentice Hall Publishing Company
1 Lake Street
Upper Saddle River, NJ 07458

The best ones submitted will appear in the next edition (along with credit to the problem poser).

CHAPTERS 1–10   Cumulative Review

Calculus is sometimes divided into *single-variable calculus* and *multivariable calculus*. The end of this chapter marks the transition between these major divisions of calculus, and as such it is a good time to take a look back at what we have done. There are three main ideas in single-variable calculus. The first is the notion of *limit*, which was introduced in Chapter 2. In Chapter 3 we introduced the idea of a *derivative*, the second major topic of calculus. In Chapter 5 we introduced one of the most important and revolutionary ideas in the history of mathematics—namely, that of a Riemann sum, and *integration*.

Definition of limit   The limit statement

$$\lim_{x \to c} f(x) = L$$

means that for each $\epsilon > 0$, there corresponds a number $\delta > 0$ with the property that

$$|f(x) - L| < \epsilon \quad \text{whenever} \quad 0 < |x - c| < \delta$$

The notion of a limit is fundamental for many of the ideas of calculus, primarily in the definitions of both the derivative and integral.

Definition of derivative   The derivative of f at x is given by

$$f'(x) = \lim_{\Delta x \to 0} \frac{f(x + \Delta x) - f(x)}{\Delta x}$$

provided this limit exists. If this limit exists the function f is said to be differentiable.

There are many applications of derivative, including related rates, curve sketching, and optimization.

Definition of integral   If f is defined on the closed interval $[a, b]$, we say f is integrable on $[a, b]$ if

$$I = \lim_{\|P\| \to 0} \sum_{k=1}^{n} f(x_k^*) \Delta x_k$$

exists, where $\|P\| = \max \Delta x_k, k = 1, 2, \ldots, n$. This limit is called the definite integral of f from a to b. The definite integral is denoted by

$$I = \int_a^b f(x)\, dx$$

Table 10.3 summarizes this relationship between modeling and the Riemann sum.

In the last two chapters we considered vectors in $\mathbb{R}^2$ and $\mathbb{R}^3$, as well as vector-valued functions. We summarize these ideas in Table 10.4.

TABLE 10.3 Modeling Formulas Involving Integration

Section	Situation	Riemann Sum Model	Outcome
5.3	**Introduction** Model a quantity in terms of one or more continuous functions on a closed interval $[a, b]$.	1. Partition interval. 2. Choose a number x_k^* arbitrarily from each subinterval of width Δx_k. 3. Form a sum of the type $$R_n = \sum_{k=1}^{n} f(x_k^*) \Delta x_k.$$	The approximations improve as the norm of the partitions goes to 0. The Riemann sums approach a limiting integral. Use this integral to define and calculate what we originally wanted to measure.
5.2	**Area** Find the area under a curve defined by $y = f(x)$, where $f(x) \geq 0$, above the x-axis and bounded by the lines $x = a$ and $x = b$.	Find the sum of n rectangles. $$\sum_{k=1}^{n} \underbrace{f(x_k^*) \Delta x_k}_{\text{Area of } k\text{th rectangle}}$$	$$\text{Area} = \int_a^b f(x)\, dx$$
5.3	**Displacement and distance traveled** Find the displacement and distance traveled for an object that is moving along a line having continuous velocity $v(t)$ for each time t between $t = a$ and $t = b$.	Find the sum of n distances. $$\sum_{k=1}^{n} \underbrace{\left| v[a + (k-1)\Delta t] \right| \Delta t}_{\substack{\text{Distance traveled over} \\ k\text{th time interval}}}$$	$$\text{Distance} = \int_a^b |v(t)|\, dt$$ $$\text{Displacement} = \int_a^b v(t)\, dt$$ $$= s(b) - s(a)$$
5.7	**Average value** Find the average value of a continuous function on the interval $[a, b]$.	Find the average of a weighted sum of n values. $$\frac{1}{b-a} \sum_{k=1}^{n} f(x_k^*) \Delta x, \text{ where}$$ $$\Delta x = \frac{b-a}{n}$$	$$\text{Average value} = \frac{1}{b-a} \int_a^b f(x)\, dx$$
6.1	**Area between curves** Find the area between the curves $y = f(x)$ and $y = g(x)$.	$$\sum_{k=1}^{n} \underbrace{[f(x_k^*) - g(x_k^*)]}_{\substack{\text{Top curve minus} \\ \text{bottom curve}}} \Delta x_k$$	$$\text{Area} = \int_a^b [f(x) - g(x)]\, dx$$
6.2	**Volume by cross section** Find the volume of a solid whose cross section perpendicular to the x-axis has area $A(x)$.	$$\sum_{k=1}^{n} A(x_k^*) \Delta x_k$$	$$\text{Volume} = \int_a^b A(x)\, dx$$
6.2	**Volumes of revolution** Find the volume of the region bounded by $y = f(x)$ and $y = g(x)$ revolved about the specified axis.		
	Disks: x-axis	$$\sum_{k=1}^{n} \pi [f(x_k^*)]^2 \Delta x_k$$	$$\text{Volume} = \pi \int_a^b [f(x)]^2\, dx$$
	Washers: x-axis	$$\sum_{k=1}^{n} \pi \left([f(x_k^*)]^2 - [g(x_k^*)]^2 \right) \Delta x_k$$	$$V = \pi \int_a^b \left([f(x)]^2 - [g(x)]^2 \right) dx$$
	Shells: y-axis	$$\sum_{k=1}^{n} 2\pi x_k^* f(x_k^*) \Delta x_k$$	$$\text{Volume} = 2\pi \int_a^b x f(x)\, dx$$
6.4	**Arc length** Find the length of a curve $y = f(x)$ on $[a, b]$.	$$\sum_{k=1}^{n} \sqrt{1 + [f'(x_k^*)]^2} \, \Delta x_k$$	$$\text{Length} = \int_a^b \sqrt{1 + [f'(x)]^2} \, dx$$
6.4	**Area of a surface of revolution** Find the area of a surface formed by rotating the curve $y = f(x)$ about the x-axis over $[a, b]$	$$\sum_{k=1}^{n} 2\pi f(x_k^*) \Delta s_k$$	$$\text{Area} = 2\pi \int_a^b f(x)\sqrt{1 + [f'(x)]^2} \, dx$$

TABLE 10.3 (continued)

Section	Situation	Riemann Sum Model	Outcome
6.5	**Mass** Find the mass of a thin plate with constant density ρ, bounded by $y = f(x)$ and $y = g(x)$.	$\displaystyle\sum_{k=1}^{n} \rho[f(x_k^*) - g(x_k^*)]\Delta x_k$	$\displaystyle m = \rho\int_a^b [f(x) - g(x)]\,dx$
6.5	**First moment** Find the moment of a thin plate with constant density ρ bounded by $y = f(x)$ and $y = g(x)$ (about the y-axis).	First moment about the y-axis $\displaystyle\sum_{k=2}^{n} \rho x_k^*[f(x_k^*) - g(x_k^*)]\Delta x_k$ First moment about the x-axis $\displaystyle\sum_{k=1}^{n} \frac{\rho}{2}\left\{[f(x_k^*)]^2 - [g(x_k^*)]^2\right\}\Delta x_k$	$\displaystyle M_y = \rho\int_a^b x[f(x) - g(x)]\,dx$ $\displaystyle M_x = \frac{\rho}{2}\int_a^b \left\{[f(x)]^2 - [g(x)]^2\right\}\,dx$
	Centroid Find the centroid of a homogeneous lamina. (ρ constant.)		$\displaystyle (\bar{x}, \bar{y}) = \left(\frac{M_y}{m}, \frac{M_x}{m}\right)$
6.5	**Work** Find the work done when an object moves along the x-axis from a to b when a variable force $F(x)$ is applied.	$\displaystyle\sum_{k=1}^{n} F(x_k^*)\Delta x_k$	$\displaystyle \text{Work} = \int_a^b F(x)\,dx$
6.5	**Hydrostatic force** Find the total force of a fluid against one side of a vertical plate, where h is the depth.	$\displaystyle\sum_{k=1}^{n} \rho(h_k^*)L(h_k^*)\Delta h_k$	$\displaystyle F = \int_a^b \rho h L(h)\,dh$

TABLE 10.4 Summary of Velocity, Acceleration, and Curvature

Position vector	$\mathbb{R}^2$ (Plane) $\mathbf{R}(t) = x(t)\mathbf{i} + y(t)\mathbf{j}$ $\mathbb{R}^3$ (Space) $\mathbf{R}(t) = x(t)\mathbf{i} + y(t)\mathbf{j} + z(t)\mathbf{k}$ The graph is called the **trajectory** of the object's motion.
Velocity vector	$\displaystyle \mathbf{V}(t) = \frac{d\mathbf{R}}{dt} = \mathbf{R}'(t)$ $\displaystyle \|\mathbf{V}\| = \frac{ds}{dt}$ is the object's **speed**. $\displaystyle \frac{\mathbf{V}}{\|\mathbf{V}\|}$ is the unit vector in the direction of $\mathbf{V}$ or *direction of motion*.
Unit tangent and principal unit normal vectors	$\displaystyle \mathbf{T} = \frac{\mathbf{V}}{\|\mathbf{V}\|} = \frac{\mathbf{R}'(t)}{\|\mathbf{R}'(t)\|} = \frac{d\mathbf{R}}{ds}$ is the **unit tangent vector** in the direction of *motion* $\displaystyle \mathbf{N} = \frac{\mathbf{T}'(t)}{\|\mathbf{T}'(t)\|} = \frac{1}{\kappa}\frac{d\mathbf{T}}{ds}$ is the **principal unit normal vector**.
Acceleration vector	$\displaystyle \mathbf{A}(t) = \frac{d^2\mathbf{R}}{dt^2} = \frac{d\mathbf{V}}{dt} = A_T\mathbf{T} + A_N\mathbf{N}$ where $\displaystyle A_T = \frac{d^2 s}{dt^2} = \frac{\mathbf{R}'\cdot\mathbf{R}''}{\|\mathbf{R}'\|}$ is the **tangential component**, and $\displaystyle A_N = \kappa\left(\frac{ds}{dt}\right)^2 = \frac{\|\mathbf{R}'\times\mathbf{R}''\|}{\|\mathbf{R}'\|} = \sqrt{\|\mathbf{A}\|^2 - A_T^2}$ is the **normal component**.
Curvature	$\displaystyle \kappa = \left\|\frac{d\mathbf{T}}{ds}\right\| = \frac{\|\mathbf{R}'\times\mathbf{R}''\|}{\|\mathbf{R}'\|^3}$; if $y = f(x)$ then $\displaystyle \kappa = \frac{|f''(x)|}{[1 + [f'(x)]^2]^{3/2}}$
Torsion	$\displaystyle \tau = \left\|\frac{d\mathbf{B}}{ds}\right\|$

Cumulative Review Problems for Chapters 1–10

1. **WHAT DOES THIS SAY?** In your own words, outline a procedure for integrating a given function.

2. **WHAT DOES THIS SAY?** In your own words, outline a procedure for deciding whether a given series converges or diverges.

3. **WHAT DOES THIS SAY?** What is a vector? What is a vector function? In your own words, discuss what is meant by vector calculus.

Evaluate the limits in Problems 4–9, or explain why the limit does not exist.

4. $\lim\limits_{x \to 1} \dfrac{7x^3 - 5x - 2}{3x^2 + 5x - 8}$

5. $\lim\limits_{k \to +\infty} \dfrac{(2x^2 - 3x + 1)(1 - 5x)}{5x^3 + 4x - 9}$

6. $\lim\limits_{x \to 0} \dfrac{\sin 3x}{\tan 2x}$

7. $\lim\limits_{x \to +\infty} \left(1 - \dfrac{2}{x}\right)^{3x}$

8. $\lim\limits_{x \to 0^+} \left(\dfrac{2x + 3}{x} - \csc x\right)$

9. $\lim\limits_{x \to 0} \dfrac{\cos x - 1}{e^x - x - 1}$

Find the derivatives in Problems 10–15.

10. $y = 3x^4 - 7\sqrt{2x} + 4$

11. $y = \sin^3 x + 2 \tan x$

12. $y = \ln \sqrt[3]{x} + xe^{-2x}$

13. $y = \sin^{-1} x + 2 \tan^{-1} \dfrac{1}{x}$

14. $y = \dfrac{e^{-2x}(1 - x^2)}{\sqrt[3]{x^2 - x^3 + 3x^4}}$

15. $xy^3 + x^2 e^{-y} = 4$

Find the integrals in Problems 16–21.

16. $\displaystyle\int x \ln \sqrt[3]{x}\, dx$

17. $\displaystyle\int \sin^2 x \cos^3 x\, dx$

18. $\displaystyle\int x\sqrt{16 - x}\, dx$

19. $\displaystyle\int \dfrac{dx}{1 + \cos x}$

20. $\displaystyle\int \dfrac{dx}{x^2(x^2 + 5)}$

21. $\displaystyle\int \dfrac{dx}{\sqrt{2x - x^2}}$

22. A student graphs the function $f(x) = 2x^3 + 51x^2 - 360x$ using a calculator, and the graph is shown in Figure 10.51. Is this graph sufficient to get an idea of what the function looks like? Why or why not?

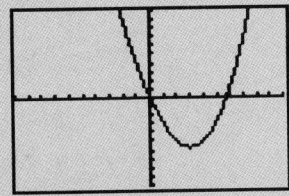

Figure 10.51 Calculator graph of $f(x) = 2x^3 + 51x^2 - 360x$

23. Let f be a continuous differentiable function with $f(0) = 0$ and $-2 \le f'(x) \le 4$ for $-3 \le x \le 3$.
    a. Can $f(2)$ be negative? Give a reason for your answer.
    b. Can $f(-2)$ be negative? Give a reason for your answer.
    c. Must f have a critical point between -3 and 3?

24. Find the area bounded by the curve $y = x\sqrt{x^2 + 8}$ and the x-axis on $[-2, 1]$.

25. Find the area bounded by the curves $y = \sin x$ and $y = \cos x$ and the lines $x = 0$ and $x = 1$.

26. Find the area of the region inside the circle $r = 4$ and to the right of the line $r = 2 \sec \theta$.

27. Find the volume of the solid formed by revolving about the x-axis the region bounded by the curve
$$y = \dfrac{2}{\sqrt{3x - 2}}$$

28. Find the equation of the line through $(-1, 2, 5)$ and perpendicular to the plane $2x - 3y + z = 11$ in symmetric form.

29. Find the equation of the plane satisfying the given conditions.
    a. passing through $(5, 1, 2)$, $(3, 1, -2)$, and $(3, 2, 5)$
    b. passing through $(-2, -1, 4)$ and perpendicular to the line
    $$\dfrac{x}{2} = \dfrac{y + 1}{5} = \dfrac{3 - z}{2}$$

Test the series in Problems 30–35 for convergence.

30. $\displaystyle\sum_{k=0}^{\infty} \dfrac{k^3}{k^4 + 2}$

31. $\displaystyle\sum_{k=1}^{\infty} \dfrac{1}{k \cdot 4^k}$

32. $\displaystyle\sum_{k=0}^{\infty} \dfrac{3k^2 - 7k + 2}{(2k - 1)(k + 3)}$

33. $\displaystyle\sum_{k=1}^{\infty} \dfrac{k!}{2^k \cdot k}$

34. $\displaystyle\sum_{k=0}^{\infty} \dfrac{(-1)^{k+1} k}{k^2 + k - 1}$

35. $1 + \dfrac{1}{8} - \dfrac{1}{27} - \dfrac{1}{64} + \dfrac{1}{125} + \dfrac{1}{216} - - + + \cdots$

36. In each case, find the sum of the convergent series
    a. $\displaystyle\sum_{k=1}^{\infty} \dfrac{2^{k-1}}{5^{k+3}}$
    b. $\displaystyle\sum_{k=1}^{\infty} \dfrac{1}{(3k - 1)(3k + 2)}$

37. In each case, determine whether the given improper integral converges, and if it does, find its value.
    a. $\displaystyle\int_1^{\infty} x^2 e^{-x}\, dx$
    b. $\displaystyle\int_0^2 \dfrac{dx}{\sqrt{4 - x^2}}$

38. Find $\mathbf{v} \cdot \mathbf{w}$ and $\mathbf{v} \times \mathbf{w}$ for the vectors $\mathbf{v} = 3\mathbf{i} - 2\mathbf{j} + 5\mathbf{k}$ and $\mathbf{w} = \mathbf{i} - 3\mathbf{j} - \mathbf{k}$.

39. Find $\mathbf{F}'$ and $\mathbf{F}''$ for $\mathbf{F}(t) = 2t\mathbf{i} + e^{-3t}\mathbf{j} + t^4\mathbf{k}$.

40. Find $\displaystyle\int [e^t\mathbf{i} - \mathbf{j} - t\mathbf{k}] \cdot [e^{-t}\mathbf{i} + t\mathbf{j} - \mathbf{k}]\, dt$

41. Find $\mathbf{T}$ and $\mathbf{N}$ for $\mathbf{R}(t) = 2(\sin 2t)\mathbf{i} + (2 + 2\cos 2t)\mathbf{j} + 6t\mathbf{k}$.

42. Show that the alternating series
$$S = \sum_{k=1}^{\infty} \dfrac{(-1)^{k+1}}{\sqrt{k}}$$
converges and determine what N must be to guarantee that the partial sum
$$S_N = \sum_{k=1}^{N} \dfrac{(-1)^{k+1}}{\sqrt{k}}$$
approximates the entire sum S with four-decimal-place accuracy.

43. a. Find the Maclaurin series representation for
    $$f(x) = x^2 e^{-x^2}.$$
    b. Use the representation in **a** to approximate
    $$\int_0^1 x^2 e^{-x^2}\, dx$$
    with three-decimal-place accuracy.

44. Let $P(x) = 7 - 3(x-4) + 5(x-4)^2 - 2(x-4)^3 + 6(x-4)^4$ be the fourth-degree Taylor polynomial for the function f about 4.

  a. Find $f(4)$ and $f'''(4)$.

  b. Use the third-degree Taylor polynomial for f' about $x = 4$ to approximate $f'(4.2)$.

  c. Write a fifth-degree Taylor polynomial for
  $$F(x) = \int_4^x f(t)\,dt \text{ about 4.}$$

45. Solve the first-order linear differential equation
$$\frac{dy}{dx} + 2y = x^2$$
subject to the condition $y = 2$ when $x = 0$.

46. During the time period from $t = 0$ to $t = 6$ seconds, a particle moves along the path given by $x(t) = 3\cos(\pi t)$, $y(t) = 5\sin(\pi t)$.

  a. What is the position of the particle when $t = 1.5$?

  b. Graph the path of the particle from $t = 0$ to $t = 6$. Show direction.

  c. How many times does the particle pass through the point found in part **a**?

  d. Find the velocity vector for the particle at any time t.

  e. What is the distance traveled by the particle from $t = 1.25$ to $t = 1.75$.

47. Find an equation in terms of x and y for the line tangent to the curve given by
$$x = t^2 - 2t - 1, \quad y = t^4 - 4t^2 + 2$$
at the point where $t = 1$.

48. A particle moves in space with position vector
$$\mathbf{R}(t) = (\sin t)\mathbf{i} - (\cos t)\mathbf{j} + \mathbf{k}$$

  a. Find the velocity and acceleration vectors for the particle and find its speed.

  b. Find a Cartesian equation for the particle's trajectory.

  c. Find the curvature κ and the tangential and normal components of acceleration for the particle's motion.

49. A mason lifts a 25-lb bucket of mortar from ground level to the top of a 50-ft building using a rope that weighs 0.25 lb/ft. Find the work done in lifting the bucket.

50. **Modeling Problem** At what speed must a satellite travel to maintain a circular orbit 1,000 mi above the surface of the earth? Assume the earth is a sphere of radius 4,000 mi and that GM in Newton's law of universal gravitation is approximately $9.56 \times 10^4 \text{ mi}^3/\text{s}^2$.

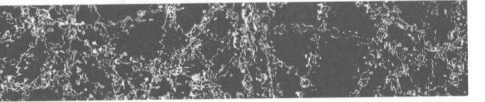

11

Partial Differentiation

PREVIEW

This chapter extends the methods of single-variable differential calculus to functions of two or more independent variables. You will learn how to take derivatives of such functions and to interpret those derivatives as slopes and rates of change. You will also learn a more general version of the chain rule and extended procedures for optimizing a function. The vector methods developed in Chapters 9 and 10 play an important role in this chapter, and indeed, we will find that the closest analogue of the single-variable derivative is a certain vector function called the *gradient*. In physics, the gradient is the rate at which a variable quantity, such as temperature or pressure, changes in value. In this chapter, we will define the *gradient of a function*, which is a vector whose components along each axis are related to the rate at which the function changes in the direction of that axis.

PERSPECTIVE

In many practical situations, the value of one quantity depends on the values of two or more others. For example, the amount of water in a reservoir depends on the amount of rainfall and on the amount of water consumed by local residents and thus may be regarded as a function of two independent variables. The current in an electrical circuit is a function of four variables: the electromotive force, the capacitance, the resistance, and the inductance. Graphical models involving functions of several variables often provide a valuable picture of what is happening in a situation of interest, as illustrated by the graphical model of Mount St. Helens shown in the accompanying figure before and after its eruption on May 18, 1980. We will analyze a variety of such models using techniques and tools that will be developed in this chapter.

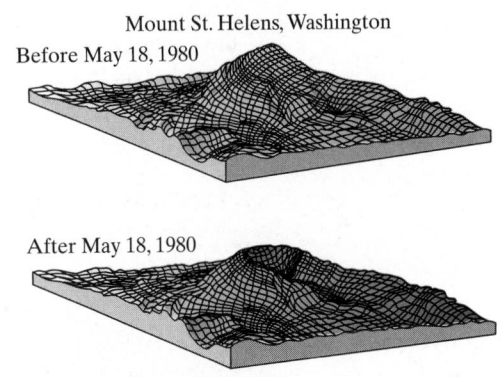

Mount St. Helens, Washington
Before May 18, 1980

After May 18, 1980

Mount St. Helens map courtesy of Bill Lennox, Humboldt State University.

11.1   Functions of Several Variables

IN THIS SECTION   basic concepts, level curves and surfaces, graphs of functions of two variables

BASIC CONCEPTS

Physical quantities often depend on two or more variables (see the Perspective at the beginning of this chapter). For example, we might be concerned with the temperature, T, at various points (x, y) on a metal plate. In this situation, T might be regarded as a function of the two location variables, x and y. Extending the notation for a function of a single variable, we can denote this relationship by $T(x, y)$.

Function of Two Variables

> A **function of two variables** is a rule f that assigns to each ordered pair (x, y) in a set D a unique number $f(x, y)$. The set D is called the **domain** of the function, and the corresponding values of $f(x, y)$ constitute the **range** of f.

Functions of three or more variables can be defined in a similar fashion. For example, the temperature in our introductory example may vary not only on the plate, but also with time t, in which case it would be denoted by $T(x, y, t)$. Occasionally, we will examine functions of four or more variables, but for simplicity, we will focus most of our attention on functions of two or three variables.

When dealing with a function f of two variables, we may write $z = f(x, y)$ and refer to x and y as the **independent variables** and to z as the **dependent variable**. Often, the functional "rule" will be given as a formula, and unless otherwise stated, *we will assume that the domain is the largest set of points in the plane (or in $\mathbb{R}^3$) for which the functional formula is defined and real-valued.* These definitions and conventions are illustrated in Example 1 for a function of two variables.

EXAMPLE 1   Domain, range, and evaluating a function of two variables

Let $f(x, y) = \sqrt{9 - x^2 - 4y^2}$.

a. Evaluate $f(2, 1)$ and $f(2t, t^2)$.
b. Describe the domain and range of f.

Solution

a. $f(2, 1) = \sqrt{9 - 2^2 - 4(1)^2} = 1$

$f(2t, t^2) = \sqrt{9 - (2t)^2 - 4(t^2)^2} = \sqrt{9 - 4t^2 - 4t^4}$

b. The domain of f is the set of all ordered pairs (x, y) for which $\sqrt{9 - x^2 - 4y^2}$ is defined. We must have $9 - x^2 - 4y^2 \geq 0$, or, equivalently, $x^2 + 4y^2 \leq 9$, in order for the square root to be defined. Thus, the domain of f is the set of all points (x, y) inside or on the ellipse $x^2 + 4y^2 = 9$, as shown in Figure 11.1.

The range of f is the set of all numbers $z = \sqrt{9 - x^2 - 4y^2}$ for (x, y) in the domain $x^2 + 4y^2 \leq 9$. Thus, the range is the interval $0 \leq z \leq 3$.   ∎

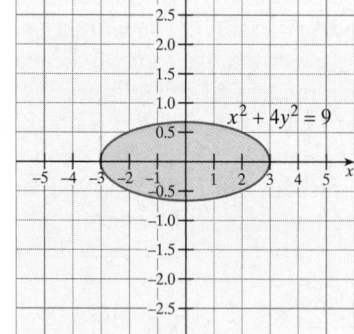

Figure 11.1 The domain of $f(x, y) = \sqrt{9 - x^2 - 4y^2}$

Functions of several variables can be combined in much the same way as functions of a single variable, as noted in the following definition.

Operations with Functions of Two Variables

> If $f(x, y)$ and $g(x, y)$ are functions of two variables with domain D, then
>
> **Sum** $(f + g)(x, y) = f(x, y) + g(x, y)$
>
> **Difference** $(f - g)(x, y) = f(x, y) - g(x, y)$

Operations with Functions of Two Variables (Continued)

Product	$(fg)(x, y) = f(x, y)g(x, y)$	
Quotient	$\left(\dfrac{f}{g}\right)(x, y) = \dfrac{f(x, y)}{g(x, y)}$	$g(x, y) \neq 0$

A **polynomial function in x and y** is a sum of functions of the form

$$Cx^m y^n$$

with nonnegative integers m and n and C a constant; for instance,

$$3x^5 y^3 - 7x^2 y + 2x - 3y + 11$$

is a polynomial in x and y. A **rational function** is a quotient of two polynomial functions. Similar notation and terminology apply to functions of three or more variables.

LEVEL CURVES AND SURFACES

By analogy with the single-variable case, we define the **graph of the function $f(x, y)$** to be the collection of all 3-tuples (ordered triples) (x, y, z) such that (x, y) is in the domain of f and $z = f(x, y)$. The graph of $f(x, y)$ is a surface in $\mathbb{R}^3$ whose projection onto the xy-plane is the domain D.

It is usually not easy to sketch the graph of a function of two variables without the assistance of technology. One way to proceed is illustrated in Figure 11.2.*

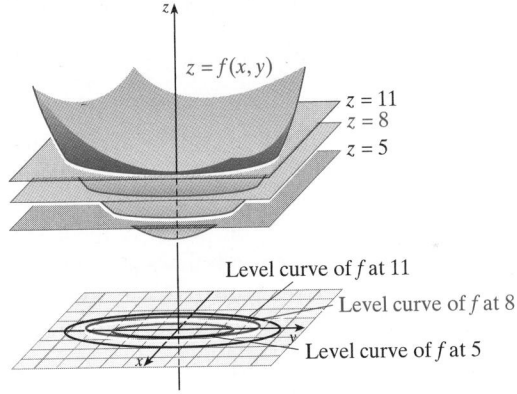

Figure 11.2   Graph of a function of two variables

Notice that when the plane $z = C$ intersects the surface $z = f(x, y)$, the result is the curve with the equation $f(x, y) = C$. Such an intersection is called the **trace** of the graph of f in the plane $z = C$. The set of points (x, y) in the xy-plane that satisfy $f(x, y) = C$ is called the **level curve** of f at C, and an entire family of level curves is generated as C varies over the range of f. We can think of a trace as a "slice" of the surface at a particular location and a level curve as its projection onto the xy-plane. By sketching members of this family on the xy-plane, we obtain a useful topographical map of the surface $z = f(x, y)$. Because level curves are used to show the shape of a surface (a mountain, for example), they are sometimes called **contour curves**.

For instance, imagine that the surface $z = f(x, y)$ is a "mountain" and that we wish to draw a two-dimensional "profile" of its shape. To draw such a profile, we indicate the paths of constant elevation by sketching the family of level curves in the plane and pinning a "flag" to each curve to show the elevation to which it corresponds,

---

*See the *Technology Manual* accompanying this book for some suggestions about using technology to help you graph functions of two variables.

as shown in Figure 11.3b. Notice that regions in the map where paths are crowded together correspond to the steeper portions of the mountain. An actual topographical map of Mount Rainier is shown in Figure 11.3c.

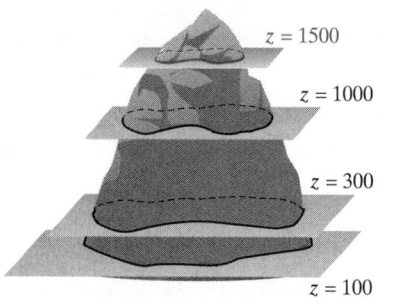

a. The surface $z = f(x, y)$ as a mountain

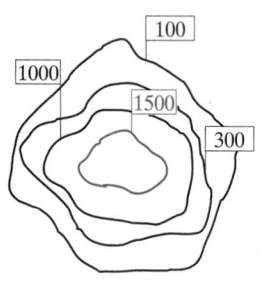

b. Level curves yield a topographic map of $z = f(x, y)$.

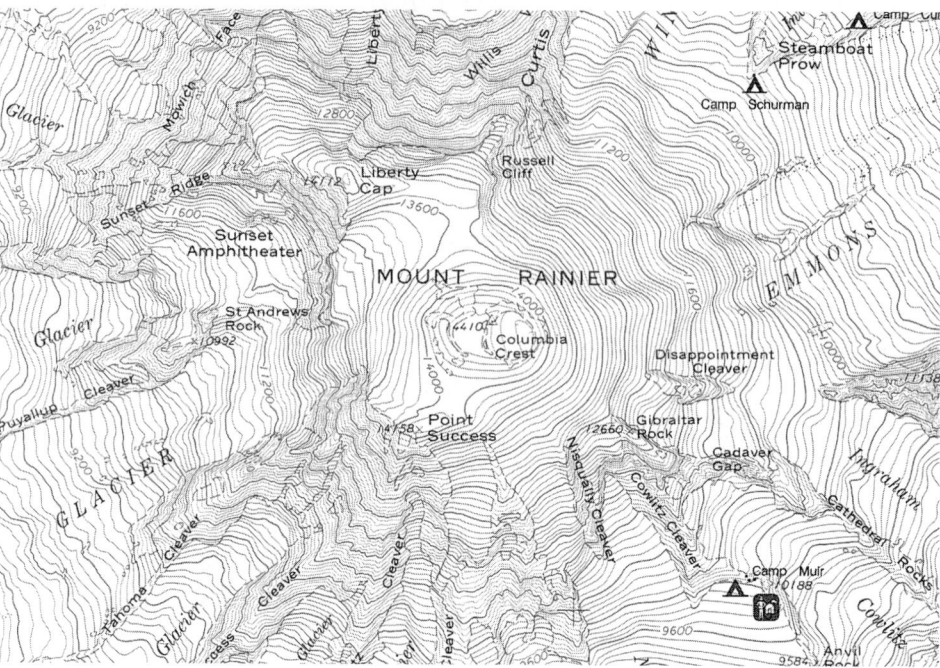

c. Topographic map of Mount Rainier

Figure 11.3   Level curves of a surface

You probably have seen level curves on the weather report in the newspaper or television news shows, where level curves of equal temperature are called **isotherms** (see Figure 11.4). Other common uses of level curves involve curves of equal pressure (called **isobars**) and curves of electric potential (called **equipotential lines**).

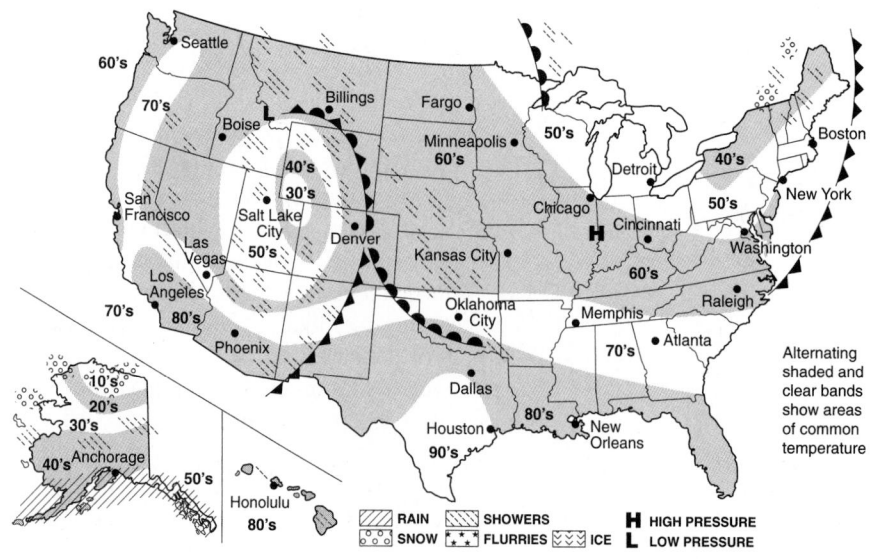

Figure 11.4   Isotherms

EXAMPLE 2   Level curves

Sketch some level curves of the function $f(x, y) = 10 - x^2 - y^2$.

Solution

A computer graph of $z = f(x, y)$ is the surface shown in Figure 11.5a. Figure 11.5b shows traces of the graph of f in the planes $z = 1$, $z = 6$, and $z = 9$, and the corresponding level curves are shown in Figure 11.5c. A table of values is shown in the margin.

k	level curve $z = k$
1	$1 = 10 - x^2 - y^2$ or $x^2 + y^2 = 9$
6	$6 = 10 - x^2 - y^2$ or $x^2 + y^2 = 4$
9	$9 = 10 - x^2 - y^2$ or $x^2 + y^2 = 1$

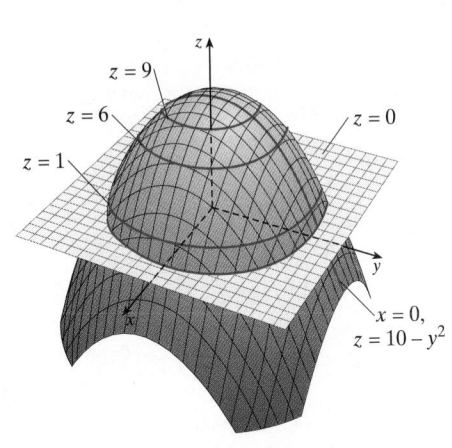

a. Computer generated graph of surface

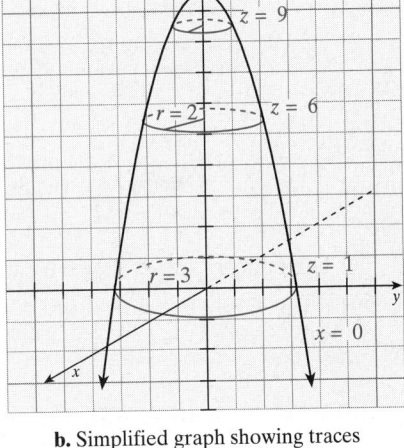

b. Simplified graph showing traces

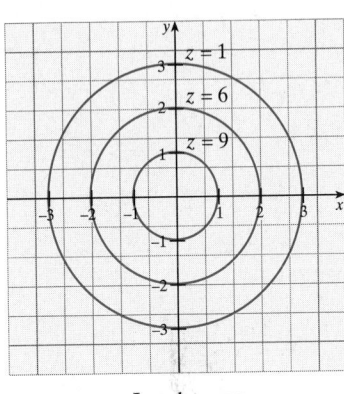

c. Level curves

Figure 11.5   Three ways of viewing the surface $z = 10 - x^2 - y^2$ ∎

GRAPHS OF FUNCTIONS OF TWO VARIABLES

The level curves of a function $f(x, y)$ provide information about the cross sections of the surface $z = f(x, y)$ perpendicular to the z-axis. However, a more complete picture of the surface can often be obtained by examining cross sections in other directions as well. This procedure is used to graph a function in Example 3.

EXAMPLE 3   Level curves

Use the level curves of the function $f(x, y) = x^2 + y^2$ to sketch the graph of f.

Solution

The level curve $x^2 + y^2 = 0$ (that is, $C = 0$) is the point $(0, 0)$, and for $C > 0$, the level curve $x^2 + y^2 = C$ is the circle with center $(0, 0)$ and radius $\sqrt{C}$ (Figure 11.6a). There are no points (x, y) that satisfy $x^2 + y^2 = C$ for $C < 0$.

We can gain additional information about the appearance of the surface by examining cross sections perpendicular to the other two principal directions; that is, to the x-axis and the y-axis. Cross-sectional planes perpendicular to the x-axis have the form $x = A$ and intersect the surface $z = x^2 + y^2$ in parabolas of the form $z = A^2 + y^2$. For example, the cross section of the plane $x = 5$ intersects the surface in the parabola $z = 25 + y^2$. That is, it is the set of point $(5, y, 25 + y^2)$ as y varies. Similarly, cross-sectional planes perpendicular to the y-axis have the form $y = B$ and intersect the surface in parabolas of the form $z = x^2 + B^2$.

To summarize, the surface $z = x^2 + y^2$ has cross sections that are circles in planes perpendicular to the z-axis and parabolas in the other two principal directions. Since the surface is formed by revolving a parabola about its axis, it is called a **circular paraboloid** or a **paraboloid of revolution**. The graph of the surface is shown in Figure 11.6b.

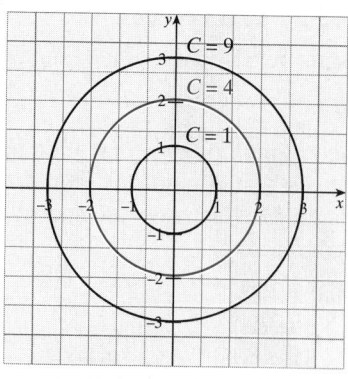
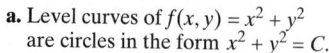
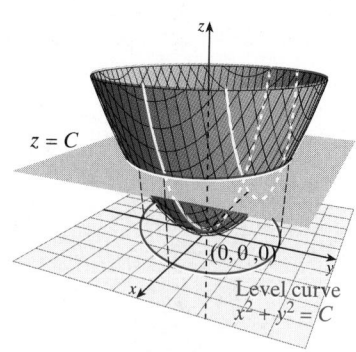

a. Level curves of $f(x, y) = x^2 + y^2$ are circles in the form $x^2 + y^2 = C$.

b. The surface $z = x^2 + y^2$. Cross sections perpendicular to the y-axis shown in white are parabolas.

Figure 11.6   The graph of the function $f(x, y) = x^2 + y^2$ ∎

The concept of level curve can be generalized to apply to functions of more than two variables. In particular, if f is a function of 3 variables x, y, and z, then the graph of the equation $f(x, y, z) = C$ is a surface of $\mathbb{R}^3$ called a **level surface** of f at C.

EXAMPLE 4   Isothermal surface

Suppose a region of $\mathbb{R}^3$ is heated so that its temperature T at each point (x, y, z) is given by $T(x, y, z) = 100 - x^2 - y^2 - z^2$ degrees Celsius. Describe the isothermal surfaces for $T > 0$.

Solution

The isothermal surfaces are given by $T(x, y, z) = k$ for constant k; that is, $x^2 + y^2 + z^2 = 100 - k$. If $100 - k > 0$, the graph of $x^2 + y^2 + z^2 = 100 - k$ is a sphere of radius $\sqrt{100 - k}$ and center $(0, 0, 0)$. When $k = 100$, the graph is a single point (the origin), and $T(0, 0, 0) = 100°$C. As the temperature drops, the constant k gets smaller, and the radius $\sqrt{100 - k}$ of the sphere gets larger. Hence, the isothermal surfaces are spheres, and the larger the radius, the cooler the surface. This situation is illustrated in Figure 11.7.

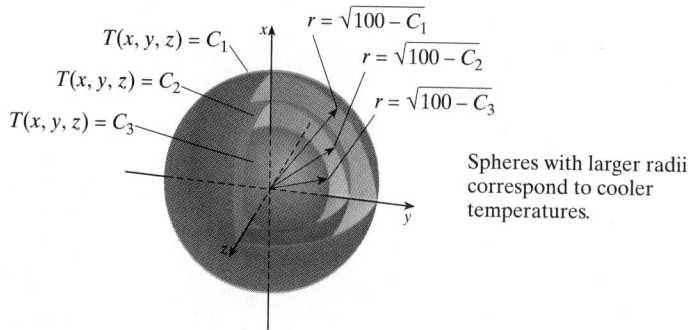

Spheres with larger radii correspond to cooler temperatures.

Figure 11.7   Isothermal surfaces for $T(x, y, z) = 100 - x^2 - y^2 - z^2$ ∎

As you can see by the examples in this section, you will need to recall the graphs of quadric surfaces (see Section 9.7). It will also help if you can recognize the surface by looking at its equation. What you will need to remember is summarized in Table 9.1, page 625.

Computer software is now available for graphing functions of two variables. Software packages such as *Mathematica*, *Maple*, MATLAB, and *Derive* will sketch very sophisticated graphs in three dimensions. Software usually allows a given graph to be visualized from different viewpoints by rotating the surface until a desired viewpoint is found. A few examples of computer generated surfaces are shown in Figure 11.8.

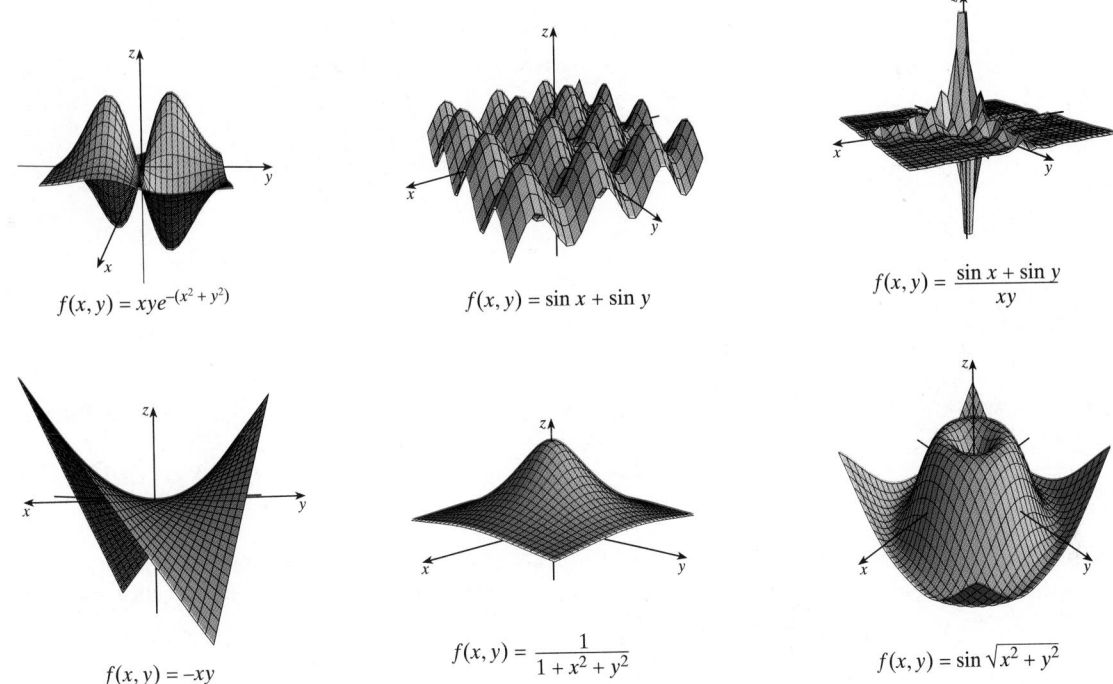

$f(x, y) = xye^{-(x^2 + y^2)}$

$f(x, y) = \sin x + \sin y$

$f(x, y) = \dfrac{\sin x + \sin y}{xy}$

$f(x, y) = -xy$

$f(x, y) = \dfrac{1}{1 + x^2 + y^2}$

$f(x, y) = \sin \sqrt{x^2 + y^2}$

Figure 11.8 Several computer generated surfaces

11.1 PROBLEM SET

A **1.** Let $f(x, y) = x^2 y + xy^2$. If t is a real number, find:

   a. $f(0, 0)$ **b.** $f(-1, 0)$ **c.** $f(0, -1)$

   d. $f(1, 1)$ **e.** $f(2, 4)$ **f.** $f(t, t)$

   g. $f(t, t^2)$ **h.** $f(1 - t, t)$

2. Let $f(x, y, z) = x^2 y e^{2x} + (x + y - z)^2$. Find

   a. $f(0, 0, 0)$ **b.** $f(1, -1, 1)$ **c.** $f(-1, 1, -1)$

   d. $\dfrac{d}{dx} f(x, x, x)$ **e.** $\dfrac{d}{dy} f(1, y, 1)$ **f.** $\dfrac{d}{dz} f(1, 1, z^2)$

3. WHAT DOES THIS SAY? Discuss what is meant by a function of two variables. Your discussion should include examples of a function of two variables not discussed in this section.

4. WHAT DOES THIS SAY? Describe how level curves can be used to sketch the graph of a function $f(x, y)$. Include some examples in your discussion (different from those in the text).

Find the domain and range for each function given in Problems 5–14.

5. $f(x, y) = \sqrt{x - y}$ **6.** $f(x, y) = \dfrac{1}{\sqrt{x - y}}$

7. $f(u, v) = \sqrt{uv}$ **8.** $f(x, y) = \sqrt{\dfrac{y}{x}}$

9. $f(x, y) = \ln(y - x)$ **10.** $f(u, v) = \sqrt{u \sin v}$

11. $f(x, y) = \sqrt{(x + 3)^2 + (y - 1)^2}$

12. $f(x, y) = e^{(x+1)/(y-2)}$

13. $f(x, y) = \dfrac{1}{\sqrt{x^2 - y^2}}$ **14.** $f(x, y) = \dfrac{1}{\sqrt{9 - x^2 - y^2}}$

Sketch some level curves $f(x, y) = C$ for $C \geq 0$ for each function given in Problems 15–20.

15. $f(x, y) = 2x - 3y$ **16.** $f(x, y) = x^2 - y^2$

17. $f(x, y) = x^3 - y$ **18.** $g(x, y) = x^2 - y$

19. $h(x, y) = x^2 + \dfrac{y^2}{4}$ **20.** $f(x, y) = \dfrac{x}{y}$

In Problems 21–26, sketch the level surface $f(x, y, z) = C$ for the given value of C.

21. $f(x, y, z) = y^2 + z^2$ for $C = 1$

22. $f(x, y, z) = x^2 + z^2$ for $C = 1$

23. $f(x, y, z) = x + y - z$ for $C = 1$

24. $f(x, y, z) = x + y - z$ for $C = 0$

25. $f(x, y, z) = (x + 1)^2 + (y - 2)^2 + (z - 3)^2$ for $C = 4$

26. $f(x, y, z) = 2x^2 + 2y^2 - z$ for $C = 1$

In Problems 27–34, describe the traces of the given quadric surface in each coordinate plane, then sketch the surface.

27. $9x^2 + 4y^2 + z^2 = 1$

28. $\dfrac{x^2}{4} + y^2 + \dfrac{z^2}{9} = 1$

29. $\dfrac{x^2}{4} + \dfrac{y^2}{9} - z^2 = 1$

30. $\dfrac{x^2}{9} - y^2 - z^2 = 1$

31. $z = x^2 + \dfrac{y^2}{4}$

32. $z = \dfrac{x^2}{9} - \dfrac{y^2}{16}$

33. $x^2 + 2y^2 = 9z^2$

34. $z^2 = 1 + \dfrac{x^2}{9} + \dfrac{y^2}{4}$

Match each family of level curves given in Problems 35–40 with one of the surfaces labeled A–F.

35. $f(x, y) = x^2 - y^2$

36. $f(x, y) = e^{1-x^2+y^2}$

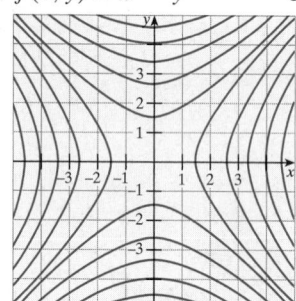

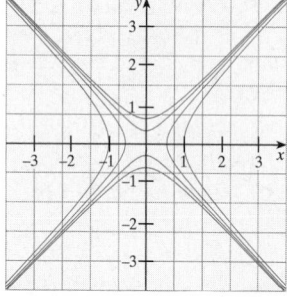

37. $f(x, y) = \dfrac{1}{x^2 + y^2}$

38. $f(x, y) = \sin\left(\dfrac{x^2 + y^2}{2}\right)$

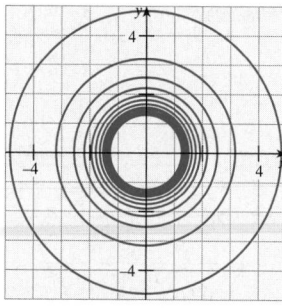

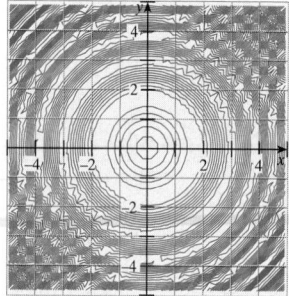

39. $f(x, y) = \dfrac{\cos xy}{x^2 + y^2}$

40. $f(x, y) = \sin\sqrt{x^2 + y^2}$

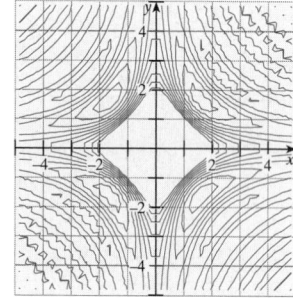

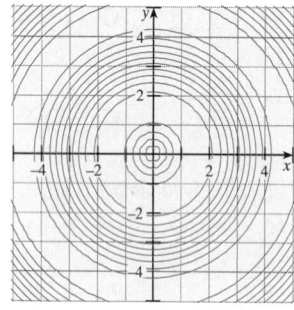

A.

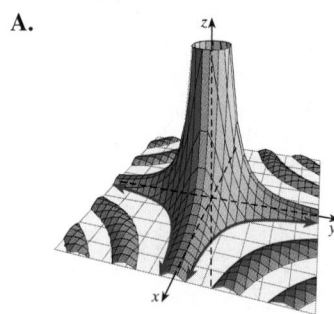

B.

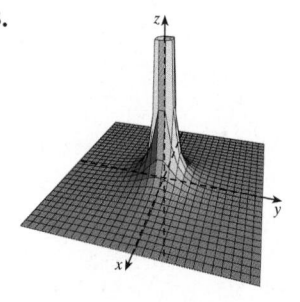

C.   **D.**

E.   **F.**

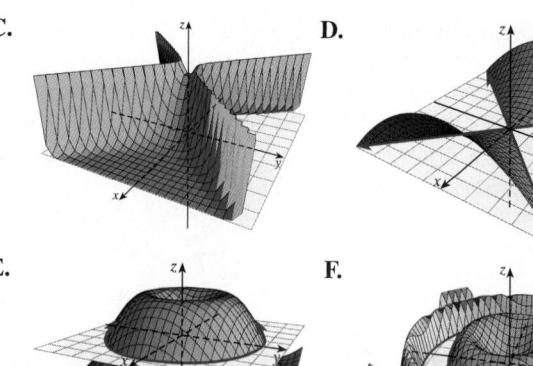

B *Sketch the graph of each function given in Problems 41–52.*

41. $f(x, y) = -4$

42. $f(x, y) = x$

43. $f(x, y) = y^2 + 1$

44. $f(x, y) = x^3 - 1$

45. $f(x, y) = 2x - 3y$

46. $f(x, y) = x^2 - y$

47. $f(x, y) = 2x^2 + y^2$

48. $f(x, y) = x^2 - y^2$

49. $f(x, y) = \dfrac{x}{y}$

50. $f(x, y) = \sqrt{x + y}$

51. $f(x, y) = x^2 + y^2 + 2$

52. $f(x, y) = \sqrt{1 - x^2 - y^2}$

53. If $E(x, y)$ is the voltage (potential) at each point (x, y) in the plane, the level curves of E are called *equipotential curves.* Suppose

$$E(x, y) = \dfrac{7}{\sqrt{3 + x^2 + 2y^2}}$$

Sketch the equipotential curves that correspond to $E = 1$, $E = 2$, and $E = 3$.

54. According to the ideal gas law, $PV = kT$, where P is pressure, V is volume, T is temperature, and k is a constant. Suppose a tank contains $3{,}500$ in.^{3} of a particular gas at a pressure of 24 lb/in.^{2} when the temperature is $270°$ K (degrees Kelvin).

a. Determine the constant of proportionality k for this gas.

b. Express the temperature T as a function of P and V using the constant found in part **a** and describe the isotherms for the temperature function.

55. The *lens equation* in optics states that

$$\dfrac{1}{d_o} + \dfrac{1}{d_i} = \dfrac{1}{L}$$

where d_o is the distance of an object from a thin, spherical lens, d_i is the distance of its image on the other side of the lens, and L is the *focal length* of the lens (see Figure 11.9). Write L as a function of d_o and d_i, and sketch some level curves of the function (these are curves of constant focal length).

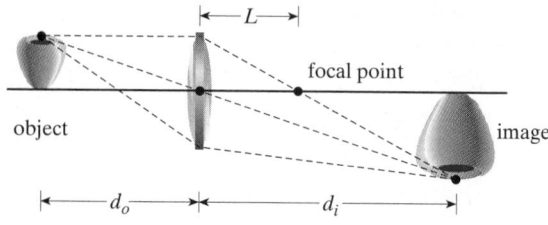

Figure 11.9 Image of an object through a lens

56. The EZGRO agricultural company estimates that when $100x$ worker-hours of labor are employed on y acres of land, the number of bushels of wheat produced is $f(x, y) = Ax^a y^b$, where A, a, and b are nonnegative constants. Suppose the company decides to double the production factors x and y. Determine how this decision affects the production of wheat in each of these cases:

a. $a + b > 1$ **b.** $a + b < 1$ **c.** $a + b = 1$

57. Suppose that when x machines and y worker-hours are used each day, a certain factory will produce $Q(x, y) = 10xy$ mobile phones. Describe the relationship between the "inputs" x and y that result in an "output" of 1,000 phones each day. *Note:* You are finding a level curve of the production function Q.

58. Modeling Problem At a certain factory, the daily output is modeled by $Q = CK^r L^{1-r}$ units, where K denotes capital investment, L is the size of the labor force, and C and r are constants, with $0 < r < 1$ (this is called a *Cobb-Douglas production function*). What happens to Q if K and L are both doubled? What if both are tripled?

59. Sketch the level curves for the graph of $f(x, y) = xy$ in the first quadrant.

60. A publishing house has found that in a certain city each of its salespeople will sell approximately

$$\frac{r^2}{2{,}000p} + \frac{s^2}{100} - s \quad \text{units}$$

per month, at a price of p dollars/unit, where s denotes the total number of salespeople employed and r is the amount of money spent each month on local advertising. Express the total revenue R as a function of p, r, and s.

61. Modeling Problem A manufacturer with exclusive rights to a sophisticated new industrial machine is planning to sell a limited number of the machines to both foreign and domestic firms. The price that the manufacturer can expect to receive for the machines will depend on the number of machines made available. It is estimated that if the manufacturer supplies x machines to the domestic market and y machines to the foreign market, the machines will sell for

$$60 - \frac{x}{5} + \frac{y}{20}$$

thousand dollars apiece at home and

$$50 - \frac{x}{10} + \frac{y}{20}$$

thousand dollars apiece abroad. Express the revenue R as a function of x and y.

11.2 Limits and Continuity

IN THIS SECTION open and closed sets in $\mathbb{R}^2$ and $\mathbb{R}^3$, limit of a function of two variables, continuity, limits and continuity for functions of three variables

Most commonly considered functions of a single variable have domains that can be described in terms of intervals. However, dealing with functions of two or more variables requires special terminology and notation that we will introduce in this section and then use to discuss limits and continuity for functions of two variables.

OPEN AND CLOSED SETS IN $\mathbb{R}^2$ AND $\mathbb{R}^3$

An **open disk** centered at the point $C(a, b)$ in $\mathbb{R}^2$ is the set of all points (x, y) such that

$$\sqrt{(x - a)^2 + (y - b)^2} < r$$

for $r > 0$ (see Figure 11.10a). If the boundary of the disk is included (that is, if $\sqrt{(x - a)^2 + (y - b)^2} \leq r$), the disk is said to be **closed** (see Figure 11.10b). Open and closed disks are analogous to open and closed intervals on a coordinate line.

A point $P_0(x_0, y_0)$ is said to be an **interior point** of a set S in $\mathbb{R}^2$ if some open disk centered at P_0 is contained entirely within S, as shown in Figure 11.11a. If S is the empty set, or if every point of S is an interior point, then S is called an **open set** (Figure 11.11b). The point P_0 is called a **boundary point** of S if every open disk centered at P_0 contains both points that belong to S and points that do not. The collection of all boundary points of S is called the **boundary** of S, and S is said to be **closed** if it contains its boundary (Figure 11.11c). The empty set and $\mathbb{R}^2$ are both open and closed.

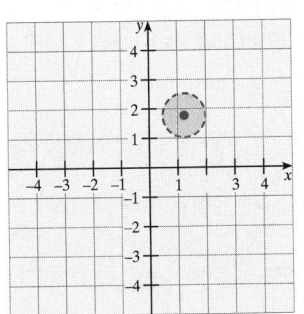

a. Open disk

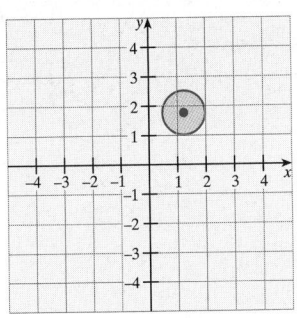

b. Closed disk

Figure 11.10 Open and closed disks

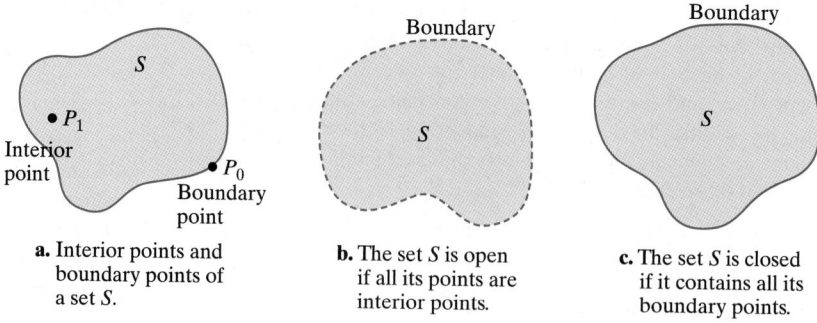

a. Interior points and boundary points of a set S.

b. The set S is open if all its points are interior points.

c. The set S is closed if it contains all its boundary points.

Figure 11.11   Open and closed sets in $\mathbb{R}^2$

Similarly, an **open ball** centered at $C(a, b, c)$ is the set of all points $P(x, y, z)$ such that

$$\sqrt{(x - a)^2 + (y - b)^2 + (z - c)^2} < r$$

for $r > 0$. A point P_0 is an **interior point** of a set S in $\mathbb{R}^3$ if there exists an open ball centered at P_0 that is contained entirely within S, and the nonempty set S is an **open set** if all its points are interior points. The point P_0 is a **boundary point** of S if every open ball centered at P_0 contains both points that belong to S and points that do not, and S is **closed** if it contains all its boundary points. As with $\mathbb{R}^2$, the set $\mathbb{R}^3$ is both open and closed.

LIMIT OF A FUNCTION OF TWO VARIABLES

In Chapter 2, we informally defined the limit statement $\lim\limits_{x \to c} f(x) = L$ to mean that $f(x)$ can be made arbitrarily close to L by choosing x sufficiently close (but not equal) to c. For a function of two variables we write

$$\lim_{(x, y) \to (x_0, y_0)} f(x, y) = L$$

to mean that the functional values $f(x, y)$ can be made arbitrarily close to the number L by choosing the point (x, y) sufficiently close to the point (x_0, y_0). The following is a more formal definition of this limiting behavior.

Limit of a Function of Two Variables

The limit statement

$$\lim_{(x, y) \to (x_0, y_0)} f(x, y) = L$$

means that for each given number $\epsilon > 0$, there exists a number $\delta > 0$ so that whenever (x, y) is a point in the domain D of f such that

$$0 < \sqrt{(x - x_0)^2 + (y - y_0)^2} < \delta$$

then

$$|f(x, y) - L| < \epsilon$$

→ **What This Says** If $\lim\limits_{(x,y)\to(x_0,y_0)} f(x,y) = L$, then given $\epsilon > 0$, the function value of $f(x,y)$ must lie in the interval $(L - \epsilon, L + \epsilon)$ whenever (x,y) is a point in the domain of f other than $P_0(x_0, y_0)$ that lies inside the disk of radius δ centered at P_0. This is illustrated in Figure 11.12.

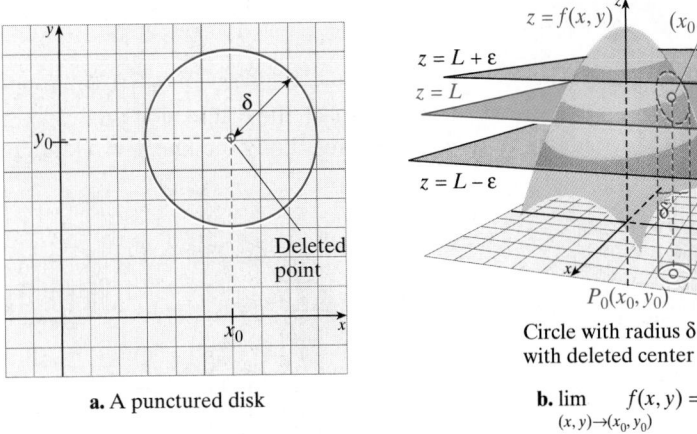

a. A punctured disk

b. $\lim\limits_{(x,y)\to(x_0,y_0)} f(x,y) = L$

Figure 11.12   Limit of a function of two variables

When considering $\lim\limits_{x\to c} f(x)$ we need to examine the approach of x to c from two directions (the left- and right-hand limits). However, for a function of two variables, we write $(x,y) \to (x_0, y_0)$ to mean that the point (x,y) is allowed to approach (x_0, y_0) along any curve in the domain of f that passes through (x_0, y_0). For example, no matter how you get to the 15th step of Denver's state capitol, you will still be at 5,280 ft when you get there. If the

$$\lim_{(x,y)\to(x_0,y_0)} f(x,y)$$

is not the same for all approaches, or **paths** within the domain of f, then *the limit does not exist.*

EXAMPLE 1   Evaluating a limit of a function of two variables

Evaluate $\lim\limits_{(x,y)\to(0,0)} \dfrac{x^2 + x - xy - y}{x - y}$.

Solution

First, note that for $x \neq y$,

$$f(x,y) = \frac{x^2 + x - xy - y}{x - y} = \frac{(x+1)(x-y)}{x - y} = x + 1$$

Therefore, since $f(x,y)$ is defined only for $x \neq y$, we have

$$\lim_{(x,y)\to(0,0)} \frac{x^2 + x - xy - y}{x - y} = \lim_{(x,y)\to(0,0)} (x + 1) = 1 \qquad \blacksquare$$

EXAMPLE 2   Showing a limit does not exist

If $f(x,y) = \dfrac{2xy}{x^2 + y^2}$, show

$$\lim_{(x,y)\to(0,0)} f(x,y)$$

does not exist by evaluating this limit along the x-axis, the y-axis, and along the line $y = x$.

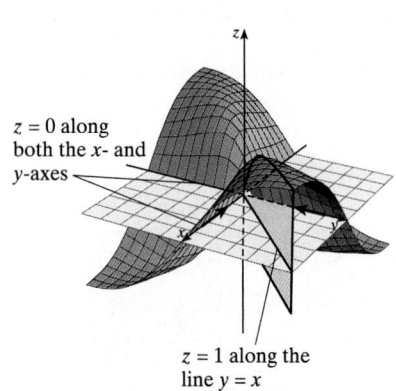

$z = 0$ along both the x- and y-axes

$z = 1$ along the line $y = x$

Figure 11.13 Graph of $z = \dfrac{2xy}{x^2 + y^2}$ and limits as $(x, y) \to (0, 0)$

Solution

First note that the denominator is zero at $(0, 0)$, so $f(0, 0)$ is not defined. If we approach the origin along the x-axis (where $y = 0$), we find that

$$f(x, 0) = \frac{2x(0)}{x^2 + 0} = 0$$

so $f(x, y) \to 0$ as $(x, y) \to (0, 0)$ along $y = 0$ (and $x \neq 0$). We find a similar result if we approach the origin along the y-axis (where $x = 0$); see Figure 11.13.

However, along the line $y = x$, the functional values are

$$f(x, y) = f(x, x) = \frac{2x^2}{x^2 + x^2} = 1 \quad \text{for} \quad x \neq 0$$

so that $f(x, y) \to 1$ as $(x, y) \to (0, 0)$ along $y = x$. Because $f(x, y)$ tends toward different numbers as $(x, y) \to (0, 0)$ along different curves, it follows that f has no limit at the origin. ∎

EXAMPLE 3   Showing a limit does not exist

Show that

$$\lim_{(x,y) \to (0,0)} \frac{x^2 y}{x^4 + y^2}$$

does not exist.

Solution

If we approach this problem as we did the one in Example 2, we would take limits as $(x, y) \to (0, 0)$ along the x-axis, the y-axis, and the line $y = x$. All these approach lines have the general form $y = mx$. We find

along $y = mx$:

$$\lim_{(x,y) \to (0,0)} \frac{x^2 y}{x^4 + y^2} = \lim_{(x,y) \to (0,0)} \frac{x^2 (mx)}{x^4 + (mx)^2}$$
$$= \lim_{(x,y) \to (0,0)} \frac{mx}{x^2 + m^2} = 0$$

However, if we approach $(0, 0)$ along the parabola $y = x^2$, we find

along $y = x^2$:

$$\lim_{(x,y) \to (0,0)} \frac{x^2 y}{x^4 + y^2} = \lim_{(x,y) \to (0,0)} \frac{x^2 (x^2)}{x^4 + (x^2)^2}$$
$$= \lim_{(x,y) \to (0,0)} \frac{x^4}{2x^4} = \frac{1}{2}$$

WARNING It is often possible to show that a limit does not exist by the methods illustrated in Examples 2 and 3. However, it is impossible to try to prove that $\lim\limits_{(x,y) \to (0,0)} f(x, y)$ exists by showing the limiting value of $f(x, y)$ is the same along every curve that passes through (x_0, y_0) because there are too many such curves.

Therefore, since approaching $(0, 0)$ along the lines $y = mx$ gives a different limiting value from approaching along the parabola $y = x^2$, we conclude that the given limit does not exist. ∎

We have just observed that it is difficult to show that a given limit exists. However, limits of functions of two variables that are known to exist can be manipulated in much the same way as limits involving functions of a single variable. Here is a list of the basic rules for manipulating such limits.

Basic Formulas and Rules for Limits of a Function of Two Variables

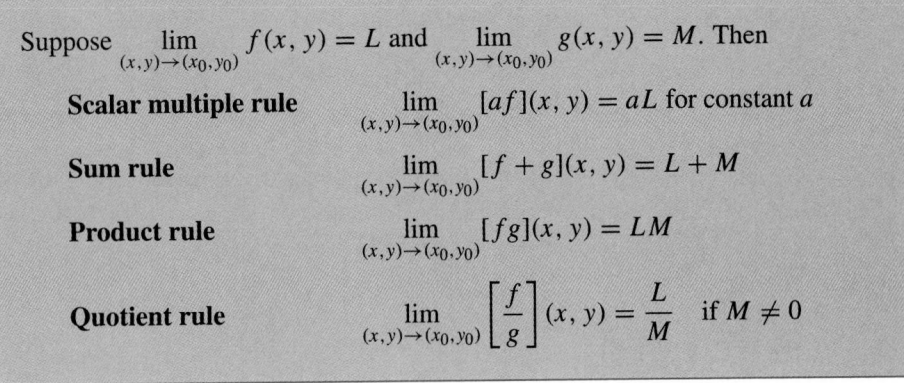

Suppose $\lim\limits_{(x,y)\to(x_0,y_0)} f(x,y) = L$ and $\lim\limits_{(x,y)\to(x_0,y_0)} g(x,y) = M$. Then

Scalar multiple rule $\qquad \lim\limits_{(x,y)\to(x_0,y_0)} [af](x,y) = aL$ for constant a

Sum rule $\qquad \lim\limits_{(x,y)\to(x_0,y_0)} [f+g](x,y) = L+M$

Product rule $\qquad \lim\limits_{(x,y)\to(x_0,y_0)} [fg](x,y) = LM$

Quotient rule $\qquad \lim\limits_{(x,y)\to(x_0,y_0)} \left[\dfrac{f}{g}\right](x,y) = \dfrac{L}{M}$ if $M \neq 0$

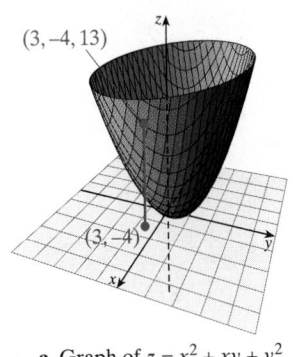

$(3, -4, 13)$

$(3, -4)$

a. Graph of $z = x^2 + xy + y^2$

$\left(1, 2, \frac{4}{5}\right)$

$(1, 2)$

b. Graph of $f(x, y) = \dfrac{2xy}{x^2 + y^2}$

Figure 11.14 Graphs showing limits

EXAMPLE 4 Manipulating limits of functions of two variables

Assuming each limit exists, evaluate:

a. $\lim\limits_{(x,y)\to(3,-4)} (x^2 + xy + y^2)$ $\qquad$ **b.** $\lim\limits_{(x,y)\to(1,2)} \dfrac{2xy}{x^2 + y^2}$

Solution

a. $\lim\limits_{(x,y)\to(3,-4)} (x^2 + xy + y^2) = (3)^2 + (3)(-4) + (-4)^2 = 13$. A graph is shown in Figure 11.14a.

b. $\lim\limits_{(x,y)\to(1,2)} \dfrac{2xy}{x^2 + y^2} = \dfrac{\lim\limits_{(x,y)\to(1,2)} 2xy}{\lim\limits_{(x,y)\to(1,2)} (x^2 + y^2)}$

$\qquad\qquad = \dfrac{2(1)(2)}{1^2 + 2^2} = \dfrac{4}{5}$

The graph is shown in Figure 11.14b. ∎

CONTINUITY

Recall that a function of a single variable x is continuous at $x = c$ if

1. $f(c)$ is defined; $\qquad$ **2.** $\lim\limits_{x\to c} f(x)$ exists; $\qquad$ **3.** $\lim\limits_{x\to c} f(x) = f(c)$.

Using the definition of the limit of a function of two variables, we can now define the continuity of a function of two variables analogously.

Continuity of a Function of Two Variables

The function $f(x, y)$ is **continuous** at the point (x_0, y_0) if

1. $f(x_0, y_0)$ is defined;

2. $\displaystyle\lim_{(x,y)\to(x_0,y_0)} f(x, y)$ exists;

3. $\displaystyle\lim_{(x,y)\to(x_0,y_0)} f(x, y) = f(x_0, y_0)$.

The function f is **continuous on a set S** if it is continuous at each point in S.

→ **What This Says**   The function f is continuous at (x_0, y_0) if the functional value of $f(x, y)$ is close to $f(x_0, y_0)$ whenever (x, y) in the domain of f is sufficiently close to (x_0, y_0). Geometrically, this means that f is continuous if the surface $z = f(x, y)$ has no "gaps" or "holes" (see Figure 11.15).

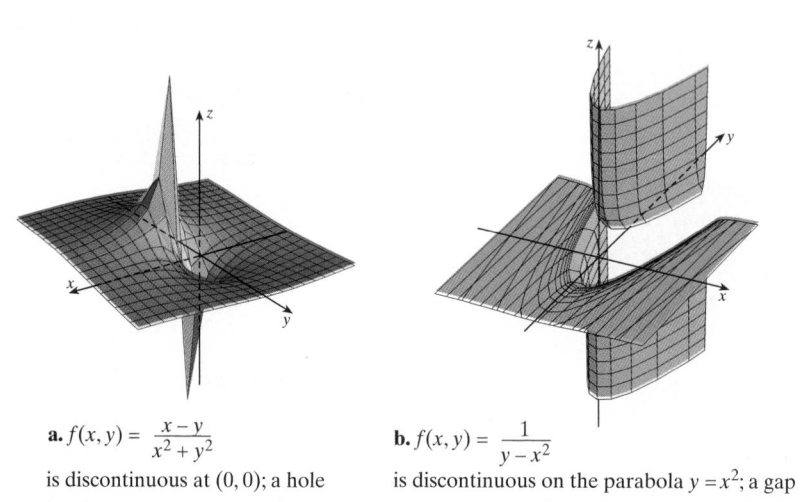

a. $f(x, y) = \dfrac{x - y}{x^2 + y^2}$ **b.** $f(x, y) = \dfrac{1}{y - x^2}$

is discontinuous at $(0, 0)$; a hole   is discontinuous on the parabola $y = x^2$; a gap

Figure 11.15   Two types of discontinuity

The basic properties of limits can be used to show that if f and g are both continuous on the set S, then so are the sum $f + g$, the multiple af, the product fg, the quotient f/g (whenever $g \neq 0$), and the root $\sqrt[n]{f}$ wherever it is defined. Also, if F is a function of two variables that is continuous at (x_0, y_0) and G is a function of one variable that is continuous at $F(x_0, y_0)$, it can be shown that the composite function $G \circ F$ is continuous at (x_0, y_0).

Many common functions of two variables are continuous wherever they are defined. For instance, a polynomial in two variables, such as $x^3 y^2 + 3xy^3 - 7x + 2$, is continuous throughout the plane, and a rational function of two variables is continuous wherever the denominator polynomial is not zero. Unless otherwise stated, the functions of two or more variables considered in this text will be continuous wherever they are defined.

EXAMPLE 5   **Testing for continuity**

Test the continuity of the functions:

a. $f(x, y) = \dfrac{x - y}{x^2 + y^2}$ **b.** $f(x, y) = \dfrac{1}{y - x^2}$

These are the functions whose graphs are shown in Figure 11.15.

Solution

a. The function f is a rational function of x and y (since $x - y$ and $x^2 + y^2$ are both polynomials), so it is discontinuous only where it is undefined; namely at $(0, 0)$.

b. Again, this is a rational function and is discontinuous only where it is undefined; that is, where

$$y - x^2 = 0$$

Thus, the function is continuous at all points except those lying on the parabola $y = x^2$. ∎

EXAMPLE 6   Continuity using the limit definition

Show that f is continuous at $(0, 0)$ where

$$f(x, y) = \begin{cases} y \sin \dfrac{1}{x} & x \neq 0 \\ 0 & x = 0 \end{cases}$$

Solution

The graph is shown in Figure 11.16. To prove continuity at $(0, 0)$, we must show that for any $\epsilon > 0$, there exists a $\delta > 0$ such that

$$|f(x, y) - f(0, 0)| = \left| y \sin \frac{1}{x} \right| < \epsilon \quad \text{whenever} \quad 0 < x^2 + y^2 < \delta^2$$

(We use $x^2 + y^2$ and δ^2 here instead of $\sqrt{x^2 + y^2}$ and δ for convenience.) Note that $\left| y \sin \frac{1}{x} \right| \leq |y|$ for all $x \neq 0$, because $\left| \sin \frac{1}{x} \right| \leq 1$ for $x \neq 0$. If (x, y) lies in the disk $x^2 + y^2 < \delta^2$, then the points $(0, y)$ that satisfy $y^2 < \delta^2$ lie in the same disk (let $x = 0$ in $x^2 + y^2 < \delta^2$). In other words, points satisfying $|y| < \delta$ lie in the disk, and if we let $\delta = \epsilon$ it follows that

$$|f(x, y) - f(0, 0)| \leq |y| < \delta = \epsilon \quad \text{whenever} \quad 0 < \sqrt{x^2 + y^2} < \delta \qquad ∎$$

LIMITS AND CONTINUITY FOR FUNCTIONS OF THREE VARIABLES

The concepts we have just introduced for functions of two variables in $\mathbb{R}^2$ extend naturally to functions of three variables in $\mathbb{R}^3$. In particular, the limit statement

$$\lim_{(x,y,z) \to (x_0, y_0, z_0)} f(x, y, z) = L$$

means that for each number $\epsilon > 0$, there exists a number $\delta > 0$ such that

$$|f(x, y, z) - L| < \epsilon$$

whenever (x, y, z) is a point in the domain of f such that

$$0 < \sqrt{(x - x_0)^2 + (y - y_0)^2 + (z - z_0)^2} < \delta$$

The function $f(x, y, z)$ is **continuous** at the point $P_0(x_0, y_0, z_0)$ if

1. $f(x_0, y_0, z_0)$ is defined;
2. $\displaystyle\lim_{(x,y,z) \to (x_0, y_0, z_0)} f(x, y, z)$ exists;
3. $\displaystyle\lim_{(x,y,z) \to (x_0, y_0, z_0)} f(x, y, z) = f(x_0, y_0, z_0)$.

Most commonly considered functions of three variables are continuous wherever they are defined. We close with an example that illustrates how to determine the set of discontinuities of a function of three variables.

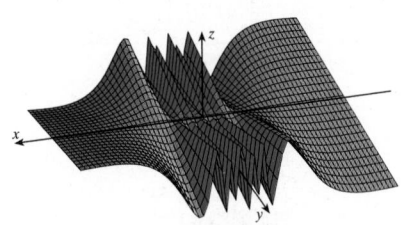

Front view

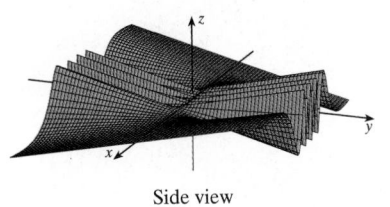

Side view

Figure 11.16 Graph of f in Example 6

EXAMPLE 7 **Determining where a function of three variables is continuous**

For what points (x, y, z) is the following function continuous?

$$f(x, y, z) = \frac{3}{\sqrt{x^2 + y^2 - 2z}}$$

Solution

The function $f(x, y, z)$ is continuous except where it is not defined; that is, for $x^2 + y^2 - 2z \leq 0$. Thus, $f(x, y, z)$ is continuous at any point not inside or on the paraboloid $z = \frac{1}{2}(x^2 + y^2)$. ∎

11.2 PROBLEM SET

A **1. WHAT DOES THIS SAY?** Describe the notion of a limit of a function of two variables.

2. WHAT DOES THIS SAY? Describe the basic formulas and rules for limits of a function of two variables.

In Problems 3–20, find the given limit, assuming it exists.

3. $\lim\limits_{(x,y)\to(-1,0)} (xy^2 + x^3y + 5)$

4. $\lim\limits_{(x,y)\to(0,0)} (5x^2 - 2xy + y^2 + 3)$

5. $\lim\limits_{(x,y)\to(1,3)} \dfrac{x+y}{x-y}$

6. $\lim\limits_{(x,y)\to(3,4)} \dfrac{x-y}{\sqrt{x^2+y^2}}$

7. $\lim\limits_{(x,y)\to(1,0)} e^{xy}$

8. $\lim\limits_{(x,y)\to(1,0)} (x+y)e^{xy}$

9. $\lim\limits_{(x,y)\to(0,1)} [e^{x^2+x} \ln(ey^2)]$

10. $\lim\limits_{(x,y)\to(e,0)} \ln(x^2+y^2)$

11. $\lim\limits_{(x,y)\to(0,0)} \dfrac{x^2-2xy+y^2}{x-y}$

12. $\lim\limits_{(x,y)\to(1,2)} \dfrac{(x^2-1)(y^2-4)}{(x-1)(y-2)}$

13. $\lim\limits_{(x,y)\to(0,0)} \dfrac{e^x \tan^{-1} y}{y}$

14. $\lim\limits_{(x,y)\to(0,0)} \dfrac{x^2y^2}{x^2+y^2}$

15. $\lim\limits_{(x,y)\to(0,0)} \dfrac{\sin(x+y)}{x+y}$

16. $\lim\limits_{(x,y)\to(0,0)} (\sin x + \cos y)$

17. $\lim\limits_{(x,y)\to(5,5)} \dfrac{x^4-y^4}{x^2-y^2}$

18. $\lim\limits_{(x,y)\to(a,a)} \dfrac{x^4-y^4}{x^2-y^2}$; a is a constant.

19. $\lim\limits_{(x,y)\to(2,1)} \dfrac{x^2-4y^2}{x-2y}$

20. $\lim\limits_{(x,y)\to(0,0)} \dfrac{x^2+y^2}{\sqrt{x^2+y^2+4}-2}$

In Problems 21–29, evaluate the indicated limit, if it exists.

21. $\lim\limits_{(x,y)\to(2,1)} (xy^2 + x^3y)$

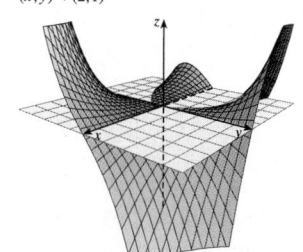

22. $\lim\limits_{(x,y)\to(1,2)} (5x^2 - 2xy + y^2)$

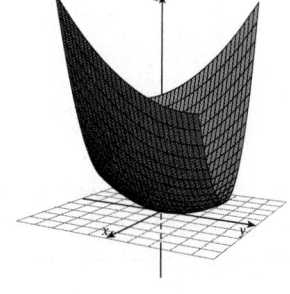

23. $\lim\limits_{(x,y)\to(0,0)} \dfrac{x+y}{x-y}$

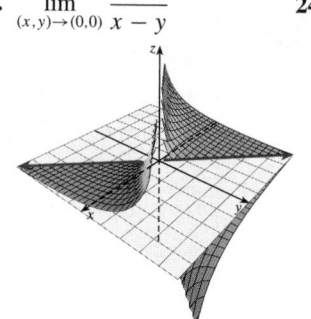

24. $\lim\limits_{(x,y)\to(0,0)} \dfrac{x-y}{\sqrt{x^2+y^2}}$

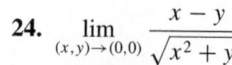
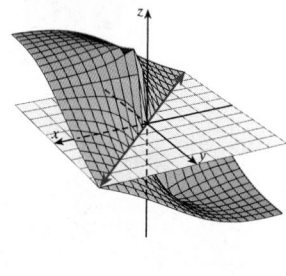

25. $\lim\limits_{(x,y)\to(0,0)} e^{xy}$

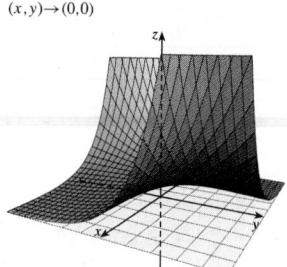

26. $\lim\limits_{(x,y)\to(1,1)} (x+y)e^{xy}$

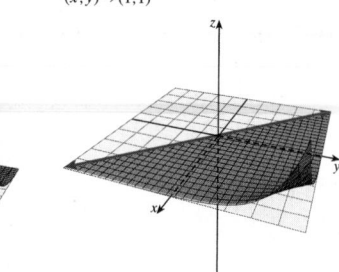
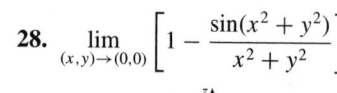

27. $\lim\limits_{(x,y)\to(0,0)} (\sin x - \cos y)$

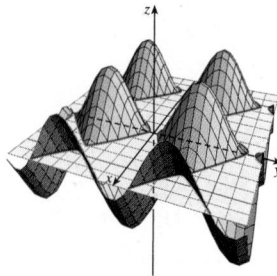

28. $\lim\limits_{(x,y)\to(0,0)} \left[1 - \dfrac{\sin(x^2+y^2)}{x^2+y^2}\right]$

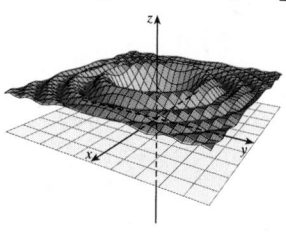

29. $\lim\limits_{(x,y)\to(0,0)} \dfrac{1-\cos(x^2+y^2)}{x^2+y^2}$

B *In Problems 30–33, show that* $\lim\limits_{(x,y)\to(0,0)} f(x, y)$ *does not exist.*

30. $f(x, y) = \dfrac{x^4 y^4}{(x^2 + y^4)^3}$

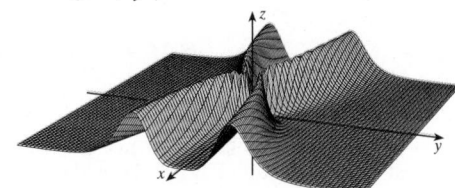

31. $f(x, y) = \dfrac{x - y^2}{x^2 + y^2}$

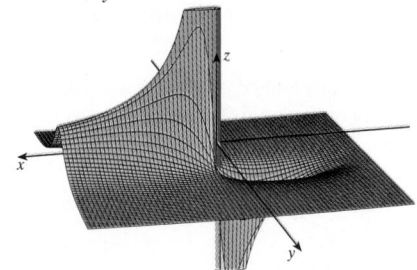

32. $f(x, y) = \dfrac{x^2 + y}{x^2 + y^2}$

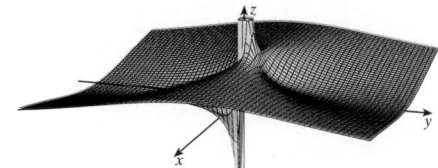

33. $f(x, y) = \dfrac{x^2 y^2}{x^4 + y^4}$

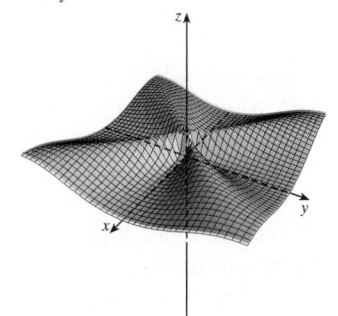

34. Let f be the function defined by

$$f(x, y) = \begin{cases} \dfrac{xy^2}{x^2 + y^4} & \text{for } (x, y) \neq (0, 0) \\ 0 & \text{for } (x, y) = (0, 0) \end{cases}$$

Is f continuous at $(0, 0)$? Explain.

35. Let f be the function defined by

$$f(x, y) = \begin{cases} \dfrac{xy^3}{x^2 + y^6} & \text{for } (x, y) \neq (0, 0) \\ 0 & \text{for } (x, y) = (0, 0) \end{cases}$$

Is f continuous at $(0, 0)$? Explain.

36. Let f be the function defined by $f(x, y) = \dfrac{x^2 - y^2}{x^2 + y^2}$ for $(x, y) \neq (0, 0)$.
 a. Find $\lim\limits_{(x,y)\to(2,1)} f(x, y)$.
 b. Prove that f has no limit at $(0, 0)$.

37. Let f be the function defined by $f(x, y) = \dfrac{x^2 + 2y^2}{x^2 + y^2}$ for $(x, y) \neq (0, 0)$.
 a. Find $\lim\limits_{(x,y)\to(3,1)} f(x, y)$.
 b. Prove that f has no limit at $(0, 0)$.

38. Given that the function

$$f(x, y) = \begin{cases} \dfrac{x^3 + y^3}{x^2 + y^2} & \text{for } (x, y) \neq (0, 0) \\ A & \text{for } (x, y) = (0, 0) \end{cases}$$

is continuous at the origin, what is A?

39. Given that the function

$$f(x, y) = \begin{cases} \dfrac{3x^3 - 3y^3}{x^2 - y^2} & \text{for } x^2 \neq y^2 \\ B & \text{otherwise} \end{cases}$$

is continuous at the origin, what is B?

40. Let

$$f(x, y) = \begin{cases} \dfrac{x^2 y^2}{x^2 + y^2} & \text{for } (x, y) \neq (0, 0) \\ 0 & \text{for } (x, y) = (0, 0) \end{cases}$$

Given that $f(x, y)$ has a limit at $(0, 0)$, is f continuous there?

41. Assuming that the limit exists, show that

$$\lim_{(x,y,z)\to(0,0,0)} \frac{xyz}{x^2 + y^2 + z^2} = 0$$

42. Let $f(x, y) = \dfrac{\sin(x^2 + y^2)}{x^2 + y^2}$ for $(x, y) \neq (0, 0)$. For what value of $f(0, 0)$ is $f(x, y)$ continuous at $(0, 0)$? *Hint*: Use polar coordinates.

43. Consider the function

$$f(x, y) = \begin{cases} \dfrac{2x^2 - x^2 y^2 + 2y^2}{x^2 + y^2} & \text{for } (x, y) \neq (0, 0) \\ A & \text{for } (x, y) = (0, 0) \end{cases}$$

Find the value of A which will make f continuous at the origin. *Hint*: Use polar coordinates.

Use polar coordinates to find the limit given in Problems 44–47.

44. $\lim\limits_{(x,y)\to(0,0)} \dfrac{\tan(x^2 + y^2)}{x^2 + y^2}$

45. $\lim\limits_{(x,y)\to(0,0)} (1 + x^2 + y^2)^{1/(x^2+y^2)}$

46. $\lim\limits_{(x,y)\to(0,0)} \dfrac{x^2 y^2}{x^2 + y^2}$ **47.** $\lim\limits_{(x,y)\to(0,0)} x \ln \sqrt{x^2 + y^2}$

Counterexample Problems *In Problems 48–50, either show that the given statement is true or find a counterexample.*

48. If $\lim\limits_{y\to0} f(0, y) = 0$, then $\lim\limits_{(x,y)\to(0,0)} f(x, y) = 0$.

49. If $f(x, y)$ is continuous for all $x \neq 0$ and $y \neq 0$, and $f(0, 0) = 0$, then $\lim\limits_{(x,y)\to(0,0)} f(x, y) = 0$.

50. If $f(x)$ and $g(y)$ are continuous functions of x and y, respectively, then

$$h(x, y) = f(x) + g(y)$$

is a continuous function of x and y.

C *Use the ϵ-δ definition of limit to verify the limit statements given in Problems 51–54.*

51. $\lim\limits_{(x,y)\to(0,0)} (2x^2 + 3y^2) = 0$ **52.** $\lim\limits_{(x,y)\to(0,0)} (x + y^2) = 0$

53. $\lim\limits_{(x,y)\to(0,0)} \dfrac{x^2 - y^2}{x + y} = 0$ **54.** $\lim\limits_{(x,y)\to(1,-1)} \dfrac{x^2 - y^2}{x + y} = 2$

55. Prove that if f is continuous and $f(a, b) > 0$, then there exists a δ-neighborhood about (a, b) such that $f(x, y) > 0$ for every point (x, y) in the neighborhood.

56. Prove the scalar multiple rule:

$$\lim\limits_{(x,y)\to(x_0,y_0)} [af](x, y) = a \lim\limits_{(x,y)\to(x_0,y_0)} f(x, y)$$

57. Prove the sum rule:

$$\lim\limits_{(x,y)\to(x_0,y_0)} [f + g](x, y) = L + M$$

where $L = \lim\limits_{(x,y)\to(x_0,y_0)} f(x, y)$ and $M = \lim\limits_{(x,y)\to(x_0,y_0)} g(x, y)$.

58. A function of two variables $f(x, y)$ may be continuous in each separate variable at $x = x_0$ and $y = y_0$ without being itself continuous at (x_0, y_0). Let $f(x, y)$ be defined by

$$f(x, y) = \begin{cases} \dfrac{xy}{x^2 + y^2} & \text{for } (x, y) \neq (0, 0) \\ 0 & \text{for } (x, y) = (0, 0) \end{cases}$$

Let $g(x) = f(x, 0)$ and $h(y) = f(0, y)$. Show that both $g(x)$ and $h(y)$ are continuous at 0 but that $f(x, y)$ is not continuous at $(0, 0)$.

11.3 Partial Derivatives

IN THIS SECTION partial differentiation, partial derivative as a slope, partial derivative as a rate, higher-order partial derivatives

PARTIAL DIFFERENTIATION

It is often important to know how a function of two variables changes with respect to one of the variables. For example, according to the ideal gas law, the pressure of a gas is related to its temperature and volume by the formula $P = \dfrac{kT}{V}$, where k is a constant. If the temperature is kept constant while the volume is allowed to vary, we might want to know the effect on the rate of change of pressure. Similarly, if the volume is kept constant while the temperature is allowed to vary, we might want to know the effect on the rate of change of pressure.

The process of differentiating a function of several variables with respect to one of its variables while keeping the other variable(s) fixed is called **partial differentiation**, and the resulting derivative is a **partial derivative** of the function.

Recall that the derivative of a function of a single variable f is defined to be the limit of a difference quotient, namely,

$$f'(x) = \lim_{\Delta x \to 0} \frac{f(x + \Delta x) - f(x)}{\Delta x}$$

Partial derivatives with respect to x or y are defined similarly.

Partial Derivatives of a Function of Two Variables

If $z = f(x, y)$, then the partial derivatives of f with respect to x and y are the functions f_x and f_y, respectively, defined by

$$f_x(x, y) = \lim_{\Delta x \to 0} \frac{f(x + \Delta x, y) - f(x, y)}{\Delta x}$$

and

$$f_y(x, y) = \lim_{\Delta y \to 0} \frac{f(x, y + \Delta y) - f(x, y)}{\Delta y}$$

provided the limits exist.

➡ **What This Says** For the partial differentiation of a function of two variables, $z = f(x, y)$, we find the partial derivative with respect to x by regarding y as constant while differentiating the function with respect to x. Similarly, the partial derivative with respect to y is found by regarding x as constant while differentiating with respect to y.

EXAMPLE 1 Partial derivatives

If $f(x, y) = x^3 y + x^2 y^2$, find: **a.** f_x **b.** f_y

Solution

a. For f_x, hold y constant and find the derivative with respect to x:

$$f_x(x, y) = 3x^2 y + 2xy^2$$

b. For f_y, hold x constant and find the derivative with respect to y:

$$f_y(x, y) = x^3 + 2x^2 y \qquad ■$$

Several different symbols are used to denote partial derivatives, as indicated in the following box.

Alternative Notation for Partial Derivatives

For $z = f(x, y)$, the partial derivatives f_x and f_y are denoted by

$$f_x(x, y) = \frac{\partial f}{\partial x} = \frac{\partial z}{\partial x} = \frac{\partial}{\partial x} f(x, y) = z_x = D_x(f)$$

and

$$f_y(x, y) = \frac{\partial f}{\partial y} = \frac{\partial z}{\partial y} = \frac{\partial}{\partial y} f(x, y) = z_y = D_y(f)$$

The values of the partial derivatives of $f(x, y)$ at the point (a, b) are denoted by

$$\left. \frac{\partial f}{\partial x} \right|_{(a,b)} = f_x(a, b) \qquad \text{and} \qquad \left. \frac{\partial f}{\partial y} \right|_{(a,b)} = f_y(a, b)$$

EXAMPLE 2 Finding and evaluating a partial derivative

Let $z = x^2 \sin(3x + y^3)$.

a. Evaluate $\left. \dfrac{\partial z}{\partial x} \right|_{(\pi/3, 0)}$. **b.** Evaluate z_y at $(1, 1)$.

Solution

a. $\dfrac{\partial z}{\partial x} = 2x \sin(3x + y^3) + x^2 \cos(3x + y^3)(3)$

$\qquad = 2x \sin(3x + y^3) + 3x^2 \cos(3x + y^3)$

Thus,

$$\left.\frac{\partial z}{\partial x}\right|_{(\pi/3,0)} = 2\left(\frac{\pi}{3}\right)\sin \pi + 3\left(\frac{\pi}{3}\right)^2 \cos \pi = \frac{2\pi}{3}(0) + \frac{\pi^2}{3}(-1) = -\frac{\pi^2}{3}$$

b. $z_y = x^2 \cos(3x + y^3)(3y^2) = 3x^2y^2 \cos(3x + y^3)$ so that

$$z_y(1, 1) = 3(1)^2(1)^2 \cos(3 + 1) = 3\cos 4 \qquad \blacksquare$$

TECHNOLOGY NOTE

Finding partial derivatives using technology is a natural extension of the way you have been finding other derivatives. The general format for most calculators and computer programs is the same: *derivative operator, function, variable of differentiation*. Evaluating the partial derivative is then accomplished by using the evaluate feature. For example, Figure 11.17a displays the computation of the partial derivative of $f(x, y) = x^3y + x^2y^2$ with respect to x from Example 1, while Figure 11.17b displays the evaluation of the partial derivative of $z = x^2 \sin(3x + y^3)$ with respect to x at the point $\left(\frac{\pi}{3}, 0\right)$ found in Example 2.

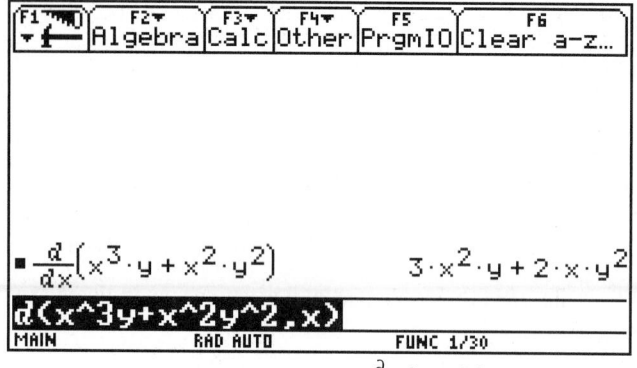

a. The partial derivative $\frac{\partial}{\partial x}(x^3y + x^2y^2)$

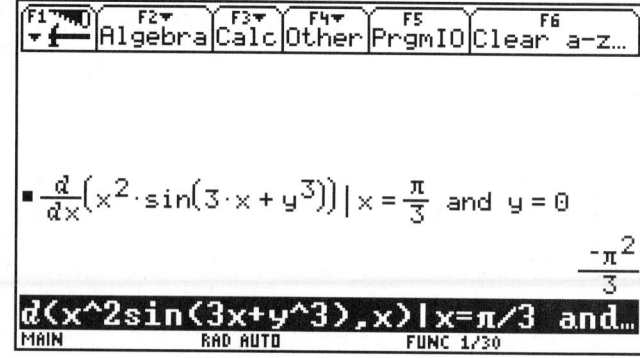

b. The partial derivative $\frac{\partial}{\partial x}(x^2 \sin(3x + y^3))$ evaluated at $\left(\frac{\pi}{3}, 0\right)$

Figure 11.17 Computing partial derivatives with technology

EXAMPLE 3   Partial derivative of a function of three variables

Let $f(x, y, z) = x^2 + 2xy^2 + yz^3$; determine: **a.** f_x **b.** f_y **c.** f_z

Solution

a. For f_x, think of f as a function of x alone with y and z treated as constants:

$$f_x(x, y, z) = 2x + 2y^2$$

WARNING In $f(x, y, z)$, z is an independent variable.

b. $f_y(x, y, z) = 4xy + z^3$
c. $f_z(x, y, z) = 3yz^2$ $\blacksquare$

EXAMPLE 4   Partial derivative of an implicitly defined function

Let z be defined implicitly as a function of x and y by the equation

$$x^2z + yz^3 = x$$

Determine $\partial z/\partial x$ and $\partial z/\partial y$.

Solution

Differentiate implicitly with respect to x, treating y as a constant:

$$2xz + x^2 \frac{\partial z}{\partial x} + 3yz^2 \frac{\partial z}{\partial x} = 1$$

Then solve this equation for $\frac{\partial z}{\partial x}$:

$$\frac{\partial z}{\partial x} = \frac{1 - 2xz}{x^2 + 3yz^2}$$

Similarly, holding x constant and differentiating implicitly with respect to y, we find

$$x^2 \frac{\partial z}{\partial y} + z^3 + 3yz^2 \frac{\partial z}{\partial y} = 0$$

so that

$$\frac{\partial z}{\partial y} = \frac{-z^3}{x^2 + 3yz^2}$$ ∎

PARTIAL DERIVATIVE AS A SLOPE

A useful geometric interpretation of partial derivatives is indicated in Figure 11.18. In Figure 11.18a, the plane $y = y_0$ intersects the surface $z = f(x, y)$ in a curve C parallel to the xz-plane. That is, C is the trace of the surface in the plane $y = y_0$. An equation for this curve is $z = f(x, y_0)$, and because y_0 is fixed, the function depends only on x. Thus, we can compute the slope of the tangent line to C at the point $P(x_0, y_0, z_0)$ in the plane $y = y_0$ by differentiating $f(x, y_0)$ with respect to x and evaluating the derivative at $x = x_0$. That is, the slope is $f_x(x_0, y_0)$, the value of the partial derivative f_x at (x_0, y_0). The analogous interpretation for $f_y(x_0, y_0)$ is shown in Figure 11.18b.

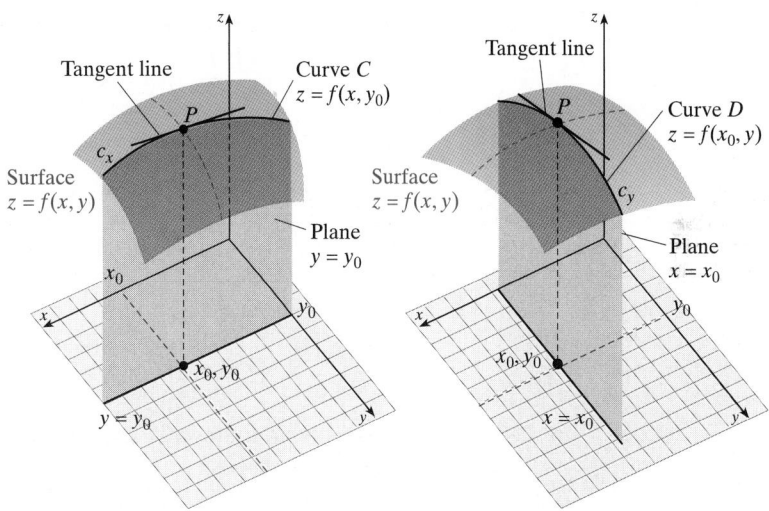

a. The tangent line in the plane $y = y_0$ to the curve C at the point P has slope $f_x(x_0, y_0)$.

b. The tangent line in the plane $x = x_0$ to the curve D at the point P has slope $f_y(x_0, y_0)$.

Figure 11.18   Slope interpretation of the partial derivative

---

Partial Derivative as the Slope of a Tangent Line

The line parallel to the xz-plane and tangent to the surface $z = f(x, y)$ at the point $P_0(x_0, y_0, z_0)$ has slope $f_x(x_0, y_0)$. Likewise, the tangent line to the surface at P_0 that is parallel to the yz-plane has slope $f_y(x_0, y_0)$.

EXAMPLE 5   **Slope of a line parallel to the xz-plane**

Find the slope of the line that is parallel to the xz-plane and tangent to the surface $z = x\sqrt{x + y}$ at the point $P(1, 3, 2)$.

Solution

If $f(x, y) = x\sqrt{x + y} = x(x + y)^{1/2}$, then the required slope is $f_x(1, 3)$.

$$f_x(x, y) = x\left(\frac{1}{2}\right)(x + y)^{-1/2}(1 + 0) + (1)(x + y)^{1/2} = \frac{x}{2\sqrt{x + y}} + \sqrt{x + y}$$

Thus, $f_x(1, 3) = \dfrac{1}{2\sqrt{1 + 3}} + \sqrt{1 + 3} = \dfrac{9}{4}$.   ∎

PARTIAL DERIVATIVE AS A RATE

The derivative of a function of one variable can be interpreted as a rate of change, and the analogous interpretation of partial derivative may be described as follows.

Partial Derivatives as Rates of Change

As the point (x, y) moves from the fixed point $P_0(x_0, y_0)$, the function $f(x, y)$ changes at a rate given by $f_x(x_0, y_0)$ in the direction of the positive x-axis and by $f_y(x_0, y_0)$ in the direction of the positive y-axis.

EXAMPLE 6   **Partial derivatives as rates of change**

In an electrical circuit with electromotive force (EMF) of E volts and resistance R ohms, the current is $I = E/R$ amperes. Find the partial derivatives $\partial I/\partial E$ and $\partial I/\partial R$ at the instant when $E = 120$ and $R = 15$ and interpret these derivatives as rates.

Solution

Since $I = ER^{-1}$, we have

$$\frac{\partial I}{\partial E} = R^{-1} \qquad \text{and} \qquad \frac{\partial I}{\partial R} = -ER^{-2}$$

and thus, when $E = 120$ and $R = 15$, we find that

$$\frac{\partial I}{\partial E} = 15^{-1} \approx 0.0667 \qquad \text{and} \qquad \frac{\partial I}{\partial R} = -(120)(15)^{-2} \approx -0.5333$$

This means that if the resistance is fixed at 15 ohms, the current is increasing (because the derivative is positive) with respect to voltage at the rate of 0.0667 ampere per volt when the EMF is 120 volts. Likewise, with the same fixed EMF, the current is decreasing (because the derivative is negative) with respect to resistance at the rate of 0.5333 ampere per ohm when the resistance is 15 ohms.   ∎

HIGHER-ORDER PARTIAL DERIVATIVES

The partial derivative of a function is a function, so it is possible to take the partial derivative of a partial derivative. This is very much like taking the second derivative of a function of one variable if we take two consecutive partial derivatives with respect to the same variable, and the resulting derivative is called the **second-order partial derivative** with respect to that variable. However, we can also take the partial derivative with respect to one variable and then take a second partial derivative with respect to a different variable, producing what is called a **mixed second-order partial derivative**. The higher-order partial derivatives for a function of two variables $f(x, y)$ are denoted as indicated in the following box:

Higher-Order Partial Derivatives

Given $z = f(x, y)$.

Second-order partial derivatives

$$\frac{\partial^2 f}{\partial x^2} = \frac{\partial}{\partial x}\left(\frac{\partial f}{\partial x}\right) = (f_x)_x = f_{xx}$$

$$\frac{\partial^2 f}{\partial y^2} = \frac{\partial}{\partial y}\left(\frac{\partial f}{\partial y}\right) = (f_y)_y = f_{yy}$$

Mixed second-order partial derivatives

$$\frac{\partial^2 f}{\partial x \partial y} = \frac{\partial}{\partial x}\left(\frac{\partial f}{\partial y}\right) = (f_y)_x = f_{yx}$$

$$\frac{\partial^2 f}{\partial y \partial x} = \frac{\partial}{\partial y}\left(\frac{\partial f}{\partial x}\right) = (f_x)_y = f_{xy}$$

WARNING   The notation f_{xy} means that we differentiate first with respect to x and then with respect to y, while $\dfrac{\partial^2 f}{\partial x \partial y}$ means just the opposite (differentiate with respect to y first and then with respect to x).

EXAMPLE 7   Higher-order partial derivatives of a function of two variables

For $z = f(x, y) = 5x^2 - 2xy + 3y^3$, determine these higher-order partial derivatives.

a. $\dfrac{\partial^2 z}{\partial x \partial y}$ **b.** $\dfrac{\partial^2 f}{\partial y \partial x}$ **c.** $\dfrac{\partial^2 z}{\partial x^2}$ **d.** $f_{xy}(3, 2)$

Solution

a. First differentiate with respect to y; then differentiate with respect to x.

$$\frac{\partial z}{\partial y} = -2x + 9y^2$$

$$\frac{\partial^2 z}{\partial x \partial y} = \frac{\partial}{\partial x}\left(\frac{\partial z}{\partial y}\right) = \frac{\partial}{\partial x}(-2x + 9y^2) = -2$$

b. Differentiate first with respect to x and then with respect to y:

$$\frac{\partial f}{\partial x} = 10x - 2y$$

$$\frac{\partial^2 f}{\partial y \partial x} = \frac{\partial}{\partial y}\left(\frac{\partial f}{\partial x}\right) = \frac{\partial}{\partial y}(10x - 2y) = -2$$

c. Differentiate with respect to x twice:

$$\frac{\partial^2 z}{\partial x^2} = \frac{\partial}{\partial x}\left(\frac{\partial z}{\partial x}\right) = \frac{\partial}{\partial x}(10x - 2y) = 10$$

d. Evaluate the mixed partial found in part **b** at the point $(3, 2)$:

$$f_{xy}(3, 2) = -2$$ ∎

Notice from parts **a** and **b** of Example 7 that $\dfrac{\partial^2 z}{\partial x \partial y} = \dfrac{\partial^2 z}{\partial y \partial x}$. This equality of mixed partials does not hold for all functions, but for most functions we will encounter, it will be true. The following theorem provides sufficient conditions for this equality to occur.

THEOREM 11.1   Equality of mixed partials

If the function $f(x, y)$ has mixed second-order partial derivatives f_{xy} and f_{yx} that are continuous in an open disk containing (x_0, y_0), then

$$f_{yx}(x_0, y_0) = f_{xy}(x_0, y_0)$$

Proof   This proof is omitted.   ❑

EXAMPLE 8   Partial derivatives of functions of two variables

Determine f_{xy}, f_{yx}, f_{xx}, and f_{xxy}, where $f(x, y) = x^2 y e^y$.

Solution

We have the partial derivatives

$$f_x = 2xye^y \qquad\qquad f_y = x^2 e^y + x^2 y e^y$$

The mixed partial derivatives (which must be the same by the previous theorem) are

$$f_{xy} = (f_x)_y = 2xe^y + 2xye^y \qquad\qquad f_{yx} = (f_y)_x = 2xe^y + 2xye^y$$

Finally, we compute the second- and higher-order partial derivatives:

$$f_{xx} = (f_x)_x = 2ye^y \qquad \text{and} \qquad f_{xxy} = (f_{xx})_y = 2e^y + 2ye^y \qquad\blacksquare$$

An equation involving partial derivatives is called a **partial differential equation**. An important partial differential equation is the *diffusion* or *heat equation*

$$\frac{\partial T}{\partial t} = c^2 \frac{\partial^2 T}{\partial x^2}$$

where $T(x, t)$ is the temperature in a thin rod at position x and time t. The constant c is called the *diffusivity* of the material in the rod. In the following example, we verify that a certain function satisfies this heat equation.

EXAMPLE 9   Verifying that a function satisfies the heat equation

Verify that $T(x, t) = e^{-t} \cos \dfrac{x}{c}$ satisfies the heat equation, $\dfrac{\partial T}{\partial t} = c^2 \dfrac{\partial^2 T}{\partial x^2}$.

Solution

$$\frac{\partial T}{\partial t} = -e^{-t} \cos \frac{x}{c}$$

and

$$\frac{\partial^2 T}{\partial x^2} = \frac{\partial}{\partial x} \left(-\frac{1}{c} e^{-t} \sin \frac{x}{c} \right)$$

$$= -\frac{1}{c^2} e^{-t} \cos \frac{x}{c}$$

Thus, T satisfies the heat equation $\dfrac{\partial T}{\partial t} = c^2 \dfrac{\partial^2 T}{\partial x^2}$.   ∎

Analogous definitions can be made for functions of more than two variables. For example,

$$f_{zzz} = \frac{\partial^3 f}{\partial z^3} = \frac{\partial}{\partial z} \left[\frac{\partial}{\partial z} \left(\frac{\partial f}{\partial z} \right) \right] \qquad \text{or} \qquad f_{xyz} = \frac{\partial^3 f}{\partial z \partial y \partial x} = \frac{\partial}{\partial z} \left[\frac{\partial}{\partial y} \left(\frac{\partial f}{\partial x} \right) \right]$$

EXAMPLE 10 **Higher-order partial derivatives of a function of several variables**

By direct calculation, show that $f_{xyz} = f_{yzx} = f_{zyx}$ for the function $f(x, y, z) = xyz + x^2y^3z^4$.

Solution

First, compute the partials:

$$f_x(x, y, z) = yz + 2xy^3z^4$$
$$f_y(x, y, z) = xz + 3x^2y^2z^4$$
$$f_z(x, y, z) = xy + 4x^2y^3z^3$$

Next, determine the mixed partials:

$$f_{xy}(x, y, z) = (yz + 2xy^3z^4)_y = z + 6xy^2z^4$$
$$f_{yz}(x, y, z) = (xz + 3x^2y^2z^4)_z = x + 12x^2y^2z^3$$
$$f_{zy}(x, y, z) = (xy + 4x^2y^3z^3)_y = x + 12x^2y^2z^3$$

Finally, obtain the required higher mixed partials:

$$f_{xyz}(x, y, z) = (z + 6xy^2z^4)_z = 1 + 24xy^2z^3$$
$$f_{yzx}(x, y, z) = (x + 12x^2y^2z^3)_x = 1 + 24xy^2z^3$$
$$f_{zyx}(x, y, z) = (x + 12x^2y^2z^3)_x = 1 + 24xy^2z^3$$

∎

11.3 PROBLEM SET

Ⓐ 1. **WHAT DOES THIS SAY?** What is a partial derivative?

2. **Exploration Problem** Describe two fundamental interpretations of the partial derivatives $f_x(x, y)$ and $f_y(x, y)$.

Determine f_x, f_y, f_{xx}, and f_{yx} in Problems 3–8.

3. $f(x, y) = x^3 + x^2y + xy^2 + y^3$
4. $f(x, y) = (x + xy + y)^3$
5. $f(x, y) = \dfrac{x}{y}$ 6. $f(x, y) = xe^{xy}$
7. $f(x, y) = \ln(2x + 3y)$ 8. $f(x, y) = \sin x^2y$

Determine f_x and f_y in Problems 9–16.

9. **a.** $f(x, y) = (\sin x^2)\cos y$ **b.** $f(x, y) = \sin(x^2\cos y)$
10. **a.** $f(x, y) = (\sin\sqrt{x})\ln y^2$ **b.** $f(x, y) = \sin(\sqrt{x}\ln y^2)$
11. $f(x, y) = \sqrt{3x^2 + y^4}$ 12. $f(x, y) = xy^2\ln(x + y)$
13. $f(x, y) = x^2e^{x+y}\cos y$ 14. $f(x, y) = xy^3\tan^{-1}y$
15. $f(x, y) = \sin^{-1}(xy)$ 16. $f(x, y) = \cos^{-1}(xy)$

Determine f_x, f_y, and f_z in Problems 17–22.

17. $f(x, y, z) = xy^2 + yz^3 + xyz$
18. $f(x, y, z) = xye^z$
19. $f(x, y, z) = \dfrac{x + y^2}{z}$
20. $f(x, y, z) = \dfrac{xy + yz}{xz}$
21. $f(x, y, z) = \ln(x + y^2 + z^3)$
22. $f(x, y, z) = \sin(xy + z)$

In Problems 23–28, determine $\dfrac{\partial z}{\partial x}$ and $\dfrac{\partial z}{\partial y}$ by differentiating implicitly.

23. $\dfrac{x^2}{9} - \dfrac{y^2}{4} + \dfrac{z^2}{2} = 1$ 24. $3x^2 + 4y^2 + 2z^2 = 5$

25. $3x^2y + y^3z - z^2 = 1$ 26. $x^3 - xy^2 + yz^2 - z^3 = 4$

27. $\sqrt{x} + y^2 + \sin xz = 2$

28. $\ln(xy + yz + xz) = 5$ $(x > 0, \quad y > 0, \quad z > 0)$

In Problems 29–32, compute the slope of the tangent line to the graph of f at the given point P_0 in the direction parallel to

   a. *the xz-plane*   **b.** *the yz-plane*

29. $f(x, y) = xy^3 + x^3y$; $P_0(1, -1, -2)$

30. $f(x, y) = \dfrac{x^2 + y^2}{xy}$; $P_0(1, -1, -2)$

31. $f(x, y) = x^2\sin(x + y)$; $P_0\left(\frac{\pi}{2}, \frac{\pi}{2}, 0\right)$

32. $f(x, y) = x\ln(x + y^2)$; $P_0(e, 0, e)$

Ⓑ 33. Determine f_x and f_y for

$$f(x, y) = \int_x^y (t^2 + 2t + 1)\, dt$$

Hint: Review the second fundamental theorem of calculus.

34. Determine f_x and f_y for

$$f(x, y) = \int_{x^2}^{2y} (e^t + 3t)\, dt$$

Hint: Review the second fundamental theorem of calculus.

A function $f(x, y)$ is said to be **harmonic** on the open set S if f_{xx} and f_{yy} are continuous and

$$f_{xx} + f_{yy} = 0$$

throughout S. Show that each function in Problems 35–38 is harmonic on the given set.

35. $f(x, y) = 3x^2 y - y^3$; S is the entire plane.

36. $f(x, y) = \ln(x^2 + y^2)$; S is the plane with the point $(0, 0)$ removed.

37. $f(x, y) = e^x \sin y$; S is the entire plane.

38. $f(x, y) = \sin x \cosh y$; S is the entire plane.

39. For $f(x, y) = \cos xy^2$, show $f_{xy} = f_{yx}$.

40. For $f(x, y) = (\sin^2 x)(\sin y)$, show $f_{xy} = f_{yx}$.

41. Find $f_{xzy} - f_{yzz}$, where $f(x, y, z) = x^2 + y^2 - 2xy \cos z$.

42. Two commodities Q_1 and Q_2 are said to be *substitute commodities* if an increase in the demand for either results in a decrease in the demand of the other. Let $D_1(p_1, p_2)$ and $D_2(p_1, p_2)$ be the demand functions for Q_1 and Q_2, respectively, where p_1 and p_2 are the respective unit prices for the commodities.

a. Explain why $\dfrac{\partial D_1}{\partial p_1} < 0$ and $\dfrac{\partial D_2}{\partial p_2} < 0$.

b. Are $\dfrac{\partial D_1}{\partial p_2}$ and $\dfrac{\partial D_2}{\partial p_1}$ positive or negative? Explain.

c. Give examples of substitute commodities.

43. Two commodities Q_1 and Q_2 are said to be *complementary commodities* if a decrease in the demand for either results in a decrease in the demand of the other. Let $D_1(p_1, p_2)$ and $D_2(p_1, p_2)$ be the demand functions for Q_1 and Q_2, respectively, where p_1 and p_2 are the respective unit prices for the commodities.

a. Is it true that $\dfrac{\partial D_1}{\partial p_1} < 0$ and $\dfrac{\partial D_2}{\partial p_2} < 0$? Explain.

b. Determine whether $\dfrac{\partial D_1}{\partial p_2}$ and $\dfrac{\partial D_2}{\partial p_1}$ are positive or negative? Explain.

c. Give examples of complementary commodities.

44. Modeling Problem   The flow (in cm^3/s) of blood from an artery into a small capillary can be modeled by

$$F(x, y, z) = \frac{c\pi x^2}{4} \sqrt{y - z}$$

for constant $c > 0$, where x is the diameter of the capillary, y is the pressure in the artery, and z is the pressure in the capillary. Compute the rate of change of the flow of blood with respect to

a. the diameter of the capillary

b. the arterial pressure

c. the capillary pressure

45. Modeling Problem   Biologists have studied the oxygen consumption of certain furry mammals. They have found that if the mammal's body temperature is T degrees Celsius, fur temperature is t degrees Celsius, and the mammal does not sweat, then its relative oxygen consumption can be modeled by

$$C(m, t, T) = \sigma(T - t)m^{-0.67}$$

(kg/h), where m is the mammal's mass (in kg) and σ is a physical constant. Compute the rate (rounded to two decimal places) at which the oxygen consumption changes with respect to

a. the mass m

b. the body temperature T

c. the fur temperature t

46. Modeling Problem   A gas that gathers on a surface in a condensed layer is said to be *adsorbed* on the surface, and the surface is called an *adsorbing surface*. The amount of gas adsorbed per unit area on an adsorbing surface can be modeled by

$$S(p, T, h) = ape^{h/(bT)}$$

where p is the gas pressure, T is the temperature of the gas, h is the heat of the adsorbed layer of gas, and a and b are physical constants. Compute the rate of change of S with respect to

a. p **b.** h **c.** T

47. The *ideal gas law* says that $PV = kT$, where P is the pressure of a confined gas, V is the volume, T is the temperature, and k is a physical constant.

a. Calculate $\dfrac{\partial V}{\partial T}$.   **b.** Calculate $\dfrac{\partial P}{\partial V}$.

c. Show that $\dfrac{\partial P}{\partial V} \cdot \dfrac{\partial V}{\partial T} \cdot \dfrac{\partial T}{\partial P} = -1$.

48. At a certain factory, the output is given by the production function $Q = 120K^{2/3}L^{2/5}$, where K denotes the capital investment (in units of $\$1,000$) and L measures the size of the labor force (in worker-hours).

a. Determine the *marginal productivity of capital*, $\partial Q/\partial K$, and the *marginal productivity of labor*, $\partial Q/\partial L$.

b. Determine the signs of the second-order partial derivatives $\partial^2 Q/\partial L^2$ and $\partial^2 Q/\partial K^2$, and give an economic interpretation.

49. The temperature at a point (x, y) on a given metal plate in the xy-plane is determined according to the formula $T(x, y) = x^3 + 2xy^2 + y$ degrees. Compute the rate at which the temperature changes with distance if we start at $(2, 1)$ and move

a. parallel to the vector $\mathbf{j}$

b. parallel to the vector $\mathbf{i}$

50. In physics, the *wave equation* is

$$\frac{\partial^2 z}{\partial t^2} = c^2 \frac{\partial^2 z}{\partial x^2}$$

and the *heat equation* is

$$\frac{\partial z}{\partial t} = c^2 \frac{\partial^2 z}{\partial x^2}$$

In each of the following cases, determine whether z satisfies the wave equation, the heat equation, or neither.

a. $z = e^{-t}\left(\sin \dfrac{x}{c} + \cos \dfrac{x}{c}\right)$ **b.** $z = \sin 3ct \sin 3x$

c. $z = \sin 5ct \cos 5x$

51. The **Cauchy-Riemann equations** are

$$\frac{\partial u}{\partial x} = \frac{\partial v}{\partial y} \quad \text{and} \quad \frac{\partial u}{\partial y} = -\frac{\partial v}{\partial x}$$

where $u = u(x, y)$ and $v = v(x, y)$. Which (if any) of the following functions satisfy the Cauchy-Riemann equations?

a. $u = e^{-x} \cos y, \ v = e^{-x} \sin y$

b. $u = x^2 + y^2, \ v = 2xy$

c. $u = \ln(x^2 + y^2), \ v = 2 \tan^{-1}\left(\frac{y}{x}\right)$

52. When two resistors R_1 and R_2 are connected in parallel, their combined resistance R satisfies

$$\frac{1}{R} = \frac{1}{R_1} + \frac{1}{R_2}$$

What is $\dfrac{\partial^2 R}{\partial R_1^2} \dfrac{\partial^2 R}{\partial R_2^2}$?

53. Show that the production function $P(L, K) = L^\alpha K^\beta$, where α and β are constants, satisfies

$$L\frac{\partial P}{\partial L} + K\frac{\partial P}{\partial K} = (\alpha + \beta)P$$

54. The kinetic energy of a body of mass m and velocity v is $K = \frac{1}{2}mv^2$. Show that

$$\frac{\partial K}{\partial m} \frac{\partial^2 K}{\partial v^2} = K$$

55. A study of ground penetration near a toxic waste dump models the amount of pollution P at a depth x (in feet) and time t (in years) by the function

$$P(x, t) = P_0 + P_1 e^{-kx} \sin(At - kx)$$

where A, k, P_0, and P_1 are constants. Show that $P(x, t)$ satisfies the diffusion equation

$$\frac{\partial P}{\partial t} = c^2 \frac{\partial^2 P}{\partial x^2}$$

for a certain constant c.

56. Counterexample Problem Let

$$f(x, y) = \begin{cases} xy\left(\dfrac{x^2 - y^2}{x^2 + y^2}\right) & \text{if } (x, y) \neq (0, 0) \\ 0 & \text{if } (x, y) = (0, 0) \end{cases}$$

Show that $f_x(0, y) = -y$ and $f_y(x, 0) = x$, for all x and y. Then show that $f_{xy}(0, 0) = -1$ and $f_{yx}(0, 0) = 1$. Why does this not violate the equality of mixed partials theorem?

57. Show that $f_x(0, 0) = 0$ but $f_y(0, 0)$ does not exist, where

$$f(x, y) = \begin{cases} (x^2 + y) \sin\left(\dfrac{1}{x^2 + y^2}\right) & \text{if } (x, y) \neq (0, 0) \\ 0 & \text{if } (x, y) = (0, 0) \end{cases}$$

58. Modeling Problem Suppose a substance is injected into a tube containing a liquid solvent and that the tube is placed so that its axis is parallel to the x-axis, as shown in Figure 11.19.

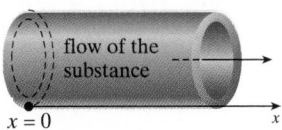

Figure 11.19 Problem 58

Assume that the concentration of the substance varies only in the x-direction, and let $C(x, t)$ denote the concentration at position x and time t. Because the number of molecules in this substance is very large, it is reasonable to assume that C is a continuous function whose partial derivatives exist. One model for the flow yields the *diffusion equation in one dimension*, namely,

$$\frac{\partial C}{\partial t} = \delta \frac{\partial^2 C}{\partial x^2}$$

where δ is the *diffusion constant*.

a. What must δ be for a function of the form

$$C(x, t) = e^{ax + bt}$$

(a and b are constants) to satisfy the diffusion equation?

b. Verify that

$$C(x, t) = t^{-1/2} e^{-x^2/(4\delta t)}$$

satisfies the diffusion equation.

59. The area of a triangle is $A = \frac{1}{2}ab \sin \gamma$, where γ is the angle between sides of length a and b.

a. Determine $\dfrac{\partial A}{\partial a}, \dfrac{\partial A}{\partial b}$, and $\dfrac{\partial A}{\partial \gamma}$.

b. Suppose a is given as a function of b, A, and γ. What is $\dfrac{\partial a}{\partial \gamma}$?

60. Journal Problem *Crux,* problem by John A. Winterink* ∎ Prove the validity of the following simple method for finding the center of a conic: For the central conic,

$$\phi(x, y) = ax^2 + 2hxy + by^2 + 2gx + 2fy + c = 0$$

$ab - h^2 \neq 0$, show that the center is the intersection of the lines $\partial \phi / \partial x = 0$ and $\partial \phi / \partial y = 0$.

---

*Problem 54, Vol. 6 (1980), p. 154.

11.4   Tangent Planes, Approximations, and Differentiability

IN THIS SECTION   tangent planes, incremental approximations, the total differential, differentiability

TANGENT PLANES

Suppose S is a surface with the equation $z = f(x, y)$, where f has continuous first partial derivatives f_x and f_y. Let $P_0(x_0, y_0, z_0)$ be a point on S, and let C_1 be the curve of intersection of S with the plane $x = x_0$ and C_2, the intersection of S with the plane $y = y_0$, as shown in Figure 11.20a. The tangent lines T_1 and T_2 to C_1 and C_2, respectively, at P_0 determine a unique plane, and in Section 11.6 we will find that this plane actually contains the tangent to every smooth curve on S that passes through P_0. We call this plane the **tangent plane** to S at P_0 (Figure 11.20b).

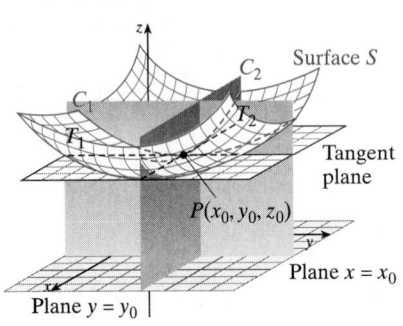

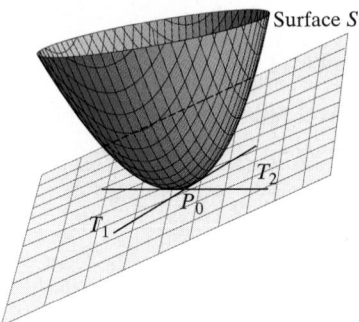

a. C_1 and C_2 are the curves of intersection of the surface S with the planes $x = x_0$ and $y = y_0$.

b. The tangent plane to S at P_0 contains the tangent lines T_1 and T_2 to C_1 and C_2, respectively.

Figure 11.20   Tangent plane to the surface S at the point P_0

To find an equation for the tangent plane, recall that the equation of a plane with normal $\mathbf{N} = A\mathbf{i} + B\mathbf{j} + C\mathbf{k}$ is

$$A(x - x_0) + B(y - y_0) + C(z - z_0) = 0$$

If $C \neq 0$, divide both sides by C and let $a = -A/C$ and $b = -B/C$ to obtain

$$z - z_0 = a(x - x_0) + b(y - y_0)$$

The intersection of this plane and the plane $x = x_0$ is the tangent line T_1, which we know has slope $f_y(x_0, y_0)$ from the geometric interpretation of partial derivatives. Setting $x = x_0$ in the equation for the tangent plane, we find that T_1 has the point-slope form

$$z - z_0 = b(y - y_0)$$

so we must have $b = f_y(x_0, y_0) = \dfrac{\partial z}{\partial y}\Big|_{(x_0, y_0)}$. Similarly, setting $y = y_0$, we obtain

$$z - z_0 = a(x - x_0)$$

which represents the tangent line T_2, with slope $a = f_x(x_0, y_0)$. To summarize:

Equation of the Tangent Plane

> Suppose S is a surface with the equation $z = f(x, y)$ and let $P_0(x_0, y_0, z_0)$ be a point on S at which a tangent plane exists. Then an **equation for the tangent plane** to S at P_0 is
>
> $$z - z_0 = f_x(x_0, y_0)(x - x_0) + f_y(x_0, y_0)(y - y_0)$$
>
> If the equation is written in the form
>
> $$Ax + By + Cz + D = 0$$
>
> we say the equation of the plane is in standard form.

EXAMPLE 1 **Equation of a tangent plane for a surface defined by** $z = f(x, y)$

Find an equation for the tangent plane to the surface $z = \tan^{-1} \dfrac{y}{x}$ at the point $P_0\left(1, \sqrt{3}, \frac{\pi}{3}\right)$.

Solution

$$f_x(x, y) = \frac{-yx^{-2}}{1 + \left(\dfrac{y}{x}\right)^2} = \frac{-y}{x^2 + y^2}; \qquad f_x\left(1, \sqrt{3}\right) = \frac{-\sqrt{3}}{1 + 3} = \frac{-\sqrt{3}}{4}$$

$$f_y(x, y) = \frac{x^{-1}}{1 + \left(\dfrac{y}{x}\right)^2} = \frac{x}{x^2 + y^2}; \qquad f_y\left(1, \sqrt{3}\right) = \frac{1}{1 + 3} = \frac{1}{4}$$

The equation of the tangent plane is

$$z - \frac{\pi}{3} = \left(\frac{-\sqrt{3}}{4}\right)(x - 1) + \frac{1}{4}\left(y - \sqrt{3}\right)$$

or, in standard form,

$$3\sqrt{3}x - 3y + 12z - 4\pi = 0 \qquad \blacksquare$$

INCREMENTAL APPROXIMATIONS

In Chapter 3, we observed that the tangent line to the curve $y = f(x)$ at the point $P(x_0, y_0)$ is the line that best fits the shape of the curve in the immediate vicinity of P. That is, if f is differentiable at $x = x_0$ and the increment Δx is sufficiently small, then

$$\Delta y = f(x_0 + \Delta x) - f(x_0) \approx f'(x_0)\Delta x$$

or, equivalently,

$$f(x_0 + \Delta x) \approx f(x_0) + f'(x_0)\Delta x$$

Similarly, the tangent plane at $P(x_0, y_0, z_0)$ is the plane that best fits the shape of the surface $z = f(x, y)$ near P, and the analogous **incremental** (or **linear**) approximation formula is as follows.

Incremental Approximation of a Function of Two Variables

If $f(x, y)$ and its partial derivatives f_x and f_y are defined in an open region R containing the point $P(x_0, y_0)$ and f_x and f_y are continuous at P, then

$$\Delta f = f(x_0 + \Delta x, y_0 + \Delta y) - f(x_0, y_0) \approx f_x(x_0, y_0)\Delta x + f_y(x_0, y_0)\Delta y$$

so that

$$f(x_0 + \Delta x, y_0 + \Delta y) \approx f(x_0, y_0) + f_x(x_0, y_0)\Delta x + f_y(x_0, y_0)\Delta y$$

A graphical interpretation of this incremental approximation formula is shown in Figure 11.21.

The tangent plane to the surface $z = f(x, y)$ has the equation

$$z - z_0 = f_x(x_0, y_0)(x - x_0) + f_y(x_0, y_0)(y - y_0)$$

or

$$z - f(x_0, y_0) = f_x(x_0, y_0)\Delta x + f_y(x_0, y_0)\Delta y$$

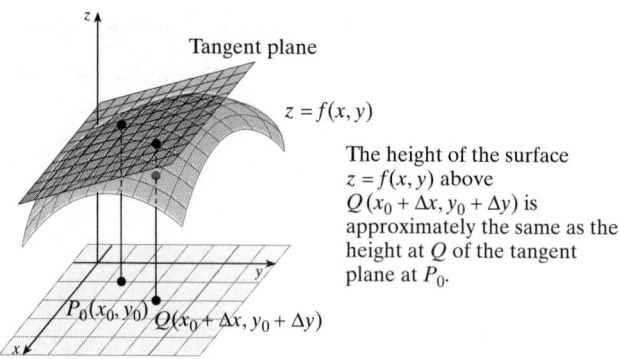

Figure 11.21   Incremental approximation to a function of two variables

As long as we are near (x_0, y_0), the height of the tangent plane is approximately the same as the height of the surface. Thus, if $|\Delta x|$ and $|\Delta y|$ are small, the point $(x_0 + \Delta x, y_0 + \Delta y)$ will be near (x_0, y_0) and we have

$$\underbrace{f(x_0 + \Delta x, y_0 + \Delta y)}_{\substack{\text{Height of } z = f(x, y) \\ \text{above } Q(x_0 + \Delta x, y_0 + \Delta y)}} \approx \underbrace{f(x_0, y_0) + f_x(x_0, y_0)\Delta x + f_y(x_0, y_0)\Delta y}_{\text{Height of the tangent plane above } Q}$$

Increments of a function of three variables $f(x, y, z)$ can be defined in a similar fashion. Suppose f has continuous partial derivatives f_x, f_y, f_z in a ball centered at the point (x_0, y_0, z_0). Then if the numbers Δx, Δy, Δz are all sufficiently small, we have

$$\Delta f = f(x_0 + \Delta x, y_0 + \Delta y, z_0 + \Delta z) - f(x_0, y_0, z_0)$$
$$\approx f_x(x_0, y_0, z_0)\Delta x + f_y(x_0, y_0, z_0)\Delta y + f_z(x_0, y_0, z_0)\Delta z$$

EXAMPLE 2   Using increments to estimate the change of a function

An open box has length 3 ft, width 1 ft, and height 2 ft and is constructed from material that costs \$2/ft² for the sides and \$3/ft² for the bottom (see Figure 11.22). Compute the cost of constructing the box, and then use increments to estimate the change in cost if the length and width are each increased by 3 in. and the height is decreased by 4 in.

Solution

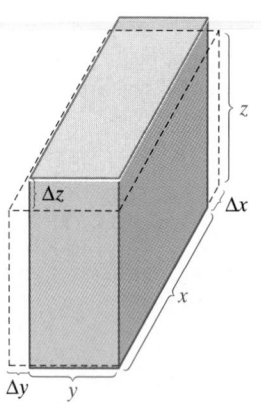

Figure 11.22 Construction of a box

An open (no top) box with length x, width y, and height z has surface area

$$S = \underbrace{xy}_{\text{Bottom}} + \underbrace{2xz + 2yz}_{\text{Four side faces}}$$

Because the sides cost \$2/ft² and the bottom \$3/ft², the total cost is

$$C(x, y, z) = 3xy + 2(2xz + 2yz)$$

The partial derivatives of C are

$$C_x = 3y + 4z \qquad C_y = 3x + 4z \qquad C_z = 4x + 4y$$

and the dimensions of the box change by

$$\Delta x = \tfrac{3}{12} = 0.25 \text{ ft} \qquad \Delta y = \tfrac{3}{12} = 0.25 \text{ ft} \qquad \Delta z = \tfrac{-4}{12} \approx -0.33 \text{ ft}$$

Thus, the change in the total cost is approximated by

$$\Delta C \approx C_x(3, 1, 2)\Delta x + C_y(3, 1, 2)\Delta y + C_z(3, 1, 2)\Delta z$$
$$= [3(1) + 4(2)](0.25) + [3(3) + 4(2)](0.25) + [4(3) + 4(1)]\left(-\tfrac{4}{12}\right)$$
$$\approx 1.67$$

That is, the cost increases by approximately \$1.67.   ∎

EXAMPLE 3   Maximum percentage error using differentials

The radius and height of a right circular cone are measured with errors of at most 3% and 2%, respectively. Use increments to approximate the maximum possible percentage error in computing the volume of the cone using these measurements and the formula $V = \frac{1}{3}\pi R^2 H$.

Solution

We are given that

$$\left|\frac{\Delta R}{R}\right| \le 0.03 \quad \text{and} \quad \left|\frac{\Delta H}{H}\right| \le 0.02$$

The partial derivatives of V are

$$V_R = \tfrac{2}{3}\pi R H \quad \text{and} \quad V_H = \tfrac{1}{3}\pi R^2$$

so the change in V is approximated by

$$\Delta V \approx \left(\tfrac{2}{3}\pi R H\right)\Delta R + \left(\tfrac{1}{3}\pi R^2\right)\Delta H$$

Dividing by the volume $V = \frac{1}{3}\pi R^2 H$, we obtain

$$\frac{\Delta V}{V} \approx \frac{\frac{2}{3}\pi R H \,\Delta R + \frac{1}{3}\pi R^2 \Delta H}{\frac{1}{3}\pi R^2 H} = 2\left(\frac{\Delta R}{R}\right) + \left(\frac{\Delta H}{H}\right)$$

so that $\left|\dfrac{\Delta V}{V}\right| \le 2\left|\dfrac{\Delta R}{R}\right| + \left|\dfrac{\Delta H}{H}\right| = 2(0.03) + (0.02) = 0.08$. Thus, the maximum percentage error in computing the volume V is approximately 8%. ∎

THE TOTAL DIFFERENTIAL

For a function of one variable, $y = f(x)$, we defined the differential dy to be $dy = f'(x)\,dx$. For the two-variable case, we make the following analogous definition.

Total Differential

> The **total differential** of the function $f(x, y)$ is
>
> $$df = \frac{\partial f}{\partial x}\,dx + \frac{\partial f}{\partial y}\,dy = f_x(x, y)\,dx + f_y(x, y)\,dy$$
>
> where dx and dy are independent variables. Similarly, for a function of three variables $w = f(x, y, z)$ the **total differential** is
>
> $$df = \frac{\partial f}{\partial x}\,dx + \frac{\partial f}{\partial y}\,dy + \frac{\partial f}{\partial z}\,dz$$

EXAMPLE 4   Total differential

Determine the total differential of the given functions:

a. $f(x, y, z) = 2x^3 + 5y^4 - 6z$ **b.** $f(x, y) = x^2 \ln(3y^2 - 2x)$

Solution

a. $df = \dfrac{\partial f}{\partial x}\,dx + \dfrac{\partial f}{\partial y}\,dy + \dfrac{\partial f}{\partial z}\,dz = 6x^2\,dx + 20y^3\,dy - 6\,dz$

b. $df = \dfrac{\partial f}{\partial x}\,dx + \dfrac{\partial f}{\partial y}\,dy$

$$= \left[2x\ln(3y^2 - 2x) + x^2\dfrac{-2}{3y^2 - 2x}\right]dx + \left[x^2\dfrac{6y}{3y^2 - 2x}\right]dy$$

$$= \left[2x\ln(3y^2 - 2x) - \dfrac{2x^2}{3y^2 - 2x}\right]dx + \dfrac{6x^2 y}{3y^2 - 2x}\,dy \qquad \blacksquare$$

EXAMPLE 5 Application of the total differential

At a certain factory, the daily output is $Q = 60K^{1/2}L^{1/3}$ units, where K denotes the capital investment (in units of $1,000) and L the size of the labor force (in worker-hours). The current capital investment is $900,000, and 1,000 worker-hours of labor are used each day. Estimate the change in output that will result if capital investment is increased by $1,000 and labor is decreased by 2 worker-hours.

Solution

The change in output is estimated by the total differential dQ. We have $K = 900$, $L = 1,000$, $dK = \Delta K = 1$, and $dL = \Delta L = -2$. The total differential of $Q(x, y)$ is

$$dQ = \dfrac{\partial Q}{\partial K}\,dK + \dfrac{\partial Q}{\partial L}\,dL$$

$$= 60\left(\tfrac{1}{2}\right)K^{-1/2}L^{1/3}\,dK + 60\left(\tfrac{1}{3}\right)K^{1/2}L^{-2/3}\,dL$$

$$= 30K^{-1/2}L^{1/3}\,dK + 20K^{1/2}L^{-2/3}\,dL$$

Substituting for K, L, dK, and dL,

$$dQ = 30(900)^{-1/2}(1,000)^{1/3}(1) + 20(900)^{1/2}(1,000)^{-2/3}(-2) = -2$$

Thus, the output decreases by approximately 2 units when the capital investment is increased by $1,000 and labor is decreased by 2 worker-hours. $\qquad \blacksquare$

EXAMPLE 6 Maximum percentage error in an electrical circuit

When two resistances R_1 and R_2 are connected in parallel, the total resistance R satisfies

$$\dfrac{1}{R} = \dfrac{1}{R_1} + \dfrac{1}{R_2}$$

If R_1 is measured as 300 ohms with a maximum error of 2% and R_2 is measured as 500 ohms with a maximum error of 3%, what is the maximum percentage error in R?

Solution

We are given that

$$\left|\dfrac{dR_1}{R_1}\right| \le 0.02 \quad \text{and} \quad \left|\dfrac{dR_2}{R_2}\right| \le 0.03$$

and we wish to find the maximum value of $\left|\dfrac{dR}{R}\right|$. Because $R = \dfrac{R_1 R_2}{R_1 + R_2}$ (solve the given equation for R), we have

$$\dfrac{\partial R}{\partial R_1} = \dfrac{R_2^2}{(R_1 + R_2)^2} \quad \text{and} \quad \dfrac{\partial R}{\partial R_2} = \dfrac{R_1^2}{(R_1 + R_2)^2} \qquad \text{Quotient rule}$$

it follows that the total differential of R is

$$dR = \dfrac{\partial R}{\partial R_1}\,dR_1 + \dfrac{\partial R}{\partial R_2}\,dR_2$$

$$= \dfrac{R_2^2}{(R_1 + R_2)^2}\,dR_1 + \dfrac{R_1^2}{(R_1 + R_2)^2}\,dR_2$$

We now find $\dfrac{dR}{R}$ by dividing both sides by R; however, since $\dfrac{1}{R} = \dfrac{R_1 + R_2}{R_1 R_2}$, it follows that

$$dR \cdot \frac{1}{R} = \left[\frac{R_2^2}{(R_1 + R_2)^2}\, dR_1 + \frac{R_1^2}{(R_1 + R_2)^2}\, dR_2 \right] \cdot \frac{R_1 + R_2}{R_1 R_2}$$

$$\frac{dR}{R} = \frac{R_2}{R_1 + R_2} \cdot \frac{dR_1}{R_1} + \frac{R_1}{R_1 + R_2} \cdot \frac{dR_2}{R_2}$$

Finally, apply the triangle inequality (Table 1.1, p. 3) to this relationship:

$$\left| \frac{dR}{R} \right| \leq \left| \frac{R_2}{R_1 + R_2} \right| \left| \frac{dR_1}{R_1} \right| + \left| \frac{R_1}{R_1 + R_2} \right| \left| \frac{dR_2}{R_2} \right|$$

$$\leq \frac{500}{300 + 500}(0.02) + \frac{300}{300 + 500}(0.03) = 0.02375$$

The maximum percentage is approximately 2.4%.   ■

DIFFERENTIABILITY

Recall from Chapter 3 that if $f(x)$ is differentiable at x_0, its increment is

$$\Delta f = f(x_0 + \Delta x) - f(x_0) = f'(x_0)\Delta x + \epsilon \Delta x$$

where $\epsilon \to 0$ as $\Delta x \to 0$ (see Figure 11.23).

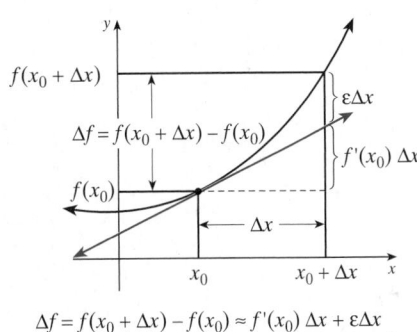

$$\Delta f = f(x_0 + \Delta x) - f(x_0) \approx f'(x_0)\,\Delta x + \underbrace{\varepsilon \Delta x}_{\substack{\text{Error when using} \\ df \text{ to estimate } \Delta f}}$$

Figure 11.23   Increment of a function f

For a function of two variables, the increment of x is an independent variable denoted by Δx, the increment of y is an independent variable denoted by Δy, and the increment of f at (x_0, y_0) is defined as

$$\Delta f = f(x_0 + \Delta x, y_0 + \Delta y) - f(x_0, y_0)$$

We use this increment representation to define differentiability as follows.

Definition of Differentiability

> The function $f(x, y)$ is **differentiable** at (x_0, y_0) if the increment of f can be expressed as
>
> $$\Delta f = f_x(x_0, y_0)\Delta x + f_y(x_0, y_0)\Delta y + \epsilon_1 \Delta x + \epsilon_2 \Delta y$$
>
> where $\epsilon_1 \to 0$ and $\epsilon_2 \to 0$ as both $\Delta x \to 0$ and $\Delta y \to 0$. In addition, $f(x, y)$ is said to be **differentiable in the region R** of the plane if f is differentiable at each point in R.

In Section 3.1, we showed that a function of one variable is continuous wherever it is differentiable. The following theorem establishes the same result for a function of two variables.

THEOREM 11.2 **Differentiability implies continuity**

If $f(x, y)$ is differentiable at (x_0, y_0), it is also continuous there.

Proof We wish to show that $f(x, y) \to f(x_0, y_0)$ as $(x, y) \to (x_0, y_0)$ or, equivalently, that

$$\lim_{(x,y)\to(x_0,y_0)} [f(x, y) - f(x_0, y_0)] = 0$$

If we set $\Delta x = x - x_0$ and $\Delta y = y - y_0$ and let Δf denote the increment of f at (x_0, y_0), we have (by substitution)

$$f(x, y) - f(x_0, y_0) = f(x_0 + \Delta x, y_0 + \Delta y) - f(x_0, y_0) = \Delta f$$

Then, because $(\Delta x, \Delta y) \to (0, 0)$ as $(x, y) \to (x_0, y_0)$, we wish to prove that

$$\lim_{(\Delta x, \Delta y)\to(0,0)} \Delta f = 0$$

Since f is differentiable at (x_0, y_0), we have

$$\Delta f = f_x(x_0, y_0)\Delta x + f_y(x_0, y_0)\Delta y + \epsilon_1 \Delta x + \epsilon_2 \Delta y$$

where $\epsilon_1 \to 0$ and $\epsilon_2 \to 0$ as $(\Delta x, \Delta y) \to (0, 0)$. It follows that

$$\lim_{(\Delta x, \Delta y)\to(0,0)} \Delta f = \lim_{(\Delta x, \Delta y)\to(0,0)} [f_x(x_0, y_0)\Delta x + f_y(x_0, y_0)\Delta y + \epsilon_1 \Delta x + \epsilon_2 \Delta y]$$

$$= [f_x(x_0, y_0)] \cdot 0 + [f_y(x_0, y_0)] \cdot 0 + 0 + 0 = 0$$

as required. ❏

WARNING Be careful about how you use the word *differentiable*. In the single-variable case, a function is differentiable at a point if its derivative exists there. However, the word is used differently for a function of two variables. In particular, the existence of the partial derivatives f_x and f_y does not guarantee that the function is differentiable, as illustrated in the following example.

EXAMPLE 7 **A nondifferentiable function for which f_x and f_y exist**

Let

$$f(x, y) = \begin{cases} 1 & \text{if } x > 0 \text{ and } y > 0 \\ 0 & \text{otherwise} \end{cases}$$

That is, the function f has the value 1 when (x, y) is in the first quadrant and is 0 elsewhere. Show that the partial derivatives f_x and f_y exist at the origin, but f is not differentiable there.

Solution

Since $f(0, 0) = 0$, we have

$$f_x(0, 0) = \lim_{\Delta x \to 0} \frac{f(0 + \Delta x, 0) - f(0, 0)}{\Delta x} = 0$$

and similarly, $f_y(0, 0) = 0$. Thus, the partial derivatives both exist at the origin.

If $f(x, y)$ were differentiable at the origin, it would have to be continuous there (Theorem 11.2). Thus, we can show f is not differentiable by showing that it is not continuous at $(0, 0)$. Toward this end, note that $\lim_{(x,y)\to(0,0)} f(x, y)$ is 1 along the line $y = x$ in the first quadrant but is 0 if the approach is along the x-axis. This means that the limit does not exist. Thus, f is not continuous at $(0, 0)$ and consequently is also not differentiable there. ■

Although the existence of partial derivatives at $P(x_0, y_0)$ is not enough to guarantee that $f(x, y)$ is differentiable at P, we do have the following sufficient condition for differentiability.

THEOREM 11.3 Sufficient condition for differentiability

If f is a function of x and y, and f, f_x, and f_y are continuous in a disk D centered at (x_0, y_0), then f is differentiable at (x_0, y_0).

WARNING Note that the function in Example 7 does not contradict Theorem 11.3. because there is no disk centered at $(0, 0)$ on which f is continuous.

Proof The proof is found in advanced calculus texts. ❏

EXAMPLE 8 Establishing differentiability

Show that $f(x, y) = x^2 y + xy^3$ is differentiable for all (x, y).

Solution

Compute the partial derivatives

$$f_x(x, y) = \frac{\partial}{\partial x}(x^2 y + xy^3) = 2xy + y^3$$

$$f_y(x, y) = \frac{\partial}{\partial y}(x^2 y + xy^3) = x^2 + 3xy^2$$

Because f, f_x, and f_y are all polynomials in x and y, they are continuous throughout the plane. Therefore, the sufficient condition for differentiability theorem assures us that f must be differentiable for all x and y. ■

11.4 PROBLEM SET

A *In Problems 1–6, determine the standard-form equations for the tangent plane to the given surface at the prescribed point P_0.*

1. $z = \sqrt{x^2 + y^2}$ at $P_0(3, 1, \sqrt{10})$

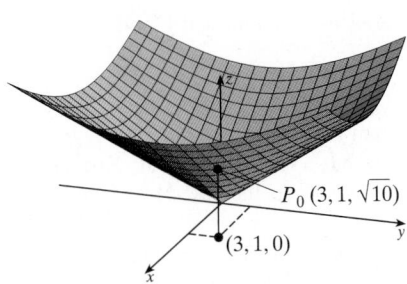

$P_0 (3, 1, \sqrt{10})$
$(3, 1, 0)$

2. $z = 10 - x^2 - y^2$ at $P_0(2, 2, 2)$

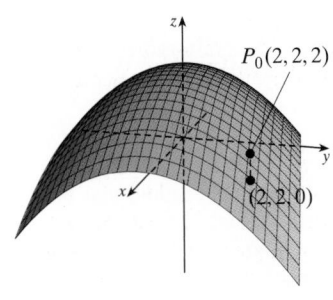

$P_0(2, 2, 2)$
$(2, 2, 0)$

3. $f(x, y) = x^2 + y^2 + \sin xy$ at $P_0 = (0, 2, 4)$

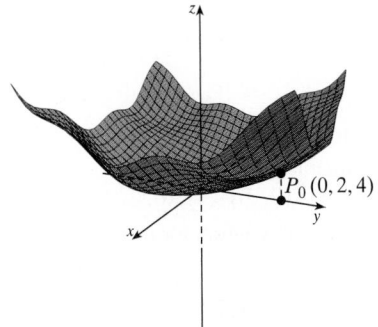

$P_0 (0, 2, 4)$

4. $f(x, y) = e^{-x} \sin y$ at $P_0 \left(0, \frac{\pi}{2}, 1\right)$

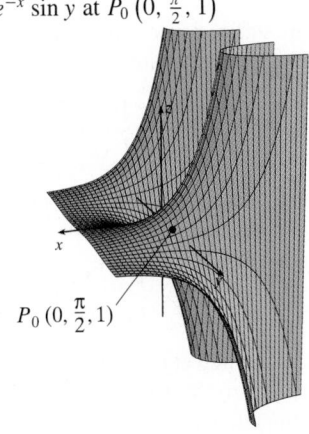

$P_0 \left(0, \frac{\pi}{2}, 1\right)$

5. $z = \tan^{-1}\frac{y}{x}$ at $P_0\left(2, 2, \frac{\pi}{4}\right)$

6. $z = \ln\left|x + y^2\right|$ at $P_0(-3, -2, 0)$

Determine the total differential of the functions given in Problems 7–18.

7. $f(x, y) = 5x^2y^3$

8. $f(x, y) = 8x^3y^2 - x^4y^5$

9. $f(x, y) = \sin xy$

10. $f(x, y) = \cos x^2 y$

11. $f(x, y) = \frac{y}{x}$

12. $f(x, y) = \frac{x^2}{y}$

13. $f(x, y) = ye^x$

14. $f(x, y) = e^{x^2+y}$

15. $f(x, y, z) = 3x^3 - 2y^4 + 5z$

16. $f(x, y, z) = \sin x + \sin y + \cos z$

17. $f(x, y, z) = z^2 \sin(2x - 3y)$

18. $f(x, y, z) = 3y^2z \cos x$

Show that the functions in Problems 19–22 are differentiable for all (x, y).

19. $f(x, y) = xy^3 + 3xy^2$

20. $f(x, y) = x^2 + 4x - y^2$

21. $f(x, y) = e^{2x+y^2}$

22. $f(x, y) = \sin(x^2 + 3y)$

Use an incremental approximation to estimate the functions at the values given in Problems 23–28. Check by using a calculator.

23. $f(1.01, 2.03)$, where $f(x, y) = 3x^4 + 2y^4$

24. $f(0.98, 1.03)$, where $f(x, y) = x^5 - 2y^3$

25. $f\left(\frac{\pi}{2} + 0.01, \frac{\pi}{2} - 0.01\right)$, where $f(x, y) = \sin(x + y)$

26. $f\left(\sqrt{\frac{\pi}{2}} + 0.01, \sqrt{\frac{\pi}{2}} - 0.01\right)$, where $f(x, y) = \sin(xy)$

27. $f(1.01, 0.98)$, where $f(x, y) = e^{xy}$

28. $f(1.01, 0.98)$, where $f(x, y) = e^{x^2y^2}$

B **29.** Find an equation for each horizontal tangent plane to the surface

$$z = 5 - x^2 - y^2 + 4y$$

30. Find an equation for each horizontal tangent plane to the surface

$$z = 4(x - 1)^2 + 3(y + 1)^2$$

31. a. Show that if x and y are sufficiently close to zero and f is differentiable at $(0, 0)$, then
$$f(x, y) \approx f(0, 0) + xf_x(0, 0) + yf_y(0, 0).$$
b. Use the approximation formula in part **a** to show that

$$\frac{1}{1 + x - y} \approx 1 - x + y$$

for small x and y.

c. If x and y are sufficiently close to zero, what is the approximate value of the expression

$$\frac{1}{(x + 1)^2 + (y + 1)^2}$$

32. When two resistors with resistances P and Q ohms are connected in parallel, the combined resistance is R, where

$$\frac{1}{R} = \frac{1}{P} + \frac{1}{Q}$$

If P and Q are measured at 6 and 10 ohms, respectively, with errors no greater than 1%, what is the maximum percentage error in the computation of R?

33. A closed box is found to have length 2 ft, width 4 ft, and height 3 ft, where the measurement of each dimension is made with a maximum possible error of ± 0.02 ft. The top of the box is made from material that costs $2/ft^2$; and the material for the sides and bottom costs only $1.50/ft^2$. What is the maximum error involved in the computation of the cost of the box?

34. A cylindrical tank is 4 ft high and has an outer diameter of 2 ft. The walls of the tank are 0.2 in. thick. Approximate the volume of the interior of the tank assuming the tank has a top and a bottom that are both also 0.2 in. thick.

35. The Higrade Company sells two brands, X and Y, of a commercial soap, in thousand-pound units. If x units of brand X and y units of brand Y are sold, the unit price for brand X is

$$p(x) = 4,000 - 500x$$

and that of brand Y is

$$q(y) = 3,000 - 450y$$

a. Find an expression for the total revenue of R in terms of p and q.

b. Suppose brand X sells for $500 per unit and brand Y sells for $750 per unit. Estimate the change in total revenue if the unit prices are increased by $20 for brand X and $18 for brand Y.

36. The output at a certain factory is

$$Q = 150K^{2/3}L^{1/3}$$

where K is the capital investment in units of $1,000 and L is the size of the labor force, measured in worker-hours. The current capital investment is $500,000 and 1,500 worker-hours of labor are used.

a. Estimate the change in output that results when capital investment is increased by $700 and labor is increased by 6 worker-hours.

b. What if capital investment is increased by $500 and labor is decreased by 4 worker-hours?

37. According to Poiseuille's law, the resistance to the flow of blood offered by a cylindrical blood vessel of radius r and length x is

$$R(r, x) = \frac{cx}{r^4}$$

for a constant $c > 0$. A certain blood vessel in the body is 8 cm long and has a radius of 2 mm. Estimate the percentage change in R when x is increased by 3% and r is decreased by 2%.

38. For 1 mole of an ideal gas, the volume V, pressure P, and absolute temperature T are related by the equation $PV = kT$, where k is a certain fixed constant that depends on the gas. Suppose we know that if $T = 400$ (absolute) and $P = 3,000$ lb/ft^2, then $V = 14$ ft^3. Approximate the change in pressure if the temperature and volume are increased to 403 and 14.1 ft^3, respectively.

39. Modeling Problem If x gram-moles of sulfuric acid are mixed with y gram-moles of water, the heat liberated is modeled by

$$F(x, y) = \frac{1.786xy}{1.798x + y} \quad \text{cal}$$

Approximately how much additional heat is generated if a mixture of 5 gram-moles of acid and 4 gram-moles of water is increased to a mixture of 5.1 gram-moles of acid and 4.04 gram-moles of water?

40. Modeling Problem A business analyst models the sales of a new product by the function

$$Q(x, y) = 20x^{3/2}y$$

where x thousand dollars are spent on development and y thousand dollars on promotion. Current plans call for the expenditure of \$36,000 on development and \$25,000 on promotion. Use the total differential of Q to estimate the change in sales that will result if the amount spent on development is increased by \$500 and the amount spent on promotion is decreased by \$500.

41. Using x hours of skilled labor and y hours of unskilled labor, a manufacturer can produce $f(x, y) = 10xy^{1/2}$ units. Currently, the manufacturer has used 30 h of skilled labor and 36 h of unskilled labor and is planning to use 1 additional hour of skilled labor. Use calculus to estimate the corresponding change that the manufacturer should make in the level of unskilled labor so that the total output will remain the same.

42. Modeling Problem A grocer's weekly profit from the sale of two brands of orange juice is modeled by

$$P(x, y) = (x - 30)(70 - 5x + 4y) + (y - 40)(80 + 6x - 7y)$$

dollars, where x cents is the price per can of the first brand and y cents is the price per can of the second. Currently the first brand sells for 50¢ per can and the second for 52¢ per can. Use the total differential to estimate the change in the weekly profit that will result if the grocer raises the price of the first brand by 1¢ per can and lowers the price of the second brand by 2¢ per can.

43. A juice can is 12 cm tall and has a radius of 3 cm. A manufacturer is planning to reduce the height of the can by 0.2 cm and the radius by 0.3 cm. Use a total differential to estimate the percentage decrease in volume that occurs when the new cans are introduced. (Round to the nearest percent.)

44. Modeling Problem It is known that the period T of a simple pendulum with small oscillations is modeled by

$$T = 2\pi \sqrt{\frac{L}{g}}$$

where L is the length of the pendulum and g is the acceleration due to gravity. For a certain pendulum, it is known that $L = 4.03$ ft. It is also known that $g = 32.2$ ft/s^2. What is the approximate error in calculating T by using $L = 4$ and $g = 32$?

45. If the weight of an object that does not float in water is x pounds in the air and its weight in water is y pounds, then the specific gravity of the object is

$$S = \frac{x}{x - y}$$

For a certain object, x and y are measured to be 1.2 lb and 0.5 lb, respectively. It is known that the measuring instrument will not register less than the true weights, but it could register more than the true weights by as much as 0.01 lb. What is the maximum possible error in the computation of the specific gravity?

46. A football has the shape of the ellipsoid

$$\frac{x^2}{9} + \frac{y^2}{36} + \frac{z^2}{9} = 1$$

where the dimensions are in inches, and is made of leather 1/8 inch thick. Use differentials to estimate the volume of the leather shell. *Hint*: The ellipsoid

$$\frac{x^2}{a^2} + \frac{y^2}{b^2} + \frac{z^2}{c^2} = 1$$

has volume $V = \frac{4}{3}\pi abc$.

47. Show that the following function is not differentiable at $(0, 0)$:

$$f(x, y) = \begin{cases} \dfrac{xy}{x^2 + y^2} & \text{if } (x, y) \neq (0, 0) \\ 0 & \text{if } (x, y) = (0, 0) \end{cases}$$

48. Compute the total differentials

$$d\left(\frac{x}{x - y}\right) \quad \text{and} \quad d\left(\frac{y}{x - y}\right)$$

Why are these differentials equal?

49. Let A be the area of a triangle with sides a and b separated by an angle θ, as shown in Figure 11.24.

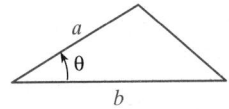

Figure 11.24 Problem 49

Suppose $\theta = \frac{\pi}{6}$, and a is increased by 4% while b is decreased by 3%. Use differentials to estimate the percentage change in A.

50. In Problem 49, suppose that θ also changes by no more than 2%. What is the maximum percentage change in A?

11.5 Chain Rules

IN THIS SECTION chain rule for one parameter, extensions of the chain rule

CHAIN RULE FOR ONE PARAMETER

We begin with a differentiable function of two variables $f(x, y)$. If $x = x(t)$ and $y = y(t)$ are, in turn, functions of a single parameter t, then $z = f(x(t), y(t))$ is a composite function of a parameter t. In this case, the chain rule for finding the derivative with respect to one parameter can now be stated.

THEOREM 11.4   The chain rule for one independent parameter

Let $f(x, y)$ be a differentiable function of x and y, and let $x = x(t)$ and $y = y(t)$ be differentiable functions of t. Then $z = f(x, y)$ is a differentiable function of t, and

$$\frac{dz}{dt} = \frac{\partial z}{\partial x}\frac{dx}{dt} + \frac{\partial z}{\partial y}\frac{dy}{dt}$$

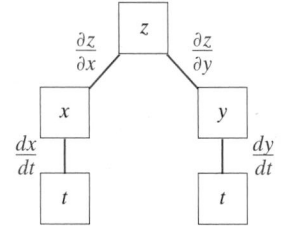

Tree diagram illustrating the chain rule

▶ **What This Says**   The tree diagram shown in the margin is a device for remembering the chain rule. The diagram begins at the top with the dependent variable z and cascades downward in two branches, first to the independent variables x and y, and then to the parameter t on which they each depend. Each branch segment is labeled with a derivative, and the chain rule is obtained by first multiplying the derivatives on the two segments of each branch and then adding to obtain

$$\frac{dz}{dt} = \underbrace{\frac{\partial z}{\partial x}\frac{dx}{dt}}_{\text{left branch}} + \underbrace{\frac{\partial z}{\partial y}\frac{dy}{dt}}_{\text{right branch}}$$

Proof   Recall that because $z = f(x, y)$ is differentiable, we can write the increment Δz in the following form:

$$\Delta z = \frac{\partial z}{\partial x}\Delta x + \frac{\partial z}{\partial y}\Delta y + \epsilon_1 \Delta x + \epsilon_2 \Delta y$$

where $\epsilon_1 \to 0$ and $\epsilon_2 \to 0$ as both $\Delta x \to 0$ and $\Delta y \to 0$. Dividing by $\Delta t \neq 0$, we obtain

$$\frac{\Delta z}{\Delta t} = \frac{\partial z}{\partial x}\frac{\Delta x}{\Delta t} + \frac{\partial z}{\partial y}\frac{\Delta y}{\Delta t} + \epsilon_1 \frac{\Delta x}{\Delta t} + \epsilon_2 \frac{\Delta y}{\Delta t}$$

Because x and y are functions of t, we can write their increments as

$$\Delta x = x(t + \Delta t) - x(t) \quad \text{and} \quad \Delta y = y(t + \Delta t) - y(t)$$

We know that x and y both vary continuously with t (remember, they are differentiable), and it follows that $\Delta x \to 0$ and $\Delta y \to 0$ as $\Delta t \to 0$, so that $\epsilon_1 \to 0$ and $\epsilon_2 \to 0$ as $\Delta t \to 0$. Therefore, we have

$$\frac{dz}{dt} = \lim_{\Delta t \to 0}\frac{\Delta z}{\Delta t} = \lim_{\Delta t \to 0}\left[\frac{\partial z}{\partial x}\frac{\Delta x}{\Delta t} + \frac{\partial z}{\partial y}\frac{\Delta y}{\Delta t} + \epsilon_1 \frac{\Delta x}{\Delta t} + \epsilon_2 \frac{\Delta y}{\Delta t}\right]$$

$$= \frac{\partial z}{\partial x}\frac{dx}{dt} + \frac{\partial z}{\partial y}\frac{dy}{dt} + 0\frac{dx}{dt} + 0\frac{dy}{dt} \qquad ❑$$

EXAMPLE 1   Verifying the chain rule explicitly

Let $z = x^2 + y^2$, where $x = \dfrac{1}{t}$ and $y = t^2$. Compute $\dfrac{dz}{dt}$ in two ways:

a. by first expressing z explicitly in terms of t
b. by using the chain rule

Solution

a. By substituting $x = \dfrac{1}{t}$ and $y = t^2$, we find that

$$z = x^2 + y^2 = \left(\dfrac{1}{t}\right)^2 + (t^2)^2 = t^{-2} + t^4 \qquad \text{for} \quad t \neq 0$$

Thus, $\dfrac{dz}{dt} = -2t^{-3} + 4t^3$.

b. Because $z = x^2 + y^2$ and $x = t^{-1}$, $y = t^2$,

$$\dfrac{\partial z}{\partial x} = 2x; \qquad \dfrac{\partial z}{\partial y} = 2y; \qquad \dfrac{dx}{dt} = -t^{-2}; \qquad \dfrac{dy}{dt} = 2t$$

Use the chain rule for one independent parameter:

$$\begin{aligned}
\dfrac{dz}{dt} &= \dfrac{\partial z}{\partial x}\dfrac{dx}{dt} + \dfrac{\partial z}{\partial y}\dfrac{dy}{dt} \\[2mm]
&= (2x)(-t^{-2}) + 2y(2t) && \textsf{Chain rule} \\[2mm]
&= 2(t^{-1})(-t^{-2}) + 2(t^2)(2t) && \textsf{Substitute} \\[2mm]
&= -2t^{-3} + 4t^3
\end{aligned}$$

∎

EXAMPLE 2 Chain rule for one independent parameter

Let $z = \sqrt{x^2 + 2xy}$, where $x = \cos\theta$ and $y = \sin\theta$. Find $\dfrac{dz}{d\theta}$.

Solution

$$\dfrac{\partial z}{\partial x} = \tfrac{1}{2}(x^2 + 2xy)^{-1/2}(2x + 2y) \qquad \text{and} \qquad \dfrac{\partial z}{\partial y} = \tfrac{1}{2}(x^2 + 2xy)^{-1/2}(2x)$$

Also, $\dfrac{dx}{d\theta} = -\sin\theta$ and $\dfrac{dy}{d\theta} = \cos\theta$. Use the chain rule for one independent parameter
to find

$$\begin{aligned}
\dfrac{dz}{d\theta} &= \dfrac{\partial z}{\partial x}\dfrac{dx}{d\theta} + \dfrac{\partial z}{\partial y}\dfrac{dy}{d\theta} \\[2mm]
&= \tfrac{1}{2}(x^2 + 2xy)^{-1/2}(2x + 2y)(-\sin\theta) + \tfrac{1}{2}(x^2 + 2xy)^{-1/2}(2x)(\cos\theta) \\[2mm]
&= (x^2 + 2xy)^{-1/2}(x\cos\theta - x\sin\theta - y\sin\theta)
\end{aligned}$$

∎

EXAMPLE 3 Related rate application using the chain rule

A right circular cylinder (see Figure 11.25) is changing in such a way that its radius r is
increasing at the rate of 3 in./min and its height h is decreasing at the rate of 5 in./min.
At what rate is the volume of the cylinder changing when the radius is 10 in. and the
height is 8 in.?

Solution

The volume of the cylinder is $V = \pi r^2 h$, and we are given $\dfrac{dr}{dt} = 3$ and $\dfrac{dh}{dt} = -5$. We
find that

$$\dfrac{\partial V}{\partial r} = \pi(2r)h \quad \text{and} \quad \dfrac{\partial V}{\partial h} = \pi r^2 (1)$$

By the chain rule for one parameter,

$$\dfrac{dV}{dt} = \dfrac{\partial V}{\partial r}\dfrac{dr}{dt} + \dfrac{\partial V}{\partial h}\dfrac{dh}{dt} = 2\pi rh\dfrac{dr}{dt} + \pi r^2\dfrac{dh}{dt}$$

Thus, at the instant when $r = 10$ and $h = 8$, we have

$$\dfrac{dV}{dt} = 2\pi(10)(8)(3) + \pi(10)^2(-5) = -20\pi$$

The volume is decreasing at the rate of about 62.8 in.^{3}/min.

∎

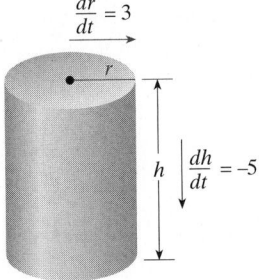

$\dfrac{dr}{dt} = 3$

$\dfrac{dh}{dt} = -5$

Figure 11.25 Right circular
cylinder

If $F(x, y) = 0$ defines y implicitly as a differentiable function x, we can regard x as a parameter and apply the chain rule to obtain

$$0 = \frac{\partial F}{\partial x}\frac{dx}{dx} + \frac{\partial F}{\partial y}\frac{dy}{dx} = \frac{\partial F}{\partial x} + \frac{\partial F}{\partial y}\frac{dy}{dx}$$

so

$$\frac{dy}{dx} = \frac{-\dfrac{\partial F}{\partial x}}{\dfrac{\partial F}{\partial y}} = -\frac{F_x}{F_y} \qquad \text{provided } F_y \neq 0$$

This formula provides a useful alternative to the procedure for implicit differentiation introduced in Section 3.6. This alternative procedure is illustrated in the following example.

EXAMPLE 4   Implicit differentiation using partial derivatives

If y is a differentiable function of x such that

$$\sin(x + y) + \cos(x - y) = y$$

find $\dfrac{dy}{dx}$.

Solution

Let $F(x, y) = \sin(x + y) + \cos(x - y) - y$, so that $F(x, y) = 0$. Then

$$F_x = \cos(x + y) - \sin(x - y)$$
$$F_y = \cos(x + y) - \sin(x - y)(-1) - 1$$

so

$$\frac{dy}{dx} = -\frac{F_x}{F_y} = \frac{-[\cos(x + y) - \sin(x - y)]}{\cos(x + y) + \sin(x - y) - 1} \qquad \blacksquare$$

When z is defined implicitly in terms of x and y by an equation $F(x, y, z) = 0$, the chain rule can be used to find $\dfrac{\partial z}{\partial x}$ and $\dfrac{\partial z}{\partial y}$ in terms of F_x, F_y, and F_z. The procedure is outlined in Problem 57.

EXAMPLE 5   Second derivative of a function of two variables

Let $z = f(x, y)$, where $x = at$ and $y = bt$ for constants a and b. Assuming all necessary differentiability, find d^2z/dt^2 in terms of the partial derivatives of z.

Solution

By using the chain rule, we have

$$\frac{dz}{dt} = \frac{\partial z}{\partial x}\frac{dx}{dt} + \frac{\partial z}{\partial y}\frac{dy}{dt}$$

and

$$\begin{aligned}
\frac{d^2z}{dt^2} &= \frac{d}{dt}\left(\frac{dz}{dt}\right) = \frac{d}{dt}\left(\frac{\partial z}{\partial x}\frac{dx}{dt} + \frac{\partial z}{\partial y}\frac{dy}{dt}\right)\\
&= \frac{\partial z}{\partial x}\left[\frac{d}{dt}\left(\frac{dx}{dt}\right)\right] + \left[\frac{d}{dt}\left(\frac{\partial z}{\partial x}\right)\right]\frac{dx}{dt} + \frac{\partial z}{\partial y}\left[\frac{d}{dt}\left(\frac{dy}{dt}\right)\right] + \left[\frac{d}{dt}\left(\frac{\partial z}{\partial y}\right)\right]\frac{dy}{dt}\\
&= \left[\frac{\partial z}{\partial x}\frac{d^2x}{dt^2} + \frac{dx}{dt}\left(\frac{\partial^2 z}{\partial x^2}\frac{dx}{dt} + \frac{\partial^2 z}{\partial x \partial y}\frac{dy}{dt}\right)\right] + \left[\frac{\partial z}{\partial y}\frac{d^2y}{dt^2} + \frac{dy}{dt}\left(\frac{\partial^2 z}{\partial y \partial x}\frac{dx}{dt} + \frac{\partial^2 z}{\partial y^2}\frac{dy}{dt}\right)\right]
\end{aligned}$$

Substituting $\dfrac{dx}{dt} = a$ and $\dfrac{dy}{dt} = b$, we obtain

$$\frac{d^2z}{dt^2} = \left[\frac{\partial z}{\partial x}(0) + a\left(\frac{\partial^2 z}{\partial x^2}a + \frac{\partial^2 z}{\partial x\partial y}b\right)\right] + \left[\frac{\partial z}{\partial y}(0) + b\left(\frac{\partial^2 z}{\partial y\partial x}a + \frac{\partial^2 z}{\partial y^2}b\right)\right]$$

$$= a^2\frac{\partial^2 z}{\partial x^2} + 2ab\frac{\partial^2 z}{\partial x\partial y} + b^2\frac{\partial^2 z}{\partial y^2} \qquad \text{Note } \frac{\partial^2 z}{\partial x\partial y} = \frac{\partial^2 z}{\partial y\partial x}. \qquad \blacksquare$$

EXTENSIONS OF THE CHAIN RULE

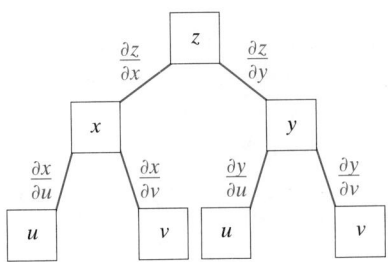

Next, we will consider the kind of composite function that occurs when x and y are both functions of two parameters. Specifically, let $z = F(x, y)$, where $x = x(u, v)$ and $y = y(u, v)$ are both functions of two independent parameters u and v. Then $z = F[x(u, v), y(u, v)]$ is a composite function of u and v, and with suitable assumptions regarding differentiability, we can find the partial derivatives $\partial z/\partial u$ and $\partial z/\partial v$ by applying the chain rule obtained in the following theorem.

THEOREM 11.5   The chain rule for two independent parameters

Suppose $z = f(x, y)$ is differentiable at (x, y) and that the partial derivatives of $x = x(u, v)$ and $y = y(u, v)$ exist at (u, v). Then the composite function $z = f[x(u, v), y(u, v)]$ is differentiable at (u, v) with

$$\frac{\partial z}{\partial u} = \frac{\partial z}{\partial x}\frac{\partial x}{\partial u} + \frac{\partial z}{\partial y}\frac{\partial y}{\partial u} \quad \text{and} \quad \frac{\partial z}{\partial v} = \frac{\partial z}{\partial x}\frac{\partial x}{\partial v} + \frac{\partial z}{\partial y}\frac{\partial y}{\partial v}$$

Proof   This version of the chain rule follows immediately from the chain rule for one independent parameter.   For example, if v is fixed, the composite function $z = f[x(u, v), y(u, v)]$ depends on u alone, and we have the situation described in the chain rule of one independent variable.   We apply this chain rule with a partial derivative (because x and y are functions of more than one variable):

$$\frac{\partial z}{\partial u} = \frac{\partial z}{\partial x}\frac{\partial x}{\partial u} + \frac{\partial z}{\partial y}\frac{\partial y}{\partial u}$$

The formula for $\dfrac{\partial z}{\partial v}$ can be established in a similar fashion.   ❑

EXAMPLE 6   Chain rule for two independent parameters

Let $z = 4x - y^2$, where $x = uv^2$ and $y = u^3v$. Find $\dfrac{\partial z}{\partial u}$ and $\dfrac{\partial z}{\partial v}$.

Solution

First find the partial derivatives:

$$\frac{\partial z}{\partial x} = \frac{\partial}{\partial x}(4x - y^2) = 4 \qquad\qquad \frac{\partial z}{\partial y} = \frac{\partial}{\partial y}(4x - y^2) = -2y$$

$$\frac{\partial x}{\partial u} = \frac{\partial}{\partial u}(uv^2) = v^2 \qquad\qquad \frac{\partial y}{\partial u} = \frac{\partial}{\partial u}(u^3v) = 3u^2v$$

and

$$\frac{\partial x}{\partial v} = \frac{\partial}{\partial v}(uv^2) = 2uv \qquad\qquad \frac{\partial y}{\partial v} = \frac{\partial}{\partial v}(u^3v) = u^3$$

Therefore, the chain rule for two independent parameters gives

$$\frac{\partial z}{\partial u} = \frac{\partial z}{\partial x}\frac{\partial x}{\partial u} + \frac{\partial z}{\partial y}\frac{\partial y}{\partial u}$$

$$= (4)(v^2) + (-2y)(3u^2v) = 4v^2 - 2(u^3v)(3u^2v) = 4v^2 - 6u^5v^2$$

and

$$\frac{\partial z}{\partial v} = \frac{\partial z}{\partial x}\frac{\partial x}{\partial v} + \frac{\partial z}{\partial y}\frac{\partial y}{\partial v}$$

$$= (4)(2uv) + (-2y)(u^3) = 8uv - 2(u^3v)u^3 = 8uv - 2u^6v \qquad \blacksquare$$

EXAMPLE 7   Implicit differentiation using the chain rule

If f is differentiable and $z = u + f(u^2v^2)$, show that $u\dfrac{\partial z}{\partial u} - v\dfrac{\partial z}{\partial v} = u$.

Solution

Let $w = u^2v^2$, so $z = u + f(w)$. Then, according to the chain rule,

$$\frac{\partial z}{\partial u} = 1 + \frac{df}{dw}\frac{\partial w}{\partial u} \qquad\qquad \frac{\partial z}{\partial v} = \frac{df}{dw}\frac{\partial w}{\partial v}$$

$$= 1 + f'(w)(2uv^2) \qquad\qquad = f'(w)(2u^2v)$$

so that

$$u\frac{\partial z}{\partial u} - v\frac{\partial z}{\partial v} = u\left[1 + f'(w)(2uv^2)\right] - v\left[f'(w)(2u^2v)\right]$$

$$= u + f'(w)\left[u(2uv^2) - v(2u^2v)\right]$$

$$= u \qquad \blacksquare$$

The chain rules can be extended to functions of three or more variables. For instance, if $w = f(x, y, z)$ is a differentiable function of three variables and $x = x(t)$, $y = y(t)$, $z = z(t)$ are each differentiable functions of t, then w is a differentiable composite function of t and

$$\frac{dw}{dt} = \frac{\partial w}{\partial x}\frac{dx}{dt} + \frac{\partial w}{\partial y}\frac{dy}{dt} + \frac{\partial w}{\partial z}\frac{dz}{dt}$$

In general, if $w = f(x_1, x_2, \ldots, x_n)$ is a differentiable function of the n variables $x_1, x_2, \ldots, x_n$, which in turn are differentiable functions of m parameters $t_1, t_2, \ldots, t_m$, then

$$\frac{\partial w}{\partial t_1} = \frac{\partial w}{\partial x_1}\frac{\partial x_1}{\partial t_1} + \frac{\partial w}{\partial x_2}\frac{\partial x_2}{\partial t_1} + \cdots + \frac{\partial w}{\partial x_n}\frac{\partial x_n}{\partial t_1}$$

$$\vdots$$

$$\frac{\partial w}{\partial t_m} = \frac{\partial w}{\partial x_1}\frac{\partial x_1}{\partial t_m} + \frac{\partial w}{\partial x_2}\frac{\partial x_2}{\partial t_m} + \cdots + \frac{\partial w}{\partial x_n}\frac{\partial x_n}{\partial t_m}$$

EXAMPLE 8   Chain rule for a function of three variables with three parameters

Find $\dfrac{\partial w}{\partial s}$ if $w = 4x + y^2 + z^3$, where $x = e^{rs^2}$, $y = \ln\dfrac{r+s}{t}$, and $z = rst^2$.

Solution

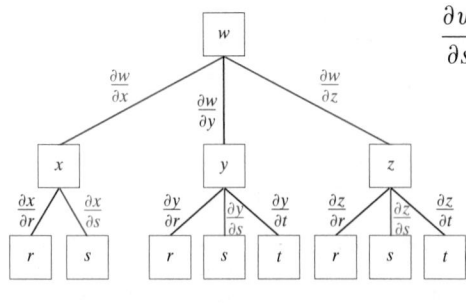

$$\frac{\partial w}{\partial s} = \frac{\partial w}{\partial x}\frac{\partial x}{\partial s} + \frac{\partial w}{\partial y}\frac{\partial y}{\partial s} + \frac{\partial w}{\partial z}\frac{\partial z}{\partial s}$$

$$= \left[\frac{\partial}{\partial x}(4x + y^2 + z^3)\right]\left[\frac{\partial}{\partial s}(e^{rs^2})\right] + \left[\frac{\partial}{\partial y}(4x + y^2 + z^3)\right]\left[\frac{\partial}{\partial s}\left(\ln\frac{r+s}{t}\right)\right]$$

$$+ \left[\frac{\partial}{\partial z}(4x + y^2 + z^3)\right]\left[\frac{\partial}{\partial s}(rst^2)\right]$$

$$= 4\left[e^{rs^2}(2rs)\right] + 2y\left(\frac{\frac{1}{r+s}}{t}\right)\left(\frac{1}{t}\right) + 3z^2(rt^2)$$

$$= 8rse^{rs^2} + \frac{2y}{r+s} + 3rt^2z^2$$

In terms of r, s, and t, the partial derivative is

$$\frac{\partial w}{\partial s} = 8rse^{rs^2} + \frac{2}{r+s}\ln\frac{r+s}{t} + 3r^3s^2t^6 \qquad \blacksquare$$

11.5   PROBLEM SET

A 1. **WHAT DOES THIS SAY?**   Discuss the various chain rules and the need for such chain rules.

2. **WHAT DOES THIS SAY?**   Discuss the usefulness of the schematic (tree) representation for the chain rules.

3. **WHAT DOES THIS SAY?**   Write out a chain rule for a function of two variables and three independent parameters.

In Problems 4–7, the function $z = f(x, y)$ depends on x and y, which in turn are each functions of t. In each case, find dz/dt in two different ways:

  a. Express z explicitly in terms of t.

  b. Use the chain rule for one parameter.

4. $f(x, y) = 2xy + y^2$, where $x = -3t^2$ and $y = 1 + t^3$

5. $f(x, y) = (4 + y^2)x$, where $x = e^{2t}$ and $y = e^{3t}$

6. $f(x, y) = (1 + x^2 + y^2)^{1/2}$, where $x = \cos 5t$ and $y = \sin 5t$

7. $f(x, y) = xy^2$, where $x = \cos 3t$ and $y = \tan 3t$

In Problems 8–11, the function $F(x, y)$ depends on x and y. Let $x = x(u, v)$ and $y = y(u, v)$ be given functions of u and v. Let $z = F[x(u, v), y(u, v)]$ and find the partial derivatives $\partial z/\partial u$ and $\partial z/\partial v$ in these two ways:

  a. Express z explicitly in terms of u and v.

  b. Apply the chain rule for two independent parameters.

8. $F(x, y) = x + y^2$, where $x = u + v$ and $y = u - v$

9. $F(x, y) = x^2 + y^2$, where $x = u \sin v$ and $y = u - 2v$

10. $F(x, y) = e^{xy}$, where $x = u - v$ and $y = u + v$

11. $F(x, y) = \ln xy$, where $x = e^{uv^2}$, $y = e^{uv}$

Write out the chain rule for the functions given in Problems 12–15.

12. $z = f(x, y)$, where $x = x(s, t)$, $y = y(s, t)$

13. $w = f(x, y, z)$, where $x = x(s, t)$, $y = y(s, t)$, $z = z(s, t)$

14. $t = f(u, v)$, where $u = u(x, y, z, w)$, $v = v(x, y, z, w)$

15. $w = f(x, y, z)$, where $x = x(s, t, u)$, $y = y(s, t, u)$, $z = z(s, t, u)$

Find the indicated derivatives or partial derivatives in Problems 16–21. Leave your answers in mixed form (x, y, z, t).

16. Find $\dfrac{dw}{dt}$, where $w = \ln(x + 2y - z^2)$ and $x = 2t - 1$, $y = \dfrac{1}{t}$, $z = \sqrt{t}$.

17. Find $\dfrac{dw}{dt}$, where $w = \sin xyz$ and $x = 1 - 3t$, $y = e^{1-t}$, $z = 4t$.

18. Find $\dfrac{dw}{dt}$, where $w = ze^{xy^2}$ and $x = \sin t$, $y = \cos t$, $z = \tan 2t$.

19. Find $\dfrac{dw}{dt}$, where $w = e^{x^3 + yz}$ and $x = \dfrac{2}{t}$, $y = \ln(2t - 3)$, $z = t^2$.

20. Find $\dfrac{\partial w}{\partial r}$, where $w = e^{2x - y + 3z^2}$ and $x = r + s - t$, $y = 2r - 3s$, $z = \cos rst$.

21. Find $\dfrac{\partial w}{\partial r}$ and $\dfrac{\partial w}{\partial t}$, where $w = \dfrac{x + y}{2 - z}$ and $x = 2rs$, $y = \sin rt$, $z = st^2$.

In Problems 22–27, assume the given equations define y as a differentiable function of x and find dy/dx using the procedure illustrated in Example 4.

22. $x^2y + \sqrt{xy} = 4$

23. $(x^2 - y)^{3/2} + x^2y = 2$

24. $x^2y + \ln(2x + y) = 5$

25. $x \cos y + y \tan^{-1} x = x$

26. $xe^{xy} + ye^{-xy} = 3$

27. $\tan^{-1}\left(\dfrac{x}{y}\right) = \tan^{-1}\left(\dfrac{y}{x}\right)$

B *Find the following higher-order partial derivatives in Problems 28–33.*

  a. $\dfrac{\partial^2 z}{\partial x \partial y}$ b. $\dfrac{\partial^2 z}{\partial x^2}$ c. $\dfrac{\partial^2 z}{\partial y^2}$

28. $x^3 + y^2 + z^2 = 5$

29. $xyz = 2$

30. $\ln(x + y) = y^2 + z$

31. $x^{-1} + y^{-1} + z^{-1} = 3$

32. $x \cos y = y + z$

33. $z^2 + \sin x = \tan y$

34. Let $f(x, y)$ be a differentiable function of x and y, and let $x = r \cos\theta$, $y = r \sin\theta$ for $r > 0$ and $0 < \theta < 2\pi$.

  a. If $z = f[x(r, \theta), y(r, \theta)]$, find $\dfrac{\partial z}{\partial r}$ and $\dfrac{\partial z}{\partial \theta}$.

  b. Show that

$$\left(\frac{\partial z}{\partial r}\right)^2 + \frac{1}{r^2}\left(\frac{\partial z}{\partial \theta}\right)^2 = \left(\frac{\partial z}{\partial x}\right)^2 + \left(\frac{\partial z}{\partial y}\right)^2$$

35. Let $z = f(x, y)$, where $x = au$ and $y = bv$, with a, b constants. Express $\partial^2 z/\partial u^2$ and $\partial^2 z/\partial v^2$ in terms of the partial derivatives of z with respect to x and y. Assume the existence and continuity of all necessary first and second partial derivatives.

36. Let (x, y, z) lie on the ellipsoid

$$\frac{x^2}{a^2} + \frac{y^2}{b^2} + \frac{z^2}{c^2} = 1$$

Without solving for z explicitly in terms of x and y, compute the higher-order partial derivatives

$$\frac{\partial^2 z}{\partial x^2} \quad \text{and} \quad \frac{\partial^2 z}{\partial x \partial y}$$

37. The dimensions of a rectangular box are linear functions of time, $\ell(t)$, $w(t)$, and $h(t)$. If the length and width are increasing at 2 in./sec and the height is decreasing at 3 in./sec, find the rates at which the volume V and the surface area S are changing with respect to time. If $\ell(0) = 10$, $w(0) = 8$, and $h(0) = 20$, is V increasing or decreasing when $t = 5$ sec? What about S when $t = 5$?

38. Van der Waal's equation in physical chemistry states that a gas occupying volume V at temperature T (Kelvin) exerts pressure P, where

$$\left(P + \frac{A}{V^2} \right)(V - B) = kT$$

for physical constants A, B, and k. Compute the following rates:

a. the rate of change of volume with respect to temperature

b. the rate of change of pressure with respect to volume

39. The concentration of a drug in the blood of a patient t hours after the drug is injected into the body intramuscularly is modeled by the Heinz function

$$C = \frac{1}{b-a}(e^{-at} - e^{-bt}) \qquad b > a$$

where a and b are parameters that depend on the patient's metabolism and the particular kind of drug being used.

a. Compute the rates $\dfrac{\partial C}{\partial a}$, $\dfrac{\partial C}{\partial b}$, and $\dfrac{\partial C}{\partial t}$.

b. Explore the assumption that $a = (\ln b)/t$, b constant for $t > (\ln b)/b$. In particular, what is dC/dt?

40. A paint store carries two brands of latex paint. An analysis of sales figures indicates that the demand Q for the first brand is modeled by

$$Q(x, y) = 210 - 12x^2 + 18y$$

gallons/month, where x, y are the prices of the first and second brands, respectively. A separate study indicates that t months from now, the first brand will cost $x = 4 + 0.18t$ dollars/gal and the second brand will cost $y = 5 + 0.3\sqrt{t}$ dollars/gal. At what rate will the demand Q be changing with respect to time 9 months from now?

41. To model the demand for the sale of bicycles, it is assumed that if 24-speed bicycles are sold for x dollars apiece and the price of gasoline is y cents per gallon, then

$$Q(x, y) = 240 - 21\sqrt{x} + 4(0.2y + 12)^{3/2}$$

bicycles will be sold each month. For this model it is further assumed that t months from now, bicycles will be selling for $x = 120 + 6t$ dollars apiece, and the price of gasoline will be $y = 80 + 10\sqrt{4t}$ cents/gal. At what rate will the monthly demand for the bicycles be changing with respect to time 4 months from now?

42. At a certain factory, the amount of air pollution generated each day is modeled by the function

$$Q(E, T) = 127E^{2/3}T^{1/2}$$

where E is the number of employees and T (°C) is the average temperature during the workday. Currently, there are 142 employees and the average temperature is 18°C. If the average daily temperature is falling at the rate of 0.23°/day and the number of employees is increasing at the rate of 3/month, what is the corresponding effect on the rate of pollution? Express your answer in units/day. For this model, assume there are 22 workdays/month.

43. The combined resistance R produced by three variable resistances R_1, R_2, and R_3 connected in parallel is modeled by the formula

$$\frac{1}{R} = \frac{1}{R_1} + \frac{1}{R_2} + \frac{1}{R_3}$$

Suppose at a certain instant, $R_1 = 100$ ohms, $R_2 = 200$ ohms, $R_3 = 300$ ohms, and that R_1 and R_3 are decreasing at the rate of 1.5 ohm/s while R_2 is increasing at the rate of 2 ohms/s. How fast is R changing with respect to time at this instant? Is it increasing or decreasing?

In Problems 44–48, assume that all functions have whatever derivatives or partial derivatives are necessary for the problem to be meaningful.

44. If $z = f(uv^2)$, show that

$$2u\frac{\partial z}{\partial u} - v\frac{\partial z}{\partial v} = 0$$

45. If $z = f(u - v, v - u)$, show that

$$\frac{\partial z}{\partial u} + \frac{\partial z}{\partial v} = 0$$

46. If $z = u + f(uv)$, show that

$$u\frac{\partial z}{\partial u} - v\frac{\partial z}{\partial v} = u$$

47. If $w = f\left(\dfrac{r-s}{s}\right)$, show that

$$r\frac{\partial w}{\partial r} + s\frac{\partial w}{\partial s} = 0$$

48. If $z = xy + f(x^2 + y^2)$, show that

$$y\frac{\partial z}{\partial x} - x\frac{\partial z}{\partial y} = y^2 - x^2$$

49. Let $w = f(t)$ be a differentiable function of t, where $t = (x^2 + y^2 + z^2)^{1/2}$. Show that

$$\left(\frac{dw}{dt}\right)^2 = \left(\frac{\partial w}{\partial x}\right)^2 + \left(\frac{\partial w}{\partial y}\right)^2 + \left(\frac{\partial w}{\partial z}\right)^2$$

50. Suppose f is a twice differentiable function of one variable, and let $z = f(x^2 + y^2)$. Find

a. $\dfrac{\partial^2 z}{\partial x^2}$ **b.** $\dfrac{\partial^2 z}{\partial y^2}$ **c.** $\dfrac{\partial^2 z}{\partial x \partial y}$

51. Find $\dfrac{d^2 z}{d\theta^2}$, where z is a twice differentiable function of one variable θ and can be written $z = f(\cos\theta, \sin\theta)$. *Hint:* Let $x = \cos\theta$ and $y = \sin\theta$. Leave your answer in terms of x and y.

52. Let f and g be twice differentiable functions of one variable, and let

$$u(x, t) = f(x + ct) + g(x - ct)$$

for a constant c. Show that $\dfrac{\partial^2 u}{\partial t^2} = c^2\dfrac{\partial^2 u}{\partial x^2}$. *Hint:* Let $r = x + ct$; $s = x - ct$.

53. Suppose $z = f(x, y)$ has continuous second-order partial derivatives. If $x = e^r\cos\theta$ and $y = e^r\sin\theta$, show that

$$\frac{\partial^2 z}{\partial x^2} + \frac{\partial^2 z}{\partial y^2} = e^{-2r}\left[\frac{\partial^2 z}{\partial r^2} + \frac{\partial^2 z}{\partial \theta^2}\right]$$

54. If $f(u, v, w)$ is differentiable and $u = x - y$, $v = y - z$, and $w = z - x$, what is

$$\frac{\partial f}{\partial x} + \frac{\partial f}{\partial y} + \frac{\partial f}{\partial z}?$$

C 55. The *Cauchy-Riemann equations* are

$$\frac{\partial u}{\partial x} = \frac{\partial v}{\partial y} \quad \text{and} \quad \frac{\partial u}{\partial y} = -\frac{\partial v}{\partial x}$$

(See Problem 51, Section 11.3.) Show that if x and y are expressed in terms of polar coordinates, the Cauchy-Riemann equations become

$$\frac{\partial u}{\partial r} = \frac{1}{r}\frac{\partial v}{\partial \theta} \quad \text{and} \quad \frac{\partial v}{\partial r} = -\frac{1}{r}\frac{\partial u}{\partial \theta}$$

56. Let $T(x, y)$ be the temperature at each point (x, y) in a portion of the plane that contains the ellipse $x = 2\cos t$, $y = \sin t$ for $0 \le t \le 2\pi$. Suppose

$$\frac{\partial T}{\partial x} = y \quad \text{and} \quad \frac{\partial T}{\partial y} = x$$

a. Find $\dfrac{dT}{dt}$ and $\dfrac{d^2 T}{dt^2}$ by using the chain rule.

b. Locate the maximum and minimum temperatures on the ellipse.

57. Let $F(x, y, z)$ be a function of three variables with continuous partial derivatives F_x, F_y, F_z in a certain region where $F(x, y, z) = C$ for some constant C. Use the chain rule for two parameters and the fact that x and y are independent variables to show that (for $F_z \ne 0$)

$$\frac{\partial z}{\partial x} = \frac{-F_x}{F_z} \quad \text{and} \quad \frac{\partial z}{\partial y} = -\frac{F_y}{F_z}$$

Use these formulas to find $\dfrac{\partial z}{\partial x}$ and $\dfrac{\partial z}{\partial y}$ if z is defined implicitly by the equation $x^2 + 2xyz + y^3 + e^z = 4$.

58. Suppose the system

$$\begin{cases} xu + yv - uv = 0 \\ yu - xv + uv = 0 \end{cases}$$

can be solved for u and v in terms of x and y, so that $u = u(x, y)$ and $v = v(x, y)$. Use implicit differentiation to find the partial derivatives $\dfrac{\partial u}{\partial x}$ and $\dfrac{\partial v}{\partial x}$.

59. A function $f(x, y)$ is said to be *homogeneous of degree n* if

$$f(tx, ty) = t^n f(x, y) \qquad \text{for all } t > 0$$

a. Show that $f(x, y) = x^2 y + 2y^3$ is homogeneous and find its degree.

b. If $f(x, y)$ is homogeneous of degree n, show that

$$x\frac{\partial f}{\partial x} + y\frac{\partial f}{\partial y} = nf$$

60. Suppose that F and G are functions of three variables and that it is possible to solve the equations $F(x, y, z) = 0$ and $G(x, y, z) = 0$ for y and z in terms of x, so that $y = y(x)$ and $z = z(x)$. Use the chain rule to express dy/dx and dz/dx in terms of the partial derivatives of F and G. Assume these partials are continuous and that

$$\frac{\partial F}{\partial y}\frac{\partial G}{\partial z} \ne \frac{\partial F}{\partial z}\frac{\partial G}{\partial y}$$

11.6   Directional Derivatives and the Gradient

IN THIS SECTION   the directional derivative, the gradient, maximal property of the gradient, functions of three variables, normal property of the gradient, tangent planes and normal lines

Suppose $z = T(x, y)$ gives the temperature at each point (x, y) in a region R of the plane, and let $P_0(x_0, y_0)$ be a particular point in R. Then we know that the partial derivative $T_x(x_0, y_0)$ gives the rate at which the temperature changes for a move from P_0 in the x-direction, while the rate of temperature change in the y-direction is given by $T_y(x_0, y_0)$. Suppose we want to find the direction of greatest temperature change, which may be in a direction not parallel to either coordinate axes. To answer this question, we will introduce the concept of *directional derivative* in this section and examine its properties.

THE DIRECTIONAL DERIVATIVE

In Chapter 3 we defined the *slope of a curve* at a point to be the ratio of the change in the dependent variable to the change in the independent variable at the given point. To determine the slope of the tangent line at a point $P_0(x_0, y_0)$ on a surface defined by $z = f(x, y)$, we need to specify the *direction* in which we wish to measure. We do this by using vectors. In Section 11.3 we found the slope parallel to the xz-plane to be the partial derivative $f_x(x_0, y_0)$. We could have specified this direction in terms of the unit vector $\mathbf{i}$ (x-direction), while $f_y(x, y)$ could have been specified in terms of the unit vector $\mathbf{j}$. Finally, to measure the slope of the tangent line in an *arbitrary* direction, we use a unit vector $\mathbf{u} = u_1\mathbf{i} + u_2\mathbf{j}$ in that direction.

To find the desired slope, we look at the intersection of the surface with the vertical plane passing through the point P_0 parallel to the vector $\mathbf{u}$, as shown in Figure 11.26. This vertical plane intersects the surface to form a curve C, and we define the slope of the surface at P_0 in the direction of $\mathbf{u}$ to be the slope of the tangent line to the curve C defined by $\mathbf{u}$ at that point.

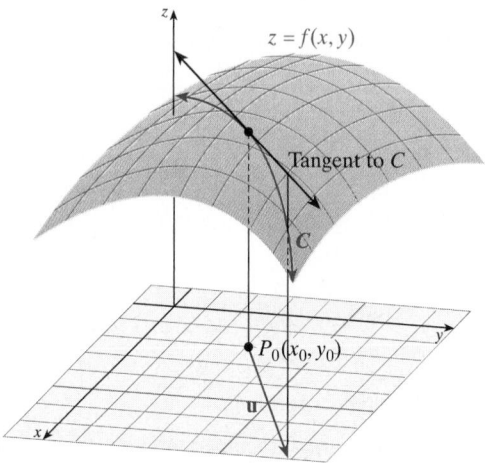

Figure 11.26 The directional derivative $D_u f(x_0, y_0)$ is the slope of the tangent line to the curve on the surface $z = f(x, y)$ in the direction of the unit vector $\mathbf{u}$ at $P_0(x_0, y_0)$.

We summarize this idea of slope *in a particular direction* with the following definition.

Directional Derivative

> **WARNING** Remember, $\mathbf{u}$ must be a *unit* vector.

Let f be a function of two variables, and let $\mathbf{u} = u_1\mathbf{i} + u_2\mathbf{j}$ be a unit vector. The **directional derivative of f at $P_0(x_0, y_0)$** in the direction of $\mathbf{u}$ is given by

$$D_{\mathbf{u}} f(x_0, y_0) = \lim_{h \to 0} \frac{f(x_0 + hu_1, y_0 + hu_2) - f(x_0, y_0)}{h}$$

provided the limit exists.

At a particular point $P_0(x_0, y_0)$, there are infinitely many directional derivatives to the graph of $z = f(x, y)$, one for each direction radiating from P_0. Two of these are the partial derivatives $f_x(x_0, y_0)$ and $f_y(x_0, y_0)$. To see this, note that if $\mathbf{u} = \mathbf{i}$ (so $u_1 = 1$ and $u_2 = 0$), then

$$D_{\mathbf{i}} f(x_0, y_0) = \lim_{h \to 0} \frac{f(x_0 + h, y_0) - f(x_0, y_0)}{h} = f_x(x_0, y_0)$$

and if $\mathbf{u} = \mathbf{j}$ (so $u_1 = 0$ and $u_2 = 1$),

$$D_{\mathbf{j}} f(x_0, y_0) = \lim_{h \to 0} \frac{f(x_0, y_0 + h) - f(x_0, y_0)}{h} = f_y(x_0, y_0)$$

The definition of the directional derivative is similar to the definition of the derivative of a function of a single variable. Just as with a single variable, it is difficult to apply the definition directly. Fortunately, the following theorem allows us to find directional derivatives more efficiently than by using the definition.

THEOREM 11.6 Directional derivatives using partial derivatives

Let $f(x, y)$ be a function that is differentiable at $P_0(x_0, y_0)$. Then f has a directional derivative in the direction of the unit vector $\mathbf{u} = u_1\mathbf{i} + u_2\mathbf{j}$ given by

$$D_{\mathbf{u}} f(x_0, y_0) = f_x(x_0, y_0)u_1 + f_y(x_0, y_0)u_2$$

Proof We define a function F of a single variable h by $F(h) = f(x_0 + hu_1, y_0 + hu_2)$, so that

$$D_{\mathbf{u}} f(x_0, y_0) = \lim_{h \to 0} \frac{f(x_0 + hu_1, y_0 + hu_2) - f(x_0, y_0)}{h}$$

$$= \lim_{h \to 0} \frac{F(h) - F(0)}{h} = F'(0)$$

Apply the chain rule with $x = x_0 + hu_1$ and $y = y_0 + hu_2$:

$$F'(h) = \frac{dF}{dh} = \frac{\partial f}{\partial x}\frac{dx}{dh} + \frac{\partial f}{\partial y}\frac{dy}{dh} = f_x(x, y)u_1 + f_y(x, y)u_2$$

When $h = 0$, we have $x = x_0$ and $y = y_0$, so that

$$D_{\mathbf{u}} f(x_0, y_0) = F'(0) = \frac{\partial f}{\partial x}u_1 + \frac{\partial f}{\partial y}u_2 = f_x(x_0, y_0)u_1 + f_y(x_0, y_0)u_2 \qquad \square$$

EXAMPLE 1 Finding a directional derivative using partial derivatives

Find the directional derivative of $f(x, y) = 3 - 2x^2 + y^3$ at the point $P(1, 2)$ in the direction of the unit vector $\mathbf{u} = \frac{1}{2}\mathbf{i} - \frac{\sqrt{3}}{2}\mathbf{j}$.

Solution

First, find the partial derivatives $f_x(x, y) = -4x$ and $f_y(x, y) = 3y^2$. Then since $u_1 = \frac{1}{2}$ and $u_2 = -\frac{\sqrt{3}}{2}$, we have

$$D_{\mathbf{u}} f(1, 2) = f_x(1, 2)\left(\frac{1}{2}\right) + f_y(1, 2)\left(-\frac{\sqrt{3}}{2}\right)$$

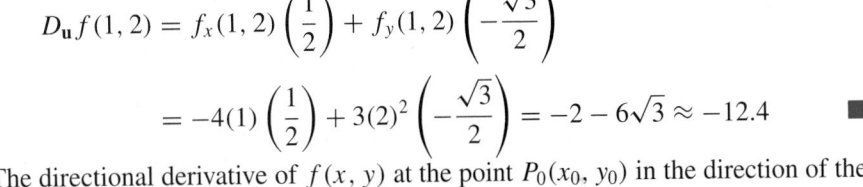

$$= -4(1)\left(\frac{1}{2}\right) + 3(2)^2\left(-\frac{\sqrt{3}}{2}\right) = -2 - 6\sqrt{3} \approx -12.4 \qquad \blacksquare$$

The directional derivative of $f(x, y)$ at the point $P_0(x_0, y_0)$ in the direction of the unit vector $\mathbf{u} = \langle u_1, u_2 \rangle$ can be interpreted as both a rate of change and a slope. For instance, in Example 1, the intersection of the surface $z = 3 - 2x^2 + y^3$ with the vertical plane through the point $P(1, 2)$ parallel to the unit vector $\mathbf{u} = \left\langle \frac{1}{2}, \frac{-\sqrt{3}}{2} \right\rangle$ is a curve C, and the directional derivative $D_{\mathbf{u}} f(1, 2) = -12.3$ is the slope of C at the point $Q(1, 2, 9)$ on the surface above P, as shown in Figure 11.27. The directional derivative also gives the rate at which the function $f(x, y) = 3 - 2x^2 + y^3$ changes as a point (x, y) moves from P in the direction of $\mathbf{u}$.

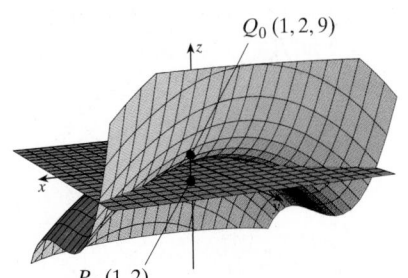

Figure 11.27 The graph of the surface $z = 3 - 2x^2 + y^3$

THE GRADIENT

The directional derivative $D_{\mathbf{u}} f(x, y)$ can be expressed concisely in terms of a vector function called the *gradient*, which has many important uses in mathematics. The gradient of a function of two variables may be defined as follows.

Gradient

Let f be a differentiable function at (x, y) and let $f(x, y)$ have partial derivatives $f_x(x, y)$ and $f_y(x, y)$. Then the **gradient** of f, denoted by ∇f (pronounced "del eff"), is a vector given by

$$\nabla f(x, y) = f_x(x, y)\mathbf{i} + f_y(x, y)\mathbf{j}$$

The value of the gradient at the point $P_0(x_0, y_0)$ is denoted by

$$\nabla f_0 = f_x(x_0, y_0)\mathbf{i} + f_y(x_0, y_0)\mathbf{j}$$

Note: Think of the symbol ∇ as an "operator" on a function that produces a vector. Another notation for ∇f is **grad** $f(x, y)$.

EXAMPLE 2 Finding the gradient of a given function

Find $\nabla f(x, y)$ for $f(x, y) = x^2 y + y^3$.

Solution

Begin with the partial derivatives:

$$f_x(x, y) = \frac{\partial}{\partial x}(x^2 y + y^3) = 2xy \quad \text{and} \quad f_y(x, y) = \frac{\partial}{\partial y}(x^2 y + y^3) = x^2 + 3y^2$$

Then

$$\nabla f(x, y) = 2xy\mathbf{i} + (x^2 + 3y^2)\mathbf{j} \qquad \blacksquare$$

The following theorem shows how the directional derivative can be expressed in terms of the gradient.

THEOREM 11.7 The gradient formula for the directional derivative

If f is a differentiable function of x and y, then the directional derivative of f at the point $P_0(x_0, y_0)$ in the direction of the unit vector $\mathbf{u}$ is

$$D_{\mathbf{u}}f(x_0, y_0) = \nabla f_0 \cdot \mathbf{u}$$

Proof Because $\nabla f_0 = f_x(x_0, y_0)\mathbf{i} + f_y(x_0, y_0)\mathbf{j}$ and $\mathbf{u} = u_1\mathbf{i} + u_2\mathbf{j}$, we have

$$D_{\mathbf{u}}f(x_0, y_0) = \nabla f_0 \cdot \mathbf{u} = f_x(x_0, y_0)u_1 + f_y(x_0, y_0)u_2 \qquad \square$$

EXAMPLE 3 Using the gradient formula to compute a directional derivative

Find the directional derivative of $f(x, y) = \ln(x^2 + y^3)$ at $P_0(1, -3)$ in the direction of $\mathbf{v} = 2\mathbf{i} - 3\mathbf{j}$.

Solution

$$f_x(x, y) = \frac{2x}{x^2 + y^3}, \quad \text{so} \quad f_x(1, -3) = -\frac{2}{26}$$

$$f_y(x, y) = \frac{3y^2}{x^2 + y^3}, \quad \text{so} \quad f_y(1, -3) = -\frac{27}{26}$$

$$\nabla f_0 = \nabla f(1, -3) = -\tfrac{2}{26}\mathbf{i} - \tfrac{27}{26}\mathbf{j}$$

A unit vector in the direction of $\mathbf{v}$ is

$$\mathbf{u} = \frac{\mathbf{v}}{\|\mathbf{v}\|} = \frac{2\mathbf{i} - 3\mathbf{j}}{\sqrt{2^2 + (-3)^2}} = \frac{1}{\sqrt{13}}(2\mathbf{i} - 3\mathbf{j})$$

Thus,

$$D_{\mathbf{u}}(x, y) = \nabla f \cdot \mathbf{u} = \left(-\frac{2}{26}\right)\left(\frac{2}{\sqrt{13}}\right) + \left(-\frac{27}{26}\right)\left(-\frac{3}{\sqrt{13}}\right)$$

$$= \frac{77\sqrt{13}}{338} \qquad \blacksquare$$

Although a differentiable function of one variable $f(x)$ has exactly one derivative $f'(x)$, a differentiable function of two variables $F(x, y)$ has two partial derivatives and an infinite number of directional derivatives. Is there any single mathematical concept for functions of several variables that is the analogue of the derivative of a function of a single variable? The properties listed in the following theorem suggest that the gradient plays this role.

THEOREM 11.8 **Basic properties of the gradient**

Let f and g be differentiable functions. Then

Constant rule	$\nabla c = \mathbf{0}$ for any constant c
Linearity rule	$\nabla(af + bg) = a\nabla f + b\nabla g$ for constants a and b
Product rule	$\nabla(fg) = f\nabla g + g\nabla f$
Quotient rule	$\nabla\left(\dfrac{f}{g}\right) = \dfrac{g\nabla f - f\nabla g}{g^2}, \; g \neq 0$
Power rule	$\nabla(f^n) = nf^{n-1}\nabla f$

Proof **Linearity rule**

$$\nabla(af + bg) = (af + bg)_x\mathbf{i} + (af + bg)_y\mathbf{j} = (af_x + bg_x)\mathbf{i} + (af_y + bg_y)\mathbf{j}$$
$$= af_x\mathbf{i} + bg_x\mathbf{i} + af_y\mathbf{j} + bg_y\mathbf{j} = a(f_x\mathbf{i} + f_y\mathbf{j}) + b(g_x\mathbf{i} + g_y\mathbf{j})$$
$$= a\nabla f + b\nabla g$$

Power rule

$$\nabla f^n = [f^n]_x\mathbf{i} + [f^n]_y\mathbf{j} = nf^{n-1}f_x\mathbf{i} + nf^{n-1}f_y\mathbf{j}$$
$$= nf^{n-1}[f_x\mathbf{i} + f_y\mathbf{j}] = nf^{n-1}\nabla f$$

The other rules are left for the problem set (Problem 57). ❑

MAXIMAL PROPERTY OF THE GRADIENT

In applications, it is often useful to compute the greatest rate of increase (or decrease) of a given function at a specified point. The direction in which this occurs is called the direction of **steepest ascent** (or **steepest descent**). For example, suppose the function $z = f(x, y)$ gives the altitude of a skier coming down a slope, and we want to state a theorem that will give the skier the *compass direction* of the path of steepest descent (see Figure 11.28b). We emphasize the words "compass direction" because the gradient gives direction in the xy-plane and does not itself point up or down the mountain. The following theorem shows how the direction of maximum change is determined by the gradient (see Figure 11.28).

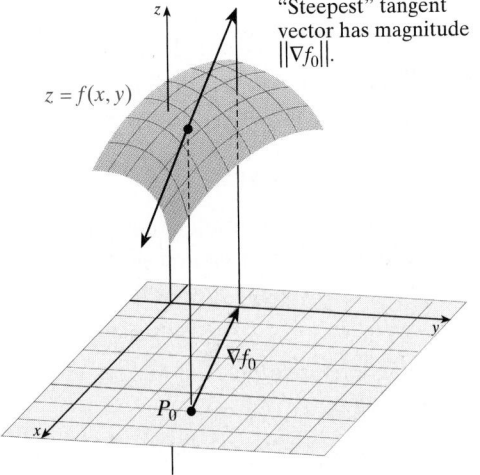

a. The optimal direction property of the gradient

b. Skier on a slope

Figure 11.28 Steepest ascent or steepest descent

THEOREM 11.9   Maximal direction property of the gradient

Suppose f is differentiable at the point P_0 and that the gradient of f at P_0 satisfies $\nabla f_0 \neq \mathbf{0}$. Then

a. The largest value of the directional derivative $D_{\mathbf{u}} f$ at P_0 is $\|\nabla f_0\|$ and occurs when the unit vector $\mathbf{u}$ points in the direction of ∇f_0.

b. The smallest value of $D_{\mathbf{u}} f$ at P_0 is $-\|\nabla f_0\|$ and occurs when $\mathbf{u}$ points in the direction of $-\nabla f_0$.

Proof   If $\mathbf{u}$ is any unit vector, then

$$D_{\mathbf{u}} f = \nabla f_0 \cdot \mathbf{u} = \|\nabla f_0\| \, (\|\mathbf{u}\| \cos \theta) = \|\nabla f_0\| \cos \theta$$

where θ is the angle between ∇f_0 and $\mathbf{u}$. But $\cos \theta$ assumes its largest value 1 at $\theta = 0$; that is, when $\mathbf{u}$ points in the direction ∇f_0. Thus, the largest possible value of $D_{\mathbf{u}} f$ is

$$D_{\mathbf{u}} f = \|\nabla f_0\|(1) = \|\nabla f_0\|$$

Statement **b** may be established in a similar fashion by noting that $\cos \theta$ assumes its smallest value -1 when $\theta = \pi$. This value occurs when $\mathbf{u}$ points toward $-\nabla f_0$, and in this direction

$$D_{\mathbf{u}} f = \|\nabla f_0\|(-1) = -\|\nabla f_0\|$$ ❑

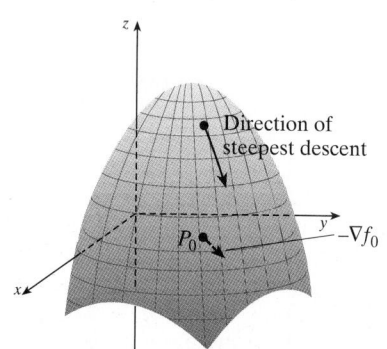

Figure 11.29 The direction of steepest descent

➡ **What This Says**   The theorem states that at P_0 the function f increases most rapidly in the direction of the gradient ∇f_0 and decreases most rapidly in the opposite direction (see Figure 11.29).

EXAMPLE 4   Maximal rate of increase and decrease

In what direction is the function defined by $f(x, y) = xe^{2y-x}$ increasing most rapidly at the point $P_0(2, 1)$, and what is the maximum rate of increase? In what direction is f decreasing most rapidly?

Solution

We begin by finding the gradient of f:

$$\nabla f = f_x \mathbf{i} + f_y \mathbf{j} = [e^{2y-x} + xe^{2y-x}(-1)]\mathbf{i} + [xe^{2y-x}(2)]\mathbf{j}$$
$$= e^{2y-x}[(1-x)\mathbf{i} + 2x\mathbf{j}]$$

At $(2, 1)$, $\nabla f_0 = e^{2(1)-2}[(1-2)\mathbf{i} + 2(2)\mathbf{j}] = -\mathbf{i} + 4\mathbf{j}$. The most rapid rate of increase is $\|\nabla f_0\| = \sqrt{(-1)^2 + (4)^2} = \sqrt{17}$ and it occurs in the direction of $-\mathbf{i} + 4\mathbf{j}$. The most rapid rate of decrease occurs in the direction of $-\nabla f_0 = \mathbf{i} - 4\mathbf{j}$.   ∎

FUNCTIONS OF THREE VARIABLES

The directional derivative and gradient concepts can easily be extended to functions of three or more variables. For a function of three variables, $f(x, y, z)$, the gradient ∇f is defined by

$$\nabla f = f_x \mathbf{i} + f_y \mathbf{j} + f_z \mathbf{k}$$

and the directional derivative $D_{\mathbf{u}} f$ of $f(x, y, z)$ at $P_0(x_0, y_0, z_0)$ in the direction of the unit vector $\mathbf{u}$ is given by

$$D_{\mathbf{u}} f = \nabla f_0 \cdot \mathbf{u}$$

where, as before, ∇f_0 is the gradient ∇f evaluated at P_0. The basic properties of the gradient of $f(x, y)$ (Theorem 11.8) are still valid, as is the maximal direction property of Theorem 11.9. Similar definitions and properties are valid for functions of more than three variables.

EXAMPLE 5   Directional derivative of a function of three variables

Let $f(x, y, z) = xy \sin(xz)$. Find ∇f_0 at the point $P_0(1, -2, \pi)$ and then compute the directional derivative of f at P_0 in the direction of the vector $\mathbf{v} = -2\mathbf{i} + 3\mathbf{j} - 5\mathbf{k}$.

Solution

Begin with the partial derivatives:

$$f_x = y \sin(xz) + xy(z \cos(xz)); \quad f_x(1, -2, \pi) = -2 \sin \pi - 2\pi \cos \pi = 2\pi$$
$$f_y = x \sin(xz); \quad f_y(1, -2, \pi) = 1 \sin \pi = 0$$
$$f_z = xy(x \cos(xz)); \quad f_z(1, -2, \pi) = (1)(-2)(1) \cos \pi = 2$$

Thus, the gradient of f at P_0 is

$$\nabla f_0 = 2\pi \mathbf{i} + 2\mathbf{k}$$

To find $D_{\mathbf{u}} f$ we need $\mathbf{u}$, the unit vector in the direction of $\mathbf{v}$:

$$\mathbf{u} = \frac{\mathbf{v}}{\|\mathbf{v}\|} = \frac{-2\mathbf{i} + 3\mathbf{j} - 5\mathbf{k}}{\sqrt{(-2)^2 + (3)^2 + (-5)^2}} = \frac{1}{\sqrt{38}}(-2\mathbf{i} + 3\mathbf{j} - 5\mathbf{k})$$

Finally,

$$D_{\mathbf{u}} f(1, -2, \pi) = \nabla f_0 \cdot \mathbf{u} = \frac{1}{\sqrt{38}}(-4\pi - 10) \approx -3.66 \quad \blacksquare$$

NORMAL PROPERTY OF THE GRADIENT

Suppose S is a level surface of the function defined by $f(x, y, z)$; that is, $f(x, y, z) = K$ for some constant K. Then if $P_0(x_0, y_0, z_0)$ is a point on S, the following theorem shows that the gradient ∇f_0 at P_0 is a vector that is **normal** (that is, orthogonal) to the tangent plane surface at P_0 (see Figure 11.30).

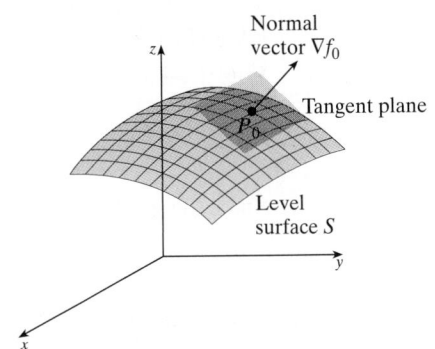

Figure 11.30   The normal property of the gradient

THEOREM 11.10   The normal property of the gradient

Suppose the function f is differentiable at the point P_0 and that the gradient at P_0 satisfies $\nabla f_0 \neq \mathbf{0}$. Then ∇f_0 is orthogonal to the level surface of f through P_0.

Proof   Let C be any smooth curve on the level surface $f(x, y, z) = K$ that passes through $P_0(x_0, y_0, z_0)$, and describe the curve C by the vector function $\mathbf{R}(t) = x(t)\mathbf{i} + y(t)\mathbf{j} + z(t)\mathbf{k}$ for all t in some interval I. We will show that the gradient ∇f_0 is orthogonal to the tangent vector $d\mathbf{R}/dt$ at P_0.

Because C lies on the level surface, any point $P(x(t), y(t), z(t))$ on C must satisfy $f[x(t), y(t), z(t)] = K$, and by applying the chain rule, we obtain

$$\frac{d}{dt}[f(x(t), y(t), z(t))] = f_x(x, y, z)\frac{dx}{dt} + f_y(x, y, z)\frac{dy}{dt} + f_z(x, y, z)\frac{dz}{dt}$$

Suppose $t = t_0$ at P_0. Then

$$\frac{d}{dt}[f(x(t), y(t), z(t))]\Big|_{t=t_0}$$

$$= f_x(x(t_0), y(t_0), z(t_0))\frac{dx}{dt} + f_y(x(t_0), y(t_0), z(t_0))\frac{dy}{dt} + f_z(x(t_0), y(t_0), z(t_0))\frac{dz}{dt}$$

$$= \nabla f_0 \cdot \frac{d\mathbf{R}}{dt}$$

since $\dfrac{d\mathbf{R}}{dt} = \dfrac{dx}{dt}\mathbf{i} + \dfrac{dy}{dt}\mathbf{j} + \dfrac{dz}{dt}\mathbf{k}$. We also know that $f(x(t), y(t), z(t)) = K$ for all t in I (because the curve C lies on the level surface $f(x, y, z) = K$). Thus, we have

$$\frac{d}{dt}\{f[x(t), y(t), z(t)]\} = \frac{d}{dt}(K) = 0$$

and it follows that $\nabla f_0 \cdot \dfrac{d\mathbf{R}}{dt} = 0$. We are given that $\nabla f_0 \neq \mathbf{0}$, and $d\mathbf{R}/dt \neq \mathbf{0}$ because the curve C is smooth. Therefore, ∇f_0 is orthogonal to $d\mathbf{R}/dt$, as required. ❏

→ What This Says   The gradient ∇f_0 at each point P_0 on the surface $f(x, y, z) = K$ is orthogonal at P_0 to the tangent vector $\mathbf{T} = \dfrac{d\mathbf{R}}{dt}$ of each curve C on the surface that passes through P_0. Thus, all these tangent vectors lie in a single plane through P_0 with normal vector $\mathbf{N} = \nabla f_0$. This plane is the *tangent plane* to the surface at P_0.

EXAMPLE 6   Finding a vector that is normal to a level surface

Find a vector that is normal to the level surface $x^2 + 2xy - yz + 3z^2 = 7$ at the point $P_0(1, 1, -1)$.

Solution

Since the gradient vector at P_0 is perpendicular to the level surface, we have

$$\nabla f = f_x\mathbf{i} + f_y\mathbf{j} + f_z\mathbf{k} = (2x + 2y)\mathbf{i} + (2x - z)\mathbf{j} + (6z - y)\mathbf{k}$$

At the point $(1, 1, -1)$, $\nabla f_0 = 4\mathbf{i} + 3\mathbf{j} - 7\mathbf{k}$ is the required normal. ∎

Here is an example in which f involves only two variables, so $f(x, y) = K$ is a level curve in the plane instead of a level surface in space.

EXAMPLE 7   Finding a vector normal to a level curve

Sketch the level curve corresponding to $C = 1$ for the function $f(x, y) = x^2 - y^2$ and find a normal vector at the point $P_0(2, \sqrt{3})$.

Solution

The level curve for $C = 1$ is a hyperbola given by $x^2 - y^2 = 1$, as shown in Figure 11.31. The gradient vector is perpendicular to the level curve. We have

$$\nabla f = f_x\mathbf{i} + f_y\mathbf{j} = 2x\mathbf{i} - 2y\mathbf{j}$$

so at the point $(2, \sqrt{3})$, $\nabla f_0 = 4\mathbf{i} - 2\sqrt{3}\mathbf{j}$ is the required normal. This normal vector and a few others are shown in Figure 11.31. ∎

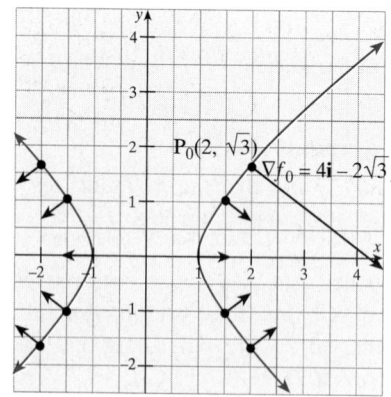

Plane $z = 1$

Figure 11.31 The level curve $x^2 - y^2 = 1$

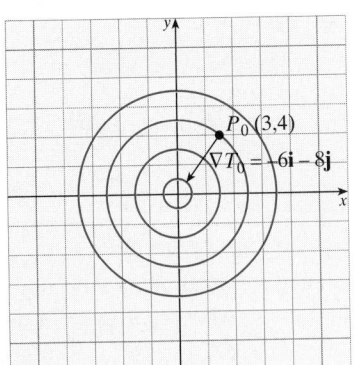

Figure 11.32 Isotherms of $T(x, y) = x^2 + y^2$. Heat flow at P_0 is in the direction of $-\nabla T_0 = -6\mathbf{i} - 8\mathbf{j}$.

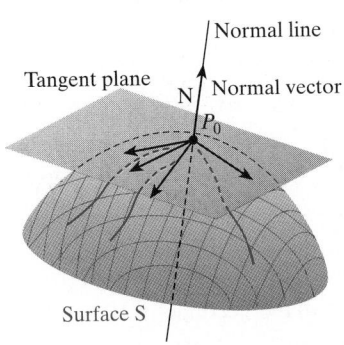

Figure 11.33 Tangent plane and normal line

Tangent Plane and Normal Line to a Surface

EXAMPLE 8 Heat flow application

The set of points (x, y) with $0 \le x \le 5$ and $0 \le y \le 5$ is a square in the first quadrant of the xy-plane. Suppose this square is heated in such a way that $T(x, y) = x^2 + y^2$ is the temperature at the point $P(x, y)$. In what direction will heat flow from the point $P_0(3, 4)$?

Solution

The flow of heat in the region is given by a vector function $\mathbf{H}(x, y)$, whose value at each point (x, y) depends on x and y. From physics it is known that $\mathbf{H}(x, y)$ will be perpendicular to the isothermal curves $T(x, y) = C$ for C constant. The gradient ∇T and all its multiples point in such a direction. Therefore, we can express the heat flow as $\mathbf{H} = -k\nabla T$, where k is a positive constant (called the *thermal conductivity*). The negative sign is introduced to account for the fact that heat flows "downhill" (that is, in the direction of decreasing temperature).

Because $T(3, 4) = 25$, the point $P_0(3, 4)$ lies on the isotherm $T(x, y) = 25$, which is part of the circle $x^2 + y^2 = 25$, as shown in Figure 11.32. We know that the heat flow $\mathbf{H}_0$ at P_0 will satisfy $\mathbf{H}_0 = -k\nabla T_0$, where ∇T_0 is the gradient at P_0. Because $\nabla T = 2x\mathbf{i} + 2y\mathbf{j}$, we see that $\nabla T_0 = 6\mathbf{i} + 8\mathbf{j}$. Thus, the heat flow at P_0 satisfies

$$\mathbf{H}_0 = -k\nabla T_0 = -k(6\mathbf{i} + 8\mathbf{j})$$

Because the thermal conductivity k is positive, we can say that heat flows from P_0 in the direction of the unit vector $\mathbf{u}$ given by

$$\mathbf{u} = \frac{-(6\mathbf{i} + 8\mathbf{j})}{\sqrt{(-6)^2 + (-8)^2}} = -\frac{3}{5}\mathbf{i} - \frac{4}{5}\mathbf{j} \qquad \blacksquare$$

TANGENT PLANES AND NORMAL LINES

Tangent planes and normal lines to a surface are the natural extensions to $\mathbb{R}^3$ of the tangent and normal lines we examined in $\mathbb{R}^2$. Suppose S is a surface and $\mathbf{N}$ is a vector normal to S at the point P_0. We would intuitively expect the normal line and the tangent plane to S at P_0 to be, respectively, the line through P_0 with the direction of $\mathbf{N}$ and the plane through P_0 with normal $\mathbf{N}$ (see Figure 11.33). These observations lead us to the following definition.

> Suppose the surface S has a nonzero normal vector $\mathbf{N}$ at the point P_0. Then the line through P_0 parallel to $\mathbf{N}$ is called the **normal line** to S at P_0, and the plane through P_0 with normal vector $\mathbf{N}$ is the **tangent plane** to S at P_0.

We would expect a surface S with the representation $z = f(x, y)$ to have a non-vertical tangent plane at each point where $\nabla f \ne \mathbf{0}$. In particular, if S has an equation of the form $F(x, y, z) = C$, where C is a constant and F is a function differentiable at P_0, the normal property of a gradient tells us that the gradient ∇F_0 at P_0 is normal to S (if $\nabla F_0 \ne \mathbf{0}$) and that S must therefore have a tangent plane at P_0.

EXAMPLE 9 Finding the tangent plane and normal line to a given surface

Find equations for the tangent plane and the normal line at the point $P_0(1, -1, 2)$ on the surface S given by $x^2y + y^2z + z^2x = 5$.

Solution

We need to rewrite this problem so that the normal property of the gradient theorem applies. Let $F(x, y, z) = x^2y + y^2z + z^2x$, and consider S to be the level surface $F(x, y, z) = 5$. The gradient ∇F is normal to S at P_0. We find that

$$\nabla F(x, y, z) = (2xy + z^2)\mathbf{i} + (x^2 + 2yz)\mathbf{j} + (y^2 + 2xz)\mathbf{k}$$

so a normal vector at P_0 is

$$\mathbf{N} = \nabla F_0 = \nabla F(1, -1, 2) = 2\mathbf{i} - 3\mathbf{j} + 5\mathbf{k}$$

Hence, the required tangent plane is

$$2(x - 1) - 3(y + 1) + 5(z - 2) = 0 \qquad \text{or} \qquad 2x - 3y + 5z = 15$$

The normal line to the surface at P_0 is

$$x = 1 + 2t, \qquad y = -1 - 3t, \qquad z = 2 + 5t \qquad \blacksquare$$

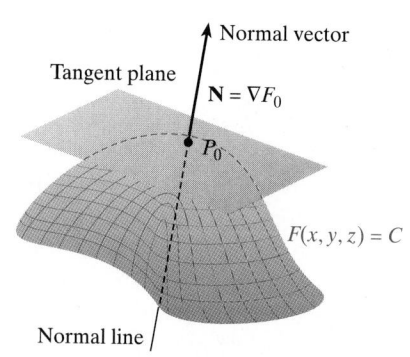

Figure 11.34 The tangent plane and normal line to a surface

By generalizing the procedure illustrated in the preceding example, we are led to the following formulas for the tangent plane and normal line. (Also see Figure 11.34.)

Formulas for the Tangent Plane and Normal Lines to a Surface

Suppose S is a surface with the equation $F(x, y, z) = C$ and let $P_0(x_0, y_0, z_0)$ be a point on S where F is differentiable with $\nabla F_0 \neq \mathbf{0}$. Then the **equation of the tangent plane** to S at P_0 is

$$F_x(x_0, y_0, z_0)(x - x_0) + F_y(x_0, y_0, z_0)(y - y_0) + F_z(x_0, y_0, z_0)(z - z_0) = 0$$

and the **normal line** to S at P_0 has parametric equations

$$x = x_0 + F_x(x_0, y_0, z_0)t$$
$$y = y_0 + F_y(x_0, y_0, z_0)t$$
$$z = z_0 + F_z(x_0, y_0, z_0)t$$

Note if $z = f(x, y)$, we have $F(x, y, z) = f(x, y) - z = 0$. Then $F_x = f_x$, $F_y = f_y$, and $F_z = -1$ and the equation of the tangent plane becomes

$$f_x(x_0, y_0, z_0)(x - x_0) + f_y(x_0, y_0, z_0)(y - y_0) - (z - z_0) = 0$$

which is equivalent to the tangent plane formula given in Section 11.4.

EXAMPLE 10   Equations of the tangent plane and the normal line

Find the equations for the tangent plane and the normal line to the cone $z^2 = x^2 + y^2$ at the point where $x = 3$, $y = 4$, and $z > 0$.

Solution

If $P_0(x_0, y_0, z_0)$ is the point of tangency and $x_0 = 3$, $y_0 = 4$, and $z_0 > 0$, then

$$z_0 = \sqrt{x_0^2 + y_0^2} = \sqrt{9 + 16} = 5$$

If we consider $F(x, y, z) = x^2 + y^2 - z^2$, then the cone can be regarded as the level surface $F(x, y, z) = 0$. The partial derivatives of F are

$$F_x = 2x \qquad F_y = 2y \qquad F_z = -2z$$

so at $P_0(3, 4, 5)$,

$$F_x(3, 4, 5) = 6, \qquad F_y(3, 4, 5) = 8, \qquad F_z(3, 4, 5) = -10$$

Thus the tangent plane has the equation

$$6(x - 3) + 8(y - 4) - 10(z - 5) = 0$$

or $3x + 4y - 5z = 0$, and the normal line is given parametrically by the equations

$$x = 3 + 6t, \qquad y = 4 + 8t, \qquad z = 5 - 10t \qquad \blacksquare$$

11.6   PROBLEM SET

A *Find the gradient of the functions given in Problems 1–10.*

1. $f(x, y) = x^2 - 2xy$

2. $f(x, y) = 3x + 4y^2$

3. $f(x, y) = \dfrac{y}{x} + \dfrac{x}{y}$

4. $f(x, y) = \ln(x^2 + y^2)$

5. $f(x, y) = xe^{3-y}$

6. $f(x, y) = e^{x+y}$

7. $f(x, y) = \sin(x + 2y)$

8. $f(x, y, z) = xyz^2$

9. $g(x, y, z) = xe^{y+3z}$

10. $f(x, y, z) = \dfrac{xy - 1}{z + x}$

Compute the directional derivative of the functions given in Problems 11–16 at the point P_0 in the direction of the given vector **v**.

Function	Point P_0	Vector v
11. $f(x, y) = x^2 + xy$	$(1, -2)$	$\mathbf{i} + \mathbf{j}$
12. $f(x, y) = \dfrac{e^{-x}}{y}$	$(2, -1)$	$-\mathbf{i} + \mathbf{j}$
13. $f(x, y) = \ln(x^2 + 3y)$	$(1, 1)$	$\mathbf{i} + \mathbf{j}$
14. $f(x, y) = \ln(3x + y^2)$	$(0, 1)$	$\mathbf{i} - \mathbf{j}$
15. $f(x, y) = \sec(xy - y^3)$	$(2, 0)$	$-\mathbf{i} - 3\mathbf{j}$
16. $f(x, y) = \sin xy$	$(\sqrt{\pi}, \sqrt{\pi})$	$3\pi\mathbf{i} - \pi\mathbf{j}$

Find a unit vector that is normal to each surface given in Problems 17–24 at the prescribed point, and the standard form of the equation of the tangent plane at that point.

17. $x^2 + y^2 + z^2 = 3$ at $(1, -1, 1)$

18. $x^4 + y^4 + z^4 = 3$ at $(1, -1 - 1)$

19. $\cos z = \sin(x + y)$ at $\left(\frac{\pi}{2}, \frac{\pi}{2}, \frac{\pi}{2}\right)$

20. $\sin(x + y) + \tan(y + z) = 1$ at $\left(\frac{\pi}{4}, \frac{\pi}{4}, -\frac{\pi}{4}\right)$

21. $\ln\left(\dfrac{x}{y - z}\right) = 0$ at $(2, 5, 3)$

22. $\ln\left(\dfrac{x - y}{y + z}\right) = x - z$ at $(1, 0, 1)$

23. $ze^{x+2y} = 3$ at $(2, -1, 3)$

24. $ze^{x^2 - y^2} = 3$ at $(1, 1, 3)$

Find the direction from P_0 in which the given function f increases most rapidly and compute the magnitude of the greatest rate of increase in Problems 25–34.

25. $f(x, y) = 3x + 2y - 1$; $P_0(1, -1)$

26. $f(x, y) = 1 - x^2 - y^2$; $P_0(1, 2)$

27. $f(x, y) = x^3 + y^3$; $P_0(3, -3)$

28. $f(x, y) = ax + by + c$; $P_0(a, b)$

29. $f(x, y, z) = ax^2 + by^2 + cz^2$; $P_0(a, b, c)$; assume $a^4 + b^4 + c^4 \neq 0$.

30. $f(x, y) = ax^3 + by^3$; $P_0(a, b)$; assume $a^6 + b^6 \neq 0$.

31. $f(x, y) = \ln\sqrt{x^2 + y^2}$; $P_0(1, 2)$

32. $f(x, y) = \sin xy$; $P_0\left(\frac{\sqrt{\pi}}{3}, \frac{\sqrt{\pi}}{2}\right)$

33. $f(x, y, z) = (x + y)^2 + (y + z)^2 + (x + z)^2$; $P_0(2, -1, 2)$

34. $f(x, y, z) = z\ln\left(\frac{y}{x}\right)$; $P_0(1, e, -1)$

In Problems 35–38, find a unit vector that is normal to the given graph at the point $P_0(x_0, y_0)$ on the graph. Assume that a, b, and c are constants.

35. the line $ax + by = c$

36. the circle $x^2 + y^2 = a^2$

37. the ellipse $\dfrac{x^2}{a^2} + \dfrac{y^2}{b^2} = 1$

38. the hyperbola $\dfrac{x^2}{a^2} - \dfrac{y^2}{b^2} = 1$

39. Find the directional derivative of $f(x, y) = x^2 + y^2$ at the point $P_0(1, 1)$ in the direction of the unit vector **u** shown in Figure 11.35.

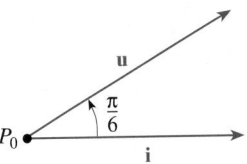

Figure 11.35   Problem 39

40. Find the directional derivative of $f(x, y) = x^2 + xy + y^2$ at $P_0(1, -1)$ in the direction toward the origin.

41. Find the directional derivative of $f(x, y) = e^{x^2 y^2}$ at $P_0(1, -1)$ in the direction toward $Q(2, 3)$.

42. Let $f(x, y, z) = 2x^2 - y^2 + 3z^2 - 8x - 4y + 201$, and let P_0 be the point $\left(2, -\frac{3}{2}, \frac{1}{2}\right)$

    a. Find ∇f_0.

    b. Find $\cos\theta$, where θ is the angle between ∇f_0 and the vector toward the origin from P_0.

B **43.** Let $f(x, y, z) = xyz$, and let **u** be a unit vector perpendicular to both $\mathbf{v} = \mathbf{i} - 2\mathbf{j} + 3\mathbf{k}$ and $\mathbf{w} = 2\mathbf{i} + \mathbf{j} - \mathbf{k}$. Find the directional derivative of f at $P_0(1, -1, 2)$ in the direction of **u**.

44. Let $f(x, y, z) = ye^{x+z} + ze^{y-x}$. At the point $P(2, 2, -2)$, find the unit vector pointing in the direction of most rapid increase of f.

45. Modeling Problem   Suppose a box in space given by $0 \leq x \leq 2$, $0 \leq y \leq 2$, $0 \leq z \leq 2$ is temperature-controlled so that the temperature at a point $P(x, y, z)$ in the box is modeled by $T(x, y, z) = xy + yz + xz$. A heat-seeking missile is located at $P_0(1, 1, 1)$. In what direction will the missile move for the temperature to increase as quickly as possible? What is the maximum rate of change of the temperature at the point P_0?

46. Modeling Problem   A metal plate covering the rectangular region $0 < x \leq 6, 0 < y \leq 5$ is charged electrically in such a way that the potential at each point (x, y) is inversely proportional to the square of its distance from the origin. If an object is at the point $(3, 4)$, in which direction should it move to increase the potential most rapidly?

47. A hiker is walking on a mountain path when it begins to rain. If the surface of the mountain is modeled by $z = 1 - 3x^2 - \frac{5}{2}y^2$ (where x, y, and z are in miles) and the rain begins when the hiker is at the point $P_0\left(\frac{1}{4}, -\frac{1}{2}, \frac{3}{16}\right)$, in what direction should she head to descend the mountainside most rapidly?

48. Let f have continuous partial derivatives, and assume the maximal directional derivative of f at $(0, 0)$ is equal to 100 and is attained in the direction toward $(3, -4)$. Find the gradient ∇f at $(0, 0)$.

49. Suppose at the point $P_0(-1, 2)$, a certain function $f(x, y)$ has directional derivative 8 in the direction of $\mathbf{v}_1 = 3\mathbf{i} - 4\mathbf{j}$ and 1 in the direction of $\mathbf{v}_2 = 12\mathbf{i} + 5\mathbf{j}$. What is the directional derivative of f at P_0 in the direction of $\mathbf{v} = 3\mathbf{i} - 5\mathbf{j}$?

50. The directional derivative of $f(x, y, z)$ at the point P_0 is greatest in the direction of $\mathbf{v} = \mathbf{i} + \mathbf{j} - \mathbf{k}$ and has value $5\sqrt{3}$ in this direction. What is the directional derivative of f at P_0 in the direction of $\mathbf{w} = \mathbf{i} + \mathbf{j}$?

51. Let f have continuous partial derivatives and suppose the maximal directional derivative of f at $P_0(1, 2)$ has magnitude 50 and is attained in the direction from P_0 toward $Q(3, -4)$. Use this information to find $\nabla f(1, 2)$.

52. Let $T(x, y) = 1 - x^2 - 2y^2$ be the temperature at each point $P(x, y)$ in the plane. A heat-loving bug is placed in the plane at the point $P_0(-1, 1)$. Find the path that the bug should take to stay as warm as possible. *Hint*: Assume that at each point on the bug's path, the tangent line will point in the direction in which T increases most rapidly.

53. **a.** Show that the ellipsoid

$$\frac{x^2}{a^2} + \frac{y^2}{b^2} + \frac{z^2}{c^2} = 1$$

has a tangent plane at $P_0(x_0, y_0, z_0)$ with the equation

$$\frac{x_0 x}{a^2} + \frac{y_0 y}{b^2} + \frac{z_0 z}{c^2} = 1$$

   b. Find the equation for the tangent plane to the hyperboloid of one sheet

$$\frac{x^2}{a^2} + \frac{y^2}{b^2} - \frac{z^2}{c^2} = 1$$

   at the point $P_0(x_0, y_0, z_0)$.

   c. Find the equation for the tangent plane to the elliptic paraboloid

$$\frac{z}{c} = \frac{x^2}{a^2} + \frac{y^2}{b^2}$$

   at the point $P_0(x_0, y_0, z_0)$.

54. **Spy problem**   Just as the Spy is about to catch up with Scélérat (Problem 70 of Chapter 10 Supplementary Problems), the snow gives way and he falls into a cavern. He staggers to his feet and removes his skis. Why is it so warm? Good grief— the cave is a large roasting oven! Fortunately, he is wearing his heat-detector ring, which indicates the direction of greatest temperature decrease. Suppose the bunker is coordinatized so that the temperature at each point (x, y) on the floor of the bunker is given by

$$T(x, y) = 3(x - 6)^2 + 1.5(y - 1)^2 + 41$$

degrees Fahrenheit, where x and y are in feet. The Spy begins at the point $(1, 5)$ and stumbles across the room at the rate of 4 ft/min, always moving in the direction of maximum temperature decrease. But he can last no more than 2 minutes under these conditions! Assuming that there is an escape hole at the point where the temperature is minimal, does he make it or is the Spy toast at last?

55. Recall that an ellipse is the set of all points $P(x, y)$ such that the sum of the distances from P to two fixed points (the *foci*) is constant. Let $P(x, y)$ be a point on the ellipse, and let r_1 and r_2 denote the respective distances from P to the two foci, F_1 and F_2 as shown in Figure 11.36.

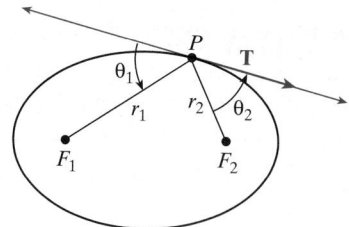

Figure 11.36   Unit tangent to an ellipse

   a. Show that $\mathbf{T} \cdot \nabla(r_1 + r_2) = 0$, where $\mathbf{T}$ is a unit tangent to the ellipse at P.

   b. Use part **a** to show that the tangent line to the ellipse at P makes equal angles with the lines joining P to the foci (that is, $\theta_1 = \theta_2$ in Figure 11.36).

56. **Modeling Problem**   A particle P_1 with mass m_1 is located at the origin, and a particle P_2 with mass 1 unit is located at the point (x, y, z). According to Newton's law of universal gravitation, the force P_1 exerts on P_2 is modeled by

$$\mathbf{F} = \frac{-Gm_1(x\mathbf{i} + y\mathbf{j} + z\mathbf{k})}{r^3}$$

where r is the distance between P_1 and P_2, and G is the gravitational constant.

   a. Starting from the fact that $r^2 = x^2 + y^2 + z^2$, show that

$$\frac{\partial}{\partial x}\left(\frac{1}{r}\right) = \frac{-x}{r^3}, \quad \frac{\partial}{\partial y}\left(\frac{1}{r}\right) = \frac{-y}{r^3}, \quad \frac{\partial}{\partial z}\left(\frac{1}{r}\right) = \frac{-z}{r^3}$$

   b. The function $V = -Gm_1/r$ is called the *potential energy* function for the system. Show that $\mathbf{F} = -\nabla V$.

57. Verify each of the following properties for functions of two variables.

   a. $\nabla c = \mathbf{0}$ for constant c

   b. $\nabla(f + g) = \nabla f + \nabla g$

   c. $\nabla(f/g) = \dfrac{g\nabla f - f\nabla g}{g^2}$, $g \neq 0$

   d. $\nabla(fg) = f\nabla g + g\nabla f$

58. Find the parametric equations for the tangent line to the curve of intersection of the paraboloid $z = x^2 + y^2$ and the ellipsoid $2x^2 + 2y^2 + z^2 = 8$ at $P_0(-1, 1, 2)$.

59. Find a general formula for the directional derivative $D_{\mathbf{u}} f$ of the function $f(x, y)$ at the point $P(x_0, y_0)$ in the direction of the unit vector $\mathbf{u} = (\cos\theta)\mathbf{i} + (\sin\theta)\mathbf{j}$. Apply your formula to obtain the directional derivative of $f(x, y) = xy^2 e^{x-2y}$ at $P_0(-1, 3)$ in the direction of the unit vector

$$\mathbf{u} = \left(\cos\tfrac{\pi}{6}\right)\mathbf{i} + \left(\sin\tfrac{\pi}{6}\right)\mathbf{j}$$

60. Suppose that $\mathbf{u}$ and $\mathbf{v}$ are unit vectors and that f has continuous partial derivatives. Show that

$$D_{\mathbf{u}+\mathbf{v}} f = \frac{1}{\|\mathbf{u} + \mathbf{v}\|} (D_{\mathbf{u}} f + D_{\mathbf{v}} f)$$

61. **Counterexample Problem**   If f, f_x, and f_y are continuous and $\nabla f(x, y) = \mathbf{0}$ inside the disk $x^2 + y^2 < 1$, then either show that $f(x, y)$ is a constant function inside the disk or find a counterexample.

62. **Counterexample Problem**   If f is differentiable at $P_0(x_0, y_0)$ and $D_{\mathbf{u}} f(x_0, y_0) = 0$ for unit vectors $\mathbf{u}_1$ and $\mathbf{u}_2$, where $\mathbf{u}_1 \times \mathbf{u}_2 \neq \mathbf{0}$, then show that $D_{\mathbf{u}} f(x_0, y_0) = 0$ for every unit vector $\mathbf{u}$, or find a counterexample.

63. Let $\mathbf{R} = x\mathbf{i} + y\mathbf{j} + z\mathbf{k}$, and let $r = \|\mathbf{R}\| = \sqrt{x^2 + y^2 + z^2}$.

   a. Show that ∇r is a unit vector in the direction of $\mathbf{R}$.

   b. Show that $\nabla(r^n) = nr^{n-2}\mathbf{R}$, for any positive integer n.

64. Suppose the surfaces $F(x, y, z) = 0$ and $G(x, y, z) = 0$ both pass through the point $P_0(x_0, y_0, z_0)$ and that the gradients ∇F_0 and ∇G_0 both exist. Show that the two surfaces are tangent at P_0 if and only if $\nabla F_0 \times \nabla G_0 = \mathbf{0}$.

11.7   Extrema of Functions of Two Variables

IN THIS SECTION relative extrema, second partials test, absolute extrema of continuous functions, least squares approximation of data

There are many practical situations in which it is necessary or useful to know the largest and smallest values of a function of two variables. For example, if $T(x, y)$ is the temperature at a point (x, y) in a plate, where are the hottest and coldest points in the plate and what are these extreme temperatures? If a hazardous waste dump is bounded by the curve $F(x, y) = 0$, what are the largest and smallest distances to the boundary from a given interior point P_0? We begin our study of extrema with some terminology.

Absolute Extrema

> The function $f(x, y)$ is said to have an **absolute maximum** at (x_0, y_0) if $f(x_0, y_0) \geq f(x, y)$ for all (x, y) in the domain D of f. Similarly, f has an **absolute minimum** at (x_0, y_0) if $f(x_0, y_0) \leq f(x, y)$ for all (x, y) in D. Collectively, absolute maxima and minima are called **absolute extrema**.

In Chapter 4, we located absolute extrema of a function of one variable by first finding *relative extrema*, those values of $f(x)$ that are larger or smaller than those at all nearby points. The relative extrema of a function of two variables may be defined as follows.

Relative Extrema

> Let f be a function defined on a region containing (x_0, y_0). Then
>
> $f(x_0, y_0)$ is a **relative maximum** if $f(x, y) \leq f(x_0, y_0)$ for all (x, y) in an open disk containing (x_0, y_0).
>
> $f(x_0, y_0)$ is a **relative minimum** if $f(x, y) \geq f(x_0, y_0)$ for all (x, y) in an open disk containing (x_0, y_0).
>
> Collectively, relative maxima and minima are called **relative extrema**.

RELATIVE EXTREMA

In Chapter 4, we observed that relative extrema of the function f correspond to "peaks and valleys" on the graph of f, and the same observation can be made about relative extrema in the two-variable case, as seen in Figure 11.37.

For a function f of one variable, we found that the relative extrema occur where $f'(x) = 0$ or $f'(x)$ does not exist. The following theorem shows that the relative extrema of a function of two variables can be located similarly.

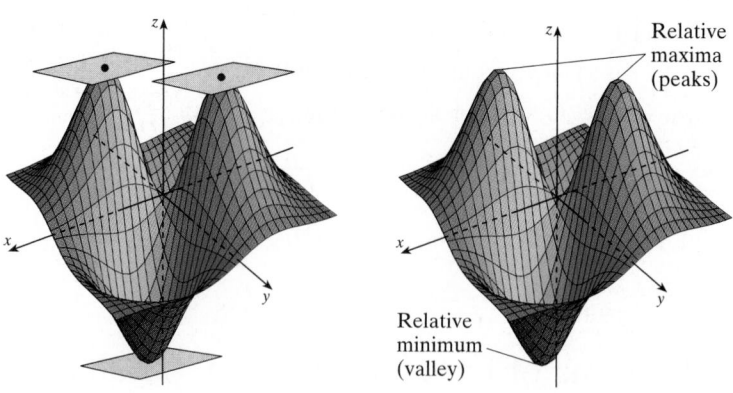

Figure 11.37 Relative extrema correspond to peaks and valleys

THEOREM 11.11 **Partial derivative criteria for relative extrema**

If f has a relative extremum (maximum or minimum) at $P_0(x_0, y_0)$ and partial derivatives f_x and f_y both exist at (x_0, y_0), then

$$f_x(x_0, y_0) = f_y(x_0, y_0) = 0$$

Proof Let $F(x) = f(x, y_0)$. Then $F(x)$ must have a relative extremum at $x = x_0$, so $F'(x_0) = 0$, which means that $f_x(x_0, y_0) = 0$. Similarly, $G(y) = f(x_0, y)$ has a relative extremum at $y = y_0$, so $G'(y_0) = 0$ and $f_y(x_0, y_0) = 0$. Thus, we must have both $f_x(x_0, y_0) = 0$ and $f_y(x_0, y_0) = 0$, as claimed. ❑

WARNING There is a horizontal tangent plane at each extreme point where the first partial derivatives exist. However, this **does not** say that whenever a horizontal tangent plane occurs at a point P, there must be an extremum there. All that can be said is that such a point P is a possible location for a relative extremum.

In single-variable calculus, we referred to a number x_0, where $f'(x_0)$ does not exist or $f'(x_0) = 0$ as a *critical number*. This terminology is extended to functions of two variables as follows.

Critical Points

A **critical point** of a function f defined on an open set D is a point (x_0, y_0) in D where either one of the following is true:

a. $f_x(x_0, y_0) = f_y(x_0, y_0) = 0$.
b. At least one of $f_x(x_0, y_0)$ or $f_y(x_0, y_0)$ does not exist at (x_0, y_0).

EXAMPLE 1 **Distinguishing critical points**

Discuss the nature of the critical point $(0, 0)$ for the quadric surfaces

a. $z = x^2 + y^2$ **b.** $z = 1 - x^2 - y^2$ **c.** $z = y^2 - x^2$

Solution

The graphs of these quadric surfaces are shown in Figure 11.38. Let $f(x, y) = x^2 + y^2$, $g(x, y) = 1 - x^2 - y^2$, and $h(x, y) = y^2 - x^2$. We find the critical points:

a. $f_x(x, y) = 2x$, $f_y(x, y) = 2y$; critical point $(0, 0)$. The function f has a relative minimum at $(0, 0)$ because x^2 and y^2 are both nonnegative, yielding $x^2 + y^2 > 0$ for all nonzero x and y.

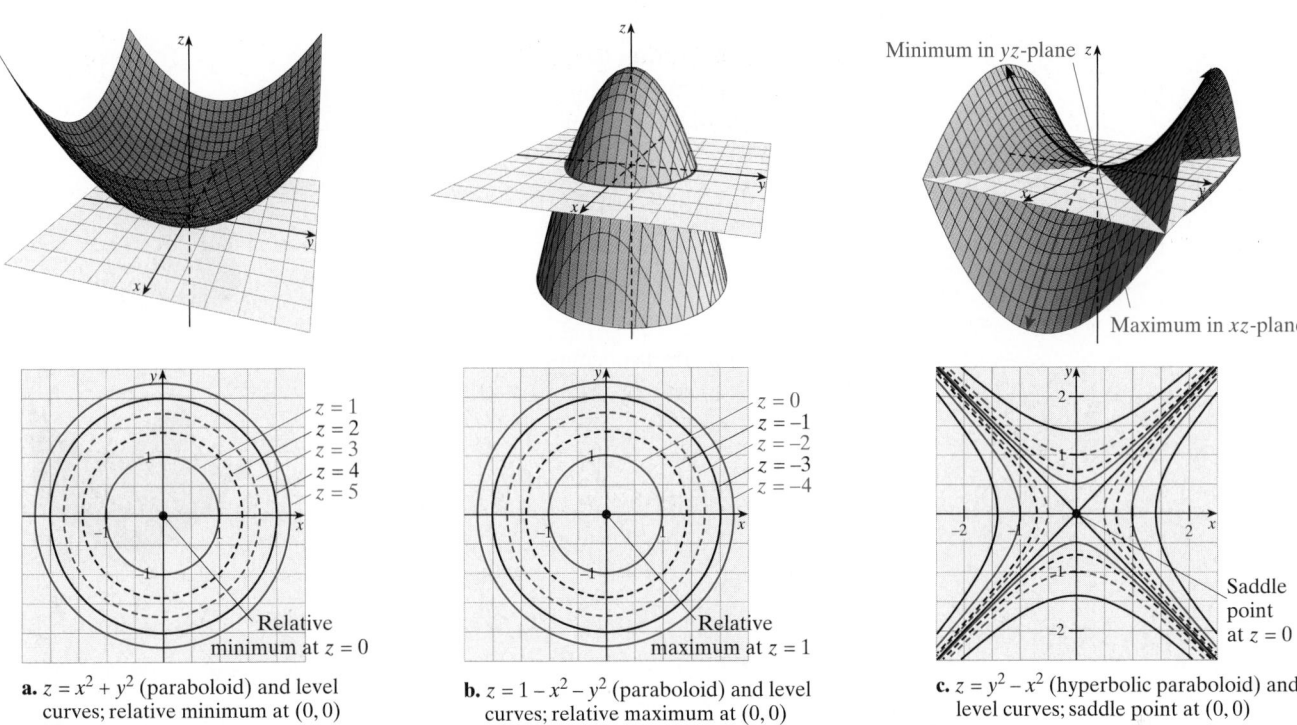

a. $z = x^2 + y^2$ (paraboloid) and level curves; relative minimum at $(0, 0)$

b. $z = 1 - x^2 - y^2$ (paraboloid) and level curves; relative maximum at $(0, 0)$

c. $z = y^2 - x^2$ (hyperbolic paraboloid) and level curves; saddle point at $(0, 0)$

Figure 11.38 Classification of critical points

b. $g_x(x, y) = -2x$, $g_y(x, y) = -2y$; critical point $(0, 0)$. Since $z = 1 - x^2 - y^2$, it follows that $z \leq 1$ with a relative maximum occurring where x^2 and y^2 are both 0; that is, at $(0, 0)$.

c. $h_x(x, y) = -2x$, $h_y(x, y) = 2y$; critical point $(0, 0)$. The function h has neither a relative maximum nor a relative minimum at $(0, 0)$. When $z = 0$, h is a minimum on the y-axis (where $x = 0$) and a maximum on the x-axis (where $y = 0$). ∎

A critical point $P_0(x_0, y_0)$ is called a **saddle point** of $f(x, y)$ if every open disk centered at P_0 contains points in the domain of f that satisfy $f(x, y) > f(x_0, y_0)$ as well as points in the domain of f that satisfy $f(x, y) < f(x_0, y_0)$. An example of a saddle point is $(0, 0)$ on the hyperbolic paraboloid $z = y^2 - x^2$, as shown in Figure 11.38c.

SECOND PARTIALS TEST

The previous example points to the need for some sort of a test to determine the nature of a critical point. In Chapter 4, we developed the second derivative test for functions of one variable as a means for determining whether a particular critical number c of f corresponds to a relative maximum or minimum. If $f'(c) = 0$, then according to this test, a relative maximum occurs at $x = c$ if $f''(c) < 0$ and a relative minimum occurs if $f''(c) > 0$. If $f''(c) = 0$, the test is inconclusive. The analogous result for the two-variable case may be stated as follows.

THEOREM 11.12 Second partials test

Let $f(x, y)$ have a critical point at $P_0(x_0, y_0)$ and assume that f has continuous second-order partial derivatives in a disk centered at (x_0, y_0). The *discriminant* of f is the expression

$$D = f_{xx} f_{yy} - f_{xy}^2$$

Then

A **relative maximum** occurs at P_0 if
$D(x_0, y_0) > 0$ and $f_{xx}(x_0, y_0) < 0$
(or, equivalently, $D(x_0, y_0) > 0$ and
$f_{yy}(x_0, y_0) < 0$).

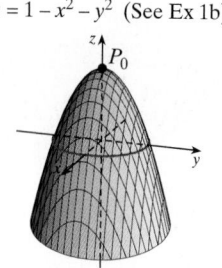

$z = 1 - x^2 - y^2$ (See Ex 1b)

A **relative minimum** occurs at P_0 if
$D(x_0, y_0) > 0$ and $f_{xx}(x_0, y_0) > 0$
(or $f_{yy}(x_0, y_0) > 0$).

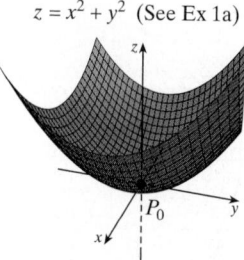

$z = x^2 + y^2$ (See Ex 1a)

A **saddle point** occurs at P_0 if $D(x_0, y_0) < 0$.

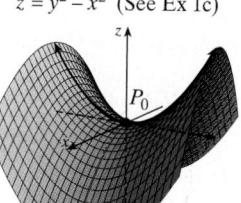

$z = y^2 - x^2$ (See Ex 1c)

Summary: For a critical point (a, b):

$D(a, b)$	$f_{xx}(a, b)$	Type
$+$	$-$	Rel. max.
$+$	$+$	Rel. min.
$-$	NA	Saddle point
0	NA	Inconclusive

If $D(x_0, y_0) = 0$, then the test is **inconclusive**. Nothing can be said about the nature of the surface at (x_0, y_0) without further analysis.

Proof   The second partials test can be proved by using an extension of the Taylor series expansion (Section 8.8) that applies to functions of two variables $f(x, y)$. Details can be found in most advanced calculus texts (also see Problem 60).   ❑

The discriminant $D = f_{xx} f_{yy} - f_{xy}^2$ may be easier to remember in the equivalent determinant form

$$D = \begin{vmatrix} f_{xx} & f_{xy} \\ f_{xy} & f_{yy} \end{vmatrix}$$

Note that if $D > 0$ at the critical point $P_0(x_0, y_0)$, then f_{xx} and f_{yy} must have the same sign. This is the reason that when $D > 0$, either $f_{xx} > 0$ or $f_{yy} > 0$ is enough to guarantee that a relative minimum occurs at P_0 (or a relative maximum if $f_{xx} < 0$ or $f_{yy} < 0$).

Geometrically, if $D > 0$ and $f_{xx} > 0$ and $f_{yy} > 0$ at P_0, then the surface $z = f(x, y)$ curves upward in all directions from the point $Q(x_0, y_0, z_0)$, so there is a relative minimum at Q. Likewise, if $D > 0$ and $f_{xx} < 0$ and $f_{yy} < 0$ at P_0, then the surface curves downward in all directions from P_0, which must therefore be a relative maximum. However, if $D < 0$ at P_0, the surface curves up from Q in some directions, and down in others, so Q must be a saddle point.

WARNING   The second partials test says nothing about the geometry of the surface at Q if $D = 0$ at P_0. Example 4 and Problem 54 show that a relative minimum, a relative maximum, a saddle point, or something entirely different may occur if $D = 0$.

EXAMPLE 2   Using the second partials test to classify critical points

Find all relative extrema and saddle points of the function

$$f(x, y) = 2x^2 + 2xy + y^2 - 2x - 2y + 5$$

Solution

First, find the critical points:

$$f_x = 4x + 2y - 2 \qquad f_y = 2x + 2y - 2$$

Setting $f_x = 0$ and $f_y = 0$, we obtain the system of equations

$$\begin{cases} 4x + 2y - 2 = 0 \\ 2x + 2y - 2 = 0 \end{cases}$$

and solve to obtain $x = 0$, $y = 1$. Thus, $(0, 1)$ is the only critical point. To apply the second partials test, we obtain

$$f_{xx} = 4 \qquad f_{yy} = 2 \qquad f_{xy} = 2$$

and form the discriminant

$$D = f_{xx} f_{yy} - f_{xy}^2 = (4)(2) - 2^2 = 4$$

For the critical point $(0, 1)$ we have $D = 4 > 0$ and $f_{xx} = 4 > 0$, so there is a relative minimum at $(0, 1)$. ∎

EXAMPLE 3   Second partials test with a relative minimum and a saddle point

Find all critical points on the graph of $f(x, y) = 8x^3 - 24xy + y^3$, and use the second partials test to classify each point as a relative extremum or a saddle point.

Solution

$$f_x(x, y) = 24x^2 - 24y, \qquad f_y(x, y) = -24x + 3y^2$$

To find the critical points, solve

$$\begin{cases} 24x^2 - 24y = 0 \\ -24x + 3y^2 = 0 \end{cases}$$

From the first equation, $y = x^2$; substitute this into the second equation to find

$$-24x + 3(x^2)^2 = 0$$
$$x(x^3 - 8) = 0$$
$$x(x - 2)(x^2 + 2x + 4) = 0$$
$$x = 0, 2 \qquad \text{The solutions of } x^2 + 2x + 4 = 0 \text{ are not real.}$$

If $x = 0$, then $y = 0$, and if $x = 2$, then $y = 4$, so the critical points are $(0, 0)$ and $(2, 4)$. To obtain D, we first find $f_{xx}(x, y) = 48x$, $f_{xy}(x, y) = -24$, and $f_{yy}(x, y) = 6y$ to find $D(x, y) = (48x)(6y) - (-24)^2$ and then compute:

$$D = \begin{vmatrix} f_{xx} & f_{xy} \\ f_{xy} & f_{yy} \end{vmatrix} = \begin{vmatrix} 48x & -24 \\ -24 & 6y \end{vmatrix} = 288xy - 576$$

At $(0, 0)$, $D = -576 < 0$, so there is a saddle point at $(0, 0)$.

At $(2, 4)$, $D = 288(2)(4) - 576 = 1{,}728 > 0$ and $f_{xx}(2, 4) = 96 > 0$, so there is a relative minimum at $(2, 4)$.

To view the situation graphically, we calculate the coordinates of the saddle point $(0, 0, 0)$, and the relative minimum $(2, 4, -64)$, as shown in Figure 11.39.

Critical point

(a, b)	$D(a, b)$	$f_{xx}(a, b)$	type
$(0, 0)$	Neg.		Saddle
$(2, 4)$	Pos.	Pos.	Rel. min.

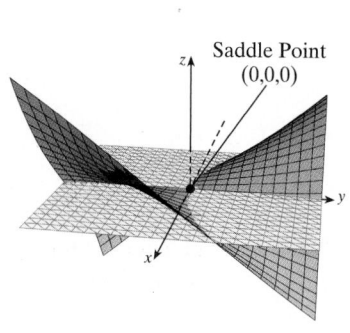

a. View near the origin (showing the saddle point)

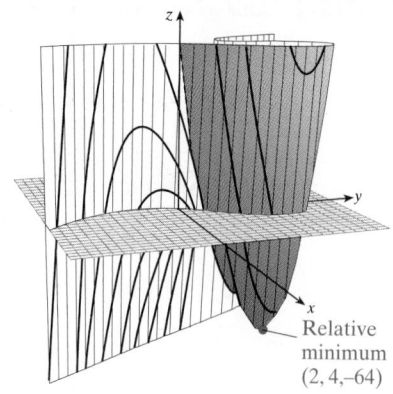

b. View away from the origin (showing the relative minimum point)

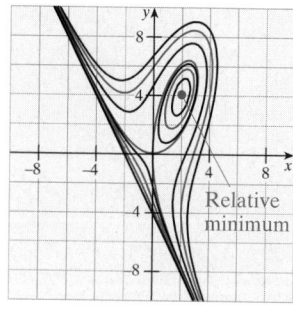

c. Level curves

Figure 11.39 Graph of $f(x, y) = 8x^3 - 24xy + y^3$

EXAMPLE 4   Extrema when the second partials test fails

Find all relative extrema and saddle points on the graph of

$$f(x, y) = x^2 y^4$$

The graph is shown in Figure 11.40.

Solution

Since $f_x(x, y) = 2xy^4$, $f_y(x, y) = 4x^2y^3$, we see that the critical points occur only when $x = 0$ or $y = 0$; that is, every point on the x-axis or y-axis is a critical point. Because

$$f_{xx}(x, y) = 2y^4, \qquad f_{xy}(x, y) = 8xy^3, \qquad f_{yy}(x, y) = 12x^2y^2$$

the discriminant is

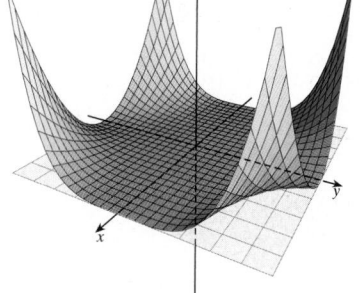

Figure 11.40 Graph of $f(x, y) = x^2 y^4$

$$D = \begin{vmatrix} f_{xx} & f_{xy} \\ f_{xy} & f_{yy} \end{vmatrix} = \begin{vmatrix} 2y^4 & 8xy^3 \\ 8xy^3 & 12x^2y^2 \end{vmatrix} = 24x^2y^6 - 64x^2y^6 = -40x^2y^6$$

Since $D = 0$ for any critical point $(x_0, 0)$ or $(0, y_0)$, the second partials test fails. However, $f(x, y) = 0$ for every critical point (because either $x = 0$ or $y = 0$, or both), and because $f(x, y) = x^2y^4 > 0$ when $x \neq 0$ and $y \neq 0$, it follows that each critical point must be a relative minimum.

ABSOLUTE EXTREMA OF CONTINUOUS FUNCTIONS

The extreme value theorem (Theorem 4.1) says that a function of a single variable f must attain both an absolute maximum and an absolute minimum on any closed, bounded interval $[a, b]$ on which it is continuous. In $\mathbb{R}^2$, a nonempty set S is **closed** if it contains its boundary (see the introduction to Section 11.2) and is **bounded** if it is contained in a disk. The extreme value theorem can be extended to functions of two variables in the following form.

THEOREM 11.13   Extreme value theorem for a function of two variables

A function of two variables $f(x, y)$ attains both an absolute maximum and an absolute minimum on any closed, bounded set S where it is continuous.

Proof   The proof is found in most advanced calculus texts. ◻

To find the absolute extrema of a continuous function $f(x, y)$ on a closed, bounded set S, we proceed as follows:

Procedure for Determining Absolute Extrema

Given a function f that is continuous on a closed, bounded set S,

Step 1. Find all critical points of f in S.
Step 2. Find all points on the boundary of S where absolute extrema can occur.
Step 3. Compute the value of $f(x_0, y_0)$ for each of the points (x_0, y_0) found in steps 1 and 2.

Evaluation: The absolute maximum of f on S is the largest of the values computed in step 3, and the absolute minimum is the smallest of the computed values.

EXAMPLE 5 Finding absolute extrema

Find the absolute extrema of the function $f(x, y) = e^{x^2 - y^2}$ over the disk $x^2 + y^2 \leq 1$. The graph is shown in Figure 11.41.

Solution

Step 1. $f_x(x, y) = 2xe^{x^2 - y^2}$ and $f_y(x, y) = -2ye^{x^2 - y^2}$. These partial derivatives are defined for all (x, y). Because $f_x(x, y) = f_y(x, y) = 0$ only when $x = 0$ and $y = 0$, it follows that $(0, 0)$ is the only critical point of f and it is inside the disk.

Step 2. Examine the values of f on the boundary curve $x^2 + y^2 = 1$. Because $y^2 = 1 - x^2$ on the boundary of the disk, we find that

$$f(x, y) = e^{x^2 - (1 - x^2)} = e^{2x^2 - 1}$$

We need to find the largest and smallest values of $F(x) = e^{2x^2 - 1}$ for $-1 \leq x \leq 1$. Since

$$F'(x) = 4xe^{2x^2 - 1}$$

we see that $F'(x) = 0$ only when $x = 0$ (since $e^{2x^2 - 1}$ is always positive). At $x = 0$, we have $y^2 = 1 - 0^2$, so $y = \pm 1$; thus $(0, 1)$ and $(0, -1)$ are boundary critical points. At the endpoints of the interval $-1 \leq x \leq 1$, the corresponding points are $(1, 0)$ and $(-1, 0)$.

Step 3. Compute the value of f for the points found in steps 1 and 2:

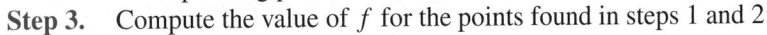

Points to check	Compute $f(x_0, y_0) = e^{x_0^2 - y_0^2}$
$(0, 0)$	$f(0, 0) = e^0 = 1$
$(0, 1)$	$f(0, 1) = e^{-1}$; minimum
$(0, -1)$	$f(0, -1) = e^{-1}$; minimum
$(1, 0)$	$f(1, 0) = e$; maximum
$(-1, 0)$	$f(-1, 0) = e$; maximum

Evaluation: As indicated in the preceding table, the absolute maximum value of f on the given disk is e, which occurs at $(1, 0)$ and $(-1, 0)$, and the absolute minimum value is e^{-1}, which occurs at $(0, 1)$ and $(0, -1)$. ∎

In general, it can be difficult to show that a relative extremum is actually an absolute extremum. In practice, however, it is often possible to make the determination using physical or geometric considerations. Consider the following example.

EXAMPLE 6 Minimum distance from a point to a plane

Find the point on the plane $x + 2y + z = 5$ that is closest to the point $P(0, 3, 4)$.

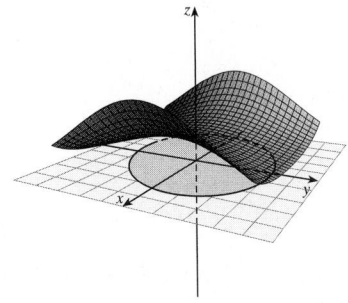

Figure 11.41 Graph of $f(x, y) = e^{x^2 - y^2}$ over the disk $x^2 + y^2 \leq 1$

Solution

If $Q(x, y, z)$ is a point on the plane $x + 2y + z = 5$, then $z = 5 - x - 2y$ and the distance from P to Q is

$$d = \sqrt{(x - 0)^2 + (y - 3)^2 + (z - 4)^2}$$
$$= \sqrt{x^2 + (y - 3)^2 + (5 - x - 2y - 4)^2}$$

Instead of minimizing d, we minimize

$$f(x, y) = d^2 = x^2 + (y - 3)^2 + (1 - x - 2y)^2$$

since the minimum of d will occur at the same points where d^2 is also minimized.

To minimize $f(x, y)$, we first determine the critical points of f by solving the system

$$f_x = 2x - 2(1 - x - 2y) = 4x + 4y - 2 = 0$$
$$f_y = 2(y - 3) - 4(1 - x - 2y) = 4x + 10y - 10 = 0$$

We obtain $x = -\frac{5}{6}$, $y = \frac{4}{3}$, and since

$$f_{xx} = 4, \qquad f_{yy} = 10, \qquad f_{xy} = 4$$

we find that

$$D = f_{xx}f_{yy} - f_{xy}^2 = 4(10) - 4^2 > 0 \quad \text{and} \quad f_{xx} = 4 > 0$$

so a relative minimum occurs at $\left(-\frac{5}{6}, \frac{4}{3}\right)$.

Intuitively, we see that this relative minimum must also be an absolute minimum because there must be exactly one point on the plane that is closest to the given point. The corresponding z-value is $z = 5 - \left(-\frac{5}{6}\right) - 2\left(\frac{4}{3}\right) = \frac{19}{6}$. Thus, the closest point on the plane is $Q\left(-\frac{5}{6}, \frac{4}{3}, \frac{19}{6}\right)$, and the minimum distance is

$$d = \sqrt{\left(\frac{5}{6}\right)^2 + \left(\frac{4}{3} - 3\right)^2 + \left[1 + \frac{5}{6} - 2\left(\frac{4}{3}\right)\right]^2} = \sqrt{\frac{25}{6}} = \frac{5}{\sqrt{6}}$$

Check: You might want to check your work by using the formula for the distance from a point to a plane in $\mathbb{R}^3$ (Theorem 9.9):

$$d = \left| \frac{Ax_0 + By_0 + Cz_0 - D}{\sqrt{A^2 + B^2 + C^2}} \right| = \left| \frac{0 + 2(3) + 4 - 5}{\sqrt{1^2 + 2^2 + 1^2}33} \right| = \frac{5}{\sqrt{6}} \qquad ■$$

LEAST SQUARES APPROXIMATION OF DATA

In the following example, calculus is applied to justify a formula used in statistics and in many applications in the social and physical sciences.

EXAMPLE 7 Least squares approximation of data

Suppose data consisting of n points $P_1, \ldots, P_n$ are known, and we wish to find a function $y = f(x)$ that fits the data reasonably well. In particular, suppose we wish to find a line $y = mx + b$ that "best fits" the data in the sense that the sum of the squares of the vertical distances from each data point to the line is minimized.

Solution

We wish to find values of m and b that minimize the sum of the squares of the differences between the y-values and the line $y = mx + b$. The line that we seek is called the **regression line**. Suppose that the point P_k has components (x_k, y_k). At this point the value on the regression line is $y = mx_k + b$ and the value of the data point is y_k. The "error" caused by using the point on the regression line rather than the actual data point can be measured by the difference

$$y_k - (mx_k + b)$$

The data points may be above the regression line for some values of k and below the regression line for other values of k. We see that we need to minimize the function that represents the sum of the *squares* of all these differences:

$$F(m, b) = \sum_{k=1}^{n}[y_k - (mx_k + b)]^2$$

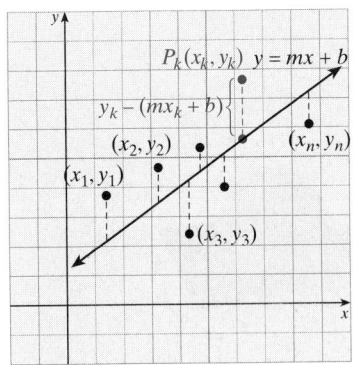

Figure 11.42 Least squares approximation of data

The situation is illustrated in Figure 11.42. To find where F is minimized, we first compute the partial derivatives.

$$F_m(m, b) = \sum_{k=1}^{n} 2[y_k - (mx_k + b)](-x_k)$$

$$= 2m\sum_{k=1}^{n} x_k^2 + 2b\sum_{k=1}^{n} x_k - 2\sum_{k=1}^{n} x_k y_k$$

$$F_b(m, b) = \sum_{k=1}^{n} 2[y_k - (mx_k + b)](-1)$$

$$= 2m\sum_{k=1}^{n} x_k + 2b\sum_{k=1}^{n} 1 - 2\sum_{k=1}^{n} y_k$$

$$= 2m\sum_{k=1}^{n} x_k + 2bn - 2\sum_{k=1}^{n} y_k$$

Set each of these partial derivatives equal to 0 to find the critical values (see Problem 61).

$$m = \frac{n\sum_{k=1}^{n} x_k y_k - \left(\sum_{k=1}^{n} x_k\right)\left(\sum_{k=1}^{n} y_k\right)}{n\sum_{k=1}^{n} x_k^2 - \left(\sum_{k=1}^{n} x_k\right)^2} \quad \text{and} \quad b = \frac{\sum_{k=1}^{n} x_k^2 \sum_{k=1}^{n} y_k - \left(\sum_{k=1}^{n} x_k\right)\left(\sum_{k=1}^{n} x_k y_k\right)}{n\sum_{k=1}^{n} x_k^2 - \left(\sum_{k=1}^{n} x_k\right)^2}$$

It can be shown that these values of m and b yield an absolute minimum for $F(m, b)$. ■

Most applications of the **least squares formula** stated in Example 7 involve using a calculator or computer software. The following technology note provides an example.

TECHNOLOGY NOTE

Many calculators will carry out the calculations required by the least squares approximation procedure. Look at your owner's manual for specifics. Most calculators allow you to input data with keys labeled $\boxed{\text{STAT}}$ and $\boxed{\text{DATA}}$. After the data are input, the m and b values are given by pressing the $\boxed{\text{LinReg}}$ choice. For example, ten people are given a standard IQ test. Their scores are then compared with their high school grades:

IQ:	117	105	111	96	135	81	103	99	107	109
GPA:	3.1	2.8	2.5	2.8	3.4	1.9	2.1	3.2	2.9	2.3

A calculator output shows: $m = .0224144711$ and $b = .3173417224$. A scatter diagram with the least squares line is shown in Figure 11.43.

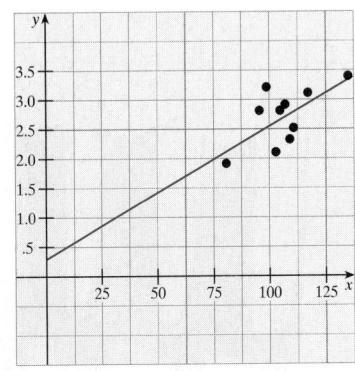

Figure 11.43 Scatter diagram and least squares line

11.7 PROBLEM SET

A 1. **WHAT DOES THIS SAY?** Describe what is meant by a critical point.

2. **WHAT DOES THIS SAY?** Describe a procedure for classifying relative extrema.

3. **WHAT DOES THIS SAY?** Describe a procedure for determining absolute extrema on a closed, bounded set S.

Find the critical points in Problems 4–23, and classify each point as a relative maximum, a relative minimum, or a saddle point.

4. $f(x, y) = 2x^2 - 4xy + y^3 + 2$

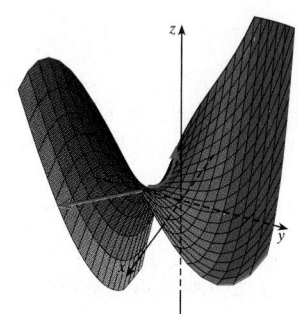

5. $f(x, y) = (x - 2)^2 + (y - 3)^4$

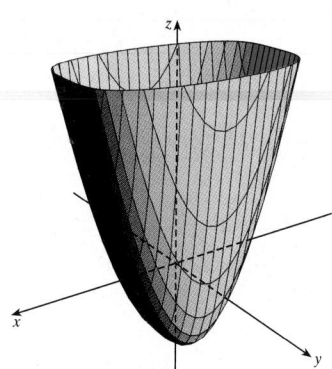

6. $f(x, y) = e^{-x} \sin y$

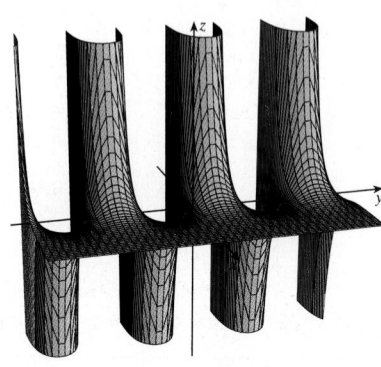

7. $f(x, y) = (1 + x^2 + y^2)e^{1-x^2-y^2}$

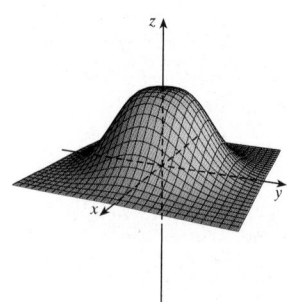

8. $f(x, y) = \dfrac{9x}{x^2 + y^2 + 1}$

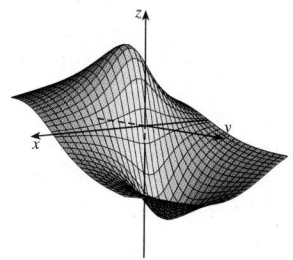

9. $f(x, y) = x^2 + xy + y^2$ 10. $f(x, y) = xy - x + y$

11. $f(x, y) = -x^3 + 9x - 4y^2$ 12. $f(x, y) = e^{-(x^2+y^2)}$

13. $f(x, y) = (x^2 + 2y^2)e^{1-x^2-y^2}$

14. $f(x, y) = e^{xy}$

15. $f(x, y) = x^{-1} + y^{-1} + 2xy$

16. $f(x, y) = (x - 4)\ln(xy)$

17. $f(x, y) = x^3 + y^3 + 3x^2 - 18y^2 + 81y + 5$

18. $f(x, y) = 2x^3 + y^3 + 3x^2 - 3y - 12x - 4$

19. $f(x, y) = x^2 + y^2 - 6xy + 9x + 5y + 2$

20. $f(x, y) = x^2 + y^2 + \dfrac{32}{xy}$

21. $f(x, y) = x^2 + y^3 + \dfrac{768}{x + y}$

22. $f(x, y) = 3xy^2 - 2x^2y + 36xy$

23. $f(x, y) = 3x^2 + 12x + 8y^3 - 12y^2 + 7$

B *Find the absolute extrema of f on the closed bounded set S in the plane as described in Problems 24–30.*

24. $f(x, y) = 2x^2 - y^2$; S is the disk $x^2 + y^2 \le 1$.

25. $f(x, y) = xy - 2x - 5y$; S is the triangular region with vertices $(0, 0)$, $(7, 0)$, and $(7, 7)$.

26. $f(x, y) = x^2 + 3y^2 - 4x + 2y - 3$; S is the square region with vertices $(0, 0)$, $(3, 0)$, $(3, -3)$, and $(0, -3)$.

27. $f(x, y) = 2 \sin x + 5 \cos y$; S is the rectangular region with vertices $(0, 0)$, $(2, 0)$, $(2, 5)$, and $(0, 5)$.

28. $f(x, y) = e^{x^2+2x+y^2}$; S is the disk $x^2 + 2x + y^2 \le 0$.

29. $f(x, y) = x^2 + xy + y^2$; S is the disk $x^2 + y^2 \le 1$.

30. $f(x, y) = x^2 - 4xy + y^3 + 4y$; S is the square region $0 \le x \le 2$, $0 \le y \le 2$.

Find the least squares regression line for the data points given in Problems 31–34.

31. $(-2, -3)$, $(-1, -1)$, $(0, 1)$, $(1, 3)$, $(3, 5)$

32. $(0, 1)$, $(1, 1.6)$, $(2.2, 3)$, $(3.1, 3.9)$, $(4, 5)$

33. $(3, 5.72)$, $(4, 5.31)$, $(6.2, 5.12)$, $(7.52, 5.32)$, $(8.03, 5.67)$

34. $(-4, 2)$, $(-3, 1)$, $(0, 0)$, $(1, -3)$, $(2, -1)$, $(3, -2)$

35. Find all points on the surface $y^2 = 4 + xz$ that are closest to the origin.

36. Find all points in the plane $x + 2y + 3z = 4$ in the first octant where $f(x, y, z) = x^2yz^3$ has a maximum value.

37. A rectangular box with no top is to have a fixed volume. What should its dimensions be if we want to use the least amount of material in its construction?

38. A wire of length L is cut into three pieces that are bent to form a circle, a square, and an equilateral triangle. How should the cuts be made to minimize the sum of the total area?

39. Find three positive numbers whose sum is 54 and whose product is as large as possible.

40. A dairy produces whole milk and skim milk in quantities x and y pints, respectively. Suppose the price (in cents) of whole milk is $p(x) = 100 - x$ and that of skim milk is $q(y) = 100 - y$, and also assume that $C(x, y) = x^2 + xy + y^2$ is the joint-cost function of the commodities. Maximize the profit

$$P(x, y) = px + qy - C(x, y)$$

41. Let R be the triangular region in the xy-plane with vertices $(-1, -2)$, $(-1, 2)$, and $(3, 2)$. A plate in the shape of R is heated so that the temperature at (x, y) is

$$T(x, y) = 2x^2 - xy + y^2 - 2y + 1$$

(in degrees Celsius). At what point in R or on its boundary is T maximized? Where is T minimized? What are the extreme temperatures?

42. A particle of mass m in a rectangular box with dimensions x, y, z has *ground state energy*

$$E(x, y, z) = \frac{k^2}{8m}\left(\frac{1}{x^2} + \frac{1}{y^2} + \frac{1}{z^2}\right)$$

where k is a physical constant. If the volume of the box is fixed (say $V_0 = xyz$), find the values of x, y, and z that minimize the ground state energy.

43. A manufacturer produces two different kinds of graphing calculators, A and B, in quantities x and y (units of 1,000), respectively. If the revenue function (in dollars) is $R(x, y) = -x^2 - 2y^2 + 2xy + 8x + 5y$, find the quantities of A and B that should be produced to maximize revenue.

44. Suppose we wish to construct a closed rectangular box with volume 32 ft^3. Three different materials will be used in the construction. The material for the sides costs $1 per square foot, the material for the bottom costs $3 per square foot, and the material for the top costs $5 per square foot. What are the dimensions of the least expensive such box?

45. **Modeling Problem** A store carries two competing brands of bottled water, one from California and the other from upstate New York. To model this situation, assume the owner of the store can obtain both at a cost of $2/bottle. Also assume that if the California water is sold for x dollars per bottle and the New York water for y dollars per bottle, then consumers will buy approximately $40 - 50x + 40y$ bottles of California water and $20 + 60x - 70y$ bottles of the New York water each day. How should the owner price the bottled water to generate the largest possible profit?

46. **Modeling Problem** A telephone company is planning to introduce two new types of executive communications systems that it hopes to sell to its largest commercial customers. To create a model to determine the maximum profit, it is assumed that if the first type of system is priced at x hundred dollars per system and the second type at y hundred dollars per system, approximately $40 - 8x + 5y$ consumers will buy the first type and $50 + 9x - 7y$ will buy the second type. If the cost of manufacturing the first type is $1,000 per system and the cost of manufacturing the second type is $3,000 per system, how should the telephone company price the systems to generate maximum profit?

47. **Modeling Problem** A manufacturer with exclusive rights to a sophisticated new industrial machine is planning to sell a limited number of the machines to both foreign and domestic firms. The price the manufacturer can expect to receive for the machines will depend on the number of machines made available. For example, if only a few of the machines are placed on the market, competitive bidding among prospective purchasers will tend to drive the price up. It is estimated that if the manufacturer supplies x machines to the domestic market and y machines to the foreign market, the machines will sell for $60 - 0.2x + 0.05y$ thousand dollars apiece at home and $50 - 0.1y + 0.05x$ thousand dollars apiece abroad. If the manufacturer can produce the machines at a total cost of $10,000 apiece, how many should be supplied to each market to generate the largest possible profit?

48. A college admissions officer, Dr. Westfall, has compiled the following data relating students' high-school and college GPAs:

HS GPA	2.0	2.5	3.0	3.0	3.5	3.5	4.0	4.0
College GPA	1.5	2.0	2.5	3.5	2.5	3.0	3.0	3.5

Plot the data points on a graph and find the equation of the regression line for these data. Then use the regression line to predict the college GPA of a student whose high school GPA is 3.75.

49. It is known that if an ideal spring is displaced a distance y from its natural length by a force (weight) x, then $y = kx$, where k is the so-called spring constant. To compute this constant for a particular spring, a scientist obtains the following data:

x (lb)	5.2	7.3	8.4	10.12	12.37
y (in.)	11.32	15.56	17.44	21.96	26.17

Based on these data, what is the "best" choice for k?

50. **Exploration Problem** The following table gives the approximate U.S. census figures (in millions):

Year:	1900	1910	1920	1930	1940
Population:	76.2	92.2	106.0	123.2	132.1

Year:	1950	1960	1970	1980	1990
Population:	151.3	179.3	203.3	226.5	248.7

a. Find the least squares regression line for the given data and use this line to "predict" the population in 1997. (The actual population was about 266.5 million.)

b. Use the least squares linear approximation to estimate the population at the present time. Check your answer by looking up the population using the Internet. Comment on the accuracy (or inaccuracy) of your prediction.

51. Exploration Problem The following table gives the Dow Jones Industrial Average (DJIA) Stock Index along with the per capita consumption of wine (in gallons) for those years.

Year:	1965	1970	1975	1980	1985	1990	1995
DJIA Index:	911	753	802	891	1,328	2,796	3,838
Consumption:	0.98	1.31	1.71	2.11	2.43	2.05	1.79

a. Plot these data on a graph, with the DJIA Index on the *x*-axis and consumption on the *y*-axis.

b. Find the equation of the least squares line.

c. Determine whether the consumption figures predicted by the least squares line in part **b** are approximately correct by using the most recent figures available at the time of this writing: The DJIA opened 1997 at 6,442 and U.S. wine consumption was 1.95 gallons. Interpret your findings.

d. In 2001 the stock market began the year at 10,790. Use the least squares line to predict per capita wine consumption that corresponds to this stock value.

52. Linearizing nonlinear data In this problem, we turn to data that do *not* tend to change linearly. Often we can "linearize" the data by taking the logarithm or exponential of the data and then doing a linear fit as described in this section.

a. Suppose we have, or suspect, a relationship $y = kx^m$. Show that by taking the natural logarithm of this equation we obtain a linear relationship: $Y = K + mX$. Explain the new variables and constant K.

b. Following are data relating the periods of revolution t (in days) of the six inner planets and their semimajor axis a (in 10^6 km). Kepler conjectured the relationship $t = ka^m$, which is very accurate for the correct k and a. You are to "transform" the data as in part **a** (thus obtaining $T_i = \ln t_i, \ldots$) and do a linear fit to the new data, thus finding k and m.

t-data: $(87.97, 224.7, 365.26, 686.98, 4332.59, 10759.2)$
a-data: $(58, 108, 149, 228, 778, 1426)$

53. Following are data pertaining to a recent Olympic weight-lifting competition. The x-data are the "class data" giving eight weight classes (in kg) from featherweight to heavyweight-2. The w-data are the combined weights lifted by the winners in each class. Theoretically, we would expect a relationship $w = kx^m$, where $m = 2/3$. (Can you see why?)

a. Linearize the data as in Problem 52 and use the least squares approximation to find k and m.

x-data: $(56, 60, 67.5, 75, 82.5, 90, 100, 110)$
w-data: $(292.5, 342.5, 340, 375, 377.5, 412.5, 425, 455)$

b. Comment on the 60-kg entry. Do you see why this participant (N. Suleymanoglu of Turkey) was referred to as the strongest man in the world?

C 54. This problem is designed to show, by example, that if $D = 0$ at a critical point, then almost anything can happen.

a. Show that $f(x, y) = x^4 - y^4$ has a saddle point at $(0, 0)$.

b. Show that $g(x, y) = x^2 y^2$ has a relative minimum at $(0, 0)$.

c. Show that $h(x, y) = x^3 + y^3$ has no extremum or saddle point at $(0, 0)$.

55. Counterexample Problem If f is a continuous function of one variable with two relative maxima on a given interval, there must be a relative minimum between the maxima. By considering the function*

$$f(x, y) = 4x^2 e^y - 2x^4 - e^{4y}$$

show that it is possible for a continuous function of two variables to have only two relative maxima and no relative minima.

56. Counterexample Problem If a continuous function of one variable has only one critical number on an interval, then a relative extremum must also be an absolute extremum. Show that this result does not extend to functions of two variables by considering the function†

$$f(x, y) = 3xe^y - x^3 - e^{3y}$$

In particular, show that it has exactly one critical point, which corresponds to a relative maximum. Is this also an absolute maximum? Explain.

57. Tom, Dick, and Mary are participating in a cross-country relay race. Tom will trudge as fast as he can through thick woods to the edge of a river, and then Dick will take over and row to the opposite shore. Finally, Mary will take the baton and run along the river road to the finish line. The course is shown in Figure 11.44.

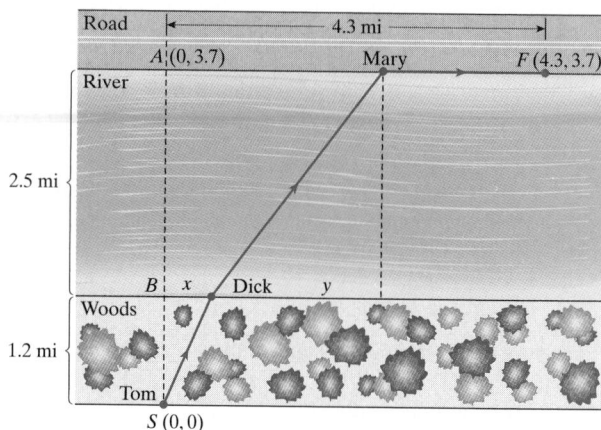

Figure 11.44 Course for the relay

Teams must start at point S and finish at point F, but they may position one member anywhere along the shore of the river and another anywhere along the river road. Suppose Tom can trudge at 2 mi/h, Dick can row at 4 mi/h, and Mary can run at 6 mi/h. Where should Dick and Mary wait to receive the baton in order for the team to finish the course as quickly as possible?

---

*Based on the problem "Two Mountains Without a Valley," by Ira Rosenholtz, *Mathematics Magazine*, 1987, Vol. 60, No. 1, p. 48.

†Based on material in the article, "The Only Critical Point in Town Test" by Ira Rosenholtz and Lowell Smythe, *Mathematics Magazine*, 1985, Vol. 58, No. 3, pp. 149–150.

58. Exploration Problem Consider the function $f(x, y) = (y - x^2)(y - 2x^2)$. Discuss the behavior of this function at $(0, 0)$.

59. Exploration Problem Sometimes the critical points of a function can be classified by looking at the level curves. In each case shown in Figure 11.45, determine the nature of the critical point(s) of $z = f(x, y)$ at $(0, 0)$.

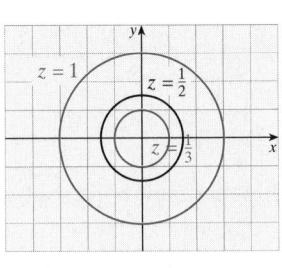
a.

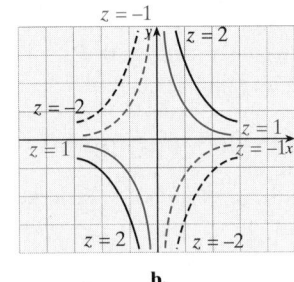
b.

Figure 11.45 Problem 59

60. Prove the second partials test. *Hint:* Compute the second directional derivative of f in the direction of the unit vector $\mathbf{u} = h\mathbf{i} + k\mathbf{j}$ and complete the square.

61. Verify the formulas for m and b associated with the least squares approximation.

62. This problem involves a generalization of the least squares procedure, in which a "least squares plane" is found to produce the best fit for a given set of data. A researcher knows that the quantity z is related to x and y by a formula of the form $z = k_1 x + k_2 y$, where k_1 and k_2 are physical constants. To determine these constants, she conducts a series of experiments, the results of which are tabulated as follows:

x	1.20	0.86	1.03	1.65	−0.95	−1.07
y	0.43	1.92	1.52	−1.03	1.22	−0.06
z	3.21	5.73	2.22	0.92	−1.11	−0.97

Modify the method of least squares to find a "best approximation" for k_1 and k_2.

11.8 Lagrange Multipliers

IN THIS SECTION method of Lagrange multipliers, constrained optimization problems, Lagrange multipliers with two parameters, a geometric interpretation of Lagrange's theorem

METHOD OF LAGRANGE MULTIPLIERS

In many applied problems, a function of two variables is to be optimized subject to a restriction or **constraint** on the variables. For example, consider a container heated in such a way that the temperature at the point (x, y, z) in the container is given by the function $T(x, y, z)$. Suppose that the surface $z = f(x, y)$ lies in the container, and that we wish to find the point on $z = f(x, y)$ where the temperature is the greatest. In other words, *What is the maximum value of T subject to the constraint $z = f(x, y)$, and where does this maximum value occur?*

THEOREM 11.14 Lagrange's theorem

Assume that f and g have continuous first partial derivatives and that f has an extremum at $P_0(x_0, y_0)$ on the smooth constraint curve $g(x, y) = c$. If $\nabla g(x_0, y_0) \neq \mathbf{0}$, there is a number λ such that

$$\nabla f(x_0, y_0) = \lambda \nabla g(x_0, y_0)$$

Proof Denote the constraint curve $g(x, y) = c$ by C, and note that C is smooth. We represent this curve by the vector function

$$\mathbf{R}(t) = x(t)\mathbf{i} + y(t)\mathbf{j}$$

for all t in an open interval I, including t_0 corresponding to P_0, where $x'(t)$ and $y'(t)$ exist and are continuous. Let $F(t) = f(x(t), y(t))$ for all t in I, and apply the chain rule to obtain

$$F'(t) = f_x(x(t), y(t))\frac{dx}{dt} + f_y(x(t), y(t))\frac{dy}{dt} = \nabla f(x(t), y(t)) \cdot \mathbf{R}'(t)$$

Because $f(x, y)$ has an extremum at P_0, we know that $F(t)$ has an extremum at t_0, the value of t that corresponds to P_0 (that is, P_0 is the point on C where $t = t_0$). Therefore, we have $F'(t_0) = 0$ and

$$F'(t_0) = \nabla f(x(t_0), y(t_0)) \cdot \mathbf{R}'(t_0) = 0$$

If $\nabla f(x(t_0), y(t_0)) = 0$, then $\lambda = 0$, and the condition $\nabla f = \lambda \nabla g$ is satisfied trivially. If $\nabla f(x(t_0), y(t_0)) \neq 0$, then $\nabla f(x(t_0), y(t_0))$ is orthogonal to $\mathbf{R}'(t_0)$. Because $\mathbf{R}'(t_0)$ is tangent to the constraint curve C, it follows that $\nabla f(x_0, y_0)$ is normal to C. But $\nabla g(x_0, y_0)$ is also normal to C (because C is a level curve of g), and we conclude that ∇f and ∇g must be *parallel* at P_0. Thus, there is a scalar λ such that $\nabla f(x_0, y_0) = \lambda \nabla g(x_0, y_0)$, as required.   ❑

CONSTRAINED OPTIMIZATION PROBLEMS

The general procedure for the method of Lagrange multipliers may be described as follows.

Procedure for the Method of Lagrange Multipliers

Suppose f and g satisfy the hypotheses of Lagrange's theorem, and that $f(x, y)$ has an extremum subject to the constraint $g(x, y) = c$. Then to find the extreme value, proceed as follows:

1. Simultaneously solve the following three equations for x, y, and λ:

$$f_x(x, y) = \lambda g_x(x, y) \qquad f_y(x, y) = \lambda g_y(x, y) \qquad g(x, y) = c$$

2. Evaluate f at all points found in step 1 and all points on the boundary of the constraint. The extremum we seek must be among these values.

EXAMPLE 1   Optimization with Lagrange multipliers

Given that the largest and smallest values of $f(x, y) = 1 - x^2 - y^2$ subject to the constraint $x + y = 1$ with $x \geq 0$, $y \geq 0$ exist, use the method of Lagrange multipliers to find these extrema.

Solution

Because the constraint is $x + y = 1$, let $g(x, y) = x + y$

$$f_x(x, y) = -2x \qquad f_y(x, y) = -2y \qquad g_x(x, y) = 1 \qquad g_y(x, y) = 1$$

Form the system

$$\begin{cases} -2x = \lambda(1) & \leftarrow f_x(x, y) = \lambda g_x(x, y) \\ -2y = \lambda(1) & \leftarrow f_y(x, y) = \lambda g_y(x, y) \\ x + y = 1 & \leftarrow g(x, y) = 1 \end{cases}$$

The only solution is $x = \frac{1}{2}$, $y = \frac{1}{2}$.

$$f\left(\tfrac{1}{2}, \tfrac{1}{2}\right) = 1 - \left(\tfrac{1}{2}\right)^2 - \left(\tfrac{1}{2}\right)^2 = \tfrac{1}{2}$$

The endpoints of the line segment

$$x + y = 1 \qquad \text{for } x \geq 0, y \geq 0$$

are at $(1, 0)$ and $(0, 1)$, and we find that

$$f(1, 0) = 1 - 1^2 - 0^2 = 0$$
$$f(0, 1) = 1 - 0^2 - 1^2 = 0$$

Therefore, the maximum value is $\frac{1}{2}$ at $\left(\frac{1}{2}, \frac{1}{2}\right)$, and the minimum value is 0 at $(1, 0)$ and $(0, 1)$. (See Figure 11.46.)   ■

SMH This system is solved as Example 3.4 in Section 3.1 of the *Student Mathematics Handbook.*

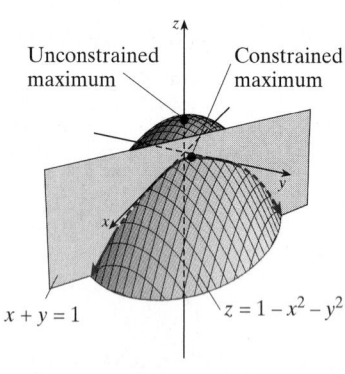

Figure 11.46 The maximum is the high point of the curve of intersection of the surface and the plane.

The method of Lagrange multipliers extends naturally to functions of three or more variables. If a function $f(x, y, z)$ has an extreme value subject to a constraint $g(x, y, z) = c$, then the extremum occurs at a point (x_0, y_0, z_0) such that $g(x_0, y_0, z_0) = c$ and $\nabla f(x_0, y_0, z_0) = \lambda \nabla g(x_0, y_0, z_0)$ for some number λ. Here is an example.

EXAMPLE 2 Hottest and coldest points on a plate

A container in $\mathbb{R}^3$ has the shape of the cube given by $0 \le x \le 1, 0 \le y \le 1, 0 \le z \le 1$. A plate is placed in the container in such a way that it occupies that portion of the plane $x + y + z = 1$ that lies in the cubical container. If the container is heated so that the temperature at each point (x, y, z) is given by

$$T(x, y, z) = 4 - 2x^2 - y^2 - z^2$$

in hundreds of degrees Celsius, what are the hottest and coldest points on the plate? You may assume these extreme temperatures exist.

Solution

The cube and plate are shown in Figure 11.47. We will use Lagrange multipliers to find all critical points in the interior of the plate, and then we will examine the plate's boundary. To apply the method of Lagrange multipliers, we must solve $\nabla T = \lambda \nabla g$, where $g(x, y, z) = x + y + z$. We obtain the partial derivatives.

$$T_x = -4x \qquad T_y = -2y \qquad T_z = -2z \qquad g_x = g_y = g_z = 1$$

We must solve the system

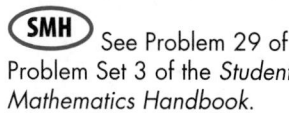 See Problem 29 of Problem Set 3 of the *Student Mathematics Handbook.*

$$\begin{cases} -4x = \lambda & \leftarrow T_x = \lambda g_x \\ -2y = \lambda & \leftarrow T_y = \lambda g_y \\ -2z = \lambda & \leftarrow T_z = \lambda g_z \\ x + y + z = 1 & \leftarrow g(x, y, z) = 1 \end{cases}$$

The solution of this system is $\left(\frac{1}{5}, \frac{2}{5}, \frac{2}{5}\right)$. The boundary of the plate is a triangle with vertices $A(1, 0, 0)$, $B(0, 1, 0)$, and $C(0, 0, 1)$. The temperature along the edges of this triangle may be found as follows:

$$T_1(x) = 4 - 2x^2 - (0)^2 - (1 - x)^2 = 3 - 3x^2 + 2x, \quad 0 \le x \le 1$$
$$T_2(x) = 4 - 2x^2 - (1 - x)^2 - (0)^2 = 3 - 3x^2 + 2x, \quad 0 \le x \le 1$$
$$T_3(y) = 4 - 2(0)^2 - y^2 - (1 - y)^2 = 3 + 2y - 2y^2, \quad 0 \le y \le 1$$

Edge AC: Differentiating, $T_1'(x) = T_2'(x) = -6x + 2$, which equals 0 when $x = \frac{1}{3}$. If $x = \frac{1}{3}$, then $z = \frac{2}{3}$ (because $x + z = 1$, $y = 0$ on edge AC), so we have the critical point $\left(\frac{1}{3}, 0, \frac{2}{3}\right)$.

Edge AB: Because $T_2 = T_1$, we see $x = \frac{1}{3}$. If $x = \frac{1}{3}$, then $y = \frac{2}{3}$ (because $x + y = 1$, $z = 0$ on edge BC), so we have another critical point $\left(\frac{1}{3}, \frac{2}{3}, 0\right)$.

Edge BC: Differentiating, $T_3'(y) = 2 - 4y$, which equals 0 when $y = \frac{1}{2}$. Because $y + z = 1$ and $x = 0$, we have the critical point $\left(0, \frac{1}{2}, \frac{1}{2}\right)$.

Endpoints of the edges: $(1, 0, 0)$, $(0, 1, 0)$, and $(0, 0, 1)$.

The last step is to evaluate T at the critical points and the endpoints:

$$T\left(\tfrac{1}{5}, \tfrac{2}{5}, \tfrac{2}{5}\right) = 3\tfrac{3}{5};$$
$$T\left(\tfrac{1}{3}, 0, \tfrac{2}{3}\right) = 3\tfrac{1}{3}; \qquad T\left(\tfrac{1}{3}, \tfrac{2}{3}, 0\right) = 3\tfrac{1}{3}; \qquad T\left(0, \tfrac{1}{2}, \tfrac{1}{2}\right) = 3\tfrac{1}{2};$$
$$T(1, 0, 0) = 2; \qquad T(0, 1, 0) = 3; \qquad T(0, 0, 1) = 3$$

Comparing these values (remember that the temperature is in hundreds of degrees Celsius), we see that the highest temperature is 360°C at $\left(\frac{1}{5}, \frac{2}{5}, \frac{2}{5}\right)$ and the lowest temperature is 200°C at $(1, 0, 0)$. ∎

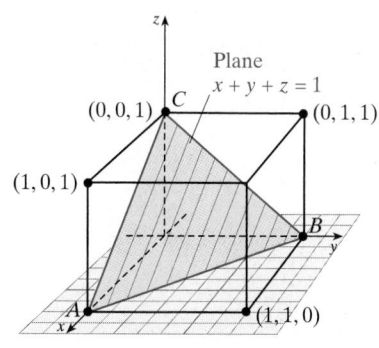

Figure 11.47 Find the hottest and coldest points on the plate inside the cube.

Edge AC: $x + z = 1, y = 0$

Edge AB: $x + y = 1, z = 0$

Edge BC: $y + z = 1, x = 0$

Notice that the multiplier is used only as an intermediary device for finding the critical points and plays no role in the final determination of the constrained extrema. However, the value of λ is more important in certain problems, thanks to the interpretation given in the following theorem.

THEOREM 11.15 Rate of change of the extreme value

Suppose E is an extreme value (maximum or minimum) of f subject to the constraint $g(x, y) = c$. Then the Lagrange multiplier λ is the rate of change of E with respect to c; that is, $\lambda = dE/dc$.

Proof Note that at the extreme value (x, y) we have

$$f_x = \lambda g_x, \quad f_y = \lambda g_y, \quad \text{and} \quad g(x, y) = c$$

The coordinates of the optimal ordered pair (x, y) depend on c (because different constraint levels will generally lead to different optimal combinations of x and y). Thus,

$$E = E(x, y) \quad \text{where } x \text{ and } y \text{ are functions of } c$$

By the chain rule for partial derivatives:

$$
\begin{aligned}
\frac{dE}{dc} &= \frac{\partial E}{\partial x}\frac{dx}{dc} + \frac{\partial E}{\partial y}\frac{dy}{dc} \\
&= f_x\frac{dx}{dc} + f_y\frac{dy}{dc} && \text{Because } E = f(x, y) \\
&= \lambda g_x\frac{dx}{dc} + \lambda g_y\frac{dy}{dc} && \text{Because } f_x = \lambda g_x \text{ and } f_y = \lambda g_y \\
&= \lambda\left(g_x\frac{dx}{dc} + g_y\frac{dy}{dc}\right) \\
&= \lambda\frac{dg}{dc} && \text{Chain rule} \\
&= \lambda && \text{Because } \frac{dg}{dc} = 1 \text{ (remember } g = c\text{)} \quad \square
\end{aligned}
$$

This theorem can be interpreted as saying that the multiplier estimates the change in the extreme value E that results when the constraint c is increased by 1 unit. This interpretation is illustrated in the following example.

EXAMPLE 3 Maximum output for a Cobb-Douglas production function

If x thousand dollars is spent on labor, and y thousand dollars is spent on equipment, it is estimated that the output of a certain factory will be

$$Q(x, y) = 50x^{2/5}y^{3/5}$$

units. If \$150,000 is available, how should this capital be allocated between labor and equipment to generate the largest possible output? How does the maximum output change if the money available for labor and equipment is increased by \$1,000? In economics, an output function of the general form $Q(x, y) = x^\alpha y^{1-\alpha}$ is known as a *Cobb-Douglas production function*.

Solution

Because x and y are given in units of \$1,000, the constraint equation is $x + y = 150$. If we set $g(x, y) = x + y$, we wish to maximize Q subject to $g(x, y) = 150$. To apply the method of Lagrange multipliers, we first find

$$Q_x = 20x^{-3/5}y^{3/5} \qquad Q_y = 30x^{2/5}y^{-2/5} \qquad g_x = 1 \qquad g_y = 1$$

Next, solve the system

$$\begin{cases} 20x^{-3/5}y^{3/5} = \lambda(1) \\ 30x^{2/5}y^{-2/5} = \lambda(1) \\ x + y = 150 \end{cases}$$

From the first two equations we have

$$20x^{-3/5}y^{3/5} = 30x^{2/5}y^{-2/5}$$
$$20y = 30x$$
$$y = 1.5x$$

Substitute $y = 1.5x$ into the equation $x + y = 150$ to find $x = 60$. This leads to the solution $y = 90$, so that the maximum output is

$$Q(60, 90) = 50(60)^{2/5}(90)^{3/5} \approx 3,826.273502 \quad \text{units}$$

We also find that

$$\lambda = 20(60)^{-3/5}(90)^{3/5} \approx 25.50849001$$

Thus, the maximum output is about 3,826 units and occurs when $\$60,000$ is allocated to labor and $\$90,000$ to equipment. We also note that an increase of $\$1,000$ (1 unit) in the available funds will increase the maximum output by approximately $\lambda \approx 25.51$ units (from 3,826.27 to 3,851.78 units). ∎

LAGRANGE MULTIPLIERS WITH TWO PARAMETERS

The method of Lagrange multipliers can also be applied in situations with more than one constraint equation. Suppose we wish to locate an extremum of a function defined by $f(x, y, z)$ subject to two constraints, $g(x, y, z) = c_1$ and $h(x, y, z) = c_2$, where g and h are also differentiable and ∇g and ∇h are not parallel. By generalizing Lagrange's theorem, it can be shown that if (x_0, y_0, z_0) is the desired extremum, then there are numbers λ and μ such that $g(x_0, y_0, z_0) = c_1$, $h(x_0, y_0, z_0) = c_2$, and

$$\nabla f(x_0, y_0, z_0) = \lambda \nabla g(x_0, y_0, z_0) + \mu \nabla h(x_0, y_0, z_0)$$

As in the case of one constraint, we proceed by first solving this system of equations simultaneously to find λ, μ, x_0, y_0, z_0 and then evaluating $f(x, y, z)$ at each solution and comparing to find the required extremum. This approach is illustrated in our final example of this section.

EXAMPLE 4   Optimization with two constraints

Find the point on the intersection of the plane $x + 2y + z = 10$ and the paraboloid $z = x^2 + y^2$ that is closest to the origin (see Figure 11.48). You may assume that such a point exists.

Solution

The distance from a point (x, y, z) to the origin is $s = \sqrt{x^2 + y^2 + z^2}$, but instead of minimizing this quantity, it is easier to minimize its square. That is, we will minimize

$$f(x, y, z) = x^2 + y^2 + z^2$$

subject to the joint constraints

$$g(x, y, z) = x + 2y + z = 10 \quad \text{and} \quad h(x, y, z) = x^2 + y^2 - z = 0$$

Compute the partial derivatives of f, g, and h:

$$f_x = 2x \quad f_y = 2y \quad f_z = 2z$$
$$g_x = 1 \quad g_y = 2 \quad g_z = 1$$
$$h_x = 2x \quad h_y = 2y \quad h_z = -1$$

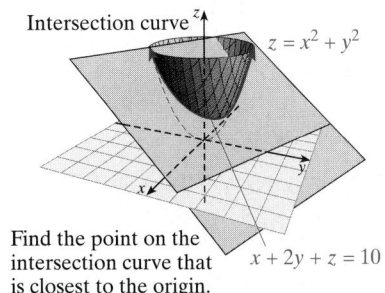

Find the point on the intersection curve that is closest to the origin.

Figure 11.48 Graphical representation of Example 4

To apply the method of Lagrange multipliers, we use the formula
$$\nabla f(x_0, y_0, z_0) = \lambda \nabla g(x_0, y_0, z_0) + \mu \nabla h(x_0, y_0, z_0)$$
which leads to the following system of equations:
$$\begin{cases} 2x = \lambda(1) + \mu(2x) \\ 2y = \lambda(2) + \mu(2y) \\ 2z = \lambda(1) + \mu(-1) \\ x + 2y + z = 10 \\ z = x^2 + y^2 \end{cases}$$

This is not a linear system, so solving it requires ingenuity.

Multiply the first equation by 2 and subtract the second equation to obtain
$$4x - 2y = (4x - 2y)\mu$$
$$(4x - 2y) - (4x - 2y)\mu = 0$$
$$(4x - 2y)(1 - \mu) = 0$$
$$4x - 2y = 0 \quad \text{or} \quad 1 - \mu = 0$$

CASE I: **If $4x - 2y = 0$**, then $y = 2x$. Substitute this into the two constraint equations:

$x + 2y + z = 10$	$x^2 + y^2 - z = 0$
$x + 2(2x) + z = 10$	$x^2 + (2x)^2 - z = 0$
$z = 10 - 5x$	$z = 5x^2$

By substitution we have $5x^2 = 10 - 5x$, which has solutions $x = 1$ and $x = -2$. This implies

$x = 1$	$x = -2$
$y = 2x = 2(1) = 2$	$y = 2x = 2(-2) = -4$
$z = 5x^2 = 5(1)^2 = 5$	$z = 5x^2 = 5(-2)^2 = 20$

Thus, the points $(1, 2, 5)$ and $(-2, -4, 20)$ are candidates for the minimal distance.

CASE II: **If $1 - \mu = 0$**, then $\mu = 1$, and we look at the system of equations involving x, y, z, λ, and μ.
$$\begin{cases} 2x = \lambda(1) + \mu(2x) \\ 2y = \lambda(2) + \mu(2y) \\ 2z = \lambda(1) + \mu(-1) \\ x + 2y + z = 10 \\ z = x^2 + y^2 \end{cases}$$

The top equation becomes $2x = \lambda + 2x$, so that $\lambda = 0$. We now find z from the third equation:
$$2z = -1 \quad \text{or} \quad z = -\tfrac{1}{2}$$

Next, turn to the constraint equations:

$x + 2y + z = 10$	$x^2 + y^2 - z = 0$
$x + 2y - \tfrac{1}{2} = 10$	$x^2 + y^2 + \tfrac{1}{2} = 0$
$x + 2y = 10 + \tfrac{1}{2}$	$x^2 + y^2 = -\tfrac{1}{2}$

There is no solution because $x^2 + y^2$ cannot equal a negative number.

We check the candidates for the minimal distance:
$$f(x, y, z) = x^2 + y^2 + z^2 \quad \text{so that}$$
$$f(1, 2, 5) = 1^2 + 2^2 + 5^2 = 30$$
$$f(-2, -4, 20) = (-2)^2 + (-4)^2 + 20^2 = 420$$

Because $f(x, y, z)$ represents the square of the distance, the minimal distance is $\sqrt{30}$ and the point on the intersection of the two surfaces nearest to the origin is $(1, 2, 5)$. ∎

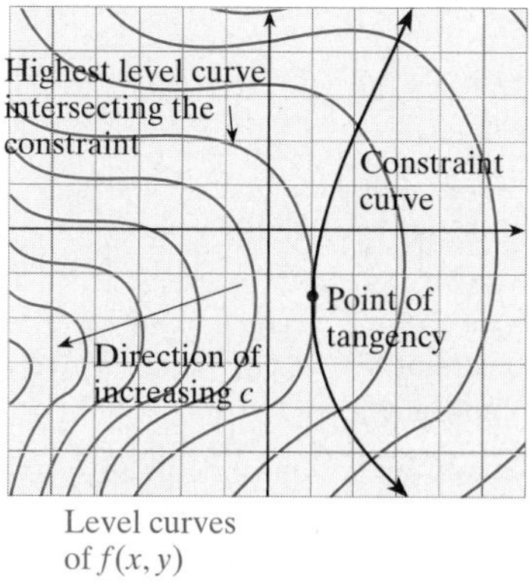

A GEOMETRIC INTERPRETATION

Lagrange's theorem can be interpreted geometrically. Suppose the constraint curve $g(x, y) = c$ and the level curves $f(x, y) = k$ are drawn in the xy-plane, as shown in Figure 11.49.

To maximize $f(x, y)$ subject to the constraint $g(x, y) = c$, we must find the "highest" (leftmost, actually) level curve of f that intersects the constraint curve. As Figure 11.49 suggests, this critical intersection occurs at a point where the constraint curve is tangent to a level curve—that is, where the slope of the constraint curve $g(x, y) = c$ is equal to the slope of a level curve $f(x, y) = k$. According to the formula derived in Section 11.5 (p. 732),

$$\text{Slope of constraint curve } g(x, y) = c \text{ is } \frac{-g_x}{g_y}.$$

$$\text{Slope of each level curve is } \frac{-f_x}{f_y}.$$

The condition that the slopes are equal can be expressed by

$$\frac{-f_x}{f_y} = \frac{-g_x}{g_y}, \qquad \text{or, equivalently,} \qquad \frac{f_x}{g_x} = \frac{f_y}{g_y}$$

Let λ equal this common ratio,

$$\lambda = \frac{f_x}{g_x} \qquad \text{and} \qquad \lambda = \frac{f_y}{g_y}$$

so that

$$f_x = \lambda g_x \qquad \text{and} \qquad f_y = \lambda g_y$$

and

$$\nabla f = f_x \mathbf{i} + f_y \mathbf{j} = \lambda(g_x \mathbf{i} + g_y \mathbf{j}) = \lambda \nabla g$$

Because the point in question must lie on the constraint curve, we also have $g(x, y) = c$. If these equations are satisfied at a certain point (a, b), then f will reach its constrained *maximum* at (a, b) if the *highest* level curve that intersects the constraint curve does so at this point. On the other hand, if the *lowest* level curve that intersects the constraint curve does so at (a, b), then f achieves its constrained *minimum* at this point.

Highest level curve intersecting the constraint

Constraint curve

Point of tangency

Direction of increasing c

Level curves of $f(x, y)$

Figure 11.49 Increasing level curves and the constraint curve

11.8 PROBLEM SET

In the problems in this set, you may assume that the requested extreme value(s) exist.

A *Use the method of Lagrange multipliers to find the required constrained extrema in Problems 1–14.*

1. Maximize $f(x, y) = xy$ subject to $2x + 2y = 5$.
2. Maximize $f(x, y) = xy$ subject to $x + y = 20$.
3. Maximize $f(x, y) = 16 - x^2 - y^2$ subject to $x + 2y = 6$.
4. Minimize $f(x, y) = x^2 + y^2$ subject to $x + y = 24$.
5. Minimize $f(x, y) = x^2 + y^2$ subject to $xy = 1$.
6. Minimize $f(x, y) = x^2 - xy + 2y^2$ subject to $2x + y = 22$.
7. Minimize $f(x, y) = x^2 - y^2$ subject to $x^2 + y^2 = 4$.
8. Maximize $f(x, y) = x^2 - 2y - y^2$ subject to $x^2 + y^2 = 1$.
9. Maximize $f(x, y) = \cos x + \cos y$ subject to $y = x + \frac{\pi}{4}$.
10. Maximize $f(x, y) = e^{xy}$ subject to $x^2 + y^2 = 3$.
11. Maximize $f(x, y) = \ln(xy^2)$ subject to $2x^2 + 3y^2 = 8$ for $x > 0$.

12. Maximize $f(x, y, z) = xyz$ subject to $3x + 2y + z = 6$.
13. Minimize $f(x, y, z) = x^2 + y^2 + z^2$ subject to $x - 2y + 3z = 4$.
14. Minimize $f(x, y, z) = x^2 + y^2 + z^2$ subject to $4x^2 + 2y^2 + z^2 = 4$.

B 15. Find the smallest value of $f(x, y, z) = 2x^2 + 4y^2 + z^2$ subject to $4x - 8y + 2z = 10$. What, if anything, can be said about the largest value of f subject to this constraint?

16. Let $f(x, y, z) = x^2 y^2 z^2$. Show that the maximum value of f on the sphere $x^2 + y^2 + z^2 = R^2$ is $R^6/27$.

17. Find the maximum and minimum values of $f(x, y, z) = x - y + z$ on the sphere $x^2 + y^2 + z^2 = 100$.

18. Find the maximum and minimum values of $f(x, y, z) = 4x - 2y - 3z$ on the sphere $x^2 + y^2 + z^2 = 100$.

19. Use Lagrange multipliers to find the distance from the origin to the plane $Ax + By + Cz = D$ where at least one of A, B, C is nonzero.

20. Find the maximum and minimum distance from the origin to the ellipse $5x^2 - 6xy + 5y^2 = 4$.

21. Find the point on the plane $2x + y + z = 1$ that is nearest to the origin.

22. Find the largest product of positive numbers x, y, and z such that their sum is 24.

23. Write the number 12 as the sum of three positive numbers x, y, z in such a way that the product xy^2z is a maximum.

24. A rectangular box with no top is to be constructed from 96 ft^2 of material. What should be the dimensions of the box if it is to enclose maximum volume?

25. The temperature T at point (x, y, z) in a region of space is given by the formula $T = 100 - xy - xz - yz$. Find the lowest temperature on the plane $x + y + z = 10$.

26. A farmer wishes to fence off a rectangular pasture along the bank of a river. The area of the pasture is to be 3,200 yd^2, and no fencing is needed along the river bank. Find the dimensions of the pasture that will require the least amount of fencing.

27. There are 320 yd of fencing available to enclose a rectangular field. How should the fencing be used so that the enclosed area is as large as possible?

28. Use the fact that 12 oz is approximately 6.89π in.^{3} to find the dimensions of the 12-oz Coke can that can be constructed using the least amount of metal. Compare your answer with an actual can of Coke. Explain what might cause the discrepancy.

29. A cylindrical can is to hold 4π in.^{3} of orange juice. The cost per square inch of constructing the metal top and bottom is twice the cost per square inch of constructing the cardboard side. What are the dimensions of the least expensive can?

30. Find the volume of the largest rectangular parallelepiped that can be inscribed in the ellipsoid

$$x^2 + \frac{y^2}{4} + \frac{z^2}{9} = 1$$

31. A manufacturer has \$8,000 to spend on the development and promotion of a new product. It is estimated that if x thousand dollars is spent on development and y thousand is spent on promotion, sales will be approximately $f(x, y) = 50x^{1/2}y^{3/2}$ units. How much money should the manufacturer allocate to development and how much to promotion to maximize sales?

32. Modeling Problem If x thousand dollars is spent on labor and y thousand dollars is spent on equipment, the output at a certain factory may by modeled by

$$Q(x, y) = 60x^{1/3}y^{2/3}$$

units. Assume \$120,000 is available.

a. How should money be allocated between labor and equipment to generate the largest possible output?

b. Use the Lagrange multiplier λ to estimate the change in the maximum output of the factory that would result if the money available for labor and equipment is increased by \$1,000.

33. Modeling Problem An architect decides to model the usable living space in a building by the volume of space that can be used comfortably by a person 6 feet tall—that is, by the largest 6-foot-high rectangular box that can be inscribed in the building. Find the dimensions of an A-frame building y ft long with equilateral triangular ends x ft on a side that maximizes usable living space if the exterior surface area of the building cannot exceed 500 ft^2.

34. Find the radius of the largest cylinder of height 6 in. that can be inscribed in an inverted cone of height H, radius R, and lateral surface area 250 in.^{2}.

35. In Problem 42 of Problem Set 11.7, you were asked to minimize the ground state energy

$$E(x, y, z) = \frac{k^2}{8m}\left(\frac{1}{x^2} + \frac{1}{y^2} + \frac{1}{z^2}\right)$$

subject to the volume constraint $V = xyz = C$. Solve the problem using Lagrange multipliers.

36. Modeling Problem A university extension agricultural service concludes that, on a particular farm, the yield of wheat per acre is a function of water and fertilizer. Let x be the number of acre-feet of water applied, and y the number of pounds of fertilizer applied during the growing season. The agricultural service then concludes that the yield B (measured in bushels), can be modeled by the formula $B(x, y) = 500 + x^2 + 2y^2$. Suppose that water costs \$20 per acre-foot, fertilizer costs \$12 per pound, and the farmer will invest \$236 per acre for water and fertilizer. How much water and fertilizer should the farmer buy to maximize the yield?

37. How would the farmer of Problem 36 maximize the yield if the amount spent is \$100 instead of \$236?

38. Present post office regulations specify that a box (that is, a package in the form of a rectangular parallelepiped) can be mailed parcel post only if the sum of its length and girth does not exceed 108 inches, as shown in Figure 11.50. Find the maximum volume of such a package. (Compare your solution here with the one you might have given to Problem 17, Section 4.6, page 246.)

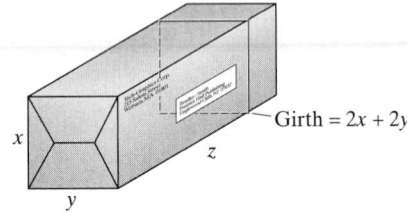

Figure 11.50 Maximum volume for a box mailed by U.S. parcel post

39. *Heron's formula* says that the area of a triangle with sides a, b, c is

$$A = \sqrt{s(s - a)(s - b)(s - c)}$$

where $s = \frac{1}{2}(a + b + c)$ is the semiperimeter of the triangle. Use this result and the method of Lagrange multipliers to show that of all triangles with a given fixed perimeter P, the equilateral triangle has the largest area.

40. If x, y, z are the angles of a triangle, what is the maximum value of the product $P(x, y, z) = \sin x \sin y \sin z$? What about $Q(x, y, z) = \cos x \cos y \cos z$?

Use the method of Lagrange multipliers in Problems 41–44 to find the required extrema for the two given constraints.

41. Find the minimum of $f(x, y, z) = x^2 + y^2 + z^2$ subject to $x + y = 4$ and $y + z = 6$.

42. Find the maximum of $f(x, y, z) = xyz$ subject to $x^2 + y^2 = 3$ and $y = 2z$.

43. Maximize $f(x, y, z) = xy + xz$ subject to $2x + 3z = 5$ and $xy = 4$.

44. Minimize $f(x, y, z) = 2x^2 + 3y^2 + 4z^2$ subject to $x + y + z = 4$ and $x - 2y + 5z = 3$.

45. Modeling Problem A manufacturer is planning to sell a new product at the price of $150 per unit and estimates that if x thousand dollars is spent on development and y thousand dollars on promotion, then approximately

$$\frac{320y}{y + 2} + \frac{160x}{x + 4}$$

units of the product will be sold. The cost of manufacturing the product is $50 per unit.

a. If the manufacturer has a total of $8,000 to spend on the development and promotion, how should this money be allocated to generate the largest possible profit?

b. Suppose the manufacturer decides to spend $8,100 instead of $8,000 on the development and promotion of the new product. Estimate how this change will affect the maximum possible profit.

c. If unlimited funds are available, how much should the manufacturer spend on development and promotion to maximize profit?

d. What is the Lagrange multiplier in part **c**? Your answer should suggest another method for solving the problem in part **c**. Solve the problem using this alternative approach.

46. Modeling Problem A jewelry box with a square base has an interior partition and is required to have volume 800 cm³ (see Figure 11.51).

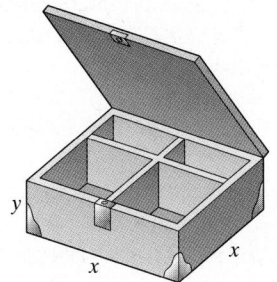
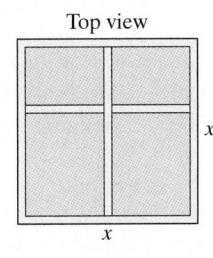

Top view

Figure 11.51 Constructing a jewelry box

a. The material in the top costs twice as much as that in the sides and bottom, which in turn, costs twice as much as the material in the partitions. Find the dimensions of the box that minimize the total cost of construction. *Does it matter that you have not been told where the partitions are located?*

b. Suppose the volume constraint changes from 800 cm³ to 801 cm³. Estimate the appropriate effect on the minimal cost.

47. Three alleles, A, B, and O, determine the four blood types A, B, O, and AB. The *Hardy-Weinberg law* says that the proportions of individuals in a population who carry two different alleles is

$$P = 2pq + 2pr + 2rq$$

where p, q, and r are the proportions of blood types A, B, and O in the population. Given that $p + q + r = 1$, what is the largest value of P?

Ⓒ 48. A farmer wants to build a metal silo in the shape of a right circular cylinder with a right circular cone on the top (the bottom of the silo will be a concrete slab). What is the least amount of metal that can be used if the silo is to have a fixed volume V_0?

49. Find the volume of the largest rectangular parallelepiped (box) that can be inscribed in the ellipsoid

$$\frac{x^2}{a^2} + \frac{y^2}{b^2} + \frac{z^2}{c^2} = 1$$

(See Problem 30.)

50. Exploration Problem The method of Lagrange multipliers gives a constrained extremum only if one exists. If the method is applied to optimizing $f(x, y) = x + y$ subject to $xy = 1$, the method yields two candidates for an extremum. Is one a maximum and the other a minimum? Explain.

In Problems 51–54, let $Q = f(x, y)$ be a production function in which x and y represent units of labor and capital, respectively. If p and q represent unit costs of labor and capital, respectively, then $C(x, y) = px + qy$ represents the total cost of production.

51. Use Lagrange multipliers to show that subject to a fixed production level Q_0, the total cost is smallest when

$$\frac{f_x}{p} = \frac{f_y}{q} \quad \text{and} \quad Q = f(x, y) = Q_0$$

(provided $\nabla f \neq \mathbf{0}$, and $p \neq 0$, $q \neq 0$). This is often referred to as the *minimum cost problem*, and its solution is called the *least cost combination of inputs*.

52. Show that the inputs x, y that maximize the production level $Q = f(x, y)$ subject to a fixed cost k satisfy

$$\frac{f_x}{p} = \frac{f_y}{q} \quad \text{with } px + qy = k$$

(assume $p \neq 0$, $q \neq 0$). This is called a *fixed-budget problem*.

53. A Cobb-Douglas production function is an output function of the form $Q(x, y) = cx^\alpha y^\beta$, with $\alpha + \beta = 1$.

a. Show that such a function is maximized with respect to the fixed cost $px + qy = k$ when $x = \alpha k/p$ and $y = \beta k/q$.

b. Where does the maximum occur if we drop the condition $\alpha + \beta = 1$? How does the maximum output change if k is increased by 1 unit?

54. Show that the cost function

$$C(x, y) = px + qy$$

is minimized subject to the fixed production level $Ax^\alpha y^\beta = k$, with $\alpha + \beta = 1$ when

$$x = \frac{k}{A}\left(\frac{\alpha q}{\beta p}\right)^\beta \qquad y = \frac{k}{A}\left(\frac{\beta p}{\alpha q}\right)^\alpha$$

55. HISTORICAL QUEST Joseph Lagrange is generally acknowledged as
one of the two greatest mathematicians of the eighteenth century, along
with Leonhard Euler (see HISTORI-
CAL QUEST #84 of the Supplementary Problems of Chapter 4).   There
is a distinct difference in style between
Lagrange and Euler.   Lagrange has
been characterized as the first true analyst in the sense that he attempted to
write concisely and with rigor. On the other hand, Euler wrote
using intuition and with an abundance of detail.   Lagrange
was described by Napoleon Bonaparte as "the lofty pyramid
of the mathematical sciences," and followed Euler as the court
mathematician for Frederick the Great. He was the first to use
the notation $f'(x)$ and $f''(x)$ for derivatives. In this section we
were introduced to the method of Lagrange multipliers, which
provide a procedure for constrained optimization. This method
was contained in a paper on mechanics that Lagrange wrote
when he was only 19 years old.* ∎

JOSEPH LAGRANGE
1736–1813

For this Quest, we consider Lagrange's work with solving *algebraic* equations. You are familiar with the quadratic
formula, which provides a general solution for any second-
degree equation $ax^2 + bx + c = 0$, $a \neq 0$. Lagrange made
an exhaustive study of the general solution for the first four
degrees. Here is what he did. Suppose you are given a general
algebraic expression involving letters $a, b, c, \ldots$; how many
different expressions can be derived from the given one if the
letters are interchanged in all possible ways? For example,
from $ab + cd$ we obtain $ad + cb$ by interchanging b and d.

This problem suggests another closely related problem,
also part of Lagrange's approach. Lagrange solved general
algebraic equations of degrees 2, 3, and 4. It was proved later
(not by Lagrange, but by Galois and Abel) that no general solution for equations of degree greater than 4 can be found. Do
some research and find the general solution for equations of
degrees 1, 2, 3, and 4.

───────
*From *Men of Mathematics* by E. T. Bell, Simon & Schuster, New York,
1937, p. 165.

CHAPTER 11 REVIEW

Proficiency Examination

CONCEPT PROBLEMS

1. What is a function of two variables?

2. What are the domain and range of a function of two variables?

3. What is a level curve of the function defined by $f(x, y)$?

4. What do we mean by the limit of a function of two variables?

5. State the following properties of a limit of functions of two
variables.

    a. scalar rule   **b.** sum rule

    c. product rule   **d.** quotient rule

6. Define the continuity of a function defined by $f(x, y)$ at a
point (x_0, y_0) in its domain and continuity on a set S.

7. If $z = f(x, y)$, define the first partial derivatives of f with
respect to x and y.

8. What is the slope of a tangent line to the surface defined by
$z = f(x, y)$ that is parallel to the xy-plane at a point P_0 on f?

9. If $z = f(x, y)$, represent the second partial derivatives.

10. If $z = f(x, y)$, what are the increments of x, y, and z?

11. What does it mean for a function of two variables to be differentiable at (x_0, y_0)?

12. State the incremental approximation of $f(x, y)$.

13. Define the total differential of $z = f(x, y)$.

14. State the chain rule for a function of one parameter.

15. State the chain rule for a function of two independent parameters.

16. Define the directional derivative of a function defined by
$z = f(x, y)$.

17. Define the gradient $\nabla f(x, y)$.

18. State the following basic properties of the gradient.

    a. constant rule   **b.** linearity rule

    c. product rule   **d.** quotient rule

    e. power rule

19. Express the directional derivative in terms of the gradient.

20. State the optimal direction property of the gradient (that is, the
steepest ascent and steepest descent).

21. State the normal property of the gradient.

22. Define the normal line and tangent plane to a surface S at a
point P_0.

23. Define the absolute extrema of a function of two variables.

24. Define the relative extrema of a function of two variables.

25. What is a critical point of a function of two variables?

26. State the second partials test.

27. State the extreme value theorem for a function of two variables.

28. What is the least squares approximation of data, and what is a
regression line?

29. State Lagrange's theorem.

30. State the procedure for the method of Lagrange multipliers.

PRACTICE PROBLEMS

31. If $f(x, y) = \sin^{-1} xy$, verify that $f_{xy} = f_{yx}$.

32. Let $w = x^2 y + y^2 z$, where $x = t \sin t$, $y = t \cos t$, and $z = 2t$.
Use the chain rule to find $\dfrac{dw}{dt}$, where $t = \pi$.

33. Let $f(x, y, z) = xy + yz + xz$, and let P_0 denote the point
$(1, 2, -1)$.

    a. Find the gradient of f at P_0.

    b. Find the directional derivative of f in the direction from
P_0 toward the point $Q(-1, 1, -1)$.

c. Find the direction from P_0 in which the directional derivative has its largest value. What is the magnitude of the largest directional derivative at P_0?

34. Show that the function defined by

$$f(x, y) = \begin{cases} \dfrac{x^2 y}{x^3 + y^3} & \text{if } (x, y) \neq (0, 0) \\ 0 & \text{if } (x, y) = (0, 0) \end{cases}$$

is not continuous at $(0, 0)$.

35. If $f(x, y) = \ln\left(\dfrac{y}{x}\right)$, find f_x, f_y, f_{yy}, and f_{xy}.

36. Show that if $f(x, y, z) = x^2 y + y^2 z + z^2 x$, then

$$\frac{\partial f}{\partial x} + \frac{\partial f}{\partial y} + \frac{\partial f}{\partial z} = (x + y + z)^2$$

37. Let $f(x, y) = (x^2 + y^2)^2$. Find the directional derivative of f at $(2, -2)$ in the direction that makes an angle of $\frac{2\pi}{3}$ with the positive x-axis.

38. Find all critical points of $f(x, y) = 12xy - 2x^2 - y^4$ and classify them using the second partials test.

39. Use the method of Lagrange multipliers to find the maximum and minimum values of the function

$$f(x, y) = x^2 + 2y^2 + 2x + 3$$

subject to the constraint $x^2 + y^2 = 4$.

40. Find the largest and smallest values of the function

$$f(x, y) = x^2 - 4y^2 + 3x + 6y$$

on the region defined by $-2 \leq x \leq 2, 0 \leq y \leq 1$.

Supplementary Problems

Describe the domain of each function given in Problems 1–4.

1. $f(x, y) = \sqrt{16 - x^2 - y^2}$ **2.** $f(x, y) = \dfrac{x^2 - y^2}{x - y}$

3. $f(x, y) = \sin^{-1} x + \cos^{-1} y$ **4.** $f(x, y) = e^{x+y} \tan^{-1}\left(\dfrac{y}{x}\right)$

Find the partial derivatives f_x and f_y for the functions defined in Problems 5–10.

5. $f(x, y) = \dfrac{x^2 - y^2}{x + y}$ **6.** $f(x, y) = x^3 e^{3y/(2x)}$

7. $f(x, y) = x^2 y + \sin\dfrac{y}{x}$ **8.** $f(x, y) = \ln\left(\dfrac{xy}{x + 2y}\right)$

9. $f(x, y) = 2x^3 y + 3xy^2 + \dfrac{y}{x}$ **10.** $f(x, y) = xye^{xy}$

For each function given in Problems 11–15, describe the level curve or level surface $f = c$ for the given values of the constant c.

11. $f(x, y) = x^2 - y; c = 2, c = -2$

12. $f(x, y) = 6x + 2y; c = 0, c = 1, c = 2$

13. $z = f(x, y) = \begin{cases} \sqrt{x^2 + y^2} & \text{if } x \geq 0 \\ -|y| & \text{if } x < 0 \end{cases}$

$c = 0, c = 1, c = -1$

14. $f(x, y, z) = x^2 + y^2 + z^2; c = 16, c = 0, c = -25$

15. $f(x, y, z) = x^2 + \dfrac{y^2}{2} + \dfrac{z^2}{9}; c = 1, c = 2$

Evaluate the limits in Problems 16 and 17, assuming they exist.

16. $\displaystyle\lim_{(x,y)\to(1,1)} \dfrac{xy}{x^2 + y^2}$ **17.** $\displaystyle\lim_{(x,y)\to(0,0)} \dfrac{x + ye^{-x}}{1 + x^2}$

Show that each limit in Problems 18 and 19 does not exist.

18. $\displaystyle\lim_{(x,y)\to(0,0)} \dfrac{x^3 - y^3}{x^3 + y^3}$ **19.** $\displaystyle\lim_{(x,y)\to(0,0)} \dfrac{x^3 y^2}{x^6 + y^4}$

Find the derivatives in Problems 20–23 using the chain rule. You may leave your answers in terms of x, y, t, u, and v.

20. Find $\dfrac{dz}{dt}$, where $z = -xy + y^3$, and $x = -3t^2$, $y = 1 + t^3$.

21. Find $\dfrac{dz}{dt}$, where $z = xy + y^2$, and $x = e^t t^{-1}$, $y = \tan t$.

22. Find $\dfrac{\partial z}{\partial u}$ and $\dfrac{\partial z}{\partial v}$, where $z = x^2 - y^2$, and $x = u + 2v$, $y = u - 2v$.

23. Find $\dfrac{\partial z}{\partial u}$ and $\dfrac{\partial z}{\partial v}$, where $z = x \tan\dfrac{x}{y}$, and $x = uv$, $y = \dfrac{u}{v}$.

Use implicit differentiation to find $\dfrac{\partial z}{\partial x}$ and $\dfrac{\partial z}{\partial y}$ in Problems 24–27.

24. $x^2 + 6y^2 + 2z^2 = 5$ **25.** $e^x + e^y + e^z = 3$

26. $x^3 + 2xz - yz^2 - z^3 = 1$ **27.** $x + 2y - 3z = \ln z$

In Problems 28–33, find f_{xx} and f_{yx}.

28. $f(x, y) = \tan^{-1} xy$ **29.** $f(x, y) = \sin^{-1} xy$

30. $f(x, y) = x^2 + y^3 - 2xy^2$ **31.** $f(x, y) = e^{x^2 + y^2}$

32. $f(x, y) = x \ln y$ **33.** $f(x, y) = \displaystyle\int_x^y \sin(\cos t)\, dt$

Find equations for the tangent plane and normal line to the surfaces given in Problems 34–36 at the prescribed point.

34. $x^2 y^3 z = 8$ at $P_0(2, -1, -2)$

35. $x^3 + 2xy^2 - 7x^3 + 3y + 1 = 0$ at $P_0(1, 1, 1)$

36. $z = \dfrac{-4}{2 + x^2 + y^2}$ at $P_0(1, 1, -1)$

Find all critical points of $f(x, y)$ in Problems 37–42 and classify each as a relative maximum, a relative minimum, or a saddle point.

37. $f(x, y) = x^2 - 6x + 2y^2 + 4y - 2$

38. $f(x, y) = x^3 + y^3 - 6xy$

39. $f(x, y) = (x - 1)(y - 1)(x + y - 1)$

40. $f(x, y) = x^2 + y^3 + 6xy - 7x - 6y$

41. $f(x, y) = x^3 + y^3 + 3x^2 - 18y^2 + 81y + 5$

42. $f(x, y) = \sin(x+y) + \sin x + \sin y$ for $0 < x < \pi, 0 < y < \pi$
(See Figure 11.52.)

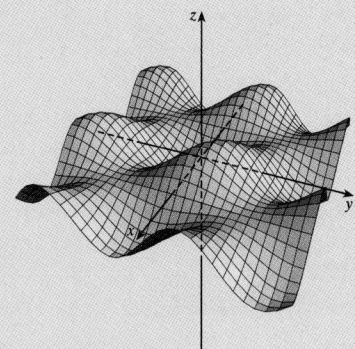

Figure 11.52 Graph of $f(x, y) = \sin(x + y) + \sin x + \sin y$

In Problems 43–46, find the largest and smallest values of the function f on the specified closed, bounded set S.

43. $f(x, y) = xy - 2y$; S is the rectangular region $0 \leq x \leq 3$, $-1 \leq y \leq 1$

44. $f(x, y) = x^2 + 2y^2 - x - 2y$; S is the triangular region with vertices $(0, 0)$, $(2, 0)$, $(2, 2)$

45. $f(x, y) = x^2 + y^2 - 3y$; S is the disk $x^2 + y^2 \leq 4$

46. $f(x, y) = 6x - x^2 + 2xy - y^4$; S is the square $0 \leq x \leq 3$, $0 \leq y \leq 3$

47. Use the chain rule to find $\dfrac{dz}{dt}$ if $z = x^2 - 3xy^2$; $x = 2t$, $y = t^2$.

48. Use the chain rule to find $\dfrac{dz}{dt}$ if $z = x \ln y$; $x = 2t$, $y = e^t$.

49. Let $z = ue^{u^2 - v^2}$, where $u = 2x^2 + 3y^2$ and $v = 3x^2 - 2y^2$. Use the chain rule to find $\dfrac{\partial z}{\partial x}$ and $\dfrac{\partial z}{\partial y}$.

50. Use implicit differentiation to find $\dfrac{\partial z}{\partial x}$ and $\dfrac{\partial z}{\partial y}$, where x, y, and z are related by the equation $x^3 + 2xz - yz^2 - z^3 = 1$.

51. Find the slope of the level curve of $x^2 + y^2 = 2$, where $x = 1$, $y = 1$.

52. Find the slope of the level curve of $xe^y = 2$, where $x = 2$.

53. Find the equations for the tangent plane and normal line to the surface $z = \sin x + e^{xy} + 2y$ at the point $P_0(0, 1, 3)$.

54. The electric potential at each point (x, y) in the disk $x^2 + y^2 < 4$ is $V = 2(4 - x^2 - y^2)^{-1/2}$ volts. Draw the equipotential curves $V = c$ for $c = \sqrt{2}$, $2/\sqrt{3}$, and 8.

55. Let $f(x, y, z) = x^3 y + y^3 z + z^3 x$. Find a function $g(x, y, z)$ such that $\dfrac{\partial f}{\partial x} + \dfrac{\partial f}{\partial y} + \dfrac{\partial f}{\partial z} = x^3 + y^3 + z^3 + 3g(x, y, z)$.

56. Let $u = \sin \dfrac{x}{y} + \ln \dfrac{y}{x}$. Show that $y \dfrac{\partial u}{\partial y} + x \dfrac{\partial u}{\partial x} = 0$.

57. Let $w = \ln(1 + x^2 + y^2) - 2 \tan^{-1} y$, where $x = \ln(1 + t^2)$ and $y = e^t$. Use the chain rule to find $\dfrac{dw}{dt}$.

58. Let $f(x, y) = \tan^{-1} \dfrac{y}{x}$. Find the directional derivative of f at $(1, 2)$ in the direction that makes an angle of $\frac{\pi}{3}$ with the positive x-axis.

59. Let $f(x, y) = y^x$. Find the directional derivative of f at $P_0(3, 2)$ in the direction toward the point $Q(1, 1)$.

60. According to postal regulations, the largest cylindrical can that can be sent has a girth ($2\pi r$) plus length ℓ of 108 inches. What is the largest volume cylindrical can that can be mailed?

61. Let $f(x, y, z) = z(x - y)^5 + xy^2 z^3$.

   a. Find the directional derivative of f at $(2, 1, -1)$ in the direction of the outward normal to the sphere $x^2 + y^2 + z^2 = 6$.

   b. In what direction is the directional derivative at $(2, 1, -1)$ largest?

62. Find positive numbers x and y for which xyz is a maximum, given that $x + y + z = 1$. Assume that the extreme value exists.

63. Maximize $f(x, y, z) = x^2 yz$ given that x, y, and z are all positive numbers and $x + y + z = 12$. Assume that the extreme value exists.

64. If $z = f(x^2 - y^2)$, evaluate $y \dfrac{\partial z}{\partial x} + x \dfrac{\partial z}{\partial y}$.

65. Find the shortest distance from the origin to the surface $z^2 = 3 + xy$. Assume the extreme value exists.

66. Modeling Problem A plate is heated in such a way that its temperature at a point (x, y) measured in centimeters on the plate is given in degrees Celsius by

$$T(x, y) = \frac{64}{x^2 + y^2 + 4}$$

   a. Find the rate of change in temperature at the point $(3, 4)$ in the direction $2\mathbf{i} + \mathbf{j}$.

   b. Find the direction and the magnitude of the greatest rate of change of the temperature at the point $(3, 4)$.

67. Modeling Problem The beautiful patterns on the wings of butterflies have long been a subject of curiosity and scientific study. Mathematical models used to study these patterns often focus on determining the level of morphogen (a chemical that affects change). In a model dealing with eyespot patterns, a quantity of morphogen is released from an eyespot and the morphogen concentration t days later is modeled by

$$S(r, t) = \frac{1}{\sqrt{4\pi t}} e^{-(\gamma kt + r^2/(4t))} \qquad t > 0$$

where r measures the radius of the region on the wing affected by the morphogen, and k and γ are positive constants.[*]

   a. Find t_m so that $\partial S/\partial t = 0$. Show that the function $S_m(t)$ formed from $S(r, t)$ by fixing r has a relative maximum at t_m. Is this the same as saying that the function of two variables $S(r, t)$ has a relative maximum?

   b. Let $M(r)$ denote the maximum found in part **a**; that is, $M(r) = S(r, t_m)$. Find an expression for M in terms of $z = (1 + 4\gamma kr^2)^{1/2}$.

   c. Show that $\dfrac{dM}{dr} < 0$ and interpret this result.

68. Modeling Problem Certain malignant tumors that do not respond to conventional methods of treatment (surgery, chemotherapy, etc.) may be treated by *hyperthermia*, a process involving the application of extreme heat using microwave transmission (see Figure 11.53). For one particular kind of microwave application used in such therapy, the temperature at each point located r units from the central axis of the tumor and h units inside it is modeled by the formula

$$T(r, h) = Ke^{-pr^2}[e^{-qh} - e^{-sh}]$$

where K, p, q, and s are positive constants that depend on the properties of the patient's blood and the heating application.[†]

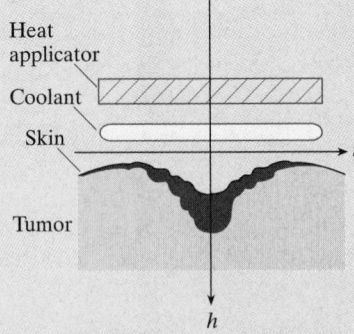

Figure 11.53 Hyperthermia treatment

[*]J. D. Murray, *Mathematical Biology*, 2nd edition, Springer-Verlag, New York, 1993, p. 464.

[†]"Heat Therapy for Tumors," by Leah Edelstein-Keshet, *UMAP Modules 1991: Tools for Teaching*, Consortium for Mathematics and Its Applications, Inc., Lexington, MA, 1992, pp. 73–101.

a. At what depth inside the tumor does the maximum temperature occur? Express your answers in terms of K, p, q, and s.

b. The article on which this problem is based discusses the physiology of hyperthermia in addition to raising several other interesting mathematical issues. Read this article and discuss assumptions made in the model.

69. Modeling Problem The marketing manager for a certain company has compiled the following data relating monthly advertising expenditure and monthly sales (in units of $1,000).

Advertising	3	4	7	9	10
Sales	78	86	138	145	156

a. Plot the data on a graph and find the least squares line.

b. Use the least squares line to predict monthly sales if the monthly advertising expenditure is $5,000.

70. Find $f_{xx} - f_{xy} + f_{yy}$, where $f(x, y) = x^2y^3 + x^3y^2$.

71. Find f_{xyz}, where $f(x, y, z) = \cos(x^2 + y^3 + z^4)$.

72. Let $z = f(x, y)$, where $x = t + \cos t$ and $y = e^t$.

a. Suppose $f_x(1, 1) = 4$ and $f_y(1, 1) = -3$. Find $\dfrac{dz}{dt}$ when $t = 0$.

b. Suppose $f_x(0, 2) = -1$ and $f_y(0, 2) = 3$. Find $\dfrac{\partial z}{\partial r}$ and $\dfrac{\partial z}{\partial \theta}$ at the point where $r = 2$, $\theta = \frac{\pi}{2}$, and $x = r\cos\theta$, $y = r\sin\theta$.

73. Suppose f has continuous partial derivatives in some region D in the plane, and suppose $f(x, y) = 0$ for all (x, y) in D. If $(1, 2)$ is in D and $f_x(1, 2) = 4$ and $f_y(1, 2) = 6$, find dy/dx when $x = 1$ and $y = 2$.

74. Suppose $\nabla f(x, y, z)$ is parallel to the vector $x\mathbf{i} + y\mathbf{j} + z\mathbf{k}$ for all (x, y, z). Show that $f(0, 0, a) = f(0, 0, -a)$ for any a.

75. Find two unit vectors that are normal to the surface given by $z = f(x, y)$ at $(0, 1)$, where $f(x, y) = \sin x + e^{xy} + 2y$.

76. Let $f(x, y) = 3(x - 2)^2 - 5(y + 1)^2$. Find all points on the graph of f where the tangent plane is parallel to the plane $2x + 2y - z = 0$.

77. Let z be defined implicitly as a function of x and y by the equation $\cos(x + y) + \cos(x + z) = 1$. Find $\dfrac{\partial^2 z}{\partial y \partial x}$ in terms of x, y, and z.

78. Suppose F and F' are continuous functions of t and that $F'(t) = C$. Define f by $f(x, y) = F(x^2 + y^2)$. Show that the direction of $\nabla f(a, b)$ is the same as the direction of the line joining (a, b) to $(0, 0)$.

79. Let $f(x, y) = 12x^{-1} + 18y^{-1} + xy$, where $x > 0$, $y > 0$. How do you know that f must necessarily have a minimum in the region $x > 0$, $y > 0$? Find the minimum.

80. Let $f(x, y) = 3x^4 - 4x^2y + y^2$. Show that f has a minimum at $(0, 0)$ on every line $y = mx$ that passes through the origin. Then show that f has no relative minimum at $(0, 0)$.

In Problems 81–83, you may assume the required extremum exists.

81. Find the minimum of $x^2 + y^2 + z^2$ subject to the constraint $ax + by + cz = 1$ (with $a \neq 0$, $b \neq 0$, $c \neq 0$).

82. Suppose $0 < a < 1$ and $x \geq 0$, $y \geq 0$. Find the maximum of $x^a y^{1-a}$ subject to the constraint $ax + (1 - a)y = 1$.

83. The **geometric mean** of three positive numbers x, y, z is $G = (xyz)^{1/3}$ and the **arithmetic mean** is $A = \frac{1}{3}(x + y + z)$. Use the method of Lagrange multipliers to show that $G(x, y, z) \leq A(x, y, z)$ for all x, y, z.

84. Liquid flows through a tube with length L centimeters and internal radius r centimeters. The total volume V of fluid that flows each second is related to the pressure P and the viscosity a of the fluid by the formula $V = \dfrac{\pi P r^4}{8aL}$. What is the maximum error that can occur in using this formula to compute the viscosity a, if errors of $\pm 1\%$ can be made in measuring r and L, $\pm 2\%$ in measuring V, and $\pm 3\%$ in measuring P?

85. Suppose the functions f and g have continuous partial derivatives and satisfy

$$\frac{\partial f}{\partial x} = \frac{\partial g}{\partial y} \quad \text{and} \quad \frac{\partial f}{\partial y} = -\frac{\partial g}{\partial x}$$

These are called the *Cauchy-Riemann equations*.

a. Show that level curves of f and g intersect at right angles provided $\nabla f \neq \mathbf{0}$ and $\nabla g \neq \mathbf{0}$.

b. Assuming that the second partials of f and g are continuous, show that f and g satisfy Laplace's equations

$$f_{xx} + f_{yy} = 0 \quad \text{and} \quad g_{xx} + g_{yy} = 0$$

86. Show that if $z = f(r, \theta)$, where r and θ are defined as functions of x and y by the equations $x = r\cos\theta$, $y = r\sin\theta$, then the equation $\dfrac{\partial^2 z}{\partial x^2} + \dfrac{\partial^2 z}{\partial y^2} = 0$ becomes $\dfrac{\partial^2 z}{\partial r^2} + \dfrac{1}{r^2}\dfrac{\partial^2 z}{\partial \theta^2} + \dfrac{1}{r}\dfrac{\partial z}{\partial r} = 0$. This is Laplace's equation in polar coordinates.

87. A circular sector of radius r and central angle θ has area $A = \frac{1}{2}r^2\theta$. Find θ for the sector of fixed area A_0 for which the perimeter of the sector is minimized. Use the method of Lagrange multipliers and assume that the minimum exists.

88. For the production function given by $Q(x, y) = x^a y^b$, where $a > 0$ and $b > 0$, show that

$$x\frac{\partial Q}{\partial x} + y\frac{\partial Q}{\partial y} = (a + b)Q$$

In particular, if $b = 1 - a$ with $0 < a < 1$,

$$x\frac{\partial Q}{\partial x} + y\frac{\partial Q}{\partial y} = Q$$

89. The diameter of the base and the height of a closed right circular cylinder are measured, and the measurements are known to have errors of at most 0.5 cm. If the diameter and height are taken to be 4 cm and 8 cm, respectively, find bounds for the propagated error in

a. the volume V of the cylinder

b. the surface area S of the cylinder

90. A right circular cone is measured and is found to have base radius $r = 40$ cm and altitude $h = 20$ cm. If it is known that each measurement is accurate to within 2%, what is the maximum percentage error in the measurement of the volume?

91. An elastic cylindrical container is filled with air so that the radius of the base is 2.02 cm and the height is 6.04 cm. If the container is deflated so that the radius of the base reduces to 2 cm and the height to 6 cm, approximately how much air has been removed? (Ignore the thickness of the container.)

92. Suppose f is a differentiable function of two variables with f_x and f_y also differentiable, and assume that f_{xx}, f_{yy} and f_{xy} are continuous. The **second directional derivative** of f at the point (x, y) in the direction of the unit vector $\mathbf{u} = a\mathbf{i} + b\mathbf{j}$ is defined by $D_\mathbf{u}^2 f(x, y) = D_\mathbf{u}[D_\mathbf{u} f(x, y)]$. Show that

$$D_\mathbf{u}^2 f(x, y) = a^2 f_{xx}(x, y) + 2ab f_{xy}(x, y) + b^2 f_{yy}(x, y)$$

93. A capsule is a cylinder of radius r and length ℓ, capped on each end by a hemisphere. Assume that the capsule dissolves in the stomach at a rate proportional to the ratio $R = S/V$, where V is the volume and S is the surface area of the capsule. Show that

$$\frac{\partial R}{\partial r} < 0 \quad \text{and} \quad \frac{\partial R}{\partial \ell} < 0$$

94. Spy Problem Gasping for breath, the Spy tumbles through the escape hole in the cave (Problem 54, Section 11.6) and is immediately knocked unconscious. He awakens tied to a chair, alone, except for a rather large ticking bomb less than 10 feet away. "So my friend," whispers the icy voice of Coldfinger, "you plan to eliminate Scélérat and me for Blohardt, but it appears you are the one about to be eliminated. Still, for old times' sake, I'll give you a chance. Pick a number, S, then I'll pick a number, C, and the value of the expression

$$N = \frac{\exp[(C + S)^2 + 4S + 22]}{(C + S)^2(e^{40} + e^{8S})}$$

will be the number of minutes I'll wait before pressing this little red button." Assuming Coldfinger does his best to minimize the expression once S has been chosen, what number should the Spy pick, and how many minutes will he have to escape and defuse the bomb?

95. Counterexample Problem Find the minimum distance from the origin to the paraboloid $z = 4 - x^2 - 4y^2$. The graph is shown in Figure 11.54.

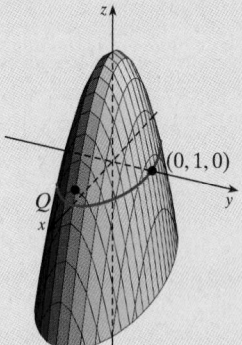

Figure 11.54

The distance from $P(x, y, z)$ to the origin is

$$d = \sqrt{x^2 + y^2 + z^2}$$

This distance will be minimized when d^2 is minimized. Thus, the function to be minimized (after replacing x^2 by $4 - 4y^2 - z$) is $D(x, y) = 4 - 4y^2 - z + y^2 + z^2 = 4 - 3y^2 + z^2 - z$. Setting

the partial derivatives D_y and D_z to 0 gives the critical point $y = 0$, $z = 0.5$. Solving for x on the paraboloid gives the points $Q_1(\sqrt{3.5}, 0, 0.5)$ and $Q_2(-\sqrt{3.5}, 0, 0.5)$. These points are *not* minimal because $(0, 1, 0)$ is closer. Explain what is going on here. Our thanks to Herbert R. Bailey, who presented this problem in *The College Mathematics Journal* (" 'Hidden' Boundaries in Constrained Max-Min Problems," May 1991, Vol. 22, p. 227).

96. It can be shown that if $z = f(x, y)$ has the least surface area of all surfaces with a given boundary, then

$$(1 + z_y^2)z_{xx} - zz_{xy} + (1 + z_x^2)z_{yy} = 0$$

A surface satisfying such an equation is called a **minimal surface**.

a. Find constants A, B so that

$$z = \ln\left(\frac{A\cos y}{B\cos x}\right)$$

is a minimal surface.

b. Is it possible to find C and D so that $z = C\ln(\sin x) + D\ln(\sin y)$ is a minimal surface?

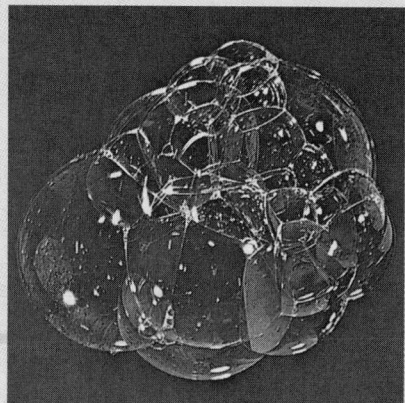

Soap bubbles form minimal surfaces. For an interesting discussion, see "The Geometry of Soap Films and Soap Bubbles," by Frederick J. Almgren, Jr., and Jean E. Taylor, *Scientific American*, July 1976, pp. 82–93.

97. Putnam Examination Problem Let f be a real-valued function having partial derivatives defined for $x^2 + y^2 < 1$ that satisfies $|f(x, y)| \leq 1$. Show that there exists a point (x_0, y_0) in the interior of the unit circle such that
$$[f_x(x_0, y_0)]^2 + [f_y(x_0, y_0)]^2 \leq 16.$$

98. Putnam Examination Problem Find the smallest volume bounded by the coordinate planes and a tangent plane to the ellipsoid

$$\frac{x^2}{a^2} + \frac{y^2}{b^2} + \frac{z^2}{c^2} = 1$$

99. Putnam Examination Problem Find the shortest distance between the plane $Ax + By + Cz + 1 = 0$ and the ellipsoid

$$\frac{x^2}{a^2} + \frac{y^2}{b^2} + \frac{z^2}{c^2} \leq 1$$

Desertification

This project is to be done in groups of three or four students. Each group will submit a single written report.

A friend of yours named Maria is studying the causes of the continuing expansion of deserts (a process known as *desertification*). She is working on a biological index of vegetation disturbance, which she has defined. By seeing how this index and other factors change through time, she hopes to discover the role played in desertification. She is studying a huge tract of land bounded by a rectangle. This piece of land surrounds a major city but does not include the city. She needs to find an economical way to calculate for this piece of land the important vegetation disturbance index $J(x, y)$.

Maria has embarked upon an ingenious approach of combining the results of photographic and radar images taken during flights over the area to calculate the index J. She is assuming that J is a smooth function. Although the flight data do not directly reveal the values of the function J, they give the rate at which the values of J change as the flights sweep over the landscape surrounding the city. Maria's staff has conducted numerous flights, and from the data she believes she has been able to find actual formulas for the rates at which J changes in the east-west and north-south directions. She has given these functions the names M and N. Thus, $M(x, y)$ is the rate at which J changes as one sweeps in the positive x-direction and $N(x, y)$ is the corresponding rate in the y-direction. Maria shows you these formulas:

$$M(x, y) = 3.4e^x(y - 7.8)^2 \qquad \text{and} \qquad N(x, y) = 22\sin(75 - 2xy)$$

Convince her that these two formulas cannot possibly be correct. Do this by showing her that there is a condition that the two functions M and N must satisfy if they are to be the east-west and north-south rates of change of the function J and that her formulas for M and N do not meet this condition. However, show Maria that if she can find formulas for M and N that satisfy the condition that you showed her, it is possible to find a formula for the function J from the formulas for M and N.

MATHEMATICS in its pure form, as arithmetic, algebra, geometry, and the applications of the analytic method, as well as mathematics applied to matter and force, or statics and dynamics, furnishes the peculiar study that gives to us, whether as children or as men, the command of nature in this its quantitative aspect; mathematics furnishes the instrument, the tool of thought, which we wield in this realm.

——W. T. Harris
Psychological Foundations of Education
(New York, 1898), p. 325.

---

[*]Marcus S. Cohen, Edward D. Gaughan, R. Arthur Knoebel, Douglas S. Kurtz, and David J. Pengelley, "Priming the Calculus Pump: Innovations and Resources," *MAA Notes* 17(1991).

12

Multiple Integration

PREVIEW

The *single integral* $\int_a^b f(x)\,dx$ introduced in Chapter 5 has many uses, as we have seen. In this chapter, we will generalize the single integral to define *multiple* integrals in which the integrand is a function of several variables. We will find that multiple integration is used in much the same way as single integration, by "adding" small quantities to define and compute area, volume, surface area, moments, centroids, and probability.

PERSPECTIVE

What is the volume of a doughnut (torus)? Given the joint probability density function for the amount of time a typical shopper spends shopping at a particular store and the time spent in the checkout line, how likely is it that a shopper will spend no more than 30 minutes altogether in the store? If the temperature in a solid body is given at each point (x, y, z) and time t, what is the average temperature of the body over a particular time period? Where should a security watch tower be placed in a parking lot to ensure the most comprehensive visual coverage? We will answer these and other similar questions in this chapter using multiple integration.

12.1   Double Integration over Rectangular Regions

IN THIS SECTION   definition of the double integral, properties of double integrals, volume interpretation, iterated integration, an informal argument for Fubini's theorem

DEFINITION OF THE DOUBLE INTEGRAL

Recall that in Chapter 5, we defined the definite integral of a single variable $\displaystyle\int_a^b f(x)\,dx$ as a limit involving Riemann sums

$$\sum_{k=1}^n f(x_k^*)\Delta x_k, \quad \text{where } a = x_0 < x_1 < x_2 < \cdots < x_n = b$$

are points in a partition of the interval $[a, b]$ and x_k^* is a representative point in the subinterval $[x_{k-1}, x_k]$. We now apply the same ideas to define a definite integral of two variables $\displaystyle\iint_R f(x, y)\,dA$, over the rectangle $R : a \leq x \leq b, c \leq y \leq d$.

The definition requires the ideas and notation described in the following three steps:

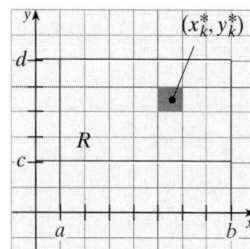

Figure 12.1 A partition of the rectangle R into mn cells showing the kth cell representative.

Step 1.   Partition the interval $a \leq x \leq b$ into m subintervals and the interval $c \leq y \leq d$ into n subintervals. Using these subdivisions, partition the rectangle R into $N = mn$ **cells** (subrectangles), as shown in Figure 12.1. Call this partition P.

Step 2.   Choose a representative point (x_k^*, y_k^*) from each cell in the partition of the rectangle. Form the sum

$$\sum_{k=1}^N f(x_k^*, y_k^*)\Delta A_k$$

where ΔA_k is the area of the kth representative cell. This is called the **Riemann sum** of $f(x, y)$ with respect to the partition P and cell representatives (x_k^*, y_k^*).

Step 3.   To measure the size of the rectangles in the partition P, we define the **norm** $\|P\|$ of the partition to be the length of the longest diagonal of any rectangle in the partition. We **refine** the partition by subdividing the cells in such a way that the norm decreases.

When this process is applied to the Riemann sum and the norm decreases indefinitely to zero, we write

$$\lim_{\|P\| \to 0} \sum_{k=1}^N f(x_k^*, y_k^*)\Delta A_k$$

If this limit exits, its value is called the *double integral* of f over the rectangle R.

Double Integral

> If f is defined on a closed, bounded rectangular region R in the xy-plane, then the **double integral of f over R** is defined by
>
> $$\iint_R f(x, y)\,dA = \lim_{\|P\| \to 0} \sum_{k=1}^N f(x_k^*, y_k^*)\Delta A_k$$
>
> provided this limit exists, in which case, f is said to be **integrable** over R.

More formally, the limit statement

$$I = \lim_{\|P\| \to 0} \sum_{k=1}^{N} f(x_k^*, y_k^*) \Delta A_k$$

means that for any $\epsilon > 0$, there exists a $\delta > 0$ such that

$$\left| I - \sum_{k=1}^{N} f(x_k^*, y_k^*) \Delta A_k \right| < \epsilon$$

whenever $\sum_{k=1}^{N} f(x_k^*, y_k^*) \Delta A_k$ is a Riemann sum whose norm satisfies $\|P\| < \delta$. In this process, the number of cells N depends on the partition P, and as $\|P\| \to 0$, it follows that $N \to \infty$.

It can be shown that if $f(x, y)$ is continuous on a rectangle R, then it must be integrable on R, although it is also true that certain discontinuous functions are integrable as well. Moreover, it can also be shown that if the limit that defines the definite integral exists, then it is unique in the sense that the same limiting value results no matter how the partitions and subinterval representatives are chosen. We will extend the definition of the definite integral to nonrectangular regions in Section 12.2. However, issues involving the existence and uniqueness of the definite integral are generally dealt with in a course in advanced calculus.

PROPERTIES OF DOUBLE INTEGRALS

Double integrals have many of the same properties as single integrals. Three of these properties are contained in the following theorem.

THEOREM 12.1 Properties of double integrals

Assume that all the given integrals exist on a rectangular region R.

Linearity rule: For constants a and b,

$$\iint\limits_{R} [af(x, y) + bg(x, y)] \, dA = a \iint\limits_{R} f(x, y) \, dA + b \iint\limits_{R} g(x, y) \, dA$$

Dominance rule: If $f(x, y) \geq g(x, y)$ throughout a rectangular region R, then

$$\iint\limits_{R} f(x, y) \, dA \geq \iint\limits_{R} g(x, y) \, dA$$

Subdivision rule: If the rectangular region of integration R is subdivided into two subrectangles R_1 and R_2, then

$$\iint\limits_{R} f(x, y) \, dA = \iint\limits_{R_1} f(x, y) \, dA + \iint\limits_{R_2} f(x, y) \, dA$$

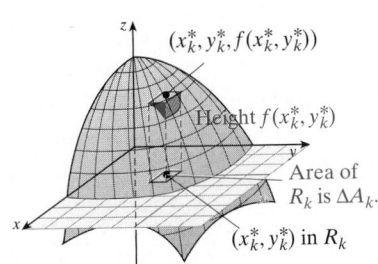

Region R

Proof This proof is omitted. ❑

VOLUME INTERPRETATION

If $g(x) \geq 0$ on the interval $[a, b]$, the single integral $\int_a^b g(x) \, dx$ can be interpreted as the area under the curve $y = g(x)$ over $[a, b]$. The double integral $\iint\limits_{R} f(x, y) \, dA$ has a similar interpretation in terms of volume. To see this, note that if $f(x, y) \geq 0$ on the rectangular region R and we partition R, then the product $f(x_k^*, y_k^*) \Delta A_k$ is the volume of a parallelepiped (a box) with height $f(x_k^*, y_k^*)$ and base area ΔA_k, as shown in Figure 12.2.

Figure 12.2 The approximating parallelepiped has volume $\Delta V_k = f(x_k^*, y_k^*) \Delta A_k$

The Riemann sum

$$\sum_{k=1}^{N} f(x_k^*, y_k^*) \Delta A_k$$

provides an estimate of the total volume under the surface $z = f(x, y)$ over R, and if f is continuous, we expect the approximation to improve by using more refined partitions (that is, more rectangles with smaller norm). Thus, it is natural to *define* the total volume under the surface as the limit of Riemann sums as the norm tends to 0. That is, the volume under $z = f(x, y)$ over the domain R is given by

$$V = \lim_{\|P\| \to 0} \sum_{k=1}^{N} f(x_k^*, y_k^*) \Delta A_k = \iint\limits_{R} f(x, y) \, dA$$

The approximation by the Riemann sum is illustrated in Figure 12.3.

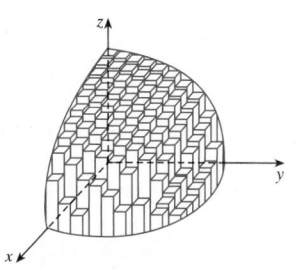

Figure 12.3 Volume approximated by rectangular parallelepipeds

EXAMPLE 1   Evaluating a double integral by relating it to a volume

Evaluate $\iint\limits_{R} (2 - y) \, dA$, where R is the rectangle in the xy-plane with vertices $(0, 0)$, $(3, 0)$, $(3, 2)$, and $(0, 2)$.

Solution

Because $z = 2 - y$ satisfies $z \geq 0$ for all points in R, the value of the double integral is the same as the volume of the solid bounded above by the plane $z = 2 - y$ and below by the rectangle R. The solid is shown in Figure 12.4. Looking at it endwise, it has a triangular cross section of area B and has length 3. We use the formula $V = Bh$.

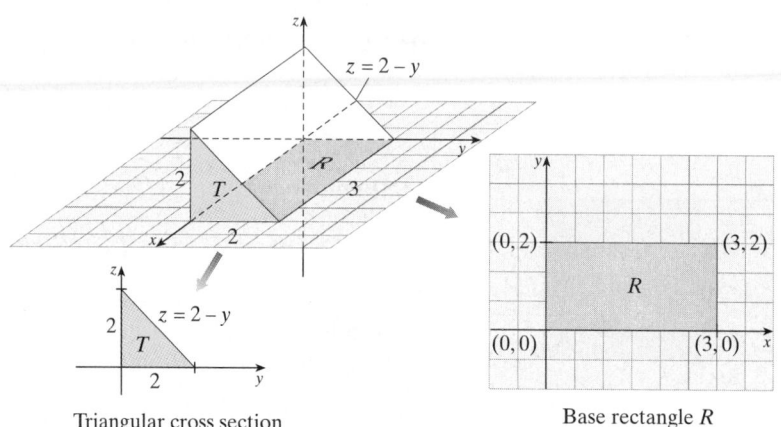

Triangular cross section   Base rectangle R

Figure 12.4   Evaluation of $\iint\limits_{R} (2 - y) \, dA$ as a volume

Because the base is a triangle of side 2 and altitude 2, we have

$$V = Bh = \left[\frac{1}{2}(2)(2) \right](3) = 6$$

Therefore, the value of the integral is also 6; that is,

$$\iint\limits_{R} (2 - y) \, dA = 6$$

■

ITERATED INTEGRATION

As with single integrals, it is often not practical to evaluate a double integral even over a simple rectangular region by using the definition. Instead, we will compute double integrals by a process called **iterated integration**, which is like partial differentiation in reverse.

Suppose $f(x, y)$ is continuous over the rectangle R: $a \leq x \leq b, c \leq y \leq d$. Then we write $\int_c^d f(x, y)\, dy$ to denote the integral obtained by integrating $f(x, y)$ with respect to y over the interval $[c, d]$ with x held constant. The integral obtained by this partial integration is a function of x alone, $G(x) = \int_c^d f(x, y)\, dy$, which we integrate over the interval $[a, b]$ to obtain the **iterated integral**

$$\int_a^b G(x)\, dx = \int_a^b \left[\int_c^d f(x, y)\, dy \right] dx \qquad \text{Integrate with respect to } y \text{ first, keeping } x \text{ constant, and then integrate with respect to } x.$$

Similarly, if we integrate $f(x, y)$ first with respect to x over $[a, b]$ holding y constant, and then with respect to y over $[c, d]$, we obtain the iterated integral

$$\int_c^d \left[\int_a^b f(x, y)\, dx \right] dy \qquad \text{Integrate with respect to } x \text{ first, keeping } y \text{ constant, and then integrate with respect to } y.$$

The following theorem, which shows how the double integral

$$\iint\limits_R f(x, y)\, dA$$

can be evaluated in terms of iterated integrals, was proved in a more general form by the Italian mathematician Guido Fubini (1879–1943) in 1907.

THEOREM 12.2 Fubini's theorem over a rectangular region

If $f(x, y)$ is continuous over the rectangle R: $a \leq x \leq b, \ c \leq y \leq d$, then the double integral

$$\iint\limits_R f(x, y)\, dA$$

may be evaluated by either iterated integral; that is,

$$\iint\limits_R f(x, y)\, dA = \int_c^d \int_a^b f(x, y)\, dx\, dy = \int_a^b \int_c^d f(x, y)\, dy\, dx$$

➡ **What This Says**   Instead of using the definition of a double integral of $f(x, y)$ over the rectangle R: $a \leq x \leq b, c \leq y \leq d$, evaluate either of the iterated integrals:

Limits of x (variable outside brackets)   Limits of y (variable outside brackets)

$$\int_a^b \left[\int_c^d f(x, y)\, dy \right] dx \qquad \text{or} \qquad \int_c^d \left[\int_a^b f(x, y)\, dx \right] dy$$

Limits of y (variable inside brackets)   Limits of x (variable inside brackets)

Note that Fubini's theorem applies only when $a, b, c,$ and d are constants.

Proof   We will provide an informal, geometric argument at the end of this section. The formal proof may be found in most advanced calculus textbooks.   ❑

Let us see how Fubini's theorem can be used to evaluate double integrals. We begin by taking another look at Example 1.

EXAMPLE 2   Evaluating a double integral by using Fubini's theorem

Use an iterated integral with y-integration first to compute $\displaystyle\iint_R (2 - y)\, dA$, where R is the rectangle with vertices $(0, 0)$, $(3, 0)$, $(3, 2)$, and $(0, 2)$.

Solution

The region of integration is the rectangle $0 \le x \le 3$, $0 \le y \le 2$ (see Example 1 and Figure 12.4). Thus, by Fubini's theorem, the double integral can be evaluated by the iterated integral:

$$\iint_R (2 - y)\, dA = \int_0^3 \int_0^2 (2 - y)\, dy\, dx \qquad \text{Integrate inner integral}$$
$$\text{with respect to } y.$$

$$= \int_0^3 \left[2y - \frac{y^2}{2} \right]\Big|_0^2 dx$$

$$= \int_0^3 \left[4 - \frac{4}{2} - (0) \right] dx$$

$$= \int_0^3 2\, dx = 2x\big|_0^3 = 6$$

which is the same as the result obtained geometrically in Example 1.   ■

EXAMPLE 3   Double integral using an iterated integral

Evaluate $\displaystyle\iint_R x^2 y^5\, dA$, where R is the rectangle $1 \le x \le 2$, $0 \le y \le 1$, using an iterated integral with

a. y-integration first   **b.** x-integration first

Solution

a. The graph of the surface $z = x^2 y^5$ over the rectangle is shown in Figure 12.5a, and the rectangular region of integration in Figure 12.5b.

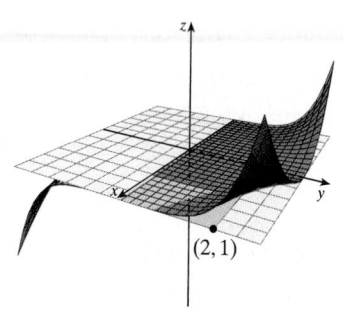
a. Graph of surface $z = x^2 y^5$

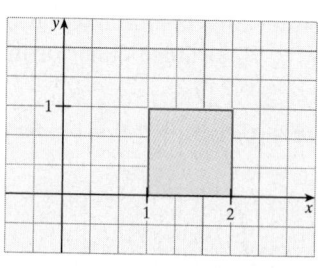
b. Sketch of rectangular region

Figure 12.5 Graph of the surface over a rectangle

$$\iint_R x^2 y^5\, dA = \int_1^2 \int_0^1 x^2 y^5\, dy\, dx \qquad \text{Read this as } \int_1^2 \left[\int_0^1 x^2 y^5\, dy \right] dx.$$

$$= \int_1^2 \left[x^2 \frac{y^6}{6} \right]\Big|_0^1 dx$$

$$= \int_1^2 \left[x^2 \left(\frac{1}{6} - \frac{0}{6} \right) \right] dx = \frac{x^3}{18}\Big|_1^2 = \frac{8}{18} - \frac{1}{18} = \frac{7}{18}$$

b.
$$\iint_R x^2 y^5\, dA = \int_0^1 \int_1^2 x^2 y^5\, dx\, dy = \int_0^1 y^5 \left[\frac{x^3}{3} \right]\Big|_1^2 dy$$

$$= \int_0^1 \left[y^5 \left(\frac{8}{3} - \frac{1}{3} \right) \right] dy = \frac{7y^6}{18}\Big|_0^1 = \frac{7}{18} - \frac{0}{18} = \frac{7}{18} \qquad ■$$

TECHNOLOGY NOTE

Using technology for multiple integrals offers no special difficulties. You simply integrate with respect to one variable and then with respect to the other variable. You must be careful, however, to input properly the correct limits of integration for each integral. Notice that for $\int_1^2 \int_0^1 x^2 y^2 \, dy \, dx$, most calculators and software programs require the following syntax: *integration operator, function, variable of integration, lower limit of integration, upper limit of integration.*

$$\int\left(\left(\int\underbrace{(x^2 y^5)}_{function},\underset{\underset{\substack{inner\ variable \\ of\ integration}}{\uparrow}}{y},\overbrace{0,1}^{\substack{inner\ limits \\ of\ integration}}\right),\underset{\underset{\substack{outer\ variable \\ of\ integration}}{\uparrow}}{x},\overbrace{1,2}^{\substack{outer\ limits \\ of\ integration}}\right)$$

"inside" integral is the function
for the "outside" integration

The result of this operation is shown in Figure 12.6 (compare with Example 3).

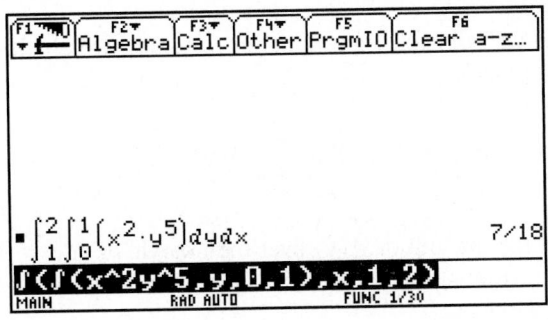
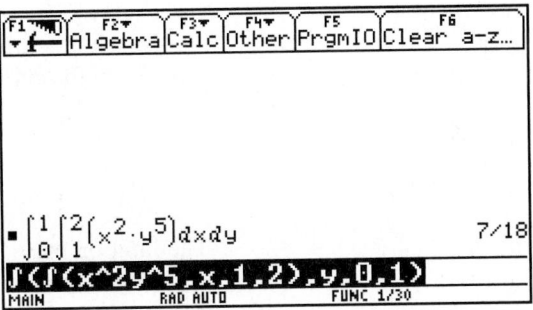

Figure 12.6   Calculator output for Example 3

In many problems, the order of integration in a double integral is largely a matter of personal choice, but occasionally, choosing the order correctly makes the difference between a straightforward evaluation and one that is either difficult or impossible. Consider the following example.

EXAMPLE 4   Choosing the order of integration for a double integral

Evaluate $\iint\limits_R x \cos xy \, dA$ for R: $0 \le x \le \frac{\pi}{2}, 0 \le y \le 1$.

Solution

Suppose we integrate with respect to x first:

$$\int_0^1 \left[\int_0^{\pi/2} x \cos xy \, dx \right] dy$$

The inner integral requires integration by parts. However, integrating with respect to y first is much simpler:

$$\int_0^{\pi/2} \left[\int_0^1 x \cos xy \, dy \right] dx = \int_0^{\pi/2} \left[\frac{x \sin xy}{x} \right]\Big|_0^1 dx$$

$$= \int_0^{\pi/2} (\sin x - \sin 0) \, dx = -\cos x \Big|_0^{\pi/2} = 1 \qquad \blacksquare$$

AN INFORMAL ARGUMENT FOR FUBINI'S THEOREM

We can make Fubini's theorem plausible with a geometric argument in the case where $f(x, y) \geq 0$ on R. If $\iint\limits_{R} f(x, y) \, dA$ is defined on a rectangle R: $a \leq x \leq b$, $c \leq y \leq d$, it represents the volume of the solid D bounded above by the surface $z = f(x, y)$ and below by the rectangle R. If $A(y_k^*)$ is the cross-sectional area perpendicular to the y-axis at the point y_k^*, then $A(y_k^*)\Delta y_k$ represents the volume of a "slab" that approximates the volume of part of the solid D, as shown in Figure 12.7.

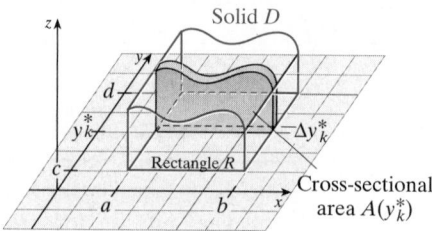

Figure 12.7   Cross-sectional volume parallel to the xz-plane

By using a limit to "add up" all such approximating volumes, we obtain the volume, V, of the entire solid D; that is,

$$\iint\limits_{R} f(x, y) \, dA = V = \lim_{\|P\| \to 0} \sum_{k=1}^{N} A(y_k^*)\Delta y_k$$

The limit on the right is just the integral of $A(y)$ over the interval $c \leq y \leq d$, where $A(y)$ is the area of a cross section with fixed y. In Chapter 5, we found that the area $A(y)$ can be computed by the integral

$$A(y) = \int_a^b f(x, y) \, dx \qquad \text{Integration with respect to } x \ (y \text{ is fixed})$$

We can now make this substitution for $A(y)$ to obtain

$$\iint\limits_{R} f(x, y) \, dA = V = \lim_{\|P\| \to 0} \sum_{k=1}^{N} A(y_k^*)\Delta y_k$$

$$= \int_c^d A(y) \, dy$$

$$= \int_c^d \underbrace{\left[\int_a^b f(x, y) \, dx \right]}_{A(y)} dy \qquad \text{Substitution}$$

The fact that

$$\iint\limits_{R} f(x, y) \, dA = \int_a^b \int_c^d f(x, y) \, dy \, dx$$

can be justified in a similar fashion (you are asked to do this in Problem 46). Thus, we have

$$\int_c^d \left[\int_a^b f(x, y) \, dx \right] dy = \iint\limits_{R} f(x, y) \, dA = \int_a^b \left[\int_c^d f(x, y) \, dy \right] dx$$

12.1 PROBLEM SET

A *In Problems 1–6, evaluate the iterated integrals.*

1. $\int_0^2 \int_0^1 (x^2 + xy + y^2)\, dy\, dx$

2. $\int_1^2 \int_0^\pi x \cos y\, dy\, dx$

3. $\int_1^{e^2} \int_1^2 \left[\frac{1}{x} + \frac{1}{y}\right]\, dy\, dx$ **4.** $\int_0^{\ln 2} \int_0^1 e^{x+2y}\, dx\, dy$

5. $\int_3^4 \int_1^2 \frac{x}{x-y}\, dy\, dx$ **6.** $\int_2^3 \int_{-1}^2 \frac{1}{(x+y)^2}\, dy\, dx$

Use an appropriate volume formula to evaluate the double integral given in Problems 7–12.

7. $\iint_R 4\, dA;$ **8.** $\iint_R 5\, dA;$

$R: 0 \le x \le 2, 0 \le y \le 4$ $R: 2 \le x \le 5, 1 \le y \le 3$

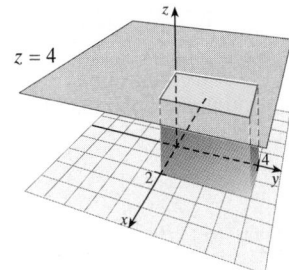

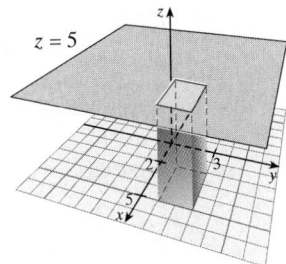

9. $\iint_R (4-y)\, dA;$ **10.** $\iint_R (4-2y)\, dA;$

$R: 0 \le x \le 3, 0 \le y \le 4$ $R: 0 \le x \le 4, 0 \le y \le 2$

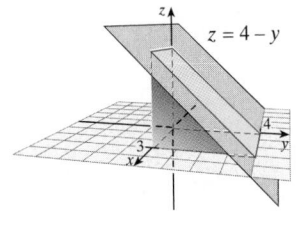

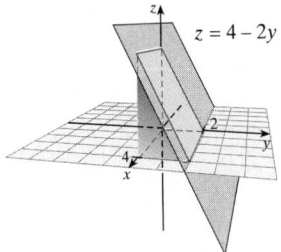

11. $\iint_R \frac{y}{2}\, dA;$ **12.** $\iint_R \frac{y}{4}\, dA;$

$R: 0 \le x \le 6, 0 \le y \le 4$ $R: 0 \le x \le 2, 0 \le y \le 8$

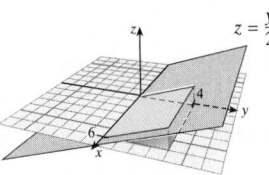

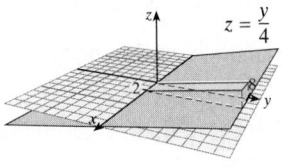

Use iterated integration to compute the double integrals in Problems 13–20 over the specified rectangle.

13. $\iint_R x^2 y\, dA; \; R: 1 \le x \le 2, 0 \le y \le 1$

14. $\iint_R \left(\frac{4+x^2}{1+y^2}\right)\, dA; \; R: 0 \le x \le 1, 0 \le y \le 1$

15. $\iint_R 2xe^y\, dA; \; R: -1 \le x \le 0, 0 \le y \le \ln 2$

16. $\iint_R x^2 e^{xy}\, dA; \; R: 0 \le x \le 1, 0 \le y \le 1$

17. $\iint_R \frac{2xy\, dA}{x^2+1}; \; R: 0 \le x \le 1, 1 \le y \le 3$

18. $\iint_R y\sqrt{x-y^2}\, dA; \; R: 1 \le x \le 5, 0 \le y \le 1$

19. $\iint_R \sin(x+y)\, dA; \; R: 0 \le x \le \frac{\pi}{4}, 0 \le y \le \frac{\pi}{2}$

20. $\iint_R x \sin xy\, dA, \; R: 0 \le x \le \pi, 0 \le y \le 1$

Find the volume of the solid bounded below by the rectangle R in the xy-plane and above by the graph of $z = f(x, y)$ in Problems 21–31.

21. $f(x, y) = 2x + 3y; \; R: 0 \le x \le 1, 0 \le y \le 2$

22. $f(x, y) = 5x + 2y; \; R: 0 \le x \le 1, 0 \le y \le 2$

23. $f(x, y) = \frac{x}{y} + \frac{y}{x}, \; R: 1 \le x \le 2, 1 \le y \le 2$

24. $f(x, y) = x \ln(xy); \; R: 1 \le x \le 2, 1 \le y \le e$

25. $f(x, y) = \sqrt{xy}; \; R: 0 \le x \le 1, 0 \le y \le 4$

26. $f(x, y) = \frac{\ln x}{y}; \; R: 1 \le x \le e, 1 \le y \le 2$

27. $f(x, y) = \frac{xy}{\sqrt{x^2+y^2+1}}; \; R: 0 \le x \le 1, 0 \le y \le 1$

28. $f(x, y) = xe^{xy}; \; R: 0 \le x \le 1, 0 \le y \le \ln 3$

29. $f(x, y) = (x+y)^5; \; R: 0 \le x \le 1, 0 \le y \le 1$

30. $f(x, y) = \sqrt{x+y}; \; R: 0 \le x \le 1, 0 \le y \le 1$

31. $f(x, y) = x \cos y + y \sin x; \; R: 0 \le x \le \frac{\pi}{2}, 0 \le y \le \frac{\pi}{2}$

B **32. WHAT DOES THIS SAY?** Discuss the definition of the double integral.

33. WHAT DOES THIS SAY? Explain how Fubini's theorem is used to evaluate double integrals.

34. Modeling Problem Suppose R is a rectangular region within the boundary of a certain national forest that contains 600,000 trees per square mile. Model the total number of trees, T, per square mile in the forest as a double integral. Assume that x and y are measured in miles.

35. Modeling Problem Suppose mass is distributed on a rectangular region R in the xy-plane so that the density (mass per unit area) at the point (x, y) is $\delta(x, y)$. Model the total mass as a double integral.

36. Modeling Problem Let R be a rectangular region within the boundary of a certain city defined by $R: -3 \le x \le 2, -1 \le y \le 1$, where units are in miles and $(0, 0)$ is the city center. Assume the population density is $12e^{-0.07r}$ thousand people per square mile, where $r = \sqrt{x^2+y^2}$. Model the total population of the region of the city as a double integral, but do not evaluate the integral.

In Problems 37–40, evaluate the integral. Note that one order of integration may be considerably easier than the other.

37. Compute $\iint\limits_{R} x\sqrt{1-x^2}\,e^{3y}\,dA$, where R is the rectangle $0 \le x \le 1, 0 \le y \le 2$.

38. Compute $\iint\limits_{R} \dfrac{\ln\sqrt{y}}{xy}\,dA$, where R is the rectangle $1 \le x \le 4$, $1 \le y \le e$.

39. Compute (correct to the nearest hundredth) $\iint\limits_{R} \dfrac{xy}{x^2+y^2}\,dA$, where R is the rectangle $1 \le x \le 3, 1 \le y \le 2$.

40. Evaluate $\iint\limits_{R} xe^{xy}\,dA$, where R is the rectangle $0 \le x \le 1$, $1 \le y \le 2$.

41. Explain why $\iint\limits_{R} (4 - x^2 - y^2)\,dA > 2$, where R is the rectangular domain in the plane given by $0 \le x \le 1, 0 \le y \le 1$.

42. Use a grid with 16 cells to approximate the volume of the solid lying between the surface $f(x, y) = 4 - x^2 - y^2$ and the square region R given by $0 \le x \le 1, 0 \le y \le 1$.

43. Use a grid with 16 cells to approximate the volume of the solid lying between the surface $f(x, y) = x^2 + y^2 + 1$ and the square region R given by $0 \le x \le 1, 0 \le y \le 1$.

44. HISTORICAL QUEST Guido Fubini taught at the Institute for Advanced Study in Princeton. He was nicknamed the "Little Giant," because of his small body but large mind. Even though the conclusion of Fubini's theorem was known for a long time and successfully applied in various instances, it was not satisfactorily proved in a general setting until 1907. His most important work was in differential projective geometry. In 1938 he was forced to leave Italy because of the Fascist government, and he immigrated to the United States. ∎

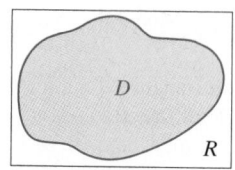

GUIDO FUBINI
1879–1943

For this Historical Quest, write several paragraphs about the nature of differential projective geometry.

45. Let f be a function with continuous second partial derivatives on a rectangular domain R with vertices (x_1, y_1), (x_1, y_2), (x_2, y_2), and (x_2, y_1), where $x_1 < x_2$ and $y_1 < y_2$. Use the fundamental theorem of calculus to show that

$$\iint\limits_{R} \frac{\partial^2 f}{\partial y \partial x}\,dA = f(x_1, y_1) - f(x_2, y_1) + f(x_2, y_2) - f(x_1, y_2)$$

46. Let f be a continuous function defined on the rectangle $R: a \le x \le b, c \le y \le d$. Show that

$$\iint\limits_{R} f(x, y)\,dA = \int_a^b \int_c^d f(x, y)\,dy\,dx$$

Hint: Modify the argument given in the text by taking cross-sectional areas perpendicular to the x-axis.

47. Counterexample Problem Show that the iterated integrals

$$\int_0^1 \int_0^1 \frac{y - x}{(x + y)^3}\,dy\,dx \quad \text{and} \quad \int_0^1 \int_0^1 \frac{y - x}{(x + y)^3}\,dx\,dy$$

have different values. Why does this not contradict Fubini's theorem?

48. Exploration Problem You want to evaluate

$$\iint\limits_{D} y \sin(xy) \sin^2(\pi y)\,dA$$

over the rectangle $D: 0 \le x \le \pi, 0 \le y \le \frac{1}{2}$. Which order of integration is easier?

12.2   Double Integration over Nonrectangular Regions

IN THIS SECTION   double integrals over Type I and Type II regions, more on area and volume, choosing the order of integration in a double integral

Let $f(x, y)$ be a function that is continuous on the region D that can be contained in a rectangle R. (See Figure 12.8.)

Define the function $F(x, y)$ on R as $f(x, y)$ if (x, y) is in D and 0 otherwise. That is,

Figure 12.8 The region D is bounded by a rectangle R.

$$F(x, y) = \begin{cases} f(x, y) & \text{for } (x, y) \text{ in } D \\ 0 & \text{for } (x, y) \text{ in } R, \text{ but not in } D \end{cases}$$

Then, if F is integrable over R, we say that f is **integrable over D**, and the **double**

integral of f over D is defined as

$$\iint\limits_{D} f(x, y)\, dA = \iint\limits_{R} F(x, y)\, dA$$

The function $F(x, y)$ may have discontinuities on the boundary of D, but if $f(x, y)$ is continuous on D and the boundary of D is fairly "well behaved," then it can be shown that $\iint\limits_{R} F(x, y)\, dA$ exists and hence that $\iint\limits_{D} f(x, y)\, dA$ exists. This procedure is valid for the type I and type II regions we discuss next, although a general notion of what constitutes a "well-behaved" boundary is a topic for advanced calculus.

DOUBLE INTEGRALS OVER TYPE I AND TYPE II REGIONS

A type I, or vertically simple region, D, in the plane is a region that can be described by the inequalities

type I D_1: $a \leq x \leq b$, $g_1(x) \leq y \leq g_2(x)$

where $g_1(x)$ and $g_2(x)$ are continuous functions of x on $[a, b]$.

Likewise, a type II, or horizontally simple region, D, is one that can be described by the inequalities

type II D_2: $c \leq y \leq d$, $h_1(y) \leq x \leq h_2(y)$

where $h_1(y)$ and $h_2(y)$ are continuous functions of y on $[c, d]$. Vertically and horizontally simple regions are illustrated in the following box.

Type I Region (vertically simple)

A **type I** region is the set of all points (x, y) such that for each fixed x between $x = a$ and $x = b$, the vertical line segment $g_1(x) \leq y \leq g_2(x)$ lies in the region.

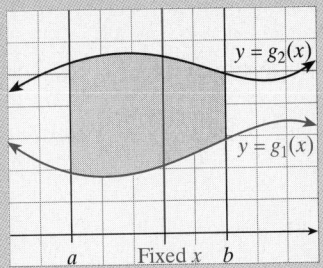

Type II Region (horizontally simple)

A **type II** region is the set of all points (x, y) such that for each fixed y between $y = c$ and $y = d$, the horizontal line segment $h_1(y) \leq x \leq h_2(y)$ lies in the region.

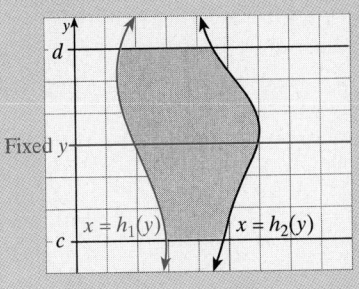

To evaluate a double integral $\int_{D_1} f(x, y)\, dA$ when D_1 is a type I region, first note that D_1 is contained in the rectangle R: $a \leq x \leq b$, $c \leq y \leq d$. Then, if

$$F(x, y) = \begin{cases} f(x, y) & \text{for } (x, y) \text{ in } D_1 \\ 0 & \text{for } (x, y) \text{ in } R \text{, but not in } D_1 \end{cases}$$

we have

$$\int_{c}^{d} F(x, y)\, dy = \int_{g_1(x)}^{g_2(x)} f(x, y)\, dy$$

because for each fixed x in the interval $[a, b]$, $F(x, y) = 0$ if $y < g_1(x)$ and also if $y > g_2(x)$ and $F(x, y) = f(x, y)$ for $g_1(x) \leq y \leq g_2(x)$. Therefore,

$$\iint\limits_{D_1} f(x, y)\, dA = \iint\limits_{R} F(x, y)\, dA = \int_a^b \left[\int_c^d F(x, y)\, dy \right] dx$$

$$= \int_a^b \int_{g_1(x)}^{g_2(x)} f(x, y)\, dy\, dx$$

Similarly, if D_2 is a type II region, then

$$\iint\limits_{D_2} f(x, y)\, dA = \int_c^d \left[\int_a^b F(x, y)\, dx \right] dy$$

$$= \int_c^d \int_{h_1(y)}^{h_2(y)} f(x, y)\, dx\, dy$$

These observations are summarized in the following theorem.

THEOREM 12.3   Fubini's theorem for nonrectangular regions
If D_1 is a type I region, then

TYPE I (vertically simple):
x fixed, y varies (form $dy\, dx$)

$$\iint\limits_{D_1} f(x, y)\, dA = \int_a^b \int_{g_1(x)}^{g_2(x)} f(x, y)\, dy\, dx$$

whenever both integrals exist. Similarly, for a type II region, D_2,

TYPE II (horizontally simple):
y fixed, x varies (form $dx\, dy$)

$$\iint\limits_{D_2} f(x, y)\, dA = \int_c^d \int_{h_1(y)}^{h_2(y)} f(x, y)\, dx\, dy$$

whenever both integrals exist.

Proof   This proof is found in most advanced calculus textbooks.   ❑

EXAMPLE 1   Evaluation of a double integral
Evaluate $\displaystyle\int_0^1 \int_{x^2}^{\sqrt{x}} 160xy^3\, dy\, dx$.

Solution

$$\int_0^1 \int_{x^2}^{\sqrt{x}} 160xy^3\, dy\, dx = \int_0^1 \left[40xy^4 \Big|_{y=x^2}^{y=\sqrt{x}} \right] dx \quad \text{Since } x \text{ is treated as a constant}$$

$$= \int_0^1 [40x \left(\sqrt{x} \right)^4 - 40x(x^2)^4]\, dx$$

$$= \int_0^1 [40x^3 - 40x^9]\, dx$$

$$= [10x^4 - 4x^{10}] \Big|_0^1$$

$$= 6 \qquad\qquad \blacksquare$$

When using Fubini's theorem for nonrectangular regions, it helps to sketch the region of integration D and to find equations for all boundary curves of D. Such a sketch often provides the information needed to determine whether D is a type I or type II region (or neither, or both) and to set up the limits of integration of an iterated integral.

EXAMPLE 2   Double integral over a triangular region

Let T be the triangular region enclosed by the lines $y = 0$, $y = 2x$, and $x = 1$. Evaluate the double integral

$$\iint_T (x + y)\,dA$$

using an iterated integral with

a. y-integration first   **b.** x-integration first

Solution

a. To set up the limits of integration in the iterated integral, we draw the graph as shown in Figure 12.9 and note that for fixed x, the variable y varies from $y = 0$ (the x-axis) to the line $y = 2x$. These are the limits of integration for the inner integral (with respect to y first). The outer limits of integration are the numerical limits of integration for x; that is, x varies between $x = 0$ and $x = 1$.

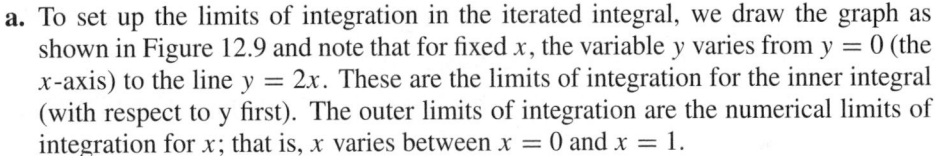

$$\iint_T (x + y)\,dA = \int_0^1 \int_0^{2x} (x + y)\,dy\,dx = \int_0^1 \left[xy + \tfrac{1}{2}y^2\right]\Big|_{y=0}^{y=2x}\,dx$$

$$= \int_0^1 \left[x(2x) + \tfrac{1}{2}(2x)^2 - \left(x(0) + \tfrac{1}{2}(0)^2\right)\right]\,dx$$

$$= \int_0^1 4x^2\,dx = \tfrac{4}{3}\,x^3\Big|_{x=0}^{x=1} = \tfrac{4}{3}$$

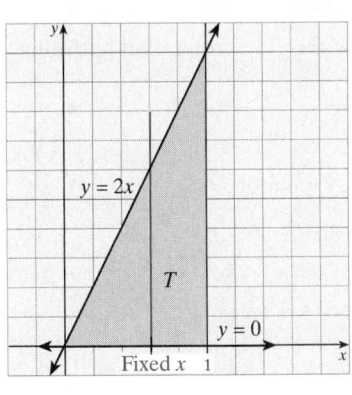

Figure 12.9 For each fixed x $(0 \le x \le 1)$, y varies from $y = 0$ to $y = 2x$.

b. Reversing the order of integration, we see from Figure 12.10 that for each fixed y, the variable x varies (left to right) from the line $x = y/2$ to the vertical line $x = 1$. The outer limits of integration are for y as y varies from $y = 0$ to $y = 2$.

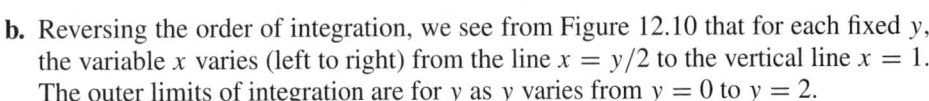

$$\iint_T (x + y)\,dA = \int_0^2 \int_{y/2}^1 (x + y)\,dx\,dy$$

$$= \int_0^2 \left[\tfrac{1}{2}x^2 + xy\right]\Big|_{x=y/2}^{x=1}\,dy = \int_0^2 \left[\tfrac{1}{2} + y - \tfrac{y^2}{8} - \tfrac{y^2}{2}\right]\,dy$$

$$= \left[\tfrac{y}{2} + \tfrac{y^2}{2} - \tfrac{5y^3}{24}\right]\Big|_{y=0}^{y=2} = \left[1 + 2 - \tfrac{5(8)}{24}\right] - [0] = \tfrac{4}{3} \qquad ■$$

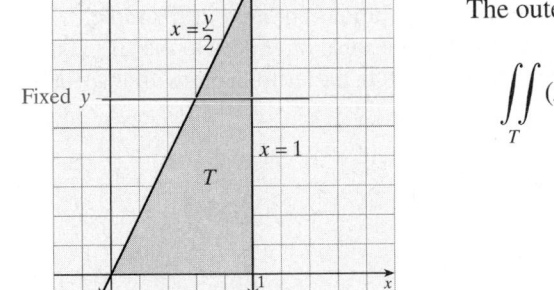

Figure 12.10 For each fixed y $(0 \le y \le 2)$, x varies from $y/2$ to 1.

MORE ON AREA AND VOLUME

Even though we can find the area between curves with single integrals, it is often easier to compute area using a double integral. If $f(x, y) \ge 0$ over a region D in the xy-plane, then $\iint_D f(x, y)\,dA$ gives the **volume of the solid** bounded above by the surface $z = f(x, y)$ and below by the region D. In the special case where $f(x, y) = 1$, we have $\iint_D 1\,dA = $ AREA OF D.

> ### The Double Integral as Area and Volume
>
> The **area** of the region D in the xy-plane is given by
>
> $$A = \iint\limits_{D} dA$$
>
> If f is continuous and $f(x, y) \geq 0$ on the region D, the **volume** of the solid under the surface $z = f(x, y)$ above the region D is given by
>
> $$V = \iint\limits_{D} f(x, y) \, dA$$

EXAMPLE 3 Area of a region in the xy-plane using a double integral

Find the area of the region D between $y = \cos x$ and $y = \sin x$ over the interval $0 \leq x \leq \frac{\pi}{4}$ using

a. a single integral **b.** a double integral

Solution

a. The graph is shown in Figure 12.11. We find that

$$\int_{0}^{\pi/4} (\cos x - \sin x) \, dx = [\sin x + \cos x]\big|_{0}^{\pi/4} = \sqrt{2} - 1$$

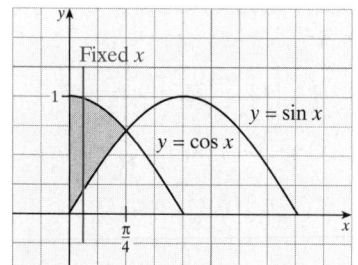

b.
$$A = \iint\limits_{D} dA = \int_{0}^{\pi/4} \int_{\sin x}^{\cos x} 1 \, dy \, dx = \int_{0}^{\pi/4} [y]\Big|_{y=\sin x}^{y=\cos x} dx$$
$$= \int_{0}^{\pi/4} [\cos x - \sin x] \, dx = \sqrt{2} - 1$$

Figure 12.11 The area of the region between $y = \cos x$ and $y = \sin x$

The area is $\sqrt{2} - 1 \approx 0.41$ square unit. ∎

In comparing the single and double integral solutions for area in Example 3, you might ask, "Why bother with the double integral, because it reduces to the single integral case after one step?" The answer is that it is often easier to begin with the double integral

$$A = \iint\limits_{D} dA$$

and then let the *evaluation* lead to the proper form.

EXAMPLE 4 Volume using a double integral

Find the volume of the solid bounded above by the plane $z = y$ and below in the xy-plane by the part of the disk $x^2 + y^2 \leq 1$ in the first quadrant.

Solution

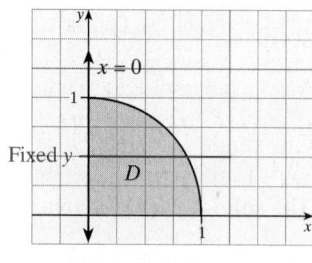

Figure 12.12 The quarter disk $x^2 + y^2 \leq 1, x \geq 0, y \geq 0$

The projection in the xy-plane is shown in Figure 12.12. We can regard D as either a type I or type II region, and because we worked with a type I (vertical) region in Example 3, we will use a type II (horizontal) region for this example. Accordingly, note that for each fixed number y between 0 and 1, x varies between $x = 0$ on the left and $x = \sqrt{1 - y^2}$ on the right. Thus,

$$
\begin{aligned}
V &= \iint\limits_D f(x, y)\, dA \\[2mm]
&= \int_0^1 \int_0^{\sqrt{1-y^2}} y\, dx\, dy \qquad f(x, y) = y \text{ is given; } dA = dx\, dy. \\[2mm]
&= \int_0^1 [yx]\Big|_{x=0}^{x=\sqrt{1-y^2}}\, dy \\[2mm]
&= \int_0^1 y\sqrt{1 - y^2}\, dy \qquad \text{Let } u = 1 - y^2 \text{ to integrate.} \\[2mm]
&= \left[-\frac{1}{3}(1 - y^2)^{3/2} \right]\Big|_{y=0}^{y=1} = \frac{1}{3}
\end{aligned}
$$

The volume is $\frac{1}{3}$ cubic unit. ■

CHOOSING THE ORDER OF INTEGRATION IN A DOUBLE INTEGRAL

Often a region D is both vertically and horizontally simple, and to evaluate an integral $\int_D f(x, y)\, dA$ you have a choice between performing x-integration before y-integration, or vice versa. In the following example, you are given one order of integration and are asked to reverse the order of integration.

EXAMPLE 5 Reversing order of integration in a double integral

Reverse the order of integration in the iterated integral

$$
\int_0^2 \int_1^{e^x} f(x, y)\, dy\, dx
$$

Solution

Draw the region D by looking at the limits of integration for both x and y in the double integral. For this example, we see that the y-integration is done first, so D is a type I region. The inner limits are

$$
y = e^x \quad \text{(top curve)} \qquad \text{and} \qquad y = 1 \quad \text{(bottom curve)}
$$

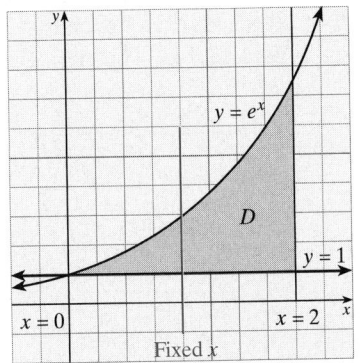

a. D as a type I region; y varies from 1 to e^x

These are shown in Figure 12.13a. Next, draw the appropriate limits of integration for x:

$$
x = 0 \quad \text{(left point)} \qquad \text{and} \qquad x = 2 \quad \text{(right point)}
$$

The vertical lines $x = 0$ and $x = 2$ are also drawn in Figure 12.13a.

To reverse the order of integration, we need to regard D as a type II region (Figure 12.13b). Note that the region varies from $y = 1$ to $y = e^2$ (corresponding to where $y = e^x$ intersects $x = 0$ and $x = 2$, respectively). For each fixed y between 1 and e^2, the region extends from the curve $x = \ln y$ (that is, $y = e^x$) on the left to the line $x = 2$ on the right. Thus, reversing the order of integration, we find that the given integral becomes

$$
\int_1^{e^2} \int_{\ln y}^2 f(x, y)\, dx\, dy
$$

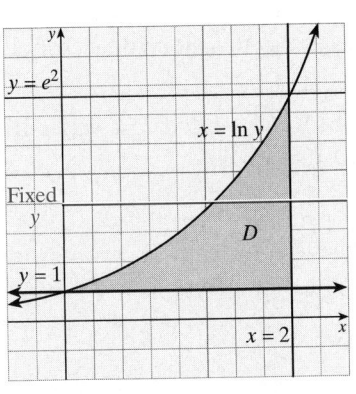

b. D as a type II region; x varies from $\ln y$ to 2

Figure 12.13 The region of integration for Example 5

The two different ways of representing the integral in this example may be summarized as follows:

Type I: x fixed (vertically simple)   **Type II: y fixed (horizontally simple)**

y-integration first; x-integration first;
varies from $y = 1$ to $y = e^x$ varies from $x = \ln y$ to $x = 2$

$$\int_0^2 \int_1^{e^x} f(x, y)\, dy\, dx \quad = \quad \int_1^{e^2} \int_{\ln y}^2 f(x, y)\, dx\, dy$$

x varies from 0 to 2 y varies from 1 to e^2

EXAMPLE 6   Choosing the order of integration

The region D bounded by the parabola $y = x^2 - 2$ and the line $y = x$ is both vertically and horizontally simple. To find the area of D, would you prefer to use a type I or a type II description?

Solution

The parabola and the line intersect where

$$x^2 - 2 = x$$
$$x^2 - x - 2 = 0$$
$$(x - 2)(x + 1) = 0$$
$$x = 2, -1$$

Thus, they intersect at $(2, 2)$ and $(-1, -1)$. The graph of D is shown in Figure 12.14.

As a type I region, D can be described as the set of all points (x, y) such that for each fixed x in $[-1, 2]$, y varies from $x^2 - 2$ to x (see Figure 12.14). The area, A, of D is given by

$$A = \int_{-1}^2 \int_{x^2-2}^x dy\, dx$$
$$= \int_{-1}^2 [x - (x^2 - 2)]\, dx$$
$$= \left[\frac{x^2}{2} - \frac{x^3}{3} + 2x \right]\Big|_{-1}^2$$
$$= \frac{9}{2}$$

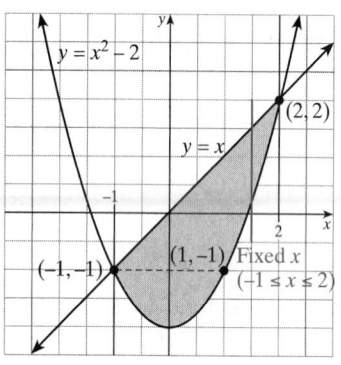

a. Type I description

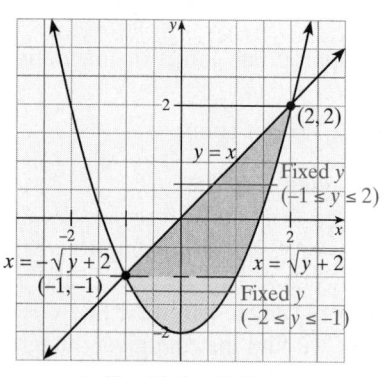

b. Type II description

Figure 12.14 The region between the parabola $y = x^2 - 2$ and the line $y = x$.

If, however, D is regarded as a type II region, it is necessary to split up the description into two parts (see Figure 12.14b):

> The set of all (x, y) such that for each fixed y between -1 and 2, x varies from the line $x = y$ to the right branch of the parabola $x = \sqrt{y + 2}$;

and

> The set of all (x, y) such that for each fixed y between -2 and -1, x varies from the left branch of the parabola $x = -\sqrt{y + 2}$ to the right branch $x = \sqrt{y + 2}$.

Thus, the area of D is given by the sum of the integrals

$$A = \int_{-2}^{-1} \int_{-\sqrt{y+2}}^{\sqrt{y+2}} dx\, dy + \int_{-1}^2 \int_y^{\sqrt{y+2}} dx\, dy$$

Clearly, it is preferable to use the type I representation, although both methods give the same result (you might wish to verify this fact).

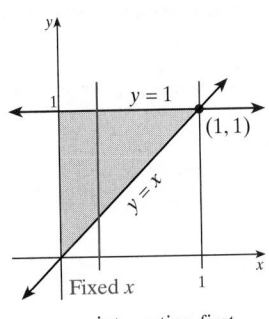

a. *y*-integration first

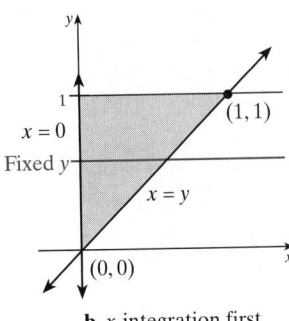

b. *x*-integration first

Figure 12.15 The region of integration for Example 7

As illustrated in Example 6, the shape of the region of integration D may determine which order of integration is more suitable for a given integral. However, our final example of this section shows that the integrand also plays a role in determining which order of integration is preferable.

EXAMPLE 7 **Evaluating a double integral by reversing the order**

Evaluate $\displaystyle\int_0^1 \int_x^1 e^{y^2}\, dy\, dx$

Solution

We cannot evaluate the integral in the given order (y-integration first) because the integrand e^{y^2} has no elementary antiderivative. We will evaluate the integral by reversing the order of integration. The region of integration is sketched in Figure 12.15a. Note that for any fixed x between 0 and 1, y varies from x to 1.

To reverse the order of integration, observe that for each fixed y between 0 and 1, x varies from 0 to y, as shown in Figure 12.15b.

$$\int_0^1 \int_x^1 e^{y^2}\, dy\, dx = \int_0^1 \int_0^y e^{y^2}\, dx\, dy$$

$$= \int_0^1 xe^{y^2}\Big|_{x=0}^{x=y}\, dy = \int_0^1 ye^{y^2}\, dy \qquad Let\ u = y^2.$$

$$= \left[\frac{1}{2}e^{y^2}\right]\Big|_0^1 = \frac{1}{2}(e^1 - e^0) = \frac{1}{2}(e - 1) \qquad \blacksquare$$

12.2 PROBLEM SET

Ⓐ **1. Exploration Problem** Describe the process for finding volume using a double integral.

2. WHAT DOES THIS SAY? What is Fubini's theorem for nonrectangular regions?

Sketch the region of integration in Problems 3–16, and compute the double integral (either in the order of integration given or with the order reversed).

3. $\displaystyle\int_0^4 \int_0^{4-x} xy\, dy\, dx$

4. $\displaystyle\int_0^4 \int_{x^2}^{4x} dy\, dx$

5. $\displaystyle\int_0^1 \int_{-x^2}^{x^2} dy\, dx$

6. $\displaystyle\int_1^e \int_0^{\ln x} xy\, dy\, dx$

7. $\displaystyle\int_0^{2\sqrt{3}} \int_{y^2/4}^{\sqrt{12-y^2}} dx\, dy$

8. $\displaystyle\int_{-2}^1 \int_{y^2+4y}^{3y+2} dx\, dy$

9. $\displaystyle\int_0^3 \int_1^{4-x} (x+y)\, dy\, dx$

10. $\displaystyle\int_0^1 \int_{x^3}^1 (x+y^2)\, dy\, dx$

11. $\displaystyle\int_0^1 \int_0^x (x^2+2y^2)\, dy\, dx$

12. $\displaystyle\int_{-1}^1 \int_{-1}^x (3x+2y)\, dy\, dx$

13. $\displaystyle\int_0^2 \int_0^{\sin x} y\cos x\, dy\, dx$

14. $\displaystyle\int_0^{\pi/2} \int_0^{\sin x} e^y \cos x\, dy\, dx$

15. $\displaystyle\int_0^{\pi/3} \int_0^{y^2} \frac{1}{y}\sin\frac{x}{y}\, dx\, dy$

16. $\displaystyle\int_0^1 \int_0^y y^2 e^{xy}\, dx\, dy$

Evaluate the double integrals in Problems 17–20.

17. $\displaystyle\int_0^1 \int_0^{y^3} e^{x/y}\, dx\, dy$

18. $\displaystyle\int_{\pi/3}^\pi \int_0^{y^2} \frac{1}{y}\cos\frac{x}{y}\, dx\, dy$

19. $\displaystyle\int_0^1 \int_{\tan^{-1} y}^{\pi/4} \sec x\, dx\, dy$

20. $\displaystyle\int_0^1 \int_{\sin^{-1} y}^{\pi/2} \sqrt{1+\cos^2 x}\, \cos x\, dx\, dy$

Evaluate the double integral given in Problems 21–32 for the specified region of integration D.

21. $\displaystyle\iint_D (x+y)\, dA$; D is the triangle with vertices $(0,0)$, $(0,1)$, $(1,1)$.

22. $\displaystyle\iint_D (2y-x)\, dA$; D is the region bounded by $y = x^2$ and $y = 2x$.

23. $\displaystyle\iint_D y\, dA$; D is the region bounded by $y = \sqrt{x}$, $y = 2 - x$, and $y = 0$.

24. $\displaystyle\iint_D 4x\, dA$; D is the region bounded by $y = 4 - x^2$, $y = 3x$, and $x = 0$.

25. $\displaystyle\iint_D 2x\, dA$; D is the region bounded by $x^2 y = 1$, $y = x$, $x = 2$, and $y = 0$.

26. $\displaystyle\iint_D \frac{dA}{y^2+1}$; D is the triangle bounded by $x=2y$, $y=-x$, and $y=2$.

27. $\displaystyle\iint_D 12x^2 e^{y^2}\,dA$; D is the region in the first quadrant bounded by $y=x^3$ and $y=x$.

28. $\displaystyle\iint_D \cos e^x\,dA$; D is the region bounded by $y=e^x$, $y=-e^x$, $x=0$, and $x=\ln 2$.

29. $\displaystyle\iint_D \frac{\sin x}{x}\,dx\,dy$; D is the triangle bounded by the lines $x=0$, $y=\pi$, and $y=x$.

30. $\displaystyle\iint_D x\sqrt{y^2-x^2}\,dx\,dy$; D is the triangle with vertices $(0,0)$, $(1,1)$, and $(0,1)$.

31. $\displaystyle\iint_D x\,dy\,dx$; D is the region between the parabola $y=x^2$ and the line $y=2x+3$.

32. $\displaystyle\iint_D \frac{4-2x}{y^2}\,dy\,dx$; D is the triangle with vertices $(0,-2)$, $(3,-2)$, and $(0,4)$.

Sketch the region of integration in Problems 33–40, and then compute the integral in two ways:

a. *with the given order of integration, and*
b. *with the order of integration reversed.*

33. $\displaystyle\int_0^4\int_0^{4-x} xy\,dy\,dx$

34. $\displaystyle\int_0^4\int_{x^2}^{4x} dy\,dx$

35. $\displaystyle\int_0^1\int_x^{2x} e^{y-x}\,dy\,dx$

36. $\displaystyle\int_0^4\int_0^{\sqrt{x}} 3x^5\,dy\,dx$

37. $\displaystyle\int_0^1\int_{-x^2}^{x^2} dy\,dx$

38. $\displaystyle\int_1^e\int_0^{\ln x} xy\,dy\,dx$

39. $\displaystyle\int_0^{2\sqrt{3}}\int_{y^2/6}^{\sqrt{16-y^2}} dx\,dy$

40. $\displaystyle\int_{-2}^1\int_{y^2+4y}^{3y+2} dx\,dy$

Sketch the region of integration in Problems 41–50, and write an equivalent integral with the order of integration reversed.

41. $\displaystyle\int_0^1\int_0^{2y} f(x,y)\,dx\,dy$

42. $\displaystyle\int_0^1\int_{x^2}^{\sqrt{x}} f(x,y)\,dy\,dx$

43. $\displaystyle\int_0^4\int_{y/2}^{\sqrt{y}} f(x,y)\,dx\,dy$

44. $\displaystyle\int_1^{e^2}\int_{\ln x}^2 f(x,y)\,dy\,dx$

45. $\displaystyle\int_0^3\int_{y/3}^{\sqrt{4-y}} f(x,y)\,dx\,dy$

46. $\displaystyle\int_0^1\int_x^{2-x} f(x,y)\,dy\,dx$

47. $\displaystyle\int_{-3}^2\int_{x^2}^{6-x} f(x,y)\,dy\,dx$

48. $\displaystyle\int_2^4\int_x^{16/x} f(x,y)\,dy\,dx$

49. $\displaystyle\int_0^7\int_{x^2-6x}^x f(x,y)\,dy\,dx$

50. $\displaystyle\int_0^1\int_{\tan^{-1}x}^{\pi/4} f(x,y)\,dy\,dx$

B *Set up a double integral for the volume of the solid region described in Problems 51–57.*

51. The tetrahedron that lies in the first octant and is bounded by the coordinate planes and the plane $z=7-3x-2y$

52. The solid bounded above by the paraboloid $z=6-2x^2-3y^2$ and below by the plane $z=0$

53. The solid that lies inside both the cylinder $x^2+y^2=3$ and the sphere $x^2+y^2+z^2=7$

54. The solid that lies inside both the sphere $x^2+y^2+z^2=3$ and the paraboloid $2z=x^2+y^2$

55. The solid bounded by the ellipsoid $\dfrac{x^2}{a^2}+\dfrac{y^2}{b^2}+\dfrac{z^2}{c^2}=1$

56. The solid bounded above by the plane $z=2-3x-5y$ and below by the region shown in Figure 12.16.

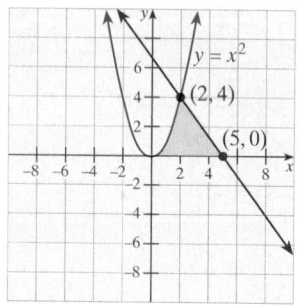

Figure 12.16 Region for Problem 56

57. The solid that remains when a square hole of side 2 is drilled through the center of a sphere of radius $\sqrt{2}$.

Express the area of the region D bounded by the curve given in Problems 58–59 as a double integral in two different ways (with different orders of integration). Evaluate one of these integrals to find the area.

58. Let D denote the region in the first quadrant of the xy-plane that is bounded by the curves $y=\dfrac{4}{x^2}$ and $y=5-x^2$.

59. Let D denote the region bounded by the ellipse $\dfrac{x^2}{a^2}+\dfrac{y^2}{b^2}=1$.

60. Find the volume under the surface $z=x+y+2$ and above the region D bounded by the curves $y=x^2$ and $y=2$.

61. Find the volume under the plane $z=4x$ and above the region D given by $y=x^2$, $y=0$, and $x=1$.

62. Evaluate

$$\int_0^1\int_0^y (x^2+y^2)\,dx\,dy+\int_1^2\int_0^{2-y} (x^2+y^2)\,dx\,dy$$

by reversing the order of integration.

63. Reverse the order of integration in

$$\int_1^2\int_x^{x^3} f(x,y)\,dy\,dx+\int_2^8\int_x^8 f(x,y)\,dy\,dx$$

64. Evaluate $\displaystyle\iint\limits_{D} xy\,dA$, where D is the triangular region in the xy-plane with vertices $(0,0)$, $(1,0)$, and $(4,1)$.

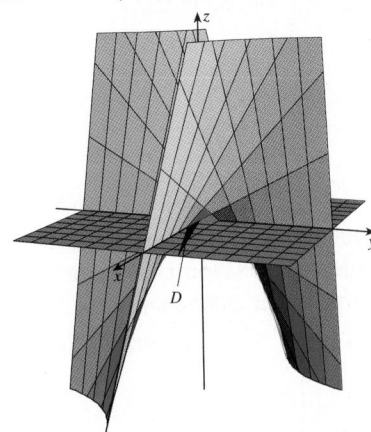

65. Compute $\displaystyle\iint\limits_{D} (x^2 - xy - 1)\,dA$, where D is the triangular region bounded by the lines $x - 2y + 2 = 0$, $x + 3y - 3 = 0$, and $y = 0$.

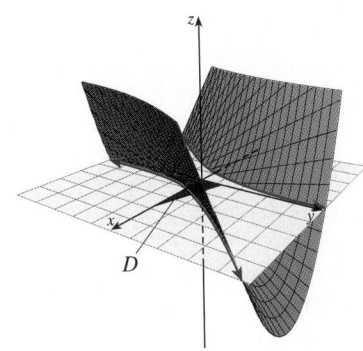

66. Find the volume under the plane $z = x + 2y + 4$ and above the region D bounded by the lines $y = 2x$, $y = 3 - x$, and $y = 0$.

67. Find the volume under the plane $3x + y - z = 0$ and above the elliptic region bounded by $4x^2 + 9y^2 \le 36$, with $x \ge 0$ and $y \ge 0$.

68. Find the volume under the surface $z = x^2 + y^2$ and above the square region bounded by $|x| \le 1$ and $|y| \le 1$.

Evaluate each integral in Problems 69–71 by relating it to the volume of a simple solid.

69. Evaluate $\displaystyle\iint\limits_{R} \left(3 - \sqrt{x^2 + y^2}\right)\,dA$, where R is the disk $x^2 + y^2 \le 9$ in the xy-plane.

70. Evaluate $\displaystyle\iint\limits_{R} \left(1 - \sqrt{x^2 + z^2}\right)\,dA$, where R is the disk $x^2 + z^2 \le 1$ in the xz-plane.

71. Evaluate $\displaystyle\iint\limits_{R} \left(4 - \sqrt{y^2 + z^2}\right)\,dA$, where R is the disk $y^2 + z^2 \le 16$ in the yz-plane.

C 72. Show that if $f(x, y)$ is continuous on a region D and $m \le f(x, y) \le M$ for all points (x, y) in D, then

$$mA \le \iint\limits_{D} f(x, y)\,dA \le MA$$

where A is the area of D.

73. Use the result of Problem 72 to estimate the value of the double integral

$$\iint\limits_{D} e^{y \sin x}\,dA$$

where D is the triangle with vertices $(-1, 0)$, $(2, 0)$, and $(0, 1)$.

74. The region D shown in Figure 12.17 is the union of a type I and a type II region. Evaluate

$$\iint\limits_{D} xy\,dA$$

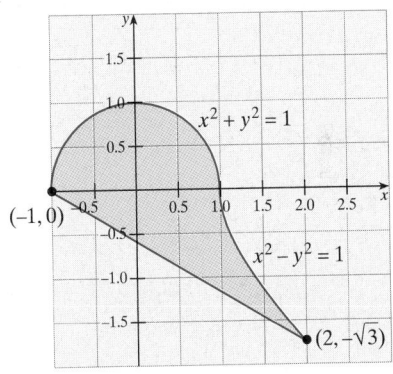

Figure 12.17 Union of type I and type II regions

12.3   Double Integrals in Polar Coordinates

IN THIS SECTION   change of variables to polar form, area and volume in polar form

In general, changing variables in a double integral is more complicated than in a single integral. In this section, we focus attention on using polar coordinates in a double integral, and in Section 12.8, we examine changing variables from a more general standpoint.

CHANGE OF VARIABLES TO POLAR FORM

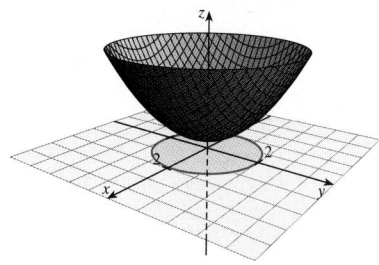

Figure 12.18 Graph of the surface $f(x, y) = x^2 + y^2 + 1$ along with the region R shown in the xy-plane

Polar coordinates are used in double integrals primarily when the integrand or the region of integration (or both) have relatively simple polar descriptions. As a preview of the ideas we plan to explore, consider Figure 12.18 and let us examine the double integral

$$\iint_R (x^2 + y^2 + 1) \, dA$$

where R is the region (disk) in the xy-plane bounded by the circle $x^2 + y^2 = 4$.

Interpreting R as a vertically simple region (type I), we see that for each fixed x between -2 and 2, y varies from the lower boundary semicircle with equation $y = -\sqrt{4 - x^2}$ to the upper semicircle $y = \sqrt{4 - x^2}$, as shown in Figure 12.19a. Using the type I description, we have

$$\iint_R (x^2 + y^2 + 1) \, dA = \int_{-2}^{2} \int_{-\sqrt{4-x^2}}^{\sqrt{4-x^2}} (x^2 + y^2 + 1) \, dy \, dx$$

The iterated integral on the right is difficult to evaluate, but both the integrand and the domain of integration can be represented quite simply in terms of polar coordinates. Specifically, using the polar conversion formulas

$$x = r \cos \theta \qquad y = r \sin \theta \qquad r = \sqrt{x^2 + y^2} \qquad \tan \theta = \frac{y}{x}$$

we find that the integrand $f(x, y) = x^2 + y^2 + 1$ can be rewritten

$$f(r \cos \theta, r \sin \theta) = (r \cos \theta)^2 + (r \sin \theta)^2 + 1 = r^2 + 1$$

and the region of integration R is just the interior of the circle $r = 2$. Thus, R can be described as the set of all points (r, θ) so that for each fixed angle θ between 0 and 2π, r varies from the origin ($r = 0$) to the circle $r = 2$, as shown in Figure 12.19b.

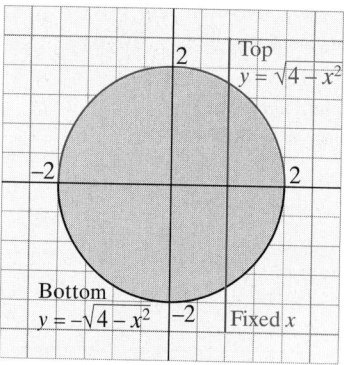

a. Type I description:
For fixed x between -2 and 2
y varies from $y = -\sqrt{4 - x^2}$
to $y = \sqrt{4 - x^2}$

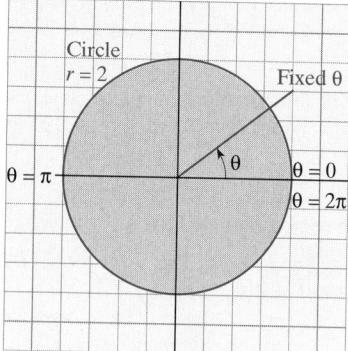

b. Polar description:
For fixed θ between 0 and 2π,
r varies from 0 to 2.

Figure 12.19 Two interpretations of a region R

But what is the differential of integration dA in polar coordinates? Can we simply substitute "$dr \, d\theta$" for dA and perform the integration with respect to r and θ? The answer is no, and the correct formula for expressing a given double integral in polar form is given in the following theorem.

THEOREM 12.4 **Double integral in polar coordinates**

If f is continuous in the polar region D described by $r_1(\theta) \leq r \leq r_2(\theta)$ $(r_1(\theta) \geq 0$, $r_2(\theta) \geq 0)$, $\alpha \leq \theta \leq \beta$ $(0 \leq \beta - \alpha \leq 2\pi)$, then

$$\iint_D f(r, \theta)\, dA = \int_\alpha^\beta \int_{r_1(\theta)}^{r_2(\theta)} f(r, \theta)\, r\, dr\, d\theta$$

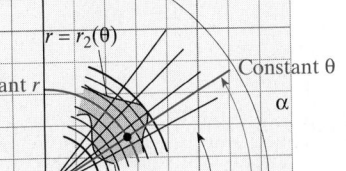

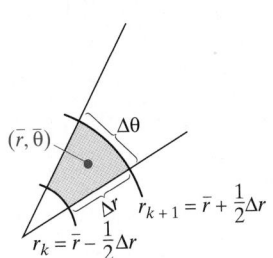

a. A partition of a region into polar coordinates

b. A typical polar rectangle in the partition

Figure 12.20 A polar rectangle

➡ **What This Says** The procedure for changing from a Cartesian integral

$$\iint_R f(x, y)\, dA$$

into a polar integral requires two steps. First, substitute $x = r\cos\theta$ and $y = r\sin\theta$, $dx\, dy = r\, dr\, d\theta$ into the Cartesian integral. Then convert the region of integration R to polar form D. Thus,

$$\iint_R f(x, y)\, dA = \iint_D f(r\cos\theta, r\sin\theta)\, r\, dr\, d\theta$$

Proof A polar region described by $r_1(\theta) \leq r \leq r_2(\theta)$, $\alpha \leq \theta \leq \beta$ can be subdivided into **polar rectangles**. A typical polar rectangle is shown in Figure 12.20.

We begin by subdividing the region of integration into polar rectangles. Next we pick an arbitrary polar-form point (r_k^*, θ_k^*) in each polar rectangle in the partition and then take the limit of an appropriate Riemann sum

$$\sum_{k=1}^{N} f(r_k^*, \theta_k^*) \Delta A_k,$$

where ΔA_k is the area of the kth polar rectangle.

To find the area of a typical polar rectangle, let (r_k^*, θ_k^*) be the center of the polar rectangle—that is, the point midway between the arcs and rays that form the polar rectangle, as shown in Figure 12.20b. If the circular arcs that bound the polar rectangle are Δr apart, then the arcs are given by

$$r_1 = r_k^* - \tfrac{1}{2}\Delta r_k \qquad \text{and} \qquad r_2 = r_k^* + \tfrac{1}{2}\Delta r_k$$

SMH See Section 1.2 of the *Student Mathematics Handbook.*

In Chapter 6 we used the fact that a circular section of radius r and central angle θ has area $\frac{1}{2}r^2\theta$ (see the *Student Mathematics Handbook* for details). Thus, a typical polar rectangle has area

$$\Delta A_k = \left[\tfrac{1}{2}\underbrace{(r_k^* + \tfrac{1}{2}\Delta r_k)^2}_{\text{Radius of outside arc}} - \tfrac{1}{2}\underbrace{(r_k^* - \tfrac{1}{2}\Delta r_k)^2}_{\text{Radius of inside arc}} \right] \Delta\theta_k = r_k^* \Delta r_k \Delta\theta_k$$

Finally, we compute the given double integral in polar form by taking the limit

$$\iint_D f(r, \theta)\, dA = \lim_{\|P\| \to 0} \sum_{k=1}^{N} f(r_k^*, \theta_k^*) \Delta A_k = \lim_{\|P\| \to 0} \sum_{k=1}^{N} f(r_k^*, \theta_k^*) r_k^* \Delta r_k \Delta\theta_k$$

$$= \int_\alpha^\beta \int_{r_1(\theta)}^{r_2(\theta)} f(r, \theta)\, r\, dr\, d\theta \qquad \square$$

It can be shown that under reasonable conditions, the change of variable $x = x(u, v)$, $y = y(u, v)$ transforms the integral $\iint f(x, y)\, dA$ into $\iint f(u, v)\, |J(u, v)|\, du\, dv$, where

$$J(u, v) = \begin{vmatrix} \dfrac{\partial x}{\partial u} & \dfrac{\partial x}{\partial v} \\[2mm] \dfrac{\partial y}{\partial u} & \dfrac{\partial y}{\partial v} \end{vmatrix}$$

This determinant is known as the **Jacobian** of the transformation. In the case of polar coordinates, we have $x = r\cos\theta$ and $y = r\sin\theta$, so the Jacobian is

$$J(r, \theta) = \begin{vmatrix} \dfrac{\partial}{\partial r}(r\cos\theta) & \dfrac{\partial}{\partial \theta}(r\cos\theta) \\[2mm] \dfrac{\partial}{\partial r}(r\sin\theta) & \dfrac{\partial}{\partial \theta}(r\sin\theta) \end{vmatrix}$$

$$= \begin{vmatrix} \cos\theta & -r\sin\theta \\ \sin\theta & r\cos\theta \end{vmatrix} = r\cos^2\theta + r\sin^2\theta = r$$

This yields the result of Theorem 12.4:

$$\iint\limits_{R} f(x, y)\, dA = \iint\limits_{D} f(r, \theta)\, r\, dr\, d\theta = \int_{\alpha}^{\beta} \int_{r_1(\theta)}^{r_2(\theta)} f(r\cos\theta, r\sin\theta)\, r\, dr\, d\theta$$

We discuss this more completely in Section 12.8.

If you carefully compare the result in the preview box with the result of Theorem 12.4, you will see that they are not *exactly* the same. The region D in Theorem 12.4 already is in polar coordinates. The more common situation is that we are given f and a region R in rectangular coordinates that we need to change to polar coordinates.

AREA AND VOLUME IN POLAR FORM

You will need to be familiar with the graphs of many polar-form curves. These can be found in Table 6.2 on page 379, and also in the *Student Mathematics Handbook*. We now present the example we promised in the introduction.

SMH See Chapter 5 of the *Student Mathematics Handbook*.

EXAMPLE 1 **Double integral in polar form**

Evaluate $\displaystyle\iint\limits_{R} (x^2 + y^2 + 1)\, dA$, where D is the region inside the circle $x^2 + y^2 = 4$.

Solution

In this example, the region R is given in rectangular form. We will describe this as a polar region D. Earlier, we observed that in D, for each fixed angle θ between 0 and 2π, r varies from $r = 0$ (the pole) to $r = 2$ (the circle). Thus,

$$\iint\limits_{R} \underbrace{(x^2 + y^2 + 1)}_{f(x,y)}\, dA = \int_{0}^{2\pi} \int_{0}^{2} \underbrace{(r^2 + 1)}_{f(r\cos\theta,\, r\sin\theta)}\ \underbrace{r\, dr\, d\theta}_{dA}$$

$$= \int_{0}^{2\pi} \int_{0}^{2} (r^3 + r)\, dr\, d\theta = \int_{0}^{2\pi} \left[\frac{r^4}{4} + \frac{r^2}{2} \right]_{0}^{2} d\theta = \int_{0}^{2\pi} 6\, d\theta = 6\theta\big|_{0}^{2\pi} = 12\pi \quad \blacksquare$$

EXAMPLE 2 Computing area in polar form using a double integral

Compute the area of the region D bounded above by the line $y = x$ and below by the circle $x^2 + y^2 - 2y = 0$.

Solution

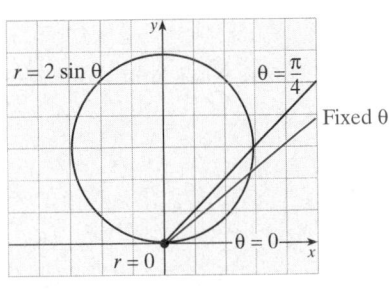

Figure 12.21 The region D

The circle $x^2 + y^2 - 2y = 0$ and the line $y = x$ are shown in Figure 12.21. The polar form for the line $y = x$ is $\theta = \pi/4$ and for the circle is

$$x^2 + y^2 = 2y$$
$$r^2 = 2r \sin \theta$$
$$r = 2 \sin \theta$$

Thus, the region D is determined as r varies from 0 (the pole) to $2 \sin \theta$ (the circle) for θ between 0 and $\pi/4$. The area is given by the integral

$$A = \iint\limits_D dA = \int_0^{\pi/4} \int_0^{2 \sin \theta} r \, dr \, d\theta$$

$$= \int_0^{\pi/4} \left[\frac{1}{2} r^2 \right] \Big|_{r=0}^{r=2 \sin \theta} d\theta$$

$$= \int_0^{\pi/4} \frac{1}{2} (4 \sin^2 \theta) \, d\theta$$

$$= 2 \int_0^{\pi/4} \frac{1 - \cos 2\theta}{2} \, d\theta$$

$$= \left[\theta - \frac{\sin 2\theta}{2} \right] \Big|_0^{\pi/4} = \frac{\pi - 2}{4}$$ ∎

EXAMPLE 3 Volume in polar form

Use a polar double integral to show that a sphere of radius a has volume $\frac{4}{3} \pi a^3$.

Solution

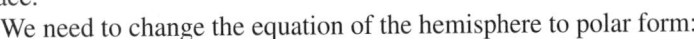

We will compute the required volume by doubling the volume of the solid hemisphere $x^2 + y^2 + z^2 \le a^2$, with $z \ge 0$. This hemisphere (see Figure 12.22) may be regarded as a solid bounded below by the circular disk $x^2 + y^2 \le a^2$ and above by the spherical surface.

We need to change the equation of the hemisphere to polar form:

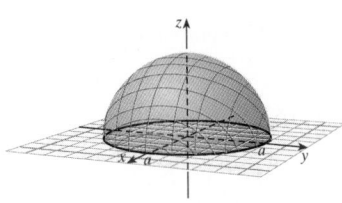

Figure 12.22 The solid hemisphere $z \le \sqrt{a^2 - x^2 - y^2}$ is bounded above by the sphere and below by the disk $x^2 + y^2 \le a^2$.

In rectangular form: $z = \sqrt{a^2 - x^2 - y^2}$

In polar form: $z = \sqrt{a^2 - r^2}$ *Because $r^2 = x^2 + y^2$*

Describing the disk D in polar terms, we see that for each fixed θ between 0 and 2π, r varies from the origin to the circle $x^2 + y^2 = a^2$, which has the polar equation $r = a$, as shown in Figure 12.23. Thus, the volume is given by the integral

$$V = 2 \iint\limits_D z \, dA \qquad \text{Rectangular form}$$

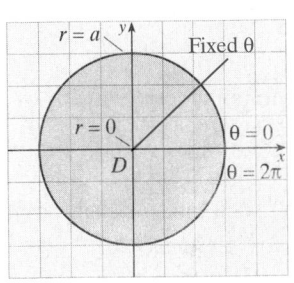

Figure 12.23 The disk D: for θ between 0 and 2π, r varies from 0 to a.

$$= 2 \int_0^{2\pi} \int_0^a \sqrt{a^2 - r^2} \, r \, dr \, d\theta \qquad \boxed{\text{Let } u = a^2 - r^2; \, du = -2r \, dr}$$

$$= 2 \int_0^{2\pi} \left[-\frac{1}{3} (a^2 - r^2)^{3/2} \right] \Big|_{r=0}^{r=a} d\theta$$

$$= -\frac{2}{3} \int_0^{2\pi} [(a^2 - a^2)^{3/2} - (a^2 - 0)^{3/2}] \, d\theta$$

$$= \frac{2}{3} \int_0^{2\pi} a^3 \, d\theta = \frac{2}{3} a^3 \theta \Big|_0^{2\pi} = \frac{4}{3} \pi a^3$$ ∎

EXAMPLE 4   Region of integration between two polar curves

Evaluate $\iint_D \dfrac{1}{x}\, dA$, where D is the region that lies inside the circle $r = 3\cos\theta$ and outside the cardioid $r = 1 + \cos\theta$.

Solution

Begin by sketching the given curves, as shown in Figure 12.24. Next, find the points of intersection:

$$3\cos\theta = 1 + \cos\theta$$
$$2\cos\theta = 1$$
$$\cos\theta = \tfrac{1}{2}$$
$$\theta = -\tfrac{\pi}{3}, \tfrac{\pi}{3}$$

Notice that D is the region such that, for each fixed angle θ between $-\pi/3$ and $\pi/3$, r varies from $1 + \cos\theta$ (the cardioid) to $3\cos\theta$ (the circle). This gives us the limits of integration, and in polar form, the integrand becomes

$$\underbrace{\dfrac{1}{x}}_{\text{Rectangular form}} = \underbrace{\dfrac{1}{r\cos\theta}}_{\text{Polar form}}$$

Thus,

$$\iint_D \frac{1}{x}\, dA = \iint_D \frac{1}{r\cos\theta}\, r\, dr\, d\theta$$

$$= \int_{-\pi/3}^{\pi/3} \int_{1+\cos\theta}^{3\cos\theta} \frac{1}{\cos\theta}\, dr\, d\theta$$

$$= 2\int_0^{\pi/3} \left[\frac{r}{\cos\theta}\right]\Big|_{r=1+\cos\theta}^{r=3\cos\theta}\, d\theta \qquad \text{By symmetry}$$

$$= 2\int_0^{\pi/3} \frac{1}{\cos\theta}\,[3\cos\theta - (1+\cos\theta)]\, d\theta$$

$$= 2\int_0^{\pi/3} (2 - \sec\theta)\, d\theta$$

$$= 2\,[2\theta - \ln|\sec\theta + \tan\theta|]\big|_0^{\pi/3}$$

$$= \frac{4\pi}{3} - 2\ln(2 + \sqrt{3}) \qquad\blacksquare$$

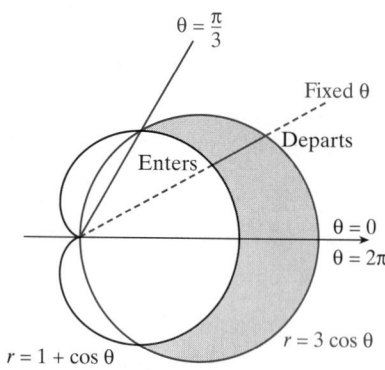

Figure 12.24 Region D

EXAMPLE 5   Converting an integral to polar form

Evaluate $\displaystyle\int_0^2 \int_0^{\sqrt{2x-x^2}} y\sqrt{x^2 + y^2}\, dy\, dx$ by converting to polar coordinates.

Solution

The region of integration D is the set of all points (x, y) such that for each point x in the interval $[0, 2]$, y varies from $y = 0$ to $y = \sqrt{2x - x^2}$. Note that

$$y = \sqrt{2x - x^2}$$
$$y^2 = 2x - x^2$$
$$x^2 - 2x + y^2 = 0$$
$$(x - 1)^2 + y^2 = 1$$

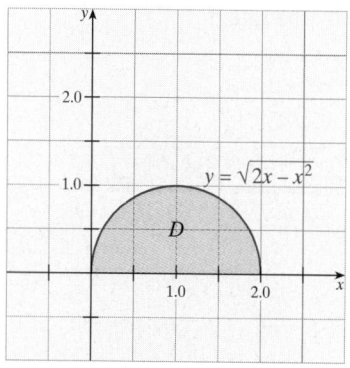

Figure 12.25 Region of integration in Example 5

This is the equation of a circle of radius 1 centered at $(1,0)$. Thus, $y = \sqrt{2x - x^2}$ is the semicircle shown in Figure 12.25. The top boundary of this region is the semicircle

$$y = \sqrt{2x - x^2}$$
$$y^2 = 2x - x^2$$
$$x^2 + y^2 = 2x$$

which has the polar form

$$r^2 = 2r\cos\theta$$
$$r = 2\cos\theta$$

In polar coordinates, D is the region in which r varies from 0 to $2\cos\theta$ for θ between 0 and $\frac{\pi}{2}$. Thus, the integral is

$$\int_0^2 \int_0^{\sqrt{2x-x^2}} y\sqrt{x^2+y^2}\,dy\,dx = \iint_D y\sqrt{x^2+y^2}\,dA$$
$$= \int_0^{\pi/2}\int_0^{2\cos\theta}(r\sin\theta)\,r\,(r\,dr\,d\theta) = \int_0^{\pi/2}\sin\theta\left[\frac{r^4}{4}\right]_0^{2\cos\theta}d\theta$$
$$= \frac{1}{4}\int_0^{\pi/2}16\cos^4\theta\sin\theta\,d\theta = 4\left[-\frac{1}{5}\cos^5\theta\right]_0^{\pi/2} = \frac{4}{5}$$ ∎

12.3   PROBLEM SET

 In Problems 1–8, sketch the region D and then evaluate the double integral $\iint_D f(r,\theta)\,dr\,d\theta$.

1. $\int_0^{\pi/2}\int_1^3 re^{-r^2}\,dr\,d\theta$

2. $\int_0^{\pi/2}\int_1^2 \sqrt{4-r^2}\,r\,dr\,d\theta$

3. $\int_0^\pi\int_0^4 r^2\sin^2\theta\,dr\,d\theta$

4. $\int_0^{\pi/2}\int_1^3 r^2\cos^2\theta\,dr\,d\theta$

5. $\int_0^{2\pi}\int_0^4 2r^2\cos\theta\,dr\,d\theta$

6. $\int_0^{2\pi}\int_0^{1-\sin\theta}\cos\theta\,dr\,d\theta$

7. $\int_0^{\pi/2}\int_0^{2\sin\theta}dr\,d\theta$

8. $\int_0^\pi\int_0^{1+\sin\theta}dr\,d\theta$

Use a double integral to find the area of the shaded region in Problems 9–22.

9. $r = 4$

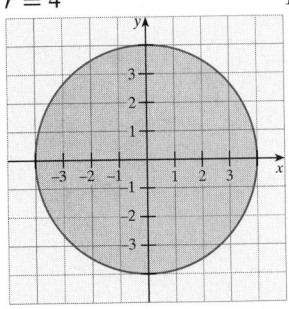

10. $r = 2\cos\theta$

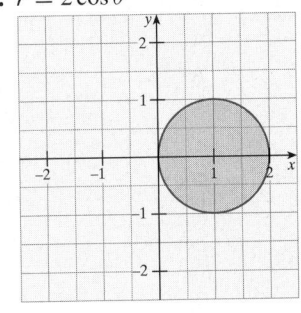

11. $r = 2(1-\cos\theta)$

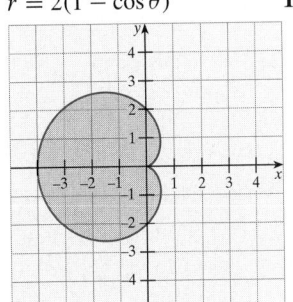

12. $r = 1+\sin\theta$

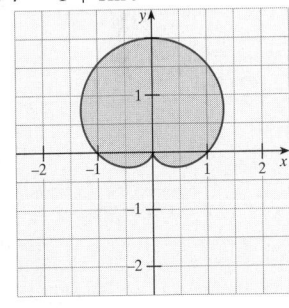

13. $r = 4\cos 3\theta$

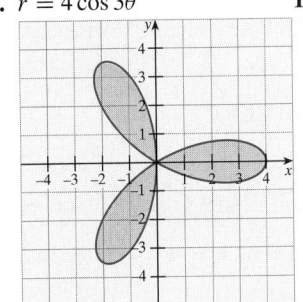

14. $r = 5\sin 2\theta$

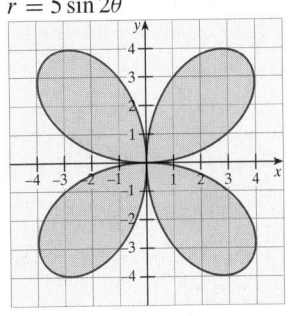

15. $r = \cos 2\theta$

16. $r = 1$ and $r = 2\sin\theta$
Hint: Consider $0 < \theta < \frac{\pi}{6}$ and $\frac{\pi}{6} < \theta < \frac{\pi}{2}$ separately.

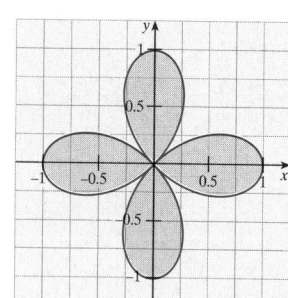

25. $f(x, y) = y^2$

26. $f(x, y) = x^2 + y^2$

27. $f(x, y) = \dfrac{1}{a^2 + x^2 + y^2}$

28. $f(x, y) = e^{-(x^2 + y^2)}$

29. $f(x, y) = \dfrac{1}{a + \sqrt{x^2 + y^2}}$

30. $f(x, y) = \ln(a^2 + x^2 + y^2)$

Use polar coordinates in Problems 31–36 to evaluate the given double integral.

31. $\displaystyle\iint_D y\, dA$, where D is the disk $x^2 + y^2 \le 4$

32. $\displaystyle\iint_D (x^2 + y^2)\, dA$, where D is the region bounded by the x-axis, the line $y = x$, and the circle $x^2 + y^2 = 1$

33. $\displaystyle\iint_D e^{x^2 + y^2}\, dA$, where D is the region inside the circle $x^2 + y^2 = 9$

34. $\displaystyle\iint_D \sqrt{x^2 + y^2}\, dA$, where D is the region inside the circle $(x - 1)^2 + y^2 = 1$ in the first quadrant

35. $\displaystyle\iint_D \ln(x^2 + y^2 + 2)\, dA$, where D is the region inside the circle $x^2 + y^2 = 4$ in the first quadrant

36. $\displaystyle\iint_D \sin(x^2 + y^2)\, dA$, where D is the region bounded by the circles $x^2 + y^2 = 1$ and $x^2 + y^2 = 4$, and the lines $y = 0$ and $x = \sqrt{3}\, y$

17. $r = 1$ and $r = 2\sin\theta$

18. $r = 1$ and $r = 1 + \cos\theta$

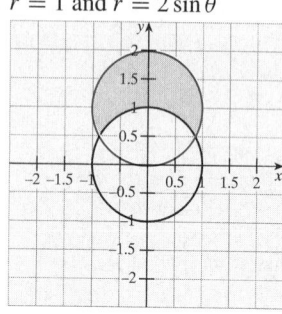
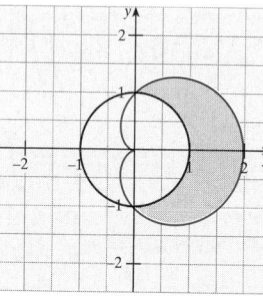

19. $r = 1$ and $r = 1 + \cos\theta$

20. $r = 1$ and $r = 1 + \cos\theta$

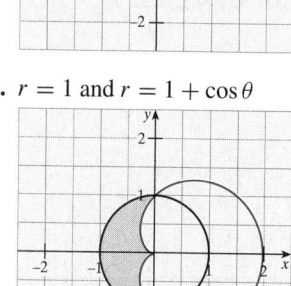

37. Find the volume of the solid bounded by the paraboloid $z = 4 - x^2 - y^2$ and the xy-plane.

38. Find the volume of the solid bounded above by the cone $z = 6\sqrt{x^2 + y^2}$ and below by the circular region $x^2 + y^2 \le a^2$ in the xy-plane, where a is a positive constant.

In Problems 39–48, evaluate the given integral by converting to polar coordinates.

39. $\displaystyle\int_0^3 \int_0^{\sqrt{9 - x^2}} x\, dy\, dx$

40. $\displaystyle\int_0^2 \int_y^{\sqrt{8 - y^2}} \frac{1}{\sqrt{1 + x^2 + y^2}}\, dx\, dy$

41. $\displaystyle\int_0^2 \int_0^{\sqrt{4 - y^2}} e^{x^2 + y^2}\, dx\, dy$

42. $\displaystyle\int_0^3 \int_0^{\sqrt{9 - x^2}} \cos(x^2 + y^2)\, dy\, dx$

43. $\displaystyle\int_0^4 \int_0^{\sqrt{4y - y^2}} \frac{1}{\sqrt{x^2 + y^2}}\, dx\, dy$

44. $\displaystyle\int_2^4 \int_0^{\sqrt{4y - y^2}} \frac{1}{\sqrt{x^2 + y^2}}\, dx\, dy$

45. $\displaystyle\int_0^2 \int_0^{\sqrt{4 - y^2}} \frac{1}{\sqrt{9 - x^2 - y^2}}\, dx\, dy$

21. $r = 3\cos\theta$ and $r = 1 + \cos\theta$

22. $r = 3\cos\theta$ and $r = 2 - \cos\theta$

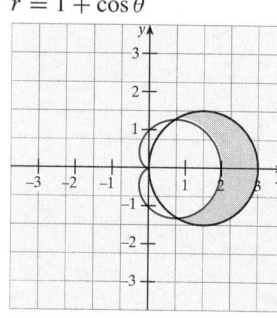
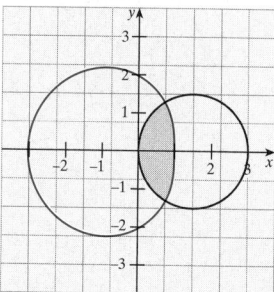

23. Use a double integral to find the area inside the inner loop of the limaçon $r = 1 + 2\cos\theta$.

24. Use a double integral to find the area bounded by the parabola

$$r = \frac{5}{1 + \cos\theta}$$

and the lines $\theta = 0$, $\theta = \frac{\pi}{3}$, and $r = \frac{5}{2}\sec\theta$.

Use polar coordinates in Problems 25–30 to find $\iint_D f(x, y)\, dA$, where D is the circular disk defined by $x^2 + y^2 \le a^2$ for constant $a > 0$.

46. $\displaystyle\int_{-3}^{3}\int_{-\sqrt{9-x^2}}^{\sqrt{9-x^2}} \ln(x^2 + y^2 + 9)\, dy\, dx$

47. $\displaystyle\int_{0}^{2}\int_{0}^{\sqrt{2x-x^2}} \frac{x-y}{x^2+y^2}\, dy\, dx$

48. $\displaystyle\int_{0}^{1}\int_{x}^{\sqrt{x}} (x^2+y^2)^{3/2}\, dy\, dx$

B **49.** Use polar coordinates to evaluate $\iint_D xy\, dA$, where D is the intersection of the circular disks $r \le 4\cos\theta$ and $r \le 4\sin\theta$. Sketch the region of integration.

50. Let D be the region formed by intersecting the regions (in the xy-plane) described by $y \le x$, $y \ge 0$, and $x \le 1$.

    a. Evaluate $\iint_D dA$ as an iterated integral in Cartesian coordinates.

    b. Evaluate $\iint_D dA$ in terms of polar coordinates.

51. Example 9 of Section 6.3 used a single integral to find the area of the region common to the circles $r = a\cos\theta$ and $r = a\sin\theta$. Rework this example using double integrals.

52. Example 10 of Section 6.3 used a single integral to find the area between the circle $r = 5\cos\theta$ and the limaçon $r = 2 + \cos\theta$. Use double integrals to find the same area.

In Problems 53–58, find the volume of the given solid region.

53. The solid that lies inside the sphere $x^2 + y^2 + z^2 = 25$ and outside the cylinder $x^2 + y^2 = 9$

54. The solid bounded above by the sphere $x^2 + y^2 + z^2 = 4$ and below by the paraboloid $3z = x^2 + y^2$

55. The solid region common to the sphere $x^2 + y^2 + z^2 = 4$ and the cylinder $x^2 + y^2 = 2x$

56. The solid region common to the cylinder $x^2 + y^2 = 2$ and the ellipsoid $3x^2 + 3y^2 + z^2 = 7$

57. The solid bounded above by the paraboloid $z = 1 - x^2 - y^2$, below by the plane $z = 0$, and on the sides by the cylinder $x^2 + y^2 = x$

58. The solid region bounded above by the cone $z = x^2 + y^2$, below by the plane $z = 0$, and on the sides by the cylinder $x^2 + y^2 = y$

59. Use polar coordinates to evaluate the double integral $\iint_D x\, dA$ over the shaded region.

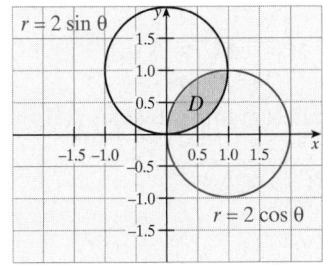

60. Use polar coordinates to evaluate the double integral $\iint_D (x^2 + y^2)\, dA$ over the shaded region.

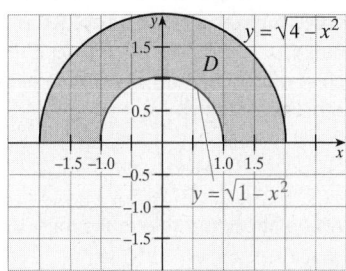

C **61.** **Exploration Problem** If we evaluate the integral $\iint_R r^2\, dr\, d\theta$, where R is the region in the xy-plane bounded by $r = 2\cos\theta$, we obtain

$$\int_0^{\pi}\int_0^{2\cos\theta} r^2\, dr\, d\theta = \int_0^{\pi} \frac{r^3}{3}\Big|_0^{2\cos\theta}\, d\theta$$

$$= \frac{8}{3}\int_0^{\pi} \cos^3\theta\, d\theta = \frac{8}{3}\left[\sin\theta - \frac{\sin^3\theta}{3}\right]\Big|_0^{\pi} = 0$$

Alternatively, we can set up the integral as

$$\iint_R r^2\, dr\, d\theta = \int_0^{\pi/2}\int_0^{2\cos\theta} r^2\, dr\, d\theta$$

$$+ \int_{\pi/2}^{\pi}\int_0^{2\cos\theta} r^2(-dr)\, d\theta = \frac{32}{9}$$

Both of these answers cannot be correct. Which procedure (if either) is correct and why?

62. HISTORICAL QUEST   Newton and Leibniz have been credited with the discovery of calculus, but much of its development was due to the mathematicians Pierre-Simon Laplace, Lagrange (Historical Quest 55, Section 11.8), and Gauss (Historical Quest 59, Supplementary Problems to Chapter 5). These three great mathematicians of calculus were contrasted by W.W. Rouse Ball:

PIERRE-SIMON LAPLACE 1749–1827

The great masters of modern analysis are Lagrange, Laplace, and Gauss, who were contemporaries. It is interesting to note the marked contrast in their styles. Lagrange is perfect both in form and matter, he is careful to explain his procedure, and though his arguments are general they are easy to follow. Laplace on the other hand explains nothing, is indifferent to style, and, if satisfied that his results are correct, is content to leave them either with no proof or with a faulty one. Gauss is exact and elegant as Lagrange, but even more difficult to follow than Laplace, for he removes every trace of the analysis by which he reached his results, and strives to give a proof which while rigorous will be as concise and synthetical as possible.*

*A Short Account of the History of Mathematics, as quoted in Mathematical Circles Adieu, by Howard Eves (Boston: Prindle, Weber & Schmidt, Inc., 1977).

Pierre-Simon Laplace has been called the Newton of France. He taught Napoleon Bonaparte, was appointed for a time as Minister of Interior, and was at times granted favors from his powerful friend. Today, Laplace is best known as the major contributor to probability, taking it from gambling to a true branch of mathematics. He was one of the earliest to evaluate the improper integral

$$I = \int_{-\infty}^{\infty} e^{-x^2} \, dx$$

which plays an important role in the theory of probability. ∎

Show that $I = \sqrt{\pi}$. *Hint:* Note that

$$\int_{-\infty}^{\infty} e^{-x^2} \, dx \cdot \int_{-\infty}^{\infty} e^{-y^2} \, dy = \int_{-\infty}^{\infty} \int_{-\infty}^{\infty} e^{-(x^2+y^2)} \, dx \, dy$$

where the integral on the right is over the entire xy-plane, described in polar terms by $0 \le r < \infty$ and $0 \le \theta \le 2\pi$.

63. For constant a where $0 \le a \le R$, the plane $z = R - a$ cuts off a "cap" from the hemisphere

$$z = \sqrt{R^2 - x^2 - y^2}$$

Use a double integral in polar coordinates to find the volume of the cap. For what value of a is the volume of the cap half the volume of the hemisphere?

12.4 Surface Area

IN THIS SECTION definition of surface area, surface area projections, area of a surface defined parametrically

In Chapter 6, we found that if f has a continuous derivative on the closed, bounded interval $[a, b]$, then the length L of the portion of the graph of $y = f(x)$ between the points where $x = a$ and $x = b$ may be defined by

$$L = \int_a^b \sqrt{1 + [f'(x)]^2} \, dx$$

The goal of this section is to study an analogous formula for the surface area of the graph of a differentiable function of two variables.

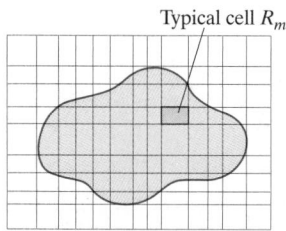

Typical cell R_m

a. The region R is partitioned by a rectangular grid.

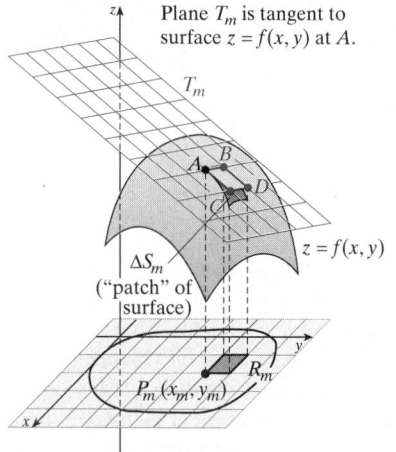

Plane T_m is tangent to surface $z = f(x, y)$ at A.

T_m

ΔS_m ("patch" of surface)

$z = f(x, y)$

R_m

$P_m(x_m, y_m)$

b. The surface area above R_m is approximated by the area of the parallelogram on the tangent plane.

Figure 12.26 Surface area

DEFINITION OF SURFACE AREA

Consider a surface defined by $z = f(x, y)$ defined over a region R of the xy-plane. Enclose the region R in a rectangle partitioned by a grid with lines parallel to the coordinate axes, as shown in Figure 12.26a. This creates a number of cells, and we let $R_1, R_2, \ldots, R_n$ denote those that lie entirely within R.

For $m = 1, 2, \ldots, n$, let $P_m(x_m^*, y_m^*)$ be any corner of the rectangle R_m, and let T_m be the tangent plane above P_m on the surface of $z = f(x, y)$. Finally, let ΔS_m denote the area of the "patch" of surface that lies directly above R_m. The rectangle R_m projects onto a parallelogram $ABDC$ in the tangent plane T_m, and if R_m is "small," we would expect the area of this parallelogram to approximate closely the element of surface area ΔS_m (see Figure 12.26b).

If Δx_m and Δy_m are the lengths of the sides of the rectangle R_m, the approximating parallelogram will have sides determined by the vectors

$$\mathbf{AB} = \Delta x_m \mathbf{i} + [f_x(x_m^*, y_m^*) \Delta x_m] \mathbf{k} \quad \text{and} \quad \mathbf{AC} = \Delta y_m \mathbf{j} + [f_y(x_m^*, y_m^*) \Delta y_m] \mathbf{k}$$

In Chapter 9, we showed that such a parallelogram with sides $\mathbf{AB}$ and $\mathbf{AC}$ has area

$$\|\mathbf{AB} \times \mathbf{AC}\|$$

This is shown in Figure 12.27.

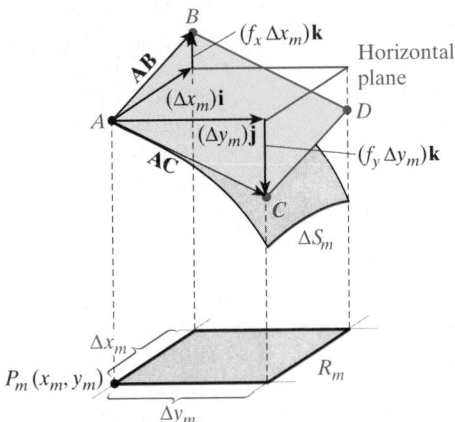

Figure 12.27 An element of surface area has area $\|\mathbf{AB} \times \mathbf{AC}\|$.

If K_m is the area of the approximating parallelogram, we have

$$K_m = \|\mathbf{AB} \times \mathbf{AC}\|$$

To compute K_m, we first find the cross product:

$$\mathbf{AB} \times \mathbf{AC} = \begin{vmatrix} \mathbf{i} & \mathbf{j} & \mathbf{k} \\ \Delta x_m & 0 & f_x(x_m^*, y_m^*)\Delta x_m \\ 0 & \Delta y_m & f_y(x_m^*, y_m^*)\Delta y_m \end{vmatrix}$$

$$= -f_x(x_m^*, y_m^*)\Delta x_m \Delta y_m \,\mathbf{i} - f_y(x_m^*, y_m^*)\Delta x_m \Delta y_m \,\mathbf{j} + \Delta x_m \Delta y_m \,\mathbf{k}$$

Then, we calculate the norm:

$$K_m = \|\mathbf{AB} \times \mathbf{AC}\|$$

$$= \sqrt{[f_x(x_m^*, y_m^*)]^2 \Delta x_m^2 \Delta y_m^2 + [f_y(x_m^*, y_m^*)]^2 \Delta x_m^2 \Delta y_m^2 + \Delta x_m^2 \Delta y_m^2}$$

$$= \sqrt{[f_x(x_m^*, y_m^*)]^2 + [f_y(x_m^*, y_m^*)]^2 + 1} \,\Delta x_m \Delta y_m$$

Finally, summing over the entire partition, we see that the surface area over R may be approximated by the sum

$$\Delta S_n = \sum_{m=1}^{n} \sqrt{[f_x(x_m^*, y_m^*)]^2 + [f_y(x_m^*, y_m^*)]^2 + 1} \,\Delta A_m$$

where $\Delta A_m = \Delta x_m \Delta y_m$. This is a Riemann sum, and by taking an appropriate limit (as the partitions become more and more refined), we find that surface area, S, satisfies

$$S = \lim_{n \to \infty} \sum_{m=1}^{n} \sqrt{[f_x(x_m^*, y_m^*)]^2 + [f_y(x_m^*, y_m^*)]^2 + 1} \,\Delta A_m$$

$$= \iint\limits_{R} \sqrt{[f_x(x, y)]^2 + [f_y(x, y)]^2 + 1} \,dA$$

Surface Area as a Double Integral

Assume that the function $f(x, y)$ has continuous partial derivatives f_x and f_y in a region R of the xy-plane. Then the portion of the surface $z = f(x, y)$ that lies over R has **surface area**

$$S = \iint\limits_R \sqrt{[f_x(x, y)]^2 + [f_y(x, y)]^2 + 1} \, dA$$

The region R may be regarded as the projection of the surface $z = f(x, y)$ on the xy-plane. If there were a light source with rays perpendicular to the xy-plane, R would be the "shadow" of the surface on the plane. You will notice the shadows drawn in the figures shown in this section. It is also worthwhile to make the following comparisons:

Length on x-axis: **Arc length:**

$$\int_a^b dx \qquad\qquad \int_a^b ds = \int_a^b \sqrt{[f'(x)]^2 + 1} \, dx$$

Area in xy-plane: **Surface area:**

$$\iint\limits_R dA \qquad\qquad \iint\limits_R dS = \iint\limits_R \sqrt{[f_x(x, y)]^2 + [f_y(x, y)]^2 + 1} \, dA$$

EXAMPLE 1   Surface area of a plane region

Find the surface area of the portion of the plane $x + y + z = 1$ that lies in the first octant (where $x \geq 0$, $y \geq 0$, $z \geq 0$).

Solution

The plane $x + y + z = 1$ and the triangular region T that lies beneath it in the xy-plane are shown in Figure 12.28. We begin by letting $f(x, y) = 1 - x - y$. Then $f_x(x, y) = -1$ and $f_y(x, y) = -1$, and

$$S = \iint\limits_T \sqrt{[f_x(x, y)]^2 + [f_y(x, y)]^2 + 1} \, dA$$

$$= \iint\limits_T \sqrt{(-1)^2 + (-1)^2 + 1} \, dA$$

$$= \int_0^1 \int_0^{1-x} \sqrt{3} \, dy \, dx \qquad \text{Look at Figure 12.28 to see the region } T \text{ and the limits for both } x \text{ and } y.$$

$$= \sqrt{3} \int_0^1 [y]\big|_0^{1-x} \, dx$$

$$= \sqrt{3} \int_0^1 (1 - x) \, dx$$

$$= \sqrt{3} \left[x - \frac{x^2}{2} \right]\Big|_0^1 = \frac{\sqrt{3}}{2}$$

The surface area is $\sqrt{3}/2 \approx 0.866$ square units. ∎

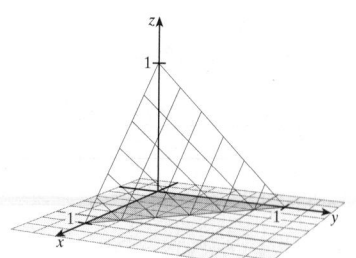

a. The surface of the plane $x + y + z = 1$ in the first octant

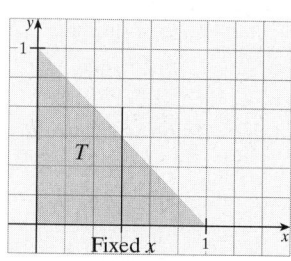

b. The surface projects onto a triangle in the xy-plane.

Figure 12.28 Surface area

EXAMPLE 2   Surface area by changing to polar coordinates

Find the surface area (to the nearest hundredth square unit) of that part of the paraboloid $x^2 + y^2 + z = 5$ that lies above the plane $z = 1$.

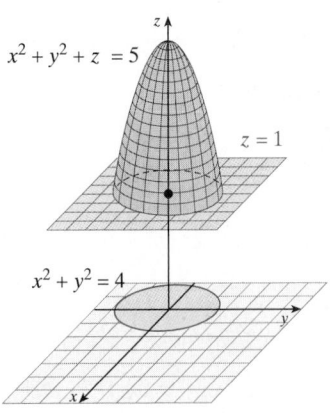

$x^2 + y^2 + z = 5$

$z = 1$

$x^2 + y^2 = 4$

Projected region D

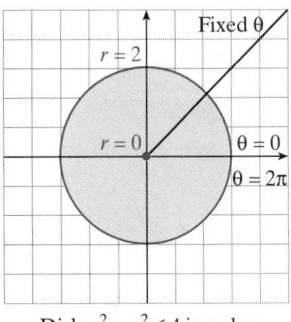

Fixed θ

$r = 2$

$r = 0$

$\theta = 0$

$\theta = 2\pi$

Disk $x^2 + y^2 \le 4$ in polar
coordinates

Figure 12.29 The surface
$x^2 + y^2 + z = 5$ above
$z = 1$ projects onto a disk.

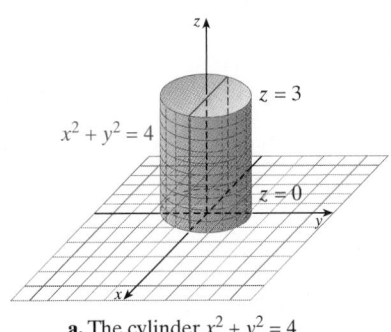

$z = 3$

$x^2 + y^2 = 4$

$z = 0$

a. The cylinder $x^2 + y^2 = 4$

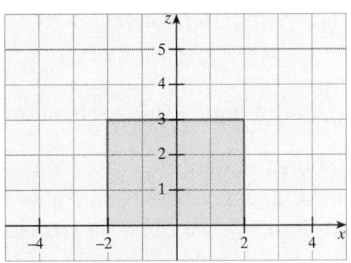

b. The projection of the
cylinder on the xz plane

Figure 12.30 Surface area of a cylinder

Solution

Let $f(x, y) = 5 - x^2 - y^2$. Then $f_x(x, y) = -2x$, $f_y(x, y) = -2y$, and

$$S = \iint_D \sqrt{[f_x(x, y)]^2 + [f_y(x, y)]^2 + 1}\, dA = \iint_D \sqrt{4x^2 + 4y^2 + 1}\, dA$$

To determine the limits for the region D note that the paraboloid intersects the plane $z = 1$ in the circle $x^2 + y^2 = 4$. Thus, the part of the paraboloid whose surface area we seek projects onto the disk $x^2 + y^2 \le 4$ in the xy-plane, as shown in Figure 12.29 (note the shadow).

It is easier if we convert to polar coordinates by letting $x = r\cos\theta$, $y = r\sin\theta$. Because the region is bounded by $0 \le r \le 2$ and $0 \le \theta \le 2\pi$, we have

Note: It is usually best to set up an integral first in rectangular coordinates and then switch to polar form, if appropriate.

$$S = \iint_D \sqrt{4x^2 + 4y^2 + 1}\, dA$$

$$= \int_0^{2\pi} \int_0^2 \sqrt{4r^2 + 1}\, r\, dr\, d\theta$$

Let $u = 4r^2 + 1$, so $du = 8r\, dr$. If $r = 2$, then $u = 17$ and if $r = 0$, $u = 1$.

$$= \int_0^{2\pi} \int_1^{17} u^{1/2}\, \frac{du}{8}\, d\theta$$

$$= \int_0^{2\pi} \frac{1}{8} \cdot \frac{2}{3} u^{3/2}\Big|_1^{17}\, d\theta$$

$$= \frac{1}{12} \int_0^{2\pi} (17^{3/2} - 1)\, d\theta$$

$$= \frac{1}{12}(17^{3/2} - 1)(2\pi - 0) \approx 36.18$$

The surface area is approximately 36.18 square units. ∎

SURFACE AREA PROJECTIONS

We have been projecting the given surface onto the xy-plane, but we can easily modify our procedure to handle other cases. For instance, if the surface $y = f(x, z)$ is projected onto the region Q in the xz-plane, the formula for surface area becomes

$$S = \iint_Q \sqrt{[f_x(x, z)]^2 + [f_z(x, z)]^2 + 1}\, dx\, dz$$

An analogous formula for projection onto the region T in the yz-plane would be

$$S = \iint_T \sqrt{[f_y(y, z)]^2 + [f_z(y, z)]^2 + 1}\, dy\, dz$$

EXAMPLE 3 Surface area of a cylinder

Find the lateral surface area of the cylinder $x^2 + y^2 = 4$, $0 \le z \le 3$.

Solution

The cylinder is shown in Figure 12.30a. We can find the lateral surface area using the formula for a rectangle by imagining the cylinder "opened up." The length of one side is the height of the cylinder (3 units), and the length of the other side of the rectangle is the circumference of the bottom, namely, $2\pi(2) = 4\pi$. Thus, the lateral surface area is 12π.

We will illustrate our integral formula by using it to recompute this surface area. Specifically, we will compute the surface area of the right half of the cylinder and then double it to obtain the required area. If we project the half-cylinder onto the xy-plane, we will not be accounting for the height of the cylinder. Instead, we will project the surface onto the xz-plane to obtain the rectangle Q bounded by $x = 2$, $x = -2$, $z = 0$, and $z = 3$, as shown in Figure 12.30b. Because we are projecting onto the xz-plane, we solve for y to express the surface as $y = f(x, z)$. Since

$$y = f(x, z) = \sqrt{4 - x^2}$$

we have $f_x(x, z) = \dfrac{-x}{\sqrt{4 - x^2}}$ and $f_z(x, z) = 0$ so that

$$[f_x(x, z)]^2 + [f_z(x, z)]^2 + 1 = \frac{x^2}{4 - x^2} + 1 = \frac{4}{4 - x^2}$$

Finally, we note the limits of integration:

$$-2 \leq x \leq 2 \qquad \text{and} \qquad 0 \leq z \leq 3$$

The surface area can now be calculated:

$$S = \iint\limits_{Q} \sqrt{\frac{4}{4 - x^2}}\, dA = \int_{-2}^{2} \int_{0}^{3} \frac{2}{\sqrt{4 - x^2}}\, dz\, dx$$

$$= 6 \sin^{-1} \frac{x}{2} \Big|_{-2}^{2} = 6\pi$$

The lateral surface area of the whole cylinder is $2(6\pi) = 12\pi$. ∎

AREA OF A SURFACE DEFINED PARAMETRICALLY

Suppose a surface S (see Figure 12.31) is defined parametrically by the vector function

$$\mathbf{R}(u, v) = x(u, v)\mathbf{i} + y(u, v)\mathbf{j} + z(u, v)\mathbf{k}$$

for parameters u and v.

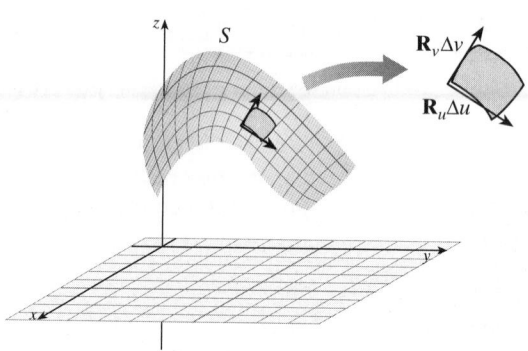

Figure 12.31   Area of a parametrically defined function

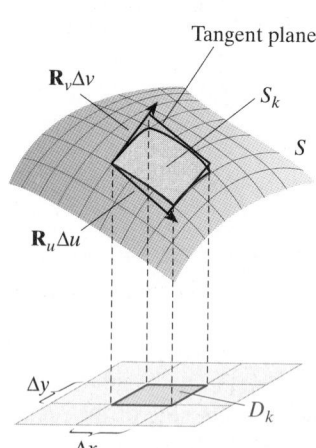

Figure 12.32 Area of a surface defined by a vector function

Let D be a region in the xy-plane on which x, y, and z, as well as their partial derivatives with respect to u and v, are continuous. The partial derivatives of $\mathbf{R}(u, v)$ are given by

$$\mathbf{R}_u = \frac{\partial \mathbf{R}}{\partial u} = \frac{\partial x}{\partial u}\mathbf{i} + \frac{\partial y}{\partial u}\mathbf{j} + \frac{\partial z}{\partial u}\mathbf{k} \qquad \mathbf{R}_v = \frac{\partial \mathbf{R}}{\partial v} = \frac{\partial x}{\partial v}\mathbf{i} + \frac{\partial y}{\partial v}\mathbf{j} + \frac{\partial z}{\partial v}\mathbf{k}$$

Suppose the region D is subdivided into cells, as shown in Figure 12.32. Consider a typical rectangle in this partition, with dimensions Δx and Δy, where Δx and Δy are small. If we project this rectangle onto the surface $\mathbf{R}(u, v)$, we obtain a **curvilinear** parallelogram with adjacent sides $\mathbf{R}_u(u, v)\Delta u$ and $\mathbf{R}_v(u, v)\Delta v$. The area of this rectangle is approximated by

$$\Delta S = \|\mathbf{R}_u(u, v)\Delta u \times \mathbf{R}_v(u, v)\Delta v\| = \|\mathbf{R}_u(u, v) \times \mathbf{R}_v(u, v)\| \Delta u \Delta v$$

By taking an appropriate limit, we find the surface area to be a double integral.

Surface Area Defined Parametrically

> Let S be a surface defined parametrically by
>
> $$\mathbf{R}(u, v) = x(u, v)\mathbf{i} + y(u, v)\mathbf{j} + z(u, v)\mathbf{k}$$
>
> on the region D in the uv-plane, and assume that S is smooth in the sense that $\mathbf{R}_u$ and $\mathbf{R}_v$ are continuous with $\mathbf{R}_u \times \mathbf{R}_v \neq \mathbf{0}$ on D. Then the **surface area**, S, is defined by
>
> $$S = \iint\limits_{D} \|\mathbf{R}_u \times \mathbf{R}_v\|\, du\, dv$$
>
> The quantity $\mathbf{R}_u \times \mathbf{R}_v$ is called the **fundamental cross product**.

EXAMPLE 4 Area of a surface defined parametrically

Find the surface area (to the nearest square unit) of the surface given parametrically by $\mathbf{R}(u, v) = (u \sin v)\mathbf{i} + (u \cos v)\mathbf{j} + u^2\mathbf{k}$ for $0 \leq u \leq 3, 0 \leq v \leq 2\pi$.

Solution

We find that

$$\mathbf{R}_u = \sin v\,\mathbf{i} + \cos v\,\mathbf{j} + 2u\mathbf{k}$$
$$\mathbf{R}_v = u \cos v\,\mathbf{i} + (-u \sin v)\mathbf{j}$$

so the fundamental cross product is

$$\mathbf{R}_u \times \mathbf{R}_v = \begin{vmatrix} \mathbf{i} & \mathbf{j} & \mathbf{k} \\ \sin v & \cos v & 2u \\ u \cos v & -u \sin v & 0 \end{vmatrix} = (2u^2 \sin v)\mathbf{i} + (2u^2 \cos v)\mathbf{j} - u\mathbf{k}$$

We find that

$$\|\mathbf{R}_u \times \mathbf{R}_v\| = \sqrt{4u^4 \sin^2 v + 4u^4 \cos^2 v + u^2} = \sqrt{4u^4 + u^2} = u\sqrt{4u^2 + 1}$$

and we can now compute the surface area:

$$S = \int_0^{2\pi} \int_0^3 u\sqrt{4u^2 + 1}\, du\, dv = \int_0^{2\pi} \left[\frac{1}{12}(4u^2 + 1)^{3/2} \right]\Big|_{u=0}^{u=3} dv$$

$$= \int_0^{2\pi} \left[\frac{1}{12}(37^{3/2} - 1) \right] dv = \frac{37^{3/2} - 1}{12}[2\pi - 0] \approx 117.3187007$$

The surface area is approximately 117 square units. ∎

Notice that in the special case where the surface under consideration has the explicit representation $z = f(x, y)$, it can also be represented in the vector form

$$\mathbf{R}(x, y) = x\mathbf{i} + y\mathbf{j} + f(x, y)\mathbf{k}$$

where x and y are used as parameters ($x = u$ and $y = v$). With this vector representation, we find that

$$\mathbf{R}_x = \mathbf{i} + f_x\mathbf{k} \quad \text{and} \quad \mathbf{R}_y = \mathbf{j} + f_y\mathbf{k}$$

so the fundamental cross product is

$$\mathbf{R}_x \times \mathbf{R}_y = \begin{vmatrix} \mathbf{i} & \mathbf{j} & \mathbf{k} \\ 1 & 0 & f_x \\ 0 & 1 & f_y \end{vmatrix} = -f_x\mathbf{i} - f_y\mathbf{j} + \mathbf{k}$$

Therefore, in the case where $z = f(x, y)$, the surface area over the region D is given by

$$S = \iint_D \| \mathbf{R}_x \times \mathbf{R}_y \| \, dx \, dy$$

$$= \iint_D \sqrt{(-f_x)^2 + (-f_y)^2 + 1^2} \, dx \, dy$$

$$= \iint_D \sqrt{f_x^2 + f_y^2 + 1} \, dx \, dy$$

which is the formula obtained at the beginning of this section.

12.4 PROBLEM SET

A *Find the surface area of each surface given in Problems 1–19.*

1. The portion of the plane $2x + y + 4z = 8$ that lies in the first octant

2. The portion of the plane $4x + y + z = 9$ that lies in the first octant

3. The portion of the paraboloid $z = x^2 + y^2$ that lies inside the cylinder $x^2 + y^2 = 1$. *Hint:* Convert to polar coordinates after setting up the integral.

4. The portion of the paraboloid $z = 3x^2 + 3y^2$ that lies inside the cylinder $x^2 + y^2 = 4$. *Hint:* Convert to polar coordinates after setting up the integral.

5. The portion of the plane $3x + 6y + 2z = 12$ that is above the triangular region in the plane with vertices $(0, 0, 0)$, $(1, 0, 0)$, and $(1, 1, 0)$

6. The portion of the plane $2x + 2y - z = 0$ that is above the square region in the plane with vertices $(0, 0, 0)$, $(1, 0, 0)$, $(0, 1, 0)$, $(1, 1, 0)$

7. The portion of the surface $x^2 + z = 9$ above the square region in the plane with vertices $(0, 0, 0)$, $(2, 0, 0)$, $(0, 2, 0)$, $(2, 2, 0)$

8. The portion of the surface $z = x^2$ that lies over the triangular region in the plane with vertices $(0, 0, 0)$, $(0, 1, 0)$, and $(1, 0, 0)$

9. The portion of the surface $z = x^2$ over the square region with vertices $(0, 0, 0)$, $(0, 4, 0)$, $(4, 0, 0)$, $(4, 4, 0)$

10. The portion of the surface $z = 2x + y^2$ over the square region with vertices $(0, 0, 0)$, $(3, 0, 0)$, $(0, 3, 0)$, $(3, 3, 0)$

11. The portion of the paraboloid $z = x^2 + y^2$ that lies below the plane $z = 1$

12. The portion of the sphere $x^2 + y^2 + z^2 = 25$ that lies above the plane $z = 3$

13. The portion of the cylinder $x^2 + z^2 = 4$ that is in the first octant and is bounded by the plane $y = 2$

14. The portion of the plane $x + y + z = 4$ that lies inside the cylinder $x^2 + y^2 = 16$

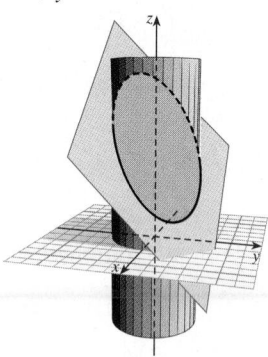

15. The portion of the sphere $x^2 + y^2 + z^2 = 8$ that is inside the cone $x^2 + y^2 - z^2 = 0$

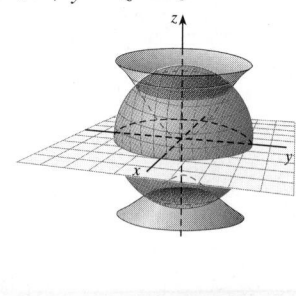

16. The portion of the sphere $x^2 + y^2 + z^2 = 4$ that lies inside the cylinder $x^2 + y^2 = 2y$

17. The portion of the surface $z = x^2 + y$ above the rectangle $0 \le x \le 2, 0 \le y \le 5$

18. The portion of the surface $z = x^2 - y^2$ that lies inside the cylinder $x^2 + y^2 = 9$

19. The portion of the paraboloid $z = 4 - x^2 - y^2$ that lies above the xy-plane

B 20. **WHAT DOES THIS SAY?** Describe the process for finding a surface area.

21. **WHAT DOES THIS SAY?** Describe what is meant by a surface area projection.

22. On a given map, a city parking lot is shown to be a rectangle that is 300 ft by 400 ft. However, the parking lot slopes in the 400-ft direction. It rises uniformly 1 ft for every 5 ft of horizontal displacement. What is the actual surface area of the parking lot?

23. Find the surface area of the portion of the plane $Ax + By + Cz = D$ (A, B, C, and D all positive) that lies in the first octant.

24. Find the portion of the plane $x + 2y + 3z = 12$ that lies over the triangular region in the xy-plane with vertices $(0, 0, 0)$, $(0, a, 0)$, and $(a, a, 0)$.

25. Find the surface area of that portion of the plane

$$x + y + z = a$$

that lies between the concentric cylinders $x^2 + y^2 = \dfrac{a^2}{4}$ and $x^2 + y^2 = a^2$ $(a > 0)$.

26. Find the surface area of the portion of the cylinder $x^2 + z^2 = 9$ that lies inside the cylinder $y^2 + z^2 = 9$.

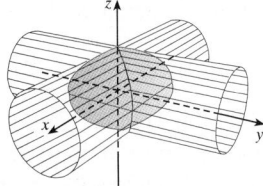

27. Find a formula for the area of the conical surface $z = \sqrt{x^2 + y^2}$ between the planes $z = 0$ and $z = h$.

28. Find a formula for the surface area of the frustum of the cone $z = 4\sqrt{x^2 + y^2}$ between the planes $z = h_1$ and $z = h_2$, where $h_1 > h_2$.

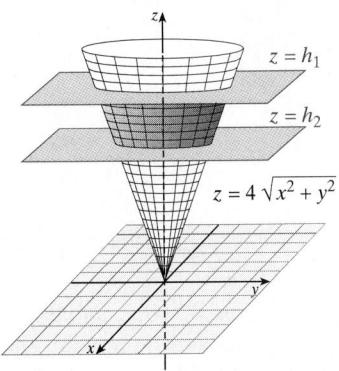

29. Find the surface area of that portion of the sphere $x^2 + y^2 + z^2 = 9z$ that lies inside the paraboloid $x^2 + y^2 = 4z$.

30. Find the surface area of that portion of the cylinder $x^2 + z^2 = 4$ that is above the triangle with vertices $(0, 0, 0)$, $(1, 1, 0)$, and $(1, 0, 0)$.

*In Problems 31–36, **set up** (but do not evaluate) the double integral for the surface area of the given portion of surface.*

31. The surface given by $z = e^{-x} \sin y$ over the triangle with vertices $(0, 0, 0)$, $(0, 1, 1)$, $(0, 1, 0)$

32. The surface given by $x = z^3 - yz + y^3$ over the square $(0, 0, 0)$, $(0, 0, 2)$, $(0, 2, 0)$, $(0, 2, 2)$

33. The surface given by $z = \cos(x^2 + y^2)$ over the disk $x^2 + y^2 \le \frac{\pi}{2}$

34. The surface given by $z = e^{-x} \cos y$ over the disk $x^2 + y^2 \le 2$

35. The surface given by $z = x^2 + 5xy + y^2$ over the region in the xy-plane bounded by the curve $xy = 5$ and the line $x + y = 6$

36. The surface given by $z = x^2 + 3xy + y^2$ over the region in the xy-plane bounded by $0 \le x \le 4$, $0 \le y \le x$

Compute the magnitude of the fundamental cross product for the surface defined parametrically in Problems 37–40.

37. $\mathbf{R}(u, v) = (2u \sin v)\mathbf{i} + (2u \cos v)\mathbf{j} + u^2\mathbf{k}$

38. $\mathbf{R}(u, v) = (4 \sin u \cos v)\mathbf{i} + (4 \sin u \sin v)\mathbf{j} + (5 \cos u)\mathbf{k}$

39. $\mathbf{R}(u, v) = u\mathbf{i} + v^2\mathbf{j} + u^3\mathbf{k}$

40. $\mathbf{R}(u, v) = (2u \sin v)\mathbf{i} + (2u \cos v)\mathbf{j} + (u^2 \sin 2v)\mathbf{k}$

41. Find the area of the surface given parametrically by the equation

$$\mathbf{R}(u, v) = uv\mathbf{i} + (u - v)\mathbf{j} + (u + v)\mathbf{k}$$

for $u^2 + v^2 \le 1$. *Hint*: Use polar coordinates with $u = r \cos\theta$ and $v = r \sin\theta$.

42. A *spiral ramp* has the vector parametric equation

$$\mathbf{R}(u, v) = (u \cos v)\mathbf{i} + (u \sin v)\mathbf{j} + v\mathbf{k}$$

for $0 \le u \le 1, 0 \le v \le \pi$. Find the surface area of this ramp.

43. The surface given parametrically by

$$\mathbf{R}(u, v) = (u \sin v)\mathbf{i} + (u \cos v)\mathbf{j} + v\mathbf{k}$$

for $0 \le u \le a$ and $0 \le v \le b$ is called a *helicoid*.

   a. Compute $\mathbf{R}_u \times \mathbf{R}_v$

   b. Find the surface area of the helicoid. *Hint*: Express your answer in terms of a and b.

44. Verify that a sphere of radius a has surface area $4\pi a^2$.

45. Verify that a cylinder of radius a and height h has surface area $2\pi a h$.

46. Find the surface area of the torus defined by

$$\mathbf{R}(u, v) = (a + b \cos v) \cos u\mathbf{i} + (a + b \cos v) \sin u\mathbf{j} + b \sin v\mathbf{k}$$

for $0 < b < a, 0 \le u \le 2\pi, 0 \le v \le 2\pi$.

47. Suppose a surface is given implicitly by $F(x, y, z) = 0$. If the surface can be projected onto a region D in the xy-plane, show that the surface area is given by

$$A = \iint\limits_{D} \frac{\sqrt{F_x^2 + F_y^2 + F_z^2}}{|F_z|} \, dA$$

where $F_z \ne 0$. Use this formula to find the surface area of a sphere of radius R.

48. Let S be the surface defined by $f(x, y, z) = C$, and let R be the projection of S on a plane. Show that the surface area of S can be computed by the integral

$$\iint\limits_{R} \frac{\|\nabla f\|}{|\nabla f \cdot \mathbf{u}|} \, dA$$

where $\mathbf{u}$ is a unit vector normal to the plane containing R and $\nabla f \cdot \mathbf{u} \ne 0$. This is a practical formula sometimes used in calculating the surface area.

12.5   Triple Integrals

IN THIS SECTION   definition of the triple integral, iterated integration, volume by triple integrals

DEFINITION OF THE TRIPLE INTEGRAL

A double integral $\iint\limits_{D} f(x, y)\, dA$ is evaluated over a closed, bounded region in the plane, and in essentially the same way, a **triple integral** $\iiint\limits_{D} f(x, y, z)\, dV$ is evaluated over a closed, bounded solid region D in $\mathbb{R}^3$. Suppose $f(x, y, z)$ is defined on a closed region D, which in turn is contained in a "box" B in space. Partition B into a finite number of smaller boxes using planes parallel to the coordinate planes, as shown in Figure 12.33.

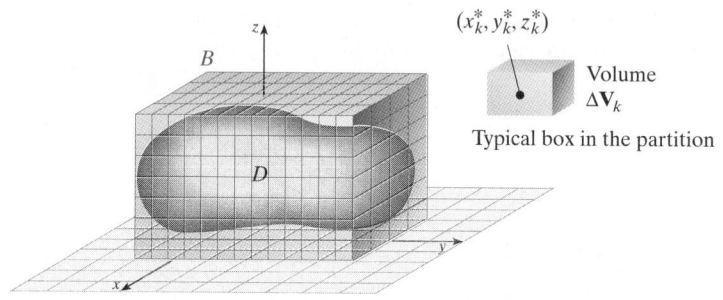

Figure 12.33   The box B contains D and is subdivided into smaller boxes.

We exclude from consideration any boxes with points outside S. Let $\Delta V_1, \Delta V_2, \ldots, \Delta V_n$ denote the volumes of the boxes that remain, and define the norm $\|P\|$ of the partition to be the length of the longest diagonal of any box in the partition. Next, choose a representative point (x_k^*, y_k^*, z_k^*) from each box in the partition and form the Riemann sum

$$\sum_{k=1}^{n} f(x_k^*, y_k^*, z_k^*)\Delta V_k$$

If we repeat the process with more subdivisions, so that the norm approaches zero, we are led to the following definition.

Triple Integral

> If f is a function defined over a closed bounded solid region D, then the **triple integral of f over D** is defined to be the limit
>
> $$\iiint\limits_{D} f(x, y, z)\, dV = \lim_{\|P\| \to 0} \sum_{k=1}^{n} f(x_k^*, y_k^*, z_k^*)\Delta V_k$$
>
> provided this limit exists.

A surface is said to be **piecewise smooth** if it is made up of a finite number of smooth surfaces. It can be shown that the triple integral exists if $f(x, y, z)$ is continuous on D and the surface of D is piecewise smooth. It can also be shown that triple integrals have the following properties, which are analogous to those of double integrals listed in Theorem 12.1. In each case, assume the indicated integrals exist.

Linearity rule For constants a and b

$$\iiint_D [af(x, y, z) + bg(x, y, z)] \, dV$$

$$= a \iiint_D f(x, y, z) \, dV + b \iiint_D g(x, y, z) \, dV$$

Dominance rule If $f(x, y, z) \geq g(x, y, z)$ on D, then

$$\iiint_D f(x, y, z) \, dV \geq \iiint_D g(x, y, z) \, dV$$

Subdivision rule If the solid region of integration D can be subdivided into two solid subregions D_1 and D_2 (see Figure 12.34), then

$$\iiint_D f(x, y, z) \, dV = \iiint_{D_1} f(x, y, z) \, dV + \iiint_{D_2} f(x, y, z) \, dV$$

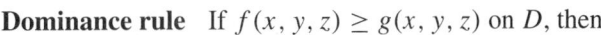

Figure 12.34 Dividing the solid D into two solid subregions

ITERATED INTEGRATION

As with double integrals, we evaluate triple integrals by iterated integration. However, setting up the limits of integration in an iterated triple integral is often difficult, especially if the solid region of integration, D, is hard to visualize. The relatively simple case where B is a rectangular solid (box) may be handled by applying the following theorem.

THEOREM 12.5 Fubini's theorem over a parallelepiped in space

If $f(x, y, z)$ is continuous over a rectangular box B: $a \leq x \leq b, c \leq y \leq d, r \leq z \leq s$, then the triple integral may be evaluated by the iterated integral

$$\iiint_B f(x, y, z) \, dV = \int_r^s \int_c^d \int_a^b f(x, y, z) \, dx \, dy \, dz$$

The iterated integration can be performed in any order, with appropriate adjustments to the limits of integration:

$$
\begin{array}{ccc}
dx \, dy \, dz & dx \, dz \, dy & dz \, dx \, dy \\
dy \, dx \, dz & dy \, dz \, dx & dz \, dy \, dx
\end{array}
$$

Proof The proof, which is similar to the two-dimensional case, can be found in an advanced calculus course. ❏

EXAMPLE 1 Evaluating a triple integral using Fubini's theorem

Evaluate $\displaystyle\iiint_B z^2 y e^x \, dV$, where B is the box given by

$$0 \leq x \leq 1, \quad 1 \leq y \leq 2, \quad -1 \leq z \leq 1$$

This box is shown in Figure 12.35.

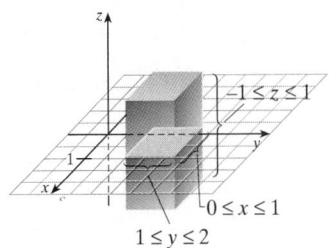

Figure 12.35 Region B

Solution

We will evaluate the integral in the order $dx\,dy\,dz$.

$$\iiint\limits_{B} f(x, y, z)\,dV = \int_{-1}^{1}\int_{1}^{2} \underbrace{\int_{0}^{1} z^2 y e^x\,dx}\,dy\,dz$$

Treat y and z as constants.

$$= \int_{-1}^{1}\int_{1}^{2} z^2 y\,\left[e^x\right]\big|_{x=0}^{x=1}\,dy\,dz = \int_{-1}^{1}\underbrace{\int_{1}^{2} z^2 y\,[e-1]\,dy}\,dz$$

Treat z as a constant.

$$= (e-1)\int_{-1}^{1} z^2 \left[\frac{y^2}{2}\right]\bigg|_{y=1}^{y=2}\,dz = (e-1)\int_{-1}^{1} z^2 \left[\frac{2^2}{2} - \frac{1^2}{2}\right]\,dz$$

$$= \frac{3}{2}(e-1)\int_{-1}^{1} z^2\,dz = \frac{3}{2}(e-1)\,\frac{z^3}{3}\bigg|_{z=-1}^{z=1}$$

$$= \frac{3}{2}(e-1)\left[\frac{1^3}{3} - \frac{(-1)^3}{3}\right] = e-1$$

As an exercise, verify that the same result is obtained by using any other order of integration—for example, $dz\,dy\,dx$.   ∎

Next, we will see how triple integrals can be evaluated over solid regions that are not rectangular boxes. We will assume the solid region of integration D is *z-simple* in the sense that it has a lower bounding surface $z = u(x, y)$ and an upper bounding surface $z = v(x, y)$, and that it projects onto a region A in the xy-plane that is of either type I or type II. Such a solid is shown in Figure 12.36.

The region D can be described as the set of all points (x, y, z) such that $u(x, y) \leq z \leq v(x, y)$ for all (x, y) in A. Then the triple integral of $f(x, y, z)$ over the solid region D can be expressed as an iterated integral with inner limits of integration (with respect to z) $u(x, y)$ and $v(x, y)$. We summarize in the following theorem.

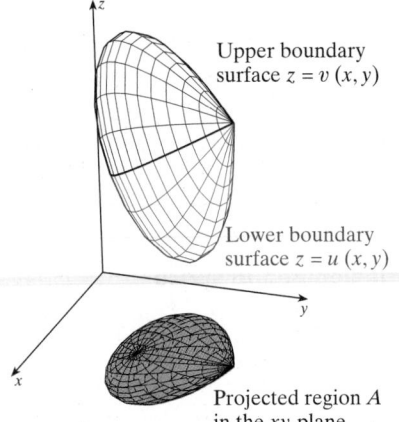

Upper boundary surface $z = v(x, y)$

Lower boundary surface $z = u(x, y)$

Projected region A in the xy-plane

Figure 12.36 A z-simple solid D

THEOREM 12.6   Triple integral over a z-simple solid region

Suppose D is a solid region bounded below by the surface $z = u(x, y)$ and above by $z = v(x, y)$ that projects onto the region A in the xy-plane. If A is of either type I or type II, then the integral of the continuous function $f(x, y, z)$ over D is

$$\iiint\limits_{D} f(x, y, z)\,dV = \iint\limits_{A}\left(\int_{u(x,y)}^{v(x,y)} f(x, y, z)\,dz\right)\,dA$$

Proof   Even though a proof is beyond the scope of this text, we note that if A is vertically simple (type I), then for each fixed x in an interval $[a, b]$, y varies from $g_1(x)$ to $g_2(x)$, and the triple integral of $f(x, y, z)$ over D can be expressed as

$$\iiint\limits_{D} f(x, y, z)\,dV = \int_{a}^{b}\int_{g_1(x)}^{g_2(x)}\int_{u(x,y)}^{v(x,y)} f(x, y, z)\,dz\,dy\,dx$$

Likewise, if A is horizontally simple (type II), then for each fixed y in an interval $[c, d]$, x varies from $h_1(y)$ to $h_2(y)$, and

$$\iiint\limits_{D} f(x, y, z)\,dV = \int_{c}^{d}\int_{h_1(y)}^{h_2(y)}\int_{u(x,y)}^{v(x,y)} f(x, y, z)\,dz\,dx\,dy$$ ❑

We illustrate this procedure in the following example.

EXAMPLE 2 Evaluating a triple integral over a general region

Evaluate $\iiint\limits_{D} x\, dV$, where D is the solid in the first octant bounded by the cylinder $x^2 + y^2 = 4$ and the plane $2y + z = 4$.

Solution

The solid is shown in Figure 12.37. The upper boundary surface of D is the plane $z = 4 - 2y$, and the lower boundary surface is the xy-plane, $z = 0$. The projection A of the solid on the xy-plane is the quarter disk $x^2 + y^2 \le 4$ with $x \ge 0$, $y \ge 0$ (because D lies in the first octant). This projection may be described in type I form as the set of all (x, y) such that for each fixed x between 0 and 2, y varies from 0 to $\sqrt{4 - x^2}$. Thus, we have

$$
\iiint\limits_{D} x\, dV = \iint\limits_{A} \int_{0}^{4-2y} x\, dz\, dA = \int_{0}^{2} \int_{0}^{\sqrt{4-x^2}} \int_{0}^{4-2y} x\, dz\, dy\, dx
$$

$$
= \int_{0}^{2} \int_{0}^{\sqrt{4-x^2}} x[(4 - 2y) - 0]\, dy\, dx = \int_{0}^{2} \int_{0}^{\sqrt{4-x^2}} (4x - 2xy)\, dy\, dx
$$

$$
= \int_{0}^{2} \left[4xy - xy^2 \right]\Big|_{y=0}^{y=\sqrt{4-x^2}}\, dx = \int_{0}^{2} \left[4x\sqrt{4 - x^2} - x(4 - x^2) \right]\, dx
$$

$$
= \left[-\frac{4}{3}(4 - x^2)^{3/2} - 2x^2 + \frac{1}{4}x^4 \right]\Big|_{0}^{2} = \left[0 - 8 + 4 + \frac{32}{3} + 0 - 0 \right] = \frac{20}{3}
$$ ∎

VOLUME BY TRIPLE INTEGRALS

Just as a double integral can be interpreted as the area of the region of integration, a triple integral may be interpreted as the **volume** of a solid. That is, if V is the volume of the solid region D, then

$$
V = \iiint\limits_{D} dV
$$

EXAMPLE 3 Volume of a tetrahedron

Find the volume of the tetrahedron T bounded by the plane $2x + y + 3z = 6$ and the coordinate planes $x = 0$, $y = 0$, and $z = 0$.

Solution

The tetrahedron T is shown in Figure 12.38a. The upper surface of T is the plane $z = \frac{1}{3}(6 - 2x - y)$ and its lower surface is $z = 0$. Note that T projects onto a triangle, A, in the xy-plane, as shown in Figure 12.38b. Described in type I form, the triangle A is the set of all (x, y) such that for each fixed x between 0 and 3, y varies from 0 to $6 - 2x$. Thus,

$$
V = \iiint\limits_{T} dV = \iint\limits_{A} \int_{0}^{\frac{1}{3}(6-2x-y)} dz\, dA
$$

$$
= \int_{0}^{3} \int_{0}^{6-2x} \int_{0}^{\frac{1}{3}(6-2x-y)} dz\, dy\, dx
$$

$$
= \int_{0}^{3} \int_{0}^{6-2x} \left[\tfrac{1}{3}(6 - 2x - y) - 0 \right]\, dy\, dx
$$

$$
= \int_{0}^{3} \left[2y - \tfrac{2}{3}xy - \tfrac{1}{6}y^2 \right]\Big|_{y=0}^{y=6-2x}\, dx
$$

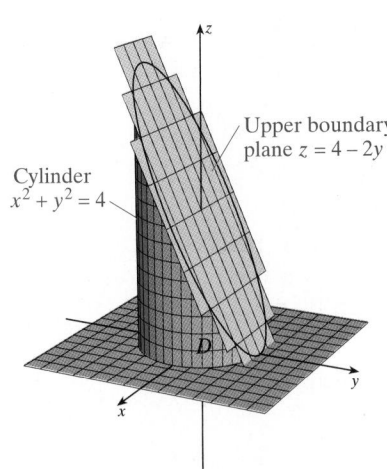

a. The solid D

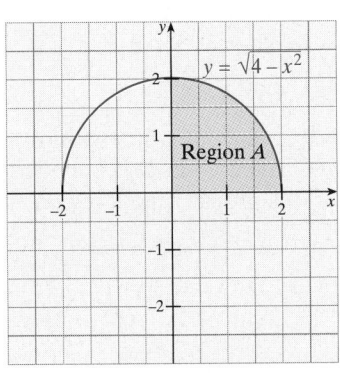

$y = \sqrt{4 - x^2}$

Region A

b. The region A

Figure 12.37 The solid D and its projection A in the xy-plane

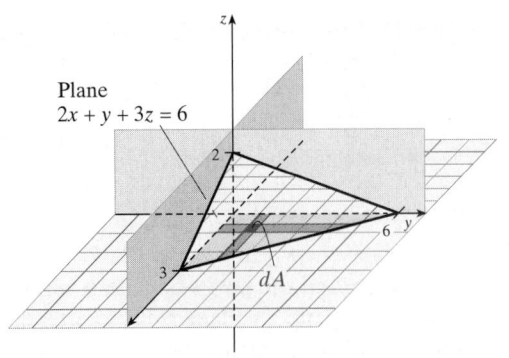

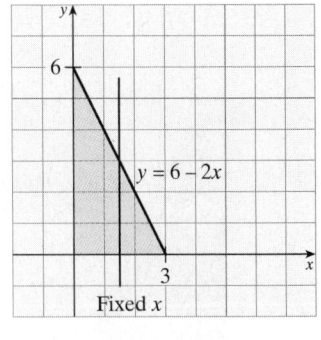

a. The tetrahedron bounded by the plane $2x + y + 3z = 6$ and the positive coordinate planes.

b. The region projected onto the xy-plane is a triangle.

Figure 12.38   Volume of a tetrahedron

$$= \int_0^3 \left[2(6 - 2x) - \tfrac{2}{3}x(6 - 2x) - \tfrac{1}{6}(6 - 2x)^2 - 0 \right] dx$$

$$= \int_0^3 \tfrac{1}{6}[36 - 24x + 4x^2] \, dx = 6$$

The volume of the tetrahedron is 6 cubic units.   ∎

Sometimes it is easier to evaluate a triple integral by integrating first with respect to x or y instead of z. For instance, if the solid region of integration D is bounded by $x = x_1(y, z)$ and $x = x_2(y, z)$, and the boundary surfaces project onto a region A in the yz-plane, as shown in Figure 12.39a, then

$$\iiint_D f(x, y, z) \, dV = \iint_A \int_{x_1}^{x_2} f(x, y, z) \, dx \, dA$$

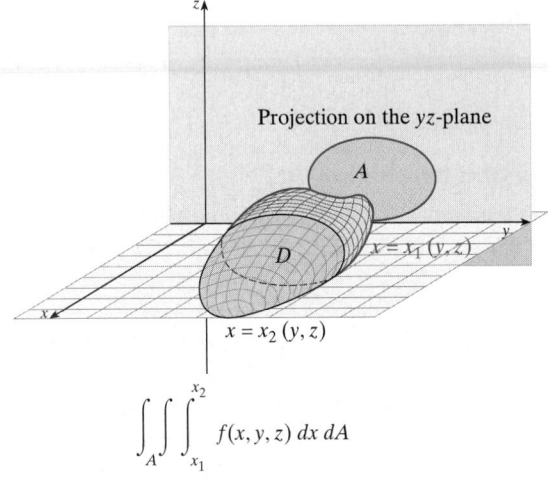

$$\int_A \int \int_{x_1}^{x_2} f(x, y, z) \, dx \, dA$$

a. A solid D with "front" surface $x = x_2(y, z)$ and "back" surface $x = x_1(y, z)$

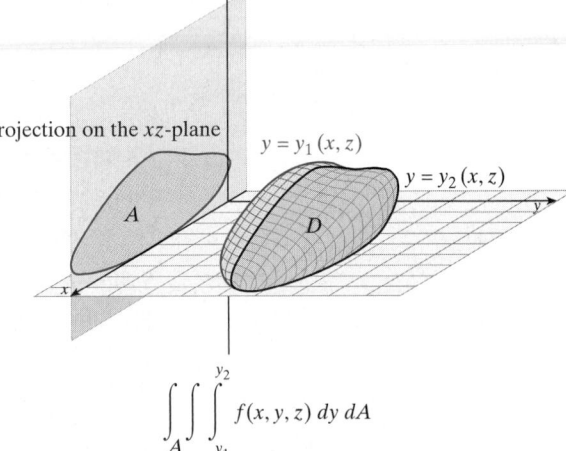

$$\int_A \int \int_{y_1}^{y_2} f(x, y, z) \, dy \, dA$$

b. A solid D with "side" surfaces $y = y_2(x, z)$ and $y = y_1(x, z)$

Figure 12.39   Iterated integration with respect to x or y first

On the other hand, if the solid region of integration D is bounded by the surfaces $y = y_1(x, z)$ and $y = y_2(x, z)$, and the boundary surfaces project onto a region A in the xz-plane as shown in Figure 12.39b, then

$$\iiint_D f(x, y, z) \, dV = \iint_A \int_{y_1}^{y_2} f(x, y, z) \, dy \, dA$$

As an illustration, we will now rework Example 3 by projecting the tetrahedron T onto the yz-plane.

EXAMPLE 4 Volume of a tetrahedron by changing the order of integration

Find the volume of the tetrahedron T bounded by the coordinate planes and the plane $2x + y + 3z = 6$ in the first octant by projecting onto the yz-plane.

Solution

Note that T is bounded by the yz-plane and the plane $2x + y + 3z = 6$, which we express as $x = \frac{1}{2}(6 - y - 3z)$. (See Figure 12.40a.) The volume is given by

$$V = \iiint_T dV = \iint_B \int_0^{\frac{1}{2}(6-y-3z)} dx\, dA$$

where B is the projection in the yz-plane. This projection is the triangle bounded by the lines $z = 0$, $y = 0$, and $z = \frac{1}{3}(6 - y)$, as shown in Figure 12.40b.

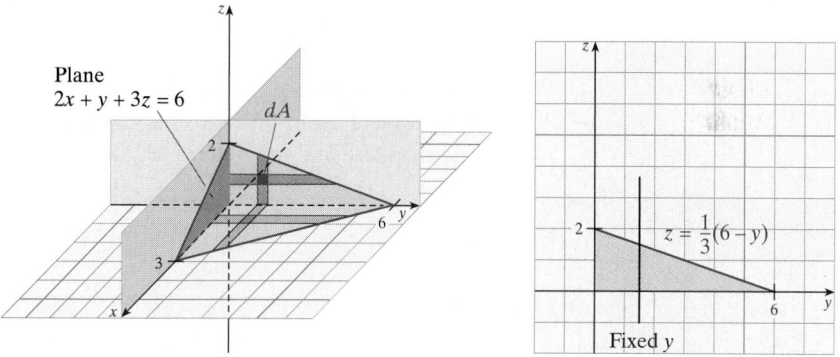

a. The tetrahedron bounded by the plane $2x + y + 3z = 6$ and the positive coordinate planes.

b. The region projected onto the yz-plane is a triangle.

Figure 12.40 Volume of a tetrahedron; alternative projection

Thus, for each fixed y between 0 and 6, z varies from 0 to $\frac{1}{3}(6 - y)$, and we have

$$V = \int_0^6 \int_0^{\frac{1}{3}(6-y)} \int_0^{\frac{1}{2}(6-y-3z)} dx\, dz\, dy = \int_0^6 \int_0^{\frac{1}{3}(6-y)} \frac{1}{2}(6 - y - 3z)\, dz\, dy$$

$$= \int_0^6 \left[3z - \frac{1}{2}yz - \frac{3}{4}z^2 \right]\Big|_{z=0}^{z=\frac{1}{3}(6-y)} dy$$

$$= \int_0^6 \left[(6 - y) - \frac{1}{6}y(6 - y) - \frac{1}{12}(6 - y)^2 - 0 \right] dy = 6$$

This is the same result we obtained in Example 3 by projecting onto the xy-plane. ∎

EXAMPLE 5 Setting up a triple integral to find a volume

Set up (but do not evaluate) a triple integral for the volume of the solid D that is bounded above by the sphere $x^2 + y^2 + z^2 = 4$ and below by the plane $y + z = 2$. The projection on the xy-plane is shown as a shadow in Figure 12.41.

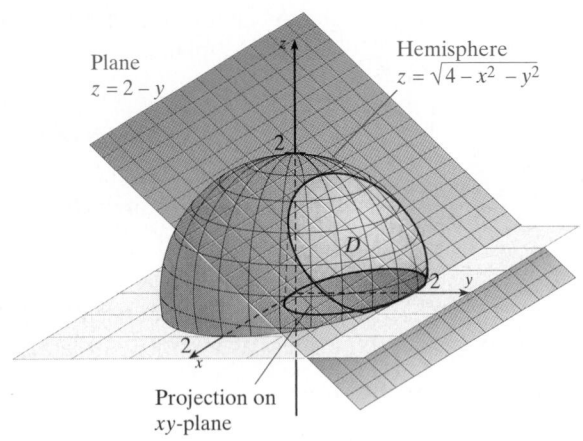

Figure 12.41 Region bounded above by a sphere and below by a plane

Solution

First, note that the intersection of the plane and the sphere occurs above the xy-plane (where $z \geq 0$), so the sphere can be represented by the equation

$$z = \sqrt{4 - x^2 - y^2}$$

(the upper hemisphere). To find the limits of integration for x and y we consider the projection of D onto the xy-plane. To this end, consider the intersection of the hemisphere and the plane $z = 2 - y$:

$$\sqrt{4 - x^2 - y^2} = 2 - y$$
$$4 - x^2 - y^2 = 4 - 4y + y^2$$
$$x^2 + 2y^2 - 4y = 0$$
$$x^2 + 2(y - 1)^2 = 2$$

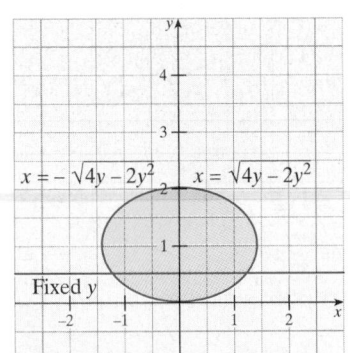

Figure 12.42 The projection of D onto the xy-plane

Although this intersection occurs in $\mathbb{R}^3$, its equation does not contain z. Therefore, the equation serves as a projection on the xy-plane, where $z = 0$. This is an ellipse centered at $(0, 1)$, as shown in Figure 12.42.

We consider this as a type II region, which means we will integrate first with respect to x, then with respect to y. Because $x^2 + 2(y - 1)^2 = 2$ we see that for fixed y between 0 and 2, x varies from $-\sqrt{2 - 2(y - 1)^2} = -\sqrt{4y - 2y^2}$ to $\sqrt{4y - 2y^2}$. However, using symmetry, we see the required volume V is twice the integral as x varies from 0 to $\sqrt{4y - 2y^2}$. This leads us to evaluate V by the following triple integral.

$$V = 2 \int_0^2 \int_0^{\sqrt{4y - 2y^2}} \int_{2 - y}^{\sqrt{4 - x^2 - y^2}} dz \, dx \, dy \qquad \blacksquare$$

EXAMPLE 6 **Choosing an order of integration to compute volume**

Find the volume of the solid D bounded below by the paraboloid $z = x^2 + y^2$ and above by the plane $2x + z = 3$.

Solution

The graph of the solid D is shown in Figure 12.43a. The projection of the solid onto the xy-plane is the graph of the equation

$$x^2 + y^2 = 3 - 2x \qquad \text{Substitute the second equation into the first.}$$
$$(x + 1)^2 + y^2 = 4 \qquad \text{Complete the square for } x.$$

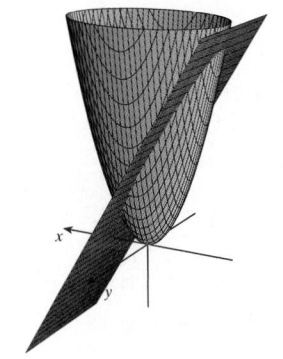

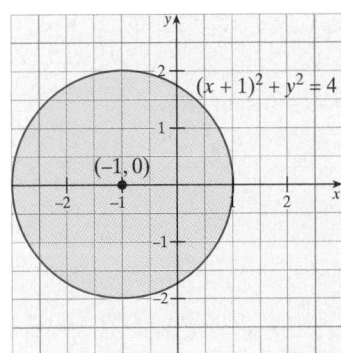

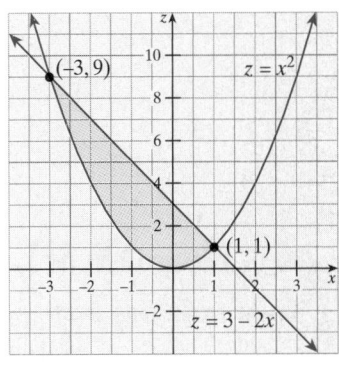

a. The solid D bounded by $z = x^2 + y^2$ and $2x + z = 3$

b. The projection of D on the xy-plane

c. The projection of D on the xz-plane

Figure 12.43   The solid D bounded by $z = x^2 + y^2$ and $2x + z = 3$ and projections on two coordinate planes.

This is a circle of radius 2 centered at $(-1, 0)$, as shown in Figure 12.43b. Proceeding as in Example 5, we find that the volume is given by the integral

$$V = 2 \int_{-3}^{1} \int_{0}^{\sqrt{3-2x-x^2}} \int_{x^2+y^2}^{3-2x} dz \, dy \, dx$$

which is not especially easy to integrate (try it!).

However, if we project the solid D onto the xz-plane, the projection A is the region bounded by the line $2x + z = 3$ and the parabola $z = x^2$ (take $y = 0$ in the equation $z = x^2 + y^2$), which intersect at the points $(1, 1)$ and $(-3, 9)$, as shown in Figure 12.43c. The solid D is symmetric with respect to the xz-plane, so we can integrate with respect to y from $y = 0$ to $y = \sqrt{z - x^2}$ and double the result. We can then describe A as the following type I region.

$A:$ set of all (x, z) such that for each fixed x in the interval
$\quad\quad -3 \le x \le 1, z$ varies from $z = x^2$ to $z = 3 - 2x$

The volume of D is given by the integral

$$V = 2 \int_{-3}^{1} \int_{x^2}^{3-2x} \int_{0}^{\sqrt{z-x^2}} dy \, dz \, dx$$

$$= 2 \int_{-3}^{1} \int_{x^2}^{3-2x} \sqrt{z - x^2} \, dz \, dx$$

$$= 2 \int_{-3}^{1} \frac{2}{3} (z - x^2)^{3/2} \Big|_{x^2}^{3-2x} dx$$

$$= \frac{4}{3} \int_{-3}^{1} (3 - 2x - x^2)^{3/2} \, dx$$

$$= \frac{4}{3} \int_{-3}^{1} [4 - (x + 1)^2]^{3/2} \, dx \quad\quad \textit{Complete the square.}$$

$$\boxed{\text{Let } x + 1 = 2 \sin\theta; \, dx = 2\cos\theta \, d\theta}$$

$$= \frac{4}{3} \int_{-\pi/2}^{\pi/2} 8 \cos^3 \theta \, (2 \cos\theta \, d\theta)$$

$$= \frac{128}{3} \int_{0}^{\pi/2} \cos^4 \theta \, d\theta \quad\quad \textit{Symmetry}$$

$$= \frac{128}{3}\left(\frac{3\pi}{16}\right) \qquad \text{Formula 320}$$

$$= 8\pi$$

∎

12.5 PROBLEM SET

Ⓐ **1. WHAT DOES THIS SAY?** State Fubini's theorem for a continuous function over a parallelepiped in $\mathbb{R}^3$.

2. Exploration Problem Set up integrals, with appropriate limits of integration for the six possible orders of integration for $\iiint\limits_D f(x, y, z)\, dV$, where D is the solid described by

$$D : y^2 \le x \le 4, \quad 0 \le y \le 2, \quad 0 \le z \le 4 - x$$

Compute the iterated triple integrals in Problems 3–14.

3. $\displaystyle\int_1^4 \int_{-2}^3 \int_2^5 dx\, dy\, dz$

4. $\displaystyle\int_{-1}^3 \int_0^2 \int_{-2}^2 dy\, dz\, dx$

5. $\displaystyle\int_1^2 \int_0^1 \int_{-1}^2 8x^2 yz^3\, dx\, dy\, dz$

6. $\displaystyle\int_4^7 \int_{-1}^2 \int_0^3 x^2 y^2 z^2\, dx\, dy\, dz$

7. $\displaystyle\int_0^2 \int_0^x \int_0^{x+y} xyz\, dz\, dy\, dx$

8. $\displaystyle\int_0^1 \int_{\sqrt{x}}^{\sqrt{1+x}} \int_0^{xy} y^{-1} z\, dz\, dy\, dx$

9. $\displaystyle\int_{-1}^2 \int_0^\pi \int_1^4 yz \cos xy\, dz\, dx\, dy$

10. $\displaystyle\int_0^\pi \int_0^1 \int_0^1 x^2 y \cos xyz\, dz\, dy\, dx$

11. $\displaystyle\int_0^1 \int_0^y \int_0^{\ln y} e^{z+2x}\, dz\, dx\, dy$

12. $\displaystyle\int_1^3 \int_0^{2z} \int_0^{\ln y} ye^{-x}\, dx\, dy\, dz$

13. $\displaystyle\int_1^4 \int_{-1}^{2z} \int_0^{\sqrt{3}x} \frac{x-y}{x^2+y^2}\, dy\, dx\, dz$

14. $\displaystyle\int_0^1 \int_{x-1}^{x^2} \int_{-x}^y (x+y)\, dz\, dy\, dx$

Evaluate the triple integrals in Problems 15–22.

15. $\iiint\limits_D (x^2 y + y^2 z)\, dV$, where D is the box $1 \le x \le 3$, $-1 \le y \le 1, 2 \le z \le 4$

16. $\iiint\limits_D (xy + 2yz)\, dV$, where D is the box $2 \le x \le 4$, $1 \le y \le 3, -2 \le z \le 4$

17. $\iiint\limits_D xyz\, dV$, where D is the tetrahedron with vertices $(0, 0, 0), (1, 0, 0), (0, 1, 0)$, and $(0, 0, 1)$

18. $\iiint\limits_D x^2 y\, dV$, where D is the tetrahedron with vertices $(0, 0, 0), (3, 0, 0), (0, 2, 0)$, and $(0, 0, 1)$

19. $\iiint\limits_D xyz\, dV$, where D is the region given by $x^2 + y^2 + z^2 \le 1, y \ge 0, z \ge 0$

20. $\iiint\limits_D x\, dV$, where D is bounded by the paraboloid $z = x^2 + y^2$ and the plane $z = 1$

21. $\iiint\limits_D e^z\, dV$, where D is the region described by the inequalities $0 \le x \le 1, 0 \le y \le x$, and $0 \le z \le x + y$

22. $\iiint\limits_D yz\, dV$, where D is the solid in the first octant bounded by the hemisphere $x = \sqrt{9 - y^2 - z^2}$ and the coordinate planes

Find the volume V of the solids bounded by the graphs of the equations given in Problems 23–32 by using triple integration.

23. $x + y + z = 1$ and the coordinate planes

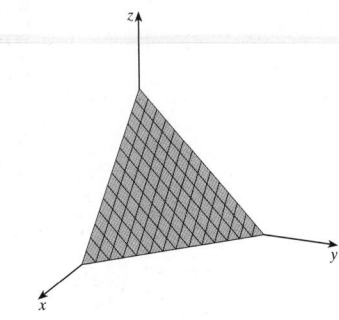

24. $y = 9 - x^2, z = 0, z = y$

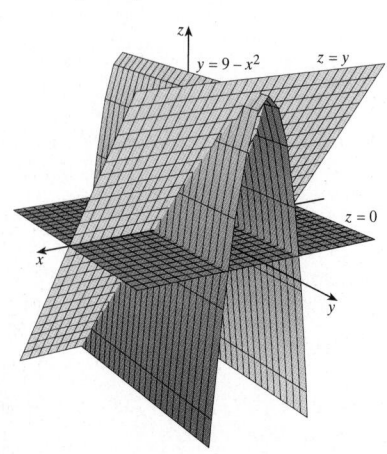

25. $(x-1)^2 + (y-2)^2 + (z-3)^2 = 1$

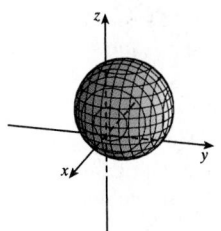

26. $z = 4 - 4x^2 - 4y^2, z = 0$

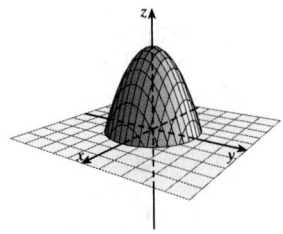

27. $x^2 + 3y^2 = z$ and the cylinder $y^2 + z = 4$

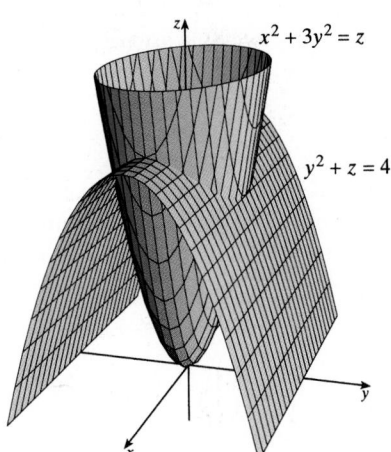

28. $x^2 + y^2 + z^3 = 9, z = 0$

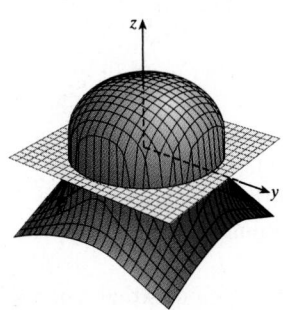

29. The solid bounded above by the paraboloid $z = 6 - x^2 - y^2$ and below by $z = 2x^2 + y^2$

30. The solid bounded by the sphere $x^2 + y^2 + z^2 = 2$ and the paraboloid $x^2 + y^2 = z$

31. The solid region common to the cylinders $x^2 + z^2 = 1$ and $x^2 + y^2 = 1$

32. The solid bounded by the cylinders $y = z^2$ and $y = 2 - z^2$ and the planes $x = 1$ and $x = -2$

For each given iterated integral there are five other equivalent iterated integrals. Find the one with the requested order in Problems 33–38.

33. $\displaystyle\int_0^1 \int_0^x \int_0^y f(x, y, z)\, dz\, dy\, dx$;
change the order to $dz\, dx\, dy$.

34. $\displaystyle\int_1^2 \int_0^{z-1} \int_0^x f(x, y, z)\, dy\, dx\, dz$;
change the order to $dy\, dz\, dx$.

35. $\displaystyle\int_0^2 \int_0^{\sqrt{4-x^2}} \int_0^{\sqrt{4-x^2-y^2}} f(x, y, z)\, dz\, dy\, dx$;
change the order to $dx\, dy\, dz$.

36. $\displaystyle\int_0^2 \int_0^{\sqrt{4-x^2}} \int_0^{\sqrt{4-x^2}} f(x, y, z)\, dz\, dy\, dx$;
change the order to $dy\, dx\, dz$.

37. $\displaystyle\int_0^1 \int_0^{1-y} \int_0^{y^3} f(x, y, z)\, dx\, dz\, dy$;
change to the order $dz\, dy\, dx$.

38. $\displaystyle\int_0^{1/2} \int_0^{1-4x^2} \int_0^{1-2x} f(x, y, z)\, dz\, dy\, dx$;
change to the order $dy\, dx\, dz$.

B 39. Find the volume of the ellipsoid $\dfrac{x^2}{4} + \dfrac{y^2}{9} + \dfrac{z^2}{16} = 1$.

40. Find the volume of the region between the two elliptic paraboloids
$$z = \frac{x^2}{9} + y^2 - 4 \quad \text{and} \quad z = -\frac{x^2}{9} - y^2 + 4$$

41. Find the volume of the region bounded by the paraboloids $z = 16 - x^2 - 2y^2$ and $z = 3x^2 + 2y^2$.

42. A wedge is cut from a right-circular cylinder of radius R by a plane perpendicular to the axis of the cylinder and a second plane that meets the first on the axis at an angle of θ degrees, as shown in Figure 12.44.

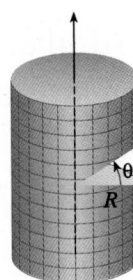

Figure 12.44 Cutting a wedge from a cylinder

Set up and evaluate a triple integral for the volume of the wedge.

43. Find the volume of the region that is bounded above by the elliptic paraboloid
$$z = \frac{x^2}{9} + y^2$$
on the sides by the cylinder
$$\frac{x^2}{9} + y^2 = 1$$
and below by the xy-plane.

44. Find the volume of the solid region in the first octant that is bounded by the planes $z = 8 + 2x + y$ and $y = 3 - 2x$.

C **45.** Use triple integration to find the volume of a sphere.

46. Use triple integration to find the volume of a right pyramid with height H and a square base of side S.

47. Use triple integration to find the volume of the ellipsoid

$$\frac{x^2}{a^2} + \frac{y^2}{b^2} + \frac{z^2}{c^2} = 1$$

(assume $a > 0$, $b > 0$, $c > 0$).

48. Find the volume of the solid region common to the paraboloid $z = k(x^2 + y^2)$ and the sphere

$$x^2 + y^2 + z^2 = 2k^{-2}, \quad \text{where } k > 0$$

49. **Counterexample Problem** Let B be the box defined by $a \le x \le b, c \le y \le d, r \le z \le s$. Is it true that

$$\iiint_B f(x)g(y)h(z)\,dV$$

$$= \left[\int_a^b f(x)\,dx\right]\left[\int_c^d g(y)\,dy\right]\left[\int_r^s h(z)\,dz\right],$$

if f, g, and h are continuous? Either show that this equation is generally true or find a counterexample.

50. Change the order of integration to show that

$$\int_0^x \int_0^v f(u)\,du\,dv = \int_0^x (x - u)f(u)\,du$$

Also, show that

$$\int_0^x \int_0^v \int_0^u f(w)\,dw\,du\,dv = \frac{1}{2}\int_0^x (x - w)^2 f(w)\,dw$$

51. Evaluate the triple integral

$$\iiint_D \sin(\pi - z)^3\,dz\,dy\,dx$$

where D is the solid region bounded below by the xy-plane, above by the plane $x = z$, and laterally by the planes $x = y$ and $y = \pi$. *Hint: See Problem 50.*

52. One of the following integrals has the value 0. Which is it and why?

A. $\displaystyle\int_{-2}^2 \int_{-\sqrt{4-y^2}}^{\sqrt{4-y^2}} \int_{-\sqrt{4-x^2-y^2}}^{\sqrt{4-x^2-y^2}} (x + z^2)\,dz\,dx\,dy$

B. $\displaystyle\int_0^1 \int_x^{2-x^2} \int_{-3}^3 z^2 \sin xz\,dz\,dy\,dx$

Higher-dimensional multiple integrals can be defined and evaluated in essentially the same way as double integrals and triple integrals. Evaluate the given multiple integrals in Problems 53–54.

53. $\displaystyle\iiiint_H xyz^2 w^2\,dx\,dy\,dz\,dw,$

where H is the four-dimensional "hyperbox" defined by $0 \le x \le 1, 0 \le y \le 2, -1 \le z \le 1, 1 \le w \le 2$

54. $\displaystyle\iiiint_H e^{x-2y+z+w}\,dw\,dz\,dy\,dx,$

where H is the four-dimensional region bounded by the hyperplane $x + y + z + w = 4$ and the coordinate spaces $x = 0$, $y = 0$, $z = 0$, and $w = 0$ in the first hyperoctant (where $x \ge 0, y \ge 0, z \ge 0, w \ge 0$)

12.6 Mass, Moments, and Probability Density Functions

IN THIS SECTION mass and center of mass, moments of inertia, joint probability density functions

MASS AND CENTER OF MASS

A (planar) **lamina** is a flat plate that occupies a region R in the plane and is so thin it can be regarded as two dimensional. If m is the lamina's mass and A is the area of the region R, then $\delta = \frac{m}{A}$ is the density of the lamina. The lamina is **homogeneous** if its density $\delta(x, y)$ is constant over R and **nonhomogeneous** if $\delta(x, y)$ varies from point to point. We considered homogeneous lamina in Section 6.5, and in this section, we examine nonhomogeneous lamina.

Figure 12.45 shows a lamina covering a region R that has been partitioned into a number of rectangles. Choose a representative point (x_k^*, y_k^*) in each rectangle of the partition, and note that the mass of the part of the lamina that lies in the kth subrectangle is approximated by

$$\Delta m_k \approx \delta(x_k^*, y_k^*)\Delta A_k$$

We then approximate the total mass m by the Riemann sum

$$m \approx \sum_{k=1}^n \delta(x_k^*, y_k^*)\Delta A_k$$

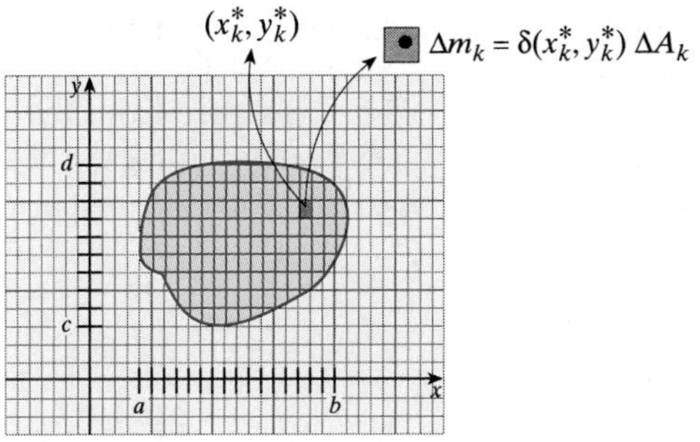

(x_k^*, y_k^*) $\Delta m_k = \delta(x_k^*, y_k^*) \, \Delta A_k$

Figure 12.45 Partition of a lamina in the plane

so that

$$m = \lim_{\|P\| \to 0} \sum_{k=1}^{n} \delta(x_k^*, y_k^*) \Delta A_k = \iint_R \delta(x, y) \, dA$$

We use these observations as the basis for the following definition.

Mass of a Planar Lamina of Variable Density

If δ is a continuous density function on the lamina corresponding to a plane region R, then the mass m of the lamina is given by

$$m = \iint_R \delta(x, y) \, dA$$

EXAMPLE 1 Mass of a planar lamina

Find the mass of the lamina of density $\delta(x, y) = x^2$ that occupies the region R bounded by the parabola $y = 2 - x^2$ and the line $y = x$.

Solution

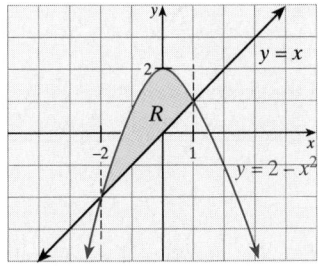

Figure 12.46 A lamina over the region R bounded by $y = 2 - x^2$ and $y = x$

Begin by drawing the parabola and the line, and by finding their points of intersection, as shown in Figure 12.46. By substitution,

$$x = 2 - x^2$$
$$x^2 + x - 2 = 0$$
$$x = -2, 1$$

We see that the region R is the set of all (x, y) such that for each x between -2 and 1, y varies from x to $2 - x^2$. Thus, we have

$$m = \iint_R x^2 \, dA = \int_{-2}^{1} \int_{x}^{2-x^2} x^2 \, dy \, dx$$

$$= \int_{-2}^{1} x^2 (2 - x^2 - x) \, dx = \int_{-2}^{1} (2x^2 - x^4 - x^3) \, dx$$

$$= \left[\frac{2x^3}{3} - \frac{x^5}{5} - \frac{x^4}{4} \right]\Bigg|_{-2}^{1} = \frac{63}{20} = 3.15 \qquad \blacksquare$$

The *moment* of an object about an axis measures the tendency of the object to rotate about the that axis. It is defined as the product of the object's mass and the signed distance from the axis (see Figure 12.47). Thus, by partitioning the region R as before (with mass), we see that the moments M_x and M_y of the lamina about the x-axis and y-axis, respectively, are approximated by the Riemann sums

$$M_x \approx \sum_{k=1}^{n} y_k^* \,\delta(x_k^*, y_k^*)\Delta A_k \quad \text{and} \quad M_y \approx \sum_{k=1}^{n} x_k^* \,\delta(x_k^*, y_k^*)\Delta A_k$$

Distance to x-axis   Distance to y-axis

By taking the limit as the norm of the partition tends to 0, we obtain

$$M_x = \iint\limits_{R} y\delta(x, y)\, dA \quad \text{and} \quad M_y = \iint\limits_{R} x\delta(x, y)\, dA$$

The *center of mass* of the lamina covering R is the point $(\overline{x}, \overline{y})$ where the mass m can be concentrated without affecting the moments M_x and M_y; that is,

$$m\overline{x} = M_y \quad \text{and} \quad m\overline{y} = M_x$$

The center of mass $(\overline{x}, \overline{y})$ may also be thought of as the point from which the lamina may be suspended without movement. For future reference, these observations are summarized in the following box.

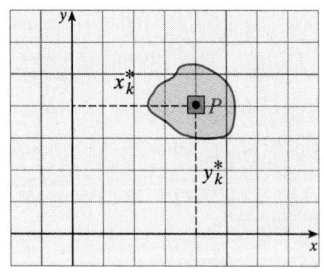

Figure 12.47 The distance from P to the x-axis is y and the distance to the y-axis is x.

M_x has a factor of y and M_y has a factor of x.

Moments and Center of Mass of a Variable Density Planar Lamina

If $\delta(x, y)$ is a continuous density function on a lamina corresponding to a plane region R, then the **moments of mass** with respect to the x- and y-axes, respectively, are

$$M_x = \iint\limits_{R} y\delta(x, y)\, dA \quad \text{and} \quad M_y = \iint\limits_{R} x\delta(x, y)\, dA$$

Furthermore, if m is the mass of the lamina, the **center of mass** is $(\overline{x}, \overline{y})$, where

$$\overline{x} = \frac{M_y}{m} \quad \text{and} \quad \overline{y} = \frac{M_x}{m}$$

If the density δ is constant, the point $(\overline{x}, \overline{y})$ is called the **centroid** of the region.

EXAMPLE 2   Finding a center of mass

Locate the center of mass of the lamina of density $\delta(x, y) = x^2$ that occupies the region R bounded by the parabola $y = 2 - x^2$ and the line $y = x$. This is the lamina defined in Example 1.

Solution

In Example 1 we found that for each fixed x between -2 and 1, y varies from x to $2 - x^2$ (see Figure 12.47). Thus, we have

$$M_x = \iint\limits_{R} y(x^2)\, dA \qquad\qquad M_y = \iint\limits_{R} x(x^2)\, dA$$

$$= \int_{-2}^{1}\int_{x}^{2-x^2} yx^2\, dy\, dx \qquad\qquad = \int_{-2}^{1}\int_{x}^{2-x^2} x^3\, dy\, dx$$

$$= \int_{-2}^{1} \left[\tfrac{1}{2}x^2 y^2\right]\Big|_{y=x}^{y=2-x^2}\, dx \qquad\qquad = \int_{-2}^{1} x^3[(2-x^2) - x]\, dx$$

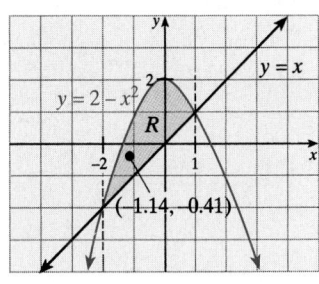

Figure 12.48 Showing the center of mass for a lamina

$$= \frac{1}{2} \int_{-2}^{1} x^2(x^4 - 5x^2 + 4)\, dx \qquad = \int_{-2}^{1} (2x^3 - x^5 - x^4)\, dx$$

$$= \frac{1}{2} \left[\frac{1}{7}x^7 - x^5 + \frac{4}{3}x^3 \right]\Big|_{-2}^{1} \qquad = \left[\frac{2x^4}{4} - \frac{x^6}{6} - \frac{x^5}{5} \right]\Big|_{-2}^{1}$$

$$= -\frac{9}{7} \qquad\qquad = -\frac{18}{5}$$

From Example 1, $m = \frac{63}{20}$, so the center of mass is $(\overline{x}, \overline{y})$, where

$$\overline{x} = \frac{M_y}{m} = \frac{-\frac{18}{5}}{\frac{63}{20}} = -\frac{8}{7} \approx -1.14 \qquad \overline{y} = \frac{M_x}{m} = \frac{-\frac{9}{7}}{\frac{63}{20}} = -\frac{20}{49} \approx -0.41$$

The center of mass for Example 1 is shown in Figure 12.48. ∎

In a completely analogous way, we can use the triple integral to find the mass and center of mass of a solid in $\mathbb{R}^3$ with density $\delta(x, y, z)$. The mass m, moments M_{yz}, M_{xz}, M_{xy} about the yz-, xz-, and xy-planes, respectively, and coordinates $\overline{x}, \overline{y}, \overline{z}$, of the center of mass (see Figure 12.49) are given by:

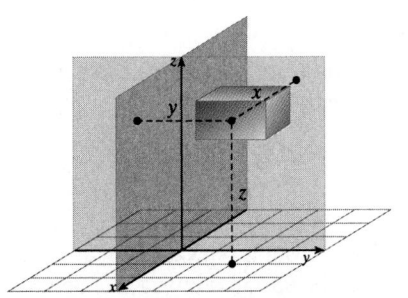

Figure 12.49 Note the distances to the coordinate axes.

Mass
$$m = \iiint_R \delta(x, y, z)\, dV$$

Moments
$$M_{yz} = \iiint_R x\delta(x, y, z)\, dV$$
$$\uparrow$$
Distance to the yz-plane

$$M_{xz} = \iiint_R y\delta(x, y, z)\, dV$$
$$\uparrow$$
Distance to the xz-plane

$$M_{xy} = \iiint_R z\delta(x, y, z)\, dV$$
$$\uparrow$$
Distance to the xy-plane

Center of mass
$$(\overline{x}, \overline{y}, \overline{z}) = \left(\frac{M_{yz}}{m}, \frac{M_{xz}}{m}, \frac{M_{xy}}{m} \right)$$

As before, if the density is constant, the center of mass is called the **centroid**. Example 3 illustrates how this point can be found by multiple integration.

EXAMPLE 3   Centroid of a tetrahedron

A solid tetrahedron has vertices $(0, 0, 0)$, $(1, 0, 0)$, $(0, 1, 0)$, and $(0, 0, 1)$ and constant density $\delta = 6$. Find the centroid.

Solution

The tetrahedron may be described as the region in the first octant that lies beneath the plane $x + y + z = 1$, as shown in Figure 12.50a. The boundary of the projection of the top face of the tetrahedron in the xy-plane is found by solving the equations $x + y + z = 1$ and $z = 0$ simultaneously. We find that the projection is the region bounded by the coordinate axes and the line $x + y = 1$, as shown in Figure 12.50b. This means that for each fixed x between 0 and 1, y varies from 0 to $1 - x$.

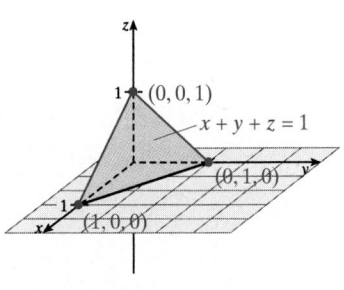

a. A tetrahedron

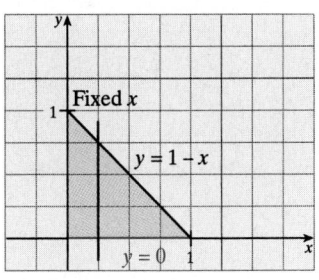

b. Projection on the xy-plane

Figure 12.50 The centroid of a tetrahedron

$$m = \iiint_R \delta\, dV = \int_0^1 \int_0^{1-x} \int_0^{1-x-y} 6\, dz\, dy\, dx$$

$$= \int_0^1 \int_0^{1-x} 6(1 - x - y)\, dy\, dx = \int_0^1 [6y - 6xy - 3y^2]\Big|_{y=0}^{y=1-x}\, dx$$

$$= \int_0^1 3(x - 1)^2\, dx = [x^3 - 3x^2 + 3x]\Big|_0^1 = 1$$

Similarly, we find that

$$M_{yz} = \iiint\limits_R 6x\,dV = \int_0^1 \int_0^{1-x} \int_0^{1-x-y} 6x\,dz\,dy\,dx = \frac{1}{4}$$

$$M_{xz} = \iiint\limits_R 6y\,dV = \int_0^1 \int_0^{1-x} \int_0^{1-x-y} 6y\,dz\,dy\,dx = \frac{1}{4}$$

$$M_{xy} = \iiint\limits_R 6z\,dV = \int_0^1 \int_0^{1-x} \int_0^{1-x-y} 6z\,dz\,dy\,dx = \frac{1}{4}$$

(Verify the details of these integrations.) Thus,

$$\bar{x} = \frac{M_{yz}}{m} = \frac{\frac{1}{4}}{1} = 0.25, \qquad \bar{y} = \frac{M_{xz}}{m} = \frac{\frac{1}{4}}{1} = 0.25, \qquad \bar{z} = \frac{M_{xy}}{m} = \frac{\frac{1}{4}}{1} = 0.25$$

The centroid is $(0.25, 0.25, 0.25)$. ∎

MOMENTS OF INERTIA

In general, a lamina of density $\delta(x, y)$ covering the region R in the first quadrant of the plane has (first) moment about a line L given by the integral

$$M_L = \iint\limits_R s\,dm$$

where $dm = \delta(x, y)\,dA$ and $s = s(x, y)$ is the distance from a typical point $P(x, y)$ in R to L. Similarly, the *second* moment, or *moment of inertia*, of R about L is defined by

$$I_L = \iint\limits_R s^2\,dm$$

In physics, the moment of inertia measures the tendency of the lamina to resist a change in rotational motion about the axis L. Moments of inertia about the coordinate axes are given by the formulas listed in the following box.

Moments of Inertia

The **moments of inertia** of a lamina of density δ covering the planar region R about the x-, y-, and z-axes, respectively, are given by

$$I_x = \iint\limits_R y^2 \delta(x, y)\,dA$$

$$I_y = \iint\limits_R x^2 \delta(x, y)\,dA$$

$$I_z = \iint\limits_R (x^2 + y^2)\delta(x, y)\,dA = I_x + I_y$$

EXAMPLE 4   Finding the moments of inertia

A lamina occupies the region R in the plane that is bounded by the parabola $y = x^2$ and the lines $x = 2$ and $y = 1$. The density of the lamina at each point (x, y) is $\delta(x, y) = x^2 y$. Find the moments of inertia of the lamina about the x-axis and the y-axis.

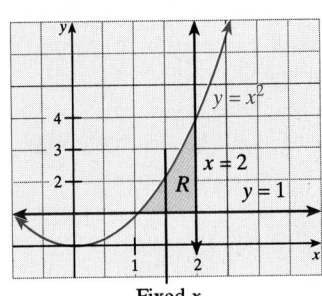

Figure 12.51 Moments of inertia of a lamina

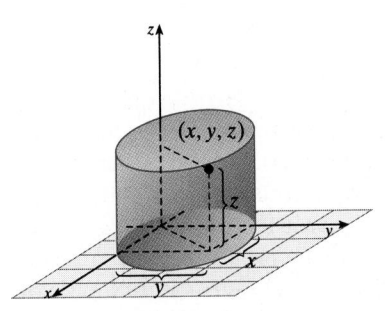

Figure 12.52 A typical solid, R

Solution

The graph of R is shown in Figure 12.51. We see that for each fixed x between 1 and 2, y varies from 1 to x^2.

$$I_x = \iint_R y^2 \, dm = \iint_R y^2 \delta(x, y) \, dA = \iint_R y^2 (x^2 y) \, dA$$

$$= \int_1^2 \int_1^{x^2} x^2 y^3 \, dy \, dx = \frac{1}{4} \int_1^2 x^2 (x^8 - 1) \, dx = \frac{1,516}{33} \approx 45.94$$

$$I_y = \iint_R x^2 \, dm = \iint_R x^2 \delta(x, y) \, dA = \iint_R x^2 (x^2 y) \, dA$$

$$= \int_1^2 \int_1^{x^2} x^4 y \, dy \, dx = \frac{1}{2} \int_1^2 x^4 (x^4 - 1) \, dx = \frac{1,138}{45} \approx 25.29 \qquad \blacksquare$$

A simple generalization enables us to compute the moment of inertia of a solid figure about an arbitrary axis L. Specifically, suppose the solid occupies a region R (see Figure 12.52) and that the density at each point (x, y, z) in R is given by $\delta(x, y, z)$. Because the square of the distance of a typical cell in R from the x-axis is $y^2 + z^2$, the moment of inertia about the x-axis is

$$I_x = \iiint_R \underbrace{(y^2 + z^2)}_{\substack{\uparrow \\ \text{Square of the distance to the } x\text{-axis}}} \underbrace{\delta(x, y, z) \, dV}_{\text{Increment of mass}}$$

Similarly, the moments of inertia of the solid about the y-axis and the z-axis are, respectively,

$$I_y = \iiint_R \underbrace{(x^2 + z^2)}_{\substack{\uparrow \\ \text{Square of the distance to the } y\text{-axis}}} \underbrace{\delta(x, y, z) \, dV}_{\text{Increment of mass}}$$

$$I_z = \iiint_R \underbrace{(x^2 + y^2)}_{\substack{\uparrow \\ \text{Square of the distance to the } z\text{-axis}}} \underbrace{\delta(x, y, z) \, dV}_{\text{Increment of mass}}$$

EXAMPLE 5   Moment of inertia of a solid

Find the moment of inertia about the z-axis of the solid tetrahedron S with vertices $(0, 0, 0)$, $(0, 1, 0)$, $(1, 0, 0)$, $(0, 0, 1)$, and density $\delta(x, y, z) = x$.

Solution

In Example 3, we observed that the solid S can be described as the set of all (x, y, z) such that for each fixed x between 0 and 1, y lies between 0 and $1 - x$, and $0 \le z \le 1 - x - y$. Thus,

$$I_z = \iiint_S (x^2 + y^2)\delta(x, y, z) \, dV = \int_0^1 \int_0^{1-x} \int_0^{1-x-y} x(x^2 + y^2) \, dz \, dy \, dx$$

$$= \int_0^1 \int_0^{1-x} x(x^2 + y^2)(1 - x - y) \, dy \, dx = \int_0^1 \left[\frac{x^3(1 - x)^2}{2} + \frac{x(1 - x)^4}{12} \right] dx = \frac{1}{90} \qquad \blacksquare$$

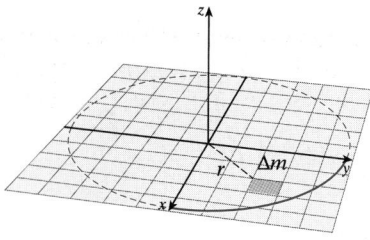

Figure 12.53 Kinetic energy of a rotating disk

Moments of inertia have a useful interpretation in physics. The **kinetic energy** of a body of mass m moving with velocity v along a straight line is defined in physics as $K = \frac{1}{2}mv^2$. Suppose a lamina covering a circular disk R centered at the origin (see Figure 12.53) is rotating around the z-axis with angular speed ω radians/second.

A cell of mass Δm located r units from the origin has linear velocity $v = r\omega$ and linear kinetic energy $K_{\text{lin}} = \frac{1}{2}(\Delta m)v^2$, and by integrating, we find that the entire disk R has kinetic energy of rotation

$$K_{\text{rot}} = \iint\limits_{R} \tfrac{1}{2}\omega^2 r^2 \, dm = \tfrac{1}{2}\omega^2 \iint\limits_{R} r^2 \, dm$$

Since $r^2 = x^2 + y^2$, we see that the integral in this formula is just the moment of inertia of R about the z-axis, so the rotational kinetic energy can be expressed as

$$K_{\text{rot}} = \tfrac{1}{2}I_z\omega^2$$

Comparing this formula to the kinetic energy formula $K_{\text{lin}} = \frac{1}{2}mv^2$, we see that the moment of inertia may be thought of as the rotational analogue of mass or, equivalently, as rotational inertia.

JOINT PROBABILITY DENSITY FUNCTIONS

Suppose we consider the useful life of a randomly chosen automobile of a particular type, or the weight of an infant chosen at random from a certain hospital, or the level of CO_2 pollution in the air of a city randomly selected from a region in India. These quantities are called **continuous random variables** because their values range over an interval of real numbers. It is often important to know the probability that a random variable takes on a given set of values. For instance, if X represents the useful life of a Honda Accord, then the probability that a randomly selected Accord will last no more than 10 years may be denoted by $P(0 \leq X \leq 10)$.

Every continuous random variable X has a **probability density function** f with the property that the probability of X lying between the numbers a and b is given by the integral

$$P(a \leq X \leq b) = \int_a^b f(x) \, dx$$

In general, $f(x) \geq 0$ for all x, and since the value of X is always some real number, it follows that $P(-\infty < X < \infty) = 1$, so

$$\int_{-\infty}^{\infty} f(x) \, dx = 1$$

In geometric terms, the probability $P(a \leq X \leq b)$ is the area under the graph of f over the interval $a \leq x \leq b$. (See Figure 12.54.)

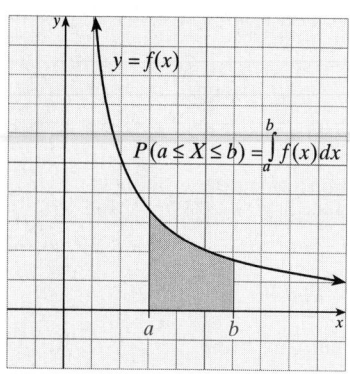

Figure 12.54 Probability as the area under the graph of the probability density function

If X and Y are both continuous random variables, then the **joint probability density function** for two random variables X and Y is a function of two variables $f(x, y)$ such that $f(x, y) \geq 0$ for all (x, y) and

$$P[(X, Y) \text{ in } D] = \iint\limits_{D} f(x, y) \, dA$$

where $P[(X, Y) \text{ in } D]$ denotes the probability that (X, Y) is in the region D. Note that

$$P[(X, Y) \text{ in the } xy\text{-plane}] = \int_{-\infty}^{\infty} \int_{-\infty}^{\infty} f(x, y) \, dx \, dy = 1$$

Geometrically, $P[(X, Y) \text{ in } D]$ may be thought of as the volume under the surface $z = f(x, y)$ above the region D.

The techniques for constructing joint probability density functions from experimental data are outside the scope of this text and are discussed in many texts on probability and statistics. The use of a double integral to compute a probability with a given joint density function is illustrated in the next example.

EXAMPLE 6   Compute a probability

Suppose X measures the time (in minutes) that a randomly selected customer at a particular grocery store spends shopping and Y measures the time the customer spends in the checkout line. A study suggests that the joint probability function for X and Y may be modeled by

$$f(x, y) = \begin{cases} \frac{1}{200} e^{-x/10} e^{-y/20} & \text{for } x \geq 0 \text{ and } y \geq 0 \\ 0 & \text{otherwise} \end{cases}$$

Find the probability that the customer's total time in the store will be no greater than 30 min.

Solution

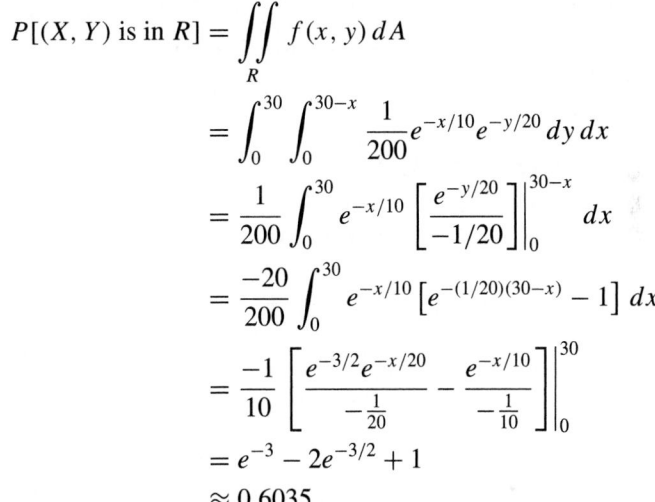

Figure 12.55 Triangle comprised of all points (X, Y) such that $X + Y \leq 30$, $X \geq 0$, $Y \geq 0$

The goal is to find the probability that $X + Y \leq 30$. Stated geometrically, we wish to find the probability that a randomly selected point (x, y) lies in the region R in the first quadrant that is bounded by the coordinate axes and the line $x + y = 30$ (see Figure 12.55). This probability is given by the double integral

$$P[(X, Y) \text{ is in } R] = \iint\limits_{R} f(x, y)\, dA$$

$$= \int_0^{30} \int_0^{30-x} \frac{1}{200} e^{-x/10} e^{-y/20}\, dy\, dx$$

$$= \frac{1}{200} \int_0^{30} e^{-x/10} \left[\frac{e^{-y/20}}{-1/20} \right]_0^{30-x} dx$$

$$= \frac{-20}{200} \int_0^{30} e^{-x/10} \left[e^{-(1/20)(30-x)} - 1 \right] dx$$

$$= \frac{-1}{10} \left[\frac{e^{-3/2} e^{-x/20}}{-\frac{1}{20}} - \frac{e^{-x/10}}{-\frac{1}{10}} \right]_0^{30}$$

$$= e^{-3} - 2e^{-3/2} + 1$$

$$\approx 0.6035$$

Thus, it is about 60% likely that the shopper will spend no more than 30 minutes in the store. ∎

A useful property of probability states that

$$P(E) + P(\overline{E}) = 1$$

where E and $\overline{E}$ together constitute the set of all possible outcomes (that is, they are *complementary events*). For Example 6, since the events $E = \{$the shopper will spend no more than 30 minutes in the store$\}$ and $\overline{E} = \{$the shopper will spend more than 30 minutes in the store$\}$ are complementary, we can find the probability that the shopper will spend more than 30 minutes in the store by using this complementary property:

$$1 - 0.6035 = 0.3965$$

12.6   PROBLEM SET

A 1. **WHAT DOES THIS SAY?** Discuss the procedure for finding the center of mass of a lamina.

2. **WHAT DOES THIS SAY?** Discuss a procedure for finding moments in three dimensions.

3. **WHAT DOES THIS SAY?** How is probability related to a joint probability function?

4. **WHAT DOES THIS SAY?** Discuss moments of inertia.

Find the centroid for the regions described in Problems 5–12.

5. A lamina with $\delta = 5$ over the rectangle with vertices $(0, 0)$, $(3, 0)$, $(3, 4)$, $(0, 4)$

6. A lamina with $\delta = 4$ over the region bounded by the curve $y = \sqrt{x}$ and the line $x = 4$ in the first quadrant

7. A lamina with $\delta = 2$ over the region between the line $y = 2x$ and the parabola $y = x^2$

8. A lamina with $\delta = 4$ over the region bounded by $y = \sin \frac{\pi}{2} x$, $x = 0$, $y = 0$, $x = \frac{1}{2}$

9. A thin homogeneous plate of density $\delta = 1$ with the shape of the region bounded above by the parabola $y = 2 - 3x^2$ and below by the line $3x + 2y = 1$

10. The part of the spherical solid with density $\delta = 2$ described by $x^2 + y^2 + z^2 \leq 9$, $x \geq 0$, $y \geq 0$, $z \geq 0$

11. The solid tetrahedron of density $\delta = 4$ bounded by the plane $x + y + z = 4$ in the first octant

12. The solid bounded by the surface $z = \sin x$, $x = 0$, $x = \pi$, $y = 0$, $z = 0$, and $y + z = 1$, where the density is $\delta = 1$

Use double integration in Problems 13–18 to find the center of mass of a lamina covering the given region in the plane and having the specified density δ.

13. $\delta(x, y) = x^2 + y^2$ over $x^2 + y^2 \leq 9$, $y \geq 0$

14. $\delta(x, y) = k(x^2 + y^2)$ over $x^2 + y^2 \leq a^2$, $y \geq 0$

15. $\delta(x, y) = 7x$ over the triangle with vertices $(0, 0)$, $(6, 5)$, and $(12, 0)$

16. $\delta(x, y) = 3x$ over the region bounded by $y = 0$, $y = x^2$, and $x = 6$

17. $\delta(x, y) = x^{-1}$ over the region bounded by $y = \ln x$, $y = 0$, $x = 2$

18. $\delta(x, y) = y$ over the region bounded by $y = e^{-x}$, $x = 0$, $x = 2$, $y = 0$

19. A lamina in the xy-plane has the shape of the semicircular region $x^2 + y^2 \leq a^2$, $y \geq 0$. Find the center of mass if the density at any point in the lamina is:
   a. directly proportional to the distance of the point from the origin
   b. directly proportional to the polar angle

20. A lamina has the shape of a semicircular region $x^2 + y^2 \leq a^2$, $y \geq 0$. Find the center of mass of the lamina if the density at each point is directly proportional to the square of the distance from the point to the origin.

21. Find the centroid of a homogeneous lamina that covers the region bounded by the curve $y = \ln x$ and the lines $x = e^2$, and $y = 0$.

22. Find I_x, the moment of inertia about the x-axis, of the lamina that covers the region bounded by the graph of $y = 1 - x^2$ and the x-axis, if the density is $\delta(x, y) = x^2$.

23. Find I_z, the moment of inertia about the z-axis, of the lamina that covers the square in the plane with vertices $(-1, -1)$, $(1, -1)$, $(1, 1)$, and $(-1, 1)$, if the density is $\delta(x, y) = x^2 y^2$.

B 24. Find the center of mass of the cardioid $r = 1 + \sin \theta$ if the density at each point (r, θ) is $\delta(r, \theta) = r$.

25. Find the centroid (correct to the nearest hundredth) of the loop of the lemniscate $r^2 = 2 \sin 2\theta$ that lies in the first quadrant.

26. Find the centroid (correct to the nearest hundredth) of the part of the large loop of the limaçon $r = 1 + 2 \cos \theta$ that does not include the small loop.

27. Find the center of mass of the lamina that covers the triangular region with vertices $(0, 0)$, $(a, 0)$, (a, b), if a and b are both positive and the density at $P(x, y)$ is directly proportional to the distance of P from the y-axis.

28. A rectangular lamina has vertices $(0, 0)$, $(a, 0)$, (a, b), $(0, b)$, and its density at any point (x, y) is the product $\delta(x, y) = xy$. Find the center of mass of the plate.

29. A homogeneous lamina covers the circular disk with boundary $x^2 + y^2 = ax$. Find the moment of inertia of this circular plate about the vertical line passing through the center of the lamina. *Hint:* Use polar coordinates.

30. Show that a homogeneous lamina of mass m that covers the circular region $x^2 + y^2 = a^2$, will have moment of inertia $ma^2/4$ with respect to both the x- and y-axes. What is the moment of inertia of the lamina with respect to the z-axis?

31. Show that a homogeneous lamina of density δ and mass m that covers the ellipse

$$\frac{x^2}{a^2} + \frac{y^2}{b^2} \leq 1$$

has moment of inertia about the x-axis equal to

$$I_x = \frac{\pi}{4} ab^3 \delta = \frac{1}{4} mb^2$$

where $m = \delta \underbrace{(\pi ab)}_{\text{Area of ellipse}}$.

32. Find the center of mass of the tetrahedron in the first octant bounded by the plane

$$\frac{x}{a} + \frac{y}{b} + \frac{z}{c} = 1$$

where a, b, and c are all positive constants. Assume the density is $\delta = x$.

33. A solid has the shape of the homogeneous sphere $x^2 + y^2 + z^2 \leq a^2$. Find the centroid of the part of the solid in the first octant $(x \geq 0, y \geq 0, z \geq 0)$.

34. Suppose the joint probability density function for the random variables X and Y is

$$f(x, y) = \begin{cases} 2e^{-2x}e^{-y} & \text{if } x \geq 0, y \geq 0 \\ 0 & \text{otherwise} \end{cases}$$

Find the probability that $X + Y \leq 1$.

35. Suppose the joint probability density function for the random variables X and Y is

$$f(x, y) = \begin{cases} xe^{-x}e^{-y} & \text{if } x \geq 0, y \geq 0 \\ 0 & \text{otherwise} \end{cases}$$

Find the probability that $X + Y \leq 1$.

36. **Modeling Problem** Suppose X measures the length of time (in days) that a person stays in the hospital after abdominal surgery, and Y measures the length of time (in days) that a person stays in the hospital after orthopedic surgery. On Monday, the patient in bed 107A undergoes an emergency appendectomy (abdominal surgery), while the patient's roommate in bed 107B undergoes orthopedic surgery for the repair of torn

knee cartilage. Suppose the joint probability density function for X and Y is

$$f(x, y) = \begin{cases} \frac{1}{6}e^{-x/2}e^{-y/3} & \text{if } x \geq 0, y \geq 0 \\ 0 & \text{otherwise} \end{cases}$$

Find the probability (to the nearest hundredth) that both patients will be discharged from the hospital within 3 days.

37. **Modeling Problem** Suppose X measures the time (in minutes) that a person stands in line at a certain bank and Y, the duration (in minutes) of a routine transaction at the teller's window. You arrive at the bank to deposit a check. If the joint probability density function for X and Y is modeled by

$$f(x, y) = \begin{cases} \frac{1}{8}e^{-x/2}e^{-y/4} & \text{if } x \geq 0, y \geq 0 \\ 0 & \text{otherwise} \end{cases}$$

Find the probability that you will complete your business at the bank within 8 min.

38. **Modeling Problem** Suppose X measures the time (in minutes) that a person spends with an insurance agent choosing a life insurance policy and Y, the time (in minutes) that the agent spends doing the paperwork once the client has decided. If the joint probability density function for X and Y is

$$f(x, y) = \begin{cases} \frac{1}{300}e^{-x/30}e^{-y/10} & \text{if } x \geq 0, y \geq 0 \\ 0 & \text{otherwise} \end{cases}$$

Find the probability that the entire transaction will take less than half an hour.

39. **Modeling Problem** Racing yachts, such as those in the America's Cup competition, benefit from sophisticated, computer-enhanced construction techniques.* For example, define the *center of pressure* on a boat's sail as the point $(\overline{x}, \overline{y})$ where all aerodynamic forces appear to act. Suppose a sail occupies the triangular region R in the plane, as illustrated in Figure 12.56, and that $\overline{x}$ and $\overline{y}$ are modeled by the formulas

$$\overline{x} = \frac{\iint_R xy \, dA}{\iint_R y \, dA} \qquad \overline{y} = \frac{\iint_R y^2 \, dA}{\iint_R y \, dA}$$

Calculate the center of pressure on this sail.

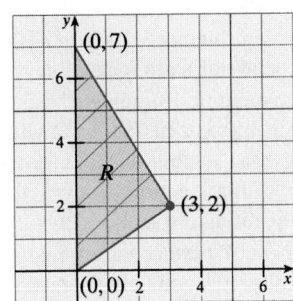

Figure 12.56 Triangular sail

*See *Scientific American* (August 1987).

The **average value** of the continuous function f over R is given by

$$\text{One variable}: \quad \frac{1}{\text{length of segment } R} \int_R f(x) \, dx$$

$$\text{Two variables}: \quad \frac{1}{\text{area of region } R} \iint_R f(x, y) \, dA$$

$$\text{Three variables}: \quad \frac{1}{\text{volume of solid } R} \iiint_R f(x, y, z) \, dV$$

Use these definitions in Problems 40–43.

40. Find the average value of $f(x, y) = e^{x^3}$, where R is the region in the first quadrant bounded by $y = x^2$, $y = 0$, and $x = 1$.

41. Find the average value of $f(x, y) = e^x y^{-1/2}$ where R is the region in the first quadrant bounded by $y = x^2$, $x = 0$, and $y = 1$.

42. Find the average value of the function $f(x, y, z) = x + 2y + 3z$ over the solid region S bounded by the tetrahedron with vertices $(0, 0, 0)$, $(1, 0, 0)$, $(0, 1, 0)$, and $(0, 0, 1)$.

43. Find the average value of the function $f(x, y, z) = xyz$ over the solid sphere $x^2 + y^2 + z^2 \leq 1$.

44. In a psychological experiment, x units of stimulus A and y units of stimulus B are applied to a subject, whose performance on a certain task is modeled by the function

$$f(x, y) = 10 + xye^{1 - x^2 - y^2}$$

Suppose the stimuli are controlled in such a way that the subject is exposed to every possible combination (x, y) with $x \geq 0$, $y \geq 0$, and $x + y \leq 1$. What is the subject's average response to stimuli?

The **radius of gyration** for revolving a region R with mass m about an axis of rotation L, with moment of inertia I, is

$$d = \sqrt{\frac{I}{m}}$$

Note that if the entire mass m of R is located at a distance d from the axis of rotation L, then R would have the same moment of inertia. Use this definition in Problems 45–47.

45. A homogeneous lamina has the shape of the right triangle in the xy-plane with vertices $(0, 0)$, $(a, 0)$, and $(0, b)$, $a > 0$, $b > 0$. Find the radius of gyration of the lamina about the z-axis.

46. Find the radius of gyration about the x-axis of the semicircular region $x^2 + y^2 \leq a$, $y \geq 0$ given that the density at (x, y) is directly proportional to the distance of the point from the x-axis.

47. Let R be the lamina bounded by the parabola $y = x^2$ and the lines $x = 2$ and $y = 1$, with density $\delta(x, y) = x^2 y$. What is the radius of gyration (to four decimal places) about the x-axis?

48. EXPLORATION PROBLEM A solid has the shape of the rectangular parallelepiped given by $-a \leq x \leq a$, $-b \leq y \leq b$, $-c \leq z \leq c$, and its density is $\delta(x, y, z) = x^2 y^2 z^2$.

a. Guess the location of the center of mass and value of the moment of inertia about the z-axis.

b. Check your response to part **a** by direct calculation.

49. Modeling Problem An industrial plant is located on a narrow river. Suppose C_0 units of pollutant are released into the river at time $t = 0$ and that the concentration of pollutant t hours later at a point x miles downstream from the plant is modeled by the diffusion function

$$C(x, t) = \frac{C_0}{\sqrt{k\pi t}} e^{-x^2/(4kt)}$$

where k is a physical constant.

a. At what time $t_m(x_0)$ does the maximum pollution occur at point $x = x_0$ miles from the plant? What is the maximum concentration $C_m(x_0)$?

b. Define the *danger zone* to be the portion of the riverbank such that $0 \leq x \leq x_m$ where x_m is the largest value of x such that $C_m(x_m) \geq 0.25C_0$. Find x_m.

c. Set up a double integral for the average concentration of pollutant over the set of all (x, t) such that $0 \leq t \leq t_m(x)$ for each fixed x between $x = 0$ and $x = x_m$.

d. How would you define the "dangerous period" for the pollution spill?

50. Modeling Problem The *stiffness* of a horizontal beam is modeled to be proportional to the moment of inertia of its cross section with respect to a horizontal line L through its centroid, as illustrated for three shapes shown in Figure 12.57.

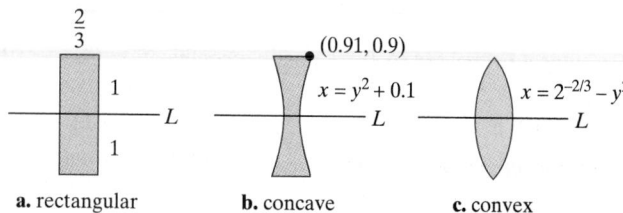

a. rectangular   b. concave   c. convex

Figure 12.57 Cross sections of horizontal beams with area 4/3

Which of the illustrated beams is the stiffest? For this model, assume the constant of proportionality is the same for all three cases and $\delta = 1$.

Often the knowledge of the center of mass allows us to greatly simplify a problem, but sometimes it can lead us to an incorrect answer. We explore this in Problems 51–52.

51. Exploration Problem *Centers of mass in physics* ■

a. Suppose a volume of liquid (or granular solid) is located so that its center of mass is at the origin. The material is to be lifted to a height of h units above the center of mass. Starting with a small element of volume, ΔV, to be lifted to height h, derive the formula for the total work done:

$$\text{Work} = \delta \iiint (h - z)\, dV$$

where δ is the weight (density) of the material.

b. Explain why the integral in part **a** simplifies to the formula

$$\text{Work} = \delta V h = \text{Force} \times \text{distance}$$

where h is the distance between the center of mass and the level to which the material is lifted.

c. Picture a cylindrical tank of radius 6 ft and height 10 ft positioned so its center of mass is at the origin. Compute the work required to lift (that is, pump) the contents (of density δ) to a level of 15 ft above the center of mass. Compute this two ways: by the integral in part **a** (suggestion—do the $dx\, dy$ integral by inspection), and also by simply lifting the center of mass to the required height. These results should agree.

52. Exploration Problem *Newton's inverse square law* ■ Recall that if two masses m and M are each concentrated at (or nearly at) a point and are separated by a distance p, then the attractive force is expressed by $F = GmM/p^2$. What physicists and others prefer to do in the case of real-life masses (which occupy some volume) is to use p, the distance between the two centers of mass. The question you are to explore here (and again in Section 12.7) is whether, and when, this simplifying way of computing attractive forces is justified.

a. Suppose one point mass, m, is located at $(0, 0, h)$ and the second, M, at $(0, 0, 0)$. We are interested in the total *resultant* force that M exerts on m, and we assume this to be in the z-direction. Hence we will sum the vertical components of the forces acting on m. Consider, in M, a small element of volume ΔV (at x, y, z) and argue that the magnitude of the force exerted on m and its vertical component are

$$\Delta F_{\text{mag}} = \frac{Gm\Delta V}{p^2}$$

$$\Delta F = \frac{Gm\Delta V (h - z)^2}{p^3}$$

where $p^2 = x^2 + y^2 + (h - z)^2$. Note that the term $(h - z)/p$ projects the force vector onto the z-axis, giving the vertical component. Do you see why?

b. Form the usual Riemann sum and obtain the following force acting between m and M.

$$F = Gm\delta \iiint \frac{(h - z)\, dV}{p^3}$$

c. Consider a solid (with density $\delta = 5$) positioned at $-2 \leq x \leq 2$, $-4 \leq y \leq 4$, and $-1 \leq z \leq 1$. (Note the center of mass is at the origin.) Compute the attractive force between this mass and a point mass, m, at $(0, 0, 8)$ using the center of mass formula $F = GmM/p^2$.

d. For the masses in **c**, compute F using the integration formula in part **b**; compare the result with that of **c**.

e. Repeat the last calculation with $h = 200$ and compare with the center of mass approximation. Comment on the role that the separating distance p plays.

53. Find the moment of inertia of a rectangular homogeneous lamina with dimensions h and l about an axis L through its center of mass.

54. Prove the following area theorem of Pappus: Let C be a curve of length L in the plane. Then the surface obtained by rotating C about the axis L in the plane has area $2\pi Lh$, where h is the distance from the centroid of C to the axis of rotation.

55. A torus (doughnut) can be formed by rotating the circle $(x - b)^2 + y^2 = a^2$ for $b > a$ about the y-axis. Find the surface area of the torus by applying Pappus' area theorem (see Problem 54 and Figure 12.58). Compare your result with the area found parametrically in Problem 46, Section 12.4.

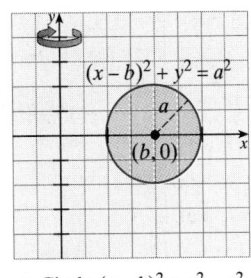

a. Circle $(x - b)^2 + y^2 = a^2$

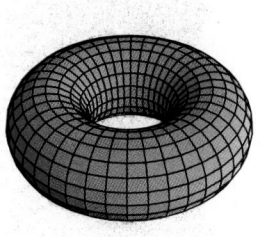

b. Torus

Figure 12.58 Torus

12.7 Cylindrical and Spherical Coordinates

IN THIS SECTION cylindrical coordinates, integration with cylindrical coordinates, spherical coordinates, integration with spherical coordinates

CYLINDRICAL COORDINATES

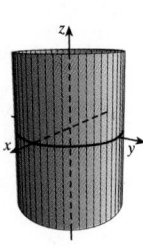

Figure 12.59 The cylindrical coordinate system

Cylindrical coordinates are a generalization of polar coordinates to surfaces in $\mathbb{R}^3$. Recall that the point P with rectangular coordinates (x, y, z) is located z units above the point $Q(x, y, 0)$ in the xy-plane (below if $z < 0$). In cylindrical coordinates, we measure the point in the xy-plane in polar coordinates, with the same z-coordinate as in the Cartesian coordinate system. These relationships are shown in Figure 12.59.

Cylindrical coordinates are convenient for representing cylindrical surfaces and surfaces of revolution for which the z-axis is the axis of symmetry. Some examples are shown in Figure 12.60.

We have the following conversion formulas, which follow directly from the rectangular-polar conversions.

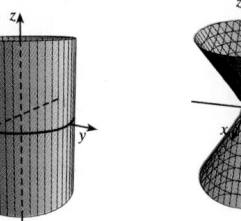
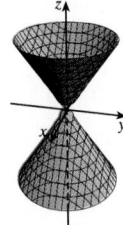
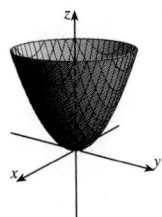
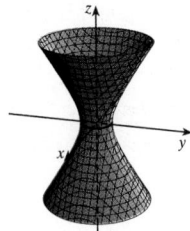

a. Cylinder	**b.** Cone	**c.** Paraboloid	**d.** Hyperboloid
Rectangular equation: $x^2 + y^2 = a^2$	$x^2 + y^2 = z^2$	$x^2 + y^2 = az$	$x^2 + y^2 - z^2 = 1$
Cylindrical equation: $r = a$	$r = z$	$r^2 = az$	$r^2 = z^2 + 1$

Figure 12.60 Surfaces with convenient cylindrical coordinates

Conversion Formulas for Rectangular/Cylindrical Coordinates

Cylindrical to rectangular: $x = r\cos\theta$
(r, θ, z) to (x, y, z) $y = r\sin\theta$
$z = z$

Rectangular to cylindrical: $r = \sqrt{x^2 + y^2}$
(x, y, z) to (r, θ, z) $\tan\theta = \dfrac{y}{x}$
$z = z$

EXAMPLE 1 Rectangular-form equation converted to cylindrical-form equation

Find an equation in cylindrical coordinates for the elliptic paraboloid $z = x^2 + 3y^2$.

Solution

We use the conversion formulas $x = r\cos\theta$ and $y = r\sin\theta$.

$$z = x^2 + 3y^2 = (r\cos\theta)^2 + 3(r\sin\theta)^2$$
$$= r^2(\cos^2\theta + 3\sin^2\theta)$$
$$= r^2[(1 - \sin^2\theta) + 3\sin^2\theta]$$
$$= r^2(1 + 2\sin^2\theta)$$

■

INTEGRATION WITH CYLINDRICAL COORDINATES

A triple integral $\iiint_D f(x, y, z)\, dV$ can often be evaluated by transforming to cylindrical coordinates if the region of integration D is z-simple and the projection of D onto the xy-plane is a region A that can be described more naturally in terms of polar coordinates than rectangular coordinates. Suppose $f(x, y, z)$ is continuous over the region of integration D, where

$$D = \{(x, y, z)\quad \text{such that}\quad u(x, y) \le z \le v(x, y)\quad \text{for all } (x, y) \text{ in } A\}$$

Then

$$\iiint_R f(x, y, z)\, dV = \iint_R \left[\int_{u(x,y)}^{v(x,y)} f(x, y, z)\, dz\right] dA$$

$$= \iint_D \int_{u(r\cos\theta, r\sin\theta)}^{v(r\cos\theta, r\sin\theta)} f(r\cos\theta, r\sin\theta, z)\, r\, dz\, dr\, d\theta$$

since in polar coordinates $x = r\cos\theta$, $y = r\sin\theta$, and $dA = r\, dr\, d\theta$ (recall Theorem 12.4 and see Figure 12.61). Thus, in cylindrical coordinates $dV = r\, dr\, d\theta\, dz$. Finally, the projected region is A, where

$$A = \{(r, \theta)\quad \text{such that}\quad g_1(\theta) \le r \le g_2(\theta)\quad \text{for}\quad \alpha \le \theta \le \beta\}$$

Transforming the given integral to cylindrical coordinates yields the form shown in the following box.

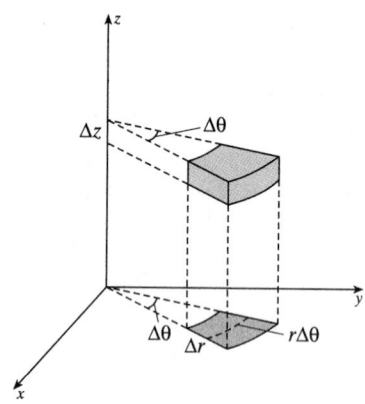

Figure 12.61 Volume element in cylindrical coordinates

Triple Integral in Cylindrical Coordinates

Let R be a solid with upper surface $z = v(r, \theta)$ and lower surface $z = u(r, \theta)$, and let D be the projection of the solid onto the xy-plane expressed in polar coordinates. Then, if $f(x, y, z)$ is continuous on R, the **triple integral of f over S** is given by

$$\iiint\limits_{R} f(x, y, z)\, dV = \int_{\alpha}^{\beta} \int_{g_1(\theta)}^{g_2(\theta)} \int_{u(r,\theta)}^{v(r,\theta)} f(r\cos\theta, r\sin\theta, z)\, r\, dz\, dr\, d\theta$$

Figure 12.62 illustrates how the region of integration D can be determined by using cylindrical coordinates.

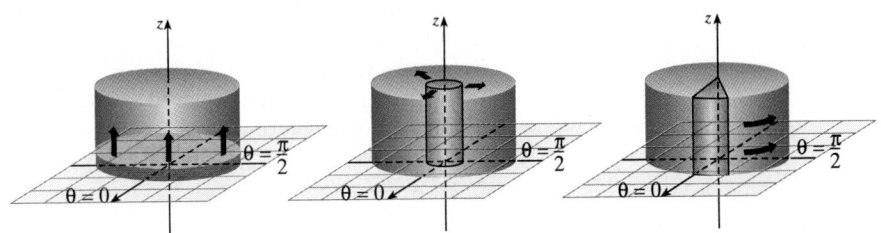

a. Integrate with respect to z.   **b.** Integrate with respect to r.   **c.** Integrate with respect to θ.

Figure 12.62   Determining regions of integration in cylindrical coordinates

EXAMPLE 2   Finding volume in cylindrical coordinates

Find the volume of the solid in the first octant that is bounded by the cylinder $x^2 + y^2 = 2y$, the half-cone $z = \sqrt{x^2 + y^2}$, and the xy-plane.

Solution

Let S be the region occupied by the solid as shown in Figure 12.63. This surface is most easily described in cylindrical coordinates.

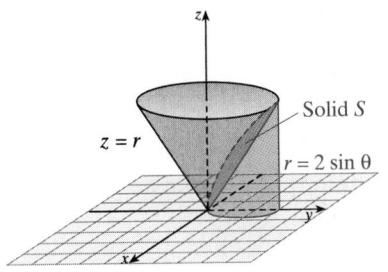

Figure 12.63 The solid bounded by $x^2 + y^2 = 2y$, $z = \sqrt{x^2 + y^2}$, and the xy-plane

Cylinder:	Cone:
$x^2 + y^2 = 2y$	$z = \sqrt{x^2 + y^2}$
$r^2 = 2r\sin\theta$	$z = r$
$r = 2\sin\theta$	

Since the region S lies in the first octant, we have $0 \le \theta \le \frac{\pi}{2}$, so S may be described by

$$0 \le z \le r \qquad 0 \le r \le 2\sin\theta \qquad 0 \le \theta \le \frac{\pi}{2}$$

$$V = \iiint\limits_{R} dV = \iint\limits_{D} \int_{u(r,\theta)}^{v(r,\theta)} r\, dz\, dr\, d\theta = \int_{0}^{\pi/2} \int_{0}^{2\sin\theta} \int_{0}^{r} r\, dz\, dr\, d\theta$$

$$= \int_{0}^{\pi/2} \int_{0}^{2\sin\theta} r^2\, dr\, d\theta = \int_{0}^{\pi/2} \frac{r^3}{3}\Big|_{r=0}^{r=2\sin\theta}\, d\theta = \frac{8}{3}\int_{0}^{\pi/2} \sin^3\theta\, d\theta$$

$$= \frac{8}{3}\int_{0}^{\pi/2} (1 - \cos^2\theta)\sin\theta\, d\theta$$

$$= \frac{8}{3}\left[-\cos\theta + \frac{\cos^3\theta}{3}\right]\Big|_{0}^{\pi/2} = \frac{16}{9}$$ ∎

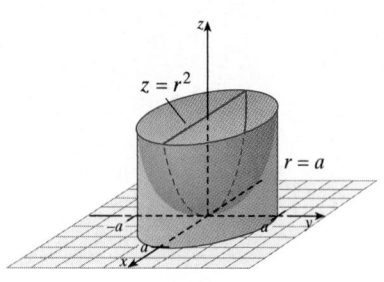

Figure 12.64 The solid bounded by $x^2 + y^2 = a^2$ and $z = x^2 + y^2$

EXAMPLE 3   Centroid in cylindrical coordinates

A homogeneous solid S with constant density δ is bounded below by the xy-plane, on the sides by the cylinder $x^2 + y^2 = a^2$ $(a > 0)$, and above by the surface $z = x^2 + y^2$. Find the centroid of the solid.

Solution

The solid S is shown in Figure 12.64. Because the solid is bounded by a cylinder, we will carry out the integration in cylindrical coordinates.

Cylinder: Paraboloid:
$$x^2 + y^2 = a^2 \qquad\qquad z = x^2 + y^2$$
$$r^2 = a^2 \qquad\qquad\qquad z = r^2$$
$$r = a \quad (a > 0)$$

Let $(\overline{x}, \overline{y}, \overline{z})$ denote the centroid. Using symmetry and the fact that the density function is constant, we have $\overline{x} = \overline{y} = 0$. Let m denote the mass of S. Since the projected region is $r = a$ for $0 \le \theta \le 2\pi$, we find that

$$\overline{z} = \frac{M_{xy}}{m} = \frac{\displaystyle\iiint_S zr \, dz \, dr \, d\theta}{\displaystyle\iiint_S r \, dz \, dr \, d\theta} = \frac{\displaystyle\int_0^{2\pi}\int_0^a\int_0^{r^2} zr \, dz \, dr \, d\theta}{\displaystyle\int_0^{2\pi}\int_0^a\int_0^{r^2} r \, dz \, dr \, d\theta} = \frac{\frac{\pi}{6}a^6}{\frac{\pi}{2}a^4} = \frac{a^2}{3}$$

Verify the details of the integration. The centroid is $\left(0, 0, \frac{a^2}{3}\right)$.   ∎

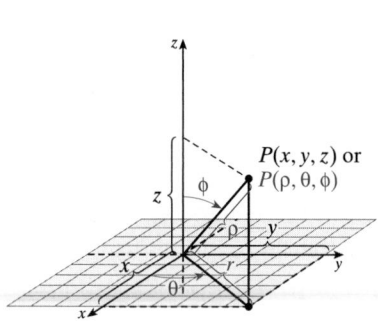

Figure 12.65 The spherical coordinate system

SPHERICAL COORDINATES

In **spherical coordinates** we label a point P by a triple (ρ, θ, ϕ), where ρ, θ, and ϕ are numbers determined as follows (refer to Figure 12.65):

$\rho = $ the distance from the origin to the point P; we require $\rho \ge 0$.

$\theta = $ the polar angle (as in polar coordinates); we require $0 \le \theta \le 2\pi$.

$\phi = $ the angle measured down from the positive z-axis to the ray from the origin through P; we require $0 \le \phi \le \pi$.

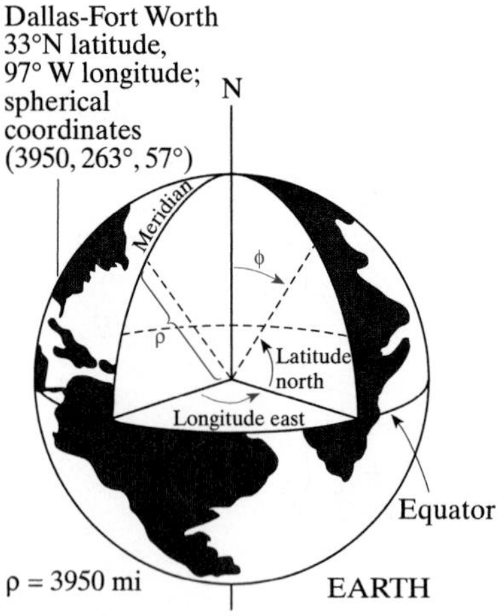

$\rho = 3950$ mi   EARTH

Figure 12.66 Spherical coordinates on the earth's surface

You might recognize that spherical coordinates are related to the longitude and latitude coordinates used in navigation. To be more specific, consider a rectangular coordinate system with the origin at the center of the earth, with the positive z-axis passing through the north pole and the xz-plane passing through the prime meridian. Then, a particular location on the surface is denoted by (ρ, θ, ϕ), where ρ is the distance from the center of the earth, θ is the longitude, and $\frac{\pi}{2} - \phi$ is the latitude (since latitude is the angle up from the equator). For example, Dallas-Fort Worth has coordinates $(\rho, \theta, \phi) = (3950, 263°, 57°)$, as shown in Figure 12.66.

Spherical coordinates are desirable when representing spheres, cones, or certain planes. Some examples are shown in Figure 12.67.

We use the relationships in Figure 12.67 to obtain the remaining conversion formulas. All of these formulas can be derived by considering the relationships among the variables as shown in Figure 12.68.

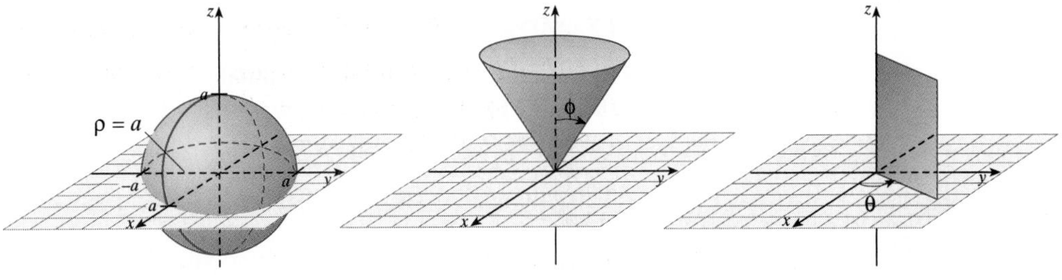

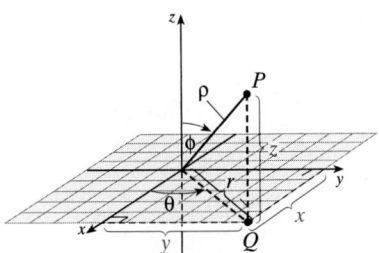

a. Sphere, $\rho = a$ $(a > 0)$ **b.** Half-cone, $\phi = a$ $(0 < a < \frac{\pi}{2})$ **c.** Vertical half-plane, $\theta = a$

Figure 12.67   Surfaces with convenient spherical coordinates

---

Conversion Formulas Involving Spherical Coordinates

Spherical to rectangular: (ρ, θ, ϕ) to (x, y, z)	$x = \rho \sin \phi \cos \theta$ $y = \rho \sin \phi \sin \theta$ $z = \rho \cos \phi$
Rectangular to spherical: (x, y, z) to (ρ, θ, ϕ)	$\rho = \sqrt{x^2 + y^2 + z^2}$ $\tan \theta = \dfrac{y}{x}$ $\phi = \cos^{-1}\left(\dfrac{z}{\sqrt{x^2 + y^2 + z^2}} \right)$
Spherical to cylindrical: (ρ, θ, ϕ) to (r, θ, z)	$r = \rho \sin \phi$ $\theta = \theta$ $z = \rho \cos \phi$
Cylindrical to spherical: (r, θ, z) to (ρ, θ, ϕ)	$\rho = \sqrt{r^2 + z^2}$ $\theta = \theta$ $\phi = \cos^{-1}\left(\dfrac{z}{\sqrt{r^2 + z^2}} \right)$

Figure 12.68 Relations among coordinate systems

EXAMPLE 4   Converting rectangular-form equations to spherical-form

Rewrite each of the given equations in spherical form.

a. the sphere $x^2 + y^2 + z^2 = a^2$ $(a > 0)$ **b.** the paraboloid $z = x^2 + y^2$

Solution

a. Because $\rho = \sqrt{x^2 + y^2 + z^2}$, we see $x^2 + y^2 + z^2 = \rho^2$, so we can write

$$\rho^2 = a^2$$
$$\rho = a \qquad \text{Because } \rho \geq 0$$

b.
$$z = x^2 + y^2$$
$$\rho \cos \phi = (\rho \sin \phi \cos \theta)^2 + (\rho \sin \phi \sin \theta)^2$$
$$\rho \cos \phi = \rho^2 \sin^2 \phi \cos^2 \theta + \rho^2 \sin^2 \phi \sin^2 \theta$$
$$= \rho^2 \sin^2 \phi (\cos^2 \theta + \sin^2 \theta)$$
$$\rho = \frac{\cos \phi}{\sin^2 \theta} = \cot \phi \csc \phi$$

INTEGRATION WITH SPHERICAL COORDINATES

For a solid S in spherical coordinates, the fundamental element of volume is a spherical "wedge" bounded in such a way that

$$\rho_1 \leq \rho \leq \rho_1 + \Delta\rho \qquad \phi_1 \leq \phi \leq \phi_1 + \Delta\phi, \qquad \theta_1 \leq \theta \leq \theta_1 + \Delta\theta$$

This "wedge" is shown in Figure 12.69 and has volume $\rho^2 \sin\phi \, \Delta\rho \, \Delta\phi \, \Delta\theta$.

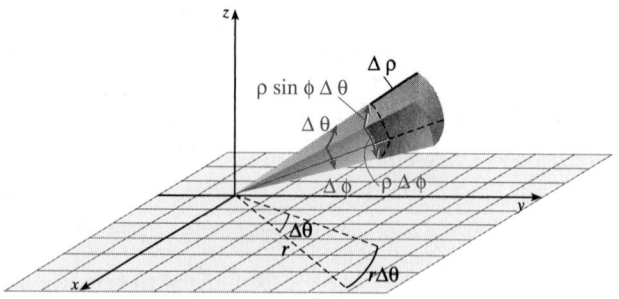

Figure 12.69 A spherical wedge

In Section 12.8 we show that the element of volume in spherical coordinates is

$$dV = \rho^2 \sin\phi \, d\rho \, d\phi \, d\theta$$

Using this formula, we can form partitions and take a limit of a Riemann sum as the partitions are refined to obtain the integral form shown in the following box.

Triple Integral in Spherical Coordinates

> If f is continuous on the bounded solid region S, then the **triple integral of f over S** is given by
>
> $$\iiint\limits_{S} f(x, y, z) \, dV$$
>
> $$= \iiint\limits_{S'} f(\rho \sin\phi \cos\theta, \rho \sin\phi \sin\theta, \rho \cos\phi) \rho^2 \sin\phi \, d\rho \, d\theta \, d\phi$$
>
> where S' is the region S expressed in spherical coordinates.

EXAMPLE 5   Volume of a sphere

In geometry, it is shown that a sphere of radius R has volume $V = \frac{4}{3}\pi R^3$. Verify this formula using integration.

Solution

It seems clear that we should work in spherical coordinates with the origin of the coordinate system at the center of the sphere, because the equation of the sphere is $\rho = R$ for $0 \leq \theta \leq 2\pi$ and $0 \leq \phi \leq \pi$.

$$V = \iiint\limits_{S} dV = \int_0^{2\pi} \int_0^{\pi} \int_0^R \underbrace{\rho^2 \sin\phi \, d\rho \, d\phi \, d\theta}_{dV}$$

$$= \int_0^{2\pi} \int_0^{\pi} \frac{\rho^3}{3} \sin\phi \Big|_{\rho=0}^{\rho=R} \, d\phi \, d\theta = \frac{R^3}{3} \int_0^{2\pi} \int_0^{\pi} \sin\phi \, d\phi \, d\theta$$

$$= \frac{R^3}{3} \int_0^{2\pi} (-\cos\phi)\Big|_0^{\pi} \, d\theta = \frac{R^3}{3} \int_0^{2\pi} 2 \, d\theta$$

$$= \frac{2R^3}{3} [\theta]\Big|_0^{2\pi} = \frac{2R^3}{3}(2\pi) = \frac{4}{3}\pi R^3 \qquad \blacksquare$$

EXAMPLE 6   Moment of inertia using spherical coordinates

A toy top of constant density δ_0 is constructed from a portion of a solid hemisphere with a conical base, as shown in Figure 12.70. The center of the spherical cap is at the point where the top spins, and the height of the conical base is equal to its radius. Find the moment of inertia of the top about its axis of symmetry.

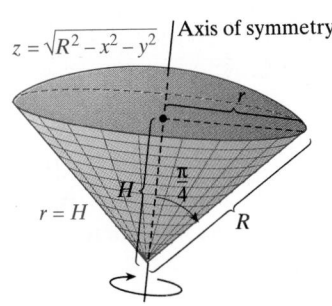

Figure 12.70 Moment of inertia for a spinning top

Solution

We use a Cartesian coordinate system in which the z-axis is the axis of symmetry of the top. Suppose the cap is part of the hemisphere $z = \sqrt{R^2 - x^2 - y^2}$. Since the height of the conical base is equal to its radius, the cone makes an angle of $\pi/4$ radians (45°) with the z-axis. Let S denote the solid region occupied by the top. Then the moment of inertia I_z with respect to the z-axis is given by

$$I_z = \iiint_S (x^2 + y^2)\, dm = \iiint_S (x^2 + y^2)\delta_0\, dV$$

The shape of the top suggests that we convert to spherical coordinates, and we find that S can be described as

$$0 \le \theta \le 2\pi \qquad 0 \le \phi \le \frac{\pi}{4} \qquad 0 \le \rho \le R$$

Also,

$$x^2 + y^2 = \rho^2 \sin^2 \phi \cos^2 \theta + \rho^2 \sin^2 \phi \sin^2 \theta = \rho^2 \sin^2 \phi$$

We now evaluate the integral using spherical coordinates:

$$I_z = \iiint_S (x^2 + y^2)\delta_0\, dV$$

$$= \delta_0 \int_0^{\pi/4} \int_0^{2\pi} \int_0^R \underbrace{\rho^2 \sin^2 \phi}_{x^2 + y^2}\, \underbrace{\rho^2 \sin \phi\, d\rho\, d\theta\, d\phi}_{dV}$$

$$= \delta_0 \int_0^{\pi/4} \int_0^{2\pi} \int_0^R \rho^4 \sin^3 \phi\, d\rho\, d\theta\, d\phi$$

$$= \delta_0 \int_0^{\pi/4} \int_0^{2\pi} \frac{\rho^5}{5} \sin^3 \phi \Big|_{\rho=0}^{\rho=R} d\theta\, d\phi = \frac{R^5 \delta_0}{5} \int_0^{\pi/4} (2\pi - 0) \sin^3 \phi\, d\phi$$

$$= \frac{2R^5 \delta_0 \pi}{5} \left[-\cos \phi + \frac{1}{3} \cos^3 \phi \right]\Big|_0^{\pi/4} = \frac{2R^5 \delta_0 \pi}{5} \left[-\frac{1}{2}\sqrt{2} + \frac{1}{12}\sqrt{2} + 1 - \frac{1}{3} \right]$$

$$= \frac{\pi \delta_0 R^5}{30} (8 - 5\sqrt{2}) \approx 0.09728 \delta_0 R^5 \qquad \blacksquare$$

It was clear in Example 5 that we should use the spherical coordinate system to find the volume of a sphere. However, sometimes it is not obvious which coordinate system to use. We address this question with the following example.

EXAMPLE 7   Deciding which coordinate system to apply to an integral

Evaluate the integral

$$I = \int_{-1}^1 \int_{-\sqrt{1-x^2}}^{\sqrt{1-x^2}} \int_{x^2+y^2}^{\sqrt{2-x^2-y^2}} z\, dz\, dy\, dx$$

using the given rectangular form, or by transforming to either cylindrical or spherical coordinates.

Solution

The region of integration is D, where

$$D = \Big\{(x, y, z) \quad \text{such that } x^2 + y^2 \le z \le \sqrt{2 - x^2 - y^2} \text{ for}$$
$$-\sqrt{1 - x^2} \le y \le \sqrt{1 - x^2} \text{ and } -1 \le x \le 1\Big\}$$

Geometrically, D is the region bounded above by the sphere $x^2 + y^2 + z^2 = 2$ and below by the paraboloid $z = x^2 + y^2$. The bounding surfaces intersect where

$$z = x^2 + y^2 \quad \text{and} \quad x^2 + y^2 + z^2 = 2$$

so

$$z + z^2 = 2 \quad \text{Substitute the first into the second.}$$
$$(z - 1)(z + 2) = 0$$
$$z = 1 \quad \text{Reject } z = -2, \text{ since } z \ge 0.$$

It follows that the projected region in the xy-plane is the disk $x^2 + y^2 \le 1$ (see Figure 12.71).

It may seem that transforming to spherical coordinates may result in a less complicated integration, since the upper boundary of D has the simple form $\rho = \sqrt{2}$, but the lower boundary $z = x^2 + y^2$ has the form

$$z = x^2 + y^2 = r^2$$
$$\rho \cos \phi = (\rho \sin \phi)^2$$
$$\rho = \frac{\cos \phi}{\sin^2 \phi} = \cot \phi \csc \phi$$

Moreover, for $0 \le \phi \le \frac{\pi}{4}$, we have $0 \le \rho \le \sqrt{2}$, but $0 \le \rho \le \cot \phi \csc \phi$ for $\frac{\pi}{4} \le \phi \le \frac{\pi}{2}$, which means we need two integrals to evaluate the integral in spherical coordinates:

$$I = \int_0^{2\pi} \int_0^{\pi/4} \int_0^{\sqrt{2}} (\rho \cos \phi) \rho^2 \sin \phi \, d\rho \, d\phi \, d\theta$$

$$+ \int_0^{2\pi} \int_{\pi/4}^{\pi/2} \int_0^{\cot \phi \csc \phi} (\rho \cos \phi) \rho^2 \sin \phi \, d\rho \, d\phi \, d\theta$$

However, if we use cylindrical coordinates, the integral has the relatively simple form

$$I = \int_0^{2\pi} \int_0^1 \int_{r^2}^{\sqrt{2-r^2}} zr \, dz \, dr \, d\theta = \int_0^{2\pi} \int_0^1 r \left[\tfrac{1}{2}z^2\right]\Big|_{r^2}^{\sqrt{2-r^2}} \, dr \, d\theta$$

$$= \int_0^{2\pi} \int_0^1 \tfrac{1}{2} r \left[(2 - r^2) - r^4\right] dr \, d\theta = \tfrac{1}{2} \int_0^{2\pi} \left[r - \tfrac{1}{4} r^3 - \tfrac{1}{6} r^6\right]\Big|_0^1 \, d\theta$$

$$= \tfrac{1}{2} \left(\tfrac{7}{12}\right) \int_0^{2\pi} d\theta = \tfrac{7}{24} (2\pi) = \tfrac{7\pi}{12}$$ ■

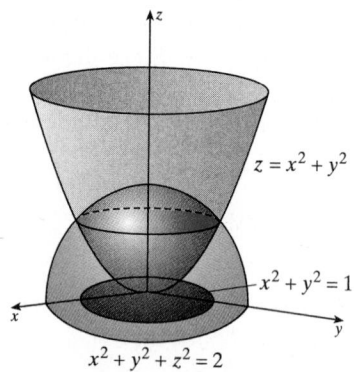

Figure 12.71 The solid D and the projected region in the xy-plane

---

12.7 PROBLEM SET

A **1. WHAT DOES THIS SAY?** Compare and contrast the rectangular, cylindrical, and spherical coordinate systems.

2. Exploration Problem Suppose you need to evaluate a particular triple integral. Discuss some criteria for choosing a coordinate system.

In Problems 3–6, convert from rectangular coordinates to
a. cylindrical   b. spherical

3. $(0, 4, \sqrt{3})$

4. $(\sqrt{2}, -2, \sqrt{3})$

5. $(1, 2, 3)$

6. (π, π, π)

In Problems 7–10 convert from cylindrical coordinates to **a.** *rectangular* **b.** *spherical*

7. $(3, \frac{2\pi}{3}, -3)$

8. $(4, \frac{\pi}{6}, -2)$

9. $(2, \frac{\pi}{4}, \pi)$

10. (π, π, π)

In Problems 11–14, convert from spherical coordinates to **a.** *rectangular* **b.** *cylindrical*

11. $(2, \frac{\pi}{6}, \frac{2\pi}{3})$

12. $(1, \frac{\pi}{6}, 0)$

13. $(1, 2, 3)$

14. (π, π, π)

Convert each equation in Problems 15–18 to cylindrical coordinates and sketch its graph in $\mathbb{R}^3$.

15. $z = x^2 - y^2$

16. $x^2 - y^2 = 1$

17. $\dfrac{x^2}{4} - \dfrac{y^2}{9} + z^2 = 0$

18. $z = x^2 + y^2$

Convert each equation in Problems 19–22 to spherical coordinates and sketch its graph in $\mathbb{R}^3$.

19. $z^2 = x^2 + y^2, z \geq 0$

20. $2x^2 + 2y^2 + 2z^2 = 1$

21. $4z = x^2 + 3y^2$

22. $x^2 + y^2 - 4z^2 = 1$

Convert each equation in Problems 23–28 to rectangular coordinates and sketch its graph in $\mathbb{R}^3$.

23. $z = r^2 \sin 2\theta$

24. $r = \sin \theta$

25. $z = r^2 \cos 2\theta$

26. $\rho^2 \sin^2 \phi = 1$

27. $\rho^2 \sin \phi \cos \phi \cos \theta = 1$

28. $\rho = \sin \phi \cos \theta$

Evaluate each iterated integral in Problems 29–36.

29. $\displaystyle\int_0^\pi \int_0^2 \int_0^{\sqrt{4-r^2}} r \sin \theta \, dz \, dr \, d\theta$

30. $\displaystyle\int_0^{\pi/4} \int_0^1 \int_0^{\sqrt{r}} r^2 \sin \theta \, dz \, dr \, d\theta$

31. $\displaystyle\int_0^{\pi/2} \int_0^{2\pi} \int_0^2 \cos \phi \sin \phi \, d\rho \, d\theta \, d\phi$

32. $\displaystyle\int_0^{\pi/2} \int_0^{\pi/4} \int_0^{\cos \phi} \rho^2 \sin \phi \, d\rho \, d\theta \, d\phi$

33. $\displaystyle\int_0^{2\pi} \int_0^4 \int_0^1 zr \, dz \, dr \, d\theta$

34. $\displaystyle\int_{-\pi/4}^{\pi/3} \int_0^{\sin \theta} \int_0^{4\cos \theta} r \, dz \, dr \, d\theta$

35. $\displaystyle\int_0^{\pi/2} \int_0^{\cos \theta} \int_0^{1-r^2} r \sin \theta \, dz \, dr \, d\theta$

36. $\displaystyle\int_0^{\pi/3} \int_0^{\cos \theta} \int_0^\phi \rho^2 \sin \theta \, d\rho \, d\phi \, d\theta$

B 37. The point (x, y, z) lies on an ellipsoid if

$$x = aR \sin \phi \cos \theta$$
$$y = bR \sin \phi \sin \theta$$
$$z = cR \cos \phi$$

for a constant R. Find an equation for this ellipsoid in rectangular coordinates.

38. Use cylindrical coordinates to compute the integral

$$\iiint_R xy \, dx \, dy \, dz$$

where R is the cylindrical solid $x^2 + y^2 \leq 1$ with $0 \leq z \leq 1$.

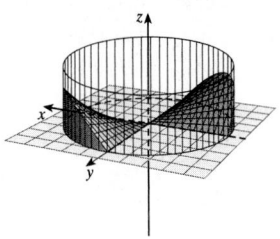

39. Use cylindrical coordinates to compute the integral

$$\iiint_R (x^4 + 2x^2y^2 + y^4) \, dx \, dy \, dz$$

where R is the cylindrical solid $x^2 + y^2 \leq a^2$ with $0 \leq z \leq \frac{1}{\pi}$

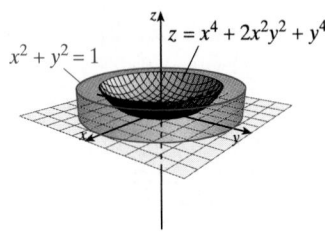

40. Use cylindrical coordinates to compute the integral

$$\iiint_D z(x^2 + y^2)^{-1/2} \, dx \, dy \, dz$$

where D is the solid bounded above by the plane $z = 2$ and below by the surface $2z = x^2 + y^2$.

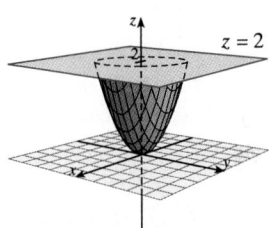

41. Find the centroid of the solid bounded by the surface $z = \sqrt{x^2 + y^2}$ and the plane $z = 9$.

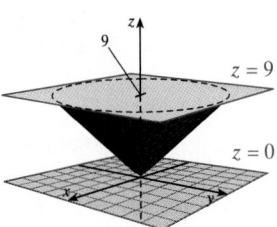

42. Find the centroid of the region bounded by the cone $z = \sqrt{x^2 + y^2}$ and the plane $z = 1$.

43. Suppose the density at each point in the hemisphere $z = \sqrt{9 - x^2 - y^2}$ is $\delta(x, y, z) = xy + z$. Set up integrals for the following quantities:
   a. the mass of the hemisphere
   b. the x-coordinate of the center of mass
   c. the moment of inertia about the z-axis

44. Find the moment of inertia about the z-axis of the portion of the homogeneous hemisphere $z = \sqrt{4 - x^2 - y^2}$ that lies between the cones $z = \sqrt{x^2 + y^2}$ and $2z = \sqrt{x^2 + y^2}$. Assume $\delta = 1$.

Recall (from Problems 40–43 of Section 12.6) that the average value of a function $f(x, y, z)$ over a solid region D is given by

$$\text{AVERAGE VALUE} = \frac{1}{\text{VOLUME OF } D} \iiint\limits_{D} f(x, y, z)\, dV$$

Use this definition in Problems 45–46.

45. Find the average value of the function $f(x, y, z) = x + y + z$ over the sphere $x^2 + y^2 + z^2 = 4$.

46. Exploration Problem What do you think the average values of θ and ϕ are over the solid sphere $\rho \le a$ for $a > 0$? Prove your conjecture.

47. Find the mass of the torus $\rho = 2 \sin \phi$ if the density is $\delta = \rho$.

48. Evaluate $\displaystyle\iiint\limits_{R} \sqrt{x^2 + y^2 + z^2}\, dx\, dy\, dz$ where R is defined by $x^2 + y^2 + z^2 \le 2$.

49. Evaluate $\displaystyle\iiint\limits_{R} (x^2 + y^2 + z^2)\, dx\, dy\, dz$ where R is defined by $x^2 + y^2 + z^2 \le 2$.

50. Evaluate $\displaystyle\iiint\limits_{D} z^2\, dx\, dy\, dz$ where D is the solid hemisphere $x^2 + y^2 + z^2 \le 1, z \ge 0$.

51. Evaluate $\displaystyle\iiint\limits_{D} \frac{dx\, dy\, dz}{\sqrt{x^2 + y^2 + z^2}}$ where D is the solid sphere $x^2 + y^2 + z^2 \le 3$.

Find the volume of the solid D given in Problems 52–56 by using integration in any convenient system of coordinates.

52. D is bounded by the paraboloid $z = 1 - 4(x^2 + y^2)$ and the xy-plane.

53. D is bounded above by the paraboloid $z = 4 - (x^2 + y^2)$, below by the plane $z = 0$, and laterally by the cylinder $x^2 + y^2 = 1$.

54. D is the intersection of the solid sphere $x^2 + y^2 + z^2 \le 9$ and the solid cylinder $x^2 + y^2 \le 1$.

55. D is the region bounded laterally by the cylinder $r = 2 \sin \theta$, below by the plane $z = 0$, and above by the paraboloid $z = 4 - r^2$.

56. D is the region that remains in the spherical solid $\rho \le 4$ after the solid cone $\phi \le \frac{\pi}{6}$ has been removed.

57. Spy Problem The Spy figures out Coldfinger's puzzle (Supplementary Problem 94 of Chapter 11), but just as his bonds come free, the door bursts open and a group of thugs rush in, led by ... the Flamer! "Why?" pleads the Spy as he is tied wrist to ankle, even more securely than before. "Don't you know?" gloats the former Chief of Spies. "I thought you knew everything! You with your fancy suits and fancy cars and fancy ... other things—let's see how fancily you die!" He pulls a lever by the door, and with a mocking salute to the Spy, leaves with his men. The cave begins to fill with water. The Spy is able to pull himself into a sitting position, with his nose 3 feet above the floor. He looks around desperately and sees that the cave has a beehive shape, something like the part of the surface $\rho = 4(1 + \cos \phi)$ that lies above the xy-plane (where ρ is measured in ft). If the Spy needs at least 10 minutes to free himself, and if water is entering at the rate of 25 ft^3/min, will he drown or survive?

© 58. In Problem 52 of Section 12.6, we noted that it is not always accurate to compute the attractive force between two masses by simply using the distance between their centers of mass. This approximation was applied first in astronomy, where the bodies are typically spherical in shape. As we will see, in this case the simple calculation is very appropriate. Consider a sphere of radius a with density δ centered at the origin and a point mass m located at $(x, y, z) = (0, 0, R)$. In this problem you are to set up the integral to compute the attractive force between the masses; and in the next problem you will do some computing.

a. Show that the distance p between point $(x, y, z) = (0, 0, R)$ and a point in the sphere, (ρ, θ, ϕ), can be expressed $p^2 = R^2 + \rho^2 - 2R\rho \cos \phi$. *Hint:* Use the law of cosines.

b. In the sphere, consider a small element of volume ΔV at point (ρ, θ, ϕ). Argue that the magnitude of the force exerted on m, and the vertical component, are

$$\Delta F_{\text{mag}} = Gm(\delta \Delta V)/p^2$$

$$\Delta F = Gm(\delta \Delta V)(R - \rho \cos \phi)/p^3$$

Note that the term $(R - \rho \cos \phi)/p$ projects the force vector onto the z-axis, giving the vertical component. Do you see why?

c. Form the Riemann sum involving ΔF and get the following for the force acting between point mass m and the sphere of radius a:

$$F = \iiint \frac{Gm\delta(R - \rho \cos \phi)\, dV}{p^3}$$

$$= 2\pi Gm\delta \int_0^a \int_0^\pi p^2 \frac{(R - \rho \cos \phi) \sin \phi}{(R^2 + \rho^2 - 2R\rho \cos \phi)^{3/2}}\, d\phi\, dp$$

Note: The integrand is independent of θ.

59. Exploration Problem

a. For an unspecified sphere of radius a and $R > a$, compute the attractive force between the masses in the previous problem using the center of mass calculation.

b. Set a and R to numerical values and compute the attractive force by the integral in part **c** of the previous problem. Try two or three different values of R until you are satisfied that the center of mass "approximation" is exact in this case.

c. Compare this result with the corresponding calculations of Section 12.6 and conjecture why the center of mass argument is sound in the case of the sphere and not for the rectangular region.

60. Let D be a homogeneous solid (with density 1) that has the shape of a right circular cylinder with height h and radius r. Use cylindrical coordinates to find the moment of inertia of S about its axis of symmetry.

61. Find the sum $I_x + I_y + I_z$ of the moments of inertia of the solid sphere

$$x^2 + y^2 + z^2 \le 1$$

about the coordinate axes. Assume the density is 1.

62. How much volume remains from a spherical ball of radius a when a cylindrical hole of radius b $(0 < b < a)$ is bored out of its center? (See Figure 12.72.)

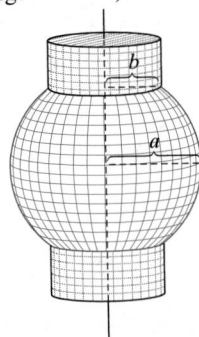

Figure 12.72 Boring a hole in a spherical ball

63. Journal Problem *UMAP Journal** ■ Tumors can be modeled by what are called *bumpy spheres* or *wrinkled spheres* (see Figure 12.73). Find the volume of the bumpy sphere $\rho = 1 + 0.2 \sin 4\theta \sin 3\phi$ $(0 \leq \theta \leq 2\pi, 0 \leq \phi \leq \pi)$ as follows:

*"Heat Therapy for Tumors" by Leah Edelstine-Keshet, Summer 1991.

a. by direct evaluation (exact value)

b. by calculator or computer (approximate value)

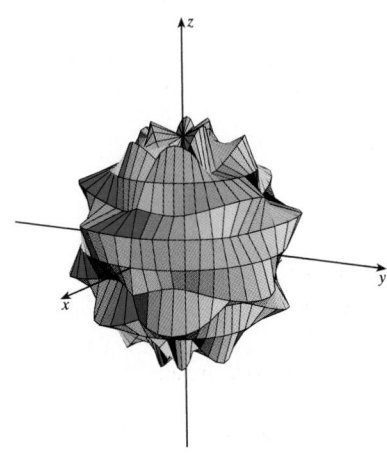

Figure 12.73 Bumpy sphere

12.8   Jacobians: Change of Variables

IN THIS SECTION   change of variables in a double integral, change of variables in a triple integral

CHANGE OF VARIABLES IN A DOUBLE INTEGRAL

When the change of variable $x = g(u)$ is made in the single integral, we know

$$\int_a^b f(x)\,dx = \int_c^d f(g(u))g'(u)\,du$$

where the limits of integration c and d satisfy $a = g(c)$ and $b = g(d)$. By changing variables in a double integral $\iint_D f(x, y)\,dA$, we want to transform the integrand $f(x, y)$ and the region of integration D so that the modified integral is easier to evaluate than the original. In general, this process involves introducing a "mapping factor" analogous to the term $g'(u)$ in the single-variable case. This factor is called a *Jacobian* in honor of the German mathematician Karl Gustav Jacobi (1804–1851; see Historical Quest Problem 57), who made the first systematic study of change of variables in multiple integrals in the middle of the nineteenth century.

Suppose we want to evaluate the double integral $\iint_D f(x, y)\,dy\,dx$ by converting it to an equivalent integral involving the variables u and v. This conversion is determined by a transformation (function) T that maps the uv-plane onto the xy-plane. If $T(u, v) = (x, y)$, then (x, y) is the *image* of (u, v) under T, and if no two points in the uv-plane map into the same point (x, y) in the xy-plane, then T is *one-to-one*. In this case, it may be possible to solve the equations $x = x(u, v)$ and $y = y(u, v)$ for u and v in terms of x and y to obtain the equations $u = u(x, y)$ and $v = v(x, y)$, which defines a **transformation** from the xy-plane back to the the uv-plane, called the **inverse transformation** of T, and is denoted by T^{-1}. This terminology is illustrated in Figure 12.74. The basic result we will use for changing variables in a double integral is stated in the following theorem.

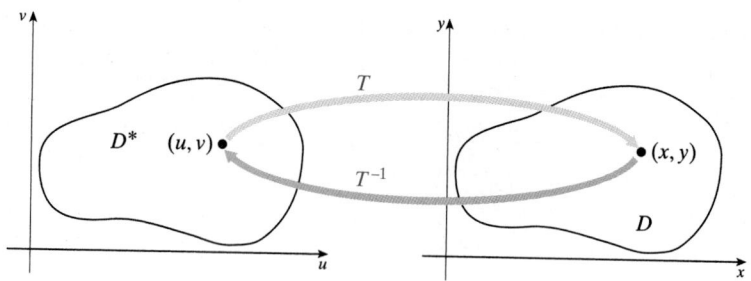

Figure 12.74   A one-to-one transformation T and its inverse T^{-1}

THEOREM 12.7   Change of variables in a double integral

Let f be a continuous function on a region D in the xy-plane, and let T be a one-to-one transformation that maps the region D^* in the uv-plane onto D under the change of variables $x = g(u, v)$, $y = h(u, v)$, for functions g and h continuously differentiable function in D^*. Then

$$\iint_D f(x, y)\, dy\, dx = \iint_{D^*} f[g(u, v), h(u, v)]\, |J(u, v)|\, du\, dv$$

where

$$J(u, v) = \begin{vmatrix} \dfrac{\partial x}{\partial u} & \dfrac{\partial x}{\partial v} \\[2ex] \dfrac{\partial y}{\partial u} & \dfrac{\partial y}{\partial v} \end{vmatrix} = \frac{\partial x}{\partial u}\frac{\partial y}{\partial v} - \frac{\partial y}{\partial u}\frac{\partial x}{\partial v}$$

is nonzero and does not change sign on D^*. The mapping factor $J(u, v)$ is called the **Jacobian** and is also denoted by $\dfrac{\partial(x, y)}{\partial(u, v)}$.

Proof   A formal proof is a matter for advanced calculus, but a geometric argument for this theorem is presented in Appendix B.   ❏

EXAMPLE 1   Finding a Jacobian

Find the Jacobian for the change of variables from rectangular to polar coordinates, namely, $x = r \cos \theta$ and $y = r \sin \theta$.

Solution

The Jacobian of the change of variables is

$$\frac{\partial(x, y)}{\partial(r, \theta)} = \begin{vmatrix} \dfrac{\partial x}{\partial r} & \dfrac{\partial x}{\partial \theta} \\[2ex] \dfrac{\partial y}{\partial r} & \dfrac{\partial y}{\partial \theta} \end{vmatrix} = \begin{vmatrix} \cos \theta & -r \sin \theta \\ \sin \theta & r \cos \theta \end{vmatrix} = r \cos^2 \theta + r \sin^2 \theta = r \qquad \blacksquare$$

This result justifies the formula we have previously used:

$$\iint_D f(x, y)\, dy\, dx = \iint_{D^*} f(r \cos \theta, r \sin \theta)\, r\, dr\, d\theta$$

where D^* is the region in the (r, θ) plane that is mapped into the region D in the (x, y) plane by the polar transformation $x = r \cos \theta$, $y = r \sin \theta$, as illustrated in Figure 12.75.

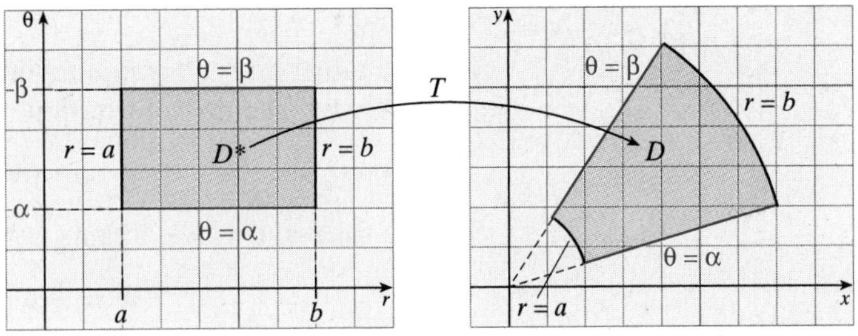

Figure 12.75 Transformation of a region D^* by $T : x = r \cos \theta, \, y = r \sin \theta$

Sometimes it is easier to express u and v in terms of x and y, and to compute the Jacobian $\dfrac{\partial(u, v)}{\partial(x, y)}$. The Jacobian $\dfrac{\partial(x, y)}{\partial(u, v)}$ needed for converting the integral $\iint\limits_{D} f(x, y) \, dy \, dx$ can then be computed by the formula

$$\frac{\partial(x, y)}{\partial(u, v)} \frac{\partial(u, v)}{\partial(x, y)} = 1$$

(see Problem 58). This procedure is illustrated by the following example.

EXAMPLE 2 **Finding the Jacobian when $u = u(x, y)$ and $v = v(x, y)$ are given**

If $u = xy$ and $v = x^2 - y^2$, express the Jacobian $\dfrac{\partial(x, y)}{\partial(u, v)}$ in terms of u and v.

Solution

It is not easy to express x and y in terms of u and v. However,

$$\frac{\partial(u, v)}{\partial(x, y)} = \begin{vmatrix} \dfrac{\partial u}{\partial x} & \dfrac{\partial u}{\partial y} \\ \dfrac{\partial v}{\partial x} & \dfrac{\partial v}{\partial y} \end{vmatrix} = \begin{vmatrix} y & x \\ 2x & -2y \end{vmatrix} = -2y^2 - 2x^2 = -2(x^2 + y^2)$$

Since

$$\begin{aligned}
(x^2 - y^2)^2 + 4x^2 y^2 &= (x^2 + y^2)^2 \\
v^2 + 4u^2 &= (x^2 + y^2)^2 \quad \text{Substitute } v = x^2 - y^2 \text{ and } u^2 = x^2 y^2. \\
x^2 + y^2 &= \sqrt{4u^2 + v^2} \quad \text{Note: } x^2 + y^2 \text{ is nonnegative.}
\end{aligned}$$

Therefore, since $\dfrac{\partial(x, y)}{\partial(u, v)} \dfrac{\partial(u, v)}{\partial(x, y)} = 1$, we have

$$\frac{\partial(x, y)}{\partial(u, v)} = \frac{1}{\dfrac{\partial(u, v)}{\partial(x, y)}} = \frac{1}{-2(x^2 + y^2)} = \frac{-1}{2\sqrt{4u^2 + v^2}} \qquad \blacksquare$$

EXAMPLE 3 **Calculating a double integral by changing variables**

Compute $\displaystyle\iint\limits_{D} \left(\frac{x - y}{x + y} \right)^4 dy \, dx$, where D is the triangular region bounded by the line $x + y = 1$ and the coordinate axes.

Solution

This is a rather difficult computation if no substitution is made. The form of the integral suggests we make the substitution

$$u = x - y, \qquad v = x + y$$

Solving for x and y, we obtain

$$x = \tfrac{1}{2}(u + v), \qquad y = \tfrac{1}{2}(v - u)$$

and the Jacobian is

$$\frac{\partial(x, y)}{\partial(u, v)} = \begin{vmatrix} \dfrac{\partial}{\partial u}\left(\dfrac{u + v}{2}\right) & \dfrac{\partial}{\partial v}\left(\dfrac{u + v}{2}\right) \\[2mm] \dfrac{\partial}{\partial u}\left(\dfrac{v - u}{2}\right) & \dfrac{\partial}{\partial v}\left(\dfrac{v - u}{2}\right) \end{vmatrix} = \begin{vmatrix} \dfrac{1}{2} & \dfrac{1}{2} \\[2mm] -\dfrac{1}{2} & \dfrac{1}{2} \end{vmatrix} = \frac{1}{2}$$

To find the image D^* of D in the uv-plane, note that the boundary lines $x = 0$ and $y = 0$ for D map into the lines $u = -v$ and $u = v$, respectively, while $x + y = 1$ maps into $v = 1$. Therefore, the transformed region of integration D^* is the triangular region shown in Figure 12.76b, with vertices $(0, 0)$, $(1, 1)$, and $(-1, 1)$.

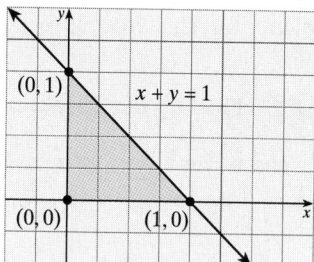

a. The region of integration D

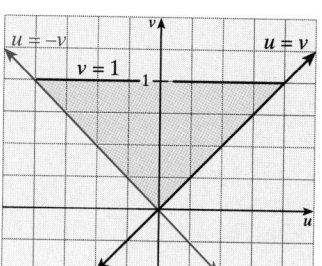

b. The transformed region D^*

Figure 12.76   Transformation of D to D^*

We now evaluate the given integral:

$$\iint_D \left(\frac{x - y}{x + y}\right)^4 dy\, dx = \iint_{D^*} \left(\frac{u}{v}\right)^4 \left|\frac{1}{2}\right| du\, dv = \frac{1}{2}\int_0^1 \int_{-v}^v u^4 v^{-4}\, du\, dv = \frac{1}{10} \quad \blacksquare$$

In Example 3, the change of variables was chosen to simplify the integrand, but sometimes it is useful to introduce a change of variables that simplifies the region of integration.

EXAMPLE 4   Change of variables to simplify a region

Find the area of the region E bounded by the ellipse $\dfrac{x^2}{a^2} + \dfrac{y^2}{b^2} = 1$.

Solution

The area is given by the integral

$$A = \iint_E dy\, dx$$

where E is the region shown in Figure 12.77a. Because E can be represented by

$$\left(\frac{x}{a}\right)^2 + \left(\frac{y}{b}\right)^2 \le 1$$

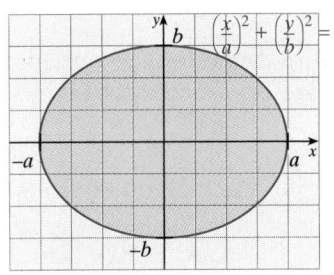

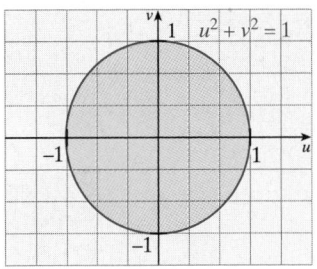

a. The elliptical region E

b. The transformed region C is a circular disk.

Figure 12.77   Transformation of the ellipse E to the circle C

we consider the substitution $u = \dfrac{x}{a}$ and $v = \dfrac{y}{b}$, which will map the elliptical region E onto the circular disk

$$C: u^2 + v^2 \le 1$$

as shown in Figure 12.77b. Then $x = au$ and $y = bv$, and the Jacobian is

$$\frac{\partial(x, y)}{\partial(u, v)} = \begin{vmatrix} \dfrac{\partial}{\partial u}(au) & \dfrac{\partial}{\partial v}(au) \\ \dfrac{\partial}{\partial u}(bv) & \dfrac{\partial}{\partial v}(bv) \end{vmatrix} = \begin{vmatrix} a & 0 \\ 0 & b \end{vmatrix} = ab$$

Because $ab > 0$, we have $|ab| = ab$, and the area of E is given by

$$\iint\limits_{E} dy\, dx = \iint\limits_{C} ab\, du\, dv$$

$$= ab \iint\limits_{C} du\, dv$$

$$= ab \iint\limits_{C} 1\, dA$$

$$= ab \left[\pi (1)^2 \right] \qquad \textit{Because } C \textit{ is a circle of radius } 1$$

$$= \pi ab \qquad\qquad\qquad\qquad\qquad\qquad \blacksquare$$

EXAMPLE 5   Using a change of variables to find a centroid

Find the centroid of the region D^* in the xy-plane that is bounded by the lines $y = \frac{1}{4}x$ and $y = \frac{5}{2}x$ and the hyperbolas $xy = 1$ and $xy = 5$.

Solution

If A is the area of D^*, the centroid is $(\bar{x}, \bar{y})$, where

$$\bar{x} = \frac{1}{A} \iint\limits_{D^*} x\, dA \quad \text{and} \quad \bar{y} = \frac{1}{A} \iint\limits_{D^*} y\, dA$$

We wish to find a transformation that simplifies the boundary curves of the region of integration, so we let $u = \dfrac{y}{x}$ and $v = xy$ and the boundaries of the transformed region D become

$$u = \tfrac{1}{4} \qquad\qquad u = \tfrac{5}{2} \qquad\qquad v = 1 \qquad\qquad v = 5$$

$$\left(y = \tfrac{1}{4}x \right) \qquad \left(y = \tfrac{5}{2}x \right) \qquad (xy = 1) \qquad (xy = 5)$$

The regions D^* and D are shown in Figure 12.78.

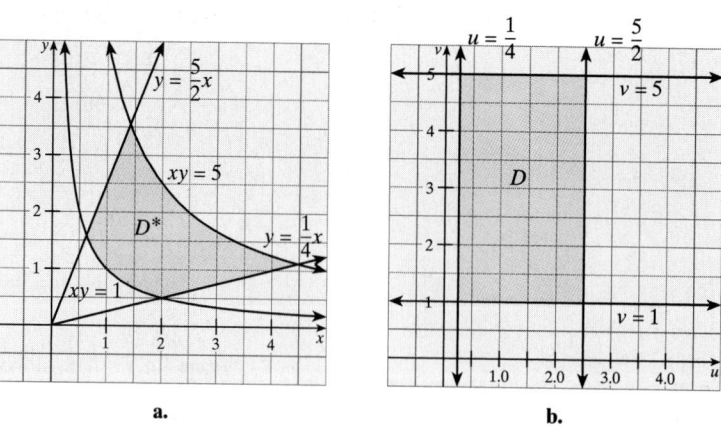

Figure 12.78   The regions D^* and D

Solving the equations $u = y/x$ and $v = xy$ for x and y, we obtain $x = \sqrt{v/u}$ and $y = \sqrt{uv}$, so the Jacobian is

$$\frac{\partial(x, y)}{\partial(u, v)} = \begin{vmatrix} \dfrac{\partial x}{\partial u} & \dfrac{\partial x}{\partial v} \\[2mm] \dfrac{\partial y}{\partial u} & \dfrac{\partial y}{\partial v} \end{vmatrix} = \begin{vmatrix} -\dfrac{1}{2}\dfrac{1}{u}\sqrt{\dfrac{v}{u}} & \dfrac{1}{2}\dfrac{1}{\sqrt{uv}} \\[3mm] \dfrac{1}{2}\sqrt{\dfrac{v}{u}} & \dfrac{1}{2}\sqrt{\dfrac{u}{v}} \end{vmatrix} = \frac{-1}{4u} - \frac{1}{4u} = \frac{-1}{2u}$$

The area of the region D^* is

$$\begin{aligned}
A &= \iint\limits_{D^*} dy\, dx \\[2mm]
&= \int_1^5 \int_{1/4}^{5/2} \left| \frac{-1}{2u} \right| du\, dv \\[2mm]
&= \frac{1}{2} \int_1^5 \ln u \Big|_{1/4}^{5/2}\, dv \\[2mm]
&= \frac{1}{2} \left[\ln \frac{5}{2} - \ln \frac{1}{4} \right] \int_1^5 dv \\[2mm]
&= \frac{1}{2} \ln \left(\frac{5/2}{1/4} \right) v \Big|_1^5 = 2 \ln 10
\end{aligned}$$

To find the centroid $(\overline{x}, \overline{y})$, we compute

$$\overline{x} = \frac{1}{A} \iint\limits_{D^*} x\, dA = \frac{1}{2 \ln 10} \int_1^5 \int_{1/4}^{5/2} \sqrt{\frac{v}{u}} \left| \frac{-1}{2u} \right| du\, dv \approx 2.0154$$

$$\overline{y} = \frac{1}{A} \iint\limits_{D^*} y\, dA = \frac{1}{2 \ln 10} \int_1^5 \int_{1/4}^{5/2} \sqrt{uv} \left| \frac{-1}{2u} \right| du\, dv \approx 1.5933$$

Thus, the centroid is at approximately $(2.0154, 1.5933)$ in the xy-plane.   ∎

CHANGE OF VARIABLES IN A TRIPLE INTEGRAL

The change of variables formula for triple integrals is similar to the one given for double integrals. Let T be a change of variables that maps a region R^* in uvw-space onto a region R in xyz-space, where

$$T: x = x(u, v, w) \quad y = y(u, v, w) \quad z = z(u, v, w)$$

Then the Jacobian of T is the determinant

$$\frac{\partial(x, y, z)}{\partial(u, v, w)} = \begin{vmatrix} \dfrac{\partial x}{\partial u} & \dfrac{\partial x}{\partial v} & \dfrac{\partial x}{\partial w} \\[2mm] \dfrac{\partial y}{\partial u} & \dfrac{\partial y}{\partial v} & \dfrac{\partial y}{\partial w} \\[2mm] \dfrac{\partial z}{\partial u} & \dfrac{\partial z}{\partial v} & \dfrac{\partial z}{\partial w} \end{vmatrix}$$

and the change of variable yields

$$\iiint_R f(x, y, z)\, dx\, dy\, dz$$

$$= \iiint_{R^*} f[x(u, v, w), y(u, v, w), z(u, v, w)] \left| \frac{\partial(x, y, z)}{\partial(u, v, w)} \right| du\, dv\, dw$$

EXAMPLE 6 **Formula for integrating with spherical coordinates**

Obtain the formula for converting a triple integral in rectangular coordinates to one in spherical coordinates.

Solution

The conversion formulas from rectangular coordinates to spherical coordinates are

$$x = \rho \sin \phi \cos \theta \qquad y = \rho \sin \phi \sin \theta \qquad z = \rho \cos \phi$$

The Jacobian of this transformation is

$$\frac{\partial(x, y, z)}{\partial(\rho, \theta, \phi)} = \begin{vmatrix} \dfrac{\partial}{\partial \rho}(\rho \sin \phi \cos \theta) & \dfrac{\partial}{\partial \theta}(\rho \sin \phi \cos \theta) & \dfrac{\partial}{\partial \phi}(\rho \sin \phi \cos \theta) \\[2mm] \dfrac{\partial}{\partial \rho}(\rho \sin \phi \sin \theta) & \dfrac{\partial}{\partial \theta}(\rho \sin \phi \sin \theta) & \dfrac{\partial}{\partial \phi}(\rho \sin \phi \sin \theta) \\[2mm] \dfrac{\partial}{\partial \rho}(\rho \cos \phi) & \dfrac{\partial}{\partial \theta}(\rho \cos \phi) & \dfrac{\partial}{\partial \phi}(\rho \cos \phi) \end{vmatrix}$$

$$= \begin{vmatrix} \sin \phi \cos \theta & -\rho \sin \phi \sin \theta & \rho \cos \phi \cos \theta \\ \sin \phi \sin \theta & \rho \sin \phi \cos \theta & \rho \cos \phi \sin \theta \\ \cos \phi & 0 & -\rho \sin \phi \end{vmatrix}$$

$$= -\rho^2 \sin \phi \qquad \text{(SMH)} \quad \begin{array}{l} \textit{See Problem 91 of Problem Set 2} \\ \textit{of the Student Mathematics Handbook.} \end{array}$$

Since $0 \le \phi \le \pi$, we have $\sin \phi \ge 0$, so

$$\left| \frac{\partial(x, y, z)}{\partial(\rho, \theta, \phi)} \right| = \left| -\rho^2 \sin \phi \right| = \rho^2 \sin \phi$$

$$\iiint_R f(x, y, z)\, dz\, dx\, dy$$

$$= \iiint_{R^*} f(\rho \sin \phi \cos \theta, \rho \sin \phi \sin \theta, \rho \cos \phi) \rho^2 \sin \phi\, d\rho\, d\theta\, d\phi \quad \blacksquare$$

12.8 PROBLEM SET

A *Find the Jacobian* $\dfrac{\partial(x, y)}{\partial(u, v)}$ *or* $\dfrac{\partial(x, y, z)}{\partial(u, v, w)}$ *in Problems 1–12.*

1. $x = u - v$, $y = u + v$ **2.** $x = u + 2v$, $y = 3u - 4v$

3. $x = u^2$, $y = u + v$ **4.** $x = u^2 v^2$, $y = v^2 - u^2$

5. $x = e^{u+v}$, $y = e^{u-v}$ **6.** $x = u \cos v$, $y = u \sin v$

7. $x = e^u \sin v$, $y = e^u \cos v$ **8.** $x = \dfrac{v}{u^2 + v^2}$, $y = \dfrac{u}{u^2 + v^2}$

9. $x = u + v - w$; $y = 2u - v + 3w$; $z = -u + 2v - w$

10. $x = 2u - w$, $y = u + 3v$, $z = v + 2w$

11. $x = u \cos v$, $y = u \sin v$, $z = we^{uv}$

12. $x = \dfrac{u}{v}$, $y = \dfrac{v}{w}$, $z = \dfrac{w}{u}$

Find the Jacobian $\dfrac{\partial(x, y)}{\partial(u, v)}$ *in Problems 13–18 either by solving the given equations for x and y or by first computing* $\dfrac{\partial(u, v)}{\partial(x, y)}$. *Express your answers in terms of u and v.*

13. $u = 2x - 3y$, $v = x + 4y$ **14.** $u = 3x + y$, $v = -x + 2y$

15. $u = ye^{-x}$, $v = e^x$

16. $u = xy$, $v = \dfrac{y}{x}$ for $x > 0$, $y > 0$

17. $u = x^2 - y^2$, $v = x^2 + y^2$

18. $u = \dfrac{x}{x^2 + y^2}$, $v = \dfrac{y}{x^2 + y^2}$

A region R is given in Problems 19–22. Sketch the corresponding region R^* in the uv-plane using the given transformations.

19.

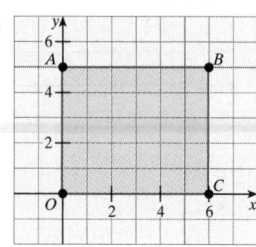

$u = x + y, v = x - y$

20.

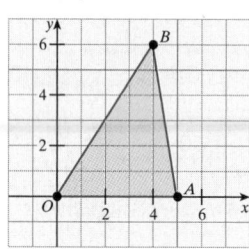

$u = 2x, v = x + y$

21.

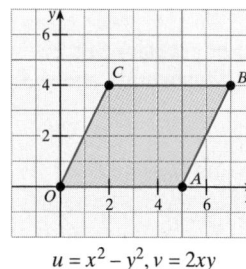

$u = x^2 - y^2, v = 2xy$

22.

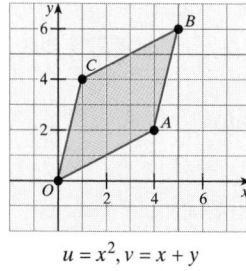

$u = x^2, v = x + y$

23. Suppose the uv-plane is mapped onto the xy-plane by the equations $x = u(1 - v)$, $y = uv$. Express $dx\, dy$ in terms of $du\, dv$.

24. Suppose the uv-plane is mapped onto the xy-plane by the equations $x = u^2 - v^2$, $y = 2uv$. Express $dx\, dy$ in terms of $du\, dv$.

Use a suitable change of variables to find the area of the region specified in Problems 25 and 26.

25. The region R bounded by the hyperbolas $xy = 1$ and $xy = 4$, and the lines $y = x$ and $y = 4x$

26. The region R bounded by the parabolas $y = x^2$, $y = 4x^2$, $y = \sqrt{x}$, and $y = \frac{1}{2}\sqrt{x}$

Let D be the region in the xy-plane that is bounded by the coordinate axes and the line $x + y = 1$. Use the change of variables $u = x - y$, $v = x + y$ to compute the integrals given in Problems 27–30.

27. $\displaystyle\iint_D \left(\frac{x - y}{x + y}\right)^5 dy\, dx$ **28.** $\displaystyle\iint_D \left(\frac{x - y}{x + y}\right)^4 dy\, dx$

29. $\displaystyle\iint_D (x - y)^5 (x + y)^3 dy\, dx$ **30.** $\displaystyle\iint_D (x - y)e^{x^2 + y^2} dy\, dx$

B **31. WHAT DOES THIS SAY?** Discuss the process of changing variables in a triple integral.

32. Exploration Problem Discuss the necessity of including the Jacobian when changing variables in a double integral.

Under the transformation

$$u = \tfrac{1}{5}(2x + y) \qquad v = \tfrac{1}{5}(x - 2y)$$

the square D in the xy-plane with vertices $(0, 0)$, $(1, -2)$, $(3, -1)$, $(2, 1)$ is mapped onto a square in the uv-plane. Use this information to find the integrals in Problems 33–38.

33. $\displaystyle\iint_D \left(\frac{2x + y}{x - 2y + 5}\right)^2 dy\, dx$

34. $\displaystyle\iint_D (2x + y)(x - 2y)^2 dy\, dx$

35. $\displaystyle\iint_D (2x + y)^2 (x - 2y)\, dy\, dx$

36. $\displaystyle\iint_D \sqrt{(2x + y)(x - 2y)}\, dy\, dx$

37. $\displaystyle\iint_D (2x + y) \tan^{-1}(x - 2y)\, dy\, dx$

38. $\displaystyle\iint_D \cos(2x + y) \sin(x - 2y)\, dy\, dx$

39. Evaluate

$$\iint_R e^{(2y-x)/(y+2x)}\, dA$$

where R is the trapezoid with vertices $(0, 2)$, $(1, 0)$, $(4, 0)$, and $(0, 8)$.

40. Let R be the region in the xy-plane that is bounded by the parallelogram with vertices $(0, 0)$, $(1, 1)$, $(2, 1)$ and $(1, 0)$. Use the linear transformation $x = u + v$, $y = v$ to compute $\iint_R (2x - y)\, dy\, dx$.

41. Use a suitable linear transformation $u = ax + by$, $v = rx + sy$ to evaluate the integral

$$\iint_R \left(\frac{x + y}{2}\right)^2 e^{(y-x)/2}\, dy\, dx$$

where R is the region inside the square with vertices $(0, 0)$, $(1, 1)$, $(0, 2)$, and $(-1, 1)$.

42. Under the change of variables $x = s^2 - t^2$, $y = 2st$, the quarter circular region in the st-plane given by $s^2 + t^2 \le 1$, $s \ge 0$, $t \ge 0$ is mapped onto a certain region D^* of the xy-plane. Evaluate

$$\iint_{D^*} \frac{dy \, dx}{\sqrt{x^2 + y^2}}$$

43. Use the change of variable $x = ar \cos \theta$, $y = br \sin \theta$ to evaluate

$$\iint_{D^*} \exp\left(-\frac{x^2}{a^2} - \frac{y^2}{b^2}\right) dy \, dx$$

where D^* is the region bounded by the quarter ellipse

$$\frac{x^2}{a^2} + \frac{y^2}{b^2} = 1, \qquad \text{in the first quadrant}$$

44. Evaluate

$$\iint_{D^*} \frac{2x - 5y}{3x + y} \, dA$$

where D^* is the region bounded by the lines $2x - 5y = 1$, $2x - 5y = 3$, $3x + y = 1$, $3x + y = 4$.

45. Evaluate

$$\iint_{D^*} e^{-(4x^2 + 5y^2)} \, dA$$

where D^* is the elliptical disk $\dfrac{x^2}{5} + \dfrac{y^2}{4} \le 1$.

46. Evaluate

$$\iint_{D^*} y^3 (2x - y) \cos(2x - y) \, dy \, dx$$

where D^* is the region bounded by the parallelogram with vertices $(0, 0)$, $(2, 0)$, $(3, 2)$, and $(1, 2)$.

47. Find the centroid of the region D^* bounded by the curves $y = x$, $y = 2x$, $xy^3 = 3$, and $xy^3 = 6$.

48. Evaluate

$$\iint_{D^*} (x^4 - y^4) e^{xy} \, dA$$

where D^* is the region bounded by the hyperbolas $xy = 1$, $xy = 2$, $x^2 - y^2 = 1$, and $x^2 - y^2 = 4$.

49. Use the change of variables $x = au$, $y = bv$, $z = cw$ to find the volume of the ellipsoid

$$\frac{x^2}{a^2} + \frac{y^2}{b^2} + \frac{z^2}{c^2} = 1$$

50. Use a change of variables to find the moment of inertia about the z-axis of the solid ellipsoid with $\delta = 1$.

$$\frac{x^2}{a^2} + \frac{y^2}{b^2} + \frac{z^2}{c^2} = 1$$

51. Evaluate

$$\iint_{R} \ln\left(\frac{x - y}{x + y}\right) dy \, dx$$

where R is the triangular region with vertices $(1, 0)$, $(4, -3)$, and $(4, 1)$.

52. A rotation of the xy-plane through the fixed angle θ is given by

$$x = u \cos \theta - v \sin \theta$$
$$y = u \sin \theta + v \cos \theta$$

(See Figure 12.79.)

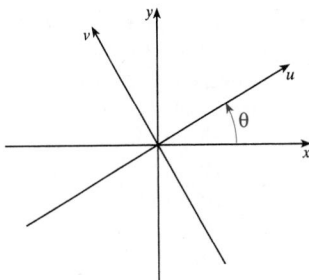

Figure 12.79 Rotational transformation

a. Compute the Jacobian $\dfrac{\partial(x, y)}{\partial(u, v)}$.

b. Let E denote the ellipse

$$x^2 + xy + y^2 = 3$$

Use a rotation of $\frac{\pi}{4}$ to obtain an integral that is equivalent to $\iint_E y \, dy \, dx$. Evaluate the transformed integral.

53. Find the area of the rotated ellipse

$$5x^2 - 4xy + 2y^2 = 1$$

Note that $5x^2 - 4xy + 2y^2 = Au^2 + Bv^2$, where A and B are constants and $u = x + 2y$, $v = 2x - y$.

54. Find the Jacobian of the cylindrical coordinate transformation

$$x = r \cos \theta, \qquad y = r \sin \theta, \qquad z = z$$

55. Exploration Problem Let R be the region bounded by the parallelogram with vertices $(0, 0)$, $(2, 0)$, $(1, 1)$, and $(-1, 1)$. Show that under a suitable change of variables of the form $x = au + bv$, $y = cu + dv$, we have

$$\iint_{R} f(x + y) \, dy \, dx = \int_0^2 f(t) \, dt$$

where f is continuous on $[0, 2]$.

56. Find the volume of the solid shown in Figure 12.80 that is under the surface

$$z = \frac{xy}{1 + x^2 y^2}$$

over the region bounded by $xy = 1$, $xy = 5$, $x = 1$, and $x = 5$.

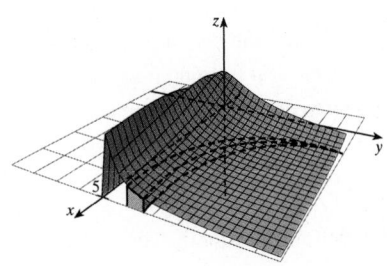

Figure 12.80 Problem 56

57. HISTORICAL QUEST   Karl G. Jacobi was a gifted teacher and one of Germany's most distinguished mathematicians during the first half of the nineteenth century. He made major contributions to the theory of elliptic functions, but his work with functional determinants is what secured his place in history. In 1841 he published a long memoir called "De determinantibus functionalibus," devoted

KARL G. JACOBI
1804–1851

to what we today call the Jacobian and pointing out that this determinant is in many ways the multivariable analogue to the differential of a single variable. The memoir was published in what is usually known as *Crelle's Journal*, one of the first journals devoted to serious mathematics. It was begun in 1826 by August Crelle (1780-1855) with the title *Journal für die reine und angewandte Mathematik*. ∎

For this Quest, set up an integral for the circumference of the ellipse

$$\frac{x^2}{a^2} + \frac{y^2}{b^2} = 1$$

This is an example of an elliptic integral.

58. Let $T : x = x(u, v)$, $y = y(u, v)$ be a one-to-one transformation on a set D so that T^{-1} has the form $u = u(x, y)$, $v = v(x, y)$. Use the multiplicative property of determinants, along with the chain rule, to show that

$$\frac{\partial(x, y)}{\partial(u, v)} \frac{\partial(u, v)}{\partial(x, y)} = 1$$

You may assume that all the necessary partial derivatives exist.

 Properties of determinants are found in Section 2.8 of the Student Mathematics Handbook.

CHAPTER 12 REVIEW

Proficiency Examination

CONCEPT PROBLEMS

1. Define a double integral.
2. State Fubini's theorem over a rectangular region.
3. What is a type I region? State Fubini's theorem for a type I region.
4. What is a type II region? State Fubini's theorem for a type II region.
5. State the formula for finding an area using a double integral.
6. State the formula for finding a volume using a double integral.
7. State the following properties of a double integral.
   a. linearity rule
   b. dominance rule
   c. subdivision rule
8. What is the formula for a double integral in polar coordinates?
9. State the double integral formula for surface area.
10. State the formula for the area of a surface defined parametrically.
11. State Fubini's theorem over a parallelepiped in space.
12. Give a triple integral formula for volume.
13. Explain how to use a double integral to find the mass of a planar lamina of variable density.
14. How do you find the moment of a lamina with respect to the x-axis?
15. What are the formulas for the centroid of a region?
16. Define moment of inertia.
17. What is a joint probability density function?

18. Complete the following table for the conversion of coordinates.

From \ To	(x, y, z) Rectangular	(r, θ, z) Cylindrical	(ρ, θ, φ) Spherical
(x, y, z) Rectangular	$x = x$ $y = y$ $z = z$	$r = $ ___? $\tan\theta = $ ___? $z = $ ___?	$\rho = $ ___? $\tan\theta = $ ___? $\phi = $ ___?
(r, θ, z) Cylindrical	$x = $ ___? $y = $ ___? $z = $ ___?	$r = r$ $\theta = \theta$ $z = z$	$\rho = $ ___? $\theta = $ ___? $\phi = $ ___?
(ρ, θ, φ) Spherical	$x = $ ___? $y = $ ___? $z = $ ___?	$r = $ ___? $\theta = $ ___? $z = $ ___?	$\rho = \rho$ $\theta = \theta$ $\phi = \phi$

19. a. State the formula for a triple integral in cylindrical coordinates.
    b. State the formula for a triple integral in spherical coordinates.
20. Define the Jacobian for a mapping $x = x(u, v)$, $y = y(u, v)$ from u, v variables to x, y variables.
21. State the formula for the change of variables in a double integral.

PRACTICE PROBLEMS

22. Evaluate $\displaystyle\int_0^{\pi/3} \int_0^{\sin y} e^{-x} \cos y \, dx \, dy$.

23. Evaluate $\displaystyle\int_{-1}^1 \int_0^z \int_y^{y-z} (x + y - z) \, dx \, dy \, dz$.

24. Use a double integral to compute the area of the region R that is bounded by the x-axis and the parabola $y = 9 - x^2$.

25. Use polar coordinates to evaluate

$$\int_0^1 \int_0^{\sqrt{1-x^2}} \cos(x^2 + y^2) \, dy \, dx$$

26. Use a triple integral to find the volume of the tetrahedron that is bounded by the coordinate planes and the plane

$$\frac{x}{a} + \frac{y}{b} + \frac{z}{c} = 1$$

with $a > 0, b > 0, c > 0$.

27. A certain appliance consisting of two independent electronic components will be usable as long as either one of its components is still operating. The appliance carries a warranty from the manufacturer guaranteeing replacement if the appliance becomes unusable within one year of the date of purchase. To model this situation, let the random variables X and Y measure the life span (in years) of the first and second components, respectively, and assume that the joint probability density function for X and Y is

$$f(x, y) = \begin{cases} \frac{1}{4} e^{-x/2} e^{-y/2} & \text{if } x \ge 0, y \ge 0 \\ 0 & \text{otherwise} \end{cases}$$

Suppose the quality assurance department selects one of these appliances at random. What is the probability that the appliance will fail during the warranty period?

28. Set up and evaluate a triple integral for the volume of the solid region in the first octant that is bounded above by the plane $z = 4x$ and below by the paraboloid $z = x^2 + 2y^2$. See Figure 12.81.

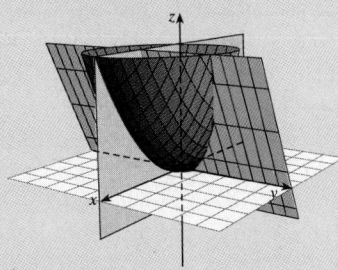

Figure 12.81 Problem 28

29. A solid D is bounded above by the plane $z = 4$ and below by the surface $z = x^2 + y^2$. Its density $\rho(x, y, z)$ at each point P is equal to the distance from P to the z-axis. Find the total mass of S.

30. Use a linear change of variables to evaluate the double integral

$$\iint_R (x + y) e^{x-2y} \, dy \, dx$$

where R is the triangular region with vertices $(0, 0)$, $(2, 0)$, $(1, 1)$.

Supplementary Problems

In Problems 1–10, sketch the region of integration, exchange the order, and evaluate the integral using either order of integration.

1. $\displaystyle\int_0^1 \int_0^{3x} x^2 y^2 \, dy \, dx$ **2.** $\displaystyle\int_0^4 \int_0^1 \sqrt{\frac{y}{x}} \, dx \, dy$

3. $\displaystyle\int_1^2 \int_0^y \frac{1}{x^2 + y^2} \, dx \, dy$ **4.** $\displaystyle\int_0^{\pi/2} \int_0^{\pi/2} \cos(x + y) \, dx \, dy$

5. $\displaystyle\int_0^1 \int_0^1 x \sqrt{x^2 + y} \, dx \, dy$ **6.** $\displaystyle\int_0^{\pi/2} \int_0^{\sqrt{\sin x}} xy \, dy \, dx$

7. $\displaystyle\int_0^3 \int_0^{9-x^2} \frac{xe^{y/3}}{9 - y} \, dy \, dx$ **8.** $\displaystyle\int_0^1 \int_{\sqrt{y}}^1 \sqrt{1 - x^3} \, dx \, dy$

9. $\displaystyle\int_0^1 \int_{x^2}^1 x^3 \sin y^3 \, dy \, dx$

10. $\displaystyle\int_0^2 \int_0^{\sqrt{4-x^2}} \sqrt{4 - x^2 - y^2} \, dy \, dx$

Evaluate the integrals given in Problems 11–34.

11. $\displaystyle\int_0^1 \int_{\sqrt{x}}^1 e^{y^3} \, dy \, dx$

12. $\displaystyle\int_0^2 \int_x^2 \frac{y}{(x^2 + y^2)^{3/2}} \, dy \, dx$

13. $\displaystyle\int_0^1 \int_1^4 \int_x^y z \, dz \, dy \, dx$

14. $\displaystyle\int_1^2 \int_0^1 \int_0^{\sqrt{1-x^2}} e^{\sqrt{x^2+y^2}} \, dy \, dx \, dz$

15. $\displaystyle\int_0^{\pi/4} \int_0^{2\pi} \int_0^\theta r^2 \sin \phi \, dr \, d\theta \, d\phi$

16. $\displaystyle\int_0^1 \int_0^x \int_0^y x^2 y \, dz \, dy \, dx$

17. $\displaystyle\int_1^2 \int_x^{x^2} \int_0^{\ln x} xe^z \, dz \, dy \, dx$

18. $\displaystyle\int_0^1 \int_{1-x}^{1+x} \int_0^{xy} xz \, dz \, dy \, dx$

19. $\displaystyle\int_{-\sqrt{3}}^{\sqrt{3}} \int_{-\sqrt{3-y^2}}^{\sqrt{3-y^2}} \int_{(x^2+y^2)^2}^9 y^2 \, dz \, dx \, dy$
Hint: Change to cylindrical coordinates.

20. $\displaystyle\iint_D x^2 y \, dA$, where D is the circular disk $x^2 + y^2 \le 4$

21. $\displaystyle\iint_D (x^2 + y^2 + 1) \, dA$, where D is the circular disk $x^2 + y^2 \le 4$

22. $\displaystyle\iint_D e^{x^2+y^2} \, dA$, where D is the circular disk $x^2 + y^2 \le 4$

23. $\displaystyle\iint_D (x^2 + y^2)^n \, dA$, where D is the circular disk $x^2 + y^2 \le 4$, $n \ge 0$

24. $\displaystyle\iint_D \frac{2y}{x} \, dA$, where D is the region above the line $x + y = 1$ and inside the circle $x^2 + y^2 = 1$

25. $\displaystyle\iint_D x^3 \sqrt{4 - y^2} \, dA$, where D is the circular disk $x^2 + y^2 \le 4$

26. $\iint\limits_D x^3\,dA$, where D is the shaded portion shown in Figure 12.82

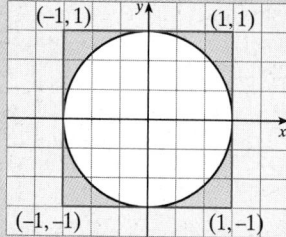

Figure 12.82 Problem 26

27. $\iint\limits_D xy^2\,dA$, where D is the shaded portion shown in Figure 12.83

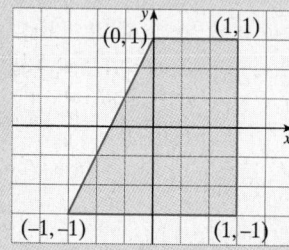

Figure 12.83 Problem 27

28. $\iint\limits_D \exp\left(\dfrac{y-x}{y+x}\right)dy\,dx$, where D is the triangular region with vertices $(0,0)$, $(2,0)$, $(0,2)$ *Hint:* Make a suitable change of variables.

29. $\iint\limits_R \dfrac{\partial^2 f}{\partial x\,\partial y}\,dx\,dy$, where R is the rectangle $a \le x \le b$, $c \le y \le d$ and $\dfrac{\partial^2 f}{\partial x\,\partial y}$ is continuous over R with $f(a,c)=4$, $f(a,d)=-3$, $f(b,c)=1$, $f(b,d)=5$

30. $\iiint\limits_D \sqrt{x^2+y^2+z^2}\,dV$, where D is the portion of the solid sphere $x^2+y^2+z^2 \le 1$ that lies in the first octant

31. $\iiint\limits_H z^2\,dV$, where H is the solid hemisphere $x^2+y^2+z^2 \le 1$ with $z \ge 0$

32. $\iiint\limits_H \dfrac{dV}{\sqrt{x^2+y^2+z^2}}$, where H is the solid hemisphere $x^2+y^2+z^2 \le 1$, with $z \ge 0$

33. $\iiint\limits_D \dfrac{dV}{x^2+y^2+z^2}$, where D is the solid region bounded below by the paraboloid $2z = x^2+y^2$ and above by the sphere $x^2+y^2+z^2 = 8$

34. $\iiint\limits_D z(x^2+y^2)^{-1/2}\,dV$, where D is the solid bounded by the surface $2z = x^2+y^2$ and the plane $z = 2$

35. Set up (but do not evaluate) an integral for the mass of a lamina with density δ that covers the region outside the circle $r = \sqrt{2}\,a$ and inside the lemniscate $r^2 = 4a^2 \sin 2\theta$ in the first quadrant.

36. Rewrite the triple integral $\displaystyle\int_0^1 \int_0^x \int_0^{\sqrt{xy}} f(x,y,z)\,dz\,dy\,dx$ as a triple integral in the order $dy\,dx\,dz$.

37. Convert the double integral
$$\int_0^{\pi/2} \int_0^{2a\cos\theta} r \sin 2\theta\,dr\,d\theta$$
to rectangular coordinates and evaluate.

38. Reverse the order of integration
$$\int_1^2 \int_{y^2}^{y^5} e^{x/y^2}\,dx\,dy$$
and evaluate using either order.

39. Express the integral
$$\int_0^1 \int_0^y f(x,y)\,dx\,dy + \int_1^4 \int_0^{(4-y)/3} f(x,y)\,dx\,dy$$
as a double integral with the order of integration reversed.

40. Express the integral
$$\int_0^1 \int_{-\sqrt{y}}^{\sqrt{y}} f(x,y)\,dx\,dy + \int_1^3 \int_{-1}^{2-y} f(x,y)\,dx\,dy$$
as a double integral with the order of integration reversed.

41. Use a double integral to find the area inside the circle $r = \cos\theta$ and outside the cardioid $r = 1 - \cos\theta$.

42. Use a double integral to find the area outside the cardioid $r = 1 + \cos\theta$ and inside the cardioid $r = 1 + \sin\theta$.

43. Use a double integral to find the area outside the small loop of the limaçon $r = 1 + 2\sin\theta$ and inside the large loop.

44. Use a double integral to compute the volume of the tetrahedral region in the first octant that is bounded by the coordinate planes and the plane $3x + y + 2z = 6$.

45. Use a double integral to find the volume of the solid that is bounded above by the paraboloid $z = x^2 + y^2$ and below by the square region $0 \le x \le 1$, $0 \le y \le 1$, $z = 0$.

46. Find the volume of the solid that is bounded above by the surface $z = xy$, below by the xy-plane, and on the sides by the circular disk $x^2 + y^2 \le a^2$ $(a > 0)$ that lies in the first quadrant.

47. Find the volume of the solid that is bounded above by the paraboloid $z = 4 - x^2 - y^2$ and below by the plane $z = 4 - 2x$.

48. Find the surface area of that portion of the cone $z = \sqrt{x^2 + y^2}$ that is contained in the cylinder $x^2 + y^2 = 1$.

49. Find the surface area of the portion of the paraboloid $z = x^2 + y^2$ that lies below the plane $z = 9$.

50. Find the surface area of the portion of the cylinder $x^2 + z^2 = 4$ that is bounded by the planes $x = 0$, $x = 1$, $y = 0$, and $y = 2$.

51. Find the volume of the region bounded by the paraboloid $y^2 + z^2 = 2x$ and the plane $x + y = 1$.

52. Find the volume of the region bounded above by the paraboloid $z = 4 - x^2 - y^2$ and below by the plane $z + 2y = 4$.

53. Find the volume of the region bounded by the ellipsoid $z^2 = 4 - 4r^2$ and the cylinder $r = \cos\theta$.

54. Find the volume of the region bounded above by the hemisphere $z = \sqrt{9 - x^2 - y^2}$, below by the xy-plane, and on the sides by the cylinder $x^2 + y^2 = 1$.

55. Show that the solid bounded below by the cone $z = \sqrt{x^2 + y^2}$ and above by the sphere $x^2 + y^2 + z^2 = 2az$ for $a > 0$ has volume $V = \pi a^3$.

56. Find the volume of the solid region bounded above by the sphere given in spherical coordinates by $\rho = a\ (a > 0)$ and below by the cone $\phi = \phi_0$ where $0 < \phi_0 < \frac{\pi}{2}$.

57. A homogeneous solid S is bounded above by the sphere $\rho = a$ $(a > 0)$ and below by the cone $\phi = \phi_0$ where $0 < \phi_0 < \frac{\pi}{2}$. Find the moment of inertia of S about the z-axis. Assume $\delta = 1$.

58. The region between the circles $x^2 + y^2 = 1$ and $x^2 + y^2 = 4$ with $0 \le z \le 5$ forms a "washer." Find the moment of inertia of the washer about the z-axis if the density δ is given by
  a. $\delta = k$ (k a constant)   **b.** $\delta(x, y) = x^2 + y^2$
  c. $\delta(x, y) = x^2 y^2$

59. Find $\bar{x}$, the x-coordinate of the center of mass, of a triangular lamina with vertices $(0, 0)$, $(1, 0)$, and $(0, 1)$ if the density is $\delta(x, y) = x^2 + y^2$.

60. Find the mass of a cone of top radius R and height H if the density at each point P is proportional to the distance from P to the tip of the cone.

61. Find $\bar{z}$, the z-coordinate of the centroid of a homogeneous right circular cone with height H and base radius R. Assume the cone is positioned with its vertex at the origin and the z-axis is its axis of symmetry.

62. Find the Jacobian $\dfrac{\partial(u, v, w)}{\partial(x, y, z)}$ of the change of variables $u = 2x - 3y + z$, $v = 2y - z$, $w = 2z$.

63. Find the Jacobian $\dfrac{\partial(u, v, w)}{\partial(x, y, z)}$ of the change of variables $u = x^2 + y^2 + z^2$, $v = 2y^2 + z^2$, $w = 2z^2$.

64. Let $u = 2x - y$ and $v = x + 2y$. Find the image of the unit square given by $0 \le x \le 1, 0 \le y \le 1$.

65. Find the mass of a lamina with density $\delta = r\theta$ that covers the region enclosed by the rose $r = \cos 3\theta$ for $0 \le \theta \le \frac{\pi}{6}$.

66. Suppose $u = \frac{1}{2}(x^2 + y^2)$ and $v = \frac{1}{2}(x^2 - y^2)$, with $x > 0$, $y > 0$.
  a. Find the Jacobian $\dfrac{\partial(u, v)}{\partial(x, y)}$.
  b. Solve for x and y in terms of u and v, and find the Jacobian $\dfrac{\partial(x, y)}{\partial(u, v)}$.
  c. Verify that $\dfrac{\partial(u, v)}{\partial(x, y)} \dfrac{\partial(x, y)}{\partial(u, v)} = 1$.

67. Let D be the region given by $u \ge 0, v \ge 0, 1 \le u + v \le 2$.
  a. Show that under the transformation $u = x + y, v = x - y$, D is mapped into the region R such that $-x \le y \le x$, $\frac{1}{2} \le x \le 1$.
  b. Find the Jacobian $\dfrac{\partial(u, v)}{\partial(x, y)}$, and compute $\displaystyle\iint_D (u + v)\, du\, dv$.

68. Use a change of variables after a transformation of the form $x = Au, y = Bv, z = Cw$ to find the volume of the region bounded by the surface $\sqrt{x} + \sqrt{2y} + \sqrt{3z} = 1$ and the coordinate planes.

69. Find the centroid of a homogeneous lamina that covers the part of the plane $Ax + By + Cz = 1, A > 0, B > 0, C > 0$ that lies in the first quadrant.

70. A homogeneous plate has the shape of the region in the first quadrant of the xy-plane that is bounded by the circle $x^2 + y^2 = 1$ and the lines $y = x$ and $x = 0$. Sketch the region and find $\bar{x}$, the x-coordinate of the centroid.

71. Let R be a lamina covering the region in the xy-plane that is bounded by the parabola $y = 1 - x^2$ and the positive coordinate axes. Assume the lamina has density $\delta(x, y) = xy$.
  a. Find the center of mass of the lamina.
  b. Find the moment of inertia of the plate about the z-axis.

72. A solid has the shape of the cylinder $x^2 + y^2 \le a$, with $0 \le z \le b$. Assume the solid has density $\delta(x, y, z) = x^2 + y^2$.
  a. Find the mass of the solid.
  b. Find the center of mass of the solid.

73. Use cylindrical coordinates to find the volume of the solid bounded by the circular cylinder $r = 2a \cos\theta\ (a > 0)$, the cone $z = r$, and the xy-plane.

74. Let u be everywhere continuous in the plane, and define the functions f and g by

$$f(x) = \int_a^x u(x, y)\, dy \qquad g(y) = \int_y^b u(x, y)\, dx$$

Show that

$$\int_a^b f(x)\, dx = \int_a^b g(y)\, dy$$

Hint: Show that both integrals equal $\displaystyle\iint_D u(x, y)\, dA$ for a certain region D.

75. Find the volume of the solid region bounded by the surface

$$x^{2/3} + y^{2/3} + z^{2/3} = a^{2/3}$$

where a is a positive constant.

76. Modeling Problem The parking lot for a certain shopping mall has the shape shown in Figure 12.84.

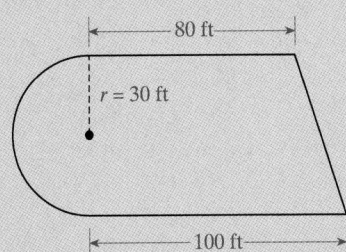

Figure 12.84 Shopping mall parking lot

Assuming a security observation tower can be located anywhere in the parking lot, where would you put it? State all assumptions made in setting up and analyzing your model.

77. Find the centroid of the solid common to the cylindrical solids $x^2 + z^2 \le 1$ and $y^2 + z^2 \le 1$.

78. Show that if $z = f(r, \theta)$ is the equation of a surface S in polar coordinates, the surface area of S is given by

$$\iint\limits_R \sqrt{1 + \left(\frac{\partial z}{\partial r}\right)^2 + \frac{1}{r^2}\left(\frac{\partial z}{\partial \theta}\right)^2}\, r\, dr\, d\theta$$

where R is the projected region in the $r\theta$-plane.

79. Find the center of mass of the solid S that lies inside the sphere $x^2 + y^2 + z^2 = 1$ in the first octant $x \geq 0$, $y \geq 0$, $z \geq 0$ if the density is $\delta(x, y, z) = (x^2 + y^2 + z^2 + 1)^{-1}$.

80. Suppose we drill a square hole of side c through the center of a sphere of radius c, as shown in Figure 12.85. What is the volume of the solid that remains?

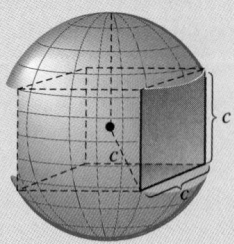

Figure 12.85 Sphere with a square hole drilled out

81. A cube of side 2 is surmounted by a hemisphere of radius 1, as shown in Figure 12.86.

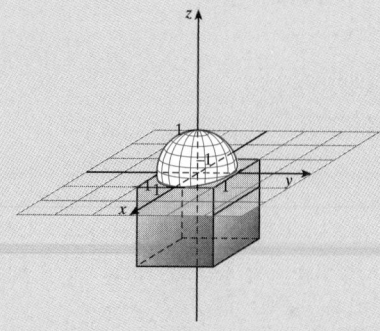

Figure 12.86 Center of mass of a complex solid

Suppose the origin is at the center of the hemispherical dome. If the entire solid is made of the same material with density $\delta = 1$, where is the centroid?

82. Putnam Examination Problem The function $K(x, y)$ is positive and continuous for $0 \leq x \leq 1$, $0 \leq y \leq 1$ and the functions $f(x)$ and $g(x)$ are positive and continuous for $0 \leq x \leq 1$. Suppose that for all $0 \leq x \leq 1$, we have

$$\int_0^1 f(y)K(x, y)\, dy = g(x)$$

and $$\int_0^1 g(y)K(x, y)\, dy = f(x)$$

Show that $f(x) = g(x)$ for $0 \leq x \leq 1$.

83. Putnam Examination Problem A circle of radius a is revolved through 180° about a line in its plane, distant b from the center of the circle ($b > a$). For what value of the ratio b/a does the center of gravity of the solid thus generated lie on the surface of the solid?

84. Putnam Examination Problem For $f(x)$ a positive, monotone, decreasing function defined in $0 \leq x \leq 1$, prove that

$$\frac{\int_0^1 x[f(x)]^2\, dx}{\int_0^1 xf(x)\, dx} \leq \frac{\int_0^1 [f(x)]^2\, dx}{\int_0^1 f(x)\, dx}$$

85. Putnam Examination Problem Show that the integral equation

$$f(x, y) = 1 + \int_0^x \int_0^y f(u, v)\, du\, dv$$

has at most one continuous solution for $0 \leq x \leq 1$, $0 \leq y \leq 1$.

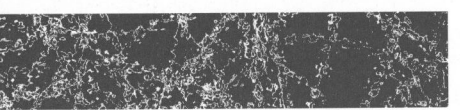
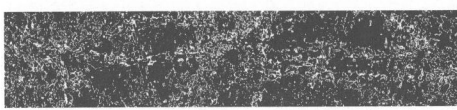
Space-Capsule Design

This project is to be done in groups of three or four students. Each group will submit a single written report.

S uppose you were part of a team of engineers designing the *Apollo* space capsule. The capsule is composed of two parts:

1. A cone with a height of 4 meters and a base of radius 3 meters.
2. A reentry shield in the shape of a parabola revolved about the axis of the cone, which is attached to the cone along the edge of the base of the cone. Its vertex is a distance D below the base of the cone. Find values of the design parameters D and δ so that the capsule will float with the vertex of the cone pointing up and with the waterline 2 m below the top of the cone, in order to keep the exit port $1/3$ m above water.

   You may make the following assumptions:

   a. The capsule has uniform density δ.
   b. The center of mass of the capsule should be below the center of mass of the displaced water because this will give the capsule better stability in heavy seas.
   c. A body floats in a fluid at the level at which the weight of the displaced fluid equals the weight of the body (Archimedes' principle).

THE SCIENCE OF MATHEMATICS has grown to such vast proportion that probably no living mathematician can claim to have achieved its mastery as a whole.

——A. N. Whitehead
An Introduction to Mathematics
(New York, 1911), p. 252

Your paper is not limited to the following questions but should include these concerns: Show the project director that the task is impossible; that is, there are no values of D and δ that satisfy the design specifications. However, you can solve this dilemma by incorporating a flotation collar in the shape of a torus. The collar will be made by taking hollow plastic tubing with a circular cross section of radius 1 m and wrapping it in a circular ring about the capsule, so that it fits snugly. The collar is designed to float just submerged with its top tangent to the surface of the water. Show that this flotation collar makes the capsule plus collar assembly satisfy the design specifications. Find the density δ needed to make the capsule float at the 2 meter mark. Assume that the weight of the tubing is negligible compared to the weight of the capsule, that the design parameter D is equal to 1 meter, and the density of the water is 1.

MAA Notes 17 (1991), "Priming the Calculus Pump: Innovations and Resources," by Marcus S. Cohen, Edward D. Gaughan, R. Arthur Knoebel, Douglas S. Kurtz, and David J. Pengelley.

13

Vector Analysis

PREVIEW

In this chapter, we combine what we have learned about differentiation, integration, and vectors to study the calculus of vector functions defined on a set of points in $\mathbb{R}^2$ or $\mathbb{R}^3$. We introduce **line integrals** and **surface integrals** to study such things as fluid flow and then obtain a result called **Green's theorem** that enables line integrals to be computed in terms of ordinary double integrals. This result is extended into $\mathbb{R}^3$ to obtain **Stokes' theorem** and the **divergence theorem**, which have extensive applications in areas such as fluid dynamics and electromagnetic theory.

PERSPECTIVE

How much work is done by a variable force acting along a given curve in space? How can the amount of heat flowing across a particular surface in unit time be measured, and is the measurement similar to measuring the flow of water or electricity? We will use line integrals and surface integrals to answer these and other questions from physics and engineering mathematics.

13.1   Properties of a Vector Field: Divergence and Curl

IN THIS SECTION   definition of a vector field, divergence, curl

DEFINITION OF A VECTOR FIELD

The satellite photograph in Figure 13.1 shows wind measurements over the Atlantic Ocean. Wind direction is indicated by directed line segments. This is an example of a *vector field*, in which every point in a given region of the plane or space is assigned a vector. Here is the definition of a vector field in $\mathbb{R}^3$.

Vector Field

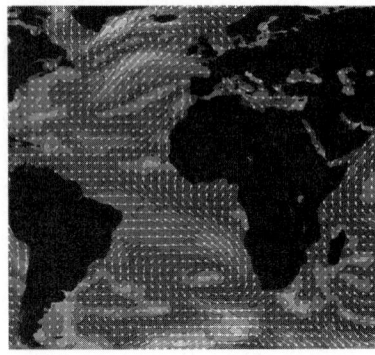

Figure 13.1 A wind-velocity map of the Atlantic Ocean

> A **vector field** in $\mathbb{R}^3$ is a function $\mathbf{F}$ that assigns a vector to each point in its domain. A vector field with domain D in $\mathbb{R}^3$ has the form
>
> $$\mathbf{F}(x, y, z) = M(x, y, z)\mathbf{i} + N(x, y, z)\mathbf{j} + P(x, y, z)\mathbf{k}$$
>
> where the scalar functions M, N, and P are called the **components** of $\mathbf{F}$. A **continuous** vector field $\mathbf{F}$ is one whose components M, N, and P are continuous.

For example,

$$\mathbf{F} = 2x^2 y\mathbf{i} + e^{yz}\mathbf{j} + \left(\tan \frac{x}{2}\right)\mathbf{k}$$

is a vector field with $\mathbf{i}$-component $2x^2 y$, $\mathbf{j}$-component e^{yz}, and $\mathbf{k}$-component $\tan \frac{x}{2}$.

A vector field in $\mathbb{R}^2$ can be thought of as a special case where there are no z-coordinates and no $\mathbf{k}$-components. That is, a vector field in $\mathbb{R}^2$ has the form

$$\mathbf{F}(x, y) = M(x, y)\mathbf{i} + N(x, y)\mathbf{j}$$

To visualize a particular vector field $\mathbf{F}(x, y, z)$, it often helps to select a number of points in the domain of $\mathbf{F}$ and then draw an arrow emanating from each point $P(a, b, c)$ with the direction of $\mathbf{F}(a, b, c)$ and length representing the magnitude $\|\mathbf{F}(a, b, c)\|$. We will refer to such a representation as the **graph of F**. Here is an example involving the graph of a vector field in $\mathbb{R}^2$.

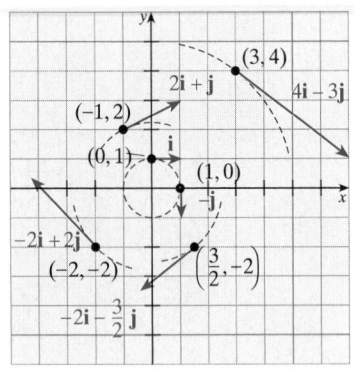

Figure 13.2 The graph of the vector field $\mathbf{F}(x, y) = y\mathbf{i} - x\mathbf{j}$

EXAMPLE 1   Graph of a vector field

Sketch the graph of the vector field $\mathbf{F}(x, y) = y\mathbf{i} - x\mathbf{j}$.

Solution

We will evaluate $\mathbf{F}$ at various points. For example,

$$\mathbf{F}(3, 4) = 4\mathbf{i} - 3\mathbf{j} \qquad \text{and} \qquad \mathbf{F}(-1, 2) = 2\mathbf{i} - (-1)\mathbf{j} = 2\mathbf{i} + \mathbf{j}$$

We can generate as many such vector values of $\mathbf{F}$ as we wish. Several are shown in Figure 13.2.   ■

The graph of a vector field often yields useful information about the properties of the field. For instance, suppose $\mathbf{F}(x, y)$ represents the velocity of a compressible fluid (like a gas) at a point (x, y) in the plane. Then $\mathbf{F}$ assigns a velocity vector to each point in the plane, and the graph of $\mathbf{F}$ provides a picture of the fluid flow. Thus, the flow in Figure 13.4a is a constant, whereas Figure 13.4b suggests a circular flow.

Gravitational, electrical, and magnetic vector fields play an important role in physical applications. We will discuss gravitational fields now, and electrical and magnetic fields later in this section. Accordingly, we begin with Newton's law of gravitation,

The examples in Figure 13.3 show some vector fields obtained using computer software.

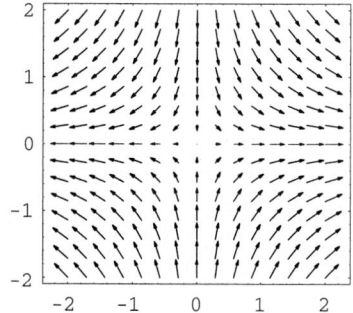

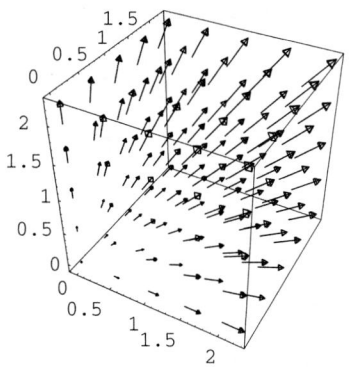

Figure 13.3 Computer generated vector fields

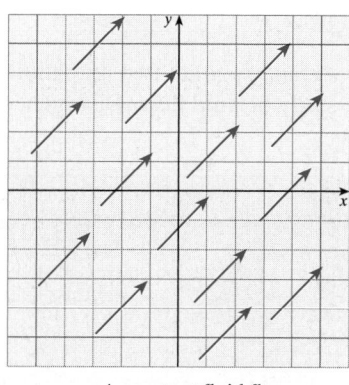

a. A constant fluid flow

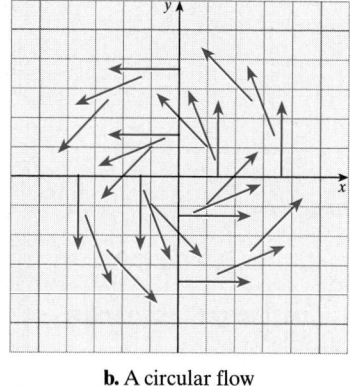

b. A circular flow

Figure 13.4 Flow diagrams

which says that a point mass (particle) m at the origin exerts on a unit point mass located at the point $P(x, y, z)$ a force $\mathbf{F}(x, y, z)$ given by

$$\mathbf{F}(x, y, z) = \frac{Gm}{x^2 + y^2 + z^2}\mathbf{u}(x, y, z)$$

where G is a constant (the universal gravitational constant) and $\mathbf{u}$ is the unit vector extending from the point P toward the origin. The vector field $\mathbf{F}(x, y, z)$ is called the **gravitational field** of the point mass m. Because

$$\mathbf{u}(x, y, z) = \frac{-1}{\sqrt{x^2 + y^2 + z^2}}(x\mathbf{i} + y\mathbf{j} + z\mathbf{k})$$

it follows that

$$\mathbf{F}(x, y, z) = \frac{-Gm}{(x^2 + y^2 + z^2)^{3/2}}(x\mathbf{i} + y\mathbf{j} + z\mathbf{k})$$

Note that the gravitational field $\mathbf{F}$ always points toward the origin and has the same magnitude for any point m located $r = \sqrt{x^2 + y^2 + z^2}$ units from the origin. Such a vector field is called a **central force field**. This force field is shown in Figure 13.5a. Other physical vector fields are shown in Figures 13.5b and 13.5c.

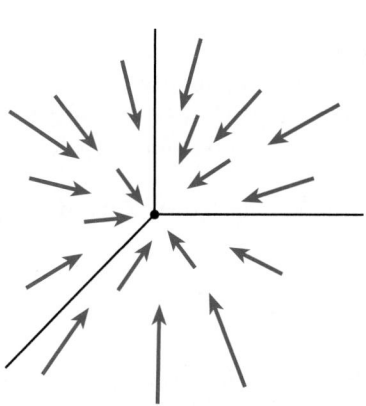

a. A central force field

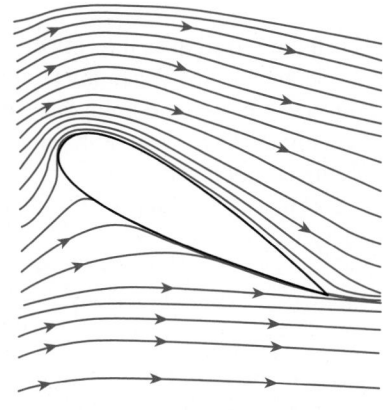

b. Air flow vector field

c. Wind velocity on a map

Figure 13.5 Examples of physical vector fields

DIVERGENCE

Divergence and *curl* are two operations on vector fields that originated in connection with the study of fluid flow. Divergence may be defined as follows.

Divergence

> The **divergence** of a vector field
> $$\mathbf{V}(x, y, z) = u(x, y, z)\mathbf{i} + v(x, y, z)\mathbf{j} + w(x, y, z)\mathbf{k}$$
> is denoted by div $\mathbf{V}$ and is given by
> $$\text{div } \mathbf{V} = \frac{\partial u}{\partial x}(x, y, z) + \frac{\partial v}{\partial y}(x, y, z) + \frac{\partial w}{\partial z}(x, y, z)$$

EXAMPLE 2   Divergence of a vector field

Find the divergence of each of the following vector fields.

a. $\mathbf{F}(x, y) = x^2 y\mathbf{i} + xy^3\mathbf{j}$
b. $\mathbf{G}(x, y, z) = x\mathbf{i} + y^3 z^2\mathbf{j} + xz^3\mathbf{k}$

Solution

a. $\text{div } \mathbf{F} = \dfrac{\partial}{\partial x}(x^2 y) + \dfrac{\partial}{\partial y}(xy^3) = 2xy + 3xy^2$

b. $\text{div } \mathbf{G} = \dfrac{\partial}{\partial x}(x) + \dfrac{\partial}{\partial y}(y^3 z^2) + \dfrac{\partial}{\partial z}(xz^3) = 1 + 3y^2 z^2 + 3xz^2$ ∎

Suppose the vector field

$$\mathbf{V}(x, y, z) = u(x, y, z)\mathbf{i} + v(x, y, z)\mathbf{j} + w(x, y, z)\mathbf{k}$$

div $\mathbf{D} > 0$

Fluid flows from a *source point.*

div $\mathbf{D} < 0$

Fluid flows toward a *sink point.*

div $\mathbf{D} = 0$

Fluid is *incompressible.*

Figure 13.6 Flow of a fluid across a plane region, **D**

represents the velocity of a fluid with density $\delta(x, y, z)$ at a point (x, y, z) in a certain region R in $\mathbb{R}^3$. Then the vector field $\delta\mathbf{V}$ is called the **flux density** and is denoted by **D**. We can think of $\mathbf{D} = \delta\mathbf{V}$ as measuring the "mass flow" of the liquid.

Assuming there are no external processes acting on the fluid that would tend to create or destroy fluid, it can be shown that div $\mathbf{D}$ gives the negative of the time rate change of the density, that is,

$$\text{div } \mathbf{D} = -\frac{\partial \delta}{\partial t}$$

This is often referred to as the **continuity equation** of fluid dynamics. (A derivation is given in Section 13.7.) When div $\mathbf{D} = 0$, **D** is said to be **incompressible**. If div $\mathbf{D} > 0$ at a point (x_0, y_0, z_0), the point is called a **source**; if div $\mathbf{D} < 0$, the point is called a **sink** (see Figure 13.6). The terms *sink*, *source*, and *incompressible* apply to any vector field **F** and are not reserved only for fluid applications.

A useful way to think of the divergence div $\mathbf{V}$ is in terms of the **del operator** defined by

$$\nabla = \frac{\partial}{\partial x}\mathbf{i} + \frac{\partial}{\partial y}\mathbf{j} + \frac{\partial}{\partial z}\mathbf{k}$$

Recall (from Section 11.6) that applying the del operator to the differentiable function $f(x, y, z)$ produces the **gradient field**

$$\nabla f = \frac{\partial f}{\partial x}\mathbf{i} + \frac{\partial f}{\partial y}\mathbf{j} + \frac{\partial f}{\partial z}\mathbf{k}$$

Similarly, by taking the dot product of the operator ∇ with the vector field $\mathbf{V} = u(x, y, z)\mathbf{i} + v(x, y, z)\mathbf{j} + w(x, y, z)\mathbf{k}$, we obtain the divergence

$$\nabla \cdot \mathbf{V} = \left(\frac{\partial}{\partial x}\mathbf{i} + \frac{\partial}{\partial y}\mathbf{j} + \frac{\partial}{\partial z}\mathbf{k}\right) \cdot (u\mathbf{i} + v\mathbf{j} + w\mathbf{k})$$

$$= \frac{\partial}{\partial x}(u) + \frac{\partial}{\partial y}(v) + \frac{\partial}{\partial z}(w)$$

$$= \frac{\partial u}{\partial x} + \frac{\partial v}{\partial y} + \frac{\partial w}{\partial z}$$

$$= \text{div } \mathbf{V}$$

CURL

The del operator may also be used to describe another derivative operation for vector fields, called the *curl*.

Curl

The **curl** of a vector field
$$\mathbf{V}(x, y, z) = u(x, y, z)\mathbf{i} + v(x, y, z)\mathbf{j} + w(x, y, z)\mathbf{k}$$
is denoted by curl $\mathbf{V}$ and is defined by
$$\text{curl } \mathbf{V} = \left(\frac{\partial w}{\partial y} - \frac{\partial v}{\partial z}\right)\mathbf{i} + \left(\frac{\partial u}{\partial z} - \frac{\partial w}{\partial x}\right)\mathbf{j} + \left(\frac{\partial v}{\partial x} - \frac{\partial u}{\partial y}\right)\mathbf{k}$$

Note that

$$\text{curl } \mathbf{V} = \left(\frac{\partial w}{\partial y} - \frac{\partial v}{\partial z}\right)\mathbf{i} - \left(\frac{\partial w}{\partial x} - \frac{\partial u}{\partial z}\right)\mathbf{j} + \left(\frac{\partial v}{\partial x} - \frac{\partial u}{\partial y}\right)\mathbf{k}$$

$$= \begin{vmatrix} \mathbf{i} & \mathbf{j} & \mathbf{k} \\ \dfrac{\partial}{\partial x} & \dfrac{\partial}{\partial y} & \dfrac{\partial}{\partial z} \\ u & v & w \end{vmatrix} \quad \begin{matrix} \leftarrow \text{ Standard basis vectors} \\ \leftarrow \nabla \\ \leftarrow \mathbf{V} \end{matrix}$$

$$= \nabla \times \mathbf{V}$$

The determinant form of curl $\mathbf{V}$ is a convenient device for remembering the definition and is helpful in organizing computations.

Del Operator Forms for Divergence and Curl

Consider a vector field
$$\mathbf{V}(x, y, z) = u(x, y, z)\mathbf{i} + v(x, y, z)\mathbf{j} + w(x, y, z)\mathbf{k}$$
The divergence and curl of $\mathbf{V}$ are given by
$$\text{div } \mathbf{V} = \nabla \cdot \mathbf{V} \quad \text{and} \quad \text{curl } \mathbf{V} = \nabla \times \mathbf{V}$$

WARNING Notice that div $\mathbf{V}$ is a scalar, and curl $\mathbf{V}$ is a vector.

EXAMPLE 3   Curl of a vector field

Find the curl of each of the following vector fields:

$$\mathbf{F} = x^2 yz\mathbf{i} + xy^2 z\mathbf{j} + xyz^2\mathbf{k} \quad \text{and} \quad \mathbf{G} = (x \cos y)\mathbf{i} + xy^2\mathbf{j}$$

Solution

$$\text{curl } \mathbf{F} = \begin{vmatrix} \mathbf{i} & \mathbf{j} & \mathbf{k} \\ \dfrac{\partial}{\partial x} & \dfrac{\partial}{\partial y} & \dfrac{\partial}{\partial z} \\ x^2yz & xy^2z & xyz^2 \end{vmatrix}$$

$$= \left(\frac{\partial}{\partial y}xyz^2 - \frac{\partial}{\partial z}xy^2z \right)\mathbf{i} - \left(\frac{\partial}{\partial x}xyz^2 - \frac{\partial}{\partial z}x^2yz \right)\mathbf{j}$$
$$+ \left(\frac{\partial}{\partial x}xy^2z - \frac{\partial}{\partial y}x^2yz \right)\mathbf{k}$$

$$= (xz^2 - xy^2)\mathbf{i} + (x^2y - yz^2)\mathbf{j} + (y^2z - x^2z)\mathbf{k}$$

$$\text{curl } \mathbf{G} = \begin{vmatrix} \mathbf{i} & \mathbf{j} & \mathbf{k} \\ \dfrac{\partial}{\partial x} & \dfrac{\partial}{\partial y} & \dfrac{\partial}{\partial z} \\ x\cos y & xy^2 & 0 \end{vmatrix}$$

$$= \left[0 - \frac{\partial}{\partial z}xy^2 \right]\mathbf{i} - \left[0 - \frac{\partial}{\partial z}(x\cos y) \right]\mathbf{j} + \left[\frac{\partial}{\partial x}xy^2 - \frac{\partial}{\partial y}(x\cos y) \right]\mathbf{k}$$

$$= (y^2 + x\sin y)\mathbf{k} \qquad \blacksquare$$

EXAMPLE 4   A constant vector field has divergence and curl zero

Let $\mathbf{F}$ be a constant vector field. Show that div $\mathbf{F} = 0$ and curl $\mathbf{F} = \mathbf{0}$.

Solution

Let $\mathbf{F} = a\mathbf{i} + b\mathbf{j} + c\mathbf{k}$ for constants a, b, and c. Then

$$\text{div } \mathbf{F} = \frac{\partial}{\partial x}(a) + \frac{\partial}{\partial y}(b) + \frac{\partial}{\partial z}(c) = 0$$

$$\text{curl } \mathbf{F} = \begin{vmatrix} \mathbf{i} & \mathbf{j} & \mathbf{k} \\ \dfrac{\partial}{\partial x} & \dfrac{\partial}{\partial y} & \dfrac{\partial}{\partial z} \\ a & b & c \end{vmatrix} = 0\mathbf{i} - 0\mathbf{j} + 0\mathbf{k} = \mathbf{0} \qquad \blacksquare$$

WARNING   Example 4 shows that the divergence and curl of a constant vector field are zero, but this does **not** mean that if div $\mathbf{F} = 0$ and curl $\mathbf{F} = \mathbf{0}$, then $\mathbf{F}$ must be a constant. For instance, the nonconstant vector field

$$\mathbf{F}(x, y, z) = x\mathbf{i} + y\mathbf{j} - 2z\mathbf{k}$$

has both div $\mathbf{F} = 0$ and curl $\mathbf{F} = \mathbf{0}$.

TECHNOLOGY NOTE

Derive, Maple, MATLAB, and *Mathematica* will carry out most vector operations. For Example 2, we define $\mathbf{G}(x, y, z) = x\mathbf{i} + y^3z^2\mathbf{j} + xz^3\mathbf{k}$, and use one of these programs:

$$\text{Div}[x, y^3z^2, xz^3] \quad \text{simplifies to} \quad 3xz^2 + 3y^2z^2 + 1$$

You may need to enter a zero, as with $\mathbf{F}(x, y) = x^2y\mathbf{i} + xy^3\mathbf{j}$, as shown here:

$$\text{Div}[x^2y, xy^3, 0] \quad \text{simplifies to} \quad x(3y^2 + 2y)$$

Finally, consider the vector field $\mathbf{F}$ from Example 3, $\mathbf{F} = x^2yz\mathbf{i} + xy^2z\mathbf{j} + xyz^2\mathbf{k}$. We can find the curl:

$$\text{Curl}[x^2yz, xy^2z, xyz^2] \quad \text{simplifies to} \quad [x(z^2 - y^2), y(x^2 - z^2), z(y^2 - x^2)]$$

Combinations of the gradient, divergence, and curl appear in a variety of applications. In particular, note that if f is a differentiable scalar function, its gradient ∇f is a vector field, and we can compute

$$\text{div } \nabla f = \left(\frac{\partial}{\partial x}\mathbf{i} + \frac{\partial}{\partial y}\mathbf{j} + \frac{\partial}{\partial z}\mathbf{k} \right) \cdot \left(\frac{\partial f}{\partial x}\mathbf{i} + \frac{\partial f}{\partial y}\mathbf{j} + \frac{\partial f}{\partial z}\mathbf{k} \right)$$

$$= \frac{\partial^2 f}{\partial x^2} + \frac{\partial^2 f}{\partial y^2} + \frac{\partial^2 f}{\partial z^2}$$

$$= \nabla \cdot \nabla f$$

In the following box, we introduce some special notation and terminology for this operation.

The Laplacian Operator

The Laplacian is named for the French mathematician Pierre Laplace (1749–1827). See the Historical Quest, Section 12.3, Problem 62.

Let $f(x, y, z)$ define a function with continuous first and second partial derivatives. Then the **Laplacian of f** is

$$\nabla^2 f = \nabla \cdot \nabla f = \frac{\partial^2 f}{\partial x^2} + \frac{\partial^2 f}{\partial y^2} + \frac{\partial^2 f}{\partial z^2} = f_{xx} + f_{yy} + f_{zz}$$

The equation $\nabla^2 f = 0$ is called **Laplace's equation**, and a function that satisfies such an equation in a region D is said to be **harmonic** in D.

EXAMPLE 5 Showing a function is harmonic

Show that $f(x, y) = e^x \cos y$ is harmonic.

Solution
$$f_x(x, y) = e^x \cos y \quad \text{and} \quad f_{xx}(x, y) = e^x \cos y$$
$$f_y(x, y) = -e^x \sin y \quad \text{and} \quad f_{yy}(x, y) = -e^x \cos y$$

The Laplacian of f is given by
$$\nabla^2 f(x, y) = f_{xx}(x, y) + f_{yy}(x, y) \qquad\qquad f_{zz} = 0$$
$$= e^x \cos y - e^x \cos y = 0$$

Thus, f is harmonic. ∎

TECHNOLOGY NOTE

Derive, *Maple*, MATLAB, and *Mathematica* will find the Laplacian of a given function. For Example 5, we obtain

$$\text{LAPLACIAN}(e^x \cos(y), [x, y]) \quad \text{which gives} \quad 0$$

If you have access to this technology, verify that

$$\text{LAPLACIAN}(x^2 y^3 z, [x, y, z]) \quad \text{yields} \quad 6x^2 yz + 2y^3 z$$

In many ways, the study of electricity and magnetism is analogous to that of fluid dynamics, and the curl and divergence play an important role in this study. In electromagnetic theory, it is often convenient to regard interaction between electrical charges as forces somewhat like the gravitational force between masses and then to seek quantitative measure of these forces.

One of the great scientific achievements of the nineteenth century was the discovery of the laws of electromagnetism by the English scientist James Clerk Maxwell (see Historical Quest, Section 13.7, Problem 32). These laws have an elegant expression in terms of the divergence and curl. It is known empirically that the force acting on a charge due to an electromagnetic field depends on the position, velocity, and amount of the particular charge, and not on the number of other charges that may be present or how those other charges are moving. Suppose a charge is located at the point (x, y, z) at time t, and consider the electric intensity field $\mathbf{E}(x, y, z, t)$ and the magnetic intensity field $\mathbf{H}(x, y, z, t)$. Then the behavior of the resulting electromagnetic field is determined by

$$\text{div } \mathbf{E} = \frac{Q}{\epsilon} \qquad\qquad \text{div}(\mu\mathbf{H}) = 0$$

$$\text{curl } \mathbf{E} = -\frac{\partial}{\partial t}(\mu\mathbf{H}) \qquad c^2(\text{curl } \mathbf{B}) = \frac{\partial \mathbf{E}}{\partial t} + \frac{\mathbf{J}}{\epsilon}$$

where Q is the *electric charge density* (charge per unit volume), $\mathbf{J}$ is the *electric current density* (rate at which the charge flows through a unit area per second), $\mathbf{B}$ is the magnetic flux density, c is the speed of light, and μ and ϵ are constants called the *permeability* and *permittivity*, respectively. Working with these equations and terms is beyond the scope of this course, but if you are interested there are many references you can consult. One of the best (despite being almost 40 years old) is the classic *Feynman Lectures in Physics* (Reading, Mass.: Addison-Wesley, 1963), by Nobel laureate Richard Feynman, Robert Leighton, and Matthew Sands.

13.1   PROBLEM SET

Ⓐ 1. Exploration Problem   Discuss the del operator and its use in computing the divergence and curl.

2. Exploration Problem   Discuss the difference between a vector valued function and a vector field.

In Problems 3–6, find div $\mathbf{F}$ *and* curl $\mathbf{F}$ *for the given vector function.*

3. $\mathbf{F}(x, y) = x^2\mathbf{i} + xy\mathbf{j} + z^3\mathbf{k}$ **4.** $\mathbf{F}(x, y) = \mathbf{i} + (x^2 + y^2)\mathbf{j}$

5. $\mathbf{F}(x, y, z) = 2y\mathbf{j}$ **6.** $\mathbf{F}(x, y, z) = z\mathbf{i} - \mathbf{j} + 2y\mathbf{k}$

In Problems 7–12, find div $\mathbf{F}$ *and* curl $\mathbf{F}$ *for each vector field $\mathbf{F}$ at the given point.*

7. $\mathbf{F}(x, y, z) = \mathbf{i} + \mathbf{j} + \mathbf{k}$ at $(2, -1, 3)$

8. $\mathbf{F}(x, y, z) = xz\mathbf{i} + y^2z\mathbf{j} + xz\mathbf{k}$ at $(1, -1, 2)$

9. $\mathbf{F}(x, y, z) = xyz\mathbf{i} + y\mathbf{j} + x\mathbf{k}$ at $(1, 2, 3)$

10. $\mathbf{F}(x, y, z) = (\cos y)\mathbf{i} + (\sin y)\mathbf{j} + \mathbf{k}$ at $\left(\frac{\pi}{4}, \pi, 0\right)$

11. $\mathbf{F}(x, y, z) = e^{-xy}\mathbf{i} + e^{xz}\mathbf{j} + e^{yz}\mathbf{k}$ at $(3, 2, 0)$

12. $\mathbf{F}(x, y, z) = (e^{-x}\sin y)\mathbf{i} + (e^{-x}\cos y)\mathbf{j} + \mathbf{k}$ at $(1, 3, -2)$

Find div $\mathbf{F}$ *and* curl $\mathbf{F}$ *for each vector field $\mathbf{F}$ given in Problems 13–28.*

13. $\mathbf{F} = (\sin x)\mathbf{i} + (\cos y)\mathbf{j}$ **14.** $\mathbf{F} = (-\cos x)\mathbf{i} + (\sin y)\mathbf{j}$

15. $\mathbf{F} = x\mathbf{i} - y\mathbf{j}$ **16.** $\mathbf{F} = -x\mathbf{i} + y\mathbf{j}$

17. $\mathbf{F} = \dfrac{x}{\sqrt{x^2 + y^2}}\mathbf{i} + \dfrac{y}{\sqrt{x^2 + y^2}}\mathbf{j}$

18. $\mathbf{F} = x^2\mathbf{i} - y^2\mathbf{j}$

19. $\mathbf{F} = ax\mathbf{i} + by\mathbf{j} + c\mathbf{k}$ for constants a, b, and c

20. $\mathbf{F} = (e^x \sin y)\mathbf{i} + (e^x \cos y)\mathbf{j} + \mathbf{k}$

21. $\mathbf{F} = x^2\mathbf{i} + y^2\mathbf{j} + z^2\mathbf{k}$

22. $\mathbf{F} = y\mathbf{i} + z\mathbf{j} + x\mathbf{k}$

23. $\mathbf{F} = xy\mathbf{i} + yz\mathbf{j} + xz\mathbf{k}$

24. $\mathbf{F} = 2xz\mathbf{i} + 2yz^2\mathbf{j} - \mathbf{k}$

25. $\mathbf{F} = xyz\mathbf{i} + x^2y^2z^2\mathbf{j} + y^2z^3\mathbf{k}$

26. $\mathbf{F} = (\ln z)\mathbf{i} + e^{xy}\mathbf{j} + \tan^{-1}\left(\dfrac{x}{z}\right)\mathbf{k}$

27. $\mathbf{F} = (z^2e^{-x})\mathbf{i} + (y^3 \ln z)\mathbf{j} + (xe^{-y})\mathbf{k}$

28. $\mathbf{F} = \dfrac{x\mathbf{i} + y\mathbf{j} + z\mathbf{k}}{\sqrt{x^2 + y^2 + z^2}}$

Determine whether each scalar function in Problems 29–32 is harmonic.

29. $u(x, y, z) = e^{-x}(\cos y - \sin y)$

30. $v(x, y, z) = (x^2 + y^2 + z^2)^{1/2}$

31. $w(x, y, z) = (x^2 + y^2 + z^2)^{-1/2}$

32. $r(x, y, z) = xyz$

33. Show that the vector field $\mathbf{B} = y^2z\mathbf{i} + xz^3\mathbf{j} + y^2x^2\mathbf{k}$ is incompressible (that is, div $\mathbf{B} = 0$).

34. Find div $\mathbf{F}$, given that $\mathbf{F} = \nabla f$, where $f(x, y, z) = xy^3z^2$.

35. Find div $\mathbf{F}$, given that $\mathbf{F} = \nabla f$, where $f(x, y, z) = x^2yz^3$.

36. If $\mathbf{F}(x, y, z) = 2\mathbf{i} + 2x\mathbf{j} + 3y\mathbf{k}$ and $\mathbf{G}(x, y, z) = x\mathbf{i} - y\mathbf{j} + z\mathbf{k}$, find curl$(\mathbf{F} \times \mathbf{G})$.

37. If $\mathbf{F}(x, y, z) = xy\mathbf{i} + yz\mathbf{j} + z^2\mathbf{k}$ and $\mathbf{G}(x, y, z) = x\mathbf{i} + y\mathbf{j} - z\mathbf{k}$, find curl$(\mathbf{F} \times \mathbf{G})$.

38. If $\mathbf{F}(x, y, z) = 2\mathbf{i} + 2x\mathbf{j} + 3y\mathbf{k}$ and $\mathbf{G}(x, y, z) = x\mathbf{i} - y\mathbf{j} + z\mathbf{k}$, find div$(\mathbf{F} \times \mathbf{G})$.

39. If $\mathbf{F}(x, y, z) = xy\mathbf{i} + yz\mathbf{j} + z^2\mathbf{k}$ and $\mathbf{G}(x, y, z) = x\mathbf{i} + y\mathbf{j} - z\mathbf{k}$, find div$(\mathbf{F} \times \mathbf{G})$.

Ⓑ 40. Let $\mathbf{A}$ be a constant vector and let $\mathbf{R} = x\mathbf{i} + y\mathbf{j} + z\mathbf{k}$. Show that div$(\mathbf{A} \times \mathbf{R}) = 0$.

41. Let $\mathbf{A}$ be a constant vector and let $\mathbf{R} = x\mathbf{i} + y\mathbf{j} + z\mathbf{k}$. Show that curl$(\mathbf{A} \times \mathbf{R}) = 2\mathbf{A}$.

42. If $\mathbf{F}(x, y) = u(x, y)\mathbf{i} + v(x, y)\mathbf{j}$, show that curl $\mathbf{F} = \mathbf{0}$ if and only if $\dfrac{\partial u}{\partial y} = \dfrac{\partial v}{\partial x}$.

43. Consider a rigid body that is rotating about the z-axis (counterclockwise from above) with constant angular velocity $\omega = a\mathbf{i} + b\mathbf{j} + c\mathbf{k}$. If P is a point in the body located at $\mathbf{R} = x\mathbf{i} + y\mathbf{j} + z\mathbf{k}$, the velocity at P is given by the vector field $\mathbf{V} = \omega \times \mathbf{R}$.
  a. Express $\mathbf{V}$ in terms of the vectors $\mathbf{i}$, $\mathbf{j}$, and $\mathbf{k}$.
  b. Find div $\mathbf{V}$ and curl $\mathbf{V}$.
44. Exploration Problem If $\mathbf{F} = \langle f, g, h \rangle$ is an arbitrary vector field whose components are twice differentiable, what can be said about curl(curl $\mathbf{F}$)?
45. Which (if any) of the following is the same as div($\mathbf{F} \times \mathbf{G}$) for all vector fields $\mathbf{F}$ and $\mathbf{G}$?

  I. $(\text{div } \mathbf{F})(\text{div } \mathbf{G})$
  II. $(\text{curl } \mathbf{F}) \cdot \mathbf{G} - \mathbf{F} \cdot (\text{curl } \mathbf{G})$
  III. $\mathbf{F}(\text{div } \mathbf{G}) + (\text{div } \mathbf{F})\mathbf{G}$
  IV. $(\text{curl } \mathbf{F}) \cdot \mathbf{G} + \mathbf{F} \cdot (\text{curl } \mathbf{G})$

In Problems 46–55, prove the given property for the vector fields $\mathbf{F}$ and $\mathbf{G}$, scalar c, and scalar functions f and g. Assume that all required partial derivatives exist and are continuous.

46. $\text{div}(c\mathbf{F}) = c \text{ div } \mathbf{F}$
47. $\text{div}(\mathbf{F} + \mathbf{G}) = \text{div } \mathbf{F} + \text{div } \mathbf{G}$
48. $\text{curl}(\mathbf{F} + \mathbf{G}) = \text{curl } \mathbf{F} + \text{curl } \mathbf{G}$
49. $\text{curl}(c\mathbf{F}) = c \text{ curl } \mathbf{F}$
50. $\text{curl}(f\mathbf{F}) = f \text{ curl } \mathbf{F} + (\nabla f \times \mathbf{F})$
51. $\text{div}(f\mathbf{F}) = f \text{ div } \mathbf{F} + (\nabla f \cdot \mathbf{F})$
52. $\text{curl}(\nabla f + \text{curl } \mathbf{F}) = \text{curl}(\nabla f) + \text{curl}(\text{curl } \mathbf{F})$
53. $\text{div}(f\nabla g) = f \text{ div } \nabla g + \nabla f \cdot \nabla g$
54. The curl of the gradient of a function is always $\mathbf{0}$. That is, $\nabla \times (\nabla f) = \mathbf{0}$.
55. The divergence of the curl of a vector field is 0. That is, $\text{div}(\text{curl } \mathbf{F}) = 0$.

In Problems 56–60, $\mathbf{R} = \langle x, y, z \rangle$, and $r = \|\mathbf{R}\| = \sqrt{x^2 + y^2 + z^2}$. In each case, verify the given identity or answer the question.

56. $\text{curl } \mathbf{R} = \mathbf{0}$; what is div $\mathbf{R}$?
57. $\text{div}\left(\dfrac{1}{r^3}\mathbf{R}\right) = 0$
58. $\text{curl}\left(\dfrac{1}{r^3}\mathbf{R}\right) = \mathbf{0}$
59. $\text{div}(r\mathbf{R}) = 4r$
60. $\text{div}(\nabla r) = \dfrac{2}{r}$
61. Exploration Problem State and prove an identity for $\text{div}(\nabla(fg))$, where f and g are differentiable scalar functions of x, y, and z.
62. Counterexample Problem Let $\mathbf{F} = \langle x^2 y, yz^2, zy^2 \rangle$. Either find a vector field $\mathbf{G}$ such that $\mathbf{F} = \text{curl } \mathbf{G}$, or show that no such $\mathbf{G}$ exists.

13.2 Line Integrals

IN THIS SECTION definition of a line integral; line integrals with respect to x, y, and z; line integrals of vector fields; applications of line integrals: mass and work

A line integral is an integral whose integrand is evaluated at points along a curve in $\mathbb{R}^2$ or in $\mathbb{R}^3$. We will introduce line integrals in this section and show how they can be used for a variety of purposes in mathematics and physics.

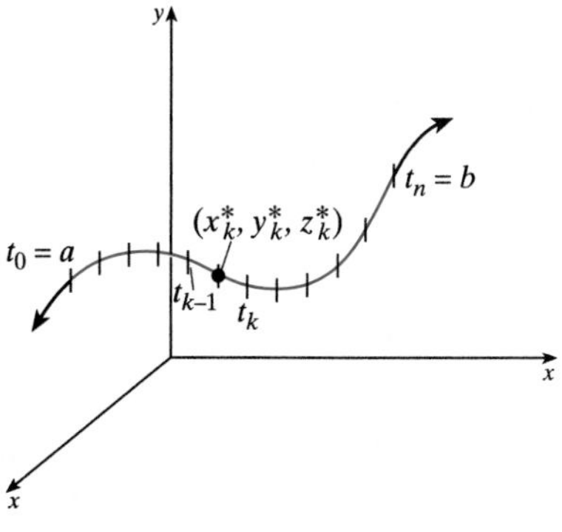

DEFINITION OF A LINE INTEGRAL

Let C be a smooth curve, with parametric equations $x = x(t)$, $y = y(t)$, $z = z(t)$ for $a \leq t \leq b$, that lies within the domain of a function $f(x, y, z)$. We say that C is **orientable** if it is possible to describe direction along the curve for increasing t.
  To define a line integral, we begin by partitioning C into n subarcs, the kth of which has length Δs_k. Let (x_k^*, y_k^*, z_k^*) be a point chosen arbitrarily from the kth subarc (see Figure 13.7). Form the Riemann sum

$$\sum_{k=1}^{n} f(x_k^*, y_k^*, z_k^*)\Delta s_k$$

and let $\|\Delta s\|$ denote the largest subarc length in the partition. Then, if the limit

$$\lim_{\|\Delta s\| \to 0} \sum_{k=1}^{n} f(x_k^*, y_k^*, z_k^*)\Delta s_k$$

Figure 13.7 The curve C partitioned into subarcs

exists, we call this limit the *line integral* of f over C and denote it by $\displaystyle\int_C f(x, y, z)\,ds$.

Line Integral over a Smooth Curve

> If $f(x, y, z)$ is defined on the smooth curve C with parametric equations $x = x(t), y = y(t), z = z(t)$, then the **line integral** of f over C is given by
>
> $$\int_C f(x, y, z)\, ds = \lim_{\|\Delta s\| \to 0} \sum_{k=1}^{n} f(x_k^*, y_k^*, z_k^*) \Delta s_k$$
>
> provided that this limit exists. If C is a closed curve, we indicate the line integral of f around C by $\displaystyle\oint_C f\, ds$.

It can be shown that the limit that defines the line integral $\displaystyle\int_C f\, ds$ always exists if f is continuous at each point of C. Also, since the curve C is smooth, the component functions $x(t)$, $y(t)$, and $z(t)$ will all be continuously differentiable. Thus, we have

$$ds = \sqrt{[x'(t)]^2 + [y'(t)]^2 + [z'(t)]^2}\, dt$$

so the line integral can be written entirely in terms of t:

$$\int_C f(x, y, z)\, ds = \int_a^b f(x(t), y(t), z(t)) \sqrt{[x'(t)]^2 + [y'(t)]^2 + [z'(t)]^2}\, dt$$

Similarly, if $f(x, y)$ is a function of only two variables and C is a curve in the plane, then

$$\int_C f(x, y)\, ds = \int_a^b f(x(t), y(t)) \sqrt{[x'(t)]^2 + [y'(t)]^2}\, dt$$

EXAMPLE 1 Evaluating a line integral in three variables

Evaluate the line integral $\displaystyle\int_C x^2 z\, ds$, where C is the helix $x = \cos t, y = 2t, z = \sin t$, for $0 \le t \le \pi$.

Solution

Since $x'(t) = -\sin t$, $y'(t) = 2$, $z'(t) = \cos t$, the line integral is

$$\int_C x^2 z\, ds = \int_0^\pi [x(t)]^2 z(t) \sqrt{[x'(t)]^2 + [y'(t)]^2 + [z'(t)]^2}\, dt$$

$$= \int_0^\pi (\cos t)^2 (\sin t) \sqrt{(-\sin t)^2 + (2)^2 + (\cos t)^2}\, dt$$

$$= \int_0^\pi \sqrt{5} \cos^2 t \sin t\, dt$$

$$= \left. \frac{-\sqrt{5}}{3} \cos^3 t \right|_0^\pi$$

$$= \frac{2\sqrt{5}}{3} \qquad \blacksquare$$

The definition of a line integral can be extended to curves that are *piecewise smooth* in the sense that they are the union of a finite number of smooth curves with only endpoints in common, as shown in Figure 13.8.

In particular, if C is comprised of a number of smooth subarcs $C_1, C_2, \ldots, C_n$, then

$$\int_C f(x, y, z)\, ds = \int_{C_1} f(x, y, z)\, ds + \int_{C_2} f(x, y, z)\, ds + \cdots + \int_{C_n} f(x, y, z)\, ds$$

This definition of line integration is illustrated in the following example.

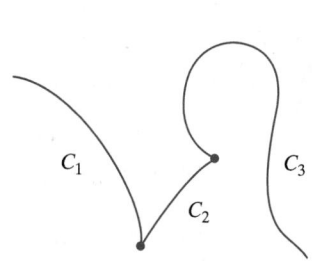

Figure 13.8 Piecewise smooth curve

EXAMPLE 2 **Evaluating a line integral over a union of curves**

Evaluate the line integral $\int_C xy\,ds$, where C consists of the line segment C_1 from $(-3, 3)$ to $(0, 0)$, followed by the portion of the curve C_2: $16y = x^4$ between $(0, 0)$ and $(2, 1)$.

Solution

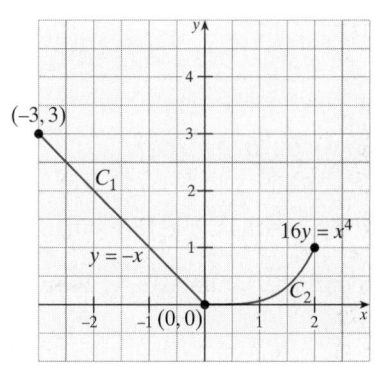

Figure 13.9 The curve C in Example 2

The curve C is shown in Figure 13.9. The segment C_1 is part of the line $y = -x$ and can be parameterized by the equations $x = t$, $y = -t$ over the interval $-3 \le t \le 0$. On this curve, we have

$$x'(t) = 1, \quad y'(t) = -1, \quad \text{so} \quad ds = \sqrt{(1)^2 + (-1)^2}\,dt = \sqrt{2}\,dt$$

and the line integral of $f(x, y) = xy$ over C_1 is

$$\int_{C_1} xy\,ds = \int_{-3}^{0} (t)(-t)\sqrt{2}\,dt$$

$$= \int_{-3}^{0} -\sqrt{2}\,t^2\,dt$$

$$= -9\sqrt{2}$$

The curve C_2, $16y = x^4$, can be parameterized by the equations $x = 2t$, $y = \frac{1}{16}x^4 = \frac{1}{16}(2t)^4 = t^4$ for $0 \le t \le 1$. We find that

$$x'(t) = 2, \quad y'(t) = 4t^3, \quad \text{so} \quad ds = \sqrt{(2)^2 + (4t^3)^2}\,dt$$

and the line integral over C_2 is

$$\int_{C_2} xy\,ds = \int_{0}^{1} (2t)(t^4)\sqrt{4 + 16t^6}\,dt$$

$$= \frac{1}{9}(1 + 4t^6)^{3/2}\Big|_{0}^{1}$$

$$= \frac{1}{9}(5\sqrt{5} - 1)$$

Thus, the line integral over C is given by the sum

$$\int_C xy\,ds = \int_{C_1} xy\,ds + \int_{C_2} xy\,ds = -9\sqrt{2} + \frac{1}{9}(5\sqrt{5} - 1) \quad\blacksquare$$

THEOREM 13.1 **Properties of line integrals**

Let f be a given scalar function defined on a piecewise smooth, orientable curve C. Then, for any constant k,

Constant multiple rule: $\int_C kf\,ds = k\int_C f\,ds$

Sum rule: $\int_C (f_1 + f_2)\,ds = \int_C f_1\,ds + \int_C f_2\,ds$
where f_1 and f_2 are scalar functions defined on C.

Opposite direction rule: $\int_{-C} f\,ds = -\int_C f\,ds$
where $-C$ denotes the curve C traversed in the opposite direction.

Subdivision rule: $\int_C f\,ds = \int_{C_1} f\,ds + \int_{C_2} f\,ds + \cdots + \int_{C_n} f\,ds$
where C is the union of smooth orientable subarcs $C = C_1 \cup C_2 \cup \cdots \cup C_n$ with only endpoints in common.

Proof The proof follows directly from the properties of limits and the definition of a line integral. ❏

LINE INTEGRALS WITH RESPECT TO $x, y,$ AND z

If Δs is replaced by Δx in the discussion leading to the definition of the line integral $\int_C f(x, y, z)\, ds$, we obtain a definition for the line integral $\int_C f(x, y, z)\, dx$. Since $x = x(t)$ is differentiable, we have $dx = x'(t)\, dt$ and the line integral of f with respect to x can be evaluated as follows:

$$\int_C f(x, y, z)\, dx = \int_a^b f[x(t), y(t), z(t)]x'(t)\, dt$$

Similarly, if g and h are continuous on C, then

$$\int_C g\, dy = \int_a^b g[x(t), y(t), z(t)]y'(t)\, dt$$

$$\int_C h\, dz = \int_a^b h[x(t), y(t), z(t)]z'(t)\, dt$$

By combining the line integrals with respect to the coordinate variables x, y, and z, we obtain a line integral of the form

$$\int_C [f(x, y, z)\, dx + g(x, y, z)\, dy + h(x, y, z)\, dz]$$

EXAMPLE 3   Evaluating a line integral with respect to coordinate variables

Evaluate the line integral

$$\int_C [y\, dx - z\, dy + x\, dz]$$

where C is the curve with parametric equations $x = t^2$, $y = e^{-t}$, $z = e^t$ for $0 \leq t \leq 1$.

Solution

Since $x'(t) = 2t$, $y'(t) = -e^{-t}$, and $z'(t) = e^t$, we have

$$\int_C [y\, dx - z\, dy + x\, dz] = \int_0^1 e^{-t}(2t\, dt) - e^t(-e^{-t}\, dt) + t^2(e^t\, dt)]$$

$$= \int_0^1 [2te^{-t} + 1 + t^2 e^t]\, dt$$

$$= \left[-2e^{-t}(t+1) + t + e^t(t^2 - 2t + 2) \right]\Big|_0^1$$

$$= [-4e^{-1} + 1 + e(1 - 2 + 2)] - [-2 + 0 + 2]$$

$$= e - 4e^{-1} + 1 \qquad \blacksquare$$

LINE INTEGRALS OF VECTOR FIELDS

We will now discuss what it means to compute the *line integral of a vector field*.

Line Integral of a Vector Field

Let $\mathbf{F}(x, y, z) = u(x, y, z)\mathbf{i} + v(x, y, z)\mathbf{j} + w(x, y, z)\mathbf{k}$ be a vector field, and let C be a piecewise smooth orientable curve with parametric representation

$$\mathbf{R}(t) = x(t)\mathbf{i} + y(t)\mathbf{j} + z(t)\mathbf{k} \qquad \text{for } a \leq t \leq b$$

Using $d\mathbf{R} = dx\mathbf{i} + dy\mathbf{j} + dz\mathbf{k}$, we define the **line integral of F along C** by

$$\int_C \mathbf{F} \cdot d\mathbf{R} = \int_C (u\, dx + v\, dy + w\, dz) = \int_C \mathbf{F}[\mathbf{R}(t)] \cdot \mathbf{R}'(t)\, dt$$

$$= \int_a^b \left[u[x(t), y(t), z(t)]\frac{dx}{dt} + v[x(t), y(t), z(t)]\frac{dy}{dt} + w[x(t), y(t), z(t)]\frac{dz}{dt} \right] dt$$

EXAMPLE 4   Evaluating a line integral of a vector field

Evaluate $\int_C \mathbf{F} \cdot d\mathbf{R}$, where $\mathbf{F} = (y^2 - z^2)\mathbf{i} + (2yz)\mathbf{j} - x^2\mathbf{k}$ and C is the curve defined parametrically by $x = t^2$, $y = 2t$, and $z = t$ for $0 \leq t \leq 1$.

Solution

Rewrite $\mathbf{F}$ using the parameter t:

$$\mathbf{F} = [(2t)^2 - (t)^2]\mathbf{i} + [2(2t)(t)]\mathbf{j} - [(t^2)^2]\mathbf{k} = 3t^2\mathbf{i} + 4t^2\mathbf{j} - t^4\mathbf{k}$$

Because $\mathbf{R}(t) = t^2\mathbf{i} + 2t\mathbf{j} + t\mathbf{k}$, we have $d\mathbf{R} = (2t\,dt)\mathbf{i} + (2\,dt)\mathbf{j} + dt\mathbf{k}$, so

$$\mathbf{F} \cdot d\mathbf{R} = (3t^2)(2t\,dt) + (4t^2)(2\,dt) + (-t^4)(dt)$$
$$= (6t^3 + 8t^2 - t^4)\,dt$$

Thus,

$$\int_C \mathbf{F} \cdot d\mathbf{R} = \int_0^1 (6t^3 + 8t^2 - t^4)\,dt = \left[\frac{3}{2}t^4 + \frac{8}{3}t^3 - \frac{1}{5}t^5\right]\Big|_0^1 = \frac{119}{30} \qquad \blacksquare$$

A line integral over a curve C does not depend on the parameterization used for C. This property of line integrals is illustrated in the following example.

EXAMPLE 5   The value of a line integral is independent of parameterization

Let $\mathbf{F} = y\mathbf{i} + x\mathbf{j}$ and let C be the top half of the circle $x^2 + y^2 = 4$ traversed counterclockwise from $(2, 0)$ to $(-2, 0)$, as shown in Figure 13.10. Evaluate the line integral $\int_C \mathbf{F} \cdot d\mathbf{R}$ for each of the following parameterizations of the curve C.

a. $x = 2\cos\theta$, $y = 2\sin\theta$, $0 \leq \theta \leq \pi$
b. $x = -t$, $y = \sqrt{4 - t^2}$, $-2 \leq t \leq 2$

Solution

a. With the parameterization $x = 2\cos\theta$, $y = 2\sin\theta$, we find that $x'(\theta) = -2\sin\theta$, $y'(\theta) = 2\cos\theta$

$$\int_C \mathbf{F} \cdot d\mathbf{R} = \int_C [y\,dx + x\,dy]$$
$$= \int_0^\pi [(2\sin\theta)(-2\sin\theta) + (2\cos\theta)(2\cos\theta)]\,d\theta$$
$$= \int_0^\pi 4(\cos^2\theta - \sin^2\theta)\,d\theta$$
$$= \int_0^\pi 4\cos 2\theta\,d\theta$$
$$= 0$$

b. For the parameterization $x = -t$, $y = \sqrt{4 - t^2}$, we have $x'(t) = -1$, $y'(t) = \dfrac{-t}{\sqrt{4 - t^2}}$. We find that

$$\int_C [y\,dx + x\,dy] = \int_{-2}^2 \left[\sqrt{4 - t^2}(-1) + (-t)\left(\frac{-t}{\sqrt{4 - t^2}}\right)\right]\,dt$$
$$= \int_{-2}^2 \frac{-4 + 2t^2}{\sqrt{4 - t^2}}\,dt$$
$$= \left[-t\sqrt{4 - t^2}\right]\Big|_{-2}^2$$
$$= 0$$

This is the same result that was obtained using the parameterization in part **a.** $\qquad \blacksquare$

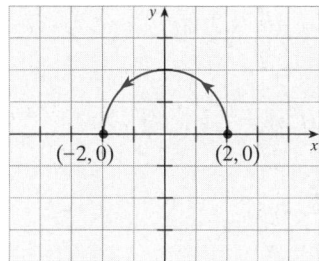

Figure 13.10 Graph of the semicircle C

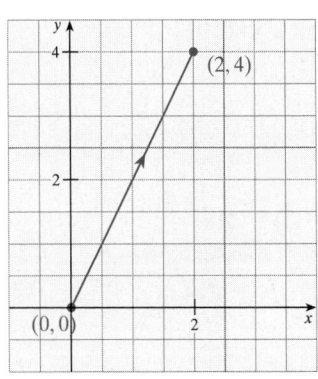

a. The line segment path

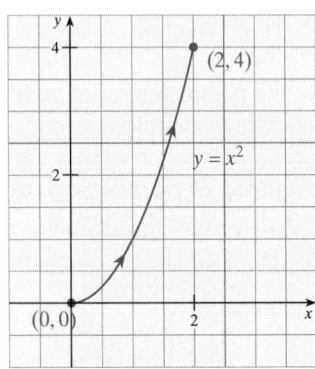

b. The parabolic path

Figure 13.11 A line integral along different paths

EXAMPLE 6 Evaluating line integrals along different paths

Let $\mathbf{F} = xy^2\mathbf{i} + x^2 y\mathbf{j}$ and evaluate the line integral $\displaystyle\int_C \mathbf{F} \cdot d\mathbf{R}$ between the points $(0, 0)$ and $(2, 4)$ along the following paths:

a. the line segment connecting the points
b. the parabolic arc $y = x^2$ connecting the points

Solution

The two paths we are considering are shown in Figure 13.11.

a. The line joining the given points has equation $y = 2x$, which may be parameterized by setting $x = t$, $y = 2t$ for $0 \le t \le 2$. Thus,

$$\mathbf{R}(t) = t\mathbf{i} + 2t\mathbf{j} \qquad \text{so that} \quad d\mathbf{R} = dt\,\mathbf{i} + 2\,dt\,\mathbf{j}$$

In terms of t, we find $\mathbf{F} = 4t^3\mathbf{i} + 2t^3\mathbf{j}$ and

$$\mathbf{F} \cdot d\mathbf{R} = 4t^3\,dt + 4t^3\,dt = 8t^3\,dt$$

$$\int_C \mathbf{F} \cdot d\mathbf{R} = \int_0^2 8t^3\,dt = \left[2t^4\right]\Big|_0^2 = 32$$

b. The parabola $y = x^2$ can be parameterized by setting $x = t$, $y = t^2$ for $0 \le t \le 2$. Thus,

$$\mathbf{R}(t) = t\mathbf{i} + t^2\mathbf{j} \qquad \text{so that} \quad d\mathbf{R} = dt\,\mathbf{i} + 2t\,dt\,\mathbf{j}$$

In terms of t,

$$\mathbf{F} = xy^2\mathbf{i} + x^2 y\mathbf{j} = (t)(t^2)^2\mathbf{i} + (t)^2(t^2)\mathbf{j} = t^5\mathbf{i} + t^4\mathbf{j}$$

and

$$\mathbf{F} \cdot d\mathbf{R} = t^5\,dt + 2t^5\,dt = 3t^5\,dt$$

$$\int_C \mathbf{F} \cdot d\mathbf{R} = \int_0^2 3t^5\,dt = \left[\frac{1}{2}t^6\right]\Big|_0^2 = 32 \qquad \blacksquare$$

Note: The "line" integral should be thought of as the "curve" integral. The equation(s) of a curve are needed so that the integral can be expressed in terms of a single variable.

In Example 6 we see that the value of the line integral is the same for both paths. Indeed, it can be shown that for the vector field $\mathbf{F} = xy^2\mathbf{i} + x^2 y\mathbf{j}$, the line integral $\displaystyle\int_C \mathbf{F} \cdot d\mathbf{R}$ along any path C joining $(0, 0)$ to $(2, 4)$ has the same value. This is not true for every $\mathbf{F}$ (see Problem 58) but when it is true, the line integral is said to be **independent of path** or **path independent**. Path independence is an important feature of certain vector fields and will be discussed in detail in the next section.

APPLICATIONS OF LINE INTEGRALS: MASS AND WORK

Line integrals were developed in the nineteenth century, primarily to deal with problems in physics involving force, fluid flow, electricity, and magnetism. We will show how line integration can be used to compute the mass of a thin wire and the work performed by an object moving along a curve in a force field. Additional applications are examined in the problem set and in Sections 13.3 and 13.4.

Consider a thin wire with the shape of a curve C and let $\delta(x, y, z)$ be the density (mass per unit length) at each point $P(x, y, z)$ on the wire. Suppose the curve is described by parametric equations $x = x(t)$, $y = y(t)$, $z = z(t)$ for $a \le t \le b$, and subdivide the parameter interval $[a, b]$ into n equal parts. This induces a partition of the portion of the curve covered by the wire into n subarcs. Let Δs_k be the length of the kth subarc, and let $P_k(x_k^*, y_k^*, z_k^*)$ be a point chosen arbitrarily from this subarc. Then, the mass of the subarc is approximately

$$\Delta m_k = \delta(x_k^*, y_k^*, z_k^*)\Delta s_k$$

and the sum $\sum_{k=1}^{n} \Delta m_k$ approximates the total mass of the wire. We improve the approximation by taking more and more subdivision points, and the actual mass of the wire is given by the limiting value

$$m = \lim_{n \to \infty} \sum_{k=1}^{n} \delta(x_k^*, y_k^*, z_k^*) \Delta s_k = \int_C \delta(x, y, z) \, ds$$

The **center of mass** of the wire is then the point $(\bar{x}, \bar{y}, \bar{z})$, where

$$\bar{x} = \frac{1}{m} \int_C x\delta(x, y, z) \, ds \qquad \bar{y} = \frac{1}{m} \int_C y\delta(x, y, z) \, ds \qquad \bar{z} = \frac{1}{m} \int_C z\delta(x, y, z) \, ds$$

EXAMPLE 7 Computing the mass of a thin wire using line integration

A wire has the shape of the curve

$$x = \sqrt{2} \sin t \qquad y = \cos t \qquad z = \cos t \qquad \text{for } 0 \leq t \leq \pi$$

If the wire has density $\delta(x, y, z) = xyz$ at each point (x, y, z), what is its mass?

Solution

We note that $x'(t) = \sqrt{2} \cos t$, $y'(t) = z'(t) = -\sin t$. The mass is given by the line integral

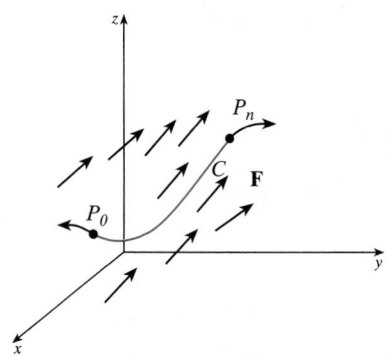

a. An object moving along a curve C in a force field $\mathbf{F}$

$$\begin{aligned}
m &= \int_C \delta(x, y, z) \, dx \\
&= \int_C xyz \sqrt{[x'(t)]^2 + [y'(t)]^2 + [z'(t)]^2} \, dt \\
&= \int_C \sqrt{2} \sin t \cos^2 t \sqrt{(\sqrt{2} \cos t)^2 + (-\sin t)^2 + (-\sin t)^2} \, dt \\
&= \int_0^\pi \sqrt{2} \sin t \cos^2 t \sqrt{2(\cos^2 t + \sin^2 t)} \, dt \\
&= 2 \int_0^\pi \cos^2 t \sin t \, dt \\
&= \frac{4}{3}
\end{aligned}$$

In Problem 49, you are asked to determine the center of mass of this wire. Note that the center of mass may not lie on the curve, or wire, itself. ∎

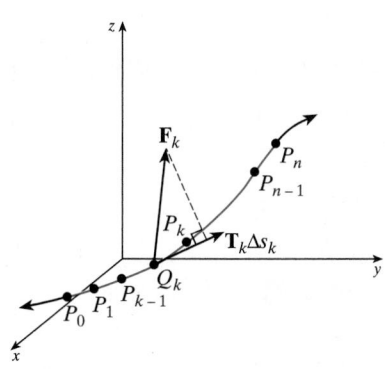

b. The work performed as the object moves along the kth subarc is $W_k = \mathbf{F}_k \cdot \mathbf{T}_k \Delta s_k$

Figure 13.12 Work performed as an object moves in a force field $\mathbf{F}$ along a curve C

One of the most important physical applications of line integration is in computing work. Recall from Section 9.3, that if an object moves along a line with displacement $\mathbf{D}$ in a constant force field $\mathbf{F}$, the work done is $W = \mathbf{F} \cdot \mathbf{D}$. We now consider the case where $\mathbf{F}$ is a variable force field and the object moves along an orientable curve C. Assume that C is parameterized by $\mathbf{R}(t)$ and that the object moves in the direction of increasing t. Partition C with subdivision points $P_0, P_1, \ldots, P_n$, as shown in Figure 13.12.

For $k = 1, 2, \ldots, n$, let $Q_k(x_k^*, y_k^*, z_k^*)$ be a point chosen arbitrarily from the kth subarc C_k (the one with endpoints P_{k-1} and P_k), and let $\mathbf{F}_k = \mathbf{F}(x_k^*, y_k^*, z_k^*)$. If the length Δs_k of the subarc C_k is small, the force will be approximately constant and we assume it has the constant value $\mathbf{F}_k$ on the subarc. Also, the direction of motion will not change much over the subarc, so we can assume that the object will move a distance of Δs_k in the direction of the unit tangent $\mathbf{T}_k = \mathbf{T}(x_k^*, y_k^*, z_k^*)$, for a linear displacement of $\mathbf{T}_k \Delta s_k$. Therefore, we can approximate the work performed over the kth subarc by

$$W_k \approx \mathbf{F}_k \cdot \mathbf{T}_k \Delta s_k$$

By adding the contributions along all n subarcs, we obtain the sum $\displaystyle\sum_{k=1}^{n} \mathbf{F}_k \cdot \mathbf{T}_k \Delta s_k$ as an approximation to the total work performed as the object moves along C in the force field $\mathbf{F}$. As the length of the largest subarc $\|\Delta s\|$ tends to 0, this approximating sum approaches the value of the line integral $\displaystyle\int_C \mathbf{F} \cdot \mathbf{T}\, ds$; that is,

$$W = \lim_{\|\Delta s\| \to 0} \sum_{k=1}^{n} \mathbf{F}_k \cdot \mathbf{T}_k \Delta s_k = \int_C \mathbf{F} \cdot \mathbf{T}\, ds$$

These observations lead us to consider **work as a line integral**.

Work as a Line Integral

Let $\mathbf{F}$ be a continuous force field over a domain D. Then the work W performed as an object moves along a smooth curve C in D is given by the integral

$$W = \int_C \mathbf{F} \cdot \mathbf{T}\, ds$$

where $\mathbf{T}$ is the unit tangent at each point on C.

Recall (from Section 10.4) that $\mathbf{T} = \dfrac{d\mathbf{R}}{ds}$ where $\mathbf{R}$ is the position vector of the object moving on C. Thus, the work can also be given by the line integral

$$W = \int_C \mathbf{F} \cdot \frac{d\mathbf{R}}{ds}\, ds = \int_C \mathbf{F} \cdot d\mathbf{R}$$

This form of the line integral for work is used in the following example.

EXAMPLE 8   **Work as a line integral**

An object moves in the force field $\mathbf{F} = y^2 \mathbf{i} + 2(x+1)y\mathbf{j}$. How much work is performed as the object moves from the point $(2, 0)$ counterclockwise along the elliptical path $x^2 + 4y^2 = 4$ to $(0, 1)$, then back to $(2, 0)$ along the line segment joining the two points, as shown in Figure 13.13.

Solution

If C is the trajectory of the moving object, the work performed is $W = \displaystyle\oint_C \mathbf{F} \cdot d\mathbf{R}$. Let C_1 be the top (elliptical) part of C, and let C_2 be the bottom (linear) part.

The curve C_1 can be parameterized by the equations

$$x = 2\cos t \qquad y = \sin t \qquad \text{for } 0 \le t \le \frac{\pi}{2}$$

(since $x^2 + 4y^2 = 4$), so the position vector for C_1 is $\mathbf{R}_1 = \langle 2\cos t, \sin t \rangle$. Thus, we have $\mathbf{R}_1' = \langle -2\sin t, \cos t \rangle$ and the work performed as the object moves along C_1 is

$$
\begin{aligned}
W_1 = \int_{C_1} \mathbf{F} \cdot d\mathbf{R}_1 &= \int_0^{\pi/2} \mathbf{F}[\mathbf{R}_1(t)] \cdot \mathbf{R}_1'(t)\, dt \\
&= \int_0^{\pi/2} [(\sin^2 t)(-2\sin t) + 2(2\cos t + 1)\sin t(\cos t)]\, dt \\
&= \int_0^{\pi/2} (-2\sin^3 t + 4\cos^2 t \sin t + 2\sin t \cos t)\, dt \\
&= \int_0^{\pi/2} (-2\sin^2 t + 4\cos^2 t + 2\cos t)\sin t\, dt
\end{aligned}
$$

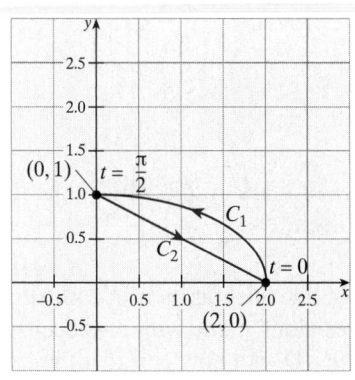

Figure 13.13 The curve C

$$= \int_0^{\pi/2} (6\cos^2 t + 2\cos t - 2) \sin t \, dt$$

$$= -\int_1^0 (6u^2 + 2u - 2) \, du$$

$$= 1$$

> Let $u = \cos t$;
> $du = -\sin t \, dt$.
> If $t = 0, u = 1$,
> and if $t = \frac{\pi}{2}, u = 0$.

For the line segment C_2, a parameterization is

$$x = 2t \qquad y = 1 - t \qquad 0 \le t \le 1$$

The position vector is $\mathbf{R}_2 = \langle 2t, 1 - t \rangle$, so $\mathbf{R}_2' = \langle 2, -1 \rangle$ and the work performed as the object moves along C_2 is

$$W_2 = \int_{C_2} \mathbf{F} \cdot d\mathbf{R}_2 = \int_0^1 \mathbf{F}[\mathbf{R}_2(t)] \cdot \mathbf{R}_2'(t) \, dt$$

$$= \int_0^1 [(1-t)^2(2) + 2(2t+1)(1-t)(-1)] \, dt$$

$$= \int_0^1 [6t^2 - 6t] \, dt$$

$$= -1$$

Thus, the total work performed as the object moves along the curve $C = C_1 \cup C_2$ is

$$W = \oint_C \mathbf{F} \cdot d\mathbf{R} = \int_{C_1} \mathbf{F} \cdot d\mathbf{R} + \int_{C_2} \mathbf{F} \cdot d\mathbf{R} = 1 + (-1) = 0 \qquad \blacksquare$$

It can be shown that the work performed as an object moves around any closed path in the force in Example 8 will always be 0. When this occurs, the force is said to be **conservative**. We will discuss conservative force fields in Sections 13.3 and 13.4.

13.2 PROBLEM SET

Ⓐ 1. WHAT DOES THIS SAY? Explain the difference between $\int_C f \, ds$ and $\int_C f \, dx$.

2. WHAT DOES THIS SAY? Discuss the evaluation of the line integral $\int_C \mathbf{F} \cdot d\mathbf{R}$.

In Problems 3–12, evaluate the given line integral over the curve C with the prescribed parameterization.

3. $\displaystyle\int_C \frac{1}{3+y} \, ds$ for $C: x = 2t^{3/2}, y = 3t, 0 \le t \le 1$

4. $\displaystyle\int_C (3x - 2y) \, ds$ for $C: x = \sin t, y = \cos t, 0 \le t \le \pi$

5. $\displaystyle\int_C \frac{y^2}{x^3} \, ds$ for $C: x = 2t, y = t^4, 0 \le t \le 1$

6. $\displaystyle\int_C (x^2 + y^2) \, ds$ for $C: x = e^{-t} \cos t, y = e^{-t} \sin t, 0 \le t \le \frac{\pi}{2}$

7. $\displaystyle\int_C (-y \, dx + x \, dy)$ for $C: y = 4x^2$ from $(-1, 4)$ to $(0, 0)$

8. $\displaystyle\int_C (-y \, dx + 3x \, dy)$ for $C: y^2 = x$ from $(1, 1)$ to $(9, 3)$

9. $\displaystyle\int_C (x \, dy - y \, dx)$ for $C: 2x - 4y = 1, 4 \le x \le 8$

10. Evaluate $\displaystyle\int_C [(y - x) \, dx + x^2 y \, dy]$, where C is the curve defined by $y^2 = x^3$ from $(1, -1)$ to $(1, 1)$.

11. Evaluate $\displaystyle\int_C [(x + y)^2 \, dx - (x - y)^2 \, dy]$, where C is the curve defined by $y = |2x|$ from $(-1, 2)$ to $(1, 2)$.

12. Evaluate $\displaystyle\int_C [(y^2 - x^2) \, dx - x \, dy]$, where C is the quarter-circle $x^2 + y^2 = 4$ from $(0, 2)$ to $(2, 0)$.

13. Evaluate $\displaystyle\int_C [(x^2 + y^2) \, dx + 2xy \, dy]$ for these choices of the curve C:

    a. C is the quarter circle $x^2 + y^2 = 1$ from $(1, 0)$ to $(0, 1)$.

    b. C is the straight line $y = 1 - x$ from $(1, 0)$ to $(0, 1)$.

14. Evaluate $\displaystyle\int_C [x^2 y \, dx + (x^2 - y^2) \, dy]$ for these choices of the curve C:

    a. C is the arc of the parabola $y = x^2$ from $(0, 0)$ to $(2, 4)$.

    b. C is the segment of the line $y = 2x$ for $0 \le x \le 2$.

15. Evaluate the integral in Problem 14 for the path C that consists of the horizontal line segment $(0, 0)$ to $(2, 0)$, followed by the vertical segment from $(2, 0)$ to $(2, 4)$.

16. Evaluate $\int_C (-xy^2\,dx + x^2\,dy)$, where C is the path shown in Figure 13.14.

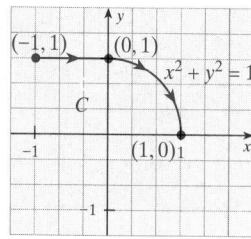

Figure 13.14   Path of C for Problem 16

17. Evaluate $\int_C (-y^2\,dx + x^2\,dy)$, where C is the path shown in Figure 13.15.

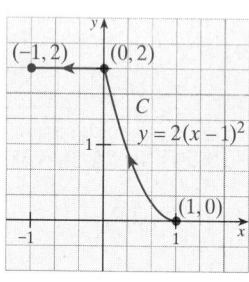

Figure 13.15   Path of C for Problem 17

18. Evaluate $\oint_C [(x^2 - y^2)\,dx + x\,dy]$, where C is the circular path given by $x = 2\cos\theta$, $y = 2\sin\theta$, $0 \le \theta \le 2\pi$.

19. Evaluate $\oint_C (x^2 y\,dx - xy\,dy)$, where C is the path that begins at $(0, 0)$, goes to $(1, 1)$ along the parabola $y = x^2$, and then returns to $(0, 0)$ along the line $y = x$.

In Problems 20–22, evaluate $\int_C \mathbf{F} \cdot d\mathbf{R}$*, where* $\mathbf{F} = (5x + y)\mathbf{i} + x\mathbf{j}$ *and* C *is the specified curve.*

20. C is the straight line segment from $(0, 0)$ to $(2, 1)$.

21. C is the curve given by $\mathbf{R}(t) = 2t\mathbf{i} + t\mathbf{j}$ for $0 \le t \le 1$.

22. C is the vertical line from $(0, 0)$ to $(0, 1)$, followed by the horizontal line from $(0, 1)$ to $(2, 1)$.

Evaluate the line integrals in Problems 23–38.

23. $\int_C \mathbf{F} \cdot d\mathbf{R}$, where $\mathbf{F} = \left\langle \dfrac{x}{\sqrt{x^2 + y^2}}, \dfrac{-y}{\sqrt{x^2 + y^2}} \right\rangle$ and C is the quarter circle path $x^2 + y^2 = a^2$, traversed from $(a, 0)$ to $(0, a)$

24. $\int_C (y\,dx - x\,dy + dz)$, where C is the helical path given by
   a. $x = 3\sin t$, $y = 3\cos t$, $z = t$ for $0 \le t \le \frac{\pi}{2}$
   b. $x = a\sin t$, $y = a\cos t$, $z = t$ for constant a and $0 \le t \le \frac{\pi}{2}$

25. $\int_C (x\,dx + y\,dy + z\,dz)$, where C is the following path:
   a. the helix defined by $x = \cos t$, $y = \sin t$, $z = t$ for $0 \le t \le \frac{\pi}{2}$
   b. the straight line segment from $(1, 0, 0)$ to $\left(0, 1, \frac{\pi}{2}\right)$

26. $\int_C (-y\,dx + x\,dy + xz\,dz)$, where C is the following path:
   a. the helix defined by $x = \cos t$, $y = \sin t$, $z = t$ for $0 \le t \le 2\pi$
   b. the unit circle $x^2 + y^2 = 1$, $z = 0$, traversed once counterclockwise as viewed from above

27. $\int_C (5xy\,dx + 10yz\,dy + z\,dz)$, where C is the following path:
   a. the parabolic arc $x = y^2$ from $(0, 0, 0)$ to $(1, 1, 0)$ followed by the line segment given by $x = 1$, $y = 1$, $0 \le z \le 1$
   b. the straight line segment from $(0, 0, 0)$ to $(1, 1, 1)$

28. $\int_C \mathbf{F} \cdot d\mathbf{R}$, where $\mathbf{F} = (y - 2z)\mathbf{i} + x\mathbf{j} - 2xy\mathbf{k}$ and C is the path given by $\mathbf{R}(t) = t\mathbf{i} + t^2\mathbf{j} - \mathbf{k}$ for $1 \le t \le 2$

29. $\oint_C \mathbf{F} \cdot d\mathbf{R}$, where $\mathbf{F} = x\mathbf{i} + xy\mathbf{j} + x^2yz\mathbf{k}$, and C is the elliptical path given by $x^2 + 4y^2 - 8y + 3 = 0$ in the xy-plane, traversed once counterclockwise as viewed from above

30. $\oint_C [(y + z)\,dx + (x + z)\,dy + (x + y)\,dz]$, where C is the circle of radius 1 centered on the z-axis in the plane $z = 2$, traversed once counterclockwise as viewed from above

31. $\int_C 2xy^2z\,ds$ for C: $x = t$, $y = t^2$, $z = \frac{2}{3}t^3$ for $0 \le t \le 1$

32. $\int_C ye^{xz}\,ds$, where C is the line segment from $(0, 0, 0)$ to $(2, 1, 3)$

33. $\oint_C \mathbf{F} \cdot d\mathbf{R}$, where $\mathbf{F} = y^2\mathbf{i} + x^2\mathbf{j} - (x + z)\mathbf{k}$ and C is the boundary of the triangle with vertices $(0, 0, 0)$, $(1, 0, 0)$, $(1, 1, 0)$, traversed once clockwise, as viewed from above

34. $\int_C \mathbf{F} \cdot \mathbf{T}\,ds$, where $\mathbf{F} = -3y\mathbf{i} + 3x\mathbf{j} + 3x\mathbf{k}$ and C is the straight line segment from $(0, 0, 1)$ to $(1, 1, 1)$

35. $\oint_C \mathbf{F} \cdot \mathbf{T}\,ds$, where $\mathbf{F} = -x\mathbf{i} + 2\mathbf{j}$, and C is the boundary of the trapezoid with vertices $(0, 0)$, $(1, 0)$, $(2, 1)$, $(0, 1)$, traversed once clockwise as viewed from above

36. $\int_C y\,ds$, where C is the curve given by $\mathbf{R}(t) = t\mathbf{i} + 2t^3\mathbf{j}$ $0 \le t \le 2$

37. $\int_C (x + y)\,ds$, where C is given by $\mathbf{R}(t) = (\cos^2 t)\mathbf{i} + (\sin^2 t)\mathbf{j}$, $-\frac{\pi}{4} \le t \le 0$

38. $\int_C \dfrac{x^2 + xy + y^2}{z^2}\,ds$, where C is the path given by $\mathbf{R}(t) = (\cos t)\mathbf{i} + (\sin t)\mathbf{j} - \mathbf{k}$ for $0 \le t \le 2\pi$

B 39. Evaluate the line integral
$$\oint_C \frac{x\,dy - y\,dx}{x^2 + y^2}$$
where C is the unit circle $x^2 + y^2 = 1$ traversed once counterclockwise.

40. $\oint_C \dfrac{dx + dy}{|x| + |y|}$, where C is the square $|x| + |y| = 1$, traversed once counterclockwise.

41. How much work is done by a constant force $\mathbf{F} = a\mathbf{i} + \mathbf{j}$ when a particle moves along the line $y = ax$ from $x = a$ to $x = 0$?

42. A force field in the plane is given by $\mathbf{F} = (x^2 - y^2)\mathbf{i} + 2xy\mathbf{j}$. Find the total work done by this force in moving a point mass counterclockwise around the square with vertices $(0, 0)$, $(2, 0)$, $(2, 2)$, $(0, 2)$.

43. Find the work done by the force field $\mathbf{F} = (x^2 + y^2)\mathbf{i} + (x + y)\mathbf{j}$ as an object moves counterclockwise along the circle $x^2 + y^2 = 1$ from $(1, 0)$ to $(-1, 0)$, and then back to $(1, 0)$ along the x-axis.

44. A force acting on a point mass located at (x, y) is given by $\mathbf{F} = y\mathbf{i} + 2x\mathbf{j}$. Find the work done by this force as the point mass moves along a straight line from $(1, 0)$ to $(0, 1)$.

Find the work done by the force $\mathbf{F}(x, y, z)$ on an object moving along the curve C in Problems 45–48.

45. $\mathbf{F} = (y^2 - z^2)\mathbf{i} + 2yz\mathbf{j} - x^2\mathbf{k}$, and C is the path given by $x(t) = t$, $y(t) = t^2$, $z(t) = t^3$, for $0 \le t \le 1$.

46. $\mathbf{F} = 2xy\mathbf{i} + (x^2 + 2)\mathbf{j} + y\mathbf{k}$, and C is the line segment from $(1, 0, 2)$ to $(3, 4, 1)$.

47. $\mathbf{F} = x\mathbf{i} + y\mathbf{j} + (xz - y)\mathbf{k}$, and C is the line segment from $(0, 0, 0)$ to $(2, 1, 2)$.

48. $\mathbf{F} = x\mathbf{i} + y\mathbf{j} + (xz - y)\mathbf{k}$, and C is the path given by $\mathbf{R}(t) = t^2\mathbf{i} + 2t\mathbf{j} + 4t^3\mathbf{k}$ for $0 \le t \le 1$.

49. A wire has the shape of the curve $C: x = \sqrt{2} \sin t$, $y = \cos t$, $z = \cos t$ for $0 \le t \le \pi$, and the density at the point (x, y, z) on the curve is $\delta(x, y, z) = xyz$. The mass of this wire was computed in Example 7. Find the center of mass.

50. Find the center of mass of a wire in the shape of the helix $x = 3 \sin t$, $y = 3 \cos t$, $z = 2t$ for $0 \le t \le \pi$ and the following choices of density $\delta(x, y, z)$:
 a. $\delta(x, y, z) = z$ **b.** $\delta(x, y, z) = x$

51. Find the centroid of a thin wire in the shape of the curve $x = 2t$, $y = t^2$, $z = \frac{1}{3}t^3$ for $0 \le t \le 2$.

52. Find the centroid of the arch of the cycloid $C: x = t - \sin t$, $y = 1 - \cos t$ for $0 \le t \le 2\pi$. *Note:* The centroid may be thought of as the center of mass of a wire of constant density.

53. A 180-lb laborer carries a bag of sand weighing 40 lb up a circular helical staircase (Figure 13.16) on the outside of a tower 50 ft high and 20 ft in diameter. How much work is done as the laborer climbs to the top in exactly five revolutions?

Figure 13.16 A circular helical staircase

54. Repeat Problem 53, assuming that the bag leaks 1 lb of sand for every 10 ft of ascent. How much work is done during the laborer's climb to the top?

55. A 5,000-lb satellite orbits the earth in a circular orbit 5,000 mi from the center of the earth. How much work is done as the satellite moves through one complete revolution?

56. Suppose a particle with charge Q and mass m moves with velocity $\mathbf{V}$ under the influence of an electric field $\mathbf{E}$ and a magnetic field $\mathbf{B}$. Then the total force on the particle is $\mathbf{F} = Q(\mathbf{E} + \mathbf{V} \times \mathbf{B})$, called the *Lorentz force*. Use Newton's second law of motion, $\mathbf{F} = m\mathbf{A}$, to show that

$$m\frac{d\mathbf{V}}{dt} \cdot \mathbf{V} = Q\mathbf{E} \cdot \frac{d\mathbf{R}}{dt}$$

and then evaluate the line integral $\displaystyle\int_C \mathbf{E} \cdot d\mathbf{R}$, where C is the trajectory of a particle traveling with constant speed.

57. Counterexample Problem If $\displaystyle\int_C f(x, y, z)\, ds = 0$, is it true that $f(x, y, z) = 0$ on C? Either prove that it is, or find a counterexample.

58. Counterexample Problem This problem shows that not all line integrals are path independent. Let $\mathbf{F} = \langle y, -x \rangle$, and let C_1 and C_2 be the following two paths joining $(0, 0)$ to $(1, 1)$.

$$C_1: y = x \text{ for } 0 \le x \le 1 \quad \text{and} \quad C_2: y = x^2 \text{ for } 0 \le x \le 1$$

Show that

$$\int_{C_1} \mathbf{F} \cdot d\mathbf{R} \ne \int_{C_2} \mathbf{F} \cdot d\mathbf{R}$$

13.3 The Fundamental Theorem and Path Independence

IN THIS SECTION fundamental theorem for line integrals, conservative vector fields, independence of path

In general, the value of the line integral $\int_C \mathbf{F} \cdot d\mathbf{R}$ depends on the path of integration C, but in certain cases, the integral will be the same for all paths in a given region D with the same initial point P and terminal point Q. In this case, we say the line integral is **independent of path** in D (see Figure 13.17). In this section, we will study path independence and characterize the kind of vector field $\mathbf{F}$ for which it occurs.

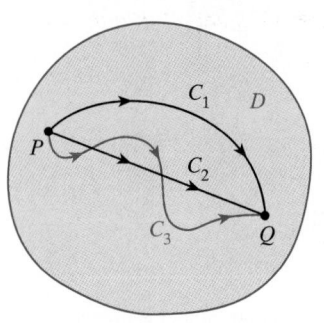

Figure 13.17 A line integral $\int_C \mathbf{F} \cdot d\mathbf{R}$ is independent of path in D if its value is the same for all curves joining any two points in D.

FUNDAMENTAL THEOREM FOR LINE INTEGRALS

The fundamental theorem of calculus (Section 5.4) says that if the function f is continuous on $[a, b]$, then

$$\int_a^b f(x)\, dx = F(b) - F(a)$$

where F is any antiderivative of f; that is, $F'(x) = f(x)$. For a function of two or three variables, the analogue of the derivative is the gradient, and the corresponding analogue of the fundamental theorem is the following theorem.

THEOREM 13.2   Fundamental theorem for line integrals

Let C be a piecewise smooth curve that is parameterized by the vector function $\mathbf{R}(t)$ for $a \leq t \leq b$, and let $\mathbf{F}$ be a vector field that is continuous on C. If f is a scalar function such that $\mathbf{F} = \nabla f$, then

$$\int_C \mathbf{F} \cdot d\mathbf{R} = f(Q) - f(P)$$

where $Q = \mathbf{R}(b)$ and $P = \mathbf{R}(a)$ are the endpoints of C.

Proof   We will prove this theorem for the case where $f(x, y, z)$ is a function of three variables, such that $\mathbf{F} = \nabla f(x, y, z)$. Suppose $\mathbf{R}(t) = \langle x(t), y(t), z(t)\rangle$ and let G be the composite function $G(t) = f[x(t), y(t), z(t)]$. Then, according to the chain rule

$$\frac{dG}{dt} = \frac{\partial f}{\partial x}\frac{dx}{dt} + \frac{\partial f}{\partial y}\frac{dy}{dt} + \frac{\partial f}{\partial z}\frac{dz}{dt}$$

and we have

$$\int_C \mathbf{F} \cdot d\mathbf{R} = \int_C \nabla f \cdot d\mathbf{R}$$

$$= \int_C \left[\frac{\partial f}{\partial x}\, dx + \frac{\partial f}{\partial y}\, dy + \frac{\partial f}{\partial z}\, dz\right]$$

$$= \int_a^b \left[\frac{\partial f}{\partial x}\frac{dx}{dt} + \frac{\partial f}{\partial y}\frac{dy}{dt} + \frac{\partial f}{\partial z}\frac{dz}{dt}\right] dt$$

$$= \int_a^b \frac{dG}{dt}\, dt \qquad \text{Substitution}$$

$$= G(b) - G(a) \qquad \text{Fundamental theorem of calculus}$$

$$= f[x(b), y(b), z(b)] - f[x(a), y(a), z(a)] \qquad \text{Substitution}$$

$$= f[R(b)] - f[R(a)] \qquad \text{Substitution}$$

$$= f(Q) - f(P) \qquad \qquad \square$$

EXAMPLE 1   Using the fundamental theorem to evaluate a line integral

Evaluate the line integral $\displaystyle\int_C \mathbf{F} \cdot d\mathbf{R}$, where

$$\mathbf{F} = \nabla(e^x \sin y - xy - 2y)$$

and C is the path described by $\mathbf{R}(t) = \left[t^3 \sin \frac{\pi}{2}t\right]\mathbf{i} - \left[\frac{\pi}{2}\cos\left(\frac{\pi}{2}t + \frac{\pi}{2}\right)\right]\mathbf{j}$ for $0 \leq t \leq 1$.

Solution

First, note that the hypotheses of the fundamental theorem for line integrals are satisfied since

$$f(x, y) = e^x \sin y - xy - 2y$$

has continuous partial derivatives on the smooth curve C. At the endpoints of C, we find

$$\textit{left endpoint} \quad (t = 0); \quad \mathbf{R}(0) = \langle 0, 0 \rangle$$
$$f(0, 0) = e^0 \sin 0 - 0 - 0 = 0$$

$$\textit{right endpoint} \quad (t = 1); \quad \mathbf{R}(1) = \left\langle 1, \frac{\pi}{2} \right\rangle$$
$$f\left(1, \frac{\pi}{2}\right) = e^1 \sin \frac{\pi}{2} - \frac{\pi}{2} - 2\left(\frac{\pi}{2}\right) = e - \frac{3\pi}{2}$$

Thus, according to the fundamental theorem for line integrals, we have

$$\int_C \mathbf{F} \cdot d\mathbf{R} = f(Q) - f(P) = f\left(1, \frac{\pi}{2}\right) - f(0, 0)$$
$$= \left(e - \frac{3\pi}{2}\right) - 0 = e - \frac{3\pi}{2} \qquad \blacksquare$$

CONSERVATIVE VECTOR FIELDS

A key requirement for evaluating the line integral $\int_C \mathbf{F} \cdot d\mathbf{R}$ by the fundamental theorem of line integrals is that $\mathbf{F}$ be the gradient of some scalar function f; that is, $\mathbf{F} = \nabla f$. Our next goal is to learn how to determine when a given vector field $\mathbf{F}$ can be expressed as a gradient field, and we begin by introducing some terminology.

Conservative Vector Field

A vector field $\mathbf{F}$ is said to be **conservative** in a region D if $\mathbf{F} = \nabla f$ for some scalar function f in D. The function f is called a **scalar potential** of $\mathbf{F}$ in D. That is,

$$\mathbf{F} = \nabla f \quad \text{for } (x, y) \text{ on } D$$
$$\uparrow \qquad \uparrow$$
Conservative vector field   Scalar potential

The term *conservative* comes from physics and is related to the law of conservation of energy (see Problem 54).

EXAMPLE 2 Verifying that a vector field is conservative

Verify that the vector field $\mathbf{F} = 2xy\mathbf{i} + x^2\mathbf{j}$ is conservative, with scalar potential $f = x^2 y$.

Solution

$\nabla f = 2xy\mathbf{i} + x^2\mathbf{j}$ and this is the same as $\mathbf{F}$, so $\mathbf{F}$ is conservative. $\qquad \blacksquare$

It is one thing to verify that a vector field is conservative as we did in Example 2, but it is more common to be given a vector field $\mathbf{F}$ and then be asked to determine whether it is conservative without knowing the answer in advance. We will establish a simple criterion for $\mathbf{F}$ to be conservative on any set D in the plane that has these properties:

1. Any two points P and Q in D can be joined by a piecewise-smooth curve entirely within D.
2. Every closed curve in D encloses only points that are also in D.

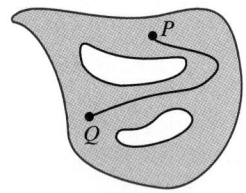

a. A region that is simply connected (no holes)

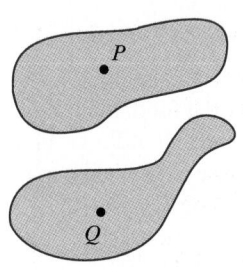

b. A connected region that is *not* simply connected

c. A region that is not connected

Figure 13.18 Regions that are connected and not connected

A region D with property (1) is **connected**, and a connected region with property (2) is **simply connected**. Roughly speaking, a simply connected region is one with no "holes," as shown in Figure 13.18.

THEOREM 13.3   Cross-partials test for a conservative vector field in the plane

Consider the vector field $\mathbf{F}(x, y) = u(x, y)\mathbf{i} + v(x, y)\mathbf{j}$, where u and v have continuous first partials in the open, simply connected region D in the plane. Then $\mathbf{F}(x, y)$ is conservative in D if and only if

$$\frac{\partial u}{\partial y} = \frac{\partial v}{\partial x} \qquad \text{throughout } D$$

Proof   We outline the proof in Problem Set 13.4 after our discussion of Green's theorem. ❑

EXAMPLE 3   Finding a scalar potential function

Show that the vector field $\mathbf{F} = (e^x \sin y - y)\mathbf{i} + (e^x \cos y - x - 2)\mathbf{j}$ is conservative and then find a scalar potential function f for $\mathbf{F}$.

Solution

First note that the component functions $u(x, y) = e^x \sin y - y$ and $v(x, y) = e^x \cos y - x - 2$ have continuous partial derivatives. Then

$$\frac{\partial u}{\partial y} = e^x \cos y - 1 \quad \text{and} \quad \frac{\partial v}{\partial x} = e^x \cos y - 1$$

Since $\dfrac{\partial u}{\partial y} = \dfrac{\partial v}{\partial x}$, it follows that $\mathbf{F}$ is conservative. To find a scalar potential function f such that $\nabla f = \mathbf{F}$, we note that f must satisfy $u(x, y) = f_x(x, y)$ and $v(x, y) = f_y(x, y)$.

$$f(x, y) = \int u(x, y)\, dx = \underbrace{\int (e^x \sin y - y)\, dx}$$

This is the "partial integral" in the sense that y is held constant while the integration is performed with respect to x alone.

$$= e^x \sin y - xy + k(y)$$

Note that $k(y)$ is a function of y alone—a "constant" as far as x-integration is concerned.

Because f must also satisfy $f_y(x, y) = v(x, y)$, we compute the partial derivative of this f with respect to y:

$$f_y(x, y) = \frac{\partial}{\partial y}[e^x \sin y - xy + k(y)] = e^x \cos y - x + \frac{dk}{dy}$$

Set this equal to $v = e^x \cos y - x - 2$ and solve for $\dfrac{dk}{dy}$:

$$e^x \cos y - x + \frac{dk}{dy} = e^x \cos y - x - 2$$

$$\frac{dk}{dy} = -2$$

$$k(y) = -2y + C$$

Thus, any function $f(x, y) = e^x \sin y - xy - 2y + C$. Any such function is a scalar potential of $\mathbf{F}$ and, for simplicity, we pick $C = 0$:

$$f(x, y) = e^x \sin y - xy - 2y$$

∎

In Example 3, we began by using the fact that $u = f_x$. In general, the issue of whether to start with $u = f_x$ or $v = f_y$ is often determined by which equation leads to the simpler integration.

EXAMPLE 4 Testing for a conservative vector field in the plane

Determine whether the vector field $\mathbf{F} = ye^{xy}\mathbf{i} + (xe^{xy} + x)\mathbf{j}$ is conservative; if it is, find a scalar potential.

Solution

We have $u(x, y) = ye^{xy}$ and $v(x, y) = xe^{xy} + x$.

$$\frac{\partial u}{\partial y} = xye^{xy} + e^{xy} \qquad \frac{\partial v}{\partial x} = xye^{xy} + e^{xy} + 1$$

so $\dfrac{\partial u}{\partial y} \neq \dfrac{\partial v}{\partial x}$, and $\mathbf{F}$ is not conservative. ∎

In $\mathbb{R}^3$, the following generalization of the cross-partials test may be used as a criterion for determining whether a given vector field is conservative.

THEOREM 13.4 The curl criterion for a conservative vector field in $\mathbb{R}^3$

Suppose the vector field $\mathbf{F}$ and curl $\mathbf{F}$ are both continuous in the simply connected region D of $\mathbb{R}^3$. Then $\mathbf{F}$ is conservative in D if and only if curl $\mathbf{F} = \mathbf{0}$.

Proof As in $\mathbb{R}^2$, a simply connected region in $\mathbb{R}^3$ can be described informally as one with no "holes." A proof using Stokes' theorem is given in Section 13.6. ❑

Note that a vector field $\mathbf{F} = \langle u(x, y), v(x, y) \rangle$ in $\mathbb{R}^2$ can be regarded as the vector field $\mathbf{G} = \langle u(x, y, 0), v(x, y, 0), 0 \rangle$ in $\mathbb{R}^3$. Since

$$\text{curl } \mathbf{G} = \begin{vmatrix} \mathbf{i} & \mathbf{j} & \mathbf{k} \\ \dfrac{\partial}{\partial x} & \dfrac{\partial}{\partial y} & \dfrac{\partial}{\partial z} \\ u(x, y, 0) & v(x, y, 0) & 0 \end{vmatrix}$$

$$= 0\mathbf{i} + 0\mathbf{j} + \left(\frac{\partial v}{\partial x} - \frac{\partial u}{\partial y} \right)\mathbf{k}$$

we have curl $\mathbf{G} = \mathbf{0}$ if and only if $\dfrac{\partial v}{\partial x} = \dfrac{\partial u}{\partial y}$. Thus, Theorem 13.4 becomes the cross-partials test if $\mathbf{F}$ is in $\mathbb{R}^2$.

EXAMPLE 5 Determining a scalar potential for a conservative vector field in $\mathbb{R}^3$

Show that the vector field

$$\mathbf{F} = \langle 20x^3z + 2y^2, 4xy, 5x^4 + 3z^2 \rangle$$

is conservative in $\mathbb{R}^3$ and find a scalar potential function for $\mathbf{F}$.

Solution

To show that $\mathbf{F}$ is conservative in $\mathbb{R}^3$, note that the components of $\mathbf{F}$ are continuous with continuous partial derivatives and that

$$\text{curl } \mathbf{F} = \begin{vmatrix} \mathbf{i} & \mathbf{j} & \mathbf{k} \\ \dfrac{\partial}{\partial x} & \dfrac{\partial}{\partial y} & \dfrac{\partial}{\partial z} \\ 20x^3z + 2y^2 & 4xy & 5x^4 + 3z^2 \end{vmatrix}$$

$$= (0 - 0)\mathbf{i} - (20x^3 - 20x^3)\mathbf{j} + (4y - 4y)\mathbf{k}$$

$$= \mathbf{0}$$

Therefore, according to Theorem 13.4, the vector field **F** is conservative.

To determine a scalar potential function for **F**, we proceed as in Example 3, except that now we have three component equations, each involving three variables:

$$\frac{\partial f}{\partial x} = 20x^3z + 2y^2 \qquad \frac{\partial f}{\partial y} = 4xy \qquad \frac{\partial f}{\partial z} = 5x^4 + 3z^2$$

Integrating the first equation with respect to x (holding y and z constant), we obtain

$$f(x, y, z) = 5x^4z + 2xy^2 + g(y, z)$$

where $g(y, z)$ is a constant with respect to x-integration. Taking the partial derivative of this expression with respect to y, and then comparing the result to the required equation $\frac{\partial f}{\partial y} = 4xy$, we see that

$$4xy + \frac{\partial g}{\partial y} = 4xy$$

Thus,

$$\frac{\partial g}{\partial y} = 0 \quad \text{and} \quad g(y, z) = h(z)$$

where $h(z)$ is a constant with respect to x- and y-integration, so

$$f(x, y, z) = 5x^4z + 2xy^2 + h(z)$$

Finally, we compute the partial derivative of f with respect to z from this equation, and compare it to the required equation $\frac{\partial f}{\partial z} = 5x^4 + 3z^2$:

$$5x^4 + h'(z) = 5x^4 + 3z^2$$
$$h'(z) = 3z^2$$
$$h(z) = z^3 + C$$

Therefore, any function of the form

$$f(x, y, z) = 5x^4z + 2xy^2 + z^3 + C$$

is a scalar potential for the vector field **F**. ∎

INDEPENDENCE OF PATH

We now have the tools to discuss path independence for a line integral. Here are the definition and notation we will use.

Independence of Path

> The line integral $\int_C \mathbf{F} \cdot d\mathbf{R}$ is **independent of path** in a region D if for any two points P and Q in D the line integral along every piecewise smooth curve in D from P to Q has the same value.

The following theorem provides three equivalent ways of determining whether a given line integral is path independent.

THEOREM 13.5 Equivalent conditions for path independence

If **F** is a continuous vector field on the open connected set D, then the following three conditions are either all true or all false:

i. **F** is conservative on D; that is, $\mathbf{F} = \nabla f$ for some function f defined on D.

ii. $\oint_C \mathbf{F} \cdot d\mathbf{R} = 0$ for every piecewise smooth closed curve C in D.

iii. $\displaystyle\int_C \mathbf{F} \cdot d\mathbf{R}$ is independent of path within D.

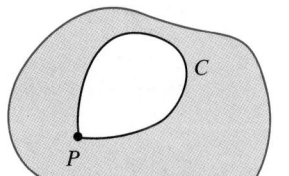

a. (i) implies (ii)

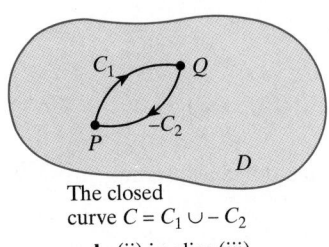

The closed
curve $C = C_1 \cup -C_2$

b. (ii) implies (iii)

Figure 13.19 Equivalent conditions for path independence

Proof   To prove this theorem, it is enough to prove that (i) implies (ii), that (ii) implies (iii), and that (iii) implies (i). Then, if any one is true, all are true.

(i) implies (ii)   Assume that $\mathbf{F}$ is conservative, and let C be a closed curve in D, as shown in Figure 13.19a. Then any point P on C can serve as both the initial point and the terminal point of the curve, and according to the fundamental theorem of line integrals, we have

$$\oint_C \mathbf{F} \cdot d\mathbf{R} = f(P) - f(P) = 0$$

where f is a scalar potential for $\mathbf{F}$.

(ii) implies (iii)   Let C_1 and C_2 be two curves in D with the same initial point P and terminal point Q. Then the curve C formed by C_1 followed by $-C_2$ (the reverse of C_2) is a closed curve beginning and ending at P. According to condition (ii), the line integral around this closed curve must be 0, so we have

$$0 = \underbrace{\oint_C \mathbf{F} \cdot d\mathbf{R}}_{\text{Condition (ii)}} = \underbrace{\int_{C_1} \mathbf{F} \cdot d\mathbf{R} + \int_{-C_2} \mathbf{F} \cdot d\mathbf{R}}_{\text{Additivity of line integrals}}$$

and it follows that (see Figure 13.19b)

$$\int_{C_1} \mathbf{F} \cdot d\mathbf{R} = -\int_{-C_2} \mathbf{F} \cdot d\mathbf{R} = \int_{C_2} \mathbf{F} \cdot d\mathbf{R}$$

Since C_1 and C_2 were chosen as any two curves in D with the same endpoints, it follows that $\displaystyle\oint_C \mathbf{F} \cdot d\mathbf{R}$ is independent of path in D.

(iii) implies (i)   For this implication, we assume that $\displaystyle\oint_C \mathbf{F} \cdot d\mathbf{R}$ is independent of path in D and construct a scalar function f such that $\mathbf{F} = \nabla f$ in order to show that $\mathbf{F}$ must be conservative. Details of this implication are outlined in Problem 55.   ❑

EXAMPLE 6   Work along a closed path in a conservative force field

Show that no work is performed when an object moves along a closed path in a connected domain where the force field is conservative.

Solution

In such a force field $\mathbf{F}$, we have $\nabla f = \mathbf{F}$, where f is a scalar potential of $\mathbf{F}$, and because the path of motion is closed, it begins and ends at the same point P. Thus, the work is given by

$$W = \oint_C \mathbf{F} \cdot d\mathbf{R} = f(P) - f(P) = 0$$ ■

We now have several ways for evaluating a given line integral $\int_C \mathbf{F} \cdot d\mathbf{R}$. We can

1. Parameterize C and use the parameterization to convert the line integral into an "ordinary" integral in t over an interval $a \le t \le b$.
2. Check to see whether $\mathbf{F}$ is conservative. If it is, find a scalar potential function f and then use the fundamental theorem of line integrals.
3. If $\mathbf{F}$ is conservative, find a convenient path C_1 with the same endpoints as C and use the fact that $\int_{C_1} \mathbf{F} \cdot d\mathbf{R} = \int_C \mathbf{F} \cdot d\mathbf{R}$ since the line integral is independent of path.

Here is an example that illustrates these options.

EXAMPLE 7   Strategy for evaluating a line integral

Evaluate the line integral $\int_C \mathbf{F} \cdot d\mathbf{R}$, where

$$\mathbf{F} = [(2x - x^2 y)e^{-xy} + \tan^{-1} y]\mathbf{i} + \left[\frac{x}{y^2 + 1} - x^3 e^{-xy}\right]\mathbf{j}$$

for each of the following curves:

a. C_1: the ellipse $9x^2 + 4y^2 = 36$
b. C_2: the curve with parametric equations $x = t^2 \cos \pi t$, $y = e^{-t} \sin \pi t$, $0 \le t \le 1$

Solution

First, we check to see whether $\mathbf{F}$ is conservative using the cross-partials test:

$$\frac{\partial}{\partial x}\left[\frac{x}{y^2 + 1} - x^3 e^{-xy}\right] = \frac{1}{y^2 + 1} + (x^3 y - 3x^2)e^{-xy}$$

$$= \frac{\partial}{\partial y}\left[(2x - x^2 y)e^{-xy} + \tan^{-1} y\right]$$

Thus, $\mathbf{F}$ is conservative and we could answer both questions by finding a potential function for $\mathbf{F}$, but it isn't really necessary.

a. Since $\mathbf{F}$ is conservative, and the ellipse C_1 is a closed curve, we must have

$$\oint_C \mathbf{F} \cdot d\mathbf{R} = 0.$$

b. The curve C_2 has initial point $P(0, 0)$, where $t = 0$, and terminal point $Q(-1, 0)$, where $t = 1$. Since $\mathbf{F}$ is conservative, the line integral $\int_C \mathbf{F} \cdot d\mathbf{R}$ is independent of path, so the given line integral has the same value as $\int_{C_3} \mathbf{F} \cdot d\mathbf{R}$, where C_3 is the line segment from P to Q. A parameterization for C_3 is $x = -t$, $y = 0$. Thus, if $\mathbf{R} = \langle -t, 0 \rangle$, we have $\mathbf{R}' = \langle -1, 0 \rangle$ and

$$\int_{C_2} \mathbf{F} \cdot d\mathbf{R} = \int_{C_3} \mathbf{F} \cdot d\mathbf{R} = \int_0^1 \mathbf{F}[\mathbf{R}(t)] \cdot \mathbf{R}'(t)\, dt$$

$$= \int_0^1 \left\{\left[(2(-t) - 0)e^0 + \tan^{-1} 0\right](-1) + \left[\frac{-t}{0 + 1} - (-t)^3 e^0\right](0)\right\} dt$$

$$= \int_0^1 2t\, dt$$

$$= 1 \qquad\blacksquare$$

In the next section, we will develop another criterion for path independence as part of our study of an important result known as Green's theorem.

13.3   PROBLEM SET

Ⓐ **1. Exploration Problem**   What is a conservative vector field?

2. WHAT DOES THIS SAY?   Describe the fundamental theorem of line integrals.

3. WHAT DOES THIS SAY?   Explain what is meant by independence of path. Describe various equivalent conditions for path independence.

Determine whether or not each vector field in Problems 4–9 is conservative, and if it is, find a scalar potential.

4. $y^2\mathbf{i} + 2xy\mathbf{j}$ **5.** $2xy^3\mathbf{i} + 3y^2 x^2\mathbf{j}$

6. $(xe^{xy}\sin y)\mathbf{i} + (e^{xy}\cos xy + y)\mathbf{j}$

7. $(-y + e^x \sin y)\mathbf{i} + [(x + 2)e^x \cos y]\mathbf{j}$

8. $(y - x^2)\mathbf{i} + (2x + y^2)\mathbf{j}$ **9.** $(e^{2x}\sin y)\mathbf{i} + (e^{2x}\cos y)\mathbf{j}$

Evaluate the line integrals in Problems 10–13 for each of the given paths.

10. $\int_C [(3x + 2y)\,dx + (2x + 3y)\,dy]$

a.

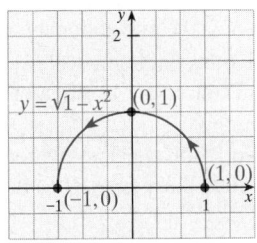

b.

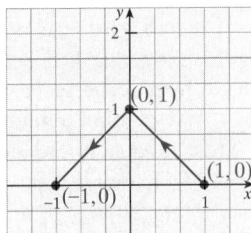

c.

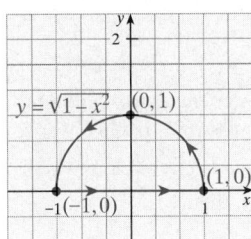

11. $\int_C [(3x + 2y)\,dx - (2x + 3y)\,dy]$

a.

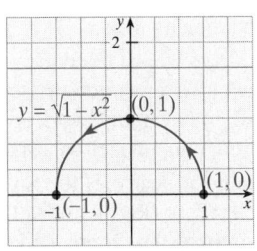

b.

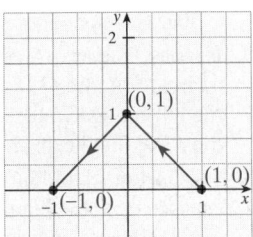

c.

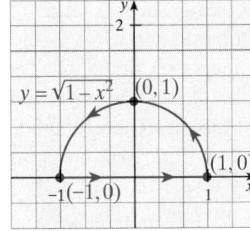

12. $\int_C [2x^2 y\,dx + x^3\,dy]$

a.

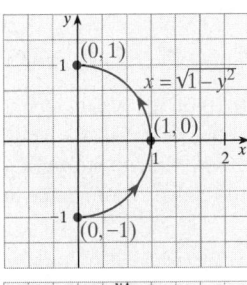

b.

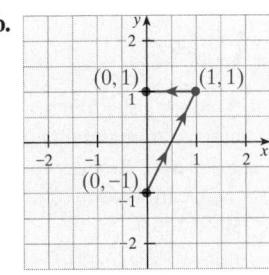

c.

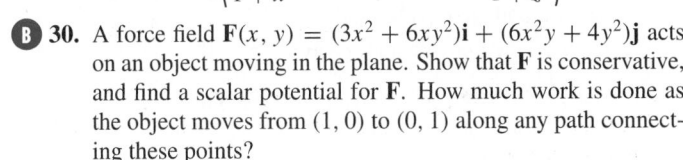

13. $\int_C [2xy\,dx + x^2\,dy]$

a.

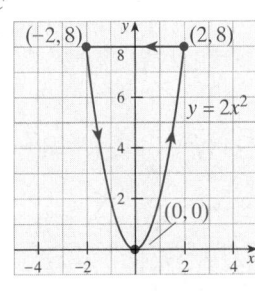

b.

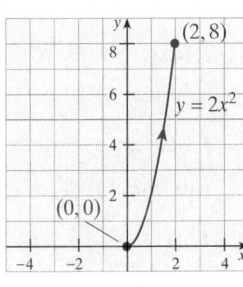

c.

In each of Problems 14–19, show that the vector field $\mathbf{F}$ is conservative and find a scalar potential f for $\mathbf{F}$. Then evaluate the line integral $\int_C \mathbf{F} \cdot d\mathbf{R}$, where C is any smooth path connecting $A(0, 0)$ to $B(1, 1)$.

14. $\mathbf{F}(x, y) = (x + 2y)\mathbf{i} + (2x + y)\mathbf{j}$

15. $\mathbf{F}(x, y) = 2xy\mathbf{i} + x^2\mathbf{j}$

16. $\mathbf{F}(x, y) = (y - x^2)\mathbf{i} + (x + y^2)\mathbf{j}$

17. $\mathbf{F}(x, y) = (2x - y)\mathbf{i} + (y^2 - x)\mathbf{j}$

18. $\mathbf{F}(x, y) = e^{-y}\mathbf{i} - xe^{-y}\mathbf{j}$

19. $\mathbf{F}(x, y) = \dfrac{(y + 1)\mathbf{i} - x\mathbf{j}}{(y + 1)^2}$

Show that the given vector field $\mathbf{F}$ in Problems 20–25 is conservative and find a scalar potential function f for $\mathbf{F}$.

20. $yz^2\mathbf{i} + xz^2\mathbf{j} + 2xyz\mathbf{k}$

21. $e^{xy}yz\mathbf{i} + e^{xy}xz\mathbf{j} + e^{xy}\mathbf{k}$

22. $yz^{-1}\mathbf{i} + xz^{-1}\mathbf{j} - xyz^{-2}\mathbf{k}$

23. $(x^2 + y^2 + z^2)(x\mathbf{i} + y\mathbf{j} + z\mathbf{k})$

24. $(y \sin z)\mathbf{i} + (x \sin z + 2y)\mathbf{j} + (xy \cos z)\mathbf{k}$

25. $(xy^2 + yz)\mathbf{i} + (x^2 y + xz + 3y^2 z)\mathbf{j} + (xy + y^3)\mathbf{k}$

In Problems 26–29, show that the vector field $\mathbf{F}$ is conservative and evaluate $\int_C \mathbf{F} \cdot d\mathbf{R}$ for any piecewise smooth path joining $A(1, 0, -1)$ to $B(0, -1, 1)$.

26. $\mathbf{F}(x, y, z) = \langle 3x^2 y^2 z, 2x^3 yz, x^3 y^2 - e^{-z} \rangle$

27. $\mathbf{F}(x, y, z) = \langle \sin z, -z \sin y, x \cos z + \cos y \rangle$

28. $\mathbf{F}(x, y, z) = \langle 2xz^3 - e^{-xy}y \sin z, -xe^{-xy} \sin z, 3x^2 z^2 + e^{-xy} \cos z \rangle$

29. $\mathbf{F}(x, y, z) = \left\langle \dfrac{y}{1 + x^2} + \tan^{-1} z, \tan^{-1} x, \dfrac{x}{1 + z^2} \right\rangle$

B **30.** A force field $\mathbf{F}(x, y) = (3x^2 + 6xy^2)\mathbf{i} + (6x^2 y + 4y^2)\mathbf{j}$ acts on an object moving in the plane. Show that $\mathbf{F}$ is conservative, and find a scalar potential for $\mathbf{F}$. How much work is done as the object moves from $(1, 0)$ to $(0, 1)$ along any path connecting these points?

Verify that each line integral in Problems 31–36 is independent of path and then find its value.

31. $\int_C [(3x^2 + 2x + y^2)\,dx + (2xy + y^3)\,dy]$, where C is any path from $(0, 0)$ to $(1, 1)$

32. $\int_C [(xy \cos xy + \sin xy)\,dx + (x^2 \cos xy)\,dy]$, where C is any path from $\left(0, \frac{\pi}{18}\right)$ to $\left(1, \frac{\pi}{6}\right)$

33. $\int_C [(y - x^2)\,dx + (x + y^2)\,dy]$, where C is any path from $(-1, -1)$ to $(0, 3)$

34. $\int_C [(3x^2y + y^2)\,dx + (x^3 + 2xy)\,dy]$, where C is the path given parametrically by $\mathbf{R}(t) = t\mathbf{i} + (t^2 + t - 2)\mathbf{j}$ for $0 \le t \le 2$

35. $\int_C [(\sin y)\,dx + (3 + x \cos y)\,dy]$, where C is the path given parametrically by $\mathbf{R}(t) = 2\sin\left(\frac{\pi t}{2}\right)\cos(\pi t)\mathbf{i} + (\sin^{-1} t)\mathbf{j}$ for $0 \le t \le 1$.

36. $\int_C [(e^x \cos y)\,dx + (-e^x \sin y)\,dy]$, where C is the path given parametrically by $\mathbf{R}(t) = (\cos t)\mathbf{i} + (\sin t)\mathbf{j}$ for $0 \le t \le \frac{\pi}{2}$.

Evaluate the line integrals given in Problems 37–41 using the fundamental theorem of line integrals.

37. $\int_C (y\mathbf{i} + x\mathbf{j}) \cdot d\mathbf{R}$, where C is any path from $(0, 0)$ to $(2, 4)$

38. $\int_C (xy^2\mathbf{i} + x^2y\mathbf{j}) \cdot d\mathbf{R}$, where C is any path from $(4, 1)$ to $(0, 0)$

39. $\int_C (2y\,dx + 2x\,dy)$, where C is the line segment from $(0, 0)$ to $(4, 4)$

40. $\int_C (e^x \sin y\,dx + e^x \cos y\,dy)$, where C is any smooth curve from $(0, 0)$ to $(0, 2\pi)$

41. $\int_C \left\{\left[\tan^{-1}\frac{y}{x} - \frac{xy}{x^2 + y^2}\right]dx\right.$
$\left. + \left[\frac{x^2}{x^2 + y^2} + e^{-y}(1 - y)\right]dy\right\}$,
where C is any smooth curve from $(1, 1)$ to $(-1, 2)$

42. Find a function g so $g(x)\mathbf{F}(x, y)$ is conservative, where
$$\mathbf{F}(x, y) = (x^2 + y^2 + x)\mathbf{i} + xy\mathbf{j}$$

43. Find a function g so $g(x)\mathbf{F}(x, y)$ is conservative, where
$$\mathbf{F}(x, y) = (x^4 + y^4)\mathbf{i} - (xy^3)\mathbf{j}$$

44. a. Over what region in the xy-plane will the line integral
$$\int_C [(-yx^{-2} + x^{-1})\,dx + x^{-1}\,dy]$$
be independent of path?

b. Evaluate the line integral in part **a** if C is defined by
$$\mathbf{R}(t) = (\cos^3 t)\mathbf{i} + (\sin 3t)\mathbf{j}$$
for $0 \le t \le \frac{\pi}{3}$.

45. The **gravitational force field** $\mathbf{F}$ between two particles of masses M and m separated by a distance r is modeled by
$$\mathbf{F}(x, y, z) = -\frac{KmM}{r^3}\mathbf{R}$$
where $\mathbf{R} = x\mathbf{i} + y\mathbf{j} + z\mathbf{k}$ and K is the gravitational constant.
a. Show that $\mathbf{F}$ is conservative by finding a scalar potential for $\mathbf{F}$. The scalar potential function f is often called the **Newtonian potential**.
b. Compute the amount of work done against the force field $\mathbf{F}$ in moving an object from the point $P(a_1, b_1, c_1)$ to $Q(a_2, b_2, c_2)$.

46. Let $\mathbf{F}(x, y) = \dfrac{-y\mathbf{i} + x\mathbf{j}}{x^2 + y^2}$.
a. Compute the line integral $\int_{C_1} \mathbf{F} \cdot d\mathbf{R}$, where C_1 is the upper semicircle $y = \sqrt{1 - x^2}$ traversed counterclockwise. What is the value of $\int_{C_2} \mathbf{F} \cdot d\mathbf{R}$ if C_2 is the lower semicircle $y = -\sqrt{1 - x^2}$ also traversed counterclockwise?
b. Show that if $\mathbf{F} = M\mathbf{i} + N\mathbf{j}$, then
$$\frac{\partial}{\partial y}\left(\frac{-y}{x^2 + y^2}\right) = \frac{\partial}{\partial x}\left(\frac{x}{x^2 + y^2}\right)$$
but $\mathbf{F}$ is not conservative on the unit disk $x^2 + y^2 \le 1$.

47. Modeling Problem A person whirls a bucket filled with water in a circle of radius 3 ft at the rate of 1 revolution per second. If the bucket and water weigh 30 lb, how much work is done by the force that keeps the bucket moving in a circular path?

48. Spy Problem Holding his breath for dear life, the Spy finally escapes from the Flamer's watery trap (Problem 57 of Section 12.7). He and the water spill into the next room, and the door slams shut. He finds himself looking across a large, rectangular room at the Flamer and Blohardt. He takes a step toward his nemeses but finds his movements restricted by a force field that appears to sap his strength. "I see you have noticed the Death Force my new assistant has designed for you," crows Blohardt with an evil laugh. "It will do you no good to stay still," boasts the Flamer. "The rays will eventually kill you even if you never move!" One more peal of laughter, and they leave together. Alone, the Spy quickly presses the stem on his wristwatch and the equation of the force field appears on the face:
$$\mathbf{F}(x, y) = (ye^{xy} + 2xy^3)\mathbf{i} + (xe^{xy} + 3x^2y^2 + \cos y)\mathbf{j}$$
Assuming that the Spy is at $(0, 0)$ on the wristwatch's coordinate system and that the door (and safety) is at $(10, 10)$, what path should he take to minimize the work of struggling against the Death Force Field while crossing the room in the least possible time?

In Problems 49 and 50, you are to experiment with the notion of computing work along a path, with and without the benefit of independence of path. Suppose you are to power a boat of some kind from point $A(0, 0)$ to point $B(2, 1)$, and the primary consideration is the force of the wind, which generally opposes you. You are to investigate the effect of taking different paths from A to B.

49. a. Suppose the wind force is $\mathbf{F} = \langle -a, -b \rangle$, for a and b positive. Compute the work involved along the straight line path between A and B; then along a second path of your choice. Does the path matter here? Why or why not?

b. Due to the effect of the harbor you are entering, suppose the wind force is $\langle -a, -ae^{-y} \rangle$. Again, compute the work along two paths as in part **a**. Does the path matter here? Why or why not?

c. Repeat part **b** for $\langle -a, -ae^{-y+x/9} \rangle$.

50. Exploration Problem An important type of problem in several fields of application is, "Can we find the optimal path to minimize the work?" You are to explore this issue in regard to the wind force in Problem 49**c**,

$$\mathbf{F} = \langle -a, -ae^{-y+x/9} \rangle$$

a. You should have the work computed for two different paths from the previous problem. By looking at these numbers and carefully studying $\mathbf{F}$, you should see that we will be rewarded (or punished) by changing the path slightly from the straight-line path. What do your observations suggest regarding trying to minimize the work?

b. Attempt to find an (approximate) optimal path, starting with your observations in part **a** and common sense. For example, the path could be described by a parabola (or higher-degree polynomial) or by some trigonometric function. Find a "good" path for this purpose.

c. Explore the following question: "Is there a realistic optimal path from A to B?" Consider two conditions: First, there is no restriction on the path; second, suppose there is a shoreline at $y = 1$ so that one's path cannot exceed this limit. *Hint*: One approach might be to consider all parabolic paths of the form $y = x(b - ax)$, where a and b are nonnegative, and $y(2) = 1$. In this case, you can eliminate b and do a one-parameter study.

d. Assume the path in part **c** cannot go above $y = 1$. You may have discovered the optimal path. What is it? If you did the parabolic study suggested in part **c**, there is an optimal path in this case. What is it?

C **51.** Show that if the vector field

$$\mathbf{F}(x, y, z) = M(x, y, z)\mathbf{i} + N(x, y, z)\mathbf{j} + P(x, y, z)\mathbf{k}$$

is conservative, then

$$\frac{\partial P}{\partial y} = \frac{\partial N}{\partial z} \qquad \frac{\partial M}{\partial z} = \frac{\partial P}{\partial x} \qquad \frac{\partial N}{\partial x} = \frac{\partial M}{\partial y}$$

52. Let f and g be differentiable functions of one variable. Show that the vector field $\mathbf{F} = [f(x) + y]\mathbf{i} + [g(y) + x]\mathbf{j}$ is conservative, and find the corresponding potential function.

53. Let $\mathbf{R} = x\mathbf{i} + y\mathbf{j} + z\mathbf{k}$ and $r = \|\mathbf{R}\|$. Show that the work done in moving an object from a distance r_1 to a distance r_2 in the central force field $\mathbf{F} = \mathbf{R}/r^3$ is given by

$$W = \frac{1}{r_1} - \frac{1}{r_2}$$

54. An object of mass m moves along a trajectory $\mathbf{R}(t)$ with velocity $\mathbf{V}(t)$ in a conservative force field $\mathbf{F}(t_1)$. Let $\mathbf{R}(t_0) = \mathbf{Q}_0$ and $\mathbf{R}(t_1) = \mathbf{Q}_1$ be the initial and terminal points on the trajectory.

a. Show that the work done on the object is $W = K(t_1) - K(t_0)$, where $K(t) = \frac{1}{2}m\|\mathbf{V}(t)\|^2$ is the object's *kinetic energy*.

b. Let f be a scalar potential for $\mathbf{F}$. Then $P(t) = -f(t)$ is the *potential energy* of the object. Prove the *law of conservation of energy*—namely,

$$P(t_0) + K(t_0) = P(t_1) + K(t_1)$$

55. Complete the proof of Theorem 13.5 by showing that if $\int_C \mathbf{F} \cdot d\mathbf{R}$ is independent of path in the open connected set D, then $\mathbf{F}$ is conservative. Do this by completing the following steps:

a. Let $P(a, b)$ be a fixed point in D, and let $Q(x, y)$ be any point in D. Define the function $f(x, y)$ by

$$f(x, y) = \int_P^Q \mathbf{F} \cdot d\mathbf{R}$$

Let $Q_1(x, y)$ be a point in D other than Q that lies on the same horizontal line as Q. Let C_1 be any curve in D from P to Q_1, and let C_2 be the horizontal line segment joining Q_1 to Q. Show that if $\mathbf{F} = M(x, y)\mathbf{i} + N(x, y)\mathbf{j}$, then $\frac{\partial f}{\partial x} = M(x, y)$.

b. Using a similar argument (only with vertical line segments), show that $\frac{\partial f}{\partial y} = N(x, y)$. Conclude that since $\mathbf{F} = \nabla f$, $\mathbf{F}$ must be conservative in D.

13.4 Green's Theorem

IN THIS SECTION Green's theorem, area as a line integral, Green's theorem for multiply-connected regions, alternative forms of Green's theorem, normal derivatives

The fundamental theorem of calculus, $\displaystyle\int_a^b \frac{dF}{dx} \, dx = F(b) - F(a)$, can be described

as saying that when the derivative $\dfrac{dF}{dx}$ is integrated over the closed interval $a \leq x \leq b$, the result is the same as that obtained by evaluating $F(x)$ at the "boundary points" a and b and forming the difference $F(b) - F(a)$. We obtained the analogous result

$$\int_C \nabla f \cdot d\mathbf{R} = f(Q) - f(P)$$

in Section 13.3, and our next goal is to obtain a different kind of analogue to the fundamental theorem of calculus called **Green's theorem** after the English mathematician George Green (Historical Quest in Problem 39).

GREEN'S THEOREM

Green's theorem relates a line integral around a closed curve to a double integral over the region contained by the curve. We begin with some terminology. A **Jordan curve**, named for the French mathematician Camille Jordan (1838–1922), is a closed curve C that does not intersect itself (see Figure 13.20). A simply connected region *D* in the plane has the property that it is connected and the interior of every Jordan curve *C* in *D* also lies in *D*, as shown in Figure 13.20.

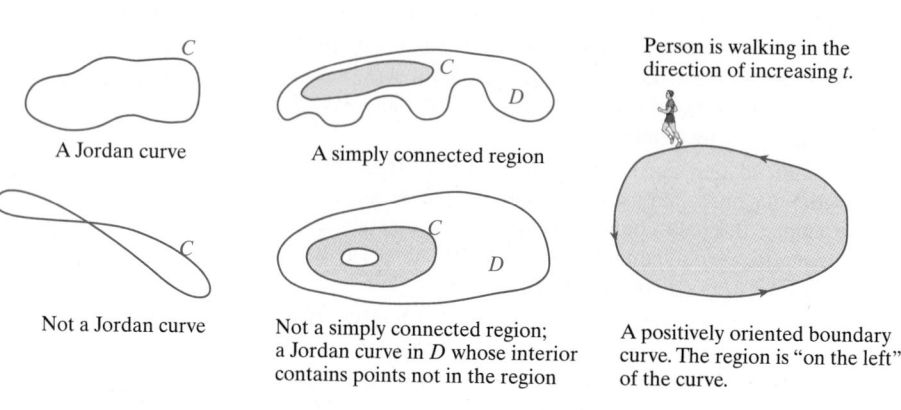

A Jordan curve

A simply connected region

Person is walking in the direction of increasing *t*.

Not a Jordan curve

Not a simply connected region; a Jordan curve in *D* whose interior contains points not in the region

A positively oriented boundary curve. The region is "on the left" of the curve.

Figure 13.20 A Jordan curve is a closed curve with no self-intersections. A region is simply connected if every Jordan curve has all its interior points in *D*.

Picture yourself as a point moving along a curve. If the region D stays on your left as you, the point, move along the curve *C* with increasing *t*, then *C* is said to be **positively oriented** (see Figure 13.20). Now we are ready to state Green's theorem.

THEOREM 13.6 Green's theorem

Let *D* be a simply connected region that is bounded by the positively oriented piecewise smooth Jordan curve *C*. Then if the vector field $\mathbf{F}(x, y) = M(x, y)\mathbf{i} + N(x, y)\mathbf{j}$ is continuously differentiable on *D*, we have

$$\oint_C (M\, dx + N\, dy) = \iint_D \left(\frac{\partial N}{\partial x} - \frac{\partial M}{\partial y} \right) dA$$

Graffiti on the wall of a high school playground in Ramat Gan (a suburb of Tel Aviv). Courtesy of Eli Maor.

> **→ What This Says** This theorem expresses an important relationship between a line integral around a simple closed curve (a curve is **simple** if there are no self-intersections and **closed** if there are no endpoints) in the plane and a double integral over the region bounded by the curve. It is one of the most important and elegant theorems in calculus. Take special note that *D* is required to be simply connected with a *positively oriented* boundary *C*.

Proof A **standard region** is one in which no vertical or horizontal line can intersect the boundary curve more than twice (see Figure 13.21). We will prove Green's theorem for the special case where *D* is a standard region, and then we will indicate how to extend the proof to more general regions. Suppose D is a standard region with boundary curve C. We begin by showing that

$$\iint_D \frac{\partial M}{\partial y} \, dx \, dy = -\int_C M \, dx$$

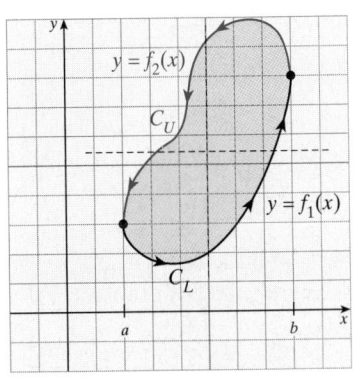

Figure 13.21 Standard region: No vertical or horizontal line intersects the boundary more than twice.

Because D is a standard region, as shown in Figure 13.21, the boundary curve C is composed of a lower portion C_L and an upper portion C_U, which are the graphs of functions $f_1(x)$ and $f_2(x)$, respectively, on a certain interval $a \le x \le b$. Then we can evaluate the double integral by iterated integration:

$$\iint_D \frac{\partial M}{\partial y} \, dx \, dy = \iint_D \frac{\partial M}{\partial y} \, dy \, dx = \int_a^b \left[\int_{f_1(x)}^{f_2(x)} \frac{\partial M}{\partial y} \, dy \right] dx$$

$$= \int_a^b M[x, f_2(x)] \, dx - \int_a^b M[x, f_1(x)] \, dx = \int_{-C_U} M \, dx - \int_{C_L} M \, dx$$

$$= -\left[\int_{C_U} M \, dx + \int_{C_L} M \, dx \right] = -\oint_C M \, dx$$

A similar argument shows that $\displaystyle\iint_D \frac{\partial N}{\partial x} \, dx \, dy = \oint_C N \, dy$. Thus,

$$\iint_D \left(\frac{\partial N}{\partial x} - \frac{\partial M}{\partial y} \right) dA = \iint_D \frac{\partial N}{\partial x} \, dx \, dy - \iint_D \frac{\partial M}{\partial y} \, dx \, dy$$

$$= \oint_C N \, dy - \oint_C (-M) \, dx = \oint_C (M \, dx + N \, dy)$$

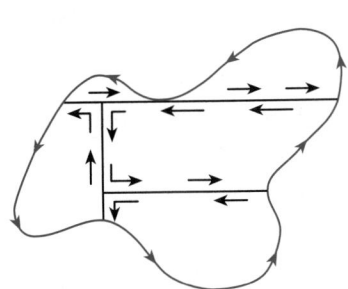

Figure 13.22 General case: The region is decomposed into a finite number of standard regions by cuts.

This completes the proof for a standard region. If D is not a standard region, it can be decomposed into a number of standard subregions by using horizontal and vertical "cuts," as shown in Figure 13.22. The proof for the standard region is then applied to each of these subregions, and the results are added. The line integrals along the cuts cancel in pairs, and after cancellation, the only remaining line integral is the one along the outer boundary C. Thus,

$$\oint_C (M \, dx + N \, dy) = \iint_R \left(\frac{\partial N}{\partial x} - \frac{\partial M}{\partial y} \right) dA$$

The case where there is one cut is considered in Problem 40. ❑

EXAMPLE 1   Using Green's theorem

Show that Green's theorem is true for the line integral $\displaystyle\oint_C (-y \, dx + x \, dy)$, where C is the closed path shown in Figure 13.23.

Solution

First, evaluate the line integral directly. The curve C consists of the line segment C_1 from $(-1, 0)$ to $(1, 0)$, followed by the semicircular arc C_2 from $(1, 0)$ back to $(-1, 0)$.

We parameterize each of these:

$$C_1 : \quad x = t, \qquad\qquad y = 0 \qquad -1 \le t \le 1$$
$$dx = dt, \qquad\qquad dy = 0$$
$$C_2 : \quad x = \cos u, \qquad\quad y = \sin u \qquad 0 \le u \le \pi$$
$$dx = -\sin u\, du, \quad dy = \cos u\, du$$

$$\oint_C (-y\, dx + x\, dy) = \int_{C_1} (-y\, dx + x\, dy) + \int_{C_2} (-y\, dx + x\, dy)$$

$$= \int_{-1}^{1} [-0\, dt + t \cdot 0] + \int_0^\pi [-\sin u(-\sin u\, du) + \cos u(\cos u\, du)]$$

$$= \int_0^\pi (\sin^2 u + \cos^2 u)\, du = \int_0^\pi 1\, du = \pi$$

Next, we use Green's theorem to evaluate this integral. Note that the boundary C is a Jordan curve and $M = -y$, $N = x$, so that $\mathbf{F}(x, y) = -y\mathbf{i} + x\mathbf{j}$ is continuously differentiable. We now apply Green's theorem:

$$\oint_C (-y\, dx + x\, dy) = \iint_D \left(\frac{\partial}{\partial x}(x) - \frac{\partial}{\partial y}(-y) \right) dA = \iint_D 2\, dA$$

$$= 2(\text{AREA OF SEMICIRCLE}) = 2\left[\tfrac{1}{2}\pi(1)^2 \right] = \pi \qquad \blacksquare$$

EXAMPLE 2   Computing work with Green's theorem

A closed path C in the plane is defined by Figure 13.24. Find the work done by an object moving along C in the force field $\mathbf{F}(x, y) = (x + xy^2)\mathbf{i} + 2(x^2 y - y^2 \sin y)\mathbf{j}$.

Solution

The work done, W, is given by the line integral $\oint_C \mathbf{F} \cdot d\mathbf{R}$. Note that $\mathbf{F}$ is continuously differentiable on the region D enclosed by C, and since D is simply connected with a positively oriented boundary (namely, C), the hypotheses of Green's theorem are satisfied. We find that

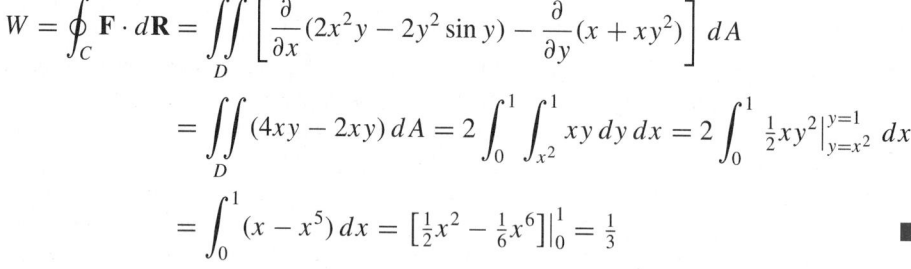

$$W = \oint_C \mathbf{F} \cdot d\mathbf{R} = \iint_D \left[\frac{\partial}{\partial x}(2x^2 y - 2y^2 \sin y) - \frac{\partial}{\partial y}(x + xy^2) \right] dA$$

$$= \iint_D (4xy - 2xy)\, dA = 2 \int_0^1 \int_{x^2}^1 xy\, dy\, dx = 2 \int_0^1 \tfrac{1}{2}xy^2 \big|_{y=x^2}^{y=1}\, dx$$

$$= \int_0^1 (x - x^5)\, dx = \left[\tfrac{1}{2}x^2 - \tfrac{1}{6}x^6 \right] \big|_0^1 = \tfrac{1}{3} \qquad \blacksquare$$

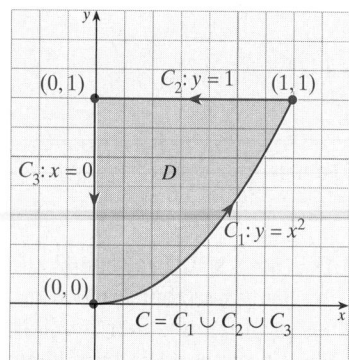

Figure 13.24 Closed path C

AREA AS A LINE INTEGRAL

A line integral can be used to compute an area of a region in the plane by applying the following theorem.

THEOREM 13.7   Area as a line integral

Let D be a simply connected region in the plane with piecewise smooth, positively oriented closed boundary C, as shown in Figure 13.25. Then the area A of region D is given by each of the following line integrals:

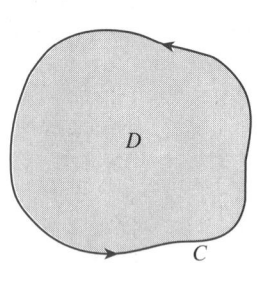

Figure 13.25 Area of region D

$$A = \oint_C x\, dy = -\oint_C y\, dx = \frac{1}{2} \oint_C [x\, dy - y\, dx]$$

Proof   We will prove that

$$A = \frac{1}{2} \oint_C [x\,dy - y\,dx]$$

and leave the other two area formulas for the reader (see Problem 44).

Let $\mathbf{F}(x, y) = -y\mathbf{i} + x\mathbf{j}$. Then since $\mathbf{F}$ is continuously differentiable on D, Green's theorem applies. We have

$$\oint_C (-y\,dx + x\,dy) = \iint_D \left[\frac{\partial}{\partial x}(x) - \frac{\partial}{\partial y}(-y) \right] dA = \iint_D 2\,dA = 2A$$

so that $A = \dfrac{1}{2} \oint_C (-y\,dx + x\,dy)$.   ❑

EXAMPLE 3   Area enclosed by an ellipse

Show that the ellipse $\dfrac{x^2}{a^2} + \dfrac{y^2}{b^2} = 1$ has area πab.

Solution

The elliptical path E is given parametrically by $x = a\cos\theta$, $y = b\sin\theta$ for $0 \le \theta \le 2\pi$. We find $dx = -a\sin\theta\,d\theta$, $dy = b\cos\theta\,d\theta$. If A is the area of this ellipse, then

$$\begin{aligned}
A &= \tfrac{1}{2} \oint_C (-y\,dx + x\,dy) \\
&= \tfrac{1}{2} \int_0^{2\pi} [-(b\sin\theta)(-a\sin\theta\,d\theta) + (a\cos\theta)(b\cos\theta\,d\theta)] \\
&= \tfrac{1}{2} \int_0^{2\pi} ab(\sin^2\theta + \cos^2\theta)\,d\theta \\
&= \tfrac{1}{2} \int_0^{2\pi} ab\,d\theta \\
&= \tfrac{1}{2}ab(2\pi - 0) \\
&= \pi ab
\end{aligned}$$
■

GREEN'S THEOREM FOR MULTIPLY-CONNECTED REGIONS

In the statement of Green's theorem, we require the region R inside the boundary curve C to be simply connected, but the theorem can be extended to multiply-connected regions, that is, regions with one or more "holes." A region with a single hole is shown in Figure 13.26a. The boundary of this region consists of an "outer" curve C_1 and an "inner" curve C_2, oriented so that the region R is always on the left as we travel around the boundary, which means that C_1 is oriented counterclockwise and C_2 clockwise.

We now make cuts AB and CD through the region to the hole, as indicated in Figure 13.26b. Let R_1 be the simply connected region contained by the closed curve C_3 that begins at A, extends along the cut to B, and then clockwise along the bottom of the curve C_2 to C, along the cut to D, and counterclockwise along the bottom of C_1 back to A. Similarly, let R_2 be the region contained by the curve C_4 that begins at D and extends to C along the cut, to B along the top of C_2, to A along the second cut, and back to D along the top part of C_1. Then, if the vector field $\mathbf{F} = M\mathbf{i} + N\mathbf{j}$ is continuously differentiable on R, we can apply Green's theorem to show

$$\iint_R \left(\frac{\partial N}{\partial x} - \frac{\partial M}{\partial y} \right) dA = \iint_{R_1} \left(\frac{\partial N}{\partial x} - \frac{\partial M}{\partial y} \right) dA + \iint_{R_2} \left(\frac{\partial N}{\partial x} - \frac{\partial M}{\partial y} \right) dA$$

$$= \oint_{C_3} (M\,dx + N\,dy) + \oint_{C_4} (M\,dx + N\,dy)$$

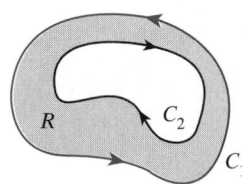

a. A doubly-connected region with oriented boundary curves C_1 and C_2.

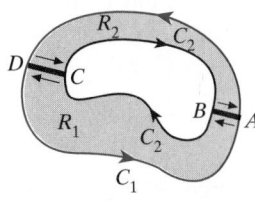

b. Two "cuts" are made through the hole.

Figure 13.26 Multiply-connected region

But the line integrals from A to B and C to D cancel those from B to A and D to C, leaving only the line integrals along the original boundary curves C_1 and C_2. Thus, we have

$$\iint\limits_R \left(\frac{\partial N}{\partial x} - \frac{\partial M}{\partial y}\right) dA = \oint_{C_1} (M\,dx + N\,dy) + \oint_{C_2} (M\,dx + N\,dy)$$

Green's Theorem for Doubly-Connected Regions

Let R be a doubly-connected region (one hole) in the plane, with outer boundary C_1 oriented counterclockwise and boundary C_2 of the hole oriented clockwise. If the boundary curves and $\mathbf{F}(x, y) = M(x, y)\mathbf{i} + N(x, y)\mathbf{j}$ satisfy the hypotheses of Green's theorem, then

$$\iint\limits_R \left(\frac{\partial N}{\partial x} - \frac{\partial M}{\partial y}\right) dA = \oint_{C_1} (M\,dx + N\,dy) + \oint_{C_2} (M\,dx + N\,dy)$$

Example 4 illustrates one way this result can be used.

EXAMPLE 4   Green's theorem for a region containing a singular point

Show that $\displaystyle\oint_C \frac{-y\,dx + x\,dy}{x^2 + y^2} = 2\pi$, where C is any piecewise smooth Jordan curve enclosing the origin $(0, 0)$.

Solution

Let $M(x, y) = \dfrac{-y}{x^2 + y^2}$ and $N = \dfrac{x}{x^2 + y^2}$. Then

$$\frac{\partial N}{\partial x} = \frac{y^2 - x^2}{(x^2 + y^2)^2} = \frac{\partial M}{\partial y}$$

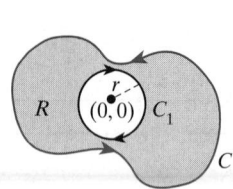

Figure 13.27 The region R for doubly-connected regions

at any point (x, y) other than the origin. Next, let C_1 be a circle centered at the origin with radius r so small that the entire circle is contained in C, and let R be the region between the curve C and the circle C_1, as shown in Figure 13.27.

We know that $\dfrac{\partial N}{\partial x} = \dfrac{\partial M}{\partial y}$ throughout R (since R does not contain the origin) and Green's theorem for doubly-connected regions tells us that

$$\oint_C \frac{-y\,dx + x\,dy}{x^2 + y^2} + \oint_{C_1} \frac{-y\,dx + x\,dy}{x^2 + y^2} = \iint\limits_R \left(\frac{\partial N}{\partial x} - \frac{\partial M}{\partial y}\right) dA = 0$$

so that

$$\oint_C \frac{-y\,dx + x\,dy}{x^2 + y^2} = -\oint_{C_1} \frac{-y\,dx + x\,dy}{x^2 + y^2} = \oint_{-C_1} \frac{-y\,dx + x\,dy}{x^2 + y^2}$$

where $-C_1$ is the circle C_1 traversed counterclockwise instead of clockwise. In other words, we can find the value of the given line integral about the curve C by finding the line integral about the circle $-C_1$. To do this, we parameterize $-C_1$ by

$$x = r\cos\theta, \qquad y = r\sin\theta \qquad \text{for } 0 \le \theta \le 2\pi$$

and find that

$$\oint_{-C_1} \frac{-y\,dx + x\,dy}{x^2 + y^2} = \int_0^{2\pi} \frac{-r\sin\theta(-r\sin\theta\,d\theta) + r\cos\theta(r\cos\theta\,d\theta)}{r^2\cos^2\theta + r^2\sin^2\theta}$$

$$= \int_0^{2\pi} \frac{r^2(\sin^2\theta + \cos^2\theta)}{r^2(\sin^2\theta + \cos^2\theta)}\,d\theta = \int_0^{2\pi} 1\,d\theta = 2\pi$$

Thus,

$$\oint_C \frac{-y\,dx + x\,dy}{x^2 + y^2} = \oint_{-C_1} \frac{-y\,dx + x\,dy}{x^2 + y^2} = 2\pi \qquad\blacksquare$$

Note that the line integral in Example 4 is not independent of path in R because there are closed paths (like C_1) along which the line integral is not 0.

ALTERNATIVE FORMS OF GREEN'S THEOREM

Green's theorem can be expressed in two forms that generalize nicely to $\mathbb{R}^3$. For the first, note that the curl of the vector field $\mathbf{F}(x, y) = M(x, y)\mathbf{i} + N(x, y)\mathbf{j}$ is given by

$$\text{curl } \mathbf{F} = \begin{vmatrix} \mathbf{i} & \mathbf{j} & \mathbf{k} \\ \dfrac{\partial}{\partial x} & \dfrac{\partial}{\partial y} & \dfrac{\partial}{\partial z} \\ M(x, y) & N(x, y) & 0 \end{vmatrix}$$

$$= 0\mathbf{i} + 0\mathbf{j} + \left[\frac{\partial N}{\partial x} - \frac{\partial M}{\partial y}\right]\mathbf{k}$$

$$= \left[\frac{\partial N}{\partial x} - \frac{\partial M}{\partial y}\right]\mathbf{k} \qquad \begin{array}{l}\textit{Because } M \textit{ and } N \textit{ are}\\ \textit{functions of only } x \textit{ and } y\end{array}$$

so

$$\iint\limits_D \left(\frac{\partial N}{\partial x} - \frac{\partial M}{\partial y}\right) dA = \iint\limits_D (\text{curl } \mathbf{F} \cdot \mathbf{k})\,dA$$

On the other hand, the line integral in Green's theorem can be expressed as

$$\oint_C \mathbf{F} \cdot d\mathbf{R} = \oint_C \mathbf{F} \cdot \frac{d\mathbf{R}}{ds}\,ds = \oint_C \mathbf{F} \cdot \mathbf{T}\,ds$$

By combining these results, we obtain

$$\oint_C \mathbf{F} \cdot d\mathbf{R} = \iint\limits_D \left(\frac{\partial N}{\partial x} - \frac{\partial M}{\partial y}\right) dA \qquad \textit{Green's theorem}$$

$$\oint_C \mathbf{F} \cdot \mathbf{T}\,ds = \iint\limits_D (\text{curl } \mathbf{F} \cdot \mathbf{k})\,dA$$

When we extend this result to surfaces in $\mathbb{R}^3$ it will be called *Stokes' theorem*. We will examine Stokes' theorem in Section 13.6 and show how it can be interpreted in terms of the circulation of a fluid flow.

We have just seen how Green's theorem can be written in terms of $\mathbf{F} \cdot \mathbf{T}$, the tangential component of the vector field $\mathbf{F}$. The following example shows how Green's theorem can also be expressed in terms of $\mathbf{F} \cdot \mathbf{N}$, the normal component of $\mathbf{F}$. When this result is extended to $\mathbb{R}^3$ in Section 13.7, it will be called the *divergence theorem*.

EXAMPLE 5 The divergence theorem in the plane

Suppose $\mathbf{F}(x, y) = M(x, y)\mathbf{i} + N(x, y)\mathbf{j}$ with a piecewise smooth boundary C. Show that

$$\oint_C \mathbf{F} \cdot \mathbf{N}\,ds = \iint\limits_D \text{div } \mathbf{F}\,dA$$

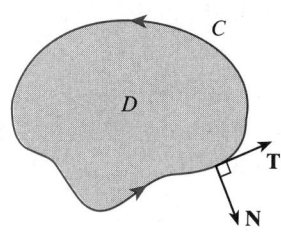

Figure 13.28 The outward unit normal to $\mathbf{R}(s) = \langle x(s), y(s) \rangle$ is $\mathbf{N} = \langle y'(s), -x'(s) \rangle$

Solution

Parameterize C with the arc length parameter s, so that $\mathbf{R}(s) = x(s)\mathbf{i} + y(s)\mathbf{j}$ is the position vector on C. A unit tangent vector $\mathbf{T}$ to the curve C is $\mathbf{T} = \mathbf{R}'(s) = x'(s)\mathbf{i} + y'(s)\mathbf{j}$, which means that an outward normal vector is $\mathbf{N} = y'(s)\mathbf{i} - x'(s)\mathbf{j}$ (see Figure 13.28).

We now apply Green's theorem to find a representation using div $\mathbf{F}$.

$$
\begin{aligned}
\oint_C \mathbf{F} \cdot \mathbf{N}\, ds &= \int_a^b (M\mathbf{i} + N\mathbf{j}) \cdot [y'(s)\mathbf{i} - x'(s)\mathbf{j}]\, ds \\
&= \int_a^b \left(M\frac{dy}{ds} - N\frac{dx}{ds} \right) ds \\
&= \oint_C (-N\, dx + M\, dy) \\
&= \iint_D \left(\frac{\partial M}{\partial x} + \frac{\partial N}{\partial y} \right) dx\, dy \qquad \text{Green's theorem} \\
&= \iint_D \operatorname{div} \mathbf{F}\, dA
\end{aligned}
$$

■

We list these alternative forms of Green's theorem for easy reference.

Alternative Forms of Green's Theorem

Let D be a simply connected region with a positively oriented boundary C. Then if the vector field $\mathbf{F} = M\mathbf{i} + N\mathbf{j}$ is continuously differentiable on D, we have

$$
\underbrace{\oint_C \mathbf{F} \cdot d\mathbf{R}}_{\text{Tangential component of } \mathbf{F}} = \oint_C (M\, dx + N\, dy)
$$

$$
= \iint_D \left(\frac{\partial N}{\partial x} - \frac{\partial M}{\partial y} \right) dA = \iint_D (\operatorname{curl} \mathbf{F} \cdot \mathbf{k})\, dA
$$

$$
\underbrace{\oint_C \mathbf{F} \cdot \mathbf{N}\, ds}_{\text{Normal component of } \mathbf{F}} = \iint_D \left(\frac{\partial M}{\partial x} + \frac{\partial N}{\partial y} \right) dA = \iint_D \operatorname{div} \mathbf{F}\, dA
$$

NORMAL DERIVATIVES

In physics, some important applications of Green's theorem involve the *normal derivative* of a scalar function f, which is defined as the directional derivative of f in the direction of the outward normal vector $\mathbf{N}$ to some curve or surface.

Normal Derivative

The **normal derivative** of f, denoted by $\partial f/\partial n$, is the directional derivative of f in the direction of the normal vector pointing to the exterior of the domain of f. In other words,

$$
\frac{\partial f}{\partial n} = \nabla f \cdot \mathbf{N}
$$

where $\mathbf{N}$ is the outward unit normal vector.

The following example illustrates how Green's theorem can be used in connection with the normal derivative. Additional examples are found in the problem set.

EXAMPLE 6   Green's formula for the integral of the Laplacian

Suppose f is a scalar function with continuous first and second partial derivatives in the simply connected region D. If the piecewise smooth closed curve C bounds D, show that

$$\iint_D \nabla^2 f \, dx \, dy = \oint_C \frac{\partial f}{\partial n} \, ds$$

where $\nabla^2 f = f_{xx} + f_{yy}$ is the Laplacian of f and $\frac{\partial f}{\partial n} = \nabla f \cdot \mathbf{N}$ is the normal derivative vector.

Solution

Let $u = -\dfrac{\partial f}{\partial y}$ and $v = \dfrac{\partial f}{\partial x}$. Then we have

$$\nabla^2 f = f_{xx} + f_{yy} = \frac{\partial v}{\partial x} - \frac{\partial u}{\partial y}$$

$$\iint_D \nabla^2 f \, dx \, dy = \iint_D \left(\frac{\partial v}{\partial x} - \frac{\partial u}{\partial y} \right) dx \, dy$$

$$= \oint_C (u \, dx + v \, dy) \qquad \text{Green's theorem}$$

$$= \oint_C \left(u \frac{dx}{ds} + v \frac{dy}{ds} \right) ds$$

$$= \oint_C \left(-\frac{\partial f}{\partial y} \frac{dx}{ds} + \frac{\partial f}{\partial x} \frac{dy}{ds} \right) ds$$

$$= \oint_C \left(f_x \frac{dy}{ds} - f_y \frac{dx}{ds} \right) ds$$

$$= \oint_C \nabla f \cdot \left(\frac{dy}{ds} \mathbf{i} - \frac{dx}{ds} \mathbf{j} \right) ds$$

$$= \oint_C \nabla f \cdot \mathbf{N} \, ds \qquad \text{Where } \mathbf{N} = \frac{dy}{ds} \mathbf{i} - \frac{dx}{ds} \mathbf{j} \text{ is the outward unit normal vector to } C$$

$$= \oint_C \frac{\partial f}{\partial n} \, ds \qquad\qquad\qquad \blacksquare$$

13.4   PROBLEM SET

Ⓐ *In Problems 1–6, use Green's theorem to evaluate the given line integral around the indicated closed curve C. Then check your answer by parameterizing C.*

1. $\oint_C (y^2\,dx + x^2\,dy)$

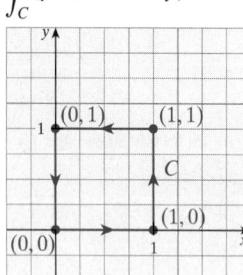

2. $\oint_C (y^3\,dx - x^3\,dy)$

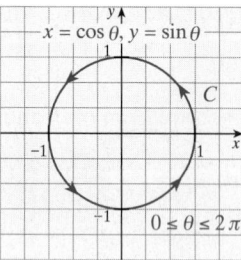

3. $\oint_C [(2x^2 + 3y)\,dx - 3y^2\,dy]$

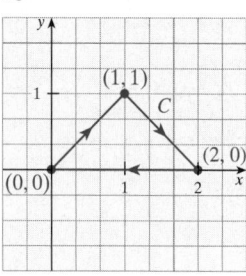

4. $\oint_C (y^2\,dx + 3xy^2\,dy)$

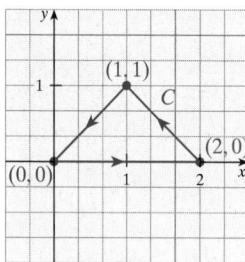

5. $\oint_C 4xy\,dx$

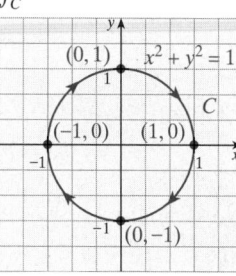

6. $\oint_C (4y\,dx - 3x\,dy)$

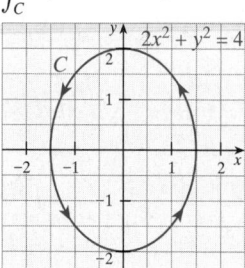

In Problems 7–14, use Green's theorem to evaluate the given line integral around the indicated closed curve C.

7. $\oint_C (2y\,dx - x\,dy)$

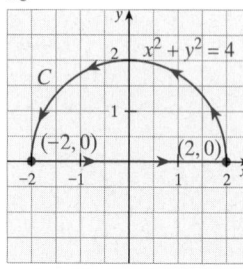

8. $\oint_C (e^x\,dx - \sin x\,dy)$

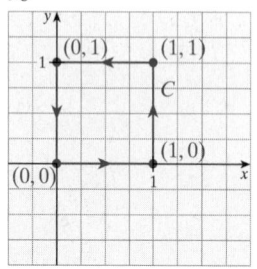

9. $\oint_C (x \sin x\,dx - e^{y^2}\,dy)$

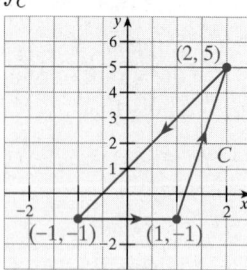

10. $\oint_C [(x + y)\,dx - (3x - 2y)\,dy]$

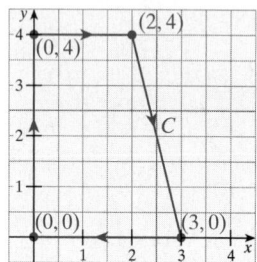

11. $\oint_C [(x - y^2)\,dx + 2xy\,dy]$

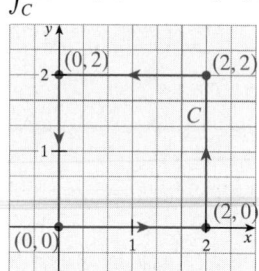

12. $\oint_C (y^2\,dx + x\,dy)$

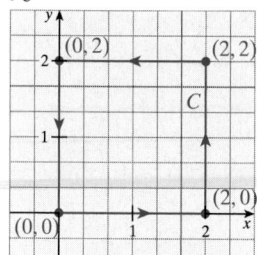

13. $\oint_C [\sin x \cos y\,dx + \cos x \sin y\,dy]$

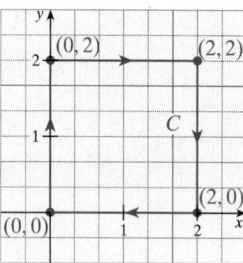

14. $\oint_C \left[2x \tan^{-1} y\,dx - \dfrac{x^2 y^2}{1 + y^2}\,dy \right]$

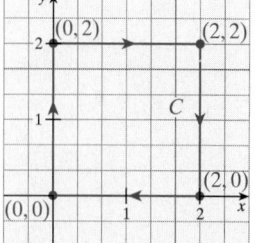

15. Use Green's theorem to find the work done by the force field

$$\mathbf{F}(x, y) = (3y - 4x)\mathbf{i} + (4x - y)\mathbf{j}$$

when an object moves once counterclockwise around the ellipse $4x^2 + y^2 = 4$.

16. Find the work done when an object moves in the force field $\mathbf{F}(x, y) = y^2\mathbf{i} + x^2\mathbf{j}$ counterclockwise around the circular path $x^2 + y^2 = 2$.

Use Theorem 13.7 to find the area enclosed by the regions described in Problems 17–20, and then check by using an appropriate formula.

17. circle $x^2 + y^2 = 4$

18. triangle with vertices $(0, 0)$, $(1, 1)$, and $(0, 2)$

19. trapezoid with vertices $(0, 0)$, $(4, 0)$, $(1, 3)$, and $(0, 3)$

20. semicircle $y = \sqrt{4 - x^2}$

B 21. Evaluate the line integral $\oint_C (x^2 y \, dx - y^2 x \, dy)$, where C is the boundary of the region between the x-axis and the semicircle $y = \sqrt{a^2 - x^2}$, traversed counterclockwise (including the x-axis).

22. Evaluate the line integral

$$\oint_C (3y \, dx - 2x \, dy)$$

where C is the cardioid $r = 1 + \sin\theta$, traversed counterclockwise.

23. Show that

$$\oint_C [(5 - xy - y^2) \, dx - (2xy - x^2) \, dy] = 3\overline{x}$$

where C is the square $0 \le x \le 1$, $0 \le y \le 1$ traversed counterclockwise and $\overline{x}$ is the x-coordinate of the centroid of the square.

24. Find the work done by the force field $\mathbf{F}(x, y) = (x + 2y^2)\mathbf{j}$ as an object moves once counterclockwise about the circle $(x - 2)^2 + y^2 = 1$.

25. Let D be the region bounded by the Jordan curve C, and let A be the area of D. If $(\overline{x}, \overline{y})$ is the centroid of D, show that

$$\overline{x} = \frac{1}{2A} \oint_C x^2 \, dy \quad \text{and} \quad \overline{y} = -\frac{1}{2A} \oint_C y^2 \, dx$$

where C is traversed counterclockwise.

26. Use Theorem 13.7 and the polar transformation formulas $x = r\cos\theta$, $y = r\sin\theta$ to obtain the area formula in polar coordinates, namely,

$$A = \frac{1}{2} \int_{\theta_1}^{\theta_2} r^2 \, d\theta = \frac{1}{2} \int_{\theta_1}^{\theta_2} [g(\theta)]^2 \, d\theta$$

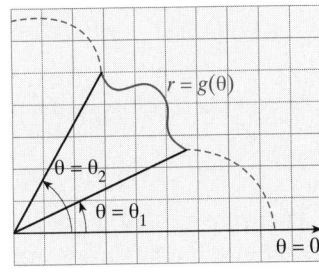

27. Evaluate $\oint_C \left[\left(\dfrac{-y}{x^2} + \dfrac{1}{x} \right) dx + \dfrac{1}{x} \, dy \right]$, where C is any Jordan curve that does not intersect the y-axis, traversed counterclockwise.

28. Evaluate $\oint_C \dfrac{x \, dx + y \, dy}{x^2 + y^2}$, where C is any Jordan curve whose interior does not contain the origin, traversed counterclockwise.

29. Evaluate the line integral

$$\oint_C \frac{x \, dx + y \, dy}{x^2 + y^2}$$

where C is any piecewise smooth Jordan curve enclosing the origin, traversed counterclockwise.

30. Evaluate $\oint_C \dfrac{-y \, dx + (x - 1) \, dy}{(x - 1)^2 + y^2}$, where C is any Jordan curve whose interior does not contain the point $(1, 0)$, traversed counterclockwise.

31. Evaluate $\oint_C \dfrac{-(y + 2) \, dx + (x - 1) \, dy}{(x - 1)^2 + (y + 2)^2}$, where C is any Jordan curve whose interior does not contain the point $(1, -2)$, traversed counterclockwise.

32. Evaluate $\oint_C \dfrac{\partial z}{\partial n} \, ds$, where $z(x, y) = 2x^2 + 3y^2$, and C is the circular path $x^2 + y^2 = 16$, traversed counterclockwise.

33. Evaluate $\oint_C \dfrac{\partial f}{\partial n} \, ds$, where $f(x, y) = x^2 y - 2xy + y^2$, and C is the boundary of the unit square $0 \le x \le 1$, $0 \le y \le 1$, traversed counterclockwise.

34. Evaluate $\oint_C x \dfrac{\partial x}{\partial n} \, ds$, where C is the boundary of the unit square $0 \le x \le 1$, $0 \le y \le 1$, traversed counterclockwise.

35. If C is a Jordan curve, show that

$$\oint_C [(x - 3y) \, dx + (2x - y^2) \, dy] = 5A$$

where A is the area of the region D enclosed by C.

36. Use line integration to find the area of the region bounded by the curve C: $x = \cos^3 t$, $y = \sin^3 t$ for $0 \le t \le 2\pi$.

C 37. Prove the following theoretical application of Green's theorem: Let $\mathbf{F}(x, y) = u(x, y)\mathbf{i} + v(x, y)\mathbf{j}$ be continuously differentiable on the simply connected region D. Then $\mathbf{F}$ is conservative if and only if

$$\frac{\partial u}{\partial y} = \frac{\partial v}{\partial x}$$

throughout D.

38. Recall that a scalar function f with continuous first and second partial derivatives is said to be *harmonic* in a region D if $\nabla^2 f = 0$ (that is, if $f_{xx} + f_{yy} = 0$). If f is such a function and D is a simply connected region enclosed by the Jordan curve C, show that

$$\iint_D (f_x^2 + f_y^2) \, dx \, dy = \oint_C f \frac{\partial f}{\partial n} \, ds$$

39. HISTORICAL QUEST   George Green (1793–1841) was the son of a baker who worked in his father's mill and studied mathematics and physics in his spare time, using only books he obtained from the library. In 1828, he published a memoir titled "An Essay on the Application of Mathematical Analysis to the Theories of Electricity and Magnetism," which contains the result that now bears his name. Very few copies of the essay were printed and distributed, so few people knew of Green's results. In 1833, at the age of 40, he entered Cambridge University and graduated just four years before his death. His 1828 paper was discovered and publicized in 1845 by Sir William Thompson (later known as Lord Kelvin, 1824–1907), and Green finally received proper credit for his work. ∎

In this Quest, use Green's theorem to prove the following two important results, known as **Green's formulas**. In both cases, D is a simply connected region enclosed by the Jordan curve C.

a. Green's first formula.

$$\iint_D \left[f \nabla^2 g + \nabla f \cdot \nabla g \right] dx \, dy = \oint_C f \frac{\partial g}{\partial n} \, ds$$

b. Once again start with the line integral and derive what is known as **Green's second formula.**

$$\iint_D \left[f \nabla^2 g - g \nabla^2 f \right] dx \, dy = \oint_C \left(f \frac{\partial g}{\partial n} - g \frac{\partial f}{\partial n} \right) ds$$

40. HISTORICAL QUEST   The result known as "Green's theorem" in the West is called "Ostrogradsky's theorem" in Russia, after Mikhail Ostrogradsky. Although Ostrogradsky published over 80 papers during a successful career as a mathematician, today he is known, even in his homeland, only for his version of Green's theorem, which appeared as part of a series of results presented to the Academy of Sciences in 1828. ∎

MIKHAIL OSTROGRADSKY
1801–1862

In this Quest you are asked to prove Green–Ostrogradsky's theorem in the plane for the nonstandard region D shown in Figure 13.29.

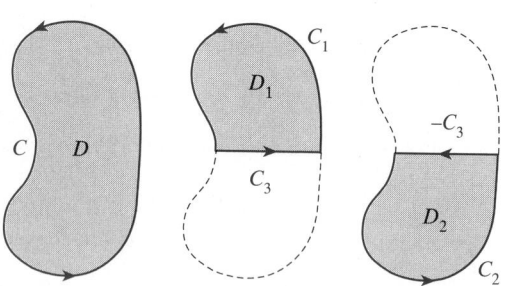

Figure 13.29   Green's theorem cut by a line L

Specifically, suppose that the line C_3 "cuts" the region D into two standard subregions D_1 and D_2. Apply Green's theorem to D_1 and D_2, and then combine the results to show that the theorem applies to the non-standard region D. *Hint*: The key is what happens along the "cut line" C_3.

41. Extend Green's theorem to a "triply-connected" region (two holes), such as the one shown in Figure 13.30.

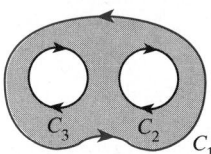

Figure 13.30   A triply-connected region

42. Suppose $\mathbf{F} = M(x, y)\mathbf{i} + N(x, y)\mathbf{j}$ is continuously differentiable in a doubly-connected region R and that

$$\frac{\partial N}{\partial x} = \frac{\partial M}{\partial y}$$

throughout R. How many distinct values of I are there for the integral

$$I = \oint_C [M(x, y) \, dx + N(x, y) \, dy]$$

where C is a piecewise smooth Jordan curve in R?

43. Answer the question in Problem 42 for the case where R is triply-connected (two holes). See Figure 13.30.

44. Let D be a simply connected region in the plane with a piecewise smooth closed boundary C. Complete the proof of Theorem 13.7 by showing that the area of D is given by

$$A = \oint_C x \, dy \quad \text{and} \quad A = -\oint_C y \, dx$$

13.5   Surface Integrals

IN THIS SECTION   surface integration, flux integrals, integrals over parametrically defined surfaces

SURFACE INTEGRATION

A surface is said to be **smooth** if there is a nonzero normal vector at each of its points, and it is **piecewise smooth** if it is composed of a finite number of smooth pieces. A

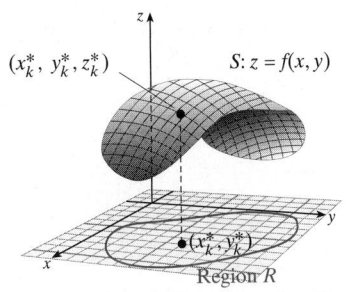

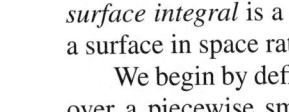

a. A piecewise smooth surface S

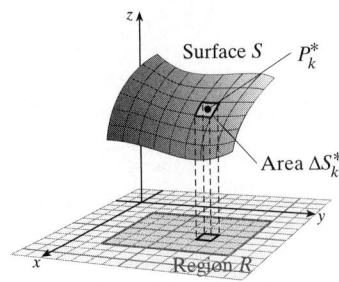

b. Construction of a Riemann sum

Figure 13.31 Definition of a surface integral

Surface Integral

surface integral is a generalization of the line integral in which the integration is over a surface in space rather than a curve.

We begin by defining the surface integral of a continuous scalar function $g(x, y, z)$ over a piecewise smooth surface S, as shown in Figure 13.31a. Partition S into n subregions, the kth of which has area ΔS_k, and let $P_k^*(x_k^*, y_k^*, z_k^*)$ be a point chosen arbitrarily from the kth subregion, for $k = 1, 2, \ldots, n$ (see Figure 13.31b). Form the Riemann sum

$$\sum_{k=1}^{n} g(P_k^*) \Delta S_k$$

and take the limit as the largest of the ΔS_k tends to 0, just as we did with surface area in Section 12.4. If this limit exists, it is called the **surface integral of g over S** and is denoted by

$$\iint\limits_{S} g(x, y, z) \, dS$$

Recall from Section 12.4 that when the surface S projects onto the region R in the xy-plane and S has the representation $z = f(x, y)$, then $dS = \sqrt{f_x^2 + f_y^2 + 1} \, dA$, where dA is either $dx \, dy$ or $dy \, dx$. We can now state the formula for evaluating a surface integral.

Let S be a surface defined by $z = f(x, y)$ and R be its projection on the xy-plane. If f, f_x, and f_y are continuous in R and g is a continuous function of three variables on S, then the **surface integral** of g over S is

$$\iint\limits_{S} g(x, y, z) \, dS = \iint\limits_{R} g(x, y, f(x, y)) \sqrt{[f_x(x, y)]^2 + [f_y(x, y)]^2 + 1} \, dA$$

EXAMPLE 1   Evaluating a surface integral

Evaluate the surface integral

$$\iint\limits_{S} g \, dS$$

shown in Figure 13.32, where $g(x, y, z) = xz + 2x^2 - 3xy$ and S is that portion of the plane $2x - 3y + z = 6$ that lies over the unit square $R: 2 \le x \le 3, 2 \le y \le 3$.

Solution

First, note that the equation of the plane can be written as $z = f(x, y)$ where $f(x, y) = 6 - 2x + 3y$. We have $f_x(x, y) = -2$ and $f_y(x, y) = 3$, so that

$$dS = \sqrt{f_x^2 + f_y^2 + 1} \, dA = \sqrt{(-2)^2 + (3)^2 + 1} \, dA = \sqrt{14} \, dA$$

Consequently,

$$\iint\limits_{S} g \, dS = \iint\limits_{R} (xz + 2x^2 - 3xy) \sqrt{14} \, dA$$

$$= \iint\limits_{R} [x(6 - 2x + 3y) + 2x^2 - 3xy] \sqrt{14} \, dy \, dx \quad \text{Since } z = 6 - 2x + 3y$$

$$= \sqrt{14} \iint\limits_{R} 6x \, dy \, dx$$

$$= 6\sqrt{14} \int_{2}^{3} \int_{2}^{3} x \, dy \, dx = 6\sqrt{14} \int_{2}^{3} x \, dx = 15\sqrt{14} \qquad \blacksquare$$

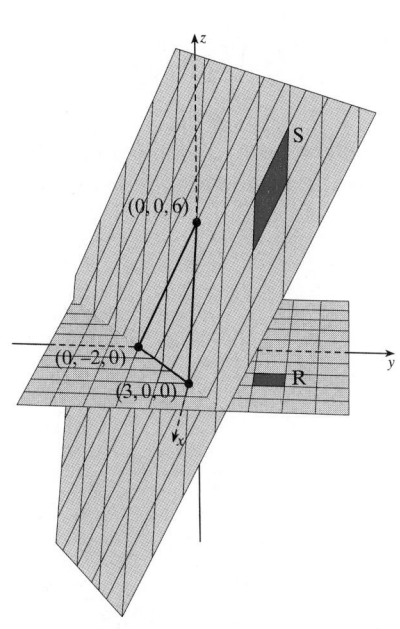

Figure 13.32 The portion of the plane that lies above the unit square R

If the function g defined on S is simply $g(x, y, z) = 1$, then the surface integral gives the surface area of S.

Surface Area Formula

If S is a piecewise smooth surface, its area is given by

$$A = \iint\limits_{S} dS$$

A useful application of surface integrals is to find the center of mass of a thin curved lamina whose shape is part of a given surface S, as shown in Figure 13.33.

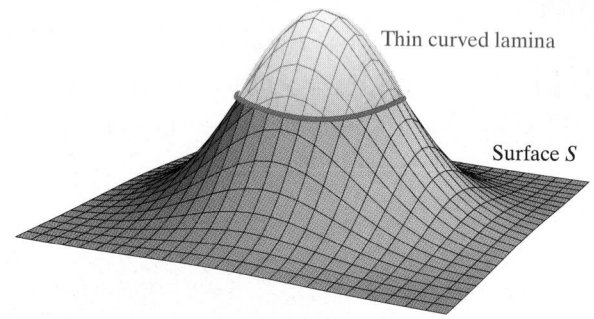

Figure 13.33 A thin lamina whose shape is the surface S

If $\delta(x, y, z)$ is the density (mass per unit area) at each point (x, y, z) on the lamina, then the *total mass*, m, of the lamina is given by the surface integral

MASS OF A LAMINA

$$m = \iint\limits_{S} \delta(x, y, z) \, dS$$

and the center of mass of the surface is the point $C(\overline{x}, \overline{y}, \overline{z})$, where

CENTER OF MASS

$$\overline{x} = \frac{1}{m} \iint\limits_{S} x\delta \, dS, \qquad \overline{y} = \frac{1}{m} \iint\limits_{S} y\delta \, dS, \qquad \overline{z} = \frac{1}{m} \iint\limits_{S} z\delta \, dS$$

These formulas may be derived by essentially the same approach used in our previous work with moments and centroids of solid regions. (See, for example, Sections 6.5 and 12.6.)

EXAMPLE 2   Mass of a curved lamina

Find the mass of a lamina of density $\delta(x, y, z) = z$ in the shape of the hemisphere $z = (a^2 - x^2 - y^2)^{1/2}$, as shown in Figure 13.34.

Solution

We begin by calculating dS.

$$z_x = \tfrac{1}{2}(a^2 - x^2 - y^2)^{-1/2}(-2x) = -x(a^2 - x^2 - y^2)^{-1/2}$$
$$z_y = \tfrac{1}{2}(a^2 - x^2 - y^2)^{-1/2}(-2y) = -y(a^2 - x^2 - y^2)^{-1/2}$$

$$dS = \sqrt{z_x^2 + z_y^2 + 1} \, dA = \sqrt{\frac{x^2}{a^2 - x^2 - y^2} + \frac{y^2}{a^2 - x^2 - y^2} + 1} \, dA$$

$$= \sqrt{\frac{a^2}{a^2 - x^2 - y^2}} \, dA = a(a^2 - x^2 - y^2)^{-1/2} \, dA$$

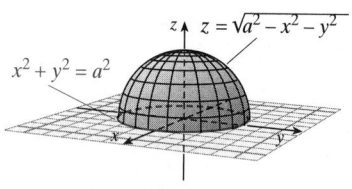

Figure 13.34 The hemisphere $z = \sqrt{a^2 - x^2 - y^2}$

The surface projects onto the disk $x^2 + y^2 \leq a^2$ in the xy-plane, so the mass of the hemisphere S is given by

$$
\begin{aligned}
m &= \iint\limits_{S} \delta(x, y, z)\, dS = \iint\limits_{S} z\, dS \\
&= \iint\limits_{R} (a^2 - x^2 - y^2)^{1/2} a (a^2 - x^2 - y^2)^{-1/2}\, dA \\
&= a \iint\limits_{R} dA = a(\pi a^2) = \pi a^3 \qquad \text{Since this integral represents the area of a circle of radius } a \quad \blacksquare
\end{aligned}
$$

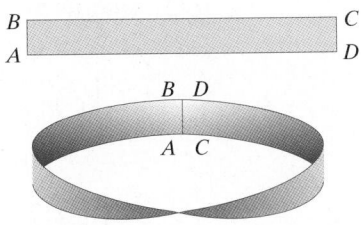

a. One-sided (non-orientable) surface: a Möbius strip.

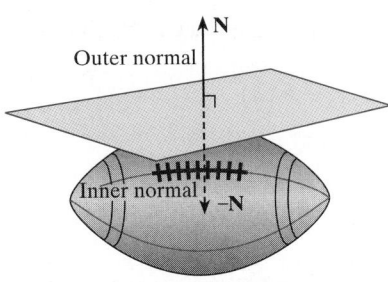

b. Two-sided (orientable) surface: a football. This is also a closed surface.

Figure 13.35 Surfaces in space

FLUX INTEGRALS

An important application of surface integrals involves the flow of a fluid through a surface. To discuss such applications, we define a surface S to be **orientable** if S has a unit normal vector field $\mathbf{N}$ that varies continuously over S. Most common surfaces, such as spheres, cones, cylinders, ellipsoids, and paraboloids, are orientable, but it is not difficult to construct a fairly simple surface that is not. For example, the **Möbius strip**, formed by twisting a long rectangular strip before joining the ends, is not orientable (see Figure 13.35a). If S is an orientable surface, there will be two possibilities for $\mathbf{N}$, which can be thought of as **outward** (pointing toward the exterior of S) or **inward** (pointing toward the interior), as illustrated in Figure 13.35b.

Consider a fluid of density δ flowing steadily through a surface S with the continuous unit normal field $\mathbf{N}$. If $\mathbf{V}$ is the velocity of the fluid flow, then the vector field $\mathbf{F} = \delta \mathbf{V}$ is the **flux density**, which measures the volume of fluid crossing the surface per unit area in unit time. Think of water flowing through a net, as shown in Figure 13.36.

If ΔS is the area of a small patch of the surface S, then the amount of fluid crossing this patch in unit time in the direction of $\mathbf{N}$ may be estimated by the volume of the cylinder of height $\mathbf{F} \cdot \mathbf{N}$, and base area ΔS (see Figure 13.37); that is,

$$
\Delta V \approx (\mathbf{F} \cdot \mathbf{N})\Delta S
$$

Thus, we can measure the total volume crossing the surface in unit time by computing the surface integral of $\mathbf{F} \cdot \mathbf{N}$, which is called a *flux integral*.

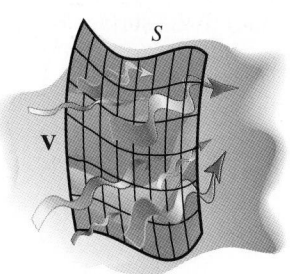

Figure 13.36 Water flowing through a net

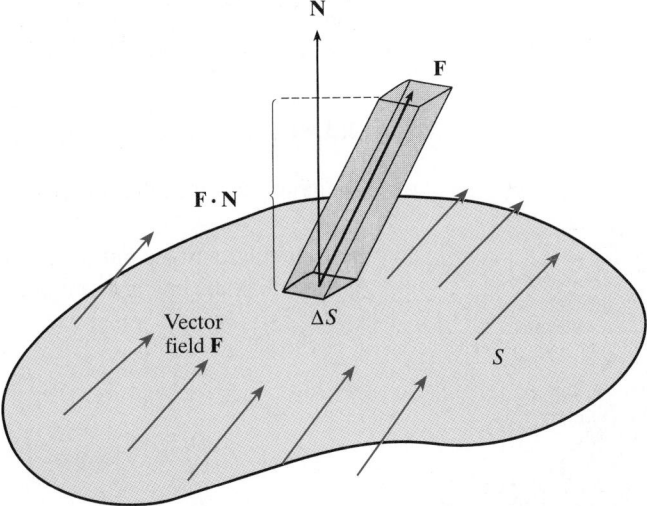

Figure 13.37 The cylinder of fluid crossing the patch of area ΔS in the direction of $\mathbf{N}$ has height $\mathbf{F} \cdot \mathbf{N}$ and volume $(\mathbf{F} \cdot \mathbf{N})\Delta S$

Flux Integral

Let $\mathbf{F}$ be a vector field whose components have continuous partial derivatives on the surface S, which is oriented by the unit normal field $\mathbf{N}$. Then the **flux** of $\mathbf{F}$ across S is given by the surface integral

$$\text{Flux} = \iint_S \mathbf{F} \cdot \mathbf{N} \, dS$$

Suppose we have a surface S described by the equation $z = f(x, y)$ that projects onto a region D in the xy-plane. Then we have $G(x, y, z) = z - f(x, y)$ and an upward unit normal (the one with positive k-component) to the surface is given by

$$\mathbf{N} = \frac{\nabla G}{\|\nabla G\|} \quad \text{where } \nabla G = \langle -f_x, -f_y, 1 \rangle$$

Therefore,

$$\mathbf{F} \cdot \mathbf{N} \, dS = \mathbf{F} \cdot \left(\frac{\nabla G}{\|\nabla G\|} \right) \sqrt{f_x^2 + f_y^2 + 1} \, dA$$

and since $\|\nabla G\| = \sqrt{(-f_x)^2 + (-f_y)^2 + 1}$, the flux integral of $\mathbf{F}$ over S can be written as

$$\iint_S \mathbf{F} \cdot \mathbf{N} \, dS = \iint_D \mathbf{F}(x, y, f(x, y)) \cdot \nabla G \, dA$$

$$= \iint_D \mathbf{F}(x, y, f(x, y)) \cdot \langle -f_x, -f_y, 1 \rangle \, dA$$

Similarly, a downward unit normal (negative k-component) to the surface is given by

$$\mathbf{N} = \frac{-\nabla G}{\|\nabla G\|}$$

and the flux integral has the form

$$\iint_S \mathbf{F} \cdot \mathbf{N} \, dS = \iint_D \mathbf{F}(x, y, f(x, y)) \cdot \langle f_x, f_y, -1 \rangle \, dA$$

Note that it is always necessary to specify the orientation of $\mathbf{N}$ (upward or downward) when describing a flux integral.

EXAMPLE 3 Evaluating a flux integral

Compute the flux integral $\displaystyle\iint_S \mathbf{F} \cdot \mathbf{N} \, dS$, where $\mathbf{F} = xy\mathbf{i} + z\mathbf{j} + (x + y)\mathbf{k}$ and S is the triangular surface cut off from the plane $x + y + z = 1$ by the coordinate planes. Assume $\mathbf{N}$ is the upward unit normal.

Solution

Let $f(x, y) = z = 1 - x - y$. Then $f_x = -1$, $f_y = -1$, and the flux integral is

$$\iint_S \mathbf{F} \cdot \mathbf{N} \, dS = \iint_D \mathbf{F}(x, y, f(x, y)) \cdot \langle -f_x, -f_y, 1 \rangle \, dA$$

where D is the projection of S on the xy-plane. Setting $z = 0$, we find that D is the triangular region bounded by the lines $x + y = 1$, $x = 0$, and $y = 0$, as shown in Figure 13.38. Thus, we have

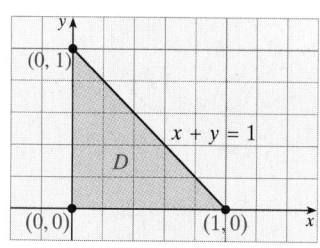

Figure 13.38 Projection D of $x + y + z = 1$ on the xy-plane

$$\iint_S \mathbf{F} \cdot \mathbf{N}\, dS = \iint_D \langle xy,\, 1-x-y,\, x+y \rangle \cdot \langle -(-1),\, -(-1),\, 1 \rangle\, dA$$

$$= \int_0^1 \int_0^{1-x} [xy + (1-x-y) + x + y]\, dy\, dx$$

$$= \int_0^1 \int_0^{1-x} [xy + 1]\, dy\, dx$$

$$= \int_0^1 \left[\tfrac{1}{2}xy^2 + y \right]\Big|_0^{1-x}\, dx$$

$$= \int_0^1 \tfrac{1}{2}(x^3 - 2x^2 - x + 2)\, dx$$

$$= \tfrac{13}{24} \qquad\blacksquare$$

EXAMPLE 4 Computing heat flow as a flux integral

Let R be the region that is bounded above by the paraboloid $z = 9 - x^2 - y^2$ and below by the xy-plane. Experiments indicate that the velocity of heat flow is given by the vector field $\mathbf{H} = -K\nabla T$, where

$$T(x, y, z) = 2x + y - 3z^2$$

is the temperature at each point $P(x, y, z)$ in the region and K is a constant (the *heat conductivity*, which is obtained experimentally for each different substance). Find the total heat flow $\iint_R \mathbf{H} \cdot \mathbf{N}\, dS$ out of the region (that is, $\mathbf{N}$ is the outer unit normal, the one pointing away from the origin).

Solution

The surface is shown in Figure 13.39. Note also that $\nabla T = \langle 2, 1, -6z \rangle$ and that the surface S is composed of a top surface S_1 and a bottom surface S_2. The top surface is S_1: $z = 9 - x^2 - y^2$ and the bottom surface is the disk S_2: $x^2 + y^2 \le 9$, which is also the projection D of S_1 on the xy-plane.

For S_1: Let $G = z + x^2 + y^2 - 9$; then, $\nabla G = \langle 2x, 2y, 1 \rangle$. The top surface S_1 has upward pointing normal, and the flux integral over S_1 is

$$\iint_{S_1} \mathbf{H} \cdot \mathbf{N}_1\, dS = \iint_{S_1} -K\nabla T \cdot \nabla G\, dS$$

$$= \iint_D -K\langle 2, 1, -6z \rangle \cdot \langle 2x, 2y, 1 \rangle\, dA$$

$$= \iint_D -K[4x + 2y - 6(9 - x^2 - y^2)]\, dA \qquad \text{Since} \atop z = 9 - x^2 - y^2 \text{ on } S$$

$$= -K \int_0^{2\pi} \int_0^3 [4r\cos\theta + 2r\sin\theta - 6(9 - r^2)]\, r\, dr\, d\theta$$

$$= -K \int_0^{2\pi} \left[36\cos\theta + 18\sin\theta - \frac{243}{2} \right]\, d\theta$$

$$= 243\pi K$$

For S_2: The outer normal $\mathbf{N}_2 = -k = \langle 0, 0, -1 \rangle$ points downward and the flux

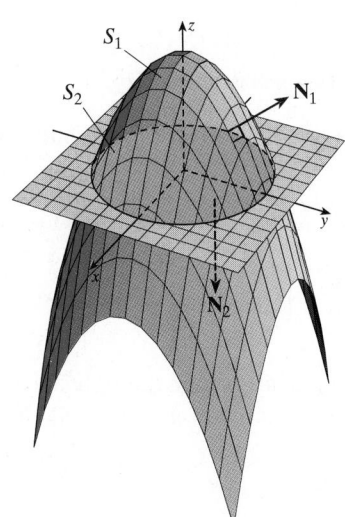

Figure 13.39 The surface S of the region bounded above by $z = 9 - x^2 - y^2$ and below by the xy-plane

integral is

$$\iint\limits_{S_2} \mathbf{H} \cdot \mathbf{N}_2 \, dS = \iint\limits_{D} -K \langle 2, 1, -6z \rangle \cdot \langle 0, 0, -1 \rangle \, dA$$

$$= -K \iint\limits_{D} 6z \, dA$$

$$= -K \iint\limits_{D} 0 \, dA \quad \text{Since } z = 0 \text{ on } S_2$$

$$= 0$$

Thus, the total heat flow is

$$\iint\limits_{S} \mathbf{H} \cdot \mathbf{N} \, dS = \iint\limits_{S_1} \mathbf{H} \cdot \mathbf{N}_1 \, dS + \iint\limits_{S_2} \mathbf{H} \cdot \mathbf{N}_2 \, dS$$

$$= 243\pi K + 0 = 243\pi K \qquad \blacksquare$$

INTEGRALS OVER PARAMETRICALLY DEFINED SURFACES

In Section 12.4, we showed that if a surface S is defined parametrically by the vector function

$$\mathbf{R}(u, v) = x(u, v)\mathbf{i} + y(u, v)\mathbf{j} + z(u, v)\mathbf{k}$$

over a region D in the uv-plane, the surface area of S is given by the integral

$$\iint\limits_{D} \|\mathbf{R}_u \times \mathbf{R}_v\| \, du \, dv$$

Similarly, if f is continuous on D, the surface integral of f over D is given by

$$\iint\limits_{S} f(x, y, z) \, dS = \iint\limits_{D} f(\mathbf{R}) \|\mathbf{R}_u \times \mathbf{R}_v\| \, du \, dv$$

EXAMPLE 5   Surface integral for a surface defined parametrically

Evaluate $\displaystyle\iint\limits_{S} (x + y + z) \, dS$, where S is the surface defined parametrically by $\mathbf{R}(u, v) = (2u + v)\mathbf{i} + (u - 2v)\mathbf{j} + (u + 3v)\mathbf{k}$ for $0 \leq u \leq 1, 0 \leq v \leq 2$.

Solution

$$\iint\limits_{S} (x + y + z) \, dS = \iint\limits_{D} f(\mathbf{R}) \|\mathbf{R}_u \times \mathbf{R}_v\| \, du \, dv$$

First, we need to find the component parts for the surface integral on the right. Using $\mathbf{R} = x\mathbf{i} + y\mathbf{j} + z\mathbf{k}$, we see that $x = 2u + v$, $y = u - 2v$, and $z = u + 3v$, and since $f(x, y, z) = x + y + z$, we have

$$f(\mathbf{R}) = f(2u + v, u - 2v, u + 3v)$$

$$= (2u + v) + (u - 2v) + (u + 3v)$$

$$= 4u + 2v$$

Next, we find that

$$\mathbf{R}_u = 2\mathbf{i} + \mathbf{j} + \mathbf{k} \quad \text{and} \quad \mathbf{R}_v = \mathbf{i} - 2\mathbf{j} + 3\mathbf{k}$$

so

$$\mathbf{R}_u \times \mathbf{R}_v = \begin{vmatrix} \mathbf{i} & \mathbf{j} & \mathbf{k} \\ 2 & 1 & 1 \\ 1 & -2 & 3 \end{vmatrix} = (3 + 2)\mathbf{i} - (6 - 1)\mathbf{j} + (-4 - 1)\mathbf{k} = 5\mathbf{i} - 5\mathbf{j} - 5\mathbf{k}$$

Thus, $\|\mathbf{R}_u \times \mathbf{R}_v\| = \sqrt{5^2 + (-5)^2 + (-5)^2} = 5\sqrt{3}$. We now substitute these values into the surface integral formula:

$$\iint_S (x + y + z)\, dS = \iint_D f(\mathbf{R})\|\mathbf{R}_u \times \mathbf{R}_v\|\, du\, dv$$

$$= \int_0^2 \int_0^1 (4u + 2v)(5\sqrt{3})\, du\, dv = 5\sqrt{3}\int_0^2 \left[2u^2 + 2uv\right]\Big|_0^1 dv$$

$$= 5\sqrt{3}\int_0^2 (2 + 2v)\, dv = 5\sqrt{3}\left[2v + v^2\right]\Big|_0^2 = 5\sqrt{3}(8) = 40\sqrt{3}$$

∎

For a flux integral over a surface S parameterized by $\mathbf{R}(u, v)$ that projects onto a region D in the uv-plane, we have

$$\iint_S \mathbf{F} \cdot \mathbf{N}\, dS = \iint_D \mathbf{F} \cdot \mathbf{N}\|\mathbf{R}_u \times \mathbf{R}_v\|\, dA$$

$$= \iint_D \mathbf{F} \cdot \left(\frac{\mathbf{R}_u \times \mathbf{R}_v}{\|\mathbf{R}_u \times \mathbf{R}_v\|}\right)\|\mathbf{R}_u \times \mathbf{R}_v\|\, dA$$

$$= \iint_D \mathbf{F} \cdot (\mathbf{R}_u \times \mathbf{R}_v)\, dA$$

The use of this formula is demonstrated in the next example.

EXAMPLE 6 Computing flux through a parameterized surface

Find the flux of the vector field $\mathbf{F} = z\mathbf{i} + x\mathbf{j} + (y + z)\mathbf{k}$ through the parameterized surface

$$\mathbf{R}(u, v) = (uv)\mathbf{i} + (u - v)\mathbf{j} + (2u + v)\mathbf{k}$$

over the triangular region D in the uv-plane that is bounded by $u = 0$, $v = 0$, and $u + v = 1$.

Solution

First, note from $\mathbf{R}(u, v)$ that $x = uv$, $y = u - v$, and $z = 2u + v$, so we have

$$\mathbf{F}(u, v) = (2u + v)\mathbf{i} + (uv)\mathbf{j} + [(u - v) + (2u + v)]\mathbf{k}$$
$$= (2u + v)\mathbf{i} + (uv)\mathbf{j} + (3u)\mathbf{k}$$

Moreover, since $\mathbf{R}_u = v\mathbf{i} + \mathbf{j} + 2\mathbf{k}$ and $\mathbf{R}_v = u\mathbf{i} - \mathbf{j} + \mathbf{k}$, it follows that

$$\mathbf{R}_u \times \mathbf{R}_v = \begin{vmatrix} \mathbf{i} & \mathbf{j} & \mathbf{k} \\ v & 1 & 2 \\ u & -1 & 1 \end{vmatrix}$$
$$= 3\mathbf{i} - (v - 2u)\mathbf{j} + (-v - u)\mathbf{k}$$

Thus, the flux is given by

$$\iint_S \mathbf{F} \cdot \mathbf{N}\, dS = \iint_D \mathbf{F} \cdot (\mathbf{R}_u \times \mathbf{R}_v)\, dA$$

$$= \int_0^1 \int_0^{1-u} \langle 2u + v, uv, 3u \rangle \cdot \langle 3, 2u - v, -(u + v) \rangle\, dv\, du$$

$$= \int_0^1 \int_0^{1-u} [(2u + v)(3) + (uv)(2u - v) + 3u(-u - v)]\, dv\, du$$

$$= \int_0^1 \int_0^{1-u} (2u^2v - 3u^2 - uv^2 - 3uv + 6u + 3v)\, dv\, du$$

$$= \int_0^1 \frac{1}{6}(u-1)(8u^3 - u^2 - 16u - 9)\, du$$

$$= \frac{137}{120}$$

■

13.5 PROBLEM SET

Ⓐ *In Problems 1–4, evaluate* $\iint_S xy\, dS.$

1. $S: z = 2 - y, 0 \le x \le 2, 0 \le y \le 2$
2. $S: z = 4 - x - y, 0 \le x \le 4, 0 \le y \le 4$
3. $S: z = 5, x^2 + y^2 \le 1$
4. $S: z = 10, \dfrac{x^2}{4} + \dfrac{y^2}{1} \le 1$

In Problems 5–8, evaluate $\iint_S (x^2 + y^2)\, dS.$

5. $S: z = 4 - x - 2y, 0 \le x \le 4, 0 \le y \le 2$
6. $S: z = 4 - x, 0 \le x \le 2, 0 \le y \le 2$
7. $S: z = 4, x^2 + y^2 \le 1$
8. $S: z = xy, x^2 + y^2 \le 4, x \ge 0, y \ge 0$

Let S be the hemisphere $x^2 + y^2 + z^2 = 4$, *with* $z \ge 0$, *in Problems 9–14. Evaluate each surface integral.*

9. $\displaystyle\iint_S z\, dS$

10. $\displaystyle\iint_S z^2\, dS$

11. $\displaystyle\iint_S (x - 2y)\, dS$

12. $\displaystyle\iint_S (5 - 2x)\, dS$

13. $\displaystyle\iint_S (x^2 + y^2)z\, dS$

14. $\displaystyle\iint_S (x^2 + y^2)\, dS$

In Problems 15–18, suppose S is the portion of the paraboloid $z = x^2 + y^2$ *for which* $z \le 4$. *Evaluate the given surface integral.*

15. $\displaystyle\iint_S z\, dS$

16. $\displaystyle\iint_S (4 - z)\, dS$

17. $\displaystyle\iint_S \sqrt{1 + 4z}\, dS$

18. $\displaystyle\iint_S \frac{dS}{\sqrt{1 + 4z}}$

19. Evaluate $\displaystyle\iint_S (x^2 + y^2)\, dS$, where S is the surface of the hemisphere $z = \sqrt{1 - x^2 - y^2}$.

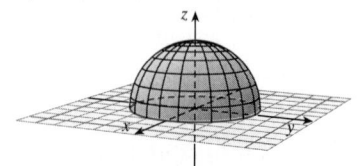

20. Evaluate $\displaystyle\iint_S 2x\, dS$, where S is the portion of the plane $x + y + z = 1$ with $x \ge 0, y \ge 0, z \ge 0$.

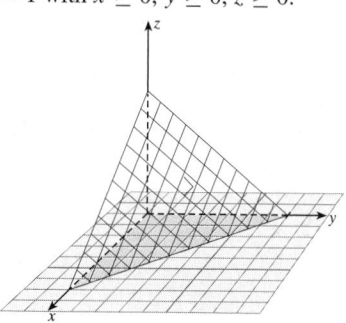

21. Evaluate $\displaystyle\iint_S (x^2 + y^2 + z^2)\, dS$, where S is the portion of the plane $z = x + 1$ that lies inside the cylinder $x^2 + y^2 = 1$.

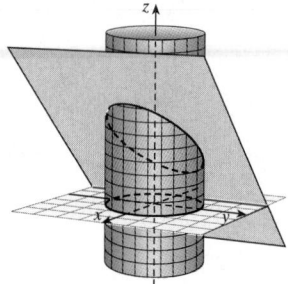

Evaluate $\displaystyle\iint_S \mathbf{F} \cdot \mathbf{N}\, dS$ *for the vector fields* $\mathbf{F}$ *and surfaces S given in Problems 22–29. Assume* $\mathbf{N}$ *is the outward directed normal field.*

22. $\mathbf{F} = x\mathbf{i} + 2y\mathbf{j} + z\mathbf{k}$, and S is the triangular region bounded by the intersection of the plane $x + 2y + z = 1$ with the positive coordinate planes.

23. $\mathbf{F} = x\mathbf{i} + 2y\mathbf{j} - 3z\mathbf{k}$, and S is that part of the plane $15x - 12y + 3z = 6$ that lies above the unit square $0 \le x \le 1$, $0 \le y \le 1$.

24. $\mathbf{F} = x\mathbf{i} + y\mathbf{j} + 2z\mathbf{k}$, and S is the surface of the cube bounded by the planes $x = 0, x = 1, y = 0, y = 1, z = 0$, and $z = 1$.

25. $\mathbf{F} = x\mathbf{i} + y\mathbf{j}$, and S is the hemisphere $z = \sqrt{1 - x^2 - y^2}$.

26. $\mathbf{F} = 2x\mathbf{i} - 3y\mathbf{j}$, and S is the part of the hemisphere given by $x^2 + y^2 + z^2 = 5$, for $z \ge 1$.

27. $\mathbf{F} = x^2\mathbf{i} + y^2\mathbf{j} + z^2\mathbf{k}$, and S is the portion of the plane $z = y + 1$ that lies inside the cylinder $x^2 + y^2 = 1$.

28. $\mathbf{F} = x^2\mathbf{i} + y^2\mathbf{j} + z^2\mathbf{k}$, and S is the part of the cone $z = \sqrt{x^2 + y^2}$ below the plane $z = 2$.

29. $\mathbf{F} = y\mathbf{i} + z^2\mathbf{j} - 2z\mathbf{k}$, and S is the part of the surface cut from the cylinder $z = 3 - x^2$ by $y = 0$, $y = 1$, and $z = 0$.

B **30.** Evaluate $\displaystyle\iint_S (3x - y + 2z)\,dS$, where S is the surface determined by $\mathbf{R}(u, v) = u\mathbf{i} + u\mathbf{j} - v\mathbf{k}$, $0 \le u \le 1$, $1 \le v \le 2$.

31. Evaluate $\displaystyle\iint_S (x - y^2 + z)\,dS$, where S is the surface defined by $\mathbf{R}(u, v) = u^2\mathbf{i} + v\mathbf{j} + u\mathbf{k}$, $0 \le u \le 1$, $0 \le v \le 1$.

32. Evaluate $\displaystyle\iint_S (\tan^{-1} x + y - z^2)\,dS$, where S is the surface defined by $\mathbf{R}(u, v) = u\mathbf{i} + v^2\mathbf{j} - v\mathbf{k}$, $0 \le u \le 1$, $0 \le v \le 1$.

33. Evaluate $\displaystyle\iint_S (x^2 + y - z)\,dS$, where S is the surface defined by $\mathbf{R}(u, v) = u\mathbf{i} - u^2\mathbf{j} + v\mathbf{k}$, $0 \le u \le 2$, $0 \le v \le 1$.

34. Evaluate $\displaystyle\iint_S (x + y + z)\,dS$, where S is the surface of the cube $0 \le x \le 1$, $0 \le y \le 1$, $0 \le z \le 1$.

35. Evaluate $\displaystyle\iint_S \mathbf{F} \cdot \mathbf{N}\,dS$, where $\mathbf{F} = x^2\mathbf{i} + z\mathbf{k}$ and S is the parametric surface

$$x = \sin u \cos v \qquad y = \sin u \sin v \qquad z = \cos u$$

for $0 \le u \le \pi$, $0 \le v \le 2\pi$.

36. Evaluate $\displaystyle\iint_S \mathbf{F} \cdot \mathbf{N}\,dS$, where $\mathbf{F} = x\mathbf{i} + y\mathbf{j} + z^4\mathbf{k}$ and S is the parametric surface

$$x = u \cos v \qquad y = u \sin v \qquad z = u$$

for $0 \le u \le 2$, $0 \le v \le 2\pi$.

In Problems 37–42 find the mass of the homogeneous lamina that has the shape of the given surface S.

37. S is the surface $z = 4 - x - 2y$, with $z \ge 0$, $x \ge 0$, $y \ge 0$; $\delta = x$.

38. S is the surface $z = 10 - 2x - y$, with $z \ge 0$, $x \ge 0$, $y \ge 0$; $\delta = y$.

39. S is the surface $z = x^2 + y^2$, with $z \le 1$; $\delta = z$. *Hint*: Use cylindrical coordinates.

40. S is the surface $z = 1 - x^2 - y^2$, with $z \ge 0$; $\delta = x^2 + y^2 + z^2$. *Hint*: Use cylindrical coordinates.

41. S is the surface $r^2 + z^2 = 5$, with $z \ge 1$; $\delta = \theta^2$.

42. S is the triangular surface with vertices $(1, 0, 0)$, $(0, 1, 0)$, and $(0, 0, 1)$; $\delta = x + y$.

43. A fluid with constant density ρ flows with velocity $\mathbf{V} = (xy)\mathbf{i} + (yz)\mathbf{j} + (xz)\mathbf{k}$. Find the upward rate of fluid flow through the paraboloid $z = 9 - x^2 - y^2$.

44. The temperature at each point (x, y, z) in a region D is $T = 3x^2 + 3z^2$. If the heat conductivity is $K = 5.8$, find the rate of heat flow outward across the cylinder $x^2 + z^2 = 4$ for $0 \le y \le 3$.

C **45. a.** A lamina has the shape of the portion of the sphere $x^2 + y^2 + z^2 = a^2$ that lies within the cone $z = \sqrt{x^2 + y^2}$. Determine the mass of the lamina if $\delta(x, y, z) = x^2 y^2 z$.

b. Let S be the spherical shell centered at the origin with radius a, and let C be the right circular cone whose vertex is at the origin and whose axis of symmetry coincides with the z-axis. Suppose the vertex angle of the cone is ϕ_0, with $0 \le \phi_0 < \pi/2$. Determine the mass of that portion of the sphere that is enclosed in the intersection of S and C. Assume $\delta(x, y, z) = 1$.

46. Recall the formula

$$I_z = \iint_S (x^2 + y^2)\delta(x, y, z)\,dS$$

for the moment of inertia about the z-axis. Show that the moment of inertia of a conical shell about its axis is $\frac{1}{2}ma^2$, where m is the mass and a is the radius of the cone. Assume $\delta(x, y, z) = 1$.

47. Recall the formula

$$I_z = \iint_S (x^2 + y^2)\delta(x, y, z)\,dS$$

for the moment of inertia about the z-axis. Show that the moment of inertia of a spherical shell of uniform density about its diameter is $\frac{2}{3}ma^2$, where m is the mass and a is the radius. Assume $\delta(x, y, z) = 1$.

48. HISTORICAL QUEST   August Möbius studied under Karl Gauss (1777–1855), as well as Gauss' own teacher Johann Pfaff (1765–1825). He was a professor at the University of Leipzig and is best known for his work in topology, especially for his conception of the Möbius strip (a two-dimensional surface with only one side). ■

AUGUST MÖBIUS
1790–1868

An example of a **Möbius strip** is given parametrically by:

$$x = \cos v + u \cos \frac{v}{2} \cos v$$

$$y = \sin v + u \cos \frac{v}{2} \sin v$$

$$z = u \sin \frac{v}{2}$$

where $-\frac{1}{2} \le u \le \frac{1}{2}$, $0 \le v \le 2\pi$. Construct a three-dimensional model of a Möbius strip and show that a Möbius strip is not orientable. If you have access to a CAS program, sketch the graph of this surface.

13.6   Stokes' Theorem

IN THIS SECTION   Stokes' theorem, theoretical applications of Stokes' theorem, physical interpretation of Stokes' theorem

In Section 13.4, we observed that Green's theorem can be written

$$\oint_C \mathbf{F} \cdot d\mathbf{R} = \iint_A (\operatorname{curl} \mathbf{F} \cdot \mathbf{k}) \, dA$$

where A is the plane region bounded by the Jordan curve C. Stokes' theorem is a generalization of this result to surfaces in space and their boundaries.

STOKES' THEOREM

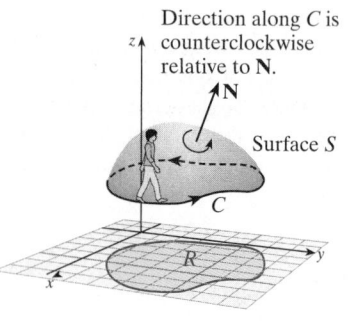

Direction along C is counterclockwise relative to **N**.

Surface S

Before stating Stokes' theorem, we need to explain what is meant by a *compatible orientation*. We say that the orientation of a closed path C on the surface S is **compatible with the orientation on S** if the positive direction on C is *counterclockwise* in relation to the outward normal vector **N** of the surface (see Figure 13.40). That is, if a person walks around C in a positive (counterclockwise) direction with her head pointing in the direction of **N**, then the surface will always be on her left.

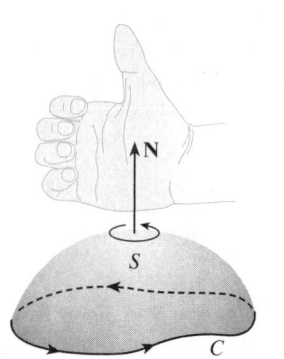

THEOREM 13.8   Stokes' theorem

Let S be an oriented surface with unit normal vector field **N**, and assume that S is bounded by a piecewise smooth Jordan curve C whose orientation is compatible with that of S. If **F** is a vector field that is continuously differentiable on S, then

$$\oint_C \mathbf{F} \cdot d\mathbf{R} = \iint_S (\operatorname{curl} \mathbf{F} \cdot \mathbf{N}) \, dS$$

Figure 13.40 Compatible orientation: The surface S is on the left of someone walking in a counterclockwise direction around the boundary curve C.

Proof   A proof assuming **F**, S, and C are "well behaved" is given in Appendix B.   ❑

EXAMPLE 1   Using Stokes' theorem to evaluate a line integral

Evaluate $\oint_C (\frac{1}{2} y^2 \, dx + z \, dy + x \, dz)$, where C is the curve of intersection of the plane $x + z = 1$ and the ellipsoid $x^2 + 2y^2 + z^2 = 1$, oriented counterclockwise as viewed from above (see Figure 13.41).

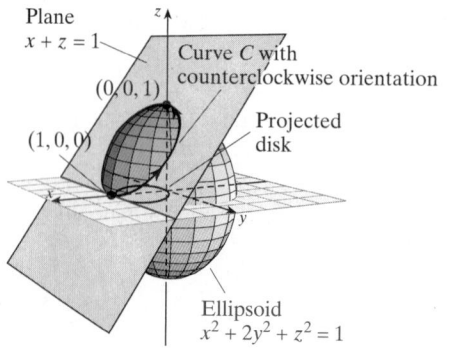

Plane $x + z = 1$

Curve C with counterclockwise orientation

$(0, 0, 1)$

$(1, 0, 0)$

Projected disk

Ellipsoid $x^2 + 2y^2 + z^2 = 1$

Figure 13.41   The surface bounded by the curve of intersection projects onto a disk in the xy-plane.

Solution

If we set $\mathbf{F} = \frac{1}{2}y^2\mathbf{i} + z\mathbf{j} + x\mathbf{k}$, the given line integral can be expressed as

$$\oint_C \mathbf{F} \cdot d\mathbf{R}$$

According to Stokes' theorem, we have

$$\oint_C \mathbf{F} \cdot d\mathbf{R} = \iint_S (\text{curl } \mathbf{F} \cdot \mathbf{N}) \, dS$$

There are many surfaces bounded by the curve C. We choose the surface S that is part of the plane $x + z = 1$. We find the required parts of the surface integral; namely, $\text{curl } \mathbf{F}$, $\mathbf{N}$, and dS.

$$\text{curl } \mathbf{F} = \begin{vmatrix} \mathbf{i} & \mathbf{j} & \mathbf{k} \\ \dfrac{\partial}{\partial x} & \dfrac{\partial}{\partial y} & \dfrac{\partial}{\partial z} \\ \frac{1}{2}y^2 & z & x \end{vmatrix} = -\mathbf{i} - \mathbf{j} - y\mathbf{k}$$

The upward unit normal vector to the plane $x + z = 1$ is $\mathbf{N} = \dfrac{1}{\sqrt{2}}(\mathbf{i} + \mathbf{k})$, so that

$$\text{curl } \mathbf{F} \cdot \mathbf{N} = \langle -1, -1, -y \rangle \cdot \left\langle \frac{1}{\sqrt{2}}, 0, \frac{1}{\sqrt{2}} \right\rangle$$

$$= -\frac{1}{\sqrt{2}} - \frac{y}{\sqrt{2}}$$

$$= \frac{-1}{\sqrt{2}}(1 + y)$$

and since $z = 1 - x$ on S, we have $z_x = -1$, $z_y = 0$, and

$$dS = \sqrt{z_x^2 + z_y^2 + 1} \, dA = \sqrt{(-1)^2 + (0)^2 + 1} \, dA = \sqrt{2} \, dA$$

Finally, to describe C we substitute $z = 1 - x$ into the equation for the ellipsoid:

$$x^2 + 2y^2 + z^2 = 1$$
$$x^2 + 2y^2 + (1 - x)^2 = 1$$
$$x^2 - x + y^2 = 0$$
$$\left(x - \tfrac{1}{2}\right)^2 + y^2 = \tfrac{1}{4}$$

Thus, the projection of C on the xy-plane is the disk D bounded by the circle $\left(x - \tfrac{1}{2}\right)^2 + y^2 = \tfrac{1}{4}$ shown in Figure 13.42. Note that this circle has the polar equation $r = \cos\theta$.

We now calculate the desired line integral using Stokes' theorem.

$$\oint_C \left(\frac{1}{2}y^2 \, dx + z \, dy + x \, dz \right) = \oint_C \mathbf{F} \cdot d\mathbf{R}$$

$$= \iint_S (\text{curl } \mathbf{F} \cdot \mathbf{N}) \, dS \qquad \text{Stokes' theorem}$$

$$= \iint_D \frac{-1}{\sqrt{2}}(1 + y)(\sqrt{2} \, dA)$$

$$= -\int_0^\pi \int_0^{\cos\theta} (1 + r\sin\theta) \, r \, dr \, d\theta \qquad \begin{array}{l}\text{Change to}\\\text{polar coordinates.}\end{array}$$

$$= -\int_0^\pi \left[\frac{1}{2}\cos^2\theta + \frac{1}{3}\cos^3\theta \sin\theta \right] d\theta = -\frac{\pi}{4} \qquad \blacksquare$$

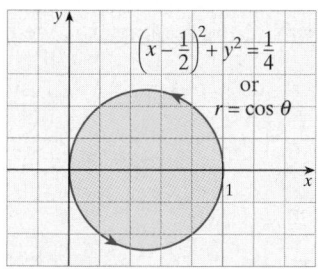

Figure 13.42 The projection D of the surface S on the xy-plane.

EXAMPLE 2 Verifying Stokes' theorem for a particular surface

Let S be the portion of the plane $x + y + z = 1$ that lies in the first octant, and let C be the boundary of S, traversed counterclockwise as viewed from above. Verify Stokes' theorem for the surface S and the vector field

$$\mathbf{F} = -\tfrac{3}{2}y^2\mathbf{i} - 2xy\mathbf{j} + yz\mathbf{k}$$

Solution

The surface S is the triangle with vertices $(1, 0, 0)$, $(0, 1, 0)$, $(0, 0, 1)$, whose boundary C is traversed in that order, as shown in Figure 13.43. We will show that the line integral $\oint_C \mathbf{F} \cdot d\mathbf{R}$ and the surface integral $\iint_S (\text{curl } \mathbf{F} \cdot \mathbf{N}) \, dS$ have the same value.

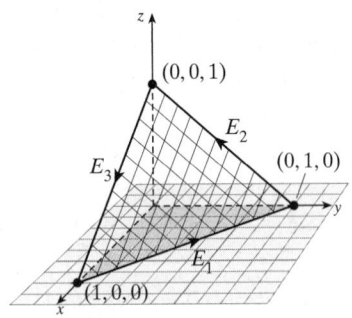

Figure 13.43 The curve C bounds the triangular surface S.

I. *Evaluation of* $\oint_C \mathbf{F} \cdot d\mathbf{R}$

The three edges of the boundary curve C are expressed as

$$
\begin{aligned}
E_1: \quad & x + y = 1, \; z = 0 \\
E_2: \quad & y + z = 1, \; x = 0 \\
E_3: \quad & x + z = 1, \; y = 0
\end{aligned}
$$

We traverse C in a counterclockwise direction (see Figure 13.43).

Edge E_1: Parameterize with $x = 1 - t$, $y = t$, $z = 0$, for $0 \le t \le 1$, so $\mathbf{R}(t) = (1 - t)\mathbf{i} + t\mathbf{j}$ and $d\mathbf{R} = -dt\mathbf{i} + dt\mathbf{j}$. Finally, in terms of the parameter t, we have $\mathbf{F}(t) = -\tfrac{3}{2}t^2\mathbf{i} - 2t(1 - t)\mathbf{j}$.

$$
\begin{aligned}
\int_{E_1} \mathbf{F} \cdot d\mathbf{R} &= \int_0^1 \left(\tfrac{3}{2}t^2 - 2t + 2t^2\right) dt \\
&= \int_0^1 \left(\tfrac{7}{2}t^2 - 2t\right) dt = \left(\tfrac{7}{6}t^3 - t^2\right)\Big|_0^1 = \tfrac{1}{6}
\end{aligned}
$$

Edge E_2: Parameterize with $x = 0$, $y = 1 - s$, $z = s$, for $0 \le s \le 1$, so $\mathbf{R}(s) = (1 - s)\mathbf{j} + s\mathbf{k}$ and $d\mathbf{R} = -ds\mathbf{j} + ds\mathbf{k}$. In terms of the parameter s, we have $\mathbf{F}(s) = -\tfrac{3}{2}(1 - s)^2\mathbf{i} + (1 - s)s\mathbf{k}$.

$$
\int_{E_2} \mathbf{F} \cdot d\mathbf{R} = \int_0^1 (1 - s)s \, ds = \left(\frac{s^2}{2} - \frac{s^3}{3}\right)\Big|_0^1 = \frac{1}{6}
$$

Edge E_3: Parameterize with $x = r$, $y = 0$, $z = 1 - r$, for $0 \le r \le 1$, so $\mathbf{R}(r) = r\mathbf{i} + (1 - r)\mathbf{k}$ and $d\mathbf{R} = dr\mathbf{i} - dr\mathbf{k}$. In terms of the parameter r, we have $\mathbf{F}(r) = \mathbf{0}$.

$$
\int_{E_3} \mathbf{F} \cdot d\mathbf{R} = 0
$$

Combining these results, we find

$$
\int_C \mathbf{F} \cdot d\mathbf{R} = \int_{E_1} \mathbf{F} \cdot d\mathbf{R} + \int_{E_2} \mathbf{F} \cdot d\mathbf{R} + \int_{E_3} \mathbf{F} \cdot d\mathbf{R} = \frac{1}{6} + \frac{1}{6} + 0 = \frac{1}{3}
$$

II. *Evaluation of* $\iint_S (\text{curl } \mathbf{F} \cdot \mathbf{N}) \, dS$

$$
\text{curl } \mathbf{F} =
\begin{vmatrix}
\mathbf{i} & \mathbf{j} & \mathbf{k} \\
\dfrac{\partial}{\partial x} & \dfrac{\partial}{\partial y} & \dfrac{\partial}{\partial z} \\
-\tfrac{3}{2}y^2 & -2xy & yz
\end{vmatrix}
= z\mathbf{i} + y\mathbf{k}
$$

The triangular region S on the surface of the plane $x + y + z = 1$ has outward unit normal vector

$$\mathbf{N} = \frac{1}{\sqrt{3}}(\mathbf{i} + \mathbf{j} + \mathbf{k})$$

Because $z = 1 - x - y$, we find

$$\text{curl } \mathbf{F} \cdot \mathbf{N} = (z\mathbf{i} + y\mathbf{k}) \cdot \frac{1}{\sqrt{3}}(\mathbf{i} + \mathbf{j} + \mathbf{k})$$

$$= \frac{1}{\sqrt{3}}(1 - x - y + y) = \frac{1}{\sqrt{3}}(1 - x)$$

and since $z_x = -1$, $z_y = -1$, it follows that

$$dS = \sqrt{z_x^2 + z_y^2 + 1}\, dA = \sqrt{(-1)^2 + (-1)^2 + 1}\, dA = \sqrt{3}\, dA$$

Finally, the surface S projects onto the triangular region D in the xy-plane that is bounded by the lines $x = 0$, $y = 0$, and $x + y = 1$ (see Figure 13.44). Thus, we have

$$\iint\limits_{S} (\text{curl } \mathbf{F} \cdot \mathbf{N})\, dS = \iint\limits_{D} \frac{1}{\sqrt{3}}(1 - x)\sqrt{3}\, dA = \int_0^1 \int_0^{1-x} (1 - x)\, dy\, dx$$

$$= \int_0^1 (1 - x)[(1 - x) - 0]\, dx = -\frac{(1 - x)^3}{3}\bigg|_0^1 = \frac{1}{3}$$

We see that for this example,

$$\oint_C \mathbf{F} \cdot d\mathbf{R} = \frac{1}{3} = \iint\limits_{S} (\text{curl } \mathbf{F} \cdot \mathbf{N})\, dS$$

as claimed by Stokes' theorem. ∎

Sometimes it is possible to exchange a particularly difficult surface integration over one surface for a less difficult integration over another surface with the same boundary curve. Suppose two surfaces S_1 and S_2 are bounded by the same curve C and induce the same orientation on C. Stokes' theorem tells us that

$$\iint\limits_{S_1} (\text{curl } \mathbf{F} \cdot \mathbf{N}_1)\, dS_1 = \oint_C \mathbf{F} \cdot d\mathbf{R} = \iint\limits_{S_2} (\text{curl } \mathbf{F} \cdot \mathbf{N}_2)\, dS_2$$

for any function $\mathbf{F}$ whose components have continuous partial derivatives on both S_1 and S_2.

EXAMPLE 3   Using Stokes' theorem to evaluate a surface integral

Evaluate $\displaystyle\iint\limits_{S} (\text{curl } \mathbf{F} \cdot \mathbf{N})\, dS$, where $\mathbf{F} = x\mathbf{i} + y^2\mathbf{j} + ze^{xy}\mathbf{k}$ and S is that part of the surface $z = 1 - x^2 - 2y^2$ with $z \geq 0$.

Solution

By setting $z = 0$ in the equation of the surface, we find that the boundary curve C for S is the ellipse $x^2 + 2y^2 = 1$, and the upward unit normal vector $\mathbf{N}$ on S induces a counterclockwise orientation on C, as shown in Figure 13.45. Let S^* be the elliptical disk defined by $x^2 + 2y^2 \leq 1$, $z = 0$. We see that S and S^* have the same boundary and the same orientation. Since the upward unit normal to S^* is $\mathbf{k}$, we have

$$\iint\limits_{S} (\text{curl } \mathbf{F} \cdot \mathbf{N})\, dS = \iint\limits_{S^*} (\text{curl } \mathbf{F} \cdot \mathbf{k})\, dS^*$$

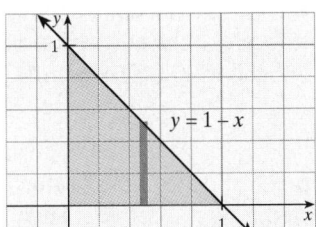

Figure 13.44 The projected region in the xy-plane is a triangle bounded by $y = 1 - x$ and the positive coordinate axes.

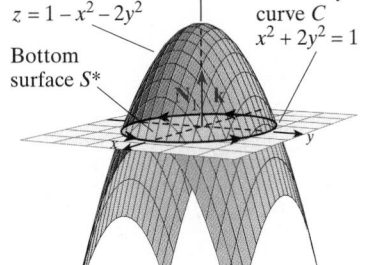

Surface S
$z = 1 - x^2 - 2y^2$

Bottom surface S^*

Boundary curve C
$x^2 + 2y^2 = 1$

Figure 13.45 Surface $z = 1 - x^2 - 2y^2$ and boundary curve C

and we use this second integral to calculate the required integral. We obtain

$$\text{curl } \mathbf{F} = \begin{vmatrix} \mathbf{i} & \mathbf{j} & \mathbf{k} \\ \dfrac{\partial}{\partial x} & \dfrac{\partial}{\partial y} & \dfrac{\partial}{\partial z} \\ x & y^2 & ze^{xy} \end{vmatrix} = (zxe^{xy})\mathbf{i} - (zye^{xy})\mathbf{j}$$

Since $z = 0$ on S^*, we have $\text{curl } \mathbf{F} \cdot \mathbf{k} = 0$ on S^* and

$$\iint\limits_{S} (\text{curl } \mathbf{F} \cdot \mathbf{N}) \, dS = \iint\limits_{S^*} (\text{curl } \mathbf{F} \cdot \mathbf{k}) \, dS^* = \iint\limits_{S^*} 0 \, dS^* = 0 \qquad \blacksquare$$

THEORETICAL APPLICATIONS OF STOKES' THEOREM

In physics and other applied areas, Stokes' theorem is often used as a device for establishing general properties. For instance, we now use it to prove the curl criterion for a conservative vector field in $\mathbb{R}^3$ stated without proof in Section 13.3 (Theorem 13.4), and whose proof was promised at this time.

The curl criterion for a conservative vector field in $\mathbb{R}^3$ Suppose the vector field $\mathbf{F}$ and $\text{curl } \mathbf{F}$ are both continuous in the simply connected region D of $\mathbb{R}^3$. Then $\mathbf{F}$ is conservative in D if and only if $\text{curl } \mathbf{F} = \mathbf{0}$ in D.

Proof of Theorem 13.4

If $\mathbf{F}$ is conservative, let f be a scalar potential function, so that $\nabla f = \mathbf{F}$. Then $\text{curl } \mathbf{F} = \nabla \times \mathbf{F} = \nabla \times (\nabla f) = \mathbf{0}$. (See Problem 54, Section 13.1 for a proof of this property.)

Conversely, if $\text{curl } \mathbf{F} = \mathbf{0}$, we will show that $\mathbf{F}$ is conservative by proving that it is independent of path. Let P_1 and P_2 be any two points in the simply connected region D and let C_1 and C_2 be two nonintersecting paths in D from P_1 to P_2. Let C be the Jordan curve from P_1 back to P_1 formed by C_1 followed by $-C_2$. Since D is simply connected (no holes), there is a piecewise smooth surface S whose boundary is C. Then, by Stokes' theorem

$$\oint_C \mathbf{F} \cdot d\mathbf{R} = \int_{C_1} \mathbf{F} \cdot d\mathbf{R} - \int_{C_2} \mathbf{F} \cdot d\mathbf{R}$$

$$= \iint\limits_{S} \text{curl } \mathbf{F} \cdot \mathbf{N} \, dS$$

$$= 0$$

so that

$$\int_{C_1} \mathbf{F} \cdot d\mathbf{R} = \int_{C_2} \mathbf{F} \cdot d\mathbf{R}$$

It follows that the line integral $\oint_C \mathbf{F} \cdot d\mathbf{R}$ is independent of path, so $\mathbf{F}$ must be conservative. $\qquad \square$

Maxwell's equations describing the behavior of electromagnetic phenomena were discussed briefly at the end of Section 13.1. The following example shows how Stokes' theorem can be used to establish one of Maxwell's equations, the *current density equation*.

EXAMPLE 4 **Maxwell's current density equation**

In physics, it is shown that if I is the current crossing any surface S bounded by the closed curve C, then

$$\oint_C \mathbf{H} \cdot d\mathbf{R} = I \quad \text{and} \quad \iint_S \mathbf{J} \cdot \mathbf{N} \, dS = I$$

where $\mathbf{H}$ is the magnetic intensity, and $\mathbf{J}$ is the electric current density. Use this information to derive Maxwell's current density equation curl $\mathbf{H} = \mathbf{J}$.

Solution

Equating the two equations of current, we obtain

$$\oint_C \mathbf{H} \cdot d\mathbf{R} = I = \iint_S \mathbf{J} \cdot \mathbf{N} \, dS$$

By Stokes' theorem,

$$\oint_C \mathbf{H} \cdot d\mathbf{R} = \iint_S (\text{curl } \mathbf{H} \cdot \mathbf{N}) \, dS$$

Equating the two surface integrals that equal $\displaystyle\oint_C \mathbf{H} \cdot d\mathbf{R}$, we have

$$\iint_S \mathbf{J} \cdot \mathbf{N} \, dS = \iint_S (\text{curl } \mathbf{H} \cdot \mathbf{N}) \, dS$$

or, equivalently,

$$\iint_S (\mathbf{J} - \text{curl } \mathbf{H}) \cdot \mathbf{N} \, dS = \mathbf{0}$$

Because this equation holds for *any* surface S bounded by C, it can be shown that

$$\mathbf{J} - \text{curl } \mathbf{H} = \mathbf{0}$$
$$\mathbf{J} = \text{curl } \mathbf{H} \qquad \blacksquare$$

PHYSICAL INTERPRETATION OF STOKES' THEOREM

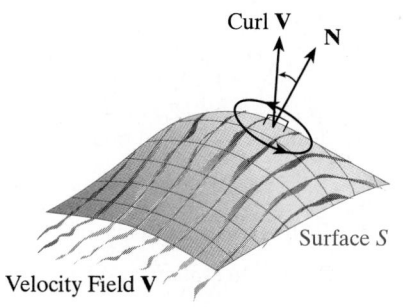

Curl $\mathbf{V}$ $\mathbf{N}$

Surface S

Velocity Field $\mathbf{V}$

Figure 13.46 The tendency of a fluid to swirl across the surface S is measured by curl $\mathbf{V} \cdot \mathbf{N}$.

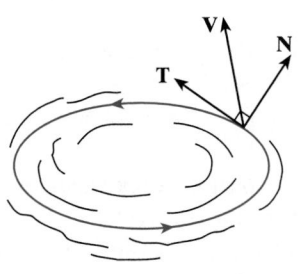

If $\mathbf{V}$ is the velocity field of a fluid flow, then curl $\mathbf{V}$ measures the tendency of the fluid to rotate, or swirl (see Figure 13.46). If the fluid flows across the surface S, the rotational tendency usually will vary from point to point on the surface, and the surface integral $\iint_S (\text{curl } \mathbf{V} \cdot \mathbf{N}) \, dS$ provides a measure of the *cumulative* rotational tendency over the entire surface.

Stokes' theorem tells us that this cumulative measure of rotational tendency equals the line integral $\displaystyle\oint_C \mathbf{V} \cdot d\mathbf{R}$. To interpret this line integral, recall that it can be written $\displaystyle\oint_C \mathbf{V} \cdot \mathbf{T} \, ds$ in terms of the arc length parameter s and the unit tangent $\mathbf{T}$ to the curve. Since the line integral sums the *tangential component* of the velocity field $\mathbf{V}$, it measures the rate of flow of fluid mass around C and for this reason is called the **circulation of V** around C. If curl $\mathbf{V} = \mathbf{0}$, the circulation is zero and $\mathbf{V}$ is said to be **irrotational**. To summarize,

$$\underbrace{\iint_S (\text{curl } \mathbf{V} \cdot \mathbf{N}) \, dS}_{\substack{\textit{The cumulative tendency} \\ \textit{of a fluid to swirl across} \\ \textit{the surface S}}} = \underbrace{\oint_C \mathbf{V} \cdot \mathbf{T} \, ds}_{\substack{\textit{The circulation of} \\ \textit{a fluid around the} \\ \textit{boundary curve C}}}$$

13.6 PROBLEM SET

ⒶⒶ *Verify Stokes' theorem for the vector functions and surfaces given in Problems 1–5.*

1. $\mathbf{F} = z\mathbf{i} + 2x\mathbf{j} + 3y\mathbf{k}$; S is the upper hemisphere $z = \sqrt{9 - x^2 - y^2}$.

2. $\mathbf{F} = (y + z)\mathbf{i} + x\mathbf{j} + (z - x)\mathbf{k}$; S is the triangular region of the plane $x + 2y + z = 3$ in the first octant.

3. $\mathbf{F} = (x + 2z)\mathbf{i} + (y - x)\mathbf{j} + (z - y)\mathbf{k}$; S is the triangular region with vertices $(3, 0, 0)$ $(0, \frac{3}{2}, 0)$, $(0, 0, 3)$.

4. $\mathbf{F} = 2xy\mathbf{i} + z^2\mathbf{k}$; S is the portion of the paraboloid $y = x^2 + z^2$, with $y \leq 4$.

5. $\mathbf{F} = 2y\mathbf{i} - 6z\mathbf{j} + 3x\mathbf{k}$; S is the portion of the paraboloid $z = 4 - x^2 - y^2$ and above the xy-plane.

Use Stokes' theorem to evaluate the line integrals given in Problems 6–13.

6. $\oint_C (x^3y^2\,dx + dy + z^2\,dz)$, where C is the circle $x^2 + y^2 = 1$ in the plane $z = 1$, counterclockwise when viewed from the origin

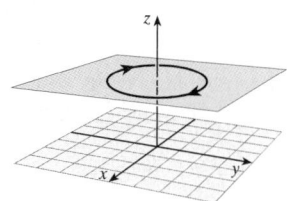

7. $\oint_C (z\,dx + x\,dy + y\,dz)$, where C is the triangle with vertices $(3, 0, 0)$, $(0, 0, 2)$, and $(0, 6, 0)$, traversed in the given order

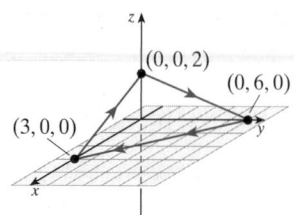

8. $\oint_C (y\,dx - 2x\,dy + z\,dz)$, where C is the intersection of the surface $z = x^2 + y^2$ and the plane $x + y + z = 1$ considered counterclockwise when viewed from the origin

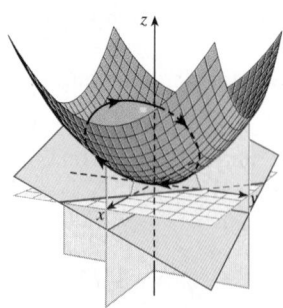

9. $\oint_C [2xy^2z\,dx + 2x^2yz\,dy + (x^2y^2 - 2z)\,dz]$, where C is the curve given by $x = \cos t$, $y = \sin t$, $z = \sin t$, $0 \leq t \leq 2\pi$, traversed in the direction of increasing t

10. $\oint_C (y\,dx + z\,dy + y\,dz)$, where C is the intersection of the sphere $x^2 + y^2 + z^2 = 4$ and the plane $x + y + z = 0$, traversed counterclockwise when viewed from above

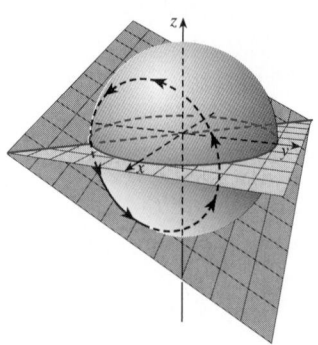

11. $\oint_C (y\,dx + z\,dy + x\,dz)$, where C is the intersection of the plane $x + y = 2$ and the surface $x^2 + y^2 + z^2 = 2(x + y)$, traversed counterclockwise as viewed from the origin

12. $\oint_C [(z + \cos x)\,dx + (x + y^2)\,dy + (y + e^z)\,dz]$, where C is the intersection of the sphere $x^2 + y^2 + z^2 = 4$ and the cone $z = \sqrt{x^2 + y^2}$, traversed counterclockwise as viewed from above

13. $\oint_C (3y\,dx + 2z\,dy - 5x\,dz)$, where C is the intersection of the xy-plane and the hemisphere $z = \sqrt{1 - x^2 - y^2}$, transversed counterclockwise as viewed from above

14. $\oint_C \mathbf{F} \cdot d\mathbf{R}$, where $\mathbf{F} = \langle x - z, y - x, z - y \rangle$ and C is the boundary of the triangular region with vertices $(12, 0, 0)$, $(0, 3, 0)$, $(0, 0, 12)$ traversed counterclockwise as viewed from above

15. $\oint_C \mathbf{F} \cdot d\mathbf{R}$, where $\mathbf{F} = \langle y^2 + z^2, x^2 + y^2, x^2 + y^2 \rangle$ and C is the triangle $(1, 0, 0)$, $(0, 1, 0)$, $(0, 0, 1)$ traversed in that order

In Problems 16–23, use Stokes' theorem to evaluate

$$\iint_S (\text{curl } \mathbf{F} \cdot \mathbf{N})\,dS$$

for the prescribed vector fields and surfaces. In each case, use the upward unit normal for S.

16. $\mathbf{F} = x\mathbf{i} + y^2\mathbf{j} + xyz\mathbf{k}$, and S is the part of the paraboloid $z = 4 - x^2 - y^2$ with $z \geq 0$. Use the upward unit normal vector.

17. $\mathbf{F} = xy\mathbf{i} - z\mathbf{j}$, and S is the surface of the cube $0 \leq x \leq 1$, $0 \leq y \leq 1$, $0 \leq z \leq 1$ except for the face where $z = 0$.

18. $\mathbf{F} = y\mathbf{i} + z\mathbf{j} + x\mathbf{k}$, and S is the part of the plane $x + y + z = 1$ that lies in the first octant.

19. $\mathbf{F} = xy\mathbf{i} + x^2\mathbf{j} + z^2\mathbf{k}$, and S is the part of the plane $z = y$ that is inside the paraboloid $z = x^2 + y^2$.

20. $\mathbf{F} = xz\mathbf{i} + y^2\mathbf{j} + x^2\mathbf{k}$, and S is the part of the plane $x + y + z = 3$ inside the cylinder $9x^2 + y^2 = 9$.

21. $\mathbf{F} = 4y\mathbf{i} + z\mathbf{j} + 2y\mathbf{k}$, and S is the hemisphere $z = \sqrt{4 - x^2 - y^2}$.

22. $\mathbf{F} = \langle x \tan^{-1} e^{-x}, y \ln(1 + y^{3/2}), ze^{-1/z} \rangle$, and S is the part of the sphere $x^2 + y^2 + z^2 = 9$ that lies inside the cone $z = \sqrt{2x^2 + 2y^2}$.

23. $\mathbf{F} = \langle 6x^2 e^{yz}, 2x^3 z e^{yz}, 2x^3 y e^{yz} \rangle$, and S is the part of the cone $z = \sqrt{x^2 + y^2}$ that lies above the inner loop of the limaçon $r = 1 + 2\cos\theta$.

B *In Problems 24–26, use Stokes' theorem to evaluate the line integral*

$$\oint_C [(1 + y)z\,dx + (1 + z)x\,dy + (1 + x)y\,dz]$$

for the given closed path C.

24. C is the elliptic path $x = 2\cos\theta$, $y = \sin\theta$, $z = 1$ for $0 \le \theta \le 2\pi$.

25. C is the boundary of the triangle with vertices $(1, 0, 0)$, $(0, 1, 0)$, $(0, 0, 1)$.

26. C is any closed path in the plane $2x - 3y + z = 1$.

In Problems 27–30, the vector field $\mathbf{V}$ represents the velocity of a fluid flow. In each case, find the circulation

$$\oint_C \mathbf{V} \cdot d\mathbf{R}$$

around the boundary C, assuming a counterclockwise orientation as viewed from above.

27. $\mathbf{V} = x\mathbf{i} + (z - x)\mathbf{j} + y\mathbf{k}$, and C is the intersection of the cylinder $x^2 + y^2 = y$ and the hemisphere $z = \sqrt{1 - x^2 - y^2}$.

28. $\mathbf{V} = y\mathbf{i} + \ln(x^2 + y^2)\mathbf{j} + (x + y)\mathbf{k}$, and C is the triangle with vertices $(0, 0, 0)$, $(1, 0, 0)$, and $(0, 1, 0)$.

29. $\mathbf{V} = (e^{x^2} + z)\mathbf{i} + (x + \sin y^3)\mathbf{j} + [y + \ln(\tan^{-1} z)]\mathbf{k}$, and C is the intersection of the sphere $x^2 + y^2 + z^2 = 1$ and the cone $z = \sqrt{x^2 + y^2}$.

30. $\mathbf{V} = y^2\mathbf{i} + \tan^{-1} z\mathbf{j} + (x^2 + 1)\mathbf{k}$, and C is the intersection of the plane $z = y$ and the cylinder $x^2 + y^2 = 2x$.

31. Let $\mathbf{F} = y^2\mathbf{i} + xy\mathbf{j} + xz\mathbf{k}$, and suppose S is the hemisphere $x^2 + y^2 + z^2 = 1$ with $z \ge 0$. Use Stokes' theorem to express

$$\iint_S (\operatorname{curl} \mathbf{F} \cdot \mathbf{N})\,dS$$

as a line integral, and then evaluate the surface integral by evaluating this line integral.

32. Let $\mathbf{F} = z\mathbf{i} + x\mathbf{j} + y\mathbf{k}$, and suppose S is a smooth surface in $\mathbb{R}^3$ whose boundary is given by $x = 2\cos\theta$, $y = 3\sin\theta$, $z = \sin\theta$, $0 \le \theta \le 2\pi$. Use Stokes' theorem to evaluate

$$\iint_S (\operatorname{curl} \mathbf{F} \cdot \mathbf{N})\,dS$$

33. **Counterexample Problem** Let C_1 and C_2 be positively oriented Jordan curves in the plane $5x + 3y + 2z = 4$ that contain the same area, and let $\mathbf{F} = \langle 4z, -3x, 2y \rangle$. Either prove that

$$\oint_{C_1} \mathbf{F} \cdot d\mathbf{R} = \oint_{C_2} \mathbf{F} \cdot d\mathbf{R}$$

or find a counterexample.

34. HISTORICAL QUEST   George Stokes was an English mathematical physicist who made important contributions to fluid mechanics, including the Navier-Stokes equations, which are important for modeling fluid flow. Most of his research was done before 1850, after which he held the Lucasian chair of mathematics at Cambridge for the better part of a half-century. William Thomson (Lord Kelvin) knew the result now known as Stokes' theorem in 1850 and sent it to Stokes as a challenge. Stokes proved the theorem, and then included it as an exam question in 1854. One of the students taking this particular examination was James Clerk Maxwell (Historical Quest #32, Section 13.7), who derived the famous electromagnetic wave equations ten years later. ∎

GEORGE STOKES
1819–1903

For this Quest, write a history of the Lucasian chair, which was deeded in 1663 as a gift of Henry Lucas. The first and second appointees were Isaac Barrow (Historical Quest #6, page 48) and Isaac Newton (Historical Quest #1, page 48); and the chair is currently held by Stephen Hawking.

C 35. Let S be the ellipsoid $\dfrac{x^2}{4} + \dfrac{y^2}{9} + z^2 = 1$, and let $\mathbf{F}$ be a vector field whose component functions have continuous partial derivatives on S. Use Stokes' theorem to show that

$$\iint_S (\operatorname{curl} \mathbf{F} \cdot \mathbf{N})\,dS = 0$$

Does it matter that S is an ellipsoid? State and prove a more general result based on what you have discovered in the first part of this problem.

36. **Faraday's law** of electromagnetism says that if $\mathbf{E}$ is the electric intensity vector in a system, then

$$\oint_C \mathbf{E} \cdot d\mathbf{R} = -\frac{\partial\phi}{\partial t}$$

around any closed curve C, where t is time and ϕ is the total magnetic flux directed outward through any surface S bounded by C. Given that

$$\phi = \iint_S \mathbf{B} \cdot \mathbf{N}\,dS$$

where $\mathbf{B}$ is the magnetic flux density, show that

$\operatorname{curl} \mathbf{E} = -\dfrac{\partial \mathbf{B}}{\partial t}$. *Hint:* It can be shown that

$$\frac{\partial}{\partial t} \iint_S \mathbf{B} \cdot \mathbf{N}\,dS = \iint_S \frac{\partial \mathbf{B}}{\partial t} \cdot \mathbf{N}\,dS.$$

37. The current I flowing across a surface S bounded by the closed curve C is given by

$$I = \iint_S \mathbf{J} \cdot \mathbf{N}\,dS$$

where $\mathbf{J}$ is the current density. Given that $\mu\mathbf{J} = \operatorname{curl} \mathbf{B}$, where $\mathbf{B}$ is magnetic flux density and μ is a constant, show that

$$\oint_C \mathbf{B} \cdot d\mathbf{R} = \mu I$$

Suppose f and g are functions of x, y, and z with continuous first- and second-order partial derivatives and C is a closed curve bounding the surface S. Use Stokes' theorem to verify the formulas given in Problems 38–39.

38. $\oint_C (f\nabla g) \cdot d\mathbf{R} = \iint_S (\nabla f \times \nabla g) \cdot \mathbf{N}\,dS$

39. $\oint_C (f\nabla g + g\nabla f) \cdot d\mathbf{R} = 0$

13.7   The Divergence Theorem

IN THIS SECTION   the divergence theorem, applications of the divergence theorem, physical interpretation of divergence

THE DIVERGENCE THEOREM

We used Green's theorem to show that $\int_C \mathbf{F} \cdot \mathbf{N}\,dS = \iint_D \operatorname{div} \mathbf{F}\,dA$, where D is a simply connected domain with the closed boundary curve C. The *divergence theorem* (also known as **Gauss' theorem**) is a generalization of this form of Green's theorem that relates an integral over a closed surface to a volume integral.

THEOREM 13.9   The divergence theorem

Let S be a smooth, orientable surface that encloses a solid region D in $\mathbb{R}^3$. If $\mathbf{F}$ is a continuous vector field whose components have continuous partial derivatives in an open set containing D, then

$$\iint_S \mathbf{F} \cdot \mathbf{N}\,dS = \iiint_D \operatorname{div} \mathbf{F}\,dV$$

where $\mathbf{N}$ is the outward unit normal field for the surface S.

Proof   An important special case is proved in Appendix B.   ❑

EXAMPLE 1   Evaluating a surface integral using the divergence theorem

Evaluate $\iint_S \mathbf{F} \cdot \mathbf{N}\,dS$, where $\mathbf{F} = x^2\mathbf{i} + xy\mathbf{j} + x^3y^3\mathbf{k}$ and S is the surface of the tetrahedron bounded by the plane $x + y + z = 1$ and the coordinate planes, with outward unit normal vector $\mathbf{N}$ (see Figure 13.47).

Solution

We will use the divergence theorem. Note that

$$\operatorname{div} \mathbf{F} = \frac{\partial}{\partial x}(x^2) + \frac{\partial}{\partial y}(xy) + \frac{\partial}{\partial z}(x^3y^3) = 2x + x + 0 = 3x$$

The tetrahedron is the set

$$R : \quad \text{all } (x, y, z) \text{ such that } 0 \leq z \leq 1 - x - y$$
$$\text{whenever } 0 \leq y \leq 1 - x \text{ for } 0 \leq x \leq 1$$

This projects onto the triangular region in the xy-plane described by

$$D : \quad \text{all } (x, y) \text{ such that } 0 \leq y \leq 1 - x \text{ for } 0 \leq x \leq 1$$

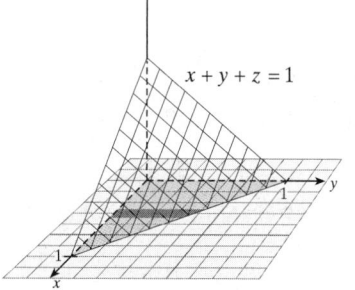

a. The surface S

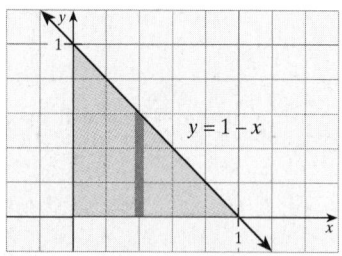

b. Projected region in the xy-plane

Figure 13.47 A tetrahedron in $\mathbb{R}^3$

(See Figure 13.47b.) Then, by applying the divergence theorem, we find that

$$\iint\limits_{S} \mathbf{F} \cdot \mathbf{N}\, dS = \iiint\limits_{R} \operatorname{div} \mathbf{F}\, dV = \int_0^1 \int_0^{1-x} \int_0^{1-x-y} 3x\, dz\, dy\, dx$$

$$= \int_0^1 \int_0^{1-x} 3x(1 - x - y)\, dy\, dx = 3 \int_0^1 \left[x(1-x)y - \tfrac{1}{2}xy^2 \right]\Big|_0^{1-x} dx$$

$$= 3 \int_0^1 \left[x(1-x)^2 - \tfrac{1}{2}x(1-x)^2 \right] dx = \tfrac{1}{8} \qquad \blacksquare$$

EXAMPLE 2   Verifying the divergence theorem for a particular solid

Let $\mathbf{F} = 2x\mathbf{i} - 3y\mathbf{j} + 5z\mathbf{k}$, and let S be the hemisphere $z = \sqrt{9 - x^2 - y^2}$ together with the disk $x^2 + y^2 \le 9$ in the xy-plane. Verify the divergence theorem.

Solution

The solid is shown in Figure 13.48. We will show that the surface integral $\iint\limits_{S} \mathbf{F} \cdot \mathbf{N}\, dS$ and the triple integral $\iiint\limits_{R} \operatorname{div} \mathbf{F}\, dV$ have the same value, where R is the solid bounded by S.

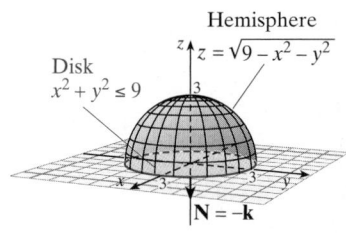

Disk
$x^2 + y^2 \le 9$

Hemisphere
$z = \sqrt{9 - x^2 - y^2}$

$\mathbf{N} = -\mathbf{k}$

Figure 13.48 The surface of the hemisphere $z = \sqrt{9 - x^2 - y^2}$

  I. *Evaluation of* $\displaystyle\iiint\limits_{R} \operatorname{div} \mathbf{F}\, dV$

$$\operatorname{div} \mathbf{F} = \frac{\partial}{\partial x}(2x) + \frac{\partial}{\partial y}(-3y) + \frac{\partial}{\partial z}(5z) = 2 - 3 + 5 = 4$$

Therefore, $\iiint\limits_{R} \operatorname{div} \mathbf{F}\, dV = \iiint\limits_{R} 4\, dV$, but $\iiint\limits_{R} dV$ is just the volume of the hemisphere $z = \sqrt{9 - x^2 - y^2}$. A hemisphere of radius 3 has volume $\tfrac{1}{2}\left[\tfrac{4}{3}\pi(3)^3 \right] = 18\pi$, so

$$\iiint\limits_{R} \operatorname{div} \mathbf{F}\, dV = \iiint\limits_{R} 4\, dV = 4V = 4(18\pi) = 72\pi$$

 II. *Evaluation of* $\displaystyle\iint\limits_{S} \mathbf{F} \cdot \mathbf{N}\, dS$

S consists of two parts: S_1, the disk on the bottom of the hemisphere, and S_2, the hemisphere. We will consider these separately and then use

$$\iint\limits_{S} \mathbf{F} \cdot \mathbf{N}\, dS = \iint\limits_{S_1} \mathbf{F} \cdot \mathbf{N_1}\, dS_1 + \iint\limits_{S_2} \mathbf{F} \cdot \mathbf{N_2}\, dS_2$$

The surface S_1: The disk $x^2 + y^2 \le 9$ with $z = 0$ has outward (downward) unit normal $\mathbf{N} = -\mathbf{k}$, so

$$\iint\limits_{S_1} \mathbf{F} \cdot \mathbf{N}\, dS_1 = \iint\limits_{S_1} \langle 2x, -3y, 5z \rangle \cdot \langle 0, 0, -1 \rangle\, dS_1$$

$$= \iint\limits_{S_1} (-5z)\, dS_1 = 0 \quad \text{Because } z = 0 \text{ on } S_1$$

The surface S_2: Since $z = \sqrt{9 - x^2 - y^2}$, we have

$$z_x = \frac{-x}{\sqrt{9 - x^2 - y^2}} \quad \text{and} \quad z_y = \frac{-y}{\sqrt{9 - x^2 - y^2}}$$

and the projection of S_2 onto the xy-plane is the disk $D : x^2 + y^2 \leq 9$ or $r \leq 3$ in polar form. (See Figure 13.49.) We find that

$$\iint_{S_2} \mathbf{F} \cdot \mathbf{N} \, dS_2 = \iint_D \langle 2x, -3y, 5z \rangle \cdot \left\langle -\left(\frac{-x}{\sqrt{9 - x^2 - y^2}} \right), -\left(\frac{-y}{\sqrt{9 - x^2 - y^2}} \right), 1 \right\rangle dA$$

$$= \iint_D \left[\frac{2x^2 - 3y^2}{\sqrt{9 - x^2 - y^2}} + 5z \right] dA$$

$$= \iint_D \left[\frac{2x^2 - 3y^2}{\sqrt{9 - x^2 - y^2}} + 5\sqrt{9 - x^2 - y^2} \right] dA \qquad \text{Since } z = \sqrt{9 - x^2 - y^2} \text{ on } S$$

$$= \int_0^{2\pi} \int_0^3 \left[\frac{2r^2 \cos^2 \theta - 3r^2 \sin^2 \theta}{\sqrt{9 - r^2}} + 5\sqrt{9 - r^2} \right] r \, dr \, d\theta \qquad \text{Changing to polar coordinates}$$

$$= \int_0^{2\pi} \left[81 - 90 \sin^2 \theta \right] d\theta$$

$$= 72\pi$$

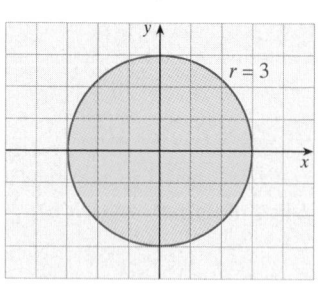

Figure 13.49 The hemisphere projects onto the disk $x^2 + y^2 \leq 9$, or $r \leq 3$ in polar form

Adding the surface integrals for S_1 and S_2, we obtain

$$\iint_S \mathbf{F} \cdot \mathbf{N} \, dS = \iint_{S_1} \mathbf{F} \cdot \mathbf{N} \, dS_1 + \iint_{S_2} \mathbf{F} \cdot \mathbf{N} \, dS_2 = 0 + 72\pi = 72\pi$$

Thus, we have

$$\iint_S \mathbf{F} \cdot \mathbf{N} \, dS = 72\pi = \iiint_R \operatorname{div} \mathbf{F} \, dV$$

as required by the divergence theorem.   ■

The divergence theorem applies only to closed surfaces. However, if we wish to evaluate $\iint_{S_1} \mathbf{F} \cdot \mathbf{N} \, dS$ where S_1 is *not* closed, we may be able to find a closed surface S that is the union of S_1 and some other surface S_2. Then, if the hypotheses of the divergence theorem are satisfied by $\mathbf{F}$ and S, we have

$$\iint_{S_1} \mathbf{F} \cdot \mathbf{N} \, dS + \iint_{S_2} \mathbf{F} \cdot \mathbf{N} \, dS = \iint_S \mathbf{F} \cdot \mathbf{N} \, dS = \iiint_D \operatorname{div} \mathbf{F} \, dV$$

where D is the solid region bounded by S. Thus, if we can compute $\iiint_D \operatorname{div} \mathbf{F} \, dV$ and $\iint_{S_2} \mathbf{F} \cdot \mathbf{N} \, dS$, we can compute $\iint_{S_1} \mathbf{F} \cdot \mathbf{N} \, dS$ by the equation

$$\iint_{S_1} \mathbf{F} \cdot \mathbf{N} \, dS = \iiint_D \operatorname{div} \mathbf{F} \, dV - \iint_{S_2} \mathbf{F} \cdot \mathbf{N} \, dS$$

This equation can also be used as a device for trading the evaluation of a difficult surface integral for that of an easier volume integral. Here is an example of this procedure.

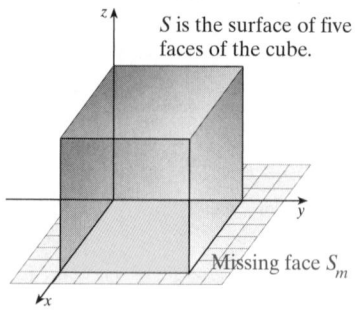

S^* is the closed surface of the entire cube.

S is the surface of five faces of the cube.

Missing face S_m

Figure 13.50 An open surface: a cube with a missing face

EXAMPLE 3   Evaluating a surface integral over an open surface

Evaluate $\displaystyle\iint_S \mathbf{F} \cdot \mathbf{N} \, dS$, where $\mathbf{F} = xy\mathbf{i} - z^2\mathbf{k}$ and S is the surface of the upper five faces of the unit cube $0 \leq x \leq 1, 0 \leq y \leq 1, 0 < z \leq 1$, as shown in Figure 13.50.

Solution

Note that the surface S is not closed, but we can close it by adding the missing face S_m, thus forming a closed surface S^* that satisfies the conditions of the divergence theorem. The strategy is to evaluate the surface integral of S^* and then subtract the surface integral over the added face S_m.

$$\iint\limits_{S^*} \mathbf{F} \cdot \mathbf{N} \, dS = \iiint\limits_{\text{cube}} \operatorname{div} \mathbf{F} \, dV = \int_0^1 \int_0^1 \int_0^1 (y - 2z) \, dx \, dy \, dz$$

$$= \int_0^1 \int_0^1 (y - 2z) \, dy \, dz = \int_0^1 \left(\tfrac{1}{2} - 2z\right) dz = -\tfrac{1}{2}$$

Also, because the outward unit normal vector to the added face S_m is $\mathbf{N} = -\mathbf{k}$ and $z = 0$ on this face, it follows that

$$\iint\limits_{S_m} \mathbf{F} \cdot \mathbf{N} \, dS = \iint\limits_{S_m} (xy\mathbf{i} - z^2\mathbf{k}) \cdot (-\mathbf{k}) \, dS = \iint\limits_{S_m} z^2 \, dS = 0$$

Therefore,

$$\iint\limits_{S} \mathbf{F} \cdot \mathbf{N} \, dS = \iiint\limits_{D} \operatorname{div} \mathbf{F} \, dV - \iint\limits_{S_m} \mathbf{F} \cdot \mathbf{N} \, dS = -\tfrac{1}{2} - 0 = -\tfrac{1}{2} \qquad \blacksquare$$

APPLICATIONS OF THE DIVERGENCE THEOREM

Like Stokes' theorem, the divergence theorem is often used for theoretical purposes, especially as a tool for deriving general properties in mathematical physics. The following example deals with an important property of fluid dynamics.

EXAMPLE 4 Continuity equation of fluid dynamics

Suppose a fluid with density $\delta(x, y, z, t)$ flows in some region of space with velocity $\mathbf{F}(x, y, z, t)$ at the point (x, y, z) at time t. Assuming there are no sources or sinks, show that

$$\operatorname{div} \delta \mathbf{F} = -\frac{\partial \delta}{\partial t}$$

Solution

Recall from Section 13.1 that a point is called a *source* if $\operatorname{div} \delta \mathbf{F} > 0$, a *sink* if $\operatorname{div} \delta \mathbf{F} < 0$, and *incompressible* if $\operatorname{div} \delta \mathbf{F} = 0$. Let S be a smooth surface in $\mathbb{R}^3$ that encloses a solid region D. In physics, it is shown that the amount of fluid flowing out of D across S in unit time is $\iint\limits_{S} \delta \mathbf{F} \cdot \mathbf{N} \, dS$, which must equal the net decrease in density of the fluid; namely $\iiint\limits_{D} \dfrac{\partial \delta}{\partial t} \, dV$. Equating these two quantities, we have

$$\iint\limits_{S} \delta \mathbf{F} \cdot \mathbf{N} \, dS = -\iiint\limits_{D} \frac{\partial \delta}{\partial t} \, dV$$

By the divergence theorem, it follows that

$$\iint\limits_{S} \delta \mathbf{F} \cdot \mathbf{N} \, dS = \iiint\limits_{D} \operatorname{div} \delta \mathbf{F} \, dV$$

so that

$$\iiint\limits_{D} \operatorname{div} \delta \mathbf{F} \, dV + \iiint\limits_{D} \frac{\partial \delta}{\partial t} \, dV = 0$$

$$\iiint\limits_{D} \left[\operatorname{div} \delta \mathbf{F} + \frac{\partial \delta}{\partial t} \right] dV = 0$$

This equation must hold for any region D, no matter how small, which means that the integrand of the integral must be 0. That is,

$$\text{div } \delta\mathbf{F} = -\frac{\partial \delta}{\partial t}$$ ∎

It is known that the total heat contained in a body with uniform density δ and specific heat σ is $\iiint_D \sigma\delta T\, dV$, where T is the temperature. Thus, the amount of heat leaving D per unit of time is given by the derivative

$$-\frac{\partial}{\partial t}\left[\iiint_D \sigma\delta T\, dV\right] = \iiint_D -\sigma\delta\frac{\partial T}{\partial t}\, dV$$

In the following example, we use this result to obtain an important formula from mathematical physics.

EXAMPLE 5   Derivation of the heat equation

Let $T(x, y, z, t)$ be the temperature at each point (x, y, z) in a solid body D at time t. Given that the velocity of heat flow in the body is $\mathbf{F} = -K\nabla T$ for a positive constant K (called the **thermal conductivity**), show that

$$\frac{\partial T}{\partial t} = \frac{K}{\sigma\delta}\nabla^2 T$$

where σ is the specific heat of the body and δ is its density.

Solution

Let S be the closed surface that bounds D. Because $\mathbf{F}$ is the velocity of heat flow, the amount of heat leaving D per unit time is $\iint_S \mathbf{F} \cdot \mathbf{N}\, dS$, and the divergence theorem applies:

$$\iint_S \mathbf{F} \cdot \mathbf{N}\, dS = \iiint_D \text{div}(-K\nabla T)\, dV = \iiint_D (-K\nabla \cdot \nabla T)\, dV$$

$$= \iiint_D -K\nabla^2 T\, dV$$

Since this is the amount of heat leaving D per unit of time, it must equal the heat integral from physics derived just before this example. Thus,

$$\iiint_D -K\nabla^2 T\, dV = \iiint_D -\sigma\delta\frac{\partial T}{\partial t}\, dV$$

This equation holds not only for the body as a whole, but for every part of the body, no matter how small. Thus, we can shrink the body to a single point, and it then can be shown that when this occurs the integrands are equal; that is,

$$-K\nabla^2 T = -\sigma\delta\frac{\partial T}{\partial t}$$

$$\frac{\partial T}{\partial t} = \frac{K}{\sigma\delta}\nabla^2 T$$ ∎

Recall from Section 13.4 that the *normal derivative* $\partial g/\partial n$ of a scalar function g defined on the closed surface S is the directional derivative of f in the direction of the outward unit normal vector $\mathbf{N}$ to S; that is,

$$\frac{\partial g}{\partial n} = \nabla g \cdot \mathbf{N}$$

We will use this equation in the following example, which is a generalization of a property we first obtained for $\mathbb{R}^2$ in Example 6 of Section 13.4.

EXAMPLE 6   Derivation of Green's first identity

Show that if f and g are scalar functions such that $\mathbf{F} = f\nabla g$ is continuously differentiable in the solid domain D bounded by the closed surface S, then

$$\iiint_D [f\nabla^2 g + \nabla f \cdot \nabla g]\, dV = \iint_S f \frac{\partial g}{\partial n}\, dS$$

This is called **Green's first identity**.

Solution

We will apply the divergence theorem to the vector field $\mathbf{F}$ (note that $\mathbf{F}$ is continuously differentiable), but first we need to express div $\mathbf{F}$ in a more useful form.

$$\begin{aligned}
\operatorname{div}(f\nabla g) &= \nabla \cdot (f\nabla g) \\
&= \left[\frac{\partial}{\partial x}\mathbf{i} + \frac{\partial}{\partial y}\mathbf{j} + \frac{\partial}{\partial z}\mathbf{k} \right] \cdot \left[f\frac{\partial g}{\partial x}\mathbf{i} + f\frac{\partial g}{\partial y}\mathbf{j} + f\frac{\partial g}{\partial z}\mathbf{k} \right] \\
&= \frac{\partial}{\partial x}\left[f\frac{\partial g}{\partial x} \right] + \frac{\partial}{\partial y}\left[f\frac{\partial g}{\partial y} \right] + \frac{\partial}{\partial z}\left[f\frac{\partial g}{\partial z} \right] \\
&= \left[\frac{\partial f}{\partial x}\frac{\partial g}{\partial x} + f\frac{\partial^2 g}{\partial x^2} \right] + \left[\frac{\partial f}{\partial y}\frac{\partial g}{\partial y} + f\frac{\partial^2 g}{\partial y^2} \right] + \left[\frac{\partial f}{\partial z}\frac{\partial g}{\partial z} + f\frac{\partial^2 g}{\partial z^2} \right] \\
&= \left[\frac{\partial f}{\partial x}\frac{\partial g}{\partial x} + \frac{\partial f}{\partial y}\frac{\partial g}{\partial y} + \frac{\partial f}{\partial z}\frac{\partial g}{\partial z} \right] + f\left[\frac{\partial^2 g}{\partial x^2} + \frac{\partial^2 g}{\partial y^2} + \frac{\partial^2 g}{\partial z^2} \right] \\
&= (\nabla f) \cdot (\nabla g) + f\nabla^2 g
\end{aligned}$$

This calculation gives us the first step in the following computation.

$$\begin{aligned}
\iiint_D [f\nabla^2 g + \nabla f \cdot \nabla g]\, dV &= \iiint_D \operatorname{div}(f\nabla g)\, dV \\
&= \iint_S (f\nabla g) \cdot \mathbf{N}\, dS \qquad \textsf{Divergence theorem} \\
&= \iint_S f(\nabla g \cdot \mathbf{N})\, dS \\
&= \iint_S f\frac{\partial g}{\partial n}\, dS \qquad \textsf{Because } \nabla g \cdot \mathbf{N} = \dfrac{\partial g}{\partial n} \\
& \hspace{5.3cm} \textsf{by definition} \qquad \blacksquare
\end{aligned}$$

PHYSICAL INTERPRETATION OF DIVERGENCE

In Section 13.6, we used Stokes' theorem to give an interpretation of the curl as a measure of the tendency of a fluid to swirl (the circulation). Our last example gives an analogous interpretation of divergence. In particular, we show that the net rate of fluid mass flowing away (that is, "diverging") from point P_0 is given by div $\mathbf{F}_0$. This is the reason P_0 is a source if div $\mathbf{F}_0 > 0$ (mass flowing out from P_0) and a sink if div $\mathbf{F}_0 < 0$ (mass flowing back into P_0).

EXAMPLE 7   Physical interpretation of divergence

Let $\mathbf{F} = \delta\mathbf{V}$ be the flux density associated with a fluid of density δ flowing with velocity $\mathbf{V}$ and let P_0 be a point inside a solid region where the conditions of the divergence theorem are satisfied. Prove that

$$\operatorname{div}\mathbf{F}_0 = \lim_{r \to 0} \frac{1}{V(r)} \iint_{S(r)} \mathbf{F} \cdot \mathbf{N}\, dS$$

where div $\mathbf{F}_0$ denotes the value of div $\mathbf{F}$ at P_0, and $S(r)$ is a sphere centered at P_0 with volume $V(r) = \frac{4}{3}\pi r^3$.

Solution

Applying the divergence theorem to the solid sphere (ball) $B(r)$ with surface $S(r)$, we obtain

$$\iint_{S(r)} \mathbf{F} \cdot \mathbf{N} \, dS = \iiint_{B(r)} \text{div} \, \mathbf{F} \, dV$$

The mean value theorem (for triple integrals) tells us that

$$\frac{1}{V(r)} \iiint_{B(r)} \text{div} \, \mathbf{F} \, dV = \text{div} \, \mathbf{F}^*$$

where $\text{div} \, \mathbf{F}^*$ denotes the value of $\text{div} \, \mathbf{F}$ at some point P^* in the ball $B(r)$. Combining these results, we find that

$$\iint_{S(r)} \mathbf{F} \cdot \mathbf{N} \, dS = \iiint_{B(r)} \text{div} \, \mathbf{F} \, dV = V(r) \, \text{div} \, \mathbf{F}^*$$

or

$$\frac{1}{V(r)} \iint_{S(r)} \mathbf{F} \cdot \mathbf{N} \, dS = \text{div} \, \mathbf{F}^*$$

Since the point P^* is inside the ball $B(r)$ centered at P_0, it follows that $P^* \to P_0$ as $r \to 0$, so $\text{div} \, \mathbf{F}^* \to \text{div} \, \mathbf{F}_0$ and we have

$$\lim_{r \to 0} \frac{1}{V(r)} \iint_{S(r)} \mathbf{F} \cdot \mathbf{N} \, dS = \lim_{r \to 0} \text{div} \, \mathbf{F}^* = \text{div} \, \mathbf{F}_0$$

as claimed.   ∎

13.7 PROBLEM SET

Ⓐ *Verify the divergence theorem for the vector function* $\mathbf{F}$ *and solid D given in Problems 1–4. Assume $\mathbf{N}$ is the unit normal vector pointing away from the origin.*

1. $\mathbf{F} = xz\mathbf{i} + y^2\mathbf{j} + 2z\mathbf{k}$; D is the ball $x^2 + y^2 + z^2 \leq 4$.

2. $\mathbf{F} = x\mathbf{i} - 2y\mathbf{j}$; D is the interior of the paraboloid $z = x^2 + y^2$, $0 \leq z \leq 9$.

3. $\mathbf{F} = 2y^2\mathbf{j}$; D is the tetrahedron bounded by the coordinate planes and the $x + 4y + z = 8$.

4. $\mathbf{F} = 3x\mathbf{i} + 5y\mathbf{j} + 6z\mathbf{k}$; D is the tetrahedron bounded by the coordinate planes and the plane $2x + y + z = 4$.

Use the divergence theorem in Problems 5–19 to evaluate the surface integral $\iint_S \mathbf{F} \cdot \mathbf{N} \, dS$ for the given choice of $\mathbf{F}$ and closed boundary surface S. Assume $\mathbf{N}$ is the outward unit normal vector field.

5. $\mathbf{F} = x\mathbf{i} + y\mathbf{j} + z\mathbf{k}$; S is the cube $0 \leq x \leq 1$, $0 \leq y \leq 1$, $0 \leq z \leq 1$.

6. $\mathbf{F} = xyz\mathbf{j}$; S is the cylinder $x^2 + y^2 = 9$, for $0 \leq z \leq 5$.

7. $\mathbf{F} = (\cos yz)\mathbf{i} + e^{xz}\mathbf{j} + 3z^2\mathbf{k}$; S is the hemisphere $z = \sqrt{4 - x^2 - y^2}$ together with the disk $x^2 + y^2 \leq 4$ in the xy-plane.

8. $\mathbf{F} = \text{curl}[e^{xz}\mathbf{i} - 4\mathbf{j} + (\sin xyz)\mathbf{k}]$; S is the ellipsoid $2x^2 + 3y^2 + 7z^2 = 1$.

9. $\mathbf{F} = (x^2 + y^2 - z^2)\mathbf{i} + x^2y\mathbf{j} + 3z\mathbf{k}$; S is the surface comprised of the five faces of the unit cube $0 \leq x \leq 1$, $0 \leq y \leq 1$, $0 \leq z \leq 1$, missing $z = 0$.

10. $\mathbf{F} = 2y\mathbf{i} - zj + 3x\mathbf{k}$; S is the surface comprised of the five faces of the unit cube $0 \leq x \leq 1$, $0 \leq y \leq 1$, $0 \leq z \leq 1$, missing $z = 0$.

11. $\mathbf{F} = x\mathbf{i} + y\mathbf{j} + z\mathbf{k}$; S is the paraboloid $z = x^2 + y^2$ for $0 \leq z \leq 9$.

12. $\mathbf{F} = \text{curl}(y\mathbf{i} + x\mathbf{j} - z\mathbf{k})$; S is the hemisphere $z = \sqrt{4 - x^2 - y^2}$ together with the disk $x^2 + y^2 \leq 4$ in the xy-plane.

13. $\mathbf{F} = x^2\mathbf{i} + y^2\mathbf{j} + z^2\mathbf{k}$; S is the sphere $x^2 + y^2 + z^2 = 4$.

14. $\mathbf{F} = xyz\mathbf{i} + xyz\mathbf{j} + xyz\mathbf{k}$; S is the surface of the box $0 \leq x \leq 1$, $0 \leq y \leq 2$, $0 \leq z \leq 3$.

15. $\mathbf{F} = x\mathbf{i} + y\mathbf{j} + (z^2 - 1)\mathbf{k}$; S is the surface of a solid bounded by the cylinder $x^2 + y^2 = 4$ and the planes $z = 0$ and $z = 1$.

16. $\mathbf{F} = (x^5 + 10xy^2z^2)\mathbf{i} + (y^5 + 10yx^2z^2)\mathbf{j} + (z^5 + 10zx^2y^2)\mathbf{k}$; S is the closed hemispherical surface $z = \sqrt{1 - x^2 - y^2}$ together with the disk $x^2 + y^2 \leq 1$ in the xy-plane.

17. $\mathbf{F} = xy^2\mathbf{i} + yz^2\mathbf{j} + x^2y\mathbf{k}$; S is the surface bounded above by the sphere $\rho = 2$ and below by the cone $\phi = \frac{\pi}{4}$ (in spherical coordinates). *Note*: S is the surface of an "ice cream cone."

18. $\mathbf{F} = xy^2\mathbf{i} + yz^2\mathbf{j} + x^2z\mathbf{k}$; S is the surface bounded above by the sphere $\rho = 2$ and below by the cone $\phi = \frac{\pi}{4}$ (in spherical coordinates). *Note*: S is the surface of an "ice cream cone."

19. $\mathbf{F} = x^3\mathbf{i} + y^3\mathbf{j} + 3a^2z\mathbf{k}$ (constant $a > 0$); S is the surface bounded by the cylinder $x^2 + y^2 = a^2$ and the planes $z = 0$ and $z = 1$.

B 20. Suppose that S is a closed surface that encloses a solid region D.

a. Show that the volume of D is given by

$$V(D) = \frac{1}{3}\iint\limits_{S} (x\mathbf{i} + y\mathbf{j} + z\mathbf{k}) \cdot \mathbf{N}\, dS$$

where $\mathbf{N}$ is an outward unit normal vector to S.

b. Use the formula in part **a** to find the volume of the hemisphere

$$z = \sqrt{R^2 - x^2 - y^2}$$

21. Use the divergence theorem to evaluate

$$\iint\limits_{S} \|\mathbf{R}\|\mathbf{R} \cdot \mathbf{N}\, dS$$

where $\mathbf{R} = x\mathbf{i} + y\mathbf{j} + z\mathbf{k}$ and S is the sphere $x^2 + y^2 + z^2 = a^2$, with constant $a > 0$.

22. **Counterexample Problem** Let $\mathbf{F} = \langle f(y, z), g(x, z), h(x, y)\rangle$ and let S be the surface of a solid G. Either prove that the flux of $\mathbf{F}$ across S is zero or find a counterexample.

23. **Exploration Problem** Let $f(x, y, z)$ be a differentiable nonzero scalar function. State an additional property of f that will guarantee

$$\iint\limits_{S} f\nabla f \cdot \mathbf{N}\, dS = \iiint\limits_{G} \|\nabla f\|^2\, dV$$

for any solid region G bounded by the closed oriented surface S.

24. The moment of inertia about the z-axis of a solid D of constant density $\delta = a$ is given by

$$I_z = \iiint\limits_{T} a(x^2 + y^2)\, dV$$

Express this integral as a surface integral over the surface S that bounds D.

C 25. Let u be a scalar function with continuous second partial derivatives in a region containing the solid region D, with closed boundary surface S.

a. Show that $\displaystyle\iint\limits_{S} \frac{\partial u}{\partial n}\, dS = \iiint\limits_{D} \nabla^2 u\, dV$.

b. Let $u = x + y + z$ and $v = \frac{1}{2}(x^2 + y^2 + z^2)$. Evaluate $\displaystyle\iint\limits_{S} (u\nabla v) \cdot \mathbf{N}\, dS$, where S is the boundary of the cube $0 \le x \le 1, 0 \le y \le 1, 0 \le z \le 1$.

26. Let f and g be scalar functions such that $\mathbf{F} = f\nabla g$ is continuously differentiable in the region D, which is bounded by the closed surface S. Prove *Green's second identity* using the divergence theorem:

$$\iiint\limits_{D} (f\nabla^2 g - g\nabla^2 f)\, dV = \iint\limits_{S} \left(f\frac{\partial g}{\partial n} - g\frac{\partial f}{\partial n}\right)\, dS$$

27. Show that if g is harmonic in the region D, then

$$\iint\limits_{S} \frac{\partial g}{\partial n}\, dS = 0$$

where the closed surface S is the boundary of D. (Recall that g harmonic means $\nabla^2 g = 0$.)

28. Show that $\displaystyle\iint\limits_{S} \mathbf{F} \cdot \mathbf{N}\, dS = 0$ if S is a closed surface and $\mathbf{F} = \text{curl } \mathbf{U}$ throughout the interior of S for some vector field $\mathbf{U}$ with continuous second partial derivatives. A vector field $\mathbf{U}$ with this property is said to be a **vector potential** for $\mathbf{F}$.

29. In our derivation of the heat equation in this section, we assumed that the coefficient of thermal conductivity K is constant (no sinks or sources). If $K = K(x, y, z)$ is a variable, show that the heat equation becomes

$$K\nabla^2 T + \nabla K \cdot \nabla T = \sigma\delta\frac{\partial T}{\partial t}$$

30. An electric charge q located at the origin produces the electric field

$$\mathbf{E} = \frac{q\mathbf{R}}{4\pi\epsilon\|\mathbf{R}\|^3}$$

where $\mathbf{R} = x\mathbf{i} + y\mathbf{j} + z\mathbf{k}$ and ϵ is a physical constant, called the **electric permittivity.**

a. Show that

$$\iint\limits_{S} \mathbf{E} \cdot \mathbf{N}\, dS = 0$$

if the closed surface S does not enclose the origin. This is **Gauss' law.**

b. Show that

$$\iint\limits_{S} \mathbf{E} \cdot \mathbf{N}\, dS = \frac{q}{\epsilon}$$

in the case where the closed surface S encloses the origin. Note that the divergence theorem does not apply directly to this case.

31. Gauss' law can be expressed as

$$\iint\limits_{S} \mathbf{D} \cdot \mathbf{N}\, dS = q$$

where $\mathbf{D} = \epsilon\mathbf{E}$ is the electric flux density, with electric intensity $\mathbf{E}$, permittivity ϵ, and q a constant. Show that div $\mathbf{D} = Q$, where Q is the charge density; that is,

$$\iiint\limits_{V} Q\, dV = q$$

32. HISTORICAL QUEST   James Clerk Maxwell was one of the greatest physicists of all time. Using the experimental discoveries of Michael Faraday as a basis, he was able to express the governing rules for electrical and magnetic fields in precise mathematical form. In 1871, he published his *Theory of Heat and Magnetism*, which formed the basis for modern electromagnetic theory and contributed to quantum theory and special relativity. Maxwell was influential  in convincing other mathematicians and scientists to use vectors and was interested in areas as diverse as the behavior of light and the statistical behavior of molecular motion. He was sometimes referred to as dp/dt because in thermodynamics, $dp/dt = JCM$, a unit of measurement named for him. ∎

JAMES CLERK
MAXWELL
1831–1879

For this Quest you are to derive **Maxwell's equation for the electric intensity E:**

$$(\nabla \cdot \nabla)\mathbf{E} = \mu\sigma \frac{\partial \mathbf{E}}{\partial t} + \mu\epsilon \frac{\partial^2 \mathbf{E}}{\partial t^2}$$

To derive this equation, you need to know that $\operatorname{curl} \mathbf{E} = -\dfrac{\partial \mathbf{B}}{\partial t}$ and $\operatorname{curl} \mathbf{H} = \sigma\mathbf{E} + \epsilon\dfrac{\partial \mathbf{E}}{\partial t}$ where **E** is electric intensity, **B** is magnetic flux density, **H** is magnetic intensity, and σ, ϵ, and μ are positive constants.

a. Use the fact that $\mathbf{B} = \mu\mathbf{H}$ to show that

$$\operatorname{curl}(\operatorname{curl}\mathbf{E}) = -\mu\frac{\partial}{\partial t}(\operatorname{curl}\mathbf{H})$$

b. Next, show that for any vector field $\mathbf{F} = \langle f, g, h \rangle$,

$$\operatorname{curl}(\operatorname{curl}\mathbf{F}) = \nabla(\operatorname{div}\mathbf{F}) - \nabla \cdot \nabla\mathbf{F}$$

c. Use the formula in **b** to show that

$$\nabla(\operatorname{div}\mathbf{E}) - (\nabla \cdot \nabla)\mathbf{E} = -\mu\frac{\partial}{\partial t}\left(\sigma\mathbf{E} + \epsilon\frac{\partial \mathbf{E}}{\partial t}\right)$$

d. Complete the derivation of *Maxwell's electric intensity equation*, assuming that the charge density Q is 0 so that div **E** = 0. (See Problem 31.)

CHAPTER 13 REVIEW

Chapter Checklist

In the following statements, assume that all required conditions are satisfied. Main results are collected here (without hypotheses) so that you can compare and contrast various results and conclusions.

Scalar function: $f(x, y, z)$

Vector field: $\mathbf{F}(x, y, z) = u(x, y, z)\mathbf{i} + v(x, y, z)\mathbf{j} + w(x, y, z)\mathbf{k}$

Notation:

Del operator: $\nabla = \dfrac{\partial}{\partial x}\mathbf{i} + \dfrac{\partial}{\partial y}\mathbf{j} + \dfrac{\partial}{\partial z}\mathbf{k}$

Gradient: $\nabla f = \dfrac{\partial f}{\partial x}\mathbf{i} + \dfrac{\partial f}{\partial y}\mathbf{j} + \dfrac{\partial f}{\partial z}\mathbf{k}$
$= f_x\mathbf{i} + f_y\mathbf{j} + f_z\mathbf{k}$

Laplacian: $\nabla^2 f = \dfrac{\partial^2 f}{\partial x^2} + \dfrac{\partial^2 f}{\partial y^2} + \dfrac{\partial^2 f}{\partial z^2}$
$= f_{xx} + f_{yy} + f_{zz}$

Normal derivative: $\dfrac{\partial f}{\partial n} = \nabla f \cdot \mathbf{N}$

Derivatives of a vector field:

$\operatorname{div}\mathbf{F} = \dfrac{\partial u}{\partial x} + \dfrac{\partial v}{\partial y} + \dfrac{\partial w}{\partial z}$ *This is a scalar derivative.*
$= \nabla \cdot \mathbf{F}$

If P is a point (x_0, y_0, z_0), then P is a
source if div **F** > 0
sink if div **F** < 0
F is incompressible if div **F** = 0

$\operatorname{curl}\mathbf{F} = \begin{vmatrix} \mathbf{i} & \mathbf{j} & \mathbf{k} \\ \dfrac{\partial}{\partial x} & \dfrac{\partial}{\partial y} & \dfrac{\partial}{\partial z} \\ u & v & w \end{vmatrix}$ *This is a vector derivative.*
$= \nabla \times \mathbf{F}$

F is irrotational if curl **F** = **0**

Line Integral: If $f(x, y, z)$ is defined on the smooth curve C with parametric equations $x = x(t)$, $y = y(t)$, $z = z(t)$, then the line integral of f over C is given by

$$\int_C f(x, y, z)\, ds$$
$$= \int_a^b f[x(t), y(t), z(t)]\sqrt{[x'(t)]^2 + [y'(t)]^2 + [z'(t)]^2}\, dt$$

Green's Theorem expresses an important relationship between a line integral over a Jordan (simple closed) curve in the plane and a double integral over the region bounded by the curve. Let D be a simply connected region with a positively oriented piecewise smooth boundary C. Then if the vector field $\mathbf{F}(x, y) = M(x, y)\mathbf{i} + N(x, y)\mathbf{j}$ is continuously differentiable on D, we have

$$\oint_C (M\, dx + N\, dy) = \iint_D \left(\frac{\partial N}{\partial x} - \frac{\partial M}{\partial y}\right) dA$$

Conservative Vector Fields and Path Independence: Let **F** be a continuous vector field on the open connected set D. Then the following three conditions are either all true or all false:

a. $\mathbf{F}$ is conservative on D; that is, $\mathbf{F} = \nabla f$ for some function f defined on D.

b. $\oint_C \mathbf{F} \cdot d\mathbf{R} = 0$ for every piecewise smooth closed curve in D.

c. $\int_C \mathbf{F} \cdot d\mathbf{R}$ is independent of path within D.

Also, if D is simply connected (no holes), then $\mathbf{F}$ is conservative if and only if curl $\mathbf{F} = \mathbf{0}$ in D.

Fundamental Theorem for Line Integrals: Let C be a piecewise smooth curve that is parameterized by the vector function $\mathbf{R}(t)$ for $a \le t \le b$. If f is a differentiable function of two or three variables whose gradient $\mathbf{F} = \nabla f$ is continuous on C, then

$$\int_C \mathbf{F} \cdot d\mathbf{R} = f(Q) - f(P)$$

where $Q = \mathbf{R}(b)$ and $P = \mathbf{R}(a)$ are the endpoints of C.

EVALUATION OF LINE INTEGRALS: $\int_C \mathbf{F} \cdot d\mathbf{R}$

Step 1. Check to see whether $\mathbf{F}$ is conservative; if it is, then

$$\oint_C \mathbf{F} \cdot d\mathbf{R} = 0 \quad \text{if } C \text{ is closed}$$

$$\oint_C \mathbf{F} \cdot d\mathbf{R} = f(Q) - f(P) \quad \begin{array}{l}\text{Initial point } P,\\ \text{terminal point } Q\end{array}$$

Step 2. If $\mathbf{F}$ is not conservative, and C is a closed curve bounding a surface S, use Stokes' theorem (or Green's theorem in $\mathbb{R}^2$) to equate the given integral to a surface integral, namely,

$$\int_C \mathbf{F} \cdot d\mathbf{R} = \iint_S (\text{curl}\,\mathbf{F} \cdot \mathbf{N})\,dS$$

Step 3. As a last resort, parameterize $\mathbf{F}$ and $\mathbf{R}$. Let $\mathbf{R}(t) = x(t)\mathbf{i} + y(t)\mathbf{j} + z(t)\mathbf{k}$ for $a \le t \le b$.

$$\int_C f(x, y, z)\,dx = \int_a^b f[x(t), y(t), z(t)]\frac{dx}{dt}\,dt$$

$$\int_C f(x, y, z)\,ds$$
$$= \int_a^b f[x(t), y(t), z(t)]\sqrt{[x'(t)]^2 + [y'(t)]^2 + [z'(t)]^2}\,dt$$

Surface Integral: Let S be a surface defined by $z = f(x, y)$ and D its projection on the xy-plane. If f, f_x, and f_y are continuous in D and g is continuous on S, then the surface integral of g over S is

$$\iint_S g(x, y, z)\,dS$$
$$= \iint_D g(x, y, f(x, y))\sqrt{[f_x(x, y)]^2 + [f_y(x, y)]^2 + 1}\,dA$$

Stokes' theorem: Let S be an oriented surface with unit normal vector field $\mathbf{N}$, and assume that S is bounded by a piecewise smooth Jordan curve C whose orientation is compatible with that of S. If $\mathbf{F}$ is a vector field that is continuously differentiable on S, then

$$\oint_C \mathbf{F} \cdot d\mathbf{R} = \iint_S (\text{curl}\,\mathbf{F} \cdot \mathbf{N})\,dS$$

The divergence theorem: Let S be a smooth, orientable surface that encloses a solid region D in $\mathbb{R}^3$. If $\mathbf{F}$ is a continuous vector field whose components have continuous partial derivatives in an open set containing D, then

$$\iint_S \mathbf{F} \cdot \mathbf{N}\,dS = \iiint_D \text{div}\,\mathbf{F}\,dV$$

where $\mathbf{N}$ is the outward unit normal field for the surface S.

EVALUATION OF FLUX INTEGRALS: $\iint_S \mathbf{F} \cdot \mathbf{N}\,dS$

Step 1. If the surface S is a closed surface bounding the solid region D, use the divergence theorem to write the flux integral as a triple integral.

$$\iint_S \mathbf{F} \cdot \mathbf{N}\,dS = \iiint_D \text{div}\,\mathbf{F}\,dV$$

Step 2. If step 1 does not apply, parameterize $\mathbf{F}$, $\mathbf{N}$, and dS. In the special case where S has the form $z = f(x, y)$, we have

$$\iint_S \mathbf{F} \cdot \mathbf{N}\,dS = \iint_D F(x, y, f(x, y)) \cdot \langle -f_x, -f_y, 1 \rangle\,dA$$

for an upward normal and

$$\iint_S \mathbf{F} \cdot \mathbf{N}\,dS = \iint_D F(x, y, f(x, y)) \cdot \langle f_x, f_y, -1 \rangle\,dA$$

for a downward normal.

Proficiency Examination

CONCEPT PROBLEMS

1. What is a vector field?
2. What is the divergence of a vector field?
3. What is the curl of a vector field?
4. What is the del operator?
5. What is Laplace's equation?
6. What is the difference between the Riemann integral and a line integral? Discuss.
7. What is the formula for a line integral of a vector field?
8. How do we find work as a line integral?
9. What is the formula for a line integral in terms of arc length parameter?
10. State the fundamental theorem for line integrals.
11. Define a conservative vector field.
12. What is the scalar potential of a conservative vector field?

13. What is a Jordan curve?
14. State Green's theorem.
15. How can you use Green's theorem to find area as a line integral?
16. What is a normal derivative?
17. Define a surface integral.
18. What is the formula for a surface integral of a surface defined parametrically?
19. What is a flux integral?
20. State Stokes' theorem.
21. State the conservative vector field theorem.
22. State the divergence theorem.

PRACTICE PROBLEMS

23. Show that $yz\mathbf{i} + xz\mathbf{j} + xy\mathbf{k}$ is conservative and find a scalar potential function.

24. Compute div $\mathbf{F}$ and curl $\mathbf{F}$ for $\mathbf{F} = x^2y\mathbf{i} - e^{yz}\mathbf{j} + \frac{1}{2}x\mathbf{k}$.

25. Use Green's theorem to evaluate the line integral $\oint_C \mathbf{F} \cdot d\mathbf{R}$, where $\mathbf{F} = (2x + y)\mathbf{i} + 3y^2\mathbf{j}$ and C is the boundary of the triangle T with vertices $(-1, 2)$, $(0, 0)$, $(1, 2)$, traversed in the given order.

26. Use Stokes' theorem to evaluate the line integral $\oint_C \mathbf{F} \cdot d\mathbf{R}$, where $\mathbf{F} = 2y\mathbf{i} + z\mathbf{j} + y\mathbf{k}$ and C is the intersection of the plane $z = x + 2$ and the sphere $x^2 + y^2 + z^2 = 4z$, traversed counterclockwise as viewed from above.

27. Use the divergence theorem to evaluate the surface integral $\iint_S \mathbf{F} \cdot \mathbf{N}\, dS$, where $\mathbf{F} = x^2\mathbf{i} + (y + z)\mathbf{j} - 2z\mathbf{k}$, and S is the surface of the unit cube $0 \le x \le 1, 0 \le y \le 1, 0 \le z \le 1$.

28. Evaluate $\oint_C \dfrac{x\, dx + y\, dy}{(x^2 + y^2)^2}$, where C is the path shown in Figure 13.51, traversed counterclockwise.

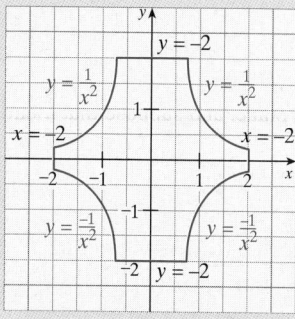

Figure 13.51 Curve C

29. An object with mass m travels counterclockwise (as viewed from above) in the circular orbit $x^2 + y^2 = 9$, $z = 2$, with angular speed ω. The mass is subject to a centrifugal force $\mathbf{F} = m\omega^2\mathbf{R}$, where $\mathbf{R} = x\mathbf{i} + y\mathbf{j} + z\mathbf{k}$. Show that $\mathbf{F}$ is conservative, and find a scalar potential function for $\mathbf{F}$.

30. Find the work done as an object moves in the force field given in Problem 29 from point $(3, 0, 2)$ to $(-3, 0, 2)$ along the circle $x^2 + y^2 = 9$ in the plane $z = 2$.

Supplementary Problems

In Problems 1–6, determine whether the given vector field is conservative, and if it is, find a scalar potential function.

1. $\mathbf{F} = 2\mathbf{i} - 3\mathbf{j}$
2. $\mathbf{F} = xy^{-2}\mathbf{i} + x^{-2}y\mathbf{j}$
3. $\mathbf{F} = y^{-3}\mathbf{i} + (-3xy^{-4} + \cos y)\mathbf{j}$
4. $\mathbf{F} = y^2\mathbf{i} + (2xy)\mathbf{j}$
5. $\mathbf{F} = \left(\dfrac{1}{y} + \dfrac{y}{x^2}\right)\mathbf{i} - \left(\dfrac{x}{y^2} - \dfrac{1}{x}\right)\mathbf{j}$
6. $\mathbf{F} = \left[2x \tan^{-1}\left(\dfrac{y}{x}\right) - y\right]\mathbf{i} + \left[2y \tan^{-1}\left(\dfrac{y}{x}\right) + x\right]\mathbf{j}$

In Problems 7–12, find $\displaystyle\int_C \mathbf{F} \cdot d\mathbf{R}$, where C is the curve $\mathbf{R}(t) = t\mathbf{i} + t^2\mathbf{j}$, $1 \le t \le 2$. Note that these are the same as the vector fields in Problems 1–6.

7. $\mathbf{F} = 2\mathbf{i} - 3\mathbf{j}$
8. $\mathbf{F} = xy^{-2}\mathbf{i} + x^{-2}y\mathbf{j}$
9. $\mathbf{F} = y^{-3}\mathbf{i} + (-3xy^{-4} + \cos y)\mathbf{j}$
10. $\mathbf{F} = y^2\mathbf{i} + (2xy)\mathbf{j}$
11. $\mathbf{F} = \left(\dfrac{1}{y} + \dfrac{y}{x^2}\right)\mathbf{i} - \left(\dfrac{x}{y^2} - \dfrac{1}{x}\right)\mathbf{j}$
12. $\mathbf{F} = \left[2x \tan^{-1}\left(\dfrac{y}{x}\right) - y\right]\mathbf{i} + \left[2y \tan^{-1}\left(\dfrac{y}{x}\right) + x\right]\mathbf{j}$

In Problems 13–16, find div $\mathbf{F}$ and curl $\mathbf{F}$.

13. $\mathbf{F} = x\mathbf{i} + y\mathbf{j} + z\mathbf{k}$
14. $\mathbf{F} = \left(\tan^{-1}\dfrac{y}{x}\right)\mathbf{i} - 3\mathbf{j} + z^2\mathbf{k}$
15. $\mathbf{F} = \dfrac{1}{r}(x\mathbf{i} + y\mathbf{j} + z\mathbf{k})$, where $r = \sqrt{x^2 + y^2 + z^2}, r \ne 0$
16. $\mathbf{F} = (xy \sin z)\mathbf{i} + (x^2 \cos yz)\mathbf{j} + (z \sin xy)\mathbf{k}$

Evaluate the line integrals in Problems 17–18 by parameterization.

17. $\displaystyle\int_C [(\sin \pi y)\, dx + (\cos \pi x)\, dy]$, where C is the line segment from $(1, 0)$ to $(\pi, 0)$, followed by the line segment from $(\pi, 0)$ to (π, π)

18. $\displaystyle\int_C (z\, dx - x\, dy + dz)$, where C is the arc of the helix $x = 3 \sin t, y = 3 \cos t, z = t$ for $0 \le t \le \frac{\pi}{4}$

In Problems 19–33, evaluate the line integral or the surface integral. In each surface integral, assume that $\mathbf{N}$ is the outward unit normal vector field.

19. $\displaystyle\int_C [yz\, dx + xz\, dy + (xy + 2)\, dz]$, where C is the curve $\mathbf{R}(t) = (\tan^{-1} t)\mathbf{i} + t^2\mathbf{j} - 3t\mathbf{k}, 0 \le t \le 1$

20. $\displaystyle\int_C [(x^2 + y)\, dx + xz\, dy - (y + z)\, dz]$, where C is the curve $\mathbf{R}(t) = t\mathbf{i} + t^2\mathbf{j} + 2\mathbf{k}, 0 \le t \le 1$

21. $\displaystyle\iint_S (3x^2 + y - 2z)\, dS$, where S is the surface $\mathbf{R}(u, v) = u\mathbf{i} + (u + v)\mathbf{j} + u\mathbf{k}, 0 \le u \le 1, 0 \le v \le 1$

22. $\displaystyle\iint_S \mathbf{F} \cdot \mathbf{N}\, dS$, where $\mathbf{F} = 3x\mathbf{i} + z^2\mathbf{j} - 2y\mathbf{k}$ and S is the surface of the hemisphere $z = \sqrt{4 - x^2 - y^2}$

23. $\int_C (x\,dx + x\,dy - y\,dz)$, where C is the curve
$\mathbf{R}(t) = t\mathbf{i} + t^2\mathbf{j} + t\mathbf{k}, 0 \le t \le 1$

24. $\int_C (x^2\,dx - 3y^2\,dz)$, where C is the line segment from $(0, 1, 1)$ to $(1, 1, 2)$

25. $\int_C (x^2\,dx + y\,dy)$, where C is the curve
$\mathbf{R}(t) = (t \sin t)\mathbf{i} + (1 - t \cos t)\mathbf{j}, 0 \le t \le 2\pi$

26. $\oint_C (xy\,dx - x^2\,dy)$, where C is the square with vertices $(1, 0)$, $(0, 1)$, $(-1, 0)$, $(0, -1)$ traversed counterclockwise

27. $\oint_C (y\,dx + x\,dy - 2\,dz)$, where C is the curve of intersection of the cylinder $x^2 + y^2 = 2x$ and the plane $x = z$, traversed counterclockwise as viewed from above

28. $\oint_C [(y + z)\,dx + (x + z)\,dy + (x + y)\,dz]$, where C is the curve of intersection of the sphere $x^2 + (y - 3)^2 + z^2 = 9$ and the plane $x + 2y + z = 3$, traversed counterclockwise as viewed from above

29. $\oint_C (-2y\,dx + 2x\,dy + dz)$, where C is the circle $x^2 + y^2 = 1$ in the plane $z = 3$, traversed counterclockwise as viewed from above

30. $\iint_S (\text{curl } y\mathbf{i}) \cdot \mathbf{N}\,dS$, where S is the hemisphere
$z = \sqrt{1 - x^2 - y^2}$

31. $\iint_S (2x^3\mathbf{i} + y^3\mathbf{j} + z^3\mathbf{k}) \cdot \mathbf{N}\,dS$, where S is the surface of the ellipsoid $2x^2 + y^2 + z^2 = 1$

32. $\iint_S (y^2\mathbf{i} + y^2\mathbf{j} + yz\mathbf{k}) \cdot \mathbf{N}\,dS$, where S is the surface of the tetrahedron bounded by the plane $2x + 3y + z = 1$ and the coordinate planes, in the first octant

33. $\iint_S \nabla\phi \cdot \mathbf{N}\,dS$, where $\phi(x, y, z) = 2x + 3y$ and S is the portion of the plane $ax + by + cz = 1$ ($a > 0, b > 0, c > 0$) that lies in the first octant

In Problems 34–38 find $\iint_S \mathbf{F} \cdot \mathbf{N}\,dS$. *Assume* $\mathbf{N}$ *is the outward unit normal vector field for* S.

34. $\mathbf{F} = x^2\mathbf{i} + y^2\mathbf{j} + x^2\mathbf{k}$, and S is the surface of the unit cube $0 \le x \le 1, 0 \le y \le 1, 0 \le z \le 1$.

35. $\mathbf{F} = 2yz\mathbf{i} + (\tan^{-1} xz)\mathbf{j} + e^{xy}\mathbf{k}$, and S is the surface of the sphere $x^2 + y^2 + z^2 = 1$.

36. $\mathbf{F} = x\mathbf{i} - 4\mathbf{j} + 3\mathbf{k}$, and S is the paraboloid $y = x^2 + z^2$ with $x^2 + z^2 < 9$. The disk $x^2 + z^2 = 9$ is omitted; that is, the paraboloid is open on the right.

37. $\mathbf{F} = xyz\mathbf{i} + xyz\mathbf{j} + xyz\mathbf{k}$, and S is the surface of the five faces of the unit cube $0 \le x \le 1, 0 \le y \le 1, 0 < z \le 1$, missing $z = 0$.

38. $\mathbf{F} = xy\mathbf{i} - 2z\mathbf{j}$, and S is the surface defined parametrically by $\mathbf{R}(u, v) = u\mathbf{i} + v\mathbf{j} + u\mathbf{k}$ for $0 \le u \le 1, 0 \le v \le 1$.

Find all real numbers c for which each vector field in Problems 39–41 is conservative.

39. $\mathbf{F}(x, y) = (\sqrt{x} + 3xy)\mathbf{i} + (cx^2 + 4y)\mathbf{j}$

40. $\mathbf{F}(x, y) = \left(\dfrac{cy}{x^3} + \dfrac{y}{x^2}\right)\mathbf{i} + \left(\dfrac{1}{x^2} - \dfrac{1}{x}\right)\mathbf{j}$

41. $\mathbf{F}(x, y, z) = e^{yz/x}\left[\left(\dfrac{cyz}{x^2}\right)\mathbf{i} + \left(\dfrac{z}{x}\right)\mathbf{j} + \left(\dfrac{y}{x}\right)\mathbf{k}\right]$

42. Let $\mathbf{F} = (y^2 + x^{-2}ye^{x/y})\mathbf{i} + (2xy + z - x^{-1}e^{x/y})\mathbf{j} + y\mathbf{k}$. Is $\mathbf{F}$ conservative?

43. Find the work done when an object moves in the force field $\mathbf{F} = 2x\mathbf{i} - (x + z)\mathbf{j} + (y - x)\mathbf{k}$ along the path given by $\mathbf{R}(t) = t^2\mathbf{i} + (t^2 - t)\mathbf{j} + 3\mathbf{k}, 0 \le t \le 1$.

44. Show that the force field $\mathbf{F} = yz^2\mathbf{i} + (xz^2 - 1)\mathbf{j} + (2xyz - 1)\mathbf{k}$ is conservative, and determine the work done when an object moves in the force field from the origin to the point $(1, 0, 1)$.

45. Find a region R in the plane where the vector field $\mathbf{F} = \dfrac{1}{x + y}(\mathbf{i} + \mathbf{j})$ is conservative. Then evaluate $\int_C \mathbf{F} \cdot d\mathbf{R}$, where C is any path in R from the point $P_0(a, b)$ to $P_1(c, d)$.

46. If u is a scalar function and $\mathbf{F}$ is a continuously differentiable vector field, show that $\text{curl}(u\mathbf{F}) = u\,\text{curl }\mathbf{F} + (\nabla u \times \mathbf{F})$.

47. Show that $\text{div}(\mathbf{F} \times \mathbf{G}) = \mathbf{G} \cdot \text{curl }\mathbf{F} - \mathbf{F} \cdot \text{curl }\mathbf{G}$, for any continuously differentiable vector fields $\mathbf{F}$ and $\mathbf{G}$.

48. A vector field $\mathbf{F}$ is *incompressible* in a region D if $\text{div }\mathbf{F} = 0$ throughout D. If $\mathbf{F}$ and $\mathbf{G}$ are both conservative vector fields in D, show that $\mathbf{F} \times \mathbf{G}$ is incompressible.

49. If $\mathbf{F} = \text{curl }\mathbf{G}$, show that $\mathbf{F}$ is incompressible. (See Problem 48.)

50. Suppose $\mathbf{F} = f(x, y, z)\mathbf{A}$, where $\mathbf{A}$ is a constant vector and f is a scalar function. Show that $\text{curl }\mathbf{F}$ is orthogonal to $\mathbf{A}$ and to ∇f.

51. If $\mathbf{A}$ is a constant vector and $\mathbf{F}$ is a continuously differentiable vector field, show that $\text{div}(\mathbf{A} \times \mathbf{F}) = -\mathbf{A} \cdot \text{curl }\mathbf{F}$.

52. Evaluate the line integral $\int_C \dfrac{x\,dx - y\,dy}{x^2 - y^2}$, where C is any path in the xy-plane that is interior to the region $x > 0, y < x$, $y > -x$ and connects the point $(5, 4)$ to $(2, 0)$.

53. Evaluate $\oint_C \left(\dfrac{-y}{x^2}\,dx + \dfrac{1}{x}\,dy\right)$, where C is the closed path $(x - 2)^2 + y^2 = 1$, traversed once counterclockwise.

54. **Counterexample Problem** Let $u(x, y)$ and $v(x, y)$ be functions of two variables with continuous partial derivatives everywhere in the plane, and suppose that u and v satisfy the equation

$$\frac{\partial u}{\partial y} = \frac{\partial v}{\partial x}$$

for all (x, y). Are u and v necessarily harmonic? Either show that they are or find a counterexample.

55. **a.** Find a region in the plane where the vector field

$$\mathbf{F} = \left(\frac{1 + y^2}{x^3}\right)\mathbf{i} - \left(\frac{y + x^2 y}{x^2}\right)\mathbf{j}$$

is conservative, and find a scalar potential for $\mathbf{F}$.

b. Evaluate $\int_C \mathbf{F} \cdot d\mathbf{R}$, where C is a path from $(1, 1)$ to $(3, 4)$. Are there any limitations on the path C? Explain.

56. Determine the most general function $u(x, y)$ for which the vector field $\mathbf{F} = u(x, y)\mathbf{i} + (2ye^x + y^2e^{3x})\mathbf{j}$ will be conservative.

57. Consider the line integral $\int_C \left(\dfrac{dx}{y} + \dfrac{dy}{x} \right)$, where C is the closed triangular path formed by the lines $y = 2x$, $x + 2y = 5$, and $x = 2$, traversed counterclockwise. First evaluate the line integral directly (by parameterizing C) and then by using Green's theorem.

58. If S is a closed surface in a region R and $\mathbf{F}$ is a twice continuously differentiable vector field on R, show that

$$\iint_S (\operatorname{curl} \mathbf{F} \cdot \mathbf{N})\, dS = 0$$

where $\mathbf{N}$ is the outward unit normal vector to S.

59. A certain closed path C in the plane $2x + 2y + z = 1$ is known to project onto the unit circle $x^2 + y^2 = 1$ in the xy-plane. Let c be a constant, and let $\mathbf{R} = x\mathbf{i} + y\mathbf{j} + z\mathbf{k}$. Use Stokes' theorem to evaluate

$$\oint_C (c\mathbf{k} \times \mathbf{R}) \cdot d\mathbf{R}$$

60. a. Show that if the scalar function w is harmonic, then

$$\nabla \cdot (w\nabla w) = \|\nabla w\|^2$$

b. Let $w = x - y + 2z$, and let S be the surface of the sphere $x^2 + y^2 + z^2 = 9$. Evaluate

$$\iint_S w\frac{\partial w}{\partial n}\, dS$$

61. A particle moves along a curve C in space that is given parametrically by $\mathbf{R}(t) = x(t)\mathbf{i} + y(t)\mathbf{j} + z(t)\mathbf{k}$ for $a \le t \le b$. A force field $\mathbf{F}$ is applied to the particle in such a way that $\mathbf{F}$ is always perpendicular to the path C. How much work is performed by the force field $\mathbf{F}$ when the particle moves from the point where $t = a$ to the point where $t = b$?

62. If $\mathbf{D}$ is the electric displacement field, then $\operatorname{div} \mathbf{D} = \phi$, where ϕ is the *charge density*. A region of space is said to be *charge-free* if $\phi = 0$ there. Describe the charge-free regions of the electric displacement field $\mathbf{D} = 2x^2\mathbf{i} + 3y^2\mathbf{j} - 2z^2\mathbf{k}$.

63. A satellite weighing $10{,}000$ kg travels in a circular orbit $7{,}000$ km from the center of the earth. How much work is done by gravity on the satellite during half a revolution?

64. If $\mathbf{F}$ is a conservative force field, the scalar function f such that $\mathbf{F} = -\nabla f$ is called the *potential energy* (see Problem 54, Section 13.3). Suppose an object with mass 10 g moves in the force field in such a way that its speed decreases from 3 cm/s to 2.5 cm/s. What is the corresponding change in the potential energy of the object?

65. Find the work done by the force field

$$\mathbf{F} = 2xyz\mathbf{i} + \left(x^2z - \frac{1}{z}\tan^{-1}\frac{y}{z} \right)\mathbf{j} + \left(x^2y + \frac{y}{z^2}\tan^{-1}\frac{y}{z} \right)\mathbf{k}$$

in moving an object along the circular helix

$$\mathbf{R}(t) = (\sin \pi t)\mathbf{i} + (\cos \pi t)\mathbf{j} + (2t + 1)\mathbf{k}$$

for $0 \le t \le \frac{1}{2}$.

66. Find the work done when an object moves against the force field $\mathbf{F} = 4y^2\mathbf{i} + (3x + y)\mathbf{j}$ from $(1, 0)$ to $(-1, 0)$ along the top half of the ellipse $x^2 + \dfrac{y^2}{k^2} = 1$. Which value of k minimizes the work?

67. Evaluate the line integral

$$\oint_C \frac{-y\, dx + x\, dy}{x^2 + y^2}$$

where C is the limaçon given in polar coordinates by $r = 3 + 2\cos\theta$, $0 \le \theta \le 2\pi$, traversed counterclockwise.

68. Suppose f and g are both harmonic in the region R with boundary surface S. Show that

a. $\displaystyle\iint_S f\frac{\partial g}{\partial n}\, dS = \iint_S g\frac{\partial f}{\partial n}\, dS$

b. $\displaystyle\iint_S f\frac{\partial f}{\partial n}\, dS = \iiint_D \|\nabla f\|^2\, dV$

69. Show that $\operatorname{curl}(\operatorname{curl} \mathbf{F}) = \nabla(\operatorname{div} \mathbf{F}) - \nabla^2\mathbf{F}$ if the components of $\mathbf{F}$ have continuous second-order partial derivatives.

70. Evaluate the surface integral $\displaystyle\iint_S \frac{\partial f}{\partial n}\, dS$, where S is the surface of the unit sphere $x^2 + y^2 + z^2 = 1$ and f is a scalar field such that $\|\nabla f\|^2 = 3f$ and $\operatorname{div}(f\nabla f) = 7f$.

71. Evaluate the surface integral $\displaystyle\iint_S dS$, where S is the torus

$$\mathbf{R}(u, v) = [(a + b\cos v)\cos u]\mathbf{i} + [(a + b\cos v)\sin u]\mathbf{j} + (b\sin v)\mathbf{k}$$

for $0 < b < a$ and $0 \le u \le 2\pi$, $0 \le v \le 2\pi$.

72. Evaluate $\displaystyle\iint_S \mathbf{F} \cdot \mathbf{N}\, dS$, where $\mathbf{F} = x\mathbf{i} + y\mathbf{j} + z\mathbf{k}$ and S is the closed cubic surface with a corner block removed, as shown in Figure 13.52.

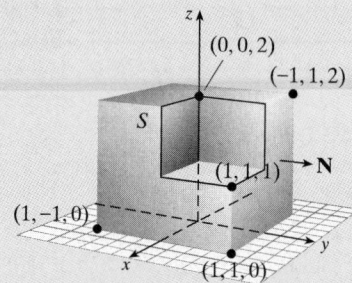

Figure 13.52   Cube with a corner removed

73. Counterexample Problem   Prove or disprove that it does not matter which corner is removed in Problem 72.

74. Show that a lamina that covers a standard region D in the plane with density $\delta = 1$ has moment of inertia

$$I = \frac{1}{3}\oint_C (-y^3\, dx + x^3\, dy)$$

with respect to the z-axis, where C is the boundary curve of D.

75. Use vector analysis to find the centroid of the conical surface $z = \sqrt{x^2 + y^2}$ between $z = 0$ and $z = 3$.

76. Putnam Examination Problem   A force acts on the element ds of a closed plane curve. The magnitude of this force is $r^{-1}\, ds$, where r is the radius of curvature at the point considered, and the direction of the force is perpendicular to the curve; it points to the convex side. Show that the system of such forces acting on all elements of the curve keeps it in equilibrium.

Continuous versus Discrete Mathematics

William F. Lucas is professor emeritus of mathematics and former department chairman at The Claremont Graduate University. He is known for his research in game theory, which provides a mathematical approach to the study of conflict, cooperation, and fairness. Dr. Lucas has also been active in educational reform efforts with a goal toward introducing more recently discovered topics into the mathematics curriculum.

Mathematicians often distinguish between *discrete* and *continuous* mathematics. The latter is illustrated by the calculus and its many descendants, including the subject of differential equations. Continuous mathematics deals with "solid" infinite sets such as the real number line $\mathbb{R}$ and functions defined on $\mathbb{R}$. One of the primary concerns is with the solutions of differential equations, which are typical families of such solid curves or surfaces. The many applications of such differential equations to discoveries in the physical sciences and engineering over the past three centuries has been one of the greatest intellectual success stories of all time.

Prior to the invention of calculus by Newton and Leibniz, most mathematics was of a discrete nature. It dealt with sets that had a finite number of elements and with infinite but "countable" sets such as the natural numbers. These sets often include continuous curves such as the conics which can be characterized by a small number of conditions. Discrete mathematics also deals with the solutions to algebraic equations, which are usually discrete sets. The twentieth century has witnessed the creation of many additional subjects in the discrete direction. This development was spurred on by the rapidly increasing use of mathematics in the social, behavioral, decisional, and system sciences, where the items under investigation are typically finite in number and not readily approximated by some continuous idealization. Moreover, nearly all aspects of the ongoing revolution in *digital* computers involve discrete considerations.

A metal bar on a minute level is composed of discrete molecules, atoms, and elementary particles. Many of its physical properties, however, can be determined by viewing the bar as a solid continuum and employing the analytical techniques of calculus. One applies the basic laws of physics to express the local (infinitesimal) properties of the bar in terms of differential equations. The solutions of these equations, in turn, provide an excellent description of the observed global behavior of the bar.

One of the greatest mathematical discoveries of the twentieth century in continuous mathematics is the famous fixed point theorem, published in 1912 by the Dutch mathematician L. E. J. Brouwer (1881–1966). It states that any continuous function f from a set S (with certain desirable properties) into the same set S has at least one *fixed point* x_0, that is $f(x_0) = x_0$. For example, for any continuous function $y = f(x)$ from the set $S = \{x \in \mathbb{R} : 0 \le x \le 1\}$ into S there is some number $x_0 \in S$ such that the curve $y = f(x)$ crosses the line $y = x$ at x_0. A head of hair must either have a seam (a parting of the hair, a discontinuity) or else a cowlick (where the hair stands straight up, a fixed point). Fixed points are realized in many physical and social phenomena such as equilibrium states in mechanics or stable prices in economics.

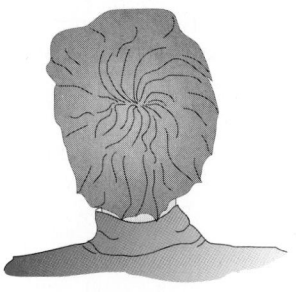

Most human heads have a fixed point, in the form of a whorl, sometimes called a cowlick, from which all the hair radiates. It would be impossible to cover a sphere with hair (or with radiating lines) without at least one such fixed point.

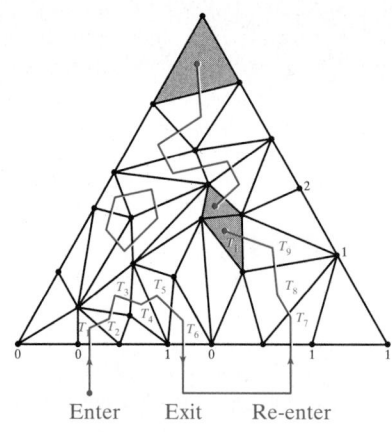

Enter   Exit   Re-enter

Figure 13.53 Arbitrary partitioning of a triangle

Like many of the outstanding results in continuous mathematics, Brouwer's theorem has an analogue in discrete mathematics, known as the labeling lemma of the German mathematician Emanuel Sperner, which appeared in 1928. Given a triangle with vertices 0, 1, and 2 (called $\triangle 012$) as shown in Figure 13.53, one can partition the interior of this triangle into (nonoverlapping) smaller triangles in any possible way.

One can then label each of the newly created vertices with any one of the numbers 0, 1, or 2. There is only one stipulation on how the new vertices on the perimeter of the triangle can be labeled: No vertex on a particular side of $\triangle 012$ can be labeled with the number appearing on the *main* vertex opposite (disjoint from) this side. For example, the side 01 of $\triangle 012$ cannot contain a vertex with the label 2. Sperner's lemma states that there must exist at least one elementary triangle inside $\triangle 012$ (or an *odd* number, in general) whose three vertices are "completely labeled" in the sense that they have all three labels 0, 1, and 2. There are three such triangles (shown in color) in Figure 13.53.

There is an elementary constructive proof of Sperner's lemma that uses the idea of a "path-following algorithm" published by Daniel I. A. Cohen in 1967. This proof is illustrated by the line shown in color Figure 13.53. One can enter into $\triangle 012$ from outside via some elementary triangle T_1 whose perimeter edge carries the labels 0 and 1. The third vertex on this elementary triangle T_1 must be either 2 (in which case T_1 is a completely labeled elementary triangle), or else it is 0 or 1. In the latter cases, one can exit T_1 via a second 01 edge. One can continue to enter and exit subsequent elementary triangles $T_2, T_3, \ldots$ through successive 01 edges until one finally reaches an elementary triangle T_n that has completely labeled vertices 0, 1, and 2. (If this path were ever to exit $\triangle 012$, then there must be still another 01 edge on the perimeter of $\triangle 012$ since there is an odd number of 01 edges on the boundary of $\triangle 012$ where one can reenter the main triangle and continue along the path, as did occur once in Figure 13.53.)

This path-following method also extends to a proof of Sperner's labeling lemma for dimensions higher than two. Furthermore, this approach is used in practical problems to arrive at a "very small" elementary triangle that can serve as an approximation to a fixed point, when it is excessively difficult or impossible to determine the precise location of the fixed point itself. In such cases, the broken path in Figure 13.53 can be viewed as the analogue in discrete mathematics of the continuous curves one arrives at when solving differential equations.

Around 1945, the great Hungarian-American mathematician John von Neumann (1903–1957) pointed out the need for approximating paths in a discrete manner when it proves too difficult to arrive at the exact continuous solutions to certain ordinary or partial differential equations. Cohen's constructive proof of Sperner's lemma, and work in the late 1960s by the mathematical economist Herbert Scarf on approximating equilibrium points, have paved the way for one very rich and extensive discrete theory that provides numerical approximations for continuous phenomena when the latter problems cannot be solved directly by the many analytic techniques of continuous mathematics.

Mathematical Essays

1. If your college offers a course on discrete mathematics, interview an instructor of the course, and using that interview as a basis, write an essay comparing continuous and discrete mathematics.

2. Draw several triangles and attempt to draw a counterexample for Sperner's labeling lemma. In each case, show how this lemma is satisfied.

3. Consider two sheets of paper containing the numbers 1 to 120, as shown in the photograph on the left.

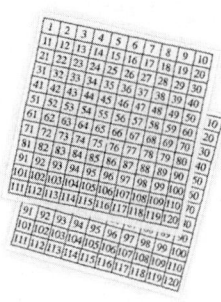 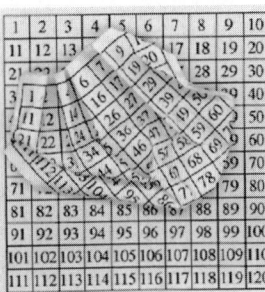

If the top sheet is crumpled and dropped on the bottom sheet, the fixed point theorem tells us that one point must still be over its starting point. In the photograph on the right, it is a point in the region of the number 78. Perform this experiment several times in an attempt to find a counterexample. In each case, show how the fixed point theorem is satisfied.

4. HISTORICAL QUEST   William Rowan Hamilton has been called the most renowned Irish mathematician. He was a child prodigy who read Greek, Hebrew, and Latin by the time he was five, and by the age of ten he knew over a dozen languages. Many mathematical advances are credited to Hamilton.   For example, he developed vector methods in analytic geometry and calculus, as well as a system

WILLIAM ROWAN
HAMILTON
1805–1865

of algebraic quantities called **quaternions**, which occupied his energies for the last 22 years of his life. Hamilton pursued the study of quaternions with an almost religious fervor, but by the early twentieth century, the notation and terminology of vectors dominated. Much of the credit for the eventual emergence of vector methods goes not only to Hamilton, but also to the scientists James Clerk Maxwell (1831–1879), J. Willard Gibbs (1839–1903), and Oliver Heaviside (1850–1925). ∎

For this Quest, write a paper on quaternions.

5. Write a 500-word essay on the history of Green's theorem, Stokes' theorem, and the divergence theorem.

6. Write a report on four-dimensional geometry.

7. **Book Report**   "We often hear that mathematics consists mainly of 'proving theorems.' Is a writer's job mainly that of 'writing sentences'? A mathematician's work is mostly a tangle of guesswork, analogy, wishful thinking and frustration, and proof, far from being the core of discovery, is more often than not a way of making sure that our minds are not playing tricks. Few people, if any, had dared write this out loud before Davis and Hersh. Theorems are not to mathematics what successful courses are to a meal. The nutritional analogy is misleading. To master mathematics is to master an intangible view." This quotation comes from the introduction to the book *The Mathematical Experience* by Philip J. Davis and Reuben Hersh (Boston: Houghton Mifflin, 1981). Read this book and prepare a book report.

8. Make up a word problem involving vector fields. Send your problem and solution to

> Strauss, Bradley, and Smith
> Prentice Hall Publishing Company
> 1 Lake Street
> Upper Saddle River, NJ 07458

The best ones submitted will appear in the next edition (along with credit to the problem poser).

CHAPTERS 11–13   Cumulative Review

TABLE 13.1   Comparison of important integral theorems

Riemann Integral (Section 5.3)	Line Integral (Section 13.2)

$$\int_a^b f(x)\,dx$$

Subdivisions on
the x-axis

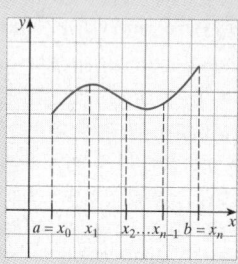

$$\int_C f(x, y, z)\,ds$$

Subdivisions on a
curve C in space

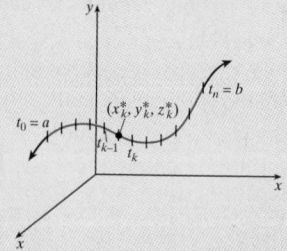

Fundamental theorem of calculus (Section 5.4)

$$\int_a^b f(x)\,dx = F(b) - F(a)$$

F is an antiderivative of f

Fundamental theorem for line integrals (Section 13.3)

$$\int_C \mathbf{F} \cdot d\mathbf{R} = f(Q) - f(P)$$

If $\mathbf{F}$ is conservative with scalar potential f; that is, $\nabla f = \mathbf{F}$

Green's theorem (Section 13.4): $\mathbf{F}(x, y) = M(x, y)\mathbf{i} + N(x, y)\mathbf{j}$ is continuously differentiable on the simply connected region D with positively oriented piecewise smooth boundary curve C. Then

$$\oint_C (M\,dx + N\,dy) = \iint_D \left(\frac{\partial N}{\partial x} - \frac{\partial M}{\partial y}\right) dA$$

Alternate forms include: $\displaystyle\oint_C \mathbf{F} \cdot \mathbf{T}\,ds = \iint_D (\mathrm{curl}\,\mathbf{F} \cdot \mathbf{k})\,dA$; $\displaystyle\oint_C \mathbf{F} \cdot \mathbf{N}\,ds = \iint_D \mathrm{div}\,\mathbf{F}\,dA$

Double Integral (Section 12.1)	Surface Integral (Section 13.5)

$$\iint_R f(x, y)\,dA$$

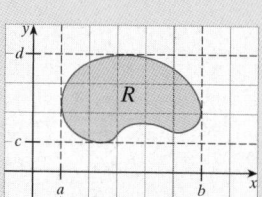

Partition of R into mn cells in the xy-plane

$$\iint_S g(x, y, z)\,dS = \iint_R g(x, y, z)\sqrt{f_x^2 + f_y^2 + 1}\,dA$$
where $z = f(x, y)$

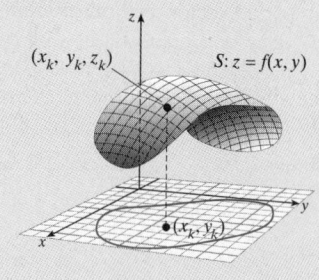

Partition of the surface S
into n subregions

Stokes' theorem (Section 13.6)

$$\oint_C \mathbf{F} \cdot d\mathbf{R} = \iint_S (\mathrm{curl}\,\mathbf{F} \cdot \mathbf{N})\,dS$$

where C is the positively
oriented boundary curve of the
surface S with outward unit
normal field $\mathbf{N}$

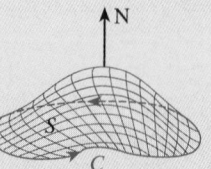

The divergence theorem
(Section 13.7; also known as
Gauss' theorem)

$$\iint_S \mathbf{F} \cdot \mathbf{N}\,dS = \iiint_D \mathrm{div}\,\mathbf{F}\,dV$$

where D is the solid region
with closed boundary
surface S.

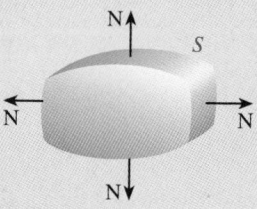

Cumulative Review Problems for Chapters 11–13

1. **WHAT DOES THIS SAY?** Suppose you tell a fellow college student that you are about to finish a calculus course. The student has not had any mathematics beyond high school and asks you, "What is calculus?" Answer this question using your own words.

2. **WHAT DOES THIS SAY?** There are three great fundamental ideas in calculus: the limit, the derivative, and the integral. In your own words, explain each of these concepts.

3. **WHAT DOES THIS SAY?** Chapters 11-13 were concerned with functions of several variables. This is often referred to as **multivariable calculus**. In your own words, discuss what is meant by multivariable calculus.

Find f_x, f_y, and f_{xy} for the functions whose equations are given in Problems 4–9.

4. $f(x, y) = 2x^2 + xy - 5y^3$

5. $f(x, y) = x^2 e^{y/x}$

6. $f(x, y) = \dfrac{x^2 - y^2}{x - y}$

7. $f(x, y) = y \sin^2 x + \cos xy$

8. $f(x, y) = e^{x+y}$

9. $f(x, y) = \dfrac{x^2 + y^2}{x - y}$

Evaluate the integrals in Problems 10–17.

10. $\displaystyle \int_0^1 \int_x^{2x} e^{y-x} \, dy \, dx$

11. $\displaystyle \int_0^4 \int_0^{\sqrt{x}} 3x^5 \, dy \, dx$

12. $\displaystyle \int_0^1 \int_0^z \int_y^{y-z} (x + y + z) \, dx \, dy \, dz$

13. $\displaystyle \int_0^{15\pi} \int_0^{\pi} \int_0^{\sin\phi} \rho^3 \sin\phi \, d\rho \, d\theta \, d\phi$

14. $\displaystyle \iint_R e^{x+y} \, dA; \ R: 0 \le x \le 1; 0 \le y \le 1$

15. $\displaystyle \iint_R y e^{xy} \, dA; \ R: 0 \le x \le 1; 0 \le y \le 2$

16. $\displaystyle \iint_R \sin(x + y) \, dA; \ R: 0 \le x \le \frac{\pi}{2}; 0 \le y \le \frac{\pi}{4}$

17. $\displaystyle \iint_R x \sin xy \, dA; \ R: 0 \le x \le \pi; 0 \le y \le 1$

Evaluate the line integrals in Problems 18–21.

18. $\displaystyle \int_C (y^2 z \, dx + 2xyz \, dy + xy^2 \, dz)$, where C is any path from $(0, 0, 0)$ to $(1, 1, 1)$

19. $\displaystyle \int_C (5xy \, dx + 10yz \, dy + z \, dz)$, where C is given by $x = t^2$, $y = t, z = 2t^3$ for $0 \le t \le 1$

20. $\displaystyle \oint_C \mathbf{F} \cdot d\mathbf{R}$, where $\mathbf{F} = yz\mathbf{i} - x\mathbf{k}$, and C is the boundary of the triangle $(1, 1, 1)$, $(1, 0, 1)$, $(0, 0, 1)$, traversed once counterclockwise as viewed from the origin

21. $\displaystyle \oint_C (x^3 + y^3) \, ds$, where C is given by $\mathbf{R}(t) = (\cos^3 t)\mathbf{i} + (\sin^3 t)\mathbf{j}$, for $0 \le t \le 2\pi$

22. Find the equations for the tangent plane and the normal line to $z = x^2 + y^2 + \sin xy$ at $P = (0, 2, 4)$. The graph of this surface is shown in Figure 13.54.

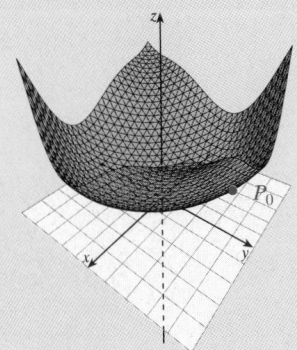

Figure 13.54 Graph of $z = x^2 + y^2 + \sin xy$

23. What are the dimensions of the closed rectangular box of fixed volume V_0 that has minimum surface area?

24. A manufacturer is planning to sell a new product at the price of $350 per unit and estimates that if x thousand dollars is spent on development and y thousand dollars is spent on promotion, consumers will buy approximately

$$\frac{250y}{y + 2} + \frac{100x}{x + 5}$$

units of the product. If manufacturing costs for this product are $150 per unit, how much should the manufacturer spend on development and how much on promotion to generate the largest possible profit, given the following circumstances?

a. Unlimited funds are available

b. The manufacturer has only $11,000 to spend on development and promotion of the new product

25. A heat-seeking missile moves in a portion of space where the temperature (in degrees Celsius) at the point (x, y, z) is given by

$$T(x, y, z) = \tfrac{1}{10}(x^2 + y + z^3)$$

(x, y, and z are measured in kilometers).

a. Find the rate at which the temperature is changing as (x, y, z) moves from the point $P_0(-2, 9, 1)$ toward $Q(1, -3, 5)$.

b. If the heat-seeking missile is at P_0, in what direction will it travel to maximize the rate of heat increase?

c. What is the maximal rate of increase (in degrees Celsius per kilometer)?

26. Find the volume of the solid bounded above by the surface $z = x^2 + y^2 + 1$, below by the xy-plane, and on the sides by the cylinder $x^2 + y^2 = 1$.

27. Find the surface area of that portion of the paraboloid $z = x^2 + y^2$ that lies below the plane $z = 16$.

28. Find the center of mass of the lamina that covers the region R inside the circle $x^2 + y^2 = 4$ in the first quadrant, given that the density at any point (x, y) is $\delta(x, y) = x + y$.

29. A force field $\mathbf{F}(x, y) = (x - 2y)\mathbf{i} + (y - 2x)\mathbf{j}$ acts on an object moving in the plane. Show that $\mathbf{F}$ is conservative, and find a scalar potential for $\mathbf{F}$. How much work is done as the object moves from $(1, 0)$ to $(0, 1)$ along any path connecting these points?

30. A particle of weight w is acted on only by the constant gravitational force $\mathbf{F} = -w\mathbf{k}$. How much work is done in moving the weight along the helical path given by $x = \cos t$, $y = \sin t$, $z = t$ for $0 \le t \le 2\pi$?

14

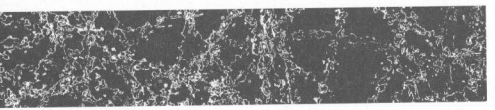

Introduction to Differential Equations

PREVIEW

We introduced and examined separable differential equations in Section 5.6 and first-order linear equations in Section 7.6. We examined applications such as orthogonal trajectories, flow of a fluid through an orifice, escape velocity of a projectile, carbon dating, the diastolic phase of blood pressure, learning curves, population models, dilution problems, and the flow of current in an *RL* circuit. In this chapter, we will extend our study of first-order differential equations by examining *homogeneous* and *exact* equations and then will investigate *second-order differential equations*.

PERSPECTIVE

The study of differential equations is such an extensive topic that even a brief survey of its methods and applications usually occupies a full course. Our goal in this chapter is to preview such a course by introducing some useful techniques for solving differential equations and by examining a few important applications.

14.1   First-Order Differential Equations

IN THIS SECTION   review of separable differential equations, homogeneous differential equations, review of first-order linear differential equations, exact differential equations, Euler's method

We have discussed several different kinds of first-order differential equations so far in this text. In this section, we review our previous methods and introduce two new forms, *homogeneous* and *exact* differential equations.

REVIEW OF SEPARABLE DIFFERENTIAL EQUATIONS

Recall that a differential equation is just an equation involving derivatives or differentials. In particular, an *n***th-order differential equation** in the dependent variable y with respect to the independent variable x is an equation in which the highest derivative of y that appears is $d^n y/dx^n$. A **general solution** of a differential equation is an expression that completely characterizes all possible solutions of the equation, and a **particular solution** is obtained by assigning specific values to the constants that appear in the general solution. An **initial value problem** involves solving a given differential equation subject to one or more initial conditions, such as $y(x_0) = y_0$, $y'(x_0) = y_1, \ldots$.

In Section 5.6, we defined a **separable differential equation** as one that can be written in the form

$$\frac{dy}{dx} = \frac{g(x)}{f(y)}$$

and observed that such an equation can be solved by separating the variables and integrating each side; that is,

$$\int f(y)\,dy = \int g(x)\,dx$$

EXAMPLE 1   Separable differential equation

Find the general solution of the differential equation

$$\frac{dy}{dx} = e^{-y}\sin x$$

Solution

Separate the variables and integrate:

$$\frac{dy}{dx} = e^{-y}\sin x$$
$$e^y\,dy = \sin x\,dx$$
$$\int e^y\,dy = \int \sin x\,dx$$
$$e^y = -\cos x + C \qquad \textsf{Combine constants of integration.}$$

This can also be written as $y = \ln|C - \cos x|$.   ∎

From the standpoint of applications, one of the most important separable differential equations is

$$\frac{dy}{dx} = ky$$

which occurs in the study of exponential growth and decay. You might review Table 7.3 on page 466, which gives the solution for uninhibited growth or decay, logistic (or inhibited) growth, and limited growth functions. In this section, we consider an application of separable differential equations from chemistry.

EXAMPLE 2   Chemical conversion

Experiments in chemistry indicate that under certain conditions, two substances A and B will convert into a third substance C in such a way that the rate of conversion with respect to time is jointly proportional to the unconverted amounts of A and B. For simplicity, assume that one unit of C is formed from the combination of one unit of A and one unit of B, and assume that initially there are α units of A, β units of B, and no units of C present. Set up and solve a differential equation for the amount $Q(t)$ of C present at time t, assuming $\alpha \neq \beta$.

Solution

Since each unit of C is formed from one unit of A and one unit of B, it follows that at time t, $\alpha - Q(t)$ units of A and $\beta - Q(t)$ units of B remain unconverted. The specific rate condition can be expressed mathematically as

$$\frac{dQ}{dt} = k(\alpha - Q)(\beta - Q)$$

where k is a constant ($k > 0$ because $Q(t)$ is increasing).

To solve this equation, we separate the variables and integrate.

$$\int \frac{dQ}{(\alpha - Q)(\beta - Q)} = \int k\, dt$$

$$\int \frac{1}{\alpha - \beta}\left[\frac{-1}{\alpha - Q} + \frac{1}{\beta - Q}\right] dQ = \int k\, dt \qquad \text{\textit{Partial fraction}}$$
$$\text{\textit{decomposition}}$$

$$\frac{1}{\alpha - \beta}[\ln(\alpha - Q) - \ln(\beta - Q)] = kt + C_1$$

$$\ln\left|\frac{\alpha - Q}{\beta - Q}\right| = (\alpha - \beta)kt + C_2$$

$$\frac{\alpha - Q}{\beta - Q} = Me^{(\alpha - \beta)kt} \qquad \text{Where } M = e^{C_2}$$

$$\alpha - Q = \beta Me^{(\alpha - \beta)kt} - QMe^{(\alpha - \beta)kt}$$

$$QMe^{(\alpha - \beta)kt} - Q = \beta Me^{(\alpha - \beta)kt} - \alpha$$

$$Q = \frac{\beta Me^{(\alpha - \beta)kt} - \alpha}{Me^{(\alpha - \beta)kt} - 1}$$

The initial condition tells us that $Q(0) = 0$, so that

$$0 = \frac{\beta Me^0 - \alpha}{Me^0 - 1}$$

$$0 = \beta M - \alpha$$

$$M = \frac{\alpha}{\beta}$$

Thus, $Q(t) = \dfrac{\beta \dfrac{\alpha}{\beta} e^{(\alpha - \beta)kt} - \alpha}{\dfrac{\alpha}{\beta} e^{(\alpha - \beta)kt} - 1} = \dfrac{\alpha\beta[e^{(\alpha - \beta)kt} - 1]}{\alpha e^{(\alpha - \beta)kt} - \beta}$. ∎

HOMOGENEOUS DIFFERENTIAL EQUATIONS

Sometimes a first-order differential equation that is not separable can be put into separable form by a change of variables. A differential equation of the form

$$M(x, y)\, dx + N(x, y)\, dy = 0$$

is called a **homogeneous differential equation** if it can be written in the form

$$\frac{dy}{dx} = f\left(\frac{y}{x}\right)$$

In other words, dy/dx is isolated on one side of the equation and the other side can be expressed as a function of y/x. We can then solve the differential equation by substitution.

To see how to solve such an equation, set $v = y/x$, so that

$$vx = y$$

$$\frac{d}{dx}(vx) = \frac{d}{dx}(y) \qquad \textit{Take the derivative of both sides.}$$

$$v + x\frac{dv}{dx} = \frac{dy}{dx} \qquad \textit{Product rule}$$

$$v + x\frac{dv}{dx} = f(v) \qquad \textit{Substitution, } \frac{dy}{dx} = f\left(\frac{y}{x}\right) = f(v)$$

$$x\frac{dv}{dx} = f(v) - v$$

$$\frac{dv}{f(v) - v} = \frac{dx}{x}$$

The equation can now be solved by integrating both sides; remember to express your answer in terms of the original variables x and y (use $v = y/x$).

EXAMPLE 3   Homogeneous differential equation

Find the general solution of the equation $2xy\,dx + (x^2 + y^2)\,dy = 0$.

Solution

First, show that the equation is homogeneous by writing it in the form $\dfrac{dy}{dx} = f\left(\dfrac{y}{x}\right)$:

$$2xy\,dx + (x^2 + y^2)\,dy = 0$$

$$\frac{dy}{dx} = \frac{-2xy}{x^2 + y^2}$$

$$= \frac{-2\left(\dfrac{y}{x}\right)}{1 + \left(\dfrac{y}{x}\right)^2}$$

Let $v = \dfrac{y}{x}$ and $f(v) = \dfrac{-2v}{1 + v^2}$.

$$\frac{dv}{f(v) - v} = \frac{dx}{x}$$

$$\frac{dv}{\dfrac{-2v}{1 + v^2} - v} = \frac{dx}{x}$$

$$-\int \frac{(1 + v^2)\,dv}{v^3 + 3v} = \int x^{-1}\,dx$$

$$\int \left[\frac{\frac{1}{3}}{v} + \frac{\frac{2}{3}v}{v^2 + 3}\right]dv = -\int x^{-1}\,dx \qquad \textit{Partial fraction decomposition}$$

$$\tfrac{1}{3}\ln|v| + \tfrac{2}{3}\left[\tfrac{1}{2}\ln|v^2 + 3|\right] = -\ln|x| + C_1$$

$$\tfrac{1}{3}\ln|v(v^2 + 3)| + \ln|x| = C_1$$

$$\ln\left|\frac{y}{x}\left[\left(\frac{y}{x}\right)^2 + 3\right]\right| + \ln|x^3| = C_2 \qquad \begin{array}{l}\textit{Substituting}\\ v = \dfrac{y}{x};\, C_2 = 3C_1\end{array}$$

$$\ln\left|\frac{y^3 + 3x^3}{x^3} \cdot x^3\right| = C_2$$

$$y^3 + 3x^3 = C \qquad\qquad \text{Where } C = e^{C_2}$$

This is the general solution of the given differential equation. ∎

REVIEW OF FIRST-ORDER LINEAR DIFFERENTIAL EQUATIONS

In Section 7.6, we considered differential equations of the form

$$\frac{dy}{dx} + p(x)y = q(x)$$

WARNING Note that the coefficient of dy/dx is 1. If it is not, then divide by that nonzero coefficient.

Such an equation is said to be **first-order linear**, and we showed that its general solution is given by

$$y = \frac{1}{I(x)}\left[\int I(x)q(x)\,dx + C\right]$$

where $I(x)$ is the *integrating factor*

$$I(x) = e^{\int p(x)\,dx}$$

EXAMPLE 4　First-order linear differential equation

Find the solution of the differential equation

$$\frac{dy}{dx} + y\tan x = \sec x$$

that passes through the point $(\pi, 2)$.

Solution

Comparing the given first-order linear differential equation to the general first-order form, we see

$$p(x) = \tan x \quad\text{and}\quad q(x) = \sec x$$

The integrating factor is

$$I(x) = e^{\int \tan x\,dx} = e^{-\ln|\cos x|} = e^{\ln\left|(\cos x)^{-1}\right|} = (\cos x)^{-1} = \sec x$$

and the general solution is

$$y = \frac{1}{\sec x}\left[\int (\sec x)(\sec x)\,dx + C\right]$$

$$= \cos x\,[\tan x + C]$$

$$= \sin x + C\cos x$$

The initial condition gives

$$2 = \sin \pi + C\cos \pi$$

$$2 = -C$$

so

$$y = \sin x - 2\cos x \qquad\qquad\blacksquare$$

First-order linear differential equations appear in a variety of applications. In Section 7.6, we showed how first-order linear equations may be used to model mixture (dilution) problems as well as problems involving the current in an RL circuit (one with only a resistor, an inductor, and an electromotive force). In this section, we consider the motion of a body that falls in a resisting medium.

EXAMPLE 5 Motion of a body falling in a resisting medium

Consider an object with mass m that is initially at rest and is dropped from a great height (for example, from an airplane). Suppose the body falls in a straight line and the only forces acting on it are the downward force of the earth's gravitational attraction and a resisting upward force due to air resistance in the atmosphere. Assume that the resisting force is proportional to the velocity v of the falling body. Find equations for the velocity and position of the body's motion. Assume the distance $s(t)$ is measured down from the drop point.

Solution

The downward force is the weight mg of the body and the upward force is $-kv$, where k is a positive constant (the negative sign indicates that the force is directed upward). According to Newton's second law, the sum of the forces acting on a body at any time equals the product ma, where a is the acceleration of the body, that is

$$\underbrace{ma}_{\substack{\text{Sum of forces} \\ \text{on the body}}} = \underbrace{mg}_{\substack{\text{Force due} \\ \text{to gravity}}} - \underbrace{kv}_{\substack{\text{Resisting} \\ \text{force}}}$$

$$m\frac{dv}{dt} = mg - kv \qquad \text{Since } a = \frac{dv}{dt}$$

$$\frac{dv}{dt} = g - \frac{k}{m}v$$

$$\frac{dv}{dt} + \frac{k}{m}v = g$$

This is a first-order linear differential equation, where $p(t) = \dfrac{k}{m}$ and $q(t) = g$. The integrating factor is

$$I(t) = e^{\int k/m \, dt} = e^{kt/m}$$

so that the solution is

$$v = \frac{1}{e^{kt/m}}\left[\int e^{kt/m}(g)\,dt + C\right] = e^{-kt/m}\left[\frac{ge^{kt/m}}{k/m} + C\right] = \frac{mg}{k} + Ce^{-kt/m}$$

Because $v = 0$ when $t = 0$ (the body is initially at rest), it follows that

$$0 = \frac{mg}{k} + Ce^0 = \frac{mg}{k} + C$$

Solving, we obtain $C = -\dfrac{mg}{k}$, so

$$v = \frac{mg}{k} + \left(-\frac{mg}{k}\right)e^{-kt/m}$$

Now, to find the position $s(t)$, we use the fact that $v(t) = \dfrac{ds}{dt}$:

$$\frac{ds}{dt} = \frac{mg}{k} - \frac{mg}{k}e^{-kt/m}$$

$$\int ds = \int \left[\frac{mg}{k} - \frac{mg}{k}e^{-kt/m}\right] dt$$

$$s(t) = \frac{mg}{k}t - \frac{mg}{k}\frac{e^{-kt/m}}{-k/m} + C$$

$$= \frac{mg}{k}t + \frac{m^2 g}{k^2}e^{-kt/m} + C$$

Because $s(0) = 0$ (the position s is measured from the point where the object is dropped), we find that

$$0 = \frac{mg}{k}(0) + \frac{m^2g}{k^2}e^0 + C \quad \text{so that} \quad -\frac{m^2g}{k^2} = C$$

Thus, the position is

$$s(t) = \frac{mg}{k}t + \frac{m^2g}{k^2}\left(e^{-kt/m} - 1\right) \qquad \blacksquare$$

In the problem set, you are asked to show that no matter what the initial velocity may be, the velocity reached by the object in the long run (as $t \to +\infty$) is mg/k.

EXACT DIFFERENTIAL EQUATIONS

Sometimes a first-order differential equation can be written in the general form

$$M(x, y)\,dx + N(x, y)\,dy = 0$$

where the left side is an exact differential, namely,

$$df = M(x, y)\,dx + N(x, y)\,dy$$

for some function f. In this case, the given differential equation is appropriately called **exact** and since $df = 0$, its general solution is given by $f(x, y) = C$.

But how can we tell whether a particular first-order equation is exact, and if it is, how can we find f? Since

$$df = \frac{\partial f}{\partial x}\,dx + \frac{\partial f}{\partial y}\,dy$$

for a total differential (see Section 11.4), we must have

$$df = \frac{\partial f}{\partial x}\,dx + \frac{\partial f}{\partial y}\,dy = M(x, y)\,dx + N(x, y)\,dy$$

so

$$\frac{\partial f}{\partial x} = M(x, y) \quad \text{and} \quad \frac{\partial f}{\partial y} = N(x, y)$$

This will be true if and only if f satisfies the *cross-derivative* test

$$\frac{\partial N}{\partial x} = \frac{\partial M}{\partial y}$$

and then the function $f(x, y)$ is found by partial integration, exactly as we found the potential function of a conservative vector field in Section 13.3. The procedure for identifying and then solving an exact differential equation is illustrated in Example 6.

EXAMPLE 6   Exact differential equation

Find the general solution for $(2xy^3 + 3y)\,dx + (3x^2y^2 + 3x)\,dy = 0$.

Solution

Let $M(x, y) = 2xy^3 + 3y$ and $N(x, y) = 3x^2y^2 + 3x$, and apply the cross-derivative test

$$\frac{\partial M}{\partial y} = 6xy^2 + 3 \quad \text{and} \quad \frac{\partial N}{\partial x} = 6xy^2 + 3$$

Because $\dfrac{\partial M}{\partial y} = \dfrac{\partial N}{\partial x}$, the equation is exact. To obtain a general solution, we must find a function f such that

$$\frac{\partial f}{\partial x} = 2xy^3 + 3y \quad \text{and} \quad \frac{\partial f}{\partial y} = 3x^2y^2 + 3x$$

To find f, we integrate the first partial on the left with respect to x:

$$f(x, y) = \int (2xy^3 + 3y)\, dx = x^2 y^3 + 3xy + u(y)$$

where u is a function of y. Taking the partial derivative of f with respect to y and comparing the result with $\partial f/\partial y$, we obtain

$$\frac{\partial f}{\partial y} = \frac{\partial}{\partial y}[x^2 y^3 + 3xy + u(y)] = 3x^2 y^2 + 3x + u'(y)$$

so that

$$3x^2 y^2 + 3x = 3x^2 y^2 + 3x + u'(y)$$
$$0 = u'(y)$$

This implies that u is a constant. Taking $u = 0$, we have $f = x^2 y^3 + 3xy$, and the general solution to the exact differential equation is

$$x^2 y^3 + 3xy = C$$

A summary of strategies for identifying and solving various kinds of first-order differential equations is displayed in Table 14.1.

TABLE 14.1 Summary of strategies for solving first-order differential equations

Form of Equation	Method	Solution
$\dfrac{dy}{dx} = \dfrac{g(x)}{f(y)}$	Separate the variables.	$\displaystyle\int f(y)\, dy = \int g(x)\, dx$
$\dfrac{dy}{dx} = f\left(\dfrac{y}{x}\right)$	Homogeneous—use a change of variable $v = y/x$.	$\displaystyle\int \frac{dv}{f(v) - v} = \int \frac{dx}{x}$
$\dfrac{dy}{dx} + p(x)y = q(x)$	Use the integrating factor $I(x) = e^{\int p(x)\, dx}$	$y = \dfrac{1}{I(x)}\left[\displaystyle\int I(x)q(x)\, dx + C\right]$
$M(x, y)\, dx + N(x, y)\, dy = 0$, where $\dfrac{\partial M}{\partial y} = \dfrac{\partial N}{\partial x}$	Exact—use partial integration to find f, where $\dfrac{\partial f}{\partial x} = M$ and $\dfrac{\partial f}{\partial y} = N$	$f(x, y) = C$

EULER'S METHOD

In Section 5.6, we introduced direction fields as a means for obtaining a "picture" of various solutions to a differential equation, but sometimes we need more than a rough graph of a solution. We now consider approximating a solution by numerical means. **Euler's method** is a simple procedure for obtaining a table of approximate values for the solution of a given initial value problem*

$$\frac{dy}{dx} = f(x, y) \qquad y(x_0) = y_0$$

The key idea in Euler's method is to increment x_0 by a small quantity h and then to estimate $y_1 = y(x_1)$ for $x_1 = x_0 + h$ by assuming x and y change by so little over the

---

*In our discussion of Euler's method, we assume that the given initial value problem has a unique solution. It can be shown that such an initial value problem always has a unique solution if f and $\partial f/\partial y$ are both continuous in a neighborhood of (x_0, y_0). The proof of this result is beyond the scope of this text but can be found in most elementary differential equations texts.

interval $[x_0, x_1]$ that $f(x, y)$ can be replaced by $f(x_0, y_0)$ for this interval. Solving the approximating initial value problem

$$\frac{dy}{dx} = f(x_0, y_0) \qquad y(x_0) = y_0$$

we obtain,

$$y - y_0 = f(x_0, y_0)(x - x_0)$$

In other words, we are approximating the solution curve $y = y(x)$ near (x_0, y_0) by the tangent line to the curve at this point, as shown in Figure 14.1a. We then repeat this process with (x_1, y_1) assuming the role of (x_0, y_0) to obtain an approximation of the solution $y = y(x)$ over the interval $x_1 \le x \le x_2$, where $x_2 = x_1 + h$ and

$$y_2 = y_1 + hf(x_1, y_1)$$

Continuing in this fashion, we obtain a sequence of line segments that approximates the shape of the solution curve as shown in Figure 14.1b. Euler's method is illustrated in the following example.

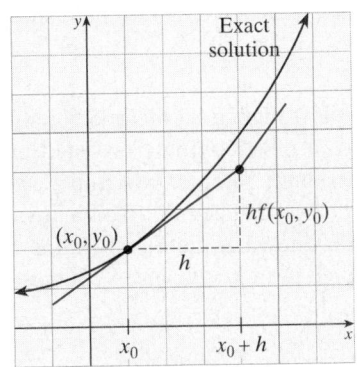

a. The first Euler approximation

EXAMPLE 7   Euler's method

Use Euler's method with $h = 0.1$ to estimate the solution of the initial value problem

$$\frac{dy}{dx} = x + y^2 \qquad y(0) = 1$$

over the interval $0 \le x \le 0.5$.

Solution

Before using Euler's method, we might first look at a graphical solution. The slope field is shown in Figure 14.2a, and the particular solution through the point $(0, 1)$ is shown in Figure 14.2b.

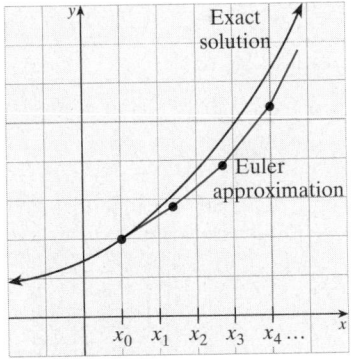

b. A sequence of Euler approximations

Figure 14.1 Graphical representation of Euler's method

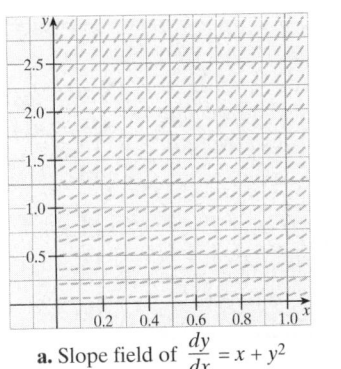

a. Slope field of $\frac{dy}{dx} = x + y^2$

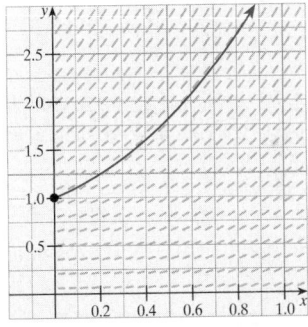

b. Particular solution through $(0, 1)$

Figure 14.2   Graphical solution using a direction field

To use Euler's method for this example, we note

$$f(x, y) = x + y^2, \quad x_0 = 0, \quad y_0 = 1, \quad \text{and} \quad h = 0.1$$

We show the calculator (or computer) solution correct to four decimal places:

$$y_0 = y(0) = 1$$

$$y_1 = y_0 + hf(x_0, y_0) = 1 + 0.1(0 + 1^2) = 1.1000$$

$$y_2 = y_1 + hf(x_1, y_1) = 1.1000 + 0.1(0.1 + 1.1000^2) = 1.2310$$

$$y_3 = y_2 + hf(x_2, y_2) = 1.2310 + 0.1(0.2 + 1.2310^2) \approx 1.4025$$

$$y_4 = y_3 + hf(x_3, y_3) = 1.4025 + 0.1(0.3 + 1.4025^2) \approx 1.6292$$

$$y_5 = y_4 + hf(x_4, y_4) = 1.6292 + 0.1(0.4 + 1.6292^2) \approx 1.9347$$

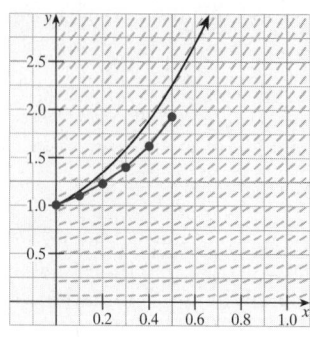

These points can be plotted to approximate the solution, as shown in Figure 14.3. Notice that we plotted these points by superimposing them on the direction field shown in Figure 14.2b.   ■

Euler's method has educational value as the simplest numerical method for solving ordinary differential equations and can be found in most computer-assisted programs. However, as you might guess by looking at Figure 14.3, as you move away from (x_0, y_0), the error may accumulate. The Euler method can be improved in a variety of ways, most notably by a collection of procedures known as the *Runge-Kutta* and *predictor-corrector* methods. These methods are studied in more advanced courses.

Figure 14.3 Solution by Euler's method

14.1 PROBLEM SET

A *Find the general solution of the differential equations in Problems 1–6 by separating variables.*

1. $xy\, dx = (x - 5)\, dy$

2. $\dfrac{dy}{dx} = y \tan x$

3. $(e^{2x} + 9)\dfrac{dy}{dx} = y$

4. $y\dfrac{dy}{dx} = e^{x-3y}\cos x$

5. $9\, dx - x\sqrt{x^2 - 9}\, dy = 0$

6. $xy\dfrac{dy}{dx} = x^2 + y^2 + x^2y^2 + 1$

In Problems 7–12, solve the given first-order linear initial value problem. Compare your answer to the given graphical solution.

7. $\dfrac{dy}{dx} + 2xy = 4x,$
passing through $(0, 0)$

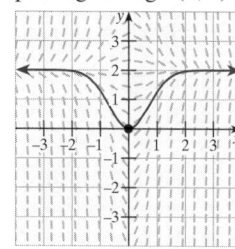

8. $\dfrac{dy}{dx} + \dfrac{y}{x} = \dfrac{\sin x}{x},$
passing through $(-2, 0)$

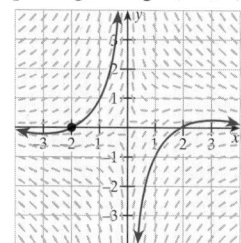

9. $\dfrac{dy}{dx} + y = \cos x,$
passing through $(0, 0)$

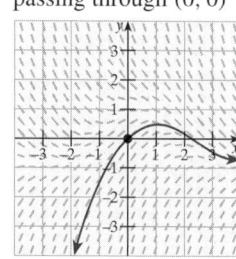

10. $\dfrac{dy}{dx} + y = \dfrac{e^x}{1 + e^{2x}},$
passing through $(0, 2)$

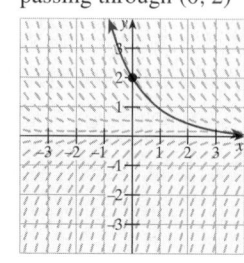

11. $x\dfrac{dy}{dx} - 2y = x^3,$
passing through $(2, -1)$

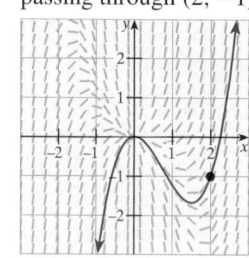

12. $\dfrac{dy}{dx} - 3xy = 5xe^{x^2},$
passing through $(0, -3)$

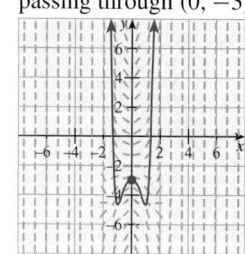

Show that each differential equation in Problems 13–18 is homogeneous and then find the general solution.

13. $(3x - y)\, dx + (x + 3y)\, dy = 0$

14. $xy\, dx - (2x^2 + y^2)\, dy = 0$

15. $(3x - y)\, dx + (x - 3y)\, dy = 0$

16. $(x^2 + y^2)\, dx - 2xy\, dy = 0$

17. $(-6y^2 + 3xy + 2x^2)\, dx + x^2\, dy = 0$

18. $x\, dy - (y + \sqrt{xy})\, dx = 0$

Show the differential equations in Problems 19–24 are exact and find the general solution.

19. $(3x^2y + \tan y)\, dx + (x^3 + x\sec^2 y)\, dy = 0$

20. $(3x^2 - 10xy)\, dx + (2y - 5x^2 + 4)\, dy = 0$

21. $\left[\dfrac{1}{1 + x^2} + \dfrac{2x}{x^2 + y^2}\right] dx + \left[\dfrac{2y}{x^2 + y^2} - e^{-y}\right] dy = 0$

22. $(2xy^3 + 3y - 3x^2)\, dx + (3x^2y^2 + 3x)\, dy = 0$

23. $[2x\cos 2y - 3y(1 - 2x)]\, dx$
$\quad - [2x^2\sin 2y + 3(2 + x - x^2)]\, dy = 0$

24. $\left[(x + xy - 3)(1 + y) - x^2\sqrt{y}\right] dx$
$\quad + \left[x^2(y + 1) - 3x - \dfrac{x^3}{6\sqrt{y}}\right] dy = 0$

B **25.** Consider the differential equation

$$\frac{dy}{dx} = x + y$$

a. Find the particular solution that contains the point $(1, 2)$.

b. Use the direction field for the given differential equation to sketch the solution through $(1, 2)$. Compare the result with part **a**.

c. Use Euler's method to approximate a solution for $x_0 = 1$, $y_0 = 2$, and $h = 0.2$. Compare this result with part **b**.

26. Consider the differential equation

$$\frac{dy}{dx} = x^2 - y$$

a. Find the particular solution that contains the point $(2, 1)$.

b. Use the direction field for the given differential equation to sketch the solution through $(2, 1)$. Compare the result with part **a**.

c. Use Euler's method to approximate a solution for $x_0 = 2$, $y_0 = 1$, and $h = 0.2$.

Estimate a solution for Problems 27–30 using Euler's method. For each of these problems, a direction field is given. Superimpose the segments from Euler's method on the given direction field.

27. $\dfrac{dy}{dx} = \dfrac{x + y}{y - x}$,
passing through $(0, 1)$
for $0 \le x \le 0.5$, $h = 0.1$

28. $\dfrac{dy}{dx} = 2x(x^2 - y)$,
passing through $(0, 4)$
for $0 \le x \le 1$, $h = 0.2$

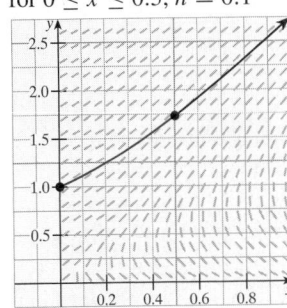

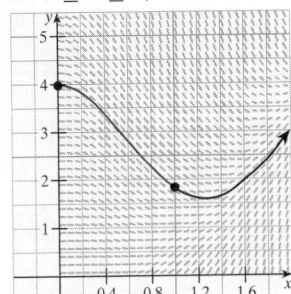

29. $\dfrac{dy}{dx} = \dfrac{5x - 3xy}{1 + x^2}$,
passing through $(0, 0)$
for $0 \le x \le 0.5$, $h = 0.1$

30. $\dfrac{dy}{dx} = \dfrac{y^2 + 2x}{3y^2 - 2xy}$,
passing through $(0, 1)$
for $0 \le x \le 0.5$, $h = 0.1$

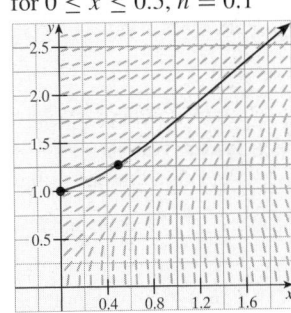

*An **integrating factor** of the differential equation $M\,dx + N\,dy = 0$ is a function $g(x, y)$ such that*

$$g(x, y)M(x, y)\,dx + g(x, y)N(x, y)\,dy = 0$$

is exact. In Problems 31–32, find an integrating factor of the specified type for the given differential equations, then solve the equation.

31. $y\,dx + (y - x)\,dy = 0$; $g(x, y) = y^n$

32. $(x^2 + y^2)\,dx + (3xy)\,dy = 0$; $g(x, y) = x^n$

Identify each equation given in Problems 33–44 as separable, homogeneous, first-order linear, or exact, and then solve. A change of variable may be needed to put the given equation into one of these forms.

33. $(2xy^2 + 3x^2y - y^3)\,dx + (2x^2y + x^3 - 3xy^2)\,dy = 0$

34. $(1 + x)\,dy + \sqrt{1 - y^2}\,dx = 0$

35. $\left(\dfrac{2x}{y} - \dfrac{y^2}{x^2}\right)dx + \left(\dfrac{2y}{x} - \dfrac{x^2}{y^2} + 3\right)dy = 0$

36. $(x^2 - xy - x + y)\,dx - (xy - y^2)\,dy = 0$

37. $e^{y-x}\sin x\,dx - \csc x\,dy = 0$

38. $x^2\dfrac{dy}{dx} + 2xy = \sin x$

39. $(3x^2 - y\sin xy)\,dx - (x\sin xy)\,dy = 0$

40. $\dfrac{dy}{dx} = \dfrac{y}{x} + x\cos\dfrac{y}{x}$ *Hint: Let* $u = \dfrac{y}{x}$

41. $(y - \sin^2 x)\,dx + (\sin x)\,dy = 0$

42. $(y^3 - y)\,dx + (x^2 + x)\,dy = 0$

43. $x\dfrac{dy}{dx} = y - \sqrt{x^2 + y^2}$

44. $(2x + \sin y - \cos y)\,dx + (x\cos y + x\sin y)\,dy = 0$

In Problems 45–52, solve the given initial value problem.

45. $\left(x\sin^2\dfrac{y}{x} - y\right)dx + x\,dy = 0$; $x = \dfrac{4}{\pi}$, $y = 1$

46. $y(5x - y)\,dx - x(5x + 2y)\,dy = 0$; $x = 1$, $y = 1$

47. $x\dfrac{dy}{dx} - 3y = x^3$; $x = 1$, $y = 1$

48. $\dfrac{dy}{dx} = 1 + 3y\tan x$; $x = 0$, $y = 2$

49. $[\sin(x^2 + y) + 2x^2\cos(x^2 + y)]\,dx + [x\cos(x^2 + y)]\,dy = 0$; $x = 0$, $y = 0$

50. $y\dfrac{dy}{dx} = e^{x+2y}\sin x$; $x = 0$, $y = 0$

51. $ye^x\,dy = (y^2 + 2y + 2)\,dx$; $x = 0$, $y = -1$

52. $(2xy + y^2 + 2x)\,dx + (x^2 + 2xy - 1)\,dy = 0$; $x = 1$, $y = 3$

53. In the chemical conversion analyzed in Example 2, what happens to $Q(t)$ as $t \to +\infty$ in the case where $\alpha \ne \beta$? What if $\alpha = \beta$?

54. a. Find an equation for the velocity of the falling body in Example 5 in the case where the body has initial velocity $v_0 \ne 0$.

b. Show that for any initial velocity (zero or nonzero) the velocity reached by the object "in the long run" (as $t \to +\infty$) is always mg/k.

55. A population of foxes grows logistically until authorities decide to allow hunting at the constant rate of h foxes per month. The population $P(t)$ is then modeled by the differential equation

$$\frac{dP}{dt} = P(k - \ell P) - h$$

where $P(0) = P_0$.

a. Solve this equation in terms of k, ℓ, h, and P_0 for the case where $h < k^2/(4\ell)$.

b. What happens to $P(t)$ as $t \to \infty$?

56. A chemical in a solution diffuses from a compartment where the concentration is $C_0(t) = 7e^{-t}$ across a membrane with diffusion coefficient $k = 1.75$. The concentration $C(t)$ in the second compartment is modeled by

$$\frac{dC}{dt} = 1.75[C_0(t) - C(t)]$$

Solve this equation for $C(t)$, assuming that $C(0) = 0$.

57. The formula for the solution of a first-order linear equation requires the differential equation to be linear in x. Suppose, instead, that the equation is linear in y; that is, it can be written in the form

$$\frac{dx}{dy} + R(y)x = S(y)$$

a. Find a formula for the general solution of an equation that is first-order linear in y.

b. Use the formula obtained in part **a** to solve

$$y\,dx - 2x\,dy = y^4 e^{-y}\,dy$$

58. Modeling Problem A man is pulling a heavy sled along the ground by a rope of fixed length L. Assume the man begins walking at the origin of a coordinate plane and that the sled is initially at the point $(0, L)$. The man walks to the right (along the positive x-axis), dragging the sled behind him. When the man is at point M, the sled is at S as shown in Figure 14.4. Find a differential equation for the path of the sled and solve this differential equation.

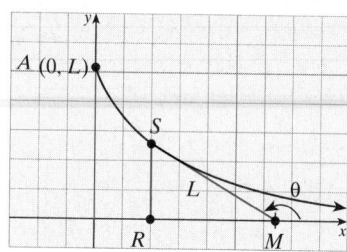

Figure 14.4 Sled problem

59. Spy Problem Having conserved as much energy as possible after his escape from the Death Ray (Problem 48, Section 13.3), the Spy is once again hot on the trail of Blohardt and the Flamer. He enters an open field and sees Blohardt pursuing the Flamer in the distance. Why? Could his old friend have had a change of heart? His mathematical mind visualizes the field as a coordinate plane (units in yards) with himself at $(100, 0)$, the Flamer at $(0, 0)$, and Blohardt at $(0, -80)$. The Spy and Blohardt both run directly at the Flamer, who is running along the positive y-axis at the rate of 12 ft/s. If Blohardt runs at the rate of 15 ft/s, how fast must the Spy run in order to reach his friend before the villain?

C 60. Almost homogeneous equations Sometimes a differential equation is not quite homogeneous but becomes homogeneous with a linear change of variable. Specifically, consider a differential equation of the form

$$\frac{dy}{dx} = f\left(\frac{ax + by + c}{rx + sy + t}\right)$$

a. Suppose $as \neq br$. Make the change of variable $x = X + A$ and $y = Y + B$, where A and B satisfy

$$\begin{cases} aA + bB + c = 0 \\ rA + sB + t = 0 \end{cases}$$

Show that with these choices for A and B the differential equation becomes homogeneous.

b. Apply the procedure outlined in part **a** to solve the differential equation

$$\frac{dy}{dx} = \left(\frac{-3x + y + 2}{x + 3y - 5}\right)$$

61. A **Riccati equation** is a differential equation of the form

$$\frac{dy}{dx} = P(x)y^2 + Q(x)y + R(x)$$

Suppose we know that $y = u(x)$ is a solution of a given Riccati equation.

a. Change variables by setting

$$z = \frac{1}{y - u(x)}$$

Show that the given equation is transformed by this change of variables into the separable form

$$\frac{dz}{dx} + [2P(x)u(x) + Q(x)]z = -P(x)$$

b. Solve the first-order linear equation in z obtained in part **a** and explain how to find the general solution of the given Riccati equation.

c. Use the method outlined in parts **a** and **b** to solve the Riccati equation

$$\frac{dy}{dx} = \frac{1}{x^2}y^2 + \frac{2}{x}y - 2$$

Hint: There is a solution of the general form $y = Ax$.

62. Journal Problem *The American Mathematical Monthly** ∎ Find all solutions of the Riccati equation

$$u' = u^2 + \frac{a}{x}u - b$$

$a, b \neq 0$, that are real rational functions of x.

*Problem E3055, Vol. 91, 1984, p. 515.

14.2 Second-Order Homogeneous Linear Differential Equations

IN THIS SECTION linear independence, solutions of the equation $ay'' + by' + cy = 0$, higher-order homogeneous linear equations, damped motion of a mass on a spring, reduction of order

LINEAR INDEPENDENCE

A **linear differential equation** is one of the general form

$$a_n(x)y^{(n)} + a_{n-1}(x)y^{(n-1)} + \cdots + a_0(x)y = R(x)$$

and if $a_n(x) \neq 0$, it is said to be of **order** n. It is *homogeneous* if $R(x) = 0$ and *nonhomogeneous* if $R(x) \neq 0$. In this section we focus attention on the homogeneous case, and we examine nonhomogeneous equations in the next section.

To characterize all solutions of the homogeneous equation

$$a_n(x)y^{(n)} + a_{n-1}(x)y^{(n-1)} + \cdots + a_0(x)y = 0$$

we require the following definition.

Linear Dependence and Independence

The functions $y_1, y_2, \ldots, y_n$ are said to be **linearly independent** if the equation

$$C_1 y_1 + C_2 y_2 + \cdots + C_n y_n = 0 \qquad \text{for constants } C_1, C_2, \ldots, C_n$$

has only the trivial solution $C_1 = C_2 = \cdots = C_n = 0$ for all x in the interval I. Otherwise the y_k's are **linearly dependent**.

→ **What This Says** A set of equations is *linearly independent* if none of the y_i can be written as a linear combination of the remaining y_j's ($j \neq i$). Recall that for two functions to be equal, they must be equal at every point x.

The functions $y_1 = \cos x$ and $y_2 = x$ are linearly independent because the only way we can have $C_1 \cos x + C_2 x = 0$ for all x is for C_1 and C_2 both to be 0. However, $y_1 = 1$, $y_2 = \sin^2 x$, and $y_3 = \cos 2x$ are linearly dependent, because

$$C_1(1) + C_2(\sin^2 x) + C_3(\cos 2x) = 0 \qquad \text{for } C_1 = 1, C_2 = -2, C_3 = -1$$

It can be quite difficult to determine whether a given collection of functions $y_1, y_2, \ldots, y_n$ is linearly independent using the definition. An alternate approach to settling the issue of linear independence involves the following determinant function, which is named after Josef Hoëné de Wronski (see the Historical Quest in Problem 47).

Wronskian

The **Wronskian** $W(y_1, y_2, \ldots, y_n)$ of n functions $y_1, y_2, \ldots, y_n$ having $n-1$ derivatives on an interval I is defined to be the determinant function

$$W(y_1, y_2, \cdots, y_n) = \begin{vmatrix} y_1 & y_2 & \cdots & y_n \\ y_1' & y_2' & \cdots & y_n' \\ \vdots & \vdots & & \vdots \\ y_1^{(n-1)} & y_2^{(n-1)} & \cdots & y_n^{(n-1)} \end{vmatrix}$$

THEOREM 14.1 **Determining linear independence with the Wronskian**

Suppose the functions $a_n(x), a_{n-1}(x), \ldots, a_0(x)$ in the nth order homogeneous linear differential equation

$$a_n(x)y^{(n)} + a_{n-1}(x)y^{(n-1)} + \cdots + a_0(x)y = 0$$

are all continuous on a closed interval $[c, d]$. Then solutions $y_1, y_2, \ldots, y_n$ of this differential equation are linearly independent if and only if the Wronskian is nonzero; that is,

$$W(y_1, y_2, \ldots, y_n) \neq 0$$

throughout the interval $[c, d]$.

Proof The proof can be found in most differential equations texts. ❏

EXAMPLE 1 **Showing linear independence**

The functions $y_1 = e^{-x}$, $y_2 = xe^{-x}$, and $y_3 = e^{3x}$ are solutions of a certain homogeneous linear differential equation with constant coefficients. Show that these solutions are linearly independent.

Solution

$$W(e^{-x}, xe^{-x}, e^{3x}) = \begin{vmatrix} e^{-x} & xe^{-x} & e^{3x} \\ -e^{-x} & (1-x)e^{-x} & 3e^{3x} \\ e^{-x} & (x-2)e^{-x} & 9e^{3x} \end{vmatrix}$$

$$= e^{-x}[9e^{3x}(1-x)e^{-x} - 3e^{3x}(x-2)e^{-x}]$$
$$\quad - xe^{-x}[-9e^{3x}e^{-x} - 3e^{-x}e^{3x}]$$
$$\quad + e^{3x}[-e^{-x}(x-2)e^{-x} - e^{-x}(1-x)e^{-x}]$$

$$= 16e^x$$

Because $16e^x \neq 0$, the functions are linearly independent. ∎

The general solution of an nth-order homogeneous linear differential equation with constant coefficients can be characterized in terms of n linearly independent solutions. Here is the theorem that applies to the second-order case.

THEOREM 14.2 **Characterization theorem**

Suppose y_1 and y_2 are linearly independent solutions of the differential equation $ay'' + by' + cy = 0$; that is, $W(y_1, y_2) \neq 0$. Then the general solution of the equation is

$$y = C_1 y_1 + C_2 y_2 \qquad \text{for arbitrary constants } C_1, C_2$$

Proof We will prove that if y_1 and y_2 are linearly independent solutions, then $y = C_1 y_1 + C_2 y_2$ is also a solution. However, the proof that all solutions are of this form is beyond the scope of this book. Suppose y_1 and y_2 are solutions, so that

$$ay_1''(x) + by_1'(x) + cy_1(x) = 0$$
$$ay_2''(x) + by_2'(x) + cy_2(x) = 0$$

If $y = C_1 y_1 + C_2 y_2$, we have

$$ay'' + by' + cy = a[C_1 y_1'' + C_2 y_2''] + b[C_1 y_1' + C_2 y_2'] + c[C_1 y_1 + C_2 y_2]$$
$$= C_1[ay_1'' + by_1' + cy_1] + C_2[ay_2'' + by_2' + cy_2]$$
$$= 0 + 0 = 0$$

Thus, $y = C_1 y_1 + C_2 y_2$ is also a solution. ❏

SOLUTIONS OF THE EQUATION $ay'' + by' + cy = 0$

Thanks to the characterization theorem, we now know that once we have two linearly independent solutions y_1, y_2 of the equation $ay'' + by' + cy = 0$, we have them all because the general solution can be characterized as $y = C_1 y_1 + C_2 y_2$. Therefore, the whole issue of how to represent the solution of a second-order homogeneous linear equation with constant coefficients depends on finding two linearly independent solutions.

Recall that the general solution of the first order equation $y' + ay = 0$ is $y = Ce^{-ax}$. Therefore, it is not unreasonable to expect the second-order equation $ay'' + by' + cy = 0$ to have one or more solutions of the form $y = e^{rx}$. If $y = e^{rx}$, then $y' = re^{rx}$ and $y'' = r^2 e^{rx}$, and by substituting these derivatives into the equation $ay'' + by' + cy = 0$, we obtain

$$ay'' + by' + cy = 0$$
$$a(r^2 e^{rx}) + b(re^{rx}) + ce^{rx} = 0$$
$$e^{rx}(ar^2 + br + c) = 0$$
$$ar^2 + br + c = 0 \qquad e^{rx} \neq 0$$

Thus, $y = e^{rx}$ is a solution of the given second-order differential equation if and only if $ar^2 + br + c = 0$. This equation is called the **characteristic equation** of $ay'' + by' + cy = 0$ and $ar^2 + br + c$ is the **characteristic polynomial**.

EXAMPLE 2   Characteristic equation with distinct real roots

Find the general solution of the differential equation $y'' + 2y' - 3y = 0$.

Solution

Begin by solving the characteristic equation:

$$r^2 + 2r - 3 = 0$$
$$(r - 1)(r + 3) = 0$$
$$r = 1, -3$$

The particular solutions are $y_1 = e^x$ and $y_2 = e^{-3x}$. Next, determine whether these equations are linearly independent by looking at the Wronskian.

$$W(e^x, e^{-3x}) = \begin{vmatrix} e^x & e^{-3x} \\ e^x & -3e^{-3x} \end{vmatrix} = e^x(-3e^{-3x}) - e^x e^{-3x} = -4e^{-2x}$$

Because $W(e^x, e^{-3x}) = -4e^{-2x} \neq 0$, the functions are linearly independent, and the characterization theorem tells us that the general solution is

$$y = C_1 y_1 + C_2 y_2 = C_1 e^x + C_2 e^{-3x} \qquad \blacksquare$$

When a characteristic polynomial $r^2 + ar + b$ does not factor as easily as the one in Example 2, it may be necessary to find the roots r_1 and r_2 of the characteristic equation by applying the quadratic formula to obtain

$$r = \frac{-b \pm \sqrt{b^2 - 4ac}}{2a}$$

The *discriminant* for this equation, $b^2 - 4ac$, figures prominently in the following theorem.

THEOREM 14.3 **Solution of** $ay'' + by' + cy = 0$

If the characteristic equation $ar^2 + br + c = 0$ of the homogeneous linear differential equation $ay'' + by' + cy = 0$ has roots

$$r_1 = \frac{-b + \sqrt{b^2 - 4ac}}{2a} \quad \text{and} \quad r_2 = \frac{-b - \sqrt{b^2 - 4ac}}{2a}$$

then the general solution of the differential equation can be expressed in exactly one of the three following forms, depending on the sign of the discriminant $b^2 - 4ac$:

$b^2 - 4ac > 0$: The roots r_1 and r_2 are real and distinct and the general solution is

$$y = C_1 e^{r_1 x} + C_2 e^{r_2 x}$$

for arbitrary constants C_1 and C_2.

$b^2 - 4ac = 0$: The roots r_1 and r_2 are real and equal, $r_1 = r_2 = -\dfrac{b}{2a}$. The general solution is

$$y = C_1 e^{r_1 x} + C_2 x e^{r_1 x} = (C_1 + C_2 x) e^{r_1 x}$$

$b^2 - 4ac < 0$: The roots r_1 and r_2 are complex conjugates,

$$r_1 = \alpha + \beta i \quad \text{and} \quad r_2 = \alpha - \beta i,$$

where $\quad \alpha = -\dfrac{b}{2a}, \quad \beta = \dfrac{\sqrt{4ac - b^2}}{2a}, \quad \text{and} \quad i = \sqrt{-1}.$

The general solution is

$$y = e^{\alpha x} (C_1 \cos \beta x + C_2 \sin \beta x)$$

Proof We have just seen that the solutions of the differential equation of the form $y = e^{rx}$ correspond to the solutions of the characteristic equation $ar^2 + br + c = 0$. The quadratic formula characterizes the three cases according to the discriminant of this equation, namely, $b^2 - 4ac$. For each case, we must find two linearly independent solutions.

$b^2 - 4ac > 0$: Let $y_1 = e^{r_1 x}$, and $y_2 = e^{r_2 x}$. Then

$$W(e^{r_1 x}, e^{r_2 x}) = \begin{vmatrix} e^{r_1 x} & e^{r_2 x} \\ r_1 e^{r_1 x} & r_2 e^{r_2 x} \end{vmatrix} = r_2 e^{(r_1 + r_2)x} - r_1 e^{(r_1 + r_2)x} = (r_2 - r_1) e^{(r_1 + r_2)x}$$

Because $r_2 \neq r_1$ and $e^{(r_1 + r_2)x} > 0$, we see $W(e^{r_1 x}, e^{r_2 x}) \neq 0$, so the functions are linearly independent. The characterization theorem tells us that the general solution is

$$y = C_1 y_1 + C_2 y_2 = C_1 e^{r_1 x} + C_2 e^{r_2 x}$$

$b^2 - 4ac = 0$: In this case, the characteristic equation has one repeated root, $r = r_1 = r_2 = -\dfrac{b}{2a}$. Thus, $y_1 = e^{rx}$ is one solution, and it can be shown that $y_2 = x e^{rx}$ is a second, linearly independent solution (see Problem 31), so the general solution is

$$y = C_1 e^{rx} + C_2 x e^{rx}$$

$b^2 - 4ac < 0$: We must show that

$$y_1 = e^{\alpha x} \cos \beta x \quad \text{and} \quad y_2 = e^{\alpha x} \sin \beta x$$

are linearly independent and satisfy the given differential equation. You are asked to verify these facts in Problem 51. ❏

EXAMPLE 3   Characteristic equation with repeated roots

Find the general solution of the differential equation $y'' + 4y' + 4y = 0$.

Solution

Solve the characteristic equation

$$r^2 + 4r + 4 = 0$$
$$(r + 2)^2 = 0$$
$$r = -2 \qquad \text{(multiplicity 2)}$$

The roots are $r_1 = r_2 = -2$. Thus, $y_1 = e^{-2x}$ and $y_2 = xe^{-2x}$, so the general solution of the differential equation is

$$y = C_1 e^{-2x} + C_2 x e^{-2x} \qquad \blacksquare$$

EXAMPLE 4   Characteristic equation with complex roots

Find the general solution of the differential equation $2y'' + 3y' + 5y = 0$.

Solution

Solve the characteristic equation:

$$2r^2 + 3r + 5 = 0$$
$$r = \frac{-3 \pm \sqrt{9 - 4(2)(5)}}{2(2)}$$
$$= \frac{-3 \pm \sqrt{31}\, i}{4}$$

The roots are

$$r_1 = -\frac{3}{4} + \frac{\sqrt{31}}{4}i, \quad r_2 = -\frac{3}{4} - \frac{\sqrt{31}}{4}i$$

Thus, the general solution is

$$y = e^{(-3/4)x}\left[C_1 \cos\frac{\sqrt{31}}{4}x + C_2 \sin\frac{\sqrt{31}}{4}x \right] \qquad \blacksquare$$

EXAMPLE 5   Second-order initial value problem

Solve $4y'' + 12y' + 9y = 0$ subject to $y(0) = 3$ and $y'(0) = -2$.

Solution

Solve

$$4r^2 + 12r + 9 = 0$$
$$(2r + 3)^2 = 0$$
$$r_1 = r_2 = -\frac{3}{2}$$

Thus, the general solution is

$$y = C_1 e^{(-3/2)x} + C_2 x e^{(-3/2)x}$$

Because $y(0) = 3$ we have

$$3 = C_1 e^0 + C_2(0)e^0$$
$$3 = C_1$$

Since $y'(0) = -2$, we find y':

$$y' = -\tfrac{3}{2}C_1 e^{(-3/2)x} - \tfrac{3}{2}C_2 x e^{(-3/2)x} + C_2 e^{(-3/2)x}$$

$$y'(0) = -\tfrac{3}{2}C_1 e^0 - \tfrac{3}{2}C_2(0)e^0 + C_2 e^0$$

$$-2 = -\tfrac{3}{2}C_1 + C_2$$

$$-2 = -\tfrac{3}{2}(3) + C_2 \qquad \text{Because } C_1 = 3$$

$$\tfrac{5}{2} = C_2$$

Thus, the particular solution is

$$y = 3e^{(-3/2)x} + \tfrac{5}{2}x e^{(-3/2)x} \qquad \blacksquare$$

HIGHER-ORDER HOMOGENEOUS LINEAR EQUATIONS

Homogeneous linear differential equations of order 3 or more with constant coefficients can be handled in essentially the same way as the second-order equations we have analyzed. As in the second-order case, some of the roots of the characteristic equations may be real and distinct, some may be real and repeated, and some may occur in complex conjugate pairs. But now, roots of the characteristic equation may occur more than twice, and when this happens, the linearly independent solutions are obtained by multiplying by increasing powers of x. For example, if 2 is a root of multiplicity 4 in the characteristic equation, the corresponding linearly independent solutions are e^{2x}, xe^{2x}, $x^2 e^{2x}$, and $x^3 e^{2x}$. The procedure for obtaining the general solution of an nth order linear homogeneous equation with constant coefficients is illustrated in the next two examples.

EXAMPLE 6 Characteristic equation with repeated roots

Solve $y^{(4)} - 5y''' + 6y'' + 4y' - 8y = 0$.

Solution

Solve the characteristic equation:

$$r^4 - 5r^3 + 6r^2 + 4r - 8 = 0$$

Because this is 4th degree, we use synthetic division and the rational root theorem (or a calculator) to find the roots -1, 2, 2, and 2. The general solution is

$$y = C_1 e^{-x} + C_2 e^{2x} + C_3 x e^{2x} + C_4 x^2 e^{2x} \qquad \blacksquare$$

EXAMPLE 7 Characteristic equation with repeated roots (some not real)

Solve $y^{(7)} + 8y^{(5)} + 16y''' = 0$.

Solution

Solve the characteristic equation:

$$r^7 + 8r^5 + 16r^3 = 0$$

$$r^3(r^4 + 8r^2 + 16) = 0$$

$$r^3(r^2 + 4)^2 = 0$$

$$r = 0 \text{ (multiplicity 3)}, \pm 2i \text{ (multiplicity 2)}$$

WARNING The general solution of an nth order linear homogeneous differential equation involves n arbitrary constants $C_1, C_2, \ldots, C_n$. Always check to make sure your solution has the correct number of constants.

The roots (showing multiplicity) are 0, 0, 0, $2i$, $2i$, $-2i$, $-2i$. The general solution is

$$y = C_1 + C_2 x + C_3 x^2 + C_4 \cos 2x + C_5 \sin 2x + C_6 x \cos 2x + C_7 x \sin 2x \qquad \blacksquare$$

DAMPED MOTION OF A MASS ON A SPRING

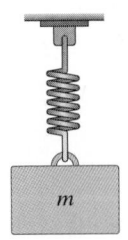

Figure 14.5 Oscillating spring

To illustrate an application of a second-order homogeneous linear differential equation, we will consider the motion of an oscillating spring, which we illustrate in Figure 14.5. Suppose an object suspended at the end of a spring is pulled down and then released. Hooke's law in physics says that a spring that is stretched or compressed x units from its natural length tends to restore itself to its natural length by a force whose magnitude F is proportional to x. Specifically, $F(x) = kx$, where the constant of proportionality k is called the **spring constant** and depends on the stiffness of the spring.

Suppose the mass of the spring is negligible compared to the mass m of the object on the spring. When the object is pulled down and released, the spring begins to oscillate, and its motion is determined by two forces, the weight mg of the object and the restoring force $F(x) = k_1 x$ of the spring. According to Newton's second law of motion, the force acting on the object is ma, where $a = x''(t)$ is the acceleration of the object. If there are no other external forces acting on the object, the motion is said to be **undamped**, and the motion is governed by the second-order homogeneous equation

$$mx''(t) = -k_1 x(t) \qquad k_1 > 0$$
$$mx''(t) + k_1 x(t) = 0$$

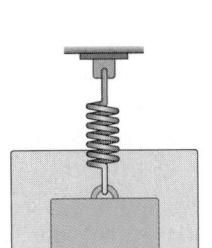

Figure 14.6 A damped spring system

Next, suppose the object is connected to a dashpot, or a device that imposes a damping force. A good example is a shock absorber in a car, which forces a spring to move through a fluid (see Figure 14.6). Experiments indicate that the shock absorber introduces a damping force proportional to the velocity $v = x'(t)$. Thus, the total force in this case is $-k_1 x(t) - k_2 x'(t)$, and Newton's second law tells us

$$mx''(t) = -k_1 x(t) - k_2 x'(t) \qquad k_1 > 0, \; k_2 > 0$$
$$mx''(t) + k_2 x'(t) + k_1 x(t) = 0$$

The constant k_2 is called the *damping constant* to contrast it from the spring constant k_1. The characteristic equation is

$$mr^2 + k_2 r + k_1 = 0$$

$$r = \frac{-k_2 \pm \sqrt{k_2^2 - 4k_1 m}}{2m}$$

The three cases that can occur correspond to different kinds of motion for the object on the spring.

overdamping: $k_2^2 - 4k_1 m > 0$ In this case, both roots are real and negative, and the solution is of the form

$$x(t) = C_1 e^{r_1 t} + C_2 e^{r_2 t}$$

where

$$r_1 = -\frac{k_2}{2m} + \frac{1}{2m}\sqrt{k_2^2 - 4k_1 m} \qquad \text{and}$$
$$r_2 = -\frac{k_2}{2m} - \frac{1}{2m}\sqrt{k_2^2 - 4k_1 m}$$

Note that the motion dies out eventually as $t \to +\infty$:

$$\lim_{t \to +\infty} x(t) = \lim_{t \to +\infty} \left(C_1 e^{r_1 t} + C_2 e^{r_2 t} \right) = 0, \quad \text{because } r_1 < 0 \text{ and } r_2 < 0$$

Overdamping is illustrated in Figure 14.7a.

critical damping: $k_2^2 - 4k_1 m = 0$ The solution has the form

$$x(t) = (C_1 + C_2 t)e^{rt}$$

where $r_1 = r_2 = r = -\dfrac{k_2}{2m}$. In this case, the motion also eventually dies out (as $t \to +\infty$), because $r < 0$. This solution is shown in Figure 14.7b.

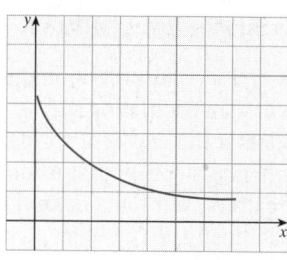
a. Overdamping $k_2^2 - 4k_1 m > 0$

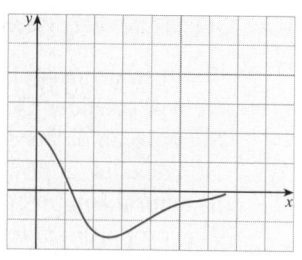
b. Critical damping $k_2^2 - 4k_1 m = 0$

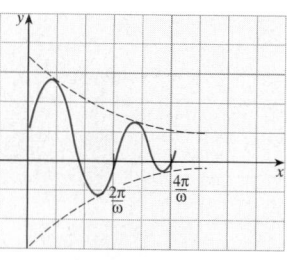
c. Underdamping $k_2^2 - 4k_1 m < 0$

Figure 14.7   Damping motion

underdamping: $k_2^2 - 4k_1 m < 0$ In this case, the characteristic equation has complex roots, and the solution has the form

$$x(t) = e^{-k_2 t/(2m)} \left[C_1 \cos\left(\frac{t}{2m} \sqrt{4k_1 m - k_2^2} \right) + C_2 \sin\left(\frac{t}{2m} \sqrt{4k_1 m - k_2^2} \right) \right]$$

This can be written as

$$x(t) = A e^{\alpha t} \cos(\omega t - C)$$

where

$$A = \sqrt{C_1^2 + C_2^2}; \quad \alpha = -\frac{k_2}{2m}; \quad \omega = \frac{1}{2m} \sqrt{4k_1 m - k_2^2}; \quad C = \tan^{-1} \frac{C_2}{C_1}$$

Because k_2 and m are both positive, α must be negative and we see that $x(t) \to 0$ as $t \to +\infty$. Notice that as the motion dies out, it oscillates with frequency $2\pi/\omega$, as shown in Figure 14.7c.

REDUCTION OF ORDER

Theorem 14.2 applies even when a, b, and c are functions of x instead of constants. In other words, the general solution of the equation

$$a(x)y'' + b(x)y' + c(x)y = 0$$

can be expressed as

$$y = C_1 y_1 + C_2 y_2$$

where $y_1(x)$ and $y_2(x)$ are any two linearly independent solutions. Sometimes, we can find one solution y_1 by observation and then obtain a second linearly independent solution y_2 by assuming that $y_2 = v y_1$, where $v(x)$ is a twice differentiable function of x. This procedure is called **reduction of order** because it involves solving the given second-order equation by solving two related first-order equations. The basic ideas of reduction of order are illustrated in the following example.

EXAMPLE 8   Reduction of order

Show that $y = x^2$ is a solution of the equation $y'' - \dfrac{3}{x}y' + \dfrac{4}{x^2}y = 0$ for $x > 0$, then find the general solution.

Solution

If $y_1 = x^2$, then $y_1' = 2x$ and $y_1'' = 2$. We have

$$y_1'' - \frac{3}{x}y_1' + \frac{4}{x^2}y_1 = 2 - \frac{3}{x}(2x) + \frac{4}{x^2}(x^2) = 0$$

so y_1 is a solution.

Next, let $y_2 = v(x)x^2$ and compute

$$y_2' = 2xv + x^2 v' \quad \text{and} \quad y_2'' = 2v + 4xv' + x^2 v''$$

Substitute these derivatives into the given equation:

$$(2v + 4xv' + x^2v'') - \frac{3}{x}(2xv + x^2v') + \frac{4}{x^2}(vx^2) = 0$$

$$x^2v'' + xv' = 0$$

$$\frac{v''}{v'} = \frac{-1}{x}$$

Integrate both sides of this equation:

$$\ln|v'| = -\ln x$$

$$v' = \frac{1}{x}$$

$$v = \ln x$$

Thus, $y_2 = vx^2 = x^2 \ln x$ is a second solution. To show that the solutions $y_1 = x^2$ and $y = x^2 \ln x$ are linearly independent, we compute the Wronskian:

$$W(x^2, x^2 \ln x) = \begin{vmatrix} x^2 & x^2 \ln x \\ 2x & x + 2x \ln x \end{vmatrix} = x^3 \neq 0 \quad \text{Since } x > 0$$

It follows that the general solution of the given differential equation is

$$y = C_1 x^2 + C_2 x^2 \ln x \qquad \blacksquare$$

14.2 PROBLEM SET

A *Find the general solution of the second-order homogeneous linear differential equations given in Problems 1–14.*

1. $y'' + y' = 0$
2. $y'' + y' - 2y = 0$
3. $y'' + 6y' + 5y = 0$
4. $y'' + 4y = 0$
5. $y'' - y' - 6y = 0$
6. $y'' + 8y' + 16y = 0$
7. $2y'' - 5y' - 3y = 0$
8. $3y'' + 11y' - 4y = 0$
9. $y'' - y = 0$
10. $6y'' + 13y' + 6y = 0$
11. $y'' + 11y = 0$
12. $y'' - 4y' + 5y = 0$
13. $7y'' + 3y' + 5y = 0$
14. $2y'' + 5y' + 8y = 0$

Find the general solution of the given higher-order homogeneous linear differential equations in Problems 15–20.

15. $y''' + y'' = 0$
16. $y''' + 4y' = 0$
17. $y^{(4)} + y''' + 2y'' = 0$
18. $y^{(4)} + 10y'' + 9y = 0$
19. $y''' + 2y'' - 5y' - 6y = 0$
20. $y^{(4)} + 2y''' + 2y'' + 2y' + y = 0$

Find the particular solution that satisfies the differential equations in Problems 21–26 subject to the specified initial conditions.

21. $y'' - 10y' + 25y = 0$; $y(0) = 1$, $y'(0) = -1$
22. $y'' + 6y' + 9y = 0$; $y(0) = 4$; $y'(0) = -3$
23. $y'' - 12y' + 11y = 0$; $y(0) = 3$, $y'(0) = 11$
24. $y'' + 4y' + 5y = 0$; $y(0) = -2$, $y'(0) = 1$
25. $y''' + 10y'' + 25y' = 0$; $y(0) = 3$, $y'(0) = 2$, $y''(0) = -1$
26. $y^{(4)} - y'' = 0$; $y(0) = 3$, $y'(0) = 0$, $y''(0) = 3$, $y'''(0) = 4$

In Problems 27–30, find the Wronskian, W, of the given set of functions and show that $W \neq 0$.

27. $\{e^{-2x}, e^{3x}\}$
28. $\{e^{-x}, xe^{-x}\}$
29. $\{e^{-x} \cos x, e^{-x} \sin x\}$
30. $\{xe^x \cos x, xe^x \sin x\}$

B 31. If $a^2 = b$, one solution of $y'' - 2ay' + by = 0$ is $y_1 = e^{ax}$. Use reduction of order to show that $y_2 = xe^{ax}$ is a second solution, and then show that y_1 and y_2 are linearly independent.

In Problems 32–37, a second-order differential equation and one solution $y_1(x)$ are given. Use reduction of order to find a second solution $y_2(x)$. Show that y_1 and y_2 are linearly independent and find the general solution.

32. $y'' + 6y' + 9y = 0$; $y_1 = e^{-3x}$
33. $2y'' - y' - 6y = 0$; $y_1 = e^{2x}$
34. $xy'' + 4y' = 0$; $y_1 = 1$
35. $x^2y'' + xy' - 4y = 0$; $y_1 = x^{-2}$
36. $x^2y'' + 2xy' - 12y = 0$; $y_1 = x^3$
37. $(1-x)^2y'' - (1-x)y' - y = 0$; $y_1 = 1 - x$

Suppose a 16-lb weight stretches a spring 8 in. from its natural length. Find a formula for the position of the weight as a function of time for the situations described in Problems 38–43.

38. The weight is pulled down an additional 6 in. and is then released with an initial upward velocity of 8 ft/s.

39. The weight is pulled down 10 in. and is released with an initial upward velocity of 6 ft/s.

40. The weight is raised 8 in. above the equilibrium point and the compressed spring is then released.

41. The weight is raised 12 in. above the equilibrium point and the compressed spring is then released.

42. The weight is pulled 6 in. below the equilibrium point and is then released. The weight is connected to a dashpot that imposes a damping force of magnitude $0.4|v|$ at all times.

43. The weight is pulled 12 in. below the equilibrium point and is then released. The weight is connected to a dashpot that imposes a damping force of magnitude $0.08 |v|$ at all times.

44. Characterize the solution of the second-order equation

$$y'' - 2ay' + (a^2 - b)y = 0 \qquad b > 0$$

in terms of the functions $\cosh kx$ and $\sinh kx$, where $k = \sqrt{b}$.

45. Verify that $y_1 = e^{2x}$, $y_2 = xe^{2x}$, and $y_3 = x^2e^{2x}$ are linearly independent solutions of the third-order differential equation $y''' - 6y'' + 12y' - 8y = 0$.

46. Modeling Problem A 100-lb object is projected vertically upward from the surface of the earth with initial velocity 150 ft/s.

   a. Modeling the object's motion with negligible air resistance, how long does it take for the object to return to earth?

   b. Change the model to assume air resistance equal to half the object's velocity. Before making any computation, does your intuition tell you the object takes less or more time to return to earth this time than in part **a**? Now set up and solve a differential equation to actually determine the round-trip time. Were you right?

47. HISTORICAL QUEST Josef Hoëné (1778–1853) adopted the name Wronski when he was 32 years old, around the time he was married. Today, he is remembered for determinants now known as Wronskians, named by Thomas Muir (1844–1934) in 1882. Wronski's main work was in the philosophy of mathematics. For years his mathematical work, which contained many errors, was dismissed as unimportant, but in recent years closer study of his work revealed that he had some significant mathematical insight. ∎

JOSEPH HOËNÉ DE WRONSKI 1778–1853

For this Historical Quest you are asked to write a paper on one of the great philosophical issues in the history of mathematics. Here are a few quotations to get you started:

Mathematics is discovered:

"... what is physical is subject to the laws of mathematics, and what is spiritual to the laws of God, and the laws of mathematics are but the expression of the thoughts of God."

——Thomas Hill,
The Uses of Mathesis; Bibliotheca Sacra, p. 523.

"Our remote ancestors tried to interpret nature in terms of anthropomorphic concepts of their own creation and failed. The efforts of our nearer ancestors to interpret nature on engineering lines proved equally inadequate. Nature has refused to accommodate herself to either of these man-made molds. On the other hand, our efforts to interpret nature in terms of the concepts of pure mathematics have, so far, proved brilliantly successful ... from the intrinsic evidence of His creation, the Great Architect of the Universe now begins to appear as a pure mathematician."

——James H. Jeans,
The Mysterious Universe, p. 142.

Mathematics is invented:

"There is an old Armenian saying, 'He who lacks sense of the past is condemned to live in the narrow darkness of his own generation.' Mathematics without history is mathematics stripped of its greatness: for, like the other arts-and mathematics is one of the supreme arts of civilization-it derives its grandeur from the fact of being a human creation."

——G. F. Simmons,
Differential Equations with Applications and Historical Notes, Second Edition, McGraw-Hill, Inc., 1991, p. xix.

Discuss whether the significant ideas in mathematics are *discovered* or *invented*.

C 48. The motion of a pendulum subject to frictional damping proportional to its velocity is modeled by the differential equation

$$mL\frac{d^2\theta}{dt^2} + kL\frac{d\theta}{dt} + mg\sin\theta = 0$$

where L is the length of the pendulum, m is the mass of the bob at its end, and θ is the angle the pendulum arm makes with the vertical (see Figure 14.8). Assume θ is small, so $\sin\theta$ is approximately equal to θ.

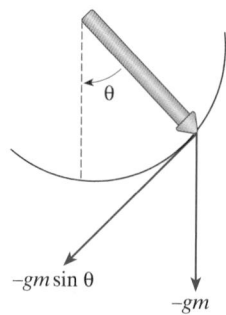

Figure 14.8 Damped Pendulum

   a. Solve the resulting differential equation for the case where $k^2 \geq 4gm^2/L$. What happens to $\theta(t)$ as $t \to \infty$?

   b. If $k^2 < 4gm^2/L$, show that

$$\theta(t) = Ae^{-kt/(2m)}\cos\left(\sqrt{\frac{B}{L}}t + C\right)$$

   for constants A, B, and C. What happens to $\theta(t)$ as $t \to \infty$ in this case?

   c. For the situation in part **b**, show that the time difference between successive vertical positions is approximately

$$T = 2\pi m\sqrt{\frac{L}{4gm^2 - k^2L}}$$

49. If there is no damping and there are no external forces, the motion of an object of mass m attached to a spring with spring constant k is governed by the differential equation $mx'' + kx = 0$. Show that the general solution of this equation is given by

$$x(t) = A\cos\left(\sqrt{\frac{k}{m}}t + C\right), \qquad k > 0$$

where A and C are constants. This is called **simple harmonic motion** with frequency $\dfrac{1}{2\pi}\sqrt{\dfrac{k}{m}}$.

50. Consider the motion of an object of mass m on a spring with spring constant k_1 and damping constant k_2 for the case where there is critical damping.

a. Describe the motion of the object assuming that it begins at rest: $x'(0) = 0$ at $x(0) = x_0$. How is this different from the case where the object begins at $x(0) = 0$ with initial velocity $x'(0) = v_0$? How do initial velocity and initial displacement affect the motion?

b. If $x(0) = x'(0)$, what is the maximum displacement? Show that the time at which the maximum displacement occurs is independent of the initial displacement $x(0)$. Assume $x(0) \neq 0$.

51. Suppose the characteristic equation of the differential equation $ay'' + by' + cy = 0$ has complex conjugate roots $r_1 = \alpha + \beta i$ and $r_2 = \alpha - \beta i$. Show that $y_1 = e^{\alpha x} \cos \beta x$ and $y_2 = e^{\alpha x} \sin \beta x$ are both solutions and are linearly independent. This is Theorem 14.3 for the case where $b^2 - 4ac < 0$.

52. Pendulum motion Suppose a ball of mass m is suspended at the end of a rod of length L and is set in motion swinging back and forth like a pendulum, as shown in Figure 14.9.

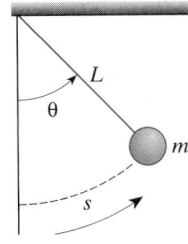

Figure 14.9 Pendulum motion

Let θ be the angle between the rod and the vertical at time t, so that the displacement of the ball from the equilibrium position is $s = L\theta$ and the acceleration of the ball's motion is

$$\frac{d^2s}{dt^2} = L\frac{d^2\theta}{dt^2}$$

a. Use Newton's second law to show that

$$mL\frac{d^2\theta}{dt^2} + mg \sin \theta = 0$$

Assume that air resistance and the mass of the rod are negligible.

b. When the displacement is small (θ close to 0), $\sin \theta$ may be replaced by θ. In this case, solve the resulting differential equation

$$\frac{d^2\theta}{dt^2} + \frac{g}{L}\theta = 0$$

How is the motion of the pendulum like the simple harmonic motion discussed in Problem 49?

53. Path of a projectile with variable mass A rocket starts from rest and moves vertically upward, along a straight line. Assume the rocket and its fuel initially weigh w kilograms and that the fuel initially weighs w_f kilograms. Further assume that the fuel is consumed at a constant rate of r kilograms per second (relative to the rocket). Finally, assume that gravitational attraction is the only external force acting on the rocket.

a. If $m(t)$ is the mass of the rocket and fuel at time t and $s(t)$ is the height above the ground at time t, it can be shown that

$$m(t)s''(t) + m'(t)v_0 + m(t)g = 0$$

where v_0 is the velocity of the exhaust gas in relation to the rocket. Express $m(t)$ in terms of $w, r, v_0,$ and g, then integrate this differential equation to obtain the velocity $s'(t)$. Note that $s'(0) = 0$ because the rocket starts from rest.

b. Integrate the velocity $s'(t)$ to obtain $s(t)$.

c. At what time is all the fuel consumed?

d. How high is the rocket at the instant the fuel is consumed?

54. Journal Problem *Canadian Mathematical Bulletin**[*] ■ Solve the differential equation

$$x^4y'' - (x^3 + 2axy)y' + 4ay^2 = 0$$

---
[*]Problem 331 by Murray S. Klamkin, Vol. 26, 1983, p. 126.

14.3 Second-Order Nonhomogeneous Linear Differential Equations

IN THIS SECTION nonhomogeneous equations, method of undetermined coefficients, variation of parameters, an application to *RLC* circuits

NONHOMOGENEOUS DIFFERENTIAL EQUATIONS

Next we will see how to solve a nonhomogeneous second-order linear equation of the general form $ay'' + by' + cy = F(x)$, where $F(x) \neq 0$. The key to our results is the following theorem.

THEOREM 14.4 Characterization of the general solution of $ay'' + by' + cy = F(x)$

Let y_p be a particular solution of the nonhomogeneous second-order linear equation $ay'' + by' + cy = F(x)$. Let y_h be the general solution of the related homogeneous equation $ay'' + by' + cy = 0$. Then the general solution of $ay'' + by' + cy = F(x)$ is given by the sum

$$y = y_h + y_p$$

Proof First, the sum $y = y_h + y_p$ is a solution of the nonhomogeneous equation $ay'' + by' + cy = F(x)$, because

$$\begin{aligned}
ay'' + by' + cy &= a(y_h + y_p)'' + b(y_h + y_p)' + c(y_h + y_p) \\
&= ay_h'' + ay_p'' + by_h' + by_p' + cy_h + cy_p \\
&= (ay_h'' + by_h' + cy_h) + (ay_p'' + by_p' + cy_p) \\
&= 0 + F(x) \\
&= F(x)
\end{aligned}$$

Conversely, if y is any solution of the nonhomogeneous equation, then $y - y_p$ is a solution of the related homogeneous equation because

$$\begin{aligned}
a(y - y_p)'' + b(y - y_p)' + c(y - y_p) &= a(y'' - y_p'') + b(y' - y_p') + c(y - y_p) \\
&= (ay'' + by' + cy) - (ay_p'' + by_p' + cy_p) \\
&= F(x) - F(x) \\
&= 0
\end{aligned}$$

Thus, $y - y_p = y_h$ (because it is a solution of the homogeneous equation). Therefore, because y was *any* solution of the nonhomogeneous equation, it follows that $y = y_h + y_p$ is the general solution of the nonhomogeneous equation. ❑

> ➡ **What This Says** We can obtain the general solution of the nonhomogeneous equation $ay'' + by' + cy = F(x)$ by finding the general solution y_h of the related homogeneous equation $ay'' + by' + cy = 0$ and just one particular solution y_p of the given nonhomogeneous equation.

We can use the methods of the preceding section to find the general solution of the related homogeneous equation. We now develop two methods for finding particular solutions of the nonhomogeneous equation.

METHOD OF UNDETERMINED COEFFICIENTS

Sometimes it is possible to find a particular solution y_p of the nonhomogeneous equation $ay'' + by' + cy = F(x)$ by assuming a **trial solution** $\overline{y}_p$ of the same general form as $F(x)$. This procedure, called the **method of undetermined coefficients**, is illustrated in the following three examples, each of which has the related homogeneous equation $y'' + y' - 2y = 0$ with the general solution $y_h = C_1 e^x + C_2 e^{-2x}$.

EXAMPLE 1 Method of undetermined coefficients

Find $\overline{y}_p$ and the general solution for $y'' + y' - 2y = 2x^2 - 4x$.

Solution

The right side $F(x) = 2x^2 - 4x$ is a quadratic polynomial. Because derivatives of a polynomial are polynomials of lower degree, it seems reasonable to consider a trial solution that is also a polynomial of degree 2. That is, we "guess" that this equation has a particular solution $\overline{y}_p$ of the general form $\overline{y}_p = A_1x^2 + A_2x + A_3$. To find the constants A_1, A_2, and A_3, calculate

$$\overline{y}'_p = 2A_1x + A_2 \quad \text{and} \quad \overline{y}''_p = 2A_1$$

Substitute the values for $\overline{y}_p$, $\overline{y}'_p$, and $\overline{y}''_p$ into the given equation:

$$y'' + y' - 2y = 2x^2 - 4x$$
$$2A_1 + 2A_1x + A_2 - 2(A_1x^2 + A_2x + A_3) = 2x^2 - 4x$$
$$-2A_1x^2 + (2A_1 - 2A_2)x + (2A_1 + A_2 - 2A_3) = 2x^2 - 4x$$

Since this must be true for *every* x, we see that this is true only when the coefficients of each power of x on each side of the equation match, so that

$$\begin{cases} -2A_1 = 2 & (x^2 \text{ terms}) \\ 2A_1 - 2A_2 = -4 & (x \text{ terms}) \\ 2A_1 + A_2 - 2A_3 = 0 & (\text{constant terms}) \end{cases}$$

SMH See Problem 30 of Problem Set 3 of the *Student Mathematics Handbook*.

Solve this system of equations simultaneously to find $A_1 = -1$, $A_2 = 1$, and $A_3 = -\frac{1}{2}$. Thus, a particular solution of the given nonhomogeneous equation is

$$y_p = A_1x^2 + A_2x + A_3 = -x^2 + x - \tfrac{1}{2}$$

and the general solution for the nonhomogeneous equation is

$$y = y_h + y_p = C_1e^x + C_2e^{-2x} - x^2 + x - \tfrac{1}{2} \qquad \blacksquare$$

Comment: Notice that even though the constant term is zero in the polynomial function $F(x)$, we cannot assume that $y = A_1x^2 + A_2x$ is a suitable trial solution. In general, all terms of the same or lower degree that could possibly lead to the given right-side function $F(x)$ must be included in the trial solution.

EXAMPLE 2 Method of undetermined coefficients

Solve $y'' + y' - 2y = \sin x$.

Solution

Because the trial solution $\overline{y}_p$ is to be "like" the right-side function $F(x) = \sin x$, it seems that we should choose the trial solution to be $\overline{y}_p = A_1 \sin x$, but a sine function can have either a sine or a cosine in its derivatives, depending on how many derivatives are taken. Thus, to account for the $\sin x$ term, it is necessary to have both $\sin x$ and $\cos x$ in the trial solution, so we set

$$\overline{y}_p = A_1 \sin x + A_2 \cos x$$

Differentiating, we find

$$\overline{y}'_p = A_1 \cos x - A_2 \sin x \quad \text{and} \quad \overline{y}''_p = -A_1 \sin x - A_2 \cos x$$

Substitute the values into the given equation:

$$y'' + y' - 2y = \sin x$$
$$(-A_1 \sin x - A_2 \cos x) + (A_1 \cos x - A_2 \sin x) - 2(A_1 \sin x + A_2 \cos x) = \sin x$$
$$(-3A_1 - A_2) \sin x + (A_1 - 3A_2) \cos x = \sin x$$

This gives the system

$$\begin{cases} -3A_1 - A_2 = 1 & (\sin x \text{ terms}) \\ A_1 - 3A_2 = 0 & (\cos x \text{ terms}) \end{cases}$$

with the solution $A_1 = -\frac{3}{10}$, $A_2 = -\frac{1}{10}$. Thus, the particular solution of the non-homogeneous equation is $y_p = -\frac{3}{10}\sin x - \frac{1}{10}\cos x$, and the general solution is $y = y_h + y_p = C_1 e^x + C_2 e^{-2x} - \frac{3}{10}\sin x - \frac{1}{10}\cos x$. ∎

Note: It can be shown that if y_1 is a solution of $ay'' + by' + cy = F(x)$ and y_2 is a solution of $ay'' + by' + cy = G(x)$, then $y_1 + y_2$ will be a solution of $ay'' + by' + cy = F(x) + G(x)$. (See Problem 54.) This is called the **principle of superposition**. For instance, by combining the results of Examples 1 and 2, we see that a particular solution of the nonhomogeneous linear equation

$$y'' + y' - 2y = 2x^2 - 4x + \sin x$$

is

$$y_p = \overbrace{-x^2 + x - \frac{1}{2}}^{\text{Solution for } F = 2x^2 - 4x} \underbrace{- \frac{3}{10}\sin x - \frac{1}{10}\cos x}_{\text{Solution for } G = \sin x}$$

EXAMPLE 3 Method of undetermined coefficients

Solve $y'' + y' - 2y = 4e^{-2x}$.

Solution

At first glance (looking at $F(x) = 4e^{-2x}$), it may seem that the trial solution should be $\overline{y}_p = Ae^{-2x}$. However, $y_1 = e^{-2x}$ is a solution of $y_1'' + y_1' - 2y_1 = 0$, so it cannot possibly also satisfy the given nonhomogeneous equation.

To deal with this situation, multiply the usual trial solution by x and consider the trial solution $\overline{y}_p = Axe^{-2x}$. Differentiating, we find

$$\overline{y}_p' = A(1 - 2x)e^{-2x} \quad \text{and} \quad \overline{y}_p'' = A(4x - 4)e^{-2x}$$

and by substituting into the given equation, we obtain

$$y'' + y' - 2y = 4e^{-2x}$$
$$A(4x - 4)e^{-2x} + A(1 - 2x)e^{-2x} - 2Axe^{-2x} = 4e^{-2x}$$
$$(4Ax - 4A + A - 2Ax - 2Ax)e^{-2x} = 4e^{-2x}$$
$$-3Ae^{-2x} = 4e^{-2x}$$
$$A = -\frac{4}{3}$$

Thus, $\overline{y}_p = -\frac{4}{3}xe^{-2x}$, so that the general solution is

$$y = y_h + y_p = C_1 e^x + C_2 e^{-2x} - \frac{4}{3}xe^{-2x}$$ ∎

The procedure illustrated in Examples 1–3 can be applied to a differential equation $y'' + ay' + by = F(x)$ only when $F(x)$ has one of the following forms:

a. $F(x) = P_n(x)$, a polynomial of degree n
b. $F(x) = P_n(x)e^{kx}$
c. $F(x) = e^{kx}[P_n(x)\cos\alpha x + Q_n(x)\sin\alpha x]$, where $Q_n(x)$ is another polynomial of degree n

We can now describe the **method of undetermined coefficients**.

Method of Undetermined Coefficients

To solve $ay'' + by' + cy = F(x)$ when $F(x)$ is one of the forms in the preceding list:

1. The solution is of the form $y = y_h + y_p$, where y_h is the general solution of the related homogeneous equation and y_p is a particular solution.
2. Find y_h by solving the related homogeneous equation

$$ay'' + by' + cy = 0$$

3. Find y_p by picking an appropriate trial solution $\overline{y}_p$:

Form of $F(x)$	Corresponding trial expression $\overline{y}_p$
a. $P_n(x) = c_n x^n + \cdots + c_1 x + c_0$	$A_n x^n + \cdots + A_1 x + A_0$
b. $P_n(x)e^{kx}$	$[A_n x^n + A_{n-1}x^{n-1} + \cdots + A_0]e^{kx}$
c. $e^{kx}[P_n(x)\cos \alpha x + Q_n(x)\sin \alpha x]$	$e^{kx}[(A_n x^n + \cdots + A_0)\cos \alpha x$ $+ (B_n x^n + \cdots + B_0)\sin \alpha x]$

4. If no term in the trial expression $\overline{y}_p$ appears in the general homogeneous solution y_h, the particular solution can be found by substituting $\overline{y}_p$ into the equation $ay'' + by' + cy = F(x)$ and solving for the undetermined coefficients.
5. If any term in the trial expression $\overline{y}_p$ appears in y_h, multiply $\overline{y}_p$ by x^k, where k is the smallest integer such that no term in $x^k\overline{y}_p$ is a solution of $ay'' + by' + cy = 0$. Then proceed as in step 4, using $x^k\overline{y}_p$ as the trial solution.

EXAMPLE 4   Finding trial solutions

Determine a suitable trial solution for undetermined coefficients in each of the given cases.

a. $y'' - 4y' + 4y = 3x^2 + 4e^{-2x}$
b. $y'' - 4y' + 4y = 5xe^{2x}$
c. $y'' + 2y' + 5y = 3e^{-x}\cos 2x$

Solution

a. The related homogeneous equation $y'' - 4y' + 4y = 0$ has the characteristic equation $r^2 - 4r + 4 = 0$, which has the root 2 of multiplicity two. Thus, the general homogeneous solution is

$$y_h = C_1 e^{2x} + C_2 x e^{2x}$$

The part of the trial solution for the nonhomogeneous equation that corresponds to $3x^2$ is $A_0 + A_1 x + A_2 x^2$ and the part that corresponds to $4e^{-2x}$ is Be^{-2x}. Since neither part includes terms in y_h, we apply the principle of superposition to conclude that

$$\overline{y}_p = A_0 + A_1 x + A_2 x^2 + Be^{-2x}$$

b. We know from part **a** that the general homogeneous solution is

$$y_h = C_1 e^{2x} + C_2 x e^{2x}$$

The expected trial solution for $5xe^{2x}$ would be $(A_0 + A_1 x)e^{2x}$, but this expression is contained in y_h. If we multiply by x, part of $(A_0 + A_1 x)xe^{2x}$ is still contained in y_h, so we multiply by x again to obtain

$$\overline{y}_p = (A_0 + A_1 x)x^2 e^{2x}$$

c. The related homogeneous equation $y'' + 2y' + 5y = 0$ has the characteristic equation $r^2 + 2r + 5 = 0$. This has complex conjugate roots $r = -1 \pm 2i$, so the general homogeneous solution is

$$y_h = e^{-x}[C_1 \cos 2x + C_2 \sin 2x]$$

Ordinarily, the trial solution for the nonhomogeneous equation would be of the form $e^{-x}[A \cos 2x + B \sin 2x]$, but part of this expression is in y_h. Therefore, we multiply by x to obtain the trial solution

$$\overline{y}_p = xe^{-x}[A \cos 2x + B \sin 2x] \qquad \blacksquare$$

VARIATION OF PARAMETERS

The method of undetermined coefficients applies only when the coefficients a, b, and c are constant in the nonhomogeneous linear equation $ay'' + by' + cy = F(x)$ and the function $F(x)$ has the same general form as a solution of a second-order homogeneous linear differential equation with constant coefficients. Even though many important applications are modeled by differential equations of this type, there are other situations that require a more general procedure.

Our next goal is to examine a method of J. L. Lagrange (see Historical Quest, Problem 55 in Section 11.8) called **variation of parameters**, which can be used to find a particular solution of any nonhomogeneous equation

$$y'' + P(x)y' + Q(x)y = F(x) \quad \text{Note the leading coefficient is 1.}$$

where P, Q, and F are continuous.

To use variation of parameters assumes that we must be able to find two linearly independent solutions $y_1(x)$ and $y_2(x)$ of the related homogeneous equation,

$$y'' + P(x)y' + Q(x)y = 0$$

In practice, if $P(x)$ and $Q(x)$ are not both constants, these may be difficult to find, but once we have them, we assume there is a solution of the nonhomogeneous equation of the form

$$y_p = uy_1 + vy_2$$

Differentiating this expression y_p, we obtain

$$y_p' = u'y_1 + v'y_2 + uy_1' + vy_2'$$

To simplify, assume that

$$u'y_1 + v'y_2 = 0$$

Remember, we need to find only *one* particular solution y_p, and if imposing this side condition makes it easier to find such a y_p, so much the better! With the side condition, we have

$$y_p' = uy_1' + vy_2'$$

and by differentiating again, we obtain

$$y_p'' = uy_1'' + u'y_1' + vy_2'' + v'y_2'$$

Next, we substitute our expressions for y_p' and y_p'' into the given differential equation:

$$
\begin{aligned}
F(x) &= y_p'' + P(x)y_p' + Q(x)y_p \\
&= (uy_1'' + u'y_1' + vy_2'' + v'y_2') + P(x)(uy_1' + vy_2') + Q(x)(uy_1 + vy_2)
\end{aligned}
$$

This can be rewritten as

$$u[y_1'' + P(x)y_1' + Q(x)y_1] + v[y_2'' + P(x)y_2' + Q(x)y_2] + u'y_1' + v'y_2' = F(x)$$

Because y_1 and y_2 are solutions of $y'' + P(x)y' + Q(x)y = 0$, we have

$$u\underbrace{[y_1'' + P(x)y_1' + Q(x)y_1]}_{0} + v\underbrace{[y_2'' + P(x)y_2' + Q(x)y_2]}_{0} + u'y_1' + v'y_2' = F(x)$$

or

$$u'y_1' + v'y_2' = F(x)$$

Thus, the parameters u and v must satisfy the system of equations

$$\begin{cases} u'y_1 + v'y_2 = 0 \\ u'y_1' + v'y_2' = F(x) \end{cases}$$

Solve this system to obtain

$$u' = \frac{-y_2 F(x)}{y_1 y_2' - y_2 y_1'} \quad \text{and} \quad v' = \frac{y_1 F(x)}{y_1 y_2' - y_2 y_1'}$$

where in each case the denominator is not zero, because it is the Wronskian of the linearly independent solutions y_1, y_2 of the related homogeneous differential equation. Integrating, we find

$$u(x) = \int \frac{-y_2 F(x)}{y_1 y_2' - y_2 y_1'}\, dx \quad \text{and} \quad v(x) = \int \frac{y_1 F(x)}{y_1 y_2' - y_2 y_1'}\, dx$$

and by substituting into the expression

$$y_p = uy_1 + vy_2$$

we obtain a particular solution of the given differential equation. Here is a summary of the procedure we have described.

WARNING The coefficient of y'' must be 1 for this method.

Variation of Parameters

To find the general solution of $y'' + P(x)y' + Q(x)y = F(x)$,

Step 1. Find the general solution, $y_h = C_1 y_1 + C_2 y_2$ to the related homogeneous equation, $y'' + P(x)y' + Q(x)y = 0$.

Step 2. Set $y_p = uy_1 + vy_2$ and substitute into the formulas:

$$u' = \frac{-y_2 F(x)}{y_1 y_2' - y_2 y_1'} \qquad v' = \frac{y_1 F(x)}{y_1 y_2' - y_2 y_1'}$$

Step 3. Integrate u' and v' to find u and v.

Step 4. A particular solution is $y_p = uy_1 + vy_2$, and the general solution is $y = y_h + y_p$.

These ideas are illustrated in the next example.

EXAMPLE 5 Variation of parameters

Solve $y'' + 4y = \tan 2x$.

Solution

Notice that this problem cannot be solved by the method of undetermined coefficients, because the right-side function $F(x) = \tan 2x$ is not one of the forms for which the procedure applies.

To apply variation of parameters, begin by solving the related homogeneous equation $y'' + 4y = 0$. The characteristic equation is $r^2 + 4 = 0$ with roots $r = \pm 2i$. These complex roots have $\alpha = 0$ and $\beta = 2$ so that the general solution is

$$y = e^0[C_1 \cos 2x + C_2 \sin 2x] = C_1 \cos 2x + C_2 \sin 2x$$

This means $y_1(x) = \cos 2x$ and $y_2(x) = \sin 2x$. Set $y_p = uy_1 + vy_2$, where

$$u' = \frac{-y_2 F(x)}{y_1 y_2' - y_2 y_1'} = \frac{-\sin 2x \tan 2x}{2 \cos 2x \cos 2x + 2 \sin 2x \sin 2x} = -\frac{\sin^2 2x}{2 \cos 2x}$$

and

$$v' = \frac{y_1 F(x)}{y_1 y_2' - y_2 y_1'} = \frac{\cos 2x \tan 2x}{2 \cos 2x \cos 2x + 2 \sin 2x \sin 2x} = \frac{1}{2} \sin 2x$$

Integrating, we obtain

$$u(x) = \int -\frac{\sin^2 2x}{2 \cos 2x} \, dx \qquad\qquad v(x) = \int \frac{1}{2} \sin 2x \, dx$$

$$= -\frac{1}{2} \int \frac{1 - \cos^2 2x}{\cos 2x} \, dx \qquad\qquad = -\frac{1}{4} \cos 2x$$

$$= -\frac{1}{2} \int (\sec 2x - \cos 2x) \, dx$$

$$= -\frac{1}{2} \left[\frac{1}{2} \ln |\sec 2x + \tan 2x| - \frac{\sin 2x}{2} \right]$$

Thus, a particular solution is

$$y_p = uy_1 + vy_2$$

$$= \left[-\frac{1}{4} \ln |\sec 2x + \tan 2x| + \frac{1}{4} \sin 2x \right] \cos 2x + \left(-\frac{1}{4} \cos 2x \right) \sin 2x$$

$$= -\frac{1}{4} (\cos 2x) \ln |\sec 2x + \tan 2x|$$

Finally, the general solution is

$$y = y_h + y_p = C_1 \cos 2x + C_2 \sin 2x - \frac{1}{4} (\cos 2x) \ln |\sec 2x + \tan 2x| \qquad \blacksquare$$

AN APPLICATION TO *RLC* CIRCUITS

An important application of second-order linear differential equations is in the analysis of electric circuits. Consider a circuit with constant resistance R, inductance L, and capacitance C. Such a circuit is called an **RLC circuit** and is illustrated in Figure 14.10.

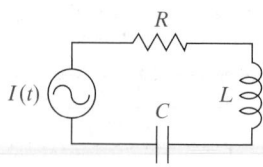

Figure 14.10 An *RLC* circuit

If $I(t)$ is the current in the circuit at time t and $Q(t)$ is the total charge on the capacitor, it is shown in physics that IR is the voltage drop across the resistance, Q/C is the voltage drop across the capacitor, and $L \, dI/dt$ is the voltage drop across the inductance. According to Kirchhoff's second law for circuits, the impressed voltage $E(t)$ in a circuit is the sum of the voltage drops, so that the current $I(t)$ in the circuit satisfies

$$L \frac{dI}{dt} + RI + \frac{Q}{C} = E(t)$$

By differentiating both sides of this equation and using the fact that $I = \dfrac{dQ}{dt}$, we can write

$$L \frac{d^2 I}{dt^2} + R \frac{dI}{dt} + \frac{1}{C} I = \frac{dE}{dt}$$

For instance, suppose the voltage input is sinusoidal—that is, $E(t) = A \sin \omega t$. Then we have $dE/dt = A\omega \cos \omega t$, and the second-order linear differential equation used in the analysis of the circuit is

$$L \frac{d^2 I}{dt^2} + R \frac{dI}{dt} + \frac{1}{C} I = A\omega \cos \omega t$$

To solve this equation, we proceed in the usual way, solving the related homogeneous equation and then finding a particular solution of the nonhomogeneous system. The solution to the related homogeneous equation is called the **transient current** because the current described by this solution usually does not last very long. The part of the nonhomogeneous solution that corresponds to transient current 0 is called the **steady-state current**. Several problems dealing with *RLC* circuits are outlined in the problem set.

14.3 PROBLEM SET

A *In Problems 1–8, find a trial solution $\overline{y}_p$ for use in the method of undetermined coefficients.*

1. $y'' - 6y' = e^{2x}$

2. $y'' + 6y' + 8y = 2 + e^{-3x}$

3. $y'' + 2y' + 2y = e^{-x}$

4. $y'' + 2y' + 2y = \cos x$

5. $y'' + 2y' + 2y = e^{-x} \sin x$

6. $2y'' - y' - 6y = x^2 e^{2x}$

7. $y'' + 4y' + 5y = e^{-2x}(x + \cos x)$

8. $y'' + 4y' + 5y = (e^{-x} \sin x)^2$

For the differential equation

$$y'' + 6y' + 9y = F(x)$$

find a trial solution $\overline{y}_p$ for undetermined coefficients for each choice of $F(x)$ given in Problems 9–16.

9. $3x^3 - 5x$

10. $2x^2 e^{4x}$

11. $x^3 \cos x$

12. $xe^{2x} \sin 5x$

13. $e^{2x} + \cos 3x$

14. $2e^{3x} + 8xe^{-3x}$

15. $4x^3 - x^2 + 5 - 3e^{-x}$

16. $(x^2 + 2x - 6)e^{-3x} \sin 3x$

Use the method of undetermined coefficients to find the general solution of the nonhomogeneous differential equations given in Problems 17–28.

17. $y'' + y' = -3x^2 + 7$

18. $y'' + 6y' + 5y = 2e^x - 3e^{-3x}$

19. $y'' + 8y' + 15y = 3e^{2x}$

20. $2y'' - 5y' - 3y = 5e^{3x}$

21. $y'' + 2y' + 2y = \cos x$

22. $y'' - 6y' + 13y = e^{-3x} \sin 2x$

23. $7y'' + 6y' - y = e^{-x}(x + 1)$

24. $2y'' + 5y' = e^x \sin x$

25. $y'' - y' = x^3 - x + 5$

26. $y'' - y' = (x - 1)e^x$

27. $y'' + 2y' + y = (4 + x)e^{-x}$

28. $y'' - y' - 6y = e^{-2x} + \sin x$

Use variation of parameters to solve the differential equations given in Problems 29–38.

29. $y'' + y = \tan x$

30. $y'' + 8y' + 16y = xe^{-2x}$

31. $y'' - y' - 6y = x^2 e^{2x}$

32. $y'' - 3y' + 2y = \dfrac{e^x}{1 + e^x}$

33. $y'' + 4y = \sec 2x \tan 2x$

34. $y'' + y = \sec^2 x$

35. $y'' + 2y' + y = e^{-x} \ln x$

36. $y'' - 4y' + 4y = \dfrac{e^{2x}}{1 + x}$

37. $y'' - y' = \cos^2 x$

38. $y'' - y' = e^{-2x} \cos e^{-x}$

B *In each of Problems 39–45, use either undetermined coefficients or variation of parameters to find the particular solution of the differential equation that satisfies the specified initial conditions.*

39. $y'' - y' = 2\cos^2 x; \ y(0) = y'(0) = 0$

40. $y'' - y' = e^{-2x} \cos e^{-x}; \ y(0) = y'(0) = 0$

41. $y'' + 9y = 4e^{3x}; \ y(0) = 0, \ y'(0) = 2$

42. $y'' - 6y = x^2 - 3x; \ y(0) = 3, \ y'(0) = -1$

43. $y'' + 9y = x; \ y(0) = 0, \ y'(0) = 4$

44. $y'' + y' = 2\sin x; \ y(0) = 0, \ y'(0) = -4$

45. $y'' + y = \cot x; \ y(\frac{\pi}{2}) = 0, \ y'\left(\frac{\pi}{2}\right) = 5$

46. Find the general solution of the differential equation $y'' + y' - 6y = F(x)$, where F is the function whose graph is shown in Figure 14.11. *Hint*: Set up and solve two separate differential equations.

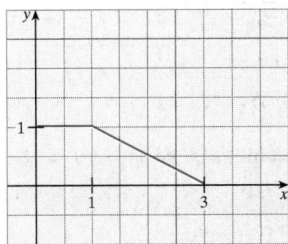

Figure 14.11 Graph of F for Problem 46

47. Find the general solution of the differential equation $y'' + 5y' + 6y = F(x)$ where F is the function whose graph is shown in Figure 14.12. *Hint*: Set up and solve three separate differential equations.

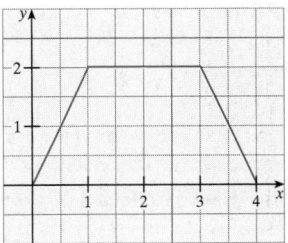

Figure 14.12 Graph of F for Problem 47

48. Find the steady-state current and the transient current in an RLC circuit with $L = 4$ henries, $R = 8$ ohms, $C = \frac{1}{8}$ farad, and $E(t) = 16 \sin t$ volts. You may assume that $I(0) = 0$ and $I'(0) = 0$.

49. Find the steady-state current and the transient current in an RLC circuit with $L = 1$ henry, $R = 10$ ohms, $C = \frac{1}{9}$ farad, and $E(t) = 9 \cos t$ volts. You may assume that $I(0) = 0$ and $I'(0) = 0$.

50. Work Problem 48 for the case where $E(t) = 10te^{-t}$.

51. Work Problem 49 for the case where $E(t) = 5t \sin t$.

C **52.** Theorem 14.4 is also valid when the coefficients a and b are continuous functions of x. Solve the differential equation

$$x^2 y'' - 3xy + 4y = x \ln x$$

by completing the following steps:

a. The related homogeneous equation

$$x^2 y'' - 3xy' + 4y = 0$$

has one solution of the form $y_1 = x^n$. Find n, and then use reduction of order to find a second, linearly independent solution y_2.

b. Use variation of parameters to find a particular solution y_p of the given nonhomogeneous equation. Then use Theorem 14.4 to write the general solution. *Hint*: Divide the differential equation by x^2.

53. Repeat Problem 52 for the equation

$$(1 + x^2)y'' + 2xy' - 2y = \tan^{-1} x$$

54. The principle of superposition Let y_1 be a solution to the second-order linear differential equation

$$y'' + P(x)y' + Q(x)y = F_1(x)$$

and let y_2 satisfy

$$y'' + P(x)y' + Q(x)y = F_2(x)$$

Show that $y_1 + y_2$ satisfies the differential equation

$$y'' + P(x)y' + Q(x)y = F_1(x) + F_2(x)$$

CHAPTER 14 REVIEW

Proficiency Examination

CONCEPT PROBLEMS

1. What is a separable differential equation?
2. What is a homogeneous differential equation?
3. What is the form of a first-order linear differential equation?
4. What is an exact differential equation?
5. Describe Euler's method.
6. Define what it means for a set of functions to be linearly independent.
7. What is the Wronskian, and how is it used to test for linear independence?
8. **a.** What is the characteristic equation of $ay'' + by' + cy = 0$?
   b. What is the general solution of a second-order homogeneous equation?
9. Describe the form of the general solution of a second-order nonhomogeneous equation.
10. Describe the method of undetermined coefficients.
11. Describe the method of variation of parameters.

PRACTICE PROBLEMS

Solve the differential equations in Problems 12–18.

12. $\dfrac{dy}{dx} = \sqrt{\dfrac{1 - y^2}{1 + x^2}}$ **13.** $\dfrac{x}{y^2}\,dx - \dfrac{x^2}{y^3}\,dy = 0$

14. $\dfrac{dy}{dx} = \dfrac{2x + y}{3x}$ **15.** $xy\,dy = (x^2 - y^2)\,dx$

16. $x^2\,dy - (x^2 + y^2)\,dx = 0$

17. $y'' + 2y' + 2y = \sin x$

18. $(3x^2 e^{-y} + y^{-2} + 2xy^{-3})\,dx$
$\quad + (-x^3 e^{-y} - 2xy^{-3} - 3x^2 y^{-4})\,dy = 0$

19. A spring with spring constant $k = 30$ lb/ft hangs in a vertical position with its upper end fixed and an 8-lb object attached to its lower end. The object is pulled down 4 in. from the equilibrium position of the spring and is then released. Find the displacement $x(t)$ of the object, assuming that air resistance is $0.8v$, where $v(t)$ is the velocity of the object at time t.

20. An RLC circuit has inductance $L = 0.1$ henry, resistance $R = 25$ ohms, and capacitance $C = 200$ microfarads (i.e., 200×10^{-6} farad). If there is a variable voltage source of $E(t) = 50 \cos 100t$ in the circuit, what is the current $I(t)$ at time t? Assume that when $t = 0$, there is no charge and no current flowing.

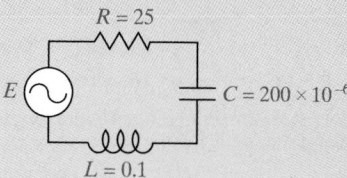

Supplementary Problems

1. Consider the differential equation

$$\frac{dy}{dx} = 2x - 3y$$

   a. Use the slope field to sketch the particular solution that passes through $(0, 1)$.
   b. Use Euler's method to find a solution for the initial value problem in part **a** for $0 \le x \le 1$ and $h = 0.2$.

2. Consider the differential equation

$$\frac{dy}{dx} = x^2 y$$

   a. Use the slope field to sketch the particular solution that passes through $(1, 2)$.
   b. Use Euler's method to find a solution for the initial value problem in part **a** for $1 \le x \le 2$ and $h = 0.2$.

Find the general solution of the given first-order differential equations in Problems 3–20.

3. $\dfrac{dy}{dx} = \dfrac{-4x}{y^3}$

4. $x\,dy + (3y - xe^{x^2})\,dx = 0$

5. $y^2\,dy - (x^2 + \dfrac{y^3}{x})\,dx = 0$

6. $\dfrac{x}{y}\,dy + \left(\dfrac{3y}{x} - 5\right)\,dx = 0$

7. $y\dfrac{dy}{dx} = e^{2x - y^2}$

8. $dy = (3y + e^x + \cos x)\,dx$

9. $dy - (5y + e^{5x} \sin x)\, dx = 0$

10. $x^2 \, dy = (x^2 - y^2)\, dx$

11. $(1 - xe^y)\, dy = e^y \, dx$

12. $xy \, dx + (1 + x^2)\, dy = 0$

13. $x \, dy = (y + \sqrt{x^2 - y^2})\, dx$

14. $2xye^{x^2} \, dx - e^{x^2} \, dy = 0$

15. $(y - xy)\, dx + x^3 \, dy = 0$

16. $\dfrac{dy}{dx} = 2y \cot 2x + 3 \csc 2x$

17. $\left(4x^3 y^3 + \dfrac{1}{x}\right) dx + \left(3x^4 y^2 - \dfrac{1}{y}\right) dy = 0$

18. $(-y \sin xy + 2x)\, dx + (3y^2 - x \sin xy)\, dy = 0$

19. $\sin y \, dx + (e^x + e^{-x}) \sin y \, dy = 0$

20. $\dfrac{dy}{dx} + 2y \cot x + \sin 2x = 0$

In Problems 21–28, find

a. *the general solution y_h of the related homogeneous equation*

b. *a particular solution y_p of the nonhomogeneous equation*

21. $y'' - 9y = 1 + x$

22. $y'' - 2y' + y = e^x$

23. $y'' - 5y' + 6y = x^2 e^x$

24. $y'' + 2y' + y = \sinh x$

25. $y'' - 3y' + 2y = x^3 e^x$

26. $14y'' + 29y' - 15y = \cos x$

27. $y'' + y = \tan^2 x$

28. $y'' + y = \sec x$

29. Solve $\dfrac{d^2 y}{dx^2} = e^{-3x}$ subject to the initial conditions $y(0) = y'(0) = 0$.

30. Use the substitution $p = dy/dx$ to solve the differential equation
$$\frac{d^2 y}{dx^2} = \left(\frac{dy}{dx}\right)^3 + \frac{dy}{dx}$$

31. Solve the system of differential equations
$$\frac{dx}{dt} = -2x \qquad \frac{dy}{dt} = -3y + 2x \qquad \frac{dz}{dt} = 3y$$
subject to the initial conditions $x(0) = 1$, $y(0) = 0$, $z(0) = 0$.

32. Find a curve $y = f(x)$ that passes through $(1, 2)$ and has the property that the y-intercept of the tangent line at each point $P(x, y)$ is equal to y^2.

33. Find a curve that passes through the point $(1, 2)$ and has the property that the length of the part of the tangent line between each point $P(x, y)$ on the curve and the y-axis is equal to the y-intercept of the tangent line at P.

34. Find a curve that passes through $(1, 2)$ and has the property that the normal line at any point $P(x, y)$ on the curve and the line joining P to the origin form an isosceles triangle with the x-axis as its base.

Orthogonal trajectories   *Recall from Section 5.6 that the orthogonal trajectories of a given family of curves are another family with the following property. Every time a member of the second family intersects a member of the given family, the tangent lines to the two curves at the common point intersect at right angles. Find the orthogonal trajectories for the families of curves in Problems 35–38.*

35. $e^x + e^{-y} = C$

36. $3x^2 + 5y^2 = C$

37. $x^2 - y^2 = Cx$

38. $y = \dfrac{Cx}{x^2 + 1}$

39. Use reduction of order to find the general solution of the Legendre equation
$$(1 - x^2)y'' - 2xy' + 2y = 0$$
given that $y_1 = x$ is one solution.

40. Find functions $x = x(t)$ and $y = y(t)$ that satisfy the linear system
$$\frac{dx}{dt} = x + y \qquad \frac{dy}{dt} = x^2 - y^2$$
Sketch the solution curve $(x(t), y(t))$ that contains the point $(0, 2)$. *Hint*: Note that $\dfrac{dy}{dx} = \dfrac{y'(t)}{x'(t)}$.

41. Solve the second-order differential equation $xy'' + 2y' = x$ by setting $p = y'$ to convert it to a first-order equation in p.

42. Find an equation for a curve for which the radius of curvature is proportional to the slope of the tangent line at each point $P(x, y)$.

43. Solve the differential equation
$$\frac{dx}{dy} - \frac{x}{y} = ye^y$$

44. A ship weighing 64,000 tons [mass = $(64,000)(2,000)/32$ slugs] starts from rest and is driven by the constant thrust of its propellers. Suppose the propellers supply 250,000 lb of thrust and the resistance of the water is $12,000v$ lb, where $v(t)$ is the velocity of the ship. Set up and solve a differential equation for $v(t)$.

45. A 10-ft uniform chain (see Figure 14.13) of mass m is hanging over a peg so that 3 ft are on one side and 7 ft are on the other. Set up and solve a differential equation to find how long it takes for the chain to slide off the peg. Neglect the friction.

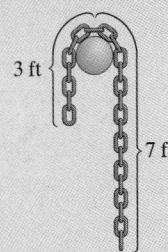

3 ft

7 ft

Figure 14.13   Problem 45

46. When an object weighing 10 lb is suspended from a spring, the spring is stretched 2 in. from its equilibrium position. The upper end of the spring is given a motion of $y = 2(\sin t + \cos t)$ ft. Find the displacement $x(t)$ of the object.

47. A horizontal beam is freely supported at both ends, as shown in Figure 14.14.

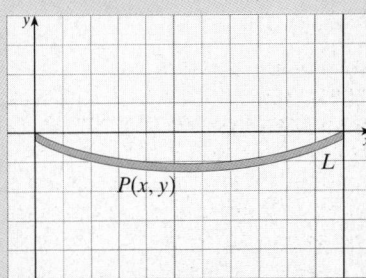

$P(x, y)$ L

Figure 14.14   Problem 47

Suppose the load on the beam is W pounds per foot and one end of the beam is at the origin, and the other end of the beam is at $(L, 0)$. Then the deflection y of the beam at point x is modeled by the differential equation

$$EI\frac{d^2y}{dx^2} = WLx - \frac{1}{2}Wx^2$$

for positive constants E and I.

a. Solve this equation to obtain the deflection $y(x)$. Note that $y(0) = y(L) = 0$.

b. What is the maximum deflection in the beam?

48. Consider the **Clairaut equation**

$$y = xy' + f(y')$$

a. Differentiate both sides of this equation to obtain

$$[x + f'(y')]y'' = 0$$

Because one of the two factors in the product on the left must be 0, we have two cases to consider. What is the solution if $y'' = 0$? This is the *general solution*.

b. What is the solution if

$$x + f'(y') = 0$$

(This solution is called the *singular solution*.) *Hint*: Use the parameterization $y' = t$.

c. Find the general and singular solutions for the Clairaut equation

$$y = xy' + \sqrt{4 + (y')^2}$$

49. A differential equation of the form

$$x^2y'' + Axy' + By = F(x)$$

with $x \neq 0$ is called an **Euler equation**. To find a general solution of the related homogeneous equation

$$x^2y'' + Axy' + By = 0$$

we assume that there are solutions of the form $y = x^m$.

a. Show that m must satisfy

$$m^2 + (A - 1)m + B = 0$$

This is the characteristic equation for the Euler equation.

b. **Distinct real roots.** Characterize the solutions of the related homogeneous equation in the case where

$$(A - 1)^2 > 4B$$

c. **Repeated real roots.** Characterize the solutions of the related homogeneous equation in the case where

$$(A - 1)^2 = 4B$$

d. **Complex conjugate roots.** Suppose that

$$(A - 1)^2 < 4B$$

and that $\alpha \pm \beta i$ are the roots of the characteristic equation. Verify that $y_1 = x^\alpha \cos(\beta \ln |x|)$ is one solution. Use reduction of order to find a second solution y_2, then characterize the general solution.

50. Find the general solution of the Euler equation

$$x^2y'' + 7xy' + 9y = \sqrt{x}$$

Hint: Use the result of Problem 49 along with variation of parameters.

51. In certain biological studies, it is important to analyze *predator-prey* relationships. Suppose $x(t)$ is the prey population and $y(t)$ is the predator population at time t. Then these populations change at rates

$$\frac{dx}{dt} = a_{11}x - a_{12}y \qquad \frac{dy}{dt} = a_{21}x - a_{22}y$$

where a_{11} is the natural growth rate of the prey, a_{12} is the predation rate, a_{21} measures the food supply of the predators, and a_{22} is the death rate of the predators. Outline a procedure for solving this system.

52. Consider the almost homogeneous differential equation

$$\frac{dy}{dx} = f\left(\frac{ax + by + c}{rx + sy + t}\right)$$

with $as = br$ (recall Problem 60, Section 14.1).

a. Let $u = \dfrac{ax + by}{a}$. Show that $u = \dfrac{rx + sy}{r}$ and

$$\frac{du}{dx} = \frac{a}{b}\left(\frac{du}{dx} - 1\right).$$

b. Verify that by making the change of variable suggested in part **a**, you can rewrite the given differential equation in the separable form

$$\frac{du}{1 + \dfrac{b}{a}f\left(\dfrac{au + c}{ru + t}\right)} = dx$$

c. Use the procedure outlined in parts **a** and **b** to solve the almost homogeneous differential equation

$$\frac{dy}{dx} = \frac{2x + y - 3}{4x + 2y + 5}$$

53. **Putnam Examination Problem** Find all solutions of the equation

$$yy'' - 2(y')^2 = 0$$

that pass through the point $x = 1$, $y = 1$.

54. **Putnam Examination Problem** A coast artillery gun can fire at any angle of elevation between $0°$ and $90°$ in a fixed vertical plane. If air resistance is neglected and the muzzle velocity is constant $(v(0) = v_0)$, determine the set H of points in the plane and above the horizontal that can be hit.

55. **Putnam Examination Problem** Show that

$$x + \frac{2}{3}x^3 + \frac{2 \cdot 4}{3 \cdot 5}x^5 + \frac{2 \cdot 4 \cdot 6}{3 \cdot 5 \cdot 7}x^7 + \cdots = \frac{\sin^{-1} x}{\sqrt{1 - x^2}} + \frac{x}{2}$$

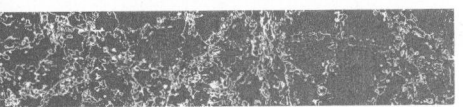

Group Research Project*

Save the Perch Project

This project is to be done in groups of three or four students. Each group will submit a single written report.

Happy Valley Pond is currently populated by yellow perch. A map is shown in Figure 14.15. Water flows into the pond from two springs and evaporates from the pond, as shown by the following table.

Spring	Dry Season	Rainy Season
A	50 gal/h	60 gal/h
B	60 gal/h	75 gal/h
Evaporation:	110 gal/h	75 gal/h

Figure 14.15 Happy Valley Pond is fed by two springs A and B

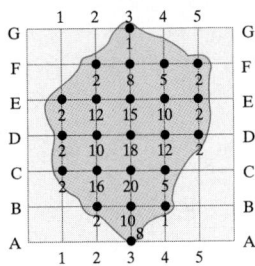

AMONG all the mathematical disciplines the theory of differential equations is the most important .... It furnishes the explanation of all those elementary manifestations of nature which involve time ....

——Sophus Lie
Leipziger Berichte, 47 (1895).

Unfortunately, spring B has become contaminated with salt and is now 10% salt, which means that 10% of a gallon of water from spring B is salt. The yellow perch will start to die if the concentration of salt in the pond rises to 1%. Assume that the salt will not evaporate but will mix thoroughly with the water in the pond. There was no salt in the pond before the contamination of spring B. Your group has been called upon by the Happy Valley Bureau of Fisheries to try to save the perch.

Your paper should include the number of gallons of water in the pond when the water level is exactly even with the top of the spillover dam. The overflow goes over the dam into Bubbling Brook. The following table gives a series of measurements of the depth of the pond at the indicated points when the water level was exactly even with the top of the spillover dam.

DEPTH OF HAPPY VALLEY POND (Location/depth)

A3/8 ft	B2/2 ft	B3/10 ft	B4/1 ft	C1/2 ft	C2/16 ft	C3/20ft
C4/5 ft	D1/2 ft	D2/10 ft	D3/18 ft	D4/12 ft	D5/2 ft	E1/2 ft
E2/12 ft	E3/15 ft	E4/10 ft	E5/2 ft	F2/2 ft	F3/8 ft	F4/5 ft
F5/2 ft	G3/1 ft					

Let $t = 0$ hours correspond to the time when spring B became contaminated. Assume it is the dry season and that at time $t = 0$ the water level of the pond was exactly even with the top of the spillover dam. Write a differential equation for the amount of salt in the pond after t hours. Draw a graph of the amount of salt in the pond versus time for the next 3 mo. How much salt will there be in the pond in the long run, and do the fish die? If so, when do they start to die? It is very difficult to find where the contamination of spring B originates, so the Happy Valley Bureau of Fisheries proposed to flush the pond by running 100 gal of pure water per hour through the pond. Your report should include an analysis of this plan and any modifications or improvements that could help save the perch.

*This group project is courtesy of Diane Schwartz from Ithaca College, New York.

Appendices

Introduction to the Theory of Limits

In Section 2.1 we defined the limit of a function as follows:
The notation

$$\lim_{x \to c} f(x) = L$$

is read "the limit of $f(x)$ as x approaches c is L" and means that the function values $f(x)$ can be made arbitrarily close to L by choosing x sufficiently close to c but not equal to c.

This informal definition was valuable because it gave you an intuitive feeling for the limit of a function and allowed you to develop a working knowledge of this fundamental concept. For theoretical work, however, this definition will not suffice, because it gives no precise, quantifiable meaning to the terms "arbitrarily close to L" and "sufficiently close to c." The following definition, derived from the work of Cauchy and Weierstrass, gives precision to the limit definition and was also first stated in Section 2.1.

**Limit of a Function
(Formal definition)**

> The limit statement
>
> $$\lim_{x \to c} f(x) = L$$
>
> means that for each number $\epsilon > 0$, there corresponds a number $\delta > 0$ with the property that
>
> $$|f(x) - L| < \epsilon \qquad \text{whenever} \qquad 0 < |x - c| < \delta$$

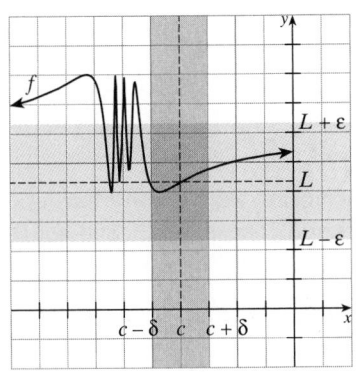

Figure A.1 The epsilon-delta definition of limit

Behind the formal language is a fairly straightforward idea. In particular, to establish a specific limit, say $\lim_{x \to c} f(x) = L$, a number $\epsilon > 0$ is chosen first to establish a desired degree of proximity to L, and then a number $\delta > 0$ is found that determines how close x must be to c to ensure that $f(x)$ is within ϵ units of L.

The situation is illustrated in Figure A.1, which shows a function that satisfies the conditions of the definition. Notice that whenever x is within δ units of c (but not equal to c), the point $(x, f(x))$ on the graph of f must lie in the rectangle (shaded region) formed by the intersection of the horizontal band of width 2ϵ centered at L and the vertical band of width 2δ centered at c. The smaller the ϵ-interval around the proposed limit L, generally the smaller the δ-interval will need to be in order for $f(x)$ to lie in the ϵ-interval. If such a δ can be found no matter how small ϵ is, then L must be the limit.

THE BELIEVER/DOUBTER FORMAT

The limit process can be thought of as a "contest" between a "believer" who claims that $\lim_{x \to c} f(x) = L$ and a "doubter" who disputes this claim. The contest begins with the doubter choosing a positive number ϵ and the believer countering with a positive number δ.

When will the believer win the argument and when will the doubter win? As you can see from Figure A.1, if the believer has the "correct limit" L, then no matter how the doubter chooses ϵ, the believer can find a δ so that the graph of $y = f(x)$ for $c - \delta < x < c + \delta$ will lie inside the heavily shaded rectangle in Figure A.1 (with the possible exception of $x = c$); that is, inside the rectangular region

$$R: \quad \text{width: } [c - \delta, c + \delta]; \quad \text{height: } [L - \epsilon, L + \epsilon]$$

On the other hand, if the believer tries to defend an incorrect value w (for "wrong") as the limit, then it will be possible for the doubter to choose an ϵ so that at least part of the curve $y = f(x)$ will lie outside the heavily shaded rectangle R, no matter what value of δ is chosen by the believer (see Figure A.2).

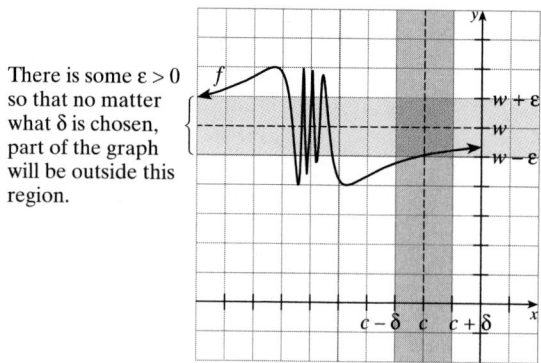

There is some $\epsilon > 0$ so that no matter what δ is chosen, part of the graph will be outside this region.

Figure A.2   False limit scenario

To avoid an endless chain of ϵ-δ challenges, the believer usually tries to settle the issue by producing a formula relating the choice of δ to the doubter's ϵ that will satisfy the requirement no matter what ϵ is chosen. The believer/doubter format is used in Example 1 to verify a given limit statement (believer "wins") and in Example 2 to show that a certain limit does not exist (doubter "wins").

EXAMPLE 1   Verifying a limit claim (believer wins)

Show that $\lim_{x \to 2} (2x + 1) = 5$.

Solution

Let $f(x) = 2x + 1$. To verify the given limit statement, we begin by having the doubter choose a positive number ϵ. To help the believer, choose $\delta > 0$, and note the computation in the following box.

> $|(2x + 1) - 5| = |2x - 4| = 2|x - 2|$
> Thus, if $0 < |x - c| < \delta$ or $0 < |x - 2| < \delta$, then
> $|(2x + 1) - 5| < 2\delta$

The believer *wants* $|f(x) - L| < \epsilon$, so we see that the believer should choose $2\delta = \epsilon$, or $\delta = \frac{\epsilon}{2}$

With the information shown in this box, we can now make the following argument, which uses the formal definition of limit:

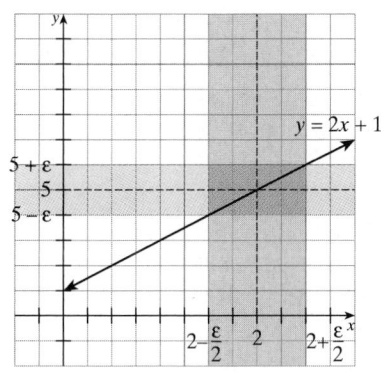

Figure A.3 Verifying $\lim\limits_{x \to 2}(2x + 1) = 5$:
Given $\epsilon > 0$, choose $\delta = \dfrac{\epsilon}{2}$.

Let $\epsilon > 0$ be given. The believer chooses $\delta = \frac{\epsilon}{2} > 0$ so that

$$|f(x) - L| = |(2x + 1) - 5| < 2\delta = 2\left(\frac{\epsilon}{2}\right) = \epsilon$$

whenever $0 < |x - 2| < \delta$, and the limit statement is verified. The graphical relationship between ϵ and δ is shown in Figure A.3. Notice that no matter what ϵ is chosen by the doubter, by choosing a number that is one-half of that ϵ, the believer will force the function to stay within the shaded portion of the graph, as shown in Figure A.3. ■

EXAMPLE 2   **Disproving a limit claim (doubter wins)**

Determine whether $\lim\limits_{x \to 2} \dfrac{2x^2 - 3x - 2}{x - 2} = 6$.

Solution

Let $f(x) = \dfrac{2x^2 - 3x - 2}{x - 2} = \dfrac{(2x + 1)(x - 2)}{x - 2} = 2x + 1,\ x \neq 2$. Once again, the doubter will choose a positive number ϵ and the believer must respond with a δ. As before, the believer does some preliminary work with $f(x) - L$:

$$\left|\frac{2x^2 - 3x - 2}{x - 2} - 6\right| = \left|\frac{2x^2 - 3x - 2 - 6x + 12}{x - 2}\right|$$

$$= \left|\frac{2x^2 - 9x + 10}{x - 2}\right|$$

$$= \left|\frac{(2x - 5)(x - 2)}{x - 2}\right|$$

$$= |2x - 5|$$

The believer wants to write this expression in terms of $x - c = x - 2$. This example does not seem to "fall into place" as did Example 1. Let's analyze the situation shown in Figure A.4.

The doubter observes that if $\epsilon > 0$ is small enough, at least part of the line $y = 2x + 1$ for $0 < |x - 2| < \delta$ lies outside the shaded rectangle

$$R: \quad \text{width:} \quad [2 - \delta, 2 + \delta]; \qquad \text{height:} \quad [6 - \epsilon, 6 + \epsilon]$$

regardless of the value of $\delta > 0$. For instance, suppose $\epsilon < 1$. Then, if δ is any positive number, we have

$$\left|f\left(2 - \frac{\delta}{2}\right) - 6\right| = \left|\left[2\left(2 - \frac{\delta}{2}\right) + 1\right] - 6\right| = |-\delta - 1| > 1$$

so $|f(x) - 6| < \epsilon$ is not satisfied for all $0 < |x - 2| < \delta$ (in particular, not for $x = 2 - \frac{\delta}{2}$). Thus, $\lim\limits_{x \to 2} \dfrac{2x^2 - 3x - 2}{x - 2} = 6$ is false. ■

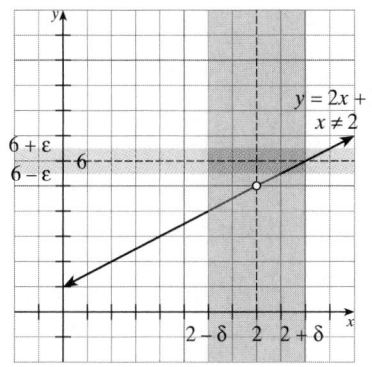

Figure A.4 Example of an incorrect limit statement

The believer/doubter format is a useful device for dramatizing the way certain choices are made in epsilon-delta arguments, but it is customary to be less "chatty" in formal mathematical proofs.

EXAMPLE 3   **An epsilon-delta proof of a limit of a rational function**

Show that $\lim\limits_{x \to 2} \dfrac{x^2 - 2x + 2}{x - 4} = -1$.

Solution

Let $f(x) = \dfrac{x^2 - 2x + 2}{x - 4}$. We have

$$|f(x) - L| = \left| \dfrac{x^2 - 2x + 2}{x - 4} - (-1) \right|$$

$$= \left| \dfrac{x^2 - x - 2}{x - 4} \right|$$

$$= \underbrace{|x - 2| \left| \dfrac{x + 1}{x - 4} \right|}$$

This must be less than the given ϵ
whenever x is near 2, but not equal to 2.

Certainly $|x - 2|$ is small if x is near 2, and the factor $\left| \dfrac{x + 1}{x - 4} \right|$ is not large (it is close to $\frac{3}{2}$). Note that if $|x - 2|$ is small it is reasonable to assume

$$|x - 2| < 1 \quad \text{so that} \quad 1 < x < 3$$

Let $g(x) = \dfrac{x + 1}{x - 4} = 1 + \dfrac{5}{x - 4}$; $g'(x) = -\dfrac{5}{(x - 4)^2} < 0$ on $(1, 3)$. Thus $g(x)$ is decreasing on $(1, 3)$ and

$$g(3) = \dfrac{4}{-1} < \dfrac{x + 1}{x - 4} < \dfrac{2}{-3} = g(1)$$

Hence, if $|x - 2| < 1$, then

$$-4 < \dfrac{x + 1}{x - 4} < 4 \qquad \text{Because} \quad -\dfrac{2}{3} < 4$$

and

$$\left| \dfrac{x + 1}{x - 4} \right| < 4$$

Now let $\epsilon > 0$ be given. If simultaneously

$$|x - 2| < \dfrac{\epsilon}{4} \quad \text{and} \quad \left| \dfrac{x + 1}{x - 4} \right| < 4$$

then

$$|f(x) - L| = |x - 2| \left| \dfrac{x + 1}{x - 4} \right| < \dfrac{\epsilon}{4}(4) = \epsilon$$

Thus, we have only to take δ to be the smaller of the two numbers 1 and $\frac{\epsilon}{4}$ in order to guarantee that

$$|f(x) - L| < \epsilon$$

That is, given $\epsilon > 0$, choose δ to be the smaller of the numbers 1 and $\frac{\epsilon}{4}$. We write this as $\delta = \min\left(1, \frac{\epsilon}{4}\right)$. We can confirm this result by looking at the graph of $y = f(x)$ in Figure A.5). ∎

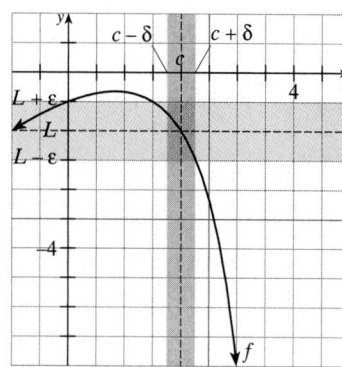

Figure A.5 $\lim\limits_{x \to 2} \dfrac{x^2 - 2x + 2}{x - 4} = -1$

EXAMPLE 4 An epsilon-delta proof that a limit does not exist

Show that $\lim\limits_{x \to 0} \dfrac{1}{x}$ does not exist.

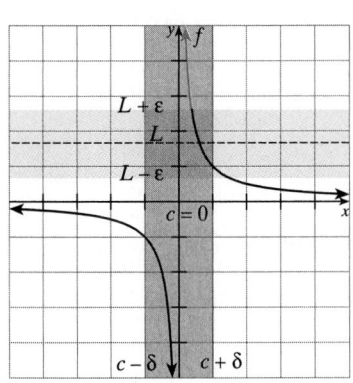

Figure A.6 $\lim\limits_{x\to 0} \dfrac{1}{x}$

Solution

Let $f(x) = \dfrac{1}{x}$ and L be any number. Suppose that $\lim\limits_{x\to 0} f(x) = L$. Look at the graph of f, as shown in Figure A.6. It would seem that no matter what value of ϵ is chosen, it would be impossible to find a corresponding δ. Consider the absolute value expression required by the definition of limit: If

$$|f(x) - L| < \epsilon, \qquad \text{or, for this example,} \qquad \left| \frac{1}{x} - L \right| < \epsilon$$

then

$$-\epsilon < \frac{1}{x} - L < \epsilon \qquad \text{\textit{Property of absolute value}}$$
$$\text{\textit{(Table 1.1, p. 3)}}$$

and

$$L - \epsilon < \frac{1}{x} < L + \epsilon$$

If $\epsilon = 1$ (not a particularly small ϵ), then

$$\left| \frac{1}{x} \right| < |L| + 1$$

$$|x| > \frac{1}{|L| + 1}$$

and thus x is not close to zero which proves (since L was chosen arbitrarily) that $\lim\limits_{x\to 0} \dfrac{1}{x}$ does not exist. In other words, since $|x|$ can be chosen so that $0 < |x| < \dfrac{1}{|L|+1}$, then $\dfrac{1}{|x|}$ will be very large, and it will be impossible to squeeze $\dfrac{1}{x}$ between $L - \epsilon$ and $L + \epsilon$ for any L. ∎

SELECTED THEOREMS WITH FORMAL PROOFS

Next, we will prove two theoretical results using the formal definition of the limit. These two theorems are useful tools in the development of calculus. The first states that the points on a graph that are on or above the x-axis cannot possibly "tend toward" a point *below* the axis, as shown in Figure A.7.

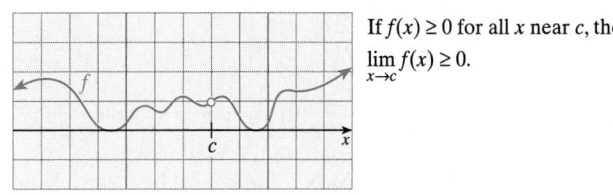

If $f(x) \geq 0$ for all x near c, then $\lim\limits_{x\to c} f(x) \geq 0.$

Figure A.7 Limit limitation theorem

THEOREM A.1 **Limit limitation theorem**

Suppose $\lim\limits_{x\to c} f(x)$ exists and $f(x) \geq 0$ throughout an open interval containing the number c, except possibly at c itself. Then

$$\lim\limits_{x\to c} f(x) \geq 0$$

Proof   Let $L = \lim\limits_{x \to c} f(x)$. To show that $L \geq 0$, assume the contrary; that is, assume $L < 0$. According to the definition of limit (with $\epsilon = -L$), there is a number $\delta > 0$ such that

$$|f(x) - L| < -L \qquad \text{whenever} \qquad 0 < |x - c| < \delta$$

Thus,

$$f(x) - L < -L$$
$$f(x) < 0$$

whenever $0 < |x - c| < \delta$, which contradicts the hypothesis that $f(x) \geq 0$ throughout an open interval containing c (with the possible exception of $x = c$). The contradiction forces us to reject the assumption that $L < 0$, so $L \geq 0$, as required.   ❏

WARNING   It may seem reasonable to conjecture that if $f(x) > 0$ throughout an open interval containing c, then $\lim\limits_{x \to c} f(x) > 0$. This is not necessarily true, and the most that can be said in this situation is that $\lim\limits_{x \to c} f(x) \geq 0$, if the limit exists. For example, if

$$f(x) = \begin{cases} x^2 & \text{for } x \neq 0 \\ 1 & \text{for } x = 0 \end{cases}$$

then $f(x) > 0$ for all x, but $\lim\limits_{x \to 0} f(x) = 0$.

Useful information about the limit of a given function f can often be obtained by examining other functions that bound f from above and below. For example, in Section 2.1 we discovered

$$\lim_{x \to 0} \frac{\sin x}{x} = 1$$

by using a table. We justified the limit statement in Section 2.2 by using a geometric argument to show that

$$\cos x \leq \frac{\sin x}{x} \leq 1$$

for all x near 0 and then noting that since $\cos x$ and 1 both tend toward 1 as x approaches 0, the function

$$\frac{\sin x}{x}$$

which is "squeezed" between them, must converge to 1 as well. Theorem A.2 provides the theoretical basis for this method of proof.

THEOREM A.2   The squeeze rule

If $g(x) \leq f(x) \leq h(x)$ for all x in an open interval containing c (except possibly at c itself) and if

$$\lim_{x \to c} g(x) = \lim_{x \to c} h(x) = L$$

then $\lim\limits_{x \to c} f(x) = L$. (This is stated, without proof, in Section 2.2.)

Proof   Let $\epsilon > 0$ be given. Since $\lim\limits_{x \to c} g(x) = L$ and $\lim\limits_{x \to c} h(x) = L$, there are positive numbers δ_1 and δ_2 such that

$$|g(x) - L| < \epsilon \quad \text{and} \quad |h(x) - L| < \epsilon$$

whenever

$$0 < |x - c| < \delta_1 \quad \text{and} \quad 0 < |x - c| < \delta_2$$

respectively. Let δ be the smaller of the numbers δ_1 and δ_2. Then, if x is a number that satisfies $0 < |x - c| < \delta$, we have

$$-\epsilon < g(x) - L \leq f(x) - L \leq h(x) - L < \epsilon$$

and it follows that $|f(x) - L| < \epsilon$. Thus, $\lim\limits_{x \to c} f(x) = L$, as claimed.   ❏

The geometric interpretation of the squeeze rule is shown in Figure A.8. Notice that since $g(x) \le f(x) \le h(x)$, the graph of f is "squeezed" between those of g and h in the neighborhood of c. Thus, if the bounding graphs converge to a common point P as x approaches c, then the graph of f must also converge to P as well.

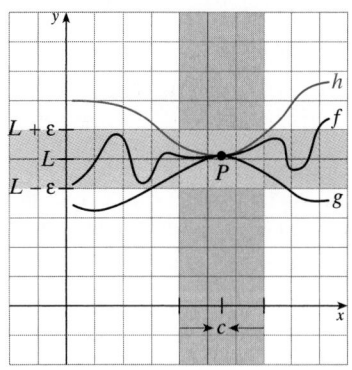

Figure A.8   The squeeze rule

A.1   PROBLEM SET

B *In Problems 1–6, use the believer/doubter format to prove or disprove the given limit statement.*

1. $\lim\limits_{x \to 1}(2x - 5) = -3$

2. $\lim\limits_{x \to -2}(3x + 7) = 1$

3. $\lim\limits_{x \to 1}(3x + 1) = 5$

4. $\lim\limits_{x \to 2}(x^2 - 2) = 5$

5. $\lim\limits_{x \to 2}(x^2 + 2) = 6$

6. $\lim\limits_{x \to 1}(x^2 - 3x + 2) = 0$

In Problems 7–12, use the formal definition of the limit to prove or disprove the given limit statement.

7. $\lim\limits_{x \to 2}(x + 3) = 5$

8. $\lim\limits_{t \to 0}(3t - 1) = 0$

9. $\lim\limits_{x \to -2}(3x + 7) = 1$

10. $\lim\limits_{x \to 1}(2x - 5) = -3$

11. $\lim\limits_{x \to 2}(x^2 + 2) = 6$

12. $\lim\limits_{x \to 2}\dfrac{1}{x} = \dfrac{1}{2}$

13. Prove that $f(x) = \begin{cases} \sin\dfrac{1}{x} & \text{if } x \ne 0 \\ 0 & \text{if } x = 0 \end{cases}$

is not continuous at $x = 0$. *Hint*: To show that $\lim\limits_{x \to 0} f(x) \ne 0$, choose $\epsilon = 0.5$ and note that for any $\delta > 0$, there exists an x of the form $x = \dfrac{2}{\pi(2n + 1)}$ with n a natural number for which $0 < |x| < \delta$.

C *In Problems 14–19, construct a formal ϵ-δ proof to show that the given limit statement is valid for any number c.*

14. If $\lim\limits_{x \to c} f(x)$ exists and k is a constant, then $\lim\limits_{x \to c} kf(x) = k \lim\limits_{x \to c} f(x)$.

15. If $\lim\limits_{x \to c} f(x)$ and $\lim\limits_{x \to c} g(x)$ both exist, then $\lim\limits_{x \to c}[f(x) - g(x)] = \lim\limits_{x \to c} f(x) - \lim\limits_{x \to c} g(x)$.

16. If $\lim\limits_{x \to c} f(x)$ and $\lim\limits_{x \to c} g(x)$ both exist and a and b are constants, then $\lim\limits_{x \to c}[af(x) + bg(x)] = a \lim\limits_{x \to c} f(x) + b \lim\limits_{x \to c} g(x)$.

17. If $\lim\limits_{x \to c} f(x) = 0$ and $\lim\limits_{x \to c} g(x) = 0$, then $\lim\limits_{x \to c} f(x)g(x) = 0$.

18. If $f(x) \ge g(x) \ge 0$ for all x and $\lim\limits_{x \to c} f(x) = 0$, then $\lim\limits_{x \to c} g(x) = 0$.

19. If $f(x) \ge g(x)$ for all x in an open interval containing the number c and $\lim\limits_{x \to c} f(x)$ and $\lim\limits_{x \to c} g(x)$ both exist, then $\lim\limits_{x \to c} f(x) \ge \lim\limits_{x \to c} g(x)$. *Hint*: Apply the limit limitation theorem (Theorem A.1) to the function $h(x) = f(x) - g(x)$.

Problems 20–23 lead to a proof of the product rule for limits.

20. If $\lim\limits_{x \to c} f(x) = L$, show that $\lim\limits_{x \to c} |f(x)| = |L|$. *Hint*: Note that $||f(x)| - |L|| \le |f(x) - L|$.

21. If $\lim\limits_{x \to c} f(x) = L$, $L \ne 0$, show that there exists a $\delta > 0$ such that

$$\tfrac{1}{2}|L| < |f(x)| < \tfrac{3}{2}|L|$$

for all x for which $0 < |x - c| < \delta$. *Hint*: Use $\epsilon = \tfrac{1}{2}|L|$ in Problem 20.

22. If $\lim\limits_{x \to c} f(x) = L$ and $L \ne 0$, show that $\lim\limits_{x \to c}[f(x)]^2 = L^2$ by completing these steps:

a. Use Problem 21 to show that there exists a $\delta_1 > 0$ so that

$$|f(x) + L| < \tfrac{5}{2}|L|$$

whenever $0 < |x - c| < \delta_1$.

b. Given $\epsilon > 0$, show that there exists a $\delta_2 > 0$ such that

$$\left|[f(x)]^2 - L^2\right| < \tfrac{5}{2}|L|\epsilon$$

whenever $0 < |x - c| < \delta_2$.

c. Complete the proof that

$$\lim_{x \to c}[f(x)]^2 = L^2$$

23. Prove the product rule for limits: If $\lim_{x \to c} f(x) = L$ and $\lim_{x \to c} g(x) = M$, then $\lim_{x \to c} f(x)g(x) = LM$. *Hint:* Use the result of Problem 22 along with the identity

$$fg = \tfrac{1}{4}[(f+g)^2 - (f-g)^2]$$

24. Show that if f is continuous at c and $f(c) > 0$, then $f(x) > 0$ throughout an open interval containing c. *Hint:* Note that $\lim_{x \to c} f(x) = f(c)$ and use $\epsilon = \tfrac{1}{2} f(c)$ in the definition of limit.

25. Show that if f is continuous at L and $\lim_{x \to c} g(x) = L$, then $\lim_{x \to c} f[g(x)] = f(L)$ by completing the following steps:

a. Explain why there exists a $\delta_1 > 0$ such that $|f(w) - f(L)| < \epsilon$ whenever $|w - L| < \delta_1$.

b. Complete the proof by setting $w = g(x)$ and using part **a.**

26. For linear functions, the relation between ϵ and δ is clear; but for complicated functions, it is not. However, the correct graph can illustrate this relationship. For the following function, illustrate not only that f is continuous at $x = 3$, but determine graphically how you would pick δ to accommodate a given ϵ. (For example, $\delta = K^{-1}\epsilon$.)

$$f(x) = \frac{x^4 - 2x^3 + 3x^2 - 5x + 2}{x - 2}$$

APPENDIX B   Selected Proofs

CHAIN RULE (Chapter 3)

Suppose f is a differentiable function of u and u is a differentiable function of x. Then, $f[u(x)]$ is a differentiable function of x and

$$\frac{df}{dx} = \frac{df}{du}\frac{du}{dx}$$

Proof   Define an auxiliary function g by

$$g(t) = \frac{f[u(x)+t] - f[u(x)]}{t} - \frac{df}{du} \quad \text{if} \quad t \neq 0 \quad \text{and} \quad g(t) = 0 \quad \text{if} \quad t = 0$$

You can verify that g is continuous at $t = 0$. Notice that for $t = \Delta u$ and $t \neq 0$,

$$g(\Delta u) = \frac{f[u(x)+\Delta u] - f[u(x)]}{\Delta u} - \frac{df}{du}$$

$$g(\Delta u) + \frac{df}{du} = \frac{f[u(x)+\Delta u] - f[u(x)]}{\Delta u}$$

$$\left[g(\Delta u) + \frac{df}{du}\right]\Delta u = f[u(x)+\Delta u] - f[u(x)]$$

We now use the definition of derivative for f.

$$\frac{df}{dx} = \lim_{\Delta x \to 0} \frac{f[u(x+\Delta x)] - f[u(x)]}{\Delta x}$$

$$= \lim_{\Delta x \to 0} \frac{f[u(x)+\Delta u] - f[u(x)]}{\Delta x} \qquad \text{Where } \Delta u = u(x+\Delta x) - u(x)$$

$$= \lim_{\Delta x \to 0} \frac{\left[g(\Delta u) + \dfrac{df}{du}\right]\Delta u}{\Delta x} \qquad \text{Substitution}$$

$$= \lim_{\Delta x \to 0} \left[g(\Delta u) + \frac{df}{du}\right]\frac{\Delta u}{\Delta x}$$

$$= \lim_{\Delta x \to 0} \left[g(\Delta u) + \frac{df}{du}\right] \lim_{\Delta x \to 0} \frac{\Delta u}{\Delta x}$$

$$= \left[\lim_{\Delta x \to 0} g(\Delta u) + \lim_{\Delta x \to 0} \frac{df}{du}\right] \lim_{\Delta x \to 0} \frac{\Delta u}{\Delta x}$$

$$= \left[0 + \frac{df}{du} \right] \frac{du}{dx}$$

$$= \frac{df}{du} \frac{du}{dx}$$

Since g is continuous at $t = 0$

❑

CAUCHY'S GENERALIZED MEAN VALUE THEOREM (Chapter 4)

Let f and g be functions that are continuous on the closed interval $[a, b]$ and differentiable on the open interval (a, b). If $g(b) \neq g(a)$ and $g'(x) \neq 0$ on (a, b), then

$$\frac{f(b) - f(a)}{g(b) - g(a)} = \frac{f'(c)}{g'(c)}$$

for at least one number c between a and b.

Proof We begin by defining a special function, just as in the proof of the MVT as presented in Section 4.2. Specifically, let

$$F(x) = f(x) - f(a) - \frac{f(b) - f(a)}{g(b) - g(a)} [g(x) - g(a)]$$

for all x in the closed interval $[a, b]$. In the proof of the MVT in Section 4.2 we show that F satisfies the hypotheses of Rolle's theorem, which means that $F'(c) = 0$ for at least one number c in (a, b). For this number c, we have

$$0 = F'(c) = f'(c) - \frac{f(b) - f(a)}{g(b) - g(a)} g'(c)$$

and the result follows from this equation.

❑

L'HÔPITAL'S RULE*(Chapter 4)

For any number a, let f and g be functions that are differentiable on an open interval (a, b), where $g'(x) \neq 0$. If $\lim\limits_{x \to a^+} f(x) = 0$, $\lim\limits_{x \to a^+} g(x) = 0$, and $\lim\limits_{x \to a^+} \dfrac{f'(x)}{g'(x)}$ exists, then

$$\lim_{x \to a^+} \frac{f(x)}{g(x)} = \lim_{x \to a^+} \frac{f'(x)}{g'(x)}$$

Proof First, define auxiliary functions F and G by

$$F(x) = f(x) \qquad \text{for } a < x \leq b \text{ and } F(a) = 0$$
$$G(x) = g(x) \qquad \text{for } a < x \leq b \text{ and } G(a) = 0$$

These definitions guarantee that $F(x) = f(x)$ and $G(x) = g(x)$ for $a < x \leq b$ and that $F(a) = G(a) = 0$. Thus, if w is any number between a and b, the functions F and G are continuous on the closed interval $[a, w]$ and differentiable on the open interval (a, w). According to the Cauchy generalized mean value theorem, there exists a number t between a and w for which

$$\frac{F(w) - F(a)}{G(w) - G(a)} = \frac{F'(t)}{G'(t)}$$

$$\frac{F(w)}{G(w)} = \frac{F'(t)}{G'(t)} \qquad \text{Because } F(a) = G(a) = 0$$

$$\frac{f(w)}{g(w)} = \frac{f'(t)}{g'(t)} \qquad \text{Because } F(x) = f(x) \text{ and } G(x) = g(x)$$

---

*This is a special case of l'Hôpital's rule. The other cases can be found in most advanced calculus textbooks.

$$\lim_{w \to a^+} \frac{f(w)}{g(w)} = \lim_{w \to a^+} \frac{f'(t)}{g'(t)}$$

$$\lim_{w \to a^+} \frac{f(w)}{g(w)} = \lim_{t \to a^+} \frac{f'(t)}{g'(t)} \qquad \text{Because } t \text{ is "trapped" between } a \text{ and } w$$

$$\lim_{x \to a^+} \frac{f(x)}{g(x)} = \lim_{x \to a^+} \frac{f'(x)}{g'(x)}$$

❑

LIMIT COMPARISON TEST (Chapter 8)

Suppose $a_k > 0$ and $b_k > 0$ for all sufficiently large k and that

$$\lim_{k \to \infty} \frac{a_k}{b_k} = L \qquad \text{where } L \text{ is finite and positive } (0 < L < \infty)$$

Then Σa_k and Σb_k either both converge or both diverge.

Proof   Assume that $\displaystyle\lim_{k \to \infty} \frac{a_k}{b_k} = L$, where $L > 0$. Using $\epsilon = \dfrac{L}{2}$ in the definition of the limit of a sequence, we see that there exists a number N so that

$$\left| \frac{a_k}{b_k} - L \right| < \frac{L}{2} \qquad \text{whenever } k > N$$

$$-\frac{L}{2} < \frac{a_k}{b_k} - L < \frac{L}{2}$$

$$\frac{L}{2} < \frac{a_k}{b_k} < \frac{3L}{2}$$

$$\frac{L}{2} b_k < a_k < \frac{3L}{2} b_k \qquad b_k > 0$$

This is true for all $k > N$. Now we can complete the proof by using the direct comparison test. Suppose Σb_k converges. Then the series $\displaystyle\sum \frac{3L}{2} b_k$ also converges, and the inequality

$$a_k < \frac{3L}{2} b_k$$

tells us that the series Σa_k must also converge since it is dominated by a convergent series.

Similarly, if Σb_k diverges, the inequality

$$0 < \frac{L}{2} b_k < a_k$$

tells us that Σa_k dominates the divergent series $\displaystyle\sum \frac{L}{2} b_k$, and it follows that Σa_k also diverges.

Thus Σa_k and Σb_k either both converge or both diverge.   ❑

TAYLOR'S THEOREM (Chapter 8)

If f and all its derivatives exist in an open interval I containing c, then for each x in I

$$f(x) = f(c) + \frac{f'(c)}{1!}(x - c) + \frac{f''(c)}{2!}(x - c)^2 + \cdots + \frac{f^{(n)}(c)}{n!}(x - c)^n + R_n(x)$$

where the remainder function $R_n(x)$ is given by

$$R_n(x) = \frac{f^{(n+1)}(z_n)}{(n+1)!}(x - c)^{n+1}$$

for some z_n that depends on x and lies between c and x.

Proof   We will prove Taylor's theorem by showing that if f and its first $n + 1$ derivatives are defined in an open interval I containing c, then for each fixed x in I

$$f(x) = f(c) + \frac{f'(c)}{1!}(x - c) + \frac{f''(c)}{2!}(x - c)^2 + \cdots + \frac{f^{(n)}(c)}{n!}(x - c)^n + \frac{f^{(n+1)}(z)}{(n + 1)!}(x - c)^{n+1}$$

where z is some number between x and c.   In our proof, we will apply Cauchy's generalized mean value theorem to the auxiliary functions F and G defined for all t in I as follows:

$$F(t) = f(x) - f(t) - \frac{f'(t)}{1!}(x - t) - \cdots - \frac{f^{(n)}(t)}{n!}(x - t)^n$$

$$G(t) = \frac{(x - t)^{n+1}}{(n + 1)!}$$

Note that $F(x) = G(x) = 0$, and thus Cauchy's generalized mean value theorem tells us

$$\frac{F'(z)}{G'(z)} = \frac{F(x) - F(c)}{G(x) - G(c)} = \frac{F(c)}{G(c)}$$

for some number z between x and c. Rearranging the sides of this equation and finding the derivatives gives

$$\frac{F(c)}{G(c)} = \frac{F'(z)}{G'(z)}$$

$$= \frac{\dfrac{-f^{(n+1)}(z)}{n!}(x - z)^n}{\dfrac{-(x - z)^n}{n!}}$$

$$= f^{(n+1)}(z)$$

$$F(c) = f^{(n+1)}(z)G(c)$$

$$f(x) - f(c) - \frac{f'(c)}{1!}(x - c) - \cdots - \frac{f^{(n)}(c)}{n!}(x - c)^n = f^{(n+1)}(z)\left[\frac{(x - c)^{n+1}}{(n + 1)!}\right]$$

Rearranging these terms, we obtain the required equation.

$$f(x) = f(c) + \frac{f'(c)}{1!}(x - c) + \cdots + \frac{f^{(n)}(c)}{n!}(x - c)^n + f^{(n+1)}(z)\left[\frac{(x - c)^{n+1}}{(n + 1)!}\right]$$

$\qquad\qquad\qquad\qquad\qquad\qquad\qquad\qquad\qquad\qquad\qquad\qquad\qquad\qquad\qquad$ ❏

SUFFICIENT CONDITION FOR DIFFERENTIABILITY (Chapter 11)

If f is a function of x and y and f, f_x, and f_y are continuous in a disk D centered at (x_0, y_0), then f is differentiable at (x_0, y_0).

Proof   If (x, y) is a point in D, we have

$$f(x, y) - f(x_0, y_0) = f(x, y) - f(x_0, y) + f(x_0, y) - f(x_0, y_0)$$

The function $f(x, y)$ with y fixed satisfies the conditions of the mean value theorem, so that

$$f(x, y) - f(x_0, y) = f_x(x_1, y)(x - x_0)$$

for some number x_1 between x and x_0, and similarly, there is a number y_1 between y and y_0 such that

$$f(x_0, y) - f(x_0, y_0) = f_y(x_0, y_1)(y - y_0)$$

Substituting these expressions we obtain:

$$f(x, y) - f(x_0, y_0) = [f(x, y) - f(x_0, y)] + [f(x_0, y) - f(x_0, y_0)]$$
$$= [f_x(x_1, y)(x - x_0)] + [f_y(x_0, y_1)(y - y_0)]$$
$$= [f_x(x_1, y)(x - x_0)] + \underbrace{f_x(x_0, y_0)(x - x_0) - f_x(x_0, y_0)(x - x_0)}_{\text{This is zero}}$$
$$+ [f_y(x_0, y_1)(y - y_0)] + \underbrace{f_y(x_0, y_0)(y - y_0) - f_y(x_0, y_0)(y - y_0)}_{\text{This is also zero}}$$
$$= f_x(x_0, y_0)(x - x_0) + f_y(x_0, y_0)(y - y_0)$$
$$+ [f_x(x_1, y) - f_x(x_0, y_0)](x - x_0)$$
$$+ [f_y(x_0, y_1) - f_y(x_0, y_0)](y - y_0)$$

Let $\epsilon_1(x, y)$ and $\epsilon_2(x, y)$ be the functions

$$\epsilon_1(x, y) = f_x(x_1, y) - f_x(x_0, y_0) \quad \text{and} \quad \epsilon_2(x, y) = f_y(x_0, y_1) - f_y(x_0, y_0)$$

Then since x_1 is between x and x_0, and y_1 is between y and y_0, and the partial derivatives f_x and f_y are continuous at (x_0, y_0), we have

$$\lim_{(x,y)\to(x_0,y_0)} \epsilon_1(x, y) = \lim_{(x,y)\to(x_0,y_0)} [f_x(x_1, y) - f_x(x_0, y_0)] = 0$$

$$\lim_{(x,y)\to(x_0,y_0)} \epsilon_2(x, y) = \lim_{(x,y)\to(x_0,y_0)} [f_y(x_0, y_1) - f_y(x_0, y_0)] = 0$$

so that f is differentiable at (x_0, y_0), as required. ❏

CHANGE OF VARIABLES FORMULA FOR MULTIPLE INTEGRATION (Chapter 12)

Suppose f is a continuous function of a region D in $\mathbb{R}^2$ and let D^* be the image of the domain D under the change of variables $x = g(u, v)$, $y = h(u, v)$ where g and h are continuously differentiable on D^*. Then

$$\iint_D f(x, y)\, dy\, dx = \iint_{D^*} f[g(u, v), h(u, v)] \underbrace{\left| \frac{\partial(x, y)}{\partial(u, v)} \right|}_{\text{absolute value of Jacobian}} dv\, du$$

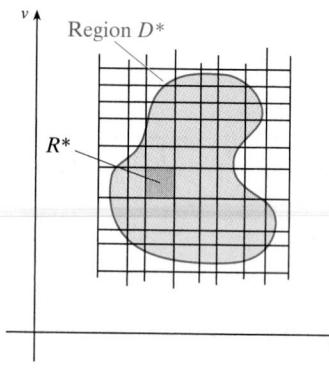

a. A rectangular grid in the uv-plane.

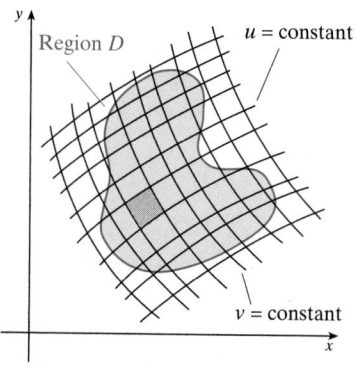

b. Corresponding grid in the xy-plane is curvilinear.

Figure B.1

Proof A proof of this theorem is found in advanced calculus texts, but we can provide a geometric argument that makes this formula plausible in the special case where $f(x, y) = 1$. In particular, we shall show that in order to find the area of a region D in the xy-plane using the change of variables $x = X(u, v)$ and $y = Y(u, v)$, it is reasonable to use the formula for area, A:

$$A = \iint_D dy\, dx = \iint_{D^*} \left| \frac{\partial(x, y)}{\partial(u, v)} \right| dv\, du$$

where D^* is the region in the uv-plane that corresponds to D.

Suppose the given change of variables has an inverse $u = u(x, y)$, $v = v(x, y)$ that transforms the region D in the xy-plane into a region D^* in the uv-plane. To find the area of D^* in the uv-coordinate system, it is natural to use a rectangular grid, with vertical lines $u = $ constant and horizontal lines $v = $ constant, as shown in Figure B.1. In the xy-plane, the equations $u = $ constant and $v = $ constant will be families of parallel curves, which provide a curvilinear grid for the region D (Figure B.1).

Next, let R^* be a typical rectangular cell in the uv-grid that covers D^*, and let R be the corresponding set in the xy-plane (that is, R^* is the image of R under the given change of variables). Then, as shown in Figure B.2, if R^* has vertices $A(\overline{u}, \overline{v})$,

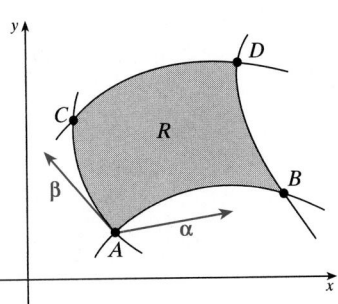

a. R^* is a typical rectangular cell in the grid covering D^*.

b. The image of R under the change of variables is a curvilinear rectangle R.

Figure B.2

$B(\overline{u} + \Delta u, \overline{v})$, $C(\overline{u}, \overline{v} + \Delta v)$, and $D(\overline{u} + \Delta u, \overline{v} + \Delta v)$, the set R will be the interior of a curvilinear rectangle with vertices

$$A[X(\overline{u}, \overline{v}), Y(\overline{u}, \overline{v})],$$
$$B[X(\overline{u} + \Delta u, \overline{v}), Y(\overline{u} + \Delta u, \overline{v})],$$
$$C[X(\overline{u}, \overline{v} + \Delta v), Y(\overline{u}, \overline{v} + \Delta v)]$$
$$D[X(\overline{u} + \Delta u, \overline{v} + \Delta v), Y(\overline{u} + \Delta u, \overline{v} + \Delta v)]$$

Note that the curved side of R joining A to B may be approximated by the secant vector

$$\mathbf{AB} = [X(\overline{u} + \Delta u, \overline{v}) - X(\overline{u}, \overline{v})]\mathbf{i} + [Y(\overline{u} + \Delta u, \overline{v}) - Y(\overline{u}, \overline{v})]\mathbf{j}$$

and by applying the mean value theorem, we find that

$$\mathbf{AB} = \left[\frac{\partial x}{\partial u}(a, \overline{v})\Delta u\right]\mathbf{i} + \left[\frac{\partial y}{\partial u}(b, \overline{v})\Delta u\right]\mathbf{j}$$

for some numbers a, b between $\overline{u}$ and $\overline{u} + \Delta u$. If Δu is very small, a and b are approximately the same as $\overline{u}$, and we can approximate $\mathbf{AB}$ by the vector

$$\boldsymbol{\alpha} = \left[\frac{\partial x}{\partial u}\Delta u\right]\mathbf{i} + \left[\frac{\partial y}{\partial u}\Delta u\right]\mathbf{j}$$

where the partials are evaluated at the point $(\overline{u}, \overline{v})$. Similarly, the curved side of R joining A and C may be approximated by the vector

$$\boldsymbol{\beta} = \left[\frac{\partial x}{\partial v}\Delta v\right]\mathbf{i} + \left[\frac{\partial y}{\partial v}\Delta v\right]\mathbf{j}$$

The area of the curvilinear rectangle R is approximately the same as that of the parallelogram determined by $\boldsymbol{\alpha}$ and $\boldsymbol{\beta}$; that is,

$$\|\boldsymbol{\alpha} \times \boldsymbol{\beta}\| = \begin{vmatrix} \mathbf{i} & \mathbf{j} & \mathbf{k} \\ \dfrac{\partial x}{\partial u}\Delta u & \dfrac{\partial y}{\partial u}\Delta u & 0 \\ \dfrac{\partial x}{\partial v}\Delta v & \dfrac{\partial y}{\partial v}\Delta v & 0 \end{vmatrix}$$

$$= \left\| \begin{vmatrix} \mathbf{i} & \mathbf{j} & \mathbf{k} \\ \dfrac{\partial x}{\partial u} & \dfrac{\partial y}{\partial u} & 0 \\ \dfrac{\partial x}{\partial v} & \dfrac{\partial y}{\partial v} & 0 \end{vmatrix} \Delta v \Delta u \right\|$$

$$= \left| \frac{\partial x}{\partial u} \frac{\partial y}{\partial v} - \frac{\partial y}{\partial u} \frac{\partial x}{\partial v} \right| \Delta v \Delta u$$

$$= \left| \frac{\partial (x, y)}{\partial (u, v)} \right| \Delta v \Delta u$$

By adding the contributions of all cells in the partition of D, we can approximate the area of D as follows:

$$\text{APPROXIMATE AREA OF } D = \sum \begin{array}{c} \text{APPROXIMATE AREA OF} \\ \text{CURVILINEAR RECTANGLES} \end{array}$$

$$= \sum \left| \frac{\partial (x, y)}{\partial (u, v)} \right| \Delta v \Delta u$$

Finally, using a limit to "smooth out" the approximation, we find

$$A = \iint_D dy \, dx = \lim \sum \left| \frac{\partial (x, y)}{\partial (u, v)} \right| \Delta v \Delta u = \iint_{D^*} \left| \frac{\partial (x, y)}{\partial (u, v)} \right| dv \, du \qquad \square$$

STOKES' THEOREM (Chapter 13)

Let S be an oriented surface with unit normal vector field $\mathbf{N}$, and assume that S is bounded by a piecewise smooth Jordan curve C whose orientation is compatible with that of S. If $\mathbf{F}$ is a vector field that is continuously differentiable on S, then

$$\int_C \mathbf{F} \cdot d\mathbf{R} = \iint_S (\text{curl } \mathbf{F} \cdot \mathbf{N}) \, dS$$

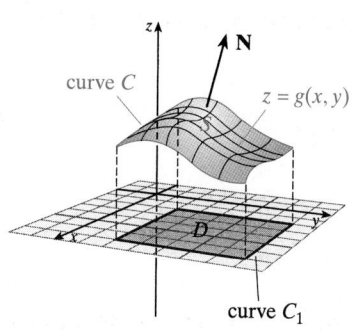

Figure B.3

Proof   The general proof requires the methods of advanced calculus. However, a proof for the case where S is a graph and $\mathbf{F}$, S and C are "well behaved" can be given. Let S be given by $z = g(x, y)$ where (x, y) is in a region D of the xy-plane. Assume g has continuous second-order partial derivatives. Let C_1 be the projection of C in the xy-plane, as shown in Figure B.3. Also let $\mathbf{F}(x, y, z) = f(x, y, z)\mathbf{i} + g(x, y, z)\mathbf{j} + h(x, y, z)\mathbf{k}$ where the partial derivatives of f, g, and h are continuous.

We will evaluate each side of Stokes's theorem separately and show that the results for each are the same. If $x = x(t)$, $y = y(t)$, and $z = z(t)$ for $a \le t \le b$ and $\mathbf{R}(t) = x(t)\mathbf{i} + y(t)\mathbf{j} + z(t)\mathbf{k}$, then

$$\int_C \mathbf{F} \cdot d\mathbf{R} = \int_a^b \left[f\frac{dx}{dt} + g\frac{dy}{dt} + h\frac{dz}{dt} \right] dt$$

$$= \int_a^b \left[f\frac{dx}{dt} + g\frac{dy}{dt} + h\left(\frac{\partial z}{\partial x}\frac{dx}{dt} + \frac{\partial z}{\partial y}\frac{dy}{dt} \right) \right] dt \qquad \text{Chain rule}$$

$$= \int_a^b \left[\left(f + h\frac{\partial z}{\partial x} \right)\frac{dx}{dt} + \left(g + h\frac{\partial z}{\partial y} \right)\frac{dy}{dt} \right] dt$$

$$= \int_{C_1} \left[\left(f + h\frac{\partial z}{\partial x} \right) dx + \left(g + h\frac{\partial z}{\partial y} \right) dy \right]$$

$$= \iint_D \left[\frac{\partial}{\partial x}\left(g + h\frac{\partial z}{\partial y} \right) - \frac{\partial}{\partial y}\left(f + h\frac{\partial z}{\partial x} \right) \right] dA \qquad \text{Green's theorem}$$

$$= \iint_D \left[\left(\frac{\partial g}{\partial x} + \frac{\partial g}{\partial z}\frac{\partial z}{\partial x} + \frac{\partial h}{\partial x}\frac{\partial z}{\partial y} + \frac{\partial h}{\partial z}\frac{\partial z}{\partial x}\frac{\partial z}{\partial y} + h\frac{\partial^2 z}{\partial y \partial x} \right) \right.$$

$$\left. - \left(\frac{\partial f}{\partial y} + \frac{\partial f}{\partial z}\frac{\partial z}{\partial y} + \frac{\partial h}{\partial y}\frac{\partial z}{\partial x} + \frac{\partial h}{\partial z}\frac{\partial z}{\partial y}\frac{\partial z}{\partial x} + h\frac{\partial^2 z}{\partial y \partial x} \right) \right] dA$$

$$= \iint_D \left[-\frac{\partial h}{\partial y}\frac{\partial z}{\partial x} + \frac{\partial g}{\partial z}\frac{\partial z}{\partial x} - \frac{\partial f}{\partial z}\frac{\partial z}{\partial y} + \frac{\partial h}{\partial x}\frac{\partial z}{\partial y} + \frac{\partial g}{\partial x} - \frac{\partial f}{\partial y} \right] dA$$

Next, we start over by evaluating the flux integral:

$$\iint\limits_{S} \text{curl } \mathbf{F} \cdot d\mathbf{S} = \iint\limits_{D} \left\langle -\left(\frac{\partial h}{\partial y} - \frac{\partial g}{\partial z}\right), \left(\frac{\partial f}{\partial z} - \frac{\partial h}{\partial x}\right), \left(\frac{\partial g}{\partial x} - \frac{\partial f}{\partial y}\right) \right\rangle \cdot \left\langle \frac{-\partial z}{\partial x}, \frac{-\partial z}{\partial y}, 1 \right\rangle dA$$

$$= \iint\limits_{D} \left[-\frac{\partial h}{\partial y}\frac{\partial z}{\partial x} + \frac{\partial g}{\partial z}\frac{\partial z}{\partial x} - \frac{\partial f}{\partial z}\frac{\partial z}{\partial y} + \frac{\partial h}{\partial x}\frac{\partial z}{\partial y} + \frac{\partial g}{\partial x} - \frac{\partial f}{\partial y} \right] dA$$

Since these results are the same, we have

$$\int_{C} \mathbf{F} \cdot d\mathbf{R} = \iint\limits_{S} (\text{curl } \mathbf{F} \cdot \mathbf{N})\, dS \qquad \square$$

DIVERGENCE THEOREM (Chapter 13)

Let D be a region in space bounded by a smooth, orientable closed surface S. If $\mathbf{F}$ is a continuous vector field whose components have continuous partial derivatives in D, then

$$\iint\limits_{S} \mathbf{F} \cdot \mathbf{N}\, dS = \iiint\limits_{D} \text{div } \mathbf{F}\, dV$$

where $\mathbf{N}$ is an outward unit normal to the surface S.

Proof   Let $\mathbf{F}(x, y, z) = f(x, y, z)\mathbf{i} + g(x, y, z)\mathbf{j} + h(x, y, z)\mathbf{k}$. If we state the divergence theorem using this notation for $\mathbf{F}$, we have

$$\iint\limits_{S} [f(\mathbf{i} \cdot \mathbf{N}) + g(\mathbf{j} \cdot \mathbf{N}) + h(\mathbf{k} \cdot \mathbf{N})]\, dS = \iiint\limits_{D} \left(\frac{\partial f}{\partial x} + \frac{\partial g}{\partial y} + \frac{\partial h}{\partial z}\right) dV$$

$$\iint\limits_{S} f(\mathbf{i} \cdot \mathbf{N})\, dS + \iint\limits_{S} g(\mathbf{j} \cdot \mathbf{N})\, dS + \iint\limits_{S} h(\mathbf{k} \cdot \mathbf{N})\, dS = \iiint\limits_{D} \frac{\partial f}{\partial x}\, dV + \iiint\limits_{D} \frac{\partial g}{\partial y}\, dV + \iiint\limits_{D} \frac{\partial h}{\partial z}\, dV$$

This result can be verified by proving

$$\iint\limits_{S} f(\mathbf{i} \cdot \mathbf{N})\, dS = \iiint\limits_{D} \frac{\partial f}{\partial x}\, dV$$

$$\iint\limits_{S} g(\mathbf{j} \cdot \mathbf{N})\, dS = \iiint\limits_{D} \frac{\partial g}{\partial y}\, dV$$

$$\iint\limits_{S} h(\mathbf{k} \cdot \mathbf{N})\, dS = \iiint\limits_{D} \frac{\partial h}{\partial z}\, dV$$

Since the proof of each of these is virtually identical, we will show the verification for the last equation; the other two can be done in a similar fashion. We will evaluate this third integral by separately evaluating the left and right sides to show they are the same.

We will restrict our proof to a standard region; that is, a solid bounded above by a surface S_T with equation $z = u(x, y)$ and below by a surface S_B with equation $z = v(x, y)$. We assume that both S_T and S_B project onto the region R in the xy-plane. The lateral surface S_L of the region is the set of all (x, y, z) such that $v(x, y) \leq z \leq u(x, y)$ on the boundary of R, as shown in Figure B.4. The upward flux across the top surface S_T is

$$\iint_{S_T} h(\mathbf{k} \cdot \mathbf{N}_T) \, dS = \iint_R h\langle 0, 0, 1 \rangle \cdot \left\langle -\frac{\partial u}{\partial x}, -\frac{\partial u}{\partial y}, 1 \right\rangle dA$$

$$= \iint_R h(x, y, z) \, dA$$

$$= \iint_R h(x, y, u(x, y)) \, dA$$

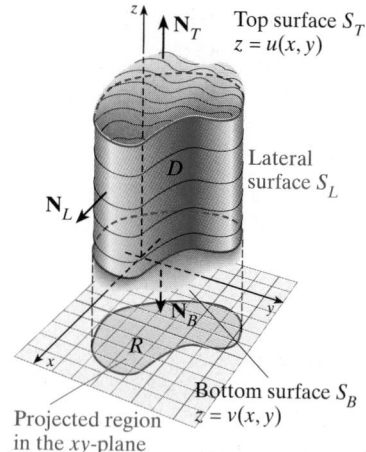

Figure B.4 A standard solid region in $\mathbb{R}^3$

Similarly, the downward flux across the bottom surface S_B is

$$\iint_{S_B} h(\mathbf{k} \cdot \mathbf{N}_B) \, dS = \iint_R h\langle 0, 0, 1 \rangle \cdot \left\langle \frac{\partial u}{\partial x}, \frac{\partial v}{\partial y}, -1 \right\rangle dA$$

$$= -\iint_R h(x, y, z) \, dA$$

$$= -\iint_R h(x, y, v(x, y)) \, dA$$

Because the outward unit normal $\mathbf{N}_L$ is horizontal on the lateral surface S_L, it is perpendicular to k, and

$$\iint_{S_L} h(\mathbf{k} \cdot \mathbf{N}_L) \, dS = 0$$

To find the flux integral over the entire closed surface S, add the separate flux integrals over the top, the bottom, and the sides:

$$\iint_S h(\mathbf{k} \cdot \mathbf{N}) \, dS = \iint_{S_T} h(\mathbf{k} \cdot \mathbf{N}_T) \, dS + \iint_{S_B} h(\mathbf{k} \cdot \mathbf{N}_B) \, dS + \iint_{S_L} h(\mathbf{k} \cdot \mathbf{N}_L) \, dS$$

$$= \iint_R h[x, y, u(x, y)] \, dA - \iint_R h[x, y, v(x, y)] \, dA + 0$$

$$= \iint_R \{h[x, y, u(x, y)] - h[x, y, v(x, y)]\} \, dA$$

Next, we start over by evaluating the triple integral $\iiint_D \frac{\partial h}{\partial z} \, dV$. Notice that we can describe the solid S as the set of all (x, y, z) for (x, y) in R and $v(x, y) \leq z \leq u(x, y)$. Thus,

$$\iiint_D \frac{\partial h}{\partial z} \, dV = \iint_R \left[\int_{v(x,y)}^{u(x,y)} \frac{\partial h}{\partial z}(x, y, z) \, dz \right] dA$$

$$= \iint_R \{h[x, y, u(x, y)] - h[x, y, v(x, y)]\} \, dA$$

$$= \iint_S h(\mathbf{k} \cdot \mathbf{N}) \, dS$$

By applying similar arguments to the integrals $\iiint\limits_{D} \dfrac{\partial f}{\partial x}\,dV$ and $\iiint\limits_{D} \dfrac{\partial g}{\partial y}\,dV$ and adding, we obtain

$$\iiint\limits_{D} \left[\frac{\partial f}{\partial x} + \frac{\partial g}{\partial y} + \frac{\partial h}{\partial z}\right] dV = \iint\limits_{S} [f(\mathbf{i}\cdot\mathbf{N}) + g(\mathbf{j}\cdot\mathbf{N}) + h(\mathbf{k}\cdot\mathbf{N})]\,dS$$

or

$$\iiint\limits_{D} \operatorname{div}\mathbf{F}\,dV = \iint\limits_{S} \mathbf{F}\cdot\mathbf{N}\,dS \qquad \square$$

APPENDIX C   Significant Digits

Throughout this book, various Technology Notes appear, and in the answers to the problems you will frequently find approximate (decimal) answers. Sometimes your answer may not exactly agree with the answer found in the back of the book. This does not necessarily mean that your answer is incorrect, particularly if your answer is very close to the given answer.

To use your calculator intelligently and efficiently, you should become familiar with its functions and practice doing problems with the same calculator, whenever possible. Read the Technology Notes provided throughout this text, and consult the owner's manual for your particular calculator when you have questions. In addition, there are *Technology Manuals* accompanying this text which are available for TI and HP graphic calculators, as well as for Mathematica and for Maple.

SIGNIFICANT DIGITS

Applications involving measurements can never be exact. It is particularly important that you pay attention to the accuracy of your measurements when you use a computer or calculator, because using available technology can give you a false sense of security about the accuracy in a particular problem. For example, if you measure a triangle and find the sides are approximately 1.2 and 3.4 and then find the ratio of $1.2/3.4 \approx 0.35294117$, it appears that the result is more accurate than the original measurements! Some discussion about accuracy and significant digits is necessary.

The digits known to be correct in a number obtained by a measurement are called **significant digits**. The digits 1, 2, 3, 4, 5, 6, 7, 8, and 9 are always significant, whereas the digit 0 may or may not be significant.

1. Zeros that come between two other digits are significant, as in 203 or 10.04.
2. If the zero's only function is to place the decimal point, it is not significant, as in

$$0.00000\,\underbrace{23} \qquad \text{or} \qquad 23{,}\underbrace{000}$$
$$\text{Placeholders} \qquad\qquad \text{Placeholders}$$

If a zero does more than fix the decimal point, it is significant, as in

$$0.0023\,\underset{\uparrow}{0} \qquad \text{or} \qquad 23{,}\underbrace{000}.01$$
$$\text{This digit is significant.} \qquad\qquad \text{These are significant.}$$

This second rule can, of course, result in certain ambiguities, such as 23,000 (measured to the exact unit). To avoid such confusion, we use scientific notation in this case:

$$2.3 \times 10^4 \quad \text{has two significant digits}$$
$$2.3000 \times 10^4 \quad \text{has five significant digits}$$

Numbers that come about by counting are considered to be exact and are correct to any number of significant digits.

When you compute an answer using a calculator, the answer may have 10 or more digits. In the Technology Notes we generally show the 10 or 12 digits that result from the numerical calculation but frequently the number in the answer section will have only 5 or 6 digits in the answer. It seems clear that if the first 3 or 4 nonzero digits of the answer coincide, you probably have the correct method of doing the problem.

However, you might ask why there are discrepancies and how many digits you should use when you write down your final answer. Roughly speaking, the significant digits in a number are the digits that have meaning. To clarify the concept, we must for the moment assume that we know the exact answer. We then assume that we have been able to compute an approximation to this exact answer.

Usually we do this by some sort of iterative process, in which the answers are getting closer and closer to the exact answer. In such a process, we hope that the number of significant digits in our approximate answer is increasing at each trial. If our approximate answer is, say, 6 digits long (some of those digits might even be zero), and the difference between our answer and the exact answer is 4 units or less in the last place, then the first 5 digits are significant.

For example, if the exact answer is 3.14159 and our approximate answer is 3.14162, then our answer has 6 significant digits but is correct to 5 significant digits. Note that saying that our answer is correct to 5 significant digits does not guarantee that all of those 5 digits exactly match the first 5 digits of the exact answer. In fact, if an exact answer is 6.001 and our computed answer is 5.997, then our answer is correct to 3 significant digits and not one of them matches the digits in the exact answer. Also note that it may be necessary for an approximation to have more digits than are actually significant for it to have a certain number of significant digits. For example, if the exact answer is 6.003 and our approximation is 5.998, then it has 3 significant digits, but only if we consider the total 4-digit number and do not strip off the last nonsignificant digit.

Again, suppose you know that all digits are significant in the number 3.456; then you know that the exact number is less than 3.4565 and at least 3.4555. Some people may say that the number 3.456 is correct to 3 decimal places. This is the same as saying that it has 4 significant digits. Why bother with significant digits? If you multiply (or divide) two numbers with the same number of significant digits, then the product will generally be at least twice as long, but will have roughly the same number of significant digits as the original factors. You can then dispense with the unneeded digits. In fact, to keep them would be misleading about the accuracy of the result.

Frequently we can make an educated guess of the number of significant digits in an answer. For example, if we compute an iterative approximation such as

$$2.3123, \quad 2.3125, \quad 2.3126, \quad 2.31261, \quad 2.31262, \ldots$$

we would generally conclude that the answer is 2.3126 to 5 significant digits. Of course, we may very well be wrong, and if we continued iterating, the answer might end up as 2.4.

ROUNDING AND RULES OF COMPUTATION USED IN THIS BOOK

In hand and calculator computations, rounding a number is done to reduce the number of digits displayed and make the number easier to comprehend. Furthermore, if you suspect that the digit in the last place is not significant, then you might be tempted to round and remove this last digit. This can lead to error. For example, if the computed value is 0.64 and the true value is known to be between 0.61 and 0.67, then the computed value has only 1 significant digit. However, if we round it to 0.6 and the true value is really 0.66, then 0.6 is not correct to even 1 significant digit. In the interest of making the text easier to read, we have used the following rounding procedure:

Rounding Procedure

To round off numbers,

1. Increase the last retained digit by 1 if the remainder is greater than or equal to 5; or
2. Retain the last digit unchanged if the remainder is less than 5.

Elaborate rules for computation of approximate data can be developed when needed (in chemistry, for example), but in this text we will use three simple rules:

Rules For Significant Digits

Addition-subtraction: Add or subtract in the usual fashion, and then round off the result so that the last digit retained is in the column farthest to the right in which both given numbers have significant digits.

Multiplication-division: Multiply or divide in the usual fashion, and then round off the results to the smaller number of significant digits found in either of the given numbers.

Counting numbers: Numbers used to count or whole numbers used as exponents are considered to be correct to any number of significant digits.

Rounding Rule   We use the following rounding procedure in problems requiring rounding by involving several steps: Round only once, at the end. *That is, do not work with rounded results, because round-off errors can accumulate. If the problem does not ask for an approximate answer, but requires a calculator result, we will show the calculator result and leave it to the reader to write the appropriate number of digits.*

CALCULATOR EXPERIMENTS

You should be aware that you are much better than your calculator at performing certain computations. For example, almost all calculators will fail to give the correct answer to

$$(10.0 \text{ EE} + 50.0) + 911.0 - (10.0 \text{ EE} + 50.0)$$

Calculators will return the value of 0, but you know at a glance that the answer is 911.0. We must reckon with this poor behavior on the part of calculators, which is called *loss of accuracy* due to *catastrophic cancellation*. In this case, it is easy to catch the error immediately, but what if the computation is so complicated (or hidden by other computations) that we do not see the error?

First, we want to point out that the order in which you perform computations can be very important. For example, most calculators will correctly conclude that

$$(10.0 \text{ EE} + 50.0) - (10.0 \text{ EE} + 50.0) + 911.0 = 911$$

There are other cases besides catastrophic cancellation where the order in which a computation is performed will substantially affect the result. For example, you may not be able to calculate

$$(10.0 \text{ EE} + 50.0) * (911.0 \text{ EE} + 73.0)/(20.0 \text{ EE} + 60.0)$$

but rearranging the factors as

$$((10.0 \text{ EE} + 50.0)/(20.0 \text{ EE} + 60.0)) * (911.0 \text{ EE} + 73.0)$$

should provide the correct answer of 4.555 EE 65. So, for what do we need to watch? If you subtract two numbers that are close to each other in magnitude, you may obtain an inaccurate result. When you have a sequence of multiplications and divisions in a string, try to arrange the factors so that the result of each intermediate calculation stays as close as possible to 1.0.

Second, since a calculator performs all computations with a finite number of digits, it is unable to do exact computations involving nonterminating decimals. This enables us to see how many digits the calculator actually uses when it computes a result. For example, the computation

$$(7.0/17.0) * (17.0)$$

should give the result 7.0, but on most calculators it does not. The size of the answer gives an indication of how many digits "Accuracy" the calculator uses internally. That is, the calculator may display decimal numbers that have 10 digits, but use 12 digits internally. If the answer to the above computation is something similar to 1.0 EE − 12, then the calculator is using 12 digits internally.

TRIGONOMETRIC EVALUATIONS

In many problems you will be asked to compute the values of trigonometric functions such as the sine, cosine, or tangent. In calculus, trigonometric arguments are usually assumed to be measured in radians. You must make sure the calculator is in radian mode. If it is in radian mode, then the sine of a small number will almost be equal to that number. For example,

$$\sin(0.00001) = 1\,E - 5 \quad \text{(which is 0.00001)}$$

If not, then you are not using radian mode. Make sure you know how to put your calculator in radian mode.

GRAPHING BLUNDERS

When you are using the graphing features, you must always be careful to choose reasonable scales for the domain (horizontal scale) and range (vertical scale). If the scale is too large, you may not see important wiggles. If the scale is too small, you may not see important behavior elsewhere in the plane. Of course, knowing the techniques of graphing discussed in Chapter 4 will prevent you from making such blunders. Some calculators may have trouble with curves that jump suddenly at a point. An example of such a curve would be

$$y = \frac{e^x}{x}$$

which jumps at the origin. Try plotting this curve with your calculator using different horizontal and vertical scales, making sure that you understand how your calculator handles such graphs.

TECHNOLOGY NOTE

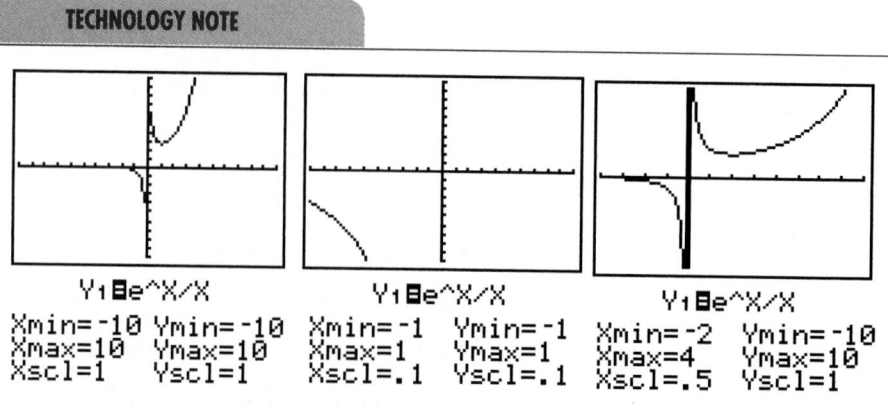

Y₁▤e^X/X	Y₁▤e^X/X	Y₁▤e^X/X
Xmin=-10 Ymin=-10	Xmin=-1 Ymin=-1	Xmin=-2 Ymin=-10
Xmax=10 Ymax=10	Xmax=1 Ymax=1	Xmax=4 Ymax=10
Xscl=1 Yscl=1	Xscl=.1 Yscl=.1	Xscl=.5 Yscl=1

APPENDIX D   Short Table of Integrals

Each formula is numbered for easy reference. The numbers in this short table are not sequential because this short table is truncated from the table of integrals found in the *Student Mathematics Handbook*.

BASIC FORMULAS

1. Constant rule $\int 0\,du = 0 + C$

2. Power rule $\int u^n\,du = \dfrac{u^{n+1}}{n+1}; \quad n \neq -1$

$\int u^n\,du = \ln|u|; \quad n = -1$

3. Natural Exponential rule $\int e^u\,du = e^u$

4. Logarithmic rule $\int \ln|u|\,du = u\ln|u| - u$

Trigonometric rules

5. $\int \sin u\,du = -\cos u$ **6.** $\int \cos u\,du = \sin u$

7. $\int \tan u\,du = -\ln|\cos u|$ **8.** $\int \cot u\,du = \ln|\sin u|$

9. $\int \sec u\,du = \ln|\sec u + \tan u|$ **10.** $\int \csc u\,du = -\ln|\csc u + \cot u|$

11. $\int \sec^2 u\,du = \tan u$ **12.** $\int \csc^2 u\,du = -\cot u$

13. $\int \sec u \tan u\,du = \sec u$ **14.** $\int \csc u \cot u\,du = -\csc u$

Exponential rule

15. $\int a^u\,du = \dfrac{a^u}{\ln a} \quad a > 0, a \neq 1$

Hyperbolic rules

16. $\int \cosh u\,du = \sinh u$ **17.** $\int \sinh u\,du = \cosh u$

18. $\int \tanh u\,du = \ln\cosh u$ **19.** $\int \coth u\,du = \ln|\sinh u|$

20. $\int \operatorname{sech} u\,du = \tan^{-1}(\sinh u)$ **21.** $\int \operatorname{csch} u\,du = \ln\left|\tanh \dfrac{u}{2}\right|$

$= 2\tan^{-1}(e^u)$

Inverse rules

22. $\int \dfrac{du}{\sqrt{a^2 - u^2}} = \sin^{-1}\dfrac{u}{a}$ **23.** $\int \dfrac{du}{\sqrt{u^2 - a^2}} = \cosh^{-1}\dfrac{u}{a}$

24. $\int \dfrac{du}{a^2 + u^2} = \dfrac{1}{a}\tan^{-1}\dfrac{u}{a}$

25. $\displaystyle\int \frac{du}{a^2 - u^2} = \begin{cases} \dfrac{1}{a} \tanh^{-1} \dfrac{u}{a} & \text{if } \left|\dfrac{u}{a}\right| < 1 \\[3mm] \dfrac{1}{a} \coth^{-1} \dfrac{u}{a} & \text{if } \left|\dfrac{u}{a}\right| > 1 \end{cases}$

26. $\displaystyle\int \frac{du}{u\sqrt{u^2 - a^2}} = \frac{1}{a} \sec^{-1} \left|\frac{u}{a}\right|$

27. $\displaystyle\int \frac{du}{u\sqrt{a^2 - u^2}} = -\frac{1}{a} \text{sech}^{-1} \left|\frac{u}{a}\right| = -\frac{1}{a} \ln \left|\frac{a + \sqrt{a^2 - u^2}}{u}\right|$

28. $\displaystyle\int \frac{du}{\sqrt{a^2 + u^2}} = \ln\left(u + \sqrt{a^2 + u^2}\right) = \sinh^{-1} \frac{u}{a}$

29. $\displaystyle\int \frac{du}{u\sqrt{a^2 + u^2}} = -\frac{1}{a} \ln \left|\frac{\sqrt{a^2 + u^2} + a}{u}\right| = -\frac{1}{a} \text{csch}^{-1} \left|\frac{u}{a}\right|$

INTEGRALS INVOLVING $au + b$

30. $\displaystyle\int (au + b)^n \, du = \frac{(au + b)^{n+1}}{(n + 1)a}$

31. $\displaystyle\int u(au + b)^n \, du = \frac{(au + b)^{n+2}}{(n + 2)a^2} - \frac{b(au + b)^{n+1}}{(n + 1)a^2}$

32. $\displaystyle\int u^2(au + b)^n \, du = \frac{(au + b)^{n+3}}{(n + 3)a^3} - \frac{2b(au + b)^{n+2}}{(n + 2)a^3} + \frac{b^2(au + b)^{n+1}}{(n + 1)a^3}$

33. $\displaystyle\int u^m(au + b)^n \, du = \begin{cases} \dfrac{u^{m+1}(au + b)^n}{m + n + 1} + \dfrac{nb}{m + n + 1} \displaystyle\int u^m(au + b)^{n-1} \, du \\[4mm] \dfrac{u^m(au + b)^{n+1}}{(m + n + 1)a} - \dfrac{mb}{(m + n + 1)a} \displaystyle\int u^{m-1}(au + b)^n \, du \\[4mm] \dfrac{-u^{m+1}(au + b)^{n+1}}{(n + 1)b} + \dfrac{m + n + 2}{(n + 1)b} \displaystyle\int u^m(au + b)^{n+1} \, du \end{cases}$

34. $\displaystyle\int \frac{du}{au + b} = \frac{1}{a} \ln |au + b|$

35. $\displaystyle\int \frac{u \, du}{au + b} = \frac{u}{a} - \frac{b}{a^2} \ln |au + b|$

36. $\displaystyle\int \frac{u^2 \, du}{au + b} = \frac{(au + b)^2}{2a^3} - \frac{2b(au + b)}{a^3} + \frac{b^2}{a^3} \ln |au + b|$

37. $\displaystyle\int \frac{u^3 \, du}{au + b} = \frac{(au + b)^3}{3a^4} - \frac{3b(au + b)^2}{2a^4} + \frac{3b^2(au + b)}{a^4} - \frac{b^3}{a^4} \ln |au + b|$

INTEGRALS INVOLVING $u^2 + a^2$

55. $\displaystyle\int \frac{du}{u^2 + a^2} = \frac{1}{a} \tan^{-1} \frac{u}{a}$

56. $\displaystyle\int \frac{u \, du}{u^2 + a^2} = \frac{1}{2} \ln(u^2 + a^2)$

57. $\displaystyle\int \frac{u^2\,du}{u^2+a^2} = u - a\tan^{-1}\frac{u}{a}$

58. $\displaystyle\int \frac{u^3\,du}{u^2+a^2} = \frac{u^2}{2} - \frac{a^2}{2}\ln(u^2+a^2)$

59. $\displaystyle\int \frac{du}{u(u^2+a^2)} = \frac{1}{2a^2}\ln\left(\frac{u^2}{u^2+a^2}\right)$

60. $\displaystyle\int \frac{du}{u^2(u^2+a^2)} = -\frac{1}{a^2u} - \frac{1}{a^3}\tan^{-1}\frac{u}{a}$

61. $\displaystyle\int \frac{du}{u^3(u^2+a^2)} = -\frac{1}{2a^2u^2} - \frac{1}{2a^4}\ln\left(\frac{u^2}{u^2+a^2}\right)$

INTEGRALS INVOLVING $u^2 - a^2$, $u^2 > a^2$

74. $\displaystyle\int \frac{du}{u^2-a^2} = \frac{1}{2a}\ln\left|\frac{u-a}{u+a}\right| \text{ or } -\frac{1}{a}\coth^{-1}\frac{u}{a}$

75. $\displaystyle\int \frac{u\,du}{u^2-a^2} = \frac{1}{2}\ln\left|u^2-a^2\right|$

76. $\displaystyle\int \frac{u^2\,du}{u^2-a^2} = u + \frac{a}{2}\ln\left|\frac{u-a}{u+a}\right|$

77. $\displaystyle\int \frac{u^3\,du}{u^2-a^2} = \frac{u^2}{2} + \frac{a^2}{2}\ln\left|u^2-a^2\right|$

78. $\displaystyle\int \frac{du}{u(u^2-a^2)} = \frac{1}{2a^2}\ln\left|\frac{u^2-a^2}{u^2}\right|$

79. $\displaystyle\int \frac{du}{u^2(u^2-a^2)} = \frac{1}{a^2u} + \frac{1}{2a^3}\ln\left|\frac{u-a}{u+a}\right|$

80. $\displaystyle\int \frac{du}{u^3(u^2-a^2)} = \frac{1}{2a^2u^2} - \frac{1}{2a^4}\ln\left|\frac{u^2}{u^2-a^2}\right|$

INTEGRALS INVOLVING $a^2 - u^2$, $u^2 < a^2$

93. $\displaystyle\int \frac{du}{a^2-u^2} = \frac{1}{2a}\ln\left|\frac{a+u}{a-u}\right| \text{ or } \frac{1}{a}\tanh^{-1}\frac{u}{a}$

94. $\displaystyle\int \frac{u\,du}{a^2-u^2} = -\frac{1}{2}\ln\left|a^2-u^2\right|$

95. $\displaystyle\int \frac{u^2\,du}{a^2-u^2} = -u + \frac{a}{2}\ln\left|\frac{a+u}{a-u}\right|$

96. $\displaystyle\int \frac{u^3\,du}{a^2-u^2} = -\frac{u^2}{2} - \frac{a^2}{2}\ln\left|a^2-u^2\right|$

97. $\displaystyle\int \frac{du}{u(a^2-u^2)} = \frac{1}{2a^2}\ln\left|\frac{u^2}{a^2-u^2}\right|$

98. $\displaystyle\int \frac{du}{u^2(a^2-u^2)} = -\frac{1}{a^2u} + \frac{1}{2a^3}\ln\left|\frac{a+u}{a-u}\right|$

99. $\displaystyle\int \frac{du}{u^3(a^2-u^2)} = -\frac{1}{2a^2u^2} + \frac{1}{2a^4}\ln\left|\frac{u^2}{a^2-u^2}\right|$

100. $\displaystyle\int \frac{du}{(a^2-u^2)^2} = \frac{u}{2a^2(a^2-u^2)} + \frac{1}{4a^3}\ln\left|\frac{a+u}{a-u}\right|$

101. $\displaystyle\int \frac{u\,du}{(a^2-u^2)^2} = \frac{1}{2(a^2-u^2)}$

102. $\displaystyle\int \frac{u^2\,du}{(a^2-u^2)^2} = \frac{u}{2(a^2-u^2)} - \frac{1}{4a}\ln\left|\frac{a+u}{a-u}\right|$

103. $\displaystyle\int \frac{u^3\,du}{(a^2-u^2)^2} = \frac{a^2}{2(a^2-u^2)} + \frac{1}{2}\ln\left|a^2-u^2\right|$

104. $\displaystyle\int \frac{du}{u(a^2-u^2)^2} = \frac{1}{2a^2(a^2-u^2)} + \frac{1}{2a^4}\ln\left|\frac{u^2}{a^2-u^2}\right|$

105. $\displaystyle\int \frac{du}{u^2(a^2-u^2)^2} = \frac{-1}{a^4u} + \frac{u}{2a^4(a^2-u^2)} + \frac{3}{4a^5}\ln\left|\frac{a+u}{a-u}\right|$

106. $\displaystyle\int \frac{du}{u^3(a^2-u^2)^2} = \frac{-1}{2a^4u^2} + \frac{1}{2a^4(a^2-u^2)} + \frac{1}{a^6}\ln\left|\frac{u^2}{a^2-u^2}\right|$

INTEGRALS INVOLVING $\sqrt{au+b}$

135. $\displaystyle\int \frac{du}{\sqrt{au+b}} = \frac{2\sqrt{au+b}}{a}$

136. $\displaystyle\int \frac{u\,du}{\sqrt{au+b}} = \frac{2(au-2b)}{3a^2}\sqrt{au+b}$

137. $\displaystyle\int \frac{u^2\,du}{\sqrt{au+b}} = \frac{2(3a^2u^2 - 4abu + 8b^2)}{15a^3}\sqrt{au+b}$

138. $\displaystyle\int \frac{du}{u\sqrt{au+b}} = \begin{cases} \dfrac{1}{\sqrt{b}}\ln\left|\dfrac{\sqrt{au+b}-\sqrt{b}}{\sqrt{au+b}+\sqrt{b}}\right| \\[4ex] \dfrac{2}{\sqrt{-b}}\tan^{-1}\sqrt{\dfrac{au+b}{-b}} \end{cases}$

139. $\displaystyle\int \frac{du}{u^2\sqrt{au+b}} = -\frac{\sqrt{au+b}}{bu} - \frac{a}{2b}\int \frac{du}{u\sqrt{au+b}}$

140. $\displaystyle\int \sqrt{au+b}\,du = \frac{2\sqrt{(au+b)^3}}{3a}$

141. $\displaystyle\int u\sqrt{au+b}\,du = \frac{2(3au-2b)}{15a^2}\sqrt{(au+b)^3}$

142. $\displaystyle\int u^2\sqrt{au+b}\,du = \frac{2(15a^2u^2 - 12abu + 8b^2)}{105a^3}\sqrt{(au+b)^3}$

INTEGRALS INVOLVING $\sqrt{u^2 + a^2}$

168. $\displaystyle \int \sqrt{u^2 + a^2}\, du = \frac{u\sqrt{u^2 + a^2}}{2} + \frac{a^2}{2} \ln\left(u + \sqrt{u^2 + a^2}\right)$

169. $\displaystyle \int u\sqrt{u^2 + a^2}\, du = \frac{(u^2 + a^2)^{3/2}}{3}$

170. $\displaystyle \int u^2\sqrt{u^2 + a^2}\, du = \frac{u(u^2 + a^2)^{3/2}}{4} - \frac{a^2 u\sqrt{u^2 + a^2}}{8} - \frac{a^4}{8} \ln\left(u + \sqrt{u^2 + a^2}\right)$

171. $\displaystyle \int u^3\sqrt{u^2 + a^2}\, du = \frac{(u^2 + a^2)^{5/2}}{5} - \frac{a^2(u^2 + a^2)^{3/2}}{3}$

172. $\displaystyle \int \frac{du}{\sqrt{u^2 + a^2}} = \ln\left(u + \sqrt{u^2 + a^2}\right) \text{ or } \sinh^{-1}\frac{u}{a}$

173. $\displaystyle \int \frac{u\, du}{\sqrt{u^2 + a^2}} = \sqrt{u^2 + a^2}$

174. $\displaystyle \int \frac{u^2\, du}{\sqrt{u^2 + a^2}} = \frac{u\sqrt{u^2 + a^2}}{2} - \frac{a^2}{2} \ln\left(u + \sqrt{u^2 + a^2}\right)$

175. $\displaystyle \int \frac{u^3\, du}{\sqrt{u^2 + a^2}} = \frac{(u^2 + a^2)^{3/2}}{3} - a^2\sqrt{u^2 + a^2}$

176. $\displaystyle \int \frac{du}{u\sqrt{u^2 + a^2}} = -\frac{1}{a} \ln\left|\frac{a + \sqrt{u^2 + a^2}}{u}\right|$

177. $\displaystyle \int \frac{du}{u^2\sqrt{u^2 + a^2}} = -\frac{\sqrt{u^2 + a^2}}{a^2 u}$

178. $\displaystyle \int \frac{du}{u^3\sqrt{u^2 + a^2}} = -\frac{\sqrt{u^2 + a^2}}{2a^2 u^2} + \frac{1}{2a^3} \ln\left|\frac{a + \sqrt{u^2 + a^2}}{u}\right|$

179. $\displaystyle \int \frac{\sqrt{u^2 + a^2}}{u}\, du = \sqrt{u^2 + a^2} - a \ln\left|\frac{a + \sqrt{u^2 + a^2}}{u}\right|$

180. $\displaystyle \int \frac{\sqrt{u^2 + a^2}}{u^2}\, du = -\frac{\sqrt{u^2 + a^2}}{u} + \ln\left(u + \sqrt{u^2 + a^2}\right)$

INTEGRALS INVOLVING $\sqrt{u^2 - a^2}$

196. $\displaystyle \int \frac{du}{\sqrt{u^2 - a^2}} = \ln\left|u + \sqrt{u^2 - a^2}\right|$

197. $\displaystyle \int \frac{u\, du}{\sqrt{u^2 - a^2}} = \sqrt{u^2 - a^2}$

198. $\displaystyle \int \frac{u^2\, du}{\sqrt{u^2 - a^2}} = \frac{u\sqrt{u^2 - a^2}}{2} + \frac{a^2}{2} \ln\left|u + \sqrt{u^2 - a^2}\right|$

199. $\displaystyle \int \frac{u^3\, du}{\sqrt{u^2 - a^2}} = \frac{(u^2 - a^2)^{3/2}}{3} + a^2\sqrt{u^2 - a^2}$

200. $\displaystyle \int \frac{du}{u\sqrt{u^2 - a^2}} = \frac{1}{a} \sec^{-1}\left|\frac{u}{a}\right|$

201. $\displaystyle\int \frac{du}{u^2\sqrt{u^2-a^2}} = \frac{\sqrt{u^2-a^2}}{a^2 u}$

202. $\displaystyle\int \frac{du}{u^3\sqrt{u^2-a^2}} = \frac{\sqrt{u^2-a^2}}{2a^2 u^2} + \frac{1}{2a^3}\sec^{-1}\left|\frac{u}{a}\right|$

203. $\displaystyle\int \sqrt{u^2-a^2}\,du = \frac{u\sqrt{u^2-a^2}}{2} - \frac{a^2}{2}\ln\left|u+\sqrt{u^2-a^2}\right|$

204. $\displaystyle\int u\sqrt{u^2-a^2}\,du = \frac{(u^2-a^2)^{3/2}}{3}$

205. $\displaystyle\int u^2\sqrt{u^2-a^2}\,du = \frac{u(u^2-a^2)^{3/2}}{4} + \frac{a^2 u\sqrt{u^2-a^2}}{8} - \frac{a^4}{8}\ln\left|u+\sqrt{u^2-a^2}\right|$

206. $\displaystyle\int u^3\sqrt{u^2-a^2}\,du = \frac{(u^2-a^2)^{5}/2}{5} + \frac{a^2(u^2-a^2)^{3/2}}{3}$

INTEGRALS INVOLVING $\sqrt{a^2-u^2}$

224. $\displaystyle\int \frac{du}{\sqrt{a^2-u^2}} = \sin^{-1}\frac{u}{a}$

225. $\displaystyle\int \frac{u\,du}{\sqrt{a^2-u^2}} = -\sqrt{a^2-u^2}$

226. $\displaystyle\int \frac{u^2\,du}{\sqrt{a^2-u^2}} = -\frac{u\sqrt{a^2-u^2}}{2} + \frac{a^2}{2}\sin^{-1}\frac{u}{a}$

227. $\displaystyle\int \frac{u^3\,du}{\sqrt{a^2-u^2}} = \frac{(a^2-u^2)^{3/2}}{3} - a^2\sqrt{a^2-u^2}$

228. $\displaystyle\int \frac{du}{u\sqrt{a^2-u^2}} = -\frac{1}{a}\ln\left|\frac{a+\sqrt{a^2-u^2}}{u}\right|$ or $-\frac{1}{a}\operatorname{sech}^{-1}\left|\frac{u}{a}\right|$

229. $\displaystyle\int \frac{du}{u^2\sqrt{a^2-u^2}} = -\frac{\sqrt{a^2-u^2}}{a^2 u}$

230. $\displaystyle\int \frac{du}{u^3\sqrt{a^2-u^2}} = -\frac{\sqrt{a^2-u^2}}{2a^2 u^2} - \frac{1}{2a^3}\ln\left|\frac{a+\sqrt{a^2-u^2}}{u}\right|$

231. $\displaystyle\int \sqrt{a^2-u^2}\,du = \frac{u\sqrt{a^2-u^2}}{2} + \frac{a^2}{2}\sin^{-1}\frac{u}{a}$

232. $\displaystyle\int u\sqrt{a^2-u^2}\,du = -\frac{(a^2-u^2)^{3/2}}{3}$

233. $\displaystyle\int u^2\sqrt{a^2-u^2}\,du = -\frac{u(a^2-u^2)^{3/2}}{4} + \frac{a^2 u\sqrt{a^2-u^2}}{8} + \frac{a^4}{8}\sin^{-1}\frac{u}{a}$

234. $\displaystyle\int u^3\sqrt{a^2-u^2}\,du = \frac{(a^2-u^2)^{5/2}}{5} - \frac{a^2(a^2-u^2)^{3/2}}{3}$

235. $\displaystyle\int \frac{\sqrt{a^2-u^2}}{u}\,du = \sqrt{a^2-u^2} - a\ln\left|\frac{a+\sqrt{a^2-u^2}}{u}\right|$

INTEGRALS INVOLVING cos *au*

311. $\displaystyle\int \cos au\, du = \frac{\sin au}{a}$

312. $\displaystyle\int u \cos au\, du = \frac{\cos au}{a^2} + \frac{u \sin au}{a}$

313. $\displaystyle\int u^2 \cos au\, du = \frac{2u}{a^2}\cos au + \left(\frac{u^2}{a} - \frac{2}{a^3}\right)\sin au$

314. $\displaystyle\int u^3 \cos au\, du = \left(\frac{3u^2}{a^2} - \frac{6}{a^4}\right)\cos au + \left(\frac{u^3}{a} - \frac{6u}{a^3}\right)\sin au$

315. $\displaystyle\int u^n \cos au\, du = \frac{u^n \sin au}{a} - \frac{n}{a}\int u^{n-1}\sin au\, du$

316. $\displaystyle\int u^n \cos au\, du = \frac{u^n \sin au}{a} + \frac{nu^{n-1}}{a^2}\cos au - \frac{n(n-1)}{a^2}\int u^{n-2}\cos au\, du$

317. $\displaystyle\int \cos^2 au\, du = \frac{u}{2} + \frac{\sin 2au}{4a}$

INTEGRALS INVOLVING sin *au*

342. $\displaystyle\int \sin au\, du = -\frac{\cos au}{a}$

343. $\displaystyle\int u \sin au\, du = \frac{\sin au}{a^2} - \frac{u \cos au}{a}$

344. $\displaystyle\int u^2 \sin au\, du = \frac{2u}{a^2}\sin au + \left(\frac{2}{a^3} - \frac{u^2}{a}\right)\cos au$

345. $\displaystyle\int u^3 \sin au\, du = \left(\frac{3u^2}{a^2} - \frac{6}{a^4}\right)\sin au + \left(\frac{6u}{a^3} - \frac{u^3}{a}\right)\cos au$

346. $\displaystyle\int u^n \sin au\, du = -\frac{u^n \cos au}{a} + \frac{n}{a}\int u^{n-1}\cos au\, du$

347. $\displaystyle\int u^n \sin au\, du = -\frac{u^n \cos au}{a} + \frac{nu^{n-1}\sin au}{a^2} - \frac{n(n-1)}{a^2}\int u^{n-2}\sin au\, du$

348. $\displaystyle\int \sin^2 au\, du = \frac{u}{2} - \frac{\sin 2au}{4a}$

349. $\displaystyle\int u \sin^2 au\, du = \frac{u^2}{4} - \frac{u \sin 2au}{4a} - \frac{\cos 2au}{8a^2}$

350. $\displaystyle\int \sin^3 au\, du = -\frac{\cos au}{a} + \frac{\cos^3 au}{3a}$

351. $\displaystyle\int \sin^4 au\, du = \frac{3u}{8} - \frac{\sin 2au}{4a} + \frac{\sin 4au}{32a}$

INTEGRALS INVOLVING sin *au* and cos *au*

373. $\displaystyle\int \sin au \cos au \, du = \frac{\sin^2 au}{2a}$

374. $\displaystyle\int \sin pu \cos qu \, du = -\frac{\cos(p-q)u}{2(p-q)} - \frac{\cos(p+q)u}{2(p+q)}$

375. $\displaystyle\int \sin^n au \cos au \, du = \frac{\sin^{n+1} au}{(n+1)a}$

376. $\displaystyle\int \cos^n au \sin au \, du = -\frac{\cos^{n+1} au}{(n+1)a}$

377. $\displaystyle\int \sin^2 au \cos^2 au \, du = \frac{u}{8} - \frac{\sin 4au}{32a}$

378. $\displaystyle\int \frac{du}{\sin au \cos au} = \frac{1}{a} \ln |\tan au|$

379. $\displaystyle\int \frac{du}{\sin^2 au \cos au} = \frac{1}{a} \ln \left| \tan \left(\frac{\pi}{4} + \frac{au}{2} \right) \right| - \frac{1}{a \sin au}$

380. $\displaystyle\int \frac{du}{\sin au \cos^2 au} = \frac{1}{a} \ln \left| \tan \frac{au}{2} \right| + \frac{1}{a \cos au}$

INTEGRALS INVOLVING tan *au*

403. $\displaystyle\int \tan au \, du = -\frac{1}{a} \ln |\cos au| \text{ or } \frac{1}{a} \ln |\sec au|$

404. $\displaystyle\int \tan^2 au \, du = \frac{\tan au}{a} - u$

405. $\displaystyle\int \tan^3 au \, du = \frac{\tan^2 au}{2a} + \frac{1}{a} \ln |\cos au|$

406. $\displaystyle\int \tan^n au \, du = \frac{\tan^{n-1} au}{(n-1)a} - \int \tan^{n-2} au \, du$

407. $\displaystyle\int \tan^n au \sec^2 au \, du = \frac{\tan^{n+1} au}{(n+1)a}$

INTEGRALS INVOLVING cot *au*

414. $\displaystyle\int \cot au \, du = \frac{1}{a} \ln |\sin au|$

415. $\displaystyle\int \cot^2 au \, du = -\frac{\cot au}{a} - u$

416. $\displaystyle\int \cot^3 au \, du = -\frac{\cot^2 au}{2a} - \frac{1}{a} \ln |\sin au|$

417. $\displaystyle\int \cot^n au \, du = -\frac{\cot^{n-1} au}{(n-1)a} - \int \cot^{n-2} au \, du$

INTEGRALS INVOLVING sec *au*

425. $\displaystyle\int \sec au\, du = \frac{1}{a}\ln|\sec au + \tan au| = \frac{1}{a}\ln\left|\tan\left(\frac{au}{2}+\frac{\pi}{4}\right)\right|$

426. $\displaystyle\int \sec^2 au\, du = \frac{\tan au}{a}$

427. $\displaystyle\int \sec^3 au\, du = \frac{\sec au\,\tan au}{2a} + \frac{1}{2a}\ln|\sec au + \tan au|$

428. $\displaystyle\int \sec^n au\, du = \frac{\sec^{n-2} au\,\tan au}{a(n-1)} + \frac{n-2}{n-1}\int \sec^{n-2} au\, du$

INTEGRALS INVOLVING csc *au*

435. $\displaystyle\int \csc au\, du = \frac{1}{a}\ln|\csc au - \cot au| = \frac{1}{a}\ln\left|\tan\frac{au}{2}\right|$

436. $\displaystyle\int \csc^2 au\, du = -\frac{\cot au}{a}$

437. $\displaystyle\int \csc^3 au\, du = -\frac{\csc au\,\cot au}{2a} + \frac{1}{2a}\ln\left|\tan\frac{au}{2}\right|$

438. $\displaystyle\int \csc^n au\, du = -\frac{\csc^{n-2} au\,\cot au}{a(n-1)} + \frac{n-2}{n-1}\int \csc^{n-2} au\, du$

INTEGRALS INVOLVING INVERSE TRIGONOMETRIC FUNCTIONS

445. $\displaystyle\int \cos^{-1}\frac{u}{a}\, du = u\cos^{-1}\frac{u}{a} - \sqrt{a^2 - u^2}$

446. $\displaystyle\int u\cos^{-1}\frac{u}{a}\, du = \left(\frac{u^2}{2}-\frac{a^2}{4}\right)\cos^{-1}\frac{u}{a} - \frac{u\sqrt{a^2-u^2}}{4}$

447. $\displaystyle\int u^2\cos^{-1}\frac{u}{a}\, du = \frac{u^3}{3}\cos^{-1}\frac{u}{a} - \frac{(u^2+2a^2)\sqrt{a^2-u^2}}{9}$

448. $\displaystyle\int \frac{\cos^{-1}(u/a)}{u}\, du = \frac{\pi}{2}\ln|u| - \int \frac{\sin^{-1}(u/a)}{u}\, du$

449. $\displaystyle\int \frac{\cos^{-1}(u/a)}{u^2}\, du = -\frac{\cos^{-1}(u/a)}{u} + \frac{1}{a}\ln\left|\frac{a+\sqrt{a^2-u^2}}{u}\right|$

450. $\displaystyle\int \left(\cos^{-1}\frac{u}{a}\right)^2 du = u\left(\cos^{-1}\frac{u}{a}\right)^2 - 2u - 2\sqrt{a^2-u^2}\cos^{-1}\frac{u}{a}$

451. $\displaystyle\int \sin^{-1}\frac{u}{a}\, du = u\sin^{-1}\frac{u}{a} + \sqrt{a^2-u^2}$

452. $\displaystyle\int u\sin^{-1}\frac{u}{a}\, du = \left(\frac{u^2}{2}-\frac{a^2}{4}\right)\sin^{-1}\frac{u}{a} + \frac{u\sqrt{a^2-u^2}}{4}$

453. $\displaystyle\int u^2\sin^{-1}\frac{u}{a}\, du = \frac{u^3}{3}\sin^{-1}\frac{u}{a} + \frac{(u^2+2a^2)\sqrt{a^2-u^2}}{9}$

454. $\displaystyle\int \frac{\sin^{-1}(u/a)}{u}\, du = \frac{u}{a} + \frac{(u/a)^3}{2\cdot3\cdot3} + \frac{1\cdot3(u/a)^5}{2\cdot4\cdot5\cdot5} + \frac{1\cdot3\cdot5(u/a)^7}{2\cdot4\cdot6\cdot7\cdot7} + \cdots$

455. $\displaystyle\int \frac{\sin^{-1}(u/a)}{u^2}\, du = -\frac{\sin^{-1}(u/a)}{u} - \frac{1}{a} \ln\left|\frac{a + \sqrt{a^2 - u^2}}{u}\right|$

456. $\displaystyle\int \left(\sin^{-1}\frac{u}{a}\right)^2 du = u \left(\sin^{-1}\frac{u}{a}\right)^2 - 2u + 2\sqrt{a^2 - u^2}\, \sin^{-1}\frac{u}{a}$

457. $\displaystyle\int \tan^{-1}\frac{u}{a}\, du = u \tan^{-1}\frac{u}{a} - \frac{a}{2}\ln\left(u^2 + a^2\right)$

458. $\displaystyle\int u \tan^{-1}\frac{u}{a}\, du = \frac{1}{2}(u^2 + a^2)\tan^{-1}\frac{u}{a} - \frac{au}{2}$

459. $\displaystyle\int u^2 \tan^{-1}\frac{u}{a}\, du = \frac{u^3}{3}\tan^{-1}\frac{u}{a} - \frac{au^2}{6} + \frac{a^3}{6}\ln(u^2 + a^2)$

INTEGRALS INVOLVING e^{au}

483. $\displaystyle\int e^{au}\, du = \frac{e^{au}}{a}$

484. $\displaystyle\int u e^{au}\, du = \frac{e^{au}}{a}\left(u - \frac{1}{a}\right)$

485. $\displaystyle\int u^2 e^{au}\, du = \frac{e^{au}}{a}\left(u^2 - \frac{2u}{a} + \frac{2}{a^2}\right)$

486. $\displaystyle\int u^n e^{au}\, du = \frac{u^n e^{au}}{a} - \frac{n}{a}\int u^{n-1} e^{au}\, du$

$\displaystyle\qquad = \frac{e^{au}}{a}\left(u^n - \frac{n u^{n-1}}{a} + \frac{n(n-1)u^{n-2}}{a^2} - \cdots + \frac{(-1)^n n!}{a^n}\right)$

if $n = $ positive integer

487. $\displaystyle\int \frac{e^{au}}{u}\, du = \ln|u| + \frac{au}{1 \cdot 1!} + \frac{(au)^2}{2 \cdot 2!} + \frac{(au)^3}{3 \cdot 3!} + \cdots$

488. $\displaystyle\int \frac{e^{au}}{u^n}\, du = \frac{-e^{au}}{(n-1)u^{n-1}} + \frac{a}{n-1}\int \frac{e^{au}}{u^{n-1}}\, du$

489. $\displaystyle\int \frac{du}{p + q e^{au}} = \frac{u}{p} - \frac{1}{ap}\ln\left|p + q e^{au}\right|$

490. $\displaystyle\int \frac{du}{(p + q e^{au})^2} = \frac{u}{p^2} + \frac{1}{ap(p + q e^{au})} - \frac{1}{ap^2}\ln\left|p + q e^{au}\right|$

491. $\displaystyle\int \frac{du}{p e^{au} + q e^{-au}} = \begin{cases} \dfrac{1}{a\sqrt{pq}}\tan^{-1}\left(\sqrt{\dfrac{p}{q}}\, e^{au}\right) \\[3mm] \dfrac{1}{2a\sqrt{-pq}}\ln\left|\dfrac{e^{au} - \sqrt{-q/p}}{e^{au} + \sqrt{-q/p}}\right| \end{cases}$

492. $\displaystyle\int e^{au}\sin bu\, du = \frac{e^{au}(a\sin bu - b\cos bu)}{a^2 + b^2}$

493. $\displaystyle\int e^{au}\cos bu\, du = \frac{e^{au}(a\cos bu + b\sin bu)}{a^2 + b^2}$

494. $\displaystyle\int u e^{au}\sin bu\, du = \frac{u e^{au}(a\sin bu - b\cos bu)}{a^2 + b^2}$

$\displaystyle\qquad\qquad - \frac{e^{au}[(a^2 - b^2)\sin bu - 2ab\cos bu]}{(a^2 + b^2)^2}$

495. $\int u e^{au} \cos bu\, du = \dfrac{u e^{au}(a \cos bu + b \sin bu)}{a^2 + b^2}$

$$- \dfrac{e^{au}[(a^2 - b^2) \cos bu + 2ab \sin bu]}{(a^2 + b^2)^2}$$

INTEGRALS INVOLVING $\ln |u|$

499. $\displaystyle\int \ln |u|\, du = u \ln |u| - u$

500. $\displaystyle\int (\ln |u|)^2\, du = u(\ln |u|)^2 - 2u \ln |u| + 2u$

501. $\displaystyle\int (\ln |u|)^n\, du = u(\ln |u|)^n - n \int (\ln |u|)^{n-1}\, du$

502. $\displaystyle\int u \ln |u|\, du = \dfrac{u^2}{2}(\ln |u| - \dfrac{1}{2})$

503. $\displaystyle\int u^m \ln |u|\, du = \dfrac{u^{m+1}}{m+1}\left(\ln |u| - \dfrac{1}{m+1}\right)$

APPENDIX E   Trigonometric Formulas

 See Chapter 4 of the *Student Mathematics Handbook* for a review of trigonometry.

Definition of the Trigonometric Functions

Let θ be any angle in standard position and let $P(x, y)$ be any point on the terminal side of the angle a distance of r from the origin ($r \neq 0$). Then

$$\cos \theta = \frac{x}{r} \qquad \sin \theta = \frac{y}{r}$$

$$\tan \theta = \frac{y}{x} \qquad \sec \theta = \frac{r}{x}$$

$$\csc \theta = \frac{r}{y} \qquad \cot \theta = \frac{x}{y}$$

Definition of the Inverse Trigonometric Functions

Inverse Trigonometric Function	Domain	Range
$y = \arccos x$ or $y = \cos^{-1} x$	$-1 \le x \le 1$	$0 \le y \le \pi$
$y = \arcsin x$ or $y = \sin^{-1} x$	$-1 \le x \le 1$	$-\frac{\pi}{2} \le y \le \frac{\pi}{2}$
$y = \arctan x$ or $y = \tan^{-1} x$	All reals	$-\frac{\pi}{2} < y < \frac{\pi}{2}$
$y = \operatorname{arccot} x$ or $y = \cot^{-1} x$	All reals	$0 < y < \pi$
$y = \operatorname{arcsec} x$ or $y = \sec^{-1} x$	$|x| \ge 1$	$0 \le y \le \pi, y \neq \frac{\pi}{2}$
$y = \operatorname{arccsc} x$ or $y = \csc^{-1} x$	$|x| \ge 1$	$-\frac{\pi}{2} \le y \le \frac{\pi}{2}, y \neq 0$

The principal values of the inverse trigonometric relations are those values defined by these inverse trigonometric functions. These are the values obtained when using a calculator.

Trigonometric Identities   Fundamental identities

Reciprocal identities

1. $\sec\theta = \dfrac{1}{\cos\theta}$ **2.** $\csc\theta = \dfrac{1}{\sin\theta}$ **3.** $\cot\theta = \dfrac{1}{\tan\theta}$

Ratio identities

4. $\tan\theta = \dfrac{\sin\theta}{\cos\theta}$ **5.** $\cot\theta = \dfrac{\cos\theta}{\sin\theta}$

Pythagorean identities

6. $\cos^2\theta + \sin^2\theta = 1$ **7.** $1 + \tan^2\theta = \sec^2\theta$ **8.** $\cot^2\theta + 1 = \csc^2\theta$

Cofunction identities

9. $\cos\left(\dfrac{\pi}{2} - \theta\right) = \sin\theta$ **10.** $\sin\left(\dfrac{\pi}{2} - \theta\right) = \cos\theta$ **11.** $\tan\left(\dfrac{\pi}{2} - \theta\right) = \cot\theta$

Opposite-angle identities

12. $\cos(-\theta) = \cos\theta$ **13.** $\sin(-\theta) = -\sin\theta$ **14.** $\tan(-\theta) = -\tan\theta$

Addition laws

15. $\cos(\alpha + \beta) = \cos\alpha\cos\beta - \sin\alpha\sin\beta$

16. $\cos(\alpha - \beta) = \cos\alpha\cos\beta + \sin\alpha\sin\beta$

17. $\sin(\alpha + \beta) = \sin\alpha\cos\beta + \cos\alpha\sin\beta$

18. $\sin(\alpha - \beta) = \sin\alpha\cos\beta - \cos\alpha\sin\beta$

19. $\tan(\alpha + \beta) = \dfrac{\tan\alpha + \tan\beta}{1 - \tan\alpha\tan\beta}$ **20.** $\tan(\alpha - \beta) = \dfrac{\tan\alpha - \tan\beta}{1 + \tan\alpha\tan\beta}$

Double-angle identities

21. $\begin{aligned}\cos 2\theta &= \cos^2\theta - \sin^2\theta \\ &= 2\cos^2\theta - 1 \\ &= 1 - 2\sin^2\theta\end{aligned}$ **22.** $\sin 2\theta = 2\sin\theta\cos\theta$

23. $\tan 2\theta = \dfrac{2\tan\theta}{1 - \tan^2\theta}$

Half-angle identities

24. $\cos\dfrac{1}{2}\theta = \pm\sqrt{\dfrac{1 + \cos\theta}{2}}$ **25.** $\sin\dfrac{1}{2}\theta = \pm\sqrt{\dfrac{1 - \cos\theta}{2}}$

26. $\begin{aligned}\tan\dfrac{1}{2}\theta &= \dfrac{1 - \cos\theta}{\sin\theta} \\[2mm] &= \dfrac{\sin\theta}{1 + \cos\theta}\end{aligned}$

Product-to-sum identities

27. $2\cos\alpha\cos\beta = \cos(\alpha - \beta) + \cos(\alpha + \beta)$

28. $2\sin\alpha\sin\beta = \cos(\alpha - \beta) - \cos(\alpha + \beta)$

29. $2\sin\alpha\cos\beta = \sin(\alpha + \beta) + \sin(\alpha - \beta)$

30. $2\cos\alpha\sin\beta = \sin(\alpha + \beta) - \sin(\alpha - \beta)$

Sum-to-product identities

31. $\cos\alpha + \cos\beta = 2\cos\left(\dfrac{\alpha + \beta}{2}\right)\cos\left(\dfrac{\alpha - \beta}{2}\right)$

32. $\cos\alpha - \cos\beta = -2\sin\left(\dfrac{\alpha + \beta}{2}\right)\sin\left(\dfrac{\alpha - \beta}{2}\right)$

33. $\sin\alpha + \sin\beta = 2\sin\left(\dfrac{\alpha + \beta}{2}\right)\cos\left(\dfrac{\alpha - \beta}{2}\right)$

34. $\sin\alpha - \sin\beta = 2\sin\left(\dfrac{\alpha-\beta}{2}\right)\cos\left(\dfrac{\alpha+\beta}{2}\right)$

Hyperbolic identities

35. $\operatorname{sech} x = \dfrac{1}{\cosh x}$

36. $\operatorname{csch} x = \dfrac{1}{\sinh x}$

37. $\coth x = \dfrac{1}{\tanh x}$

38. $\tanh x = \dfrac{\sinh x}{\cosh x}$

39. $\coth x = \dfrac{\cosh x}{\sinh x}$

40. $\cosh^2 x - \sinh^2 x = 1$

41. $1 - \tanh^2 x = \operatorname{sech}^2 x$

42. $\coth^2 x - 1 = \operatorname{csch}^2 x$

43. $\sinh(-x) = -\sinh x$

44. $\cosh(-x) = \cosh x$

45. $\tanh(-x) = -\tanh x$

46. $\sinh(x \pm y) = \sinh x \cosh y \pm \cosh x \sinh y$

47. $\cosh(x \pm y) = \cosh x \cosh y \pm \sinh x \sinh y$

48. $\tanh(x \pm y) = \dfrac{\tanh x \pm \tanh y}{1 \pm \tanh x \tanh y}$

49. $\begin{aligned}\cosh 2x &= \cosh^2 x + \sinh^2 x \\ &= 2\cosh^2 x - 1 \\ &= 1 + 2\sinh^2 x\end{aligned}$

50. $\sinh 2x = 2\sinh x \cosh x$

51. $\tanh 2x = \dfrac{2\tanh x}{1 + \tanh^2 x}$

52. $\cosh\dfrac{1}{2}x = \pm\sqrt{\dfrac{\cosh x + 1}{2}}$

53. $\sinh\dfrac{1}{2}x = \pm\sqrt{\dfrac{\cosh x - 1}{2}}$

54. $\tanh\dfrac{1}{2}x = \dfrac{\cosh x - 1}{\sinh x} = \dfrac{\sinh x}{\cosh x + 1}$

55. $\sinh^{-1} x = \ln(x + \sqrt{x^2 + 1})$

56. $\operatorname{csch}^{-1} x = \ln\left(\dfrac{1 + \sqrt{1 + x^2}}{x}\right)$ if $x > 0$

57. $\cosh^{-1} x = \ln(x + \sqrt{x^2 - 1})$

58. $\operatorname{sech}^{-1} x = \ln\left(\dfrac{1 + \sqrt{1 - x^2}}{x}\right)$ if $0 < x \le 1$

59. $\tanh^{-1} x = \dfrac{1}{2}\ln\left(\dfrac{1 + x}{1 - x}\right)$ if $-1 < x < 1$

60. $\coth^{-1} x = \dfrac{1}{2}\ln\left(\dfrac{x + 1}{x - 1}\right)$ if $x^2 > 1$

APPENDIX F   Answers to Selected Problems

Many problems in this book are labeled WHAT DOES THIS SAY? *These problems solicit answers in your own words or a statement for you to rephrase as given statement in your own words. For this reason, it seems inappropriate to include the answers to these questions.* COUNTEREXAMPLE PROBLEMS *generally ask for counterexamples for which answers may vary so these answers are also not given.*

   We also believe that an answer section should function as a check on work done, so for that reason, when an answer has both an exact answer and an approximate solution (from technology), we usually show only the approximate solution in this appendix. The exact solution (which may be the more appropriate answer) can be **checked** *by using the given approximation.*

   The Student Survival and Solutions Manual *offers some review, survival hints, and added explanations for selected problems.*

Chapter 1: Functions and Graphs

1.1 Preliminaries (Pages 10–13)

1. a. $(-3, 4)$ **b.** $3 \le x \le 5$ **c.** $-2 \le x < 1$ **d.** $(2, 7]$

3. a.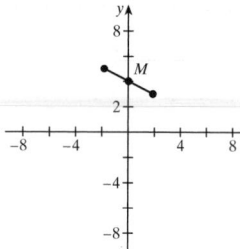

b.

c.

d.

5. a.   **b.**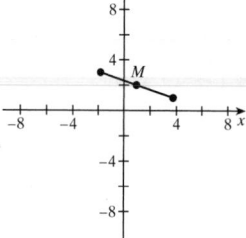

$M = (0, 4); d = 2\sqrt{5}$ $M = (1, 2); d = 2\sqrt{10}$

7. $x = 0, 1$ **9.** $y = 7, -2$ **11.** $x = \dfrac{b \pm \sqrt{b^2 + 12c}}{6}$

13. $x = 6, -10$ **15.** $w = -2, 5$ **17.** $\varnothing$

19. $x = \frac{7\pi}{6}, \frac{11\pi}{6}$ **21.** $x = \frac{3\pi}{4}, \frac{5\pi}{4}, \frac{\pi}{3}, \frac{5\pi}{3}$ **23.** $x = \frac{2\pi}{3}$

25. $\left(-\infty, -\frac{5}{3}\right)$ **27.** $\left(-\frac{5}{3}, 0\right)$ **29.** $(-8, -3]$

31. $[-1, 3]$ **33.** $[7.999, 8.001]$

35. $(x + 1)^2 + (y - 2)^2 = 9$ **37.** $x^2 + (y - 1.5)^2 = 0.0625$

39. Center $(1, -1); r = 1$ **41.** Center $(-1, 5); r = 1$

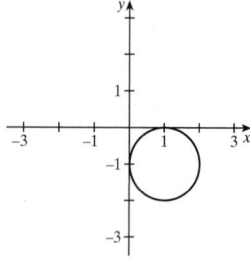

43. $\dfrac{\sqrt{2} - \sqrt{6}}{4} \approx -0.2588$ **45.** $2 - \sqrt{3} \approx 0.2679$

51. a. period 2π **b.** period 2π

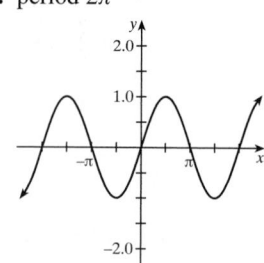   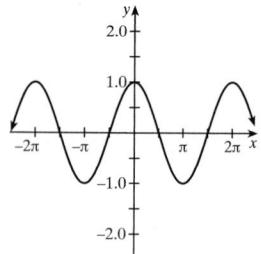

c. period π

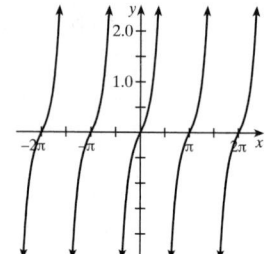

53. period $\pi/2$ **55.** period 4π

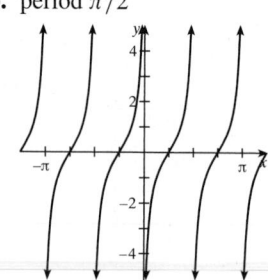   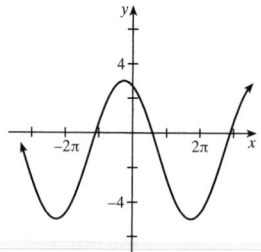

57.

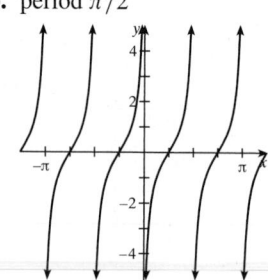

$A = 0, B = 60, C = \frac{\pi}{15}$, and $D = 7.5$

59. sun curve: $y = \cos \frac{\pi}{6}x$; moon curve: $y = 4\cos \frac{\pi}{6}x$; combined curve: $y = 5 \cos \frac{\pi}{6}x$

61. a. The apparent depth is 3.4 m.

b. The angle of incidence is 59°.

1.2 Lines in the Plane (Pages 17–19)

3. $2x + y - 5 = 0$ **5.** $2y - 1 = 0$

7. $x + 2 = 0$ **9.** $8x - 7y - 56 = 0$

11. $3x + y - 5 = 0$ **13.** $3x + 4y - 1 = 0$

15. $4x + y + 3 = 0$

17. $m = -5/7$;

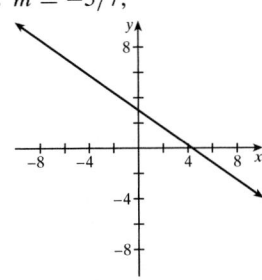

$(0, 3), \left(\frac{21}{5}, 0\right)$

19. $m = 6.001$;

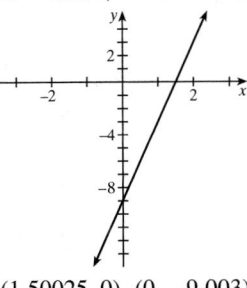

$(1.50025, 0), (0, -9.003)$

21. $y = -\frac{3}{5}x - 3$; $m = -3/5$ **23.** $y = \frac{3}{5}x - 0.3$; $m = 3/5$

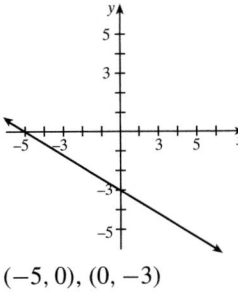

$(-5, 0), (0, -3)$

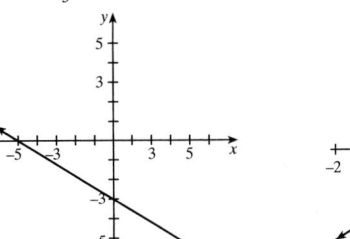

$(0.5, 0), (0, -0.3)$

25. $m = 3/2$ **27.** $y = \frac{1}{5}x$; $m = 1/5$

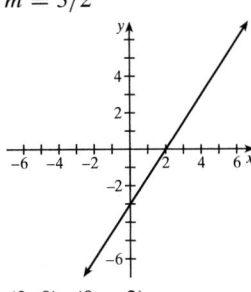

$(2, 0), (0, -3)$

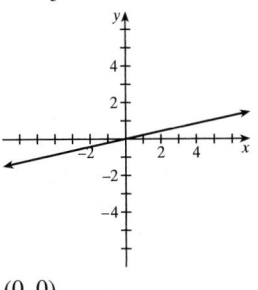

$(0, 0)$

29. no slope

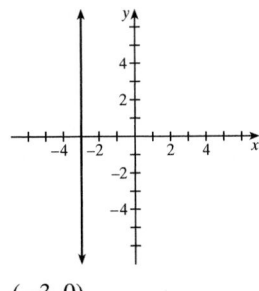

$(-3, 0)$

31. $y = 0$ and $y = 6$

33. $D(6, 6)$ or $E(2, 16)$; two parallelograms can be found

35. no values   **37.** $(4, -1)$

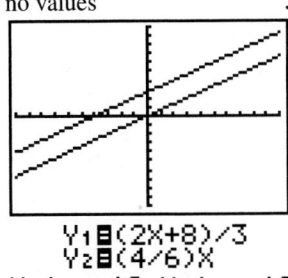

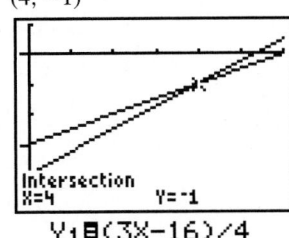

39. $\left(\frac{3}{4}, \frac{7}{2}\right)$ **41.** $\left(-\frac{64}{3}, \frac{100}{3}\right)$

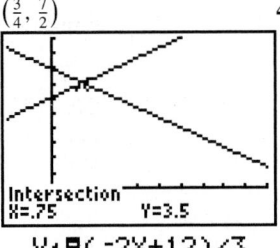

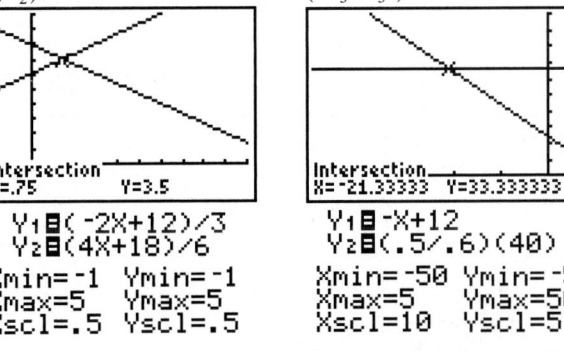

43. $(\sqrt{2}, \sqrt{2}), (-\sqrt{2}, -\sqrt{2})$ **45.** $\left(-\frac{15}{8}, \frac{7\sqrt{15}}{8}\right), \left(-\frac{15}{8}, -\frac{7\sqrt{15}}{8}\right)$

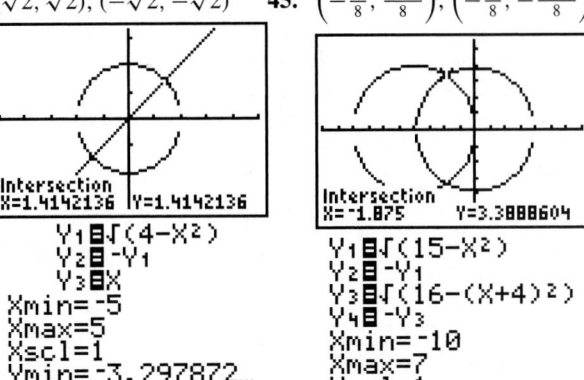

47. a. $-38.2°F$ **b.** $-17.8°C$ **c.** $-40°$

49. The Spy escapes since freedom is reached at the border after only 83.8 km.

51. $V(t) = -19{,}000t + 200{,}000$

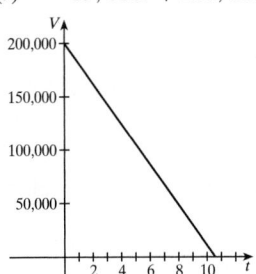

The value in 4 years is $\$124{,}000$.

55. For the 8th month, 216 gallons

57. a. $\$48$ **b.** not linear

59. $x = \dfrac{a \pm \sqrt{a^2 - 4}}{2}$, $y = \dfrac{2}{a \pm \sqrt{a^2 - 4}}$

1.3 Functions and Graphs (Pages 31–33)

Let D represent the domain in Problems 1–11.

1. $D = (-\infty, \infty)$; $f(-2) = -1$; $f(1) = 5$; $f(0) = 3$

3. $D = (-\infty, \infty)$; $f(1) = 6$; $f(0) = -2$; $f(-2) = 0$

5. $D = (-\infty, -3) \cup (-3, \infty)$; $f(2) = 0$; $f(0) = -2$; $f(-3)$ is undefined

7. $D = (-\infty, -2] \cup [0, \infty)$; $f(-1)$ is undefined; $f\left(\frac{1}{2}\right) = \frac{\sqrt{5}}{2}$; $f(1) = \sqrt{3}$

9. $D = (-\infty, \infty)$; $f(-1) = \sin 3 \approx 0.1411$; $f\left(\frac{1}{2}\right) = 0$; $f(1) = \sin(-1) \approx -0.8415$

11. $D = (-\infty, \infty)$; $f(3) = 4$; $f(1) = 2$; $f(0) = 4$

13. 9   **15.** $10x + 5h$ **17.** -1 **19.** $\dfrac{-1}{x(x+h)}$

21. not equal   **23.** equal   **25.** not equal

27. even   **29.** neither   **31.** neither   **33.** even

35. $(f \circ g)(x) = 4x^2 + 1$; $(g \circ f)(x) = 2x^2 + 2$

37. $(f \circ g)(t) = |t|$; $(g \circ f)(t) = t$

39. $(f \circ g)(x) = \sin(2x + 3)$; $(g \circ f)(x) = 2\sin x + 3$

41. $u(x) = 2x^2 - 1$; $g(u) = u^4$

43. $u(x) = 2x + 3$; $g(u) = |u|$

45. $u(x) = \tan x$; $g(u) = u^2$

47. $u(x) = \sqrt{x}$; $g(u) = \sin u$

49. $u(x) = \dfrac{x+1}{2-x}$; $g(u) = \sin u$

51. $P(5, f(5))$; $Q(x_0, f(x_0))$

53. $-\frac{1}{3}, 2$ **55.** $15, -\frac{25}{2}, \frac{65}{3}, -\frac{1}{4}$

57. 0   **59.** ± 1

61. a. The cost is $4,500.   **b.** The cost of the 20th unit is $371.

63. a. $I = \dfrac{30}{t^2(6-t)^2}$ **b.** $I(1) = \frac{6}{5}$ candles; $I(4) = \frac{15}{32}$ candles

65. a. $625t^2 + 25t + 900$ **b.** $6,600   **c.** 4 hours

67. a.   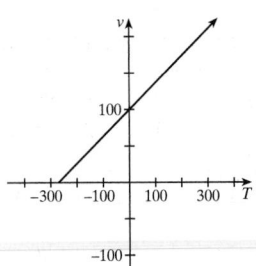   **b.** $T = 273$

69. a. The maximum height of the cannonball is 280 ft.

  b. It hits the ground approximately 1,243 ft from the firing point.

  c. The basic shape of a parabola (standard quadratic function).

71. a. 19,400 people   **b.** 67 people

  c. The population will tend to 20,000 people in the long run.

73. Pythagorean theorem: $\triangle ABC$ with sides a, b, and c is a right triangle if and only if $c^2 = a^2 + b^2$. Proofs vary.

1.4 Inverse Functions; Inverse Trigonometric Functions (Pages 41–42)

3. These are inverse functions.

5. These are not inverse functions.

7. These are not inverse functions.

9. $\{(5, 4), (3, 6), (1, 7), (4, 2)\}$

11. $y = \frac{1}{2}x - \frac{3}{2}$ **13.** $y = \sqrt{x+5}$

15. $y = (x - 5)^2$ **17.** $y = \dfrac{3x+6}{2-3x}$

19. a. $\frac{\pi}{3}$ **b.** $-\frac{\pi}{3}$ **21. a.** $-\frac{\pi}{4}$ **b.** $\frac{5\pi}{6}$

23. a. $-\frac{\pi}{3}$ **b.** π **25.** $\frac{\sqrt{3}}{2}$ **27.** 3   **29.** $-\frac{2\sqrt{6}}{5} \approx -0.9798$

33. no inverse

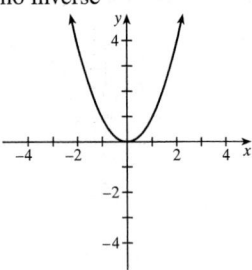

35. no inverse

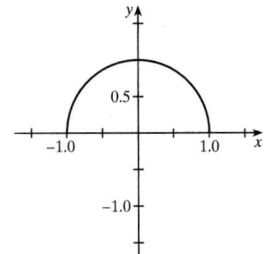

37. inverse exists

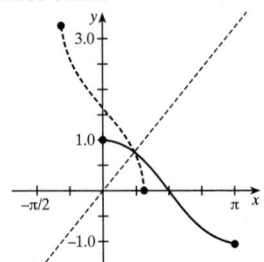

39. $\dfrac{2x}{x^2+1}$ **41.** $\dfrac{\sqrt{1-x^2}}{x}$ **43.** 1

47. a. 0.588   **b.** 2.5536   **c.** 2.1997   **d.** -0.5746

49. $h = \dfrac{x \tan \beta \tan \alpha}{\tan \alpha - \tan \beta}$

Chapter 1 Review
Proficiency Examination (Page 42–43)

18. a. $6x + 8y - 37 = 0$ **b.** $3x + 10y - 41 = 0$

  c. $3x - 28y - 12 = 0$ **d.** $2x + 5y - 24 = 0$

  e. $4x - 3y + 8 = 0$

19. $y = -\frac{3}{2}x + 6$

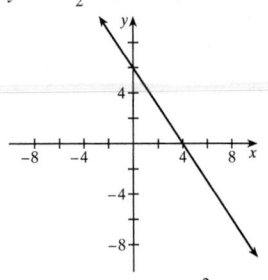

20. $y - 3 = |x + 1|$

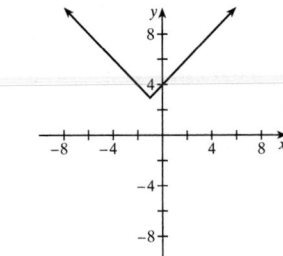

21. $y - 3 = -2(x - 1)^2$

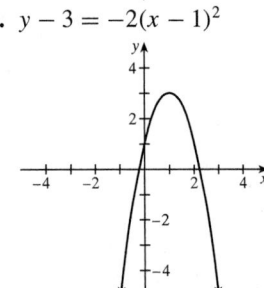

22. $y = (x - 2)^2 - 14$

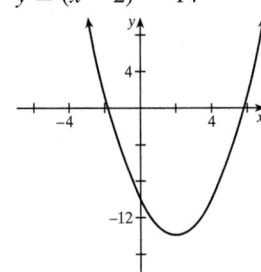

23. $y = 2\cos(x - 1)$

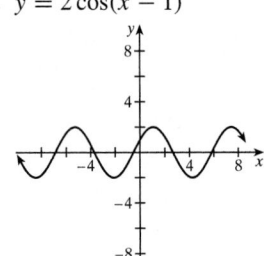

24. $y + 1 = \tan 2\left(x + \frac{3}{2}\right)$

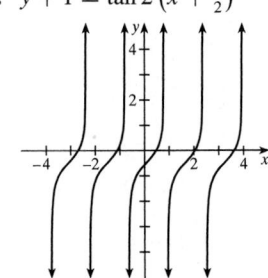

25. $y = \sin^{-1}(2x)$ **26.** $y = \tan^{-1} x^2$

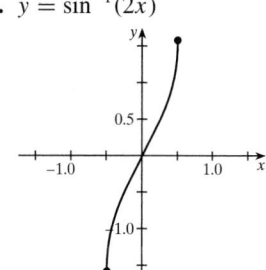   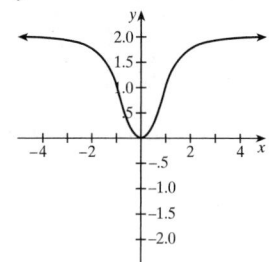

27. $-\frac{3}{2}, 1$

28. The two functions are not the same.

29. $f \circ g = \sin \sqrt{1 - x^2}$; $g \circ f = |\cos x|$

30. $V = \frac{2}{3}x(12 - x^2)$

Supplementary Problems (Pages 43–45)

1. $P = 30$; $A = 30$ **3.** $P \approx 27.1$; $A = 40$

5. $(x - 5)^2 + (y - 4)^2 = 16$ **7.** $5x - 3y + 3 = 0$

9. $A = -\frac{1}{4}$ and $B = \frac{3}{4}$

11. The medians meet at the point $\left(2, \frac{5}{3}\right)$.

13. 1,024 ft

15. a. 1.107149   **b.** 0.463647609   **c.** 1.899250945

17. $\frac{\pi^2}{4}$ **19.** $\frac{1}{2}(x^7 - 1)$ **21.** $\frac{7x + 5}{x - 1}$ **23.** $\frac{b - dx}{cx - a}$

27. a. 15 inches **b.** 21 inches **c.** 29 inches **d.** 19 inches

29. a. The domain consists of all $x \neq 300$.

  b. x represents a percentage, so $0 \leq x \leq 100$ in order for $f(x) \geq 0$

  c. 120   **d.** 300

  e. The percentage of households should be 60%.

31. a. $V = \frac{256}{3}\pi$; $S = 64\pi$ **b.** $V = 30$; $S = 62$

  c. $V = 16\pi$; $S = 24\pi$ **d.** $V = 15\pi$; $A = 3\pi \sqrt{34}$

35. $c = -\frac{4}{5}$; $(-2, 0)$, $(2, 0)$

37. $\theta = \frac{\pi}{4} - \tan^{-1} \frac{5}{12} \approx 0.3906$

39. a. $6 < p < 8$ **b.** $N(7) = 1$ is the maximum profit

41. The glass should be taken in on the 11th or 12th day.

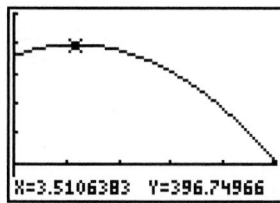

X=3.5106383   Y=396.74966

Y₁⊟-3X²+21X+360
Xmin=0   Ymin=-100
Xmax=15   Ymax=500
Xscl=3   Yscl=100

43. $C(x) = 4x^2 + 1,000x^{-1}$

45. This is Putnam Examination Problem 4 in the morning session for 1959.

Chapter 2: Limits and Continuity

2.1 The Limit of a Function (Pages 59–61)

1. a. 0   **b.** 2   **c.** 6

3. a. 2   **b.** 7   **c.** 7.5

5. a. 6   **b.** 6   **c.** 6

7. 15   **9.** 10   **11.** 8

13. 2   **15.** -1 **19.** 1.00

21. 5.00   **23.** -0.17 **25.** does not exist

27. a. 0.00   **b.** 0.64

29. 8.00   **31.** -2.00 **33.** 0.17

35. 0.25   **37.** does not exist   **39.** 2.00

41. 1.00   **43.** does not exist

45. a. $-32t + 40$ **b.** 40 ft/s

  c. 3; impact velocity is -56 ft/s

  d. $t = 1.25$ seconds

47. 228

2.2 Algebraic Computation of Limits (Pages 68–69)

1. -9 **3.** -8 **5.** $-\frac{1}{2}$ **7.** 2   **9.** $\frac{\sqrt{3}}{9}$

11. 4   **13.** -1 **15.** $\frac{1}{9}$ **17.** $\frac{1}{2}$ **19.** $\frac{1}{2}$

21. 0   **23.** 2   **25.** $\frac{5}{2}$ **27.** 0   **29.** 1

31. 0   **35.** a **37.** -1 **39.** 0

41. the limit does not exist   **43.** the limit does not exist

49. the limit does not exist   **51.** the limit does not exist

53. the limit does not exist   **55.** 4   **57.** 8

2.3 Continuity (Pages 78–80)

1. Temperature is continuous, so TEMPERATURE $= f(\text{TIME})$ would be a continuous function. The domain could be midnight to midnight say, $0 \leq t < 24$.

3. The charges (range of the function) consist of rational numbers only (dollars and cents to the nearest cent), so the function CHARGE $= f(\text{MILEAGE})$ would be a step function (that is, not continuous). The domain would consist of the mileage from the beginning of the trip to its end.

5. No suspicious points and no points of discontinuity with a polynomial.

7. The denominator factors to $x(x - 1)$, so suspicious points would be $x = 0, 1$. There will be a hole discontinuity at $x = 0$ and a pole discontinuity at $x = 1$.

9. $x = 0$ is suspicious point and is a point of discontinuity.

11. $x = 1$ is a suspicious point; there are no points of discontinuity.

13. The sine and cosine are continuous on the reals, but the tangent is discontinuous at $x = \pi/2 + n\pi$, n an integer. Each of these values will have a pole type discontinuity.

15. 3   **17.** π **19.** no value

21. a. continuous   **b.** discontinuous on $[0, 1]$

23. discontinuous at $t = 0$ **25.** discontinuous at $x = 0$

39. $a = 1$; $b = -18/5$ **41.** $a = 1$; $b = \frac{1}{2}$

43. $a = 5$; $b = 5$ **45.** 0

47. a. 1.25872   **b.** 0.785398

2.4 Exponential and Logarithm Functions (Pages 89–91)

1.   **3.**

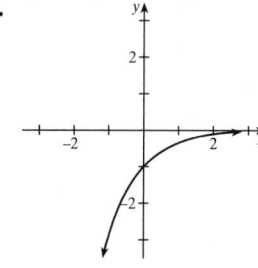

5. 31   **7.** 200.33681   **9.** 9,783.225896

11. 38,523.62544   **13.** 0   **15.** 2

17. -2 **19.** 3.5   **21.** $\frac{3}{10}$

23. 4   **25.** 0.23104906   **27.** -1.391662509

29. 729   **31.** $2, -1$ **33.** 3

35. $2, -\frac{5}{3}$ **37.** $-\frac{3}{2}$ **39.** 1

41. a. 0   **b.** e^{-1} **43. a.** e **b.** 2

45. $2e$ **47.** 27   **49.** 0.4

51. logarithmic   **53.** exponential

55. 3 m below surface   **57.** $0.7/r$ years to double

59. 6.9%

61. a. 793.7   **b.** 2 hr 40 min

63. a. $E^{1.5M+11.4}$ **b.** 1,000 times more energy

65. a.

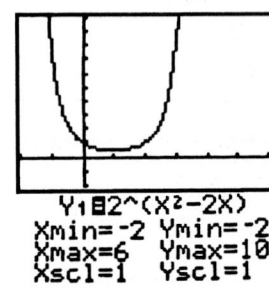

Y₁■2^(X²−2X)
Xmin=-2 Ymin=-2
Xmax=6 Ymax=10
Xscl=1 Yscl=1

   b. It crosses the y-axis at $(0, 1)$. As $x \to +\infty$, $y \to +\infty$. As $x \to -\infty$, $y \to +\infty$.

   c. The smallest value of $y = E$ is $E = 0.5$.

67. a. \$10,285.33   **b.** \$10,285.29

69. a. $\frac{4}{7}$ **b.** 59°   **c.** 70°

Chapter 2 Review
Proficiency Examination (Page 92)

19. $\frac{3}{2}$ **20.** $\frac{1}{4}$ **21.** $-\frac{1}{4}$

22. 0   **23.** $\frac{9}{5}$ **24.** -1

25. a. exponential   **b.** exponential
   c. logarithmic   **d.** logarithmic

26. We have suspicious points where the denominators are 0 at $t = 0, -1$. There are pole discontinuities at each of these points.

27. Suspicious points $x = -2$ and $x = 1$ are also points of discontinuity (since the denominator is 0).

28. a. 11 years, 3 quarters   **b.** 11 years, 6 months
   c. 11 years, 166 days

29. $A = -1; B = 1$

30. Let $f(x) = x + \sin x - \dfrac{1}{\sqrt{x+3}}$. This function is continuous on $[0, \infty)$, and $f(0) = -\frac{1}{3}$, $f(\pi) = \pi - \dfrac{1}{\sqrt{\pi+3}} \approx 2.93$. So by the root location theorem there must be some value c in $(0, \pi)$ where $f(c) = 0$.

Supplementary Problems (Pages 92–95)

1. a. 1.504077397   **b.** 16.44464677   **c.** π **d.** $\sqrt{2}$

3. -2 **5.** $16, -1$ **7.** 1.46085

9. 5   **11.** 1   **13.** 0

15. $-\frac{1}{2}$ **17.** e^4 **19.** 5

21. $\frac{3}{2}$ **23.** 0.8415   **25.** 1

27. 3   **29.** 0   **31.** $\dfrac{1}{\sqrt{2x}}$

33. $\dfrac{-4}{x^2}$ **35.** e^x **37.** continuous on $[-5, 5]$

39. discontinuity is removable   **41.** not continuous anywhere

43. a. continuous on $[0, 5]$ **b.** not continuous at $x = -2$
   c. not continuous at $x = -2$ **d.** continuous on $[-5, 5]$

45. a.

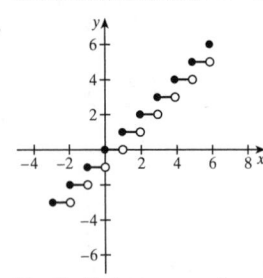

   b. $\lim\limits_{x \to 3} [\![x]\!]$ does not exist

   c. The limit exists for all nonintegral values.

47. does not exist   **49.** $a = 2$ and $b = 1$

51. a. 0.2973   **b.** 0.8232   **c.** 0.07955

53. The rock concert is one million times as intense as normal conversation.

67. a. The windchill for 20 mi/h is 3.75° and for 50 mi/h is $-7°$.
   b. $v \approx 25.2$
   c. at $v = 4$, $T \approx 91.4$; at $v = 45$, $T \approx 868$

71. This is a Problem A1 of the morning session of the 1956 Putnam Examination.

Chapter 3: Differentiation

3.1 An Introduction to the Derivative: Tangents
(Pages 107–110)

1. Some describe it as a five-step process:
   (1) Find $f(x)$
   (2) Find $f(x + \Delta x)$
   (3) Find $f(x + \Delta x) - f(x)$
   (4) Find $\dfrac{f(x + \Delta x) - f(x)}{\Delta x}$
   (5) Find $\lim\limits_{\Delta x \to 0} \dfrac{f(x + \Delta x) - f(x)}{\Delta x}$

3. Answers vary; continuity does not imply differentiability, but differentiability implies continuity.

5.

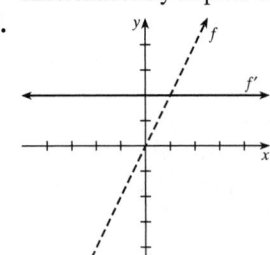

7.

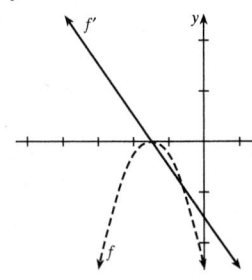

9.

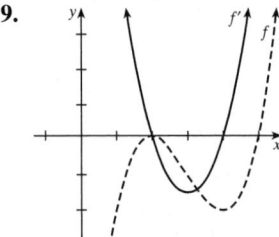

11. a. 0   **b.** 0   **13. a.** 2   **b.** 2

15. a. $-\Delta x$ **b.** 0   **17.** 0; differentiable for all x

19. 3; differentiable for all x **21.** $6x$; differentiable for all x

23. $2x - 1$; differentiable for all x

25. $2s - 2$; differentiable for all real s

27. $\dfrac{\sqrt{5x}}{2x}$; differentiable for $x > 0$

29. $3x - y - 7 = 0$ **31.** $3s - 4y + 1 = 0$

33. $x + 25y - 7 = 0$ **35.** $x + 3y - 9 = 0$

37. $216x - 6y - 647 = 0$ **39.** 2

41. 0   **43. a.** -3.9 **b.** -4

45. The derivative is 0 when $x = \frac{1}{2}$; the graph has a horizontal tangent at $\left(\frac{1}{2}, -\frac{1}{4}\right)$.

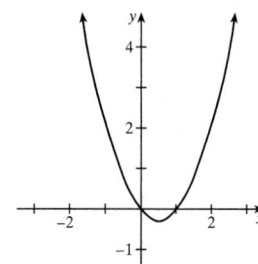

47. a. $-4x$ **b.** $y - 4 = 0$ **c.** $\left(\frac{2}{3}, \frac{28}{9}\right)$ **49.** yes

51. a.

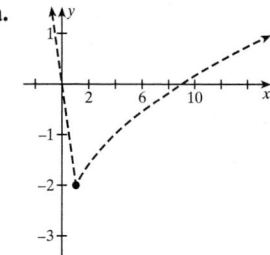

b. f is not differentiable at $x = 1$, because the difference quotient has different limits from the left and right.

53. 4   **55.** $\frac{1}{2}$ **57.** $\frac{1}{4}$

59. The y-intercept is $\left(0, -Ac^2\right)$.   **61. a.** $2x$ **b.** $2x$

63. For $x < 0$, the tangent lines have negative slope and for $x > 0$ the tangent lines have positive slope. There is a corner at $x = 0$, and there is no tangent at $x = 0$, and consequently no derivative at that point.

65. Yes, the equation of the tangent line is $y = 1$.

67. The point $(6, 0)$ on the x-axis is the point through which the normal to the parabola at $(4, 4)$ passes. The required tangent is then the line through $(4, 4)$ perpendicular to this normal.

69. The equation of the normal line is $f'(c)y - f(c)f'(c) + x - c = 0$. If $f'(c) = 0$, then the normal line is vertical with equation $x = c$.

3.2 Techniques of Differentiation (Pages 117–118)

1. (11) 0   (12) 1   (13) 2   (14) 4   (15) 0   (16) -4

3. (23) $2x - 1$ (24) $-2t$ (25) $2s - 2$ (26) $-\frac{1}{2}x^{-2}$ (27) $\dfrac{\sqrt{5x}}{2x}$

5. a. $12x^3$ **b.** -1 **7. a.** $3x^2$ **b.** 1

9. $2t + 2t^{-3} - 20t^{-5}$ **11.** $-14x^{-3} + \frac{2}{3}x^{-1/3}$

13. $1 - x^{-2} + 14x^{-3}$ **15.** $-32x^3 - 12x^2 + 2$

17. $\dfrac{22}{(x + 9)^2}$ **19.** $4x^3 + 12x^2 + 8x$

21. $f'(x) = 5x^4 - 15x^2 + 1$; $f''(x) = 20x^3 - 30x$; $f'''(x) = 60x^2 - 30$; $f^{(4)}(x) = 120x$

23. $f'(x) = 4x^{-3}$; $f''(x) = -12x^{-4}$; $f'''(x) = 48x^{-5}$; $f^{(4)}(x) = -240x^{-6}$

25. $\dfrac{d^2y}{dx^2} = 18x - 14$ **27.** $7x + y + 9 = 0$

29. $6x + y - 6 = 0$ **31.** $x - 6y + 5 = 0$

33. $(1, 0)$ and $\left(\frac{4}{3}, -\frac{1}{27}\right)$ **35.** $\left(\frac{29}{6}, -\frac{361}{12}\right)$

37. $(1, -2)$ **39.** no horizontal tangents

41. d. $-4x^{-3} + 9x^{-4}$ **43.** $2x - y - 2 = 0$

45. a. $4x + y - 1 = 0$ **b.** $x = 0$

47. $(0, 0)$ and $(4, 64)$

49. The equation is not satisfied.

51. This function satisfies the given equation.

53. $\pi \approx \frac{62,832}{20,000} \approx 3.1416$ **63.** $y = x + 3$

3.3 Derivatives of Trigonometric, Exponential, and Logarithmic Functions (Page 125)

1. $\cos x - \sin x$ **3.** $2t - \sin t$ **5.** $\sin 2t$

7. $-\sqrt{x}\,\sin x + \frac{1}{2}x^{-1/2}\cos x - x\csc^2 x + \cot x$

9. $-x^2 \sin x + 2x \cos x$ **11.** $\dfrac{x\cos x - \sin x}{x^2}$

13. $e^t \csc t(1 - \cot t)$ **15.** $x + 2x \ln x$

17. $e^{2x}(3\sin x - \cos x)$ **19.** $e^{-x}(\cos x - \sin x)$

21. $\dfrac{\sec^2 x - 2x\sec^2 x + 2\tan x}{(1 - 2x)^2}$

23. $\dfrac{t\cos t + 2\cos t - 2 - \sin t}{(t + 2)^2}$

25. $\dfrac{1}{\cos x - 1}$ **27.** $\dfrac{2\cos x - \sin x - 1}{(2 - \cos x)^2}$

29. $\dfrac{-2}{(\sin x - \cos x)^2}$ **31.** $-\sin x$

33. $-\sin\theta$ **35.** $2\sec^2\theta\tan\theta$

37. $\sec^3\theta + \sec\theta\tan^2\theta$ **39.** $-\sin x - \cos x$

41. $-2e^x\sin x$ **43.** $-\frac{1}{4}t^{-3/2}\ln t$

45. $4x - 2y - \pi + 2 = 0$

47. $\sqrt{3}x - 2y + \left(1 - \frac{\sqrt{3}\pi}{6}\right) = 0$

49. $2x - y = 0$ **51.** $x - y + 1 = 0$

53. a. yes   **b.** yes   **c.** no   **d.** no

55. $A = 0$, $B = -\frac{3}{2}$; $y = -\frac{3}{2}x\sin x$

3.4 Rates of Change: Modeling Rectilinear Motion (Pages 134–137)

1. A mathematical model is a mathematical framework whose results approximate the real-world situation. It involves abstractions, predictions, and then interpretations and comparisons with real world events. An excellent example of real world modeling from *Scientific American* (March 1991) is mentioned on page 129.

3. 1   **5.** -3 **7.** $\frac{13}{4}$

9. -1 **11.** $\frac{1}{2}$ **13.** -1 **15.** -6

17. a. $2t - 2$ **b.** 2   **c.** 2

d. Because $a(t) > 0$, the object is always accelerating.

19. a. $3t^2 - 18t + 15$ **b.** $6t - 18$ **c.** 46

d. decelerating on $[0, 3)$; accelerating on $(3, 6]$

21. a. $-2t^{-2} - 2t^{-3}$ **b.** $4t^{-3} + 6t^{-4}$

  c. $\frac{20}{9}$ **d.** accelerating on [1, 3]

23. a. $-3\sin t$ **b.** $-3\cos t$ **c.** 12

  d. decelerating on $\left[0, \frac{\pi}{2}\right)$ and on $\left(\frac{3\pi}{2}, 2\pi\right]$; accelerating on $\left(\frac{\pi}{2}, \frac{3\pi}{2}\right)$

25. quadratic model   **27.** exponential model

29. quadratic model   **31.** cubic model

33. logarithmic model

35. a. -6 **b.** The decline will be the same each year.

37. 136   **39. a.** 9.91 m/min   **b.** 9.961 m

41. a. 64 ft/s   **b.** 336 ft   **c.** $-32t + 64$ ft/s   **d.** -160 ft/s

43. 30 ft   **45.** 144 ft   **47.** $v_0 = 24$ ft/s; 126 ft

49. a. $200t + 50\ln t + 450$ newspapers per year.

  b. 1,530 newspapers per year   **c.** 1,635 newspapers

51. a. 0.2 ppm/yr   **b.** 0.15 ppm   **c.** 0.25 ppm

53. 91 thousand/hr

55. a. 20 persons per mo   **b.** 0.39% per mo

57. 7.5% per year   **59.** $\dfrac{dP}{dT} = -\dfrac{4\pi\mu^2 N}{9k} T^{-2}$

61. a. $v(t) = -7\sin t; a(t) = -7\cos t$ **b.** 2π **c.** 7

63. The Spy is on Mars.

3.5 The Chain Rule (Pages 143–145)

3. $6(3x - 2)$ **5.** $\dfrac{-8x}{(x^2 - 9)^3}$

7. $[\tan u + u\sec^2 u]\left[3 - \dfrac{6}{x^2}\right]$

9. a. $3u^2$ **b.** $2x$ **c.** $6x(x^2 + 1)^2$

11. a. $7u^6$ **b.** $-8 - 24x$ **c.** $-56(3x + 1)(12x^2 + 8x - 5)^6$

13. $25(5x - 2)^4$ **15.** $8(3x - 1)(3x^2 - 2x + 1)^3$

17. $4\cos(4\theta + 2)$ **19.** $(-2x + 3)e^{-x^2 + 3x}$

21. $e^{\sec x}\sec x\tan x$ **23.** $(2t + 1)\exp(t^2 + t + 5)$

25. $5x\cos 5x + \sin 5x$ **27.** $6(1 - 2x)^{-4}$

29. $(1 - 2x)e^{1 - 2x}$ **31.** $2x\cos 2x^2$

33. $3x^2(2 - 3x)(2 - 5x)$

35. $\dfrac{1}{2}\left(\dfrac{x^2 + 3}{x^2 - 5}\right)^{-1/2}\left[\dfrac{-16x}{(x^2 - 5)^2}\right]$

37. $\dfrac{1}{3}(x + \sqrt{2x})^{-2/3}\left(1 + \dfrac{1}{\sqrt{2x}}\right)$

39. $\dfrac{\cos x - \sin x}{\sin x + \cos x}$ **41.** $\frac{2}{9}$ **43.** 1, 7   **45.** $0, \frac{2}{3}$

47. a. 1   **b.** $\frac{3}{2}$ **c.** 1.5

49. a. $\frac{9}{40}$ **b.** $-\frac{3}{8}$ **c.** $\frac{3}{8}$

51. $-\frac{2}{3}$ **53.** 0.31 ppm/yr

55. decreasing by 6 lb/wk

57. a. increasing by 0.035 lux/s.   **b.** 7.15 m

61. $T'(2) \approx 5.23$; it is getting hotter

63. $I'(\theta) = \dfrac{2a\pi I_0}{\lambda\beta^3}\sin\beta(\beta\cos\beta - \sin\beta)\cos\dfrac{\theta}{\lambda}$

67. a. $\dfrac{3}{(3x - 1)^2 + 1}$ **b.** $\dfrac{-1}{x^2 + 1}$

71. $\dfrac{d}{dx}[f'(f(x))] = f''(f(x))f'(x)$ and

  $\dfrac{d}{dx}[f(f'(x))] = f'(f'(x))f''(x)$

3.6 Implicit Differentiation (Pages 155–157)

1. $-\dfrac{x}{y}$ **3.** $-\dfrac{y}{x}$

5. $\dfrac{-(2x + 3y)}{3x + 2y}$ **7.** $-\dfrac{y^2}{x^2}$

9. $\dfrac{1 - \cos(x + y)}{\cos(x + y) + 1}$ **11.** $\dfrac{2x - y\sin xy}{x\sin xy}$

13. $(2e^{2x} - x^{-1})y$

15. a. $-\dfrac{2x}{3y^2}$ **b.** $\dfrac{-2x}{3(12 - x^2)^{2/3}} = -\dfrac{2x}{3y^2}$

17. a. y^2 **b.** $\dfrac{1}{(x - 5)^2} = y^2$

19. $\dfrac{1}{\sqrt{-x^2 - x}}$ **21.** $\dfrac{x}{(x^2 + 2)\sqrt{x^2 + 1}}$

23. $\dfrac{6(\sin^{-1} 2x)^2}{\sqrt{1 - 4x^2}}$ **25.** $\dfrac{-1}{\sqrt{e^{-2x} - 1}}$

27. $\dfrac{-1}{x^2 + 1}$ **29.** ± 1

31. $\dfrac{1 - \sin^{-1} y - \dfrac{y}{1 + x^2}}{\dfrac{x}{\sqrt{1 - y^2}} + \tan^{-1} x}$

33. $2x - 3y + 13 = 0$ **35.** $(\pi + 1)x - y + \pi = 0$

37. $y = 0$ **39.** $y' = 0$

41. $y' = \frac{5}{4}$ **43.** $x - 1 = 0$

45. $y'' = -\dfrac{49}{100y^3}$

51. $\dfrac{dy}{dx} = y\left[\dfrac{10}{2x - 1} - \dfrac{1}{2(x - 9)} - \dfrac{2}{x + 3}\right]$

53. $\dfrac{dy}{dx} = y\left[6x - \dfrac{6x^2}{x^3 + 1} + \dfrac{8}{4x - 7}\right]$

55. $\dfrac{dy}{dx} = \dfrac{y\ln x}{x}$ **57.** $(3, -4), (-3, 4)$

61. c. The derivative does not exist.

63. $(2, 0), \left(-\frac{1}{4}, \frac{\sqrt{3}}{4}\right), \left(-\frac{1}{4}, -\frac{\sqrt{3}}{4}\right)$

65. 0.44 rad/s   **69.** $\dfrac{d^2y}{dx^2} = -\dfrac{ac}{b^2y^3}$

73. The student was correct.

3.7 Related Rates and Applications (Pages 162–165)

1. -3 **3.** 1,000   **5.** 15

7. $\frac{4}{5}$ **9.** $\frac{30}{13}$ **11.** -3

13. $-10\sqrt{3}$ units/s   **15.** 0.637 ft/s

17. increasing at \$34,000/yr

19. -30 lb/in.^{2}/s   **23.** -3π cm^3/s   **25.** 7.2 ft/s

27. decreasing at 7.5 ft/min

29. 200 ft/s toward the light.   **31.** 2.78 rad/s

33. Assume a sphere of radius r. The volume is changing at the rate of 60.3 cm^3/min.

35. 74.35 ft^3/min.

37. a. $\dfrac{dH}{dt} = \dfrac{3,125t - 6,250}{\sqrt{3,125t^2 - 12,500t + 62,500}}$

b. $t = 2$ **c.** 224 mi

39. 1 rad/min **41.** 3.927 mi/h

43. At $t = 2$ P.M., 8.875 knots; at $t = 5$ P.M., 10.417 knots

45. 0.001925 ft/min or 0.02310 in./min

47. a. $\theta = \cot^{-1}\dfrac{x}{150}$

b. $d\theta/dt$ approaches 0.27 rad/s

c. As v increases so will $d\theta/dt$ and it becomes more difficult to see the seals.

3.8 Linear Approximation and Differentials (Pages 173–176)

1. $6x^2\,dx$ **3.** $x^{-1/2}\,dx$

5. $(\cos x - x \sin x)\,dx$ **7.** $\dfrac{3x \sec^2 3x - \tan 3x}{2x^2}\,dx$

9. $\cot x\,dx$ **11.** $\dfrac{e^x}{x}(1 + x \ln x)\,dx$

13. $\dfrac{(x-3)(x^2 \sec x \tan x + 2x \sec x) - x^2 \sec x}{(x-3)^2}\,dx$

15. $\dfrac{x+13}{2(x+4)^{3/2}}\,dx$

19. 0.995; by calculator, 0.9949874371

21. 217.69; by calculator, 217.7155882 so we can see an error of approximately 0.0255882

23. 0.06 or 6% **25.** 0.03 or 3%

27. 0.05 parts per million **29.** reduced by 12,000 units

31. 28.37 in.³

33. decrease of 2 beats every 3 minutes

35. ±2%

37. S increases by 2% and the volume increases by 3%

39. 0.0525 ft

41. −6.93 (or about 7) particles/unit area

43. a. 472.7 **b.** 468.70

45. 1.2 units **47.** −1.4142 **49.** 0.5671

51. b. $x \approx 1.367$ **53.** 0.5183

57. $\Delta x = -3$, $f(97) = 9.85$; by calculator 9.848857802; if $\Delta x = 16$, $f(97) \approx 9.89$

61. $x_n = x_{n+1} = x_{n+2} = \cdots$

Chapter 3 Review
Proficiency Examination (Page 177)

21. $\dfrac{dy}{dx} = 3x^2 + \dfrac{3}{2}x^{1/2} - 2 \sin 2x$

22. $\dfrac{dy}{dx} = \dfrac{\sqrt{3x}}{2x} - \dfrac{6}{x^3}$

23. $\dfrac{dy}{dx} = -x[\cos(3 - x^2)][\sin(3 - x^2)]^{-1/2}$

24. $\dfrac{dy}{dx} = \dfrac{-y}{x + 3y^2}$ **25.** $y' = \tfrac{1}{2}xe^{-\sqrt{x}}(4 - \sqrt{x})$

26. $y' = \dfrac{\ln 1.5}{x(\ln 3x)^2}$ **27.** $y' = \dfrac{3}{\sqrt{1 - (3x + 2)^2}}$

28. $y' = \dfrac{2}{1 + 4x^2}$ **29.** $\dfrac{dy}{dx} = 0$

30. $y' = y\left[\dfrac{2x}{(x^2 - 1)\ln(x^2 - 1)} - \dfrac{1}{3x} - \dfrac{9}{3x - 1}\right]$

31. $y'' = 2(2x - 3)(40x^2 - 48x + 9)$

32. $\dfrac{dy}{dx} = 1 - 6x$ **33.** $14x - y - 6 = 0$

34. tangent line $y - \tfrac{1}{2} = \tfrac{\pi}{4}(x - 1)$; normal line $y - \tfrac{1}{2} = -\tfrac{4}{\pi}(x - 1)$

35. 2π ft²/s

Supplementary Problems (Pages 177–180)

1. $y' = 4x^3 + 6x - 7$

3. $y' = \dfrac{-4x}{(x^2 - 1)^{1/2}(x^2 - 5)^{3/2}}$

5. $y' = \dfrac{4x - y}{x - 2}$

7. $y' = 10(x^3 + x)^9(3x^2 + 1)$

9. $y' = \dfrac{(x^3 + 1)^4(46x^3 + 1)}{3x^{2/3}}$

11. $y' = 8x^3(x^4 - 1)^9(2x^4 + 3)^6(17x^4 + 8)$

13. $y' = \dfrac{-\sin\sqrt{x}}{4\sqrt{x}\sqrt{\cos\sqrt{x}}}$

15. $y' = 5(x^{1/2} + x^{1/3})^4\left(\tfrac{1}{2}x^{-1/2} + \tfrac{1}{3}x^{-2/3}\right)$

17. $y' = (4x + 5)\exp(2x^2 + 5x - 3)$

19. $y' = 3^{2-x}(1 - x \ln 3)$ **21.** $y' = \dfrac{y(1 + xye^{xy})}{x(1 - xye^{xy})}$

23. $y' = e^{\sin x}(\cos x)$ **25.** $y' = \dfrac{e^{-x}}{x \ln 5}(1 - x \ln 3x)$

27. $y' = \dfrac{2x^2 + 2xy^2 - 1}{2y - 2x - 2y^2}$ **29.** $y' = [\cos(\sin x)]\cos x$

31. $y' = \dfrac{2\sqrt{xy} - \sqrt{y}}{\sqrt{x}}$ **33.** $y' = \dfrac{1 - y \cos xy}{x \cos xy - 1}$

35. $\dfrac{dy}{dx} = \dfrac{\sin^{-1} x - x(1 - x^2)^{-1/2}}{(\sin^{-1} x)^2} + \dfrac{1}{x^2}\left(\dfrac{x}{1 + x^2} - \tan^{-1} x\right)$

37. $\dfrac{d^2 y}{dx^2} = 20x^3 - 60x^2 + 42x - 6$

39. $y'' = -\dfrac{2(3y^3 + 4x^2)}{9y^5}$

41. $y'' = -2[1 + y^2 - 4x^2 y - 4x^2 y^3]$

43. $33x - y - 32 = 0$ **45.** $2\pi x + 4y - \pi^2 = 0$

47. $x + y - 2 = 0$ **49.** $4x - 2y - 1 = 0$

51. $y - 1 = 0$ **53.** $4x - y - 3 = 0$

55. tangent line, $12x - y - 11 = 0$; normal line, $x + 12y - 13 = 0$

57. $\dfrac{dy}{dt} = (3x^2 - 7)(t \cos t + \sin t)$
or $(3t^2 \sin^2 t - 7)(t \cos t + \sin t)$

59. $f'(x) = 4x^3 + 4x^{-5}$; $f''(x) = 12x^2 - 20x^{-6}$; $f'''(x) = 24x + 120x^{-7}$; $f^{(4)}(x) = 24 - 840x^{-8}$

61. $y' = \dfrac{-4x^3}{(x^4 - 2)^{4/3}(x^4 + 1)^{2/3}}$

63. $y' = \dfrac{x + 2y}{y - 2x}$; $y'' = \dfrac{5y^2 - 20xy - 5x^2}{(y - 2x)^3}$

65. a. $f'(0) = 0$ **b.** $f'(x) = 2x \sin \tfrac{1}{x} - \cos \tfrac{1}{x}$

c. f' is not continuous at $x = 0$

67. 0.8634074099; calculator 0.8633955506

69. 0.012 rad/min

71. $\dfrac{d}{dx} f(x^2 + x) = (2x + 1)(x^4 + 2x^3 + 2x^2 + x)$

73. $4x \cos 2x^2 - 6x \sin 3x^2$

75. 75 mi/h

77. a. $\frac{4}{5}x + 3$ **b.** \$4.00   **c.** \$11.00   **d.** \$11.40

81. 0.09 radians/s $\approx 5°/s$

83. a. -0.2 **b.** -0.4 **c.** 0.3

85. $\frac{d\theta}{dt} = 0.05$ **87.** $\frac{dx}{dt} = 20\pi$ mi/min

93. For the velocity, $\frac{dx}{dt} = \frac{12\pi x \sin\theta}{2\cos\theta - x}$; for acceleration,

$$\frac{d^2x}{dt^2} = \frac{144\pi^2 x}{(2\cos\theta - x)^3}\left[2\sin^2\theta\cos\theta + (2\cos\theta - x)(1 - \tfrac{1}{2}x\cos\theta)\right]$$

95. This is Putnam Problem 1, morning session in 1946.

97. This is Putnam Problem 6, morning session in 1946.

Chapter 4: Additional Applications of the Derivative

4.1 Extreme Values of a Continuous Function (Pages 193–195)

1. critical number $x = 5$ is not in the interval; maximum value is 26 and the minimum value is -34

3. critical numbers, $x = 0$, $x = 2$; maximum value is 0 and minimum value is -4

5. critical number $x = 0$; maximum value is 1 and minimum value is $-\frac{1}{8}$

7. critical numbers $x = 0$, $\frac{4}{5}$; maximum value is 0 and minimum value is -2

9. critical number, $t = 1$; maximum value is e^{-1} and minimum value is 0

11. critical number $x = 0$; maximum value is 1 and minimum value is 0

13. critical numbers 0, $\frac{\pi}{3}$; maximum value is 1.25 and minimum value is approximately 0.41067

15. a. Find the value of the function at the endpoints of an interval.

  b. Find the critical points, that is, points at which the derivative of the function is zero or undefined.

  c. Find the value of the function at each critical point.

  d. State the absolute extrema.

17. The calculator does not seem to take the derivative at $x = 0$ and $x < 0$ into account. The derivative is not defined at $x = 0$, but it certainly is defined for $x < 0$. If you enter $(x^2)^\wedge(1/3)(5 - 2x)$ you will obtain the correct graph.

19. not defined at $t = -50$; the maximum value is 16 and the minimum value is 0.

21. the maximum value is 76 and the minimum value is -32

23. the maximum value is $\frac{5}{6}$ and the minimum value is $\frac{1}{6}$

25. the maximum value is 2π and the minimum value is $-\pi$

27. the maximum value is 0.2898 and the minimum value is -0.2898

29. the maximum value is 11 and the minimum value is -4

31. the smallest value is 3

33. the largest value is $\frac{9}{4}$

35. the largest value of g on $[2, 3]$ is approximately -1.1

37. the maximum value is approximately 1.819 and the minimum value is 0

39. the maximum value is 6,496 and the minimum value is 0

41. the maximum value is 1.59 and the minimum value is -2.52

43. the maximum value is 1 and the minimum value is $-e^{-\pi}$

45. a. $f(x) = \begin{cases} x^2 & \text{for } -0.5 \leq x \leq 1 \\ -x + 3 & \text{for } 1 < x \leq 1.5 \end{cases}$

  The minimum is 0, but there is no maximum.

  b. $f(x) = \begin{cases} -x^2 & \text{for } -1 < x \leq 1 \\ x - 3 & \text{for } 1 < x \leq 1.5 \end{cases}$

  The maximum is 0, but there is no minimum.

  c. $f(x) = \begin{cases} \sin x & \text{for } -\pi \leq x \leq \frac{\pi}{2} \\ 0.5 & \text{for } \frac{\pi}{2} < x \leq 3 \end{cases}$

  The maximum is 1 and the minimum is -1.

  d. $f(x) = \begin{cases} (1 + x)/2 & -1 \leq x < 1 \\ 0 & 1 \leq x \leq 2 \\ (x - 4)/2 & 2 < x \leq 4 \end{cases}$

  There is no maximum and there is no minimum.

47. a. No such function can be found because of the extreme value theorem (Theorem 4.1).

  b. No such function can be found because of the extreme value theorem.

  c. $f(x) = \sin x$ for $[0, 2\pi]$.

  d. No such function can be found because of the extreme value theorem.

49. $f(x) = x^{-1}$ on $(0, 1)$ has no extremum.

51. The maximum velocity is 60 when $t = 0$.

53. The largest product occurs when $x = 3$ and $y = 6$.

55. The largest product occurs when $x = 21$ and $y = 63$.

57. The largest area occurs when the length of a side is one-fourth of the length of the perimeter.

59. a. The greatest difference occurs at $x = \frac{1}{2}$.

  b. The greatest difference occurs at $x = 1/\sqrt{3}$.

  c. The greatest difference occurs at $x = \left(\dfrac{1}{n}\right)^{1/(n-1)}$.

4.2 The Mean Value Theorem (Pages 199–201)

3. $c = 1$ **5.** $c \approx 1.5275$ **7.** $c \approx 1.0772$

9. $c = 9/4$ **11.** $c \approx 0.73$ **13.** $c \approx 0.6901$

15. $c \approx 0.54$ **17.** $c \approx 1.082$ **19.** $c \approx 0.5227$

21. does not apply   **23.** applies   **25.** does not apply

27. does not apply   **29.** applies

31. $f(x) = 8x^3 - 6x + 10$ **33.** does not apply

35. applies   **37.** $c = 2.5$ and $c = 6.25$

41. does not apply   **43.** does not apply

47. does not apply   **55.** does not apply

4.3 Using Derivatives to Sketch the Graph of a Function (Pages 214–217)

7. The black curve is the function and the one in color is the derivative.

9.   **11.**

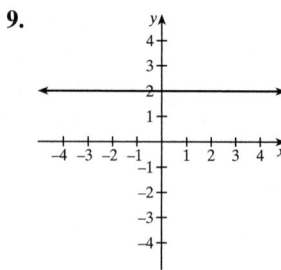

13. a. $x = 0, \quad x = -2$

   b. increasing on $(-\infty, -2) \cup (0, +\infty)$; decreasing on $(-2, 0)$

   c. critical points: $(0, 1)$, relative minimum; $(-2, 5)$, relative maximum

   d. $x = -1$; concave down on $(-\infty, -1)$; concave up on $(-1, \infty)$

   e.
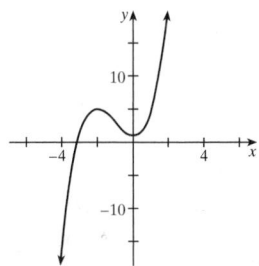

15. a. critical numbers: $x = \frac{5}{3}, x = -25$

   b. increasing on $(-\infty, -25) \cup (\frac{5}{3}, +\infty)$; decreasing on $(-25, \frac{5}{3})$

   c. critical points: $(\frac{5}{3}, -9,481)$, relative minimum; $(-25, 0)$, relative maximum

   d. $x = -\frac{35}{3}$; concave down on $(-\infty, -\frac{35}{3})$; concave up on $(-\frac{35}{3}, \infty)$

   e.
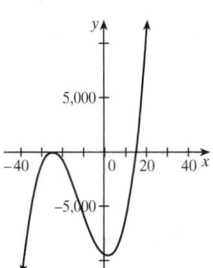

17. a. critical numbers: $x = -1, x = 3$

   b. increasing on $(-1, 3)$; decreasing on $(-\infty, -1) \cup (3, +\infty)$

   c. critical points: $(-1, -\frac{1}{2})$, relative minimum; $(3, \frac{1}{6})$, relative maximum

   d. $x \approx -2.1, x \approx 0.3, x \approx 4.8$; concave down on $(-\infty, -2.1)$ and $(0.3, 4.8)$; concave up on $(-2.1, 0.3)$

   e.
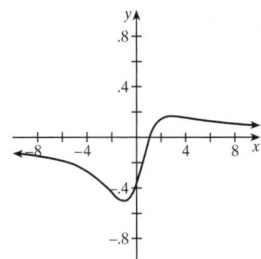

19. a. critical numbers: $t = -1, t = 3$

   b. increasing on $(-\infty, -1) \cup (3, +\infty)$; decreasing on $(-1, 3)$

   c. critical points: $(3, -32)$, relative minimum; $(-1, 0)$, relative maximum

   d. $t = 1$; concave down on $(-\infty, 1)$; concave up on $(1, \infty)$

   e.
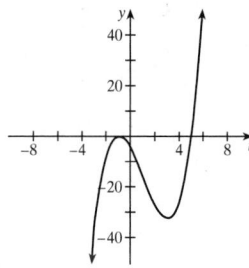

21. critical points: $(-3, -11)$, relative maximum; $(3, 13)$, relative minimum; increasing on $(-\infty, -3) \cup (3, +\infty)$; decreasing on $(-3, 0) \cup (0, 3)$; concave up on $(0, +\infty)$; concave down on $(-\infty, 0)$

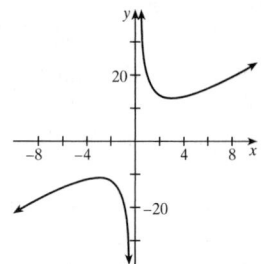

23. critical points: $(0, 26)$, relative maximum; $(-6.38, -852.22)$, relative minimum; $(1.88, -6.47)$, relative minimum; inflection points $(-4, -486)$, $(1, 9)$; increasing on $(-6.38, 0) \cup (1.88, +\infty)$; decreasing on $(-\infty, -6.38) \cup (0, 1.88)$; concave up on $(-\infty, -4) \cup (1, +\infty)$; concave down on $(-4, 1)$

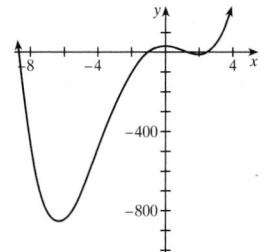

25. critical point: $(0, 0)$, relative minimum; increasing on $(0, +\infty)$; decreasing on $(-\infty, 0)$; concave up on $(-\infty, +\infty)$

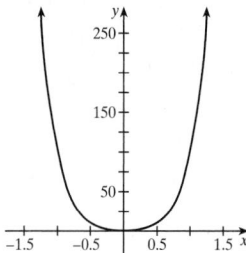

27. critical points: $(-1, -\frac{1}{2})$, relative minimum; $(1, \frac{1}{2})$, relative maximum; $(0, 0)$ is a point of inflection; points of inflection: $(\sqrt{3}, \frac{\sqrt{3}}{4})$, $(-\sqrt{3}, -\frac{\sqrt{3}}{4})$; increasing on $(-1, 1)$; decreasing on $(-\infty, -1) \cup (1, +\infty)$; concave up on $(-\sqrt{3}, 0) \cup (\sqrt{3}, +\infty)$; concave down on $(-\infty, -\sqrt{3}) \cup (0, \sqrt{3})$

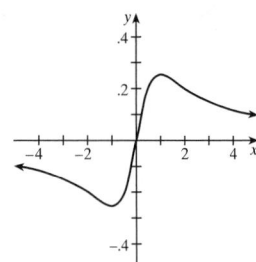

29. critical points: $(0, 0)$, relative minimum; $(0.67, 0.06)$, relative maximum; $(0.195, 0.021)$, point of inflection; $(1.138, 0.043)$, point of inflection; decreasing on $(-\infty, 0)$, $(0.67, +\infty)$; increasing on $(0, 0.67)$; concave up on $(-\infty, 0.195) \cup (1.138, +\infty)$; concave down on $(0.195, 1.138)$

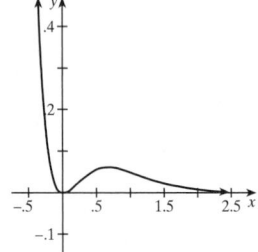

31. critical points $(1, 0)$, relative minimum; $(e, 1)$, point of inflection; decreasing on $(0, 1)$; increasing on $(1, +\infty)$; concave up for $(0, e)$; concave down for $(e, +\infty)$

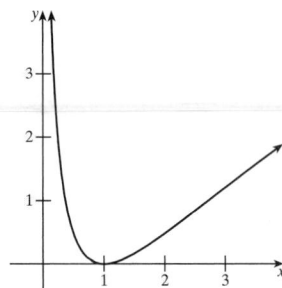

33. critical points: $(\frac{\pi}{12}, 1.13)$, relative maximum; $(\frac{5\pi}{12}, 0.44)$, relative minimum; inflection points: $(\frac{\pi}{4}, 0.79)$, $(\frac{3\pi}{4}, 2.36)$; increasing on $(0, \frac{\pi}{12}) \cup (\frac{5\pi}{12}, \pi)$; decreasing on $(\frac{\pi}{12}, \frac{5\pi}{12})$; concave up on $(\frac{\pi}{4}, \frac{3\pi}{4})$; concave down on $(0, \frac{\pi}{4}) \cup (\frac{3\pi}{4}, \pi)$

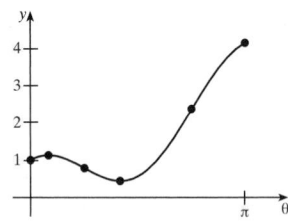

35. There are no critical points; the function is increasing for all x. Inflection point $(0, 0)$ concave down $(-1.57, 0)$; concave up $(0, 1.57)$

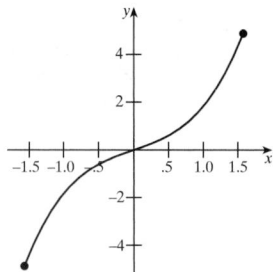

37. At $x = \frac{1}{2}$, relative maximum; at $x = 1$, relative minimum

39. At $x = 4$, relative minimum

41. $f(x) = \dfrac{x^2 - x + 5}{x + 4}$; $f'(x) = \dfrac{x^2 + 8x - 9}{(x + 4)^2}$; $f''(x) = \dfrac{50}{(x + 4)^3}$; $f''(1) = \frac{2}{5} > 0$; relative minimum $f''(-9) = -\frac{2}{5} < 0$; relative maximum

43. $f(x) = \sin x + \frac{1}{2} \cos 2x$; $f'(x) = \cos x - \sin 2x$; $f''(x) = -2 \cos 2x - \sin x$; $f''(\frac{\pi}{2}) = 1 > 0$; relative minimum; $f''(\frac{\pi}{6}) = -\frac{3}{2} < 0$; relative maximum

Answers for Problems 45–49 may vary.

45.

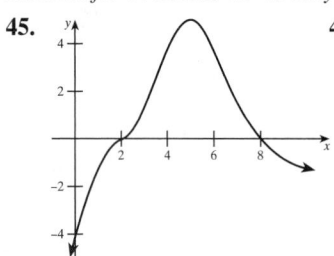

47.

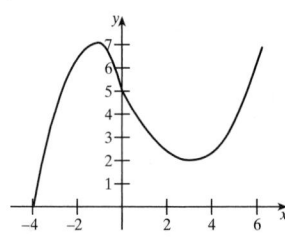

49.

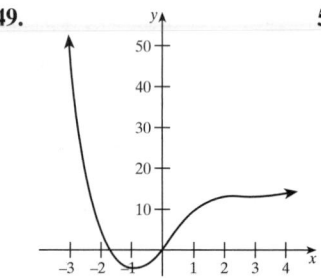

51.

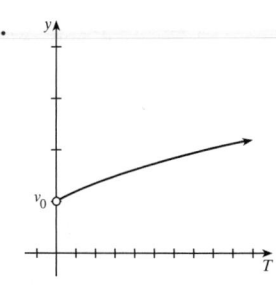

53. a. $-(2)^3 + 6(2)^2 + 13(2) = 42$; $-\frac{1}{3}(2)^3 + \frac{1}{2}(2)^2 + 25(2) = 49\frac{1}{3}$

　　b. $N(x) = -x^3 + 6x^2 + 13x - \frac{1}{3}(4-x)^3 + \frac{1}{2}(4-x)^2 + 25(4-x)$

　　c. $N'(x) = -2x^2 + 5x = 0$ when $x = 2.5$, so the optimum time for the break is 10:30 A.M. The optimum time is half the value for the diminishing return; $N''(2.5) < 0$.

55. Maximum deflection at $x = \dfrac{2\ell}{3}$

61. $f(x) = -3x^3 + 9x^2 - 1$

4.4 Curve Sketching with Asymptotes: Limits Involving Infinity (Pages 227–228)

5. 0　　　　　　**7.** 3　　　　　　**9.** 9

11. 1　　　　　　**13.** 0　　　　　**15.** $-\frac{1}{2}$

17. $+\infty$　　　　**19.** 1　　　　　**21.** $-\infty$

23. 0

25. asymptotes: $x = 7$, $y = -3$; graph rising on $(-\infty, 7) \cup (7, +\infty)$; concave up on $(-\infty, 7)$; concave down on $(7, +\infty)$; no critical points; no points of inflection;

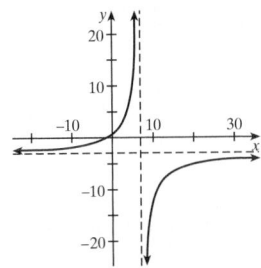

27. asymptotes: $x = 3$, $y = 6$; graph falling on $(-\infty, 3) \cup (3, +\infty)$; concave up on $(3, +\infty)$; concave down on $(-\infty, 3)$; no critical points; no points of inflection;

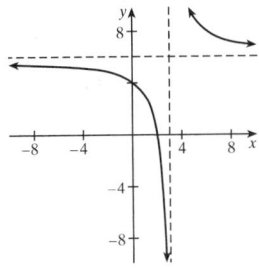

29. asymptotes: $x = 2$, $y = 1$; graph falling on $(-\infty, 2) \cup (2, +\infty)$; concave up on $(-\sqrt[3]{4}, 0)$ or $(2, +\infty)$; concave down on $(-\infty, -\sqrt[3]{4})$ or $(0, 2)$; critical point is $(0, -\frac{1}{8})$; points of inflection $(0, -\frac{1}{8})$, $(-\sqrt[3]{4}, \frac{1}{4})$;

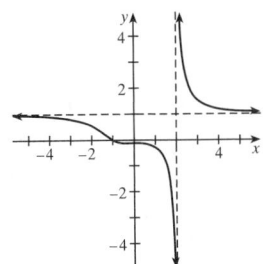

31. asymptotes: $x = -4$, $x = 1$, $y = 0$; graph falling on $(-\infty, -4) \cup (-4, 1) \cup (1, +\infty)$; concave up on $(-4, -1)$ or $(1, +\infty)$; concave down on $(-\infty, -4)$ or $(-1, 1)$; no critical points; point of inflection is $(-1, 5)$;

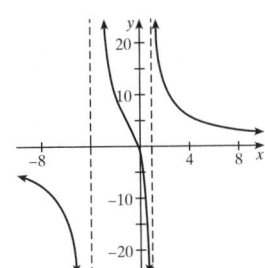

33. no asymptotes; graph rising on $(0, +\infty)$; graph falling on $(-\infty, 0)$; concave up on $(-\infty, +\infty)$; critical point is $(0, 0)$, which is a relative minimum; no points of inflection;

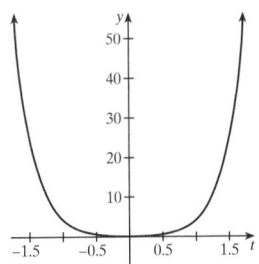

35. no asymptotes; graph rising on $(-3, 0) \cup (3, +\infty)$; graph falling on $(-\infty, -3) \cup (0, 3)$; concave up on $(-\infty, -\sqrt{3}) \cup (\sqrt{3}, +\infty)$; concave down on $(-\sqrt{3}, \sqrt{3})$; critical points are $(-3, 0)$, relative minimum; $(0, 81)$, relative maximum; $(3, 0)$, relative minimum; points of inflection are $(-\sqrt{3}, 36)$, $(\sqrt{3}, 36)$;

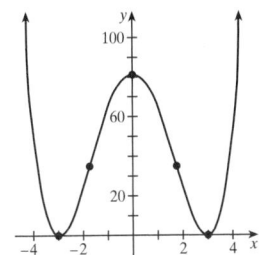

37. no asymptotes; graph rising on $(1, +\infty)$; graph falling on $(-\infty, 1)$; concave up on $(-\infty, -2) \cup (0, +\infty)$; concave down on $(-2, 0)$; critical points are $(1, -3)$, relative minimum; $(0, 0)$, vertical tangent; $(0, 0)$ and $(-2, 6\sqrt[3]{2})$ are points of inflection;

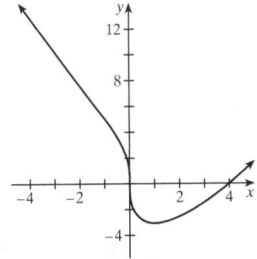

39. horizontal asymptote at $y = \frac{\pi}{2}$; relative minimum at $x = 0$;

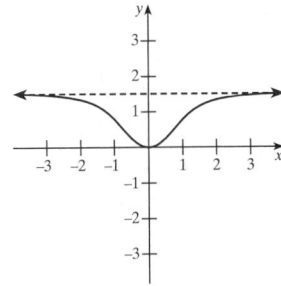

41. no asymptotes; graph rising on $(0, \frac{3\pi}{4}) \cup (\frac{7\pi}{4}, 2\pi)$; graph falling on $(\frac{3\pi}{4}, \frac{7\pi}{4})$; concave up on $(0, \frac{\pi}{4})$ or $(\frac{5\pi}{4}, 2\pi)$; concave down on $(\frac{\pi}{4}, \frac{5\pi}{4})$; critical points are $(\frac{3\pi}{4}, \sqrt{2})$, relative maximum; $(\frac{7\pi}{4}, -\sqrt{2})$, relative minimum; points of inflection: $(\frac{\pi}{4}, 0)$, $(\frac{5\pi}{4}, 0)$;

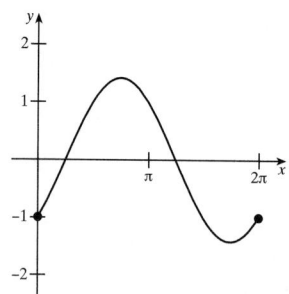

43. critical number at $x = \frac{\pi}{2}$; no asymptotes; graph rising on $(\frac{\pi}{2}, \pi)$; graph falling on $(0, \frac{\pi}{2})$; concave up on $(0, \pi)$; critical points are $(\frac{\pi}{2}, 0)$, relative minimum; $(0, 1)$, and $(\pi, 1)$ relative maxima; no points of inflection;

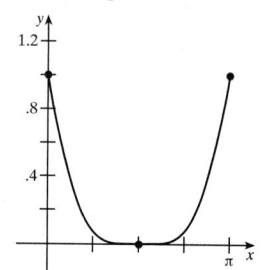

45.   **47.**

49. Frank is not correct.

51. a. $+\infty$ **b.** $+\infty$ **c.** $-\infty$
   d. $-\infty$ **e.** $+\infty$

53. $a = \frac{9}{5}, b = \frac{3}{5}$ **55.** ∞ **57.** True   **59.** False

4.5 l'Hôpital's Rule (Pages 236–237)

1. a. The limit is not an indeterminate form. The correct limit is $\frac{2}{\pi}$.

   b. The limit is not an indeterminate form. The correct limit is $\frac{2}{\pi}$.

3. $\frac{3}{2}$ **5.** 10   **7.** not defined

9. $\frac{1}{2}$ **11.** 0   **13.** $\frac{1}{2}$

15. 3   **17.** $\frac{3}{2}$ **19.** 2

21. $+\infty$ **23.** 2   **25.** $\frac{1}{2}$

27. 0   **29.** $-\infty$ **31.** 0

33. $e^{3/2}$ **35.** e^2 **37.** $+\infty$

39. $+\infty$ **41.** $+\infty$ **43.** $-\infty$

45. 1   **47.** 0   **49.** limit does not exist   **51.** $\frac{1}{120}$

53. horizontal asymptote, $y = 0$

55. horizontal asymptote, $y = 1$

61. b. 1   **63.** $a = -2; b = \frac{7}{3}$ **65.** If $C = \frac{1}{4}$, the limit is $\frac{5}{4}$.

67. $\lim\limits_{\beta \to \alpha} \left[\dfrac{C}{\beta^2 - \alpha^2} (\sin \alpha t - \sin \beta t) \right] = \dfrac{-Ct}{2\alpha} \cos \alpha t$

4.6 Optimization in the Physical Sciences and Engineering (Pages 245–250)

3. The dimensions of the garden should be 8 ft by 8 ft.

7. The largest rectangle has sides of length $R/\sqrt{2}$ and $\sqrt{2}\,R$.

9. The dimensions are $h = \dfrac{R}{3}\sqrt{3}$ and $r = \dfrac{R}{3}\sqrt{6}$.

11. A circumscribed square of side $s = \dfrac{L}{\sqrt{2}} + \dfrac{L}{\sqrt{2}} = \sqrt{2}L$ yields a maximum area.

13. The minimum distance is 200 mi.

15. The minimal perimeter is obtained when the rectangle is a square.

17. $11{,}664$ in.$^3 = 6.75$ ft^3

19. a. When $s = 4$, Missy should row all the way.

   b. When $s = 6$, she should land at a point 4.5 km from point B and run the rest of the way (1.5 km).

21. \$60.00

23. He has about 5 minutes 17 seconds to defuse the bomb.

25. $r \approx 3.84$ and $h \approx 7.67$ cm

27. b. When $p = 12$, the largest value of f is 6.

29. $x = \dfrac{Md}{\sqrt{4m^2 - M^2}}$

31. a. $T'(x) = -T \left[\dfrac{c}{(kx + c)x} + \ln p \right]$

   b. $x = \dfrac{-c \ln p + \sqrt{c^2 (\ln p)^2 - 4kc \ln p}}{2k \ln p}$

   c.

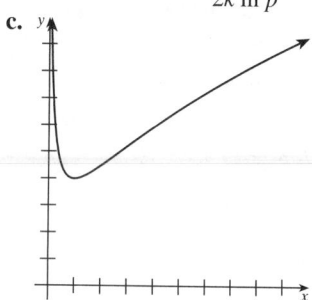

33. a. The maximum height occurs when $x = \dfrac{mv^2}{32(m^2 + 1)}$

   b. The maximum height occurs when $y' = 0$ or when $m = v^2/(32x_0)$.

35.

As $\lambda \to +\infty$, $E(\lambda) \to m_0 c^2$.

37. 26 cm is a minimum.

39. The minimum value occurs when $T \approx 4°$.

41. 270 cm^3

43. b. $D'(\alpha) = 2 - 4 \left[\dfrac{\cos \alpha}{1.33 \cos \beta} \right]$

   c. The rainbow angle is 0.742 (or about 42.5°).

4.7 Optimization in Business, Economics, and the Life Sciences (Pages 259–263)

1. $x = 26$
3. $x = 20$

5. The minimum average cost is 25.

7. a. $C(x) = 5x + \dfrac{x^2}{50}$; $R(x) = x\left(\dfrac{380 - x}{20}\right)$;
$P(x) = -0.07x^2 + 14x$

b. The maximum profit occurs when the price is \$14/item. The maximum profit is \$700.

9. Profit is maximized when $x = 60$.

11. a. 1.22 million people/yr   **b.** The percentage rate is 2%.

13. 208 years from now   **15.** 45 times per year

17. a. $x = 8$
c.

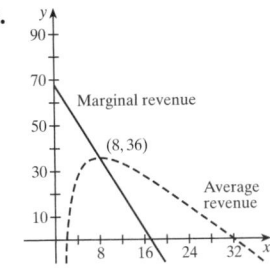

19. Since the optimum solution is over 100 years, you should will the book to your heirs so they can sell it in 117.19 years.

21. Sell the boards at a price of \$42, sell 39 per month, and have the maximum profit of \$507.

23. Lower the fare \$250.

25. Plant 80 total trees, have an average yield per tree of 320 oranges, and a maximum total crop of 25,600 oranges.

27. 62 vines

29. a. The most profitable time to conclude the project is 10 days from now.

b. Assume R is continuous over $[0, 10]$.

31. a. $R(x) = xp(x) = \dfrac{bx - x^2}{a}$ on $[0, b]$; R is increasing on $\left(0, \dfrac{b}{2}\right)$ and decreasing on $\left(\dfrac{b}{2}, b\right)$

b.

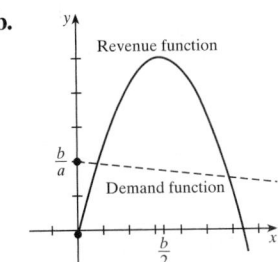

33. $v = \dfrac{kv_1}{k - 1}$

35. a. $x = r$ is a maximum

b.

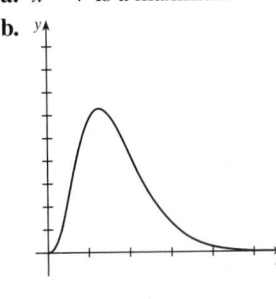

c.

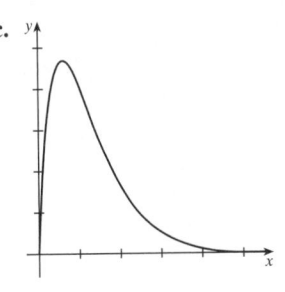

37. $v = 39$

39. a.

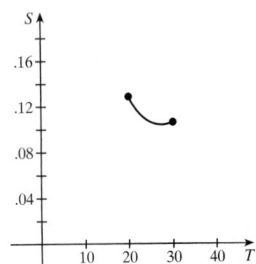

The largest survival percentage is 60.56%, and the smallest survival percentage is 22%.

b. $S'(T) = -(-0.06T + 1.67)(-0.03T^2 + 1.67T - 13.67)^{-2}$; $T \approx 27.83$

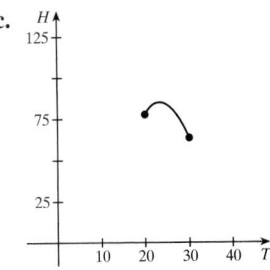

c.

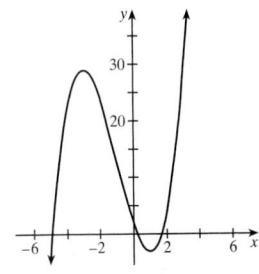

The largest hatching occurs when $T \approx 23.58$ and the smallest when $T = 30$.

41. a. $C = Sx + \dfrac{pQ}{nx}$; $x = \sqrt{\dfrac{pQ}{nS}}$

51. $\theta \approx 0.9553$; this is about 55°.

Chapter 4 Review
Proficiency Examination (Page 263)

18. 2   **19.** $-\frac{1}{2}$ **20.** 0   **21.** e^6

22. Relative maximum at $(-3, 29)$; relative minimum at $(1, -3)$; inflection point at $(-1, 13)$;

23. inflection points at approximately $\left(-\frac{27}{2}, -96.43\right)$ and $(0, 0)$; relative maximum at $\left(\frac{27}{4}, 38.27\right)$;

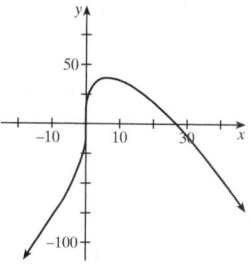

24. relative maximum at $\left(0, \frac{1}{4}\right)$

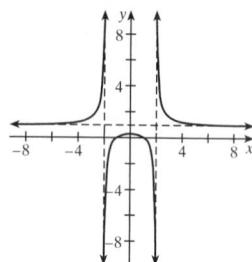

25. relative minimum at $(-1, -2e)$; relative maximum at $(3, 6e^{-3})$;

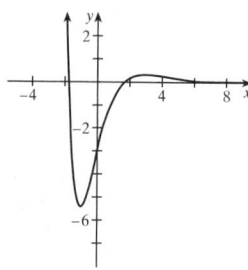

26. $(0, 0)$ is a point of infection; the graph is concave up for $x < 0$ and down for $x > 0$.

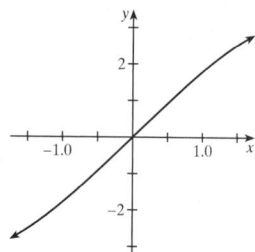

27. relative maximum where $x = \pi$; inflection points at $x = \frac{\pi}{3}$ and $x = \frac{5\pi}{3}$

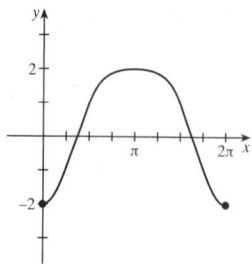

28. absolute maximum at $(0.4, 5.005)$; absolute minimum at $(1, 4)$

29. The dimensions of the box are 19 in. × 19 in. × 10 in.

30. hire 7 people

Supplementary Problems (Pages 263–268)

1.

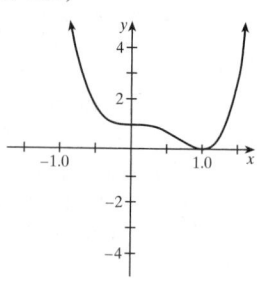

3.

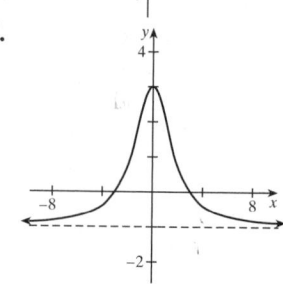

5.

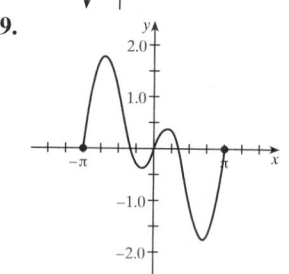

7.

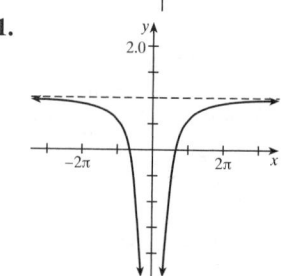

9.

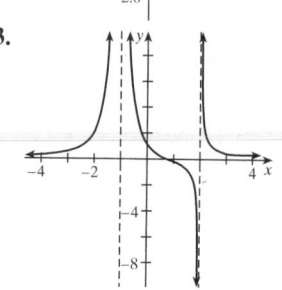

11.

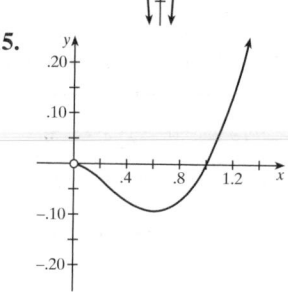

13.

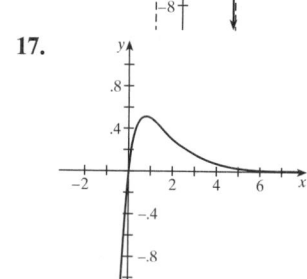

15.

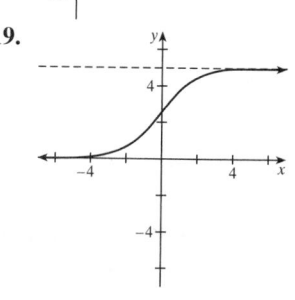

17.

19.

21. c   **23.** b

25. maximum $f(0) = 12$; minimum $f(2) = -4$

27. minimum $f(0) = 0$; maximum $f(\sqrt{3}/2) \approx 0.68$

29. 0   **31.** $-\frac{1}{2}$ **33.** 0

35. This limit does not exist.

37. 1   **39.** 9   **41.** 0

43. e^4 **45.** 1   **47.** 0

49. $+\infty$ **51.** f is the function and g is the derivative

55. $A = \frac{1}{2}, B = 0, C = -\frac{3}{2}, D = 0$

57. The maximum profit of \$108,900 is reached when 165 units are rented at \$740 each.

59. maximum yield of 6,125 for 35 trees per acre

61. 28,072 ft of pipe laid on the shore gives the minimum cost.

63. $c = 4ab$

65. The price is 90 and the maximum profit is 1,100.

73. $x = \sqrt{ab}$ leads to a relative minimum; $x = -\sqrt{ab}$ leads to a relative maximum.

75. a. The highest value is 165,000 when $N = 20$; this is in the year 2002.

    b. The model predicts that the highest point occurs when $x \approx 11.21$ or in the year 1991. This model predicts it will reach 0 when $x \approx 15.25$, or in the year 1995.

    c. This model seems to do a better job of fitting the data.

    d. Linear model: $y = 5,122x - 16,387$;
exponential model: $y = 347e^{0.4888x}$;
logarithmic model: $y = -21,712 \ln(12 - x) + 49,700$

77. a. $f'(x) > 0$ on $\left(-\frac{3}{2}, -\frac{1}{3}\right) \cup (1, 2)$ **b.** $f'(x) < 0$ on $\left(-\frac{1}{3}, 1\right)$

    c. $f''(x) > 0$ on $\left(\frac{1}{3}, +\infty\right)$ **d.** $f''(x) < 0$ on $\left(-\infty, \frac{1}{3}\right)$

    e. $f'(x) = 0$ at $x = -\frac{1}{3}, 1$ **f.** $f'(x)$ exists everywhere

    g. $f''(x) = 0$ at $x = -\frac{1}{3}$

79. a. $f'(x) > 0$ on $(-2, -0.876) \cup (0.876, 2)$

    b. $f'(x) < 0$ on $(-0.876, 0) \cup (0, 0.876)$

    c. $f''(x) > 0$ on $(0, 2)$ **d.** $f''(x) < 0$ on $(-2, 0)$

    e. $f'(x) = 0$ at $x \approx \pm 0.876$

    f. $f'(x)$ does not exist at $x = 0$ **g.** $f''(x) \neq 0$

81. Distance is minimized in the neighborhood of $x = 0.460355$.

83. a. Cost is minimized in the neighborhood of 27 mi/hr.

    b. The total cost is minimized at $x = 55$ mi/hr.

85. This is Putnam Problem 11 of the afternoon session of 1938.

87. This is Putnam Problem 1 of the morning session of 1987.

89. This is Putnam Problem 15 of the afternoon session of 1940.

Chapter 5: Integration

5.1 Antidifferention (Pages 281–282)

1. $2x + C$

3. $x^2 + 3x + C$

5. $t^4 + t^3 + C$

7. $\frac{1}{2}\ln|x| + C$

9. $2u^3 - 3\sin u + C$

11. $\tan\theta + C$

13. $-2\cos\theta + C$

15. $5\sin^{-1} y + C$

17. $\frac{2}{5}u^{5/2} - \frac{2}{3}u^{3/2} - \frac{1}{9}u^{-9} + C$

19. $\frac{1}{3}x^3 + \frac{2}{5}x^{5/2} + C$

21. $-t^{-1} + \frac{1}{2}t^{-2} - \frac{1}{3}t^{-3} + C$

23. $\frac{4}{5}x^5 + \frac{20}{3}x^3 + 25x + C$

25. $-x^{-1} - \frac{3}{2}x^{-2} + \frac{1}{3}x^{-3} + C$

27. $x + \ln|x| + 2x^{-1} + C$

29. $x - \sin^{-1} x + C$

31. $F(x) = \frac{1}{3}x^3 + \frac{3}{2}x^2$

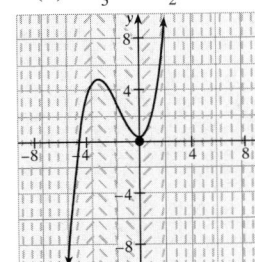

33. $F(x) = \frac{1}{2}x^2 + 4x^{3/2} + 9x - 40$

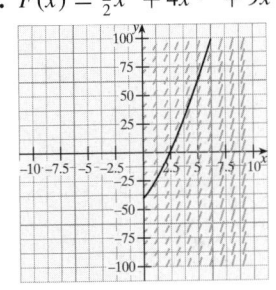

35. $F(x) = \ln|x| - x^{-1} - 1$

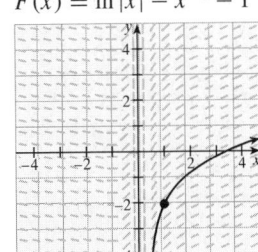

37. $F(x) = \frac{1}{2}x^2 + e^x + 1$

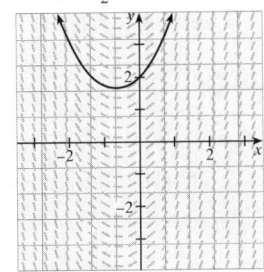

39. a. $F(x) = 2\sqrt{x} - 4x + 2$

    b.

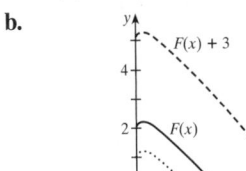
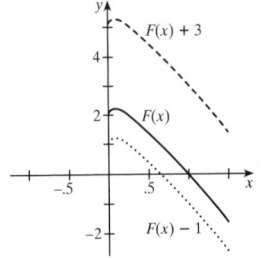

    c. $C_0 = -\frac{9}{4}$

41. $249

43. The population in 8 months will be 10,128.

45. $k = 20$ ft/s^2

47. The acceleration of the plane at liftoff is 4.3 ft/s^2

49. $k = -32$ ft/s^2 **51.** 28.8 **53.** 21

55. $e^2 - 3$ **57.** 1

59. a. $\frac{1}{2}\sec^{-1} y + C$ **b.** $\frac{1}{2}\tan^{-1}\sqrt{y^2 - 1}$

    c. Technology does not use "+C," and to reconcile the inverse trigonometric functions, use a reference triangle where $\theta = \sec^{-1} y$, so $y = \sec\theta$. Then $\tan\theta = \sqrt{y^2 - 1}$ so that $\tan^{-1}(y^2 - 1) = \sec^{-1} y$.

61. $A = \frac{1}{2}(d - c)[m(d + c) + 2b]$

5.2 Area as the Limit of a Sum (Pages 288–290)

1. 6 **3.** 120 **5.** 225 **7.** 9,800

9. $\frac{1}{2}$ **11.** 3 **13. a.** 3.5 **b.** 3.25

15. a. 2.71875 **b.** 2.58796

17. 0.795 **19.** 1.269 **21.** 1.2033 **23.** 18

25. 68 **27.** 2 **29.** false **31.** true

33. true **37. a.** $\frac{14}{3}$ **c.** The statement is true.

39. 21.3646 **41.** 0.6018907 **43.** 0.5038795

45. a. 2 **c.** The statement is true.

49. $A = \displaystyle\lim_{n \to +\infty} \left[\sum_{k=1}^{n} f\left(a + \frac{(2k+1)(b-a)}{2n}\right)\left(\frac{b-a}{n}\right) \right]$

5.3 Riemann Sums and the Definite Integral (Pages 301–302)

1. 2.25 **3.** 10.75 **5.** −0.875

7. 1.18 **9.** 1.94 **11.** 28.875

13. 1.896 **15.** 0.556 **17.** $-\frac{1}{3}$

19. $\frac{3}{2}$ **21.** $-\frac{1}{2}$ **23.** $\frac{1}{2}$

25. $\displaystyle\int_{-2}^{4} f(x)\,dx = 1$; $\displaystyle\int_{-2}^{4} g(x)\,dx = 1$ **27.** 10

29.

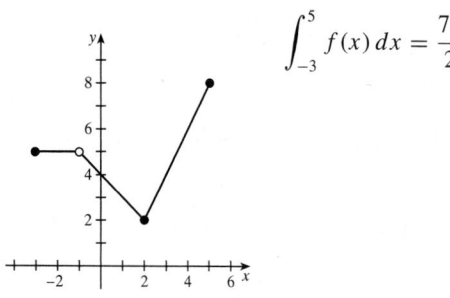

$$\int_{-3}^{5} f(x)\,dx = \frac{71}{2}$$

35. 2.3; $\|P\| = 1.1$

5.4 The Fundamental Theorems of Calculus (Pages 308–309)

1. 140

3. $16 + 8a$

5. $\frac{15}{4}a$

7. $\frac{3}{8}c$

9. 18

11. $\frac{5}{8} + \pi^2$

13. $\dfrac{2^{2a+1} - 1}{2a + 1}$

15. 15

17. $\frac{272}{15}$

19. 2

21. $\dfrac{a\pi}{2}$

23. 5

25. $2 - e$

27. $\frac{5}{2}$

29. 4

31. $\frac{8}{3}$

33. 1

35. $e - \frac{3}{2}$

37. $3\ln 2 - \frac{1}{2}$

39. $(x - 1)\sqrt{x + 1}$

41. $\dfrac{\sin t}{t}$

43. $\dfrac{-1}{\sqrt{1 + 3x^2}}$

55. $\frac{1}{8}(8 + 3\pi^2) \approx 4.7011$

57. a. relative minimum   **b.** $g(1) = 0$ **c.** $x = 0.75$

d.

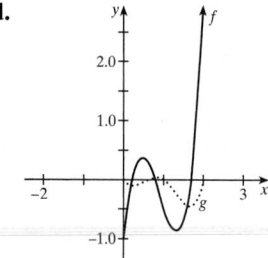

61. $8x^7 - 12x^3$

63. $y = \frac{1}{2}(x - 1)$

65. $F'(x) = f(v)\dfrac{dv}{dx} - f(u)\dfrac{du}{dx}$

5.5 Integration by Substitution (Pages 315–316)

1. a. 32   **b.** $2\sqrt{3} - 2$ **3. a.** 0   **b.** 0

5. a. $\frac{128}{5}$ **b.** $\frac{128}{5}$

7. a. $\frac{2}{9}\sqrt{2}\,x^{9/2} + C$ **b.** $\frac{1}{9}(2x^3 - 5)^{3/2} + C$

9. $\frac{1}{10}(2x + 3)^5 + C$

11. $-\ln\left|\cos(x^2 + 5x + 3)\right| + C$ or $\ln\left|\sec(x^2 + 5x + 3)\right| + C$

13. $\frac{1}{3}x^3 - \frac{1}{3}\sin 3x + C$ **15.** $\cos(4 - x) + C$

17. $\frac{1}{6}(t^{3/2} + 5)^4 + C$ **19.** $-\frac{1}{2}\cos(3 + x^2) + C$

21. $\frac{1}{4}\ln(2x^2 + 3) + C$ **23.** $\frac{1}{6}(2x^2 + 1)^{3/2} + C$

25. $\frac{2}{3}e^{x^{3/2}} + C$ **27.** $\frac{1}{3}(x^2 + 4)^{3/2} + C$

29. $\frac{1}{2}(\ln x)^2 + C$ **31.** $2\ln(\sqrt{x} + 7) + C$

33. $\ln(e^t + 1) + C$ **35.** $\frac{5}{6}\ln 3$

37. 0   **39.** $e - e^{1/2}$

41. $\frac{1}{2}\ln 2$ **43.** 1.80

45. a. We take 1 Frdor as the variable so the note from the students reads "Because of illness I cannot lecture between Easter and Michaelmas."

b. The Dirichlet function is defined as a function f so that $f(x)$ equals a determined constant c (usually 1) when the variable x takes a rational value, and equals another constant d (usually 0) when this variable is irrational. This famous function is one which is discontinuous everywhere.

47. $\frac{16}{3}$ **49.** $\sqrt{10} - \sqrt{2}$ **51.** 0   **53.** 0

55. a. true   **b.** true   **c.** false   **57.** $F(x) = -\frac{1}{3}\ln\left|1 - 3x^2\right| + 5$

59. The amount of water at 4 seconds is 2 ft^3. The depth at that time is about $\frac{1}{4}$ in.

61. a. $L(t) = 0.03\sqrt{36 + 16t - t^2} + 3.82$

b. The highest level is 4.12 ppm.

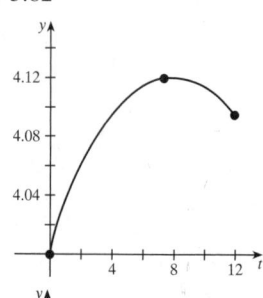

c. It is the same as 11:00 A.M. ($t = 4$) at 7:00 P.M. (when $t = 12$).

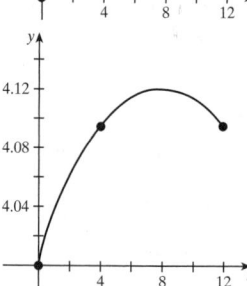

5.6 Introduction to Differential Equations (Pages 325–328)

9. $x^2 + y^2 = 8$ **11.** $y = \tan\left(x - \frac{3\pi}{4}\right)$ **13.** $x^{3/2} - y^{3/2} = 7$

15.

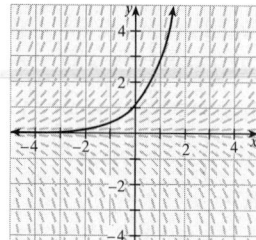

17.

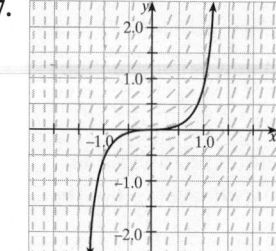

19.

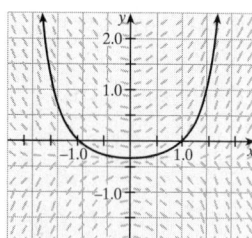

21. $y = Be^{(3/2)x^2}$

23. $2(1 - x^2)^{3/2} + 3y^2 = C$

25. $x^{3/2} + 3y^{1/2} = C$

27. $\cos x + \sin y = C$

29. $-\frac{1}{3}(1 - y^2)^{3/2} = \frac{1}{2}(\ln x)^2 + C$ **31.** $xy = C$ **33.** $y = Cx$

35.

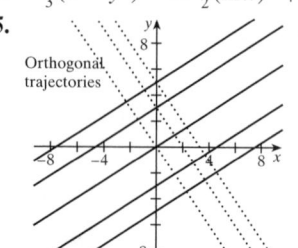

Orthogonal trajectories

37.

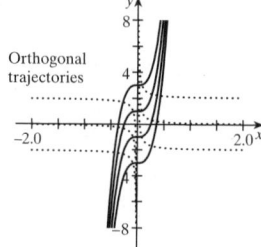

Orthogonal trajectories

39.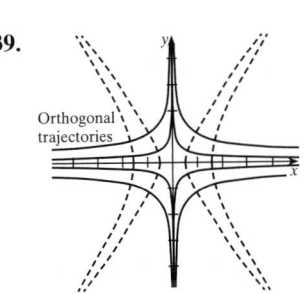

41.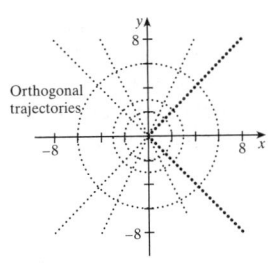

43. $\dfrac{dQ}{dt} = kQ$ **45.** $\dfrac{dT}{dt} = c(T - T_m)$ **47.** $\dfrac{dQ}{dt} = kQ(B - Q)$

49. Conjecture: The orthogonal trajectories are circles.

51. There was still 78% of the ^{14}C still present.

53. 1326 A.D.   **55.** 28 min

57. a. 98.5 ft/s **b.** $s = 3{,}956.067$; $h \approx 352$ ft

59. a. 33,000 **b.** 42,000

61. 10 years from now   **63.** 2 hr and 53 min

65. It will take about 65 hr for 43% to be left. Neptunium-139 has a half-life of 53.70 hours.

67. 7.182%; the percentage lost is always the same.

5.7 The Mean Value Theorem for Integrals; Average Value (Pages 332–333)

1. 1.55 is in the interval [1, 2].

3. $\sqrt{5} \approx 2.24$ is in the interval.

5. The mean value theorem does not apply.

7. 0.0807 is in the interval.

9. −0.187 is in the interval.

11. $A = 25$

13. $A = 38/3$

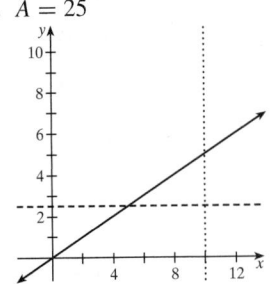

15. $A \approx 1.839$

17. $\dfrac{3}{2}$ **19.** 0

21. 0.3729   **23.** $\dfrac{4}{3}$

25. −10   **27.** −25.375

29. 2.36

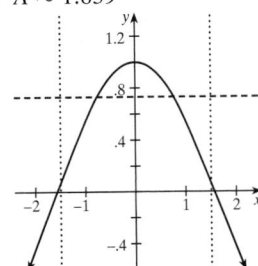

33. Avg temperature = 49.4 °F

35. a. 1,987.24

b. The average population is reached at just under 14 minutes.

37. $f(x) = (x + 1)\cos x + \sin x$

5.8 Numerical Integration: The Trapezoidal Rule and Simpson's Rule (Pages 339–342)

1. Trapezoidal rule; 2.34375; Simpson's rule, 2.33333; exact value, $\dfrac{7}{3}$

3. a. 0.7825   **b.** 0.785

5. a. 2.037871   **b.** 2.048596

7. a. 0.584   **b.** 0.594

11. $A \approx 0.775$; the exact answer is between $0.775 - 0.05$ and $0.775 + 0.05$

13. $A \approx 0.455$; the exact answer is between $0.455 - 0.0005$ and $0.455 + 0.0005$

15. $A \approx 3.25$; the exact answer is between $3.25 - 0.01$ and $3.25 + 0.01$

17. $A \approx 0.44$; the exact answer is between $0.44 - 0.01$ and $0.44 + 0.01$

19. a. $n = 164$ **b.** $n = 18$ **21. a.** $n = 184$ **b.** $n = 22$

23. a. $n = 82$ **b.** $n = 8$ **25. a.** 3.1 **b.** 3.1

27. 430   **29.** 613 ft^2 **31.** 79.17

33. a. Simpson error is 0. **b.** $f^{(4)}(x)$ is unbounded near $x = 2$

35. The inscribed circles have diameter $13\frac{1}{3}$ and $8\frac{1}{3}$.

39. $\dfrac{32}{3}$ **41.** Error is zero.

5.9 An Alternative Approach: The Logarithm as an Integral (Pages 345–346)

3. $E \approx 0.00104$; the number of subintervals should be 18

Chapter 5 Review
Proficiency Examination (Pages 346–347)

22. $-\dfrac{3}{5}$ **23.** $x^5 \sqrt{\cos(2x + 1)}$

24. $\dfrac{1}{2}\tan^{-1}(2x) + C$ **25.** $-\dfrac{1}{2}e^{-x^2} + C$ **26.** $\dfrac{17}{3}$

27. $-\dfrac{35}{3}$ **28.** $\dfrac{1}{2}$ **29.** 0   **30.** 36

31. $\displaystyle\int_1^2 e^{x^2}\, dx$ does not have a closed form, so we must use approximate integration or technology to find

$$\int_1^2 e^{x^2}\, dx \approx 14.99.$$

32. 0

33. The percent is approximately 1.33×10^{-184}, which exceeds the accuracy of most calculators and measuring devices.

34. 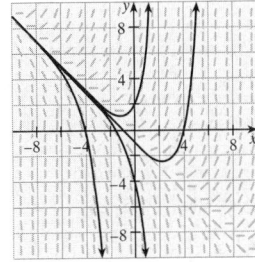   **e.** $y = -x - 1$

35. a. $n \geq 26$ **b.** $n \geq 4$

Supplementary Problems (Pages 347–350)

1. 25   **3.** 6   **5.** 1,710

7. $\dfrac{6-2\sqrt{2}}{3}$ **9.** $\sqrt{3}-1$ **11.** $-\frac{3}{4}(1-\sqrt[3]{9})$

13. $2x^{5/2} - \frac{4}{3}x^{3/2} + 2x^{1/2} + C$ **15.** $3\sin^{-1}x + \sqrt{1-x^2} + C$

17. $-\ln|\sin x + \cos x| + C$ **19.** $\frac{1}{3}(x-1)^3 + C$ **21.** $x + C$

23. $\dfrac{x^3(x^2+1)^{3/2}}{3} + C$ **25.** $-\frac{1}{15}(1-5x^2)^{3/2} + C$

27. $\frac{1}{3}(1+x^2)^{3/2} - (1+x^2)^{1/2} + C$

29. $\frac{2}{5}(1+\ln 2x)^{5/2} - \frac{2}{3}(1+\ln 2)(1+\ln 2x)^{3/2} + C$ **31.** 0

33. 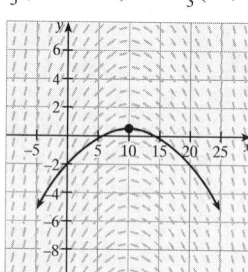   **35.**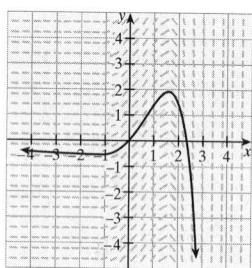

37. $\ln 4$ **39.** $\frac{1}{4}(e^8 - 1)$

41. $f(t) = -\frac{1}{16}\sin 4t + \frac{1}{4}\cos 2t + \frac{5}{4}t + \frac{5}{4} - \frac{5}{8}\pi$

43. $y = 1 - \dfrac{1}{x - C}$ **45.** $\tan y + \cot x = C$

47. $y = Ce^{(1/3)x^3 + x}$ **49.** $y = \tan^{-1}(C - \ln|\cos x|)$

51. 0.5274   **53.** 1.9541   **55.** 0.9091   **57.** $n = 6$

59. Number of primes less than x

x	$\pi(x)$	Gauss
10^3	168	178
10^4	1,229	1,246
10^5	9,592	9,628
10^6	78,498	78,628
10^{10}	455,052,511	455,055,614

61. 1.01297   **63. b.** ± 8 m/s

65. The revenue for the five years is $7,666.67.

67. The tree was 2.33 ft tall when it was transplanted.

69. $y = \frac{1}{3}(x^2 + 5)^{3/2} + 1$ **71.** 4.45 ppm   **73.** 126 people

75. The average price was $1.32 per pound.

77. about 2 min, 45 seconds

81. a. 51.7%

    b. The time for 90% to disintegrate is about $17\frac{1}{2}$ years.

83. 35 years   **85.** 1:44 P.M.

87. This is Putnam Problem 1 from the morning session in 1958.

Cumulative Review for Chapters 1–5 (Pages 353–354)

5. $\frac{7}{5}$ **7.** $\frac{1}{2}$ **9.** 0   **11.** 1   **13.** 1

15. $6(x^2+1)^2(3x-4)(2x-1)^2$ **17.** $\dfrac{\cos x + x\sin x}{(x+\cos x)^2}$

19. $6\sec^2 3x \tan 3x$ **21.** $\dfrac{10x + 3}{5x^2 + 3x - 2}$

23. 5   **25.** $\sqrt{10} - 3$ **27.** $\ln(e^x + 2) + C$ **29.** 1.812

31.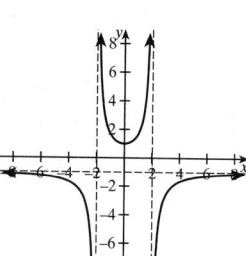

33. $y = \dfrac{9}{2(4-x^3)^{3/2}} + C$

35. $y = 5 \pm 2e^{-2x}$

37. a. $\frac{9}{4}\pi - 8$ **b.** 3

    c. $4x + y - 20 - \frac{9}{4}\pi = 0$

    d. $x = 0$ and $x = 7$

39. 0.1 rad/s

41. a. $y = -\frac{4}{\pi}x + 2$ **b.** $y = -2x + \pi$

    c. $x \approx 0.690$; mean value theorem

43. a. relative maximum at $(0, k)$; relative minimum at $(4, k-32)$

    b. $0 < k < 32$ **c.** $k = \frac{27}{4}$

45. $y = \dfrac{3}{\cos 3x + C}$

Chapter 6: Additional Applications of the Integral

6.1 Area Between Two Curves (Pages 361–362)

1. vertical strip; $\frac{125}{48}$ **3.** vertical strip; 2

5. horizontal strip; $\frac{125}{6}$

7. 1   **9.** $\frac{1}{12}$ **11.** $\frac{8}{3}$

13. $\frac{324}{5}$ **15.** $\frac{9}{2}$ **17.** $\frac{253}{12}$

19. $\frac{5}{2}$ **21.** $\frac{323}{12}$ **23.** $\frac{131}{4}$

25. $2\ln 1.6 - \sin^{-1}0.6$ **27.** $k \approx 0.34$ **29.** π

31. c. The V values are approximately 72.5299, 196.539, 344.337, 502.655, 660.972, 808.77, 932.78, 1,005.31

6.2 Volume (Pages 372–375)

The given volumes are all in cubic units.

1. 9   **3.** $\frac{1}{30}$ **5.** $36\sqrt{3}$

7. $\frac{\sqrt{3}}{2}$ **9.** $\frac{64\pi}{15}$ **11.** $\frac{\pi}{8}\left(1 - \frac{\pi}{4}\right)$

13. $\frac{\pi}{2}$ **15.** π **17.** 2,555

19. $\frac{\pi}{2}$ **21.** $\frac{\pi}{12}$ **23.** $\frac{\pi}{2}$ **25.** $\frac{\pi}{2}$

27. a. $\pi \displaystyle\int_0^4 (4-x)^2\,dx$ **b.** $2\pi \displaystyle\int_0^4 x(4-x)\,dx$

    c. $\pi \displaystyle\int_0^4 [24 - 10x + x^2]\,dx$ **d.** $2\pi \displaystyle\int_0^4 (x+2)(4-x)\,dx$

29. a. $2\pi \displaystyle\int_0^2 y\sqrt{4-y^2}\,dy$ **b.** $\pi \displaystyle\int_0^2 (4-y^2)\,dy$

    c. $2\pi \displaystyle\int_0^2 (y+1)\sqrt{4-y^2}\,dy$

    d. $\pi \displaystyle\int_0^2 \left[4 - y^2 + 4\sqrt{4-y^2}\right]\,dy$

31. a. $\pi \displaystyle\int_0^1 \left(e^{-x}\right)^2\,dx$ **b.** $2\pi \displaystyle\int_0^1 xe^{-x}\,dx$

    c. $\pi \displaystyle\int_0^1 \left(e^{-2x} + 2e^{-x}\right)\,dx$ **d.** $2\pi \displaystyle\int_0^1 (x+2)e^{-x}\,dx$

33. a. $2\pi \displaystyle\int_0^{\pi/2} y(1 - \sin y)\,dy$ **b.** $\pi \displaystyle\int_0^{\pi/2} [1^2 - \sin^2 y]\,dy$

    c. $2\pi \displaystyle\int_0^{\pi/2} (y+1)(1 - \sin y)\,dy$

    d. $\pi \displaystyle\int_0^{\pi/2} [5 - \sin^2 y - 4\sin y]\,dy$

35. a. $V = \pi \displaystyle\int_0^1 \left[\left(\sqrt{x}\right)^2 - \left(x^2\right)^2\right]\,dx$

b. $V = \pi \int_0^1 \left[(\sqrt{y})^2 - (y^2)^2 \right] dy$

37. a. $V = \pi \int_0^2 [(x^2 + 1)^2 - 1^2] \, dx$

b. $V = \pi \int_1^5 \left[(2)^2 - \left(\sqrt{y-1} \right)^2 \right] dy$

39. a. $V = \pi \int_{1.138}^{3.566} \left[(\ln x)^2 - (0.1x^2)^2 \right] dx$

b. $V = \pi \int_{0.130}^{1.271} \left[\left(\sqrt{10y} \right)^2 - (e^y)^2 \right] dy$

41. $\frac{2\pi}{35}$ **43.** $\frac{\pi}{3}$ **45.** $\frac{4}{3}\pi r^3$

47. $36\sqrt{3}$ **49.** 18π **51.** $\frac{32\sqrt{3}}{3}$

53. $90{,}000{,}000 \text{ ft}^3$ **55. a.** $\pi \ln 4$ **b.** $\frac{32\pi}{3}$ **c.** $\pi(8 + \ln 4)$

57. 63.187 ft^3 **59.** 20.13 **61.** $\frac{4}{3}\pi r^3$

6.3 Polar Forms and Area (Pages 384–385)

3. a. lemniscate   **b.** circle

c. rose (3 petals)   **d.** none (spiral)

e. cardioid   **f.** line

g. lemniscate   **h.** limaçon

5. a. rose (4 petals)   **b.** circle

c. limaçon   **d.** cardioid

e. line   **f.** line

g. rose (5 petals)   **h.** line

7.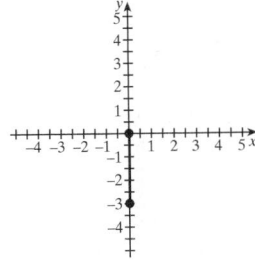

9.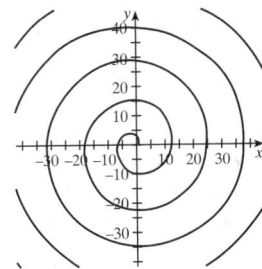

11.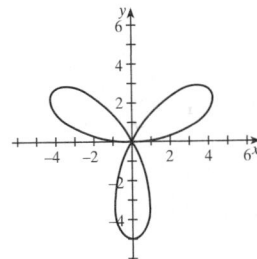

13.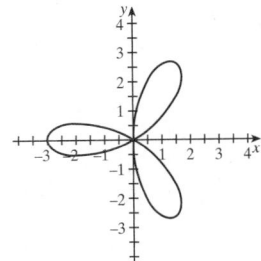

15.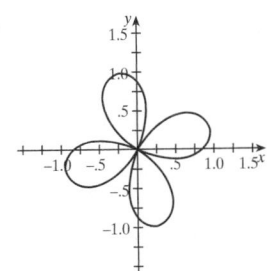

17.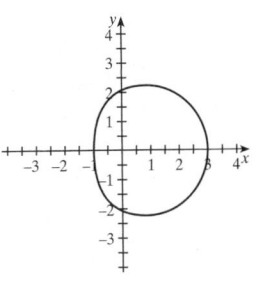

19.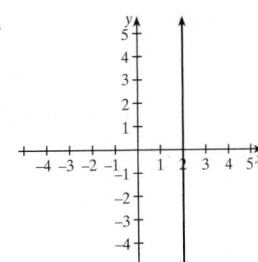

21.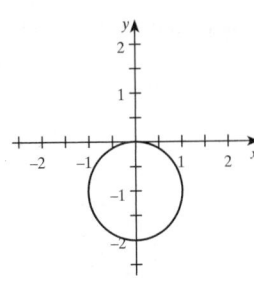

23. $P_1 \left(2, \frac{\pi}{6} \right)$ and $P_2 \left(2, \frac{5\pi}{6} \right)$ **25.** $P_1(0, 0)$, $P_2(2, 0)$, $P_3(2, \pi)$

27. $P_1(0, 0)$, $P_2 \left(1, \frac{\pi}{4} \right)$

29. There are no intersection points.

31. $\frac{\pi}{24} + \frac{\sqrt{3}}{16} \approx 0.2392$ **33.** $\frac{\sqrt{3}}{4} \approx 0.4330$

35. $\frac{1}{8}(\pi + 2) \approx 0.6427$ **37.** $\frac{16\pi^3}{5} \approx 99.2201$

39.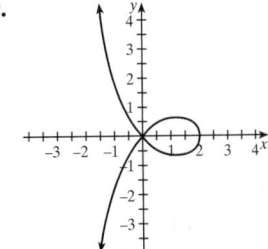

41.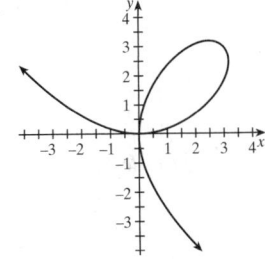

43. $\frac{\pi a^2}{4}$ **45.** $a^2 \left(2 - \frac{\pi}{4} \right)$ **47.** 4π

49. $4\pi + 12\sqrt{3} \approx 33.3510$ **51.** 0.0674

53. The maximum value of x is $9\sqrt{3}/4 \approx 3.8971$.

55.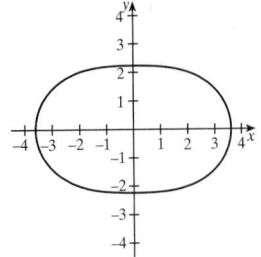

59. a. $-\cot\theta$ **b.** $\frac{1 - \cos\theta}{\sin\theta}$ **c.** $\frac{1}{3}$

6.4 Arc Length and Surface Area (Pages 393–395)

1. $3\sqrt{10}$ **3.** $2\sqrt{5}$ **5.** $\frac{10\sqrt{5}}{3} - \frac{2}{3}$

7. $\frac{331}{120}$ **9.** $\frac{123}{32}$ **11.** $\frac{14}{3}$

13. $12\pi\sqrt{5}$ **15.** 25.28 **17.** π

19. $\frac{\sqrt{10}}{3}\left[e^{3\pi/2} - 1 \right]$ **21.** $\frac{1}{3}\left(5^{3/2} \right) - \frac{8}{3}$

23. 25π **25.** $\frac{2\pi}{3}\left(3 - \sqrt{3} \right)$

27. It appears the arc length is approximately 3.82.

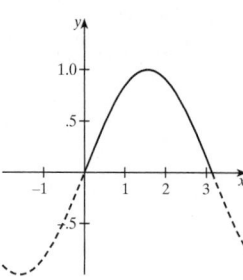

Y = SIN(X)

# OF TERMS	ARC LENGTH OVER [0, π]
2	3.724192
4	3.790091
8	3.812529
16	3.818275
32	3.819717
64	3.820077
128	3.820168
256	3.82019
512	3.820196
THIS IS THE FINAL ESTIMATE	

29. a. $\frac{1,505\pi}{18}$ **b.** 127.4

31. $3\pi\sqrt{10}$ **33.** $\pi\left(\frac{28\sqrt{3}}{5} - \frac{16}{15}\right)$

35. 6   **37.** 8.6322   **39.** 141.6974

45. $L = C\left[b^{2n} - a^{2n}\right] - D\left[b^{2(1-n)} - a^{2(1-n)}\right]$

47. $f(x) = \pm\ln|\cos x|$

6.5 Physical Applications: Work, Liquid Force, and Centroids (Pages 405–407)

5. 12,750 ft-lb   **7.** 6,500 ft-lb

9. $\frac{10}{3}$ ft-lb   **11.** 2,000 ft-lb

13. 4 ergs   **15.** 192 lb   **17.** 59.7 lb

19. $F = 64.5\int_0^{1/24} 2\left(x + \frac{1}{24}\right)\sqrt{\left(\frac{1}{24}\right)^2 - x^2}\, dx$

21. $F = 51.2\int_{-2}^0 2(x+3)\sqrt{4 - x^2}\, dx$

23. $\left(0, -\frac{18}{5}\right)$ **25.** $\left(\frac{1}{\ln 2}, \frac{1}{4\ln 2}\right)$ **27.** $\left(\frac{7}{3}, \frac{1}{2}\ln 2\right)$

29. about $y = -1$, $V = \frac{200\pi}{3}$ **31.** $V = \frac{8\pi}{3}(4 + 3\pi)$

33. a. 4.284 ft-lb   **b.** 12,603 ft-lb

35. The amount of work is approximately 345,800 ft-lb.

37. 24,881 ft-lb   **39.** 2,932.8 lb   **41.** 152,381 mi-lb

43. a. −7.5 ergs   **b.** −37.5 ergs

45. The total force on the bottom is about 85,169 lb.

47. $I_x = \frac{64}{15}$, $I_y = \frac{256}{7}$ **49.** $\rho = \frac{2}{3}\sqrt{6}$

53. $V = \pi(2sL^2 + L^3)$

6.6 Applications to Business, Economics, and Life Sciences (Pages 414–417)

5. a. 0.75 **b.** 0   **7. a.** 75 **b.** 432

9. a. $468.00   **b.**

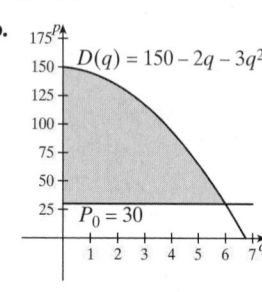

$D(q) = 150 - 2q - 3q^2$

$P_0 = 30$

11. a. $12.46   **b.**

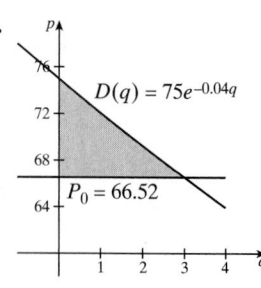

$D(q) = 75e^{-0.04q}$

$P_0 = 66.52$

13. $6.25   **15.** $2.84   **17.** $5.33   **19.** $42.67

21. a. $FV = \$10,171.84$ **b.** $PV = \$8,001.46$

23. a. The machine will be profitable for 9 years.

   b. $12,150; in geometric terms, the net earnings is presented by the area of the region between the curves $y = R'(x)$ and $y = C'(x)$ from $x = 0$ to $x = 9$.

25. a. The second plan is more profitable for the first 18 years.

   b. $7,776; in geometric terms, the net extra profit generated by the second plan is the area of the region between the curves $y = P_2(x)$ and $y = P_1(x)$ from $x = 0$ to $x = 18$.

27. a. $x = 20$ is a maximum   **b.** $400

29. a. The revenue function is $R(q) = qp(q) = \frac{1}{4}q(10 - q)^2$; the marginal revenue function is $R'(q) = \frac{1}{4}(10 - q)(10 - 3q)$.

   b. $q = 2$

   c. The consumer's surplus is $8.67.

31. $\frac{8}{3}$

33. The number of people entering the fair during the prescribed time period is 1,220 people.

35. The total future revenue is $176,256.

37. $4,081,077

39. a. The second plan will be profitable for 12 years.

   b. $100,800   **c.**

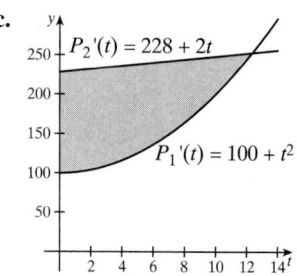

$P_2'(t) = 228 + 2t$

$P_1'(t) = 100 + t^2$

41. a. The second plan will be more profitable for about 24.5 years.

   b. The excess profit is about $3.2 million.

43. a. The machine will be profitable for 8 years.

   b. The net earnings are $7,168.

   c.

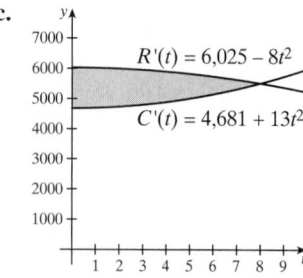

$R'(t) = 6,025 - 8t^2$

$C'(t) = 4,681 + 13t^2$

45. a. $\frac{184}{3}$ **b.**

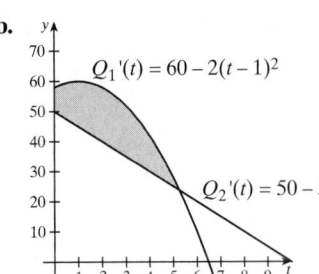

$Q_1'(t) = 60 - 2(t-1)^2$

$Q_2'(t) = 50 - 5t$

47. There would be approximately 208,128 people living in the ring.

49. 0.04π or 0.126 cm^3/s.

51. The population will increase by about 98 people.

53. The demand is approximately 515.48 billion barrels.

55. There are about 240 spies still alive.

57. There should be approximately 4,207 active members.

59. a. $f(t_k)e^{-rt_{k-1}}$

b. $\sum_{k=1}^{n} f(t_k)e^{-rt_{k-1}}\Delta_n t$, where $\Delta_n t = \dfrac{N}{n}$

c. $PV = \lim_{n\to\infty} \sum_{k=1}^{n} f(t_k)e^{-rt_{k-1}}\Delta_n t = \int_0^N f(t)e^{-rt}\,dt$

Chapter 6 Review
Proficiency Examination (Pages 417–418)

20. The definite integrals could represent the following:
A. Disks revolved about the y-axis.
B. Disks revolved about the x-axis.
C. Slices taken perpendicular to the x-axis.
D. Slices taken perpendicular to the y-axis.
E. Mass of a lamina with density π.
F. Washers taken along the x-axis.
G. Washers taken along the y-axis.
a. All but E are formulas for volumes of solids.
b. A, B, F, G   **c.** F, G   **d.** C, D   **e.** B, F   **f.** A, G

21. $8\sqrt{2}$ **22.** $\frac{1}{2}$ **23.** $\frac{256}{3}$

24. a. $\frac{32}{3}$ **b.** $\frac{256\pi}{5}$ **c.** $\frac{128\pi}{3}$

25. $a^2\left(\frac{\pi}{2} - 1\right) \approx 0.5708a^2$

26. $\frac{1}{27}\left(13^{3/2} - 8\right) \approx 1.4397$

27. $\frac{\pi}{6}\left(5\sqrt{5} - 1\right) \approx 5.33$

28. $M = \frac{5}{12}$; $M_y = \frac{13}{60}$; $M_x = \frac{3}{140}$; the centroid is $\left(\frac{13}{25}, \frac{9}{175}\right)$

29. $F = 128\int_0^2 (5-x)(1+\sqrt{1-x^2})\,dx$

30. The amount in the account will be $7,377.37.

Supplementary Problems (Pages 418–423)

1. circle   **3.** line

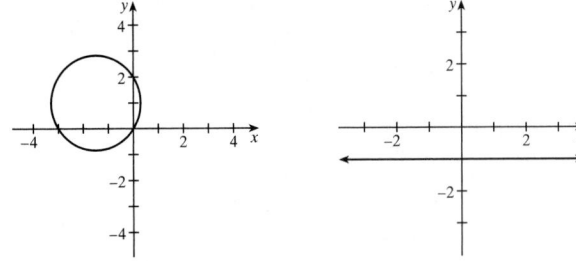

5. circle   **7.** parabola

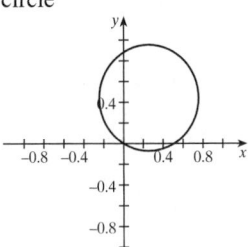   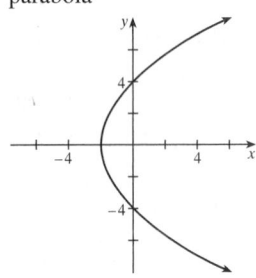

9. $P_1(0,0),\ P_2(2,0)$ **11.** $P_1(2.24, 0.464)$

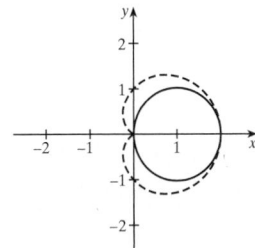   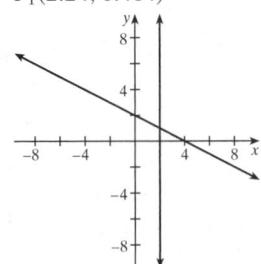

13. $\frac{9}{4}$ **15.** $\frac{4}{15}$ **17.** 8π

19. $\frac{1}{2}$ **21.** $a^2\left(\dfrac{\sqrt{3}}{2} + \dfrac{\pi}{3}\right)$ **23.** $\frac{81\pi}{4}$

25. $\frac{\pi}{2}(\sqrt{3} - \sqrt{2})$ **27.** $\frac{\pi}{240}$ **29.** 225 in.-lb

31. $V_1 = \frac{16}{15}$; $V_2 = 2$; S_2 has greater volume.

33. $S = \pi r\sqrt{r^2 + h^2}$ **35.** 30,264 ft-lb

37. 2,954.67 ft-lb   **39.** 44.108 ft-lb

41. The spring should be stretched about 14 in.

43. 5.625×10^{-5} **45.** $\left(\frac{7}{3}, \frac{1}{3}\right)$

47. $7,191.64   **49.** 309,030 people

51. a. 3 units   **b.** $31.50

53. 17,500 ft-lb   **55.** 135 lb   **57.** $F(t) = \frac{1}{2}t + \frac{2}{3}$

59. The total work is $6,176\pi$.

61. The desired distances are 4.88 cm, 11.12 cm from the right, 10.34 cm from the top, and 5.66 cm from the bottom.

63. a. $\frac{35\pi}{3}$ ft-lb   **b.** $\frac{70}{9}\pi$ ft-lb

65. The force is approximately 1,321 ft-lb.   **67.** $S = 2\pi\sqrt{2}$

69. $W = (4,000)^2 P\left(\dfrac{1}{4,000} - \dfrac{1}{t}\right)$ mi-lb   **71.** 344π

73. a. $h \approx -0.644391$ **b.** $h \approx 0.865202$

75. $W \approx 1.728 \times 10^{12}$ ft-lb

77. 4.7999   **79.** $\frac{\pi}{4}$ **81.** 1.3833

83. This is Putnam Examination Problem 1 of the morning session in 1939.

85. This is Putnam Examination Problem 1 of the morning session in 1993.

Chapter 7: Methods of Integration

7.1 Review of Substitution and Integration by Table
(Pages 433–435)

1. $2(x^2 + 5x)^{1/2} + C$ **3.** $\ln|\ln x| + C$

5. $\frac{1}{4}\tan^{-1}\dfrac{x^2}{2} + C$ **7.** $-\frac{1}{5}(1 + \cot x)^5 + C$

9. $-\frac{1}{4}(x^4 - 2x^2 + 3)^{-1} + C$ **11.** $\ln(x^2 + x + 1) + C$

13. $\dfrac{\sqrt{x^2 - a^2}}{a^2 x} + C$ **15.** $\frac{1}{2}x^2\left(\ln x - \frac{1}{2}\right) + C$

17. $a^{-1}e^{ax}(x - a^{-1}) + C$

19. $\frac{1}{2}x\sqrt{x^2 + 1} - \frac{1}{2}\ln\left|x + \sqrt{x^2 + 1}\right| + C$

21. $\frac{1}{4}\sqrt{4x^2 + 1} + C$ 23. $\frac{-4\sin 5x - 5\cos 5x}{41e^{4x}} + C$

25. $b^{-1}\ln|1 + bx| + C$ 27. $\frac{1}{20}(x + 1)^4(4x - 1) + C$

29. $\frac{1}{4}e^{4x}\left(x - \frac{1}{4}\right) + C$ 31. $x - \frac{1}{2}\ln|1 + e^{2x}| + C$

33. $\frac{1}{8}(4x^4 + 1)^{1/2} + C$

35. $\sec\frac{x}{2}\tan\frac{x}{2} + \ln\left|\sec\frac{x}{2} + \tan\frac{x}{2}\right| + C$

37. $-\frac{1}{3(3x + 1)} + C$

39. $-\sin x + \ln\left|\tan\left(\frac{x}{2} + \frac{\pi}{4}\right)\right| + C$

41. $\frac{1}{2}x + \frac{1}{4}\sin 2x + C$ 43. $-\frac{1}{5}\cos^5 x + \frac{1}{7}\cos^7 x + C$

45. If m is odd, let $u = \cos x$. If n is odd, let $u = \sin x$. If both m and n are even, use the identities shown in Problems 40 and 41 until one exponent is odd.

47. $4\left[\frac{x^{1/2}}{2} - x^{1/4} + \ln(x^{1/4} + 1)\right] + C$

49. $-6(2 + \tan^3 t)^{-1} + C$ 51. $\frac{1}{e^x + e^{-x}} + C$

53. 94.68   55. 40.3053   57. 0.7207   59. 3.8097

7.2 Integration by Parts (Pages 439–441)

1. $-\frac{1}{2}xe^{-2x} - \frac{1}{4}e^{-2x} + C$ 3. $\frac{1}{2}x^2\ln x - \frac{1}{4}x^2 + C$

5. $x\sin^{-1}x + \sqrt{1 - x^2} + C$

7. $\frac{4}{25}e^{-3x}\sin 4x - \frac{3}{25}e^{-3x}\cos 4x + C$

9. $\frac{1}{3}x^3\ln x - \frac{1}{9}x^3 + C$

11. $\frac{x}{2}[\sin(\ln x) - \cos(\ln x)] + C$

13. $x\ln(x^2 + 1) - 2x + 2\tan^{-1}x + C$

15. $\frac{-xe^{-x}}{x - 1} + e^{-x} + C$ 17. $\frac{32}{3}\ln 2 - \frac{28}{9}$

19. $e - 2$ 21. $\frac{1}{4}(e^{2\pi} - 1)$

25. $\frac{1}{2}\cos^2 x - (\cos^2 x)\ln(\cos x) + C$

27. $-(2 + \cos x)\ln(2 + \cos x) + (2 + \cos x) + C$

29. $\frac{x}{2} + \frac{1}{4}\sin 2x + C$

31. $\frac{1}{4}x^2 + \frac{1}{4}x\sin 2x + \frac{1}{8}\cos 2x + C$

33. $\frac{x^{n+1}}{n + 1}\ln x - \frac{x^{n+1}}{(n + 1)^2} + C$

35. 177 units   37. 3.73218

39. a. 2.2565   b. 13.1775   41. (0.68, 1.27)

43. $2y^{1/2} = \frac{2}{3}x^{3/2}(\ln x - \frac{2}{3}) + C$

45. $y = \exp(1 - \cos x - x\sin x)$

47. 65 miles   49. 0.07   51. $1.558nRT$

7.3 Trigonometric Methods (Page 447)

5. $\sin x - \frac{1}{3}\sin^3 x + C$ 7. $\frac{1}{3}\sin^3 x - \frac{1}{5}\sin^5 x + C$

9. $-\frac{2}{3}(\cos t)^{3/2} + C$ 11. $-e^{\cos x} + C$

13. $\frac{1}{8}x - \frac{1}{32}\sin 4x + C$ 15. $-\frac{1}{2}\ln|\cos 2\theta| + C$

17. $\frac{1}{6}\tan^6 x + \frac{1}{4}\tan^4 x + C$ 19. $2\tan x - x + C$

21. $\frac{1}{2}\sec u\tan u - \frac{1}{2}\ln|\sec u + \tan u| + C$

23. $\frac{3}{4}(\tan x)^{4/3} + C$ 25. $\frac{1}{4}\sin^2 x^2 + C$

27. $\frac{1}{4}\sec^3 t\tan t - \frac{5}{8}\sec t\tan t + \frac{3}{8}\ln|\sec t + \tan t| + C$

29. $-\frac{1}{3}\csc^3 x + C$ 31. $-\csc x + C$

33. $2\sin^{-1}\frac{t}{2} + \frac{1}{2}t\sqrt{4 - t^2} + C$

35. $\sqrt{4 + x^2} + \ln\left|\sqrt{4 + x^2} + x\right| + C$

37. $\ln\left|x + \sqrt{x^2 - 7}\right| + C$ 39. $\sin^{-1}\frac{x}{\sqrt{5}} + C$

41. $-\frac{\sqrt{4 - x^2}}{4x} + C$ 43. $\sqrt{x^2 - 4} - 2\sec^{-1}\frac{x}{2} + C$

45. $\frac{1}{3}\ln\left|\frac{x + 4}{\sqrt{9 - (x + 1)^2}}\right| + C$

47. $\ln\left|\sqrt{x^2 - 2x + 6} + x - 1\right| + C$

49. $\frac{1}{4}\tan^4 u + C$ 51. $\frac{1}{2}$ 53. 15.5031

55. $\pm 2\sqrt{2}\sin\frac{x}{2} + C$

57. $-\frac{1}{3}\cos\left(\frac{3}{2}x\right) - \frac{1}{5}\cos\left(\frac{5}{2}x\right) + C$

59. $\frac{1}{8}\sin 4x - \frac{1}{8}\sin 2x - \frac{1}{40}\sin 10x + C$

61. $-\ln\left|\sqrt{9 - x^2} - 1\right| + C$

7.4 Method of Partial Fractions (Pages 455–457)

1. $\frac{-1}{3x} + \frac{1}{3(x - 3)}$ 3. $3 - \frac{1}{x}$

5. $\frac{4}{x} + \frac{-8}{2x + 1}$

7. $\frac{3}{x} + \frac{-1}{x^2} + \frac{1}{x + 1} + \frac{-2}{(x + 1)^2}$

9. $\frac{-4}{9x^2} + \frac{17}{27x} - \frac{13}{9(x + 3)^2} + \frac{10}{27(x + 3)}$

11. $\frac{1}{4(1 - x)} + \frac{1}{4(1 + x)} + \frac{1}{2(1 + x^2)}$

13. $\frac{1}{x} - \frac{1}{3(x + 1)} - \frac{1}{3(2x - 1)}$

15. $\frac{1}{3}\ln\left|\frac{x - 3}{x}\right| + C$ 17. $3x - \ln|x| + C$

19. $4\ln|x| - 4\ln|2x + 1| + C$

21. $-9\ln|x| - x^{-1} + 6\ln|x + 1| + 5\ln|x - 1| + C$

23. $x - \frac{5}{3}\ln|x + 2| + \frac{2}{3}\ln|x - 1| + C$

25. $x + \frac{1}{2}\ln|x - 1| - \frac{1}{2}\ln|x + 1| - \tan^{-1}x + C$

27. $\ln|x + 1| + (x + 1)^{-1} + C$

29. $-\frac{1}{2}\ln|x| + \frac{1}{3}\ln|x + 1| + \frac{1}{6}\ln|x - 2| + C$

31. $\ln\left|\frac{x + 2}{x + 1}\right| - \frac{2}{x + 2} + C$

33. $3\ln|x - 1| + 2\ln|x + 3| + C$

35. $\ln\left|x^3 - x^2 + 4x - 4\right| + C$

39. $\frac{1}{7}\ln|e^x - 3| - \frac{1}{7}\ln(2e^x + 1) + C$

41. $\frac{1}{1 + \cos x} + C$ 43. $\ln|\tan x + 4| + C$

45. $3x^{1/3} + 6x^{1/6} + 6\ln\left|x^{1/6} - 1\right| + C$

47. $-\frac{1}{5}\ln\left|\tan\frac{x}{2} - 3\right| + \frac{1}{5}\ln\left|3\tan\frac{x}{2} + 1\right| + C$

49. $-\ln|\sin x + \cos x| + C$

51. $-\ln(1 - \sin x) + C$ 53. $\frac{1}{\tan\frac{x}{2} - 2} + C$

55. $\frac{1}{2}\ln|\ln x - 3| - \frac{1}{2}\ln|\ln x - 1| + C$

57. 0.6931   **59. a.** 1.0888   **b.** 7.6402

61. $\frac{1}{2}\ln|x^2 - 9| + C$ **65.** $\frac{1}{b}\ln\left|\dfrac{x}{ax + b}\right| + C$

7.5 Summary of Integration Techniques (Pages 460–461)

1. $\dfrac{1}{2x^2(x - 1)^2} + C$ **3.** $\frac{1}{4}\ln\left|\sec 2x^2 + \tan 2x^2\right| + C$

5. $\ln|\sin e^x| + C$ **7.** $-\ln|\cos(\ln x)| + C$

9. $3\ln|\sec t + \tan t| + 2\ln|\sec t| + C$

11. $\frac{1}{2}\tan^{-1} e^{2t} + C$ **13.** $x + \frac{1}{2}\ln(x^2 + 9) - \frac{8}{3}\tan^{-1}\frac{x}{3} + C$

15. $-x - 2\ln\left|e^{-x} - 1\right| + C$

17. $\frac{2}{3}\sin^{-1} t^3 + C$ **19.** $x - \frac{1}{2}\ln(e^{2x} + 1) + C$

21. $\tan^{-1}(x + 1) + C$ **23.** $\dfrac{2}{\sqrt{3}}\tan^{-1}\dfrac{1}{\sqrt{3}}(2x + 1) + C$

25. $x\tan^{-1} x - \frac{1}{2}\ln(x^2 + 1) + C$

27. $\frac{1}{2}e^{-x}(\sin x - \cos x) + C$

29. $x\cos^{-1}(-x) + \sqrt{1 - x^2} + C$

31. $-\cos x + \frac{1}{3}\cos^3 x + C$ **33.** $\frac{1}{5}\cos^5 x - \frac{1}{3}\cos^3 x + C$

35. $\frac{1}{16}x - \frac{1}{64}\sin 4x + \frac{1}{48}\sin^3 2x + C$

37. $-\frac{1}{9}\cos^9 x + \frac{2}{7}\cos^7 x - \frac{1}{5}\cos^5 x + C$

39. $\frac{1}{8}\tan^8 x + \frac{1}{6}\tan^6 x + C$

41. $\sqrt{1 - x^2} - \ln\left|\dfrac{1 + \sqrt{1 - x^2}}{x}\right| + C$

43. $\sqrt{2x^2 - 1} + \dfrac{3}{\sqrt{2}}\ln\left|\sqrt{2}x + \sqrt{2x^2 - 1}\right| + C$

45. $\ln|x| - \ln\left|1 + \sqrt{x^2 + 1}\right| + C$

47. $-2\sqrt{4x - x^2 - 2} + 5\sin^{-1}\dfrac{x - 2}{\sqrt{2}} + C$

49. $\ln(\sin x + \sqrt{1 + \sin^2 x}) + C$

51. $-\dfrac{\cos^5 x}{5} + \dfrac{2\cos^3 x}{3} - \cos x + C$

53. $\frac{1}{3}\tan^3 x - \tan x + x + C$

55. π **57.** 1.8101   **59.** 0.1353   **61.** 113.4327

63. $\ln\left(\sqrt{1 + e^{2x}} + e^x\right) + C$

65. $3\ln|x| - \ln\left|x^2 + x + 1\right| + \dfrac{4}{\sqrt{3}}\tan^{-1}\dfrac{\sqrt{3}}{3}(2x + 1) + C$

67. $5\ln|x - 7| + 2(x + 2)^{-1} + C$

69. $3\ln|x + 1| - 2(x + 1)^{-1} + C$

71. $-\frac{1}{2}\ln|x + 1| + 2\ln|x + 2| - \frac{3}{2}\ln|x + 3| + C$

73. 0.09   **77.** 2.9579   **79.** 4   **81.** 101.7876

83. $(0.71, 0.12)$ **87.** $-\frac{1}{16}\sin^3 4x\cos 4x + \frac{3}{8}x - \frac{3}{64}\sin 8x + C$

7.6 First-Order Differential Equations (Pages 469–472)

1. $\frac{1}{5}x^2 + Cx^{-3}$ **3.** $-5x^{-3} + Cx^{-2}$

5. $\frac{1}{3}x^{-2}e^{x^3} + Cx^{-2}$ **7.** $\left(\dfrac{1}{2}x + \dfrac{1}{2x}\right)\tan^{-1} x - \dfrac{1}{2} + \dfrac{C}{x}$

9. $y = -\cos x\ln|\cos x| + C\cos x$

11. $y = x^2 - 1$ for $x > -1$ **13.** $y = 2x^3 - 6x^2$

15. $2X^2 + Y^2 = C$ **17.** $Y = CX$

19. The GDP in the year 2010 will be about \$17,828 billion.

21. The predicted number of divorces in 2005 is about 2,378,000.

23. a. $Q(t) = 30 - 20e^{-t/15}$ **b.** 4 minutes, 19 seconds

25. In the "long run" (as $t \to +\infty$), the concentration will be $\displaystyle\lim_{t \to +\infty}\dfrac{\alpha}{\beta}(1 - e^{-\beta t}) = \dfrac{\alpha}{\beta}$; the "half-way point" is reached when $t = \dfrac{\ln 2}{\beta}$.

27. 46.8 million   **29.** $M(t) = \dfrac{k}{r}(1 - e^{-rt})$

31. It will take about an hour to drain.

33. a. $y = -\dfrac{k}{24}(x^4 - 2Lx^3 + L^3 x)$

    b. maximum deflection occurs where $y_m \approx -0.0130kL^4$

    c. The maximum deflection is $y_m \approx -0.0054kL^4$; the maximum deflection in the cantilevered case is less than that in part **b.**

35. a. $S_1(t) = 200(1 - e^{-t/100})$

    b. $S_2(t) = 200 - 2te^{-t/100} - 200e^{-t/100}$

    c. The maximum excess is $S(100) \approx 73.58$ lb.

37. $P(t) = P_\infty \exp\left[-\left(\ln\dfrac{P_\infty}{P_0}\right)e^{-kt}\right]$

39. $x = \dfrac{1}{2}(y + 1)e^y + \dfrac{Ce^y}{y + 1}$

41. a. $I(t) = \frac{3}{2}(1 - e^{-2t})$ **b.** $I(t) = e^{-2t}(1 - \cos t)$

43. 9.872 days   **45.** $N = \left(\dfrac{1}{m} + Ce^{pt}\right)S$

47. a. $v(t) = \dfrac{-mg}{k} + \left(\dfrac{mg}{k} + v_0\right)e^{-kt/m}$;

    $s(t) = \dfrac{-mg}{k}t + \dfrac{m}{k}\left(\dfrac{mg}{k} + v_0\right)(1 - e^{-kt/m})$

    b. The object reaches its maximum height when $v(t) = 0$. The maximum height is
$$s_{\max} = \dfrac{mv_0}{k} - \dfrac{m^2 g}{k^2}\ln\left(1 + \dfrac{kv_0}{mg}\right).$$

    c. The maximum height is 82.98 ft; the object hits the ground when $t \approx 5.51$ seconds.

    d. 9.38 seconds

7.7 Improper Integrals (Pages 479–481)

3. $\frac{1}{2}$ **5.** diverges   **7.** 10   **9.** diverges

11. $\frac{1}{10}$ **13.** $\frac{5}{2}$ **15.** $\frac{1}{9}$ **17.** diverges

19. $\dfrac{2}{e}$ **21.** 0   **23.** diverges   **25.** 2

27. diverges   **29.** diverges   **31.** 0   **33.** $\frac{5}{4}$ **35.** 2

37. $\frac{3}{2}\left[(1 - e^{-1})^{2/3} - (1 - e)^{2/3}\right]$

39. -1 **41.** 1   **43.** 2   **45.** diverges   **47.** $\frac{1}{4}$

49. There will be 100,000 millirads.

51.

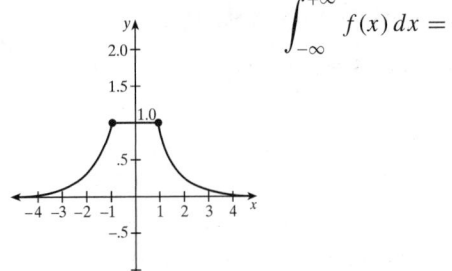

$$\int_{-\infty}^{+\infty} f(x)\,dx = 4$$

53. $(1 - p)^{-1}$ if $p < 1$, and diverges if $p \geq 1$

55. both diverge   **57.** 8   **59.** $\frac{3}{40}$

65. b. $\dfrac{s^2 - 4}{(s^2 + 4)^2}$

67. b. $\mathcal{L}(y) = \dfrac{-\frac{2}{13}s}{s^2 + 4} + \dfrac{\frac{6}{13}}{s^2 + 4} + \dfrac{\frac{28}{13}}{s + 3}$

   c. $y = -\frac{2}{13}\cos 2t + \frac{3}{13}\sin 2t + \frac{28}{13}e^{-3t}$

7.8 Hyperbolic and Inverse Hyperbolic Functions (Pages 486–487)

1. 3.6269   **3.** -0.7616 **5.** 1.1995   **7.** 0.9624

9. 1.6667   **11.** 0.6481   **13.** $3\cosh 3x$

15. $(4x + 3)\sinh(2x^2 + 3x)$ **17.** $-x^{-2}\cosh x^{-1}$

19. $\dfrac{3x^2}{\sqrt{1 + x^6}}$ **21.** $\sec x$ **23.** $\sec x$

25. $\dfrac{x - \sqrt{1 + x^2}\,\sinh^{-1}x}{x^2\sqrt{1 + x^2}}$ **27.** $\cosh^{-1}x$

29. $\left[e^x - 2e^{2x}\sinh^{-1}x - \dfrac{e^x}{\sqrt{1 + x^2}}\right]\sinh(e^x - e^{2x}\sinh^{-1}x)$

31. $-\cosh x^{-1} + C$ **33.** $\ln|\sinh x| + C$

35. $\frac{1}{3}\cosh^{-1}\dfrac{3t}{4} + C$ **37.** $\sinh^{-1}(\sin x) + C$

39. $\frac{1}{3}\tanh^{-1}x^3 + C$ **41.** -0.2027 **43.** 1.0311

45. 0.3808   **47.** 1

49. The curve is rising for all x. The curve is concave up on $(-\infty, 0)$ and concave down on $(0, +\infty)$.

53. b. $y = \cosh 2x + \sinh 2x$ **55.** $2.3504a$ **57.** 17.68

Chapter 7 Review
Proficiency Examination (Pages 487–488)

12. a. 0.5493   **b.** $\frac{4}{3}$ **c.** 0.5493

13. $2\sqrt{x^2 + 1} + 3\sinh^{-1}x + C$

14. $-\dfrac{x}{2}\cos 2x + \dfrac{1}{4}\sin 2x + C$

15. $-\frac{1}{2}\cosh(1 - 2x) + C$ **16.** $\sin^{-1}\dfrac{x}{2} + C$

17. $\frac{1}{4}\ln(x^2 + 1) + \frac{1}{2}\tan^{-1}x + \frac{1}{2}\ln|x - 1| + C$

18. $\dfrac{x^2}{2} + \dfrac{1}{2}\ln|x^2 - 1| + C$

19. 1.9089   **20.** 0.1144   **21.** -0.2027

22. 0.6095   **23.** $\frac{1}{4}$ **24.** 2

25. diverges   **26.** $\frac{1}{2}$

27. $\dfrac{1}{\sqrt{\tanh^{-1}2x}}\left[\dfrac{1}{1 - 4x^2}\right]$ **28.** 4.7999

29. $y = \dfrac{x + 1}{e^x}(\ln|x + 1| + 1)$ **30.** 485.2 lb

Supplementary Problems (Pages 488–490)

1. $(1 - x^2)^{-1}$ **3.** e^{-2x}

5. $x\cosh x + \sinh x + (e^x - e^{-x})\cosh(e^x + e^{-x})$

7. $-\dfrac{x}{2}\sqrt{4 - x^2} + 2\sin^{-1}\dfrac{x}{2} + C$

9. $-\ln|x| - x^{-1} + \ln|x - 2| + C$

11. $4x^{1/4} - 4\ln(1 + x^{1/4}) + C$

13. $\dfrac{x^3}{3}\tan^{-1}x - \dfrac{x^2}{6} + \dfrac{1}{6}\ln(1 + x^2) + C$

15. $\dfrac{1}{2}e^x\sqrt{4 - e^{2x}} + 2\sin^{-1}\left(\dfrac{e^x}{2}\right) + C$

17. $-\frac{1}{5}(1 + x^{-2})^{5/2} + \frac{1}{3}(1 + x^{-2})^{3/2} + C$

19. $-2\sqrt{1 - \sin x} + C$

21. $\dfrac{x}{2}[\sin(\ln x) - \cos(\ln x)] + C$

23. $\ln(e^{2x} + 4e^x + 1) - x + C$

25. $\dfrac{x^3}{3}\cot^{-1}x + \dfrac{x^2}{6} - \dfrac{1}{6}\ln(1 + x^2) + C$

27. $\frac{1}{3}\ln|x^3 + 6x + 1| + C$

29. $2\cos\sqrt{x + 2} + 2\sqrt{x + 2}\sin\sqrt{x + 2} + C$

31. $\frac{1}{4}\ln(x^4 + 4x^2 + 3) + C$

33. $\sqrt{5 - x^2} - \sqrt{5}\ln\left|\dfrac{\sqrt{5} + \sqrt{5 - x^2}}{x}\right| + C$

35. $\frac{1}{3}\sqrt{x^2 + 4}\,(x^2 - 8) + C$ **37.** $\dfrac{\sec^3 x}{3} + C$

39. $\frac{3}{2}x^{2/3} - 2x^{1/2} + 3x^{1/3} - 6x^{1/6} + 6\ln|x^{1/6} + 1| + C$

41. $-\ln|1 + \cos x - \sin x| + C$

43. $-2e^{x/2} - 3e^{x/3} - 6e^{x/6} - 6\ln|e^{x/6} - 1| + C$

45. $y = \dfrac{1}{x + 1}[x + C]$

47. $y = \sin x + \frac{1}{3}\cos x\tan^3 x + C\cos x$

49. 2   **51.** 0.8101   **53.** $\dfrac{n!}{a^{n+1}}$

57. -1 **59.** $T = T_0 + Be^{kt}$ **63.** (0.65, 1)

65. 2.848   **67.** 1.2876   **69.** 4.739

71. 23.38   **73.** $A_1 = A_2 = \ln|a|$

75. $3|a| + \dfrac{b^2}{8|a|}\ln 2$ **81.** 0.5199   **83.** $\dfrac{3\pi}{16}$

85. a. $v(t) = \left(\dfrac{W - B}{k}\right)\left(1 - e^{-(kg/W)t}\right)$

   b. $S(t) = \dfrac{W - B}{k}\left[t + \dfrac{W}{kg}e^{-(kg/W)t} - \dfrac{W}{kg}\right]$

   c. The critical depth is 269.07 m.

87. about 5.6 years

89. This is Putnam Examination Problem 3 in the morning session of 1980.

Chapter 8: Infinite Series
8.1 Sequences and Their Limits (Pages 503–505)

3. 0, 2, 0, 2, 0   **5.** $1, \frac{1}{2}, \frac{1}{3}, \frac{1}{4}, \frac{1}{5}$

7. $\frac{4}{3}, \frac{7}{4}, \frac{10}{5}, \frac{13}{6}, \frac{16}{7}$ **9.** $256, 16, 4, 2, \sqrt{2}$

11. 1, 3, 13, 183, 33673   **13.** 5

15. -7 **17.** 0   **19.** $\frac{1}{2}$

21. 4   **23.** 0   **25.** 1

27. 1   **29.** 1   **31.** $\frac{1}{2}$

33. 1   **35.** 1   **47.** $a_4 = 6.25\%,\ a_n = 100(\frac{1}{2})^n\%$

49. $N = 100$ **51.** $N = 1{,}001$

8.2 Introduction to Infinite Series; Geometric Series (Pages 511–514)

3. 5   **5.** 3   **7.** diverges

9. $\frac{5}{27}$ **11.** 4.51665   **13.** $-\frac{2}{45}$

15. $\frac{1}{3}$ **17.** $\frac{16}{63}$ **19.** $2(2 + \sqrt{2})$

21. $\frac{1}{2}(4 + 3\sqrt{2})$ **23.** converges to 1   **25.** converges to 1

27. diverges   **29.** The series converges to 1   **31.** $\frac{1}{99}$

33. $\frac{52}{37}$ **35. a.** $A = 1, B = 1$ **b.** $\frac{1}{2}$

37. 0   **39.** 9.14   **41.** 4.858   **43.** $\dfrac{1}{a}$

45. 2   **47.** 1,500   **49.** 3 ft

51. The total depreciation is \$10,000.

53. The patient will have about 30.8 units of the drug.

55. In the long run there will be 33 members on the board.

59. 4 miles   **63. a.** false   **b.** true   **65. d.** $\frac{3}{4}$ **67.** 3

8.3 The Integral Test; p-Series (Pages 520–521)

3. $p = 3$; converges   **5.** $p = \frac{1}{3}$; diverges

7. converges   **9.** diverges   **11.** converges

13. diverges   **15.** diverges

17. diverges   **19.** converges   **21.** diverges

23. converges   **25.** diverges   **27.** diverges

29. converges   **31.** diverges   **33.** converges

35. converges   **37.** diverges   **39.** diverges

41. diverges   **43.** diverges   **45.** diverges

47. converges   **49.** converges   **51.** diverges

53. diverges

55. converges if $p > 1$ and diverges if $p \le 1$

57. converges if $p > 1$ and diverges if $p \le 1$

59. converges if $p > 1$ and diverges if $p \le 1$

61. false

8.4 Comparison Tests (Pages 526–527)

1. converges if $|r| < 1$ and diverges if $|r| \ge 1$

3. geometric; converges   **5.** geometric; diverges

7. p-series; diverges   **9.** p-series; converges

11. geometric; diverges   **13.** converges

15. diverges   **17.** diverges   **19.** converges

21. converges   **23.** converges   **25.** diverges

27. converges   **29.** converges   **31.** converges

33. converges   **35.** diverges   **37.** converges

39. converges   **41.** converges   **43.** diverges

45. converges   **47.** converges   **49.** converges

51. diverges   **53.** converges   **55.** converges

8.5 The Ratio Test and the Root Test (Pages 532–533)

3. converges   **5.** diverges   **7.** converges

9. converges   **11.** diverges   **13.** converges

15. converges   **17.** converges   **19.** diverges

21. converges   **23.** converges   **25.** converges

27. diverges   **29.** converges   **31.** diverges

33. converges   **35.** converges   **37.** diverges

39. converges   **41.** converges   **43.** converges

45. converges for $0 \le x < 1$

47. converges for $0 \le x \le 0.5$

49. converges for $x \ge 0$

51. converges for $0 \le x < a^{-1}$

53. The integral also converges.

8.6 Alternating Series; Absolute and Conditional Convergence (Pages 542–544)

5. converges conditionally   **7.** diverges

9. converges absolutely   **11.** converges conditionally

13. converges absolutely   **15.** diverges

17. converges absolutely   **19.** converges conditionally

21. converges conditionally   **23.** converges conditionally

25. diverges   **27.** converges conditionally

29. converges conditionally   **31.** converges absolutely

33. a. $\frac{5}{8}$ **b.** $S_7 \approx 0.632$ **35. a.** 0.0823   **b.** 0.083

37. a. -0.1664 **b.** $S_5 \approx -0.167$

39. The interval of convergence is $\left[-\frac{1}{2}, \frac{1}{2}\right)$.

41. The interval of convergence is $[-1, 1]$.

43. The interval of convergence is $(-1, 1)$ for all $p > 0$.

45. $E_{max} = \dfrac{1}{6^2} \approx 0.0278$ **47.** $E_{max} = \dfrac{7}{2^7} \approx 0.0547$

49. converges absolutely

8.7 Power Series (Pages 552–553)

1. $(-1, 1)$ **3.** $(-1, 1)$ **5.** $\left(\frac{8}{3}, \frac{10}{3}\right)$

7. $\left(-\frac{13}{3}, -\frac{5}{3}\right)$ **9.** $x = 1$ **11.** $(-1, 3)$

13. $\left[1, \frac{5}{3}\right)$ **15.** $(-7, 7)$ **17.** $x = 0$

19. $[-1, 1]$ **21.** $(-\infty, \infty)$ **23.** $x = 0$

25. $(-\infty, \infty)$ **27.** $[-1, 1]$ **29.** $R = 1$

31. $R = e$ **33.** $R = \dfrac{1}{|a|}$

35. $f'(x) = \displaystyle\sum_{k=1}^{\infty} \dfrac{kx^{k-1}}{2^k}$ **37.** $f'(x) = \displaystyle\sum_{k=1}^{\infty} k(k+2)x^{k-1}$

39. $F(x) = \displaystyle\sum_{k=1}^{\infty} \dfrac{x^k}{k(2)^{k-1}}$ **41.** $F(x) = \displaystyle\sum_{k=0}^{\infty} \dfrac{(k+2)x^{k+1}}{(k+1)}$

47. $|x| > 1$ **49.** $(-1, 1)$ **51.** $R = \sqrt{2}$

8.8 Taylor and Maclaurin Series (Pages 564–566)

3. $e^{2x} = \displaystyle\sum_{k=0}^{\infty} \dfrac{(2x)^k}{k!}$ **5.** $e^{x^2} = \displaystyle\sum_{k=0}^{\infty} \dfrac{x^{2k}}{k!}$

7. $\sin x^2 = \displaystyle\sum_{k=0}^{\infty} \dfrac{(-1)^k x^{4k+2}}{(2k+1)!}$

9. $\sin ax = \displaystyle\sum_{k=0}^{\infty} \dfrac{(-1)^k (ax)^{2k+1}}{(2k+1)!}$

11. $\cos 2x^2 = \displaystyle\sum_{k=0}^{\infty} \dfrac{(-1)^k (2x^2)^{2k}}{(2k)!}$

13. $x^2 \cos x = \displaystyle\sum_{k=0}^{\infty} \dfrac{(-1)^k x^{2k+2}}{(2k)!}$

15. $x^2 + 2x + 1$ is its own Maclaurin series.

17. $xe^x = \displaystyle\sum_{k=0}^{\infty} \dfrac{x^{k+1}}{k!}$

19. $e^x + \sin x = 1 + 2x + \dfrac{x^2}{2!} + \dfrac{x^4}{4!} + \dfrac{2x^5}{5!} + \dfrac{x^6}{6!}$
$$+ \dfrac{x^8}{8!} + \dfrac{2x^9}{9!} + \cdots$$

21. $\dfrac{1}{1 + 4x} = \displaystyle\sum_{k=0}^{\infty} (-4)^k x^k$ **23.** $\dfrac{1}{a + x} = \displaystyle\sum_{k=0}^{\infty} \dfrac{(-1)^k x^k}{a^{k+1}}$

25. $\ln(3 + x) = \ln 3 + \displaystyle\sum_{k=0}^{\infty} \dfrac{(-1)^k x^{k+1}}{(k+1)3^{k+1}}$

27. $\tan^{-1}(2x) = \sum_{k=0}^{\infty} \dfrac{(-1)^k 2^{2k+1} x^{2k+1}}{2k+1}$

29. $e^{-x^2} = \sum_{k=0}^{\infty} \dfrac{(-1)^k x^{2k}}{k!}$

31. $e^x \approx e + e(x-1) + \dfrac{1}{2!}e(x-1)^2 + \dfrac{1}{3!}e(x-1)^3$

33. $\cos x \approx \cos\dfrac{\pi}{3} - \left(x - \dfrac{\pi}{3}\right)\sin\dfrac{\pi}{3} - \dfrac{\left(x - \dfrac{\pi}{3}\right)^2}{2!}\cos\dfrac{\pi}{3}$
$\qquad + \dfrac{\left(x - \dfrac{\pi}{3}\right)^3}{3!}\sin\dfrac{\pi}{3}$

35. $\tan x \approx 0 + 1 \cdot x + \dfrac{0x^2}{2!} + \dfrac{2x^3}{3!}$

37. $f(x) = (x-2)^3 + 4(x-2)^2 + 5(x-2) - 3$

39. $f(x) \approx -\dfrac{1}{3} + \dfrac{1}{9}(x-5) - \dfrac{1}{27}(x-5)^2 + \dfrac{1}{81}(x-5)^3$

41. $f(x) \approx 1 - \dfrac{2}{3}(x-2) + \dfrac{4}{9}(x-2)^2 - \dfrac{8}{27}(x-2)^3$

43. $f(x) = 1 + \dfrac{1}{2}x - \dfrac{1}{8}x^2 + \dfrac{1}{16}x^3 - \dfrac{5}{128}x^4 + \cdots$
Interval of convergence is $[-1, 1]$.

45. $f(x) = 1 + \dfrac{2}{3}x - \dfrac{1}{9}x^2 + \dfrac{4}{81}x^3 - \cdots$ Interval of convergence is $[-1, 1]$.

47. $f(x) = x + \dfrac{1}{2}x^3 + \dfrac{3}{8}x^5 + \dfrac{5}{16}x^7 + \cdots$ Interval of convergence is $(-1, 1)$.

51. $x + \dfrac{1}{3!}x^3 + \dfrac{1}{5!}x^5 + \cdots = \sum_{k=0}^{\infty} \dfrac{x^{2k+1}}{(2k+1)!}$

53. $n = 4$ **55.** $f(x) = \sum_{k=0}^{\infty}\left[1 - \dfrac{1}{2^{k+1}}\right]x^k$

57. $f(x) = \sum_{k=0}^{\infty} \dfrac{(-1)^k 2^{2k} x^{2k+1}}{(2k+1)!}$

59. $f(x) = \dfrac{1}{2}\sum_{k=0}^{\infty}(-1)^k\left[\dfrac{1+2^{2k}}{(2k)!}\right]x^{2k}$

61. $f(x) = \sum_{k=0}^{\infty}[(-1)^k 2^{k+1} + 2^{k+1} + 1]\dfrac{x^{k+1}}{k+1}$

63. 1   **69.** 0.499514

Chapter 8 Review
Proficiency Examination (Pages 566–567)
31. This is the definition of e.   **32. a.** 0 **b.** converges
33. diverges   **34.** diverges   **35.** diverges
36. diverges   **37.** converges absolutely
38. The interval of convergence is $(-1, 1)$.

39. $\sin 2x = \sum_{k=0}^{\infty} \dfrac{(-1)^k (2x)^{2k+1}}{(2k+1)!}$

40. $f(x) = -\dfrac{2}{5}\sum_{k=0}^{\infty}\left(\dfrac{2}{5}\right)^k\left(x - \dfrac{1}{2}\right)^k$

Supplementary Problems (Pages 567–569)
1. does not exist   **3.** converges to e^{-2}
5. converges to 1   **7.** converges to $\dfrac{5}{3}$
9. converges to 0   **11.** converges to 0
13. converges to e^4 **15.** converges
17. $\dfrac{1}{3}$ **19.** $\dfrac{e}{3-e}$ **21.** $\dfrac{1}{2}$

23. $\dfrac{15-e}{9(6-e)}$ **25.** $\dfrac{-1}{\ln 2}$ **27.** $\dfrac{1}{4}$
29. diverges   **31.** diverges   **33.** converges
35. converges   **37.** converges   **39.** converges
41. diverges   **43.** diverges   **45.** converges
47. converges absolutely   **49.** converges absolutely
51. diverges   **53.** converges absolutely
55. converges absolutely
57. $(0, 2)$ **59.** $(-1, 1)$ **61.** $(-\infty, \infty)$
63. $[-3, -1]$ **65.** $x = 0$ **67.** $(-\infty, \infty)$

69. $f(x) = \sum_{k=0}^{\infty}(-1)^k \dfrac{x^{2k+4}}{(2k+1)!}$

71. $f(x) = x + x^2 + \sum_{k=1}^{\infty} \dfrac{(-1)^k x^{2k+1}}{2k+1}$

73. $f(x) = \sum_{k=0}^{\infty}\left[2 + \dfrac{5(-1)^{k+1}}{2}\left(\dfrac{3}{2}\right)^k\right]x^k$

75. 0.000022   **77.** $\dfrac{20}{9}$ ft   **79.** $p = 0.95$

81. $a_k = (-1)^k(4k+1)\left[\dfrac{1\cdot 3\cdot 5\cdots(2k-1)}{2\cdot 4\cdot 6\cdots(2k)}\right]^3$

There is an interesting discussion of this identity, as well as biographical information on Ramanujan, in the article "Ramanujan the Phenomenon," by S.G. Gindikin, *Quantum*, pp. 4–9, April 1998.

85. $\int \sqrt{x^3+1}\,dx = x + \dfrac{1}{8}x^4 - \dfrac{1}{56}x^7 + \dfrac{1}{160}x^{10} - \cdots$

89. 0.1986693   **91.** $R_3(x) < 10^{-12}$ **93.** $|x| < 0.187$

95. a. $t \approx \dfrac{\lambda}{\ln 2}\left[\dfrac{S(t) - S(0)}{R(t)}\right]$
b. $t \approx 5.61 \times 10^7$ years (56 million years)

97. This is Putnam Problem 3 in the morning session of 1951.

Cumulative Review for Chapters 6–8 (Page 571)
5. $\dfrac{1}{2}x\ln x - \dfrac{1}{2}x + C$ **7.** $\dfrac{1}{2}(\tan^{-1}x)^2 + C$

9. $2\sin^{-1}\left(\dfrac{x}{2}\right) + \dfrac{1}{2}x\sqrt{4-x^2} + C$

11. a. $\dfrac{3}{x-1} + \dfrac{2}{(x-1)^2} - \dfrac{5}{2x+3}$
b. $3\ln|x-1| - \dfrac{2}{x-1} - \dfrac{5}{2}\ln|2x+3| + C$ **c.** diverges

13. converges   **15.** diverges   **17.** converges
19. -6 **21.** $-1 \le x \le 1$ **23.** 16,937 ft-lb
25. 9.7828
27. a. $y = x\tan^{-1}x + Cx$ **b.** $y = 1 + 2\cos x$

29. a. $x^2 - \dfrac{x^6}{3!} + \dfrac{x^{10}}{5!} - \cdots = \sum_{k=0}^{\infty} \dfrac{(-1)^k x^{4k+2}}{(2k+1)!}$
b. $\sum_{k=0}^{\infty} \dfrac{1}{k!}\left(\dfrac{1}{2}\right)^k x^k$ **c.** $\dfrac{3}{2} - \dfrac{19}{10}\sum_{k=0}^{\infty}\left(-\dfrac{2}{5}x\right)^k$

Chapter 9: Vectors in the Plane and in Space

9.1 Introduction to Vectors (Pages 580–582)

1.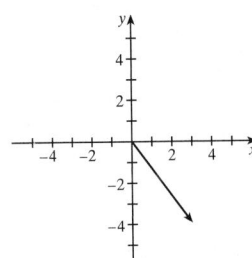

3.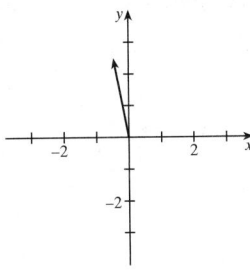

5. $\langle 4, 3 \rangle$; $\|\mathbf{PQ}\| = \sqrt{4^2 + 3^2} = 5$ **7.** $\langle -5, 0 \rangle$; $\|\mathbf{PQ}\| = 5$

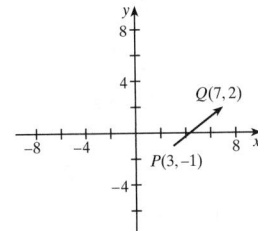

9. $\mathbf{PQ} = 2\mathbf{i}$; $\|\mathbf{PQ}\| = 2$ **11.** $\mathbf{PQ} = 4\mathbf{i} + 2\mathbf{j}$; $\|\mathbf{PQ}\| = 2\sqrt{5}$

13. $\dfrac{1}{\sqrt{2}}(\mathbf{i} + \mathbf{j})$ **15.** $\dfrac{3}{5}\mathbf{i} - \dfrac{4}{5}\mathbf{j}$

17. $s = 6; t = 24$ **19.** $s = -5; t = -1$

21. $17\mathbf{i} - 18\mathbf{j}$ **23.** $35\mathbf{i} - 35\mathbf{j}$

25. $(3, 2)$ **27.** $(2, 4), (-4, -2)$

29. $\dfrac{\sqrt{3}}{2}\mathbf{i} + \dfrac{1}{2}\mathbf{j}$ **31.** $\dfrac{4}{\sqrt{17}}\mathbf{i} - \dfrac{1}{\sqrt{17}}\mathbf{j}$

33. $\dfrac{5}{\sqrt{26}}\mathbf{i} + \dfrac{1}{\sqrt{26}}\mathbf{j}$ **35.** $(3, 10)$

37. a. $6\mathbf{i} + 3\mathbf{j}$ **b.** $10\mathbf{i} + 5\mathbf{j}$

39. $\|\mathbf{v}\| = \sqrt{\cos^2 \theta + \sin^2 \theta} = 1$ **41.** Not necessarily equal.

43. a. This is the set of points on the circle with center (x_0, y_0) and radius 1.

  b. $\|\mathbf{u} - \mathbf{u}_0\| \le r$ is the set of points on or interior to the circle with center (x_0, y_0) and radius r.

45. $a = -2t, b = t$, and $c = t$, for any t

47. $-6\mathbf{i} + 3\mathbf{j}$ **49.** 5.22 mi/hr; N53.6°W

9.2 Coordinates and Vectors in $\mathbb{R}^3$ (Pages 587–588)

1. a. $\langle 2, 2, 4 \rangle$ **b.** $\langle 6, -8, -2 \rangle$ **c.** $\langle 10, -\frac{15}{2}, \frac{5}{2} \rangle$ **d.** $\langle 2, 9, 11 \rangle$

3. a. $\langle 1, -3, 8 \rangle$ **b.** $\langle 1, -1, 2 \rangle$ **c.** $\langle \frac{5}{2}, -5, \frac{25}{2} \rangle$ **d.** $\langle 2, -7, 19 \rangle$

5. $d = \sqrt{149}$

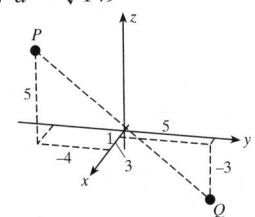

7. $d = \sqrt{382}$

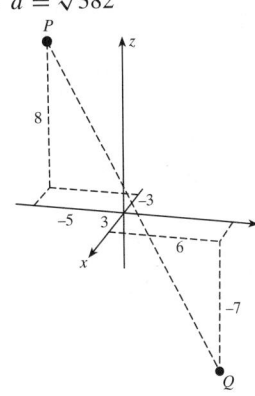

9. $x^2 + y^2 + z^2 = 1$

11. $x^2 + (y - 4)^2 + (z + 5)^2 = 9$

13. $C(0, 1, -1,); r = 2$

15. $C(3, -1, 1); r = 1$

17. $\mathbf{PQ} = -2\mathbf{i} + 2\mathbf{j} + \mathbf{k}$; $\|\mathbf{PQ}\| = 3$

19. $\mathbf{PQ} = -4\mathbf{i} - 4\mathbf{j} - 4\mathbf{k}$; $\|\mathbf{PQ}\| = 4\sqrt{3}$

21. $-7\mathbf{i} - 16\mathbf{k}$

23. $13\mathbf{i} - 4\mathbf{j} + 19\mathbf{k}$

25. $\dfrac{1}{\sqrt{14}}\langle 3, -2, 1 \rangle$

27. $\dfrac{1}{5\sqrt{2}}\langle -5, 3, 4 \rangle$

29.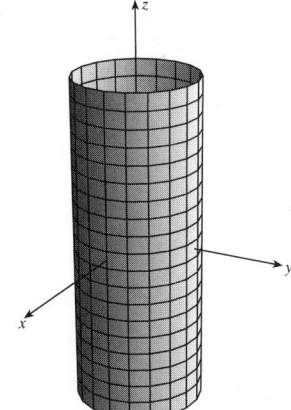

31.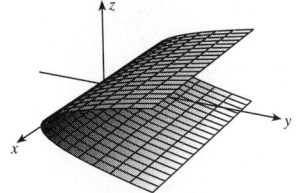

33. $(2x + 1)^2 + (2y - 5)^2 + 4z^2 = 46$

35. $\sqrt{3}$ **37.** 66   **39.** $6\mathbf{i} + 12\mathbf{j} - 3\mathbf{k}$

41. $\sqrt{46}\,(3\mathbf{i} + 2\mathbf{j} + \mathbf{k})$ **43.** no   **45.** yes

47. $\triangle ABC$ is right, but not isosceles

49. $\triangle ABC$ is neither right nor isosceles

51. collinear

53. $\mathbf{F}_1 = \frac{25}{3}\langle 0, -2, -6 \rangle$, $\mathbf{F}_2 = \frac{25}{3}\langle -\sqrt{3}, 1, -6 \rangle$, $\mathbf{F}_3 = \frac{25}{3}\langle \sqrt{3}, 1, -6 \rangle$

55. $P\left(\frac{1}{3}, \frac{7}{3}, \frac{13}{3}\right)$

9.3 The Dot Product (Pages 595–597)

3. -16 **5.** 5 **7.** orthogonal

9. orthogonal **11.** 11 **13.** 0

15. $71°$ **17.** $114°$ **19.** $1; \mathbf{k}$

21. $0; \mathbf{0}$

23. $\mathbf{u}_1 = \langle \frac{\sqrt{2}}{2}, 0, \frac{\sqrt{2}}{2} \rangle$, $\mathbf{u}_2 = \langle -\frac{\sqrt{2}}{2}, 0, -\frac{\sqrt{2}}{2} \rangle$

25. $\mathbf{u} = -\dfrac{1}{\sqrt{17}}(2\mathbf{i} + 3\mathbf{j} - 2\mathbf{k})$

27. $x = -1$, $y = -1$, and $z = 4$ **29.** $a = \frac{3}{2}$

31. $\cos\alpha = \dfrac{2}{\sqrt{38}}$, $\alpha \approx 1.24$ or $71°$; $\cos\beta = \dfrac{-3}{\sqrt{38}}$, $\beta \approx 2.08$ or $119°$; $\cos\gamma = \dfrac{-5}{\sqrt{38}}$, $\gamma \approx 2.52$ or $144°$

33. $\cos\alpha = \dfrac{1}{\sqrt{2}}$, $\alpha \approx 0.79$ or $45°$; $\cos\beta = \dfrac{-4}{5\sqrt{2}}$, $\beta \approx 2.17$ or $124°$; $\cos\gamma = \dfrac{3}{5\sqrt{2}}$, $\gamma \approx 1.13$ or $65°$

35. $\cos\theta = -\frac{1}{6}; -\frac{1}{6}\mathbf{w}$

37. a. 26 **b.** $\frac{26}{35}$ **c.** $\frac{49}{26}$ **d.** $\frac{-26}{25}$

39. 10

41. The force has magnitude $\|\mathbf{F}\| \approx 49.53$ lbs and points in the direction of the unit vector $\langle 0.979, -0.025, 0.202 \rangle$

43. a. 500 ft-lb **b.** $500\sqrt{2}$ ft-lb

47. The region inside a sphere with center (a, b, c) and radius r.

9.4 The Cross Product (Pages 604–606)

1. $\mathbf{k}$ **3.** $-2\mathbf{i} + 4\mathbf{j} + 3\mathbf{k}$

5. $-2\mathbf{i} + 25\mathbf{j} + 14\mathbf{k}$ **7.** $-2\mathbf{i} + 16\mathbf{j} + 11\mathbf{k}$

9. $-14\mathbf{i} - 4\mathbf{j} - \mathbf{k}$ **11.** $\dfrac{\sqrt{3}}{2}$ **13.** $\dfrac{\sqrt{3}}{2}$

15. $\dfrac{1}{\sqrt{14}}\mathbf{i} + \dfrac{3}{\sqrt{14}}\mathbf{j} - \dfrac{2}{\sqrt{14}}\mathbf{k}$

17. $\dfrac{-16}{\sqrt{386}}\mathbf{i} + \dfrac{7}{\sqrt{386}}\mathbf{j} + \dfrac{9}{\sqrt{386}}\mathbf{k}$

19. $\sqrt{26}$ **21.** $2\sqrt{59}$ **23.** $\frac{1}{2}\sqrt{3}$

25. $\frac{3}{2}\sqrt{3}$ **27. a.** does not exist **b.** scalar

29. a. scalar **b.** vector

31. 5 **33.** 8 **37.** $s = 2$

39. Cross product is not an associative operation.

41. $\mathbf{w} = \mathbf{0}$ **43.** $\mathbf{T} = -40\sqrt{3}\mathbf{i}$ **45.** $40°$

9.5 Parametric Representation of Curves; Lines in $\mathbb{R}^3$ (Pages 614–615)

3. $y = x - 2$; $1 \le x \le 3$ **5.** $y = \frac{4}{3}x - \frac{1}{225}x^2$; $0 \le x \le 180$

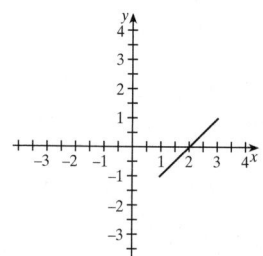

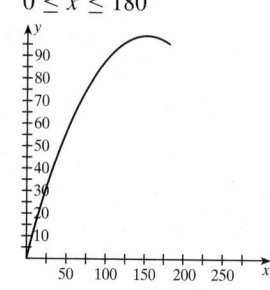

7. $y = x^{2/3}$; $x \ge 0$

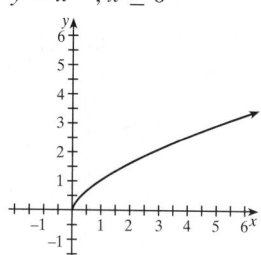

9. $x^2 + y^2 = 9$; $-3 \le x \le 3$

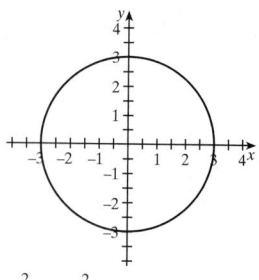

11. $(x - 1)^2 + (y + 2)^2 = 1$; $0 \le x \le 2$

13. $\dfrac{y^2}{9} - \dfrac{x^2}{16} = 1$; $-\infty < x < \infty$

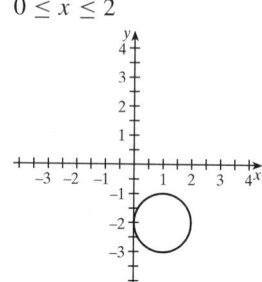

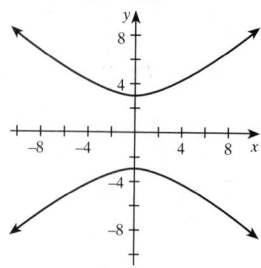

15. $y = \ln x$; $x > 0$

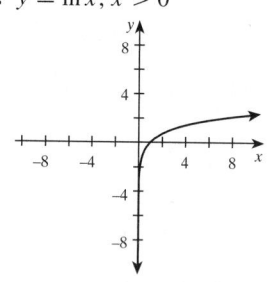

17. $x = 1 + 3t$, $y = -1 - 2t$, $z = -2 + 5t$; $\dfrac{x - 1}{3} = \dfrac{y + 1}{-2} = \dfrac{z + 2}{5}$

19. $x = 1 + t$, $y = -1 + 2t$, $z = 2 + t$; $\dfrac{x - 1}{1} = \dfrac{y + 1}{2} = \dfrac{z - 2}{1}$

21. $x = 1 + t$, $y = -3 - 3t$, $z = 6 - 5t$; $\dfrac{x - 1}{1} = \dfrac{y + 3}{-3} = \dfrac{z - 6}{-5}$

23. $x = 11t$, $y = 4 - 3t$, $z = -3 + 5t$; $\dfrac{x}{11} = \dfrac{y - 4}{-3} = \dfrac{z + 3}{5}$

25. $x = -1 + 3t$, $y = 1 + t$, $z = 6 - 2t$; $\dfrac{x + 1}{3} = \dfrac{y - 1}{1} = \dfrac{z - 6}{-2}$

27. $(0, -6, -3)$, $(8, 0, -1)$, $(12, 3, 0)$

29. $(0, 4, 9)$, $(8, 0, -3)$, $(6, 1, 0)$

31. parallel **33.** parallel **35.** $(1, 2, 3)$

37. $\pm\dfrac{1}{\sqrt{21}}(4\mathbf{i} + 2\mathbf{j} + \mathbf{k})$

39. $x = \sqrt{3}\cos t$, $y = \sqrt{3}\sin t$; $0 \le t \le 2\pi$

41. $x = 3\cos t$, $y = 2\sin t$; $0 \le t \le 2\pi$

43. $x = \dfrac{4}{\cos t}$, $y = 3\tan t$, $0 \le t \le 2\pi$, $t \ne \frac{\pi}{2}$, $t \ne \frac{3\pi}{2}$

45. parabolic arc

49. $a = 0$, $b = 5$; other choices will work

51. $x = -1 - 23t$, $y = 3 + 2t$, $z = 1 - 19t$

53. The Spy should travel from $Q(0, 0, 1)$ in the direction of the vector $\mathbf{v} = 674.35\mathbf{i} + 337.68\mathbf{j} + 4.34\mathbf{k}$

9.6 Planes in $\mathbb{R}^3$ (Pages 621–622)

5. $5x - 3y + 4z - 4 = 0$ **7.** $x - 2y + 4z + 7 = 0$

9. $x - z + 1 = 0$

11. $x + 2y - 3z - 6 = 0$

13. $x = 0$

15. $\pm \dfrac{1}{\sqrt{38}}(5\mathbf{i} - 3\mathbf{j} + 2\mathbf{k})$

17. $\dfrac{5\sqrt{38}}{19}$

19. $\dfrac{\sqrt{26}}{26}$

21. $\dfrac{2a^2 + 1}{|a|\sqrt{14}}$

23. $\dfrac{29}{\sqrt{1,265}}$

25. 2

27. $\dfrac{47}{5}$

29. $\dfrac{4\sqrt{3}}{\sqrt{14}}$

31. $\dfrac{\sqrt{65}}{3}$

33. $\dfrac{65}{\sqrt{122}}$

35. $\dfrac{2}{\sqrt{6}}$ **37. b.** $\dfrac{1}{\sqrt{6}}$

39. $(x + 1)^2 + (y - 2)^2 + (z - 4)^2 = \frac{1}{38}(2x - 5y + 3z - 7)^2$

41. a. $\cos\theta = \dfrac{aA + bB + cC}{\sqrt{a^2 + b^2 + c^2}\,\sqrt{A^2 + B^2 + C^2}}$ **b.** $\theta \approx 52°$

43. $3\mathbf{i} - 2\mathbf{j} - 11\mathbf{k}$

45. $\cos\alpha = \dfrac{-4}{\sqrt{26}}$, $\alpha \approx 2.47$ or $142°$; $\cos\beta = \dfrac{3}{\sqrt{26}}$, $\beta \approx 0.94$ or $54°$; $\cos\gamma = \dfrac{1}{\sqrt{26}}$, $\gamma \approx 1.37$ or $79°$

47. $\dfrac{x - 1}{2} = \dfrac{y + 5}{-3} = \dfrac{z - 3}{1}$

49. The unit vectors are $\mathbf{N} = \pm \dfrac{1}{\sqrt{2}}(\mathbf{i} - \mathbf{k})$

51. $2x - y + 3z + 3 = 0$ **53.** $P(9, -5, 12)$

55. $\dfrac{x - 2}{1} = \dfrac{y - 3}{1} = \dfrac{z - 1}{1}$

9.7 Quadric Surfaces (Pages 626–627)

3. circular cone; B **5.** hyperboloid of one sheet; E

7. sphere; A **9.** paraboloid, G

11. hyperboloid of two sheets; I

13. ellipsoid: xy-plane, ellipse; yz-plane, ellipse; xz-plane, ellipse

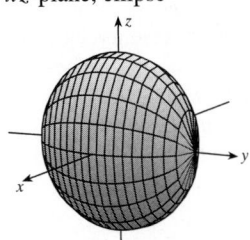

15. hyperboloid of one sheet: xy-plane, ellipse; yz-plane, hyperbola; xz-plane, hyperbola

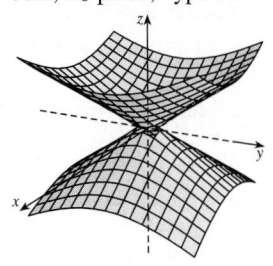

17. elliptic paraboloid: parallel to xy-plane, $z > 0$, ellipse; yz-plane, parabola; xz-plane, parabola

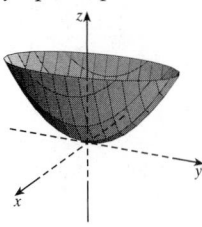

19. elliptic cone: parallel to xy-plane, $z \neq 0$, ellipse; parallel to yz-plane, $x \neq 0$, hyperbola; parallel to xz-plane, $z \neq 0$; hyperbola

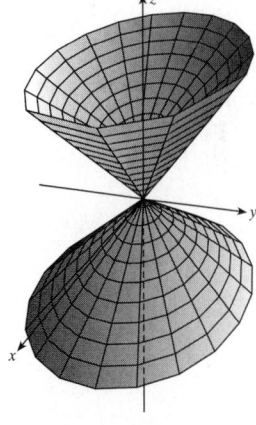

21. elliptic paraboloid: xy-plane, parabola; yz-plane, parabola; xz-plane, ellipse

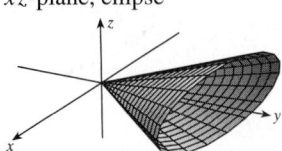

23. elliptic cone: xy-plane, hyperbola; yz-plane, hyperbola; xz-plane, ellipse

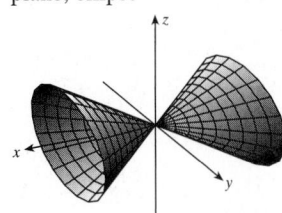

25. ellipsoid centered at $(1, -2, 3)$ with semi-axes 2, 1, and 3.

27. ellipsoid centered at $\left(\frac{9}{14}, -2, -\frac{7}{6}\right)$ with semi-axes approximately 1.31, 3.46, and 2.00.

29. elliptic paraboloid with vertex $\left(\frac{1}{2}, \frac{9}{2}, -\frac{1}{2}\right)$ and the y-axis as the axis of symmetry.

31. $\dfrac{8}{45}x^2 + \dfrac{7}{20}y^2 = 1$; this is an ellipse in the xy-plane

35. $x^2 + 2y^2 = 1$; this is the equation of an ellipse.

37. a. The equatorial radius is $a = 6{,}278.2$ and the polar radius is $b = 6{,}356.5$.

b. The volume is approximately 1.08319×10^{12} km^3.

39. $20x^2 + 36y^2 + 36z^2 = 45$ is an ellipsoid.

Chapter 9 Review
Proficiency Examination (Page 628–629)

33. a. $13\mathbf{i} - 12\mathbf{j} + 2\mathbf{k}$ **b.** 1

    c. 12   **d.** $2\mathbf{i} + 3\mathbf{j} + 5\mathbf{k}$

    e. $\frac{12}{13}(3\mathbf{i} - 2\mathbf{j})$ **f.** $\frac{6\sqrt{14}}{7}$

34. a. 40   **b.** not possible

    c. $25\mathbf{i} - 10\mathbf{j} - 15\mathbf{k}$ **d.** not possible

35. $\frac{x}{1} = \frac{y+2}{-6} = \frac{z-1}{4}$ **36.** $2x + 3z - 11 = 0$

37. $x = -\frac{13}{2} - 10t,\ y = 5 + 6t,\ z = 2t$

38. $17x + 19y + 13z - 25 = 0$

39. $\cos\alpha = \frac{-2}{\sqrt{14}},\ \alpha \approx 2.13$ or $122°$; $\cos\beta = \frac{3}{\sqrt{14}},\ \beta \approx 0.64$ or

    $37°$; $\cos\gamma = \frac{1}{\sqrt{14}},\ \gamma \approx 1.30$ or $74°$

40. a. skew   **b.** intersect at $(2, 2, 3)$

41. a. 6   **b.** $\sqrt{2}$

42. $\frac{2\sqrt{30}}{15}$ **43.** $\frac{6}{\sqrt{26}}$ **44.** $\frac{5\sqrt{6}}{\sqrt{35}}$

45. 168.4 mph   **46.** 130 ft-lb

47. a.

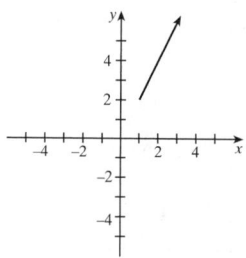

    b. $\frac{y}{x} = \frac{2^{t+1}}{2^t} = 2$ or $y = 2x,\ x \geq 1$

48. a.

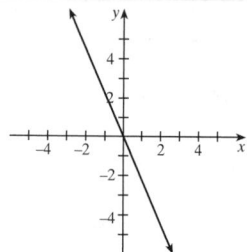

    b. $\frac{x}{4} = t$, so $x = 4t$, $\frac{y}{-9} = t$, so $y = -9t$

49. a.

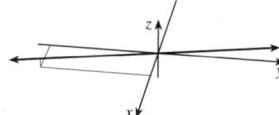

    b. $x = 4t,\ y = -9t,\ z = t$

50. a. elliptic cone   **b.** hyperbolic paraboloid

    c. hyperboloid of two sheets

    d. hyperboloid of one sheet   **e.** plane   **f.** line

    g. sphere   **h.** elliptic (circular) paraboloid

    i. hyperboloid of two sheets

    j. hyperboloid of two sheets

Supplementary Problems (Pages 629–631)

1. a. $8\sqrt{2} + \sqrt{14}$ **b.** $\frac{1}{2}\sqrt{171}$

    c. $A \approx 125°,\ B \approx 26°,\ C \approx 30°$ **d.** $p = \frac{205}{6}$

3. $\frac{x-1}{2} = \frac{z}{1}$ and $y = 4$; $x = 1 + 2t,\ y = 4,\ z = t$; answers vary for the two points

5. $z = 0$ **7.** $3x + 4y - z + 13 = 0$

9. $5x - 2y + 3z - 32 = 0$ **11.** $3x + 2y - 11z + 19 = 0$

17. $(\mathbf{u} - \mathbf{v}) \cdot \mathbf{w} = 3$; $(2\mathbf{u} + \mathbf{v}) \times (\mathbf{u} - \mathbf{w}) = 6\mathbf{i} - 10\mathbf{j} - 10\mathbf{k}$

19. $\cos\alpha = \frac{-3}{\sqrt{46}}$; $\cos\beta = \frac{6}{\sqrt{46}}$; $\cos\gamma = \frac{1}{\sqrt{46}}$

21. $\theta = 74°$

23. The center is $\left(0, -\frac{3}{2}, \frac{1}{2}\right)$ and the radius is $\frac{3}{2}$.

25. $P(3, -2, 1)$

27. $37X + 20Y - 21Z = 61$ and $67X - 20Y + 99Z = 121$

29. $x = 2\cos t,\ y = 2\sin t$ is a circle.

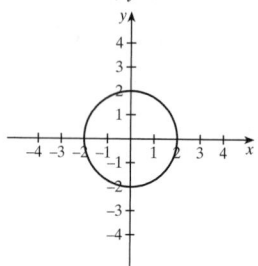

31. 13

33. $\frac{1}{2}\left(\|\mathbf{u} \times \mathbf{v}\| + \|\mathbf{u} \times \mathbf{w}\| + \|\mathbf{v} \times \mathbf{w}\| + \|(\mathbf{u} - \mathbf{v}) \times (\mathbf{w} - \mathbf{v})\|\right)$

37. $a_1 + 2b_1 + c_1 = 0$ **39.** $\frac{9\sqrt{2}}{2}$ **41.** $\frac{\sqrt{26}}{2}$

43. $2x - 3y - 7z = 0$

45. $\frac{x+1}{1} = \frac{y-2}{1}$ and $z = 0$ **47.** $\mathbf{N} = \frac{\pm 1}{\sqrt{37}}(-6\mathbf{i} + \mathbf{j})$

49. Let P have coordinates (a, b, c); then $\mathbf{r} = \mathbf{v} + \mathbf{w}t$ is the set of position vectors in the line $x = a + At,\ y = b + Bt$, and $z = c + Ct$.

51. linearly independent

55. $M\left(\frac{1}{3}, \frac{16}{3}, 1\right)$

57. Let S denote the position where the snowman had been, and let W and F denote the positions of the woodpile and flagpole. Also, for any vector $\mathbf{v}$, let $\mathbf{v}_L$ and $\mathbf{v}_R$ denote the vectors obtained by rotating $\mathbf{v}$ through 90° counterclockwise and clockwise, respectively. (Note that $\mathbf{v}_R = -\mathbf{v}_L$.) Then, the two stakes are driven at points A and B, where $\mathbf{SA} = \mathbf{SW} + \mathbf{SW}_L$ and $\mathbf{SB} = \mathbf{SF} + \mathbf{SF}_R$. Find the digging point from W by pacing off half the distance from W to F, turning right, and pacing off an equal distance.

59. c. The result is still true.

61. Let M_1 be the midpoint of $\overline{AB}$. To divide $\overline{AB}$ into thirds, drop the perpendicular from the intersection of $\overline{AM}$ and $\overline{CM_1}$ to $\overline{AB}$. The point R_1 at the foot of the perpendicular satisfies $\mathbf{AR}_1 = \frac{1}{3}\mathbf{AB}$. Then drop the perpendicular from the intersection of $\overline{AM}$ and $\overline{CR_1}$ to obtain R_2, which divides $\overline{AB}$ into fifths. The process may be continued as far as desired.

63. This is Putnam Problem 5 of the afternoon session of 1959.

Chapter 10: Vector-Valued Functions
10.1 Introduction to Vector Functions (Pages 640–641)

1. $t \neq 0$ **3.** $t \neq \frac{(2n+1)\pi}{2}$, n an integer

5. $t \neq \dfrac{n\pi}{2}$, n an integer   **7.** $t > 0$

9. parabolic cylinder; in $\mathbb{R}^2$, the graph is a parabola in the xy-plane

11. cylinder; in $\mathbb{R}^2$, the graph is a circle in the xy-plane

13. plane; in $\mathbb{R}^2$, the graph is a line in the xz plane parallel to and four units below the x-axis

15. a circular helix; in $\mathbb{R}^2$, the graph is a circle in the xy-plane

17. the curve is in the intersection of the parabolic cylinder $y = (1-x)^2$ with the plane $x + z = 1$; in $\mathbb{R}^2$, the graph is a parabola in the xy-plane

19. the curve is the intersection of the cylinder $y = x^2 + 1$ and the plane $y = z + 1$; in $\mathbb{R}^2$, the graph is a parabola in the xy-plane

21. $(7t - 3)\mathbf{i} - 10\mathbf{j} + \left(2t^2 - \dfrac{3}{t}\right)\mathbf{k}$

23. $3t - 2t^2$ **25.** $(1-t)\sin t$

27. $-t^2 e^t \mathbf{i} + (t^2 \sin t)\mathbf{j} + (2te^t + 5\sin t)\mathbf{k}$

29. $(4te^t - t^2 + t + 10\sin t)\mathbf{i} + (2e^t t^2 + 1)\mathbf{k}$

31. $t^2 e^t - t^3 e^t - 2e^t - \dfrac{5}{t} - \sin t$

37. $\mathbf{F}(t) = t\mathbf{i} + t^2\mathbf{j} + 2\mathbf{k}$

39. $\mathbf{F}(t) = 2t\mathbf{i} + (1-t)\mathbf{j} + (\sin t)\mathbf{k}$

41. $\mathbf{F}(t) = t^2\mathbf{i} + t\mathbf{j} + \sqrt{9 - t^2 - t^4}\,\mathbf{k}$

43. a. no   **b.** yes   **c.** yes

45. $2\mathbf{i} - 3\mathbf{j} + e\mathbf{k}$ **47.** $\mathbf{0}$ **49.** $-\mathbf{i} + e^{-1}\mathbf{j}$ **51.** $\frac{3}{2}\mathbf{i} + \mathbf{j}$

53. continuous for all t **55.** continuous for $t \neq 0, t \neq -1$

57. continuous for all $t \neq 0$ **59.** $x - y + z = 1$

65. a. The function is continuous at t_0.
   b. The function is continuous at t_0.
   c. The function is discontinuous at $t_0 = 0$ if $h(t) = t$.
   d. The function is continuous at t_0.

10.2 Differentiation and Integration of Vector Functions (Pages 650–651)

1. $\mathbf{F}'(t) = \mathbf{i} + 2t\mathbf{j} + (1 + 3t^2)\mathbf{k}$

3. $\mathbf{F}'(s) = (1 + \ln s)\mathbf{i} + 5s^{-1}\mathbf{j} - e^s(\ln s + s^{-1})\mathbf{k}$

5. $\mathbf{F}'(t) = 2t\mathbf{i} - t^{-2}\mathbf{j} + 2e^{2t}\mathbf{k}$; $\mathbf{F}''(t) = 2\mathbf{i} + 2t^{-3}\mathbf{j} + 4e^{2t}\mathbf{k}$

7. $\mathbf{F}'(s) = (\cos s)\mathbf{i} - (\sin s)\mathbf{j} + 2s\mathbf{k}$; $\mathbf{F}''(s) = (-\sin s)\mathbf{i} - (\cos s)\mathbf{j} + 2\mathbf{k}$

9. $f'(x) = -9x^2 - 2x$ **11.** $g'(x) = \dfrac{4x}{\sqrt{1 + 4x^2}}$

13. $\mathbf{V}(1) = \mathbf{i} + 2\mathbf{j} + 2\mathbf{k}$; $\mathbf{A}(1) = 2\mathbf{j}$; speed $= 3$; direction of motion is $\frac{1}{3}\mathbf{i} + \frac{2}{3}\mathbf{j} + \frac{2}{3}\mathbf{k}$

15. $\mathbf{V}(\frac{\pi}{4}) = -\dfrac{\sqrt{2}}{2}\mathbf{i} + \dfrac{\sqrt{2}}{2}\mathbf{j} + 3\mathbf{k}$; $\mathbf{A}(\frac{\pi}{4}) = -\dfrac{\sqrt{2}}{2}\mathbf{i} - \dfrac{\sqrt{2}}{2}\mathbf{j}$; speed $= \sqrt{10}$; direction of motion $-\dfrac{1}{2\sqrt{5}}\mathbf{i} + \dfrac{1}{2\sqrt{5}}\mathbf{j} + \dfrac{3}{\sqrt{10}}\mathbf{k}$

17. $\mathbf{V}(\ln 2) = 2\mathbf{i} - \frac{1}{2}\mathbf{j} + 8\mathbf{k}$; $\mathbf{A}(\ln 2) = 2\mathbf{i} + \frac{1}{2}\mathbf{j} + 16\mathbf{k}$; speed $= \dfrac{\sqrt{273}}{2}$; direction of motion $\dfrac{1}{\sqrt{273}}(4\mathbf{i} - \mathbf{j} + 16\mathbf{k})$

19. $\mathbf{F}'(0) = 2\mathbf{j}$; $\mathbf{F}'(1) = 2\mathbf{i} + 2\mathbf{j} + 5\mathbf{k}$; $\mathbf{F}'(-1) = -2\mathbf{i} + 2\mathbf{j} + \mathbf{k}$

21. $\mathbf{F}'(0) = \mathbf{0}$; $\mathbf{F}'(\frac{\pi}{2}) = \pi\mathbf{i} - \mathbf{j} - \frac{\pi^2}{4}\mathbf{k}$

23. $x = -1 - 3t$, $y = 1 + 2t$, $z = -1 - t$

25. $\dfrac{t^2}{2}\mathbf{i} - \dfrac{e^{3t}}{3}\mathbf{j} + 3t\mathbf{k} + \mathbf{C}$ **27.** $(t\ln t - t)\mathbf{i} - \frac{1}{2}t^2\mathbf{j} + 3t\mathbf{k} + \mathbf{C}$

29. $\dfrac{t^2}{2}\left(\ln t - \dfrac{1}{2}\right)\mathbf{i} - \cos(1-t)\mathbf{j} + \dfrac{t^2}{2}\mathbf{k} + \mathbf{C}$

31. $\mathbf{R}(t) = \left(\frac{1}{3}t^3 + 1\right)\mathbf{i} + \left(-\frac{1}{2}e^{2t} + \frac{9}{2}\right)\mathbf{j} + \left(\frac{2}{3}t^{3/2} - 1\right)\mathbf{k}$

33. $\mathbf{R}(t) = \left(\frac{4}{3}t^{3/2} + 1\right)\mathbf{i} + (\sin t + 1)\mathbf{j}$

35. $\mathbf{V}(t) = \langle 2 + \sin t, 0, 3 + t\cos t - \sin t\rangle$; $\mathbf{R}(t) = \langle 2 + 2t - \cos t, -2, -1 + 3t + 2\cos t + t\sin t\rangle$

37. $\mathbf{R}(t) = e^t\mathbf{i} + (\frac{1}{3}t^3 - 1)\mathbf{j}$ **39.** $\mathbf{R}(t) = \langle 2t^4 + 1, 2t^2 + 2\rangle$

43. $-180t^2$ **45.** $3t^2(-7\mathbf{i} + 11\mathbf{j} + 5\mathbf{k})$ **49.** $a = \frac{\pi}{4}$

53. not smooth

61. $[\mathbf{F} \times (\mathbf{G} \times \mathbf{H})]' = [(\mathbf{H} \cdot \mathbf{F})\mathbf{G}]' - [(\mathbf{G} \cdot \mathbf{F})\mathbf{H}]'$ **63.** false

10.3 Modeling Ballistics and Planetary Motion (Pages 657–660)

1. 4.6 sec; 481 ft   **3.** 129.9 sec; 73,175 m   **5.** 1.9 sec; 41 m

7. 1.5 sec; 148 ft   **9.** $\mathbf{V}(t) = \sqrt{5}\,\mathbf{u}_r$; $\mathbf{A}(t) = \mathbf{0}$

11. $\mathbf{V} = (2\cos 2t)\mathbf{u}_r + (2\sin 2t)\mathbf{u}_\theta$; $\mathbf{A} = (-8\sin 2t)\mathbf{u}_r + (8\cos 2t)\mathbf{u}_\theta$

13. $\mathbf{V} = -10\sin(2t+1)\mathbf{u}_r + 10[1 + \cos(2t+1)]\mathbf{u}_\theta$; $\mathbf{A} = [-40\cos(2t+1) - 20]\mathbf{u}_r - 40\sin(2t+1)\mathbf{u}_\theta$

15. 140 m/s   **17.** 21.7°

19. The maximum height is 85 ft; the ball will land at a distance of 568 ft; the distance to the fence is 560 ft

21. 52.3 ft   **23.** 387.8 ft/s   **25.** 5.5 sec

27. The Spy should wait one minute before releasing the canister.

29. 18.13 ft   **31.** $\mathbf{V} = (-a\omega\sin\omega t)\mathbf{i} + (a\omega\cos\omega t)\mathbf{j}$; $\mathbf{R} \cdot \mathbf{V} = 0$

33. $-a\omega^2\mathbf{R}$

35. a. 1,533.33 m   **b.** 142.41 m/s

37. 21.8°   **39.** 37.2°; 471.77 ft/s

43. a. $R_f = v_0\cos\alpha\sec\beta\, T_f$ **b.** $\alpha = \frac{\pi}{4} - \frac{1}{2}\beta$

10.4 Unit Tangent and Principal Unit Normal Vectors; Curvature (Pages 671–673)

1. $\mathbf{T}(t) = \dfrac{2}{\sqrt{4 + 9t^2}}\mathbf{i} + \dfrac{3t}{\sqrt{4 + 9t^2}}\mathbf{j}$; $\mathbf{N}(t) = \dfrac{-3t}{\sqrt{4 + 9t^2}}\mathbf{i} + \dfrac{2}{\sqrt{4 + 9t^2}}\mathbf{j}$

3. $\mathbf{T}(t) = \dfrac{\sqrt{2}}{2}[(\cos t - \sin t)\mathbf{i} + (\cos t + \sin t)\mathbf{j}]$; $\mathbf{N}(t) = -\dfrac{\sqrt{2}}{2}[(\sin t + \cos t)\mathbf{i} + (\sin t - \cos t)\mathbf{j}]$

5. $\mathbf{T}(t) = \dfrac{1}{\sqrt{2}}(-\sin t\mathbf{i} + \cos t\mathbf{j} + \mathbf{k})$; $\mathbf{N}(t) = -\cos t\mathbf{i} - \sin t\mathbf{j}$

7. $\mathbf{T}(t) = \dfrac{1}{\sqrt{1 + 4t^4}}(\mathbf{i} + 2t^2\mathbf{k})$; $\mathbf{N}(t) = \dfrac{1}{\sqrt{1 + 4t^4}}(-2t^2\mathbf{i} + \mathbf{k})$

9. $4\sqrt{5}$ **11.** $\dfrac{3\sqrt{2}\pi}{2}$ **13.** $\sqrt{41}\pi$

15. $\kappa = 0$ **17.** $\kappa = 2$ **19.** $\kappa = 2^{-3/2}$

21. $\mathbf{R}(s) = \left\langle \dfrac{\sqrt{2} - s}{\sqrt{2}}, \dfrac{s}{\sqrt{2}} \right\rangle$

23. $\mathbf{R}(s) = \left\langle 2 - \dfrac{3s}{\sqrt{26}}, 1 + \dfrac{s}{\sqrt{26}}, \dfrac{-4s}{\sqrt{26}} \right\rangle$

27. $\mathbf{T} = \dfrac{1}{\sqrt{10}}(\mathbf{i} - 3\mathbf{j})$

29. a. $T(\pi) = \dfrac{\sqrt{2}}{2}(-\mathbf{i} + \mathbf{k})$ **b.** $\frac{1}{2}$ **c.** $\sqrt{2}\pi$

31. The points at which a maximum occurs are $P(0, 3)$, and $Q(0, -3)$.

33. $\rho(0) = \frac{1}{6}$; $\rho(1) = \rho(-1) = \frac{1}{24}$

35. $\kappa = \dfrac{2\sqrt{9t^4 + 9t^2 + 1}}{(1 + 4t^2 + 9t^4)^{3/2}}$ **37.** $\kappa = \dfrac{2}{(1 + 4x^2)^{3/2}}$

39. $\kappa = \dfrac{6x^5}{(x^6 + 4)^{3/2}}$ **41.** $\dfrac{1}{\sqrt{2}\,e^\theta}$

43. The fly's speed at time t is $4t^2 + 4t + 1$; 4 sec

51. c. $\lim\limits_{s \to +\infty} \kappa(s) = +\infty$, so the spiral keeps winding tighter and tighter.

55. The total length of the ramp is about 7 units.

57. $\kappa = \dfrac{1}{2^{3/2}} \dfrac{1}{\sqrt{1 - \cos t}}$; the minimum is $\frac{1}{4}$ and there is no maximum value.

10.5 Tangential and Normal Components of Acceleration (Pages 678–679)

1. $A_T = \dfrac{4t}{\sqrt{1 + 4t^2}}$; $A_N = \dfrac{2}{\sqrt{1 + 4t^2}}$

3. $A_T = \dfrac{t}{\sqrt{1 + t^2}}$; $A_N = \dfrac{t^2 + 2}{\sqrt{t^2 + 1}}$

5. $A_T = \dfrac{4t}{\sqrt{2 + 4t^2}}$; $A_N = \dfrac{2}{\sqrt{1 + 2t^2}}$

7. $A_T = -\dfrac{\sin t \cos t}{\sqrt{1 + \cos^2 t}}$; $A_N = \sqrt{\dfrac{2}{1 + \cos^2 t}}$

9. $A_T = \dfrac{-13}{\sqrt{10}}$; $A_N = \dfrac{11}{\sqrt{10}}$ **11.** $A_T = \dfrac{-19}{\sqrt{14}}$; $A_N = \sqrt{\dfrac{59}{14}}$

13. $\dfrac{5}{\sqrt{8}}$ **15.** 0

17. The maximum speed is 8 at $t = 0$, and the minimum speed is 6 at $t = \pi/4$.

19. $\mathbf{V}(t) = (-2\sin 2t)\mathbf{i} + (2\cos 2t)\mathbf{j}$; $\mathbf{A}(t) = (-4\cos 2t)\mathbf{i} - (4\sin 2t)\mathbf{j}$; $A_T = 0$; $A_N = 4$

21. $A_T\left(\dfrac{\sqrt{399}}{8}\right) \approx 7.98999$; $A_N\left(\dfrac{\sqrt{399}}{8}\right) = 0.4$

23. $\omega = 0.52$ rev/s

25. a. the maximum safe speed is 47 ft/s (about 32 mi/h)
   b. 65.94 ft/s (about 45 mi/h)   **c.** 23.1°

27. 14 rev/min

29. $A_T = \dfrac{4t}{\sqrt{5 + 4t^2}}$; $A_N = \dfrac{2\sqrt{5}}{\sqrt{5 + 4t^2}}$

31. $A_T = \sqrt{3}\,e^t$; $A_N = \sqrt{2}\,e^t$ **33.** 42.43 units/s

37. $A_T = \dfrac{\mathbf{V} \cdot \mathbf{A}}{\|\mathbf{V}\|} = 0$ and $A_N = \dfrac{\|\mathbf{V} \times \mathbf{A}\|}{\|\mathbf{V}\|} = g$

39. b. About 36,000 km   **c.** About 200 km/h

Chapter 10 Review
Proficiency Examination (Page 679–680)

24.

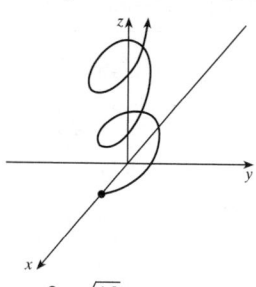

$s = 2\pi\sqrt{10}$

25. $\mathbf{F}' = \dfrac{1}{(1 + t)^2}\mathbf{i} + \dfrac{t \cos t - \sin t}{t^2}\mathbf{j} + (-\sin t)\mathbf{k}$;

$\mathbf{F}'' = -\dfrac{2}{(1 + t)^3}\mathbf{i} + \dfrac{-t^2 \sin t - 2t \cos t + 2\sin t}{t^3}\mathbf{j} - (\cos t)\mathbf{k}$

26. $(3 - 6\ln 2)\mathbf{i} + \frac{45}{4}\mathbf{j} + \left(6\ln 2 - \frac{9}{4}\right)\mathbf{k}$

27. $(e^t - t)\mathbf{i} - \left(\dfrac{t^4}{12} + 2\right)\mathbf{j} + \left(\dfrac{3t^2}{2} + 3t\right)\mathbf{k}$

28. $\mathbf{V} = \mathbf{i} + 2\mathbf{j} + e^t(t + 1)\mathbf{k}$; speed is $\sqrt{5 + e^{2t}(t + 1)^2}$; $\mathbf{A} = e^t(t + 2)\mathbf{k}$

29. $\mathbf{T} = \dfrac{2t\mathbf{i} + 3\mathbf{j} - 3\mathbf{k}}{\sqrt{4t^2 + 18}}$; $\mathbf{N} = \dfrac{3\mathbf{i} - t\mathbf{j} + t\mathbf{k}}{(2t^2 + 9)^{1/2}}$; $A_T = \dfrac{2\sqrt{2}t}{\sqrt{2t^2 + 9}}$; $A_N = \dfrac{6}{\sqrt{2t^2 + 9}}$

30. a. The maximum height is 9.77 ft.
   b. $\frac{25}{16}$ sec; maximum range is 67.7 ft

Supplementary Problems (Pages 680–683)

1. $2\mathbf{k}$ **3.** -5 **5.** $\mathbf{i} - \mathbf{j}$

7. $\mathbf{F}'(t) = (1 + t)e^t\mathbf{i} + 2t\mathbf{j}$; $\mathbf{F}''(t) = (2 + t)e^t\mathbf{i} + 2\mathbf{j}$

9. $\mathbf{F}'(t) = -2t^{-2}\mathbf{i} - 2\mathbf{j} + (1 - t)e^{-t}\mathbf{k}$; $\mathbf{F}''(t) = 4t^{-3}\mathbf{i} + (t - 2)e^{-t}\mathbf{k}$

11. $\mathbf{F}'(t) = (2t + ae^{at})\mathbf{i} + (1 - at)e^{-at}\mathbf{j} + ae^{at+1}\mathbf{k}$; $\mathbf{F}''(t) = (2 + a^2 e^{at})\mathbf{i} + (a^2 t - 2a)e^{-at}\mathbf{j} + a^2 e^{at+1}\mathbf{k}$

13.

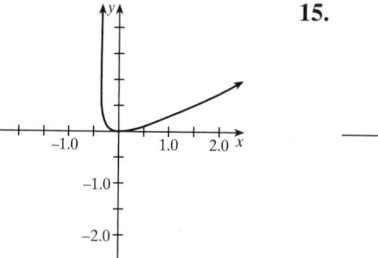

15.

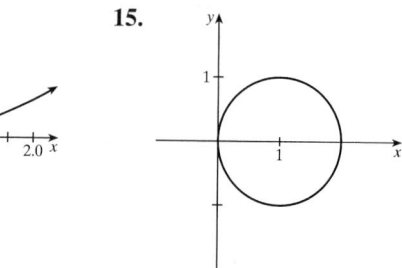

17. The graph is a circular helix of radius 2, traversed clockwise. It begins ($t = 0$) at $(0, 2, 0)$ and rises 10π units with each revolution.

19. $\dfrac{d}{dt}[\mathbf{F}(t) \cdot \mathbf{F}(t)] = 2\mathbf{F} \cdot \mathbf{F}'$

21. $\dfrac{d}{dt}\left[\dfrac{\mathbf{F}(t)}{\|\mathbf{F}(t)\|}\right] = \dfrac{\|\mathbf{F}\|^2 \mathbf{F}' - (\mathbf{F} \cdot \mathbf{F}')\mathbf{F}}{\|\mathbf{F}\|^3}$

23. $\dfrac{d}{dt}[\mathbf{F}(t) \times \mathbf{F}(t)] = \mathbf{0}$ **25.** $(e - e^{-1})\mathbf{i} + 6\mathbf{k}$

27. $(te^t - e^t)\mathbf{i} + \dfrac{\cos 2t}{2}\mathbf{j} + \dfrac{t^3}{3}\mathbf{k} + \mathbf{C}$

29. $(te^t - e^t)\mathbf{i} + \dfrac{1}{4}t^2(2\ln t - 1)\mathbf{j} + \dfrac{3t^2}{2}\mathbf{k} + \mathbf{C}$

31. $\mathbf{V}(t) = \mathbf{i} - \mathbf{j}; \dfrac{ds}{dt} = \sqrt{2}; \mathbf{A}(t) = \mathbf{0}$

33. $\mathbf{V}(t) = (t\cos t + \sin t)\mathbf{i} + (1 - t)e^{-t}\mathbf{j} + \mathbf{k};$

$\dfrac{ds}{dt} = \sqrt{t^2\cos^2 t + t\sin 2t + \sin^2 t + (1-t)^2 e^{-2t} + 1};$

$\mathbf{A}(t) = (2\cos t - t\sin t)\mathbf{i} + e^{-t}(t-2)\mathbf{j}$

35. $\mathbf{T}(t) = \dfrac{\mathbf{i} - 2t\mathbf{j}}{\sqrt{4t^2 + 1}}; \mathbf{N}(t) = \dfrac{-2t\mathbf{i} - \mathbf{j}}{\sqrt{4t^2 + 1}}$

37. $\mathbf{T}(t) = \frac{1}{5}(-4\sin t\,\mathbf{i} - 3\mathbf{j} + 4\cos t\,\mathbf{k});$
$\mathbf{N}(t) = (-\cos t)\mathbf{i} + (-\sin t)\mathbf{j}$

39. $A_T = \dfrac{4t + e^{2t}}{\sqrt{4 + 4t^2 + e^{2t}}}$; $A_N = 2\sqrt{\dfrac{t^2 e^{2t} - 2te^{2t} + 2e^{2t} + 4}{4 + 4t^2 + e^{2t}}};$

$\kappa = \dfrac{2\sqrt{t^2 e^{2t} - 2te^{2t} + 2e^{2t} + 4}}{(4t^2 + 4 + e^{2t})^{3/2}}$

41. $A_T = 0; A_N = 4; \kappa = \frac{1}{8}$

43. $\kappa = \frac{1}{2}$ **45.** $\kappa \approx 1.9221$ **47.** $\kappa = \frac{1}{6}$

49. $\mathbf{F}(t)$ is continuous for $t \neq 1.$

51. $\mathbf{F}(t) = (2t - \sin t + 1)\mathbf{i} + \left(\dfrac{3t^2}{2} + \cos t - 1\right)\mathbf{j} + \left(\dfrac{t^4}{24\pi} + \dfrac{t^2}{2}\right)\mathbf{k}$

53. **a.** $x = 1 + s, y = 1 + s, z = 1 + 3s$
 b. $(-2, -2, -8)$

55. $\mathbf{T}(s) = \dfrac{1}{\sqrt{5}}\left[\left(-\sin\dfrac{s}{a}\right)\mathbf{i} + \left(\cos\dfrac{s}{a}\right)\mathbf{j} + 2\mathbf{k}\right];$

$\mathbf{N} = -\left(\cos\dfrac{s}{a}\right)\mathbf{i} - \left(\sin\dfrac{s}{a}\right)\mathbf{j}$

57. At $t = 0, \rho = \dfrac{b^2}{a};$ at $t = \dfrac{\pi}{2}, \rho = \dfrac{a^2}{b}$

59. **a.** $\mathbf{V}(t) = e^{-t}(-\cos t - \sin t)\mathbf{i} + e^{-t}(-\sin t + \cos t)\mathbf{j} - e^{-t}\mathbf{k};$
 $\mathbf{A}(t) = e^{-t}(2\sin t)\mathbf{i} + e^{-t}(-2\cos t)\mathbf{j} + e^{-t}\mathbf{k}$

 b. $\kappa = \dfrac{\sqrt{2}}{3}e^t$

61. 4,537.5 lb

63. $\mathbf{V}(t) = -a\sin at\,\mathbf{u}_r - ae^{-at}(1 + \cos at)\mathbf{u}_\theta;$
 $\mathbf{A}(t) = [-a^2\cos at - a^2 e^{-2at}(1 + \cos at)]\mathbf{u}_r$
 $\quad + [a^2 e^{-at}(1 + \cos at) + 2a^2 e^{-at}\sin at]\mathbf{u}_\theta$

65. $\qquad\qquad x = \frac{2}{3} - \frac{5}{9}t, y = \frac{4}{3} - \frac{4}{9}t$

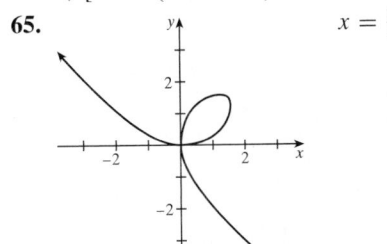

67. 20.888 μm

69. **a.** At $t = 0, \mathbf{V}(0) = 10\mathbf{u}_r$
 b. At $t = 0.25, \mathbf{V}(0.25) = 10\mathbf{u}_r + 5\pi\,\mathbf{u}_\theta$

71. $\sin x\mathbf{i} - \cos 2x\mathbf{j} + e^{-x}\mathbf{k}$

73. $\mathbf{F}(t) = \left(\dfrac{t^2}{2} + 1\right)\mathbf{i} + \left(\dfrac{t^2}{2} + 2\right)\mathbf{j} - \left(\dfrac{t^2}{2} + 3\right)\mathbf{k}$

75. $\mathbf{F}(t) = \left[\left(\dfrac{1}{2}\right)(3 - \cos 2t)\right]\mathbf{i}$

$\qquad + \left[\left(\dfrac{e^t}{2}\right)(\sin t + \cos t) - \dfrac{1}{2}\right]\mathbf{j} - [3\ln|t + 1| + 3]\mathbf{k}$

77. This is Putnam Problem 6ii of the morning session of 1939.

79. This is Putnam Problem 6 of the afternoon session of 1946.

Cumulative Review for Chapters 1-10 (Pages 691–692)

5. -2 **7.** e^{-6} **9.** -1

11. $y' = 3\sin^2 x\cos x + 2\sec^2 x$ **13.** $y' = \dfrac{1}{\sqrt{1 - x^2}} - \dfrac{2}{x^2 + 1}$

15. $y' = \dfrac{-(y^3 + 2xe^{-y})}{3xy^2 - x^2 e^{-y}}$ **17.** $\frac{1}{3}\sin^3 x - \frac{1}{5}\sin^5 x + C$

19. $-\cot x + \csc x + C$ **21.** $\sin^{-1}(x - 1) + C$

23. **a.** yes   **b.** yes   **c.** no

25. 0.4467   **27.** 5.8069

29. **a.** $2x + 7y - z - 15 = 0$ **b.** $2x + 5y - 2z + 17 = 0$

31. converges by the ratio test

33. diverges by the ratio test

35. converges by the absolute convergence test

37. **a.** converges; $5e^{-1}$ **b.** converges; $\frac{\pi}{2}$

39. $\mathbf{F}'(t) = 2\mathbf{i} - 3e^{-3t}\mathbf{j} + 4t^3\mathbf{k}; \mathbf{F}''(t) = 9e^{-3t}\mathbf{j} + 12t^2\mathbf{k}$

41. $\mathbf{T} = \dfrac{1}{\sqrt{13}}[2(\cos 2t)\mathbf{i} - 2(\sin 2t)\mathbf{j} + 3\mathbf{k}];$
 $\mathbf{N} = -\sin 2t\mathbf{i} - \cos 2t\mathbf{j}$

43. **a.** $\displaystyle\sum_{k=0}^{\infty} \dfrac{(-1)^k x^{2k+2}}{k!}$ **b.** 0.189

45. $y = \dfrac{x^2}{2} - \dfrac{x}{2} + \dfrac{1}{4} + \dfrac{7}{4}e^{-2x}$ **47.** $x = -2$

49. 1,562.5 ft-lb

Chapter 11: Partial Differentiation

11.1 Functions of Several Variables (Pages 699–701)

1. **a.** 0   **b.** 0   **c.** 0   **d.** 2
 e. 48   **f.** $2t^3$ **g.** $t^4 + t^5$ **h.** $t - t^2$

5. The domain is $x - y \geq 0$, and the range is $f(x, y) \geq 0.$

7. The domain is $uv \geq 0$, and the range is $f(u, v) \geq 0.$

9. The domain is $y - x > 0$, and the range is $\mathbb{R}.$

11. The domain is $\mathbb{R}^2$, and the range is $f(x, y) \geq 0.$

13. The domain is $x^2 - y^2 > 0$, and the range is $f(x, y) > 0.$

15. Sketch $C = 0: 2x - 3y = 0; C = 1: 2x - 3y = 1;$
 $C = 2: 2x - 3y = 2$, and $C = 3: 2x - 3y = 3.$

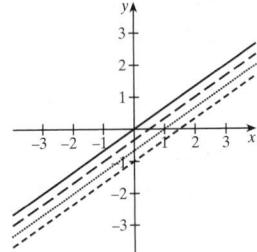

17. Sketch $C = 0: x^3 - y = 0; C = 1: x^3 - y = 1;$
 $C = 2: x^3 - y = 2; C = 3: x^3 - y = 3.$

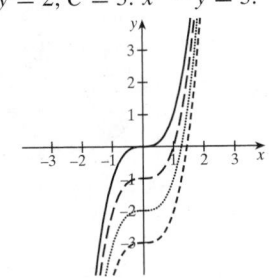

19. Sketch $C = 1$: $x^2 + \dfrac{y^2}{4} = 1$; $C = 2$: $x^2 + \dfrac{y^2}{4} = 2$;

$C = 3$: $x^2 + \dfrac{y^2}{4} = 3$.

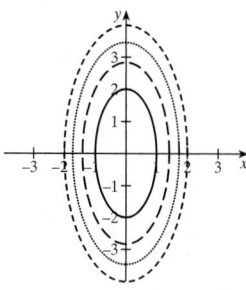

21. This is a cylinder, $y^2 + z^2 = 1$, which has the x-axis as its axis.

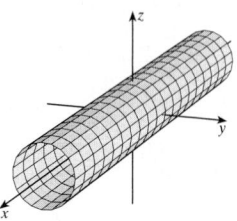

23. This is a plane: $x + y - z = 1$; its trace in the xy-plane is the line $x + y = 1$; its trace in the xz-plane is $x - z = 1$; and its trace in the yz-plane is $y - z = 1$. We show this plane (along with the xy-plane for reference).

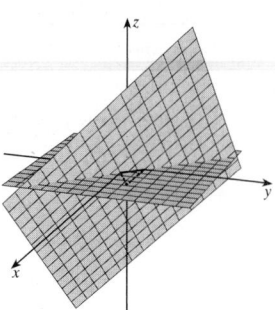

25. This is a sphere: $(x + 1)^2 + (y - 2)^2 + (z - 3)^2 = 4$; its cross sections in the planes $x = -1$, $y = 2$, and $z = 3$ are circles.

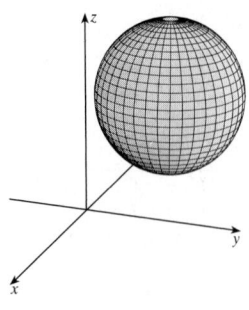

27. ellipsoid; traces are ellipses in all three coordinate planes

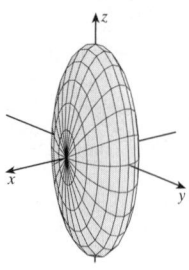

29. hyperboloid of 1 sheet: the trace in the xy-plane is an ellipse; in the xz- and yz-planes the traces are hyperbolas

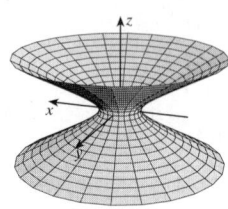

31. elliptic paraboloid: traces in the xz- and yz-planes are parabolas; the trace in the xy-plane is an ellipse

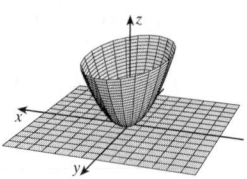

33. elliptic cone: traces in the xz- and yz-planes are pairs of lines; the trace in the xy-plane is the origin if $z = 0$ and is an ellipse if $z \neq 0$

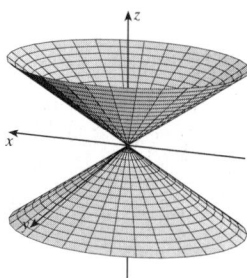

35. D   **37.** B   **39.** A

41. This is a plane parallel to the xy-plane.

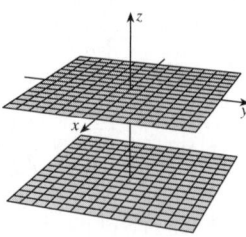

43. This is a cylinder which bends upward from the xy-plane.

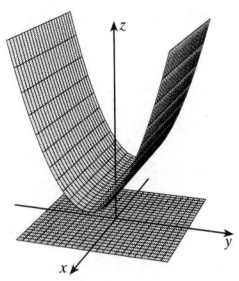

45. This is a plane which intersects the xy-plane along the line $2x - 3y = 0$.

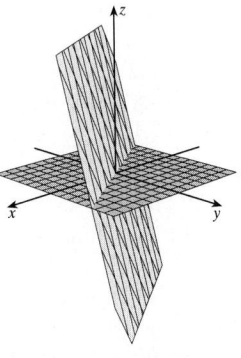

47. This is an elliptic paraboloid with vertex at the origin and which rises upward from the xy-plane.

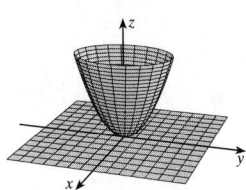

49. This is a surface that lies close to the xy-plane as it moves away from the origin, but "peels" upward close to the z-axis.

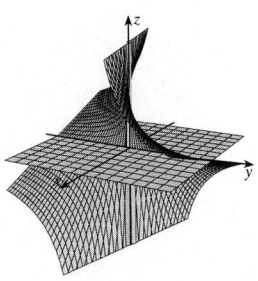

51. This is a paraboloid with vertex $(0, 0, 2)$ and rises upward from that point.

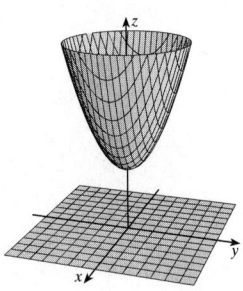

53. Equipotential curves are ellipses.
$$E = 1: x^2 + 2y^2 = 46$$
$$E = 2: x^2 + 2y^2 = \frac{37}{4}$$
$$E = 3: x^2 + 2y^2 = \frac{22}{9}$$

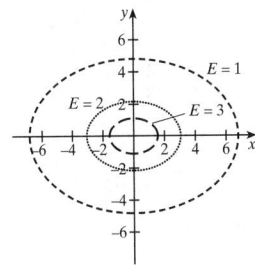

55. These level curves are hyperbolas. **57.** $y = \dfrac{100}{x}$

59.

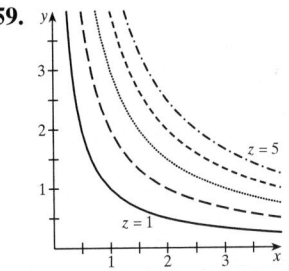

61. $R = (60 - \dfrac{x}{5} + \dfrac{y}{20})x + (50 - \dfrac{x}{10} + \dfrac{y}{20})y$

11.2 Limits and Continuity (Pages 708–710)

3. 5   **5.** -2 **7.** 1   **9.** 1   **11.** 0

13. 1   **15.** 1   **17.** 50   **19.** 4   **21.** 10

23. The limit does not exist.

25. 1   **27.** -1 **29.** 0

31. The limit does not exist.   **33.** The limit does not exist.

35. f is not continuous at $(0, 0)$.

37. a. $\frac{11}{10}$ **b.** The limit does not exist.

39. $B = 0$ **41.** 0   **43.** 2   **45.** e **47.** 0

49. The limit does not exist.

51. Choose $\delta = \dfrac{\epsilon}{3}$.   **53.** Choose $\delta = \dfrac{\epsilon}{\sqrt{2}}$.

11.3 Partial Derivatives (Pages 717–719)

3. $f_x = 3x^2 + 2xy + y^2$; $f_y = x^2 + 2xy + 3y^2$; $f_{xx} = 6x + 2y$; $f_{yx} = 2x + 2y$

5. $f_x = \dfrac{1}{y}$; $f_y = \dfrac{-x}{y^2}$; $f_{xx} = 0$; $f_{yx} = \dfrac{-1}{y^2}$

7. $f_x = \dfrac{2}{2x + 3y}$; $f_y = \dfrac{3}{2x + 3y}$; $f_{xx} = \dfrac{-4}{(2x + 3y)^2}$; $f_{yx} = \dfrac{-6}{(2x + 3y)^2}$

9. a. $f_x = (2x \cos x^2)(\cos y)$; $f_y = -(\sin x^2)(\sin y)$

b. $f_x = \cos(x^2 \cos y)(2x \cos y)$; $f_y = \cos(x^2 \cos y)(-x^2 \sin y)$

11. $f_x = \dfrac{3x}{(3x^2 + y^4)^{1/2}}$; $f_y = \dfrac{2y^3}{(3x^2 + y^4)^{1/2}}$

13. $f_x = xe^{x+y}(x+2)\cos y$; $f_y = x^2 e^{x+y}(\cos y - \sin y)$

15. $f_x = \dfrac{y}{\sqrt{1 - x^2 y^2}}$; $f_y = \dfrac{x}{\sqrt{1 - x^2 y^2}}$

17. $f_x = y^2 + yz$; $f_y = 2xy + z^3 + xz$; $f_z = 3yz^2 + xy$

19. $f_x = \dfrac{1}{z}$; $f_y = \dfrac{2y}{z}$; $f_z = -\dfrac{x + y^2}{z^2}$

21. $f_x = \dfrac{1}{x + y^2 + z^3}$; $f_y = \dfrac{2y}{x + y^2 + z^3}$; $f_z = \dfrac{3z^2}{x + y^2 + z^3}$

23. $z_x = -\dfrac{2x}{9z}$; $z_y = \dfrac{y}{2z}$

25. $z_x = -\dfrac{6xy}{y^3 - 2z}$; $z_y = -\dfrac{3x^2 + 3y^2 z}{y^3 - 2z}$

27. $z_x = -\dfrac{1}{2x^{3/2}\cos xz} - \dfrac{z}{x}$; $z_y = -\dfrac{2y}{x\cos xz}$

29. a. $f_x = y^3 + 3x^2 y$; $f_x(1, -1) = -4$
   b. $f_y = 3xy^2 + x^3$; $f_y(1, -1) = 4$

31. a. $f_x = x^2 \cos(x + y) + 2x\sin(x + y)$; $f_x\left(\frac{\pi}{2}, \frac{\pi}{2}\right) = -\frac{\pi^2}{4}$
   b. $f_y = x^2 \cos(x + y)$; $f_y\left(\frac{\pi}{2}, \frac{\pi}{2}\right) = -\frac{\pi^2}{4}$

33. $f_x = -(x^2 + 2x + 1)$; $f_y = y^2 + 2y + 1$

35. $f_x = 6xy$; $f_{xx} = 6y$; $f_y = 3x^2 - 3y^2$; $f_{yy} = -6y$; thus, $f_{xx} + f_{yy} = 0$.

37. $f_x = e^x \sin y$; $f_{xx} = e^x \sin y$; $f_y = e^x \cos y$; $f_{yy} = -e^x \sin y$; thus, $f_{xx} + f_{yy} = 0$.

41. $2(\sin z - x\cos z)$

45. a. $C_m = -0.67\sigma(T - t)m^{-1.67}$
   b. $C_T = \sigma m^{-0.67}$ **c.** $C_t = -\sigma m^{-0.67}$

47. a. $\dfrac{\partial V}{\partial T} = \dfrac{k}{P}$ **b.** $\dfrac{\partial P}{\partial V} = -\dfrac{P}{V}$

49. a. 9   **b.** 14

51. a. not satisfied   **b.** not satisfied   **c.** satisfied

11.4 Tangent Planes, Approximations, and Differentiability (Pages 727–729)

1. $3x + y - \sqrt{10}z = 0$ **3.** $2x + 4y - z - 4 = 0$

5. $x - y + 4z - \pi = 0$ **7.** $df = 10xy^3\,dx + 15x^2 y^2\,dy$

9. $df = y(\cos xy)\,dx + x(\cos xy)\,dy$

11. $df = -\dfrac{y}{x^2}\,dx + \dfrac{1}{x}\,dy$ **13.** $df = ye^x\,dx + e^x\,dy$

15. $df = 9x^2\,dx - 8y^3\,dy + 5\,dz$

17. $df = 2z^2 \cos(2x - 3y)\,dx - 3z^2 \cos(2x - 3y)\,dy + 2z\sin(2x - 3y)\,dz$

19. f, f_x, and f_y are all continuous, so the function is differentiable.

21. f, f_x, and f_y are all continuous, so the function is differentiable.

23. 37.04   **25.** 0   **27.** 2.691   **29.** $z = 9$

31. c. $\frac{1}{2}(1 - x - y)$

33. The maximum possible error will cost \$1.14.

35. a. $R = \left(\dfrac{4,000 - p}{500}\right)p + \left(\dfrac{3,000 - q}{450}\right)q$
   b. The revenue is increased by approximately \$180.

37. R increases by approximately 11%.

39. 0.0360 cal

41. The manufacturer should decrease the level of unskilled labor by about 2.4 hours.

43. 22%

45. The maximum possible error in the measurement of S is 0.014.

47. The function is not continuous.

49. A increases by about 1%.

11.5 Chain Rules (Pages 735–737)

5. $8e^{2t}(1 + e^{6t})$ **7.** $\dfrac{-3\sin^3 3t + 6\sin 3t}{\cos^2 3t}$

9. $\dfrac{\partial F}{\partial u} = 2u\sin^2 v + 2u - 4v$;

$\dfrac{\partial F}{\partial v} = 2u^2 \sin v\cos v - 4u + 8v$

11. $\dfrac{\partial F}{\partial u} = v^2 + v$; $\dfrac{\partial F}{\partial v} = 2uv + u$

13. $\dfrac{\partial w}{\partial s} = \dfrac{\partial w}{\partial x}\dfrac{\partial x}{\partial s} + \dfrac{\partial w}{\partial y}\dfrac{\partial y}{\partial s} + \dfrac{\partial w}{\partial z}\dfrac{\partial z}{\partial s}$;

$\dfrac{\partial w}{\partial t} = \dfrac{\partial w}{\partial x}\dfrac{\partial x}{\partial t} + \dfrac{\partial w}{\partial y}\dfrac{\partial y}{\partial t} + \dfrac{\partial w}{\partial z}\dfrac{\partial z}{\partial t}$

15. $\dfrac{\partial w}{\partial s} = \dfrac{\partial w}{\partial x}\dfrac{\partial x}{\partial s} + \dfrac{\partial w}{\partial y}\dfrac{\partial y}{\partial s} + \dfrac{\partial w}{\partial z}\dfrac{\partial z}{\partial s}$;

$\dfrac{\partial w}{\partial t} = \dfrac{\partial w}{\partial x}\dfrac{\partial x}{\partial t} + \dfrac{\partial w}{\partial y}\dfrac{\partial y}{\partial t} + \dfrac{\partial w}{\partial z}\dfrac{\partial z}{\partial t}$;

$\dfrac{\partial w}{\partial u} = \dfrac{\partial w}{\partial x}\dfrac{\partial x}{\partial u} + \dfrac{\partial w}{\partial y}\dfrac{\partial y}{\partial u} + \dfrac{\partial w}{\partial z}\dfrac{\partial z}{\partial u}$

17. $\dfrac{dw}{dt} = \cos(xyz)[-3yz - e^{1-t}xz + 4xy]$

19. $\dfrac{dw}{dt} = (e^{x^3 + yz})\left[\dfrac{-6x^2}{t^2} + 2ty + \dfrac{2z}{2t - 3}\right]$

21. $\dfrac{\partial w}{\partial r} = \dfrac{2s + t\cos(rt)}{2 - z}$;

$\dfrac{\partial w}{\partial t} = \dfrac{(2 - z)[r\cos(rt)] + 2st(x + y)}{(2 - z)^2}$

23. $\dfrac{dy}{dx} = \dfrac{-[3x(x^2 - y)^{1/2} + 2xy]}{-\frac{3}{2}(x^2 - y)^{1/2} + x^2}$

25. $\dfrac{dy}{dx} = \dfrac{(1 - \cos y)(1 + x^2) - y}{(1 + x^2)(-x\sin y + \tan^{-1} x)}$ **27.** $\dfrac{dy}{dx} = \dfrac{y}{x}$

29. a. $\dfrac{z^2}{2}$ **b.** $\dfrac{4}{x^3 y}$ **c.** $\dfrac{4}{xy^3}$

31. a. $\dfrac{2z^3}{x^2 y^2}$ **b.** $\dfrac{2z^2(x + z)}{x^4}$ **c.** $\dfrac{2z^2(y + z)}{y^4}$

33. a. $\dfrac{\sec^2 y\cos x}{4z^3}$ **b.** $\dfrac{2z^2 \sin x - \cos^2 x}{2z^3}$

   c. $\dfrac{4z^2 \sec^2 y\tan y - \sec^4 y}{4z^3}$

35. $\dfrac{\partial^2 z}{\partial u^2} = a^2 z_{xx}$; $\dfrac{\partial^2 z}{\partial v^2} = b^2 z_{yy}$

37. volume and surface area both decreasing

39. a. $\dfrac{\partial C}{\partial a} = \dfrac{[1 - t(b - a)]e^{-at} - e^{-bt}}{(b - a)^2}$;

$\dfrac{\partial C}{\partial b} = \dfrac{[(b - a)t + 1]e^{-bt} - e^{-at}}{(b - a)^2}$;

$\dfrac{\partial C}{\partial t} = \dfrac{1}{b - a}\left[-ae^{-at} + be^{-bt}\right]$

b. $\dfrac{dC}{dt} = \left[\dfrac{(1 - bt + \ln b)\left(\frac{1}{b}\right) - e^{-bt}}{(bt - \ln b)^2}\right]\dfrac{(-\ln b)}{1}$

$\qquad + \dfrac{t}{bt - \ln b}\left[\dfrac{-\ln b}{bt} + be^{-bt}\right]$

41. The monthly demand for bicycles will be increasing at the rate of about 31 bicycles per month (4 months from now).

43. The joint resistance is decreasing at the approximate rate of 0.3471 ohms/second.

51. $\dfrac{d^2z}{d\theta^2} = y^2 f_{xx} + x^2 f_{yy} - 2xy f_{xy} - x f_x - y f_y$

57. $\dfrac{\partial z}{\partial x} = \dfrac{-F_x}{F_z} = \dfrac{-(2x + 2yz)}{2xy + e^z};$

$\qquad \dfrac{\partial z}{\partial y} = \dfrac{-F_y}{F_z} = \dfrac{-(2xz + 3y^2)}{2xy + e^z}$

59. a. The degree is $n = 3$.

11.6 Directional Derivatives and the Gradient (Pages 747–749)

1. $\nabla f = (2x - 2y)\mathbf{i} - 2x\mathbf{j}$

3. $\nabla f = \left(-\dfrac{y}{x^2} + \dfrac{1}{y}\right)\mathbf{i} + \left(\dfrac{1}{x} - \dfrac{x}{y^2}\right)\mathbf{j}$

5. $\nabla f = e^{3-v}(\mathbf{i} - u\mathbf{j})$ **7.** $\nabla f = \cos(x + 2y)(\mathbf{i} + 2\mathbf{j})$

9. $\nabla f = e^{y+3z}(\mathbf{i} + x\mathbf{j} + 3x\mathbf{k})$ **11.** $\dfrac{\sqrt{2}}{2}$

13. $\dfrac{5\sqrt{2}}{8}$ **15.** 0

17. $\mathbf{N_u} = \pm\dfrac{\sqrt{3}}{3}(\mathbf{i} - \mathbf{j} + \mathbf{k})$; the tangent plane is $x - y + z - 3 = 0$.

19. $\mathbf{N_u} = \pm\dfrac{\sqrt{3}}{3}(-\mathbf{i} - \mathbf{j} + \mathbf{k})$; the tangent plane is $x + y - z - \frac{\pi}{2} = 0$.

21. $\mathbf{N_u} = \pm\dfrac{\sqrt{3}}{3}(\mathbf{i} - \mathbf{j} + \mathbf{k})$; the tangent plane is $x - y + z = 0$.

23. $\mathbf{N_u} = \pm\dfrac{1}{\sqrt{46}}(3\mathbf{i} + 6\mathbf{j} + \mathbf{k})$; the tangent plane is $3x + 6y + z - 3 = 0$.

25. $\nabla f(1, -1) = 3\mathbf{i} + 2\mathbf{j}$; $\|\nabla f\| = \sqrt{13}$

27. $\nabla f(3, -3) = 27(\mathbf{i} + \mathbf{j})$; $\|\nabla f\| = 27\sqrt{2}$

29. $\nabla f(a, b, c) = 2(a^2\mathbf{i} + b^2\mathbf{j} + c^2\mathbf{k})$; $\|\nabla f\| = 2\sqrt{a^4 + b^4 + c^4}$

31. $\nabla f(1, 2) = \dfrac{1}{5}(\mathbf{i} + 2\mathbf{j})$; $\|\nabla f\| = \dfrac{1}{\sqrt{5}} = \dfrac{\sqrt{5}}{5}$

33. $\nabla f(2, -1, 2) = 2(5\mathbf{i} + 2\mathbf{j} + 5\mathbf{k})$; $\|\nabla f\| = \sqrt{216} = 6\sqrt{6}$

35. $\mathbf{u} = \pm\dfrac{a\mathbf{i} + b\mathbf{j}}{\sqrt{a^2 + b^2}}$ **37.** $\mathbf{u} = \pm\dfrac{b^2 x_0\mathbf{i} + a^2 y_0\mathbf{j}}{\sqrt{b^4 x_0^2 + a^4 y_0^2}}$

39. $D_\mathbf{u} f = \sqrt{3} + 1$ **41.** $D_\mathbf{u} f = -\dfrac{6e}{\sqrt{17}}$

43. $D_\mathbf{u} f = \dfrac{11\sqrt{3}}{15}$

45. Maximum rate of temperature change is $\|\nabla T_0\| = 2\sqrt{3}$ in the direction of $\mathbf{u} = \dfrac{\sqrt{3}}{3}(\mathbf{i} + \mathbf{j} + \mathbf{k})$.

47. For the most rapid decrease, she should head in the direction $\frac{3}{2}\mathbf{i} - \frac{5}{2}\mathbf{j}$.

49. 8.06   **51.** $\nabla f(1, 2) = 5\sqrt{10}(\mathbf{i} - 3\mathbf{j})$

59. $D_\mathbf{u} f = f_x \cos\theta + f_y \sin\theta$; for $f = xy^2 e^{x-2y}$, $D_\mathbf{u} f = 6e^{-7}$

11.7 Extrema of Functions of Two Variables (Pages 758–761)

5. a minimum occurs at $(2, 3)$

7. a maximum occurs at $(0, 0)$

9. $(0, 0)$, relative minimum

11. $(\sqrt{3}, 0)$, relative maximum; $(-\sqrt{3}, 0)$, saddle point

13. $(0, 0)$, relative minimum; $(1, 0)$, saddle point; $(-1, 0)$, saddle point; $(0, 1)$, relative maximum; $(0, -1)$, relative maximum

15. $(2^{-1/3}, 2^{-1/3})$, relative minimum

17. $(0, 3)$, saddle point; $(0, 9)$, relative minimum; $(-2, 9)$, saddle point; $(-2, 3)$, relative maximum

19. $\left(\frac{3}{2}, 2\right)$, saddle point

21. $(6, 2)$, relative minimum; $(8.99, -2.45)$, saddle point

23. $(-2, 0)$, saddle point; $(-2, 1)$, relative minimum

25. The largest value of f on S is 0 and the smallest is -14.

27. The largest value of f on S is 7 and the smallest is -5.

29. 0 is minimum, $\frac{3}{2}$ is maximum

31. $y = 1.62x + 0.68$ **33.** $y = -0.02x + 5.54$

35. The closest points are $(0, 2, 0)$ and $(0, -2, 0)$.

37. The dimensions for the minimum construction occur when the sides measure $x = \sqrt[3]{2V}$, $y = \sqrt[3]{2V}$, and $z = \sqrt[3]{0.25V}$.

39. The product is maximized when all three numbers are 18.

41. The temperature is greatest $(13°C)$ at $(3, 2)$ and is least $\left(-\frac{1}{7}°C\right)$ at $\left(\frac{2}{7}, \frac{8}{7}\right)$.

43. The revenue is maximized at $\left(\frac{21}{2}, \frac{13}{2}\right)$.

45. The owner should charge $2.70 for California water and $2.50 for New York water.

47. 200 machines should be supplied to the domestic market and 300 to the foreign market.

49. 1.35

51. a.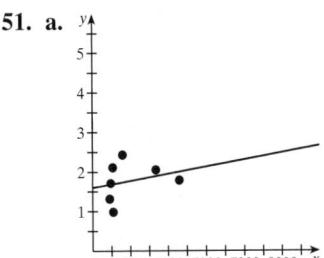

b. $y = 0.0001064x + 1.5965$

c. 2.28 gal/person (not even close to the actual)

53. a. $W = 3.42674 + 0.573164X$

57. The minimum time of travel occurs when Dick waits 0.4243 miles from the line AS and Mary waits 1.6396 miles from the finish line.

11.8 Lagrange Multipliers (Pages 767–770)

1. $\frac{25}{16}$ **3.** $\frac{44}{5}$ **5.** 2   **7.** 4

9. 1.8478   **11.** 0.72   **13.** $\frac{8}{7}$ **15.** $\frac{25}{7}$

17. 17.3 is the constrained maximum and -17.3 is the constrained minimum.

19. The minimum distance is $\dfrac{|D|}{\sqrt{A^2 + B^2 + C^2}}$.

21. The nearest point is $\left(\frac{1}{3}, \frac{1}{6}, \frac{1}{6}\right)$, and the minimum distance is 0.4082.

23. $x = z = 3$, $y = 6$; the largest product is 324.

25. The lowest temperature is $\frac{200}{3}$.

27. The maximum value of A is 6,400 yd^2.

29. the radius $x = 1$ in. and the height $y = 4$ in.

31. \$2,000 to development and \$6,000 to promotion gives the maximum sales of about $1,039$ units.

33. $x \approx 13.87$ and $y \approx 12.04$

35. $x = y = z = \sqrt[3]{C}$

37. The farmer should apply 4.24 acre-ft of water and 1.27 lb of fertilizer to maximize the yield.

39. The triangle with maximum area is equilateral.

41. $\frac{56}{3}$ **43.** $\frac{121}{24}$

45. a. \$3,000 for development and \$5,000 for promotion.
   b. The actual increase in profit is \$29.68.
   c. \$4,000 should be spent on development and \$6,000 should be spent on promotion to maximize profit.
   d. $\lambda = 0$

47. $\frac{2}{3}$ **49.** $\dfrac{8abc}{3\sqrt{3}}$ **53. b.** $x = \dfrac{k\alpha}{p(\alpha + \beta)}$, $y = \dfrac{k\beta}{q(\alpha + \beta)}$

Chapter 11 Review
Proficiency Examination (Pages 770–771)

31. $f_{xy} = f_{yx} = \dfrac{1}{(1 - x^2 y^2)^{3/2}}$ **32.** $\dfrac{dw}{dt} = 6\pi^2$

33. a. $\nabla f = \mathbf{i} + 3\mathbf{k}$ **b.** $D_{\mathbf{u}}(f) = \dfrac{-2\sqrt{5}}{5}$

   c. $\mathbf{u} = \dfrac{\mathbf{i} + 3\mathbf{k}}{\sqrt{10}}$; $\|\nabla f\| = \sqrt{10}$

34. $\displaystyle\lim_{(x,y) \to (0,0)} f(x, y)$ along the line $y = x$ is

$\displaystyle\lim_{x \to 0} \frac{x^3}{x^3 + x^3} = \frac{1}{2}$. The limit does not equal $f(0, 0)$ so the function is not continuous.

35. $f_x = -\dfrac{1}{x}$, $f_y = \dfrac{1}{y}$, $f_{yy} = -\dfrac{1}{y^2}$, $f_{xy} = 0$

36. $f_x = 2xy + z^2$; $f_y = x^2 + 2yz$; $f_z = y^2 + 2zx$
   $f_x + f_y + f_z = 2xy + z^2 + x^2 + 2yz + y^2 + 2zx = (x + y + z)^2$

37. $D_{\mathbf{u}}(f) \approx -87.4$

38. $(0, 0)$, saddle point; $(9, 3)$, relative maximum; $(-9, -3)$, relative maximum

39. maximum of 12; minimum of 3

40. The largest value of f is 49/42 at $\left(2, \frac{3}{4}\right)$ and the smallest is $-9/4$ at $(-3/2, 0)$.

Supplementary Problems (Pages 771–774)

1. The domain consists of the circle with center at the origin, radius 4, and its interior.

3. $-1 \le x \le 1$ and $-1 \le y \le 1$ is the domain

5. $f_x = 1$; $f_y = -1$

7. $f_x = 2xy - \dfrac{y}{x^2} \cos \dfrac{y}{x}$; $f_y = x^2 + \dfrac{1}{x} \cos \dfrac{y}{x}$

9. $f_x = 6x^2 y + 3y^2 - \dfrac{y}{x^2}$; $f_y = 2x^3 + 6xy + \dfrac{1}{x}$

11. For $c = 2$, $x^2 - y = 2$ is a parabola opening up, with vertex at $(0, -2)$. For $c = -2$, $x^2 - y = -2$ is a parabola opening up, with vertex at $(0, 2)$.

13. For $c = 0$, $\sqrt{x^2 + y^2} = 0$ is the origin and half-line $y = 0$, $x < 0$. For $c = 1$, $\sqrt{x^2 + y^2} = 1$ is a semicircle (to the right of the y-axis). For $c = -1$, $|y| = 1$ is a pair of half-lines, 1 unit above or below the x-axis, to the left of the y-axis.

15. For $c = 1$, $x^2 + \dfrac{y^2}{2} + \dfrac{z^2}{9} = 1$ is an ellipsoid. For $c = 2$, $x^2 + \dfrac{y^2}{2} + \dfrac{z^2}{9} = 2$ is an ellipsoid.

17. 0   **19.** The limit does not exist.

21. $\dfrac{dz}{dt} = ye^t(-t^{-2} + t^{-1}) + (x + 2y) \sec^2 t$

23. $\dfrac{\partial z}{\partial u} = \left(\tan \dfrac{x}{y} + \dfrac{x}{y} \sec^2 \dfrac{x}{y}\right)v + \left(-\dfrac{x^2}{y^2} \sec^2 \dfrac{x}{y}\right)v^{-1}$;
   $\dfrac{\partial z}{\partial v} = \left(\tan \dfrac{x}{y} + \dfrac{x}{y} \sec^2 \dfrac{x}{y}\right)u + \left(-\dfrac{x^2}{y^2} \sec^2 \dfrac{x}{y}\right)(-uv^{-2})$

25. $\dfrac{\partial z}{\partial x} = -\dfrac{e^x}{e^z} = -e^{x-z}$; $\dfrac{\partial z}{\partial y} = -\dfrac{e^y}{e^z} = -e^{y-z}$

27. $\dfrac{\partial z}{\partial x} = \dfrac{z}{3z + 1}$; $\dfrac{\partial z}{\partial y} = \dfrac{2z}{3z + 1}$

29. $f_{xx} = \dfrac{xy^3}{(1 - x^2 y^2)^{3/2}}$; $f_{yx} = (1 - x^2 y^2)^{-3/2}$

31. $f_{xx} = 2e^{x^2 + y^2}(2x^2 + 1)$; $f_{yx} = 4xye^{x^2 + y^2}$

33. $f_{xx} = \sin x \cos(\cos x)$; $f_{yx} = 0$

35. normal line: $\dfrac{x - 1}{16} = \dfrac{y - 1}{-7}$ and $z = 1$; tangent plane: $-16(x - 1) + 7(y - 1) = 0$

37. relative minimum at $(3, -1)$

39. $(1, 0)$, saddle point; $(0, 1)$, saddle point; $\left(\frac{2}{3}, \frac{2}{3}\right)$, relative maximum; $(1, 1)$, saddle point

41. $(0, 9)$, relative minimum; $(0, 3)$, saddle point; $(-2, 9)$ saddle point; $(-2, 3)$, relative maximum

43. The largest value is 2 at $(0, -1)$ and the smallest is -2 at $(0, 1)$.

45. The largest value of f is 10 at $(0, -2)$ and the smallest is $-9/4$ at $(0, 3/2)$.

47. $\dfrac{dz}{dt} = (2x - 3y^2)(2) + (-6xy)(2t)$

49. $\dfrac{\partial z}{\partial x} = e^{u^2 - v^2}(8xu^2 + 4x - 12uvx)$;
   $\dfrac{\partial z}{\partial y} = e^{u^2 - v^2}(12yu^2 + 6y + 8uvy)$

51. $\dfrac{dy}{dx} = -1$ at $(1, 1)$

53. normal line: $\dfrac{x}{2} = \dfrac{y - 1}{2} = \dfrac{z - 3}{-1}$; tangent plane: $2x + 2y - z + 1 = 0$

55. $g(x, y, z) = x^2 y + y^2 z + z^2 x$

57. $\dfrac{dw}{dt} = \left[\dfrac{2x}{1 + x^2 + y^2}\right]\left(\dfrac{2t}{1 + t^2}\right)$
   $+ \left[\dfrac{2y}{1 + x^2 + y^2} - \dfrac{2}{1 + y^2}\right]e^t$

59. $D_{\mathbf{u}} f = \dfrac{1}{\sqrt{5}}(-16 \ln 2 - 12)$

61. a. $D_{\mathbf{u}} f = -\dfrac{18}{\sqrt{6}}$ **b.** $\dfrac{1}{\sqrt{86}}(-6\mathbf{i} + \mathbf{j} + 7\mathbf{k})$

63. $x = 6$, $y = z = 3$; maximum is 324.

65. The minimum distance is $\sqrt{3}$.

67. a. $t_m = \dfrac{-1 + \sqrt{1 + 4k\gamma r^2}}{4k\gamma}$ **b.** $M(r) = \sqrt{\dfrac{k\gamma}{\pi}} \dfrac{e^{-z/2}}{\sqrt{z - 1}}$

    c. The darkest part of the eyespot pattern occurs near the center.

69. a.

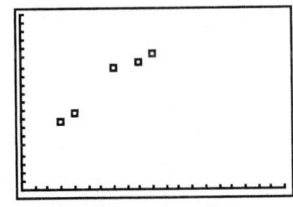

    b.

The least squares line is $y = 11.54x + 44.45$. If $x = 5{,}000$, the sales are $y \approx 102.15$.

71. $24xy^2z^3 \sin(x^2 + y^3 + z^4)$

73. $\dfrac{dy}{dx} = -\dfrac{2}{3}$ **75.** $\mathbf{u} = \pm\frac{1}{3}(2\mathbf{i} + 2\mathbf{j} - \mathbf{k})$

77. $\dfrac{\partial^2 z}{\partial x \partial y}$

$= -\dfrac{\sin^2(x + z)\cos(x + y) + \sin^2(x + y)\cos(x + z)}{\sin^3(x + z)}$

79. $f(2, 3) = 12$ is a relative minimum.

81. $x = \dfrac{a}{a^2 + b^2 + c^2}$; $y = \dfrac{b}{a^2 + b^2 + c^2}$; $z = \dfrac{c}{a^2 + b^2 + c^2}$

87. $\theta = 2$ and $r = \sqrt{A_0}$

89. a. 10π cm^3 **b.** 8π cm^2

91. Approximately 2.01 cm^3 has been removed.

97. This is Putnam Problem 6 in the afternoon session of 1967.

99. This is Putnam Problem 13 in the afternoon session of 1938.

Chapter 12: Multiple Integration

12.1 Double Integration Over Rectangular Regions
(Pages 785–786)

1. $\frac{13}{3}$ **3.** $(e^2 - 1)(\ln 2) + 2$ **5.** $\frac{15}{2}\ln 3 - 10\ln 2 + \frac{1}{2}$

7. 32   **9.** 24   **11.** 24   **13.** $\frac{7}{6}$ **15.** -1

17. $4\ln 2$ **19.** 1   **21.** 8   **23.** $3\ln 2$ **25.** $\frac{32}{9}$

27. $\sqrt{3} - \frac{4}{3}\sqrt{2} + \frac{1}{3}$ **29.** 3   **31.** $\dfrac{\pi^2}{4}$

35. $M = \displaystyle\iint_R \delta(x, y)\, dA$ **37.** $\dfrac{e^6}{9} - \dfrac{1}{9}$

39. 0.91   **43.** 1.44

47. $\displaystyle\int_0^1 \int_0^1 \dfrac{y - x}{(x + y)^3}\, dx\, dy = \dfrac{1}{2}$; $\displaystyle\int_0^1 \int_0^1 \dfrac{y - x}{(x + y)^3}\, dy\, dx = -\dfrac{1}{2}$; Fubini's theorem does not apply because the integrand is not continuous at $(0, 0)$.

12.2 Double Integration Over Nonrectangular Regions
(Pages 793–795)

3. $\frac{32}{3}$ **5.** $\frac{2}{3}$ **7.** $3\pi - 2\sqrt{3}$ **9.** $\frac{27}{2}$

11. $\frac{5}{12}$ **13.** $\frac{1}{6}\sin^3 2$ **15.** $\dfrac{\pi}{3} - \dfrac{\sqrt{3}}{2}$ **17.** $\frac{1}{2}e - 1$

19. $\sqrt{2} - 1$ **21.** $\frac{1}{2}$ **23.** $\frac{5}{12}$ **25.** $\frac{2}{3} + 2\ln 2$

27. $2e - 4$ **29.** 2   **31.** $\frac{32}{3}$ **33.** $\frac{32}{3}$ **35.** $e - 2$

37. $\frac{2}{3}$ **39.** $\dfrac{8\pi}{3} + \dfrac{2\sqrt{3}}{3}$

41. $\displaystyle\int_0^2 \int_{x/2}^1 f(x, y)\, dy\, dx$ **43.** $\displaystyle\int_0^2 \int_{x^2}^{2x} f(x, y)\, dy\, dx$

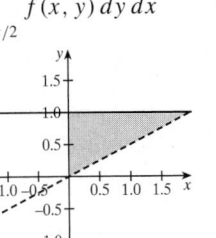

45. Intersection: $(1, 3)$

$$\int_0^1 \int_0^{3x} f(x, y)\, dy\, dx + \int_1^2 \int_0^{4-x^2} f(x, y)\, dy\, dx$$

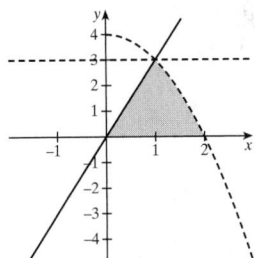

47. Intersections: $(2, 4)$ and $(-3, 9)$

$$\int_0^4 \int_{-\sqrt{y}}^{\sqrt{y}} f(x, y)\, dx\, dy + \int_4^9 \int_{-\sqrt{y}}^{6-y} f(x, y)\, dx\, dy$$

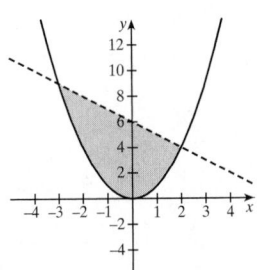

49. Intersections: $(0, 0)$ and $(7, 7)$

$$\int_{-9}^{0} \int_{3-\sqrt{9+y}}^{3+\sqrt{9+y}} f(x, y)\,dx\,dy + \int_{0}^{7} \int_{y}^{3+\sqrt{9+y}} f(x, y)\,dx\,dy$$

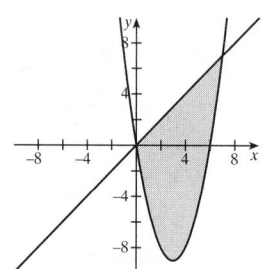

51. $V = \int_{0}^{7/3} \int_{0}^{(7-3x)/2} (7 - 3x - 2y)\,dy\,dx$

53. $V = 8 \int_{0}^{\sqrt{3}} \int_{0}^{\sqrt{3-x^2}} \sqrt{7 - x^2 - y^2}\,dy\,dx$

55. $V = 8 \int_{0}^{a} \int_{0}^{(b/a)\sqrt{a^2-x^2}} c\sqrt{1 - \dfrac{x^2}{a^2} - \dfrac{y^2}{b^2}}\,dy\,dx$

57. $V = \dfrac{4}{3}\pi(\sqrt{2})^3 - 8 \int_{0}^{1} \int_{0}^{1} \sqrt{2 - x^2 - y^2}\,dy\,dx$

59. πab **61.** 1 **63.** $\int_{1}^{8} \int_{\sqrt[3]{y}}^{y} f(x, y)\,dx\,dy$

65. $\frac{5}{24}$ **67.** 22 **69.** 18π **71.** $\frac{128\pi}{3}$

73. The value of the integral is between 1.10 and 2.15. (The actual value is approximately 1.63.)

12.3 Double Integrals in Polar Coordinates (Pages 801–804)

1. $\dfrac{\pi}{4}\left(\dfrac{1}{e} - \dfrac{1}{e^9}\right)$ **3.** $\dfrac{32\pi}{3}$

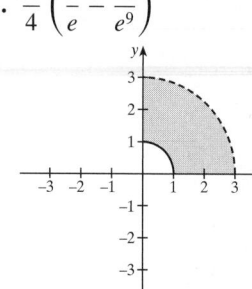 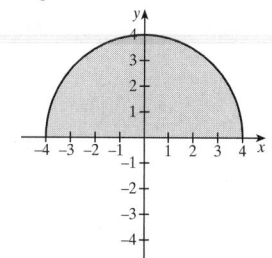

5. 0 **7.** 2

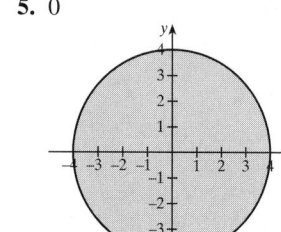 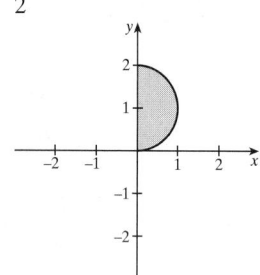

9. 16π **11.** 6π **13.** 4π **15.** $\dfrac{\pi}{2}$

17. $\frac{1}{6}(2\pi + 3\sqrt{3})$ **19.** $\dfrac{5\pi}{4} - 2$ **21.** π

23. $\pi - \dfrac{3\sqrt{3}}{2}$ **25.** $\dfrac{a^4\pi}{4}$ **27.** $\pi \ln 2$

29. $2\pi a(1 - \ln 2)$ **31.** 0 **33.** $\pi(e^9 - 1)$

35. $\frac{3}{2}\pi \ln 3 + \pi \ln 2 - \pi$ **37.** 8π **39.** 9

41. $\frac{\pi}{4}(e^4 - 1)$ **43.** 4

45. $(3 - \sqrt{5})\left(\dfrac{\pi}{2}\right)$ **47.** $\dfrac{\pi - 2}{2}$

49. $\dfrac{8}{3}$ **51.** $\dfrac{a^2}{8}(\pi - 2)$

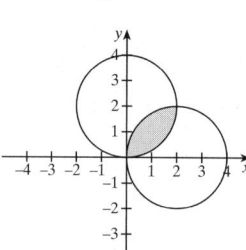

53. $\dfrac{128\pi}{3}$ **55.** $\frac{16}{9}(3\pi - 4)$ **57.** $\dfrac{5\pi}{16}$

59. $\dfrac{\pi}{4} - \dfrac{1}{2}$ **63.** $\frac{1}{3}\pi a^2(3R - a)$; $a \approx 0.6527R$

12.4 Surface Area (Pages 810–811)

1. $4\sqrt{21}$ **3.** $\frac{\pi}{6}(5\sqrt{5} - 1)$ **5.** $\frac{7}{4}$

7. $2\sqrt{17} + \frac{1}{2}\ln(4 + \sqrt{17})$ **9.** $8\sqrt{65} + \ln(8 + \sqrt{65})$

11. $\frac{\pi}{6}(5\sqrt{5} - 1)$ **13.** 2π **15.** $16\pi(2 - \sqrt{2})$

17. $15\sqrt{2} + \frac{5}{2}\ln(2\sqrt{2} + 3)$ **19.** $\frac{\pi}{6}(17\sqrt{17} - 1)$

23. $S = \dfrac{D^2}{2ABC}\sqrt{A^2 + B^2 + C^2}$ **25.** $S = \dfrac{3\sqrt{3}\pi a^2}{4}$

27. $\sqrt{2}\,\pi h^2$ **29.** 36π

31. $S = \int_{0}^{1} \int_{0}^{y} \sqrt{\csc^2 y + z^{-2}}\,dz\,dy$

33. $S = \int_{0}^{2\pi} \int_{0}^{\sqrt{\pi/2}} \sqrt{4r^2 \sin^2 r^2 + 1}\,r\,dr\,d\theta$

35. $S = \int_{1}^{5} \int_{5/x}^{6-x} \sqrt{(2x + 5y)^2 + (2y + 5x)^2 + 1}\,dy\,dx$

37. $4|u|\sqrt{u^2 + 1}$ **39.** $2|v|\sqrt{9u^4 + 1}$

41. $\frac{2\pi}{3}(3\sqrt{6} - 4)$

43. a. $(\cos v)\mathbf{i} - (\sin v)\mathbf{j} - u\mathbf{k}$

  b. $\dfrac{b}{2}\left[\ln(a + \sqrt{1 + a^2}) + a\sqrt{1 + a^2}\right]$

47. $4\pi R^2$

12.5 Triple Integrals (Pages 820–822)

3. 45 **5.** 45 **7.** $\dfrac{68}{9}$ **9.** $-\dfrac{15}{\pi}$

11. $\frac{1}{8}(5 - e^2)$ **13.** $6\pi - 18\ln 2$ **15.** 8 **17.** $\dfrac{1}{720}$

19. 0 **21.** $\dfrac{e^2}{2} - e$ **23.** $\frac{1}{6}$ **25.** $\dfrac{4\pi}{3}$

27. 4π **29.** $3\sqrt{6}\pi$ **31.** $\dfrac{16}{3}$

33. $\int_{0}^{1} \int_{y}^{1} \int_{0}^{y} f(x, y, z)\,dz\,dx\,dy$

35. $\int_{0}^{2} \int_{0}^{\sqrt{4-z^2}} \int_{0}^{\sqrt{4-y^2-z^2}} f(x, y, z)\,dx\,dy\,dz$

37. $\int_{0}^{1} \int_{\sqrt[3]{x}}^{1} \int_{0}^{1-y} f(x, y, z)\,dz\,dy\,dx$

39. 32π **41.** 32π **43.** $\dfrac{3\pi}{2}$ **45.** $\frac{4}{3}\pi R^3$

47. $\dfrac{4\pi abc}{3}$ **51.** $\dfrac{1 - \cos \pi^3}{6}$ **53.** $\frac{14}{9}$

12.6 Mass, Moments, and Probability Density Functions (Pages 829–833)

5. $\left(\frac{3}{2}, 2\right)$ **7.** $\left(1, \frac{8}{5}\right)$ **9.** $\left(\frac{1}{4}, \frac{4}{5}\right)$ **11.** $(1, 1, 1)$

13. $\left(0, \dfrac{24}{5\pi}\right)$ **15.** $\left(7, \frac{5}{3}\right)$ **17.** $(1.608, 0.231)$

19. a. $\left(0, \dfrac{3a}{2\pi}\right)$ **b.** $\left(-\dfrac{8a}{3\pi^2}, \dfrac{4a}{3\pi}\right)$

21. $(4.9110, 0.7616)$ **23.** $\frac{8}{15}$ **25.** $(0.56, 0.56)$

27. $\left(\dfrac{3a}{4}, \dfrac{3b}{8}\right)$ **29.** $\dfrac{a^4 \pi}{64}$ **31.** $\dfrac{mb^2}{4}$

33. $\left(\dfrac{3a}{8}, \dfrac{3a}{8}, \dfrac{3a}{8}\right)$ **35.** $1 - \frac{5}{2}e^{-1}$

37. The probability is roughly 75%.   **39.** $\left(\frac{11}{12}, \frac{67}{18}\right)$

41. $3(e - 2)$ **43.** 0 **45.** $\sqrt{\dfrac{a^2 + b^2}{6}}$ **47.** 2.4107

49. a. $t_m = \dfrac{x_0^2}{2k}$; $C_m(x_0) = \sqrt{\dfrac{2}{\pi}}\, C_0 \dfrac{e^{-1/2}}{x_0}$

   b. $x_m \le 1.9358$; the danger zone is approximately 1.9 miles

   c. $AV = \dfrac{1}{A} \displaystyle\int_0^{1.9358} \int_0^{x^2/(2k)} \dfrac{C_0}{\sqrt{k\pi t}} \exp\left(\dfrac{-x^2}{4kt}\right) dt\, dx$

51. c. $5{,}400\pi\,\delta$ **53.** $\dfrac{h\ell(h^2 + \ell^2)}{12}$ **55.** $4\pi^2 ab$

12.7 Cylindrical and Spherical Coordinates (Pages 840–843)

3. a. $(4, \pi/2, \sqrt{3})$ **b.** $(\sqrt{19}, \pi/2, \cos^{-1}(\sqrt{3}/\sqrt{19}))$

5. a. $(\sqrt{5}, \tan^{-1} 2, 3)$ **b.** $(\sqrt{14}, \tan^{-1} 2, \cos^{-1}(3/\sqrt{14}))$

7. a. $(-3/2, 3\sqrt{3}/2, -3)$ **b.** $(\sqrt{18}, 2\pi/3, \cos^{-1}(-3/\sqrt{18}))$

9. a. $(\sqrt{2}, \sqrt{2}, \pi)$ **b.** $(\sqrt{\pi^2 + 4}, \pi/4, \cos^{-1}(\pi/\sqrt{\pi^2 + 4}))$

11. a. $(3/2, \sqrt{3}/2, -1)$ **b.** $\left(\sqrt{3}, \dfrac{\pi}{6}, -1\right)$

13. a. $(\sin 3 \cos 2, \sin 3 \sin 2, \cos 3)$ **b.** $(\sin 3, 2, \cos 3)$

15. $z = r^2 \cos 2\theta$

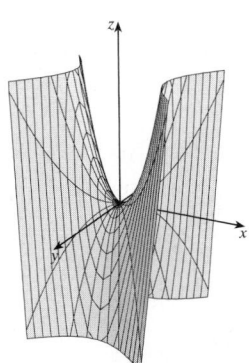

17. $r = \dfrac{6z}{\sqrt{4 - 13\cos^2\theta}}$ or $9r^2 \cos^2\theta - 4r^2 \sin^2\theta + 36z^2 = 0$

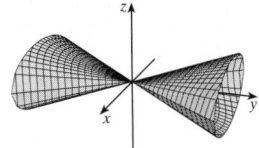

19. $\phi = \dfrac{\pi}{4}$

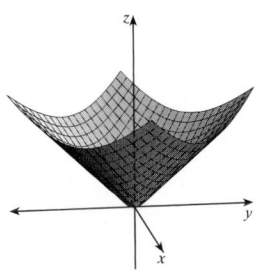

21. $\rho = \dfrac{4 \cot\phi \csc\phi}{3 - 2\cos^2\theta}$ or $4\rho \cos\phi = \rho^2 \sin^2\phi(\cos^2\theta + 3\sin^2\theta)$

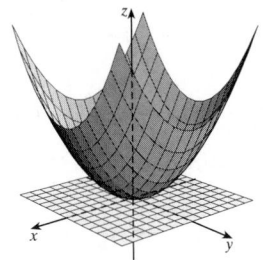

23. $z = 2xy$ **25.** $z = x^2 - y^2$

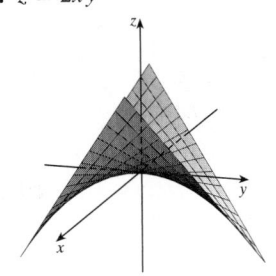   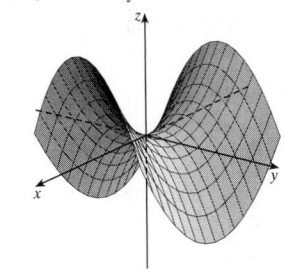

27. $xz = 1$

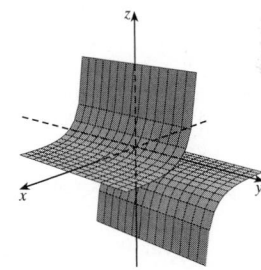

29. $\frac{16}{3}$ **31.** 2π **33.** 8π **35.** $\frac{7}{60}$

37. $\dfrac{x^2}{a^2} + \dfrac{y^2}{b^2} + \dfrac{z^2}{c^2} = R^2$ **39.** $\dfrac{a^6}{3}$ **41.** $\left(0, 0, \frac{27}{4}\right)$

43. a. $m = \displaystyle\int_0^{2\pi} \int_0^3 \int_0^{\sqrt{9-r^2}} (r^2 \sin\theta \cos\theta + z)\, r\, dz\, dr\, d\theta$

   b. $\bar{x} = \dfrac{1}{m} \displaystyle\int_0^{2\pi} \int_0^3 \int_0^{\sqrt{9-r^2}} r \cos\theta (r^2 \sin\theta \cos\theta + z) r\, dz\, dr\, d\theta$

   c. $I_z = \displaystyle\int_0^{2\pi} \int_0^3 \int_0^{\sqrt{9-r^2}} r^2 (r^2 \sin\theta \cos\theta + z) r\, dz\, dr\, d\theta$

45. 0 **47.** $\dfrac{128\pi}{15}$ **49.** $\dfrac{16\pi\sqrt{2}}{5}$ **51.** 6π

53. $\dfrac{7\pi}{2}$ **55.** $\dfrac{5\pi}{2}$ **57.** He should survive.

61. $\frac{8\pi}{5}$ **63. a.** $\frac{3,608\pi}{2,625}$ **b.** 4.31445

12.8 Jacobians: Change of Variables (Pages 850–852)

1. 2   **3.** $2u$ **5.** $-2e^{2u}$ **7.** $-e^{2u}$ **9.** -9

11. ue^{uv} **13.** $\frac{1}{11}$ **15.** -1 **17.** $\frac{1}{8xy}$

19. $A(0, 5) \rightarrow (5, -5)$;
$B(6, 5) \rightarrow (11, 1)$;
$C(6, 0) \rightarrow (6, 6)$;
$O(0, 0) \rightarrow (0, 0)$

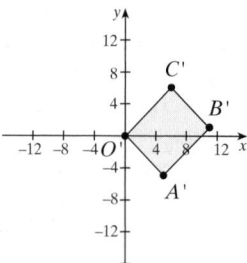

21. $A(5, 0) \rightarrow (25, 0)$;
$B(7, 4) \rightarrow (33, 56)$;
$C(2, 4) \rightarrow (-12, 16)$;
$O(0, 0) \rightarrow (0, 0)$

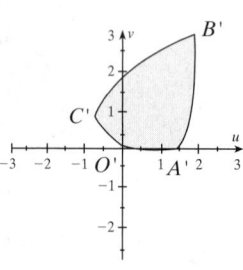

23. $dx\,dy = u\,du\,dv$ **25.** $3\ln 2$ **27.** 0   **29.** 0

33. $\frac{5}{6}$ **35.** $\frac{625}{6}$ **37.** $\frac{25}{2}\tan^{-1}5 - \frac{5}{4}\ln 26$

39. $6(e^2 - e^{-1/2})$ **41.** $\frac{2}{3}(e-1)$

43. $\frac{ab\pi}{4}(1 - e^{-1})$ **45.** $\frac{8\sqrt{5}}{40}(1 - e^{-20})(2\pi)$

47. $(1.1430, 1.5690)$ **49.** $\frac{4}{3}\pi abc$

51. $\frac{1}{4}\left(49\ln 7 - \frac{75}{2}\ln 5 - 27\ln 3 + 6\right)$ **53.** $\frac{\pi\sqrt{6}}{6}$

57. $C = 4\int_0^a \frac{1}{a\sqrt{a^2 - x^2}}\sqrt{a^4 + (b^2 - a^2)x^2}\,dx$

Chapter 12 Review
Proficiency Examination (Pages 852–853)

22. $e^{-\sqrt{3}/2} + \frac{\sqrt{3}}{2} - 1$ **23.** 0   **24.** 36   **25.** $\frac{\pi}{4}\sin 1$

26. $\frac{abc}{6}$ **27.** 0.15   **28.** $2\pi\sqrt{2}$

29. $\frac{128\pi}{15}$ **30.** $\frac{1}{3}\left(e^2 + \frac{8}{e} - 3\right)$

Supplementary Problems (Pages 853–856)

1. $\frac{3}{2}$ **3.** $\frac{\pi}{4}\ln 2$

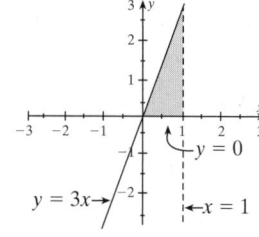

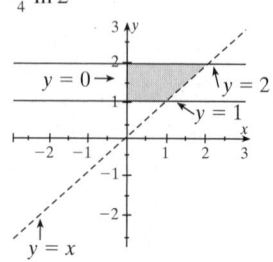

5. $\frac{8\sqrt{2} - 4}{15}$ **7.** $\frac{3}{2}(e^3 - 1)$

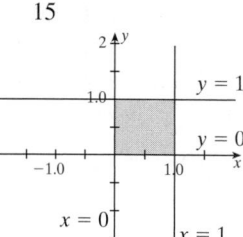

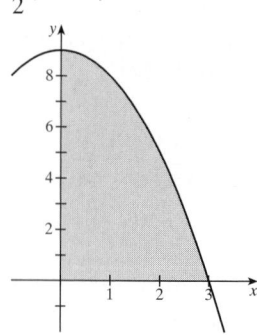

9. $\frac{1 - \cos 1}{12}$

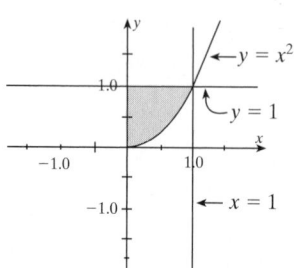

11. $\frac{1}{3}(e - 1)$ **13.** 10   **15.** $\frac{2}{3}\pi^4(2 - \sqrt{2})$ **17.** $\frac{31}{30}$

19. $\frac{81\pi}{8}$ **21.** 12π **23.** $\frac{2^{2n+2}\pi}{n+1}$ **25.** 0

27. $\frac{1}{5}$ **29.** 11   **31.** $\frac{2\pi}{15}$ **33.** $2\pi(\ln 2 + 2\sqrt{2} - 2)$

35. $m = \int_{\pi/12}^{5\pi/12} \int_{\sqrt{2}a}^{2a\sqrt{\sin 2\theta}} \delta r\,dr\,d\theta$

37. a^2 **39.** $\int_0^1 \int_x^{4-3x} f(x, y)\,dy\,dx$

41. $\sqrt{3} - \frac{\pi}{3}$ **43.** $\pi + 3\sqrt{3}$ **45.** $\frac{2}{3}$ **47.** $\frac{\pi}{2}$

49. $\frac{\pi}{6}\left(37\sqrt{37} - 1\right)$ **51.** $\frac{9\pi}{4}$ **53.** $\frac{4(3\pi - 4)}{9}$

55. πa^3 **57.** $\frac{2\pi a^5}{15}(\cos^3\phi_0 - 3\cos\phi_0 + 2)$

59. $\frac{2}{5}$ **61.** $\frac{3}{4}H$ **63.** $32xyz$ **65.** $\frac{3\pi - 7}{243}$

67. a. $-x \leq y \leq x; \frac{1}{2} \leq x \leq 1$

   b. $\frac{\partial(u, v)}{\partial(x, y)} = -2; \iint_D (u + v)\,du\,dv = \frac{7}{3}$

69. $\left(\frac{1}{3A}, \frac{1}{3B}, \frac{1}{3C}\right)$ **71. a.** $\left(\frac{16}{35}, \frac{1}{2}\right)$ **b.** $\frac{11}{240}$

73. $\frac{32a^3}{9}$ **75.** $\frac{4a^3\pi}{35}$ **77.** $(0, 0, 0)$

79. $\left(\frac{1 - \ln 2}{4 - \pi}, \frac{1 - \ln 2}{4 - \pi}, \frac{1 - \ln 2}{4 - \pi}\right)$ **81.** $(0, 0, -0.71)$

83. This is Putnam Problem 5 in the afternoon session of 1942.

85. This is Putnam Problem 5 in the morning session of 1958.

Chapter 13: Vector Analysis

13.1 Properties of a Vector Field: Divergence and Curl (Pages 866–867)

3. $\text{div } \mathbf{F} = 3x + 3z^2$; $\text{curl } \mathbf{F} = y\mathbf{k}$ **5.** $\text{div } \mathbf{F} = 2$; $\text{curl } \mathbf{F} = \mathbf{0}$

7. At $(2, -13)$ $\text{div } \mathbf{F} = 0$; $\text{curl } \mathbf{F} = \mathbf{0}$

9. At $(1, 2, 3)$ $\text{div } \mathbf{F} = 7$; $\text{curl } \mathbf{F} = \mathbf{j} - 3\mathbf{k}$

11. At $(3, 2, 0)$, $\text{div } \mathbf{F} = 2 - 2e^{-6}$; $\text{curl } \mathbf{F} = -3\mathbf{i} + 3e^{-6}\mathbf{k}$

13. $\text{div } \mathbf{F} = \cos x - \sin y$; $\text{curl } \mathbf{F} = \mathbf{0}$

15. $\text{div } \mathbf{F} = 0$; $\text{curl } \mathbf{F} = \mathbf{0}$ **17.** $\text{div } \mathbf{F} = \dfrac{1}{\sqrt{x^2 + y^2}}$; $\text{curl } \mathbf{F} = \mathbf{0}$

19. $\text{div } \mathbf{F} = a + b$; $\text{curl } \mathbf{F} = \mathbf{0}$

21. $\text{div } \mathbf{F} = 2(x + y + z)$; $\text{curl } \mathbf{F} = \mathbf{0}$

23. $\text{div } \mathbf{F} = x + y + z$; $\text{curl } \mathbf{F} = -y\mathbf{i} - z\mathbf{j} - x\mathbf{k}$

25. $\text{div } \mathbf{F} = yz + 2x^2yz^2 + 3y^2z^2$;
$\text{curl } \mathbf{F} = (2yz^3 - 2x^2y^2z)\mathbf{i} + xy\mathbf{j} + (2xy^2z^2 - xz)\mathbf{k}$

27. $\text{div } \mathbf{F} = -x^2e^{-x} + 3y^2 \ln z$;
$\text{curl } \mathbf{F} = \left(\dfrac{-y^3}{z} - xe^{-y}\right)\mathbf{i} + (2ze^{-x} - e^{-y})\mathbf{j}$

29. harmonic   **31.** harmonic   **35.** $2yz^3 + 6x^2yz$

37. $(xy - 3xz)\mathbf{i} - (y^2 + 3yz)\mathbf{j} + (yz + 3z^2)\mathbf{k}$ **39.** $xz - xy$

43. a. $(bz - cy)\mathbf{i} + (cx - az)\mathbf{j} + (ay - bx)\mathbf{k}$
b. $\text{div } \mathbf{V} = 0$; $\text{curl } \mathbf{V} = 2\boldsymbol{\omega}$

45. II only   **61.** $\text{div}(\nabla f g) = f\,\text{div}(\nabla g) + 2\nabla f \cdot \nabla g + g\,\text{div}(\nabla f)$

13.2 Line Integrals (Pages 875–877)

3. $2\sqrt{2} - 2$ **5.** $\frac{1}{144}(257^{3/2} - 5^{3/2})$ **7.** $\frac{4}{3}$ **9.** 1

11. $\frac{26}{3}$ **13. a.** $-\frac{1}{3}$ **b.** $-\frac{1}{3}$ **15.** $-\frac{16}{3}$ **17.** $\frac{77}{15}$

19. $-\frac{7}{60}$ **21.** 12   **23.** $-a$ **25. a.** $\dfrac{\pi^2}{8}$ **b.** $\dfrac{\pi^2}{8}$

27. a. $\frac{5}{2}$ **b.** $\frac{11}{2}$ **29.** $\frac{\pi}{2}$ **31.** $\frac{116}{297}$ **33.** $-\frac{1}{3}$ **35.** 0

37. $\dfrac{\sqrt{2}}{2}$ **39.** 2π **41.** $-2a^2$ **43.** $\frac{\pi}{2} - \frac{4}{3}$

45. $\frac{1}{35}$ **47.** $\frac{25}{6}$

49. The center of mass is $\left(\dfrac{3\sqrt{2}\,\pi}{16}, 0, 0\right)$.

51. The centroid is $\left(\dfrac{12}{5}, \dfrac{44}{25}, \dfrac{14}{15}\right)$.

53. The work done is 11,000 ft-lb.

55. 0   **57.** No; answers vary.

13.3 The Fundamental Theorem and Path Independence (Pages 884–887)

5. $f(x, y) = x^2y^3$; conservative

7. not conservative   **9.** not conservative

11. a. -2π **b.** -4 **c.** -2π **13. a.** 0 **b.** 32 **c.** 32

15. 1   **17.** $\frac{1}{3}$ **19.** $\frac{1}{2}$ **21.** ze^{xy}

23. $\frac{1}{4}(x^2 + y^2 + z^2)^2$ **25.** $\frac{1}{2}x^2y^2 + xyz + y^3z$

27. $\cos 1 + \sin 1 + 1$ **29.** $\frac{\pi}{4}$

31. $\frac{13}{4}$ **33.** 8   **35.** $\frac{1}{2}(3\pi - 4)$ **37.** 8   **39.** 32

41. $-\tan^{-1}(-2) + 2e^{-2} - \frac{\pi}{4} - e^{-1}$

43. $g(x) = Cx^{-5}$

45. a. $f(x, y, z) = kmM\left(\dfrac{1}{r}\right)$

b. $W = \dfrac{kmM}{\sqrt{a_2^2 + b_2^2 + c_2^2}} - \dfrac{kmM}{\sqrt{a_1^2 + b_1^2 + c_1^2}}$

47. No work is performed.

49. a. $W = -(2a + b)$; the path does not matter
b. $W_1 = a(e^{-1} - 3)$; the path does not matter
c. $W_2 = \frac{a}{7}(9e^{-7/9} - 23)$; $W_3 = -ae^{-7/9}(2e^{7/9} + e - 1)$; the path does matter here

13.4 Green's Theorem (Pages 896–898)

1. 0   **3.** 3   **5.** 0   **7.** -6π **9.** 0

11. 16   **13.** 0   **15.** 2π **17.** 4π **19.** $\frac{15}{2}$

21. $-\dfrac{\pi a^4}{4}$ **27.** 0   **29.** 0   **31.** 0   **33.** 3

41. $\displaystyle\int_C M\,dx + N\,dy = \iint_D \left(\dfrac{\partial N}{\partial x} - \dfrac{\partial M}{\partial y}\right) dA$
$$= \int_{C_1} M\,dx + N\,dy + \int_{C_2} M\,dx + N\,dy + \int_{C_3} M\,dx + N\,dy$$

43. There are a total of seven possible values.

13.5 Surface Integrals (Pages 906–907)

1. $4\sqrt{2}$ **3.** 0   **5.** $\dfrac{160\sqrt{6}}{3}$ **7.** $\dfrac{\pi}{2}$ **9.** 8π

11. 0   **13.** 16π **15.** $\frac{\pi}{60}\left(391\sqrt{17} + 1\right)$

17. $\frac{\pi}{6}(17\sqrt{17} - 1)$ **19.** $\frac{4\pi}{3}$ **21.** $\dfrac{7\pi\sqrt{2}}{4}$

23. -6 **25.** $\frac{4\pi}{3}$ **27.** π

29. $\frac{49}{32}\ln(25 - 4\sqrt{39}) - \frac{23}{8}\sqrt{39}$

31. $-\dfrac{19\ln(\sqrt{5} + 2)}{192} + \dfrac{17\sqrt{5}}{32} - \dfrac{1}{12}$

33. $-\frac{1}{8}[4\sqrt{17} + \ln(4 + \sqrt{17})]$

35. $\frac{4\pi}{3}$ **37.** $\dfrac{16\sqrt{6}}{3}$ **39.** $\frac{\pi}{60}(25\sqrt{5} + 1)$

41. $\frac{8}{3}\pi^3(5 - \sqrt{5})$ **43.** $\dfrac{243\pi\rho}{2}$

45. a. $\dfrac{\pi a^7}{192}$ **b.** $2\pi a^2(1 - \cos \phi_0)$ **47.** $\frac{2}{3}ma^2$

13.6 Stokes' Theorem (Pages 914–916)

1. 18π **3.** $\frac{9}{2}$ **5.** -8π **7.** -18 **9.** 0

11. $2\sqrt{2}\,\pi$ **13.** -3π **15.** $\frac{1}{3}$ **17.** $-\frac{1}{2}$ **19.** 0

21. -16π **23.** 0   **25.** $\frac{3}{2}$ **27.** $-\frac{\pi}{4}$ **29.** $\frac{\pi}{2}$ **31.** 0

13.7 The Divergence Theorem (Pages 922–924)

1. $\dfrac{64\pi}{3}$ **3.** $\dfrac{128}{3}$ **5.** 3   **7.** 24π **9.** $\dfrac{13}{3}$

11. $\dfrac{81\pi}{2}$ **13.** 0   **15.** 12π **17.** $\dfrac{8(16 - 7\sqrt{2})}{15}\pi$

19. $\dfrac{9\pi a^4}{2}$ **21.** $4\pi a^4$ **23.** $\text{div } \nabla f = 0$ **25. b.** 6

Chapter 13 Review
Proficiency Examination (Pages 925–926)

23. $f = xyz$

24. $\text{div } \mathbf{F} = 2xy - ze^{yz}$; $\text{curl } \mathbf{F} = ye^{yz}\mathbf{i} - \frac{1}{2}\mathbf{j} - x^2\mathbf{k}$

25. -2 **26.** $-4\pi\sqrt{2}$ **27.** 0   **28.** 0

29. $\phi = \dfrac{m\omega^2}{2}(x^2 + y^2 + z^2)$ **30.** 0

Supplementary Problems (Pages 926–928)

1. $\mathbf{F}$ is conservative; $f = 2x - 3y$.

3. $\mathbf{F}$ is conservative; $f = xy^{-3} + \sin y$.

5. $\mathbf{F}$ is not conservative.

7. -7 **9.** $\sin 4 - \sin 1 - \dfrac{31}{32}$ **11.** $\dfrac{5}{2}$

13. $\operatorname{div}\mathbf{F} = 3$; $\operatorname{curl}\mathbf{F} = \mathbf{0}$

15. $\operatorname{div}\mathbf{F} = \dfrac{2}{\sqrt{x^2 + y^2 + z^2}}$; $\operatorname{curl}\mathbf{F} = \mathbf{0}$

17. $\pi \cos \pi^2$ **19.** $-\dfrac{3\pi}{4} - 6$ **21.** $\sqrt{2}$

23. $\dfrac{5}{6}$ **25.** $2\pi(\pi - 1)$ **27.** 0 **29.** 4π

31. $\dfrac{6\sqrt{2}\,\pi}{5}$ **33.** $\dfrac{2a + 3b}{2abc}$ **35.** 0 **37.** $\dfrac{3}{4}$

39. $\dfrac{3}{2}$ **41.** -1 **43.** $\dfrac{5}{6}$

45. $\mathbf{F}$ is conservative in any region of the plane where $x + y \neq 0$;
$W = \ln \left| \dfrac{c + d}{a + b} \right|$.

53. 0

55. a. D is any region that does not contain the y-axis;
$f(x, y) = -\dfrac{1 + y^2}{2x^2} - \dfrac{y^2}{2}$.

b. $\dfrac{-67}{9}$; C is any curve that does not intersect the y-axis.

57. $\dfrac{5}{4} + \ln \dfrac{2}{9}$ **59.** $2\pi c$ **61.** 0

63. 0 **65.** $\dfrac{\pi}{4} - \dfrac{1}{2}\ln 2$ **67.** 2π

71. $4\pi^2 ab$ **73.** 21 **75.** $(0, 0, 2)$

Cumulative Review for Chapters 11–13 (Pages 933–934)

5. $f_x = e^{y/x}(2x - y)$; $f_y = xe^{y/x}$; $f_{xy} = e^{y/x}(1 - y/x)$

7. $f_x = 2y \sin x \cos x - y \sin xy$; $f_y = \sin^2 x - x \sin xy$;
$f_{xy} = \sin 2x - xy \cos xy - \sin xy$

9. $f_x = \dfrac{x^2 - 2xy - y^2}{(x - y)^2}$; $f_y = \dfrac{x^2 + 2xy - y^2}{(x - y)^2}$; $f_{xy} = \dfrac{-4xy}{(x - y)^3}$

11. $\dfrac{49{,}152}{13}$ **13.** $\dfrac{4\pi}{15}$ **15.** $e^2 - 3$ **17.** π **19.** 8

21. 0 **23.** $x = y = z = \sqrt[3]{V_0}$

25. a. $-\dfrac{6}{65}$ **b.** $\dfrac{1}{10}(-4\mathbf{i} + \mathbf{j} + 3\mathbf{k})$ **c.** $\dfrac{1}{10}\sqrt{26}$

27. $\dfrac{\pi}{6}(65\sqrt{65} - 1)$ **29.** 0

Chapter 14: Introduction to Differential Equations

14.1 First-Order Differential Equations (Pages 944–946)

1. $\ln |y| = x + \ln |x - 5|^5 + C$

3. $\ln |y| = -\dfrac{1}{18}[\ln(e^{2x} + 9) - 2x] + C$

5. $y = 3 \sec^{-1}\left|\dfrac{x}{3}\right| + C$ **7.** $y = 2(1 - e^{-x^2})$

9. $y = \dfrac{1}{2}(\cos x + \sin x) - \dfrac{1}{2}e^{-x}$ **11.** $y = x^3 - \dfrac{9}{4}x^2$

13. $-\ln\sqrt{x^2 + y^2} - \dfrac{1}{3}\tan^{-1}\dfrac{y}{x} = C$

15. $(y + x)^2(y - x) = C$ **17.** $\dfrac{y - x}{3y + x} = Cx^8$

19. $x^3 y + x \tan y = C$

21. $\tan^{-1} x + \ln(x^2 + y^2) + e^{-y} = C$

23. $x^2 \cos 2y - 3xy + 3x^2 y - 6y = C$

25. a. $y = -x - 1 + 4e^{x-1}$

b. 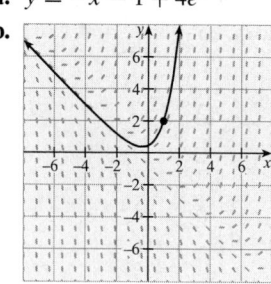   **c.**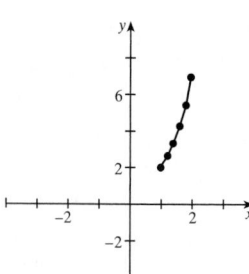

27. 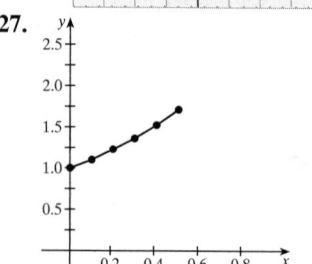   **29.**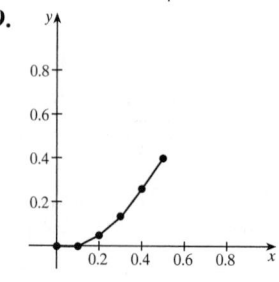

31. $\dfrac{x}{y} + \ln |y| = C$ **33.** $x^2 y^2 + x^3 y - xy^3 = C$

35. $\dfrac{x^2}{y} + \dfrac{y^2}{x} + 3y = C$

37. $5e^x = e^y(2 \sin x \cos x + \sin^2 x + 2) + Ce^{x+y}$

39. $x^3 + \cos xy = C$

41. $y = (\csc x + \cot x)[(-\sin x + x) + C]$

43. $\sqrt{x^2 + y^2} + y = B$ **45.** $\cot \dfrac{y}{x} = \ln\left(\dfrac{\pi x}{4}\right) + 1$

47. $y = x^3 \ln |x| + x^3$ **49.** $x \sin(x^2 + y) = 0$

51. $\dfrac{1}{2}\ln(y^2 + 2y + 2) - \tan^{-1}(y + 1) + e^{-x} = 1$

53. If $\alpha > \beta$, $\displaystyle\lim_{t \to +\infty} Q(t) = \beta$; if $\alpha < \beta$, $\displaystyle\lim_{t \to +\infty} Q(t) = \alpha$,
and if $\alpha = \beta$, $\displaystyle\lim_{t \to +\infty} Q(t) = \alpha$

55. a. $P(t) = \dfrac{r_1(P_0 - r_2) - r_2(P_0 - r_1)e^{-Dt}}{(P_0 - r_2) - (P_0 - r_1)e^{-Dt}}$ **b.** $\displaystyle\lim_{t \to +\infty} P(t) = r_1$

57. a. $x = \dfrac{1}{I(y)}\left[\displaystyle\int I(y)S(y)\,dy + C\right]$

b. $x = -y^2[(y + 1)e^{-y} + C]$

59. The Spy must run at 4.674 yd/s or about 14 ft/s.

61. b. $y = u(x) + \dfrac{1}{z(x)}$ **c.** $y = \dfrac{3Cx + 2x^4}{3C - x^3}$

14.2 Second-Order Homogeneous Linear Differential Equations (Pages 955–957)

1. $y = C_1 + C_2 e^{-x}$ **3.** $y = C_1 e^{-5x} + C_2 e^{-x}$

5. $y = C_1 e^{3x} + C_2 e^{-2x}$ **7.** $y = C_1 e^{(-1/2)x} + C_2 e^{3x}$

9. $y = C_1 e^x + C_2 e^{-x}$ **11.** $y = C_1 \cos \sqrt{11}\,x + C_2 \sin \sqrt{11}\,x$

13. $y = e^{(-3/14)x}\left[C_1 \cos\left(\dfrac{\sqrt{131}}{14}x\right) + C_2 \sin\left(\dfrac{\sqrt{131}}{14}x\right)\right]$

15. $y = C_1 + C_2 x + C_3 e^{-x}$

17. $y = C_1 + C_2 x + e^{-(1/2)x}\left[C_3 \cos\left(\dfrac{\sqrt{7}}{2}x\right) + C_4 \sin\left(\dfrac{\sqrt{7}}{2}x\right)\right]$

19. $y = C_1 e^{2x} + C_2 e^{-3x} + C_3 e^{-x}$

21. $y = e^{5x} - 6xe^{5x}$ **23.** $y = \dfrac{11}{5}e^x + \dfrac{4}{5}e^{11x}$

25. $y = \dfrac{94}{25} - \dfrac{19}{25}e^{-5x} - \dfrac{9}{5}xe^{-5x}$

27. $5e^x$ **29.** e^{-2x} **33.** $y = C_1 e^{2x} + C_2 e^{-3x/2}$

35. $y = C_1 x^{-2} + C_2 x^2$ **37.** $y = C_1(1-x) + C_2(1-x)^{-1}$

39. $y = \frac{5}{6}\cos(4\sqrt{3}\,t) - \frac{1}{2}\sqrt{3}\sin(4\sqrt{3}\,t)$

41. $y = -\cos(4\sqrt{3}\,t)$

43. $y = e^{-0.08t}\,[\cos 6.93t + 0.0115\sin 6.93t]$

53. a. $m(t) = \dfrac{w - rt}{g}$; $s'(t) = -v_0 \ln\left(\dfrac{w - rt}{w}\right) - gt$

b. $s(t) = \dfrac{v_0(w - rt)}{r}\ln\left(\dfrac{w - rt}{w}\right) - \dfrac{1}{2}gt^2 + v_0 t$

c. The fuel is consumed when $rt = w_f$; that is, when $t = w_f/r$.

d. The height is

$$\frac{v_0(w - w_f)}{r}\ln\left(\frac{w - w_f}{w}\right) - \frac{1}{2}\frac{gw_f^2}{r^2} + \frac{v_0 w_f}{r}$$

14.3 Second-Order Nonhomogeneous Linear Differential Equations (Pages 965–966)

1. $\overline{y}_p = Ae^{2x}$ **3.** $\overline{y}_p = Ae^{-x}$

5. $\overline{y}_p = xe^{-x}(A\cos x + B\sin x)$

7. $\overline{y}_p = (A + Bx)e^{-2x} + xe^{-2x}(C\cos x + D\sin x)$

9. $\overline{y}_p = A_3 x^3 + A_2 x^2 + A_1 x + A_0$

11. $\overline{y}_p = (A_3 x^3 + A_2 x^2 + A_1 x + A_0)\cos x$
$\qquad + (B_3 x^3 + B_2 x^2 + B_1 x + B_0)\sin x$

13. $\overline{y}_p = A_0 e^{2x} + B_0 \cos 3x + C_0 \sin 3x$

15. $\overline{y}_p = A_3 x^3 + A_2 x^2 + A_1 x + A_0 + B_0 e^{-x}$

17. $y = C_1 + C_2 e^{-x} - x^3 + 3x^2 + x$

19. $y = C_1 e^{-3x} + C_2 e^{-5x} + \frac{3}{35}e^{2x}$

21. $y = e^{-x}(C_1 \cos x + C_2 \sin x) + \frac{1}{5}\cos x + \frac{2}{5}\sin x$

23. $y = C_1 e^{x/7} + C_2 e^{-x} + e^{-x}\left(-\frac{1}{16}x^2 - \frac{15}{64}x\right)$

25. $y = C_1 + C_2 e^x - \left(\frac{1}{4}x^4 + x^3 + \frac{5}{2}x^2 + 10x\right)$

27. $y = C_1 e^{-x} + C_2 x e^{-x} + e^{-x}(\frac{1}{6}x^3 + 2x^2)$

29. $y = C_1 \cos x + C_2 \sin x - \cos x \ln|\sec x + \tan x|$

31. $y = C_1 e^{3x} + C_2 e^{-2x} - \frac{1}{32}(8x^2 + 12x + 13)e^{2x}$

33. $y = C_1 \cos 2x + C_2 \sin 2x + \frac{1}{2}x\cos 2x - \frac{1}{4}\sin 2x(\ln|\cos 2x|)$

35. $y = C_1 e^{-x} + C_2 x e^{-x} + \frac{1}{4}x^2(2\ln x - 3)e^{-x}$

37. $y = C_1 + C_2 e^x - \frac{1}{20}\sin 2x - \frac{1}{2}x - \frac{1}{5}\cos^2 x$

39. $y = -\frac{4}{5} + \frac{6}{5}e^x - \frac{1}{10}\sin 2x - x - \frac{2}{5}\cos^2 x$

41. $y = -\frac{2}{9}\cos 3x + \frac{4}{9}\sin 3x + \frac{2}{9}e^{3x}$

43. $y = \frac{35}{27}\sin 3x + \frac{1}{9}x$

45. $y = -4\cos x - \sin x \ln|\csc x + \cot x|$

47. $y = C_1 e^{-2x} + C_2 e^{-3x} + G(x)$

where $G(x) = \begin{cases} \frac{1}{3}x - \frac{5}{18} & \text{for } 0 \le x \le 1 \\ \frac{1}{3} & \text{for } 1 < x < 3 \\ -\frac{1}{3}x + \frac{29}{18} & \text{for } 3 \le x \le 4 \end{cases}$

49. $I(t) = \frac{81}{656}e^{-9t} - \frac{9}{16}e^{-t} + \frac{18}{41}\cos t + \frac{45}{82}\sin t$

51. $I(t) = 0.312e^{-t} - 0.015e^{-9t} - 0.297\cos t - 0.067\sin t + t(0.244\cos t + 0.305\sin t)$

53. $y = C_1 x + C_2(x\tan^{-1} x + 1) - \frac{1}{2}\tan^{-1} x$

Chapter 14 Review
Proficiency Examination (Page 966)

12. $\sin^{-1} y = \sinh^{-1} x + C$ **13.** $y = Bx$

14. $y = x + C\sqrt[3]{x}$ **15.** $x^2(x^2 - 2y^2) = C$

16. $\dfrac{2}{\sqrt{3}}\tan^{-1}\left[\dfrac{2}{\sqrt{3}}\left(\dfrac{y}{x} - \dfrac{1}{2}\right)\right] = \ln|x| + C$

17. $y = e^{-x}(C_1 \cos x + C_2 \sin x) - \frac{2}{5}\cos x + \frac{1}{5}\sin x$

18. $x^3 e^{-y} + xy^{-2} + x^2 y^{-3} = C$

19. $x(t) = e^{-1.60t}[0.33\cos 10.84t + 0.05\sin 10.84t]$

20. $I(t) = e^{-125t}[-0.562\cos 185.4t + 2.79\sin 185.4t]$
$\qquad + 0.562\cos 100t - 0.899\sin 100t$

Supplementary Problems (Pages 966–968)

1. a. 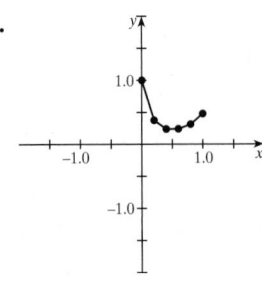   **b.**

3. $\frac{1}{4}y^4 = -2x^2 + C$ **5.** $\dfrac{y^3}{3x^3} = \ln|x| + C$

7. $e^{y^2} = e^{2x} + C$ **9.** $y = -e^{5x}\cos x + Ce^{5x}$

11. $x = e^{-y}[y + C]$ **13.** $\dfrac{y}{x} = \sin(\ln|x| + C)$

15. $y = Be^{(1-2x)/(2x^2)}$ **17.** $x^4 y^3 + \ln|x| - \ln|y| = C$

19. $y = -\tan^{-1} e^x + C$

21. a. $y_h = C_1 e^{3x} + C_2 e^{-3x}$ **b.** $y_p = -\frac{1}{9}(x+1)$

23. a. $y_h = C_1 e^{2x} + C_2 e^{3x}$ **b.** $y_p = \left(\frac{1}{2}x^2 + \frac{3}{2}x + \frac{7}{4}\right)e^x$

25. a. $y_h = C_1 e^x + C_2 e^{2x}$ **b.** $y_p = \left(-\frac{1}{4}x^4 - x^3 - 3x^2 - 6x\right)e^x$

27. a. $y_h = C_1 \cos x + C_2 \sin x$

b. $y_p = \sin x \ln|\sec x + \tan x| - 2$

29. $y = \frac{1}{9}e^{-3x} + \frac{1}{3}x - \frac{1}{9}$ **31.** $z(t) = -3e^{-2t} + 2e^{-3t} + 1$

33. $y^2 = 5x - x^2$ **35.** $e^{X+Y} = 1 + Ke^X$

37. $Y(Y^2 + 3X^2) = K$

39. $y = C_1 x + C_2\left[\dfrac{x}{2}\ln\left|\dfrac{x-1}{x+1}\right| + 1\right]$

41. $\dfrac{1}{6}x^2 - \dfrac{C_1}{x} + C_2$

43. $x = y[e^y + C]$ **45.** 0.62 sec

47. a. $y(t) = \dfrac{WLx^3}{6EI} - \dfrac{Wx^4}{24EI} - \dfrac{WL^3 x}{8EI}$

b. $y_{\max} \approx \dfrac{WL^4}{EI}(-0.045)$

49. b. $y = C_1 x^{m_1} + C_2 x^{m_2}$

c. $y = C_1 x^{m_0} + C_2 x^{m_0}\ln|x|$

d. $y = x^\alpha[C_1 \cos(\beta \ln|x|) + C_2 \sin(\beta \ln|x|)]$

53. This is Problem 9 of the afternoon session of the 1938 Putnam Examination.

55. This is Problem 6ii of the morning session of the 1948 Putnam Examination.

Appendix A (Pages A-7–A-8)

1. $\delta = \frac{\epsilon}{2}$ **3.** false   **5.** $\delta = \min(1, \frac{\epsilon}{5})$

7. $\delta = \epsilon$ **9.** $\delta = \frac{\epsilon}{3}$ **11.** $\delta = \min(1, \frac{\epsilon}{5})$

APPENDIX G   Credits

This page constitutes an extension of the copyright page.

CHAPTER 1

12   Problems 59 and 60 from *Introductory Oceanography*, 5th ed., by H. V. Thurman, p. 253. Reprinted with permission of Merrill, an imprint of Macmillan Publishing Company. Copyright ©1988 Merrill Publishing Company, Columbus, Ohio.

12   Problem 61 adapted from R. A. Serway, *Physics*, 3rd ed., Philadelphia: Saunders, 1992, p. 1007.

12   Journal problem (#62) by Murray Klamkin reprinted from *The Mathematics Student Journal*, Vol. 28, 1980, issue 3, p. 2.

18–19   Babylonian system of equations in Problem 58 and 59 taken from *A History of Mathematics*, 2nd ed., by Carl B. Boyer, revised by Uta C. Merzbach, John Wiley and Sons, Inc., New York, 1968.

19   Journal problem (#64) reprinted from *Ontario Secondary School Mathematics Bulletin*, Vol. 18, 1982, issue 2. p. 7.

33   Journal problem (#72) reprinted from *The Mathematics Student Journal*, Vol. 28, 1980, issue 3, p. 2.

45   Putnam examination problem (#45) 1959, reprinted by permission from The Mathematical Association of America.

45   Putnam examination problem (#46) 1960, reprinted by permission from The Mathematical Association of America.

46–47   Guest essay, "Calculus Was Inevitable," by John L. Troutman.

48   Historical Quest (#9) information from *Ethnomathematics* by Marcia Ascher, (Pacific Grove: Brooks/Cole, 1991) pp. 128–129 and 188–189.

CHAPTER 2

78   Graph (#36) from Michael D. La Grega, Philip L. Buckingham, and Jeffery C. Evans, *Hazardous Waste Management*, New York: McGraw-Hill, 1994, pp. 565–566.

79   Modeling problem (#37) from E. Batschelet, *Introduction to Mathematics for Life Scientists*, 2nd ed., New York: Springer-Verlag, 1976, p. 280.

95   Modeling problem (#67) from William Bosch and L. G. Cobb, "Windchill," *UMAP Module No. 658*, (1984), pp. 244–247.

95   Putnam examination problem (#71) 1956, reprinted by permission from The Mathematical Association of America.

95   Putnam examination problem (#72) 1986, reprinted by permission from The Mathematical Association of America.

CHAPTER 3

129   Global modeling illustration from *Scientific American*, March 1991.

157   Journal problem (#73) by Bruce W. King from *The Pi Mu Epsilon Journal*, Volume 7 (1981), p. 346.

174   Modeling problem (#30) by John A. Helms, "Environmental Control of Net Photosynthesis in Naturally Grown Pinus Ponderosa Nets," *Ecology* (Winter 1972) p. 92.

174   Modeling problems (#35, #36) from *Introduction to Mathematics for Life Scientists*, 2nd ed. New York: Springer-Verlag (1976), pp. 102–103.

178   Problem 65 from 1982 BC AP Examination.

180   Putnam examination problem (#95) 1946, reprinted by permission from The Mathematical Association of America.

180   Putnam examination problem (#96) 1939, reprinted by permission from The Mathematical Association of America.

180   Putnam examination problem (#97) 1946, reprinted by permission from The Mathematical Association of America.

181   Chaos example is by Jack Wadhams of Golden West College.

181   Photo courtesy of Gregory Sams/Photo Researchers, Inc.

CHAPTER 4

183   Energy expended by a pigeon by Edward Batschelet, *Introduction to Mathematics for Life Scientists*, 2nd ed., New York: Springer-Verlag, 1979, pp. 276–277.

209   MAL cartoon, © 1974, by permission from the estate of Malcolm Hancock.

216   Problem 54 from "The Mechanics of Bird Migration," by C. J. Pennycuick, *Ibis III*, pp. 525–556.

216   Journal problem (#57) from *Mathematics Magazine*, Volume 55 (1982), p. 300.

228   Journal problem (#54) from *Parabola*, Vol. 20, Issue 1, 1984.

228   Historical Quest (#55) from "Mathematics in India in the Middle Ages," by Chandra B. Sharma, *Mathematical Spectrum*, Volume 14(1), pp. 6–8, 1982.

237   Historical Quest (#58) from *A Source Book in Mathematics, 1200–1800* by D. J. Struik, Cambridge, MA: University Press, 1969, pp. 313–316.

245   Journal problem (#6) from *Parabola*, Vol. 19, Issue 1, 1983, p. 22.

248   Modeling problem (#31) by Paul J. Campbell, "Calculus Optimization in Information Technology," *UMAP Module 1991: Tool for Teaching*, Lexington, MA, CUPM Inc., 1992, pp. 175–199.

248   Modeling problem (#32) by John C. Lewis and Peter P. Gillis, "Packing Factors in Diatomic Crystals," *American Journal of Physics*, Vol. 61, No. 5 (1993), pp. 434–438.

249–250   Modeling problem (#42) by Thomas O'Neil, "A Mathematical Model of a Universal Joint," *UMAP Modules 1982: Tools for Teaching*. Lexington, MA: Consortium for Mathematics and Its Applications, Inc., 1983, pp. 393–405.

250   Modeling problem (#43) is based on an article by Steve Janke, "Somewhere Within the Rainbow," *UMAP Modules 1992: Tools for Teaching*. Lexington, MA: Consortium for Mathematics and Its Applications, Inc., 1993.

256   Concentration of drugs in the bloodstream application adapted from E. Heinz, "Probleme bei der Diffusion kleiner Substanzmengen innerhalb des menschlichen Körpers," *Biochem.*, Vol. 319 (1949), pp. 482–492.

257   Modeling vascular branching is adapted from *Introduction to Mathematics for Life Scientists*, 2nd ed., by Edward Batschelet, New York: Springer-Verlag, 1976, pp. 278–280.

261   Modeling problem (#35) from "A Blood Cell Population Model, Dynamical Diseases, and Chaos," by W. B. Gearhart and M. Martelli, *UMAP Modules 1990: Tools for Teaching*, Arlington, MA: Consortium for Mathematics and Its Applications (CUPM) Inc., 1991.

261   Modeling problem (#37) adapted from "Flight of Birds in Relation to Energetics and Wind Directions," by V. A. Tucker and K. Schmidt-Koening, *The Auk*, Vol. 88, 1971, pp. 97–107.

261   Modeling problem (#39) adapted from P. L. Shaffer and H. J. Gold, "A Simulation Model of Population Dynamics of the Codling Moth Cydia Pomonella," *Ecological Modeling*, Vol. 30, 1985, pp. 247–274.

262   Problem #47 adapted from "Price Elasticity of Demand: Gambling, Heroin, Marijuana, Prostitution, and Fish," by Yves Nievergelt, *UMAP Modules 1987: Tools for Teaching*. Arlingon, MA, CUPM Inc., 1988, pp. 153–181.

263   Photo of a beehive, courtesy of Scott Camazine/Photo Researchers, Inc.

264   Journal problem (#51) from the *Mathematics Teacher*, December 1990, p. 718.

265   Journal problem (#63) from the *AMATYC Review*, Spring 1995, pp. 67–68.

265   Journal problem (#64) from *Quantum*, 1997, Vol. 7, No. 4, pp. 50–53.

266   Modeling problem (#75) adapted from "Modeling the AIDS Epidemic," by Allyn Jackson, *Notices of the American Mathematical Society*, Vol. 36., No. 8 (October 1989), pp. 981–983.

267   Historical Quest (#84) quotation about Euler from *Elements of Algebra, 5th Ed*, by Leonhard Euler, London: Longman, Orme, and Co., 1840.

268   Putnam examination problem (#85) 1938, reprinted by permission from The Mathematical Association of America.

268   Putnam examination problem (#86) 1941, reprinted by permission from The Mathematical Association of America.

268   Putnam examination problem (#87) 1987, reprinted by permission from The Mathematical Association of America.

268   Putnam examination problem (#88) 1985, reprinted by permission from The Mathematical Association of America.

268   Putnam examination problem (#89) 1940, reprinted by permission from The Mathematical Association of America.

268   Putnam examination problem (#90) 1961, reprinted by permission from The Mathematical Association of America.

269   Photograph of a wine cellar showing wooden cask, courtesy of Peter Menzel/Stock Boston.

269   Group research project is from Elgin Johnston of Iowa State University. This group research project comes from research done at Iowa State University as part of a National Science Foundation grant.

CHAPTER 5

285   Software output from *Converge* by John R. Mowbray, JEMware, 567 South King Street, Suite 178, Honolulu, HI 96813.

308   Journal problem (#52) from *FOCUS*, February 1995, p. 15.

315   Historical Quest (#45) quotation from "A Short Account of the History of Mathematics," as quoted in *Mathematical Circles Adieu* by Howard Eves, Boston: Prindle, Weber & Schmidt, Inc., 1977.

316   Journal problem (#60) by Murray Klamkin from the *College Mathematics Journal*, Sept. 1989, p. 343. Problem by Murray Klamkin.

327   Shroud of Turin, courtesy of Gianni Tortoli/Science Source/Photo Researches, Inc.

341   Historical Quest (#34) Early Asian Calculus from *Mathematics*, by David Bergamini, p. 108. Reprinted by permission of Time, Incorporated, 1963.

349   Modeling problem (#76) adapted from "Flight Speeds of Birds in Relation to Energies and Wind Directions," by V. A. Tucker and K. Schmidt-Koenig, *The Auk*, Vol. 88 (1971), pp. 97–107.

350   Putnam examination problem (#86) 1951, reprinted by permission from The Mathematical Association of America.

350   Putnam examination problem (#87) 1958, reprinted by permission from The Mathematical Association of America.

351–352 Guest essay, "Kinematics of Jogging," by Ralph Boas.

CHAPTER 6

374   Photograph of the great pyramid of Cheops, courtesy of Paul W. Liebhardt.

385   Journal problem (#60) from *School Science and Mathematics*, Problem 3949 by V. C. Bailey, Vol. 83, 1983, p. 356.

395   *Blondie* cartoon reprinted with special permission of King Features Syndicate.

418   Journal problem (#20) *Mathematics Teacher*, December 1990, p. 695.

422   Putnam examination problem (#83) 1939, reprinted by permission from The Mathematical Association of America.

422   Putnam examination problem (#84) 1938, reprinted by permission from The Mathematical Association of America.

423   Putnam examination problem (#85) 1993, reprinted by permission from The Mathematical Association of America.

424   Photograph of Harry Houdini, courtesy of AP/Wide World Photos.

424   Group research project is from *MAA Notes*, Vol. 17, 1991, "Priming the Calculus Pump: Innovations and Resources," by Marcus S. Cohen, Edward D. Gaughan, R. Arthur Knoebel, Douglas S. Kurtz, and David J. Pengelley.

CHAPTER 7

456   Historical Quest (#61) from "Pólya, Problem Solving, and Education," by Alan H. Schoenfeld, *Mathematics Magazine*, Vol. 60, No. 5, December 1987, p. 290.

480   Journal problem (#56) by Peter Lindstrom from the *College Mathematics Journal*, Vol. 24, No. 4, September 1993, p. 343.

489   Modeling problem (#60) adapted from "The Learning Function," by L. L. Thurstone, *J. of General Psychology 3* (1930), pp. 469–493.

490   Putnam examination problem (#88) 1968, reprinted by permission from The Mathematical Association of America.

490   Putnam examination problem (#89) 1980, reprinted by permission from The Mathematical Association of America.

490   Putnam examination problem (#90) 1985, reprinted by permission from The Mathematical Association of America.

491   Photograph of buoy, courtesy of G. Walts/The Image Works.

491   Group research project is adapted from a computer project used at the U.S. Coast Guard Academy.

CHAPTER 8

543   Journal problem (#54) by Michael Brozinsky, *School Science and Mathematics*, Vol. 82, 1982, p. 175.

565   Historical Quest (#68) from *The Historical Development of the Calculus* by C. H. Edwards, Jr., Springer-Verlag, 1979, p. 292.

566   Journal problem (#75) by Robert C. Gebhardt, *The Pi Mu Epsilon Journal*, Vol. 8, 1984, Problem 586.

568   Ramanujan's series (#81) from *Quantum*, March/April, 1998.

569   Modeling problem (#95) adapted, "How Old Is the Earth?" by Paul J. Campbell, *UMAP Modules 1992: Tools for Teaching*, Lexington, MA: Consortium for Mathematics and Its Applications, Inc., 1993, pp. 105–137.

569   Putnam examination problem (#96) 1984, reprinted by permission from The Mathematical Association of America.

569   Putnam examination problem (#97) 1951, reprinted by permission from The Mathematical Association of America.

569   Putnam examination problem (#98) 1982, reprinted by permission from The Mathematical Association of America.

570   Photograph of a tightrope walker, courtesy of Paul Conklin, PhotoEdit.

570   Group research project is from David Pengelley of New Mexico State University.

CHAPTER 9

609   Photograph of a bicycle, courtesy of David Young-Wolff, PhotoEdit.

615   Journal problem (#56) by Frank Kocher, *The MATYC Journal*, Problem 148, Vol. 14, 1980, p. 155.

631   Putnam examination problem (#62) 1939, reprinted by permission from The Mathematical Association of America.

631   Putnam examination problem (#63) 1959, reprinted by permission from The Mathematical Association of America.

631   Putnam examination problem (#64) 1983, reprinted by permission from The Mathematical Association of America.

632   Photograph of the Starship Enterprise from *Star Trek: The Next Generation* © Paramount Pictures, courtesy of CorbisSygma.

632   Group research project is from *MAA Notes*, Vol. 17, 1991, "Priming the Calculus Pump: Innovations and Resources," by Marcus S. Cohen, Edward D. Gaughan, R. Arthur Knoebel, Douglas S. Kurtz, and David J. Pengelley.

CHAPTER 10

635   Drawing of double helix of DNA, courtesy of *Scientific American*, October 1985, p. 60.

678   Photograph of a Ferris wheel, courtesy of Marc D. Longwood.

682   Putnam examination problem (#77) 1939, reprinted by permission from The Mathematical Association of America.

683   Putnam examination problem (#78) 1947, reprinted by permission from The Mathematical Association of America.

683   Putnam examination problem (#79) 1946, reprinted by permission from The Mathematical Association of America.

684   Quotation by Johann Kepler from *The World of Mathematics*, Vol. I, James R. Newman, New York: Simon & Schuster, 1956, p. 220.

684–686 Guest essay, "The Simulation of Science," by Howard Eves. This article is reprinted by permission from *Great Moments in Mathematics Before 1650*, published by The Mathematical Association of America, 1983, p. 194.

CHAPTER 11

693   Computer-generated graph of Mount St. Helens, courtesy of Bill Lennox, Humboldt State University.

696   Typographic map of Mount Ranier, courtesy of U.S. Geological Survey.

696   Map showing isotherms, courtesy of Accu-Weather, Inc.

719   Journal problem (#60) by John A. Winterink, *CRUX Mathematicorum*, problem number 546, Vol. 6, 1980, p. 154.

741   Photograph of a downhill skier, courtesy of Jean Y. Ruszniewski, Stone.

760   Counterexample problem (#55) based on the problem, "Two Mountains Without a Valley," by Ira Rosenholtz, *Mathematics Magazine*, 1987, Vol. 60, No. 1, p. 48.

760   Counterexample problem (#56) based on material in the article "The Only Critical Point in Town Test" by Ira Rosenholtz and Lowell Smythe, *Mathematics Magazine*, 1985, Vol. 58, No. 3, pp. 149–150.

770   Historical Quest (#55) from *Men of Mathematics* by E. T. Bell, New York: Simon & Schuster, 1937, p. 165.

772   Modeling problem (#67) from *Mathematical Biology*, 2nd ed., by J. D. Murray, New York: Springer-Verlag, 1993, p. 464.

772   Modeling problem (#68) from "Heat Therapy for Tumors," by Leah Edelstein-Keshet, *UMAP Modules 1991: Tools for Teaching*, Lexington MA: Consortium for Mathematics and Its Applications, Inc., 1992, pp. 73–101.

774   Counterexample problem (#95) adapted from " 'Hidden' Boundaries in Constrained Max-Min Problems," by Herbert R. Bailey from *The College Mathematics Journal*, May 1991, p. 227.

774   Photograph of soap bubbles from *Scientific American*, "The Geometry of Soap Films and Soap Bubbles," by Frederick Almgren, Jr. and Jean Taylor, July 1976, pp. 82–93.

774   Putnam examination problem (#97) 1967, reprinted by permission from The Mathematical Association of America.

774   Putnam examination problem (#98) 1946, reprinted by permission from The Mathematical Association of America.

774   Putnam examination problem (#99) 1938, reprinted by permission from The Mathematical Association of America.

775   Photograph of a desert, courtesy of Scott T. Smith.

775   Group research project is from *MAA Notes*, Vol. 17, 1991, "Priming the Calculus Pump: Innovations and Resources," by Marcus S. Cohen, Edward D. Gaughan, R. Arthur Knoebel, Douglas S. Kurtz, and David J. Pengelley.

CHAPTER 12

803   Quotation in Historical Quest (#62) by W. W. Rouse Ball from *A Short Account of the History of Mathematics* as quoted in *Mathematical Circles Adieu* by Howard Eves, Boston: Prindle, Weber & Schmidt, Inc., 1977.

843   Journal problem (#63) from "Heat Therapy for Tumors" by Leah Edelstine-Keshet (*UMAP Journal*, summer 1991).

856   Putnam examination problem (#82) 1993, reprinted by permission from The Mathematical Association of America.

856   Putnam examination problem (#83) 1942, reprinted by permission from The Mathematical Association of America.

856   Putnam examination problem (#84) 1957, reprinted by permission from The Mathematical Association of America.

856   Putnam examination problem (#85) 1958, reprinted by permission from The Mathematical Association of America.

857   Photograph of an Apollo spacecraft, courtesy of NASA.

857   Group research project is from *MAA Notes*, Vol. 17, 1991, "Priming the Calculus Pump: Innovations and Resources," by Marcus S. Cohen, Edward D. Gaughan, R. Arthur Knoebel, Douglas S. Kurtz, and David J. Pengelley.

CHAPTER 13

860   Photograph of a wind-velocity map of the Atlantic Ocean, courtesy of NASA.

888   Graffiti on the wall of a high school playground in Ramat Gan (a suburb of Tel Aviv), courtesy of Regev Nathansohn of Ramat Gan, Israel. Source: Eli Maor.

928   Putnam examination problem (#76) 1948, reprinted by permission from The Mathematical Association of America.

929   Guest essay, "Continuous versus Discrete Mathematics," by William Lucas.

CHAPTER 14

940   Photograph of a skydiver, courtesy of Getty Images.

946   Journal problem (#62) from *The American Mathematical Monthly*, Vol. 91, 1984, p. 515.

956   *Mathematics is discovered*, quotation by James H. Jeans, *The Mysterious Universe*, p. 142. *Mathematics is invented* quotation by G. F. Simmons, *Differential Equations with Applications and Historical Notes*, 2nd ed., New York: McGraw-Hill, Inc., 1991, p. xix.

957   Journal problem (#54) by Murray S. Klamkin, Problem 331 in the *Canadian Mathematical Bulletin*, Vol. 26, 1983, p. 126.

968   Putnam examination problem (#53) 1938, reprinted by permission from The Mathematical Association of America.

968   Putnam examination problem (#54) 1947, reprinted by permission from The Mathematical Association of America.

968   Putnam examination problem (#55) 1948, reprinted by permission from The Mathematical Association of America.

969   Photograph of a dam, courtesy of Tennessee Valley Authority.

969   Group research project, "Save the Perch Project," by Diane Schwartz, Ithaca College, Ithaca, NY.

Index

DIFFERENTIATION FORMULAS

PROCEDURAL RULES

Constant multiple rule $\quad (cf)' = cf'$

Sum rule $\quad (f+g)' = f' + g'$

Difference rule $\quad (f-g)' = f' - g'$

Linearity rule $\quad (af + bg)' = af' + bg'$

Product rule $\quad (fg)' = fg' + f'g$

Quotient rule $\quad \left(\dfrac{f}{g}\right)' = \dfrac{gf' - fg'}{g^2}$

Chain rule $\quad \dfrac{dy}{dx} = \dfrac{dy}{du}\dfrac{du}{dx}$

BASIC FORMULAS

Extended power rule $\quad \dfrac{d}{dx}u^n = nu^{n-1}\dfrac{du}{dx}$

Trigonometric rules

$$\frac{d}{dx}\sin u = \cos u\,\frac{du}{dx} \qquad\qquad \frac{d}{dx}\cos u = -\sin u\,\frac{du}{dx}$$

$$\frac{d}{dx}\tan u = \sec^2 u\,\frac{du}{dx} \qquad\qquad \frac{d}{dx}\cot u = -\csc^2 u\,\frac{du}{dx}$$

$$\frac{d}{dx}\sec u = \sec u\tan u\,\frac{du}{dx} \qquad\qquad \frac{d}{dx}\csc u = -\csc u\cot u\,\frac{du}{dx}$$

Inverse trigonometric rules

$$\frac{d}{dx}\sin^{-1} u = \frac{1}{\sqrt{1-u^2}}\,\frac{du}{dx} \qquad\qquad \frac{d}{dx}\cos^{-1} u = \frac{-1}{\sqrt{1-u^2}}\,\frac{du}{dx}$$

$$\frac{d}{dx}\tan^{-1} u = \frac{1}{1+u^2}\,\frac{du}{dx} \qquad\qquad \frac{d}{dx}\cot^{-1} u = \frac{-1}{1+u^2}\,\frac{du}{dx}$$

$$\frac{d}{dx}\sec^{-1} u = \frac{1}{|u|\sqrt{u^2-1}}\,\frac{du}{dx} \qquad\qquad \frac{d}{dx}\csc^{-1} u = \frac{-1}{|u|\sqrt{u^2-1}}\,\frac{du}{dx}$$

Logarithmic rules

$$\frac{d}{dx}\ln u = \frac{1}{u}\frac{du}{dx} \qquad\qquad \frac{d}{dx}\log_b u = \frac{\log_b e}{u}\frac{du}{dx} = \frac{1}{u\ln b}\frac{du}{dx}$$

Exponential rules

$$\frac{d}{dx}e^u = e^u\frac{du}{dx} \qquad\qquad \frac{d}{dx}b^u = b^u\ln b\,\frac{du}{dx}$$

Hyperbolic rules

$$\frac{d}{dx}\sinh u = \cosh u\,\frac{du}{dx} \qquad\qquad \frac{d}{dx}\cosh u = \sinh u\,\frac{du}{dx}$$

$$\frac{d}{dx}\tanh u = \operatorname{sech}^2 u\,\frac{du}{dx} \qquad\qquad \frac{d}{dx}\coth u = -\operatorname{csch}^2 u\,\frac{du}{dx}$$

$$\frac{d}{dx}\operatorname{sech} u = -\operatorname{sech} u\tanh u\,\frac{du}{dx} \qquad\qquad \frac{d}{dx}\operatorname{csch} u = -\operatorname{csch} u\coth u\,\frac{du}{dx}$$

Inverse hyperbolic rules

$$\frac{d}{dx}\sinh^{-1} u = \frac{1}{\sqrt{u^2+1}}\,\frac{du}{dx} \qquad\qquad \frac{d}{dx}\cosh^{-1} u = \frac{1}{\sqrt{u^2-1}}\,\frac{du}{dx}$$

$$\frac{d}{dx}\tanh^{-1} u = \frac{1}{1-u^2}\,\frac{du}{dx} \qquad\qquad \frac{d}{dx}\coth^{-1} u = \frac{1}{1-u^2}\,\frac{du}{dx}$$

$$\frac{d}{dx}\operatorname{sech}^{-1} u = \frac{-1}{u\sqrt{1-u^2}}\,\frac{du}{dx} \qquad\qquad \frac{d}{dx}\operatorname{csch}^{-1} u = \frac{-1}{|u|\sqrt{1+u^2}}\,\frac{du}{dx}$$

INTEGRATION FORMULAS

PROCEDURAL RULES

Constant multiple rule
$$\int cf(u)\,du = c\int f(u)\,du$$

Sum rule
$$\int [f(u) + g(u)]\,du = \int f(u)\,du + \int g(u)\,du$$

Difference rule
$$\int [f(u) - g(u)]\,du = \int f(u)\,du - \int g(u)\,du$$

Linearity rule
$$\int [af(u) + bg(u)]\,du = a\int f(u)\,du + b\int g(u)\,du$$

BASIC FORMULAS

Constant rule
$$\int 0\,du = C$$

Power rules
$$\int u^n\,du = \frac{u^{n+1}}{n+1} + C; \qquad n \neq -1$$
$$\int u^{-1}\,du = \ln|u| + C$$

Exponential rules
$$\int e^u\,du = e^u + C$$
$$\int a^u\,du = \frac{a^u}{\ln a} + C \quad a > 0, a \neq 1$$

Logarithmic rule
$$\int \ln u\,du = u\ln u - u + C, u > 0$$

Trigonometric rules

$$\int \sin u\,du = -\cos u + C \qquad\qquad \int \cos u\,du = \sin u + C$$

$$\int \tan u\,du = -\ln|\cos u| + C \qquad\qquad \int \cot u\,du = \ln|\sin u| + C$$
$$= \ln|\sec u| + C$$

$$\int \sec u\,du = \ln|\sec u + \tan u| + C \qquad \int \csc u\,du = -\ln|\csc u + \cot u| + C$$

$$\int \sec^2 u\,du = \tan u + C \qquad\qquad \int \csc^2 u\,du = -\cot u + C$$

$$\int \sec u \tan u\,du = \sec u + C \qquad\qquad \int \csc u \cot u\,du = -\csc u + C$$

Cosine squared formula
$$\int \cos^2 u\,du = \tfrac{1}{2}u + \tfrac{1}{4}\sin 2u + C$$

Sine squared formula
$$\int \sin^2 u\,du = \tfrac{1}{2}u - \tfrac{1}{4}\sin 2u + C$$

Hyperbolic rules

$$\int \sinh u\,du = \cosh u + C \qquad\qquad \int \cosh u\,du = \sinh u + C$$

$$\int \tanh u\,du = \ln(\cosh u) + C \qquad\qquad \int \coth u\,du = \ln|\sinh u| + C$$

Inverse rules

$$\int \frac{du}{\sqrt{a^2 - u^2}} = \sin^{-1}\frac{u}{a} + C \qquad\qquad \int \frac{du}{\sqrt{u^2 - a^2}} = \cosh^{-1}\frac{u}{a} + C$$

$$\int \frac{du}{a^2 + u^2} = \frac{1}{a}\tan^{-1}\frac{u}{a} + C \qquad\qquad \int \frac{du}{a^2 - u^2} = \begin{cases} \dfrac{1}{a}\tanh^{-1}\dfrac{u}{a} + C & \text{if } \left|\dfrac{u}{a}\right| < 1 \\[2mm] \dfrac{1}{a}\coth^{-1}\dfrac{u}{a} + C & \text{if } \left|\dfrac{u}{a}\right| > 1 \end{cases}$$

$$\int \frac{du}{u\sqrt{u^2 - a^2}} = \frac{1}{a}\sec^{-1}\frac{|u|}{a} + C$$

$$\int \frac{du}{u\sqrt{a^2 - u^2}} = -\frac{1}{a}\operatorname{sech}^{-1}\left|\frac{u}{a}\right| + C = -\frac{1}{a}\ln\left|\frac{a + \sqrt{a^2 - u^2}}{u}\right| + C$$

$$\int \frac{du}{\sqrt{a^2 + u^2}} = \sinh^{-1}\frac{u}{a} + C = \ln\left(\sqrt{a^2 + u^2} + u\right) + C$$

$$\int \frac{du}{u\sqrt{a^2 + u^2}} = -\frac{1}{a}\operatorname{csch}^{-1}\left|\frac{u}{a}\right| + C = -\frac{1}{a}\ln\left|\frac{\sqrt{a^2 + u^2} + a}{u}\right| + C$$